Cicero's *Academici libri* and *Lucullus*

Cicero's *Academici libri* and *Lucullus*

A Commentary with Introduction and Translations

TOBIAS REINHARDT

Great Clarendon Street, Oxford, OX2 6DP,
United Kingdom

Oxford University Press is a department of the University of Oxford.
It furthers the University's objective of excellence in research, scholarship,
and education by publishing worldwide. Oxford is a registered trade mark of
Oxford University Press in the UK and in certain other countries

© Tobias Reinhardt 2023

The moral rights of the author have been asserted

First Edition published in 2023

All rights reserved. No part of this publication may be reproduced, stored in
a retrieval system, or transmitted, in any form or by any means, without the
prior permission in writing of Oxford University Press, or as expressly permitted
by law, by licence or under terms agreed with the appropriate reprographics
rights organization. Enquiries concerning reproduction outside the scope of the
above should be sent to the Rights Department, Oxford University Press, at the
address above

You must not circulate this work in any other form
and you must impose this same condition on any acquirer

Published in the United States of America by Oxford University Press
198 Madison Avenue, New York, NY 10016, United States of America

British Library Cataloguing in Publication Data

Data available

Data is available at the Library of Congress

ISBN 978–0–19–927714–8

Printed and bound by
CPI Group (UK) Ltd, Croydon, CR0 4YY

Links to third party websites are provided by Oxford in good faith and
for information only. Oxford disclaims any responsibility for the materials
contained in any third party website referenced in this work.

Für Eva, Anna und Arthur Reinhardt

Acknowledgements

The aims of this commentary are adumbrated in the initial sections of the introduction. I began work on it and on the critical edition which it accompanies in 1999; completion has taken longer than originally anticipated. Secondary literature is considered up to September 2021, no doubt incompletely.

On the way I have accumulated many debts of gratitude to individuals who gave me the benefit of their advice, made me think harder, or shared forthcoming publications with me; they include Jim Adams, Michael I. Allen, Sophie Aubert-Baillot, David Blank, Mauro Bonazzi, George Boys-Stones, Ada Bronowski, Lesley Brown, Felix Budelmann, Myles Burnyeat, Riccardo Chiaradonna, Ursula Coope, Paolo Crivelli, Serafina Cuomo, Kilian Fleischer, Therese Fuhrer, Dorothea Frede, Michael Frede, Miriam Griffin, Stephen Heyworth, Gregory Hutchinson, Brad Inwood, George Karamanolis, Arnd Kerkhecker, David Langslow, Jane Lightfoot, Ermanno Malaspina, Wolfgang-Rainer Mann, Anna Marmodoro, Wolfgang De Melo, Ernest Metzger, Ben Morison, Anna Morpurgo Davies, Hindy Najman, Reviel Netz, Giuseppe Pezzini, Harm Pinkster, Oliver Primavesi, Donald Russell, Barnaby Taylor, Malcolm Schofield, David Sedley, Gisela Striker, Harold Tarrant, Teun Tielemann, Katja Maria Vogt, Katharina Volk, James Warren, Gareth Williams, and Jim Zetzel. Michael Winterbottom took the time to comment on the translations in the summer of 2021; his friendship and encouragement have been an enrichment. I have learnt a great deal from exchanges with James Allen.

There are a number of scholars with whose published work I am frequently in dialogue, notably Charles Brittain, John Glucker, Woldemar Görler, and Carlos Lévy. This commentary owes much to their insights and arguments.

During my work I have been a member of three different Oxford colleges, Merton, Somerville, and Corpus Christi. I am indebted to all of them and to the colleagues who made them congenial and stimulating places.

I was fortunate to have access to the Bodleian Library, the Weston Library, the Taylorian Library, and the libraries of the three colleges named above. Colleagues working in these institutions have been very helpful, especially Julia Walworth, Pauline Adams, Joanna Snelling, Charlotte Goodall, and Martin Kauffmann.

Much appreciated financial assistance came from the Craven Committee, the Loeb Foundation, and the Leverhulme Trust (in the form of a Major Research Fellowship, awarded for the years 2014–17).

Revised versions of Reinhardt (2018a) and (2021a) appear here as sections 6 and 8; revised material from Reinhardt (2018b) appears in section 10; and revised material from Reinhardt (2018) in the commentary on *Ac.* 1.30–4 and 1.40–2. I am grateful to Cambridge University Press, Walter de Gruyter GmbH, and Brepols Publishers, respectively.

At Oxford University Press, the Classics editors past and present, Hilary O'Shea and Charlotte Loveridge, the project editor, Henry Clarke, and the production editor,

Meghan Watson, have been unfailingly patient and supportive. Timothy Beck's attentive copy-editing has done much to enhance the volume.

Others who have aided this project, sometimes in ways that may not be apparent to them, are Audrey Cahill, Raúl Lafuente Sánchez, Edgar Scharf, my parents Sabine and Mathias Reinhardt, and Andrea and Sebastian Reinhardt.

The dedication is to my wife and our children, with love.

T.R.

Oxford,
July 2022

Contents

Note on the Text — xi
Note on Translations — xv
Abbreviations — xvii
Introduction — xxi
  1. Opening — xxi
  2. Philosophy and History in *Acad.* — xxii
  3. *Acad.* within the Ciceronian Corpus — xxvi
  4. Academic Positions and Academic Arguments — xxxvii
    4.1 The Clitomachean Position — xli
    4.2 Mitigated Scepticism — xliv
    4.3 The Roman Books View — xlvii
    4.4 Metrodorus' Position — xlviii
  5. The Debate about the Cataleptic Impression — l
    5.1 Definitions — li
    5.2 The Interpretation of the Second Clause — liv
    5.3 The Stoics: Epistemological Internalists, Externalists, or Something in Between? — lvi
    5.4 The Interpretation of the Third Clause — lx
    5.5 Cataleptic Impression: Perceptual or also Non-perceptual? — lxiii
    5.6 Ἀπαραλλαξία — lxiv
      5.6.1 Dreams and Madness — lxix
      5.6.2 Very Similar Objects — lxxii
    5.7 Arrangement — lxxvi
    5.8 Generalization — lxxvi
    Appendix—Ἀπαραλλαξία in the Different Versions of the Core Argument in *Acad.* — lxxviii
  6. The Carneadean πιθανόν and Cicero's *probabile* — lxxx
    6.1 The Evidence from Sextus — lxxxi
    6.2 ἔμφασις before Carneades — lxxxix
    6.3 Back to Sextus, *M.* 7 — xci
    6.4 Stoic πιθανά — xcvii
    6.5 The Evidence from Cicero — ci
    6.6 The πιθανόν/*probabile*, Clitomacheanism, and Mitigated Scepticism — cvi
  7. Constructions of History and of Historical Figures in *Acad.* — cviii
    7.1 Sceptical Histories — cix
    7.2 Antiochus' Construction of the Old Academy — cxiv
    7.3 Socrates — cxxiv
    7.4 Plato — cxxvii
    7.5 Arcesilaus — cxxviii

8. Cicero's Clitomacheanism	cxlii
9. Editions of *Acad.* and Their Reconstruction	clvii
9.1 Evidence from Cicero's Letters to Atticus on the Creation of *Acad.*	clviii
9.2 Ciceronian Editions of *Acad.* and Their Reconstruction	clxvi
9.3 Sources	clxxii
9.3.1 *Luc.*	clxxii
9.3.2 *Ac.* 1	clxxv
9.3.3 Earlier Scholarship	clxxvii
9.4 The Title(s)	clxxviii
9.5 The *Hortensius* and *Acad.*	clxxx
10. The Linguistic Form of *Acad.*	clxxxii
10.1 Impressions I: *uidere, uideri, uisum*	clxxxii
10.2 Impressions II: *uisio, species, nota, signum*	clxxxix
10.3 'Beliefs'	cxci
11. Table of Contents for *Ac.* 1 and *Luc.*	cxciii

Translations

Letters Documenting the Creation of *Acad.*	3
Academicus Primus	15
Fragments and Testimonia	25
Lucullus	33

Commentary

Academicus Primus	79
Fragments and Testimonia	265
Lucullus	295

Appendix 1: Non-Ciceronian Texts on the Sceptical Academy	805
Texts	805
Translations	809
Commentary	812
Appendix 2: Numenius on the Academy	817
Texts	817
Translations	823
Commentary	830
Bibliography	837
General Index	885
Index Locorum	895
Index of Greek Terms	913
Index of Latin Terms	916

Note on the Text

The text to which the commentary refers is that of the Oxford Classical Text, whose preface explains the transmission of *Ac.* 1 and *Luc.* and gives full references.

The stemma of *Ac.* 1 is bipartite. On one side there is manuscript P. On the other side, there is a reconstructed manuscript (Γ), whose closest descendants relate to one another as follows:

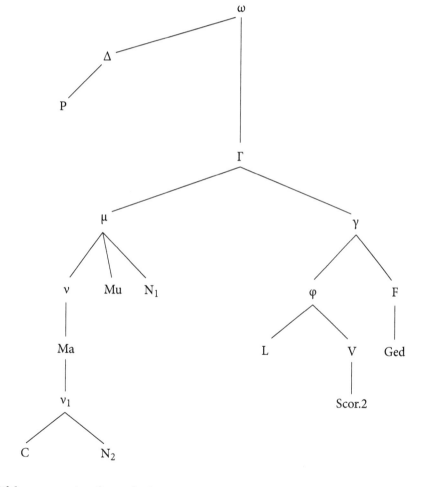

Of the manuscripts from which μ is reconstructed only Mu offers the entire text. Two descendants of Ma, C and N_2, can be used in its place where it is not available.

The stemma of *Luc.* is bipartite too, with B representing one branch and three other manuscripts (AVS), whose agreement I call ζ, representing the other, as follows:

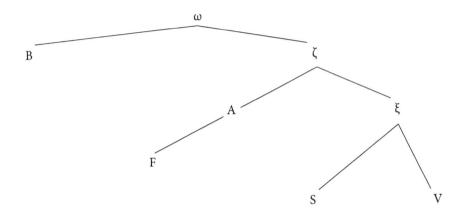

In §104 V breaks off and its readings must be reconstructed from descendants of V which reflect V before mutilation. A and B were cross-corrected in the ninth century, and V was corrected *ope ingenii* as well as against ξ and another lost witness (V^m), which, however, did not offer vertically transmitted readings not attested elsewhere. There is also a ninth-century copy of—for the text of *Luc.*—A after correction (F). The commentary on occasion discusses not just variants and emendations, but also places which speak to the nature of the corrections in A, B, and V.

I have not examined manuscripts of Nonius, Augustine, or any of the other authors preserving fragments of the *Academici libri*.

The sigla referred to above are resolved as follows:

Ac. 1
P   Paris, Bibl. Nationale Lat. 6331, saec. 12
Ma   Madrid, Bibl. Nacional 9116, saec. 14 (§§1–38 *in ratione esse dicerent*)
C   Cesena, Bibl. Malatestiana, S.12,6, saec. 14
N₂   Naples, Bibl. Nazionale IV.G.46, saec. 15
Mu   Modena, Bibl. Estense Lat. 213, saec. 14
N₁   Naples, Bibl. Nazionale IV.G.43, saec. 15 (§19 *prauumue quid*–§26 *itaque aer*, §32 *ad probandum–fin.*)
L   Firenze, Bibl. Medicea Laurenziana, Strozzi 37, saec. 15
V   Vatican, Bibl. Apostolica Vaticana, Lat. 1720, saec. 15
Scor.2   Madrid, El Escorial, Real Bibl. de San Lorenzo T.III.18, saec. 15
F   Firenze, Bibl. Nazionale Centrale, Magliabecchi XXXI 30, saec. 15
ω   agreement of PΓ
Γ   agreement of μγ
γ   agreement of φF
φ   agreement of LV

μ   agreement of **MaMu** (§§1–19 *rectum in oratione*) or **MaMuN$_1$** (§§19 *prauumue quid*–26 *itaque aer*) or **MaMu** (§§26 *hoc quoque utimur*–32 *notis ducibus utebantur*) or **MaMuN$_1$** (§§32–8 *in ratione esse dicerent*) or **CN$_2$MuN$_1$** (§§38 *sed quasdam uirtutes–fin.*)
v   a lost manuscript once owned by Petrarch
v$_1$ agreement of CN$_2$

Luc.
A   Leiden, Universiteitsbibl. Voss. Lat. F84, saec. 9
B   Leiden, Universiteitsbibl. Voss. Lat. F86, saec. 9
V   Vienna, Österreichische Nationalbibl. 189, saec. 9 (§§1–104 . . . *aut etiam aut non*)
𝒱   agreement of witnesses derived from V
S   Madrid, El Escorial (Antolin. R.I.2), saec. 14
F   Florence, Bibl. Medicea Laurenziana, San Marco 257, saec. 9
ω   agreement of **ABVS** (or **AB𝒱S**)
ζ   agreement of **AVS** (or **A𝒱S**)
ξ   agreement of **VS** (or **𝒱S**)

Note on Translations

This volume contains my own translations of all texts included in the Oxford Classical Text.[1] In the introduction I translate quotations in Greek and Latin as a matter of course, whereas in the commentary I give translations of longer Greek quotations, while leaving longer Latin quotations untranslated except when a particular point of interpretation needs to be illustrated (so that consultation of an existing translation would not necessarily be informative). For longer quotations I have sometimes cited published translations with acknowledgement, and sometimes offered my own translation. Quotations of Latin and Greek words and phrases are only translated when their meaning does not emerge from the context.

In the translation of *Luc.* I have attempted to render, as far as possible, the flexibility of the terminology Cicero uses to speak about impressions (see section 10.1 on uses of *uidere, uideri, uisum, quod uidetur*, etc.). The Latin term *probabile*, corresponding to Greek πιθανόν, is translated 'plausible'; this choice is justified in section 6 of the introduction.

---

[1] I have benefitted from comparing the translations of Reid[2], Rackham (1951), Schäublin et al., Gigon, Brittain (2006), Kany-Turpin and Pellegrin (2010), as well as those of particular passages in Dörrie (1987), Long and Sedley (1987), and Hülser (1987–8).

Abbreviations

Editions and translations not included in the following list of abbreviations are cited by author and date. A detailed discussion of important editions from the *editio princeps* (i.e. the Roman edition of 1471) onwards with reference to *Ac.* 1 is in Hunt (1998: 225–59).

Section (1): Editions, Translations, Commentaries

Aldina	*M.T. Ciceronis de philosophia volumen primum*, Venice 1523 (published by Andreas Asulanus).
Alleemudder	Asraff Alleemudder, *A Philosophical Commentary on Cicero, Academica Priora II, 1–62*, Ph.D. thesis, University of London, 1979.
Baiter	*M. Tullii Ciceronis opera quae supersunt omnia ediderunt J. G. Baiter, C. L. Kayser*, vol. VI, Leipzig 1863.
Camerarius	*Opera Marci Tullii Ciceronis quotquot ab interitu vindicari summorum virorum industria potuerunt cum veterum exemplarium, tum recentiorum collatione restituta et recognitione Ioachimi Camerarii Pabergensis elaborata: cuius et locorum aliquot praecipuorum annotationes subiunguntur*, Basel 1540.
Davies	*M. Tullii Ciceronis Academica. Recensuit, variorum notis suas immiscuit, et Hadr. Turnebi Petrique Fabri commentarios adiunxit Ioannes Davisius*, Cambridge 1725.
Durand	*Académiques de Ciceron avec le texte latin de l'édition de Cambrige, et les remarques nouvelles, outre les conjectures de Davis et de Bentley, suivies du commentaire latin de Pierre Valence. Par David Durand*, Paris 1740.
Ernesti	*M. Tullii Ciceronis ex recensione Jo. Aug. Ernesti qui et notas suas adjecit. Voluminis quarti pars prima. Opera philosoph.*, Halle 1776.
Gigon	*Hortensius, Lucullus, Academici libri.* Herausgegeben, übersetzt und kommentiert von Laila Straume-Zimmermann, Ferdinand Broemser und Olof Gigon. Düsseldorf and Zürich 1997.
Goerenz	*M.T. Ciceronis philosophica omnia, ex scriptis recens collatis editisque libris castigatius et explicatius edidit Io. Aug. Goerenz, volumen secundum*, Leipzig 1810.
Gruter	*M. Tullii Ciceronis opera omnia quae exstant, xx sola fere codd. mss. fide emendata studio atque industria Jani Gulielmii et Jani Gruteri*, Hamburg 1618.
Halm	*M. Tullii Ciceronis opera quae supersunt omnia ex recensione Io. Casp. Orellii, editio altera emendatior, opus morte Orellii interruptum continuaverunt I. G. Baiterus et Car. Halmius, volumen quartum*, Zurich 1861.
Haltenhoff	Andreas Haltenhoff, *Kritik der akademischen Skepsis: ein Kommentar zu Cicero, Lucullus 1–62*, Frankfurt 1998.
Klotz	*M. Tullii Ciceronis scripta quae manserunt omnia recognovit Reinholdus Klotz, partis iv. vol. i*, Leipzig 1854.

Lambinus	*Tomus quartus operum M. Tullii Ciceronis philosophicos libros a Dionys. Lambino Monstroliensi ex auctoritate codicum manuscr. emendatos*, Paris 1565.
'Lambinus'	*M.T. Ciceronis philosophicorum librorum pars prima*, Paris 1573.
Manutius	*M. Tullii Ciceronis de philosophia prima pars*, Venice 1541 and 1565 ('Paulus Manutius Aldi filius').
Mueller	*M. Tullii Ciceronis scripta quae manserunt omnia, recognovit C. F. W. Mueller, partis IV volumen I*, Leipzig 1878.
Plasberg[1]	Otto Plasberg, *M. Tulli Ciceronis Paradoxa Stoicorum, Academicorum Reliquiae cum Lucullo, Timaeus, De Natura Deorum, De Divinatione, De Fato*, fasc. 1, Leipzig 1908.
Plasberg[2]	Otto Plasberg, *Academicorum Reliquiae cum Lucullo*, Leipzig 1922.
Reid[1]	James S. Reid, *M. Tulli Ciceronis Academica*, a text revised and explained, London 1885.
Reid[2]	*The Academics of Cicero*, translated by James S. Reid, London 1885.
Schäublin et al.	Marcus Tullius Cicero, *Akademische Abhandlungen—Lucullus*. Text und Übersetzung von Christoph Schäublin. Einleitung von Andreas Graeser und Christoph Schäublin. Anmerkungen von Andreas Bächli und Andreas Graeser. Hamburg 1995.
Schütz	*M. Tullii Ciceronis opera quae supersunt omnia ac deperditorum fragmenta, recognovit potiorem lectionis diversitatem adnotavit, indices rerum ac verborum copiosissimos adiecit Christianus Godofr. Schütz*, Leipzig 1816.
Sigonius	*Fragmenta Ciceronis in variis locis dispersa, Caroli Sigonii diligentia collecta, et scholiis illustrata*, Venice 1559.

Section (2): Grammars, Dictionaries, Encyclopaedias

Heumann-Seckel	H. G. Heumann, *Handlexikon zu den Quellen des römischen Rechts*, in 9. Auflage neu bearbeitet von E. Seckel, Jena 1926.
Hofmann-Szantyr	J. B. Hofmann and Anton Szantyr, *Lateinische Syntax und Stilistik*, Munich 1972.
Kühner-Gerth	Raphael Kühner and Bernhard Gerth, *Ausführliche Grammatik der Griechischen Sprache*, 2 vols, Hannover 1992 [reprint of the 3rd edn, Hannover and Leipzig 1898] [cited by volume number and page].
Kühner-Stegmann	Raphael Kühner and Carl Stegmann, *Ausführliche Grammatik der Lateinischen Sprache, Zweiter Teil: Satzlehre*, 2 vols, Hannover 1992 [reprint of the 2nd rev. edn, Hannover 1914] [cited by volume number and page].
LGPN	*The Lexicon of Greek Personal Names*, edited by P. M. Fraser and E. Matthews (et al.), Oxford 1987–.
Löfstedt	Einar Löfstedt, *Syntactica—Studien und Beiträge zur historischen Syntax des Lateins*, Lund 1928 and 1933 [cited by volume number and page].
LSJ	*A Greek-English Lexicon*. Compiled by Henry George Liddell and Robert Scott, revised and augmented throughout by Sir Henry Stuart

	Jones with the Assistance of Roderick McKenzie and with the Co-operation of many Scholars, with a Supplement. Oxford 1968.
Merguet	H. Merguet, *Lexikon zu den philosophischen Schriften Cicero's*, 3 vols, Jena 1887–94.
OLD	*Oxford Latin Dictionary*, edited by P. G. W. Glare, Oxford 1994.
Pinkster	Harm Pinkster, *The Oxford Latin Syntax*, Volume I: *The Simple Clause*; Volume 2: *The Complex Sentence and Discourse*, Oxford 2015 and 2021 [cited by volume number and page].
RE	*Pauly's Real-Encylopädie der classischen Altertumswissenschaft*. Neubearbeitung, begonnen von Georg Wissowa, fortgeführt von Wilhelm Kroll und Karl Mittelhaus. Stuttgart 1894–1963 (1. Reihe I–XXIX), 1914–72 (2. Reihe I–X), and 1912–78 (Supplementbände).
TLL	*Thesaurus linguae latinae, editus iussu et auctoritate consilii ab academiarum quinque germanicarum Berolinensis Gottingensis Lipsiensis Monacensis Vindobonensis.* Leipzig 1900–.

Section (3): Collections of Texts

DDG	Hermann Diels, *Doxographi Graeci*, Berlin 1879.
DK	*Die Fragmente der Vorsokratiker*, griechisch und deutsch von Hermann Diels. Herausgegeben von Walther Kranz. 12th edn, 3 vols. Dublin and Zurich 1966.
DM	K. Döring, *Die Megariker- Kommentierte Sammlung der Testimonien*, Amsterdam 1972.
DNO	S. Kansteiner, K. Hallof, L. Lehmann, B. Seidensticker, and K. Stemmer (eds) *Der Neue Overbeck (DNO)—die antiken Schriftquellen zu den bildenden Künsten der Griechen*, Berlin and New York 2014.
FDS	K. Hülser, *Die Fragmente zur Dialektik der Stoiker: Neue Sammlung der Texte mit deutscher Übersetzung*, 4 vols, Stuttgart 1987–8.
LS	A. A. Long and D. N. Sedley, *The Hellenistic Philosophers*, Vol. 1: *Translations of the Principal Sources with Philosophical Commentary*; Vol. 2: *Greek and Latin Texts with Notes and Bibliography*, Cambridge 1987 [cited either by section and text or by volume number and page number].
SH	*Supplementum Hellenisticum ediderunt H. Lloyd-Jones, P. Parsons*, Berlin and New York 1983.
SSR	*Socratis et Socraticorum Reliquiae collegit, disposuit, apparatibus notisque instruxit G. Giannantoni*, 4 vols, Naples 1990.
SVF	Hans von Arnim (ed.), *Stoicorum Veterum Fragmenta*, 3 vols, Leipzig 1903–5. Index volume by M. Adler, Stuttgart 1924.

Introduction

1. Opening

The remains of the *Academici libri* and the *Lucullus* (the second book of their two-volume predecessor), which are jointly referred to as '*Acad.*' in this commentary,[1] are as fascinating as they are complex. They were composed near the end point of a two-hundred-year debate between sceptical Academic philosophers and Stoics, by which time discussion had reached a considerable level of intricacy. While much of ancient philosophical writing situates itself self-consciously within a historical context, *Acad.* is an unusual case, in that the opposing philosophical positions in play each cast themselves as the legitimate representative of the same tradition. If these historical claims are not just deemed assertions, the question arises whether ancient readers would have found them credible, how a modern reader should evaluate them, and whether the text as we have it provides information on the grounds for the claims which would have been cited. *Acad.* is of course written in Latin, and while Latin authors, notably in dramatic genres and in didactic poetry, had begun to write about perceptual phenomena with a more than intuitive awareness of the challenges involved, Cicero did have to develop ways of talking about his subject in his native language.

For the creation of *Acad.* sources were used, albeit with autonomous creativity and variability regarding the notional distance between source and Ciceronian text. It is one of the contentions of this commentary that Antiochus of Ascalon underpinned his construction of the history of philosophy by developing it where possible from Platonic texts. If this is correct, a particular kind of elucidation will be required in the commentary, viz. the identification of possible references to particular Platonic texts in the Ciceronian text even when some of the normal cues are absent.

As a work of Roman literature, *Acad.* is a set of dialogues. Thus it needs to be read against other dialogues by Cicero as well as Greek philosophical dialogues, and there is a small set of passages which are central to the philosophical interpretation of the text whose appraisal in the round requires attention to their literary form. First-person speakers called Cicero are a presence throughout the Ciceronian corpus, and they demand to be considered together.

For the cultural history of Europe *Acad.* is significant, as a substantial and self-contained body of evidence for one of two sceptical schools in antiquity, as evidence for Stoic thought presented on its own terms and in interaction with objections as opposed to, say, in occasionally hostile doxographical reports, as a key text in a broader tradition which is devoted to the possibility of knowledge arising from

---

[1] The letters documenting the creation of *Acad.*, which are included in the Oxford Classical Text, are referred to by 'T' and a number. The fragments and testimonia of *Acad.*, likewise included in the edition, are referred to by 't.' and a number.

perceptual experience, and as evidence for the fate of Plato's Academy in its final phase as a functioning school. *Acad.* had an extensive reception in late antique, Renaissance, early modern, and even twentieth-century thought, and it is to be hoped that work on this reception will be facilitated by this commentary, whose aim it is to explain *Acad.* in its complexity, without trying to replace the elementary linguistic and stylistic elucidation which Reid[1] provided in an exemplary way.

2. Philosophy and History in *Acad.*

Acad. offers insights into the debate two and a half centuries long between Stoics and Academics on the nature and possibility of knowledge, and into the chronologically overlapping inner-Academic debate about the most consistent sceptical response to the Stoic conception of knowledge.[2] It does this through the format of a dialogue featuring Roman characters, modelled on historical individuals, who make the competing views in the debate their own and thereby re-enact aspects of it, in a Roman context and in the medium of Latin. Only parts of two different editions of *Acad.* have come down to us, featuring different interlocutors, and set at different dramatic dates and consequently in somewhat different historical contexts.

The inner-Academic debate is fairly overtly the subject of the conversation in *Acad.*; e.g. different speakers in the first edition represent two of the available options, explain their origins and articulate them, while a third one is explicitly considered and dismissed. By contrast, the debate between Stoics and Academics is over long stretches of text presented in a synchronic fashion, as one about issues and problems, to which philosophers whom we can place chronologically contribute a consideration or new turn. Thus key moments in the historical development of the debate are only occasionally marked or stylized as such,[3] and the sequence of moves and countermoves over time has to be pieced together, as far as this is possible, by selecting evidence from *Acad.* and contextualizing it with information from elsewhere.

One way in which a historical dimension does come into view in *Acad.* is through different constructions of the history of philosophy deployed by both sides to underpin their stance. These are largely kept separate from the substantial debate, and while the Antiochian speakers did not attempt to recount the period from Arcesilaus down to Antiochus (instead ending with Zeno), the Academic speakers did offer sketches of the main protagonists on the Academic side in chronological order. However, this appears to have been done, as is suggested by *Ac.* 1.44–6 on Arcesilaus (the text breaks off after that), in a manner which did not closely trace the sequential steps of the debate. Relatedly, in *Ac.* 1.40–2 the Antiochian speaker Varro introduces the concept of κατάληψις, but does so without citing the definition of the cataleptic impression on which some of the debate focused. That the definition features explicitly in *Luc.* suggests that in the final edition it was introduced in a later, synchronic

---

[2] With this section, cf. Brittain (2006: xiii–xv).
[3] This is partly a function of the fact that the speakers deliver long speeches rather than have quick-fire exchanges, but it is not altogether clear whether Cicero or his source material had a detailed notion of the development of the debate about the cataleptic impression over time.

part of the dialogue.⁴ The dialogue (or dialogues) thus exhibits a fairly clear separation between accounts of history and argumentative back-and-forth.

One can distinguish the following phases in the debate between Stoics and Academics:

(i) Zeno (born c.334/3; died 262/1),⁵ before he founded the Stoa a pupil of Polemo in the Academy like Arcesilaus (*Ac.* 1.34), develops the conception of κατάληψις and formulated the two-clause definition of the cataleptic impression. Arcesilaus (born c.316/15; died in the period 244–240), who eventually became head of the Academy between 268 and 264,⁶ challenged the doctrine, arguing that there could be an impression 'just like' a cataleptic one but which was false (the ἀπαραλλαξία objection); see *Luc.* 77 and section 5 of this introduction. Zeno, or so the story goes, responded by adding a third clause to the initial two-clause definition, which, however, did nothing to stop Academics from continuing the challenge. Zeno and later Stoics went on to make the cataleptic impression the basis for other central components of their thought (*Luc.* 19–39).

(ii) After Arcesilaus the sceptical stance and argument practices introduced by him may not have solidified immediately (see on *Luc.* 16 and appendix 2 on Numenius).

(iii) Chrysippus (born between 281 and 277; died at the age of 73 in the period 208–204)⁷ continued the debate with the Academics, possibly reinterpreted the Zenonian definition slightly, and devised further arguments to counter the Academic challenge. See again section 5. Overall, Chrysippus has a smaller presence in the extant parts of *Acad.* than might have been expected.

(iv) Carneades (born 214/13; died 129/28)⁸ reinvigorated and expanded the Academic challenge, which in turn prompted a response from younger, unnamed Stoics, notably the addition of a constraint on cataleptic impressions winning assent (Sextus, *M.* 7.253–7; see section 6.4). Crucially, drawing on Stoic theory, Carneades proposed the πιθανόν as an alternative to the cataleptic impression (see ibid. and on *Luc.* 32–6, 98–111). Diogenes of Babylon, head of the Stoa in the mid-second century BC, may have been a contributor to the debate, even though his fragments in the field of epistemology are concerned with other matters.⁹

(v) Antipater, who may have succeeded Diogenes as scholarch and who died in 129 BC,¹⁰ continued the engagement with Carneades, as is clear from *Luc.* 28–9 and 109. Antipater may have been one of the younger Stoics mentioned in (iv).

---

⁴ These features of the dialogue may in part be inherited from the sources used by Cicero, and when Cicero sat at the feet of Philo and Antiochus (sc. at different times), each will have strived to present their chosen stance as reasoned and warranted in itself.
⁵ On his dates, see Dorandi (1991a: 7–10) and the modification in Dorandi (1999: 32); Vezzoli (2016: 10); Gourinat (2018: 364).
⁶ See Dorandi (1999: 32).
⁷ See Dorandi (1999: 40).
⁸ See Dorandi (1994d: 225).
⁹ See Aubert-Baillot (2009); Guérard et al. (2018).
¹⁰ See Dorandi (1999: 41).

(vi) In the 90s BC, while still in the Academy, Antiochus adopted Stoic epistemology as one element within his Old Academic position; see on *Luc.* 69–71. This pitted him against his teacher Philo of Larissa, head of the Academy at the time. In *Acad.* speakers representing Antiochus (Hortensius, Lucullus; Varro) assume the role of the dogmatists/Stoics.

The inner-Academic debate arose amongst the pupils of Carneades, notably Clitomachus and Metrodorus, who were viewed or declared themselves as privileged interpreters of Carneades (see on *Luc.* 78, 98, and 139), and was continued by the generation of Academics after them (cf. phase vi above) at least until the end of the Academy as a functioning school—and then amongst the Roman speakers in *Acad.* Three positions are in evidence, but their precise distinguishing features are contentious, as is the exact status of one of the positions within the Academy. Each of the three, of which the first two are attested to have been formulated by Carneades as an ad hominem response to the Stoics, is advanced as the most consistent sceptical response to the Stoic theory and the claim that only it is able to account for human action inter alia (see section 4). They are:

(a) the Clitomachean position, so called because it represents Clitomachus' interpretation of Carneades' stance. It is crucially characterized by a commitment to universal suspension of judgement.[11] This is the position Cicero maintained throughout his life in first-person statements in his writings (see section 8). I also think that it was the position Philo of Larissa maintained until he conceived view (c) below (*pace* Brittain 2001: passim and 2006: xiv), as well as the overall position of the Academy prior to the formulation of view (c), and that Antiochus' (and Aenesidemus') departure from the Academy happened partly in response to the Clitomachean position. I further believe that the Clitomachean position evolved over time, accommodating many of the features ascribed to view (b) by others until it differed from view (b) primarily on what alternative to dogmatic belief it permitted.

(b) a position of mitigated scepticism, which abandons universal suspension of judgement and instead allows for self-aware assent (i.e. acceptance of certain impressions as true with the proviso that one might be mistaken). This position is clearly adopted by the younger Catulus in *Luc.* 148, and has been linked—less convincingly, I think—with 'Philo or Metrodorus' in *Luc.* 78. It has been claimed that it represented the official position of the Academy and of Philo in the period of *c.*100–87 BC and the reference point for hostile or dismissive statements about the Academics as quasi-dogmatists,[12] but in this commentary it is assumed that it represented a philosophical option which had some currency but was not endorsed by Philo, and that the attacks mentioned may equally have been directed at the Clitomachean position.

---

[11] The Clitomachean position has also been given other designations, e.g. 'radical scepticism'; I shall discuss these in section 4.

[12] All relevant texts are assembled, translated, and discussed in appendix 1.

(c) the position Philo advanced in the Roman Books, which appears to have claimed a form of κατάληψις for the Academics, albeit one which the Stoics would not have recognized and would instead have categorized as opinion (δόξα). It apparently operated the first two clauses of the Zenonian definition only and permitted assent as well.[13] This stance is only characterized in outline in *Acad.* (see on *Luc.* 12 and 18; *Ac.* 1.13) and dismissed by all sides, including—reportedly—Antiochus (*Luc.* 11). There is reason to believe that Philo only formulated this position after his arrival in Rome and that he did not immediately present it as his official view. It is likely that the Roman Books view led Antiochus to modify his account of the history of philosophy and that Varro's speech in *Ac.* 1 reflects a post-Roman Books version of it. I do not think that there is evidence that Philo, before he died in 84/3 BC,[14] reverted to position (a) after the perceived failure of the Roman Books,[15] or that he adopted yet another position.[16]

In *Acad.* it is of course Roman speakers who speak to the philosophical issues and the historical constructions which underpin them—a different set in both partially extant editions, with Cicero the only recurrent character, as an active *consularis* in the late 60s BC and as a politically sidelined elder statesman in the mid-40s respectively; see section 3. In the first edition Hortensius and Lucullus spoke for Antiochus, Catulus the son for the Academic position (b) above, and Cicero for the Academic position (a), while in the final edition Antiochus was represented by one speaker only, Varro, and the Academic side by Cicero only. However, already in the first edition, i.e. in *Luc.*, Lucullus can attack the Academy generally, without distinguishing clearly between positions (a) and (b), and Cicero can reply on behalf of the Academy generally; see esp. on *Luc.* 27–8, 40–4. How this 'conflation' of two positions manifests itself demands careful study and illuminates the very nature of position (a).

Attention also needs to be paid to who introduces certain pieces of information. It is for instance striking that it is the Antiochian Lucullus who furnishes some unique pieces of information on the *probabile* within the remains of *Acad.* (*Luc.* 32–6). Here one can glimpse an earlier discussion by an Academic speaker in the lost *Catulus*. Equally striking, but probably not to be explained in the same way, is that it is again Lucullus who surveys leading figures of the sceptical Academy in *Luc.* 17.

How the speakers invoke authorities is another interesting feature of the text, which in turn informs the status of *Acad.* as evidence for these authorities. Thus the character Cicero uses Arcesilaus as a philosophical model in passages which provide a fundamental characterization of position (a); see sections 7.5, 8, and *Luc.* 65–7. And while much or possibly all of the exposition on κατάληψις in Lucullus' speech (*Luc.* 19–39) is orthodox Stoic, Chrysippus is not there invoked, and the fact that he

---

[13] See Barnes (1997: 70–6); Brittain (2001: 154–8) and (2006: xiv and xxx–xxxi).
[14] See Fleischer (2017) and (2017b).
[15] *Pace* Glucker (1978) and (2004), who is led to his view by assumptions about the source which underlies Cicero's speech in *Luc.*; see section 9.3. See also Barnes (1997: 76–8).
[16] The Roman Books view has been characterized as a form of fallibilism by some, while others use the term to describe mitigated scepticism.

is invoked occasionally elsewhere obscures the degree to which he and his writings must have been the ultimate origin for large parts of the Stoic dogmatic sections.

In the introduction to the commentary I have tried to adopt a 'Cicero first' approach whenever possible,[17] since my purpose is of course to elucidate *Acad.* in the first instance. This distinguishes the commentary in its *intentio operis* from e.g. studies of particular Academic philosophers, including collections of fragments and testimonia, or of the history of the Academy. In many cases the 'Cicero first' approach raises a problem of method. While it is never true that writing a commentary involves taking a text which is perceived as a problem and explaining it with reference to other texts which are unproblematic (so that all they want is for parts of them to be gestured at by 'cf.'), in the case of *Acad.* most other texts to be drawn on are opaque, and problematic in their status, form, content, and intent, so that the task of explaining *Acad.* becomes one of creating a hopefully accessible account of the dynamic interrelationship of intertexts and target text from the perspective of *Acad.* Section 7.5 on Arcesilaus might serve as a particularly telling illustration of these challenges.

3. *Acad.* within the Ciceronian Corpus

In this section I propose to contextualize *Acad.* with the factual evidence concerning Cicero's literary activity in the 50s and 40s BC as well as with higher-level statements in his writings about the purpose of this activity.[18]

I shall not here discuss the details of the compositional and editorial history of *Acad.* (for which see section 9.1 on the relevant letters to Atticus). Nor shall I analyse here how Cicero's dialogues function pragmatically, i.e. by what means or to what extent Cicero accomplishes the stated aims of his literary activity which are the subject of the present section, as well as possibly additional ones not recoverable from first-person statements in the texts. To be sure, how Ciceronian dialogues demand to be read tells us something about Cicero's intentions including as an Academic sceptic creating such texts. Passages in the texts which appear to speak to these issues explicitly need to be measured against observations regarding the structure and stylization of the dialogues. In this book the pragmatics of *Acad.* as a dialogue are a running theme in the commentary. They are also covered in section 8, where I give a summary of my views on the matter.

In *Ac.* 1.11, having asked Varro why he had written nothing about philosophy when he had contributed to so many areas of knowledge, Cicero states that for him

---

[17] A subject where this is not easily possible is section 6, on the πιθανόν/*probabile*, given that our evidence from Sextus is much more extensive than that from Cicero, partly due to the loss of relevant passages of *Acad.*

[18] Discussions which centre on *Acad.* include Reid¹ pp. 20–8; Bringmann (1971: 111–37); Alleemudder (1979: 38–45); Griffin (1997: 1–14); Brittain (2006: xi–xii). Studies devoted to the whole corpus of Cicero's dialogues are Hirzel (1895: 457–552); Philippson (1939: 1104–92); Bringmann (1971); Görler (1974); Schmidt (1978–9); Steinmetz (1989). Gildenhard (2007) is devoted to *Tusc.* in the wider corpus, and Baraz (2012) is a study of the prefaces of the philosophical works.

philosophy had remained a private pursuit while he was still active as a politician and statesman, but that now (the dramatic date of *Ac.* 1 is the same as the date of composition) grief over his daughter's death, the desire to do something honourable, the wish to educate his fellow citizens, or the sheer absence of anything better to do have lead him to compose philosophical works.

The passage illustrates neatly some of the problems one faces in reconstructing Cicero's motivation for writing his dialogues. Four different reasons are mentioned, connected by *aut*—thus Cicero almost invites the interlocutor and the reader to select the most important (or convincing) one rather than identifying it himself. In context this vagueness about Cicero's purpose partly serves a dramatic function. It signals a certain weariness on Cicero's part, due to personal grief and political despondency, and it would also have been discourteous to Varro if he had suggested that he, Cicero, was pursuing an admirable cause to which he was unqualifiedly committed (and which Varro could pursue, too, but does not want to). Nonetheless, there is a general point here: in his published works, and up to a point also in his letters, Cicero often talks about his motivations, but rarely in a way which can make the modern reader confident that a stable hierarchy of the historical Cicero's reasons can be drawn up. Unsurprisingly, it is easier to identify and describe justificatory themes and motifs in the texts than to reach beyond them to the author's intention.[19] Moreover, depending on context and date of composition, Cicero's own accounts of his literary activity may vary. In *Ac.* 1.11 Cicero chooses to present his own philosophical writing as a recent development,[20] whereas in the preface to *Div.* 2, the famous review of Cicero's philosophical work to date written after Caesar's death, the two substantial dialogues written between 55 and 51 BC (*De orat.*; *Rep.*) are included among the philosophical works (as well more recent works), albeit at one remove.[21]

The works of the 50s influence the way modern scholars look at the works of the following decade. *De orat.* and especially *Rep.* were overtly concerned with political subjects and thus can straightforwardly be read as intended to be beneficial to Cicero's fellow Romans.[22] So when Cicero repeats in the works of the 40s that it is his

---

[19] Wiseman (2009: 128) notes that both Cicero and Varro actually turned to historical writing after the Ides of March. And Cicero returned to the political stage when the opportunity arose.

[20] The point is specifically about writing: in *N.D.* 1.6 Cicero rejects the claim that he was a new convert to philosophy, citing his personal contact with philosophers; cf. *Brut.* 306, 309, 315.

[21] Discussions of the 'catalogue' in *Div.* 2 *init.* include Fox (2007: 218–20); Baraz (2012: 188–94); Schofield (2012c).

[22] Cf. the end of the preface of *Rep.* 1 (§12), *Q.fr.* 3.5.1 (= SB 25; *sermo autem in nouem et dies et libros distributus de optimo statu ciuitatis et de optimo ciue*, 'The conversation, distributed over nine days and nine books, was concerned with the ideal constitution and the ideal citizen') from end of October or beginning of November of 54 BC, and *Fam.* 9.2.5 (= SB 177; to Varro, written shortly after 20 April 46, before Cicero embarked on his major philosophical works): *Sed haec tu melius, modo nobis stet illud: una uiuere in studiis nostris, a quibus antea delectationem modo petebamus, nunc uero etiam salutem; non deesse, si quis adhibere uolet, non modo ut architectos, uerum etiam ut fabros, ad aedificandam rem publicam, et potius libenter accurrere; si nemo utetur opera, tamen et scribere et legere* πολιτείας *et, si minus in curia atque in foro, at in litteris et libris, ut doctissimi ueteres fecerunt, gnauare* [see Hunt 1981: 219; *nauare s, grauare* MVDH] *rem publicam et de moribus ac legibus quaerere*, 'But you will judge better than me. Let us just establish the following: to live together in our literary studies, from which we used to seek pleasure and now seek salvation; not to decline if anybody cares to call us in as architects or even as workmen to help build a commonwealth, but rather to apply ourselves to the task readily. If nobody requires our help, we must still read and write "Republics". Like the most learned men of the past used to, we must serve the

desire to benefit the citizens of Rome, without ever clarifying in the prefaces of the dialogues what precisely this benefit should consist in, the door is opened for a political interpretation of the *philosophica* (see p. xxxvi). One feature of the prefaces of the works of the 50s is that, although they were written at a time when Cicero was largely sidelined politically and restricted in his activities as an advocate, they present the dialogues as the product of an *otium* which Cicero struggles to secure given the enormous demands of his public career.[23] The works of the 40s, by contrast, are overtly written during an *otium* enforced by dicatorship, when the question of whether it is honourable to pursue projects which do not directly advance the business of the *negotium* has become marginal. This is one reason why different justificatory concerns come to the fore in the later group.

Let us recall the chronological sequence of some of Cicero's planned and actually executed works under the dictatorship:[24]

46 BC

- [Cicero's exchange of letters with Varro began in late 47 or early 46 with *Fam.* 9.1 and ended in the second half of June 46 with 9.6.]
- *Brutus*: composed between January and April.
- *Paradoxa Stoicorum*: beginning of April. *De optimo genere oratorum*: composed in the spring.
- *Cato* (which prompted Caesar's *Anticato*): composed in the summer.
- *Orator*: soon after the *Cato*.
- *Pro Marcello* (composed around mid-October, delivered in September).
- *Pro Ligario* (November).

45 BC

- [some scholars date the *uolumen prooemiorum* to January or February,[25] but there is no solid evidence to support this early date, and we have no independent grounds for thinking that Cicero's plans for a series of dialogues were sufficiently advanced at the very beginning of 45 BC for him to draw up the *uolumen* then. The *uolumen* is better placed right after the decision to move away from the initial cast of speakers featuring in *Hort.*, *Catul.*, and *Luc.* The attractive idea (see below) that the *uolumen* was not a file of disparate texts but an attempt to pursue the themes of self-justification and of the difficulty of writing

---

state in our libraries, if we cannot in Senate House and Forum, and enquire into customs and laws'. Against this background it is also readily understandable that *De orat.* and *Rep.* (as well as *Leg.*), unlike those of the 40s, offer explanations for their existence cast in terms of the *otium/negotium* distinction (Schmidt 1978–9: 120 even sees a 'lack of apologia' in the prefaces of the works in question). Gildenhard (2007: 45–63) offers a sequential reading of the prefaces from *De orat.* to *Fin.*

[23] See Gildenhard (2007: 51 n. 184) for scholarship on whether the claim is credible.
[24] Cf. Steinmetz (1990: 142–3) for a similar table; Marinone (2004²), who lists relevant bibliography for the dating of each work.
[25] See Marinone (2004²: 213).

- philosophy in Latin across a number of prefaces would seem to require the opening-up of Cicero's project which arises from the replacement of the original speakers.] See on t. 20 (Cic., *Att.* 16.6.4 = SB 414).
- [mid-February: Tullia dies].
- around 7–11 March:[26] *consolatio* (to himself) completed. *Hortensius* probably completed in the course of March, but some assume completion in February prior to Tullia's death.[27]
- 13 May: *Catulus* and *Lucullus* completed (*Att.* 12.44.4 = SB 285 = T12).
- 20 May: συμβουλευτικόν (a political letter) to Caesar completed in draft; work begins on the second, intermediate version of *Acad.*
- 28 May: συμβουλευτικόν aborted; mentions plan of a σύλλογος πολιτικός (*dialogus more Dicaearchi*) (*Att.* 13.30.2 = SB 303), probably not completed.
- 29 May: *Fin.* 1 completed in draft (*Att.* 13.32.3 = SB 305 = T15).
- 24 June: works begins on the final version of *Acad.* (*Att.* 13.13.1–2 = SB 321 = T19).
- 30 June: final version of *Acad.* completed; *Fin.* 1–5 completed (*Att.* 13.21a.1 = SB 327 = T24).
- August: *Laudatio Porciae* completed (*Att.* 13.37.3 = SB 346; *Att.* 13.48.2 = SB 345).[28] *Tusc.* 1–5 in progress (already on Cicero's mind when he worked on the first edition of *Acad.*, cf. *Luc.* 135; completed after *Fin.* but before *N.D.*, probably end of July/August); dialogue on natural philosophy, incorporating *Tim.*, in progress (after the final version of *Acad.* and *Fin.*, before *N.D.*, presumably autumn 45), see below, p. xxxii.
- November: *Pro rege Deiotaro. N.D.* 1–3 (completed probably near the end of 45; work on it first attested in August).[29]

44 BC

- *Cato maior* (probably early 44, certainly before Caesar's assassination).[30] *Div.* in progress before Caesar's death; preface to Book 2 composed after his death.[31]
- 15 March: Caesar assassinated.
- since March: Ἡρακλείδειον, a dialogue in justification of Caesar's assassins; not completed.[32] Thus Cicero attempted a return to political subjects when the opportunity seemed to arise.
- June: *Fat.* completed (presupposes the situation after the Ides of March).[33]
- 27 June: work on *De gloria* begins.
- 11 July: first version of *De gloria* completed.
- 17 July: *De gloria* 1–2 sent to Atticus.
- 20–8 July: *Topica* composed during the journey to Regium.

[26] See Marinone (2004^2: 213–14).
[27] On the Hortensius, see section 9.5.
[28] See Marinone (2004^2: 215).
[29] See Dyck (2003: 2–3).
[30] See Powell (1988: 1).
[31] See Wardle (2006: 37–43).
[32] See Marinone (2004^2: 237).
[33] See Sharples (1991: 5–6).

The first apparent reference to a plan to write philosophical works is to be found in *Or.* 148, where Cicero announces works on *grauiora et maiora* than are contained in *Or.* itself.³⁴ In addition, Bringmann (1971: 88–9) has argued for a preoccupation with the themes of *Acad.* in *Or.* 237, where Cicero professes that he follows the *ueri simile* and is free to change his mind on the subject he has been discussing, but Griffin (1997) has observed that in its context the passage does not gratuitously insert an issue Cicero happens to be thinking about but serves a very specific purpose in Cicero's conclusion.³⁵ It is not possible for us to tell how developed a plan is hinted at in *Or.* 148, but the fact that the projected work (or works) in question are placed above the rhetorical writings shows that Cicero is at least clear about the scale of his ambition. It is a stereotype that arguments from silence are never compelling, but the exchange of letters with Varro in the first half of 46 would have been a good opportunity to mention plans for a cycle of philosophical works if such a plan had already taken firm shape then, and when Cicero appears to come close to talking about future plans in these letters, he is rather vague.³⁶

There are no letters for the period from the end of November 46 to 6 March 45 during which Cicero wrote the *Hortensius*. The *Hortensius*, *Catulus*, and *Lucullus* feature the same set of speakers in all three dialogues, which are also connected by their setting (*Hort.* takes place at Lucullus' villa at Tusculum, *Catul.* at Catulus' villa at Cumae, *Luc.* at Hortensius' villa at Bauli). While this does not prove that the three dialogues were conceived as a unity,³⁷ such an assumption is plausible. The extant

---

³⁴ On Cic., *Or.* 148 (= T0) see section 9.1; Reid¹ p. 29 n. 6 overstates the import of the passage when he says that the passage 'makes it probable that [*Acad.*] was begun in 46'. See also Steinmetz (1990: 146); Goerler (1994: 1019–20). Dyck (2004: 213) has an interesting discussion of a forward reference (*mox uidero*) in *Leg.* 1.54 which appears to be not intended to be specific.

³⁵ Griffin (1997: 2): 'It is important to remember, however, that Cicero was trying there to be tactful to Brutus, whose views on oratory he knew he had just been contradicting, and that he therefore had every reason to emphasize how tentative they were.' Prima facie similar statements in the philosophical works which are not in the same way explicable with reference to living persons are discussed in section 8.

³⁶ See *Fam.* 9.2.4–5 (= SB 177, dated shortly after 20 April 46; quoted above, n. 22), where Cicero suggests (§5) that, if nobody calls on Varro and him to get involved actively, they can continue to 'read and write "Republics"... and enquire into customs and laws'. It seems unlikely that Cicero would have characterized his literary activity in these terms if the philosophical writings were already firmly planned. See also Rösch-Binde (1998: 139–40); Baraz (2012: 84–6). The *Brutus*, a dialogue written earlier in 46 BC, offers a historical survey of Roman orators with Cicero as the culminating point (and interlocutor, resulting in a first-person narrative over long stretches). The survey itself is not agenda-free: it does not just end with himself, but places Cicero's position of moderate Asianism against a history which itself shows the tension of a more restrained approach to oratory (what one might call Atticist tendencies) and a fuller style (Asianist tendencies). Where might Cicero have encountered a historical survey coupled with a self-justification in dialogue form? Possibly in Antiochus' *Sosus*. The title suggests that the *Sosus* was a dialogue, and the context in which Antiochus wrote it suggests that it advanced a historical claim about the Academic tradition as well as said something on the doctrines which Antiochus himself endorsed (which were Stoic in the field of epistemology, Old Academic with a Stoic influence in the field of physics, and a complex conglomerate in the field of ethics). There is no evidence suggesting that Antiochus was himself a character in the dialogue, but the position which Antiochus needed to defend against Philo was that there is a continuous line of development from Plato through the Old Academics to the Stoics, and that he resurrected that tradition after the aberration of the sceptical Academics (Arcesilaus to Philo). It is thus conceivable that through its overall concept the *Brutus* provides early indirect evidence for Cicero's return to one eventual source of *Acad.*

³⁷ In *Fin.* 1.2 Cicero says that the positive response to the *Hortensius* made him pursue philosophical writing further. This would of course be compatible with having a plan for further works at the time of writing *Hort.*, to be actioned if appropriate and possible, and it could also be a version of the familiar

fragments of *Hort.* do not contain clear forward references to *Catul.* and *Luc.* (of the kind which would demonstrate that the three dialogues were conceived as a set), but frg. 107 Grilli = 91 Straume-Zimmermann and 51 G. = 92 S.-Z. of *Hort.* suggest that the discussion was detailed enough to introduce not just Academic scepticism generally but the Clitomachean position, and in *N.D.* 1.11 Cicero presents *Acad.* as offering a justification of his personal stance.[38] In the *Catulus*, Hortensius, who was hostile to philosophy in *Hort.* and needed to be converted by Cicero, appears to have introduced the material given to Varro in his speech in *Ac.* 1, or possibly a less developed version of it. This need not mean that he was cast as an Antiochian in *Catul.*, but suggests that his interest was stimulated sufficiently for him to present material on the subject (compare the less than total commitment of Lucullus to Antiochian thought expressed in *Luc.* 10). There was thus a degree of narrative progression and character development from *Hort.* to *Catul.* However, this unity was removed when Cicero decided to replace Hortensius, Lucullus, and Catullus as interlocutors.

Luc. 147, which is sometimes read as an announcement of further dialogues on ethics and physics, is in fact a meta-philosophical comment on the debate represented in *Luc.*; see the commentary ad loc. It thus offers no clue as to Cicero's further plans. The chronology of the dialogues suggests that *Fin.* 1 was being composed (see the table above) while Cicero finalized the first edition of *Acad.* In *Luc.* 135 Cicero's speech shows close correspondences with a passage in *Tusc.* 4, suggesting that Cicero was planning or composing that work, too, while writing *Luc.* Now *Tusc.* is formally sui generis amongst Cicero's late works, showing minimal indications of setting and adopting the older Academic (i.e. Arcesilaen) format of arguments against a thesis.[39] *Fin.* 1, set in 52 BC, is from the beginning closer in its setting to the final edition of *Acad.* (as well as the aborted intermediate version) than to *Catul.* and *Luc.*, in that contemporaries of Cicero (albeit deceased ones) debate with him rather than men of an earlier generation. The overall impression is that Cicero was experimenting with different formats while expanding the thematic range of his writings *pedetemptim progrediens*.

So rather than think in terms of an encylopaedia of philosophy, conceived as early as the summer of 46, announced in *Or.* 148 and then executed, in which *Acad.* deals with λογική, *Fin.* (as well as, according to some, *Tusc.*) with ethics, and *N.D.* as well as *Div.* with natural philosophy (i.e. physics), of which theology is a part, one should think in terms of a more serendipitous emergence of works, with only the triptych as a tightly organized core that was conceived at some point in the second half of 46. This would be compatible with interpreting the interconnections between the works in the finished cycle teleologically after the event. It is, however, notable that, on the several occasions when Cicero refers to *Acad.* in later works (*Tusc.* 2.4, *Tim.* 1, *N.D.* 1.11, *Div.* 2.1, *Off.* 2.8) or indeed when he expresses a desire to cover large areas

---

proem topos which presents a work as an attempt to meet a request or demand; see Goldberg (1999: 224–6).

[38] On *Hort.*, see section 9.5.

[39] *Tusc.* is clearly identified as an Academic work (as opposed to a dogmatic one) e.g. in 4.7, *pace* Griffin (1997: 6).

of philosophy (*N.D.* 1.9; see below), he does not present the work's purpose as an introduction to epistemology.[40]

The works created in the second half of 45 BC are in line with this. The *Timaeus* mentions (§1) only *Acad.* as a work in which Cicero has written *contra physicos*, which is one reason for placing it earlier than *N.D.* Another reason is that *N.D.* 2.47 repeat verbatim a snippet from the translation of Plato's *Tim.* 33a–b, which is best explained by assuming that the translation was already in existence when *N.D.* was composed.[41] Now Cicero's *Timaeus* is in fact not just a translation, but part of an aborted and rather experimental dialogue on natural philosophy:[42] the setting was Cilicia in 51 BC (Cicero was on his way to take up his provincial governorship), and the interlocutors appear to be the Pythagorean Nigidius Figulus and the Peripatetic philosopher Cratippus.[43] *Fin.* 5 is famously the only extant Ciceronian dialogue not set in Italy (but in Athens), and the work to which the translation of *Tim.* belongs would have moved further afield and would uniquely have involved a Greek philosopher as speaker.[44] The format, combining dialogue with a translation, would clearly have been highly unusual, too.[45] However, Cicero appears not to have completed the work, and it is absent from the catalogue of his writings in the preface in *Div.* 2. The ensemble *N.D.*, *Div.*, and *Fat.* is more likely to be an alternative project and a new departure than what remains of a larger scheme which had the *Timaeus* at its centre. The latter was not the only dialogue project Cicero abandoned during this period; see the list above.

The preface of *N.D.* 1 references *Acad.* as a text where Cicero has explained and justified his allegiance to the sceptical Academy (§11; cf. *Tusc.* 2.4); in §6 Cicero had commented on some reader's bemusement that he subscribes to a philosophy which 'robs people of the light' and is in fact defunct. The context in which *Acad.* is mentioned is thus quite specific, and the question of how the dialogue might sit with Cicero's other works does not come into view. *N.D.* 1.9 mentions a desire to cover philosophy in its totality as one motivating factor, without, however, presenting *Acad.* as the part of that enterprise devoted to logic.[46]

---

[40] See also Schofield (2012c: 77).
[41] See Ax (1938: vi–vii); Sedley (2013: 192–3).
[42] See Gawlick and Görler (1994: 1052).
[43] Linderski (1995a: 49) rejects the possibility that Cratippus might have been cast as an actual participant in the discussion. With the setting of *Tim.* two further considerations with bearings on chronology emerge. Nigidius Figulus died in 45 BC; although we cannot pinpoint the time, his recent death may have been one reason for making him an interlocutor. And if *Tusc.* 5.10 is an announcement of the dialogue featuring the translation of *Tim.*, this would be consistent with the date of publication usually assumed for *Tusc.*: *Nec uero Pythagoras nominis solum inuentor, sed rerum etiam ipsarum amplificator fuit. Qui cum post hunc Phliasium sermonem in Italiam uenisset, exornauit eam Graeciam, quae magna dicta est, et priuatim et publice praestantissumis et institutis et artibus. Cuius de disciplina aliud tempus fuerit fortasse dicendi*, 'Nor was Pythagoras simply the inventor of the name, but he expanded the actual content of philosophy as well. After his arrival in Italy, following this conversation at Phlius, he enriched the private and public life of the area known as Magna Graecia with the most excellent institutions and arts—perhaps there will be another time to talk about his doctrines.'
[44] It is conceivable that the work was projected to have more than one book, that the interlocutors mentioned in the preface are only those of e.g. the first book, and that a Stoic was to join the debate later.
[45] There are some reasons for thinking that Antiochus anticipated Middle Platonism in one important respect, viz. by promoting a close engagement with Platonic texts; see e.g. on *Ac.* 1.30–2.
[46] Cf. Gawlick and Görler (1994: 1020): 'In "De natura deorum" I 9 (Anfang März 44) wird deutlicher, dass eine umfassende systematische Darstellung geplant ist.'

In the preface of *Div.* 2, most probably composed—unlike the bulk of *Div.*—soon after Caesar's death,[47] Cicero reviews his philosophical works written up to that point (*Fat.* is only announced, and none of the other later works—*De gloria*, *Topica*, *Laelius*, and *Off.*—is mentioned as projected). While *Ac.* 1.11 offered four possible reasons for Cicero's philosophical writing without firmly committing to one, Cicero now singles out the desire to continue his public service. It is difficult to avoid the impression that this sense of purpose after the event is connected to the fact that Caesar's assassination has once more opened up the vague prospect of actual political engagement. The *Hortensius* is named first, as an invitation to engage in the study of philosophy. *Acad.* is presented as an advertisement of an approach to philosophy which is least arrogant and most consistent. This dovetails with remarks in *Acad.* itself that the dogmatist's position routinely overreaches in its claims (*Luc.* 114, 126), as well as with Varro's remark in *Ac.* 1 that philosophy, even though he does not write on the subject in Latin, helps him achieve *constantia uitae* (*Ac.* 1.7). The emphasis is thus on what philosophy, and Academic scepticism in particular, can do for those who adopt it; there is no indication that *Acad.* is intended to cover a part of philosophy. *Fin.* is introduced as addressing the foundation of philosophy, i.e. the question of what counts as good and evil, and as setting out the arguments for and against the different views (leaving the audience to take an informed decision). *Tusc.* is said to be devoted to questions which are central to the happy life, and Cicero provides a detailed table of contents, stressing the importance of Book 5, which, as he says, teaches (*docet*) that virtue is sufficient for happiness.[48] It is at this point that we might expect a reference to the *Timaeus*, but no such reference is forthcoming, and instead Cicero introduces *N.D.* as devoted to the subject of the title, *Div.* as a clarification of and expansion on *N.D.*, and the projected *Fat.* as what is needed to cover 'that entire issue' (*toti huic quaestioni*). This sounds deliberately vague, but is in any event not a natural way of saying that the three works together cover physics. Cicero then makes a point of moving on to philosophical works in a wider, looser sense, but he does not simply add the three great dialogues of the 50s (*Leg.* is in fact not mentioned at all, probably because it was unpublished);[49] rather, his criterion for inclusion seems to be whether the work in question can be plausibly claimed to be of use to his fellow citizens as per his initial remark in 2.1. He wants *Rep.* to be seen as a philosophical work, given that governance is a subject eminently fit for philosophical discussion, 'as Plato, Aristotle, Theophrastus, and the whole Peripatetic school thought'. He also hopes the *De consolatione* will be of use to others, and adds the *De senectute* to the list. Then, somewhat surprisingly, he names a, for all we know, smaller work, the *Cato*, 'because it is by philosophy that a man becomes virtuous and strong'; it prompted a written response from Caesar, which may be one reason for its inclusion.[50] From here he moves to rhetorical works (*De orat.*, *Brut.*, *Or.*), which

---

[47] See Wardle (2006: 37–43).
[48] In a context where the Academic format of *Acad.* and *Fin.* is stressed, the remark about 'teaching' is best taken as a comment on the format of *Tusc.* rather than as a suggestion that it is a work of dogmatic philosophy, which *Tusc.* does not purport to be; cf. 4.7.
[49] See Dyck (2004: 10).
[50] On the *Anticato*, see *Top.* 64; Tschiedel (1981).

should count towards the project on the grounds that rhetoric and philosophy are conjoined according to Aristotle and Theophrastus.

In *Div.* 2 Cicero would have had ample opportunity to highlight to what extent he has achieved coverage of the different parts of philosophy. Yet even here where he attempts to impose order on his work with hindsight, achieving coverage is not a primary consideration, and when Cicero comes close to making such a claim for part of the project, it is not entirely credible.[51]

Cicero's aspiration to benefit his fellow citizens by writing philosophy in Latin raises a number of questions.[52] While it seems entirely appropriate to the political works of the 50s, its restatement in the works of the 40s requires more explanation, especially because the most obviously programmatic passages on the subject do not provide any detail.

Two texts from the 40s (*Tusc.* 1.1–8 and 4.1–7) and one from the 50s (*Rep.* 1.1–23) are germane to the question, because in them Cicero turns cultural historian and tells three different but related stories about the conditions under which Greek science and philosophy were received at Rome. In the first two, the subject of writing philosophy is addressed, in interestingly different ways. *Tusc.* 1.1–8 combines the notions that philosophy is the art of living well (1.1) and that there is a cultural competition between Greece and Rome to engage in and win, concerned with the production of literary artefacts inter alia; the first notion makes attending to philosophical doctrine desirable and beneficial, the second makes writing about it in Latin desirable, too. The work is marked as a return to writing philosophy (linked to the *uia recta uiuendi*) from the beginning. It is acknowledged that the subject can be pursued in Greek, but anything Greek the Romans put their mind to is improved, either by being added to or by being made better. For the Romans were better at everything, including with respect to their moral qualities, except in the field of *litterae* where they chose not to compete for a long time (§2). Poetry arrived late, but since it was appropriated, the best Roman poetry has been a match for the best Greek efforts (§3). Other disciplines where Romans chose not to compete were painting, music, and geometry (§§4–5a), but rhetoric they embraced, and thus Roman oratory excels. Philosophy has not been properly adopted, and here Cicero needs to make amends (§5b), all the more actively given that there are now sub-standard Epicurean

---

[51] Cf. Schofield (2012c: 83): 'Cicero's claim that he will have done full justice to the whole theological issue when he completes the trilogy he has in mind sounds as though he may be meaning to imply that he will thereby have covered the whole of philosophy in the sequence of writings beginning with the *Academic Books* (and prefaced by *Hortensius*), an encyclopaedic ambition he does occasionally profess (e.g. *N.D.* 1.9, cf. *Div.* 2.4). On the other hand, there is more to physics than theology and its physical and cosmological underpinnings. And the preface to *On the Nature of the Gods* provides a strong clue as to what especially tempted him to write on theology. It is an issue, he says, on which there are a great number of different views, and one which prompts a lot of debate—with Carneades in particular having held forth provocatively and at length on the subject (*N.D.* 1.1–5): in short, the ideal topic for the systematically opposed arguments of an Academic dialogue.'

[52] Cf. *Rep.* 1.33; *Luc.* 6; *Ac.* 1.11; *Tusc.* 1.5; *Fin.* 1.10; *Div.* 2.1 and 2.4; see also Gawlick and Görler (1994: 1018). Whether the historical Cicero actually thought his writings would benefit other Romans is not the question which I seek to answer here; cf. Zetzel (2016: 56): 'One doubts whether even he [i.e. Cicero] thought that his writings actually made either government or individual life better or more tolerable.' Rather, I shall examine his various statements for coherence and mutual illumination.

writers (§6). Aristotle is Cicero's model, and the old Socratic technique of arguing against a thesis is his format (§§7–8).

Some of these themes reappear in a different way in *Tusc.* 4. Cicero expresses admiration for the genius of his ancestors, especially in a field they adopted late, i.e. philosophy. But actually, because of the Pythagorean tradition in Rome, even philosophy was already an early presence in Roman culture (§§1–3a). King Numa was deemed to be a scholar of Pythagoras. There is then a restatement of the notion that the Romans excelled in any field as soon as they tried their hand at it (§§3b–5a). While the study of wisdom was of long standing, there were no *sapientes* in the technical sense before the age of Scipio and Laelius. Carneades and Diogenes of Babylon must have been chosen as ambassadors in 155 BC because familiarity with and interest in philosophy on the part of the Romans was (rightly) assumed. Yet the Roman *sapientes* promoted philosophy, dubbed *bene uiuendi disciplina*, through their life rather than their writings. Consequently, there are no writings on Academic philosophy (unusually broadly construed as including the Old Academy, the Peripatetics, the Stoa, and the sceptical Academy). This created a cultural vacuum, which Roman writers on Epicurean philosophy filled. They gave rise to many followers (sc. who also wrote about the subject in Latin) so that Epicureanism with its false appeal is now a threat. Cicero now writes philosophy to diffuse this threat (§§5b–7a). Here it clearly suits him not to pretend that he is the first to write philosophy in Latin: the allure of Epicureanism needs to be countered. In §7b Cicero expresses his own commitment to Academic scepticism, which is evidently compatible with presenting the *bene uiuendi disciplina* for the benefit of Romans.

In *Rep.* 1 the guiding questions are what the best state is and what qualities the best leading man must possess. Philosophers (or at least respectable ones) are said to teach virtue in their classrooms, but that is not enough. Virtue needs to be enacted to be good. And just as the Romans are able to turn abstract astronomical knowledge into a battle-winning military advantage, because they wield military power, so only Romans can enact virtue, because only they are required and able to perform moral actions on a grand scale. Philosophical expertise is uncomplicatedly linked to being virtuous, but the connection is not problematized further.[53]

Even if philosophy is linked to the *recta uiuendi uia*, this still leaves a range of options for how exactly philosophy might benefit Cicero's fellow Romans.[54] One possibility would be that philosophical theory helps Romans to rationalize their traditional behaviour, thus allowing them to become more or more reflectively Roman as it were; cf. e.g. *Luc.* 146 where Cicero suggests that Academic scepticism is natural in the sense that it formalizes and expresses inclinations which Romans had all along. One of the attractions of this kind of interpretation would be that it could be extended to *N.D.* and *Div.*,[55] and beyond this to moral behaviour and works like *Fin.*

---

[53] *Rep.* is not presented as a work of philosophy in the strong sense (but it will be with hindsight in *Div.* 2). And without the idea of cultural competition which looms large in *Tusc.*—in *Rep.* Rome's position is one of towering strength—the need to *write* philosophy (rather than devote time to it) is less likely to come into view.

[54] Only in *Off.* 1.1–3 the suggestion seems to be that the benefit *consists* in Cicero's excelling in the cultural competition with the Greeks and winning as it were on the Romans' behalf; cf. Schofield (2012c: 75). Cultural competition and usefulness feature as separate points in e.g. *Fin.* 1.1–12.

[55] Thus the character Cotta in *N.D.* conveys not just why a commitment to Academic scepticism is compatible with his being a *pontifex*, but why it makes him a good *pontifex*; see Wynne (2014).

and *Tusc*. Perhaps something like this is also meant by Varro when he says in *Ac.* 1.7 that he avails himself of the study of philosophy for the sake of *constantia uitae*. Ethical theory, on such a reading, would help Cicero's readers to understand themselves better and e.g. make decisions in a more accountable way, rather than improve them morally directly.[56] However, there are also ways in which Cicero may have regarded his fellow citizens as in need of philosophical help to change their ways while assuming they are at their core well disposed. Given the wider historical context, one wonders if Cicero wanted to imply at least in certain places that the dictatorship could be interpreted as an objectionable form of government imposed on the Roman people without their doing. In *Marc.* 13, broadly of the same period (see above), the civil war is described in terms reminiscent of Greek tragedy, almost as a curse which has affected the Roman people rather than something they brought upon themselves through moral failings of their own. Cicero might have been thinking (and was arguably thinking in *Tusc.*) of the trope of philosophy as therapy, not of ingrained flaws but of momentary disturbances.

Another attempt to conceptualize benefit bestowed looks to the political dialogues of the 50s, which include potentially useful general reflections as well as concrete proposals,[57] and proceeds to offer a political reading of the dialogues of the 40s. On a very general level, a version of this view is widely held; cf. e.g. Wiseman (1994: 89): 'There is no overt opposition, but the whole tone and ethos of the essays is a tacit reproach of the world of power politics.' A more specific thesis that the dialogues are a sustained critical engagement with Caesar's dictatorship has been defended by Strasburger (1990), whose argument turns on the biography of many of the interlocutors chosen by Cicero, on *exempla* employed, and on passages which are supposed to be veiled references to contemporary criticism of Caesar.[58] Independently but along similar lines, Lévy (1992: 633) has proposed the following reading specifically with respect to *Acad.*:

La condamnation du dogmatisme philosophique sera donc aussi pour Cicéron celle du régime césarien:

—le tyran et le dogmatique sont tous deux animés par la *temeritas*, qui, lorsqu'elle est envisagée d'un point de vue moral s'identifie à l'*audacia*. Parce qu'ils cherchent avant tout à se mettre en avant, à s'affirmer eux-mêmes, ils n'ont d'autre temps que le présent. La réflexion cicéronienne réhabilite au contraire la durée, la recherche peut-être infinie, mais confiante;

—le tyran et le dogmatique imposent leur vérité et n'ont aucun égard pour ceux qui rejettent ou critiquent celle-ci. Pour Cicéron, au contraire, le critère de la vérité

---

[56] Cf. *Fin.* 3.4 (1.3; 1.11–12). In *Tusc.* 1.2 Cicero explicitly says that Romans have always outdone Greeks with respect to their *mores*.

[57] See e.g. Atkins (2013).

[58] See also Wassmann (1996), who develops Strasburger's approach further. Cf. Baraz (2012: 96–103), whose view is crisply summarized on p. 101: 'Thus, the philosophical content of Cicero's work is identified as a source of critical qualities that the Roman state in its current condition lacks. The implied conclusion is that there exists a natural link between the practice of philosophy and a state that deserves praise and exhibits dignity.'

est le *consensus*, l'acceptation universelle et tout ce qui suscite un dissentiment relève, au mieux, du probable, du vraisemblable;

—le tyran et le dogmatique ont leur propre définition et leur propre hiérarchie des valeurs morales. A l'inverse, la démarche cicéronienne sera, non de bouleverser le système de valeurs du *mos maiorum*, mais de donner une expression philosophique de celui-ci et d'établir entre les deux domaines un échange fécond.[59]

Against this view, richly supported by Lévy, Griffin (1997: 12–13) has urged inter alia that *temeritas*, rash assent leading to (mere) opinion, associated with Caesar's desire for the *principatus* in *Off.* 1.26, is not an error (or, if habituated, a flaw) in the eyes of the Academics alone, but in those of the Stoics, too. So the mapping of, respectively, the tyrant and the Republican onto dogmatist and Academic with reference to this feature is problematic. Moreover, the Academic's use of *dissensio* among dogmatists issuing in suspension of judgement does not allow for the inference that universal agreement was the criterion; consistent aberration within a given domain is a possibility.

4. Academic Positions and Academic Arguments

Cicero's writings, especially *Acad.*, are our most important source for Academic scepticism.[60] The majority of them are dialogues, and a distinction can be drawn between the scepticism exhibited by Cicero in these writings (the man, the author who emerges from these writings, the narrator, or the character) on the one hand, and sceptical positions and modes of argument which feature in them on the other. This section is about the latter, while section 8 is devoted to the former. In addition and relatedly, one can of course ask what can be inferred from Cicero's writings about the philosophical positions of individuals other than Cicero.

Academic philosophy is characterized by a set of argumentative practices, notably arguing against a thesis and arguing on either side. In principle, a philosopher could adopt these practices consistently for various reasons, which include a flippant desire to be difficult, a policy of attempting to induce suspension of judgement in himself and/or others (which would itself require a motivation, cf. the notion that ἀταραξία can be found through ἐποχή, as the Pyrrhonists held),[61] a firmly held conviction that

---

[59] 'The condemnation of philosophical dogmatism will therefore also be for Cicero that of the Caesarean regime: the tyrant and the dogmatic are both animated by *temeritas*, which, when viewed from a moral point of view, is identified with *audacia*. Because they seek above all to advance themselves, to assert themselves, they have no other time than the present. By contrast, Ciceronian reflection rehabilitates spending time on issues, enquiry that is perhaps infinite, but confident; the tyrant and the dogmatist impose their truth and have no regard for those who reject or criticize it. For Cicero, by contrast, the criterion of truth is the consensus, universal acceptance, and anything that gives rise to dissent is, at best, *probabile*, *ueri simile*; the tyrant and the dogmatist have their own definition and their own hierarchy of moral values. Conversely, the Ciceronian approach will not be to upset the system of values, of the *mos maiorum*, but to give a philosophical expression to it and to establish a fruitful exchange between the two domains.'

[60] Other evidence is exemplified by the texts in appendices 1 and 2.

[61] On tranquillity as happiness achieved through ἐποχή, see e.g. Striker (1996e: 188–95).

nothing can be known (coupled with the inclination to demonstrate to dogmatic philosophers that this is so), a commitment to the search for the truth (however conceptualized), which requires submitting views to scrutiny, and didactic intent, e.g. to induce a reflective attitude in the audience. It is in any event reasonable to expect some rationale for confining one's philosophical activity to engaging in argument in this way, as the Academy did for a substantial period of time. Cicero, speaking in the framing parts of dialogues or as a character, cites the desire to find the truth when he explains what Academics do.[62] In *Ac.* 1.45 the Cicero character appears to ascribe meta-philosophical views to Arcesilaus, which motivate his argumentative practice.[63] Opponents of the Academy, in Cicero's works and elsewhere, tend to present Academics as negative dogmatists, obstructionists, or at least as intent on inducing ἐποχή.[64]

Argument on either side or against a thesis is often called 'dialectical', a designation by which scholars may mean a number of different things but arguably chiefly that the proponent of an argument is not committed and is not committing to it.[65] In this way Academics can freely argue for and against a position; this is how Carneades' speeches for and against justice (whether they are deemed historical or not) would appear to be understood by most interpreters.[66] The Academics are also often said to argue from the opponent's premisses, on which they themselves take no view, to a conclusion that is unacceptable to him.[67] In fact not many Academic arguments which are attested match this description. Rather, the Academic arguments in question tend to include at least one premiss which *ought* to carry weight with the opponent, because of the considerations the Academic is able to cite in support of it and which the opponent should feel unable to dismiss (the ἀπαραλλαξία thesis is a case in point).[68] Faced with a challenge by the dogmatist (e.g. the ἀπραξία charge; see section 6.1), the Academic can also build complex alternatives to the dogmatist's position, indeed can develop them in stages in response to dogmatic criticism. But the alternative 'doctrines' need not carry the Academic's endorsement in any way. Rather, they may be offered to the dogmatist as an alternative to his theory which ought to be equally compelling by the dogmatist's standards.[69] At times any philosopher can and will argue dialectically in this sense of course; what is distinctive of the Academics is that such argument, and other types of argument which can be called 'dialectical', is the essence of their philosophizing. This means inter alia that as philosophers they are fundamentally different from dogmatists in an important respect: one cannot say

---

[62] See on *Luc.* 7b–9a, where Cicero speaks as first-person narrator in the 'frame' before the dialogue starts.

[63] See ad loc. and section 7.5.

[64] See on *Luc.* 65, where the character Cicero explains his allegiance to the Academy. On the different question of what gives rise to suspension of judgement according to Academics and Pyrrhonists respectively, see Striker (1996b: 95–6).

[65] See Castagnoli (2019), who also notes that 'dialectic' and 'dialectical' were not so used by the Academics themselves. For the Academic policy of concealment, see on *Ac.* 1.44–6 and *Luc.* 60.

[66] See on *Luc.* 137.

[67] This interpretation was famously advanced by Couissin (1929) and has since been embraced by most interpreters with respect to Arcesilaus, Carneades, and Clitomachus. Görler (1994: 804, 816–19) is the only significant voice who rejects the possibility of ad hominem argument completely.

[68] See Castagnoli (2019: 194).

[69] Once accepted, they could themselves become the object of scrutiny.

of them that 'as Academics' they are firmly committed to certain tenets, e.g. that nothing can be known, in the way in which one can say of e.g. the Stoics that 'as Stoics' they are committed to the view that virtue is the end. However, many of the Academics' opponents, including in *Acad.*, treat the Academics as if they were in this respect like the dogmatists, i.e. as if they were negative dogmatists.[70]

Yet the record, notably *Acad.*, provides evidence for conceptualizations of attitudes the Academic might adopt to impressions and the corresponding propositions below the level of dogmatic endorsement. These conceptualizations may first have been formulated in a non-committal way but became characterizations of attitudes actually adopted by Academics at some point.[71] In this connection it is important to acknowledge that texts on the subject use Stoic conceptual categories as a frame of reference and description.[72] For the Stoics 'opinion' (δόξα) arises from assent given by the non-sage,[73] with the understanding that assent involves accepting impressions as true unqualifiedly. Clitomacheans try and avoid opinions in this sense, while mitigated sceptics allow for opinions only with the rider that the assent given is self-aware, i.e. given with an appreciation that the impression assented to may always be false (cf. *Luc.* 148). While Clitomacheans hold no opinions in the sense outlined, they do 'follow' impressions or—in Cicero—'approve' them.[74] This does not leave them with δόξαι in one of the senses indicated but does leave them with views or beliefs of a kind as we would call them.[75] The record preserves no noun for the kind of views or quasi-beliefs Clitomacheans permit themselves, in Greek or in Latin. The πιθανόν-scheme comes into this as a characterization of the impressions involved. Clitomacheans follow or approve (sc. some) πιθανά, while mitigated sceptics assent to some πιθανά qualifiedly.[76] For the evaluation of the evidence from Cicero and also for characterizations of the Academics preserved in other writers, much depends on the difference between the views Clitomacheans and mitigated sceptics permit themselves, as well as on how philosophers hostile to the Academics would choose (or not choose) to present this difference. It is one of the contentions of this commentary that the Clitomacheanism which we encounter in *Acad.* and in the works of Cicero

---

[70] On this point see Allen (1997: 219–23). From an outside perspective it remains of course reasonable to observe that Academic scepticism is generally characterized by the advancement of a thesis (that nothing can be known) as well as a logically independent recommendation (that one should suspend judgement on all matters), although the recommendation was qualified by some later Academics; so Striker (1996b: 92).

[71] See also Frede (1987b: 222). Statements about what the (Academic) sage does and does not do are open to a dialectical reading as well as to being read as an account of the kind of epistemic behaviour the Academic aspires to on his own terms (although in practice he may often fall short; see on *Luc.* 66). The question of chronology, i.e. of when exactly Academics began to adopt accounts of their cognitive attitudes as opposed to just formulate such accounts for the sake of the argument, is pursued in the commentary; see also below. Castagnoli (2019) doubts if there was ever any scope for Academic argument which did not require a degree of commitment from its proponents. Obdrzalek (2006: 271) argues that Carneades' own attitude towards e.g. the πιθανόν is largely irretrievable from the existing evidence, i.e. primarily Cicero and Sextus.

[72] See Couissin (1983), first published in 1929.
[73] See Meinwald (2005); and the commentary on *Ac.* 1.40-2.
[74] For the conceptualization of approval, see on *Luc.* 104.
[75] See also Striker (1996b: 114).
[76] See p. cvi on whether Clitomacheans and mitigated sceptics are likely to have operated different conceptions of the πιθανόν.

generally is rich in the sense that it accommodates many of the features associated with mitigated scepticism by others.⁷⁷

The Academic response to the Stoic doctrine of cataleptic impression is encapsulated in three interconnected arguments, which Brittain has dubbed the 'core Academic argument', 'the corollary argument', as well as an alternative to the corollary argument.⁷⁸ The core argument (esp. *Luc.* 40-4) goes back to Arcesilaus and is directed at the definition of the cataleptic impression (*Luc.* 77); cf. *Luc.* 78 *init.*, where the character Cicero states that the one point of contention remaining from the dispute of Zeno and Arcesilaus was whether the condition demanded by the third clause of Zeno's definition was ever met:

(1) There are true and false impressions.
(2) False impressions are not cataleptic.
(3) If there can be a false impression which is exactly like a true one, the true impression will not be cataleptic.
(4) For any true impression there can be one exactly like it which is false.
(5) There are no cataleptic impressions.

Premiss (1) is a Stoic view, premiss (2) corresponds to the first clause of Zeno's definition, (3) corresponds to the third clause of Zeno's definition, (4) is the Academic ἀπαραλλαξία thesis, which the Stoics had to disarm.

The 'corollary argument', which also goes back to Arcesilaus (see on *Luc.* 66-7), starts from the conclusion of the core argument and invokes the Stoic conception of rationality as embodied by the sage (here 6 is a Stoic tenet):

(5) There are no cataleptic impressions.
(6) The sage will not assent to non-cataleptic impressions.
(7) The sage will not assent to any impression.

The Stoic rejoinder is a version of the ἀπραξία argument, which posits that action presupposes assent, and that action is evidently possible, so either premiss 6 or premiss 5 must be false (and the Stoics regard 6 as true).⁷⁹ The three Academic

---

⁷⁷ The most detailed attempted reconstruction of mitigated scepticism so understood is offered by Brittain (2001), but see also Wynne (2014: 256-7 and passim), who also assembles predecessors for Brittain's analysis (p. 250 n. 8). The literature on Academic scepticism sometimes describes the evolution from rigid Clitomacheanism towards mitigated scepticism (and Philo's Roman Books view) in prima facie contradictory terms without there being material disagreement, i.e. as a hardening (of a stance which allows for views which progressively become more like Stoic 'opinions'), as well as a softening (of an originally total commitment to suspension of judgement). Brittain (2001) is followed e.g. by Thorsrud (2012) in claiming that Cicero was a radical sceptic in *Acad.* and a mitigated sceptic elsewhere, which, if true, would make much of the Ciceronian corpus evidence for mitigated scepticism. (Contrast, however, Brittain 2015.) Relatedly, not every reference to 'mitigated scepticism' in the literature presupposes that qualified assent is the key definer of it; rather, a willingness to hold a view, if only tentatively or qualifiedly in some sense, is enough for some to warrant use of the phrasal term.

⁷⁸ See Brittain (2006: xix-xxxi). For my interpretation of ἀπαραλλαξία as non-distinctness rather than indistinguishability, see section 5.6.

⁷⁹ A distinction between two types of ἀπραξία argument is drawn by Striker (1996b: 99-104, 109); further distinctions in Vogt (2010a). See also on *Luc.* 37-9.

positions which are in evidence in *Acad.* can be characterized with reference to the core and corollary arguments. The Clitomachean position rejects the connection between assent and action assumed by the Stoics and thus upholds the corollary argument; in so doing, it could and did look to Arcesilaus as a model.⁸⁰ Mitigated scepticism—see especially on *Luc.* 148—accepts the Stoic objection and jettisons (6) and therefore (7); however, this does not mean that the link between action and assent is accepted unqualifiedly, but only that a happy life (as lived by the sage) requires some δόξαι.⁸¹ In taking this position, mitigated sceptics are able to invoke an alternative to the corollary argument which Carneades had occasionally put forward (*Luc.* 59, 67, 78; cf. 112):⁸²

(5) There are no cataleptic impressions.
(8) The sage will sometimes assent.
(9) The sage will sometimes hold opinions.

The Roman Books view allows for assent and introduces an alternative conception of κατάληψις; this, however, does not amount to a straightforward rejection of the core argument, since the Philo of the Roman Books must have continued his opposition to the Stoic conception of κατάληψις. Further, Roman Books καταλήψεις are opinions as per the alternative to the corollary argument. Thus I assume that the Philo of the Roman Books used the core argument and the alternative to the corollary argument as part of an account of the origin of his position in the Academic tradition.⁸³

I shall now survey how the three different stances are fleshed out in the available evidence.

4.1 The Clitomachean Position

I believe that Cicero's position throughout his works was the Clitomachean one, a view for which I argue in detail in section 8 below.⁸⁴ Cicero's works are, in any event, our best source for Clitomacheanism, and the Clitomachean characters he has created (including e.g. Cicero in *Acad.*; Cotta in *N.D.*; the narrators in *Tusc.* and *Off.*) are given plenty of scope to explain themselves on their own terms in what seem to be personal statements—no non-Ciceronian text has Clitomacheans speak about their attitude at length.⁸⁵

---

⁸⁰ See on *Luc.* 65–7.
⁸¹ See Brittain (2006: xxv n. 42).
⁸² I believe that in *Luc.* 78, unlike in the other passages cited, the alternative to the corollary argument is used to reference Philo's Roman Books view as well as a similar one held by Metrodorus; see ad loc. and below.
⁸³ See on *Luc.* 78. Cf. Philod., *Index Acad.* col. xxvi.9, who reports that Metrodorus (see below), whose view is referenced alongside Philo's in *Luc.* 78, said everyone had misunderstood Carneades, which makes it likely that he (M.) constructed a Carneadean ancestry for his own view. Brittain (2006: xxx–xxxi) holds that Philo's Roman Books view involved a rejection of the Academic alternative to the corollary argument.
⁸⁴ Contrast e.g. Frede (1987b: 218): '[Cicero]...was a dogmatic sceptic'; Brittain (2001: 218): '...the sceptical history Cicero expounds in the *Academica* is not his settled view. His customary characterization of Academic philosophy and his own practice as an Academic is Philonian/Metrodorian [references]'; Thorsrud (2012).
⁸⁵ See appendix 1.

Academics had mounted arguments against dogmatic views since the time of Arcesilaus, but Carneades represented a new phase in the Academy's history, for a number of reasons. He had the whole body of developed Stoic doctrine to engage with, he advanced arguments against other schools' doctrines, his argumentative finesse and the power of his personality made him the most prominent philosopher of his time in Athens, and he innovated by introducing the πιθανόν. He did not write, like Arcesilaus, and so found both chroniclers and interpreters amongst his pupils, notably Clitomachus, Metrodorus, and Charmadas.[86] The inscrutability of Carneades' views is illustrated by the different interpretations his immediate pupils could place on his pronouncements, and indeed by the suggestion that he needed an interpreter at all. No statements by Carneades on the motivation for his argumentative activity or its aims are attested, nor are there other traces of a self-conception on which inferences could be based; contrast Arcesilaus' apparent invocation of Socrates (see section 7.3), and Cicero's repeated claim that Academics search for the truth.

Clitomachus is on record as saying that he took Carneades to argue ad hominem at least with respect to specific cases (*Luc.* 78) and that he did not know what his view on anything was (*Luc.* 139),[87] but he also relayed Carneadean pronouncements which are open to a non-dialectical reading and which are deployed by Cicero in accounts of his own attitude and habits as a Clitomachean. A case in point is the account of approval in *Luc.* 104–5, a section which is a rare translation from a work by Clitomachus and which purports to set out how Carneades explained that it was possible for the Academic to endorse certain impressions in a qualified way under general ἐποχή, with respect to impressions which could give rise to action and in philosophical exchanges. Carneades could consistently say that this was possible and how, as well as the Academic way, and yet never overtly give this kind of endorsement himself.

Beyond that, much depends on the assessment of the evidence from Cicero. If one regards it as distorted, as some do for different reasons (see below), one will of course be hesitant to infer from the Ciceronian texts what Clitomacheanism certainly in its late form looked like, but, or so I think, this would mean dismissing or partially dismissing our best source for Academic philosophical practice on the basis of either perceived inconsistencies which are actually capable of resolution or of non-Ciceronian evidence which bears comparatively little weight. If one takes Cicero to represent Clitomacheanism legitimately in his works, then it will have to be acknowledged that the 'search for the truth' as the motive for the Academic practice of arguing on either side (and indeed arguing against a thesis), as well as the notion that argument on either side might allow either the truth or the *probabile/ueri simile* to emerge, are

---

[86] For Clitomachus, see on *Luc.* 139; for Metrodorus, on *Luc.* 78; for Charmadas, see on *Luc.* 16. Consider also Cic., *Or.* 51 (= Carneades F4b Mette = Clitomachus T7a Mette): *Scitum est enim, quod Carneades noster dicere solebat, Clitomachum eadem dicere, Charmadam autem eodem etiam modo dicere*, 'For it is well known that Clitomachus said the same as Carneades used to, but Charmadas said it also in the same way', with Brittain (2014: 314).

[87] The Latin in *Luc.* 139 is *quamquam Clitomachus affirmabat numquam se intellegere potuisse quid Carneadi probaretur*. The verb *probare* is here most likely vague but can certainly not denote assent (see ad loc.). Striker (1996b: 97) indicates how someone who wanted to read Carneades as a mitigated sceptic would have to explain the evidence of *Luc.* 139: 'One might be inclined to discount Clitomachus' testimony as coming from a sceptic over-anxious to avoid all appearance of dogmatism.'

part of the Clitomachean position as it had evolved by the beginning of the first century BC.[88] If already Carneades had made remarks to that effect, this ought to have left a trace in the non-Ciceronian record, and given Clitomachus' reputation for being a faithful chronicler of Carneades' arguments, he may not have innovated himself. In any event the emergence of both features is hard to date precisely. The Academy had always been a tolerant school,[89] so that the change need not have emanated from the scholarch. Clitomachus' contemporary Metrodorus clearly felt entitled to offer an interpretation of the Carneadean stance which was quite different from Clitomachus'.[90] It is therefore not inconceivable that Clitomacheanism was already being developed further while Clitomachus was still scholarch, possibly even by Philo among others. Now there is reason to believe that Philo's Clitomachean credentials helped him secure the headship of the Academy.[91] The question is then whether the feature with reference to which Clitomacheanism and mitigated scepticism were distinguished was the assent/approval distinction alone (as I believe it was, at least by the early 80s BC; see below). If it was, then Philo may already have adopted essentially the stance which Cicero exhibits before he became scholarch. If it was not, then it is more likely that Philo formulated or adopted the developed Clitomachean position after he became head of the Academy.[92] The evidence, or so I think, does not allow us to decide between these options since non-Ciceronian texts do not speak to the issue directly; see appendix 1.[93] A relevant consideration is also that all one can say with certainty about mitigated scepticism is furnished by *Luc.* 148, i.e. we have no positive evidence on which practices and attitudes accreted around self-aware assent exclusively, in contradistinction to those which were associated with developed Clitomacheanism.

It has been claimed that a particular conception of the πιθανόν was distinctive of Clitomacheanism in non-dialectical contexts, viz. that the πιθανόν could be used and

---

[88] For the former notion, see above; for the latter one, see *Luc.* 7; *Tusc.* 1.8, 2.9; *Fat.* 1; cf. *De orat.* 1.158. Gawlick and Görler (1994: 1024–5) point to other Ciceronian texts which emphasize, apparently inconsistently, the Academic concealment of views. In *Sto. Rep.* Plutarch reports (1037b = *SVF* ii.128–9) that Chrysippus stated in his Περὶ τῆς τοῦ λόγου χρήσεως that λόγος should be deployed only in search of the truth and to impose order on one's findings, not with the opposite end in mind, although many did so use it. Plutarch (ibid.) comments that Chrysippus was thinking of those who suspend judgement, and continues, apparently in their defence (1037c): ἀλλ' ἐκεῖνοι μὲν οὐδέτερον καταλαμβάνοντες εἰς ἑκάτερον ἐπιχειροῦσιν, ὡς εἴ τι καταληπτόν ἐστιν οὕτως ἂν μόνως ἢ μάλιστα κατάληψιν ἑαυτῆς τὴν ἀλήθειαν παρέχουσαν. Although Plutarch was able to and did read Ciceronian works, the passage suggests that it is due to the accidents of survival that only Cicero (and texts informed by his works) mention the search for the truth as the Academics' rationale. On the passage see appendix 1; Opsomer (1998a: 187–90, 239), who compares *Tusc.* 2.9 and *Luc.* 7–9; Bénatouïl (2007: 86).

[89] See Tarrant (2020: 202–3).

[90] See on *Luc.* 78; Brittain (2001: 47–8).

[91] See Numenius frg. 28 Des Places (included in appendix 2).

[92] Brittain (2001: 53–8) dates the phase of mitigated scepticism in Philo's life to the same period, i.e. assumes that it began some time after he became scholarch and lasted until he formulated the Roman Books view. I give my main objections to this reading in the discussion of mitigated scepticism below.

[93] The Clitomachean work from which Cicero translates in §104 presented the distinction between assent and approval as Carneadean in all likelihood (cf. on *Luc.* 99). If this was correct, one would need to assume that the distinction and its conceptualization was first advanced dialectically by Carneades and then at some point adopted by Clitomachean Academics (or even already by Clitomachus himself). An innovator in our or somebody else's view might of course genuinely believe that he is acting in the spirit of Carneades.

was used for psychological self-reports, indicating the grounds for choices made, decisions and options taken, as opposed to the πιθανόν being taken as evidence for the truth. I do not regard this as plausible for several reasons. First, it is unlikely on general grounds that Clitomacheanism and mitigated scepticism could be as neatly separated as this scenario envisages; rather, even if one assumed the basic validity of the distinction, a gradual merging of one position into the other would be more credible. Second, as I will explain in section 6.1, the most detailed extant discussion of the Carneadean πιθανόν in *M.* 7 presents the phenomenal properties of persuasive impressions as functions of impressions' relationship with the external world. In ad hominem arguments this feature of the scheme would not enable an inference to the use of the πιθανόν as evidence by Clitomacheans, but as soon as the πιθανόν is invoked outside of ad hominem arguments, the interpretation of it as evidence for the truth will be unavoidable—unless one wanted to argue that *M.* 7.166–89 already reflected the outlook of mitigated scepticism (see section 4.2 below).[94] Note how my reading relates to the widely held view that Cicero presented himself, at least in certain works, as a mitigated sceptic: I suggest that Cicero's brand of Academic scepticism exhibits features usually assigned to mitigated scepticism, but accommodates them within his Clitomachean stance, which is crucially characterized by a commitment to universal suspension of judgement.

I further believe that Philo presented himself as a Clitomachean *in that sense* when Cicero started attending his lectures, on the grounds that this is the best explanation for why Cicero adopted Clitomacheanism in his works from *Inv.* onwards as well as created a second character, Cotta in *N.D.*, who purportedly heard Philo at about the same time and who is a Clitomachean, too;[95] see section 8.

4.2 Mitigated Scepticism

A position of mitigated scepticism as characterized above existed on the evidence of *Luc.* 148. It is the position which the younger Catulus adopted in *Catul.* and *Luc.*, following, so he is made to say, his father. It is positively characterized exclusively by a licence to give assent in a self-aware fashion (as well as an attendant story of origin for that permission). Beyond that it may have shared the features of rich Clitomacheanism, but the extant evidence does not provide confirmation on this point. It is unlikely that mitigated scepticism is a Ciceronian invention, although no non-Ciceronian text proves beyond doubt that the position existed outside the works of Cicero (see appendix 1).[96]

Other claims which have been made about mitigated scepticism, usually understood to be characterized by a licence to give qualified assent *as well as* many of the

---

[94] Thus Hirzel (1883: 174 n. 3); Burnyeat (unpublished); Brittain (2001: 95–6).
[95] Wynne (2018: 98) takes Philo to have been a mitigated sceptic (in the period before he advanced the view of the Roman Books), but not Cicero.
[96] Burnyeat (1997: 308) thinks that mitigated scepticism 'won', a statement which is not explained further; its meaning may be gleaned from the fact that in Burnyeat (unpublished) the account of the πιθανόν in Sext. *M.* 7 is taken to be composed from a mitigated point of view. Brittain (2001) takes mitigated scepticism to be the reference point of several of the texts assembled in appendix 1.

features which I would assign already to Clitomacheanism, seem less than compelling to me:

(i) that it was the position of Philo at one point: the main piece of evidence cited in support of this claim, *Luc.* 78, is open to other interpretations, and as argued in section 8, the narrative of how Cicero came to be an Academic, developed in the Ciceronian corpus, does not sit well with the notion that he was first exposed to Philo when the latter was a mitigated sceptic (or argued for the Roman Books view).

(ii) that, because it was Philo's view for a period while he was scholarch, mitigated scepticism was the official view of the Academy from about 100 BC into the early 80s. The evidence for the period is sparse, but it seems unlikely that the Academics' hostile critics would not have exploited two substantial changes of position on Philo's part with glee.[97] Abandoning the commitment to universal ἐποχή was a non-trivial change of position.

(iii) that there was a discernible group of people who advocated mitigated scepticism, and that they can be identified as the 'Philonian/Metrodorians': it is likely that there was a group of Academics who expressed a preference for this view, but the fact that the first edition of *Acad.* took some care to build up Catulus the father as the main authority for it rather suggests that one should think of a loose grouping of proponents without a discernible leader.[98] Catulus the father is said to have challenged Philo himself over the Roman Books, calling him a liar, probably for claiming that the epistemological view advanced in the Roman Books had been held by the Academy all along (*Luc.* 18; cf. *Luc.* 12). If *Philo* had been the source and inspiration for the elder Catulus' position of mitigated scepticism, then a charge of fickleness rather than of mendacity would have made more sense.[99] *Luc.* 78, which is the only potential piece of evidence for the second claim, is better read as stating that Philo and Metrodorus, while holding different views, converged at one time on one narrow point, viz. the idea that Carneades advocated assent under certain circumstances. I argue further at *Luc.* 78 that the views in question were most likely Philo's Roman Books view and a position which was similar in outline and formulated by Metrodorus.[100] *Luc.* 148, on my reading, is also concerned with the possibility of assent, but speaks to a different position than those referenced in *Luc.* 78.

---

[97] A point also made by Glucker (2004: 130–1).

[98] In *Luc.* 59 Lucullus states that *nonnulli* promote this stance. Would one expect Lucullus to have named Philo if he had been one of the proponents of this view? Perhaps it is too much to ask of Cicero the author to allow an Antiochian character to deliver a significant blow against Cicero the character, by pointing out that the latter occupied a position which was at variance with the one Philo adopted before he unveiled the Roman Books. Glucker (2004: 118) also disputes that there ever was a group of Philonians/Metrodorians as conceived by Brittain (2001).

[99] Büttner (1893: 125–59) provides an illustration of how an Academic identity might have been constructed for the elder Catulus.

[100] *Luc.* 11b, where Antiochus is reported to have suggested that the claims of the Roman Books were unheard of, requires an explanation on this reading: briefly, I suggest that the philosophical claim of the Roman Books and Metrodorus' position fitted under the same high-level description but were articulated differently.

(iv) that later texts which are critical of the Academics target specifically the position of mitigated scepticism, thus providing indirect evidence for its substantial *Sitz im Leben*: while this cannot be ruled out, and while it is a possible reading for some texts, the same texts can equally be aiming at a developed form of Clitomacheanism as found in the works of Cicero, or indeed at both positions at the same time; see appendix 1. That there was a genuine difference between the two need not have been accepted or recognized by the opponents of the Academy.[101]

(v) that it was distinctive of mitigated scepticism to regard the persuasiveness of a given impression as evidence for its truth and to use the method of arguing on either side to get as close as possible to the truth:[102] as explained in the previous section, all the Ciceronian evidence suggests that the Clitomachean position accommodates both features, and the evidence from non-Ciceronian texts does not suggest otherwise (see appendix 1). Relatedly, I do not regard talk of the πιθανόν as a 'criterion' as evidence of mitigated scepticism exclusively (*Luc.* 33), although mitigated sceptics may have talked in this way.

(vi) that the evidence permits us to distinguish between the ways in which developed Clitomacheanism on the one hand and mitigated scepticism on the other would view practical and theoretical arts.[103]

(vii) that the evidence permits us to conclude that Aenesidemus and Antiochus left the Academy—for different intellectual destinations—in the 90s BC in reaction to mitigated scepticism. Rather, developed Clitomacheanism may have been an equally potent push factor, although the existence of mitigated scepticism as a view (which I acknowledge) may have had an aggravating effect.

(viii) that Lucullus' arguments, notably in *Luc.* 40-4, only make sense if they are read as directed against a position of mitigated scepticism. Rather, I take them to be directed either at the developed Clitomachean position only, or at it *and* mitigated scepticism at the same time (as I try to show step by step in the commentary).

As a result, I would distinguish Clitomacheanism as found in the works of Cicero and mitigated scepticism primarily with reference to a difference in the conception of permitted belief (in the modern sense, not in the Stoic sense of δόξα): Clitomacheans 'approve', mitigated sceptics assent in a self-aware fashion, sc. in suitable circumstances. And consequently I would reconstruct the philosophical pressures which led Philo to propose the theses of the Roman Books somewhat differently from what has been suggested.

While the difference between 'beliefs' arising from approval and those arising from assent may seem negligible to opponents of the Academy, it is arguably substantial and raises profound philosophical questions. Proponents of mitigated

---

[101] Thus also Striker (1996b: 94–5).
[102] Thus Brittain (2008a: section 3.3), who developed an interpretation of Frede (1987b).
[103] *Pace* Brittain (2001: 160–5); see on *Luc.* 145–6.

scepticism might have broken away from Clitomacheanism over this issue alone.[104] Further, while it is not difficult to envisage the kind of qualified endorsement which approval represents with respect to particular views, it is harder to see how this model would be applied to all one's views, as it would have to; for typically, qualified endorsement of particular views happens against a background of unqualified endorsement of a host of background assumptions in the relevant domain. I believe that the conception of approval would allow for an explanation of why background assumptions can be treated as if they were true even though any one of them could if necessary be problematized, but one can also understand why in a context in which Stoic philosophy of mind was the dominant framework some Academics may have been persuaded that background beliefs need to be taken to be true as envisaged by the Stoic conception of assent.

4.3 The Roman Books View

Even allowing for artistic licence, the description of Antiochus' reaction to the Roman Books in *Luc.* 11–12 precludes the possibility that they merely recorded established Academic practice. That Cicero extols suspension of judgement in his earliest work in *Inv.* 2.9 makes it likely that Philo initially lectured on Clitomacheanism when he came to Rome in 88–7 BC and only unveiled the Roman Books view later.[105] The crucial texts on the Roman Books—*Luc.* 12 and 18, *Ac.* 1.13, and Sextus, *P.H.* 1.235—jointly suggest that the Roman Books contained at least two main claims, a historical claim and an epistemological one. The latter (see on *Luc.* 18) was that, while κατάληψις as conceived by the Stoics is beyond reach, some form of κατάληψις is possible; on this alternative construal, κατάληψις was most likely conceived as arising from an impression meeting the stipulations of the first two clauses of the Zenonian definition coupled with (dogmatic) assent.[106] The historical claim was that this had been the view of the Academy all along. Brittain (2001: 129–219) stands out for showing how these bare outlines might have amounted to a substantial and historically aware position, albeit one which, as is universally agreed, did not find supporters.[107]

While this reconstruction does, or so I believe, best justice to the evidence, there are features in said evidence which seem not immediately compatible with it. Sextus groups the Philo who advanced the claim I link to the Roman Books with Charmadas (*P.H.* 1.220), who heard Carneades in person and was certainly dead by the time Philo came to Rome. Further, Cicero ascribes to Peripatetics an epistemological view which in outline corresponds to the Roman Books view.[108] If the reference to

---

[104] See Wynne (2018: 95–9) on the 'ethics of belief'; and more generally Perin (2010). How Clitomachean 'belief' would be theorized, as well as the relevant terminology, is discussed at *Luc.* 104–5.
[105] An idea considered and dismissed by Barnes (1997: 74 n. 84), but Barnes does not consider *Inv.* 2.9.
[106] Thus Frede (1987b: 218); Barnes (1997: 70–6); Striker (1997: 257–1); and Brittain (2001: 19 and 129–68).
[107] How far back exactly Philo would have traced back his philosophical thesis is not clear; see also Lévy (2010: 89).
[108] I discuss both questions in the commentary on *Luc.* 18 and appendix 1.

Charmadas is not just an error, apt to undermine our confidence that Sextus had historically and philosophically accurate insight into the Academy (whatever his intentions), it may suggest that Philo invoked Charmadas as an Academic authority for the suggestion that the Academy had, outside of dialectical contexts, held the Roman Books view for a long time.[109] As to the Peripatetics' epistemological views, the charge against the Roman Books was not that the view advanced there was altogether new, but that no Academic had held it before. Moreover, the requirement contained in the second clause of Zeno's definition is open to more than one articulation, so that the actual identity of the Roman Books view with the one ascribed to the Peripatetics is not a given.[110]

The term 'fallibilism' is used by some in connection with mitigated scepticism, and by others in connection with the Roman Books. If by fallibilism one understands a position which does not hold that knowledge is unavailable but that it is always provisional, then only the Roman Books view deserves to be so characterized, since no mitigated sceptic (let alone a Clitomachean) would have laid claim even to provisional knowledge while characterizing his own attitude, whereas on the Roman Books view any purported instance of κατάληψις might turn out to be a (false) opinion.[111]

4.4 Metrodorus' Position

Scholarship on *Acad.* which surveys the different Academic stances in evidence in the dialogues does not usually recognize a separate Metrodorean position, on the grounds that it tends to equate it with one of the other stances clearly attested. However, on my reading the evidence (*Luc.* 78; a passage in Augustine's *Contra Acad.* which is probably informed by lost parts of the final edition of *Acad.*; a passage in Philodemus' *Index Acad.*) offers a glimpse of Metrodorus' own distinctive position, which appears to have been similar to Philo's Roman Books view in its general outline but must have been articulated differently. In order to posit a reference to a uniquely Metrodorean view, one must assume that *aut* in *Luc.* 78 (*equidem Clitomacho plus quam Philoni aut Metrodoro credens*) is not equivalent to *et*, and that *Luc.* 148, concerned with the possibility of opinion resulting from self-aware assent, speaks to a view which is different from the two gestured at in *Luc.* 78.

I shall now briefly survey some of the fundamental interpretative choices scholars have made with respect to the question of how Academic scepticism is presented in *Acad.*; these choices can be used to group existing work on the text into strands.

A crucial issue is the status which is accorded to *Acad.* and to other Ciceronian works as evidence. On one end of the spectrum there is the view that *Acad.* is a fair

---

[109] Thus also Tarrant (2018: 83).
[110] For the reasons why mitigated scepticism can itself be viewed as a precarious construct, thus giving rise to a view like that of the Roman Books, see Frede (1987b: 216); Brittain (2001: 132–8); and on *Luc.* 18.
[111] In the context of the debate between Academics and dogmatists, the term ἐπιστήμη/*scientia* is confined to the overall disposition of the sage or to his καταλήψεις; see on *Luc.* 145–6.

record of Academic practice and that, with due care, one can retrieve from the dialogue and other Ciceronian texts a consistent and articulated philosophical position especially of 'Cicero' (whether deployed as narrator or as interlocutor), which allows for fairly immediate inferences as to how Academic scepticism would have been enacted at least by certain proponents, and possibly also for inferences regarding written sources used by Cicero. This is in essence the approach taken in this commentary, although I am cautious about what can be said about Cicero's sources (see section 9.3). Alternatively, the evidence from Cicero has been deemed or treated as problematic in one of several ways: Gawlick and Görler (1994: 1089–118) argue that the entire notion that argument *in utramque partem* could be deployed 'in search of the truth' and in order to uncover the *probabile* is a Ciceronian invention, not unrelated to his occupation as an advocate who appeared in adversarial settings, whereas Academic dialectic was in essence destructive.[112] Brittain (2001: 112–14, 218), who is otherwise optimistic about using *Acad.* as evidence and indeed pioneering in the manner in which he does so, cites a statement of the narrator in *Luc.* 7 about the Academic aspiration to find the truth as evidence for mitigated scepticism while acknowledging that the character Cicero in *Acad.* is a Clitomachean, thus assuming either that the narrator Cicero takes a different position from the character Cicero or that the narrator/character Cicero, while a Clitomachean, exhibits features which actually were owned by mitigated scepticism. Ioppolo (2017: 192–3) argues that the evidence from Cicero, when compared with Sextus, suggests that Carneades tended towards a mitigated position whereas Clitomachus was more radical; see on *Luc.* 104. Tarrant (2018: 82) holds that the speaker of the frame in *Luc.* (who professes to be searching for the truth) is informed by Philo's lectures on the Roman Books, which would be compatible with him being a Clitomachean only if there was no difference between the two positions in this regard. What is at stake here is what kind of attention Cicero demands or bears as a source for Academic scepticism, a question not always confronted in scholarship on Academic scepticism.[113]

A number of interpretations of *Acad.* recognize that the character Cicero is committed to suspension of judgement while the character Catulus is not (*Luc.* 148), although they differ in the conclusions they draw from this observation. Sometimes Cicero's remark in *Luc.* 78 is drawn in, viz. that 'Philo or Metrodorus' thought that Carneades held as opposed to argued that the sage would sometimes opine. Hirzel (1883: 170, 194–5) assumed that *Luc.* 78 and 148 referred to Philo's Roman Books view, which was represented by Catulus (against this see *Luc.* 12 and 18). Frede (1987b: 213) took Catulus' position not to be the general view of the Academy and as not presented as such in *Acad.*,[114] while linking it with *Luc.* 78 and 'Philo and Metrodorus'; he did not address how a position that is not the Roman Books view could be Philo's without also being the general view of the Academy. Striker (1996b: 93) and Burnyeat (1997: 308), linking *Luc.* 78 with 148, recognize Catulus' position as committed to qualified assent and assume that Catulus' position is Philo's

---

[112] See Galen, *Opt. doctr.* 1, discussed in appendix 1.
[113] Woolf (2015) does consider Cicero as a philosopher in his own right, but seems vague as to whether he regards him as a Clitomachean or a mitigated sceptic.
[114] Cf. Görler (2004c: 288), who speaks of 'one of two current interpretations of the master's doctrine'.

referenced in *Luc.* 78. Burnyeat adds, as noted above, that the position of *Luc.* 148 'won' in the end and that it was found to be superior. Brittain (2001: 73–128) argues that mitigated scepticism, in virtue of being Philo's view for a time, was the official view of the Academy prior to the publication of the Roman Books (or the public presentation of the views contained in them).[115] A fair amount of especially older scholarship does not recognize the distinction between assent and approval as important and is vague regarding the manner in which variations of Academic argumentative practice may have been associated with the three different stances.

Of the position Philo argued for in the Roman Books there exist four quite different types of interpretation: (i) in them Philo tried to return the Academy to a form of dogmatic Platonism; (ii) the Roman Books did set out a shift from Clitomacheanism to mitigated scepticism as invoked by Catulus in *Luc.* 148; (iii) they upheld ἀκαταληψία under the Stoic criterion for human beings but allowed for the notional possibility of κατάληψις; (iv) they upheld ἀκαταληψία under the Stoic criterion for human beings but allowed for the actual possibility of a differently conceived kind of κατάληψις. In this case I think that two of the options which have been proposed (i and ii) can very straightforwardly be shown to be impossible to reconcile with the extant evidence on the Roman Books, while (iv) offers a clearly better interpretation of said evidence than (iii); see on *Luc.* 18.

Reconstructions of Philo's position prior to the Roman Books tend to correlate with a particular reconstruction of the key tenets of the latter, and consequently with a particular reading of *Acad.*, in the following way: those who think that Philo held only two positions in the course of his life tend to identify them as Clitomacheanism and mitigated scepticism, assuming the latter to be the view of the Roman Books (Hirzel 1883; Glucker 1978; Sedley 1981; Lévy 1992 and 2010), while those who posit three tend to reconstruct the Roman Books view as a fallibilism (Frede 1987b; Barnes 1989; Striker 1997; Brittain 2001) or dogmatic Platonism (Krische 1845).[116] In this commentary it is assumed that Philo held two positions in the course of his life, the Clitomachean one and the fallibilist position of the Roman Books.

5. The Debate about the Cataleptic Impression

The debate between Stoics and Academics centres on the cataleptic impression (cf. *Luc.* 83), the main point of philosophical dispute between the Antiochian and the Academic characters in *Acad.*[117] The Stoics claimed that there are self-warranting

---

[115] I argue at *Luc.* 78 and 148 that different positions are referred to in *Luc.* 78 and 148, respectively—positions which, however, share the property of envisaging a role for assent.

[116] This classification is informed by the one offered by Brittain (2008a: section 2.), who, however, takes Tarrant (1985) to posit three positions but to view the Roman Books as a return to dogmatic Platonism (against this see Tarrant 2018). Glucker (1978: 415 and 2004: 111–17) in addition believes that Philo returned to his Clitomachean stance after the failure of the Roman Books; see also section 9.3. Earlier scholarship is often not fully alive to the interpretative options made available by the text and is consequently difficult to categorize.

[117] *Acad.* touches on Zeno's definition of the cataleptic impression several times, but due to the accidents of survival neither of the introductory discussions which must have featured in both editions has come down to us. The passages in *Luc.* presuppose an earlier discussion in the lost *Catulus* (e.g. §18, §77),

true impressions which provide human beings with an infallible grasp of reality, notably of objects or states of affairs in the perceptible world.[118] Against this, the Academics advanced arguments from ἀπαραλλαξία, i.e. the claim that, given how the cataleptic impression is defined, there could be 'one just like it' which is false (*Luc.* 77). In our sources this alikeness of allegedly cataleptic and false impressions is sometimes construed with reference to the imprints on or alterations of the soul's ruling part to which impressions amount, sometimes with reference to representational content, and sometimes with reference to properties of impressions like clarity and strikingness (thus two impressions which are alike in type only, i.e. which differ qua imprints and have different representational content, can be called ἀπαράλλακτοι, too).[119]

Providing a detailed reconstruction of the debate in terms of relative or absolute chronology is not possible given the state of the sources, but it is possible to identify a couple of crucial junctures and particular exchanges with certainty (notably Zeno's addition of the third clause under pressure from Arcesilaus), and there are further contributions to the debate which due to considerations of charity should be located at some points rather than others. In any case, the evidence does show that considerations of ἀπαραλλαξία provided a complex and flexible set of strategies capable of different combinations, thus helping to make intelligible why the debate could continue over two centuries and why it took a different path from modern debates e.g. about internalism and externalism.

5.1 Definitions

Zeno initially defined the cataleptic impression in the following way:[120]

καταληπτικὴ (sc. φαντασία) δέ ἐστιν ἡ (i) ἀπὸ ὑπάρχοντος καὶ (ii) κατ' αὐτὸ τὸ ὑπάρχον ἐναπομεμαγμένη καὶ ἐναπεσφραγισμένη.

A cataleptic impression is (i) from what is and (ii) imprinted and sealed on in accordance with that which is itself.

---

while *Ac.* 1.40–1 is part of a historical survey introduced by Varro from an Antiochian point of view. As a consequence, it introduces the main elements of Zeno's epistemology only qua 'corrections' or 'modifications' of the epistemology of the Old Academy (1.30–2). The actual definition must have featured in the final edition in the lost part of *Ac.* 1 for the first time.

[118] On the question of whether the Stoics took perceptual cataleptic impressions to be primary (in a sense to be clarified), see section 5.5.

[119] In using the notion of 'representational content' here, I am following Frede (1987c: 155–7 and passim). The distinction between representational content and properties like clarity and strikingness, to be clarified below, does not map neatly on the distinction between representational content and phenomenal character which one finds in contemporary epistemological debate, e.g. Gendler and Hawthorne (2006: 17–20). The distinction between propositional and representational content is rejected by Shogry (2019). On impressions as thoughts which are entertained and a 'candidate for endorsement', see *Ac.* 1.40 and Meinwald (2011: 363).

[120] Sextus, *M.* 7.248 (= *SVF* i.59, p. 18.7–9 = *FDS* 247); see also the commentary on *Ac.* 1.40–2. Cf. Sextus, *M.* 11.183; D.L. 7.46.

A second definition, in which Zeno added a third clause in response to an objection by Arcesilaus (*Luc.* 77), is also attested:[121]

καταληπτικὴ (sc. φαντασία) δέ ἐστιν ἡ (i) ἀπὸ ὑπάρχοντος καὶ (ii) κατ' αὐτὸ τὸ ὑπάρχον ἐναπομεμαγμένη καὶ ἐναπεσφραγισμένη, (iii) ὁποία οὐκ ἂν γένοιτο ἀπὸ μὴ ὑπάρχοντος.

A cataleptic impression is (i) from what is and (ii) imprinted and sealed on in accordance with that which is itself, (iii) such as could not come about from what is not.

Two quite different interpretations of the two-clause definition of the cataleptic impression are attested (phases I and II below), a fact which has plausibly been explained in developmental terms by Sedley (2002a). Such a development would have been enabled by two ambiguities in the initial two-clause definition, that of ἀπό and that of ὑπάρχειν. The preposition ἀπό may be used in a causal sense or in a representational sense. Assuming a perceptual impression, an impression which is 'ἀπό X' may be caused by X, or it may have X for its representational content.[122] The two relevant meanings of the polysemous verb ὑπάρχειν are 'to exist' (used by the Stoics e.g. of objects in the perceptible world) and 'to obtain', in which case the verb denotes the particular mode of existence characteristic of facts, specifically the status of λεκτά when they are true, in virtue of a predicate's being true of a body.[123]

There would then have been four phases:

(I) Possibly under the influence of the wax-tablet simile in Plt., *Tht.* (191a–195b),[124] Zeno formulated the original two-clause definition. It relied on the causal interpretation of ἀπό and used ὑπάρχειν to designate the existence of objects. The first clause would not stipulate veridicality but would

---

[121] See Sextus, *M.* 7.402 and 426; *P.H.* 2.4; D.L. 7.50. I shall discuss ways in which these definitions have been translated as I proceed.

[122] See Sedley (2002a: 142), who cites the characterization of Orestes' impression of Electra (who is standing in front of him) as 'from the Furies' (Sextus, *M.* 8.67: ἀπὸ τῶν Ἐρινύων) as an instance of the representational use of ἀπό.

[123] Cf. Hadot (1969: 126) on the second sense of ὑπάρχειν: 'Aristoteles und die Stoiker haben also ὑπάρχειν zur Bezeichnung der Beziehung eines Prädikates zu einem Subjekt verwendet. Aber sie unterscheiden sich darin, daß für Aristoteles ὑπάρχειν vor allem das Anhaften eines Prädikates an einem Subjekt bedeutet, während bei den Stoikern ὑπάρχειν vielmehr die Gegenwärtigkeit eines Geschehens oder eines Vorganges, die Aktualität einer Auswirkung, die aus einer Ursache resultiert, also eine Tätigkeit, bezeichnet. Indem es die Seinsweise bezeichnet, die einem Geschehen oder einem Prädikat eignet, bezeichnet es in ihren Augen die Seinsweise, die einem Unkörperlichen im Gegensatz zur körperlichen Substanzhaftigkeit eigen ist.' See below (p. liii) on how the representational interpretation of the definition can at all be viable given Stoic metaphysical and physical assumptions. Stojanović (2019: 168) argues that in the definition ὑπάρχειν is intended to mean 'to be present' or 'to be there', 'in both temporal and spatial sense', with what counts as present being determined by the context; if this was so, one stratum of our evidence (the one which locates the requirement of veridicality in the first clause, i.e. *Acad.* and Sextus, *M.* 7.152) would need to be discounted, and the position of μή in the third clause would be hard to explain (see below). Further insightful discussion is in Bronowski (2019: 127–8, 334–40). In *M.* 8.85–6 Sextus suggests that the meaning of ὑπάρχειν in the definition is unclear and that the Stoics use the notion in a circular way. Other substantial studies on ὑπάρχειν include Goldschmidt (1972); Glucker (1994).

[124] Cf. Ioppolo (1990: 438–41); Long (2002: 120); Reinhardt (2018).

merely require that a cataleptic impression be of an existing object; veridicality and catalepticity would be secured through the detailed correspondence between object and impression referred to in the second clause.[125]

(II) Zeno would then come to reinterpret the two-clause definition, give ἀπό the representational sense, and use ὑπάρχειν as of the mode of existence of facts. This would shift veridicality to the first clause and leave it to the second clause to require the precise correspondence between fact represented and impression, thereby making the impression self-warranting. While the reasons for this development can only be speculated about, the next phase provides strong support for the view that such a development did occur.[126]

(III) Arcesilaus is reported (*Luc.* 77) to have challenged Zeno by asking if there could not be an impression which was just like one which satisfied the second clause of the two-clause definition but was false.[127] Put differently, Zeno questions whether the second clause succeeds in picking out a property of impressions which belongs to a subset of true impressions exclusively. Since the sources do not record an example with which Arcesilaus supported this intervention, the exact import of his challenge is at this stage not clear. In reaction to this, Zeno added the third clause. For this to be an effective response, as Sedley (2002a: 137, 148) has shown, the first clause of the definition must have been understood by Zeno to require veridicality, and ὑπάρχειν must have been used to denote the mode of existence of facts. For only in that case is it intelligible that the third clause reuses material from the first clause and that the negation μή stands after the preposition in the phrase ἀπὸ μὴ ὑπάρχοντος, so that it comes to mean 'from that which is not so' (i.e. from a different fact than the one it is actually 'from'); if τὸ ὑπάρχον meant 'that sc. object which exists' here, the negation would naturally precede the preposition.

(IV) This phase is Chrysippus' interpretation of Zeno's three-clause definition. He reverts to a causal interpretation of ἀπό. Now given that facts cannot be causes according to Stoic physics and that the formulation of the third clause requires veridicality to be stipulated by the first clause, Chrysippus comes to interpret (τὸ) ὑπάρχον in the first clause as 'a *particular* object'. To state that an impression can only be caused by a particular object is to require that it be true. The second clause then identifies a species of true impressions: those which exactly correspond to the impression's object. The third clause comes to mean 'such as could not be caused by what is not that

---

[125] On this interpretation the first clause rules out delusions (hallucinations, dreams), while the second clause rules out illusions and misperceptions (which involve an object in the external world); cf. e.g. Reed (2002: 150).

[126] On the question of whether facts can, according to Stoic thinking, be the kind of thing that gives rise to impressions, see below.

[127] Cf. Cic., *Luc.* 77: *post requisitum, etiamne si eius modi esset uisum uerum quale uel falsum*; Sextus, *M.* 7.252 (where reference is made to the Academics in general and not to Arcesilaus): τὸ δὲ 'οἵα οὐκ ἂν γένοιτο ἀπὸ μὴ ὑπάρχοντος' προσέθεσαν, ἐπεὶ οὐχ ὥσπερ οἱ ἀπὸ τῆς Στοᾶς ἀδύνατον ὑπειλήφασι **κατὰ πάντα ἀπαράλλακτόν** τινα εὑρεθήσεσθαι, οὕτω καὶ οἱ ἀπὸ τῆς Ἀκαδημίας, 'they added the clause "of such a kind as could not arise from what is not the case" because the Academics did not, as the Stoics did, regard it as impossible that a presentation exactly alike in all respects could be found.'

very object', a strained reading of ἀπὸ μὴ ὑπάρχοντος which is only explicable against the background of the developments of phase (III). A reason for the reinterpretation of phase (IV) may have been the presence of Zeno's causal *Ur*-theory (phase I) in early works of his and the need to reconcile it with the three-clause definition. As indicated above, the reasons for rejecting the notion that this was an extension of the interpretation Zeno had intended all along include that in our evidence there is material which locates the requirement of veridicality in the second clause of the definition, as well as the manner in which the third clause is formulated.[128]

Later generations may not have appreciated the diachronic developments of Zeno's position, and they may have been unaware that Chrysippus had reinterpreted the three-clause definition (in general, Chrysippus tried to reinterpret rather than replace doctrines of Zeno's which he found problematic). As a result, for those later generations both the two-clause theory of phase I and Chrysippus' reinterpretation (phase IV) would have had sound Zenonian credentials, and although they arose in sequence, they co-existed in the record.

In *Acad.* Cicero presupposes the three-clause definition (*Luc.* 18, 77), he locates veridicality in the first clause (*Luc.* 77: *uisum a uero*), he interprets the third clause as meaning 'and which does not come from this very object' (*Luc.* 18: *quale esse non posset ex eo unde non esset*), and he assumes the theory to be a causal one (*Ac.* 1.40:...*e quadam quasi impulsione oblata extrinsecus*). He thus relies on the interpretation of phase (IV). In Sextus arguments against the cataleptic impression are sometimes formulated with reference to the phase (I) reading, and sometimes with reference to the phase (IV) reading.

5.2 The Interpretation of the Second Clause

The texts ascribe distinctive properties to cataleptic impressions, the most prominent of which is 'clarity'.[129] In some of these sources the feature described in the second clause seems to be equated with clarity. In others 'clarity' in a suitable technical sense as well as 'strikingness', a distinct property (see below), are treated jointly as a peculiar but not a defining feature of cataleptic impressions (an ἰδίωμα).[130]

The apparent inconsistency in the evidence can be explained with reference to the different interpretations of the definition of the cataleptic impression. On a representational reading (phase II), an impression would naturally be deemed clear if and only if its representational content is uniquely detailed. An impression's (supreme)

---

[128] Evidence that later Stoics grappled with the problems Sedley's four phases are intended to explain is also furnished by *P. Berol.* 16545, on which see Backhouse (2000).

[129] I have tried to reconstruct, from evidence in Galen, the Stoic conception of clarity in Reinhardt (2011); see also sections 6.1 and 6.3 for the competing Academic conception.

[130] On ἐνάργεια, see Lefebvre (2007) and Ierodiakonou (2012); τρανής 'clear' and ἔκτυπος 'distinct' function as synonyms of ἐναργής. Lefebvre also assembles the evidence for an impression's being striking, πληκτικός. On the notion of an ἰδίωμα, see Allen (1997: 233); cf. e.g. Arist., *Top.* A5, 102a18–19; and Barnes (2003: 213–19). In Sextus, *M.* 7.408 (discussed below, p. lxix) the cataleptic impression is called ἔντονος, 'intense'.

clarity and its uniquely detailed representational content would be equivalent. On a causal interpretation the second clause would refer to physical properties of the soul's ruling part, whether the impression's object is deemed to give rise to an 'imprint' or an 'alteration'.[131] The impression's representational content and its clarity would be distinct from the imprint/alteration.[132] Of course the Stoics would insist that the impression qua modification of the soul's ruling part and its representational content/clarity can only be separated notionally, but the Academics tried to go beyond that.[133]

Strikingness is by its nature a property which manifests itself in the effect a particular perceptual experience has on the perceiving subject, in that the subject finds it very difficult, though not impossible, to avoid ending up with a perceptual belief as a consequence (the sources, e.g. Sextus, M. 7.257, speak of cataleptic impressions dragging the perceiving subject by the hair, sc. towards assent).[134] Human beings are naturally prone to assent to cataleptic impressions, which, we must assume, they experience frequently and regularly (the Stoics actually define perception as assent to a cataleptic impression);[135] their epistemic difficulties arise mostly not from missing epistemic opportunities by failing to assent to cataleptic impressions,[136] but from assenting to non-cataleptic ones, notably false ones. Since assent is a movement of the soul's ruling part, a causal interpretation of the definition is in a better position than the representational one to explain in terms of Stoic physics how objects in the world can give rise to assent by means of an impression. However, it would seem to require very unlikely contortions to *locate* strikingness in the second clause.

Thus once the causal interpretation of phase (IV) became standard, it was appropriate to treat clarity and strikingness jointly as a peculiar but not essential property of cataleptic impressions.[137]

I submit here, and will discuss in detail below, that Arcesilaus' challenge, which reportedly gave rise to the addition of the third clause (phase III and n. 127 above), is formulated in Cicero (*si eius modi esset uisum uerum quale uel falsum*) and in Sextus (κατὰ **πάντα** ἀπαράλλακτον) in a way which is ambiguous with respect to whether a supposedly cataleptic impression could be matched by one which offers the same imprint on the soul's ruling part or the same representational content, or by one

---

[131] On Chrysippus' correction of 'imprint' (τύπωσις) to 'alteration' (ἑτεροίωσις) see Sextus, M. 7.228–31 (*SVF* ii.56).

[132] Cf *Ac.* 1.41, where the causal mechanism which gives rise to all impressions is referred to first and then…*quae propriam quandam haberent declarationem earum rerum quae uiderentur* is added (of cataleptic impressions).

[133] In *Luc.* 58 (*non uos id dicere, inter ipsas impressiones nihil interesse, sed inter species et quasdam formas eorum*) the Academics suggest to the Stoics that two impressions may be different from one another qua imprints but identical with regard to their representational content. The Stoic reply is that any distinction of impressions can only be made with reference to their representational content (so that representational content must be different, too, if impressions qua imprints differ).

[134] See Brittain (2012: 121) and (2014) for a full discussion.

[135] Cf. D.L. 7.52 (= *SVF* ii.71): Αἴσθησις δὲ λέγεται κατὰ τοὺς Στωικοὺς τό τ' ἀφ' ἡγεμονικοῦ πνεῦμα ἐπὶ τὰς αἰσθήσεις διῆκον καὶ ἡ δι' αὐτῶν κατάληψις…, 'According to the Stoics, the term "perception" is applied to the breath which extends from the commanding faculty to the senses, to the apprehension which comes about through the senses…'; and Aët., *Plac.* 4.8 (= *SVF* ii.72).

[136] This happens when human beings (i.e. non-sages) antecedently hold false beliefs which are incompatible with the propositional content of cataleptic impressions they experience (see Sextus, M. 7.254–5), as well as possibly when they fail to attend to their impressions or their content (see on *Luc.* 46).

[137] Cf. e.g. *Luc.* 38: *sic animum perspicuis cedere.*

which is identical with respect to clarity and strikingness. The phrase in Sextus signals a definite scope, but without specifying what is comprised by 'all respects'.[138]

5.3 The Stoics: Epistemological Internalists, Externalists, or Something in Between?

Neither the first nor the second clause give any explicit indication that an awareness requirement is being placed on cataleptic impressions, in the sense that the perceiver has to be aware of the cataleptic impression's catalepticity (however construed), or in the sense that the exact and unique detail of what is represented in the impression has to be available to the perceiver. However, as will be clear after the discussion of the previous section, the question needs to be considered diachronically, with respect to each of the four phases.

In contemporary epistemology, one fundamental way of classifying a given conception of knowledge is with reference to the internalism/externalism distinction.[139] And, as we shall see presently, considerations of access to one's own conscious states in general and to the self-warranting nature of cataleptic impressions in particular do feature in the ancient debate, but we cannot just assume that the issue of access entered the stage fully formed as it were, and it is plain that access would have to be construed quite differently depending on how exactly the second clause of Zeno's definition is understood. We can also observe that the debate between Stoics and Academics does not simply anticipate the relevant debates of the twentieth century, although as so often points of contact emerge in interestingly unpredictable ways.

I propose to consider phase (IV) first because most of our extant evidence, including *Acad.*, relates to it. The causal interpretation allows for a distinction between the physical aspect of an impression (its being an imprint on the soul's ruling part, or an alteration of it) and an impression's representational content which on the representational interpretation is merely notional.[140] An impression is cataleptic if it is true and if it corresponds to the object exactly. Clarity and strikingness are jointly a peculiar but, as one might put it in Aristotelian terms, non-essential property of cataleptic impressions. Clarity is a function of an impression's representational content. It is, one might think, a property which is more directly available to us than strikingness, which we only notice by its effect (i.e. that we find ourselves with a perceptual belief). After all, we are able modify the conditions under which we receive impressions, e.g. by improving the lighting, moving closer to the object, and so on, and thereby we improve clarity.[141] At the same time, clarity is not a quality which we can observe independently of the representational content of an impression, as opposed to being

---

[138] The texts hint at a debate about how far-reaching this correspondence should be supposed to be, i.e. whether it should extend to all properties or just to salient ones, perhaps of a particular sense modality; see the commentary on *Ac.* 1.41. Κατὰ πάντα is also ambiguous between 'relative to every feature that the object (and thus the impression) has' and 'relative to every respect with reference to which one can characterize an impression' (imprint, representational content, clarity, strikingness).

[139] See e.g. Pappas (2014).

[140] See *Luc.* 58 (*inter ipsas impressiones nihil interesse, sed inter species et quasdam formas eorum*), cited above (n. 133).

[141] Cf. *Luc.* 19, with Allen (1994: 106).

a way in which what the impression is of is represented (Cicero's phrase *propriam... declarationem... rerum* in *Ac.* 1.41 captures this well).[142] It has been suggested that the ascription of the property of clarity by itself settles the question of whether a perceiving subject can tell if he is experiencing a cataleptic impression.[143] That this cannot have been the developed Stoic view (i.e. phase IV) is plain. Otherwise the epistemic situation of the non-sage, which the Stoics regarded as precarious, not easy to improve, and near impossible to improve to the point of sagehood, would be different. One important difference between sages and non-sages is that non-sages can be reasoned out of their perceptual beliefs which have arisen from assent to cataleptic impressions (*Ac.* 1.41); this ought to be impossible if clarity was a feature that was straightforwardly and consciously available, for in that case no amount of argumentative pressure should suffice to dislodge the belief in question. Moreover, if cataleptic impressions were straightforwardly recognizable for anyone in virtue of their clarity, then epistemic progress towards sagehood could follow a simple strategy: assent to cataleptic impressions, withhold assent to non-cataleptic impressions, and let go of those beliefs which have not arisen from cataleptic impressions or else are incompatible with cataleptic impressions. But that is evidently not how the Stoics conceive of it; they regarded epistemic and, relatedly, moral progress as very difficult, and sages as either extremely rare or a theoretical construct. However, the cataleptic impression is the one thing which does offer hope to the non-sage, for cataleptic impressions are available to non-sages and sages alike,[144] and any epistemic improvement must involve the gradually more judicious use of cataleptic impressions and the gradual phasing-out of misguided assent to non-cataleptic impressions.[145] There is evidence that the Stoics did envisage such a gradual process of getting better at using cataleptic impressions. Thus they counter arguments (to be discussed in greater detail below) that, as most people would say, identical objects like twins and eggs cannot be told apart by saying that every object in the world is in fact unique (so that the discrimination not of identical but of very similar objects is at issue) and that a mother can tell her twin children apart (evidently because of familiarity with them). They also claim that Delian poultry farmers cannot just tell apart eggs but can also say from which hen a particular egg came. Given that the question of discrimination is at issue, this last remark might seem beside the point, but it would make good sense if it meant that as part of the process of learning to use cataleptic impressions to the best effect, human beings do not just get better at telling very similar looking things apart (by becoming appreciative of minute details of the representational content of their impressions),[146] but are actually able to retrieve at

---

[142] For a different way of conceiving of clarity, which the Academics tried to force upon the Stoics, see below on the strong interpretation of the third clause.

[143] So Reed (2002: 159): 'In fact, they [the Stoics] seem to characterize the causal feature in phenomenal terms so that it cannot operate in a blind way', who then refers to *Luc.* 38: *sic animum perspicuis cedere* (see below, p. lxi). Nawar (2014) also argues that the clarity of cataleptic impressions settles the question of whether the perceiving subject is, or can easily be, aware of their being cataleptic.

[144] See *Ac.* 1.42 and Meinwald (2005).

[145] The 'judiciousness' at issue need not be a conscious one, i.e. a subject may be judicious in his assent patterns but unable to account for the behaviour in question.

[146] Cf. *Luc.* 46, where a failure to appreciate cataleptic impressions for what they are is put down to a lack of application or attention on the part of the perceiver.

least in part and in suitable circumstances the causal history of a particular impression. What does this mean for the conception of clarity, specifically in what way can the experienced Delian poultry farmer and a farmer's apprentice be said to have the same kind of impression, given their very different ability to make use of them, what does that difference in ability consist in, and how should we make sense of the prima facie counterintuitive notion that an impression is clear but its representational content not fully available to us? The Stoics did apparently take the view that 'the discriminatory power of the senses far outruns the ability of the mind ability to conceptualize the object.'[147] This means that an impression has an object, whether we think of it as a physical object or as a state of affairs represented, and relatedly a propositional content, but the latter is situated in (to use as flat a metaphor as possible) an abundance of perceptual information which goes far beyond an impression's propositional content.[148] To the extent that an impression is an imprint on or an alteration of the soul's ruling part, it is this abundance of perceptual information, and not the impression's propositional content, which properly corresponds to the imprint or alteration.[149] And as far as this perceptual information is concerned, sage and non-sage are placed in the same position, in that they have the same kind of impression.[150] But sage and (untrained) non-sage are able to do different things with this perceptual information. The texts, which link an improved ability to use and access perceptual information not just to training but to expert knowledge in particular, suggest that this might work in the following way. Consider an orthopaedic surgeon who looks, together with a patient, at an X-ray image of the patient's healthy but slightly worn shoulder joint. The surgeon will be able to see the early traces of arthrosis, in the form of minute variations in the shades of grey in evidence in the image, and she will have this ability because she is able to conceptualize aspects of the perceptual information to which the image gives rise in her which the patient

---

[147] Thus Frede (1987c: 161); see also Reinhardt (2011).
[148] See Brennan (2005: 57).
[149] See Frede (1987c: 154–7). The question might be raised how such a 'mass of perceptual information' *can* actually be the kind of thing that is true or false. I believe it does not pose itself in precisely this form because impressions are propositions thought in a certain way, and rational beings assent to the propositional content of impressions. However, we learn from Sextus, *M.* 7.151–7, that Arcesilaus criticized Zeno's theory of the cataleptic impression inter alia because it was intended to deliver apprehension as a result of assent to a cataleptic impression—and Arcesilaus raised the question of whether assent could not only be given to a proposition rather than an impression (see Ioppolo 1990); this seems to be a related issue.
[150] The claim that sages and non-sages alike can experience cataleptic impressions does not mean that two minds could ever experience two impressions which are identical qua tokens. This is so because a particular mind, with its own unique history and disposition, will always conceptualize the object of an impression in its own unique way; on this point, see Frede (2011: 38). The definition of the cataleptic impression takes no stance, even on the interpretation of phases (II) and (III), on the degree to which the representational content of an impression is conceptualized. That Stoics are capable of talking of concepts by using linguistic expressions connected with the notion of printing and that the second clause of the definition uses such expressions, too, is coincidental, for the assumption cannot be that the representational content of an impression is fully conceptualized. Meinwald (2011: 363) recounts an anecdote of Nabokov's in which two different observers, one with a certain grasp of botany and one without it, end up with impressions of the same tree whose propositional content can be given as 'this is an American elm' and 'this is a shade tree [tree providing shade]' respectively. Arguably, for the latter observer to have impressions whose truth is warranted by their uniquely rich representational detail, representational content should not need to be conceptualized throughout. (There is no evidence that the Stoics recognized indexical concepts, so that e.g. shades of green could be deemed conceptualized as '*that* green'.)

cannot conceptualize. The patient may either be unable to advance beyond the observation that there are minute differences in the shades of grey in evidence, or—more likely and more to the point—will be unable to make out these minute differences in the first place, precisely because of a much-reduced or non-existent ability to conceptualize the relevant information. The surgeon is able to point to and describe in words these minute differences, because of her increased ability to conceptualize. An analogous account could be given of the Delian poultry farmer's ability to distinguish eggs.[151] One question raised by this account is to what extent perception in everyday contexts can be aligned with perception in contexts where a technical skill (a τέχνη) is brought to bear on an impression. The texts do not record an Academic objection to the effect that only a rather peculiar kind of clarity could be unavailable to the perceiver, but then the fact that experts 'perceive more' in their particular fields and that training improves what one can do with one's impressions generally was well recognized.[152] What the texts do record is a concern that the Stoics turn everyday perception into a complicated task which requires unlikely levels of expertise and technical skill (*Luc.* 86).

On the account given above, the mature Stoic position (phase IV) was an externalist one, inasmuch as experiencing a cataleptic impression carried no awareness requirement, i.e. no requirement that the subject is directly aware or could be directly aware that the impression in question is self-warranting.[153] Still less did experiencing a cataleptic impression carry a reason-giving requirement such that the subject should be able to specify relevant grounds for regarding a given impression as self-warranting, e.g. the particular way the impression represents its object. It is hard to see where in the definition either of these requirements should be located, once they came to be appreciated as an issue.

However, this does not mean that the Stoics took an avowedly externalist position, i.e. that they declared an awareness of one's epistemic standing to be irrelevant and asserted that what mattered was only that this standing was good as a matter of fact. Even if it was only a coincidental feature of cataleptic impressions that the perceiving subject could become aware of them, they must have felt that dismissing this possibility as not part of the definition would have left them with a position that was jejune. For they recognized that, for cataleptic impressions to fulfil the role ascribed to them, it was desirable that one was at least able to progress from (A) an inability to discriminate between a cataleptic and a non-cataleptic impression, over (B) an ability to discriminate without being able to say what one's discrimination is based on, to (C) an ability to discriminate and specify reasons for it.[154] Stage (B) envisages

---

[151] One might ask at this point why heightened awareness of elements of the representational content of an impression should correlate with a higher degree of conceptualization of perceptual information. Could one not, through learning, become more attentive without increased conceptualization playing a role? While this seems a valid question, the textual evidence, which assigns an important role to expertise and craft knowledge in particular, points to the scenario I have laid out, especially considering how the knowledge to which the possession of a τέχνη amounted was construed. See the commentary on *Luc.* 86.

[152] The 'experts' cited by the Stoics include painters and musicians (*Luc.* 20; cf. Cicero's response in 86 from an Academic point of view), family members (*Luc.* 56), and poultry farmers (*Luc.* 57).

[153] It is consistent with this larger picture that on the Stoic view the προκόπτων is assumed not to notice immediately when he becomes a sage (i.e. when all his καταλήψεις are true and he has become wholly rational) and that his becoming a sage (or remaining one) is in no way conditional on him noticing the transformation. See Brouwer (2014: 51–91).

[154] Cf. Reinhardt (2011: 313–14).

discrimination on the part of the perceiving subject but clearly stops short of what one might call full conscious awareness of the state the subject is in; the subject would be able to tell when he behaves in a distinctive way (including when he identifies the 'correct' egg), but would not be able to grasp the nature of his behaviour beyond that. At stage (C) the situation would be different in that the subject would be able to refer to aspects of the particular impression's representational content or to parts of its causal history;[155] that is suggested by the Stoic response to the argument from eggs and twins (i.e. the Delian poultry farmer and his ability to tell hens from eggs).[156] The discrimination-related terminology used in the sources is ambiguous and could refer to either stage (B) or stage (C).[157]

I have suggested that by the time of phase (IV) the Zenonian definition was interpreted in an externalist way. This raises the question of whether the definition was originally so conceived. Relatedly, how exactly did considerations of access and awareness enter the debate? I shall pursue these questions in the section on ἀπαραλλαξία below.

5.4 The Interpretation of the Third Clause

I continue with the discussion of phase (IV). As has been noticed, the third clause of Zeno's definition is open to two interpretations, a weak and a strong one. On the weak one, it reasserts that impressions of the kind characterized by the first two clauses could not but be true; given that on some level the debate is a clash of fundamental yet incompatible intuitions about perception, such a reassertion would not be a pointless one. On the strong one, it amounts to the statement that cataleptic impressions could not but be true in virtue of possessing a unique feature over and above those posited or implied by the first two clauses, without specifying what this difference in kind is. The most obvious candidate is the conjunction of clarity and strikingness, but now construed as a defining feature. If clarity and strikingness are allowed to pull in different directions, then one might conceivably end with a messy picture of clarity as a feature which is immediately available (on other interpretations than the one adopted here) or potentially available (on the interpretation adopted here), and strikingness as a feature that can only ever be available through its effect. However, there is no reason to allow them to pull apart: Sextus speaks of clarity and

---

[155] An impression's causal history could never be fully retrievable, though. Moreover, much of what we think we know about causal processes is based on inference, and it would be problematic to rely on inferential knowledge to make the case that a particular impression is self-warranting.

[156] For a distinction like mine between option (B) and option (C), see Reed (2002: 159).

[157] Cf. *discernere* in *Luc.* 22, *internoscere* in *Luc.* 33 and 47 and elsewhere (see the *index uerborum* s.v.) and διορίζειν / διάκρισις in Sextus, *M.* 7.409 (to be discussed below), where, however, these terms feature in the sceptical argument. The terms are open to further ambiguities depending on who their focalizer is taken to be (e.g. the perceiving subject, the narrator), or depending on whether a logical or grammatical object *uisum* is taken to refer to object seen and visual experience had at the same time, or only to the latter. When the frame of reference is the sage, or an expert within a narrowly circumscribed domain, then the discrimination at issue is usually what others call 'conscious discrimination' (e.g. Brittain 2001: 99–100 n. 42).

strikingness jointly as the ἰδίωμα, and the Antiochian speaker Lucullus uses phrases like *sic animum perspicuis cedere* in *Acad.* (*Luc.* 38), which is consistent with the evidence from Sextus. The fact that the Stoics continued to use the two-clause definition after the introduction of the three-clause definition and after the interpretation of phase (IV) became the prevailing view strongly suggests that the weak interpretation corresponds to the official Stoic position.[158]

However, it is plausible to think that the Academics tried to use arguments from ἀπαραλλαξία to force the Stoics into adopting the strong interpretation (see the separate section below). That the strong interpretation was open to devastating objections in a way in which the weak interpretation was not provides a rationale for this; it also provides independent grounds for assuming that the strong interpretation was not the official Stoic position.

In order to appreciate a vulnerability of the Stoic position, we must look more closely at how the distinction between the weak and the strong interpretations of the third clause is to be articulated given the position of phase (IV). One way of construing the strong interpretation of the third clause would be to say that the feature it refers to is clarity,[159] but not the kind of clarity which is located at the end of a spectrum from dim or murky to clear.[160] Rather, it is a categorically separate feature, distinctive irrespective of the content of the impression, and not just a property of the impression qua representation.[161] Thus understood, the third clause would have left the Stoics with an indefensible position, for a number of reasons: one is that, on this reading, clarity, and not the cataleptic impression as a whole, should be the criterion, another is that clarity would be used as a sign from which one infers the truth of a given impression, 'an awkward combination of alleged self-evidence with knowledge reached by inference'.[162] The problem is now that the notion that one could learn to discriminate cataleptic impressions by becoming more sensitive to how changes in conditions affect the clarity of our impressions sets up a drift towards the strong interpretation as I have described it which is very difficult to halt. This happens in the following way. While it is obvious that a perceiving subject can track the way in which changes in conditions affect the clarity of one's impressions, e.g. when one moves closer or further away, changes one's stance, modifies the lighting, and so on, it is not the case that the perceiving subject can be certain that, when conditions have been reached which feel as if they cannot be improved upon and which cannot be

---

[158] So Frede (1999: 308), who is aware that there are texts in which the two-clause definition is relied on, but is interpreted in a way which locates the requirement of veridicality in the second clause.

[159] Another way of construing it, left to one side for now, would be to take it to refer to the assent-inducing property of cataleptic impressions. I have stated above why I think that clarity and strikingness cannot be separated.

[160] Clarity, thus understood, would be a property perceiving subjects have access to or could have access to; cf. Bergmann's awareness requirement (cited p. lxii below).

[161] Cf. Striker (1997: 272), characterizing the weak interpretation by contrasting it with the strong interpretation: 'This would mean that [sc. on the weak interpretation: TR] the distinguishing characteristic was not some additional feature, like a blue ribbon or perhaps a watermark, discernible only with due training.'

[162] Again Striker (1997: 272). Striker herself holds that in *Luc.* the Antiochian Lucullus, possibly following some later Stoics, held a position like this one when he speaks of a *nota* of cataleptic impressions. Brittain (2012: 118–20) concludes that this is unlikely to be the case, without committing fully to a rejection of Striker's view. See the commentary on *Luc.* 33–4 and 84.

improved upon at that moment as a matter of fact, these conditions do really mark end-of-the-scale clarity rather than slightly less than that.[163] In order for this problem to be overcome, the clarity of cataleptic impressions needs to be conceptualized as categorically different from a very high degree but still sub-optimal degree of clarity—but that is then the strong interpretation.[164]

It may be helpful, finally, to tabulate interpretations of the Stoic position which have been advanced or are conceivable, so as to place the one defended here, i.e. an externalist interpretation which adopts the weak interpretation of the third clause, in a context; the reference point will be phase (IV). An interpretation is deemed internalist if access to, or the (easy) possibility of having access to, what makes an impression self-warranting is part of the definition of a cataleptic impression. Cf. Bergmann's formulation of an awareness requirement in the case of knowledge defined as justified true belief (Bergmann 2006: 9):

S's belief B is justified only if (i) there is something, X, that contributes to the justification of B—e.g. evidence for B or a truth-indicator for B or the satisfaction of some necessary condition of B's justification—and (ii) S is aware (or potentially aware) of X.

	internalist	externalist
weak interpretation of the third clause	The clarity of cataleptic impressions, which is a function of the precise correspondence between object and impression referred to in the second clause, is construed as a feature whose presence one can establish by attending to the way in which the impression represents its object. The third clause reasserts that all and only impressions which meet the first two clauses are guaranteed to be true.[165]	Clarity and strikingness are jointly a peculiar, non-essential feature of cataleptic impressions, which are defined as true and corresponding precisely to the impression's object. Human beings can learn to appreciate the peculiar feature to various degrees, but their doing so is not a necessary condition for their experiencing a cataleptic impression.[166] The third clause functions as in the option to the left.

[163] It is only at the very end of the murkiness–clarity spectrum that the problem formulated by Reed (2002: 160) arises: 'This, however, leads us into epistemic circularity, for both the following must be true: (1) before the subject can learn which of his impressions are cognitive, he first must have a proper awareness of the conditions in which his impressions arise, and (2) before the subject can have a proper awareness of the conditions in which his impressions arise, he must first learn which of his impressions are cognitive. But, of course, the subject cannot satisfy *both* of these requirements.'
[164] See below under section 5.8 'Generalization' for other situations during the debate when the 'pull' of the strong interpretation might be felt by the Stoics or Antiochus.
[165] Cf. e.g. Reed (2002), with the qualification that he takes the Stoic position on veridical, self-warranting perception to be a direct realist one. Overall, Reed defends a disjunctivist interpretation, but on what theory false impressions are explained is not at issue at the moment.
[166] Cf. Allen (1997), whose position is largely the same as that of Frede (1999), except for a greater degree of precision on how the defining feature spelt out in the second clause of Zeno's definition relates to the ἰδίωμα.

	internalist	externalist
strong interpretation of the third clause	The clarity of cataleptic impressions is construed as a feature which one can identify irrespective of representational content.[167] The third clause states that all and only impressions which meet the first two clauses are guaranteed to be true in virtue of their distinctive feature, which makes them different in kind from the type of impression cited in Arcesilaus' objection.	The distinctive feature of cataleptic impressions, clarity combined with strikingness, is a causal one which induces assent. Human beings can track their behaviour when experiencing cataleptic impressions but do not have direct access to the feature.[168] The third clause functions as in the option to the left.

The considerations in favour of an externalist interpretation of the Stoic position (phase IV) which assumes a weak interpretation of the third clause have hopefully emerged from the discussion above. One might think, in addition, that the interpretation in the top left quadrant would struggle to accommodate the fact that Sextus as well as Cicero present cataleptic impressions as clear *as well as striking*, and that in Sextus these two features *jointly* make up the ἰδίωμα. Strikingness is naturally read as an externalist feature, in that it could never be directly accessible and would only ever reveal itself through the effect an impression has on a perceiving subject.

I take it that the bracket in Bergmann's (ii)—'S is aware (or potentially aware) of X'—relates to e.g. situations in which a subject's being unaware of X is due to a failure to attend to X, so that awareness of X could be easily achieved. If one could appreciate X only after an enormously laborious training process, then that would amount to potential awareness of X in quite a different sense (and arguably make the whole externalism/internalism distinction specious). This is the reason why the two options in the left half of the table only speak of an ability to identify, and not also of the possibility of learning to identify.

5.5 Cataleptic Impression: Perceptual or also Non-perceptual?

The sources seem to say different things about whether cataleptic impressions in the primary sense must be perceptual, so that non-perceptual καταλήψεις would owe their status to being derived, ultimately, from perceptual experiences; alternatively, cataleptic impressions may simply be either perceptual or non-perceptual. If, as I shall explore in greater detail in the next section, certain passages in Plato's *Theaetetus* inspired the formulation of the definition of the cataleptic impression and informed the debate as time went on, then there would be ways of locating the origin of the

---

[167] This is the position into whose adoption some Academic arguments aim to pressure the Stoics and which Striker (1997: 265–72) posits for Antiochus. *Pace* Reed (2002: 153), the adoption of the strong interpretation of the third clause does not necessarily yield an 'externalist' position.

[168] Cf. Frede (1987c).

question in that dialogue, too, namely in the manner in which the wax-tablet simile as a model for explaining false belief is rejected through a reference to false beliefs about arithmetic, which it is unable to account for (195e).

Once again the fact that there were phases (I)–(IV) can help explain the uneven record. A causal interpretation, as in phase (I) and (IV), would naturally restrict cataleptic impressions in the primary sense to perceptual impressions (since only objects in the world have the required metaphysical status to function as impressors), while a representational interpretation, as in phase (II) and (III), would allow for non-perceptual cataleptic impressions in addition.[169] The formulation of the second clause of the Zenonian definition, evoking the mechanics of imprinting and suggesting a heavily textured impressor, would also seem to discourage the assumption that cataleptic impressions were from the beginning intended to include non-perceptual impressions.[170]

For our purposes the issue is not a major one, given that even on the causal interpretation derivatively cataleptic impressions are recognized (cf. *Luc.* 21-7), but it does raise one question which has rarely been considered: how should we conceive of non-perceptual ἀπαραλλαξία? Is there such a thing, and if so what role if any did it play in the debate?

5.6 Ἀπαραλλαξία

In order to appreciate the nature of the objection from ἀπαραλλαξία which Arcesilaus is reported to have made against the definition of the cataleptic impression in phase (II), thereby prompting Zeno to add the third clause (phase III), we need start from Zeno's original conception (phase I).

Put very generally, when Plato thinks about knowledge, he tends to be more interested in expertise, complex bodies of knowledge, rather than individual items of knowledge, knowledge that *p*. Socratic exchanges in the early dialogues are predicated on the assumption that an expert ought to have consistent beliefs within the domain of his expertise. In order to be able to tell if his beliefs are consistent, they would normally be expected to be transparent to him: he must be able to tell if he has them. The debate in the *Theaetetus* approaches the subject of knowledge via the subject of expertise (145c–e): Socrates asks Theaetetus what knowledge is, and Theaetetus cites a range of fields of expertise in reply (geometry and mathematics; cobbling and other crafts). At the same time, perception looms large in *Tht.* Many of the examples are perceptual, and the question whether perception itself is knowledge is considered. The wax-tablet section (191a-195b) explores whether false belief can be explained as a failure to match an experience arising from an encounter with an object in the world with a memory imprint formed earlier.[171] At the end of the

---

[169] This point is made by Sedley (2002a: 150–1). Brennan (1996) argues plausibly that the Stoics recognized cataleptic impressions whose propositional content can be rendered as 'it is reasonable [εὔλογον] that *p*'. Such impressions cannot be perceptual.

[170] Those who favour an internalist causal reading of the doctrine of the cataleptic impression will naturally incline to excluding non-perceptual impressions from the class of cataleptic impressions.

[171] Long (2002: 120) links *Tht.* 191a–195b with the definition of the cataleptic impression.

dialogue (206c2–210a9), where the question is whether knowledge could be true δόξα with an account (λόγος), different conceptions of the 'account' are considered. The third option is that to give the account of an object is to cite its διαφορά (e.g. 208e4), which has left a distinct μνημεῖον 'imprinted' in us (ἐνσημηναμένη: 209c6–7). The participle recalls the term σημεῖον from the wax-tablet section (194d4), where it denoted the memory imprint on the soul, but here μνημεῖον relates to a feature, or set of features, which uniquely belongs to the object (the example given is Theaetetus' snub-nosedness, which is different from everybody else's snub-nosedness).

If we posited that Zeno took his cue from these passages, we might assume that the theory of the cataleptic impression during phase (I) was *unreflectively internalist*, in the sense that, given Plato's general thoughts about expertise and transparency of expertise and the individual items of knowledge which constitute it, Zeno may have seen no problem initially in telling, say, a particular human being apart from other people with reference to peculiar distinctive features. In this case it would have been implicit in the definition that a subject can tell if an impression of his is cataleptic. There is no conception of clarity to be found in *Tht.*

However, although the relative chronology of the formulation of Stoic doctrines by Zeno is uncertain, the issue mentioned earlier to do with the difficulties of becoming a sage cannot have taken long to arise. If Zeno came up against them early, phase (I) may not even have been 'uncomplicatedly internalist'. If he came up against them later, then we should be hesitant to assume that Zeno had not recognized, by phase (II), a need for the assumption that a perceiving subject can be in the *state* described in the definition of the cataleptic impression without being *aware* that this is so. What seems unlikely to me is that it took the intervention by Arcesilaus which reportedly gave rise to the third clause to make Zeno aware that access to one's own mental states was a problem. In this connection it is relevant that Arcesilaus was some eighteen years younger than Zeno, and that the former became head of the Academy in the years 268–264 while Zeno died in 262/1.[172] Of course their debates may have started well before Arcesilaus became head of the Academy, but it is plausible to assume that the definition of the cataleptic impression had to withstand various tests before Arcesilaus started to tackle it.

Now Arcesilaus is said to have argued against Zeno's two-clause definition that there could be an impression 'just like' the one the Stoics regard as cataleptic which was false, a statement which is capable of several interpretations (see the section on the second clause above). Arguments which fall under this general description are in the Greek sources described as involving ἀπαραλλαξία (on the term see p. lxvi), whereas Cicero employs the periphrastic 'just like it' locution or similar expressions.[173]

---

[172] See Mette (1984: 78–9); Dorandi (1989a); Steinmetz (1994: 518–21); Görler (1994: 787–96); Vezzoli (2016: 10–11).

[173] See Cic., *Luc.* 77: *post requisitum etiamne si eius modi esset uisum uerum quale uel falsum*; cf. *Luc.* 34: *in eo autem, si erit* **communitas** *cum falso*, and 42: *uolunt efficere iis omnibus quae uisa sint ueris* **adiuncta** *esse falsa quae a ueris nihil differant* (similarly *N.D.* 1.12). See the commentary on *Luc.* 48 (the apparent exception to the rule): *quia nulla in uisis distinctio appareat*. A passage from the Greek evidence which exhibits similar terminology is Sextus, *M.* 7.438: ὡς γὰρ διαβάλλοντες τὴν καταληπτικὴν φαντασίαν ἔφασκον μὴ εἶναι κριτήριον ταύτην τῆς ἀληθείας τῷ καὶ ἄλλας ἀπαραλλάκτους **παρακεῖσθαι** αὐτῇ ψευδεῖς,

It is not possible to say whether it was a Stoic or an Academic who first used the noun, and it is not attested prior to being used in the context of the debate.¹⁷⁴

Two basic types of arguments are attested, one involving very similar objects like eggs and twins, to which reference had already been made above, and one involving abnormal states of mind (dreams, madness, drunkenness), during which the perceiving subject is said to experience impressions just like a cataleptic impression which are, however, false. How exactly these arguments are formulated and what their precise purpose is will be discussed below.

The main evidence for these arguments comes from Sextus (*M.* 7.402–11) and Cicero (*Luc.* 40–58 and 83–90).¹⁷⁵ A difference between the two discussions is that Cicero's offers not just the initial arguments, but also versions modified so as to take Stoic responses on board. The account in Sextus, by contrast, mostly gives the initial Academic challenges to the Stoic position, but shows no awareness of the moves and countermoves which followed.¹⁷⁶

The term ἀπαραλλαξία is frequently rendered 'indistinguishability' or 'indiscernibility', and its cognate adjective as 'indistinguishable'.¹⁷⁷ However, the meaning of these terms is better captured by Cicero's 'just like' formulation, i.e. 'non-distinctness', and 'precisely alike', respectively. Lexically, the noun refers to the relational property, of an impression or of two impressions relative to each other, of being exactly alike; it does not denote a different property, their being incapable of being distinguished by the perceiving subject.¹⁷⁸ This might be a vacuous and pedantic point to make, e.g. if it could be shown that, even if 'non-distinctness' was the correct translation, independent evidence suggested that the perceiving subject's ability to discriminate, whether in sense (B) or (C) distinguished above (see p. lix), was invariably and from

---

οὕτως οὐκ ἀπέοικε καὶ τοῖς διεξωδευμένοις πράγμασιν ἡμῖν ἐν τῷ διαθεωρεῖν τὴν πιθανὴν φαντασίαν ἄλλα τινὰ ψευδῆ **παρακεῖσθαι**..., 'For just as, in their disparagement of the apprehensive representation, they kept saying that this is not the criterion of truth since other non-distinct representations lie beside which are false, so it is not unlikely that, during our examination of the persuasive representation, certain false things lie beside those which have been scrutinised' (transl. Bury, modified).

¹⁷⁴ However, once again we look to the wax-tablet section in Plt. *Tht.*, where misidentifying one (familiar) person A as another person B is described as a case of mismatching (παραλλάττειν) an αἴσθησις (of A) with an imprint (σημεῖον) of B in 194d3–4 (cf. also 193c5–6, 194a3, 196c5). If Zeno's definition was inspired by passages in the *Tht.*, one would expect a leading philosopher of the Academy to be aware of it, and to have looked to the same dialogue for ammunition.

¹⁷⁵ See, however, also Plut., *Comm. not.*, ch. 36.

¹⁷⁶ One might be tempted to explain this in terms of the relative chronology of the sources used, and this would dovetail with the manner in which evidence on Arcesilaus is presented in Sextus and Cicero, respectively (cf. p. cxxviii). Alternatively, Sextus may have wanted to set out the main battle-lines in stark simplicity; what supports this second reading is that one of the ἀπαραλλαξία scenarios considered in Sextus is from the start more complex than the corresponding scenario in Cicero (see on *Luc.* 88–90).

¹⁷⁷ See e.g. LSJ s.v.; Long and Sedley (i.1987: 171); Schofield (1999: 342); Görler (2004c: 274); Brittain (2006: xxxiii).

¹⁷⁸ In general, nouns of the same formation as ἀπαραλλαξία do not typically denote an ability or inability to do something, but a condition or a state: ἀταραξία denotes a state in which one is unperturbed, not an inability to be perturbed (similarly ἀναισθησία); that ἀπραξία means 'not-acting' as opposed to an inability to act is clear from its first occurrence in Greek literature (Eur., *Or.* 426: τὸ μέλλον ἴσον ἀπραξίᾳ λέγω, 'intending to act is the same as doing nothing', on which see Willink 1989: 157). See Buck and Petersen (1944: 120–1). The verb παραλλάττω means, in its intransitive uses, 'to deviate from one another, to miss each other', 'to alternate', 'to differ', and 'to vary from'; ἀπαραλλάττω is then simply the negation of these senses. It seems unlikely that those who render the term as 'indistinguishable' mean 'indistinguishable for the narrator' as opposed to the perceiving subject.

the very beginning the issue. If this cannot be shown, then two worthwhile observations will be possible: first, the earliest invocation of ἀπαραλλαξία might not actually mark the moment when 'internalist considerations', considerations of what the perceiving subject is aware of, enter the debate; second, given that the definition of the cataleptic impression does not explicitly invoke considerations of awareness and that the reply that there could be a false one 'just like it' need not do so either, there are prima facie grounds for thinking that Stoics and Academics saw eye to eye on the meaning of the second clause (if not on its success). And while we have reason to assume that the Academics, at least from a certain point onwards and sometimes, employed considerations of access to one's conscious states, there would be no grounds for thinking e.g. that Arcesilaus' initial move amounted to urging considerations of awareness against a position which gave no room to awareness ex hypothesi, and that he and Zeno were thus at cross purposes.[179]

If, on the one hand, when Arcesilaus mounted his challenge, the Stoics assumed that access to the fact that one is in a cataleptic state was unproblematic, then the possibility that there might be an impression 'just like' a cataleptic impression but which is false could address representational content/clarity, strikingness, *as well as access*. It would not be a suitable formulation for pressing for access alone, and once the Stoics exclude access, it would be an unsuitable formulation for raising the issue of access (rather, access would be a separate consideration not covered by ἀπαραλλαξία).

If, on the other hand, when Arcesilaus mounted his challenge, the Stoics assumed that access to the fact that one is in a cataleptic state was neither a given nor required (for a subject to experience a cataleptic impression), then the challenge would address representational content/clarity and strikingness. It would again be an unsuitable formulation for raising the issue of access.

I have given my reasons above why I regard the second of these scenarios as the more likely one. Following Sedley, I have assumed that Arcesilaus' challenge was made when Zeno operated the representational interpretation of the definition (phase II). Once phase (IV) became the standard interpretation, it was possible to distinguish the physical aspect of an impression (its being an imprint or an alteration), its representational content, and the ἰδίωμα.

In any event, the evidence shows that the question of whether perceiving subjects are aware of an impression's self-warranting nature (in either sense B or sense C distinguished above, p. lix) did come into view at some point, and one can only speculate how. When Cicero tells the overly neat story of how Arcesilaus' objection that there might be an impression just like the one characterized by Zeno's two-clause definition but which was false (*Luc.* 77), he does not, as was already observed above, give an example which Arcesilaus used to support his point. This makes our evidence for the very beginning of the debate vague on a crucial point. It seems unlikely that Arcesilaus began by arguing from dreams (or hallucinations), given that the Stoics

---

[179] For this interpretative option, see Annas (1990). It is also worth noting that even later the Stoics are not on record as dismissing considerations of awareness as positively irrelevant, and that the Academics were capable of arguing against the claim that every object in the world is unique (*Luc.* 85).

could have made the point that on their view dream appearances were not even impressions in the narrow sense (rather, they were φαντάσματα).[180]

Twins or eggs, by contrast, would have provided counterexamples involving what the Stoics recognized as φαντασίαι, and the identity of the objects could have been invoked *directly* as evidence that two impressions at issue must be identical in terms of representational content, i.e. without any consideration of or reference to the perceiving subject's awareness of his own epistemic standing, and also without an intermediate step referring to an absent ἰδίωμα.[181] The Stoics could have pointed out at *that* point, as we know they did at *some* point, that they held the view that all objects in the world were individuals and that consequently impressions of them were unique.[182] Note that this consideration is a precise rejoinder to the Academic challenge only as long as access to one's own epistemic standing is not at issue (for whatever reason);[183] charity would thus suggest to assign this move a place in the debate where it is not beside the point. The Academics might then have pulled back to saying that, even if that was so, one could not tell the difference. At that point the evidence suggests that the Stoics could have given two different responses: first, they could have suggested that the sage will refrain from assenting to impressions of very similar objects (a move attested in *Luc.* 57); second, they could have revealed (or devised) the view that cataleptic impressions have a peculiar feature, clarity and strikingness, which one can learn to appreciate, as indeed mothers do with regard to their twins.[184] What is not attested is a confident Stoic assertion that access is irrelevant, i.e. that they are committed externalists and that being in a cataleptic state is all that matters; on the contrary, the Stoics thought that, in order to be wise, one must know that one is wise.[185]

With this, or so I suggest, it had become an option to argue that the perceiving subject cannot tell what state he is in and whether a given impression is self-warranting and why (see B and C above, p. lix), but the point did not supplant other

---

[180] Ioppolo (1993: 199–200 n. 60) also suspects that Arcesilaus concentrated on ἀπαραλλαξία turning on very similar objects, whereas Carneades 'insisted more on the inner conditions of the subject'. See on *Luc.* 87b.

[181] Cf. the example cited in Sextus, *M.* 7.409, discussed below, and the late mentioning of the ἰδίωμα in 7.411.

[182] I will argue in section 5.6.2 that not all attested Academic arguments from ἀπαραλλαξία acknowledge this Stoic metaphysical assumption. Does this tell against a reconstruction in which the invocation of that principle features so early in the debate, i.e. at a point which likely predates most of our evidence for arguments from ἀπαραλλαξία? I do not think it does, because this principle was unlikely to pass unchallenged (cf. *Luc.* 85), and we will also encounter other situations in which the Academic attacks are modified by sometimes rejecting and sometimes accepting (for the sake of the argument) certain elements of Stoic doctrine.

[183] Cf. Reed (2002: 152): '[Context: the Academics might argue that impressions could appear to be indiscernible, even though they are actually, qua imprints or in terms of representational content, different.] Notice, finally, that this sort of case cannot be ruled out even by applying the principle of the identity of indiscernibles directly to impressions as well as to objects. Such a move only highlights the fact that the perfect correlation in detail between cognitive impressions and their objects is of no use epistemically.'

[184] We will see below that decisive considerations against the first of these responses are attested quite early, which may suggest that the second response was advanced after the first had been found wanting.

[185] Cf. *Luc.* 24, 27; and the so-called 'disappearing argument' (διαλεληθὼς λόγος), which was designed to show—against the Stoics—that, even if one had achieved a state in which one only held apprehensions, there would be no way of acquiring second-order knowledge that this is so. Chrysippus wrote a book on this argument (D.L. 7.198 = *SVF* ii.15). See Burnyeat (1997: 288–9).

considerations as we shall see, and there are no grounds for thinking that this has to be explained in terms of relative chronology. Rather, the second clause of the Zenonian definition, understood as a description of a state the subject is in, remained a valid target, and the issue of access to cataleptic states and others can feature in various ways.

Let us now take a closer look at the two groups of ἀπαραλλαξία arguments, those from abnormal mental states (dreams, madness) and those from very similar objects (eggs, twins, etc.). In Sextus these are referred to in the following way (*M.* 7.408):

> ἀλλὰ γὰρ αὕτη μὲν ἡ ἀπαραλλαξία τῶν τε καταληπτικῶν καὶ τῶν ἀκαταλήπτων φαντασιῶν κατὰ τὸ ἐναργὲς καὶ ἔντονον ἰδίωμα παρίσταται. οὐδὲν δὲ ἧττον δείκνυται τοῖς ἀπὸ τῆς Ἀκαδημίας καὶ ἡ κατὰ χαρακτῆρα καὶ [ἡ] κατὰ τύπον.
>
> This type of non-distinctness of cataleptic and non-cataleptic impressions, with respect to the clear and striking peculiar property, is set out; that with respect to stamp and impress is shown to obtain no less surely by the Academics.

On the most natural reading, this sentence is concerned with non-distinctness in respect of 'the clear and striking peculiar property' and 'stamp/impress', not with non-distinctness in some other sense established by invoking both. It is notable, then, that only one of the two types of argument is explicitly associated with the distinctive feature of cataleptic impressions, clarity coupled with strikingness. I shall try and see if the arguments as reported in Sextus naturally fall under these headings, if the evidence from Cicero is consistent with such a reading, and why Sextus refers to the two types of argument in the way he does.

5.6.1 Dreams and Madness

Consider the following passage from Sextus' discussion of the impressions experienced by madmen and dreamers, which gives an Academic argument (*M.* 7.403):

> καὶ τεκμήριον τῆς ἀπαραλλαξίας τὸ ἐπ' ἴσης ταύτας ἐναργεῖς καὶ πληκτικὰς εὑρίσκεσθαι, τοῦ δὲ ἐπ' ἴσης πληκτικὰς καὶ ἐναργεῖς εἶναι τὸ τὰς ἀκολούθους πράξεις ἐπιζεύγνυσθαι.
>
> And it is evidence for ἀπαραλλαξία that these impressions are found to be as clear and as striking, and it is evidence for them being as striking and clear that the corresponding actions are linked to them.

Here one inference (note τεκμήριον) is made from a certain kind of behaviour exhibited by dreamers and madmen (which according to the Stoics arises only from cataleptic impressions) to the impressions of such people being equally clear and striking, and another inference from those impressions 'being found to be' equally clear and striking to their ἀπαραλλαξία.[186] It is difficult to see how the verb εὑρίσκεσθαι could

---

[186] The shift from εἶναι to εὑρίσκεσθαι between the two inferences is probably not meaningful. The context after the quote illuminates what is meant by 'actions' of people who dream (they feel relief when they dream that they are drinking from a spring, or terror when they dream of horrors encountered).

be focalized by someone other than the perceiving subject: it is *to them* that impressions had while dreaming appear equally clear and striking (i.e. equally, sc. compared to purported cataleptic impressions). Given that ἀπαραλλαξία cannot possibly be defined as 'to be found to be equally clear and striking by the perceiving subject',[187] the second inference is from a feeling on the part of the perceiving subject that the impressions are equally clear and striking to the objective equivalence of purported cataleptic impressions and others. Access features only in the intermediate step and is access to a subjective state.

An example provided by Sextus (*M*. 7.405-7) is illuminating: Heracles saw his children and, stricken with madness, ended up with the false belief that they were the children of his enemy Eurystheus. He also received a true impression of his bow and arrows and proceeded to kill his children with them. Both impressions, Sextus continues, were followed by the corresponding action—the killing of Heracles' children and the deployment of the bow—and hence must have been ἀπαράλλακτος (7.407). We can note, first, that the example is consistent with the above analysis but omits the intermediate step turning on clarity and strikingness. Second, the two impressions at issue are of different objects and have different representational content; if they are nonetheless ἀπαράλλακτος, then this can only mean non-distinctness in type, a relationship readily covered by Cicero's 'just like it'-formulation, which corresponds to one of Sextus' in 7.406 (μία γὰρ καὶ ἡ αὐτὴ προϋπέκειτο καὶ ὡσαύτως ἔχοντι φαντασία). Third, the example posits that Hercules, while in a state of madness, has a cataleptic impression and a false impression, both of which give rise to relevant actions;[188] at least in the example no comparison between impressions had while awake and sane and others experienced while insane is drawn, and I will consider below how exactly the scenario could be exploited to advance the Academics' argumentative goals.

We can further observe that the impression arising from Heracles' children and in which they appear as Eurystheus' could only meet the first clause of the definition if it was read as 'from a real object' and would not meet it on the reading of 'from a particular object' or 'from an actually obtaining state of affairs', while dream appearances do not meet the first clause on any construal.[189]

The evidence from *Luc.* complements that from Sextus. There is one noticeable difference, in that there is initially no explicit invocation of the distinctive feature (Sextus' ἰδίωμα). Thus in *Luc.* 48 Lucullus reports an Academic argument to the effect that the mind is moved by things one merely imagines as well as by what

---

[187] Ἀπαραλλαξία cannot be thus defined because, as argued above, the term does not denote the property of being indistinguishable; moreover, the second inference would be from the *definiens* to the *definiendum*, which would be oddly redundant. We shall also see that arguments from similar objects aim to show inter alia that purported cataleptic impressions do not have a distinguishing feature, not that the feature belongs to purported cataleptic impressions *as well as others*. Any definition of ἀπαραλλαξία needs to be general enough to cover both classes of argument.

[188] The argument as cited by Sextus does not endorse that the impression of the bow is cataleptic; rather, it is implied that it ought to be deemed cataleptic by the opponent due to the successful outcome (7.405): εἰ οὖν καταληπτικαί τινές εἰσι φαντασίαι παρόσον ἐπάγονται ἡμᾶς εἰς συγκατάθεσιν καὶ εἰς τὸ τὴν ἀκόλουθον αὐταῖς πρᾶξιν συνάπτειν..., 'if, then, some presentations are cataleptic inasmuch as they attract us to apprehension and to attaching to them the attendant action....'

[189] See above, p. lii on the different interpretations of Zeno's definition.

appears to those who are dreaming or gripped by madness just as much as by real events, which shows not just that it cannot distinguish between true and false but that there is as a matter of fact no difference between them (... *ut non modo* **non** **internoscat** *uera illa uisa sint anne falsa, sed ut in iis* **nihil intersit** *omnino*). Likewise (ibid.), the Academics are reported as saying that there was no way of telling whether physiological reactions associated with anxiety (trembling, turning pale) could occur without an external object inducing them and that there was no difference between an internally and externally induced reaction (*Luc.* 48). In both cases a direct inference from behaviour to the equivalence (in type) of the impressions is made. However, clarity and strikingness are not far away. Amongst the Stoic objections to these Academic arguments, Lucullus singles out the assertion that impressions experienced while mad or dreaming lack the *perspicuitas* (i.e. ἐνάργεια) of cataleptic impressions (*Luc.* 51), a tenet to which the Stoics must cling with tenacity (*mordicus*); this—taken as an insistence on objective clarity—would also be a fitting rejoinder to the Heracles scenario in Sextus.[190] And it is reminiscent of strikingness that the text seems to make a point of not describing the situation in terms of what the perceiving subject is consciously aware of, speaking instead in depersonalized terms of how the mind is moved. Sextus' and Cicero's accounts can thus in this respect be reconciled without much difficulty.

Unlike Sextus, Cicero provides various responses to the Academic arguments; these are given to the character Lucullus, and as an interlocutor Cicero gives the Academic responses to these responses. Apart from the insistence that the impressions of dreamers and madmen do not have the *perspicuitas* of cataleptic impressions, as is evidenced by the limited confidence which drunks often exhibit with regard to their impressions and with which they accept them if they do so (*Luc.* 52),[191] Lucullus notes that human beings no longer give credence to the impressions in question, or the beliefs arising from them, once they have recovered (*Luc.* 51; cf. 90). To that the Academics reply that what matters is whether these impressions were assent-inducing at the time (*Luc.* 88–9). A Stoic rejoinder is not attested, but the Stoics might have replied that all that this shows is that most human beings' corrupted state, which accounts for their assenting to non-cataleptic impressions on occasion while awake and under ideal conditions, accounts for their behaviour at times of drunkenness and madness, too; and they will have clung onto objective clarity '*mordicus*'. That one cannot be sure of one's mental health and might be insane while taking oneself to be of sound mind is treated in *Luc.* 54 as 'an absurd consequence of the Academic position, not as a point raised by the Academics themselves'.[192]

Overall, Academic arguments from dreams and madness are in the first instance intended to establish that false impressions experienced by dreamers or madmen are—in type—like purported cataleptic impressions with respect to their capacity to

---

[190] Thus the insistence on *perspicuitas* suggests that the Stoics might grant that some impressions are 'found' to be clear and striking by perceiving subjects, but that they would distinguish this subjective clarity from an objective clarity which they regard as peculiar to cataleptic impressions.

[191] Sextus' example of Heracles (*M.* 7.407), who has—on the Academic argument—cataleptic impressions and false ones while mad, could have been used in reply.

[192] Striker (1997: 268 n. 13).

trigger assent. This is used as evidence that purported cataleptic impressions and others are non-distinct. Considerations of access need not be part of the reasoning and can be applied to subjective states.

5.6.2 Very Similar Objects

Arguments from objects like eggs and twins are in Sextus introduced with the remark that ἀπαραλλαξία, sc. of cataleptic and non-cataleptic impressions is shown with reference to 'stamp and impress' (κατὰ χαρακτῆρα καὶ κατὰ τύπον; *M.* 7.408 quoted above). This way of referring to the group of arguments in question does not feature in any other text, and it is not elucidated further in the course of Sextus' discussion. The two terms must refer to the object perceived and the imprint or alteration it leaves on the perceiving subject's mind respectively.[193] However, the former is not an established technical term for 'object' and seems to have been chosen in order to evoke the idea of the causal mechanics of imprinting. On the most natural reading, the aim of these arguments is to show the equivalence of purported cataleptic impressions and others with respect to the property referred to in the second clause of Zeno's definition qua description of a physical alteration of the mind. The physical alteration of the mind is not the kind of thing a perceiving subject can have direct access to, and it would have to be inferred in the course of the relevant argument.

The designation of this group of arguments does provide a meaningfully contrasting characterization with the first group, for two reasons: first, arguments from dreams and madness related to cases where either no such causal process is envisaged or only a partially effective one (i.e. in the event that an object is causally responsible for an impression, but only partially so, since it is not represented as what it is); second, whereas arguments from dreams and madness aimed at arguing that the distinguishing feature attaches to purported cataleptic impressions as well as others, here it is concluded that purported cataleptic impressions have no such feature (*M.* 7.411). It is not part of the record who formulated the designations of the arguments, but there is no good reason for the Stoics to devise them.

The first examples aim at showing that it is not possible to distinguish (διορίζειν) cataleptic impressions from false or acataleptic ones (*M.* 7.409):[194] the Stoic, presented with two eggs or with twins in succession, would not be able to tell them apart and say which one was which. In the case of twins, if the sage mistook one twin for the other, he would have an impression which met the first two clauses of Zeno's definition and yet was false (this only holds if the first clause is construed as 'arising from a real object'). Two aspects of Sextus' discussion which are worth noting are, first, that it makes no mention of the Stoic response to such arguments, namely the

---

[193] Striker (1997: 272) translates 'accuracy and precision', which levels out that the two terms denote impressor and imprint. Cf. LSJ s.v. χαρακτήρ no. I; the use of the word to denote an imprint is secondary.

[194] Sextus, *M.* 7.409: ἐπὶ γὰρ τῶν ὁμοίων μὲν κατὰ μορφήν, διαφερόντων δὲ κατὰ τὸ ὑποκείμενον, ἀμήχανόν ἐστι διορίζειν τὴν καταληπτικὴν φαντασίαν ἀπὸ τῆς ψευδοῦς καὶ ἀκαταλήπτου· οἷον δυεῖν ᾠῶν ἄκρως ἀλλήλοις ὁμοίων ἐναλλὰξ τῷ Στωικῷ δίδωμι πρὸς διάκρισιν, εἰ ἐπιβαλὼν ὁ σοφὸς ἰσχύσει λέγειν ἀδιαπτώτως, πότερον ἕν ἐστι τὸ δεικνύμενον ᾠὸν ἢ ἄλλο καὶ ἄλλο; 'For in the case of things similar in shape but differing in substance, it is not feasible to distinguish the cataleptic impression from the one that is false and not cataleptic; if for example I offer, of two eggs which are exactly alike, each one in turn to the Stoic for discrimination, will the sage upon inspection be able to say in an incontrovertible way whether the egg shown is this one or that one?'

observation that no two distinct things, however similar, are identical, as in general the section gives the Academic challenge but not the Stoic reply. Second, Sextus' example makes no reference to the ἰδίωμα, but *M.* 7.403 (discussed above) illustrates readily enough how it could have been referred to, namely for its absence: the sage is not able to tell apart twins, so the impression of neither twin can be marked by the feature, and so the two impressions at issue must be identical.

The verb διορίζειν is an ambiguous term (see above, n. 157), but here it seems clear that it is used to refer to a perceiving subject's inability to distinguish impressions; however, given how Sextus calls the type of argument, an inference from the absence of a distinctive feature to the equivalence of impressions qua physical states is still intended. In *M.* 7.409 Sextus talks first about the impossibility of distinguishing purported cataleptic from false and non-cataleptic impressions, and then introduces the sage who is invited to discriminate eggs.[195] The use of the sage as a frame of reference (absent in the arguments from abnormal states of mind) is significant because one might wonder how one could infer equivalence of physical states from inability to distinguish very similar objects if access is not part of the definition. The answer must be that for the sage the Stoics assumed a privileged epistemic standing and an enhanced ability to discriminate. They may thus have been reluctant to counter such arguments by observing that what matters is the state one is in, not access to it.[196]

The discussion in Cicero, *Luc.* 83–5, is interestingly complementary. In its context, it is the Academic response to the dogmatist's response to the first wave of such arguments, which must have featured in the lost first book of the first edition of *Acad.* (i.e. in the *Catulus*); see ad loc. The presentation is quasi-dialogical, in that it features interventions by the dogmatist, but in a way which favours the Academic side: given that it is the last word on the subject in the first edition of *Acad.*, Cicero arguably could not resist the temptation to give himself the last word. So the script is written by an Academic in more than one sense. While this limits its evidential value for the Stoic position, it offers lessons on the complexity of our evidence. I begin in *Luc.* 83 with the restatement of what Brittain (2006: xxii) calls the 'core Academic argument', divided into four *capita* which jointly lead to the conclusion that nothing can be apprehended. The first two of these are that there are false impressions and that false impressions cannot be apprehended;[197] the third is that, if there is no difference between impressions, then it cannot be that some of them are cataleptic and the others are not. The fourth, the main subject of contention, is formulated in this way:

nullum esse uisum uerum a sensu profectum cui non appositum sit uisum aliud quod ab eo nihil intersit quodque percipi non possit.

---

[195] Unlike in Cicero (*Luc.* 48), this is not cast in the depersonalized terms of his mind being unable to make discriminations. It is possible, but would seem forced in this case, to say that διορίζειν is focalized by an observer who notes that the sage is unable to make discriminations between eggs as a matter of fact.
[196] See on §58: *Habeo enim regulam....*
[197] See Reinhardt (2018b) as well as section 10 on Cicero's renderings of terminology relating to the cataleptic impression, notably his apparent habit of talking of impressions (as opposed to objects) which are apprehended.

According to this, for every true sense impression, there is one which is 'juxtaposed' with it (*appositum*), does not differ from it, and cannot be grasped (i.e. is false).[198] The phrase *a sensu profectum* might suggest a restriction to instances of perception here (which would exclude dreams), but comparison with *Luc.* 40–2, where the same argument features, shows no such restriction can be intended. Any reference to what is available to the perceiving subject is avoided, with Cicero speaking instead objectively of 'juxtaposed' impressions which 'lack a difference'. The two impressions in question can either be alike with regard to the distinctive feature (by exhibiting it or by not exhibiting it, while differing in representational content) or be identical qua imprints or have the same representational content: Cicero's formulation is neutral in this respect.

In *Luc.* 84 Cicero then gives the example of the Servilii twins, who had earlier been introduced as hard to tell apart for strangers but easily distinguished by relatives (*Luc.* 56). If one has a good view of Publius Servilius Geminus but ends up with the impression (i.e. perceptual belief) that this is Quintus Servilius Geminus, then Publius was not the kind of object one could apprehend, i.e. have a cataleptic impression of, and what is true is not marked off from what is false by a distinguishing feature (a *nota*, which I take to correspond to Sextus' ἰδίωμα).[199] Cicero continues that, with the difference between true and false removed, the same person would not be able to identify Gaius Cotta, who was twice Geminus' colleague as consul but who— it is understood—has no twin, since he and his impression carried no distinguishing feature of such a kind which could not be false,[200] and thus the impression might be of someone else (a move to be explained presently). There is then a Stoic objection: the metaphysical claim that every object in the world, including a twin or an egg, is unique, which implies that two impressions, each arising from a different Servilius, would differ (presumably qua imprints and in terms of their representational content, but neither is mentioned). Strikingly, the objection is formulated in a way which marks its applicability to the Servilii only (*Luc.* 84: *Negas tantam similitudinem in rerum natura esse*), which requires explanation, given that Cicero's argument included a second step involving Cotta. In reply Cicero insists that two very similar objects, featuring in two impressions, may nonetheless *appear* identical (cf. *Luc.* 58).

To appreciate the force of Cicero's argument we need to look back at the discussion of twins in Sextus. His version of the argument reveals no awareness of the Stoic invocation of the metaphysical principle, thereby establishing no more than that twins—assumed to be identical—give rise to impressions which are identical (qua imprints/alterations and representational content). By contrast, in *Luc.* 84–5 the principle is not just invoked in the course of the back-and-forth of Academic argument and Stoic response, but it is arguably factored in by Cicero (as speaker) from the start so that its irrelevance to the Academic argument and the slow-footedness of

---

[198] See Reinhardt (2019: 156–7) on Cicero's use of factive expressions (like *percipere*) in *Acad.*

[199] We saw above that in Sextus' discussion of ἀπαραλλαξία in the case of objects which are alike the ἰδίωμα is only mentioned in the concluding remark (*M.* 7.411), for its absence and thus in a manner which can readily be reconciled with what Cicero writes in *Luc.* 84. See the general note on *Luc.* 33–34a for a discussion of terminology used for the distinguishing feature in *Acad.*

[200] I take it to be due to looseness of expression, rather than a substantial doctrinal shift, that it is now the distinguishing feature 'which cannot be false'.

the Stoics are dramatized. There are three reasons for reading the text in this way. First, the Servilii had featured before as capable of being told apart by relatives, which suggests that at this stage of the debate they are not assumed to be identical;[201] second, in the second half of *Luc.* 84 and 85 *init.* Cicero simply restates his argument, implying that the Stoic citation of the principle shows that they are one step behind; third, the principle enables the otherwise baffling claim of Cicero's that, if one can be left with an impression of one Servilius when one is faced with the other Servilius, then one will not be certain that, when seeing Cotta, one is not in fact seeing someone completely different. The Academics' point is that, in the absence of a distinguishing feature, we cannot tell apart what the Stoics regard as individuals, and if we cannot do it in the case of the two individuals who are the Servilii, we cannot be certain with respect to any individual that he or she is actually that individual. One cannot be certain, the argument goes, that one is not looking at somebody else, because *as a class* supposedly self-warranting impressions do not have a distinguishing feature. That is why someone's impression of Cotta may be, for all one knows, an impression of someone completely different. Once more, we are dealing with ἀπαραλλαξία in type, but in this case characterized by the absence of a *nota* (cf. Sextus, *M.* 7.411). The Stoics, who follow the weak interpretation, think that the uniqueness of the object of the impression transfers to imprint/representational content, and from there to the way the object is represented in the impression. And because for them the *nota* is a function of how the impression presents its object, they regard the move to Cotta as blocked by observing that the Servilii are unique individuals, and thus do not address it. One may not have learnt to appreciate the *nota*, but one could learn it, or so they think. To this the Academics would reply that their example *assumes* a scenario in which one has not learnt to appreciate it, and that the very possibility of such a scenario is the issue. Notice now how obvious responses to the Academic argument are not available to a Stoic: the Stoic can neither reply that he knows that Cotta does not have a twin, nor can he reply that he can see that the person he is looking at is Cotta (and not, say, Torquatus, who looks completely different). The former is not an option because the Stoics take such considerations to be irrelevant to an impression's catalepticity (though not to its prospects of winning assent);[202] the latter is not an option because when pressed how he knows, the Stoic would have to refer, ultimately, to the unique detail represented in his impression, i.e. the distinguishing feature.

What kind of inability to distinguish between impressions is at issue in Cicero's argument? The case is less clear than it seemed (to me) with respect to Sextus. In principle, one can read the exchange in causal terms, as a story about impressions which fail to make the perceiving subject discriminate. Arguably, Cicero does not need more than this to mount a powerful objection. The closest Cicero comes to using expressions comparable to Sextus' διορίζειν above is when he suggests that the case of the Servilii has shown that one does not judge by a *nota* when one identifies someone as who he appears to be (§84 *fin.*: ... *tamen non ea nota iudicabis*...).

---

[201] That every representative of a given species was a unique individual was in fact not just a Stoic view; see the commentary on *Luc.* 84–5.
[202] See Allen (1997: 249).

5.7 Arrangement

Allen (1997: 246) has observed that in both Sextus and in Lucullus' speech in *Luc.* arguments from dreams and madness precede those from very similar objects,[203] and that this sequence can be read as enabled by a concession made by the Academics, and thus not random. One way of describing the concession at issue would be to ask in what sense, given that a cataleptic impression is on any account defined as a true impression which meets additional criteria, there could be 'one just like it' which is false. Dream impressions and impressions experienced while mad are 'just like' purported cataleptic impressions (as a class) in that they have the ἰδίωμα and meet the second clause of the definition, i.e. they have supremely rich and detailed representational content; they do not meet the first clause if this is interpreted as 'of an actually obtaining state of affairs', and an external object is only partially responsible for their representational content in the case of madness, and not even that in the case of dreams or hallucinations.

If we then turn to impressions experienced while awake and sane, and of objects which come in very similar pairs or multiples, the concession would be that there is a class of impressions which meet the first clause and the second clause. However, this class of impressions is then shown to lack the ἰδίωμα, so that there could be, for a given impression, a false one 'just like it'.

5.8 Generalization

Let us briefly assemble the generalizing strategies which we either find attested or have reason to posit.[204] It is plain that the Academics did not confine themselves to arguing that only some purported cataleptic impressions could be false, even though the Stoic insistence on the extreme coherence of their system would have made that a possible line of attack.[205] Rather, the Academics intended to mount a more general challenge, as e.g. the move from the Servilii to Cotta in *Luc.* 84 showed.[206] That was predicated on a concession, the Stoic claim that every object in the world is a unique individual, and presumably became an argumentative option some way into the debate, for we have evidence of a reply to the Academic challenge from very similar objects which did not involve the invocation of this metaphysical principle: the suggestion that the sage should withhold assent to impressions representing objects which are known to be very similar to others (p. 499). That this rejoinder was of limited effect is suggested by two passages, D.L. 7.162 and 7.177:[207] both of these involve the deliberate tricking of somebody claiming to be a sage, in one case by sending the wrong twin to collect a sum of money previously deposited by the other

---

[203] In his reply, the Cicero character inverts the order, as is noted by Allen (1997: 246 n. 31).
[204] On the need to identify such generalizing strategies, see Perin (2006).
[205] Allen (1997) shows how many Academic arguments can be read as urging not that human beings are in dire epistemic straits, but that they would be given the extremist demands of the Stoics.
[206] The Stoic argumentative posture assumes and increasingly articulates standard conditions for instances of perception, while the Academics press special cases and seek to generalize from them.
[207] See the discussion in Ioppolo (1996: 67–71); Striker (1997: 268–9).

twin, in the second case by placing wax pomegranates in front of someone, who is promptly duped into mistaking them for real ones. Now given that it is impossible to predict when the sage might find himself the victim of such a deception and that a determined individual might manufacture duplicate objects which are very hard to categorize in general terms (scenarios cited in discussions of the Gettier problem come to mind), the possibility of deception has to be reckoned with at almost any moment: there is no neatly delineated class of objects which come in pairs or multiples.[208] This, then, is a second generalizing strategy.

It is less clear how the Academic would generalize from scenarios turning on the impressions of dreamers and madmen, simply because no attempt at generalization is attested. That such scenarios were, as a matter of fact, not used to argue that we might be dreaming or mad now was mentioned above (p. lxxi). The Stoics did recognize the possibility of false impressions experienced while awake and of sound mind, and they did assume that non-sages sometimes assent to them. Why did they not refer to such cases instead?[209] The reason may be that the circumstances under which human beings experience false impressions while awake and sane are contingent, whereas dreams and madness make for scenarios in which the subject invariably experiences some false impressions, notably on the view of the Academics, who have no reason to follow the Stoics in regarding false impressions experienced while awake and sane as simply less clear than cataleptic ones. We saw above that the Academics infer from actions carried out by dreamers and madmen that false impressions experienced by such people must be—to them—as clear and striking as purported cataleptic impressions. One way in which one might generalize from this to impressions experienced while awake is suggested by the example from Heracles. He experiences a true impression (of the bow), which gives rise to the action it would give rise to under normal circumstances, alongside a false impression (of his children as Eurystheus'). Now if true impressions and false impressions which both have the ἰδίωμα can be experienced alongside each other while insane, it becomes reasonable to argue that this is so also while one is awake and sane.[210] For it would seem difficult for the Stoics to argue that the perceiving subject's mental state is part of the causal history of a cataleptic impression (referred to in the second clause), so that impressions experienced while insane are excluded, when the impression of the bow was true and gave rise to relevant action (see above, n. lxx, for Sextus pressing this point). Lucullus' own injunction to cling to the (supreme) clarity of cataleptic impressions 'mordicus' (§51), which would be cited to rule true impressions experienced while insane as non-cataleptic, sounds somewhat desperate.

When the Academics say that there is no true impression of such a kind that there is not one just like it which is false (cf. *Luc.* 77, see below), this should not be read as the claim that for every object of a purported cataleptic impression X, there is an

---

[208] As Striker (1997: 270) observes, such scenarios might have been used to create pressure on the Stoics to adopt the strong interpretation of the third clause, so that impressions which are cataleptic would be marked by a sign.
[209] Cf. Perin (2005: 507) [author's emphasis]: 'What work is being done here by the fact that the false impressions to which the Academics appeal occur in *dreams* and *madness*?'
[210] Note that *for the Stoics* the ἰδίωμα is bound up with the defining property specified in the second clause of Zeno's definition.

object X′ which is indistinguishable from it,²¹¹ or—consequently—that for every purported cataleptic impression A experienced while awake and sane, there is an impression A′ of the same representational content which is false. Both of these claims could only ever be made for some impressions. The general claim the Academics do make is better characterized as: 'Any given purported cataleptic impression may in fact be false' (see above, p. lxxvi), i.e. there is the epistemic possibility that the proposition it contains is false.²¹² This is a possible reading of e.g. *Luc.* 77: *Incubuit autem in eas disputationes ut doceret nullum tale esse uisum a uero ut non eiusdem modi etiam a falso possit esse.* What is more, this way of interpreting the ἀπαραλλαξία-claim also makes non-perceptual ἀπαραλλαξία a straightforward notion; see on *Luc.* 43–4.

Appendix—Ἀπαραλλαξία in the Different Versions of the Core Argument in *Acad.*

The core argument features in several places in *Acad.*, and there is some variation to the way in which the ἀπαραλλαξία consideration is worded. I shall survey the passages in question in the light of the distinctions drawn above (and leave aside contexts in which ἀπαραλλαξία is invoked without the ostensible purpose of setting out or discussing the core argument).

§40
(a) quae ita uidentur ut etiam alia eodem modo uideri possint nec in iis quicquam intersit, non posse eorum alia percipi, alia non percipi; nihil interesse autem non modo, si omni ex parte eiusdem modi sint, sed etiam si discerni non possint.
(b) quod autem uerum uisum est id omne tale est ut eiusdem modi falsum etiam possit uideri; et quae uisa sint eius modi ut in iis nihil intersit....

§41
(a) inter quae uisa nihil intersit, ex iis non posse alia talia esse ut percipi possint alia ut non possint.
(b) alterum, omne uisum quod sit a uero tale esse quale etiam a falso possit esse.

---

²¹¹ Cf. Perin (2006): 'But in conceding this much the Stoics need not concede, and it is not easy to see how the Academics have given them reason to concede, that for any object A there is in fact a second object B that is "indiscriminable" from A and, therefore, that for any object A, no impression of A is a "cataleptic" impression.'

²¹² Perin (2005) shows how devastating Academic objections to the Stoic position would be if these objections turned on the counterfactual possibility that there *could have been* an impression 'just like' a cataleptic impression which was false, as opposed to the epistemic possibility that there *could be* an impression 'just like' a cataleptic impression which is false. However, the Stoics had no reason at all to allow such objections (and consequently it is unlikely that the Academics did make them). For the third clause of the definition, given its mood (aorist optative with ἄν), can only be read as ruling out epistemic possibility, and not as ruling out counterfactual possibility (which would require the imperfect or aorist indicative with ἄν, cf. Kühner-Gerth i.232). For the distinction between epistemic and counterfactual possibility see DeRose (1991: 581). Epistemic possibility is neutral to the internalism/externalism distinction. I assume that a possibility is an epistemic possibility in case it is not known whether it obtains in the actual world. See also on *Luc.* 119.

§42
—uolunt efficere iis omnibus quae uisa sint ueris adiuncta esse falsa quae a ueris nihil differant.

§83
—tertium, inter quae uisa nihil intersit, fieri non posse ut eorum alia percipi possint alia non possint.

An initial observation to make is that discrimination (in some sense) is only mentioned once in this set of passages, in §40(a). It features there in a gloss on a phrasal term in the previous sentence (i.e. on *nihil interesse*). 'There being no difference between two impressions' would not just apply, sc. on the understanding of the Academics if two impressions were 'of the same kind in every respect' but 'also if they could not be distinguished'. On one reading, this suggests that the ἀπαραλλαξία-relationship proper is about equivalence or non-distinctness, and that the gloss introduces a conceptual extension of sorts, itself not part of non-distinctness in the narrow sense (and perhaps to be invoked in suitable circumstances). On a second reading, Cicero is being elliptic here, so that the distinction at issue would be between impressions 'being *eiusdem modi* (and being indiscriminable)' and '(not being *eiusdem modi* but) being indiscriminable'. Two considerations tell against the second reading: (i) if Cicero had intended it, it would have been clearer if he had written e.g. *sed etiam si **tantummodo** discerni non possint* in §40(a); (ii) in §58 *fin*. Lucullus ascribes to the Academics, in apparent backward reference to the *Catulus*, the following claim:... *non uos id dicere, inter ipsas impressiones nihil interesse, sed inter species et quasdam formas eorum*. This suggests that arguing from identical 'look' does not carry an assumption of non-distinctness qua imprint/alteration.

Should one feel entitled or even compelled to expand the earlier part of the sentence in §40(a) to 'being *eiusdem modi* (and being indiscriminable)'? I do not think so. Cicero is careful to avoid discriminability talk with respect to the ἀπαραλλαξία claim proper, and instead speaks of equivalences, juxtapositions, etc. as I hope to have shown, which does seem to signal that indiscriminability is not part of the concept of ἀπαραλλαξία/being *eiusdem modi*. This, I submit, holds true when Cicero talks about impressions (*uisa*) being no different from each other (e.g. in §83; cf. §42 where, however, *uisa* feels more like a genuine participle than a substantivated one), *and* when he uses expressions like *eodem modo uideri* (§40a). Further, I hesitate to take *uideri* in these passages to mean only 'to appear phenomenally', since in the core argument ἀπαραλλαξία should cover cases of non-distinctness in type, i.e. cases where an impression is deemed to be 'just like' another one with respect to clarity and strikingness while being different in terms of representational content (see p. lxxviii above). However, the *eodem modo uideri* expression (or equivalents) does not invite a reading on which equivalents of imprints on/alterations of the soul's leading part are meant, since one would assume that these cannot directly form the content of our impressions. In §83, where the Academic speaks, a formulation is used which *could* cover equivalence of imprints, too (*inter quae uisa nihil intersit*).

6. The Carneadean πιθανόν and Cicero's *probabile*

In addition to mounting arguments against the cataleptic impression, Carneades also devised an alternative account of how human beings might successfully function using persuasive impressions (πιθανά), whereby the latter could be perceptual or non-perceptual impressions (including philosophical theses).[213]

Along with the majority of interpreters, I believe that Carneades himself formulated this alternative account ad hominem, as one which the Stoic opponent ought to find at least as compelling as the doctrine of the cataleptic impression but on which Carneades himself did not take a view.[214]

In the case of the πιθανόν the evidence from Sextus is, on the specific issue of how persuasiveness was conceived, more detailed than that from Cicero, partly because Cicero appears to have opted for certain simplifications, and partly because relevant sections from the first and the final edition of *Acad.* are not extant. Hence it seems methodologically sound to evaluate the evidence from Sextus first and then to establish whether the evidence from Cicero is consistent with the picture emerging from Sextus and ideally also confirms it. I shall also consider briefly how the Carneadean conception of πιθανότης relates to the Stoic one.[215]

I will begin by asking what accounts for the initial persuasiveness of impressions which Carneades termed πιθανά; the answer to this question then has implications for other issues. I will argue that an impression's initial persuasiveness, prior to any testing or scrutiny, is taken to be due to the fact that its propositional content is consistent with views antecedently held by the subject, and that an impression's phenomenal clarity is an enabling not a constitutive property of persuasiveness as conceived by Carneades. The rational persuasiveness which is owed to the fact that a πιθανόν is congruous in the sense described will be called *plausibility*.

I will consequently reject a number of alternative conceptions of persuasiveness, which include: that the initial persuasiveness of a persuasive impression is a brute fact, not capable of explanation or analysis; that it is exclusively or primarily due to the phenomenal clarity of an impression; or that it is linked to probability, pre-theoretical or otherwise (where probability is defined in terms of statistical likelihood, evidence, or a combination of the two).[216] I will also argue against the view that the πιθανόν

---

[213] It is a matter of contention whether the Carneadean πιθανόν was first conceived to describe human behaviour in everyday situations involving perceptual impressions only or whether it was conceived from the beginning as capable of ranging over perceptual impressions *and* non-perceptual ones as they might feature in philosophical debate; I believe the latter. In Cicero the *probabile* is envisaged to be used for both purposes, by the character Cicero and the character Lucullus (*Luc.* 32 *fin.*, in an apparent report of what one of the Academic speakers said in the *Catulus*). Crucially, it is also envisaged to be so used in *Luc.* 104, where Cicero translates from a work by Clitomachus (see ad loc., notably on *item ea quae interrogati in utramque partem*), who is not usually taken to innovate on Carneades (but see Ioppolo 2017). See also the beginning of section 6.1 and section 6.6. Striker (1996b: 106) argues that the scheme as laid out in Sextus is readily extendable beyond perceptual impressions.

[214] For a different view, see Castagnoli (2019: 199).

[215] Arcesilaus' εὔλογον, which is sometimes compared to the Carneadean πιθανόν, is in my view absent from the Ciceronian record; on it see section 7.

[216] That initial persuasiveness might be a brute fact seems to be suggested by scholarly discussions which fail to confront the question where it comes from. The idea that the initial persuasiveness of the πιθανόν is due to the clarity of its phenomenal content is found e.g. in Brittain (2001: 105): 'Carneades had

was first conceived in one way and then re-interpreted by later Academics; however, differences in the use of the πιθανόν are attested.

6.1 The Evidence from Sextus

The Carneadean πιθανόν, the subject of this section, was developed, as has long been recognized, with reference to the Stoic conception of the πιθανόν. I propose to discuss the latter in section 6.4 below, even though some of the evidence for it predates Carneades and my discussion in this section will inevitably refer to other aspects of Stoic thought on occasion. The reasons for this are threefold. An immanent re-examination of the Sextan material is warranted, the pre-Carneadean Stoic evidence is disparate and more reliably put into context if the Carneadean evidence is considered first, and the most significant Stoic material arguably post-dates Carneades and reacts to him.

The main reference point in this section will be Sextus' discussion of the Carneadean πιθανόν in *M.* 7.166–89, although the briefer account *P.H.* 1.227–30 will be considered, too.[217] The discussion of the πιθανόν from *M.* 7.166 is preceded by a section (§§159–65) on Carneades' arguments in favour of the non-existence of the criterion; the πιθανόν itself is then introduced as Carneades' 'criterion for the conduct of life and for the attainment of happiness' (κριτήριον πρός τε τὴν τοῦ βίου διεξαγωγὴν καὶ πρὸς τὴν τῆς εὐδαιμονίας περίκτησιν) and apparently functions as a rebuttal to the Stoic ἀπραξία argument.[218] Striker (1996b: 105) suggests that the πιθανόν was first conceived as a reply to the Stoic claim that the Academics make everything obscure in criticizing the cataleptic impression (cf. *Luc.* 105 *init.*).

The discussion in *M.* 7 poses, as evidence, two types of broader problems which are well recognized. The first is that some of the examples given do not seem to fit very well with what they are supposed to illustrate; this has been explained as evidence of Carneadean ingenuity by some, and as the result of poorly executed editing by others.[219] The second is that those who employ the πιθανόν are said to 'assent' to persuasive impressions on a number of occasions where one would expect assent at least in the Stoic sense to be withheld.[220] One explanation which has been offered for this is assumed Sextan bias (i.e. the desire to present Carneades as a dogmatist compared to the Pyrrhonist); alternatively, some believe that the section presents the use

---

isolated the subjective clarity of an impression as the principal assent-inducing (or 'persuasive') characteristic it could bear prior to assessment.' For an explanation of persuasiveness in terms of an early notion of probability, see Obdrzalek (2006). Ioppolo (2017) holds that it is possible to distinguish between a Clitomachean and a Carneadean conception of the πιθανόν, neither of which corresponds to the one I posit.

[217] I will not touch on the criticism offered by Sextus in *M.* 7.435–8 here, but see on *Luc.* 35b–36.
[218] See e.g. Bett (1989); on the flexibility of the ἀπραξία argument, see Vogt (2010).
[219] Görler (1994: 868–9) argues for Carneadean ingenuity; infelicitous adaptation of examples is assumed by Mutschmann (1911); Allen (1994: 94); and Brittain (2001: 101–2 n. 46). That misadaptation must have occurred is clear from the fact that some of the examples not just fail to illustrate with reasonable precision what they are supposed to illustrate, but also jar with their immediate introductions (e.g. *M.* 7.180).
[220] See e.g. *M.* 7.172, 188.

of the πιθανόν from the perspective of mitigated scepticism involving self-aware assent which was available in the Academy as an option, for the sake of the argument or as the actual stance adopted by some Academics (cf. *Luc.* 148).[221] However, in either case one would still assume that Sextus' account has an undoubtedly Carneadean core which would be unaffected by secondary reinterpretations and modifications.

In *M.* 7.166–89, Sextus reports that Carneades distinguished four types of πιθανά:[222]

- persuasive impressions ('top-level πιθανά');
- persuasive impressions which meet the further criterion of being clear ('first-level πιθανά');

and first-level πιθανά which have undergone two different types of test:[223]

- 'second-level πιθανά' (which are found to be ἀπερίσπαστος, 'unreversed', after testing);
- 'third-level πιθανά' (which are found to be διεξ- or περιωδευμένος, 'examined thoroughly', in addition).[224]

Of these, the last three are said to serve as a 'criterion' (173, 176, 184).[225] The first of the two tests in question, relating to the content of the impression,[226] is a test for compatibility with a 'syndrome' (συνδρομή) of impressions of which the impression under investigation forms part, while the second test is intended to establish that the impression under examination and the impressions in the syndrome meet the criterion of clarity,[227] which is construed as a function of the circumstances under which the perceiver had the impression (e.g. distance to object, time constraints, mental state of the perceiver). Top-level πιθανά are easily, and have often been, construed as

---

[221] Thus Hirzel (1883: 174 n. 3); Burnyeat (unpublished); Brittain (2001: 95–6); we shall return to the question of possible different attitudes to the πιθανόν adopted within the sceptical Academy in section 6.6.
[222] I have been using the term πιθανόν because it is conventional to speak of the Carneadean πιθανόν. The term features for the first time in *M.* 7.174; before that apparent synonyms are used (see below). The hopefully not too misleading distinction between 'top-level' and 'first-level' πιθανά is intended to dovetail with the terminology employed by Allen (1994).
[223] From the discussion in *M.* 7, one might draw the conclusion that these two types of test, which feature in reverse order in *P.H.* 1.227–30, are to be carried out sequentially. Quite possibly, however, they are to be carried out simultaneously; see Schofield (1999: 350).
[224] On the variation, which may not just be terminological, see Allen (1994: 91 and 97–9).
[225] That types of πιθανόν are called a 'criterion' (see p. lxxxi above) raises the same kind of question as the assent which agents are said to give in Sextus' discussion; cf. p. lxxxvi below. Compare also the unequivocal references to the truth of an impression (e.g. §179 *fin.*).
[226] I shall be distinguishing between an impression's propositional and its phenomenal content (without specifying which is meant where the context makes it clear), along the lines of the distinction between propositional and representational content employed by Frede (1987: 152–7); cf. also Brittain (2014: 335 n. 9).
[227] We call impressions 'clear' instead of 'evident', since the former conveys better that ἐνάργεια is a property of impressions owing to which they represent their subject in a certain way. On Hellenistic conceptions of ἐνάργεια, see Ierodiakonou (2012).

uncharacterized and undetermined with respect to content, as impressions which appear true to us, i.e. are apt to persuade us of their truth, as a matter of fact. First-level πιθανά are often construed in the same way but are assumed to be very clear in the phenomenal sense in addition.

An important point to appreciate is that the two types of test one is to perform on first-level πιθανά test for properties which *account for* the persuasiveness of top-level and first-level πιθανά, respectively, in that these properties are deemed to be the *reasons* why top-level πιθανά appear true, and first-level πιθανά appear true to a higher degree.

In §§169–75 Sextus discusses the Academic division of impressions, as well as top-level πιθανά and first-level πιθανά. In §169 presentations are divided into those which appear true (πιθανότης; πιθανὴ φαντασία; ἔμφασις; 'top-level πιθανά') and those which do not appear true (ἀπειθής or ἀπίθανος φαντασία; ἀπέμφασις).[228] The ἀπίθανος φαντασία is here the contradictory not the contrary of the πιθανὴ φαντασία;[229] such impressions either fail to be persuasive or are positively unpersuasive. The class of impressions which appear true is then divided further into impressions which intensely appear true (171; first-level πιθανά), which may serve as the criterion, and ones which are dim (ἀμυδρός, ἔκλυτος, both opposites of ἐναργής, but that term is not repeated here from 161),[230] but πιθανά nonetheless.

The term 'ἔμφασις' occurs in Stoic texts, and I will discuss those occurrences below. By contrast, 'ἀπέμφασις' and the verb from which it derives, 'ἀπεμφαίνω', are not found in Stoic texts. Failure to appreciate what the term 'ἀπέμφασις' means, or so I shall argue, has prevented earlier scholars from recognizing salient features of the Carneadean scheme.[231]

If one looks beyond Stoic texts, both the verb and the noun are not without relevant history. I begin with an example of 'ἀπεμφαίνω'. Polybius 6.47.7–10 compares the constitutions of various Greek city states, and dismisses the idea that Plato's *Rep.* might be considered in this context, on the grounds that in the competition for prizes artists or athletes who have not been registered and formally trained are not admitted either. Plato's constitution has, so Polybius, not been tested in practice, and considering it would be like running a beauty contest between a human being and a statue. Observers would regard this as 'an entirely incongruous comparison' (σύγκρισις τελείως ἀπεμφαίνουσα). Strabo attempts to explain the history and geographic location of a particular tribe, the Cauconians (8.3.17). Here as elsewhere, the geographer is faced with incompatible accounts and has to devise ways of either reconciling them through interpretation or excluding some so as to retain one or more, provided they are compatible. Thus agreement of pieces of information is a relevant consideration, as is the resolution of inconsistencies (cf. 8.3.17 = p. 345.19–20 Casaubon: καὶ δὴ τοῖς ὑφ᾽ Ὁμήρου λεγομένοις **ὁμολογεῖ** μᾶλλον ἡ ὑστάτη ἀπόφασις, τό τε ζητούμενον πρότερον λαμβάνει **λύσιν**, 'That last opinion fits better with what

---

[228] The resumption of §169 ἔμφασις in §173 ἐμφαινομένη, discussed below, confirms that ἔμφασις and ἀπέμφασις is indeed the top-level distinction.
[229] Noted by Burnyeat (unpublished). The Stoic conception is tellingly different, as we will see below.
[230] On the terms describing phenomenal properties of impressions, see Lefebvre (2007).
[231] Cf. e.g. Bury (1935), who merely transliterates the term; Bett (2005), who renders it 'non-reflection'; Long and Sedley (i.1987: 451): 'non-manifestation'; Schofield (1999: 346 n. 60): 'anti-appearance'.

Homer says, and the problem raised previously thereby receives a solution, too'). The splitting of an ethnic group so that the two subgroups ended up in different locations would mean that accounts of Athene departing from a location into a different direction from the one where one might expect to find the Cauconians 'would no longer be incongruous' (p. 346.9 C. οὐκ ἂν ἔχοι τι ἀπεμφαῖνον). In 10.2.12 both 'ἔμφασις' and 'ἀπέμφασις' occur in close proximity. A Homeric line is quoted (*Od.* 9.21), according to which Ithaca is at the same time 'on the ground' and 'high up', and we are told that Homer's narrative at times does contain this kind of ἀπέμφασις (p. 454.32 C.; cf. p. 454.25 ὑπεναντιότης), but that it is usually not problematic because it can be explained by reinterpreting one of the supposedly inconsistent phrases. Shortly after it is said of such a reconciliation attempt (which is ultimately rejected in favour of another) that it ἔχει ἔμφασιν, which translators into English render as 'has plausibility'. Sextus himself uses 'ἀπέμφασις' as a methodological term. In *M.* 8.192–6 he argues that with regard to the indicative sign 'we put ourselves into a position of greatest inconsistency' (195: εἰς τὴν μεγίστην ἀπέμφασιν περιστησόμεθα) if we posit that each of the things such a sign can indicate exists, since it is not possible 'for causes which are incompatible to such a degree and mutually refuting to co-exist' (τὰς γὰρ οὕτω μαχομένας καὶ ἀνασκευαστικὰς ἀλλήλων αἰτίας οὐχ οἷόν τε συνυπάρχειν). In *M.* 11.162–4 Sextus defends the sceptic against two charges, that of inactivity (ἀνενεργησία) and that of inconsistency (ἀπέμφασις). (In passing, we can observe that Sextus does not just cite 'ἀπέμφασις' as a consideration of his own against dogmatic positions, but gives the impression that opponents of the Pyrrhonist would use the term, too; this is borne out by occurrences in contemporary authors.)[232] A situation of inconsistency is said to arise when the sceptic finds himself in the power of a tyrant who forces him to commit an unspeakable act. In that case he will either refuse the order and die a terrible death, or he will avoid such a fate by following the order. In either case 'he will no longer be unmoved by choice and avoidance' (οὐκέτι ἀφυγὴς καὶ ἀναίρετος ἔσται), as he claims to be.[233]

I hope that this short survey has shown that 'incongruence' or 'inconsistency' deserve to be considered as renderings of 'ἀπέμφασις', and that 'non-reflection', 'non-manifestation', and 'anti-appearance' are ad hoc renderings, merely based on the morphological formation of the term. They are also without explanatory power regarding the passage in which they feature.

The section on the first kind of test to which first-level πιθανά are to be subjected, so as to yield second-level πιθανά, is §§175–81. It begins with a statement which is very general and may thus guide us on how top-level πιθανά are conceived of. No impression is ever μονοειδής, 'simple in form'; rather, like a link in a chain it is always interconnected with others (§176). The example given is that of seeing a man whom we know, Socrates. Our perceptual belief that this is Socrates is the result (§178: πιστεύομεν ἐκ τοῦ πάντα αὐτῷ προσεῖναι τὰ εἰωθότα) of receiving a series of impressions on typical features of his as well as the setting in which Socrates is usually found. In §179 this is compared to a doctor who diagnoses a particular condition on the basis of a συνδρομή of symptoms and not just because of the presence of one

---

[232] e.g. Clem., *Strom.* 1.17.82.6, 4.12.85.2; Origen, *Contra Celsum* 4.45.16, 4.68.9, 7.12.11.
[233] See e.g. Spinelli (2008: 38) on the passage.

symptom;²³⁴ the notion of a 'syndrome' is then reused in the following section (§182), which suggests that it is not a one-off illustration but intended to capture a key aspect of the Carneadean conception of an impression. Now surely Carneades allows for the possibility of a top-level πιθανόν that this is Socrates, which, on the explanation offered here, means that already a substantial number of impressions are involved in generating this top-level impression. If Socrates was wearing a new coat, or conversing with Phaedrus outside of the city where we do not normally expect to find him, this would produce a top-level impression which one could call incongruous, i.e. an ἀπέμφασις, as well as an ἀπίθανος φαντασία, one which fails to persuade us that this is Socrates, without necessarily persuading us that this is not Socrates (see above on the ἀπίθανος φαντασία being the contradictory not the contrary of the πιθανὴ φαντασία in the Academic division). An impression which is not incongruous in this sense appears true even if it is not clear.²³⁵

The statement that we believe that this is Socrates 'from' (ἐκ) his properties should not be taken to mean that the individual impressions about Socrates' height, shape, and so on lead us to infer that this is Socrates; no inferences ought to be involved in perceiving a person within one's ken. This one would assume on independent grounds, but also because Sextus' formulation of the analogy between doctor and Academic perceiver suggests that on this point the analogy gives out. Consider M. 1.179:

> And just as some doctors do not assume on the basis of one symptom only (ἐξ ἑνὸς λαμβάνουσι συμπτώματος) that they are dealing with a genuine fever patient, such as an excessive pulse or a severe high temperature, but on the basis of a syndrome, such as a high temperature as well as pulse and soreness to the touch and flushing and thirst and similar things, so also the Academic makes his judgement as to the truth by a syndrome of appearances, and when none of the appearances in the syndrome turns him away as being false (μηδεμιᾶς τε τῶν ἐν τῇ συνδρομῇ φαντασιῶν περισπώσης αὐτὸν ὡς ψευδοῦς), he says the impression which strikes him (τὸ προσπίπτον) is true.

What a doctor does is form a hypothesis, a provisional diagnosis upon an initial appraisal of the patient's condition, which he then aims to verify by testing for each of the symptoms associated with the illness from which he suspects the patient to suffer. If all of the symptoms are found to be in evidence, then the provisional diagnosis is confirmed. How does the doctor formulate his initial diagnosis, i.e. how does he arrive at what is at the level of the illustrandum a top-level πιθανόν, which can then be tested? On rational grounds, one would assume, because his rational nature and his experience lead him, before any testing takes place, to the view that the subset

---

²³⁴ Galen uses the notion of a condition defined by an 'assemblage of symptoms', i.e. an ἄθροισμα τῶν συμπτωμάτων, frequently. The concept is already in use substantially earlier: in De plenitudine 8 (VII.554–5 K.) Erasistratus (fourth–third century BC) is reported to have recorded the whole of the Empiricists' 'syndrome of symptoms' (τὴν τῶν ἐμπειρικῶν συνδρομήν); see von Staden (1989: 383–4).

²³⁵ Contrast Brittain (2001: 100 n. 43), who takes the apparent truth of first-level πιθανά to 'allow for cases of perceptual illusion etc., where the impression is per se clear, but also incredible'; contrast also Brittain (2001: 117 n. 69).

of symptoms immediately in evidence is consistent with a certain condition. That this condition, which is itself not directly observable, is indeed present in the patient is then grasped not from one symptom (ἐξ ἑνὸς λαμβάνουσι συμπτώματος) but from all symptoms whose concurrence defines the condition in question. By contrast, the mental operations performed by the Academic are not described in a way which suggests that an inference is being performed (μηδεμιᾶς τε τῶν ἐν τῇ συνδρομῇ φαντασιῶν περισπώσης αὐτὸν ὡς ψευδοῦς λέγει ἀληθὲς εἶναι τὸ προσπίπτον).

As to the relationship of the impression under consideration (the 'target impression'; τὸ προσπίπτον in M. 1.179) with the syndrome, Carneades evidently had two different ways of thinking about it. In one sense the target impression dissolves into the impressions which jointly make up the syndrome and which must appear true for the target impression to be a πιθανόν, so that the syndrome thus conceived no longer contains an impression whose content could be characterized as 'this is Socrates' or 'Socrates is there' (rather, that is what the impressions in the syndrome jointly amount to, as also the medical analogy would suggest). In another sense, however, Carneades does, on the evidence of Sextus' report, speak of a target impression that this is Socrates, in such a way that minimally several of the impressions of the relevant syndrome are somehow contained in it; this fits with the conception of ἔμφασις on which Sextus relies (discussed below), which independently suggests that the πιθανόν is assumed to 'contain' its syndrome in a sense to be clarified. As a result, one of the functions of the notion of the syndrome seems to be that it amounts to a competing coherentist conception for the Stoic foundationalist conception of the richness of impressions,[236] i.e. to a different way of accounting for such richness.

Sextus does not spell out what the doctor does when he finds one of the expected symptoms not to be in evidence, but he does say that the Academic would declare an impression as true if none of the impressions in the syndrome gives an appearance of its falsehood.[237] The appearance of falsehood, one assumes, would consist in a lack of fit both with an expectation which the Academic has when he embarks on the testing procedure, and with the other impressions in the syndrome which were,[238] after all, sufficient to give rise to the equivalent of the doctor's hypothetical diagnosis—the

---

[236] Compare Frede (1987: 155) on Stoic richness: 'If one perceives an object, it tends, at least under normal conditions, to be represented in one's thought in such a way that just on the basis of this very representation one could go on to say lots of things about the object in addition to what one thinks about it, and these things that one could say about it may or may not be things one antecedently believed to be true of the object'; and Allen (2001: 250-1) on Carneades: 'The burden of Carneades' argument is that using the evidence of the senses is not a matter of grasping self-evident impressions, but rather of appreciating the complicated relations among impressions and between impressions and the conditions in which they are formed in virtue of which they add to or detract from each other's plausibility.' An assumption which seems to be common to Stoics and Academics is that the object an impression is about is a given, however its richness is construed; see Brennan (2005: 57). One might object that Stoic richness was about a lot more detail than even an extensive syndrome could account for; an Academic might reply that this is one reason why non-dogmatic acceptance of an impression is only ever provisional: testing *could* be continued for a very long time.

[237] This assertion of the truth of an impression after testing (§179 *fin.*) must be added to the list of features which make the Academics sound rather dogmatic in Sextus' account: the talk of assent, the notion that the πιθανόν was a criterion. See above, n. 225.

[238] Cf. M. 7.177: ὅταν οὖν μηδεμία τούτων τῶν φαντασιῶν περιέλκῃ ἡμᾶς τῷ φαίνεσθαι ψευδής, ἀλλὰ πᾶσαι **συμφώνως** φαίνωνται ἀληθεῖς, μᾶλλον πιστεύομεν, 'So when none of these impressions pulls us away in virtue of appearing false, but all appear true in unison, we have more faith.'

impression that this is Socrates. So a new coat, *even if it was Socrates who was wearing one*, would give rise to an impression within the syndrome which appeared false, which in turn would remove the πιθανότης of the target impression, just as the absence of an expected symptom would remove (or at least diminish), as it ought to, a doctor's confidence in his diagnosis. A target impression of Socrates in a new coat may be called incongruous, on the grounds that it is incongruous for someone to be Socrates and to wear a new coat, or it may be said to be incongruous when judged against our antecedently held belief that Socrates' coat is worn.

In §§181-3 Sextus discusses the second kind of test. All the coordinated impressions in the 'syndrome' are to be subjected to a test of the conditions under which they have arisen,[239] a process which is likened to a δοκιμασία. This procedure of vetting candidates for public office is associated with the Greek city state and was defunct by the time Sextus wrote; it may, however, still have been in use in Carneades' lifetime.[240] It was not intended to establish the qualifications of the candidate, but was a standardized process aimed at establishing eligibility against set criteria. I suggest that what the examination envisaged tests for in the syndrome of impressions is the same qualities which Sextus cites earlier when he distinguishes dim persuasive and intensely persuasive impressions, identifying the latter as first-level πιθανά. Consider:

M. 7.171-3	M. 7.183
Of the apparently true kind of presentation, one kind is dim (ἀμυδρά)—like the kind received in a confused and not distinct way because of (i) the smallness of the object looked at or (ii) the distance to it or (iii) even the weakness of the perceiver's sense of vision—while the other, in addition to appearing true, also has that appearance of truth to a high degree. Of these the dim and fuzzy (ἀμυδρὰ καὶ ἔκλυτος) presentation would not be the criterion; for because it indicates neither itself nor its cause it is not apt to persuade us and draw us towards assent.	So, for example, as there are present at the seat of judgement the subject which judges and the object which is being judged and the medium through which the judgement is made, and distance and interval, place, time, mood, disposition, activity, we judge the nature of each of these—concerning the subject, (iii) whether its vision is not dulled (for vision of that kind is unsuitable for judging), (i) concerning the object judged, whether it is not too small, concerning the medium through which the subject is made, whether the atmosphere is not gloomy, (ii) concerning the distance, whether it is not too great, concerning the interval, whether it is not too short, concerning the place, whether it is not immense, (iv) concerning the time, whether it is not short, (v) concerning the disposition, whether it is not found to be mad, and (vi) concerning the activity, whether it is not unacceptable.

What I have tried to indicate through number-coding is that some of the properties for which impressions are to be tested in §183 are also invoked to effect the distinction between dim persuasive impressions and first-level πιθανά in §§171-3, while §183 proceeds to add further criteria, on the time taken to consider an impression

---

[239] There is no mention of the target impression here, only of tests to be performed on the impressions which make up the syndrome. This is consistent with the 'dissolution', for testing purposes, of a 'rich' target impression (see above, p. lxxxvi), in such a way that the syndrome contains no impression whose content is, by itself, the same as that of the target impression.

[240] The procedure is attested in Ephesus in the second century BC (*SIG*³ 838).

(iv), and on the perceiver's mental state (v).²⁴¹ The consideration of time comes up a little later (§§185–6), as one of the constraints under which a perceiver may go along with a first-level πιθανόν as opposed to running a full testing routine.

How to explain this partial overlap between the criteria in §§171-3 and §183, and how to conceptualize the relationship between first-level πιθανά and second- and third-level testing? An economical explanation would seem to be the following. The cognitive limitations of human beings, and contingent circumstances in a given situation (e.g. the need to make a quick appraisal, as envisaged in §186, possibly our practical interests), mean that consistency and clarity account for the initial persuasiveness of impressions to a degree which is smaller than the reach of the testing routines. If we have only seconds to form an impression, then a smaller number of constituent impressions in the syndrome will account for the impression's persuasiveness or lack of it than if we have more time.²⁴² And while a first-level πιθανόν's appearing intensely true is a function of factors like the size of the object or the distance between perceiver and object, reflecting on these properties for the syndrome of impressions would take longer, as indeed would assessing one's own mental state.²⁴³

The Academics do allow for a true impression, received under ideal conditions, which fails to be persuasive,²⁴⁴ whereas the Stoics do not (as I shall argue in section 6.4).²⁴⁵ If one (veridically and clearly) sees Socrates who is wearing a new coat, then the Academic would call my impression ἀπίθανόν: the Academic view is that sometimes we do not trust our eyes or ears because what we perceive is incongruous. If, however, the segment of the syndrome on which the initial appraisal of a πιθανόν is based does not feature an impression which is incompatible with his antecedent beliefs, as is apparently envisaged in P.H. 1.228 (n. 242), then an Academic may regard an impression as persuasive which on closer examination proves not to be persuasive. This means that the Carneadean model is not *predictive*: Socrates in a

---

²⁴¹ I am uncertain as to what is meant by criterion (vi).

²⁴² In P.H. 1.228 Sextus also uses the example of Admetus, in ways which require explanation given my reading. The example is once more poorly integrated (see p. lxxxi above), which limits its evidential value. Still, we are told that Admetus receives an impression of Alcestis which is 'persuasive and tested' (i.e. in terms of the distinctions made in M. 7, meeting the criteria for first- and third-level *pithana*), and that Admetus' mind recoils from assent because he 'knew that Alcestis was dead'. Here one might wonder if Alcestis should, on my construal, have given rise to a persuasive impression at all. In reply, I would observe that it is not stated explicitly that the belief that Alcestis is dead is not brought to bear on the impression until well into the scrutiny process, after the impression has been identified as a first-level πιθανόν and after third-level testing has been carried out. This suggests that the offending impression in a syndrome may well not come into view immediately, but only in the course of testing and after reflection.

²⁴³ The wording of §§175–81 suggests that it is one and the same impression which is initially received, then tested and used, etc., as opposed to the tested impression being a new impression with the same content (on the issue see Allen 1994: 96 n. 18). Perhaps one can think of this as farther-reaching conceptualization of the same impression. Presumably Carneades would have regarded it as undesirable to incur further doctrinal commitments, if only for the sake of the argument, in this area.

²⁴⁴ One might object here that the Carneadean division of πιθανά does not subdivide ἀπίθανά into clear and dim ones. But since persuasiveness is only secondarily for Carneades a function of the conditions under which an impression has been received (and the resulting phenomenal properties of the impression), this omission seems to be due to Carneades' (or his reporter's) focus being elsewhere in the present discussion. The examples of Admetus seeing Alcestis and of Menelaus seeing Helen (P.H. 1.228-9; M. 7.180) would seem to allow, possibly even to require, for clear unpersuasive impressions because no reference is made e.g. to a need to take a closer or more careful look.

²⁴⁵ Cf. Allen (1994: 107–13).

new coat may strike Carneades as πιθανόν as long as he has not brought the belief that Socrates' coat is worn to bear on his perceptual experience, although it is entirely possible that another perceiver will do so from the start and thus find the top-level impression of Socrates in a new coat to be ἀπίθανόν.[246] The Carneadean model *explains* why top-level and first-level πιθανά are persuasive for the perceiving subject.

6.2 ἔμφασις before Carneades

That the Carneadean division of πιθανά represents a response to and an adaptation of a Stoic division of πιθανά was first shown in detail by Couissin (1983), originally published in 1929, and I will consider this issue in section 6.4 below. How the distinction of ἔμφασις and ἀπέμφασις relates to Stoic thought, and how it relates to the division of πιθανά, has received less attention. I believe it can be shown that Carneades looked to Stoic usage when he adopted the concept of ἔμφασις, but that further influences are detectable, too.

As already mentioned, the term ἀπέμφασις does not occur in Stoic texts,[247] while the term ἔμφασις occurs in two quite different places, once in connection with impressions and once in connection with a type of conditional. The term has a different meaning in both cases.

It occurs in Diocles of Magnesia's account of the Stoic concept of φαντασία (D.L. 7.49–51 = SVF ii.52, 55, 61 = LS 39A = frg. 255 Hülser). In the text leading up to the instance of ἔμφασις impressions are assigned a place within the wider framework, the distinction between φαντασία and φάντασμα is introduced, the question of whether impressions are imprints on or alterations of the ruling part of the soul and the distinction between sensory and non-sensory impressions are covered. The text continues:

> Of the perceptual impressions, some arise from what is the case and involve yielding and assent; but among the impressions are also ἐμφάσεις. They arise as if from what is the case.[248]

Some perceptual impressions come about from what is the case and attract assent; other impressions are ἐμφάσεις and come about 'as if from what is the case'. The extract is clear, and the wider context where φαντάσματα were dealt with earlier does not suggest otherwise: ἐμφάσεις are impressions (i.e. an external object was involved

---

[246] Individuals will differ with regard to factual knowledge of course, but the general epistemological optimism inherent in the Carneadean model, which is inherited from the model it opposes (that built around the cataleptic impression), points to an assumption of substantial overlap between the antecedently held beliefs of perceivers.

[247] Adler's index to *SVF* lists one of the Sextus passages I have discussed above, though.

[248] Τῶν δὲ αἰσθητικῶν ⟨αἱ μὲν⟩ ἀπὸ ὑπαρχόντων μετὰ εἴξεως καὶ συγκαταθέσεως γίνονται· εἰσὶ δὲ τῶν φαντασιῶν καὶ ἐμφάσεις, αἱ ὡσανεὶ ἀπὸ ὑπαρχόντων γινόμεναι. Long and Sedley (ii.1987: 239) comment: '*emphaseis*: The Stoic use of this term (contrast the Academic, e.g. 69D2) is exemplified in SVF 2.673 by the face of the man in the moon.' On 69D2 they write (p. 446): '*emphasis*: This use of the term, with the coinage of *apemphasis* as its opposite, is an Academic initiative. By itself *emphasis* simply means "appearance", and can be used as a synonym for *phantasia*; cf. Sextus, *M*. 10.300. In Stoicism (cf. 39A18) it even stands for *phantasiai* which are "mere appearances" and have no corresponding object.'

in their coming into being), not figments of the mind.²⁴⁹ However, they cannot be said to derive, as a matter of fact, from what is the case, i.e. to be true impressions, but appear to be such. These would seem to be persuasive impressions by a different description. The passage itself does not provide further clues as to whether impressions which are persuasive and false are meant here (cf. Hülser's 'Illusionen', a meaning which 'ἔμφασις' does not normally have), but given that Sextus can use 'ἔμφασις' as a synonym for 'φαντασία' (e.g. M. 10.300), it seems preferable to regard ἐμφάσεις here as persuasive impressions which could be either true or false.

The second context in which 'ἔμφασις' occurs is in connection with conditionals, whose truth-conditions Sextus discusses in P.H. 2.110–12. Four types are distinguished. The first two are truth-functional and associated with Philo of Megara and Diodorus Cronus respectively. The third one is not assigned by name but is likely to be Chrysippus'. It is not truth-functional and assumes a 'connection' (συνάρτησις) between antecedent and consequent, which means that a conditional of the type at issue is true if the antecedent and the contradictory of the consequent are incompatible.²⁵⁰ The fourth type, which is otherwise unattested, is described in the following terms (P.H. 2.112–13):

> And those who judge by ἔμφασις say that a conditional is true when its consequent is contained implicitly in its antecedent (ἐν τῷ ἡγουμένῳ περιέχεται δυνάμει). According to them, 'if it is day, it is day', and every duplicated conditional statement, will no doubt be false; for it is impossible for anything to be contained in itself (αὐτὸ γάρ τι ἐν ἑαυτῷ περιέχεσθαι ἀμήχανον).

As Frede notes (1974: 92), Plutarch's collocation of συνάρτησις and ἔμφασις in a Stoicizing context (De E apud Del. 387a) suggests that the fourth type of conditional is Stoic. He interprets it as an attempt to clarify the kind of connection between antecedent and consequent which the third type posits, which turns on the semantic content of the simple propositions involved.

In order to elucidate the use of ἔμφασις, Frede (1974: 90–3) cites Eustathius' explanation of the term (Il. 5.576):²⁵¹ ἔμφασίς ἐστι λέξις δι' ὑπονοίας αὔξουσα τὸ ζητούμενον, ὥστε τὸ τοιοῦτον περὶ μίαν μόνην λέξιν θεωρεῖται, 'An *emphasis* is an expression which enhances the topic by means of a subtext, such that it is plain through one word [or: expression] only'. This is very similar to the explanation given in a treatise *De tropis* transmitted under the name of the late Hellenistic grammarian Tryphon.²⁵²

---

²⁴⁹ The verb φαίνειν is causative in meaning: 'to make something appear'; ἐμφαίνειν means 'to make something appear in something (a medium)'. An ἔμφασις is the act of making something appear in something, and then the appearance of something in something. (Such a shift in meaning is not unusual in *nomina actionis*: δόσις 'the act of giving' and 'the gift'.) To call an impression, a mental item, an ἔμφασις is readily intelligible, because it is the appearance of something in the mind. Similarly, ἔμφασις can mean 'reflection' qua appearance of something in a reflective surface (LSJ s.v. no. I.1).
²⁵⁰ See e.g. Bobzien (1996: 185–7).
²⁵¹ ἔμφασίς ἐστι λέξις δι' ὑπονοίας αὔξουσα τὸ ζητούμενον, ὥστε τὸ τοιοῦτον περὶ μίαν μόνην λέξιν θεωρεῖται.
²⁵² Cf. Tryphon (Rhet.Gr. III p. 199.15–20 Spengel), who gives the expressions 'we descended into the horse' (Hom., Od. 11.523) and 'being poured out of the horse' (Hom., Od. 8.515) as instances of ἔμφασις: the former is suggestive of the size of the horse, the latter of the large number of people contained in it; Quint. 8.3.83–4 apparently draws on Tryphon and replaces the examples with Vergilian ones.

As a figure of style, an ἔμφασις is an expression which is suggestive, which implies (or presupposes) something that is not explicitly stated.[253] That there is some connection between the application of the term within syllogistic and its occurrence in stylistic theory is supported by the treatment of the figure in *Rhet. Her.* 4.67, who, having defined the figure (*significatio est res, quae plus in suspicione relinquit, quam positum est in oratione*, 'a *significatio* is something which leaves more to the imagination than is actually set down in words'), identifies *consequentia* as one of its subtypes.[254]

Now given that for Carneades an impression is always associated with a syndrome of impressions, that he seemed to account for an impression's lack of persuasiveness in the first instance by referring to a lack of coherence amongst the impressions within that syndrome, and that the Stoics seemed to use the term of ἔμφασις to designate persuasive impressions, it is tempting to think that Carneades was happy to adopt the Stoic notion of ἔμφασις as a starting point but reinterpreted it by invoking the stylistic notion of ἔμφασις which either some Stoics or indeed others used in connection with conditionals: ἐμφάσεις are persuasive impressions because they are suggestive of the content of impressions in the syndrome.[255] These exhibit the compatibility with one another whose absence accounts, in Carneades' initial distinction, for the lack of persuasiveness of ἀπίθανά. By the same token, ἀπίθανά 'contain' (cf. περιέχεται in *P.H.* 2.112 above) their syndrome, too, but in their case there is an inconsistency within it, in that they do not appear true συμφώνως (*M.* 1.177).

6.3 Back to Sextus, *M.* 7

One might argue that something like this 'suggestive' conception of ἔμφασις is already present in Sextus' account simply in virtue of the juxtaposition of the term with ἀπέμφασις, but we think one can do better and find positive evidence in *M.* 7 for the conception of ἔμφασις which we posit. Having established the distinction between ἐμφάσεις and ἀπεμφάσεις in *M.* 7.169–70, Sextus goes on to make a distinction within the class of ἐμφάσεις, in the course of which the participle of 'ἐμφαίνεσθαι' occurs. It arguably throws light on the initial distinction. Consider *M.* 7.171–3, part of which was already quoted above:

---

[253] See also Thomas (2000) for the Roman first-century BC context and Ahl (1984) for the first century AD; Croissant (1984) discusses some of the literary material, too, but without firm conclusions for the fourth type of implication. The evidence from Tryphon takes us sufficiently far into the Hellenistic period to make it possible for Stoics (or others) to have adopted the term from contemporary stylistic theory. Janko's claim (1984: 203) that the term already occurred in the sense at issue in Aristotle has been shown to be false by Nesselrath (1990: 122–5). I had mentioned the sense 'appearance' (of ἔμφασις) above (n. 248). From this there developed expressions like 'the appearance of youth' (e.g. Plut., *Comm. not.* 1073b: ἔμφασις κάλλους), where the property observed is not itself directly in evidence but is conveyed by other physical properties. The stylistic sense can naturally be explained as derived from expressions like 'the appearance of youth'.

[254] Another subtype of *significatio* is *ambiguum*; ambiguity is of course another area of cross-fertilization between Stoic philosophy and rhetorical theory. Cf. Atherton (1993: 175–214) on a Stoic classification of ambiguity in Theon's *Progymnasmata*; Riesenweber (2009) on a Stoic definition of πραότης in Cic. *Inv.*

[255] Cf. the adoption of the Stoic conception of δόξα by the Academics, on which see e.g. Burnyeat (1997: 305).

Of the apparently true kind of presentation, one kind is obscure—like the kind received in a confused and not distinct way because of the smallness of the object looked at or the distance to it or even the weakness of the perceiver's sense of vision—while the other, in addition to appearing true, also has that appearance of truth to a high degree. Of these the obscure and fuzzy presentation would not be the criterion; for because it indicates neither itself nor its cause it is not apt to persuade us and draw us towards assent. But the impression which appears true and **makes itself sufficiently apparent** (ἡ δὲ φαινομένη ἀληθὴς καὶ ἱκανῶς ἐμφαινομένη) is the criterion of truth according to those around Carneades. And being the criterion, it has a large extension, and when extended one impression has a more persuasive and striking appearance than another (καὶ ἐπιτεινομένης αὐτῆς ἄλλη ἄλλης ἐν εἴδει πιθανωτέραν τε καὶ πληκτικωτέραν ἴσχει φαντασίαν).[256]

Ἐμφαίνεσθαι is a verb not requiring completion. It neither requires nor normally allows for a complement. So the translation by Bury (1935) 'but that which appears true, *and appears so vividly*, is the criterion of truth' is wrong.

The adverb ἱκανῶς can mean 'sufficiently' or 'fully'.[257] On either reading impressions which are πιθαναί and clear have the property designated by ἐμφαίνεσθαι to a higher degree than top-level πιθανά (= ἐμφάσεις), which as a class include, after all, clear and dim πιθανά. That being so, ἐμφαίνεσθαι cannot mean 'to be clear' in the phenomenal sense. For otherwise dim πιθανά would be taken to be clear to a lower degree than clear πιθανά, as opposed to not having the property of clarity. The text, however, uses contraries of 'clear' to refer to dim πιθανά (ἄμυδρος, ἔκλυτος). Ἐμφαίνεσθαι must refer to a property which is gradable across the clear/dim boundary (in the phenomenal sense).

Bett (2005) translates 'but the one that is apparently true and makes itself sufficiently apparent', capturing the medio-passive of ἐμφαινόμενη. This seems to us to be correct, provided it is understood that the conventional property (of an impression) of 'presenting itself',[258] referenced in the previous sentence in §172, cannot be meant, for it does not seem gradable in the required sense: a dim πιθανόν would seem to be no less an appearance than one which is not dim. Minimally, a dim πιθανόν would have to be an appearance of something to be a top-level πιθανόν.

Rather, the suggestive sense of ἔμφασις for which we have argued above carries over into ἱκανῶς ἐμφαινομένη ('...and makes itself sufficiently apparent', sc. as an appearance of a certain kind). On this reading one can see how a dim impression of Socrates would have the same property as one which is not dim, but would have it to a lesser degree. If someone sees Socrates from a long distance (at his usual place somewhere on the agora), their impression that this is Socrates will be based on a smaller syndrome of impressions, i.e. one with fewer component impressions, than when they can see him from up close. But if the syndrome in question includes no impression which appears false, their target impression will still be a πιθανόν.

---

[256] See below, p. xciv on why Sextus never says that testing increases the persuasiveness of impressions; the comparatives here obviously require a different explanation.

[257] 'Sufficiently' is recommended by the fact that Sextus assumes a class of πιθανά to have a πλάτος, an extension; see just below.

[258] Cf. Aët. IV.12 = SVF II.54 = LS 39B: φαντασία μὲν οὖν ἐστι πάθος ἐν τῇ ψυχῇ γιγνόμενον, ἐνδεικνύμενον ἐν αὑτῷ καὶ τὸ πεποιηκός..., 'An impression is thus an affection occurring in the soul, revealing in itself also that which effected it....'

Another detail of Sextus' discussion is that according to the Carneadean view the class of πιθανά is said to have an extension (πλάτος), such that the elements in it can be placed on a spectrum of πιθανότης (see *M.* 7.173 quoted above).²⁵⁹ This notion of an extension occurs again later, in *M.* 7.181, in the last sentence on second-level testing for coherence. It is stated there that of impressions which are ἀπερίσπαστοι, i.e. have passed second-level tests, some are more ἀπερίσπαστοι than others. The adjective is sometimes translated as 'irreversible', which does not allow for degrees and which, as Allen (1994: 93) has shown, would also be hard to reconcile with Carneades' conception of impressions, according to which impressions are only ever provisionally accepted, liable to possible further review, and in that sense never 'irreversible'. For this second reason ἀπερίσπαστος is better translated as 'not reversed', sc. for the time being.²⁶⁰ The comparative remains difficult to explain, though, especially if we consider that on the first occurrence of the notion of an extension (πλάτος) different positions on the spectrum amounted to different degrees of πιθανότης. So it would not do to say, for instance, that experience suggests that some impressions get reversed eventually while others prove irreversible in the long run, and that degrees of not being reversed are to be distinguished in this way, because at a given point in time impressions which will be reversed eventually are not, one would think, less persuasive than those which will remain unreversed. (It would be helpful if they were.) Sextus (and Carneades) may mean no more than that, as a matter of fact and for reasons unknown, some πιθανά, tested or not, turn out to be more plausible than others, but one wonders if the presuppositive sense of ἔμφασις might not suggest a different explanation: that the syndromes of impressions associated with particular impressions under consideration may vary in extent even under ideal conditions and after testing due to the content of the target impression, in such a way that some impressions are associated with numerous other impressions, while others are grounded in a much smaller syndrome.²⁶¹ The latter might then be less persuasive.²⁶²

In this connection, a comparison with medical texts gives rise to further questions. One is whether apart from the extent of the syndrome considerations of domain or subject matter ought to be significant, too. If a medical condition is defined with reference to a definite number of specific symptoms, then all of them obtaining ought to make for a high degree of evidential force, even if they are few in number. Similarly, some objects of perception are naturally likely to give rise to less extensive syndromes than others. Another is to ask if there ought to be allowance for differences in salience between component impressions within the syndrome. Galen

---

²⁵⁹ The textual difficulty at the end of §173, that an impression is said to have an impression (πιθανωτέραν τε καὶ πληκτικωτέραν ἴσχει φαντασίαν), does not seem to affect the problem in hand.

²⁶⁰ This is, of course, an entirely conventional sense for a verbal adjective of this formation; see Schwyzer (1953: 501).

²⁶¹ For a different interpretation of 'extension', see Ioppolo (2017: 205).

²⁶² The notion of an extension, however related to the concept of the syndrome, also suggests that the remarks about the persuasive impression being a criterion, which are found in several places in the section (§§173, 176, 184; see p. lxxxvi), are to be taken in one of two ways: since a criterion, on the Stoic view, does not admit of degrees (as noted e.g. by Ioppolo 2007: 248), one has to assume either a Sextan attempt to make the Academic material he is reporting sound more dogmatic, or an implicit Academic assertion that a criterion can never allow for yes/no decisions.

is capable of criticizing other doctors for leaving out 'the crucial ones' (τὰ κυριώτατα) in a list of symptoms (*De loc. aff.* VIII.187–8 K.). Similarly, one wonders if an impression of Socrates in a new coat should be assessed differently from one of Socrates with an inconspicuous and elegant nose. A third is whether the stipulation that all impressions within a syndrome must appear true for an impression to survive second-level testing is not so extreme as to lead to a loss of epistemic opportunities. After all, Socrates may for once be wearing a new coat, and it ought to be possible to have a persuasive impression of him. (This, needless to say, is a problem not just for my account of the πιθανόν.) However, the evidence suggests that, at least where diagnosis with reference to an 'assemblage of symptoms' in medical contexts was concerned, only the presence of all expected symptoms was deemed sufficient to warrant the treatment prescribed for the condition in question.[263]

Two further terms (one of them phrasal) which feature in Sextus' discussion need to be considered, in order to show how the properties which they ascribe to πιθανά relate to the latter's persuasiveness. Πιθανά are said to be true 'for the most part' (ὡς ἐπὶ τὸ πολύ); and they are called πιστά, 'deserving of credence', which is significant because attaching this property to them might be taken to signal the step from 'is' to 'ought'. Both notions have played a significant role in the discussion of the question if Carneades can be regarded as a probabilist (see the end of this section). For about a generation that question has been answered negatively by most, but the probabilist interpretation has recently enjoyed a revival. We can note that, while Carneades assumed the πιθανά within the same class (first-, second-, or third-level) to vary in πιθανότης (§173), there is no suggestion of a correlation between relative persuasiveness and statistical likelihood of being true. Rather, πιθανά generally are said to be true for the most part (in §175, at the end of the section on first-level πιθανά). Second- and third-level πιθανά are not distinguished from first-level πιθανά in terms of relative persuasiveness—what is said is that second- and third-level πιθανά are more πιστά than first-level πιθανά (see below). That they are held to be more frequently true than first-level πιθανά would seem compatible with the account as a whole, but it is nowhere stated.

The notion of εἰκός has been drawn into the debate about the Carneadean πιθανόν in the following way. It has been suggested that Cicero's use of *ueri simile* as a synonym for *probabile* ought to lead us to assume that the εἰκός was part of the Greek record on the Carneadean scheme and that the state of our sources is to blame for its absence from it. Obdrzalek (2006: 269–71), who argues for an interpretation of the Carneadean πιθανόν according to which it is a pre-theoretical anticipation of the modern conception of probability in terms of statistical likelihood and evidence, accepts Glucker's view (1995: 126–7; 2004: 149–50) that the εἰκός must have been part of the picture, i.e. was either a synonym of πιθανόν or used for the πιθανόν conceived in a certain way. She cites, in support of her overall thesis, passages which link the εἰκός to being true for the most part. Now it can be shown that the εἰκός was

---

[263] Cf. e.g. *De plen.* VII.560 K.: τῶν συμπτωμάτων ἄθροισμα τῶν ἔμπροσθεν εἰρημένων ὀνομάζεται πληθωρικὴ συνδρομή, οὐδένα χρὴ φλεβοτομεῖν πρὶν **ἅπαντα** ἔχειν αὐτά, 'The assemblage of the previously named symptoms is called the plethoric syndrome; one must not open a vein before all of them are in evidence.'

originally conceived as a special type of rationally persuasive or plausible item, too, and that frequency considerations come in only secondarily. Consider Arist., *An. Pr.* B27, 70a2-6, cited by Obdrzalek (2006: 270):

⟨An enthymeme is a syllogism from likelihoods and signs,⟩ a likelihood and a sign are not the same thing, but the likelihood is a reputable premiss (πρότασις ἔνδοξος); for what people know happens for the most part or not, or is the case or not, that is a likelihood, e.g., 'the envious feel hatred' or 'those who show affection feel love'.[264]

The proof from the εἰκός is the oldest element of Greek rhetorical theory that we know of.[265] It arose in a forensic context and was there typically used to mount a particular kind of argument, designed to establish motive: whether it was 'likely' or not that an attribute attached to a particular individual or group of people given a known characteristic which they have. The etymology of εἰκός played a role in this, in that the question was quite literally whether, as one might say, it was 'like' the truth that x committed y, or 'like' x that x committed y. Killing a rival in a jealous rage is something that is εἰκός for a young man, because young men are deemed to be impulsive. Aristotle would, in *Rhet.* B23, 1397b12-27, and *Top.* B10, 115a6-24, turn this into what he calls the τόποι ἐκ τοῦ μᾶλλον καὶ τοῦ ἧττον and ἐκ τοῦ ὁμοίως, and there are some passages where he makes it plain that in an εἰκός argument a predicate is ascribed to the subject because of a specific quality which the subject has and which is itself unstated in the propositions involved (*Rhet.* B23, 1397b18-20 and 24-5).[266] In the *Rhetorica ad Alexandrum*, which is pre-Aristotelian in substance, we find a different explanation, one which also plays on the etymology of εἰκός and which has left a reflection in Plato's *Phaedrus* 273d-274a: an εἰκός is something of which the audience has παραδείγματα (instances, models) in their minds (i.e. something which is 'like' those παραδείγματα; 1428a25-6).[267] Here again rational grounds—coherence with antecedent beliefs—account for the εἰκός. It seems economical to assume that in *An. pr.* Aristotle does not have something like the modern conception of probability in mind, but that 'being true for the most part' is for him a property which attaches to the εἰκός because that is how we can secondarily rationalize things appearing plausible to us, just as this property attaches to πιθανά secondarily in Sextus' account of the Carneadean scheme. The εἰκός is a πρότασις ἔνδοξος inasmuch as it can be seen as a species of the ἔνδοξον.[268] So even in the unlikely event

---

[264] ⟨Ἐνθύμημα δὲ ἐστὶ συλλογισμὸς ἐξ εἰκότων ἢ σημείων,⟩ εἰκὸς δὲ καὶ σημεῖον οὐ ταὐτόν ἐστιν, ἀλλὰ τὸ μὲν εἰκός ἐστι πρότασις ἔνδοξος· ὃ γὰρ ὡς ἐπὶ τὸ πολὺ ἴσασιν οὕτω γινόμενον ἢ μὴ γινόμενον ἢ ὂν ἢ μὴ ὄν, τοῦτ' ἐστὶν εἰκός, οἷον τὸ μισεῖν τοὺς φθονοῦντας ἢ τὸ φιλεῖν τοὺς ἐρωμένους.

[265] Evidence is collected in Radermacher (1951: BII (Corax et Tisias), frg. 15-20); see also Goebel (1989); Schmitz (2000); Hoffman (2008).

[266] Smith (1989: 226) comments on 70a5-6: 'Note that the examples here concern conduct typical of people who have certain emotional attitudes towards others and provide a basis for inferring those attitudes: we infer X loves Y because X shows affection for Y, we infer that X is envious of Y because X hates (expresses hatred for) Y.' Later Greek rhetorical manuals classify the εἰκός as a species of the πιθανόν, which applies to a person, i.e. they retain a sense of the original conception (cf. e.g. Anonymus Seguerianus pp. 28.15-29.3 Graeven). See also Primavesi (1996: 252-66) on *Top.* B10, 115a6-24.

[267] See Reinhardt (2010a).

[268] Cf. Smith (1989: 226): 'As with Aristotle's other definitions, this is not intended to explain the term for those (like us) who are ignorant of its meaning, but to accommodate it in the deductive theory of the figures.'

that the Academics used the term εἰκός alongside πιθανόν, there are no good reasons for assuming that the former gave rise to an interpretation of the latter in terms of statistical likelihood.²⁶⁹

The differences between first-, second-, and third-level πιθανά are, however, characterized in terms of degrees of being πιστόν.²⁷⁰ The adjective πιστόν refers to an attitude which either the perceiver or a third party (like the narrator) adopts towards a πιθανόν: that it is deserving of credence. As an adjective πιστόν attaches to impressions of course, but focalization by the perceiver is possible (i.e. that a narrator calls an impression deserving of credence from the viewpoint of the perceiver he describes, as opposed to his own viewpoint, or both).²⁷¹ Indeed, in the context of a wholly dialectical argument, even focalization by the narrator would not mean that an objective statement that πιθανά are πιστά was forthcoming.²⁷² Being πιθανόν and being πιστόν go hand in hand in Sextus' report on Carneades,²⁷³ whereas there is at least one instance of them coming apart in a relevant Stoic context.²⁷⁴ This is in line with the Stoic and the Academic positions on πιθανά representing fundamental but incompatible intuitions about visual perception, a view for which I will argue in section 6.4. So much for πιθανά 'being true for the most part' and 'deserving of credence'.

I take the Carneadean πιθανόν to be applicable, and to have been conceived to be applicable, to action-guiding impressions, to non-perceptual impressions, and to factual perceptual ones. It is easy to see why the first and the second category will minimally require a conception of the πιθανόν which takes it to be the plausible in some sense. However, even if one wants the πιθανόν to be something an agent can engage with and use in a conscious rational way, it is not a given that factual perceptual impressions would be made πιθανόν by features other than phenomenal ones, in particular clarity.²⁷⁵ Specifically, even a perceptual experience which is eventually

---

²⁶⁹ In fact, the discussion in Sextus, *M.* 7, says of persuasive impressions that they 'appear true' often enough to make it unnecessary to posit a gap in the Greek record where τὸ εἰκός once stood.

²⁷⁰ Cf. *M.* 7.181–2: Τῆς δὲ ἀπερισπάστου φαντασίας **πιστοτέρα** μᾶλλόν ἐστι καὶ τελειοτάτη ἡ ποιοῦσα τὴν κρίσιν, ἢ σὺν τῷ ἀπερίσπαστος εἶναι ἔτι καὶ διεξωδευμένη καθέστηκεν, 'Even more deserving of credence than the impression which is not turned away and most complete is the one which brings about judgement, which together with not being turned away is also carefully scrutinized'; 188–9.

²⁷¹ Thus Burnyeat (unpublished: 48).

²⁷² Similarly, remarks which Sextus makes in his own voice about Stoics and Academics are open to various interpretations, depending on whether one assumes Sextan bias, a particular Academic interpretation of Carneades, etc.; cf. *M.* 7.401: Λείπεται ἄρα τὰς μὲν πιστὰς τὰς δὲ ἀπίστους ἀξιοῦν, ὅπερ οἱ ἀπὸ τῆς Στοᾶς καὶ οἱ ἀπὸ τῆς Ἀκαδημίας ἔλεγον, οἱ μὲν ἀπὸ τῆς Στοᾶς τὰς καταληπτικὰς φαντασίας ἀποδεχόμενοι, οἱ δὲ ἀπὸ τῆς Ἀκαδημίας τὰς πιθανὰς εἶναι δοκούσας, 'It remains therefore to require that some (impressions) are deserving of credence and others are not, as the Stoics and the representatives of the Academy have said, the former approving cataleptic impressions, the latter those which appear persuasive.'

²⁷³ This has led some to the erroneous view that the latter is simply used as a synonym of the former; see e.g. Svavarsson (2014: 356 n. 2), and earlier Görler (1994: 861), who consequently finds it hard to understand why some can regard the πιθανόν as that which is merely persuasive.

²⁷⁴ Sextus, *M.* 7.253–5, to be discussed below.

²⁷⁵ Third-level testing is difficult to interpret as turning on features other than phenomenal ones. The continued appeal of the notion that the πιθανόν might be the probable in some sense is in part due to the fact that perceptual impressions are uncharacterized with respect to their content if they are only seen as persuasive, whereas they appear sufficiently substantial to do the philosophical work they are supposed to do if they are probable (in a pre-theoretical sense which nonetheless turns on statistical frequency and evidence); see Obdrzalek (2006: 257) and passim. Between these two positions I would locate the plausible in the specific sense defended above.

dismissed as inconsistent with the subject's beliefs could be πιθανόν in that sense. That is not the Carneadean view, which, on the interpretation offered above, makes consistency with antecedently held beliefs and concurrent impressions a necessary condition for an impression's being πιθανόν in the first place (i.e. on the top level). This conception of the πιθανόν is more readily applicable across all three categories. Moreover, it clearly allows for more than rationally blind action, i.e. a scenario where the perceiver or agent is led by his πιθανά in an unconscious way or can only rationalize his behaviour after the event.[276] One might think that the one proposed here is too thin a conception of πιθανότης to preclude e.g. perceptual judgements and courses of action which are plausible only from the perspective of an utterly corrupt human being, but it would appear that, in the contexts in which the scheme is put forward and used, Carneades helps himself to the epistemological optimism which characterizes the Stoic position with regard to the sage, implicitly urging that one will be able to devise an entirely sensible account of human behaviour if one excises from the Stoic one specifically the notion of a cataleptic impression and replaces it with the πιθανόν.[277] Another objection which seems to be forestalled by Carneades' background assumptions is that we cannot be sure if our experience and behaviour is not entirely divorced from a reality and a—coherent—figment of our imagination: on the available evidence ancient sceptics were not sceptics about the external world itself,[278] so this possibility was not envisaged. We shall turn to the subject of different Academic interpretations of the scheme in the overall conclusion to this article.

We have deliberately avoided talk of objective and subjective conceptions of the πιθανόν, since both notions are very hard to pin down. One might think that only a πιθανόν grounded in statistical likelihood alone (sc. which was not entertained in antiquity) would merit being called 'objective', since already the modern conception of 'evidence' cuts across the subjective/objective distinction, at least where the evaluation of evidence from the senses is concerned. (If a dermatologist calls a suspicious-looking mole 'probably cancerous', meaning that it looks like many other cancerous moles she has seen before, in person and in the classificatory literature, then her appraisal will be based on evidence without thereby being unequivocally objective.) What matters for now is that Carneades, or rather his conception of the πιθανόν, assumes that there are discernible reasons why impressions have πιθανότης, reasons which can be stated, and while there is allowance for the notion that different things are persuasive to different people, there is at the same time an assumption that the same things tend to be persuasive to rational and sensible individuals. In that sense there is an objective side, one that obtains in an intersubjective way, to the Carneadean πιθανόν.

6.4 Stoic πιθανά

The Academic use and conception of the πιθανόν takes Stoic thinking on the πιθανόν as its starting point, as was first shown by Coussin (1983: 44–51), first published in

---

[276] I have borrowed the expression 'rationally blind' from Vogt (2010: 171).
[277] For analogous reasons Carneades' account is in no way applicable to animal behaviour, a feature which it shares with the Stoic view on the uses of πιθανά.
[278] See Burnyeat (1982: 19); Frede (1988: 70); contrast Fine (2003).

1929, and is now widely accepted. In this section we want to look again at the πιθανόν in Stoic thought, at definitions given, and at the uses to which πιθανά are put, with a view to describing Stoic–Academic interaction in this area.[279]

The Stoics recognize persuasive impressions as well as, unsurprisingly, persuasive propositions (simple as well as complex ones). Various characterizations or 'definitions' are in evidence.[280] According to one, the πιθανόν is 'a proposition which leads in the direction of assent' (D.L. 7.75: πιθανὸν δέ ἐστιν ἀξίωμα τὸ ἄγον εἰς συγκατάθεσιν), and the example given is the conditional 'if someone gave birth to something (ἔτεκεν), she is its mother', which is taken to be persuasive but false, given that a hen is not the mother of an egg it has laid. No further explanation is given. It is presumably a moot point whether ἔτεκεν is ambiguous here, given that 'to lay an egg' could reasonably be classed as a metaphorical use of τίκτειν, for ambiguity is recognized as a source of πιθανότης by the Stoics.[281] It is tempting to think that the example given was deemed πιθανόν because most people could think of many true instances without being able to think of a counterexample, and to assume consequently that non-perceptual πιθανότης was construed by Stoics in much the same way as it was by the Academics or Aristotle in his *Rhet.*,[282] as consistency with propositions in the relevant domain, but the 'definition' actually given does no more than translate 'persuasiveness' into the categories of Stoic philosophy of mind, while restricting the domain of the πιθανόν to human beings (who alone possess the faculty of assent). A characterization of the πιθανὴ φαντασία is that it 'causes a smooth motion in the soul' (Sextus, *M.* 7.242: αἱ λεῖον κίνημα περὶ ψυχὴν ἐργαζόμεναι = *SVF* ii.25), and the examples given are perceptual (but possibly provided by Sextus himself rather than part of his source: 'it is now day', 'I am conversing'). One would think that, for an impression to have this effect, its propositional content (whether aided by phenomenal features of the impression or not) must be involved, given Stoic metaphysical assumptions,[283] although the effect caused seems to be of a different order compared to that caused by a falsehood, which is said to give rise to 'upheaval' in the mind (D.L. 7.110: ἐκ δὲ τῶν ψευδῶν ἐπιγίνεσθαι τὴν διαστροφὴν ἐπὶ τὴν διάνοιαν... = *SVF* iii.99). The immediately following class of unpersuasive impressions is illustrated with non-perceptual examples (i.e. obviously false conditionals), as in general no Stoic text gives an instance of a perceptual ἀπίθανόν.[284] Is it possible that coherence-related considerations might account for the persuasiveness of a Stoic *perceptual* πιθανόν just as they do in the case of their Academic counterpart, i.e. that propositional content could account for perceptual persuasiveness *in that way*?

We do not think so. To see this, we need to turn to the Stoic division of impressions reported in Sextus, *M.* 7.241–51 (already used above),[285] and to a reply to

---

[279] Relevant studies include Burnyeat (unpublished); Sedley (1982); Barnes (1985); Bett (1989: 78–88); Tieleman (1996: 264–87).
[280] I use inverted commas because the status of a given characterization is rarely stated or deducible from the context with certainty.
[281] See Atherton (1993: 56); Burnyeat (2012: 110 n. 51).
[282] See Rapp (2002: 104); Allen (2014).
[283] Cf. Brittain (2001: 97 n. 35).
[284] Cf. Allen (1994: 96 n. 18).
[285] My remarks on the division are much indebted to Burnyeat (unpublished).

Carneades ascribed to younger Stoics (7.253–7). The Stoics divide impressions into four classes (πιθανόν, ἀπίθανον, both πιθανόν and ἀπίθανον, neither πιθανόν nor ἀπίθανον), whereby the ἀπίθανον is, unlike in the Academic division, the contrary not the contradictory of the πιθανόν, while impressions which leave the subject indifferent, in the Academic division included alongside those which deter assent (= Stoic ἀπίθανά) in the category 'ἀπίθανον', appear as 'neither πιθανόν nor ἀπίθανον'. Impressions which are πιθανόν are then divided further according to whether they are true, false, both true and false, or neither true or false. Cataleptic impressions are a species of impressions which are πιθανόν and true. The ἀπίθανον is not divided further so that we do not have explicit confirmation, but it seems reasonable to assume that the Stoics did not recognize an ἀπίθανον which is true. At the same time, we are told in §247 that not every true impression gains assent. This would suggest that such impressions are deemed to be πιθανόν but fail to win assent nonetheless, for reasons which are unconnected to their πιθανότης, a reading which the evidence from later Stoics will lend support to. Another question one could pose is where in this division a requirement for coherence with antecedent beliefs or concurrent impressions could be placed upon the πιθανόν: cataleptic impressions themselves are not defined in a way which invokes this kind of coherence, nor is the truth of propositions or impressions defined by the Stoics with reference to it (so that a coherence requirement cannot be introduced at the next level up). That means that, if cataleptic impressions were to meet a coherence requirement as the Academics envisage it, this would have to be part of the conception of the πιθανόν two levels up. Conversely, if cataleptic impressions are possible which do not meet the coherence requirement, this will show that no such requirement was placed upon πιθανά to begin with. It thus seems safe to conclude that the Stoics explain the persuasiveness of perceptual impressions with reference to their phenomenal properties, as their foundationalist convictions would lead one to expect.

In *M*. 7.253 Sextus refers to 'younger Stoics', who add to Zeno's definition of the cataleptic impression a constraint on such impressions winning assent: '...and which has no obstacle (ἔνστημα).' The addition is likely to have been made in response to Carneades' point that an impression can only be persuasive if it is consistent with one's beliefs.[286] Consider *M*. 7.253–5 (part of LS 40K), mentioned earlier (p. xcvi) as a Stoic passage where being πιθανόν and being πιστόν come apart:

> The older Stoics say that the cataleptic impression thus defined is the criterion of truth, but the younger ones add 'and which does not have an obstacle' (καὶ τὸ μηδὲν ἔχουσαν ἔνστημα). For it is possible that a cataleptic impression occurs, but is found to be undeserving of credence because of external circumstances (ἄπιστος δὲ διὰ τὴν ἔξωθεν περίστασιν), as when Heracles stood with Admetus having led Alcestis up from the underworld, Admetus received a cataleptic impression from Alcestis, but did not trust it (τότε ὁ Ἄδμητος ἔσπασε μὲν καταληπτικὴν φαντασίαν ἀπὸ τῆς Ἀλκήστιδος, ἠπίστει δ' αὐτῇ).

---

[286] See Allen (1994: 107–9) on *M*. 7.253–7, to whose discussion my account is much indebted. We differ in that I take coherence to be a necessary condition already for Carneadean top-level πιθανότης, and in the evaluation of the younger Stoics' stance: I take their view to be a restatement of the position inherent in the division of impressions in *M*. 7.241–51.

The younger Stoics regard Admetus' impression of Alcestis as a cataleptic one; as such, it must also be a πιθανόν, on the grounds that cataleptic impressions are a species of persuasive impressions. At the same time, the impression in question is undeserving of credence (ἄπιστος). That this is said from the perceiver's perspective is suggested by the phrase 'διὰ τὴν ἔξωθεν περίστασιν', since the obstacle envisaged in the addition is, one would assume, an antecedently held belief (that Alcestis is dead), not external circumstances. What the obstacle seems to do is derail or block the belief-forming mechanism through which cataleptic impressions, when assented to, normally lead to apprehensions: assent is not forthcoming.[287] I take this to be confirmation of my contention that, for the Stoics, πιθανότης in the field of perceptual impressions does not already have consistency with antecedently held views as a necessary condition. The Stoics take the view that every veridical perceptual experience had under ideal conditions can be deemed persuasive, while the Academic view is that if what is perceived is incongruous it will not be persuasive however clearly perceived. The two positions reflect two fundamental but incompatible intuitions about perceptual experience.[288]

Another point of contact between the Stoics and the Academics is the term Carneades uses to refer to an impression which had survived the first kind of test (ἀπερίσπαστος). This term is formed from 'περισπᾶν', 'to draw away from', a verb which Chrysippus used in a context where he comments on the uses and effects of dialectical argument *in utramque partem* (Plut., *Sto. rep.* 1036d–e = SVF iii.271).[289] Specifically, he warns against the persuasive power of πιθανά which are employed in support of the other side of a given view, and which are capable of 'drawing listeners away' from their apprehensions because they are insufficiently fastened (as they would be in anyone who is not a sage). Did Carneades coin the term 'ἀπερίσπαστος' with polemical intent, as if to say that what the Stoics call cognitions (καταλήψεις), i.e. mental items which are the result of cataleptic impressions which have been assented to, are at best πιθανά which are undiverted (for now)?[290] Yet regarding the nature of the πιθανά employed in the context envisaged by Chrysippus, what persuasiveness they have would be due to their coherence with other πιθανά in the relevant domain, including those cited in the arguments mounted in support of them.[291]

---

[287] On this point I am in agreement with Brittain (2014: 352–3); Allen (1994: 108–13) argues that in situations like those envisaged in the Admetus example assent is given but immediately revoked. The text in *M.* 7.253–5 speaks of 'giving credence', which creates an opening for different interpretations.

[288] The point at which coherence with the subject's other beliefs becomes crucial is when a προκόπτων becomes a sage, which means that all his καταλήψεις become ἐπιστῆμαι because they are secure due to their consistency with all other beliefs the individual in question holds; see Brouwer (2002) and (2007). Nonetheless, I take it that, on the Stoic view, many impressions of sages and non-sages alike are dismissed, often unconsciously, at the stage where beliefs are formed, precisely because they conflict with the subject's antecedently held beliefs, but that has nothing to do with the persuasiveness an impression has to begin with.

[289] On the passage, see Bett (1989: 79); Tielemann (1996: 264–8); and Bénatouïl (2007: 79–89).

[290] For this claim, see *Luc.* 105a; and cf. Galen, *Plac. Hipp.* 9.7.3 (p. 778 Kühn = p. 586 De Lacy) and 9.9.37 (p. 802 Kühn = p. 606 De Lacy). For Galen's views on the πιθανόν in general, see Chiaradonna (2014).

[291] I do not have the space here to engage with Tielemann (1996: 264–87), who argues that the Carneadean πιθανόν, despite acknowledged differences in meta-philosophical status relative to the Stoic view, is essentially taken over from Chrysippus, notably the requirement for coherence with associated impressions (Tieleman 1996: 287 n. 90), but I would note that this impression can arise if Stoic attitudes to non-perceptual and perceptual πιθανά are not adequately distinguished, and if the question of what

6.5 The Evidence from Cicero

I had argued above that, according to Sextus' account of the Carneadean πιθανόν, top-level πιθανά are persuasive because their propositional content is congruous, while first-level πιθανά are clear in addition, with clarity being an enabling or facilitating property, and that the two types of test distinguished are intended to examine first-level πιθανά for these properties (incongruity and clarity). In this section I want to consider how the Ciceronian evidence can be related to this interpretation; for detail, see the commentary.

Cicero's chosen rendering for 'πιθανόν', 'probabile', is etymologically connected with '(ap)probare', a term Cicero uses for dogmatic assent as well as non-dogmatic 'approval' (see below on *Luc.* 104). This might lead one to think that the *probabile* is semantically nothing beyond that which we can approve of, in much the same way in which the πιθανόν has been regarded by some as what is, as a matter of fact, persuasive to us without being capable of further analysis. However, if one surveys uses of '*probabilis*' in non-philosophical texts, it is plain that there are numerous grounds on which something can be called '*probabilis*' and that these can be inferred from the context with reasonable accuracy. To say that these grounds do not contribute to the meaning of '*probabile*' seems arbitrary, and is certainly not the view of lexicographers. The etymology of a term is, trivially, but one clue as to its meaning, and one needs to ask whether Cicero provides further information regarding the sense of '*probabilis*' he has in mind. Nor is the link with '(*ap)probare*' necessarily straightforward, since there are *probabilia* which we cannot approve of.[292] It follows that instances of *probabile* must be looked at in their wider context.

Two different interpretations of Carneades' overall philosophical stance are mentioned in *Acad.*[293] This could complicate the interpretation of the Ciceronian evidence, in that different conceptions of the *probabile* might be found side by side. If, however, as suggested in section 6.1, the πιθανόν was rationally persuasive (or plausible) from the very beginning and the different Academic positions differed from one another primarily in the type of endorsement of impressions envisaged or permitted, and if Cicero took the same view, then only one interpretation of the *probabile*, and one sense of '*probabile*', would be likely to be at issue. This I believe to be the case.

---

accounts for initial persuasiveness prior to any scrutiny is not posed. On the Stoic use of 'πιθανά' for argumentative purposes, see also Sedley (1982: 252), who refrains from 'suggesting that Chrysippus had a separate and systematic theory of extra-logical discourse'; and Brunschwig (1991: 95), who suggests that the Stoics engaged in ethical argument *more Aristotelico*, i.e. from commonly held views, alongside their argument 'from a particular view of the place of human beings in divine cosmic nature'.

[292] In *Div. Caec.* 64 Cicero says that it is *probabile* but insufficiently *honestum* for someone who has been wronged to mount his own legal challenge, because the wronged are likely to lose sight of the common good, and that it is better for someone else to act on their behalf. '*Probabile*' here means 'understandable (but misguided)', which we may compare with the sense 'persuasive (but dubious)' which 'πιθανόν' can have. This is one reason why it cannot plausibly be claimed that Academic scepticism in its Latin representation in Cicero offers a more optimistic outlook on the possibility of obtaining knowledge on the grounds that it replaces 'that which persuades us' with 'that which merits approval', *pace* Görler (2004b: 71–2).

[293] On the Clitomachean position, represented by Cicero, as well as that of mitigated scepticism, see sections 4 and 8. Philo's Roman Books' view is mentioned but explicitly excluded from the discussion; see on *Luc.* 18.

Before I look at the detailed correspondences between Sextus and Cicero, I want to draw attention to an important motif which Cicero uses to locate the refusal to make or endorse excessive knowledge claims within pre-philosophical Roman practice and which, as I shall argue, is in the background of some of the statements Cicero makes about *probabilia*. Consider *Luc.* 146 (Cicero the character, a Clitomachean, speaking in reply to Lucullus):

> But just as you said that craft skills collapse if nothing can be apprehended, and did not concede that what is plausible is of sufficient power to sustain the arts, so I now retort that craft is not possible without knowledge. Can it really be that Zeuxis or Phidias or Polyclitus would tolerate this, that they knew nothing, even though they had such great skill? Yet if someone then informed them what force 'knowledge' is said to have, they would stop being enraged; they would not even be angry with us on learning that we were only removing what is nowhere to be found in any case, yet leaving untouched what was sufficient for their purposes [i.e. the *probabile*]. This way of thinking is also sanctioned by the diligence shown by our ancestors, who first wanted everyone to swear 'to the best of their belief' (*ex sui animi sententia*), then to be held guilty of perjury only 'if one knowingly misled', on the grounds that there was much ignorance in our life, then that someone who offered testimony should say that 'he was of the view' (*arbitrari*) even when he had seen something himself, and that the findings of judges were couched in such a way that they did not say *x* was the case ⟨or not the case⟩ but 'appeared to them to be such-and-such (*quaeque iurati iudices cognouissent, ut ea non aut esse* ⟨*aut non esse*⟩ *facta sed ut* **uideri** *pronuntiarentur*).'

In this passage Cicero turns the tables on the dogmatist by suggesting that, given their views about the epistemic position of sages and non-sages, craft knowledge is only to be had by the sage. Thus famous artists, clearly in possession and complete command of their respective craft, would refrain from claiming technical knowledge if knowledge (ἐπιστήμη, *scientia*) was defined as the Stoics defined it. By the same token, the ancestors stipulated that witnesses should swear using a formula which allowed for their fallibility, even if they had witnessed an event with their own eyes, and judges would qualify their verdicts by saying that 'it appeared to them that *x* or *y* was the case'.[294] In Rome judges were not members of a specially trained judiciary, and prosopographical studies have shown that it was unusual for a *iurisconsultus* to act as a judge or advocate (see Kunkel 1952). Rather, the judges were laymen who met certain formal criteria and who, in some cases after receiving instructions from a magistrate on terms of reference and the like, carried out their duties by relying on their own good sense and what experience they had. And given how the passage moves from outstanding artists to witnesses to judges, the witnesses in question are surely understood to be rational agents, too. In *Acad.* there are passages where *uisa* which correspond to the loaded sense of *uideri* employed by judges issuing their

---

[294] See *OLD* s.v. *uideo* no. 22: '(pass., in legal and other technical contexts) to appear after due consideration, or sim., be deemed'; for a more detailed account by a legal historian, see Daube (1956: 73–7), cited on *Luc.* 104.

verdict are identified as *probabilia*, specifically the kind of *probabilia* an Academic follows (see below on *Luc.* 103–5, p. cvii). We recall that Sextus, too, as has been urged by Burnyeat in particular, presents the scheme of the πιθανόν as an abstraction from how rational people behave as a matter of fact—people whose epistemic habits can be likened to a procedure like the δοκιμασία or to a doctor making a diagnosis.²⁹⁵ The *probabile* as understood in *Luc.* 146 is what deserves the acceptance of rational individuals who decide on rational grounds following a due process. Especially in the field of legal decision-making considerations of coherence, of making pieces of evidence fit with each other as well as explaining them in terms of each other, are obviously central to the process.²⁹⁶

I continue with the review of what Cicero says about *probabilia*. He is aware that Carneades, unlike the Stoics, divided impressions into persuasive ones and those which are not persuasive.²⁹⁷ *Non probabilia* are not characterized further, and there is no trace of the ἔμφασις/ἀπέμφασις distinction in Cicero, which makes the evidence from Cicero indeterminate on an important point on which Sextus was specific.²⁹⁸

Lucullus says, speaking ironically, that the Academics had drawn up 'an entire *ars* of impressions', involving a division and definitions of the items in it (*Luc.* 40); if the division which we find in Sextus has been secondarily and not entirely successfully imposed, as Allen (1994: 103) has plausibly argued, then *Luc.* 40 would suggest that Cicero's source material was nonetheless in this respect similar to Sextus'. What Cicero actually says about *probabilia* would not suggest a distinction between top- and first-level πιθανά, nor an association of different types of test with different levels of πιθανόν. Rather, a distinction is drawn between impressions which immediately strike us as *probabile* and *probabilia* which have been examined and tested in some way. Consider Lucullus, representing Antiochus' views (*Luc.* 35–6):

> So what is this persuasive impression of yours (*uestrum probabile*)? For if that which strikes people and appears persuasive to them, as it were, on first glance (*primo quasi aspectu*) is affirmed, what could be flimsier than that? If they say they follow that which appears to be the case on the basis of a certain scrutiny and careful consideration (*ex circumspectione aliqua et accurata consideratione*), then they will nonetheless not find a way out.

---

²⁹⁵ On a fully dialectical reading, I would expect Carneades to mount the strongest possible rejoinder to the ἀπραξία charge, which would involve replacing the cataleptic impression with the persuasive impression while retaining a highly rational agent.

²⁹⁶ It does not matter for present purposes if the character Cicero endorses what he says in *Luc.* 146 or if he retains his dialectical posture and argues ad hominem, since what is said is consistent with other, non-dialectical pronouncements elsewhere.

²⁹⁷ Cf. *Luc.* 99: *Duo placet esse Carneadi genera uisorum; in uno hanc diuisionem: alia uisa esse quae percipi possint ⟨alia quae non possint⟩, in altero autem: alia uisa esse probabilia alia non probabilia*, 'Carneades holds that there are two main classes of impressions: in one, there is this division, into impressions which can be apprehended ⟨and impressions which cannot be apprehended⟩; in the other, there is this division, into persuasive ones and others which are not persuasive.' The term *improbabile* is attested later (in legal texts inter alia, e.g. D. 50.14.3.1). I can see no linguistic or stylistic reason why Cicero could not have used or coined the word had he wanted to; see Frisk (1966: 214–23).

²⁹⁸ Schofield (1999: 346 n. 60) suspects ἔμφασις behind *species* in *Luc.* 58; for a different explanation see Striker (1997: 271).

Relying on what is *probabile* 'at first sight, as it were' is clearly unsatisfactory in the opinion of Lucullus, but relying on a *probabile* which has undergone testing is not much better. The two terms used to describe the testing can be linked to terms we find in Sextus in connection with second- and third-level testing. '*Circumspectio*' is reminiscent of 'περιοδεύω' (see above, p. lxxxii). '*Consideratio*' is less straightforward. It has been linked to 'διεξοδεύω' which we also find in Sextus, but a correspondence is barely recognizable, and there are reasons for thinking that we should connect it with an impression's being ἀπερίσπαστος when none of the impressions within a syndrome appears false in virtue of being incompatible with antecedently held beliefs and in disagreement with the others. '*Consideratio*' can rather generically mean 'careful consideration', of course, but etymologically, as ancient and modern philologists agree, it comes from '*sidus*', which means 'constellation' (and only secondarily 'star', the proper term for which is *stella*). *Consideratio* is thus the comprehensive (*con-*) application of a critical gaze to something which is an ordered set of items.[299] It became a technical term for rational scrutiny exercised by augurs and *haruspices* and was used in legal contexts, too (like *circumspectio*). Cicero himself nowhere makes explicit reference to the etymology, but may well be thinking of it in *Fin.* 5.58 *consideratio cognitioque rerum caelestium*. In the required sense the noun or the verb from which it derives do not occur again, but I submit that we have some reason to think that the material from which he worked made reference to a syndrome, too, and that Cicero 'translated' it by replacing the notion of a syndrome with that of a constellation.[300] This move would have been facilitated by the use of '*consideratio*' in medical texts, of the appraisal of symptoms.[301] It would be preferable if this was not done in quite such a subtle way, but at least on this occasion the fragmentary state of *Acad.* must be invoked. Is it really credible that the Carneadean types of testing featured only once, briefly, and then in the speech of the Antiochian Lucullus? What is the force of the indefinite pronoun in *aliqua circumspectione* in *Luc.* 35 quoted above? It could have its normal alienating sense, but it may equally well be dismissive, of something that had been said before. There can be little doubt that a detailed exposition of

---

[299] Cf. Paul. Fest., *verb. signif.* p. 33 Müller = p. 37 Lindsay: *considerare a contemplatione siderum uidetur appellari*; Thurneysen (1906: 183): 'die zu einem Sternbild (*sidus*) gehörigen Sterne mit dem Blick zusammensuchen und vereinigen'; Walde-Hofmann (1938: i. 263): 'die Gestirne beobachten bzw. mit dem Blick zusammenfassen'; further views to the same effect in Pârvulescu (1980: 159 n.1); see also de Meo (1983: 244–5) on ancient and modern conceptions of what a constellation is. The etymology in Festus, in line with ancient convention, does not account for every component of '*consideratio*', but one can glean the force that *con-* was deemed to have by different means. '*Consideratio*' occurs a number of times from the archaic period onwards in an alliterative pair with '*contemplatio*' (cf. the Festus quote above), and we know that Varro offered an analysis of the latter (in *L.L.* 7.9, which was written at the same time as the *Academica* and is dedicated to Cicero) which sheds light on the interpretation he would have given the prefix *con-*: '*contemplari*' was taken to mean originally 'to draw together the *templum* with one look', whereby *templum* means 'an area in the sky'; see e.g. Linderski (1986: 2270–3). See also Latte (1968: 97–9) on the force of *con-* in other broadly cognitive terms in augural language (e.g. *colligere*). A passage where the 'etymological' sense of '*considerare*' may be taken to be at issue is Gellius, *N.A.* 2.21.1–11 (esp. 2: *sedebamus ergo in puppi simul uniuersi et lucentia sidera considerabamus*), on a group of people looking at the night sky, identifying constellations and pointing them out to each other.
[300] Note also *Luc.* 66, where Cicero (as interlocutor, beginning his reply to Lucullus' speech) alludes to his (Clitomachean) way of following *probabilia* by means of the image of a navigator who is guided by one type of constellation rather than another.
[301] See *TLL* s.v. *considero* col. 427.54–61 and Celsus 8.10.1ff.

the *probabile* scheme was offered in the *Catulus*, by Catulus the younger or Cicero (see p. clxviii).

Nearby in *Luc.* 33 (and elsewhere) a distinction is drawn between *probabilia* without further qualification and *probabilia* 'which are not impeded' (see below, section 6.5). The latter is, as has been shown by Allen (1994: 97), a general expression covering any test that might be performed, as opposed to, specifically, the test for coherence with the syndrome of impressions whose successful passing leads in Sextus to second-level πιθανά.³⁰² Thus 'and which are unimpeded' is in fact a shorthand for 'and which are unimpeded after testing'. This is significant because otherwise passages like *Luc.* 33 might be used to argue that Cicero's plain *probabile* is not itself already plausible and congruous:

> Therefore whether you offer a persuasive impression or one which is persuasive and not impeded (*siue tu probabilem uisionem siue [in]probabilem et quae non impediatur*), as Carneades wanted, or something else that you can follow, you will have to return to the sort of persuasive impression which we are discussing.

This passage employs the same distinction as *Luc.* 35–6 above. Overall, the situation in the *Academica* encourages the interpretation, formulated on the basis of inconsistencies with Sextus' account in *M.* and the reversed order of tests for a persuasive impression in *P.H.* relative to *M.* that the tests are not necessarily supposed to be performed in succession, but that they represent two different ways of scrutinizing an impression.³⁰³

Acad. as we have it is not concerned with explaining what makes a plain *probabile probabile* to begin with. Minimally, the testimony of §146 discussed above, with its reference to the evaluation of evidence and decision-making in legal contexts, and what Cicero says about plain *probabilia* in particular, is compatible with what Sextus said (on my construal) about what makes a first-level πιθανόν persuasive (congruence in the first instance, with clarity acting as an enabling property). But we argued above that the notion of a constellation (*sidus*) in Cicero may correspond to that of a syndrome in Sextus' account, so that *consideratio* amounts to the careful examination of a set of *uisa* with which a target impression is associated or into which it dissolves. And since a plain *probabile* of, say, *Ursa Maior* must be possible, just as a top- or first-level πιθανόν of Socrates must be possible—we do not see a cluster of stars, and a constellation only upon testing, just as we do not see features of Socrates, and Socrates only upon testing—, a plain *probabile* may well have been conceived of as congruous by Cicero in the sense in which first-level πιθανόν are in Sextus on my argument. If someone sees a group of stars in the night sky and provisionally identifies it as constellation *x*, only to discover upon closer examination that she must be mistaken because she can make out a star where there should not be one (or fails to see one which she is expecting), then a plain *probabile* has been found to be impeded upon testing. In confirming that all and only the individual stars which make up the

---

³⁰² Consider e.g. the variant formulation in *Luc.* 99: (*Sic quidquid acciderit specie probabile, si nihil se offeret quod sit probabilitati illi contrarium*), which surely covers clarity or its absence, too.
³⁰³ Schofield (1999: 349), citing Allen (1994).

constellation are present, the individual performs a test not just for specific features but for ones which account for her original plain *probabile* that she is looking at constellation *x*.

6.6 The πιθανόν/*probabile*, Clitomacheanism, and Mitigated Scepticism

Carneadean πιθανά are persuasive and appear true on rational grounds, primarily because of the relationship of their propositional content with that of other impressions which we hold to be true and which are associated with them. The clarity of perceptual πιθανά is, as we have argued, construed by Carneades as an independent feature, but also as further enabling this rational πιθανότης and in that sense secondary to it. That the Carneadean πιθανόν is thus at bottom characterized by a logical property—fit with other impressions—explains why it can also be employed in the discussion of non-perceptual impressions, as was clearly envisaged from the beginning: non-perceptual πιθανά are *plausible* (see p. lxxxv). The tests for the conditions under which a πιθανόν is experienced (cf. *M*. 7.181–3) do not seem applicable to non-perceptual items,[304] while tests for coherence are.[305]

In *Acad*. we find evidence of three different Academic positions: Clitomacheanism, mitigated scepticism, and the view of Philo's Roman Books, which we shall leave to one side here.[306] Is there reason to think that Clitomacheans and mitigated sceptics viewed, treated, or used the πιθανόν in different ways, e.g. by placing different metaphilosophical interpretations on it? In order to answer this question, one must first note that the division of persuasive impressions into ἐμφάσεις and ἀπεμφάσεις is integral to the scheme and in all likelihood original, i.e. goes back to Clitomachus' records of Carneadean pronouncements;[307] likewise the manner in which phenomenal properties are accounted for, i.e. as dynamically determined by external conditions.[308] Thus the notion that a πιθανόν provides evidence for a state of affairs in the world is present from the very beginning, including in ad hominem arguments, given that the phenomenal properties of a πιθανόν are construed from the very beginning as predicated on sensorimotor interaction with the world. With a πιθανόν thus conceived, the notion that in describing one's actions in response to πιθανά one describes the psychological histories of one's views only, and does not also give (tentative, undogmatic) epistemic justifications for them, is hard (for this interpreter) to make sense of.[309] Cicero, describing eyewitness accounts and legal decision-making

---

[304] *Pace* Tieleman (1996: 264).
[305] On a conception of the πιθανόν which takes top-level πιθανά to be persuasive as a matter of fact and for no specifiable reason, and first-level πιθανά to be more persuasive because they have the phenomenal feature of clarity in addition, this easy applicability to non-perceptual impressions would be harder to explain.
[306] Strictly speaking, there is evidence for a fourth one, viz. that of Metrodorus, which I unlike other scholars do not identify with one of the three positions mentioned; see on *Luc*. 78.
[307] This is widely accepted but contested by Ioppolo (2017).
[308] By contrast, the assent which persuasive impressions receive in Sextus' discussion (see above, n. 225) is not integrated into the scheme.
[309] Thus Brittain (2008: section 3.3) and the characterization of Cotta's behaviour in Cic. *N.D.* by Wynne (2014: 247).

in §146 (p. cii), evidently feels entitled to operate such a conception of πιθανά as evidence concurrently with a disavowal of knowledge claims.³¹⁰

An attested difference between radical and mitigated scepticism lies in the type of acceptance or endorsement of impressions permitted: Clitomacheans withhold assent but are able to 'approve' (*Luc.* 104–105a), while mitigated sceptics give qualified assent, i.e. take impressions to be true in suitable circumstances with the *caueat* that they might be false (*Luc.* 148). The conception of the πιθανόν/*probabile* as the rationally persuasive or plausible is relied on in the former passage, which represents a rare point of contact between Academic dialectic as codified in Aristotle's *Top.* and sceptical Academic argument practice as documented in Cicero's dialogue. While our information on the reception of *Top.* itself in the Hellenistic period is scant, we can assume that question-and-answer λόγοι continued to be used for practice purposes and that philosophers retained familiarity with it and its conventions, acquired through actual experience and not through perusal of *Top.*³¹¹ Dialectical exchanges can also provide a presentational framework for issues which were not dialectical, as in Chrysippus' discussion of the Sorites.³¹² Similarly, or so we hold, the rules and mechanisms of dialectical exercise influenced the debate between Stoics and Sceptics in some ways, by providing conceptual categories or by helping to articulate conceptual distinctions. A case in point is the kind of acceptance of premises (offered in a dialectical exchange) and of impressions respectively, at issue in *Luc.* 103–5. In this passage, on the two types of endorsement distinguished by Carneades according to Clitomachus,³¹³ we are told that the person who withholds dogmatic assent is nonetheless moved by impressions and acts on them, in which case he 'approves' of them. The impressions which have this effect are *probabilia*. However, he will not use all the impressions which are apt to give rise to action, but only those 'which are not impeded', i.e. have been tested. This subclass of persuasive impressions is then said to appear in what must be the technical legal sense of *uideri* touched on above (*Luc.* 146).³¹⁴ Plain *probabilia*, given that they can give rise to action (even if they are not to be used), resemble first-level πιθανά in Sextus' account; for top-level πιθανά 'do not induce assent' (*M.* 7.172).

The passage likens approval to respondent behaviour in a question-and-answer λόγος when it is said that the Academic sage would follow *probabilia*, in practical matters relating to action, as well as on theoretical matters when questioned on either side (cf. *Luc.* 32). If Cicero had wanted to present theoretical *probabilia* as the outcome of speeches on either side, he could have done so, but here, it seems, his point was a different one: that giving approval is like replying 'yes' in a dialectical exchange.³¹⁵ Now there can of course be exchanges in question and answer where

---

³¹⁰ Whether or not the character Cicero is speaking ad hominem in this passage, it seems plain that he could easily speak in this manner in a non-dialectical context as a Clitomachean.

³¹¹ See *Tusc.* 1.7–17, whose similarity to the procedures described in *Top.* Θ8 is striking, as Moraux (1968: 300–7) has shown.

³¹² Galen, *De exp. med.* XVI.1–2, XVII.102 Walzer; *Luc.* 93–4; see Bobzien (2002: 217–18).

³¹³ Burnyeat (1997: 303–4) notes that, strictly, the passage has Clitomachus distinguish between non-assent and qualified non-assent.

³¹⁴ See on *Luc.* 104–5.

³¹⁵ See on *Luc.* 104: *item ea quae interrogati in utramque partem respondere possimus.*

saying 'yes' is equivalent to Stoic assent (Chrysippus on the Sorites in *Luc.* 93–4 being an example), in the sense that in answering 'yes' the respondent can be taken to adopt or proclaim a belief that *p*, as is recognized by Aristotle at the end of his main discussion of the rules governing the behaviour of respondents when offered premisses (*Top.* Θ5, 159b25–7). But in *Luc.* 103–5 Cicero cannot mean this, given that it is stated three times that the Academic reaction amounts to a withholding of assent. Instead, Cicero must be referring to the normal case (on which Aristotle seeks to legislate in *Top.* Θ5, 159a38–159b25), where the respondent in a dialectical exchange combines a full application of his rational self to the activity of appraising propositions with a simultaneous detachment from the issue, such that it can be articulated why a premiss to which the answer was 'yes' does not amount to a belief acquired or expressed. *That* attitude is meant to elucidate the concept of approval.[316] In a dialectical exchange one may well find oneself debating questions on which one personally does not have a view ('Is the cosmos eternal or not?'), and yet the rules of the game dictate that the respondent has to select one proposition of the contradictory pair as his thesis, which the questioner will then seek to refute by arguing for the thesis he is landed with by the respondent's decision. Crucially, in an exchange in question and answer a respondent answers 'yes' in a suitably detached way not for reasons which are opaque to himself and just because he finds himself feeling so inclined, but for specifiable reasons, like other premisses granted earlier which jointly support a more general premiss inductively, or the fact that the respondent granted another premiss earlier which entails the one he is now asked to accept.[317] It is no coincidence that the 'endoxality' of ἔνδοξα in Aristotle's *Top.* is construed in a manner which makes them close relatives of Carneadean πιθανά.

7. Constructions of History and of Historical Figures in *Acad.*

In *Acad.* philosophical positions are developed and defended against a background of particular constructions of the history of philosophy. In this section my aim is to introduce the scenarios in evidence, with detail to be provided in the commentary. Academics on the one hand and Antiochus on the other had only partially overlapping needs when it came to characterizing their philosophical ancestry: the Academics sought to trace their approach as far back as the Presocratics and to present their scepticism as the final evolutionary stage of sceptical concerns, while Antiochus sought to root his stance in the outlook of the Old Academics and that of the Stoics. Relatedly, Antiochian speakers have an interest in the Presocratics only in rebuttal, whereas Academics have no interest in Plato's immediate successors. However, Socrates and Plato become contentious figures, because both sides need to place distinctive interpretations on them.

---

[316] This conception of approval raises problems of its own, like the question of whether approval as it appears to be construed in *Luc.* 103–5 would not require a large number of actual beliefs as a background; on this problem, see e.g. Perin (2010: 149–50). See also Thorsrud (2010: 73).

[317] On the rationale for accepting premisses in dialectical exchanges as described in Arist. *Top.*, see Reinhardt (2015: 232–6).

The picture is complicated by the fact that the relevant narratives are distributed over several passages and that at least one of them is prima facie not internally consistent. The latter feature may be due to a number of reasons, including the specific argumentative aims of a given passage or the use of more than one source.

The section is organized in such a way that the two narratives, the Academic and the Antiochian one, are laid out first, followed by a discussion of particular characters which feature in different ways in the two narratives or else require a separate introduction for different reasons, e.g. because they are deployed for specific purposes by one side in addition to being characterized on their own terms.[318]

7.1 Sceptical Histories

We have reason to believe that from Arcesilaus onwards sceptical Academics put forward partial accounts of the history of philosophy,[319] either in a tentative and non-dialectical fashion or dialectically, i.e. without endorsing them themselves but with the implicit assumption that they ought to make an impression on their opponents given the esteem in which these opponents held certain earlier figures and given their doctrinal commitments and standards of rationality. Our main source for such Academic constructions of history is Cicero's *Acad.*, but there are also short and isolated Greek texts which provide context.

In the extant parts of *Acad.* the narrative of Academic views on the history of philosophy is sustained by an Academic speaker (Cicero in *Ac.* 1.44–6 and *Luc.* 72–6) as well as a non-Academic speaker (Lucullus in *Luc.* 13–15), the latter in evident response to the two Academic speakers of the previous book (*Catul.*), i.e. Catulus and Cicero. Lucullus both rehearses what the Academics say and offers his alternative reading of the *ueteres physici*.

Since what Lucullus' reports on the Academic account of the Presocratics does not completely overlap with what we can read in the extant part of Cicero's speech in *Ac.* 1,[320] and since a backward reference to *Catul.* (*Luc.* 13 *init.*) strongly suggests that Cicero's speech there (where it was the third and final speech of the book, or so I think; see p. clxviii) also included some historical considerations, the question arises how the Academic narrative develops. An important clue in this connection is tone: Cicero's invocation of the *ueteres physici* in *Ac.* 1.44 is matter-of-fact, while Lucullus argues somewhat polemically, likening the Academics' invocation of the Presocratics to the unwarranted invocation, made by seditious politicians, of venerable political figures of the past. If we assumed that Catulus' words in the first edition which corresponded to Cicero's in *Ac.* 1.44 were equally unemotive, then the polemical tone of

---

[318] Where the discussion turns mainly on passages from *Acad.*, I will offer minimal annotation in this section and details in the commentary; where evidence from outside of *Acad.* plays a decisive role, I provide secondary references in the footnotes.

[319] The most important study on the subject is Brittain and Palmer (2001); see also Bringmann (1971: 262–3); Brittain (2001: passim); Allen (2018); Bonazzi (2018); Lévy (2018a). For Arcesilaus' interest in the history of scepticism, cf. Plut., *Adv. Col.* 1121e–2a, on which see Warren (2002); Vezzoli (2016: 190–5).

[320] Lucullus names—while reciting the figures named by the Academics (*Luc.* 14: *profertis*)—Xenophanes and Parmenides among the *ueteres physici* invoked, but these two do not feature in the extant part of Cicero's speech in *Ac.* 1 (= Catulus' in *Catul.*).

Lucullus in *Luc.* 13–15 would come out of nowhere, and it would be natural to assume that, when the character Cicero made his historical remarks in *Catul.*, he did not just cite additional Presocratics (i.e. the ones named in *Luc.* 14 but absent in *Ac.* 1.44) but also commented on the manner in which the historical considerations are deployed, perhaps in a mildly provocative way (e.g. by gesturing to the dogmatist's fondness for *auctoritas*, cf. *Luc.* 60–2).[321]

The immediate prompt for Cicero's speech in *Ac.* 1.44–6 is Varro's invitation to explain the Academy's departure from its dogmatic heritage under Arcesilaus; this departure is characterized by Varro as a *discidium* (1.43). Cicero's response is designed to provide a rationale for Arcesilaus' actions, while rejecting the notion that he broke with earlier Academic tradition. Zeno was deliberately selected as an opponent—apparently for his confident knowledge claims (see ad loc.)—by Arcesilaus,[322] who was troubled by the *obscuritas rerum*, which had led Socrates to his famed profession of ignorance and before him 'almost all the ancients' (Democritus, Anaxagoras, and Empedocles are named) to say (*dixerunt*) that nothing can be known, that the senses and reason are weak, and truth was hidden in an abyss (so Democritus in particular) and everything shrouded in darkness. Therefore (*itaque* in *Ac.* 1.45 *init.*), i.e. presumably not because these thinkers made these claims but because of the *obscuritas rerum*, Arcesilaus denied (*negabat*) that there was anything that can be known.

The sceptical pronouncements ascribed to the Presocratics presuppose no particular conception of knowledge, as is signalled by the use of several semantically similar terms (*cognosci, percipi, sciri*).[323] They relate to both reason and the senses. Cicero relays this as something he has learnt about (*accepimus*), and the larger context—in which the Cicero character is invited to explain Arcesilaus' *discidium* by Varro—makes it natural to favour a non-dialectical reading of the passage: Cicero presents this account not so much because the dogmatist should find it compelling given his own assumptions (although the conception of Socrates invoked is not incompatible with that introduced by Varro in *Ac.* 1.15; contrast *Luc.* 15) as because he himself traces Arcesilaus' argumentative practice back to Socrates and from there to the Presocratics, who all responded to the *obscuritas rerum*, albeit in different ways: Arcesilaus' position is explicitly described as different from Socrates', and no equivalence of the Presocratics' and Arcesilaus' positions is suggested.[324] *Obscuritas rerum* is assumed to exist, but the epistemic status of this claim is not explicitly

---

[321] The argument against gauging the tone of Catulus' historical remarks in *Catul.* from Cicero's in *Ac.* 1.44 is that the political analogy employed by Lucullus in *Luc.* 13–15 would be less relevant in 45 BC (when Caesar was dictator), and that the character Cicero would respond to the character Varro in as unprovocative a fashion as possible (given Cicero's difficult personal relationship with Varro; see p. 88), whereas the younger Catulus may have tackled Hortensius more forcefully. Already in *Hort.* the character Cicero used the term *consularis* to refer to respected philosophers; see frg. 114 Grilli = 83 Straume-Zimmermann.

[322] However, while Arcesilaus engaged with Zeno in particular, he also argued *contra omnium sententias* (1.45).

[323] When used in a terminological sense, *scire* is used in *Acad.* of the knowledge which only the sage has (see on *Luc.* 144–5); its being juxtaposed with *cognoscere* and *percipere* shows that Cicero intends to speak of knowledge generally here.

[324] Castagnoli (2019: 210) suggests that accumulating sceptical pronouncements ought to be viewed as the marshalling of *evidence* that certain knowledge is not to be had; cf. the way *placita* are pitted against each other by Academics (*Luc.* 112–46).

characterized; it is not cast as anyone's dogma, but more as an impression arising from difficulty repeatedly encountered. As to Plato, nothing is said to be affirmed in his works, much is discussed on either side, everything is interrogated, and nothing certain said. This is a sceptical reading of Plato which, by identifying features of the texts only, seems to avoid any statement on authorial intention and as a consequence characterization of *Plato's* position. However, because the Cicero character appears to advance a developmental view of Academic thought, there is reason to ask whether Plato's position is supposed to be different from Arcesilaus'.[325]

In *Luc.* 13, having finished the description of the Alexandrian scene (Antiochus taking delivery of the Roman Books), Lucullus turns to his subject proper ('Arcesilaus and Carneades'). He specifically addresses Cicero when he introduces the political analogy which likens the Academics to subversives, and the well-established republic to the doctrinal edifice of philosophy which had gradually developed over time. Speaking of the subversives, he says that they cite their political ancestors *ut eorum ipsi similes uideantur*, which may be seen as an acknowledgement that the Academics do not present the outlook of the Presocratics as identical to their own. The rest of §13 expands the political side of the analogy. In §14 Lucullus lists the thinkers the Academics cite (*profertis*, apparently now in address to Catulus *and* Cicero) to undermine *philosophia bene iam constituta*, which means doctrinal philosophy as it had developed in the Old Academy (in Antiochus' sense). The list of Presocratics now cited includes Parmenides and Xenophanes who do not feature in *Ac.* 1.44; see above, n. 320. Lucullus acknowledges that the Presocratics made the sceptical pronouncements which Cicero refers to in *Ac.* 1.44, but he gives two alternative explanations for them: (a) 'modesty' (*uerecundia*), in particular Democritus', which he contrasts with Arcesilaus' deliberate trickery (*calumnia*); (b) momentary frustration after encountering particular difficulties, as one would only expect during the first beginnings of philosophy. If anything, Lucullus suggests, the Presocratics claimed too much, by which he means presumably not that they knew that they'knew nothing. Rather, their substantial philosophical views are meant, which, the modern reader would agree, often involved quite fantastic claims about obscure subjects. In §15 Lucullus restates that much time has passed between the first beginnings of philosophy (i.e. the Presocratics) and the *constituta philosophia*, which Arcesilaus chose to attack. Plato and Socrates, claimed by the Academics to be predecessors like the Presocratics, cannot be so interpreted. The last reference to the Presocratics may be *illa uetera* in §16, which Lucullus is happy to leave aside as being *incognita*.

Lucullus, as we saw, does not try to deny that the Presocratics made sceptical pronouncements, but suggests that these are not due to fundamental problems like a perceived *obscuritas rerum*. We have no reason to think that Antiochus' own construction of the history of philosophy featured the Presocratics; rather, for him they were philosophical pre-history, and he allocates a place to them only because they mattered for the Academics and their understanding of the Academic tradition. If it is correct to assume that Lucullus does not supply additional Presocratics from his own resources but because they featured in a second set of historical comments by

---

[325] I pursue this question further in my detailed notes on *Ac.* 1.46.

the second Academic speaker in *Catul.*, then it will have to be acknowledged that his remarks do not suggest that the two Academic speakers in any way disagreed on the Presocratics (e.g. because they adopted different Academic stances). This facilitated the creation of the final edition.

With the account of Socrates and Plato in *Ac.* 1.44–6 (and, I assume, *Catul.*) Lucullus contrasts his own: Plato left a *perfectissima disciplina*, which sounds as if Lucullus pictures him as a straightforward dogmatist (see below, p. cxxvii), while Socrates said one thing, thought another, and was merely ironic (in his disavowal of knowledge claims, or so one would naturally assume; see below, p. cxxiv).

In *Luc.* 72 Cicero engages directly with Lucullus' remarks in §§13–15. He recapitulates them accurately and then rejects them: *Illi cum res ⟨non⟩ bonas tractent, similes bonorum uideri uolunt. Nos autem ea dicimus nobis uideri quae uosmet ipsi nobilissimis philosophis placuisse conceditis*, 'These men, when they engage in endeavours which are ⟨not⟩ good, want to appear like good men. We by contrast say that things seem to be the case to us which you concede were actually held by the most noble of philosophers.' Despite certain formal correspondences between the two halves of this sentence, they do not map particularly closely on one another (*uideri* is used in two different senses, *placuisse* and *tractare* are unrelated; see ad loc.). This, however, does not affect the overall sense: the analogy between seditious politicians and the Academics is rejected, and Cicero observes that Lucullus conceded that sceptical pronouncements were statements of belief for the Presocratics, but are the recording of mere appearances for the Academics. With this Cicero picks up on *Luc.* 14a (*et tamen isti*...) and Lucullus' concession that the Presocratics do make sceptical pronouncements, but it is a somewhat rhetorical overstatement that Lucullus thereby conceded that the Presocratics' pronouncements reflected their doctrines (cf. *placuisse*).

There is then a sense break in the text, for Cicero's next point about Anaxagoras is not (directly) concerned with the possibility of obtaining knowledge. Anaxagoras claimed that snow was black because of preconceptions about the nature of things, and yet he was deemed a celebrated thinker (and not a sophist).

In §73 Democritus follows, who is well respected by the dogmatists, although he makes more sweeping statements than the Academics. Metrodorus is cited as a respected privileged interpreter of Democritus, apparently to reinforce the point about Democritus' extremism.

Empedocles, addressed in §74, was described as raving by Lucullus in *Luc.* 14, but Cicero suggests he spoke appropriately for the subjects he chose (presumably natural philosophy is meant, the area of philosophy which is especially unclear in the eyes of the Academic). Yet he, Cicero complains, is never subjected to the stock accusations levelled against the Academics (which are listed). Socrates and Plato, Cicero adds, were rightly claimed by the Academics, because Socrates was not ironic, and Plato would not have sustained an ironic Socrates over so many dialogues. Here Cicero is very brief, but what he says is consistent with what Cicero says in *Ac.* 1.44–6.[326]

---

[326] In *Luc.* 142–3 Cicero comes to talk about Plato again (and Xenocrates), but I would be hesitant to read the passage as necessarily continuous with *Luc.* 72–6; see below.

Luc. 75 begins with a meta-philosophical comment: Cicero does not just name reputable people as models, but also imitates only famous and noble ones. Note that Cicero does not say that he imitates all the ones named, but that those he imitates are famous and noble, i.e. he explains the original primarily non-dialectical appeal to the Presocratics as we can read it in *Ac.* 1.44–5, whereby what immediately precedes *Luc.* 75 served to reveal the credentials of the Presocratics in the eyes of the dogmatists (as well as the unfair treatment of the Academics at the hands of the dogmatists).

With this the rebuttal of Lucullus' criticism of the Academic appeal to the Presocratics ends. Cicero then begins a *praeteritio*, which, as this rhetorical figure often tends to do, develops into a fuller argument: he observes that he has refrained from citing people like the dialecticians, or Chrysippus (for his sceptical pronouncements), whom he could cite if mischief-making was his purpose. However, Chrysippus does then receive a more detailed treatment after all, and in §76 Cicero adds the Cyrenaics for good measure: as it is presented, they had a competing conception of apprehension, conceptually much thinner than the Stoic one (inter alia, it was non-representational). Why, Cicero asks, would the Stoic one be superior, sc. in the Stoics' eyes?

I have noted above that *Ac.* 1.44–6, while open to a dialectical reading, is best read in a non-dialectical fashion, while *Luc.* 72–6 is equally open to both readings, but invites a dialectical one; on this point I am indebted to Brittain and Palmer (2001).

The relationship between the remarks made on the *ueteres physici* in *Ac.* 1.44–6 and *Luc.* 72–6 is not simply that of general characterization and elaborating detail, although there is a degree of elaboration. Rather, the purpose to which the invocation of the Presocratics is put is modified due to Cicero's exposition in *Luc.* 72–6 being more open to a dialectical reading. On this reading the dogmatist's respect for the Presocratics is invoked, who are then shown to be more extreme in their views than the Academics, and yet it is the Academics who are attacked by the dogmatists. The combined effect of the sheer diversity of Presocratic views is that their efforts are presented as a casting about for the truth, while Academic scepticism is different in virtue of being a continuous, open-ended search for the truth. Overall, I assume that the passages surveyed can be read coherently as reflections of one perspective on the history of philosophy.[327]

This picture comprises, i.e. allocates a historical position to, the Presocratics, Socrates, Plato, and Arcesilaus (as well as Carneades).[328] There are two other passages where the character Cicero comments on historical figures: in *Ac.* 1.43 Cicero expresses agreement with Varro's claim, itself a cornerstone of Antiochian theorizing, that Zeno's epistemological views laid out in *Ac.* 1.40–2 represented a mere correction of the *prima forma* of philosophy formulated by the Old Academics. Here the question is whether this prima facie baffling statement needs to be explained in terms of the characterization as created by Cicero the author, i.e. whether he deemed it undesirable to have his character flatly disagree with the Varro character. The real-life relationship between Varro and Cicero makes this a genuine possibility. The

---

[327] A different way of conceptualizing the relationship of *Ac.* 1.44–6 and *Luc.* 72–6 has been proposed by Allen (2018). He argues that the former passage presents the Presocratics as negative dogmatists, whereas the latter presents them as being in a state of genuine *aporia*.

[328] Donini (2011a: 370 n. 28) notes the absence of Pythagoras, the Pythagoreans, and Aristotle.

alternative would be that here we glimpse a version of Academic history which was handed down to Cicero and which covered further parties. If so, it would need to be a late one, i.e. one responding to the formulation of Antiochus' Old Academy. Earlier Academics had no reason to account for Plato's immediate successors or for the Stoics,[329] whereas both groups needed to be fitted into the picture after the emergence of Antiochus. In *Luc.* 142 Plato's view on the criterion is relayed by the Cicero character, which is at variance with what we learn about Plato's views in *Ac.* 1.44–6 and *Luc.* 72–6; this is best explained by assuming that in *Luc.* 142 Cicero is relying on a doxographical source whose outlook on Plato is different from that presupposed by the sceptical Academy.

I have assumed above that the two Academic speakers in *Catul.* both remarked on the history of philosophy, and we know that they were of different persuasion: Catulus was cast as a mitigated sceptic (see *Luc.* 148), Cicero as a Clitomachean. I believe on independent grounds that in *Catul.* there was an opening remark by Catulus and that the sequence of speakers was Hortensius, Catulus, and Cicero (see section 9.2). Given what we know about the recasting process (see p. clxviii), it is therefore likely that the material introduced by Cicero in *Ac.* 1 had been introduced by Catulus in *Catul.* Now considering that we have found the evidence of *Ac.* 1.44–6 and *Luc.* 72–6 to be of a piece, one can either assume that mitigated sceptics and Clitomacheans operated essentially the same version of Academic history or that Cicero revised Catulus' remarks when he made them Cicero's in *Ac.* 1. On the face of it, the justificatory needs of the two Academic positions would differ only with respect to the status of (self-aware) assent, which in the extant parts of *Acad.* is firmly linked with Carneades.

A historical view which is only gestured to but not expounded in detail in *Acad.* is the one set out by Philo in his Roman Books. According to it, the Academy from Plato onwards held one consistent epistemological position, i.e. the one articulated by Philo in said books. See on *Luc.* 18 and section 9.3 on the sources of *Acad.*

7.2 Antiochus' Construction of the Old Academy

Cicero's *Acad.* and *De finibus* are our most important sources for Antiochian thought, while Philodemus' *Index Acad.* tells us more about the institutional existence of the group formed by Antiochus.[330]

---

[329] Another text which speaks to the Academic account but draws in the Old Academics is t. 64* (Aug., *Contra Acad.* 2.6.14–15), which I classify as a *dubium* of the indirect tradition; see p. 292.

[330] Important recent studies on Antiochus' Old Academy include Glucker (1978: 13–120); Dörrie (1987: 188–211 and 448–83); Frede (1987f: 1040–2); Lévy (1992); Görler (1994: 938–80) with full earlier bibliography; Barnes (1997); Reydams-Schils (1999: 117–33); Görler (2004a); Karamanolis (2006: 44–84); Donini (2010), first published in 1979; Bonazzi (2012); Sedley (2012b) and (2012) in general; Tsouni (2018) and (2018a); Petrucci (2021). These studies share, for all their differences, a desire to look at Antiochus' attempt to construct a particular version of the history of philosophy charitably; earlier scholarship was more inclined to charge Antiochus with an inept form of syncretism, often echoing Cicero's speech in *Luc.* (which of course is not an unbiased account), or with eclecticism (but Antiochus did not take himself to 'select' elements of doctrine from different schools so as to arrive at his *disciplina*). On the evidence from Philodemus' *Index Acad.*, see the edition by Dorandi (1991), now superseded by Fleischer (forthcoming); Glucker (1978: 98–120); Blank (2007); Hatzimichali (2012: 25–30); Polito (2012); Fleischer (2015). Antiochus' known works are listed by Görler (1994: 945–7).

In *Acad.* there feature two different historical accounts of the Old Academy, both by Antiochian speakers, i.e. Lucullus' in *Luc.* 13–15, and Varro's in *Ac.* 1.15–42 (with Cicero's response in 1.43). We shall survey them both so as to identify what is distinctive about them, before we evaluate them in their larger context and try to explain the variation.

At the beginning of *Luc.* 13 Lucullus refers back to the *Catulus*, where Cicero—who is addressed in person—cited the *ueteres physici* (i.e. the Presocratics) as intellectual ancestors, in the way in which political revolutionaries of today cite—implausibly— earlier by comparison moderate figures.[331] It is not stated how exactly this was done, i.e. whether Cicero had claimed that the posture of the *ueteres physici* was exactly like his or merely relevantly similar: the last sentence of the paragraph is open to both readings, and evidence from elsewhere in *Acad.* suggests that the Academics presented the Presocratics as negative dogmatists rather than sceptics. That is, they assumed a genuine development over time which culminated in their own view.

In §14 Lucullus elaborates on the analogy between the Academic historical arguments and those of contemporary demagogues. In both cases the earlier model invoked, so Lucullus argues, is in fact unable to serve its intended purpose. The Presocratics may have had occasional outbursts at the difficulty and impenetrability of it all, but—if anything—they were too confident in their positive views (final sentence of the paragraph; see ad loc.). The Academics, presumably from Arcesilaus onwards, want to undermine what Lucullus calls *philosophia bene constituta*, which is more naturally read as an assault on doctrines rather than on the institutions which promoted them (Arcesilaus was of course head of the Academy), but could mean either or indeed both. However, organized philosophy as practised in schools ought to be an indirect target only in the present context on Lucullus' view—the Academics' primary target should be doctrine.

In §15 Lucullus dismisses philosophical pre-history as in any case irrelevant, since there were centuries of development after the Presocratics. Thus Arcesilaus appeared on the scene when there was a *constituta philosophia* (a resumption of the phrase in the previous paragraph) which he sought to subvert. The same applies as above— 'body of doctrines' is a more natural reading than 'philosophy as practised in schools'. Arcesilaus is said to have hidden behind Socrates and Plato (mentioned already in §14). Then there comes a shift in perspective (from *quorum e numero*), and Lucullus rejects that Plato and Socrates can serve in any way as models for the Academics. Plato cannot because he left behind a *perfectissima disciplina*, Socrates because he was being ironic. On the face of it, this means that Plato left behind an organized body of doctrines, and that Socrates held substantial beliefs but was being ironic when he professed otherwise.

One might wonder if §15 could be saying something slightly different and *in extremis* a lot less.[332] *Disciplina* can mean something like 'body of doctrines', but it

---

[331] Pronouncements on the Presocratics in Antiochian sections of *Acad.* represent reactions to sceptical Academic accounts of the history of philosophy (see p. cix above; also on *Ac.* 1.15); Antiochus appears to have attributed no independent positive role to them as ancestors of the Academic tradition as he saw it.

[332] One might argue that in *Luc.* 15 Lucullus aims to give a nutshell account, which naturally elides historical nuance, whereas Varro's speech in *Ac.* 1 is a complex, developmental story of Antiochus' Old Academy in chronological sequence.

can also mean 'sect' or 'school' in an informal sense (cf. the similar ambiguity of *philosophia* noted just above). Given how the sentence continues after *disciplinam*, with a reference to the Peripatetics and the Academics as groups of people rather than to their doctrines, the sense 'sect' does at least get a look-in, although sects are identified by their doctrines (and there is such a thing as metonymy in philosophical texts, too). As for Socrates, it seems at least possible that the claim is not that the historical Socrates or the character in Plato's dialogues actually endorsed most or all of the views of Plato (and concealed this behind irony), but that he made one firm knowledge claim—that he knew nothing—which might be enough to put him on the dogmatic side of the dogmatist–sceptic divide. Especially the first of these alternative readings—*disciplina* in the sense of 'sect'—would have significant implications, in that Plato's exact role in the formulation of the doctrines which Peripatetics and Academics share would be left in the dark. However, we believe that what Cicero says in *Luc.* 74b discourages both alternative readings (see on Socrates p. cxxiv below, and ad loc.). Rather, in *Luc.* 15 Plato is viewed as simply having passed on a body of doctrines formulated by him.

In *Ac.* 1.15–17, as a first and programmatic statement on the subject in the final edition, Varro, representing Antiochus, gives an account of Socrates, Plato, and the *antiqui*.

Socrates is here the enquirer and investigator, who has moral intuitions and concerns which do, however, not come up to being, or issue in, firm views—in fact, this is the Socrates whom the sceptical Academics posited.[333] There is no mention of irony, nor is there space for it: anyone who characterizes Socrates as Varro does cannot consistently ascribe substantial beliefs to him, and in §16 Socrates is presented as explicit about claiming that he knows only one thing, that he knows nothing—so he cannot be ironic about that claim, either. And while §15 speaks about Socrates in a way which *implies* an equivalence between the historical Socrates and Socrates the literary character, as did the *Luc.* passage discussed earlier, §16 *init.* makes plain that there is a meaningful distinction to be drawn between the historical individual and the character as he features in dialogues written by various people—but the representation is portrayed as accurate.

§17 is then devoted to Plato and his successors. For Varro's distinctive understanding of the Old Academy it is the key text, whose meaning I shall try to pin down and then examine how one would read the rest of Varro's speech coherently with it. We learn that a first 'form' (*forma*) of philosophy was instituted by Plato's authority, namely that of the Academics and the Peripatetics. No agent is named, the sentence is cast in the passive. Plato provides authority but does not uncomplicatedly deliver a set of doctrines, to be adopted and possibly honed by his successors; rather, he himself is 'many-sided, complex, and rich in content' (*uarius et multiplex et copiosus*). This is not a characterization of his style: his dialogues, as we might say, represent a sea of philosophical options. That Speusippus is left as the 'heir of Plato's philosophy' might be seen to ascribe to Plato himself rather more agency, but as we read on, we see that it merely sets up the accommodation of a historical fact—that Speusippus

---

[333] This has been widely noted; see ad loc.

alone was Plato's chosen heir—while Xenocrates and Aristotle are his chief interpreters.[334] They are linked to different schools for, Varro implies, quite coincidental reasons. The crucial sentence is then the one beginning with *sed utrique...*: Academics and Peripatetics (note the plural of *utrique*) were filled with Plato's *ubertas*—again, this is not a stylistic term (as e.g. in Quintilian's characterization of Livy's style as *lactea ubertas* in 10.1.32), but a richness of content. What they did was, filled with such richness, assemble a *formula*. The noun *formula* is a technical legal term that Cicero can be seen to appropriate for (different) philosophical purposes elsewhere. It is associated with a particular type of conducting trials in matters of private law, where a magistrate (the *praetor*) selects, devises, or has someone else devise, a general outline of the matter under dispute (the *formula*), which he then refers to a judge for decision. Cicero's (correct) assumption here is that such a *formula* is itself the result of an attempt to isolate the core issue in many, similar cases which, however, will differ significantly in their non-salient details (see ad loc.). The *formula* that the Peripatetics and Old Academics created, while itself the result of the exercising of interpretative judgement, is, however, not reductive: hence it is called *plenam ac refertam*. In creating this *formula*, they left Socrates' mode and practice of arguing behind and arrived at an *ars philosophiae* and a *descriptio disciplinae* (the latter evidently a variation on *disciplinae formula*). There can be no suggestion that the *philosophia* which Plato is earlier said to have left to Speusippus was already such a *disciplina*—rather, the *disciplina* is only the result of the interpretative efforts of the Old Academics and the Peripatetics.[335] This is a connotation also carried by the term *formula*: while some *formulae* were straightforward to formulate, other legal problems were not easy to capture, and individual efforts to do so were associated with the name of the jurisconsult who devised the *formula* that ended up being deemed satisfactory.

Nothing Varro says later in his speech requires us to modify this reading. I shall first consider passages where Plato is mentioned. After *Ac.* 1.15–17 Varro gives a survey of the teachings of the *antiqui* arranged according to the tripartite division of ethics, physics, and logic (in the broad sense of λογική).[336] The latter section is *Ac.* 1.30–2. We refer to the commentary for details but observe that a rapid list of views in this area is ascribed to *utrique*, Old Academics and Peripatetics alike, and the third-person plural is sustained throughout. Plato is mentioned, but if one does not already approach the passage with the preconception that Plato *is* one of the *antiqui* (and *Ac.* 1.15–17 suggests otherwise), the text itself does not say this: the ancients took the mind to see *id quod semper esset simplex et unius modi et tale quale esset* (*hanc illi ἰδέαν appellabant, iam a Platone ita nominatam, nos recte speciem possumus dicere*). That is, the ἰδέα is a concept owned by the *antiqui*, though the term and thus the conception (however it is to be understood here) comes from Plato.

---

[334] The transmitted text requires a supplement in *Ac.* 1.17; see the commentary ad loc.
[335] The abandoning of Socratic method is supposed to be the precondition for the Old Academy's arriving at its doctrinal framework. One might wonder if Varro can really mean that the departure from Socrates came with the Old Academics and Peripatetics rather than with Plato himself, but grammatically that is what the text says (*reliquerunt*, of Socrates' argumentative practice). The last sentence of §17 does not explicitly restate the point because it is cast in the passive (*facta est*).
[336] The tripartite division is dubbed *accepta a Platone philosophandi ratio triplex* in *Ac.* 1.19. By itself, it does not constitute a distinctive doctrinal commitment since it is universally accepted in *Acad.*

In §33 *init.* Varro makes a concluding remark on the entire first part of his speech: *haec forma* [Madvig's emendation: *om.* P; *prima Γ*] *erat illis prima a Platone tradita; cuius quas acceperim immutationes* [Davies' emendation: *disputationes ω*] *si uultis exponam.*[337] There are two issues in the first part of this sentence, one of perspective ('Whose view is being given, Varro's or that of the *antiqui*?') as well as the force of the dative *illis*. They are connected. If the dative is a normal object dative, then the sentence is best read as giving Varro's perspective: 'this was the first form of philosophy, handed over to them by Plato (sc. or so I, Varro, think)'. We argue ad loc. that the dative is better read as what is called a dative of the person judging: 'this was in their view the first form of philosophy, handed on by Plato.' The phrase *a Platone tradita* inherits the focalization of *illis*: the *antiqui* took what Varro calls the *forma* to derive from Plato, and, as we might actually say, to be Plato's view. And that is consistent with what we suggested above about *Ac.* 1.15–17: on Antiochus' construal, the *antiqui* do not do away with authorial intention; rather, they take the result of their interpretative efforts to be what Plato intended.

After the section on epistemology Varro discusses the *immutationes*—changes, if the emendation is correct—made by Peripatetics and Stoics (*Ac.* 1.33b–39). *Accipere* in *Ac.* 1.33 *init.* (see *acceperim* above) means 'to learn about' not 'to accept', for some of the later proposals he rejects. He continues (*Ac.* 1.33b):

> Aristoteles igitur primus species quas paulo ante dixi labefactauit, quas mirifice Plato erat amplexatus, ut in iis quiddam diuinum esse diceret.

> Aristotle then was the first to undermine the forms which I have mentioned a little earlier, which Plato had embraced in an astonishing way, so much so that he said in them there was something divine.

Several ambiguities in this passage make it a very difficult one to interpret. I explain in the commentary why Aristotle can be presented as a critic of *species* here when he was earlier, at least on my reading, one of the architects of the *formula/prima forma* of philosophy which included *species* in some sense. I also explain why I think that *mirifice amplexari* is better translated as 'to endorse in a striking fashion' than as 'to endorse in an admirable fashion'.

In *Ac.* 1.34, in the context of a discussion of changes to the *prima forma* suggested by the various 'stakeholding' schools, which differed from one another in their readiness to break away from the *prima forma* and which included the occasional maverick, Varro writes:

> Speusippus autem et Xenocrates, qui primi Platonis rationem auctoritatemque susceperant, et post eos Polemo et Crates unaque Crantor in Academia congregati diligenter ea quae a superioribus acceperant tuebantur.

The sentence might seem patently at variance with *Ac.* 1.17, given the different role accorded to Speusippus and the absence of Aristotle. Arguably, it is not and instead

---

[337] For the textual problems, see the commentary.

makes a point on a different level of description: Plato's successors in the Academy prior to Arcesilaus were, on the whole, conservative, or so Varro claims. Nor does the sentence speak to the issue of how precisely the *prima forma* came about: by itself, it is compatible with both construals in evidence in *Acad.*, the handing down of a *disciplina* as envisaged in *Luc.* 15 and that of *Ac.* 1.17.

In *Ac.* 1.43, after the end of Varro's speech, the Cicero character expresses agreement with Varro that the Stoics merely offered corrections of the *uetus Academia* (a term which here covers the Peripatetics, too). (It is surprising that Cicero, who represents Academic scepticism, professes to agree with Varro, but that is of no concern at present.) Stoic epistemology, discussed in the preceding two paragraphs, is thus a correction of the *prima forma* described in *Ac.* 1.30–2 rather than a *noua disciplina*. The passage gives out nothing for the question of whether Plato was one of the *antiqui* in a narrower sense.

In *Ac.* 1, or so we have argued, Plato's role is not that of one of the *antiqui* whom Antiochus invokes as the founders of the Academic tradition as he sees it.[338] To be sure, anything 'the ancients' undertake or devise derives its authority from Plato, and Plato's *ubertas* means that nothing which his successors come up with is not in some sense 'in' Plato, but the actual body of doctrines which Antiochus regards as distinctive of the Old Academy in its early phase is the result of interpretative work done by Plato's successors in the Academy and the Peripatetics from Aristotle onwards. What Plato does is provide philosophical options as well as *auctoritas*. However, this should not be taken to mean that assumed authorial intention (on Plato's part, in his dialogues) is out of the picture. While the ancients are clearly accorded a role as privileged interpreters, the assumption is more likely to be that what they are retrieving in assembling their *formula* is their best guess of what Plato intended.[339] They are not—sc. in their own mind, on Antiochus' construal—postmodern theorists who propagate the death of the author and come up with 'readings' of Platonic dialogues. If this is correct, then successful corrections offered by later representatives of the Academic tradition—like the Stoic doctrine of the cataleptic impression and what belongs with it, e.g. the faculty of assent—take on a particular complexion: they are not corrections of Plato, but of the *formula* composed by the *antiqui*. Plato, on this model, can never be wrong, nor can he ever be corrected, although one can be more or less good at isolating and identifying his meaning.[340] Contrast here two famous statements on

---

[338] Thus correctly Dörrie (1987: 466–8), *pace* Barnes (1997: 78 n. 98). Varro also does not class Plato as one of the *Academici*—that term is being polemically reclaimed by him in *Ac.* 1.17, since it is in *Acad.* properly owned by the sceptical Academics and used to describe themselves; see Glucker (1978: 103–5).

[339] Contrast e.g. Brittain (2006a: 534) [author's emphases]: 'In the case of his rival Antiochus, however, it meant an appeal to the authoritative *consensus* of the ongoing Platonic tradition—the old Academic and Peripatetic doctrines which the sceptical Academics had misguidedly rejected—to validate the *truth* of the dogmatic philosophical system that Plato himself had established.'

[340] Contrast Sedley (2002: 49) [my emphasis]: 'It would be nearer the truth to say that he [sc. Antiochus] considers the Platonists to be the real philosophical giants, and the Stoics to be dwarves on their shoulders. To use the image, the dwarves' position may enable them to see more of or in Plato than the *antiqui* saw, or indeed more of "*how things really are*".' On my reading, it would still be Plato who, on Antiochus' construal of his meaning, saw how things really are, but it would be the Stoics who spotted this (sc. in relation to certain specific issues). Cf. also Sedley (1997b: 122 n. 37): 'Antiochus saw Stoic epistemology as an innovation on Plato (*Acad.* 1. 40, 43) but did nevertheless endorse it (ibid. 2 passim)'; Sedley (2012b: 81).

Antiochus' Stoicism.[341] Cicero says, in his Academic persona and intent on demolishing the Antiochian case made by Lucullus, that Antiochus was a 'most genuine Stoic' (*Luc.* 132: *Qui appellabatur Academicus, erat quidem, si perpauca mutauisset, germanissimus Stoicus*). Sextus, in *P.H.* 1.235, begins in a manner which rhymes with what Cicero says, but then adds that Stoic doctrines were, on Antiochus' argument, 'present' or 'there' in Plato.[342] This kind of talk rather fits with the idea of the Platonic corpus as a furnisher of options, of which the right ones need to be isolated by competent interpreters.[343]

If this picture of the Academic tradition as Antiochus construed it—at least in the text on which Varro's speech in *Ac.* 1 is based—is plausible, a question will arise: what exactly was the role Antiochus accorded to himself in this? To be sure, de facto he is on my reading acting as the ultimate arbiter of what Plato really intended, evaluating the *prima forma* and then further modifications of it by Peripatetics, Old Academics, and Stoics. He is the one who really gets to determine what Plato actually meant (not unlike modern interpreters of philosophical texts, who will often take themselves to reconstruct what philosopher *x* 'really' meant). But he may have been, indeed is more likely to have been, a character in the play so to speak in addition: precisely because he had been active as a member of the Academy at a time when the Academy was still a functioning school, he may have presented himself as the legitimate heir of the Academic tradition even after his departure from the Academy. And this would have distinguished him from later Platonists who had to operate without such a concrete connection with the Academy as an institution.[344]

That Antiochus cast himself in this way is prima facie likely: Varro's speech may be based on Antiochus' reply to Philo's Roman Books, in which Philo must have cast himself similarly—as he would, for he was scholarch of the Academy. But Philo claimed that his particular stance regarding the possibility of knowledge had been accepted all along by those who preceded him. So Antiochus would have a reason to create a mirror position at least as far as making authoritative claims about the Academy goes. However, in *Acad.* this would have been obscured by the fact that Cicero cast the difficult Varro as an Antiochian in his own right so that it is Varro's known erudition and independent thinking about the issues which, within the logic of the dialogue, elevates him above the level of a mouthpiece. Yet there is an interesting parallel in Cicero. In the dialogue *Brutus*, written in 46 just before Cicero embarked on the triptych of *Hortensius*, *Catulus*, and *Lucullus*, Cicero shows how a

---

[341] All relevant passages are collected at *Luc.* 132.

[342] Ἀλλὰ καὶ ὁ Ἀντίοχος τὴν Στοὰν μετήγαγεν εἰς τὴν Ἀκαδημίαν, ὡς καὶ εἰρῆσθαι ἐπ' αὐτῷ ὅτι ἐν Ἀκαδημίᾳ φιλοσοφεῖ τὰ Στωικά· ἐπεδείκνυε γὰρ ὅτι παρὰ Πλάτωνι **κεῖται** τὰ τῶν Στωικῶν δόγματα, 'Moreover, Antiochus actually transferred the Stoa to the Academy, so that it was even said of him that "In the Academy he teaches Stoic philosophy"; for he tried to show that the tenets of the Stoics **are** already **present** in Plato' (transl. Bury, modified).

[343] It is consistent with this that the particular move at issue can be seen to be anticipated by Antipater of Tarsus, who shifted from attacking Plato, as earlier Stoics had done, to stressing common ground between the Stoa and Plato—Antiochus, or so I think, saw himself as the proper owner of the Academic tradition, and thus entitled to help himself to and claim as his own interpretative choices first devised by others as long as they related to Plato. See Clem., *Strom.* 5.14.97.6 (= Antipater, *SVF* iii. 56); Sedley (2003: 20–4); Bonazzi and Helmig (2007: viii); Long (2013: 7).

[344] The speaker of e.g. Anon. *in Theat.* is self-effacing and comments on what Socrates/Plato intends without an indication who he is and where his authority comes from (sc. in the extant parts).

historical survey (in that case of the history of oratory) would culminate with the person laying out the survey (he himself) as the brightest representative of and heir to the preceding tradition, so that one wonders if Antiochus' dialogue *Sosus* had a similar narrative arc.[345]

So far we have covered the theory as it is presented but, without an actual practice to underpin it, it would have to be found wanting, in the eyes of contemporaries of Antiochus and later Platonists, and probably also in our eyes. The practice would consist in actually showing in some detail and nuance how the elements of doctrine which Antiochus takes to be part of the *forma*, whether the first one or the final one which he accepts as his own view, can be derived from Platonic dialogues. In other words, it would need to go some way to being text-based in the way in which later Platonism was, albeit without availing itself of the crucial device of the commentary and with the added complication that certain Peripatetic and Stoic doctrines would need to be recovered from Platonic dialogues.[346] Do we have reason to think that this was indeed Antiochus' approach? It is quite possible that behind the sections of Varro's speech which lay out the *prima forma* of philosophy there lie sources which meet the description that I have just given, and for 1.30–2 which I touched on earlier it is quite obvious that there are passages in Plato which could be linked to the various tenets assembled there (though often not through verbal correspondences, i.e. standard intertextual cues); I have tried to show this in the commentary and in Reinhardt (2018).[347] Cicero's way of writing would have obscured this: he has Varro address a Roman audience and is therefore relaying the main text not including the footnotes as it were, i.e. he wants to convey the substance of the doctrine rather than reveal the textual influences which lie behind his Greek sources. Moreover, the material which Varro delivers here was in the first edition of *Acad.*, i.e. in the *Catulus*, given to the speaker Hortensius (see section 9.2), who had only been converted to philosophy in *Hort.* (see section 9.5). For Hortensius to cite chapter and verse would have been incongruous, and we know from Cicero's letters to *Att.* (see section 9.1) that he only took a few days to recast the two-book edition into four books and change the speakers. The consequence of this for my reading of Cicero's *Acad.* as evidence for Antiochus is that we should feel encouraged to contemplate references to Platonic texts even in the absence of clear allusive markers. This is not an approach which one would adopt if one pictured Antiochus as a clunking syncretist or as an eclectic who worked from handbooks.

It has been observed, by readers of *Ac.* 1.15–17 who acknowledge the 'sceptical' Socrates but take Plato to be the straightforward architect of the *disciplina* as in *Luc.* 15, that a wide separation between the (historical) Socrates and Plato is unusually modern and in fact found nowhere else in antiquity.[348] (Later Platonists tend to minimize the aporetic side of Socrates and not to invoke the notion of irony.)[349] In fact,

---

[345] Hatzimichali (2012: 23) entertains the possibility that Antiochus featured as a speaker in the *Sosus*.
[346] On the significance of the commentary format for the emergence of Platonism, see Sedley (1997b).
[347] Cf. the views of the *antiqui* (*Ac.* 1.24–9), which on any reading show a strong influence of Plato's *Tim.* (see Sedley 2002: 80–1), and Zeno's corrections in the domain of physics (*Ac.* 1.39).
[348] See Sedley (2012b: 83), who also notes (ibid. p. 82): 'It was typical of ancient Platonism to merge the philosophical positions of Plato and Socrates, and Antiochus can be indirectly witnessed doing so himself in Cicero, *Lucullus* 15.'
[349] See Long (2010).

Antiochus is—on my construal—even more modern than that: he adds to a historical Socrates who in his outline is not unlike the one many would posit today a Plato who is open to many readings and is read selectively (that is one of the ideas implied by the notion of a *formula*). We might add 'and in a manner that is guided by one's own concerns' (like fitting in the Stoics somehow), but that is not what Antiochus would need to think: for him there may well have been something *in re* which the interpreters of Plato have been reaching for—something that the author intended—rather than something that they are creating or fashioning out of Platonic material.[350] Still, the avowed acknowledgement of selective interpretation is by itself distinctive in its ancient context. If Antiochus is looked at in this manner, one might say that one thing which stood in the way of a significant Antiochian reception in antiquity was that he was too transparent about the handling of Plato.

If we assume that the historical scenario of *Ac*. 1.15–17 is materially different from that developed in *Luc*. 15, the question arises if the difference between the two Antiochian accounts is one of chronology. This has in fact been argued by Sedley (2012b: 82–4) with respect to the conception of Socrates. By itself, it is plain that the account in *Luc*. is very black-and-white, while that in *Ac*. 1 is much more nuanced. As a result the model in *Luc*. requires bigger interpretational trade-offs to account for the entire tradition Antiochus wants to account for. The Stoics do end up correcting Plato's own *disciplina*, and one has to say that to get from Platonic forms to Stoic empiricism requires some correction. Moreover, an ironic Socrates is also not easy to reconcile with Antiochus' Stoicism in the field of epistemology: the Stoics rejected irony, just as they rejected much less egregious violations of σαφήνεια, and while Antiochus' model in *Luc*. does not make Socrates into a Stoic, he has to be recruited as a philosophical hero. I find it tempting to think that *Luc*. 15 reflects the viewpoint of the young iconoclast, while *Ac*. 1.15–17 is a more mature and reflected position. Notice how much Antiochus gives to the other side in *Ac*. 1.15–17, i.e. he gives them their Socrates as well as a Plato who poses genuine problems of interpretation due to features which would lead the Academics to view him a sceptic.[351] These concessions increase the plausibility of the picture and might even be seen to allow for a glimpse of Antiochus' own philosophical development. If the assumed chronology was correct, then Antiochus ended up abandoning an earlier historical construction which

---

[350] Roman jurisconsults who composed *formulae* relating to legal problems presumably took themselves to be identifying an issue that exists *in re*, too.

[351] Cicero's works include one other passage where an Antiochian account of the Old Academy (including the Peripatetics and the Stoics) is given, arranged by part of philosophy as in Varro's speech, is *Fin*. 4.3–10. Since it does not explicitly mention Socrates or Plato and it only makes vague reference to how Plato's successors came by its original doctrinal edifice (4.3: 'Existimo, igitur,' inquam, 'Cato, ueteres illos Platonis auditores, Speusippum, Aristotelem, Xenocratem, deinde eorum, Polemonem, Theophrastum, satis et copiose et eleganter habuisse constitutam disciplinam, ut non esset causa Zenoni, cum Polemonem audisset, cur et ab eo ipso et a superioribus dissideret', 'Here, then, Cato is my view: Plato's original disciples, namely Speusippus, Aristotle and Xenocrates, and then their pupils Polemo and Theophrastus, put together a system of thought full of richness and refinement. So there was no reason at all for Zeno, as a pupil of Polemo, to dissent from Polemo and his predecessors', transl. Woolf), it offers fewer immediate points of comparison than it might. However, it exhibits a marked desire to minimize and play down doctrinal disagreements between early Academics, Peripatetics, and Stoics, and as such looks early and inchoate, as Sedley (2012b: 87–8) has plausibly argued. On the passage, see further Reinhardt (2018: 65–6).

was closer to that of later Platonists in the way in which it conceived of Socrates and Plato.

I end this section with some miscellaneous observations. Passages purporting to present Antiochian material may exhibit what one might call different modes of Antiochian argument. When an Antiochian speaker presents the history of the Academic tradition on his own terms and unchallenged, he will be inclined to adopt certain strategies of reconciliation, e.g. (famously) that Stoics and Old Academics substantially agree but use different terminology (see below). When he is, however, faced with an actual or imagined objection to such a harmonizing line of argument, he may argue from the opponent's assumptions e.g. in a reductio ad absurdum. This need not suggest that Antiochus remained wedded to dialectical argument as it was practised in the sceptical Academy, to which Antiochus of course initially belonged;[352] for any dogmatic philosopher is free to use arguments which start from the opponent's assumptions on occasion as one weapon in his arsenal. Prima facie contradictory statements can arise from these two modes of arguing.

The status of promoted indifferents illustrates the difference between a harmonizing and a quasi-dialectical mode of argument. On the former view, 'promoted indifferents' is just a different designation for what the Old Academy calls 'goods' (see e.g. Fin. 5.81, 5.88–91; Leg. 1.55).[353] Yet if the Stoics insist that 'promoted indifferents' really are not goods, then an Antiochian speaker will respond that the Stoics reduce human beings to their minds by recognizing no other good than virtue (see e.g. Fin. 4.26, 32, and 4.41).

Even within sections that are overall detailed and developmental, there may at times be strategic emphasis on continuity. In Ac. 1.33–4 the Peripatetics after Aristotle are said to include Strato, an outlier in most respects, while Plato's successors in the Academy are presented as faithful and apparently uniform custodians of the Platonic heritage. Elsewhere, by contrast, the successors of Plato are given individual identities, and Polemo is singled out (e.g. Fin. 4.45). And while the Antiochian ethical τέλος is in most contexts ascribed to the antiqui (i.e. Academic and Peripatetics) without a suggestion of disagreements amongst the Peripatetics, in Fin. 5.72–3 the Antiochian speaker Piso attempts to offer an explanation why within the Carneadea diuisio of ethical ends there feature several Peripatetics with 'personal' views which are at variance with the view Antiochus posits as the end for his Old Academy. Piso seems to explain this with a slightly desperate and not entirely

---

[352] Lévy (1992: 187–94) argues that Lucullus in his speech in Luc. gives Stoic arguments against the Academics, without actually subscribing to them. Polito (2012: 40) argues that Antiochus continued to use 'conceptual categories' employed by the Academics after his departure from the Academy.

[353] I do, however, not believe that the claim of the unity of Old Academics and Peripatetics is in Antiochian passages confined to this issue; consider e.g. that the material in Ac. 1.30–2 is ascribed to both schools, or the general claim made in Fin. 4.3. Contrast Sedley (2002: 48): 'The one, repeated claim which will strike most of us as manifestly unsatisfactory is that the old Academy and the Peripatos were de facto one and the same school (18, 22). But at both its occurrences Varro is quite honest about the perspective from which he feels the claim is legitimised: on the classification of goods, a topic of absolutely pivotal importance to any Antiochean, the Platonists and the Peripatetics were in agreement. When on the other hand it comes to Aristotle's rejection of the theory of Forms, to Theophrastus' ethical innovations, and the Strato's exclusive concentration on physics, Varro is equally ready to brand them as deserters from the Platonist camp (33–4). There is nothing either simplistic or palpably dishonest about this evaluation.'

committed striving for originality (5.72 *fin.*): *Hinc ceteri particulas arripere conati suam quisque uidero uoluit afferre sententiam*, 'From this body of doctrines all the other schools have attempted to snatch fragments, which each has hoped may pass as their teaching.'[354]

Finally and trivially, one must of course distinguish between attempts to devise plausible readings of Antiochian narratives on their own terms, i.e. as we think they might have been intended, and the vantage point of the historian of philosophy, who may feel that some of Antiochus' construals fly in the face of available evidence or of plausible readings of canonical texts.[355]

7.3 Socrates

As we saw, Socrates features in *Acad.* in a number of roles: as an important figure in the history of philosophy on both the Antiochian and the Academic account(s), and as an important intellectual ancestor of Arcesilaus in particular, and therefore indirectly for Cicero, since Cicero casts himself as a Clitomachean, and the Clitomachean position seems to have invoked Arcesilaus in particular for his unqualified commitment to suspension of judgement (mitigated scepticism, by contrast, allows for qualified assent).

Above I have endorsed the widely held view that in *Acad.* there is an Academic (i.e. sceptical) conception of Socrates in evidence, and a dogmatic one, on which Socrates holds dogmatic views but hides them behind the mask of irony.[356] The latter conception is assumed to be found in *Luc.* 15, while the former is found in Academic contexts as well as in one Antiochian context, Varro's speech in *Ac.* 1. Against this, Burnyeat (1997) has argued that the accounts of Socrates found in *Acad.* can be read so as to be consistent with each other, and that the reference to irony in *Luc.* 15 is a presentational rather than a substantial difference. I shall survey all four passages and explain my reasons for adopting the traditional view, which does not emerge from *Luc.* 15 alone but only from a comparison of *Luc.* 15 and 74.

Varro begins his speech, a historical survey of the Old Academy as conceived by Antiochus, with Socrates in *Ac.* 1.15–17. In line with a central theme of the biographical tradition, Socrates is said to have directed the concerns of philosophy from cosmology and physics to real life and questions of virtue, of what counts as a good, etc. In all his conversations, as they are 'reported' (not 're-imagined') by various

---

[354] Differently Barnes (1997c: 86): 'But in this later section Aristotle and Theophrastus appear in a somewhat different light—at least, they are named first among those who "snatched pieces" from the system Antiochus has described (74) [i.e. 72 *fin.*]: they are not its originators.' In 5.73 Piso describes how later Peripatetics (and others: Aristo the Stoic is named, too) fastened on and magnified particular remarks of the *antiqui* in order to arrive at their views.

[355] See Inwood (2012: 217–18); Sedley (2002: 77), who argues that Varro's physics is anti-Xenocratean.

[356] On different interpretations placed on Socrates by philosophers in antiquity, see Long (1989), (1999a), and (2010); on Academic interpretations of Socrates, see Opsomer (1998a: 83–126) and Warren (2002); on Socrates in Cicero, see Gorman (2005) and McConnell (2019a); on Socrates in *Acad.*, see Ioppolo (1995: 89–123, esp. 118–21); Glucker (1997); Brittain (2001: 182–3); and see on *Ac.* 1.44–6 and on *Luc.* 15.

Socratics (not just Plato), his argumentative posture is such that he affirms nothing, refutes others, and says he knows nothing except this one thing, that he knows nothing (so the scope of 'affirms nothing' must relate to subjects discussed other than Socrates' state of knowledge). He says that he is better than others for knowing he knows nothing, while others are unaware of their ignorance, and that this was presumably why the Delphic oracle declared him to be the wisest: because human wisdom consists in having no false beliefs that one knows something. This posture he maintained throughout, and he continued to extol virtue and to encourage others to pursue it.

In *Ac.* 1.44–5 Cicero picks up from Varro, who had ended in *Ac.* 1.40–2 on Zeno's modifications to the *prima forma* (1.33) of Old Academic philosophy in the field of logic. Arcesilaus is presented as having characterized his position with reference to Socrates: he knew nothing, not even that one thing which Socrates had left himself, viz. that he knew nothing.[357] The section is about Arcesilaus, but what information it offers on Socrates is consistent with Varro's earlier exposition.

In *Luc.* 14–15, near the beginning of the Antiochian Lucullus' speech, Socrates is named as one of those cited by the Academics alongside the Presocratics and Plato, evidently in a line of philosophical predecessors for the Academic position. (This must refer to a section of the *Catulus* which has no counterpart in the extant part of *Ac.* 1.) Lucullus rejects the suggestion that Socrates and Plato can be counted among this number: not Plato because he left a *perfectissima disciplina* behind, and not Socrates because—and at this point Lucullus speaks not of beliefs of Socrates but of his practice to guide the discussion away from himself (and by implication any beliefs he might hold) and instead to ascribe to others whom he wanted to refute 'more' (presumably knowledge or wisdom). In saying one thing but thinking another, he used the dissimulation which the Greeks call irony. What was he thinking? If it is assumed that Socrates had substantial beliefs which he concealed (though beliefs jointly falling short of a *perfectissima disciplina*, given the contrast with Plato), then Socrates is a dogmatist who uses irony to conceal his position. If, however, Socrates makes one knowledge claim only, that he knows nothing, affects to grant his interlocutors knowledge which he suspects they do not have, all the while thinking he is wise, then his irony masks the same attitude as in *Ac.* 1.15–17 and 1.44–5.[358] On the latter reading, it is the making of one second-order knowledge claim which is enough for Lucullus to group Socrates together with Plato, as well as possibly a certain confidence on Socrates' part that he is wise because he knows his limitations unlike everyone else.

What might seem to point in the direction of Socratic dogmatism concealed behind irony is that Socrates is said to have 'wanted' to refute his interlocutors.

---

[357] We take the Socratic position described in *Ac.* 1.44–5 not to be self-refuting; see ad loc.

[358] Cf. Burnyeat (1997: 293): 'We tend to think of Socrates as talking ironically, on a variety of themes. But suppose the irony of which Lucullus speaks here is more specific. Suppose it consists in Socrates saying to his interlocutors "I'm not wise like you are" while thinking "I am much wiser than you". He thinks this, however, not in the sense that he thinks he knows important truths about the subjects he discusses— the virtues and vices, and good and evil generally (*Ac.* 1.15)—but in the sense ascribed to him by Varro at [*Ac.* 1.16:...*ob eamque rem se arbitrari ab Apolline omnium sapientissimum esse dictum, quod haec esset una hominis sapientia, non arbitrari sese scire quod nesciat*]. He says he is not wise, but thinks he is, simply because he does not think he knows what he does not know.'

However, even such a desire need not spring from firm but concealed beliefs which one wants to prove correct, but could arise from a non-dogmatic commitment to rationality, which gives rise to the wish to shake other people's beliefs if and when, as one suspects, they are not firmly grounded.

In *Luc.* 74 the Cicero character responds to *Luc.* 14–15. Thus he could offer an insight into what kind of stance precisely Socrates' irony masks on Lucullus' view and resolve the ambiguity of *Luc.* 14–15, or at least offer an insight into how Cicero the character chooses to take Lucullus' point. After a couple of remarks about the Presocratics, including that their sceptical pronouncements may in part have been an angry reaction to the over-optimistic knowledge claims of others (thus aligning them with Socrates), Cicero rejects Lucullus' suggestion that Plato and Socrates should be set apart from the Presocratics, citing his in-depth familiarity with both. Socrates is credited with the familiar claim that he knows nothing, except this one thing, 'nothing more' (*nihil amplius*). On one reading, *nihil amplius* by itself suggests that Cicero takes Lucullus to have ascribed further knowledge claims to Socrates, a notion which Cicero rejects. On an alternative reading, Cicero's emphasis is on Socrates' first-order claim that he knows nothing, and the one (second-order) knowledge claim is dismissed as insignificant by *nihil amplius*. Plato's categorization as the inventor of a dogmatic system (§15: *perfectissima disciplina*) is rejected on the grounds that he would not have 'recorded' (*persequi*) Socrates' disavowal of knowledge in so many books if he had not approved it. The paragraph ends with this sentence: *ironiam enim alterius, perpetuam praesertim, nulla fuit ratio persequi*. Burnyeat (and Rackham) introduce an 'otherwise' into the sentence, so that irony remains a feature of Socrates as it was in *Luc.* 15; thus Burnyeat (1997: 298) translates: 'Otherwise there was no reason for the one to keep on depicting the irony of the other, particularly since it was unremitting', adding in n. 58: 'In its context, this confirms from the Academic side that Socrates' irony has to do with his wisdom and ignorance'. Yet there is no 'otherwise' in the text, and thus the sentence gives an explanation for why on Cicero's reading Socrates was not being ironic. This leaves the question of why it is inconceivable for the Cicero character that Plato would go along with an ironic Socrates. One might think that, especially if what is provided is merely a faithful record, this should not be a problem. The point only makes sense if irony is supposed to conceal substantial beliefs—*those* Plato would have had no reason to suppress, and the fact that Socrates disavows them consistently in Plato's works should accordingly be taken at face value in the Cicero character's view. Suppressing that Socrates thought he was wise relatively speaking because he knew his limitations, i.e. that he knew nothing except that one thing, should not give rise to bafflement. On the Cicero character's reading, Socrates' disavowal of knowledge (with the one exception) was genuine, and Plato affirmed nothing. For this reason the two of them should not be separated from the Presocratics. And Lucullus, on the Cicero character's view, did hint at (further) substantial beliefs which he took to be concealed behind Socrates' irony. Thus I opt for the first of the two readings of *nihil amplius* referred to above.

If Cicero the character does justice to Lucullus the character, then the Antiochian passage *Luc.* 15 operates a conception of Socrates which is different from that in the Antiochian passage *Ac.* 1.15–17, where the speaker Varro relies on the Academic conception. In terms of the economy of the debate, it is hard to see what Cicero the character (or the author) would gain by misinterpreting Lucullus' point.

Glucker (1997) is a synoptic study of substantial Ciceronian passages featuring Socrates. The four crucial passages from *Acad.* which I have discussed above are illuminated in various ways (see the commentary), but perhaps most interestingly, the other material does not directly speak to the central question pursued above with respect to *Luc.* 15—whether Socratic irony can be used to conceal substantial beliefs as opposed to an awareness of Socrates' ignorance, which is, however, seen as wisdom. To be sure, one encounters a Socrates who is elegantly ironic and attributes wisdom to others while presenting himself as *inscius omnium rerum* and *rudis* (*Brut.* 292, Atticus speaking; Glucker 1997: 66), as well as a Socrates who argues against others while not showing what he himself thinks (*De orat.* 3.67 on Arcesilaus, who behaved in the same way—*id fuit Socraticum maxime*—, and *Tusc.* 5.11; Glucker 1997: 77 and 81, respectively), but there is no specific parallel for the Socrates who holds dogmatic beliefs and uses irony to conceal them. Glucker (1997: 70–1) wonders if this was because Cicero took this conception of Socrates to be a peculiarly Antiochian one, which he did not want to endorse in his own voice (even though he must have been familiar with it since the time when he first heard about Antiochus' response to the Roman Books). What is plain in any event is that Cicero was familiar with a range of conceptions of Socrates, including ones employed in the rhetorical tradition, and of course he knew many of Plato's dialogues directly and thus will have thought independently and creatively about him.[359]

Although the philosophical reception of Socrates acknowledges irony as one of his features from the very beginning, irony is not generally a prominent feature of Socrates in the Hellenistic period, as Long (1988) has shown inter alia. Philosophical schools which aspired to plain and direct speaking—in any event a heavily constructed concept—would either acknowledge Socrates' irony and regard it as a serious flaw (thus the Epicureans), or dispute that Socrates was ironic since irony was seen as a weakness which a wise man, or aspiring wise man, would never exhibit (thus the Stoics). Given the latter, it is remarkable that Antiochus would deploy a Socrates who is a dogmatist and uses irony. For Antiochus appears otherwise to have adopted Stoic epistemology without qualification,[360] and the Stoic rejection of irony is at least in part grounded in considerations which fall under the heading of λογική. See the commentary on *Luc.* 15 for further discussion.

7.4 Plato

How Plato features in the two competing narratives has been discussed in some detail above. Here I want to develop briefly one observation which is central to how I see the relationship between the two narratives. The dogmatic narrative has, or so

---

[359] See DeGraff (1940).
[360] See Brittain (2012).

I contend, an internal tension (*Luc.* 14–15; *Ac.* 1.16–17, 19, 30, 33, 34), whereas the sceptical narrative does not (*Luc.* 74 and *Ac.* 1.44–6).

There seems to be little scope for mediation between the Plato who created a *perfectissima disciplina* according to Lucullus (*Luc.* 15) and the sceptical Plato of *Ac.* 1.46, 'in whose books nothing is affirmed and many issues are discussed on either side, every matter is investigated, and nothing certain is said' according to the Cicero character. However, the Plato of Varro's speech who is rich in content and resistant to easy retrieval of authorial intention (*Ac.* 1.17) to the point where that intention is only definitively recovered by Antiochus, superior interpreter and arbiter on earlier attempts to hone the *prima forma* of Old Academic philosophy further, is a different case. That Plato can have many of the features posited by Cicero in *Ac.* 1.44–6, in fact his having them could be construed as the reason why he can only be understood through a joint effort over time and incrementally.

Cicero's characterization of Plato's works in *Ac.* 1.46, strikingly cast in the passive and thereby refraining from ascribing a stance to the author, could actually be endorsed by Varro as it stands, provided that he insisted in addition that the features described by Cicero, while present, do not prevent one from discerning Plato's favoured views and theories. In this he would be similar to modern readers who feel able to isolate a 'theory of *x*' (e.g. belief) in the dialogues and to call it 'Plato's' (meaning something stronger than merely 'found in Plato'), although there would be disagreement on what the substance of the theory is. Such dogmatic readings of Plato are not blind to the features Cicero mentions, but hold that ultimately they do not prevent the construction of an overall meaning.

If the difference I posit between Lucullus' and Varro's account of Plato is real, then Varro's must appear the more sophisticated one, not just for its explanatory power regarding the tradition Varro seeks to explain but also because it is able to concede to the Academics non-trivial features of Plato which Lucullus' account would have to dismiss as irrelevant. In philosophical debate nuance increases over time. Hence my assumption that Varro's speech in *Ac.* 1 reflects a relatively later version of Antiochian thinking compared to Lucullus' speech; see sections 7.2 and 9.3.

7.5 Arcesilaus

The historical Arcesilaus and the nature of his scepticism have been the subject of detailed and penetrating studies, and there exist judicious surveys of this scholarship.[361] Arcesilaus wrote nothing or at least nothing that revealed his outlook and shaped his reception in antiquity.[362] There is no universally accepted account of the

---

[361] See Görler (1994: 786–824); Brittain (2008). Important studies include: Glucker (1978: 31–47); Couissin (1983); Ioppolo (1984); Ioppolo (1986) with Maconi (1988); Long (1986); Frede (1987b); Long (1989); Annas (1992a); Striker (1996b); Cooper (2006); Brittain (2008); Perin (2013); Ioppolo (2018); Tarrant (2020). The sources are collected in Mette (1984) and Vezzoli (2016: 153–268); the latter also offers an overall interpretation of the evidence. In this section I cite scholarship to which my view is indebted and acknowledge other interpretations in the commentary.

[362] See the evidence assembled by Görler (1994: 786–7).

historical Arcesilaus with which one could simply compare the role accorded to him in *Acad.*; rather, *Acad.* is one important component of the primary evidence.

Before one can attempt a reconstruction of the historical Arcesilaus' position, recurrent pieces of information on his views (in a suitably qualified sense), as well as disagreements and omissions, need to be identified in the relevant sources. The way in which each source constructs Arcesilaus, in line with whatever agenda it may pursue, needs to be described. What emerges needs to be contextualized with what one can reasonably expect of the head of the Academy, albeit an unusual one deliberately breaking with the immediate past. It may then be possible to devise a genealogy of these different constructions and to speculate how the historical Arcesilaus' stance is best characterized. The task of illuminating Arcesilaus' role in *Acad.* is thus a necessary component of a reconstruction of the historical Arcesilaus.

It has been observed that two of our primary sources on Arcesilaus appear to be in disagreement: while Sextus in *M.* has Arcesilaus mount arguments against the Stoics ad hominem, Cicero in *Acad.* presents Arcesilaus as endorsing (in a sense to be clarified) the same arguments. However, we shall argue in the present section that this view needs to be qualified and that in fact both conceptions of Arcesilaus' activities are present in *Acad.*: in *Ac.* 1 we encounter Arcesilaus arguing ad hominem against a range of opponents including the Stoics, whereas in *Luc.* the same speaker—Cicero— presents him as endorsing anti-Stoic arguments in a qualified way.

The best explanation of this prima facie baffling state of affairs is that Cicero, who deploys Arcesilaus for a particular purpose (namely as a figurehead for the particular variety of Academic scepticism adopted by him, i.e. the Clitomachean position; see on *Luc.* 65–7), presents Arcesilaus as having attacked the Stoics ad hominem initially but as having qualifiedly endorsed those same arguments at a later stage.[363] This means that within the narrative developed in *Acad.* Cicero's Arcesilaus eventually also gave his approval to certain Stoic conceptions relied on in the anti-Stoic arguments. The reason for this shift on Arcesilaus' part, for the qualified licence he granted to the Stoics, was, or so Cicero may be taken to imply, that Stoicism held out a deeply attractive hope for Arcesilaus.

Our main evidence for Arcesilaus within *Acad.* comes from the character Cicero's contributions to the conversation.

Lucullus refers to Academic scepticism in general, by way of a shorthand, as 'Arcesilaus and Carneades' (*Luc.* 12 *fin.*), which raises the question of how each contributes to the Academic stance as Lucullus sees it. Otherwise references to Arcesilaus made by the character Lucullus are not very informative, either: in *Luc.* 14 Arcesilaus' 'vexatious trickery' (*calumnia*) is referred to as different from the sincere (sc. but misguided) sceptical pronouncements of Democritus; similarly in §15 Arcesilaus is said to have subverted 'well-ordered philosophy' (*constituta philosophia*). In §16 there is a passing reference to Arcesilaus among the various heads of the Academy. In §60 the success of Academic scepticism is put down not to its substance as a

---

[363] This endorsement, which issues in what are, in the terms in which the debate is conducted, non-beliefs which are based on reasons, is characterized as 'approval' (see on *Luc.* 104).

philosophical approach but to the rhetorical abilities of Arcesilaus and Carneades. Overall, the Arcesilaus who emerges from Lucullus' references to him is not clearly delineated: he is a rhetorically effective but philosophically insubstantial rebel without a cause. If Cicero's position is in an important sense indebted to Arcesilaus, then Lucullus flatly refuses to recognize this; however, it is arguable that Lucullus' outlook prevents him from getting into the Academic position in general and appreciating it on its own terms.[364] The character Varro's only two comments on Arcesilaus come in *Ac.* 1.34 *fin.*, where Arcesilaus is merely mentioned, alongside Zeno, as a student of Polemo, and in *Ac.* 1.43, where he blames him for the *discidium* from the earlier Academic tradition which Academic scepticism represents from an Antiochian point of view.

By contrast, Arcesilaus features substantially in Cicero's contributions in *Luc.* 66–7 and 77, and in *Ac.* 1.44–6. While *Ac.* 1 was composed later than the sections in *Luc.*, logically the historical survey which takes up the bulk of the extant part of *Ac.* 1 precedes the largely synchronic discussion of philosophical issues covered in the two speeches in *Luc.* One would expect the character Cicero to be consistent in his accounts of Arcesilaus across both editions,[365] and consequently the initial approach would be to try and reconcile any differences. We shall indeed see that *Ac.* 1.44–6 and *Luc.* 66–7 differ in their account of Arcesilaus in a crucial respect.

In *Ac.* 1.44–6 Varro, speaking on behalf of Antiochus, has just completed his historical survey of the Old Academy, the Peripatos, and the Stoa, presenting various epistemological doctrines of the latter as corrections of Old Academic views rather than completely new departures. He invites Cicero to explain the break (*discidium*) between the Old and the sceptical Academy, including Arcesilaus' 'innovations' (1.43). Cicero is thus challenged to present Arcesilaus' stance as not emerging ex nihilo and as credibly motivated. We learn that Arcesilaus 'set up' (*instituit*) his entire conflict (*omne certamen*) with Zeno. *Instituere* is suggestive of the deliberate choosing of one opponent when Arcesilaus could conceivably have picked another opponent (or additional ones, as Carneades later did); if this was correct, then something may be assumed to have guided Arcesilaus' choice of opponent. We are also told that he was not motivated by stubbornness and ambition, but that he engaged Zeno on account of the same *obscuritas rerum* which had led the Presocratics and Socrates to professions of ignorance. The obscurity of things, one would think, is only concerning for those who want to know and understand. On account of said obscurity, Arcesilaus 'held' (the verb used is *censere*; *negare* also features, with respect to the

---

[364] See the commentary on *Luc.* 110–11; Polito (2012: 46–7). Antiochus (and hence Lucullus) did not just adopt Stoic doctrines in the field of epistemology but also Stoic defensive postures; in the record there is almost complete silence on how, i.e. as a result of which insights, recognitions, or even epiphanies Antiochus shifted from an Academic outlook to his dogmatic stance; see on *Luc.* 69–71.

[365] I discuss the possibility that Cicero's first speech in *Ac.* 1 and his later statements in the final edition presented different views of *Carneades* in section 9.3. For Cicero's first speech in *Ac.* 1 is in all likelihood based on that of Catulus the son's in the first edition, who is like his father a mitigated sceptic, and is thus likely to have construed Carneades in a different way compared to the Clitomachean character. Cf. also the case of two apparently different conceptions of Socrates in two Antiochian passages in *Acad.*, *Luc.* 15 (Socrates as an εἴρων), and *Ac.* 1.16–17 (Socrates' genuine disavowal of knowledge); see the commentary ad loc.

claim that anything can be known) that (i) nothing can be known and that (ii) one should suspend judgement as a consequence. Conferring assent and approval (*assensio, approbatio*) in cases where this did not lead to apprehension he deemed (still *censebat*) to be shameful (no reason is given, nor is the status of this view characterized further). However, 'in line with this stance' (*huic rationi quod erat consentaneum*), he argued against everyone's views, and led most of his hearers away from their view and to his own *ratio*, with the effect that assent was easier withheld from either side, when the case for any view was found to be as strong as the case against it.[366] Crucially, this description of Arcesilaus' practice, on the back of his rejection of 'assent and approval' (which in the present context seem intended to exhaust possible modes of endorsement), ought to mean that Arcesilaus confronted opponents with arguments to whose premises these opponents are committed as a matter of fact or ought to be committed given their standards of rationality and known appreciation of evidence, and whose conclusions they ought to accept as a consequence— it is *the opponents'* suspension of judgement that is to be induced (when both sides of a question are found to be equipollent, or when there are powerful considerations on either side).[367] The general account of how Arcesilaus tackled interlocutors also qualifies the earlier remark that his *omne certamen* was with Zeno.

The passage as just summarized does not quite give us a motivation for Arcesilaus' engaging in debate with Zeno in particular, but joining the dots on this point at least seems straightforward: Zeno must have appeared intriguing in that he made unequivocal knowledge claims. (Other Ciceronian passages on Arcesilaus speak of his desire to find the truth; within *Acad.* cf. *Luc.* 76 *fin.*, and the point made above about *obscuritas rerum* only being a problem for those who want to know.) The term used in *Ac.* 1.45 to describe the manner in which Arcesilaus holds his views (i) and (ii), viz. *censere* (*negare* is not a doxastic term), does not have settled terminological meaning in *Acad.* Without good reason, one should not regard them as negative dogmatic views, which would put Arcesilaus in an obviously self-refuting position: it may just be that (i) and (ii) strike him as true, time and again, faced with the *obscuritas rerum*.[368] Further, Cicero seems to go out of his way to formulate (i) in a way which is not predicated on and thus confined to a particular conception of knowledge (e.g. the Stoic one), and in the case of (ii) there is also an accumulation of semantically similar terms, suggesting that it is not Stoic assent that is advised against in isolation, even though the term *assensio* is used (among others), or assent and

---

[366] On the textual problem after *disserens*, see the commentary (unlike Brittain 2006: 107 n. 62 I am not attracted by Madvig's emendation *in eam* for *de sua*).

[367] Thus also Brittain (2001: 201).

[368] This point is made by Cooper (2006); cf. Brittain (2008: section 6) on view (i): 'The Socratic interpretation suggests that we should understand the first view as a way of expressing the cumulative results of Arcesilaus' method, rather than as the beliefs that motivated it. The suggestion is that, like Socrates, Arcesilaus was engaged in a search for the truth about philosophical questions. But, like Socrates, he found that the arguments in favor of any position were always inadequate, or balanced by equally convincing arguments against it (cf. Diogenes Laertius 4.28, Cicero *Academica* 1.45). The view that nothing can be known is thus not the conclusion of an argument relying on a theory about knowledge or our cognitive faculties; it is not a *theoretical* or rationally warranted belief, but just the way things strike him.' The use of the imperfect tense (§45: *negabat, censebat*) may suggest that (i) and (ii) were not antecedently held views but were what he came to think as a result of arguments leading, time and again, to the recognition that the case pro was as strong as the case contra. For different readings, see the commentary ad loc.

Clitomachean approval (cf. *Luc.* 104).³⁶⁹ At this stage in the final edition, a reference to Clitomachean approval could not be understood by any reader, and even in *Luc.* Cicero uses *assensio* (and related expressions) in the terminological sense only occasionally, leaving the reader to work out in each instance whether the technical sense or a looser one is at issue.³⁷⁰ Thus in *Ac.* 1.45 Cicero is clearly aiming to speak generally in characterizing Arcesilaus' views (i) and (ii). According to the description of his argumentative practice, asserting (i) and (ii), or arguing for them, was not part of Arcesilaus' approach. This raises the question of why Cicero (and the tradition he represents) feels able to tell that Arcesilaus held (i) and (ii), and how exactly they informed his argumentative practice. The text provides no answer. And while *Ac.* 1.44–6 does tell us that Arcesilaus engaged Zeno as well as hints at possible reasons, it tells us nothing about what form exactly this engagement took, i.e. 1.44–6 turns to Arcesilaus' general approach after a reference to Zeno. However, on the basis of the description of Arcesilaus' practice in *Ac.* 1.45 *fin.*, we would expect Arcesilaus to have engaged Zeno (like everyone else) with ad hominem arguments at least in the first instance.

References to Arcesilaus in other works of Cicero are consistent with this picture and allow us to go a little further. In *De orat.* 3.67, written in 55 BC but set in 91 BC, Arcesilaus is said to have derived view (i) from reading 'works of Plato and from *sermones Socratici*', which probably means dialogues in which Socrates features, not just Platonic ones (so that the connective 'and' is not explicative); this is compatible with *obscuritas rerum* being cited in *Acad.* as giving rise to (i), in that one can follow Socratic conversations in works by Plato and others, regard the topics as substantial, and be struck, time and again, where they end (rather than, say, be dissatisfied that obvious solutions are missed). Arcesilaus' argumentative practice of concealing his own view and arguing against the views of those he is engaging with is mentioned and linked to Socrates, too.³⁷¹ The impression which emerges is that of Arcesilaus consciously modelling himself on Socrates, or at least of him being conceived in this way by others. In *N.D.* 1.11, written not long after *Acad.*, the latter work is referred to as the place where Cicero explains his allegiance to the sceptical Academy. Distinctive

---

³⁶⁹ Cf. *Ac.* 1.45: *Itaque Arcesilas negabat* (i) **esse quicquam quod sciri posset**, *ne illud quidem ipsum quod Socrates sibi reliquisset; sic omnia latere censebat in occulto* **neque esse quicquam quod cerni aut intellegi posset**; (ii) *quibus de causis nihil oportere* **neque profiteri neque affirmare quemquam neque assensione approbare**, *cohibereque semper et ab omni lapsu continere temeritatem, quae tum esset insignis cum aut falsa aut incognita res approbaretur, neque hoc quicquam esse turpius quam cognitioni et perceptioni assensionem approbationemque praecurrere.* See the translation and also section 10.

³⁷⁰ But Stoic assent had been introduced in *Ac.* 1.40–2, so it is naturally taken to be one of notions excluded.

³⁷¹ *De orat.* 3.67: *Arcesilas primum, qui Polemonem audierat, ex uariis Platonis libris sermonibusque Socraticis hoc maxime arripuit, nihil esse certi quod aut sensibus aut animo percipi possit; quem ferunt eximio quodam usum lepore dicendi aspernatum esse omne animi sensusque iudicium primumque instituisse—quamquam id fuit Socraticum maxime—non quid ipse sentiret ostendere, sed contra id, quod quisque se sentire dixisset, disputare*, 'Polemo's pupil Arcesilas, to begin with, selected from the various writings of Plato and the Socratic dialogues the notion that nothing can be apprehended either by the senses or by the mind; and he, deploying a remarkably attractive style of speaking, is said to have rejected judgement of the mind and of sense perception entirely and to have initiated the practice—an entirely Socratic one to be sure—of not showing his own opinion but arguing against the opinions put forward by everyone else.'

of the latter is said to be an argumentative practice of arguing against everything and judging nothing overtly which starts from Socrates, is resumed by Arcesilaus (*profecta a Socrate, repetita ab Arcesila*), and affirmed by Carneades. A little later in the same paragraph the Academic argumentative practice is linked to the pursuit of finding the truth.

The evidence on Arcesilaus in Sextus' doxographical survey on epistemology from Plato onwards is in important respects consistent with that from Cicero reviewed so far. Sextus reports that Arcesilaus argued in the following way that the wise man will suspend judgement (Sextus, *M*. 7.155):

> Μὴ οὔσης δὲ καταληπτικῆς φαντασίας οὐδὲ κατάληψις γενήσεται· ἦν γὰρ αὕτη καταληπτικῇ φαντασίᾳ συγκατάθεσις. μὴ οὔσης δὲ καταλήψεως πάντ' ἔσται ἀκατάληπτα. Πάντων δὲ ὄντων ἀκαταλήπτων ἀκολουθήσει **καὶ** κατὰ τοὺς Στωικοὺς ἐπέχειν τὸν σοφόν.
>
> But if there is no cataleptic impression, apprehension will not come to pass either; for it was assent to a cataleptic impression. If there is no apprehension, everything will be inapprehensible. And if everything is inapprehensible, it will follow according to the Stoics **too** that the sage will suspend judgement.

As has been widely recognized, this is most naturally read as an argument made ad hominem: given Stoic assumptions and commitments (e.g. to the existence of cataleptic impressions), if there are no cataleptic impressions, the Stoic wise man will suspend judgement, as *the Stoics* ought to hold. There is a question whether the highlighted καί points to the argument being not just ad hominem, i.e. whether 'the sage will suspend judgement' will follow according to Arcesilaus *as well as* the Stoics,[372] but it seems tenuous to posit endorsement on this basis (let alone assent, which would put Arcesilaus into a self-refuting position; see below, p. cxl), and there are other and more plausible explanations.[373]

Sextus does not credit Arcesilaus with views (i) and (ii) referred to above, nor does he tell us that Arcesilaus consciously followed the practice of Socrates or modelled himself on him, but what he does tell us is not just compatible with, but easier to understand against the background of, the Socratic self-conception which is in evidence in *Ac*. 1.44–6 (and other Ciceronian passages mentioned above).[374]

It is safe to assume that Sextus takes Arcesilaus to adopt the stance (in some sense) that nothing can be known. However, when Sextus comes to characterize the Academics as negative dogmatists in *P.H*. 1.226, he does not name Arcesilaus. And when he says that Carneades took all things to be non-cataleptic in a way that differs from the sceptic (i.e. the Pyrrhonist), it is tempting to conclude that Sextus took

---

[372] Thus Ioppolo (1986: 59) on καί: '... in cui *anche* sottolinea che al saggio stoico non resta che uniformarsi all'attegiamento di quello accademico.'

[373] *Kaí* could mean 'even' or 'actually', see Maconi (1988: 241 n. 32); Schofield (1999: 326): 'Arcesilaus' claim that the Stoics "too" must agree to the rationality of *epochē* suggests an attempt to recommend to all and sundry, as one that *even* the Stoics—the most deeply entrenched dogmatists—ought to see that they are committed to accepting.'

[374] This has been shown by Cooper (2006: 184–5).

Arcesilaus to be like the sceptic in this respect, i.e. 'nothing can be known' was not a philosophical position for Arcesilaus (on Sextus' view) for which he would argue and which he would uphold like a dogmatic view.³⁷⁵ Cooper (2006) suggests plausibly that this fits with the evidence on view (i) in *Ac.* 1.44–6.

A little later, in *P.H.* 1.232–4, Sextus addresses the similarity between Arcesilaus and Pyrrho (as he sees it) directly. Cooper (2006) shows how the information furnished in 1.233 that Arcesilaus took individual acts of suspension of judgement to be good, and acts of assent to be bad, is explicable in terms of Arcesilaus' conscious following of Socrates (as documented in Cicero): his commitment to reason, coupled with the fact that investigation and scrutiny has so far not revealed any knowledge, is what leads Arcesilaus to the claim that individual acts of suspension are good.³⁷⁶ This commitment to reason does again not have the status of a doctrine and is not something which one could expect Arcesilaus to have defended with arguments as his considered position, just as Socrates never defended it and is never made to articulate it.³⁷⁷

We now turn to the evidence from *Luc.* As far as the treatment of Arcesilaus is concerned, there is a sense in which *Luc.* 66–7 and 77, the two passages where he features, complement each other: both are concerned with the avoidance of opinion, but given that in a debate with the Stoics assent to the non-cataleptic is opinion, §§66–7 focuses on the desirability of avoiding assent, while §77 is primarily about all impressions being non-cataleptic. We thus would not expect both passages to cover precisely the same ground.

In §§66–7 Arcesilaus is said to 'hold' (*censet*), in this respect 'agreeing with Zeno' (*Zenoni assentiens*), that the sage is uniquely placed to avoid being tricked or misled, which in the context means accepting a view or impression when he should not. The wider context is a characterization of Clitomacheanism as contrasted with Stoic thinking, as well as—by implication—with mitigated scepticism. It is a mission statement of sorts for Cicero qua Clitomachean, and it is suggestive that Arcesilaus features so prominently in it, notably as someone who rejected assent and opinions (like the Clitomacheans). As an intellectual ancestor Arcesilaus is important for Cicero's personal view in *Acad.* in a way in which he could not be for mitigated scepticism.³⁷⁸ The sage is a Stoic concept, which is not mentioned in *Ac.* 1.44–6, and views (i) and (ii) were not in any sense restricted to particular subjects or persons; rather, their general formulation made it natural to read them as applying to all human beings. *Assentire alicui* could in principle be used in a case where the agreeing subject held

---

³⁷⁵ Cf. Numenius frg. 26 Des Places, where Arcesilaus is categorized a Pyrrhonist; see appendix 2.

³⁷⁶ When Sextus claims that Arcesilaus took individual acts of assent to be bad, and acts of suspension to be good, 'in the nature of things' (πρὸς τὴν φύσιν), then this is arguably marked as Sextus' interpretation, and not part of Sextus' report; contrast Cooper (2006: 185): 'According to Sextus, Arcesilaus said that each act of suspension is really good, good in the nature of things…'.

³⁷⁷ The notion that Arcesilaus traced his view to Socrates and Plato is in evidence as early as the third century BC; cf. Plut., *Adv. Col.* 1121e–1122a, discussed in the commentary on *Ac.* 1.44–6, and the secondary references collected by Warren (2002a: 17 n. 23).

³⁷⁸ Cooper (2006: 175–6) fails to consider *Luc.* 66–7; this omission enables him to link Arcesilaus as presented in *Acad.* with mitigated scepticism.

the same view antecedently, but nothing we have heard so far suggests this, and 'the sage will not be tricked' is not an instantiation of view (ii) ascribed to Arcesilaus in *Ac.* 1.44–6. Holding view (ii) could conceivably dispose one favourably towards 'the sage will not be tricked', but it would depend on how 'tricking' is construed. *Censere* is used of views (i) and (ii) in *Ac.* 1.44–6, but it remains the case that it cannot be placed with certainty among the various notions of believing (and quasi-believing) which are in evidence in *Acad.*,[379] and the fact that we are now dealing with evidence from the first edition which on first approach looks to be at variance with that from the second should induce further caution. The context in §§66–7, which builds towards the corollary argument, is one which emphasizes agreements and similarities between Zeno and the Academics, only to lead eventually to the observation that there is a single issue which separates them (§67 *fin.*): the stance on the third clause of the Zenonian definition and on ἀπαραλλαξία.

In §67 Arcesilaus is said to 'confirm' (*confirmabat*) the premises of the corollary argument and to 'approve' (*probabat*) the argument as a whole (see the commentary). This argument is of course anti-Stoic and relies on Stoic assumptions (e.g. that there are impressions, which come about in a certain way, or that the mind has the faculty of assent, cf. *Ac.* 1.40). Given what *Ac.* 1.45 *fin.* said about Arcesilaus' argumentative practice, one would have expected Arcesilaus to mount the corollary argument ad hominem, as something that ought to impress the Stoics. So what is the nature of Arcesilaus' 'approval', and how do we relate the conclusion of the corollary argument to his view (ii), which (like i) was marked as a general attitude in *Ac.* 1.44–5 and not predicated on the thinking of a particular school? Given the overall context, we should not just assume that 'approval' means that Arcesilaus assented to the argument. Rather, §67 seems to be a sufficiently marked context for 'approval' to be the technical kind of approval explained in detail in *Luc.* 104 and no doubt mentioned in passing in the *Catulus*—approval thus understood is like saying 'yes' to propositions which appear true in a dialectical exchange in which one's personal beliefs are not at stake (cf. on *Luc.* 78, 104). One might wonder if it does not represent an anachronism, within the logic of the text, to have Arcesilaus give approval as it is distinctive for the Clitomachean position (which is supposed to reflect Carneades' views), but this worry is allayed by observing that the account given of approval in *Luc.* 104 is intended to capture and clarify a pre-existing phenomenon.[380] It is a separate question whether the modern historian of philosophy would want to credit the historical Arcesilaus with different conceptions of belief as they are distinguished by the pupils of Carneades.[381] For the corollary argument to get started, the conclusion of the core argument needs to be assumed to obtain. The core argument is also formulated with

---

[379] See also section 10.

[380] Castagnoli (2019: 200) suggests that behind Arcesilaus' approval the εὔλογον ('reasonable') hides, which in other sources (Sextus, *M.* 7.158) features as Arcesilaus' reply to the ἀπραξία-charge, in a manner which seems similar to the Carneadean πιθανόν. This suggestion need not be incompatible with my reading, though the absence of any explicit references to the εὔλογον in the Ciceronian record makes me wonder if Cicero was aware of it.

[381] On this point, see Maconi (1988: 244–5); Schofield (1999: 332). I use 'belief' here not in the Stoic sense of δόξα or in the Academic sense derived from it, i.e. δόξα which is aware of its own limitations (cf. *Luc.* 148), but in the broader sense of view arising either from assent or from approval. See also section 10.

reference to Stoic doctrine. So although §67 does not comment on the subject, it is likely that one should read it to imply that Arcesilaus approved the core argument, too. Since the text is silent on whether and how views (i) and (ii) inform in some loose sense Arcesilaus' posture, I postpone the consideration of the issue. What we can note in any case is that Arcesilaen endorsement of an anti-Stoic argument, even if it is endorsement in a qualified sense that does not involve or issue in belief as it is construed within the context of the debate, stands in tension with the account of the Arcesilaus in *Ac.* 1.44–6 who argues ad hominem.

In §76 *fin.* Cicero claims that Arcesilaus engaged Zeno not out of a sheer desire for confrontation, but because he wanted to find the truth. This is new information on Arcesilaus' motives, but compatible with what is said in *Ac.* 1.44–5 (see above on Arcesilaus' motives, stated as well as hinted at). In §77 *init.* Cicero identifies a unique insight of Zeno's and one which Arcesilaus appreciated: nobody had said before that it was possible to live without opinions and, what is more, that living in this way was necessary for the sage. Arcesilaus' reaction is strikingly described: *uisa est Arcesilae cum uera sententia tum honesta et digna sapiente.* While *uisa est* can be seen as indicative of restraint on Arcesilaus' part, the rest of the sentence signals enthusiasm. Here we must recall that in *Ac.* 1.44–6 Arcesilaus is reported to have thought that it is shameful to grant approval when certainty is not to be had (= view ii), but this leaves room for a life in shamefulness, so to speak, even if one aspires to something better. Thus one can see why Cicero brands Zeno's insights as unique, and why Arcesilaus reacts the way he does: Stoicism appears to offer a hope and a prospect, and one which has obvious affinity with his view (ii). Arcesilaus then poses the question of what to do if the sage did not apprehend anything and is not to hold opinions. To this Zeno replies that there is something which can be apprehended, namely the cataleptic impression; the celebrated account of how Arcesilaus' questioning gave rise to the third clause follows. At the end of §77 Arcesilaus is presented as pressing on the issue of ἀπαραλλαξία, but the syntax is such that it remains open whether he intended to show that ἀπαραλλαξία obtains, or whether this was the outcome of his arguments (as Cicero, the speaker, holds, while the character Lucullus would disagree). Nonetheless, given that we are told in §67 *init.* that Arcesilaus approved the corollary argument, he must have approved the premiss of the core argument which claims ἀπαραλλαξία, too (sc., again, on Cicero's construal).

It is unlikely that, in a text as philosophically complex as *Acad.* and as reliant on historical arguments, there should have been no mediation between the Arcesilaus of *Ac.* 1 who argues ad hominem against everyone and that of *Luc.* who approves anti-Stoic arguments. Cicero may have mediated between the two in the following way.[382] If we assume that Arcesilaus was committed to rationality like Socrates, had formed the tentative views that nothing can be known and that one should not make unwarranted knowledge claims as a consequence, but remained committed to the search for the truth, then Zeno's doctrines must have appeared as not just intriguing for their optimism about the possibility of knowledge at least on the Stoic conception of

---

[382] I would expect such mediation to have been attempted in the *Catulus* (by Catulus or Cicero) and at some point (earlier rather than later) in the final edition.

knowledge, but must also have offered the hope of a rational life. We can glimpse such a hope in Arcesilaus' reaction to the claim that a life without opinions was possible and even mandatory for the sage (*Luc.* 77 *init.*, quoted above). This hope might have prompted Arcesilaus—sc. on Cicero's construal—to give Stoicism a chance, as it were, in particular a chance which issued in the approval of the framework within which the Stoics are operating: impressions, assent, the possibility of κατάληψις, etc.[383] For in approving Stoic premises, Arcesilaus approved their presuppositions. Approval, we recall, is explained in terms of the mechanisms of a dialectical exchange, invoked in Clitomachus' account of approval in *Luc.* 104: it is like saying 'yes' in such an exchange. If a respondent is offered the question of whether the cosmos is eternal or not, then either possible answer requires the (at least hypothetical) acceptance of the notion that there is a cosmos at all.[384] Arcesilaus' approval of the premises of the core and corollary arguments, where they straightforwardly present propositions which are Stoic positions, is granted in the same spirit. That is compatible with observing that the attitude a subject might take to a proposition which appears true to him and thus attracts approval can vary in degree: some propositions may appear true rather than false without the subject being in any way invested in them, whereas others—still without amounting to the contents of settled views of the subject—may appear intensely true. The Stoics are issued with a licence of sorts, which is very different from commitment on Arcesilaus' part to elements of Stoic doctrine presupposed in the arguments.[385] However, there is no direct path from the views (i) and (ii) in *Ac.* 1.44–6 to the approval of the conclusions of the core and corollary arguments: the latter are not simply instantiations of the former.

On this reconstruction, Arcesilaus would have engaged Zeno with ad hominem arguments like every other opponent in the first instance, but would have issued his licence in a second step once the hope held out by Stoicism came into view. One might wonder if an objection to this scenario can be built on the fact that the enthusiastic response of §77 *init.* is supposed to form the starting point of an attack on Zeno which only lead to the addition of the third clause of the definition of the cataleptic impression (and core and corollary arguments presuppose the three-clause definition), but to this I would reply that the scene depicted in §77 wears its fictional character on its sleeve. Arcesilaus would end up approving the core and corollary arguments because, unlike the Stoics, he approves the premiss which makes the claim of ἀπαραλλαξία.

---

[383] Note *Luc.* 77 *fin.*, where Arcesilaus is reported to have said that the third clause was 'correctly' (*recte*) added to the Zenonian definition, while going on to argue that the condition the clause stipulates is never met; cf. also *Luc.* 113 *fin.*

[384] Ordinary dialectical exchanges are *not* about the beliefs of the questioners and the respondent; rather, they are about what appears true to them for the purposes of a dialectical exchange. Aristotle distinguishes these two scenarios very clearly in *Top.* Θ5 and declares the latter to be the normal one sc. in the pre-existing type of question-and-answer λόγος which he intended to impose firm rules on in *Top.* (and whose conventions continued to be understood throughout the Hellenistic period whether or not philosophers knew Aristotle's *Top.*); see Moraux (1968: 304–7).

[385] Contrast Görler (1994: 816–17), who considers whether Arcesilaus accepted, i.e. dogmatically assented to, elements of Stoic theory, like the definition of the cataleptic impression (cf. §77, on the third clause: *recte consensit Arcesilas ad definitionem additum*): sc. on this construal 'Arkesilaos hat sich wesentliche Teile der stoischen Erkenntnistheorie zu eigen gemacht, aber von den gleichen Voraussetzungen aus ist er zu einem anderen Ergebnis gelangt.'

We can note further that both Arcesilaus as depicted in *Ac.* 1.44–6, tackling everyone (and by clear implication Zeno) with ad hominem arguments, and the Arcesilaus who approves the core and corollary argument in *Luc.*, are compatible. The former disavows even the one knowledge claim Socrates had left himself with, holds view (i) (and view ii) not as a dogmatic position, and suggests that the conclusion of the core argument ought to impress the Stoics while he himself takes no view on it; the latter escapes the charge that he cannot consistently assert (= regard as true) that nothing can be known and assert that one should suspend judgement universally in the absence of knowledge by operating a mode of endorsement that falls short of assertion (namely, approval).[386] However, the former stance raises questions about Arcesilaus' commitment to rationality, which underpins his continued search for the truth,[387] while the latter may be deemed anachronistic as an interpretation of the historical Arcesilaus.

Brittain (2008) has set out, with admirable clarity, which interpretative choices underlie the different modern reconstructions of the position of the historical Arcesilaus. He distinguishes between:

(a) a dialectical (ad hominem) interpretation, under which Arcesilaus advances premisses the Stoics are committed to as a matter of fact, as well as ones to which they ought to be committed given their standards of rationality, leading to conclusions to which they ought to be committed, too;
(b) an Academic interpretation (which is primarily characterized by a commitment, on the part of Arcesilaus, to the claims that nothing can be known and that one should suspend judgement as a consequence); and
(c) a Socratic interpretation (according to which Arcesilaus is committed to reason, searches for truth, but entertains—for now and undogmatically—views i and ii).

The Academic interpretation can be divided further, depending on the kind of commitment assumed to be involved.

One arrives at the dialectical interpretation if one gives primacy to the evidence from Sextus discussed above, while the Academic interpretation is primarily based on the evidence from *Luc.* surveyed above.[388] The Socratic interpretation is mainly grounded in *Ac.* 1.44–6, other texts by Cicero, as well as the evidence from Sextus

---

[386] See Schofield (1999: 331–2). Ibid., p. 331 n. 24, Schofield notes that the ancient text which advances this charge in particular is Lact., *Inst.* 3.6.7–12 (= my t. 61), and he speculates plausibly that Lactantius probably draws on a lost section of *Acad.* To this one can add that Antiochus, on the evidence of *Luc.* 43–4, tried to force the Academics into a choice between assent as he conceived it and complete suspension of judgement. He would thus not recognize an Arcesilaus who 'approves' anti-Stoic arguments, and would instead treat approval as if it was assent. Cf. also *Luc.* 111.

[387] Cf. Brittain (2008: §6): '[On the Socratic interpretation of Arcesilaus]...the basic philosophical puzzle about Arcesilaus' skepticism is not whether it is possible to live without beliefs, but whether it is possible to be committed to rationality and yet sufficiently detached from it to recognise that, whatever it is, it may not work.'

[388] Cf. Numenius frg. 27 (Eus., *Praep. Ev.* XIV.8.3 = part of T2 Mette and of F93 Vezzoli), who claims that Arcesilaus unlike Carneades 'thought that what he said was the truth', likening Arcesilaus to a Hydra which destroys itself in frg. 25 (XIV.6.3); but see n. 393 below and appendix 2 on the evidence from Numenius as a whole.

read in a certain way.³⁸⁹ Notably, the Socratic interpretation naturally accommodates the notion that Arcesilaus' arguments against particular schools were made ad hominem. Some proponents of the Academic interpretation have argued, from evidence relating to the intellectual environment in which Arcesilaus and Zeno operated, that some of the Stoic assumptions relied on in the core and corollary arguments, and some of the supposedly Stoic premises, were either genuinely embraced by Arcesilaus or were in fact common ground and widely accepted at the time (and in that sense mischaracterized as Stoic);³⁹⁰ on either view, Arcesilaus made the same assumptions as the Stoics, made them in the same way, but arrived at different conclusions (whatever the consequences), and at the price of internal consistency.

While a substantial contribution to the debate about the historical Arcesilaus lies beyond the scope of this commentary, we can make the following observations in the light of the discussion above. The purely dialectical interpretation rests primarily on the evidence from Sextus, and on the assumptions that everything we know about Arcesilaus ultimately goes back to one tradition, and that Sextus reflects this tradition more purely than anyone else.³⁹¹ Dissatisfaction with this picture, whatever further evidence it has been grounded in, has usually been motivated by the view that a purely dialectical Arcesilaus was a jejune, obstructionist figure, hard to explain with reference to the traditions of the Academy. While there is evidence that Arcesilaus argued ad hominem against the Stoics in Sextus, and while this is a natural implication of Ac. 1.45, there are enough footholds in Sextus and especially Cicero for thinking that this is not all there was to Arcesilaus.

That Arcesilaus modelled himself and his activities on Socrates has detailed and nuanced support from Cicero, a degree of support from D.L. (see n. 368 above), and allows for a more profound reading of the evidence from Sextus. Notably, the Socratic interpretation has room for ad hominem argumentation, but underpins it with a plausible rationale, and one that is credible in terms of Academic traditions.³⁹²

---

³⁸⁹ Long (1986: 441) suggests that D.L., in his biography of Arcesilaus (4.28–45), also presents him as 'someone who wanted to identify the Academy with its Socratic tradition'. In support of such a view, one might cite Diogenes' emphasis on the argumentative practices which were distinctive of Arcesilaus' approach (although concealment of his own views is not mentioned explicitly), as well as the fact that Aristo of Chios called Arcesilaus a 'corruptor of youth and shameless teacher of immorality' (§40; the ostensible reason given by D.L. is Arcesilaus' fondness for boys).

³⁹⁰ See Görler (1994: 816).

³⁹¹ This point is made by Maconi (1988: 246). The εὔλογον, which features in Sextus but is not mentioned in Cicero, features in a dialectical argument, too; see Brittain (2008: §5). If Cicero was aware of it, he may have omitted it on the grounds that he considered it to be unhelpfully similar to the Carneadean πιθανόν. See also n. 380 above.

³⁹² Perin (2013) has argued that even on the Socratic interpretation Arcesilaus relies on beliefs, minimally about what constitutes the difference between a philosophical belief and a non-philosophical view one is 'left with', and that consequently the interpretative choice is only between a dogmatic interpretation and a dialectical interpretation of the historical Arcesilaus. This might be so if there was no way of conceptualizing a form of belief weak enough to avoid being subsumed under the dogmatic interpretation. Perin does not consider the particular conception of weak belief which is suggested in *Luc.* 104 and ascribed to Arcesilaus in *Luc.* 67 (like his target Cooper 2006, Perin does not take *Luc.* 67 into account). However, it is plain that Cicero (and the Academics he followed when writing *Acad.*) thought Arcesilaus relied on a form of weak belief, and it is conceivable that the historical Arcesilaus took himself to do the same thing with respect to views (i) and (ii). Modern scholars may of course choose to evaluate Arcesilaus against the set of interpretative options laid out by Perin.

I have suggested above that *Luc.* hints at an account of how Arcesilaus came to 'approve' the Stoic assumptions which underlie the core and corollary arguments, as well as these arguments themselves, and that this approval is presented as growing out of the Socratic stance which represents Arcesilaus' overall posture in *Acad.* While this approval serves a certain purpose in *Acad.*, i.e. to legitimize and conceptualize Cicero's own Clitomachean position, and while the term itself is clearly marked as Carneadean or Clitomachean, it does offer a plausible way of describing Arcesilaus' engagement with Zeno. If the historical Arcesilaus was a Socratic, he could have fastened on the Stoics as opponents in this way. However, it is worth repeating that on this scenario Arcesilaus does start out as a Socratic who argues against everyone he encounters ad hominem, and that the endorsement he gives to anti-Stoic arguments and those Stoic assumptions on which they rely is not dogmatic assent. Consequently, we see no reason for interpreting the evidence cited in support of the Academic interpretation of Arcesilaus in a manner which assumes that Arcesilaus started from Stoic assumptions, either because he accepted them or because they were in fact common ground, and that he ever assented to them: we have discussed the evidence from Cicero in some detail (and refer to the commentary on *Ac.* 1.44–6; *Luc.* 66–7, and 77–8), and the evidence from Numenius lands Arcesilaus with a position which is flatly self-contradictory, as Numenius himself observes, and which is explicitly dismissed in *Acad.*[393]

Long (1986) is an insightful study of the biography of Arcesilaus in D.L., who drew on the near-contemporary (with Arcesilaus), fairly reliable, yet philosophically uninterested Antigonus of Carystus, but used other sources, too.[394] Long notes (pp. 440–4) that the critical engagement with the Stoa, and with Zeno in particular, is not mentioned in the biography. Instead, debates with another Stoic, Aristo of Chios, are hinted at in vague terms, and he is also cited for his famous epigram characterizing Arcesilaus, which casts doubt on the latter's Platonic allegiance (and presumably by implication Socratic credentials) while supporting the notion that Arcesilaus was seeking both.[395] Long further observes that in other biographies of Stoics (Herillus,

---

[393] On the evidence from Numenius, see appendix 2. I am not confident that it can be pressed on the nuances of the Academic attitudes to ἐποχή. Thus ἐποχή is referred to generically in *Praep. Ev.* XIV.5.1, and is linked to Arcesilaus' refusal to state opinions of his own and likened to the ink with which the cuttlefish shrouds itself (*P.E.* XIV.6.6 = Num. frg. 25 Des Places). In the satirical story about Lacydes and his slaves, the former is said to have recommended ἐποχή to a friend after he had studied with Arcesilaus (*P.E.* XIV.7.4 = frg. 26 Des Places). Numenius does state clearly that Arcesilaus placed himself in a self-refuting position, presumably by asserting that nothing can be known in *P.E.* XIV.8.3 = frg. 27 Des Places (ἐκεῖνος μέν γε περιερχόμενος τῇ φαρμάξει τοὺς συγκορυβαντιῶντας ἔλαθεν ἑαυτὸν πρῶτον ἐξηπατηκὼς μὴ ᾐσθῆσθαι, πεπεῖσθαι δ' ἀληθῆ εἶναι, ἃ λέγει, διὰ τῆς ἁπαξαπάντων ἀναιρέσεως χρημάτων; see transl. p. 829), which is consistent with Numenius' comparison of Arcesilaus to a Hydra which decapitates itself (*P.E.* XIV.6.3 = frg. 25 Des Places). However, in the appendix I express some doubts about the consistency of frg. 25 and 27, and what is said in frg. 27 is at variance with what Cicero says in *Ac.* 1.45: *Itaque Arcesilas negabat esse quicquam quod sciri posset, ne illud ipsum quod Socrates sibi reliquisset*. There are no good grounds for giving more credence to Numenius frg. 27 than to the evidence from Cicero here.
[394] See Wilamowitz (1881: 45–77).
[395] Cf. Sextus, *P.H.* 1.234 (= SVF i.343 (Aristo) = LS 68E2 = F86 Mette and Vezzoli (Arcesilaus)): πρόσθε Πλάτων, ὄπιθεν Πύρρων, μέσσος Διόδωρος, 'Plato in front, Pyrrho behind, Diodorus in the middle', adapted from the description of the chimaera in Hom., *Il.* 6.181; D.L. 4.33; Num. frg. 25 Des Places (cf. appendix 2). Sextus, in line with his overall portrayal of Academic scepticism as dogmatic, interprets the

Dionysius) Aristo appears as an opponent of Arcesilaus', debating issues which on the evidence of Cicero we might have expected Arcesilaus to debate with Zeno. This makes Long wonder if Zeno displaced Aristo in the tradition reflected in Cicero and if it was Aristo whom Arcesilaus engaged in anti-Stoic argument. If that was indeed the case, one would be even more hesitant to speculate about the position of the historical Arcesilaus, simply because there would be reason to suspect our sources for the debate between Zeno and Arcesilaus.

However, it is arguable that the evidence cited by Long does not support the drastic conclusion which he draws. Consider D.L. 7.162, from the biography of Aristo (see Long 1986: 442–3):

Μάλιστα δὲ προσεῖχε Στωικῷ δόγματι τῷ τὸν σοφὸν ἀδόξαστον εἶναι. πρὸς ὃ Περσαῖος ἐναντιούμενος διδύμων ἀδελφῶν τὸν ἕτερον ἐποίησεν αὐτῷ παρακαταθήκην δοῦναι, ἔπειτα τὸν ἕτερον ἀπολαβεῖν· καὶ οὕτως ἀπορούμενον διήλεγξεν. ἀπετείνετο δὲ πρὸς Ἀρκεσίλαον· ὅτε θεασάμενος ταῦρον τερατώδη μήτραν ἔχοντα, 'οἴμοι,' ἔφη, 'δέδοται Ἀρκεσιλάῳ ἐπιχείρημα κατὰ τῆς ἐναργείας.'

The Stoic doctrine to which he attached most importance was the wise man's refusal to hold mere opinions. And against this doctrine Persaeus was contending when he induced one of a pair of twins to deposit a certain sum with Aristo and afterwards got the other to reclaim it. Aristo being thus reduced to perplexity was refuted. He was at variance with Arcesilaus; and one day when he saw an abomination in the shape of a bull with a uterus, he said: 'Alas, here Arcesilaus has had given into his hand an argument against the evidence of the senses.' (transl. Hicks, modified)

The extract begins with Aristo's commitment to the Stoic view that the sage should not opine. While this view features prominently in *Luc.* 77 as one which intrigued Arcesilaus and which led him to engage Zeno in the exchange about the cataleptic impression, it is perfectly consistent with this to say that Aristo was fully committed to it, especially if Ioppolo (1980) is right that the tradition presents him unfairly as an eccentric.[396] By the same token, if he made mocking remarks about self-evidence to Arcesilaus, this is misrepresented by saying that 'Diogenes attaches to Aristo the controversy with Arcesilaus over κατάληψις that Cicero credits to Zeno' (Long 1986: 442): *Luc.* 77 is a pointed exchange about a specific issue, the definition of the cataleptic impression. It is true that in §77 Cicero inserts cautious parentheses (*fortasse, credo* twice), but these arguably signal the transparent fictionality of the short dialogue rather than express doubt that it puts the debate between Arcesilaus and Zeno

---

line as supportive of the notion that Arcesilaus secretly held 'Platonic' doctrines and passed them on to suitable pupils. More plausibly, Diogenes and Numenius interpret the line as meaning that Arcesilaus was an avowed follower of Plato, advanced many arguments which sounded Pyrrhonist, and appeared to use devices associated with dialecticians. See also Glucker (1978: 31–47, esp. 35); Ioppolo (1986: 40–9); Long and Sedley (i.1987: 446); Görler (1994: 811–12); Wyss (2005: 119); Ioppolo (2018: 37); Castagnoli (2019: 170–1); Tarrant (2020: 218–19). Timon of Phlius, alluding to Hom., *Od.* 5.360–4, cast Arcesilaus as Odysseus suffering shipwreck (with his dogmatic approach to philosophy) and intending to seek refuge with Pyrrho and Diodorus (frg. 806 SH = 32 Diels); see Lurie (2014).

[396] Cf. Mansfeld (1985: 210): 'It is clear that A. [Aristo] had a theory of knowledge, or rather that he accepted Zeno's and sided with the school against Arcesilaus (*SVF* I 346–7) [= D.L. 7.162, quoted above].'

in a nutshell. As Long (1986: 443 with n. 19) says, for Cicero 'Aristo was a deviant Stoic of the distant past' (cf. *Fin.* 2.43, 5.23; *Tusc.* 5.85). We see no good reason to suspect that Aristo has been systematically displaced by Zeno in our sources.[397]

8. Cicero's Clitomacheanism

When characterizing Cicero's position, one must be clear who is meant. There is, first, the historical individual Cicero (cos. 63 BC), whose beliefs and attitudes one can try to reconstruct and infer, while acknowledging that they are ultimately as irretrievable (sc. for others) as the beliefs and attitudes of any 'real' individual, alive or dead. It is of course the historical individual who gave the character Piso a long Antiochian speech in *Fin.* 5, but did not juxtapose it with the kind of detailed reply the Epicurean view receives in *Fin.* 2 or the Stoic view in *Fin.* 4. Second, there is the author persona, whose overall attitude one may want to describe e.g. when looking at a dialogue like *Acad.* or *Fin.* and asking what overall stance of the author emerges given that he wrote such a work or works. 'Cicero' so understood may well be different from the historical individual Cicero; consider e.g. that the latter may have *wanted* to be an Academic sceptic but failed, whereas the former may emerge as a successful or consistent Academic sceptic. Or else Cicero the implied author may have been a deliberate construct, designed to make the reader think, while the historical Cicero may have held views of some description, which he, however, did not want to map on those which can be hypothesized for the implied author. Third, there is the first-person speaker who features in the frames of Cicero's dialogues and who is presented as explaining and justifying what he is doing and why in writing philosophy in Latin, or in pursuing philosophy at all when 'men like him' are not supposed to indulge in supposedly meaningless endeavours. We should not simply equate him with 'Cicero' in the two senses distinguished earlier, because we would not expect the historical individual to speak directly through a first-person individual in the text and because it is one of the hallmarks of implied authors that they are significantly underdetermined by what is on the page. Fourth and finally, there is another first-person speaker, the character called Cicero, who features as an interlocutor in some dialogues of Cicero, for instance in *Hort.*, *Catul.*, and *Luc.* Cicero in that sense is in important respects different from Cicero speaking in the frame; e.g. the speaker in the frame appears to operate in the now, i.e. the time of composition, whereas the character Cicero is the *consularis* who has just dealt with Catilina.[398] I shall treat the speaker in *Ac.* 1 as continuous with the Cicero character in the first edition, but note here that *Ac.* 1 has no frame and launches straight into the dialogue setting, so that the Cicero character is conflated with the speaker who comments on the subject of writing philosophy in Latin and compares his own literary efforts with those of the character Varro.

[397] See also Long (2018) for further discussion of the Life of Zeno in D.L.
[398] Cicero the author may choose to play with these distinctions, but this does not erase them (or invalidate attending to them). Thus e.g. in *Div.* 1.7 Cicero, in a frame, comments on what he did as an author in *N.D.* Compare also Brittain (2011: 83–4) on Augustine's practice of distinguishing different '*personae*' in Cicero.

For the last two senses of 'Cicero', the discussion will largely but not exclusively draw on first-person statements in the texts. Yet in order to get, however imperfectly, at Cicero the historical individual and Cicero the author, one needs to reflect on the pragmatics of the Ciceronian dialogue more generally and ask to what extent the structure of the dialogues and the interaction between characters reflect or are expressive of a sceptical outlook, and possibly of Cicero's Clitomachean outlook in particular. It is also at least conceivable that tensions emerge between choices Cicero made as an author and the statements Ciceronian characters make in the text.[399]

Other characters in the dialogues may make statements which illuminate the position of the Cicero character indirectly. Thus Lucullus in *Luc.* delivers a speech against the Academic position, and in the process of attacking it, arguably fashions a new one, namely when he can clearly be shown to distort the Academic position to make his refutation more easily achievable.[400] Further, in *N D.* we encounter another sceptical character, Cotta, who also features in *De orat.*, although there he is not clearly identified as an Academic and is given nothing to do that would reveal him as one. Cotta is a creation of the historical Cicero and is, like the Cicero character in *Acad.*, a Clitomachean, although this need not mean that his position is articulated exactly like Cicero's; thus the fact that he is a priest means that he has certain deeply held convictions in areas to which the Cicero character has no reason to speak.[401]

It is against this background—statements in the text as well as formal and compositional features of the dialogues—that one can try and delineate Cicero's stance or stances.[402] I believe it that the evidence from Cicero's works is most plausibly read as suggesting that he adopted the same position from his first statement on the subject onwards throughout his life. Note, however, that said statements vary greatly in the amount of detail they furnish, so that in a number of cases one can demonstrate consistency with evidence from elsewhere but not detailed correspondence. I further believe that Cicero's position both as an author and as a speaker in the text is best characterized as radical scepticism in terms of the distinctions drawn by the Cicero character in *Acad.*, but that it is able to encompass many of the features modern scholars associate with mitigated scepticism.[403]

Another question is to what extent sceptical positions which we find in Cicero's works are distinct from those of e.g. his philosophical teacher Philo of Larissa, either because Cicero failed to follow his teacher in adopting the position which the latter held when Cicero attended his lectures, or because his scepticism ended up being different from any position Philo ever took e.g. due to Cicero's being a Roman or writing in Latin (to name but two reasons which have been entertained). I hold that

---

[399] This is a set of issues which is pursued throughout the commentary.
[400] Distortion occurs in places where Lucullus attacks the Academics as if they were negative dogmatists (e.g. in *Luc.* 28-9), which they are not, thereby creating—somewhat paradoxically, for he is an Antiochian—the most extreme form of scepticism found in Cicero's works (see Allen 1997: 219-21); when these attacks are rebutted by the Cicero character in his speech in *Luc.* (e.g. in *Luc.* 109-11), the rebuttals illuminate Cicero's actual position.
[401] Cicero was a member of the college of augurs (see Linderski 1986a), but this is not an important component of his persona in the philosophical works of the 40s BC.
[402] For a survey of scholarly attempts to characterize Cicero's position, see section 4.
[403] Contra e.g. Brittain (2001) and Thorsrud (2012), who hold that Cicero outside of *Acad.* casts himself as a mitigated sceptic; see, however, Brittain (2016).

Cicero inherited the position Philo held when Cicero was his pupil and before he developed the view of the Roman Books, but that the precise manner in which he enacted or articulated this position is peculiar to him and his circumstances (see on *Luc.* 146).

The earliest text in the Ciceronian corpus in which the subject of scepticism features is the preface of the second book of *De inventione*.[404] This treatise is likely to be Cicero's first extant work, dating from the mid-80s BC,[405] and unlike later compositions, including on the subject of rhetorical theory, it is comparatively unoriginal (which makes it invaluable in its own way, as evidence for Hellenistic rhetorical theory).[406] The only sections in it which have the appearance of independent compositions (albeit closely informed by a number of sources) are the prefaces of the two books. The sense of enthusiasm projected by these prefaces, when set against the soberness and derivativeness of the material in the body of both books of *Inv.*, is apt to move the reader to believe that in the former the historical Cicero speaks to us through the first-person narrator about some of his most profound personal commitments at the time, but this supposed immediateness may of course just be an aggregate of stylistic properties of the text. Still, it represents as choice on the part of the historical Cicero. The proem of *Inv.* 2 begins with a famous story about the artist Zeuxis, who selected several beautiful women as partial models in order to create a representation of the perfect woman, the mythical Helen.[407] This sets up the idea in §4 that Cicero selected, by exercising judgement, the best elements from earlier treatises, while rejecting an approach which would have had him follow some one treatise. One cannot but think of remarks in *Acad.* which pit the judgement Academics exercise (and seek to foster in their pupils) against the blind following of a randomly and prematurely selected authority practised by the dogmatists (*Luc.* 8–9). In §§6–8 Cicero then characterizes the tradition on which he draws, which has Aristotle and Isocrates as its fountainheads. In §9 he states that he hopes to have chosen individual precepts well, but if he made a mistake (omitting something important, or selecting the wrong thing), he will gladly change his mind. He continues:

> Non enim parum cognosse, sed in parum cognito stulte et diu perseuerasse turpe est, propterea quod alterum communi hominum infirmitati, alterum singulari cuiusque uitio est attributum. (10) Quare nos quidem **sine ulla affirmatione** simul quarentes dubitanter unum quidque dicemus, ne, dum paruulum consequamur, ut satis haec commode perscripsisse uideamur, illud amittamus, quod maximum est, **ut ne cui rei temere atque arroganter assenserimus**. Verum hoc quidem nos **et in hoc tempore et in omni uita** studiose, **quoad facultas feret**, consequemur: nunc

---

[404] *Inv.* 2 is often not attended to in the scholarship on Cicero's scepticism and on Cicero as evidence for Academic scepticism (not cited in e.g. in Glucker 1978; Inwood and Mansfeld 1997; Brittain 2001); see, however, Gawlick and Görler (1994: 1084–5).
[405] See Achard (1994: 5–10); Schwameis (2014: 169–81).
[406] The standard source-critical analysis is Adamietz (1960); see also Hirsch (forthcoming).
[407] On the anecdote and its uses in antiquity, see Sutton (2009: 274–5); for the Renaissance reception, see Lee (1940). Contrast *Rhet. Her.* 4.4–9 for a rather different treatment of the question of how an author of an *ars* selects examples.

autem, ne longius oratio progressa uideatur, de reliquis, quae praecipienda uidentur esse, dicemus.

For not understanding too little, but persisting stupidly and continuously in what is inadequately understood is disgraceful, because the first is attributed to the weakness common to all humanity, while the latter is attributed to everyone's very own fault. (10) Therefore we shall, without any affirmation, continuously enquire and make each statement with a degree of hesitation, in order to avoid that, while we achieve the small point of having written a reasonably useful book, we miss the most important one, not to give assent rashly rashly and arrogantly to anything. This principle we shall pursue now and in our whole life diligently, as far as we are able to.

Cicero's stance is here characterized by universal suspension of judgment, not by a rejection of rash assent (which would leave scope for assent that was not rash but self-aware and cautious, as envisaged in *Luc.* 148, possibly to a suitably defined subset of impressions); on these grounds, one would call him a radical sceptic, not a mitigated sceptic.[408] And yet Cicero feels able to put forward rhetorical precepts, not as injunctions he regards as unqualifiedly true, but as ones which he endorses with a particular kind of proviso.[409] This suggests that he thinks there is a mode (or modes) of endorsement available to him which falls short of assent, i.e. of accepting something as true. Moreover, the context here does not suggest that Cicero is speaking ad hominem, setting out an alternative which an opponent should find as compelling as his own avowedly held one, given his own assumptions. Rather, the speaker sets out his stance on his own terms. Note also that Cicero undertakes to keep enquiring,[410] and that he undertakes to conduct his whole life, and not only, say, the composition of rhetorical treatises, along the lines he is setting out.[411] Finally, *quoad facultas feret* hints at doubts that the speaker might be able to sustain a policy of universal ἐποχή; compare the similar but more elaborate remarks of the Cicero character in *Luc.* 66. While the passage is manifestly a statement 'in the text' which does not afford an insight into the historical Cicero's mind, it certainly rhymes with the manner in which Cicero characterizes his formative encounter with Philo approximately forty years later.[412]

---

[408] See section 4.
[409] In saying this, Cicero does not so much elide as reinterpret the fact that rhetorical precepts generally offer guidelines rather than hard injunctions.
[410] See *OLD* s.v. *quaero* no. 9b; cf. *Luc.* 7: *neque nos studium exquirendi defatigati relinquemus.*
[411] It is less attractive to think that in *et in hoc tempore et in omni uita* the second conjunct is purely temporal in scope.
[412] See *Brut.* 306: *Eodemque tempore, cum princeps Academiae Philo cum Atheniensium optimatibus Mithridatico bello domo profugisset Romamque uenisset, totum ei me tradidi admirabili quodam ad philosophiam studio concitatus; in quo hoc etiam commorabar attentius—etsi rerum ipsarum uarietas et magnitudo summa me delectatione retinebat—, sed tamen sublata iam esse in perpetuum ratio iudiciorum uidebatur,* 'At the same time Philo, then head of the Academy, had come to Rome as a refugee from his home city because of the Mithridatic war along with a group of the best of the Athenians. I devoted myself entirely to him, filled with a miraculous enthusiasm for philosophy. In this enthusiasm I persisted all the more attentively as, although the variety of the issues themselves and their significance held me with great enjoyment, it appeared that the whole system of the courts had been removed in perpetuity.'

Thus we derive from *Inv.* a starting point—that Cicero chose to cast himself in *Inv.* in a first-person statement as a radical sceptic in the 80s BC—against which one can judge later pronouncements in other works.

From the 80s BC down to the mid-50s, Cicero pursued his career as an advocate and politician. Only letters (beginning with *Att.* 1.5 = SB 1, from November 68) and speeches are extant for this period. While the letters do make frequent reference to philosophical subjects, they do not contain any clear first-person statements on a philosophical stance comparable to *Inv.* 2.9–10. We do find numerous instances of Cicero rehearsing, *in utramque partem*, a difficult political problem on which he must take a view, clearly in the hope that this will help him opt for the right course of action. In *Att.* 2.3.3 (= SB 23), written in late 60 BC, Cicero calls arguing *in utramque partem* (sc. in private) on Caesar's first agrarian reform bill 'speaking on either side in the Socratic manner' (in Greek, not by coincidence, and marking the practice out as philosophical rather than rhetorical), and says that he will state his preferred position at the end, 'as those men used to do' (*ut illi solebant*)—'those men' are surely Academics, on the most plausible reading.[413] That a preference for a view may be given after the *in utramque partem* procedure is also cast in Greek terms, which suggests that it was not a Ciceronian innovation and addition to the Academic practice.[414]

The speeches rarely mention philosophy positively and in a manner which informatively characterizes the speaker persona, since a Roman jury and larger audience would have taken against an orator who casts himself as an intellectual. The dialogues written in the mid-50s, i.e. *De orat.*, *Rep.*, and *Leg.* (the latter not released at the time and not mentioned in the survey in *Div.* 2 *init.*),[415] are indebted to Platonic models in terms of their format. This was interpreted by some as evidence that Cicero was during that phase of his life a follower of Antiochus of Ascalon,[416] whom he encountered around 79 BC, i.e. after Philo,[417] but programmatic passages which might seem to support this reading have been shown to offer no actual support (*Ac.* 1.13; *N.D.* 1.6),[418] and the three works contain enough gestures to a sceptical stance as well as suitable formal features to make it preferable to view them as exploring vaguely Platonic themes in a Platonizing format from a sceptical standpoint. In *De orat.* 3.145 Cotta says in reply to Crassus' final contribution to the conversation that

---

[413] *Att.* 2.3.3: *Venio nunc ad mensem Ianuarium et ad* ὑπόστασιν *nostram ac* πολιτείαν, *in qua* Σωκρατικῶς εἰς ἑκάτερον, *sed tamen ad extremum, ut illi solebant,* τὴν ἀρέσκουσαν, 'I come now to the month of January and *la base de ma politique*. I shall argue thereupon *in utramque partem à la Socrate*, but in the end, according to the practice of the school, shall declare my preference' (transl. Shackleton Bailey), with Shackleton Bailey (1965: 357). The tense of *solebant* need not imply that the sceptical Academy was defunct in 60 BC (although it probably was), but may be used to refer to Cicero's past experience ('they used to do this', sc. when I knew them, or at least one of them, Philo). On the letters, see McConnell (2014: passim), but esp. p. 8 n. 19, pp. 51–2 on *Att.* 2.3.3, and ch. 4.
[414] Gawlick and Görler (1994: 1089–1118) argue for Ciceronian innovation.
[415] On *Leg.*, see Schmidt (2001).
[416] See Hirzel (1883: 488–9); Glucker (1988); Steinmetz (1989).
[417] See Hatzimichali (2012) for the chronology of Antiochus.
[418] See Görler (1995).

he has now been won over by the Academy;[419] nothing Crassus said would associate him with Antiochus' Old Academy in particular, sceptical Academic techniques of argument are mentioned (*ancipites uias rationesque*), and Cotta features as a proponent of scepticism ten years later in *N.D.*[420] In *Rep.* 3.8 Philus assumes that enquiry on either side is a format familiar to interlocutors and audience alike, and that it is used for enquiry into justice.[421] In *Leg.* 1.36 Atticus alludes to Cicero's freedom to form his own view guided by reason and his avowed lack of dependence on authority (a theme we first encountered in the preface to *Inv.* 2).[422]

In the 40s, after Caesar's victory over Pompeius in the Roman civil war and during his dictatorship, Cicero returned to philosophical writing and produced a substantial number of works in quick succession (see section 3). The first of these was the dialogue *Hortensius* (*Hort.*), conceived and probably begun in the second half of 46. It has the same ensemble of speakers and (roughly) dramatic date as the first edition of the *Acad.* (i.e. *Catul.* and *Luc.*). The three dialogues thus did form a triptych, whether or not they were first so conceived; they were in any event written in succession. What is relevant for my purposes is that in *Hort.*, in which the eponymous character is converted to philosophy after other areas of expertise to which he might equally devote his spare time are found to have a less strong claim (art, poetry, history), the character Cicero (no first-person statements belonging to a frame are preserved among the fragments of *Hort.*).[423] wins the protreptic competition for philosophy generally and makes statements which dovetail with *Inv.* 2.9–10, as well with first-person statements made in the frame and ones made by the character Cicero in *Luc.* Thus Augustine has himself say in *Contra Acad.* 3.14.31 (cf. text no. 28 of the indirect transmission):

---

[419] *De orat.* 3.145: *Quo cum ingressus esses, repente te quasi quidam aestus ingenii tui procul a terra abripuit atque in altum a conspectu paene omnium abstraxit; omnem enim rerum scientiam complexus non tu quidem eam nobis tradidisti; neque enim fuit tam exigui temporis; sed apud hos quid profeceris nescio, me quidem in Academiam totum compulisti. In qua uelim sit illud, quod saepe posuisti, ut non necesse sit consumere aetatem atque ut possit is illa omnia cernere, qui tantum modo aspexerit; sed etiam si est aliquando spissius aut si ego sum tardior, profecto numquam conquiescam neque defatigabor ante, quam illorum ancipites uias rationesque et pro omnibus et contra omnia disputandi percepero*, 'And after you had started, the great swell of your genius carried you away from land to the high sea, almost out of everybody's sight. You embraced the entire knowledge of the art, and though you did not convey it to us (which was impossible in such a short amount of time), nevertheless, although I do not know what progress you made with our friends, *I* was compelled to come over entirely to the side of the Academy. And I should be glad to think that your frequent claims hold—that one need not spend a lifetime on it, that it is possible to take in the entire approach if one is prepared to look; but even if it is more heavy-going than that, or if I myself am slow, without question I shall never rest and not give up exhausted before I have grasped the Academics' twofold approach and way of thinking and of arguing on either side of every proposition'. On the passage, see Wisse, Winterbottom, and Fantham (2008: 165 and 168–9) and Mankin (2011: 232–3).
[420] The dramatic date of *De orat.* (91 BC) precedes the historical Cotta's encounter with Philo (cf. *N.D.* 1.59, 93; p. clvi below)—so Cicero is fashioning a starting point for Cotta's interest in the Academy.
[421] On the fact that *De re publica* does not relinquish Philus' or the Academic perspective after Philus' speech, see also Lévy (1992: 506) and Atkins (2013: 37–43).
[422] *Leg.* 1.36: *Et scilicet tua libertas disserendi amissa est, aut tu is es qui in disputando non tuum iudicium sequare, sed auctoritati aliorum pareas!*, 'And, of course, you have lost your freedom to argue in any direction, or else you are the kind of man not to follow your own judgment in a debate, but to accept the authority of others!'; see Dyck (2004: 166); Schofield (2017: 62).
[423] See p. clxxx; given that *Luc.* has a proem with a frame, it seems likely that *Hort.* had one, too.

> Clamat Cicero se ipsum magnum esse opinatorem [cf. *Luc.* 66], sed de sapiente se quaerere. Quod si adhuc uos, adulescentes, ignotum habetis, certe in Hortensio [frg. 51 Grilli = 92 Straume-Zimmermann] legistis: 'Si igitur nec certi est quidquam nec opinari sapientis est, nihil umquam sapiens approbabit.'
>
> Cicero loudly declares that, while he himself may be a great holder of opinions, he is enquiring about the sage. If you young people do not know this work yet, you have certainly read in the *Hortensius*: 'If there is nothing certain and holding opinions is not what the sage does, the sage will never approve anything.'

Note the manner in which a programmatic statement made by the character Cicero in his speech in *Ac.* 4 (corresponding to the second half of *Luc.*) is linked to a statement of the character Cicero in *Hort.* The latter was committed to universal suspension of judgement.[424]

I now turn to *Acad.*, whose final edition is cited in later dialogues as a foundational work and as the place where Cicero's philosophical position is set out.[425] The first edition, as shown by *Att.* 13.32.2–3 (= SB 305 = T15) and *Luc.*, had a frame. The latter offers first-person statements, and the body of the dialogue contains statements by Cicero the character; in addition, it features another Academic speaker, Catulus the younger, who adopts a different position from Cicero, i.e. mitigated scepticism (see section 4 and on *Luc.* 148). In the final edition of *Acad.* in four books, i.e. in *Ac.* 1 which in all likelihood draws on the first part of *Catul.*, there is no frame, and the Cicero character assumes features confined to the first-person speaker in the proem of *Luc.*, notably the property of being an author who reflects on the practice of writing philosophy in Latin. Moreover, the material presented by Catulus in *Catul.* was introduced by the Cicero character (see section 9.2), which must mean that he introduced a position which was different from his own in one part of the text (i.e. the lost part of *Ac.* 1) and actually advocated the one his character adopts in *Luc.* (and elsewhere, or so I believe).

In the preface of *Luc.* there are first-person comments by Cicero on the nature of his stance, which one can examine for consistency with those found in earlier works. Having dismissed criticism on account of his portraying distinguished Romans as engaging in philosophy or as having more expertise in it than the real-life individuals could conceivably have had, Cicero responds to those who criticize him for adopting an Academic stance in particular (*Luc.* 7 *fin.*–8). In doing so, he characterizes it, in a manner that is most plausibly read as non-dialectical, even though it involves a contrast with the dogmatist's view; what is more, while Cicero appears to speak generally, the preface of *Luc.* of course presupposes *Catul.*, from which it must have

---

[424] See further section 9.5; cf. also *Contra Acad.* 1.3.7 (ll. 15–27 Green), with Schlapbach (2003: 95–7) for the probable ascription to *Hort.* By itself frg. 51 Grilli may seem open to a reading on which it just refers to the 'corollary argument' (see section 4), advanced dialectically by Carneades, as opposed to characterizing a view which the Cicero character embraces, but in his speech in *Luc.* the Cicero character endorses the argument (i.e. 'approves it' in the sense characterized in *Luc.* 104–5a). (The figure of the 'sage' functions as an idealized reference point or embodiment of aspirations.) It is also unlikely on independent grounds that *Hort.* offered an in-depth account of the genesis of the Clitomachean position; see Grilli (2010: 243).

[425] See e.g. *N.D.* 1.11–12 (T39) and *Div.* 2.1 (T40).

emerged that, while Academics are ready to scrutinize anyone's knowledge claims as well as the theory underpinning them, it is the Stoic epistemological theory as promoted by Antiochus which is in *Acad.* identified as the main target of the Academic speakers.[426] Cicero contrasts those *qui se scire arbitrantur*, which should be taken to mean 'those who think they have knowledge of certain things' (rather than 'those who have the exalted disposition of knowledge', sc. which one would credit a sage with), with himself or people like him 'who are in possession of many plausible impressions, which we can follow easily, but which we cannot affirm' (*nos probabilia multa habemus, quae sequi facile, affirmare uix possumus*). Just before that (*Luc.* 7 *fin.*) he had stated that in his discussions (*disputationes*)—deliberately ambiguous between real-life discussions as depicted in the dialogues and the discussions in the dialogues qua artistic creations—he has but one goal, to extract (*elicere, exprimere*), by presenting arguments on either side and by listening to them, what is either true or comes to it as close as possible.

As in *Inv.* 2.9–10, Cicero's position is characterized by a commitment to suspension of judgement. He is looking for the truth, sc. on philosophical questions, as the context makes clear, and he deploys the technique of argument on either side to reach them, or failing that, to get close to them. While he hopes to find the truth by this method, he is prepared to settle for what comes as close as possible to it. He does not believe he has knowledge, in general and—or so the context suggests—as the Stoics understand it, and this view of his is quite likely to be underpinned by his qualified endorsement of the so-called core argument (see section 4). To be sure, some endorsement of the argument is required, or else it would not leave Cicero with a view in a non-dialectical context. But the endorsement does not translate into a belief as conceived by the Stoic framework, since such a belief requires assent, and assent is explicitly rejected as we saw. Instead, Cicero claims for himself the possibility of a lesser form of belief, which has two components: the content of his beliefs has the status of a *probabile* rather than of a truth, and the endorsement he is entitled to is characterized as *sequi*, 'to follow'.[427] All of this is consistent with *Inv.* 2.9–10.

As mentioned above, the second Academic speaker in the first edition of *Acad.*, Catulus the younger, adopts a different position from Cicero's ('mitigated scepticism'; see section 4). From *Luc.* 148 there emerges one respect in which it is different from Cicero's (i.e. the first-person speaker in the preface of *Luc.* and the Cicero character). While Cicero is committed to universal suspension of judgement, tries to avoid assenting consistently (although as a matter of fact he does not always succeed, see below), and regards the form of endorsement of impressions to which he is entitled as a form of non-assent, Catulus is ready to assent and therefore have beliefs or opinions as the Stoics define 'opinion' (see on *Ac.* 1.40–2),[428] but his assent is qualified by an awareness that the impressions which he takes to be true in assenting to them may in fact be false.[429]

---

[426] One can extrapolate this from what Varro says in *Ac.* 1.40–2.
[427] On the conception of a *probabile* employed here see section 6; on the endorsement (referred to by *sequi*, 'to follow', in *Luc.* 8) envisaged in the quasi-beliefs Cicero permits to the Academic, see the commentary on *Luc.* 104–105a.
[428] See on *Luc.* 78.
[429] See on *Luc.* 148 for the construal of self-aware assent.

In a passage early in his speech in *Luc.*, Cicero relates his stance on the question of endorsement of impressions to one which envisages assent. He says that, as a matter of fact and because he is not a wise man, he will often assent to impressions (*Luc.* 66, whose counterpart in the final edition of *Acad.* is cited by Augustine in *Contra Acad.* 3.14.31, quoted above).[430] This, however, is not due to a hold which the alternative Academic view has on him as a theoretical position, i.e. it is not due to a rational appeal of said view, but because due to human weakness he cannot help but assent on many occasions when he should suspend judgement (cf. *Luc.* 68, 108, 115).

It is a striking feature of the Cicero character's stance in *Luc.* that it is linked to Arcesilaus as a kind of figurehead (see section 7.5). For it was Arcesilaus who urged that, if there are no cataleptic impressions, one should suspend judgement universally (*Luc.* 66–7). By contrast, the position promoted by Catulus would not be able to invoke Arcesilaus in the same way.[431] Search for the truth as a motif is linked to Arcesilaus' and Carneades' argumentative practice alike (*Luc.* 76 and *N.D.* 1.4, respectively).

One can now ask whether Cicero, the implied author of *Acad.*, can either be aligned with the first-person speaker Cicero in the proem of *Luc.* or Cicero the character, or has to be characterized differently. Relevant evidence would consist in a favouring, e.g. by means of structural features or through the rhetorical effectiveness of the proponent, of Antiochianism over Academic scepticism (or vice versa), or in a favouring of mitigated scepticism over Clitomacheanism. A natural heuristic assumption would be that the implied author Cicero agrees with the first-person speaker in the prefaces and the Cicero character. We can note that *Luc.* ends with Catulus (for one) saying (*Luc.* 148) that he sides with his father's view introduced in the discussion on the previous day (*Catul.*), so the historical Cicero has built a character into the text who is not won over by Cicero the character's reply to Lucullus; this should make one hesitant to see the Cicero character as being made to prevail by the implied author because he speaks last (a formal feature sometimes cited). In one of the letters to Atticus which document the conversion of the first edition of *Acad.* into the final version (*Att.* 13.25.3 = SB 333 = T30), Cicero worries that Varro (cast as the Antiochian speaker in that edition, who replaced Hortensius and Lucullus) might feel that Cicero had given himself the upper hand in the exchange with the Varro character. Cicero, it is implied, would regard this as unwarranted, but he also seems to think that Varro might take this view in any event, without there being an actual reason for it. On the evidence of *Acad.* it is arguable that the implied author should be taken to present, or to aim to present, both sides equally compellingly, leaving it—in line with the avowed intention of Academic characters in the dialogue—to the

---

[430] Brittain (2015: 12–13, 39) argues that in this passage Cicero signals that he is torn between radical and mitigated scepticism qua philosophical positions; if this was correct, the consequences for the overall interpretation of Cicero's stance would be far-reaching. I disagree because I interpret passages establishing the supposed pull of mitigated scepticism felt by the Cicero character differently (notably *Luc.* 66).

[431] One might think that this 'use' of Arcesilaus by a Clitomachean is motivated by the existence of mitigated scepticism as a serious alternative Academic stance and thus evidence for the significance of the latter. However, Arcesilaus would be equally useful to a Clitomachean who wants to maintain that the possibility of the sage opining was floated by Carneades merely as a dialectical option (see on *Luc.* 78), and of course prior to the emergence of Carneades Academic scepticism would naturally be characterized by both ἀκαταληψία and a commitment to universal ἐποχή.

iudicium of the reader to make up his mind. This may, however, be a deliberate ploy on the part of the implied author, who could 'actually' and 'secretly' be favouring the stance of the first-person speaker in the preface of *Luc.* and the Cicero character.

Against this background, one can now turn to the philosophical works composed at the same time as and after *Acad.* and ask if they can be read in a manner which is consistent with the picture which has emerged. Once again formal features of the texts, including how compelling the various contributions are, should be taken into account, inasmuch as they might illuminate the (or any) scepticism of Cicero the historical individual and Cicero the implied author. By contrast, first-person statements in the texts will again illuminate the position of Cicero the narrator or speaker in the frame or in frame-like contexts, as well as the outlook of the Cicero character. In connection with first-person statements, it will be helpful to introduce two further considerations. First, whether the issue is Academic methodology, so that the speaker's epistemic behaviour is the topic, or whether attitudes to substantial philosophical tenets are at issue, of the kind which a dogmatist might affirm, thereby turning them into philosophical beliefs. Second, whether the particular context is one in which ostensibly instruction is taking place; this is relevant because the Academic, when in instruction mode, does not disclose, in the spirit of Socrates, so as not to influence others with his *auctoritas*,[432] what seems *probabile* to him personally.

For *Fin.* there exist very detailed studies which place rather different interpretations on the whole dialogue, seeing the work either as a 'doxographical' rehearsal of opposing views held by different schools, as involving the finger of Cicero the author on the scales which leads to an endorsement of the Antiochian position through Piso's exposition in *Fin.* 5 and the rebuttal of the Stoic view in *Fin.* 4, or as a dramatization of a radically sceptical outlook on issues which are fundamentally intractable.[433] The interpretative choices which make scholars incline to one of these views cannot be rehearsed here. My reading would be closest to the third of these options, with the qualification that I view the whole work as a teaching context in which the author would be obligated to conceal any leanings towards a particular view. Two first-person remarks in the frame of *Fin.* 1 are relevant in this connection (1.6, 1.12):

> Quid? Si nos non interpretum fungimur munere, sed tuemur ea, quae dicta sunt ab iis quos probamus, iisque nostrum iudicium et nostrum scribendi ordinem adiungimus, quid habent, cur Graeca anteponant iis, quae et splendide dicta sint neque sint conuersa de Graecis?

> Assuming that we do not act as a mere translator, but, while representing what has been said by those whom we rate, apply our own judgement and our own arrangement, on what grounds do these critics rank works in Greek above compositions that are at once stylistically brilliant and not mere translations from Greek originals?

> Nos autem hanc omnem quaestionem de finibus bonorum et malorum fere a nobis explicatam esse his litteris arbitramur, in quibus, quantum potuimus, non modo

---

[432] See *Ac.* 1.45 (on Arcesilaus); Aug., *Contra Acad.* 3.20.43 (= t. 63* of the indirect tradition). In *Luc.* 60 Lucullus seems to be mockingly referencing a statement to similar effect made in *Catul.*

[433] See Brittain (2015) for a discussion of these options with respect to *Fin.*

quid nobis probaretur, sed etiam quid a singulis philosophiae disciplinis diceretur, persecuti sumus.

In this work we believe we have given a near-exhaustive exposition of the whole question of highest good and the worst evil. The book is intended to contain as far as possible an account not only of the views that we approve of, but also of the doctrines formulated by all the different schools of philosophy.

The first passage contrasts what Cicero does with mere translation, which discourages a reading of the dialogue that makes the dialogical form, the setting, and the characterizations mere embellishments of a text which could have formally reproduced a 'source'. *Tueri* is used as of the advocate taking on a brief on behalf of a client,[434] which of course does not involve a direct and unmediated use of the 'facts of the case' or the information furnished by the client, but judgement, skill, and tact on the part of the advocate and, in the analogy, on the part of the author; *iudicium* arguably encompasses all three and is thus neither simply judgement passed on the views and doctrines introduced nor judgement exercised in evaluation. *Quid nobis probaretur* illustrates the flexibility of *probabile*-related terminology, in that the sense of the verb must be broad enough to include Epicurean views on the nature of pleasure: these are views which appear to have standing on the speaker's view, which merit engagement, which have plausibility without necessarily inviting or commanding endorsement.[435] In the second passage *non modo quid nobis probaretur* manifestly refers to something else, viz. to doctrines or components thereof which the speaker deems plausible. However, it would be rash to think of these as the speaker's views in some sense.

As a literary creation *Fin.* would, on this reading, be consistent with the Clitomachean persona Cicero adopts elsewhere. It could be shown that *N.D.* and *Div.*, which are comparable in formal terms, as well as *Tusc.* and *Off.*, which are formally different, are open to similar readings and feature statements by Cicero as speaker in the frame which are consistent with the picture that emerges from *Acad.* and *Fin.* Especially the preface of *N.D.* 1 (§§1–12), delivered by Cicero, is full of points of contact with *Acad.* and refers to the latter as the place where Cicero has explained why he is an Academic (§11). *N.D.* 1.1 and 1.12, while not explicitly precluding that Cicero allowed for self-aware assent, are plausibly read as a commitment to universal suspension of judgment;[436] importantly, 1.1 is a parallel to *Fin.* 1.6 qua statement in the frame on how the dialogue might be approached by a reader. Relevant first-person statements in *Div.* include 2.8 and 2.28.

The five books of the *Tusculans* are not dialogues like *Fin.* and *N.D.*; instead, a pupil character formulates a thesis, and a speaker who may be taken to be Cicero but is not identified argued against them. The format is identified as Socratic and designed to discover what is *ueri simillimum* in 1.8 (cf. 3.46, 4.7), where, however, it

---

[434] See *OLD* s.v. *tueor* no. 4b.
[435] On the passage, see the slightly different interpretations of Patzig (1979: 308) and Brittain (2015: 16 n. 9).
[436] See the discussion of *N.D.* 1.12 in Wynne (2019: 38–9).

is also called a σχολή. In 2.5 the speaker declares: 'We follow *probabilia* and cannot advance beyond what is *ueri simile*.' In *Off.*, a treatise rather than a dialogue, Cicero (as a first-person speaker comparable to that in the prefaces of *Luc.*, *Fin.*, and *N.D.*) professes to follow the Stoics on a specific point 'today' (*hoc quidem tempore*, 1.6), but explains elsewhere that the Academy allows him to defend what strikes him as *ueri simile* at a given time (3.20) and that being an Academic does not mean that his mind wanders around aimlessly and that he has nothing at all which he could follow (2.7–8). The latter point is arguably an important corrective and qualification to the former: the Academic is not saying that he is free to judge pleasure the highest good today and virtue tomorrow, that this is what the freedom of the Academic amounts to, and that this was his way of living successfully. Similarly, *Tusc.* 5.33, superficially an expression of the utterly ephemeral nature of quasi-beliefs claimed by the Academic, is a context-specific comment on the force of a view felt during an Academic argument in front of an audience.[437] This is different from 'disclosing his view' in a stronger sense, which the Academic avoids even if he has one. With this I conclude the brief survey of works composed after *Acad.*

What makes the works of Cicero unique as evidence for Academic scepticism is that they contain a number of second-order statements on what we might call the enactment or the living practice of an Academic sceptical stance and argument practice.[438]

In *Luc.* 112 Cicero presents the behaviour of the Cicero character in a given debate context as a function of the position and attitude adopted by his opponent. When he is talking to Stoics or an Antiochian who embraces the Stoic conception of the cataleptic impression, he will play defensively and deny that there is knowledge, but when faced with a Peripatetic, who operates a more relaxed conception of knowledge, there is less reason to disagree. Similarly, in *Luc.* 98 he proposes to leave behind the nitpicking mode of argument which the Stoics adopt in the field of logic, and instead proposes to show 'who we are'. He goes on to cite a Clitomachean division of impressions. Arguably, there are two separate points being made: when arguing ad hominem, the Academic's stance will be determined by the opponent's stance up to a point. An unrealistically stringent conception of knowledge will be met with a punctilious and unforgiving counterargument, which, if one does not attend to the adversarial context, can make the Academic look extreme, i.e. committed to the view that, if there is no knowledge on the Stoic conception of knowledge, there is no knowledge generally speaking. The second point is that a non-dialectical exposition of the Academic's self-conception will only be possible in an environment which is not hostile as it were: the Academic will not lay out how he operates cognitively on his own terms when he feels he has to adopt a defensive posture.

---

[437] With *Tusc.* 5.33, cf. 5.83. I am indebted to James Allen for a discussion of passages which reference the freedom of the Academic. See Allen (2022). I would read the much-discussed passage *N.D.* 3.95, where the Cicero character appears to express a preference for the Stoic view because 'it appears to tilt closer to what seems like the truth' (*mihi Balbi ad ueritatis similitudinem uideretur esse propensior*), in a similar way; see Pease (1913); Taran (1987); Filippo (2000); and Wynne (2019: 39, 270–1).

[438] Two studies which are particularly sensitive to this aspect of Cicero's scepticism are Görler (2004c) and (2016); cf. Wynne (2014) on the self-conception of the Clitomachean Cotta in *N.D.*

The Academic is also happy to be refuted by rational means, i.e. he is not the obstructionist he is often painted as by his opponents, nor does he have the personal ambition of winning for the sake of it. This is so because he genuinely searches for the truth. A counterargument against the dogmatist which cannot be sustained deserves to fail, or so he thinks. Thus in *Tusc.* 4.4 Cicero says that he does not just not mind when others oppose him in writing, he positively hopes for it (because scrutiny can never be bad), and in 2.55 he says that he follows what is *probabile* and cannot advance beyond the *ueri simile*, which is why he is happy to be refuted, will not show misplaced persistence, and is prepared to be proven wrong without any danger of him getting irate. In 3.51 he says that he will happily yield to those who tell the truth (leaving it open how often he encounters such people). More teasingly Cotta says to Balbus in *N.D.* 3.95 that he is happy to be refuted and that he knows Balbus will be able to do so easily.[439]

However, there are some passages where Cicero (or Cotta) maintains his sceptical stance while expressing a hope or a wish that a particular view is true. In *Tusc.* 5.20 Cicero wishes to reward those who enable him to believe more firmly in the sufficiency of virtue for happiness. In *N.D.* 1.61 Cotta wishes to be firmly convinced of the existence of the gods (cf. 3.7). Such passages are indicative of background intuitions and convictions which the speakers in question entertain, but which do not come up to the firmness or quality of doctrinal beliefs, and are therefore compatible with a sceptical outlook. However, they do form part of the make-up of the particular speakers, and it is in every case worth asking where the particular intuition comes from. Cotta is a Roman priest, and *N.D.* dramatizes (among many other things) the question of how one can be a priest as well as an Academic at the same time, given that a priest may be assumed to believe ex officio a great many things on which an Academic may prefer not to take a view. Conceivably some of these background intuitions may also be what makes the characters in question distinctively Roman,[440] given that priesthood and its obligations were conceptualized in culturally contingent ways.

In general, the fact that the characters in Cicero's dialogues are representations of real people may explain some of their behaviour. Brittain (2015: 34–6) observes that Cicero's commitment to the Roman *mos maiorum* and to a philosophical life of some description leads to a series of commitments, notably that virtue is the primary good and that there are also goods of fortune (thus the *mos maiorum*), and that there are rational means for securing happiness. The first and the third considerations jointly lead one to favour the Stoic $\tau\acute{\epsilon}\lambda os$ (virtue as the sole good) over the Antiochian one (virtue guarantees the happy life, but virtue and the goods of fortune the happiest), while the second consideration is only accommodated by the Antiochian $\tau\acute{\epsilon}\lambda os$. It is tempting to think that the historical Cicero will have leant at different times of his life to one or the other of these options—e.g. the consular humbled by exile and his own moments of weakness to the Antiochian view, but the politically sidelined ex-Pompeian of 45 BC to whom fortune had done her worst (and who would go for

---

[439] For Socrates' avowed happiness to be refuted if he is wrong, cf. e.g. Plt., *Grg.* 458a; it is natural for a Clitomachean to invoke Socrates because Arcesilaus invoked Socrates, and the Clitomachean position shares with Arcesilaus' stance the commitment to suspension of judgement.

[440] See Wynne (2014).

broke in his speeches against Antony) to the Stoic view—and that, when he created the Cicero character in *Fin.*, he had the insight to allow for these shifts of outlook.[441] Clitomacheanism so understood would be responsive to life experiences.

I contend that in first-person statements Cicero maintained essentially the same philosophical outlook in all his works,[442] but characterize this outlook in a way that differs from existing accounts. My account is at variance with the view that Cicero presented himself at least in some works as a mitigated sceptic. Rather, I would say that Cicero was a radical sceptic whose scepticism accommodated many of the features which others would associate with mitigated scepticism, like the use of argument *in utramque partem* in search of the truth and in the hope that a *ueri simile* might emerge, or the holding of views (in a suitably qualified way, i.e. not as a result of assent or self-aware assent). This is so because, on the evidence of Cicero's texts, radical and mitigated scepticism differed mainly on the fairly narrow question of what conception of belief they allowed for.[443] Further, it has been suggested that the conception of the πιθανόν/*probabile* employed by radical sceptics is different from that of mitigated sceptics, in that the former, in invoking persuasiveness, give psychological self-reports, or merely the grounds for their (qualified) acceptance of a πιθανόν, while mitigated sceptics regard persuasiveness of πιθανόν as evidence for the truth of the propositional content of the impressions in question.[444] I recognize the conceptual distinction, but do not think it can be used to differentiate radical and mitigated scepticism, sc. as both stances present themselves in Cicero, because I think that a radical sceptic using and citing πιθανά outside of a dialectical context will already be treating them as (albeit ultimately inconclusive) evidence, given how persuasiveness was construed in the Carneadean scheme.[445]

According to an influential view, Cicero's teacher Philo adopted three Academic positions in the course of his life, the Clitomachean one, a position of mitigated scepticism (which permitted self-aware assent, cf. *Luc.* 148), and the position of the Roman Books.[446] Now it is possible that Philo promoted mitigated scepticism or the Roman Books view when Cicero first encountered him, that he merely mentioned Clitomacheanism, and that after the failure of the Roman Books Cicero came away thinking that the Clitomachean position was superior, but it is not a natural assumption to make, unless the evidence requires it.[447]

---

[441] See also Gawlick and Görler (1994: 1113–14).

[442] So also Gawlick and Görler (1994), but they characterize Cicero's position differently (notably, they do not treat the distinction between assent and approval as pivotal); *pace* Brittain (2001), who takes Cicero to be a mitigated sceptic outside *Acad.* Brittain (2015) signals a qualified change of opinion, in that it adds *Fin.* to the list of works where Cicero qua implied author is not a mitigated but a radical sceptic.

[443] Note that according to the categories found in ancient texts, a belief arising from approval as opposed to assent was not a belief (δόξα) in the technical sense; see on *Luc.* 78 and 148.

[444] See Frede (1987b: 209–10); Brittain (2008: §3.3); Wynne (2014: 247).

[445] See section 6.1.

[446] This is a central contention of Burnyeat (1997) and Brittain (2001); cf. Striker (2016). See, however, Glucker (2004).

[447] *Luc.* 78 is the one Ciceronian passage which might suggest that Philo ever was a mitigated sceptic, but, as I argue ad loc., the fact that a view of Philo's is linked to Metrodorus' suggests that the reference is to the Roman Books view.

My suggestion is that *Brut.* 306 casts the encounter with Philo as deeply formative, that Cicero the historical individual appears to reveal himself to us with unusual immediacy through the words of the first-person speaker in *Inv.* 2.9–10, and that this sense of a deeply personal experience being disclosed is strengthened by the fact that the profession of a commitment to universal ἐποχή is somewhat out of place in a work like *Inv.*, although Cicero took care to motivate it in its immediate context. Of course one might object that it is carefully calculated features of the text which I am describing and that it is impossible for us to reach through to historical reality as it were.

It is also worth repeating in this connection that, some forty years after he first identified himself as a radical sceptic in *Inv.* 2.9–10, Cicero created, with Cotta in *N.D.*, another Clitomachean character. The historical Cotta heard Philo at some point between 91 and 89/8 BC, prior to the conception of the Roman Books view and at a time when Philo was supposedly a mitigated sceptic.[448] When Cicero was working on *Acad.*, before he embarked on composing on *N.D.* (for all we know), and quite possibly before he conceived of the grouping *N.D.*, *Div.*, and *Fat.*, Atticus raised the question of whether Cotta might become one of the interlocutors;[449] Cicero rejected this because it would make him, i.e. the Cicero character, a κωφὸν πρόσωπον. This at least suggests that he (i.e. the first-person speaker in the letters) viewed Cotta as a Clitomachean already then. Was the character Cotta deliberately created by Cicero the historical individual, e.g. to shore up the position of Clitomacheanism as the true form of Academic scepticism? Or was the historical Cotta another Roman who heard Philo advancing one position but came away adopting a different one? Or did the historical Cotta, like—on my argument—the historical Cicero, hear Philo articulate and promote Clitomacheanism and found his outlook compelling?

There is further evidence from within *Acad.*, and what significance one attaches to it will again depend on similar considerations. In *Luc.* 69, in a context where Antiochus' abandoning of scepticism is at issue, the Cicero character says of Antiochus that the latter learnt from Philo *haec ipsa quae a me defenduntur*, which would be somewhat misleading if a period when Philo was a mitigated sceptic was being elided. In *Luc.* 18 Lucullus reports that Catulus the father, a mitigated sceptic, accused Philo of lying (in the Roman Books) not of changing his mind, which suggests that he did not see him as a creator or proponent of mitigated scepticism (and that in the *Catulus* the elder Catulus did not derive his Academic outlook from Philo himself). The Catulus character evidently did not think that the mitigated view derived its authority from Philo.

I do not believe that evidence from outside the Ciceronian corpus can be used to settle this question,[450] viz. whether Philo himself ever was a mitigated sceptic,

---

[448] According to *N.D.* 1.17, Cotta and Cicero 'learnt to know nothing from Philo' (in the character Velleius' words). Cotta was exiled under the *Lex Varia* in 91 BC and did not return to Rome until after Sulla's victory in 82 BC; cf. Cic., *Brut.* 205 and Gruen (1965: 64). He heard Philo in Athens (*N.D.* 1.59), where the latter instructed him to attend lectures by the Epicurean Zeno inter alia, whose lectures Cicero later attended, too (*Fin.* 1.16). On Cotta, see also Dyck (2003: 6–7); Mankin (2011: 34–5); and Wynne (2014: 245 n. 1).

[449] See *Att.* 13.19.3–4 (= SB 326 = T23).

[450] I review relevant texts in appendices 1 and 2.

although it seems unlikely to me that the mostly hostile reporters of Academic views and arguments would not have fastened on two rather than one change of position by a scholarch. Numenius frg. 28 Des Places and, less clearly because of the damaged state of the text, Philod., *Index Acad.* col. xxxiii, suggest one major change in Philo's outlook not two.

What is ultimately at stake here is not which of two to an outsider marginally different positions Philo held for a period of at most fifteen years, although I would argue that the difference between the two views is substantial. Rather, I think broad agreement is possible on the view that Cicero was a radical sceptic throughout his documented life and that this position was richly articulated across his various works (whether or not one thinks Clitomacheanism can be 'lived'). This being so, it matters for our attitude towards the Ciceronian corpus as evidence for Academic scepticism whether one sees continuity between Cicero and Philo. Notice that our evidential base for mitigated scepticism is tiny: *all* we know for certain about what was distinctive for it is that it allowed for self-aware assent (*Luc.* 148). If we wanted to recreate mitigated scepticism through imaginative reconstruction using the Ciceronian corpus, as one might given that it is our most substantial body of evidence for Academic scepticism, then we would end up offering imaginative reconstructions on the basis of passages which are unequivocally Clitomachean. Put differently, such a project of fleshing out mitigated scepticism would require us to take the corpus not at face value in an important sense.

Thus I assume in this commentary that in one respect Cicero's Academic scepticism is not uniquely Cicero's, in that Philo's stance at the time when the historical Cicero became his pupil is likely to have fallen on the radical side of the radical vs mitigated scepticism divide, in virtue of its attitude to assent, and that Philo formulated or at least publicly proposed the Roman Books view not immediately upon arrival in Rome. Philo would have discussed mitigated scepticism as an option upheld by some, in a manner comparable to the Cicero character in the final edition of *Acad.* (who assumed, in addition to his own, the role Catulus had played in the first edition).

9. Editions of *Acad.* and Their Reconstruction

In this section I discuss a number of issues to do with the creation of the extant and missing parts of *Acad.* Section 9.1 surveys the letters, mostly to Atticus, which Cicero wrote in the first half of 45 BC while finalizing the first edition of *Acad.* (i.e. *Catul.* and *Luc.*), briefly entertaining and setting down a second edition which removed Catulus, Lucullus, and Hortensius as characters, and finally settling on an edition in four books featuring Varro, himself, and Atticus in a small role.[451] In section 9.2 I give indicative reconstructions of the *Catulus*, using the backward references to it in *Luc.* and information offered by the fragments of the final edition,[452] as well as of

---

[451] The fragments and testimonia of this final edition are included on pp. 39–64 of the Oxford Classical Text and translated on pp. 25–32 of the present volume.

[452] These backward references are assembled on pp. 65–70 of the Oxford Classical Text.

clviii INTRODUCTION

the missing parts of the *Academici libri*.[453] Section 9.3 considers in general terms whether Cicero followed continuous sources for parts of *Acad.*, and what the outlook and relative date of any sources used might have been. Section 9.4 discusses the terminology Cicero used to refer to all or parts of *Acad.* while they were in the process of being created. *Catul.* and *Luc.* were preceded by the dialogue *Hortensius*, with which they formed an ensemble; continuities between the three dialogues are the subject of section 9.5.

9.1 Evidence from Cicero's Letters to Atticus on the Creation of *Acad.*

The broader context of *Acad.* within Cicero's philosophical works is discussed in section 3. Here I survey the series of letters mostly to Atticus dating from the spring and summer of 45 BC which Cicero wrote while working on *Acad.*, *Fin.*, and *Tusc.* as well as a couple of smaller projects which he eventually abandoned.[454] The latter illustrate, together with likely modifications of the arrangement of *N.D.* while it was being composed later in the same year,[455] that the changes of mind which account for the complex editorial history of *Acad.* were not peculiar to *Acad.*

It is not possible to trace the conception of the plan for an ensemble of dialogues (*Hort.*, *Catul.*, *Luc.*) with precision. When Cicero corresponded with Varro in the first half of 46,[456] no such plan is mentioned, although it would have been an obvious subject to raise.[457] *Or.* 148 (T0) may hint at some plan for philosophical works, but given Cicero's documented changes of mind on works in progress in 45, it is not possible to be confident what is meant. There is a gap in the correspondence with Atticus from the end of November 46 to 6 March 45. It is reasonable to presume that *Hort.* was completed and 'published' in the first part of this period,[458] and that preparations for, and quite possibly work on, *Catul.* and *Luc.* were also in progress at the same time. The less likely alternative is that Cicero's (justly) famed productivity allowed him to start work on *Catul.* and *Luc.* only after the death of his beloved daughter Tullia in the mid-February of 45.

When the correspondence resumes (T1), Cicero is in mourning, slightly defensive since he knows he is being criticized for it by political opponents and also allies (the theme becomes more prominent in subsequent letters), and engaged in unspecified

---

[453] For the commentary on the testimonia and fragments of the final edition, see pp. 265–94.
[454] I also touch on passages from later works of Cicero's which make reference to *Acad.* All these texts are collected in the Oxford Classical Text, pp. 1–15; they are translated in the present volume, pp. 3–14.
[455] See Dyck (2003: 2–4). On the possibility of two editions of *Tusc.*, see Giusta (1969).
[456] See the general note on *Ac.* 1.1–8 for the history of their relationship.
[457] Note also *Fam.* 9.8 (= SB 254 = T29): *Puto fore ut, cum legeris, mirere nos id locutos esse inter nos quod numquam locuti sumus; sed nosti morem dialogorum*, 'I think you will be surprised when you find that we have discussed a subject which we in fact never discussed; but you know the convention of dialogues.'
[458] *Fam.* 9.26.4 (= SB 197), in preparation towards the end of 46 BC, is widely regarded as a reference to work on *Hort.*: *Sic igitur uiuitur. Cottidie aliquid legitur aut scribitur*, 'And so life passes. Every day a bit of reading and a bit of writing'; see Ruch (1958: 35–7); Bringmann (1971: 118–19); and Marinone (2004[2]: 213). A remark in *Att.* 12.12.2 (= SB 259; my T6), dated 16 March, probably gestures to reactions to *Hort.* after publication (see below).

literary activity at his villa near Astura, where he says he has everything he needs for that purpose. On the next day (T2) Cicero mentions a *consolatio* which he has written for himself and which he will forward to Atticus once it is copied, but other writing is clearly going on at the same time (*totos dies scribo*)—a distraction from his pain, but not as effective as the *consolatio*. That this 'other writing' at least includes *Acad.* is suggested by Cicero's remark in (T3), dated the following day (9 March), that he spends his days in 'thick, rough woods' (*cumque mane me in siluam abstrusi densam et asperam, non exeo inde at uesperum*), which is reminiscent of Cicero's remark in *Luc.* that Stoic preoccupations force him into the thicket of dialectic (§112: *Cum sit enim campus, in quo exultare possit oratio, cur eam tantas in angustias et Stoicorum dumeta compellimus?*). (T4) and (T5) attest continued writing.

In (T6), from 16 March, there is the first reference to *Fin.*, which has evidently been in planning and production alongside *Acad.* The name *Epicurus* characterizes the subject matter of *Fin.* 1 and 2 (metonymically, or as a provisional title), and it appears that one of Atticus' Epicurean friends made a request. It is usually and reasonably assumed that the request was for the person himself to be cast as a character, or mentioned.[459] One might wonder, alternatively, if the request was made on behalf of someone else, in which case one would think first of the two Epicureans who do feature in *Fin.* 1 and 2, Torquatus or Triarius (the former had died at Thapsus, the latter at Pharsalus). However, the sentence *incredibile est quam ea quidam requirant* points to the first option, since even an insistent request made on behalf of a deceased Epicurean friend would be an act of *pietas*.[460] Cicero seems intent on complying, albeit grudgingly, then undertakes to return to the *antiqui* in the future. By this he must mean the characters of an older generation who featured in the dialogues of the previous decade (and not Lucullus, Catulus, Hortensius, et al., i.e. the suggestion is not that he is turning his mind back to *Acad.*). If Cicero did include an Epicurean friend of Atticus who was alive at the time of writing, then he must have changed his mind by the time he completed *Fin.*, for no such character features in the version we are able to read.

In (T7) Cicero asks Atticus about the purpose of the philosophical embassy of 155 BC and about the head of the Epicurean school at the time.[461] The embassy is mentioned in *Luc.* 137 and also in *Fin.* 2.59. The two items of information requested do not feature in either passage, but the headship of the Garden could conceivably have been mentioned in *Fin.* while it would have been extraneous to the discussion in *Luc.*[462]

In (T8) Cicero expresses pride in the work(s) he has been engaged in producing, as well as resuming the theme of loss (of liberty and of his daughter) and of a refusal

---

[459] Thus Shackleton Bailey (1966: 316).

[460] So understood, the sentence can be read as an indirect reference to *Hort.*, which was likely to have been the work which signalled that Cicero had shifted to younger speakers; thus Bringmann (1971: 92); Griffin (1997: 8). This would also be consistent with the view that *Hort.* was composed in the autumn and winter of 46.

[461] One would have thought that the author of *Rep.* knew precisely what the purpose of the embassy was, and the fact that he did not raises questions about the historicity of other information in *Rep.*, as Powell (2013) argues.

[462] The letter is linked to *Luc.* e.g. by Reid¹ p. 338 and Shackleton Bailey (1966: 320), and to *Fin.* by Glucker (1978: 410–11 n. 40).

to accept criticism for excessive grieving. In April Cicero stayed with Atticus at his Nomentanum, and thus there are no letters for that month. In (T9) Cicero again addresses whispering about his prolonged absence from Rome, and shows himself satisfied with the volume of his output and the complexity of the subject matter (the latter is suggestive of *Acad.*). At the end of the letter (not quoted), he comments on reading to do with the Συμβουλευτικόν to Caesar,[463] which is the subject of §2 in (T10), where it is already discussed in terms which convey doubts about the appropriateness and benefit of the endeavour. §1 of (T10) is concerned with a pamphlet Cicero wrote in praise of Cato, which gave rise to Caesar's *Anticato* (extant fragments of the latter, on Cato's alleged fondness for drink, bear out what Cicero says).[464] One can see why Cicero ponders the futility of advisory letters.

In (T12) Cicero announces the completion of two large συντάγματα. These must be *Catul.* and *Luc.*, rather than *Acad.* and *Fin.* or *Hort.* and *Acad.*[465] *Hic* (*duo magna*) is usually taken to mean 'here where I am writing', but might mean 'here' used in pointing out or offering (*OLD* s.v. *hic*², no. 1b), in which case the two items might have been enclosed with the letter. In any event we learn from (T15) that Cicero had sent both books earlier, i.e. either with (T12) or soon after: (T15) was only written a fortnight after (T12). (T15) was accompanied by new proems for *Catul.* and *Luc.*,[466] designed to enhance the credibility of the eponymous characters as lead interlocutors. *Luc.* as it has come down to us has such a proem. As to the meaning of σύνταγμα, the term is used by Cicero of books as part of a treatise, with σύνταξις being used of works made up of συντάγματα.[467]

(T13) comments on Cicero's undiminished activity and, in the part not quoted, on a planned journey from Astura to Lanuvium and then to Tusculum, from where Cicero begins to write on 16 May (*Att.* 12.47 = SB 288).

(T14) is dated a week later. It is frequently quoted in connection with Cicero's philosophical works in general and the final edition of *Acad.* in particular. After a reference to the advisory letter to Caesar, mentioned also in a section of (T13) not quoted here, which Cicero had drafted but apparently not send in the end, and some Roman gossip, §3 contains a well-known corruption which hampers interpretation.[468] Refraining from an attempt to restore the train of thought of the paragraph as a whole, I observe that the phrase *de lingua Latina* is highly unlikely to be a reference to Varro's work, in preparation at the time:[469] if Cicero had known that the work Varro had undertaken to dedicate to him was concerned with the Latin language, he

---

[463] See McConnell (2014: 195–219).
[464] See e.g. Plin., *Epist.* 3.12.2, with Tschiedel (1977); Corbeill (2017).
[465] See Hunt (1998: 11 n. 6).
[466] See the general note on *Luc.* 1–9a on the proems of *Luc.*
[467] See Reid¹ p. 31 n. 1, quoted with approval by Shackleton Bailey (1966: 335); Hunt (1998: 11 n. 6). The term σύνταγμα is used of another work, probably the *Laelius*, in *Att.* 16.3.1 (= SB 413). On σύγγραμμα, see Landolfi (2018). On the difference between a σύνταγμα and a ὑπόμνημα, see also Simpl. *in Arist. Cat.* pp. 18.23–6 and 44.3–4 Kalbfleisch.
[468] The fullest discussion of the passage is Bringmann (2012). See also Shackleton Bailey (1960: 61–2) and (1966: 341–2).
[469] Thus Shackleton Bailey (1966: 341–2); Glucker (1978: 407–12). The most likely alternative is that the phrase relates to the issue of rendering Greek philosophy, notably technical terms, in Latin; see also (T33) for Atticus' interest in this aspect of Cicero's project.

would have characterized Varro's literary production in the final edition of *Acad.* in different terms, a fortiori so if he had known that Varro would be using a Stoic framework. Rather, he is much more likely to have known the *De lingua Latina* only under the description of a 'major work' (cf. T18), i.e. without an inkling of its contents or even its title. As to the statement about his philosophical works being ἀπόγραφα, Cicero is routinely at his most unconvincing when he affects to be modest. The letters which document the composition of *Acad.* contain expressions of satisfaction about the difficulties being mastered in the process and about the intellectual merits of the outcome (T19).[470] So whatever the import of the paragraph as a whole was, it did not end in a candid but considered disclosure of what Cicero's works (or more narrowly *Acad.*) 'really' are.[471]

(T15) begins with requests for works which most likely relate to *Tusc.*, which was at least in preparation, and quite possibly in the process of being composed at the time; see the commentary on *Luc.* 135. The inquiry in the second half of §3 may relate to *Luc.* 89, where the son of C. Sempronius Tuditanus features as an example of mental illness (see also *Att.* 13.30 = SB 303). It is unclear whether 'Torquatus' refers to *Fin.* 1 or *Fin.* 1–2; the sentence *ita confeci quinque libros* περὶ τελῶν *ut Epicurea L. Torquato, Stoica M. Catoni,* περιπατητικά *M. Pisoni darem* in (T23) shows that the latter is at least an option. *Catul.* and *Luc.* are named here for the first time after the generic reference in (T12); see above on when Cicero may have sent them to Atticus, and on the secondary addition of laudatory proems. The *litterae* mentioned here (*eas litteras uolo habeas*) are probably not the two dialogues, but the new proems.[472] That Cicero forwarded the two dialogues and their new proems to Atticus does not mean that he deemed them fit for release, but as we shall see, there was scope for misunderstandings.

In (T16) Cicero mockingly complains to Atticus that he was not included when Tyrannio read from his work on prosody, then lauds Atticus for his intellectual interests, only to end by saying that prosody is a trifling subject compared to the subject of the highest good, sc. with which he is preoccupied inter alia.

(T17) probably means that after copying (cf. T15) the 'Torquatus' was erroneously sent to Tusculum where Cicero was rather than to Atticus as planned.

(T18)–(T21) are the key texts for the conception of the different editions of *Acad.*, including an intermediate one, soon superseded, which is, however, only mentioned in (T21), i.e. out of strictly chronological sequence.[473] In (T18) Cicero makes reference to a letter of Atticus which mentioned a request of Varro's to be included in a work of Cicero's. (A similar request had been made nine years earlier; cf. *Att.* 4.16.2 = SB 89.) When Cicero says that his speeches and earlier dialogues, which featured interlocutors of an older generation, afforded no opportunity to 'weave in' (*intexere*) Varro, this seems to preclude that the request was understood to be for a mere dedication or reference to Varro. (In T21 Cicero effectively asks how precisely Atticus

---

[470] Cf. also the proem of *Fin.* 1.
[471] See also Barnes (1997: 66–7).
[472] Thus Shackleton Bailey (1966: 351).
[473] Glucker (1978: 422) proposed to change the relative chronology of (T18) and (T21), but I think it is more plausible that Cicero submits a fuller account with delay.

learnt of Varro's wish, which might imply that he suspected that the request was Atticus' idea.)[474] Cicero proceeds to cite a reason why there is no urgency to accommodate Varro—he promised the dedication of a serious work two years ago,[475] but had not acted on it—and observes as well that the dedication of *Fin.* has been promised to Brutus. Thus he proposes to transfer the Ἀκαδημική (sc. σύνταξις) to Varro, which would also be apt because Varro approves of *Antiochia*; this is loosely put of course, since the Antiochian position is only one side in the dialogue. Cicero seeks a reaction to this proposal from Atticus.

In (T19), written just one day after (T18), Cicero announces that he has made the change considered in (T18), but (T21) shows that this is not the whole story. When Cicero claims that he has transferred the 'entire Academy' from most noble men to 'our friend Varro', the plural *ab hominibus nobilissimis* implies that Antiochus was represented by two main speakers in the first edition, Lucullus in *Luc.* as we know and Hortensius in the *Catul.* (contrast the slightly different formulation in T21). This is significant because the backward references to *Catul.* in *Luc.* are not very informative on the role of Hortensius, and some reconstructions assume that Hortensius did not offer an extended speech at all.[476] The change from the first to the final edition also involved a change of format from two to four books. One might wonder if the manner in which information on the intermediate edition is supplied later would make it possible that it already had the four-book layout; *eosdem illos sermones ad Catonem Brutumque transtuli* in (T21) seems to tell against it, if only ex silentio. The final edition is characterized as more substantial, although Cicero says he removed material, too; so the additions outweighed the omissions.[477] The pride expressed at the end of §1 is at variance with the claim that *Acad.*, or *Acad.* and *Fin.*, are mere ἀπόγραφα (T14). As indicated, Cicero's question about how Atticus learnt of Varro's wish does convey uncertainty about whether the request was really Varro's and perhaps also uneasiness about the possibility of meeting his 'requirements' even if it was clear what they are. Varro's jealousy of someone must have been mentioned by Atticus, and Brutus is indeed the only obvious candidate—unless Varro was misinformed about characters featuring in works which were in production at the time. (T20) continues the theme of hesitation about whether *Acad.* as now conceived should be sent to Varro. Atticus, Cicero says, is now a stakeholder since he has become a character (see also T25). If *nomina iam facta sunt* was a transactional joke,[478] it would hint that a function of the dedication would be to extract the promised dedication of a Varronian work in return (a point also made in somewhat clunking fashion in the 'dedicatory letter', T29).

(T21) then provides the chronology of the intermediate edition and shows that what had been given so far was a streamlined account. Cicero did not execute the changes from first to final edition in a single day. His doubts about the suitability of Catulus, Lucullus, and Hortensius as interlocutors, not allayed by the secondary addition of

---

[474] Suggested by Rösch-Binde (1997: 177).
[475] The general terms in which the work Varro promised is described here rather supports the notion that Cicero had at this stage no knowledge of its likely contents.
[476] See section 9.2.
[477] See e.g. my t. 51 (= Aug., *Contra Acad.* 3.7.15–16).
[478] See Shackleton Bailey (1966: 368).

laudatory proems, led him to replace the three with Cato and Brutus.[479] The sequence of the names does not seem to reflect the structure of either edition; one consideration which could have given rise to the order of the five names would be date of birth in descending order, but this may be coincidental. Cicero does not tell us how exactly the re-allocation of roles worked, but what is said here is compatible with assuming that Brutus took on Hortensius' material in *Catul.*, Cato Lucullus' speech in *Luc.*, and Cicero Catulus'.[480] Brutus would be a very credible speaker for the historical survey given to Varro in *Ac.* 1, the almost entirely Stoic speech delivered by Lucullus would not sound peculiar if delivered by an actual Stoic, and having one Academic speaker instead of two was a sensible rationalization. If this was correct, the main structural differences which set the first and final edition of *Acad.* apart were actually implemented in the intermediate edition already. At any rate, when this intermediate edition had been set down, Atticus' letter about Varro's request arrived, and Cicero could think of nobody who would more credibly represent Antiochus' thought. Then hesitation sets in again and Cicero asks if a dedication to Varro and of this work in particular was a good idea. (T22) reiterates these questions: how Atticus became aware of the fact that Varro was hoping for something from Cicero (the formulation, *eum desiderare a me*, is studiedly vague and still leaves it unclear what precisely the request was), and who Varro was jealous of (cf. T19). That Varro, 'although he wrote much', had never 'challenged' (*lacessisset*) Cicero to do something must mean that he had not actually made a dedication himself, not that he did not ask Cicero directly.[481]

In (T23) Cicero replies to a consideration which Atticus had raised, that Cicero might appear φιλένδοξος to Varro if he sent him *Acad.*, or possibly might appear so to everyone if he was seen to send it. The Greek term is a hapax, and its import is not clear. Atticus' point may have been that Varro's and Cicero's relationship was not cordial enough to justify a public dedication, and that this might give rise to a perception that he made the dedication not out of personal devotion but to associate himself with the renowned scholar.[482] Cicero then retraces how he came to put together the final edition when prompted by Atticus against the background of his general thinking on the subject of the dialogue form (eliding the intermediate edition again). The possibility of replacing himself with Cotta, the Clitomachean speaker of *N.D.*, is rejected because in that case Cicero would have had to be a silent character (as he almost is in *N.D.*).[483] This is fine when the interlocutors belong to an earlier

---

[479] (T15), mentioning the new proems for *Catul.* and *Luc.*, dates from 29 May. On 21–2 June Cicero left Tusculum and went to Arpinum, where he made the change to Brutus and Cato 'as soon as he arrived at the villa' (T21). On 24 June he reports that he made the changes necessary for the final edition (T19). So the life-span of the intermediate edition was only two or three days, but Cicero may have been toying with the idea of removing Hortensius, Catulus, and Lucullus since the end of May. See Griffin (1997: 15 and 20); Rösch-Binde (1997: 182–3).

[480] What happened to Catulus' contribution is left somewhat unclear by only Cato and Brutus being named, but assuming that a dogmatist speaker was temporarily entrusted with Academic material does not seem an option.

[481] See the general note on *Ac.* 1.1–8 on Cicero's and Varro's relationship.

[482] This is a version of the second of the options considered by Shackleton Bailey (1966: 369): 'Does it = φιλόδοξος, "vain", or (as suits the context here) "fond of notabilities (ἔνδοξοι)"?'. The adjective ἔνδοξος in φιλένδοξος is unlikely to mean 'of high social status' (rather than 'of high renown'), because Varro was a knight like Cicero.

[483] On Cotta as a second Clitomachean character created by Cicero (apart from the character 'Cicero') see section 8, p. clvi.

generation alive when Cicero was a young man, but unacceptable when the characters are contemporary. Cicero reiterates how qualified, considerations of appropriateness aside, Varro is as a representative of Antiochus. Nor could he take offence over being 'defeated' in the dialogue, since his arguments are persuasive in themselves and further enhanced by Cicero's style. The letter ends again with the question if the work should be passed on to Varro. Cicero says he can see a case against, having just made the case for it.

At the beginning of (T24) and in §2 of the same letter Cicero expresses irritation that parts of *Fin.* had reached third parties before Brutus had been presented with his copy, and before Cicero considered it complete; see also §3 of (T25). At the end of §1 Cicero makes it clear that he does not want the same to happen to *Acad.* This is of interest for my purposes because it suggests a route by which *Luc.* has come down to us—as an unauthorized release, or a release whose authorization Cicero withdrew too late.[484] In line with the gist of (T23) Cicero is keen on presenting *Acad.* to Varro, whereas in (T25) he is hesitant again and keen to know Atticus' views.

Strikingly, (T26) mentions an unannounced and inconvenient visit of Varro's at Tusculum around 8 July (*Att.* 13.33a = SB 330).[485] No connection with the ongoing discussions about the dedication is made, but the silence is highlighted by Cicero's 'speak of the devil' comment (*lupus in fabula*).

(T27) begins a new phase in Cicero's agonizing over the dedication of *Acad.*: he wants to pass responsibility for not just the actual handover but also the dedication as a whole to Atticus. The latter apparently did not jump with alacrity at this notion (see T28) and must have asked what Cicero wanted him to do. Cicero restates his anxieties, but professes to be relaxed (*in alteram aurem*) since Atticus is assuming responsibility (*tu suscipis*).[486] That Atticus might not present Varro with *Acad.* is apparently only a theoretical possibility from Cicero's point of view at this point.

(T29) is the so-called 'dedicatory letter' which no doubt accompanied the personal copy of *Acad.* which was presented to Varro. The very end of the letter tells against publication with *Acad.*, though,[487] and it is certainly transmitted with the *Fam.* collection. Its tone is stilted; Cicero says in (T30) how much trouble he took over it and that he dictated it syllable by syllable (sc. to ensure that there was not a wrong word in it). Cicero likens the four books of *Acad.* to a group of people engaging in a *flagitatio*, a small public demonstration designed to pressure and shame a debtor or borrower into the return of a sum of money or an item lent.[488] The dedication of a work of Varro's, promised two years earlier, is what Cicero thereby wants to extract. To the modern reader the *flagitatio* motif seems somewhat inelegant, but it is conceivable that Varro had written about the custom in one of his antiquarian works.[489] Academia

---

[484] Thus also Hunt (1998: 13). As noted above, our version of *Luc.* is the second one, which includes the expanded proem on Lucullus.
[485] Not included by Plasberg¹ and Plasberg², and Griffin (1997), but see Rösch-Binde (1997: 205–6).
[486] On the meaning of διφθέραι, see Shackleton Bailey (1966: 379).
[487] *Pace* Plasberg² p. xi n. 3.
[488] Cf. also *Q.fr.* 2.10.1 (= SB 14) with Marshall (1968), and 2.11 (= SB 15) with Lintott (1967); *Dom.* 14–15; Catul. 42; and Usener (1901).
[489] Cf. Varro, *L.L.* 5.153, with Richlin (2017: 174).

adulescentior is a reference to the 'new', sceptical Academy; for the emergence of the notion of a New Academy and related divisions of the Academy generally see on *Ac.* 1.18. With the remark that Varro's slow progress over the promised work was due to the care he applied cf. *Ac.* 1.3: *audiui enim e Libone…non te ea intermittere sed accuratius tractare nec de manibus umquam deponere* (and the less understanding remarks in T18). The statement that Varro has been given the Antiochian part and Cicero the Philonian gives out nothing for the question of which particular Academic position Philo took when Cicero first met him, or which position Cicero took to be his primary one, leaving the aberration of the Roman Books aside (see section 8, p. clv);[490] rather, it signals only quite generally that Cicero speaks for the sceptical Academy. Cicero does not go so far as to credit Varro with being an Antiochian as opposed to being sympathetic to Antiochus' stance and approach, and Cicero candidly says that the subjects covered in *Acad.* were never the subject of conversation between him and Varro. The remarks about shared interests near the end of the letter pointedly revisit the subjects discussed in the correspondence of 46 BC (*Fam.* 9.1–7 = SB 175–81).

(T30) was written when Atticus had received (T29) to be passed on, but when the presentation had not yet been made, and Cicero's vacillations continue. Atticus had signalled concern that he should pass on *Acad.* alongside (T29) 'at his own risk', and Cicero simultaneously asks for remaining worries to be disclosed now and expresses his confidence in the quality of the work and in Varro's openness to receiving it. Cicero had shown himself uncertain about Varro's wishes earlier as we saw, and thus one might wonder if Varro's visit, even if the possible dedication was not discussed, had given Cicero a sense of how Varro would feel about it, but the letter continues *in utramque partem*: on the one hand Varro is like Achilles prone to take offence at nothing, e.g. because he feels, unreasonably, that Cicero has given himself more space in the dialogue (and Cicero pictures Varro's expression which would go with the rebuke), on the other Atticus and he have had Varro's copy expensively produced (a reason for not letting the expense be in vain). He briefly contemplates one more editorial change, which would give Brutus Varro's role; this is apparently not the intermediate edition envisaged earlier, where the Antiochian part was to be split between Cato and Brutus.[491] After a self-conscious comment on his indecisiveness (which resembles that of the sceptical Academy) he asks what Varro thought of the dedicatory letter (T29); the question is the reason for the latter's relative position in my sequence of testimonia. (T31), written after Atticus had indicated that he will present the work, conveys Cicero's anticipation and sounds almost taunting at the same time (*hui, si scias quanto periculo tuo*).[492] (T32) finally reveals that the presentation to Varro has been made by Atticus.[493]

The silence in the correspondence regarding Varro's reaction is anticlimactic. A month later *Acad.* features one more time (T33). Varro's reaction is not touched

---

[490] *Pace* Griffin (1997: 12).

[491] Such a change would of course not just require a change of names: the preface of *Ac.* 1 is very much tailored to Varro as an individual, and the digression on writing philosophy in Latin in 1.25 is connected with it. See also on Aug., *Contra Acad.* 3.7.15–16 (t. 51).

[492] On the exclamation *hui*, see Ricottilli (2003: 120–1).

[493] Rösch-Binde (1997: 224) speculates about the precise date.

on, but evidently there was no Achillean μῆνις. At some point between the handover of *Acad.* and this letter Cicero was persuaded by Atticus to replace the term *sustinere* for 'to withhold assent', i.e. suspend judgement, with *inhibere*. There are several instances of *sustinere* in this sense in *Luc.*, used elliptically or with an object,[494] while there is none of *inhibere*. *Inhibere* is a nautical term, which Cicero had thought was used in the imperative to order the crew to stop rowing when a ship approaches the jetty; in fact, as he realized the previous day while observing a docking manoeuvre, the crew do not stop rowing and hold still but perform a countermovement, intended to further slow the ship right before it makes contact with the jetty.[495] This countermovement makes *inhibere* unsuitable to convey the suspension of judgement, which is pointedly not the positive or active rejection of an impression, but just a standing-back, a non-acceptance of it. At some point during the month preceding the composition of (T33), Atticus or Cicero himself must have invited Varro to change instances of *sustinere* to *inhibere*—Cicero suggests that Varro might have made the change (*si forte mutauit*), so *inhibere* cannot have been in the version formally presented—,[496] and Cicero now asks Atticus to write to Varro to change the text back if indeed he implemented the changes in the first place.[497]

(T34)—(T40) and (T42) show how Cicero fitted *Acad.* into his larger programme of philosophical writings, but see the commentary on (T34), which is chronologically out of sequence. (T41) is discussed on p. 275.

9.2 Ciceronian Editions of *Acad.* and Their Reconstruction

Acad. was first composed as an edition in two books (*Catul.* and *Luc.*, of which the latter is extant), then recast with a new set of speakers (probably in two books as well), and then recast again as an edition in four books, of which we have the first part of the first book, *Ac.* 1. Our information on all three editions comes from the extant parts (*Luc.* and *Ac.* 1), Cicero's letters, mostly to Atticus, written during the later part of the creation of *Acad.*, the backward references to *Catul.* in *Luc.*, and the indirect tradition of the final edition.[498] In this section I outline how I would reconstruct the lost parts.[499]

---

[494] See *Luc.* 48, 53, 68, 94, 98, 104, 107, 108.

[495] The necessity of the countermovement is implicitly recognized in *De orat.* 1.153: *Vt concitato nauigio, cum remiges inhibuerunt, retinet tamen ipsa nauis motum et cursum.*

[496] Bringmann (2013: 35) argues that Atticus must have made the suggestion during his stay at Tusculum on 18 or 19 May, but this is too early, given that Varro is asked to reverse changes he had been invited to make earlier.

[497] It is usually assumed, e.g. by Shackleton Bailey (1966: 394), that the suggested change relates only to the *Ac.* 4 counterpart of *Luc.* 94 (see ad loc.), where Cicero compares the suspension of judgement adopted by a respondent facing a series of soritical questions to a charioteer stopping his chariot before a precipice (*ego enim, ut agitator callidus, prius quam ad finem ueniam equos sustinebo*). Lucilius (l. 1305 Marx) is quoted in (T33) to bestow authority on *sustinere*. (*Inhibere equos* is idiomatic Latin, too.) However, whether assent amounts to active resistance is clearly a general issue.

[498] The Latin text of the letters, the backward references to *Catul.* in *Luc.*, and of the indirect tradition is given in the Oxford Classical Text. Translations and commentary are included in the present volume; on the letters, see section 9.1 above.

[499] My views on the subject are *derived* from *Luc./Ac.* 1 and the letters; they *determine* the order of some of the fragments and testimonia.

On a general level, much is clear about how the first edition of *Acad.* relates to the final one, including—in my view—some issues which have proved contentious unnecessarily.⁵⁰⁰ This means that the weight of the evidence points to one particular account of that relationship, to be described in the next paragraph, and the salient question is whether there is anything in the evidence which suggests a modification of this account.

From fragments and testimonia of *Ac.* 3 and *Ac.* 4 it is plain that *Luc.* was recast as these two books, with Lucullus' Antiochian speech (*Luc.* 11–62) becoming a speech of Varro's in *Ac.* 3, and Cicero's Academic speech of *Luc.* 64–147 being placed in *Ac.* 4. Cicero added, took away, and modified material locally, without rewriting the material extant in *Luc.* systematically. Thus it is a natural assumption, to be modified only if the evidence requires it, that the *Catulus* was recast as *Ac.* 1 and 2 on the same pattern. *Ac.* 1 begins (after a preface) with a speech presenting a historical account of the history of philosophy from an Antiochian point of view, with Varro as speaker, explaining his conception of the Old Academy as encompassing Old Academic (in the narrow sense), Peripatetic, and Stoic thought. Given that even on the Academic view Arcesilaus and his Academic successors reacted to dogmatic philosophy, notably Stoic innovations in the field of epistemology,⁵⁰¹ that it would be exceedingly difficult to give an account of Academic scepticism and its overall rationale without providing a dogmatic reference point first, and that the pattern 'dogmatic exposition followed by sceptical reply' is used elsewhere in Cicero's dialogues to good effect, notably in *Fin.* which Cicero worked on overlappingly with *Acad.*,⁵⁰² the initial assumption ought to be that the first substantial speech in *Catul.* was an exposition of Old Academic thought roughly corresponding to Varro's speech. We know that three main speakers featured in *Catul.*: Catulus the son, Cicero, and Hortensius (Lucullus was present but restricted to one or more short contributions).⁵⁰³ Of them the only credible presenter of Varro's material in *Ac.* 1 is Hortensius, since he is cast as an Antiochian in *Luc.* 10 (cf. 148), where he says that 'yesterday' he said more than he intended to; by contrast, to have Catulus, i.e. an Academic speaker, rather than Hortensius present the Antiochian point of view would be very peculiar indeed.⁵⁰⁴ In addition, based on *Luc.* 28 we assume that Hortensius also made at least one

---

⁵⁰⁰ Discussions of the likely structure of *Catul.* include Goerenz (1810.ii: xiii–xxxviii); Krische (1845); Reid¹ pp. 39–46; Lörcher (1911: 240–95); Plasberg² pp. xii–iii; Plezia (1936); Philippson (1939: 1127–34); Emonds (1941: 265–77); Glucker (1978: 406–20); Alleemudder pp. 60–3; Lévy (1992: 180–201); Görler (1994: 918–20 and 945–7); Gigon pp. 371–3; Griffin (1997); Mansfeld (1997); Haltenhoff pp. 79–81; Rösch-Binde (1998: 350–9); Lévy (1999).

⁵⁰¹ Cf. *Ac.* 1.44:...*cum Zenone...ut accepimus Arcesilas sibi omne certamen instituit*...; *Luc.* 77–8. That Academic scepticism is reactive in this sense is compatible with a (historically accurate or manufactured) assumption that there existed sceptical leanings in the Academy prior to Arcesilaus.

⁵⁰² On this point, see Mansfeld (1997: 66); cf. Griffin (1997: 18–20) on other compositional principles adhered to in Cicero's dialogues.

⁵⁰³ On Catulus, see *Luc.* 11, 12, 18; on Cicero, *Luc.* 13, 22, 79; on Hortensius, *Luc.* 10; on Lucullus, *Luc.* 9 (he was present), 10 (the promise of a speech made good in *Luc.*).

⁵⁰⁴ When Cicero expresses dissatisfaction with the initial set of speakers in his correspondence with *Att.*, it is over the general expertise of the historical individuals and hence their credibility as characters (*Att.* 13.16.1–2 = SB 323 = T21). The intermediate edition had an Antiochian speaker, too, namely Brutus (ibid.); on Brutus as an Antiochian, see Sedley (1997a); Osorio (2021).

intervention outside of his speech.[505] As for Cicero's speech, a large part of it was devoted to arguments against the senses, as Cicero says in *Luc.* 79 (cf. *Luc.* 42). These arguments cannot just have been set forth by themselves but must have been accompanied by an indication of what lesson is to be learnt from conflicting appearances. In addition, we learn that Cicero translated the term ἔννοιαι as *notitiae* (*Luc.* 22), but there is no indication of the context in which the rendering was proposed.[506] *Luc.* 13 (cf. 72) shows that Cicero also spoke about the *ueteres physici*, i.e. philosophers earlier than Socrates.[507] A speech of this kind would naturally follow upon another speech setting out the broader Academic position, the conception of the history of philosophy in general (i.e. not just on the *ueteres physici*) which underpins it, the different Academic stances and their evolution (see on *Luc.* 59b), and an account of the πιθανόν.[508] The latter kind of speech follows Varro's in *Ac.* 1 (but is cut short in 1.46 at the moment when Carneades comes into view),[509] is delivered by Cicero, and must correspond to one given to Catulus, who replied to Hortensius in the *Catulus*. This would give Catulus a role weighty enough to warrant the naming of the dialogue after him, who was also exalted in a secondarily composed proem corresponding to the one at the beginning of *Luc.* (*Att.* 13.32.2-3 = SB 305 = T15), and who may have started off proceedings with an account of Philo's period in Rome, the controversy of the Roman Books, and his father's challenge to, or criticism of, Philo over the latter.[510] Catulus and Cicero, while both speaking for the Academic side, differed from one another in that Catulus adopted a position of mitigated scepticism, following his father in this respect, while Cicero adopted the Clitomachean position, as he already did in *Hort.*[511] We are not explicitly told if the intermediate edition (for which see

---

[505] Those who assume that Hortensius was not the first speaker of *Catul.* might try and derive support from their view from *Luc.* 28, on the grounds that *postulabat* (ibid.) suggests that Hortensius reacted to somebody else's claim. While I agree that Hortensius was probably reacting to someone else when he made the point, I also observe that in *Ac.* 1.40-2 there would not be a natural place for such a remark, because Varro introduces the concepts 'impression', 'assent', and κατάληψις newly, and the Hortensian point requires more context. This suggests that its natural place is later in the relative chronology of the debate. Scholars disagree on whether Hortensius' demand shows common sense or exhibits philosophical sophistication not in keeping with the character (see ad loc.).

[506] The term *notitiae* does not feature in the extant part of *Ac.* 1, but *notiones* occurs in *Ac.* 1.32 and 1.42 (where 'notions' are said to arise from apprehension), where Varro is the speaker. Those who think that in *Catul.* Cicero presented the material given to Varro in *Ac.* 1 will derive encouragement from this; see n. 518 below on *Ac.* 1.46 *exposui* vs *exposuisti*.

[507] Note the second-person plural addresses in §13 and in §14, but a personal address to Cicero in §13.

[508] Mansfeld (1997: 55) rejects that 'either of the two Catuli defended the doctrine of the "probable".'

[509] *Luc.* 32-6 presupposes a treatment of the πιθανόν in *Catul.*, in that it alludes somewhat dismissively (see on §36: *ex circumspectione aliqua*) but all too briefly to testing procedures for *probabilia* which are described in elaborate detail by Sextus (*M.* 7.166-89). In *Luc.* 98-9 Cicero introduces further material on *probabilia* which suggests that the source material at his disposal was rather like Sextus' and not severely truncated.

[510] This would correspond to the Alexandrian episode in *Luc.* 11-12, which furnishes a personal connection of Lucullus' with Antiochus and thus creates credibility for the character Lucullus. Note that the speaker of *Luc.* 11-12 is Lucullus, but that his speech properly starts in §13; a similar brief section might have been given to Catulus, to precede Hortensius' longer speech. According to *Luc.* 18, the elder Catulus accused Philo of lying (in his Roman Books) rather than of changing his mind, which suggests that he acquired his outlook of mitigated scepticism from an Academic other than Philo; if so, these historical connections might have been explained early in *Catul.*

[511] For Catulus the crucial passage is *Luc.* 148, which has, however, given rise to alternative interpretations; see below and ad loc. For Cicero the character as a Clitomachean, see esp. *Luc.* 65-7. For fragments from the *Hortensius* which speak to Cicero's position in that dialogue, see section 9.5.

Att. 13.16.1–2 = SB 323 = T21), in which Brutus and Cato were introduced, had two books like the first or four books like the final edition,[512] and we are not provided with details on the re-allocation of roles, but given that Brutus was an Antiochian, that Lucullus' speech in *Luc.* is largely concerned with epistemology on which Antiochus agreed with the Stoics, and that Cicero took over Catulus' role in addition to his own in the final edition, the most natural interpretation of the evidence would be that Brutus assumed Hortensius' role, that Cato assumed Lucullus' role, and that it was already the intermediate and not only the final edition which reduced the number of Academic speakers from one to two and thus expanded Cicero's role.[513]

If one leaves aside mere statements of opinion, a number of alternative views on aspects of the picture just laid out have been defended. These alternative views differ by assuming different structural and compositional features of the missing parts of *Acad.*, or by assuming different meta-philosophical attitudes for one or more interlocutors than I have assumed. I do not aim for completeness or appropriate classification of all views expressed on the subject.

Mansfeld (1997) is the most detailed attempt to date at a reconstruction of the *Catulus*. That reconstruction, like mine, assumes that Catulus the son used Philo's Roman Books as an entry point for the discussion, that Hortensius gave the first longer speech, an account of Antiochian philosophy, followed by Catulus and Cicero. It further assumes that both Catulus and Cicero spoke as Academic sceptics. It differs from my account above by assuming that Catulus the son did not argue from a position of mitigated scepticism and instead presented the Roman Books view with a degree of endorsement, and that he criticized Antiochian philosophy as presented by Hortensius from a Roman Books perspective.[514] The argument mounted in support is intricate, full of acute observations on details of the Latin text, and thus difficult to do justice to in a summary, but it does seem fair to say that it rests on two interpretative decisions in particular: (i) that it would be inappropriate for Catulus the son to do no more than rehearse the view of his father; (ii) that Catulus' statement in *Luc.* 148 that, having heard the speeches by Lucullus and Cicero, he would 'return' to the view of his father, must imply a return from the position of the Roman Books, which Catulus would have embraced at least to such a degree that he could 'return' from it to a different view. On (i), I disagree that adopting the viewpoint of the distinguished father would be a mark against Catulus the son: the latter following the former on such an issue is surely deeply unproblematic in a Roman context, a fortiori if the

---

[512] *Eosdem illos* sermones ad Catonem Brutumque transtuli in *Att.* 13.16.1–2 (= SB 323 = T21) perhaps discourages the assumption that already the intermediate edition had four books.

[513] The published view which comes closest to mine is that of Lévy, developed in Lévy (1999) on the structure of *Catul.*, expanding on Lévy (1992: 180–201), and Lévy (1992: 191) on the likely shape of the intermediate edition. A survey of earlier views on the intermediate edition is in Griffin (1997: 15–16, 20–7), who opts for a different pattern of rearrangement. That Antiochus' position in the field of epistemology was probably entirely Stoic is argued by Brittain (2012). On the possible setting of the intermediate edition, see Griffin (1997: 24): Brutus was a neighbour of Cicero's at Cumae (*Brut.* 300), and 'Cato, after the death of Lucullus in 56 or 55, became a trustee of his property for his son.'

[514] Mansfeld further assumes that the Roman Books themselves were directed at Antiochus, so that *Catul.* reproduced the set-up of the Roman Books in that respect (rather than, say, presented previously differently configured material in this way).

younger Catulus had presented his adoption of the view as a reasoned choice and if I am right in thinking that Philo never was a mitigated sceptic himself—then the outlook becomes a family trait.[515] On (ii), I do not believe that *ad patris reuoluor sententiam* in *Luc.* 148 suggests that in *Catul.* Catulus the younger adopted the position of the Roman Books (sc. with a sufficient degree of endorsement to warrant speaking in terms of a return from it to the position of his father). It would be in keeping with the tone of the interlude in §§63–4 (where Catulus comments on the effect Lucullus' speech might have had on Cicero) if Catulus affected to have been swayed by both Lucullus' and Cicero's speeches, in each case while they were being delivered, due to a suspension of disbelief induced by the sheer quality of the 'performances',[516] but returned now to his original position. Consider also that the Roman Books are dismissed by all in *Luc.*; as such, they are not in need of a character promoting them in *Catul.*, and making the younger Catulus defend them would border on besmirching his memory. Mansfeld (1997: 58–60) also argues that in *Luc.* 12 (...*is* [i.e. Philo] *qui ista quae sunt heri defensa negat Academicos omnino dicere*) the reference of *quae sunt heri defensa* is to Hortensius' Antiochian speech, the first of *Catul.* on Mansfeld's view, against which Catulus argued from the perspective of the Roman Books. Yet the term *Academicus* also occurs earlier in *Luc.* 12 and before that in *Luc.* 11, in both cases in the sense of 'sceptical Academic'. Thus on the most natural reading it has this meaning in the contentious sentence, too, and what 'was defended yesterday' is the Academic claim of ἀκαταληψία, viz. that nothing can be known.[517]

An influential earlier reconstruction is Reid[1] pp. 39–46. He assumed that some kind of account of Philo's lectures on the Roman Books must have provided an entry point for the discussion as well as established credentials for Catulus the son, but that the first speech was then delivered by Catulus, who rejected the thesis of the Roman Books and instead argued that a satisfactory account of knowledge was provided by the Carneadean πιθανόν as interpreted by mitigated sceptics. To this Hortensius then responded, arguing that a satisfactory account had already been achieved by the *ueteres* and was misguidedly abandoned by Arcesilaus and Carneades. A speech by Cicero, mostly against the senses, followed. This means that in terms of subjects presumed to have been covered in the three speeches, there is substantial overlap between Reid's reconstruction and my own, but I do not believe that an intelligible explanation of the philosophical and historical theses of the Roman Books would have been possible without a preceding speech like Varro's in *Ac.* 1 as reference point, nor do I find Reid's suggestion plausible that Catulus argued that 'the Carneadean theory of the *pithanon*' provided 'a satisfactory basis for *episteme*' (p. 43), although he may well have argued, as Cicero does from a Clitomachean standpoint e.g. in *Luc.* 103, that human beings are not epistemically in a position akin to blindness if one adopts a position of mitigated scepticism. Reid[1] p. 43 observes perceptively that

---

[515] Cf. on *Luc.* 146, where the Cicero character argues that scepticism has always been encoded in Roman thought.
[516] This option is considered by Mansfeld (1997: 56 n. 26).
[517] For Philo's Roman Books view, which allowed for a non-Stoic conception of κατάληψις, see on *Luc.* 18.

'those parts of Lucullus' speech which deal with the constructive part of Academicism seem to be intended for Catulus', whereas 'all the counter arguments of Lucullus which concern the destructive side of Academic teaching appear to be distinctly aimed at Cicero', which would fit with the fact that the speech which begins in *Ac.* 1.44 was Catulus' in *Catul.*, and that Cicero mostly argued 'against the senses' (*Luc.* 79). Plasberg² pp. xii–xiii offers a brief reconstruction of *Catul.*, largely in agreement with Reid's regarding the order of the speeches and the topics featuring in each, but does not pronounce on the question of how exactly Catulus would engage with the thesis of the Roman Books.

Philippson (1939: 1131–2) assumes that Varro's and Cicero's speech in *Ac.* 1 corresponded to one long speech of Cicero's in *Catul.*,[518] which was followed by a speech of Catulus' on 'Karneades' reine Lehre', a speech of Hortensius' arguing for the truth of the deliverances of the senses also featuring the remark mentioned in *Luc.* 28, followed by a speech of Cicero's against the senses, and a promise by Lucullus to rehearse what he had heard Antiochus say against Carneades—a reconstruction which is significantly underdetermined by the evidence and would, inter alia, have an Academic introduce Antiochian material.

Glucker (1978: 419–20) maps his reconstruction of Antiochus' dialogue *Sosus* onto one of the first and of the final edition of *Acad.* For *Catul.* he assumes that the dialogue began with a speech containing the material given to Varro in *Ac.* 1, presented by Lucullus, followed by a speech of Cicero 'expounding Philo's Roman view of the history of the one indivisible Academy, and based on the Roman Books' and a speech by Catulus, 'reproving Philo for his innovations and refuting Antiochus from a more traditional Academic position' (thus Glucker's characterization of a speech by Sosus in the *Sosus*, which he assumes to be the source of Catulus' speech). I note that the extant evidence does not suggest that Lucullus had an extended speaking role in *Catul.*, and wonder (again) how the Roman Books view could have been characterized effectively without the Clitomachean and mitigated positions as background.

Characters in the three editions of *Acad.*

First edition	Second edition	Third edition
Hortensius	Brutus	Varro
Lucullus	Cato	Varro
Catulus	Cicero	Cicero
Cicero	Cicero	Cicero

---

[518] One consideration cited in favour of the prima facie baffling view that Cicero should have introduced (a version of) the Antiochian material given to Varro in *Ac.* 1 is the reading *exposui* in *Ac.* 1.46. However, while I agree that *exposui* cannot be correct, I take the genesis of the corruption to be different; see ad loc.

Structure of the first and third editions of *Acad.* (extant parts in bold)

First edition: *Catul.* and *Luc.*

Catulus:
preface about Catulus the father
(Possibly brief remarks by Catulus the son, cf. *Luc.* 11–12)
Hortensius' speech
Catulus the son's speech
Cicero's speech

Lucullus:
account of the Alexandrian episode
Lucullus' speech
Cicero's speech

Final edition: *Academici Libri* (four bks)

Ac. 1:
preface about Varro not writing philosophy
Varro's first speech
first speech of Cicero's (two §§ of it)
Ac. 2:
second speech of Cicero's
Ac. 3:
proem, reused in *De gloria* by mistake (see T41)
Varro's second speech
Ac. 4:
Cicero's third speech

9.3 Sources

I shall begin with an account of the likely sources of *Luc.* and *Ac.* 1, followed by a review of earlier scholarship on the subject. It is assumed to be uncontroversial that Lucullus' and Cicero's speeches in *Luc.* are Antiochian and Academic in outlook respectively, that they draw on sources in some way (though not mechanically so that they could be viewed as translations or paraphrases except in particular places, and not necessarily on continuous single sources), and that Varro's speech and the extant beginning of Cicero's speech in *Ac.* 1 are also Antiochian and Academic in outlook respectively.[519]

9.3.1 *Luc.*

Considerations which should enter into any account include: (i) Lucullus' speech, i.e. the sections which expound doctrine and which rebut counterarguments, is orthodox Stoic and of Stoic habitus.[520] By 'of Stoic habitus' I mean that Lucullus does not just argue for Stoic positions, but does so in a manner which assumes Stoic defensive postures, rather than to defend Stoic views from the vantage point of a 'reformed' Academic sceptic.[521] (ii) Lucullus' speech is directed at a form of Clitomacheanism

---

[519] Surveys of the evidence for known publications of Philo and Antiochus are provided by Görler (1994: 918–20 and 945–7); however, except for Antiochus' *Sosus*, part of which may lie behind Varro's speech in *Ac.* 1, there are no good grounds for identifying the sources of *Acad.* with known works of either philosopher.

[520] See Brittain (2012).

[521] See passages where Lucullus claims the Academics blind human beings through a stance they adopt (e.g. *Luc.* 103), an allegation that can only begin to make sense if one defines, as the Stoics did, perception as assent to a cataleptic impression (*Luc.* 108). A defence of the cataleptic impression from the vantage point of a reformed Academic would e.g. signal why ἀπαραλλαξία-considerations were in the end found to

which envisages 'approval' (cf. *Luc.* 104–105a) as a non-dialectical option as well as, secondarily, at mitigated scepticism.⁵²² (iii) Lucullus does not make a particular effort to differentiate between counterarguments to either Academic position; rather, he appears intent to want to engage with Academic scepticism in its two significant varieties at the same time. (iv) Cicero's speech is a carefully constructed, relevant, point-by-point reply to Lucullus.⁵²³ (v) The character Cicero tries to refute Lucullus from his own Clitomachean position.⁵²⁴ (vi) His Clitomacheanism is assertive, in that he does not withdraw to a position of pure ad hominem argumentation when replying on the core argument (see on *Luc.* 43–4 and 111), and to the extent that his stance is pessimistic about the epistemic situation of human beings, he presents this as a function of Old Academic/Stoic extremism.⁵²⁵ (vii) There are passages whose tone would be appropriate in a rebuke of Antiochus' issued by Philo, but out of keeping with Cicero the character addressing Lucullus the character;⁵²⁶ it is these passages in particular which stand in the way of a dismissal of the notion that the two speeches closely follow sources at least in places. (viii) In Cicero's speech Clitomachus is quoted/translated directly (*Luc.* 98–9, 103–4), against Cicero's usual practice; this direct quotation may be secondary, i.e. inherited from a source, or not. (ix) The Roman Books are pointedly not included by either side as a substantial subject for discussion, which, however, need not preclude the possibility of passing references to them in the body of the speeches.⁵²⁷ (x) The *Sosus*, Antiochus' reply to the Roman Books, is reported to have consisted of one book only;⁵²⁸ this would seem to preclude that it was a refutation of Academic scepticism in all its varieties, even if it was assumed that a reply to the Roman Books would have been a natural place for such a fundamental refutation.⁵²⁹ (xi) Cicero had contact with Antiochus, as is well known, after he had contact with Philo. This raises the possibility that the source of Lucullus' speech, if it did make sense to posit a single one, might post-date the Roman Books.⁵³⁰ Antiochus' view, taken with hindsight sometime after the end of the debate,

---

be uncompelling, or would present the Academic stance as second-best and wanting but not as *omnis uitae euersio* (*Luc.* 99).

⁵²² *Luc.* 148 secures the existence of mitigated scepticism as an actual option rather than a stance entertained for the sake of the argument; cf. also on *Luc.* 78. I use the phrasal term 'non-dialectical option' to convey that it is assumed by Lucullus that his Academic opponent would actually deploy approval himself rather than entertain it in an ad hominem argument.

⁵²³ See the commentary passim; Ruch (1969); Bringmann (1971: 111–37 and 261–5); Glucker (1978: 391–420).

⁵²⁴ This asymmetry—Lucullus attacks Clitomacheanism and mitigated scepticism, but Cicero only defends the former view—is unsurprising: in *Catul.*, two different sceptical positions were presented, but the character Cicero has no reason to stand up for the one presented by Catulus. Moreover, except for the fairly narrow issue on which Clitomacheans and mitigated sceptics disagree, followers of either Academic position would cite the same points against Lucullus.

⁵²⁵ See Görler (2004c: 270–3) on *Luc.* 98b.

⁵²⁶ See *Luc.* 69–70, 98, 102, 132, 133–4, 143, with Glucker (2004: 114 n. 22).

⁵²⁷ See *Luc.* 18 and 78 (on my reading); Allen (1997: 218–19) on Carneades as a creator of philosophical positions for the sake of the argument.

⁵²⁸ See *Luc.* 12: ...*quin contra suum doctorem librum etiam ederet, qui Sosus inscribitur*; Glucker (1978: 392 n. 5).

⁵²⁹ Lévy (1992: 391–423) argues that the *Sosus* is the source for all parts of *Acad.*

⁵³⁰ See Görler (1994: 946) on *N.D.* 1.16 (= Antiochus frg. 11 Mette): an Antiochian work dedicated to Balbus would, if the fictional date of *N.D.* is used as a guide, need to be dated to 78 BC.

might have been that Academic scepticism proper was conceived by Arcesilaus, shaped by Carneades, and comprised Clitomacheanism as well as mitigated scepticism, and that Philo's Roman Books view was an aberration without afterlife and consequently without long-term corrosive potential, thus not warranting engagement beyond the *Sosus*.

It is in any event to be acknowledged that finding fault with existing accounts of the sources of *Acad.* is easier than devising a plausible positive account which combines simplicity and explanatory power. The options which follow are given in decreasing order of plausibility.

If one assumed that *Luc.* simply reflects sources of the same outlook as the Ciceronian text itself, with the source of Cicero's speech having been composed as a reply to the source of Lucullus' speech, then the latter would either be pre-Roman Books or written after the Roman Books when the thesis of the Roman Books was deemed to have misfired, for it is primarily directed against Clitomacheanism.[531] Cicero's speech is delivered from a position of Clitomacheanism. If one tries to place the purported sources of both speeches jointly and chronologically, there will be implications, deriving from the outlook of Cicero's speech: the source for it would come either from a time when Philo was still a Clitomachean and had not yet devised the Roman Books view, or from a time when he had reverted to Clitomacheanism after the failure of the Roman Books. In the latter case, one would assume that hostile critics of the sceptical Academy would have told us of Philo's second about-turn (sc. after the shift towards the Roman Books view).[532] The former would not be compatible with an assumption that just before 100 or shortly after Philo turned to mitigated scepticism, and that Antiochus was reacting—like Aenesidemus, if in a quite different way—to mitigated scepticism when he formed the Old Academy. It would, however, be compatible with the assumption that Philo was a Clitomachean in the period before he devised the Roman Books, and that mitigated scepticism was presented as an option by Philo rather than his or the Academy's official position.[533] In connection with this chronology, i.e. that the source for Lucullus' speech dates from the period between, roughly, the mid-90s and the early 80s BC, as does the source for Cicero's speech, with the Roman Books as a terminus ante quem, it may be cited that the historical account of the Old Academy as Antiochus conceives of it in *Luc.* 15 looks to be earlier than the rather different account in Varro's speech in *Ac.* 1, which is more nuanced and which would have represented a more powerful reply to the historical thesis of the Roman Books.[534] Against this account, one might want to cite the fact that the frame for Lucullus' speech in *Luc.* is the Alexandrian scene (i.e. Antiochus' angry reaction when he receives the Roman Books), and that Lucullus' speech is presented as relaying points made by Antiochus in discussion in the days following the receipt of the Roman Books. Yet given that Lucullus' speech avowedly does not address the Roman Books in detail and is instead directed against a different, earlier Academic stance (or stances), and that the *Sosus* is referred to in terms

---

[531] See, however, on *Luc.* 43–4.
[532] See Glucker (2004: 130–1).
[533] See section 8, p. clvi.
[534] See sections 7.1 and 7.2.

which suggest it had one book only, inferences about the date of the source of Lucullus' speech from its frame seem hazardous.[535]

One might, alternatively, take the view that only Lucullus' speech is closely based on a single continuous source. In that case it is still more likely to have been written before the publication of the Roman Books (because of various intrinsic features like the nature of the historical account of *Luc.* 15), but if the arguments cited in favour of an early date were found not to be compelling, one might posit that it was written at any time after Antiochus conceived of his Old Academy—provided we assume that Antiochus took the Roman Books view to be an aberration once it had been formulated, and Clitomacheanism and mitigated scepticism to represent 'genuine' Academic scepticism (on this construal, the *Sosus* would have been a one-off rebuttal). Cicero's speech in turn might then be a genuine Ciceronian composition, drawing on multiple sources (including the Clitomachean work cited in *Luc.* 98, a doxographical source used in *Luc.* 112–46), selected and harnessed to advance his Clitomachean agenda. This scenario cannot be ruled out, but I do not regard it as the most economical explanation of the evidence in its totality.[536]

If one is open to the assumption that Cicero's speech draws on a number of sources but is essentially a Ciceronian composition, in that it was him who assembled material to support his Clitomachean outlook, one might make a similar assumption for Lucullus' speech.[537] However, Lucullus' speech includes fewer sections which are clearly marked as drawing on a source than Cicero's, and I hesitate to embrace an account which combines reduced explanatory power and increased complexity. Deriving general conclusions regarding the final phase of the sceptical Academy or Antiochus' Old Academy from *Luc.* would also become precarious.

9.3.2 *Ac.* 1

Varro's speech in *Ac.* 1 is avowedly Antiochian in content (*Ac.* 1.14). As always, this does not mean that it is a continuous translation of a Greek source, but e.g. the survey of the views which jointly amount to the *prima forma* of Old Academic philosophy stands out within Cicero's oeuvre through the manner in which it gives the appearance of closely following a Greek model.[538] The speech is tightly organized in the way in which it places compressed exposition of doctrine against the background of a narrative theme about how the *antiqui* devised a *prima forma* of philosophy drawing on Plato's works and how that *forma* was then honed further by Plato's successors, Peripatetics, and Stoics, with Antiochus as the final arbiter and heir to the tradition. If the speech was a composite drawing on multiple sources, it would be an ingenious one. I have explained in some detail in section 7.2 why the historical account given by Varro strikes me as showing features of mature reflection and why I regard it as a credible component of an Antiochian post-Roman Books position. This makes Antiochus' dialogue *Sosus* one possible source of Varro's speech, but it is possible that

---

[535] See below on the suggestion, advanced by some, that the *Sosus* is the source of Lucullus' speech in *Luc.*, but that the actual arguments and views expressed predate the Roman Books.
[536] Note also the spread of passages cited under point (vii) above.
[537] Glucker (1978: 391–420) has argued that Lucullus' speech is based on two different sources; see below.
[538] See e.g. *Ac.* 1.24–9 and 1.30–2.

the speech draws on another work by Antiochus—composed, in any event, after the Roman Books. I believe further that the material introduced by Varro in *Ac.* 1 was presented by Hortensius in the first major speech in the *Catulus* and regard it as possible that the speech was extended and strengthened—Hortensius was a recent convert to philosophy in *Catul.*,[539] whereas Varro is an expert on matters Antiochian in his own right.[540] There is, however, no positive reason to assume that Hortensius' speech in *Catul.* and Varro's speech in *Ac.* 1 drew on different sources.

Cicero's speech in *Ac.* 1, or rather the extant beginning of it, which is concerned with Arcesilaus (1.44), picks up chronologically from Varro's preceding speech, which concluded with Zeno. Thus it does not respond to Varro's speech in the manner in which Cicero's speech in *Luc.* addresses issues raised by Lucullus' point by point, which means that there is no positive reason even to consider the possibility that the source of Cicero's speech was conceived as a reply to the source of Varro's speech. *Ac.* 1.44–6 raises, however, a different question: given that its counterpart in the *Catulus* was probably delivered by Catulus the son, and that he was cast like his father as a mitigated sceptic (see on *Luc.* 148), one must wonder if the passage portrays Arcesilaus in a manner that could be seen as distinctive for the position adopted by Catulus, e.g. by presenting him as a proto-mitigated-sceptic. If that was the case, one would have some reason to posit a source of the same outlook, which would complement the likely Clitomachean source behind Cicero's speech in *Luc.* and would provide further information on the *Sitz im Leben* of mitigated scepticism (i.e. that it was a sufficiently established view to give rise to Academic texts predicated on it). However, I do not think that *Ac.* 1.44–6 speaks to these issues as a matter of fact, nor do I think that there is a reasonable expectation that the text would do so. To take the second point first, the Academics can be shown to have operated a model of history according to which their position is the result of evolution and development; thus there is no necessary expectation that a mitigated sceptic would have sought to legitimize his position by tracing it as far back as possible.[541] Further, in *Ac.* 1 the technical notion of approval (see *Luc.* 104) has not been introduced yet, and Arcesilaus is presented as approving anti-Stoic arguments in Cicero's speech in *Luc.* So the difference between a proto-mitigated-sceptical view and a Clitomachean view (and corresponding modes of endorsement) would be indiscernible. Most fundamentally, however, *Ac.* 1.44–6 arguably does not speak to the issue at all. Arcesilaus is presented as having broad, undogmatic, and 'Socratic' views (arising from the sum of his experiences rather than being convictions or beliefs with which he starts out), and as engaging in ad hominem arguments loosely guided by these views.[542] There is no suggestion or implication that he endorses (in whatever sense) specifically anti-Stoic arguments which presuppose elements of Stoic theory (see on *Ac.* 1.44–6). This means that we cannot characterize the likely source of the beginning of Cicero's speech beyond it being 'Academic'.[543] In Catulus' speech in *Catul.* the first conception of mitigated scepticism will have been associated with Carneades (cf. *Luc.* 67, 78). In

---

[539] *Hort.* told, on one level of description, the story of Hortensius' conversion; see section 9.5.
[540] See the general note on *Ac.* 1.1–8.
[541] See section 7.1 on the historical accounts deployed by the Academics.
[542] See section 7.5 on Arcesilaus.
[543] However, *partes...Philonis* in *Fam.* 9.8 (= SB 254 = T29; the dedicatory letter to Varro) suggests that one should feel entitled to call the source not just Academic but Philonian.

adapting Catulus' speech for the final edition, Cicero must have changed the presentation since mitigated scepticism could no longer be introduced and endorsed in a first-person perspective by a character embracing it. That Cicero proceeded to talk about Carneades in the lost part of *Ac.* 1 is shown by t. 8 (= Nonius p. 65 M.).

9.3.3 Earlier Scholarship

The serious debate about the sources of *Acad.* stretches back into the nineteenth century.[544] Useful surveys of it exist, esp. by Glucker (1978: 391–420), Görler (1994: 918–20 and 945–7), and Glucker (2004: 111–17), which have jointly eliminated some long-standing hypotheses without any one account agreeing precisely with the picture laid out above (but I take my account to be consistent with that favoured by Görler 1994). Rather than offer another survey, I will highlight significant insights or fundamentally different assessments of the source background of *Acad.* A remark of Cicero's which has played a significant role in the debate comes from one of his letters to Atticus, written while he was composing *Acad.* (*Att.* 12.52.3 = SB 294 = T14): ἀπόγραφα sunt, minore labore fiunt, uerba tantum affero, quibus abundo.[545]

Bringmann (1971: 111–37 and 261–5) and Glucker (1978: 391–420) comprehensively refute the influential hypothesis of Hirzel (1883: 251–341) that Cicero's speech in *Luc.* is based on a source to which the source of Lucullus' speech was the reply. They do this by showing that in fact Cicero's speech very relevantly addresses, point by point, Lucullus'. But Bringmann assumes that Lucullus' speech is based on Antiochus' *Sosus*, while Glucker regards it is partly based on the *Sosus*, partly on a 'later Antiochian source' (§§40–60), adding a speculative reconstruction of the contents and structure of the *Sosus*.[546] Bringmann (1971: 265) argues that, since we know of no reply of Philo's to the *Sosus*, Cicero must himself have assembled his character's speech in *Luc.* from various sources (notably works of Clitomachus); by contrast, Glucker (1978: 406–20) assumes that Philo did respond to the *Sosus*,[547] that the reply to the *Sosus* is the basis for Cicero's speech in *Luc.*, and that Philo reverted to the position he held before he devised the Roman Books (for Glucker, this is a position I would characterize as Clitomachean).[548] One consideration which weighs with Glucker and which I regard as significant, too, is that passages in Cicero's speech which exhibit severe 'reproof' do not suit the character Cicero replying to the older Lucullus, but do suit the teacher Philo replying to a renegade pupil. Thus they point to a continuous underlying source for Cicero's speech in *Luc.*[549] Glucker (1978: 419)

---

[544] Substantial earlier contributions to the debate usually discuss the question of sources in connection with a reconstruction of the missing parts of *Acad.*; see the bibliography assembled on p. clxvii, n. 500, as well as Barnes (1997: 64–8, 70–6); Polito (2012: 41–4).

[545] I explain on p. clxi why I do not think that the sentence affords an insight into Cicero's working method.

[546] See the summary in the form of a table in Glucker (1978: 419), and earlier Lörcher (1911: 246) on *Luc.* 40–60; on the possible contents of the *Sosus*, see also Hatzimichali (2012: 11, 23).

[547] See Glucker (1978: 84–7 and 413–15), citing *Luc.* 17 and Aug., *Contra Acad.* 3.18.41 (= t. 58); on both passages, see Görler (1994: 919), on *Contra Acad.* 3.18.41 only Barnes (1997: 76–7), and the further thoughts of Glucker (2004: 111–17).

[548] See also Glucker (1988: 64–5).

[549] See Glucker (1978: 415), citing Plezia (1937: 19) on *Luc.* 69–70: 'Hunc locum, quo Antiochus acerrime reprehenditur, Ciceroni adscribi aegre ferrem. Indignum enim mihi uidetur humanissimo scriptore acerbissimis probris defunctum iam magistrum suum insectari, a quo prorsus numquam sit offensus. Potius igitur Philoni sunt haec tribuenda, cuius contra Antiochum indignationis causae satis sunt perspicuae.'

assumes, as I do, that Varro's speech in *Ac.* 1 draws on the *Sosus*. He further suggests (p. 69, cf. p. 419) that the Academic reply to Varro, or rather the continuation of the chronological narrative in *Ac.* 1.44–6, derives from the Roman Books.⁵⁵⁰

Sedley (1981: 69) and (2012b: 83), like Bringmann and Glucker, takes the view that the source for Lucullus' speech in *Luc.* is the *Sosus*,⁵⁵¹ but acknowledges that the arguments themselves are old in the sense that they target an earlier, more conventional Academic position. Sedley justifies this view with reference to the frame, i.e. the Alexandrian scene and the manner in which it is referenced in the body of Lucullus' speech (*Luc.* 49, cf. 12).⁵⁵² While I acknowledge that the Alexandrian scene is likely to have featured in the *Sosus* and that it may allow for inferences as to the speakers who featured in that text, I do think that it is deployed by Cicero to create credibility for the character Lucullus, and that it allows for no inference regarding the origin of the bulk of Lucullus' speech.⁵⁵³ As noted above, the fact that the *Sosus* appears to have consisted of one book only and that the evidence suggests that Antiochus objected to quite specific aspects of the Roman Books makes it unlikely that it contained a fundamental engagement with Academic scepticism in all its forms. Sedley (2012b: 83) assumes, as I do, that the source of Varro's speech in *Ac.* 1 postdates the Roman Books, on the grounds that the account of the Academic tradition developed in Varro's speech allows for discontinuities in a manner which is best explained by assuming that it is a response to the historical claim of the Roman Books.⁵⁵⁴

Brittain (2001) argues in detail that the official position of the Academy in the 90s BC and prior to the composition of the Roman Books was one of mitigated scepticism. Partly as a consequence of this he rejects some of Glucker's (1978) views on the sources of *Acad.* (see Brittain 2001: 189–90 n. 27), in particular that Philo would revert to the Clitomachean position after the failure of the Roman Books (cf. the source behind Cicero's speech), rather than to a position of mitigated scepticism. As suggested above, the silence of later, mostly hostile, sources on a purported return of Philo's to any earlier position after the failure of the Roman Books seems telling.

9.4 The Title(s)

Cicero refers to the two books of the first edition as *Catulus* and *Lucullus* (*Att.* 13.32.2–3 = SB 305; dated 29 May).⁵⁵⁵ Their forming an ensemble with the *Hortensius*,

---

⁵⁵⁰ See the persuasive arguments cited by Brittain (2001: 173–91) against this view, and the reply by Glucker (2004: 115–16).
⁵⁵¹ Sedley (1981: 74 n. 2) also accepts Glucker's suggestion that Catulus' speech in the *Catulus* was based on that of Heraclitus in the *Sosus*.
⁵⁵² Thus also earlier Lörcher (1911: 246, 251).
⁵⁵³ Sosus is not mentioned as present in Alexandria. Hatzimichali (2012: 23) raises the possibility that there was an embedded dialogue in the *Sosus* in which he featured.
⁵⁵⁴ Thus on this reading both the 'earlier' passage *Luc.* 15 and the more recent passage *Ac.* 1.15–17 (in terms of outlook) are supposed to come from the *Sosus*.
⁵⁵⁵ On the subject of the title(s), see Krische (1845: 12); Reid¹ p. 38; Plasberg² p. x; Philippson (1939: 1129, 1132); Emonds (1941: 265–6); Griffin (1997: 33–4), which is the best discussion of the issue; Hunt (1998: 13–16), who also surveys titles used by editors.

through the characters and the dramatic date, suggests that these were not just working titles. Quintilian's knowledge of (at least) the titles suggests this, too (3.6.64 = t. 65).[556] No collective title for the first edition is attested (but see below).

To the final edition he refers as *Academici (libri)* in *Tusc.* 2.4, *N.D.* 1.11, and *Div.* 2.1, which makes *Ac.* 1 the *Academicus primus*; cf. *in Academico tertio* sc. *libro* and *Academicos* sc. *libros* in *Att.* 16.6.4 = SB 414, dated 25 July 44. I take *Academici libri* to be the official title of the final edition. Concurrently with *Acad.*, he also worked on what is now *Fin.* 1 (or *Fin.* 1 and 2), and initially called it *Torquatus* (*Att.* 13.32.2–3 = SB 305); so Cicero performed a general shift away from book titles based on the names of individuals.

No title is mentioned when Cicero briefly refers to the intermediate edition which he entertained for a couple of days (*Att.* 13.16.1–2 = SB 323), but Griffin (1997: 33) rightly observes that, because Cicero had already published books entitled *Cato* and *Brutus*, the notion that the books needed an overall title may have been formed by Cicero then.

Cicero uses the expression Ἀκαδημικὴ σύνταξις in *Att.* 13.16.1–2 (= SB 323), shortened to Ἀκαδημική in *Att.* 13.12.3 (= SB 320), which is in fact the earliest reference to the work as a whole, and says he 'transferred it to Varro' sc. in creating the final edition; in 13.12.3 he also mentions a Περὶ τελῶν σύνταξις, i.e. what was to become *Fin.* The Greek phrases were evidently not intended as titles. Other expressions used to refer to the work without being titles are *tota Academia* (13.13.1 = SB 321) used of the first edition, and *Academica quaestio* (13.19.3 = SB 326) used of the final edition.

Academica, influentially promoted as the original collective title of the work at all stages by Reid[1] p. 38,[557] occurs in the phrase *haec Academica*, with reference to the first edition, in 13.19.5 (= SB 326), cf. *illa quae habes de Academicis* in 13.13.1 (= SB 321), where, as indicated, the phrase *tota Academia* features, too. (Other texts cited by Reid may equally be read as evidence for the collective title *Academici libri*, i.e. *Off.* 2.8 *in Academicis nostris*, *Tim.* 1 *in Academicis*; even 13.13.1 *de Academicis* could be so read.) This means that the other later references to the work quoted above all but secure that *Academici libri* was Cicero's collective title for the final edition. *Academica* is unlikely to have been the collective title for the first edition since it is one of several generic references to the work which are descriptive of content (see above). Thus in 13.19.5 (= SB 326), the relatively speaking best evidence for *Academica* as the overall title of the work, Cicero uses other neuter plurals to refer to the content of *Fin.* just before the occurrence of '*Academica*': *Ita confeci quinque libros* περὶ τελῶν *ut Epicurea L. Torquato, Stoica M. Catoni,* περιπατητικά *M. Pisoni darem*. The demonstrative *haec* in 13.19.5 *haec Academica* also points to *Academica* not being a title.

Some other titles which have a degree of currency in the literature were devised by modern scholars (*Academica priora* for *Catul.* and *Luc.*; *Academica posteriora* for the final edition; *Varro* for *Ac.* 1).[558]

---

[556] See also Plut., *Luc.* 42 (= t. 66), *Cic.* 40 (= t. 67).
[557] Davies (1725) also speaks of '*Academica*'.
[558] Hunt (1998: 16) traces '*Academica posteriora*' back to the edition of Schütz.

9.5 The *Hortensius* and *Acad.*

The three dialogues *Hort.*, *Catul.*, and *Acad.* were connected through its cast of characters and, probably loosely, through its dramatic date (see below).[559] (*Catul.* and *Luc.* are staged on subsequent days.) I discuss the rather vague references to work on *Hort.*, as opposed to those to the finished dialogue, and its date in the winter 46/45 in section 3. By the time Cicero wrote *Fin.* 1.2, where Cicero cites the positive reception of *Hort.* as a reason for his continuing to write philosophical works, *Hort.* must have been available to readers.

Evidence for *Hort.* comes from references to it in Cicero's own works, as well as from later authors, notably Seneca, Tacitus, Nonius Marcellus, Lactantius, and Augustine. Much of this evidence would naturally be classed as testimonia, but Nonius offers brief verbatim quotations.

Hort. probably had a proem like *Catul.* and *Luc.*, in which Cicero spoke as author before the dialogue started. Hortensius praised Lucullus' villa (frgs 2, 5, 18 Grilli = 22–4 Straume-Zimmermann), and Catulus asked about the library (frg. 8 G. = 35 S.-Z.). Lucullus spoke in favour of historiography (frg. 11 G. = 26 S.-Z.),[560] and Hortensius extolled rhetoric (frg. 19 G. = 103 S.-Z.). The fragments are too exiguous to determine the length of these contributions and whether they should be thought of as speeches. There appears also to have been a series of exchanges, rather than opposing speeches, on the merits of rhetoric (represented by Hortensius) and philosophy (represented by Cicero). A longer speech in praise of philosophy by Cicero concluded the dialogue. In *Catul.* Hortensius appears as an Antiochian and delivered a (possibly shorter) version of the material given to Varro in *Ac.* 1. Thus either *Hort.* or *Catul.* must have furnished an account of or at least a statement on Hortensius' conversion.[561] I also believe that the dramatic dates of *Hort.* and *Catul.* cannot have been successive days,[562] since a brand-new convert to philosophy could not credibly have presented the material given to Varro in *Ac.* 1 without some preparation. If this is correct, then Lucullus' *Tusculanum*, the grandest of his villas known for its excellent library,[563] becomes a possible setting for *Hort.* next to his *Neapolitanum*, given the distance between Tusculum and Campania, which could not be traversed by the characters if the dramatic dates of *Hort.* and *Catul.* were continuous.[564]

---

[559] Modern editions with commentary of *Hort.* are Plasberg (1892); Ruch (1958); Straume-Zimmermann (1976) and (1997²); and Grilli (2010²); discussion of aspects of its editorial history is in Brink (1961) and Görler (1980). A judicious survey of what is known about the dialogue from the perspective of its reception in Augustine is Schlapbach (2006); see also Schlapbach (2003) passim. Other useful studies include Hagendahl (1967: 79–94 and 486–97); Bringmann (1971: 111–37); Doignon (1983). On the setting of the dialogue, see Gigon (1962) and Voss (1966). On Aristotle's *Protrepticus*, which influenced *Hort.*, see Hirzel (1876) and Hutchinson and Johnson (2005).

[560] See Gildenhard (2013a: 251–3).

[561] *Luc.* 61, quoted below, cannot be that account and comes too late in the work.

[562] So also Griffin (1997: 4); Schofield (2012c: 76) assumes the action of *Hort.* and *Catul.* takes place on successive days.

[563] In this library Cicero finds Cato in *Fin.* 3.7 'surrounded by Stoic works'. See also Plut., *Luc.* 42; McCracken (1942).

[564] Thus Gigon (1962: 227–8); Voss (1966) argues for the *Neapolitanum* as setting for *Hort.* See also Grilli (2010²: 129–30) on *Contra Acad.* 3.16.35. Fuhrer (1997: 38–9) suggests that the week-long gap in dramatic date between Augustine's *Contra Acad.* 1, which draws on *Hort.*, and *Contra Acad.* 2–3, which draw on the *Academici libri*, signals awareness of the triptych structure *Hort.*–*Catul.*–*Luc.* on Augustine's

The evidence for a series of exchanges is frgs 26-32 G. = 55, 60-1, 63, 67-8, 93 S.-Z., esp. frg. 32 G. = 68 S.-Z., where Cicero offers to Hortensius that he may withdraw an earlier concession, likening the withdrawal to a move in a board game.[565] Hortensius appears to have attacked dialectic as a component discipline of philosophy. This is remarkable given that, as an Antiochian, he must have endorsed it in *Catul.* There is reason to suspect that Cicero offered a more detailed account of how Hortensius came to change his mind on this specific issue, probably in *Catul.*

When Cicero refers to *Hort.*,[566] he presents the dialogue as an exhortation to philosophy, an overall characterization which must have been largely determined by his character's final speech in it; cf. *Luc.* 61 (Lucullus addressing Cicero): *cum tantis laudibus philosophiam extuleris Hortensiumque nostrum dissentientem commoueris.* Crucially, it is to be acknowledged that Cicero's speech in *Hort.*, or Cicero's contributions in the dialogue more generally, combined statements which knowledgeable readers of Cicero have deemed to be at odds with Academic scepticism with expressions of commitment to Academic scepticism and Clitomacheanism in particular.[567] Thus Cicero appears to make the assumption that all human beings want to be happy (frg. 58 G. = 69 S.-Z.; 59 G. = 69A S.-Z.), that philosophy is a prerequisite for happiness, and that consequently all human beings should engage with it. He also considered three possible domains from which happiness might accrue: external goods (frg. 67 G. = 40D S.-Z.), fame (frg. 78 G. = 94 S.-Z.; 82 G. = 98 S.-Z.), and the search for truth (frg. 93 G. = 50 S.-Z.; and see below). At the end (frg. 112 G. = 99A S.-Z.; 115 G. = 102 S.-Z.) there was also extensive discussion of eschatological themes (112 G. = 99 S.-Z.; 105 G. = 100 S.-Z.; 110 G. = 101 S.-Z.; 115 G. = 102 S.-Z.; 19 G. = 103 S.-Z.). Against this one needs to set statements that the search for the truth could give rise to happiness even if the truth was not discovered, and that the sage would have to suspend judgement on all matters if all that was to be had was opinion.[568] If one ignored the latter set of fragments, then the first set might sound generically dogmatic. If one operated a conception of Academic scepticism and Clitomacheanism

---

part, even though Augustine ended up not using *Catul.* and *Luc.* The difference in dramatic date may mirror the one I posit for *Hort.* on the one hand and *Catul.* and *Luc.* on the other. On the dramatic date of *Luc.*, see Griffin (1997: 10): 'He [sc. Cicero] could only just manage to appear alongside Catulus as an ex-consul by choosing the dramatic date of BCE 62/1, since he was consul in 63 and Catulus died in the autumn of 61.'

[565] Nonius p. 170.22 M. (frg. 32 G. = 68 S.-Z.): *SCRIPTA, puncta tesserarum. M. Tullius in Hortensio:* '*Itaque tibi concedo, quod in duodecim scriptis solemus, ut calculum reducas, si te alicuius dati paenitet*', 'Therefore I permit you, as we usually do during a board game, to move a piece back if you regret to have granted something'. Frg. 30 G. = 93 S.-Z. may describe—in accounting terminology—the refusal to accept a conclusion after the concession of the premisses from which it is derived: Nonius p. 193.11 M. (frg. 30 G. = 93 S.-Z.): *AERA neutri generis. M. Tullius in Hortensio:* '*Quid? Tu, inquam, soles, cum rationem a dispensatore accipis, si aera singula probasti, summam, quae ex his confecta sit, non probare?*', 'What? Are you saying you are of the habit that, when the you get the final calculation from the cashier, you don't approve the sum, even if you have approved the individual items which add up to it?'.

[566] See *Fin.* 1.1-3, *Tusc.* 2.1-2 and 4, and 3.1-3 and 6, *Div.* 2.1, *Off.* 2.4-6.

[567] Pace Griffin (1997: 7): 'A plausible conclusion to draw from all these considerations would be that Cicero in the summer of 46 planned only the trilogy *Hortensius, Catulus, Lucullus*, in which the main function of the latter two books would be to answer the obvious question which would occur to readers of the *Hortensius*: which school did Cicero himself favour? For *Luc.* 61 shows that Cicero had not made it clear in that earlier work what system he himself followed, no doubt because, as Lucullus is made to hint here, it could have weakened the effectiveness of the case of philosophy which he was pleading here.'

[568] See also Schlapbach (2003: 95-7) on Aug., *Contra Acad.* 1.7; Grilli (2010^2: 243-4).

in particular which is similar to the caricature Lucullus develops in his speech in *Luc.*, then there might be a temptation to dismiss frg. 107 G. = 91 S.-Z. and 51 G. = 92 S.-Z.,[569] but while editors ascribe the former to *Hort.* only due to contextual considerations,[570] the latter fragment references *Hort.* explicitly and is formulated as a conditional.[571] Overall the fragments suggest that Cicero, while not having his character conceal his position, emphasized the positive outlook Academic scepticism affords outside of adversarial contexts; see on *Luc.* 98, which characterizes the perceived extremism of the Academic position as a defensive posture adopted in the face of the dogmatic challenge.

10. The Linguistic Form of *Acad.*

Cicero had an excellent grasp of the philosophical issues discussed in his dialogues, but he also used sources. The uses of such sources can be placed on a spectrum which ranges from actual translation in exceptional cases to a much looser connection between the Ciceronian text and the Greek model including free and independent composition informed by earlier reading. While studies of the language of Cicero's philosophical works have often focused on one-to-one correspondences between Greek technical terms and their Roman counterparts created (in the case of neologisms) or repurposed (in the case of existing expressions not previously used for philosophical purposes) by Cicero, an appreciation of the linguistic form of Cicero's philosophical dialogues must arguably take a broader view.[572] In many cases Cicero clearly reflected on the existing resources of the Latin language and then chose to negotiate and invoke certain philosophical concepts in a manner which is not amenable to an analysis or description in terms of word-for-word translation.[573]

10.1 Impressions I: *uidere, uideri, uisum*

The central philosophical subject of *Acad.* is whether a particular type of impression posited by the Stoics, i.e. the cataleptic impression, exists. Forms of *uidere* play a crucial role in the presentation of this debate.

---

[569] The texts assembled as frg. 107 G. = 91 S.-Z. are too numerous to cite here. Frg. 51 G. = 92 S.-Z. = Aug., *Contra Acad.* 3.14.31 (translated in section 8, p. cxlviii; cf. my t. 28): *Clamat Cicero se ipsum magnum esse opinatorem, sed de sapiente se quaerere. Quod si adhuc uos, adulescentes, ignoti habetis, certe in Hortensio legistis: 'Si igitur nec certi est quidquam nec opinari sapientis est, nihil umquam sapiens approbabit'*. Diels (1888: 488) and Plasberg (1892: 40) found the notion that the Cicero character might have appeared as an Academic in *Hort.* so intolerable that they assign frg. 51 G. to Hortensius, who would have been ridiculing the Academy.

[570] The speaker Licentius in Aug., *Contra Acad.* 1.2.7 professes to know *Hort.* only; see Philippson (1932: 1127).

[571] See also Hagendahl (1967: 490–2).

[572] Important studies on linguistic aspects of Cicero's philosophical works include Hartung (1970); Moreschini (1979); Puelma (1986); Lévy (1992a); Powell (1995); Glucker (2012). Merguet (1887–94) remains an invaluable resource. Adams (1995) and Langslow (2000) are primarily concerned with medical texts but contain much that is applicable to or illuminating of philosophical works written in Latin.

[573] On Cicero's statements about the prospects of writing philosophy in Latin, see the general note in *Ac.* 1.1–8 and Fögen (2000: 77–141).

I contend, and argue in detail in Reinhardt (2015) and (2018b), that the prototypical sense of active *uidere* in Latin ('to see an object in the world veridically') is achieved by combining two senses—(a) 'to look at an object in the world' and (b) 'to have a visual awareness of it'—, but that both senses (a) and (b) can also occur in isolation, in which case sense (a) designates a gazing and sense (b) what we call phenomenal seeing (the having of a visual experience caused by an object, whether or not the object is accurately represented).[574] Accordingly, when it corresponds to the prototypical sense of *uidere*, the term *uisum* denotes simultaneously an object seen and an accurate (veridical) visual experience had of it.[575] While *uisum* in this sense has two distinct referents, the suggestion is that *uisa* in the sense at issue are so called because external objects present themselves in the experience of the perceiver.

However, just as *uidere* has other senses than the prototypical one, so *uisum* (or expressions like *quod uidetur*) can have other meanings, too. For present purposes only some of them are relevant. *Visum* can have dual reference in at least two further ways: it can also denote (i) an object or state of affairs perceived *and* the veridical experience thereof in a sense modality other than vision, as well as (ii) an object or state of affairs perceived *and* the experience thereof in any sense modality without the explicit presumption of veridicality.[576]

Visum can also denote an experience only, i.e. a perceptual thought. This sense comes closest in meaning to the Greek term φαντασία.

Consider the following two passages:

---

[574] The gazing sense is sparsely attested in Latin; see Reinhardt (2015: 65, 76). 'To gaze at something deliberately' is *aspicere* in Latin.

[575] *Visum* can have two distinct referents at the same time, but whether it should be so construed in a given case depends on complex factors, including the meaning of any verb whose grammatical object *uisum* is and the artistic intent of the author. This may be illustrated by two occurrences of *uisum* outside of a philosophical context. A case where the assumption of two referents feels necessary is Prop. 2.6.27–30 (P. is speaking of obscene wall paintings): *quae manus obscenas depinxit prima tabellas | et posuit casta turpia* **uisa** *domo | illa puellarum ingenuos corrupit ocellos | nequitiaeque suae noluit esse rudes*, 'It was the artist who first painted lewd panels and set up indecent pictures in a virtuous house, who corrupted the innocent eyes of girls, refusing to leave them ignorant of his own depravity' (transl. Goold). On first approach, *uisa* are the paintings qua object seen; this is suggested by *posuit (casta...domo)*. And yet, Fedeli (2005: 212) comments on the passage: 'nel v. 28 *visa* non perde qui del tutto il senso proprio di "apparizioni", "visioni", by which, I assume, he means that the paintings are not just tableaux on the wall: an indecent image must do more than be on display to have its corrupting force: it must register with the observer (this is arguably stated in lines 29–30). Here it would seem that both perspectives are required and are to be taken simultaneously. Contrast Dido's ill-omened sacrifice (Verg., *A*. 4.450–6): *tum uero infelix fatis exterrita Dido | mortem orat; taedet caeli conuexa tueri. | quo magis inceptum peragat lucemque relinquat, |* **uidit**, *turicremis cum dona imponeret aris,| (horrendum dictu) latices nigrescere sacros | fusaque in obscenum se uertere uina cruorem; | hoc* **uisum** *nulli, non ipsi effata sorori*, 'Then it was that unhappy Dido prayed for her death. She had seen her destiny and was afraid. She could bear no longer to look up to the bowl of heaven, and her resolve to leave the light was strengthened when she was laying offerings on the incense-breathing altars and saw to her horror the consecrated milk go black and the wine, as she poured it, turn to filthy gore. No one else saw it and she did not even tell her sister' (transl. West). Here *uidit* initially suggests that we are dealing with an instance of prototypical seeing, while *uisum* raises at least the question whether Dido's imagination has in fact played a trick on her and she is hallucinating (in which case *uidit* would be seeing qua perceptual experience only); cf. Pease (1935) on 4.456: 'Virgil may think of this *uisum* as an hallucination on the part of Dido.' Here it is either one or the other, for the text is delicately balanced on the edge between the two possibilities, and its effect depends on the reader sharing Dido's uncertainty about what she has seen.

[576] In Greek one could achieve similar though not identical effects with φαίνεσθαι / τὸ φαινόμενον.

Luc. 18: si illud esset, sicut Zeno definiret, tale uisum (iam enim hoc pro φαντασίᾳ uerbum satis hesterno sermone triuimus)....

Luc. 108: Alterum est quod negatis actionem ullius rei posse in eo esse, qui nullam rem assensu suo conprobet. Primum enim uideri oportet, in quo sit etiam assensus (dicunt enim Stoici sensus ipsos assensus esse, quos quoniam appetitio consequatur actionem sequi)—tolli autem omnia si uisa tollantur.

The first passage informs us that *uisum* is Cicero's translation for the term φαντασία,[577] i.e. here *uisum* denotes a perceptual thought, at least in the first instance. In the second passage the sense requires *uisa* to mean not just 'true impressions' but 'cataleptic impressions' (sc. a species of true impressions).[578] Here one might be surprised that this shift in meaning is not more clearly marked, but one might also wonder how exactly it is achieved given existing uses of *uideri*. In response to the latter question, we recall that in cases of prototypical (sc. veridical) seeing two notions are present at the same time: that there is an object within the ken of the perceiver, and that the perceiver has a visual experience of this object. That is, in instances of veridical seeing objects in the world present themselves in the experience of the perceiver (sc. as they are). Correspondingly, the term *uisum*, if construed with reference to prototypical *uidere*, refers to object perceived and veridical visual experience had of it at the same time. And the Stoics define an individual perception as an assent to a cataleptic impression.[579]

Our contention is that the phrase *percipere uisum* (or *comprehendere uisum*; see below), whereby *uisum* has the sense of 'cataleptic impression' in the way just described, has to be considered as the fundamental reference point in interpreting Cicero's account of the debate between Stoics and Academics. *Percipere uisum* so understood means to grasp the object and the impression it causes at the same time, by assenting to it.[580] This formulation is explicit on one important point which the corresponding Greek formulations do not convey: that in assenting to a cataleptic impression we acquire a secure hold of not just the object, but also of the impression it causes, in such a way that it is excluded that what we have actually assented to is an impression just like the one we took ourselves to assent to.[581] The phrase *percipere uisum* thus construed is intended to convey that the Stoic position is supposed to be immune to the charge of ἀπαραλλαξία.[582]

---

[577] *Visum* was probably used before Cicero in the sense of 'appearance' (see *OLD* s.v. a), which cites *CIL* I².1423 (see Kragelund 2001: 81 n. 83). An 'appearance' so understood may or may not be something 'outside' of the perceiving subject.

[578] The subject under dispute between Stoics/Antiochus and Academics is whether cataleptic impressions exist, not whether impressions exist.

[579] Cf. Cic., *Ac.* 1.41: *quod autem erat sensu comprehensum, id ipsum sensum appellabat, et si ita erat comprensum ut conuelli ratione non posset scientiam*; Aët., *Plac.* 4.8.12 and 4.9.4 (= *SVF* ii.72 and ii.78).

[580] For an occurrence of *percipere uisum* in a negative context, see *Luc.* 84: ...*incidebat in eius modi uisum quod percipi non posset.*

[581] However, as Brittain (2006: xliii n. 84) notes, the later Stoic Hierocles (second century AD) states that the apprehension (ἀντίληψις) of something white has to be coordinated with a perception (αἴσθησις) of oneself being whitened, which suggests that he took two cataleptic impressions to be involved in one's conscious perception of something white ('Ηθικὴ στοιχείωσις, 6.1–6); see also Ramelli and Konstan (2009: 16, 53).

[582] Whether the Stoic position was *originally* meant to be insulated against the kind of objection which was later formulated as the (various types of) argument from ἀπαραλλαξία is a separate question. Within

However, while *percipere uisum* in its archetypal sense is an elegant way of referring to the grasping of mind-independent facts through perception, Cicero may find himself in situations where he needs to talk about impressions or even cataleptic impressions qua mental items only, e.g. when he reports Zeno's definition (which is of a mental item, not of objects and the impressions caused by them at the same time), or when his focus is on our secure grasp of an impression as opposed to one just like it. In this case he may use expressions like *percipere uisum* and mean the grasping of a mental item only, without thereby implying or being committed to the view that such impressions do not represent objects in the world or are, in the case of cataleptic impressions, veridical and self-warranting representations of them. In general, ancient sceptics, Academics or Pyrrhonists, have been appropriately characterized as property sceptics, not external world sceptics: they do not take the step which later philosophers will take, of doubting that there is an external world beyond our consciousness, and instead query whether the external world is appropriately and accurately presented in our experience.[583] A passage which illustrates this is *Luc.* 105 (see ad loc.), in which the sceptic refuses to ascribe a particular colour to the sea, but has no hesitation to refer to the sea with a deictic pronoun (*illud*).[584]

Using cognates of the verb καταλαμβάνειν,[585] the Stoics say we experience impressions which are capable of grasping or of affording a grasp (καταληπτικός). In Stoic fragments we also find the term καταληπτός, 'capable of being grasped',

---

Acad., Cicero does not present the doctrine as one which has, in this respect, evolved over time. Annas (1990: 184–203) argues that the Stoic position was originally indeterminate regarding an awareness requirement being placed on one's self-warrantingly true perceptions and was forced into an externalist position—one which does without an awareness requirement—by the considerations from ἀπαραλλαξία. See also section 5.6.

[583] See Burnyeat (1982) and Frede (1988); contrast Fine (2003). In saying that ancient sceptics are not external world sceptics, I intend to make a comment on the evidence we have. If a sceptic had found himself in a suitable dialectical situation, it is likely that he would have argued against the existence of a world external to our minds.

[584] It seems safe to exclude the possibility that in *Luc.* 105 the object—the sea—is itself meant to be taken as a mind-dependent component of the perceptual experience of the Academic sage at that moment, because of the communicative situation (the speaker invites the addressee to share focus). But it will be as well to note that the mere presence of deictic and other spatial expressions does not by itself establish the reference to the outside world (cf. also *OLD* s.v. *uideo* no. 3a: '(emphasizing the presence of the obj. of the vb.) To see; (also indicating the presence of the subj. in the locality of the obj.)'). When we read, of Hector's dream appearance to Aeneas, in Verg., *A.* 2.270–3, *in somnis ecce ante oculos maestissimus Hector | uisus adesse mihi largosque effundere fletus, raptatus bigis ut quondam aterque cruento | puluere perque pedes traiectus lora tumentis*, 'in slumbers, I dreamed that Hector, most sorrowful and shedding floods of tears, stood before my eyes, torn by the car, as once of old, and black with gory dust, his swollen feet pierced with thongs' (transl. Fairclough/Goold), the phrase *ante oculos* should give us pause. It seems unsatisfactory to explain it with the rigid conventions of epic language, which supposedly allow for the paradoxical inclusion of *ante oculos* just because it is conventional, even in cases where there is nothing there to be seen *ante oculos* and any eyes are, one would think, closed. It seems preferable to think that *ante oculos* characterizes the subjective feel of the dream appearance—it is *as if* Hector was before Aeneas' eyes. Contrast Verg., *A.* 2.772–3: *infelix simulacrum atque ipsius umbra Creusae | uisa mihi ante oculos et nota maior imago*, 'there rose before my eyes the sad phantom and ghost of Creüsa herself, a form larger than her wont' (transl. Fairclough/Goold), where real seeing takes place and where there is something *ante oculos*, but it is a *simulacrum*. See also Joffre (2005: 91–9, at 96–7).

[585] Already Plato uses verbs from the semantic field 'to grasp', though not καταλαμβάνειν, in connection with the mental grasp of something; see Long (2002: 115–31), at 123 on λαμβάνειν, ἀναλαμβάνειν, προσλαμβάνειν, and ἐφάπτεσθαι. Long also observes that in Stoic texts καταλαμβάνειν is used of true items only, while the terms used by Plato can be applied to truths and falsehoods alike.

i.e. morphologically the passive counterpart of the active καταληπτικός, but while the latter is a frequently attested attribute of impressions, the former is a rarely attested attribute of objects in the world, not because these are not grasped by means of cataleptic impressions (they are), but because objects in the world are not problematic for Stoics—to call them capable of being grasped would, outside of dialectical debate, be a statement of the obvious. The few instances where καταληπτός is used of objects in Stoic texts confirm this: e.g. someone is said to be καταληπτός as a sage, i.e. it is not someone's graspability qua object which is at issue, but whether one can apprehend through perception if someone is a sage.[586] Cataleptic impressions by themselves do not lead to beliefs; for beliefs to ensue from them, the mind has to assent to them. Once they have been assented to, they are called a 'grasp' (κατάληψις), sc. of the object. Κατάληψις is a *nomen actionis*, and its sense is active. At the same time, because καταλήψεις are impressions which have been assented to, they are mental items; this is not an unusual shift in meaning for nouns of this formation.[587] The verb καταλαμβάνειν, unless it is modally qualified, goes with κατάληψις rather than καταληπτικὴ φαντασία: we grasp an object when we have a cataleptic impression of it and assent to it, not just by having a καταληπτικὴ φαντασία, in which case we merely entertain the object in thought. A formulation which is not present in the Greek record on the Stoics is that we grasp impressions by assenting to them, but I will later discuss material which suggests that later Stoics, or a Stoicizing Academic like Antiochus, might have used such an expression.

In connection with the καταληπτ-*/καταληπτικ-* distinction there are two passages which need to be explained if we are to contend plausibly that Cicero's terminological choices in this area are the result of careful deliberation and acute analysis rather than the combined product of an insufficient understanding of the issues and hasty production. In these two passages Cicero introduces a Greek term (καταληπτόν) but gives an explanation of its reference which is at variance with the Greek record.

One of these is *Luc*. 18, on which see the commentary. The other is *Ac*. 1.40–2, where Varro, in the account of the history of philosophy from Socrates to the Stoics, explains the modifications which Zeno made to the epistemology of the *ueteres*:

> Plurima autem in illa tertia philosophiae parte mutauit. In qua primum de sensibus ipsis quaedam dixit noua, quos iunctos esse censuit e quadam quasi impulsione oblata extrinsecus, quam ille φαντασίαν, nos uisum appellemus licet, et teramus hoc uerbum quidem, erit enim utendum in reliquo sermone saepius—sed ad haec quae uisa sunt et quasi accepta sensibus assensionem adiungit animorum, quam esse uult in nobis positam et uoluntariam. (41) **Visis non omnibus adiungebat fidem, sed iis solum quae propriam quandam haberent declarationem earum rerum quae uiderentur; id autem uisum cum ipsum per se cerneretur, comprehendibile—feretis haec?**' 'Nos uero' inquit; 'quonam enim alio modo καταληπτὸν diceres?'—'Sed cum acceptum iam et approbatum esset, **comprehensionem appellabat, similem iis rebus quae manu prenderentur**; ex quo etiam nomen hoc duxerat [at], cum eo

---

[586] Aët., *Plac*. 4.9.17 (= *SVF* i.204).
[587] Consider δόσις = the giving ⟩ gift, payment, with Benveniste (1993: 76); cf. *natatio* = the swim ⟩ swimming pool.

uerbo antea nemo tali in re usus esset, plurimisque idem nouis uerbis (noua enim dicebat) usus est. Quod autem erat sensu comprehensum, id ipsum sensum appellabat, et si ita erat comprehensum ut conuelli ratione non posset, scientiam, sin aliter, inscientiam nominabat, ex qua existeret etiam opinio, quae esset imbecilla ⟨assensio⟩ et cum falso incognitoque communis. (42) Sed inter scientiam et inscientiam comprehensionem illam quam dixi collocabat, eamque neque in rectis neque in prauis numerabat, sed soli credendum esse dicebat. E quo sensibus etiam fidem tribuebat, quod ut supra dixi **comprehensio facta sensibus et uera esse illi et fidelis uidebatur, non quod omnia quae essent in re comprehenderet**, sed quia nihil quod cadere in eam posset relinqueret....'

What is in need of explanation in this passage, in general and also given what I have said above, is that Cicero says that an impression of the kind which he has just introduced (a cataleptic impression, sc. a mental item), considered by itself, i.e. before it has been assented to, is to be called *comprehendibile*, 'that which can be grasped'.[588] In reply to the question if this was tolerable, Atticus asks how else one is supposed to render καταληπτόν. Cicero's translation of the Greek term is correct as far as the sense of the term is concerned, but he applies it to (cataleptic) impressions rather than objects in the world, and in a context where we would expect him to introduce impressions which are capable of grasping, sc. objects in the world (i.e. καταληπτικαὶ φαντασίαι).

I had explained above that *percipere uisum*, where *uisum* is used for 'cataleptic impression', means 'to grasp an external object by means (or: in) an impression'. That this conception of what it means to have a cataleptic impression is in the background in our passage, too, is suggested by a rather inconspicuous detail: *comprehensio* (= κατάληψις), the deverbative noun of a synonym of *percipere*, is used in a passive sense (41: **comprehensionem** appellabat, similem iis rebus quae manu **prenderentur**), i.e. the mental item which is grasped, and in an active sense (**comprehensio** facta sensibus et uera esse illi et fidelis uidebatur, non quod omnia quae essent in re **comprehenderet**...), i.e. the mental item which grasps, sc. objects (*res*).[589] (That in the latter case *comprehenderet* features in a negated clause introducing a rejected reason seems unproblematic, since what is rejected is the notion that a *comprehensio* grasps all features of the object as opposed to salient ones.) The presence of the double perspective on grasping in our passage tells against a simple mistake on Cicero's part,[590] because he does even here show awareness that the καταλήψεις resulting from cataleptic impressions are held to grasp objects.

Given that there was no confusion in Cicero's mind as to how the notion of grasping relates to impressions in Stoic thought, his use of καταληπτόν with reference to an impression must have struck him as not problematic. Three possible reasons for this are the following. First, the terminological cluster centring on καταλαμβάνειν

---

[588] The context precludes the possibility that *comprehendibilis* is instrumental/active in meaning; see Leumann (1977: 348–9) for this option in principle.

[589] This is recognized by the *OLD* s.v. compr(eh)ensio no. 5a and b, but not by the *TLL*. The shift between grasping an object (of some sort) with the mind and grasping the mental item corresponding to an object is anticipated in *Rhet. Her.*: contrast 2.30: *res breuis est, ut facile memoria comprehendatur* and 3.33: *rei...memoriam...una nota et imagine simplici comprehendimus*. See Puelma (1986: 55 n. 20).

[590] Confusion on Cicero's part is assumed by von Staden (1978: 98–9).

became, already in the Hellenistic period, common currency in philosophical debate generally and was used in ways which represented a deviation from their original Stoic usage. The Cyrenaics held that the only thing we can be certain of are our bodily affections as opposed to representational states like impressions, and in the Greek sources this position is reported as the view that only these affections can be grasped;[591] Cicero was familiar with the Cyrenaic position, as is clear from references to it in *Acad.* (e.g. *Luc.* 142). Second, the debates about ἀπαραλλαξία mentioned above, which postdate the formulation of the definition of the cataleptic impression of course, at times created the need to claim that one was undergoing an impression A as opposed to an impression B which was exactly like it in every respect,[592] and it seems conceivable that this was expressed in Greek as 'grasping an impression A', even if no such formulation happens to have survived. Third, the Stoic view is that we have impressions which reveal themselves and their object, while we assent to impressions not objects represented by them. If one does not conceive of the possibility that there might be no world external to ourselves at all, as nobody in classical antiquity did (see above), then saying that one grasps an impression, used as a shorthand for grasping an object by means of an impression, would not sound like 'being certain about the content of one's perceptual beliefs qua subjective states only' as it does to the modern reader, conditioned as we are through brain-in-the-vat scenarios and the like.[593]

It also seems relevant that Cicero, had he wanted to render καταληπτικός, would have encountered various problems. One is the absence of an active verbal adjective meaning 'capable of ϕ-ing' in Latin. A *uisum comprehendens* would have meant an impression which actually grasps as opposed to being able to, and thus might at best have been suitable as a rendering of κατάληψις, for which, as we saw, Cicero uses deverbative *nomina actionis* matching the Greek term morphologically. A phrasal term involving a clause, like *uisum quod comprehendere potest*, would have sat uncomfortably with the archetypal *percipere uisum*: the potential for misunderstanding that objects perceived can grasp would have been too great. *Visum quod comprehendere potest* would also have run into the problem that *uisum* probably had an established sense of 'apparition' before Cicero.[594] So the ridiculous notion of ghosts being able to seize things would not have been far off, and we remember in this connection that Cicero himself made fun of the Epicurean Catius who rendered the term εἴδωλον as *spectra*, which is the origin of English 'spectre' and is likely to have evoked the association with 'ghost' already in Cicero's time.[595]

---

[591] See Tsouna (1998: 30–61, esp. 32 n. 2).
[592] See above, p. clxxxiv, and section 5.6. Impressions can conceivably be different from one another qua alterations of the ἡγεμονικόν and yet be indistinguishable regarding their phenomenal content; see *Luc.* 58.
[593] This would also answer the question why Cicero used Greek terms at all if he knew his application of the term to impressions to be a deviant one: he did not take this view, as is also suggested by the fact that Cicero has the character Atticus supply the Greek term καταληπτόν in dialogue.
[594] It must be due to the accidents of survival that chronologically the earliest instances of *uisum* come from Cicero; cf. Verg., *A.* 4.450–6 (n. 575 above), which surely is not evidence for the early reception of *Acad.*
[595] See Cic., *Fam.* 15.16.1–2 (= SB 215, with the reply by Cassius, 15.19.1 = SB 216): I am assuming that Cicero's point that it was unlikely that *spectra* were in our power (so that they can be summoned at will) combines substantial philosophical criticism with a joke (*in meane potestate ut sit spectrum tuum, ut, simul ac mihi collibitum sit de te cogitare, illud occurrat?*). See also Reinhardt (2005: 156); McConnell (2019) for a different account of Cicero's objections to *spectra*.

10.2 Impressions II: *uisio, species, nota, signum*

In *Acad.* there are a number of expressions which have been regarded as synonyms of *uisum*, although they can in fact be shown to overlap in meaning only with that term. One such expression is *uisio*, which occurs twice in *Luc.* 33, including in a marked contrast at the end of the paragraph (see ad loc.). There *uisio* is used of a non-cataleptic impression qua mental item, in contradistinction to a *uisum* = sub-class of impressions which is the subject of Lucullus' discussion (i.e. the cataleptic impression). (*Visio* may carry a hint of dismissiveness in addition; cf. the other uses below.) However, an earlier occurrence in the same paragraph the term is ambiguous, in that *uisio* can either be used in the same sense or denote a mental faculty, which is one of the senses φαντασία can have in Greek and indeed the use the *OLD* s.v. *uisio* deems primary (citing as the earliest instance Apul., *Met.* 8.6). The matter is, however, not clear-cut, and I suspect that even a native speaker would not just read over the paragraph and settle for one meaning confidently; arguably there is method to this, in that Cicero appears to have used some expressions with a particular didactic intent, viz. to make the reader work to retrieve the correct reading (or possible readings).[596] The other two instances of *uisio* occur in *Luc.* 49 and 90. In *Luc.* 49 the term is used in the plural modified by the adjective *inanes* and denotes either misperceptions of the insane (i.e. an object is encountered by the perceiving subject, but ends up being represented as something other than what it is) or experiences divorced from reality, i.e. hallucinations experienced while awake and without input from the external world or dream images. In any event, *uisio* seems deliberately used to describe an experience only, rather than have the double reference to object represented and experience had of it. In this respect the usage is aligned with *Luc.* 33. In *Luc.* 90 the force of *uisio* as a *nomen actionis* is invoked once again in that the term is used to describe the mind's activity in having *inanes uisiones* in the sense in evidence in *Luc.* 49, but because *uisio* qua faculty of the mind is neutral or indeterminate, the term is modified by the phrase *aut furentium aut somniantium* in *Luc.* 90.[597]

There are also four passages in *Acad.* where the term *species* is deployed in connection with impressions,[598] in the sense of their 'look'.[599] In *Luc.* 52 the speaker is Lucullus, but the word occurs in a piece of direct speech giving the objection of the Academic interlocutor. For the objection to have the best effect, it should rely on a conception of the look of an impression which is dogmatic or Stoic rather than Academic. From the Stoic perspective a cataleptic impression is marked out by a supreme phenomenal clarity which is distinct from the clarity non-cataleptic

---

[596] Cf. e.g. Lucr. 4.353–7, discussed in Reinhardt (2016: 88–9).

[597] For *uisio* = Epicurean εἴδωλον, see e.g. Cic., *N.D.* 1.109.

[598] Plasberg² p. 122 notes in his index s.v. species: '*fere* φαντασία'. Not germane are instances of *species* where it is used in a physical sense of form (*Ac.* 1.27) or of Platonic forms (*Ac.* 1.30, 33).

[599] For this sense, see *OLD* s.v. *species* no. 3a; cf. *OLD* s.v. *aspectus* no. 5a and s.v. *uisus* no. 3c. See also Ernout and Robin (1932: 921). Outside of *Acad.* there is one instance of *uisus, -ūs* used in a very similar way (*N.D.* 1.12: *Ex quo exsistit et illud, multa esse probabilia, quae quamquam non perciperentur, tamen, quia uisum quendam haberent insignem et illustrem, his sapientis uita regeretur*, 'From this followed that many sensations are persuasive; they, although they are not grasped, nonetheless enable the sage's life to be guided by them, because they have a certain distinct and clear aspect').

impressions might have.⁶⁰⁰ *Luc.* 58 has Lucullus engage with a different objection made by the Academic opponent: that impressions may be different from one another qua imprints on the human mind, and yet have the same look. This is dismissed as absurd, on the grounds that the look provides the means of discrimination; consequently, a difference in imprint must, for Lucullus, correspond to a difference in look. However, the term *species* can be invested with different conceptions of what determines an impression's look. In *Luc.* 99 Cicero argues against Lucullus that even the sage will have nothing to act on but *quidquid acciderit specie probabile*, and so he will act on it; this refers to the alternative conception of the Academic sage, as is clear from the fact that Cicero continues by asserting that the Stoic sage has to do the same on occasion.⁶⁰¹ For the Academics, as I have argued in section 6.1, the look of a *probabile* must be 'congruous' and would be enabled not constituted by clarity in a phenomenal sense. In any event, the look of a *probabile* is at issue, which is different from the look of a cataleptic impression, as both sides agree. In *Luc.* 111 Cicero states against Lucullus and Antiochus that he recognizes true as well as false impressions, i.e. that the rejection of the cataleptic impression does not mean that the distinction between true and false is rejected by or unavailable to him. He ends by saying: *sed probandi species est, percipiendi signum nullum habemus*, which contrasts a look that gives rise to approval (cf. on *Luc.* 104) with the cataleptic's impression hypothesized distinctive feature signalling the possibility of apprehension (consequent upon assent). Once more this would need to be a 'congruous' look.⁶⁰²

Cicero uses the term *nota* in contexts where the distinctive feature cataleptic impressions are supposed to have is at issue. There has been a debate about the philosophical interpretation of the feature in *Acad.*, i.e. whether Lucullus (and Cicero in his reply) takes the feature to enable the impression to function as a natural criterion or whether he interprets it as a sign from which the certain truth of an impression can be inferred.⁶⁰³ Here I cite a selection of telling instances, in order to show that they once more seem to demand effort on the part of the reader if their meaning is to be retrieved. While in some places the *nota* seems to be a mark which could attach to cataleptic impressions independently of their content (so that it could serve as a sign to infer the truth of the impression),⁶⁰⁴ in others the cataleptic impression as a whole seems to be called a *nota* (in *Luc.* 71 one is said to apprehend through a *nota*); in *Luc.* 58 the 'look' of impressions is associated with the *nota* (*Quasi uero non specie uisa iudicentur, quae fidem nullam habebunt sublata ueri et falsi nota*), which sounds rather like the orthodox Stoic view; in *Luc.* 57 objects are said to be 'marked out', which suggests that it is the manner in which they are represented which is distinctive (*res similes…dinotatas*);⁶⁰⁵ and sometimes the *nota* is called 'a mark of assent',

---

⁶⁰⁰ On the Stoic conception of clarity, see sections 5.2 and 5.3; on the Academic conception, see section 6.1 and Reinhardt (2018a).
⁶⁰¹ For the notion that what the Stoics call cataleptic impressions *are* persuasive impressions which have been tested, see *Luc.* 105a.
⁶⁰² For the phrase involving a gerund, see ad loc. and below on *nota*.
⁶⁰³ See Striker (1997: 262–5) and Brittain (2012: 118–20).
⁶⁰⁴ Consider *Luc.* 33: *nec potest is, cui uisio ueri falsique communis, ullum habere iudicium aut ullam omnino ueritatis notam*, where *habere* is instrumental in enabling the inferential interpretation.
⁶⁰⁵ Cf. *Ac.* 1.41 (Varro speaking, on Zeno): *Visis non omnibus adiungebat fidem, sed iis solum quae propriam quandam haberent declarationem earum rerum quae uiderentur*.

which seems to emphasize the causal effect of cataleptic impressions.[606] *Signum* has been held to be a synonym of *nota*;[607] I believe it means 'impression' in a literal sense, evoking the etymological association with *signare* and related compounds as they feature in passages which translate Zeno's definition of the cataleptic impression. See the full discussion in the general note on *Luc.* 33–34a.

10.3 'Beliefs'

In *Acad.* the term 'belief' (*opinio*; δόξα) and the corresponding verb *opinari* occur in a technical Stoic sense, on which more below. However, much of the discussion is arguably about beliefs or belief-like attitudes and commitments in a more general sense. These, or rather the manner in which they are talked about, are the subject of the present section. Under this heading there fall Stoic (or Antiochian) καταλήψεις, Stoic δόξαι and the version of them which mitigated sceptics regarded as permissible, the views which arise from 'approval' in the technical sense of *Luc.* 104 and which in *Acad.* are equated by the character Cicero with the attitudes which come about if one 'follows' an impression, as well as the less narrowly circumscribed intuitions which governed Arcesilaus' argumentative practice on the Cicero character's construal, themselves modelled on Socrates' epistemic behaviour interpreted in a certain way.

The beliefs of the Stoic sage are, on one level of description and in terms of their coming into being, καταλήψεις (see below), but they are also individual items of knowledge, ἐπιστήμαι or *scientiae*, which are characterized by their firmness, i.e. it is impossible to dislodge them by argument; see on *Ac.* 1.41 and *Luc.* 145–6. The corresponding verb is *scire*; cf. *Luc.* 115, 145. The epistemic states of non-sages are not called knowledge or described in terms of knowing in *Acad.*

Apprehension has already been touched on above in connection with *uidere*, *uideri*, *uisum*, and *uisum percipere*. Cicero deploys a range of nouns and verbs in order to talk about apprehension, but not in a mutually exchangeable way. Moreover, the relevant expressions are used with some consistency in Cicero's philosophical works beyond *Acad.* The following two passages are a useful entry point:

> *Luc.* 17: Nec definiri aiebant necesse esse quid esset cognitio aut perceptio aut, si uerbum e uerbo uolumus, comprehensio, quam κατάληψιν illi uocant.

> *Luc.* 23: Quaero etiam, ille uir bonus, qui statuit omnem cruciatum perferre, intolerabili dolore lacerari potius quam aut officium prodat aut fidem, cur has sibi tam graues leges imposuerit, cum quam ob rem ita oporteret nihil haberet **comprehensi percepti cogniti constituti**.

---

[606] Consider *N.D.* 1.12: *Non enim sumus ii, quibus nihil uerum esse uideatur, sed ii, qui omnibus ueris falsa quaedam adiuncta esse dicamus tanta similitudine, ut in iis nulla insit certa iudicandi et assentiendi nota*, 'For we are not people to whom nothing appears to be true, but rather ones who say that all true impressions are associated with false ones of such similarity that in them there is no certain mark enabling judgement and assent.'

[607] *Nota* and *signum* do overlap semantically when they denote a natural peculiar feature of a person or a thing (see *OLD* s.v. *nota* no. 1d, s.v. *signum* no. 3a), but I do not believe that the uses of both terms in *Acad.* converge on this sense.

In *Luc.* 17 the three nouns *cognitio*, *perceptio*, and *comprehensio* appear to be treated as equivalent in meaning, with the only noticeable difference being that *comprehensio* is said to be a word-for-word translation of the Greek term, i.e. formed from a prefix and from the Latin verb matching λαμβάνειν most closely semantically. In *Luc.* 23 the four participles seem to be given for clarification and emphasis,[608] without a suggestion that they differ in meaning, nor can we discern a grouping of the cluster of four terms into e.g. pairs. The nouns and the verbs from which they are derived are, however, only partially exchangeable; see on *Ac.* 1.41.

When the Stoic sage assents to an impression which is not cataleptic, this leads to an 'opinion' (δόξα, *opinio*). The corresponding verb is *opinari*. A Clitomachean like Cicero may profess, when accounting for his own epistemic behaviour, that at times he will give assent and therefore opine because he cannot help it (*Luc.* 66), whereas a mitigated sceptic will be ready to assent and therefore opine as a matter of policy, albeit with the rider that any impression thus assented to may turn out to be false (*Luc.* 148).

For expressions used to designate 'assent' (*assensio*, *assensus*, occasionally *approbatio*; συγκατάθεσις), from which apprehension and opinion arise, see on *Luc.* 37 and *Ac.* 1.40–2.

When Academic speakers explain how one might be guided by impressions, or act on them, without assenting, or when they explain on their own terms how they see their epistemic practices, they may use the verb *sequi*, 'to follow'.[609] There is no corresponding noun to designate a state which arises from following, which one might regard as belief-like (but see below).

Relatedly, in *Luc.* 103–4 Cicero translates from a work by Clitomachus, in which the latter purported to relay a Carneadean distinction between two types of non-assent, one of which is 'approval', a mode of endorsement which the character Cicero deploys. How approval is conceptualized is explained in the commentary ad loc. Verbs used for approving are *approbare*, *probare*, and *sequi*. There is no corresponding noun designating a state arising from approval; in *Luc.* 99, *Qua re ita placere, tale uisum nullum esse ut perceptio consequeretur, ut autem probatio multa*, the terms *perceptio* and *probatio* seem to designate the acts of apprehending and approving, respectively. When Lucullus uses *approbatio* occasionally (*Luc.* 52, 61), a generic act of endorsement is most likely to be meant; in such cases *probare* and related expressions are used non-terminologically,[610] or else with polemical intent, i.e. so as to signal that Lucullus rejects that there is such a thing as approval and that the only available options are suspension of judgement and assent.[611] One might speculate whether a reason for the absence of a noun designating (grammatically) a state arising from approval or following is that (epistemologically) approving and following

---

[608] One function such a cluster of synonyms might have is to establish equivalence, which would then enable the interchangeable use of the individual terms; however, one would suspect such a thing earlier in the work.

[609] See e.g. on *Luc.* 8, 99, 104, 108.

[610] Thus Striker (1996b: 98 n. 23): 'It is true that Cicero does not always observe the terminological distinction between "*adsentiri*" and "*adprobare*", but he emphasizes it in crucial passages.'

[611] This would require the—reasonable—assumption that the basic concept of approval was introduced though not fully explained in the *Catulus*.

does not issue in epistemic states as they are usually conceived, whatever one's particular notion of belief. While Academic following is construed by some in a manner which would be consistent with this view, *Luc.* 103–4 appears to suggest that many impressions which attract approval would issue in belief-like states which are retained as long as the relevant impressions remain unobstacled, in the domain of everyday life and actions as well as in relation to (some) philosophical impressions as they feature in exchanges in question and answer.

Another term and concept which ought to feature here is *decretum*/δόγμα. A *decretum* is a substantial view dogmatically held. Cicero, speaking in the frame of *Luc.* before the dialogue starts (*Luc.* 8–9), explains, without using the actual term, that dogmatists come by their *decreta* by coincidence and are then forced to cling to them blindly, while he is free to exercise judgement and to refrain from forming *decreta*, though not from an attitude of negative dogmatism and while retaining an open mind. According to Lucullus the Stoic sage obviously has and requires *decreta*, which arise from acts of assent to cataleptic impressions and are, qua apprehensions of the sage, ἐπιστῆμαι (*Luc.* 27). It is a charge levelled by the dogmatist, notably Antiochus, against the Academics that despite their pronouncements they actually entertain at least one *decretum*, that nothing can be known (*Luc.* 29). In *Luc.* 133 the character Cicero says he and Lucullus share a δόγμα, viz. that one should not assent to the incognitive. This is either meant as a joke (the Clitomachean and the Stoic hold this view, but only for the dogmatist is it a δόγμα in the technical sense) or it gestures to §109, where Cicero responds to *Luc.* 29 by saying the Academic sage has plenty of *decreta* and could not function without them: in §109 the Cicero character polemically claims the term for the quasi-beliefs the Clitomachean is permitted to hold as a result of approvals (see *Luc.* 104).

Finally, in *Ac.* 1.45, where Arcesilaus' outlook is described, he is said to deny (*negare*) that nothing can be known and to 'hold' (*censere*) that everything was shrouded in darkness. I think that there something like Socratic intuitions, which are different from reasoned views, are at issue.[612] These intuitions do not have the status of one of the 'formal' categories of belief distinguished in *Acad.* and are therefore deemed consistent with a sceptical stance—at least on the view of the Academics.

Terminology related to a perceiving subject's discrimination between impressions or of cataleptic impressions is discussed in section 5.3, expressions used in connection with suspension of judgement (ἐποχή) in the commentary on *Luc.* 94.

11. Table of Contents for *Ac.* 1 and *Luc.*

In this section I present the structure of *Ac.* 1 and *Luc.* Individual sections could be characterized differently, and the reader is encouraged to compare the similar treatments in Reid[1] (pp. 74–83); Schäublin et al. (pp. lxv–lxxxv); and Brittain (2006: liv–lviii).

---

[612] See section 7.3 and Cooper (2006: 180).

Ac. 1:

§§1–14: Proem

§1: Cicero, Atticus, and Varro meet at Cumae

§§2–3: Cicero asks why Varro has not written philosophy

§§4–6: Varro does not see much point in writing philosophy in Latin

§§7–8: Varro encourages friends to study philosophy in Greece, while he writes about subjects not covered by Greek writers

§§9–12: Cicero defends writing philosophy in Latin and encourages Varro to take it on

§§13–14: Varro accuses Cicero of deserting the Old Academy for the New, whereupon Cicero insists (citing Philo) that the New Academy is in agreement with the old; Varro is prevailed upon to speak on the matter

§§15–42: Antiochus' view of the history of philosophy (Varro's speech)

§§15–18: Presocratics, Socrates, Plato; Plato's successors in the Academy and Aristotle (collectively called the *antiqui*); Academy and Peripatos in essential agreement on the *prima forma* of philosophy

§§19–23: Ethical views of the *antiqui*

§§24–9: Physical views of the *antiqui*

§§30–2: Logical views of the *antiqui*

§§33–42: Proposed changes to the *prima forma*, some of which may count as adopted

§§33–4: Peripatetic changes

§33: Aristotle 'undermines' Forms

§33: Theophrastus deems virtue insufficient for happiness

§34: Strato abandoned ethics and concentrates on heterodox physics

§§35–39a: Stoic changes in the area of ethics

§35: Only virtue is good

§§36–7: Indifferents and their selection

§37: Appropriate actions as intermediate

§38: All virtues are rational

§§38–9: Emotions are bad judgements and immoral

§§40–2: Zeno's changes in the field of logic: impressions and assent; apprehension; apprehension, opinion, knowledge, ignorance

§43: Cicero's response (expression of agreement that the Stoics made corrections to the *prima forma* but were not a new school)

§§44–6: Cicero's speech

§44: Arcesilaus, the Presocratics, and Socrates

§45: Arcesilaus' position

§46: Arcesilaus' views were in agreement with Plato and taken forward by Carneades

Luc.:

§§1–6: Lucullus' biography, personal qualities, interest in philosophy, familiarity with Antiochus

§§7–9: Cicero, not yet in character, on his commitments as a Clitomachean

§10a: A look back to *Catul.*

§10b: Lucullus' attitude to the material he relies on
§§11–12: Purported context in which Lucullus learnt of what he relays in his speech—Antiochus' reaction to the Roman Books (Lucullus' speech)
§§13–15: Presocratic predecessors of Academic scepticism; Plato, Socrates, Arcesilaus
§§16–17: Academic scepticism did not immediately supplant the dogmatic approach in the Academy but required consolidation by Carneades
§18: The Roman Books view
§§19–29: Arguments in support of apprehension; it enables:
 §19: Perception
 §19: Perception informed by craft knowledge
 §20: Internal touch
 §§21–2: Conceptions
  §22: Memory
  §22: Craft knowledge
 §23: Virtue
 §24: Wisdom
 §25: Action
 §26: Enquiry
 §§27–9: Meaningful philosophical engagement (which excludes the Academic position)
§§30–1: Teleological justification for §§19–29
§§32–6: Rebuttal of the *probabile*
 §32: Different negative attitudes to apprehension
 §§33–4: Impressions one can go by need a distinctive feature
 §§34–5: Distinction between *percepta* and *perspicua* unsustainable
 §§35–6: Scrutiny of impressions is pointless if they have no distinctive feature
§§37–9: Assent is indispensable for
 §37: Apprehension
 §§37–8: Action, incl. in accordance with nature
 §38: Memory, conceptions, art
 §§38–9: Freedom to act
§§40–60: Counterarguments to the Academics
 §§41–4: Regarding the core argument, which is inconsistent (as deployed by the Academics)
 §§45–6: Defensive strategy for the dogmatist: remain committed to apprehension and reject counterarguments
 §§47–8: Regarding three Sorites-type arguments:
  Involving an ordered series of impressions fashioned by god
  Involving movement of the mind by an ordered series of impressions
  Involving an ordered series of impressions
 §§49–51: Counterpoints to §§47–8
  §§49–50: Progress of the argument depends on acceptance of each step
  §50: Similarity and identity are not the same thing
  §51: Vacuous impressions lack clarity

§52: Regarding the supposed non-distinctness of cataleptic impressions and those experienced while asleep
§53: Regarding impressions experienced while insane
§53: Academic arguments end up confusing everything
§§54–8: Similarities
    §54: Similarities
    §§55–6: Democritus and countless worlds
    §56: Twins
    §§57–8: Difficult cases and how to handle them
§§59–60: Suspension of judgement
    §59: Arcesilaus vs Carneades
    §60: Academic method: *in utramque partem dicere*, not following authority
§§61–2: Conclusion: Cicero is happy to make knowledge claims as a politician and orator, and extol philosophy to Hortensius (in *Hort*.), while following an absurd caricature of philosophy
§63: interlude, attending to tensions between the pronouncements of the Cicero character (and the first-person speaker in the frame) and pronouncements and actions of the historical Cicero
[§§64–147: Cicero's speech]
§§64–8: Introductory section
    §64: Cicero is going to speak about himself and his character
    §65: He is genuine in everything he says
    §66: He tries to avoid assent, but cannot help assenting on many occasions
    §§66–8: Assent is irrational and reprehensible, as Arcesilaus argued; Carneades sometimes granted that the wise man may assent to the non-cataleptic; the Stoics, Antiochus, and Cicero agree that he may not
§§69–71: Inconsistency of Antiochus: while a follower of Philo he argued for non-distinctness of true and false impressions; under the influence of the Stoics he shifted to the endorsement of apprehension, but ascribed his position to the Old Academy; he is proof that nothing can arise from what is the case which could not also arise from what is not the case
§§72–6a: Actual and possible sceptical authorities
    §§72–4: Presocratics, Socrates, Plato
    §§75–6a: Dialecticians, Chrysippus, Cyrenaics
§§76b–78: Zeno and Arcesilaus: the nature and origin of their dispute over the cataleptic impression; the possibility of opinion as an inner-Academic dispute
§§79–98a: The impossibility of apprehension
    §§79–82: The senses are unreliable
    §83: Commitment to the Academic core argument
    §§84–90: Arguments for ἀπαραλλαξία
    §§91–98a: Dialectic—nothing can be apprehended by reason
§§98b–111: The Carneadean *probabile*, its uses, and its function
    §98b: Clitomachus as a source
    §§99–102: The place of the *probabile* relative to other impressions and the sage's use of it
    §103: The senses are not done away with, only certainty

§§104–105a: The Academic mode of endorsement according to Clitomachus: approval
§105: Perception not abolished or impossible
§106: Memory does not require apprehension
§107: Crafts do not require apprehension
§§107–9: Suspension of judgement is possible, as is action without assent
§§109a: In many situations nothing better than the *probabile* is available
§§109–10: The Academic philosopher can and does operate without a *decretum* as defined by the dogmatist, but has *decreta* (arising from approval of *probabilia*)
§111: The core argument is not inconsistent
§§112–46: Disagreement among dogmatic philosophers
    §§112–13: No philosopher before Zeno defined apprehension as Zeno did and stipulated that the sage does not opine; a Peripatetic agreement on the possibility of opining would be easier to reach for Cicero, given the Peripatetic's more relaxed understanding of apprehension; invocation of the Old Academy for the Antiochian view is unwarranted
    §§114–15: It is difficult to understand how the ban on opining and dogmatizing in the area of ethics and physics are to go together
    §§116–28: Physics
        §§116–17: Results unclear
        §§117–21: Disagreements about first principles
        §§122–4: Disagreements about the human body, heavenly bodies, the mind
        §§125–8: Reasons against opting for any one possibility
    §§129–41: Ethics
        §§129–31: Disagreements about ends
        §§132–7: Disagreements between the Old Academics and the Stoics
        §§138–41: Chrysippus on ends
    §§142–6: Logic
        §§142–3: Protagoras, the Cyrenaics, Epicurus, and Plato disagree on the criterion
        §143: Disagreements about conditionals
        §§144–6: The Stoic and Antiochian conception of (craft) knowledge ought to confine it to the sage; Romans naturally incline towards a sceptical posture
§147: Conclusion
§148: End of the dialogue: Catulus remains attached to the mitigated position that was also his father's

TRANSLATIONS

Letters Documenting the Creation of *Acad.*

(T0) *Orat.* 148 July–September 46[1]

Literature was once my companion in the courts and in the Curia, now it gives me pleasure at home. I am not devoting myself to matters such as are contained in this book, but to much more serious and grander ones. If they are completed, then my literary work carried out at home will truly match my forensic activities.

(T1) *Att.* 12.13.1 (= SB 250) 7 March 45[2]

I am troubled by Attica, though I agree with Craterus. Brutus' letter, although it was tactful and friendly, nonetheless moved me to many tears. The loneliness here irks me less than the busyness there. Only you I want to see, but devoting myself to my studies is not more difficult here than if I were at home. Nonetheless the old agony haunts me and persists. I do not yield to it but rather resist.

(T2) *Att.* 12.14.3 (= SB 251) 8 March 45[3]

I have even done what nobody has ventured before: I have written a consolation to myself. I shall send the book to you when the copyists have finished it. I tell you with confidence that there is no consolation like it. I write all day every day—not that it helps, but it distracts me….

(T3) *Att.* 12.15 (= SB 252) 9 March 45

Please see to it that my apologies are given to Appuleius on a daily basis since a blanket apology is deemed not acceptable. In this lonely place I do not talk to anyone, and when I have withdrawn in the morning to a dense and rough forest, I do not come back out until the evening. After you I have no better friend than solitude. In solitude all my conversation is with my studies. It is however interrupted by crying. I fight it as far as I am able to, but up to now I am not equal to it. I shall write back to Brutus as you advise. You shall have the letter tomorrow. Please forward it when you have the opportunity.

(T4) *Att.* 12.16 (= SB 253) 10 March 45

Reading and writing do not make it better but distract me.

---

[1] T22 in Griffin (1997); for the date, see Marinone (2004²: 192).   [2] T1 in Griffin (1997).
[3] T2 in Griffin (1997).

(T5) *Att.* 12.20.1 (= SB 258) 15 March 45

It seems you still do not appreciate that Antony has not disturbed me at all and that nothing of this kind disturbs me anymore. I wrote to you about Terentia in the letter I sent off yesterday. You say I should conceal the extent of my pain and that others expect this of me, too. Can I do this in a better way than by spending all my time on literary work? Admittedly I do not do this to conceal but in order to soothe and cure my soul, but even if this does not benefit me very much, I should think that I am doing enough to disguise my feelings.

(T6) *Att.* 12.12.2 (= SB 259) 16 March 45[4]

Regarding Epicurus, as you please; though in the future I shall change my practice with regard to this kind of character. It is incredible how keen certain people are to feature. Therefore back to the ancients, for no wrath is incurred there.

(T7) *Att.* 12.23.2 (= SB 262) 19 March 45[5]

Just so that you see that, though I am grieving, I am not altogether cast down by it in your *liber Annalis* it is written down under which consuls Carneades and the embassy came to Rome. Now I am asking what the reason for their coming was—something to do with Oropus, I think, but I know nothing definite; and, if that is correct, what was the point at issue. Morever, tell me who the eminent Epicurean at that time was, head of the Garden at Athens, also who were the outstanding politicians in Athens. I believe you can obtain this information from Apollodorus' book among others.

(T8) *Att.* 12.28.2 (= SB 267) 24 March 45[6]

You suggest I go back to my usual ways. For a long time I used to mourn the republic, which I did, but in moderation for there was a place of comfort for me. Now I can no longer follow that way of life nor do I think I should care what others feel I should do; my conscience matters more to me than what everyone says. Regarding my literary consolation of myself, I am not dissatisfied with what I have accomplished. I reduced the visible part of grief; the pain I could not reduce, nor would I want to if I could.

[During April Cicero was with Atticus at his Nomentanum.]

(T9) *Att.* 12.38a.1 (= SB 279) 7 May 45[7]

You say that it is the right time for my strength of spirit to be clearly seen and that some speak in a more severe tone about me than your and Brutus's letters are cast in. If those who think that I am broken in spirit and impaired know the amount and

---

[4] T3 in Griffin (1997).   [5] T4 in Griffin (1997).   [6] T5 in Griffin (1997).
[7] Plasberg (1908 28, ll. 1–6).

nature of my literary production, then I believe they would, if they are at all decent human beings, hold that I am undeserving of reproach, whether it is because I am so far restored that I can turn my susceptive mind to writing on these difficult subjects, or because I have chosen the distraction from my pain which is most free and appropriate for an educated man. Rather they would think that I deserve some praise.

(T10) *Att.* 12.40.1–2 (= SB 281) 9 May 45[8]

Of what kind Caesar's denunciation, directed against my eulogy, is going to be I have seen clearly from the book which Hirtius sent to me. In it he assembles Cato's flaws, while praising me highly at the same time. Thus I have sent the book to Musca, so that he can pass it on to your copyists. I want it be distributed widely; please instruct your people accordingly so that this happens.

I continue to take stabs at the 'letter of advice'. I find nothing I can say, though I have both Aristotle's and Theompompus' letter to Alexander with me. But where is the similarity? They wrote things which were a credit to them and welcome to Alexander. Can you think of something of this kind? Nothing comes to my mind.

You write that you fear that my standing and authority are diminished by my grief. I do not know what people criticize or demand. That I do not hurt? How is that possible? That I do not lie defeated? Has anyone ever been less defeated? While I was seeking comfort in your house, whom did I refuse to see? Did anyone come who was unwelcome to me? From you I travelled to Astura. Those happy people who criticize me could not very well read as much as I have written—how well is irrelevant. But the kind of writing was such that nobody could do it whose spirit was broken. For thirty days I was at the place in the country. Who wanted to meet me or talk to me? Now I read, I write, and those who are in my company find it harder to relax than I find it to work.

(T11) *Fam.* 5.15.4–5 (= SB 252; addressed to Lucceius) written at Astura and sent in reply to SB 251, sent by Lucceius on or around 9 May 45[9]

So I turn to literature, on which I spend all my time, not to seek lasting medicine, but brief forgetfulness of my pain. But if you and I had done what did not even cross our minds because of the daily terrors and spent all our time together, your health would not be a burden to me nor my grief to you. Let us accomplish this, as far as is possible. For what would be better suited to the both of us? So I shall see you soon.

(T12) *Att.* 12.44.4 (= SB 285) 13 May 45[10]

Here I have finished two large compositions; for there is no other way in which I can divert myself from my unhappiness.

---

[8] Plasberg (1908: 28, ll. 7–11). [9] Plasberg (1908: 28, ll. 12–14).
[10] Plasberg (1908: 28, ll. 15–6) and (1922: iii, ll. 1–3); T6 in Griffin (1997).

(T13) *Att.* 13.26.2 (= SB 286) 14 May 45[11]

It is hardly believable how much I am writing, even at night.

[On 16 May Cicero left Astura and went briefly to Lanuuium, then to Tusculum.]

(T14) *Att.* 12.52.2–3 (= SB 294) 21 May 45[12]

I am waiting to hear what you have done about the letter to Caesar. About Silius I am less concerned. You must get me either Scapula's or Clodia's (gardens). You seem to be in some doubt about Clodia: is it about when she will return or whether they are for sale? And what is it that I am hearing about Spinther, that he has got divorced? Do not worry about the Latin language. You will say †...†. They are transcripts and do not require much work; I merely contribute the words, of which I have plenty.

(T15) *Att.* 13.32.2–3 (= SB 305) 29 May 45[13]

Please send me Dicaearchus' two books on the soul and the Descent; I cannot find the Tripoliticus and his letter to Aristoxenus. I would dearly like to have these three books now; they would help with what I am thinking about.

'Torquatus' is in Rome. I have sent word that it be handed over to you. I have sent 'Catulus' and 'Lucullus' earlier, I believe. New proems have been added to these books, in which each of them is eulogized. I would like you to have these works, and there are some others. You did not quite understand what I wrote to you about the ten commissioners, I think, since I had used abbreviations. I was asking about C. Tuditanus, who I learnt from Hortensius was one of the commissioners. I see it mentioned by Libo that he was praetor when P. Popilius and P. Rupilius were consuls. How could he have been a commissioner fourteen years before he was made praetor? Unless he became praetor very late, which I don't believe. For I see that he obtained curule magistracies at the legally permitted time without any difficulty. As for Postumius, whose statue at the Isthmus you say you remember, I did not know that he was Aulus. It was him who was consul with L. Lucullus. You have made him an appropriate addition to my conference. If you are able to, please look out for the others, so that my personae may join the procession.

(T16) *Att.* 12.6.2 (= SB 306) 31 May 45 (?)[14]

But, I ask you, what is the relevance of a disquisition on the grave and the acute to the highest good?

(T17) *Att.* 13.5 (= SB 312) 5 June 45[15]

I have sent you 'Torquatus'.

---

[11] Plasberg (1908: 28, ll. 17–18). [12] Plasberg (1908: 28, ll. 19–21); T7 in Griffin (1997).
[13] Plasberg (1908: 28, ll. 22–5) and (1922: iii, ll. 4–8); T8 in Griffin (1997).
[14] T9 in Griffin (1997). [15] T10 in Griffin (1997).

[On 21–2 June Cicero left Tusculum for his estate at Arpinum.]

(T18) *Att.* 13.12.3 (= SB 320) 23 June 45[16]

Regarding what you're writing about Varro, you know that earlier I wrote speeches and other kinds of material which would not allow me to weave in Varro. But after I had begun to undertake these more learned compositions, Varro promised the dedication of a major and weighty work to me. Two years have gone by where this slow-coach has run hard but not advanced a foot, while I prepared myself to reciprocate to what he would send me 'either by the same measure or better still', if I was at all able to; for that qualification Hesiod added as well, 'if you can'. Now I have pledged the work on the ends, which I quite like, to Brutus, and you approved; he is not averse, as you have indicated in your letter. Therefore let me transfer the Academic treatise, in which noble men but in no sense scholars speak all too acutely, to Varro. The subject is Antiochian matters, of which he very much approves. We will make it up to Catulus and Lucullus some other time, that is, if you approve of the idea. Please write back to me about it.

(T19) *Att.* 13.3.1–2 (= SB 321) 24 June 45[17]

Moved by your letter about Varro, I have taken away the whole Academy from these most noble men and have transferred it to our friend, converting the two books into four. They are altogether bigger than the earlier two, though much has been taken away. I would very much appreciate if you told me how you understood that he would like that; one thing I would dearly like to know in particular is who you think he is jealous of, unless perhaps it is Brutus. That would be the one thing that was missing! Still, I would very much like to know. The books themselves, unless fondness for myself deceives me, have turned out so well that not even among the Greeks there is something similar of this kind. I am sure you will bear the waste of your copyists' time with equanimity now that what you already have on Academic matters has been copied in vain. These books will be finer, more concise, and better.

Right now, though, I do not know where to turn first. I want to write something for Dolabella, who would like this very much; I cannot find a suitable topic, and at the same time 'I fear the Trojans', and will not be able to escape criticism if I give him something different. So I must either pause or think of something.

(T20) *Att.* 13.14.1 (= SB 322) 25 June 45[18]

I should like you to consider again and yet again whether you think it is a good idea to send to Varro what I have written—though the matter affects you too. For you should know that you are connected with the dialogue as a third speaker. I do think we need to reflect. The names have already been set down, but they can be cancelled or altered.

---

[16] Plasberg (1908: 28, l. 26–9, l. 6) and (1922: iii, ll. 9–24); T11 in Griffin (1997).
[17] Plasberg (1908: 29, ll. 7–17) and (1922: iii, l. 25–iv, l. 38); T12 in Griffin (1997).
[18] Plasberg (1908: 29, ll. 18–22) and (1922: iv, ll. 39–44); T13 in Griffin (1997).

(T21) *Att.* 13.16.1–2 (= SB 323) 26 June 45[19]

Although I am drawn to streams and solitude to keep my spirits up, I have so far hardly set foot out of the door because of heavy and constant rain. We have transferred the entire Academic work to Varro. First the participants were Catulus, Lucullus, and Hortensius. Then, because this did not seem right since it is well known these characters lacked the familiarity with these matters though not the general cultured disposition, I transferred these conversations to Cato and Brutus. At that moment your letter about Varro came. The Antiochian stance is uniquely suitable to him. But please write back to me to say if I should dedicate something to him and, if yes, if it should be this work.

(T22) *Att.* 13.18 (= SB 325) 28 June 45[20]

Meanwhile, following your advice, I have finished some clever little books to Varro, but I am nonetheless waiting for your answers to my questions, first how you got the sense that he would like a dedication from me since he himself, very prolific as he is, never challenged me to do this; then who you think he is jealous of. If not Brutus, much less can it be Hortensius or the men who conversed in *On the Republic*. What I would primarily like you to say clearly is whether you remain of the view that I send my writings to him or whether you regard this as unnecessary. But let us discuss this.

(T23) *Att.* 13.19.3–5 (= SB 326) 29 June 45[21]

In connection with Varro I am unconcerned that I might look like someone who is in search of appreciation. The fact is that I had resolved not to feature living persons in my dialogues, but because you wrote that it was Varro's desire and that this meant much to him, I have composed this work and have dealt with the entire Academic question in four books, I do not know how well, but at least as conscientiously as possible. In them I have given to Varro what had been splendidly gathered together by Antiochus against the claim that there is no apprehension. To that I myself respond; you are the third man in this conversation. If I had let Cotta and Varro have this conversation, as you suggested in your last letter, then I would be a *muta persona*. This works when the characters are historical; Heraclides has done this in many books, and we have done this in the six books *On the Republic*. And there are the three books *On the Ideal Orator*, of which I think highly. In them the characters were such that I had to remain silent. Crassus speaks, Antonius, the older Catulus, C. Julius, the brother of Catulus, Cotta, and Sulpicius. The conversation is set at a time when I was a boy, so I could not take part. But what I have written recently follows the Aristotelian manner, in which the other characters in the dialogue are introduced in such a way that the author takes the lead. In this manner I have completed five books on limits, giving the Epicurean material to Torquatus, the Stoic material to

---

[19] Plasberg (1908: 29, ll. 23–30) and (1922: iv, ll. 45–53); T14 in Griffin (1997).
[20] Plasberg (1908: 29, ll. 31–8) and (1922: iv, ll. 54–63); T15 in Griffin (1997).
[21] Plasberg (1908: 29, l. 39–30, l. 24) and (1922: iv, l. 64–v, l. 98); T16 in Griffin (1997).

Cato, the Peripatetic material to Piso. I thought that this would not give rise to jealousy since all of them were dead. The Academic work, as you know, I had given to Catulus, Lucullus, and Hortensius. Admittedly this did not fit the characters; for the work was more argumentative than they could ever have dreamt of. Thus, when I read your letter about Varro, I seized upon the opportunity as a godsend. Nothing could have been better suited to that type of philosophy, which he seems to enjoy particularly, and his role is such that I have not succeeded in making my side of the argument appear stronger. For Antiochus thought is very persuasive; I have expressed them carefully, so that they have Antiochus' acumen, but the splendor of our oratory, assuming it has any. But please consider yet again if this work should be given to Varro. I can see considerations against; but let us talk about them.

(T24) *Att.* 13.21a.1–2 (= SB 327) 30 June/1 July 45[22]

Now tell me, do you approve of publication without my instruction? Not even Hermodorus did that, who used to flock Plato's books, whence the standing expression. And another point: do you think it was right to give the book to anyone before Brutus, whom I made the dedicatee on your suggestion? Balbus writes to me that he has copied out Book 5 from your exemplar; in that I have not made many changes but nonetheless some. You will do me a favour by holding the others back, so that Balbus does not get them uncorrected and Brutus already perused. But enough of that; I do not want to seem preoccupied with trivialities. Still, these things are matters of the highest importance for me nowadays, for what else is there?

I am in such a hurry to send to Varro what I have written at your instigation that I have already sent it to Rome for copying. If you want it, you will get it at once. I have written to the copyists to let your people take a copy if you wish. Please keep it to yourself until I see you, as you routinely do most diligently when I ask you to.

But how did I forget to tell you? Quite astonishingly, Caerellia, undoubtedly burning with zeal for philosophy, copying from your people, has the very work *On Ends*. I assure you, though I may be mistaken like any man, that she does not have it from my people. I kept it close, so that they could not have made two copies when they barely managed one. Still, I do not think there has been foul play by your people, and neither should you; I neglected to say that I did not want them to go out yet. Dear me, how much time I have spent on trifles. I actually have nothing to say on serious matters.

(T25) *Att.* 13.22.1 and 3 (= SB 329) 4(?) July 45[23]

It is not without a reason that I ask with such persistence what you think should be done with regard to Varro. Some objections occur to me. We will talk about them. I have woven you in with the greatest pleasure and will do so frequently in the future. From your last letter I understood for the first time that you do not object to this....

---

[22] Plasberg (1908: 30, ll. 25–9) and (1922: v, ll. 99–104); T17 in Griffin (1997).
[23] Plasberg (1908: 30, ll. 30–5) and (1922: v, ll. 105–11); T18 in Griffin (1997).

Back to the first topic. Nowhere would I rather want my writings to be than in your care, but I want them to be shared out when both of us think the time is right. I exonerate your copyist and do not accuse you, but I did write to you about something else, that Caerellia is in possession of works which she cannot have received from my people. I realized Balbus' wishes had to be satisfied; I merely did not want Brutus to be given something already perused or Balbus something that was not finished. I shall send my book to Varro as soon as if I have seen you, if you think that is right. You shall know the reason for my hesitation when I see you.

[On 6/7 July Cicero travelled to Tusculum from Arpinum.]

(T26) *Att.* 13.33a.1 (= SB 330) 9(?) July 45

We were talking about Varro: speak of the devil. He came to visit me, at an hour when I had to make him stay. But I ensured that I did not tear his coat. For I remember your phrase: 'there were many, and we were unprepared.' No use! Soon after C. Capito arrives with T. Carrinas. I barely touched their coat. But they stayed and it turned out rather well.

(T27) *Att.* 13.23.2 (= SB 331) 10 July 45[24]

My work in several books dedicated to Varro will not be delayed, they are almost finished, as you saw; only the copyists' mistakes are being removed. You know I have my doubts about this work, but you know best. The copyists also have the work I am sending to Brutus in hand.

(T28) *Att.* 13.24.1 (= SB 332) 11 July 45[25]

What is this that Clodius Hermogenes tells me that Andromenes had told him that he had seen Marcus Cicero on Corcyra? I should have thought you heard of it. Did he fail to give something to include in a letter even to him? Or did he not see him? Please let me know. What am I to reply to you on Varro? The four books are at your disposal. Whatever you do I shall approve. Still, it is not that 'I fear the Trojans?'— why would I—and was more concerned what he would make of the dedication. But since it is your responsibility, I shall simply roll on my other side.

(T29) *Fam.* 9.8 (= SB 254; the dedicatory letter to Varro) app. 11 July 45[26]

Although to demand a gift, even if someone has created an expectation, is something not even the crowd does unless it has been provoked, I am nonetheless moved by the expectation of your fulfilling your promise to remind you, though not to make a demand. I have sent you four reminders who are not overly shy; you of course know that this younger Academy has a bit of a mouth on it. The reminders I have sent you

---

[24] Plasberg (1908: 30, ll. 36–9) and (1922: v, ll. 112–16).
[25] Plasberg (1908: 30, l. 40–31, l. 2) and (1922: v, ll. 117–21).
[26] Plasberg (1908: 31, ll. 3–27) and (1922: v, ll. 122–52).

have been mustered from Academy central; I am afraid they may make demands, but I have charged them to ask nicely. I have been waiting quite a while and holding back so that I would not write for you one thing before I had received another, in order to be able to pay you back in the same coin. But since you are making slow progress, which I interpret as being considered, I could not restrain myself from making plain, by means of a composition that lay within my powers, that there is between us a bond of common pursuits and affection. So I have mounted a conversation between us at Cumae, with Pomponius also present; I have given you the Antiochian part, which I believe you approve of, and have taken on the Philonian part myself. I think you will be surprised when you find that we have discussed a subject which we have in fact never discussed; but you know the convention of dialogues. In future, dear Varro, we shall have plenty of conversations if so minded, between ourselves and to please ourselves—perhaps late in the day. But may the fortune of the republic stand for what is past, the present we must take care of ourselves. Wish we could pursue these mutual interests in calmer times and while the country was if not in a good then at least a settled state. Though in that case there would be other demands placed on us, calling us to honourable attention and action; now what reason is there for us to want to live without our studies? I for one have little desire for life with them, and none at all if they were taken away. But we will talk this over when we are together and often. Good luck with your move and the purchase; I think what you are doing is wise. Take care of your health.

(T30) *Att.* 13.25.3 (= SB 333) 12 July 45[27]

Why is is that you are aghast that I have directed that the books be given to Varro at your risk? If you have any concerns even at this stage, let me know what they are. I think it is a really neat piece of work. I want Varro as a dedicatee, especially because he asked for it; but he is, as you know, 'a man to be feared; quickly he'd blame even a blameless man'. I have often imagined his expression complaining, perhaps, on the grounds that my parts in the books are better argued than his, which you will certainly find not to be the case if you ever get to Epirus. Right now I am devoting attention to Alexio's letters. However, I have not given up in the idea that Varro will approve, and since we have gone to the expense of a folio edition, I readily stick to the plan. But I say it again and again, it will be at your risk. If you have any concerns, let us transfer to Brutus; since he, too, is an Antiochian. The Academy, always changing her mind—this is quite like her! Soon this view, then that one. But tell me, did you not quite like my letter to Varro? I curse myself if I should ever make such an effort over anything again. For that reason I did not dictate it to Tiro, who tends to take down entire periods in one go, but syllable by syllable to Spintharus.

(T31) *Att.* 13.35-6.2 (= SB 334) 13 July 45[28]

You say you will present it to Varro as soon as he arrives. So it is done and there is no way back; ah, if only you knew what danger you're in. Or perhaps my letter made you

---

[27] Plasberg (1908: 31, ll. 3–27) and (1922: vi, ll. 153–71); T19 in Griffin (1997).
[28] Plasberg (1908: 31, ll. 43–4) and (1922: vii, ll. 172–7).

hesitate if you had not read it when you wrote your last. I am eager to know how the matter stands.

(T32) *Att.* 13.44.2 (= SB 336) 28(?) July 45[29]

You dared to give it to Varro. I am awaiting his judgement. When will he read it?

[On 25 August Cicero returned to Astura.]

(T33) *Att.* 13.21.3 (= SB 351) 27 August 45[30]

To return to business, your term *inhibere*, which seemed most attractive to me, I know profoundly dislike. The term is entirely nautical. I knew this of course, but I thought the oarsmen stopped rowing on the command *inhibere*. That is not the case, as I learnt yesterday, when a boat put in at my house. They do not stop rowing but row in a different way. That is furthest removed from suspension of judgement. So could you please put it back into the book as it was. And could you ask the same thing of Varro if he indeed made the change. One cannot put it better than Lucilius: 'Hold in, like a good driver, the car and the horses.' And Carneades always compared a boxer's posture and a driver's holding in to suspension of judgement. But *inhibitio* of oarsmen involves movement and quite powerful movement, too, rowing the boat astern.

(T34) *Luc.* 147 March–May 45[31]

Next time when we investigate such matters, we should rather talk about the disagreement among so many leading men, about the obscurity of physical issues and about the mistake made by so many philosophers (who disagree about goods and evils to such a degree that, because more than one claim on a given matter cannot be true, so many noble systems must lie shattered), rather than about lies of the eyes and the remaining senses, about the sorites and about the liar—hunting nets which the Stoics have woven for themselves.

(T35) *Fin.* 1.2 March–May 45[32]

Since this work appeared to find your and Brutus' approval as well as that of those whom I regard as able to make a judgement, I have embarked on further endeavours....

(T36) *Tusc.* 2.4 July–August 45[33]

In the *Hortensius* we replied to those who are critical of philosophy in general. What can be said in support of the Academy we believe we have laid out in detail in the

---

[29] Plasberg (1908: 32, ll. 5–6) and (1922: vii, ll. 178–80); T20 in Griffin (1997).
[30] Plasberg (1908: 32, l. 33–33, l. 2) and (1922: vii, ll. 181–96); T21 in Griffin (1997).
[31] T23 in Griffin (1997).   [32] T24 in Griffin (1997).
[33] Plasberg (1908: 32, ll. 7–9); for the date, see Marinone (2004²: 215).

four *Academici libri*; but we are so far from not wanting to be criticized that we very much welcome criticism. For even in Greece itself philosophy would never have been held in such regard if it had not flourished due to the disputes and disagreements of the most learned men.

(T37) *Tim.* 1 composed just before *N.D.*(?)[34]

In my *Academici libri* I have made many points against the natural philosophers and have often had discussions with P. Nigidius in the Carneadean manner.

(T38) *N.D.* 1.9 August 45[35]

But I had no better way of enjoying even this (consolation) than to devote myself not just to reading books but also to treating the whole of philosophy in writing. All of its parts and all of its branches are most readily known if all the issues raised in philosophy are explained in writing. For philosophy is an admirable interlinked and joined-up body of issues, so that everything is connected with something else and is mutually connected and bound together.

(T39) *N.D.* 1.11–12[36]

To those who are surprised that I follow this school in particular, a sufficient reply is given in the four *Academici libri*. Nor is it the case that we have undertaken the guardianship of a lost and abandoned cause; views do not die with the passing of individuals, but they do perhaps suffer the loss of an authoritative exponent. Take for instance in philosophy the approach of arguing against everything and not passing judgement openly on anything, which arises from Socrates, was resumed by Arcesilaus, strengthened by Carneades, and flourished right down to our age; I understand it is now almost without a champion in Greece. But this I ascribe not to the fault of the Academy, but to the mental slowness of mankind. If it is a considerable task to understand any one system of philosophy, how much greater a task is it to understand them all. Yet this those must do whose mission it is to speak against all philosophers and for all philosophers in order to find the truth. In an endeavour so large and difficult I do not claim to have reached complete facility, but I do point out that I have sought it. At the same time it is not possible that those who do engage in philosophy in this manner have nothing that they could follow. I have discussed this matter elsewhere more thoroughly, but because certain people are dull and slow to grasp things, it seems right to remind them frequently.

---

[34] For the date, see Marinone (2004^2: 215).
[35] T25 in Griffin (1997); for the date, see Marinone (2004^2: 215–16).
[36] Plasberg (1908: 32, ll. 7–9).

(T40) *Div.* 2.1 November 45–after 15 March 44[37]

In my work entitled *Hortensius* I encouraged readers as best I could to take up the study of philosophy, and I showed in the four *Academici libri* which type of philosophizing I regard as the least arrogant, and the most consistent and sophisticated.

(T41, cf. t. 20) Cicero, *Att.* 16.6.4 (= SB 414) 25 July 44

[Translation included as t. 20 amongst the fragments and testimonia.]

(T42) *Off.* 2.7–8 Autumn 44[38]

We encounter criticism, from learned and educated people at that, who ask if we think we are being consistent when, although we say that nothing can be apprehended, we discuss all sorts of topics and are at this very moment concerned with precepts on duty. I wish that those critics understood our position adequately. For we Academics are not people whose mind wanders in a state of aimlessness, having nothing that it could follow. For what sort of mindset would it be and indeed what sort of life, after all rules not just of reasoning and also of living are removed? But we call some things persuasive, other things the opposite, just others, with whom we disagree, call some things certain, other things uncertain. What then prevent me from following those impressions which appear to be persuasive to me, and not to approve those which appear to be the opposite, and to evade rashness by avoiding the arrogance of assent, which is most distant from wisdom? Our side argues against all propositions because that which is persuasive cannot possibly shine forth unless there is a contest of both cases argued from either side. But these matters are explained in our *Academici libri* quite carefully, as I think.

---

[37] Plasberg (1908: 32, ll. 15–17); for the date, see Marinone (2004^2: 216).
[38] Plasberg (1908: 32, ll. 15–17); for the date, see Marinone (2004^2: 236–7).

Academicus Primus

(I) (§1) Recently, when my friend Atticus was staying with me at the villa near Cumae, we received a message from M. Varro that he had come from Rome the previous evening and, if he was not too tired from the journey, would come to us straightaway. When we heard this, we thought we must not delay to see a man bound to us by an interest in the same studies and by the length of our friendship; thus we set off immediately to go to him. When we were but a small distance away from his villa, we saw the man himself coming towards us; and we embraced him, as is the custom among friends, and after quite a while led him back to his villa. (§2) Once we were there, there was a bit of preliminary conversation, and I enquired if there was any news from Rome.

Then Atticus said: 'Please pass over all this we cannot enquire and hear about without distress, and rather ask whether *he* has any news. Varro's Muses have been silent for longer than usual, but I do not believe he is at a standstill as much as concealing what he is writing.'

'Not at all', he said, 'I think it is the mark of a heedless man to write something with the intention of hiding it; but I have on hand an expansive work, on which I have been working for quite some time; for I have undertaken something dedicated to him'—he meant me—'which is quite big and is being polished carefully by me.'

(§3) And I said: 'This work that you mention, Varro, I have been expecting for long time, but I do not dare to demand it; for I have heard from our friend Libo, whose zeal you know (we cannot conceal anything of this kind), that you are working on it without interruption, are taking great care over it, and never put it down. There is, however, something that to ask you has never entered my mind before now. But now that I have embarked on writing up things I learnt with you and on illuminating in Latin that ancient brand of philosophy which took its rise from Socrates, I ask why it is that you, although you write voluminously, pass over this genre, especially considering that you are an expert in it and that the passion for that pursuit and the whole subject is far superior to other arts and fields of study.'

(II) (§4) Then he said: 'You are asking about a subject I have often thought about and pondered this way and that. So I shall not be hesitant in replying, but say things I have ready to hand, for I have thought about this very issue often, as I say, and long. For when I saw that philosophy had been most carefully expounded in Greek, I thought that, if some of our fellow countrymen had a real interest in this subject, they would rather read Greek works than any of mine in Latin, if they were educated in Greek learning, but if they were repelled by Greek arts and subjects, they would not pay attention to writings in Latin which cannot be understood in themselves unless one is versed in Greek learning. Therefore I did not want to write what the uneducated could not understand and the educated did not care to read. (§5) You are able to see—for you have learnt the same things yourself—that we cannot be like

Amafinius and Rabirius, who talk about subjects which are in plain sight in common language without employing formal method, define nothing, offer no divisions, do not arrive at conclusions by asking appropriate questions, and in sum do not believe that there is either an art of rhetoric or of philosophical argument. But *we* obey the precepts of the dialecticians and of the orators in addition (since our people deem both faculties to be virtues) as if they were laws, and are forced to use new terms as well; those precepts the learned as I say will prefer to obtain from the Greeks, while the unlearned will not accept them from us either, so that the whole effort is undertaken in vain. (§6) Now about physics I could write in as plain a manner as Amafinius, if I approved of Epicurus, that is, of Democritus. For what is remarkable in talking about the random collision of "small bodies" (for that is what he calls atoms), because he has done away with the causes which bring about effects? You know our teachings on physics: since they are comprising of effective force and matter which the effective force shapes and forms, geometry has to be attended to as well—in what language is someone supposed to make pronouncements on that and whom is one going to get to understand it? Then, again, these questions about life, behaviour, and what one should strive for and what shun, these they deal with in a basic way, for they think that there is the same good for animals and humans, while with our people you know well what remarkable subtlety there is on the subject. (§7) For if you follow Zeno, it is a large task to make someone understand what this true and simple good is which cannot be detached from the honourable (Epicurus says that he cannot even have an inkling of the nature of this good without pleasures which stimulate the senses); but if we follow the Old Academy, which we approve of as you know, how shrewdly will it have to be explained by us, how cleverly and even obscurely will one have to argue against the Stoics. Thus I pursue the study of philosophy as a whole both with a view to consistency in my life, as far as I am able, and to delight my mind, and I do not regard, as we read in Plato, any gift from the gods to man as greater or better. (§8) But my friends, who are interested in philosophy, I send to Greece, i.e. I tell them to seek out Greeks as teachers, so that they may drink from the spring rather than go for the secondary channels. But what nobody had taught until now and where there was no resource from which those who were interested could obtain the information, there I have done what I could (none of my books I admire excessively) to make it familiar to our fellow Romans; for from the Greeks such information could not be obtained and after the death of our L. Aelius not from Latin writers either. Still, in those earlier works of mine, over which—imitating Menippus but not translating him—we have sprinkled a certain lightheartedness, many profoundly philosophical points have been woven in, much is said dialectically, and to help the less learned to understand it, they have been invited to read by a dose of charm: while in the encomia, indeed in these very proems of the *Antiquitates* our intention was to write in a philosophical manner, if indeed we have achieved that.'

(III) (§9) Then I said: 'That is so, Varro. For when we were feeling like foreigners and wandering aimlessly in our own city, your books escorted us, as it were, home, so that we could at last understand who and where we are. The age of our homeland, its chronology, the sacred laws and customs relating to the priesthoods, the rules obtaining during peace time and in times of war, the names, types, functions, and origins of locations, regions, and places, of all divine and human things—it is you who has opened all these things for us. You have brought much light to our poets and in general to Latin literature and Latin vocabulary, and have yourself composed poetic work which is varied, elegant, and cast in almost every metre available, and you have begun to deal with philosophy in many places, enough to encourage readers, though not enough to serve as instruction. (§10) But you do indeed cite a plausible reason for this: either those who are educated will prefer to read Greek texts, or, in the case of those who do not know Greek, they will not read on the subject in Latin either. But you do not quite carry your point: for those who can read Greek and those who cannot will actually not spurn what is written in their native language. For why should those who are instructed in Greek learning read Latin poets, but not philosophers? Further, considering that Ennius, Pacuvius, Accius, and many others who have not translated Greek poets literally but conveyed their sense, give rise to enjoyment, how much more will philosophers delight if, just as those imitate Aeschylus, Sophocles, and Euripides, so they imitate Plato, Aristotle, and Theophrastus. Indeed, I see orators of ours lauded if they imitate Hyperides or Demosthenes. (§11) But, Varro—for I will tell you how things are—while ambition, posts, legal cases, while not just concern for the welfare of the state but to a degree also its administration held me tied up and committed by many obligations, I kept philosophy in my mind and refreshed it when I could by reading so that it would not go stale; but now that fortune has inflicted a most severe wound on me and that I am free from the running of the state, I seek a cure for my pain from philosophy and judge it to be the most noble delight of my leisure time. For either it is most fitting for me at my age, or best in agreement with any actions of mine which may have been deserving of praise, or else nothing is more useful for educating one's fellow citizens, or if none of these applies, I do not see anything else that we could do. (§12) Our friend Brutus, who is outstanding in every kind of praiseworthy activity, pursues philosophy in Latin in such a way that one feels the need for nothing in Greek on the same subject, and he follows the same view as you. For he once heard Aristus in Athens, whose brother Antiochus you had heard. Thus I ask you, devote yourself to this kind of literature, too.'

(IV) (§13) Then he said: 'I will certainly consider this, but not without involving you. But what is it that I hear about *you*?'

'In what connection?', I say.

'That you have left behind the Old Academy', he said, 'and that you are now treating of the New one.'

'What of it?', I said. 'Is Antiochus, our friend, to have more freedom to move back into the old house from the new one than we to move from the old one into the new? Certainly the most recent thing is always the most correct and improved. Philo, though, Antiochus' teacher, a great man as you yourself think, denies in his books what I used also to hear him say personally, that there are two Academies, and showed up the error of those who thought this.'

'It is as you say', he said. 'But I don't think you are ignorant of what Antiochus wrote against Philo's books.'

(§14) 'Indeed', I said, 'these matters and the whole of the Old Academy, from which I have been absent for such a long time, I would like to see treated afresh by you, if it is not inconvenient', and at the same time: 'Let us sit down if it suits.'

'By all means, yes', he said. 'For I am fairly tired. But let us see if Atticus agrees that I do what, as I see, you want me to do.'

'Yes, I do', Atticus said. 'What could I like better than to recall what I heard from Antiochus a long time ago, and to see at the same time if it can be said in Latin satisfactorily?'

After these remarks we all sat down facing one another.

(§15) Then Varro began like this: 'It seems to me that Socrates, as is agreed by all, was the first to call philosophy away from obscure subjects, wrapped up by nature herself, with which all previous philosophers were preoccupied, and brought it to everyday life. Thus he inquired into the virtues and vices and in general into things good and bad, but deemed matters of the heavens to be far beyond human cognition or, if they were known as well as can be, irrelevant to living well. (§16) In almost all his conversations, which were written down by those who heard him in colourful and eloquent works, he argues in such a way that he affirms nothing, refutes others, says that he knows nothing except this itself, and that he exceeds others precisely because they think they know what they do not know while he himself knows this one thing, that he knows nothing; and that he thinks he was called the wisest of all men by Apollo because human wisdom consisted in not thinking that one knows what one does not know. While he said this habitually and persisted in this view, all his talk was nonetheless about praising virtue and exhorting people to the study of virtue, as can be understood from the books of the Socratics and of Plato in particular. (§17) By the authority of Plato, who was many-sided, complex, and eloquent, one form of philosophy was established, uniform and in agreement with itself but carrying two names, that of the Academics and that of the Peripatetics, who agreed in substance but had different names. For after Plato had left Speusippus, the son of his sister, in charge as the heir of his philosophy as it were, but the two who stood out for zeal and learning, Xenocrates of Calchedon and Aristotle of Stageira, ⟨as caretakers so to speak⟩, those who were with Aristotle were called Peripatetics, because they held discussions while walking around in the Lyceum, but those who, because by a custom established by Plato they used to meet in the Academy, which is the other gymnasium, and hold conversations there, took their name from the place. But both, filled with Plato's richness of thought, assembled a certain distinct formula of his doctrines, and a plentiful and comprehensive one at that, but the custom of Socrates' of discussing all subjects in a doubtful manner and without applying any firm endorsement, that they left behind. So there was fashioned what Socrates used to disapprove of completely, a kind of philosophical craft, an order of subjects, and a clear outline of the body of doctrines. (§18) This was initially one, albeit with two names as I said; for there was no difference between the Peripatetics and that Old Academy. Aristotle stood out, it seems to me, by a certain wealth of innate talent, but both had the same fountain head and the same division of things to be pursued and to be avoided.

(V) But what am I doing', he said, 'or am I of sound mind that I teach you about these matters? For even if it is not a case of a pig teaching Minerva as the saying goes, nonetheless anyone who endeavours to teach Minerva is being silly.'

Then Atticus said: 'By all means continue, Varro; I take great delight in our subjects and our people, and these topics bring me joy when they are stated in Latin and in this manner.'

'What joy do you think *I* take', I said, 'given that I have already declared that I will put philosophy on display for our fellow Romans.'

(§19) 'Let us continue then', he said, 'since that is what you want. There was then already, handed down from Plato, a tripartite division of philosophy, one about how to live and how to behave, the second about nature and matters which are hidden, the third about discourse and judging what is true, what false, what correct in speech and what false, what is consistent and what inconsistent.

But they looked to nature for the first part about the good life from nature and said one should obey her, and that nowhere else but in nature that highest good should be sought which is the reference point for everything, and they determined that the thing that is to be pursued the most and the end was the obtainment of all goods deriving from nature with respect to soul, body, and life. As to the goods of the body, they put some in the whole, and some in the parts, health, strength, and beauty into the whole, but into the parts unimpaired senses and a kind of excellence of the individual parts, like swiftness in the feet, strength in the hands, clarity in the voice, also in language a fully developed ability of expression. (§20) The goods of the soul they made what was suitable to grasping virtue with one's innate disposition, and these were divided by them into what is part of one's nature and what are acquired forms of behaviour. To nature they accorded the ability to learn quickly and memory, both of which are peculiar to the mind and to one's innate talent; belonging with "acquired forms of behaviour" they thought were application and as it were habit, which they formed partly by regular practice and partly by a reasoned approach, in which lay philosophy herself. In it what has begun and is not yet ⟨complete⟩ is called progress towards virtue, but what is complete, i.e. virtue, is as it were the perfection of one's nature and the single best thing of all they situate in the soul. So much for the goods of the soul. (§21) These, then, are the goods of the soul. But the goods of life (for this was the third item), which were significant for the use of virtue, were associated with them, they said. Now virtue is manifest in the goods of the mind and of the body and in certain things which are not so much connected with nature as with the happy life. For they judged that man is as it were a certain part of a commonwealth and of the whole of the human race, and that he is connected with other human beings in a kind of human fellowship. About the highest and natural good they say this, then; but other goods are on their view relevant to enhancing or maintaining it, like wealth, resources, glory, and influence. In this manner the doctrine of the three goods is introduced by them, (VI) (§22) and these are the three goods regarding which most people think they were meant by the Peripatetics. That is not a false view; for this division does belong to the Peripatetics. Rash is, however, if one thinks that the Academics who then bore this title and the Peripatetics were separate groups. The doctrine belonged to both, and to both the following appeared to be the highest good, to obtain the first advantages of nature and things of value pursued on their own account, either all of them or the most important ones; but the most important ones are those, which reside in the soul itself and in virtue itself. Therefore that entire ancient brand of philosophy deemed the happy life to be placed in virtue alone, but not the most happy one, unless the goods of the body and what was named above as suitable to support the use of virtue are added as well. (§23) From that outline a starting point for action in life and for appropriate action was derived, which lay in the preservation of all the things which nature prescribed. From this there arose an avoidance of idleness and a disdain for pleasures, also the willingness to shoulder burdens and endure great and varied pain, for the sake of what was right and honourable and of those things which were in agreement with the stipulations of nature; from this there arose also friendship, justice, and fairness, and these things were put ahead of pleasures and the many advantages of life. Such then was in their view an organized system of moral behaviour, and the form and outline of the part of philosophy which I put first.

(§24) About nature (this subject comes next) they spoke in such a way that they divided it into two things, so that one was effective, the other as it were offered itself to the first, and it was made into something. They thought that there was a force in the thing which was effective, but in the one which was affected there was only a certain kind of matter. Nonetheless, (they thought) both were in one another; for neither could matter hang together if it was not held together by any force, nor could force exist without any matter; for there is nothing which is not necessarily somewhere. But what arises from both, that they now called a body and as it were a certain "quality"—you will allow, I hope, that on unfamiliar subjects we use sometimes words never heard before, which is what the Greeks themselves do who have been discussing such matters for a long time.'

(VII) (§25) 'Of course we will allow you to do that', said Atticus. 'You can even use Greek words when you want to, if you run out of Latin ones.'

'That is good of you; but I shall strive to speak Latin, with the exception of those words—to name "philosophy", "rhetoric", "physics", or "dialectic" as examples—which like many others are already conventionally used instead of Latin ones. Thus I have called "qualities" what the Greeks call *poiotêtes*, a word which even among the Greeks is not used by the many but by the philosophers, and this applies in many cases; but dialecticians have no terms at all which are in public use, they use their own. And this is indeed common to almost all arts; for either one has to create new words for new things or one has to transfer them from others. If the Greeks do this, who have occupied themselves with these matters for so many ages, how much more does one need to concede it to us, who are trying to deal with them for the first time now?'

(§26) 'But you, Varro', I said, 'will be deserving well of your fellow citizens, if you do not just enrich them with a wealth of new subjects, as you have done, but also of new terms.'

'We shall dare then', he said, 'use new words with you to back us if it is necessary: Of those qualities then some are primary, others have arisen from them. The primary ones are of one kind and simple; those which have arisen from them are varied and as it were multiform. Therefore *aer* (we use this term too instead of a Latin one), fire, water, and earth are primary; but from them there arise the forms of animals and of the things that spring from the earth. Thus they are called principles and, to translate from the Greek, elements; of these, *aer* and fire have the power to move and to bring about an effect, the remaining ones play the roles of receiving and as it were allowing (that something be done to them), I mean water and earth. A fifth kind, out of which stars and minds are fashioned, Aristotle deemed to stand alone and to be something different from the other four which I named above. (§27) But underlying all things, they thought, was a certain matter which had no form and lacked all quality (for let us make this term more familiar and broken in by using it), out of which all things are modelled and fashioned, which can take on everything in its entirety and undergo change in all kinds of ways and from any quarter and thereby also disappear, not into nothing but into its parts, which can be cut up and divided indefinitely, since there is absolutely no minimum in nature which cannot be divided further; but all things which move move in virtue of intervals, which themselves can be divided indefinitely. (§28) And since that force which we called quality is moved in such a way, and since it shifts back and forth, they think that matter itself in its totality is fundamentally altered and that that is fashioned which we call "qualified items"; and that from them, in nature as a whole which coheres and is coextensive with all its parts, one world was created, outside of which there is no part of matter and no body. (They also think that) the parts of the world are all the things in it, which are held together by a thinking nature, in which there resides perfect reason, which is at the same time eternal (for there is nothing more powerful due to which it might perish); (§29) that force, they say, is the world soul—and it is at the same time perfect mind and perfect wisdom—which they call "god", and a kind of providence reigning over all the things which are subject to it, attending to heavenly matters especially, then also on earth to those matters which concern human beings; they sometimes also called it necessity, because nothing can possibly be in a different way than is determined by it, sometimes a, so to speak, fated chain of causes and an unchangeable continuation of the eternal order, and sometimes they also called it fortune, since it brings about many events unforeseen and unexpected by us because of the obscurity of the underlying causes and our ignorance of them.'

(VIII) (§30) Hereafter the third part of philosophy, which was concerned with reason and argument, was treated by both groups in the following way. They held that the judgement of what is true, although it arose from the senses, nonetheless does not lie in them. They wanted the mind to be the judge of things, and thought it alone was fit to be trusted, since it alone saw what was always simple, of the same kind, and such as it was (this they called an *idea*, already thus dubbed by Plato; we can rightly call it "form" [*species*]). (§31) They took the view that all the senses are blunt and slow, and incapable of perceiving in any way the things which presented themselves to the senses and appeared to them, because they were either so small that they could not fall within the ken of sense, or so mobile and swift that nothing was ever one and persistent, and not even identical with itself, since everything was persistently in motion and in flux. Therefore they called that whole class of things "subject to opinion"; (§32) but knowledge, they held, did not exist anywhere except in the notions of the mind and in reasonings. Therefore they approved of definitions of things and applied them to everything about which they held disquisitions; the explication of words was approved, too, i.e. for what reason everything was called as it was, which they called etymology; later they used certain arguments and signs of things as it were as guides for proving and bringing to a conclusion that which they wanted explained. In this (part) was passed on the entire discipline of dialectic, i.e. of speech brought to a conclusion methodically; to it, so to speak from the other side, the rhetorical power of speaking was adjoined, which unfolds continuous speech geared towards persuasion. (§33) This was the first form of philosophy for them, handed down by Plato; I shall set out modifications of it of which I have learnt if you like.'

'We *would* like that', I said, 'if I may answer for Atticus, too.'

'That is the right answer', he said. 'For the opinion of the Peripatetics and of the Old Academy is being explained splendidly.'

(IX) 'Aristotle then was the first to undermine the forms which I mentioned a little earlier, which Plato had embraced in an astonishing way, so much so that he said there was something divine in them. But Theophrastus, a man whose speech is delightful and whose character is such that he exhibits a certain goodness and nobility, in a way broke even more forcefully with the view of the old doctrine; for he stripped virtue of its beauty and rendered her weak, because he denied that living happily resided in virtue alone. (§34) Strato, his pupil, although of sharp intellect, needs to be separated from this school altogether; after he left behind the most necessary part of philosophy, which lies in virtue and morality, and turned entirely to the investigation of nature, he set himself apart completely in this field from the members of his school. But Speusippus and Xenocrates, who were the first to embrace Plato's thinking and authority, and after them Polemo and Crates together with Crantor, all of them gathered in the Academy, carefully guarded what they had received from their predecessors. Polemon in turn had been heard assiduously by Zeno and Arcesilaus. (§35) But Zeno, because he was older than Arcesilaus, most subtle in discussion, and very acute in his responses, attempted to correct the body of doctrines. This correction I shall explain as well if you like, as Antiochus used to.'

'I should like that very much', I said, 'and you see that Pomponius indicates the same.'

(X) 'Zeno, then, was in no way the kind of man who like Theophrastus would sever the muscles of virtue at any time, but on the contrary someone who constantly placed everything which belonged to the happy life in virtue alone, counted nothing else among the goods, and called honourable only that which was something simple and the sole and only good. (§36) Of the remaining things, even though they were neither goods nor evils, he said that some are in accordance with nature, and others contrary to it; and he counted some which were in between the two and in a middle position. He taught that those things which were in accordance with nature are to be sought and deserving of some esteem, and that those which were against nature were the opposite. Those which were neither he left in the middle, attaching absolutely no significance to them. (§37) But of the things which are to be sought, some are to be rated higher, others lower, and conversely those which are opposite. Those which are to be valued higher he called "promoted", but "rejected" those which are to be valued lower. And just as he made these changes less with respect to the actual subjects than with respect to terminology, so he placed between right action and sin "appropriate action" and "against what is appropriate action" as certain intermediate items, situating right actions solely in good actions, evil actions, i.e. sin, in bad actions. Appropriate actions honoured and passed on he put in the middle as I said. (§38) And while the predecessors said that not every virtue was situated in reason, but that certain virtues are brought to perfection by nature or character, he located them all within reason. And while they took the view that the virtues which I mentioned earlier can be separated, he argued that this could not come to pass in any way, and that not just the actual use of virtue as the predecessors had assumed but the disposition itself was excellent by itself, but that nonetheless nobody was in possession of virtue who did not use it all the time. And while they did not remove emotion from man and said that human beings feel pain, desire, fear, and joy by nature, but curtailed them and confined them, he wanted the sage to be free of all of these emotions as if they were illnesses. (§39) And although the ancients said these states of turmoil were natural and irrational, and placed desire in one part of the soul and reason in another, he did not even agree with them; for he thought that such states of turmoil were voluntary, that they were undergone due to a judgement of opinion, and that the mother of all states of turmoil was a certain unbridled lack of self-control. This is the essence of Zeno's stance on ethics.

(XI) About natural principles he thought the following: first, he did not add to the four beginnings of things (i.e. the elements) that fifth natural principle, from which the predecessors thought the senses and the mind were made; for he stated that fire was the very element which brought forth everything, the mind as well as the senses. He also differed from them in that he held that in no way could something be brought about by a nature that was itself not in possession of a body—of that kind Xenocrates and the predecessors had said the soul was, too—, and that nothing that brought about or experienced an effect could be something other than a body.

(§40) But the largest number of changes he made in the third part of philosophy. Here he first said new things about the senses themselves, which he deemed to be a combination of a kind of blow dealt from the outside, which he called *phantasia*, and which we may call it "appearance", and let us go on using this word, for we shall have to deploy it frequently in the rest of our discussion—but to those things which have appeared to us and are as it were received by the senses he added assent given by our minds, assent which he wanted to lie within us and to be voluntary. (§41) He did not attach reliability to all appearances, but only to those which had a certain peculiar way of making the things clear which appeared; but this appearance, when it was considered by itself, (he called) "apprehensible"—can you bear this?' 'Yes, indeed', Atticus said, 'for how else would you say *katalêpton*?' 'But once it was received and approved, he called it an apprehension, similar to those things which were grasped by a hand; from there he had also drawn the term itself, since nobody has used this word before in connection with such an application, and he used plenty of new words (for he was saying new things). But what had been apprehended by sense perception, that he called sense perception itself, and if something had been apprehended in such a way that it could not be dislodged by reasoning, he called it science, and if it *could* still be dislodged, ignorance, taking this to be the source of opinion as well, which was weak ⟨assent⟩ and common with what was false and non-apprehensible. (§42) But between science and ignorance he located the apprehension which I mentioned, but he counted it neither among the good things nor among the bad things, and said that it alone should be given credence. On this basis he also attributed reliability to the senses, because as I said above an apprehension brought about by the senses appeared to him to be true and reliable, not because it apprehended every feature a given thing had, but because it left nothing out which could fall under it, and because nature had given it (i.e. apprehension) as a yardstick for knowledge and as the starting point for understanding her. Later notions of things arising from apprehensions are imprinted on the mind, he held. From them not just the starting points but also certain broader ways of discovering reason are found. But error and rashness and ignorance and opining and guessing and in a word all the things which were alien to firm and consistent assent he removed from virtue and wisdom. And in these points consisted the change and Zeno's entire disagreement from his predecessors.'

(XII) (§43) When he had said this, I replied: 'You, Varro, have expounded the thinking of the Old Academy and of the Stoics briefly and in a manner that is not obscure at all. But I take the view, as seemed right to our friend Antiochus, that the doctrines of the Stoics are to be deemed a correction of the Old Academy rather than a new system.'

Then Varro said: 'Now is your turn: you are departing from the doctrine of the ancients and approving of Arcesilaus' innovations; tell us of what kind the separation was and for what reasons it took place, so that we can see whether that defection was adequately justified.'

(§44) Then I said: 'We have been told that Arcesilaus embarked on his entire contest with Zeno, not out of stubbornness or a mere desire to win, it seems to me, but because of that obscurity of things which had led Socrates to a profession of ignorance and already before Socrates Democritus, Anaxagoras, Empedocles, and almost all older philosophers, who said that nothing can be cognized, nothing perceived, nothing be known, that the senses are limited, our minds weak, and our lifespan short, and who said like Democritus that the truth has been hidden in an abyss, that everything was confined by opinions and conventions, that nothing was left for truth, finally that all things were shrouded in darkness. (§45) Therefore Arcesilaus used to deny that there was anything that could be known, not even that which Socrates had left himself; so he held that everything was hidden in the dark and that there was nothing which could be discerned or understood; that for these reasons nobody should profess, affirm, or approve by assent anything, one should always curb blind rashness and prevent it from giving rise to any lapse, which was manifest when either a false or an inapprehensible thing was approved, and that nothing was more disgraceful than for assent and approval to run ahead of cognition and perception. He routinely acted in a manner that was in agreement with this reasoning: while arguing against the views of everyone, he drew most people away from their views, so that, when on the same subject equally weighty considerations in favour of either side were found, assent could more easily be withheld from both sides. (§46) They call this Academy the new one, which seems old to me, if indeed we count as a member of that old Academy Plato, in whose books nothing is affirmed, many things are discussed on either side, everything is questioned, nothing certain is said—still, that Academy which you have set out, let us call it the Old one, and this the New Academy. The New Academy continued in this vein until Carneades, who was the fourth (scholarch) starting with Arcesilaus, and persisted in Arcesilaus' approach. But Carneades was not ignorant of any part of philosophy and (as I learnt from those who had heard him and especially from the Epicurean Zeno, who, although he disagreed with him most strongly, admired him uniquely beyond all others) was possessed of an incredible talent and....'

Fragments and Testimonia

Indirectly transmitted material corresponding either to a passage in the extant part of *Ac.* 1 or to one in *Luc.* is left untranslated here; see, however, the translations of *Ac.* 1 and *Luc.*

Ac. 1

t. 8. *Digladiari* is a term used for disagreeing and being of a different opinion: it comes from *gladii* (swords). Cicero in the first book of the *Academici libri*: But why does Mnesarchus rail, why does Antipater cross swords in disagreement with Carneades in so many volumes?

Ac. 2

t. 9. Plumb lines and squares. Cicero in the second book of the *Academici libri*: Yet if we believed this, we would have no need for plumb lines, squares, and rulers.

t. 10. *Hebes* ('dull') is used for 'obscure' and 'blunt'. Cicero in the second book of the *Academici libri*: What? Are you able to say what the outlines of the moon are, whose horns appear blunter at one time and more pointed at another as it waxes and wanes?

t. 11. *Aequor*, from what is level and plane. What appears as level as the sea? For this reason the poets also call it *aequor*.

t. 12. *If the image never deceives*: for nothing deceives as much as an image; in the mirror it shows everything with left and right reversed, and in water we see the intact oar as broken, as he also lays out in the *Tusculans* in some detail.

t. 13. 'Turns purple.' Cicero in the second book of the *Academici libri*. What? The sea is blue, is it not? Yet when its wave is stirred by oars, it turns purple, and indeed the ⟨body⟩ of the water is coloured and dyed in a certain way.

t. 14. *Siccus* is how sober and restrained is also called.…Cicero in the second book of the *Academici libri*: There is one (perceived taste)[1] for grown-ups, another for youths, another for sick people, another for those who are sober (*siccus*), and another for those who are drunk.

t. 15. 'Box'. Cicero in the second book of the *Academici libri*. To them even a box full of perfumed ointment appears to be rotting.

---

[1] Alternatively, 'perceived colour' or 'complexion' (i.e. *color*) is to be supplied; see the commentary ad loc.

t. 16. 'Listen then', he (sc. Licentius) said, 'to what I would have put forward yesterday if you had not interrupted: To me error seems to be giving approval to what is false as if it was true. He who regards the truth as something to be sought runs in no way into this problem. For the man who approves nothing cannot approve what is false; so he cannot err, but he can easily be happy.'

t. 17. Who does not know that he (sc. Cicero) affirmed emphatically that nothing is perceived by man, and that nothing is left for the sage to do but the most careful investigation of the truth, because, if there was assent to uncertain things, even if they happened to be true, he could not be freed from error, which is the greatest crime for the sage? Therefore, if one must believe that the wise man is necessarily happy and that the perfect task for wisdom is the search for truth alone, why do we hesitate to believe that a happy life is possible through the very investigation of the truth?

t. 18. *Exponere* is used for holding up examples of what is good. Cicero, in the second book of the *Academici libri*:…to break greed, to punish sins, to put forward one's own life as something for the young to imitate.

t. 19. *Adamare* (is used by) Cicero, in the second book of the *Academici libri*: Those who developed a liking for public offices too late would not normally be admitted to them, and they cannot be recommended to the many to a sufficient degree.

Ac. 3

t. 20. Now learn about an instance of carelessness on my part. I sent the book *On Glory* to you. Yet in it is the same preface which is also in the third book of the *Academici libri*. This happened because I have a collection of prefaces. From that I usually make a selection when I set down a work. And so when at Tusculum and when I did not remember that I had already used this preface, I slotted it into the work which I sent you. But when I read the *Academica* while on board, I realized my mistake. Therefore I immediately wrote a new proem and sent it to you. Will you cut off the old one, and glue the new one on.

t. 21. Nonetheless one should not be discouraged or lose hope in oneself if defeated by desire, driven by lust, deceived by error, or driven by force one has slipped and got on the path of injustice. For one can be led back to the right path and liberated if the agent in question feels regret and does right by god having been turned himself to better things. Cicero thought this could not happen. These are his words in the third book of the *Academici libri*: But if it was permitted, as with those who have gone the wrong way on a journey, for those who have followed the wrong path of life to put right their mistake through regret, then a correction of previous blindness would be easier.

t. 22. *Vindicare* means to defend a bad deed…*uindicare*, 'to draw', 'to set free.'…Cicero in the third book of the *Academici libri*: There would be some capacity (or: power), he would set himself free.

t. 23. *Digladiari* is a term used for disagreeing and being of a different opinion: it comes from *gladii* (swords)….[frg.]…Cicero in the third book of the *Academici libri*: But always crossing swords and fighting persistently among criminals and desperados—who would not call this most miserable and, what is more, most stupid?

t. 24. (See the translation of *Luc.*)

t. 25. *Ingeneratur* in the sense of 'might be inborn'. Cicero in the third book of the *Academici libri*: That in man alone, given so large a variety of living beings, there should be an innate desire for learning and knowledge.

t. 26–7. (See the translation of *Luc.*)

Ac. 4

t. 28–9. (See the translation in *Luc.*)

t. 30. As the matter stood, the Old Academy seemed enhanced rather than beleaguered. Then Philo's pupil Antiochus arose, who, as it seemed to some, was more desiring of fame than of truth and brought the views of the two Academies into conflict.

t. 31–3. (See the translation of *Luc.*)

t. 34. 'They dive'. Cicero in the fourth [my emendation; 'second' is transmitted] book of the *Academici libri*: For when we submerge ourselves, like divers, we see either nothing of what is above or very obscurely.

t. 35–46. (See the translation of *Luc.*)

t. 47. *Exultare* is a word for 'to leap out'. Cicero in the third book of the *Academici libri*: And as we sit now at the Lucrine lake and see the fish leap out....

t. 48–50. (See the translation of *Luc.*)

t. 51. There is, in the books which Cicero wrote in support of the Academic case, a certain passage which, it seems to me, to be spiced with remarkable wit, and to no small number of others also armoured with strength. It is difficult for anyone not to be moved by what is said there, that to the Academic sage second place is granted by all members of the others schools, who think of themselves as sages, because everyone claims first place for himself necessarily. From this one can infer plausibly that he who in everyone else's judgement is second rightly occupies the first rank by his own judgement. (16) Suppose that the Stoic sage was here; for the brilliance of the Academics is keen to engage them in particular. If then either Zeno or Chrysippus is asked who is wise, he will reply that it is the one whom he himself has described. In reply, Epicurus or another of the opponents will deny this and will claim that the sage is he who is the most knowledgeable catcher of pleasures for himself. Then it descends into a squabble. Zeno screams, with the whole Porch in uproar, that man is borne for no other thing than what is honourable. It attracted minds to itself in virtue of its own splendour and without any external good being offered and acting as a kind of alluring reward, and that pleasure of Epicurus was common only among mere beasts, and that it was a sin for man and sage to enter into association with them. Against this he (sc. Epicurus) stands up, like Liber, having called a drunken crowd from the gardens, which is looking for someone whom they can tear apart with their long fingernails and cruel mouths, raving. He elevates the name of pleasure as sweetness and tranquillity, citing the people as his witness, and urges strenuously that without it nobody can be happy. If the Academic walked in on their squabble, he will listen to both parties attempting to draw him on their side, but if he concedes to one side or the other, he will be loudly denounced as insane, ignorant, and blind by those whom he deserted. Therefore when he has carefully listened to this side as well as the other, he will say in response to the question of what seemed to him to be the case that he is in doubt. Ask then the Stoic who is better, Epicurus who he says is mad, or an Academic who professes that he needs to think about a matter of such weight; nobody doubts that it is the Academic who is going to be preferred. Now turn to the Epicurean again and ask whom he likes better, Zeno who calls him a beast, or the Academic from whom he hears: 'Maybe you are telling the truth but I shall investigate more thoroughly'; is it not plain that the whole Porch appears as insane, but the Academics as modest ahead of them and as cautious people to Epicurus? In this way Cicero presents to his readers a most enjoyable display as it were, featuring almost all philosophical schools in great detail, showing that there is none among them which would not, although it awarded first place to itself as it has to, grant him second place, seeing that he did not fight back but exhibit doubt. On this score I will not make objects nor take away from their glory in any way. (17) Cicero may seem to some not to be speaking facetiously, but, because he was repulsed by the frivolity of the Greeklings themselves, to have held that inane and vapid consequences follow.

t. 52. (See the translation of *Luc.*)

Ex incertis libris

t. 53. *Concinnare* means 'to bring about'…but the force of this word is such because among the ancients *cinnus* is a term for a drink made from numerous substances. Correctly *concinnare* can also be understood as 'to agree', 'to be in unison' as it were, like when one tune is achieved by many singing in different ways…. Likewise in the first book of the *Academici libri*: …who, since [or: while, although] he appeared to be completely consistent with himself due to what is similar to what is true….

t. 54. The Academics call plausible ('approvable') or truth-like that which is able to entice us to acting without assent. By 'without assent' I mean that we do not hold that what we do is true nor believe that we had knowledge of it, but act all the same: for example, if someone asked me whether after last night, clear and pure as it was, today such a bright sun would rise, then we would deny, I think, that we knew this, but would nonetheless say that it appeared so. In this fashion, said the Academic, everything appears to me, and I thought one should call such appearances plausible or truth-like; if you want to call such appearances by another name, I do not resist. It is enough for me that you have properly taken on board what I am saying, that is, which things I designate in this way. For it is right that the sage should not be someone who fashions terms but who enquires into things. Now do you understand how these playthings with which I have been stirring you up have been shaken out of my hands? When both of them had responded that they understood and demanded through their expression my response, I said: 'Why do you think that Cicero, whose words these are, was so poor in his Latin expression that he assigned less suitable terms to the things he was considering?'

t. 55. Tell us, therefore, what you have learnt, or in what sect you have discovered the truth. In the Academy, no doubt, which followed, of which you approved. But it teaches nothing, excepting that you know that you know nothing. Therefore your own books argue how little can be learnt from your philosophy for our life—nothing. These are your words: **But to me we seem not only blind to wisdom, but also dull and blunt with respect to those things which can be seen to a certain degree.**

t. 56. Who has investigated these matters more eagerly than Marcus Varro? Who has been engaged in discovery in a more learned way? Who has considered things with more application? Who has drawn distinctions more crisply? Who has written more careful and more complete summaries of issues? Although he may be less smooth in his expression, he is nonetheless so full of learning and wise statements that in every domain of knowledge which we call 'secular' but the pagans 'liberal', he teaches the student of subjects as much as Cicero delights the student of words. Finally also Tullius himself bears such witness to this man that he says in his *Academici libri* that he had the conversation which features in this book with '**Marcus Varro, a man who was easily the most acute of all and without any doubt the most learned**'. He does not say 'the most eloquent' or 'the most fluent', for in that area he is much inferior; but he does say 'easily the most acute of all', and adds in those books, the Academic ones, where he claims that everything is to be doubted, 'without any doubt the most learned'. Indeed about this issue he was so certain that he removed doubt, which he tends to apply to all things, as if on this one matter he had forgotten that he was an Academic, even when he was about to speak in defence of the doubt of the Academics. In the first book he praises the literary efforts of this same Varro in these words.

t. 57. *Figor* is inflected differently amongst the ancients in the perfect tense: we find *fictus* and *fixus*.... [example for *fictus*]...Varro, in the third book of the work dedicated to Cicero, uses '*fixus*', and Cicero writes in the third book of the *Academici libri* [...] '**malcho in opera affixa**' and Vergil [in A. 4.15] 'If (that resolution) was not firmly fastened in my heart'.

t. 58. Indeed Antiochus, the pupil of Philo, a most cautious man as I think, who had begun to open the gates at a time when, as it were, the enemy was retreating and to call back the Academy and its laws to Plato's authority—although **Metrodorus, too, had tried to do that earlier, who is said to have been the first to profess that the Academics do not accept the tenet that nothing can be apprehended, but had of necessity taken up arms of this kind against the Stoics**—Antiochus, then, as I had started to say, **who had been a student of the Academic Philo and the Stoic Mnesarchus,** sneaked, like a citizen offering assistance, into the Old Academy when it was undefended and untroubled as it were by any enemy, bringing with him some kind of evil out of the ashes of Stoicism, to violate Plato's inner sanctuary.

t. 59. So if individual sects are convicted of stupidity by the judgement of many sects, then all sects will be found to be vapid and insubstantial: in this way philosophy consumes and finishes herself. Because Arcesilaus, the founder of the (sceptical) Academy, understood this, he collected the rebukes all famous philosophers had issued to one another and their professions of ignorance and armed himself against all of them: it was in this manner that he established a new philosophy of not philosophizing.

t. 60. When he was under pressure from all sides on the grounds that, if the sage was not assenting to anything, he would never act—what a wondrous man, but then not so wondrous, for he was a stream flowing from the springs of Plato—, Carneades wisely focused on what actions his opponents approved. When he saw that they were like some truths or other, he called what he followed in this world to guide his actions 'truth-like'. What such truths are like he did know well and concealed cleverly. He also called it 'the plausible'. For someone who looks at a model approves also the likeness of it. For how does the sage approve and how does he follow the truth-like when he does not know what the true itself is? Therefore the Academics knew the truth and approved falsehoods in which they saw a praiseworthy imitation of true things. But since it was neither right nor feasible to reveal this to the uninitiated, so to speak, they left some sign of their view to those who would come after them as well as to those for whom they could do this at the time. They were well able to prevent dialecticians from raising questions about words, insulting them and making fun of them.

t. 61. But Arcesilaus, the teacher of ignorance, when he was maligning Zeno, the leader of the Stoics, so that he might overthrow philosophy altogether, assumed the following view, under the authority of Socrates: he affirmed that nothing can be known. Thus he disproved the belief the philosophers had of themselves that the truth was drawn out and discovered by their talents. That is to say, because that wisdom was mortal and, having been created only fairly recently, had reached its point of highest development, so that it was necessarily now ageing and dying, the Academy arose suddenly, the old age of philosophy as it were, which might dispatch it now that it was withering away. And Arcesilaus rightly saw that they are arrogant or rather foolish who think that knowledge of the truth can be grasped by conjecture. But nobody can refute another as speaking falsely except someone who has known antecedently what is true. Yet Arcesilaus, attempting to do this without knowledge of the truth, introduced a kind of philosophy which is called *asystatum*, unstable and inconstant we may say in Latin. For in order to know nothing, something must necessarily be known: if you know nothing at all, then this, that nothing can be known, will be taken away. Therefore he who proclaims as a belief that nothing is known, will profess something as grasped and apprehended: therefore something can be known.

Dubia

t. 62*. Here one may reproach their vapidity: they, when wanting to show that the senses are false, collect many scenarios in which the eyes are tricked, among which there is also situation that to people who are enraged and to those who are drunk everything appears double.

t. 63*. But whosoever thinks that the Academics thought this [sc. that the truth could not be discovered by man], should hear Cicero himself. For he says that they had the habit of concealing their view and of not revealing it to anyone except those who had lived with them into their old age. But what that view was a god may be able to see; I for one think it was the view of Plato.

t. 64*. Then, after we had eaten as much as was needed to still our hunger, Alypius said to us upon our return to the meadow: I shall follow your idea and will not dare to resist. For if nothing has escaped me, the credit will be to your teaching and my memory. Yet if I were to slip up on some issue, you will remedy this, so that from here onwards I am not afraid of this kind of assignment. I believe that the 'split' of the New Academy was not so much devised against the Old one as a move against the Stoics. One should not regard it as a split if there really was a necessity to resolve and discuss a new issue introduced by Zeno. Although the view about not perceiving had been treated without giving rise to conflicts, it has not unreasonably been thought to occupy the minds of Old Academics, too. This can easily be proved by the authority of Socrates himself, and of Plato, and the other Older Ones, who thought that they could defend themselves against any error as long as they did not blindly hand themselves over to assent, although they had not inserted a discussion properly devoted to this subject into their lectures, nor had they asked at any point expressly if the truth can be perceived or not. When Zeno introduced this notion as something untried and new and claimed that nothing could be perceived except what was true in such a way that it could be distinguished from other things by peculiar marks, and that the sage must not engage in opining, and Arcesilaus heard this, he denied that something like this could be found by man and said that the sage must not entrust his life to that shipwreck of opinion. From that he also derived the conclusion that one should not assent to anything.

(15) But although this was the situation—that the Old Academy seemed shored up rather than beleaguered—, Philo's pupil Antiochus turned up who, as some people thought, was more desiring of glory than of truth and drew the views of the two Academies into conflict. He said that the New Academics had tried to introduce a view that was unheard of and very far removed from the opinion of the ancients. With respect to this topic he beseeched us to trust the old natural thinkers and other great philosophers, opposing the New Academics themselves, who said that they were following what is truth-like, while professing to be ignorant of the truth itself, and he had assembled many arguments, which I think I should leave aside for now, defending above all else the claim that the sage can apprehend. This, I think, was the dispute between New and Old Academics. If things are actually different, I would ask you to inform Licentius on the subject in full detail on behalf of both of us. But if things are as I have been able to explain them, continue with the discussion which you had begun.

Apparent Testimonia of the *Catulus* and *Lucullus*

t. 65. Marcus Tullius did not hesitate to condemn some books which were already issued after he had later written others, such as the *Catulus* and the *Lucullus* as well as those about which I have just spoken, the *De inventione*.

t. 66. He enjoyed all philosophy, and was well-disposed and friendly towards every kind, but from the beginning he loved and had a keen interest in the Academy, not the so-called New Academy, although it flourished at the time through Carneades' sayings, with Philo as a proponent, but the Old Academy, which had Antiochus of Ascalon as chief, a persuasive and rhetorically powerful man. Lucullus made an effort to befriend this man and made him his friend and companion, and put him up against the pupils of Philo, of whom Cicero also was one. Cicero wrote a very fine treatise on this school, in which he gave the argument in support of 'apprehension' to Lucullus and assumed the opposing role himself. The book is entitled 'Lucullus'.

t. 67. After this, after the state had turned into a monarchy, Cicero withdrew from public service and spent his time with young men who wanted to study philosophy, and mainly from his familiarity with these, since they were of very high birth and leading, he once more exercised influence in the state. He also devoted himself to composing and translating philosophical dialogues, and to render into Latin a number of terms pertaining to dialectic and physics; for it was him, as they say, who first, or principally, provided Latin terms for 'impression', 'assent', 'suspension of judgement', and 'apprehension', as well as for 'atom', 'that which has no component parts', 'void', and many others like these, managing partly by metaphors and partly by neologisms to make them intelligible and familiar.

Lucullus

(I) (§1) The great natural talent of Lucius Lucullus and his great devotion to the best fields of expertise, as well all the learning he had acquired, becoming of a free man and befitting of one of noble birth, were entirely deprived of their natural surroundings in the city at a time when he could have enjoyed his greatest success on the public stage. For when he had, as quite a young man, together with his brother, endowed with equal familial devotion and application, avenged the enmities his father was subjected to in an altogether glorious manner, he went to Asia as a quaestor and directed the province for many years so as to win admiring praise. He was then made an aedile in his absence, right after that praetor (faster than was usual, as was granted to him by statute), after that to Africa, and on to the consulship; this he discharged in such a way that everyone admired his careful fulfilment of his duty and recognized his natural talent. After that he was dispatched to the war against Mithridates by the senate and surpassed not just everyone's opinion regarding his valour, but also the glory of those who came before him. (§2) This was all the more miraculous because military achievement was not particularly expected of him, for he had spent his youth occupied with work on the forum, and the long period of his quaestorship in peacetime Asia while Murena was on campaign in Pontus.

However, the really incredible scale of his gifts did not require the training which only actual practice provides and which cannot be taught. Thus when he had spent the whole journey on land and on sea either questioning experienced men or reading of military achievements, he came to Asia as a fully formed general, although he had departed from Rome a mere novice in war. For he had an almost divine memory for facts—Hortensius' was better regarding words, but as much as in conducting practical matters facts are of greater benefit than words, the former kind of memory was superior. They say that Themistocles, whom we would easily rank as Greece's most eminent man, was possessed of a unique memory of this kind. He is said to have replied to a man who promised him 'the art of memory', which was first put forward at that time, that he would rather learn to forget (I think because whatever he had heard or seen remained stuck in his recollection). Lucullus, endowed with such a talent, had added also the training which Themistocles had spurned; thus just as we put down in writing what we want to commit to memory, so he held facts engraved in his mind.

(§3) And so he proved to be a general of such calibre in every type of warfare, hostile encounters, sieges, and sea battles, involving every tool and device of warfare, that that king, the greatest after Alexander, professed that he recognized Lucullus as a greater commander than anyone of those he had read about. In him there was such wisdom in establishing and ordering states, such fairness that today Asia persists in adhering to the arrangements Lucullus had made and by following, as it were, in his footsteps. But even if it was very beneficial to the state, the absence of such a force of excellence and talent from the gaze of the forum and the senate house lasted for longer than I would have wanted. What is more, even when he had returned victorious from the war against Mithridates, he obtained his triumph three years later than it was owed thanks to the machinations of his enemies. It was I as consul who practically led the chariot of this most splendid man into the city. I would say how I benefitted from his advice and influence in most important matters if I did not thereby have to talk about myself, which is unnecessary at this point. Thus I shall rather deprive him of the tribute due to him than to combine it with praise of my own person.

(II) (§4) But the achievements of his life which deserved to be extolled by public praise have been fairly well celebrated in Greek and Latin writings. I often had the opportunity to get to know his public achievements along with many, his private qualities along with few others from the man himself. For Lucullus was devoted to every kind of literature and in particular philosophy more ardently than those who did not know him assumed, and not only during his youth but also for years of his quaestorship and during times of war itself, when military matters tend to require so much time that little leisure is left to the general when he is actually under canvas. But because Antiochus, Philo's pupil, was deemed to stand out among philosophers for his talent and knowledge, Lucullus kept him by his side both as quaestor and some years later as general, and since he had the kind of memory I described earlier, he easily learned from hearing often what he would have remembered had he heard it but once. He enjoyed enormously reading books which he had heard mentioned.

(§5) Sometimes I fear that, in wanting to enhance the glory of such figures, I may actually diminish it. For there are many who have no love for Greek literature at all, even more who have none for philosophy, and as for the rest, even though they have nothing against either, they think that the discussion of such matters ill befits the leading men of the state. But since I have heard that Marcus Cato learnt about Greek literature in his old age, since historiographical works say that Panaetius was the sole companion of Publius Africanus during that noble embassy which he undertook before his censorship, I require no other champion of Greek literature or philosophy.

(§6) It remains for me to reply to those who do not want the involvement of figures so eminent in conversations of this kind. As if it was a requirement that famous men either meet in silence, or restrict themselves to joking, or exchanges over lightweight matters! For if in a certain book of mine I was right to praise philosophy, then engaging in it is indeed most worthy of the best and greatest man, and we whom the Roman people have placed in this elevated position, only have to see to this one thing, that we do not let our private studies distract us from public business. And since, when I had an official duty to discharge, I not just never drew my attention away from the assemblies of the people, but did not ever write anything unless if it was connected with my work in the forum, who will criticize my leisure time now? In it I do not just want to avoid becoming blunted and slack, but am striving to be of use to many. We think that we do not diminish but even enhance the glory of those whose public and celebrated praises we supplement with these less familiar and less widely broadcast ones.

(§7) There are also those who deny that the characters who conduct discussions in our books had knowledge of the subjects discussed. They seem to me to be jealous not just of the living but also of the dead.

(III) There remains one type of critic who disapproves of the Academy's way of thinking and arguing. We would be more concerned about this if anyone approved any sect of philosophy except for the one he himself followed. We, however, since we routinely say against everyone else what appears to us to be the case, cannot object if others disagree with us. In any event, *our* case is straightforward to present: we want to find the truth without any contentiousness, and we strive for this with the greatest diligence and commitment. For even if all cognition is obstructed by many difficulties, and there is such darkness in the things themselves, and such weakness in our judgements that not without reason the oldest and most learned thinkers distrusted their ability to find what they wanted to find, nonetheless they did not give up, and nor will we, out of weariness, let go of our desire to investigate. Nor do our discussions pursue something other than that, by speaking [and listening] on either side, they elicit and as it were squeeze out what either is true or comes as close as possible to the truth. (§8) There is also no difference between us and those who believe they have knowledge, except that they have no doubt that what they defend is true, while we regard many things as plausible which we can easily follow, but hardly affirm. For that reason we are freer and less constrained, because our ability to make judgements is unimpaired and we are not forced by any necessity to defend all the things which are prescribed by certain people and as it were commanded. For, first, the others were already kept in bondage before they could judge what the best doctrine was; then, in the weakest period of their life, they either yield to some friend or are overcome by a single speech given by whoever they happen to hear first, and so make a judgement about things that are not apprehended, and cling to whatever system they have been carried to, so to speak, by a storm, as they would to a rock. (§9) For as to their claim that their trust in the man whom they judge to have been wise is total, I would approve if they, unformed and uneducated as they are, could have made that judgement (to establish who is wise seems particularly the province of the wise man). But granted they were able to make this judgement, they could have done so after all matters had been listened to, also after the views of the others had been ascertained. But instead they made their judgement after they heard about the matter once and submitted themselves to the authority of a single person. But somehow most people prefer erring and defending the view that has become dear to them aggressively to enquiring without obstinacy what is said with the greatest consistency.

About these matters we had much inquiry and discussion on many occasions and especially once at Hortensius' villa near Bauli, when Catulus and Lucullus and I had come there the day after we met at Catulus's. We came there quite early, because it had been decided that, if there was wind, Lucullus would sail to his place in Naples, and I to mine in Pompeii. So when we had talked a little in the colonnade, we sat down in the same space.

(IV) (§10) Here Catulus said: 'Although yesterday the issue had been almost completely explained, so that nearly the entire question seems to have been dealt with, I am still waiting for you, Lucullus, to tell us what you promised, namely what you had heard from Antiochus.'

'Indeed', Hortensius said, 'I did more than I meant to; the whole subject should have been preserved untouched for Lucullus, Catulus. Nonetheless, perhaps it *has* been so preserved: for I said only the things which were the most obvious; from Lucullus I desire something more recherché.'

Then Lucullus said: 'Your expectation, Hortensius, does not trouble me too much, even if there is nothing as awkward for those who want to please, but because I am unconcerned about the extent to which I am going to prove what I say, I am even less troubled. For what I will be saying neither belongs to me nor is it of such a kind that I should not prefer being defeated, if it does not obtain, to being victorious. But certainly, as the case presents itself now, although it has been shaken by yesterday's discussion, it appears to me to be very true. I shall argue as Antiochus used to. The subject is familiar to me, because I listened to him without prejudice and with great attention, even about the same issue repeatedly. And so I create even greater expectation for me than Hortensius created just now.'

After he had begun in this way, we concentrated on listening. (§11) He said: 'When I was in Alexandria as a proquaestor, Antiochus was with me, and Heraclitus from Tyre, a friend of Antiochus, had already been there since before we arrived. He had heard Clitomachus as well as Philo for many years, and was thus a man who was well recognized and distinguished in that brand of philosophy which after almost becoming defunct is now being revived. I heard Antiochus debate with him often, but both of them proceeded gently. And indeed, those two books of Philo, about which Catulus spoke yesterday, were brought to Alexandria at this time and first made their way then into Antiochus' hands. And this most forgiving of men (for nothing could be gentler than him) nonetheless started to get angry. I was amazed, for I had never seen him like that before.

Yet he, calling on Heraclitus' recollection, asked him whether these claims appeared to be Philo's, or whether he had heard them ever before either from Philo or from any other Academic. He said he had not, but recognized Philo's way of writing. Nor can this be cast into doubt, for my friends, the learned P. and C. Selius as well as Tetrilius Rogus were there, who said that they had heard these claims from Philo in Rome and that they themselves had transcribed those two books from Philo's copy. (§12) Then Antiochus said the same things as Catulus recalled yesterday his father said to Philo, and other things more. Nor did he restrain himself from actually issuing a book directed at his teacher, entitled *Sosus*. On this occasion, when I heard Heraclitus argue with commitment against Antiochus and likewise Antiochus against the Academics, I attended to Antiochus more carefully so that I would understand the whole issue from what he said. So we spent much time for several days on this one discussion, drawing in Heraclitus and a number of other learned men, among them Antiochus' brother Aristus and furthermore Aristo and Dio, whom Antiochus rated most highly after his brother. But the part which was directed at Philo is to be left aside here. For he is a less fierce adversary who says that those claims which were defended yesterday are not made at all by the Academics. He may be lying, but he is a less serious adversary. Let us proceed to Arcesilaus and Carneades.'

(V) (§13) When he had said this, he resumed in the following manner: 'First, it seems to me that when you'—and he addressed me by name—'name the old natural philosophers, you do the same thing as seditious citizens when they hold up certain famous men from amongst the ancients, who they say were "friends of the people", so that they themselves might appear similar to them. They go back to P. Valerius, who was consul in the first year after the expulsion of the kings. Then they cite others who on their view brought in laws "in the interest of the people" about appeals when they were consuls. Then they go on to those more familiar figures, C. Flaminius, who as tribune brought in a land law against the will of the senate some years before the second Punic war and was later made consul twice, and to L. Cassius and Q. Pompeius. These people even tend to count P. Africanus among the same number, but say that two most wise and famous brothers, P. Crassus and P. Scaevola, encouraged Tiberius Gracchus in his legislation, the former, as we know, publicly, the other, as is suspected, more secretively. They add also C. Marius, and as far as he is concerned, they are not mistaken. Having set forth the names of these men—so many and so distinguished—, they say that they are following the principle established by them.

(§14) Similarly, when you, just as they do with respect to the state, want to throw the already well-organized field of philosophy into confusion, you adduce Empedocles, Anaxagoras, Democritus, Parmenides, Xenophanes, Plato even and Socrates. However, neither did Saturninus, to name a particular enemy of my family, resemble in any way those earlier men, nor may the trickery of Arcesilaus be compared to the modesty of Democritus. And yet, for all you say, those natural philosophers do but rarely, when they are stuck on a particular point, cry out as if they are highly upset (indeed Empedocles does this in such a way that he sometimes seems to me to be mad) that everything is hidden, that we perceive nothing, that we make out nothing, that we cannot find out with respect to anything at all what it is really like; but for the most part, it seems to me, these men affirm certain things too strongly and proclaim to know more than they do.

(§15) But if at that time those men moved unsteadily in unfamiliar terrain in the manner of young children, do we think that nothing has been uncovered over so many centuries, by the greatest intellects and by immense enthusiasm? Is it not the case that, when the most authoritative schools of philosophy had already been set up, there arose, as in the best state Tiberius Gracchus to disturb the peace, so Arcesilaus to overthrow established philosophy and to hide behind the authority of those who, he said, denied that something could be known and apprehended? From their number both Plato and Socrates are to be removed, one because he left to posterity the most perfect system, the Peripatetics and the Academics who differ in name but coincided in substance, with whom the Stoics in turn disagreed more with respect to terminology than with respect to their beliefs—Socrates, however, disparaged himself and attributed more (sc. knowledge) to those whom he wanted to refute. And so, by saying one thing and thinking another, Socrates freely used to avail himself of the kind of pretence which the Greeks call "irony". Fannius said that irony was also present in Africanus, and that this trait was not to be considered a flaw in him because Socrates had it, too.

(VI) (§16) Granted, if you wish, that those ancient matters were not known: was there no advance, given their further investigations, after Arcesilaus, as it is held, disparaged Zeno for making no new discoveries himself and instead tinkering with his predecessors' work by changing terms, and tried to smother in darkness matters which are most clear in wanting to undermine his definitions? Initially his way of thinking found little approval (although he stood out for his acumen and even more for a certain admirable charm of speech) and was next after him upheld by Lakydes only, but later brought to perfection by Carneades. He is the fourth successor after Arcesilaus; for he was a pupil of Hegesinus, who was a pupil of Euandrus, who was a disciple of Lakydes, after Lakydes had been one of Arcesilaus. But Carneades himself held his position for a long time, for he lived ninety years, and his pupils attained considerable distinction. Of them Clitomachus had the most industry (as the large number of his books indicates), Hagnon had no less talent, Charmadas no less eloquence, Melanthius of Rhodes no less charm; but Metrodorus of Stratonikeia was thought to have known Carneades particularly well. (§17) More recently Philo of your school devoted attention to Clitomachus for many years. But while Philo lived, the Academy did not lack advocacy.

But what we are now undertaking to do—to argue against the Academics—, some philosophers, and no mediocre ones at that, regarded as something one should not do at all, and they thought that there were no grounds for debating with those who approved of nothing, and they criticized the Stoic Antipater because he was very active in doing so. Nor, they said, was it necessary to define what "cognition" or "perception" was, or—to translate literally—what apprehension was, which the Greeks call *katalêpsis* (i.e. grasp). And those, they said, who wanted to convince others that there was such a thing as to be capable of being apprehended and perceived were acting without proper knowledge because there was nothing clearer than *enargeia*— thus the Greeks; we may call it "transparency" or "evidence" if that is acceptable, and manufacture words if need be; I say this so that he', and he addressed me jokingly, 'does not think only he is allowed to do that. In any event, they thought that no pronouncement could be found that was more lucid than evidence itself, nor were those things which were so clear in need of definition. But others said that they would not say anything in support of that evidence of their own accord, but felt that something had to be said in response to the arguments cited against it, so that nobody would be misled. (§18) Yet most do not object to definitions even of evident things and regard the issue as a legitimate subject for inquiry, and the people in question as worthy interlocutors.

But Philo, when he pushed certain novelties revolutionary claims, because he had been unable to withstand what were being said about the obstinacy of the Academics, lied openly, for which Catulus the father criticized him, and, as Antiochus showed, placed himself in the very position which he feared. For when he denied that there was something apprehensible (for in this way we want to render *katalêpton*) if it was an "appearance" of such a kind as Zeno defined it (we already deployed this word for *phantasia* in our conversation yesterday)—i.e. an appearance thus impressed and moulded from that object from which it derived as could not arise from that object from which it did not arise (we say that this definition of Zeno's is absolutely correct; for how can anything be apprehended in such a way that you may be confident that it has been perceived and cognized which is such that it might as well be false?)—by weakening and removing this [i.e. Zeno's definition, or specifically the third clause], he removes the capacity to distinguish between what cannot be cognized and what can. Consequently, nothing can be apprehended. Thus, without foreseeing it, he is returned to the position where he wants to be least of all. Therefore the whole case against the Academy is taken on by us so that we retain that definition which

Philo wanted to overthrow; unless we secure it, we concede that nothing can be apprehended.

(VII) (§19) Let us then begin with the senses. Their judgements are so clear and certain that, if our entire nature were given a choice and were asked by some deity if it was satisfied with its senses when they are sound and uncorrupted or if it wanted something more, I cannot see what better it could ask for. And you cannot at this point want for me to give an answer involving the bent oar or the pigeon's neck. For I am not the sort who claims that whatever appears to us is such as it appears to us; Epicurus may see to this claim and many others. But in my judgement there is the highest degree of truth in the senses if they are sound and functioning and if everything that obstructs and impedes them is removed. For that reason we often want to change the lighting and the position of the things we are looking at, and either reduce or increase the distance to the object, and do many things until our vision itself gives rise to warranted confidence in its judgement. The same thing happens with respect to sounds, smells, and taste, so that there is none of us who requires a more acute judgement in any of his senses. (§20) But when practice and skill are applied, so that the eyes dwell on a painting, and the ears on song, is there anyone who does not see what power resides in the senses? How many things do painters see in areas which are apparently set back and in ones which apparently protrude that we do not see? How many things which elude *us* in a piece of music can be heard by those who are practised in this kind of skill, who say at the first note of the fluteplayer that it is Antiope or Andromache, when *we* do not even yet suspect this? It is not in any way necessary to speak of taste or smell, in which a certain intelligence, albeit faulty, resides. About touch, and that kind in particular which the philosophers call internal, of either pleasure or pain, wherein the Cyrenaics think the criterion of truth alone resides, as it is felt immediately—can then anyone say that there is no difference between the person who is in pain and the one who is in a state of pleasure, or that someone who thinks that way is not manifestly insane?

(§21) Such are the things which we say are perceived by the senses. They are followed by things like them which, however, are not said to be perceived by the senses themselves, but by the senses in a way, like these: "That is white, this is sweet, that other thing well-sounding, this one pleasant-smelling, and that one rough to the touch." We regard these as apprehended by means of the mind, not the senses. Then: "that is a horse, that is a dog." There follows another string linking up larger elements, like the ones which comprise an, as it were, filled-out apprehension of things: "If someone is a human being, he is a living being which is mortal and partakes in reason." From that kind notions of things are imprinted on our minds, without which nothing can be understood, examined, or discussed. (§22) Suppose there were false notions (for you seemed to call *ennoiai* "notions")—so if there were false notions or ones imprinted on us by impressions of such a kind as could not be discriminated from false ones, how would we make use of them, how would we see what was in agreement with each thing and what in conflict with it? For memory certainly, which principally holds not just philosophy but the business of our entire life and all arts to the highest degree, there is then no place left. For what memory of falsehoods could there be, or how could someone remember what he does not grasp and hold in his mind? What art could exist if not one which is not made up of one or two but many apprehensions of the mind? If you take it away, how will you distinguish the expert from someone who is not skilled? For it is not randomly that we call that man an artist and say that other man is not one, but only when we see that the first is in possession of perceptions and apprehensions while the other one is not in the same way. And because of the arts one type is such that it only sees its subject with the mind, while the other sets something in motion and creates something, how can either a geometer make out things which are not the case or cannot be told apart from false ones, or how can the lyre player hit the right notes and complete his lines; the same will also hold in similar arts, whose entire occupation lies in making things and in action. For what can be brought about by means of a craft if he who practises it has not perceived many things?

(VIII) (§23) But it is particularly the appraisal of the virtues that confirms that many things can be perceived and apprehended. In them alone we say that knowledge resides, which we take to be not just apprehension of things but apprehension which is stable and unchangeable, and so we speak of wisdom again, the art of living, which has steadfastness from its own resources. If this steadfastness was not in possession of something that is perceived and cognized, then, I ask, where does it arise from and how? I also ask, that good man, who has resolved to endure any kind of torture, and be torn apart by unbearable pain rather than betray either his duty or his word, why does he impose such harsh laws on himself when why he should act in this way is not something which he has apprehended, perceived, cognized, and which is settled. Consequently it cannot be that anyone regards equity and trust so highly that for their preservation he would decline no punishment, unless he has assented to things which cannot be false. (§24) Wisdom herself, if she does not know whether she is wisdom or not, how will she obtain the title of wisdom to begin with? Then, how will she dare to undertake anything or act with confidence, when there is nothing certain that she can follow? But when she doubts if there is a highest and ultimate good, and is ignorant of what the reference point for everything is, how can she be wisdom? It is also plain that there needs to be an initial thing which wisdom can follow when she embarks on a course of action, and that this beginning is in agreement with nature. For otherwise impulse (for that term we want to stand for ὁρμή by means of which we are driven to action and seek to obtain what has appeared to us) cannot be aroused. (§25) Now that which gives rise to an impulse must first appear veridically and be given credence; this cannot come to pass if the appearance experienced cannot be distinguished from a false one. But how can the mind be moved to seek to obtain something if it does not perceive, with respect to that which appears to us, whether it is in agreement with nature or alien to it? By the same token, if what is an appropriate course of action for it does not present itself to the mind, he [i.e. the sage] will never act in any way at all, will never receive an impulse to do anything, and will never be moved. So if he is ever to act in any way at all, it is necessary for that true impression which he encounters to appear so to him.

(§26) What of the fact that, if their claims hold true, all reason is undone, the guiding light of life as it were? Will you nonetheless persist in this wrongheadedness? For reason bestowed the starting point of enquiry, and carried virtue to perfection, after reason herself had been made solid by enquiry. Now enquiry is the striving for cognition, and the end of enquiry is discovery. But nobody "discovers" falsehoods, nor can those things which remain uncertain be "discovered", but when those things which had been, as it were, wrapped up are opened, then they are called "discovered". Thus reason encapsulates the beginning of enquiry and the outcomes of perceiving and apprehending. Therefore proof, *apodeixis* in Greek, is defined thus: "An argument which starts from things which are apprehended and leads to that which was not included amongst the apprehensions."

(IX) (§27) If all impressions are as those people say, so that they might possibly be false, and that no faculty could tell them apart, how will we say that anyone brought an argument to a conclusion or found something, or what trust will there be in a proof once reached? Philosophy herself must proceed through reasonings: what way out will remain open to her? What will happen to wisdom? Wisdom must neither have doubts about herself nor about her tenets (which the philosophers call *dogmata*), none of which can be betrayed without transgression. For when a tenet is betrayed, the law of truth and rectitude is betrayed, from which flaw in turn betrayals of friendships and of countries tend to arise. Consequently one cannot doubt that no tenet of the sage can be false, and that it not being false is not enough, for it must also be stable, fixed, and considered, such that no reasoning can dislodge it. Such tenets can, however, neither exist nor appear to exist on the reasoning of those who deny that those impressions from which all tenets arise differ at all from false ones.

(§28) Out of this arises what Hortensius demanded, that you grant at least that the sage has perceived this one thing, that nothing can be grasped. But when Antipater demanded just that—he said that it was consistent for someone who affirms that nothing can be perceived to say that that one thing could be perceived, even though other things cannot—, Carneades resisted rather cleverly. For he said that, far from this being consistent, it would stand in complete conflict. That was so because he who denied that anything could be perceived made no exception; thus it was necessary that not even that one claim, for which no exception had been made, could be apprehended and perceived in any way. (§29) Antiochus appeared to move in more closely on this point. He argued that, because the Academics had this tenet (you understand by this time that I am using "tenet" for *dogma*), that nothing can be perceived, they must not waver with respect to their tenet as they do on other subjects, especially because this is the upshot of their position: for this is the guiding rule of their philosophy, the establishment of what is true and what is false, of what is apprehensible and what is not. Because they accepted this mechanism as their own and wanted to teach which appearances should be accepted and which rejected, they certainly ought to have accepted this thing itself from which every judgement of what is true and what is false arises. For, he argued, there are these two crucial reference points in philosophy, the judgement of what is true and the highest good, and there cannot be a sage who does not know either the starting point of cognizing or the end he is ultimately striving for, so that he does not know either from where to start or where he has to arrive. To be in doubt about these two issues and not feel sure about them in such a manner that they cannot be moved was completely alien to wisdom. So in this manner one had to demand from them that they say at least this one thing, that nothing can be apprehended, was apprehended by them. But to say this about the inconsistency of their entire stance—if there is such a thing as a stance of someone who approves of nothing—should, as I think, suffice.

(X) (§30) There follows a debate which is rich but somewhat more recondite—this is so because it owes something to the area of natural philosophy—, so that I fear that I am granting more freedom and unbounded license to the person who will make the opposite case; for what am I to think will the person who tries to take the light away from us do about subjects which are hidden and obscure? Now one could have discussed in a nuanced way with how much, as it were, craftsmanship nature manufactured first every living being and then man in particular, what power resided in the senses, how first appearances hit us, then how impulse triggered by them arose, and then how we direct the senses towards the perception of things. For the mind, which is the source of the senses and even a sense itself, has a natural capacity which it directs to things by which it is moved. Therefore it seizes some appearances in such a way that it makes immediate use of them, and stores away others as it were; from them memory arises. The rest it constructs from similarities, from which the notions of things arise, which the Greeks call *ennoiai* or *prolêpseis*. When to that reason, formal proof, and an uncountable number of facts has been added, then also apprehension of all these things appears and reason thus perfected has reached wisdom by these steps. (§31) Thus since the human mind is most suited to knowledge of things and consistency in life, it especially embraces cognition and that *katalêpsis*, which as I said we shall translate literally as "apprehension", when it loves it by itself (for nothing is sweeter to it than the light of truth) and because of the use to which it can be put. Therefore the mind uses the senses and creates the crafts as other senses of sorts and strengthens philosophy herself to the point where it brings about virtue, the one thing on which our life in its entirety depends. Thus those who deny that anything can be grasped rip out those tools and equipment of life, or rather turn the whole of life upside down and deprive the living being itself of its soul, so that it is difficult to talk about the blindness of these people in the manner required by the case.

(§32) Nor can I altogether establish what their plan is or what they want. Sometimes when we approach them with a line to the effect that, if what they argue is true, then everything will be uncertain, they reply: "What does that have to do with us? Is it our fault? Accuse nature who has hidden truth deep in an abyss, as Democritus says." But others are more elegant. They actually complain that we accuse them wrongfully of saying that everything is uncertain, and try to teach how great the difference is between what is uncertain and what cannot be apprehended, and try to distinguish the two. Let us therefore deal with those who make this distinction, and leave behind as hopeless cases those who say that everything is as uncertain as whether the number of stars is odd or even. For these other people (and this, I have noticed, has made the strongest impact with you) want there to be something which is plausible and truth-like as it were, and want to follow it as a guide both in the contact of their life and in philosophical inquiry and debate. (XI) (§33) What is that device for judging what is true and false if we have no concept of true and false because they cannot be distinguished? For if we have such a concept, then there must be a difference between true and false just as there is one between straight and crooked. If there is no such difference, there is no device, nor can someone to whom true and false appear in the same way have any kind of judgement or be in possession of any mark of truth. For when they say that they remove only this one assumption that something can appear to us in such a way that something false could not also appear in the same way, while granting us everything else, they behave childishly. Having removed the means by which everything is judged, they deny that they are removing everything else: this is as if someone who deprived another person of his eyes claimed that he had not removed the objects of sight. Just as these objects are recognized only by means of the eyes, so "everything else" is by means of appearances, and in particular by a mark which is peculiar to what is true, not common to what is true and false. Therefore whether you put forward a plausible appearance or one that is plausible and unimpeded, as Carneades wanted, or something else that you can follow, you will have to return to the appearance about which we are talking. (§34) But if in that appearance there is a commonality of the true with the false, no judgement will reside in it, since what is peculiar to one thing cannot be discerned in a sign that is shared with other things. If, however, there is no shared sign, then I have what I want; for I ask for this one thing, that what is true appears to me in such a way that the same thing cannot equally appear to be false. They make a similar error when, forced by the loud protest of the truth, they want to distinguish what is perspicuous from what is perceived and try to show that there is such a thing as "the perspicuous", namely something that is true and imprinted on the soul and the mind, yet nonetheless it cannot be perceived and apprehended. For how can you say that something is perspicuously white when it is possible that something which is black appears white? Or how can we call these appearances either perspicuous or subtly imprinted when it is uncertain if the mind is moved by a true appearance or deceptively? In this way neither colour nor body nor truth nor argument nor sense perception nor anything "perspicuous" is left. (§35) As a result it happens to the Academics that, whatever they say, they are asked by some: "So what you have just said you do perceive, do you?" But those who ask these questions are laughed at by them. For they (i.e. the Academics) do not set out to prove that nobody can make any claim about anything or affirm it without some certain and peculiar mark of the thing each person is advocating. What then is the nature of that "plausible" you talk of? If what just happens to occur to each man and appears, as it were, at first glance plausible is affirmed, what could be more frivolous? (§36) But if they say they follow what appears to them on the basis of a certain scrutiny and precise consideration, they will nonetheless not have an escape route, first because all those appearances which do not differ are denied credibility in the same way; second, when they say that it can happen to the sage that, after he has done everything and has applied the most careful scrutiny, there may yet arise something which both appears truth-like and is furthest away from the truth, they will not be able to trust themselves even if, as they are fond of saying, they get at the truth itself in most cases or come as close to it as possible. For in order for them to trust this judgement, the mark of truth will have to be familiar to them; when that is obscured and suppressed, what truth will they attain in the end on their own view? Yet what can be said as absurdly as when they say: "This is indeed the sign or the proof of that, and for this reason I follow it; but it can happen that what is marked by the sign is either false or does not exist at all"?

But enough of perception. If someone wants to undermine what has been said, then the truth will easily defend herself even in our absence.

(XII) (§37) Now that the issues which have just been laid out are sufficiently understood, we shall make a few remarks about assent and approval, which the Greeks call *sugkatathesis*, and while this topic is broad, the basis for such a discussion was provided a little earlier. For when we were explaining what power resides in the senses, that related issue was being opened up at the same time, that many things are apprehended and perceived with the senses, which cannot happen without assent. Then, because the biggest difference between a being which does not have a soul and a living being is that the living being acts as rational beings do (if it did not act in this way, one could not even imagine what kind of thing it is), one must either take sense perception away from it or must restore assent to us as something that is in our power. (§38) Yet the mind is in a manner of speaking torn out of those whom they want neither to perceive nor to assent. Just as it necessary for the pan of the scale to be pressed down once weights have been placed on it, so the mind must yield to perspicuous appearances. For just as any living being cannot fail to pursue what is in agreement with its nature (that the Greeks call *oikeion*), so the mind cannot fail to approve a perspicuous thing which it is confronted with. Nevertheless, if what has been discussed is true, it is beside the point to talk about assent at all; for someone who perceives anything assents at once. But these consequences also follow, that memory cannot subsist without assent, or notions of things or the crafts; and what is the most important thing, that something is in our power, in that state someone who assents to nothing will not be. (§39) Consequently, where is virtue if nothing rests with ourselves? But it is most absurd to hold that flaws are within our power and that nobody sins unless by giving assent, yet that this is not so in the case of virtue, whose entire steadfastness and strength comes from the things to which she assented and which she approved. Speaking generally, it is necessary that something appears to us (veridically) before we act and that that which has appeared is assented to. Therefore someone who removes either (self-warranting) appearance or assent, removes all action from life.

(XIII) (§40) Let us now see what arguments they (sc. the Academics) muster against this. But before that, you have the opportunity to understand the, as it were, basis of their entire way of thinking. First, then, they put together a kind of craft to do with what we call appearances, and define their capacity and kinds, among them what the kind of appearance is that can be perceived and apprehended, with the same number of words as the Stoics. Then they set out the following two claims which almost, they say, encapsulate the whole issue: with respect to what appears in such a way that something else could appear in the same way, without there being a difference between them, it is not possible that some of these appearances are perceived, but others are not; and there would "be no difference" not just if the appearances at issue were the same in kind in all respects but also if they could not be distinguished. Once these two assumptions have been set forth, then by conclusion of a single argument, the entire case (sc. as they see it) is gathered up starting from the two claims. But the concluding argument is put together thus: "of the things which appear, some are true and others are false; and what is false cannot be perceived; but everything which is a true appearance is of such a kind that something false which is exactly alike could appear in the same way; and with respect to appearances which are such that there is no difference between them, it cannot come to pass that some of them can be perceived and others cannot. Thus there is no appearance which can be perceived." (§41) With respect to the assumptions which they make in order to arrive at their intended conclusion, they think that two are granted to them (for nobody argues against them). These are: "those appearances which are false cannot be perceived"; and: "with respect to appearances which are no different from one another, it cannot be that some of them are such that they can be perceived, while others are such that they cannot". The other assumptions they defend with rich and varied discourse; these are likewise two: first, "of those things which appear, some are true and some are false"; second, "every appearance which derives from something that is the case is such that it can also derive from something that is not the case." (§42) They do not just skim over these two propositions but expand on them in such a way that they apply to them no mean degree of care and diligence. For they divide their discourse into parts, indeed quite substantial ones, first the senses, then those things which are derived from the senses and from general experience, which they want to be plunged into darkness. Then they reach the part of the discourse devoted to the idea that nothing can be perceived either by a rational method or by conjecture. These more general subjects they then divide up in even smaller sections. Just as you saw with respect to the senses yesterday, they do the same thing with the rest, and with respect to every single subject, which they divide down to its smallest parts, they want to bring it about that to all true appearances there are adjoined false appearances which are no different from true ones; and because they are of such a nature, they cannot be apprehended.

(XIV) (§43) This kind of subtlety in argument I judge to be most fitting for philosophy, but most remote from the case these people are arguing. Definitions, partitions, and a discourse that uses them as highlights, then similarities, differences, and the delicate and sharp discrimination between the two properly belongs to people who are confident that these things are true, stable, and certain, not to those who scream that these things are no more true than false. For what would they do if, when they have defined something, someone asked them whether this definition can be transferred to another subject? If they said it was possible, what would they possibly have to say as to why that definition is true? If they deny that it is possible, one would have to confess that, because this true definition cannot be applied to a wrong subject, what is explained by this definition can be perceived. Yet this they do not want at all. The same can be said with respect to all other parts of their discourse. (§44) For if they say that they have a clear view of the subjects they are discussing and are not impeded by any commonality of (true and false) appearances, then they will be confessing that they apprehend the appearances; but if they deny that true appearances can be distinguished from false ones, how will they be able to proceed further? They will be met again as they have been met already. For an argument cannot be brought to a conclusion unless the assumptions made in it to reach the conclusion are approved in such a way that there can be no false assumptions which are just like them. Thus if a reasoning based on what has been apprehended and perceived reaches this conclusion, that nothing can be apprehended, what can possibly be found that is more in conflict with itself? And while the very nature of formal argument professes that she would make manifest what is not plain, and that, in order to achieve this more easily, she would avail herself of sense perceptions and of what is perspicuous, what are we to think of that discourse of theirs who want that everything is not as it appears? But they are completely defeated when they take these two assumptions to be compatible with each other which are vehemently in conflict, first that there are false impressions (in wanting this to obtain, they make it plain that certain claims are true), then in the same breath, that there is no difference between false and true appearances. Yet you had made the first assumption as if there was a difference; so the later claim is not linked to the former, nor the former to the later one.

(§45) But let us now proceed further and act in such a way that we do not give the impression of being unduly biased in favour of our own views, and let us pursue what is said by them in such a way that we do not pass over anything. First of all, then, that perspicuity which we have mentioned has sufficient power that it indicates by itself the things as they are. But in order to stick to what is perspicuous more firmly and securely, greater skill or, if you will, care is needed, so that we are not driven away from the things which are clear as such by certain tricks and attempts to dupe us. He who wanted to address those errors which appear to confuse the cognition of what is true and who said that it was the job of the sage to separate opinion from perspicuity, achieved nothing; for he in no way removed the error which resides in opinion itself.

(XV) (§46) Therefore, since two causal factors work against perspicuous and evident matters, the same number of countermeasures are accordingly to be prepared. The first difficulty is that people do not make their minds focus on and attend to what is perspicuous, so that they cannot appreciate the amount of light they are surrounded by; the other is that, constrained and deceived by fallacious and specious question-and-answer games, certain people when they cannot resolve the fallacies veer from the truth. Thus one must have at hand those considerations which can be cited in favour of perspicuity by way of response, about which I have just spoken, and be armed, so that we can counter the interrogations and expose their attempts to get us. This I have resolved to do in what follows.

(§47) Thus I will set out each class of their arguments, because even these people tend to express themselves in a manner which is not confused. First they attempt to show that many things can appear to us to be the case which in fact are not the case at all, because our minds are moved vacuously in the same manner by those things which are not the case at all as they are by those which are. "For when you state", they say, "that certain appearances are sent by a deity, like those which appear in dreams and which are made plain in oracles, bird signs, and entrails"—these matters, they say, are approved by the Stoics, against whom they are arguing—then they ask how god can make what are in fact false appearances plausible, but not bring about the same effect for appearances which come very close to being true; or if he can do this as well, why he cannot do it for appearances which can—albeit with great difficulty—be told apart; and if that, why not for those for which there is no difference at all.

(§48) "Then, because the mind is moved by itself, as is plain is the case from things we imagine or from apparitions sometimes experienced by people who are asleep or insane, it is likely that the mind too is moved in such a way that it does not just not discriminate whether those appearances are true or false, but also that there is no difference between them at all"—e.g. if, when people tremble and turn white either from a movement of the mind itself or from some terrible thing that has been thrust upon them from outside, in such a way that there was no way of distinguishing that first quivering and paleness, nor of finding any difference between an internally generated appearance and one brought to the subject from the outside.

"Finally, if there are no false appearances which are plausible, then another reasoning applies; if there are some, however, then why should there not also be some which are not easily told apart, or indeed some which exhibit no difference whatsoever? Especially considering that you yourselves say that the sage will refrain from all assent while in a state of insanity because no difference of (true and false) appearances is in evidence."

(XVI) (§49) With respect to all these empty apparitions Antiochus said a lot, and the discussion of an entire day was devoted to this one subject. Yet *I* do not think I have to do the same thing, but I do have to address the headings in question. First, a rebuke must be issued that they use the most deceptive type of argument by interrogation, which tends to enjoy the smallest amount of approval in the field of philosophy, when something is added or taken away little by little and in small steps. They call this kind of argument *Sorites*, because they create a heap by adding just one grain. It is certainly a reasoning which is designed to ensnare and deceive! This is how you make the climb: "if a sleeping man has been confronted by a god with an appearance of such quality as to be plausible, why not also as to be *very* truthlike; why, then, not as to be such that it can only with difficulty be distinguished from a true one, why, then, not as cannot be distinguished at all, why not finally as to be such that there is no difference between this (true) and that (false) one?" If you reach this point owing to my conceding you every step, then it will be my mistake, if you proceed of your own accord, it will be your mistake. (§50) For who will concede to you that god can do anything or that he would act in that way if he could? And on what basis do you assume agreement that, if something can be similar to something else, it follows that it is also difficult to distinguish, then that it cannot be distinguished at all, finally that it is identical? And if wolves are similar to dogs, you will say in the end that they are the same. And indeed honourable things are similar to those which are not honourable, and goods to things which are not goods, and skilful things to things which are not skilful—why do we hesitate then to say that there is no difference between them? Do we not even see that they are incompatible? For there is nothing which can be transferred from the class to which it belongs into another class. Yet if it was proved that there was no difference between appearances which belong to different classes, then some would be found that were in their own class and also in another class. How can that possibly happen? (§51) There is one way of rejecting all empty apparitions, whether they are formed by thinking, which we have conceded does commonly happen, or when we sleep or as a consequence of wine or of insanity: we must say that all appearances of this kind lack perspicuity, to which we must stick tooth and nail. For who does not perceive, when he imagines something and sketches it in his imagination, as soon as he has stirred and collected himself, what the difference is between perspicuous and empty appearances? The same rationale applies to dreams. Do you really think that Ennius, after he had taken a walk with his neighbour Servius Galba in his gardens, said: "It appeared to me that I was taking a walk with Galba"? Yet when he dreamt, he put it thus:

> It appeared to me that the poet Homer was in my presence.

So too Ennius in the *Epicharmus*:

> It appeared to me when I was dreaming that I was dead.

Therefore we attach no value to these appearances once we have woken up and do not regard them as on a par with business we conducted on the forum. (XVII) (§52) "Yet *while* they appear to us, the same look is to be found in those dream appearances as is exhibited by the things we see while awake." First of all, there *is* a difference, but let us leave that to one side. For we say this, that people who sleep and people who are awake do not have the same power and soundness with respect to either the mind or their senses. Not even drunk people do what they do with the same kind of approval as the sober: they are not sure, they hesitate, they stop themselves sometimes and give weaker assent to the things which appear to them, and when they have slept it off they realise how insubstantial these appearances were. The same thing happens to the insane when they are at the beginning (of an episode of madness): they are aware that they are raving and say that something which is not the case appears to them to be the case, and when the severity of the disease lessens they are aware of it and utter these famous words of Alcmeon:

> …but my heart does not agree with what my eyes saw.

(§53) "Yet the sage restrains himself while in a state of madness so as to avoid approving false appearances as true." And indeed on many other occasions, if in his senses there lies a certain heaviness or slowness, or if what appears is rather obscure, or if the sage is prevented from gaining perspicuity due to lack of time. Nonetheless, the whole idea that the sage sometimes suspends assent works against you; for if there were no difference between true and false appearances. He would either suspend judgement either always or never. But from this whole type of consideration one can see through the flippancy of the talk of those who desire to bring everything into disorder. We look for judgement characterized by seriousness, steadfastness, constancy, and wisdom—yet we use examples of dreamers, madmen, and drunks. Do we appreciate how inconsistently we speak in this entire area? For we would not put forward examples of people who are drunk, sleepy, or insane in this absurd fashion, only to say at one moment that there was a difference between the appearances of people who are awake, sober, and sane and those who are in other states, and at another moment that there was no difference. (§54) They do not even see that they make everything unclear, which they do not want. (I call those things "uncertain" which the Greeks call *adêla*.) For if the situation is such that there is no difference in whether an appearance was had by an insane person or a sane one, who could be confident of his own sanity? To want to bring this about is the hallmark of no small measure of madness. They also go on childishly about similarities either of twins or of sealmarks imprinted with rings. Which of us denies that there are similarities when these are in evidence in most things? But, if it suffices for removing cognition that many things are similar to many others, why are you not content with this, especially given that we concede the point, and why do you claim beyond that something which the nature of things does not allow for, that not every thing is of its own kind in its make-up, and that there is a common and in no way different disposition to any two or three things? It may be so that there are eggs most similar to others, or bees most similar to others: why fight on, and what do you want from the twins? For it is granted that they are similar, a concession which might have satisfied you; but you want them to be absolutely identical, not similar, which just cannot be the case. (§55) Then you seek refuge with the natural philosophers, who are most derided within the Academy, from whom not even you will stay away, and say that Democritus claims that there are countless worlds, and indeed ones amongst them which are not just similar, but completely and absolutely equivalent in all respects so that there is no difference whatsoever.[1] Next you demand that, if one world is entirely equal to another so that there is not the smallest difference between them, let it be granted to you that, in this our world, there exists something which is equal to something in such a way that there is no difference and distinction. "Why", you will ask, "should it be the case that out of those indivisible bodies from which Democritus affirms everything is made, in the other worlds, countless ones at that, countless Q. Lutatii Catuli could not only come about but actually do exist, but in our world, vast as it is, another Catulus could not be brought about?" (XVIII) (§56) First you draw my attention to Democritus. I do not agree with him and reject him rather, because of what is taught most clearly by the more sophisticated natural philosophers, that there are properties peculiar to each individual thing. Let us assume those Servilii brothers of old, who were twins, were as similar as it is claimed—do you really think they were identical too? "They were not recognized in public"—but at home. "Not by strangers"—but by their own family. Do we not see that it is a familiar phenomenon that those whom we never thought we could tell apart we can with practice so easily tell apart that they do not appear similar to the slightest degree? (§57) Here you may put up a fight, but I will not fight back. Indeed I will even concede that that sage himself, with whom our conversation is entirely concerned, when he encounters similar things which he does not have marked out, will refrain from assent and will never assent to any appearance unless it is such as a false one could not be. But for the other matters he does have a certain craft by means of which he can distinguish true from false (appearances), and on these similarities practice is to be brought to bear: just as a mother is able to tell her twins apart due to the experience of her eyes, so you will tell them apart once you have become adapted. Do you see how in the proverb eggs exhibit similarity with each other? Nonetheless we gather that on Delos, when it was still prosperous, there were people who used to breed lots of hens commercially; when they had examined an egg, they were able to say which hen had laid it. (§58) And this last point is not a valid point against us since we are content not to be able to tell those eggs apart; for I would not be any more inclined to say that this egg is that one than if there was no difference at all between them. For I have a rule such that I judge those appearances as true which cannot be false; from that I must not diverge by as much as a finger's breadth as they say, for fear of confounding everything; for not just the cognition but also the nature of the true and the false will be removed if there is no difference, so that also the claim which you sometimes make is absurd that, when

---

[1] I regard *et eo quidem innumerabiles itemque homines* as intruded and do not translate it.

appearances are imprinted on the mind, you do not say that there is no difference between the imprints themselves, but between their look and as it were form. As if we did not judge appearances by their look; they will have no credibility when the mark of truth and falsehood is removed. (§59) That other claim of yours is most absurd, that you follow plausible impressions if you are not impeded by anything. First, how can you *not* be impeded when false appearances do not differ from true ones? Then what criterion of truth is there when it is shared with the false? From these considerations the notion of *epochê* is born, i.e. suspension of judgement, in which Arcesilaus was more consistent if what a number of people think about Carneades is true. For if nothing can be perceived, as appeared to be the case to both, assent is to be removed altogether; for what is so pointless as to approve something which has not been apprehended? We heard also yesterday that Carneades sometimes slipped into talk to the effect that the sage would opine, i.e. commit a transgression. That there is something which can be apprehended, a subject which I have been talking about for too long, is not as certain for me as that the sage does not opine, i.e. does not assent to any matter that is either false or incognitive. (§60) What remains is their claim that in order to find the truth one must argue against everything and for everything. So I would like to see what they have found. "We are not in the habit of showing it", they say. What are these mysteries, and why do you conceal your view as if it was something reprehensible? "So that those who will listen to us may be guided by their own reason rather than authority", they say. What if both factors come into it, is that really worse? Nonetheless, that one claim they do not conceal, that nothing can be known. Does not authority stand in the way of that? Very much, as I think. For who would have followed this tenet, plainly and perspicuously perverse and false as it is, if Arcesilaus had not had such wealth of content and power of expression, and even more so Carneades?

(XIX) (§61) Antiochus made roughly these points then in Alexandria and many years later even more forcefully, when he was with me in Syria shortly before he died. But now that the case has been set out firmly, I shall not hesitate to admonish you, since you are a close friend'—he was addressing me—'and a man who is some years younger than me. Will you really, having extolled philosophy with such weighty laudatory remarks and having driven our Hortensius, who was in disagreement, from his opinion, follow that philosophy which conflates the true with the false, takes away our own judgement, deprives us of any approval, and robs us of our senses? Even for the Cimmerians, from whom either a god or nature herself had taken away the sight of the sun, or indeed the location of the place which they inhabited, there were nonetheless fires whose glow they were able to use. But those whom you approve of, having poured such darkness upon us, have not left us any glimmer of light so that we might see something; if we follow them, we shall be constrained by such shackles that we cannot move at all. (§62) For by removing assent, they have removed both any movement of the mind and any practical action; this cannot just be not right but is not possible at all. Take care also that you do not find yourself the one who is least of all permitted to defend such a stance. Will you, who have opened up the most obscure matters, brought them into the light, and confirmed under oath that you had "understood" them (which was by the same token granted to me, who had learnt these things from you), say that nothing can be learnt, apprehended, and perceived? I also ask you repeatedly that you see to it that the standing of your most beautiful actions is not diminished by you yourself.' Having said this, he stopped.

(§63) Hortensius signalled his admiration emphatically (as he had already done throughout Lucullus' speech, so much so that he even often raised his hands—unsurprisingly, for I do not think anyone ever spoke more with more subtlety against the Academy) and likewise began to encourage me to give up my stance, whether in jest or in earnest (I could not quite tell).

Then Catulus said to me: 'If Lucullus' speech has made you waver, which showed recall, precision, and richness, I shall be silent and will hold that I should not put you off changing your mind if that seems right to you. One thing, though, I would not regard as right: that you be influenced by his authority. He only reminded you', he said with a smile, 'that you should be careful that some wicked tribune, of whom as you know there will always be many, may seize you and ask you in the assembly how you can consistently deny that anything certain can be found and yet say that you had "understood" something. Make sure, I ask you, that this does not frighten you. On the issue itself I would prefer you to disagree with him; yet if you yield, I shall not be particularly surprised. For I recall that Antiochus himself, although he had thought differently for many years, gave up his view as soon as it seemed right to him.'

When Catulus had said this, everyone looked at me. (XX) (§64). Then I, no less nervous than I usually am in big court cases, began a speech in this way:

'Catulus, on the issue itself Lucullus' speech has moved me as that of a learned man who has a grasp of all the facts, is prepared, and leaves nothing out of the things which can be said in support of his case, yet not in such a way that I would distrust my ability to respond to him. Authority as great as his was likely to move me if you had not set against it your own authority, which is not smaller. I shall make a start then, beginning with a few words as it were about my own reputation. (§65) If either due to an impulse towards ostentation or out of eagerness for quarrelling I devoted myself to this philosophy in particular, then, I think, one should not just condemn my stupidity but also my character and entire nature. For if in very small matters stubbornness is criticized, and intention to deceive is actively reigned in, why would I want to either fight with others bitterly, or mislead others and even more so myself about the general condition and plan of life as a whole? Therefore, if I did not regard it as silly to do during such a discussion what sometimes happens when the debate is about the state, I would swear by god and the Penates that I am burning with desire to find the truth and that I mean what I say. (§66) For how can I not desire to find the truth when I am already happy if I find something that is truth-like? But just as I judge it to be the most beautiful thing to see the truth, so to approve as true what is false is the most disgraceful thing. Nonetheless I am not someone who never approves anything false, never assents, never opines; but we are asking about the sage. However, I myself am a great opiner (for I am no sage) and I direct my thoughts not at that tiny Little Bear,

> on which "the Phoenicians rely as a guide at sea by night",

as Aratus says, thereby steering a more direct course, because they stick to her,

> who "turns on an inner course in a small orbit"

—but instead at Helice and the very bright Septemtriones, i.e. patterns of a wider appearance and not explored to the finest point. So it comes that I err and roam more widely. But as I said, the question is not about me, but about the sage. These appearances (sc. corresponding to the Septemtriones), when they have struck the mind and the senses sharply, I accept, and I sometimes even assent to them. Nonetheless, I do not perceive: for I hold that nothing can be perceived. I am not a sage; therefore I give in to appearances and cannot resist. Arcesilaus, agreeing with Zeno on this point, thought that that this was the principal power of the sage, to ensure that he is not caught out, to see to it that he is not tricked. For nothing is further removed from our conception of the sage's seriousness, than error, rashness, and blind action. What shall I say, then, about the strength of the sage? You, too, concede that he never opines. Because this is approved by you—to deal with the last of your statements first; I shall soon return to the proper order—, consider first the following argument: (XXI) (§67) "If the sage ever assents to anything, he will also sometimes opine; yet he will never opine; therefore he will never assent to anything." Arcesilaus used to approve this argument; for he affirmed the first premiss and the second one. Carneades occasionally granted that second premiss, that the sage at times assents; so it followed that he also opines, something that you do not want, and rightly so, it seems to me. But that first premiss, that the sage will also opine if he assents, is false, the Stoics say, as does their supporter Antiochus, on the grounds that the sage can distinguish false appearances from true ones, and appearances which cannot be perceived from ones that can. (§68) Yet to me the habit itself of giving assent, even if something can be apprehended, seems dangerous and slippery. Therefore, since it is well known assenting to something that is false or not cognitive is such a significant mistake, all assent must rather be suspended, so that he (the sage) does not fall over if he proceeds with blind rashness. For false appearances are so close to true ones, and ones which cannot be perceived ⟨to those which can be⟩ (if the latter exist; we shall see), that the sage must not entrust himself to such steeply descending ground. But if I advance the premiss on my own account that there is nothing at all which can be perceived, and accept that other premiss which you grant me, that the sage does not opine, the conclusion will be that the sage restrain his assent in all cases. In this way you will have to see whether you prefer this view, or the view that the sage will opine. "Neither", you will say, "of the two." Let us then work to show that nothing can be perceived; for the whole controversy is about that question.

(XXII) (§69) But before that let us have a few words with Antiochus, who learnt the very things which I am defending under Philo for, as is a matter of record, a longer period than anyone else, wrote about these matters with the greatest acumen, and attacked this stance no more keenly than anyone else in his old age than he had previously defended it. Consequently, although he was acute, as he indeed was, his authority is lessened by his inconsistency. For, I ask, what the day was that dawned on him and showed him that mark of truth and falsehood whose existence he had denied for so many years? He thought something up? Well, he says the same things as the Stoics. He regretted holding these earlier views? Why has he not joined another group of philosophers, and the Stoics in particular? For that difference of opinion was peculiar to them. Why was he dissatisfied with an association with Mnesarchus, or with Dardanus? They were the leaders of the Stoics in Athens at the time. He never left Philo, not until after he began to have pupils of his own. (§70) From where has the Old Academy suddenly been called up from the dead? It seems he wanted to retain the dignity of the name while wanting to secede from the thing itself. There were also some who said that he did this out of a desire for fame, and that he also hoped that those who followed him would be called Antiochians; to me it seems rather that he could not bear being besieged by all philosophers. (For amongst them there are a number of shared opinions on all other matters; this one view of the Academics is the only one which of the remaining philosophers nobody approves.) Therefore he yielded, and like those who cannot bear the sun under the New Shops (on the forum), he kept to, when he felt hot, the shadow of the Academics as others keep to the shadow of the Maenian balconies. (§71) When he held that nothing can be perceived, he used to argue by asking which of the two views Dionysius of Herakleia had apprehended due to the definite mark by which you say one should assent, the claim which he had held for many years and with respect to which he had believed his teacher Zeno, that what is honourable is the sole good, or the claim which he defended later, that the honourable was a vacuous term, and that pleasure was the highest good—he who strove to teach, on the basis of Dionysius' change of opinion, that nothing is imprinted on our minds from what is true in such a way that it cannot also come from what is false, saw to it that others could derive from him the argument which he himself had derived from Dionysius. But I shall deal with Antiochus on another occasion in greater detail; now on to these things said by you, Lucullus.

(XXIII) (§72) Let us first examine the claim you made at the beginning: that the old philosophers are cited by us in a manner which is similar to the way in which seditious citizens used to name distinguished but nonetheless "popular" men. These men, when they engage in endeavours which are ⟨not⟩ good, want to appear like good men; we by contrast say that things seem to be the case to us which you concede were actually held by the most noble of philosophers. Anaxagoras said that snow is black. Would you tolerate it if I said the same thing? No, not even if I wondered with hesitation if it might be true. But who is this Anaxagoras? A sophist (as those people were called who engaged in philosophy to show off or for money)? Well, no: he enjoyed the highest fame for seriousness and talent. (§73) What shall I say about Democritus? Whom can we compare not just for the magnitude of his talent but also of his spirit with one who was brave enough to begin thus: "What follows I say about everything"? There is no exception to his promise. For what can lie beyond the scope of "everything"? Who does not place this philosopher ahead of Cleanthes, Chrysippus, and the other representatives of an inferior age? Compared to him they seem to me to belong to the fifth class. And he did not say what we say—we do not deny that there is something true, but deny that it can be perceived. He by contrast denies straightforwardly that it exists. The senses he calls not "obscure" but "dark"; that is the expression he uses. The man who admired him most, Metrodorus of Chios, said at the beginning of his book about nature: "I deny that we know whether we know something or know nothing, that we know not even that itself, nor whether anything or nothing is the case." (§74) Empedocles appears to rave to you—yet to me it seems he sends forth the kind of noise most appropriate to the subjects he is talking about. Does he really blind us or deprive us of the senses if he holds there is insufficient power in them to judge the matters which are subjected to them? Parmenides, Xenophanes, in less good verse but in verse nonetheless, rail as if in wrath against the arrogance of those who, although nothing can be known, dare to say that they have knowledge. From them, he said, Socrates and Plato are to be removed. Why? Is there anyone about whom I could speak more confidently? Indeed, it seems to me that I have lived with them: so many conversations have been recorded, which allow for no doubt that it appeared to Socrates that nothing could be known. He made just one exception, that he "knew (this one thing) that he knew nothing", nothing more. What shall I say about Plato? He would not have gone along with this in so many books unless he had approved it. For there was no reason to follow the irony of someone else, especially when it was consistent. (XXIV) (§75) Do you not get the impression that I do not, like Saturninus, name only famous men, but that I actually imitate only ever those who are distinguished and noble? Yet I had at my disposal those characters who are irritating to you but less significant, Stilpo, Diodorus, and Alexinus, whose province is certain twisted and needling "sophisms" (for so they call treacherous little arguments). But why should I marshal them when I have Chrysippus, who is deemed to be the pillar for the porch of the Stoics? How many arguments has he advanced against the senses, how many against everything that is approved in the realm of ordinary experience! "Yet he took these arguments apart, too." That is not my view, but let us assume he did do so. Certainly he would not have collected so many arguments which tricked us with their great plausibility, if he had not seen that one cannot easily resist them. (§76) What do you make of the Cyrenaics, philosophers who are not looked down on at all? They deny that there could be anything which can be perceived from the outside: they claim to perceive only those things which they feel through an internal touch, like pain and pleasure, and that they do know of which colour or of which sound something is, but that they feel only that they are affected in a certain way.

But enough about authorities. Still, you had asked me if I did not think that after the efforts of those ancients over so many centuries what is true could have been found when so many talented minds and such zeal had searched for it. What has been found I shall see in a moment, and you yourself will be the judge. Arcesilaus did not fight with Zeno in order to disparage him; rather, he wanted to find what is true, as is understood from the following. (§77) Nobody of those who came before had ever as much as said let alone stated in detail that it was possible that a man could hold no opinions, and that it was not just possible but actually necessary for the wise man. This appeared to Arcesilaus to be a true view as well as one that was honourable and befitting the sage. Perhaps he asked Zeno what would happen if the sage could perceive nothing and if to opine was unbecoming for the sage. He replied, I believe, that the sage would not opine because there was something that could be perceived. What this was, then? "An appearance", I think he said. "What kind of appearance?" Then he defined it like this, an appearance imprinted, stamped, and formed from what was as it was. Then it was asked whether this was so even if an appearance which was true was of such a kind that it could also be false. Here Zeno is said to have seen acutely that there was no appearance which could be perceived if, arising from what is, it was such as it could be arising from what is not. Arcesilaus agreed that this addition to the definition was correct, for neither what is false could be perceived nor what is true if the latter was such that it could also be false. He concentrated in conversations on the point that there was no appearance which arose from something true as could not in the same way arise from what is false.

(§78) This is the one point of contention which has lasted until the present day. For that other claim, that the sage will assent to nothing, has nothing to do with this dispute. As you know, it was possible to perceive nothing and nonetheless opine, a view which Carneades is said to have approved; I personally believe Clitomachus rather than Philo or Metrodorus, and think that this view was advanced by him for the sake of the argument rather than approved. But let us leave this to one side. Once opining and perception have been removed, this follows, the suspension of all assent, so that, if I show that nothing can be perceived, you concede that the sage will never assent.

(XXV) (§79) What is it then that can be perceived if not even the senses report the truth? You defend them with a commonplace, Lucullus. In order for you to be unable to do this, I went out of my way yesterday to say so many things against the senses. But you deny that you are moved by the bent oar or the neck of the dove. First, why? For in the case of the oar I sense that what appears to be the case is not the case, and in the case of the dove that there appear more colours but that there is not more than one. Then, did we say nothing else? If all these points were to stand, your case lies defeated. His senses tell the truth, he says. In that case you always have an authority you can invoke, and one at that who argues his case at great risk to himself; for Epicurus lets the case rest on the point that, if one sense has lied once in one's entire life, one must never trust any of them again. (§80) This is being true to oneself, having confidence in one's witnesses and to stick with such perversity; therefore the Epicurean Timagoras denies that he had ever seen two flames arising from one lamp when he pressed on his eye; the lie belonged to opinion, not to the eyes. As if the question was what actually was the case, not what appears to be the case. So he argued, like his ancestors (i.e. Epicurus and his immediate followers); but you, who say that of the things which appear to the senses some are true and others false, how do you distinguish them? And, I beg you, forego the commonplaces; we grow those at home. "If", you say, "some god were to ask you 'if your senses are healthy and intact, do you want something else,' what would you reply?" If only a god did ask: you will hear how badly he has done by us. For assuming we see the truth, how far will we see? I can make out Catulus' Cumanum from here; I see the area (sc. of the Pompeianum), but I cannot make out the Pompeianum, and there is no obstacle blocking my line of sight, but rather the gaze cannot be cast further. What a delightful view! We see Puteoli, but our friend Gaius Avianius, who is perhaps just walking in the arcade of Neptune, we do not see. (§81) "Yet there was this man, who is usually mentioned in lectures, who could see things that were 1,800 stadia away." And some birds can see even further. Consequently I would boldly reply to this god of yours that I am not at all satisfied with these eyes. He says that my sight is sharper than that of those fishes perhaps. They are not seen by us (and they are now right before our eyes) and cannot themselves see us from below. So just as their view is smothered by water, so is ours by thick air. "But we desire nothing more." What? Do you think the mole desires the light? Nor would I complain to your deity because I do not see far enough so much as because I see what is false. Do you see that ship? To us it appears to be standing still, but to those who are on the ship this villa appears to be moving. Search out the reason why it appears in this way; yet however completely you could find it (and I doubt you would be able to), you would not show that you have a truthful witness, but at best one which gives false testimony not without a reason. (XXVI) (§82) Why do I bring up the ship? I saw that you look down on the oar; perhaps you want more substantial examples. What could be more substantial than the sun? The mathematicians confirm that it is eighteen times larger than the earth. Yet how small it appears to us! About one foot across, I would say. Epicurus thinks it is possible that it could even be slightly smaller than it appears to be, but not much; nor does he think it is much larger, or it may be as large as it appears to be, so that the eyes either do not lie or do not lie much. What then becomes of this "only once" of yours? But let us move away from this gullible man who thinks that the senses never lie, who does not even think that they lie now, when the sun right there, which is carried around with such rapidity that its speed cannot even be conceived of, appears to us to be motionless. (§83) But in order to reduce the dispute in scope, consider, I ask you, on how small an issue it turns. There are four heads, which jointly lead to the conclusion that nothing can be known, perceived, apprehended—the claim which is the subject of this whole debate. The first of them is that there is such a thing as a false appearance; the second, that a false appearance cannot be perceived; the third, that if two kinds of appearances are no different, it is not possible that some of them can be perceived and others cannot; fourth, that there is no true appearance arising from sense perception with which another appearance is not juxtaposed which is no different from it and which cannot be perceived. Of those four, the second and the third everyone concedes. The first one Epicurus does not grant; you, who I am dealing with, concede it, too. The entire fight is about the fourth. (§84) Consequently someone who was looking at P. Servilius Geminus, but thought he was looking at Quintus, happened upon the kind of appearance which could not be perceived because what is true was not distinguished from what is false by any sign. And after that difference was removed, what sign which could not be false would he have for identifying C. Cotta, who was consul twice with Geminus? You deny that such similarity exists in the nature of things. Certainly, you fight, but with a compliant adversary. The similarity may not exist, admittedly—but it can certainly appear that way; it will thus deceive sense perception. And once one similarity has thus deceived, it will have rendered everything doubtful. For once the means of judgement, required for identifying, is removed, even if who you look at is the person he appears as, you will not be making your judgement with reference to the sign which you say is required in order to prevent there possibly being a false one which is exactly the same. (§85) So since Publius Geminus can appear to you as Quintus, what certainty do you have why someone who is not Cotta could not appear to you as Cotta, since there is something that does appear to be the case while not being the case? You say that everything is of its own unique kind, and that nothing is the same as something else. This is indeed a Stoic tenet and not a particularly credible one, that no hair is in all respects the same as another hair, no grain like another grain. These claims could be refuted, but I do not want to fight. For with respect to the matter in hand it makes no difference whether something that features in an appearance is in no respect different (from another thing) or whether it cannot be distinguished even if it is different. But if the similarity of two human beings cannot be so great, not even that of statues? Tell me, could Lysippus not with the same bronze, the same blend of metals, the same chisel, the same water, and identical conditions, make a hundred Alexanders exactly the same in kind? By what measure would you distinguish them? (§86) What? If I press in wax of the same type one hundred seal marks with this ring, what difference will there be in the process of telling them apart? Will you have to look for a ring expert since you found that expert Delian chicken farmer who is capable of recognizing eggs? (XXVII) Then you also apply technical skill, recruited to assist the senses: "The painter sees things that we do not see", and "as soon as the fluteplayer starts, the song is at once recognized by the expert." What? Do you not think that it counts against you if without great artistic finesse, which few people reach, at least of our race, we can neither see nor hear? Now for those splendid words regarding the skill with which nature had crafted our senses, the mind, and the whole construction of a human being—(§87) why should I not fear the rashness of opining? Are you really able to affirm this, Lucullus, that there is some power, in possession of prudence and wise planning of course, which has made or, to use your term, has crafted man? What is the nature of this craft, where is it applied, when, why, and how? These things are dealt with brilliantly, they are also discussed elegantly; indeed, let them appear to you to be the case, just don't affirm them. But I shall talk about the natural philosophers soon, particularly in order to ensure that you, who said a little earlier that this is what I would be doing, don't look to have misled me.

But in order to move to matters which are clearer, I shall expand on matters of general import, about which entire books have been filled not only by our people, but also by Chrysippus (about whom the Stoics tend to complain that, when he carefully collected all arguments against the senses, clarity, all experience, and reason, he was actually weaker when he replied to himself, and that for this reason Carneades was supplied with weapons by him). (§88) These points, which were most diligently discussed by you, are of the following kind. You said repeatedly that the appearances of people who are asleep, drunk or insane are weaker than those of people who are awake, sober, and sane. How so? Because Ennius, after he had woken up, did not say that he had seen Homer, but that he had appeared to him, while Alcmaeon said:

but my mind does not agree with me…

Similarly about drunk people. As if anyone denied that he who had woken up thought that he had dreamt, and that the man whose madness had subsided thought that the things that appeared to him while insane were not true. But that is not the issue; how things appeared to you when they appeared to you, that is the question. Unless of course we think that Ennius did not hear the whole speech beginning:

O you devotion of the soul…

when he dreamt it as clearly as if he were hearing it while awake. Having woken up, he was able to regard these appearances for what they were, dreams: when he was asleep they were approved by him as he would have approved them while awake. What? When Iliona while having that dream said:

Mother, I am calling you…,

did she not so strongly think that her son was speaking, that she even thought it once she had woken up? And where else would the following come from:

Come on, stay here, remain, and listen: say this again to me?

Do she really seem to place less confidence in her appearances than people who are awake usually do? (XXVIII) (§89) What shall I say about insane people? What was your relation Tuditanus like, Catulus? Does any perfectly sane person think what he sees is as certain as Tuditanus thought the things were that appeared to him? What of him who said:

I see you, I see you. Live, Odysseus, as long as you can?

Did he not actually exclaim twice that he saw something when he saw nothing at all? What? In Euripides, was not Hercules moved as much by false appearances as by true ones when he was piercing his own children with arrows as if they were Eurystheus', when he was dispatching his wife, when he was trying to kill his father, too? What? Your Alcmaeon himself, who denies that his "mind agrees with his eyes", does he not say in the same context when his madness grew intense:

where does this flame arise from?

And then these words next:

come, come; they are here, they are seeking me—

what of the scene in which he appeals to the maiden's loyalty for support?

Offer me succour; drive the pestilence away from me,
that flame-carrying force which tortures me,
dark, girded with snakes they advance,
and stand around me with burning torches.

Do you really doubt that it appeared to him that he saw these things? Likewise the rest:

Apollo, with flowing locks, bends
the gilded bow, leaning on the moon,
Diana throws a torch from the left.

(§90) How could he have given these appearances more credence if they had been real than he did because they appeared to be so? For here it is plain that "the mind agrees with the eyes." All these instances are put forward to obtain the conclusion—and nothing could be more certain—that with respect to the mind's assent there is no difference between true and false appearances. But you are engaged in a futile exercise when you try to refute the false appearances of the insane or of dreamers by invoking their own later recollection. For it is not a question of what kind the recollection is of people who have woken up, or of those who have ceased to be insane, but of what quality the visual experience was of the insane or of the dreamers at the time when they were moved by the impression. With this I leave the subject of the senses.

(§91) What can be grasped by reason? You say that dialectic was invented as an, as it were, arbitress and judge of the true and the false. Of which true and false thing, and with respect to what? Will the dialectician decide what is true and false in the field of geometry or in letters or in music? But he does not know any of these things. In philosophy, then: but what concern is to him (i.e. the dialectician) what the size of the sun is? And by what means could he judge what the highest good is? So what will he judge? Which conditional and which disjunction is true, what is said ambiguously, what follows from what, what is incompatible with it. If these matters and ones like them are what dialectic judges, it makes judgements about itself; but it promised more than that. For to make judgements on these issues is not enough if we look to the many and important matters philosophy is concerned with. (§92) But since you put so much stock in that craft (i.e. dialectic), see to it that it is not entirely set against you. On first setting out the craft gaily bestows the parts of speech, the understanding of ambiguity, and the theory of argument, then by means of a few small additions it arrives at the sorites, a slippery and dangerous place surely, which you said just now is a corrupt type of interrogation. (XXIX) What then? Are *we* really to blame for this corruptness? The nature of things has given us no cognition of boundaries, so that we could fix with respect to each thing how far it extends, and not just with respect to a heap of grain, from which the term comes, but with respect to no subject on which we are interrogated in a step-by-step sort of way, whether someone is rich, poor, famous, obscure, whether an amount is many, few, large, small, long, short, wide, narrow. We are not able to know how much one has to add or take a way for us to give a definitive reply. (§93) "But soritical arguments are flawed." Break them up then if you can, so that they are no longer awkward; for that is what they are going to be if you are not careful. "Precautions have been taken", he says. "Chrysippus thinks that, when he is asked questions proceeding step by step whether, say, three is few or many, one should rest"—(that is what they call *hêsychazein*)—"at some point before one comes to 'many'." "You may even snore as far as I am concerned", says Carneades, "and not just rest. But what good does it do? For next there comes someone who is bent on rousing you from your sleep and who asks you in the same manner: 'And if I add to the number at which you fell silent one more, will that be many?' You will go forward again then for as long as seems fit." What more do I need to say? For you confess that you cannot specify in reply the last of "few" or the first of "many". This kind of problem seeps so far that I cannot see where it cannot go. (§94) "It does not hurt me", he says. "For I will, like a clever charioteer, make the horses stop before

I reach the boundary, and all the more so if the place to which the horses are carried is a steep slope. In the same manner I", he says, "restrain myself and not give further replies to the questioner intent on trickery." If you have something clear at your disposal and you do not reply, you will be acting arrogantly; if you do not, then not even you are able to perceive something. If that is because things are obscure, I allow it; but you deny that you will proceed up to the point where things are obscure; if so, you always halt where things are clear. If you only stop in order to be silent, you achieve nothing; for what difference does it make to someone who wants to catch you whether he ensnares you while you are silent or while you talk? But if you answer up to nine in the sequence, let us say, without hesitation that it is "few", and halt at ten, then you are withholding assent also from matters which are certain and perfectly clear; yet that same thing you do not let me do with respect to matters which are obscure. So that craft of yours (i.e. dialectic) helps you nothing against soritical arguments, as it does not teach what is first or what is last in an ascending or descending series. (§95) What of the fact that this craft, like Penelope undoing what she has woven, destroys in the end what it has done before? Are you to blame for this or are we? It is surely the basis of dialectic that anything asserted (this they call *axioma*, which is an "utterance" as it were) is either true or false. What then—is the following true or false: if you say that you are telling a falsehood [and say so truthfully], are you lying or telling the truth? True, your school call such arguments "inexplicable"; this is more invidious than the things which we call not apprehended and not perceived.

(XXX) But I leave this aside and ask the following instead: if these arguments cannot be explained and no means of judging them is found to enable you to reply whether they are true or false, then what becomes of that definition, that anything asserted is something that is either true or false. Once certain assumptions are made, I will add that other things must follow from them which are to be rejected—which properties are contradictory. (§96) How in your judgement has this argument been brought to a conclusion: "if you say it is day now and you tell the truth, ⟨it is day; you say that it is day now and you tell the truth⟩; thus it is day now"? Your school certainly approve the type of argument and say it reaches a conclusion most correctly, and therefore you pass on in your teaching that first type of argument. Now either you will approve of any argument brought to a conclusion in this fashion or your craft of dialectic is worthless. Consider now whether you will approve the following argument: "if you say you are telling a falsehood and you are telling the truth, you are telling a falsehood; you say that you are telling a falsehood and you are telling the truth; thus you are telling a falsehood"? How can you not approve this when you have approved the earlier argument of the same type? These are Chrysippean arguments, resolved not even by him? What would he do in the face of this argument: "If it is day, it is day; it is day; therefore it is day"? He would of course agree to it; the nature of the conditional compels you to accept the second when you have accepted the first. So how does it differ from this argument: "if you tell a falsehood, you tell a falsehood; but you tell a falsehood; so you tell a falsehood"? You say that you can neither approve nor reject this; why then is this more readily possible with the earlier argument? If the craft, the rationale, the method, the power of the argument has any force, it is the same in both cases. (§97) But this move is what they come to at last: they demand that an exception is made for these inexplicable arguments. I think they should see some tribune: from me they will never obtain this exception. And since they do not obtain from Epicurus, who despises and derides the whole of dialectic, his concession that the statement "either Hermarchus will be alive tomorrow or he will not be alive" is true, whereas the dialecticians state that every disjunction of the form "either p or not-p" is not just true but even necessary (consider how careful the man is whom they consider slow: "for if", he says, "I concede that either of the two is necessary, it will be necessary either that Hermarchus is alive tomorrow or that he is not alive; yet no such necessity exists in the nature of things"), let the dialecticians, i.e. Antiochus and the Stoics, fight against him: for he overthrows the whole of dialectic. For if a disjunction composed of contradictories (I call contradictories those propositions where one affirms something and the other denies it), if such a distinction can be false, none is true. (§98) But what dispute do they have with me when I am only following their method? When something like this had occurred, Carneades used to joke: "If I have obtained the conclusion correctly, I keep to it; if in a flawed way, Diogenes will give me back my *mine*." From that Stoic philosopher he had learnt dialectic, and that was the standard fee for dialecticians. Consequently I follow the procedures I have learnt from Antiochus, and I find no grounds why I judge "if it is day, it is day" to be true for the reason which I have learnt, that every conditional in which antecedent and consequent are the same is true, while I do not judge "if you are speaking a falsehood, you are speaking a falsehood" to be a conditional formed in the same way. So I will either judge this one to be just as that one, or that if the latter is not true, then the former will not be true either.

(XXXI) But to leave all those pointed tools and the whole tortuous type of argumentation behind and to show who we are on our own terms: once the whole view of Carneades is explained, all these teachings of Antiochus will collapse on themselves. And I shall not say anything in such a way that someone might suspect that I have made it up; I will take what I am going to say from Clitomachus, who was with Carneades until old age, a man who was sharp, as one would expect from a Carthaginian, and very studious and painstaking; and there are four books of his on the withholding of assent. What I am going to say is taken from the first. (§99) Carneades holds there are two kinds of appearances: in one division, there are some appearances which can be perceived, ⟨and others which cannot be perceived⟩, but in the other division there are some appearances which are plausible, and others which are not plausible. Therefore everything that is said against the senses and against perspicuity pertains to the former division, but no objection ought to be brought against the latter division. Thus, he says, his view was this: there was no appearance such that perception followed upon it, but appearances which attract approval there were many. For it would be against nature if there were nothing plausible; upon it there follows the overturning of all aspects of life which you were talking about, Lucullus. Therefore there are many appearances to approve for the senses, but just this one thing should be kept in mind, that there is amongst them never one which was such that there could not be a false one which did not differ from it at all—so whatever appearance happened to arise with a plausible look, if nothing presented itself which was opposed to that plausibility, the sage will use, and so the whole scheme of his life will be governed. And indeed that sage who is cited by you follows many plausible appearances which are not apprehended, not perceived, and not assented to, but which are truth-like, and if he does not approve them, life in its entirety would be abolished. (§100) What? Has your sage boarding a ship really apprehended and perceived with his mind that he will have a safe journey according to his plan? How can he? But if he were to set off from this place to Puteoli, a distance of thirty stades, with a good ship, a fine helmsman, and this kind of calm, it would appear plausible to him that he will arrive there safely. So he will resolve on plans for action or inaction on the basis of such appearances and will be more amenable to approving that snow is white than Anaxagoras was, who not only denied that it was white, but said it did not even appear white to him because he knew that the water from which it had formed was black. (§101) And whatever thing affects him in such a way that the appearance is plausible and not impeded by anything, he will be moved by. For he is not sculpted from rock or carved from oak, he has a body, a mind, he is moved with respect to the mind, is moved with respect to the senses, so that many true things appear to him and yet do not appear to him to have that extraordinary and peculiar sign of perceiving. And for that reason, he says, the sage does not assent because there could be a false appearance just like that true appearance. Nor do we, when we speak against the senses, say anything that is different from what the Stoics say, who say that many things are false and that they are quite different from how they appear to the senses. (XXXII) But if this is so, that there is just one false thing which appears to the senses, there is immediately someone who denies that anything can be perceived by the senses. Therefore, without us saying a word, perception and apprehension are overturned by one Epicurean assumption and one that belongs to you. What is the Epicurean assumption? "If any sense appearance is false, nothing can be perceived." What is yours? "There are false sense appearances." What follows? The conclusion itself speaks, without a word from me: "Nothing can be perceived." "I do not give way to Epicurus' point", he says. Fight with him then, who is completely different in outlook from you, not with me, who agrees with you certainly on this point, that there is something false in the senses. (§102) Nothing, though, seems so strange to me as that these claims are made at all, especially by Antiochus, to whom what I said a little earlier was deeply familiar. For though anyone is free to reproach us, if he sees fit, because we deny that anything can be perceived, certainly the blame is to us of little significance because we say that certain appearances are plausible. That does not seem enough to you. Let it be insufficient; yet these charges we are bound to escape which have emphatically been pursued by you: "Consequently you see nothing, hear nothing, nothing is clear to you." I explained a little earlier, relying on Clitomachus' authority, how Carneades spoke on these issues; hear now how the same points are made by Clitomachus in the book he dedicated to the poet C. Lucilius, after he had written on the same issues in a work dedicated to L. Censorinus who was consul with M'. Manilius—they are familiar to me because the basic groundwork and lessons as it were on these very subjects with which we are dealing are contained in that work—in any event, here is what is written there:

(§103) The Academics hold that there are differences between things such that some appear plausible and others do not. That, however, is not sufficient ground for you to say that some things are perceived and others are not, because many false appearances are plausible while nothing which is false can be perceived and cognized. Therefore, he says, those are very much mistaken who say that the senses are rooted out by the Academics: the Academics had never said that colour, taste, or sound do not exist. What they did argue was that those things had no mark of what is true and certain which is peculiar to them and which is nowhere else to be found.

(§104) After he had explained this, he added that "the sage withholds assent" is said in two senses, in one sense where it is understood that he assents to nothing whatsoever, and another where he does ⟨not⟩ check himself from responding so as to approve or disapprove, in such a way that he neither denies or affirms anything. Since this is so, he says that the sage adopts the former, so that he never assents, and goes with the latter, in such a way that, following plausibility, wherever it obtains or is absent, he can answer either "I suppose so" or "no". And since he holds that he who checks himself from assenting about everything is nonetheless moved and acts, he left those impressions through which we are stirred to action, likewise those with respect to which we, when interrogated on either side, can respond, following only what appears to be so, provided we do this without assent. However, not all impressions of this kind are approved but only those which are not impeded by anything. (§105) If we fail to prove these points to you, they may be false, but they are certainly not invidious. For we do not snatch daylight away from you, but say that the things of which you say that they are perceived and apprehended, "appear" to us so long as they are plausible.

(XXXIII) With the plausible appearance thus introduced and established, and unencumbered, unshackled, and free at that, not entangled with anything, you surely see, Lucilius, that your entire attempt to defend clarity lies in tatters. The sage about whom I am talking will look with the same eyes as your sage at the sky, the earth, and the sea, and will take cognizance with the same senses of all the other things which fall under each sense. The sea there, which now that Favonius picks up appears purple, will appear the same to our sage, but he will nonetheless not assent, since even to ourselves it appeared blue just now, and grey in the morning, and because it is now white and shimmers where the sun lights it up, it is different from the area that is immediately adjacent to it, so that, even if you can give an explanation why this happens, you can nonetheless not defend the claim that the appearance it gave to the eyes is true.

(§106) "Where does memory come from if we perceive nothing?" This was your question. What? We cannot remember appearances unless they are apprehended? What? Polyaenus, who is said to have been a great mathematician, thought, after he accepted the view of Epicurus, that geometry in its entirety was false—do you really think he had also forgotten what he once knew? Yet what is false cannot be perceived, as you yourselves hold. Consequently if memory is of things which are perceived and apprehended, then everything which someone remembers he holds apprehended and perceived. But nothing false can be apprehended, and Siron remembers all of Epicurus' tenets; thus all of them are true as things stand. That is fine with me—but you must either concede that this is so, which you do not want at all, or you must grant memory to me and admit that there is room for it, even if there is no apprehension and perception.

(§107) "What happens to the arts?" To which ones? To those which by their own admission rely on conjecture more than knowledge, or to those which merely follow what appears to be the case and do not have your art at their disposal to enable them to distinguish true and false?

But the following two considerations are the highlights which encapsulate your case in particular. First, you deny that it is possible that anyone assents to nothing. Yet it is clear that it is possible, because Panaetius, close to being the leading Stoic at least in my judgement, says he has doubts that about something which all Stoics apart from him regard as most certain, that the appraisals of the entrail-inspectors, the auspices, the oracles, the dream appearances, and the prophecies are true, and he restrains himself from assenting—if he can do this with respect to matters which his own teachers regard as most certain, why could the sage not do it with respect to all other matters? Or is there anything which, once it is set forth, he can reject or approve, but not have doubts about? Can you do this in soritical arguments when you want to, but the sage will not be able to restrain himself from assenting in the same way with respect to other matters, especially because he can—without assent—follow truth-likeness itself when it is not impeded?

(§108) The other point is that you deny that any kind of action is possible by someone who approves of nothing with his assent. For first something must appear veridically [i.e. through a cataleptic impression], in which there lies also assent (the Stoics say that instances of sense perception are themselves instances of assent, upon which, because impulse follows them, there follows action)—but everything would be abolished if (cataleptic) appearances are abolished. (XXXIV) On this issue many things have been said and written on either side, but the whole topic can be settled briefly. For even though I regard it as an action of the highest order to fight appearances, to withstand opinions, and to refrain from slippery assents, as well as believe Clitomachus when he writes that a Herculean labour was completed by Carneades when he tore assent, as it were some wild and enormous monster, from our minds, that is opinion and rashness, nonetheless, to leave this part of the defence to one side, (I still ask) what will bar the action of someone who follows plausible impressions while there is no impediment? (§109) "Precisely that", he says, "will bar action that he claims that not even what he approves can be perceived." Well, then the same thing will also bar you when you embark on a voyage, when you sow your crop, when you take a wife, when you have children, and in many other areas where one does not follow anything other than the plausible.

Nonetheless you put forward this much-used and often rejected argument, not like Antipater, but as you say "more closely"; for Antipater was reproached for saying that it was consistent for someone who affirmed that nothing can be apprehended to say that this one thing at least could be apprehended. That seemed to Antiochus to be stupid and self-contradictory; for it cannot be said consistently that nothing can be apprehended if it is said at the same time that something can be apprehended. Rather, he thinks one should have exercised pressure on Carneades in such a way that, because there cannot be such a thing as a tenet of the sage unless it is apprehended, perceived, and cognized, he admitted that this tenet itself, that nothing can be perceived by the sage, was perceived—as if the sage had no tenet of any other kind that was his and could conduct his life without tenets. (§110) But just as he regards these appearances as plausible ones, not as ones which have been (cataleptically) perceived, so he regards this one, that nothing can be (cataleptically) perceived. For if he had a sign of cognition in this case, he would use it in other cases, too. Because he does not have it, he uses plausible impressions. Therefore he is not afraid that he might appear to confuse everything and render everything uncertain. For if he is asked about appropriate action and many other things in which he has had experience and practice, he would not say he does not know as he would if asked if the number of stars is even or odd. For with respect to matters which are uncertain there are no plausible appearances. In areas where they are available, however, the sage will not be at a loss what to do and how to respond.

(§111) Not even did you, Lucullus, pass over *that* reproach made by Antiochus' (unsurprisingly, since he enjoys especially good repute), by which Antiochus used to say Philo was very troubled indeed: it was that when one assumption is made, that there are false appearances, and another, that they do not differ from true appearances, he (sc. Philo) did not take into account that the earlier assumption was conceded because some difference between (true and false) appearances was in evidence, which, however, was done away with by the other, by which he denies that true appearances differ from false ones—nothing was as inconsistent as this. This would come to pass if we (sc. Academics) abolished the true altogether. That is not what we do; for we see true as well as false appearances. Yet the look gives rise to approval only, we do not have a mark of perception.

(XXXV) (§112) It seems to be that I am dealing with this in too restrictive a fashion at the moment. For although there is a broad field in which our speech could frolic, why do we drive it into such narrow corners, i.e. the thickets belonging to the Stoics? For if I were dealing with a Peripatetic, who would say that "what is imprinted from what is true" could be perceived without attaching the significant further clause "as could not be imprinted from what is false", I would be dealing with a straightforward man in a straightforward fashion, I should not greatly dispute the matter, and even if, after I had said that nothing could be apprehended, he said that the sage would sometimes opine, I would not resist, especially because Carneades does not put up much of a fight on this point, either. As it is, what can I do?

(§113) For I ask what it is that can be apprehended. Aristotle or Theophrastus do not reply to me, nor Xenocrates or Polemo either, but a younger man: "a true appearance which is such that it could not be false." I encounter nothing of the kind. Therefore, unsurprisingly, I shall assent to what is not apprehended, i.e. opine. That the Peripatetics and the Old Academy grant to me; you and your friends deny it, Antiochus in particular. He influences me a great deal, because I loved the man just as he loved me, or because I judge him to be the most polished and the sharpest philosopher of all whom we can remember. First I would ask him how he can be a member of the Academy to which he professes to belong. To pass over other issues, those two claims we are discussing, who of either the Old Academy or of the Peripatetics ever made them, that only a true appearance can be perceived which is such that it could not be false, or that the sage did not opine? Nobody, certainly. Neither of the two was much defended before Zeno. Nonetheless I think both of them are true, and I do not say this merely to serve the occasion, but I approve of them entirely.

(XXXVI) (§114) One thing I cannot bear (sc. about Antiochus): you ban me from assenting to the incognitive and say that it is most reprehensible and full of blind rashness, and yet you take so much upon yourself as to set out a doctrinal system, i.e. explain the nature of all things, create norms, set the highest good and the worst evil, outline appropriate action, define what kind of life I am to embark on, and also say that you will hand over a criterion and method of argument and understanding—will you bring it about that I, having embraced these countless topics, will never slip, will never opine? What kind of philosophical system is it, then, to which you are guiding me if you have succeeded in dragging me away from the one I am following? I fear you are acting somewhat arrogantly when you say that it is your philosophical system; and yet it is necessary for you to say that. Nor are you alone in this, and everyone will rush me off to his own system. (§115) Fine then, let us assume that I resist the Peripatetics, who say that they are akin to the orators, that famous men trained by them have often held the helm of the state, that I stave off the Epicureans, so many of whom are my friends, and who are such good men and devoted to each other—what shall I do about Diodotus the Stoic, whose pupil I have been from boyhood, who has associated with me for so many years, who lives in my house in fact, whom I both admire and love, and who looks down on these Antiochian teachings? "Our doctrines alone", you will say, "are true." Certainly yours alone if they are indeed true; for there cannot be several true doctrines if they are at variance with each other. So are we shameless, who do not want to slip, or are they arrogant, who have convinced themselves that they alone know everything? "Not me personally, to be sure", you say, "but I say that the sage knows." Perfect: to be sure, you mean "know the things that constitute your doctrine". First of all, what sort of admission is this, that wisdom is explained by the non-sage? But let us leave ourselves aside, and let us talk about the sage, about whom as I have often said this entire dispute is.

(§116) Wisdom is divided into three parts by most people and by you (the Antiochians). First, if you agree, let us see which inquiries there have been into the nature of things—or rather, to take this point first: is there anyone so bloated with erroneous thinking that he has brought himself to believe he has knowledge of these matters? I am not asking about reasonings which depend on conjecture, which in discussion are dragged hither and thither, which do not involve persuasive cogency. No, let the geometers supply us, who proclaim that they do not persuade but compel and who "prove" to you everything that they draw in their diagrams. I do not ask them about the first principles of mathematics—if these are not granted they cannot advance as much as a finger's width—, about the point which has no extension, about an area and, as it were, a plane which has no thickness, about a line which is a length without width and height. When I grant that these are true, if I put the sage to the oath (but not before Archimedes, while he looks on, has outlined all the steps by which it is shown how many times the sun is larger than the earth), do you think he will take the oath? If he does, he will have shown contempt for the sun itself, which he regards as a god. (§117) But if he is not likely to give credence to the reasonings of the geometers, given that it is these reasonings which exercise cogent force in their teachings, as you yourselves say, verily he will be far from giving credence to the arguments of the philosophers—or if he is to give credence, to whom in particular? Here one could lay out all the doctrines of the natural philosophers, but it would take a long time; nonetheless I ask whom he follows. Assume now someone is in the process of becoming a sage, but is not one yet: which view and which doctrine will he select in particular? Though whatever doctrine he selects, he will select as a non-sage; but let us assume he is of divine talent: whom among the natural philosophers will he approve particularly? He cannot approve more than one. I am not pursuing open-ended questions here. Let us merely see with respect to the principles of things, from which everything is made up, whom he approves. For amongst the leading figures there is the strongest disagreement.

(XXXVII) (§118) The first is Thales, one of the Seven, to whom the other six are said to have granted the leading role; he said that everything consists of water. But that did not persuade Anaximander, his fellow citizen and associate; he said that there was an indeterminate nature from which all things are created. After came his pupil, Anaximenes, who said it was the infinite air, but that the things which arose from it were finite; what arose was earth, water, and fire, and then all the things which derive from them. Anaxagoras said it was infinite matter, small particles which are similar to each other; these were first mixed up, and then later arranged in an orderly way by a divine mind. Xenophanes, who was a little older, said everything was one, and it was not changeable, and it was a god, unborn and eternal, of spherical shape. Parmenides named the fire, which moves the earth and shapes by it; Leucippus the empty and the full. Democritus was similar to him in this respect, and more detailed in the other respects. Empedocles named his widely familiar and well-known four elements. Heraclitus, fire. Melissus, what was infinite and unchangeable, and what existed always and will always exist. Plato thought that from matter which took on everything in itself the world was created by a god so as to be everlasting. The Pythagoreans want everything to arise from numbers and mathematical principles.

From these your sage, I believe, will select one to follow; the rest, numerous and great as they are, will walk away, rejected and condemned. (§119) But whichever view he approves, he will have apprehended with his mind in the same way as what he apprehends with the senses, and he will not approve more strongly that it is now day than, because he is a Stoic, that this world is wise, that it has a mind, which had constructed both itself and the world and which guides, moves, and governs everything. He will be convinced that also the sun, the moon, all the stars, the earth and the sea are gods, because a certain soul-like intelligence permeates and penetrates all these things; and that nonetheless there will come a day when this entire world will be burnt up in a conflagration. These claims may be true (you see surely by this time that I admit that there is something true), but I nonetheless deny that they are apprehended and perceived. For when your Stoic sage has said these things, syllable by syllable, Aristotle will appear, pouring forth a golden river of a speech—to say the Stoic is out of his mind. For the world had neither come into being ever, because there was no beginning for such a splendid creation requiring the conception of a new plan, and it is so well-organized in all respects that no force could bring about such enormous motions and effect change, no old age due to the length of time could exist for it, so that this cosmos could ever fall down and expire. *You* must then necessarily reject this, and defend that earlier construct like your life and your reputation: and to *me* it won't be granted even that I feel some doubt? (§120) Let me leave aside the lack of seriousness of those who give assent blindly: how highly is the freedom itself to be priced that what is necessary for you is not necessary for me. Is there a reason why god, although he was creating everything for our sake (for so you want it to be), created watersnakes and vipers in such great supply, why he has distributed them, many, deadly, and pernicious as they are, across land and sea? You deny that these things could have been brought about in such an accomplished and delicate way without some kind of divine technical skill; and that skill's majesty you indeed stretch to the point where it includes the exquisite creation of bees and ants, so that it would appear as if amongst the gods there was some Myrmecides who manufactured tiny artefacts. (§121) You deny that without a divine being there could be anything. Look, Strato of Lampsacus appears from left field, to give your god dispensation—from a large burden indeed, but seeing that priests of the gods take vacations, then how much more equitable is it for the gods themselves to take them—: he denies that he relies on the help of the gods in fashioning the world. Rather, he teaches that all that there is was brought about by nature herself, and not in such a way as that man claims that everything is put together from rough, smooth, and hooked particles, with void in between (he thinks these are dreams on the part of Democritus, his wishes rather than things that can be shown to be so). Attending to the individual parts of the world, whatever either exists or comes to be, he himself teaches that they arise or were made by masses and their movements. Indeed, he liberates god from a great task and me from my fear! For who would not, because he thinks that he is watched over by god, live in dread of the divine power day and night, as well as fear that, if something adverse happened—and to whom does such a thing not happen?—it may happen deservedly? Still, I do not agree with Strato nor do I agree with you; now this appears more plausible to me, now that. (XXXIX) (§122) All these things, Lucullus, are hidden, obscured and cloaked by thick darkness, so that no human talent is sharp enough to advance into the sky, to enter into the earth. We do not know our own bodies, where its organs are located, we do not know which role which organ plays. Therefore the doctors themselves, to whom it mattered to know these things, have opened bodies so that the organs could be seen, but the empiricists say that the parts of the body do not become better known that way, because it may be that, once opened up and laid open, they change. But are we able to cut up, open and partition component parts of nature in the same way, in order to see if the earth has deep foundations and hangs on by its roots as it were or whether it is suspended in mid-air? (§123) Xenophanes says the moon is inhabited, and that it is another earth with many cities and mountains: that seems a fantasy. Still, neither could he who said this give an oath that this is how things are, nor could I that it was not so. Your friends also say that opposite us, on the other side of the earth, there are people whom you call antipodes, who stand such that the soles of their feet face ours. Why are you angrier with me, who do not spurn these claims, than with those who, upon hearing this claim, think you're insane? Hicetas of Syracuse, as Theophrastus says, thinks that the sky, the sun, the moon, the stars, indeed everything in the realm above stands still and that nothing except for earth moves at all; because it turns and spins around its axis at the highest speed, all the same effects were brought about as would arise if the earth stood still and the sky moved. Some think that Plato said the same thing in his *Timaeus*, but in a more obscure manner. What is your opinion, Epicurus? Tell us: do you think the sun is of such a small size? "Me? I think it is as large as indicated." And then you are derided by him and you yourselves make fun of him in turn. Free of such derision is Socrates, free is Aristo of Chius, who thinks that none of these things can be known. (§124) But I return to the mind and the body. Can we grasp what the nature of the muscles is, what of the blood vessels? Do we have a grasp of what the mind is, where it is, finally if it exists or, as appeared to Dicaearchus, whether it has no existence at all? If it exists, whether it has three parts, as Plato thought, reason, anger, and desire, or whether it is simple and one; if it is one, whether it is fire or breath or blood or, as Xenocrates held, a number without bodily existence (what kind of thing that is supposed to be can hardly be understood); and, whatever it is, whether it is mortal or eternal? For on either side many things are said. Some one view of these appears certain to your sage, to our sage nothing has occurred that was even the most plausible, so exactly even is for him the weight of the opposite considerations on most issues. (XL) (§125) If, however, you act with more respect and accuse me not that I do not assent to your reasonings but that I do not assent to any at all, I shall overcome my inclinations and choose someone to assent to—but whom in particular, whom? Democritus; for I have always been, as you know, a devotee of nobility. At once I shall be put under pressure by the accusations of all of you: "You would be inclined to believe, then, that there is such a thing as void, although everything is so compacted and filled that any body which is moved gives place and something else follows immediately in the direction in which each thing yielded, or that there are atoms, from which everything is made that is so very unlike them, or that without the action of some rational mind something so splendid could be brought about? And that, because in one world the order is so wonderful, there are countless other worlds above, below, right, before, after, some very different, others of the same kind? And that, just as we are now at Bauli and look to Puteoli, so there are countless other persons in the same kind of place, with the same names, the same status, who have the same achievements, have the same talents, look the same as well as being the same age, and talk about the same things? And that images impinge upon our minds from the outside, penetrating our body, either now or even if we are asleep? But you must not claim these things for yourself or give your assent to such fairytales; to hold no views at all is better than having ones which are so profoundly wrong."

(§126) So the issue is not that I should approve something with my assent; in asking that I approve the same things as you, make sure that you are not just not shameless but also not arrogant in your demands, especially given that your views do not even appear plausible to me. For I do not think that divination which you approve of exists at all, and I take a dim view of that "fate" of yours which supposedly holds together everything; I do not even think that this world was constructed by divine planning, and I don't know whether it is in fact true; but why am I held up as an object of disapprobation? Do I have your permission not to know what I do not know, or is it acceptable for the Stoics to dispute amongst themselves, but not for others to dispute with them? To Zeno and almost all the other Stoics the ether appears to be the highest god, endowed with a mind by which everything is governed; Cleanthes, a Stoic from, as it were, the best stock, a pupil of Zeno, thinks that the sun rules and is in charge of things; thus we are forced, because of the disagreement amongst the sages, not to know who our master is, since we do not know if we are slaves of the sun or the ether. Indeed, the size of the sun (it seems to gaze at me now crowned with rays, reminding me that I should refer to it more often)—so you indicate its size as if you had measured it with a ten-foot ruler; I refuse to put confidence in your measurements, as if you were bad architects. It is not at all clear who of us, to put it mildly, is showing more respect. (§127) Still, I do not think that one should do away with these enquiries carried out by the natural philosophers. For the consideration and contemplation of nature is, as it were, the natural food for the mind and the intellect. We stretch ourselves and appear taller, look down on human affairs, and by considering things up above and heavenly matters, we come to despise our concerns as tiny and exceedingly small. The mere investigation of things which are at once of the highest significance but also profoundly hidden holds delight; but if something comes up which appears truth-like, the soul is filled with the most human type of pleasure. (§128) Thus your as well as our sage will be looking for this, but yours in such a way as to assent, give credence, and affirm, while ours will do it in such a way as to be afraid that he might opine rashly, and he will think that he has been exceedingly well done by if he finds among these matters something that is truth-like.

Let us proceed to the notion of good and evil; yet a small prefatory remark is necessary. It appears that they do not consider that, when they affirm these things so very positively, they also lose their authority with respect to matters which are less obscure. For just as they assent to the idea and approve that it is now day, they hold that, when the crow caws, it commands or forbids something; and they will lend no greater endorsement to the claim that this statue—once they have measured it—is six feet tall than to the other claim, that the sun, which they cannot measure, is more than twenty-two times larger than the earth. From this the following argument springs: "If it cannot be perceived how large the sun is, then he who approves these other things in the same manner in which he approves the size of the sun does not perceive them; but the size of the sun cannot be perceived; thus he who approves this, as if he perceived it, perceives nothing whatsoever." They may reply that it can be perceived how large the sun is; I will not put up resistance, as long as they say that everything else is perceived and apprehended by the same token. For they cannot say that one thing is more or less apprehended than another, because for everything there is just one definition of apprehension.

(XLII) (§129) But to continue with what I had started: what certainty do we have in matters good and evil? Indeed, endpoints are to be established with reference to which the calculation about good and evil may be made. About which subject, then, is there more disagreement amongst the leading men? And I leave aside those positions which appear to have been left by the wayside: Erillus, who sets knowledge and scientific understanding as the highest good; although he was Zeno's pupil, you see how far he diverged from him and how little from Plato. The Megarians had a noble school, whose founder, as I read, was Xenophanes, whom I mentioned just now, then following him Parmenides and Zeno (for that reason they were called the Eleatics by them), then Euclides, Socrates' pupil from Megara, after whom those Megarians are named, who said that the only good was that which was one, ever like itself, and always the same; they also held many views derived from Plato. After Menedemos, however, because he was from Eretria, the Eretrians were named, who thought that every good was located in the mind and in the mind's keenness, by means of which the truth might be seen; similar views were held by the Erillians, but I think formulated in a richer and more adorned style. (§130) If we look down on these people and regard them as already discarded, then we should certainly show less contempt for the following: Aristo, who, having been Zeno's pupil, actually approved what Zeno merely paid lip service to, that there was no other good than virtue and no other evil than what was opposed to virtue; the items in between which Zeno posited he thought did not exist at all. For him the highest good is a state in which one is moved in neither direction on such questions, a state which he calls *adiaphoria*. But Pyrrho held that the sage did not even perceive these things with the senses, a state he called *apatheia*. So, to pass over these views, let us now look at the ones which have been defended for a long time and with many arguments.

(§131) Some wanted the highest good to be pleasure; in this category ranked first is Aristippus, who had been a pupil of Socrates, from whom the Cyrenaics descend; then Epicurus, whose doctrine is now more famous, although he does not agree with the Cyrenaics on the subject of pleasure itself. Callipho held that pleasure and the honourable were the end, to be free from any kind of discomfort was Hieronymus' view, Diodorus thought it was that same thing coupled with the honourable; the last two were Peripatetics. That the end was to live honourably while enjoying those things which nature commends in particular for man was the view of not only of the Old Academy, as the writings of Polemo indicate of whom Antiochus approves particularly, but Aristotle and his friends appear to come very close to it too. Further, Carneades introduced the view, not because he approved it but in order to set it against the Stoics, that the highest good was the enjoyment of those things which nature had commended in particular for man. But to live honourably, which has as its starting point this commendation of nature, Zeno stated was the highest good; he was the founder and first head of the Stoics.

(XLIII) (§132) Next, this is plain, that opposed to all the highest goods which I have set out there are worst evils. Now I turn to you to ask whom I should follow; just let no one give me that uneducated and absurd reply of "anyone, as long as you follow someone"; nothing can be called less thought-out. I would very much like to follow the Stoics. Is that allowed—I leave aside "as far as Aristotle is concerned", an almost unique figure in philosophy, or so I judge—as far as Antiochus is concerned, who was called an Academic, but would have been a most genuine Stoic if he had made some very small changes. So the matter will already be at the point where a decision is required: for *either* the Stoic sage is to be installed *or* that of the Old Academy. For between them the dispute is not about boundaries, but about possession of the whole. For every way of life is encapsulated in the definition of the highest good; those who disagree about it disagree about the entire way of life. So they cannot both be sages, since they disagree so profoundly, but only one can: if it is Polemo's, then the Stoic sage errs by assenting to something false (but you say that there is nothing which is so alien to the sage); if Zeno's views are true, the same is to be said against the Old Academics and the Peripatetics. So he who agrees with neither if it is never apparent who of the two is wise, is he not more prudent than either?

(§133) What? Does not Antiochus himself, when he disagrees with the Stoics, beloved by him, on certain things, indicate that the sage cannot approve these things? The Stoics hold that all transgressions are equal; yet Antiochus does not like this at all. So let me consider whose view I want to follow. "Be brief", he says, "give a reply, any reply, for once." What? When what has been said on either side appears to me to be clever and evenly balanced, shall I not take care that I do not commit a crime? For a crime, as you said, Lucullus, is to betray one's "dogma"; so I restrain myself, in order to avoid assent to the incognitive, which is the dogma that you share with me.

(§134) But see now, there comes a much larger disagreement. Zeno believes that the happy life lies in virtue alone. What does Antiochus think? "Yes", he says, "the happy life, but not the happiest life." The former, who thought that virtue is lacking in nothing, was a god, a puny man, though, is he who believes that for man there are many things apart from virtue which are partly dear and partly even necessary. But I fear that the first one attributes more to virtue than nature permits (Theophrastus in particular says much on the subject, in a learned and detailed way), and I am afraid that the second one is scarcely consistent, who, although he says that there are some evils both of the body and of fortune, nonetheless regards someone who is afflicted with them all as happy if he is a sage: I am being dragged in different directions here, and at one time the former view appears to be more plausible to me, and at another the latter, and nonetheless, unless one of them obtains, I believe that virtue will be altogether laid low. Yet in this lies their disagreement.

(XLIV) (§135) What? With respect to the issues on which they agree, can we really approve those as true, that the mind of the sage is never moved by desire or elated by happiness? Well, these may certainly be plausible claims. What about *those*, that the sage never experiences fear, never pain? Would the sage not fear that his homeland may be destroyed, not feel pain if it is destroyed? Harsh claims, but ones to which Zeno is necessarily committed, for whom nothing except the honourable counts among the goods, though you, Antiochus, would not be committed to them at all, to whom apart from the honourable many things appear to have the status of goods, and many things the status of evils besides wickedness, whose future arrival the sage must fear and over whose actual arrival he must feel pain. But I ask when such harshness reigned in the Old Academy, that they denied that the mind of the sage is moved and perturbed? They approved of "means" and wanted there to be a natural amount in every emotion. We have all read Crantor the Old Academic's book on grief; for it is a small but golden work, to be committed to memory word for word, as Panaetius recommended to Tubero. And they also said that those types of emotion had been given by nature to our minds for a purpose, fear so that one would be careful, compassion and sorrow so that we showed mildness; they said that anger itself was as it were the whetstone of courage—whether this was right or wrong, we shall consider another time. (§136) In any event, I do not know how that harshness of yours is forced itself into the Old Academy. The following claims I cannot bear (not because I dislike them, for they are most of extraordinary sayings of the Stoics, which are called paradoxes, are Socratic in nature): but where did Xenocrates even touch on them, where Aristotle (those two you want to be virtually the same)? Would they ever say that sages alone are kings, are rich, are beautiful? That everything that was anywhere belonged to the sage? That nobody was a consul, a praetor, and imperator, well not even a member of a commission of fifteen men unless he was a sage? Finally, that the sage alone is a citizen, that he alone is free, that the non-sages are all foreigners, exiled men, slaves, and lunatics? Lastly, that the writings of Lycurgus and of Solon, that our Twelve Tables are not laws, that there were not even cities and states except for those of the sages? (§137) If you agree with your friend Antiochus, then you must defend these claims, Lucullus, as if they were the walls of your city, whereas I have to defend anything only to a reasonable degree and to the extent that the claim appears true to me. (XLV) I have read in Clitomachus that, when Carneades and the Stoic Diogenes stood on the Capitol, waiting for the senate to receive them, Aulus Albinus—who was praetor in the year when P. Scipio and M. Marcellus were consuls, the same man who was consul with your grandfather, Lucullus, and who, on the evidence of his history written in Greek, was clearly a learned man—said to Carneades in jest: "I do not give the appearance of being a praetor to you [because I am not a sage], nor this a city, nor that there is a citizen-body in it." To which Carneades replied: "You do not appear thus to this Stoic." Aristotle or Xenocrates, whom Antiochus wanted to follow, would not have doubted that he was a praetor and that Rome was a city inhabited by the Roman citizen-body. But our man here is, as I said above, very much a Stoic, who, however, stumbles over his words on very rare occasions.

(§138) For me who am afraid that I lapse and end up with an opinion, that I adopt and approve something that is incognitive, which you do not want at all, what advice do you give? Chrysippus declares that there are only three views concerning the highest good which can be defended: he truncates and prunes the number of views. Either the honourable, or pleasure, or a combination of the two is the highest good, he says. For those who say that the highest good is the freedom from any discomfort are only shunning the hated name of pleasure but linger in the vicinity. That same thing is also done by those who couple freedom from any discomfort with the honourable, and not much different are those who conjoin to the honourable the first advantages of nature. So he leaves three views which he thinks can be defended plausibly. (§139) This may well be so, although I am not easily torn away from Polemo's, the Peripatetics', and Antiochus' ends, and I do not as yet have something more plausible. Still, I see how agreeably pleasure flatters our senses; I am drifting into agreeing with Epicurus and Aristippus. Virtue calls me back, or rather pulls me back with her hand, says that these movements of the soul are fitting for field animals, and links man to god. I can take up a position in the middle; thus, because Aristippus only looks at the body as if we had no mind, and Zeno embraces only the mind, as if we had no bodies, I would follow Calliphon, whose view Carneades used to defend with so much application that he even appeared to approve it (Clitomachus, though, asserted that he had never been able to understand what Carneades actually did approve); but if I wanted to follow that view of the end, would not truth herself, and serious, right reason, appear before me and say: "Since being honourable consists in looking down on pleasure, will you really create a union of both, like that of a man with a beast?"

(XLVI) (§140) Thus just one pair of adversaries is left to fight it out, pleasure matched with the honourable; on this matter there was for Chrysippus, as far as I can see, no real contest. If you follow one of them, many things fall down, notably the community together with mankind, loving care, friendship, and justice, the other virtues, none of which can exist unless they did everything without reward. For virtue which is driven to appropriate action by pleasure as if by some kind of remuneration it receives is not virtue, but a deceptive imitation and pretence of it. Hear by contrast those who say that they do not even understand what the term "the honourable" means (unless we want to dub "honourable" that which gives rise to glory among the masses), that the source of all goods lies in the body, that it is nature's rule, yardstick, and injunction, and that anyone who diverged from it would never have anything in life that he could follow.

(§141) Do you think I am in no way moved when I hear things like this and countless others? I am moved as much as you, Lucullus, and please do not regard me as less of a human being than you are. The only difference is that you, when you have been moved by something, are content, assent, and approve, want that truth to be certain, apprehended, perceived, settled, firm, and fixed, and cannot be shifted or moved from it by any reasoning. Whereas I think that there is nothing which is such that I, if I have assented to it, do not often assent to something false, because true impressions are not separated from false ones by any difference, especially considering that your criteria of dialectic are non-existent.

(§142) I come now to the third part of philosophy. One criterion is that of Protagoras, who thinks that that thing is true for anyone which appears to him to be so; another is that of the Cyrenaics, who think there is no criterion other than the innermost movements of the soul; another that of Epicurus, who locates the criterion only in the senses, our notions of things, and in pleasure. Plato wanted any criterion of truth and the truth itself to be removed from opinion and the senses, belonging entirely to thinking itself and the mind. (§143) Does your Antiochus approve any of these positions? None, not even the view which was held by his own ancestors. For where does he follow either Xenocrates, whose books on argument theory are many and widely approved, or Aristotle himself, compared to whom nobody is more acute and more polished? Nowhere does he move even a foot away from Chrysippus. (XLVII) How come we are called Academics then? Are we just misusing the repute in which the name is held? Or why are we forced to follow people who disagree with one another? In the very subject which the dialecticians teach in their introductory lectures, how one should judge whether a conditional like "if it is day, it is light" is true or not, what controversy there is: Diodorus believes one thing, Philo another, Chrysippus yet another. What? Consider on how many issues Chrysippus disagrees with his teacher Cleanthes. What? Antipater and Archidemus, the two who are certainly leaders amongst the dialecticians, very opinionated individuals, do they not disagree on a great many things?

(§144) So why, Lucullus, do you incite hostility against me and call me before the people as it were, and indeed, as seditious tribunes are wont to do, order the closing of the shops? For what is the point of your complaint that we do away with the products of crafts if not to upset the craftsmen? If they come together from everywhere, they will easily be whipped up against you. I shall first expound those unpopular claims of yours, that you say all those who stand there assembled are exiles, slaves, and insane; then I shall come to those which relate not to the crowd but to you who are present here. Zeno denies, and Antiochus denies, that you know anything. "In what way?", you will say. "We defend the claim that even the fool apprehends many things." (§145) Yet you say that no one knows anything unless he is a sage. And Zeno used to show that by gesture. For when he had shown his stretched-out hand with straight fingers, he said: "Appearance is like this." Then, after he had bent his fingers a little, he said: "Assent is like that." Then when he had closed his hand entirely and had made a fist, he said this was apprehension, and because of the resemblance assigned the term *katalêpsis* to it, which had not existed before. However, when he had moved the left hand close and had squeezed together the other hand, now a fist, closely and forcefully, he said such was knowledge, in which nobody partakes apart from the sage. But who is or was a sage not even they themselves usually say. And so it follows that you, Catulus, do not know now that it is day, nor you, Hortensius, that we are in your villa. (§146) Are these remarks less liable to stir resentment? Still, they are not very elegantly put; the earlier points were more subtle. But just as you said that craft skills collapse if nothing could be apprehended, and did not concede that what is plausible is of sufficient power to sustain the crafts, so I now retort that craft is not possible without knowledge. Can it really be that Zeuxis or Phidias or Polyclitus would tolerate this, that they knew nothing, even though they had such great skill? Yet if someone then informed them what force "knowledge" was said to have, they would stop being enraged; they would not even be angry with us once they learned that we were only removing what was nowhere to be found in any case, yet leaving untouched what was sufficient for their purposes. This way of thinking is also sanctioned by the diligence shown by our ancestors, who first wanted everyone to swear "to the best of their belief", then to be held guilty of perjury only "if one knowingly misled", on the grounds that there was much ignorance in our life, then that someone who offered testimony should say that "he was of the view" even concerning something he had seen something himself, and that the findings of judges under oath should be couched in such a way that they did not say *x* was the case ⟨or not the case⟩ but "appeared to them to be such-and-such."

(XLVIII) (§147) But since not just the boatman is giving the sign, but also Favonius itself is whispering that it is time for us to sail, Lucullus, and since I have already said enough, I should come to a close. Next time when we investigate such matters, we should rather talk about the disagreement among so many leading men, about the obscurity of physical issues and about the mistake made by so many philosophers (who disagree about goods and evils to such a degree that, because more than one claim on a given matter cannot be true, so many noble systems must lie in ruins), rather than about lies of the eyes and the remaining senses, about the sorites and about the liar—hunting nets which the Stoics have woven for themselves.'

(§148) Then Lucullus said: 'I do not regret at all that we have discussed all this. We shall meet more often and enquire into such questions as they present themselves to us, especially on our estates near Tusculum.'

'Excellent', I said, 'but what does Catulus think, what Hortensius?'

Then Catulus said: 'What do I think? I revert to my father's view, which he used to say was indeed the Carneadean one: I believe that nothing can be apprehended, but that the sage will assent to what is not apprehended, i.e. opine—but in such a way that he understands that he opines and knows that there is nothing which can be apprehended and perceived; rejecting that suspension of judgement about all things, I assent emphatically to that other view, that there is nothing that can be perceived.'

I said: 'I understand your view and do not very greatly object to it. But what do you think, Hortensius?'

To which he replied: 'Away with it.'

I said: 'I have you on my side; for this view is peculiar to the Academy.' And so, with the conversation concluded, Catulus stayed; we made our way down to our boats.

COMMENTARY

Academicus Primus

§§1–8

The dialogue starts without a preface: from the beginning Cicero is already in character as one of the interlocutors.[1] While staying with Atticus at the *Cumanum*, news comes that Varro had arrived the previous evening from Rome, sc. at his own villa nearby, and that he would come to see them soon if he was not too tired. The time of day is not specified, as in general the setting is characterized in broad outline only.[2] Cicero continues that he and Atticus set off to see Varro immediately, whose longstanding friendship and interests shared with Cicero are referred to. This is the closest Cicero can come to mentioning the dedication in the dialogue, given the absence of a frame and that he is a character in it.[3] In reality Cicero's personal relationship with Varro had never been cordial, their political stances, while broadly similar, had been motivated in quite different ways, and Cicero had agonized over the dedication as well as over making Varro an interlocutor.[4]

Cicero then describes their meeting—Varro was already on his way to them—somewhat stiltedly (they embrace, '*ut mos amicorum est*'), and how he and Atticus escorted Varro back to his villa. The political situation in Rome is briefly mentioned (§2 *init.*), in very general terms which do not suggest a particular fictional date for the dialogue beyond it being close to the time of composition, and then immediately dropped as a subject of conversation on Atticus' intervention.[5] Atticus notes that Varro had not published anything for an unusually long time, 'no doubt because he is hiding what he is writing rather than not writing'. Varro, with a hint of the angularity the real Varro must have had, replies that it would be the mark of a fool to write something without the desire to make it available to others, and that he has been working on a

---

[1] Contrast the preface of *Luc.* (executed in two phases, like that of *Catul.*; see the general note on *Luc.* 1–9a) and that of *Fin.* 1, whose composition overlaps with *Acad.* For a crisp survey of Cicero's prefaces in the dialogues, see Schmidt (1978–9); Steel (2013), esp. pp. 223 n. 11 and 225; Gildenhard (2013a), esp. pp. 253 and 256. For the selection of characters in *Acad.*, see also sections 9.1 and 9.2.

[2] See on t. 47, i.e. Nonius pp. 65–6 M. (frg. 13 Reid; Plasberg[1] p. 140 and Plasberg[2] p. 90). The extant fragments of the edition in four books do not allow us to tell if the action was spread over two days (as in the *Catulus* and *Luc.*, where the location is a different villa for each of the two books). A crisp survey of the settings of Cicero's dialogues is in Linderski (1995a).

[3] Contrast the manner in which Brutus is directly addressed in *Fin.* 1.1.

[4] See below on Cicero's relationship with Varro and section 9.1 on the dedicatory letter (*Fam.* 9.8 = SB 254 = T29).

[5] This replicates the situation at the beginning of *Brut.* (46 BC), where Atticus also intervenes when the political situation is mentioned in conversation, dismissing it as distressing (*Brut.* 11). There the history of Roman oratory is then discussed. The structural similarity is no coincidence, in that many of the writings of this period are avowedly situated in an *otium* imposed by the political situation, whereas *De orat.*, *Rep.*, and *Leg.* are presented as the product of an *otium* Cicero struggles to find in the face of the obligations of his *negotium*. On this point, see Gildenhard (2007: 51), who in n. 184 surveys the scholarship on whether Cicero's claim that he is exceedingly busy in the second half of the 50s is credible; see also section 3.

work dedicated to Cicero, which was substantial and was now being polished. The reference is to the *De lingua Latina*, which, however, Cicero knew only under the description of a substantial work in progress when he wrote *Acad.*[6]

Cicero intervenes, in direct speech (§3): He has been expecting the work eagerly for a long time, but did not dare to ask for it, and he has it on good authority—from their mutual friend Libo, who, Cicero avers, passed on the information out of *studium* (keen interest in literary matters, rather than out of personal devotion, or as an indiscretion)—how committedly Varro has been working on it. Again, this feels slightly more circumspect than normal proem style would require, hinting at Varro's quickness to take offence.[7] From here Cicero moves to the subject of philosophy. Now that he has embarked on writing about philosophy, about which both he and Varro know, in Latin, Cicero asks himself what he had not asked before:[8] why Varro, who had contributed to many genres, had not written philosophy, in which he was an expert, and a passion for which was superior to other interests.

In §§4–8 Varro responds to Cicero's question. The passage is frequently cited as evidence for the challenges of writing philosophy in Latin in the late Republic, but it is of course Varro who is made to speak here, he is introduced as defending why he is not himself writing strictly philosophical works, and Cicero the author has an interest in presenting his project as trailblazing. (See below on other texts in which Cicero speaks on the subject in his own voice.) Varro begins by stating, somewhat ponderously, that Cicero's question addresses an issue he has given much thought to, so that the 'omission' appears quite deliberate and considered. Varro argues that, given the high quality of philosophical writing in Greek, there are two possible responses to philosophical writing in Latin: (i) those who are instructed in Greek *doctrinae* (i.e. familiar with Greek doctrines, and only by implication in possession of a grasp of Greek) will prefer to read Greek works; (ii) those who reject Greek learning will not care for philosophy written in Latin. He adds the secondary point that such writings would not be intelligible without antecedent familiarity with the Greek content. This raises interesting questions: one can certainly point to passages in *Acad.* where correspondences of Greek and Latin terms are used to key the Latin discussion to its Greek background in a manner which is only transparent to someone who is fully familiar with the latter (*Luc.* 17–18; *Ac.* 1.40–1);[9] however, such passages seem to be the exception rather than the norm.[10] In any event, the main thrust of Varro's argument is plain: there would be no market for philosophy written in Latin.[11]

---

[6] See on *Ac.* 1.2: *Silent enim diutius Musae Varronis...quae scribat existimo*.

[7] Whether Varro would have regarded the reference to a planned dedication of his major work in progress, i.e. *L.L.*, as an attempt to exercise pressure on him is impossible to say; see below, p. 91.

[8] Cf. *Fam.* 9.8 (= SB 254 = T29; to Varro): *Puto fore ut, cum legeris, mirere nos id locutos esse inter nos quod numquam locuti sumus, sed nosti morem dialogorum.*

[9] For both passages, see the commentary ad loc. and Reinhardt (2017).

[10] Similarly, scholars working on Lucretius face the question of whether they should try and elucidate the poem with reference to the poetic tradition in which Lucretius (who is avowedly writing for an educated Roman who is not familiar with the Greek background) stands, or whether they should try to explain the poem with reference to the Greek texts which must have been on the poet's desk when he composed *De rerum natura*.

[11] I shall argue below that Cicero himself suppresses part of the evidence for contemporary writing in philosophy. Depending on how transparent this suppression was, what Varro says here may be at variance with what the first audience knows.

In §§5–7, having surmised that philosophy in Latin would have no audience, Varro provides a secondary reason for why he has had no wish to write philosophy: his particular philosophical persuasion would make such an endeavour exceedingly difficult or even impossible. The passage has the appearance of being one of Cicero's variations on the 'poverty topos' (sc. of the Latin language),[12] but what Varro is made to say is of course undermined by the very work in which Varro appears as an interlocutor, and some of the arguments which he cites cannot but strike the reader as less than compelling.[13] Varro refers to what must be prose works by Epicurean writers in Latin (see below, p. 87), which he dismisses for being cast in *uulgaris sermo*, as well as for exhibiting the absence of proper philosophical method often associated with Epicureanism; thus Epicureans reject definitions, partitions, and theory of argument, i.e. dialectic and rhetoric (see the notes below). It is not immediately clear that the two points of criticism are connected: the works in question could, one might think, be stylistically artless, as well as exhibit the philosophical flaws which vitiate, on Varro's view, all of Epicurean philosophy. Here, however, Varro's point appears to be that, as it were, *res* and *uerba* are linked, and any attempt to write Epicurean philosophy in Latin is bound to end up as *uulgaris sermo* in virtue of its subject matter.[14] This is suggested by the way in which Varro proceeds to cover the different areas of philosophy: 'we', i.e. either he and Cicero as followers of the Academy in the broader sense, or he and Cicero as men who have been exposed to Antiochus' Old Academic teachings, would find it much more difficult to write philosophy in Latin because— in the area of λογική—they would need to adhere to the strict rules according to which Academic philosophy proceeds, could not, unlike the Epicureans, use ordinary language, and instead would have to use newly created technical terminology, which would make the *docti* resort to the Greek original and which the *indocti* would not accept to begin with. It is not obvious why the acceptance of a formal theory of argument should make a difference to philosophical discourse in general, and on the occasions when Lucullus introduces formal arguments in his speech in *Luc.* (§§92–8), these do not seem to pose particular challenges as far as Latin expression is concerned. That it should be the use of technical terms, and of neologisms in particular,[15] which characterizes philosophical discourse, may not appear compelling to the modern reader—indeed, Cicero's skill as a writer of philosophy in Latin is evident less on the occasions where he coins a new word to render a Greek term than in his deployment of existing Latin words in a terminological way.[16] However, in this case there

---

[12] The phrase is used by Farrell (2001: 28), who comments: 'Most obviously, poverty connotes deficient semantic power.'

[13] Once again it is tempting to compare Lucretius, whose didactic strategies include the creation of passages which invite the reader's disagreement in some form, and thus reinforce their 'actual' didactic message obliquely.

[14] See the note ad loc. for the use of the phrase *uulgaris sermo*; Reinhardt (2005: 174–5) on how disapproval of the Epicurean doctrine of pleasure in particular affected the appreciation of other elements of Epicurean doctrine in antiquity.

[15] The phrase *noua uerba* suggests neologisms rather than ordinary Latin words used in novel (e.g. metaphorical) ways (see the n. below), but new (metaphorical) uses of existing words are acknowledged elsewhere. The *Glossarium Epicureum* (= Usener 1977) suggests that Epicureanism was as prone to jargon as other schools.

[16] See Reinhardt (2016).

are grounds for thinking that ancient and modern views come apart, in that Cicero, in passages which deal overtly with the alleged poverty of Latin, never addresses the issue of philosophical discourse as a mere variety of natural discourse. In the area of physics, Varro suggests that it is easy to describe the banal doctrine of atoms in Latin, whereas Old Academic physics, which posits an efficient cause and relies on geometry, is not so easily rendered. Both require linguistic, in particular lexical resources in order to be presented clearly, which Latin supposedly does not have. Here one is tempted to observe that a conception of efficient causation was used by Roman jurists long before philosophy came to Rome,[17] and that it is difficult to see why causal theory should pose particular challenges for a Latin writer; Cicero's later efforts in that direction, notably the *De fato*, are impressive but did not require unlikely feats of ingenuity. The case of geometry is slightly less clear-cut: at least a certain amount of geometrical terminology was used by *agrimensores* (whose writings date from the early empire onwards, but whose field of expertise arose before that time, when Rome started expanding significantly beyond a city state), but Cicero notes elsewhere that geometry was an art held in high esteem by the Greeks and adopted by the Romans only as far as it was required to meet elementary practical purposes.[18] It would, however, require a separate argument to show that higher-level geometry is particularly difficult to represent in Latin. Finally, in ethics the Epicurean conception of the goal is dismissed as applicable for animals and humans alike, whereas the Stoa and Antiochus' Old Academy take positions which are enormously subtle, and even more subtle are arguments directed against the Stoics from an Old Academic point of view. On a charitable reading, the Epicurean view is here presented as easy to present in simple terms because the doctrine is elementary. Yet again, *Fin.* 1 and 2, which must have been well advanced when Cicero wrote *Ac.* 1,[19] shows that Epicurean teachings on pleasure were much more nuanced than the caricatures suggest.[20] At the end of this general note I shall compare what Varro says with other Ciceronian passages which speak to the subject of writing philosophy in Latin, but I note already here that the remarks about the particular difficulty of rendering dogmatic philosophy other than Epicureanism in Latin are not paralleled elsewhere and that some of the objections they give rise to seem obvious (see further p. 85 below). Moreover, in the section on physics (*Ac.* 1.24 *fin.*–26) Varro is made to resume the issue, with particular examples, so even if the text here seems to invite a degree of scepticism on the part of the reader, Varro's views are presented as a reasoned position in *Acad.* Another function of Varro's remarks may be to explain certain omissions. The section on physics (*Ac.* 1.24–9) draws heavily on Plato's *Timaeus* (though not directly), where geometry features as a central subject.[21] Geometry is, however,

---

[17] See tab. VIII.13 in Crawford (1996.ii: 692–4) and Reinhardt (2003: 331–4) on *Top.* 64.
[18] Cf. *Tusc.* 1.5: *In summo apud illos honore geometria fuit, itaque nihil mathematicis illustrius; at nos metiendi ratiocinandique utilitate huius artis terminauimus modum*; and Horace's comparison of the Greek pursuit of knowledge out of desire for glory and the Roman teaching of arithmetics out of *cura peculi* (*A.P.* 323–32).
[19] On the relative chronology of the creation of *Acad.* and *Fin.*, see section 9.1.
[20] In *Fin.* 3.3 (where Cicero addresses the dedicatee Brutus) there is, however, the same gesture to the plainness of Epicurean thought and its presentation in Latin.
[21] See e.g. White (1975); Burnyeat (1999); Paparazzo (2013).

omitted from Varro's discussion, perhaps—or so would be the implication—because Varro deems it too difficult to communicate in Latin.

In *Ac.* 1.7b Varro then clarifies his attitude to philosophy as such. He uses it to bring steadfastness to his life (*constantia uitae*) as well as for intellectual enjoyment, and regards it as the greatest and best divine gift to man. On the first point, which credits philosophical activity with a kind of usefulness, see the wider discussion of Cicero's repeatedly stated aspiration to benefit his fellow citizens through his philosophical writings.[22] However (§8a), those who have an interest in the subject Varro sends to study with the Greeks, so that they may drink from the sources directly rather than from (secondary) runlets. By this point Varro's focus no longer seems to be the Old Academy,[23] and instead Greek philosophy in general is meant.

In §8b Varro then articulates the rationale for his own literary activity while observing that there are some philosophical elements in his work to date.[24] The fragments of Varro's writings do not contain one in which he explains himself in a similar fashion, but what Cicero puts in his mouth here is, given what we know about Varro's oeuvre, a fair representation of his approach.[25] He writes about matters for which there are no Greek sources to use, nor—since the death of his teacher L. Aelius Stilo—Roman ones, i.e. Roman subjects which have not been covered yet and which he wishes to bring to the attention of his fellow Romans.[26] Varro then qualifies what he has just said (*tamen*): his Menippean satires, among his early works and inspired rather than closely based on Menippus of Gadara's works, include profound elements of philosophy, as well as dialectical arguments. Similarly, his *Laudationes* (for the problem of identification, see below) and the *Antiquitates* were written with philosophers in mind (the former, presumably, because funeral speeches inevitably contain consolatory themes, and thus reflection on the human condition, the shape of a human life and the extent to which it is disrupted by death, etc.). Varro is not contradicting himself here, but making the point that, while he has not written anything which might count as philosophical instruction in a narrow sense, it would be wrong to say that philosophy did not inform a number of his works, and sometimes quite profoundly. Cicero's reply in §9 politely complements what Varro says, in that Cicero supplies a summary list of contents of the *Antiquitates* which bears out Varro's remarks.

Of the works mentioned here, the Menippean satires are the earliest work; see the notes for details. On the date of composition of the *Antiquitates rerum humanarum et diuinarum*, see Cardauns (2001a: 50–4) and earlier Horsfall (1972). Publication of both parts preceded *Ac.* 1, and Lactantius (*Inst.* 1.6.7) and Augustine (*C.D.* 7.35) report that the *Res diuinae* were dedicated to Caesar as *pontifex maximus*. It is not

---

[22] See the end of section 3.

[23] Apart from the fact that Varro is now speaking generally, we have no reason to think that Antiochian Old Academic philosophy was still taught in Athens in the mid-40s. On Antiochus' pupils, see Cic. *Luc.* 12; Philod., *Index Acad.* cols xxxiv–v, Görler (1994: 967–75); Puglia (2000); Hatzimichali (2011: 40–52) and (2012: 24–6).

[24] I list all known Varronian works published by 45 BC in the notes below.

[25] The desire to be useful to his fellow citizens (*praestare se ciuibus suis*) is mentioned in Aug., *C.D.* 4.22 = Varro, *Antiquitates diuinae* frg. 3 Cardauns; cf. *Res rusticae* 1.1.3. That bestowing such benefit was one of Varro's stated aims may be an additional reason for Cicero claiming the same for his own output; see the introduction, section 3.

[26] Cicero will echo these words in *Ac.* 1.26a.

certain which larger body of works is referred to as the *laudationes* here. Scholars have either seen a reference to the *Logistorici* or to a less clearly delineated body of speeches (see n.). The arguments are considered by Gwyn Morgan (1974: 117–22), who makes a strong case for the view that that the reference is more likely to be to epideictic and panegyric speeches of some kind and that the *Logistorici*, which would not naturally be referred to as speeches, were written later than 45 BC.[27] *Laudatio* is a generic term for panegyric speech. When Cicero talks about funeral speeches, he tends to qualify *laudatio* further (see n.). This is compatible with the assumption that a particular *laudatio* is on Cicero's mind here. We know that Varro (like Cicero and an otherwise unknown Ollius) wrote a *laudatio* on the younger Cato's sister Porcia, who had died in late 46 or early 45 BC. In August 45, i.e. after the extended exchange over *Acad.* and without any reference to it, Cicero asks Atticus to send him the *laudationes* written by Ollius and Varro (*Att.* 13.48.2 = SB 345). His own version is at advanced revision stage, and he wants to refresh his memory (*regustare* is the term used) of Varro's version. Except for the information contained in the letter, we know nothing about this *laudatio* of Varro's or of any series of works with which it might have formed a larger whole. Given the timeline, it is conceivable that Cicero and Varro talked about the *laudatio* when Varro paid Cicero a visit in early July 45 (*Att.* 13.33a(33).1 = SB 330 = T26). In this case Cicero would have created a reference whose specificity was transparent to Varro only, adding a personal touch to the preface. That the *laudatio* is mentioned before the *Antiquitates* might be due to Cicero wanting to end with Varro's main work.

The reasons which Varro cites in §§4–8 for not having written strictly philosophical works overlap with the possible criticisms which philosophy written in Latin might face according to *Fin.* 1.1–12, composed while Cicero was also working on *Acad.* (see sections 3, 9.1). Peculiar to the latter passage are objections to philosophy itself, or philosophy as a suitable occupation for the Roman statesman, which the historical Varro and the character created by Cicero would not have recognized in any case. Cicero's replies here in *Ac.* 1 are thus in part a function of Varro's narrower focus.

In *Fin.* 1, Cicero cites four possible objections or types of criticism:[28]

(i) Some people show a general interest in *litterae* but reject philosophy.
(ii) Others do not mind philosophy being pursued, but only if it is done in an amateurish way.
(iii) A third group prefers to read philosophy in Greek but rejects it in Latin. Varro, as we saw, thought nothing at all could be done for those without any interest in philosophy, but cited this consideration as the main reason for why philosophy in Latin would have no audience.
(iv) A fourth group does not object to Cicero writing, but rejects philosophy as a subject (favouring law or possibly historiography instead). Although not cast

---

[27] The arguments of Gwyn Morgan (1974) have not been universally accepted; see e.g. Wiseman (2009: 126), and more cautiously Cardauns (2001a: 72).
[28] A discussion of the proem of *Fin.* 1 which attends to its status as evidence for interaction between Greek and Roman culture is Baraz (2012: 113–27). Gildenhard (2007: 52–63) surveys the prefaces of the philosophical works qua literary apologiae.

in precisely those terms, this objection can see no benefit in writing philosophy, but assumes the usefulness of other types of literary output.

To these points Cicero has himself reply:

(i´) The indiscriminate rejection of philosophy was already addressed in the *Hortensius*, to which Cicero refers without repeating himself. (He also credits the favourable response which *Hort.* received as a reason for continuing to write philosophical works. This notion provides at least a counterbalance to any suggestion that the dialogues of the 40s were the result of a grand plan which, once conceived, was carried out with minor modifications. See sections 3, 9.5.)

(ii´) The attraction exercised by philosophy is so profound that it is unrealistic to assume one could pursue it with moderate commitment.

(iii´) Here Cicero expands on a point which he also makes in *Ac.* 1.10 in reply to Varro. Even word-for-word translations of Greek drama find readers as a matter of fact (note that Cicero is not speaking of audiences of dramatic performances),[29] and even bad translations deserve the attention of Romans as Roman cultural accomplishments. By implication, it is un-Roman, and prejudice directed at one's own culture, if one rejects philosophy written in Latin. The notion that even poor Latin translations of Greek plays deserve to be read is, as Baraz (2012: 116–17) observes, 'a domesticating, nationalistic impulse taken to its logical extreme'. However, Cicero continues, he provides more than word-for-word translation: using his superior organizational and presentational skills as an orator, he adds value to the contents of the Greek texts which inform his writings (1.6).[30]

(iv´) Cicero suggests an equivalence of some kind between the benefit bestowed upon the commonwealth by his activities as a statesman on the one hand, and his literary activities on the other. The implication is that writing philosophy is Cicero's way of continuing to benefit his fellow citizens. The same point is cited in *Ac.* 1.11 *fin.* as one of several possible motivations, and it recurs elsewhere in the dialogues (e.g. *Div.* 2.1–2), but always without further detail, so that the possible benefits which Cicero had in mind require speculative reconstruction;[31] see section 3.

In §§5–7 Varro had also claimed that respectable dogmatic philosophy was, unlike Epicureanism, very difficult to present in Latin, which makes the section part of the

---

[29] Cicero, who had reflected deeply on translation practice, was undoubtedly aware that Roman dramatic texts were not word-for-word translation, either.

[30] Relevant in this connection is also a series of texts (the beginnings of *Rep.* 1, *Tusc.* 1, and *Tusc.* 4) which tell in different ways the story of how Greek learning and more specifically philosophy arrived at Rome and were adopted and put to beneficial use in a way which contemporary Greeks were, for political and broader cultural reasons, were incapable of. In the process, Cicero develops a number of paradigms of cultural interaction; see on *Ac.* 1.10.

[31] The works of the 50s are a special case. They are more overtly a continuation of political service by different means, and only ex post facto included among the philosophical works.

patrii sermonis egestas narrative, whose primary exponents are Lucretius (who coined the phrase: 1.832, 3.260), Cicero, Quintilian, and Aulus Gellius.[32]

Lucretius appears to present the poverty of the Latin language as a constraint on his work in some passages (e.g. 1.136–9), but mostly employs the notion in contexts which seem designed either to induce the reader's rejection of the complaint as unwarranted,[33] or to make qualities other than richness emerge as most desirable in didactic discourse, or even to valorize a relative lack of richness (1.830–3, where Latin is found to be incapable of rendering the supposedly bizarre Anaxagorean notion of ὁμοιομερία)—yet without ever rejecting overtly that Latin exhibits *egestas*. Cicero acknowledges the fact that Latin is widely perceived to suffer from relative *inopia*, and he concedes that the absence of Latin 'counterparts' for certain Greek terms poses challenges, as do Greek neologisms, but he never grants as a first-person speaker that these challenges are due to inherent weaknesses of the Latin language, and treats supposed cases in point as evidence that the Roman practitioner in question is at fault, either because he is an inferior *interpres*, or (as in the case of Epicureanism here in *Ac.* 1.5–6) because his Latin version has inherited the flaws of the underlying doctrine. Rather, the resources of the Latin language, according to Cicero, exceed those of Greek.[34]

Thus the notion that the Latin language is suffering from *inopia* features as a widely held view in speeches (e.g. *Caec.* 51) or in the philosophical works (e.g. *N.D.* 1.8: the false perception that certain things cannot be said in Latin has prevented other Roman from promulgating their expertise in philosophy; *Fin.* 3.5). It is sometimes introduced by characters other than Cicero, e.g. by Cato in *Fin.* 3.51: in connection with promoted indifferents Zeno uses neologisms *quod nobis in hac inopi lingua non conceditur*, adding that Cicero disagrees and often calls Latin the richer language. The remark given to Cato shows that perceived *inopia* does not just manifest itself in the absence of terms where the Greek language has a term, but also in constraints on creating new terms—constraints which seem to be due less to the inherent resources of Latin than to what is accepted by the community of language users (note *conceditur*).[35]

Although Cicero does not quite claim to be the first to write philosophy in Latin, he does present himself as the first who genuinely confronted the challenges of the task as he saw it. This allows him to pass over some potential predecessors as different in intention, and others as failing in the endeavour. Earlier Roman drama would presumably be judged like Varro's works, as merely containing philosophical

---

[32] See Fögen (2000), the most comprehensive treatment of the subject to date; Farrell (2001: 28–51).
[33] See the wider context of 1.136–45, with Farrell (2001: 41–2).
[34] Cf. *N.D.* 1.8: *Complures enim Graecis institutionibus eruditi ea, quae didicerant, cum ciuibus suis communicare non poterant, quod illa, quae a Graecis accepissent, Latine dici posse diffiderent; quo in genere tantum profecisse uidemur, ut a Graecis ne uerborum quidem copia uinceremur*; *Fin.* 1.10: *Sed ita sentio et saepe disserui, Latinam linguam non modo ⟨non⟩ inopem, ut uulgo putarent, sed locupletiorem etiam esse quam Graecam*; *Fin.* 3.5: *...et quoniam saepe diximus, et quidem cum aliqua querela non Graecorum modo, sed eorum etiam, qui se Graecos magis quam nostros haberi uolunt, nos non modo non uinci a Graecis uerborum copia, sed esse in ea etiam superiores...*; *Fin.* 3.51. See also Fögen (2000: 81–2) and Adams (2003a: 202).
[35] See section 10 for a partial appraisal of Cicero's use of the resources of the Latin language in writing philosophical Latin.

elements, and is of course contrasted with philosophy in the present context. Lucilius is treated as a social commentator, who addresses himself to philosophy inasmuch as it is part of the cultural habitus of upper-class Romans (see esp. *Fin.* 1.8–10). Lucretius is not overtly engaged with in Cicero's works, but various suggestions have been made that he has an intertextual presence.[36] Brutus is warmly acknowledged here, but his works appear to have been too small in scale to gain him more than an honorable mention,[37] or else inconvenient for the argument made. What qualifies in Cicero's eyes seem to be works (i) in prose, (ii) of some bulk, which (iii) set out and expound doctrine, and (iv) do so in an elegant manner and with charm (*Tusc.* 1.6). Here the only reference point which Cicero fully acknowledges is Roman Epicurean writers, whom he seems to hold partly responsible for the perception that the overall project is unpromising (because their writings are inadequate while having significant reach). A relevant text, which complements *Ac.* 1.5–6, is *Tusc.* 4.6–7:

> Itaque illius uerae elegantisque philosophiae, quae ducta a Socrate in Peripateticis adhuc permansit et idem alio modo dicentibus Stoicis, cum Academici eorum controuersias disceptarent, nulla fere sunt aut pauca admodum Latina monumenta siue propter magnitudinem rerum occupationemque hominum, siue etiam quod imperitis ea probari posse non arbitrabantur, cum interim illis silentibus C. Amafinius extitit dicens, cuius libris editis commota multitudo contulit se ad eam potissimum disciplinam, siue quod erat cognitu perfacilis, siue quod inuitabantur illecebris blandis uoluptatis, siue etiam, quia nihil erat prolatum melius, illud quod erat tenebant. Post Amafinium autem multi eiusdem aemuli rationis multa cum scripsissent, Italiam totam occupauerunt, quodque maximum argumentum est non dici illa subtiliter, quod et tam facile ediscantur et ab indoctis probentur, id illi firmamentum esse disciplinae putant.

In the almost complete (*nulla fere*; *pauca admodum*) absence of Latin works on respectable philosophical schools, Amafinius' work found warm reception as well as many successors. The success is explained because Epicureanism presented in Latin was simple to understand even by the *indocti*, had (sc. reprehensible) appeal due to its promotion of pleasure, and was without competitors. (Other passages criticize Epicureanism generally for its lack of method, without making the connection with writing on the subject in Latin.)[38] While Cicero does not here comment on the style of the writings in question in the narrow sense, the appeal to the *indocti* and the failure to write *subtiliter* come close.[39]

Evidence for Stoic writers is harder to find, but Griffin (1995: 344 n. 85), who also refers to *nulla fere* and *pauca admodum* in *Tusc.* 4.6, and in greater detail Zetzel (2016: 51–2) have drawn attention to the fact that the recently converted Epicurean Cassius, in an exchange of letters dating from December 46 and January 45 (Cic., *Fam.*

---

[36] On the issue, see e.g. André (1964); Pucci (1966); Zetzel (1998), who suggests that the six-book structure of Lucretius' poem informed that of Cicero's *Rep.*; Fögen (2000: 83–4) and Hardie (2007: 113), with further literature.
[37] See Hendrickson (1939); Osorio (2021).
[38] Cf. e.g. *Luc.* 97; *Fin.* 1.22, 2.3–5, 2.18; Taylor (2016); Sedley (2018).
[39] See also MacGillivray (2015).

15.16–19), responds to Cicero's mockery of another Roman Epicurean's rendering of εἴδωλα (*spectra* used by Catius: *Fam.* 15.16.1-2 = SB 215) by threatening to 'toss so many rustic Stoics at you [i.e. Cicero] that you'll say that Catius was a true Athenian' (*Fam.* 15.19.1 = SB 216: *pro quo tibi proxima epistula tot rusticos Stoicos regeram ut Catium Athenis natum esse dicas*).[40] Here Stoics writing in Latin must be meant.[41]

Our passage goes a step further than *Tusc.* 4.6-7 in implying that artful discourse on Epicureanism is hard to achieve in virtue of its subject matter. This point is evidently polemical, and if true Cicero himself ought to find it difficult to overcome it when he writes on Epicurean subjects (*Fin.* 1–2 and *N.D.* 1 do not speak to the matter, and the character Torquatus' exposition is praised in *Fin.* 3.3). Varro then takes the notion that philosophical subject matter and a particular way of doing philosophy, as opposed to the skill of the translator, have an effect on its Latin rendering, and applies it to dogmatic philosophy, whose superior technique and demanding doctrines pose exceptional challenges for the *interpres*.[42] As we saw, Cicero does not address the claim in his reply, and it is de facto refuted by Varro's speech (and *Acad.* as a whole). One of its functions in the narrative may be to signal the achievement the work represents in the author's eyes.[43]

Elsewhere Cicero highlights the fact that he is able to bring his rhetorical skills to bear on his philosophical works and[44] invokes philosophers who were also great writers as his models (Plato, Aristotle, Theophrastus; cf. *Fin.* 1.14). Moreover, a sceptical Academic has to be versed in dogmatic method of course, since his mode of arguing depends heavily on the opponent's.

In the survey of *Ac.* 1.1-8 I identified some places where Cicero's handling of the character Varro seems overly circumspect. Such circumspection would be expected given what we know of Cicero's personal relationship with Varro.[45] The earliest

---

[40] Suggestions why *spectra* was deemed to be unsatisfactory in Reinhardt (2005: 160-1); McConnell (2019).

[41] Zetzel (2016: 52), in response to Shackleton Bailey's suggestion that the 'notoriously poor stylist' Chrysippus was meant, writes: 'Chrysippus may not have been a great writer, but he was scarcely a *rusticus*, and the context in any case makes it perfectly clear that Cassius is threatening to swap country Stoics for the Insubrian Gaul Catius, and for the joke to work, they must be Latin-speaking rustics. The point is that these rustic Stoics will make even the Gaul Catius seem as urbane as an Athenian.' A passage where Cicero first declares philosophy written in Latin as non-existent, only to declare it a moment later as widely practised but unsatisfactory, is *Tusc.* 1.5-6.

[42] Cicero does on occasion comment on the awkwardness of the style of the Stoics (*Luc.* 112; *Fin.* 3.3, 3.15, 3.26, 3.40, 4.2, 4.5-10, 4.79) and that they create new concepts or doctrines which then require new terms (*Ac.* 1.41), but this is the closest he comes to the idea that dogmatic philosophy is special in the way claimed by Varro.

[43] Cf. *Att.* 13.13.1 = SB 321 = T19: *libri quidem* [i.e. the *Academici libri*] *ita exierunt, nisi forte me communis* φιλαυτία *decipit, ut in tali genere ne apud Graecos quidem simile quicquam*.

[44] Cf. e.g. *Fin.* 4.10 (where the contrast with poetry suggests that the skills of the orator are referenced in the contrast): *Quod etsi ingeniis magnis praediti quidam dicendi copiam sine ratione consequuntur, ars tamen est dux certior quam natura. Aliud est enim poetarum more uerba fundere, aliud ea, quae dicas, ratione et arte distinguere*. Baraz (2012: 112 n. 37) suggests that in *Ac.* 1.5 the Epicureans are criticized for inferior rhetorical organization, too; I believe the contrast to be a different one.

[45] The most detailed study of the subject is Rösch-Binde (1998), to whom my precis is indebted. See also Baier (1997: 15-70), who offers a broader discussion of shared intellectual interests, Wiseman (2009) (who suggests on p. 126: 'There is no sign of any...friction [sc. between Cicero and Varro] in the revised *Academica*'); Kronenberg (2009: 88-9); Rühl (2018: 201-9). Earlier studies include Kumaniecki (1962) and Della Corte (1970: 89-103, 135-76).

evidence for a connection between the two men dates from 59 BC,[46] when Cicero tried to secure, with Atticus acting as middleman, Varro's support at a time when Clodius was about to become tribune.[47] Cicero ended up finding Varro's attitude in the face of the first Triumvirate too adaptive.[48] In the following two years, i.e. during Cicero's exile and after his return, there are no more than seven references to Varro in *Att.*, and Varro appears not to have played a significant role in Cicero's recall. The letters dating from 57-51 suggest that in the period 57-51 BC contact was no less sporadic. In 54 (*Att.* 4.14 (16) = SB 88). Cicero asks Atticus, in connection with his work on *Rep.*, for a copy of a work of Varro's (presumably the *Antiquitates rerum humanarum*, but the work is not named—Cicero's references to Varro in works of the 40s, i.e. *Brut.* 60 and 205, as well as *Ac.* 1.9, emphasize almost exclusively the antiquarian aspect of his work). Here for the first time we glimpse appreciation for Varro's work on Cicero's part, and it is tempting to speculate that Atticus notified Varro of Cicero's interest. A month and a half later Cicero mentions (*Att.* 4.16 (17) = SB 89) a request of Varro's (or, what is less likely, Atticus', who may have acted in accordance with an unstated and merely suspected desire of Varro's) that Varro may be 'included somewhere' ('have a place', Shackleton Bailey) in one of Cicero's works (*Varro, de quo ad me scribis, includetur in aliquem locum, si modo erit locus*).[49] Although no further details are given, the request may well have been connected with Cicero's request to Atticus for sight of a work of Varro's. Cicero goes on to explain why the setting of the work in production at the time would not allow for Varro's inclusion (neither *De orat.* nor *Rep.* feature living speakers), even though he appears ready to meet the request (perhaps for Atticus' sake more than for Varro's). He then wonders if the prefaces might provide an opportunity to mention Varro. The fragmentary state of *Rep.* does not allow us to verify whether Cicero enacted this possibility when he eventually finished the dialogue, but that a similar request is made nine years later (cf. *Att.* 13.12(24).3 = SB 320, dated 23 or 24 June 45 = T18) tells against it.[50] While this tells us little about their personal relationship in the second half of the 50s, the role of Atticus as an intermediary suggests that Varro's and Cicero's relationship had not become any closer. Varro is mentioned only once more in this decade (*Att.* 5.11.3 = SB 104, dated 6 July 51), as the source for a piece of information on Pompey (again according to Atticus), but the *Att.* collection has a

---

[46] The *quas* (sc. *res*) *tecum simul didici* in *Ac.* 1.3, about Antiochus' teachings, seems too restrained to suggest that they were contemporaries as Antiochus' pupils, which is also unlikely given their age difference. *Audiebamus* in *Ac.* 1.13, used in connection with Philo's Roman Books, is of course phraseological, i.e. refers to Cicero only.

[47] See *Att.* 2.20.1 (= SB 40), 2.21.6 (= SB 41), 2.22.4 (= SB 42), 2.25.1 (= SB 45).

[48] See Wiseman (2007: 110-12). Note, however, Varro's work Τρικάρανος ('Three-headed monster'), of which we only know the title (*Men. Sat.* frg. 556 Buecheler), and his attack on Crassus' greed in frg. 36 Buecheler.

[49] *Includetur* may be unspecific as to whether a mere mention and inclusion as a character in a dialogue is meant; in *Att.* 13.19.3-5 (= SB 326 = T23) dated 29 June 45, the verb can only denote inclusion as a character.

[50] Thus e.g. Shackleton Bailey (1965: 200). When Cicero mentions the renewed request in 13.12(24).3 (= SB 320 = T18), he remarks that his speeches and his other works to date were such *ut Varronem nusquam possem intexere*. This does not conclusively settle the question if Varro was ever mentioned in a work of the 50s because *intexere* ('to weave, sc. as a character') is more specific than *includere*; see Rösch-Binde (1998: 167 n. 2).

gap extending from the end of November 54 (4.19(21) = SB 93) to the beginning of May 51 (5.1 = SB 94) when Cicero departs for Cilicia. During the civil war Cicero and Varro found themselves politically aligned as followers of Pompey (Varro committed earlier and more formally, serving as a legate in Spain), and both acted on a sense of personal obligation rather than ideologically entrenched Republicanism or genuine commitment to Pompey.[51] Cicero reflects on their shared fate in a series of seven letters sent directly to Varro and dating from 46 BC (= *Fam.* 9.1–7 = SB 175–81).[52] The first of these letters either triggered the renewal of Varro's request to feature in some way in one of Cicero's works or, as is more likely, was preceded by such a request.[53] The series begins when both men were awaiting the outcome of Caesar's campaign in Africa and ends when Caesar is about to return after the battle of Thapsus.[54] The letters stand out not just because they are addressed to Varro himself, but also because they reveal an in some respects temporary change of attitude to Varro on Cicero's part. While still formal, they are markedly different in tone. Cicero reflects on their shared love of learning and scholarship, on his and Varro's position in the civil war and the lack of a reasonable alternative at the time, whereby he acknowledges that Varro had been the more consistent of the two. Early on in the series he also expresses a desire for a meeting (apparently Varro was unlike Cicero not in Italy at the time, but able to travel to Italy if he wanted to), but it is not clear if such a meeting came to pass at the time. The next we hear of Varro is in the series of letters to Atticus which represent the evidence for the editorial history of *Acad.* dating from 45 BC and are preserved in *Att.* 13 (see section 9.1). These show that Cicero, while he was confident that Varro was a more suitable representative of Antiochian thought than Hortensius, Lucullus, or Brutus/Cato, was far from certain that the dedication of the edition in four books would please Varro and considered it possible that he might even be offended by the work. And while Atticus is seen to move the project along with gentle encouragement, this ends when Cicero, having completed the edition in four books and having agonized further over Varro's likely reaction, tries to pass on to Atticus all responsibility for what happens when Varro receives the work (e.g. *Att.* 13.24(35).1 = SB 332 = T28: *sed quoniam tu suscipis, in alteram aurem*).[55] This responsibility Atticus rejects (*Att.* 13.25(36) = SB 333 = T30), which causes a kind of inversion of argumentative positions: Cicero now argues that he wants Varro as a dedicatee (having regarded him as a suitable interlocutor in any case). It is in this context that Cicero says (*Att.* 13.25.3 = SB 333 = T30; dated 12 July 45): *uolo Varronem, praesertim cum ille desideret; sed est, ut scis,* δεινὸς ἀνήρ· τάχα κεν καὶ ἀναίτιον αἰτιόῳτο (= Hom., *Il.* 11.654). While the comparison of Varro with Achilles gives some indication of what Cicero thinks about Varro, in context the

---

[51] See Rösch-Binde (1998: 109–18), with perceptive remarks on the references to Varro in Caes. B.C.
[52] See, in addition to the broader studies named above, Leach (1999: 165–8) and Baraz (2012: 78–86). *Fam.* 9.1 may date from late 47; see Rösch-Binde (1998: 125 n. 2).
[53] On this point see Rösch-Binde (1998: 125–6), with discussion of earlier scholarship.
[54] On the battle of Thapsus, cf. Varro, *Men. Sat.* frg. 225 Buecheler: *Africa terribilis, contra concurrere ciuis* | ⟨*ciui*⟩ *atque Aeneae misceri sanguine sanguen*, echoing Ennius, *Ann.* 309 Skutsch.
[55] Varro unexpectedly visited Cicero on 8 or 9 July, cf. *Att.* 13.33a.1 (= SB 330 = T 26), but the letter does not connect the visit with the narrative about the composition and dedication of *Acad.* beyond the acknowledgement that Varro had been a topic of conversation (*lupus in fabula*).

quote is intended to take the edge off Cicero's attempt to pass on responsibility for Varro's reaction to the dedication to Atticus: in the end, Cicero's attempted shift of responsibility is to be taken with a pinch of salt, since he knows that Varro might take offence. It is almost futile (given ἀναίτιον) to ask which aspects of the work might have given rise to offence on Varro's part. Envy of Brutus, dedicatee of a series of works of Cicero, is mentioned as a possibility at one point (*Att.* 13.13–14(25).1 = SB 321 = T19); also that Varro might find that in the dialogue Cicero's case is more fully argued than the Antiochian one (*Att.* 13.25(36).3 = SB 333 = T30), which Cicero says is untrue.[56] There is no letter documenting or mentioning Varro's reaction, but it can be inferred that Varro took no offence, from the silence as well as the fact that in *Att.* 13.21(43).3 (= SB 351 = T33), dated around 27 August 45, Cicero asks Atticus to pass on a small change to Varro (relating to the verb used to render the act of suspending judgement; see the commentary on *Luc.* 94), so that he can implement it in his (expensively produced; see *Att.* 13.25.3 = SB 333 = T30) copy if he so wishes (*dices hoc idem Varroni, si forte mutauit*).[57] In *Phil.* 2.102–5 Cicero was to extol the venerable and cultured endeavours which used to be pursued in Varro's villa—where now Antonius was engaging in debauchery, having seized his estates.[58]

It is tempting to speculate briefly about the nature of the preface of the *Catulus* on the basis of the preface to *Ac.* 1. As regards topics like the supposed difficulties of expounding philosophy in Latin, possible objections to the project, and—although this can only have been a secondary issue—the question of whether statesmen should devote their *otium* to philosophy, one would expect considerable continuity with *Ac.* 1. The *Hortensius* was only a protreptic to philosophy, not to the writing of it in Latin. Moreover, if it is right to think that Cicero's famed *uolumen prooemiorum* (*Att.* 16.6.4 = SB 414) did not just represent a collection of disparate items, but enabled him—and was designed—to develop and balance prefatorial themes over a series of prefaces, then, even if it only came into existence when Cicero aborted the first edition of *Acad.* (see the introduction, section 9.1),[59] it will be plausible to assume that the issues which are not specific to Varro featured in the *Catulus*, too (contrast e.g. antiquarian writings and their intended benefit to fellow Romans). For a desire to pursue themes across text boundaries is a precondition for the *uolumen*'s coming into being.

Further, since the interlocutors were the same as in the *Hortensius*, there will have been a reference to the earlier discussion, when Hortensius was 'converted' to philosophy (the location changed from Lucullus' villa, probably the one near Tusculum rather than one near Naples, to Catulus' villa at Cumae).[60] Lucullus does not seem to have had a major speaking role in the *Catulus*, and the other two speakers were

---

[56] See, however, *Div.* 2.1: *Nam et cohortati sumus ut maxime potuimus ad philosophiae studium eo libro qui est inscriptus Hortensius, et, quod genus philosophandi minime arrogans maximeque et constans et elegans arbitraremur, quattuor Academicis libris ostendimus.*

[57] With reference to *Att.* 13.19.3 (= SB 326 = T23), Wiseman (2009: 125) suggests implausibly that the main reason for unease between Cicero and Varro 'was no doubt literary rivalry'.

[58] See Ramsey (2003: 311–16). After Caesar's death both Cicero and Varro turned to historiographical work (in Cicero's case inter alia), on which, see Wiseman (2009: 128), but this need not have given rise to further contact.

[59] Cf. Gildenhard (2007: 89–90); Baraz (2012: 5–8).

[60] On the question whether *Hort.* could have been set at Lucullus' *Tusculanum* rather than the *Neapolitanum*, see Gigon (1962: 227); Voss (1966); and Bringmann (1971: 112); see also section 9.5.

Academics of slightly different persuasion (Catulus the younger, Cicero): none of the three is a likely presenter of the historical account of the Old Academy as conceived by Antiochus which Varro's speech here in *Ac.* 1 contains (see section 9.2). Thus Hortensius presented the material (or at least a less developed version of it) given to Varro here. This being so, the *Catulus* would have had to explain how Hortensius, having only been converted in the dialogue that bears his name, came to know enough about Antiochian thought to present a historical account of it, or even embrace it if that is what he did. Since Hortensius' expertise was presumably presented as the result of a period of study (although his phenomenal memory will have enabled him to acquire expertise quickly; cf. *Luc.* 2), one would expect that some time elapsed between the conversation in the *Hortensius* and that in the *Catulus*, and that this period was specified at least vaguely.[61] Moreover, we can tell from fragments of the *Hortensius* that Cicero did not just speak for philosophy generally (although he did that, too) but identified himself as a sceptical Academic (see section 9.5). This would make it natural for Hortensius to state not just how he came to know about Antiochian philosophy (e.g. by reading works furnished by Cicero?), but also why he was attracted enough by it to immerse himself in it or even to make it his own (cf. *Luc.* 10 on the degree of Lucullus' commitment to Antiochian thought).

At the same time, there must of course have been material in the proem of *Catul.* which could not be re-used in the proem of *Ac.* 1. Here I would include an explanation of Catulus' Academic credentials, somehow invoking the elder Catulus and his exposure to Academic scepticism; cf. the quite detailed material on Lucullus' personal connection with Antiochus in the proem of *Luc.*[62]

§1

In Cumano nuper...continuo ad nos uenturum fuisse: Cicero speaks for the attention of the reader as a character in the narrative; see p. 79 above and section 8 *init.* The choice of venue allows Cicero inter alia to retain the maritime setting which the *Catulus* must have had and which *Luc.* has (e.g. 105, 147); see Griffin (1997: 24). On Cicero's *Cumanum*, also the setting for the conversation of *Fin.* 1–2 and located on the eastern slope of the *lacus Lucrinus* (*Att.* 14.16.1 = SB 370), see Schmidt (1899: 99); D'Arms (1970: 198–200); as well as M. Tullius Laurea's poem preserved by Pliny, *N.H.* 31.6–8, on which see Hollis (2007: 326–9).

On Varro's *Cumanum*, see D'Arms (1970: 197–8). It appears to have been within sight of the *lacus Lucrinus* on the evidence of Nonius pp. 65–6 M. = my t. 47 (from *Ac.* 4): *Et ut nos nunc sedemus ad Lucrinum pisculosque exultantes uidemus...*, unless there was a change of location from *Ac.* 1–2 to *Ac.* 3–4 as there was from *Catul.* to *Luc.* Cicero's *uilla* can be located with some precision on independent evidence (see

---

[61] Griffin (1997: 4) appears to assume a gap between the dramatic dates of *Hort.* and *Catul.*, while Schofield (2012c: 76) takes the two dialogues to have been set on successive days.

[62] On the question of whether we can discern two different layers in the proem of *Luc.*, reflecting a desire on Cicero's part to strengthen Lucullus' credentials, see ad loc.

Morgan 2007: 117–18), but Varro's cannot. There is no reason to doubt that the two *uillae* were within walking distance of each other.

The dramatic date is identical with, or very near to, the time of composition; this is suggested by Atticus' intervention in *Ac.* 1.2.

Reid¹ p. 85 has various good linguistic points. For the collocation *cum mecum* there are ample parallels. The juxtaposition of *mecum* and *noster* is unproblematic, even though *noster* = *meus* as opposed to 'our (i.e. Varro's and Cicero's)' mutual friend. *De uia fessus*, e.g. in *Rep.* 6.1; cf. *Phil.* 1.5 (*languere de uia*). *A M. Varrone* means 'from Varro's house' and is not a replacement of a dative of the agent; cf. *TLL* s.v. *a, ab* col. 15.56–62. The *praenomen* (*M.*) is given for reasons of formality and because this is the first reference to Varro.

Translators disagree on whether Varro's reported remark is a present counterfactual (so Brittain 2006) or past counterfactual (so Gigon). *Fessus esset* shows it must be the former.

Quod cum audissemus...perreximus: on the history and nature of Cicero's relationship with Varro, and the somewhat stagey feel of the scene, see above, pp. 79, 88.

Moram interponere just 'delay', not 'impose an obstacle'. Reid¹ p. 85 notes that *audissemus* is transmitted and unobjectionable, and thus should not be changed to *audiuissemus*; he also defends *eisdem* over *isdem* (and *iisdem*). Plasberg¹ put a full stop, Plasberg² a semicolon after *coniunctum*.

Paulumque cum ab eius uilla...ad suam uillam reduximus: Morgan (2007: 118) has a map indicating the location of Cicero's *Cumanum*. For embraces as a greeting among Roman men of higher social status, cf. Hor., *S.* 1.5.43: *o qui complexus et gaudia quanta fuerunt. Ire* could by itself refer to being carried in a litter, but the description of the actual encounter suggests that Cicero presents himself and Atticus as walking. The formality of *ut mos amicorum est* is neatly illustrated by a comparison with *De orat.* 2.13: *qui cum inter se, ut ipsorum usus ferebat, amicissime consalutassent.*

Reid¹ p. 86 observes that Davies's emendation *se uisentium* for *satis enim/eum*, while linguistically unproblematic, would work against the sense of the passage. Cicero wishes to stress the warmth of his relationship with Varro, and a remark that they had not seen each other for a long time would thus jar, in that it would amount to an apology for an—on that reading—overcordial embrace. *Interuallum* cannot have the physical sense of 'space' (thus Goerenz p. 2), and the transmitted *satis eum* is the best text. *Satis longum interuallum* is otherwise attested in the sense of 'tolerably long period of time' (e.g. *Fam.* 5.17.1 = SB 23). The position of *eum* after *satis* is the only awkwardness. Reid cites parallels of phrases where a pronoun splits *satis* from the word modified by *satis*, and points out that the series of pronouns *eum, eius, illum, eum* supports the emendation *eum*. There are two Ciceronian instances of *satis longo interuallo* (*Clu.* 177; *Arch.* 6). Plasberg¹ opted for *enim* over *eum*, posited a lacuna after *interuallo*, and treated the whole of *satis enim longo interuallo* as a parenthesis (in brackets) to *ut mos amicorum est*. In the apparatus he listed Reitzenstein's insertion *non uideramus inter nos* and his own *aduenerat* (both to go after after *interuallo*), thus assuming the sense to be similar to that posited by Davies. See also the discussion in Ruch (1970: 76–7).

For *ad suam uillam* 'to his own *uilla*' despite *ab eius uilla* above, see Hofmann-Szantyr p. 175.

§2

Hic pauca primo…ecquid forte Roma noui: with *pauca primo* and ellipsis, at the beginning of a Ciceronian dialogue, cf. *Fin.* 1.14: *Nam cum ad me in Cumanum salutandi causa uterque uenisset, pauca primo inter nos de litteris….* For the format of the question, cf. Suet. *Nero* 48: *ecquid in urbe noui de Nerone?* But note that *Roma* is most likely nominative (sc. *agat* or *faciat*). *Nobis* must strictly refer to Cicero only (unlike the first person plural of *reduximus*), given Atticus' *omitte ista*.

With the request for news more generally cf. Cic., *De orat.* 2.13; *Brut.* 10. With *atque ea* used to introduce a specification, cf. Cic., *Dom.* 98; *Fat.* 2: *idque (et saepe alias et quodam liberiore)* and Christ's emendation below. *Percontari* does not suggest particular inquisitiveness or insistence (despite *per-*). There is no suggestion that Cicero's question relates to a particular event which would signal a more specific dramatic date, or hints at privileged insight on Varro's part due to a particular role or function. Reference is to what had become the normal situation under the dictatorship.

Percunctantibus is in P, *percontantibus* in *Γ* (not included in the app. since I regard it as an orthographical variation). *Percunctari* is probably a hypercorrect secondary formation to *percontari*. No diachronic difference between the two appears to have been felt by native speakers, and it is impossible to say what Cicero wrote. See Donatus *ad Ter. Hec.* 77.2 on the currency of both spellings in his day. The correction *ecquid* is made in Lambinus' edition of 1565, *pace* Hunt (1998: 236), who ascribes it to Paulus Manutius.

⟨**Tum**⟩ **Atticus…ecquid ipse noui:** for the character Atticus closing down a similar question about 'news from Rome' on the grounds that it only gives rise to *molestia*, thus enabling the dialogue to get started, cf. *Brut.* 11 (referred to ibid. 157). *Quae* in *quae nec percontari* is internal object, and the formulation alternative to *de quibus percontari*. *Ecquid ipse noui*, sc. *agit*.

For *tum*, printed by Reid and adopted by Plasberg, cf. *Fin.* 3.10: *tum ille*, 5.2 *tum Piso*; *Rep.* 1.17: *tum Furius…tum ille*, 1.19: *tum Philus*; contrast *Fin.* 1.14: *deinde Torquatus*. The suggestion *Atticus (autem)* is first found in the scholia to the 1573 (posthumous) edition by Lambinus, as Hunt (1998: 246) notes.

Silent enim diutius Musae Varronis…quae scribat existimo: *Musae* is conventionally used metonymically of poetic composition (cf. Lucr. 4.589; Verg., *A.* 10.191), as well as of scholarly composition (see *TLL* s.v. cols 1693.75–1694.17). With the use of *silere*, cf. *Brut.* 19: *iampridem conticuerunt tuae litterae*; *Off.* 2.3. Scholarly debate has centred on the question of whether Atticus is referring to a particular, esp. wide-ranging work, the *Disciplinae*, on which, it is assumed, progress had halted and which is otherwise not securely dated (thus e.g. Buchwald 1966; Shanzer 2007); or whether the remark is unspecific, and a pause in the publication of works generally is meant (Reid[1] p. 87; Dahlmann 1978). That the latter is meant is quite plain from Varro's reply, which indicates that he has been working on a large work dedicated to Cicero, whose dedication had been announced by Varro some time ago as we know from Cicero's letters (cf. esp. *Att.* 13.12(24).3 = SB 320 = T18, where Cicero expresses impatience) and which Varro is made to acknowledge here (*ad hunc enim ipsum— me autem dicebat—quaedam institui*). That the former view could gain credence is due not just to the use of the phrase *Musae Varronis* by Arnobius in apparent reference to a work which could well be the *Disciplinae* (Arnob., *Nat.* 6.11), but also to *Musae Varronis* being deemed to be a playful, ironic expression which would have been inappropriate for Atticus to use in conversation with Varro (thus Buchwald 1966: 216; Fussl 1999; Shanzer 2007: 86) if *Musae* was not an official or unofficial title used by Varro himself. The latter reasoning, I believe, underestimates the finesse employed by Cicero in the characterization of the interlocutors here: Cicero is carefully polite, Varro's demeanour borders on the gruff (*intemperantis enim esse arbitror esse scribere quod occultari uelit*; see next note), and Atticus is relaxed and urbane. This is in keeping with what we know of Atticus, including in his dealings with Varro. When the conversation turns to Varro's works as the dialogue progresses, the *Disciplinae* are not mentioned (*Ac.* 1.8), and at least a book on dialectic or logic would have been a counterexample to the claim that Varro had not yet produced works which offer philosophical instruction (1.3). By the same reasoning, Cicero cannot have known what the *De lingua Latina* would be about when he composed *Ac.* 1.

For a defence of *istum cessare* over *ipsum cessare*, see Reid[1] p. 87. *Cessare* used in the sense of 'to write nothing' e.g. in Cic., *Fam.* 16.22.1 (= SB 185). The mood of *scribat* is due to the relative clause being consecutive. See also Hieronymus, *Apol. adv. Lib. Ruf.* 1.1 (= t. 1).

'Minime uero'...sed habeo magnum opus in manibus, quae iam pridem: cf. *Tusc.* 1.6:...*sed mandare quemquam litteris cogitationes suas, qui eas nec disponere nec illustrare possit nec delectatione aliqua allicere lectorem, hominis est intemperanter abutentis et otio et litteris*, where the context is criticism of the Epicurean writers who also feature in *Ac.* 1.5. They publish inferior works, and Cicero makes the point that artless writing without proper disposition and stylistic finesse indicates a lack of self-control. That writing which deserves the name meets these criteria is assumed by Varro, and the *intemperantia* which lies in not publishing such works is not lack of self-control, but extravagance (because no benefit will be bestowed on anyone). On *Tusc.* 1.6, see Gildenhard (2007: 145–8).

For the phrase *in manibus habere* of literary production, cf. Cic., *Sen.* 22 (with Powell 1988: 152); for the sense 'peruse', cf. *Tusc.* 2.62 (of Greek works which are read). With *opus magnum* here, cf. *Luc.* 121: *opere magno*. The transmitted *quae iam pridem*, both with respect to the resumption and to the shift from singular to plural is justified by Plasberg[1] ad loc.; Christ's emendation *idque* is unnecessary. Reid[1] p. 88 notes that *occultari* means 'to conceal studiously' and is thus stronger than *celare* above.

Ad hunc enim ipsum...et limantur a me politius: *ad hunc* alludes to the format of dedications in book titles; see Schröder (1999: 24–5). For *instituere* of literary production, cf. Varro, *R.* 3.1.9. Reid[1] p. 88 has a collection of parentheses similar to *me autem dicebat*; for the avoidance of Cicero's name (*me autem dicebat*), cf. *Luc.* 13, 17, 61; and Dickey (1997). The relative clause cites two reasons for the long gestation, the size of the work and Varro's desire to polish the work appropriately. For *lima* and related terms used in connection with literary production, see Reid[1] p. 255 on *Luc.* 66; Brink (1971: 321) on Hor. *A.P.* 291 *poetarum limae labor*.

In *Att.* 13.12(24).3 (= SB 320 = T18), dated 23 or 24 June 45, Cicero mentions Varro's announcement of the dedication of a major work to Cicero 'two years ago', and expresses his dissatisfaction that Varro has not made good on his undertaking since then. In addition to the information contained in our passage consider also the dedicatory epistle to Varro (*Fam.* 9.8.1 = SB 254 = T29; see section 9.1), in which Cicero fails to conceal his impatience successfully; Lörcher (1911: 80–1). Studies devoted to the dedication of *L.L.* to Cicero include Barwick (1957); Rösch-Binde (1998: 394–469); de Melo (2019: 4–5).

§3

Et ego 'Ista quidem'...nec de manibus umquam deponere: in the game of politeness, Cicero responds to the two reasons cited for the delay of the Varro's work that he would not dare to ask for it. The period referred to by *iam diu* cannot be specified beyond the *biennium* mentioned in *Att.* 13.12(24).3 = SB 320 = T18 (see previous n.), and *biennium* is hardly to be taken as a precise indication, but a period of roughly two years would suggest that the promise of a dedication was made before Cicero wrote *Fam.* 9.1 = SB 175 in late 47 or early 46 (the first in the series of letters to Varro, see the general note above), and it may actually have been the trigger for Cicero's making direct contact. Cicero does not seem to be using his own enormous rate of production as a yardstick. *Flagitare* suggests a request passionately made, rather than a request for something one feels one is entitled to; cf. the use of the verb in the dedicatory epistle *Fam.* 9.8.1 = SB 254 = T29 (see previous n.). *De manibus deponere* neatly resumes Varro's *habeo...in manibus*, just as *accuratius tractare* gestures to *limantur a me politius*.

Kronenberg (2009: 119 n. 26) suggests that in *R.R.* 3.1.9 Varro might be alluding to the fact that Cicero felt he (Varro) owed him a dedication. Gurd (2007: 72) thinks that 'Cicero wants to bring Varro into the fold of his literary society by making the case for collective revision'; there is no hint of this in the text.

Lucius Scribonius Libo (cos. 34 BC), *RE* s.v. Scribonius no. 20, a Pompeian and father-in-law of Sextus Pompeius, is only mentioned here in the dialogues, but a number of times in the letters. See Kondratieff (2015). The first-person plural of *possumus* is presumably meant to include Libo, Cicero, and Varro—the latter so as to forestall any impression that Libo had been indiscrete.

Reid[1] pp. 88–9 comments on *et* in *Et ego*, on *studium* meaning *studium litterarum* rather than personal devotion, and observes that *nihil enim...* gives the reason for *audiui*.

Illud autem...a te requirere: *a te requirere* just 'to ask of you', not 'to demand' and not 'to seek again'. *Illud* is proleptic of *quaero quid sit* below, as Reid[1] p. 89 correctly observes, but it tells against the idea 'that in this sentence Cic. practically admits (what his letters show) that he had again and again thought of pressing Varro about the dedication of the *De lingua latina*' (ibid.). In *Fam.* 9.8 (= SB 254 = T29), the dedicatory epistle, *puto fore, ut, cum legeris, mirere nos id locutos esse inter nos, quod numquam locuti sumus; sed nosti morem dialogorum*, relates to the dialogue as a whole, not narrowly to the question of writing philosophy in Latin, but it does seem unlikely that the Cicero character could have said what he says here if it was not actually true.

Sed nunc postea...ceteris et studiis et artibus antecedat: *ingressus* suggests that Cicero here does not count *De orat.* and *Rep.* among the philosophical works, as he does in *Div.* 2.3–4 (see the introduction, section 3). Cicero's philosophical project is characterized as 'illuminating in Latin that ancient kind of philosophy which arose from Socrates'. What kind of philosophy is meant? The dialogues written up to this point (*Hort.*, *Acad.*) or in progress (*Fin.*; possibly *Tusc.*, see on *Luc.* 135) are not devoted to Antiochian philosophy primarily or exclusively, and Socrates plays a foundational role for Antiochus and Academics alike. On the other hand, *ueterem* points to Old Academic thought, and *quas tecum simul didici* does the same, even though the clause should not be taken to suggest that Varro and Cicero were pupils of Antiochus in Athens at the same time (so also Jocelyn 1977: 339); this is so because of their age difference and the loose way in which expressions like *tecum simul discere* are used (see Reid[1] p. 89), and because the letters to Atticus which discuss the suitability of Varro as an interlocutor and a proponent of Antiochian thought in particular would surely have mentioned if Cicero and Varro had studied philosophy together in some sense. In §§5–6 Varro speaks of philosophers as *nostri* who, to judge from their views summarily referred to, are followers of Antiochus. In §13 the belonging to one Academy rather than another becomes the subject of an ironic exchange between Cicero and Varro. It is possible that the character Cicero speaks of the broader Academic tradition here, to which they both belonged, while the character Varro speaks, or is presented as choosing to speak, in terms of the Old Academy.

For the inference from what Cicero says here that Varro's philosophical works postdate *Acad.*, i.e. notably the *De philosophia*, see the general note above. That philosophy is to be ranked higher as other *artes* was the upshot of the *Hortensius* (see section 9.5), where the competitors were historiography and oratory. Whether the antiquarian type of scholarship with which Varro is particularly associated would be classed with the former is not quite clear, but *studiis* here would appear to cover it as well.

Statements by Cicero on Varro's commitment to Antiochian thought are confined to the present passage and to *Att.* 13.12(24).3 (= SB 320 = T18), where Cicero explains that Varro is a suitable presenter of Antiochian thought because he is a *philologus* (unlike Lucullus) and because he *Antiochia...ualde probat*, which suggests more than a mere interest but less than dogmatic commitment. On Varro's use of Antiochus, see also the general note on *Ac.* 1.19–23 and Blank (2012).

Mandare monumentis means 'to commit to writing', with slight stylistic elevation; cf. e.g. Cic., *Sest.* 102; *Brut.* 26. *Praetermittas* is qualified in *Ac.* 1.8–9. The Latin loanword *philosophia* is first attested in the mid-second century BC in C. Cassius Hemina,

Ann. frg. 35 *FRHist*, and used by Cicero as early as *Inv.* 1.33; see Mankin (2011: 151) on *De orat.* 3.60, also von Staden (1999: 262); Hine (2016). With *genus hoc* something like *scriptorum* or *litterarum* is to be supplied; see Reid[1] p. 89 on elliptical uses of *genus*. With *totaque ea res*, cf. *Ac.* 1.7 *totum illud studium*.

§4

Tum ille: 'Rem a me saepe deliberatam…multum ut dixi et diu cogitaui': Cicero avoids any impression that Varro's refraining from writing on philosophical subjects was not a reasoned position. At the same time Varro conveys why he is able to speak on the subject in a way which fits neatly with the themes of other Ciceronian prefaces.

With *tum ille* marking speaker change, cf. §14: *mihi uero, ille. Non* negates *haesitans* not the sentence; Reid[1] p. 90 notes the slight illogicality in following up positive *respondebo* with *sed…dicam* (Bake 1852: 305 emended *sed* to *et*). Schütz (1816) deleted *quod ista…cogitaui*, while Goerenz had deleted *sed ea…cogitaui*.

Nam cum philosophiam uiderem…quae sine eruditione Graeca intellegi non possunt: Varro begins with the claim that there is philosophical writing in Greek which is satisfactory, in that it is carefully and adequately set out (Cicero does not react to this claim in *Ac.* 1 but asserts in *Fin.* 1.6 that he goes beyond providing the services of a mere translator and adds value by offering a better arrangement of material as well as his own judgement). He then offers a dilemma: (i) if one is *Graecis doctrinis eruditus*, one will read the Greek philosophical works; (ii) if one has no interest in or even actively rejects Greek learning, one will not read Latin translations, esp. if they are unintelligible without *eruditio Graeca*. 'Being versed in Greek learning' does not mean 'knowing Greek' (cf. *Brut.* 173, 236; *Tusc.* 1.3) but entails it. The notion that one could just know the language to a sufficiently high level to read Greek philosophical treatises without a broader interest in Greek learning is unfamiliar to Cicero. In *Ac.* 1.12 Brutus is cited as someone who writes philosophy in Latin *nihil ut iisdem de rebus Graeca desideres*, and Cicero has the same aspiration.

The actual practice of Cicero is of course more complex than these position statements suggest; cf. *Ac.* 1.40-2, which can on one level be read as referencing Greek texts on a particular subject.

For the loanword *philosophia*, see on *Ac.* 1.3. Reid[1] pp. 90-1 notes that *si qui de nostris…si essent Graecis doctrinis eruditi* should not count as an example of a double protasis since the first *si*-clause barely has conditional force and amounts to 'anyone who…'. *Artes et disciplinae* is not a hendiadys since not all fields of expertise are crafts in the technical sense.

Itaque ea nolui scribere…nec docti legere curarent: the conclusion to Varro's argument: he did not want to write something for which there is no market, since the *indocti* could not understand philosophy written in Latin (and would reject it on those grounds), and the *docti* did not care to read it. For *intellegere* rather than a verb meaning 'to read', see the previous n. See Reid[1] p. 91 on the subjunctive of *possent*.

§5

Vides autem...artem esse nec dicendi nec disserendi putant: at the beginning of the paragraph Reid[1] and Plasberg[1] print a different text, with Reid moving *enim* forward and assuming a parenthesis (*uides autem—eadem enim ipse didicisti—non posse nos*), and Plasberg maintaining the transmitted word order and assuming a short clause followed by strong punctuation (*uides autem eadem ipse; didicisti enim non posse...*). (Reid's text, suggested by Davies, was first printed by Baiter; for details on earlier editions, which vary in punctuation and in the position of *ipse* and *enim*, see Plasberg[1] p. 35.)

On Plasberg's reading, which is the transmitted text, the reasoning of §§5–7 is intended to bear out the conclusion of the dilemmatic argument in §4, and there is some support for this in §5 (*uerbis...nouis cogimur uti, quae docti, ut dixi, a Graecis petere malent, indocti ne a nobis quidem accipient, ut frustra omnis suscipiatur labor*). *Eadem* would refer back to the conclusion of the dilemmatic argument, with the plural perhaps being due to the fact that said conclusion dismisses two considerations at once (possible readers who are *docti* and those who are not).

However, in §§5–7 more weight seems to be accorded to a new consideration, that writing proper philosophy in Latin is exceedingly difficult. This is what Reid's text effectively conveys. *Eadem* (sc. as the speaker Varro) *enim ipse didicisti* would then refer to Cicero's having absorbed Antiochian philosophy; it cannot have forward reference and, given the uses of *discere*, cannot mean that Cicero like Varro read the writings of Amafinius and Rabirius. See also *Tusc.* 2.7: *Est enim quoddam genus eorum qui se philosophos appellari uolunt, quorum dicuntur esse Latini sane multi libri; quos non contemno equidem, quippe quos numquam legerim; sed quia profitentur ipsi illi qui eos scribunt se neque distincte neque distribute neque eleganter neque ornate scribere, lectionem sine ulla delectatione neglego.*

Cicero's reply to Varro in §10 disputes the claim that people who like Greek *doctrina* will read Greek while those who dislike it will not be tempted by a Latin version of it. However, Cicero the character does not seem to address that writing on philosophy other than Epicureanism in Latin is supposed to be difficult, or to acknowledge the connection. Rather, Cicero the author has the character Varro refute himself through the speech he is given to deliver (on 'genuine' philosophy).

Amafinius is also mentioned in the quasi-historiographical passage *Tusc.* 4.6–7 on the arrival of philosophy in Rome (quoted p. 87 above). His date has been the subject of some debate, and *Tusc.* 4.7 at least suggests that he was early enough to give rise to a whole generation of followers known to Cicero. See e.g. Eckerman (2013); Maso (2008: 62) and (2016: 178) places him as early as the middle of the second century BC. Given that *Tusc.* 4.7 mentions only Amafinius, it seems reasonable to consider Rabirius (mentioned here) as one of his *aemuli*. A third one would be Catius (see above, p. 88). On Rabirius and Catius, see Castner (1988: 63 and 24–32), as well as pp. 7–11 on Amafinius. The correction of the ω reading to *Amafanii* in *ς* was aided by the occurence just below (that readers would recall *Tusc.* 4.6–7, quoted above, is less likely); Jerome, *Comm. in Osee Proph.* 2.180, who either made the correction or, as is perhaps more likely, had access to a text which was not corrupt on this point, is t. 3.

100 COMMENTARY

Posse is used of feasibility as well as acceptability. *Nulla arte adhibita* creates an effect of *copia*, whether it anticipates *artem...dicendi...disserendi* below (so Reid[1] p. 91) or *uulgari sermone* earlier in the sentence. *Res ante oculos positae* are things which are plain (cf. e.g. Cic., *De orat.* 2.79), but elsewhere *ante oculos ponere* is used of making things ἐναργῆ (thus e.g. *Verr.* 2.5.78; *Rhet. Her.* 4.61). *Vulgaris sermo* here probably neither the 'language of the common man' (for this sense, see Ricottilli 2003: 91-2) nor 'language without rhetorical finesse' (e.g. *Rhet. Her.* 4.69; see Ferri and Probert 2010: 46), but rather aimed at the Epicurean fondness for ordinary language in devising ethical terms; cf. *uerbis...nouis cogimur uti* below, *Fin.* 2.6-19, 48-50, with Taylor (2016). On this reading Varro moves from terms to definitions to entire arguments (a principle of organization also present in *Ac.* 1.30-2, the section on λογική in the Old Academy). *Nihil definiunt* and *nihil partiuntur* presumably go together, in that *partitio* is an analytical technique associated with definition; for the Epicurean rejection of definition, see *Fin.* 2.3-5. *Nihil apta interrogatione concludunt* relates to the Epicurean rejection of formal argument; see on *Luc.* 97, *N.D.* 1.70; Bown (2016); Sedley (2018). Reid[1] p. 92 correctly comments: '*Interrogatione* has exactly the same meaning as *ratione*', and gives parallels; this is so because formal argument retained the association with question-answer exchanges which it had had since the time of Socrates (see on *Luc.* 104). Reid[1] p. 92 suggests that *nullam in nullam denique artem* means 'worthless', which is a rare slip, given **nec dicendi nec disserendi**. In Stoic texts in particular rhetoric and dialectic differ in the presentation of discourse, but not with respect to the standard of cogency expected; for dialectic defined as τὴν διαλεκτικὴν ἐπιστήμην τοῦ εὖ λέγειν, τὸ δὲ εὖ λέγειν ἐν τῷ τὰ ἀληθῆ καὶ τὰ προσήκοντα λέγειν εἶναι τιθέμενοι, 'the science of speaking well, whereby they locate speaking well in saying what is true and appropriate', see Alex. Apr. *in Top.* p. 1.10-11 Wallies (= *SVF* ii.124). The reading *scribendi* in μ is a misguided emendation and can be stemmatically eliminated.

Nos autem praeceptis dialecticorum et oratorum...ut frustra omnis suscipiatur ⟨labor⟩: see the general note above on the claim that dogmatic philosophy poses particular problems for a translator into Latin. *Nos* may be intended to include Cicero (see on §3 *res eas quas tecum simul didici* above), but see also §13; as an Academic Cicero would of course not obey the *praecepta* of dialecticians and rhetoricians as if they were laws. That rhetoric and dialectic are virtues is a Stoic view in origin (see Reinhardt and Winterbottom 2006: 361-77 on Quint. 2.20), but one which Antiochus—on the evidence of the present passage—adopted alongside Stoic epistemology more generally; on the latter point, see Brittain (2012). On a different level of description, the Stoics took dialectic and rhetoric to be dispositions of the human mind (διαθέσεις); see on *Ac.* 1.40-2.

Oratorum is used in the sense of *rhetorum* (cf. *Or.* 113), from which it is distinguished in other contexts (*De orat.* 3.54); hence the emendation *rhetorum* by Pearce (1810[6]: 87) is unnecessary. On *et...etiam*, see Reid[1] p. 92. *Quoque* signals that Varro thinks he would face two distinct difficulties about the kind of philosophy he approves of in Latin: the rigours of the doctrine (cf. Reid[1] p. 93: 'the need of attending to logical and rhetorical rules'), and the need to use *noua uerba*. *Quae* picks up *praeceptis*. Orelli as reported in Halm (p. 58) thought *indocti ne a nobis quidem accipient*, suggested by Davies (p. 8), to be arrogant and reordered to *a nobis ne accipient quidem* (cf. the Roman edition of 1471), but Reid[1] p. 93 points out that *ne...quidem* need not imply the gradation of 'not even' and may just be negative ('auch nicht'), and Varro's point need not be taken to be arrogant: he is uniquely concerned with Roman matters in his writings (cf. §8 and Cicero's reply in §9), so it is saying something if he reckons philosophy in Latin would not be accepted even if it came from him. *Labor* was compellingly added in ms. Ged by emendation; see Hunt (1998: 94).

§6

Iam uero physica, si Epicurum...ut Amafinius: *iam* marks the transition; cf. Reid[1] p. 280 on *iam illa praeclara*. On *iam uero* 'nun vollends', see Hofmann-Szantyr p. 494. Epicurean physics, banal as it is, would be easy to convey in Latin (cf. *Fin.* 3.3 for a similar point made about the Epicurean doctrine of pleasure). The self-correction *id est, si Democritum probarem* is polemical; it is an anti-Epicurean trope that Epicurean physics is stolen from Democritus. Cf. *Fin.* 1.17 (subject is Epicurus): *Principio, inquam, in physicis, quibus maxime gloriatur, primum totus est alienus: Democritea dicit perpauca mutans, sed ita, ut ea, quae corrigere uult, mihi quidem deprauare uideatur*; Reinhardt (2005: 170). For *planus/plane* to describe the opposite of stylistic elevation (which is only a fault in suitable contexts), cf. e.g. *Top.* 97: *...itemque narrationes ut ad suos fines spectent, id est ut planae sint, ut breues, ut euidentes, ut credibiles, ut moderatae, ut cum dignitate*. Here *plane* seems to pick up on *uulgari sermone* above, and the interpretation offered above is supported by Varro's addressing not just Epicurean physics in general but the use of *corpusculum* for 'atom'. On *physica*, cf. *TLL* s.v. col. 2065.7–23 on the neuter adjective in the singular and the plural; for the latter, cf. *Rep.* 5.5; *Tusc.* 1.71.

Quid est enim magnum...concursione fortuita loqui? As indicated in the general note, Varro does not pause long enough to explain the gap in sophistication which he sees between a physical theory employing a notion of efficient causation and atomic theory. The term *corpusculum* and the phrase *concursione fortuita* (which balances *causas rerum efficientium*) suggest two possible weaknesses: a concern that explanations turning on atoms and their primary qualities seem to lack the explanatory power to illuminate events in the perceptible world, and the supposedly implausible notion of an uncaused event (the swerve of atoms which gives rise to collisions between them). The swerve is criticised also in *Fin.* 1.20 and *Fat.* 46, whereas the atoms' inability to bear weight metaphorical speaking is conveyed by the connotation of 'feeble body' which *corpusculum* has (see *N.D.* 1.66, 1.67, 2.94; *Tusc.* 1.22); see Reinhardt (2005: 158–72). That Amafinius used *corpusculum*, an original Latin word attested once before in an erotic context in Plautus (*Cas.* 843), for 'atom' is our only piece of evidence on his actual translation practice and would be an instance of the *uulgaris sermo* mentioned in §5, as an emotive diminutive (see Ricottilli 2003[3]: 381). On translations of Epicurean statements in the Ciceronian corpus, see Traglia (1971).

Reid[1] p. 94 glosses *magnum* rightly as *egregium* and cites parallels, as well as other uses of *magnum* in similar phrases. *Loqui* is used of conversation as opposed to formal speech (see *OLD* s.v. no. 3b); cf. §5: *uulgari sermone*.

That Varro should talk dismissively about using an original Latin word for a Greek concept which he himself designates with a Greek loanword (*atomus*) may seem ironic, but *atomus* with Latin inflection may have been treated as established by Cicero; see Reinhardt (2005: 155–8).

'Lambinus', followed in recent times by Gigon, proposed emendation to *causas rerum efficientes*, but *rerum efficientium* may be taken as a *genitiuus epexegeticus*; cf. Cic., *Top*. 58: *Proximus est locus rerum efficientium, quae causae appellantur*. See also Ruch (1970: 78–80).

Nostra tu physica nosti...aut quem ad intellegendum poterit adducere: Varro's remarks about Antiochian physics complement the survey provided in *Ac.* 1.24–9 in various ways (see ad loc.). While the initial bipartite division there envisages an active entity and a passive one 'in' which matter is, here the latter is identified with matter, without it being clear whether the difference matters. Geometry is not mentioned in the later passage, and since philosophical physical theory and geometry make contact only in a limited number of places in ancient theorizing, it is plausible to think that Varro is thinking in particular about the application of geometry to physics in Plato's *Tim.*, on any account an important model for 1.24–9, where, however, geometry is not touched on. The present passage may be seen to provide an explanation for this fact—geometry is just too difficult to render in Latin, or so the suggestion is. Cicero's translation of *Tim.* is not securely dated beyond a reference to the *Academici libri* in the preface (*Tim.* 1), which provides a terminus post quem, but Cicero may well have been thinking about the project already when he created the final edition of *Acad.*; see Sedley (2013: 189). This means that he would have been able to link the physical views rehearsed by Varro in *Ac.* 1.24–9 with Plato's *Tim.* See also below on §7: *Totum igitur illud philosophiae studium...maius aut melius a diis datum munus homini*.

On Roman interest in geometry, see *Tusc.* 1.5: *In summo apud illos* (i.e. the Greeks) *honore geometria fuit, itaque nihil mathematicis illustrius; at nos metiendi ratiocinandique utilitate huius artis terminauimus modum*; Geymonat (2009); and above, p. 82 on land surveying as a field in which Romans had to adopt some geometrical concepts and terminology. Cf. Cicero's invocation of geometry in an argument against abstruse physical theorizing in *Luc.* 116–17, and ibid. 106 on Epicurus' rejection of geometry. See also Guillaumin (2003) on Sen., *Ep.* 88.10–13.

Nostra refers to Antiochian physics and means either 'mine' or 'yours and mine', cf. on §5: *eadem enim ipse didicisti.... Nos autem*, above. Varro is appealing to Cicero as a fellow Antiochian (of sorts), i.e. fellow pupil of Antiochus. For *effectio, materia*, and *fingit et format*, see on *Ac.* 1.24–9 below (p. 176 in particular). Reid[1] p. 95 spells out the answers to anti-Epicurean questions *quibusnam uerbis* and *quem...adducere* and refers to *Tusc.* 4.7, where the simplicity of Epicureanism is cited as the reason for its popularity.

Above on §2 *Musae Varronis* I considered the suggestion that the work that was being delayed was the *Disciplinae*. If that was the implication, which is implausible on independent grounds, the present passage would suggest that not just the book on logic but also that on geometry could not have been written yet.

Haec ipsa de uita et moribus...apud nostros autem non ignoras quae sit et quanta subtilitas: Reid[1] p. 95 explains compellingly why the sentence cannot run on after *adducere* and end with *rebus*. However, *haec ipsa...fugiendisque rebus* is awkward. Reid inserts *ecce*, follows P on the position of *enim*, and puts a question mark after *rebus*. Some have suspected a lacuna after *rebus*, assuming that something like *quam uarie tractantur* has dropped out (see Plasberg[1] p. 36). What the sentence does is introduce a new topic. I take it, with hesitation, to be an 'isoliert-emphatischer Nominativ', on which see Hofmann and Szantyr p. 29 as well as Norberg (1943: 79), and put a comma after *rebus*. Cf. Cato, *Agr.* 34.2: *ager rubicosus et terra pulla, materina, rudecta, harenosa, item quae aquosa non erit, ibi lupinum bonum fiet*. Plasberg[1] puts a comma after *simpliciter* (assuming an ellipsis of *tractant?*). *Ipsa*, on any account, emphasizes *haec*.

For the phrase *de uita ac moribus* to refer to ethics, see *Ac.* 1.19; with *de expetendis fugiendisque rebus*, cf. 1.18: *rerum expetendarum fugiendarumque partitio*. *Simpliciter* may mean 'frankly' but could also stand in opposition to *quanta subtilitas* (which signals precision and accuracy rather than pedantry and overcleverness; cf. *OLD* s.v. no. 4a). For the point of criticism, cf. *Fin.* 2.111.

§7

Siue enim Zenonem sequare...sine uoluptatibus sensum mouentibus ne suspicari ⟨quidem⟩: Varro turns to Stoicism and the difficulty of expressing its central ethical doctrine (concerned with the good) in Latin, but returns to Old Academic thought and the challenges posed by conveying it in Latin in §7b. On the Stoic conception of the good, see *Fin.* 3.20–1; Frede (1999b); Inwood (2005c); for Epicurus' criticism of Zeno's conception of the good, cf. *Luc.* 140; *Fin.* 2.38. One might think that the Antiochian Varro could run the Old Academy and Stoicism together on the subject of the good in the present context, using the device of 'substantial agreement but difference in terminology', but (i) the desired contrast seems to be between Epicureanism and rigorous dogmatic philosophy generally (sc. and the presentation of either in Latin), and (ii) Varro goes on to make the point in §7b that the difference between the Stoics and the Old Academy requires particular nuance. The difficulty singled out here is intelligibility (*quis intellegat*); elsewhere stylistic acceptability is a secondary concern (cf. e.g. *Ac.* 1.41: *feretis haec?*).

For the view of Epicurus' referred to, cf. D.L. 10.6 (= frg. 67 Usener): ἔν τε τῷ Περὶ τέλους γράφειν οὕτως· Οὐ γὰρ ἔγωγε ἔχω τί νοήσω τἀγαθόν, ἀφαιρῶν μὲν τὰς διὰ χυλῶν ἡδονάς, ἀφαιρῶν δὲ τὰς δι' ἀφροδισίων καὶ τὰς δι' ἀκροαμάτων καὶ τὰς διὰ μορφῆς, 'In *On the Ethical End* he writes the following: I do not know how to conceive the good, apart from the pleasures of taste, sexual pleasures, the pleasures of sound and the pleasures of beautiful form' (transl. Hicks, adjusted), as well as the other texts collected by Usener ibid., notably *Tusc.* 3.41, which offers a translation of the passage beyond the point where D.L. stops.

On Zeno of Citium, cf. *Ac.* 1.40–2, 1.44; *Luc.* 66, 77; section 5; Gourinat (2018) is a survey of his life and work with further references.

Sequi here of allegiance in general; contrast e.g. *Luc.* 104: *sequens probabilitatem*. For the tense/mood pattern *si* + present subjunctive/present indicative, cf. *Luc.* 140: *si sequare…ruunt. Magnum est*, 'it is difficult' (parallels collected by Reid¹ p. 96); contrast *Quid est magnum…* in §6. With *uerum et simplex bonum*, cf. *Ac.* 1.35: *simplex et solum et unum bonum*. For the phrase *ab honestate seiungere*, cf. *Off.* 3.101. Lambinus inserted *se* after *Epicurus* to give *negat* its customary accusative-with-infinitive construction, but Reid¹ p. 96 shows the insertion to be unnecessary. *Omnino* should not here modify *negat*, so the word order *negat omnino* is correct. The emendation by Durand (1740), i.e. *ne suspicari quidem* for *nec suspicari*, is most likely correct because *nec = nec…quidem* is not Ciceronian; see Reid¹ p. 96; Hofmann-Szantyr p. 450.

Si uero Academiam ueterem persequemur…quam argute quam obscure etiam contra Stoicos disserendum: Varro's focus returns to the Old Academy (i.e. the *antiqui* of 1.17), whose different stance on the good compared to the Stoics, or different stance in certain unspecified respects, is not played down (see previous n.). On *si uero* for an expected *siue enim*, see Reid¹ pp. 96–7. For *persequi*, see his note on *Ac.* 1.12 (p. 105); the verb suggests not so much philosophical allegiance to a school than close attention to something (cf. *Att.* 13.12(24).3 = SB 320 = T18, of Varro: *Antiochia…ualde probat*). Contrast the end of §12: *eandem…sententiam sequitur quam tu*. It is possible that **totum** *illud philosophiae studium* below is intended to convey that Varro reads well beyond 'his' school. *Argute* ('smartly'; *De orat.* 2.250; *Brut.* 322) and *obscure* qualify one another: unavoidable obscurity given a complex subject is meant.

Totum igitur illud philosophiae studium…maius aut melius a diis datum munus homini: for the role accorded to philosophy here see section 3, and the previous n. on the possible implication of *totum* (*totaque ea res* in §3 means 'the whole field, sc. of philosophy'). With *constantia uitae*, cf. *Luc.* 31; *Fin.* 3.50: *Quod si de artibus concedamus, uirtutis tamen non sit eadem ratio, propterea quod haec plurimae commentationis et exercitationis indigeat, quod idem in artibus non sit, et quod uirtus stabilitatem, firmitatem, constantiam totius uitae complectatur, nec haec eadem in artibus esse uideamus*. Cicero stressed the enjoyment of the life of scholarship as lived by Varro in a letter to him in 46 BC (*Fam.* 9.6.4–5 = SB 181).

The reference to Plato is to *Tim.* 47b: φιλοσοφίας γένος, οὗ μεῖζον ἀγαθὸν οὔτ' ἦλθεν οὔτε ἥξει ποτὲ τῷ θνητῷ γένει δωρηθὲν ἐκ θεῶν, translated by Cicero in *Tim.* 52: *philosophiam adepti sumus, quo bono nullum optabilius nullum praestantius neque datum est mortalium generi deorum concessu atque munere neque dabitur*. Contrast with the vague paraphrase here (and its variations in *Leg.* 1.58; *Lael.* 47; *Sen.* 40; *Tusc.* 1.64; *Off.* 2.5; *Fam.* 15.4.16 = SB 110) the apparent quote from the *Tim.* translation in *N.D.* 2.47, with Sedley (2013: 192–3, 200–1).

§8

Sed meos amicos...potius hauriant quam riuulos consectentur: we are not able to identify individuals who studied philosophy with Greeks or in Greece on Varro's suggestion, but the general practice is of course deeply familiar (see e.g. *Off.* 1.1, with Dyck 1996 ad loc.; and the material assembled by Jocelyn 1977). With *studium* cf. §3 *cuius nosti studium*. *Iubeo* need not be stronger than 'to invite, to suggest to' (see OLD s.v. no. 7a). The image is that of drinking from a source vs drinking from man-made irrigation channels; see Reid[1] p. 98. For the different image of small tributary vs large river, see *Rep.* 2.34. For the phrase *riuolos consectari* (alongside *fontes non uidere*), cf. *De orat.* 2.117. The pronoun in the transmitted *ea a fontibus*, printed by Reid[1], has no reference.

Quae autem nemo adhuc docuerat...ne a Latinis quidem: the characterization of Varro as primarily an antiquarian writer also in *Brut.* 205 (written in 46 BC, see section 3): *Fuit is* [i.e. Aelius Stilo] *omnino uir egregius et eques Romanus cum primis honestus idemque eruditissimus et Graecis litteris et Latinis, antiquitatisque nostrae et in inuentis rebus et in actis scriptorumque ueterum litterate peritus. Quam scientiam Varro noster acceptam ab illo auctamque per sese, uir ingenio praestans omnique doctrina, pluribus et illustrioribus litteris explicauit*. As stated in the general note above, this tells against the possibility that the *De philosophia* or the philosophical parts of the *Disciplinae* had already been composed by 45 BC. Varro did of course work from sources in the antiquarian works (see Ferenczy 1989), but these are presented as not being literary works by an author who intends to inform (*nemo...docuerat*, and Reid[1] p. 98 on *nec erat unde* = *nec erat quisquam a quo*); for the implication of value added by Varro as author cf. Cic., *Fin.* 1.6, on his own works. On *nihil...meorum*, see Reid[1] p. 98.

On Varro's antiquarian works generally, see Cardauns (2001: 50–63); on the recently completed—see Horsfall (1972) on the likely precise date—*Antiquitates rerum*, see Cardauns (1978).

With Varro's implication of the ambitious scope of his work, cf. also Cicero's statement on Varro's *uilla* in *Phil.* 2.105: *Quae in illa uilla antea dicebantur, quae cogitabantur, quae litteris mandabantur! Iura populi Romani, monumenta maiorum, omnis sapientiae ratio omnisque doctrina*; and Quint. 12.11.24: *Quam multa, paene omnia tradidit Varro*; Volk (2019) on the nature of Varro's attempts to impose order on disparate bodies of knowledge.

On L. Aelius Stilo (Praeconinus) (c.150–85 BC), see Cic., *De orat.* 1.193 (*Aeliana studia*) with Leeman, Pinkster, and Nelson (1985: 100-1); *Brut.* 205-7 (with Gell. 16.8.2); *Leg.* 2.59 with Dyck (2004: 399–408); *Top.* 10 with Reinhardt (2003: 212–13); Suet. *Gramm.* 3 with Kaster (1995: 68–70); De Melo (2019) on Varro, *L.L.* 5.18; Lehmann (1985). Cicero (*Brut.* 207) like Varro counted himself among his pupils (in an informal sense, as he is unlikely to have offered formal instruction). Varro refers to him as a friend in *Ant. rer. div.* frg. 89 Cardauns (= Gell. 1.18.2); cf. also the reference to Aelius as *magister Varronis* in Gell. 16.8.2 and Charisius 106.8 Barwick. His works included an interpretation of the *carmen saliare* (Varro, *L.L.* 7.2) and linguistic-etymological analyses of legal and religious Latin, notably from the Twelve Tables (frgs 5-46 Funaioli). The emendation *L. Aelii* is made in Camerarius (1552: 20), as Hunt (1998: 240 n. 33) notes.

Nostri = 'the Romans', unlike *nos* and *nobis* in §7b. The distribution of *occasus*, as Reid[1] p. 99 notes, suggests it is poetic, but the intended effect here is presumably just one of mild stylistic elevation ('passing'). On *Latini* = 'writers in Latin', see Adams (2003a: 195); Kramer (1998).

Et tamen in illis ueteribus nostris...si modo consecuti sumus: *tamen* signals the qualification of the claim that Varro focused on previously untaught, antiquarian subjects: philosophical themes are nonetheless present in his *Menippea*.

Several fragments of the *Menippea*, edited with commentary by Cèbe (1972-99), have been dated to around 80 BC (see Cichorius 1922: 207-26; Krenkel 1997), which would warrant *ueteribus*; see also Cèbe (1972: XVI). For general orientation, see Cardauns (2001: 40-9); Wiseman (2009a); on philosophical elements, see Sigsbef (1976); Messina (2011). Cf. also Cicero's claim in *N.D.* 1.6b that, while he may only have taken up writing on philosophical topics recently, he had always been interested in them, as is evident from his speeches, which are filled with philosophical *sententiae*.

By *imitati non interpretati* Varro asserts his originality; cf. *Fin.* 1.6 for Cicero's rejection of the notion that he is a mere *interpres*; *Off.* 1.6, 2.60. *Multa dicta sunt dialectice* suggests clipped argumentative points; cf. the contrast with rhetorical argument in *Fin.* 2.17 and 5.10. Reid[1] p. 99 assembles expressions similar to *ex intima philosophia*.

The thesis that *laudationes* refers to the *Logistorici* has been most fully developed by Dahlmann (in Dahlmann 1935: 1262; Dahlmann and Heisterhagen 1957: 15-20; and Dahlmann and Speyer 1959: 15-18). Since the *Logistorici* cannot be dated on internal grounds (see Gwyn Morgan 1974: 118-19 on some largely uninformative termini post quem arising from the fragments), the identification, if correct, would provide a terminus ante quem for at least a substantial body of them. However, it is now widely assumed that the *Logistorici* were dialogues, which makes *laudatio* an unsuitable term to refer to them, even though it is true that a dialogue in which a central speaking role is accorded to a character and his achievements is de facto panegyric. Gwyn Morgan (1974: 121) has good grounds for following Ritschl (1857: 496-7) in connecting the *Laudationes* with e.g. the *orationum libri XXII* listed in Jerome's partial catalogue of Varro's works (on which see Cardauns 2001a: 85-7). Cicero dismisses traditional Roman funeral speeches, a different kind of writing, in *Brut.* 62 for their dishonesty.

Reid[1] pp. 99-100 emends *quae quo* to *quae cum*, on invalid grounds. He also inserts *sunt* after *multa dicta* without marking it as supplied. The ellipsis after *multa dicta* puts the one after *inuitati* in context (Gigon emends to *inuitauimus*); Varro is finishing up briskly. Reid[1] also emends *philosophiae* as in ω to *philosophis* ('for philosophers') and dismisses earlier solutions, but the one suggested by Plasberg[1] is compelling.

§§9–12

Cicero's reply to Varro begins with an appreciation of his writings, frequently cited from antiquity onwards as a mission statement for Varro's scholarship (in the absence of a suitable statement by Varro himself). Cicero proceeds to a list of contents rather than work titles as Varro had provided, showing that he is familiar with Varro's scholarship (he had probably used the *Antiquitates* for *Rep.* in 54 BC, cf. *Att.* 4.14 (16) (= SB 88), and referred to Varro's antiquarian writings in *Brut.* 60 and 205; see on §8 above). That it is Cicero who provides this information allows Varro's dialogue persona to be modest. At the end of §9 Cicero acknowledges the philosophical themes in Varro's published work to date, while noting that they did not amount to actual instruction in philosophy, which, it is implied, is Cicero's aspiration.[63]

In §10 Cicero turns to Varro's arguments against writing philosophy in Latin, calling them a *causa probabilis*, which could mean 'deserving of approval' but also means 'superficially deserving of approval' (see n.). He then briefly summarizes them and casts douby on whether Varro has actually succeeded in proving his point (*ea mihi non sane probas*). This may be intended as a mild assertion of Cicero's philosophical identity as an Academic sceptic: despite the common ground with Varro (who had bracketed himself with Cicero in 1.6: *nostra* and *apud nostros*), he subjects everything to the same scrutiny. In respect of the claim that philosophy in Latin would have no audience, Cicero simply points to poetry, especially drama, and oratory in Latin, both of which are based on Greek models (see the related discussion in *Fin.* 1.4–6, and the notes below). Strikingly, he offers no reply to §§5–7 where Varro argued that respectable dogmatic, i.e. Old Academic and Stoic, philosophy was very difficult to present in Latin, unlike the banal Epicurean teachings. Arguably *Acad.* as a whole addresses the point, though.

In §11 Cicero turns to his own reasons for writing philosophy. The emphasis is here on personal reasons, which need not mean that personal reasons were overriding for Cicero at the time of writing. Rather, the focus on the personal means that there is less of a suggestion that one ought to write philosophy, or that it is an omission if one does not although one could. While he was occupied with his legal and political career, all he could do was keep au fait with philosophy and refresh his knowledge of the arguments from time to time. Now that he is shattered by personal misfortune (the death of his daughter Tullia) and sidelined as a politician (because Caesar is dictator), he uses (i) philosophy as a cure for his pain and (ii) as the most honourable way to spend his *otium*. In context, these considerations are offered as reasons for writing, but by themselves they are only sufficient to explain why Cicero *thinks* about philosophy. He adds (iii) that nothing is more useful for educating citizens than writing philosophy,[64] and (iv), somewhat disarmingly, that he has nothing

---

[63] Kronenberg (2009: 88) regards it as implicit criticism, and Zetzel (2015: 54) as patronizing, when Cicero points out that Varro has made a start on philosophy but has provided no instruction. The sentence ending *ad impellendum satis, ad edocendum parum* (§9) does seem glib.

[64] See section 3 on the benefits Cicero hopes to bestow on his fellow citizens by writing philosophy.

else to do. Cicero introduces (iii) and (iv) at the end of the paragraph in a stylistically interesting way, as part of a list of alternatives introduced by *aut...aut*, almost as if leaving it to the reader to select the option or options which appeal most.

In §12 he adds an argument *ex auctoritae*: Brutus writes on philosophy, too, in Latin and in a manner which does not require reference to the Greek 'sources'—and he is a follower of the Old Academy like Varro. The existence of Brutus' *De uirtute* of course somewhat undermines Cicero's claim to a singular status as a writer of serious philosophy in Latin, but Cicero is punctilious in acknowledging it (cf. also *Fin.* 1.8, *Tusc.* 5.12; see n. below), and Brutus is used to counter a point made by Varro which Cicero could not easily have derived from *Hort.* without seeming arrogant. Cicero ends by asking Varro to write on philosophical subjects, too.

§9

Tum ego 'Sunt', inquam 'ista, Varro...tu omnium diuinarum humanarumque rerum nomina genera officia causas aperuisti': the general characterization of Varro's antiquarian works is widely quoted in modern scholarship as offering an insight into the immediate reception of Varro; see e.g. Murphy (2004: 134); Jenkyns (2013: 154); Hardie (2013: 110). MacRae (2017: 350): '...the Ciceronian statement stands as a potential map of Varro's (lost) learning.' Augustine quotes the sentence from *Nos...in nostra urbe peregrinantes...* in *C.D.* 6.2 (text 56 of the indirect transmission) and indicates against his usual practice (which is to paraphrase without acknowledgement) that his source is the first book (sc. of the *Academici libri*). Hunt (1998: 23 n. 19) notes further quotations of the paragraph in Claudianus Mamertus, John of Salisbury, and Guglielmo da Pastrengo. Augustine goes on to list the contents of the *Antiquitates* in *C.D.* 6.3.

It is tempting to think that Cicero is presenting Varro's antiquarian scholarship not just as the conveying of previously unfamiliar historical information, but as also having a moral dimension, in the sense that contemporary Rome had seen a political and moral decline so that learning about institutions of old was apt to lead to moral restitution, and in that sense to knowledge of who the Romans really are. The Menippean satires are full of critical remarks about contemporary Rome and its institutions (see Robinson 1976: 481–3 for a rapid survey). Intriguing and a possible candidate for a secondary allusion in our passage is a Menippean satire, the *Sexagesis* (or *Sexagessis*), the remains of which are collected as frgs 485–505 Buecheler (Robinson loc. cit., and Cebè 1998: 1895–1941). Varro casts himself as a Rip van Winkle figure who comes to Rome after falling asleep for fifty years at the age of 10, struggles to recognize his city among all the depravity and corruption, and gets thrown into the Tiber for his accusations—and for bringing up again, and going on about, *antiquitates*, 'how things used to be' (frg. 505, text and punctuation as in Cebè: '*erras*', inquit, '*Marce; accusare noli: ruminaris antiquitates*'). (Varro would have been 60 in 56 BC; Wiseman 2009a: 147 thinks the satires were written between 85 and 60 BC.) If the larger assumption was accurate, Cicero would choose not to present Varro's antiquarianism as moralistic in intent.

With *sunt ista*, 'this is true', cf. *Lael.* 6 with Neuhausen (1992: 209), *Rep.* 1.16; no insertion of *uerum* (or *ita*) is warranted. Reid[1] p. 100 assembles Ciceronian parallels on the *hospes* theme; being ignorant of politics and political institutions is sometimes compared to being a stranger in one's own country (*De orat.* 1.249), and not being familiar with the politics of the day to being a stranger in Rome (*Att.* 4.13.2 = SB 87). He also suggests (p. 101) that *qui et ubi* refers to two different kinds of work, those on Roman history and on topography, but given what we know of the varied content of the *Antiquitates*, it is more likely that aspects of the same work are meant. The further notes on subject areas covered by Varro deserve attention, and I have tried to do justice to them in the translation. The correspondence of the phrase *diuinarum humanarumque rerum* with the definitions of *sapientia* in *Off.* 1.153 (*illa autem sapientia, quam principem dixi, rerum est diuinarum et humanarum scientia, in qua continetur deorum et hominum communitas et societas inter ipsos*) and 2.5 (*sapientia autem est... rerum diuinarum et humanarum causarumque quibus eae res continentur scientia*) is curious (not noted by Dyck 1996: 367–8 on 2.5 in an otherwise informative note), but if it is more than coincidence, Cicero does not develop the point.

In *C.D.* 6.2 (t. 56) Augustine reads *reduxerunt* for *deduxerunt*, and *publicam* for *bellicam*; numerous manuscripts of *C.D.* also have *sedum* (see the app. crit. in Hoffmann 1899: 272, who, however, prints *sedem* with his b² and e) for *sedem* transmitted in *Ac.* 1 tradition. Reid[1] prints *sedem*, Plasberg[1] *sedum*. The former deems the asyndetic string of three genitives awkward, but it is arguably no more awkward than the string of accusatives later in the sentence. There are phrases like *Leg. agr.* 1.18, *sedem urbis atque imperii*, which, however, are apt to demonstrate that *regionum locorum* make for an inherently redundant phrase if dependent on *sedem*. In Cicero *sedes* is sometimes paired with *locus*, sometimes with *regio*. *Deducere* is often used of escorting someone home (see Reid[1] pp. 100–1); in support of *bellicam* Plasberg[1] p. 38 cites *Off.* 1.76: *haec quidem res non solum ex domestica est ratione, attingit etiam bellicam*. Ruch (1970: 82–3) makes the case for *sacerdotem*.

Plurimum quidem poetis nostris...ad impellendum satis, ad edocendum parum: Reid[1] punctuates with a comma before *plurimum* and prints *plurimumque idem*. Cicero now changes perspective and attends to the aid Varro has provided for the understanding of poets and writers generally (his own poetry—*atque ipse*—will be the final subject of the paragraph); thus I print *plurimum*, stressed by *quidem*. *Idem* cannot be right in direct address to Varro, and the sense break is marked enough to place a full stop before *plurimum* (without *-que*). For *lumen* = 'light', understanding shed on a subject', cf. *OLD* s.v. no. 10b. *Verbis* shows that *poetis, Latinis litteris*, and *uerbis* are normal dative objects, not *datiui commodi*. One wonders if the interlaced word order, with *luminis* depending on *plurimum*, is supposed to depict excitement on the part of the speaker. The illumination of words cannot refer to the *De lingua Latina*, which is unpublished at the time of writing, and Cicero most likely did not know its subject (see p. 80 above).

For the sense *omni fere numero poema*, 'a poem in almost every metre', see Reid[1] p. 102; the loanword *poema* is in evidence from Plautus onwards and is used as a standard term for 'poem'. *Varium et elegans* would be a natural attribute of a body of poems in most contexts, but is especially appropriate to Menippean satires. *Incohare* here 'to begin to deal with', as is shown by the rest of the sentence; Cicero confirms Varro's point made in §8 that the Menippean satires contain a fair amount of philosophy, but suggests that it is only enough to serve as protreptic (with *impellendum*, cf. *Fin.* 1.2: *mouere hominum studia*) and not enough to instruct. Reid[1] p. 102, following Ritschl, sees a reference to the *Logistorici* here.

§10

Causam autem probabilem…non contemnent sua: Cicero seems to acknowledge the force of Varro's argument (cf. §4 *fin.*) by calling it a *causa probabilis*. However, *probabile* turns out to mean 'plausible but unpersuasive', due to *ea mihi non sane probas* below (noted by Reid[1] pp. 102–3, who glosses it as 'specious' and gives further parallels; he, however, prints *da mihi nunc: satisne probas?*, using P's *da* = *dic* and *nunc* on erasure). Cf. e.g. *Div. Caec.* 64. Cicero is here speaking as an Academic who weighs every argument carefully. As before, *eruditum esse* with respect to Greek matters is taken to entail knowledge of Greek. For *non sane*, see *OLD* s.v. *sane* no. 4a.

Cicero then directly rejects Varro's two claims: both those who are not able to read Greek (ellipsis of *legere*) and those who are will not spurn what is written in their language (*sua*); see Reid[1] p. 103 on *contemnere* not being as strong as 'despise'. In §10b Cicero overtly rejects only the notion that the learned will spurn philosophy written in Latin, but perhaps the implication of the reference to Roman drama is that plays were performed to mixed audiences. Reid prints P's *nesciunt*, but *erunt* in the first part of the sentence supports the future tense.

Quid enim causae est cur poetas Latinos…philosophos non legant: the format of this question and the next is reminiscent of Greek πρόβλημα style (διὰ τί; … ἢ ὅτι …), often taken to represent the teacher's question and the tentative reply given by the student. The mood in the *cur*-clause corresponds to a present indicative in direct speech, as the next sentence shows (*delectat*). However, as *delectabunt* below suggests, what he means is that he fails to see why Romans would not read Latin philosophical works if someone composed them.

In the preface to *Fin.* 1 Cicero argues somewhat differently. There he expresses bafflement but concedes that Romans would read Greek drama translated into Latin but philosophy less so (*Fin.* 1.4: *in quibus hoc primum est in quo admirer, cur in grauissimis rebus non delectet eos sermo patrius, cum idem fabellas Latinas ad uerbum e Graecis expressas non inuiti legant*) and adds that he feels obliged to read even poor representatives of the dramatic genre *because* they are written in Latin (1.5); note also the different characterizations of translation practice. For the notion of cultural competition driving translation and appropriation activity, see the general note above.

An quia delectat Ennius…sic hi Platonem imitentur Aristotelem Theophrastum: the success of Roman dramatic writers is due to the fact that they provide enjoyment. They are, moreover, misrepresented as translators since they are not literal translators; this contradicts what is said in *Fin.* 1.4 and 1.7. Reid[1] p. 103, following Madvig (1876: 12) on *Fin.* 1.4, resolves the contradiction by assuming that only some writers are meant here. Complementarily, one can observe that the rhetorical strategies employed in both passages are not identical (see previous n.). Presumably philosophy would delight more than drama because it ranks higher (for Cicero).

On the sentence's change of direction after *poetarum* Plasberg[1] p. 39 aptly comments: '*Debebat pergere* philosophi non delectant, *sed spem significaturus mutauit orationem*'. For the sequence *delectabunt…imitentur*, see Reid[1] p. 103. Some *deteriores* offer Greek inflections in transliteration (*Sophoclen, Euripiden*); see section 6 of the preface of the Oxford Classical Text on my spelling choices.

Oratores quidem laudari uideo…aut Demosthenem imitati: Cicero does not pause long enough to specify what exactly he has in mind. Some Roman orators imitated Greek orators in public speeches, political or forensic, cf. Weische (1972) on Cicero generally, and Stroh (1982) on Cic. *Phil.*, but this would not normally involve close translation of longer passages, as the contexts here seems to require. Thus Cicero may be thinking of exercises in which an orator rendered Greek speeches in Latin (cf. *De orat.* 1.155, with Leeman and Pinkster 1981: 260), which may have involved a small audience of friends. In *De opt. gen. orat.* 18, written in 46 BC, Cicero talks about those who accept translations of Greek drama but reject translations of Greek oratory ('*Quid istas* [sc. *orationes*] *potius legam quam Graecas?' Idem Andriam et Synephebos nec minus Andromacham aut Antiopam aut Epigonos Latinos recipiunt. Quod igitur est eorum in orationibus e Graeco conuersis fastidium, nullum cum sit in uersibus?*').

§11

Ego autem Varro…renouabam, cum licebat, legendo: *dicam enim ut res est* (for which cf. Plt., *Merc.* 351 *dico ut res est*) and similar phrases can mark contrivance, but when the Cicero character proceeds to his own reasons for writing philosophy (on which see section 3) towards the end of §11, he does so with an air of disarming honesty. To address Varro by his name is an effective device which helps create this impression. I do agree with Plasberg[1] p. 39 that the two branches of the tradition each preserve part of the reading of the archetype (*autem* P: *Varro* Γ).

Cicero only starts presenting himself as confined to his *otium* under the dictatorship, i.e. the works of the 50s present themselves as composed when Cicero practically had no leisure time due to his public commitments. For the opposition of *cura* and *procuratio*, see *Q.fr.* 3.7.3 (= SB 27): *rei publicae statu in quo etiam si nihil procuro, tamen nihil curare uix possum*. The clause *etiam si nihil procuro* is resumed by *administratione rei publicae liberatus* below.

Animus can come close to meaning 'heart' when designating the mind as a seat of affections and intentions, but the juxtaposition with the notion (if not the term) of memory favours the translation 'mind'. With *animo haec inclusa habebam*, cf. *Tusc.* 1.1 ('philosophical studies *retenta animo* during his active career'); Sen., *Ep.* 6.4: *si cum hac exceptione detur sapientia, ut illam inclusam teneam nec enuntiem, reiciam*. On *obsolescere*, see Reid[1] p. 104. Philosophy is presented as discursive knowledge here rather than something one might 'live by', no doubt partly because writing philosophy (or not) is the issue (note the emphatic and contrastive *legendo* at the end of the sentence).

Nunc uero et fortunae grauissimo percussus uulnere...oblectationem hanc honestissimam iudico: on Tullia's death in February 45, see the introduction (sections 3, 9.1), *Fam.* 4.6.2 = SB 249: *graue uolnus*, *N.D.* 1.9, and Servius Sulpicius Rufus' famous consolatory letter (*Fam.* 4.5 = SB 248). With *percussus uulnere*, cf. Prop. 1.1.13; on *perculsus*, found in some later mss. and printed by Lambinus, see Reid[1] p. 104. For philosophy as *medicina animi*, cf. e.g. *Tusc.* 3.4–6. *Oblectatio* is somewhat weaker than *delectatio*, 'enjoyment' rather than 'pleasure'.

Aut enim huic aetati hoc maxime aptum est...nihil aliud uideo quod agere possimus: on this sentence and the notion that Cicero's philosophical writings might benefit his fellow citizens see the introduction, section 3. With the last option named, cf. *Div.* 2.6: *nec nihil agere poteram, nec quid potius, quod quidem me dignum esset, agerem reperiebam*; *Tusc.* 2.1: *necesse mihi quidem esse arbitror philosophari, nam quid possum, praesertim nihil agens, agere melius?* The term *aetas* is better taken to mean 'my age' than 'the age we live in', given that both what precedes and what follows are remarks of a more personal nature. Reid[1] p. 104 prints *eis rebus*, but *his* is secured by the pronouns in the other disjuncts, and the sense is not indefinite.

§12

Brutus quidem noster...cuius tu fratrem Antiochum: M. Iunius Brutus (85–42 BC; *RE* s.n. Iunius no. 53), the murderer of Caesar. Cicero dedicated *Brut.*, *Fin.*, *Tusc.*, and *N.D.* to him. The marginal role assigned to Brutus here in an argument justifying philosophical literature in Latin need not be due to Cicero's desire to present his own activities as pioneering. In the letters to Atticus which document the editorial history of *Acad.*, Cicero shows concern that Varro might be jealous of Brutus (*Att.* 13.13–14(25).1 = SB 321 = T19).

Brutus is used to rebut a specific point made by Varro in §4 (*quae sine eruditione Graeca intellegi non possunt*), that (respectable) philosophy written in Latin would not be intelligible for those who are not already versed in Greek learning (and by implication know the language): *nihil ut eiusdem de rebus Graeca desideres*. On the use of the neuter plural *Graeca*, and the merits of *Graecia*, see Reid[1] p. 105; on Paulus Manutius' emendation *desideres*, see Hunt (1998: 237).

Brutus' *De uirtute* was first sent to Cicero while he was awaiting Caesar's return at Brundisium (October 48–September 47), as a letter composed by Brutus in Mytilene or Samos (*Brut.* 12, 330). It is also alluded to in *Brut.* 250, as Sen., *Helv.* 9, confirms in *Fin.* 1.8, and in *Tusc.* 5.12. Two other philosophical works are mentioned elsewhere, Περὶ τοῦ καθήκοντος (Sen., *Ep.* 95.45; cf. *De officiis* in Priscian, *GL* ii.199 Keil) and *De patientia* (Diomedes, *GL* i.383 Keil). See Hendrickson (1939) and Osorio (2021) on the *De uirtute*; Sedley (1997a) on Brutus' philosophical outlook more generally and the extent to which it might have influenced his political actions; Lévy (2012: 300).

Sententiam sequitur suggests that Varro actually adopted Antiochian thought in some stronger sense, as does *Att.* 13.25.3 = T30, of Brutus: *est is quoque* [sc. like Varro] *Antiochius*; contrast *Antiochia...ualde probat* (*Att.* 13.12(24).3 = SB 320 = T18).

Antiochus' brother Aristos (*Aristus*) is also part of the Alexandrian scene in *Luc.* 11–12; see ad loc. In *Brut.* 332 he is dubbed *heres* of the *uetus Academia*; cf. his being called the recipient (διεδέξατο) of Antiochus' διατριβή in Philod., *Index Acad.* col. xxxv.2–3 (= T3 in Sedley 2012c: 335–6; see also Kalligas et al. 2020a: 375), and Blank (2007). For his relationship with Brutus, cf. *Brut.* 1; *Fin.* 5.8; *Tusc.* 5.21; Plut., *Brut.* 2.

For Cicero's views on Brutus as an orator (undoubtedly part of *excellens omni genere laudis*), as well as a precis of their relationship, see Balbo (2013). The adverb *aliquamdiu* appears only on four other occasions in Cicero.

Quam ob rem...huic etiam generi litterarum: *quam ob rem* relates to all that precedes, not the last point made. For *dare se alicui rei*, 'to devote oneself to something', cf. e.g. *Att.* 2.8.1 = SB 28: *ego me do historiae*. This passage in particular precludes that Varro had produced philosophical writings prior to the composition of *Acad.*

§§13–14

This transitional passage leaves behind the issue of writing philosophy in Latin and sets up the dialogue proper.

Varro says that it has come to his attention that Cicero has abandoned the Old Academy for the New,[65] to which Cicero replies that this should not be a problem when Antiochus abandoned the New Academy (of Philo and his predecessors) for the Old, i.e. formulated his Old Academic stance.[66] Playing on the use of the attributes 'old' and 'new', Cicero observes that the latest thing is always the most up-to-date and corrected (leaving it open whether he means the New Academy or the newly set up, i.e. Antiochian, Old Academy, ironizing his 'shift', Antiochus', or both). However (*quamquam*), i.e. against the notion that the latest thing is always best, Philo denied in his Roman Books Antiochus' thesis that there were two Academies and argued that those who thought otherwise erred. To this Varro is made to reply that Cicero will be familiar with Antiochus' response, which, it is implied but not stated, reasserted that there were two Academies (and not one). With this (§14), the main subject has almost been reached, as Cicero expresses the desire that Varro renews his acquaintance with 'these things and the whole matter of the Old Academy' (*ista et totam ueterem Academiam*), leaving it somewhat vague whether he means the dispute over the Roman Books or the dispute between the Old Academy (representing dogmatic philosophy) and the Academy more generally. (The extant part of *Ac.* 1 does not touch on the Roman Books again nor, for all we know, does it draw on their content; see section 9.3 of the introduction.) Varro eventually agrees and undertakes to relay what he has learnt from Antiochus a long time ago, as well as to see if it can be expressed in Latin in a satisfactory way (*commode*).

It is my view that Cicero's philosophical outlook as conveyed in first-person statements in his works was that of an Academic sceptic throughout his life, i.e. from his

---

[65] *Academiam* is supplied by emendation; see the note below.
[66] On the question of when Antiochus converted to dogmatism and whether his 'Old Academy' should be viewed as a school in its own right, see on *Luc.* 69–71.

first exposure to Philo onwards (cf. *Inv.* 2.9–10).[67] (I also believe him to have been a Clitomachean throughout his life, whereas others take him to have been a mitigated sceptic, but this distinction is irrelevant in the present context; see sections 4 and 8.)

A minority view, first formulated by Hirzel (1883: 488–91) and then articulated in detail and independently by Glucker (1988) and Steinmetz (1989),[68] has it that Cicero, impressed by Antiochus, shifted to the latter's dogmatic outlook and retained it for much of his life including the period in which the dialogues of the 50s were written, but returned to a sceptical outlook in the mid-40s before he composed the second cycle of philosophical works. Key passages invoked by Glucker and Steinmetz are *Leg.* 1.39 and the present passage.[69] Görler (1995) is a comprehensive refutation of Glucker (1988) and Steinmetz (1989), and has since its publication commanded almost universal assent. With respect to *Ac.* 1.13 Glucker and Steinmetz had argued that Varro's reference is to an actual conversion from Old Academic dogmatism back to Academic scepticism, thus mirroring Antiochus' conversion from Academic sceptic to dogmatist.[70] The nub of the question is the interpretation of the verb *tractari* in *relictam a te ueterem illam...tractari autem nouam*, which Glucker (1988: 44) and Steinmetz (1989: 14) interpret as 'to take up a case and deal with it thoroughly as counsel'. Against this Görler (1995: 108–9), following Reid[1] p. 106, demonstrates that *tractare* with an impersonal object (and consequently the corresponding passive construction) can only mean 'to treat of' or 'deal with sc. a subject', so that the sense would be that in his earlier works Cicero treated of issues which are characteristic of the Old Academy or even presented Old Academic views and teachings (albeit without endorsing them himself).[71] On this reading the two shifts that are being compared are not the same in kind (Görler 1995: 110 calls the argument '*a maiore ad minus*'), and Cicero's ironic remark about the perceived attractiveness of the new, which leaves it open if the New or the—in his view, synthetic—Old Academy is meant, is rather in keeping with such a reading.

According to this interpretation of the passage, the character Varro raises with the character Cicero something which the author Cicero chose to do. The fact that the Varro character does this, in a way which can be paralleled in other Ciceronian

---

[67] Cf. also Aug., *Contra Acad.* 3.18.41: *Sed huic arreptis iterum illis armis et Philo restitit, donec moreretur, et omnes eius* (sc. Antiochus') *reliquias Tullius noster oppressit se uiuo impatiens labefactari uel contaminari quidquid amauisset*, where, however, the reference is admittedly to the *Academici libri* in particular.

[68] See also Brunt (2013a: 223–5), which was published posthumously and predates Winterbottom (1994) and Dyck (1996); and the survey of earlier scholarship in Glucker (1988: 38–9 n. 18).

[69] Cf. *Leg.* 1.39: *Sibi autem indulgentes et corpori deseruientes, atque omnia quae sequantur in uita quaeque fugiant uoluptatibus et doloribus ponderantes, etiamsi uera dicunt (nihil enim opus est hoc loco litibus), in hortulis suis iubeamus dicere, atque etiam ab omni societate rei publicae, cuius partem nec norunt ullam neque umquam nosse uoluerunt, paulisper facessant rogemus. Perturbatricem autem harum omnium rerum Academiam, hanc ab Arcesila et Carneade recentem, exoremus ut sileat: nam si inuaserit in haec quae satis scite nobis instructa et composita uidentur, nimias edet ruinas; quam quidem ego placare cupio, summouere non audeo.*

[70] Brittain (2011) is in part devoted to how Augustine reconciled the Academic and Platonic elements in the Ciceronian corpus.

[71] With respect to this reading, although his overall interpretation is different, Glucker (1988: 57–69), makes a number of useful points; see also Glucker (1997: 70–1).

dialogues,⁷² does of course nothing to detract from the observation that the modern interpreter needs to distinguish, when speaking of 'Cicero' and e.g. his philosophical views, between the historical individual, the implied author, the speaker in the frame of dialogues, and the Cicero character (see section 8).

Philo's Roman Books, on which Cicero heard Philo lecture publicly as he says here,⁷³ are known to us only from *Acad.* and one passage in Sextus; see on *Luc.* 18, 78. From these passages it emerges that they contained a philosophical claim about the nature of knowledge, whose precise interpretation is a matter of dispute, and a historical claim (alluded to here) to the effect that there had only ever been one Academy, i.e. that the distinction drawn between an 'old', pre-Arcesilaen Academy and the New Academy was unwarranted.⁷⁴ Moreover, Philo connected the two claims so as to suggest that the Academy (i.e. Socrates, Plato, as well as Arcesilaus and Carneades) had held the philosophical view which he set out in the Roman Books all along: there had only ever been one Academy *in that sense*. I discuss these issues elsewhere in detail as indicated and ask here only why Cicero mentions this comparatively marginal issue at this point and whether its being mentioned here tells us anything about the rest of *Ac.* 1 and the second edition of *Acad.* as a whole.

With Cicero having concluded the account of his reasons for writing philosophy, Varro—on the reading endorsed above—indicates that he is familiar with Cicero's works just as Cicero was able to recount the contents of Varro's works in §9.⁷⁵ This represents a neat transition from what precedes.⁷⁶ The idea of two Academies between which Cicero shifted (in the sense indicated above) then allows Cicero to introduce the historical thesis of the Roman Books, on which there was only one Academy. In this way, the Roman Books come to feature briefly at the margins of the discussion just as they do in *Luc.* 18, where they are touched on before Lucullus starts his defence of κατάληψις, which pointedly omits them. In *Luc.* 18 we also learn that in the *Catulus* Catulus senior was reported as having accused Philo of openly lying in the Roman Books. While this means that for the final edition Cicero would have had to fashion a different introduction of the Roman Books view, there are no positive grounds for suspecting that this view was completely written out of the discussion.⁷⁷ However, in *Ac.* 1.44–6 where Cicero replies to Varro and begins a sceptical alternative history, he relies on a historical view of the Academy which is developmental, i.e. posits differences between Socrates and Arcesilaus. Thus speaking in his own voice he is not there adopting the historical view of the Roman Books.

---

⁷² In *Div.* 1.9 the character Quintus Cicero refers to something Marcus Cicero the author wrote in *N.D.* In 1.33 Quintus cites against Marcus a historical fact as something known to him (Marcus) which the character Balbus introduced in *N.D.* 2.10–11.

⁷³ If the first-person plural meant that Cicero and Varro had heard these lectures, Cicero would no doubt have developed the point and used it to justify Varro's selection as an interlocutor further.

⁷⁴ Since the Academics had little interest in Plato's immediate successors, who were primarily of concern to Antiochus (see section 7.2), this claim must have related to Plato primarily (as well as possibly to Socrates). For a discussion of unity views in the wider Academic tradition, see Brittain (2001: 169–219).

⁷⁵ This is in fact another consideration in favour of Görler's interpretation. *Nec uero sine te* earlier in the paragraph can be seen to set the tone for the continued display of mutual politeness.

⁷⁶ In *Luc.* the connection is partly personal, too, because Lucullus' credibility as spokesman for Antiochus is linked to the arrival of the Roman Books in Alexandria.

⁷⁷ Contrast Griffin (1997: 12).

Yet while the beginning of Cicero's reply to Varro in 1.44 shows no signs of being informed by the Roman Books, the exchange here in §§13–14 may tell us something about Varro's speech, namely that the historical account of the Old Academy which he gives in *Ac.* 1.15–42 probably draws on a particular Antiochian source, the *Sosus* (cf. *Luc.* 12), Antiochus' reply to the Roman Books which Varro refers to without mentioning the title.[78] At this level of generality, this is a widely held view, whose general plausibility derives from the fact that Varro's exposition offers the kind of history of philosophy which, given what else we know about Antiochus' views on ethics (mostly from *Fin.*) and epistemology (mostly from *Luc.*), would go well with them. Moving beyond the unresolvable question of whether the *Sosus* rather than another Antiochian text is the source for Varro's speech, Sedley (2012: 87–8) has suggested that *Fin.* 4.8–10, another but much more compressed account of the history of philosophy from an Antiochian point of view, predates the Roman books and shows Antiochus eager to emphasize common ground between the *ueteres* and the Stoics, while Varro's speech postdates the Roman books and is, in the face of Philo's 'one Academy' thesis, much more ready to accept discontinuities and developments within the Academic tradition.[79] This is attractive, and would presumably have been presented by Antiochus as less of a shift in substance than of tone or presentational strategy, although the modern interpreter may disagree (see section 9.3.2). With the later phase of Antiochus' work Sedley (2012: 101) also associates 'the close study of canonical philosophical texts', pointing to the fact that Antiochus was living and working in Alexandria, which was at this very point in time emerging as a centre for a way of doing philosophy in such a text-based way. Both the physical and the epistemological section of Varro's speech make, on any interpretation, close reference to particular Platonic texts.

§13

Tum ille 'Istud quidem considerabo…' 'Quid ergo' inquam: Varro's character promises Cicero's to consider writing on philosophical subjects, 'with Cicero's assistance' (*nec uero sine te*). The latter remark suggests once more a familiarity which the historical individuals seem not to have had.

When Varro then asks *sed de te ipso…?*, the fact that writing has just been at issue suggests that it is an enquiry about something which Cicero has written, while *quod audio* might seem to suggest a question about Cicero the man rather than the author (Reid[1] p. 106 glosses 'sc. from Atticus, who was the chief means of communicating between Cicero and Varro', which is possible but not necessary). In any event, the boundary between man and character is blurred here, and Cicero was presumably hesitant to make Varro comment too closely on e.g. the *Hortensius* (assuming Varro knew it—there is no evidence either way).

---

[78] Cicero can be very precise in his references when he wants to be; cf. *Luc.* 98 (Clitomachus' work on ἐποχή) and 102 (the work addressed to Lucilius). Cicero's conventions for identifying sources do little to lend positive support to the thesis that the *Sosus* in particular is the source for Varro's speech, but do not cast doubt on the view, either.

[79] See Reinhardt (2018) for a comparison of both passages.

The emendation *Academiam*, proposed by 'Lambinus' (not Bentley, as Hunt 1998: 246 observes) for the transmitted *iam*, is superior to *illam* suggested by Madvig (1826: 115), given that the Academy had not featured since §7 and will only be named again later in §13. *Relinquere* is easily used either of the abandoning of a philosophical position or of a subject of writing; it is, however, disambiguated by *tractari*. Reid[1] p. 106 comments on the latter: 'It is important to notice that this implies a reference to some *writing* of Cicero's, which can only be the "Academica" itself.... The illusion of the dialogue is not here carefully preserved.' Since there is reason to believe that in *Hort.* Cicero indicated that he saw himself as an Academic without going so far as to defend his position (see section 9.5), Varro might also be referring to *Hort.* On the uses of *tractare*, see Glucker (1988: 44–5) and Steinmetz (1989: 14), as well as the definitive discussion in Görler (1995: 108–10); see the general note above, and *Ac.* 1.25 *fin.* I add to Görler's arguments that, even if *tractare aliquam rem* could here have the sense which the rejected interpretation favours ('to represent as counsel'), it would not deliver Cicero as an Old Academic, since advocates have to make their client's case their own, but are not required to endorse their client's case as true; cf. the use of *tueri* in *Fin.* 1.6, with Patzig (1979: 308–9). The notion of calling another character away from the New Academy and towards the Old is present in *Fin.* 5.7: *tamen audebo te ab hac Academia noua ad ueterem illam uocare.*

I print *istuc (quidem considerabo)*, which must have been in ω; on forms of *ille* and *iste* with the deictic suffix -*c(e)*, see Adams (2013: 454–9).

Quid ergo? is printed by Reid[1], while Plasberg[1] has the question run on and only punctuates after *uetere*. On the uses of *quid ergo*, see Brink (1971: 364); on sentence questions without an interrogative particle ('wenn die Frage mit einem gewissen Affekte...ausgesprochen...wird'), see Kühner-Stegmann ii.501. Chahoud (2016: 239 and 243–4) on *quid ergo facio*.

Antiocho id magis licuerit...correcta et emendata maxime: as indicated in the general note above, no like-with-like comparison is made here, in that Antiochus' abandoning of Academic scepticism is likened to Cicero treating of topics associated with the New Academy. For Antiochus' abandonment of Academic scepticism see on *Luc.* 69–71; whether the move referred to is metaphorical only or intended to include Antiochus' physical departure from the Academy as a school (note *domum*; cf. *Fin.* 1.65; Hor., *C.* 1.29.14) is not clear. The parenthetical *nostro familiari* makes Cicero's argument sound less confrontational than it otherwise would; cf. *ut tu existimas ipse*, below. Reid[1] p. 106 notes that *remigrare* here only signals a move 'in retrograde direction', not to a position previously held by Antiochus himself.

I have argued above that *certe enim...maxime* is deliberately ambiguous in that it can refer to Antiochus' shift, Philo's shift, or both. This ambiguity is enabled by *recentissima* (rather than e.g. *nouissima*) which can refer to the New Academy or the newly introduced (or revived) Old Academy of Antiochus. It is possible that 'the latest thing is always best' is a proverbial expression of some kind, or ironizes one which makes the opposite point, but I have not found a good parallel.

For divisions of the Academy in antiquity see on *Ac.* 1.18. For *licuerit*, see Kühner-Stegmann ii.178 on the potential subjunctive in rhetorical questions. *Corrigere* means originally 'to rectify' rather than 'to free from faults' (= *emendare*), but here the two terms seem juxtaposed for stylistic fullness.

Quamquam Antiochi magister Philo…erroremque eorum, qui ita putarunt, coarguit: on *quamquam*, see Reid¹ pp. 106–7: 'Here elliptic "yet there is no need for this argument, since Philo says the Academy is really one".' Kühner-Stegmann ii.444 on *quamquam* used to introduce main clauses.

With *ut tu existimas ipse*, cf. *nostro familiari* above: both sides have mutual appreciation, despite their disagreements. For Philo's Roman Books, see on *Luc.* 18. Cicero also (*etiam*) heard from Philo himself either in a public setting or in personal conversation (*coram* can mean either) about the historical thesis of the Roman Books, i.e. he did not just read the *libri*. In *Brut.* 306 Cicero speaks of how he committed himself to philosophy when Philo came to Rome. Yet from meeting Philo he came away a Clitomachean himself, which raises the question if Philo only formulated the Roman Books view in Rome and was still a Clitomachean when he arrived (at least in his public pronouncements); cf. *Inv.* 2.9–10 and section 8.

Negaret cannot be right, but a third-person singular verb meaning 'to deny' in the indicative is broadly what sense requires. Plasberg¹ suggests *negare solet* in the app. crit. (in the text he prints *negaret* in 1908, adding a † in 1922), which is palaeographically closer to what is transmitted but *solet* would be without point here (*pace* Plasberg¹, who says of *negare solet* '*ut persaepe in opinionibus philosophorum*'; yet here no position-defining tenet is at issue). Hence I print (like Reid¹) *negat* proposed by Davies, which is historical present like *coarguit*. The latter is a success verb, but may be focalized by Philo, in which case it would not carry the endorsement of the Cicero character. The reference of *eorum* is in part clarified by *Luc.* 11–12, but the relative clause is indefinite (hence I print the transmitted *putarent*, not *putarunt* like Reid¹ and some others before him). Plasberg¹ p. 40, who also prints *putarent*, sees a lapse into historic sequence here which Cicero sometimes exhibits when rehearsing philosophers' opinions; see Madvig (1876: 459).

'Est', inquit, '…quae contra Philonis Antiochus scripserit': an important passage on Antiochus' reply to the Roman Books, the *Sosus*; see on *Luc.* 18 and section 9.3. The transmitted *Philonis* was printed by Plasberg¹, whereas Reid¹ had expanded to *ea Philonis*; yet other solutions are reported by Plasberg¹. The decision about what to print turns on whether it is deemed possible to have the elliptical expression (*contra Philonis*, sc. *libros*) in a dialogue when it is only attested once in a letter (*Att.* 12.23.2 = SB 262: *ex Apollodori*, sc. *annali*, the latter supplied from the wider context). Arguably, the dialogues admit of colloquialisms otherwise confined to the letters especially in passages featuring exchanges rather than longer speeches, and in the present context *libros* is very readily supplied. Thus I print the transmitted text.

§14

Immo uero et ista et totam Academiam…si uidetur: it is more natural to take *et ista* as a reference to the dispute over the Roman Books than to the entire debate between

Academics and Stoics, given that a generalizing colon follows (*totam ueterem Academiam*). Griffin (1997: 11–12) accepts that at least a brief account of the Roman Books is likely to have featured in the *Catulus*, but suggests that 'with the change of speakers in the final version, the treatment of Philo's innovations may have been attenuated or even dropped.' *Ista* on the reading adopted here would amount at least to an invitation to Varro to talk about the subject from an Antiochian perspective at some point, and I see no reason to doubt that Cicero's speech from *Ac.* 1.44 would eventually have lead to an account of the Roman Books, possibly with a reply by Varro. Griffin's general point, however, is not in doubt: the Roman Books remained at the margin of the discussion in both editions (nor is there reason to think that they served as a source for any part of the dialogue; see section 9.3).

The clause *a qua absum iam diu* could by itself relate to philosophical allegiance or to themes touched on in literary works; I am committed to the latter view, having sided with Reid[1] and Görler (1995) above on §13. For *renouare* in the sense of 'to restore a memory or reputation', cf. e.g. *Vat.* 28; in 45 BC the teaching of Antiochian philosophy had ceased in Athens (and elsewhere). See Hatzimichali (2012: 28).

Reid[1] p. 108 assembles parallels for speakers being seated in Ciceronian dialogues and observes on *simul*: 'as though to cut V. off from the chance of refusal'; see also ibid. on the late position of *inquam*.

Sane istud quidem...uideo: a nod to the relationship between Atticus and Varro; see the general note on *Ac.* 1.1–8. On the sequence *sane istud* (or *istuc*) *quidem*, see Reid[1] p. 108.

'Mihi uero', ille; '...satisne ea commoda dici possint Latine?': Atticus had accompanied Cicero, his brother Quintus, their cousin Lucius, and M. Pupius Piso to Athens in 79 BC, where they all attended Antiochus' lectures; cf. *Fin.* 5.1 (= F9 Mette and in Sedley 2012c) and *Brut.* 315 (= F4 Mette and in Sedley 2012c); Hatzimichali (2012: 25). If Varro were to provide what Atticus wishes to remember, then the material presented by him would postdate the Roman Books and the *Sosus* by a decade. By that time the Roman Books would presumably no longer be a suitable subject for Antiochus' anger (contrast *Luc.* 11). However, this is of course no way to determine the relative date of the source for Varro's speech.

Cf. the end of *Fin.* (5.96; Atticus speaking): *Quae enim dici Latine posse non arbitrabar, ea dicta sunt a te uerbis aptis nec minus plane quam dicuntur a Graecis.* On the absence of a *uerbum dicendi* after *ille*, see Madvig (1876: 23).

Quae cum essent dicta, in conspectu sedimus: with *in conspectu* 'in plain sight', cf. the setting in *Luc.* 9: *cum igitur pauca in xysto locuti essemus, tum eodem in spatio consedimus*; TLL s.v. *conspectus* cols 491.80–492.33. On *essent*, an emendation in ms. F, see Plasberg[1] p. 41.

§§15–18

Varro's speech begins here and ends in 1.42. In 1.15–18 Varro asserts the unity of Old Academy (i.e. Plato's immediate successors and the Peripatos) and gives an initial indication of how their thought relates to Plato's (and Socrates').[80] In 1.19-23 he introduces the Old Academic views on ethics, in 1.24-9 those on physics, and 1.30-2 those on logic. This avowedly historical survey yields a *prima forma* of Old Academic thought (1.33a).[81] In 1.33-42 Varro explains changes made to it by the Peripatetics (1.33-4) and Zeno, the founder of the Stoa (1.35-42). (Plato's successors in the Academy appear in 1.34b as a homogenous group which preserved its intellectual inheritance.) Some of these changes are accepted, others rejected, and it is not always clear in each case whether a given change is accepted or rejected.[82] In one case, or so I argue, Varro assumes two successive modifications of the *prima forma* before the position is reached which Antiochus himself takes.[83] Part of the philosophical fiction of the entire section is that successful modifications of the *prima forma* are not corrections of Plato but modifications of the *prima forma* formulated by the Old Academics (as understood by Antiochus) with reference to the authority of Platonic texts;[84] on this point see the introduction, section 7.2.

Both the Academics and Antiochus had views on philosophical pre-history, notably the Presocratics, but Antiochus' views on the subject were most likely formulated only in response to the Academy (see section 7). The natural starting point for a version of Academic history as Antiochus would require it to underpin his views is Socrates (§15). Varro begins his speech with a clear indication that what he is going to say about Socrates is both his firm belief and widely agreed. His initial point is then almost proverbial—Socrates was the first to have directed philosophy away from concern with cosmological questions as pursued by the Presocratics and towards ethical questions, on the grounds that heavenly matters were either unknowable or not concerned with the good life—, but it leads into a less universally accepted characterization, and one which one would not necessarily expect an Antiochean to endorse (§16).

In *Ac.* 1.16 Socrates is said to have proceeded in discussions recorded by his pupils (i.e. Socratics in general, not just Plato) in such a way that he made no positive affirmations himself, refuted others, and said that he knew nothing except this one thing, that he knew nothing. He also said that what made him superior to others (sc. in wisdom) is that unlike him they thought they knew things which they do not

---

[80] Important earlier discussions of the passage qua programmatic statement on Antiochus' Old Academy, in addition to the commentaries, include Hirzel (1883: 242 n. 1); Glucker (1978: passim); Dörrie (1987: 202-5, 466-8); Lévy (1992: 145-7); Barnes (1997: 82); Glucker (1997: 71-7); Sedley (1997b: 120-2); Brittain (2006a: 534-5); Karamanolis (2006: 51-7); Bonazzi (2012: 308-9); Sedley (2012: 99-100); Bryan, Wardy, and Warren (2018: 2-3); Tarrant (2018: 86); Tsouni (2018: 268-9); Tsouni (2018a: 145-6). I believe my interpretation to be different from all of these in some respects and therefore develop it here largely on its own terms.
[81] *Forma* in *Ac.* 1.33a is a modern emendation; see ad loc.
[82] Cf. Brittain (2006: 92 n. 12 and xxxi-xxxv).
[83] The issue is the central question of forms/ideas; cf. the *species* of 1.30, Aristotle's criticism of them in 1.33, and Zeno's view on *notiones* in 1.42.
[84] On the concept of modification, cf. *Ac.* 1.42 (*commutatio*), 1.33 (*immutatio*); the latter instance is an emendation, but while one cannot be certain if *com*- or *immutatio* is to be printed there, sense would seem to require *a* word meaning 'modification'. *Immutatio* in *Luc.* 16 is more narrowly about terms. That the authority of Platonic texts was invoked not just by Plato's successors but also by Antiochus emerges from the intertextual references to Platonic texts in Varro's speech down to *Ac.* 1.42. I seek to document these ad loc.

know, and that he suspects that this is why he was named the wisest by the Delphic oracle, because wisdom amounts to not thinking one knows things when one does not. This passage is well recognized as informed by Plt., *Apol.* 21b-d, where Socrates—unusually and unlike in the dialogues—comments on the rationale of his own elenctic technique.[85] Note that in *Ac.* 1.16 Socrates makes no general pronouncements (e.g. to the effect that nothing can be known by him, still less that nothing can be known generally speaking) and only claims to know one thing (that he knows nothing).[86] He is said to have persisted in this *sententia*, which cannot just mean a pronouncement but must also mean his view in some sense (see n. below), but encouraged everyone to pursue virtue. For reasons of consistency, this exhortation cannot have been grounded in views of the same status (about virtue) as the conviction that he knows nothing.[87]

In §§17–18a Varro then gives a general description of how the Old Academy as he construes it arrived at the body of doctrines which characterize it. This is cast as a new departure given the conception of Socrates in the previous paragraph. By Plato's *auctoritas*, a new *forma* of philosophy was established, which belonged to Academics and Peripatetics alike, who only differed in name.[88] Note how the text avoids identifying Plato as the creator of this *forma*, choosing instead a passive (*forma instituta est*) and the somewhat vague *Platonis... auctoritate*, and that the complex nature of

---

[85] Plt., *Apol.* 20e–21d: 'With respect to my wisdom—whether I have any and what sort it is—, I will call the god in Delphi as a witness. You know, I believe, about Chaerephon—he was a friend of mine from my youth, a friend to your democracy, went into exile with you, and returned with you—and you know what kind of man he was, how committed in pursuit of his endeavours. And once he went to Delphi and undertook to consult the oracle on this issue and—as I said, gentleman, please refrain from making noise while I speak. For he asked the oracle who was the wisest. Now the Pythian priestess thought nobody was wiser. His brother here will testify to this, since Chaerephon is dead.

Consider why I am saying this: I am about to tell you where the slanderous remarks about me come from. When I heard about the oracle's pronouncements, I thought the following: 'What is the god saying, and what is the meaning of this riddle? In nothing great or small do I have any awareness that I am wise (ἐγὼ γὰρ δὴ οὔτε μέγα οὔτε σμικρὸν σύνοιδα ἐμαυτῷ σοφὸς ὤν); why then does he say that I am the wisest? For he does not lie. That is not permitted to him.' And for a long time I was at a loss what he was saying. Then with hesitation I moved towards the following inquiry into this. I went to one of those who appeared to be wise, since there if anywhere I would be able to refute the prophecy and show to the oracle that 'this man is wiser than me, but you said it was me.' In examining this man—for I do not need to identify him by name, but it was one of the politicians I was looking at when I found myself in this situation, Athenians—and in talking to him, it seemed to me that this man was deemed wise by others and particularly by himself, but was not actually wise. As a result I became a source of annoyance for him and for the many, but as I left I thought to myself that I was wiser than this man at least. For chances are that neither of us two knew anything genuinely good, but he thought he knew something without knowing it, but I, just as I did not know, did not think I did. I therefore appeared to be wiser than him through one small respect, that I did not think I know what I do not know (ἔοικα γοῦν τούτου γε σμικρῷ τινι αὐτῷ τούτῳ σοφώτερος εἶναι, ὅτι ἃ μὴ οἶδα οὐδὲ οἴομαι εἰδέναι). From there I went on to another one of those who are deemed to be rather wise, and arrived at the same view, and then became a source of annoyance for him as well and for many others.'

[86] One might wonder why Varro emphasizes that his picture of Socrates is derived from the writings of all his pupils when he then gives an account which is closely modelled on Plt., *Apol.* 21b–d, a text which is with respect to the pronouncements made by the Delphic oracle at variance with Xen. *Ap.* 14. Varro may be suggesting that Plato's presentation of Socrates is borne out not just by his own dialogues but also by those written by other Socrates pupils.

[87] *Pace* Ioppolo (1995: 118–21); contrast Annas (1992a: 58): 'Note that Antiochus finds no problem in seeing Socrates as a moralist with convictions but no reasoned asserted views.'

[88] See section 7.2 on the various strategies employed by Antiochus to construct the history of philosophy as he sees it.

Plato is emphasized (*qui uarius et multiplex et copiosus fuit*).[89] Varro proceeds to explain why there are both Peripatetics and Academics when the difference between them is in name only: when Plato had installed his sister's son Speusippus as the 'as it were, heir of his philosophy', as well as his eminent pupils Xenocrates and Aristotle, those who were with Aristotle were called Peripatetics, while the other group (Xenocrates' followers) got their name from the gymnasium where they met and conversed, i.e. Plato's Academy. When Varro then continues with *Sed utrique...*, it is not clearly signposted whether he is offering a restatement of the account of doctrine formation (cf. *forma instituta est* above), or describing a second phase of it. The former is the more plausible reading, for reasons which I shall explain in a moment. Both groups of philosophers were filled with the richness (*ubertas*, cf. the relative clause quoted above) of Plato and formulated a *formula disciplinae plena*: the legal term *formula* suggests a process of abstraction and reduction compared to said richness (see the n. below), but the end result is nonetheless not deficiently reductive (hence *plenam ac refertam*). This is contrasted with Socratic doubt about everything, his dialectical practice, and his refusal to affirm anything. It is this remark about the abandoning of Socratic method which suggests that Varro is providing a restatement of how the Old Academy came by its doctrinal framework, for surely the departure from Socrates came with Plato according to Antiochus, not with his successors. The result was an *ars philosophiae*, an ordered body of philosophical knowledge (see n.)— precisely what Socrates did not approve of at all. Crucially (§18a), both schools relied on the same view of what should be sought and avoided (i.e. of what counts as the good and as the τέλος), it being understood that one way of individuating philosophical schools is with reference to their conception of the end. Aristotle receives a special mention for ingenuity in *Ac.* 1.18a, but is immediately brought back into the Old Academic fold through the observation that the Peripatetics' thinking derived from the same source as that of Plato's successors in the Academy.

Varro's remarks about the Old Academy are a programmatic statement, esp. given their position in the final edition of *Acad.* I discuss in the introduction (section 7.2) how Plato can be both the source and origin of Old Academic thought on Antiochus' construal as well as the inspiration for his privileged interpreters, i.e. Plato's successors in the Academy as well as Aristotle and the Peripatetics, and how this explanatory model is sustained over the course of Varro's speech.

It has been noted that *Ac.* 1.15–17 gives a characterization of Socrates which is different from that of *Luc.* 15. This requires an explanation, given that in both passages the speaker is an Antiochian (Varro here, Lucullus there). Solutions to this problem which have been proposed either assume that the difference in characterization is superficial and that the basic conception of Socrates is the same in both passages, or assume that two different conceptions of Socrates are involved and proceed to offer explanations which turn on the likely nature of the sources used or on the possibility that Cicero created his Antiochian speakers as unique individuals. Relatedly, in both *Ac.* 1 and *Luc.* the character Cicero has an opportunity to reply to the Antiochian speaker and offer his view on Socrates (see *Ac.* 1.45–6 and *Luc.* 74).

---

[89] Cf. *Ac.* 1.33: *Haec forma erat illis prima, a Platone tradita* (text restored by emendation; see ad loc.).

All four passages also mention Plato at least in the wider context, whose construal in each case has to enter into the interpretation of the passages.

I discuss all passages together in the introduction (section 7.3), where I side with the majority view that the Socrates of *Ac.* 1.15–17 is the same as the one posited by the Academics, while the Socrates of *Luc.* 15 has substantial beliefs and conceals them behind irony. Different explanations have been offered for the coexistence of two different Antiochian conceptions of Socrates. Reid[1] pp. 110–11 suggested that Varro in *Ac.* 1.17 offers a glimpse of the historical Varro, whom he takes to be 'more inclined to scepticism than his master Antiochus', referring to Varro's remarks about theology in Aug., *C.D.* 7.17.[90] Glucker (1997: 74–5; cf. 1978: 406–20, esp. 419) believes that Varro's speech in *Ac.* 1 draws on a speech by the character Antiochus in Antiochus' *Sosus*, while the first part of Lucullus' speech in *Luc.* draws on 'a speech by Sosus the Stoic, refuting the version of Academic philosophy of Heraclitus of Tyre, Philo's faithful pupil' (Glucker 1997: 74). On this view Antiochus retained the conception of Socrates which his Academic teachers relied on, while a Stoic would want to bring Socrates, too, and not just Plato into the dogmatic fold.[91] Sedley (2012: 82–4) holds—plausibly, and unlike Glucker without further assumptions about the characters who appeared in the *Sosus* like e.g. Glucker—that Varro's speech draws on that dialogue, and that in Cicero's works we can glimpse two versions of an Antiochian history of philosophy, one harmonizing and pre-Roman Books, and one post-Roman Books, directed at Philo's thesis of a unity of the whole Academic tradition and thus more ready to allow for fissures and variation within the tradition; on this reading, the sceptical Socrates of Varro's speech is a calculated sacrifice made in order to discredit Philo's unity thesis. I am attracted by the chronological element of this explanation; see section 9.3 of the introduction.

Antiochus and Aristotle

In many ways Antiochus was not an early Platonist. Most conspicuously, his epistemological views remained committed to the empiricist framework prevalent in the Hellenistic period. However, in some respects Antiochus did anticipate Platonism.[92] His attempt to integrate Aristotle with Plato's successors is a case in point, although the manner in which he tried to achieve this integration is again peculiar to him and his philosophical project.[93]

Cicero tells us practically nothing about the philosophical considerations which moved Antiochus to convert from Academic scepticism to his own brand of dogmatism (see on *Luc.* 69–70).[94] As a consequence, one can only try and infer from what

---

[90] Reid's suggestion is discussed by Glucker (1997: 73). Cf. *Att.* 13.12.3 (= SB 320 = T18).
[91] I are unable to follow, with respect to *Luc.*, the source-critical analysis on which Glucker's account is predicated; see section 9.3.
[92] See e.g. Karamanolis (2006: 44–84), with ample references to earlier literature.
[93] On the reception of Aristotle in Antiochus and Cicero, see also Long (1995); Chiaradonna (2013); Dillon (2016).
[94] We know about some arguments Antiochus uniquely cited against the Academics (*Luc.* 28–9 and 109), as well as about some of the anti-sceptical arguments he cited alongside other dogmatists (see the

we know about the Old Academy as Antiochus construed it what motivated Antiochus to include Aristotle in the first place.

Further, one may wonder (i) about the extent to which Antiochus engaged directly with Aristotelian writings and (ii) about the extent to which Cicero would have been able to form an independent view on any contribution Aristotle made to Antiochus' outlook. For—*ad* (ii)—while we know that Cicero had extensive direct knowledge of Platonic dialogues,[95] his knowledge of Aristotle appears to have been much less developed. Remarks about the attractiveness of Aristotle's style are best explained by assuming that Cicero knew dialogues of Aristotle. These have not come down to us except in fairly exiguous fragments. It has been a matter of debate if Cicero had direct knowledge of Aristotelian treatises, but in any event no plausible case has been made that Cicero drew directly and substantially on any Aristotelian treatise.[96] Contrast the close intertextual relationship of *Ac.* 1.24–9 and 1.30–2 with Platonic dialogues (see ad loc.). Nor—*ad* (i)—is there an 'Antiochian' passage in Cicero or elsewhere which the modern reader is able to link directly with a particular Aristotelian text irrespective of what was or was not transparent to Cicero the author.[97]

The question then becomes whether Antiochus' view of the history of philosophy as well as his considered position owed something to Aristotle in some looser sense and what Aristotle as a joint figurehead of the Old Academy delivered for Antiochus.

Cicero links Aristotle with argument on either side of a question, albeit not with sceptical *in utramque partem* argument in particular (*Tusc.* 2.9), a connection for which there is also non-Ciceronian evidence going back to Aristotle's own *Topics*.[98] Aristotle, and more specifically a version of Aristotelian rhetorical theory, is also associated with the rhetorical teaching of Philo to which Cicero was exposed in Rome.[99] Since we have no reason to think that Philo's interest in rhetoric only arose when he formulated the Roman Books view, it seems legitimate to push it further back chronologically, nearer the period when I assume that Antiochus began to move away from his sceptical stance while still a pupil of Philo's in the Academy. Philo will not have invoked Aristotle as a factor in the formulation of his philosophical stance in the narrow sense, e.g. by making him a sceptic, but any invocation of him, in tracing the intellectual ancestry of his rhetorical teachings or in the—to us—murky borderline area between his rhetorical and ethical lecturing, might have signalled to Antiochus that he ought to account for Aristotle.

Aristotle's most important contribution to the Antiochian view lies in the field of ethics, viz. in the τέλος favoured over the Stoic one (see on *Ac.* 1.19–23). Given our very limited knowledge of the ethical views notably of Polemo, who is accorded an important role in Antiochus' construction of the ethical views of his Old Academy, and our limited knowledge of what Antiochus knew about him, it is difficult to say to what extent Antiochus could have fashioned his ethical theory with recourse to

---

commentary on Lucullus' speech passim). Unless one interprets the former as revelatory of how Antiochus progressively acquired his dogmatic stance (see e.g. Karamanolis 2006: 49), they do not speak to the reasons for his conversion.

[95] See the collection in DeGraff (1940).
[96] See Barnes (1997c); Irwin (2012).   [97] See Chiaradonna (2013).
[98] See Alex. Aphr. *in Arist. Top.* pp. 27.11–12, 584.9–11 Wallies.
[99] See Reinhardt (2000); Brittain (2001: 296–342).

Polemo alone. As it is, the Peripatetic doctrine of the *tria genera bonorum*,[100] for which 'Aristotle' is not an illegitimate shorthand, stands as an equally important component alongside Polemo's contribution.

In the field of epistemology, Aristotle is credited with a role in the formation of the 'correct' interpretation of Forms (see on *Ac.* 1.33b); if my interpretation is correct, he took them to be not innate concepts as the *prima forma* would have it, but as concepts which have arisen from experience. The crucial passage on said *prima forma*, *Ac.* 1.30–2, has Platonic intertexts and only tags on at the end a remark about the relationship between rhetoric and dialectical argument which corresponds to the first sentence of Aristotle's *Rhet.*

§15

Tum Varro ita exorsus est: 'Socrates mihi uidetur...nihil tamen ad bene uiuendum': Varro introduces here what is the most famous item of doxography (cf. *constat inter omnes*) in the ancient biographical tradition on Socrates; it goes back to Xen., *Mem.* 1.1.4, 1.1.11–12, and 4.7.6, with which cf. *Tusc.* 5.10, 3.8; *Brut.* 31; and *Leg.* 1.56 (a shorthand reference, indicative of the deep familiarity of the motif). See also the Pyrrhonist Timon of Phlius (*c.*320–235 BC) as reported in Sextus, *M.* 7.8; on him Clayman (2009) and (2016). Further, Plt., *Phd.* 96–9, on Socrates' early aspirations in natural science (with Menn 2010), and the reaction to it in Arist., *Met.* A6, 987b1–2; *Phdr.* 229e–230a6. Finally, Sen., *Ep. mor.* 71.7; with Inwood (2007: 187).

In *Rep.* 1.15 Scipio expresses doubts about Panaetius' readiness to engage in physical speculation and to make confident pronouncements on physical matters. He cites Socrates' wise refusal to be interested in physics, on the grounds that the subject was too difficult and irrelevant to a human life. Tubero replies (1.15) that he cannot understand how tradition could hand down this conception of Socrates when it was plain from Platonic dialogues that Socrates thought moral issues could not be separated from mathematics and *harmonia* (as was also Pythagoras' practice). In reply, Scipio (1.16) insists that Socrates was only interested in moral questions, and that Plato first became impressed by Pythagoreanism on his journeys and then, out of affection for Socrates, credited him with views and interests which properly belonged to Pythagoras. This is one of the moments when the ancient evidence comes close to posing the so-called Socratic question about the dividing line between the historical Socrates and the character created by Plato. (A different, historically more influential distinction is drawn by Arist., *S.E.* 34, 183b6–8.) Burkert (1972a: 94–5) suggests that Scipio's proposal for 'reading' the Platonic Socrates reflects a sceptical Academic interpretation of Plato, on the grounds that the Academy had a need to isolate the elenctic, sceptical Socrates, but for this to be credible *Plato's* Pythagorean interests would have to be subject to some kind of sceptical proviso. For, the argument goes, while Academics must have deemed it desirable to bring Socrates into the Academic fold, it was mandatory for them to do so with respect to Plato. There is no suggestion

---

[100] See Inwood (2014).

of a sceptical Plato with mere Pythagorean interests (as opposed to beliefs) in *Rep.* 1.16, but the passage's concerns lie elsewhere so that the omission is not telling; see also Burkert (ibid.) on different responses by Platonists (broadly construed) to the Pythagorean element in Plato over time. In general, Scipio in *Rep.* 1.16 does not characterize the 'historical' Socrates as he sees him in enough detail for us to be able to tell whether he is identical with the Socrates of *Ac.* 1.16, but this possibility is not precluded, either. Glucker (1997: 83–7) suggested, contra Burkert, that Antiochus might have devised the story of *Rep.* 1.16. One can at least see why Antiochus could have done this, given what is said about the Old Academy in *Ac.* 1.15–18. In response to a question of how the conception of Socrates in evidence here would accommodate the Pythagorean-sounding pronouncements of Socrates, Antiochus might have suggested that Plato, rich in content as he was, ascribed his own Pythagorean interests (as opposed to beliefs) to Socrates. *Fin.* 5.87 is a summary statement of the story relayed in *Rep.* 1.16.

Mihi uidetur, at the very beginning of Varro's speech, should not be taken to signal qualified endorsement. *Auocare* is without the connotation of sorcery which the term can have, *pace* Reid[2] p. 17, who translates 'charmed away'. For the obscurity of the cosmological questions which exercised the Presocratics (*a rebus occultis*, with Reid[1] p. 109 on *procul esse a nostra cognitione* below) see *Ac.* 1.19; *Luc.* 122 (in §123 the further point is made that physical knowledge would be useless even if it was available, cf. *si maxime*...here). Reid[1] p. 109 rejects the suggestion by Ursinus (1581) to delete *ab* in *ab ipsa natura* with reference to the strong personification of *natura*, which requires the marked indication of agency which the instrumental ablative would not provide. Varro as an Antiochian is committed to some notion of providential organization of the universe (cf. *Ac.* 1.29), but as in the case of *mihi uidetur*, it seems not advisable to scrutinize his words for doctrinal commitments at this early stage of his speech. With *uita communis* 'ordinary life', cf. *De orat.* 1.248; *Lael.* 18. *Omnino* merely signals that the subject of goods and evils is a broader one than that of virtues and vices, *pace* Reid (1885: 109). *Caelestia* = οὐράνια and δαιμόνια in Xen., *Mem.* 1.1.4, 1.1.11–12, 4.7.6; cf. *Tusc.* 5.10; *Brut.* 31; Sen., *Ep. mor.* 71.7 (see above, p. 125). With *nihil tamen ad bene uiuendum* (which does not require the addition of an infinitive), cf. D.L. 2.21 (from the Life of Socrates): γνόντα δὲ τὴν φυσικὴν θεωρίαν μηδὲν εἶναι πρὸς ἡμᾶς, τὰ ἠθικὰ φιλοσοφεῖν ἐπί τε τῶν ἐργαστηρίων καὶ ἐν τῇ ἀγορᾷ, '[Demetrius of Byzantium relates...] that he discussed moral questions in the workshops and the market-place, being convinced that the study of nature is no concern of ours' (transl. Hicks).

§16

Hic in omnibus fere sermonibus...non arbitrari sese scire quod nesciat: Varro cites—here at the beginning and again at the end of the paragraph—dialogues written by the Socratics in general in support of his conception of Socrates (whose pupils, the implication is, agreed on what his approach was), but, as noted above, this stands in tension with Varro's alluding to one particular passage in one particular text.

The result of Varro following Plato in particular is a Socrates who is clear on the respect in which he thinks he can be called wise (*he* does not make unwarranted knowledge claims) and who disavows knowledge except for one second-order knowledge claim (i.e. that he knows nothing). However, that the Platonic version of the story is referenced here in §16 does not mean that it is accurately represented. On the question of whether *Apol.* 21b (οὔτε μέγα οὔτε σμικρὸν σύνοιδα ἐμαυτῷ σοφὸς ὤν) does actually say something other than 'I know that I know nothing', Burnyeat (1997: 290-1) comments: 'Not only are the verb phrases σύνοιδα ἐμαυτῷ and σοφὸς ὤν different from each other, but σύνοιδα ἐμαυτῷ may mean something less than "I know" and σοφὸς ὤν may mean something more than "I know", since σοφός usually indicates an expertise or specialized knowledge that most people do not have. There are plenty of reasons for thinking that in the *Apology* Socrates' declaration of ignorance is more nuanced than "I know that I know nothing".' See also Fine (2008), in part concerned with the reception history of the declaration.

According to Xenophon's *Apol.* 14, the oracle's pronouncement was somewhat different from what Varro derives from Plato here: Χαιρεφῶντος γάρ ποτε ἐπερωτῶντος ἐν Δελφοῖς περὶ ἐμοῦ πολλῶν παρόντων ἀνεῖλεν ὁ Ἀπόλλων μηδένα εἶναι ἀνθρώπων ἐμοῦ μήτε ἐλευθεριώτερον μήτε δικαιότερον μήτε σωφρονέστερον, 'Once when Chairephon made an enquiry about me in Delphi, Apollo answered, in the presence of many people, that no man was more free, more just, and more prudent than me.' Contrast Plt., *Apol.* 21a: ἀνεῖλεν οὖν ἡ Πυθία μηδένα σοφώτερον εἶναι. Brief references to the oracle tend to agree with the Platonic version (D.L. 2.37; Schol. *in Arist. Nub.* 114).

With *nisi id ipsum*, cf. the portrayal of the εἴρων in Philod., *De vitiis* col. xx.20-2 Jensen, clearly inspired by Socrates (see Opsomer 1998a: 114, esp. n. 160): ἐγὼ γὰρ | οἶδα τί πλ[ήν γε] τούτου ὅτι [οὐ-]|δὲν οἶδα, 'What do I know, except for the fact that I know nothing.'

The adverbs *uarie copioseque* modifying *perscripti* convey a different point from §17 *uarius et multiplex et copiosus* (of Plato) and *Platonis ubertate*: the dialogues of the Socratics (see next note), for all their diversity and persuasive detail, agree in their representation of Socrates. Both properties, it is implied, increase their value as evidence. Reid[1] p. 110 notes on *perscripti*: 'The word implies an assumption that the discourses ascribed to Socrates by his pupils were really delivered by him'; cf. *TLL* s.v. col. 1671.35-44 on the use in connection with the creation of formal records. For the idea that the Σωκρατικοὶ λόγοι should be filed under 'mimetic art', see already Arist., *Poet.* 6, 1449b38.

Socrates is characterized by a particular practice of arguing which is then described in a consecutive clause (not a final clause, i.e. *ita disputat ut nihil*... does not give an insight into Socrates' intention). One of the effects of Socrates' technique is that he ends up refuting others (*refellat alios*), sc. who took themselves to be experts in their fields. Contrast *Luc.* 15 (where another Antiochian speaker, Lucullus, takes Socrates to be ironic and to hold, as *Luc.* 74 shows, substantial beliefs): *Socrates...plus tribuebat iis quos uolebat refellere*. This conveys a desire to refute, which, although it need not logically stem from a conviction that one is in possession of the truth (i.e. of substantial true beliefs rather than a mere awareness of one's lack of knowledge), is probably so intended; see section 7.3 on Socrates in *Acad*. Note that *in omnibus fere sermonibus* suggests that Socrates is not presented as adopting the practice in question in all Socratic texts; see Glucker (1997: 75) on this point.

Reid[2] p. 17, like Ioppolo (1995: 119), mistranslates *id ipsum*, by making it the antecedent of *quod* as well as the object of *scire* rather than just the latter, treating *eoque praestare ceteris* as parenthetical: '...he possesses no knowledge himself but this (and this is which gives him his superiority over the rest), that men imagine themselves to know what they know not...'; as Burnyeat (1997: 291 n. 34) notes, on this translation Socrates ends up claiming knowledge of two things rather than one.

Schütz (1829) emended *dictum* to *iudicatum*, evidently assuming a gloss. I print *hominis* (*Γ*) in *quod haec esset una hominis sapientia* rather than *omnis* (P); the latter, while clearly not impossible (and printed e.g. by Reid[1] p. 111), comes close to being otiose, while *hominis* gains some point from its contrast with *Apolline*. On the tense of *quod esset*, *haec una* for *hoc unum*, and the indefinite force of *sese*, see Reid ibid.

Quae cum diceret constanter...ut e Socraticorum libris maximeque Platonis intellegi potest: *in ea sententia permanere*, a standing phrase, can in principle mean 'to persist in a view/opinion' or 'to persist in the pronouncement of a view', in which case the subject may or may not endorse the view in question (as would not be unusual in political contexts). Here the latter sense would just repeat *quae cum diceret constanter*, which does not seem to need special emphasis, and *sententia* stands in contrast with *oratio* (see below), so the former sense is more likely to be intended. There would still be only one substantial belief in Socrates' *sententia*, i.e. the one corresponding to his one knowledge claim, that he knows nothing. It is, however, in fact not true that the dialogues at least of Plato, who is singled out (*maximeque Platonis*), are full of meta-philosophical statements along the lines of Plt., Apol. 21.

Tamen (printed by Gruter), an emendation (ascribed to his *s* by Plasberg[2]) for the transmitted *tam*, yields the best sense (with Davies's *tantum* being a possibility, too; see Glucker 1997: 74). Despite having no substantial beliefs, Socrates had moral intuitions, sc. on the Socrates conception employed here. *Tamen* should not be taken to signal that, contrary to his pronouncements, substantial moral beliefs on Socrates' part governed his argumentative practice; see the general note above.

For the phrase *oratio consumitur in re*, cf. Fat. 2: *omnis fere nostra in his deliberationibus consumebatur oratio*, but the point of *oratio* here is a different one: despite making only one knowledge claim, Socrates manifestly had moral preoccupations and intuitions, and these showed up in the subjects he wanted to discuss. However, these moral intuitions did not come up to the status of a belief as defined or understood in the context of the current debate. Ioppolo (1995: 118–21) holds that the sentence suggests that Antiochus ascribed positive doctrines to Socrates, but only in the field of ethics. See also Glucker (1997: 83) on Fin. 5.84. The present passage does not say, but also does not preclude, if Socrates as construed had epistemological intuitions in addition to his moral ones, like a commitment to rationality; see on Ac. 1.44–6. On the need to motivate dialectical activity, see sections 4 and 7.5.

The Socratics as a group are mentioned in Cicero from the earliest time; cf. Inv. 1.51 and 1.61, which are well integrated with their context and do not look like attempts to enhance the rhetorical material from which Cicero was working secondarily. In general, there seems to be no single point of entry for Cicero's exposure to them. The most substantial discussion is in De orat. 3.56–73, where they feature in a brief historical account guided by the question of rhetoric's relationship to philosophy. Socrates is there made responsible for splitting rhetoric from a broader conception of wisdom, and since most schools avowedly acknowledged a debt to Socrates, their attitude to rhetoric tended to be negative. On the term, see Mankin (2011: 153): '...in Cic. *Socraticus* normally indicates a first-hand connection with the historical Socrates: it is used of philosophers who heard his *ipsa uerba* [refs.], of what they recalled of his conversations..., methods..., manner..., and ideas, and of books they wrote about these things...'; Sedley (2014: 101–2) on the term Σωκρατικοί and Hor., *A.P.* 310 *Socraticae...chartae*. Plato is explicitly counted among the Socratics also in *Tusc.* 2.8. Their fragments and testimonia are collected by Giannantoni (1991).

§17

Platonis autem auctoritate...qui rebus congruentes nominibus differebant: the sentence by itself might suggest that Plato, whose writings were varied and complex (for such was his thinking, too), devised a single *forma* of philosophy, which was then adopted by Academics and Peripatetics alike, who merely differed in name. As the paragraph continues, however, it becomes clear that this is not what is meant, that the passive *instituta est*, obscuring agency, is not just a manner of speaking and that the phrase *Platonis auctoritate* is not just a periphrasis for *a Platone*: Plato's authority is the source of the *forma*, whose actual extraction from his rich and complex writings was performed by the early Academics and Peripatetics. In their own view, they were licensed to claim that the doctrines they came up with were in some sense in Plato and had Platonic authority, but Antiochus takes them to be the product of a—quite literally creative—act of interpretation. *Auctoritate* is a causal or instrumental ablative, in that Plato's authority is the source or motivating reason for the establishment of the *forma*; e.g. Reid[2] and Gigon translate in this way, although their overall interpretation differs from my own. Brittain (2006) opts for paraphrase (and also an interpretation that differs from my own): 'Following Plato's complex and eloquent lead...'; for *auctoritas* = 'guidance, lead', see *OLD* s.v. no. 5. A legal sense, which one might consider given the occurence of *heres* below, seems precluded in that it would suggest action on instruction or with permission. Cf. *Tusc.* 5.34, where a central Stoic tenet is said to derive its weight *a Platonis auctoritate*, without the implication that it was a Platonic view: *Et si Zeno Citieus, aduena quidam et ignobilis uerborum opifex, insinuasse se in antiquam philosophiam uidetur, huius sententiae grauitas a Platonis auctoritate repetatur, apud quem saepe haec oratio usurpata est, ut nihil praeter uirtutem diceretur bonum*; Sedley (1997b) and Schofield (2018) on the construal and transfer of authority more generally in the period and in Cicero respectively; and Heinze (1925). Contrast the cluster of *auctoritas* terminology in *Ac.* 1.33–4, notably §33 *Peripateticorum et Academiae ueteris auctoritas*, where the noun means 'opinion' (see ad loc.). For Antiochus' construction of his Old Academy, see the introduction, section 7.2.

Reid[1] pp. 111–12 has a detailed note on verbal parallels for *uarius et multiplex* (and similar phrases), but none of them illustrates the specific feature which must be meant here: the rich and polysemous nature of Plato's work (which is but reflected in stylistic richness and variety). For the idea that Plato is rich and requires interpretation but that there is, ultimately, a coherent set of views to be extracted from him, cf. Stob., *Ecl.* II.7, pp. 55.5–7 Wachsmuth: Πλάτων πολύφωνος ὤν, οὐχ ὥς τινες οἴονται πολύδοξος, πολλαχῶς διῄρηται τἀγαθόν, 'Given that Plato has many voices, but not, as some think, many views, there are multiple divisions of the good' [there follow such divisions]. On the Platonic dialogue as a κόσμος that can be read on many levels, see Anon., *Proleg. phil. Plat.* 4.15.1–19 Westerink; Layne (2018: 543–54).

The phrase *duobus uocabulis* is best taken as an *ablatiuus qualitatis*, in which case *una et consentiens* = 'single and consistent (form) of two different names'; see *TLL* s.v. *consentio* col. 400.5–7. If taken as a dative going with *consentiens*, the sense could only be 'uniform and corresponding/answering to two names', for which use of *consentire* there are no good parallels. The resumption of *uocabulis* by *nominibus* below suggests that the two words are used interchangeably here; but see also on *Ac.* 1.37: *ut haec non tam rebus quam uocabulis....* With *forma philosophiae*, cf. *Ac.* 1.23 (i.e. the end of the ethics section): *haec quidem fuit apud eos morum institutio et eius partis quam primam posui forma et descriptio* (cf. *descriptio* here in §17); 1.33: *haec erat illis prima forma a Platone tradita* (where *forma* is an emendation); and section 7.2 of the introduction. For the Antiochian strategy of claiming substantial agreement but differences in terminology, here applied to schools, elsewhere to particular doctrines, cf. *De orat.* 2.136, 3.67; *Fin.* 4.5, 5.14, 5.21; *Leg.* 1.38 and 1.55. Reid[1] p. 112 rightly points to *Fin.* 4.2, where Antiochus' Old Academy is linked to an inner core of Aristotle, Theophrastus, Speusippus, Xenocrates, and Polemo, but e.g. *Ac.* 1.34 suggests that other figures esp. on the Academic side are recognized and can be included when the aim is to give, or be seen to give, a detailed account, or an account on a different level of description.

Nam cum Speusippum sororis filium ... e loci uocabulo nomen habuerunt: the sentence aims to substantiate the claim that Peripatetics and Old Academics differed only in name with reference to the biographies of the main players; secondarily, it introduces a distinction between Speusippus on the one hand and Xenocrates and Aristotle on the other. Grammatically, it is a temporal *cum*-clause followed by a main clause, with both clauses falling into roughly two halves. The subordinate clause becomes very hard to make sense of if one does not assume a lacuna after *Stagiritem* in which a characterization of Xenocrates and Aristotle stood, balancing *quasi heredem*. Witness how Reid, who does not assume that something has dropped out, translates (in Reid[2]) as if *reliquisset* was construed in the first part of the *cum*-clause with a double accusative and in the second with a simple object ('for after Plato had left behind him his sister's son Speusippus as a kind of heir to his philosophy, and two other pupils whose zeal and learning were preeminent, Xenocrates of Calchedon, and Aristotle of Stageira; those who associated with Aristotle received the name of Peripatetics, because...'); but *autem* suggests a contrast. Gigon supplies *auditores* before *Xenocratem* and translates as if Xenocrates and Aristotle had been named heirs, too. Brittain (2006: 93) moves quite far away from the Latin: 'Plato, you see, left Speusippus, his sister's son, as the heir of his philosophy, ⟨but his work was inherited⟩ by two men of outstanding energy and learning....' While Antiochian speakers can play up or play down the significance of particular Old Academics and

Peripatetics depending on context (see below), the overall rationale of the present passage and *Luc.* 137 (*Aristoteles aut Xenocrates quos Antiochus sequi uolebat*...), which may well be looking to the passage in the *Catulus* corresponding to *Ac.* 1.17 (for Aristotle and Xenocrates do not feature in Lucullus' speech), suggests that Aristotle and Xenocrates are here presented as privileged creators of the *forma philosophiae*. (Another passage which brackets the two, as creators of a *finis bonorum*, is *Fin.* 4.15.) Further, given *heredem* and *formula* below, it is reasonable to expect a legal term apt to characterize their role. This reduces the options for what could have stood in the lacuna. *Successor* in the legal sense would usually be a looser term for *heres* and not deliver a contrast. *Curatores* does contrast with *heres*, but is used of those entrusted with a caretaking role when the heir is mute, insane, or profligate. *Procuratores* (*omnium bonorum*) is a more natural term (used by Cicero in *Rep.* 2.51, but not in a contrast); see Kaser (1971: 265–6); Zimmermann (1996: 53–4, 417–18).

The downgrading which Speusippus suffers here in §17 is not paralleled in non-Ciceronian evidence. In §34 Speusippus and Xenocrates appear to be given the 'joint custody' role which Aristotle and Xenocrates have here in §17; there, however, Academics and Peripatetics are treated separately and one by one, and Varro endeavours to be comprehensive.

Reid[1] routinely assumes that *quasi* signals translations of Greek terms and thus glosses (p. 112) *quasi heredem* 'no doubt a translation of διάδοχον'. On *duo* vs *duos*, see Leumann (1977: 485–6). For the spelling of *Calchedonius*, see *TLL* s.v. col. 73.2–12; p. lxxiv of the Oxford Classical Text on that of *Stagiritem*; *OLD* s.v. no. 2 on *Lycium*. For the bilingual play on the etymology of *Peripatetici*, cf. *De orat.* 3.109. Parallels for the considerable distance between *erant* and *soliti* are assembled by Reid[1] p. 113.

The fragments of Speusippus and Xenocrates are collected in Isnardi Parente (1980) and (1981) respectively; see also *eadem* (2016) and (2018). On Xenocrates, see further Dörrie (1967); Krämer (1983: 44–72); Dillon (2003: 89–155); and Thiel (2006).

Sed utrique Platonis ubertate completi...et nulla adfirmatione adhibita consuetudinem disserendi reliquerunt: for the use of *utrique*, see *OLD* s.v. *uterque* no. 3b (contrast Gigon, who translates as if two *formulae* were being generated, which cannot be the intended meaning; cf. e.g. *Ac.* 1.23 *fin.*). For *ubertas* = 'richness in content' as opposed to stylistic richness, see *OLD* s.v. no. 3b: as the wider context makes clear (*uarius et multiplex et copiosus* above), *ubertas* is specifically the capacity to enable and support complex readings, arguments, and theories not necessarily consistent with each other (hence the need for privileged interpreters). For the collocation *ubertas/copia* in the stylistic sense, cf. e.g. *De orat.* 1.50; *Brut.* 44. *Completi* suggests a deep familiarity with Plato's writings and thinking; cf. *De orat.* 3.121: *non enim solum acuenda nobis neque procudenda lingua est, sed onerandum complendumque pectus maximarum rerum et plurimarum suauitate, copia, uarietate.*

Formula has been translated 'code of doctrine' (Reid[1]), 'rule of doctrine' (Rackham 1951), 'eine eigene Art der philosophischen Lehre (in einem vollständigen und umfassenden System)' (Gigon), 'system of teaching' (Brittain 2006), 'definitely formulated rule of doctrine' (Dillon 2016: 183). A *formula* is, in its primary meaning, 'an official instruction from the praetor to the judge hearing a particular case. It spelled out who the parties were, what the issues were, and what range of decisions could be handed down by the judge' (Riggsby 2010: 268). Inherent to the concept of a *formula* is that it distils the complexities of the case (as well as, at another remove, of similar cases like it if a pre-existent *formula* is used) into an instruction for the judge; cf. Kaser and Hackl (1996: 152): 'Die *formula* legt zwar gleichfalls [sc. like the *legis actiones*] das Streitprogramm fest, das der Magistrat und die Parteien aushandeln und dem sie sich unterwerfen. Aber die *formula* enthält nicht mehr unmittelbar die einzelnen Erklärungen der Parteien und des Magistrats, sondern faßt das Ergebnis dieser Verhandlung in einem Bericht zusammen; einem objektiv gefaßten Protokoll, das als Satzung und zugleich als Anweisung und Informationsquelle für das Urteilsgericht zu dienen hat.' The process of abstraction by which the *praetor*, having listened to the parties involved, devises (or, in practice in most cases, identifies) the *formula* under which the case presented is to be dealt with by the *iudex* is thus compared to the manner in which Plato's immediate successors as well as Aristotle (and leading Peripatetics) derive an *ars quaedam philosophiae* from the riches of Platonic thought and writing. Reid[1] p. 113 in the app. crit. wonders if *formula* is corrupted from *forma* ('nam hoc *formulae* uerbum magis aptum est ad unum quoddam praeceptum'), but as explained, a *formula* is neither a straightforward precept for a particular and specific course of action, nor is the fact that it is formally an injunction salient here. The word *descriptio* below does not support *formula* over *forma*, as one might think, given Ac. 1.23 *fin.*: *forma atque descriptio*. For another creative but different use of *formula*, cf. *Off.* 3.19–20 (with Dyck 1996: 519–21); a detailed discussion of the *actio de dolo* is in *Off.* 3.58–60, on which see ter Beek (2006). Further Kübler (1895); Mantovani (1999[2]). That the process of identifying the *ars philosophiae* is neither reductive nor yields a reductive result is signalled by *plenam ac refertam*; for the collocation of adjectives, cf. *Sest.* 23. One might ask whether *formula* corresponds closely to a term which Antiochus used; possible candidates include σχῆμα, ὑποφραφή, and ὑποτύπωσις. None of these terms appears to have had a relevant legal use (see LSJ; Preisigke 1915).

Componere, used to denote the assembling of *formulae* from components, is used in Gaius, *Inst.* 4.60 (*formula quae in factum composita est*), and D. 1.2.2.6–7 refers several times to *actiones compositae* (which can be read as references to *formulae*). Another verb used to describe the creation of a *formula* is *concipere* (cf. *TLL* s.v. *concipio* col. 55.7–21); cf. Gai., *Inst.* 4.30, which makes the point that *formulae* were assembled by selecting discrete components. I am indebted to Professor Ernest Metzger for giving me his views on §17.

With the characterization of Socratic manner abandoned by the Old Academy, cf. *Inv.* 2.10: *Quare nos quidem sine ulla affirmatione simul quaerentes dubitanter unum quicque dicemus, ne, dum paruulum consequamur, ut satis haec commode perscripsisse uideamur, illud amittamus, quod maximum est, ut ne cui rei temere atque arroganter assenserimus*, on which see section 8. Having the intuitions or interests which drive Socrates' questioning on ethical matters (see §16 *fin.*) is evidently compatible with *nullam affirmationem adhibere*, i.e. these intuitions are not the result of acts of assent (included in *affirmatio* here). It might seem surprising that Varro claims that the departure from Socrates came with the Old Academics rather than Plato himself, but grammatically that is what the text says (*reliquerunt*). Dörrie (1987: 466–8) noted that the *ueteres* do not, for Antiochus, include Plato himself; this is disputed by Barnes (1997: 78 n. 98). Reid[1] prints *dubitationem*, which takes emphasis away from the argumentative practice, *consuetudo disserendi*. Two attributes side by side (*Socraticam dubitantem*) seems inelegant. The text as corrected by Baiter (1863) has two adverbial phrases of roughly equal weight. On the conception of doubt underlying ancient sceptical practice see Vogt (2015a: 262–5).

Ita facta est...ars quaedam philosophiae et rerum ordo et descriptio disciplinae: the Socrates of this section is the Academic one, and his conception of philosophy is clearly not that of an *ars philosophiae*. This leaves it again somewhat unclear where Plato stood on these two fundamentally different conceptions of philosophy; see sections 7.3 and 7.4.

The body of doctrines which, depending on perspective, the Old Academy constructed out of or extracted from Plato's writings is in §18 referred to by a series of semantically overlapping but not coextensive terms or phrasal terms: *forma, formula*; *ars quaedam philosophiae, rerum ordo, descriptio disciplinae*. A craft or art (*ars*; τέχνη) is an ordered body of knowledge (a σύστημα καταλήψεων; see Bronowski 2019: 52–80), which is usually—depending on the domain of the art—arrived at by abstraction from countless cases which ex hypothesi order themselves into species. This is e.g. how doctors arrive at the concept of a particular medical condition, which is then articulated so as to yield a definition; see Barnes (2015b). A *descriptio* is, in its primary sense, a drawing (geometrical, architectural, astrological), which depending on subject matter carries connotations of being a representation or an abstraction from a more complex reality, then more loosely a scheme or outline; *pace* Reid[1] 114: 'the same in sense as *forma, formula* above'. *Disciplina* here 'system' rather than 'school', although dogmatic schools can be identified by their system; cf. the next sentence, the similar use of αἵρεσις, and *Luc.* 15: (Plato)... *reliquit perfectissimam disciplinam, Peripateticos et Academicos nominibus differentes re congruentes*.

Disserendi in P before *est* is mistakenly repeated from the preceding sentence.

§18

Quae quidem erat primo duobus...et illam ueterem Academiam differebat: *quae*, presumably sc. *disciplina*. Cicero uses *illam ueterem Academiam* presumably for variation, given Ac. 1.17 *Academicorum et Peripateticorum*. Outside of contexts concerned with the history of the Academy and where the speaker is an Antiochian, *Academici* is used for sceptical Academics; cf. Glucker (1978: 103–5).

Several ancient divisions of the Academy are in evidence; see the comprehensive but concise collection of material in Görler (1994: 779–81), as well as Wyss (2005: 193–204), who gives all relevant texts with German translation and commentary; Glucker (1978: 344–7); Gigante in Isnardi Parente (1980: 11–25). The character Cicero, who is an Academic, does not recognize a distinction between Old Academy and New Academy (Ac. 1.46), and his persona in the letters makes fun of the notion of a new Academy (*Fam.* 9.8.1, the dedicatory letter to Varro = SB 254 = T29: *os huius adolescentioris Academiae*); for him the Academy starts with Plato, who was a sceptic, Plato's successors are marginal figures (see section 7.1), and Arcesilaus, Carneades, etc. stand directly in Plato's tradition. Antiochian speakers obviously recognize an Old Academy and call the sceptical Academy the New Academy (*Ac.* 1.13; *Fin.* 5.7). Varro, in Augustine's report drawing on the *De philosophia* (Aug., *C.D.* 19.1–3), treats the distinction as established. There is no evidence suggesting that it goes back to someone other and earlier than Antiochus, and as long as the Academy was sceptical, the distinction could only have been made by an outsider. Another division posits an Old, a Middle, and a New Academy. There are two versions, both of which agree that the Middle Academy begins with Arcesilaus. They differ in that one lets the New Academy begin with Lacydes (*Index. Acad.* xxi.37–42 = Lakydes T 2b Mette; D.L. 1.14, 1.19, 4.59, cf. Suda s.v. Λακύδης no. 72 Adler), the other with Carneades (Sext., *P.H.* 1.220–1; Ps.-Gal., *Hist. phil.* 3 = DDG pp. 599.11–600.4; Clem., *Strom.* 1.14.64.1). Cicero shows awareness of neither, and Görler (1994: 780) suspects that both tripartite divisions were developed independently after the creation of Antiochus' Old Academy. Sextus (*P.H.* 1.220–1) and Ps.-Galen (*Hist. phil.* 3 = DDG p. 600.3–4) also know a fivefold division in which the third Academy begins with Carneades, the fourth with Philo, and the fifth with Antiochus, with traces of an earlier fourfold division which does not separate Philo from Carneades being preserved in Numenius (cf. Eus., *Praep. Ev.* XIV.7.15 = Numenius frg. 26 Des Places and XIV.9.3 = frg. 28 Des Places). Numenius used sources considerably earlier than himself (he wrote in the second half of the second century AD), but the origins of the more extensive divisions are not traceable. In *P.H.* 1.220–1 the different phases of the Academy are connected with different readings of Plato; see Vogt (2014: 483).

Abundantia quadam ingeni praestabat…et eadem rerum expetendarum fugiendarumque partitio: cf. *De orat.* 3.67 for a similar comparison of Aristotle with his contemporaries: *Reliqui sunt Peripatetici et Academici; quamquam Academicorum nomen est unum, sententiae duae; nam Speusippus Platonis sororis filius et Xenocrates, qui Platonem audierat, et qui Xenocratem Polemo et Crantor, nihil ab Aristotele, qui una audierat Platonem, magno opere dissensit; copia fortasse et uarietate dicendi pares non fuerunt*; Reid[1] p. 114 for parallels to the phrase *abundantia ingenii*.

That Plato is termed the *fons* of Academics and Peripatetics alike (*utrisque*) is compatible with the idea that the *ars philosophiae* needs to be extracted from his work by privileged interpreters; cf. *sed utrique Platonis ubertate completi* above. Reid[1] p. 114 thinks, with reference to *De orat.* 1.42 (*philosophorum greges iam ab illo fonte at capite Socrate*), that Socrates is the *fons*.

Varro ends on the shared view regarding choices and avoidances (cf. *Ac.* 1.6 above). This does not (*pace* Sedley 2002: 48) mean that the preceding two paragraphs only told the story of the Old Academy with a view to ethical questions; rather, the phrase is forward-looking and sets up the ethical discussion (§§19–23), to be continued after the intermezzo in §18b.

Reid[1] p. 114 aptly comments that the claim of a fundamental agreement of Peripatetics and Academics in the field of ethics is enabled by the jettisoning of Platonic metaphysics: 'In maintaining the identity of Platonic and Aristotelian ethics,

Antiochus left out of account the ideal theory with its Idea of the Good, which had in his time become obsolete practically, so that the similarity between the two systems seemed greater than it was'; see also Boys-Stones (2012) and on *Ac.* 1.30–33a below.

On the word order of *mihi quidem uidetur* and on *rerum expetendarum fugiendarumque* = αἱρετῶν καὶ φευκτῶν, see Reid[1] p. 114.

Sed quid ago...quisquis Mineruam docet: Reid[1] pp. 114–15 aptly comments on the conventional self-correction (*sed quid ago?*), on which see also Chahoud (2016: 219), the relative clause with causal force but an indicative verb (*qui haec uos doceo*), the ellipsis with *inepte* (sc. *facit*), and the Latin version of a Greek proverb (ὗς ποτ' Ἀθηναίαν ἔριν ἤρισεν; cf. Theocr. 5.23), which Cicero also uses in *De orat.* 2.233 and *Fam.* 9.18.3 = SB 191. On Theocr. 5.23, see also Gow (1952: 99): 'used...of those who teach their grandmothers.'

Strikingly, Cicero uses a similar proverb (in Greek) in *Fam.* 9.3 (= SB 176) in a letter to Varro written shortly before the battle of Thapsus (and the first in the series of letters to Varro preserved in *Fam.* 9), at the end of the letter, with a gesture of self-correction, and cutting short a meditation on the pursuit of scholarship (*Sed quid ego nunc haec ad te, cuius domi nascuntur,* γλαῦκ' εἰς Ἀθήνας?). It is unlikely that Cicero has forgotten this, and so it seems he is inviting the historical Varro to recall their—from Cicero's side—almost cordial exchange of 46 BC. See Rösch-Binde (1998: 132–3).

Tum Atticus...cum Latine dicuntur et isto modo: *nostra* = *Latina*; *ista* must refer to respectable dogmatic, i.e. Antiochian and Stoic, philosophy, which Varro claimed is exceedingly difficult to convey in Latin (*Ac.* 1.5–7).

'Quid me', inquam, 'putas...exhibiturum?' 'Pergamus igitur', inquit, 'quoniam placet': another ellipsis with *quid me putas*, sc. *sentire* or *dicturum esse*; *exhibiturum* (*esse*) after *professus sim* would normally require a subject accusative, i.e. *me*; see Reid[1] p. 115. *Ac.* 1.18b, unsurprisingly given that it is styled as a quick exchange, has a markedly higher density of colloquial features, thus illustrating that general statements about whether Cicero's dialogues admit of colloquial features have little validity.

§§19–23

In the preceding paragraphs Varro had offered a survey of the tradition in which the Old Academy as he conceives of it stands, covering Socrates (§15), his style and practice of argument (§16); Plato, although he is presented as a source of authority and influence on the Old Academy, to which the system itself is ascribed; as well as Aristotle and the Peripatetics, with Aristotle and Xenocrates mentioned in conjunction (rather than Plato and Aristotle). These two men, we are told, were avowed dogmatists and gave up on Socrates' doubt and non-commitment. In §18 Varro makes one of the key claims associated with Antiochus' project: that there was no difference between the—the context suggests, early—Peripatetics and the Old Academics, i.e. the immediate successors of Plato in the Academy. In §19, after another invitation,

Varro begins with the actual exposition of doctrine, with §§19–23 being devoted to ethics after an initial division of the whole of philosophy.[101]

Varro's exposition in §§19–23 is cast in the past tense. Given Varro's explicit invocation of the Old Academy (as well as of the Peripatetics) on behalf of Antiochus, one would initially assume that it retains unqualified validity until Varro's day. However, from the section on epistemology in particular (§§30–2) it is plain that in some respects the speech gives a historical picture which required modification, and §§33–42 are concerned with changes to the system of the Old Academy, without it being clear in every case whether these changes were accepted by Antiochus.[102] The present passage can be put into context by two other accounts purported to expound Antiochus' views on ethics, Piso's speech in *Fin.* 5 and the report on Antiochus' ethics in Augustine, *C.D.* 19.1–3, which draws on Varro's *De philosophia* and thus represents potentially valuable evidence which is independent of Cicero and might yield an insight into the way in which Cicero's and the historical Varro's readings of Antiochus differed.[103] The criticism of Stoic ethics in *Fin.* 4 is also likely to be informed by Antiochian views on ethics,[104] but they are difficult to separate from other strands of criticism, e.g. Academic anti-Stoic arguments (some of which helped to shape Antiochus' position and can thus be cited among his reasons for not adopting the Stoic position).[105] Looking at these other texts will also help with the interpretation of the present passage, since what is given here is a summary account which is often compressed and vague.[106]

In §19 Varro begins with the threefold division of philosophy into ethics, logics, and physics; this is said to have been 'received from Plato' (*accepta a Platone*), sc. by the Old Academics and Peripatetics, but while issues which one might classify under the three headings are the subject of various dialogues, the division itself is normally credited to Xenocrates, and a related organizational principle is employed in Arist. *Top.* Ethics is described as being *de uita ac moribus*, a generic phrase more reminiscent of oratory and descriptions of the conduct of individuals in it than of philosophy. The Stoics adopted the division, too, alongside other divisions.

Varro's starting point for the exposition of doctrine is a commitment to a kind of naturalism: the pursuit of a good life and of the highest good is to be derived from nature. What exactly is meant by nature is not immediately stated, but the phrase *omnia e natura et animo et corpore et uita* points the way: Varro is speaking of human

---

[101] General discussions of Antiochus' ethics, or discussions covering central aspects of it, include Pohlenz (1940: 88–99); White (1979); Dorandi (1989); Annas (1993: 180–7); Görler (1994: 955–65); Barnes (1997: 86–9); Karamanolis (2006: 44–84); Allen (2011); Irwin (2012); Schofield (2012a) and (2012b); Tsouni (2012); Chiaradonna (2013: 28–37); Inwood (2014); Tsouni (2019). Collections of Antiochus' testimonia, are Mette (1986–7) and Sedley (2012c), who also offers an English translation.

[102] Cf. Brittain (2006: xxxii; 92 n. 12): 'Antiochus' own philosophical commitments are not easily read off from this summary, since he accepts some, but not all, of the "corrections" in the second part.'

[103] This in turn would raise questions of characterization: might one be able to discern the historical Varro's interpretation of Antiochus in Varro's speech here, or is there more reason to think that Cicero puts 'his' Antiochus into Varro's mouth, or does the evidence not speak to these questions? A crisp survey of the classification of τέλη in Varro's *De philosophia* is in Leonhardt (1999: 172–8).

[104] See Ioppolo (2016: 168–9) with a survey of earlier scholarship on Antiochian influences in *Fin.* 4.

[105] See Striker (1996d: 268–70); Schofield (2012a).

[106] There is, of course, also evidence on the views of Plato's successors as well as those of the Hellenistic Peripatetics which is most likely unmediated by Antiochus; see below.

nature in its natural setting as opposed to e.g. the workings of nature as they reveal themselves through contemplation of non-human affairs and subjects. In this way the outline of Antiochus' stance begins to emerge. In line with the major Hellenistic schools, he adopts a position of moral naturalism, but one which has human beings and their concerns at its centre. That three types of good are acknowledged (cf. *et animo et corpore et uita* in §19a *fin.*) indicates the taking of another distinct position within the matrix of options available: the final good does not reside in virtue alone (which is chief among the goods of the soul) but includes goods relating to the body and those external to ourselves.[107] This leaves open the possibility that the three types of good contribute to the final good to different degrees. Later in §22 *init.* on Varro introduces another distinction fully set out elsewhere, i.e. that between the happy life, for which virtue is a necessary and sufficient condition, and the happiest life, which includes the other goods.

This division of three goods is then articulated in some detail in §§19b–21 (in the order of body, mind, and goods belonging to our lives). The division itself is one that is intuitive in a pre-philosophical sense. There are passages in Plato and Aristotle where this pre-philosophical division becomes an object of reflection and argument,[108] but nowhere does it harden in either thinker into something approaching a formal doctrine, and of course both Platonic and Aristotelian ethical thought includes elements which would require substantial work to be made compatible with such a notion, like the intellectualist conception of virtue in the case of Plato and the role of contemplation in the case of Aristotle. The three goods only became a formal doctrine in the hands of Peripatetics, notably Carneades' contemporary Critolaus, and it is likely that Carneades' dialectical attacks were the reason for this hardening of a common sense distinction into a doctrine, as Inwood (2014: 273–4) has suggested.[109] Cicero is not our only source for the claim that the *tria bona* were 'also' an Academic doctrine (see below), but positing *tria bona* is quite clearly not associated with Stoicism.[110]

In order to see the point of positing three types of good, we can look ahead to the 'corrections' the Stoics made to Old Academic ethics as presented here, two of which Antiochus is said to have rejected (those which he accepted do not fully come into view in our passage here because of the brevity of the exposition). The two are discussed in 1.36–7, and it is the first in particular which matters here: Zeno's treatment of bodily and external goods as 'indifferents', which for Varro is an instance of the Stoics' tendency to introduce apparent innovations to Old Academic doctrine which

---

[107] Cf. the general note on *Luc.* 129–41 on different conceptions of naturalism which underpin the debates in Hellenistic ethics. It distinguishes Antiochus' theory from the Stoic one that the former takes the first natural impulses to be included in the final end, whereas the Stoics assume that at some point in a human being's development a reorientation from the *prima naturae* to the categorically different end of virtue occurs.

[108] Virtue conceived as using other goods in Plt., *Men.* 87c–89a and *Euthyd.* 278e–282d, see Annas (1993a); Arist., *E.E.* H6, 1214a30–3.

[109] See, however, Inwood (2014: 261–2) on D.L. 5.30 (from the Life of Aristotle), where under the influence of the later Peripatetic tradition Aristotle is credited with the three goods.

[110] Chrysippus did talk loosely about goods when strictly preferred indifferents are at issue (Plut., *Sto. rep.* 1048a; Origen, *Contra Celsum* 8.51 = *SVF* iii.474; see Inwood 2014: 273), but later Stoics seem to have abandoned this practice.

are in fact mere terminological variations.¹¹¹ For the Stoics virtue is a disposition of the mind of the sage, and since virtue cannot be an inert state, happiness involves acting in a virtuous way.¹¹² This means selecting things which are of value and in agreement with nature, and rejecting things which are not of value in the corresponding sense. However, what is selected is not a good in itself; only the disposition which enables and issues in such selection is. Within Stoicism, the related issue of whether virtue would for consistency need to be isolated from the selection of things which are in themselves indifferent arose as early as with Zeno's contemporary Aristo (see below, and *Luc.* 130 with comm.). Despite the Antiochian talk about the mere verbal difference between the Old Academic/Peripatetic and the Stoic position regarding things of value (see on *Ac.* 1.37), there are passages in Cicero which connect the two different stances with the two different conceptions of naturalism at issue: on this reading, the Stoic view reduces human nature to the mind alone and is thus able to treat only virtue as a genuine good, whereas the Antiochian view accommodates the fact that human beings are not reducible to their minds but consist of soul and body.¹¹³

In §22 Varro adds that it is a mistake to think that the Peripatetics can be separated from the Old Academics (i.e. Plato's successors in the Academy). I shall review the history of this claim and its likely plausibility both to the first readers of *Acad.* and in general.¹¹⁴ Varro continues that both groups also accepted the distinction between the happy and the happiest life (§22 *fin.*; ascribed to Antiochus in *Luc.* 134; cf. *Fin.* 5.71 and 81, 3.43; Aug., *C.D.* 19.3), on which virtue (and the goods of the mind) is a necessary and sufficient condition for the happy life, whereas the happiest life includes bodily and external goods.

The concluding §23 moves on to how, on Antiochus' theory, appropriate action is conceptualized. Here Varro provides a brief version of a doctrine of οἰκείωσις, which he says flows from the framework developed in the previous paragraph.¹¹⁵ Antiochus did not simply adopt the Stoic version and instead made modifications.¹¹⁶ An impulse to conserve the objects prescribed by nature accounts for choices and avoidances, and explains why human beings are social beings, desire and seek to implement justice, and, when a conflict or the need for a choice arises, forego pleasure. However, the subject of pleasure is underdefined here, and a moral theory which grants some status to goods of the body is exposed in an obvious way.¹¹⁷

---

¹¹¹ The criticism that the Stoic view offered amounted to mere terminological variations of other views was first made by Carneades; see Cic. *Fin.* 3.41; *Tusc.* 5.120.
¹¹² See the texts collected by Long and Sedley (1987) in sections 59–61, and e.g. Schofield (2003).
¹¹³ Cf. *Fin.* 4.26, 32, and 4.41, where it is pointedly claimed that living in accordance with nature for the Stoics actually means stepping away from nature (*a natura discedere*); White (1979: 148); Algra (1990: 456); Gill (2016: 230).
¹¹⁴ See also on *Ac.* 1.18 above.
¹¹⁵ See White (1979: 155 and 167); Gill (2016); on the Stoic doctrine, see Striker (1996d); Klein (2016).
¹¹⁶ The question of whether Theophrastus' notion of οἰκειότης was a predecessor or an influence for the Stoic doctrine of οἰκείωσις has been extensively studied; see White (1979: 146–7 n. 17), and Long (1998: 367–75) for a review of the debate. No such connection can be substantiated, nor do Cicero's dialogues give any indication that Antiochus tried to invoke a connection to support his conception of the Old Academy. Note, however, *Fin.* 4.15–17 (= Xenocrates frg. 79 Heinze = frg. 152 Isnardi Parente), where an impulse towards self-preservation is ascribed to the Stoics, Xenocrates, and Aristotle.
¹¹⁷ A dismissive attitude towards pleasure emerges from the only Antiochian text on the subject, *Fin.* 5.45: *In enumerandis autem corporis commodis si quis praetermissam a nobis uoluptatem putabit, in aliud*

Piso's speech in *Fin.* 5.9-74, following arguments pro and contra Epicurean ethics (*Fin.* 1-2) and Stoic ethics (*Fin.* 3-4), is a text whose debt to Antiochus is quite explicitly signalled.[118] In both 5.8 and 5.75 Piso's personal experience of two philosophers is mentioned, Antiochus and the Peripatetic Staseas of Naples.[119] In 5.8 Cicero invites Piso to talk about the *sententia ueteris Academiae de finibus bonorum Peripateticorumque*, saying that he is well placed to do so since he knew Staseas for many years and has—in the fictional setting of the dialogue—been interrogating Antiochus on the subject for several months.[120] This might raise the question whether the Latin phrase just quoted is to be construed distributively, i.e. whether there is a suggestion to the reader that what Cicero is about to put into Piso's mouth is Cicero's view of the ethical teachings of the Old Academy, informed by Antiochus on the one hand and Staseas on the other. However, such a reading is discouraged by 5.75, where Cicero the character commends Piso for delivering a speech which was more plausible than Staseas' teachings on the subject. In reply Piso confirms that Antiochus had on his view, too, spoken *melius et fortius* on the subject. Both passages together suggest that Staseas is mentioned because from him Piso could derive insights into the Peripatetic heritage of Antiochus' construal of the Old Academy and because his theory was similar enough to Antiochus' to allow for a comparison, but that it is Antiochus' view which is laid out.[121] In 5.14 Antiochus' view is referred to as

---

tempus ea quaestio differatur. Vtrum enim sit uoluptas in iis rebus, quas primas secundum naturam esse diximus necne sit, ad id quod agimus nihil interest. Si enim, ut mihi quidem uidetur, non explet bona naturae uoluptas, iure praetermissa est; sin autem est in ea quod quidam uolunt, nihil impedit hanc nostram comprehensionem summi boni. Quae enim constituta sunt prima naturae, ad ea si uoluptas accesserit, unum aliquod accesserit commodum corporis neque eam constitutionem summi boni quae est proposita mutauerit, 'Someone may take the view that in our enumeration of bodily advantages we have overlooked pleasure. Let us postpone this issue for discussion at another time. The question whether pleasure belongs with what we have called the primary things in accordance with nature is irrelevant to what we are discussing. If, as it seems to me, pleasure adds nothing to the goods of nature, it has rightly been omitted; but if it is amongst these things as some posit, then it in no way hampers our understanding of the highest good. If we add pleasure to the first advantages of nature, then we have merely added one more bodily advantage and will not have modified the basic structure of the supreme good.' See Tsouni (2012: 133).

[118] Useful discussions of the speech include White (1979: 150-1); Steinmetz (1989); Annas (1993: 419-25); Barnes (1997: 86-7); Long (1998: 358-9); Görler (2011), who also covers source criticism; Inwood (2014a: 66-72); see also Irwin (2012); Schofield (2012a); Tsouni (2012); and Gill (2016) on particular issues within the speech (other than the *Carneadea diuisio*, for which see the commentary on *Luc.* 129-41).

[119] On Staseas see, apart from Inwood (2014a) to be cited below, Hobein (1929); Moraux (1974: 218-21); Sharples (2010: 20 and 161); Dorandi (2016).

[120] On the dramatic date and setting of *Fin.* 5, see e.g. Hatzimichali (2012: 25); Brittain (2016: 20-2); of Cicero's dialogues only it and the frame of *Tim.* are set in Greece. On the date of composition of *Fin.*, see section 9.1 and Marinone (2004[2]: 214).

[121] Cf. also *Fin.* 5.8: *Tum...Piso exorsus est. Cuius oratio attende, quaeso, Brute, satisne uideatur Antiochi complexa esse sententiam*; 5.14. Contrast Inwood (2014a: 72), who takes these passages to suggest that Piso's speech is Cicero's creation, who is signalling that its Peripatetic elements are owed to Staseas of Naples, while its Stoic elements are owed to Antiochus: 'Since the tougher-minded position on the sufficiency of virtue for happiness is associated with Antiochus (it is something he inherited from Critolaus, like him being engaged in close argument with the Stoics), and since Cicero here seems to attribute to Staseas a weaker position that allows more weight to the contingencies that afflict external and bodily goods (that is, a position closer to Theophrastus), it is possible that Staseas is the philosopher who pulled together the main account, with its richly Aristotelian version of ethical naturalism, while Antiochus is responsible for the tougher and more Stoic-sounding stance on the sufficiency thesis. That would cohere with everything else we learn about Antiochus from Cicero and would explain why Staseas, otherwise

based on the *antiqui*, i.e. the shared position of Aristotle and Polemo (sc. who is a couple of generations younger than Xenocrates).[122] The Stoics enter this picture (5.22, 5.74) as people who attached new terminology to the doctrines they had lifted wholesale from the Old Academy as Antiochus conceived of it.[123]

Having explained the central role which the highest good plays for any moral theory in 5.15, Piso introduces the *Carneadea diuisio* which Antiochus was fond to employ from 5.17 *fin*. The *diuisio* had been announced in 5.16 but was prefaced with an indication of the common ground between the theories classified, notably a commitment to a particular kind of naturalism (one which envisages that the *prima naturae* enter into the final end); see the general note on *Luc*. 129–41. This division and its origin, a simpler version of which is used in *Luc*. 131, allows for an illustration of the moves and countermoves of the debate between Stoics and Academics. As explained in the commentary on *Luc*. 129–41, the idea of a division of moral theories according to the highest good goes back to Chrysippus (cf. *Luc*. 138). He is likely to have employed one in connection with his teaching, in such a way as to argue for existing moral theories, the Stoic one and others, on either side, in order to reinforce the apprehension of the Stoic theory (assumed to be pre-existent in his pupils) and induce ἐποχή one by one about the rival theories. Carneades modified and expanded this division so as to include highest goods which were conceivable but not actually upheld by anyone, and then used it to show either that there were no rational grounds for any of these views or to argue for an alternative to the Stoic theory which he had devised for the sake of the argument (see *Fin*. 5.20). Antiochus then assumes Chrysippus' mantle and uses a version of Carneades' division, but in Chrysippus' spirit: to eliminate all theories but his preferred one. In *Fin*. 5 the *Carneadea diuisio* is partly a presentational device which also serves the purpose of characterizing Antiochus; one would not expect it to feature in Varro's speech, where the ethical views of the Old Academy are surveyed on their own terms.

Antiochus' theory is characterized through a composite τέλος which includes the *honestum*, i.e. virtue, and what Cicero calls the *prima naturae* ('the primary natural advantages'), i.e. things in agreement with their nature that human beings strive for

---

little known, is even mentioned here. And if this is so...it would mean that the overall author of Piso's account, now revealed as a composite of Aristotelian naturalism and Antiochean rigorism, is Cicero himself. Piso's speech in *Fin*. 5 is treated as a straightforward exposition of Antiochus' views e.g. by Sedley (2012c: 334). It is also a relevant consideration that Cicero's relationship with Varro was complex (see the general note on *Ac*. 1.1–8). It therefore seems unlikely that in *Ac*. 1 Cicero should have 'given' the known Antiochian Varro a speech which imposed the Peripatetic framework of the *tria bona* on an original, much more Stoic view of ethics which was Antiochus' actual position. Similarly, the invitation issued by Cicero to Brutus in *Fin*. 5.8 to check if Piso's speech properly captures Antiochus' thinking (*cuius oratio attende, Brute, satisne uideatur Antiochi complexa esse sententiam*) tells against Cicero splicing Antiochian and non-Antiochian material. Gigon (1988: 263) suggests that for Piso's speech 'fundamental is Theophrastus' *On Happiness*, from which, I believe, [*Fin*.] 5.24–70 (esp. 24–58) is a rather precise excerpt (with the addition, of course, of 5.77 and 5.86–95)'; that *Fin*. 5.12 (*Theophrastum tamen adhibeamus ad pleraque*) cannot be interpreted as an indication of a source is shown by Görler (2011), who lists on p. 334 n. 5 other studies which took the half-sentence to signal a source (without necessarily going so far as to make most of Piso's speech 'a precise excerpt').

[122] For Xenocrates, see on *Ac*. 1.17; on Polemo, see n. 131 below.
[123] *Pace* Barnes (1997: 86), I see no inconsistency in the way the origins of Antiochus' system are characterized in *Fin*. 5.9, 14, 22, and 74.

from the beginning of their lives, initially automatically, but gradually with greater understanding of themselves and their environment (see below). The Stoic position is separated from the Antiochian one in that it posits a simple τέλος, i.e. the *honestum* alone, but Antiochus' distinction between a *uita beata* and a *uita beatissima* means that virtue is sufficient for the former, whereas the latter includes the *prima naturae*. Piso does not discuss the *tria bona* distinction until 5.65–74, but it relates to the distinction of the two *uitae*: the *honestum*/virtue is associated with the goods of the mind, while the goods of the body and external goods are associated with the *prima bona*.

Piso then explains the concept of *prima naturae* further, by relating it to the notions of self-love and of living in accordance with nature (5.24–33);[124] with this he offers an alternative account to the Stoic doctrine of οἰκείωσις. There follows an account of the dual nature of human beings made up of soul and body (5.34–45), and of the excellences and ways to perfect each (5.46–64). This is of a piece with the humano-centric naturalism encountered in Varro's speech. At the end of the speech Piso turns to the status of external goods in Antiochus' theory (5.65–74). From this last section alone one could not be certain that Piso is laying out and endorsing the same view of *tria bona* and their relation to happiness as we find in Varro's speech in *Ac.* 1 (see 5.71–2 in particular), but the character Cicero in his response makes it clear—without objection from Piso—that this is what he takes Piso to be committing himself to on Antiochus' behalf (5.84).[125]

While Piso's speech and *Ac.* 1.19–23 are readily compatible with each other, the structures and presentational emphases are different, quite apart from the fact that *Fin.* 5 offers the far more substantial treatment and discusses issues not addressed or merely hinted at here in *Ac.* 1. The use of the *Carneadea diuisio* in Piso's speech has been touched on above. Having arrived at the Old Academic view, the speech lays out components of the theory in such a way that the overall impression is one of a modified Stoic framework with Peripatetic additions. The Antiochian view on *bona* comes at the very end, but as indicated above no stress is placed on the fact that the status of things which are of value is significantly different from that of preferred indifferents. By contrast, Varro's exposition in *Ac.* 1.19–23 has the *tria bona* at the centre. Thus if one draws up a hierarchy of ostensible influences for the passage, then the doctrine of the *tria bona*, which is primarily associated with Peripatetic thought in the mid-second century BC, will sit at the top, and it does encapsulate a salient difference between Stoic and Antiochian ethics.[126] This provides a rationale for Varro's emphasis in §22 and Piso's emphasis in *Fin.* 5 on the Peripatetic pedigree of Antiochus' ethics of the Old Academy and tells against the notion that the Peripatetic label was secondarily attached by Cicero to a theory whose largely Stoic origin was

---

[124] With the τέλος-formula given in the discussion of the *Carneadea diuisio*, cf. the fuller version in 5.26, intended to capture the particular type of naturalism employed by Antiochus: *uiuere ex hominis natura undique perfecta et nihil requirente.*

[125] Thus also Inwood (2014: 274). On the treatment of the *tria bona* in Piso's speech, see also Görler (2011: 336–54).

[126] It is compatible with this that Varro (and Antiochus) does not attach the same weight to all three types of *bona*; see below.

plain.¹²⁷ One effect of the prominence accorded to the *tria bona* scheme is that it creates a tie-in with the Zenonian modifications of *Ac.* 1.33b–39, where some *bona* are treated as akin to promoted indifferents. Piso's second shorter speech (*Fin.* 5.83–95) requires separate investigation and assessment.

The evidence on Antiochus' ethics from Aug., *C.D.* 19.1–3, which draws on Varro's *De philosophia* but appears to show awareness of the final edition of *Acad.*, too,¹²⁸ has recently been re-examined by Blank (2012: 250–62); see also Tarver (1997: 145–61), and the edition with commentary by Langenberg (1959), which both cite earlier literature. I shall quote relevant parallels in the notes. Like Piso in *Fin.* 5, Varro uses a *diuisio*, but his is a division of philosophical schools rather than one of actual or conceivable ends. The number of *sectae* thus distinguished is vastly expanded (to 288), but like Piso Varro eliminates all options but the Old Academic one (which Augustine then goes on to dismiss in his own voice). Several distinctive theses of Antiochus' ethics are in evidence in Augustine's report of Varro, but there are also divergences, which are plausibly explained by Blank as due to Varro's different presentational concerns and constraints arising from them. The most striking difference is that according to Varro in Augustine Antiochus held virtue to be 'implanted by instruction', whereas in Piso's speech in *Fin.* human beings are said to develop naturally towards virtue from small 'seeds' (*Fin.* 5.43, 5.60; cf. 5.18). While Varro's speech in *Ac.* 1 does not explicitly speak to the question, the fact that it mentions Antiochus' version of the doctrine of οἰκείωσις makes it likely that Varro's speech is supposed to agree with Piso's speech on this point. One might think that this means that Cicero put his own interpretation of Antiochus into Varro's mouth, but a chronological explanation is preferable, i.e. that Varro had not yet written the *De philosophia* when

---

¹²⁷ Görler (1994: 956) raises a different suspicion, i.e. that Antiochus ascribed his ethical view to the *ueteres* (conceived as including the Old Academy and the Peripatetics), whereas Cicero placed stress on the 'Peripatetic' origin. Given the prominence accorded to the *tria bona* scheme here in *Ac.* 1, one can either assume that Cicero gave particular prominence to the Peripatetic element in Antiochus ethics (in which case he did not just modify the general designation) or that the Peripatetic element was genuinely strong in Antiochus' conception (in which case acknowledging that this was so would have been a natural thing to do for Antiochus rather than Cicero). One should also remember that what became known as the Antiochian view features in the *Carneadea diuisio*, which Antiochus was fond of using (*Fin.* 5.16). The question thus arises whose view Carneades took it to be. The Old Academy was obsolete when he was active, so it is more likely that he was thinking of certain Peripatetics (other Peripatetics feature in the *diuisio* with a different view, though). There is thus a sense in which to call the Antiochian view 'Peripatetic' has historical pedigree. In Augustine's report on what Varro said about Antiochus' ethics in *C.D.* 19.1–3 the 'Old Academy' is mentioned, without an indication that it included the Peripatetics. This, I suggest, tells us more about Varro than about Antiochus. Annas (1993: 180) characterizes Antiochus' moral theory thus: 'The theory is strikingly Aristotelian in content, though Antiochus tries to incorporate important aspects of Stoic moral theory; it is most usefully viewed as an Aristotelian reaction to the Stoic challenge, and can often be fruitfully compared with the account of Aristotelian ethics to be found in Arius Didymus.'

¹²⁸ Cf. Blank (2012: 253): 'As for Augustine's notice that Varro took the description of the best life in his *De philosophia* "on the authority of Antiochus, Cicero's master and his own" (*De civ. D.* 19.3), we may suspect that Augustine has lifted the master–pupil relation from Cicero, in the light of his mention here of Cicero, and of his note that Cicero apparently contradicts the portrayal of Antiochus as an Old Academic when he makes it clear that Antiochus was more often a Stoic.' See on *Luc.* 132 for the latter point, i.e. the correspondence *C.D.* 19.3: *quem sane Cicero in pluribus fuisse Stoicum quam ueterem Academicum uult uideri* ~ *Luc.* 132:... *Antiochum? Qui appellabatur Academicus, erat quidem, si perpauca mutauisset, germanissimus Stoicus.* Augustine is, however, likely to have used the final edition. Giusta (2012²: 94–105) has good observations on similarities and differences between *Fin.* 5 and Aug., *C.D.* 19.1–3.

Cicero composed *Acad.* and that he only knew Varro to be an Antiochian in general terms.[129]

To what extent one finds merit in the broader historical claims which underpin Antiochus' construction of ethics in the Old Academy, at least as a possible view of the history of philosophy, depends on the credibility of Antiochus' repeated claims that some 'Stoic' elements of his doctrine do in fact go back to Plato's successors in the Academy and the early Peripatos. One may also ask if it is possible, as in the case of the sections on physics (1.24-9) and on epistemology (1.30-2 and 40-2), to see behind Cicero's Latin text allusions to canonical texts which, if read in a certain way, might yield textual support for Antiochus' claims.[130]

There are a number of passages in which Cicero ascribes versions of particular elements of doctrine which one would associate with Stoicism in the first instance to particular members of the Academy, notably Polemo, and for these parallels can be found in Greek sources.[131] The teacher-pupil relationship of Polemo and Zeno is invoked several times by Cicero, including in connection with particular points of doctrine.[132] (a) In Cicero Polemo is associated with agreement with nature as the end, and specifically with a naturalism that is focused on human beings and interprets living in agreement with nature as a combination of virtue as the end and the enjoyment of the 'first things granted by nature'.[133] (b) However, virtue is seen as sufficient for happiness, so that Polemo is cast as anticipating the Antiochian distinction between the *uita beata* and the *uita beatissima*.[134] (c) Several passages which either name Polemo or render the Old Academic view more generally use expressions

---

[129] In *Ac.* 1.3 Cicero the character points out to Varro that in his writings he has neglected the field of philosophy, to which Varro is made to reply in 1.4-8 that writing philosophy in Latin was either superfluous or had no market. The exchange can plausibly be taken to establish a terminus post quem for works of Varro which are taken to be narrowly philosophical; see Tarver (1997: 143-5).

[130] For epistemology and physics we have no other detailed passages in the Ciceronian corpus which we could compare; in the field of ethics it is not just *Ac.* 1.19-23 but once again Piso's speech in *Fin.* 5, too, which can scrutinized for its intertextual resonances.

[131] Biographical information on Polemo mostly comes from his biography in D.L. 4 and Philodemus' *Index Acad.* (*P.Herc.* 1021 and 164). Editions of Polemo's testimonia are Schumacher (1966) [*non uidi*]; Gigante (1976); and Marzotto (2012), the latter with commentary. A selection of texts, not all of which assignable to Polemo, with German translation and notes is in Dörrie (1987: 95-101 and 319-28). Important discussions of the extant evidence include von Fritz (1952); Krämer (1983: 151-74); Ioppolo (1986: 146-50); Dillon (2003: 156-77); Kupreeva (2012); Tarrant (2020). See also Brittain (2006: 94 n. 16). For Xenocrates, see on *Ac.* 1.17.

[132] Cf. *Ac.* 1.34 (Varro still speaking); *Fin.* 4.3 (Cicero as Clitomachean giving Antiochus' view), cf. 4.14, 4.61 (again Cicero speaking). The influence which Polemo may have exercised on several of his pupils (apart from Zeno, these included Arcesilaus, Aristo of Chios, and Crantor) is the subject of several interconnected scholarly debates; see the crisp summary by Kupreeva (2012: 1193).

[133] Cf. *Fin.* 2.34 (= frg. 127 Gigante = t. 42 Marzotto; cf. *Fin.* 4.14 = frg. 129 Gigante = t. 44 Marzotto): *Polemoni et iam ante Aristoteli ea prima uisa sunt, quae paulo ante dixi. Ergo nata est sententia ueterum Academicorum et Peripateticorum, ut finem bonorum dicerent secundum naturam uiuere, id est uirtute adhibita frui primis a natura datis*; cf. *Fin.* 5.26 *fin.*: *uiuere ex hominis natura*.

[134] Cf. *Fin.* 4.51 (= frg. 130 Gigante = t. 46 Marzotto): *Dabit hoc Zenoni Polemo, etiam magister eius et tota illa gens et reliqui qui, uirtutem omnibus rebus multo anteponentes, adiungunt ei tamen aliquid summo in bono finiendo. Si enim uirtus digna est gloriatione, ut est, tantumque praestat reliquis rebus, ut dici uix possit, et beatus esse poterit uirtute una praeditus carens ceteris, nec tamen illud tibi concedet, praeter uirtutem nihil in bonis esse ducendum. Illi autem, quibus summum bonum sine uirtute est, non dabunt fortasse uitam beatam habere, in quo iure possit gloriari, etsi illi quidem etiam uoluptates faciunt interdum gloriosas*; cf. *Tusc.* 5.30, 39, 86.

which suggest that virtue is something which needs to be enacted rather than merely amounting to a disposition of the subject, a notion which looks back to Aristotle's conception of virtue as an activity and forward to the Stoics and rational selection of preferred indifferents as what virtue actually does.[135] (d) When Cicero traces the Stoic doctrine of οἰκείωσις to the Old Academy and Polemo in particular,[136] he seems to be deliberately cautious at times (and as we shall see, independent corroborating evidence is absent);[137] here a sense of *interpretatio Antiochea* is difficult to avoid, although Cicero's (and his sources') nuance is to be acknowledged. As mentioned above (n. 116), Cicero shows no awareness of a question which has exercised modern scholars, i.e. whether Theophrastus anticipated the Stoic doctrine of οἰκείωσις.[138]

Most parallels—brief and compressed and hence open to more than one interpretation—come from Clement of Alexandria's *Strom*. The teacher–pupil relationship of Polemo and Zeno is independently attested.[139] We find the end as 'agreement with nature' (a) alluded to in a book title referred to by Clement.[140] Polemo is also

---

[135] Cf. *Ac.* 1.22: *uirtutis usus*; *frui* in *Fin.* 2.34 (quoted above), where Polemo is named, and *Luc.* 131. See Pfligersdorfer (1971) on *uti/frui* in Augustine.

[136] See *Ac.* 1.23, *Fin.* 2.33-4, 4.14-18, 5.24-33, and 74.

[137] In *Fin.* 2.33 a brief account of οἰκείωσις precedes *Fin.* 2.34 (quoted above), and the connection is made by *Atque ab isto capite fluere necesse est omnem rationem bonorum et malorum*. In *Luc.* 131 speaks of 'approximation': *Honeste autem uiuere fruentem rebus iis quas primas homini natura conciliet et uetus Academia censuit, ut indicant scripta Polemonis quem Antiochus probat maxime, et Aristoteles eiusque amici huc proxime uidentur accedere*. Cf. also Aug., *C.D.* 19.3, which as noted above is independent of Cicero: *...bona sunt tamen, et secundum istos* [scil. *ueteres*] *etiam ipsa propter se ipsa diligit uirtus utiturque illis et fruitur sicut uirtutem decet*. See the notes below on *Ac.* 1.23.

[138] In *Fin.* 2.33-4 Polemo is linked to *Aristotle*, though; in 4.15-18 (above n. 116) it is Xenocrates and Aristotle to whom a similar theory is ascribed.

[139] Cf. D.L. 7.2 (= frg. 85 Gigante), where—cf. 7.25—Hippobotus is Diogenes' source; see Wilamowitz (1881: 104 n. 2). See also frg. 86-91 Gigante.

[140] Cf. Clem., *Strom*. 7.6.32.9 Stählin (= frg. 112 Gigante = t. 64 Marzotto): Δοκεῖ δὲ Ξενοκράτης (= frg. 100 Heinze = frg. 267 Isnardi Parente) ἰδίᾳ πραγματευόμενος Περὶ τῆς ἀπὸ τῶν ζῴων τροφῆς καὶ Πολέμων ἐν τοῖς Περὶ τοῦ κατὰ φύσιν βίου συντάγμασι σαφῶς λέγειν, ὡς ἀσύμφορόν ἐστιν ἡ διὰ τῶν σαρκῶν τροφή, ⟨ἡ⟩ εἰργασμένη ἤδη καὶ ἐξομοιοῖ ταῖς τῶν ἀλόγων ψυχαῖς, 'Xenocrates, in his work "On the Food Derived from Animals", and Polemon, in his work "On Life According to Nature" appear to say clearly that nourishment through the meat of animals is not beneficial, inasmuch as it has already been elaborated and assimilated to the souls of the irrational beings.' *Strom.* 2.22.133.7 Stählin (= part of frg. 123 Gigante = t. 58 Marzotto) reports a different end (obtainment of which is equated with happiness), apparently wrongly inferred from Polemo's use of αὐτάρκεια: ὁ γὰρ Ξενοκράτους γνώριμος Πολέμων φαίνεται τὴν εὐδαιμονίαν αὐτάρκειαν εἶναι βουλόμενος ἀγαθῶν πάντων, ἢ τῶν πλείστων καὶ μεγίστων. δογματίζει γοῦν χωρὶς μὲν ἀρετῆς μηδέποτε ἂν εὐδαιμονίαν ὑπάρχειν, δίχα δὲ καὶ τῶν σωματικῶν καὶ τῶν ἐκτὸς τὴν ἀρετὴν αὐτάρκη πρὸς εὐδαιμονίαν εἶναι, 'For Polemo, the pupil of Xenocrates, seems to hold that happiness is sufficiency of all good things, or of the most and greatest. He thus holds the view that happiness never exists without virtue; and that virtue, separate from corporeal and external things, is sufficient for happiness'. Another statement of Polemo's, sometimes related to his moral naturalism, is a remark about the need for moral action in the service of self-improvement rather than dialectical prowess (i.e. adroitness in exchanges in question and answer); cf. D.L. 4.18 (= frg. 101 Gigante = part of t. 2 Marzotto; cf. Philod., *Index Acad.* col. xiv.3-10 = frg. 100 Gigante): ἔφασκε δὲ ὁ Πολέμων δεῖν ἐν τοῖς πράγμασι γυμνάζεσθαι καὶ μὴ ἐν τοῖς διαλεκτικοῖς θεωρήμασι, καθάπερ ἁρμονικόν τι τεχνίον καταπιόντα καὶ μὴ μελετήσαντα, ὡς κατὰ μὲν τὴν ἐρώτησιν θαυμάζεσθαι, κατὰ δὲ τὴν διάθεσιν ἑαυτοῖς μάχεσθαι, 'Polemo used to say that we should exercise ourselves with facts and not with mere logical speculations, which leave us, like a man who has got by heart some paltry handbook on harmony but never practised, able, indeed, to win admiration for the skill in asking questions, but utterly at variance with ourselves in the ordering of our lives' (transl. Hicks), but it is not certain that this is the sense of the passage. See Dillon (2003: 159-60) and (2020: 188-9). Krämer (1983: 157) seeks to leverage D.L. 4.18 against the evidence for Polemo's naturalism, viz. that the role

reported to have recognized goods of the body and external goods, which together with the claim of the sufficiency of virtue for happiness aligns him with the Peripatetics (see b above);[141] however, the evidence does not support the conclusion that he sought to assign to bodily and external goods less weight than to goods of the mind, in the way in which Antiochus seems to have done (cf. *Fin*. 5.71). For the notion of virtue as an activity (see c above), see Plut. (just quoted, n. 141): ⟨ἐν⟩ αὐτοῖς ἐνεργοῦσαν οἰκείως. That passage (and phrase) is also the closest the Greek evidence comes to crediting Polemo with a predecessor of the Stoic doctrine of οἰκείωσις (see d above).[142]

In times gone by when Antiochus was readily suspected to be 'behind' Greek texts which resemble Ciceronian ones, much of this evidence might have been dismissed as going back to the same sources as Cicero. Scholars are rightly much less willing to make this assumption now, and it is plausible to think that Antiochus' historical views would have been doomed to failure from the start if they had been seen to be pure constructions without a foothold in historical views others would recognize as their own. Much depends on how Polemo's naturalism was construed. The evidence which makes it the background for the stance on what counts as a good and what makes a happy life does suggest that Polemo's naturalism was (construed not just by Antiochus as) relevantly like Zeno's.[143] It would have been easier for Antiochus to posit this kind of naturalism for Polemo if forms qua transcendental entities played no role in Antiochus' reconstruction of the Old Academy—and clearly, in *Ac*. 1.19–23 or Piso's speech in *Fin*. 5 there is no mention of forms, nor could they be accommodated, nor do forms feature in *Ac*. 1.24–9 on physics. I shall argue in the com-

---

Polemo accords to nature, and to human nature in particular, is intended to preclude wilful stipulations ('willkürliche Setzungen und Ansprüche') and should not be read in a biologistic and antimetaphysical way, but D.L. 4.18 arguably speaks to something else. There is no tangible evidence for metaphysical commitments on Polemo's part, notably to Forms, in the record.

[141] Apart from *Strom*. 2.22.133.7 Stählin quoted above, see Plut., *Comm. not*. 23, 1069e–1070b (= frg. 124 Gigante = t. 56 Marzotto; part of Xenocrates frg. 233 Isnardi Parente): 'Πόθεν οὖν' φησίν 'ἄρξωμαι; καὶ τίνα λάβω τοῦ καθήκοντος ἀρχὴν καὶ ὕλην τῆς ἀρετῆς, ἀφεὶς τὴν φύσιν καὶ τὸ κατὰ φύσιν; πόθεν δ' Ἀριστοτέλης, ὦ μακάριε, καὶ Θεόφραστος ἄρχονται; τίνας δὲ Ξενοκράτης καὶ Πολέμων λαμβάνουσιν ἀρχάς; οὐχὶ καὶ Ζήνων τούτοις ἠκολούθησεν ὑποτιθεμένοις στοιχεῖα τῆς εὐδαιμονίας τὴν φύσιν καὶ τὸ κατὰ φύσιν; ἀλλ' ἐκεῖνοι μὲν ἐπὶ τούτων ἔμειναν ὡς αἱρετῶν καὶ ἀγαθῶν καὶ ὠφελίμων, καὶ τὴν ἀρετὴν προσλαβόντες ⟨ἐν⟩ αὐτοῖς ἐνεργοῦσαν οἰκείως χρωμένην ἑκάστῳ τέλειον ἐκ τούτων καὶ ὁλόκληρον ᾤοντο συμπληροῦν βίον καὶ συμπεραίνειν, τὴν ἀληθῶς τῇ φύσει πρόσφορον καὶ συνῳδὸν ὁμολογίαν ἀποδιδόντες, ' "What, then", says he, "will be my point of departure and what shall I take as duty's principle and virtue's matter, once I have abandoned nature and what is in conformity with nature?" Why, my good sir, what is the point of departure for Aristotle and for Theophrastus; and what do Xenocrates and Polemon take as principles? And has not Zeno too followed them in their assumption that nature and what is conformity with nature are basic elements of happiness? Those former men, however, held by these things as beneficial and good and objects of choice; and, having taken virtue in addition as operating ⟨among⟩ them by making proper use of each, they thought that with these constituents they were filling out and finishing off a perfect and integrated life by presenting the consistency that is truly in conformity and harmony with nature' (transl. Cherniss). That virtue is sufficient for happiness, which was not Theophrastus' view according to *Ac*. 1.35, is ascribed to other post-Platonic Academics as well (see Speusippus frgs 102–6 Isnardi Parente; Xenocrates frgs 241–5 Isnardi Parente, but contrast frg. 232), and these are figures mentioned sporadically by Cicero, too. What distinguishes them from Polemo in Cicero's texts is that the latter has arguably devoted a narrative to him in Cicero's works, which singles him out as a predecessor of Antiochus'.

[142] See also Karamanolis (2006: 77–9).

[143] See, however, Krämer (1971: 33 n. 136) for the suggestion that agreement with nature is to be linked with the Socratic conception of consistency with oneself (and thus no evidence for naturalism).

mentary on *Ac.* 1.30-2 that the forms mentioned in 1.30 are to be understood as concepts.

I shall document in the commentary on *Ac.* 1.24-9 (on physics) and 1.30-2 (on epistemology) that both passages stand in intertextual relationships with canonical Platonic texts, the *Timaeus* in the former case and the *Theaetetus* in the latter. If the views of the Old Academy as expounded by Varro are seen to be derivable from passages in Platonic dialogues, then—however concurrently present Stoic elements may be in these passages—this goes some way towards supporting the historical view which underpins Antiochus' philosophy (whether the Platonic references were meant to be available to readers of Cicero, too, or merely inherent in his source material, which forms the basis of Varro's speech, is impossible to decide). *Ac.* 1.19-23 is different, in that no particular canonical text appears to be referenced.[144] For Plato this is less surprising, given that support for the view that virtue is necessary and sufficient for happiness would be easier to find in the dialogues (which the Stoics engaged with), but *N.E.*, *E.E.*, and *M.M.* would have provided more opportunities. Irwin (2012) is a reading of Piso's speech in *Fin.* 5 against relevant 'Aristotelian' texts, with a view to the question of how one might extract an Antiochian position from them. In that speech Piso begins (5.12) by pitting Theophrastus, who held that virtue is not sufficient for the happy life (*Ac.* 1.36), against Aristotle and his son Nicomachus, who took the opposite view, thus gesturing to *N.E.* (which Piso seems to ascribe to Nicomachus) and other ethical works assigned to Aristotle (on this point see Irwin 2012: 152-5). However, while Irwin's discussion demonstrates how Antiochus could have underpinned some of his views with interpretations of canonical texts, there does not seem to be close referencing of particular identifiable passages either in Piso's speech in *Fin.* 5 or here in Varro's speech.[145] If this is a fair observation, then one reason for the absence of such an intertextual reference might be that Peripatetic texts on ethics had nothing like the familiarity and circulation which central Platonic dialogues had in the Hellenistic period. After all, the desire to ground the Antiochian position in relevant texts is documented in principle in Piso's speech. However, there may be another way in which *Ac.* 1.19-23 is designed to be read on more than one level: in several places Cicero uses verbal cues whose possible functions include the signalling of a Latin term as a translation of a Greek term (e.g. §20: *quasi consuetudinem... progressio quaedam ad uirtutem*). Such cues might have the purpose not of sending the contemporary reader away to find the particular Greek text referenced, but rather to cast the Latin text as 'translation literature' and as referring to a Greek text which *might* lie behind Cicero's Latin. The effect would be to invest Varro's exposition on ethics with the kind of authority which the physics section (*Ac.* 1.24-9) derives from its retrievable references to Plato's *Timaeus*.[146]

---

[144] See, however, Trabattoni (2022), who discusses a number of Platonic texts, notably *Symp.* 204d-206e, with a view to the question of whether they might have been cited as evidence for a Platonic origin of Antiochus' moral theory as discussed in *Fin.* 5.

[145] Scepticism that the references to Aristotle, Nicomachus, and Theophrastus indicate first-hand knowledge on Cicero's part is expressed by Barnes (1997: 58); see also Chiaradonna (2013: 31), who notes on p. 32: 'It is very difficult to detect clear traces of any first-hand reading of Aristotle in Cicero's report.'

[146] On Cicero's translation choices in the group of texts at issue in this section, see Marzotto (2012: xliv-xlviii).

While it is reasonable to construe the historical claims underpinning Antiochus' ethics with charity, esp. in a context like *Ac.* 1.19-23 where prominence is quite deliberately given to the *tria bona* scheme which properly belongs to the Peripatetics, one can also look at Antiochus' moral theory as derived from Stoic moral theory, but reflecting and being shaped by the criticisms levelled against the latter over time. The main critics were not Peripatetics, but dissident Stoics like Aristo as well as Academics, notably Carneades.

Striker (1996d: 261-70) has reconstructed the moral theory which Carneades advanced for the sake of the argument and which challenged the Stoics that this hypothetical theory should really be the one upheld by them given their commitments and concerns. In the *Carneadea diuisio* of actually held and conceivable ethical theories distinguished by their end, the τέλος associated with this theory is the obtainment of the *prima naturae*, the first advantages of nature. In *Fin.* 5 the *diuisio* is used by Piso to eliminate all theories but the Old Academic/Antiochian one, which is then set out at length, and the theory ascribed to Carneades in the *diuisio* is nowhere defended in detail—hence the need to reconstruct it. Striker's reconstruction draws on several pieces of information, but relies particularly on the prefatory material which precedes the *diuisio* in *Fin.* 5 as well as on what we know of Philus' speech against justice in *Rep.* 3. Although it seems most unlikely that Carneades actually delivered a speech even roughly matching Philus' in content in 155 BC,[147] it remains plausible to assume that for *Rep.* 3 Cicero was drawing on Academic material, and that the arguments advanced by Philus are in that sense Carneadean. As to the prefatory material to the *Carneadea diuisio* in *Fin.* 5, it is not a given that it belongs 'originally' with the division itself, because as a matter of fact it helps advance Piso's goals in his speech, viz. to allow the Antiochian theory to emerge as the last one standing, so that there is at least a question of whether it was Antiochus who included it (see the general note on *Luc.* 129-41). However, Striker shows that it is entirely apt to advance Carneades' 'for the sake of the argument' theory, so that it becomes economical to assume that Carneades devised it and Antiochus retained it.

Carneades appears to have cited three considerations, which jointly support his hypothetical theory.[148] They are described by Striker (1996d: 267) as follows:

(i) *Natural concern*: Carneades argued that the ultimate object of desire must be identical with the first. This raises the question how the Stoic theory of the good can go together with the psychological doctrine of *oikeiōsis*. If human beings were made by nature to seek self-preservation and self-realization, how can they eventually come to accept agreement with nature as their only good? If agreement with nature is not the same as self-realization, how can one get from the first object of desire to the last? Or if it is the same, how can one preserve and develop one's nature while totally neglecting bodily and external advantages?

---

[147] See Powell (2013).
[148] Even if they did not thus support it, it would remain plausible that they correspond to formative influences for Antiochus.

(ii) *Virtue as a craft*: according to Carneades, the goal of the art of living ought to be obtaining the things in accordance with nature, not just trying to obtain them. If Carneades is right on this point, it would follow that happiness consisted in precisely those things that the Stoics had taken great care to declare indifferent, not real goods, though objects of rational selection. It would also follow that happiness was a matter of chance and good luck, not something that is in our power.

(iii) *Appropriate action*: it would seem, on Carneades' account of human nature, that following nature results, not in virtue, but on the contrary in a reckless pursuit of one's own (or one's group's) advantage, at the expense of one's neighbours. This was of course an attack on the thesis that nature leads us to virtue, challenging the Stoics to show that Carneades was wrong about human nature.

The evidence that Carneades did advance these considerations consists in (i) a remark of Piso's in *Fin.* 5.17, made after the *Carneadea diuisio* has been announced but before it is actually introduced,[149] and repeated criticism levelled against the Stoic view in *Fin.* 4 that its theory of οἰκείωσις involves a shift from one end to another without mediating appropriately between the two, in (ii) passages in Plutarch and Alexander of Aphrodisias documenting Carneadean attacks on the Stoic conception of virtue as a τέχνη,[150] and (iii) the evidence for Philus' speech in *Rep.* 3.

An anti-Stoic argument which Carneades made without it being part of the justification for 'his' moral theory but which can be read as shaping Antiochus' position, too, questions the status of promoted indifferents as incoherent and confronts the Stoics with a dilemma: either they should adopt the position of Aristo, who declared virtue the sole good and rational discrimination between indifferents impossible (so that there cannot be promoted ones), or they should adopt that of the Peripatetics, who elevate what the Stoics call promoted indifferents to the status of goods (*Fin.* 4.72).[151]

Antiochus' moral theory can be seen to opt for the Peripatetic horn of the anti-Stoic dilemma in promoting things of value which the Stoics class as promoted indifferents to the status of goods. It also accommodates the three considerations (i)–(iii) by assuming the *prima naturae* to contain the 'seeds of virtue' and to enter into the composite τέλος (i + iii), and by assuming the happy life to consist in the obtainment of virtue (ii), and only the happiest life in the additional pursuit of goods of the body and external goods.[152]

---

[149] Cic., *Fin.* 5.17: *Quid autem sit quod ita moueat itaque a natura in primo ortu appetatur non constat, deque eo est inter philosophos, cum summum bonum exquiritur, omnis dissensio. Totius enim quaestionis eius, quae habetur de finibus bonorum et malorum, cum quaeritur, in his quid sit extremum et ultimum, fons reperiendus est in quo sint prima inuitamenta naturae; quo inuento omnis ab eo quasi capite de summo bono et malo disputatio ducitur.*

[150] See Plut., *Comm. not.* 26, 1070f–1071b and Alex. Aphr., *De an.* II pp. 167.13–168.20 Bruns [neither in Mette 1985]; see Striker (1996c), summarized in Striker (1996d: 239–48).

[151] See also Brittain (2001: 263) and (2015: 27). [152] See Striker (1996d: 268–70).

§19

Fuit ergo iam accepta...quid repugnet iudicando: while passages can be found in Plato's dialogues which deal with issues falling under the headings of ethics, physics, and logic, as these parts of philosophy were understood in the Hellenistic period, the division as such is of course not to be found in the dialogues. See, however, the Ps.-Platonic *Def.* 414b7–9: Φιλοσοφία τῆς τῶν ὄντων ἀεὶ ἐπιστήμης ὄρεξις· ἕξις θεωρητικὴ τοῦ ἀληθοῦς, πῶς ἀληθές· ἐπιμέλεια ψυχῆς μετὰ λόγου ὀρθοῦ, 'Philosophy is a reaching for the knowledge of eternal things; an attitude that is contemplating the true, how it is true; the care for the soul in combination with right reason.' For the ascription to Plato, see also D.L. 3.56 ('Plato added logic to the two pre-existing parts of philosophy'); Sext., *M.* 7.16 (Plato as virtual ἀρχηγός of the three parts, since he discussed many problems pertaining to them). In *Top.* A14 105b19–29 Aristotle suggests that opinions which might feature in προβλήματα or προτάσεις in dialectical exchanges be divided into ἠθικαί, φυσικαί, and λογικαί. The tripartite division of philosophy which we find here in Cicero was conventionally ascribed to Xenocrates (Sextus, *M.* 7.16 = frg. 1 Heinze = frg. 82 Isnardi-Parente); see further frgs 83–9 Isnardi Parente. Aristotle might have used the related categorization of problems and premisses because it was already current in the Academy. The Stoics used the division, too; see once more Sext., *M.* 7.16, and Ierodiakonou (1993). Here in Cicero there is no reference to another dispute, over whether logic is a tool or instrument rather than a part of philosophy; see Barnes (1997a: 140). See also the collection of Greek and Latin texts on the division of philosophy in Wildberger (2006: 355–66); Habets (1997) [*non uidi*]; Bronowski (2019: 17–52).

The sequence of ethics, physics, and logic, 'marked if not stressed' (Barnes 1997a: 140 n. 3: 1.19 *primum*, 1.22 *sequebatur*, 1.30 *tertia*), is also in Eudorus *ap.* Stob., *Ecl.* II.7, p. 42.11–13 Wachsmuth; Sen., *Ep. mor.* 99.9; and Aug., *C.D.* 8.4 (cf. *Contra Acad.* 3.17.37). In Cicero's speech in *Luc.* the places of ethics and physics are reversed (§114, and the whole doxographical section down to §146 *fin.*).

With the expression *de uita et moribus*, cf. *Tull.* 3: *proferre de uita et moribus et existimatione M. Tulli*; *Sull.* 69: *ut...de uita hominis ac de moribus dicam*. Contrast e.g. the characterization of ethics in *Fin.* 4.14. Cicero has here chosen terminology which is reminiscent of the courts (presumably because it was an established shorthand, not because there is anything 'rhetorical' in ethics). With the characterization of physics, cf. the much fuller passage *Fin.* 4.12–13. The obscurity of physical matters is noted several times in *Luc.* 118–28, as well as in 147; cf. also *Fin.* 3.37, 5.10, 5.51.

The manner in which logic is characterized has been analysed in detail by Barnes (1997a: 140–2). Cicero uses no noun to refer to the whole of what I have called 'logic', but it is clear from e.g. *Fat.* 1 that he is thinking of λογική: *totaque est λογική quam rationem disserendi uoco* (unlike *musica*, *dialectica*, etc., *logica* was never used by Cicero). *Tertia de disserendo* functions as a phrasal term, with the following epexegetic *et* setting up descriptions of areas within 'logic'. In other passages (*Fin.* 2.17; *Orat.* 113–14) Cicero treats 'logic' as a generic *uis loquendi*, divided into rhetoric and dialectic (i.e. the study of arguments); this is a different level of description and reflects the Stoic notion (also found in Arist. *Rhet.* and Plt. *Phaedr.*) that 'genuine' rhetoric is or should be relevantly like philosophical argument, merely presented in a different way. The three cola which gloss *tertia de disserendo* are suggestive of epistemology and the criterion of truth (*quid uerum sit, quid falsum* [sc. *iudicando*]), rhetoric (*quid rectum in oratione prauumue* [sc. *iudicando*]), and dialectic (*quid consentiens, quid repugnans iudicando*). Cf. *Leg.* 1.62, where the first and the third colon only are paralleled: ... *disserendi ratione, ueri et falsi iudicandi scientia, et arte quadam intellegendi quid quamque rem sequatur et quid sit quoique contrarium*; *Tusc.* 5.68: *tertius* [sc. *animi fructus*] *in iudicando, quid cuique rei sit consequens quid repugnans, in quo inest omnis cum subtilitas disserendi, tum ueritas iudicandi*. For the Greek terms corresponding to *consentiens/repugnet*, see on *Luc.* 91. The brevity of the characterization of the third part of philosophy makes it difficult to say whether a contemporary reader would have felt that λογική as conceived by the Stoics is ascribed to the Old Academy here. The evidence for Xenocrates' views on the subject, assembled by Krämer (1983: 48–9), shows that he was indebted to Aristotle and the earlier inner-Academic tradition. On logic qua theory of arguments, see also *Luc.* 26, 91–8.

Iam accepta a Platone probably means 'already received from Plato' (cf. *Brut.* 205), not 'already accepted (or: endorsed) by Plato' (cf. *Leg.* 2.14). *Accipere* is not normally used in *Acad.* of endorsements; cf., however, *Luc.* 66 *accipio* (in a contrast with endorsement by assent), 68 *accepero* (of assumptions made in the course of an argument). The uses in *Ac.* 1.26: *reliquae partes accipiendi et quasi patiendi* and 1.27: *materiam quandam ... quae tota omnia accipere possit* are quite different. The tripartite division of philosophy, one may assume, does not by itself represent a deeper doctrinal commitment on Plato's part (as opposed to a high-level formal principle) according to Varro; the division is relied on and not interrogated in Cicero's speech in *Luc*. Gigon translates: 'Die schon von Platon überkommene Art des Philosophierens verlief also auf drei Bahnen...'.

Goerenz printed *consentiens* ⟨*sit*⟩, but the ellipsis is entirely standard.

Ac primam partem...et animo et corpore et uita: this first sentence presents Old Academic theory as naturalist in that it is ultimately grounded in the observation of nature (in some sense) and represents an attempt to obey nature. Nature alone provides a guide towards the highest good, but the exposition stops short of stating that nature straightforwardly furnishes it (according to *Fin.* 5.17b the *prima inuitamenta naturae* can lead to the highest good). The highest good has been obtained when someone has reached, starting from nature, everything, sc. good in relation to soul, body, and 'life' (i.e. goods external to our physical make-up; see also on §22 below, where *Fin.* 5.68 is discussed). That the end of the sentence refers to three classes of *bona* is clear from 1.21 *fin.*: *ita tripartita ab iis inducitur ratio bonorum*. That *natura* means 'human nature' only as opposed to, say, human nature and the universe as a whole emerges gradually as Varro continues; see Burkert (1972: 35–6) on Ps.-Pythagorean texts which contain the former conception of nature (see the next note). There is no pronouncement or, as far as I can see, implication as yet that what the highest good in one's moral theory is can be directly inferred from human nature, notably observations made 'at the cradle'; on arguments about nature based on such observations, see Brunschwig (1986); Inwood (2016).

With *extremum...rerum expetendarum*, cf. τὸ ἔσχατον τῶν ὀρεκτῶν or τὸ ἔσχατον ὀρεκτόν in Sextus, *P.H.* 1.25; Arius Didymus *apud* Stob., *Ecl.* II.7, p. 76.22–3

Wachsmuth; Alex. Aphr., *Mant.* p. 150.20-1 Bruns: τὸ ἔσχατον τῶν ὀρεκτῶν; and Falcon (2012: 148-9).

Reid[1] (p. 116) wonders if *partem* could be due to *artem* having been corrupted (cf. *Fin.* 5.16), but the ethical part of philosophy is not a craft. *Primam* marks the first item in an enumeration of *partes*, with the next one beginning in §24; see previous n. Plasberg[1] prints *primum* with *Γ*; this would only be preferable if it signalled the first in a series of topics within ethics, and *pars bene uiuendi* seems to resume *de uita ac moribus* above. The evidence for Polemo's naturalism from Cicero and elsewhere is reviewed in the general note above. Reid[1] prints *repetebant* for the transmitted *petebant*. One might think that the sense is better served by a verb suggesting ultimate derivation or grounding rather than direct derivation (cf. *Leg.* 1.20 for the use: *repetam stirpem iuris a natura*, and *OLD* s.v. no. 7), but Plasberg[1] cites two instances of *petere* in similar contexts (*Fin.* 4.47, 5.33). With *referrentur* Reid[1] (p. 117) aptly compares Greek ἀναφέρειν; the subjunctive is due to indirect speech after *dicebant*. For the three classes of goods, referred to by ablatives of respect and associated with the Peripatetics in particular, see Stob., *Ecl.* II.7, p. 46 Wachsmuth; Clement, *Strom.* II, cap. XXI p. 184, 1-3 Stählin; D.L. 5.30, where it is ascribed to Aristotle in the latter's Life; *Tusc.* 5.24 (ascribing it to Theophrastus); *Tusc.* 5.76 and 84-5, where the division is claimed for the Peripatetics and the Old Academy (in line with Aristotelian thinking); *Fin.* 5.84; Inwood (2014) and (2014a: 51-72). With external goods as 'goods with respect to life', cf. 1.21 *init.*, where they are called *(bona) uitae...adiuncta*.

The seclusion of *esse* after *extremum* as implemented by Gigon would remove the copula between the subject accusative (*extremum rerum expetendarum et finem bonorum*) and the complement (the rest of the sentence from *adeptum*); while such ellipseis are possible, a convoluted sentence would be made even less clear here. *Esse* as a full verb would make no sense, since the existence of a *summum bonum* is already assumed in the preceding part of the sentence.

Corporis autem alia ponebant in toto...in lingua explanatam uocum impressionem: cf. *Fin.* 5.34-6 for the notion that human beings are made up of body and soul (with the collection of texts in Dörrie 1987: 94-101 and 319-28, who starts with *Alc. I*, 129e-130c; Burkert 1972: 36 on evidence from Ps.-Pythagorean texts apparently influenced by Antiochus), and that goods of the body and the soul taken as wholes can be distinguished from goods of parts of the body and the soul. The same distinction is to be found in Stob., *Ecl.* II.7, pp. 46-8 Wachsmuth, where it follows upon the *tria bona* distinction ascribed to the younger Peripatetics and followers of Critolaus; see previous n. and Madvig (1876: 666-7). The beginning of the Stob. passage is discussed in Inwood (2014: 260-1).

Reid[1] (p. 118) cites detailed parallels both from the thematically related passages noted above and from a broader range of texts. *Corporis*, sc. *bona* (cf. 1.21 *fin.*). For goods of the body as a whole, cf. *Fin.* 5.18. As to *in lingua...explanatam uocum impressionem*, the contrast with the singular *uoce* in the preceding colon makes it clear that words or articulated sounds are at issue here; see *TLL* s.v. *explano* col. 1713.32-4 and Luque Moreno (1996: 34), who analyses classifications of *uox* in Latin grammatical texts and suggests *explanata* = διεξοδική. *Impressionem* has been modified to *expressionem* in some later manuscripts, but the idea here is that structure is pressed upon unarticulated sounds (cf. *OLD* s.v. *impressio* nos. 3–4, not 1–2; *TLL* s.v. col. 676.22–3). The imposition of rhythmical structure, or rather structure conceived as imposed, is at issue in *De orat.* 3.185: *si numerosum est in omnibus sonis atque uocibus quod habet quasdam impressiones...*, which May and Wisse (2001: 282) translate as: 'If in all sounds and utterances rhythm is understood as the quality of having certain beats and of being measurable by regular intervals...'.

The relatively smaller value of the goods of the body is discussed by Piso in *Fin.* 5.71b–72: *Illa enim quae sunt a nobis bona corporis numerata complent ea quidem beatissimam uitam, sed ita ut sine illis possit beata uita existere. Ita enim paruae et exiguae sunt istae accessiones bonorum ut, quem ad modum stellae in radiis solis, sic istae in uirtutum splendore ne cernantur quidem. (72) Atque hoc ut uere dicitur, parua esse ad beate uiuendum momenta ista corporis commodorum, sic nimis uiolentum est nulla esse dicere; qui enim sic disputant, obliti mihi uidentur quae ipsi fecerint principia naturae. Tribuendum est igitur his aliquid, dum modo quantum tribuendum sit intellegas. Est enim philosophi non tam gloriosa quam uera quaerentis nec pro nihilo putare ea quae secundum naturam illi ipsi gloriosi esse fateantur, et uidere tantam uim uirtutis tantamque, ut ita dicam, auctoritatem honestatis ⟨esse⟩ ut reliqua non illa quidem nulla, sed ita parua sint, ut nulla esse uideantur. Haec est nec omnia spernentis praeter uirtutem et uirtutem ipsam suis laudibus amplificantis oratio; denique haec est undique completa et perfecta explicatio summi boni. Hinc ceteri particulas arripere conati suam quisque uideri uoluit afferre sententiam.* That the stars in the night sky emit light which, while being light, is so much less bright than that of the sun (§71 *fin.*) is obvious, but it is less clear how the stars can be deemed to contribute any brightness once the sun rises. So perhaps the point of the simile is that the night sky demonstrates that the stars emit light, which tells against denying them the role of a light emitter (in the analogy, the status of a good), even though their contribution is minute. One difference between Stoic indifferents and Antiochian *bona* is that, qua things of value, indifferents are different from virtue not just by degree but in kind, whereas the value of the three classes of *bona* is a (very substantial) difference of degree (see the general note on *Ac.* 1.33b–39). The latter notion is conveyed by the analogy. Cf. Klein (2015: 240–1) on *Fin.* 3.45.

§20

Animi autem quae essent...in naturam et mores diuidebantur: the goods of the soul, which inter alia enable humans to grasp virtue with their minds, are divided into those we are endowed with naturally (*natura*) and those which require training and experience (i.e. are the result of conditioning due to *mores*).

Cf. *Fin.* 5.36: *Animi autem et eius animi partis quae princeps est quaeque mens nominatur plures sunt uirtutes, sed duo prima genera, unum earum quae ingenerantur suapte natura appellanturque non uoluntariae, alterum autem earum quae in uoluntate positae magis proprio nomine appellari solent, quarum est excellens in animorum laude praestantia. Prioris generis est docilitas, memoria; quae fere omnia appellantur uno ingenii nomine, easque uirtutes qui habent ingeniosi uocantur. Alterum autem genus est magnarum uerarumque uirtutum, quas appellamus uoluntarias, ut prudentiam temperantiam fortitudinem iustitiam et reliquas eiusdem generis. Et summatim quidem haec erant de corpore animoque dicenda, quibus quasi informatum est quid hominis natura postulet.* While the thematic resemblances with *Ac.* 1.20 are obvious, *Fin.* 5.36 is formally a division of virtues or excellences, not of goods (see the general note above on the disposition of the speech in *Fin.* 5). The Aristotelian distinction between ethical and intellectual virtues (cf. *N.E.* A13) may be alluded to in *Fin.* 5.36, in part to claim Peripatetic credentials for what is said, whereas *Ac.* 1.19–23 relies on the later Peripatetic framework of the *tria bona*. Aristotle broadly holds ethical virtues to be acquired and intellectual ones to be natural, but is aware that the distinction is not clear-cut.

Reid[1] (p. 147) on *Ac.* 1.38 *natura aut more* writes as if here in *Ac.* 1.20 ethical and intellectual virtues were at issue: 'In §20 the διανοητικαὶ ἀρεταί were said to owe their development to nature, and the ἠθικαὶ ἀρεταί theirs to practice.' See on *Ac.* 1.38 for Zeno's modifications of the Old Academic scheme.

Naturae celeritatem ad discendum et memoriam dabant...proprium et ingeni: *naturae* is dative, and the *ueteres* are the subject of *dabant. Ad* introducing a purpose (*celeritatem ad discendum*) is conventional. The terms εὐμάθεια and μνήμη e.g. in 'Arist.', *M.M.* 1.5 (not *N.E.* A13, pace Reid[1] p. 118). See *Fin.* 5.36, quoted in the previous n., on the association of *ingenium* with intellectual virtues. The mood of *esset* is due to *oratio obliqua*; with the emendation *esse*, made by Orelli recorded in Halm, *quorum...ingenii* would be a main clause.

Morum autem putabant studia esse...in quibus erat philosophia ipsa: *morum* is an objective genitive: to *mores, studia* and *consuetudo* are applied. The latter in turn is partly formed by practice, and partly by reflection, which jointly are (*erat = uersabatur*) the province of philosophy (*oratio obliqua* is dropped, but there is no reason to suspect an authorial remark of Cicero's). *Ratio* is of course an ambiguous term, but the immediate context as well as the fact that Peripatetic theorizing, including in ethics, tends to start from observation arguably narrow down its meaning. Implicitly rejected is any notion that virtue is something human beings are divinely endowed with. Reid[1] (p. 119) suggests that *quasi* signals a translation of a Greek term and quotes Arist., *N.E.* B1, 1103a17: ἡ δ' ἠθικὴ (sc. ἀρετή) ἐξ ἔθους περιγίνεται, which he thinks may be behind Cicero's Latin. If so, then it will remain true that no particular Peripatetic text, e.g. the end of *N.E.* Book 1 and the beginning of Book 2, is being systemtically referenced in the wider context here. See also Stob., *Ecl.* II.7, p. 117 Wachsmuth (on the Peripatetics): τὸν δ' ἄνθρωπον, τῷ λόγῳ πλαττόμενον, ἐκ τοῦ ἐθισμοῦ μέρους τῆς ψυχῆς ἀλόγου, and Macrob. 3.8.9: *Varro de moribus morem* (*logist.* frg. 74 Bolisani) *dicit esse in iudicio animi, quem sequi debeat consuetudo*; both quoted already by Reid[1] (p. 119).

Opinions vary about the precise nature of the emphasis created by *philosophia ipsa*; cf. Reid[2] (p. 19): '...and in these methods philosophy herself was included'; Gigon (p. 287): '...auf diesen Leistungen beruht gerade auch das Philosophieren'; Brittain (2006: 95): '...practice and reason being the domain of philosophy'.

In qua quod incohatum est...Ergo haec animorum: Varro now introduces terminology (*appellatur*) in the domain of philosophy (*in qua* [sc. *philosophia*]): progress to virtue, as yet incomplete, is to be distinguished from virtue. Virtue obviously ranks first among the goods of the soul, being *una res optima*. Peripatetic theory, like the Stoic one, had a notion of progress towards virtue (see Burnyeat 1980), but the terminology here is more suggestive of the Stoic notion of προκοπή, which is, at least as a technical term, absent from our sources on Peripatetic ethics. Reid[1] (p. 119) has a complete collection of Cicero's renderings: *progressio* as here also in *Off.* 3.14 and 17; *Fin.* 4.17 and 67; *Tusc.* 4.1; *progressus* in *N.D.* 1.15 (if προκοπή is alluded to there) and *Tusc.* 4.44; *processus* in *Brut.* 232. On the doctrine itself, see Luschnat (1958); and Roskam (2005), who discusses evidence from Cicero on pp. 140–5.

Neque functions like *et non*, with *non* negating *absolutum* only. On virtue as a perfection of human nature, a pervasive idea in Aristotle's ethical thought, cf. Arist., *Phys.* H2, 246a13–6: ἀλλ' ἡ μὲν ἀρετὴ τελείωσίς τις (ὅταν γὰρ λάβῃ τὴν αὑτοῦ ἀρετήν, τότε λέγεται τέλειον ἕκαστον—τότε γὰρ ἔστι μάλιστα [τὸ] κατὰ φύσιν—ὥσπερ κύκλος τέλειος, ὅταν μάλιστα γένηται κύκλος καὶ ὅταν βέλτιστος), 'Excellence is a kind of perfection (for when a thing has acquired its appropriate excellence, then it is said to be perfect—for it is then in most complete conformity to its own nature—as a circle becomes perfect when it becomes the best possible circle)', and *SVF* iii.257 (= Galen, *De Hipp. et Plat. plac.* 5.5): μία γὰρ ἑκάστου τῶν ὄντων ἡ τελειότης, ἡ δ' ἀρετὴ τελειότης ἐστὶ τῆς ἑκάστου φύσεως, 'there is one state of perfection for each thing, and excellence is the perfection of the nature of each thing.' Cf. *Ac.* 1.42 *fin*. For *omnium rerum quas in animis ponunt* in the sense of faculties, cf. *Leg.* 1.16: *quantam uim optimarum rerum mens humana contineat*. Concluding phrases like *ergo haec animorum* (cf. 1.39 *haec fere de moribus*; more parallels in Reid[1] p. 120) structure the text for its first readers, who did not have the benefit of a modern layout; on more familiar *Gliederungsmittel* in the ancient and medieval layout of texts, see Schröder (1999: 93–159).

For statements by ancient grammarians on *incohare* vs *inchoare*, see *TLL* s.v. *incoho*, col. 966.58–67. The supplement *absolutum*, probably added in what Hunt dubs τ while other *deteriores* supply *perfectum* (see Hunt 1998: 218), seems compelling, given the attested *absolutum* later in the same sentence; for the pair *incohatum/absolutum*, cf. e.g. *Off.* 3.33.

§21

Vitae autem (id enim erat tertium)…quam beatae uitae adiuncta sunt: the relative clause, which is part of the indirect statement and consecutive in sense (in that it characterizes the *bona*), functions as the subject accusative in an accusative with infinitive governed by *dicebant*, with *uitae* (dative)…*adiuncta* serving as the complement. This is preferable to supplying *bona* after *uitae* and taking *adiuncta* only as the complement, which would make the relative clause an afterthought.

Cf. 1.19:…*et animo et corpore et uita*, where the third class of goods was announced. Elsewhere they are called *externa bona* (sc. external to the person made up of body and soul): *Tusc.* 5.76; *Part. or.* 74; *De orat.* 3.115. See also Stob., *Ecl.* II.7, p. 46 Wachsmuth, and cf. Aristotle's phrase τὰ ἐκτὸς ἀγαθά, on which see *N.E.* A8, 1098b12–16; Cooper (1985: 176–7). Parallel discussions of external goods in *Fin.* 5.65–74 and *Tusc.* 5.22–3; Inwood (2014: passim).

Virtutis usus, cf. *Ac.* 1.38, can be paralleled in principle in Peripatetic as well Stoic texts—in the former case, one thinks of activity according to virtue (cf. e.g. D.L. 5.30, where the end and happiness according to Aristotle are reported in later Peripatetic terms), see Inwood (2014: 261-2), whereas in the latter case, selection of things of value (i.e. preferred indifferents) is what virtue, which on another level of description is a disposition of the mind of the sage, actually does. See Annas (1993) on Plt., *Euthyd.* 278-282d and 288d-292e on the uses of virtue, a seminal set of passages for Stoic ethics. The phrase, like its presumptive Greek counterparts (e.g. ἀρετῆς χρῆσις), is capable of several interpretations, as Görler (1994: 962) notes: 'Neben der genannten Bedeutung: a) Tugend wird "angewandt", kann man verstehen: b) die Tugend "benutzt" anderes, nämlich die körperlichen und äusseren Güter (genitivus subiectivus); c) die Tugend "wird benutzt" (genitivus obiectivus).' He goes on to observe that the evidence from Augustine (*C.D.* 19.3) appears to confirm that Antiochus appreciated these ambiguities and did not just intend one of these senses:...*omnibus (primis naturae) simul et se ipsa utitur* [sc. *uirtus*]...(*uirtus*) *bene utitur et se ipsa et ceteris, quae hominem faciunt beatum, bonis.* See also Bénatouïl (2007: 219-43), who contrasts the Stoic and the Antiochian conception of the use of what the Stoics call indifferents.

Cernitur with ablative means 'is seen [sc. veridically] in connection with' (Reid[1] p. 120) or 'is manifest in' (Brittain 2006: 95). Whereas just above Varro was speaking in terms of the *ueteres* positing something (§20 *fin.*: *in animis ponunt*), he now talks in terms of the objectively observable. The second part of the sentence is difficult. That the goods are *adiuncta* means that they are external add-ons to something: not so much to *natura* (i.e. body and soul) as to the happy life (which is only associated with the goods of the soul and virtue in particular). Cf. §§22b-23a.

Iam uirtus was changed by Goerenz to *nam uirtus*, printed also by Reid[1] and some earlier editors (see the apparatus in Plasberg[1] p. 44), but the sentence offers no grounds for the preceding one or the claims made in it.

Hominem enim esse censebant...humana quadam societate: cf. *Fin.* 5.66 for the Aristotelian notion of man as a political animal: *Nam cum sic hominis natura generata sit, ut habeat quiddam ingenitum quasi ciuile atque populare, quod Graeci* πολιτικόν *uocant, quidquid aget quaeque uirtus, id a communitate et ea quam exposui caritate ac societate humana non abhorrebit, uicissimque iustitia, ut ipsa se fundet in ceteras uirtutes, sic illas expetet. Seruari enim iustitia nisi a forti uiro, nisi a sapiente non potest. Qualis est igitur omnis haec, quam dico, conspiratio consensusque uirtutum, tale est illud ipsum honestum, quandoquidem honestum aut ipsa uirtus est aut res gesta uirtute; quibus rebus uita consentiens uirtutibusque respondens recta et honesta et constans et naturae congruens existimari potest.* In this passage the 'transition from ethics to politics' is made plain, which Reid[1] (p. 120) feels is missing from our passage. Man's social nature is not touched on in *Luc.* 132-4, where Cicero draws attention to aspects of Antiochus' ethics deemed to be inconsistent with his Stoicism, which Cicero makes a point of emphasizing, perhaps because what Varro says here also resonates with the Stoic conception of a κοσμόπολις to which all human beings belong. See *SVF* iii.340-8, the texts collected in section 67 of Long and Sedley (1987), as well as Vogt (2008) on the Stoics; Schofield (2012b) on Antiochus' conception of social virtue.

In the report on Antiochus' ethical teachings from Varro's *De philosophia*; Aug., *C.D.* 19.3, p. 355.8–17 Dombart-Kalb writes: *Hanc uitam beatam etiam socialem perhibent esse, quae amicorum bona propter se ipsa diligat sicut sua eisque propter ipsos hoc uelit quod sibi; siue in domo sint, sicut coniunx et liberi et quicumque domestici, siue in loco ubi domus est eius, sicuti est urbs, ut sunt hi qui ciues uocantur, siue in orbe toto, ut sunt gentes quas ei societas humana coniungit, siue in ipso mundo, qui censetur nomine caeli et terrae, sicut esse dicunt deos, quos uolunt amicos esse homini sapienti, quos nos familiarius angelos dicimus.* On this passage and *Fin.* 5.65–6 see Blank (2012: 254–7).

Quasi in *quasi partem* is unlikely to function as a marker that a Greek term is being rendered, given that here the only possible candidate would be the plain μέρος. See the general note above for the suggestion that terms like *quasi* serve the function of signalling close reference to *some* Greek source, marking the section as *Übersetzungsliteratur*. Reid[1] (p. 121) surveys apparent synonyms of *humana societas* (*humanitatis societas*; *hominum societas* as in *Leg.* 1.42; *societas generis humani* as in *N.D.* 1.4) and suggests that the latter are mere characterizations of the entity whereas *humana societas* hints at 'the civilizing effect of social union' (presumably because attributes which precede the head tend to be descriptive rather than classifying).

Brittain (2006: 95 n. 17) notes: 'The Stoics construed these goods [i.e. 'relational goods such as friendships and membership in a flourishing community'] as psychological states in the good person...but the Peripatetics and Old Academics regard them as external goods, i.e. as partly contingent on other people or the state of the world.' See Stob., *Ecl.* II.7, p. 94.21 Wachsmuth = *SVF* iii.98; Vogt (2008: 148–54); and the collection of texts on the subject in Banateanu (2001).

P reads *hominem esse censebant quasi partem quandam ciuitatis*, μ *hominem enim censebant quasi partem quandam esse ciuitatis*, and γ *hominem enim esse censebant quasi partem quandam ciuitatis*. Reid[1] (p. 120) prints P's text, dismissing the μ reading because he found it in one manuscript he deemed interpolated (Ged); the μ reading is objectionable on rhythmical grounds, as Hunt (1998: 96 n. 31) notes. The text of γ, printed by Plasberg[1], is possible (for the sequence *hominem enim*, cf. e.g. *De orat.* 2.28) and has point in that *enim* is justificatory and not just interactional here (Plasberg[1] 44: '...*sed enim peraptum est, quoniam illa quae beatae uitae adiuncta sunt, i.e. patria parentes liberi amici alia, humana societate continentur*'). For γ alone to preserve the archetypal correct reading, P would have needed to drop *enim*, and μ to move *esse*. This seems as likely as the explanation for the text without *enim* furnished by Hunt (1998: 96–7 and 104–5), i.e. that P preserves the archetypal correct reading, that in Γ *enim* was mistakenly written for *esse* in the body of the text while *esse* was added in the margin (intended as a replacement of *enim*), and that *esse* was then put into the text in different places by μ and γ.

Ac de summo quidem atque naturali bono...ut gratiam: Reid[1] (p. 121) puts a colon after *sic agunt* and assumes that the *summum bonum* includes goods of the mind and bodily goods here, so that *cetera autem* describes external goods. As he himself notes, however, in §22 'the "*animi bona*" are set against the "*corporis bona*" and the "*externa*" combined', and in §19 Varro says:...*constituebantque extremum esse rerum expetendarum et finem bonorum adeptum esse omnia e natura et animo et corpore et uita*. Thus I take the first sentence to be a conclusion to what precedes, requiring strong punctuation after *sic agunt*: the *summum bonum*, obtainment of which ensures the happiest life (*Ac.* 1.23), includes the *tria bona*. What Varro turns to from *Cetera autem* is other goods, whose status is left somewhat obscure (thus also Brittain 2006: 95 n. 18). (For distinctions drawn by the Stoics between different promoted indifferents, cf. D.L. 7.107 = *SVF* iii.135 = LS 59m.)

This delivers consistency for *Ac.* 1.19–23, but behind the textual problem there lies an issue of substance. Cf. *Fin.* 5.68: *Ita fit ut duo genera propter se expetendorum reperiantur, unum, quod est in iis, in quibus completur illud extremum, quae sunt aut animi aut corporis; haec autem quae sunt extrinsecus, id est quae neque in animo insunt neque in corpore, ut amici, ut parentes ut liberi, ut propinqui, ut ipsa patria, sunt illa quidem sua sponte cara, sed eodem in genere quo illa non sunt*. Here external goods are not *propter se expetenda* and do not contribute to happiness, i.e. the *uita beatissima*. Drawing a distinction between external goods qua social goods and the kind of things mentioned in the present passage (wealth, glory, etc.) as goods of some lesser kind would not make *Fin.* 5.68 cohere with our passage. In 5.69 Piso continues with an explanation of why external goods cannot form part of the highest good: happiness would become unattainable and beyond the reach of the subject. For a full discussion of the issue, see Schofield (2012: 182–7), as well as Görler (1994: 961), who, however, does not address the tension between the accounts of *Ac.* 1 and *Fin.* 5. Piso's account in *Fin.* 5, while intelligible on its own terms, raises the question of why external goods count as goods if they do not contribute to the *uita beatissima*, still less the *uita beata*. Perhaps this is the reason why Piso seems somewhat fuzzy on the exact status of external goods, as noted by Inwood (2014: 274).

Augustine, *C.D.* 19.3, recognizes only goods of the soul and goods of the body, says the 'happy life' is associated with virtue only, the 'happier life' with virtue and some goods of the body, and the 'happiest life' with virtue and all goods of the body. External goods do not contribute, but human beings are social animals. This is consistent with the situation in *Fin.* 5.

Reid[1] (p. 121) suggests that *pertinere* is 'most likely a translation of συμβάλλεσθαι, as in *Fin.* 3.54'. *Pertinere ad* with gerund is frequent; for the gerundive, cf. e.g. *Clu.* 87: *nam id quoque ad corrumpendum iudicium pertinet*. The transmitted *tenendum* gives sense and is *difficilior* than *tuendum* (dett.), printed e.g. by Lambinus; see Plasberg[1] (p. 44) for a fuller report, and cf. *Luc.* 104: *alterum tenere*.

Ita tripertita ab his inducitur ratio bonorum: on τριγένεια as a technical term for the three Peripatetic kinds of goods, see Inwood (2014: 258). The manuscript evidence largely agrees on the spelling *tripert-**, but Plasberg[1] (p. 45) is right to note that we cannot be certain that Cicero did not write *tripart-**, which editors have tended to print. Plasberg[1] prints *his* here, Reid[1] *eis*; I have opted for the former on the grounds that it is more emphatic. This emphasis seems desirable because of the contrast with the next sentence: *his* refers to the *ueteres*, not just the Peripatetics.

§22

Atque haec illa sunt tria genera...Peripateticos arbitrantur: according to Varro the *tria genera bonorum* are rightly ascribed to the Peripatetics; however, it would be wrong to think that they are thereby peculiar to them, since the Academics and the

Peripatetics were one and the same thing. The implication is that the terminological distinction is Peripatetic, while the substantial view (hence *communis haec* **ratio** in the next sentence) is shared. This is consistent with the parallel evidence reviewed in the general note above, where it was argued that the personal relationship between Varro and Cicero made it unlikely that Cicero would have put a substantially modified 'ethics of Antiochus' into Varro's mouth.

Illud in *illud impudenter* has forward reference to *si...arbitrantur*. See Reid[1] (p. 121) on the subjunctive of *appellarentur*. For *dicere* 'set forth', see *TLL* s.v. *dico*, col. 965.52–74.

Communis haec ratio...quae in ipso animo atque in ipsa uirtute uersantur: the second purpose of the paragraph is to clarify what the highest good is for Academics and Peripatetics vis-à-vis the *tria bona* scheme. *Videbatur* is evidently not intended to introduce a qualification, and the view in question is dogmatically held. The *prima naturae* are here presented as including *either* all three kinds of goods distinguished above (*aut omnia...*), sc. and are connected with the *uita beatissima* (§23), *or* the goods of the soul (*aut maxima...*), sc. and are connected with the *uita beata*. *Aut...aut* has its exclusive sense. Cf. the commentary on *Luc.* 131.

The phrase *prima naturae*, and similar alternative formulations, has been rendered 'first advantages of nature' (vel sim.) by some (e.g. 'primary natural advantages' in Irwin 2012: 152), and 'first natural instincts' (vel sim.) by others (e.g. 'primäre Strebungen der Natur' in Burkert 1972: 31). It is clear from the various alternatives which Cicero uses for this phrasal term (see below) that strictly *prima naturae* are things (perceived to be) of value, not the impulses or instincts that make human beings go for them. This is especially plain in contexts where the *prima naturae* are the logical object of verbs like 'to enjoy' or 'to seek to reach'. Within Cicero, the notion that there are *prima naturae* features in a number of related contexts: one is in connection with so-called cradle arguments, where philosophers consider the young or not-so-young child in the cradle and affect to observe its initial attachments, which then enter into a moral theory, either as ultimate ends or in a more indirect way (e.g. *Fin.* 3.17); the second is the various *diuisiones* of ethical ends, where *prima naturae*, i.e. their obtainment or their pursuit, features in simple and compound ends (e.g. *Fin.* 5.21); the third is in accounts of οἰκείωσις, where the *prima naturae* are ascribed a role in the process of appropriation (e.g. *Fin.* 5.40). There is reason for thinking that the cradle argument, on which see Brunschwig (1986) and Inwood (2016), originated within Epicureanism, even though it does not feature in Epicurus' extant texts, and that the Stoic version is a response to it. And while Cicero, in Antiochian contexts, links the notion of *prima naturae* with the post-Platonic Academy, we saw above that probably no theory resembling that of οἰκείωσις can be claimed for it (see above, n. 116). However, in Cicero's report on the *Chrysippea diuisio* (*Luc.* 138) which probably inspired Carneades', one of the options recognized by Chrysippus, if only to be reduced to another one, is characterized as a combination of virtue and the *prima naturae* (*...eos qui ad honestatem prima naturae commoda adiungerent*). If this report is authentic, then Chrysippus was probably thinking of the Peripatetics rather than the Old Academics, but was using a Stoic expression (τὰ πρῶτα κατὰ φύσιν; see Adler's index to *SVF*, p. 160, and e.g. Plut., *Comm. not.* ch. 26) to describe the objects of our first impulses. In relation to the developed *tria bona* framework deployed in our passage here and used by Antiochus, reconciliation with the *prima naturae* is not difficult: the *prima naturae* fall under all three or under two of these *bona* (those of the soul and those of the body), although within the classes of *bona* they rank at the very bottom. For the Stoics, they would be promoted indifferents (see *Fin.* 2.34 *fin.*); see also on *Ac.* 1.33–9 and *Fin.* 4.72. Cicero at times writes as if the existence of *prima naturae* was a shared assumption between the Stoics and the Old Academy (see the ascription to Polemo and Aristotle in *Fin.* 2.34), and for all we know the Stoics and Antiochus both assumed there was such a thing, but they differed in their conception of the *prima naturae* in a crucial respect: the Stoics assumed that the first natural impulses were directed at things like health, self-preservation, and well-functioning senses (Stob., *Ecl.* II.7, pp. 47.20–48.1 Wachsmuth), and that what is truly good, i.e. virtue, appeared so to the subject only later, whereas Antiochus speaks of 'seeds' or 'sparks' of virtue which are among the *prima naturae* already (e.g. *Fin.* 5.18). This, or so he assumed, does not leave his overall theory exposed to the charge, as the Stoic one was, that his theory of οἰκείωσις involved a shift of the end mid-development which undermined the naturalistic framework on which the overall theory relied (*Fin.* 4.43). See also the discussion of the *prima naturae* in Madvig (1876: 815–25); Philippson (1932); Inwood (1985: 218–23); Long and Sedley (i.1987: 257–9); Marzotto (2012: xlv–xlviii); Gill (2016: 238); and Dillon (2003: 162–3) on *Fin.* 2.33–4.

Reid[1] (p. 122) prints *prima naturā* over the transmitted variants *prima in* and *in prima* and comments on *naturā*: 'The ablative is conditioned by *essent*', by which he means that the ablative functions as the complement, with *essent* as auxiliary. The case for dismissing both transmitted readings would be that they look like independent attempts to improve on a *prima natura* which is found wanting, or independent attempts to allocate the right place to an *in* placed in the margin or between the lines by a reader or copyist. Of the two, *prima in naturā* (so Plasberg) would be preferable to *in primā naturā*. The hypothetical *prima natura* without *in* could be the result of corruption from *prima naturae* (suggested by Bremi 1798: 154 on *Fin.* 2.33: *quae prima data sint natura*), which is used elsewhere. Against *prima naturae* one could cite that there is no obvious reason why the phrase should be introduced here; and that, even once it is established, *prima naturae* does not harden to a technical term (cf. *Fin.* 2.42: *omnia quae prima natura approbauisset*, where *natura* is subject and *prima* goes with *omnia quae*; *Luc.* 131:...*uiuere fruentem rebus iis quas primas homini natura conciliet*; see the collection of passages in Madvig 1876: 816). On balance, however, it seems likely that Cicero wrote *prima naturae*, that *naturae* was corrupted to *natura*, and that the transmitted readings are attempts to address the situation after corruption. Hence I print *prima naturae*.

For *ipse* in *in ipso animo atque in ipsa uirtute*, see Reid[1] (p. 95) on *Ac.* 1.6 *haec ipsa de uita et moribus*. For *uersari in re* 'to reside in', see *OLD* s.v. *uerso* no. 11a.

Itaque omnis illa antiqua philosophia...ad uirtutis usum idonea: this concluding sentence introduces the *uita beata–uita beatissima* distinction; cf. the general note above; *Luc.* 134, *Fin.* 5.71 and 81 (= Antiochus frg. 9 Mette); *Tusc.* 5.22 (= frg. 10 Mette); Sen., *Ep. mor.* 92.14; see also Görler (1994: 963–4), and Görler (2004e), who argues that Antipater paved the way for the Antiochian distinction. While Antiochus was prepared to classify goods of the body and external goods as good in the formal sense, evidence from elsewhere suggests a desire to downplay them relative to the goods of the soul (see above, p. 145). Chief among the latter is virtue, which is necessary and sufficient for happiness, and within our power; the other goods, while they are all natural and while some of them are 'intrinsically precious' (*sua sponte cara* in *Fin.* 5.68), are not within our power, which is cited by Piso (ibid.) as the reason why obtaining them is not part of the *uita beata*; see Schofield (2012b: 182–7). This also made it more credible to claim that the Stoic view of the end is merely a verbal variation on the Old Academic one; cf. Carneades' claim that on this issue the Stoic differed from the Peripatetics merely verbally (*Tusc.* 5.120; *Fin.* 3.41), with Lévy (1992: 391–4).

Sensit is like *uidebatur* in §22 a term which may convey limited endorsement but does not do so here. Reid[1] (p. 122) points to *N.D.* 1.27 where *sensit* and *censuit* are used interchangeably.

The phrase *omnis antiqua philosophia* allows Varro to convey that the *ueteres* include Academics as well as Peripatetics. *Antiqua* carries no connotation of being obsolete, since Varro is relaying Antiochus' view, but the overall context is of course an account of the *prima forma*. With *ad uirtutis usum*, cf. §21: *ad uirtutis usum*, with n. Virtues are active, and are used, in a way in which the bodily and external goods are not.

§23

Ex hac descriptione…quas natura praescriberet: *descriptio* initially denotes a diagram, and then any outline, account, or narrative with specified parameters (see on *Ac.* 1.17 *fin.*). The suggestion is that a framework for human action arises from the commitment to an end in virtue of said parameters; *descriptio…praescriberet* seems deliberate.

The phrase *agendi…aliquid in uita et officii ipsius initium* distinguishes action generally (as opposed to inactivity) and moral action: both arise from the *descriptio*. (The charge of ἀπραξία frequently levelled against the Academics can similarly turn on one or the other sense of πρᾶξις; see on *Luc.* 33–4.) *Reperire* (on the tense see Reid[1] p. 122) of discoveries made while following a *descriptio* in Vitr. 9.pr.4 (where, however, the primary sense of *descriptio* is at issue): *quod opus fuerit genere numeri, quod multiplicationibus non inuenitur, eo descriptionibus linearum emendatius reperitur.*

With *officium* consisting in the *conseruatio earum rerum quas natura praescriberet*, cf. Plut., *Comm. not.* 23, 1069e (= *SVF* iii.491): 'Πόθεν οὖν' φησίν 'ἄρξωμαι; καὶ τίνα λάβω τοῦ καθήκοντος ἀρχὴν καὶ ὕλην τῆς ἀρετῆς, ἀφεὶς τὴν φύσιν καὶ τὸ κατὰ φύσιν;', '"What, then," says he, "will be my point of departure and what shall I take as duty's principle and virtue's matter, once I have abandoned nature and what is in conformity with nature?"' (transl. Cherniss). Cf. e.g. *Fin.* 3.22 (= *SVF* iii.497): *Cum uero illa, quae officia esse dixi, proficiscantur ab initiis naturae, necesse est ea ad haec referri, ut recte dici possit omnia officia eo referri, ut adipiscamur principia naturae….* Plasberg[2] assumes a lacuna after *in conseruatione* and inserts *sui et in appetitione* (cf. *Fin.* 5.24), a possibility mentioned only in the apparatus in Plasberg[1], but *Fin.* 4.27 suggests that preservation may be the primary idea and obtainment of *res* implied: ...*appeteret etiam conseruationem sui earumque rerum custodiam, finemque sibi constitueret secundum naturam uiuere*. Given the remark that a notion of appropriate action flows from what preceded, the fact that one can best parallel what Varro says here with Stoic texts on the καθῆκον is perhaps not sufficient to establish that the contemporary reader would have seen a narrowly Stoic definition here. On the difference between the Stoics and Antiochus regarding what is meant by 'nature' in such contexts, see the general note above; and Gill (2016) more generally on the two different theories of οἰκείωσις, one Stoic and one Antiochian, developed in Cic. *Fin.*

Hinc gignebatur fuga desidiae uoluptatumque contemptio...et multis uitae commodis anteponebantur: this list of choices and avoidances arising from the commitment to the end ascribed to the *ueteres* anticipates the objection that the addition of the *prima naturae* to the simple end of virtue opens the door to hedonism (see the general note on *Luc.* 129–41, esp. p. 747 on *Fin.* 5.23, for this potential threat to Antiochus' view).

See Reid[1] (pp. 122–3) for parallels to the items in the list, as well as the suggestion that Cicero seeks to mention the cardinal virtues here. With *laborum dolorumque susception*, cf. *Off.* 3.117 (and *Fin.* 1.49): *fortitudo quae est dolorum laborumque contemptio*. The correspondence *uoluptatum contemptio* = σωφροσύνη becomes plausible through the context. *Congruentes* evokes the technical senses of *descriptio* (see n. above). The *commoda uitae* are the non-ranked goods of §21 *fin.*, not the *uitae...adiuncta* of §21 *init.* The phrase itself is common and has no definite technical meaning. Reid[1] tacitly omits the first *et* in *et uoluptatibus et multis uitae*.

Haec quidem fuit...forma atque descriptio: *primam posui* looks back to *Ac.* 1.19: ...*ratio triplex: una de uita*.... The pairing of *forma* and *descriptio* resumes *Ac.* 1.17 *fin.* on the one hand and provides important guidance for the textual problem in *Ac.* 1.33 *init.* on the other. The latter passage is also illuminated by the prepositional phrase *apud eos* here, in that it suggests a particular interpretation of *illis* in 1.33: *haec forma erat illis prima, a Platone tradita*; see ad loc. *Apud eos*, aptly translated by Reid[2] quoted below, must go with both cola, i.e. *morum institutio* and *eius...descriptio*.

Institutio is here better translated as 'system' (*OLD* s.v. no. 1; *TLL* s.v. col. 1996.36–7) than as 'action of teaching, method of instruction' (*OLD* s.v. no. 4), since the preceding paragraph refers to doctrines (similarly Reid[2]: 'Such then was in their minds the outline of the theory of conduct...'; contrast Brittain 2006: 'So this was their training of ethical dispositions...'). This being so, *et (eius partis)* comes close to being epexegetic. Walker's emendation *partis* is recorded by Davies (p. 28).

Varro's survey here is historical, in that he gives the view of the *antiqui*, but any view of theirs that was not modified along the way became Antiochus', or so is the construal.

§§24–29

I start with an interpretative paraphrase of the section, the one devoted to physics in Varro's historical survey, which is opaque in places, thus obscuring what the interpretative options are.[153]

1. §24 *De natura autem… efficeretur aliquid*

The section begins with an indication of the *object* of physics qua part of philosophy, *natura* 'nature'; contrast the beginning of the section on λογική in *Ac.* 1.30 (*tertia deinde philosophiae pars*).[154] In *Ac.* 1.6 Varro is made to say: *Nostra tu physica nosti: quae cum contineantur ex effectione et ex ea materia quam fingit et format effectio…*, where the neuter plural *physica* must mean something like 'physical theory'. This suggests that Varro's offering a division of nature here in *Ac.* 1.24 rather than of physical theory is not intended to be significant.

Nature is said to be divided by 'them' (the subject of *diuiderent*, i.e. the *antiqui*) into two 'things' or 'entities' (*res*). *Res* is semantically flat and does not by itself imply e.g. material components or constituents. Principles feature later in the section, and it is clear that the two *res* are not principles in the sense in which the text employs the term.[155] Neither *res* is given a name at this point, and instead both are characterized by properties which they have: one is such that it 'brings about' (*efficiens*), while the other one 'offers itself' to the first one and is made into something (see the n. below on the construction of *eaque efficeretur aliquid*).

2. §24 *In eo quod efficeret… quod non alicubi esse cogatur*

In the 'thing' which brings something about they assumed a 'force' (*uis*) to reside, while in that which is merely affected there is a certain matter (*materia quaedam*); neither *res* is identified with a force or matter respectively. (In *Ac.* 1.6 *materia* is the thing which is affected; 'it is not clear what difference this makes', as Inwood 2012: 209 observes.) The alienating *quaedam* can in principle be intended to indicate a correspondence with a particular Greek term (ὕλη or οὐσία), or it might serve to discourage a simple materialist interpretation of *materia*, or both; see n. below. Apparently because the characterization of the two *res* might suggest otherwise, Varro continues that 'nonetheless' (*tamen*) both things are in one another (and thus in some sense mutually dependent).

The mutual dependence is explained next: matter cannot 'hang together' if it is not contained by a force (*uis*), and a force cannot exist—*esse* is most likely the verb omitted—without some matter. Thus actual existence rather than notional conceivability is

---

[153] Cf. the paraphrases in Sedley (2002) and Inwood (2012: 208–12), to which mine is indebted in many ways.
[154] See Inwood (2012: 209 n. 45) on the same point.
[155] Thus correctly Inwood (2012: 210); contrast Sedley (2002: 55).

meant here: conceiving of and talking about them as distinctive entities is not a problem. Varro continues, again linking up with *enim*, that there is nothing which is not forced to be somewhere or in some place (*alicubi*). The sentence explains why the two things must be in one another if all there is are the two things: otherwise they would be in something else, i.e. a third thing.

3. §24 *Sed quod ex utroque… nominabant*

What is (made) of the two things they (i.e. the *ueteres*) at once[156] described as a 'body' (*corpus*) and a 'quality' (*qualitas*) of sorts. Following Madvig (1876: lxv n. 1), Reid[1] (p. 126) thought that Cicero had misunderstood and/or mistranslated here in that a *corpus* was a qualified item (a *quale*), not a quality. However, the term *qualia* is used below in §28, and in the immediately following section 1.24 *fin.*–26a Cicero has Varro resume the subject of the difficulty of expressing philosophical issues in Latin. *Qualitas* as a rendering of ποιότης is cited as an instance. It would be an egregious error on Cicero's part to confuse 'quality' and 'qualified item' at this very point.

One way of interpreting the sentence is to assume that Varro is talking about two different characterizations arising from the two *res* as they jointly account for a qualified item: from the viewpoint of the *res* containing or including *materia*, a qualified item is a *corpus* (i.e. *materia* which is no longer pre-bodily), while from the viewpoint of the active, effecting *res* it is a quality (the quality which accounts for it being an item qualified in a certain way).[157] *Qualia* below in §28 is on this reading a different designation for compounds, i.e. the entities formed by the two initial *res*—one which does not privilege one of the two viewpoints.

4. §26 *Earum igitur qualitatum sunt… quae gignuntur e terra*

Varro next introduces two kinds of qualities (i.e. of qualities of such things as are themselves the result of the two *res* introduced in no. 1 above coming together in

---

[156] On the force of *iam* in *sed quod ex utroque, id iam corpus et…*, see below.

[157] The notion that the quality is the item becomes more intelligible if one considers issues arising from flux: it is the quality rather than the matter which ensures the item's persistence over time. Cf. the Stoic response to the 'growing argument' (αὐξανόμενος λόγος), with Kupreeva (2003: 297–8), although (arguably) no doctrinal commitments peculiar to the Stoics would be incurred in our passage. Unlike the Stoics, the *antiqui* as presented here do not hold that a quality, in order to fulfil this role, needs to be a body; cf. Zeno's 'correction' on this point in *Ac.* 1.39. See also Sedley (2002: 57), whose reading of the passage I take to be similar to mine: 'A more palatable alternative will be to read "That which consisted of both was already, in their parlance, a body and, so to speak, a sort of quality"… as describing two *distinct* products of the principles' combination. Viewed in their own right, the passive and the active principle are, respectively, prime matter and a creative force; but when they are viewed in any actual combination the passive principle becomes some specific primitive body—whether earth, fire, air or water—and the active principle becomes some specific quality of that body, say heat or wetness.' A different interpretation is given by Inwood (2012: 210): '…the body generated by the active and passive entities is itself properly called a quality of sorts, rather than the bearer of a quality. A quality, then, is a primitive body; bodies are not bearers of qualities; neither force (neither the active nor the passive entity) considered on its own either a quality or a body.'

individual entities). The first kind is primary, the second kind are qualities arising from the primary qualities. The primary qualities are uniform and simple; they are, as is explained a moment later, the traditional four elements. The second kind of qualities are the *formae* of the animals and things which arise from the earth (i.e. non-animate things in the world). The term *formae* is open to a number of interpretations: Varro may be thinking of the species or kinds of animals and inanimate things, or he may be using *formae* to refer to the qualities which 'make' kinds of things in the sense of quality introduced above, but two levels of description down. Qualities thus understood account for kinds, too.[158] It is less likely that *formae* would be used of the forms of individuals (akin to a notion of Aristotelian particular forms—*Einzelformen*—or Stoic peculiar qualities, the latter a concept demonstrably familiar to Cicero; cf. on *Luc.* 84). That the beings and things which arise from the elements are called *quasi multiformes* could mean that they are genera with many species; if it meant that they are varied as individuals (in some sense), then *formae* and *-formis* in *multiformes* would refer to different kinds of 'form'.[159]

5. §26 Ergo illa innitia... dissimile Aristoteles quoddam esse rebatur

The four primary compounds (*illa* refers to what stands further away, i.e. not the *formae*) are now referred to as elements as well as principles (*elementa*, as well as *initia*, i.e. ἀρχαί, 'principles'). This shows that the initial bipartite distinction into an active and an affected *res* was not concerned with principles.

Air and fire have the power to move and affect, while water and earth can only be affected. One might think that this just means that the dualism of properties which obtained at the initial level of two *res* is replicated one level down, separating the elements into two groups of two. However, this is unlikely to be the intended sense because the elements would naturally be assumed to have properties of their own, even if they can be grouped in pairs along the lines indicated.[160]

---

[158] Inwood (2012: 210) holds that the qualities mentioned must be primitive bodies (see previous n.). I do not think that the text requires or invites this reading, and Zeno's modification discussed in *Ac.* 1.39—that only bodies can cause effects—would not be one if already Varro assumed here that qualities are bodies.

[159] Cf. Inwood (2012: 210): 'Other qualities are derived from them [i.e. the primary qualities]; these are differentiated and multiform. Plants and animals of various kinds ("formae") are listed. The observation that the derivative qualities are *uariae* and multiform may refer to the fact that plant as a genus and animal as a genus have multiple species ranged under them (dandelions, oak trees; rabbits, elephants). Alternatively, it may refer to the internal variety and differentiation within each species (dandelions and rabbits are pretty complex internally compared to the simplicity and uniformity of earth, air, fire, water). In favour of the former option is the occurrence of *formae*, which seems to refer to species, right after *multiformes*. It would be nice if the root *form*- had the same sense in both cases. In favour of the latter is the fact that the simplicity of the primary qualities is clearly a matter of internal structure and that the initial assertion of variety among derived qualities seems to be set in contrast to this feature of the primary qualities. Of course, both senses of "multiform" could be intended. Both are certainly applicable.'

[160] Thus also Inwood (2012: 210–11): 'The pre-elemental forces ('vis') above [i.e. in §24] seem to be completely subsumed in the quality/bodies which they underlie and seem not to be differentiated in any way beyond the one being active and the other being passive. At the present level of analysis, the forces must differ among the four elements (or at least between the active pair and the passive pair). This higher-level differentiation could, of course, be the product of features or facts about the underlying forces (the

Aristotle, we are told, thought there was a fifth element, from which the stars and minds were made. It is not stated if this is treated as Aristotle's personal opinion (not shared by others) or as the result of his superior interpretation of Platonic texts and/or thinking (see section 7.2), which was then embraced by the *ueteres*. Scholars have usually assumed the former (e.g. Inwood 2012: 211), but this does not seem to correspond to Varro's (and thus Antiochus') view. For in *Ac.* 1.39b Zeno's changes in the area of physics are named, and one of them is that Zeno 'did not avail himself of [the fifth element]' (...*non adhiberet*). This would make no sense if the fifth element was Aristotle's personal view rather than his contribution to the agreed position of the *antiqui*.[161] Varro does say (ibid.) that the existence of the fifth element was a view adopted by the *superiores* (*quintam hanc naturam ex qua superiores sensus et mentem effici rebantur*), which in its context cannot just mean 'Aristotle and the Peripatetics' as the final sentence of 1.39b makes clear (see on *Xenocrates et superiores etiam*).[162]

6. §27 *Sed subiectam patent... quod diuidi nequeat*

Varro now returns to his initial division, and characterizes the passive *res* further. Underlying all things but itself without any form (*species*) and quality at all is, according to them (i.e. again the *antiqui*), a certain *materia*, from which everything is moulded (*exprimere*) and brought about, and which can accept and shed any form (with *accipere*, cf. *reliquae partes accipiendi* in §26, of the passive elements), without disappearing completely. Although *materia* is characterized here on its own terms, this presumably should not be seen as contradicting the claim that the two basic *res* do not occur separately from each other: notional properties are at issue. The concept of moulding was not mentioned in §24, but is anticipated by *fingere* and *formare* in *Ac.* 1.6. Because matter is so eminently (*omnibus modis*) formable, it can perish, but not into nothing; rather, it is infinitely divisible because there is no minimum in the nature of things.

7. §27 *Quae autem moueantur... §28 illa effici quae appellant qualia*

Motion of things comes about due to intervals between them, which again can be divided infinitely (presumably because an interval is not void but again *materia* with a certain quality). Due to this motion (referred to by *ita* and *sic*), they think, the force which was said to be a quality is moved 'back and forth' (*ultro citroque*), and as a

---

active force being somehow more dominant in one pair of elements compared with the other). But it must be stressed that no feature of Cicero's text actually suggests this.'

[161] An alternative interpretation is to assume that Varro's account is incoherent; thus Inwood (2012: 204–8), who writes (p. 206): 'There is evidently some unclarity in Varro's (and for all we know Antiochus') mind about how general the doctrine of the fifth element was in the early Academy.' Inwood's appraisal of this particular issue informs his overall view of Varro's/Antiochus' reconstruction efforts.

[162] The term *superiores* occurs several times in *Ac.* 1.33b–43, with shifting referents; cf. 1.34, 1.38 (twice), 1.39 (twice), 1.42.

consequence *materia* itself is fundamentally or comprehensively (*penitus*) transformed so that *qualia*, things which possess a certain quality, are brought about.

8. §28 *E quibus in omni natura... sit nullumque corpus*

Out of these (sc. *qualia*, which include everything there is, for there is no unqualified matter in the world), the one world that there is is made, outside of which there is no *materia* and no qualified matter (*corpus*); see no. 2 above.

9. §28 *Partes autem esse mundi... a quo intereat*

The parts of the world are all those contained within it, which are in the hold of a thinking nature, in which there is perfect reason, and which is eternal (for there is nothing more powerful which could put an end to it).

10. §29 *Quam uim animum esse... ignorationemque causarum*

Varro now reports that 'they' provide a series of further characterizations of this force (*quae uis*, resuming *ratio perfecta*). It is 'the mind of the world' (*animus mundi*), represents perfect wisdom (*sapientia perfecta*), is a god (*deus*), is providence which governs heavenly as well as human affairs, and is necessity since nothing can turn out otherwise than was decided by it. It is also called 'chance' (*fortuna*), because its workings are not transparent to human beings, and thus many unforeseen and unexpected things arise from it due to the obscurity and our ignorance of causes.[163]

The section, which purports to give the view of the *antiqui*, was until recently among the less closely discussed in *Acad*. Its evaluation was for a long time guided by the assumption that Antiochus was a crude eclectic and in most respects a Stoic.[164] As a consequence, scholars could, avowedly or not, take the view that all the critical engagement which the passage demands, assuming its synthetic nature and that Antiochus devised it from his own resources, was the identification and separation of primarily Stoic and to a lesser extent Platonic elements (in the latter case mostly correspondences with Plato's *Tim.*), a process which would reverse, as it were, the method by which Antiochus 'devised' his physics of the Old Academy.[165] On this view, references to *Tim.*, which have always been recognized (see Reid[1] on the

---

[163] Inwood (2012: 212–13) observes that Varro makes no attempt to explain what the relationship is between (i) *uis* in the initial distinction between an active and a passive *res*, (ii) in the distinction of active and passive elements, and (iii) in the global account of §29. I have assumed in my summary that the *uis* in (i) and (iii) is the same, since the discussion in §§28–9 seems to return to the initial distinction in a ring composition of sorts. (This, of course, does not tell us how *uis* in i and iii *can* be the same kind of thing.)

[164] The latter notion was partly derived from statements of Academic speakers in Cicero's dialogues (notably *Luc.* 132; see ad loc.), who, however, are anything but unbiased reporters.

[165] See e.g. Reid (1885: 124).

section), function as transparent attempts to lend a Platonic appearance to an essentially Stoic set of views.¹⁶⁶

Ac. 1.29 can quite straightforwardly be related to a number of familiar Stoic views (see the nn. below), and with the beginning of the section (i.e. 1.24) which introduces an active and a passive *res* as well as, one level up, elements one may compare e.g. (A) D.L. 7.134 (= part of *SVF* ii.300, ii.299 = LS 44B):

Δοκεῖ δ' αὐτοῖς ἀρχὰς εἶναι τῶν ὅλων δύο, τὸ ποιοῦν καὶ τὸ πάσχον. τὸ μὲν οὖν πάσχον εἶναι τὴν ἄποιον οὐσίαν τὴν ὕλην, τὸ δὲ ποιοῦν τὸν ἐν αὐτῇ λόγον τὸν θεόν· τοῦτον γὰρ ἀΐδιον ὄντα διὰ πάσης αὐτῆς δημιουργεῖν ἕκαστα...διαφέρειν δέ φασιν ἀρχὰς καὶ στοιχεῖα· τὰς μὲν γὰρ εἶναι ἀγενήτους ⟨καὶ⟩ ἀφθάρτους, τὰ δὲ στοιχεῖα κατὰ τὴν ἐκπύρωσιν φθείρεσθαι. ἀλλὰ καὶ ἀσωμάτους εἶναι τὰς ἀρχὰς καὶ ἀμόρφους, τὰ δὲ μεμορφῶσθαι.

They take the view that there are two principles of all things, the active principle and the passive principle. The passive principle, then, is a substance without quality, that is, matter, the active principle is reason in this substance, that is, god. For he is eternal and the one who fashions everything inherent in the whole extent of matter.... They say that there is a difference between principles and elements; the former are without creation and destruction, but the elements are destroyed in the conflagration. Moreover, the principles are incorporeal and without form, but the elements have been endowed with form.

An important contribution to the debate was made by Görler (2004a), first published in 1990, who observed that three of the references to *Tim.* in the section, while representing verbal correspondences, occur in contexts which are actually at variance with the Platonic passages ostensibly referenced.¹⁶⁷ Görler described the phenomenon and ventured no explanation of it,¹⁶⁸ but in any event succeeded in showing that the standard view fails to appreciate the Platonic references in their apparent subversiveness.

More recently, a case has been made by Sedley (2002) that the physical views of the Old Academy as presented by Varro in *Ac.* 1.24-9 are not just an intellectually credible reconstruction of the physical views of Plato's successors from a first-century BC standpoint but might actually represent a summary of the physical views of the Academy under Polemo, which, however, need not mean that the views in question were formulated in their entirety by Polemo, rather than part formulated and part adopted and promoted. The argument starts from a text which was ignored or under-

---

[166] Thus e.g. Dörrie (1987: 472-7).
[167] See Görler (2004a: 92-4), who notes that (i) the phrase *animus mundi* in *Ac.* 1.29 is obviously reminiscent of the Timaean world-soul, without there being any suggestion that the *animus* in question originates from the work of the demiurge, in the manner envisaged in *Tim.*, etc.; that (ii) the claim that the active and the passive *res* are inextricably connected (1.24; no. 2 of the summary above) shows a close similarity with part of a sentence in *Tim.* 52b, where, however, it features in a context which dismisses the possibility that everything exists in such a way as to be spatially located (see the n. below); and that (iii) the claim that the two *res*, jointly constituting all there is, must consequently be in one another (1.24 *in utroque tamen utrumque*) directly contradicts *Tim.* 52c6-8 (again, see n.).
[168] Görler (2004a: 94): 'Es fällt schwer, dieses Verfahren literarisch einzuordnen und zu bewerten, aber der Befund und Antiochus' Aussage sind klar.'

appreciated in earlier literature,[169] (B) Simpl. *in Arist. Phys.* p. 26.5–15 (= Theophrastus frg. 230 FHS&G):

Καὶ Πλάτων τρία μὲν τὰ κυρίως αἴτια τίθησι τό τε ποιοῦν καὶ τὸ παράδειγμα καὶ τὸ τέλος, τρία δὲ τὰ συναίτια τήν τε ὕλην καὶ τὸ εἶδος καὶ τὸ ὄργανον. ὁ μέντοι Θεόφραστος τοὺς ἄλλους προϊστορήσας "τούτοις, φησίν, ἐπιγενόμενος Πλάτων, τῇ μὲν δόξῃ καὶ τῇ δυνάμει πρότερος τοῖς δὲ χρόνοις ὕστερος καὶ τὴν πλείστην πραγματείαν περὶ τῆς πρώτης φιλοσοφίας ποιησάμενος, ἐπέδωκεν ἑαυτὸν καὶ τοῖς φαινομένοις ἁψάμενος τῆς περὶ φύσεως ἱστορίας· ἐν ᾗ δύο τὰς ἀρχὰς βούλεται ποιεῖν τὸ μὲν ὑποκείμενον ὡς ὕλην ὃ προσαγορεύει πανδεχές [cf. Plt., *Tim.* 51a:...ἀλλ' ἀνόρατον εἶδός τι καὶ ἄμορφον, πανδεχές...], τὸ δὲ ὡς αἴτιον καὶ κινοῦν ὃ περιάπτει τῇ τοῦ θεοῦ καὶ τῇ τοῦ ἀγαθοῦ δυνάμει."

And Plato posits three causes in the strict sense, the maker, the paradigm, and the end, and also three contributory causes, matter, form, and the instrument. But Theophrastus, having first given a historical account of the others, adds: 'These were followed by Plato, who was their superior in reputation and ability but followed them chronologically. He devoted the greater part of his work to first philosophy, but also attended to appearances, undertaking enquiry into nature; in this he wants to make the principles two in number, one that which underlies as matter, which he calls "all receiving" [cf. Plt., *Tim.* 51], the other that which causes and moves, which he links to the power of god and that of the good.'

In this text Theophrastus states that Plato avowed a physical doctrine which posited two principles, an active and a passive one (the latter described in terms borrowed from the description of the receptacle in Plato's *Tim.*). Forms do not appear to enter into the account of physics (but see below on the reference to first philosophy.) This secures the possibility in principle that Varro's account here, which also does not involve forms, owes its initial assumption of two *res* as the basis of reality not to a retrojection of the Stoic view of two principles, but to an 'original' Old Academic interpretation of *Tim.* From there Sedley proceeds with a sequential reading of the whole section (minus the intermezzo on writing philosophy in Latin), examining in each case how one might arrive at the view in question on the basis of either a historically possible interpretation of a relevant section of *Tim.* or attested views of post-Platonic Academics and/or Peripatetics. Because a historically possible interpretation is not the same as the one most likely to be right, Sedley suggests that the burden of proof lies with those who want to assume Stoic elements in the account, for two reasons: first, Antiochian ethical theory, the closest thing to a comparandum, does seem to be consistent with key tenets of Polemo's ethics, on which we have substantially more independent information than on his physical views. It would seem unlikely that Antiochus was a historically aware and sophisticated syncretist (as opposed to eclectic) in his reconstruction of Old Academic ethics, but took a completely different, manifestly inferior approach in the field of physics. Second, Varro's

---

[169] However, an important earlier study on which Sedley draws is Krämer (1971: 108–31). Lefebvre (2017a) is devoted to frg. 230 in its own right.

speech is likely to be based on the *Sosus*, the dialogue which represents Antiochus' reply to Philo's Roman Books and which criticizes inter alia the historical claim that the epistemological position developed in the Roman Books was in fact the one which in the Academy had been held by Socrates, Plato, Arcesilaus, as well as Carneades all along. The historical claim was deemed to be a lie by Antiochus (*Luc.* 12 *fin.*). Against this background, so the argument, it is less than credible that Antiochus' rebuttal would involve a blunt and easily recognizable retrojection of Stoicism onto the Old Academy. Finally, Sedley cites two considerations in favour of the view that Old Academic physics as presented by Varro can actually be associated with a particular individual, Polemo: (a) the one fragment which we have on Polemo's physical views provides a piece of information which we also find in Varro's survey and which in the latter context would naturally have been put down to Stoic influence;[170] (b) in *Ac.* 1.39 Varro discusses Zeno's corrections of the Old Academic views on physics: *discrepabat etiam ab iisdem, quod nullo modo arbitrabatur quicquam effici posse ab ea quae expers esset corporis, cuius generis Xenocrates et superiores etiam animum esse dixerant*. Sedley argues (pp. 80–1) that here Polemo is a presence *in rasura* as it were, because Xenocrates and his predecessors are presented as having held that the mind is not a body. Here, or so Sedley suggests, the possibility is pointedly left open that Polemo was already shifting towards a position like Zeno's.

Whether consideration (b) carries weight largely depends on how exactly one takes *superiores*, which is not one of the standard terms to refer to the Old Academy as a group of philosophers (*antiqui, ueteres*) but occurs in the preceeding passage (*Ac.* 1.34 *fin.*, 1.38 *init.*). Sedley (p. 81) assumes that the predecessors of Xenocrates are meant (i.e. presumably Plato),[171] which would indeed yield the implication that the position of post-Xenocratean Old Academics including Polemo is left conspicuously vague. However, it is more natural to assume that the *superiores* are the predecessors of *Zeno*, who would here be seen as part of the tradition of the Old Academy (cf. *Ac.* 1.43a). In this case Polemo would be included among the *superiores* holding a different view, and Xenocrates would be mentioned separately because his is an extreme version of the view that the mind is incorporeal (as well as not part of the official *forma philosophiae*; cf. *Ac.* 1.33, and on *Luc.* 124).[172] Sedley's first argument will need to suffice to support his reading.

Sedley's proposal has been met with enthusiasm by Dillon (2003: ch. 4), who is willing to grant an even more significant role to Polemo, qualified approval by Frede (2005), who does not believe that 1.24–9 can be linked with Polemo in particular, and scepticism by Inwood (2012) and Reydams-Schils (2013).[173]

---

[170] Aët. 1.7.29 (= frg. 121 Gigante = t. 62 Marzotto): Πολέμων τὸν κόσμον θεὸν ἀπεφήνατο, 'Polemo declared the cosmos was god' (see Marzotto 2012: 419–25; Kupreeva 2012: 1194).

[171] Thus also Brittain (2006).

[172] Sedley (2002: 76 n. 81) considers the question of whether the order of topics in *Ac.* 1.24–9 might be considered Stoic rather than Academic and observes: 'We simply have no information on what ordering of physical topics had already, before the advent of Stoicism, become conventional in the Academy as a result of Xenocrates' formal systematisation of philosophy.'

[173] See also Sedley (2012: 102 n. 40); Gourinat (2009: 51–8). Of related interest is Scade (2010). Long (2005: 61), in a review of Dillon (2003), thinks retrojection of Stoic doctrine may be the best explanation after all because geometry does not feature in 1.24–9. But geometry is mentioned in *Ac.* 1.6 as one of the

At the centre of Inwood's study stands a close reading of *Ac.* 1.24–9, which shows effectively how compressed and elliptic the section is, and at the same time how many interpretative choices the reader has to make on any account, and in a somewhat precarious linear sequence of 'correct' binary choices in order to arrive at the view that the section contains genuinely Old Academic material. This, Inwood suggests, should reduce anyone's confidence about the status of the passage as evidence for Old Academic thought. Beyond that, Inwood holds that the background assumptions which lead Sedley to argue that, if it possible to read the section as a credible account of Old Academic views, it will be plausible to do so, do not stand up. He argues that Piso's speech in *Fin.* 5 is quite clearly marked as containing genuine Antiochian material, while this is less strongly emphasized with respect to Varro's speech; I disagree on the interpretation of the indications of 'sources' preceding as well as in Piso's speech,[174] and think that in *Ac.* 1 Cicero is at pains not to offend Varro. Presenting him as a mere mouthpiece by placing too much emphasis on his sources would probably have had that effect. Nor do I think that Antiochus can be shown to be guilty of extensive undeclared retrojection elsewhere: in ethics key tenets of Antiochus' theory are associated with Polemo in independent evidence, and in epistemology Antiochus' acceptance of Zeno's views over those of the *ueteres* is explicit (although it is possible that Antiochus tried to show that Zeno's doctrines are themselves developed from suggestions found in Plato; see on *Ac.* 1.40–2). Extensive deliberate but undeclared retrojection in the field of physics would therefore not be normal expectation. Inwood also suggests (pp. 205–6) that Zeno's modifications of the *prima forma* of Old Academic physics in *Ac.* 1.39 do not neatly fit with the earlier exposition, in that the first ('Zeno assumed the mind to be made of fire rather than the fifth element') modifies Aristotle's personal view rather than the official agreed one,[175] while the second ('Zeno assumed that incorporeals can exert power, which is why the soul must be a body') is pitted against the Old Academic 'and especially Xenocrates's' view that the soul is without a body, which, so the argument goes, references only Xenocrates' personal view and certainly not one shared by Aristotle. All this is deemed to show that Varro's grasp of Old Academic views on physics is not secure, and that one should feel discouraged to trace every bit of information in *Ac.* 1.24–9 to the Old Academy. I disagree on the first point and would take the second in a different way. Rather than to assume that the reference to the fifth element in *Ac.* 1.26 is coincidental, I think that Antiochus held that the Old Academy's *prima forma* of philosophy included the fifth element—as is *stated* in 1.39—, whose originator or contributor Aristotle is correctly identified.[176] By contrast, Xenocrates's notorious view that the soul is a self-moving number is indeed assumed to be his personal view (akin to the Old Academic view only in that it, too, assumes the soul not to be a body). It may be cited to signal that the issue is contested among Old Academics

things which makes Old Academic philosophy hard to render into Latin, which suggests that, if 1.24–9 was not so compressed, geometry would have featured.

[174] See the general note on *Ac.* 1.19–23.
[175] Similarly Kupreeva (2009: 139–40); and earlier Sedley (2002: 79).
[176] This does require that Aristotle's fifth element is in fact conceived as Platonic, i.e. specifically as Aristotle's interpretation of a particular Platonic text; see the n. below. On the notion of the *prima forma* see section 7.2 and on *Ac.* 1.15–17.

(despite there being an official position), or for rhetorical effect, i.e. to make Zeno's modification appear reasonable. Antiochus could not accept the Stoic positions on the cataleptic impression and on assent, as he did, without accepting Zeno's modification.[177] Inwood ends by noting that the ascription of the account of physics in *Ac.* 1.24–9 is precarious and that, if Antiochus had been drawing on genuine Old Academic source material, his account (or that of his sources) ought to have registered with the subsequent Middle and Neo-Platonic addition, which it did not. How one judges the force of this consideration depends on how in general one thinks Antiochus influenced subsequent Platonists. If it is assumed that the *ars philosophiae* (*Ac.* 1.17 *fin.*) adopted by him had no room whatsoever for forms qua transcendental entities and did not even credit Plato or the *ueteres* (sc. prior to Zeno's corrective activity) with such a view, then it is easier to imagine that Middle Platonists followed Antiochus' lead in terms of method, i.e. by engaging closely with Platonic dialogues, but chose to supplant his substantial physical views completely.

Reydams-Schils (2013) has contra Sedley provided an update of the traditional view that *Ac.* 1.24–9 represents a retrojection of Stoicism onto the *antiqui*, but she has based it on a firmer evidential footing and a more fine-grained understanding of the evolution of the particular philosophical tradition at issue than were found in earlier attempts. Acknowledging that Antiochus' construal of Old Academic physics must have had a degree of plausibility to command any assent at all, Reydams-Schils makes a number of important observations about key pieces of primary evidence. She points out that in (B) above Plato is credited with a physical theory positing an active and a passive principle, but that he is also said to have engaged extensively in first philosophy, without the latter precluding the former. She also observes that the tripartite division of philosophy which Varro/Antiochus employ can be seen as having the effect of keeping any theorizing about transcendental forms out of the picture because it will not neatly fall within any one of the three parts of philosophy (pp. 24–5). She further shows that the one physical fragment of Polemo which was cited above, fairly general and open to numerous interpretations in any event, can be read as a truncated quotation from *Tim.*, with truncation being one of the devices used in doxographical texts to fit δόξαι into the somewhat Procrustean presentational schema used in that tradition.[178] Finally, Reydams-Schils suggests that it is not a given that, despite the teacher–pupil relationship of Polemo and Zeno, any influence was only in one direction rather than the results of a genuine exchange of views. This last point, while not implausible, would seem to multiply unknown quantities unnecessarily, but the observation on Polemo's one securely attested physical view is well made and is apt to highlight just how much the evaluation of it depends on one's overall assessment and credibility of Antiochus' conception of the Old Academy. As

---

[177] On the evidence of *Ac.* 1.40–2, Antiochus accepted a causal interpretation of Zeno's doctrine of the cataleptic impression; see also section 5.

[178] With the Polemonian fragment given above (n. 170), cf. Plt., *Tim.* 92c (see Reydams-Schils 2013: 42, who inserted the brackets for illustration): [ὅδε] ὁ κόσμος [οὕτω, ζῷον ὁρατὸν τὰ ὁρατὰ περιέχον, εἰκὼν τοῦ νοητοῦ] θεὸς [αἰσθητός, μέγιστος καὶ ἄριστος κάλλιστός τε καὶ τελεώτατος γέγονεν εἰς οὐρανὸς ὅδε μονογενὴς ὤν]. Reydams-Schils comments further (ibid.): 'In this passage, Plato declares the *kosmos* to be god, most beautiful and perfect, and heaven as one of a kind. But, of course, in Plato's longer version of the dictum, the *kosmos* is also visible and sensible, and as such a mere image of the intelligible realm.'

to (B) and the reductive effect of the tripartite division of philosophy, it makes a difference whether alternative divisions really were conceivable for someone who professed to be an Academic and a dogmatist at the time when Antiochus was active.[179] If Antiochus exercised a deliberate choice while being conscious that there were other options, then it would be reasonable to suspect that one of the reasons why he adopted the tripartite division was precisely to marginalize what (B) calls first philosophy, thereby creating the appearance of substantial common ground between Old Academy and Stoa, and facilitating the retrojection of Stoic physical tenets. What tells against this scenario is that the interlocutor Cicero, in his reply to Lucullus, uses the same framework without any hesitation, which he would not do if he recognized it as a device intended to blank out an important part of philosophical theorizing in the post-Platonic Academy (or as de facto functioning in this way). In fact, it is difficult to find a passage in the Ciceronian corpus where Platonic forms are at issue *and* are interpreted as transcendental entities (see the excursus below). I thus wonder if the 'subversive' allusions to *Tim.* identified by Görler (see above) are better seen as attempts to control the meaning of certain passages in line with Antiochus' preferred way of interpreting the Platonic text. That Cicero can be seen doing something similar in his translation of *Tim.*, where—one might think—he is under no obligation to be guided by Antiochus' preferred interpretation of the dialogue, would support the assumption that Cicero himself did not construe forms as transcendental entities. While this may seem misguided from the modern point of view, it is a distinct possibility historically; see also on *Ac.* 1.30-2. What would represent positive evidence for retrojection of Stoicism is evidence for assuming that the post-Platonic Academy moved over time further away from the two-principle framework ascribed to Plato in (B).[180] Here, once again, one comes up against the problem that evidence of physical views becomes more elusive the closer one gets to Polemo chronologically.

I shall assemble relevant primary evidence in the notes, but as the above survey of scholarly reactions to the section has hopefully shown, the interpretation of that evidence is largely determined by one's broader evaluation of the Antiochian project and resulting views about the significance of parallel texts.[181] The Theophrastean fragment (B) exhibits prima facie only a couple of points of contact with *Ac.* 1.24-9, whereas the Stoic fragment speaks to more, though not all, of the section's details. This means that an argument which places the Theophrastean fragment higher in the hierarchy of parallels will need to do more to supplement it with evidence from elsewhere. Moreover, beyond the straightforward question of how many details of our passage can be related to either text (and suitable supplementary material), issues like the precise terminology used to characterize the fundamental bipartite division in *Ac.* 1.24, shifts in emphasis, and—crucially—apparently meaningful omissions enter into another level of analysis.[182]

---

[179] The tripartite division has Xenocratean credentials; see on *Ac.* 1.19.
[180] This point is made by Klein (2014).
[181] A similar point is made by Algra (2017), who is to be added to the list of sceptics regarding Sedley's hypothesis that *Ac.* 1.24-9 furnishes an account of Polemo's physical views.
[182] It has been argued by some that fragments from Book 16 of Varro's *Antiquitates rerum diuinarum* reflect Antiochian thought on physics; see e.g. Fladerer (1996: 101-35); Van Nuffelen (2010: 173-4).

Forms as Thoughts of God

A well-known doctrine of Middle Platonism and Neoplatonism, with a rich afterlife in Byzantium, the medieval period, and the Renaissance, is that of the forms as thoughts of god, viz. that the forms, rather than having independent transcendental existence, exist in the mind of god who stands apart from the perceptible world, and that they serve as a model for creation.[183] A number of scholars have argued that this doctrine predates Antiochus or that Antiochus actually developed it. In either case Cicero's writings could conceivably contain evidence for it. The footholds for such a doctrine in Plato's dialogues are limited,[184] although some ancient as well as some modern readers of Plato have thought otherwise. Those scholars who would be inclined to date the doctrine to the early Hellenistic period have suggested a number of possible origins, including the Xenocratean divine νοῦς (Aët. 1.7.30 = frg. 133 Isnardi Parente = frg. 15 Heinze), whose activity would include thinking or thinking about the forms, and the identification of Aristotelian immanent form with forms, such that the notion of form which guides the craftsman when he fashions a product would, by analogy, be likened to forms in the creator's mind which guide the process of creation.[185] (Either possibility would have been congenial to Antiochus' project.) Those who have argued that Antiochus created the doctrine tend to do so with reference to two passages in particular. In *Or.* 8–10 he speaks of perfect eloquence and how we can contemplate it by attending to a corresponding notion in our minds, just as the famous painter Phidias created representations of perfect beauty by attending to a notion of perfect beauty in his mind. This is reminiscent of the analogy between divine creator and craftsman which in later texts often serves as a vehicle for communicating how forms as thoughts of god are to be understood, but crucially lacks the actual analogy, and the notion of a form of eloquence seems markedly Ciceronian. The second passage is *Ac.* 1.24–9. Here the strongest case that can be made would cite that forms of some kind are posited in *Ac.* 1.30, that 1.33 has Varro remark that Plato said of forms that there was something divine in them (*species...quas mirifice Plato erat amplexatus, ut in iis quiddam diuinum esse diceret*; cf. *Fin.* 4.42), that god is present in this world as an active principle (1.29), and that the manner in which 1.24–9 jettisons the Timaean two-world view in favour of two principles in operation in one immanent world beyond which there is nothing requires the forms to be in

---

I regard the number of points of contact as insufficient to recommend this view. See especially the table in Fladerer (1996: 107–8).

[183] Studies include Miller Jones (1929); de Vogel (1953: 50–2); Rich (1954); Doherty (1960); Theiler (1964: 37–40), first published in 1934; Fladerer (1996: 102–3); Gersh (1996: i.180–94); Sedley (2002: 62); Dillon (2003: 120–3); Karamanolis (2006: 63–4); Inwood (2007) on Sen., *Ep.* 58 and 65; Reydams-Schils (2010: 196–9) also on Seneca; Dillon (2011); Bonazzi (2015: 50–8); on the doctrine in the Greek fathers, see Lilla (1990) [*non uidi*]; on the doctrine in Byzantium, Lilla (2003); on Aquinas, Boland (1996).

[184] Cf. e.g. Plt., *Tim.* 39e, on the demiurge contemplating an eternal model, without a suggestion that the model is situated in the demiurge's mind. Dillon (2011): 'I would argue...that really all that is required for the development of such a theory (though no doubt stimulated by both the theorizing and the gibes of Aristotle) is the postulation that the account of the nature and activities of the Demiurge in Plato's *Timaeus* is not to be taken literally; and we know this position to have been maintained, among his immediate predecessors, by both Speusippus and Xenocrates.'

[185] See Jones (1929); Rich (1954: 126–7); Donini (2011: 309–10).

this world—so that it would be economical to situate them in the mind of a god who is immanent in this world, leaving it to later thinkers to relocate god and the forms in his mind to a world beyond the perceptible one. I believe that nothing in *Or.* 8–10 invites the assumption that forms are deemed to be thoughts of god—god, or his thoughts, is simply not at issue, and assuming otherwise does not add depth or meaning to the passage.[186] *Ac.* 1.24-9 offers slightly better prospects, although I would observe that 1.30-3 introduces a conceptualist interpretation of forms on my reading and is concerned with human minds only, so that forms in the minds of god and how they give rise to or correspond to notions in human minds would be unstated in the background. Assuming this was so, the attitude ascribed to Plato in 1.33 would only make sense if they related to notions in human minds (for only on an ingenious reading would it not be banal to say that there is something divine in the thoughts of god). Overall I see no benefit in assuming that Antiochus entertained the doctrine, as doing so only multiplies unknowns *praeter necessitatem*.[187]

§24

De natura autem…eaque efficeretur aliquid: cf. A and B above; Plt., *Soph.* 247d8–e4 (= LS 44h), where the Eleatic stranger suggests that the 'capacity to act and be acted upon' exhaustively marks existing things: λέγω δὴ τὸ καὶ ὁποιανοῦν [τινα] κεκτημένον δύναμιν εἴτ' εἰς τὸ ποιεῖν ἕτερον ὁτιοῦν πεφυκὸς εἴτ' εἰς τὸ παθεῖν καὶ σμικρότατον ὑπὸ τοῦ φαυλοτάτου, κἂν εἰ μόνον εἰς ἅπαξ, πᾶν τοῦτο ὄντως εἶναι· τίθεμαι γὰρ ὅρον [ὁρίζειν] τὰ ὄντα ὡς ἔστιν οὐκ ἄλλο τι πλὴν δύναμις, 'I suggest that everything which possesses any power of any kind, either to produce a change in anything of any nature or to be affected even in the least degree by the slightest cause, though it be only on one occasion, has real existence. For I set up as a definition which defines being, that it is nothing else than power' (transl. Fowler); the Aristotelian 'translation' of a two-principle view (matter and forms) in Arist., *Met.* A7, 988a7–11; *Ac.* 1.6: *nostra tu physica nosti: quae cum contineantur ex effectione et ex materia ea quam fingit et format effectio, adhibenda etiam geometria est*; *Luc.* 118: *Plato ex materia in se omnia recipiente mundum factum esse censet a deo sempiternum*, apparently alluding to the characterization of the receptacle also referenced in B above (Plt., *Tim.* 51a: πανδεχές). The extant evidence on Speusippus' and Xenocrates' metaphysical and physical views does not provide straightforward opportunities to retrace a two-principle view to them; on Speusippus, see Krämer (1983: 22–43); Dillon (2003: 30–88); Isnardi Parente (2016); on Xenocrates, Krämer (1983: 44–72); Dillon (2003: 89–155). Sedley (2002) argues that the two-principle view may have been held in Polemo's Academy, and that Xenocrates, through his adventurous interpretations of *Tim.*, might have paved the way for it. The sole fragment on Polemo's physical views is Aët.

---

[186] See Reinhardt (2018: 51–3).

[187] Dillon (2011) also argues that Aug., *C.D.* 7.28, which comes from Varro's *Antiquitates rerum diuinarum*, is an important piece of evidence for Antiochus' advancing of the doctrine. I do not share this conviction, nor the view (ibid., n. 19) that Varro was a 'thoroughgoing disciple of Antiochus'—the evidence from Varro's *De philosophia* suggests considerable freedom on Varro's part.

1.7.29 (= frg. 121 Gigante = t. 62 Marzotto): Πολέμων τὸν κόσμον θεὸν ἀπεφήνατο (see above, n. 170; Marzotto 2012: 419–25; and Kupreeva 2012: 1194), which is consistent with *Ac.* 1.24–9 but not more; see the general note above on whether Varro should be taken to imply a link between his account of physics and Polemo in particular. Sedley (2002: 60–4) offers a reconstruction of a reading of *Tim.* by which one might have arrived at the two-principle view.

Pace Reid[1] (p. 124): 'Essentially the same systematisation of physics is adopted by Plutarch as belonging to the Academy', who apparently takes himself to rely on Volkmann (1869: 64), Plutarch's *De animae procreatione in Timaeo* does not adopt a relevantly similar two-principle reading of *Tim.*; on it see Opsomer (2004).

Luc. 118, from a passage demonstrably drawing on doxographical material (see ad loc.), probably reflects the same tradition as B and thus documents further the latter's historicity. However, it cannot readily be taken to suggest that Cicero agrees with Antiochus' construal of this particular aspect of Plato's physical theory (and thus, say, does not regard it as transparent retrojection), because here in *Ac.* 1 Varro's speech relies by universal agreement on an Antiochian source, whereas the wider context in *Luc.* 118 shows that a doxographical source is (ultimately) the basis for what Cicero says there. Nor can we be certain that what Varro says here in *Ac.* 1 corresponds in detail to Antiochian material which Hortensius presented in the *Catulus*; there is some reason for thinking that the change of speakers from the first to the final edition gave rise to an expansion of the Antiochian account of the history of philosophy. Varro was an eminently credible presenter of this material, while Hortensius had only recently (sc. in the scenario envisaged in the first edition) been persuaded (i.e. in *Hort.*) that philosophy merits serious engagement.

A comparison of Varro's opening statement with A and B shows that in our passage the two *res* are not called 'principles'. In B one cannot be sure if the use of the term is due to the way in which Theophrastus' report is itself reported, but A and a wealth of further evidence suggest that the Stoics did call the active cause and matter 'principles' (cf. *SVF* ii.299–327). Varro does, however, recognize 'principles' at the next level of description, in that he calls the elements both 'elements' and 'principles' ('a non-Stoic feature', Sedley 2002: 55). Further, Varro's way of referring to the passive *res* is not closely reminiscent of Plato's characterization of the receptacle in *Tim.* 51a as *Luc.* 118 illustrates. However, Sedley (2002: 55) suggests that the failure to name the passive *res* as opposed to characterizing it through attributes 'follows the lead of the *Timaeus*'. An apparent difference to Stoic thought is that Varro's two *res* appear to exhaust all there is, while the Stoics distinguished between the world which is 'whole' on the one hand and 'all' which comprises the world and the infinite void the world is situated in on the other; cf. Sextus, *M.* 9.332 (= part of *SVF* ii.524 = LS 44A): Καὶ δὴ οἱ μὲν ἀπὸ τῆς Στοᾶς φιλόσοφοι διαφέρειν ὑπολαμβάνουσι τὸ ὅλον καὶ τὸ πᾶν· ὅλον μὲν γὰρ εἶναι λέγουσι τὸν κόσμον, πᾶν δὲ τὸ σὺν τῷ κόσμῳ ἔξωθεν κενόν, καὶ διὰ τοῦτο τὸ μὲν ὅλον πεπερασμένον εἶναι (πεπέρασται γὰρ ὁ κόσμος), τὸ δὲ πᾶν ἄπειρον (τοιοῦτον γὰρ τὸ ἐκτὸς τοῦ κόσμου κενόν), 'Now the philosophers of the Stoic school suppose that "the Whole" differs from "the All"; for they say that the Whole is the cosmos, whereas the All is the external void together with the cosmos, and on this account the Whole is limited (for the cosmos is limited) but the All unlimited (for the void outside the cosmos is so)' (transl. Bury). Varro rejects the notion of void in §27, but could conceivably be talking about void within the world. Overall it seems fair to say that, unless one approaches the discussion already assuming that a two-principle world view is distinctive of Stoic thought, the beginning of the physical section looks at best vaguely reminiscent of it.

On *natura* as designation of the topic, see the paraphrase above. For *id enim sequebatur*, cf. the *diuisio* in *Ac.* 1.19 *init.*

Efficiens (res) here and *effectio* in 1.6 mutually illuminate each other. The term *effectio* may have been coined by Cicero and is only used here, and in *Fin.* 3.24 and 3.45. There its sense is 'accomplishment', and it retains in 3.24 some of its force as a *nomen actionis* (*nec enim gubernationi aut medicinae similem sapientiam esse arbitramur, sed actioni illi potius, quam modo dixi, et saltationi, ut in ipsa insit, non foris petatur extremum, id est artis effectio*—the acting in accordance with the art is its end). On deverbative nouns in *-tio*, see Hofmann-Szantyr pp. 741–5; Benveniste (1993: 96–104).

The implied subject of *dicebant* is the *ueteres*; see section 7.2. *Res* is semantically so flat that by itself it does not even suggest physical existence, but the next sentence which locates *uis* in one of the *res* would not make this an unnatural reading. Note, however, Inwood (2012: 208): 'We may note as well that the characteristically Stoic emphasis on the bodily nature of anything engaged in causal interaction is missing here'; comparison with 1.39 strongly suggests that this is deliberate.

The transmitted *eaque* is unobjectionable: *ea* is nominative and resumes the second *altera*. The construction corresponds to the active one with double accusative (*efficere aliquam rem aliquid* = 'to turn a thing into something'), with *aliquid* having the more specific sense of 'a particular thing' (cf. τι, and *corpus* below). Reid[1] (p. 124) prints *ex eaque* (an emendation by Mueller 1878), which he calls 'certain'. Sedley (2002: 53) gives the text as transmitted and translates: '...the other at this one's disposal, as it were, and acted upon by it in some way', which would seem to involve an unexampled use of *efficere* and the construal of *aliquid* as an adverbial accusative; cf. Brittain (2006: 96), who reads *eoque efficeretur aliquid*: '...and the other lending itself to it and thus acted on in some manner.' It is difficult to render *efficiens...efficeretur* with the same English verb.

In eo quod efficeret...materiam quandam: that the two *res* are not equated with *uis* and *materia* respectively had been noted above; rather, *uis* and *materia* are in the *res*. Note also the shift from *res* to neuter singular pronouns. As elsewhere Reid[1] (p. 125) glosses *materiam quandam* with the claim that *quidam* marks the translation of a Greek term; Sedley (2002: 56 n. 29), while acknowledging a trend, cites counterexamples (§21 *partem quandam, humana quadam societate*) and suggests that the repetition of the phrase in *Ac.* 1.27 tells against *quidam* serving to signal a translation here. This being so, there is less reason to assume that behind *materia* there must lurk its most obvious Greek counterpart, ὕλη, as Reid[1] (p. 125) assumes. While this is possible, Cicero may equally translate οὐσία as *materia*; cf. his translation of *Tim.* 21, 22, and 27. Because the term ὕλη is not peculiar to the Stoics and could already have become common property at the time when Plato's predecessors were active, and because certainty is not to be had as to which Greek term is actually rendered *materia*, the occurrence of *materia* by itself in *Ac.* 1.24–9 offers little positive indication of the origin of the division presented by Varro; see Sedley (2002: 55–7, 70–3).

In utroque tamen utrumque...neque uim sine aliqua materia: the statement overall seems to reference Plt., *Tim.* 52c6–8, but so as to contradict the Platonic passage, as Görler (2004a: 94) has observed: ἕως ἄν τι τὸ μὲν ἄλλο ᾖ, τὸ δὲ ἄλλο, οὐδέτερον ἐν οὐδετέρῳ ποτὲ γενόμενον ἓν ἅμα ταὐτὸν καὶ δύο γενήσεσθον, 'So long as one thing is one thing, and another something different, neither of the two will ever come to exist in the other so that the same thing becomes simultaneously both one and two' (transl. Bury).

Reid[1] (p. 125) comments on *in utroque tamen utrumque*: '*Vtroque* here represents τὸ σύνολον or ἡ σύνολος οὐσία of Aristotle..., i.e. the concrete object...; while *utrumque* denotes the ingredients, the formal and material elements of which the object is composed; the words mean therefore "each of these factors however [= tamen] exists in the concrete object"; i.e. only in it, not outside it.' This seems unlikely because *utrumque* would be an unnatural way to refer to the composite; see also *quod ex utroque* below. Rather, both *res* are said to be in one another; thus e.g. Brittain (2006: 96): 'both were present in each'. See Kühner-Stegmann i.616, who call *uter utrumque* for *uterque alterum* 'selten und unklassisch'.

With *cohaerere*, cf. *Ac.* 1.28: *cohaerente natura*. On *sine aliqua* 'without some', as opposed to *sine ulla* 'without any', see Reid[1] (p. 221) on *Luc.* 35. The reason why there is a qualification at all is presumably due to the conception of void touched on in §27 below.

Neque enim... esse cogatur is explanatory of *in utroque tamen utrumque*; hence the colon after *utrumque*.

Nihil est enim quod non alicubi esse cogatur: deleted by Hülsemann (1806: 87) as '*sine sensu idoneo*'.

Enim marks the sentence as explanatory of the claim that the two *res* are in one another: if they are all there is and everything must be somewhere (i.e. in some location), then the two *res* can only be in one another, for they could not be in some third *res*.

The sentence closely resembles one in *Tim.*, which, however, forms part of an argument that there is such a thing as place and that a thing's existence is only possible if it can be in some (particular) place (52a8–b5): τρίτον δὲ αὖ γένος ὂν τὸ τῆς χώρας ἀεί, φθορὰν οὐ προσδεχόμενον, ἕδραν δὲ παρέχον ὅσα ἔχει γένεσιν πᾶσιν, αὐτὸ δὲ μετ' ἀναισθησίας ἁπτὸν λογισμῷ τινι νόθῳ, μόγις πιστόν, πρὸς ὃ δὴ καὶ ὀνειροπολοῦμεν βλέποντες καί **φαμεν ἀναγκαῖον εἶναί** που τὸ ὂν ἅπαν ἔν τινι τόπῳ καὶ κατέχον χώραν τινά, τὸ δὲ μήτ' ἐν γῇ μήτε που κατ' οὐρανὸν οὐδὲν εἶναι, 'A third kind is ever-existing place, which admits not of destruction, and provides room for all things that have birth, itself being apprehensible by a kind of bastard reasoning by the aid of non-sensation, barely an object of belief; for when we regard this we dimly dream and *affirm that it is somehow necessary that all that exists should exist in some spot and occupying some place*, and that that which is neither on earth nor anywhere in the heaven is nothing' (transl. Bury). See Görler (2004a: 92–3). The sentence seems to be on Augustine's mind in *Soliloqu.* 1.15.29 and *Immort.* 1.1, as Hagendahl (1967: 55) notes.

Sed quod ex utroque, id iam corpus et quasi qualitatem quandam nominabant: Varro now brings compounds arising from the two *res* into view; the sentence is cast in the singular since he is speaking of compounds as a class. *Iam* according to Reid¹ (p. 125) '= ἤδη, at once' (i.e. 'immediately', not 'simultaneously'), 'already' according to Sedley (2002: 53); on the latter interpretation *iam* would be otiose, whereas on the former it would emphasize that the concept of body only enters at the level of compounds. Kupreeva (2009: 138 n. 21) suggests that the force of *iam* is 'adversative', but *sed* creates a strong enough contrast with what precedes. If *quidam* was used to signal that *qualitas* corresponds to a particular Greek term (ποιότης), then its function would be the same as that of *quasi*; so *qualitas quaedam* is likely to mean 'a quality of sorts'. *Nominare* = 'to describe as, count among'.

The neologism *qualitas* is used here for the first time, then in *N.D.* 2.94; Varro *ap.* Charis. p. 109.1; Ps.-Varro, *Sent.* 52; freely from Vitruvius onwards. Powell (1995: 295) notes: 'There may be a suspicion that the credit for *qualitas* should be shifted away from Cicero to his older contemporary Varro. This is based on the word's occurrence, without explanation or apology, in a fragment of Varro, and on the context of the *Acad. Post.* passage where the word is discussed, where, at any rate for the purposes of the dialogue, Varro is certainly presented as responsible for the coinage.' See earlier Meillet (1925) and Lévy (2008). On the formation of the term, see Nicolas (2005: 131).

Dabitis enim profecto...utamur uerbis interdum inauditis: the section from here down to §26...*nouis uerbis uti te auctore si necesse erit* is an instance of what Glucker (2012: 39) aptly calls 'Übersetzungsbekenntnisse'. He collects and classifies most of the passages meeting this description; see also ibid. pp. 37–9 for earlier but less informative collections. A distinctive feature of the section here is of course that it is mostly Varro who is speaking. Taking his cue from *qualitas*, Varro proposes to speak in Latin except in the case of loanwords from Greek which no longer feel foreign. This means that he will create Latin terms for newly created philosophical concepts, either ex nihilo or by using existing terms metaphorically. After all, in Greek, too, every field of expertise has its own specialized terminology, not shared by the many. In the last sentence of §25 Cicero has Varro abandon his earlier doubts about the possibility of rendering respectable dogmatic philosophy into Latin and instead asks assertively—as Cicero the man and the character would—if the Romans should not be conceded the right to coin new terminology a fortiori, given that the Greeks, who have practised philosophy so much longer, do the same thing.

I have argued elsewhere that the emphasis on a particular sub-set of terminological issues—unfamiliar concepts and how to talk about them—belies the adroitness with which Cicero and others used the existing resources of Latin to discuss philosophical subjects; see Reinhardt (2016), and section 10.

With *Graeci ipsi*, cf. Arist., *N.E.* B7, 1108a17–19 (quoted by Reid¹ p. 126): πειρατέον δ', ὥσπερ καὶ ἐπὶ τῶν ἄλλων, αὐτοὺς ὀνοματοποιεῖν σαφηνείας ἕνεκα καὶ τοῦ εὐπαρακολουθήτου, 'One must try, as in other cases, to fashion names for them ourselves, for the sake of clarity and to make things easy to follow.' A particularly rich source of reflections on the subject is Galen; see Hankinson (1994); Morison (2008). On the related subject of medical Latin, see Langslow (2000: 26–41).

§25

'Nos uero', inquit Atticus...'si te Latina forte deficient': an intervention which moves the discussion on but which Cicero could not possibly have given to himself. Ellipses with *nos uero* sc. *dabimus*, and *Graecis/Latina* sc. *uerbis/uerba*, a feature of a more conversational style. For the problem referred to in *si...forte deficient*, cf. *Fin.* 3.15; for the *patrii sermonis egestas* motif, see the general note on *Ac.* 1.1–18 above.

Bene sane facis, sed enitar ut Latin loquar...quibus ut aliis multis consuetudo iam utitur pro Latinis: for *bene facis*, which is politely conversational ('that's good of you!'), cf. *Fin.* 3.16; Hor. *S.* 1.4.17: *di bene fecerunt*; Halla-Aho and Kruschwitz (2010: 148); Hofmann-Szantyr p. 579 on *bene facis quod*. With the speaker's vow to use Latin if at all possible (*enitar ut Latine loquar*), cf. *Tusc.* 1.15. *Vt... appellem*, as Reid[1] (p. 127) notes, is explanatory of *huiusce modi uerbis*. Parallels for the use of *appello = pronuntio* are collected in the *TLL* s.v. col. 274.43–51.

For the Greek words which have become loanwords, cf. *Fin.* 3.5: *Et quoniam saepe diximus, et quidem cum aliqua querela non Graecorum modo, sed eorum etiam, qui se Graecos magis quam nostros haberi uolunt, nos non modo non uinci a Graecis uerborum copia, sed esse in ea etiam superiores, elaborandum est ut hoc non in nostris solum artibus, sed etiam in illorum ipsorum adsequamur. Quamquam ea uerba, quibus instituto ueterum utimur pro Latinis, ut ipsa philosophia, ut rhetorica, dialectica, grammatica, geometria, musica, quamquam Latine ea dici poterant, tamen, quoniam usu percepta sunt, nostra ducamus.* The word *physica* as in our passage also in *Fin.* 3.72–3. Reid[1] (pp. 126–7) rightly dismisses the suggestion that *rhetoricam* might have displaced *ethicam* (vel sim.)—the point is that there are deeply familiar loanwords for fields of expertise—and goes on to discuss their usage beyond Cicero. For a related reason the Latinized endings are preferable to Manutius' accusatives in *-en*. The *TLL* s.v. *dialectica* col. 949.63–4 records that Quintilian uses *dialectice* as well as *dialectica*, which might suggest that he did not regard the term as completely naturalized; but the transmission cannot be relied on for this kind of detail. For the personified use of *consuetudo*, see *Fin.* 2.48; *Orat.* 157; the proverbial expressions listed in *TLL* s.v. *consuetudo* col. 553.63–5. On *consuetudo* as a term occurring in descriptions of linguistic register/sociolect, see Ferri and Probert (2010: 38).

On pronouns with the deictic suffix *-c(e)* (*huiusce*), see on *Ac.* 1.13: *Tum ille 'Istud quidem considerabo'... 'Quid ergo?' inquam.*

Qualitates igitur appellaui...sed philosophorum, atque id in multis: cf. Plt., *Tht.* 182a, the first attested occurence of ποιότης, where Socrates comments on the word being unusual (...ἀλλόκοτόν τε φαίνεται ὄνομα καὶ οὐ μανθάνεις ἁθρόον λεγόμενον). Varro appears to be alluding to this passage (thus also Burnyeat 1990: 311–12 n. 37), which, given that the digression on philosophy in Latin cannot have come from Cicero's Antiochian source, suggests familiarity with *Tht.* on Cicero's part (*qualitas* from *qualis* like ποιότης from ποιός); this matters for my reading of *Ac.* 1.30 and 1.40–2, which I think refer to the *Theatetus*. Varro's comment here, from Cicero's own resources, makes it more likely that he would have been alive to allusions to the *Tht.* in the Greek source material on which the later sections draw.

Cf. also *Fin.* 3.3-4, where Cicero comments on the need to create new terms when discussing philosophy in the medium of Latin; this, he continues, is a feature of technical fields of expertise in general (examples cited are epistemology, physics, geometry, music, grammar, and rhetoric); see below on *quod si Graeci faciunt...qui haec nunc primum tractare conamur.*

Dialecticorum uero uerba nulla sunt publica...aut ex aliis transferenda: see *Top.* 53-7 for a discussion of Stoic types of argument. However, there Cicero does not create entirely new words for the neuter participles of existing verbs which the Stoics use in a technical sense to designate complex propositions. On *effatum* = ἀξίωμα, see *Luc.* 95 with Nicolas (2005: 33-4, 52-3).

With *facienda nomina aut ex aliis transferenda,* cf. *De orat.* 3.149: *Ergo utimur uerbis aut iis, quae propria sunt et certa quasi uocabula rerum, paene una nata cum rebus ipsis; aut iis, quae transferuntur et quasi alieno in loco collocantur; aut iis, quae nouamus et facimus ipsi;* and 154: *Nouantur autem uerba, quae ab eo, qui dicit, ipso gignuntur ac fiunt, uel coniungendis uerbis, ut haec: tum pauor sapientiam omnem mi exanimato expectorat. Num non uis huius me uersutiloquas malitias...uidetis enim et 'uersutiloquas' et 'expectorat' ex coniunctione facta esse uerba, non nata; sed saepe uel sine coniunctione uerba nouantur ut 'ille senius desertus', ut 'di genitales', ut 'bacarum ubertate incuruescere'.* See the excellent introduction to the section on the treatment of individual words in the *elocutio* (*De orat.* 3.148-70) in Wisse, Winterbottom, and Fantham (2008: 176-86); Mankin (2011: 239-41) on 3.154. *Translatio* in the relevant sense already in *Rhet. Her.* 4.15, 45-6, 61; cf. *Or.* 92.

Quod si Graeci faciunt...qui haec nunc primum tractare conamur: Cf. *Fin.* 3.5 (immediately preceding text referenced above), where, however, Cicero is speaking: *Quamquam ex omnibus philosophis Stoici plurima nouauerunt, Zenoque, eorum princeps, non tam rerum inuentor fuit quam uerborum nouorum. Quodsi in ea lingua, quam plerique uberiorem putant, concessum est ut doctissimi homines de rebus non peruagatis inusitatis uerbis uterentur, quanto id nobis magis est concedendum, qui ea nunc primum audemus attingere? Et quoniam saepe diximus, et quidem cum aliqua querela non Graecorum modo, sed eorum etiam, qui se Graecos magis quam nostros haberi uolunt, nos non modo non uinci a Graecis uerborum copia, sed esse in ea etiam superiores, elaborandum est ut hoc non in nostris solum artibus, sed etiam in illorum ipsorum adsequamur.* Varro's initial hesitation (cf. *Ac.* 1.4-7) appears to have given way—now that he has made a start on expounding Old Academic thought in Latin—to the kind of assertive optimism expressed in *Fin.* 3.5.

With the use of *tractare,* cf. *Ac.* 1.13: *a te...tractari autem nouam.* Reid[1] (p. 128) observes that the relative clause could well have been treated as causal and cast in the subjunctive; cf. 1.18 *qui haec uos doceo.*

§26

'Tu uero', inquam, 'Varro...si necesse erit': Cicero's intervention looks back to his description of Varro's antiquarian works in *Ac.* 1.9, which cover hitherto neglected subject matter (*res*). For the theme of the usefulness of literary activity see the introduction, section 3. Lambinus (1566) emended to *fecisti*, which is possible but not compelling; Plasberg[1] (p. 47): '*efficere laboris est*'.

Earum igitur qualitatum...quae gignuntur e terra: marking the resumption of the earlier discussion by *igitur* (cf. *Ac*. 1.35 for the use), Varro moves the discussion one level up from the active *res*/passive *res* dichotomy and distinguishes primary and secondary qualities (see above, p. 163). Primary qualities, identified with the elements, are uniform and simple, the latter are diverse and multiform: they are the *formae* of plants and animals. If *formae* means 'species', then Varro is talking about general items one level up from individuals; alternatively, Varro could be using *formae* to refer to the *qualitates* which account for a class (species) of things. On either reading *multiformes* would signal diversity at the level of the species. Less likely and unparalleled would be *formae* = forms of individuals; on that reading, to say that the qualities which correspond to the *formae* of individuals are *multiformes* could e.g. mean that they are diverse as individuals.

Reid[1] (pp. 128–9) assembles possible Greek terms and expressions behind Cicero's Latin ones, without suggesting that any one particular passage is referenced. Sedley (2002: 58) suggests that 'the emphasis on *qualia* and "qualities" is a formalisation of the argument at *Tim*. 49d–e. According to Timaeus, at least on the most favoured reading of this text, the water, air, earth and fire into which the receptacle is initially formed are too unstable to be properly designated by a demonstrative like "this" (τοῦτο, τόδε), and should rather be called "such" (τοιοῦτο), in recognition of the fact that they are merely transient characterisations of the receptacle. This insistence on Timaeus' part is, it seems, translated by our Academics into the labelling of these four stuffs, out of which the world as a whole is then structured..., as *qualia* (= ποιά).' The movement from an active and a passive principle to elements to the cosmos and things in it can indeed be paralleled from *Tim*. 49d–e, and Sedley (2002: 58 n. 36) himself cites D.L. 3.70 which also summarizes it (τραπέσθαι δὲ τὴν οὐσίαν ταύτην [sc. matter] εἰς τὰ τέτταρα στοιχεῖα, πῦρ, ὕδωρ, ἀέρα, γῆν· ἐξ ὧν αὐτόν τε τὸν κόσμον καὶ τὰ ἐν αὐτῷ γεννᾶσθαι), but it is not a distinctive one in that anyone who starts from an active and a passive 'principle' would end up performing it, and it is hard to see that the resemblance extends beyond said movement. In particular, it is not clear to me that the *qualitas/qualia* distinction could function like that of τοῦτο/τόδε and τοιοῦτο.

I consider possible meanings of *unius modi* and *simplex* (and correspondingly of *uariae* and *multiformes*) above, p. 164 (see also Reid[1] p. 128 on the possible Greek counterparts). The similarity with *Ac*. 1.30...*quia* [sc. *mens*] *sola cerneret id quod semper esset simplex et unius modi et tale quale esset* is probably coincidental.

For *aer*, cf. Enn., *Ann*. 440 Skutsch (where it is feminine), 140 (where it may be masculine), and *uar*. 55 Vahlen (masculine); see Skutsch (1985: 598–9); Plt., *Asin*. 99; Lucr. 4.132. The term was 'not naturalised much before Cicero's time' (Reid[1] p. 128), and distribution suggests it was felt to be poetic until Cicero used it; Reid goes on to compare *N.D*. 2.91: *aer, Graecum illud quidem sed perceptum iam tamen usu a nostris; tritum est enim pro Latino*. In the Lucil. fragment quoted in the next note *anima* is used. An enumeration of coordinated items in the singular with a verb in the plural (*sunt*) and a neuter complement (*prima*) is standard; the variant *primae* in some later manuscripts would mean sc. *qualitates*. On *utimur enim*, see the note in Plasberg[1] (p. 47).

The phrase *animantium forma* also in *De orat.* 3.179 and *N.D.* 1.47–8, where it means the physical shape of living beings. *Earumque rerum quae gignuntur* is due to φυτός having no exact counterpart in Latin, as Reid[1] (p. 128) notes.

Ergo illa initia et, ut e Graeco uertam, elementa dicuntur...aquam dico et terram: *initia* must be ἀρχαί, and *elementa* στοιχεῖα. This use of 'principles' is markedly different from Stoic usage (on which see Vogt 2009: 137–41), which may discourage a reading of the passage as uncomplicated retrojection; the evidence for an Academic bipartite division of principles is less informative on the precise terminology used (see the general note above). The term στοιχεῖον means 'letter' as well as 'element' in Greek (on the term's uses, see Burkert 1959). Cicero uses *elementum* in the sense of 'letter' in *De orat.* 1.163, where there is no indication that the term was not already established in this sense; cf. Lucr. 1.196 (and elsewhere). Varro's *ut e Graeco uertam* signals that he uses *elementum* in an apparently new 'Greek' sense, which is a familiar sense of στοιχεῖον. See Diels (1899: 69–70); contrast *Tusc.* 1.22: *Aristoteles, longe omnibus (Platonem semper excipio) praestans et ingenio et diligentia, cum* **quattuor nota illa genera principiorum** *esset complexus, e quibus omnia orerentur, quintam quandam naturam censet esse, e qua sit mens.* Cf. also *elementa loquendi* 'basic building blocks of speech' in *Luc.* 92; and *quod in elementis dialectici docent* of the introductory teachings of logicians (*Luc.* 143). I do not think that *et* in *initia et ut* is used in the sense of *etiam*, so that *elementa* only would become a complement (as opposed to *initia* and *elementa* being complements).

The grouping of the elements into two active and two passive ones is Stoic doctrine, but a distinction between an active element (fire) and material elements shaped by fire (earth, water, air) is attested for Xenocrates (Aët. 1.7.30 = frg. 213 Isnardi Parente; Aëtius adds ibid.: ταῦτα δὲ χορηγήσας τοῖς Στωικοῖς τὰ πρότερα παρὰ τοῦ Πλάτωνος μεταπέφρακεν). See Sedley (2002: 59), who comments: 'Whether a shift had first occurred within Academic physics [sc. from one active element to two] or was a Stoic innovation is a matter for guesswork.'

Varro's summary makes no attempt to mediate between the *uis* which is the active *res* in the initial dichotomy and the *uis mouendi et efficiendi* inherent in the two active elements. Inwood (2012: 210–11) comments: 'The important question is whether *uis* should be understood similarly here and in...[the initial division]. I suspect the answer should be "no", since the pre-elemental forces ("uis") above seem to be subsumed in the quality/bodies which they underlie and seem not to be differentiated in any way beyond the one being active and the other passive. At the present level of analysis, the forces must differ among the four elements (or at least between the active pair and the passive pair). This higher-level differentiation could, of course, be the product of features of or facts about the underlying forces (the active force being somehow more dominant in one pair of elements compared with the other). But it must be stressed that no feature of Cicero's text actually suggests this.'

Partes is nominative, not accusative and parallel to *uim*, as Reid[1] (p. 129) shows.

The equation of ἀρχαί and στοιχεῖα also in Lucilius, ll. 789–95 Krenkel [= 784–90 Marx = 'Probus' *in Vergilii eclogas* 6.31, pp. 340.23–341.4 Thilo and Hagen]:

˘ _ ˘ _ ˘ _ ˘ hoc cum feceris
cum ceteris reus una tradetur Lupo.
Non aderit: ἀρχαῖς hominem et stoicheiois simul
priuabit. Igni cum et aqua interdixerit,
duo habet stoicheia, adfuerit: anima et corpore
(γῆ corpus, anima est πνεῦμα), posterioribus
stoicheiois, si id maluerit, priuabit tamen.

Quintum genus, e quo essent astra mentesque...dissimile Aristoteles quoddam esse rebatur: on the fifth element in Cicero, see also *Tusc.* 1.22 (quoted in the previous n.); Moreschini (1979: 162-3) on Ciceronian terminology relating to it. I have explained in the general note above (p. 165) why the only way how the present passage and *Ac.* 1.39b (on Zeno's innovations in the field of physics) can be read coherently is by assuming that the fifth element is intended to be part of the *prima forma* of philosophy ascribed to the *ueteres* (*Ac.* 1.17, 1.33a) and that Aristotle is here named as the individual whose contribution it was (which was then accepted by other *antiqui*). (In 1.33b Varro seems to present a secondary correction, relating to the forms, made by Aristotle to the *prima forma* which had previously been co-formulated by him; in 1.39b Xenocrates is revealed either as someone who attempted a secondary modification of the *prima forma* which was not endorsed by others, or revealed as someone who never provided endorsement of the *prima forma* on the point at issue, viz. the nature of the soul.)

Part of this construction may well have been that Aristotle derived the idea that Plato had posited a fifth element from *Tim.* 53c-57c, as later Platonists thought; see Plut., *De E* 389f-390c; cf. *De def. orac.* 422f-423a, 428c-430b, with Karamanolis (2006: 104). Some sources appear to posit acceptance of the fifth element for Speusippus ([Iambl.], *Theol. Arithm.* pp. 82-5 = frg. 122 Isnardi Parente; see also Dillon 2003: 60-1), and Xenocrates is also reported to have ascribed this view, apparently on the basis of a reading of *Tim.* rather than by invoking oral teachings, to Plato (Simpl. *in Arist. Phys.* p. 1165.33-8 Diels = frg. 53 Heinze = frgs 264-6 Isnardi Parente), with Kotrč (1981: 216 n. 11). Cf. also [Plat.], *Epin.* 981b-c, with Tarán (1975: 36-42).

The notion, in evidence here and in *Tusc.* 1.22, that the fifth element does not just have a cosmological function but is the material stars and more importantly minds are made of is not Aristotelian; for a full discussion, see Moraux (1963), esp. cols 1245-6 on two possible origins of the notion, viz. Platonic motifs like the celestial origin of the soul, or the Stoic idea that the πνεῦμα of which individual souls are made is the same material as what stars are made of. (Bos 2003: 23-4 is a short summary of Moraux 1963 in English.) Brittain (2006: 97 n. 24) suggests another possibility: 'Cicero's error (repeated in *Tusc.* 1.22) is probably due to later Peripatetic elaborations of Aristotle's scattered remarks on the role of *pneuma* (fiery air) in human psychology, and a subsequent conflation of *pneuma* with the fifth element.'

On the doubtful ascription of the sentence to Aristotle's *De philosophia* (= frg. 27 Ross), see Sedley (2002: 79 n. 87); Kupreeva (2009: 139-40 n. 28); Lefebvre (2017: 61 n. 17 and 64 n. 28).

Reid[1] (p. 129) comments on *e quo essent*: 'This clause seems to give the *reason* for the use of the word *singulare*; otherwise *esse* might have been expected.'

§27

Sed subiectam putant omnibus sine ulla specie...quae interualla item infinite diuidi possint: Varro returns to the top-level distinction of the active and the passive *res* and elaborates on the latter, 'in' which matter is said to be. Matter underlies 'all things' (*omnibus*, sc. *rebus*, not *elementis*), which does not just mean all objects but everything that there is: the 'spaces' between moving objects are infinitely divisible like the objects, presumably because said spaces arise like objects from matter penetrated by the active force. The paragraph is grammatically one long sentence (with *quae autem* still being governed by *putant*) and largely free of indications which claim is explanatory of which; compare the rather different paraphrases in Sedley (2002: 67) and Inwood (2012: 211). On the correction *putant*, see Hunt (1998: 120).

For the Stoics the thesis of infinite divisibility is well attested; see *SVF* ii.482–91, LS 50; [Galen], *De qualitatibus incorporeis* ll. 109–61 Giusta (in Giusta 1976); Todd (1973); Scade (2010). Kupreeva (2009: 140 n. 36) points out that the 'theory of motion "by infinitely divisible intervals" has some affinities with Aristotelian theory as developed by Strato'; cf. Strato frg. 82 Wehrli.

An argument that successors of Plato may also have held matter to be indivisible cannot in the same way rely on independent evidence. Rather, Sedley (2002: 67–70) has argued that (i) we have independent reasons for thinking that *Ac.* 1.24–9 offers Old Academic material, notably the fundamental distinction between an active and a passive *res* (1.24) and (ii) that we know that Xenocrates took the creation story of Plt. *Tim.* to be a mere literary device and held the world to be eternal and consequently have reason to think that he took the Timaean primary triangles to be 'intrinsically indissoluble'. If one takes Varro by his word, as is reasonable given (i), then, so the argument goes, *Ac.* 1.27 might reflect a later Old Academic (i.e. Polemonian) view which pointedly diverges from Xenocrates and takes the world to have arisen out of the initial active and passive *res* and also accepts the infinite divisibility of matter. Whether one is attracted by this account or not depends largely on one's larger assumptions about the passage (see the general note above). In *Ac.* 1.6 Varro appears to suggest that the Old Academic account of physics in Latin would require the ability to talk about geometry; see Kupreeva (2009: 139 n. 26). This makes it likely that the source material used by Cicero for the current section featured such a discussion, which raises the question of how Antiochus dealt with the primary triangles; see Brittain (2006: 89 n. 5). See on *Luc.* 106, where Cicero touches on the Epicurean rejection of geometry.

The thesis of the indivisibility of matter puts the account provided by Varro in natural opposition to the Epicurean view, but there is no reason for thinking that the account is specifically anti-Epicurean (despite *cum sit nihil omnino in rerum natura minimum*). Rather, its ideological concerns lie elsewhere.

Inwood (2012: 211) comments on *sine ulla specie atque carentem omni illa qualitate*: 'This may just mean that it [sc. matter] is not yet (either analytically or temporally) combined with the active force so that neither is a body yet, but the focus here is emphatically on the standing of the passive entity. Yet the phrasing here ['*materiam quandam...carentem qualitate*'] suggests that the quality itself is the active force and that both the raw material and the shaping agent could be specified independently (as was not the case with the two entities [i.e. the two *res*] introduced above).' I agree that this part of the sentence is open to both readings in principle, but I do not regard the second one as more natural, and since it introduces a problem (on which see also Hatzimichali 2011: 111–12) which is absent on the first reading, I opt for the latter. *Subiectam... omnibus* above suggests that the matter in all compounds which exist in the world is meant, and matter thus understood can only be conceived of analytically; consider also that Varro speaks of *materiam quandam* as in *Ac.* 1.24.

With *faciamus... tritius*, cf. *N.D.* 1.95: *durum* [of *beatitas* and *beatitudo*], *sed usu mollienda nobis uerba sunt*. The participles *expressa* and *effecta* add to what was said earlier in that they give at least some characterization of the mechanism by which matter yields compounds: *exprimere* 'to bring out', when used of the handiwork of the craftsmen especially suggestive of three-dimensional, clearly delineated shapes (contrast *adumbrare*; see Reinhardt 2008: 134 n. 24), while *efficere* means 'to complete'. (Turnebus emended to *efficta*.) Cf. the use of διαζωγραφεῖν in Plt., *Tim.* 55c, with Kotrč (1981: 212–15).

The adjective *tota* is feminine singular and qualifies *quae*; cf. §28 *materiam ipsam totam*. *Omnia accipere* suggests that matter can take on any form when it was previously notionally shapeless, rather than it takes on actual pre-existing qualities which are already themselves forms of sorts; cf. my reading of *carentem omni illa qualitate* above.

I take *moueantur* in *quae autem moueantur* to be medio-passive; see also the next note. *Possit (omnibusque modis)* is to be found in descendants of what Hunt (1998: xiii) dubs ψ^2 (see ibid. p. 179); see also Hunt (1998: 247) on the emendation *mutari*.

§28

Et cum ita moueatur illa uis quam qualitatem esse diximus...in qua ratio perfecta insit, quae sit sempiterna: having returned to the top-level division and to one of its two elements, *materia*, in §27, Varro proceeds to the other, active one (*uis*). The connection with the immediately preceding sentence is not straightforward: *ita* can only have backward reference and mean 'in the aforementioned way', but just before the movement of objects (broadly construed) rather than of *uis* was at issue. Unless one follows Reid[1] (p. 132) in thinking that the reference is as far back as to §24 (where movement was not mentioned), the natural solution is that the *uis* is moved/moves itself when objects move. In that case the movement described in *cum sic ultro citroque uersetur* (where *sic* is equivalent in function and meaning to *ita* earlier in the sentence) is most likely the same as that of the objects: they move back and forth, but not in a regularized, vibrating manner (see Sedley 2002: 67 n. 59 and below). That being so, the profound change of matter which is mentioned next (*materiam...penitus commutari putant*) and which issues in the creation of *qualia* is not most naturally seen as the creation of the elements (*pace* Reid[1] p. 132), but of objects which arise from the interaction of the active and the passive *res* of §24 at any level (from elements to living beings and inanimate objects). *Qualia*, on this reading (see above, p. 166), are compounds arising from the active and the passive *res*. Jointly all such *qualia* make up the world (*mundus*), interconnected as it is, outside of which there is no matter and no body. In *nulla pars materiae... nullumque corpus* the latter phrase is presumably epexegetic of the former (see *OLD* s.v. *-que* no. 6a), for matter which is not a *corpus* as a consequence of interaction with the active *res* (cf. 1.24 *fin.*) should only be a notional possibility in Varro's account. (Varro takes no explicit stance on whether he—like the Stoics—assumes there to be void outside of the world, but it is more plausible to think that he does not since here he would have had another opportunity after *Ac.* 1.24 to say that he does.) The world's parts are all the things in it, which are held together by a rational being (*natura sentiens*), which is eternal. It is eternal because nothing exists which is more powerful than it and which could end its existence (uncaused expiry of the world as the reason for its eventual end is not an option). The *natura sentiens/ratio perfecta et sempiterna* is identified with the active *res/uis*, as §29 *init.* suggests.

The verb *moueatur* must be medio-passive (see *TLL* s.v. col. 1539.4–31), since the *uis* itself is the active force which is not and cannot be moved by something else. With *et cum... et cum...*, cf. *Ac.* 1.38–9: *cumque...* (four times).

For the use of *ultro* and *citro* assumed above, cf. *N.D.* 2.84: *Nam ex terra aqua ex aqua oritur aer ex aere aether, deinde retrorsum uicissim ex aethere aer inde aqua ex aqua terra infima. Sic naturis his ex quibus omnia constant sursus deorsus ultro citro commeantibus mundi partium coniunctio continetur.* The way in which our passage here follows on from the previous paragraph tells against the notion that the role assigned to *uis* is relevantly similar to the Stoic doctrine of pneumatic tension; *pace* Brittain (2006: 98 n. 25); Kupreeva (2009: 140).

Reid[1] (p. 132) explains *in omni natura* as 'by operations extending over the whole of the substance' and provides parallels; cf. also Brittain (2006: 98): 'A single world has been brought about in the totality of ⟨material⟩ nature.' With *natura cohaerente*, cf. *N.D.* 2.155 *cohaerentia mundi*; 2.82. With *natura... continuata cum omnibus suis partibus*, cf. *N.D.* 2.84: *et cum quattuor genera sint corporum, uicissitudine eorum mundi continuata natura est*; also *natura sentiente teneantur* below.

On *extra quem... nullumque corpus*, see above. The phrase *partes mundi* is used frequently in *N.D.* 2, concerned with Stoic theology; see Reid[1] (p. 132). With *natura sentiente*, cf. *N.D.* 2.85: *aut igitur nihil est quod sentiente natura regatur, aut mundum regi confitendum est*; D.L. 7.139 (= part of LS 47O): ὁ μέντοι Χρύσιππος διαφορώτερον πάλιν τὸ καθαρώτατον τοῦ αἰθέρος ἐν ταὐτῷ, ὃ καὶ πρῶτον θεὸν λέγουσιν αἰσθητικῶς ὥσπερ κεχωρηκέναι διὰ τῶν ἐν ἀέρι καὶ διὰ τῶν ζῴων ἁπάντων καὶ φυτῶν, διὰ δὲ τῆς γῆς αὐτῆς καθ' ἕξιν, 'Yet Chrysippus has a rather different account in the same book ['On Providence'], viz. the purest part of aether, which they say passes as first god perceptibly through the things in the air as well as all animals and plants, and through the earth itself, as a principle of cohesion'. With *ratio perfecta*, cf. *N.D.* 2.34, 3.22.

Nihil enim ualentius esse a quo intereat: uncaused expiry is not an option, and there is nothing stronger than the world. See Pinkster i.245 on the use of *ab* with ablative for an inanimate cause. Reid[1] (p. 133) names parallels for the commonplace (*N.D.* 2.31; Sen., *N.Q.* 6.4.1). For Xenocrates' view that the world is eternal, see above, p. 184.

§29

In this concluding paragraph of the physical section Varro provides a string of characterizations for the *uis* = *natura sentiens* = *ratio perfecta et sempiterna* of the previous paragraph. These can be linked to Stoic views, as has always been recognized, including by Cicero. Cf. e.g. *N.D.* 1.39 (part of *SVF* ii.1077 = part of LS 54B; see the general note on *Luc.* 118–26 for Cicero's likely source in *N.D.* 1): *Chrysippus... ait enim uim diuinam in ratione esse positam et in uniuersae naturae animo atque mente, ipsumque mundum deum dicit esse et eius animi fusionem uniuersam, tum eius ipsius principatum, qui in mente et ratione uersetur, communemque rerum naturam uniuersam atque omnia continentem, tum* εἱμαρμένην *et fatalem necessitatem* [so Dyck following Birt; *fatalem umbram et necessitatem* ω] *rerum futurarum, ignem praeterea et eum quem ante dixi aethera, tum ea quae natura fluerent atque manarent, ut et aquam et terram et aera solem lunam sidera uniuersitatemque rerum qua omnia continerentur, atque etiam homines eos qui immortalitatem essent consecuti*; cf. D.L. 7.135-6 (part of *SVF* i.102 = LS 46B).

However, the views in question were in part developed through creative interaction with Plt. *Tim.* Thus the question arises whether there are also reasons for thinking that said views could also have been held in the Academy, where one would naturally have looked to Plt. *Tim.*, too, and, secondarily, whether if not Cicero's first audience then Antiochus' might have been able to appreciate this. See Sedley (2002: 73-6) and Inwood (2012: 212-13).

Quam uim animum esse dicunt mundi...quae pertinent ad homines: apart from the Stoic parallels cited above, cf. *Tim.* 42: *omnem animum uniuersae naturae* = Plt., *Tim.* 41D: τὴν τοῦ παντὸς ψυχήν. For *mundi...mentem*, cf. *N.D.* 2.58; the phrase also (of the sun) in *Rep.* 6.17. With *sapientia perfecta* (of the world), cf. *N.D.* 2.36 (the Stoic view that the world is *sapiens*), and the criticism of the claim in *N.D.* 3.23. With *quasi prudentiam quandam*, cf. *N.D.* 1.18 (the speaker is Epicurean): *audite... non futtiles commenticiasque sententias, non opificem aedificatoremque mundi Platonis de Timaeo deum, nec anum fatidicam Stoicorum Pronoeam, quam Latine licet Prouidentiam dicere, neque uero mundum ipsum animo et sensibus praeditum, rutundum, ardentem, uolubilem deum, portenta et miracula non disserentium philosophorum, sed somniantium*; for *quasi* combined with *quandam*, see above, p. 178. *Procurare*, as Reid[1] (p. 134) notes, is normally a political term; for its use of divine providential action, see *TLL* s.v. col. 1582.15-21. The movement from general to particular in the sentence does not shed light on how the *uis* in question relates to that inherent in the initial active *res* or that in the active elements, but the seamless transition from §§27-8 to 29 suggests that one and the same *uis*, operating on different levels, is meant throughout. *Caelestia* (= μετέωρα) are 'heavenly matters' or 'heavenly affairs' (Brittain 2006), not just more narrowly 'Himmelskörper' (Gigon). Lambinus emended *prudentiam* to *prouidentiam*, but Plasberg[1] (p. 48) aptly cites *N.D.* 2.58.

With *quem deum appellant*, cf. Sextus, *M.* 9.75-6 (= *SVF* ii.311 = LS 44C), which offers an argument why the power which moves substance is god. However, cf. also the sole fragment on Polemo's physical views in Aët. 1.7.29 (= frg. 121 Gigante = t. 62 Marzotto): Πολέμων τὸν κόσμον θεὸν ἀπεφήνατο (see above, n. 170).

Reid¹ (p. 134) suggests that the mood of *pertinent* signals actual endorsement of the speaker's part.

Quam interdum eandem necessitatem appellant...inter⟨dum⟩ ⟨seriem causarum⟩ quasi fatalem et immutabilem continuationem ordinis sempiterni: some conception of fate as necessity (ἀνάγκη) was widespread in popular belief, but in the present context the relevant Stoic doctrine lies closer to hand; see *N.D.* 1.39 quoted above. Reid¹ (pp. 134–5) comments, citing *Tim.* 47–8, that ἀνάγκη in Plato is 'entirely unlike the *necessitas* described here as "old Academic".' Sedley (2002: 73–5) offers a reading of the same *Tim.* passage on which the Polemonian Academy, given their other commitments as reported in our passage, could equate god with necessity 'to ensure coherence in their own global interpretation of the *Timaeus*'.

With *quia...constitutum sit*, cf. this line from Cleanthes' Hymn to Zeus (Stob., *Ecl.* I.1, p. 26.4 = *SVF* i.537): οὐδέ τι γίγνεται ἔργον ἐπὶ χθονὶ σοῦ δίχα, δαῖμον, 'Nothing happens on earth without you, deity' (but Cleanthes goes on to blame evil on humans). On *possit* rather than Lambinus' *esse possit*, see Löfstedt ii.270. For the justificatory use of *inter*, see *OLD* s.v. 8c. *Quasi* in *quasi fatalem...* may only signal philosophers' parlance.

Reid¹ (p. 134) prints the text as transmitted and translates in Reid² '...since events cannot happen otherwise than by it [sc. fate] ordained, being linked in what they call the destined and changeless chain of the everlasting order', explaining: 'this use of the word [sc. *inter*], to introduce a consideration accounting for, or confirming a previous statement, is rare in Cic.' I regard *inter* in this sense as very unlikely and think that *interdum* for *inter* is compelling, given the enumerating style of the section, and that the supplement *seriem causarum*, in the app. in both Plasberg¹ and Plasberg², may well be right. There are good parallels for the idea as well as the expression in relevantly similar contexts in Cicero (*Div.* 1.125; *Fat.* 20) and beyond, and the occurrence of *causarum* later in the sentence would arguably be better motivated. There are no obvious mechnical reasons for why *seriem causarum* should have dropped out, but someone might have deemed it a gloss.

Non numquam quidem eandem fortunam...propter obscuritatem ignorationemque causarum: *necessitas* is called *fortuna* if we are ignorant of cause–effect relationships which are often (cf. *multa*, 'many events') obscure to us. See the texts collected as *SVF* ii.965–73. On fate as a chain of causes, known or otherwise, see *Div.* 1.125–6 (*SVF* ii.921 = LS 55L). *Necopinatus* e.g. in *Tusc.* 3.28 and 45, but as Reid¹ (p. 135) notes, Cicero also uses *inopinatus* in the same sense. For the phrase *causarum ignoratio*, cf. *Div.* 2.49.

§§30–33a

Like the account of physics which immediately precedes, this section on the third part of philosophy is compressed, and the connections between some of the areas of doctrine mentioned, especially in its second half, are sketchy. What is presented here is ascribed to Plato's successors prior to Arcesilaus as well as to Aristotle and the

Peripatetics in 1.30 (*ab utrisque*), while the concluding sentence in 1.33 appears to clarify that we are dealing with a set of interrelated doctrines accepted by both groups and—in *their* view—handed down to them by Plato (*haec forma erat* **illis** *prima, a Platone tradita*, and *praeclare… Peripateticorum et Academiae ueteris auctoritas*; for the interpretation see ad loc.), while the character Varro regards this *prima forma* as shaped by the interpretative work of Old Academics and Peripatetics (see on Ac. 1.15–17), who, however, in many cases came close to divining Plato's intention (see section 7.2). 1.33b will then introduce modifications of said *prima forma* proposed by Aristotle and the Peripatetics. These are to be regarded as chronologically secondary disagreements on particular points, to be seen against a background of broad agreement, given that 1.33 *illis* and 1.30 *utrisque* refer to the same people.

Varro begins with a general indication of what λογική comprises according to the *antiqui*: epistemology, as well as logic and dialectic. The two phrases *in ratione* and *in disserendo*, vague as they are, seem to refer to slightly overlapping rather than complementary fields, and *in ratione* includes, apart from theories of argument, what we would call epistemology in a more narrow sense. The *iudicium ueritatis*, although it arises from the senses, is said not to reside in the senses; the phrase *iudicium ueritatis* is often plausibly linked to the Greek κριτήριον τῆς ἀληθείας, but one should note that here the *iudicium ueritatis* is something the mind *does* in its role as *iudex*. The mind then acts as *iudex rerum*; on the most natural reading, this means that the mind judges things which present themselves in experience, having been relayed by the senses. The phrase would be unusually or elliptically used if what the mind was taken to do is contemplate, access, or recollect forms qua transcendent entities. The mind alone deserves our trust; it alone looks at (*cerneret*) what is simple, uniform, and the same as itself.[188] This object of the mind's vision is then identified as a Form (ἰδέα), and Varro adds that already Plato called it that. We then learn what the problem is with sense perception—the senses are blunt and sluggish and they are unable to grasp with accuracy the objects which present themselves to them, because these objects are either too small or in a state of perpetual flux. Given how the sentence is formulated, it is clear that the two weaknesses of the senses named (bluntness; sluggishness) map onto the properties of the objects of perception (smallness; being subject to flux), but it is not made clear whether it is the senses or the objects which are held responsible, and the properties of both senses and objects of perception are presented in the positive form grammatically. On its own, this may sound like a complete dismissal of the senses, but *quamquam oriretur a sensibus* above accords at least some role to the senses. The account then steps back and sums up this entire area of the world as associated with mere opinion,[189] and locates knowledge (*scientia*) exclusively in the *notiones animi atque rationes*, the notions in the mind and calculations, one has to assume, involving or about them.[190] An interest in definitions is then closely linked with these *notiones*, as well as one in etymology, which, it is implied, is

---

[188] *Cernere* has other senses which may be deemed to be relevant here; see the lemmatized note below.

[189] I do not think that the passage exhibits a so-called 'two-world view', viz. that there coexist a realm of the forms and the perceptible world; see below.

[190] Given what is said about the senses and their objects, it is difficult to see how—according to 1.30–33a—the *antiqui* could have seen the *notiones* as derived from sense perception.

concerned with the analysis of *uerba* as opposed to *res* designated. There follows a reference to theories of argumentation, with an emphasis on arguments used to demonstrate scientific truths. The section ends with a verbal gesture to the famous opening sentence of Aristotle's *Rhet.*, which is the only peculiarly Aristotelian element in the section; the interest in definition and theory of argument can be associated with Aristotle as much as with Speusippus and Xenocrates.

The Form (*species*) 'already called ἰδέα by Plato' is mentioned in 1.30, where I take the singular to be generic. Even though there was no reference to Forms in the sections on ethics and on physics, and though their introduction here seems somewhat unemphatic (see n. ad loc.), their presence has determined interpretative reactions to the section to a considerable extent and has given rise to some rather diverse views on the status one should accord to the section as evidence, given that Lucullus' speech in *Luc.*, which argues for the existence of κατάληψις and which is the most complete record of Antiochian epistemology, is Stoic in content (see Brittain 2012). As such Lucullus' speech does not leave room for metaphysical entities like forms and takes the things in the spatio-temporal world as natural, unproblematic and fairly stable objects of perception. The majority view is that 1.30-33a is a historical account,[191] to be superseded by Stoic views eventually, which Antiochus regarded and accepted as an outgrowth of the wider Academic tradition; it is usually part of such a reading to assume that the Forms mentioned are transcendental items.[192] Others believe that the section, for all its verbal gestures to Plato, is in fact Stoic in substance, and thus in substantial agreement with *Luc.*; on this reading, the forms are identified with concepts and have no transcendental status as a result of retrojection.[193] Yet others try to read Lucullus' speech in *Luc.* in a Platonizing manner (Fladerer 1996: 86-8) and aim to achieve reconciliation in that way. It has also been suggested that *Ac.* 1.30-33a is Platonic and anti-empiricist in content and gives Antiochus' view (or rather that of the *ueteres*, which Antiochus accepted), while Lucullus' speech is spoken dialectically (Lévy 1992: 187-91).[194]

On the interpretation given here (cf. Reinhardt 2018), *Ac.* 1.30-33a is indeed intended to be a historical account (as seems inescapable given the framing remarks of the section), but the position posited for the Old Academics and Peripatetics is a conceptualist interpretation of Platonic forms which does not involve a two-world view, notably one derived from *Timaeus* 27d-28a (quoted below). In *Ac.* 1.30-33a *init.* reason, partly but not exclusively through the application of concepts to perceptual information, cannot do entirely without the senses, even though their role is significantly diminished compared to the Stoic view exhibited in Lucullus' speech in *Luc.* The view that the senses and reason need to work together is taken to be the doctrinal thread which according to Antiochus runs through the *ueteres* and Aristotle to the Stoics. The need to identify such a thread is due to the fact that

---

[191] See e.g. Barnes (1997: 95-6); Glucker (1997: 72); Sedley (2012b: 87).

[192] Fladerer (1996: 101-6) offers a survey of scholarly opinions on Antiochus' views on Forms. Scholars who have recently assumed Antiochus/Varro to have posited transcendental Forms as a view of the *ueteres* include Karamanolis (2006: 62-3); Blank (2012: 274-5); and Bonazzi (2015: 61-4) with qualifications. See also Gildenhard (2013) on passages concerned with Forms in Cicero.

[193] Thus e.g. Görler (2004a: 95); Tsouni (2018: 274-5).

[194] On the doctrine of Forms as thoughts of god, see the general note on *Ac.* 1.24-9.

otherwise it would be impossible to understand how Zeno's 'corrections' in the field of epistemology (*Ac.* 1.40–2; cf. 1.43: *correctionem ueteris Academiae potius quam aliquam nouam disciplinam*) can be characterized in those terms: how could the doctrine of the cataleptic impression and a Stoic materialist view of the world be seen as a mere 'correction' of the two-world view and the complete dismissal of the senses?

I will also argue that Antiochus sought to secure appropriate credentials for his account by deriving key aspects of the epistemological views of the Old Academics and Peripatetics from Plato's *Theaetetus*, a dialogue which was significantly more amenable to this endeavour than dialogues of the middle period and which was an ideologically important text for the sceptical Academy, so that its reclaiming mattered to the Antiochian project.[195] Antiochus also implied that Zeno's epistemological amendments to the Platonic position were derived from the same dialogue (see on *Ac.* 1.40–2). This is suggested by a number of coordinated correspondences between Cicero's text and the *Tht.* Verbal similarities with other dialogues are detectable, too, and will be documented below, but they are not of sufficient extent and suitable ideological import to dislodge the *Tht.* in the hierarchy of models.[196]

In *Tht.* 182–7,[197] i.e. the end of the enquiry into whether perception is knowledge, the question is finally answered negatively, because knowledge is implied to reside in or consist in something other than individual episodes of perception or the results of such episodes: the 'common concepts' (κοινά) and our 'calculations' (ἀναλογίσματα) about or involving them.[198] Socrates suggests that the senses are merely used, like tools, by the soul in order to perceive (184e–185a), and that the soul unifies the αἰσθήσεις provided by the various senses into a single form (ἰδέα, 184d3). Perception is not knowledge because in what is usually called αἰσθήσεις we make use of a range of κοινά (~ *notiones*), i.e. 'commons' or 'common terms' (including being, not-being, sameness, difference, 185c9–10), which the soul invariably applies as it processes the information it receives from the senses, and which cannot have been acquired through perception (185b7–9; Cicero's *notiones* here in *Ac.* 1.30 cannot derive from perception, either). Perception by itself, i.e. perception narrowly conceived, only

---

[195] On *Tht.* and the sceptical Academy, see e.g. Anon. *in Tht.* cols 54.38–55.13; Burnyeat (1990: 235); Ioppolo (1990); Annas (1992a: 52–61); Sedley (1996: 86); Opsomer (1998a: 34, 42–9) with further secondary references. Favorinus of Arelate, a late representative of the sceptical Academy, claimed (Galen, *De opt. doct.* 1) that even the sun was unknowable. This may be a reference to the very end of the *Tht.*, where the suggestion that knowledge is true belief plus an account of how an object differs from all other things is illustrated with an account of the sun: 'the brightest of the bodies that move around the earth in the heavens' (208d). On Favorinus' stance, see Ioppolo (1993).

[196] Alternative readings to mine would either assume that a different dialogue or dialogues is a more important model than *Tht.* or would reject the notion of meaningful intertextual references altogether; for the latter view, see Brittain (2012: 107): 'Varro's presentation in *Ac.* 1.30–32 and 34 is a rapid and perhaps deliberately vague sketch, based on allusions to largely uninterpreted Platonic passages.'

[197] On this section of *Tht.*, see Frede (1989), esp. 21–4; Fine (2017); Sedley (2004: 106) observes that, strictly, the κοινά feature as predicates in *Theat.* 184. See also Silverman (1990).

[198] See especially Plt., *Tht.* 186d2–5 (Socrates speaking): Ἐν μὲν ἄρα τοῖς παθήμασιν οὐκ ἔνι ἐπιστήμη, ἐν δὲ τῷ περὶ ἐκείνων συλλογισμῷ· οὐσίας γὰρ καὶ ἀληθείας ἐνταῦθα μέν, ὡς ἔοικε, δυνατὸν ἅψασθαι, ἐκεῖ δὲ ἀδύνατον, 'Then knowledge is to be found not in the experiences but in the process of reasoning about them; it is here, seemingly, not in the experiences, that it is possible to grasp being and truth' (transl. Levett). With the use of ἐπιστήμη here contrast the use of δοξάζειν, also of the mind's reasonings about experiences, in 187a8 (Theaetetus speaking). I am assuming that, in terms of terminology, *Ac.* 1.30–2 is looking to the earlier of the two *Tht.* passages.

confers mere passive affection, and any attempt to move beyond this passive affection will involve the κοινά and 'calculations' (ἀναλογίσματα, 186c3 ~ *rationes*, cf. *OLD* s.v. *ratio* nn. 1, 2, and 4), i.e. reason brought to bear on perceptual information. Reason, or the soul, attempts to perform judgements (κρίνειν πειρᾶται, 186b8 ~ *mentem esse iudicem rerum*);[199] the soul investigates the κοινά of everything for that purpose (185e1-2 αὐτὴ δι' αὑτῆς ἡ ψυχὴ τὰ κοινά μοι φαίνεται περὶ πάντων ἐπισκοπεῖν ~ *quia sola* [sc. *mens*] *cerneret id quod semper esset simplex et unius modi et tale quale esset*).[200] As to the *rationes* (ἀναλογίσματα), these are not further glossed in Cicero, and the only illumination which the term receives comes from the context, i.e. the juxtaposition with concepts on the one hand, and definitions on the other. The *Tht.* tells us that the 'calculations regarding the being of affections and whether they are advantageous come, for those for whom they come to pass, only with effort and over time, involving a good deal of trouble and education' (186c1-5); in the first instance, the calculations clearly represent just the application of concepts, but then also comparison of concepts with one another and thereby reflection on them (186b6-9; this meaning would be readily covered by *rationes*).[201] Reflection on concepts would establish a straightforward link with definitions, since the results of conceptual analysis are encapsulated in definitions. Modern scholars disagree on whether *Tht.* 184a-187 maintains a version of the Heraclitean flux view of the

---

[199] Cf. *Tusc.* 1.46 (the only other passage in the Ciceronian corpus where *Tht.*, and again 182-7, is referenced, as noted by Long 1995: 44 n. 14): *quae numquam quinque nuntiis animus cognosceret, nisi ad eum omnia referrentur et is omnium iudex solus esset*, 'The soul could never recognize these [the deliverances of the different senses] through its five messengers, unless everything was reported to it and it alone was the judge of all things.'

[200] With the characterization of what the soul considers in Cicero compare also Socrates' concluding remark in *Tht.* 187a1-6: Ἀλλ' οὔ τι μὲν δὴ τούτου γε ἕνεκα ἠρχόμεθα διαλεγόμενοι, ἵνα εὕρωμεν τί ποτ' οὐκ ἔστ' ἐπιστήμη, ἀλλὰ τί ἔστιν. ὅμως δὲ τοσοῦτόν γε προβεβήκαμεν, ὥστε μὴ ζητεῖν αὐτὴν ἐν αἰσθήσει τὸ παράπαν ἀλλ' ἐν ἐκείνῳ τῷ ὀνόματι, ὅτι ποτ' ἔχει ἡ ψυχή, **ὅταν αὐτὴ καθ' αὑτὴν πραγματεύηται περὶ τὰ ὄντα**, 'But we did not begin this discussion in order to find out what knowledge is not, but to find out what it is. Yet we have come only so far as to stop looking for it in sense perception at all, and instead look for it *in whatever the activity is called in which the soul engages when it is busy by itself with the things which are*.' The modern unitarian reader of *Tht.* may seek support in τὰ ὄντα for the identification of κοινά and forms; I suggest that someone who regards κοινά as concepts, like, on my argument, Antiochus, would feel encouraged to apply attributes we might associate with forms (*quod semper esset simplex et unius modi et tale quale esset*) to concepts.

[201] On *Tht.* 186b6-9, see esp. the observations in Frede (1989: 23): 'The mind's "calculations and comparisons" (186a-c) may, indeed, stand for no more than our ordinary judgements, as, for instance, that this piece of clay is softer than that one; how much softer it is; what good it would do to use this harder piece of clay to make a dish rather than this softer one. But the "calculations" may also stand for an explicit and reflective concern with the concepts of hardness and softness themselves: "their being, and the being of the difference between them" (186b6-9). What speaks for the claim that Plato had a stronger interpretation in mind is not only employment of rather technical vocabulary here ("the being of their oppositeness", 186b7), but most of all Socrates' saying that these calculations are achieved "just barely, over a long time, through a lot of difficulty and education, for those who in fact do achieve them" (186c2-4).' Various non-unitarian readings of *Tht.* 184-7 have been advanced by modern scholars. My account of the section given above is meant to be compatible with several of them, since I am not confident that one can determine which of them in particular was ascribed to the *antiqui* by Antiochus (or whether it was a slightly different one still). However, I do note that one modern reading aligns the passage with others which can be interpreted as predecessors of the Stoic doctrine of appearance/impression and assent; see Moss (2014: 228-36). It would fit with my reconstruction of the use of *Tht.* by Antiochus if he deployed a version of that reading to explain Zeno's 'corrections' to the views of the *antiqui*, viz. as a superior reading of Plato. See on *Ac.* 1.40-2.

perceptible world which is assumed in the earlier part of the discussion (e.g. Chappell 2004: 141–9) or indeed abandons it in favour of ordinary stable objects of perception (thus e.g. Cooper 1970: 125 n. 4; Burnyeat 1990: 55–6). I suggest the former would have been a possible interpretation for a reader in antiquity (182b3–4 ἐν μηδὲν αὐτὸ καθ' αὑτὸ εἶναι and 182a1 πάντα δὴ πᾶσαν κίνησιν ἀεὶ κινεῖται ~ *aut ita mobiles et concitatae ut **nihil umquam unum esset** ⟨et⟩ constans, ne idem quidem, quia **continenter laberentur et fluerent omnia**).*[202]

How, then, to integrate the reference to forms with this reading of *Ac.* 1.30–33a against the *Tht.*? Initially, one might be tempted to see Antiochus pursuing a reading whereby the forms as metaphysical entities are not mentioned in the dialogue but are still assumed to be in operation in the background, and are taken to relate to the κοινά.[203] (Such a reading could be compared to a modern unitarian reading of *Tht.*, i.e. one which assumes that transcendental forms are presupposed in the dialogue, except that we cannot know if, and have no positive evidence suggesting that, Antiochus read the dialogues of the middle period in a way which involved transcendent forms.) But I think this would be mistaken; rather, I suggest that in *Ac.* 1.30–33a concepts are called forms and in that sense identified with forms.[204] The connection with *Tht.* does not in itself suggest otherwise, and it is plausible to think that Antiochus anticipated a reading of the dialogue on which no forms qua metaphysical entities are taken to be presupposed by the discussion.[205] I note in this connection that the list of κοινά in *Tht.* includes not-being (185c9: τὸ μὴ εἶναι), which discourages an interpretation that connects them with transcendent forms.[206] In *Parmenides* 129d there is a list of forms (likeness, multitude, rest, and their opposites, expanded to include ethical forms in 130b) which is reminiscent of the κοινά, but in that dialogue a conceptualist interpretation of the forms is dismissed. By the same token, I do not think that Cicero's *notiones* should make one think of the μέγιστα γένη of the *Sophistes* 254b–258e. In general, I do not see grounds for ranking *Parm.* and *Soph.* highly in the hierarchy of models for *Ac.* 1.30–33a.[207]

---

[202] Cf. Long (1995: 46 n. 18): 'No citation from Plato is given at *Acad.* 1.31, but two of Cicero's expressions in this context are virtual translations of sentences in *Tht.* 182, "nihil umquam esset constans", and "continenter laberentur et fluerent omnia". Cicero's Latin is closer to Plato's actual words here than to other Platonic contexts he could have had before him, such as *Crat.* 439d and *Tim.* 49e.' On *Tim.* 49, see e.g. Zeyl (1975); Gill (1987).

[203] I submit that such a reading would be possible only if *Ac.* 1.30–33a was allowed to be inconsistent with 1.24–9, where the account of physics as posited by the Old Academics and Peripatetics is unable to accommodate transcendental forms (see the general note on that section); mutatis mutandis the same is true of the section on ethics preceding it (*Ac.* 1.19–23).

[204] Cf. Hirzel (1883: 499 n. 2); Reid¹ (p. 138) on *Ac.* 1.32 *animi notionibus*: 'Cic. here seems to imply that there was practically little difference between Plato's ἰδέαι and Aristotle's ἔννοιαι τῶν καθόλου.' Another passage where notions and forms are mentioned side by side, frequently discussed alongside our passage here without being relevant to it, is *Tusc.* 1.56–8, on which see Reinhardt (2018: 33–9).

[205] On the two readings of *Tht.*, see e.g. Cooper (1970: 123); Burnyeat (1990: 7–10). Among later Platonists, 'unitarian' interpretations of *Tht.* were the norm in antiquity (see Sedley 1996).

[206] Bonazzi (2015: 32–50) makes a number of interpretative choices which are similar to mine, notably on the status of the senses in *Ac.* 1.30–1, but does not assign a particular role to *Tht.* as an intertext. He also appears to credit the Forms mentioned in *Ac.* 1.30 with some residual transcendent status. See also Petrucci (2018).

[207] Cic., *Or.* 8–10, discussed in Reinhardt (2018: 51–3), is frequently seen as Antiochian, on less than compelling grounds. I note, though, that, like *Ac.* 1.30–33a on my reading, it juxtaposes a flux view of the

As for *Tim.* 27d5–28a4, posited as Cicero's main model by Sedley (2012b: 84–7), the question is how close and extensive the correspondences are and how much about our passage they can explain; I quote 27d5–28a4:

Ἔστιν οὖν δὴ κατ' ἐμὴν δόξαν πρῶτον διαιρετέον τάδε· τί τὸ ὂν ἀεί, γένεσιν δὲ οὐκ ἔχον, καὶ τί τὸ γιγνόμενον μὲν ἀεί, ὂν δὲ οὐδέποτε; τὸ μὲν δὴ νοήσει μετὰ λόγου περιληπτόν, ἀεὶ κατὰ ταὐτὰ ὄν, τὸ δ' αὖ δόξῃ μετ' αἰσθήσεως ἀλόγου δοξαστόν, γιγνόμενον καὶ ἀπολλύμενον, ὄντως δὲ οὐδέποτε ὄν.

As I see it, we must begin by making the following distinction: What is *that which always is* and has no becoming, and what is *that which becomes* but never is? The former is grasped by understanding, which involves a reasoned account. It is unchanging. The latter is grasped by opinion, which involves unreasoning sense perception. It comes to be and passes away but never really is. (transl. Zeyl)

This very influential passage introduces a clear division between two domains and characterizes them in terms which resemble Cicero's wording in *Ac.* 1.30.[208] In the notes below I explain why the similarities are actually smaller than it might appear. More importantly, however, what the passage does not account for is Cicero's reference to the mind and its role as a judge, to notions and calculations about them, and to the claim that knowledge resides in them. And while the idea that the perceptible world is in flux is present, connections with *Tht.* are closer on this point, too (see above). These considerations suggest that *Tim.* is less important to the construction of the meaning of our passage than *Tht.* There is also a question of whether all points of contact are equally important if one holds that a developmental account of Academic thought is discernible in outline across the two books. *Notiones* and calculations about them feature in the section on Zeno's corrections (*Ac.* 1.40–2) as well as in Lucullus' speech in *Luc.* (19–22), while a distinction between two worlds, or of two domains within one world, is only important here.[209]

In *Phd.* 72e–78b Socrates puts forward the argument from recollection for the soul's immortality, in the course of which he argues that the notion of similarity cannot be derived from sense perception and similar objects in particular, since the objects of our experience are never precisely similar and since, in order to judge objects of experience, we need a notion of similarity to begin with.[210] It would appear that the grounds on which the senses are dismissed are different in the *Phd.* and more along the lines of why the perceptible world is deemed inferior elsewhere in Plato.[211] Moreover, and crucially, the role of the forms is conceived differently: any notions we hold in our minds derive from the soul's contact with the forms prior to incarnation (a point not made in the *Ac.* passage and impossible to supply from the

---

perceptible world and forms which are located in the mind of human beings, *pace* Gildenhard (2013: 248–62), who argues that in *Or.* 7–10 transcendental forms are envisaged.

[208] On *Tim.* 27d5–28a4, see Thesleff (1999); on *Tim.* in the Hellenistic period more generally, see Niehoff (2007).

[209] For a reading of *Tim.* which extends the non-unitarian reading of *Tht.* and the attendant interpretation of the κοινά to that dialogue, see Frede (1996).

[210] See e.g. Svavarsson (2009).   [211] See Nehamas (1975).

wider context), and it is positively incompatible with the overall argumentative purpose of the *Phd.* section that the realm of knowledge should be restricted to our notions (as in *Ac.* 1.31-2).

Since within Stoic texts on ontology (or texts reflecting Stoic thinking on the subject) forms are recognized as a philosophical proposition but functionally replaced with a type of concept (ἐννοήματα), one might wonder if we are dealing with an instance of retrojection of Stoicism after all.[212] Again, this suggestion does not seem to withstand scrutiny: the attributes which the Stoics apply to ἐννοήματα are rather different from those which Varro applies to forms in our passage, and Stoic ἐννοήματα are not assumed to be in the mind,[213] so one can accord to Stoic ontology a facilitating role at best. But one could then equally ask why *Parm.* could not have played the same enabling role.

Some other relevantly similar texts allow the distinctiveness of the present section to emerge. The first, Alcinous' *Didascalicus* or *Handbook of Platonism*, deals with the κριτήριον and with epistemology in ch. 4. This text primarily brings home how compressed and sketchy *Ac.* 1.30-33a is. The allusive density with respect to Platonic passages referenced is high, and *Tht.* is used but does not have a significant presence. Matter and forms feature in separate, later chapters (8, 9).[214] Second, *Fin.* 4.8-10, which has often been held to be informed by Antiochean thinking, provides some confirmation for the claim that Antiochus identified the need for the mind and the senses to work together to obtain knowledge as one of the continuities in the Academic tradition.[215] This passage precedes Cicero's criticism of Stoic ethics from an Antiochian point of view, and it shares with Varro's speech in *Ac.* some important general features: it is the section on epistemology in a survey of the views of the Academic tradition by area of philosophy, and it broadly argues for a unity view. However, it is also different in important respects, which complicates its use as a comparandum for *Ac.* 1.30-33a. It precedes rather than follows a discussion of physics, and it clearly plays down the doctrinal differences between the *ueteres* and the Stoics in a way in which Varro's speech does not.[216] Thus the continuity between the two groups is not argued for, at least to begin with, with respect to the areas of doctrine in which *Ac.* 1 sees discontinuity, but rather with reference to areas where common ground is easier to detect: the concern with definitions is the starting point, which is an area of agreement in *Ac.*, too, but only tacitly so. There is no reference to forms. The *ueteres* are said to have taken the view that reason and the senses must

---

[212] Thus Görler (2004a: 95): 'Antiochos' "Immerwährendes" hat mit platonischen Ideen nur sehr wenig gemein: Es handelt sich um nichts anderes als um aus der Erfahrung abgeleitete Begriffe.'

[213] See *SVF* i.65A and B; Long and Sedley (1987) section 30; Sedley (1985); Brunschwig (1994: 126-34) and (2003); Brunschwig (1999); Caston (1999); Vogt (2009: 146-7). There is disagreement about the ontological status accorded to concepts by the Stoics; compare Caston (1999) and Brunschwig (2003).

[214] See Sedley (1996a); Boys-Stones (2005).

[215] Cf. Bénatouïl (2016: 209): 'Another epistemological teaching of the Ancient Academics listed by Cicero in the following sentence [*Fin.* 4.9, quoted in n. 217 below] is to keep the senses and reason together instead of using them separately from each other: this standard is clearly applied in all those arguments where the Stoic doctrines are blamed for leading to the inconceivable idea of a pure mind with no body or nothing natural in it.'

[216] Note *Fin.* 4.8: *In his igitur partibus duabus* [i.e. 'logic' and physics] *nihil erat, quod Zeno commutare gestiret. Res enim se praeclare habebat, et quidem in utraque parte. Quid enim ab antiquis ex eo genere, quod ad disserendum ualet, praetermissum est?*

cooperate to obtain knowledge,[217] so that, it is implied, the Stoics did not need to make changes in this respect.[218] An important difference compared to Varro's speech is that Chrysippus is recognized as a significant figure, while Zeno's contribution is rated to have been much smaller than that of the *ueteres*—this should caution against aligning the two reconciliation efforts too closely (and possibly supplying missing elements by extrapolation).[219] By the same token, the following section on physics (4.13) speaks of zoological research as a shared interest between the schools, a topic that is absent from *Ac.* 1 and which one would associate with Aristotle and the Peripatos in particular. See further below on possible ways of explaining the coexistence of the two accounts. Third, there is the section on Plato's epistemology in Sextus' epistemological doxography from Plato onwards (*M.* 7.141–260). *M.* 7.141–4 references the *Tim.* passage which Sedley (2012b: 84–5) regards as the primary model for *Ac.* 1.30–33a, but develops and manipulates it so as to yield a reconciliation between Stoic confidence in perception and Platonic reliance on reason (see Sedley 2012: 93–101). The Antiochian origin of the text is disputed. Antiochus is cited twice in the wider context (7.162; 7.201–2) for what may be specific points, so that the references to him need not be indications of Sextus' source for the entire section.[220] In favour general considerations can be cited, like the fact that Antiochus is the most likely candidate we know of to have attempted the kind of reconciliation which the passage represents, given his ideological commitments, while the opposing view starts from the accurate observation that neither our passage nor anything in *Luc.* corresponds closely to *M.* 7.141–4. Since this cannot be disputed, the hypothesis of Antiochian origin can only be upheld by means of developmental assumptions, on which see more below. The passage shows some intriguing points of contact with *Ac.* 1.30–33a against *Tim.* 27d–28a, but also noticeable differences. I quote *M.* 7.141–4:

Πλάτων τοίνυν ἐν τῷ Τιμαίῳ διελόμενος τὰ πράγματα εἴς τε τὰ νοητὰ καὶ αἰσθητά, καὶ εἰπὼν περιληπτὰ μὲν λόγῳ εἶναι τὰ νοητά, δοξαστὰ δὲ τυγχάνειν τὰ αἰσθητά, προδήλως κριτήριον ὥρισε τῆς τῶν πραγμάτων γνώσεως τὸν λόγον, συμπεριλαβὼν αὐτῷ καὶ τὴν διὰ τῶν αἰσθήσεων ἐνάργειαν. λέγει δὲ οὕτως· 'τί τὸ ὂν ἀεί, γένεσιν δὲ οὐκ ἔχον, καὶ τί τὸ γινόμενον μέν, ὂν δὲ οὐδέποτε; τὸ μὲν δὴ νοήσει μετὰ λόγου

---

[217] *Fin.* 4.9: *Quid, quod plurimis locis quasi denuntiant, ut neque sensuum fidem sine ratione nec rationis sensibus exquiramus, atque ut eorum alterum ab altero ⟨ne⟩ separemus?*, 'And what of the fact that frequently they, as it were, announce that we should not seek either reliability of the senses without the mind or vice versa, and that we should not divorce one from the other?'

[218] In *Luc.* 142, where the Cicero character argues for discontinuity between Plato and Antiochus in the field of epistemology, a view is ascribed to *Plato*, and one which appears to leave no room for cooperation between reason and the senses: *Plato autem omne iudicium ueritatis ueritatemque ipsam abductam ab opinionibus et a sensibus cogitationis ipsius et mentis esse uoluit*, 'But Plato wanted the entire judgement of truth and truth itself to be removed from opinion and the senses and to belong with thought and the mind.' The passage is also consistent with a conceptualist view of forms being presented in *Ac.* 1.30–33a, although it does not mention forms—if the speaker had taken the view that forms qua independent metaphysical entities were the real objects of knowledge, it would seem inexplicable that he did not exploit the opportunity to say so in *Luc.* 142. Yet the larger context in *Luc.* is informed by a doxographical source and thus may simply follow the rationale of its immediate context, in which case the reader would not be expected to connect it with *Ac.* 1.30–33a.

[219] Tarrant (1980: 110 n. 7), in a review discussion of Glucker (1978), writes: 'Antiochus' debt to Aristotelian logic is best seen in Cic. *Fin.* 4.9–13, 5.10.'

[220] Thus Barnes (1997: 65); Brittain (2012: 108–11).

περιληπτόν, τὸ δὲ δόξῃ μετὰ αἰσθήσεως.' περιληπτικὸν δὲ καλεῖσθαί φασι λόγον παρ᾽ αὐτῷ οἱ Πλατωνικοὶ τὸν κοινὸν τῆς ἐναργείας καὶ τῆς ἀληθείας. δεῖ γὰρ τὸν λόγον ἐν τῷ κρίνειν τὴν ἀλήθειαν ἀπὸ τῆς ἐναργείας ὁρμᾶσθαι, εἴπερ δι᾽ ἐναργῶν ἡ κρίσις γίνεται τῶν ἀληθῶν. ἀλλ᾽ ἥ τε ἐνάργεια οὐκ ἔστιν αὐτάρκης πρὸς γνῶσιν ἀληθοῦς· οὐ γὰρ εἴ τι κατ᾽ οὐκ ἔστιν αὐτάρκης πρὸς γνῶσιν ἀληθοῦς· οὐ γὰρ εἴ τι κατ᾽ ἐνάργειαν φαίνεται, τοῦτο καὶ κατ᾽ ἀλήθειαν ὑπάρχει· ἀλλὰ δεῖ παρεῖναι τὸ κρῖνον τί τε φαίνεται μόνον καὶ τί σὺν τῷ φαίνεσθαι ἔτι καὶ κατ᾽ ἀλήθειαν ὑπόκειται, τουτέστι τὸν λόγον. ἀμφότερα τοίνυν συνελθεῖν δεήσει, τήν τε ἐνάργειαν ὡς ἂν ἀφετήριον οὖσαν τῷ λόγῳ πρὸς τὴν κρίσιν τῆς ἀληθείας, καὶ αὐτὸν τὸν λόγον πρὸς διάκρισιν τῆς ἐναργείας. εἰς μέντοι τὸ ἐπιβάλλειν τῇ ἐναργείᾳ καὶ τὸ ἐν ταύτῃ ἀληθὲς διακρίνειν πάλιν συνεργοῦ δεῖται ὁ λόγος τῆς αἰσθήσεως· διὰ ταύτης γὰρ τὴν φαντασίαν παραδεχόμενος ποιεῖται τὴν νόησιν καὶ τὴν ἐπιστήμην τἀληθοῦς, ὥστε περιληπτικὸν αὐτὸν ὑπάρχειν τῆς τε ἐναργείας καὶ τῆς ἀληθείας, ὅπερ ἴσον ἐστὶ τῷ καταληπτικόν.

Well then, Plato in the *Timaeus*, having divided things into intelligible and perceptible, and said that intelligible things are comprehensible by reason, while perceptible things turn out to be opinable, clearly determined the criterion of the knowledge of objects to be reason, including with it the plain experience of sense-perception as well. He says the following: 'What is that which always is and has no coming into being, and what is that which is always coming into being and never is? The one is comprehensible by intelligence, with reason, the other by opinion, with sense-perception.' And the Platonists say that the reason that is common to plain experience and the truth is called by him 'comprehensive.' For in judging the truth, reason has to start from plain experience, if indeed the judgment of true things comes about through plain things. But plain experience is not self-sufficient for knowledge of what is true. For it is not the case that if something appears in plain experience, this thing is also truly real. Rather, the thing that judges what merely appears and what, along with appearing, also truly exists—that is, reason—has to be present. So both have to come together, plain experience in the role of a starting-line for reason in its judgement of the truth, and reason itself for a determination about plain experience. However, for applying itself to plain experience and determining what is true in it, reason again needs sense-perception to work with it. For it is by receiving the appearance through sense-perception that it creates the understanding and the knowledge of what is true, so that it is comprehensive of both plain experience and the truth, which is equivalent to 'apprehensive'. (transl. Bett)

In the first sentence, Sextus refers to *Tim*. 27d–28a, by dividing 'things' into two different species, in a way which suggests that the species distinguished belong to one world rather than two. This (see the notes below) is similar to Cicero's account. That the mind judges the data provided by the senses is another point of contact, but because the senses are assumed to deliver (or represent) ἐνάργεια and their objects are presumably assumed to be comparatively unproblematic, the correspondence is partial: *quamquam oriretur a sensibus... mentem uolebant esse rerum iudicem* ~ δεῖ γὰρ τὸν λόγον ἐν τῷ κρίνειν τὴν ἀλήθειαν ἀπὸ τῆς ἐναργείας ὁρμᾶσθαι. That λόγος should include the senses in 'comprehensive reason' is peculiar to the passage, as is the relationship between ἐνάργεια and 'what underlies' (ὑπόκειται). Flux, notions, and calculations about them are absent. If the passage makes use of *Tht.* in its account of what reason does with perceptual information, then this is not clearly marked. Note, however, that Sextus unlike Varro gives Plato's views rather than an agreed position of the *ueteres* (see below).

Sedley (2012b), who reads *Ac.* 1.30–33a as anti-empiricist and espousing a two-world theory while accepting *Fin.* 4.8–10 and Sextus, *M.* 7.141–4 as Antiochian, has argued that Antiochus initially, i.e. when he first turned to dogmatism, provided an account of the development of the Academic tradition which emphasized continuities and marginalized differences, but that in response to Philo's Roman Books he devised the account in *Ac.* 1.30–33a, which, while still arguing for a unity thesis, is much readier to acknowledge fissures and discontinuities. I regard this as an attractive suggestion.[221] And while the importance of *Tim.* 27d–28a for *M.* 7.141–4 is plain, I hold that the later historical account availed itself of *Tht.*, partly because it offered a way of securing Platonic credentials for the new position (including Zeno's 'corrections' in *Ac.* 1.40–2).[222] The retention of verbal echoes of *Tim.* 27d–28a would not tell against this, suggestive as they would be of a degree of continuity between the two historical accounts. The alternative explanation assumes that Antiochus offered two incompatible readings of the same *Tim.* passage at different points in time, and that he landed himself with an impossible task regarding the tracing of any continuity between the Old Academy and the Stoa.

If we ask how bold or conventional, either in conception or in approach, the historical reconstruction employed in this passage is, we can note that there are no good grounds for assuming a retrojection of Stoicism and that the use of a Platonic dialogue, interpreted in a certain way, surpasses in its sophistication known earlier attempts and foreshadows methodologically the developments of Middle Platonism. Exactly how bold it was as a construal of Plato's position in Antiochus' historical context is, however, not easy to determine, given that some of the orthodoxies of Platonic interpretation, including a prioritization of the dialogues of the middle period over others, had not yet been formulated (see Boys-Stones 2012: 230–2). The positions on the κριτήριον which are accorded to Speusippus and Xenocrates right after the account of Plato's views in the Sextus passage cited above (*M.* 7.145–6 and 7.147–9 respectively) are separate from one another, but both remain beholden to a view which assumes a transcendental world and a perceptible world, a position which is precluded in *Ac.* 1 if one wants to read 1.24–9 and 1.30–33a coherently: the

---

[221] See also Reinhardt (2018: 66–7). The notion of a *forma/formula* created by the *ueteres* through engagement with Plato's works (see *Ac.* 1.15–17 with comm.; and section 7.2), revised further over time, and ultimately evaluated and locked down by Antiochus is only attested for the ex hypothesi later version of Antiochus' view of history. *Luc.* 15, on my reading, suggests that it was not part of the purportedly earlier version of Antiochus' historical account (see ad loc. and sections 7.3 and 7.4), while *Fin.* 4.3 would be compatible with the *formula* device (views of the *ueteres* are rehearsed while their pupil status is emphasized, without an explicit suggestion that the set of doctrines they subscribe to was simply handed over to them as a unit by Plato). See also the discussion of the sources of *Acad.* in section 9.3.

[222] If Antiochus was revising an earlier reconstruction of Academic thought under perceived pressure, he may have wanted to create unity in a way that was different from mere doctrinal agreement, namely by emphasizing the importance of a Platonic text or of Platonic thinking (as opposed to doctrine) for the Academic tradition.

former passage leaves no room for transcendental forms and assumes there to be one world only.

§30

Tertia deinde philosophiae pars...ab utrisque: corresponding to λογική. Cf. *Ac.* 1.19 *tertia* (i) *de disserendo* (ii) *et quid uerum quid falsum* (iii) *quid rectum in oratione prauumque* (iv) *quid consentiens quid repugnet iudicando* (with nn.), where (i) is generic (cf. *Fat.* 1 *ratio disserendi* = λογική), with the highlighted *et* in (ii) being epexegetic, (ii) seems to refer to epistemology, (iii) to rhetoric, and (iv) to logic in the narrow sense (so Barnes 1997a: 142). *Ratione* and *disserendo* thus suggest epistemology and theories of argument (see also Aubert-Baillot 2019: 256–8). This is consistent with what follows, and with the *diuisio* in *Ac.* 1.19. A survey of other passages where Cicero either makes reference to the third part of philosophy or even indicates what falls under it has been conducted by Barnes (1997a: 140–6), who found recurrent terminology with slight variations, e.g. concerning the inclusion of rhetoric or the apparent reduction of λογική to dialectic (i.e. logic in a narrow sense), to suit particular contexts. Of these passages, some relate to the Old Academy (e.g. *Fin.* 4.8–10), others to Stoicism. See also Dyck (2004: 232–3) on *Leg.* 1.62, and *Ac.* 1.5 on Roman Epicureans writing in Latin who reject λογική. *Ab utrisque* refers to the Peripatetics and the Old Academy, cf. *Ac.* 1.33.

Quamquam oriretur a sensibus tamen non esse iudicium ueritatis in sensibus. Mentem uolebant rerum esse iudicem: the phrase *iudicium ueritatis* must correspond to κριτήριον τῆς ἀληθείας, as Reid[1] (p. 135) notes; see also on *Luc.* 142 *iudicium ueritatis*. The Greek phrasal term only emerged in the course of the Hellenistic period, so its application to an Old Academic context, whether it is a deliberate historical fiction or a serious attempt at historical reconstruction, is strictly an anachronism. In Plato and Aristotle, the term κριτήριον means 'ability or faculty of judgement' (*Rep.* 9, 582a6; *Tht.* 178b6; Striker 1996a: 26), in the debate between Stoics and Sceptics it is 'a means for establishing what is or is not the case within the scope of perception' (Striker 1996a: 52–3). Neither of these meanings captures the sense of *iudicium ueritatis* here perfectly, since, as the grammatical subject of *oriretur*, it is said to 'arise' from the senses: the mind does not in any sense arise from the senses (e.g. the concepts in it do not arise from perceptual experience—this notion is, on my reading, only introduced in *Ac.* 1.33b as a development of the view of the *antiqui*), and *iudicium* cannot, unlike κριτήριον in Greek, denote an instrument in Latin. Rather, the *iudicium ueritatis* is best taken as the action or process of passing judgements on the deliverances of the senses, however wanting they or their objects may be. *Rerum...iudicem* points in the same direction, as does the fact that *iudicium* is picked up by *iudex*, suggesting that *iudicium* is what the *iudex* does, not what he uses or applies. The notion of a judge, and a judge of *res* at that, also discourages interpretations which see an allusion to recollection here, either in the sense that recollection without perceptual input is at issue, such that the mind contemplates or accesses forms qua transcendent entities, or in the sense that such a process was triggered by perceptual information (thus Brittain 2006: 99 n. 30). When Cicero speaks about recollection elsewhere (e.g. *Tusc.* 1.57–8, on which see Reinhardt 2018: 33–9), this is not presented as involving the passing of a judgement, and it would also be odd if a crucial concept like recollection would have to be supplied entirely by the reader.

Solam censebant idoneam cui crederetur: believing the mind must mean believing the determinations the mind makes.

Quia sola cerneret id quod semper esset simplex et unius modi et tale quale esset: cf. *OLD* s.v. *cerno* no. 6 'to discern with the intellect, perceive clearly' as well as no. 7 'to look at, examine'. I have opted to use the latter for the translation because of the correspondence with *Tht.* 185e1–2: αὐτὴ δι' αὑτῆς ἡ ψυχὴ τὰ κοινά μοι φαίνεται περὶ πάντων ἐπισκοπεῖν; see the general note above. The properties of what the mind sees, referred to in the collective singular, match very closely those which Plato ascribes in various places to forms qua transcendental items: e.g. *Phd.* 78d: ἕκαστον ὃ ἔστιν, τὸ ὄν, μή ποτε μεταβολὴν καὶ ἡντινοῦν ἐνδέχεται; ἢ ἀεὶ αὐτῶν ἕκαστον ὃ ἔστι, μονοειδὲς ὂν αὐτὸ καθ' αὑτό, ὡσαύτως κατὰ ταὐτὰ ἔχει καὶ οὐδέποτε οὐδαμῇ οὐδαμῶς ἀλλοίωσιν οὐδεμίαν ἐνδέχεται, '(Absolute equality, absolute beauty, any absolute existence, true being), do they ever admit of any change whatsoever? Or does each absolute essence, since it is uniform and exists by itself, remain the same and never in any way admit of any change?' (transl. Fowler); *Symp.* 211b: αὐτὸ καθ' αὑτὸ μεθ' αὑτοῦ μονοειδὲς ἀεὶ ὄν, 'existing by itself in a single form forever'; *Tim.* 35a: οὐσίας ἀεὶ κατὰ ταὐτὰ ἔχον (= *Tim.* 21 *materia quae est unius modi*); *Tim.* 28a: τὸ κατὰ ταὐτὰ ἔχον (= *Tim.* 4: *ea species quae semper est eadem*) (all passages in Reid[1] p. 136); and the quasi-definition of the form in Aët. 1.10: οὐσία ἀσώματος, αἰτία τῶν ⟨τοιούτων⟩ οἷά ἐστιν αὐτή, 'the form is a body-less substance, the cause of all things which are like it', with Burkert (1972: 39). However, as has been noted by Boys-Stones (2012: 222–3), they are also applicable to notions and concepts, and in *Or.* 8–10 (above, n. 207) Cicero describes forms conceived as concepts in similar terms; see esp. *Or.* 10: *Has rerum formas appellat* ἰδέας *ille non intellegendi solum sed etiam dicendi grauissimus auctor et magister Plato, easque gigni negat et ait semper esse ac ratione et intellegentia contineri; cetera nasci occidere fluere labi nec diutius esse uno et eodem statu*, 'Plato, this most authoritative master and teacher not just of thought but also of speech, calls these forms "ideas", and denies that they come into being, and says that they exist forever and that they are contained within reason and intellect; everything else, he held, was born, perished, was in flux, on the slide, and never very long in one and the same state', with Reinhardt (2018: 51–3); *Or.* 18: *Insidebat... in eius* [sc. M. Antonii] *mente species eloquentiae, quam cernebat animo, re ipsa non uidebat*. In *Luc.* 142 (above, n. 218) Platonic epistemology is characterized from a sceptical viewpoint; forms do not feature, however conceived. Cf. also *Fin.* 4.42, from the Antiochian critique of Stoic ethics: *Vt quidam philosophi, cum a sensibus profecti maiora quaedam et diuiniora uidissent, sensus reliquerunt, sic isti, cum ex appetitione rerum uirtutis pulchritudinem aspexissent, omnia, quae praeter uirtutem ipsam uiderant, abiecerunt obliti naturam omnem appetendarum rerum ita late patere, ut a principiis permanaret ad fines, neque intellegunt se rerum illarum pulchrarum atque admirabilium fundamenta subducere*, 'There are philosophers who began with the senses but then saw a grander and more divine vision, whereupon they abandoned the senses. So, too, the Stoics moved on from original desire to the beautiful vision of virtue, and cast aside all that they saw apart from virtue. But they forgot that in its entirety the nature of what is desirable has a very wide scope, from starting points to final ends. And they failed to realize that they were undermining the foundations of those beautiful objects of their admiration' (transl. Woolf), which is open to different interpretations regarding the status of *maiora quaedam et diuiniora*.

Hanc illi ἰδέαν appellabant, iam a Platone ita nominatam, nos recte speciem possumus dicere: there can be no doubt that Cicero wrote ἰδέαν here and not some other Greek word; on the occasional confusion which manuscripts show over ἰδέα vs εἶδος, see Reinhardt (2003: 268) on *Top.* 30 εἴδη, where *species* is used in the sense of 'concept' (= ἔννοια). The singular ἰδέαν is generic, for on any interpretation not just one Form is posited. The manner in which Form is introduced is striking, via its properties, with the actual designations in parenthesis; see Görler (2004a: 94). The gender of *hanc* is due to attraction. Varro is still characterizing the *prima forma* as determined by the *ueteres* (*illi*), working with the *ubertas* of Plato's dialogues (*Ac.* 1.17); since Plato is not one of the *ueteres* (note *iam*) but made pronouncements on Form, he is mentioned in his own right. Forms do not feature in *Fin.* 4.8-10 (see the general note above); cf., however, *Or.* 10 (see previous n.); *Tusc.* 1.58. With *recte* and the implication that rendering Greek terms is not just a matter of stipulation, cf. *Or.* 94; *Fin.* 4.5; *N.D.* 2.58; *Tim.* 38; *Ac.* 1.41: '...*comprehendibile—feretis haec?*'; and section 10 of the introduction. *Species*, which recurs in 1.33, is also used in other technical senses in *Acad.*; cf. *Ac.* 1.27; *Luc.* 52, 58, 99, 111.

§31

Sensus autem omnis hebetes et tardos esse arbitrabantur...quia continenter laberentur et fluerent omnia: as noted in the general note above, the two weaknesses of the senses named (bluntness, sluggishness) map onto the properties of the objects of perception (smallness, being subject to flux), but it is not made clear whether it is the senses or the objects which are held responsible, and the properties of both senses and objects of perception are presented in the positive form grammatically. On its own, this may sound like a complete dismissal of the senses, but *quamquam oriretur a sensibus* above accords at least some role to the senses. The 'correction' to the status accorded to the senses in the *prima forma* is provided in *Ac.* 1.40-2, which in turn is in agreement with the developed Antiochian position on apprehension as developed in Lucullus' speech in *Luc.* and the corresponding lost parts of *Ac.* 3. What is said about the objects of perception here ought to cohere with *Ac.* 1.24-9, but there is no marked backward reference. 1.40-2 and Lucullus in *Luc.* assume stable objects of perception.

For the claim that Plato was committed to the view that all perceptibles are always in flux and that there was no ἐπιστήμη about them, see Arist., *Met.* A6, 987a32-b1.

Percipere is in *Acad.* used in the technical sense of 'to grasp something cataleptically', i.e. to have a cataleptic impression of something and assent to it (see section 10);

this use of the term has not yet been introduced at this point of the first book of the second edition.

Reid[1] (p. 137) assembles parallels for similar uses of *subicere* and translates *quae subiectae sensibus uiderentur* 'which were commonly thought to fall within the province of the senses', but *uideri* need not be doxastic and can also designate phenomenal appearance, as in my translation.

Vnum, constans, and *idem* (a compelling emendation by Manutius for *eidem*) are semantically overlapping complements to *nihil*, with *esset* functioning as an auxiliary; before *constans* a connective is needed, and I have printed *et* with Halm. To the correspondences with *Tht.*, documented and interpreted in the general note above, add *ne idem quidem*: *Tht.* 181c–183c is concerned with the absurd consequences which the flux theory has for sensible particulars. See also Ademollo (2018: 73–5).

I print *quae* rather than *quod* (sc. *essent aut ita paruae*) for stemmatic reasons; *quae* is also *difficilior*.

Itaque hanc omnem partem rerum opinabilem appellabant: as Reid[1] (p. 137) points out, Cicero renders δοξαστόν as *opinabile* in *Tim.* 3, and Plato often contrasts δοξαστός with νοητός. Together with the reference to ἰδέαι this sentence has been used to locate a two-word view in the section, as formulated in *Tim.* 27d–28a (thus, e.g. Sedley 2012: 84). But Boys-Stones (2012: 223 n. 13) notes: 'To my ears, the phrase [sc. *hanc omnem partem rerum*] rather implies that objects of sense perception are a *subset* of the very same ontological "realm" as the mental objects distinguished from them.' Specifically, ***partem rerum*** suggests this reading. Goerenz emended to *opinabilium*, which would require *rerum opinabilium* to function as a complement; but *rerum* must go with *partem*.

§32

Scientiam autem nusquam esse censebant nisi in animi notionibus atque rationibus: *nusquam . . . nisi* is emphatic. The view implicitly excluded must be that knowledge also resides in the senses or in perceptions (= appearances), or that these appearances amount to knowledge (not that knowledge might be located elsewhere than in the mind, or in mental items other than *notiones* or mental operations other than *rationes*). Contrast *Fin.* 4.9, quoted above, p. 217. The role accorded to concepts and their employment represents a point of contact with Lucullus' speech (see esp. *Luc.* 21, 26, 30); see also *Ac.* 1.42 on Zeno's view on *notiones*. The term *notio* is not associated with a particular school in Cicero; see Dyck (2003: 89) on *N.D.* 1.27a. On its use in a Platonic context in *Tusc.* 1.56–8, see Reinhardt (2018: 33–40). *Motio* (as opposed to *permotio* or *commotio*) does not make a natural pair in Cicero, and sense requires *notio* as Turnebus saw. If Antiochus was positing Forms as thoughts of god (see the general note on *Ac.* 1.24–9), which somehow relate to concepts in human minds, then here would have been a good moment for Varro to signal this.

Qua de causa definitiones rerum probabant et has ad omnia de quibus disceptabatur adhibebant: definitions are presumably conceptual analyses of the *notiones* in the previous sentence. *Rerum* functions like a generic 'things' in English and does not specifically resume *rerum...iudicem* and *omnem partem rerum opinabilem* above. It then contrasts with *uerborum* in the next sentence; see Modrak (2010) on Aristotle's distinction between *definitio rei* and *definitio nominis* in *An. Post.* B7, and on *Ac.* 1.33b, where I suspect another indirect reference to *An. Post.* Definition and the related topic of methods of division is listed first among the areas of agreement between the Stoa and the *ueteres* in *Fin.* 4.9, and they are a credible if unspecific area of common ground between Plato's successors and the Peripatetics including Aristotle.

Verborum etiam explicatio probabatur, id est, qua de causa quaeque essent ita nominata, quam ἐτυμολογίαν appellabant: *ita*, sc. *ut sunt nominata*. Definitions articulate concepts, etymologies then explain the designations used to refer to them and to objects falling under them; see Reid[1] (p. 138) on *quaeque* = 'each set of objects'. The Greek term is not attested for the Old Academy or the Peripatetics, but this is a minor anachronism like the reference to the criterion of truth above. That Plato and Aristotle and their followers had, like the Stoics, a keen interest in etymology is well documented. See also Reinhardt (2003: 208–13 and 273–9) on arguments from etymology in Cicero and the terminology used.

Post argumentis quibusdam et quasi rerum notis ducibus utebantur ad probandum et ad concludendum id quod explanari uolebant: the adverbial *post* marks a new topic. Two interpretations of the sentence have been proposed. On the first, the reference is to arguments from etymology (Reid[1] p. 139); on the second, logic proper and arguments from signs are at issue (Barnes 1997a: 143). The former view would give arguments from etymology an unparalleled and inexplicable prominence in the field of λογική at the expense of logic qua theory of argument (see next sentence), when *Ac.* 1.19 *quid consentiens quid repugnet iudicando* created the expectation that theory of argument would feature in Varro's survey. *Top.* 35, invoked by Reid, states that words are *rerum notae*, but only as an explanation of Cicero's rendering for ἐτυμολογία, *notatio*. The phrase *argumentis quibusdam* would also lack point on this reading; it suggests certain definite arguments and thus *types* of argument. Arguments and inferences from observable signs to unobservable states of affairs naturally go together. The analysis of both is, for us and for Cicero's contemporary readers, more closely associated with Aristotle than with Plato; see Burnyeat (1982a); Allen (2001). Of Plato's successors, especially Xenocrates was credited with an interest in theory of argument; see frgs 1–10 Isnardi Parente; Krämer (1971: 32–7).

Some editors moved *quasi* before *ducibus*, perhaps because it is more markedly metaphorical than *notis*; *quasi* cannot modify *ducibus* if left in its transmitted position. Like Plasberg[1] (p. 50) I think that *quasi* modifies the phrasal term *rerum notae*; *notis* would be difficult to construe if it were not a noun (i.e. ablative of *notae*) but an adjective qualifying *ducibus*.

In qua tradebatur omnis dialecticae disciplina, id est orationis ratione conclusae: cf. *Fin.* 3.5 on the loanword *dialectica* being well established and deeply familiar. For the force of the apposition to *dialecticae*, cf. *TLL* s.v. *concludo* col. 77.6–24 (this passage l. 17), 'i.e. of speech brought to a conclusion methodically'. Dialectic never lost its association with actual spoken argument (here signified by *oratio*); cf. the prima facie unnecessary dialogical stylization of *Luc.* 93–4 (Chrysippus on the sorites), and on *Luc.* 104. That 'the whole discipline of dialectic' is summarily referred to here tells against a reference to arguments from etymology, at best a marginal subfield of dialectic however conceived, in the previous sentence.

The transmitted *in qua* has been found difficult. Varro is coming to the end of this section, and this is a suitably general remark, so that a backward reference to *tertia deinde philosophiae pars* is appropriate: it signals that the vital discipline of logic (as well as that of rhetoric) is included under this heading, as announced in *Ac.* 1.19.

Huic quasi ex altera parte oratoria uis dicendi adhibebatur: cf. Arist., *Rhet.* A1, 1354a1–6 (the beginning of the treatise): Ἡ ῥητορική ἐστιν ἀντίστροφος τῇ διαλεκτικῇ· ἀμφότεραι γὰρ περὶ τοιούτων τινῶν εἰσιν ἃ κοινὰ τρόπον τινὰ ἁπάντων ἐστὶ γνωρίζειν καὶ οὐδεμιᾶς ἐπιστήμης ἀφωρισμένης· διὸ καὶ πάντες τρόπον τινὰ μετέχουσιν ἀμφοῖν· πάντες γὰρ μέχρι τινὸς καὶ ἐξετάζειν καὶ ὑπέχειν λόγον καὶ ἀπολογεῖσθαι καὶ κατηγορεῖν ἐγχειροῦσιν, 'Rhetoric is the counterpart of Dialectic. Both alike are concerned with such things as come, more or less, within the general ken of all men and belong to no definite science. Accordingly all men make use, more or less, of both; for to a certain extent all men attempt to discuss statements and to maintain them, to defend themselves and to attack others' (transl. Solmsen). Rhetoric and dialectic are by Aristotle represented as manifestations of the same general rational ability (cf. **uis dicendi**?), which can be exercised by acting as questioner or respondent in dialectical exchange, or in prosecution or defence in a forensic context; this seems germane to the present context. Various Platonic dialogues, in particular the *Phaedr.*, offer reflections on the relationship of dialectic and rhetoric, to which Aristotle may be taken to allude in *Rhet.*; see Rapp (2002: i.212–23). Cf. also *Or.* 114: *Aristoteles principio artis rhetoricae dicit illam artem quasi ex altera parte respondere dialecticae*. We do not have grounds for thinking that Antiochus taught or had more than a historical interest in rhetoric. What Cicero knows about Aristotelian rhetorical theory is more plausibly linked to Philo of Larissa; see Brittain (2001: 296–343); Reinhardt (2000) and (2003: 49–50). On the role Aristotle generally plays for Antiochus' historical reconstruction, see the general note on *Ac.* 1.15–18. For the use of *adhibere*, see *TLL* s.v. *adhibeo* col. 644.77.

Explicatrix orationis perpetuae ad persuadendum accommodatae: *perpetuae* distinguishes continuous speech from clipped dialectical arguments. A full discussion of definitions of rhetoric is in Quint. 2.15, on which see Reinhardt and Winterbottom (2006: 225–76). The noun *explicatrix* only here in Cicero, but cf. *Inv.* 2.6: *ut... omnes, qui quod illi* [sc. *artis rhetoricae inuentores*] *praecipiant uelint intellegere, ad hunc* [sc. *Aristotelem*] *quasi ad quendam multo commodiorem explicatorem reuertantur.*

Haec forma erat illis prima, a Platone tradita; cuius quas acceperim immutationes si uultis exponam: these two sentences are important for the understanding of the overall approach adopted in Varro's speech and of how Antiochus conceived of his position in relation to the views of his intellectual ancestors.

The first sentence is manifestly corrupt, and the reading of the archetype is uncertain (though Γ may be preserving it, with P making an attempt at correction). Madvig (1860: 118–19) was right to observe that *forma* is the word which has been replaced or dropped out; he cited *Ac.* 1.17: *certam quandam disciplinae formulam*; 1.23 *fin.*: *haec quidem fuit apud eos morum institutio et eius partis, quam primam posui, forma atque descriptio*. Reid[1] opted for a different word order: *haec erat illis prima forma*, which has slightly less support from the paradosis. A number of translators appear to take *illis* as a dative object with *tradita*; see e.g. Reid[2] (p. 23): 'Such was the original system they inherited from Plato.' Similarly Brittain (2006: 100). Word order would seem to tell against this possibility. Others make *illis* a possessive dative with *erat*; cf. e.g. Kany-Turpin (2010: 101): 'Tel était le modèle, hérité de Platon, que ces philosophes appliquèrent d'abord.' This would be unobjectionable in terms of word order (assuming Madvig's text), but not in terms of sense. The *ueteres*, in constructing the *forma*, took themselves to be retrieving Plato's meaning from the *ubertas* of his dialogues (cf. *Ac.* 1.17), but did in fact, in Antiochus'/Varro's view, only partially succeed. The pronoun *illis* is best taken as a *datiuus iudicantis* ('this was in their view [or: to them] the first form of philosophy'), in which case the phrase *a Platone tradita* inherits the focalization of *illis*, i.e. this, too, reflects the perspective of the *ueteres* rather than Varro's. (On this kind of dative, see Pinkster 2015: 926–7, 1203.) I submit that this interpretation receives further support from the functionally similar *apud eos* in *Ac.* 1.23 quoted above, a remark concluding a section like the sentence under discussion. The parallelism with 1.23 can be exploited for another purpose: that *eos* there does not include Plato is confirmed by the fact that *illis* here cannot include him.

The transmitted *disputationes* has in recent times only been maintained by Dörrie (1987: 196–7), who translates 'Erörterungen'. Madvig (1860: 119) thought that 'philosophiae disputationes' could not mean 'discessiones philosophorum a Platone et nouarum disciplinarum ortus'; similarly Görler (1994: 948). The emendation *dissupationes* (Baiter 1863; rendered 'Verfallsformen' by Görler 2004a: 97 n. 25; printed by Plasberg[1] and Plasberg[2]), a variant spelling of *dissipationes* (see Leumann 1977: 87) intended to be as close as possible to what is transmitted, is without parallel in this sense (*pace TLL* s.v. *dissipatio* col. 1486.44–8) and would imply the dismissal of all the changes which follow, which is plainly not the case (some are accepted, others dismissed, and there are some uncertain cases). (For the same reason, *quas acceperim* must mean '(of) which I have heard' (*OLD* s.v. 18a), not 'which I accept'.) *Immutationes*, proposed by Davies, has been accepted by majority of scholars (including Reid[1]; Reinhardt 2018: 55), and it may certainly be right, given *Ac.* 1.37 *commutauerat*, 1.40 *mutauit*, and 1.42 *commutatio*. In particular, it is a term that Cicero might have used in this sense (cf. *De orat.* 3.114), but it is also a term which might have given rise to a gloss, either because of a reader's preconceptions of how the history of philosophy ought to be described or because *immutatio* is preferentially used for certain types of verbal change, including that involved in word play, word order change, or changes to the form of a word (cf. e.g. *De orat.* 2.256, 261; *Or.* 84; *commutatio* would be more conventional for doctrinal modifications). The question is if *disputationes* really is impossible. Madvig (1860: 119), as reported above, fails to appreciate how Varro's historical survey arrives at its destination, i.e.

Antiochus' view: by evaluating and, as appropriate, accepting or rejecting changes to the *prima forma* made by representatives of a broader Academic tradition (which includes the Stoics), whose collective aspiration is to arrive at a superior understanding of Plato's meaning; see also Barnes (1997: 95). This process of 'discussion about' or 'negotiation of' could be called *disputationes* with a *genitiuus obiectiuus* (for which cf. *De orat.* 1.96; *Luc.* 5); *disputationem* (sg.) *exponere* e.g. in *Tusc.* 2.9. However, one may think that the notion of a *prima forma* which receives modifications would better foreground what is said about Aristotle in 1.33b; cf. the somewhat subversive play on Form-related terminology in *Rep.* 2.51: *Quare prima sit haec forma et species et origo tyranni, inuenta nobis in ea re publica quam auspicato Romulus condiderit, non in illa quam [ut perscripsit Plato] sibi ipse Socrates ⟨ut perscripsit Plato⟩ illo in sermone depinxerit*, with Gildenhard (2013: 241). But the term introduced for Form in 1.30 was *species*. I print *immutationes* with hesitation.

§§33b–39

In *Ac.* 1.33a Varro concluded the first phase of his account of the Old Academy as construed by Antiochus, representing its *prima forma* 'handed down by Plato', sc. according to the *ueteres* prior to any modification through which it became fully formed. In *Ac.* 1.33b–42 he discusses changes to this *prima forma* which have been suggested by various parties, including by undisputed contributors to the *prima forma*, notably Aristotle (so that what is presented in the section under discussion must be his second thoughts). Some of these changes were deemed compelling by Antiochus and were thus adopted, while others were deemed misguided and thus ended up not shaping the whole, without it always being clear under which heading a given proposed modification falls. The section is ordered by school:

- 1.33–4: Peripatetic changes, with a statement in 1.34b that Plato's successors remained faithful to what had been handed down by their predecessors;
- 1.35–42 Stoic changes, divided into a section on ethics (1.35–39a), physics (1.39b), and logic (1.40–2).

However, the division is roughly chronological at the same time (Strato of Lampsacus and Zeno of Citium were contemporaries).

Varro begins with Aristotle, who was the first to level criticism at the *prima forma*, whose co-architect he was on the evidence of *Ac.* 1.17. The concession that there were, or emerged, tensions and disagreements amongst the *ueteres* is apt to bestow credibility on Antiochus' construction, in that the need to attend to areas of broad agreement while ignoring ultimately insignificant disagreements (and terminological variations) is established from the start. If my interpretation of *Ac.* 1.26 *fin.* is correct, then we learnt there that individual contributions to the *prima forma* which were accepted by everyone involved are discernible, too.

What Varro says about Aristotle could out of context be taken as a reference to Aristotle's criticism of forms as transcendental entities, and has been so interpreted by scholars who accept such an interpretation for *Ac.* 1.30 (see ad loc.). Given that the passage overtly looks back to *Ac.* 1.30–1, this presents a problem, because, as I have argued, such an interpretation of forms is discouraged there. One reason why I took this view was that, if Varro was crediting Plato with a theory of Forms which are transcendental entities, and Aristotle with criticism of them, it would be very difficult to see how Stoic epistemology, which Antiochus straightforwardly accepted, can be seen as a mere correction or modification of the *prima forma* of Old Academic thought, possibly modified by Aristotle and others; cf. the Cicero character in *Ac.* 1.43a: *arbitror... correctionem ueteris Academiae potius quam aliquam nouam disciplinam putandam.* Or, to put it differently, the presentation of one philosophical position as a modification of another with which is irreconcilable would be the interpretative price to be paid for positing references to forms seen as transcendental entities in *Ac.* 1.30–1 and here. Another reason why I assumed that in *Ac.* 1.30–33a no transcendental forms are ascribed to the Old Academy was the absence of forms from the ethical (*Ac.* 1.19–23) and physical sections (*Ac.* 1.24–9).

Two further Ciceronian passages are directly relevant to the assessment of this problem:

> *Luc.* 142–3 *init.*: Plato autem omne iudicium ueritatis ueritatemque ipsam abductam ab opinionibus et a sensibus cogitationis ipsius et mentis esse uoluit. Num quid horum probat noster Antiochus?

> *Fin.* 4.42: Vt quidam philosophi, cum a sensibus profecti **maiora quaedam et diuiniora** uidissent, sensus reliquerunt, sic isti, cum ex appetitione rerum uirtutis pulchritudinem aspexissent, omnia, quae praeter uirtutem ipsam uiderant, abiecerunt obliti naturam omnem appetendarum rerum ita late patere, ut a principiis permanaret ad fines, neque intellegunt se rerum illarum pulchrarum atque admirabilium fundamenta subducere.

The first passage comes from a rapid survey of dogmatist views on the criterion, none of which Antiochus accepts, so that, or so the Cicero character's argument goes, it must be reasonable for the Clitomachean not to accept any one of them (or indeed any other). Some scholars take *Luc.* 142–3 to be a restatement of Plato's view as set forth in *Ac.* 1.30–2, while I argue in the commentary on *Luc.* 142–3 that there Cicero has Plato dismiss the evidence from the senses completely in a manner which does not happen in *Ac.* 1.30–2. Note also that *Ac.* 1.30–2 does not give Plato's view, but the *prima forma*, i.e. what the *ueteres* took Plato's view to be. (That in *Luc.* 143 the Cicero character observes that Plato's view as given in *Luc.* 142 *fin.* is not actually endorsed by Antiochus is not germane to the question in hand.) In *Luc.* 142–3 the Cicero character would have had motive and opportunity to credit Plato with transcendental forms, which would have made the gulf between Plato and Antiochus even wider, but he does not do so.

In *Fin.* 4.42, in his criticism of Stoic ethics inspired by Antiochus,[223] Cicero draws an analogy: the Stoics take human ethical development to arise from the striving for

---

[223] On the criticism of Stoic ethics in *Fin.* 4 being inspired by Antiochus, see the survey of scholarship since Madvig (1876) in Ioppolo (2016: 168–9 n. 8).

the first natural advantages but then abandon the naturalist foundations of their moral theory completely by assuming that from a certain point onwards human beings recognize virtue as the sole good and pursue it instead. Similarly, certain philosophers start with the evidence from the senses but then see *maiora et diuiniora* and leave the evidence from the senses behind. If one identifies the *philosophi* as Platonists and *starts* with the assumption that Cicero took Platonists to posit transcendental forms, then the passage is consistent with such a reading, but if one does not make that assumption, then *Fin.* 4.42 may be taken to ascribe to the *philosophi* a view similar to that found in *Ac.* 1.30–2 (on my reading above).[224] On *maiora quaedam et diuiniora* in *Fin.* 4.42, see below, p. 209.

Some interpreters have detected a hint of sarcasm or at least criticism in *mirifice*, which others find wholly inappropriate in a reference to Plato. The adverb as such is used in sarcastic as well as laudatory or positive contexts. I think a laudatory use would fit the passage well, provided it is appreciated that we can respect and sincerely praise a doctrine or argumentative position and yet regard it as wrong. In order to make this intelligible, the rest of the sentence needs to be reviewed.

Labefactauit would seem to state a fact: Aristotle did 'shake' the forms rather than attempted to do that (the verb is not conative in meaning). Because of the brevity of the reference, one cannot be confident what is meant here, nor are we able to say how much Antiochus knew about Aristotle's criticism of the forms.[225] On my reading, as indicated, it is unlikely that Varro, who had discussed forms from an epistemological point of view and identified them with concepts, would suddenly shift to Aristotle's attitude to them qua metaphysical items.[226] I tentatively propose that the Aristotelian text which we should think of is not the obvious passages known to us where Aristotle criticizes the forms,[227] but *An. Post.* B19, where Aristotle takes concepts to derive from sense perception as opposed to being innate. The deliverances of the senses, or so I argued, were given *some* role in 1.30–2, but their contribution was severely constrained by the properties of the objects of perception (1.31:…*quia continenter laberentur et fluerent omnia*). So Aristotle is said to 'shake' forms as conceived in *Ac.* 1.30–2. This, I suggest, is said from the point of view of the *ueteres*: *for them* concepts derived from the senses would be problematic. On this reading the focus on concepts would be maintained, thus providing a link with the previous passage, which in turn would give point to *labefactauit*, given what had been said about the senses and their objects in 1.31: as long as the senses do not deliver self-warranting truths, linking forms (= concepts) to the senses can be described as weakening them. This solution does not require Antiochus (or Varro or Cicero) to have studied or to have had direct access to *An. Post.* (which would be unlikely given what we know about the dissemination and availability of the Aristotelian Organon in the Hellenistic period); rather, one would assume e.g. a handbook account on the epistemological views of the various schools to have stated that Aristotle took concepts

---

[224] On the passage see also Görler (2004a: 96–7); Bénatouïl (2016: 217–20).
[225] On the issue, see also Chiaradonna (2013: 30–1).
[226] This point is made by Boys-Stones (2012: 224–5).
[227] Cf. Arist., *N.E.* A6; *Met.* A9; and the Περὶ ἰδεῶν, preserved as fragments in Alex. Aphr. *in Arist. Metaph.*, on which see Fine (1993).

to derive from sense perception, as indeed he did. By itself, and without also accepting something like cataleptic impressions, this cannot have satisfied Antiochus.²²⁸ So Aristotle's modification, while a step forward and accepted by Antiochus,²²⁹ would still require Zeno's key contribution to take us to Antiochus' actual view. There is a sense that the *forma* of philosophy which Antiochus accepts is being honed step by step.

The meaning of *ut in iis quiddam diuinum esse diceret* has been described well by Boys-Stones (2012: 224 n. 15):

> But in its strained circumlocution, Varro very precisely and carefully *avoids* saying that Plato believed forms to be divine (let alone gods, or God). Indeed, it looks to me more as if he is explaining (almost *apologizing for*) the language of divinity used by Plato in a way that would hardly be necessary if he thought it literally meant: it is, he suggests, just Platonic hyperbole, a manner of speaking (note 'diceret') which reflects Plato's enthusiasm, not the nature of objects [author's emphasis].

I submit that the identification of concepts and forms is something which Antiochus regarded as unnecessary: concepts he could happily accept, calling them forms and speaking of them in quasi-religious language less so.²³⁰

In §33 Theophrastus' stance on virtue is characterized through a military metaphor (*spoliauit enim uirtutem suo decore imbecillamque reddidit*), in that virtue is likened to an opponent who is stripped of his armour and humiliated (because Theophrastus regarded virtue as necessary but not sufficient for happiness). This metaphor is picked up in the description of Zeno's position (§35: *Zeno igitur nullo modo is erat qui, ut Theophrastus, neruos uirtutis inciderit…*): Zeno did not, like Theophrastus, cut the tendons of virtue, rendering her help- or powerless. Theophrastus' innovation, as far as virtue is concerned, is evidently rejected by the speaker, and this is initially hinted at through the description and later confirmed. One might then look back to Aristotle's 'shaking' of the forms and ask whether it is an analogous case of rejected modification. It is, by implication, described as a break with the Platonic tradition (*uehementius etiam fregit*, of Theophrastus),²³¹ but that just means that it is acknowledged that in this respect Aristotle broke with tradition and does not imply, by itself, that Antiochus himself embraced the forms or criticized Aristotle for undermining them.²³²

---

²²⁸ I do not see how the text can be read in a way which leaves open the possibility that Platonic forms are to be connected with Aristotelian immanent forms (thus Donini 2011: 309–10) or with the essences of perceptible objects (thus Karamanolis 2006: 62–4).

²²⁹ Scholars who reject the notion that Antiochus approves Aristotle's modification of Plato's view on *species* include Karamanolis (2006: 61–3); Bonazzi (2012: 316–23); and Bénatouïl (2016: 218 n. 57).

²³⁰ Contrast Sedley (2012b: 84 n. 6): 'I am not taking sides in the debate…as to whether Antiochus himself took Plato's Forms to be metaphysically transcendent. However, his description of Plato as thinking there to be something divine in them (*Ac.* 1.33) suggests to me that he had in mind passages such as *Resp.* 500d, which elevate the Forms to a far higher status than the human ἐννοήματα to which Stoicism had reduced them.'

²³¹ Contrast Donini (2011: 299) and Bonazzi (2012: 317) on this point.

²³² I do not believe that the organization of the passage, from lesser modifications to more invasive or egregious ones (Aristotle, Theophrastus, Strato), points in the direction of a rejection of Aristotle's change: it merely reflects the fact that forms are lesser entities (namely concepts) than transcendent forms would

One might wonder why Theophrastus is singled out in this way, given that the Peripatetics in general are associated in many sources with the view that virtue is necessary for happiness but good fortune is required, too.[233] In the Antiochian sections Cicero allows for different weightings of the three classes of *bona* recognized by the Peripatetics. Aristotle and the Peripatetics in general, unlike Theophrastus, are assumed to rank goods other than the *bona animi* sufficiently lowly—on Antiochus' construal—to fall under the formula that virtue is sufficient and necessary for the *uita beata*, while the addition of the other goods yields the *uita beatissima* (see the general note on *Ac.* 1.19–23).[234] This distinction between a *uita beata* and a *uita beatissima* is open to various objections of course; see also below on Zeno's changes to the conception of appropriate action.

In §34a Strato of Lampsacus is named, who dismissed ethics and devoted himself to physics, but in a manner which was heterodox relative to school tradition. This is said with reference to *Ac.* 1.24–9, but holds true not just with respect to the physical doctrines laid out there but also with respect to physics as practised by Aristotle and Theophrastus. Strato's inclusion here serves in part a rhetorical purpose, in that it allows Varro to anticipate the charge that his picture of the Old Academy papers over demonstrably existing tensions. In §34b Varro turns to the Academics who came after Plato but before Arcesilaus. They are said to have 'guarded carefully' (*diligenter...tuebantur*) the teachings of their predecessors (*a superioribus*). Since the philosophers in question are again arranged in chronological sequence or in teacher/pupil relationships, it is not quite clear if *a superioribus* means 'from their predecessors in each case', or if everyone is meant who is counted amongst the *ueteres*. The former appears more likely, since Varro seems to be distinguishing a Peripatetic and an Academic line within Antiochus' Old Academy, and is now concerned with the latter. The impression of relative homogeneity within the Academic tradition may seem at variance with the privileged role accorded to Polemo as a predecessor for Stoic ethics, but Cicero provides an explanation for the latter in the next paragraph.

According to §35a, both Zeno and Arcesilaus were pupils of Polemo, but Zeno was older than Arcesilaus and—in apparent distinction to Arcesilaus—engaged with Polemo and responded acutely to his teachings, trying to correct them. A brief exchange between Varro and Cicero then marks section break.

In §35b Varro turns to Zeno, who, quite unlike Theophrastus, did not hamstring virtue and instead posited that the happy life resided in virtue alone and that nothing else was a good. Everything else was indifferent (§36; Cicero uses *nec bona nec mala*, rather than a closer rendering of ἀδιάφορον or the Greek term),[235] but some indifferents were in accordance with nature, while others were the opposite. These two classes are not jointly exhaustive, and between them there was a category of

---

be. What Antiochus took away from Aristotle's intervention was that forms (i.e. concepts) arise from sense perception, but that helped him complete only part of the journey towards Zeno's view.

[233] See Irwin (1986: 221).

[234] Cf. *Luc.* 134; *Fin.* 5.81; *Tusc.* 5.22, 28, and 76; and see Burkert (1972: 32–3); Görler (1974: 80–1), who cites *Fin.* 3.41 as a passage where the Peripatetics in general are mentioned for their laxness in ethical doctrine (*contentio...tractatam a Peripateticis mollius*); Karamanolis (2006: 54–6); Görler (2011: 353); Inwood (2014a: 27–9, 36–7).

[235] See Hartung (1970: 160–3).

indifferents which was 'intermediate' (*in mediis*). Indifferents which are in accordance with nature were 'to be selected' (*sumenda*) and 'deserving of estimation' (*quadam aestimatione dignanda*; see below), while the opposite held of those things which were not in accordance with nature, and those indifferents in between were of no significance whatsoever. In §37a, where the text is in doubt, Varro seems to introduce Latin technical terms for promoted and dis-promoted indifferents (again without naming, as Cicero does elsewhere, the Greek ones).

The extant evidence on the Stoic doctrine of indifferents is substantial and complex, reflecting extensive debate and probably changes in the Stoic position without it being clear in each case where in the relative chronology of the debate a given piece of evidence belongs.[236] It has plausibly been argued by Klein (2015) that an Old Stoic theory (i.e. Zeno's and Chrysippus') can be discerned, as well as a deviant and non-original version of that theory which is documented in Carneades' criticism, to which much of the evidence including that coming from Cicero relates. Klein argues further that scholarly opinion often mistakes Carneades' target for the Old Stoic theory and thus is not brought up against the question if the latter is misrepresented to begin with. The question of how Cicero's compressed remarks here relate to other ancient evidence and modern interpretations thus arises. Klein (2015) argues that the Old Stoic theory accords to indifferents the status of epistemic reasons, in that their selection is due to the subject's rational and probabilistic calculation as to which course of action is in agreement with nature. On this reading, for which Klein cites Chrysippean evidence from Epictetus, indifferents are not deemed to be of instrumental value for advancing what nature requires and are not selected for that value.[237] The relevant texts speak of indifferents as an indicator or metric (rather than, say, a tool or instrument). Carneades used the Socratic conception of virtue as a craft to argue that an art needs to have an end that lies outside the compass of its own tenets and injunctions, like health in the case of the art of medicine (*Fin.* 5.16). On this construal of how craft knowledge operates, individual actions in accordance with the art are undertaken because they are instrumental to advancing the art's end, and are deemed to be so by the subject and selected for that reason. Klein distinguishes ways in which indifferents could be held to be of instrumental value, i.e. they could either have the same value as virtue in kind but to a much smaller degree, or they could, by an 'axiological dualism', have value of their own but one which is different in kind from that of virtue. The latter view, which has some claim to being the prevailing interpretation of Stoic indifferents among modern scholars, fits the evidence for the Carneadean phase of the debate well, and it would be a reasonable expectation that it is also assumed by Antiochus, given that it allows for the relatively most plausible construal of two central ethical views of his: that the Stoics merely use different terms for *bona* other than virtue, and that virtue is necessary and sufficient for the *uita beata*.[238] The first view would be compatible with the value of indifferents

---

[236] See section 58 in Long and Sedley (1987), and *SVF* i.191–6 (Zeno), iii.117–68 (Chrysippus). Of the many important studies, easily accessible through companions and handbooks, see the seminal Striker (1996d); Brennan (2005: 119–33); Klein (2015) with extensive further bibliography.
[237] See Epict., *Diss.* 2.6.9 and 2.10.5–6, with Klein (2015: 267).
[238] A question not addressed by Klein (2015) is why Stoics contemporary with Carneades would not just charge Carneades with *ignoratio elenchi* if his arguments were directed at an interpretation of the Stoic

and virtue to be the same in kind but different in degree as well as with an axiological dualism, but the second view can only be made plausible if the value of virtue and indifferents is different in kind. Now given that in Piso's speech in *Fin.* 5 the *Carneadea diuisio* 'which Antiochus was fond of employing' prefaces the division with a remark about all crafts having an end 'outside of' the art itself, one would assume that Varro's account of Zeno's modifications here treats indifferents as things of value but on a different scale from virtue (the axiological dualism referred to above). *Ac.* 1.36–7 is consistent with such a reading, in that it calls indifferents *quadam aestimatione dignanda* and uses genitives *pretii* for the value and disvalue attached to promoted and dispromoted indifferents. *Aestimatio* can mean 'value' or the act of attaching a value, but is less suitable for conveying the notion that indifferents are to be used as metrics in the subject's calculations of what is in accordance with nature (contrast *Fin.* 3.60–1).

Making the familiar Antiochian point that Zeno merely changed the terminology in certain areas of Old Academic doctrine, which in context means either that the diminished status which the Old Academy accords to goods other than virtue is reflected in the Stoic category of 'indifferents' or that the Stoics accepted within their category of 'things in accordance with nature' the same gradations which the Old Academy posited for *bona* other than virtue (the text is in doubt, and I opt for the second solution; see n. below), Varro moves in §37b to right (i.e. virtuous) action and error, 'between which' appropriate and inappropriate action is located. This means not that there are four different classes of actions, but that every action is either a virtuous action (i.e. appropriate action of the sage) or an error (i.e. appropriate or inappropriate action of the non-sage); see the note below. Inappropriate action is not a concept which features frequently in Stoic texts, which tend to distinguish virtuous action, appropriate action, and vice/error, but it is plain that actions not in agreement with nature are meant, which the sage does not undertake ex hypothesi. 'Appropriate action' (*officium*) as conceived by the Old Academy featured in *Ac.* 1.23, and was there conceived as the conservation of all things which nature prescribes, which is to be seen against the Old Academy's composite τέλος of obtainment of virtue and pursuit of the *prima naturae*. The *prima naturae* are goods for Antiochus, so he rejects the avowed Zenonian position, while holding that materially it is not different from his own view, on which appropriate action involves the selection of *bona*.[239]

(i) In §§38–39a Varro turns to four further changes which Zeno made; unlike his predecessors, on whom see *Ac.* 1.20, Zeno wanted all virtues to be a disposition of reason (see n. below), a view which Antiochus accepted (see *Luc.* 31).[240] In *Fin.* 5.34 Piso, speaking for Antiochus, notes that human beings are made up of soul and body (see on §35: *Zeno igitur nullo modo...*), but

theory which philosophers like Diogenes and Antipater did not recognize as their own and if the Old Stoic theory was not actually open to Carneades's objections. Arguably, this line of reasoning suggests that what Klein identifies as the Carneadean interpretation predates Carneades. By the same token, it is difficult to believe that Carneades would not have attacked the Stoics for placing probabilistic reasoning about what is in accordance with nature at the heart of their moral theory.

[239] See Brittain (2006: xxxii); Bonazzi (2012: 328).
[240] See Plut., *Virt. mor.* 2, p. 441a (= *SVF* iii.255 = part of LS 61B).

ascribes all virtues to the soul.²⁴¹ Zeno also thought that it was not possible to separate (*seiungere*) non-rational virtues from rational ones.²⁴² The doctrine of the ἀντακολουθία of virtues,²⁴³ which Piso mentions in *Fin.* 5.67 and which Antiochus accepted, is here introduced as a modification of the view of the *superiores*. Plt., *Rep.* 443d–444c and Arist., *N.E.* Z13, are passages where the inseparability of virtues along with the separability of lower kinds of virtues is acknowledged,²⁴⁴ and there are other Platonic texts in which Socrates argues for the inseparability of virtues without further distinctions (e.g. Plt. *Prot.*). It is conceivable that Antiochus took Zeno to offer his view not simply from his own resources, but as a superior interpretation of the wider Academic tradition.²⁴⁵

(ii) He wanted not just the use or exercise of virtue to be excellent, but the disposition itself, too, while assuming that nobody had virtue who did not use it all the time. One competing view in the background is Aristotle's of virtue as an activity (ἐνέργεια). For Zeno, virtue does not consist in the selection of indifferents, even though this is what virtue invariably does; see n. below.

(iii) Unlike the Peripatetics and the Old Academy, Zeno did not favour μετριοπάθεια, but wanted the sage to be free from emotions. See *Luc.* 135, where Antiochus is said to agree with the Stoic view.²⁴⁶

(iv) Nor did he agree with the analysis of emotions as natural, irrational, and located in a part of the soul other than the mind. Rather, he took the passions to be voluntary on the grounds that they involve assent to impressions (resulting in opinions, δόξαι; see on *Ac.* 1.40–2; *Luc.* 78 and 148), and anything what is commonly called passion was the result of a lack of self-control (i.e. of rash assent). For the Stoic analysis of emotions, see again on *Luc.* 135. Antiochus has been held to adopt the original Stoic view that the soul had no parts other than the ruling part by some, and to assume a rational and an irrational part or parts by others.²⁴⁷ (Antiochus' psychological views are important for the question of the extent of his commitment to Stoicism, given that in the area of epistemology his developed position cannot be shown to ever deviate from the Stoic one.) Crucial evidence for the second view consists in *Ac.* 1.39 *ne his* **quidem** *assentiebatur* and a couple of remarks made by Piso *en passant* in his speech in *Fin.* 5 (5.36, on the ruling part: *animi autem et eius animi partis quae princeps est quaeque mens nominatur plures sunt uirtutes*; 5.38: *in homine autem summa omnis animi est et in animo rationis, ex qua uirtus est, quae rationis absolutio definitur*). Virtue is, however, as the second quote shows, deemed to be a disposition of reason alone, as it was for the Stoics.

---

²⁴¹ See also Bonazzi (2012: 325–31).
²⁴² See Plut., *Sto. rep.* 7, p. 1034c (= *SVF* i.200 = part of LS 61C).
²⁴³ See the texts collected under *SVF* iii.295–304; Irwin (2007: 328–31).
²⁴⁴ Cited by Brittain (2006: 102 n. 44).
²⁴⁵ See Alesse (2008).   ²⁴⁶ See Graver (2002: xxiii–xxv).
²⁴⁷ Primary evidence includes, apart from *Ac.* 1.39, *Luc.* 135–6; *Fin.* 5.31–2 and 5.95. The second view has recently been endorsed by Karamanolis (2006: 78) and Bonazzi (2012: 326–7). Brittain (2012: 123 n. 42) deems the evidence insufficient to make a determination.

In §39b Varro turns to two changes (signalled by *primum* and *etiam*) made by Zeno in the area of physics. He relates them both to the physical make-up of the mind although the second point is a broader one. That there are only two changes should not surprise us, since the Stoics are assumed to be essentially in agreement with the physical teachings laid out in *Ac.* 1.24–9. Zeno rejects the fifth element from which according to the *superiores* the mind is made and instead assumed that the mind was fire, i.e. the same fire from which the entire cosmos was made; the *superiores* would, on the most natural reading, be Peripatetics starting from Aristotle as well as Plato's successors (see on *Ac.* 1.26 *fin.*). Zeno also assumed the mind to be a body, 'unlike Xenocrates and other predecessors [*superiores*]', since being a body is a necessary condition for a thing's ability to effect anything. Here the separate mention of Xenocrates suggests that, while he also did not take the mind to be a body, he was actually not included with those who, in connection with the first change, assume the mind to consist of the fifth element.[248] In *Luc.* 124 the Cicero character reviews different opinions which have been held on the nature of the mind, so as to argue that suspension of judgement is reasonable given the *quot homines tot sententiae*. Xenocrates is cited for the view that the mind is a number *nullo corpore*. That section in *Luc.* is informed by a doxographical source, directly or indirectly, so it is not a given that Varro would associate Xenocrates with this view here in *Ac.* 1.39, but to have him do so makes for an economical reading of the passage.[249] This need not mean that Varro is cast as assuming the fifth element not to be material here, or that Cicero made this assumption: being material and being a body in the Stoic sense is arguably not the same thing.[250] I think it is reasonable to assume that Cicero appreciated this fact and that he had no reason to land the character Varro with the inability to appreciate it, but no passage in the Ciceronian corpus actually speaks to the issue.

The reader cannot but be struck by the fact that it is not plainly stated in each case which supposed corrections and modifications Antiochus accepted and which he rejected. Antiochus' overall position does not emerge incrementally as one reads through Varro's speech in *Ac.* 1.[251] Yet it would be rash to put this down to the speed with which Cicero composed *Acad.*, especially given that only the first part of the

---

[248] Put differently, common ground between the other *ueteres* and Xenocrates was not to regard the soul as a body in the Stoic sense; see the note below on the phrase *expers…corporis* in *Ac.* 1.39b. Inwood (2012: 204–8) offers a different reading of this passage, which affects other interpretative choices of his in the wider context. Sedley (2002: 80–1) and Dillon (2020: 197) take the absence of a reference to Polemo in 1.39b as an indication that the Varro character did not regard Polemo as wedded to the notion of incorporeal existence.

[249] Thus also Inwood (2012: 206 n. 39): 'It is hard to see why Xenocrates would be singled out by Cicero here if not for his well-documented and distinctive position.'

[250] *Pace* Reid¹ (p. 151), who comments: 'Either Cic. is here thinking of Plato only, or he does not realize that the πέμπτον σῶμα of Aristotle, however fine and subtle, is still corporeal.'

[251] On this point see also Brittain (2006: xxxii–iv); cf. Reid¹ (p. 141) on *Ac.* 1.33: 'After the preceding argument to prove that the early Academics formed one harmonious school (cf. esp. §§17, 18) it is startling to find Aristotle, Theophrastus and Strato treated as disturbers of the harmony. The words used in §§33, 34 would, if pressed, exclude the philosophers named from all connexion with the supposed old school. Cicero cannot have given here quite in full the exposition of Antiochus, who no doubt minimized the differences between Plato on the one hand and on the other Aristotle and Theophrastus.' For the view that Varro's speech draws on Antiochian material which was written after the Roman Books and which acknowledged fissures and tensions in the Old Academy (as constructed by Antiochus), see Sedley (2012b: 82–3); sections 7.2 and 9.3.

first book of the second edition is extant. Perhaps it is a deliberate compositional principle of Cicero's not to allow Antiochus' view to emerge already from Varro's survey, and to use the latter to signal points of contention which will be revisited later in the dialogue.

§33b

Nos uero uolumus...pro Attico etiam respondeam: on Atticus' role in the final edition see p. 95. *Nos uero* makes the answer emphatic (Varro's *si uultis* just above did not indicate doubt as to whether he was welcome to proceed). Reid[1] (p. 140) assembles parallels from Cicero's dialogues in which one character speaks emphatically for others at a section break (who nonetheless sometimes give a reply of their own). The purpose of the device is to convey keenness of the character answering for others, and to create the impression of an enthusiastic internal audience. Cf. e.g. *Lael.* 32: *tu uero perge, pro hoc enim respondeo.... Recte tu quidem* (sc. *respondes*).

Et recte quidem...ueteris auctoritas: Varro had ended by saying that he had set out the *prima forma* which Plato's successors and Peripatetics—including Aristotle, we should assume, given *Ac.* 1.17—took to have been handed over to them by Plato. Atticus confirms that the *Peripateticorum et Academiae ueteris auctoritas* is being explained admirably; *Academia uetus* here evidently refers to Plato's successors only; contrast e.g. *Ac.* 1.13. So when Peripatetic deviations, beginning with Aristotle's, are then introduced, these must be secondary (whether one reads *disputationes* or *immutationes* just above). See on *Ac.* 1.33a, the general note above, and section 7.2. *Auctoritas* here means, as Reid[1] (p. 141) rightly notes, 'opinion' (*OLD* s.v. no. 9; *TLL* s.v. col. 1223.3–68) as in the phrase *senatūs auctoritas*; note the two further instances of the term below, *auctoritatem ueteris disciplinae* and 1.34 *rationem auctoritatemque*, of which, however, the second requires a different interpretation in my view.

On *et recte* and related phrases in replies or the speaker's own resumption (*Verr.* 5.21: *errabas et uehementer errabas*) see Reid[1] (p. 141). On *recte* alone ('you are right'), see Ricottilli (2003: 152–3). With *et recte quidem*, cf. *Brut.* 255; *Leg.* 1.16; *Tusc.* 1.15; for *et recte* without *quidem*, printed e.g. by Reid[1], in a rejoinder, cf. *Leg.* 2.14.

Aristoteles igitur primus species...diuinum esse diceret: *primus* marks Aristotle as the first of those who floated potentially destabilizing, at least from some point of view, modifications of the *prima forma* accepted by the *ueteres* (including himself, see previous n.); *uehementius* below suggests that Aristotle's proposed modification was less egregious than Theophratus'. *Species* is the rendering for ἰδέα used in *Ac.* 1.30; see ibid. for terminology relating to the forms in Cicero. As indicated in the general note above, one constraint in determining what is meant by *species* here is what is meant in 1.30; the same conception of what an ἰδέα is must be employed in both places. On *labefactare*, see *TLL* s.v. col. 765.46–50 for passages where the verb is used in contrast with semantically similar verbs, demonstrating that *labefactare* is stronger than e.g. *temptare* but weaker than *euertere* or *funditus tollere*; Görler (2012: 380–1). Parallels for the use of the term with, broadly speaking, philosophical constructs include *Luc.* 10 (*etsi (causa) hesterno sermone labefactata est*), where the speaker Lucullus does not actually think that the *causa* (i.e. the Antiochian position) has been damaged, 16 (*dum huius* [i.e. Zenonis] *definitiones labefactare uult*), 36 *fin.* (of *perceptio*, κατάληψις); *N.D.* 2.116 (*quo labefactari possit tanta contentio grauitatis et ponderum*). These parallels show (see Merguet s.v.) that the verb is fairly generically used of the calling-into-question of claims, arguments, and positions; it is not a success verb. I have argued above that a connotation peculiar to the present context may be that *species* are 'shaken' because concepts in the mind of human beings are here assumed by Aristotle to be the result of sense perception rather than innate (*Ac.* 1.30–2 presented them as the latter according to the *antiqui*, on my reading). *Mirifice* can be sarcastic (*Catul.* 53.2) as well as laudatory (*Catul.* 71.4), and it is probably the latter here (even though Varro respectfully disagrees on my construal). Parallels in Cicero suggest that semantically it can be little more than an intensifier; cf. e.g. *Luc.* 4; *De orat.* 1.57; *N.D.* 1.58, 1.73. See also Ricottilli (2003: 205). *Amplexari* of items of doctrine which are held dear, e.g. in *Tusc.* 2.30 (*honestum*); *Fin.* 2.43 (virtue), *Fin.* 4.36 (*cognitio*, of Erillus); in its uses it only partially overlaps with *amplecti*, which, unlike *amplexari*, can mean 'to grapple with'. If *species* were transcendental items, using *amplexari* here might be seen as facetious (since forms thus understood are the most unembraceable items imaginable), especially if *mirifice* is seen to be sarcastic.

On the import of *quiddam diuinum*, see the general note above. A text in which Aristotle criticized Platonic Forms and which was more readily available in the Hellenistic period than Περὶ ἰδεῶν was Aristotle's lost dialogue *De philosophia.*

In *N.D.* Cicero reveals indirect knowledge of this text, and one might wonder if what Varro reports here can be linked with what we know about its contents, and what we may assume Cicero to have known about them. Unfortunately, neither of the two fragments in question seems illuminating. *N.D.* 1.33 (= Arist. frg. 26 Rose = 25.1 Gigon) is spoken by the Epicurean Velleius and directed at Aristotle's conception of the divine. Velleius argues (if we read the text as transmitted and do not follow Manutius in inserting *non* before *dissentiens*) that Aristotle, while not disagreeing with Plato, called a substantial number of different things divine in a manner which was implausible and self-contradictory; see Dyck (2003: 100) and Flashar et al. (2006: 138–9). *N.D.* 2.95–6 (= Arist. frg. 12 Rose = 838 Gigon; Balbus speaking), whose ascription to *De philosophia* is less certain, is Aristotle's version of the cave simile, a striking passage for many reasons, including that Cicero never talks about *Plato's* cave. Human beings do not inhabit the equivalent of a cave (the notion features only as a counterfactual), and there is no realm beyond the observable universe; see Bos (1989: 185–200) and Flashar et al. (2006: 139–40). I see no reason to link either passage with 1.33b here. Cicero's source for the relevant passage in *N.D.* is widely held to be Philodemus (see the general note on *Luc.* 118–26); see also Barnes (1997c: 47–8).

An. Post. B19, or a doxographical summary of it, was cited above as an instance of the kind of text Antiochus may have been thinking of; other candidates would be Aristotle's *De memoria*, or *Met.* A1. See Bénatouïl (2016a: 63–6) for a summary of possible Aristotelian influences on Stoic logic in the Hellenistic period, esp. p. 66 with n. 39 on the starting points of knowledge. What makes *An. Post.* B19 a particularly intriguing reference point is that it engages closely and obviously with Plato's *Phaedo*, so that it could be fitted into a narrative which presents Aristotle's view as arising from and informed by a reading of Platonic texts, and that it is concerned not with the acquisition of any knowledge, but that of first principles, which for Aristotle are universals, described in terms reminiscent of forms; cf. *An. Post.* B19, 100a6–8 ἐκ δ' ἐμπειρίας ἢ ἐκ παντὸς ἠρεμήσαντος τοῦ καθόλου ἐν τῇ ψυχῇ, τοῦ ἑνὸς παρὰ τὰ πολλά, ὃ ἂν ἐν ἅπασιν ἓν ἐνῇ ἐκείνοις τὸ αὐτό, τέχνης ἀρχὴ καὶ ἐπιστήμης, 'And from experience, or from all the universal which has come to rest in the soul (the one apart from the many, i.e. whatever is one and the same in all these items), there comes a principle of skill and understanding' (transl. Barnes) with *Ac.* 1.30:...*quia sola cerneret id quod semper esset simplex et unius modi et tale quale esset*. See esp. Adamson (2010). The evidence for the reception of *An. Post.* B19 is later; see e.g. Helmig (2010). However, the doxographical section on the Peripatetic view of the criterion in Sextus, *M.* 7.217–26, which is widely held to go back to Hellenistic material and not to be influenced by the commentary tradition, does seem reminiscent of the account of the genesis of knowledge in *An. Post.* B19 (and *Met.* A1); see e.g. Chiaradonna (2013: 34–5). On the question of whether the larger context of Sextus *M.* 7.217–26 is Antiochian, see Brittain (2012: 108–13). Alternatively, Aristotle might have been integrated into the *Theaetetus*-related narrative, such that his 'revision' would be derived from his reading of passages which suggest that concepts arise from perception, e.g. *Theaet.* 191a5–196c6 (wax tablet) or 196d1–200c6 (aviary). Both can be read as speaking to the issue of concept formation without assuming that concepts arise from self-warranting true perceptions; see Helmig (2012: 285–6).

Igitur is resumptive as in *Ac.* 1.35b: *Zeno igitur*. Reid[1] (p. 141) cites *Fin.* 1.28 and *Brut.* 204 as parallels for abrupt speaker change without as much as an *inquit*.

Theophrastus autem...quod negauit in ea sola positum esse beate uiuere: = the first part of Theophrastus frg. 497 FHS&G. On Theophrastus' view at issue here, in itself and compared to Aristotle and other Peripatetics as they appear in Cicero, see the general note above; cf. also *Fin.* 5.12, 77, 85 and *Tusc.* 5.85, but especially *Tusc.* 5.24–5 (= Theophrastus frg. 493 FHS&G). Our passage stands alongside others in which Cicero ascribes to Theophrastus the unqualified claim that the happy life did not reside in virtue alone, and non-Ciceronian evidence also suggests that Theophrastus' position was so interpreted. However, *Tusc.* 5.24–5 suggests that Cicero was aware that Theophrastus' position may actually have been more nuanced. On the passage, see Annas (1993: 385–8).

For Theophrastus' charm, cf. Gell. 13.5 (Aristotle's words on his death bed): ἡδίων ὁ Λέσβιος. This feature, along with Theophrastus' personal integrity, are here mentioned to balance what in Varro's eyes is a reprehensible move, i.e. the claim that virtue is not sufficient for happiness. (In a similar way ancient texts sometimes draw a distinction between Epicurus' personal conduct and his view that pleasure is the end; cf. e.g. *Tusc.* 3.46 = frg. 440 Usener.) Cicero's comments elsewhere on Theophrastus' sweetness relate to his style; cf. *De orat.* 1.49: *Theophrastus...Carneades...in dicendo suaues*; *Brut.* 121: *Quis...Theophrasto dulcior?* On the biographical tradition relating to Theophrastus, see Mejer (1998).

Cicero uses *spoliare* in the sense of 'to deprive' in a number of places in the philosophical works (e.g. *Tusc.* 4.23; *N.D.* 4.23), as well as in the sense of 'undress' (*Off.* 3.21), but here the more specific sense of συλᾶν is evoked through *imbecillamque reddidit*; cf. Enn., *Ann.* 618 Skutsch: *spoliantur eos et corpora nuda relinquont* (where, however, Skutsch prints *despoliantur*).

The sentence from *uehementius fregit* is a peculiar combination of emphatic statement and qualification. There are also several ambiguous terms (cf. the occasional *praeualet notio* when meanings are distinguished in the *TLL*) which are not readily disambiguated by the context. *Auctoritas* ought to retain the sense of 'view' as in *Peripateticorum et Academiae ueteris auctoritas* just above, although the senses of 'standing' and 'authority' cannot be declared to be absent. *Disciplina*, which recurs in 1.35a, has connotations both of 'doctrine/body of doctrines' and 'school', i.e. the people who hold those doctrines; see on *Luc.* 15 for the same ambiguity. *Vehementius* marks the middle stage in a progression whose culminating point is Strato (cf. *omnino* below); *quodam modo* stands too far away from *uehementius* to qualify it. So *quodam modo* qualifies *fregit*, which is hard to pin down: the sense of 'breaking with' (sc. the view of the *ueteres*) is present, but the military imagery of *spoliauit* also gives 'to take away the vigour or masculine qualities of, enervate, weaken' (*OLD* s.v. *frango* no. 8) a look-in. *Quodam modo* either merely softens the metaphor of *fregit* or hints at the fact that Theophrastus' view is actually only gradually different from the wider Peripatetic tradition. Reid[1] (p. 141) on *negauit... uiuere* aptly points out that Varro seems to be offering small print here; contrast *Ac.* 1.22: **omnis illa antiqua philosophia sensit in una uirtute esse positam beatam uitam, nec tamen beatissimam**. See also *Luc.* 134 on Theophrastus; and the survey article by Schneider (2016b).

§34

Nam Strato, eius auditor...in ea ipsa plurimum dissedit a suis: = Strato frg. 13 Wehrli. The force of *nam*, for which cf. *N.D.* 1.27, is aptly characterized by Reid[1] (p. 142) as elliptical: 'I need hardly mention Strato, for...'; Hofmann-Szantyr p. 505 ('...in Wirklichkeit als Einleitung eines Begründungssatzes zu einem unterdrückten Zwischenglied gedacht...'). For Strato, see also *Luc.* 121, esp. on his views on physics; Repici (1988); Desclos and Fortenbaugh (2010); Lefebvre (2016: 21–4); Schneider (2016). Strato is an outlier within the Peripatetic school, and Varro's open acknowledgement of this fact seems designed to counter any charge of forced harmonization on Antiochus' part. For the hypothesis that Varro's speech draws on Antiochian material composed after the Roman Books, in which Antiochus was more ready to acknowledge tensions within his conception of the Old Academy, see Sedley (2012b: 82–3) and sections 7.2 and 9.3.

For *auditor* in the sense of pupil (ἀκούστης), see *Luc* 118, 126; for the organizational principle of doxographical material by succession, see the general note on *Luc.* 118–26 and Schneider (2016a) on Sotion. *Disciplina* exhibits the same ambiguity as in the previous paragraph, between 'school' and 'doctrines which are characteristic for the school', but given that Varro treats Peripatetics and Old Academy separately, he means the Peripatetics and their doctrines, not Antiochus' Old Academy. *Omnino* signals the final stage in the progression from small changes (Aristotle) to large ones. See on *Ac.* 1.19 for Ciceronian ways of referring to the branch of philosophy which is ethics (*in uirtute et moribus*). *Relinquere* cannot mean 'neglect' and must mean 'leave behind altogether', but this a rhetorical exaggeration. There are at least book titles on ethical subjects attested, e.g. D.L. 5.59: Περὶ τἀγαθοῦ (= frg. 134) and Περὶ εὐδαιμονίας (= Strato frg. 135 Wehrli). For *dissidere* used of differences of learned opinion, see *TLL* s.v. cols 1467.47–1468.7.

Speusippus autem et Xenocrates...diligenter ea, quae a superioribus acceperant, tuebantur: = Speusippus frg. 28 Isnardi Parente = Xenocrates frg. 75 Isnardi Parente = Polemon frg. 120 Gigante = Polemon T. 41 Marzotto. Cf. Philod., *Index Acad.* col. xviii.7–13. Varro's gaze shifts to the Academics. The first four heads of the Academy after Plato are named in sequence, with Crantor (who was never scholarch) added. They are divided into two groups, with Speusippus and Xenocrates as initial recipients of the *ratio auctoritasque Platonis* (cf. the *prima forma* of *Ac.* 1.33a, but see below), and the second group of three as faithful trustees of the *superiores*' views. The effect is to signal that the inner-Academic tradition prior to Arcesilaus was very homogenous, with respect to doctrinal commitments and approach.

One might wonder if the sentence implies that Plato fully formulated the body of doctrines which characterizes the Old Academy (including the Peripatos), as envisaged in *Luc.* 15, which he then passed on to his successors. If so, the passage would be at variance with *Ac.* 1.16–17, 1.23 *fin.*, and 1.33a; see ad loc. and section 7.2. I suggest that what we are told here does not speak to, and hence cannot be at variance with, what was said about the mechanics of the formation of the *prima forma* in *Ac.* 1.17, but represents supplementary information on a different level of description; witness e.g. how Speusippus and Xenocrates are put on a par even though only one of them was scholarch (contrast 1.17). *Ratio* and *auctoritas* must stand for a way of doing philosophy (cf. *Luc.* 7: *Academiae ratio*) and the authority which flows from Plato as founder of the Academy; *auctoritas* is unlikely to mean 'view' here, as it did in *Ac.* 1.33 *Peripateticorum et Academiae ueteris auctoritas*, since the two terms would otherwise come close to being equivalent, in which case the fullness of the expression would be unwarranted. The term *superiores* here most likely designates predecessors within the Academy; it does not have a fixed reference like the term *ueteres*. See also the other instances of *superiores* in the immediate vicinity (*Ac.* 1.38 twice, 1.39 twice, 1.42). *Suscipere* suggests that Plato's successors accepted said *ratio* and *auctoritas* willingly and out of *diligentia* (cf. *OLD* s.v. *suscipio* no. 7b; cf. nos. 4 and 8); there may be an implied accusation against Arcesilaus, who did not recognize his obligations. *Rationem suscipere* also in *Rosc. Am.* 149, but there *ratio* means 'area, domain'. The point of the phrase *in Academia congregati* is not obvious: the suggestion may be that Plato's successors remained in conversation with one another in the same place, which accounts for their steadfastness in outlook; see Marzotto (2012: 236–7). The phrase may also hint at the crassness of the break with tradition implemented by Arcesilaus in its historical context, and the baselessness of his (and his successors') claim to being an 'Academic'. For *grex* of philosophical schools, cf. *Lael.* 69: *in nostro (ut ita dicam) grege*; Hor., *Epist.* 1.4.16: *Epicuri de grege porcum*, and the other parallels collected by Reid[1] (p. 142). Differences in the concerns and interests as well as the doctrines of these philosophers, which are independently attested, belie this picture as soon as one examines details, but on a sufficiently general level modern scholars would acknowledge continuities among the Academics who preceded

Arcesilaus. For Cicero's references to Plato's immediate successors, see section 7. On Crates, Polemo's successor as head of the Academy, see Dorandi (1994h). On the spelling of *Polemo*, see the Oxford Classical Text, p. lxxiv. The name of Crantor, restored by a corrector (not the first hand) in P, is also to be found in later mss.; Crantor is also mentioned in *Luc.* 135 (where the oldest manuscripts give *Grantor*) and in other philosophical works (e.g. *De orat.* 3.67; *Fin.* 5.7; *Tusc.* 1.115). The readings *eis* and *utebantur* in P go together, but the text of *Γ*, with its emphasis on custodianship, is preferable, since it fits better with *diligenter* and *susceperant* above.

Iam Polemonem audiuerant assidue Zeno et Arcesilas: *iam* 'to proceed' (Reid[1] p. 142); *OLD* s.v. no. 8a. The teacher–pupil relationship of Polemo on the one hand and Zeno and Arcesilaus on the other is attested elsewhere; see Strab. 13.1.67 (= Polemo T. 21 Marzotto) and on *Ac.* 1.19–23, Kupreeva (2012: 1192–3); Marzotto (2012: 237–8). That it is emphasized here makes the obvious point that there is continuity between the last scholarch of the Academy before it turned sceptical and the Stoa, but may also imply that Arcesilaus could so easily have been a better pupil of Polemo than he proved to be. He and Zeno had the same extensive exposure to Polemo (*assidue*). On the spelling of *Arcesilas*, see *TLL* s.v. Arcesilaus.

§35

Sed Zeno…corrigere conatus est disciplinam: that Arcesilaus 'failed' as a member of the Academy is implicitly put down to a lack of maturity, of subtlety in reasoning and argument (cf. *ualdeque subtiliter dissereret*), and to a failure to respond intelligently to his teacher (cf. *peracute moueretur*), which must appear ironic, given that the most famous Academic, Carneades, was known for his supreme argumentative dexterity. Zeno's 'corrections' in turn are presented as resulting from the zeal and restless intellectual energy of the star pupil (who is readily forgiven for occasional overreach). For the relative dates of Zeno and Arcesilaus see Gourinat (2018: 376–83) and Görler (1994: 787–96) respectively. *Arcesilas* in P and *μ* is most likely a perseveration error from the previous sentence, given that the nominative produces no satisfactory sense on any account. Translators usually render the *cum*-clause as a relative clause or as a parenthesis; it can only be causal. *Corrigere* reflects Zeno's viewpoint primarily. On *disciplina*, cf. the previous paragraph. With *peracute moueretur*, cf. *Fam.* 15.21.4 (= SB 207): *deinde ingenium eius maioribus extuli laudibus, quam tu id uere potuisse fieri putas, primum quod ita iudicabam: acute mouebatur*; see Plasberg[1] (p. 51), who hints that the use of *mouere* in connection with impressions may be alluded to (e.g. *Luc.* 34: …*cum sit incertum uere inaniterne moueatur*). If so, then this would be apparent only on re-reading, given that impressions will only be introduced in *Ac.* 1.40.

Eam quoque, si uidetur…sicut solebat Antiochus: in the immediately preceding sentence, Zeno is said to have *attempted* reform or correction. Given that Antiochus accepts only some of Zeno's modifications (see the general note above), one has to understand the attribute 'attempted' with *correctio* here, or assume that *correctio* reflects Zeno's point of view.

Solebat hints at the fact that the historical Varro heard Antiochus in person and did not learn of his views from books (or from books alone); see on *Ac.* 1.3 *Sed nunc postea... ceteris et studiis et artibus antecedat.*

Mihi uero...significare Pomponium: see above on *Ac.* 1.33a *fin.* for the use of such brief interventions at section breaks. *Pomponius* is a more formal way of referring to Atticus than *Atticus*; see Adams (1978: 159–60).

Zeno igitur nullo modo...quod esset simplex quoddam et solum et unum bonum: = *SVF* i.188 = first part of Theophrastus frg. 497 FHS&G. For *Zeno igitur*, see on *Ac.* 1.33b *Aristoteles igitur.* The expression *neruos uirtutis inciderit*, 'cut the tendons (or muscles) of virtue', resumes the second colon of *Ac.* 1.33b: *spoliauit enim uirtutem suo decore imbecillamque reddidit.* For the phrase, cf. *Leg. agr.* 2.47; *Phil.* 12.8; Liv. 37.42.5.

Omnia quae ad beatam uitam pertinerent in una uirtute poneret is a peculiar way of saying that Zeno declared virtue to be the sole good. The contrast *omnia–una* implies there is nothing reductive in the Stoic view: all that is required for a happy life is included. Cf. e.g. *Fin.* 4.41, where Cicero, as an Academic but criticizing Stoicism from an Antiochian vantage point, criticizes the Stoics for reducing human beings, who have a mind and a body, to disembodied minds. For praise of Zeno's uncompromising stance, and a comparison with Antiochus, cf. *Luc.* 134. Reid[1] (p. 143) aptly glosses the plural *in bonis* as 'in the category of good'.

On *honestum* as a rendering of τὸ καλόν, see on *Luc.* 138. For the view that only the *honestum* is the good, cf. *Fin.* 3.27 (= *SVF* iii.37), 4.48; *Tusc.* 5.43–5; Plut., *Sto. rep.* 1039c (= *SVF* iii.29); Clem., *Protr.* 6.72.7 (= *SVF* i.557 (Cleanthes) = LS 61Q3); D.L. 7.100 (= *SVF* iii.83). See also Wildberger (2006: 549 n. 291) for a collection of passages in Seneca devoted to the subject. Scholarly discussions include Irwin (1986: 210–13); Frede (1999b); Inwood (2005c). The characterization of the *honestum* as *simplex quoddam et solum et unum bonum* is reminiscent of the characterization of the Platonic ἰδέα in *Ac.* 1.30: *quod semper esset simplex et unius modi et tale quale esset.* This is unlikely to be coincidental, but Varro does not pause to explain the connection. Varro, or so I argued ad loc., took forms to be conceptions in the mind. Virtue is for Zeno a stable disposition (διάθεσις) of the mind, unassailable by argument; see on *Ac.* 1.40–2 and *Luc.* 144–5.

On Zeno's τέλος-formula, see also *Luc.* 132 *fin.* (*honeste uiuere, quod ducatur a conciliatione naturae, Zeno statuit finem esse bonorum...*) and 138 on the so-called *Chrysippea diuisio* (where *honestas* is given as the Stoic end).

On the tense pattern *erat...inciderit...poneret* Reid[1] (p. 143) aptly comments: 'The perfect *inciderit* seems to me necessary here, the sense being "he was not the man *ever at any time* to have cut the sinews of virtue, but just the man *constantly* to teach that virtue contained all that is necessary to happiness". Such changes of tense are common enough in categorical statements containing indicatives, and there can be no reason for suspecting them when the syntax requires subjunctives. Our MSS give us many examples very few of which are left untouched by editors' (author's emphasis).

According to Plasberg[1] (p. 51), Cicero omitted out of *neglegentia* after *unum bonum* what Zeno had to say about evil (*turpitudo*). Gigon posits a *lacuna*. See also the next note.

§36

Cetera autem etsi nec bona nec mala essent...et media numerabat: Varro proceeds to indifferents, i.e. all other things that are not virtue, but gives a characterization of the concept in his own words, rather than the Greek term and a close Latin translation, as he does elsewhere in similar contexts. Indifferents are either in agreement with nature, or in disagreement with nature, or neither.

Cf. D.L. 7.104–5 (= *SVF* iii.119 = LS 58B): Διχῶς δὲ λέγεσθαι ἀδιάφορα· ἅπαξ μὲν τὰ μήτε πρὸς εὐδαιμονίαν μήτε πρὸς κακοδαιμονίαν συνεργοῦντα, ὡς ἔχει πλοῦτος, δόξα, ὑγίεια, ἰσχὺς καὶ τὰ ὅμοια· ἐνδέχεται γὰρ καὶ χωρὶς τούτων εὐδαιμονεῖν, τῆς ποιᾶς αὐτῶν χρήσεως εὐδαιμονικῆς οὔσης ἢ κακοδαιμονικῆς. ἄλλως δὲ λέγεται ἀδιάφορα τὰ μήθ' ὁρμῆς μήτ' ἀφορμῆς κινητικά, ὡς ἔχει τὸ ἀρτίας ἔχειν ἐπὶ τῆς κεφαλῆς τρίχας ἢ περιττάς, ἢ ἐκτεῖναι τὸν δάκτυλον ἢ συστεῖλαι, τῶν προτέρων ἀδιαφόρων οὐκέθ' οὕτω λεγομένων· ὁρμῆς γάρ ἐστιν ἐκεῖνα καὶ ἀφορμῆς κινητικά. διὸ τὰ μὲν αὐτῶν ἐκλέγεται, ⟨τὰ δὲ ἀπεκλέγεται⟩, τῶν [δ'] ἑτέρων ἐπίσης ἐχόντων πρὸς αἵρεσιν καὶ φυγήν, '"Indifferent" is used in two senses: unconditionally, of things which contribute neither to happiness nor unhappiness, as is the case with wealth, reputation, health, strength, and the like. For it is possible to be happy even without these, though the manner of using them is constitutive of happiness and unhappiness. In another sense those things are called indifferent which activate neither impulse nor repulsion, as in the case of having an odd or even number of hairs on one's head, or stretching or contracting a finger. But the previous indifferents are not spoken of in this sense. For they are capable of activating impulse or repulsion. Hence some of them are selected and other disselected, but the second type is entirely equal with respect to choice and avoidance' (transl. Long and Sedley); see also the other texts collected under LS 58. The main discussion in the Ciceronian corpus is *Fin.* 3.51–7. For Cicero's translations of ἀδιάφορον, see Hartung (1970: 160–3); Moreschini (1979: 130–2). Ἀδιάφορον is rendered *indifferens* just once (*Fin.* 3.53: *quod enim illi ἀδιάφορον dicunt, id mihi ita occurrit ut indifferens dicerem*); Cicero's standard translation is *medium*. On the doctrine itself, its evolution, and modern interpretations, see Klein (2015).

Reid[1] (p. 144) thinks that before going on to indifferents Varro should have specified that only *malum* is a vice, but this is neither the contrast aimed for here nor does it capture the Stoic position. Moreover, the implicit reference point is the *tria bona* structure which forms the backbone of *Ac.* 1.19–23, so that the question Varro addresses here is what 'everything else' is if, as it were, one particular *bonum animi* is elevated to the status of sole good. Cf. the last note on §35. On *his ipsis*, which had troubled earlier editors, see Reid[1] (p. 144).

Quae autem secundum naturam essent...in quibus ponebat nihil omnino esse momenti: Varro expands on the three categories introduced in the previous sentence. Things in accordance with nature are *sumenda* (ληπτά), and as such contrasted elsewhere with *expetenda* (αἱρετά), things sought for their own sake, i.e. virtue. Cf. Plut., *Comm. not.* 23, 1070a (= SVF iii.123): Τὰ αὐτὰ πράγματα ληπτὰ καὶ οὐχ αἱρετὰ καὶ οἰκεῖα καὶ οὐκ ἀγαθὰ καὶ ἀνωφελῆ μὲν εὔχρηστα δέ, καὶ οὐδὲν μὲν πρὸς ἡμᾶς ἀρχὰς δὲ τῶν καθηκόντων ὀνομάζοντες, 'they call the same things "takeable" and not objects of choice and appropriate and not good and of no benefit yet useful and of no concern to us but yet starting points of our duties', with Klein (2015: 238); *Fin.* 4.20 (the Cicero character speaking, with irony): *Alia quaedam dicent, credo, magna antiquorum esse peccata, quae ille ueri inuestigandi cupidus nullo modo ferre potuerit. Quid enim peruersius, quid intolerabilius, quid stultius quam bonam ualetudinem, quam dolorum omnium uacuitatem, quam integritatem oculorum reliquorumque sensuum ponere in bonis potius quam dicerent nihil omnino inter eas res iisque contrarias interesse? Ea enim omnia, quae illi bona dicerent, praeposita esse, non bona, itemque illa, quae in corpore excellerent, stulte antiquos dixisse per se esse expetenda; sumenda potius quam expetenda. Ea denique omni uita, quae in una uirtute consisteret, illam uitam, quae etiam ceteris rebus, quae essent secundum naturam, abundaret, magis expetendam non esse, sed magis sumendam.*

See the general note above for some of the philosophical issues arising from the Stoic doctrine of indifferents; Ioppolo (2016), esp. pp. 184–92, on the inner-Stoic debate as used by Cicero against Cato in *Fin.* 4.

Cicero's renderings of Greek terms may in this case produce material differences in the understanding of the doctrines to which these terms are related. *Sumenda* is a gerundive, whereas ληπτά are merely 'takeable'; see Tronci (2013). *Aestimatio* is the act of evaluation or, secondarily, the value attached to something as a result of it, whereas ἀξία, to which *aestimatio* corresponds, just means 'value' in the first instance, although the Stoics may have revived its earlier, 'etymological' meaning; see Hartung (1970: 149–50): 'Während die Bedeutung des Substantivs ἀξία bis zu der Zeit, als die Stoiker es übernahmen, in der Tat so weit verblaßte, daß es sich mit dem deutschen "Wert" treffend substituieren läßt, aktualisierten die sprachkundigen Stoiker erneut die etymologisch gegebene Bedeutung des alten und häufig gebrauchten Wortes: "das aufwiegende Herabziehen einer Waagschale" (als abstrahierte Verbalhandlung verstanden).'

§37

Sed quae essent sumenda...quae minoris: = SVF i.193; cf. *Fin.* 3.58 = SVF iii.498 = LS 59F. The text as transmitted poses a problem. Within the category of *sumenda* introduced in the previous paragraph, some things are said to be of 'rather high' (or 'higher') value, others of 'rather low' (or 'lower value'). The former are called *praeposita*, the latter are *reiecta*—but then *reiecta* would fall paradoxically under *sumenda*. Davies's suggestion of printing *media* for *sumenda* would mean that the promoted indifferents introduced in the next sentence would come from *media* situated between things in accordance with nature and things not in accordance with nature of 1.36. In his English translation Brittain (2006: 101) suggests something like *Sed quae essent sumenda ⟨contrariaque⟩, ex iis alia pluris esse aestimanda, alia minoris.*

Quae pluris ea praeposita appellabat, reiecta autem quae minoris. This is possible, but would in part be a restatement from above in a passage which is otherwise exceedingly economical. Perhaps Cicero's point is a different one: that there are gradations within the class of things of value. This would receive support from the immediately following Antiochian trope that the Stoics merely changed terminology, in that Varro would not just be saying that the Stoics called promoted indifferents what the Old Academy calls *bona*, but that the Stoics agreed with the Old Academy also that the *bona* other than virtue include things whose value is really very limited indeed (cf. 1.22 *fin.*). While the notion of gradations among indifferents (beyond promoted, dispromoted, and what Cicero calls things *in mediis*) is thinly attested elsewhere and disputed as Stoic e.g. by Inwood (2005b: 102 n. 21), one may compare Stob., *Ecl.* II.7, p. 84.18–24 Wachsmuth (part of *SVF* i.192 and iii.128 = LS 58E): Τῶν δ' ἀξίαν ἐχόντων τὰ μὲν ἔχειν πολλὴν ἀξίαν, τὰ δὲ βραχεῖαν. Ὁμοίως δὲ καὶ τῶν ἀπαξίαν ἐχόντων ἃ μὲν ἔχειν πολλὴν ἀπαξίαν, ἃ δὲ βραχεῖαν. Τὰ μὲν ⟨οὖν⟩ πολλὴν ἔχοντα ἀξίαν προηγμένα λέγεσθαι, τὰ δὲ πολλὴν ἀπαξίαν ἀποπροηγμένα, Ζήνωνος ταύτας τὰς ὀνομασίας θεμένου πρώτου τοῖς πράγμασι, 'Some valuable things have much value and others little. So too some disvaluable things have much disvalue and others little. Those which have much value are called "preferred" and those which have disvalue "dispreferred". Zeno was the first to apply these terms to things' (transl. Long and Sedley). A Latin text which yields this sense would be: *Sed quae essent sumenda, ex iis alia pluris esse aestimanda, alia minoris, ⟨contraque contraria⟩. Quae pluris ea praeposita appellabat, reiecta autem quae minoris.* The phrase *contraque contraria* might have dropped out because it was deemed to be an erroneous repetition from above. The sentence from *quae pluris* would, in line with Stobaeus, say that within the class of things of value, those of the highest value are called promoted, sc. indifferents, while within the class of things of negative value, those with the highest negative value are called dispromoted, sc. indifferents.

On the distinction between προηγμένα and ἀποπροηγμένα, see D.L. 7.106 (= *SVF* iii.127), who characterizes προηγμένα as 'things which have value' in several spheres (the soul, like progress towards virtue; the body, like health; things external to ourselves, like renown) and ἀποπροηγμένα as their opposites; and *SVF* iii.128–39. Cf. *Fin.* 3.15: *Si enim Zenoni licuit, cum rem aliquam inuenisset inusitatam, inauditum quoque ei rei nomen imponere, cur non liceat Catoni? Nec tamen exprimi uerbum e uerbo necesse erit, ut interpretes indiserti solent, cum sit uerbum, quod idem declaret, magis usitatum. Equidem soleo etiam quod uno Graeci, si aliter non possum, idem pluribus uerbis exponere. Et tamen puto concedi nobis oportere ut Graeco uerbo utamur, si quando minus occurret Latinum, ne hoc 'ephippiis'* [a type of saddle] *et 'acratophoris'* [a type of wine jar] *potius quam 'proegmenis' et 'apoproegmenis' concedatur; quamquam haec quidem praeposita recte et reiecta dicere licebit.*

Cicero's terms *praeposita* and *reiecta* capture an important aspect of the meaning of προηγμένα and ἀποπροηγμένα which is lost if one renders the terms as '*preferred* and *dispreferred* indifferents'. With respect to the Greek term, Klein (2015: 227 n. 1) notes: 'The Greek terms do not suggest any intrinsic connection to an agent's preferences or motivating states.' Hartung (1970: 164–80) offers a close semasiological discussion of the Greek terms and their Latin counterparts, and observes (p. 169): 'So lassen sich mit προηγμένα Dinge und Handlungsweisen prädizieren, denen auf der

Wertskala ein Grad zukommt, der zwischen dem Nullpunkt und dem ἀγαθόν, also auf der—vom Nullpunkt aus gesehen—positiven Achse liegt', which is consistent with the promotedness of προηγμένα bearing no connection with an agent's motivational states, but introduces the misleading notion that the value attached to προηγμένα is on the same scale as that of virtue. See the general note above on the wider philosophical issues arising from the doctrine of indifferents.

Atque ut haec non tam rebus quam uocabulis commutauerat...media putabat ut dixi: = *SVF* i.231. Varro proceeds to the modified conception of appropriate action which Zeno introduced as a consequence of classifying *bona* other than virtue as promoted indifferents. On the motif of substantial agreement but changed terminology, which had a history in the Hellenistic period and was employed by dissident dogmatists as well as Academic sceptics before it was adopted by Antiochus, see the general note above.

For the distinction between right action (*recte factum*; τὸ κατόρθωμα), action undertaken and selections made which are in accordance with nature and flow from (only) the sage's virtuous disposition, and appropriate action (*officium*; τὸ καθῆκον), action capable of a reasonable explanation, in accordance with nature, but not flowing from a virtuous disposition, see Stob., *Ecl.* II.7, pp. 85.13–86.4 (= *SVF* iii.494 = LS 59B), which defines appropriate action as 'consequentiality in life, i.e. that which, once done, has a reasonable explanation' (τὸ ἀκόλουθον ἐν ζωῇ, ὃ πραχθὲν εὔλογον ἀπολογίαν ἔχει), and right action as 'activities in accordance with virtue' (τὰ κατ' ἀρετὴν ἐνεργήματα). On the relationship between right action, appropriate action, and vicious action, cf. Brennan (2005: 181 n. 7): 'Every action is either vicious, if done by a non-Sage, or virtuous, if done by a Sage—and there is no third class of people, either (since progressors are non-Sages).... The case is again like *katalêpsis*, which some texts say is "on the border between" or "intermediate between" knowledge and opinion, but which more careful texts clearly show divides its instances between these two types exhaustively and without remainder.'

In contexts where a word is at issue qua technical term, *uocabulum* is preferred over *uerbum* and *nomen*, but the distinction is not a firm one. In many contexts the difference between *uerba* and *uocabula* can be compared with that between 'Worte' and 'Wörter' in German, i.e. meaningful words in the context of an utterance vs words as the material a language is made of. Cf. e.g. Schultz (1856: 175); Döderlein (1852: 182); Hyman (2005). For the contrast *uocabulum–res* ('terminology-substance'), cf. also Varro, *L.L.* 10.6. Tacitus used this sense of *uocabulum* to promote attention to linguistic usage as a manifestation of the principate and its rules and mechanisms; see Haynes (2004). Cf. *Ac.* 1.17 *init.*, where *uocabula* and *nomina* feature in the same sentence (and *nomina* seems to be used for variation).

For the notion of inappropriate action see the general note above. *Contra officium* is just a prepositional phrase (also in *Off.* 1.19, 1.32, 3.43), i.e. *contra* cannot function as a negation (*pace* Reid[1] p. 151).

I print *seruata* with Lambinus rather than *conseruata* with Plasberg[1]. Cicero used both in relevant contexts with *officia* or *officium* (for *seruare*, see e.g. *Fin.* 4.15; *Off.* 1.34). 'Lambinus' also emended *putabat* to *ponebat*, but *ponere* is used in the previous and in the following sentence, and *putabat* is an innocuous variation.

§38

Cumque superiores...hic omnes in ratione ponebat: in *Ac.* 1.38–39a four changes in the field of ethics made by Zeno are introduced, but a prefatory sentence is absent. However, four instances of adversative *cum(que)* structure the passage; Reid[1] (p. 147) regards the repetition as inelegant. In *Ac.* 1.20 Varro had not spelt out how the types of goods distinguished and corresponding to virtues are connected with a particular psychology (see ad loc.). A view of the soul which envisages a rational and an irrational part (or parts) would be likely to ascribe only intellectual virtues to the former (thus Aristotle), whereas, or so Varro says, Zeno ascribed 'virtue in general' or 'virtue as a whole' (note the singular *omnem uirtutem*) to reason, i.e. the soul's ruling part.

For Antiochus' view as featured in Piso's speech in *Fin.* (5.36), see on *Ac.* 1.20 *init.* On the Stoic view, see Long (1996b).

Superiores must refer here to the *ueteres*, whose position (the *prima forma* of *Ac.* 1.33a) Zeno is diverging from (*superiores* also in §34, in the present § below, twice, §42). There is no suggestion that only the Peripatetics are meant and that the successors of Plato within the Academy already held a version of Zeno's view. See also Bonazzi (2007a: 123–4).

Gigon translates *in ratione esse* as 'haben ihren Ursprung im Verstand', which is less than Cicero has Varro say.

Cumque illi ea genera...nec id ullo modo fieri posse disserebat: the distinction between intellectual and other virtues, dispositions of different parts of the soul, allows for the possibility that a subject has, or has developed, some virtues but not others, esp. if the point of reference are ordinary decent people rather than the sage as envisaged by the Stoics. Zeno, by contrast, assumed all virtues to be mutually dependent (i.e. that there was ἀντακολουθία of virtues), and this view was adopted by Antiochus, too; cf. Piso in *Fin.* 5.67: *Atque haec coniunctio confusioque uirtutum tamen a philosophis ratione quadam distinguitur. Nam cum ita copulatae conexaeque sint, ut omnes omnium participes sint nec alia ab alia possit separari, tamen proprium suum cuiusque munus est, ut fortitudo in laboribus periculisque cernatur, temperantia in praetermittendis uoluptatibus, prudentia in dilectu bonorum et malorum, iustitia in suo cuique tribuendo. Quando igitur inest in omni uirtute cura quaedam quasi foras spectans aliosque appetens atque complectens, existit illud, ut amici, ut fratres, ut propinqui, ut affines, ut ciues, ut omnes denique—quoniam unam societatem hominum esse uolumus—propter se expetendi sint. Atqui eorum nihil est eius generis, ut sit in fine atque extremo bonorum.* See the general note above for modern studies.

The thesis that all virtues are mutually dependent and can only be possessed together raises various questions which are not addressed here or in *Fin.* 5.67. For instance, any technical expertise that the sage has will not just be a τέχνη but an ἐπιστήμη and a virtue. See e.g. Menn (1995) on physics as a virtue. This raises the question of the extent to which sagehood depends on having absorbed discursive knowledge, i.e. of having acquired certain kinds of expertise.

Reid[1] (p. 147) quotes on *seiungi* Arist., *N.E.* Z13, 1144b33–4: ...ᾧ διαλεχθείη τις ἂν ὅτι χωρίζονται ἀλλήλων αἱ ἀρεταί, 'a passage in which a close approach is made to the Stoic view'. The correspondence appears to be coincidental, given that Zeno's 'predecessors' are cited for a view which is different from Zeno's; see the previous n. on *superiores*.

Nec uirtutis usum modo…quin ea semper uteretur: = *SVF* i.199. Syntactically this is still part of what precedes, i.e. an accusative with infinitive governed by *disserebat*. The intended contrast appears to be that between virtue as an activity (ἐνέργεια, cf. *uirtutis usus* here and *Ac*. 1.21 *init*.) and virtue as a disposition (διάθεσις, cf. *ipsum habitum*), which makes Aristotle the target in particular; cf. e.g. the view that the ἔργον of a human being consists in activity of the rational part of the soul in accordance with virtue (*N.E.* A6, 1097b22–1098a20). That Aristotle regarded virtue—on a different level of description—as a ἕξις is not directly at issue, and in contrasting ἕξεις and διαθέσεις he did not rely on the same conception of διάθεσις as the Stoics (cf. *Met*. Δ19–20, 1022b1–14).

In saying that virtue is a disposition (sc. of the soul's ruling part of the sage) Zeno stresses that it is a perfectly stable state of knowledge, incapable of alteration or enhancement, to be achieved at the end point of the προκόπτων's progress towards wisdom (cf. *Fin*. 3.48:…*item qui processit aliquantum ad uirtutis habitum nihilo minus in miseria est quam ille, qui nihil processit*). See Roskam (2005). Progress towards wisdom requires the gradual elimination of beliefs which resulted from assent to non-cataleptic impressions. In that sense virtue *is* the disposition. Cf. Plut., *Virt. mor.* ch. 3, 441c–d (= *SVF* i.202); and on *Ac*. 1.40–2; *Luc*. 145–6.

But what virtue actually does is make selections, and φρόνησις is defined as knowledge of what to do and what not to do (cf. e.g. Stob., *Ecl.* II.7, p. 59.4–5 Wachsmuth = *SVF* iii.262 = LS 61H1: ἐπιστήμη ὧν ποιητέον καὶ οὐ ποιητέον καὶ οὐδετέρων). This is not purely theoretical knowledge, which the sage rejoices in while not actually doing anything. Hence the insistence that virtue is only present in those who use it. Cf. Stob., *Ecl.* II.7, p. 99.2–7 Wachsmuth (= *SVF* i.216): (There are two kinds of human beings, virtuous and wicked ones)…καὶ τὸ μὲν τῶν σπουδαίων διὰ παντὸς τοῦ βίου χρῆσθαι ταῖς ἀρεταῖς, τὸ δὲ τῶν φαύλων ταῖς κακίαις, 'The virtuous use their virtues throughout their life, bad people use wickedness.' See also Bénatouïl (2007: 154–5) on the overall import of *Ac*. 1.38. On the question of whether the art leaves the practitioner (orator, doctor) when it is not enacted, in a Stoicizing context, see Quint. 2.18.3–4.

For the ellipsis *ut superiores*, cf. *Luc*. 124: *ut Xenocrates*. For the reference of *superiores* see on *Ac*. 1.38 *cumque superiores*. The expression *nec…uirtutem cuiquam adesse*, for which cf. Quint. 2.5.23 *fin*. and Tac. *Agr*. 32.1, seems an unusual way of saying that nobody is virtuous (sc. who is not constantly behaving virtuously); Cicero may have chosen it to underline that Zeno conceived of virtue as a *habitus*.

Cumque perturbationem animi…hic omnibus his quasi morbis uoluit carere sapientem: *illi* are the *superiores* (i.e. the *ueteres*), *hic* is Zeno. The Old Academic and Stoic attitudes to emotion are the subject of *Luc*. 137 and discussed ad loc.; see also Bénatouïl (2016a: 70–1) on possible Stoic reactions to Aristotelian thinking about emotions. *Perturbatio* generically of 'emotion' (= πάθος) is paralleled elsewhere (e.g. *Tusc*. 4.8, 11, 124), and there is no need for Walker's emendation *perturbationes*, as Reid[1] (p. 148) notes. The resumption with the plural *ea* can be paralleled, too. For the fourfold Stoic division of πάθη (λύπη, ἐπιθυμία, φόβος, ἡδονή) and the Latin translations used by Cicero, see p. 227. For *in angustum deducere* and related phrases, see *OLD* s.v. *angustus* no. 1d. Reid[1] (p. 148) notes that *morbus* can sometimes function as a synonym of *perturbatio* (thus *Tusc.* 4.23, but rejected in *Fin.* 3.35 in favour of *perturbatio*), but here Varro's point clearly depends on the two being different: emotions are deemed to be almost like mental illness. Other references to mental illness in *Luc.* 48, 52, 88–9, 90. See also Leavy (1997); Nordenfelt (1997). If Antiochus had intended to link Zeno's view that the sage be free of passions with a Platonic text, so as to present Zeno's suggested modifications of the *prima forma* as informed by Plato's *ubertas* (*Ac.* 1.17), then *Phaed.* 83b would have fit the bill. (Cicero translates a short passage from the *Phaedo* in *Tusc.* 1.103.)

§39

Cumque eas perturbationes...ne his quidem assentiebatur: §38 was about tightly controlling passions; §39a is about their analysis. For general orientation, see Frede (1986: 97–110). For the philosophical issue and Antiochus' position relative to the Stoic one, see the general note above; *ne his quidem assentiebatur* signals surprise or even disapproval on the part of Varro (and hence, we may assume, Antiochus) that Zeno deviated on this point. See also Bonazzi (2007a: 123–4). With *antiqui*, cf. *superiores* in *Ac.* 1.38 and p. 226 above. For the Platonic view of the soul, cf. *Tusc.* 4.10, where the soul is said to be bipartite—cf. *aliaque in parte...*, *alia* here—according to Plato; on the further subdivision in the irrational part see *Div.* 1.61; *Tusc.* 1.20: *Eius doctor Plato triplicem finxit animum, cuius principatum, id est rationem, in capite sicut in arce posuit, et duas partes parere uoluit, iram et cupiditatem, quas locis disclusit: iram in pectore, cupiditatem supter praecordia locauit.* For general orientation on the psychological views discussed in Platonic dialogues, see Lorenz (2009). Elsewhere Cicero makes no general pronouncement on what he takes Aristotle's view on the question of the soul and its parts (or powers) to be, but see on 1.39b; Arist., *An.* B3 with Johansen (2012: 47–72). There is, however, no reason to think that Cicero's knowledge of Aristotle's psychology came from the study of Aristotle's treatises; he will have had access to summaries in doxographical handbooks. Whether the Antiochian source material which underlies the present passage was informed by a direct study of Aristotelian works is hard to say; see the general note on *Ac.* 1.19–23. Reid[1] (p. 149) on the omission of *in* before *alia (rationem)*.

Nam et perturbationes uoluntarias esse putabat...Haec fere de moribus: *perturbationes* are voluntary because assent is voluntary; see Brittain (2014) on how to reconcile this notion with the compulsion to assent at least to cataleptic impressions which is mentioned in the sources, and *Ac.* 1.40 on assent being *in nobis posita et uoluntaria*. Emotions are due to *opinio* because they are based on false judgements; for the Stoic conception of δόξα as assent to the non-cataleptic, see on *Luc.* 78 and 148, but in the case of emotions only one type of non-cataleptic impressions (i.e. false ones) are at issue. With *perturbationum...intemperantiam*, cf. *Tusc.* 4.22: *Omnium autem perturbationum fontem esse dicunt intemperantiam, quae est [a] tota mente a recta ratione defectio, sic auersa a praescriptione rationis, ut nullo modo adpetitiones animi* *nec regi nec contineri queant. Quem ad modum igitur temperantia sedat adpetitiones et efficit, ut eae rectae rationi pareant, conseruatque considerata iudicia mentis, sic huic inimica intemperantia omnem animi statum infiammat conturbat incitat, itaque et aegritudines et metus et reliquae perturbationes omnes gignuntur ex ea.* Graver (2002: 147) surveys the different uses of Greek term corresponding to *intemperantia* (ἀκολασία). With its occurrence here, cf. 'uncontrolled reason' (ἀκόλαστος λόγος) in Plut., *Virt. mor.* 441d (cited above, p. 227). Reid[1] (p. 149) assembles parallels for phrases involving *mater* with a genitive, including from contexts where Cicero is very unlikely to be working from any Greek source (e.g. *De orat.* 2.171: *luxuries auaritiae mater*). Graeser (1975: 154): 'Für den Fall, daß Cicero nicht einfach eine Formulierung wie "τὴν ἀκολασίαν εἶναι μητέρα τῶν παθῶν" vor Augen hätte, wäre diese Ausdrucksweise ja insofern glücklich, als es in der Tat die gestörte Seelenspannung ist (vgl. Galen, *De Hipp. et Plat. Plac.* 377.5–7), die zutreffenden Behauptungen im Bereich der Wert-Urteile unmöglich macht und entsprechend unangemessene ὁρμαί hervorbringt.' With *opinionisque iudicio suscipi*, cf. *Tusc.* 3.80 (on Chrysippus): *Edocuit tamen ratio, ut mihi quidem uidetur, cum hoc ipsum proprie non quaereretur hoc tempore, num quod esset malum nisi quod idem dici turpe posset, tamen ut uideremus, quicquid esset in aegritudine mali, id non naturale esse, sed uoluntario iudicio et* **opinionis errore contractum**. For *opinio*, cf. *Ac.* 1.41.

A question to which the evidence does not clearly speak is the perceived gap between what is commonly understood by 'emotional state' and the Stoic analysis of emotions, i.e. the question of whether getting worked up by a false belief *is* having the belief. With the concluding phrase, cf. *Att.* 16.4.2 (= SB 411): *haec fere de Sexto*.

De naturis autem sic sentiebat...non adhiberet: Reid[1] (p. 149) suggests that the plural *naturae* corresponds to οὐσίαι, but the sequence *naturis...initiiis...quintam hanc naturam* suggests that 'element' is meant in each case. For *naturae* = στοιχεῖα, cf. *N.D.* 2.84: *naturis his ex quibus omnia constant*; *Tusc.* 1.66. *Sentire* is used for *uariatio* and means 'to hold a view'; see also on *Luc.* 65 *fin.* The fifth element is called the *quintum genus (e quo essent astra mentesque)* in *Ac.* 1.26 and specifically ascribed to Aristotle, as, or so I think, his contribution to the *prima forma* of philosophy which was then embraced by others. What can be meant by *superiores* in *superiores...rebantur* is determined by occurrences of the term in what precedes, and by the occurrence in the next sentence: predecessors of Zeno minus Xenocrates must be at issue (see above, p. 226). Cicero and his source may have thought that αἰθήρ, recognized apparently in addition to the traditional four elements in *Tim.* 58d, anticipated the fifth element; see on *Ac.* 1.26.

On the view itself, cf. *Tusc.* 1.22, which, however, is no Antiochian context and is not strictly incompatible with *Ac.* 1.26 and the present passage: *Aristoteles, longe omnibus (Platonem semper excipio) praestans et ingenio et diligentia, cum quattuor nota illa genera principiorum esset complexus, e quibus omnia orerentur, quintam quandam naturam censet esse, e qua sit mens; cogitare enim et prouidere et discere et docere et inuenire aliquid et tam multa [alia] meminisse, amare odisse, cupere timere, angi laetari, haec et similia eorum in horum quattuor generum inesse nullo putat; quintum genus adhibet uacans nomine et sic ipsum animum* ἐνδελέχειαν *appellat nouo nomine quasi quandam continuatam motionem et perennem*; also 1.41, 1.65; *Fin.* 4.12 (= *SVF* i.134).

Once again Varro's expression is compressed, and the phrase *sensus et mentem effici* is somewhat zeugmatic, in that the fifth element accounts for or enables sense perception but constitutes the mind.

Statuebat enim ignem esse ipsam naturam...et mentem atque sensus: for *ipsam* to give suitable emphasis, it must modify not just the noun *naturam* but also the relative clause which depends on it. The view itself is abundantly documented; see the texts assembled under no. 46 in Long and Sedley (1987).

Reid[1] (p. 151) observes correctly that *et...atque* is not used by Cicero for *et...et* and that sense is best served if *et* has the force of *etiam*. However, he then emends *et* to *etiam* on the grounds that *et* for *etiam* was not Ciceronian; see contra Hofmann-Szantyr p. 483.

Discrepabat etiam ab iisdem...quod efficeretur posse esse non corpus: = *SVF* i.90. For my overall interpretation of this sentence, including the reference of *superiores*, see the general note above. For *discrepare* used of disagreements, cf. *Tusc.* 4.61. For the Stoic view that only bodies can give rise to effects because only they are capable of acting on something, see the texts collected under no. 55 in Long and Sedley (1987) (with Frede 1987e and Brunschwig 1994), and no. 45 for the conception of body involved; Antiochus would have found it easy to present the Stoic conception of a body (and of a cause) as the result of superior interpretation of Platonic texts (see section 7.2). On the discussion about whether the capacity to act and be acted upon is a defining feature of body according to the Stoics, see Betegh (2015: 136 n. 10). That Xenocrates held the soul not to be a body is presumably seen as an implication of his definition of 'soul' (Arist., *De an.* A2, 404b27–30: ἀριθμὸς ἑαυτὸν κινῶν = frg. 60 Heinze = frg. 85 Isnardi Parente); cf. *Luc.* 124. The relative clause *ab ea quae expers esset corporis* might seem a somewhat expansive way of saying 'from that (*natura*) which is not a body (sc. in the Stoic sense)', but in *Luc.* 139 Cicero speaks of two views which amount to being only body or only soul in the following way:...*Aristippus quasi animum nullum habeamus corpus solum tuetur, Zeno quasi corporis simus expertes animum solum complectitur*, and the point is only fully revealed later in the sentence here in 1.39b. The shift from *mens* 'mind' in the previous sentence to *animus* 'soul' in the present one reflects the fact that the Xenocratean view alluded to was about the soul; on this point, see Inwood (2012: 205). For collocations like *non corpus*, where the negation functions like a privative suffix, see the parallels assembled by Reid[1] (p. 151); Wackernagel (2009: 731); and Pinkster i.685–6; contrast e.g. *N.D.* 1.68 (addressed to an Epicurean): *Ita enim dicebas, non corpus esse in deo, sed quasi corpus, nec sanguinem, sed tamquam sanguinem.*

§§40–42

Varro now introduces Zeno's views on epistemology, which Cicero in §43, for reasons which are not immediately obvious (see ad loc.), characterizes as a 'correction of the Old Academy rather than a new doctrine' (*correctionem ueteris Academiae potius quam aliquam nouam disciplinam*). The conclusion of Varro's speech in §42 *fin.* suggests that the elements of Zenonian epistemology which Varro has laid out represent the extent of Zeno's disagreement with his 'predecessors' (*Atque in his fere commutatio constitit omnis dissensioque Zenonis a superioribus*).

What both terms—'correction' as well as 'modification'—suggest is that what Varro is offering here is not an account of Zeno's epistemology from first principles, but rather a characterization with reference to the earlier discussion of λογική in *Ac.* 1.30-2. *Ac.* 1.39, on the changes which Zeno made in the field of physics, does meet this expectation, in that it clearly refers back to 1.26 and keys Zeno's changes to the exposition there.[252]

There would have been various ways in which Zeno's epistemology could have been presented with reference to *Ac.* 1.30-2, including that for Zeno the objects of perception are stable, that the evidence from the senses is in most cases reliable, and that the cataleptic impression is defined in such and such a way (especially considering that this is the first time that the cataleptic impression features in the final edition). Instead we learn that according to Zeno perception in a narrow sense does not give us knowledge, that one needs the mind's contribution in the form of assent, and that in fact only a sub-set of perceptions are reliable (namely those which reveal their objects in a peculiar way). Moreover, an individual item of knowledge can only be called *scientia* when it is unassailable by argument, which means that it has to be integrated with other items of knowledge in the mind so as to issue in a knowledgeable state.[253] This is arguably a way of presenting Zeno's position which aligns it as much as is credible with that of the *prima forma* of the *ueteres* in *Ac.* 1.30-2 while modifying and correcting it (see below).[254]

I had suggested in the commentary on *Ac.* 1.30-2 that Plato's *Theaetetus* is to be placed highly in the hierarchy of Platonic intertexts referenced in that section, specifically a passage in which Socrates dismisses the notion that knowledge is to be found in perception by suggesting that, in processing the deliverances of the senses, the mind applies κοινά to αἰσθήσεις (from which said κοινά cannot have arisen, given how αἰσθήσεις are characterized). I shall be suggesting that references to Platonic dialogues and to *Tht.* in particular, notably including the section referenced in 1.30-2, can plausibly be claimed for the present passage, too. On this reading Varro is implicitly promoting the idea that Zeno's changes themselves relied on the adoption and pursuit of philosophical options which feature in *Tht.* Since that text may be assumed to have been foundational for the sceptical Academy in virtue of the fact that it is an aporetic dialogue on the possibility of knowledge,[255] Antiochus would

---

[252] Bonazzi (2012: 313-14) suggests that 'modification', 'correction', and even more so 'innovation' (1.40: *dixit noua*) are designed to invite disapproval in the present context: 'For the problem was not so much to correct the philosophy of the ancients as to recover and articulate it. Hence a better interpretation is to read these words as conveying a charge against the typically Stoic pretence of modifying the doctrines of the ancients in order to integrate them into the Stoic system. Neither here nor elsewhere are Stoic innovations ever explicitly approved.' Such a reading seems hard to reconcile with the substantial agreement of *Ac.* 1.40-2 with Lucullus' speech in *Luc.* (cf. Brittain 2012: passim), and the significant gulf between the epistemology of the Ancients in *Ac.* 1.30-2 and Zeno's here in 1.40-2. Glucker (1978: 82) speaks of a 'welcome "correction"' by Zeno (but offers an account of the nature of the correction which is different from mine).

[253] The Cicero character deploys this view against the Stoic position in *Luc.* 144-5.

[254] Existing scholarship tends not to investigate how 1.40-2 could be read as a modification of what is reported in 1.30-2 rather than as an altogether alternative approach; see, however, Reinhardt (2018).

[255] See the general note on *Ac.* 1.30-33a, esp. p. 191 n. 195.

here be trying to reclaim it for his Old Academy. He would be doing this primarily in two ways: (i) by deriving the impression/assent distinction from *Tht.* and (ii) by suggesting that in formulating his definition of the cataleptic impression Zeno took his cue from an option entertained at the very end of the dialogue, which is found wanting by Socrates, too, but which Zeno may be viewed to have developed and improved. Deriving Stoic doctrine from a Platonic dialogue, and from *Tht.* in particular, would also bolster Antiochus' claim that the Old Academy and the Stoics belong to *one* tradition.

The connection I posited between *Tht.* and *Ac.* 1.30-2 had not been fully developed before (but Long 1995 had pointed out important correspondences).[256] However, that Zeno's doctrine of the cataleptic impression is likely to be inspired by certain passages in Plato's *Tht.* has been suggested by various scholars,[257] who would then invoke *Ac.* 1.40-2 as one of the passages containing information on the doctrine. Beyond that, it is arguable that the relevant correspondences were probably *appreciated* if not by Cicero then by the Antiochian source material Cicero was relying on, and served an ideological purpose.

In 1.40 the notions of impression and assent are introduced. *De sensibus* **ipsis** makes it clear that one of the Zenonian changes relates to the conception of the senses themselves (see n. below).[258] As the following relative clause shows, *sensus* here has a broader sense, as 'the senses' are said to be a combination of the impression and assent to it. In *quasi accepta sensibus* below we then have a more narrow sense, since the reference is to the impression prior to assent being given.

In *Tht.* 184a-186, referred to in *Ac.* 1.30-2 (on my argument; see ad loc.), an initially broader and unanalysed notion of αἴσθησις is differentiated into αἰσθήσεις in a narrow sense, i.e. mere παθήματα of the body (186c2), and the mind's application of κοινά to αἰσθήσεις in perceptual judgements.[259] It is plausible to think that Varro's distinction here, while different—Zeno is assumed to be modifying the *prima forma*—, is intended to be reminiscent of that alluded to in *Ac.* 1.30-2. It is tempting to go further and note that Antiochus might have linked Stoic impressions with the mind's application of κοινά to αἰσθήσεις in perceptual judgements in *Tht.*, in virtue of the fact that Stoic impressions have propositional content.

Moreover, Antiochus could also have argued that certain Platonic texts inspired the Stoic conception of assent. One only needs to read on from *Tht.* 184a-186 and into the discussion of whether knowledge is true belief to come across a passage which could have provided inspiration for the Stoic notion of assent (189e6-190a6):

Λόγον ὃν αὐτὴ πρὸς αὑτὴν ἡ ψυχὴ διεξέρχεται περὶ ὧν ἂν σκοπῇ. ὥς γε μὴ εἰδώς σοι ἀποφαίνομαι. τοῦτο γάρ μοι ἰνδάλλεται διανοουμένη οὐκ ἄλλο τι ἢ διαλέγεσθαι, αὐτὴ ἑαυτὴν ἐρωτῶσα καὶ ἀποκρινομένη, καὶ φάσκουσα καὶ οὐ φάσκουσα. ὅταν δὲ ὁρίσασα, εἴτε βραδύτερον εἴτε καὶ ὀξύτερον ἐπάξασα, τὸ αὐτὸ ἤδη φῇ καὶ μὴ διστάζῃ, δόξαν

---

[256] See also Reinhardt (2018).   [257] See Ioppolo (1990: 438-41); Long (2002).
[258] In 1.40-2 I can detect no criticism of the enhanced role Zeno accorded to the senses, *pace* Bonazzi (2012: 318-19).
[259] See Burnyeat (1976: 45-50); Frede (1987a).

ταύτην τίθεμεν αὐτῆς. ὥστ᾽ ἔγωγε τὸ δοξάζειν λέγειν καλῶ καὶ τὴν δόξαν λόγον εἰρημένον, οὐ μέντοι πρὸς ἄλλον οὐδὲ φωνῇ, ἀλλὰ σιγῇ πρὸς αὑτόν.

[Context: Socrates had asked if Theaetetus means the same thing by 'thinking'—διανοεῖσθαι—as he does, and then clarifies.] A talk which the soul has with itself about the objects under its consideration. Of course, I'm only telling you my idea in all ignorance; but this is the kind of picture I have of it. It seems to me that the soul when it thinks is simply carrying on a discussion in which it asks itself questions and answers them itself, affirms and denies. And when it arrives at something definite, either by a gradual process or a sudden leap, when it affirms one thing consistently and without divided counsel, we call this its judgement. So, in my view, to judge is to make a statement, and a judgement is a statement which is not addressed to another person or spoken aloud, but silently addressed to oneself. (transl. Levett)

This is one of several passages in which belief formation is characterized as a three-step process, involving an appearance, an interrogation of the appearance, and an assertion based on the appearance; cf. also *Phileb.* 38b12–39a7; *Soph.* 263e3–264a2. The Stoics need not have thought that every act of assent is the result of an actual internal dialogue the perceiving subject has conducted, but this aspect of Plato's account may serve the purpose of dramatization, and any act of automatic assent could probably be rationalized into something like the dialogue Socrates envisages. It is plausible on independent grounds that the Stoics looked to passages like *Tht.* 189e6–190a6 when they devised the notion of assent,[260] and it is entirely conceivable that Antiochus was aware of this and used the insight to advance his suggestion that Zeno's changes in the area of epistemology are modifications of the *prima forma* of philosophy (*Ac.* 1.33a)—modifications which are just better than earlier attempts by the *ueteres* at isolating what is right within the *ubertas* that Plato's dialogues represent (*Ac.* 1.17).[261]

The model of perception which assumes a perceptible object or state of affairs impinging on the perceiving individual and the perceiver assenting to the resulting impression, thereby employing the mind or reason (*assensum adiungit animorum*), does thus not emerge in *Ac.* 1.40 as a flat disagreement with the *ueteres* on the value of sense perception, but as a version of the view put forward at *Ac.* 1.30–2: reason (the *animus*) has to be involved for knowledge to be obtained from the senses. When Varro says a little later *quod autem erat sensu comprensum id ipsum sensum appellabat* (i.e. the Stoics define αἴσθησις as sc. the mind's assent to a cataleptic impression; see n. below), this may be seen to underline that there is agreement between the *ueteres* and the Stoics on the point of the inertness of the senses by themselves and narrowly conceived, and that to some extent the perceived disagreement on the value of the senses is a matter of terminology only.[262]

---

[260] Thus Vogt (2012: 84–5); Togni (2013); Moss (2014: 228–36), who shows how something like the impression/assent distinction is foregrounded in *Tht.* 184–7, i.e. the section which I take to be the primary intertextual reference in *Ac.* 1.30–2.

[261] See also section 7.2.

[262] This would be a standard reconciliation strategy of Antiochus'. I had also suggested above that in *Ac.* 1.30–2 a reading of *Tht.* is presupposed which takes the objects of the senses to be subject to flux and divisible into constituents; see on 1.42.

In §41 *init.* Varro continues that not all impressions are held to be reliable by Zeno, but only a species of them. The distinguishing feature of a cataleptic impression is named here (*...is solum quae propriam quandam haberent declarationem earum rerum quae uiderentur*), and the actual term of a mark or sign which singles out the cataleptic impression is used elsewhere in *Ac.* (*nota* in e.g. *Luc.* 33). Long (2002: 124) has pointed to a correspondence between, on the one hand, the Zenonian suggestion that a cataleptic impression has a distinctive feature, namely the particular way in which it reveals the object and its features and, on the other, the third part of *Tht.*, where the claim that knowledge is 'true belief with a λόγος' is probed, and λόγος is on the third attempt explained as a mark or sign (σημεῖον, διαφορά) which uniquely characterizes a particular object (208b12–210b3). In the *Tht.* this conception of knowledge, with this interpretation of λόγος, is rejected, too—it offers no method or reasoned procedure for achieving such differentiation—,[263] but arguably the Stoics had gone some way towards providing such a method for perceptual presentations, by naming and conceptualizing properties which are distinctive of self-warranting impressions. The examples given in the *Tht.* passage are actually the kind of properties the Stoics would hope to grasp (Theaetetus' snub nose and bulging eyes, 209b10–c2), in line with the dialogue's practice of drawing its examples from the perceptible world. In *Tht.* 209c4–9 Socrates suggests that no sooner will he have a true judgement featuring Theaetetus than when Theaetetus' snubness has left a mark imprinted on him which is different from everybody else's snubness;[264] this invites comparison both with the notion that cataleptic impressions are imprints of objects or states of affairs left on the mind (see on *Luc.* 18; section 5), and the Stoic notion that there is a peculiar quality characterizing every individual (ἴδια ποιότης; see on *Luc.* 84). In the context of the suggested attempt at reclaiming the *Tht.* from the Academics, and given that Varro introduces Zeno's 'improvements', it would make good sense if Antiochus had thought that Zeno was able to overcome the final aporia of the dialogue because he did furnish a theory of the kind identified as a desideratum by Socrates.

After a dialogical interlude in which *comprehendibile* is approved as translation for καταληπτόν (see n. below), the rest of the section down to §42 *fin.* is concerned with the role the cataleptic impressions play in Stoic epistemology more generally. There are thus points of contact with Lucullus' speech in *Luc.* 20–7, which treats the issue systematically rather than historically and must have had its counterpart in Book 3 of the final edition (see section 9.2 and the relevant fragments). In introducing *comprehensio* as a translation of κατάληψις, Varro alludes to Zeno's hand simile, which is properly introduced in *Luc.* 145 (see the comm.) and is likely to have featured in a later passage in the final edition, too. Here the allusion would be recognizable only to

---

[263] See e.g. Sedley (2004: 174–5) on this point.
[264] Ἀλλ' οὐ πρότερόν γε, οἶμαι, Θεαίτητος ἐν ἐμοὶ δοξασθήσεται, πρὶν ἂν ἡ σιμότης αὕτη τῶν ἄλλων σιμοτήτων ὧν ἐγὼ ἑώρακα διάφορόν τι μνημεῖον παρ' ἐμοὶ ἐνσημηναμένη κατάθηται—καὶ τἆλλα οὕτω ἐξ ὧν εἶ σύ—ἤ με, καὶ ἐὰν αὔριον ἀπαντήσω, ἀναμνήσει καὶ ποιήσει ὀρθὰ δοξάζειν περὶ σοῦ, 'It will not, I take it, be Theaetetus who is judged in my mind until this snub-nosedness of yours has left imprinted and established in me a record that is different in some way from the other snub-nosednesses I have seen; and so with the other details of your make-up. And this will remind me, if I meet you to-morrow, and make me judge correctly about you' (transl. Levett).

someone familiar with the simile and is not taken further. In commenting that the terminology—κατάληψις—was new and that Zeno was talking about 'new things' (noua), Varro alludes to the Antiochian τόπος that Stoic innovations on the Old Academic heritage in the narrow sense were largely terminological, but in this case substantial innovation is not disputed.

When Varro then comes to relate *comprehensio* (κατάληψις), *scientia* (ἐπιστήμη), *opinio* (δόξα), and *notio* (ἔννοια) to one another, the discussion is looking back to Ac. 1.30-2, where the last three terms featured. Everything to do with the senses was there dismissed as the *pars opinabilis rerum*, and knowledge located in the notions in the mind as well as the mind's calculations about them. For Zeno a particular sense perception is a *sensus* proper only when it has issued in an apprehension, which is the result of an assent to a cataleptic impression. An apprehension is an individual *scientia* (ἐπιστήμη) only when it is deeply interconnected with other apprehensions, so that it cannot be dislodged, i.e. dismissed by the subject, through reflection and argument (both are likely to be covered by *ratio*).[265] If an apprehension is not a *scientia* (ἐπιστήμη), i.e. if it is the apprehension of a non-sage (all the sage's καταλήψεις are ἐπιστήμαι), then it is ignorance (*inscientia*, ἄγνοια), or opinion (*opinio*, δόξα), which is a weakly held state (i.e. one can readily be reasoned out of it). There is also opinion which arises from assent to false and non-cataleptic impressions, as Varro observes.[266] That apprehension should be ignorance may appear counterintuitive, given that it represents a state which one could loosely call knowledge, but is entirely in keeping with the stark division between a state of wisdom, peculiar to the sage, and the state all non-sages are in, whether all of their δόξαι are false or just some of them. When in §42 *init.* Varro states that Zeno located apprehension 'between' *scientia* and *inscientia*, what he means is not that there is a third state between the two (called apprehension), so that a subject may be in any one of the three, but rather that apprehension is notionally located between the two, and that any apprehension is either one or the other. That is why it is by itself neither good nor bad (*neque in rectis neque in prauis numerabat*). As for possible connections with *Tht.*, we had discussed above that the notion of assent could be traced to 189e6–190a6. Vogt (2012: chs 3 and 7) has argued that the entire Stoic conception of δόξα as a deficient epistemic state can be traced to the middle section of the dialogue (187b–201c). The Stoic conception of ἐπιστήμη (1.42) shows resemblance with the notion of expertise which Plato employs passim. Socratic exchanges in the early dialogues are predicated on the assumption that an expert ought to have consistent beliefs within the domain of his expertise. In order to be able to tell if his beliefs are consistent, they would normally be expected to be transparent to him: he must be able to tell if he has them. The debate in the *Theaetetus* approaches the subject of knowledge via the subject of expertise (145c-e): Socrates asks Theaetetus what knowledge is, and Theaetetus cites a range of fields of expertise in reply (geometry and mathematics; cobbling and other crafts). However, in *Tht.* expertise is not uniquely the province of the sage.

---

[265] On this point, see the discussion of Stob., *Ecl.* ii.7, p. 74.16 Wachsmuth (= *SVF* iii.112) in Brunschwig (1994b: 81–2).

[266] The present passage is one of our main pieces of evidence on the Stoic conception of δόξα.

When Varro names the reasons (1.42) why a *comprehensio* is deemed *uera et fidelis*, he says *non quod omnia quae esset in re comprehenderet, sed quia nihil quod **cadere in eam** (sc. comprehensionem) posset relinqueret*, offering first a possible reason for consideration (*non quod*), and then endorsing a different one instead (*sed quia*). Reid[1] (p. 155) noted an apparent verbal correspondence with the position of the *ueteres* in 1.31 (of the objects of perception)—*quod essent aut ita paruae ut **sub sensum cadere non possent**—*, which might be intended to invite a reading of the later passage against the former. The rejected reason might look back to the section on physics (1.24–9), in which case Zeno would be said not to derive the truth and reliability of *comprehensiones* from a human ability to grasp the constituent elements of perceivable objects. The endorsed reason might turn on the ἴδια ποιότης of individual objects (mentioned in the previous paragraph), which Zeno did indeed think can be grasped by cataleptic impressions and the apprehensions arising from them. The reference to 1.31 would mark a point of disagreement: all that needs to be grasped by apprehensions is actually grasped, and an apprehension need not grasp anything on the micro-level (where flux as posited in 1.31, or at least a degree of flux; thus flux could remain a possibility, which would, however, not vitiate apprehension).[267]

Notiones, another subject which is resumed from the earlier section, are said to derive from cataleptic impressions that have been assented to.[268] *Ac.* 1.30–2, like *Tht.* 184a–186 regarding the κοινά, was silent on how we come by the *notiones* in which knowledge alone supposedly resides, though in view of what is said about sense perception there, one would assume them to be innate. Aristotle, on my argument above, took a significant if by itself insufficient step when he derived concepts from sense perception (1.33). From there it is but a small step to claiming that only some sense perceptions give rise to *notiones*, and 1.42 *unde postea notiones rerum in animis imprimerentur* is suitably low-key. The following sentence, which refers to the role *notiones* play in the creation of doctrine and discursive knowledge, alludes to what may be deemed common ground. The *Theaetetus* might once again have been invoked for the introduction of concepts arising from sense perception: in the wax-tablet passage, false belief is explained as arising from a failure to match perceptual experiences with memory imprints (σημεῖα; 194d4) which have been formed earlier. The Stoics do use the imprinting imagery which features in the second clause of Zeno's definition for concepts, too.

The penultimate sentence of §42 briefly gestures at the import which Zeno's epistemological views have for his ethics and his conception of wisdom. Varro seems to stress that unwarranted assent qua mental act is incompatible with both (see n. below). By contrast, 1.30–2 remained confined to matters properly pertaining to the field of λογική.

The section ends with the suggestion that what has been discussed represents the extent of Zeno's changes to the earlier tradition. Subjects touched in the earlier section but not mentioned here—which one would read as areas of common ground—include argument theory broadly speaking, including the relationship of rhetoric and dialectic. One can speculate how Antiochus would have construed the historical

---

[267] Contrast my earlier interpretation of the sentence in Reinhardt (2018: 62).
[268] See Reinhardt (2018: 35–6) on Cicero's uses of the term *notio* in Platonic as well as Stoic contexts.

continuities in this area, and in doing so be guided by the account of epistemology from an Antiochian point of view in *Fin.* 4.8–10.[269] Harmonization would in any event have been easier if Plato as interpreted by the Old Academy *as well as the Peripatos* had been compared with Stoic teachings. In *Luc.* 98 Cicero cites Antiochus as his teacher in dialectic, in the conclusion of a section designed to demolish *Stoic* logic, but that may be deemed to be a synchronic context, not one concerned with developments over time. The text which comes closest to giving us an impression of how the required harmonization might have been achieved is chs 4–5 of Alcinous' *Didascalicus,* and even that text is more charitably read as stopping short of claiming that Plato e.g. invented Stoic logic because he uses arguments which can be described or analysed in terms of Stoic logic; see Barnes (2015a: 240–2).

§40

Plurima autem in illa tertia philosophiae parte mutauit: = *SVF* i.55 (cf. i.61) = LS 40B = *FDS* 253 = *FDS* 256 (–42 Zenonis a superioribus). The contrasting *autem* (Pμ) rather than *etiam* (γ) is what sense requires here. The backward reference is to the logical part of the *prima forma* (1.30 *tertia deinde philosophiae pars*...) in the first instance, and to 1.19 (*fuit ergo iam accepta a Platone philosophandi ratio triplex... tertia de disserendo et quid uerum quid falsum quid rectum in oratione prauumue quid consentiens quid repugnet iudicando*). 'Modification' (*mutauit;* cf. e.g. 1.42 *fin.: commutatio*) is one of the notions used by Antiochus to conceptualize discontinuities in what he sees as broadly one philosophical tradition; 'correction' is another (1.43: *correctionem ueteris Academiae*); 'using different terminology for the same thing' is the third. There is no indication whether Varro (or Antiochus) located Zeno's changes in what we call epistemology within a sub-field of λογική, e.g. dialectic; see Castagnoli (2010a: 161 n. 33).

In qua primum de sensibus ipsis...in nobis positam et uoluntariam: as noted by Reid[1] (p. 151) and before him Madvig (1876: 798), the sentence changes its syntactical direction after *extrinsecus*, where the notion of assent would naturally have featured as a second noun phrase parallel to the one built around *impulsione* and adjoined by a connective (Madvig suggests *et ex assensione animorum*). The parenthesis explaining the correspondence *uisum/φαντασία* has a derailing effect; cf. *Off.* 1.153. The change in syntax motivates the resumption *haec quae uisa sunt et quasi accepta sensibus,* which otherwise would have been unnecessary.

De sensibus **ipsis**, 'about the senses themselves', is presumably intended to contrast with the role καταλήψεις play in conceptualizing wisdom, expertise, etc. (1.41-2). *Sensūs* here has a broader sense, comprising—as becomes plain when one reads on—impressions and assent, whereas in *quasi accepta sensibus* below the impression alone is meant (see the general note above); cf. Frede (1987a) on the development of the technical meanings of αἰσθάνεσθαι. The plural could refer to multiple instances of

---

[269] On *Fin.* 4.8–10, see the general note on *Ac.* 1.30–33a.

impressions assented to, by different individuals rather than the same individual (note *adsensionem...animorum* below). Alternatively, different sense modalities could be meant; if so, then the thread is not picked up, and *declaratio rerum* invites a visual reading. The reading *iunctos* is clearly superior to *uinctos*; Reid[1] (p. 151) notes *Tim.* 27 as another instance of *uinctus/iunctus* confusion, and that *iunctus ex* is paralleled in *Fin.* 2.44: *Cum Epicuro autem hoc plus est negotii, quod e duplici genere uoluptatis coniunctus est....*

The phrase *e quadam quasi impulsione extrinsecus* suggests that impressions arise from something external (see *Luc.* 48 *intestinum et oblatum*, on internally and externally generated impressions); cf. Philo, *De mundi opificio* §166, vol. i p. 58.9 Wendland (= *SVF* ii.57): (Αἱ αἰσθήσεις) τὰ φανέντα ἐκτὸς εἴσω κομίζουσαι διαγγέλλουσι καὶ ἐπιδείκνυνται, '(perceptions) bring outside appearances inside, announce them and point them out.' *Impulsio* 'push, thrust' (cf. *OLD* s.v. no. 1; *TLL* s.v. col. 716.43–65) does invite a causal reading more than a representational one (see the introduction, sections 5.1 and 5.2); cf. *Fat.* 46 [subject is 'atoms']: *Aliam enim quandam uim motus habebant a Democrito impulsionis, quam plagam ille appellat, a te, Epicure, grauitatis et ponderis*; and Ioppolo (1990: 434). For the double alienation *quadam quasi*, cf. Reid[1] (p. 121) on 1.21 *hominem enim esse censebant quasi partem quandam ciuitatis*, which Cicero and other writers tend to use (in inverted order) to soften metaphors or to foreshadow translations of Greek terms. The phrase overall specifies a property of the impression rather than the impression itself, which is, depending on the level of description, a physical alteration of the perceiving subject's mind (Alex. Aphr., *De Anim.* p. 68.11 Bruns = *SVF* ii.59; D.L. 7.50) or a thought; see sections 5.2–5.4 of the introduction.

On *uisum* as a rendering of φαντασία, see section 10 and Reinhardt (2016), where it is argued that *uisum* does not just function as stand-in for the Greek term in *Acad.*; rather, Cicero deploys the full range of meanings of *uideri* in his terminological uses of the verb's parts. Thus a *uisum* may be used for a veridical experience, whether visual or not, for an impression which may be true or false, or for a merely phenomenal experience that is indeterminate with respect to veridicality. With our passage here, cf. *Luc.* 18, which refers back to the passage in the *Catulus* where the terminological correspondence was introduced. See also Hartung (1970: 31–9). On the related term *uisio*, see on *Luc.* 33. *Visum* in the sense of 'appearance' was probably used before Cicero (see Reinhardt 2016: 79 and Reinhardt 2018b: 310 n. 18 on Prop. 2.6.27–30 and Verg., *A.* 4.450–6), so *appellemus licet* relates to the deployment of *uisum* as a technical term in philosophical contexts. With *teramus hoc uerbum quidem*... Cicero assigns to Varro a quasi-authorial remark. On the use of *terere*, see *OLD* s.v. no. 4b.

If one does not treat *uisum* as a stand-in for φαντασία, then *quae uisa sunt et quasi accepta sensibus* will refer to objects or states of affairs in the world *and* the impressions they give rise to (or objects as represented in impressions); see Reed (2002) for the suggestion that the Stoics propose a kind of direct realism (for veridical perception), i.e. assume that impressions put human beings directly in touch with the external world. However, assent can only be given to the impression, or even its propositional content. The 'acceptance, as it were, by the senses' must refer to the mind's entertaining a perceptual thought prior to assent being given. Cicero may also be hinting at the fact that the entertaining of a perceptual thought is not deemed to be a purely passive affection of the mind; rather, even then the mind needs to 'do' certain things, like conceptualize the object.

Assensio, unlike *assensus*, which Cicero also uses (but in *Acad.* only in *Luc.*; see the index to the Oxford Classical Text), is a term from the political sphere, where it denotes the expression of approval given to someone's *sententia* in a meeting, notably the senate; see Hellegouarc'h (1972: 122–3). This is comparable to the Greek συγκατάθεσις, which denotes the expression of acceptance of a viewpoint or judgement (συγκατατίθεσθαι is originally transitive and takes τὸν ψῆφον as its natural object, and later becomes intransitive); see Dodds (1959: 320) on Plt., *Grg.* 501c5. The force of the prefix συν-, which originally was functional, i.e. 'to lay down e.g. an opinion with someone else', eventually no longer needed to be felt in the non-philosophical uses. One suspects the same for the Stoic uses of the term, which make no reference to another person; if a force of συγ- was felt in such cases, then the assumption would have to be that the impression represents an object as being in a certain way and the perceiving subject concurs through his assent (thus Stroux 1965: 73). Due to the political resonance, συγκατάθεσις and *assensio* are naturally suitable for communicating the notion that assent means acceptance of a proposition. The assent-related terminology used by Cicero is discussed in some detail by Hartung (1970: 72–8); see also Moreschini (1979: 120). Hartung makes a plausible case that *assensio* is primarily used to denote an individual act of assent, while *assensus* is more general and abstract (cf. *Luc.* 94 *cohibes assensum* with comm.). In *Luc.* both *assensus* and *assensio* are used, but a verbal expression only once in the final edition (1.39 *assentiebatur*). See section 10.3 on the uses of *approbatio*, which can be used in the sense of 'assent', too. Cf. on *Luc.* 104–5, where assent as a mode of endorsement is one subject of discussion; on *Luc.* 93–4, where suspension of judgement is discussed. For assent 'being located in us and voluntary', see the commentary on *Luc.* 37. Further Ioppolo (1990); Goerler (2004f); Frede (2011: 31–48); Meinwald (2011); Brittain (2014); Coope (2016). For suspension of judgement (ἐποχή), i.e. the withholding of assent, see *Luc.* 59. On *adiungit*, see the next note.

Plasberg[1] (pp. 53–4) notes that Plut., *Cic.* 40 (= t. 67) comments on Cicero's innovations in translating Greek philosophical terminology, including φαντασία, ἐποχή, συγκατάθεσις, and κατάληψις. Plut., *Luc.* 42.3–4 (= t. 66; cf. Brittain 2001: 352–3) shows that Plutarch knew *Luc.* In the absence of positive evidence that Plutarch knew the final edition of *Acad.*, it is possible that *Cic.* 40 refers not to our passage, but to its counterpart in the *Catulus*. Related, but not assignable to a particular edition, is Caelius Aurelianus, *Acut. Morb.* 3.13: *Omnis phantasia, cuius diuersitates Latini uisa uocauerunt ut Tullius, siue illa naturalia siue contra naturam fuerint, animi non corporis esse noscuntur*; cf. Macrob., *In Somn.* 1.3.2.

Regarding the variants *teramus* (Γ; Plasberg[1] and Plasberg[2]) and *teneamus* (P; Reid[1]), the former is choicer in that it gestures to the link between acceptability and actual usage.

§41

Visis non omnibus…feretis haec: = *SVF* i.60 (*Visis non omnibus*–§42 *a uirtute sapientiaque remouebat*), i.62 (*Quod autem erat sensu comprehensum…sensum* *appellabat*) = LS 41B (*Quod autem erat sensu comprehensum... a uirtute sapientiaque remouebat*), i.68 (*Si ita erat comprehensum... inscientiam nominabat*). *Adiungere* of the positing of a property in the context of a doctrine (cf. *OLD* s.v. no. 10a); something of this sense may be present in the previous sentence, too, where *adiungit* would otherwise just seem to resume *iunctos*. *Fides* may signify the property of being deserving of credence ('trustworthiness'; *OLD* s.v. no. 9) or a property on which such purported trustworthiness is based ('reliability'; cf. *OLD* s.v. no. 4b), or indeed both; cf. also the discussion of *Luc.* 19 *dum aspectus ipse fidem faciat sui iudicii*.

Declaratio corresponds to ἐνάργεια, and *propria* is reminiscent of Sextus' term ἰδίωμα for the distinctive property of cataleptic impressions, clarity combined with strikingness (cf. *M.* 7.408; *Luc.* 38: *animum perspicuis cedere*); however, *declaratio* designates the property of clarity only secondarily and primarily means the act or ability of making something clear (*haberent* is capable of actualizing both senses). Cataleptic impressions are ex hypothesi self-warranting as a class of perceptual thoughts in virtue of a property each individual impression has, and not in virtue of any relationship with other cataleptic impressions. (Coherentist considerations do, however, enter in connection with the state of *scientia*/ἐπιστήμη, which is peculiar to the sage; see below and *Luc.* 146–7.) The phrase *propriam declarationem rerum habere* captures well that for the Stoics the peculiar clarity of cataleptic impressions is not a property which they have over and above their representational content, but one which manifests itself in the manner in which the object is represented in the impression; this is not captured e.g. by Gigon (p. 303): '...die eine bestimmte eigentümliche Kennzeichnung der durch die Sinne vermittelten Dinge enthielten'. Cf., however, *Luc.* 45: *perspicuitas... magnam habet uim, ut ipsa per sese ea quae sint nobis ita ut sint indicet*. On the Stoic vs the Academic way of conceptualizing clarity, see also section 6 and Reinhardt (2018a). *Declarare* in the sense of 'revealing something that is the case' is inter alia used in physiognomical contexts; cf. Cic., *De orat.* 3.222: *oculos... natura nobis... ad motus animorum declarandos dedit, Div.* 1.2 *fin.*; Catul. 64.34: *declarant gaudia uultu*. The noun *declaratio* is attested in Cicero for the first time, and the three other instances are about the making plain of intentions or states of mind; cf. *Sest.* 122 (56 BC): *declaratio uoluntatis, Fam.* 15.21.2 (= SB 207; December 46 BC): *declaratio amoris tui; Fam.* 10.5.2 (= SB 359; January 43 BC): *declaratio animi tui*. On Greek and Latin terminology for properties of impressions generally, see Lefebvre (2007).

Id autem uisum... is elliptical, but no *erat* or *nominabat* is to be supplied, given that *feretis haec?* is missing an interrogative suffix or particle, too. Reid[1] (p. 152) suggests that *cum ipsum per se cerneretur* means 'when it is discriminated from a false impression by its own inherent characteristics', but the parallel syntax of *cum acceptum iam et approbatum esset* below suggests that 'when it is considered in itself' (*OLD* s.v. *cerno* no. 7), i.e. prior to being assented to, is the intended sense.

Nos uero... καταληπτὸν diceres: cf. *Luc.* 18: ... *id enim uolumus esse* καταληπτόν... Cicero is right that καταληπτός means *comprehendibile*, i.e. 'capable of being grasped', but our Greek sources almost universally call self-warranting impressions καταληπτικός, i.e. 'capable of grasping'. (I have found no good instances for the passive use which existed according to Sandbach 1971: 10.) Reinhardt (2018b) discusses this problem in detail (without offering a simple explanation); cf. also Reinhardt (2016). That Cicero was not confused about what cataleptic impressions are supposed to do may be inferred from the fact that much of his impression-related terminology can be explained with reference to the phrase *percipere uisum*: if *uidere* has its veridical sense here, then the phrase means 'to grasp [cataleptically] the object a cataleptic impression is of *and* the object itself'. It fits with this that the noun *comprehensio* is used in an active (42 *comprehensio... non quod omnia quae essent in re comprehenderet*) as well as a passive sense (41 *comprehensionem appellabat, similem is rebus quae manu prenderentur*) in our passage; see the introductory section on the linguistic form of *Acad.*, section 10.

Atticus' intervention, viz. that he supplies the Greek term whose meaning Varro is seeking to convey in Latin, also invites speculation regarding the communicative situation Cicero envisages with respect to his first readership. While there is no reason to doubt that the philosophical dialogues are introductory in nature and thus intended to be accessible without antecedent knowledge, they also invite readers who are familiar with the Greek background bring their knowledge to bear on the text. Some earlier editors print the emendation *inquam* (first in the Aldina of 1523) for *inquit*, but we know that Atticus was Cicero's companion at least for part of his philosophical training, and he had apparently professed to be delighted at being featured in this way; see also Plasberg[1] (p. 54). *Quonam* conveys mild urgency ('However else... tell me').

Plasberg uses the spelling καταλημπτόν in both editions. We cannot be certain what Cicero wrote; see Schulze (1958: 19–20).

Sed, cum acceptum iam et approbatum esset, comprehensionem appellabat...plurimisque idem nouis uerbis (noua enim dicebat) usus est: see section 10 on the linguistic form of *Acad*. *Accipere* and *approbare* are not synonyms and thus not used for fullness of expression; rather, *accipere* means 'to receive' of the impression only, prior to endorsement, and denotes the mere entertaining of the impression qua thought, since *accipere* is not one of the terms used for assenting. *Approbare* signifies endorsement, i.e. assent in the present case; no reference to approval as discussed in *Luc.* 104 is intended (nor would it be intelligible at this point in the final edition). The position of *iam* is due to it attaching to the focus of the *cum*-clause. On the passive sense of *comprehensio*, see the previous n. On Zeno's hand simile, see *Luc.* 145 (= *SVF* i.66), which is also cast mostly in the imperfect tense (cf. *appellabat* here).

The emphasis on the novelty of the term *comprehensio*/κατάληψις, and of the underlying concept, is not at variance with the possible connection with Plato's *Tht.*, suggested in the general note above. Rather, apprehension could be seen as part of the solution to the final aporia of the dialogue. And κατάληψις is of course a modification of the *prima forma* of philosophy; see on *Ac.* 1.17 and section 7.2 of the introduction.

The Stoics used no synonyms for καταλαμβάνειν and κατάληψις. However, *comprehendere* and *comprehensio*, which might seem to be introduced as sole renderings here, have competing terms in *Acad.*, viz. *perceptio* and *cognitio*. In the extant part of *Ac.* 1 the two occur in a pointedly non-terminological use, i.e. to designate 'knowledge on any conception' in the report of Arcesilaus' dialectical practice (1.45). By contrast, in *Luc.* the two terms feature as equivalents of *comprehensio*. There are occasions where either term by itself represents 'apprehension' generically qua mental act or resulting mental state: in *Luc.* 36 Lucullus concludes the first part of his speech, devoted to apprehension, with *sed de perceptione hactenus*, while in *Luc.* 54 the power of arguments from ἀπαραλλαξία is at issue (*si satis est ad tollendam cognitionem similia esse multa multorum*...). *Perceptio* and *comprehensio* can also occur as a doublet with a connective, apparently for stylistic fullness (*Luc.* 101 with *et*, with *perceptio* in first position; 106 with *-que*, with *comprehensio* in first position). All three terms occur side by side, connected by *aut* and in the sequence *cogn., perc.,* and *compr.*, in *Luc.* 17, and *comprehensio* is singled out there as the term which corresponds to κατάληψις *uerbum e uerbo* (which probably relates to word formation and the meaning of *prehendere*). One might wonder if Cicero reduced these options in the final edition, and if this accounts for the apparent privileging of *comprehensio* in *Ac.* 1.40–1. This seems unlikely for various reasons, one of which is that the neuter participle *incognitum*, associated with *cognoscere* and *cognitio*, has no exact counterpart associated with one of the other two terms, would need *cognoscere/cognitio* for context, and is unlikely to have been abandoned in the final edition (clauses of the form *quod percipi non potest* fulfil a similar function, but are not handy substitutes in all contexts). The remains of *Acad.* do not preserve the moment *perceptio* and *cognitio* were marshalled as synonyms of *comprehensio*. Neither *comprehensio* nor *perceptio* are neologisms: both words are attested from the early first century BC (both terms in *Inv.* 1.79 and 1.36, respectively; in *Inv.* 1.36 and *Rhet. Her.* the sense of *perceptio* is relevantly similar). *Cognitio* has an earlier application as a form of legal procedure; see Kaser and Hackl (1996: 189–90). Cf. also *Fin.* 3.17. Only *comprehensio* is recognizably used by Cicero in an active as well as a passive sense (see previous n.), and only *comprehensio* evokes the Zenonian hand simile (see *Luc.* 144–5). Of the three nouns, only *perceptiones* is used in the plural in the sense of καταλήψεις. In *Luc.* 31 there seems to be a slight contrast between *cognitio* and *comprehensio* (possibly faculty of apprehension vs instances of apprehension). *Visum* can be a grammatical or logical object of *comprehendere* and *percipere*, but not of *cognoscere*. *Comprehendere* and *percipere* have an effective aspect. The adjective *comprehendibile*, on whose relationship to καταληπτικόν and καταληπτόν see above on *nos uero*..., is used only here by Cicero, whose purpose may not have been to create a useable term of art. There are no further parallels in *Acad.* for the use of *constituere* in *Luc.* 23...*nihil haberet comprehendi percepti cogniti constituti*. See also Hartung (1970: 26–30, 34–9); Moreschini (1979: 103–9); and Glucker (2012); the relevant entries in the *TLL* and Merguet.

Quod autem erat sensu comprehensum...quae esset imbecilla ⟨assensio⟩ et cum falso incognitoque communis: see on *uisis non omnibus* above for *SVF* and LS references. For the Stoic definition of perception as assent to a cataleptic impression, cf. D.L. 7.52 (= *SVF* ii.71): Αἴσθησις δὲ λέγεται κατὰ τοὺς Στωικοὺς τό τ' ἀφ' ἡγεμονικοῦ πνεῦμα ἐπὶ τὰς αἰσθήσεις διῆκον καὶ ἡ δι' αὐτῶν κατάληψις..., 'According to the Stoics, the term "perception" is applied to the breath which extends from the commanding faculty to the senses, to the apprehension which comes about through the senses...'; and Aët., *Plac.* 4.8 (= *SVF* ii.72).

A person's apprehensions become ἐπιστῆμαι, and his state one of wisdom, when he has managed to rid himself of all δόξαι which have not arisen from cataleptic impressions and is aware that he is in such a state; see *Luc.* 23–5. In that situation all of the person's apprehensions are mutually coherent, and any new apprehension will cohere with those antecedently held by the person. Any attempt to dislodge one of the sage's apprehensions by mounting arguments against it will be futile, since it will be secured by its coherence with other apprehensions. On *ratione* (= λόγος), see *TLL* s.v. col. 170.70-3 (our passage in col. 171.9–10): 'Respiciuntur, qui *acrius* inquirunt, disputant adhibitis *fere praeceptis artis indagandi*...hic illic sublucet notio argumenti allati' [author's emphasis]. Cf. Sextus, *M.* 7.151–2 (= *SVF* i.68 = LS 41C), cf. Stob., *Ecl.* II.7, pp. 73.19–74.14 Wachsmuth = (*SVF* iii.112); D.L. 7.47, 7.165 (= *SVF* i.411).

However, an apprehension which was not an ἐπιστήμη (*scientia*), i.e. any apprehension of the non-sage, is an instance of ignorance (*inscientia*), as well as of opinion (*opinio*; δόξα), which is 'weak' (in virtue of the fact that it is not secured in the same way as the sage's apprehensions). Opinions can also arise from assent to false and non-cataleptic (true) impressions (*cum falso incognitoque communis*). What all opinions have in common is that they are weakly held (and arise from weak assent), for the said reasons; cf. the definition of ἄγνοια in Stob., *Ecl.* II.7, p. 111.20-1 Wachsmuth (= *SVF* i.68): μεταπτωτικὴ συγκατάθεσις καὶ ἀσθενής. On the interconnection of all these concepts, and the stark radicalism of Stoic thought evident in it, see Meinwald (2005) and Vogt (2012: 158–82), as well as Brouwer (2014: 29–50) on wisdom and self-knowledge. Meinwald (2006: 215) notes: 'In this set-up, the fool is not a figure of so to speak idealized ignorance. That is, the fool and the sage are not symmetrically counterpoised, not equally abstracted figures representing practically unattainable extremes with real human beings falling somewhere on a continuum between them. Rather, the fool is the complement of the sage in such a way that to him is assigned all parts of "cognitive achievement space" except the region that represents the certain, systematic, unshakeable, and unerring disposition that is wisdom, i.e. to the fool is assigned all parts of cognitive achievement space that we regular types occupy.' A text which reflects this interpretation and makes opinion not a species of ignorance but coextensive with it has comma rather than semicolon after *nominabat* and the relative clause from *ex qua* as indirect speech (hence *existeret*, an emendation found in Amst; see Hunt 1998: 53); thus Meinwald (2005: 225). Linguistically and in terms of sense *imbecilla* and *communis* look jejune without a noun, as is also illustrated by some modern translations (Long and Sedley 1987: '*something* weak'; Brittain 2006: 'weak *condition*' [my emphasis]), and as Plasberg[1] (p. 54) noted in his app. crit., (Stoic) opinion is elsewhere characterized as weak assent (e.g. *Tusc.* 4.15; Sextus, *M.* 7.151). Gigon also inserts the noun. If it did not drop out for mechanical reasons, then a reader may have been baffled by the claim that opinion *is* assent, but this is unobjectionable: by the same token, καταλήψεις can be called assents. Plasberg[1] (pp. 54–5) also wondered if *uero* had dropped out before *communis*; I take *uero* as needing to be understood.

§42

Sed inter scientiam et inscientiam...sed soli credendum esse dicebat: = *SVF* i.69 (*Inter scientiam et inscientiam...neque in prauis numerabat*). Cf. Sextus, *M.* 7.151–2

(= part of LS 41C): τρία γὰρ εἶναί φασιν ἐκεῖνοι τὰ συζυγοῦντα ἀλλήλοις, ἐπιστήμην καὶ δόξαν καὶ τὴν ἐν μεθορίῳ τούτων τεταγμένην κατάληψιν, ὧν ἐπιστήμην μὲν εἶναι τὴν ἀσφαλῆ καὶ βεβαίαν καὶ ἀμετάθετον ὑπὸ λόγου κατάληψιν, δόξαν δὲ τὴν ἀσθενῆ καὶ ψευδῆ συγκατάθεσιν, κατάληψιν δὲ τὴν μεταξὺ τούτων, ἥτις ἐστὶ καταληπτικῆς φαντασίας συγκατάθεσις, 'The Stoics say there are three things which are linked together, scientific knowledge, opinion, and cognition stationed between them. Scientific knowledge is cognition which is secure and firm and unchangeable by reason. Opinion is weak and false assent. Cognition in between these is assent belonging to a cognitive impression' (transl. Long and Sedley). Meinwald (2006: 229) explains the sense in which apprehension lies 'between' *scientia* and *inscientia*, or is 'conjoined' with ἐπιστήμη and δόξα: 'In the ur-image of *suzugounta*, a pair of animals is yoked together. This ur-image makes it obvious that the key thing about the situation is that one yoke is common to the two animals. It is not a third animal plopped into the row, but a thing of another sort lying over (at least part of) each of them and so joining them together. And while "linked together" changes the image, it is a good translation because it also features a form of overlap or jointure.' The contrast between *neque in rectis neque in prauis numerare* and *soli credendum esse dicebat* is somewhat skewed, but there is no reason to suspect the text. For the sense of *credi* 'to be given credence to', see *TLL* s.v. *credo* cols 1133.13–1134.75. See Reid[1] (p. 55) on earlier editors' doubts about *soli*.

E quo sensibus etiam fidem tribuebat...latiores quaedam ad rationem inueniendam uiae reperiuntur: see the general note above, p. 236. *E quo* refers back to *soli credendum esse dicebat* and explains the basic confidence Zeno had in the senses, which is immediately qualified, but it is not quite clear how. Brittain (2006: 105 n. 55) plausibly refers to Sextus, *M.* 7.248–51, where Sextus states that cataleptic impressions should capture πάντα τὰ ἰδιώματα of an object, which may mean all the features or, if one takes ἰδίωμα more narrowly, all (jointly or individually) peculiar features of the object. On the latter reading the suggestion of the *sed quia* clause might be that an apprehension grasps the ἰδία ποιότης of an object. The noun to be supplied with *eam* in *cadere in eam posset* is more naturally taken to be *comprehensionem* rather than *rem* (from *quae essent in re*). The notion of a property 'falling into an object' would be hard to construe with reference to Stoic metaphysics, and Platonic notions of e.g. participation in forms would have little context in *Acad.* (see on 1.30–2) and would be out of place in a section on Zeno's epistemology. See also Ioppolo (1990: 442); Annas (1990: 190–2); and Frede (1999: 305–8) on the passage.

The import of the rejected reason (...*non quod omnia*...) may be that not everything which makes up an object below the level of the ἰδία ποιότης, like its constituent matter, itself made up of elements, can be perceived. This would open the door for maintaining some kind of flux view and would thus go some way towards facilitating reconciliation with the *prima forma* (cf. 1.31: *aut ita mobiles...quia continenter laberentur and fluerent omnia*). At least from Chrysippus onwards the Stoics made the distinction between a being qua qualified individual and qua lump of matter, and assumed flux on the latter level of description; see Sedley (1982a); Celkyte (2020). These resources were apparently developed in response to Academic arguments; cf. Plut., *Comm. not.* 1083b-c (= part of LS 28A). Evidence on the role which

Antiochus accorded to Chrysippus in the shaping of philosophy as opposed to Zeno is very limited. That qualified individuals are the objects of perception and crucially of cataleptic impressions is at issue in *Luc.* 84–5; see also section 5.6.2.

Less convincingly, Reid[1] (pp. 154–5) made a connection with passages in Sextus which argue that it is impossible to say how things are like by nature (*P.H.* 1.94); all one can say is how they appear to us. Thus we cannot say whether the smell, colour, and texture of an apple are not in fact one feature to which our senses respond in different ways, or indeed whether an apple has perceptible properties which humans cannot pick up because they lack an appropriate sense.

Quodque natura quasi normam scientiae... is another causal clause on the same level as... *sed quia*... above, not a relative clause parallel to *quod cadere in eam posset*. Reid[1] (p. 155) suggests that *norma* corresponds to γνώμων or κανών, but neither term is well attested in Stoic fragments. On Cicero's ways of rendering κριτήριον, see Hartung (1970: 39–43). *Norma* is the least frequently used of them (but cf. Merguet s.v.), which may be the reason for *quasi*. The respects in which the cataleptic impression is a *principium* emerge from *Luc.* 19–26. *Principium sui* is correctly glossed 'sc. *cognoscendae*' by Reid[1] (p. 155), viz. 'as a starting point for understanding her'. *Sui* is not a *genitiuus subiectiuus* ('first principle of herself', i.e. nature, or 'first principle of itself', i.e. apprehension); for this option, see van den Hout (1999: 597); Hofmann-Szantyr (p. 61).

On conceptions (*notiones*) arising from cataleptic impressions (sc. that have been assented to) see the commentary on *Luc.* 21–2. In *Ac.* 1.32 it had been left unstated how human beings acquire their *notiones*, but the natural assumption was that they would be innate. I have argued on *Ac.* 1.33b that Aristotle is there linked with the derivation of *notiones* from perception. On my reading, the present passage closes a narrative arc which began with the account of the *prima forma* in the field of λογική; see also the general note above and section 7.2. With *imprimerentur* here, cf. *Luc.* 22 *impressae*. Brittain (2014: 264–5) raises the question if the passage needs to be read as precluding that common conceptions arise or at least start forming before the faculty of reason is developed, given that apprehension is at issue (which involves assent which is a faculty of reason). He suggests that either Cicero is claiming something for apprehension here which he should strictly claim for the cataleptic impression only or that one might posit a faculty of quasi-assent alongside the well-attested quasi-speech and quasi-emotions which the Stoics ascribed to children.

I have punctuated strongly before *E quibus* since Cicero shifts back into direct speech. For the role accorded to *notiones* by *principia solum*, cf. *Tusc.* 1.56–8 on Plato's *Meno*, with Reinhardt (2018: 33–9). I have translated *ratio* as 'reason'; the term may denote a rational though imperfect disposition, or it may designate the endpoint of human development towards reason, the rational disposition of the sage (which is a subject in the next sentence). 'Lambinus' considered emending *reperiuntur* to *aperiuntur*, but *principia solum* needs to go with the same predicate as the second half of the sentence, and *e quibus* tells against *aperiuntur*.

Errorem autem et temeritatem... a uirtute sapientiaque remouebat: = *SVF* i.53. Cf. *Luc.* 66: *Sapientis autem hanc censet Arcesilas uim esse maximam, Zenoni assentiens, cauere ne capiatur, ne fallatur uidere; nihil est enim ab ea cogitatione quam habemus* *de grauitate sapientis, errore leuitate temeritate diiunctius.* The string of nouns here suggests a desire for coverage: Cicero now talks about mental attitudes or states *as well as* mental acts or activities which are distinctive of the non-sage. If *opinatio* (cf. οἴησις in D.L. 7.23 = *SVF* i.71) is not used for *uariatio* (contrast *opinio* above), then an activity is at issue here (but note *Tusc.* 4.15: *opinationem imbecillam assensionem*). For *temeritas*, see on §31, Griffin (1997: 13); and the detailed discussion by Lévy (2018). *Ignorantia* only here in Cicero, as Reid[1] (p. 155) notes, who therefore considers emendation to *ignorationem*; cf. *N.D.* 1.2; Plasberg[1] (p. 55). *Suspicio* is not straightforward to gloss: it may be linked to ὑπόληψις, which was used by the Stoics as the genus of which δόξα and ἐπιστήμη are species (see Moss 2019: 24–5). As such, it was a neutral term close to the modern notion of belief. The other nouns with which *suspicio* is juxtaposed are pejorative; it appears to mean 'tentative idea' (cf. *OLD* s.v. *suspicio*[2] no. 2), taken as a bad thing.

We know of corresponding sub-virtues of dialectic (itself a virtue) which were recognized by the Stoics and which were stipulated to be the sole province of the sage. What these sub-virtues have in common is that they turn on assent, i.e. accepting things as true, for which human beings are accountable in a manner they could not be with respect to their impressions. D.L. 7.46–7 (= *SVF* ii.130 = LS 31B) distinguishes: ἀπροπτωσία (defined as ἐπιστήμη τοῦ πότε δεῖ συγκατατίθεσθαι καὶ μή, 'knowledge when one is must give assent and when not'), ἀνεικαιότης (defined as ἰσχυρὸς λόγος πρὸς τὸ εἰκός, ὥστε μὴ ἐνδιδόναι αὐτῷ, 'strong-mindedness with respect to the plausible so as not to give in to it'), ἀνελεγξία (defined as ἰσχὺς ἐν λόγῳ, ὥστε μὴ ἀπάγεσθαι ὑπ' αὐτοῦ εἰς τὸ ἀντικείμενον, 'strength in argument, so as not to be driven by it to the opposite'), and ἀματαιότης (defined as ἕξις ἀναφέρουσαν τὰς φαντασίας ἐπὶ τὸν ὀρθὸν λόγον, 'a disposition which refers impressions to right reason'). The first of these is characterized slightly differently in a parallel source, viz. as 'a disposition (διάθεσις) not to assent in advance of cognition' (*P.Herc.* 1020, col. IV = *SVF* ii.131 = LS 41D = frg. 88 *FDS*). Coope (2016: 247) notes (author's emphasis): 'If we put these two descriptions together, we arrive at the view that the sage's *disposition to assent only when he should* just is his *understanding of when one should and should not assent*. This is possible just because the sage, in assenting or withholding assent, is guided by his understanding of when one should and should not assent. This view thus assumes that assenting (and withholding assent) is the kind of activity that *can* be guided by such understanding.' See also *Fin.* 3.72 (frg. 90 Hülser). Long (1996a: 92) attributes the 'catalogue of dialectical virtues' to Chrysippus; so also von Arnim (1890: 489–95) in his edition of *P.Herc.* 1020. Other useful studies on them include Gourinat (2000: 73–9); on the related vices, see also Salles (2007) and, more distantly, Donini (1988).

Atque in his fere commutatio…a superioribus: see the general note above on this remark as a comment on the tradition which Varro envisages. For Zeno, see n. on *Ac.* 1.7 *init.*

§43

The tone of stilted politeness in which Cicero's reaction to Varro's speech is cast is different from the manner in which the characters in the first edition converse with one another, including how the character Cicero talks to Lucullus.²⁷⁰ Lucullus, the Antiochian spokesman there, had been dead for a decade when Cicero produced the first edition, and apart from general plausibility and propriety there was no reason why the interlocutors Lucullus and Cicero should be overly circumspect in dealing with each other. On the other hand, Cicero had no reason to present Lucullus and himself as arguing with one another, which makes it likely that the combative tone which can be found in some places was inherited from the source material.

The reader may thus take the description of Varro's speech ('certainly short and not obscure at all') and of the relationship between the views of the Academy prior to Arcesilaus and, or so seems to be the implication, of the Peripatos and the Stoic system ('a correction rather than a new body of doctrine') with a pinch of salt;²⁷¹ the parenthetical (*Antiocho*) *nostro familiari* is in part explanatory of Cicero's restraint and anticipates the charge of disingenuousness.²⁷² However, it may again capture something of the real relationship between Varro and Cicero when 'Varro' then replies in somewhat blunter terms, referring to the break with tradition which the intervention of Arcesilaus represents three times within the same sentence,²⁷³ and reserving judgement as to whether the defection was justified.²⁷⁴ The charge—levelled against Antiochus—that he defected from the Academy (cf. *Luc.* 69–70) has to be read against the claim made here that Arcesilaus broke with earlier tradition.

Brittain (2001: 183–4) suggests that, in order to explain why Cicero can go along with the identification of Old Academics (in the narrow sense) and Peripatos as well as the Antiochian notion that the Stoics merely corrected the earlier tradition they formed part of, we have to assume that Cicero offers here his personal perspective on Academic history. This seems unlikely, given what we know about Cicero's familiarity and engagement with Platonic dialogues, Aristotelian and Peripatetic texts, and Stoic material which we have no reason to regard as mediated by Antiochus. Brittain also notes that the interpretation of Academic history offered in *Luc.* 112–46 is at variance with what Cicero says here. I am inclined to explain the peculiarity of Cicero's intervention here with reference to the constraints arising from the introduction of the Varro character in the final edition.²⁷⁵

Varro's invitation to respond may merely amount to a suggestion to represent the Academic side (as in *Fam.* 9.8 = SB 254 = T29, the dedicatory letter to Varro: *partes... mihi sumpsi Philonis*), or it could, additionally, hint at Cicero's particular position, which is characterized by complete ἐποχή and adopts Arcesilaus as a figurehead; see sections 7.5 and 8 and *Luc.* 65–7.

Quae cum dixisset...'quam aliquam nouam disciplinam putandam': *disciplina* relates to doctrine; no claim about the Academy, the Peripatos, and the Stoa qua

---

²⁷⁰ See *Luc.* 69–70, 98, 102, 132, 133–4, 143, with Glucker (2004: 114 n. 22) and section 9.3 on the sources of *Acad.* See also on *Luc.* 63, which is the exchange immediately following Lucullus' speech.
²⁷¹ See section 7.2 on Antiochus' construction of the Old Academy.
²⁷² Hatzimichali (2012: 25) sees the reference as evidence for 'lasting feelings of esteem and affection'.
²⁷³ Görler (1994: 948) suggests not implausibly that the reference to Arcesilaus' *discidium* still reflects the Antiochian source material on which Varro's speech drew.
²⁷⁴ On the relationship between Cicero and Varro, see the general note on *Ac.* 1.1–8. In *Att.* 13.25.3 (SB 333 = T30) Cicero likens Varro to Achilles, citing Hom., *Il.* 11.654 (Patroclus speaking to Nestor): *sed est, ut scis,* δεινὸς ἀνήρ· τάχα κεν καὶ ἀναίτιον αἰτιόῳτο.
²⁷⁵ See section 7.1 on different Academic constructions of the history of philosophy in *Acad.*

institutions is made; cf. *Luc*. 15: *perfectissimam disciplinam*; *Fin*. 4.21: *O magnam uim ingenii causam iustam, cur noua existeret disciplina!* Reid[1] (p. 156) prints the transmitted *uerum*, but it cannot stand, and *horum*, proposed by Goerenz, is a compelling emendation; see Plasberg[1] (p. 55).

Tunc Varro, '…ista sit iusta defectio': for *tuae sunt nunc partes*, 'Now it is your turn', cf. *Div*. 1.105; *Att*. 11.14.3 (= SB 225); Sen., *Contr*. 8.6.1; cf. *Fam*. 9.8 = SB 254 = T29 quoted above. With *desciscere, discidium*, and *defectio*, on which see Hellegouarc'h (1972: 128–32), cf. the title of Numenius' book (Περὶ τῆς τῶν Ἀκαδημαϊκῶν πρὸς Πλάτωνα διαστάσεως) and appendix 2. Wyss (2005: 152) notes that only Numenius and the Antiochian parts of *Acad*. speak about the sceptical Academy's break with tradition in political metaphors. Cf. also *Luc*. 15: *Nonne, cum iam philosophorum disciplinae grauissimae constitutissent, tum exortus est ⟨ut⟩ in optima re publica Tib. Gracchus qui otium perturbaret, sic Arcesilas qui constitutam philosophiam euerteret et in eorum auctoritate delitesceret qui negauissent quicquam sciri aut percipi posse*; 27: *Cum enim decretum proditur, lex ueri rectique proditur, quo e uitio et amicitiarum proditiones et rerum publicarum nasci solent*. Consider also Aug., *Contra Acad*. 2.6.14 (with Fuhrer 1997: 167; my t. 64*): *Nouae Academiae discidium non tam contra ueterem conceptum, quam contra Stoicos arbitror esse commotum*, on which Glucker (1978: 68 n. 182) comments: 'It may not be an accident that Augustine…makes Alypius speak of a *discidium* (in this context, the nearest equivalent to the διάστασις in the title of Numenius' work), not between the "New" Academy and the "Old", but between them and the Stoa—as if Augustine knew of a version which ascribed to the "New" Academy a διάστασις πρὸς Πλάτωνα, and he is attempting to counter it.'

Tunc before consonant is rare before Livy as Reid[1] (p. 156) notes, and may be slightly more emphatic than *tum* (Gaertner 2007: 215–16); replacing it with the emendation *tum* seems unwarranted.

§§44–46

On Arcesilaus in *Acad*. in general, and on the non-Ciceronian texts used to reconstruct Arcesilaus' position, see the introduction, section 7.5. Cicero's account of Arcesilaus has no proem and gives the impression that it simply picks up the thread of Varro's speech.[276] However, rather than engage with the notion of a defection, sc. from the earlier tradition, Cicero speaks of a *certamen* which Arcesilaus 'set up' with Zeno.[277] In putting it like that, Cicero implies that Arcesilaus might have engaged someone else if things had been different. *Certamen* may also imply an engagement for the sake of the argument. When Cicero then comes to consider the reason for the

---

[276] Similarly, Varro's speech turns to the subject of discussion almost immediately (*Ac*. 1.19), while Lucullus opens with an account of the Alexandrian episode (*Luc*. 11), and Cicero gestures to themes which traditionally feature in proems (*Luc*. 64–5).

[277] Cf. Numenius frg. 25 (= Eus., *P.E*. XIV.5–6.14), p. 68.83–7 Des Places, included in appendix 2, Lact., *Inst*. 3.6.7 (= t. 61), and Aug., *Contra Acad*. 3.7.38 (the latter two probably drew on Cicero), whereas a conflict between Zeno and Arcesilaus is absent from the biographies of both in D.L. (see the introduction, p. cxl).

contest, he first dismisses one (quarrelsomeness), but then does not cite a positive one (like e.g. the desire to find the truth). Instead, he refers to the obscurity of things, which led Socrates to his famous confession of ignorance, as it had led various Presocratics to sceptical pronouncements. These are cited in all their variety, suggesting a widespread tendency among the Presocratics as well as the diverse nature of their sceptical attitudes.

When in §45 Arcesilaus' stance is then introduced by 'therefore', this primarily refers to the *obscuritas rerum* itself as a motivating force, but it could also signal that Arcesilaus was impressed by the fact that the *obscuritas rerum* had led the Presocratics and Socrates alike to a broadly sceptical attitude. There is no suggestion that the sceptical pronouncements of the Presocratics carried weight with Arcesilaus because he took them to have carried weight with Socrates. What we then learn in §45 about Arcesilaus is best read as a description of a *general* attitude (from which there issued a *particular* engagement with Zeno), i.e. §45 is not narrowly a characterization of Arcesilaus' *anti-Stoic* stance. This is suggested by the fact that Arcesilaus' sceptical pronouncements are not exclusively cast in terminology which is otherwise reserved for the Stoics, by the fact that Arcesilaus' views map onto those of the Presocratics given in §44,[278] as well as by the description of Arcesilaus' strategy as directed 'against the *sententiae* of everyone' (non-Stoics would not necessarily be vulnerable to anti-Stoic arguments).

If this picture is right, it leaves some things unexplained: what is Arcesilaus' ultimate motivation? And why the concentration on Zeno? After all, one might think that a recognition that things are obscure might issue in, say, despondency rather than relentless attacks on dogmatists, and on Zeno in particular. Cicero ascribes a desire to find the truth to the Academics in various programmatic passages, including to Arcesilaus in *Luc.*,[279] which does supply a motive for Arcesilaus' argumentative practice that is in keeping with his frequent characterization as a Socratic. Socrates as presented in Plato's early dialogues may also help explain the focus on Zeno. Some of the interlocutors in these early dialogues are self-proclaimed experts, who, if they were genuine experts, might point out a path towards knowledge as well as offer discursive knowledge, to be absorbed and used. While we have no reason to think that Zeno regarded or presented himself as a sage, he made all kinds of claims about the sage which, if true, would make being a Stoic sage a goal worth aspiring to.

Ac. 1.44–6 mentions Socrates twice, but only on the second occasion is there a suggestion that Arcesilaus consciously modelled himself on Socrates. On the first occasion (§44), the Cicero character states that Socrates made his *confessio ignorationis* in the light of the obscurity of things. On the second, which is in indirect speech and thus reflects Arcesilaus' viewpoint (1.45:...*quod Socrates sibi reliquisset*...), the latter is presented as going beyond what Socrates himself said, by

---

[278] See Brittain and Palmer (2001: 41 n. 6) on this point.
[279] Cf. *Luc.* 76 *fin.*: *Arcesilam uero non obtrectandi causa cum Zenone pugnauisse sed uerum inuenire uoluisse sic intellegitur.* In *Luc.* 77 init. Cicero then recounts—that is what *sic* refers to—that nobody before Zeno had said that it was possible for human beings to have no opinions and that this was even required for the sage. To Arcesilaus this appeared to be a *uera sententia tum honesta et digna sapienti*.

disavowing not just first- but also second-order knowledge.²⁸⁰ However, other passages from Cicero do present Arcesilaus as a follower of Socrates, and such a reading would be a natural extension of what is said about Socrates in §§44–6.²⁸¹

Arcesilaus is credited with two views in §§44–6: (i) nothing can be known, and—consequently (*quibus de causis*)—(ii) one should not assert anything.²⁸² What do we learn about these views and the manner in which Arcesilaus held them? From the wording which Cicero uses it is plain that (i) and (ii) are not the conclusions of the core and corollary arguments, respectively, but are more general; that is, they are not the conclusions of anti-Stoic arguments which rely on Stoic conceptions e.g. of knowledge and assent (contrast *Luc.* 40–2 and 65–7 with comm.).²⁸³ Views (i) and (ii) are grammatically dependent on *negabat* and *censebat*, neither of which are technical terms in *Acad.*, so that one could infer from them what type of belief is envisaged. The latter term at least makes it clear that some kind of view of Arcesilaus' is meant (as opposed to a claim he advanced for the sake of the argument).²⁸⁴ Arcesilaus would be inconsistent in 'asserting' (i) or (ii) in the sense envisaged in (ii). Whatever the historical Arcesilaus thought or did, such—unacknowledged—inconsistency does not seem plausible for Arcesilaus as constructed by the author and the character Cicero.²⁸⁵ As the reason for view (i) Arcesilaus' coming up against the *obscuritas rerum* is cited; the fact that the Presocratics felt defeated by it as well may be a secondary reason. This suggests that Arcesilaus arrived at view (i) inductively, but clearly no such induction can ever be complete. This would help explain Arcesilaus' disavowal of second-order knowledge of (i). If Arcesilaus does not dogmatically believe (i) but rather (i) appears to him to be the case, on the basis of his and other people's experience, then it is not inconsistent for (ii) to appear to him to be the case and for him to say so. However, on what grounds he would hold (ii), given (i), then becomes an issue. If it appears to someone that nothing can be known (in any sense

---

²⁸⁰ Contrast Numenius frg. 27 (= Eus., *Praep. Ev.* XIV.8.1–15 = T2 Mette), p. 76.17–18 Des Places, who claims that Arcesilaus unlike Carneades 'thought that what he said was the truth', likening Arcesilaus to a Hydra which destroys itself; cf. Favorinus frg. 26 Barigazzi (= Gell. 11.5): *Quod Academici quidem ipsum illud nihil posse comprehendi quasi comprehendunt et nihil posse decerni quasi decernunt, Pyrrhonii ne id quidem ullo pacto uerum uideri dicunt quod nihil esse uerum uidentur*; Sextus, *P.H.* 1.226. Brittain (2008a: section 3.3) regards passages like those from Favorinus and Sextus as reactions to mitigated secpticism; see also the introduction, section 4. A discussion of all images used for Arcesilaus by Numenius (Hydra, Chimaera, Empousai) is in Wyss (2005: 119–21).
²⁸¹ Consider also Annas (1992a: 52): 'It is also hard to think that Arcesilaus did not appeal to a dialogue which is clearly late, but is deliberately Socratic in form—the *Theaetetus*. Here we find that *ad hominem* reasoning has been raised to a feature of Socratic methodology. The point is made explicitly by the imagery of Socrates as the barren midwife, and by the constant repetition of the point that Socrates is not putting forward any of his own ideas, but is merely drawing ideas out of Theaetetus to see whether they work out or not. All that happens is that Theaetetus offers various definitions of knowledge; none of them do work; and so he is cured of any complacency on the subject. Socrates gets Theaetetus to see that all his definitions must be rejected because they lead to unacceptable results; he does not himself put forward any beliefs, still less use them to refute Theaetetus.'
²⁸² *Ac.* 1.45: *Itaque Arcesilas negabat esse quicquam quod sciri posset...quibus de causis nihil oporteret neque profiteri neque affirmare quemquam neque assensione approbare, cohibereque semper et ab omni lapsu continere temeritatem....*
²⁸³ On these arguments, see also section 4.
²⁸⁴ A question not addressed by the text is how we know that Arcesilaus held (i) and (ii), given his policy of concealing his views mentioned elsewhere (e.g. *De orat.* 3.67).
²⁸⁵ *Pace* e.g. Cooper (2006: 174 n. 10).

of 'knowing'), why hold (ii) as a consequence rather than, say, that one might as well say anything? The reason may be, and this point has been made forcefully and convincingly by Cooper (2006), that Arcesilaus follows Socrates as a model, who pursued a life devoted to rationality and reason, and that this Socratic attitude underpins his argumentative practice.[286] The final sentence of §45 does not indicate that Arcesilaus argued against everyone's opinion *in order to* induce suspension of judgement on their part. Rather, the first *ut* in that sentence is explicative and mentions a frequent though not universal effect of Arcesilaus' argumentative engagement, while the second *ut* is consecutive and describes the result of Arcesilaus' practice, sc. in the event of success and for his interlocutor (see n. below for further discussion).

In §46 Cicero objects to the name 'New Academy', deployed by an unspecified 'they', for the Academy from Arcesilaus onwards, on the grounds that Plato himself can be read as having sceptical leanings (see the note below on the interpretative options for the exact position ascribed to Plato). According to Cicero nothing is affirmed in Plato's works, many issues are discussed *in utramque partem*, every position is called into question, and nothing definite is stated. No comment is offered on the Academics who came between Plato and Arcesilaus, nor one on Aristotle and the Peripatos or the Stoics. However, Cicero does not dwell on whether he rejects the Antiochian view of the history of philosophy and instead grants Varro the terminological distinction: *Academia uetus* for what Varro has described, *Academia noua* for the sceptical Academy. Arcesilaus' next three successors continued with his approach. Then, it is implied, Carneades modified the school's *ratio*. The text breaks off before we are told what these modifications were (the *probabile* is the most likely candidate). What we are told of Carneades may already be intended to contrast with his predecessors at least to a degree, namely that he knew about every branch of philosophy and that he was a very powerful speaker. Carneades' rhetorical powers are widely documented, and there is extensive evidence that he engaged not just Stoics but other schools, too. This might be behind the claim of his broad knowledge of philosophy.

Acad. contains two surveys of historical figures delivered by the Academic character Cicero (*Ac.* 1.44-6; *Luc.* 72-6), as well as comments by an Antiochian character on such a survey (*Luc.* 13-16, in reference to the lost *Catul.*, and possibly reflecting at least in part remarks made by the character Catulus, whose position was different from Cicero's; see on *Luc.* 148). Questions which arise include if these accounts cohere with one another, how their differences are to be explained, how they are used to support larger argumentative strategies, whether an evolution of a broadly sceptical outlook over time is envisaged, and whether hypotheses regarding their sources can be formulated; see section 7.1 of the introduction, where I argue that all three accounts can be reconciled and that they are likely to reflect a standard account of Academic history, as opposed to e.g. going back to the Roman Books of Philo, as well as section 9.3 on the sources of *Acad*. This does mean that Cicero had the Cicero

---

[286] Cf. Cooper (2006: 185): 'On my account, Arcesilaus is a Socratic in that like Socrates he is passionately devoted to reason; reason, he thinks, is our highest faculty, the one and only thing in us with which we should in the strongest and deepest sense identify ourselves. This is not a philosophical doctrine for Arcesilaus, in that he will never announce it as his opinion, and he does not hold it in a way that places a burden on him to defend it with arguments of his own or against its denial by anyone. Nonetheless this is a very deep conviction of his'; see also Thorsrud (2009: 56).

character respond to an Antiochian account which was post-Roman Books with an Academic account which was earlier in conception. Consequently, *Ac.* 1.44–6 is unlikely to represent evidence for an (otherwise unattested) Philonian reply to Antiochus' *Sosus*. There are also later non-Ciceronian texts which are informed by Academic thinking about the history of philosophy and which may be compared with the evidence from *Acad.*, notably Plutarch and Augustine. Pyrrhonian scepticism did not conceive of itself as the legitimate heir to a complex philosophical and institutional tradition that was interpreted quite differently by others, and had less reason to allocate itself a place in a historical narrative; however, there is at least some scope for comparison, e.g. of the Academic and Pyrrhonian readings of Plato.[287]

§44

Tum ego ... circumfusa esse dixerunt: on the lack of any preface, see the general note above. With *ut accepimus* here, cf. *fortasse* and *credo* in *Luc.* 77 (on Arcesilaus' debate with Zeno about the cataleptic impression). Long (1986: 443) wonders with respect to all three passages if such qualifications indicate doubts on Cicero's part about the accuracy of what he is reporting, possibly because he has an inkling that Zeno had displaced Aristo in the accounts on which he is relying (see section 7.5, p. cxl). I think a distinction ought to be drawn. Here it seems preferable to see it as the sole function of *ut accepimus* to mark what Cicero relays as handed down by tradition; cf. also Brittain and Palmer (2001: 42 n. 7). Consider that Varro inserts similar qualifications into his speech (e.g. *Ac.* 1.33: *cuius quas acceperim immutationes*); cf. also *Luc.* 5 (Cicero speaking as author): *ego autem, cum Graecas litteras M. Catonem in senectute didicisse acceperim*.... However, the two verbs in *Luc.* 77 signal hesitation about the authenticity of the story in addition to it marking it as traditional.

We learn that Arcesilaus 'set up' (*instituit*) his entire conflict (*omne certamen*) with Zeno: *certamen instituere* can mean 'to set up public games' (cf. e.g. Suet., *Dom.* 4.4.1), but this is unlikely to be the sense here; rather, 'to engage in conflict' (cf. *Tusc.* 3.51) is meant, i.e. *certamen* has no connotation of 'mere display flight' or 'contest merely for the sake of competition'. *Instituere* is suggestive of the deliberate choosing of one opponent when Arcesilaus could conceivably have picked another opponent (or additional ones, as Carneades later did), and does not have associations of engineering a contest.

On *pertinacia*, Reid[1] (pp. 156–7) notes that *pertinacia* is the bad side of perseverance, the good side being *perseuerantia* (*Inv.* 2.165) or *constantia* (*Marc.* 31). Similar motivations are assigned, or reported or implied to be assigned, to the sceptical Academy elsewhere: *Luc.* 9: *sine pertinacia*; 65: *pertinacia ... calumnia ... studio certandi*; 14: *Arcesilae calumnia*; *N.D.* 1.13: *procax Academia*; see also Fuhrer (1997: 58) on *Contra Acad.* 2.1. Numenius suggests that Arcesilaus attacked Zeno out of jealousy over the success of the cataleptic impression; frg. 25 Des Places (= Eus., *Praep. Ev.* XIV.5.10–6.14), p. 70.132–5, included in appendix 2.

---

[287] See Bonazzi (2011).

On Socrates, see section 7.3 and the commentary on *Luc.* 15 and 74. Neither a 'profession of ignorance' nor the claim of knowledge of his own ignorance ascribed to Socrates in §45 need to amount to the self-refuting position according to which Socrates would claim to know that he knows nothing. Rather, the latter is more plausibly read, and more plausibly ascribed to Arcesilaus by the Clitomachean Cicero, as the claim that Socrates knows nothing except this one thing, that he knows nothing (see Burnyeat 1997: 290–300, esp. 295–6). A profession (§44) would by itself not naturally be read as a knowledge claim, but the interpretation of *confessio ignorationis* should cohere with the remark in §45. Socrates is said to have been 'led' (*adducere*) to the *confessio ignorationis* by the obscurity of things. The verb *adducere* is not technical in Cicero's dialogues. It is used in forensic contexts, e.g. of the conviction induced in the judges by the orator (cf. *OLD* s.v. no. 7; *Clu.* 104: *adducti iudices sunt…potuisse honeste ab eo reum condemnari*). It is a suitable term to describe a defeasible conviction someone has arrived at by an inductive mechanism. Brittain and Palmer (2001: 42–3) think Socrates is presented as dogmatic about his one (on their view, second-order) knowledge claim here, and observe that this interpretation would allow Arcesilaus' position to emerge as a development of Socrates'. I assume development, too, and that it consists in Arcesilaus' disavowal of knowledge of the only item of 'knowledge' Socrates had claimed for himself, but, as indicated, because of the associations of *adducere* and *confessio* I am not certain that Socrates' one 'knowledge' claim posited here should be read as a claim of dogmatic knowledge.

For the sceptical pronouncements of the Presocratics, see on *Luc.* 13–15, 72–6; Brittain and Palmer (2001); section 7.1 of the introduction. That the practice of constructing an intellectual ancestry for the Academic stance goes as far back as Arcesilaus emerges from Plut., *Adv. Col.* 26, 1121f–1122a (= Arcesilaus frg. 7 Mette = frg. 75 Vezzoli = part of LS 68H), 'Baustein' 12.6 in Dörrie (1987): ὁ δ' Ἀρκεσίλαος τοσοῦτον ἀπέδει τοῦ καινοτομίας τινὰ δόξαν ἀγαπᾶν καὶ ὑποποιεῖσθαί ⟨τι⟩ τῶν παλαιῶν, ὥστ' ἐγκαλεῖν τοὺς τότε σοφιστάς, ὅτι προστρίβεται Σωκράτει καὶ Πλάτωνι καὶ Παρμενίδῃ καὶ Ἡρακλείτῳ τὰ περὶ τῆς ἐποχῆς δόγματα καὶ τῆς ἀκαταληψίας οὐδὲν δεομένοις, ἀλλ' οἷον ἀναγωγὴν καὶ βεβαίωσιν αὐτῶν εἰς ἄνδρας ἐνδόξους ποιούμενος, 'Yet Arcesilaus was so far from loving any reputation for novelty or arrogating to himself anything belonging to the ancients, that the sophists of his time accused him of rubbing off his doctrines about suspension of judgement and noncognition on Socrates, Plato, Parmenides and Heraclitus, who did not need them; whereas he attributed them as it were, by way of confirmation, to famous men' (transl. Long and Sedley). Here in 1.44 Socrates and the Presocratics are presented as responding in similar fashion to the *obscuritas rerum*, and Arcesilaus' stance appears as motivated in the same way (1.45 *init.*: *Itaque Arcesilaus…*). Plutarch does not report who the sophists were, but if they were roughly contemporaries, then a similar charge as that levelled against Arcesilaus according to Plutarch's report could be advanced against any Academic who constructs Arcesilaus as Cicero does in the present passage. The information from Plutarch also suggests that the account of the Academic tradition given here in 1.44–6 is not specifically Philonian as opposed to Academic. The pronouncements ascribed to the Presocratics are arranged in three groups. The first assembles statements to the effect that nothing can be known, the second is concerned with various limitations on human cognitive faculties, and the third with the claim that there is no truth (as opposed to it being not available to humans); for a slightly different description of the three groups see Brittain and Palmer (2001: 41–2). The Academic historical account relies for what claim it has on the opposition on the Presocratic pronouncements themselves but also on the respect in which the dogmatists, notably the Stoics, held the Presocratics (cf. *Luc.* 14), but it was unlikely to have been purely dialectical, since the Academics themselves, in conceiving of Arcesilaus as a Socratic, will have been thinking of passages like Plt., *Phd.* 96a ff., which claim an interest in Presocratic natural philosophy (if not of epistemology, let alone sceptical pronouncements) for Socrates (see Cooper 2006: 176 n. 16).

The statements actually cited by Cicero are not matched to a specific individual except for Democritus' that the truth is submerged in an abyss (*in profundo ueritatem esse demersam* ~ D.L. 9.72 = 68B117 DK: ἐτεῇ δὲ οὐδὲν ἴδμεν· ἐν βυθῷ γὰρ ἡ ἀλήθεια); cf. the paraphrase of the same fragment in *Luc.* 32: *naturam accusa, quae in profundo ueritatem, ut ait Democritus, penitus abstruserit*, and see Morel (2018: 52–6). Consider also Lact., *Inst.* 3.28.10–13 (cf. 3.30.6): *Anaxagoras pronuntiat circumfusa esse tenebris omnia*; *Empedocles angustas esse sensuum semitas quaeritur*, which assigns two further pronouncements featuring here in *Ac.* 1.44 to particular individuals, in a context that exhibits knowledge of the final edition of *Acad.* (cf. t. 4 and 7 in my edition). On the ancient tradition of presenting Democritus as a sceptic generally, see Castagnoli (2010: 308–29). For Empedocles, cf. 31B2.1 DK; for the ascription of the first statement to Anaxagoras, see the different explanations in Long and Sedley (ii.1987: 433) and Brittain and Palmer (2001: 70–3); see also Plasberg[1] (p. 56). It is not impossible that Lactantius may have made these ascriptions on the basis of a passage which came later in the final edition and which is lost. However, other explanations are possible, and *Luc.* 14, i.e. Lucullus' reply to the Academic invocation of the Presocratics, is perfectly intelligible as a reply to a passage corresponding to what we read here in 1.44 (sc. and which would have featured in the *Catulus*). In the end I opted not to include Lact., *Inst.* 3.28.10–13 amongst the fragments and testimonia, since it is hard to see where the information contained in it would have featured in the *Academici libri* (the relevant part of *Ac.* 1 is obviously extant, and Anaxagoras and Empedocles are deployed in a different way in *Luc.* 72–4).

The string of near-synonymous verbs of knowing (*nihil cognosci, nihil percipi, nihil sciri*), all of which either feature or resonate with technical Stoic terms in the immediately preceding section (1.40–2), cannot carry the absurd implication that the Presocratics thought that nothing can be known in the Stoic sense of the term, or that they operated conceptions of knowledge (and wisdom) which are as a matter of fact identical with or closely similar to the Stoic position. The cluster of synonyms may be intended to signal the diversity of their statements, and the range of ways in which the precarious epistemic position of human beings was thought of by the Presocratics. Lévy apud Vezzoli (2016: 175) has suggested that it is an ordered series: 'Carlos Lévy ritiene che *cognosci, percipi* e *sciri* indichino per tutto il passo una gradazione della conoscenza.'

Instituta in *opinionibus et institutis omnia teneri* means 'conventions'; cf. *Rep.* 5.1: *ueterem morem ac maiorum instituta retinebant excellentes uiri* and Sextus, *M.* 7.135 (= DK68B9): 'νόμῳ' γάρ φησι 'γλυκὺ καὶ νόμῳ πικρόν, νόμῳ θερμόν, νόμῳ ψυχρόν, νόμῳ χροιή· ἐτεῇ δὲ ἄτομα καὶ κενόν᾽, 'By convention sweet and by convention bitter, by convention hot, by convention cold, by convention color; in truth atoms and void.'

The bracketed *uel ut* may be a half-executed gloss, or part of a gloss, that has intruded into the text, which was then garbled through changes in word separation. For the endings of the Greek names (*-em* rather than *-en*), see the Oxford Classical Text, p. lxxiv. On the force of *deinceps* in *deinceps omnia tenebris*, see Reid[1] (p. 158).

§45

Itaque Arcesilas negabat...assensionem approbationemque praecurrere: *itaque* links Arcesilaus' stance to the overarching theme of the previous paragraph, the *obscuritas rerum* which lead the Presocratics and Socrates alike to their sceptical attitude. Brittain (2006: 106 n. 60) comments on the first sentence of the paragraph: 'This account of Socrates' views seems to be inconsistent with Cicero's earlier version in Ac. 2.74 (responding to Ac. 2.15) as well as Varro's in Ac. 1.15–16. Socrates is represented there as the aporetic questioner of Plato's Socratic dialogues, whose confession of ignorance is the consequence of his method. But here his aporetic method is explained as a consequence of his acceptance of inapprehensibility for theoretical reasons set out by the Presocratics.' Because I take *itaque* to refer to the *obscuritas rerum* and because I take 1.44–5 not to contain the claim or the suggestion that the theoretical reasons set out by the Presocratics gave rise to Socrates' view that nothing can be known, I see no inconsistency with *Luc.* 74. Rather, Socrates' aporetic questioning brought him up against the *obscuritas rerum* time and again, which is why he ended up taking the view that nothing can be known, but this does not amount to 'acceptance of inapprehensibility for theoretical reasons'.

Negare is not a term that is clearly marked as dogmatic assertion, but denotes a declaration or statement of some sort (rather than a privately held view). Some texts, though not the present passage explicitly, state that Arcesilaus concealed his opinion and instead interrogated others about their opinion (e.g. *De orat.* 3.67), but perhaps this relates to particular subjects discussed, rather than to the sort of meta-view at issue when 'nothing can be known' is ascribed to Arcesilaus. Cf. Maconi (1988: 246–7).

It is true that the views attributed to Arcesilaus in §45 can be paralleled with those ascribed to the Presocratics in the previous one (see Brittain and Palmer 2001: 41 n. 6), but this gives out nothing for the question of how Arcesilaus came by them. *Scire* is a word which is surprisingly rare in *Acad.*, and *scientia* is usually used in the highly technical sense of Stoic ἐπιστήμη (which cannot be at issue here; cf. *Luc.* 145). This suggests that Arcesilaus' view is a general one, which does not presuppose any commitment to a *theory* of knowledge, or a *particular* theory of knowledge. Reid[1] (p. 158) raises the question of why *quod...sibi reliquisset* is not in the indicative (since the relative clause reflects what was probably Cicero's view), and assumes a degree of carelessness on his part; that is possible, but given what we learn elsewhere about Arcesilaus modelling himself on Socrates, the subjunctive may be functional here and reveal that Arcesilaus was looking to Socrates precisely when he diverged from him. *Reliquisset* suggests that Socrates had made an exception for the one knowledge claim he did make, rather than had claimed that he knew that nothing can be known.

As a consequence of having refrained from the one knowledge claim Socrates did make, Arcesilaus held that everything is hidden, and that there was nothing which could be known: *censere* just means 'having a view', i.e. tells us nothing about the manner in which the view is held through the use and meaning of the verb, but the imperfect tense may have iterative force, which would suggest an attitude reinforced repeatedly through experience over time as opposed to a firm resolution at one point in time. *Cernere* and *intellegere* suggest perceptual and non-perceptual knowledge, but are otherwise not technical in *Acad*. Note that Stoicism and Zeno have only been mentioned generically so far: Arcesilaus' view must be taken to be a general one at this point.

From *quibus de causis* down to *assensionem approbationemque praecurrere* Cicero states with unusual fullness that because of view (i) Arcesilaus held view (ii) and deemed it shameful to make unwarranted knowledge claims. Reid[1] (p. 158) glosses some of the terms with Greek Stoic ones or relates them to Latin ones which are used in Stoic contexts, but it seems likely that the accumulation of synonyms and the fullness of expression are once again supposed to convey that knowledge claims of any kind, within any framework, and in general are to be avoided. An indication that *cognitio, perceptio, assensio,* and *approbatio* do not refer to Stoic conceptions here may be given by the combination with *praecurrere*: Stoic apprehension cannot be outrun by assent, because assent is required to turn a cataleptic impression into apprehension (as Varro explains in *Ac.* 1.40–2). But if one talks more loosely, then Cicero's formulation effectively conveys accepting something as true before one knows it for certain.

Vt nihil se scire sciret after *reliquisset* is only in Γ; Reid[1] did not print it, unlike Plasberg (both editions). Burnyeat (1997: 295 n. 49) comments: 'Plasberg adds, with some mss. support, "ut nihil scire se sciret". Unlike Long and Sedley..., I follow Reid[1] and Rackham, on the grounds that the idea has become so familiar that "illud ipsum" can be used as a tag, without the need of explanation (cf. D.L. II.32); both here and in [*Luc*. 28–9] *illud* could import "well known, famous". But Rackham's translation has Arcesilaus' Socrates claim to know that nothing can be known, rather than that he himself knows nothing. Both Yonge and Reid (and whoever wrote the extra words 'ut nihil scire se sciret') see that *illud* looks forward to *quod*, not backwards to Arcesilaus' denial that anything can be known.' After *intellegi* Reid[1] prints *possit*, unaware that *posset* has manuscript support. For *temeritas*, see on 1.42. *Esse* for *esset* was first printed by Manutius.

Huic rationi quod erat consentaneum faciebat...facilius ab utraque parte assensio sustineretur: *ratio* does not mean 'theory' here—nothing approaching a theory has been provided—, but something less formal, like a set of views. That Arcesilaus argued against everyone's opinions confirms that above a general attitude was meant (see the previous n.). Moreover, the description of Arcesilaus' practice, on the back of his rejection of acceptance and approval (which in the present context seem to exhaust possible modes of endorsement), ought to mean that he confronted opponents with arguments to whose premisses these opponents are committed as a matter of fact or ought to be committed given their standards of rationality and known appreciation of evidence, and whose conclusions they ought to accept as a consequence—it is *the opponents'* suspension of judgement that is induced (when both sides of a question are found to be equipollent).

As to the textual problem (*disserens de sua Γ; dies iam* P; *disserens in eam* coni. Madvig 1826: 120–1; *dicens in eam* coni. Reid[1]), the reading of P is nonsensical, *de sua* would mean 'away from their own position', and *in eam* (sc. *sententiam*) 'towards his own position of (general) ἐποχή'. One might wonder if Arcesilaus' view (ii) could function as a position to which one would *want* to convert others, but that would be the wrong question to ask at this point, since the first *ut*-clause is not a purpose clause but explicative. This means that this first *ut*-clause is in any case a description of what happened as a matter of fact most of the time or rather with most interlocutors (*plerosque*). This is widely agreed among interpreters and translators; only Reid[2] (p. 26) translates 'He acted in accordance with this theory, and *strove* by speaking against the opinions of all men…' [my emphasis], but states in Reid[1] (p. 158) that he regards the first *ut*-clause as explicative. Explicative *ut*-clauses tend to have demonstrative antecedents in the main clause, but *quod erat consentaneum* can so function as well; see Hofmann-Szantyr (p. 645). For *deducere*, cf. e.g. *Tusc.* 2.60: *Quem cum Cleanthes condiscipulus rogaret, quaenam ratio eum de sententia deduxisset, respondit*…. The prepositional phrase *in eam*, judged 'tempting' by Brittain (2006: 107 n. 62) and adopted by Ioppolo (2018: 38), would dub Arcesilaus' attachment to suspension of judgement a *sententia* and thus put it on a par with other people's dogmatically held views; this is not impossible as an instance of loose writing, but I would not want to introduce it by emendation. The next question is whether the following *ut*-clause describes the outcome in such cases or the intended purpose of Arcesilaus' argumentative assault. The adverb *facilius* would seem to point to the latter reading, while *cum* rather than *si* points to the former reading. If Arcesilaus is like Socrates committed to reason and thinks that unwarranted knowledge claims are not just undesirable but reprehensible, then he can want to convert others if the conditions are right. However, the transmitted text has 'when the conditions are right' not 'if they are right' (unless one wanted to emend or regard the temporal *cum*-clause as conditional in force, cf. Kühner-Stegmann ii.430–1). Hence reading the second *ut*-clause as consecutive seems preferable. Thus also Long and Sedley (i.1987: 438); Vezzoli (2016: 175). Plasberg[1] suggested the insertion of *et efficeret* after *deduceret*, which was printed by Gigon, but there is no good reason to assume that Cicero wrote it.

Given *contra omnium sententias*, one would assume that Zeno was initially just one of the *omnes* against whom Arcesilaus argued in the envisaged scenario.

For Arcesilaus' technique of arguing against other people's views (so that their original grounds for their view and his ad hominem arguments against it end up as *paria momenta*), see *De orat.* 1.43, 3.67; *N.D.* 1.11; *Fin.* 3.2; *D.L.* 4.28; Philod., *Index Acad.* col. xx *init*. (= part of T1b Mette = F33 Vezzoli), which also mentions Arcesilaus' habit of not disclosing any view of his own (cf. the commentary on *Luc.* 60 and on Aug., *Contra Acad.* 3.20.43 = t. 63*). For the Carneadean *in utramque partem* technique, see *Tusc.* 2.9; *Fin.* 5.10; *De orat.* 3.80. In *Off.* 2.8 Cicero seems to attempt a mediation between the two: *Contra autem omnia disputantur a nostris, quod hoc ipsum probabile elucere non possit, nisi ex utraque parte causarum esset facta contentio. Sed haec explanata sunt in Academicis nostris satis, ut arbitror, diligenter.* I discuss the Carneadean conception of equal persuasiveness on either side of a question in section 6 and Reinhardt (2018a); on the Pyrrhonist notion of ἰσοσθένεια, see Svavarsson (2014) and Machuca (2017).

§46

Hanc Academiam nouam appellabant...in eadem Arcesilae ratione permansit: for divisions of the Academy and their likely date and origin, see the commentary on *Ac.* 1.13. The subject of *appellant* is not given, but since Cicero grants the distinction only for the sake of the argument, Antiochus and his followers are likely to be meant. On the sceptical (Academic) interpretation of Plato, see in particular Annas (1992a); Opsomer (1998a) on Academic thinking which survived into Middle Platonism, when anti-empiricist arguments as devised by the Academics could comfortably sit alongside, and be deployed, a renewed commitment to the transcendental; Brittain (2001: 201–13) as well as his index s.v. 'Plato, interpreted by Academics'; Bonazzi (2003) with comprehensive bibliography up to the date of publication; Wyss (2005: 205–41), who offers a thematically arranged collection of texts on the subject with German translation and commentary.

With the present passage, cf. *Luc.* 74 with comm.; *De orat.* 3.67: *Reliqui sunt Peripatetici et Academici; quamquam Academicorum nomen est unum, sententiae duae; nam Speusippus Platonis sororis filius et Xenocrates, qui Platonem audierat, et qui Xenocratem Polemo et Crantor, nihil ab Aristotele, qui una audierat Platonem, magno opere dissensit; copia fortasse et uarietate dicendi pares non fuerunt: Arcesilas primum, qui Polemonem audierat, ex uariis Platonis libris sermonibusque Socraticis hoc maxime arripuit, nihil esse certi quod aut sensibus aut animo percipi possit; quem ferunt eximio quodam usum lepore dicendi aspernatum esse omne animi sensusque iudicium primumque instituisse—quamquam id fuit Socraticum maxime—non quid ipse sentiret ostendere, sed contra id, quod quisque se sentire dixisset, disputare.* If Cicero rejects, and then accepts out of mere politeness, the distinction between Old and New Academy here, while in *De orat.* 3.67 the speaker Crassus has no problem in acknowledging *sententiae duae*, then the contradiction is superficial (*pace* Reid[1] p. 159): here Cicero claims continuity between Plato and Socrates on the one hand and Arcesilaus on the other, while in *De orat.* 3.67 the Old Academics in the narrow sense, who are out of the picture in *Ac.* 1.46 (and generally of little interest to sceptical Academics), are said to represent a separate *sententia*.

De orat. 3.67 complements our passage in another way: it tells us that Arcesilaus' stance was informed by his interpretation of Plato's dialogues, which he read in a way which is consistent with what the Cicero character says in 1.46 about them. Plut., *Adv. Col.* 26, 1121f–1122a (= Arcesilaus frg. 7 Mette = frg. 75 Vezzoli), 'Baustein' 12.6 in Dörrie (1987), cited on *Ac.* 1.44 above, indicates that Arcesilaus counted Plato amongst his predecessors, but makes no reference to texts.

On the association of Arcesilaus and Socrates, cf. also *Fin.* 2.2 (= LS 68J]; Arcesilaus quite deliberately resumed Socrates' approach); *N.D.* 1.11 (a briefer statement to the same effect).

As to the characterization of Plato's dialogues, which Cicero claims for the Academics in general (*numeramus*), four features are named: (i) *nihil affirmatur*, (ii) *in utramque partem multa disseruntur*, (iii) *de omnibus quaeritur*, (iv) *nihil certi dicitur*. A question which immediately arises is what the difference between (i) *nihil affirmatur* and (ii) *nihil certi dicitur* is. Because Cicero uses the passive voice throughout, no subject is given, but it is tempting to think that on the first occasion the reference is to Socrates the character, while *nihil certi dicitur* refers to Plato the author: in *Luc.* 74 Cicero makes the same distinction and adds that there could be no reason why Plato as author would go along with Socrates' irony (i.e. Antiochus' conception of Socrates in *Luc.* 15). Annas (1992a: 62) comments: 'How are we to distinguish the first from the third [i.e. *nihil affirmatur* and *nihil certi dicitur*]? Most plausibly, the first concerns the form of Plato's writings: claims made in the dialogues are not prefaced by expressions of certainty, but are put forward with hesitations and hedges. The third claims that in fact what is being done in the dialogues is enquiry rather than the putting forward of statements.' Brittain (2001: 204–5) has a different proposal, arising from the observation that in *Ac.* 1.44–6 Cicero's account is in part developmental, such that Socrates' position is different from Arcesilaus', and Carneades is in some respects different from Arcesilaus, so that it is reasonable to expect that Plato's purported position is not the same as Arcesilaus'. Moreover, Brittain suggests that ascribing some beliefs of some kind to Plato on the basis of the study of the dialogues, even though said beliefs do not come up to knowledge, is natural for anyone, and points out that ἀποφαίνεσθαι features in *Tht.* 150c4–7 (τοὺς μὲν ἄλλους ἐρωτῶ, αὐτὸς δὲ οὐδὲν ἀποφαίνομαι περὶ οὐδενὸς διὰ τὸ μηδὲν ἔχειν σοφόν, 'I question other people, but make no affirmations myself about anything because I have no wisdom'), a passage which can be shown to be a key piece of evidence in the ancient debate about whether Plato should be interpreted in a sceptical or a dogmatic way (Brittain 2001: 204 n. 54 cites four different texts which suggest this: Anon., *in Tht.* on 150c4–7, col. 54.38–43 Sedley and Bastianini; ibid., col. 59.19–21; D.L. 3.52; Sextus, *P.H.* 1.221–5 and 232). Against this background Brittain suggests that Cicero's *affirmare* translates ἀποφαίνεσθαι and that *nihil affirmatur* 'must mean that Plato does not *assert* his own opinion in any of the dialogues in the sense of *revealing* or *broadcasting* it' [his emphasis], which would allow for the suspicion on the part of the Cicero character that Cicero had at least some beliefs of some kind. A degree of support for this reading comes from the late antique Anon., *De phil. Plat.*, on whom see below. And it is true that *affirmare* has a number of uses in which it amounts to 'to corroborate', sc. an account which has been provided antecedently, or a view an individual might be deemed to have; it can also mean 'to provide assurance', i.e. give a formal legal undertaking when someone had previously given an informal undertaking (on this last point see Heumann-Seckel s.v.). On the other hand, *affirmare* is unlike some other terms not narrowly technical in *Acad.* and related texts from the Ciceronian corpus, and if Cicero intended the quite specific sense envisaged, he did not signal it, although the Cicero character is quite circumspect in separating Plato and Socrates. Thus one may wonder if the desire to have a progression from Plato onwards needs to issue in a distinctive philosophical position ascribed to Plato, at least at this early stage in the final edition. As noted above, the text seems to go out of its way to speak of properties of the dialogues as opposed to views of the man, and Plato was of course different from Socrates, Arcesilaus, and Carneades in virtue of the fact that he wrote.

The characterization of Plato's works given by Cicero has points of contact with that given in Anon., *De phil. Plat.*, section 10, lines 1-46 Westerink, pp. 205-6 Hermann, discussed by Tarrant (1985: 71-9); Annas (1992a: 62-72); and Brittain (2001: 208-11); see also Layne (2018): Ἀλλὰ καὶ τὴν τῶν νέων Ἀκαδημαϊκῶν ὑπερέβαλεν φιλοσοφίαν τῷ ἐκείνην ἀκαταληψίαν πρεσβεύειν, δεῖξαι δὲ τοῦτον ὡς εἰσὶν ἐπιστήμονι καὶ καταλήψεις τινές. (a) λέγουσι δέ τινες συνωθοῦντες τὸν Πλάτωνα εἰς τοὺς ἐφεκτικούς τε καὶ τοὺς Ἀκαδημαϊκοὺς ὡς καὶ αὐτοῦ ἀκαταληψίαν εἰσάγοντος· καὶ κατασκευάζουσι τοῦτο ἐκ τῶν εἰρημένων αὐτῷ ἐν τοῖς συγγράμμασιν αὐτοῦ. λέγει τοίνυν, φασίν, ἐπιρρήματά τινα ἀμφίβολά τε καὶ διστακτικὰ περὶ πραγμάτων διαλεγόμενος, οἷόν ἐστι τὸ 'εἰκὸς' καὶ τὸ 'ἴσως' καὶ 'τάχ' ὡς οἶμαι'· τοῦτο δ' οὐκ ἐπιστήμονός ἐστιν, ἀλλά τινος μὴ καταλαβόντος τὴν ἀκριβῆ γνῶσιν. πρὸς τούτους δὲ φαμεν ὡς ταῦτα φησὶν οἷον προσδιοριζόμενος, ὅπερ οὐ ποιοῦσιν οἱ ἐφεκτικοί· οὔτε γὰρ ἀκριβῶς διαλέγονται οὔτε προσδιορίζονται, εἴπερ πάντων ἀκαταληψίαν λέγουσι. (b) δεύτερον λόγον λέγουσιν ὅτι ἐξ ὧν τὰ ἐναντία περὶ τῶν αὐτῶν κατασκευάζει δῆλός ἐστιν ἀκαταληψίαν πρεσβεύων· οἷον περὶ φιλίας ἐν τῷ Λύσιδι διαλεγόμενος τἀναντία κατεσκεύασεν, καὶ περὶ σωφροσύνης ἐν τῷ Χαρμίδῃ, καὶ περὶ ὁσιότητος ἐν τῷ Εὐθύφρονι. καὶ πρὸς τούτους δὲ ἐροῦμεν ὅτι εἰ καὶ τἀναντία κατεσκεύασεν, ἀλλ᾽ οὖν τελευταῖον ἐπέκρινε τὴν ἀλήθειαν. (c) τρίτον λέγουσιν ὅτι οὐκ οἴεται ἐπιστήμην εἶναι· καὶ δῆλον ἐξ ὧν πᾶσαν ἀπόδοσιν τῆς ἐπιστήμης καὶ τὸν ἀριθμὸν ἀνεσκεύασεν ἐν Θεαιτήτῳ· πῶς οὖν κατάληψιν φήσομεν τὸν τοιοῦτον πρεσβεύειν; πρὸς οὓς ἐροῦμεν ὅτι ὁ Πλάτων οὐκ οἴεται ἀγράφῳ γραμματείῳ ἐοικέναι τὴν ψυχήν, ἀλλὰ νομίζει αὐτὴν ἀνακαλύψεως δεῖσθαι μόνης πρὸς τὸ νῆψαι καὶ ἰδεῖν τὰ πράγματα, ἐπεὶ ἔχει τὴν ἐπιστήμην ἐν αὐτῇ, ἀμβλυώττει δὲ διὰ τὴν πρὸς τὸ σῶμα συνάφειαν. μόνης οὖν ἀνακαθάρσεως δεῖται· διὸ τοὺς κακῶς εἰρημένους περὶ ἐπιστήμης λόγους ἀνεσκεύασεν, ἐάσας ψυχῇ ἀποκαθαρθείσῃ νοῆσαι τὸ ἀληθές. (d) τέταρτον λέγουσι λόγον τοιοῦτον· εἰ διττὴν οἴεται τὴν γνῶσιν ὁ Πλάτων, τὴν μὲν δι᾽ αἰσθήσεως, τὴν δὲ διὰ νοῦ γινομένην, ἑκατέραν δὲ λέγει σφάλλεσθαι, δῆλον ὡς ἀκαταληψίαν πρεσβεύει. φησὶν γὰρ 'οὐδὲν οὔτε ὁρῶμεν οὔτε ἀκούομεν ἀκριβῶς, ἀλλὰ διαμαρτάνουσιν αἱ αἰσθήσεις'· καὶ πάλιν περὶ τῶν νοητῶν φησὶν ὅτι 'ἡ ψυχὴ ἡμῶν προσπεπλεγμένη ⟨τῷ⟩ κακῷ τούτῳ, τῷ σώματι, οὐδὲν νοεῖ. πρὸς οὓς ἐροῦμεν ὅτι, ὅταν εἴπῃ ὡς αἱ αἰσθήσεις οὐκ ἀντιλαμβάνονται τῶν αἰσθητῶν, τοῦτο λέγει ὅτι τὴν οὐσίαν τῶν αἰσθητῶν οὐ γινώσκουσιν· ἐπεὶ τοῦ πάθους τοῦ εἰς αὐτὰς ἐξ αὐτῶν τῶν αἰσθητῶν γινομένου ἀντιλαμβάνονται, οὐκ ἴσασι δὲ τὴν οὐσίαν αὐτὴν καθ᾽ αὑτὰς οὖσαι. οἷον ἡ ὄψις διακρινομένη μὲν ὑπὸ λευκοῦ αἰσθάνεται, τί δ᾽ ἐστι λευκὸν καθ᾽ αὑτὴν οὐκ οἶδεν, ἀλλὰ συμπλεκομένη τῇ φαντασίᾳ διαγινώσκει· ὥσπερ καὶ ἡ δόξα οὐκ οἶδεν καθ᾽ αὑτὴν οὖσα ἅπερ οἶδεν μετὰ τῆς διανοίας. πάλιν ὅταν εἴπῃ ὅτι ἡ ψυχὴ οὐ νοεῖ συνοῦσα τῷ κακῷ τούτῳ, οὐ περὶ πάντων τῶν ἀνθρώπων λέγει τοῦτο, ἀλλὰ περὶ τῶν ἐνύλως ζώντων· ἐκεῖνοι γὰρ καὶ ἡττωμένην ἔχουσι τὴν ψυχὴν ὑπὸ τοῦ σώματος, οὓς καὶ 'σπαρτικοὺς' ἀλλαχοῦ ὀνομάζει, δίκην φυτῶν ἀποβλαστάνοντας· οἱ δὲ καθαροὶ καὶ ὑπ᾽ αὐτοῦ ἀλλαχοῦ 'οὐρανοπολῖται' λεγόμενοι, οὗτοι νοοῦσιν. (e) πέμπτος λόγος ἐστὶν οὗτος· αὐτός, φασίν, λέγει ἐν διαλόγῳ αὐτοῦ ὅτι 'οὐδὲν οἶδα οὔτε διδάσκω τι, ἀλλὰ διαπορῶ μόνον'· ὅρα οὖν πῶς ὁμολογεῖ ἰδίῳ στόματι μηδὲν κατειληφέναι, 'But he also outstripped the philosophy of the New Academics, in that they preach this so-called inapprehensibility, while Plato showed that there are apprehensions delivering knowledge. (a) Some people, aiming to press Plato into the position of the sceptics and Academics, say that he also maintained inapprehensibility; and they bring this about on the basis of certain sayings of his in his writings. In his dialogues, he uses certain adverbs, as they say, which are ambiguous and hesitating with reference to facts, e.g. 'probably' and also 'maybe' and 'perhaps I think'. This is not the way in which someone speaks who knows, but of someone who has not seized precise cognition. We say to them that he says these things as someone who is speaking precisely, which the sceptics do not do; for they neither converse with precision nor speak precisely, since they claim the inapprehensibility of all things anyway. (b) Second, they say that it is plain that he preaches inapprehensibility from the fact that he argues for opposite conclusions about the same subjects; thus he argues for opposite views about friendship in the *Lysis*, and about temperance in the *Charmides*, and about piety in the *Euthyphron*. To these people we shall say that, if he argued for opposite conclusions, he pronounced on the truth in the end. (c) Third, they say that he does not believe that there is knowledge, and that this is plain from the fact that he destroys every definition of knowledge as well as the notion of number in the *Theaetetus*; how shall we then say that he preaches apprehension? To them we shall say that Plato does not believe that the soul resembles a blank writing tablet, but believes that all the soul needs is for her veil to be taken away in order to recover herself and see the things for what they are, since it holds knowledge within herself, but her sight is blurred through her contact with the body. Therefore she is in need of purification; therefore Plato demolished the false accounts of knowledge, leaving it to the purified soul to cognize the true. (d) Fourth, they say the following: given that Plato says that cognition is twofold, one kind coming about through perception, the other through reason, and he says that each is deceived, it is plain that he preaches inapprehensibility. For he says "we neither see nor hear accurately, but perceptions commit mistakes"; and again he says about objects of reason that "our soul, entangled with the evil that is the body, cannot apprehend anything." To them we shall say that, when he says about perceptions that they do not apprehend perceptible objects, then he means by this that they do not understand the essence of perceptible things; because they do grasp the effect that registers with them from perceptible objects, but do not grasp essence itself if left to themselves. For example, sight discriminates and perceives the white, but does not know by itself what "white" is, but sight makes it out when bound up with imagination, in the same way as opinion by itself does not know what it knows when combined with reasoning. And again, when he says that the soul does not cognize anything being together as she is with that evil, he does not say this about all human beings, but about those who live bound up with matter; for their soul is in an inferior state under the body. Elsewhere he calls them "sown men", rooted in the world like plants; the pure, however, whom he calls "citizens of heaven" elsewhere, they cognize. (e) The fifth argument is this: Plato himself, they say, says in one of his dialogues: "I know nothing and I teach nothing, but wonder about things." Look how he confirms with his own mouth that he has apprehended nothing.'

For general orientation on this text, including its late date (sixth century AD) and overall purpose, see the introduction in Westerink (1962). The extract illuminates in greater detail how reading Plato as a sceptic would work, even though the five arguments distinguished do not map neatly on Cicero's four (with the exception of ii = c); Brittain (2001: 203–4) and Layne (2018: 537–40) show how one might have derived the five arguments from Platonic dialogues. Unlike the Cicero character in *Acad.*, notably *Luc.* 74, the author draws no distinction between Plato the author and thinker and Socrates qua character in the dialogues, although he does not equate the two in other parts of the text. Consideration (a) and (d) would appear to allow for beliefs of some description, although these would not amount to knowledge, as Brittain (2001: 209–10) notes. In my view this helps establish the possibility that *nihil affirmatur* in *Ac.* 1.46 hints at beliefs ascribed to Plato which are below the threshold of knowledge, but the differences between *Anon.* and Cicero are substantial enough to make the case no stronger than that.

Quae usque ad Carneadem perducta does not suggest that the New Academy was taken to end with Carneades' predecessor, just that Carneades represents a new phase; cf. *N.D.* 1.11: *Vt haec in philosophia ratio contra omnia disserendi nullamque rem aperte iudicandi profecta a Socrate, repetita ab Arcesila, confirmata a Carneade usque ad nostram uiguit aetatem; quam nunc prope modum orbam esse in ipsa Graecia intellego.* Other divisions of the Academy posit a 'Middle Academy' and let the New Academy begin with Carneades; see e.g. Sextus, *P.H.* 1.220; [Galen], *Hist. phil.* 3; Clemens, *Strom.* 1.64.1; and Görler (1994: 779–81). On *quartus* as a subject complement, see Pinkster i.766.

I print Durand's emendation *exposuisti* rather than the transmitted *exposui*. In §46 *init.* Cicero states that others call the sceptical Academy the new Academy, whereas it seems old to him, since it goes back to Plato. The question is then if *sed tamen illa*...restates this point or makes the polite concession that the Academy as construed by Antiochus may be called the old one, and the sceptical Academy the new one. That *illa* usually refers to what stands further away and that *quae usque*...picks up what has just been mentioned suggests the second option (polite concession) is right. In that case one would want *exposuisti*, since it was Varro who spoke about the Old Academy. There are a number of possible explanations for the corruption of *exposuisti* to *exposui*: a reader might have thought that Cicero is restating the point just made, viz. that 'his' Academy is actually the old one. Alternatively, Plasberg[1] (p. 57) refers in the app. to *Div.* 1.87, where something is ascribed to Quintus Cicero that had been mentioned by the first-person narrator of the frame in *Div.* 1 (Cicero); see section 8 for a distinction of senses of 'Cicero'. Philippson (1939: 1130), like Plezia (1936: 435–6), regards *exposui* not as a corruption for *exposuisti*, but as the result of an oversight on Cicero's part when he adapted *Catul.* However, it seems most unlikely that the speaker who introduced this material in *Catul.* also presented the Antiochian material which is given to Varro in the final edition; rather, Hortensius must have been given what is now *Ac.* 1.19–42, probably with some modifications. See sections 9.2 and 9.5. If one assumes, as we do, that Hortensius' role was given to the Antiochian Brutus in the intermediate edition, Cicero would have missed that *exposui* needed adjustment during both revision processes.

Carneades autem nullius philosophiae partis ignarus et...incredibili quadam fuit facultate † et to [...]: while the anti-dogmatic arguments recorded for Arcesilaus are aimed at the Stoa and Stoic epistemology and philosophy of action in particular (see 1.44 *init.*), Carneades expanded into logic, ethics, and theology, as well as engaged the Epicureans in argument (cf. e.g. *Fat.* 23). For Zeno of Sidon see the collection of his fragments by Angeli and Colaizzo (1979); von Fritz (1972); and Angeli (2018).

He is mentioned because he represents a direct link with Carneades: Cicero heard him in Athens (*Fin.* 1.16; *N.D.* 1.59, 1.93-4; *Tusc.* 3.38), and Zeno had heard Carneades; he is famous inter alia for his characterization of Socrates reported in *N.D.* 1.93: *Zeno quidem non eos solum, qui tum erant, Apollodorum Sillim ceteros, figebat maledictis, sed Socratem ipsum, parentem philosophiae, Latino uerbo utens scurram Atticum fuisse dicebat, Chrysippum numquam nisi Chrysippam uocabat.* On Zeno's use of code-switching, see Dyck (2003: 177) ad loc.

In what followed Cicero probably introduced a contrast with Arcesilaus (this is suggested by *autem*) and named the *probabile* as Carneades' major innovation. The latter point is made by both Lucullus and Cicero in *Luc.* (33-6, 59; 66-7, 77-8; cf. Aug., *Contra Acad.* 2.5.12), as Brittain (2001: 174 n. 7) observes. Numenius suggests that the Academic position needed to be salvaged by Carneades' revision of it; cf. frg. 27 (Eus., *Praep. Ev.* XIV.8.1-15), p. 76.14-32, and frg. 26 (Eus., *Praep. Ev.* XIV.7.1-13), p. 75.107-11; see appendix 2.

Another innovation that might have been mentioned is the technique of arguing *in utramque partem* of a question; cf. Numenius frg. 26 (Eus., *P.E.* XIV.7.1-13), p. 75.105-7, and contrast 1.45:...*contra omnium sententias disserens*...(on Arcesilaus). Carneades also raised the possibility that the sage might opine, and his pupils disagreed on whether he argued this ad hominem or endorsed it himself; see on *Luc.* 74, and Glucker (1997: 82) on the Carneadean changes.

Carneades' rhetorical abilities are attested to by many sources; according to D.L., his voice was so powerful that the keeper of the gymnasium asked him to tone it down (4.63), and teachers of rhetoric would suspend their classes and go and listen to him instead (4.62). See also *Luc.* 60, 67; *De orat.* 2.45, 161; 3.68. On the basis of this Krische (1845: 56 n. 1) proposed *facultate* ⟨*dicendi*⟩, not implausibly; the phrase is often used by Cicero. If Hunt (1998: 110) is right to suggest that *et to* is a catchword, intended to facilitate the assembly of a manuscript after its gatherings had been prepared separately, then the point in time when catchwords came in use is a terminus post quem for the archetype. Catchwords were common by the thirteenth century and first appear in Spain in the tenth century; see Derolez (2003: 34). *Producta* in v_1, if deliberate, is an unnecessary modification, but it may also be the result of a misunderstood abbreviation. My t. 8 is next in the sequence.

Fragments and Testimonia

In the Oxford Classical Text I have assembled evidence for the lost parts of *Acad.*, consisting of the backward references to *Catul.* in *Luc.*, as well as the fragments and testimonia of the final edition.[1] The latter are there contextualized with texts which quote from or draw on the extant part of *Ac.* 1, on the grounds that both groups of texts jointly represent the indirect tradition of the final edition. In the commentary I refer to these texts as 't', followed by a number.

The *editio princeps* of fragments of *Acad.* was that by Sigonius of 1559, whereas that of *Ac.* 1 and *Luc.* (alongside other Ciceronian *philosophica*) was the Roman edition by Conrad Sweynheym and Arnold Pannartz, published in 1471. Early editions of Cicero present the fragments of *Acad.* alongside fragments of other Ciceronian works rather than alongside *Ac.* 1 and *Luc.* Annotated editions of the fragments are included in Reid[1] and Plasberg[1]. The latter is the only editor to date who added a collection of the backward references in *Luc.* to the *Catulus*; however, annotated lists of such backward references were also drawn up by Plezia (1936: 427–9) and Mansfeld (1997).[2] Little would be gained by a full survey of the editorial history of the fragments.[3]

There are no certain fragments or testimonia of the first edition of *Acad.* other than the backward references to *Catul.* in *Luc.*[4] Our main sources for the lost parts of

---

[1] On my use of the terms 'fragment' and 'testimonium', see below.
[2] Mansfeld (1997: 46–7) seems unaware of Plasberg[1] and cites De Lacy (1984[3]: 64–71) as a model.
[3] See, however, Goerenz (vol. ii, pp. xiii–xxxviii), who surveys earlier scholarly engagement with *Acad.* and notes (p. xix) that Talon (1547: 2–6) had correctly described how *Ac.* 1, *Luc.*, and the fragments preserved in Nonius fit together (acknowledged by Sigonius from p. 96r), but that waters were muddied when Lambinus assumed that the fragments of *Ac.* 4 preserved by Nonius and corresponding to passages in *Luc.* were derived from *Luc.* itself (or that *Luc.* had become *Ac.* 4 unmodified). Misled into thinking that Cicero's concerns about *Catul.* and *Luc.* had been allayed by the addition of new proems (*Att.* 13.32.2–3 = SB 305 = T15), Lambinus posited an edition in four books, whose last two books were *Catul.* and *Luc.* De Allio (1743: 5) expanded on Lambinus' view by identifying the first two books of *Acad.* as *Varro* and *Hort.* Talon's correct insight eventually regained status (see e.g. the concise statement in Davies p. 51), but even today secondary literature occasionally refers to *Ac.* 1 as *Varro* (or to *Luc.* as *Ac.* 2). Scope for misapprehension arose from misunderstandings regarding the relative date of the letters to Atticus written while Cicero worked on *Acad.* (or from a failure to attend to all relevant letters), and from the titles under which *Ac.* 1 and *Luc.* feature in the manuscripts available to editors in the sixteenth century (see the preface of the edition). On Talon's *Academia* in its historical context, see Schmitt (1972: 81–91).
[4] Thus also Philippson (1939: 1128); Hunt (1998: 18–19). Quint. 3.6.64 (= t. 65) and Plut., *Luc.* 42.4 (= t. 66) show an awareness of the existence of *Catul.* and *Luc.*, and *Luc.* only, respectively, but we have no way of confirming that either author actually read the first edition. (Plut., *Cic.* 40 = t. 67 may be deemed a testimonium on *Catul.* if first-hand knowledge of the first edition on Plutarch's part is assumed.) Glucker (1978: 389–90) argues that Plutarch relied on a lost biography of Cicero by Cornelius Nepos; see also Philippson (1939: 1134). As to Quint., his contemporary Pliny the Elder appears to have known the final edition (cf. *N.H.* 31.6). *N.H.* 31.6 puts *N.H.* 10.155 (see on t. 27) into context. Without the information in 31.6, one might be tempted to connect 10.155 with *Luc.* 57 (for the notion that Delian poultry farmers can tell from an egg which hen laid it) and *Luc.* 86 (for the term *gallinarius*), but given 31.6, which alludes to

the final edition of *Acad.* are the late antique grammarian Nonius Marcellus and St. Augustine, followed by Lactantius.⁵ In his *De compendiosa doctrina* Nonius quotes, because he is interested in a particular word which functions as a lemma, individual sentences, parts of sentences, or phrases from the final edition of *Acad.* usually with an indication of the book.⁶ Augustine's dialogue *Contra Academicos* draws extensively on the final edition of *Acad.* but, for all we know, not in a manner which involves verbatim quotation, nor does he indicate books referred to or drawn on.⁷ It thus seems appropriate to view evidence from Nonius as fragments, and evidence from Augustine as testimonia (except in cases where Augustine seems to signal verbatim quotes; see t. 56, cf. 63*). Although I draw the distinction in my discussion where it is straightforward,⁸ I present fragments and testimonia alike in the sequence which I take to be the original one (rather than list fragments and testimonia separately).⁹ Moreover, in cases where the fragment or testimonium cannot be neatly isolated but where it is nonetheless plausible to assume that *Acad.* is reflected in a passage, I have erred on the side of fullness in giving context.¹⁰

---

the title *Academici libri* which Cicero only used for the final edition, it is more likely that Pliny derived the information in 10.155 from *Ac.* 3 and *Ac.* 4. The impossibility of positively identifying reliance on *Luc.* rather than on *Ac.* 3 and 4 in any author after Cicero's time, coupled with the fact that Lactantius and Augustine knew the edition in four books, makes it the default assumption that lesser figures of similar date in the indirect tradition of *Acad.* (Ammianus, Jerome) used the final edition.

⁵ Lactantius knew the final edition of *Acad.*; cf. *Inst.* 6.24.1 (t. 21), which puts the other quotations and reminiscences into context. Cautiously Barthel (1903: 9): '... so dass mit Sicherheit nicht gefolgert werden kann, dass Lactantius neben den *ac. poster.* auch die *priora* ausgeschrieben hat...'; Fessler (1913) and Faes De Mottoni (1982: 337 n. 10) think that Lactantius read *Ac.* 1 and *Luc.* See Kendeffy (2016) on Lactantius' engagement with Academic scepticism in general. On Ammianus' use of Cicero, see Michael (1874: 31–2) and Jenkins (1985: 128 and 172).

⁶ On Nonius' method and use of sources, see Lindsay (1901: 100–12); Fedeli (1961–4); Chahoud (2007); and Welsh (2012); on his date, see Deufert (2001); on ninth-century editorial work on the text, see von Büren (2019).

⁷ Augustine famously knew *Hort.*, and makes it plain in *C.D.* 6.2 (my t. 56) that he knew the final edition of *Acad.* I can find no positive evidence requiring the assumption that he also knew *Catul.* and *Luc.*, and one might have expected him to find a way of acknowledging the coexistence of the two editions had he been aware of it. However, Fuhrer (1997: 38–9), who observes that certainty is not to be had, notes: 'Für die ausschliessliche Benützung der *Academici Posteriores* [sc. in *Contra Acad.*] spricht der Umstand, dass Augustin den *Hortensius* offenbar nicht als Teil der *Academici Libri* betrachtet..., zu denen der *Protreptikos* in der als "Trilogie" konzipierten ersten Version noch gehörte...Die "Trilogie"-Konzeption der *Academici Priores* scheint er aber gekannt zu haben, da er sich in *c. acad.* 1 mit dem *Hortensius* auseinandersetzt...; er wollte sie offenbar selbst nachbilden, indem er die beiden (zeitlich um sieben Tage getrennten) Dialogkomplexe von *c. acad.* 1 (Hauptquelle: *Hortensius*) bzw. 2 und 3 (Hauptquelle: *Academici Libri* [*Posteriores?*]) in ein Werk zusammenfasste.' That Augustine knew only the final edition is assumed e.g. by Reid¹ (p. 168); Plasberg² (p. x); Plezia (1936: 429); Hagendahl (1967: 60 n. 1, 498–500). See also Fuhrer (1997: 37–44) on the sources of *Contra Acad.* more generally. *Contra Acad.* 3.7.15–16 (my t. 51) may represent evidence that Cicero worked allusions to Varronian material into the final edition. On how Augustine read Cicero and how he interpreted Cicero's philosophical position, see Brittain (2011).

⁸ Plasberg², unlike Plasberg¹, uses italics to indicate that he views a text as a testimonium rather than a fragment.

⁹ For Nonius I follow the edition of Lindsay (1903) but cite, as is conventional, after the pagination of the earlier edition of Mercier (1583¹ and 1614²); for Augustine I follow Green (1970) and signal divergences in the commentary. The spelling has been harmonized in line with that employed in the Oxford Classical Text.

¹⁰ On the theory and practice of collecting fragments, see Most (1997), especially the contributions by Kidd (1997); Laks (1997); and Németh (2016).

What sequence one regards as original depends on one's conception of the shape of the two (or three) editions, and that conception is in turn not unconnected with the extant fragments. However, as I argue in section 9.2, the backward references to *Catul.* in *Luc.*, taken together with what can be observed in the extant part of *Ac.* 1 and consideration of some general formal principles which Cicero adheres to in his dialogues, make one particular reconstruction of *Catul.* more likely than others, and the fragments and testimonia of the final edition offer no decisive evidence contra even if arranged slightly differently. In presenting the fragments and testimonia, I have assumed that Cicero's speech in *Ac.* 1, based on Catulus' in the *Catulus* (which was the second one after Hortensius'), contained information on Carneades, the πιθανόν and the testing procedures (see on *Luc.* 35–6), on the difference between Clitomacheanism and mitigated scepticism, and on the Roman Books, and that in *Ac.* 2, after a proem, Cicero gave a speech which included an extensive section 'against the senses' (§79), adapted from his speech in the *Catulus* (there the third and final one, delivering—in anticipation—considerations against the third clause of Zeno's definition of the cataleptic impression, which in *Luc.* is named as the remaining key point of contention; see *Luc.* 78). Most of the fragments relating to *Ac.* 2 contain considerations arising from conflicting appearances. One might think that guidance on the order of these fragments could be obtained from two different quarters. First, given that Sextus Empiricus offers extensive parallel material for such arguments,[11] one might wonder if the arrangement of the relevant passages in Sextus can, in one way or another, help in imposing order on the Ciceronian fragments. However, while patterns of arrangement can be discerned in Sextus, e.g. by the state of the perceiving subject, normal or not (the latter due to insanity, drunkenness, etc.), or by sense modality, I am not persuaded that there was a standard way of organizing the relevant material, and certainly not at the time when Cicero was writing. Second, it has been recognized for a long time that the material presented in Nonius' *De compendiosa doctrina* follows certain patterns in its organization. In particular, when Nonius draws on an excerpt which he himself created from a primary text available to him, he presents material, within a given book of his, in the order in which he found it in the excerpted text, a principle known as 'Lindsay's law' but noted before Lindsay formulated it.[12] Mueller and Reid[1] arranged the fragments of *Ac.* 2 in order of appearance in Nonius, but in a manner which extended across book divisions, i.e. beyond the applicability of the 'law'. The only fragments whose relative order falls within its domain are t. 8, t. 11, as well as probably t. 47 (see ad loc.),[13] all from the grouping 'Cicero viii' in Lindsay (1901: 16).[14] Plasberg[1] and Plasberg[2] appear to have opted—no rationale is given—for a sequence from general to particular. My arrangement is similar, though this may not be immediately apparent since I intercalate indirectly transmitted material which is also available in direct transmission. Like Plasberg I assume that Cicero did not just assemble examples of conflicting appearances, but added at least a general remark on what follows from the existence of such appearances: that assenting to the non-apprehensive is to be

---

[11] Cf. e.g. Sextus, *P.H.* 1.100–11 and 2.48–69; Burnyeat (1979).
[12] See Lindsay (1901: 1–10 and passim); Astbury (1974); Gatti (2011).   [13] See Scarsi (1986).
[14] See also Lindsay (1902).

avoided at all costs because it leads to *error*.[15] Conversely, the fragments which are explicitly ascribed to *Ac.* 2 by Nonius do not suggest that Cicero, in adapting the *Catulus*, transferred material from Catulus' speech to what was his own in the *Catulus*; there are e.g. no general remarks on Carneades or on the πιθανόν.[16] However, from the backward references to *Catul.* in *Luc.* (see esp. §13), it is also clear that the character Cicero must have made some historical remarks, too, notably on the outlook of the *ueteres physici*.

I further assume, uncontroversially, that *Ac.* 3 and *Ac.* 4 correspond to Lucullus' and Cicero's speeches in *Luc.* respectively, with occasional additions, deletions and modifications; cf. *Att.* 13.3.1 (= SB 321 = T19). This is strongly suggested by those Nonian fragments which match closely, or even verbatim, passages in *Luc.* These fragments also provide anchor points of sorts for the fragments and testimonia more loosely attributed or attributable to *Ac.* 3 and 4.[17] None of the fragments generically attributed to *Ac.* 3 by Nonius can compellingly or plausibly be linked with a passage outside of the first half of *Luc.* Some appear to derive from the proem of *Ac.* 3, others can be linked with passages within Lucullus' speech, yet others are hard to place (e.g. t. 23).

For *Ac.* 4 most fragments correspond closely to extant parts of *Luc.*; however, I have moved t. 34 and 47 here, which earlier editors have classified differently.

At the end of the collection there stand passages which one cannot confidently assign to a particular book, as well as *dubia*.[18]

Ac. 1

t. 1–7

t. 1 is one of three unacknowledged reminiscences of the *Academici libri* in Jerome, the others being t. 3 and 33; see also Hunt (1998: 22). Together all these texts represent evidence for the indirect transmission of the final edition of *Acad.*

t. 2, 4, and 7, on which see Ogilvie (1978: 58–60), are put into context by other passages in Lactantius (32, 42, 49, 55, 59; 21, which cites a particular book). As to t. 7, in its larger context, viz. *Inst.* 3.28.10–13 and 3.30.6, the sceptical proclamations ascribed to the Presocratics in general in *Ac.* 1.44–6 are allocated to particular individuals; see on *Ac.* 1.44 for possible explanations.

---

[15] This is the conclusion a Clitomachean would draw from conflicting appearances, and Cicero was cast as a Clitomachean in *Hort.*, in the *Catulus* and in *Luc.*, and in the final edition of *Acad.*; see section 9.5.

[16] My t. 18 and 19 are fragments of *Ac.* 2 which cannot be connected with the section against the senses; however, they do not permit inferences regarding other, larger themes in *Ac.* 2.

[17] Plasberg[1] prints these texts underneath the text of *Luc.*

[18] Hagendahl (1967: 60–70) lists passages in the Augustinian corpus which represent verbal reminiscences of sentences or phrases in *Luc.* or rather their counterparts in *Ac.* 3 and 4. Only substantial correspondences are included here, but the reader may want to appraise Hagendahl's collection independently (who notes on p. 499: '...I venture to say that Augustine presumably borrowed still more'). See also Testard (1958).

t. 8

Quid Antipater... tot uoluminibus is *SVF* iii.4 (Antipater); t. 8 as a whole is Carneades F18a Mette. It is plain from the extant part of *Ac.* 1 that after the end of Varro's speech Cicero continued with an account of Academic scepticism from a historical point of view, and t. 8 clearly was part of that account. In it the chronology of Antipater of Tarsus and Mnesarchus of Athens is inverted: the former, head of the Stoic school after Diogenes of Bablyon, died around 130 BC and was a high-profile opponent of Carneades (who died in 129 BC),[19] while the latter was born around 160 BC, died around 85 BC, and was a teacher of Antiochus'; see Eus., *Praep. Ev.* XIV.9.3 = T1 Mette = Numenius frg. 28 Des Places, Aug., *Contra Acad.* 3.18.41 = F8a Mette = my t. 58, Philod., *Index Acad.* col. xxxiv.23-4 Fleischer, with Fleischer (2015). Fleischer (2015: 416–17) also considers the evidence for the view that already Philo had heard Mnesarchus. Cicero refers to Mnesarchus also in *De orat.* 1.46, 1.83; *Fin.* 1.6; *Luc.* 69 (see ad loc.).

The juxtaposition of two Stoics of successive generations is suggestive of persistent conflict with the Academy. The questions *quid... quid...?* could conceivably have been genuine and enquiring ('What was the basis of their criticism?'), but are more likely to be rhetorical, inviting the answer 'none' to 'what was the point of...?'. This is suggested by the terminology in which the criticism is described. *Stomachari*, when used not of anger per se (cf. *Luc.* 12) but of criticism voiced, absolutely or with generic objects (e.g. *omnia*), often means 'to rail', i.e. to criticize loudly and in an ineffectual manner (contrast Rackham's translation, 'why is Mnesarchus resentful?'; Krische 1845: 57 sees a reference to 'mündliches Verfahren' only).[20] Antipater had the nick-name 'pen shouter' ($\kappa\alpha\lambda\alpha\mu\sigma\beta\sigma\alpha s$),[21] because he was productive in writing but less adroit in philosophical discussion. The somewhat paradoxical *iunctura* of *digladiari* and *uoluminibus* appears to allude to his nickname. One effect of including Mnesarchus is that dismissive comment on the Stoa's stance from a historical point of view becomes a criticism of Antiochus: Mnesarchus must be credited with a role in turning Antiochus away from scepticism, a shift remarked on in *Acad.* (*Luc.* 69–70); note also the imagery of pollution in Aug., *Contra Acad.* 3.18.41 (t. 58).

Brittain (2001: 53) makes a connection with Philo in particular: 'Numenius reports that Philo began his scholarchate fighting the Stoics (fr. 28). There is perhaps evidence for this in fr. 1 of the *Academici* (p. 161 Reid), which notes Mnesarchus as a Stoic opponent of the Academy.' Tarrant (1982: 21) links the fragment to the claims of Philo's Roman Books, but it is hard to see why these should be of concern to a Stoic based in Athens, i.e. Mnesarchus (Antipater had been dead for forty years).

---

[19] The year of Antipater's birth cannot be inferred with any precision; see Guérard and Puech (1989); Steinmetz (1994: 637): '...ist sicher noch im 3. Jahrhundert geboren.'

[20] *Stomachari cum aliquo* does exist and means 'to be angry at someone' (e.g. *De orat.* 2.267:...*Scipio apud Numantiam, cum stomacharetur cum C. Metello*), but in the present case, where the two philosophers each have their own predicate, and where *tot uoluminibus* seems not to apply to both, *cum Carneade* is unlikely to do double duty in both questions.

[21] See Plut., *Garr.* 514c-d = *SVF* iii.5, Antipater; Numenius frg. 27.47-56 Des Places = *SVF* iii.6, Antipater; Burnyeat (1997: 280–1).

Ac. 2

t. 9

In the form of a counterfactual conditional, this fragment appears to offer a general statement on the power, or rather lack thereof, of our senses, and is therefore plausibly placed near the beginning of Cicero's speech in *Ac.* 2, corresponding to his speech, directed against the senses inter alia, in the *Catulus*; see *Luc.* 79 and the general note above.

Early in his speech in defence of κατάληψις Lucullus states that humans are endowed with senses so exceptional that, if a god were to appear and offer something better, one could not wish for more. This claim would be a rejoinder, if not a rational consideration against, the point made in the fragment that we would not need various aids used by craftsmen for taking measurements and verifying physical properties if 'we believed "that"' (*id*). (The terms for the aids are thus not used metaphorically.) The reference of *id* is unspecified but could be the claim that our senses are sufficiently powerful. Similarly Plezia (1936: 441). The *norma* (γνώμων), fashioned from the wooden rulers, is used by carpenters and masons to make their work rectangular; see e.g. Vitr. 7.3.

t. 10

Another consideration cited 'against the senses' (cf. *Luc.* 79), which must have formed part of Cicero's speech in *Catul.* originally. Cf. *Luc.* 105, where Cicero argues that one can observe the sea to take on different colour depending on circumstances, without thereby being able to say with respect to any one appearance that it is true, sc. not as a report on momentary appearance but on the nature of the object seen; Sextus, *P.H.* 1.118–23 on the Fifth Mode.

The point made could have stood on its own or could have been the rejoinder to a claim that the power of our senses can be inferred from the clarity with which we see an object as far away as the moon (which Cicero might have introduced as the opponent's view).

A survey of ancient attitudes to the moon's phases and of the Greek and Latin terminology used to describe them is in Gundel (1933: 98–100); for speculation about the moon more generally, see Plut., *De facie quae in orbe lunae apparet*, with Coones (1983). *Potesne* shows that a question mark needs to be placed after *quid*.

t. 11

The key term must be *uidetur*, i.e. *aequor* captures, on the argument made here, how the sea appears to the poets. In Lucullus' speech in *Luc.* there are places where he relies on linguistic naturalism, suggesting that, broadly speaking, aspects of the nature of a thing can be inferred from expressions used to designate it; Cicero counters them in his speech by observing that such expressions are at best indicative of speakers' beliefs about things. See Reinhardt (2019).

On *aequor* as a poetic term (i.e. a term used in poetry, and in prose only in quotations or passages of marked elevation, where the poetic resonance is intended) see Coleman (1999: 74); Gaertner (2005: 253) on Ov., *Pont.* 1.3.53; Pilar García Ruiz (2014). *Etiam* signals that *aequor* is an alternative term, rather than being affirmative or justificatory (cf. German 'ja auch').

t. 12

Given the ascription of the salient part of the testimonium to *Tusc.*, the case for inclusion here rather than among the *dubia* (if at all) must seem weak prima facie. However, we know that the 'broken oar', i.e. the oar that appears broken when partially submerged in water but straight when not (thus counting as an instance of conflicting appearances), was mentioned in the *Catulus*, since Lucullus professes himself to be unimpressed by it (*Luc.* 19:...*dum de remo inflexo...respondeam*; cf. 79, where *infractus* replaces *inflexus*: *Tu autem te negas infracto remo neque columbae collo commoueri. Primum, cur?*). Since the issue does not feature in *Tusc.* or anywhere else in Cicero, Plasberg[1] (p. 58) cited the passage in the app. crit. to the fragments.

Cf. Tert., *De anim.* 17.2: *Itaque mendacium uisui obicitur, quod remos in aqua inflexos uel infractos adseuerat aduersus conscientiam integritatis...*, 'For this reason sight is accused of lying since it offers assurance that oars in water are bent and broken when we are conscious they are not', and the collection of parallels in Waszink (2010[2]: 241). Lucretius uses *refractus* and *reflexus* in 4.438–42. Corydon of course speaks of a reflection (*imago*) in the calm sea in *Ecl.* 2.27.

t. 13

The manuscripts used by Lindsay agree on the ascription of the fragment to *Ac.* 2, but it is of course possible that the numeral was corrupted. Plasberg[1] (p. 58) wonders (following Klotz 1854) if the fragment might come from *Ac.* 4, citing *Luc.* 105 (so that it would be a rewriting of the passage): *Mare illud, quod nunc Fauonio nascente purpureum uidetur, idem huic nostro uidebitur, nec tamen adsentietur,* **quia nobismet ipsis modo caeruleum uidebatur, mane rauum, quodque nunc qua a sole collucet** *albescit et uibrat dissimileque est proximo et continenti, ut, etiam si possis rationem reddere cur id eueniat, tamen non possis id uerum esse quod uidebatur oculis defendere*. However, t. 36 below, from *Ac.* 4, partially overlaps with *Luc.* 105 (see highlighted section) and suggests that Cicero did not substantially alter the wording of this particular passage of *Luc.* in the final edition, even though (T19) (*Att.* 13.3.1 = SB 321) makes alterations and additions in general likely.

This raises the question of whether t. 13 is actually making a slightly different point. While t. 36 is about conflicting appearances and the inability to identify any particular appearance as a true representation of how things really are, t. 13 seems to suggest a model for conceptualizing this state of affairs: the appearances of different colours are like dye applied to water, and one only ever sees the water already (sc. temporarily) dyed. To this point *Luc.* 105 would reply that, even if one were able to give an explanation for the phenomenon of changing colours (*etiam si possis rationem reddere cur id eueniat*), one cannot argue that any one of one's impressions is true (as opposed to a report on an appearance at that point in time).

Aquae has no construction as it stands. Reid[1] (p. 162) notes correctly that Cicero does not use the plural *aquae* to denote the sea (although he does use the plural of *aqua*, e.g. in *Div.* 1.111 or *N.D.* 2.27; see *TLL* s.v. cols 349.63–350.11). The sentence from *et quidem* clarifies, elaborates or explains further what came before. *Tinctum* and *infectum* (on which see OLD s.v. *inficio* no. 1b) are near-synonyms, and the latter is not pejorative (contrast Brittain 2006: 109: 'tinged or contaminated'). Especially the latter word suggests that the issue is not the colouring of a surface but of a body or substance in three dimensions. Although certainty is not to be had, a word meaning 'substance' or 'body' which is neuter and on which *aquae* depends may have dropped out. I have supplied *corpus* tentatively since the phrasal term *corpus aquae* occurs thrice in Lucretius in suitable uses (2.232, 6.854, and 863), but there is nothing about it which makes it peculiarly Lucretian.

t. 14

The fragment clearly lacks a noun, which probably stood in the wider context, to give it meaning. Reid[1] (p. 163) thought the noun was *color*, 'complexion', and cited parallels from Sextus (*M.* 7.198 and 413; *P.H.* 1.44). Reid has been followed by later scholars (e.g. Rackham 1951: 459; Brittain 2006: 109). However, only *M.* 7.413 is concerned with variations in complexion (κατὰ ὥρας ἐνεργείας φύσεις ἡλικίας περιστάσεις νόσους ὑγείαν ὕπνον ἐγρήγορσιν, 'for it changes according to seasons, activities, natures, ages, conditions, diseases, health, sleep, waking', transl. Bett).

In the other two Sextan passages it is colour *perception* that is at issue, which is said to be affected by the state a given human being is in. If we supply *color* in this sense in the present passage, it would yield an instance of conflicting appearances, too, in this case not due to changes in the object perceived, but to changes or variations in the perceiving subject (with the object perceived putatively remaining in the same state). Cf. the Fourth Mode in Sextus, *P.H.* 1.100–17. The suggestion could be that the same colour appears differently to different people (a possibility linked to the eye-colour of the perceiving subject in Sextus, *P.H.* 1.198), or that it is appealing to some but not to others.

One may wonder if, alternatively, the noun to be supplied is *sapor*, the suggestion being that the same things taste differently to people depending on the state they are in. This, too, would be covered by the Fourth Mode. If *sapor* was supplied, the fragment would differ from earlier ones by invoking a sense modality other than vision.

t. 15

On my preferred reading of t. 14 above, t. 15 can be construed as making a similar point (though for a sense modality which has not featured hitherto), that, depending on the state one is in, certain things smell differently, to the point where a perfumed ointment smells foul to people in a certain state. Alternatively, the observation made is that certain things which are pleasant to some species are repulsive to others; thus Sextus, *P.H.* 1.55, on perfume being pleasant to humans but repulsive to dung-beetles and bees. The loanword *alabaster* (cf. ἀλάβαστρος) only here in Cicero; on the form *alabastrus*, found in other authors, see Denk (1906: 279). In *Cael.* Cicero uses the term *pyxis* (πυξίς) for a similar container eight times (first in §61); while in *Cael.* the Greekness of the term may be significant, *alabaster* here is likely to be the natural *uerbum proprium*. I print *putrere* with Lindsay, which is attested in Republican tragedy; Plasberg[1] (p. 59) opted for *putre esse* (with Lindsay's L A^A B^A).

t. 16

The classification of this text as a testimonium is formally tenuous; of earlier editors, only Plasberg[1] included it. Inclusion hinges on its thematic connection with the next item. I include both texts here rather than under *Ac.* 1 since the points which t. 16 and 17 make can serve as a natural conclusion to draw from the various arguments against the senses (which must have been accompanied by some kind of evaluative section). In any event, including both texts among the information on the final edition does arguably not distort the certain evidence for the latter.

Because conflicting appearances make it difficult to judge any particular impression as certainly true, giving assent is rash, and approving something false as true amounts to *error* (*approbatio* does not seem to denote Clitomachean approval here; cf. *Luc.* 104). Cicero, a Clitomachean in *Acad.*, i.e. an Academic who rejects assent unqualifiedly rather than permits informed assent as a mitigated sceptic would, may well have concluded his speech in *Ac.* 2 (and before that his speech in *Catul.*) with, inter alia, a remark like the one contained in the present fragment; cf. *Luc.* 66, and *Luc.* 53: *ipse sapiens sustinet se in furore ne approbet falsa pro ueris*. It is difficult to see how the statement could be a profession of mitigated scepticism, given how the proviso that self-aware assent might be given to something false operated; see on *Luc.* 148. *Pro* in *pro uero*, 'on the mistaken understanding that…' rather than 'instead of'. Within *Contra Acad.*, cf. 2.5.11 and 3.14.31. On t. 16, see also the commentary by Schlapbach (2003: 123–4).

t. 17

The text complements the preceding one, but unlike it references Cicero; I consider it a testimonium, too, though there is nothing in the passage which marks it as Augustinian in phrasing (and as such not a Ciceronian 'fragment').

Suspension of judgement is not a stand-offish refusal to accept anything, but positively enables continued open-minded enquiry in search of the truth (with *inquisitio ueritatis*, cf. *Off.* 1.13: *ueri inquisitio*); see on *Luc.* 7b–9a. Assenting to anything runs the risk of not just accepting as true what is false (cf. t. 16), but also of accepting what just happens to be true. The Academic sage is a device used in various places in

Lucullus' speech in *Luc.*, in response to Lucullus' use of the Stoic sage; see e.g. *Luc.* 66, and Neuhausen (1987). On t. 17, see also the commentary by Schlapbach (2003: 96–103).

t. 18

The fragment is short, syntactically incomplete, and thus only allows for speculation. *Exponere* is most likely a good thing (being or ending up as a model as a matter of fact, rather than making a display of one's virtue), given that the other two infinitive phrases describe actions or intentions which are laudable. If the fragment formed part of someone's characterization, then being an example to the young might be thought to be reminiscent of Socrates. However, the impulse to do away with greed and to punish transgressions is less plausibly associated with him, nor did he have the political influence necessary to do either. Indeed, these considerations tell against any Greek philosopher being at issue. A Roman figure who might be so characterized is the elder Cato, who held the highest political offices of the state, as well as that of *censor*, and is widely used by Cicero (and others) as an exemplum; see van der Blom (2010), index s.v. 'Porcius Cato, M. (Cato Maior)'. In the extant parts of *Acad.* he is only mentioned in *Luc.* 5 (one of the passages which claim that he learnt Greek late in life); cf. *Fin.* 5.2 for a near-contemporary reference to him.

On my organization of the remains of *Acad.* this and the following fragment are the only ones securely attributable to *Ac.* 2 which cannot be related to conflicting appearances and the conclusion to draw from them, i.e. the part of Cicero's speech which was directed 'against the senses' (*Luc.* 79). While the two fragments show that Cicero did not confine himself to arguing against the senses, the information they provide by itself is insufficient for forming a picture of any other larger themes Cicero's speech in *Ac.* 2 may have covered. However, the backward refences to *Catul.* in *Luc.*, notably §13 (cf. §72), tell us that Cicero in his speech in *Catul.* must have gestured to the Presocratics, i.e. that the historical scenario which is developed as background to the Academic position was not introduced by Catulus alone, although on the evidence of the beginning of Cicero's speech in *Ac.* 1 *fin.*, which I take to correspond to Catulus' in *Catul.*, he did introduce it in part.

t. 19

Reid[1] (p. 162) suggested two possible readings: 'This fragment refers either to the late arrival of Stoicism on the field of philosophy or to the late period of life at which Antiochus broke away from the New Academicism.' The first of these options, while not impossible, has little to recommend it, and no third option imposes itself. The debate between Stoics and Academics had been going on for the best part of two centuries by the 80s BC, and Stoicism was the dominant school of the time. Carneades himself had earlier ironically acknowledged the Academy's debt to the Stoa (εἰ μὴ γὰρ ἦν Χρύσιππος, οὐκ ἂν ἦν ἐγώ, 'No Chrysippus, no me'; D.L. 4.62), and we have no reason to think that post-Carneadean Academics sought to diminish the Stoics or their place in the history of philosophy, although they of course continued to disagree with their views. By contrast, Antiochus' conversion to dogmatism is more credibly presented as belated aspiration to political office, and it would be an apt piece of polemic for Cicero to say that drumming up support for it was difficult. (He also benefitted from hindsight, viz. knowledge of the fact that the Old Academy did not survive Antiochus for long, be it as an institution in some sense or through high-profile second-generation proponents; see Hatzimichali 2012.) The fragment suggests that the political analogies deployed by Lucullus and Cicero in *Luc.*, where Lucullus likens dogmatism to the established, conservative position of the *optimates* (§15), were not excluded from the final edition, although they will have required adaptation: the *optimates/populares* distinction suited the late 60s, less so the mid-40s. See also on t. 18.

Ac. 3

t. 20

The letter, written about a year after Cicero completed *Acad.* (see section 9.1), shows that the *uolumen prooemiorum* pre-dated the composition of the proem of *Ac.* 3, for if the latter had been written before Cicero assembled the *uolumen*, the mistake of re-using the same proem in the *De gloria* could not have occurred. Cicero would not have added a proem that had been written for a specific purpose/work to the *uolumen*. The fragments and testimonia of *Ac.* 3 which may come from the proem of that book (t. 21–3) do not yield enough material for us to judge, by analogous reasoning, if the *uolumen* also pre-existed the composition of *Luc.*, but the manner in which Cicero speaks about the second proems of *Catul.* and *Luc.* in *Att.* 13.32.2-3 (= SB 305 = T15) of 29 May suggests that either the *uolumen* did not yet exist then or that Cicero did not use it for the new proems: rather, the new proems are described in terms which suggest that they were specifically composed for *Catul.* and *Luc.* (see also section 3 and on *Luc.* 1–10). *Att.* 13.32.2-3 provides a soft terminus post quem for the creation of the *uolumen*. In *Fin.* 1.2 Cicero implies that he embarked on the composition of further philosophical works only when *Hort.* was received well, to which *Catul.* and *Luc.* are closely connected. The natural point in time at which Cicero would have conceived of the *uolumen* would be when he decided to go beyond the triptych.

Given that the proem to *Ac.* 1 is quite carefully adapted to Varro as addressee, one should not picture the use of the collection of proems as a mechanical operation. Rather, adaptation of the prefatory material to the particular context/work will have been involved.[22] Removing a proem thus adapted was, however, straightforward, especially when a replacement was available which signalled, or from which it could be inferred, where the obsolete proem ended (hence *desecabis... adglutinabis* here). On *De gloria*, see Sullivan (1941); Alfonsi (1967: 147–53); Graver (2016: 121).

---

[22] See the commentary on the proems of *Ac.* 1 and *Luc.* for further discussion of the likely contents of the proem of *Catul.*

t. 21

Lactantius cites the lost parts of the final edition only on this occasion by book number, so we are in no position to tell how accurate he is in assigning fragments. In *Acad.* error is conceived as assent to the non-cataleptic; cf. e.g. *Luc.* 66. This is the Stoic view, which the Clitomachean, unlike the mitigated sceptic, endorses (while disagreeing with the dogmatist on whether there are cataleptic impressions); Augustine in *Contra Acad.* 1.9.24 calls this position 'the citadel of the Academics' (*ubi enim arcem locauerunt Academici... nisi in erroris definitione?*). In *Contra Acad.* we find a second, anti-sceptical use of *error*, viz. of the supposedly aimless searching for the truth which never issues in the discovery of anything; see 1.4.10–1.5.14 with Schlapbach (2003: 117–38), and 3.15.34–3.16.36 with Fuhrer (1997: 387–402). Associated images would be that of the wrong turn taken (developed into a full allegory in the second of the passages just cited) by those who are not wise, and that of wisdom as the *recta uia uitae*. The metaphor of the wrong turn taken is not found in the directly transmitted parts of *Acad.* The present fragment shows that it occurred in *Acad.*, possibly though not necessarily in its Augustinian use.

One possibility is therefore that the fragment is anti-dogmatist in import, in which case dogmatic theorizing is the error at issue, qua assent to the non-cataleptic. This is the reading of Reid[1] (p. 165), who links this fragment with *Luc.* 9 (*Sed nescio quo modo plerique errare malunt eamque sententiam quam adamauerunt pugnacissime defendere quam sine pertinacia quid constantissime dicatur exquirere*) and assigns it to the proem of *Ac.* 3 in particular (citing *Att.* 16.6.4 = t. 20 above); thus also Ruch (1950: 16). The context in *Luc.* 9 is concerned with the manner in which people form allegiance to a dogmatic school: without a proper survey of the options, but with a blind commitment to 'authority' once a decision has been made. Lactantius' introductory remarks might point to the issue being rash assent and its consequences in the conduct of life more generally, but *ad meliora conuersus satis deo faciat* suggests that Lactantius is bending the Ciceronian sentence to support his own point. The speaker of the fragment would be Cicero, specifically the character rather than the narrator 'in the frame', given that the proem of *Ac.* 1 does not have a frame, either (unlike *Luc.*).

Alternatively, the speaker would be Varro, and *error* would be what the Academics do on the dogmatist view, i.e. aimless, untethered, and unguided wandering. The presence of the motif of the wrong turn, given its anti-sceptical use in Augustine, supports this reading. The suggestion would be, as elsewhere, that the Academic is a negative dogmatist, as wedded to his outlook as the dogmatist is to the Academic view. In this case, too, the proem of *Ac.* 3 would be a good place for this fragment, in that it would set up the praise of κατάληψις given to Lucullus in *Luc.* The noun *emendatio* is used in Cicero's philosophical works only here and in *Fin.* 4.21.

t. 22

The fragment is ambiguous in several ways. It is not clear if the text quoted is syntactically complete and what the force of the present subjunctive is. The noun *potestas* may mean 'power' or 'capacity', but not 'opportunity'. A subject is not specified; the sage, man in general, or someone looking to choose a school to follow are but three options.

Editors have rarely tried to modify the paradosis, but the Aldina (of Nonius) inserted *si* before *sit*. If the subjunctive expressed a possibility, then the fragment might be a complete sentence, i.e. a grammatical asyndeton equivalent to a conditional (see Kühner-Stegmann ii.155–9). Manutius' *potestas ⟨si⟩ sit* would be a normalization. Alternatively, *aliqua potestas sit* and *uindicet...libertatem* could be the two components of an asyndetic structure that represents the apodosis, in which case Nonius omitted a preceding (or following) protasis.

The present subjunctive may also convey a wish or an injunction ('may he have the [or: such] power/the capacity, may he claim his freedom'); thus Rackham (1951: 460–1).

Two possible contexts from which the fragment might derive are: (i) an extolment of the freedom of the Academic which comes with his ability to exercise his own judgement rather than to follow an authority as the dogmatist has to, and (ii) an extolment of the freedom of the Stoic/Old Academic, which derives from the faculty of assent; cf. *Luc.* 8 (Cicero speaking) and *Luc.* 38–9 (Lucullus speaking), respectively. I thus see no reason to doubt the ascription of the fragment to *Ac.* 3, *pace* Reid[1] (p. 164): 'There are numerous parallels in Cicero's speech in the *Academica Priora*, none in that of Lucullus. If the words we have here were really put in Varro's mouth, they can only have figured as a quotation from his opponents.'

We know from *Att.* 16.6.4 (= SB 414 = t. 20) that *Ac.* 3 had a proem and did not immediately start with Varro's speech.

t. 23

Depugnare most likely means 'to fight persistently', not 'to fight to the end', since the overall import of the fragment appears to be the futility of perpetual battle. The phrase *in facinorosis et audacibus* describes the nature of the opposition, amongst whom one is forced to fight, and is not a characterization of one's own side alongside whom one fights. The fragment does not have an obvious counterpart in *Luc.* (but see below). If one assumes that it comes from Varro's speech rather than the proem, there are two possible readings: (i) Varro could be expressing bafflement about the Academics, who go on and on attacking people whom they see as *facinerosi et audaces*. The Stoics/Old Academics could be so described because their standards of knowledge are unachievable and they are thus themselves, on the Stoic view, vicious and madmen. (ii) Alternatively and preferably, the words are spoken by Varro from his own point of view, who declares it be futile to engage with *facinerosi et audaces* (i.e. the Academics) beyond a certain point; thus Reid[1] (p. 163), who cites *Luc.* 17 (...*ut contra Academicos disseramus, id quidam e philosophis et ii quidem non mediocres faciendum omnino non putabant*). For the collocation *facinerosus/audax*, cf. Cic., *Phil.* 8.16, 12.15.

t. 24

On the manner in which Augustine reworks the definition of the cataleptic impression, see the commentary on *Luc.* 18; Fuhrer (1992) and (1997: 144–58); and Reinhardt (2018a).

t. 25

This fragment has been convincingly linked to *Luc.* 31 by Reid[1] (p. 164) and Plasberg[1] (p. 61), cf. esp. ibid.: *Ad rerum igitur scientiam uitaeque constantiam aptissima cum sit mens hominis, amplectitur maxime cognitionem, et istam κατάληψιν...cum ipsam per se amat (nihil est enim ei ueritatis luce dulcius), tum etiam propter usum.* Other *animalia* are mentioned in *Luc.* 30, but *Luc.* 30-1 pose considerable problems of interpretation regarding the difference in mental faculties animals and human beings are endowed with (see ad loc.). Cicero may have tried to address this problem when he came to make the changes for the final edition (cf. Burnyeat 1997: 300); this would explain the emphasis on the special status of human beings, and indeed the fact that this is not one of the passages which were carried over with minimal change from *Luc.* With the use of *ingeneraretur*, cf. Cic., *Fin.* 5.33 and 36; *Off.* 1.12.

t. 26, 27-9, 31-3, 35-46, 48-50, 52

Taken together, these fragments confirm that Lucullus' speech in *Luc.* became a speech of Varro's in *Ac.* 3, and that Cicero's speech took up *Ac.* 4 (consider the ascriptions of t. 26 and 27, on which see below, on the one hand, and t. 29, 31, 35-9, 43-4, 46, and 52 on the other). They also suggest that over large stretches of text Cicero only carried out minimal re-writing of both speeches: the divergence in t. 26 may be due to a copying error of Nonius' or of later scribes; t. 36, 44, and 46 suggest light revision on Cicero's part; in t. 45 Cicero has modified the wording slightly and changed the character addressed from Lucullus to Varro. t. 28 is remarkable for the connection it makes between the Clitomachean Cicero character in *Luc.* and the Cicero character in *Hort.*; see section 8 and 9.5.

That the variations in these passages are so few goes some way towards explaining how Cicero could draw up the final edition within a couple of days. However, Cicero's own statement about the nature of his revision (*Att.* 13.3.1-2 = SB 321 = T19) and other texts which are minimally credible testimonia suggest he cut, added, and substantially revised in particular places when he completed the final edition.

See the general note above on the question of whether Lactantius and Augustine knew the first edition of *Acad.* (sc. in addition to the final one).

t. 27 (see above)

Pliny, *N.H.* 10.155, may appear to pick up on material presented in *Luc.* 57 and 86, and we know that Quintilian, at about the same time, was at least aware of the book titles *Catulus* and *Lucullus*. That Pliny is, however, likely to have used the final edition is suggested by *N.H.* 31.6: *Dignum memoratu, uilla est ab Auerno lacu Puteolos tendentibus imposita litori, celebrata porticu ac nemore, quam uocabat M. Cicero Academiam ab exemplo Athenarum, ibi compositis uoluminibus eiusdem nominibus,* 'It is worth while recording that there is a country seat on the coast as you go from Lake Avernus to Puteoli, with a famous portico and grove, which M. Cicero, copying

Athens, called Academia. There he wrote the volumes of the same name' (transl. Rackham, modified), on the grounds that *Catul.* and *Luc.* were only given titles by Cicero as individual books, whereas the title *Academici libri* is associated with the final edition; see section 9.4.

Ac. 4

t. 28–9 (see above, p. 278)

t. 30

t. 30 is testimonium no. XVI on Philo in Brittain (2001: 353), as well as part of F8a in Sedley (2012c: 343). *Contra Acad.* 2.6.15 represents a testimonium on a narrow point: that Antiochus conceived of the Old Academy out of desire for glory, and that Cicero retained this claim in the final edition of *Acad.*

t. 31–3 (see above, p. 278)

t. 34

The fragment itself is plain enough in sense, but in the absence of a context its import or role in a larger argument is hard to gauge. If the point made was that we should rejoice in our sense of vision because it operates in a medium less dense than water, then Nonius' ascription of the text to *Ac.* 2 could only be correct if Cicero offered an argument advanced by the dogmatist (and then went on to reject it). Cicero would have had to introduce this argument of his own accord, drawing on his familiarity with the debate; for Varro's speech in *Ac.* 1 is extant, and he did not make a related point, nor does it seem likely that Cicero himself would have cited the dogmatist's view already once before, in the lost part of his speech in *Ac.* 1.

However, comparison with *Luc.* 81 suggests that in Nonius' text the numeral has been corrupted (cf. t. 47 for another likely instance of this) and that the text comes from *Ac.* 4. In *Luc.* 81 Cicero says: *Responderem igitur audacter isti uestro deo me plane his oculis non esse contentum. Dicit me acrius uidere quam illos pisces fortasse. Qui neque uidentur a nobis (et nunc quidem sub oculis sunt) neque ipsi nos suspicere possunt. Ergo ut illis aqua, sic nobis aer crassus offunditur.* The beginning of this extract is a backward reference to *Luc.* 19, where Lucullus imagined the appearance of a *deus* who asks human nature if she could want for better senses. She could not, on Lucullus' view. When Cicero moves on to the eyesight of fish, he seems to mark the point as one which his opponent might make (*fortasse*; the conjecture *dicet* rather than the transmitted *dicit* would make it even clearer that the point had not already been made), thus suggesting that fish and what they can see have not featured before. Our fragment is likely to have formed part of the revised version of *Luc.* 81. For instance, it could have featured in an argument for the limitations of our senses: ideal visual perception would be unencumbered by any medium; the perceived superiority of human vision is due to the fact that humans are land-dwelling so that their sense of sight operates in a less dense (but still dense: *sic nobis aer crassus offunditur*) medium. That it is the different medium, rather than the inherent keenness of human vision, which is responsible for what power human eyes do have can be seen if one places oneself in the position of fish.

t. 35–9 (see above, p. 278)

t. 40

The correspondence between *C.D.* 8.2 and *Luc.* 118 appears detailed and specific enough to assume that Augustine drew on *Ac.* 4. No other passage where Cicero mentions Anaxagoras offers details of his physical theory.

t. 41

Ammianus has very few possible reminiscences of *Acad.* (I am only aware of one other passage, see below). The writers chronologically closest to him are most likely to have read the final edition only. The present passage could conceivably derive from a collection of memorable phrases and thus not represent evidence for direct familiarity with *Acad.*, but it is put into context by t. 48, where such an explanation would not possible.

t. 42

Ogilvie (1978: 59) comments: '7.4.11 is more revealing.... The relevant passage of the *Lucullus* (120) agrees except for reading "cur mortifera tam multa ⟨ac add. Reid; et add. Halm⟩ perniciosa terra...." Now it is possible that the variant is due to carelessness by Lactantius (*pes/tifera; mortifera/perniciosa*) but *pestifer* is a good Ciceronian word (e.g. *N.D.* 2.120) and it seems, therefore, more likely that Lactantius is here also quoting from the *Academica Posteriora* and not from the *Lucullus*.' Note also the occurrence of *pestifera* in *De ira dei* 13.9.

t. 43–6 (see above, p. 278)

t. 47

Reid[1] (p. 164) notes the verbal similarity with *Luc.* 125: *ut nos nunc simus ad Baulos Puteolosque uideamus* and wonders if either the numeral in Nonius has been corrupted or material has been moved from Cicero's speech in *Luc.* to Varro's in *Ac.* 3. *Luc.* 125 is about the possibility of countless other worlds, in which identical sets of people might be gazing from identical Baulis to identical Puteolis. The fragment is about the disputants looking at the *lacus Lucrinus* which is close by, i.e. close enough for them to see fish jumping out of the water. Given that the fragment seems to have been part of a sentence which involved a comparison, it might have come from the adaptation (sc. in the final edition) of the passage to which *Luc.* 125 replies, i.e. *Luc.* 55 (which needed adapting because it made reference to Catulus; Lucullus speaking): *Deinde postulas ut, si mundus ita sit par alteri mundo ut inter eos ne minimum quidem intersit, concedatur tibi ut in hoc quoque nostro mundo aliquid alicui sic sit par ut nihil differat, nihil intersit.* '*Cur enim*', *inquies*, '*ex illis indiuiduis, unde omnia Democritus gigni affirmat, in reliquis mundis et in iis quidem innumerabilibus innumerabiles Q. Lutatii Catuli non modo possint esse, sed etiam sint, in hoc tanto mundo Catulus alter non possit effici?*'. The comparison would have been with identical scenarios in innumerable other worlds, a notion which Varro must have dismissed just as Lucullus dismissed it. However, what tips the balance in favour of a place in *Ac.* 4 is that this is one of the passages in Nonius which are based on his own excerpts (in this case of the *Academici libri*). Such passages are, within a given book, normally given in the order in which they appear in the excerpted work; the present fragment would violate this rule if the transmitted numeral was allowed to stand. See Lindsay (1901: 16) on 'Cicero viii', which includes the entries 'digladiari', assigned to *Ac.* 1 (t. 8), 'aequor', assigned to *Ac.* 2 (t. 11), 'Maeniana', assigned to *Ac.* 4 (t. 31 = *Luc.* 70), 'natrices', assigned to *Ac.* 4 (t. 43 = *Luc.* 120), and 'exultare', assigned to *Ac.* 3; 'Cicero viii' continues with three entries from *Tusc.* in the right order. This was observed by Lindsay (1902: 204) and argued for in some detail by Scarsi (1986).

The fragment might also offer a clue regarding the location (otherwise quite uncertain) of Varro's *Cumanum* (i.e. within sight of the *lacus Lucrinus*) if the setting in *Ac.* 3–4 was indeed still Varro's *Cumanum* (where the discussion of *Ac.* 1–2 is situated); see D'Arms (1970: 197). If, however, in *Ac.* 3 the discussion was moved to Cicero's *Cumanum* (Philippson 1939: 1132; entertained as a possibility also by Griffin 1997: 24), which would be in line with the change of setting from *Catul.* to *Luc.*, then the information would obviously pertain to Cicero's villa, which we know to have been near the *lacus*; see *Att.* 10.16.5 (= SB 208); 10.17.1 (= SB 209). That the two *uillae* were in walking distance of one another is suggested by the proem of *Ac.* 1.[23] Passages on *pisculi exultantes* as a sign of fine weather are collected by Reid[1] (p. 164); cf. in particular *Div.* 1.24.

t. 48 (see above on t. 40)

t. 49 (see above, p. 278)

t. 50 = Antiochus F8b Mette; see also Sedley (2012c: 344)

t. 51

Clamat Zeno... nefas esse is *SVF* i.186; *roga nunc... Epicuro* is F136 in Vezzoli (2016). t. 51 has featured in editions of fragments of Cicero since the sixteenth century,

---

[23] Augustine's phrase *tamquam in gymnasio Cumano atque adeo Neapolitano* in *Contra Acad.* 3.16.35, on which see Krische (1845: 47), is another pointer that Augustine used the final edition of *Acad.*, since Catulus' *uilla* at Bauli would not be referred to as a *Cumanum*. Consider also the beginning of *Ac.* 1: *In Cumano nuper....* On Naples (i.e. Lucullus' *uilla*) as a possible setting for *Hort.*, see Fuhrer (1997: 397); on Lucullus' *Tusculanum*, Gigon (1962: 227–8).

usually in the long form given here, whereas some editors have only given a shorter extract (i.e. *Academico sapientis... iudicio sit secundus*).[24] Early editors, notably Lambinus, made a number of changes to the text, on the assumption that it is simply an embedded passage from *Acad.*, and in order to bring it in line with their notions of Ciceronian usage.[25] While the passage comes from the part of *Contra Acad.* where the fairly brief dialogical exchanges are giving way to longer speeches,[26] so that incorporation of an actual extract would be easier, it would not be in line with Augustinian practice to lift quotes from a Ciceronian text. This is also the reason why stylistic revision of the text is a misguided endeavour. The passage should thus not be viewed as a fragment, but the ascription to *Acad.* rather than another work is plausible, as I hope to show.[27]

The passage develops themes and motifs which are treated in the ethical section of *Luc.* 129–41.[28] Given that other fragments of *Ac.* 4, which correspond to the second half of *Luc.*, match the wording of *Luc.* to a large degree and that they offer numerous points of contact over a longer section of *Luc.*, the passage could either be an isolated purple passage which Cicero added in the final edition, or it could represent Augustine's own development of what he found in Cicero's text (*Ac.* 4 rather than *Luc.*). That Augustine was well capable of this kind of development is shown by a

---

[24] Detailed recent discussions include Doignon (1981), whose primary purpose is to dismiss the identification of Epicurus with *Liber* and to argue for the reading *libera*; and Fuhrer (1997: 285–302). Reid[1] (p. 167) gives the shortened text and comments: 'Halm has included a long passage which follows in Augustine, but it has so few genuine traces of Cicero's style that I do not think it worth while to give it.' The entire passage is marked out as a fragment in Green (1970), following Mueller, in the standard edition of *Contra Acad.* Supportive of connecting the entire text with Cicero are also Glucker (1978: 59 n. 161) and Zetzel (2016: 60 n. 38).

[25] Doignon (1981: 156–7) also discusses the vulgate editorial history of the passage within editions of Cicero's fragments vis-à-vis that grounded in the study of manuscripts carrying Augustine's text.

[26] See Fuhrer (1997: 284).

[27] Plasberg[1] (p. 60): 'Etsi probabile est Augustinum nonnulla in his suo more "propter faciliorem intellectum uel praetermisisse uel paululum commutasse" ut ait ipse de ciu. Dei II 9 (cf. III 15, XIX 1 med.) uel ad suum loquendi usum accommodasse (ut *quam* pro *nisi... qui* pro *uter...*; cf. *Tim.* 11,40 *de nat. d.* I 11,26 II 28,70), tamen etiam illa quae proponit [in the part omitted by Reid and others] ita mihi uisa sunt Ciceronianum leporem prae se ferre, ut ea non putauerim omittenda cum r[eid].'

[28] *Luc.* 129–41 is, like our passage, concerned with disputes amongst philosophers about the highest good and casts Cicero qua Academic not as a contributor to the discussion but—due to the narrative perspective—as an evaluator. Cf. e.g. *Luc.* 140–1: *Vnum igitur par quod depugnet reliquum est, uoluptas cum honestate.... Alteram si sequare, multa ruunt et maxime communitas cum hominum genere.... Audi contra illos qui nomen honestatis a se ne intellegi quidem dicant... ego nihil eius modi esse arbitror cui si assensus sim non assentiar saepe falso....* Augustine's prefatory remarks that Cicero spoke in great detail (*copiosissime*) and about almost all schools (*prope de omnibus sectis*) would fit *Luc.* 129–41 and thus probably its later incarnation in *Ac.* 4. With Augustine's *fac enim uerbi causa Stoicum adesse sapientem* (3.7.16 init.), cf. *Luc.* 117: *Finge aliquem nunc fieri sapientem, nondum esse; quam potissimum sententiam [melius] eliget ⟨et⟩ disciplinam?* With Augustine's *quasi lenocinante mercede*, cf. *Luc.* 140: *Nam quae uoluptate quasi mercede aliqua ad officium impellitur, ea non est uirtus, sed fallax imitatio simulatioque uirtutis.* Both correspondences noted by Fuhrer (1997) ad loc., who also comments (p. 287): 'Die Szene [sc. in Augustine] hat Züge einer Gerichtsverhandlung; dabei sind die Vertreter der verschiedenen Schulen selbst gleichzeitig Richtende und auch Konkurrenten, die für ihre Lehrmeinung werben, um die Stimmen der anderen für sich zu gewinnen. Der Akademiker erscheint abwechslungsweise in der Rolle des Mitstreiters um den ersten Rang (3, 7, 15...), als Richtender über die Konkurrenten (s. zu 3, 7, 16...), als Schüler verschiedener Lehrmeister (3, 7, 17...) und als Prozessgegner Augustins (ibid....).'

passage in *Contra Acad.* 3.10.23, which takes its cue from very brief and, except for one term which arguably acts as a trigger (*libido*), jejune remarks in *Fin.*[29]

However, there is a consideration which points in the direction of Ciceronian embellishment of his own material.[30] A number of Menippean satires of Varro were concerned with quarrels between philosophical schools and philosophers,[31] and it is possible that one (or more) satires informed Cicero's reworking of the passage in a way that would have been transparent to Varro and other contemporaries.[32] This would have enabled him to pay homage to Varro, to acknowledge a point he had given to the character Varro—that his Menippean satires, while not philosophical works as such, covered philosophical themes (*Ac.* 1.8 *fin.* and 9 *fin.*)—, and to mitigate the fact that Cicero had given himself the last word, i.e. final speech, in the dialogue. (He states in *Att.* 13.25.3 = SB 333 = T30 that he is concerned that Varro might think that the Academic position had been given favourable treatment in *Acad.*)

On balance it seems appropriate to treat the passage as a testimonium relating to *Ac.* 4.[33]

t. 52 (see above, p. 278)

De incert. lib.

t. 53

The fragment poses basic problems of interpretation which impede even vague contextualization. The transmitted phrase *similitudine uerbi* might suggest the Antiochian trope that the Stoics substantially agreed with the Old Academics (i.e. on the *res*) while deploying different terminology (i.e. *uerba*), cf. e.g. *Ac.* 1.35; *Fin.* 5.22; but if the text is sound, the exact opposite—a similarity of expression—is at issue; so correctly Reid[1] (p. 161), contra Krische (1845: 57). Tarrant (1982: 21-2) assigns the fragment to *Ac.* 1, since he takes it to contain a historical consideration, and restores the text as *qui cum similitudine uerbi concinere maxime sibi uideretur.* He further suggests that the half-sentence comes from a report on Antiochus, who defended the

---

[29] Cf. *Contra Acad.* 3.10.23: *nam iste luxuriosus cum atomos quasi ancillulas suas, id est corpuscula quae in tenebris laetus amplectitur, non tenere uiam suam sed in alienos limites passim sponte declinare permittit, totum patrimonium etiam per iurgia dissipauit* and Cic., *Fin.* 1.19: *quae cum tota* ⟨*res*⟩ *ficta pueriliter, tum ne efficit* ⟨*quidem*⟩ *quod uult. Nam et ipsa declinatio ad libidinem fingitur (ait enim declinare atomum since causa; quo nihil est turpius physico quam fieri quicquam sine causa dicere).* ... Brief discussion in Reinhardt (2005: 174–5).

[30] That such embellishment was carried out at all is suggested by Cicero's remark in *Att.* 13.3.1-2 (= SB 321 = T19): *grandiores sunt omnino quam erant illi* (sc. *libri*), *sed tamen multa detracta*, although of course nothing definite follows for the particular case in hand.

[31] Varronian references are assembled by Zetzel (2016: 59–60). The motif is of course familiar well beyond Varro; see the references collected by Fuhrer (1997: 287 n. 5).

[32] Suggested by Mras (1914: 400–1) and endorsed by Zetzel (2016: 60 n. 38).

[33] Note also the manner in which Augustine sets up the passage: *Est in libris Ciceronis, quos in huius causae patrocinium scripsit, locus quidam*...; see also Glucker (1997: 58).

claim that Plato was a dogmatist and embraced perceptual knowledge by invoking a particular expression in Plato (*qui* would thus refer to Plato, and *sibi* to Antiochus). The expression would be περιληπτά (*Tim.* 28a1, c1, 29a7, 52a7), and the suggestion would be that Plato's use of the term shows that he anticipated Stoic κατάληψις. An attempt to reveal Plato as a dogmatist using the same terminological correspondence is attested in Sextus, *M.* 7.143–4, part of a larger context linked by many with an Antiochian source (but see Brittain 2012: 108–13). While I am sympathetic to the idea that Antiochus' embrace of Stoic epistemology was underpinned by a reading of Platonic texts (see on *Ac.* 1.30–2), I doubt that *cum similitudine uerbi* is an idiomatic way of expressing in Latin that one's agreement with someone is signalled through a particular expression. I also note that the Antiochian part of *Ac.* 1 is extant, so that the point would ex hypothesi have been introduced by an Academic (i.e. the Cicero character).

Reid[1] (p. 161) asserts that '*cum* is of course conjunction, not preposition', perhaps because double complementation of *concinere* (by *sibi* and by *cum similitudine*) is not possible (cf., however, *De orat.* 2.266 for *cum similitudine* as a prepositional phrase).

In the apparatus of his Nonius edition Lindsay wondered if *uerbi* was corrupted from *ueri*. In *Luc.* 107 *fin.* Cicero notes that Chrysippus' strategy of suspending judgement in the face of a series of soritical questions would not be transferable to other situations, and that it was also possible to follow the unencumbered persuasive impression without assenting to it. That impression is referred to as a *similitudo ueri* in that context (...*praesertim cum possit sine assensione ipsam ueri similitudinem non impeditam sequi*).

Concinere sibi means 'to be (or to act) in harmony with oneself, consistent with oneself', a phrase which could be used for a state a subject is in which is, as a matter of fact, such that only true and thus mutually consistent impressions or beliefs on the part of the subject are involved. That a virtuous disposition is a harmonious one and that virtuous action arises from such a disposition is a tenet of Stoic ethics; cf. e.g. Quint. 2.20.5: *ab illis haec dicuntur: si consonare sibi in faciendis ac non faciendis uirtus est (quae pars eius prudentiae uocatur), eadem in dicendis ac non dicendis erit*, 'This is what the philosophers say. If consistency in what should and should not be done is a virtue (the part of virtue called prudence), the same virtue should appear in respect of what should and should not be said' (trans. Russell), with Reinhardt and Winterbottom (2006: 370–1).

Assuming that the half-sentence makes the point that someone (possibly an Academic sage) appeared to act in a manner consistent with himself due to the application of what is similar to the true (i.e. the persuasive impression), then *similitudine* would best be seen as an *ablatiuus causae*, in which case it could indeed not be accompanied by the preposition *cum*, and *cum* would have to be interpreted as a conjunction. *Qui* would refer to a successful agent more generally, or to the Academic sage, *cum* could be causal, adversative, or concessive.

For the association of the Carneadean πιθανόν with considerations of consistency and coherence see section 6.1. An impression is unencumbered if it is consistent with all impressions in its 'syndrome'; see Sextus, *M.* 7.176–81 and the commentary on *Luc.* 36.

t. 54

The highlighted passage was classified as a fragment by Mueller and Reid[1], who both listed it under *ex libris incertis*; it was ascribed to *Ac.* 2 in particular by Plasberg in both editions.

The case against treating the passage as a fragment, or a testimonium which reflects anything Cicero wrote closely, is made by Brittain (2006: 111 n. 8), who observes that just before *Contra Acad.* 2.11.26 Augustine had given a mistaken characterization of the *probabile*—as a device deployed by the Academics to conceal their positive doctrines from ignorant and malicious people—which cannot possibly have come from Cicero's text. He adds: 'The last sentence [*quid putatis...?*] could quite naturally be taken to mean only that Cicero used the terms *probabile* and *uerisimile....*'

The case for treating the passage as a fragment would begin with the observation that, leaving aside the context, nothing in it is manifestly mistaken or misleading, that it exhibits points of contact with extant parts of *Acad.* without simply restating them, and that it has stylistic features which are at least reminiscent of Cicero; *inquit Academicus* could signal a closer relationship with Cicero's text, and *haec uerba* might not just refer to two terms. With the example of the clear night upon which a sunny day can be expected to follow compare the Academic sage of *Luc.* 100, who boards a ship in good order, commanded by an experienced captain, on a fine day when the sea is calm, and who therefore has good reason to expect to arrive safely, without knowing for certain that he will do so. And given the contrast in the immediately preceding text between knowing that the day will be sunny and it appearing that it will be so, it is tempting to link the point about not insisting on particular terminology for the *probabile* with *Luc.* 105 *init.*, where Cicero comments that he calls those impressions *probabilia* which the dogmatists mistakenly call 'cataleptic': *non enim lucem eripimus, sed ea quae uos percipi comprehendique, eadem nos si modo probabilia sint uideri dicimus.* (The wider context in *Contra Acad.* 2.10.24–2.13.30 is also concerned with the question if the debate about the *ueri simile* is merely a terminological dispute.) Stylistically the passage has no features which clearly suggest that it is or is not Ciceronian, but the phrasal terms *uocabulorum opifex* and *rerum inquisitor* stand out, and may be compared with Cicero's self-characterization as a *magnus opinator* in *Luc.* 66 (sc. despite his commitment to suspension of judgement, which is also mentioned in the wider context of t. 51).[34]

The *probabile* is discussed twice in *Luc.*, once by Lucullus (§§32–6) and once by Cicero (§§98–103). The latter passage, one of the rare occasions where Cicero signals explicitly that he is working from a Clitomachean source, is manifestly intended to give 'chapter and verse' on some contentious issues, and as such marked as the last word on the subject in *Acad.* The former passage makes casual reference to testing procedures which *probabilia* are supposed to be subjected to, and for these testing procedures there is very detailed parallel evidence in Sextus (*M.* 7.166–89); see

---

[34] Cf. also *Tusc.* 5.34: *Zeno...ignobilis uerborum opifex*; *Fin.* 3.5, also about Zeno: *non tam rerum inuentor fuit quam uerborum nouorum.*

Reinhardt (2018a). When the Sextus passage is compared with what Lucullus says, it is plain that the latter must be picking up on an earlier discussion of the same subject in the *Catulus*. Given what we know about Catulus' and Cicero's roles in *Catul.*, it is natural to assume that it was Catulus who introduced the *probabile* and the testing procedures. His speech, as I suggest elsewhere (section 9.2), was the second in *Catul.* after Hortensius'. The material Catulus introduced was given to Cicero in the final edition, who will have presented it in his first speech, whose beginning is extant at *Ac.* 1.44–6. Thus elementary introductory points on the *probabile* would be likely to have featured in *Ac.* 2 only if Cicero's first speech extended over the book boundary, which would conflict with the formal conventions of the Ciceronian dialogue. By contrast, it would be in keeping with structural principles adhered to by Cicero elsewhere if his character's first speech ended in *Ac.* 1, and *Ac.* 2 began with a proem, followed by a new speech by Cicero. So if the passage were to be treated as a testimonium, its content would most naturally be ascribed to the lost part of *Ac.* 1 in virtue of its subject matter.[35] Said content is not closely related to t. 14 and 15 above, i.e. the issue of conflicting appearances and appropriate epistemic behaviour, but it can also not be excluded that it featured as part of the general material in Cicero's speech in *Ac.* 2.

t. 55

The character Cicero can sound optimistic about the epistemic position of man when speaking on his own terms (cf. e.g. *Luc.* 146), but pessimistic when replying to what he regards as his Antiochian interlocutor's exaggerated claims about the power of the senses or the human ability to reach knowledge (cf. e.g. *Luc.* 80, replying to *Luc.* 19). Cf. *Luc.* 112; *N.D.* 1.5.

Cicero's speech in *Luc.* offers plenty of comment on the limitations of human knowledge; thus *Ac.* 4 is one possible source for the sentence. However, *sed ad ea ipsa quae aliqua ex parte cerni uideantur* in the testimonium seems to pick up on the restriction Varro admitted for the cataleptic impression (*Ac.* 1.42:…*comprehensio facta sensibus et uera esse illi et fidelis uidebatur, non quod omnia quae essent in re comprehenderet, sed quia nihil quod cadere in eam posset relinqueret*). Cicero's point would be that impressions classified as cataleptic fail to live up to the dogmatist's standard even if the restriction is accepted. The connection between cataleptic impressions and wisdom (cf. *ad sapientiam caeci*)—the former offer a pathway to the latter—is made in *Ac.* 1.42 as well. So the fragment is best assigned to Cicero's reply to Varro's speech in *Ac.* 1, and may thus derive from *Ac.* 1 or *Ac.* 2. Ogilvie (1978: 60) assigns it to *Ac.* 2, Plasberg[1] (p. 62), however, to *Ac.* 3.

Caeci used metaphorically hints at the connection between apprehension and wisdom. *Ad ea ipsa* may emphasize that Cicero is making a connection with the

---

[35] Fuhrer (1997: 219 n. 8) argues that the ascription of the fragment to the final edition of *Acad.* is not compelling because it might derive from the *Catulus*, i.e. he (or Cicero) might be the *Academicus* cited. While this cannot be ruled out, there is not a single Augustinian passage which requires that Augustine used the first edition, and the evidence that he knew of the first edition is circumstantial.

passage on scope restriction cited above. Cf. also *Luc.* 81 on human vision being obstructed by dense air; and *Ac.* 1.31, with *hebetes* (but the passage is not connected to the fragment): *Sensus autem omnes hebetes et tardos esse arbitrabantur.*

t. 56

The apparent fragment (rather than testimonium; but see on t. *63) offers generic praise of Varro except for *sine ulla dubitatione*, which is evidently self-conscious (though seen as indicative of Ciceronian inconsistency by Augustine later in the passage which embeds the fragment). Reid[1] (p. 168) ascribes the text to the proem of *Ac.* 3 which is mentioned in *Att.* 16.6.3 (= SB 414) for having been re-used in *De gloria*, but any proem of *Ac.* 2–4 is a possibility, as are indeed Cicero's speeches in the lost part of *Ac.* 1 as well as *Ac.* 2 and 4.

I have reproduced the wider context because it shows that Augustine knew the final edition in four books. If he had known *Catul.* and *Luc.* in addition, one might have expected him to reveal this e.g. in *Contra Acad.*

t. 57

In the edition I cite the Latin text after Keil (1855) and reproduce relevant material from his app. crit. If Keil was right in positing a *lacuna*, then *malcho…affixa* may be a quote from an author other than Cicero. The latter would, like Varro, be cited for the word *fixus* only, which occurs in *Luc.* 27 and 141 (on apprehension being a *uerum fixum*, as well as a *certum comprehensum perceptum ratum firmum*). Editors of *Acad.* tend not to assume a *lacuna*.

Varro ad Ciceronem, whether with or without *tertio*, is usually taken to be a reference to Varro's *De lingua Latina*, with '*fixus*' being classed as a fragment by editors. *Malcho* is not part of a Latin word, and it could not be a name here.

Reid[1] (p. 165) has the most substantial comment to date: '*malcho* is possibly a mistake for *malleo*, a hammer; cf. Vitruu. 10, 22 naues malleolis confixae; Plaut. Men 2, 3, 52 nauem saepe fixam, saepe excusam malleo (Brix *fissam*). Opera is probably also an error for *opere*. If these words really occurred in the third book of the *Academica*, second edition, we must suppose that they formed part of a concrete illustration appended in some way to the description of a δόγμα in *Lucullus* §27 where the word *fixum* stands. But may we not suppose that Diomedes has mixed up his quotations; that he really meant to quote *fixum* only from *Academica* III and the words *malcho…adfixa* from Varro's *De lingua Latina* III?'

In the absence of further contextual information, Reid's suggestion of a confusion of two fragments cannot be substantiated or dismissed; see also Hunt (1998: 21).

Affigere is construed either with *aliquid alicui rei* or *aliquid ad aliquid*, which tells against emending *opera* to *opere*, because the participle is most likely an attribute to *opera* and not to whatever *malcho* has displaced, and *opere* has the wrong gender. Halm, as recorded in the app. by Keil (1855: 377), wondered if *malcho* was corrupted from the name Clitomachus (i.e., presumably, ⟨Clito⟩ma[l]cho), a possibility not to be dismissed given the separation of the name in ms. A on *Luc.* 11 *Clitomachum* or B on §16 *Clitomacho*. However, this would still leave the overall import of the fragment unclear.

t. 58

Part of Antiochus frg. 8a Mette, as well as part of no. 8a in Sedley (2012c: 343–4); no. XXXI in Brittain (2001: 363). This text is in some ways an obvious Augustinian flight of fancy; see the general note on *Luc.* 60 for a discussion of its larger context, as well as Brittain (2001: 69–73, 215), Glucker (2004: 123–4), and Brittain (2011: 84–91) on Augustine's overall approach in *Contra Acad.* 3. However, it contains two pieces of information which are not stated in the extant parts of *Acad.* but are either confirmed by evidence from elsewhere or are consistent with and organically expand on such evidence. t. 58 is thus a testimonium on the final edition of *Acad.*, and the Augustinian embellishment or modification is not difficult to strip away.

The first piece of information is that the Stoic Mnesarchus was the teacher of Antiochus rather than just a Stoic prominent and active during his time in Athens; see on t. 8, Eus., *Praep. Ev.* XIV.9.3 (= Numenius frg. 28 Des Places = T1 Mette), Philod., *Index Acad.* col. xxxiv.23–4 Fleischer, with Fleischer (2015). Cicero may have deployed the point to ask Varro why Antiochus did not simply go over to the Stoics (cf. *Luc.* 69, see below).

The second piece of information is that Metrodorus had stated that the Academics did not hold that nothing can be known unqualifiedly, but only in response to the Stoics. This coheres with Metrodorus' remark, reported by Philod., *Index Acad.* col. xxvi.8–11 Fleischer, that 'everyone else had misunderstood Carneades; for the latter had not regarded everything as non-apprehensible... [text breaks off]':

ὃς ἔφη [Κ]αρ-
νεά[δ]ου παρακηκ[οέν]αι
πάντας· οὐ γὰρ ἀκατ[άλη-
π[τα] ν[ε]νομ[ι]κέναι [π]άν[τα

The evidence from Philodemus and Augustine combined suggests strongly that Metrodorus anticipated in general outline, though probably not in its detailed articulation, the philosophical claim of Philo's Roman Books. See on *Luc.* 16 (which speaks to the claim that Metrodorus took himself to understand Carneades better than anyone else), 18 (on Philo's Roman Books view), 78 (where Philo and Metrodorus appear side by side in a way which is open to interpretation). See also Görler (1994: 779, 819, 849, 905).

I see no reason to assume that both pieces of information featured in the same context in *Acad.*, so while there are no grounds for classifying t. 58 as a *dubium*, assigning it to a book is not possible. The information on Mnesarchus might have featured in *Ac.* 4, in the revision of what has come down to us as *Luc.* 69–71. A natural place for the information on Metrodorus would have been Catulus' speech in

Catul., i.e. the second speech of that dialogue on my reconstruction. Of that speech we can read the initial two paragraphs in *Ac.* 1 before it breaks off (there given to the Cicero character). Thus I would assume the information on Metrodorus to have featured in the lost part of that book. *Luc.* 16 and especially 78 arguably presuppose that Metrodorus had been discussed in *Catul.*

Fuhrer (1997: 442) refers to *Luc.* 29 in support of the reading *decreto: Quoniam enim id haberent Academici decretum…nihil posse percipi, non debere eos in suo decreto sicut in ceteris rebus fluctuari.* See also *Luc.* 109 (with comm.).

t. 59

Brittain and Palmer (2001: 63–4) argue plausibly that Lact., *Inst.* 3.4.10–11, rather than reflecting *Ac.* 1.44–5 which is reproduced directly in *Inst.* 3.29.7 (see t. 7), seems to be based on a lost part of *Acad.*, one which said that Arcesilaus started collecting conflicting opinions of the wise. (On Academic scepticism as a formal influence on the doxographical tradition, see Mansfeld 1989a, esp. pp. 338–42.) As a generic remark made by Cicero in the missing part of *Ac.* 1, *Ac.* 2, or *Ac.* 4, this would set up the actual doxographical section in *Luc.* For the theme of a competition between philosophical schools, cf. t. 51.

t. 60

Part of Carneades F14b Mette. This extract, which has not featured in earlier editions, cannot be deemed a fragment or a testimonium in the conventional sense. I include it here because it contains a reasoning which one would expect to be in the background for a number of the anti-sceptical arguments which Lucullus advances in *Luc.* or which the Cicero character responds to or anticipates. I therefore suggest that it featured somewhere in the lost parts of the *Academici libri*, most naturally in *Ac.* 3. The reasoning is that the Academics cannot credibly claim to be guided by impressions which 'appear true' given their commitment to ἀπαραλλαξία.

What enables the reasoning is that both in the Greek and the Latin record πιθανά or *probabilia* are characterized as impressions which appear true or are truth-like; cf. e.g. Sextus, *M.* 7.173 (ἡ δὲ φαινομένη ἀληθής, sc. φαντασία) and *Luc.* 107 (*praesertim cum possit sine assensione ipsam ueri similitudinem non impeditam sequi*). (There is no need to assume that a synonym or near-synonym of τὸ πιθανόν used by the Academics was τὸ εἰκός; see section 6.3.)

That Augustine deploys the reasoning to advance a tenet of his own, viz. the notion that the Academics knew the truth or what is true well but concealed it for centuries because they were afraid of the Stoics, does not pose a serious problem of interpretation, since the repurposing is quite transparent.

The dogmatist might have advanced a number of different points under the deliberately generic characterization of 'the reasoning' given above: e.g., that, in the absence of or without a commitment to a theory of truth, the Academic could not identify what is truth-like; that ex hypothesi he could not have the concept of truth, since it would need to have arisen from cataleptic impressions, and he consequently could not identify what was truth-like; or that the Academic could not tell, when faced with a true impression, that it was true, and that the situation ought to be no different for truth-like impressions. The Academic could reject the notion that one needs a theory of truth in order to have impressions which strike one as true. Because the possibility that one could interact largely successfully with the world while guided by false impressions may have struck people in the Hellenistic period as being as absurd as external world scepticism, the Academic may have mounted an inference to the best explanation without feeling thereby committed to asserting the truth of any particular impression dogmatically. He might also have cited his coherentist intuition of what accounts for persuasiveness, namely a consistent appearance of truth across a syndrome of impressions, while emphasizing the possibility of an impression which did not fit with a part of the syndrome just beyond one's cognitive reach, able to come into view at any moment. Truth could then be conceptualized as universal appearance of truth across the syndrome, including any inaccessible parts—but then he would already be on his way towards a theory of truth.

The Cicero character explains why he is entitled to laying claim to experiencing true impressions in *Luc.* 111 (see ad loc.). Lucullus argues in §36: *Vt enim confidant, notum iis esse debebit insigne ueri; quo obscuro et oppresso quod tandem uerum sibi uidebuntur attingere?* Cicero's commitment in the frame of *Luc.* (§§7b–9a) to searching for the truth is relevant as well. See Görler (1994: 862–4); Fuhrer (1997: 434–9); Stroud (2014); and Wynne (2018: 94–5).

t. 61

This passage—3.6.7-19 is Arcesilaus T14b Mette and F128 Vezzoli—has been plausibly linked to the lost parts of the *Academici libri* by Schofield (1999: 331 n. 24), where, however, the reference is incorrect. On the objection to Arcesilaus' posture, see section 7.5. The section might be informed by the counterpart to *Luc.* 15 in *Ac.* 3 (cf. *Tib. Gracchus qui otium perturbaret, sic Arcesilas qui constitutam philosophiam euerteret et in eorum auctoritate delitesceret qui negauissent quicquam sciri aut percipi posse*), if *Luc.* 15 was expanded in the final edition; however, a major expansion of *Luc.* 15 would have altered the course of the narrative substantially. Alternatively, Cicero may also have used the Cicero character to rehearse and reject an anti-Academic argument.

Dubia

t. 62*

In the *editio maior* but not in the *editio minor* Plasberg treats this text as a fragment following my t. 14. Lactantius' introduction and the reference to drunks and madmen seem to encourage such a connection, although no author or work is cited as a source. However, on closer examination the differences come to the fore. That people whose state of mind is impaired see things double is a poor argument against the senses (nor is it an instance of conflicting appearances); the dogmatist would surely claim that any pronouncements on the senses' excellence relate to normal conditions (cf. *Luc.* 53; Sextus, *P.H.* 2.54). That impressions experienced while deranged or drunk do in fact differ from those experienced in a sober and healthy waking state is an argument dogmatists cite *against* Academic arguments which turn on ἀπαραλλαξία (*Luc.* 52). This raises questions about Lactantius' introduction. If the sentence or part of a sentence does in fact come from *Acad.*, it is more likely to have featured in Varro's speech in *Ac.* 3, corresponding to Lucullus' in *Luc.*, not Cicero's in *Ac.* 2.

t. 63*

Unlike some other texts from *Contra Acad.* (e.g. t. 51), which I have called testimonia rather than fragments because of general assumptions about the way in which Augustine interacted with the Ciceronian texts (see above, p. 266), this text is presented by Augustine as a Ciceronian quotation or close paraphrase (cf. t. 56). However, t. 63 seems clearly of a piece with Augustine's interpretation of the sceptical Academy as a Platonist school which closely guarded its dogmatic views and used the sceptical posture (and particular devices like the πιθανόν) to distract and conceal, as the immediately following sentence shows.[36] (The sentence also suggests that Augustine took himself to be extrapolating from or even expanding on what he read in Cicero; see Fuhrer 1997: 469.) Given that the weight of the evidence from *Acad.* and elsewhere supports the view that the Academics were genuine sceptics in the relevant sense and interpreted in this way even by Philo in his Roman Books, it is difficult to believe that Cicero could have written the entire sentence.[37] Tarrant (1981: 70), on the basis of this text, assumes that Philo exploited a pre-existing notion that the Academy secretly held dogmatic views to support the historical thesis of the Roman Books (i.e. that the philosophical views advanced in the Roman Books had been held by Academics all along), but this reading seems problematic for a number of reasons; see also Tarrant (2018: 87–8).

With *Contra Acad.* 3.20.43 one must compare *Luc.* 60; I do this in the commentary on the latter passage, where Academic concealment of one's own view is also discussed. To the evidence cited there add *Luc.* 98, where Clitomachus is cited as an authority for Carneadean distinctions though not substantial views because he remained with Carneades until old age: ... *a Clitomacho sumam, qui usque ad senectutem cum Carneade fuit, homo et acutus ut Poenus et ualde studiosus ac diligens.*[38] For the expression *uiuere cum aliquo*, see also *Luc.* 74: *Vixisse cum iis equidem uideor* (of Socrates and Plato); 115: *Diodoto ... qui mecum uiuit tot annos.*

---

[36] See also on t. 58 above.   [37] Thus also Brittain (2001: 34 n. 61).
[38] Clitomachus is also cited as intimately familiar with Carneades' thinking, though in a way which positively discourages the notion that he therefore knew of substantial Carneadean views, in *Luc.* 139: ... *ut Calliphontem sequar, cuius quidem sententiam Carneades ita studiose defensitabat ut eam probare etiam uideretur (quamquam Clitomachus affirmabat numquam se intellegere potuisse quid Carneadi probaretur).*

Earlier editors assigned this text to *Ac.* 2 if they thought that it comes from the context to which *Luc.* 60 is a reply, or to *Ac.* 3 if they thought that it comes from the revised version of *Luc.* 60 in *Ac.* 3. Since I cannot envisage a scenario in which Cicero could actually have written the entire sentence Augustine appears to be reporting, although it may contain a genuine kernel,[39] I classify it as a *dubium*.

t. 64*

Quod cum Zeno... assentiendum is F135 in Vezzoli (2016). Reid[1] (p. 168) took this text to be a testimonium for the lost part of the account of the Academy's history which Cicero begins in *Ac.* 1.44–6, but he did not include it amongst the fragments.

The speaker in *Contra Acad.* is Augustine's friend and former pupil Alypius, who takes over the defence of the sceptical Academy in 2.8.21 and only yields to Augustine in 3.7.14. He is presented as well informed and adept (having been taught by Augustine during the latter's sceptical phase), is not recruited to advance Augustine's theory of crypto-dogmatism, and cannot elsewhere be shown to relay wilfully distorted or false information.

I survey the contents of the passage before I consider if it contains information which disqualifies it from being a testimonium or indeed information which suggests classifying it as one; cf. Brittain (2001: 187–9) for a similar survey.

Alypius first speaks to the suggestion that there was a schism (*discidium*) between Old and New Academics; this he rejects, and puts the perception of it down to a new point being formulated by Zeno (the cataleptic impression, and apprehension arising from it), which had to be addressed in a novel way. As to the substantial issue of ἀκαταληψία, this had not been a subject of consideration or discussion for the Old Academics, but Alypius regards it as a reasonable assumption that they were open to it. The evidence cited is that Socrates, Plato, and Plato's immediate successors thought they could protect themselves from error by avoiding rash assent. Arcesilaus heard of Zeno's definition of the cataleptic impression and apparently accepted it, but thought no impression could ever meet the requirement, and thus concluded that the sage must not ever assent and form opinions. For Alypius this amounted to a bolstering of the Old Academy (sc. as he construed it), but when Antiochus entered the scene, he misrepresented the New Academy by claiming it had adopted a new stance. Antiochus wanted everyone to follow the ancients as he saw them rather than the New Academics and their *probabile*.

The historical account which Alypius gives has no exact counterpart in the extant parts of *Acad.* It comes close to presenting a unity thesis for the history of the Academy, in that the views of Plato and the Old Academics on the possibility of knowledge emerge as less clearly articulated versions of Arcesilaus' position, characterized by a commitment to ἀκαταληψία and to ἐποχή, and there is no suggestion that Carneades and his successors disagreed on these two points. Since the historical

---

[39] Tarrant (2020: 208–9) comments: 'There could be a certain truth here, because we are well aware that Arcesilaus was brought up in an institution where the successor did live constantly with the scholarch (D.L. 4.22).'

thesis of Philo's Roman Books amounted to the claim that his revised conception of κατάληψις was de facto the view held throughout the Academic tradition (from Plato to Philo), t. 64* cannot be presenting an expanded version of the historical view of the Roman Books.

Rather, the account is in substantial agreement with that cited by Cicero in *Luc.* 72-8 and *Ac.* 1.44-6, but omits a comment on the Presocratics while adding one on the Old Academics, who do not feature in the two parallel passages. In *Ac.* 1.43 Cicero grants—surprisingly—to Varro that Antiochus' view of the Stoics as mere correctors of the—for Varro, dogmatic—Old Academy, here meant to include the Peripatos. Cicero's concession in *Ac.* 1.43 is surprising because one would expect him to either pass over the Old Academics in silence or treat them as proto-sceptics of some description, as Alypius does, not as dogmatists whom the Stoics merely corrected (the latter is very much an Antiochian idea).[40] In the commentary on *Ac.* 1.43 I consider possible explanations for Cicero's concession, including a desire to mitigate the disagreement between his character and Varro's.

However, for anyone who reads *Acad.* with understanding, as Augustine did, the information contained in *Ac.* 1.43 sticks out in a peculiar way, and the recruitment of the Old Academics (coupled with a tacit sidelining of the Peripatos) to Cicero's Arcesilaen (and Clitomachean) agenda is an obvious move. The question is, then, whether the historical picture our fragment offers is more likely to have come from a lost part of *Acad.* or is better viewed as a synthetic summary, mainly based on what we can actually still read in 1.44-6, with the incongruent point made in 1.43 ironed out by Alypius/Augustine. I lean towards the second option because of the substantial overlap of the fragment with *Ac.* 1.44-6, and because it is hard to see where yet another account of Academic history would have featured given what we know about the final edition, and notably one which is different from an earlier one (i.e. 1.44-6) only in one comparatively negligible respect (sc. from an Academic point of view; for Antiochus the role of the Old Academics is vital of course). Nor does the text look like a revision of some part of *Luc.* 72-80 (which also does not feature the Old Academics).

Nothing in the text is suggestive of Augustine's theory of Academic scepticism as a front for crypto-dogmatism or -esotericism. The *discidium* between Old and New Academy is invoked by Varro in *Ac.* 1.43 right before Cicero's speech begins: *Tuae sunt nunc partes... qui ab antiquorum ratione desciscis et ea quae ab Arcesila nouata sunt probas, docere quod et qua de causa discidium factum est, ut uideamus satisne ista sit iusta defectio.* In our passage it is used in quotation marks as it were, since the speaker immediately rejects its applicability to the relationship of Platonic/post-Platonic dogmatic and sceptical Academy, as the character Cicero in *Acad.* would have done on both a pre- and a post-Roman-Books conception of the history of philosophy (and it is not clear that the latter featured at all in *Acad.* in detail). That Arcesilaus' stance was adopted *contra Stoicos* could conceivably serve as a general description of Augustine's view that the Academics were Platonists who sought to protect their views against the threat of Stoic materialism (see esp. *Contra Acad.*

---

[40] The Academics appeared to have had no interest in integrating Plato's immediate successors into their constructions of the history of philosophy.

3.17.38, and the commentary on *Luc.* 60), but Cicero himself in his speech in *Luc.* clearly acknowledges that the specific Stoic claims about certain knowledge prompted scrutiny on the part of the Academics (cf. esp. *Luc.* 77), and taken by itself our passage says no more than that.

Since I regard the passage as neither a fragment nor a testimonium of a lost part of *Acad.*, but rather assume that the text draws mostly or exclusively on an extant part, with a small degree of manipulation of the Ciceronian material (concerning the views of Plato's immediate successors in the Academy), I classify the passage as a *dubium*.

t. 65–7

t. 66 is Carneades T14 Mette. The three texts t. 65–7 represent the extent of what we know of the history and reception of the first edition of *Acad.* in antiquity (beyond the fact that *Luc.* evidently survived, and the possibility that the three-book structure of Augustine's *Contra Acad.* is informed by the triptych *Hort., Catul., Luc.*). Quintilian knew at least the titles of both dialogues as well as that Cicero tried to 'recall' them; cf. the similar case of the first two books of *Fin.* (*Att.* 13.21a.1–2 = SB 327 = T24). t. 66 shows that Plutarch was aware of *Luc.*, of its broad structure, and of the thrust of Lucullus' and Cicero's speeches. t. 67 mentions a number of terms which are discussed in the extant part of *Ac.* 1 and thus will have been discussed in *Catul.* However, Plutarch adds ὥς φασιν, thus leaving it in doubt if he examined the dialogue himself and noted that a number of terms of Stoic epistemology were cited, translated, and discussed there; see on *Ac.* 1.40–2. Τὸ ἀμερές is not discussed in the extant philosophical works of Cicero.

Lucullus

§§1–9a

The preface of *Luc.* covers the first nine and a half paragraphs, with §§1–9a being spoken by the Ciceronian narrator persona known from other prefaces (though not *Ac.* 1) in a manner which is not tied to a particular place and time, while §§9b–10, retaining the same speaker persona, refers to the specific settings of *Catul.* and *Luc.*[1]

There are three parts: §§1–4 is a biographical sketch of Lucullus, §§5–7a is a defence of Roman and Ciceronian engagement with philosophy, including in the form of dialogues, which is part of the larger narrative justifying writing philosophy in Latin. In §§7b–9a Cicero defends (his particular brand of) Academic scepticism, in his own voice but in a way which is continuous with his character's later speech against Lucullus' point of view. In a conversational exchange §§9b–10 will look back to discussion of the previous day (i.e. the *Catulus*).

Larger issues raised by the section include its status as evidence for Lucullus' biography, the details and background of the characterization of Academic scepticism given, and finally whether the preface, which we know to be a second version, allows us to glimpse the first version.

The Prefaces of *Luc.*

I begin with the last topic, partly because it illuminates a number of structural features of the passage. If we had only *Luc.* and the fragments of the final edition which overlap with it, then it would not be unreasonable to infer, on the basis of the fairly close correspondences, that Cicero had been broadly happy with the philosophical content of *Acad.* The letters which document the creation and editorial evolution of *Acad.* are consistent with this, in that they suggest dissatisfaction with the chosen protagonists of the dialogues, but not with the articulation of the subject matter. *Att.* 13.32.2–3 (= SB 305 = T15) of 29 May speaks to the issue and states that *Catul.* and *Luc.*, once they were completed, were furnished with new proems which praise Catulus and Lucullus. It seems unlikely in itself that the first proems insufficiently extolled the two characters, and indeed *Att.* 13.16.1–2 (= SB 323 = T21) of 26 June makes it clear that the concern was rather that the historical individuals featuring in the first edition (sc. other than Cicero) did not have the in-depth familiarity with philosophical debates that would make them credible representatives of Academic scepticism and Antiochianism respectively. *Att.* 13.19.5 (= SB 326 = T23) of 29 June states that the two dialogues were λογικώτερα for Catulus, Lucullus and Hortensius

---

[1] For an attempt to distinguish the first-person speakers in Cicero's rhetorical works, see section 8.

to have dreamt of the subject matter.[2] Consequently it is reasonable to scrutinize the proem for material which one would expect in any preface to the kind of dialogue *Luc.* is, as well as for material which specifically speaks to the issue of Lucullus' credentials. This needs to involve attention to structural features of the text, like enumerations which contain duplicates or omissions, as well as to linguistic devices which mark such structural features.

Luc. 1–3 is the biographical sketch of Lucullus. Much of what we learn here speaks to his credentials as a talented and committed politician, provincial administrator and general, as well as his personal relationship with Cicero. No reference to philosophy is made, but two claims about Lucullus are relevant for his role in the dialogue: he had a highly receptive memory, so much so that he had no use for mnemotechnics, and he was capable of picking up through suitable reading knowledge and skills that usually require practical experience. §4 then introduces the notion that Lucullus was interested in philosophy, included Antiochus in his entourage due to his reputation, and absorbed everything he said due to his exceptional memory. This means that the paragraph anticipates directly the concerns Cicero had about Lucullus as a character, but it is foregrounded in the preceding biographical section. It is plausible to identify §§1–4 as the praise of Lucullus which according to *Att.* 13.32.2–3 (= SB 305 = T15) the second proem contained. I thus speculate that the first proem of *Luc.* contained a biographical sketch, but that it did not emphasize or even feature the subject of Lucullus' memory, and that §4 includes material that was added so as to link Lucullus' memory with his philosophical expertise.

§§5–6 might on first approach look like partial duplicates of one another, given how the first sentence of each paragraph seems the address the same criticism, down to the terminology involved, viz. that Cicero diminishes the historical individuals who are his characters (*personae*) by showing them engaged in conversation on philosophical topics. However, they are not duplicates: §5 distinguishes three groups who dislike (i) Greek literature, (ii) Greek philosophy, or (iii) the denigration of historical individuals which comes from their being associated with conversation about philosophical topics. §5 then goes on to rebut the criticism of groups (i) and (ii), while §6 deals with group (iii) and is more specifically about disrespectful treatment which comes from presenting Roman nobles as engaged in discussion of such nugatory matters in their spare time.

An impression that some splicing of material has occurred arises from the repetition of a transitional device: §6 begins with *restat ut*, §7b with *restat unum genus reprehensorum*. However, this, too, cannot be put down to the rewrite of the proem: §§7b–9a is very likely to have featured already in the first proem in its substance (see below). §7a, i.e. the first two sentences of §7, resume the topic of §4 but introduce it as a new point. Here one is tempted to see a left-over from the old proem, i.e. the sole crisp and confident dismissal of this consideration in that version, formulated before Cicero had second thoughts and composed *Luc.* 1–4 in their transmitted form.

§§7b–9a, concerned with the justification of the *Academiae ratio* after it was met with criticism (or so Cicero says), must be seen as carrying an implicit reference to

---

[2] §3 of the same letter mentions Cicero's earlier decision not to use living characters apart from himself.

Hort., where Cicero identified his philosophical stance as the Academic one (see frg. 107 Grilli = 91 Straume-Zimmermann and 51 G. = 92 S.-Z. and section 9.5). For this reason I regard it as a natural part of the original conception of the proem of *Luc.* Including such material here would also fit with the compositional principle of a 'proem in the middle', typically associated with poetry: on this principle, initial proems in literary works are concerned with subject matter, while proems in the middle of a work speak to the ideological commitments of the work and of the author persona.[3] The transition to §9b claims that 'about such matters' (*quibus de rebus*) the *personae* of *Catul.* and *Luc.* debated often and especially on the day the debate represented in *Luc.* took place; some have seen this as a manifest left-over from an earlier stage of the proem, but the transition is in my view not grating, and the *Academiae ratio* of the preceding section would certainly be a suitable topic in the fictional world *Luc.* is set.[4] In §10 Lucullus expresses a limited commitment to Antiochian philosophy; this is compatible with his having a detailed understanding of what he is relaying.

Chronologically the self-justificatory narrative on writing philosophy in Latin restarts with *Luc.* 5–6—for the modern reader, but the subject may have featured in *Hort.*—and comprises the refutation of objections as well as Cicero's positive reasons for his project.[5] The 'narrative' is of course a development of earlier Ciceronian statements on producing dialogues in the works of the 50s BC and, to an extent, in *Brut.* A move which resumes a theme from these earlier works—*otium* as a space for writing—but is distinctive of the present context is to be found in *Luc.* 6: beginning, conventionally enough, with the notion that not just did his writing not interfere with his obligations in public life, it fulfilled those very same obligations in a different sphere, Cicero then makes it clear that his *otium* has been forced upon him and that he regards it as objectionable. The significance of this has been pointed out by Gildenhard (2007: 55–7), who comments (p. 57):

> This surprising turn of thought retrospectively highlights the fact that his *otium* is involuntary, which in turn renders the idea of censuring Cicero for his philosophical writings patently absurd. His apology here unfolds against the hypothetical scenario that he retired voluntarily and now devotes himself to his private intellectual passion. Even if that *were* the case, so he implies, he should not become the target of criticism, given his long and distinguished record of public commitment. But his current *otium* is not of his own choosing. On the contrary, he loathes his idleness and sees in the writing of philosophy the only means by which he can continue his public service. Thus he cannot blamed for his leisure since it is enforced; and, for two reasons, he should not be blamed for filling it with intellectual efforts:

---

[3] See the classic study by Conte (1992) on proems in the middle in Latin poetry; also Farrell (2008). For an argument that such structural devices influenced Livy in his composition of *Ab urbe condita*, see Vasaly (2014: 226–7).

[4] Earlier analyses of the proem are Krische (1845: 16–19, 35–40); Lörcher (1911: 244–6); Philippson (1939: 1130–2); Ruch (1950); Ruch (1958a: 263–7).

[5] Studies partially or wholly devoted to the section as a site of ideological and pragmatic import include Schmidt (1978–9); Linderski (1995a); Gildenhard (2007: 45–63); Steel (2013). A discussion of Cicero's prefaces and their topics is provided in the general note on *Ac.* 1.1–10; see also section 3.

first, because the alternative would be complete idleness of mind and body, an undesirable state of inactivity; and, second, his efforts are designed to benefit his fellow Romans. The passage, then, is as programmatic as it is bitter and sets up a caesura between his previous and his present writings. The former are *forenses*, the latter are not, for the simple reason that the public sphere has disappeared. (author's emphasis)

We know from *Att.* 16.6.4 (= SB 414 = t. 20) of 25 July 44 BC that (part of; see below) the proem of *Ac.* 3 came from the *uolumen prooemiorum*, which is why Cicero could make the mistake of reusing it a year later in the lost *De gloria*. The comments made in 45 BC while Cicero was re-working the proems of *Catul.* and *Luc.* do not mention a *uolumen* and focus on the credibility of *Catul.* and *Luc.* on their own terms. Hence it is plausible to assume that the *uolumen* was first conceived as an idea and actually assembled in the period between the completion of the first and the start of work on the final edition of *Acad.* The question arises what of the revised proem of *Luc.* was taken over in the proem of *Ac.* 3 and whether the former allows for guesses as to the contents of the *uolumen*. The sections devoted to Lucullus would obviously have been omitted (§§1–4). There is one point of contact between *Luc.* 9a and Lact., *Inst.* 6.24.1 (= t. 21), which suggests that the section on the *Academiae ratio* (§§7b–9a), which is not tied to the *personae* of *Luc.*, featured in *Ac.* 3, too, in revised form.[6] The observations made above about the suitability of a 'proem in the middle' would still apply. §§5–6, which are also not tied to peculiarities of the dialogue, could conceivably stand in any preface of a Ciceronian dialogue, where they would form part of the self-justification narrative. It is tempting to speculate that this section and its manifest applicability across dialogues played a role in Cicero's conception of the *uolumen*. One might even wonder if §§5–6 actually provided the kernel of the *uolumen*.[7]

Academiae ratio

I continue with §§7b–9a. According to Cicero the Academics engage in argument in the spirit of inquiry and in the desire to find the truth; this motivation stands in marked contrast with those ascribed to the Academics by their opponents.[8] Moreover, Cicero claims for the Academic position a certain kind of freedom, viz.

---

[6] A second possible candidate is *Luc.* 7: *Etsi…in iudiciis nostris* ~ Lact., *Inst.* 3.14.15: *haec tua uerba sunt: mihi autem non modo ad sapientiam caeci uidemur, sed ad ea ipsa quae aliqua ex parte cerni uideantur, hebetes et obtunsi*. I did not include it amongst the fragments since the correspondence is not close enough; it is, however, marked as a direct quote (without being assigned to a particular work).

[7] The topic of writing philosophy in Latin of course already received coverage in the proem of *Ac.* 1. Scholarship on the *uolumen* includes Philippson (1939: 1127–8) and Plezia (1989). The practice of providing a separate introduction for each book of a philosophical dialogue is linked to Aristotle's lost exoteric writings in the earlier *Att.* 4.16.5 (= SB 89): *quoniam in singulis libris utor prooemiis ut Aristoteles in iis quos ἐξωτερικοὺς uocat*. Cicero did not adopt it universally, though (cf. *Fin.* 3; *N.D.* 2 and 3).

[8] See on *Luc.* 18 and *Ac.* 1.44. Tarrant (2020: 202–3) reads *Luc.* 7b–9a as a policy statement encompassing the Academy from Plato to Philo and implicitly asserting a kind of intellectual unity of the Academy over time; I note that explicit markers of scope are absent.

the freedom to form independent views without being beholden to the authority of school doctrine or of a particular teacher and thereby committed to defending positions no matter what. Although Cicero does not do so here, he could have claimed Socratic credentials for this stance e.g. through a reference to Plato, *Alc.* 114e, where Socrates advises Alcibiades to think for himself rather than simply adopt the beliefs of others.[9]

One might think that a dogmatist would be free to explore any position for the sake of the argument and that his position does afford him freedom to think e.g. about the right course of action in a given situation. These considerations point to two restrictions which are in place in our passage: first, it is the dogmatist's actual beliefs which are at stake, not exploration of philosophical positions for the sake of the argument; second, for the dogmatist there are positions which define their outlook and which they cannot normally give up if they want to remain a dogmatist of such and such a persuasion.

The Academic is not so constrained. One may ask, though, what his freedom would actually consist in and what it would be worth.[10] If a philosopher avowedly holds no beliefs because he refrains from forming them and if he was entirely uncommitted to any views of whatever description which he does hold, then such a stance might be read as a refusal to be accountable, to himself and to others, and it may in addition point to an inability to be accountable. If so, the freedom of the Academic would be in danger of being vacuous, offering no prospect of helping him to live a life which meets any sensible description of an internally or externally successful one.

Yet the Academic speakers in Cicero's works clearly feel that they can be themselves—effective politician and advocate (Cicero); priest (Cotta in *N.D.*)—whilst being Academics. Especially Cotta makes a sustained argument to that effect, and his outlook is, like that of the Cicero speaker in *Luc.* 7 as I will show, Clitomachean.[11] Already in his earliest sceptical pronouncement (*Inv.* 2.7-10, dating to the 80s BC, on which see section 8), Cicero stressed that he had exercised careful judgement in selecting the precepts he was relaying in the treatise and that he was at the same time committed to suspension of judgement with regard to their truth—without any suggestion that this would interfere with their usefulness or his ability to apply them.[12] The Clitomachean speakers in Cicero's works may of course be mistaken about what their scepticism can afford them, but it should be acknowledged that their particular position leaves them, in their own mind, neither without any views of any description nor makes them unaccountable in the relevant sense.

In the debate between Stoics and Academics a point of reference are beliefs (δόξαι, *opiniones*) which arise from assent, from the mental act of endorsing an impression

---

[9] See Renaud and Tarrant (2015: 110–25) on whether Cicero was familiar with *Alc.*
[10] Coope (2019) investigates these two questions in a discussion of *Luc.* 7b–9a and of passages in Olympiodorus which engage with Plt., *Alc.* 114e; see also Frede (1996a); Tarrant (2018: 82–3).
[11] See Wynne (2014).
[12] However, dogmatists would have held, and the Academics might have agreed, that the status of the injunctions and normative statements which jointly form the art of rhetoric is different from that of rules by which one might live.

as true. Beliefs in this sense are not available to the Clitomachean,[13] i.e. he thinks one ought to resist forming them if at all possible. However, the Clitomachean does feel able to 'follow' impressions, and impressions one follows do give rise to beliefs of a kind, even though in *Acad.* no noun is used to designate this quasi-belief.[14] ('Following', which arises from 'approval', is conceptualized in *Luc.* 104–5.) *Probabilia*, as I argue in section 6, are rationally persuasive impressions, i.e. their persuasiveness depends primarily on their coherence with other impressions. Because *probabilia* are permanently kept under review ex hypothesi, the Academic can change his mind about them, and because they are rationally persuasive, he ought to be able to articulate why he changed his mind in a given case. Unlike a dogmatist, the Academic is not committed to certain first-order views which define his position and whose abandonment would make him a renegade in his school.[15] It is not difficult to see how Cicero might change his mind over the course of his life, possibly not just once, on, e.g., whether virtue is sufficient for happiness or if the goods of fortune were necessary in addition. There would be nothing flippant to such changes of mind, and in each case he would have been able to provide an account of his reasoning. Passages like *Tusc.* 5.33, which emphasize the transient (as opposed to provisional) nature of 'probabilities followed', are best read as concerned with propositions merely explored in argument (*Tusc.* 5.83 illuminates 5.33, and the larger context is relevant in each case).[16] Some 'probabilities followed' will, however, be more stable than others as a matter of fact, and it would be fair to say that the Academic lives by them while regarding them as open to revision. Which views these are the Academic would not disclose, under a general policy of not disclosing his own views, following the Socratic model. It is these views which Lucullus dubs *mysteria* in *Luc.* 60.[17]

An Academic like Cicero may have felt that he was free in a way in which dogmatists were not, and that his freedom was not just an empty promise never to be enacted and never to be fulfilled. It is, however, also to be acknowledged that the Academic's 'beliefs', to the extent that they arise from the approval of impressions, could to dogmatist critics appear either as too weakly held to be efficacious or as actually resulting from assent, in a manner that is not transparent to the Academic or about which he is in denial.

It is well recognized that there was more than one Academic position, and it has been a matter of contention what standing each of them had at different points in

---

[13] See sections 4 and 6.6; *Luc.* 66–7, 148 (with comm.); Wynne (2016) on the 'ethics of belief' in Cicero; cf. Friedman (2017).

[14] Cf. also Cicero's laying claim to *decreta*, sc. of a kind in *Luc.* 109–10.

[15] Seneca comments on his own school in *Ep. mor.* 117.6: the Stoa's followers are at times 'unduly concerned with orthodoxy owing to a mistaken conception of school loyalty' (Inwood 2007: 294), which can mean that he, unlike others, regards position-defining tenets as negotiable or that others feel committed even to tenets which are not position-defining. Since Academics and especially Clitomacheans are not negative dogmatists, they would not regard themselves as dogmatically committed to e.g. 'nothing can be known', even though their opponents would present them in this way.

[16] On the semantic range of *probabile*, which includes the genuinely plausible and the superficially plausible (applicable in cases where the Clitomachean is considering a proposition on its own merits), see Reinhardt (2018a: 243–4). I am indebted to James Allen for a discussion of *Tusc.* 5.33; see also Allen (forthcoming).

[17] See also Aug., *Contra Acad.* 3.20.43 (= t. 63*).

time and which one Cicero embraced. I need to secure my assumption that Cicero speaks as a Clitomachean in §§7b–9a. In the present passage Cicero offers what appears to be a general defence of Academic scepticism against presumed or actual criticisms; a passage of similar purpose and, as we shall see, outlook is *N.D.* 1.10–12. The Academic position, and the one which Cicero embraces, is characterized (i) by the citation of 'what appears to be the case' (*quae uidentur*) against things which others (i.e. dogmatic philosophers) think they know (*se scire arbitrantur*; §8 *init.*), whereby no domain is specified (e.g. perceptual thoughts, philosophical tenets), (ii) a keen pursuit of the truth, coupled with and undaunted by an awareness how difficult it is to establish anything, (iii) a practice of arguing on either side of a question, in order for the truth or what is like the truth to emerge,[18] and (iv) a particular response to what was called 'what appears to be the case' above and what is later called *probabilia*, which consists in 'following' (*sequi*) as opposed to 'affirmation' (*affirmare*; §8).

Given that allowing for assent to non-cataleptic impressions is what distinguishes the position of mitigated scepticism (*Luc.* 148) from the Clitomachean one, (iv) strongly suggests that Cicero assumes a version of the Clitomachean position here, as indeed his character does in his speech in reply to Lucullus'.[19] Further, given that assent is unqualifiedly dismissed, it seems natural to assume that in (iv) Cicero rejects not just his overt target, Stoic dogmatic assent, but also the informed, non-dogmatic assent permitted by mitigated scepticism. (It seems much less likely that Cicero felt entitled to subsume non-dogmatic assent under 'following', given that non-dogmatic assent is recognized as different from approval in *Luc.*; see on §§66–7 and 148.) That being so, Cicero appears to be laying claim to representing the Academic position in general, by presenting the Clitomachean view as its primary or even sole representative.[20]

Features (i)–(iii), addressed in Lucullus' speech in §§59–60, coupled with (iv) allow an Academic position to emerge which is in its nature positive and intended to add up to a way of life, rather than being negative and deployed to attack dogmatic positions or to show that the opposite view is equipollent. And this picture is entirely consistent with the one presented by Cicero in his speech in the second half of *Luc.* However, this does not mean that Academic scepticism thus construed would not

---

[18] On the spirit in which Academics search for the truth, see Wynne (2014: 264–5). Gawlick and Görler (1994: 1089–92) argues that the notion that an argument on either side is pursued in search of the truth was a Ciceronian invention and not part of the practice or self-conception of his Academic teacher Philo; see, however, Galen, *Opt. doctr.* 1 (included in appendix 1). Brittain (2001: 112–13, 114 n. 62, 218, 112–14, 226 n. 13) holds that the hoped-for emergence of the *ueri simile* is a hallmark of the 'Philonian/Metrodorian' position. On the Pyrrhonist rejection of the notion that the Academics were searching for the truth as opposed to being negative dogmatists, see Striker (2010: 196–8).

[19] *Luc.* 7b–9a is of course part of a frame, and continuity between the first-person speakers cannot just be assumed.

[20] In *Luc.* 66 Cicero calls himself a *magnus opinator*, which means that he frequently assents to non-cataleptic impressions, thus ending up with non-dogmatic beliefs. However, this is pointedly presented as the inevitable result of human weakness, due to the fact that Cicero is not a sage, and thus consistent with a formal position that one should not assent to non-cataleptic impressions. Cf. Wynne (2014: 256): 'A Radical *prescribes* avoidance of opinions, but might fail to live up to his own prescription' [author's emphasis].

have the option to engage in ad hominem or 'for the sake of the argument' attacks on certain positions in particular contexts, motivated solely by the desire to probe whether the dogmatic position in question is warranted by its holder's standards of rationality.

In the proem of *N.D.* 1, where *Acad.* is cross-referenced as providing the epistemological background to the dialogue (1.11), Cicero characterizes his position in very similar terms. On (i) and (iv) above, cf. *N.D.* 1.1; on (ii), cf. *N.D.* 1.4 *fin.*; on (iii), cf. *N.D.* 1.11 *fin.*

I argue in the commentary on *Luc.* 104–5a that the manner in which the Clitomachean holds views is compared to the manner in which a respondent in a dialectical exchange accepts propositions offered to him if they appear true to him, in contexts in which avowedly it is not the respondent's beliefs in a stronger sense which are at stake. Applied to our context here, this points to an asymmetry between the dogmatist and the Clitomachean. The former is, one would assume, free to think and argue 'for the sake of the argument', whereas this freedom is curtailed when his commitments are at issue. The Clitomachean is free to interrogate anything, including positions which happen to be his defeasible views (though he will not signal when that is the case), but there is no qualitative difference between the manner in which he endorses positions deemed *probabile* in discussion and the manner in which he endorses said defeasible views.

The Historical Lucullus and Cicero's Character Lucullus

While *Luc.* 1–4 is in itself an important (and early) source of biographical information on Lucullus, there are of course a number of other important texts to draw on, notably Plutarch's *Life of Lucullus*. We are also able to compare the picture of Lucullus which emerges from *Luc.* with Ciceronian statements elsewhere.[21] It would appear that Cicero exaggerated Lucullus' inexperience at the moment when he was entrusted with the campaign against Mithridates (see nn. below) and that he passed over in silence military ventures which did not yield the desired result (notably because his soldiers engaged in mutiny). That it took three years for Lucullus to be granted a triumph was in part a consequence of the loss of political support after his ordering of the cities of Asia, which had a negative impact on wealthy creditors in Rome, notably knights. Cicero omitted Lucullus' reputation for luxury, which was presumably not entirely unrelated to what interest in philosophy he had, but could hardly have been turned into a credential.[22] Lucullus and Hortensius are likely to have been included

---

[21] See Gelzer (1926); Jolivet (1987); Keaveney (1992); as well as Tröster (2008) on Plutarch's *Life of Lucullus*. Cicero's *Acad.* was known to Plutarch, so that in a number of cases a judgement needs to be made as to whether Plutarch offers independent evidence. In particular, he seems to have known of *Luc.* (cf. Plut., *Luc.* 42 = t. 66) and, on the evidence of Plut., *Cic.* 40 (= t. 67), of *Catul.*

[22] Cicero shows an awareness of this aspect of his reputation in *Sest.* 93, where he alludes to a *contio* of 67 BC in which a tribune, A. Gambinius, used a drawing of one of Lucullus' villas in order to turn public opinion against him. In *Off.* 1.40 Cicero mentions the splendour of Lucullus' country houses in a passage which calls for restraint and modesty. Earlier in *Leg.* 3.30 Lucullus' country houses are said to give rise to excessive buildings among lower classes.

among those who Cicero referred to as *piscinarii* ('fish pond devotees') for their lack of engagement with the political situation in the period 61–60 BC.[23]

§1

Magnum ingenium L. Luculli...caruit omnino rebus urbanis: the first sentence of the prefaces touches on many of the themes known from (chronologically later) Ciceronian *prooemia* and anticipates concerns one might have about the Lucullus character (which eventually prompted Cicero to create two further editions): Lucullus' *ingenium* and his devotion to the *optimae artes* were remarkable, i.e. he had the capacity and actual expertise. Said devotion was not misplaced or, worse, a waste of time or an embarrassment, but would have enabled him to stand out in the forum, i.e. the *optimae artes* actually help the Roman statesman meet his obligations. But Lucullus did not shine in the forum for extended periods of time, because he was away from Rome engaged in military activities, i.e. he was doing something even more respectable, which should secure his credentials on any account. The periods of absence which Cicero has in mind are detailed below.

The notion of a group of *optimae artes* features elsewhere in Cicero; see Mankin (2011: 117) on *De orat.* 3.21. While the phrasal term *artes liberales* does occur in Cicero (*Inv.* 1.35), it only hardened so as to designate a definite set of disciplines after Cicero. See also *TLL* s.v. *liberalis* col. 1293.8–9.

The phrase *percepta doctrina* may hint at Lucullus' having firmly grasped Antiochian philosophy (without necessarily endorsing it, cf. *Luc.* 10), with an allusion to the Stoic conception of κατάληψις; this would have been introduced in the passage of the *Catulus* corresponding to *Ac.* 1.40–2 (probably reflected in Plut., *Cic.* 40 = t. 67). Thus the first readers would have been able to make the connection. Reid[1] (p. 169) glosses as 'gained, won'. On *carere* 'to be unavoidably absent from', see Reid[1] (p. 169); also ibid. on *tum* in enumerations. For *res urbanae*, contrasted with *res bellicae*, cf. e.g. Cic., *Phil.* 12.24.

Vt enim [urbanis] admodum adulescens...ingenium agnoscerent: for all of the biographical facts enumerated here, see Gelzer (1926), to which my nn. on §§1–4 are indebted throughout.

Lucullus' father (see *RE* s.v. Licinius no. 103) had been convicted on an embezzlement charge around 101 BC, with C. Servilius Augur acting as prosecutor (Plut., *Luc.* 1.2). Lucullus and his brother Marcus (cos. 73 BC) pursued C. Servilius for dereliction of official duty *ulciscendi causa* (Cic., *Off.* 2.50; see also Dyck 1996: 433–4 ad loc.). The trial was accompanied by violent clashes and was evidently high-profile (cf. *magna cum gloria* here); see Lintott (1968: 186 and 211). On the obligations felt by upper-class Romans to prosecute enemies of family members, see Cic., *Off.* 3.90; Thomas (1984).

---

[23] See *Att.* 1.17.8–10 (= SB 17); 1.18.3–8 (= SB 18); 1.19.6–8 (= SB 19); 1.20.2–3 (= SB 20); 2.1.6–8 (= SB 21).

Having served as military tribune during the Social War, Lucullus was assigned as a quaestor to Sulla in 87 BC (Vell. 74.1) and travelled ahead to Greece when Sulla began his campaign against Mithridates (Plut., *Sulla* 11). In the winter of 87/6 Lucullus was charged with assembling a fleet in Egypt and Syria to aid Sulla; on that journey he was accompanied by the poet Archias (cf. Cicero's *Arch.*) as well as by Antiochus of Ascalon (cf. the scene in Alexandria described in *Luc.* 11–12).

When Sulla left Asia in 84 BC, Lucullus remained there, serving under the propraetor L. Licinius Murena and taking part in various military endeavours; he returned to Rome in 80 BC and was elected aedile while still on the return journey. Lucullus had delayed his application for this office in order to be able to serve with his brother Marcus; the pair arranged for lavish games in 79 BC In 78 BC Lucullus became praetor and then went as propraetor to Africa. If Cicero's *inde ad consulatum* is no exaggeration, then Lucullus remained there until 75 BC. His colleague as consul in 74 was M. Aurelius Cotta, whose older brother Gaius appears as an interlocutor in Cicero's *De orat.* as well as in *N.D.*, where he is a representative of the sceptical Academy and the Clitomachean position in particular (see section 8 of the introduction).

Quaestores of course had considerable powers and responsibilities (cf. *praefuit*), but no *imperium*. With the phrase *legis praemio*, cf. the phrase *sortium beneficio* in Caes., *B.G.* 1.53; on progression from the aedileship to the praetorship with an interval of just one year, see Astin (1958: 9–19); Badian (1964: 144–7). On *per multos annos* vs *permultos annos*, see *TLL* s.v. *permultus* col. 1572.41–3 and Oakley (2005: 593) on Livy 9.45.10; the span so described must be about ten years (Reid[1] p. 170).

Post ad Mithridaticum bellum...gloriam superiorum: at the time of Lucullus' consulship king Mithridates of Pontus was preparing for war once again, and when Nicomedes IV. of Bithynia died, leaving his kingdom to the Roman people, Mithridates seized it, claiming to assert the rights of a son of Nicomedes (Sall., *Hist.* 4.69.9). After a period of political intrigue which began when Lucullus' colleague Cotta (see previous n.), widely deemed less suitable, was allotted the proconsulship of Asia while Lucullus obtained that of *Gallia citerior* (Plut., *Luc.* 5.2), Lucullus was made *proconsul* and left for the East presumably already in the summer of 74. Cicero exaggerates that Lucullus outdid all of his predecessors in *gloria* (which may be true of L. Murena but not of Sulla). With *opinionem uincere*, cf. *expectationem uincere* in Cic., *Verr.* 2.5.5.11.

§2

Idque eo fuit mirabilius...rei militaris rudis: Lucullus was military tribune in the Social War (Plut., *Luc.* 2.1), and even if assembling a fleet (Plut., *Luc.* 3.2) does not count as military experience in a narrow sense, in his time as quaestor or proquaestor Lucullus achieved success in a naval battle near Tenedos (Cic., *Arch.* 21: *nostra semper feretur et praedicabitur L. Lucullo dimicante...incredibilis apud Tenedum pugna illa naualis*) and was involved in the siege of Mytilene (Plut., *Luc.* 4.2). So it is not credible that Lucullus left Rome as a novice in military matters (*rei militaris rudis*), as is also suggested by the senate's apparent desire to have Lucullus rather than Cotta engage Mithridates. But talking to experienced soldiers and reading historiography, inevitably concerned with accounts of war, is supposed to have made him an *imperator*. Cicero is clearly trying to establish that the talents which allowed Lucullus to be a successful general are the same as those which make him a credible spokesman for Antiochian philosophy. No forensic activities other than the trial against Servilius (§1 above) are attested.

For the passive sense of *indocilis*, see *TLL* s.v. col. 1217.18–57 (our passage at ll. 51–3). The phrase *laus imperatoria* (*laus* generically = 'praiseworthy acts') also in Cic., *Verr.* 2.15.11; in the plural in *Vatin.* 24.16. Reid[1] (pp. 170–1) has informative notes on *admodum* with verbs as opposed to adjectives and on *factus* 'trained, fully formed'. On *quaedam* in *incredibilis quaedam ingenii magnitudo*, see Pinkster i.1110; contrast Reid[1] p. 171.

Habuit enim diuinam quandam memoriam rerum…in animo res insculptas habebat: the distinction between memory for words and memory for things, and its use here, is not an obvious one. Cato's famous injunction *rem tene uerba sequentur* (Iul. Vict., *Rhet.* p. 197 Orelli) does not seem to provide the required contrast. In stylistic theory, *res* and *uerba* are distinguished as the issues one talks about, and what linguistic form the issues are presented in. So the suggestion would be that Lucullus had a real understanding of the issues, while Hortensius is better at repeating something he has committed to memory verbatim. This distinction of *res/uerba* also in *De orat.* 2.359 (part of an intertext for the present passage; see below): *Sed uerborum memoria, quae minus est nobis necessaria, maiore imaginum uarietate distinguitur; multa enim sunt uerba, quae quasi articuli conectunt membra orationis, quae formari similitudine nulla possunt; eorum fingendae sunt nobis imagines, quibus semper utamur; rerum memoria propria est oratoris; eam singulis personis bene positis notare possumus, ut sententias imaginibus, ordinem locis comprehendamus.*

If Hortensius, whose conversion to philosophy was dramatized in Cicero's *Hortensius* (see section 9.5), had a speaking role in the *Catulus* which allocated to him some of the historical material given to Varro in the second edition, then the device of a 'memory for words' could make it possible to have him report in intricate and accurate detail on something he had heard or read, even though he was only a recent convert. (On the dramatic dates of *Hort.* and *Catul.*, see section 9.5.) Elsewhere Cicero claims both *copia rerum* and *dicendi uis* for the orator (*De orat.* 3.76; cf. 60). The present passage should not be read as an appraisal of the historical Hortensius. For material relayed in a dialogue as memorized cf. *Lael.* 3.

The poet Simonides is also linked with the art of memory in *Tusc.* 1.59. According to Cic., *Fin.* 2.104, he offered to teach it to Themistocles, of whose preeminent role in the defeat of an eastern enemy the reader is supposed to think. The locus classicus on mnemotechnic in the Ciceronian corpus, with an extensive reception in the later rhetorical tradition and the Middle Ages, is *De orat.* 2.351–60, where Antonius recounts the story of how Simonides developed the technique, viz. the mental association of physical places with items to be remembered, after a collapsed roof killed a party of diners and disfigured them beyond recognition. Simonides, so the story goes, was able to identify them by remembering the position of the guests before the accident. The memory of Simonides also features in Cotta's account of how he conceives of himself as a Clitomachean sceptic in *N.D.* 1.60, specifically with respect to his command of the doctrines of all schools, which is a prerequisite for arguing *in utramque partem*; cf. Wynne (2014: 252–3, 257–61). On mnemotechnic in the medieval period (and its ancient origins), see Carruthers (2008).

Ille in animo res insculptas habebat gestures to the imagery from printing and sealing which the Stoics employ in connection with cataleptic impressions as well as concepts (see *Luc.* 18); cf. *percepta doctrina* in §1 above. With the formulation, cf. *N.D.* 2.12: *omnibus enim innatum est et in animo quasi inscriptum esse deos*.

Quo and *hoc* are *ablatiui mensurae* which go with the comparatives *plus* and *praestantior*, with *illa memoria* referring back to *memoria rerum*.

§3

Tantus ergo imperator...quos legisset fateretur: no pronouncements of Mithridates on Lucullus are attested elsewhere. That Mithridates compared Lucullus to generals he had *read* about creates a parallel with Lucullus (§2). *Proelia* and *oppugnationes* are frequently contrasted as types of military engagement. On *instrumento et apparatu*, see Reid[1] (pp. 172–3)

In eodem tanta prudentia fuit...institutis seruandis et quasi uestigiis persequendis: *in constituendis temperandisque ciuitatibus* probably refers to the granting of a constitution to the city of Cyrene (Plut., *Luc.* 2.3–5). *Aequitas* relates to the fair and reasonable financial administration; see Elkins (2017). The province Asia had become unable to meet the demands for tributes, interest payments, and duties. Lucullus instigated a program of debt consolidation and relief, which turned Roman creditors against him (Plut., *Luc.* 20.5). In 61 BC Caesar restored *Hispania ulterior* to a proper footing by similar measures. See Gelzer (1926: 394–5). In *Man.* 4, 6, 14–19 Cicero argues for Pompeius' special command with reference to the threatened financial interests of the *uiri honestissimi*. Consecutive *ut*-clauses need not follow the sequence of tenses; hence *fuit ut stet*.

Sed etsi magna cum utilitate...et fori et curiae: Cicero is glossing over the reasons for the lack of appreciation Lucullus encountered in Rome (see previous n.). For *ab oculis abesse*, cf. Cic., *Catil.* 1.13; *Rab. perd.* 16; *Sul.* 74; what makes the expression here striking is the genitives dependent on *oculis*, which refer to people only metonymically. See also Reid[1] (p. 173) on the *res pro persona* substitution in *tanta uis uirtutis*. With *etsi...tamen* cf. Kühner-Stegmann ii.440 ('mit gemeinsamem Verb für Haupt- und Nebensatz'): Cic., *Fin.* 2.45: *homines etsi aliis multis tamen hoc uno plurimum a bestiis differunt*.

Quin etiam, cum uictor a Mithridatico bello reuertisset...triumphauit: Pompeius' special command in the East, supported by Cicero against resistance from Catulus and Hortensius (*Man.* 51–60; Cass. Dio 36.30.4–36.4), de facto stripped Lucullus of his, and political supporters of Pompeius had no interest in a public display which presented Lucullus' campaign as conclusive and detracted from Pompeius' achievements. A *plebiscitum* designed to prevent a triumph, pursued by the *tribunus plebis*

C. Memmius, was thwarted by leading aristocrats (Plut., *Luc.* 37.3; *Cato min.* 29). *Calumnia* specifically 'fraudulent use of legal forms' here, as Reid[1] (p. 173) notes.

Nos enim consules introduximus…quam id cum mea laude communicem: Cicero is probably just indicating that Lucullus' triumph was delayed until the beginning of 63 (or the end of 64) rather than implying that he played a role in the conflict with C. Memmius. In addition to advising Cicero (cf. also *Luc.* 62; *Att.* 12.21.1 = SB 260), Lucullus supported Cicero during the Catilinarian conspiracy by having his veterans vote for his former legate L. Murena in the consular elections for 62 (cf. Cic., *Mur.* 37, 69). Those awaiting triumph were required to wait outside the *pomerium* (cf. *in urbem* here).

§4

Sed quae populari gloria…et Graecis litteris celebrata et Latinis: Haltenhoff (pp. 63–5) assembles the evidence for favourable literary treatments of Lucullus' achievements. The Greek poet Archias, already a protégé of Lucullus' father, accompanied Lucullus during his campaign against Mithridates and eulogized him (Cic., *Arch.* 21). It is possible that the historical works of Posidonius made reference to Lucullus, as their coverage extended into the first war against Mithridates (*FGrHist* 87, frg. 38). There are further, yet less certain Roman candidates for appreciations in the medium of historiography. Cicero himself remarks favourably on Lucullus in *Manil.* 5, 10, and 20–1 as well as *Arch.* 21.

Nos autem illa externa cum multis…lectione librorum de quibus audiebat: Cicero is now overtly diverging from the known record, using the device of public and private knowledge about the man. Lucullus undoubtedly had a genuine interest in Greek philosophy; his villa near Cicero's Tusculanum had a famously extensive library, and in *Fin.* 3.7–8 Cicero describes how he went there to consult some books and found Cato surrounded by Stoic writings. It is stressed that Lucullus pursued this interest not just as a young man as Roman aristocrats frequently would; rather, his contact with Antiochus dates from the later period when he was quaestor or proquaestor and held the *imperium* in the war against Mithridates, and Lucullus pursued this interest even when he had very little *otium* and lived in tents, i.e. was actively engaged in military endeavours. Haltenhoff (p. 64) refers to Scipio, who in *Rep.* 1.17 is reported to have engaged in theoretical discussion with P. Rutilius during the siege of Numantia and while being *sub moenibus*. The impression given is that Antiochus was selected for his philosophical expertise and acted as a philosophical interlocutor, but modern scholars rightly observe that the primary reason for Antiochus' presence is likely to have been a desire for advice on diplomatic matters (see in particular Glucker 1978: 21–7). One does not have to be a *Quellenforscher* to read the last sentence of the paragraph as hinting at the sources for Lucullus' speech.

The particular use of the *externa/interiora* contrast, while unobjectionable, seems otherwise unexampled. I have translated *sub pellibus* 'under canvas' since this is a standing English expression, but Kraner, Dittenberger, and Meusel (1960: 286–7) at

Caes., *B.G.* 3.29.2 explain that tents were covered with hides when it was cold. On *potuisset* Reid[1] (p. 175): 'A condition is wrapped up in the words "uel semel audita" = "si semel tantum audisset"...'

For the constitution of the text it gives out nothing if we take *librorum de quibus audiebat* at face value or take it with Madvig as a compressed version of *de iis rebus de quibus audiebat*. The conjecture *audierat* by Ernesti has little to recommend it.

§5

Ac uereor interdum...earum rerum disputationem principibus ciuitatis non ita decoram putent: note the somewhat misleading similarity of the first sentence of §5 with the first sentence of §6 (see the general note above). Those who (i) dislike Greek literature in general or those who (ii) dislike Greek philosophy are rebutted by (i) a reference to Cato who studied Greek and (ii) a reference to P. Scipio Africanus who relied on Panaetius as an advisor. *Persona* can be 'an individual' (*OLD* s.v. no. 5), i.e. a real person, as well as a 'character' in a work of literature; it is almost a technical term in the frames of Cicero's dialogues (*Fin.* 1.1; 3.75). See the note in Reid[1] on *non ita decoram* in the sense of *non admodum decoram*. He prints *putant*, a conjecture he had found in ms. Oxford, Balliol College 248 D (saec. xv), but the preceding grammatically coordinate verbs have the subjunctive.

Ego autem, cum Graecas litteras...nec litterarum Graecarum nec philosophiae iam ullum auctorem requiro: Astin (1978: 157–81) gives an appraisal of all the available evidence on Cato's pronouncements about Greeks and Greek culture, their chronological distribution, the context and bias of the relevant testimonia, as well as reviews extant texts by Cato and allusions to Greek texts in them. He concludes that Cato must have been exposed to Greek culture as well as texts quite early and was able to make nuanced reference to them, but that a persistent negative attitude towards things Greek is very unlikely to be a construct of the later biographical tradition. Similarly Kienast (1954: 101–16). The present passage stands alongside others in which Cicero describes Cato as turning towards Greek literature broadly construed late in life (*litterae Graecae* cannot refer to Greek language): cf. Cic., *Sen.* 3, which postdates *Acad.*, and possibly *Rep.* 5, which predates it. Grillius *in Cic. Rhet.* p. 30.11–17 Jakobi juxtaposes the *rector rei publicae* treated in *Rep.* 5 with the information about Cato, but in a way which makes it impossible to isolate a Ciceronian fragment (see the note in Powell's edition). In the introduction to his edition of *Sen.*, Powell (1988: 18–19) comments: 'Cicero seems to have known a tradition that Cato was converted to the enthusiastic study of Greek literature in his old age: the notion recurs in Nepos, Valerius Maximus and Quintilian..., although they may have obtained it from Cicero. At any rate this is not a piece of *ad hoc* tendentiousness on Cicero's part [sc. in *Sen.* 3], thought up for the purpose of this dialogue: he mentions the same tradition in *Acad. pr.* 2.5, presumably before he thought of writing the *Cato*, and both there and in the *Cato* preface he speaks of it as being common knowledge.' Scipio Africanus' association with Panaetius is well documented (and the parallel with the relationship of Lucullus and Antiochus no doubt intended); cf. e.g. *Tusc.* 1.81 and Astin (1967:

294–306); Griffin (1989). On the plural of *historiae* and the personification, see Reid[1] (p. 176).

§6

Restat ut iis respondeam qui sermonibus eius modi…has etiam minus notas minusque peruolgatas adiungimus: Reid[1] (p. 176) objects to Cicero's use of *restat ut* to introduce an intermediate rather than a final point, esp. given that the expression is repeated in §7b to introduce a final type of criticism addressed by Cicero (which, however, was not mentioned in §5 *init.*). Alleemudder (p. 70 n. 1) notes, contra, that *restat ut* can mark the transition to a new point rather than a final point; cf. *N.D.* 2.45: *restat ut qualis eorum natura sit consideremus.* In fact, Cicero now addresses the criticism raised by the third group of critics mentioned in §5 and is in that sense making a final point under that heading. Nonetheless, the duplication of *restat* in §6a and §7b seems inconsiderate; see the general note above.

In this section Cicero defends both the intellectual interests of real-life individuals and their representation in his dialogues, but not every expression he employs is capable of conveying both options at the same time: *personas illigare* is something which an author does in a work of literature.

The first point in reply (*quae uero clarorum uirorum…*) is polemically put but valid. Even if one applies the exceedingly demanding standards of *Rep.* 1.8 ('Leading Roman men are entitled to *otium* only after they have dedicated all their talents to the state and there is for the moment no further call on them'), the question arises what would be an acceptable pastime for *principes ciuitatis* with intellectual interests. The writing and discussion of nugatory poetry, as associated with the circle of Quintus Lutatius Catulus (i.e. the father of the character Catulus in *Hort.*, *Catul.*, and *Luc.*), was just as open to criticism.

Cicero cites the *Hortensius* elsewhere, too, as a work in which a general defence of philosophy is offered (*Fin.* 1.2, *Tusc.* 2.4 and 3.6, *Div.* 2.1); in *Luc.* 62 Lucullus throws this back at him, questioning if Academic scepticism could count as philosophy in the required sense. Note *a nobis laudata*: this may refer to Cicero's authorial intention in *Hort.*, or it may relate to the role played by the Cicero character. In our passage here we are, however, in the frame. Thus Cicero the author may in the present passage be treating the Cicero character and the first-person speaker of the frame as continuous. Similarly, in *Div.* 1.9 *init.* the Quintus Cicero character addresses his interlocutor, the Cicero character, and presents him as the author of *N.D.* 3. All this, of course, does not mean that it is futile to distinguish the different Ciceronian first-person speakers, as I try to do in section 8. For such equations are local and can conceivably be precarious: in some respects the Cicero of 62 BC is the same as the first-person speaker of the preface of *Luc.*, and in others he is not, as the historical Cicero would have been the first to acknowledge.

With *nisi ne quid priuatis studiis de opera publica detrahamus*, cf. *Off.* 2.3–4 where Cicero says that, while he was able to play a public role, he merely read philosophy and wrote for forensic and political purposes only. Texts which present the philosophical works as the second-best contribution to public life include *Ac.* 1.11; *Fin.*

1.10; *N.D.* 1.7; *Div.* 2.6–7; *Off.* 2.3. In *Div.* 2.3 Cicero observes that only *Rep.* was written before his enforced retirement.

See Gildenhard (2007: 55–7) on how the sentence from *Quod si* first contrasts Cicero's previous total devotion to his public duties with his current—the implication is, well-deserved—state of *otium*, only to dismiss the latter as forced upon him in the relative clause from *qui in eo*; see also the general note above.

A consideration which Cicero omits here is that philosophy in Latin allows the Romans to compete with the Greeks; cf. *Att.* 13.13.1 (= SB 321 = T19), written upon completion of the *Academici libri*: *libri quidem ita exierunt, nisi forte me communis* φιλαυτία *decepit, ut in tali genere ne apud Graecos quidem simile quicquam.*

The project of writing philosophy in Latin is also defended in *Ac.* 1.10 (cf. *Fin.* 1.4–10), which raises the possibility that in the *Catulus* the topic was remarked upon, too.

On *aut ludicros sermones*, see Reid[1] (p. 176): 'condensed for *aut quasi oporteat clarorum uirorum ludicros esse sermones*'. The term *colloquia* is more suggestive of exchanges than *sermones*, but here the two seem used for variation. *In gradu* 'in an allocated position', not necessarily with a military connotation, although it is so used elsewhere; the phrase only here in Cicero. Roman aristocrats, but not *homines noui*, did of course assume they had certain rights by birth, but political offices were (usually) granted by election through the people (= *populus* here). Plasberg[1] (p. 68) gives a careful descriptions of the manuscript evidence on [*ut*] and *cum fungi munere debebamus*; by contrast, the app. crit. of the Oxford Classical Text gives summary evaluations. Schäublin et al. print *ut ⟨quam⟩ plurimis prosimus*, but it is not obvious that the sense requires 'to be of use to as many as possible'; contrast *Off.* 2.38: *quod prodesse uult plurimis* with *Div.* 2.1: *quanam re possem prodesse quam plurimis*.

§7a

Sunt etiam qui negent…sed etiam mortuis inuidere: as Alleemudder (p. 72) notes, stating that the literary conventions are what they are, and that they include the idealization of characters, was not an option for Cicero here, especially given that the proem is phrased with delicate ambiguity, and neither just about literary creations nor just about historical individuals. The letters, however, are a different matter; thus Cicero can say in the dedicatory letter to Varro (*Fam.* 9.8 = SB 254 = T29): *Puto fore ut, cum legeris, mirere nos id locutos esse inter nos quod numquam locuti sumus; sed nosti morem dialogorum.*

Given the chronology of Cicero's works, such criticism, if it is not merely anticipated, can only have been levelled against *De orat.*, *Rep.*, or the *Hortensius* (as well as, perhaps, against material pertaining to *Acad.* informally circulated prior to publication).

Haltenhoff (p. 68) suggests that these two sentences are functionally equivalent to the eulogy of Lucullus in §§1–4, in that they dismiss grounds for thinking that he might be an unsuitable interlocutor given the topic, and that therefore we ought to regard them as left over from the first proem of *Luc.* (i.e. that Cicero failed to excise them out of carelessness). Alternatively Cicero may have felt that they are addressing a general criticism, whereas §§1–4 is only about Lucullus' credentials. And while the abruptness with which the point is dispatched is striking, it may be due to the fact that Cicero is resuming a motif familiar from *Hort*. Alleemudder (p. 72 n. 3) draws attention to the grammarian Arusianus Messius (fourth century AD), who quotes from *Hort*. (GL vii.458 Keil = frg. 17 Grilli = 19 Straume-Zimmermann): *qui hodie bellum cum mortuo gerunt*. Of the characters in *Hort*. and *Luc*., only Cicero is still living of course.

See Kaster (2005: 84–103), referring to *Att*. 5.19.3 (= SB 112), where Cicero observes that Latin *inuidia* ranges over the meanings of φθόνος and νέμεσις in Greek, which denote pain felt at somebody else's good fortune and pain felt at somebody else's good fortune given some general, often societal principle. Here we seem to have a combination of the two: envy of learning, and anger at somebody's learning given that they should be occupied with something else. *Scientia* here denotes discursive knowledge generally and has none of the technical senses to be found elsewhere in *Acad*.

§7b

Restat unum genus reprehensorum...quibus Academiae ratio non probatur: for *restat*, cf. §6 *init*. As Reid[1] (p. 177) notes, a *reprehensor* is an unfavourable critic (as opposed to an *existimator*, a favourable or neutral critic). Given the chronology of Cicero's works, these critics, if they are not just a literary device designed to motivate a mission statement, can only have responded to *Hort*. Passages which can be usefully compared, apart from the ones from within *Acad*. (esp. *Luc*. 65–7, 76–7), include *N.D.* 1.6 and 1.11–12, which explain Cicero's commitment to Academic scepticism, in the face of criticism (as envisaged here) and of the suggestion that by the dramatic date of *N.D.* (c.77–75 BC) it could be deemed defunct (a claim of course disputed by Cicero). See also section 8 of the introduction on Cicero's overall stance.

I have translated *Academiae ratio* 'the Academy's way of thinking and arguing'. Given the semantic range of *ratio*, including in phrasal terms where another component is a designation of a school or of followers of a school, one might regard this translation as tendentious, i.e. as making Cicero sound more reluctant to ascribe substantial views to the Academy than he would be on some interpretations of his Academic posture, notably those which make him a mitigated sceptic who allows for qualified assent or a negative dogmatist; cf. 'Denkweise der Akademie' (Schäublin et al.), but contrast 'Academic system' (Reid[2]). One might also regard it as an overtranslation and be content to omit 'and arguing'. The *Stoicorum ratio* of *Fin*. 3.15 is a way of going about things (and the linguistic expressions which go with it); the *ueteris Academiae ratio et Stoicorum* of *Ac*. 1.43 comes closer to being a 'system', except that for all the continuity Varro claims between the *ueteres* and the Stoics, he of course has enough historical awareness to see them as distinct contributors to a broader tradition. The *Cynicorum...ratio atque uita* of *Fin*. 3.68 is an approach to life. The *ratio Peripateticorum* of *Fin*. 5.86 is the Peripatetics' reasoning; cf. *Div*. 1.82: *quam quidem esse re uera hac Stoicorum ratione concluditur* [an argument follows]; *Div*. 2.100. Academic argument is invoked from *nos autem quoniam* below.

Quod grauius ferremus...quin alii a nobis dissentiant recusare: the manuscripts before correction read *nos autem quoniam contra omnes qui dicere quae uidentur* *solemus*; this was in the archetype and is syntactically incomplete. In F and V *qui* was then deleted. A later corrector of A, A³, also deleted *qui* (through underlining rather than expunction) but added *aliis* after *quae*. Others assume a lacuna after *qui* in which descriptive reference is made to the dogmatists: ⟨*se scire arbitrantur*⟩ Halm (1861), ⟨*docere se profitentur*⟩ Plasberg² in the apparatus. I follow the correctors of V and F, on the grounds that what is salient for the sense of our passage is that the Academics argue against everyone else and hence should be able to live with being challenged. The contrast which Halm's and Plasberg's suggestions introduce appears only in §8 *init.*, where it is suitably motivated.

On the two Academic practices of arguing against every thesis and arguing on either side, see section 4. Here the former is cited because it allows Cicero to acknowledge the legitimacy of the anti-Academic stance of others. In *N.D.* 1.11 the method of arguing against any thesis is presented as in use throughout the period when the Academy was sceptical, but not given prominence over the argument *in utramque partem*: *ut haec in philosophia ratio contra omnia disserendi nullamque rem aperte iudicandi profecta a Socrate, repetita ab Arcesila, confirmata a Carneade usque ad nostram uiguit aetatem.* With the present context, cf. also *Ac.* 1.44–5 (on Arcesilaus', who serves as a model of sorts for Cicero's Clitomachean position in particular; see also section 7.5); *Luc.* 65–7. For *recusare quin* in the sense 'to reject, oppose', see *OLD* s.v. no. 3c.

Quamquam nostra quidem causa facilis est...neque nos studium exquirendi defatigati relinquemus: Cicero's *causa* is defended easily, possibly because his stance is not that of a negative dogmatist whose position could be self-refuting (depending on its exact formulation). Rather, he is genuinely committed to finding the truth, and this commitment drives his argumentative practice. For the Academic pursuit of truth, cf. *Luc.* 60, 65–6, 76 *fin.*; *N.D.* 1.11 *fin.*; *Fin.* 1.3; *Tusc.* 3.46; Burkert (1965: 187); Wynne (2014: 265).

The attribute *omnis* in the phrase *omnis cognitio* signals that *cognitio* does not stand for Stoic κατάληψις here (the concept must have been introduced in *Catul.*, in the passage corresponding to *Ac.* 1.40–2); *eaque* is subordinative: the absence of *cognitio* is jointly accounted for by *in rebus obscuritas* and *in iudiciis infirmitas*. For both phrases cf. *Ac.* 1.44, where the ancient proto-sceptics feature, too, and where they are identified. On the invocation of Presocratics in the New Academy, see *Luc.* 13–15, 72–6; Brittain and Palmer (2001); and section 7 of the introduction. On apprehension terminology, see section 10. On the issue of judgement (*iudicia*), cf. the Academic claim that our judgements are free and reside in us in §8.

A difference between the present passage and the preface of *N.D.* 1 (see above) is that here Cicero is ready to cite the obscurity in which all things are shrouded as a reason for his Academic stance, whereas in *N.D.* 1.6 very similar expressions are offered as the (it is implied, unreasonable) criticisms of the opponents of Academic scepticism: *multis etiam sensi mirabile uideri eam nobis potissimum probatam esse philosophiam quae lucem eriperet et quasi noctem quandam rebus offunderet.* The contradiction is, however, not real: the dogmatist defines perception as apprehension, and thus equates the absence of apprehension with being epistemically comprehensively stranded, whereas the Academic cites the obscurity of things as the reason for not accepting anything as true, without thereby accepting that he has nothing to go on; cf. §8 *init.*

Contentio suggests competitiveness for the sake of it; cf. the claim that the Academics act out of *pertinacia* (*Luc.* 9, 18; *Ac.* 1.44). When Cicero turns to the indefatigability of the ancients and the Academics in the search for the truth (*nec illi defecerunt...*), the envisaged alternative seems not the acceptance of claims and impressions whose certain truth is beyond proof, but a kind of despondent indifference. This would be very different from the tranquillity Pyrrhonists claim will ensue upon suspension of judgement; see Morison (2019: § 3.3) on objections which have been levelled against said notion of tranquillity. On the subject of 'desire to find out' (*studium exquirendi*), see on §9a below.

Neque nostrae disputationes...ad id quam proxime accedat: the syntax conveys the Academics' attitude to their arguments: on the one hand the arguments themselves, rather than those who advance them, are cast as agents, signalling detachment on the part of the Academics; on the other a positive purpose is ascribed to these arguments (*agunt...ut*), i.e. the eliciting of the truth or something like it. Note further that the truth (or something like it) is presented as being inherent in the subject discussed: it is there to be elicited or 'squeezed out' (*exprimant*). Reid[1] (p. 178) on *exprimant* ('embody') is a rare misstep. Cf. *Rep.* 3.8; *Tusc.* 2.9, where eliciting what is truth-like features as a rejected reason for rhetorical effect only: *itaque mihi semper Peripateticorum Academiaeque consuetudo de omnibus rebus in contrarias partes disserendi non ob eam causam solum placuit, quod aliter non posset quid in quaque re ueri simile esset inueniri, sed etiam quod esset ea maxima dicendi exercitatio*; *Tusc.* 5.11 (where the withholding of one's own opinion is also mentioned); *Div.* 2.150; *Off.* 2.7–8 and 3.20; Plut., *Sto. rep.* 1037c, where the truth is presented as something that according to the Academics can conceivably be discovered through argument on either side (quoted in appendix 1). Note also that in *Sto. rep.* 1037c the Academics are, as in Cicero, presented as those who suspend judgement; so reference is most likely to the Clitomachean position.

Et audiendo, which was in the archetype but omitted by V, has been defended by Plasberg[1] with reference to *N.D.* 1.56, but the passage gives out little beyond the obvious point that *dicere* and *audire* make a natural pairing (which may indeed have motivated the gloss). In *Luc.* 104–105a exchanges in question and answer provide the framework for a point about 'approval', but *dicere* and *audire* are unsuitable terms for describing the activities of questioner and respondent (see ad loc.), and the idea that the emergence of the truth is somehow a collaborative project between Academic and dogmatist opponent would come out of the blue (and be at variance with **nostrae disputationes**). V may have omitted *et audiendo* fortuitously rather than deliberately. For the notion of truth-likeness, see on §8. For anti-sceptical arguments turning on the supposedly illegitimate deployment of the concept 'true' or of a 'criterion of truth' by the Academics, see on *Luc.* 32–6.

§8

Nec inter nos et eos...affirmare uix possumus: the Academic claims he can function as a human being, moral agent, and to an extent philosopher in the same way as the dogmatist, a claim of course disputed by the latter. The only difference according to the Academic is that the dogmatist makes knowledge claims, whereas the Academic regards impressions as persuasive, as capable of attracting approval, and is free to follow them. On the πιθανόν/*probabile* and its relationship to truth, or its character of being truth-like, see section 6 of the introduction; for following and approval, see on *Luc.* 104–5. The dogmatist will of course dispute that the differences are small, between cataleptic and persuasive impressions, and between the kind of endorsement which assent and approval represent, respectively; see on *Luc.* 43–4. In *Luc.* 105a the Cicero character makes the different point that (presumably, some of) the very same things which the dogmatists think they can apprehend 'appear' to the Academics. Given the terminological and conceptual options in play, *affirmare uix possumus* must mean that the Academics feel unable to give deliberate assent of any kind, including the self-aware assent of *Luc.* 148. Cf. *Inv.* 2.10 (*...sine ulla affirmatione...ut ne cui rei temere atque arroganter assenserimus*), on which see section 8.

Hoc autem liberiores et solutiores sumus...tamquam ad saxum adhaerescunt: the Academics are not beholden to authority and are instead free to exercise their judgement (cf. *Luc.* 120; *Leg.* 1.36; *N.D.* 1.10 on Pythagoras' followers; and Lucullus' response in *Luc.* 60). With reference to the present passage Brittain (2001: 113–14) suggests that 'the Philonian/Metrodorians seem to have identified the pressure of "authority" as the principal irrational factor liable to influence a rational enquiry conducted on Academic (or other strictly philosophical) lines'; as explained in the general note, I think that in this framing section, too, Cicero speaks as a Clitomachean.

Cf. the statement on 'Academic freedom' in *Tusc.* 2.5: *eamque* [sc. *philosophiam*] *nos adiuuemus nosque ipsos redargui refellique patiamur. Quod ii ferunt animo iniquo qui certis quibusdam destinatisque sententiis quasi addicti et consecrati sunt eaque necessitate constricti, ut, etiam quae non probare soleant, ea cogantur constantiae causa defendere; nos qui sequimur probabilia nec ultra quam id quod ueri simile occurrit, progredi possumus, et refellere sine pertinacia et refelli sine iracundia parati sumus*; Reid[1] (p. 179) assembles further Ciceronian parallels on the contrast between freedom and necessity in his note on *necessitate ulla cogimur*.

On *nec ut omnia...defendamus necessitate ulla cogimur* Reid[1] compares Publilius Syrus l. 282 Ribbeck: *incertus animus dimidium* [edd., coni. Bothe; *remedium* mss.] *est sapientiae*, associated with the sceptical Academy also by Lachapelle (2011: 67 n. 320). Publilius was a younger contemporary of Cicero's.

On *quae praescripta a quibusdam* Reid[1] comments that it is 'a word of the jurisconsults'. In legal contexts the logical subject of *praescribere* is the magistrate (praetor) who instructs the lay judge under formulary procedure how to conduct a trial. Cf. Heumann-Seckel (p. 449): '**praescriptio**, Voranstellung, vorangestellter Satz, insbesondere der Vormerk oder die Klausel, welche im Formularprozeß der Formel inserirt wurde.' With *tenentur astricti*, cf. the similar context in *Tusc.* 4.7: *sed defendat, quod quisque sentit; sunt enim iudicia libera: nos institutum tenebimus nullisque unius disciplinae legibus astricti, quibus in philosophia necessario pareamus, quid sit in quaque re maxime probabile, semper requiremus*.

The paragraph ends with nautical imagery: some people find their philosophical persuasion like sailors whom the storm has carried to a place at random, and to that (persuasion) they cling as to a cliff (*adhaerescere* discourages an interpretation of *saxum* as 'anchor stone'). Cf. *Fin.* 5.49, where Cicero puts the image to a different use (though there is a connection with knowledge as well).

§9a

Nam quod dicunt omnia se credere...quam sine pertinacia quid constantissime dicatur exquirere: I explain the text as I print it (largely following Lambinus) and then contrast it with other solutions. Already in §8 the independent judgement of the Academic was favourably contrasted with the behaviour of young men in particular: they either take a rash decision to follow a friend's philosophical outlook, or allow themselves to be taken in by the first speaker in favour of a particular dogmatic persuasion whom they encounter. To this persuasion they then cling with blind loyalty. §9 introduces a claim made by the same people, viz. that they have complete faith in him whom they regard as wise. This would be a legitimate position, Cicero replies, if as young and unformed people they were able to make such a judgement; for to make such determinations is something only the sage can do (*uel maxime* means 'altogether'; cf. *OLD* s.v. *uel* no. 5c; Hofmann-Szantyr p. 502). Yet as it is, if they can make such a judgement at all, they could only have made it after having looked at everyone; thus the text as restored by Lambinus in an explanatory note. *Vt* is concessive and needs the subjunctive; *potuerunt* has the force of a counterfactual subjunctive, cf. Kühner-Stegmann i.171; two different inflections of the same word side-by-side are prone to corruption. Yet (Halm's *autem* for transmitted *aut*) what they actually did was hear about the subject once, and then hand themselves over to the authority of that one person. (I do not adopt Lambinus' insertion of *atque* after *semel audita*, since the two main clauses in asyndetic juxtaposition give the sentence epigrammatic point.) The sentence beginning with *sed nescio* expresses puzzlement that dogmatists are willing to do this and err rather than adopt the Academic attitude.

Plasberg[2] places a full stop after *uidetur esse sapientis*, begins the next sentence with *sed ut potuerint* (thus merely modifying the transmitted *potuerunt*), and inserts *aut* before *omnibus rebus auditis* (retaining the transmitted *aut* before *re semel audita*). Yet it is hard to see why a complete review of dogmatic alternatives or following one person's (or school's) authority should both be live options and jointly exhaustive: only the latter was at issue in the preceding text. Schäublin et al. print a text which says that it is generally the case that the sage identifies another sage (or what a sage is) after having examined all schools. This disrupts the train of thought of the passage, and a doxographical approach is alien to the Stoic sage in particular. Gigon prints, after the transmitted *ut potuerunt*, a supplement which introduces a new group of people, those with marginally more insight who look at the various schools before taking a view.[24] See also Hermann (1852: 466-7).

[24] Cf. Plasberg[1]: *...si id ipsum rudes et indocti iudicare potuissent (statuere enim qui sit sapiens uel maxime uidetur esse sapientis); sed ut potu⟨erint aut ut debuer⟩unt,* [suppl. Plasberg] *omnibus rebus auditis cognitis etiam reliquorum sententiis iudicauerunt, aut re semel audita ad unius se auctoritatem contulerunt.*

Reid[1] sees an unequivocal reference to the Epicureans in *dicunt...sapientem*, citing Sen., *Ep.* 33.4: *non sumus sub rege; sibi quisque se uindicat. Apud istos quicquid dicit Hermarchus, quicquid Metrodorus, ad unum refertur.* However, in §60 Lucullus replies to the point made here in §9a, and thus does not seem to treat it as directed at the Epicureans only, who, in any case, play a very marginal role in *Acad.*, even though they are likely to have been a frequent target of the Academy. Moreover, the Stoics formulate most of their doctrines for an ideal scenario which involves a sage, and Lucullus emphasizes in his speech that he is expounding doctrine with reference to a sage (§57:...*illum ipsum sapientem, de quo omnis hic sermo est*). This does raise the question, reminiscent of one the sceptic poses about the criterion (cf. Sextus, *P.H.* 1.166), how anyone who is not a sage can tell whether his authority is a sage: *si id ipsum rudes et indocti iudicare potuissent—statuere enim qui sit sapiens uel maxime uidetur esse sapientis* aims at allegiance formed at a young age in particular, without the implication that anyone can hope to become so experienced as to make following an authority a viable option. In *N.D.* 1.10, the point is a less specific one, i.e. the unreflective following of authority is criticized: *obest plerumque iis, qui discere uolunt, auctoritas eorum qui se docere profitentur, desinunt enim suum iudicium adhibere, id habent ratum quod ab eo quem probant iudicatum uident.* For Epicurean uses of the concept of the sage, see Vander Waerdt (1987); Annas (2008: 15–16), and the entries under σοφός in Usener (1977).

I translate *re semel audita* 'after they heard about the matter once' rather than 'after a single hearing of the case' (so Rackham 1951), since no argument for and against is envisaged; cf. *unius alicuius oratione* above. The theme of authority (cf. *se ad auctoritatem conferre*), associated with the manner in which dogmatic philosophy is embraced, is problematized by Lucullus in §60; see also on *Ac.* 1.15–17, where Varro invokes *auctoritas* to explain how the Academic tradition works, and Schofield (2018: 288–94) for a discussion of passages from Cicero's corpus of philosophical works which qualify the rejection of authority. On a Clitomachean reconceptualization of authority and its role, see Wynne (2014: 268). *Errare malunt* means 'they prefer to persist in a state of being wrong', as opposed to '...make a one-off bad decision'; for one consideration, the adoption of a dogmatic outlook cannot be the result of a single decision. On the unrelated concept of Academic 'erwünschtes Irren', see Görler (2016).

The desire to investigate (*exquirere*), related to the desire to find the truth or what is similar to it, is distinctive of the *Academiae ratio* as Cicero presents it; it provides a meta-reason for Academic argumentative practice, which could conceivably have

---

Plasberg[2]:...*si id ipsum rudes et indocti iudicare potuissent (statuere enim qui sit sapiens uel maxime uidetur esse sapientis); sed ut potuerint,* ⟨*aut*⟩ [suppl. Plasberg] *omnibus rebus auditis, cognitis etiam reliquorum sententiis iudicauerunt, aut re semel audita ad unius se auctoritatem contulerunt.* Schäublin et al.:...*si id ipsum rudes et indocti iudicare potuissent (statuere enim qui sit sapiens uel maxime uidetur esse sapientis* [*sed ut potuerunt*] *omnibus rebus auditis, cognitis etiam reliquorum sententiis). Iudicauerunt aut*⟨*em*⟩ *re semel audita* ⟨*et*⟩ [suppl. Schäublin] *ad unius se auctoritatem contulerunt.* Gigon:...*si id ipsum rudes et indocti iudicare potuissent (statuere enim qui sit sapiens uel maxime uidetur esse sapientis). Sed ut potuerunt,* ⟨*fecerunt. Pauci quidem aut paulo instructiores*⟩ [suppl. Gigon] *omnibus rebus auditis, cognitis etiam reliquorum sententiis iudicauerunt, aut re semel audita ad unius se auctoritatem contulerunt.*

other (less respectable) motivations. Cf. *Luc.* 7: *neque nos studium exquirendi defatigati relinquemus*; *Fin.* 1.3: *tamen nec modus est ullus inuestigandi ueri nisi inueneris, et quaerendi defatigatio turpis est cum id quod quaeritur sit pulcherrimum*; *Fin.* 1.11 *fin.*; *Tusc.* 2.9. Cicero links the desire to find the truth with Arcesilaus e.g. in *Luc.* 76, Plutarch by implication with 'the Academics' (*Sto. rep.* 1037c, see appendix 1; also quoted on §7 above). See also sections 7.5 and 8 of the introduction on scholarly disagreements about whether the desire to investigate (or to find the truth) should already be linked to Arcesilaus' activity or if the suggestion is Ciceronian retrojection, or else if one can pinpoint its emergence at a post-Arcesilaen point of Academic history but before Cicero. Sextus attempts to distinguish between Pyrrhonists and Academics by presenting the former as genuine searchers and the latter as negative dogmatists; see *P.H.* 1.1–3, cf. 1.226; and e.g. Striker (2010).

§§9b–10

This transitional passage describes the setting for the debate, the occasion, and gives an indication of how what is about to follow relates to the discussion of the previous day, which was dramatized in the *Catulus*. For similar introductions, located after the proem, cf. *N.D.* 1.15; *Div.* 1.8.

The setting is Hortensius' *uilla* near Bauli,[25] after the party of Lucullus, Catullus, Hortensius, and Cicero had moved there, having met the previous day at Catulus' *uilla* (and having conducted the discussion of the *Catulus* there). That the conversation is to take place so as to fit with Lucullus' and Cicero's travel plans is a nod to the notion that making time for it when one could be doing something more useful is frowned upon (see the general note above).

The 'question' of the previous day is not specified. It might have been 'what was the debate between Philo and Antiochus about?', or 'what was the debate between the Old Academy and the New Academy about?'.[26]

Catulus' opening remark suggests that in terms of coverage already the *Catulus* was comprehensive, such that *Luc.* is designed to provide detail and depth in the form of Lucullus' speech, which is assumed to draw directly on Antiochean teachings (and Antiochian sources, we may assume). Hortensius affects to have encroached on Lucullus' space, or perhaps not, since he only touched on 'what was readily available' (*quae in promptu erant*), whereas Lucullus is expected to deal with *reconditiora*. The latter is easy to recognize as a description of Lucullus' speech, but Hortensius' contribution in the *Catulus* is harder to picture on the basis of his remarks. In §2 it is said that he had a memory for words, where Lucullus' was more for things or facts.

On the basis of *Ac.* 1, and Varro's speech in particular, I would assume that the *Catulus* must have included a historical account of the Old Academy's teachings (including any Peripatetic and Stoic 'corrections'), and that this account was the first

---

[25] This is the *uilla* where Nero had Agrippina murdered; see Katzoff (1973); Keppie (2011).
[26] Griffin (1997: 7–8) suggests the trilogy *Hort.*, *Catul.*, and *Luc.* was about the question of which school Cicero himself favoured.

substantial section in the *Catulus*. Given that Hortensius must have been the only Antiochian speaker (short interventions by Lucullus are conceivable, though), he must have relayed this material. But what sounds reasonably credible out of the mouth of Varro, a polymath with Antiochian leanings, would have sounded less credible out of Hortensius'. We know of Cicero's concerns about the appropriateness of speakers in the first edition of course, and this, together with what we know of the kind of revision undertaken between first and second edition, might lead one to assume that Hortensius presented more or less Varro's material. However, Varro's speech, with its fairly intricate detail especially on physics, can, one might think, only ironically be described as *quae in promptu erant* (even though a memory for words might explain how Hortensius could parrot material he is not deemed to have fully understood). Thus one wonders if a change implemented between the two editions was an expansion of the historical account of the Old Academy.[27] It is likely that the *Catulus* also offered a historical account of the New Academy, and given that Cicero describes his role as consisting in the accumulation of arguments against the senses (*Luc.* 79), it is likely that Catulus presented that historical account.

Another notable feature of this preliminary discussion is the extent to which Lucullus disavows what he is about to say, even though he vouches for its accuracy alluding to his good memory. This lack of investment, which is carefully stated in an otherwise conversational exchange, stands in marked contrast to Cicero's attitude and curiously subverts what preconceptions one might have with respect to the attitudes dogmatists and sceptics take to their argumentative positions. On balance, it is more likely part of the attempt to negotiate the credibility of the character Lucullus than an indication of the epistemological commitments of Antiochus (see n. below).

For the dramatic date, cf. Griffin (1997: 17) on the *Catulus*: 'The dramatic date is BCE 62 or the first half of 61, after the exposure of the Catilinarian conspiracy in the autumn of Cicero's consulship in 63 (*Luc.* 62) and just before the death of Catulus (*Att.* 1.16.5, 1.20.3).' No reference is made to *Hort.* in §§9b–10; this might be seen to support the notion that its dramatic date was not the day preceding the action of *Catul.* (see section 9.5).

§9b

Quibus de rebus et alias saepe...mihi in Pompeianum nauigare: for Hortensius' villa at Bauli, see Varro, *R.R.* 3.17.5; Pliny, *N.H.* 9.172, where Bauli is said to be a district of Baiae; D'Arms (1970: 68–9, 181–2), where the latter passage discusses the contentious location of ancient Bauli. For Lucullus' famous *Neapolitanum*, cf. Varro, *R.R.* 3.17.9; Pliny, *N.H.* 9.170; Plut., *Luc.* 39.3; D'Arms (1970: 108, 113, 185–6); Jolivet (1987). Our passage is the earliest reference to it, and the dramatic date of *Luc.* provides a terminus post quem for Lucullus owning the property (thus also Stärk 1995: 105 n. 24). Cicero's *Pompeianum* is mentioned again in *Luc.* 80, along with Catulus'

---

[27] The letters which talk about the changes made between the two editions of which parts have come down to us speak of a transfer of roles only, i.e. do not mention supplementation, but they are fairly general; cf. *Att.* 13.16.1 (= SB 323 = T21), 13.19.5 (= SB 326 = T23).

Cumanum. On the basis of *Luc*. 80 it has been suspected that Catulus had two villas, the *Cumanum* and one at Pompeii; if that was so, I would still expect participants here to have come from the *Cumanum*, and that *uilla* to be the setting for the *Catulus*, given that only it would be close enough to Bauli to reach the latter after making an early start, with a view to undertaking longer journeys later in the day. See Griffin (1997: 16–17 n. 64).

Krische (1845: 18) thought *quibus de rebus* marked the boundary between the second, younger proem of *Luc*. and the body of the dialogue; see the general note above for my view on what was carried over from the first proem.

Reid[1] (p. 181) finds it difficult to 'resist the conclusion that, in instances like this [*fuissemus*], the subjunctive is purely due to a desire for symmetry'; I think it marks the chronologically earlier event relative to the main clause after *cum historicum*. Lambinus emended *nobis* to *a nobis*, but the plain dative of the agent is unobjectionable. The main corrector of V (V²) was able to supply *quam...fuissemus* because he had access to source of VS (ξ); see the edition, p. lx.

Cum igitur pauca in xysto locuti essemus, tum eodem in spatio consedimus: see the excellent note on *in xysto* in Haltenhoff (p. 78). Two different meanings for the term *xystus* (or *xystum*; ξυστός in Greek) are attested: (i) as in Greek, the term could refer to the covered portico of a gymnasium; (ii) a garden walk or a promenade between rows of trees; both senses in Vitr. 5.11.4. The juxtaposition with *spatium* ('open space') and the fact that the interlocutors have sight of the sea and refer to it (*Luc*. 80, 105) suggest that the latter sense is intended; see Gieré (1986: 104–5).

Hic Catulus '... dicturum': Lucullus' major contribution to the debate has evidently been delayed until now, but he must have made at least one small intervention in the *Catulus* (when he undertook to report what he had heard from Antiochus), and indeed is likely to have made more. It is consistent with Catulus' forthright and somewhat provocative remarks in *Luc*. 64–5 that he is the first to speak here and announces what he expects from Lucullus. *Id quod quaerebatur* is equivalent to *quaestio* in what follows. On the content of the *quaestio*, see the introductory note above.

Equidem...a Lucullo autem reconditiora desidero: the archetype read *totam enim rem Catulo integram seruatam oportuit*, which cannot be right since Catulus stands for a version of Academic scepticism. A character cannot refer to the previous day's discussion by the title of the book which records it, and one would require *in Catulo* on this reading. So either a scribe wrote *Catulo* for *Lucullo* by a common psychological error, or a scribe found a gloss like *in Catulo* in the margin and misguidedly used it to alter the text, or there is a *lacuna* to be assumed like the one posited by Plasberg:...*rem, Catul⟨e, Lucull⟩o integram*...The correction to *Lucullo* is already made in Cant2.

On the opposition between *quae in promptu erant* and *reconditiora*, see the general note above. For *equidem* at the beginning of a speech immediately followed by parenthetical *inquit*, cf. Cic., *De orat*. 2.16, 2.26, 3.144. For *plus quam uellem*, see Hofmann-Szantyr p. 594; contrast Reid[1] (p. 181): 'Really the apodosis to a condition not expressed, such as *si modo id fieri posset*.'

Tum ille 'Non sane...quam modo fecit Hortensius': the addition of *non* before *si non fuerint* (Plasberg[1]), a *lectio singularia* in B which the corrector of B (B[a]) expunged when he brought the text in line with that of A, creates excellent sense with minimal interference. Reid[1] inserts a second *non* before *uinci*. The two cola *nec mea nec...* signal Lucullus' attitude to the Antiochian material: he would want to secure victory for something that was properly his view, and he would want to secure victory for a position to which he is leaning, but which he endorses to a lesser degree than someone who holds it to be true. What he is going to present is neither, but still appears most true and unshaken by the previous day's discussion. (An alternative interpretation of *mea* would be 'my original thoughts', which I regard as not intended, since it will have been manifest already from *Catul.* that Lucullus is speaking for Antiochus.)

Polito (2012: 45) suggests that Antiochus held a position which combined a commitment to Stoic apprehension with 'the usual Academic qualifications expressing uncertainty', and cites *sed mehercule...uerissima* as evidence: 'What Lucullus is here advocating is the (temporary and subjective) truth of Stoic apprehension, and these remarks of his bring to the fore a live possibility of reconciling yielding to apprehension with scepticism.' Given how Catulus tears into Antiochus for having abandoned scepticism after many years in *Luc.* 63, it seems unlikely that he or Cicero would not have been made to voice criticism of the unhappy hybrid position proposed by Polito. Consider also anti-Antiochian statements which cast Antiochus as a pure Stoic (*Luc.* 132; Sextus, *P.H.* 1.235), although admittedly they must be construed as sacrificing nuance for other objectives on any account. I argue in the general note above that Lucullus is signalling limited investment with the Antiochian material which he relays in order to anticipate the objection that he is not an ideal spokesman. Görler (2004c: 268 n. 1) suggests that the Lucullus character is conveying that he has been impressed by the discussion of the previous day; he adds: 'Calling Antiochus' *sententia* "true to the highest degree" (*verissima, ibid.*) is weaker than calling it simply "true": all superlatives make their adjectives "relative".' On *uerissima*, cf. Cic., *N.D.* 1.60 (of the poet Simonides, who serves as a model for the Clitomachean Cotta): *dubitantem quid eorum esset uerissimum desperasse omnem ueritatem*, with Wynne (2014: 258–9).

For *mehercule* used like an emphatic particle, see Ricottilli (2003: 137–8). Cicero uses the *conigatio periphrastica* '*probaturus sim*', rather than a plain subjunctive, because it stands in an indirect question. The tense of *agebat* gestures at Lucullus' exposure to Antiochus over a long time. Reid[1] prints *labefactata* for *labefacta*, following later manuscripts; see, however, Plasberg[1] (p. 70).

Cum ita esset exorsus, ad audiendum animos ereximus: this sentence seems to draw attention to the overtly rhetorical nature of some of what Lucullus has just said through the use of rhetorical terminology (*exoriri* of the orator; *ad audiendum animos erigere* of the audience); cf. Cic., *Or.* 122: *ordiri orationem...quo auditur erigatur*; *Inv.* 1.20 (on a type of proem, *principium*): *principium est oratio perspicue et protinus perficiens auditorem beniuolum aut docilem aut attentum*.

§§11–18

The dogmatic exposition begins in §19, and it was what Lucullus had promised on the previous day (cf. §10), i.e. in the *Catulus*. It is thus not obvious at first sight why Lucullus begins his speech in the way he does, but one can observe that the account of events in Alexandria (§11–12), whatever else its function, works to establish Lucullus' credentials as a spokesman for Antiochus, even if it creates dispositional problems elsewhere (i.e. the need to mention the doctrine of the Roman Books in §18 despite the fact that Lucullus' discussion avowedly excludes them). Since there is no suggestion that the new proem which Cicero added to *Luc.* when his concerns over the suitability of the interlocutors grew extended beyond §9a,[28] the Alexandrian scene shows that Cicero had recognized from the start that care would have to be devoted to establishing the credibility of the Lucullus character.

The dialogue begins like the final edition with historical issues. Even if Cicero decided to expand the historical material for the edition in four books, it seems likely that Lucullus is building on an Antiochian historical exposition similar to Varro's in the *Catulus*, most likely furnished by Hortensius, which received responses as *Catul.* continued from the two Academic characters, Catulus and Cicero.[29]

§§11–12

In the winter of 87/6 Sulla, on campaign against Mithridates and engaged in a siege of Athens, which had taken the side of the king of Pontus, set up winter camp near Eleusis, and sent Lucullus as proquaestor in order to assemble a fleet in Egypt and Syria (Plut., *Luc.* 2; App., *Mithr.* 33), since Mithridates had control of the sea. The situation in Athens had driven Philo to Rome (Cic., *Brut.* 306), while Antiochus joined Lucullus on his journey and reached Alexandria with him (the alternative—that Antiochus moved to Alexandria of his own accord and met Lucullus there—is less likely; see n. below), approximately twenty-six years before the dramatic date of the dialogue. Here—and this is where Lucullus' narrative starts—Antiochus received a copy of Philo's Roman Books, which, once it was established they were genuine, made him angry, because they contained 'a lie' (see below). Antiochus then criticized the claims made in the Roman Books, and there followed several days of discussion, during which Heraclitus spoke against Antiochus and Antiochus against the Academics. Lucullus observed and paid particular attention to Antiochus' exposition.

The story of how Antiochus came to know the Roman Books and his reaction to them is usually deemed to be historical,[30] but details of the account have been called into question, notably by Alleemudder (pp. 84–5) and Hatzimichali (2012: 20–5).[31]

---

[28] See the general note on *Luc.* 1–9a.
[29] See section 9.2 on the reconstruction of the missing parts of *Acad.*
[30] See e.g. Brochard (1887: 210); Dal Pra (1975: 231–2); Glucker (1978: 13–15); Lévy (1992: 49, 159); Görler (1994: 942); Barnes (1997: 70); Brittain (2001: 64–6); Lévy (2012: 290–4); Bonazzi (2020: 250); Tarrant (2020: 207).
[31] For an avowedly literary reading of the section, see Cappello (2019: 228–38).

Thus even if Lucullus was present when the Roman Books arrived, he will not have had time to follow several days of philosophical discussion.[32] That these discussions were not just about the Roman Books, but about the entire dispute between the Old Academy and the Academics, creates credibility for Lucullus qua interlocutor, but seems unlikely in itself.

Other aspects of the account do not contribute to the enhancement of Lucullus' credibility; thus their presence would, if called into question, seem to require a different explanation. That Heraclitus had never heard Philo say the kind of things he expounds in the Roman Books and yet is able to authenticate them may be due to their style (we are told that they are not autographs). And for Metrodorus of Stratonicea some statements are attested which come very close to the philosophical thesis of the Roman Books at least in outline (see on *Luc.* 18, 78), which is one reason to think that what Antiochus and Heraclitus are said never to have heard of is the historical thesis which went with it.[33]

It has been suspected that Antiochus' eventual reply to the Roman Books, the *Sosus* (mentioned here at the end of §12), included a description of the scene Cicero depicts here and that it is the source for the scene in general.[34] This is plausible: the arrival of the Roman Books in Alexandria would certainly make an excellent opening for a work directed against them, although, as already noted, the notion proves to be something of an intrusion in Lucullus' speech, who, after all, does really want to talk about 'Arcesilaus and Carneades' and passes over the Roman Books. That Philo is an *aduersarius lenior* (§12) seems to be an ad hoc attempt on Cicero's part to get the Roman Books off the stage; the claim would not fit the rationale of the *Sosus* for all we know, and elsewhere Cicero is ready to use Philo's name as shorthand for the sceptical Academy in general (cf. *Fam.* 9.8 = SB 254 = T29). As for Lucullus, in the *Sosus* Antiochus may have said no more than that he was with him.

The *Sosus* is widely assumed to have been a dialogue.[35] Some of the reasons cited for this view are good. A work named after an individual, a Stoic philosopher (see n. below), and written by a self-proclaimed heir to Plato may well have been a dialogue. The scene in Alexandria, whether used as part of a frame or not, would fit with this (but it is also conceivable as the narrative opening of a treatise). That Lucullus speaks of several days of debate about the conflict between the Old and the New Academy, involving Antiochus and Heraclitus, does not suggest, for reasons given above, that dialogical exchanges on this subject featured in the *Sosus*.

Relatedly, the *Sosus* has been assumed to be Cicero's source for Lucullus' speech as a whole, because the reference to it here was read as an indication to that effect.[36] This notion faces numerous problems, some of which are observable facts. Given that the *Sosus* is a reply to the Roman Books, it must have included a rebuttal of their historical and philosophical claims. The former may have taken the form of an

---

[32] Plut., *Luc.* 2.10, claims that Lucullus made no time for sightseeing while in Egypt.
[33] Metrodorus' statements must be assumed to predate 87 BC; see on §16 below.
[34] See section 9.3 on the sources of *Acad.*
[35] See Hirzel (1883: 265–79) and Glucker (1978: 406–20); earlier Krische (1845: 70–7) and Eble (1846–7).
[36] Glucker (1978: 417–19) argues that the *Sosus* was the source for part of Lucullus' speech.

alternative history of the Academic tradition, the latter should have been fairly swiftly refutable. Lucullus' defence of κατάληψις and its applications would not have fitted the bill. Further, Lucullus' speech is largely directed at the Clitomachean position, with occasional gestures to that of mitigated scepticism.[37] So in order to see the *Sosus* as its source one would have to assume, uneconomically, that Cicero did not use those parts of the *Sosus* which were devoted to its primary purpose—the refutation of the claims of the Roman Books—and instead used others which date from an earlier phase of the debate but which featured in the *Sosus*, too.[38] A version of this view is proposed by Sedley (2012b: 83 with n. 4), who observes that in *Luc.* 49 Lucullus notes that the account of the Academic appeal to empty impressions amounted to a summary of 'a whole day's debate', sc. of the *complures dies* mentioned here in *Luc.* 12. The suggestion is that we find in the body of Lucullus' speech references to the probably (some would say, avowedly) *Sosus*-inspired preliminary remarks of §§11–12, which tie both together. However, as indicated above, the notion of several days of discussion about the fundamental conflict between the Old and the New Academy fits Cicero's agenda in *Acad.* rather better than the *Sosus*'s and thus may well be a Ciceronian 'addition'. All one can reasonably assume that the *Sosus* was a dialogue, that the arrival of the Roman Books in Alexandria featured in it in some form, and that its rebuttal of the Roman Books addressed both their historical and their philosophical claims, by dismissing the former as a 'lie' and the latter as self-defeating (cf. *Luc.* 18).[39]

What do we learn about the *Catulus* from §§11–12, specifically about the manner in which the Catulus character was invested with credibility? The younger Catulus is cited as saying (§12 *init.*) that his father had criticized Philo on the same grounds as Antiochus. For one thing, this shows that Academics 'Old and New' agreed on the Roman Books, and Antiochus' insight into the matter is plausibly regarded as supreme. Yet even allowing for literary fiction, it is striking that a Roman aristocrat would be presented as criticizing the head of the Academy—whether in person or not (see on §12: *a patre suo dicta Philoni*)—for adopting a position on the grounds that it was out of keeping with Academic thinking and history: what insight into the history of the Academy and its positions could the elder Catulus claim? While I do think that Philo arrived in Rome as a Clitomachean, delivered lectures as a Clitomachean,[40] and only then devised the thesis of the Roman books (or committed to it) and went on to lecture on his revised views, it seems unlikely the elder Catulus'

---

[37] Cicero's characterization of the Academic position in *Luc.* 7b–9a is consistent with the one he adopts in his speech in the second half of the book, but mitigated scepticism featured as an option maintained by Catulus in the discussion of the previous day (cf. *Luc.* 148).

[38] That what we do read in §§19–62 of Lucullus' speech somehow functions as a refutation of the Roman Books seems impossible, given that the latter are expressly omitted from the debate and given some of their 'doctrinal' assumptions (on most reconstructions), notably about the role of assent.

[39] Thus also Brittain (2006: 9 n. 10), and see the full discussion in Brittain (2001: chs 3 and 4).

[40] The rhetorical teaching which impressed Cicero so much grows out of Philo's views prior to the Roman Books, however they are construed; see Brittain (2001: 296–342), Reinhardt (2000). And the stated commitment to Academic scepticism, explicitly including suspension of judgement, in Cicero's earliest extant work (*Inv.* 2.9–10) does not read like an act of emancipation from a teacher who taught that there is κατάληψις, just not of the Stoic variety; rather, it reads as if it was inspired by exposure to a very convincing Clitomachean. See section 8.

authority on matters of Academic philosophy would derive directly from what he had heard from Philo earlier; for in that case the charge of a sudden and baffling change of mind should be part of the criticism, and the elder Catulus would have struggled to be an authority for a view which he had only just acquired himself.[41] Perhaps the *Catulus* included a finely drawn account of the elder Catulus poring over books by those leading Academics who actually wrote, but I do not regard this as likely, either. These considerations point to the possibility that a back-story on the elder Catulus must have been provided, which linked him personally to either earlier Academics or Romans with credible exposure to Academic philosophy. Given his date of birth of 149 BC, he was too young to be linked with the famous embassy of philosophers of 155 BC (see on *Luc.* 137), but he was a significant literary figure, credited with introducing the epigram to Roman poetry,[42] and no doubt acquainted with the satirist Lucilius (180–c.103 BC), to whom Clitomachus had dedicated a work of his (see on *Luc.* 102). On the possibility that Lucilius had Academic leanings, and that he was connected to Catulus, see Büttner (1893: 124–59).

The views which the Roman Books are likely to have contained will be discussed in more detail in the commentary on §18. For now one would ideally only extract what can be gleaned about them from §§11–12, with a view to later contextualization and disambiguation. Yet this would require that the information contained in §18 is itself unambiguous. In fact, both what we are told here and what we learn in 18 is ambiguous, and all one can hope for is to place a plausible interpretation on the evidence of both passages considered together. On the evidence of §§11–12, the Roman Books raised the question if Philo could conceivably have argued for the views contained in them. They also prompted an angry response from Antiochus. Now all reconstructions of the Roman Books assume that they combined philosophical claims with historical claims about the emergence and the endorsement of the philosophical claims within the Academy. One can already see why this assumption is made: wrong-headed, even outlandish philosophical views, especially those held by one's opponent, can give rise to incredulity (or mirth), but not to anger. Historical claims about when and by whom these philosophical views were held are much more likely to meet with anger if they are deemed to be false and if the audience is invested in the question (as Antiochus was). At the end of §12 Philo is called a liar: again, formulating misguided views is not lying, ascribing these views to someone who did not hold them can be so described.[43] What does the lie consist in? It consists in denying that 'those things which were defended yesterday were ever said by an Academic'. The issue must be views argued for by the Academics.[44] The fact that they are said to have

---

[41] Unlike others, I think Philo never was a mitigated sceptic; if that was true, it would mean that the elder Catulus' views could at best come from a view Philo had mentioned rather than endorsed himself.

[42] See Courtney (2003: 75–8).

[43] Note Brittain (2001: 179): 'Finally, it should be observed that a plausible distinction is made in the text of the *Academica* between historical *disagreement*, and historical *fabrication*. Cicero recognises two standard interpretations of Carneades (*Ac.* 2.78), as does Lucullus (*Ac.* 2.59); but, although they believe only one of these, they do not condemn the other as fabrication. Cicero and Varro disagree over the roles of Socrates and Plato in Academic history; but, rather than insulting each other, they proffer reasons for their differing views' (author's emphasis).

[44] This is widely agreed; however, Mansfeld (1997: 58–9) makes the case for the reference being to the Antiochian position.

been 'defended' is worth noting, given that arguments made by Academic sceptics are at issue, who may not acknowledge that they defend rather than, say, advance views, but then Lucullus has a tendency of presenting the Academics as if they were negative dogmatists. As to the plural ('those things'), more than one view may be meant, or—more plausibly—a set of views, an argument, a position. It has long been recognized that Lucullus must be talking about the view that nothing can be known (*nihil posse percipi*; ἀκαταληψία), which is the conclusion of the Academic core argument. Elsewhere in his speech Lucullus presents the Academics as wedded to this view; this would fit with the remark that 'those views' were *defended* yesterday. And Philo, through his denial, must have held that something can be known.

It is widely agreed now that the situation described in §§11–12 does not describe Antiochus' 'conversion', the moment when he finally broke with the sceptical Academy institutionally, and that this break occurred some years earlier.[45] (The material which Lucullus relays from §19 onwards would in any case have been devised prior to the moment of the Roman Books coming into his hands, in the fictional world of the dialogue and by implication in real life.) What little our passage by itself gives out on the issue will be discussed in the nn. below; cf. on *Luc.* 69–70 for a fuller discussion.

At ille, 'Cum Alexandriae pro quaestore...sed utrumque lenienter': Glucker (1978: 21): 'Cicero's words are quite explicit: *fuit Antiochus mecum* must mean that Antiochus was in Lucullus' retinue.' In fact the phrase cited is ambiguous, and the preceding *cum*-clause, concerned with Lucullus' stay in Alexandria (*essem*) rather than his arrival, points if anything towards Antiochus being based in Alexandria prior to Lucullus' arrival. What strongly suggests that Antiochus travelled with Lucullus is *antea* in the following colon.

On Heraclitus of Tyre (*RE* 'Herakleitos' no. 11), see Glucker (1978: 100 n. 11, 417–19); Dorandi (2000); Hatzimichali (2012: 17, 20–1); Fleischer (2017a); speculatively Polito (2012: 41–3). Heraclitus is known only through our passage (= Antiochus F5 Mette and the translations of the Antiochian testimonia in Sedley 2012b: 341; cf., however, the mention in Philod., *Index Acad.* col. xxxiv.16). His being a pupil of Clitomachus makes it likely that he was a contemporary of Philo's. For the chronology of the Roman Books, though one has to bear the dramatic purpose of the present passage in mind, he contributes that their claims are presented as unfamiliar to someone who was a member of the Athenian Academy prior to Philo's and Antiochus' departure, while the same claims are presented as familiar to Romans who had heard Philo in Rome. (See section 8 for my view that Philo arrived a Clitomachean in Rome and only developed the Roman Books view in Rome.) In context Heraclitus' view on the Roman Books carries more weight if he continues to be an Academic sceptic, as is also suggested by his arguing the sceptical side in the debate with Antiochus; his being a *familiaris* of Antiochus' thus does not point to intellectual allegiance. See Glucker (1978: 417–19) on the question of whether Heraclitus was a character in the *Sosus* (assuming this work was a dialogue).

---

[45] See Barnes (1997: 68–70); Hatzimichali (2012: 13–14) with earlier literature; Polito (2012: 32–4) argues for Antiochus' secession from the Academy after 87 BC.

In *Luc.* 61 Lucullus also recognizes Academic scepticism as a *philosophia* (meaning a school-specific philosophical approach), if an utterly misguided one. *Nunc prope dimissa reuocatur* (sc. *a Cicerone*) relates to the resurrection of the Academy by Cicero, presumably qua character in *Acad.* and at the fictional date of the dialogue, rather than qua author in 45 BC; while there continued to be self-identified followers of Academic scepticism like Favorinus of Arelate (*c.* AD 80–AD 160), Philo was the last leader of the sceptical Academy and the last scholarch of the Academy as a school (cf. *Luc.* 17: *Philone autem uiuo patrocinium Academiae non defuit*). See Brittain (2001: 38–72) for a discussion of the evidence on Philo's life; Fleischer (2017), (2017a), (2017b). See also Opsomer (1998a) on the afterlife of Academic argument and Academic attitudes in Middle Platonism.

The transfer of *auctoritas* which the present passage is inter alia intended to achieve is plain: Heraclitus had heard Philo and Clitomachus, and Lucullus heard Heraclitus discuss things with Antiochus.

The repetition of *Alexandriae* is noted as inelegant by Reid[1] (p. 183), but there is no reason to suspect the text. See ibid. on *cum quo* for *quicum*.

I print *cum quo Antiochum*, not *cum quo et Antiochum* as in B (which may be due to *qui et Clitomachum* earlier); see, however, Madvig (1879: 788–90) and Plasberg[1] (p. 71).

Here in §11, in §12, and in §111 the name 'Philio' rather than 'Philo' has manuscript support. One might dismiss this fact with reference to the unreliability with which medieval manuscripts report Greek names, although the name 'Philio' as such undoubtedly existed and is attested for seventy-three individuals in *LGPN*. However, the name 'Philio' also occurs in a list of Athenian scholarchs given in P. Duke Inv. G. 178, whose general reliability is open to doubt (see Görler 1994: 781), in Philod. *Index Acad.* (cols xxv and xxxiii, as Kilian Fleischer has established), in the manuscripts of Eusebius' *Praep. Ev.* preserving Numenius frgs 27–8 Des Places, and in another Herculaneum papyrus, in which the Epicurean Demetrius Laco, a contemporary of Philo's, mentions a not clearly identifiable 'Philio' (*P.Herc.* 1012, col. lxxii.7–9 Puglia) in an epistemological context. On this basis Fleischer (2022) makes the case for the view that name of the last scholarch of the Academy was actually 'Philio' and that he should be so referred to; if this was correct, 'Philio' rather than 'Philo' should be read in *Ac.* 1, the fragments of the *Academici libri*, and in *Luc.*

Et quidem isti libri duo Philonis…umquam ante uideram: The younger Catulus talked about the Roman Books in the *Catulus*. Given that he is presented as embracing a position of mitigated scepticism in *Luc.* 148, he will have disapproved of them like his father, who is said—in §13, cf. §18—to have criticized them on the same grounds as Antiochus. Cicero says of his own contribution to the *Catulus*' discussion in *Luc.* 79: *idcirco heri non necessario loco contra sensus tam multa dixeram*. Both pieces of information taken together might suggest that the younger Catulus spoke about Academic positions historically and systematically, while Cicero advanced arguments against the senses without a chronological dimension. However, §13 *init.* shows that there must have been some historical dimension to Cicero's remarks in the *Catulus*.

One might wonder why Cicero uses the Greek loanword *stomachari* when there exist a number of Latin words which could equally have been used. The distribution of the term, first attested in comedy, is, however, quite wide by the middle of the 40s BC. The word suggests strong anger rather than mild annoyance; see also Hoffer (2007). In poetry it can be used to achieve an effect of bluntness, of a calculated lowering of the tone (see e.g. Gowers 2012: 167 on Hor., *S.* 1.4.55; cf. Nisbet and Hubbard 1970: 85 on Hor., *C.* 1.6.6 *stomachum*). Cf. also *Verr.* 2.2.20: *homo inimicus iis qui recitassent, hostis omnibus qui acclamassent, exarsit iracundia ac stomacho; uerum tamen fuit tum sui dissimilis*, an exception to the general rule that Greek and Greek loanwords tend to be avoided in the speeches. There may be an implicit suggestion that the kind of anger exhibited was un-Roman. Cf. also *N.D.* 1.93 and frg. 1 of *Ac.* 1.

Libri duo specifies *libri* in *Ac.* 1.13. *Et quidem* marks the shift to a new point; on *et* in *et homo* see *OLD* s.v. no. 16a. Reid[1] (p. 183) suggests *nec enim* ⟨*id*⟩ *umquam*, but note Plasberg[1] (p. 71). The tense of *mirabar* may be best explained as what Hofmann-Szantyr (p. 317) call narrative use, 'wo der Sprechende aus seiner Erinnerung erzählt oder sich an die Erinnerung des Hörenden wendet'.

At ille Heracliti memoriam implorans...dicerent descripsisse: for *implorare aliquam rem* 'to call on, to appeal to', see *OLD* s.v. 2b. *Illa Philonis*, sc. *esse*. On what we can infer about the nature of the claims made in the Roman Books, see the general note above and on §18.

The phrase *scriptum alicuius agnoscere* means 'to recognize the writing of *x*' (*OLD* s.v. *scriptum* no. 5, though the use in the singular is rare), which can mean 'recognize someone's writing style' or their handwriting. We learn from what follows that the visitors from Rome had made a copy of Philo's own exemplar. There is no suggestion of identification on the basis of Philo's handwriting, *pace* Glucker (1978: 13 n. 3), who, however, notes that Antiochus was as well placed to identify Philo's writings as Heraclitus. He suggests that seeking a second opinion must have been the point; alternatively, the contrivance under the veneer of realism is showing.

The otherwise unattested *familiares* of Lucullus—Publius Selius, Gaius Selius, and Tetrilius Rogus—serve to authenticate the views of the Roman Books as Philonian and Roman. The natural inference is that it was they who also delivered the Roman Books to Alexandria, but this is not explicitly stated. Wilhelm Heraeus (cited by Plasberg[2] p. xxviii) suggested that the *nomen gentile* of the third individual was *Etrilius*. *Etrilius* is attested on inscriptions from Praeneste from an early period onwards (e.g. *CIL* I[2].153 = XIV.3125); see Schulze (1904: 268). Lucullus' younger brother, Marcus Terentius Varro Lucullus, was tasked by Sulla with establishing a colony in Praeneste, and the older brother had clients there.

See Reid[1] (p. 184) on the -*ne* and *num* sentence questions in succession (*uidereturne*...). He also wonders if *Nec id quidem* should be emended to *ne*, but this would not deliver the required sense. *Academicus* is used in its standard sense of 'sceptical Academic'; see on *Ac.* 1.18; on the late introduction of the term σκεπτικός in Greek texts, see Striker (1996b: 92 n. 1). Reid[1] (p. 184) cites good parallels for the metonymical use of an expression denoting a person for a work: Cic., *Att.* 13.21.4 (= SB 351): *scripsit Balbus ad me, se a te quintum de finibus librum descripsisse*; Hor., *Sat.* 2.3.33: *si quid Stertinius ueri crepat, unde ego mira descripsi praecepta haec.*

§12

Tum et illa dixit...Sosus inscribitur: on *illa* the reading of the archetype is in doubt. I print, like Reid[1] and Plasberg[1], what I take to be A[a]'s (and, independently, V[2]'s) emendation, on the grounds that in a highly partisan debate an emphasis on the agreement between the elder Catulus and Antiochus regarding the Roman Books gives the best sense. The reference of *illi* would either be Heraclitus, who does feature in what follows as an interlocutor but does not deserve a special mention as addressee of Antiochus' words here, or Philo, in which case the kind of dative involved would be resumed in *Philoni* below (and the possibility that the elder Catulus had made the point to Philo in person excluded).

Mansfeld (1997) has argued that it would be a mark against Catulus the son if he merely relayed the views of his father. This need not be so depending on how the elder Catulus' authority on Academic philosophy was constructed. See the general note above and section 9.2.

The dative in *dicta Philoni* can signify that the elder Catulus made the point to Philo himself, in which case one would assume a description of the encounter featured in the *Catulus*. However, it can also mean that Catulus made the remark with reference to Philo, sc. in his absence, a usage which is more familiar though not confined to the phrases *bene/male dicere alicui*. See Reid (1925: 191) on *Fin.* 2.80 *qui maledictis insectantur eos*. Reid[1] (p. 184) suspects that *Philoni* is a gloss; if it was, the reading on which the elder Catulus spoke to Philo in person would become farfetched. See *Luc.* 18 on what the elder Catulus supposedly said.

On what little we know about the contents and the structure of the *Sosus*, see above and section 9.3. Sosus was a Stoic philosopher, a pupil of Panaetius (Philod., *Index Stoic.* col. lxxv.1–2), and came like Antiochus from Ascalon (Stephanus of Byzantium, *Ethnica* p. 132.3 Meineke = T4b in Sedley 2012c). Glucker (1978: 418–19) suggested—plausibly—that he was a character in the *Sosus* who—this is less plausible, for the reasons set out above—spoke for dogmatism and against ἀκαταληψία; this he was able to do because in the field of epistemology Antiochus was a Stoic. (We recall that in the intermediate edition of *Acad.* Lucullus' part had been given to the Stoic Cato; cf. *Att.* 13.16.1–2 = SB 323 = T21.) It is, however, notable that Sosus is not named as being present in Alexandria, considering that the Alexandrian scene can fairly plausibly be ascribed to the *Sosus*; Hatzimichali (2012: 23) thus wonders if the work included an embedded dialogue featuring Sosus. It is unclear why he could be sufficiently significant for a reply to the Roman Books to be named after him.

On the *non se tenere quin* construction, see Kühner-Stegmann ii.257; on the present tense of *inscribitur* Reid[1] (p. 184).

Tum igitur...cognoscerem: a general debate is at issue (consider *Contra Academicos*), not one about the Roman Books (whose views Heraclitus will hardly have embraced, not even for the sake of the argument): Cicero is now setting up the main discussion. Lucullus claims to have paid careful attention to Antiochus' case (so as to be a credible spokesman); he does not set himself up as a *iudex*, *pace* Glucker (1978: 14 n. 5), despite proclaiming to attend to the *causa* (which may mean 'his case', as Reid[2] has it;

contrast my 'the whole debate'). *Et cum* is a familiar transposition for *cum et*; see Reid[1] (p. 185).

Itaque complures...consumpsimus: on the group of people named here generally see Lévy (2012). For Heraclitus of Tyre, see on §11 above; for Antiochus' brother Aristos, see the n. on *Ac.* 1.12; for Aristo of Alexandria Moraux (1974: 181–93) and Caujolle-Zaslawsky and Goulet (1989), and the collection of his testimonia by Mariotti (1966). For Dio of Alexandria see Dorandi (1994e) and Fleischer (2016); his assassination in Rome is part of the background of Cicero's *Pro Caelio*. Aristo later moved from the Old Academy to the Peripatos (Philod., *Index Acad.* col. xxxv.1–14), like Cratippus (on whom see Lévy 2012: 294–6); for Dio this has been claimed, too, on the basis of *Index Acad.* col. xxxv.2–16, by Glucker (1978: 96 and 113), but Dorandi (1994e) and Fleischer (2016) are doubtful that the text allows for this reading.

With *complures dies*, cf. *Luc.* 49 *unius diei disputatio*; see the general note above and section 9.3 on whether such temporal expressions should be viewed as indications of the sources used. Reid[1] (p. 184) regards the repetition *complures/compluribus* as a sign of haste. For *adhibere* in the absolute ablative with a person, see *OLD* s.v. no. 3: 'to bring in, call in, have present.'

Sed ea pars...Carneademque ueniamus: while the omission of the Roman Books is suitably motivated, in that their theses lack heft and misrepresent Academic tradition (sc. on Lucullus' view), it is peculiar and not adequately motivated that their philosophical thesis and its problems appear, albeit briefly, in §18.

On *negat Academicos omnino dicere*, Glucker (1978: 80 n. 227) argues that there are two possible meanings, 'he denied altogether that the Academics had said these things' and 'he denied that the Academics had said such things absolutely'. He regards the second option is preferable in terms of sense. Word order suggests that only the second option is a live one, since it would be very peculiar for *omnino* to modify *negat* rather than *dicere*. That this is right is also suggested by parallel evidence from Sextus, *P.H.* 1.235: οἱ δὲ περὶ Φίλωνά φασιν ὅσον μὲν ἐπὶ τῷ Στωικῷ κριτηρίῳ, τουτέστι τῇ καταληπτικῇ φαντασίᾳ, ἀκατάληπτα εἶναι τὰ πράγματα, ὅσον δὲ ἐπὶ τῇ φύσει τῶν πραγμάτων αὐτῶν, καταληπτά; see on §18, where translations of 1.235 are discussed. I do not think that *omnino* means 'at all' here, *pace* Mansfeld (1997: 58). Haltenhoff (pp. 84–5) observes that Lucullus has no reason to present Philo's position as less absurd than he is reasonably able to, but what Lucullus says on my reading is sufficiently absurd. *Mentiri* can of course mean 'to tell a falsehood' or 'to tell a falsehood knowingly, deliberately', but in the present context the latter sense would explain Antiochus' anger much better. The 'lie' must have consisted in denying that unqualified ἀκαταληψία had consistently been argued for by the *Academici* (= sceptical Academics; cf. the two earlier occurrences in §§11–12) and, relatedly, in ascribing the philosophical thesis of the Roman Books to earlier Academics (see the general note above, and on §18); for a different interpretation, see Mansfeld (1997: 58–9).

'Arcesilaus and Carneades' stand here in contradistinction with the Philo of the Roman Books and almost function as a stand-in for 'Academic scepticism in its established varieties'. In *Fam.* 9.8 (= SB 254 = T29) Philo's name stands for the position which Cicero has claimed for himself in the final edition, i.e. Academic scepticism in general and only possibly Clitomacheanism in particular.

With *acer...aduersarius*, cf. §84 *aduersarius facilis*, of the speaker himself; such tags provide second-order comments on the discussion. Reid[1] (p. 185) glosses *heri defensa* 'sc. a Catulo', but Cicero was a speaker for the Academy in *Catul.*, too. *Academicos* can only refer to new or sceptical Academics. *Leuior* is in S, but the possibility of minim confusion makes *lenior* almost the same reading; *lenior* carries a (desirable) implication of naiveté which *leuior* does not have. See the Oxford Classical Text, p. lxxiv, for the spelling of the endings of the personal names.

§§13–14

On the basis of *Ac.* 1.44–6 we have reason to assume that in *Catul.* the Academic side constructed a history of its position, so as to contextualize and justify its outlook. That Lucullus' remarks on the subject are addressed to Cicero in particular shows that the Cicero character made historical remarks, too, and did not confine himself to arguments against the senses, as *Luc.* 79 by itself might suggest. The material of *Ac.* 1.44–6 was, however, most likely delivered by Catulus in *Catul.* A reason why both Academic speakers made historical remarks in *Catul.* may have been that they held different positions and would thus need to fashion slightly different endings to the history of the Academic position, with Catulus presumably emphasizing Carneades, and Cicero Arcesilaus.

After a clearly marked new start Lucullus addresses the Academic attempt to claim the Presocratic philosophers as ancestors. This, he suggests, is comparable with, and as illegitimate as, the attempt by populist politicians to turn statesmen of the Roman past into models for their *popularis* stance.

Having characterized the type of argument advanced by the Academics in §13 in general terms, Lucullus proceeds to describe the politicians of times past who are invoked by contemporary *populares*. In §14 Lucullus turns to the Academics themselves and to the details of the perceived analogy. Three phases are distinguished in the fields of Roman history and Greek philosophy, respectively: the present, on the side of philosophy characterized by the well-orderedness of Antiochus' philosophical system, to which the present-day Republic corresponds (one might wonder if the latter ought to be deemed well-ordered at the fictional date of the dialogue, but Lucullus is an optimate). The second phase is earlier, and here associated with Arcesilaus and Saturninus respectively. That the two were not contemporaries does not matter for the argument which is being made, and in §13 Tiberius Gracchus occupies the relative position of Saturninus—the main point seems to be to identify a game-changing intermediate phase, which links Arcesilaus to a known demagogue of the past. The third phase, yet earlier, is that of the Presocratics, Socrates, and Plato on the one hand, and of earlier Republican politicians (beginning with the first consuls elected immediately after the expulsion of Tarquinius Superbus). The suggestion is that present-day Academics aim to unsettle philosophy, just as present-day *populares* aim to unsettle the Republic.

However, Lucullus refuses to accept the tradition thus constructed: Saturninus bore no similarity with earlier historical figures, and Arcesilaus acted with malicious arrogance, whereas Democritus was modest. The Presocratics represent philosophical pre-history and would, at times and apparently ad hoc, make sceptical pronouncements because philosophical enquiry is complex and frustration consequently hard to avoid, but this should not be misinterpreted as a sceptical stance. If anything, Lucullus says, the Presocratics were too confident in some of their dogmatic pronouncements (from Antiochus' point of view they were of course often wrong). On this last point, there is actually common ground between the Academics and Antiochus: as *Luc.* 72–8 show, the Academics offer a more nuanced history of philosophy than Lucullus allows for here, and see some Presocratics as deriving their sceptical pronouncements from dogmatic assumptions about the nature of things.[46]

See section 7 on all passages reflecting the historical views of the Academics as well as Antiochus' counternarrative.

Quae cum dixisset, sic rursus exorsus est: the Alexandrian episode is quite clearly marked off and the beginning of a new 'section' signalled by *exorsus*; the term does not signal that what follows is an *exordium* of a kind, and indeed the subject matter is not suitable proem material. (Cf. also §11 *init.*) This would be consistent with, but no evidence for, the assumption that only the Alexandrian scene comes from the *Sosus*. Cf. the structural boundaries in *Luc.* 5 *init.* and 9b.

Primum mihi uidemini...ut eorum ipsi similes esse uideantur: this sentence characterizes the general strategy employed by the New Academy, through a comparison with the way in which contemporary *populares* posit a political ancestry for their views, sc. as an aristocrat like Lucullus sees it. The Academics did not claim their stance to be identical to that of certain Presocratics (cf. *Ac.* 1.44–6 and *Luc.* 72–6), and indeed Lucullus speaks of similarity with respect to the claims of *seditiosi ciues*.

On the tactics deployed by the *populares*, see van der Blom (2010: 164–5), and more generally Cic., *Sest.* 96–135, on which see Kaster (2006: 31–7, 96–135).

On the significance of the Lucullus character's turn to Cicero (*me...appellabat*), see the general note above; note, however, §14 *init.*: *similiter uos cum...Φυσικός* as a noun in the sense 'natural philosopher' occurs first in Aristotle (e.g. *De anim.* A1, 403a28); *physicus* in the same sense is used from Cicero and Varro in prose (in poetry attested since Lucilius and other contemporaries); cf. the definition in *N.D.* 1.83; and Dyck (2003: 105) on *N.D.* 1.35.

Repetunt ii a P. Valerio...Q. Pompeium: for P. Valerius Publicola (Poplicola) (cos. 509–507 and 504; *RE* s.n. Valerius no. 302) see Volkmann (1955). He introduced a *lex Valeria de prouocatione* (which enabled citizens to appeal to the *contio* in cases of coercion by a magistrate) in his first year as consul and without consulting his colleague (Plut., *Publ.* 11; Liv. 2.8–16) and was viewed as an ancestor of the *populares*

---

[46] A detailed study of the passages in *Acad.* which provide evidence for the appeal sceptical Academics made to earlier philosophers is Brittain and Palmer (2001).

because of it (Liv. 2.8.1; Cic., *Rep.* 2.53). Scipio is made to comment on this law thus (*Rep.* 2.55): *modica libertate populo data facilius tenuit auctoritatem principum*, which Haltenhoff (p. 87) identifies as the senatorial party's view of Valerius. This is consistent with Lucullus denying that Valerius is like contemporary *populares* in our passage. Haltenhoff (p. 87) also supplies the identities of the unnamed *reliqui* from Cic., *Rep.* 2.53–5: they are L. Valerius Potitus and M. Horatius Barbatus (coss. 449), who jointly passed a law *de prouocatione* (Liv. 3.55), similarly assessed as the earlier one by Scipio in *Rep.* 2.54 (*hominum concordiae causa sapienter popularium*), as well as M. Valerius Maximus, the instigator of another law (see Volkmann 1948: 2418). Liv. 10.9.3 notes the three laws *de prouocatione* supported by members of the same gens. See also Develin (1978) and Oakley (2005: 120–34).

There is then a shift to figures who are 'closer by' (a chronological use of the deictic *hoc*) and therefore more familiar (*notiores*). C. Flaminius (cos. 223, 217; *RE* s.n. Flaminius no. 2) had, when *tribunus plebis* in 232 or 228, the *ager Picenus* and the *ager Gallicus* south of Ariminum distributed among Roman citizens by lot; see Cic., *Rab. perd.* 22; Val. Max. 5.4.5; Münzer (1909); Develin (1979).

L. Cassius Longinus Ravilla (cos. 127; *RE* s.n. Cassius no. 72) introduced the *lex Cassia tabellaria* in 137 as *tribunus plebis*, which extended voting by (secret) ballot to trials before the assembly (excluding treason). Haltenhoff (p. 88) makes the connection with Cic., *Leg.* 3.34, where Q. Cicero comments on the law: *quis autem non sentit omnem auctoritatem optimatium tabellariam legem abstulisse?* Cf. ibid. 3.35: *a nobili homine lata Lucio Cassio, sed (pace familiae dixerim) dissidente a bonis atque omnes rumusculos populari ratione aucupante.*

On Q. Pompeius (cos. 141; *RE* s.n. Pompeius no. 12), see Miltner (1952). No particular 'popular' initiatives are attested for him. His son (*pace* Haltenhoff p. 88) was an opponent of Tib. Gracchus; cf. Plut., *Tib. Gracch.* 14.

Lucullus' emphasis on the different periods to which the various political models belong can be read as an acknowledgement that the Academic invocation of 'sceptical' ancestors drew analogous distinctions. Periodization and its problems is also a concern in Cicero's *Brutus*, a dialogue on the history of eloquence composed in 46 BC, which features Cicero and contemporaries as interlocutors, in which Cicero appears as the endpoint of a long tradition, and whose content and format may have been inspired by the *Sosus*.

Plasberg[1] prints *i a P. Valerio*, but my spelling policy on pronouns is different; his text seems marginally preferable on palaeographical grounds to *enim a* (Reid[1]). *Repetunt a P. Valerio* as printed by Davies strays too far from the paradosis. *Repetunt iam P. Valerium* would not give the required sense; the preposition is required (see Merguet s.v. *repeto*). *Tum ad hos notiores*, sc. *ueniunt*; see Plasberg[1] (p. 72) on the ellipsis.

Illi quidem etiam P. Africanum...obscurius: P. Cornelius Scipio Aemilianus Numantinus Africanus minor (cos. 147, 134; *RE* s.n. Cornelius no. 335), the central character of Cicero's *Rep.*, may seem an odd candidate to be routinely (*solent*) cited by the *populares* as a predecessor, but Cic., *Leg.* 3.37 and *Brut.* 97 present him as an important moving force behind the *lex Cassia tabellaria* (see above). On the eventual rift with Tib. Gracchus, see Plut., *Tib. Gracch.* 7.4.

P. Mucius Scaevola (cos. 133; *RE* s.n. Mucius no. 17) and P. Licinius Crassus Divus Mucianus (cos. 131; *RE* s.n. Licinius no. 72), brothers by birth, were both distinguished jurisconsults. The latter was adopted into the *gens Licinia* and replaced Tib. Gracchus after his death on the agrarian commission. His support of the reforms was thus public (*ut uidemus*); of his brother's stance little is known (cf. *palam...obscurius*). See Plasberg[1] (p. 72) on Gruter, who suspected *ut uidemus* and *ut suspicantur* of being glosses.

Addunt etiam C. Marium...se institutum sequi dicunt: C. Marius (cos. 107, 104–100, 86; *RE* s.n. Marius no. 14), a *homo nouus* like Cicero and famous for his re-organization of the Roman army, cooperated, at least for a time, with L. Appuleius Saturninus (see below) to secure lands for his veterans. This would have warranted the designation of *popularis* in Lucullus' eyes, as may have the *lex Maria de suffragiis* (see Cic., *Leg.* 3.38–9 with Dyck 2004: 535), which could be perceived as designed to curtail the ability of aristocrats to influence voters, but otherwise Marius' resistance to populist policies is well attested; *de hoc quidem nihil mentiuntur* implies both that it was not plain that he was a *popularis* and that some of the individuals named earlier were deliberately mischaracterized. Cicero invokes Marius frequently as a positive exemplum; see van der Blom (2010: 158–60).

The phrase *institutum sequi* should not be read as suggesting that 'popular' politicians of the present claimed that they were pursuing the exact same policies as their spiritual 'ancestors', still less that, on the other level of the analogy, the Academics claimed that earlier philosophers adopted exactly the same posture as they themselves. Lucullus speaks of similarity above (*ut eorum ipsi similes esse uideantur*), and an *institutum* is not a distinctive position but a 'programme' (*OLD* s.v. no. 1) or an 'established practice' (*OLD* s.v. no. 2). Reid[1] (p. 187) comments on *expositis* that 'this word conveys the idea of a vulgar handling, profaning, or rendering common'; this polemical tone is another reason not to press the sentence.

§14

Similiter uos...Platonem etiam et Socratem profertis: having surveyed the statesmen claimed by contemporary *populares* as political ancestors, Lucullus now completes the analogical reasoning: sceptical Academics find philosophy as well ordered as *populares* find the state, and like them they invoke supposed predecessors to bolster their position: Presocratics, even Socrates and Plato. In this analogy, both state and philosophy, i.e. the Roman republic and the Old Academy respectively, have been stable and well ordered for some time. As an appraisal of the political situation at the dramatic date of the dialogue this may sound peculiarly optimistic, but Lucullus was an optimate, and he could plausibly be credited with the view that the problems of the Roman state in the late 60s were not structural and constitutional but, e.g., caused by the *ambitio* of individuals. For the history of the citation of the Presocratics as intellectual ancestors by the sceptical Academy and Arcesilaus in particular, see the commentary on *Ac.* 1.44, *Luc.* 72–8, and sections 7.1 and 7.5 of the introduction.

For the original Roman readership the Presocratics may have been familiar, e.g. through the poem *Empedoclea* by 'Sallust' (mentioned by Cicero in *Q.fr.* 2.10(9).3 = SB 14), through the reception of Empedocles and to a lesser degree Parmenides by Lucretius (and subsequently other poets), through the significance of Empedocles for Neo-Pythagoreans based in southern Italy, and through the fairly detailed discussion on Presocratic physical doctrines in Lucretius Book 1 (on which see Piazzi 2005; cf. *isti physici* below). Those with a genuine interest in philosophy would also have been able to access doxographical texts like those which serve a source for the second part of Cicero's speech in *Luc.* (see on §73). On the ancient tradition of presenting Democritus as a sceptic generally, see Castagnoli (2010: 308–29).

For *perturbare* used of political disturbance, see *TLL* s.v. *perturbo* col. 1832.24–35. I can discern no significance in the different order in which the Presocratics are introduced here compared to *Ac.* 1.44, where Parmenides and Xenophanes do not feature; *Luc.* introduces Metrodorus of Chios. Reid[1] (p. 187) notes that the subjunctive *uelitis* 'denotes the frequent repetition of the wish, "whenever you desire".'

Sed neque Saturninus…Democriti uerecundia: just as the Presocratics are unlike Arcesilaus, so Roman politicians of the past who strengthened the position of citizens are unlike Saturninus. Hence the argument from ideological lineage fails.

L. Appuleius Saturninus (trib. pleb. 100; *RE* s.n. Apuleius no. 29), who died when Lucullus was 18 years old and was thus Lucullus' *inimicus potissimus* for what he represented ideologically and culturally rather than personally, appears in Cicero as the most extreme exponent of 'popular' policies partly because of his readiness to use force in the *concilium plebis*, triggering a *senatus consultum ultimum*. The analogy with Arcesilaus, under whom the Academy turned sceptical, seems to rest in part on the suggestion that both figures were responsible for a new quality of outrage. (In the next paragraph Tiberius Gracchus will, however, change place with Saturninus.) The death of Saturninus late in 100 BC forms the background to Cicero's *Rab. perd.*, delivered during Cicero's consulship in 63 BC (shortly before the dramatic date of *Luc.*) after Caesar had used the case to mount a proxy attack on senatorial power; see esp. *Rab. perd.* 18–24.

Arcesilaus' engagement of, in particular, Zeno is branded as vexatious and as sophistry (*calumnia*), i.e. factually baseless and motivated in a reprehensible way, while Democritus' sceptical pronouncements are the result of restraint and a conscious refusal to overreach (*uerecundia*); for the latter term, see Kaster (2005: 13–27). *Calumnia* is 'slander' in legal contexts; see Santorelli (2014: 26–32). See also on *Ac.* 1.44.

Et tamen isti physici…se scire quam sciant: as Reid[1] (p. 187) observes on *et tamen*, 'elliptic, the *tamen* modifying something implied rather than expressed. The sense is "however little I may agree with the *physici*, nevertheless they seldom hold language such as yours".' And yet the 'speaking like a madman' trope is then applied generously. There is some evidence for Presocratics being branded as deranged (cited by Reid[1]): Sen., *Ep. mor.* 79.14: *Democritus quam diu furere uidebatur*; Xen., *Mem.* 1.1.13 (Socrates of the φυσικοί): τοῖς μαινομένοις ὁμοίως διακεῖσθαι πρὸς ἀλλήλους. But overall even those who disagreed with them did not dismiss them in this way.

Lucullus is being tendentious when talking about *isti physici* generally, cf. the self-correction beginning with *maiorem autem partem* below, in a probably quite transparent way. In DK 31B112 Empedocles addresses the citizens of his native town of Acragas in the voice of a god delivering an important message to mortals. Elsewhere he describes himself as a god and a δαίμων who has been punished for some transgression committed during the phase of Strife in the cosmic cycle he expounds (DK 31B115). Lucullus is implying that this narrator persona, which is peculiar to Empedocles, reflected the mindset of all *physici* (*exclamant mente incitati*) and that Empedocles had been making sceptical pronouncements while raving. Cf. Lucr. 1.731 on Empedocles: *carmina quin etiam diuini eius uociferantur*, with Piazzi (2005: 160-3).

The sentence beginning with *maiorem autem partem* makes the point that the Presocratics are if anything overconfident in their knowledge claims most of the time; it does not mean that Lucullus is trying to land the Presocratics with the self-contradictory claim that they know that they know nothing, *pace* Burnyeat (1997: 296): 'Unlike Socrates, they did assert that nothing can be known, but not that they knew this. (Lucullus in *Luc.* 14 tries to argue that they speak as if they did know it.).' Rather, statements on other things must be meant, and we of course know that the Presocratics made plenty of apparently unqualified claims on the nature of things. (The Academics would, on the evidence of *Luc.* 72-6, not disagree.) *Omnes isti* means 'all the philosophers the Academics cite'; the comma behind *omnes* in Reid[1] seems a misprint, *pace* Plasberg[1] (p. 73), and given the translation in Reid[2].

Videntur affirmare should not be linked with passages where Lucullus appears to qualify his own endorsements; cf. on §10 *fin.*: *mihi tamen uidetur esse uerissima*. The statement is couched in the terminology which the Academics usually use (*uidentur*; the charge of *affirmare*). It is, however, possible that Lucullus is mockingly adopting an Academic persona, or else *uidentur* is phraseological and similar to English 'you may find that…'. Glucker (1997: 60 n. 6) notes that *affirmare* is preferred for 'consent' not to sense-perceptions, but to 'an abstract statement and or a philosophical view'; while this is accurate as an observation on Ciceronian usage, I would nonetheless assume that there is a unified notion of endorsement in the background (and, on occasion and in suitable contexts, in Cicero's sources), viz. assent.

For the Presocratic fragments which can be read as vocalizations of ignorance see on *Ac.* 1.44. *Cernere* presumably 'discern with the mind', given its juxtaposition with *sentire*, but it can be used of veridical seeing, too; cf. Reinhardt (2016: 88-9). On the subjunctive *sciat*, see Reid[1] (p. 204) on *Luc.* 23: *potius quam…prodat*.

§15

The paragraph continues the criticism of the Academic view of the history of philosophy, by taking a step back and interrogating the applicability of the notion of progress it relies on, and by questioning the construal of key figures (Socrates and Plato) who also feature, in quite a different way, in the Antiochian account of history. The thinking of the Presocratics, Lucullus suggests, was unformed and their ability to get themselves out of tight corners as yet undeveloped. But rather than to posit that philosophy, or philosophy that mattered, developed in the direction of scepticism, the Academics should acknowledge the significant progress that has been made due to human ingenuity and the passage of time. Instead, he suggests, Arcesilaus was merely intent on creating upheaval in a well-ordered field, looking for authority figures to hide behind, and singling out ones who disavowed certainty and knowledge. However, the Academics' two key exhibits, Plato and Socrates, cannot serve this purpose and rather fit the Antiochian narrative, the former because he formulated a system of philosophy from which even the Peripatetics and the Stoics deviated in terminology only, the latter because his disavowal of knowledge was ironic.[47] For Lucullus there is no discernible evolution from the Presocratics to Arcesilaus: the former were sui generis, the latter was intent on destruction, and Plato and Socrates were simply dogmatic philosophers.

The notion that human beings had made significant progress over time notably with respect to technical disciplines was widely though not universally held,[48] and it is no coincidence that Lucullus argues for the importance of κατάληψις for such disciplines (§22), and that Cicero responds by arguing that, given the Stoic conceptions of wisdom and ἐπιστήμη, technical disciplines ought to be the exclusive province of the sage *for the dogmatists*, who assumed there were no actual sages (§§144–6). Literary accounts (didactic poetry; the first stasimon of Sophocles' *Ant.*) sometimes view progress as a human adaptation mechanism necessary to compensate for increasing moral degradation and an increasingly hostile environment, viz. as part of a counternarrative on decline over time. That progress has been made in the field of philosophy is also countered by the long doxographical passage in Cicero's speech, where incompatible philosophical opinions on difficult matters are set against one another (§§112–43).

With the account of Socrates and Plato given here, cf. *Ac.* 1.15–18, *Luc.* 74, and sections 7.3 and 7.4.

Lucullus believes he is able to reclaim Socrates from the Academics by ascribing irony to him, characterizing what is meant by 'irony' in the process: it involves saying something other than one thinks, and deploys *dissimulatio*, the pretence not to be something. The context here, taken by itself, allows us to infer that Socrates either held at least one dogmatic view or possibly dogmatic views of some kind, which were, however, not the same thing as Plato's *perfectissima disciplina*. (The difference between Socrates and Plato cannot simply be endorsement of the *perfectissima disciplina* concealed through irony vs avowed endorsement.) Given other pronouncements on Socrates in *Acad.*, it might be deemed an option that Socrates' irony conceals a single knowledge claim, viz. that Socrates professes to know nothing except one thing, that he knows nothing, and that the Lucullus character regards this as sufficient to place Socrates on the dogmatic side of the dogmaticism/scepticism divide. However, as I explain in section 7.3, Cicero's reaction to *Luc.* 15 in *Luc.* 74

---

[47] Lucullus must here be picking up on the *Catul.* passage corresponding to *Ac.* 1.44–6; see also *Ac.* 1.15–17, where the Antiochian Varro offers a different interpretation of Plato and Socrates compared to Lucullus' here.

[48] See Edelstein (1967), with Dodds (1968).

shows that this cannot be meant, and that instead the concealment of substantial beliefs must be intended (see ad loc.).⁴⁹

The concept of irony, or of the εἴρων, is from its first occurrence in comedy characterized with respect to two parameters:⁵⁰ speech or behaviour which cannot be taken at face value, and the attitude which goes with it. In comedy irony is associated with pretence, affectation, and irritating behaviour for the sake of it. In Plato irony becomes something richer and valorized; Socrates does not simply say the opposite of what he thinks, although he may on occasion do so; his deployment of irony is grounded in moral concerns, and it is complicated and didactic. Aristotle relates ἀλήθεια to εἰρωνεία on one side and ἀλαζονεία on the other: the ἀλαζών pretends to more than the truth, the εἴρων to less (N.E. B7, 1108a19–23), cf. *dissimulatio* here. Theophrastus' εἴρων is a dissembler, but not to the point of depreciating himself, disingenuously or otherwise, and not motivated by arrogance or a desire to be awkward.

The characterization of irony given here in *Luc.* 15 is close to what we find in rhetorical handbooks, but the point that Socrates' irony involves saying something other than what he thinks rather than the opposite is notable and hints at the more complex Platonic conception. One would also assume that Lucullus regards irony so understood as something positive and beneficial, rather than a neutral device; after all, he wants to claim Socrates. There are parallels for this understanding of irony and of Socratic irony elsewhere in the Ciceronian corpus, including in relative chronological vicinity to *Acad.*⁵¹ So while the picture of Socrates is neither original nor unparalleled,⁵² it is striking to find it in a Stoicizing context. Hellenistic philosophers who saw themselves as straight-talking, i.e. Stoics and Epicureans, in each case in a suitably sublimated and idiosyncratic way,⁵³ encountered a problem with the ironic Socrates. The Epicureans granted that Socrates was ironic and disapproved of him, the Stoics denied that Socrates was ironic.⁵⁴ While the epistemological views which

---

⁴⁹ Possible candidates for dogmatic views held by Socrates include 'nobody does evil on purpose', for which *Grg.* could be cited, as well as 'virtue is knowledge' and 'only knowledge is good, and only ignorance is bad'; cf. D.L. 2.31, drawing on Plt., *Euthyd.* 281e (see also ibid. the wider context from 278e, which contains many key tenets of Stoic ethics in embryonic form).

⁵⁰ See Weinrich (1976) and Behler (1998) for general orientation; Amory (1981); Diggle (2004: 166–80) on Theophrastus' treatment and for a rapid summary of earlier scholarship.

⁵¹ Cf. Cic., *De orat.* 2.270: *Socratem opinor in hac ironia dissimulantiaque longe lepore et humanitate omnibus praestitisse* (Fannius mentioned just before, as in *Luc.* 15); *Brut.* 298–9 (Fannius also mentioned; partially quoted below); *Fam.* 4.4.1 (= SB 203).

⁵² Long (1988: 159) suggests that leading members of the Academy before it went sceptical, i.e. Polemo, Crates, and Crantor, 'were already stressing the Socratic side of Plato in contrast with the systematic and theoretical tendencies of Speusippus and Xenocrates'. If true, and if Antiochus was aware of this, which he may have been given the importance of Polemo for his ethics of the Old Academy (see on *Ac.* 1.19–23), he may have felt that he was acting in the spirit of the successors of Plato.

⁵³ On the Stoics, see Atherton (1988); on Epicurus, Sedley (2019).

⁵⁴ See Long (1989) and (2010) for general orientation and on the Stoics in particular; Döring (1979) on Socrates in later Stoicism; Opsomer (1998a: 83–126), in a chapter entitled 'Socrates Academicus' and a sub-section on 'εἰρωνεία', on Middle Platonism and Plutarch in particular; Kleve (1983) on Epicurus, cf. *Brut.* 292, quoted below, and Nardelli (1984) and Campos-Daroca (2019) on the later Epicureans. Cf. e.g. Epictetus, *Diss.* 4.5.1–4, for an 'irony-free' characterization of Socrates, and Stob., *Ecl.* II.7, p. 108.12–15 Wachsmuth (= *SVF* iii.630) for the Stoic attitude to irony.

Lucullus expounds in his speech are materially Stoic, the conception of Socrates used here, arguably to make Platonic dialogues a site for dogmatic philosophy, cannot be Stoic. Rather, Antiochus availed himself of the notion of irony in order to be able to claim Socrates. One might wonder why he did not simply follow the Stoic interpretation of Socrates, for the Stoics did interpret the Platonic Socrates as a dogmatist. A possible explanation might be that, having been an Academic first and developing his brand of dogmatism from close engagement with Platonic texts, he felt unable to dispute that Socrates disavows knowledge. This would be consistent with him, at a later stage, abandoning the dogmatic interpretation of Socrates altogether and accepting the Academic one, as Varro does in *Ac.* 1.16–17, on the grounds that it was really the understanding of Plato and Plato's texts which was at stake for the Antiochian project; see ad loc. and section 7.2.

Quod si illi tum in nouis rebus...putamus: Reid[2]: 'Now even if they at the time, set in the midst of novelties, faltered like new-born babes...'; Brittain (2006): 'But so what if they did hesitate then, like newborn children in unfamiliar territory?' *Quod si* functions as a concessive conjunction. *Nasci* here most likely 'to be in the early stages of growth' (*OLD* s.v. 1c), not 'to have been born', despite *modo*, or else one would expect the perfect participle; *haesitare* 'to move unsteadily' (*OLD* s.v. 2b): the Presocratics are being compared to toddlers, not newborns. *In nouis rebus* is not a standing phrase; 'in unfamiliar terrain', metaphorically of subject matter, seems right. The chosen terminology suggests two notions about the historical development of philosophy: that things are there to be discovered and made plain (*explicare*), and that human beings, presumably due to their rational capacity, make progress incrementally (cf. the three ablative phrases).

Nonne, cum iam...percipi posse: Lucullus continues with the theme that the periods, both in the history of philosophy and in the history of the popular politics in Rome, are very different from each other (so as to undermine any invocation of ancestors and to block any argument that posits evolution towards one's own position). Tiberius Gracchus found a state at peace which had reached constitutional perfection; he chose to introduce disorder into it for no good reason. Arcesilaus did mutatis mutandis the same.

Reid[1] (p. 188) suggests that here the target is all dogmatic schools (*philosophorum grauissimae disciplinae*). *Disciplinae* is better taken as 'sects' or 'schools', as Reid would require, than as 'branches of study', e.g. logic or physics. However, the fact that *p. g. disciplinae* is picked up by *constituta philosophia* suggests that here the Old Academy is the reference point, too, as encompassing the Academy, the Peripatos, and Stoicism up to a point. Cf. *Ac.* 1.44–5, where Arcesilaus' opposition to the Old Academic system is cited, and indeed the second half of §15.

Philosophy was fully formed when Arcesilaus tried to attack it (*euerteret* is conative). The verb *delitesceret* is here used of shamefully self-aware rather than merely defensive hiding. For the spelling with *-e-* rather than *delitiscere*, see Leumann (1977: 537). The subjunctive *negauissent* may just be *attractio modi* but could also be indirect speech and give Arcesilaus' point of view.

Quorum e numero...idem fuerit in Socrate: see the general note above for the conception of Socrates and of Plato deployed here.

During the Hellenistic period, being an εἴρων was not a prominent or significant feature of Socrates, however influential he was a 'philosophical hero'. An early exception which confirms the rule is the Pyrrhonist Timon of Phlius, frg. 799 Lloyd-Jones and Parsons (= D.L. 2.19): ἐκ δ' ἄρα τῶν ἀπέκλινεν ὁ λαξόος, ἐννομολέσχης, | Ἑλλήνων ἐπαοιδός, ἀκριβολόγους ἀποφήνας, | μυκτὴρ ῥητορόμυκτος, ὑπαττικὸς εἰρωνευτής, 'From these matters (i.e. the inquiry into nature), he turned aside, the people-chiselling moralizing chatterer, the wizard of Greece, whose assertions were sharply pointed, master of the well-turned sneer, a pretty good ironist' (translation by Long 1988: 150). For Timon, see also on *Luc.* 87b.

The attribute *perfectissima* of *disciplina* would suggest that a set or edifice of doctrines is meant, rather than a school, i.e. set of people, but Lucullus then continues by naming the Peripatetics and the Academics; schools are identified by their doctrines, and this kind of metonymical shift is not suspicious (the term αἵρεσις can be used in the same way). For Antiochus' construction of the Old Academy and the manner in which the Stoics were claimed, see section 7.2.

With our passage cf. *Brut.* 292 (Atticus speaking): *ego, inquit, ironiam illam quam in Socrate dicunt fuisse, qua ille in Platonis et Xenophontis et Aeschinis libris utitur, facetam et elegantem puto. Est enim et minime inepti hominis et eiusdem etiam faceti, cum de sapientia disceptetur, hanc sibi ipsum detrahere, iis tribuere illudentem, qui eam sibi arrogant, ut apud Platonem Socrates in caelum effert laudibus Protagoram Hippiam Prodicum Gorgiam ceteros, se autem omnium rerum inscium fingit et rudem. Decet hoc nescio quo modo illum, nec Epicuro, qui id reprehendit, assentior*, with Glucker (1997: 66–9) and Opsomer (1998a: 119). Note *detrahere* as in our passage, but not used absolutely and with *sapientia* as logical object. For *de se ipse detrahere* 'to disparage oneself', not just 'to draw attention away from oneself', see *TLL* s.v. *detraho* col. 831.25–6.

I have translated *plus tribuere* as 'to attribute more (sc. knowledge)'; contrast Reid[2] and Brittain (2006), but cf. Burnyeat (1997: 292 n. 38) and Quint. 9.2.46: *nam ideo dictus* εἴρων, *agens imperitum et admiratorem aliorum tamquam sapientium*, where §§44–6 offer a representative discussion of irony in the rhetorical tradition.

Fannius, who wrote *Annales*, is used to make the same point on Scipio in *Brut.* 299; *De orat.* 2.270; *Off.* 1.108; our passage is no. 12 Fannius, F6c FRHist. Its effect here is to valorize irony. For *e numero tollere*, cf. *Flacc.* 11; *de numero tollere* in *Phil.* 14.22. On *aliud cognoscens atque* (V^mS) for *aliud diceret atque*, see the edition p. lxii.

§§16–17a

The connection of §16 with what precedes and the Antiochian speaker Lucullus' motivation for listing leading Academics down to Philo is not obvious. Lucullus' main purpose seems to be to highlight the lack of progress made by the Academics even if one leaves the Presocratics to one side and grants that the Academics are constantly enquiring, driven by a desire to find the truth. This objection is of course predicated on a dogmatist's understanding of what progress would consist in.

At the beginning Lucullus offers that he and the Academics can agree that the views of the Presocratics did not amount to apprehension. In fact the Stoics regarded their doctrines as mostly false, even though they deemed many of their failures to be admirable. The attacks of Arcesilaus on Zeno, who stands here for the Old Academy, are branded as an attempt to obscure what had successfully been clarified.

Lucullus then asks if there has been no progress since Arcesilaus and after a long period of investigation. The suggestion seems to be that something ought to have changed, but it is not stated what it should be: presumably the securing of knowledge of some kind in at least some sub-field of philosophy. Schäublin et al. (p. 198 n. 15) wonder if Chrysippus should not represent an obvious developmental step, but progress made by the *Academics* is the issue, so that if at all progress could have consisted in an Academic response to Chrysippus. Carneades famously quipped that it was Chrysippus who provided him with his raison d'être (cf. Carneades on himself in D.L. 4.62 = T1a Mette: εἰ μὴ γὰρ ἦν Χρύσιππος, οὐκ ἂν ἦν ἐγώ), but this would not have counted as progress for Lucullus.

There follows a list of the Academics who came after Arcesilaus. It is striking that such a survey of Academic philosophers, complete with biographical details apparently coincidental to Lucullus' main purpose, should be provided by an Antiochian, and as late as at the beginning of the second book of the first edition. We know that the younger Catulus spoke about the various Academic positions in the *Catulus*, which shows that there was some historical dimension to his exposition. Is Cicero's purpose to show the New Academics as coy about their history (and Lucullus as able to spot this)? Did they adopt Arcesilaus and Carneades as figureheads, suppressing—or so would be Lucullus' suggestion—parts of their history? Lucullus' history of the New Academy is not exactly a *gradus ad Parnassum*: Arcesilaus does not seem to have commanded an immediate following (which is grist to Antiochus' mill, in that it weakens the New Academy's claim to being authentic followers of Plato), the New Academics peaked with Carneades, and later Academics had various qualities (but not Carneades' calibre or impact?). Philo's stewardship of the Academy appears valiant rather than stirring.[55] Overall, the import of the list may also be that the Academics have a line of ancestors like other schools, but little to show for it in terms of outcome.

The notion that Lucullus is aiming to highlight the Academics' failure to make any progress and consequently dent the dogmatists' position is supported by the fact that Philo's Roman Books are presented in §18 as due to his failure to tolerate the charge of stubbornness (*pertinacia*) any longer—the implication being that the Academics were rigid in their stance for centuries, and completely self-defeating once they did move. In my view, this last point also tells against the suggestion that mitigated scepticism was ever the official position of the Academy, or Philo's.

Cicero replies to Lucullus in §§76b–78, where he claims that the only remaining point of disagreement between dogmatists and Academics is over the third clause of Zeno's definition of the cataleptic impression; see ad loc.

---

[55] Compare *Luc.* 144–5 where the Cicero character introduces a Zenonian fragment which, so he argues, delivers the coup de grâce for the Stoic conception of knowledge. It is a feature of the discussion in *Acad.* that the interlocutors are steeped in their opponent's position to such an extent that they can readily produce evidence belonging to the other side. See ad loc. and Reinhardt (2020).

Sed fuerint illa uetera si uultis incognita: the paragraph begins on a similar note as the previous one—the Presocratics as early and inconsequential thinkers who stand apart from later developments—, but unlike §15 soon comes to focus on the period after Arcesilaus. The perfect subjunctive indicates a concession ('Granted, those subjects of old were not apprehended'). *Si uultis* may merely underline the concessive force of the sentence or may indicate that the Academics did indeed hold that unwarranted dogmatic assumptions were made by the Presocratics (cf. Lucullus himself in §14 *fin.*). *Incognit-** is in *Acad.* typically a property of *res*, either physical objects or states of affairs, or impressions thereof (cf. *Ac.* 1.45: *cum...incognita res approbaretur*), or more loosely impressions (i.e. thoughts) whose propositional content is an abstract tenet; cf. *uisum*, which can refer to an object seen or an impression of an object experienced (or both), with section 10 and Reinhardt (2016) and (2018b). Early editors and scholars proposed various changes to the sentence, documented and convincingly dismissed by Reid[1] (pp. 189–90) and Plasberg[1] (p. 74), including *ueteribus* for *uetera* (Bentley).

Nihilne est igitur actum, quod investigata sunt...obducere: the beginning of this sentence is well explained by Reid[1] (p. 190). *Nihil agere* = 'to achieve a worthless result', or no result at all, is amply attested; *quod* means 'in that, inasmuch as'. Cf. Sen., *Ep. mor.* 74.22: *nihil agitis quod negatis*. However, exact parallels for the sequence *nihil est actum quod* are not forthcoming. The subject of the *quod*-clause is *illa uetera* from above. *Quod inuestigata sunt* alludes to the Academics' claim that a desire to investigate and to find the truth drives their argumentative practice; cf. *Luc.* 7:...*neque nos studium exquirendi defatigati relinquemus*.

Reid[1] (p. 190) collects parallels which speak to the topic of progress in philosophy, or lack of it.

In remarking on Zeno's merely verbal changes to earlier doctrine Lucullus resumes a theme from the previous paragraph, where the essential similarity of Academic and Peripatetic doctrines was asserted, thus bringing the Stoics into the Old Academic fold. This idea of the absence of progress made by the Stoics does not go against the grain of the sentence as a whole, since progress after Arcesilaus is the issue. That the Zenonian definition of the cataleptic impression is what Lucullus is talking about in particular is suggested by *clarissimis rebus tenebras obducere* as well as *definitiones labefactare* here, the fact that §17 is devoted to attitudes to ἐνάργεια, and that the definition itself features in §18. A topical passage in Plato, which the Lucullus character/Cicero might have in mind, is *Tht.* 209c4–9, where Socrates suggests that no sooner will he have a true judgement that this is Theaetetus than when Theaetetus' snubness has left a mark imprinted on him which is different from everybody else's snubness; this invites comparison both with the notion that cataleptic impressions are imprints of objects or states of affairs left on the mind, and the Stoic notion that there is a peculiar quality characterizing every individual (ἴδια ποιότης) which is captured by cataleptic impressions; see on *Ac.* 1.40–2 and Reinhardt (2018: 39–63). It is not obvious which other definitions proposed by Zeno the Lucullus character may be thinking of.

Obtrectare means 'to criticize' (⟨ *tractare*), often on reprehensible grounds (envy, malice), cf. *Ac.* 1.44 (Arcesilaus acting *non pertinacia aut studio uincendi*), *Luc.* 76

(*Arcesilam uero non obtrectandi causa…sed uerum inuenire uoluisse*), and *Luc.* 7 on the Academics' 'actual' motivation. By *ut putatur*, if it modifies the whole sentence, Lucullus may be expressing doubt about the historicity of (details of) the argumentative encounter between Zeno and Arcesilaus; cf. Striker (1997: 265) on *Luc.* 77, about Zeno's addition of the third clause to the definition of the cataleptic impression in reaction to Arcesilaus' criticism, and part of Cicero's reply to Lucullus here (cf. §76b): 'In an anecdote that is no doubt too good to be true…'; alternatively, *ut putatur* modifies *obtrectans* and casts doubt on the motivation cited by the Academics.

For the Antiochian trope that the Stoics merely changed the terminology of earlier doctrines, see section 7.2. With *tenebras obducere*, cf. on §30: *lucem eripere*, 61; *N.D.* 1.6: *noctem offundere*; Aug., *Contra Acad.* 2.13.29: *tenebrae quae patronae Academicorum solent esse*, all noted by Reid[1] (p. 191); Fuhrer (1997: 161–2).

Cuius primo non admodum…confecta a Carneade: on Arcesilaus in general, see section 7.5, and the commentary on *Ac.* 1.44–6; on the question of when he turned sceptical, i.e. whether it was before he became head of the Academy (so that his stance was conceivably a reason for electing him) or after, see Görler (1994: 791–3). With the information provided here—that Arcesilaus' stance took hold only gradually (F8 and F9 Mette = LS 68C2) and that only Lacydes upheld it initially—compare the notice that the so-called Middle Academy led a nomadic existence like the Skythians and that Lacydes gave it stability (Philod., *Index Acad.* col. xxi.35–42 = Lacydes T2b Mette); but see below on Lacydes. (Ancient divisions of the Academy are discussed on *Ac.* 1.18.) Lactantius' remark (*Inst.* 3.6.10 = Arcesilaus F14, 44 Mette) that Arcesilaus' brand of philosophy was *asystatum, quod Latine instabile uel inconstans possumus dare* might reflect a similar view, although the interpretation Lactantius places on it is different; if Lactantius was drawing on the *Academici libri* in this case, then the revised version of our passage in *Ac.* 3 would be a possible place for it. For Arcesilaus' acumen and effectiveness as a speaker see on *Ac.* 1.44. Many of Antiochus'/Lucullus' arguments will turn on the alleged counterintuitiveness of the Academic position, so the observation that it was slow to command support fits his overall purpose.

On Lacydes, Arcesilaus' successor as head of the Academy (D.L. 4.59–61 = T1a 1–30 Mette) in 241/0 BC, see Glucker (1978: 234–5); Mette (1985: 39–51); Görler (1994: 829–48); Dorandi (2005); Lévy (2005). He probably died in 207 BC; cf. Dorandi (2005: 75); Fleischer (2020: 163–8). Only the Suda s.v. Λακύδης (λ 72 Adler = T1b Mette) mentions writings of his (ἔγραψε…φιλόσοφα καὶ Περί φύσεως); that he wrote on physics may be supported by the end of frg. 5 of Diogenes of Oinoanda's inscription if the supplement printed by Smith (1993) is correct (see Verde 2017: 68–71). D.L. 4.60 suggests that Lacydes had an interest in geometry. The testimonia include a story in which he is being tricked by clever slaves. The narrative, a truncated version of which features in D.L. 4.59, seems to blend satire and allusion to philosophical matters in a way which make it impossible to derive an insight into his thought from them; see Eusebius, *Praep. Ev.* XIV.7.1–13 = Numenius frg. 26 Des Places = T3, 1–80 Mette = appendix 2. Hirzel (1883) suspected the summary of a comedy plot behind this; Görler (1994: 833) thinks of contemporary satire. It is notable that the story presents Lacydes' commitment to inapprehensibility as shaky and has him admit in the end that what is said in school is different from what is said in real life. It may just be a piece of anti-Academic polemic, or it may originally have been intended to counter the narrative which accorded to Lacydes a stabilizing role.

For Carneades, including the notion that he completed the Academy's turn towards scepticism, see on *Ac.* 1.18, on *Luc.* 137, t. 8, and section 6.1 of the introduction; von Arnim (1921); Mette (1985); Dorandi (1994); Görler (1994: 899–904); Allen (2012); Castagnoli (2019).

With *non admodum probata* **ratio**, cf. my n. on *Luc.* 7b: *Academiae ratio.* Reid[1] (p. 191) glossed *retenta est* as 'kept from oblivion' but translated it as 'was supported by' in Reid[2]. The latter is correct, as Glucker (1997: 82) has shown. The transmitted *conficta* cannot be right, and the emendation to *confecta* (S) was not difficult.

Qui est quartus ab Arcesila…Lacydes fuisset: that only the fourth head of the Academy from Arcesilaus perfected his *ratio* marks it as less than compelling; by contrast, in Cicero's accounts of Arcesilaus Academic scepticism is presented as arriving fully formed (see *Ac.* 1.44–6), although significant new impulses given by Carneades are acknowledged. Euandrus of Phocaea, whose dates are uncertain, is in other sources (e.g. D.L. 4.60 = Lacydes T1a, 15f. Mette) named together with Telecles from the same town, with whom he may have shared the scholarchate; the notion of a collegial leadership would fit with other notices which list yet more leaders of the Academy between Lacydes and Carneades (e.g. Suda s.v. Πλάτων = Lacydes T5 Mette). See Görler (1994: 834–6); Dorandi (2000a); Fleischer (2020: 168–74).

Hegesinus is only known from lists of leading Academics; see D.L. 4.60; Numenius frg. 27.1 Des Places (see appendix 2); Suda π 1707; Glucker (1978: 234); Dorandi (2000b); Fleischer (2020: 54, 170–1). For the genitive *Lacydi*, see Reid[1] p. 191.

Sed ipse Carneades diu tenuit…in Melanthio Rhodio suauitatis: the principle for inclusion then shifts from scholarch to leading representative; several of them are philosophers whom Roman acquaintances of Cicero in his earlier life (who, in some cases, feature as characters in his dialogues) had met in person.

Clitomachus became head of the Academy not immediately after Carneades; the brief scholarchates of Polemarchus of Nicomedia and Crates of Tarsus intervened (on them, see Fleischer 2020: 191–6). (The possibility that Carneades was briefly succeeded by a younger philosopher of the same name has been excluded by Fleischer 2019 on the basis of a re-reading of three passages in Philodemus' *Index Acad.*) On Carneades, see n. above. With Carneades having written no books and his stance being open to different interpretations, notably that of radical and mitigated scepticism, Clitomachus emerged as the leading proponent of the radical interpretation, which, for all we know, arose first (see section 4 on the different Academic positions). Cicero's stance in *Acad.* is avowedly Clitomachean, and he arguably presented himself as a Clitomachean throughout his life (see section 8), although his brand of Clitomacheanism may have been his own conception up to a point (see ibid. p. clvi on a second Clitomachean in the Ciceronian corpus, the character Cotta in *N.D.*). Cicero's comments on Clitomachus' personal qualities seem flat and somewhat stereotypical (*Luc.* 98: *homo et acutus ut Poenus et ualde studiosus ac diligens*; cf. Görler 1994: 901). Clitomachus is reported to have recounted a story about a visit of Scipio Aemilianus' to Alexandria (Plut., *Prov.* 200e = F11 Mette), which fits with other evidence suggesting that he was among contemporary Athenian philosophers who were open to engagement with the Roman world (see on *Luc.* 102, and the general note on *Luc.* 11-12 on how the elder Catulus' Academic credentials might have been constructed in the *Catulus*, although his position in *Acad.* was the mitigated one; cf. *Luc.* 148). D.L. 4.67 refers to 'over 400 works'. Here in *Luc.* Cicero quotes from one (*Luc.* 98: *quattuor...libri...de sustinendis assensionibus* = Περὶ ἐποχῆς; Cicero quotes specifically from Book 1). In Cicero, and elsewhere, Clitomachus appears as a chronicler of Carneades' thought (*Luc.* 98; *Or.* 51, where Carneades' comparison of Clitomachus and Charmadas is cited; D.L. 4.67), or rather arguments (*Luc.* 139 = LS 69L: *numquam se intellegere potuisse quid Carneadi probaretur*). *Tusc.* 3.54 mentions a consolatory work of his to his fellow Carthaginians after the destruction of the city at the end of the third Punic war in 146 BC. Probably in 110 BC L. Licinius Crassus (Cic., *De orat.* 1.45, 2.365) and M. Claudius Marcellus (ibid. 1.57) heard him speak in Athens.

The identity of the next Academic in the enumeration is not certain: ω had *hac nonne* in place of a name (with *hoc quam* as A[a]'s attempt at a correction, then carried over by B[a]), which Christ (recorded in Halm) emended to *Hagnone* (the *Index Acad.* col. xxiii.4-6 lists Hagnon of Tarsus as a pupil of Carneades who took notes in his lectures, but Christ's suggestion must have been guided by Quint. 2.17.15); see Görler (1994: 909) on him. The name of the equally sparsely attested Aeschines of Naples (cf. D.L. 2.64 and Görler 1994: 910) was supplied by Davies (1725) from *De orat.* 1.45 (Crassus speaking): *audiui enim summos homines, cum quaestor ex Macedonia uenissem Athenas, florente Academia, ut temporibus illis ferebatur, cum eam Charmadas et Clitomachus et Aeschines obtinebant; erat etiam Metrodorus, qui cum illis una ipsum illum Carneadem diligentius audierat, hominem omnium in dicendo, ut ferebant, acerrimum et copiosissimum*; adopted and defended by Reid[1] (p. 191), it is palaeographically less plausible.

Charmadas—on whom, see Dorandi (1994); Görler (1994: 906-8); Brittain (2001: 312-28); Lévy (2005: 60-70); Fleischer (2014), (2015a), and (2020: 208-9)—is elsewhere in Cicero noted for his interest in rhetorical matters, even if his pronouncements suggest disapproval in line with the Academy's general tendency of hostility towards rhetoric. In *De orat.* 1.47 Crassus reports that he studied Plato's *Gorgias* carefully with Charmadas, and Antonius (ibid. 1.82-92) reports on a dispute about the value of rhetoric between Charmadas and Athenian orators. Cicero cannot have met him (*De orat.* 2.360 very strongly suggests that Charmadas was dead by 91 BC), but he was still alive when the fourth book of Apollodorus' *Chronica* was published; see Fleischer (2020: 15, 58-9, 209). He originally came from Alexandria; see Philod., *Index Acad.* xxiii.8-10 Fleischer.

Melanthius of Rhodes is another shadowy figure; see Görler (1994: 909); Dorandi (2005a); Fleischer (2020: 199-205). He is attested to have been a tragic poet before he turned to Academic philosophy (*Index Acad.* col. xxxi.3-12); the connection with poetry may explain his *suauitas* (as Charmadas' *eloquentia* seems to be associated with his interest in rhetoric).

Tenuit, as Reid[1] (p. 191) notes, may be an absolute use unparalleled in Cicero, or else 'sc. *Academiam*' from above; cf. *eam...obtinebant* in *De orat.* 1.43 quoted above.

Bene autem nosse...Metrodorus putabatur: Metrodorus of Stratonicea—on whom see Görler (1994: 905-6); Glucker (2004: 118-33); Dorandi (2005b); Lévy (2005); and Fleischer (2019a), who dates his birth 'kaum später als 170 v.Chr.' (p. 126)— stands somewhat apart in Lucullus' survey (cf. *De orat.* 1.45: *erat etiam Metrodorus qui cum illis una ipsum illum Carneadem diligentius audierat, hominem omnium in dicendo, ut ferebant, acerrimum et copiosissimum*); for his views, see on *Luc.* 78, as well as on t. 58. Unusually, he was an Epicurean before he turned to Academic philosophy (Philod., *Index Acad.* col. xxiv.9-16; D.L. 10.9). He used to be identified with an unspecified Metrodorus whose name was read in *Index Acad.* col. xxxii.16 (= Apollodorus' *Chronica* l. 103 Fleischer) among pupils of Carneades 'who did not teach in the city' (see Glucker 1978: 75, 103, 107; Görler 1994: 905), but a re-reading of the papyrus has revealed the individual named there to be a 'Zenodorus' (see Fleischer 2020: 146-7 and 217). With the information provided here, cf. *Index Acad.* col. xxvi.8-10: ἔφη Καρνεάδου παρακηκοέναι πάντας, 'he said that everyone else had misunderstood Carneades'.

§17a

Iam Clitomacho Philo uester...Academiae non defuit: by highlighting Philo's long association with Clitomachus and his role as Cicero's philosophical model and/or teacher (*uester*) Lucullus makes the connection with Cicero, his intellectual ancestry, and his stance in the dialogue. If he had wanted to exploit the fact that Cicero and Catulus actually represented different but equally valid Academic positions, here would have been an opportunity, perhaps along the lines that the Academy remained prone to unsteadiness after Arcesilaus (cf. *non admodum probata ratio* above). The positive representation of Philo here, acting figuratively as a *patronus* appearing as an advocate on behalf of the Academy, contrasts with the dismissive remarks about him in §§12 *fin.* and 18, where, however, Philo qua author of the Roman Books is at issue. Lucullus does not recognize Cicero as a representative of the Academy comparable to Philo in stature and instead implies that the Academy was defunct, or else that what advocacy was provided by others, i.e. 'professional' Greek philosophers, after Philo's death was ineffectual; Antiochus does not come into consideration, and his followers were either dead or had converted to other schools by 62/1 BC (leaving Romans like Brutus and Varro to one side). On the circumstances of the death of Philo, see Fleischer (2017): according to a re-reading of Philod., *Index Acad.* cols xxxiii.42-xxxiv.7 he died in Italy from influenza in 84/3 BC. There is no evidence that he returned to Athens for a period after his move to Rome. *Philone...uiuo* also seems to imply that Philo did not have a successor as scholarch, while the *Index Acad.* passage just cited speaks of a successor in terms which are suggestive of a caretaker rather than a person who was viewed as philosophically distinguished. See also on Aug., *Contra Acad,* 3.18.41 (= t. 55), which alludes to our passage but takes it in a different direction, with Barnes (1997: 76-8).

§§17b–18a [*-quibuscum disseratur, putant*]

Lucullus now turns to three groups of philosophers without identifying them by name. The first group deems it futile to engage with the Academics argumentatively and regards definitions of κατάληψις and ἐνάργεια as pointless, for two reasons: no *definiens* could be clearer than ἐνάργεια itself (i.e. no definition could be clearer than the concept it aims to define, or possibly the related phenomenon in this case) and no definitions of something so clear should be offered. The second group would not have offered a definition of ἐνάργεια of their own accord but would respond to arguments which are apt to question its existence. The third group uncomplicatedly believes in the illuminating power of definitions and in the benefit of debate with suitable opponents, who include the Academics. Who are these various philosophers and how does the paragraph fit into its larger context?

The first group of philosophers holds that Academics approve of nothing and are for that reason already unsuitable opponents. This does not tell us who they are, but it seems to preclude the possibility that Academics promoting mitigated scepticism or indeed adherents of the Roman books are meant, since both of these positions allowed for the possibility of assent (with qualifications). That Antipater of Tarsus was singled out for criticism may suggest that reference is to an argumentative skirmish of the mid-second century, at which point universal suspension of judgement was part of the Academic position.

The obvious candidates for philosophers who reject definitions (see n. below for possible reasons of this rejection) are Epicureans. However, it may seem peculiar that they should intrude on the debate between Academics and Antiochus/the Stoics at this point of the dialogue (only to disappear as quickly as they entered), and if the reference of *illi* in *quam* κατάληψιν *illi uocant* is taken to be the criticizing philosophers, then the problem arises that κατάληψις is a Stoic term. Therefore it has been suggested, alternatively, that the first group of philosophers must be Stoics.[56]

However, this second interpretations runs into difficulties, too. The Stoics are notorious for their fondness of definitions, for the tendency of providing different definitions of the same concepts, depending on where the concepts appear in the Stoic system, and even for using quasi-definitions ('outlines', ὑπογραφαί). So one would have to assume that fellow Stoics criticized Antipater for *overfondness* of definitions, which is implausible in itself, and whether definitions (sc. of certain concepts) are possible and desirable *in principle* is clearly the issue in the section. Moreover, there is no reason to think that Antipater defined the particular concept at issue any differently from Stoics before him and after. Finally, if Antipater qua *fellow*-Stoic was meant, then to call him *Antipater Stoicus* would be somewhat peculiar, too; the attribute makes more sense if a philosopher from a different school was delivering the criticism.[57]

Thus I return to the assumption that the first group are Epicureans. For the text to be coherent, the pronoun *illi* would have to refer to other people than the

---

[56] Cf. Reid[1] (pp. 192–3); Schäublin et al. (p. 200 n. 25); Burnyeat (1997: 282).

[57] I see no reason to suspect that Cicero/Lucullus want to exclude the reference to the historian Coelius Antipater or the poet Antipater of Sidon.

philosophers delivering the criticism—most likely to the Stoics from Lucullus' point of view. The manner in which the two Greek terms κατάληψις and ἐνάργεια are cited in the text supports this reading: Lucullus produces a string of Latin synonyms meaning 'cognition', which stand for κατάληψις, sc. in (Greek) Stoic parlance, and which the Epicureans say does not need defining, since nothing is clearer than—and here follows a term closely if not exclusively associated with Epicureanism (see n. below)—ἐνάργεια.[58]

There remains the question of why the Epicureans and their criticisms come in at this point, and here one can only speculate. One effect of the reference to the Epicureans is that the focus briefly goes off the debate between Academics and Stoics/Antiochus, which is exclusively conducted within the framework of Stoic epistemology. The result of this lifting of the gaze is that the Stoic criterion is found to be recognized beyond Stoicism, even if the Epicureans refer to the same thing as ἐνάργεια, and is regarded as so plain as not to require definition.[59] No suggestion is made that the requirements for ἐνάργεια are in any way weaker than those for κατάληψις. The Stoic criterion is thus presented as natural in the sense that it is the Stoic conceptualization of something which is recognized and appreciated for what it is beyond the school.

In the immediately following section, which returns to Philo's Roman Books, their theses, or Philo in advancing them, are said to *noua commouere*, in that he posits a new, weaker conception of κατάληψις, which he then claims to have been embraced by earlier Academics all along. §§17b-18a sets up the following section by implying that, on Philo's construal, the Academics would have been embracing an outlandish notion of κατάληψις (and not a realistic one like the Stoics).

On the two other groups of philosophers, see the lemmatized nn. below; and cf. *Luc.* 32-4, where a range of apparently Academic views without clear ascription is mentioned.[60] This passage, like the present one, is indicative of a style and level of discussion which is peculiar to *Acad.* amongst Cicero's philosophical dialogues.

Sed quod nos facere...reprehendebant: for the sentiment that it is futile to engage with the Academics, cf. t. 21 (= Nonius p. 65), with my commentary: *digladiari autem semper, depugnare in facinorosis et audacibus quis non cum miserrimum tum etiam stultissimum dixerit?* Reid[1] (p. 192) cites Epict., *Diss.* 1.27.15 ('Pyrrhonists and Academics will oppose me pointlessly, and I have no time to engage with them'), but also notes statements to the contrary (*Diss.* 1.7.25), and of course the evidence for Stoic arguments against the Academics is abundant.

That the Epicureans are not identified by name may be due to Cicero primarily aiming to set up §18. Their philosophy, while popular, enjoyed a less good reputation

---

[58] Cf. the Epicurean speaker in *Fin.* 1.30 on the good (noted by Brittain 2006: 12 n. 16): *Sentiri haec putat, ut calere ignem, niuem esse albam, dulce mel. Quorum nihil oportere exquisitis rationibus confirmare, tantum satis esse admonere. Interesse enim inter argumentum conclusionemque rationis et inter mediocrem animaduersionem atque admonitionem. Altera occulta quaedam et quasi inuoluta aperiri, altera prompta et aperta iudicari.*

[59] The possibility that Carneades engaged critically with Epicurean epistemology is raised by Vogt (2014: 493).

[60] See Allen (1997: 218-19).

than Stoicism, with their ethical views attracting the most hostile criticism of course, notably on the subject of pleasure (see Reinhardt 2005: 151–3). *Et ii quidem non mediocres* does not sound condescending as such, but does not preclude a reference to the Epicureans either, since their views need to have sufficient validity to justify their citation.

If *qui nihil probarent* is not just intended to characterize the Academics, it will give a reason for not engaging with them: they have no positions at all, by approving (which must be general here, rather than the narrow technical notion of *Luc.* 104) of nothing. Yet elsewhere Lucullus ascribes at least one *decretum* to them (*Luc.* 28–9).

Antipater of Tarsus was Diogenes of Babylon's successor as head of the Stoa (died 129 BC); his fragments are collected in *SVF* vol. iii. See von Arnim (1894); Cohn (1905); Guérard and Puech (1989); Steinmetz (1994: 637–41); Burnyeat (1997) on Antipater in *Acad.*; the commentary on *Luc.* 28, 109, 143; Annas (1997) on *Off.* 3.50–7; Striker (1996c). After the death of his predecessor Antipater was Carneades' main antagonist on the Stoic side; his disinclination to engage in live argument and preference for writing earned him the nickname 'pen-shouter' (καλαμοβόας; Plut., *De garrul.* ch. 23 = *SVF* iii.244).

On κατάληψις entering common parlance in the Hellenistic period, despite being primarily a Stoic term of art, see Reinhardt (2018b: 315–16); for the Epicureans, see Usener (1977) s.v. καταλαμβάνειν, καταληπτικός, κατάληψις. On *nec ullam rationem esse* with infinitive, see Reid[1] (p. 192); ibid. on *multus in eo = multus in ea re*.

Nec definiri aiebant necesse esse...definienda censebant: the philosophers in question said that the term κατάληψις needs no definition, and Lucullus runs through the possible Latin renderings for it. One might have thought that the term would have been required already in the *Catulus*, but in *Ac.* 1.40–2 Varro discusses related issues in some detail without using the term. The three terms are also juxtaposed in *Fin.* 3.17; cf. 5.76: *percepti comprehensi cogniti*. Lucullus is not coining these terms or establishing their terminological use, and some are indeed attested in relevantly similar uses before *Acad.*, but he makes a point of assembling them. See also section 10 on terminology. The phrase like *uerbum e uerbo* marks the calque; cf. *Luc.* 31 (where morpheme-by-morpheme rendering is at issue); *Fin.* 3.15; *Tusc.* 3.7; *Top.* 35.

On the Epicurean attitude to definitions, see Cic., *Fin.* 1.22 (= fr. 243 Usener = LS 19H): *iam in altera philosophiae parte, quae est quaerendi ac disserendi, quae λογική dicitur, iste uester plane, ut mihi quidem uidetur, inermis ac nudus est. Tollit definitiones, nihil de diuidendo ac partiendo docet, non quo modo efficiatur concludaturque ratio tradit, non qua uia captiosa soluantur, ambigua distinguantur ostendit*; Usener (1887: 178) cites the present passage for comparison. See also Taylor (2016); Sedley (2019: 108–13).

On the reference of *illi*, see the general note above. *Persuadere* in *qui persuadere uellent* is emphatic and contrasts with the equally emphatic *esset* in *esset clarius* ἐναργείᾳ below. On ἐνάργεια and related terms in Epicurean texts, see Usener (1977: 250–1). With the clarity-related terminology, cf. *declaratio rerum* in *Ac.* 1.41. I have rendered *perspicuitas* as 'transparency' to bring out the fact that such impressions allow for a uniquely clear view on and of their objects (i.e. that is how the Stoics and Antiochian speakers in *Acad.* construe clarity; see also section 6.1). Similarly,

I translate *clarius* as 'clearer' rather than, e.g., 'more luminous' because of the manner in which such impressions represent the object ex hypothesi: they are not assumed to have some kind of shine to them, nor could their clarity be observed independently of how they represent their object. *Illustris* 'lucid' when applied to speech is conventional (*OLD* s.v. no. 2). In translating *euidentia* as 'evidence', I am thinking of *OED* s.v. no. I, 'The quality or condition of being evident'.

On *aliquid* in *aliquid quod comprehendi et percipi posset* Reid[1] (p. 193) comments that it should denote the external object, but that 'object and perception were often by the ancient philosophers carelessly confused'; I see deliberate choices rather than carelessness here, resulting in expressions which are different from the Greek ones; see section 10.

Alii autem negabant...ne qui fallerentur: as indicated above, this group of philosophers cannot be identified and may have been invented for rhetorical purposes; they give the impression of being drawn into the debate. *Ne qui fallerentur* signals a concern for a wider audience. The future participle with *fuisse* for a past counterfactual in an indirect statement is standard.

§18

Plerique tamen...quibuscum disseratur putant: this sentence describes the conventional attitude most philosophers adopt with respect to the evident. It enables the resumption of the attack narrative in §18b, in that Philo's Roman Books proposal could not be taken seriously even by this last group of people and placed him outside of the *digni quibuscum disseratur*.

§18b

Lucullus now returns to the subject of the Roman Books, even though we were told at the end of §13 that the part of the conversation between Heraclitus and Antiochus which was directed against Philo would be omitted. An attempt to explain this apparent contradiction would turn on the highly allusive nature of §18, which hardly amounts to a substantial engagement. I suggested at §17 that the suggestion made in that paragraph—that the Stoic criterion was widely accepted even if it was conceptualized in different ways—can be seen as motivating a brief return to the Roman Books, which—on any interpretation—failed to recognize the Stoic criterion for human beings living in this world.

The brief remarks in §13 allowed for the inference that the Roman Books contained a philosophical thesis and a historical thesis, that the philosophical thesis could be paraphrased as 'something can be apprehended' (contrary to universal ἀκαταληψία, and which may either mean that some objects can be apprehended, or that some things can be apprehended on some understanding of κατάληψις), and that the historical claim was that Academics had held this view all along. This historical claim was found to be so absurd as to give rise to disagreement from Catulus the elder, and incredulity and anger from Antiochus, i.e. from New Academics and Old Academics alike. The philosophical claim was less apt to do so, and one of the same outline description (but not necessarily the same detailed articulation) was ascribed to Metrodorus of Stratonicea in *Acad.* (see above on §17 and below on §78), though not in the extant parts.

Before I turn to §18 itself, there are two other pieces of evidence which need to be introduced. First, Numenius frg. 28 Des Places (= Eus., *Praep. Ev.* XIV.9.1–2), of which I give the English translation (Greek text in appendix 2): '(9.1) This Philo now, who had just taken over the leadership of the school, was beside himself with joy, showed himself appreciative and showed respect to (sc. his predecessor) Clitomachus, advanced the latter's views and armed himself with gleaming steel against the Stoics. (9.2) But as time went on, due to familiarity their suspension of judgement faded, and he no longer held the view which he had held before, but the clarity and consistency of his experiences made him change his mind. Given his already significant power to discriminate, he wanted at any price (we know why) encounter some who would refute his views, in order to avoid the impression that he was turning his back and withdrawing of his own accord.' Second, in *P.H.* 1.235 Sextus provides the following characterization of a view of 'those around Philo', which, given what we know about Philo's stances, can only relate to the Roman Books:

Οἱ δὲ περὶ Φίλωνά φασιν ὅσον μὲν ἐπὶ τῷ Στωικῷ κριτηρίῳ, τουτέστι τῇ καταληπτικῇ φαντασίᾳ, ἀκατάληπτα εἶναι τὰ πράγματα, ὅσον δὲ ἐπὶ τῇ φύσει τῶν πραγμάτων αὐτῶν, καταληπτά.

Those around Philo say that, as far as the Stoic criterion is concerned, i.e. the cataleptic impression, things are inapprehensible, but as far as the nature of things themselves is concerned, they are apprehensible.

The first of these texts suggests that assent was part of the second, novel position of Philo's which is being referred to, as—see below—one would assume for the Roman Books view. However, some see a reference to mitigated scepticism here, which also permits a type of assent (cf. *Luc.* 148), but which I believe Philo never to have endorsed.[61] Rather, I read the text as an obviously biased but not necessarily uninformative account of how Philo came to shift from the Clitomachean position to the Roman Books view. Since the status of Numenius frg. 28 is contentious, I will use it with care.

The second passage comes from a larger context (1.220–35) in which Sextus discusses the differences between Academics and Pyrrhonists. In 1.220 a five-fold division of the Academy is introduced (see on *Ac.* 1.17 for such divisions), in which 'Philo and Charmadas' form the fourth element, and 'those around Antiochus' the

---

[61] See Brittain (2001: 133 n. 6): 'Numenius' comment probably refers to Philo's change to the *Roman* position, but what he gives here is an explanation of Philo's rejection of *epoche*, i.e., in the first instance, of his change to the Philonian/Metrodorian position' (author's emphasis). Brittain ibid. also notes the rather similar formulation used by Plutarch in connection with Antiochus' so-called conversion to the Old Academy (*Cic.* 4.2 = Philo test. xv Brittain), which makes Numenius' comment on Philo appear somewhat generic.

fifth. This is striking because one would not associate the Roman Books view with Charmadas (see on *Luc.* 16); unless Sextus has made a mistake here, the linking may suggest that Philo invoked Charmadas in support of the historical thesis which went with said view.[62]

Two outline reconstructions of the Roman Books have been suggested, which arguably exhaust the possibilities provided by the evidence.[63] The most nuanced and consistent proponent of the first one is Sedley (reading A), while Brittain has to be seen as the main representative of the second one (reading B). Both interpretations will be introduced with reference to the evidence from Sextus and will then be applied to the evidence from Cicero.

On reading A, Philo's assessment of the prospects of human cognition would have remained the same as it was prior to the Roman Books, while it would be conceded that infallible cognition was possible, if not for human beings.[64] Sedley makes an additional assumption, unlike some earlier proponents of this view: a different kind of perceiving subject—god—is assumed to enter the frame via an implicit reference to Plato's *Tim.*, an influential text in the Hellenistic and even more so in the post-Hellenistic period. *Tim.* 29c–d in particular is concerned with the human lack of a capacity for cognition.[65]

On reading B, the evidence from Sextus is about the possibility of cognition for human beings (including sages) of objects in the perceptible world and thus stays within the frame of reference set by the debate between Stoics and Academics up to this point. There is no invocation of textual authority like *Tim.* What is claimed is that, if one assumes the Stoic conception of cognition, things are not apprehensible, but 'in fact', i.e. minimally on a different conception of cognition, they are.[66]

---

[62] That Sextus made a mistake is assumed by Brittain (2001: 54); that Philo may have invoked Charmadas is suggested by Tarrant (2018: 83).

[63] Proponents of reading A include Brochard (1887: 196–202); Glucker (1978: 64–88); and Sedley (1981) and (2012b: 84–6). Proponents of reading B include Tarrant (1985: 57–9); Görler (1994: 922–6); Barnes (1997: 73–4); Striker (1997: 258–60); Brittain (2001: 129–68); Glucker (2004: 134–43), if I interpret him correctly; and Tarrant (2018: 87). (The rather general interpretation in Lévy 1992: 290–300, esp. 295 seems compatible with either reading.) What most of these studies share is an assumption, arising from explicit statements in the text (*Luc.* 12) inter alia, that the evidence for the Roman Books is confined to a handful of passages, and that the other parts of *Acad.* only offer occasional glimpses of the Roman Books; the exception to this consensus is Tarrant (2018), who thinks that large parts of *Acad.* are informed by the Roman Books in some way, and who consequently is ready to regard passages which in this commentary are treated as unequivocally Clitomachean (like *Luc.* 7b–9a) as somehow revealing features of Philo's final position. (While I do think that *Luc.* 7b–9a might reflect Philonian teaching delivered in Rome, I also think that the content of the passage, aligning as it does with earlier Academic pronouncements in the Ciceronian corpus, reflects Philo's thinking prior to the conception of the Roman Books; see section 8.) Detailed surveys of the earlier scholarship on Philo's Roman Books going back to the mid-nineteenth century are given by Glucker (1978: 64–88) and Brittain (2001: 24–35), which I will not attempt to replicate here.

[64] Sedley (1981) does not assume that Philo was a mitigated sceptic before he formulated the Roman Books view.

[65] Sextus' summary in *P.H.* 1.235 does, as far as I can see, not include a verbal trigger for the *Tim.* reference, but the general assumption that the head of the Academy might invoke a suitable Platonic text is of course not implausible, especially if one assumes that the tenets of Antiochus' Old Academy were formulated and justified with reference to Platonic texts.

[66] Sedley and Brittain differ in their interpretation of the phrase ὅσον δὲ ἐπὶ τῇ φύσει τῶν πραγμάτων αὐτῶν. Brittain (2001: 139–40) attempts to show, through comparison with Sextan phraseology, that the phrase means no more than 'in fact, actually'. Sedley (2012b: 86), while acknowledging that there are

I shall now go through *Luc.* 18 and examine which interpretative decisions need to be taken at various junctures on either reading. For the sceptical interpretation this has been done by Tarrant and Brittain in considerable detail; for reading A this has not been done in as detailed a fashion (Sedley argues his case exclusively with respect to the evidence from Sextus). Before that I shall appraise the general shape of the passage. (i) At the beginning Philo is said to have introduced novelties relative to earlier Academic positions, because he could not bear the charge of obstinacy any more. (ii) He lied in a transparent manner, for which he was criticized by the elder Catulus (as the younger Catulus reported in the *Catulus*; cf. §12 *init.*), and (iii) according to Antiochus placed himself in the very position which he feared (*in id ipsum se induit quod timebat*). This statement, as well as one whose import is apparently equivalent (*Ita imprudens eo quo minime uolt reuoluitur*) but which brands Philo's failure as unforeseen (quite possibly tendentiously), frame a long sentence which provides the best clue regarding the Roman Books' philosophical thesis and which offers a point of contact with the Sextus passage in that it is about engagement with the Stoic definition of the cataleptic impression.[67] (iv) The sentence introduces the Zenonian definition, placing particular emphasis on the third clause (*id nos a Zenone definitum...quale uel falsum esse possit?*). Philo, in 'weakening and removing "this"' (*hoc cum infirmat tollitque*), where 'this' must be the kind of *uisum* defined, removes the criterion. (v) The result is that nothing can be apprehended, which is glossed (see above, iii) as Philo ending up inadvertently where he did not want to be.

	Reading A	Reading B
(i) *Philo... dicebantur*	The novelty would be the acceptance of infallible cognition, for god, of a non-Stoic variety (Stoic cognition is dismissed in Sextus and *Luc.* 18). Cognition would remain out of reach for human beings. The charge of obstinacy would be met by the acceptance of a form of cognition (available to gods).	The novelty would be the acceptance of a form of cognition, weaker than the Stoic one, available to humans as per the established terms of the debate, and with respects to objects/facts in the perceptible world. The charge of obstinacy would be met by the recognition of a form of cognition (available to human beings).
(ii) *Et aperte... Catulo*	The lie would consist in ascribing the acceptance of infallible cognition available to gods to earlier Academics.	The lie would consist in ascribing the acceptance of a form of cognition which is weaker than the Stoic one and available to humans to earlier Academics.

similar phrases with that meaning, observes that αὐτῶν in particular points to a more specific sense and concludes that 'in fact' is a 'considerable under-interpretation'. (Glucker 2004: 135–6 discusses the matter, too, and argues against the translation 'in fact'.) He sees 'a statement about the way the actual putative objects of the knowledge are' (ibid.); by not assigning responsibility for the failures of cognition to the objects of perception, the sentence would hint at the actual origin of any problem, viz. the perceiving subject. I regard Sedley's (and Glucker's) point as well made and as compatible with either reading.

[67] Barnes (1997: 72) calls the whole paragraph 'artfully clumsy'.

	Reading A	Reading B
(iii) *Et ut docuit... timebat*	Assuming that the position Philo wanted to avoid was (the rigid insistence on) ἀκαταληψία as experienced by human beings, Philo finds himself in this position because the cognitive situation of human beings has not changed.	Assuming that the position Philo wanted to avoid was (the rigid insistence on) ἀκαταληψία as experienced by human beings, Philo finds himself in this position because his weaker form of cognition amounts to ἀκαταληψία on the Stoic understanding of cognition.
(iv) *Cum enim ita...et cogniti*	(Ex hypothesi the cognitive position of humans remains unchanged. Philo introduces a new version of infallible cognition for gods. See i.) He would do this by 'weakening' Stoic cognition. Yet, we are told, this leaves no criterion.	Philo removes the criterion by rejecting Stoic cognition, whose hallmark is the third clause. Together with (i) this suggests that his new kind of cognition is like Stoic cognition without the assumption of infallibility. Philo 'weakens' Stoic cognition by dropping the third clause.
(v) *Ex quo... reuoluitur*	Nothing can be apprehended, sc. by human beings, since cognition is available to gods only.	Nothing can be apprehended by human beings, since human cognition does not meet the standard of infallibility.

Reading A runs into a number of difficulties. The immediately preceding §17 suggested that the Stoic criterion is accepted by the Epicureans, too, even if they use different terminology. And Epicurean ἐνάργεια is available to humans living in this world. If the assumption of infallible cognition available to gods had been the innovation of the Roman Books, then this would be anything but foregrounded by §17 (quite apart from the fact that neither Cicero nor Sextus mention god). Further, it is difficult to see what the conceptual space for infallible cognition available to gods could be if Philo 'weakened' Stoic cognition to obtain it (iv above). In general, it seems impossible to read (iv) coherently and intelligibly on reading A. Another problem of reading A is that it seems to involve negatively dogmatic assumptions about the nature of things. Finally—but this issue is the easiest to explain away—the text presents Philo's position as the result of some kind of journey or process (*se induit, reuoluitur*), while reading A assumes that his position about the prospects of human cognition remain unchanged throughout.

Reading B, by contrast, is economical and comparatively straightforward. Philo, impressed by the charge of rigidity, devises a new conception of cognition, which amounts to the first two clauses of the Zenonian definition without the infallibility requirement. Cognition remains impossible on the Stoic conception, but is possible on the revised conception. Antiochus rejects this because cognition which is not infallible is not cognition (on the view of the Stoics as well as of others, cf. §17). Regarding the Sextan phrase ὅσον δὲ ἐπὶ τῇ φύσει τῶν πραγμάτων αὐτῶν, Sedley's examples do suggest that the phrase here means more than 'in fact', but given that it is πράγματα not φύσις which is stressed, one wonders if the point is not simply that the obstacle to cognition lies not in the things themselves, but in the Stoic conception of cognition. Even Cicero speaking as a Clitomachean can make easy and uncomplicated reference to things in the world in *Luc.* 105, while insisting that we cannot be certain that a particular property which appears to attach to them at a particular point in time actually attaches to them. The Roman Books view would allow someone to speak of cognition in a situation where, to use Cicero's example, 'the sea is grey' is true and the sea is giving rise to a minutely detailed imprint in the observer's mind, which translates into highly detailed representational content.

The nature of the historical claim made in the Roman Books emerges from *Luc.* 12 (*minus enim acer est aduersarius is qui ista quae sunt heri defensa negat Academicos omnino dicere*) and *Ac.* 1.13 (*negaret in libris quod coram ex ipso audiebamus, duas Academias esse...*). In the Roman Books Philo had claimed that the Academics had not assumed a position of universal ἀκαταληψία (= *quae sunt heri defensa*). It is not difficult to see that this claim could be deemed a 'lie' by Antiochus as well as by Academics and how it could give rise to anger. The report in *Luc.* 12 is, however, vague in two respects: it gives no positive characterization of the attitude to knowledge which the Academics did adopt according to Philo, and it does not spell out who is comprised by 'the Academics'. It is plausible to assume, but no more than consistent with the evidence, that Philo claimed his philosophical thesis had in fact been the view of some earlier Academics,[68] but perhaps not equally plausible to assume that he would have traced that exact same view all the way back, considering that historical construction in the Academy traditionally allowed for gradual development. The Academics claimed Socrates and Plato as ancestors of course (see on *Ac.* 1.44–6), but did not usually call them 'Academics'. What suggests that Philo had situated Socrates and Plato in his account as well is the evidence from *Ac.* 1.13.[69]

Luc. 18 hints at an alternative definition of the cataleptic impression. An alternative conception of knowledge (= κατάληψις in the present context) would require, in addition, a mode of endorsement by the mind. Already available types of endorsement include Clitomachean approval, self-aware assent as posited by mitigated sceptics, and dogmatic assent, i.e. the unqualified taking of an impression as true. Given that the burden of Philo's new position appears to be that my καταλήψεις simply are those of my belief-like attitudes which are (i) true and (ii) very clear (sc. on a particular construal of clarity) as a matter of fact, not having accepted them as true, i.e. merely approving and 'following' them, would be a profoundly counterintuitive view. Thus either self-aware or dogmatic assent is likely to have been a component of the Roman position; cf. Numenius frg. 28 cited above.[70]

---

[68] Tarrant (2018: 87) dismisses the possibility that Philo might have attributed his philosophical thesis to earlier Academics, on the grounds that the Academics espoused no official views and that in *Luc.* 113 a conception of knowledge amounting to the first two clauses of the Zenonian definition is ascribed to the Peripatetics. The first issue is precisely the point of contention; on the second one, see below.

[69] Tarrant (2018: 87) states: 'Philo's "lies" resided neither in the attribution of New Academic doctrine to Plato and the New Academy, nor in the attribution of Platonic, Old Academic, or even Peripatetic doctrine to the New. Rather, it lay in a theory of two strands always (or almost always) co-existing.' I believe that Antiochus would have felt vindicated by such a claim of Philo's rather than roused to anger. For a reconstruction of the unity view of the Academy advanced in the Roman Books and a comparison with other, later unity views, see Brittain (2001: 169–254).

[70] Brittain (2001: 154–8) makes a persuasive case that the Roman Books view involved dogmatic assent and that it was an externalist position, i.e. did not make awareness of one's own cognitive state part of the definition of κατάληψις.

Reading B has been criticized as implausible in itself by some,[71] so it will be as well to note that fallibilist conceptions of knowledge have fared very well for much of the twentieth century, whereas maximalist conceptions like the Stoic one have been minority views.[72] However, a difference between the modern and the ancient debate is that the latter was conducted primarily with reference to perceptual knowledge.

In the extant parts of *Acad.* Philo's Roman position is presented as singular and as singularly unsuccessful. This makes it all the more striking that there is evidence of two epistemological positions which are characterized in very similar or even identical terms, viz. that of the Peripatetics in *Luc.* 113 and that of Metrodorus in Augustine, *Contra Acad.* 3.18.41 = t. 58. I discuss them in the commentary ad loc. and on *Luc.* 78 (cf. §60) respectively and observe here only that each of these three positions may well have been articulated in its own particular way. Moreover, it is a reasonable assumption that any view endorsed by any party in the course of this debate was formulated for the sake of the argument by Carneades at some stage.

Philo autem…quod timebat: *dum noua quaedam commouet* looks back to the agreement on κατάληψις and ἐνάργεια in §18a, as well as forward to the reason given in the *quod*-clause. The phrase *noua commouere* is not among the standard Latin expressions for 'instigating a rebellion'; *OLD* s.v. *commoueo* appropriately lists our passage under n. 15: 'to raise (a point or question) in a discussion.'

That Philo gave ground because he could not tolerate the accusation of rigidity any more provides no insight into the philosophical rationale of the Roman Books, and neither Cicero's nor Cotta's Clitomacheanism comes across as anything other than self-confident and robust. Note that Numenius frg. 28 quoted above provides a different explanation: that the clarity and consistency of his perceptual experiences made him yield and give up on suspension of judgement. However, it is not universally agreed that the fragment relates to the change from Clitomacheanism to the Roman Books, as I assume.

Cf. §12 for the reference to the elder Catulus, which the younger Catulus reported in the *Catulus*. This criticism must have related to the historical thesis, for *et…et* in *et aperte mentitur…et…in id ipsum se induit quod timebat* is distributive: the first criticism relates to the historical thesis of the Roman Books, the second one to their philosophical thesis. The thing which Philo feared must have been ἀκαταληψία. *Se induere* is aptly glossed *se irretire* in *TLL* s.v. col. 1270.18-24, i.e. there is a connotation of excessive cleverness gone wrong. *Sustinere* 'to withstand', not 'to tolerate' in this construction: tenability of the position, not pique on Philo's part, is the issue. *Mentitur* as in §12 of the deliberate telling of a falsehood, not because of *aperte* (which could modify the verb in either possible sense), but because of Antiochus' anger in §11. Manutius emended to *patre Catuli* (in the scholia); see the note in Plasberg[1] (p. 75).

Cum enim ita negaret quicquam esse…nihil posse comprehendi: the overall syntactical structure of the sentence is not obvious due to various parentheses and the

---

[71] See e.g. Glucker (2004: 142-3).
[72] See Brown (2018), esp. ch. 1; on some of the problems raised by fallibilism, see Reed (2012).

resumption of initial *cum*-clause (*Cum enim ita negaret*...) through *hoc cum infirmat tollitque Philo* before the main clause finally begins (*iudicium tollit incogniti*...).

Zeno's definition features again in *Luc.* 77 (cf. 42, 112); it is likely to have featured in the *Catulus*, too, although *Ac.* 1.40 suggests that *hesterno sermone* may refer to a passage in the *Catulus* where only the correspondence *uisum* = φαντασία was introduced.

On the terminology associated with cataleptic impressions, notably the fact that Cicero talks about *uisa* being grasped as opposed to φαντασίαι affording a grasp of things in the world, as well as his uses of the Greek terms καταληπτον and ἀκαταληπτον, see section 10; Reinhardt (2016) and (2018b). I print καταληπτόν like the Aldina and Turnebus. Most editors print ἀκαταληπτόν (thus Reid[1], Plasberg[1], Schäublin et al., and Gigon following the manuscripts), citing *negaret* as the reason why the negative Greek term was needed here. However, Cicero would have written something like *diceret nihil esse quod comprehendi posset* if an assertion made by Philo that everything was non-apprehensible was at issue here. This conclusion is only reached a little further down (*nihil posse comprehendi*), while Philo's intervention is presented as a rejoinder to Zeno's definition. The Greek term is clearly meant to correspond to *quicquam esse quod comprehendi posset* only. Independently, *Ac.* 1. 41 discussed above points to the same conclusion. Our passage, like *Ac.* 1.41, gives the impression that it introduces the term.

As to the Zenonian definition, cf. Sextus, *M.* 7.248 (= *SVF* i.59 = frg. 247 Hülser): καταληπτικὴ (sc. φαντασία) δέ ἐστιν ἡ (i) ἀπὸ ὑπάρχοντος καὶ (ii) κατ' αὐτὸ τὸ ὑπάρχον ἐναπομεμαγμένη καὶ ἐναπεσφραγισμένη, (iii) ὁποία οὐκ ἂν γένοιτο ἀπὸ μὴ ὑπάρχοντος, 'A cataleptic impression is one which is from what obtains, imprinted and stamped on in exact accordance with what obtains, which could not come about from what does not obtain.'

Comparison with *Luc.* 41 *fin.*, 77, and 112 suggests that Cicero correctly takes the first clause of the definition to stipulate veridicality rather than that a cataleptic impression arise from a real object; the formulation in our passage here maps less closely on the Greek one, by pulling the second clause in front, and relating the quality of impression to its object. Aug., *Contra Acad.* 2.5.11 (= t. 24) engages closely with the passage corresponding to *Luc.* 18 in *Ac.* 3 as well as with that corresponding to *Luc.* 77 in *Ac.* 4; a detailed discussion is in Reinhardt (2018b: 317–21).

In *hoc cum infirmat tollitque Philo, hoc* must logically refer to the *uisum* which just been defined, although grammatically it may more narrowly refer to *quod est tale quale uel falsum esse possit*: the character Lucullus may be of the view that the clauses entail one another in reverse order. (Glucker 2004: 138 sees the need for an interpretative choice here.) The emphatic affirmation given to the third clause (*qui enim potest quicquam comprehendi*...*quale uel falsum esse possit*) is one important reason for thinking that the philosophical thesis of the Roman Books amounted to the Zenonian definition minus the third clause. Another is the phrase *infirmat tollitque*, where it is more plausible that the two verbs are to be parsed as 'weaken and destroy' as opposed to 'completely destroy', in which case they would function as a pairing of synonyms; cf. Brittain (2001: 142 n. 21). A third one is that §17 suggested that clarity cannot fail to be part of a conception of cognition, which is a function of the minutely detailed correspondence between object and impression stipulated in the second clause of Zeno's definition. Truth—the subject of the first clause—is a given.

The phrasal term *iudicium incogniti et cogniti* of course stands for κριτήριον, but that does not mean that it is just a stand-in for the Greek term and semantically equivalent to it. I have translated it as a 'capacity to distinguish' since such a capacity is a recurrent concern in Lucullus' speech; it may or may not be exercised in a manner which is transparent to the perceiving subject, i.e. a subject may be able to make such discriminations without being able to explain their rationale; see section 5.2 and 5.3, as well as Striker (1996a) and Hartung (1970: 39–43) on criterion terminology. For the force of *incogniti et cogniti*, see Hofmann and Szantyr (1965: 392) on the 'Möglichkeitsbedeutung' of the perfect passive participle.

On *effictum* (⟩ *effingo*), clearly superior to *effectum*, see Plasberg[1] (p. 76). Lambinus twice emended Cicero's quite deliberate *ex eo unde* to *ex eo quod*; *unde* is also in *Contra Acad.* 2.5.11, although this would not tell against an early corruption. *Quod* would cause *esset* to mean 'exist' in both cases; cf. *Luc.* 77: *ex eo quod esset sicut esset impressum et signatum et effictum*. On the use of the dative in place of an ablative in code-switches from Latin to Greek (φαντασία), see Adams (2003: 501). On *triuimus*, see the parallels assembled by Reid[1] (p. 194).

Ita imprudens...reuoluitur: as indicated above, on the reading A Lucullus would say this even though Philo's Roman Books view represented no change whatsoever over its predecessor regarding human cognition. The proponent of reading A might reply that Lucullus is not interested in valid criticism: he would present the Roman Books thesis as an attempt to avoid ἀκαταληψία, and would then blame Philo for remaining landed with ἀκαταληψία. The rejoinder of the proponent of reading B would be that on reading A the heavy emphasis on the third clause is poorly motivated. Reid[2] translates *imprudens* as 'without knowing it'; I think Lucullus' point is better made by a failure, on Philo's part, to anticipate the predictable outcome than by the unsatisfactory end state being opaque to Philo.

Quare omnis oratio...percipi posse nihil concedimus: *quare* has forward reference and correlates with *ut*: in what follows Lucullus will try and defend the Zenonian definition whose rejection unites the Philo of his Roman Books with his predecessors. *Obtinemus* is dialectical terminology (= λαμβάνειν, 'to secure consent to a proposition', 'to obtain a proposition through the opponent's consent').

§§19–29

In §§19–27 Lucullus advances arguments for the existence and indispensability of the cataleptic impression, followed by an enquiry into the question of whether someone who consistently affirms that nothing can be apprehended must at least have apprehension of that claim (§§28–9). The overall rationale of these arguments is that, for certain universally accepted facts to be explicable and for certain doctrinal assumptions of the Stoics to come out true, one must assume that there are cataleptic impressions.[73]

---

[73] A Stoic or a Stoicizing Old Academic would not necessarily situate the boundary between universally accepted facts and Stoic doctrinal assumptions in the exact same place as the modern reader.

The structure of §§19–27 is tripartite, covering the senses, their products, and reason. This scheme is used again later in Lucullus' speech (cf. on §42) as well as in Cicero's reply (§§79–98), which engages meticulously with Lucullus' arguments.[74] The section reflects orthodox Stoic thought rather than some Antiochian version of Stoic teachings in the field of epistemology,[75] and it exhibits what one might call changes of perspective: sometimes the Stoic sage is used as a point of reference, and sometimes rational beings in general.

§19

The previous section on Philo's Roman Books had ended with Lucullus stating his intention to defend Zeno's three-clause definition of the cataleptic impression.

Here in §19 Lucullus proposes to begin with the senses (*sensūs*). The term *sensus* can have several meanings in Latin (see n. below), and some of these more specific meanings are employed in what follows. However, on first approach, with the plural and *iudicia clara et certa* in the next sentence providing a degree of disambiguation, *sensūs* is most naturally taken to mean 'perceptual faculties, sc. in the various sense modalities'. And indeed, as we shall see, complex scenarios involving perceptual judgements (as opposed to, say, episodes of pre-conceptual 'sensings') are at issue in §§19–20a.

The term *iudicia*, which also has a range of potentially applicable meanings (see n. below), is qualified by two adjectives, *clara* and *certa*. Cicero has arguably the judgements about the perceptible world afforded by our perceptual faculties in mind, but these judgements are not themselves clear and certain, or at least not in the primary sense in which these terms are used in Hellenistic philosophy; rather, the perceptual experiences which issue in these judgements are normally thus described (see n. below). None of this poses a problem of understanding, and it is economical and practical for Cicero/Lucullus to phase in the close mapping of the discussion on Stoic conceptual categories gradually. Indeed, it will become clear that Lucullus shifts in his discussion between arguments which turn on everyday conceptions about e.g. knowledge, memory, and discovery and the particular Stoic conceptualizations of such things.

The introduction of a deity who offers improved perceptual equipment—unnecessarily so—is a literary device. That the deity makes the offer to 'our nature' rather than to 'us' seems to look forward to §§30–1 (cf. Alleemudder p. 118 n. 3), where the argument for κατάληψις is given a teleological dimension: that humans are equipped

---

[74] Cf. Brittain (2006: 26–7 n. 56); and the broadly similar scheme in Diocles of Magnesia as reported by D.L. 7.49 (SVF ii.52 = part of LS 39A = frg. 255 Hülser) on Stoic discussions of λογική: ἀρέσκει τοῖς Στωικοῖς τὸν περὶ φαντασίας καὶ αἰσθήσεως προτάττειν λόγον, καθότι τὸ κριτήριον, ᾧ ἡ ἀλήθεια τῶν πραγμάτων γινώσκεται, κατὰ γένος φαντασία ἐστί, καὶ καθότι ὁ περὶ συγκαταθέσεως καὶ ὁ περὶ καταλήψεως καὶ νοήσεως λόγος, προάγων τῶν ἄλλων, οὐκ ἄνευ φαντασίας συνίσταται, 'The Stoics usually put the treatment of the subject "impression" and "perception" first, inasmuch as the criterion, by means of which the truth of matters is recognized, is generically an impression, and inasmuch as the treatment of "assent", of "apprehension", and of "thinking", which precedes the rest, is not put together without "impression".'

[75] See the discussion in Brittain (2012: passim and 105 n. 3 in particular).

in a certain way is part of nature's plan not just for them but for the universe they form part of.⁷⁶ 'Our nature' could not ask for more, so even if we felt subjectively and individually that keener senses would be conceivable and desirable (as Cicero will say in reply in *Luc.* 80), this would be unwarranted.

Lucullus then dismisses a standard type of antidogmatic argument from conflicting appearances (see n. below for parallels), which cites the pigeon's neck (which shimmers in many different colours and makes it impossible to determine its 'actual' one, which is assumed to exist, cf. *Luc.* 79) and the oar which is straight but looks bent when it is partially submerged in water. These must have featured in the previous day's discussion, i.e. in the *Catulus*: Cicero says in *Luc.* 79 that he rehearsed many arguments against the senses, including these ones. Lucullus claims not to be affected by these arguments, on the grounds that, unlike the Epicureans, he does not say that what appears to be such-and-such is such-and-such (cf. *Luc.* 45). This gestures to the Epicurean tenet that all perceptions are true, whereas the Stoics and Antiochus hold that there are true as well as false impressions. In saying this, Lucullus misrepresents the Epicurean position, and commits a wilful *ignoratio elenchi* as far as his own position is concerned. The Epicureans would have no trouble in accommodating the fact that a straight oar, under the perceptual conditions obtaining when it is partially submerged, looks bent:⁷⁷ when they claim that all αἰσθήσεις are true (cf. *Luc.* 83),⁷⁸ the term is not a synonym of φαντασία as employed by the Stoics.⁷⁹ The possibility of false impressions, granted by the Stoics, does nothing to address the problem that a merely apparent state of affairs, i.e. one which does not obtain, is able to give rise to an impression which is exactly like that caused by an actual state of affairs, qua imprint, in terms of representational content, and as far as we can tell. Cicero will stress this point in his reply in *Luc.* 80 (*tu uero, qui uisa sensibus alia uera dicas esse alia falsa, qui ea distinguis?*), observing that the Epicurean view that all perceptions are true at least tries to circumvent this problem (albeit in a way which satisfies neither Lucullus nor Cicero).

Lucullus continues with the claim that there lies *maxima ueritas* in the senses, provided they are healthy, in perfect working order, and unimpeded.⁸⁰ In support of this claim, he cites the way in which we seek to modify the conditions under which we receive impressions until we obtain one which in virtue of its inherent quality induces complete confidence in its reliability; for a very similar passage see Sext.,

---

⁷⁶ *Luc.* 28–9 can be read as an aside which disrupts the continuity between *Luc.* 19–27 and 30–1.

⁷⁷ Cf. Long and Sedley (i.1987: 86) on the Epicurean theory of vision: 'The theory seems to provide a promising answer to the standard sceptical appeals to optical illusion.... The visual impression of an oar in the water as bent is perfectly true—not as an impression of the oar's intrinsic bodily shape, on which vision is not qualified to pronounce, but, we might say, as an impression of the shape of its colour through a mixed medium of water and air.'

⁷⁸ Cf. D.L. 10.147 (*K.Δ.* 24), 10.31–2; Lucr. 4.469–521.

⁷⁹ See Taylor (1980); Annas (1992: 163–73); Asmis (2009); Warren (2013a); Hahmann (2015) and (2016); Bown (2016); Vogt (2016); and Verde (2018).

⁸⁰ Optimism about the accuracy of the senses is characteristic of Stoicism. An exception to the rule are certain passages in Seneca's *N.Q.*, which invoke the weakness of the senses, including the standard examples of conflicting appearances dismissed by Lucullus here, to explain why human enquiry into the natural world can only go so far; cf. *N.Q.* 1.2.3, 1.3.9–10, 1.17.2.

M. 7.258.[81] Allen (1994: 106), who draws particular attention to *dum aspectus ipse fidem faciat sui iudicii*, characterizes how the Academics interpret the same type of behaviour:

> The Academy construes such behaviour as a search for conditions because of our satisfaction with which we incline to the impression at issue. Whereas the Stoics regard the same behaviour as a search for an impression which, in virtue of satisfying these conditions, assures us of its truth all by itself. That is, though these conditions are causally responsible for the features of the impression that command our assent, it is not *because* the impression meets these conditions that we accept it in the sense that they furnish us with our reason for so doing. To have an evident impression that P should, if you will, already amount to being in a condition where it is evident to one that P.

§19 concludes with a remark that 'the same thing happens' (*quod idem fit*) in other sense modalities, with the consequence that nobody wants for a sharper judgement of the senses. The 'same thing' seems to be the striving for ideal perceptual conditions, which continues up to the point when the corresponding impression is not just very good according to the relevant standard, but so good as to be self-warranting. Humans cannot ask for more as a consequence of their ability to reach this point (see n. below on *requirat*).

Ordiamur igitur a sensibus…non uideam quid quaerat amplius: Lucullus begins with a self-conscious rhetorical gesture (*ordiamur*). The range of meaning and uses of *sensus* in Latin is broad (cf. the *OLD* entry and Glidden 1979, esp. the notes; Morillon 1974 [*non uidi*]), encompassing inter alia a particular sense modality, perception, as well as the kind of sensing or feeling which Epicurus called πάθος, though not usually an 'impression' (φαντασία). Here the plural and the resumption in *quorum iudicia* suggests that the perceptual faculties in the various sense modalities are meant (i.e. what Lucretius calls *uarii sensūs* in 2.683–5, 6.960, and 6.984–5). The term *iudicium*, 'legal proceedings' in its basic meaning, is used in various ways which could be applicable in an epistemological context: (the action of) examination, the exercise of judgement, (a particular) decision, a judgement (in the sense of 'considered opinion'), as well as the faculty of judging. The plural of *iudicia* may be distributive, relating to several sense modalities, or may refer to a multiplicity of judgements; it also has the effect of discouraging an identification with the concept

---

[81] Sext., *M.* 7.258 (= part of LS 40K): Διὸ δὴ καὶ πᾶς ἄνθρωπος, ὅταν τι σπουδάζῃ μετὰ ἀκριβείας καταλαμβάνεσθαι, τὴν τοιαύτην φαντασίαν ἐξ ἑαυτοῦ μεταδιώκειν φαίνεται, οἷον ἐπὶ τῶν ὁρατῶν, ὅταν ἀμυδρὰν λαμβάνῃ τοῦ ὑποκειμένου φαντασίαν. ἐντείνει γὰρ τὴν ὄψιν καὶ σύνεγγυς ἔρχεται τοῦ ὁρωμένου ὡς τέλεον μὴ πλανᾶσθαι, παρατρίβει τε τοὺς ὀφθαλμοὺς καὶ καθόλου πάντα ποιεῖ, μέχρις ἂν τρανὴν καὶ πληκτικὴν σπάσῃ τοῦ κρινομένου φαντασίαν, ὡς ἐν ταύτῃ κειμένην θεωρῶν τὴν τῆς καταλήψεως πίστιν, 'And this is why every human being, when striving to apprehend something with precision, seems to pursue an impression of this kind spontaneously, such as in the case of visible things, when the appearance he receives of the underlying thing is weak. For he strains his sight and moves close to it, so as to be entirely free of error, he rubs his eyes and takes in general all (necessary) steps, until he catches an impression of the thing being judged which is clear and striking, as if considering that the trustworthiness of the apprehension lies in this.'

of a κριτήριον (τῆς ἀληθείας), which, if used in the plural, does not normally relate to different senses but rather the set of things the Stoics recognized as criteria. At the same level of generality is *Fin.* 1.64 *sensuum iudicia*; Reid[2] mistranslates *clara iudicia et certa* as 'decisions [which] are so unclouded and so emphatic', even though Reid[1] (p. 196) plausibly suggests τρανής as a Greek counterpart for *clarus*; cf. Sext., *M.* 7.403 = LS 40H (2), and Lefebvre (2007: 348), as well as on *Ac.* 1.41 *declarationem earum rerum*. One may posit βέβαιος for *certus*. (On Lucretius' use of *certus*, including in the phrase *certa ratione*, see Fowler 2002: 176.) Yet these are properly attributes of impressions and καταλήψεις turned ἐπιστήμαι respectively, as Cicero knows, so he must have Lucullus merely gesture to technical Stoic discourse at this point.

On the offer (*OLD* s.v. *optio* no. 1a) of improved perceptual faculties to our personified *natura* rather than to us, see the general note above; for *optio* as an offer of choice (of goods, notably slaves bequeathed in a will) see Kaser (1971: 745). Reid[1] (p. 196) cites parallels featuring the term *electio*. On the device of a god offering choices, cf. Gowers (2012: 67) on Hor., *S.* 1.15–22: 'A fantasy scenario, reminiscent of Menippean satire...or mime..., in which a beneficent Jupiter offers mortals the chance to change places....' Cicero responds critically in *Luc.* 80. In Cic., *Tusc.* 2.67 a deity appears to a sailor chased by pirates and makes suggestions of possible courses of action in direct speech. Favourable comments on the senses also in Cic., *Fin.* 5.59, another Antiochian context.

Reid[1] (p. 196) comments '*quaerat* for *quaesitura sit*', but the *coniugatio periphrastica* is here optional at best.

Nec uero hoc loco expectandum est...Epicurus hoc uiderit et alia multa: *hoc loco* is another self-consciously rhetorical gesture after *ordiamur*. In *Luc.* 79 Cicero returns to the arguments (i) from the oar and (ii) from the pigeon's neck, on which see Ierodiakonou (2015). For (i), cf. the texts collected as Epicurus, frg. 252 Usener; Lucr. 4.440–2; Philon Alex., *Ebr.* 182; Sen., *N.Q.* 1.3.9; Aët. 3.5.5; Sext., *P.H.* 1.119 (context is the πέμπτος λόγος or Fifth Mode), *M.* 7.244 and 414; Plut., *Adv. Col.* ch. 25; Aristocles *ap.* Eus., *Praep. Ev.* XIV.20; Tert., *De an.* 17 (see Waszink 2010: 240–2 ad loc.), who also discusses conflicting appearances in sense modalities other than vision; Synesius, *De insomn.* 136C; Nemes., *De nat. hom.* 7; Aug., *Contra Acad.* 3.11.26 and *Trin.* 15.11.21 (see Fuhrer 1997: 353 for further instances in Augustine); Hieron., *c. Ioann. Hieros.* 35. For (ii), cf. *Fin.* 3.18; Lucr. 2.801–5; Sen., *N.Q.* 1.5.6 (on peacock feathers) and 1.7.2; D.L. 9.86; Sext., *P.H.* 1.120. See on *Luc.* 79 for further examples Cicero might have included in *Catul.*, where he said *contra sensus tam multa*, beyond the two given here. Cf. also the Pyrrhonist Fifth Mode in Sext., *P.H.* 1.118–23, which exploits conflicting appearances; Burnyeat (1979).

Videri in *quidquid uidetur* and *quale uideatur* means 'to appear phenomenally, to present itself in perceptual experience'; this is evidently not a veridical use. *Videre* in *Epicurus hoc uiderit* is mildly punning: 'Epicurus may see about this matter', i.e. the notion that what appears is true (cf. *OLD* s.v. *uideo* no. 18a 'to consider, attend to'). As noted above, when the Epicureans say that all perceptions are true, they neither mean that all φαντασίαι as conceived by the Stoics are true nor that all appearances (in the everyday sense of 'appearance') are true. Rather, they seem to be relying on a narrow and quite specific conception of perceptual content; see the studies cited above, p. 379 n. 79.

The usual quasi-photographic account of the evidence from A on *non enim is sum qui* is provided by Plasberg[1] (p. 76); *rasurae* are impossible to assign to a particular corrector, but given the constant reference of A^a to B it is likely that, given that *qui* was restored from B, what precedes was corrected by the same individual.

Meo autem iudicio est…dum aspectus ipse fidem faciat sui iudicii: *meo iudicio* is arguably self-conscious, given the subject of the paragraph. *Ita* is not to be read as restrictive, and the *si*-clause sets out the conditions under which the truth which resides in the senses would be greatest, i.e. their ability to deliver an accurate representation of states of affairs or more generally ongoings in the perceptible world; see the general note above. However, the Stoics and Antiochus do of course recognize the possibility of false impressions, and of it being frequently challenging to discriminate between true and false impressions; see on *Luc.* 47–58.

The characterization of said good conditions, notably the stipulation that there be no impediments to the senses (*quae obstant et impediunt*) suggests that Lucullus (and Antiochus) is aware of a constraint imposed by 'younger Stoics' on the possibility of a cataleptic impression winning assent. Cf. Sext., *M.* 7.253–4 (part of LS 40K); on the passage, see Allen (1994: 107–9); Brittain (2014: 338–42); Reinhardt (2018a: 241–2): Ἀλλὰ γὰρ οἱ μὲν ἀρχαιότεροι τῶν Στωικῶν κριτήριόν φασιν εἶναι τῆς ἀληθείας τὴν καταληπτικὴν ταύτην φαντασίαν, οἱ δὲ νεώτεροι προσετίθεσαν καὶ **τὸ μηδὲν ἔχουσαν ἔνστημα**. ἔσθ' ὅτε γὰρ καταληπτικὴ μὲν προσπίπτει φαντασία, ἄπιστος δὲ διὰ τὴν ἔξωθεν περίστασιν. οἷον ὅτε Ἀδμήτῳ ὁ Ἡρακλῆς τὴν Ἄλκηστιν γῆθεν ἀναγαγὼν παρέστησε, τότε ὁ Ἄδμητος ἔσπασε μὲν καταληπτικὴν φαντασίαν ἀπὸ τῆς Ἀλκήστιδος, ἠπίστει δ' αὐτῇ, 'The older Stoics say that the cataleptic impression thus defined is the criterion of truth, but the younger ones add "and which does not have an obstacle". For it is possible that a cataleptic impression occurs, but is found to be undeserving of credence because of external circumstances, as when Heracles stood with Admetus having lead Alcestis up from the underworld, Admetus received a cataleptic impression from Alcestis, but did not trust it.' This constraint was apparently added in response to Carneadean criticism. It does not affect how the cataleptic impression itself is defined and thus marks no deviation from the Zenonian definition.

The background and overall rationale of this section is covered in the general note above. The clause *dum aspectus ipse fidem faciat sui iudicii* is difficult. (Cf. *TLL* s.v. 1. *fides*, notably the overall structure of the entry.) The phrase *fidem facere* usually means 'to create conviction, belief', as in Cicero's characterization of *argumentum* in his definition of a *locus* in *Top.* 8: *Licet definire locum esse argumenti sedem, argumentum autem rationem quae rei dubiae faciat fidem*, '…an argument as a reasoning that creates belief for a doubtful issue.' Here *rei dubiae* is most likely dative, and the crucial issue is the manufacture of credence (= persuasion), which may or may not mean the generation of true beliefs in the audience. In our passage *sui iudicii* is a genitive depending on *fidem*. *Fides* can denote subjective confidence or objective reliability, and *sui* could refer to *aspectus* or to an unexpressed *quisque* (thus Reid[1] p. 197; see Kühner-Stegmann i.601–2). If *fides* only meant 'confidence in', this would pose a problem: Lucullus' argumentative aim is to show the self-warranting nature of cataleptic impressions, which also supports interpreting *sui* as referring to *aspectus*. Could *fides sui iudicii* have the sense of 'proof/confirmation of its own judgement' only, with a subjective rather than an objective genitive (and *fides* used in the sense of *OLD* s.v. no. 4a), so as to avoid the notion of subjective confidence altogether? This cannot be the whole story, either, since *fides* in that sense would more naturally go with *dare* (as in *fidem dare* 'to give an undertaking', cf. e.g. Plaut., *Mil.* 455) rather than *facere*. It is thus arguable that *fides* combines the notions of objective reliability and subjective confidence, and that the genitive *sui iudicii* is subjective and objective at the same time, depending on perspective. In the *aspectus* there must then, inter alia, lie a (correct) judgement, and *sui* must refer to it. This tells against *aspectus* denoting something that is external to ourselves and as it were in the world to be perceived (as a sight to be seen), as well as against it denoting the act of looking or gazing. For a judgement to reside in *aspectus*, the word must mean 'sight' in the sense of visual experience had by the perceiving (rational) subject (*aspectus ipse* in *N.D.* 2.15, cited by Reid[1] p. 196, is different). This would also fit with the *iudicia* of the senses mentioned at the beginning of the paragraph, and with the idea that adaptations are made so as to modify our perceptual experience. Qua visual experience, *aspectus* may also give confidence in the accuracy or veridicality of what is seen, in line with the suggested ambiguity of *fidem sui iudicii facere*. This raises a final question: why, if *aspectus* means 'visual experience', did Cicero not use his standard term for 'impression', *uisum*? I suggest tentatively that this is because of a subtle difference in sense: *uisum* means 'impression' in the sense of *that which* appears, whereas *aspectus* conveys better a notion of *how* something appears (which is salient given the overall context). All of these considerations, if along the right lines, are difficult to capture in a translation simultaneously. The sentence has given rise to quite different renderings; consider e.g. 'until our survey itself gives us confidence in our own judgement' (Reid[2]) and similarly 'bis das Hinblicken selbst Vertrauen in sein eigenes Urteil schafft' (Schäublin et al.); 'until our vision itself provides the warrant for its own judgement' (Brittain 2006). Reid[1] (p. 196) links our passage with Sext., *P.H.* 1.118 and Macrobius, *Sat.* 7.14.20-3; both passages are concerned with a sceptical mode of argument from conflicting appearances.

The corrector of V (V[2]) was able to supply *aut diducimus multaque facimus*, which the scribe had omitted, because the manuscript from which V and S descend was available when correction layer V[2] was generated; see the edition, p. lx.

Quod idem fit in uocibus...iudicium requirat acrius: see *OLD* s.v. no. 5c on the use of *uox* for 'sound'. Lucullus' point would be weakened if *requirere* meant 'to demand' (Cicero will do precisely that in his reply in *Luc.* 80). Rather, the verb must mean 'to need, i.e. to require according to the judgement of an impartial observer' (cf. *OLD* s.v. no. 4). See Reid[1] (p. 197) on the case of *sui cuiusque generis* and for the suggestion that *acrius* corresponds to ἀκριβέστερον (the comparative of ὀξύς can be so used, too, though).

§20

Having covered the untutored senses, Lucullus now moves to the way in which experience (*usus*) and training (*exercitatio*) can enhance our senses and give them a role within the enactment of an art (*ars*, τέχνη). The artist perceives an astonishing amount within the domain of his art and notably more than someone who has not mastered the relevant art. A study on the Stoic concept of familiarity (συνήθεια) invoked here is Glucker (1996), who assembles most of the evidence (see also the n. below). For relevant passages in Cicero, who in the field of vision speaks of *consuetudo* or *consuetudo oculorum*, cf. *Luc.* 57, 75, and especially 86. An important parallel passage for §20 is *N.D.* 2.145–8, the section on the human mind, the senses, and the arts in a Stoic exposition on the well-orderedness of the universe (see also the commentary on *Luc.* 30–1); however, unlike our passage, *N.D.* 2.145–8 has no need to distinguish between the perceptual abilities of the expert and non-expert, and takes the former as what human beings generally are capable of in principle.

How, one must wonder, is it possible for experts to 'perceive more', given that both experts and non-experts ought to be able to experience cataleptic (i.e. uniquely clear, detailed, and rich) impressions of the same object?[82] One possibility, developed in Reinhardt (2011) from evidence in Galen, who is likely to have drawn on Stoic thought, is that experts and non-experts receive in their impressions the same amount of, as we might say, perceptual information (and can in that sense be said to have comparable impressions of a given object, though not identical ones, since impressions are formed in unique ways by the mind which experiences them), but that experts are able to access and use more of said perceptual information. In part, this will be a consequence of their being able to conceptualize more information than someone who is not in possession of an art (on the link between conceptions and art see also on *Luc.* 21b–22 below). Thus the orthopaedic surgeon, to take an example from medicine, will be able to see more than the layman on an x-ray of a healthy but somewhat worn shoulder joint. He will be able to associate minute differences between shades of grey with different qualities and properties of the cartilage-covered parts of the joint and, accordingly, different degrees of arthrosis, but he may also be able to discern shades of grey as a consequence of his training which the layman is unable to make out. Not all of these shades need to be amenable to conceptualization, i.e. to being associated with concepts peculiar to them in a perceiving subject's mind.

While a painter's heightened appreciation of a painting, specifically the ability to 'see more' than the layman, seems explicable in these terms, Lucullus' next example poses a problem. It is open to two interpretations, and only on one of them does it cohere with the example from painting and actually serve the overall purpose of the argument. If Lucullus is talking about recognizing a particular piece of music one is familiar with, then the perceiving subject is privileged not because he is able to access consciously more of the information contained in his impression(s), but because the same information means something different to him. Moreover, recognizing a particular piece of music is possible for anyone who is familiar with it,

---

[82] There is no suggestion that on the Stoic view non-experts have non-cataleptic impressions, whereas experts experience cataleptic ones. The definition of the cataleptic impression makes no reference to the notion of an art, and the fact that the cataleptic impression is supposed to offer προκόπτοντες a path to virtue tells against restricting the ability to experience such impressions (as opposed to using them effectively) to experts.

without also being in possession of the relevant art.⁸³ On this reading, Lucullus' second example is not pertinent (and it may be Cicero rather than his source who misunderstood, in view of the example from Roman dramatic poetry and its accompaniment). Hence I am attracted by the following, second interpretation: technical expertise ought to improve type recognition, i.e. recognizing a token as an instance of a type. The musical accompaniment of plays in Rome was not composed by the dramatic poets themselves; rather, it would be arranged and added by the particular troop of actors performing the play,⁸⁴ who were, however, as Cic., *De orat.* 3.102 suggests, expected to capture the moods and personalities of the characters. For the example to cohere with the preceding one, the music played by the *tibicen* would need to be the *kind* of music which would suit a given play or character, and it would need to be unfamiliar to the person who identifies it.⁸⁵ What the technical expertise would need to enable is an association between music and content, like a Wagnerian *Leitmotiv*, but one which is not due to token recognition: a play *of this subject matter* or a character *of these properties* is ex hypothesi identifiable by *this kind* of music—to the expert.⁸⁶

Lucullus then, in a *praeteritio*, claims that in the senses of taste and smell there resides an understanding (*intelligentia*) as well. In saying this, he seems to go slightly off topic, in that the issue of whether these senses can be improved through practice and experience—the topics with which the paragraph started—is not pursued. Rather, the argumentative aim now seems to be a general rejection of ἀκαταληψία. Lucullus ends with the sense of touch, though not the everyday notion of touch, but with the technical and narrow notion of an inner touch as employed by the Cyrenaics. That the former could be improved by training was well known in antiquity (cf. e.g. Galen's writings on the pulse), but is not the issue here, and it is initially surprising that the Cyrenaics are introduced, given that they were not a primary target of the Academics and relied on a notion of touch which can only have been of limited use to the Stoics or Antiochus (but see n. below). However, two consequences of their being mentioned are that Lucullus can present the view that there are clear differences between internal and externally induced (if not representational) states as widely accepted, and that he ends the paragraph with a very narrow notion of

---

⁸³ In Cic., *N.D.* 2.146, the Stoic speaker Balbus praises the ears for their ability to judge differences in tone, pitch, and key among others, but identification would occur with reference to these parameters, consciously or unconsciously, on either reading considered here.

⁸⁴ On the subject, see Manuwald (2011: 89–90), with further literature.

⁸⁵ On either reading one needs to envisage a scenario in which it is not obvious to the perceiving subject from the context which play is being performed, as noted by Reid¹ (p. 198). He quotes Donatus, *De com.* 8.11: *Huius modi carmina ad tibias fiebant, ut his auditis multi ex populo ante dicerent quam fabulam acturi scenici essent, quam omnino spectatoribus ipsis antecedens titulus pronuntiaretur*, 'Songs of this type were performed with accompaniment by the flute, so that the moment the flute was heard, many from the people could say what play the actors were about to perform, before the title of the play itself was announced ahead of time to the spectators'; Ritschl (1845: 301–4), following earlier scholarship, thought Donatus invented all this on the basis of *Luc.* 20. On the Donatus passage see also Moore (2012: 19–21).

⁸⁶ The *tibicen* was deployed to perform opening pieces ('overtures') as well as accompany actors (in what has been called their 'arias'); the latter would leave scope for capturing the personality traits of characters and might also be suggested by *teneantur aures* **cantibus**, which, however, does not preclude the first sense (see n. below). The second option is favoured by Jocelyn (1967: 253).

perceptual content (see below on §21).[87] This then serves as the starting point for the next section.[88]

Adhibita uero exercitatione et arte...quae nos non uidemus: *exercitatio* is practice over time as so often in technical contexts (cf. e.g. *Rhet. Her.* 1.3: *exercitatio est assiduus usus consuetudoque dicendi*; OLD s.v. no. 3a, which cites the present passage); *ars* is skill generally, but also craft knowledge in the technical sense. On the technical notion of an *ars* (τέχνη) see Reinhardt and Winterbottom (2006: 301–52) on Quint. 2.17, and §22 below.

The consecutive *ut*-clause *ut oculi...aures cantibus* was bracketed by some earlier editors, but has not been suspected by editors since Reid. Davies (p. 81) held that the clause was superfluous and did not aid the sense. In fact, the clause seems to offer a metaphor (*tenere*) for the enhanced engagement with the object which technical expertise affords; since *tenere* has no ingressive uses (even when it means 'to grasp intellectually', the sense is 'to have an understanding of' rather than 'to gain' it), this should be taken as attentive engagement marked by dwelling on the object (the musical example below is somewhat misleading in that respect). For *cernat* see OLD s.v. no. 6: 'to discern with the intellect, perceive clearly'.

Someone trained in the art of painting sees more *in umbris et in eminentia*, a phrase which has been translated in various ways; cf. Reid[2]: 'in background and foreground'; Rackham (1933): 'in shadows and in the foreground'; Schäublin et al.: 'in den Schattenpartien und in der plastischen Hervorhebung'; Brittain (2006): 'in shadow and relief'. The phrase corresponds to the Greek εἰσοχαί and ἐξοχαί, terms used for apparent recesses and projections which arise from the use of perspective in a two-dimensional painting. That some kind of perspective was invented and used for σκηνογραφία in Aeschylus' time is attested in Vitr. 7.*praef*.11 (who, however, uses the terms *abscedentia* and *prominentia*, sc. objects). In Greek texts the possibility of creating three-dimensional effects on a two-dimensional surface is associated with the theme of conflicting appearances (already Plt., *Rep.* 602c–603b; Sext., *P.H.* 1.92, in connection with the First Mode, ἀπὸ τῆς διαφορᾶς τῶν αἰσθήσεων; in *P.H.* 1.120, in connection with the Fifth Mode, ὁ παρὰ τὰς θέσεις καὶ τὰ διαστήματα καὶ τοὺς τόπους) and consequently the unreliability of the senses. Not being misled by such optical effects was a matter of experience and familiarity with such phenomena (συνήθεια), on which Chrysippus wrote books (both for and against); cf. Glucker (1996), and the commentary on *Luc.* 75 and 87. In our passage, however, the ability is the ability 'to see more', i.e. presumably to make out and appreciate details which elude the non-expert (cf. *Luc.* 86: *pictor uidet quae nos non uidemus*), whereby *umbrae* and *eminentia* merely function as indications of the area in the picture with respect to which such additional insight is possible. In Cic., *N.D.* 2.145, Balbus says

---

[87] It has sometimes been suspected that the source for the survey of dogmatist views on the criterion in Sextus, *M.* 7.141–260, is Antiochus, since Antiochus is mentioned on a specific issue. The Cyrenaics feature in that survey, too, though not in connection with Antiochus, as Brittain (2012: 108–13) shows. Overall he makes a very plausible case for the view that Antiochus was not Sextus' source. It is of course compatible with this that material from *M.* 7.141–260 illuminates *Luc.* 19–27 in several places.

[88] One is tempted to compare the manner in which Aristotle sometimes uses reviews of the ἔνδοξα provided by his philosophical predecessors in order to move his discussion to a particular starting point.

that the eyes can appreciate *uenustas, ordo,* and *decentia* in works of art, and adds the ability to infer moral disposition, personality, and mood from the physical features of a human being (an ability which those trained in physiognomy possess).

Quam multa quae nos fugiunt in cantu...cum id nos ne suspicemur quidem: on Pacuvius' tragedy *Antiopa*, based on Euripides' Ἀντιόπη, see Schierl (2006: 91–130). Cicero states in *Off.* 1.114 (on which see Dyck 1996: 283–4) that he saw the actor Rupilius in the role of Antiopa. Cf. Donatus, *De com.* 8.9 (p. 30 Wessner): *deuerbia* ('spoken parts') *histriones pronuntiabant, cantica uero temperabantur modis non a poeta, sed a perito artis musicae factis.* Wisse, Winterbottom, and Fantham (2008: 33) comment on *De orat.* 3.102 (*neque id actores prius uiderunt quam ipsi poetae, quam denique illi etiam, qui fecerunt modos, a quibus utrisque summittitur aliquid, deinde augetur, extenuatur, inflatur, uariatur, distinguitur,* 'The actors did not see this [sc. that performances need to be calibrated appropriately to subject matter and context] any earlier than the poets, nor earlier than the composers; they both allow things to sink, then to rise, to become thinner and then to expand, to vary and to differentiate') that passages in Cicero, incl. the present one and *Luc.* 86 (*'Pictor uidet quae nos non uidemus', et 'simul influit tibicen, a perito carmen agnoscitur'*), imply 'the assumption that, at the very least for tragedy,...the original music was still known and played.' This does not seem a clear implication, and as explained above, it would not serve Lucullus' argument, whereas the example would illustrate the desired point if the accompanying music had been secondarily arranged, but so as to capture the mood of the play. The phrase *a perito agnoscitur* in *Luc.* 86 does not settle the matter either way (cf. the Donatus quote above).

On Ennius' *Andromacha*, see Jocelyn (1967: 81–93 and 234–61), who comments on our passage (p. 253): 'Cicero is patently referring to the personage from whom the aria comes, not the play as a whole.' Again this does not seem to be patent, although it is a possibility—however, in order to obtain the required philosophical point, one would still need to assume that accompaniment was heard for the first time even by the expert, and that the identification was based on the way in which it captured mood or personality of the character, or the dramatic situation. Jocelyn also thinks that Donatus, *De com.* 8.11 (*huiusmodi carmina ad tibias fiebant...ipsius antecedens titulus pronuntiaretur*), quoted above, p. 365 n. 85, is 'a scholastic misinterpretation' of it. However, in what follows (ibid.) our passage crumbles altogether under his sceptical gaze. On references to the *Andromacha* in Cicero see Wisse, Winterbottom, and Fantham (2008: 32).

For the distinction between αὐτοφυὴς and ἐπιστημονικὴ αἴσθησις in Philodemus' *De musica*, see Neubecker (1956: 12–16); Rispoli (1983) and (1983a).

Cantus may mean 'song' (*OLD* s.v. no. 1) or 'music of instruments' (ibid. no. 5a); see p. 365 n. 86 above. *Exaudire* not 'catching a distant or faint sound' (Reid[1] p. 198), but to pick out something in particular in the act of hearing; cf. Cic., *Sull.* 30. *In eo genere exercitati* supports the interpretation I have offered above, in that technical ability rather than just familiarity is emphasized.

Nihil necesse est de gustatu...intellegentia, etsi uitiosa, est quaedam tamen: *intellegentia* is used in its primary sense of 'faculty of understanding' (cf. *OLD* s.v. no. 1). Some have attempted to replace the attribute *uitiosa* by emendation (see Plasberg[1]

p. 77), but Reid[1] (p. 198) notes that the sense 'defective, incomplete' is widespread and satisfactory. One might try to justify the sense 'flawed, corrupt' with reference to N.D. 2.146, where Balbus speaks of cosmetic arts which can be deployed to do oneself up like a prostitute, but it would suit Lucullus' overall purpose here less well. There were, of course, sceptical counterarguments to the effect that the evidence from taste and smell was relative.

Quid de tactu...non apertissime insaniat: the sources and testimonies on Cyrenaic epistemology are collected in translation in Tsouna (1998: 143–60; 149–51 on evidence from Cicero); see also Brunschwig (1999: 251–9). Lucullus deploys them here on the assumption that the Academics misguidedly abolish salient differences between impressions, and argues that what experiences the Cyrenaics recognize fall into categories whose distinctness from one another cannot be denied. Tsouna (1998: 33) notes that our passage is the only piece of non-Sextan evidence in which views on the criterion (*ueri iudicium*) are ascribed to the Cyrenaics (the implication being that the Cyrenaics are presented in those terms by authors who themselves, for different reasons, are concerned with the criterion). Cicero replies in *Luc.* 76 that they can actually more credibly be recruited to his own cause: *Quid Cyrenaici tibi uidentur, minime contempti philosophi? Qui negant esse quicquam quod percipi possit extrinsecus: ea se sola percipere quae tactu intimo sentiant, ut dolorem ut uoluptatem, neque se quo quid colore aut quo sono sit scire, sed tantum sentire affici se quodam modo.* Cyrenaic sensings (πάθη), or so Cicero thinks, do nothing for the Stoic or Antiochian cause, since the perceiving subject cannot advance beyond the bare notion that he experiences them, i.e. towards a glimpse of the world which gives rise to them, let alone towards how that world is like.

Our passage and *Luc.* 76 'relate the physiological claim that the *pathē* are the only objects of internal touch and the epistemological thesis that they are the sole criteria of the true: the only things known are those perceived by internal touch, and they are known *because* they are so perceived; and, presumably, no external object can be known, precisely *because* it cannot be perceived in that special way' (Tsouna 1998: 19). It is conceivable that both the Academics and Antiochus were hoping to find a place for the Cyrenaics in their competing accounts of the Academic tradition, since the Cyrenaics were part of the Socratic movement. Cicero makes frequent reference to them, often critically because of the status they appeared to accord to pleasure: *De orat.* 3.62; *Luc.* 76 (see above), 131, 142; *Fin.* 1.23, 1.39, 2.39, 2.114; *Tusc.* 3.28, 3.31, 3.52, 3.76, 5.112; *N.D.* 1.2; *Off.* 1.2.

Reid[1] (p. 199) comments on the change of mood in *qui sentiet non...insaniat*, which is hard to parallel but unobjectionable; for *sentire* 'to think, believe' see *OLD* s.v. no. 6. The earlier, different use in *sentiatur* is emphatic, whereas *cui assentiatur*, proposed by Davies for *quis sentiatur*, is unattractive since assent would come in oddly here; an *interpretatio Stoica* of the Cyrenaics would be unmotivated.

§§21–22

In §21 Lucullus enumerates a series of increasingly more complex types of thought, which initially arise from the senses alone but soon involve the mind, too; it is not plainly stated why this mode of presentation is chosen. §22 is concerned with conceptions (*notitiae*; ἔννοιαι), which, or so Lucullus argues, can only arise from (repeated) cataleptic impressions, and proceeds to the things that rely on conceptions, memory, and art (τέχνη). The section is LS 39C = FDS 346 (§21); LS 40M (§22 down to *quod non animo comprehendit et tenet*); SVF i.73 (§22 *Ars uero quae potest...perceptionibus constat*); LS42B (*Ars uero quae potest esse...conficere uersus*).

The account in §21 can be read in two (compatible) ways, diachronically or synchronically. On the former view, it is a developmental account, mapping out the process of becoming rational with reference to the kind of thought humans are able to entertain at each stage. In this case rationality is conceived as the state in which the mind is in possession of a sufficiently large body of conceptions which are capable of articulation and suitably interrelated;[89] the parts of *sequi* which mark the transition from one step to the next (*sequuntur, sequitur*) in §21 would then in part be indicative of relative chronology. On the synchronic view, it offers a hierarchy of thoughts as they are experienced by human beings at any one time; on this reading, it may or may not be assumed that thoughts of the first type are notionally part of any of the higher thoughts distinguished.[90]

The process of becoming rational crucially depends on the subject experiencing true impressions (which are thoughts). Initially the content of these impressions would not be even partially conceptualized, nor would the subject accept them by assenting to them (since the faculty of assent is a function of being rational and only develops after some time); rather, their acceptance would be a fully automatic process. A point of contact with the preceding paragraph, highlighted through *atqui qualia sunt haec...*, is that Cyrenaic πάθη are similar to the starting point of the series in §21b, in that they are mere affections, unconceptualized, without propositional content, and have not won assent. See the nn. below on the types of thought distinguished.

The development of the human mind and emergence of reason is described in Aët. 4.11.1–4 (= LS 39E = SVF ii.83):

Οἱ Στωικοί φασιν· ὅταν γεννηθῇ ὁ ἄνθρωπος, ἔχει τὸ ἡγεμονικὸν μέρος τῆς ψυχῆς ὥσπερ χαρτίον εὔεργον εἰς ἀπογραφήν. εἰς τοῦτο μίαν ἑκάστην τῶν ἐννοιῶν ἐναπογράφεται. πρῶτος δὲ [ὁ] τῆς ἀναγραφῆς τρόπος ὁ διὰ τῶν αἰσθήσεων· αἰσθανόμενοι γάρ τινος οἷον λευκοῦ, ἀπελθόντος αὐτοῦ μνήμην ἔχουσιν· ὅταν δ' ὁμοειδεῖς πολλαὶ μνῆμαι γένωνται, τότε φαμὲν ἔχειν ἐμπειρίαν. ἐμπειρία γάρ ἐστι τὸ τῶν ὁμοειδῶν ⟨φαντασιῶν⟩ πλῆθος. τῶν δ' ἐννοιῶν αἱ μὲν φυσικῶς γίνονται κατὰ τοὺς εἰρημένους τρόπους καὶ ἀνεπιτεχνήτως, αἱ δ' ἤδη δι' ἡμετέρας διδασκαλίας καὶ ἐπιμελείας· αὗται μὲν οὖν ἔννοιαι καλοῦνται μόνον, ἐκεῖναι δὲ καὶ προλήψεις. ὁ δὲ λόγος, καθ' ὃν προσαγορευόμεθα λογικοί, ἐκ τῶν προλήψεων συμπληροῦσθαι λέγεται κατὰ τὴν πρώτην ἑβδομάδα.

---

[89] Cf. Galen, *De Hipp. et Plat. Plac.* 5.3 = part of SVF ii. 841: [The λόγος is] ἐννοιῶν τέ τινων καὶ προλήψεων ἄθροισμα.

[90] On §21, see Sedley (1982: 259), who speaks of 'the inductive element in the human learning process' which the Stoics posited; Atherton (1993: 43 and 113–14 n. 80); Brittain (2006: 14–15 n. 25); Brittain (2012: 113–17), who shows that §21 is unlikely to reflect Peripatetic thought partially, as Barnes (1997: 83–4) and Karamanolis (2006: 65–9) hold.

> The Stoics say: when a man is born, he has the ruling part of his soul like a sheet of writing material ready to be written upon. On this he inscribes each one of his conceptions. The first mode of inscription is the one through perceptions: for by perceiving something white, they retain the memory of it once it is gone. And when many memories of similar kind have arisen, then we say he has experience. For experience is the assortment of impressions which are similar in kind. Of the conceptions some arise naturally according to the aforementioned modes and without design, while others arise through our instruction and application. The latter are called 'conceptions' only, the former are called 'preconceptions' as well. Reason, for which we are called rational, is said to be completed from our preconceptions during our first seven years.

In Long and Sedley (1987) §21 features, alongside LS 39E just quoted, in the section on impressions, although §21 does not mention impressions explicitly; however, the point must have been apparent from the discussion in the *Catulus* (cf. *Ac.* 1.40–1, to whose counterpart in the first edition Plut., *Cic.* 40 = t. 67 probably alludes). On how the Stoics conceived of reason and the emergence of rationality, see Frede (1994) and Brittain (2005: 178–85), as well as on *Luc.* 30–1.

Reid[1] (p. 199) cites Sextus, *M.* 7.344–7, as a parallel to §21, which 'must partly come from the same source'. While there are close correspondences, Sextus is concerned with something different: an argument by elimination, where he seeks to show that human beings can discover truth neither through the senses, nor through the intellect, nor through a collaboration of the two. In the course of this Sextus used inter alia a Stoic account of how humans become rational. If what Lucullus reports here and what Sextus says in the passage cited ultimately go back to the same source, this will be unilluminating for our purposes, since there is no reason to think Cicero/Antiochus and Sextus drew on the same proximate source.

§21 ends with the statement that without conceptions (*notitiae*, ἔννοιαι) understanding and inquiry are impossible. §22 runs on and states that, for rational thought to be possible, conceptions must be true and cannot have arisen from *uisa* which, while true, cannot be discriminated from false ones. The last item in the sequence in §21 was a complex proposition which contained a definition of *homo*, and although the immediately following sentence does not clarify precisely how *notitiae* are related to items which can be unfolded in this way, the 'truth' of a *notitia* must be at least related to, if not amount to, the truth of the relevant proposition. The content of this *notitia* is given in the form of a conditional, which contains no demonstrative pronouns suggesting that the conditional is meant to capture a thought arising from a human being's encounter with another human being. A natural explanation of this would be that the content of the *notitia* is meant to have come about through repeated cataleptic impressions which the subject experienced during encounters with particular human beings.[91]

---

[91] In *Luc.* 106–107a the Cicero character will rebut several of the points raised in §22, notably the alleged indispensability of the cataleptic impression for any account of memory and of craft knowledge; the significance of concepts for inquiry does not receive a rebuttal.

Memory, without which philosophy, everyday life, and the arts would be impossible, would be abolished, sc. if there were no cataleptic impressions. For, Lucullus explains, there can be no memory of *falsa*, or indeed of *uera* which could be false (i.e. memories which arise from impressions which meet the first two clauses of the Zenonian definition but not the third one). The subsequent context suggests that this is not a point about the nature of memory, but rather a linguistic point about the way in which verbs like 'I remember' are used: in a factive way, whereby factivity is understood as follows (Hazlett 2010: 3):

> Certain two-place predicates, including 'knows', 'learns', 'remembers', and 'realizes', which denote relations between persons and propositions, are factive in this sense: an utterance of 'S knows p' is true only if p, an utterance of 'S learned p' is true only if p, and so on.

On this reading, developed in Reinhardt (2019), Lucullus is making the point that his conception of knowledge, specifically the point of contention in the entire debate between Stoics and Academics (§78 *init.*)—the requirement formulated in the third clause of Zeno's definition—, is presupposed by and encoded into normal Latin usage. (Factive verbs are, however, available in Greek, too, so the argument is not contingent on the fact that Cicero is writing in Latin. Antiochus may have argued along similar lines. Cf. §27 *fin.*)

It is noteworthy that Cicero, when he replies to Lucullus (§106), does not address the linguistic consideration and instead takes the question to be whether one can remember that one experienced a false impression at a particular time (this is a possibility of course, but in that case one would not say 'I remember that *p*', where *p* expresses the content of the false impression). Modern approaches to questioning if there is such a thing as factivity typically involve the use of counterexamples, which, however, can usually be disarmed by observing that the usages in question are semantically deviant. A more promising rejoinder would have been that, while there are factive expressions in Latin, whose function is indeed predicated on a conception of knowledge which is relevantly like Antiochus', one can equally find expressions which seem to presuppose different, more relaxed assumptions (cf. *Luc.* 146). Thus a general argument that the way in which Romans talk reveals a consensus about the nature of knowledge would not be compelling.

Lucullus then suggests that there could be no art ($\tau \acute{\epsilon} \chi \nu \eta$) without cataleptic impressions—'not just one or two but many'. Cicero is here alluding a particular conception of an art, devised by the Stoics and part of their system, but found in a wide range of technical texts which are not overtly Stoic; cf. Olympiodorus *in Plat. Gorg.* pp. 53–4 Jahn (= *SVF* i.21): Ζήνων δέ φησιν ὅτι τέχνη ἐστὶ σύστημα ἐκ καταλήψεων συγγεγυμνασμένων πρός τι τέλος εὔχρηστον τῶν ἐν τῷ βίῳ.

A craft is an organized body of knowledge whose individual elements are characterized as καταλήψεις, i.e. what humans are left with when they give assent to a cataleptic impression. What a craftsman knows qua craftsman is due to apprehension, directly or indirectly (e.g. in the case of a craft learnt in part from books).[92] Craft

---

[92] On the Stoic understanding of τέχνη/ars, see Barnes (2015b).

knowledge must rely on conceptions which are the result of repeated perception, and the artist must be capable of articulating them through definitions.

However, Lucullus does not just claim this, relying—on the Cicero character's view—on assumptions about the nature of crafts which he has no reason whatsoever to share (cf. §146), but invokes—this time explicitly—linguistic usage again: we call certain people artists, while withholding the title from others (and not randomly so: *Non enim fortuito hunc artificem dicemus esse, illum negabimus*), and we do so on the grounds that we take the artists to have firmly apprehended something, unlike the laymen.

The paragraph concludes with a broadening of the point: using a conventional distinction between theoretical and creative arts, Lucullus states his point is as applicable to a theoretical art like geometry as it is to a creative art like music. He then appears to add a third type of art, which involves the physical creation of a product as well as 'action' (the latter is not characterized further).

Atqui qualia sunt haec quae sensibus percipi dicimus...non sensibus: this section of §21 introduces the first two types of perceptual thought which arise from—cataleptic, it must be assumed—impressions of some kind. *Atqui* marks a sense break, which is compatible with *atqui qualia...percipi dicimus* introducing, by means of a backward reference to Cyrenaic πάθη, a kind of perceptual thought which involves the senses only, as distinct from the mind. *Talia...animo...comprehensa non sensibus* is then concerned with the next step, which already involves the mind. On this level, things within the perceiving subject's ken (marked through deictic demonstratives) are connected with basic conceptions of sensible qualities, yielding impressions which have propositional content. However, *animo...haec tenemus comprehensa, non sensibus* seems to confirm that already the very first type of impressions was deemed capable of apprehending, albeit with the senses only; Reid[1] (p. 200) is right to explain *tenemus comprehensa* as *tenemus postquam comprehendimus*. For the *qualia...talia* correlation, cf. *Luc.* 58 and Celsus, *De med.* 1.pr.41.2.

"Ille" deinceps "...animal est mortale rationis particeps": 'we are not told what the difference between a conception like 'white' or 'sweet' on the one hand and 'dog' or 'horse' on the other is supposed to be, but Sextus, *M.* 7.346–7, furnishes this information: what a single sense delivers does not involve 'combination' (σύνθεσις), whereas 'man' is a combination of colour, size, form, and other properties; see also the report on Chrysippus in Chalcidius ch. 220, p. 233 Waszink (= LS 53G = part of *SVF* ii.879) on reason as unified consciousness. Again, the pronoun *ille* seems to indicate that impressions arising in encounters with a horse or a dog are at issue.

Series itself means 'series', i.e. the last stage in the progression is itself called a series rather than an item in a series. The conditional which relates the content of an ἔννοια can be called *maiora nectens* because it includes yet more complex conceptions (like 'mortal', 'rational') than 'dog' or 'horse' above. These conceptions—referred to in the plural (*haec, amplectuntur*)—are said to comprise an, 'as it were', filled-out apprehension of things, i.e. a κατάληψις which is capable of the kind of spelling-out provided by the conditional.

The conditional, while not including a demonstrative unlike the previous items in the series (see above), gives a standard definition of 'human being'. The idea must be that a conception formed by a human mind, having arisen from repeated cataleptic impressions, is capable of articulation so as to yield a definition. Brittain (2012: 115 n. 28) notes the correspondence between the definition of human being and *M.* 11.8-11, which is influenced by Chrysippus. Augustine uses the definition in a number of passages (listed by Hagendahl 1967: 60-1).

Two structuring devices are in an unusual position, *ut haec* (which Walker cited by Davies proposed to move behind *amplectuntur*) and *deinceps* following rather than preceding *ille*. Cf. also *primum* in §24 *init.*

Quo e genere nobis notitiae rerum imprimuntur…disputari potest: *quo e genere* might be taken to suggest that the example described a particular perceptual experience, and that experiences of this kind gave rise to *notitiae*. It would fit with this reading that the verb *imprimuntur* more naturally describes a process of imprinting rather than a state of something being inscribed. However, in that case the example's conditional form would be peculiar, and given the absence of demonstratives in said example, the sentence is more plausibly read as amounting to 'our *notitiae* are of this kind', with *imprimuntur* reminding the reader of the connection between impressions and conceptions (cf. *Ac.* 1.42 on this point). On the question of whether impressions are imprints on or alterations of the mind, see p. lv.

On *quaeri*, the role which conceptions play, according to the Stoic view, in investigation of inquiry/investigation, and the Stoic response to the Meno's paradox, see Fine (2014: 257-98); the present passage is discussed on p. 257. Inquiry is treated in greater detail in *Luc.* 26.

On *notititia* (and related terms) as a rendering for 'concept', see the commentary on *Luc.* 30-1. Reid[1] prints the corrector's *disputariue*; I have opted for the transmitted *disputari* since inquiry and debate are two quite different things.

§22

Quod si essent falsae notitiae…quid repugnaret uideremus: *falsae notitiae*, on the most natural reading, are those which, if unfolded into a conditional as in the last example of §21, involve a predicate which does not apply to its subject. Having such *notitiae* might lead to various types of cognitive failure, e.g. when we encounter an object or living being but fail to classify it appropriately. And *notitiae* which had arisen from impressions which, while true, could have been false (i.e. did not meet the third clause of Zeno's definition), would not be useable because judgements which were made involving them e.g. in the conceptualization of the object of an impression, could turn out to be false. This in turn would fundamentally impair our ability to reason and to think, in that what follows from and is consistent with a given judgement could change. Cf. Galen *in Hippocr. de med. officina* XVIII b.649-50 Kühn = *SVF* ii.135 = *FDS* 528: Τῶν αἰσθήσεων ἁπάσαις τὴν γνώμην ἐφεξῆς ἔταξεν, ὅπερ ἐστὶ τὴν διάνοιαν, ἥν τε καὶ νοῦν καὶ φρένα καὶ λόγον κοινῶς οἱ ἄνθρωποι καλοῦσιν. ἐπεὶ δὲ καὶ τῶν κατὰ φωνὴν ἐστί τις λόγος, ἀφορίζοντες οὖν τοῦτον τὸν προειρημένον λόγον οἱ φιλόσοφοι καλοῦσιν ἐνδιάθετον, ᾧ λόγῳ τά τε ἀκόλουθα καὶ τὰ μαχόμενα γιγνωσκομένοις ἐμπεριέχεται καὶ διαίρεσις καὶ σύνθεσις καὶ ἀνάλυσις καὶ ἀπόδειξις,

'He (sc. Hippocrates) attached insight to all perception, i.e. reason, which people commonly call sense, understanding, and rationality. But because there is also a certain rationality to sound formations, the philosophers separate this one out and call it "inner rationality": through it we recognise what follows what and what is incompatible, which includes division, combination, analysis, and proof.'

According to the parenthesis the Cicero character (*tu*) used the term *notitia* in the *Catulus* (it is less likely that the character is addressed about something Cicero the author did). If *uidebare* is not just phraseological, it suggests that Cicero used the Latin term but did not signal which Greek term it rendered. In the extant part of *Ac.* 1 *notitia* does not feature; rather, the term *notio* is used, on both occasions by Varro (1.32, 1.42). Thus it is plausible to assume that the reference is to a section of *Catul.* corresponding to the lost part of *Ac.* 1. The issue might have been craft knowledge (as here), but other subjects are conceivable, too. A topic on which there is a substantial amount of Pyrrhonist material but no Academic evidence, although the topic must have been of concern for both schools, is how sceptical enquiry is possible for someone who disavows concepts formed in the manner assumed by the dogmatist. See Sext., *P.H.* 2.1–12; *M.* 8.337–42; in general Vogt (2006), (2010: §4.4, subsection ii), (2012: 140–56). Vogt (2010a: 175–7) distinguishes a variety of the ἀπραξία-charge where the πρᾶξις at issue is investigation. That the Cicero character touched on the subject at all is further evidence that he did not restrict himself to arguments against the senses (cf. *Luc.* 79 *init.* and section 9.2).

Discernere 'to discriminate' need not carry the implication that the perceiving subject which makes the discrimination has conscious awareness of the properties of an impression which enable the discrimination; see section 5.3. I print *eae falsae* (like Plasberg¹ 1908; Reid¹ has *hae falsae*) and *iis modo* (like Reid¹; Plasberg¹ has *his modo*); both instances of the pronoun are resumptive, and in either case I cannot detect the 'closeness' to the speaker which a part of *hic* would convey. Reid¹ (p. 200) suggests that *uteremur* is used like *sequeremur* elsewhere, but *sequi* is a term 'owned' by the Academics and implies non-assent; the Antiochian would not use it in this sense. *Visis* must be instrumental ablative not dative; the repetition of *uisa* with *qualia* is a common clarifying device in relative clauses.

Memoriae quidem certe…quod non animo comprehendit et tenet: for both memory and craft knowledge, cf. Sext., *M.* 7.373 (= *SVF* i.64 = *FDS* 403): ἀλλ' εἰ τοῦτο, ἀναιρεῖται μὲν μνήμη, θησαυρισμὸς οὖσα φαντασιῶν, ἀναιρεῖται δὲ πᾶσα τέχνη· σύστημα γὰρ ἦν καὶ ἄθροισμα καταλήψεων, 'But if this is so, then memory, which is "a storehouse of impressions", is abolished, and any craft is abolished. For it was taken to be "a system and collection of impressions".' As noted above, the possibility of misremembering something or of remembering a false impression which one experienced at some point provide such obvious rejoinders that it is questionable that Lucullus wants to deny the existence of these phenomena. I have therefore suggested in the general note above that the point that is being made turns on the use of expressions like 'I remember that *p*', which one could make plain by using inverted commas; see Cicero's reply in §106. Brittain (2012: 112) notes that 'Lucullus accepts the Stoic account of memory, in which it is defined as the retention of a proposition rather than an irrational sensory input.' Reid¹ (p. 201) links the topic of false memory to Plt. *Soph.* and *Tht.* (cf. e.g. 196d1–200d4); while there is no marked reference here, I do assume that especially *Tht.* was important for Antiochus in articulating his epistemological position; see on *Ac.* 1.30-2 and 1.40-2, and Reinhardt (2018).

In *non animo comprehendit et tenet*, the latter verb comes close to being a synonym of *comprehendit* (which is, however, most likely perfect, not present tense); cf. *Luc.* 21 *animo…tenemus comprehensa.*

Ars uero quae potest esse…uidemus, alterum non item: cf. Sext., *M.* 7.224: ἀλλ' ὁ μὲν ἀθροισμὸς τῶν τοιούτων τοῦ νοῦ φαντασμάτων καὶ ἡ συγκεφαλαίωσις τῶν ἐπὶ μέρους εἰς τὸ καθόλου ἔννοια καλεῖται, ἐν δὲ τῷ ἀθροισμῷ τούτῳ καὶ τῇ συγκεφαλαιώσει τελευταῖον ὑφίσταται ἥ τε ἐπιστήμη καὶ τέχνη, ἐπιστήμη μὲν ⟨ἡ⟩ τὸ ἀκριβὲς καὶ ἀδιάπτωτον ἔχουσα, τέχνη δὲ ἡ μὴ πάντως τοιαύτη, 'But the gathering together of such images arising in the mind, and the encapsulation of the particulars into a universal, is called conception. Finally, in this gathering together and encapsulation knowledge and craft are constituted, knowledge being such that it has precision and freedom from error, craft being such that it is not entirely like this.' This extract illuminates, with a degree of terminological variation, why Lucullus can posit invariably true ἔννοιαι as a necessary condition for the existence of craft knowledge when the standard definition of τέχνη (cited above) states that it is a σύστημα made up from καταλήψεις. The relationship between τέχνη and ἐπιστήμη in Stoic thought is notoriously hard to pin down (see Menn 1995), and Lucullus does not raise it here, even though the sage is frequently invoked in these paragraphs; the Cicero character will argue in *Luc.* 144-6 that Lucullus' understanding of τέχνη makes it the exclusive province of the sage, with manifestly absurd consequences. Because it is obvious from the larger contexts that a craft is a disposition of the mind, *animi* might seem superfluous and a potential gloss; it is, however, protected by parallel Greek texts (see νοῦ in *M.* 7.224 above).

Quam si subtraxeris…alterum non item: Madvig (1826: 139) rightly suggested that *quam* must be picking up *perceptionem* (not *artem*), and that the shift from plural to singular is possible because the latter is generic (thus the emendation *quas si* by Walker cited by Davies is unnecessary). The broader context remains concerned with the indispensability of the cataleptic impression.

Dicemus relates to ordinary usage and the way people generally speak about craftsmen. The scope of the first-person plural is human beings, rather than philosophers or Antiochians. The illocutionary force of the future tense in *dicemus* is to invite the agreement of the audience. This reading would be untouched if one interpreted *dicemus* as 'we shall assert' and the dependent construction as an accusative with infinitive. See Reinhardt (2019: 157).

On *subtrahere*, see *OLD* s.v. no. 6. With *distingues*, cf. *discerni* above. Lambinus (1566) modified to *uidebimus* in line with the main clause.

Cumque artium aliud eius modi genus sit…in faciendo atque agendo: on the division between theoretical, practical, and 'creative' arts, see Tatarkiewicz (1963); Reinhardt and Winterbottom (2006: 353-7) on Quint. 2.18, who also discuss the origin of the division (Aristotle).

For the *uerba uidendi*, uses in the sense of 'seeing with the mind's eye' (cf. *animo cernere* here) are frequently attested. 'To see *clearly and distinctly*' is a recurrent use of *cernere*, which is etymologically connected with κρίνειν; see the notes by Piazzi (2005) on Lucr. 1.642, 1.660, and 1.915, as well as Reinhardt (2016: 88–9). On the role accorded to evidence, i.e. the property of being evident and incapable of proof (αὐτόπιστος), in ancient geometrical works, see Mueller (1991) and Netz (1999: 169–85).

Reid[1] (p. 202) notes that *explere numerum* = 'to make up a [sc. required] number' is conventional, but unparalleled in an application to music. It is likely that *explere numeros* and *conficere uersus* are to be taken together here, so that the composition of a line in such a way that it fits a metrical schema (a common use of *numerus*) is at issue.

For *in faciendo atque agendo*, cf. Quint. 2.18.1. Reid[1] (p. 202) notes that *continget* has no connotation of 'good fortune'. On *nulla sunt* for *non sunt*, see Hofmann-Szantyr p. 205.

Quid enim est quod arte effici possit...multa perceperit: in relevant discussions there is often a distinction between τέχνη and τριβή (also ἐμπειρία); cf. Plt., *Grg.* 463b4 with Dodds (1959: 225); Quint. 2.15.23: *usum dicendi (nam hoc* τριβή *significat)*, with Reinhardt and Winterbottom (2006: 258). Τριβή is a 'knack', an ability to perform tasks in a manner that is governed by intuitive experience rather than knowledge. While the outcomes thus achieved are often respectable, as is usually acknowledged, the rationale of his approach is usually not transparent to the performing agent, who is thus not properly accountable for what he does (unlike someone who proceeds *arte*). On accountability as a feature which distinguishes a craft/art from a knack, see Reinhardt (2007: 87–8).

§§23–25

This section covers virtue (§23), wisdom (§24), and action (§25), but the three topics are bound up with each other in various ways: e.g., being virtuous is the mark of the wise man, who is an explicit reference point in §23 and arguably in the background in §§24–5. Presentationally, the passage combines considerations which point to the doctrinal indispensability of the cataleptic impression with the citation of widely held opinions about the subjects under discussion which dovetail with Stoic doctrine. This continues the trend in evidence in the preceding section of presenting Lucullus' stance as ingrained in traditional Roman attitudes and conventional linguistic usage.

In §23 Lucullus begins with the assertion that the *uirtutum cognitio* in particular provides confirmation that many things can be apprehended (*percipi et comprehendi*, the passive infinitive of two of the terms which Cicero uses in the sense of 'to apprehend sc. through a cataleptic impression'). One translation of *uirtutum cognitio*, suggested by Reid[1], and adopted, e.g., by Brittain (2006), is 'the study of virtues'. This sense is in evidence elsewhere in Cicero, but would be somewhat misleading in a context where proof of the existence of cataleptic impressions is the topic, given that *cognitio* is one of the terms used to render κατάληψις. One thus wonders if *cognitio* means κατάληψις here and if *uirtutum* is a subjective genitive, so that the phrase means 'the (kind of) κατάληψις which is peculiar to virtues'. This reading, adopted also by Schäublin et al., gives good sense, in that the following sentence describes the kind of κατάληψις which is constitutive of virtue: the one which is called ἐπιστήμη, which is distinguished from the κατάληψις which non-sages experience by the fact that it is stable and immutable (which means that one cannot be reasoned out of such a κατάληψις because it is secured by its consistency with numerous other καταλήψεις—false beliefs held by a subject, by contrast, may cause the subject to let go of καταλήψεις on grounds of inconsistency).

In the various virtues wisdom (*sapientia*) is also said to reside, glossed as the art of living, which derives steadfastness (*constantia*) from itself. And for this steadfastness to arise, it must have something which is 'grasped and apprehended', sc. by means of a cataleptic impression. Now wisdom, trivially, is the state of the wise man, who is in possession of all the virtues—his steadfastness, as §24 *init.* makes clear, derives from the fact that he has second-order knowledge of his state, i.e. of the fact that all of his beliefs are true and, in virtue of being true, consistent with each other. This being so, he can be certain about his judgements and about any courses of action taken which, on the Stoic view (cf. §25), inevitably involve judgements. This is illustrated by the behaviour of the sage under torture: he would not neglect his duty or break trust precisely because of his unqualified confidence in his judgements. That wisdom is the art of living is not a manner of speaking but part of the Socratic heritage of Stoic thought: their conception of a virtue and of wisdom is an extreme form of the Socratic conception of virtue knowledge as found in the early dialogues of Plato. Acting in accordance with a virtue is deemed to resemble acting in accordance with a craft, and having a craft means having one's mind configured in a certain way so that the craft is, on one level of description, a disposition of the craftsman's mind; mutatis mutandis the same is true of virtue.[93]

§24 then takes a closer look at wisdom itself, clarifying and stating explicitly in the first sentence the point that wisdom crucially involves, on the part of the wise man, a second-order awareness of his state. That this point is only made explicit here while it is mentioned in ambiguous terms at best in §23 is due to presentational economy. The second sentence (*Deinde quo modo*...) then proceeds to the question how wisdom is supposed to do anything if it cannot be certain that the individual items of knowledge which constitute it have been apprehended: thus wisdom must be certain what the highest good is so as to select the right ones among possible courses of action, which at bottom requires assent to impressions which are cataleptic and which are in agreement with nature. The concept of nature invoked here is not explained, but Lucullus is clearly alluding to the Stoic concept of οἰκείωσις (see the n. below).

In the final sentence of §24 Lucullus asserts that 'otherwise' (*aliter*) an impulse to action (ὁρμή) was impossible 'for us' (*impellimur, appetimus*). The first sentence of §25 states that the impression which gives rise to an impulse must be such that it (is true and) must not be indistinguishable from what is false (see n. below on *discerni*). This might seem to run together two issues:[94] on the Stoic view any action, even

---

[93] There are anti-Academic arguments to the effect that scepticism leads to immorality and lawlessness; these typically turn on ἐποχή not on the rejection of κατάληψις. See on *Luc.* 37–9.
[94] Cf. Brittain (2006: 17 n. 32).

foolish and misguided ones, must be the result of assent to a hormetic impression, but in such cases the impression will not need to be cataleptic or even true for action to occur. It is only the sage's actions which are invariably the result of assent to cataleptic hormetic impressions.[95] The sage and his state—wisdom—had been the subject of §24. What might suggest that the sage has been dropped as reference point is the first-person plural of the verbs (*impellimur, appetimus*), which makes it seem as if from here human beings in general are meant. But since §25 *init.* speaks of action caused by true impressions only, it seems preferable to assume that the focus has not moved away from the sage and that action in general only momentarily comes into view.[96] This would also be in line with the stated purpose of Lucullus' speech: to show that the assumption that there are cataleptic impressions is indispensable.

On Stoic moral psychology and the Stoic view of action, see *SVF* iii.169–77; LS 56A and the texts in section 57; Inwood (1985: 42–101); Annas (1992: 89–102); Donini and Inwood (1999: 690–9); Brennan (2003); Vogt (2008: 164–78). The Stoics, and following them Antiochus, held that motivations can be analysed as types of belief, whereby misguided motivations are analysed as false beliefs. Human beings, unlike other animals, experience impulses, ὁρμαί, which are rational, i.e. arising in a mind (in the required sense). An impulse is the result of assent given to a particular kind of impression (a ὁρμητική φαντασία), and as such a belief; the particular kind of impression has as its content a proposition in which an evaluative predicate (e.g. 'good' or 'bad'), is predicated of a subject (see Arius Didymus *ap.* Stob., *Ecl.* II.7, p. 88 Wachsmuth = *SVF* iii.171 in particular). On the Stoic view, experiencing a ὁρμή after having assented to a hormetic impression is sufficient for action: once the impulse is there, action ensues. Resisting an impulse is not considered a possibility, unless it was a manner of speaking for entertaining but not assenting to a hormetic impression.

§25 contains instances of parts of *uideri* in the sense of 'to appear truly' rather than just 'to appear', which raises questions about how the *Academica* articulates its philosophical content. These are explored in Reinhardt (2016). While in Greek the distinction between cataleptic and mere impressions is easily marked by adding an attribute to the term φαντασία, in Latin the distinction is less clearly marked, though it can be inferred from the context. Cicero chose to render φαντασία by means of a pre-existing Latin term (*uisum*) which offered these semantic options, perhaps because he wanted to capture the fact that competing intuitions about perception (perceptions as representing the world, possibly in a distorted way vs perceptions as representing the world, usually truly) are encoded into Latin usage.

Maxime uero uirtutum cognitio...unde nata sit aut quo modo: cf. Cic., *De orat.* 2.348:...*oratori uirtutum omnium cognitionem, sine qua laudatio effici non possit,* where knowledge *about* virtues seems to be at issue; *Tusc.* 5.71: *hinc illa cognitio uirtutis existit, efflorescunt genera partesque uirtutum, inuenitur, quid sit quod natura*

---

[95] See §§37–9 on varieties of the the ἀπραξία-argument.
[96] This means that *aliter* in the final sentence of §24 looks back to what immediately precedes and can be spelt out as: if the content of an impression which gives rise to action for wisdom was not 'firmly established' (*constitui*) and 'in accordance with nature'.

spectet extremum in bonis, quid in malis ultimum, quo referenda sint officia, quae degendae aetatis ratio deligenda, from a description of ethics as a part of philosophy (*cognitio uirtutis* perhaps 'theoretical understanding of virtue', with *uirtutis* as a generic singular). Thus Reid[2] and Brittain (2006) here ('theory of the virtues'; 'study of the virtues'). I have argued for *uirtutum cognitio* = 'the (kind of) κατάληψις which is peculiar to virtues' in the general note above.

That only 'in virtues' there is *scientia* means, given what follows, that the καταλήψεις which constitute virtue, a disposition peculiar to the sage, are all ἐπιστῆμαι. *In quibus* picks up *multa*, not '*in percipiendo et comprehendo*', as Plasberg[1] (p. 78) suggests.

The slightly baffling series of identity statements can easily be elucidated through parallels in Cicero and elsewhere, but it might seem unlikely that a passage like this one would be transparent for the original readership. However, that the following sentence occurs in Varro's speech in *Ac.* 1.41 (see nn. ibid. for Greek parallels), in the section on Stoic 'corrections' of Old Academic doctrine, and that Plut., *Cic.* 40 (= t. 67), talks about Cicero rendering συγκατάθεσις and κατάληψις into Latin, strongly suggests that the *Catulus* had touched on the topic before: *quod autem erat sensu comprehensum, id ipsum sensum* [= αἴσθησις] *appellabat, et si ita erat comprehensum ut conuelli ratione non posset, scientiam, sin aliter, inscientiam.*

Wisdom is the state of the sage who is in possession of all virtues (in line with the Socratic demand for a unity of virtues, cf. D.L. 7.125 = *SVF* iii.295); *itemque* indicates that in the virtues there lies 'equally' (sc. to *scientia*) *sapientia*. Wisdom is called the 'art of living' because enacting virtue knowledge is assumed to be closely similar to enacting craft knowledge; on the subject, see Striker (1996c).

The sage's, or rather wisdom's, *constantia* is due to the fact that he has perfected his cognitive abilities to the point where he only assents to cataleptic impressions, and he is already in possession of a set of beliefs which are true in virtue of having arisen from cataleptic impressions and which are entirely consistent with each other. Under these circumstances he could not be reasoned out of any of his (true) beliefs (cf. *Ac.* 1.41 quoted above), nor is there scope for a 'change of mind'.

Constantia is not among the virtues independently recognized by the Stoics (cf. *SVF* iii.262–94). Rather, it is a property of the sage which he has due to the fact that he is virtuous and wise, usually signalled through attributes characterizing his disposition or that of his beliefs (ἀμετάπτωτος, βέβαιος). For *ex sese habere*, see the parallels collected by Reid[1] (p. 203).

Quaero etiam, ille uir bonus...quae falsae esse non possint: earlier commentators have shown that the terms in which the sage is characterized here are reminiscent of descriptions of M. Atilius Regulus (cos. 267 and 256 BC; *RE* s.n. Atilius no. 51), who according to Roman historical myth was captured by the Carthaginians, sent to Rome to negotiate, but advised the senate against negotiation, and was tortured and killed in Carthage when he returned, making good on his undertakings prior to departure; cf. Cic., *Off.* 3.99–115, with Dyck (1996), and *Parad.* 16, where he is presented as a paragon of *constantia* and *fides*; Leach (2014). That Regulus is invoked here is one of several strategies employed by Lucullus to connect his argument with pre-existing Roman attitudes, and the implication is that the sage is not an oddity devised by unworldly Greeks, but something that the Romans have known and which they own; see on *Luc.* 13–14. *Ille uir bonus* means either 'that particular well-known good man, i.e. 'Regulus', or 'the typical good man' (so Reid[1] p. 203).

The asyndetic string of synonyms (*comprehensi percepti cogniti constituti*) is emphatic; see the discussion on apprehension-related terminology on *Ac.* 1.41. Reid[1] (p. 204) lists parallels showing that Cicero will often combine synonyms referring to the notion of κατάληψις, but such phrases usually have two elements only.

Reid[1] (p. 204) also comments that the singular in *eius conseruandae causa* suggests that *aequitas* and *fides* form one idea. The desire to avoid an *-arum…-arum* repetition may have played a role, too.

At the very end of §23 (*…nisi eis rebus assensus sit…*) Lucullus briefly makes reference to the concept of assent. It had been assumed throughout that cataleptic impressions give rise to true beliefs when they are assented to (cf. §37), but since for now the focus is only on beliefs which the subject takes to be true unqualifiedly, assent had not been made an explicit topic in Lucullus' exposition.

See Reid[1] (p. 204) on *potius quam aut* rather than *potius quam ut* suggested by 'Lambinus'.

§24

Ipsa uero sapientia…quo modo primum obtinebit nomen sapientia: Reid[1] (p. 204) notes as peculiar that Lucullus should discuss *constantia*, 'a quality of *sapientia*', first (in §23), and should then move to *sapientia* itself. However, what *sapientia* intrinsically is was discussed in §23, and what Lucullus now adds is that the state of *sapientia*, in order to be deserving of that name, needs to have second-order awareness of itself: that is, not just should the sage hold καταλήψεις only, or rather ἐπιστήμαι, but he should be aware of the fact that this is so. This issue was perceived as a problem by the Stoics, who noticed that such second-order awareness does not simply follow from achieving wisdom; cf. the notices that Chrysippus discussed the 'Disappearing Argument' (see the general note on *Luc.* §§28–9 below), and that the sage may become wise without noticing it or being able to pinpoint the moment when he became wise. See also Brouwer (2014: 51–91) on the moment of becoming wise.

In the immediate context here, it is not clear why the issue of second-order knowledge is raised. However, the issue will re-emerge in the report about a group of anti-sceptical arguments in §§28–9. These arguments are directed at Academic arguments formulated with reference to the wise man.

Deinde quo modo suscipere aliquam rem…qui poterit esse sapientia: Lucullus now moves from second-order to first-order considerations: in order to undertake any action with confidence (*fidenter*), the sage must have something certain to follow, like a notion of what the highest good is (*quid sit extremum et ultimum bonorum*). For this reasoning to stand up, *certi nihil…quod sequatur* must be something which is objectively certain as well as something in which the agent has subjective confidence. Προκόπτοντες may have a true belief about what the highest good is, but only to the sage will it be transparent that his belief on the subject is a κατάληψις.

(I assume that non-sages will only occasionally be able to appreciate that a particular impression is cataleptic; see section 5.3.) Given their being connected by *aut*, *suscipere* and *agere* are probably not synonyms.

One might wonder if it is necessary to assume that from the second sentence of §24 onwards first-order considerations are at issue, and if the sage's confidence in his belief about the highest good could not in fact derive from his second-order awareness of his wisdom. Such a reading might take encouragement from '*qui poterit esse sapientia?*'. Against that one may observe that the sentence beginning *Deinde quo modo*...and the immediately following one stress the need for a particular 'certainty', namely a view on what the highest good is.

Sequi (cf. *quod sequatur*) means 'to act on' and has no connection with 'following without assent' which the Academics claim for themselves; see on *Luc.* 104–105a. 'Lambinus' modified the word order to *primum quo modo*, but *primum* does not mark the first item in an enumeration here (despite *deinde* below); see also the parallels assembled by Plasberg[1] (p. 79), and the position of *(ille) deinceps (equus)* and *ut haec (quae quasi)* in §21.

Atque etiam illud perspicuum est...idque initium esse naturae accommodatum: it is a rhetorical touch that Lucullus introduces the next step of his argument by means of a term (*perspicuum*) which elsewhere denotes a property of cataleptic impressions. Crucially, the subject is possible action taken by *sapientia*, i.e. the sage (*quod sapientia cum agere incipiat sequatur*). The starting-point for action (*initium*) is marked as a cataleptic impression by *constitui*, one of the four synonyms used in a relevant sense in §23—in fact the last, emphatically placed one. And this starting-point must be *naturae accommodatum*, in line with the role which human beings have in the world according to the doctrine of οἰκείωσις.

Nam aliter appetitio...moueri non potest: by retaining the focus on the sage (*quod sapientia, cum quid agere incipiat, sequatur* in the previous sentence), Lucullus is able to pass over the distinction between action and action in accordance with virtue: any action undertaken by the sage is action in accordance with virtue. The Lucullus character shifts freely between *appetitio* being moved and us (i.e. perceiving subjects) being moved by an *appetitio*. See also on *Luc.* 30.

Given the shift to the first-person plural in the parenthesis, *quod est uisum* is best read as neutral with respect to veridicality, but what precedes and what follows is concerned with the sage (on my reading), who only acts on (a species of) true impressions. On the different uses of *uideri*, see Reinhardt (2016); section 10.

§25

Illud autem quod mouet...discerni non poterit a falso: the way in which Cicero has Lucullus present the issue does not aim for absolute precision, but nonetheless *illud* must refer to the subject of the impression (which corresponds to the logical subject of the ἀξίωμα which is the propositional content of the impression). *Videri* must mean 'to appear' in a veridical sense (see Reinhardt 2016: 83–5), as is clear from *discerni non poterit a falso*, and *eique credi* must be a deliberately untechnical way of describing assent to said impression. On assent, see *Luc.* 37–9.

Expressions like *discerni* play a role in the ongoing debate about whether the Stoic theory of the cataleptic impression is internalist or externalist, or rather, whether Cicero, or Cicero's Lucullus, takes it to be internalist or externalist. The word *discernere* itself means 'to separate off' in the first instance (*OLD* s.v. no. 1), then 'to distinguish (with the mind or the senses)' and '(of things) to show the difference in or between, to distinguish practically' (*OLD* s.v. no. 2). As indicated in the introduction (see section 5.3), the Zenonian definition does not include an awareness requirement, i.e. an explicit requirement that a human being experiencing a cataleptic impression is consciously aware of precisely that feature of it which makes it self-warranting. One might think that such an awareness requirement was implicit, because it was not plain to Zeno that conceptions of knowledge are possible which manage without an awareness requirement, but against that counts the fact that cataleptic impressions are, on the Stoic view, experienced by sages and non-sages alike, and non-sages are assumed to have a tenuous hold on their καταλήψεις, which suggests that they do not recognize them for what they are. However, one might then argue that here the sage is at issue, and the sage may well have full conscious access to the feature of a cataleptic impression which makes it self-warranting. This is a possibility, but not necessarily correct despite the use of *discernere*. Due to the fact that *uideri* can refer to object seen and (visual) experience had in both its veridical and its non-veridical sense, the sentence from *quod fieri non potest*…may be about a (generic) state of affairs in the world which can (or cannot, in the counterfactual scenario) be told apart from what merely appears to be a state of affairs but is not (*falsum*, on this reading). Or even if what we are given is a description of what goes on in the mind of the perceiving subject, it may be an *outside* description, a description provided by a third party: in that case the observer does not pronounce on the exact reason for why the perceiving subject is able to discriminate.

See Reid[1] (p. 210) on *Luc.* 29 for pronoun variations like *illud*…*eique* here.

Quo modo autem moueri animus…accommodatumne naturae sit an alienum: the mind, or the sage qua owner of the mind, cannot be moved if it has not been apprehended (*percipitur*) whether what presents itself in an impression is in accordance with nature or alien to it. See Inwood (1985: 200–4) on selection amongst natural things as the first function of reason. Natural things are in agreement with nature's rational and providential plan. See the text collected in §57 of Long and Sedley (1987).

Itemque, si quid officii sui sit…necesse est id ei, uerum quod occurrit, uideri: all correct action requires an impulse, in the absence of which the sage would not only not do his duty, but would in fact do nothing at all. Lucullus is here alluding to the term ἀπραξία, a state in which one does nothing (*numquam mouebitur*), rather than an inability to act. See the general note above; cf. *Luc.* 37 (with Plut., *Adv. Col.* ch. 26, 1122a–c), and 39.

Brittain (2006: 17 n. 32) sees confusion here between the Stoic theory of action and that of happiness; I have set out my alternative interpretation in the general note above.

Accordingly I take the subject of *aget* and *acturus est* to be 'the sage', from the preceding context and implied at the beginning of the paragraph, since the passage turns out coherent on this reading. Schäublin et al. take *animus* to be the subject in both cases; Brittain (2006) translates as if the subject of *aget* was *animus*, and then shifts to 'we' as the subject of *acturus est*. Reid[1] (p. 205) suggests the subject of *acturus est* was *animus* or an indefinite *quis*.

Having used veridical *uideri* earlier in the paragraph (*prius oportet uideri*), it seems to be used again in the last sentence: on this reading, *uerum* is not a complement of *uideri*, and the latter functions as a full verb. This is suggested by the sense as well as word order (*uerum* standing apart from *uideri*, and splitting *id ei* and *quod occurrit*). Yet the matter is not clear-cut; contrast the different account in Reinhardt (2016: 84). On the genitive in *quid officii sui sit*, see Reid[1] (p. 205).

§26

The subject of this section is reason (λόγος),[97] and specifically reason as a driver of investigation (ζήτησις) and discovery, which Lucullus, in a *reductio*-type argument, suggests would be entirely done away with if the Academics were right that there are no cataleptic impressions.[98] The Academics would respond, of course, that what Lucullus says is only true by the extreme standards applied by the Stoics themselves. The subject of reason is resumed, and treated in more detail and from a slightly different perspective, in *Luc.* 30-1. The whole paragraph down to...*exitus percipiendi et comprehendi tenet* is *SVF* ii.103.

In the body of the paragraph here Lucullus advances an argument which relies on the factivity of verbs like 'to find' or 'to discover' (see p. 371) and which, in virtue of the fact that it turns on normal Latin usage, has a generalizing effect: an assumption of the existence of certain truths (cf. the requirement imposed by the third clause of Zeno's definition of the cataleptic impression) is, or so is the suggestion, invariably made by speakers of Latin when they use the relevant expressions. Lucullus argues that nobody discovers 'false things' (*falsa*) and that things which remain uncertain cannot be 'discovered', but that when things which were previously 'wrapped up, as it were' come to lie out in the open, they are—and here the argument turns overtly linguistic—'said to have been found' (*tum inuenta dicuntur*).[99] Reason is then, by way of a concluding remark, said to comprise the beginning of enquiry and the outcome which consists in apprehension (see n. below for the difficult sentence beginning *sic et initium*...).

At the end of the paragraph, Lucullus connects these points with Stoic doctrine: citing the Stoic definition of demonstration (scientific proof, *argumenti conclusio*, ἀπόδειξις), i.e. 'an argument which arrives, starting from what was apprehended, at what was not [sc. initially] apprehended', Lucullus says that it is 'for this reason defined in this way' (*itaque...ita definitur*). For what reason, one cannot but ask.

[97] See Frede (1994); Long (1996a), (1999: 572-83).
[98] For the Stoic understanding of reason, see on *Luc.* 21 and 30-1.
[99] See Reinhardt (2019) for more detail.

One possibility is that the way in which a scientific proof arrives at a conclusion which was not itself apprehended but is apprehended as a result of being derived from premisses which correspond to καταλήψεις is to be seen as an instance of what was said about *ratio* in the preceding sentence. However, a second (additional rather than alternative) possibility is tempting: Lucullus may be drawing attention to the fact that the Greek word ἀπόδειξις is a factive expression in that one can only say of truths, and certain truths at that, that they have been 'demonstrated' (ἀποδεικνύναι) or have received a 'demonstration'. For this reading to work for the Latin rendering *argumenti conclusio* as well, the latter has to be taken in a certain way. *Argumenti conclusio* is ambiguous: it may either describe, from a formal point of view, what features as the conclusion of an argument (and this conclusion may be false or not validly obtained), or it may describe the conclusion of what is undoubtedly a scientific proof (i.e. a conclusion which is true and which was validly obtained). For the passage to be coherent, Lucullus must mean the latter. The way in which in §27 *inuenire*, with respect to which Lucullus had advanced a pointedly linguistic argument turning on factivity, and *concludere* are juxtaposed and are said to be impossible, if the Academic contention of ἀπαραλλαξία was true, may count as confirmation for this interpretation. And while the argument from the use of *inuenire* was made by a Roman speaker in Latin, Lucullus extends his claim to Greek by highlighting the correspondence between *argumenti conclusio* and ἀπόδειξις (although this correspondence is of course pointed out for other reasons, too). This suggests that Cicero is applying reflections on Greek usage which he found in his source material to a Latin-speaking environment. To the best of my knowledge, no Greek text argues for the notion of κατάληψις being encoded in Greek usage in this way, and Cicero may well be offering us a glimpse at an original argument of Antiochus' advanced in support of the existence of apprehension.

Quid quod, si ista uera sunt…in ista prauitate perstabitis: *si ista uera sunt* seems deliberately vague and is best taken to refer to arguments against the existence of cataleptic impressions. For the expression, see Reid[1] (p. 182) on *Luc.* 10.

On *tollere* = ἀναιρεῖν, suggestive of dialectical argument, and its use in Sextus, see Janáček (1971: 47–60); on question-and-answer exchanges as a frame of reference for philosophical argument generally in the Hellenistic period, see on *Luc.* 104–5.

Reid[1] (pp. 205–6) offers an insightful discussion of the nuances of the terms *lux* and *lumen*, noting that, when contrasted, *lux* and *lumen* denote natural and artificial light respectively (cf. *Fin.* 3.45: *obscuratur et offunditur luce solis lumen lucernae*), and thus in context stand for a natural capacity for reason and its development through training. (Bentley cited by Davies proposed emendation to *dux lumenque*.) On the association between light and reason (understanding) see in general Bultmann (1948: 18–21), as well as the various passages where Lucullus accuses the Academics of depriving humans of the light, the senses, or the eyes. See on *Luc.* 30.

In *prauitas* there lies the charge of warped thinking, but the term also has a moral dimension: the Academic objections to Stoic epistemology touch on an intellectualist conception of virtue, too. Action in accordance with virtue was the subject of the previous paragraph.

Wichert (1856: 72) proposed emendation to *Quid? Si, si* at the beginning of the paragraph, on invalid grounds (see Plasberg[1] p. 79).

Quasi quaedam is used with metaphors, not just with translations, i.e. the passage is not marked as translated. See Reid[1] (p. 206) on *tamenne*, which explains the punctuation inter alia.

Nam quaerendi initium ratio attulit...ratio confirmata quaerendo: reason provides the starting point for enquiry, presumably in seeking out the experiences which give rise to κοιναὶ ἔννοιαι, and a virtuous disposition is created when the subject is entirely rational, which is achieved when through a process of enquiry reason is corroborated (i.e. when the items which constitute it are mutually secured); cf. *Luc.* 30-1 and the general note on *Luc.* 21-2.

Reitzenstein, cited by Plasberg[1] (p. 79), deleted the second *ratio*, and Schäublin et al. place it in square brackets, but it is more likely to have been repeated for emphasis by Cicero than mechanically repeated by a scribe (or secondarily intruded after starting out as a gloss).

Quaestio autem est appetitio cognitionis...tum inuenta dicuntur: on inquiry as directed at obtaining κατάληψις, cf. Clem., *Strom.* 6.14.121.4 St. = *SVF* ii.102: ἔστιν δὲ ἡ μὲν ζήτησις ὁρμὴ ἐπὶ τὸ καταλαβεῖν, διά τινων σημείων ἀνευρίσκουσα τὸ ὑποκείμενον, ἡ εὕρεσις δὲ πέρας καὶ ἀνάπαυσις ζητήσεως ἐν καταλήψει γενομένης, ὅπερ ἐστὶν ἡ γνῶσις. καὶ αὕτη κυρίως εὕρεσίς ἐστιν ἡ γνῶσις, κατάληψις ζητήσεως ὑπάρχουσα. σημεῖον δ' εἶναί φασι τὸ προηγούμενον ἢ συνυπάρχον ἢ ἑπόμενον, 'Inquiry is an impulse towards apprehending, which finds the subject by means of certain signs; the actual finding is the final point and cessation of the search resulting in apprehension, which is cognition. And the finding properly is the cognition, delivering the apprehension connected with the search. People say that a sign is either what precedes or happens at the same time or follows.' In §24 *fin.* above *appetitio* is used as translation for ὁρμή. That the Stoics invoke conceptions in connection with their response to Meno's paradox had been mentioned on *Luc.* 21 *fin.*:....*nec quari ⟨nec⟩ disputari potest.* Cf. further Plut. *ap.* Olympiodorum in Plat. Phaed. p. 125.7 Finckh = Plut. frgs 215f. Sandbach = *SVF* ii.104: Ὅτι ἄπορον ὄντως εἰ οἷόντε ζητεῖν καὶ εὑρίσκειν, ὡς ἐν Μένωνι [i.e. *Men.* 80e] προβέβληται· οὔτε γὰρ ἃ ἴσμεν· μάταιον γάρ· οὔτε ἃ μὴ ἴσμεν· κἂν γὰρ περιπέσωμεν αὐτοῖς, ἀγνοοῦμεν, ὡς τοῖς τυχοῦσιν....οἱ δὲ ἀπὸ τῆς Στοᾶς τὰς φυσικὰς ἐννοίας αἰτιῶνται· εἰ μὲν δὴ δυνάμει, τὸ αὐτὸ ἐροῦμεν· εἰ δὲ ἐνεργείᾳ, διὰ τί ζητοῦμεν ἃ ἴσμεν; εἰ δὲ ἀπὸ τούτων ἄλλα ἀγνοούμενα, πῶς ἅπερ οὐκ ἴσμεν, 'That it is unclear whether it is possible to inquire and make discoveries, as the *Meno* problem suggests. ⟨For we can't inquire about or discover⟩ either what we know—since it is pointless—or what we don't know—since even if we encounter the latter, we won't recognize it any more than things we encounter accidentally.... The Stoics explain this by the natural conceptions. But if they mean that these are potential, our reply will be as before [viz. that the problem concerns actualized knowledge]. And if they mean that they are actualized, why do we inquire about things we know?'. On this passage, see Brittain (2005: 179-86, esp. 180), whose translation and explanatory supplements I have quoted.

On the interpretation of the passage, see the general note above. *TLL* s.v. *inuenio* col. 134.48-83 lists ancient accounts of the precise meaning of *inuenire*, sometimes with an etymology of sorts. Cicero's remarks on factivity are not paralleled. Otherwise there is an emphasis on deliberate search (*labore*) in the case of *inuenire*, whereas *quod reperitur* is what one happens upon without deliberately seeking it (*euentu*). Cf. Aug., *Trin.* 10.7.10: *inuentio si uerbi originem retractemus, quid aliud resonat nisi quia inuenire est in id uenire quod quaeritur?*

With *quaestionis finis inuentio*, cf. Cic., *Fin.* 1.3: *nec modus est ullus inuestigandi ueri nisi inueneris.*

Regarding *inuoluta*, see *TLL* s.v. *inuoluo* col. 268.7–32 on the perfect participle *inuolutus*; relevant uses in Cicero include the association (i) with definition, where the term is used to denote conceptual analysis and articulation (*Or.* 102; *Top.* 9; *Tusc.* 4.53), and (ii) with proof as here (e.g. *Fin.* 1.30: *argumentum conclusionemque rationis... occulta quaedam et quasi inuoluta aperiri*).

On *aperta*, cf. the use of ἐκκαλύπτειν in the definitions in Sextus, *M.* 8.314 and 385 quoted below.

On *cognitionis quaestionisque finis* and *quasi inuoluta* the app. crit. gives a summary account of what mss A and V read; see Plasberg[1] (pp. 79–80) for a fuller description. Halm (1861) proposed inserting *ante* after *inuoluta*, which Plasberg[1] (p. 80) printed, citing the situation in B; but *ante* is not a word the scribe of B or Carolingian scribes generally tend to abbreviate, and it adds nothing.

Sic et initium quaerendi et exitus percipiundi et comprehendi tenet: *tenet* and *exitus* are transmitted, but editors have been attracted by Bentley's emendation *tenetur* (cited by Davies), and Reid[1] reads *exitum* with Cambridge Dd.xiii.2 (his 'Cant.'; 'Cant2' in Malaspina 2011 and the Oxford Classical Text), which cannot be vertically transmitted. *Tenetur* is taken to mean 'is grasped cataleptically' (cf. §22 *comprehendit et tenet*) by Reid or 'is retained' by Schäublin et al.: 'hält man...fest.' However, in this concluding sentence (note *sic*) the subject must be *ratio* (thus also Haltenhoff p. 159), the subject of the whole paragraph: it 'comprises' or 'encompasses' the beginning of enquiry (cf. *nam quaerendi initium ratio attulit* above) as well as the result of apprehending and grasping (the 'finding' of the immediately preceding sentence, *quaestionisque finis inuentio* above). This does require a second accusative object, i.e. *exitūs*. For the sense of *tenere*, see *OLD* s.v. n. 18a: 'to hold or keep (in a confined or limited space), prevent from leaving; (also transf.)'.

Itaque argumenti conclusio...quod non percipiebatur, adducit: on the force of *itaque*, the correspondence *argumenti conclusio*—ἀπόδειξις, and the sense of *conclusio* at issue, see the general note above. For the definition, cf. D.L. 7.45 (= *SVF* ii. 235 = *FDS* 1037): τὴν δ' ἀπόδειξιν [sc. εἶναι] λόγον διὰ τῶν μᾶλλον καταλαμβανομένων τὸ ἧττον καταλαμβανόμενον περαίνοντα, 'proof is an argument concluding through what is apprehended to a higher degree what is apprehended to a lesser degree', where the comparative is reminiscent of Aristotle's definition of scientific proof (*An. Post.* A2, 71b17–22), but dubious, since κατάληψις does not admit of degrees (although a κατάληψις can become an ἐπιστήμη); Sextus, *M.* 8.314 (= *SVF* ii.266 = *FDS* 1066): ἀπόδειξίς ἐστι λόγος δι' ὁμολογουμένων λημμάτων κατὰ συναγωγὴν [cf. *adducit* here] ἐπιφορὰν ἐκκαλύπτων ἄδηλον, 'proof is an argument which by means of agreed-upon premises uncovers by way of conclusive reasoning a conclusion which is unclear', and 8.385: λόγος...κατὰ συναγωγὴν διά τινων φαινομένων ἐκκαλύπτων τι ἄδηλον, 'an argument...which, by means of certain apparent things, uncovers something that is unclear by way of conclusive reasoning'. See also the studies by Brunschwig (1980) and Barnes (1980). It would suit the Antiochian project to use a definition of proof for which Aristotelian *and* Stoic ancestry can be invoked.

§27

This paragraph provides an interim conclusion to the preceding sections: if all impressions were such that, while true, they could be false and if no examination could mark them off, then one cannot claim to have concluded anything, cannot say to have found something, and cannot have confidence in a proof that has reached its conclusion. Philosophy itself, which must proceed by arguments/proofs, would reach no results (cf. the conclusion of Lucullus' speech in §61, where this point is restated). Nor would wisdom be possible, which must have a cataleptic second-order grasp that it is wisdom, and whose individual tenets (*decreta*, δόγματα; see n. below) must be such that doubt about them is precluded, too.

The equal importance of each of the *decreta* of the wise man is then stressed: if only one of them is betrayed (i.e. not posited as true unequivocally), then a fundamental rule for what counts as true and correct (the *lex ueri rectique*) is betrayed, a grave error from which the betrayal of friendships and entire countries may arise. Qua tenets of the sage, his *decreta* must meet the criteria set by the Stoics for individual ἐπιστῆμαι: they must be fixed and immovable by any argument, and if one of them is no longer unqualifiedly regarded as true, then the entire class of ἐπιστῆμαι is undermined, including those whose contents bear on matters of profound moral significance.

One might mistake this for a mere restatement of how important the cataleptic impression is as a foundation of Stoic doctrine, to which the Academics would reply that it is the Stoics alone who bear the risk of their assumptions, and if the cataleptic impression cannot be defended against considerations from ἀπαραλλαξία, then it will be as well that theoretical constructs which rely on it crumble, too. However, Lucullus' arguments from linguistic usage (*quo modo quemquam aut conclusisse aliquid aut inuenisse dicemus...*) make his case a slightly different and stronger one: he is implying that central concepts of Stoic doctrine are natural in the sense that they are encoded into the way everyone—Greek or Roman—speaks.[100]

Lucullus ends the paragraph by acknowledging that, given the claim of ἀπαραλλαξία, the Academics do away with *decreta*, which is indeed their stated position, viz. Clitomacheans as well as mitigated sceptics do not posit the existence of *decreta* as the Stoics or Antiochus define them. (The Roman Books do not enter the picture here, and the evidence does not speak to whether items of knowledge as recognized in them were termed *decreta*.) When in *Luc.* 28–9 three views are introduced which demand of the Academics to acknowledge that they accept one *decretum*, viz.

---

[100] See Reinhardt (2019).

that nothing can be known, this is clearly prepared for thematically here in §27, but stands in contrast to the avowed position of the Academics.

Cicero replies in *Luc.* 133 to the claim that it is a 'crime' (*scelus*) to betray a *decretum*, and explains, sc. from his Clitomachean viewpoint, in §§109–10 (primarily in response to §§28–9) that the Academy is entitled to *decreta*, understood in a certain way (sc. which is different from the Stoic, κατάληψις-based view).[101]

Quod si omnia uisa eius modi essent…Sapientiae uero quid futurum est: here Lucullus must be speaking about impressions only (and impressions which can be either true or false at that), rather than about objects and experiences had thereof (i.e. impressions), since the Academic claim referred to is one about the latter. *Notio* must have the well-established sense of 'investigation' (*OLD* s.v. no. 2) here, but this is not very clearly marked in a context where conceptions have just been the subject of discussion (for these, however, Cicero has been using the cognate term *notitia*; cf. also §30–1 below). On the legal use of *notio*, see the references collected by Kaser and Hackl (1996: 189 n. 54); for von Arnim's emendation to *ratio*, see *SVF* ii.111. On *discernere*, see on §25 above; here the telling apart of true and false impressions must be meant.

On *uel* in *uel falsa* in the sense of 'possibly', 'even', or 'actually', see Reid[1] (p. 207).

Fides in *conclusi argumenti fides* combines the notions of subjective confidence in the proof (*OLD* s.v. 9a) and objective reliability (*OLD* s.v. 9b); cf. on §20 *dum aspectus ipse fidem faciat sui iudicii*.

Philosophy, in order to make progress, needs to be able to rely on its reasonings (cf. *Luc.* 44: *rebus comprehensis et perceptis nisa et progressa ratio*). On this general level of description, most dogmatists, perhaps even the Epicureans, would agree, but the Academics would of course retort that they are not invested in this model of philosophical progress (for which, cf. also §16), perhaps not even in a notion of progress, unless the continued desire to discover the truth and the combined recollections of past failed attempts to discover it were so described. Nor would the Academics accept that wisdom is done away with either through their arguments against the cataleptic impression or through their rejection of the model of progress which Lucullus adumbrates.

Once more the reader is confronted with the question of how someone who was a sceptical Academic for much of his life—Antiochus—can hold the Academics to this standard, given that he must know that they will not recognize it as valid at all. On Antiochus having been a pupil of the Stoic Mnesarchus (cf. §67), see Fleischer (2015).

See Plasberg[1] (p. 80) on the transmitted reading *(inuenisse) dicemus* and against *diceremus* found in the *deteriores* and the *editio Romana*; see Reid[1] (p. 207) for parallels to *quem habebit exitum*.

Quae neque de se ipsa dubitare debet…negant quicquam a falsis interesse: Lucullus restates the need for wisdom to be aware and certain of its own state, and for it to be certain about its individual tenets (*decreta*, δόγματα); cf. §24, where there

---

[101] See also Allen (2022: 140).

is the same sequence. Barnes (1997b: 67–78) discusses the uses of the term δόγμα over time. In its first occurrences in the fifth century BC, in legal and political parlance, it denotes a view taken by an official, a decree, a resolution. When it first occurs in philosophical uses, i.e. in Platonic dialogues, it denotes a philosophical opinion, i.e. a view which in virtue of its subject matter may count as philosophical, but which has nothing like the status of a formal doctrine to which one commits unequivocally. This sense Barnes first discerns in Philo of Alexandria, who was born about twenty years after Cicero's death and who died around the middle of the first century AD. However, Barnes cites the present passage (p. 72, with n. 58) and appears to interpret it as an instance of the same use, but fails to acknowledge that this pulls his terminus post quem forward by the best part of a century (assuming that Antiochus himself used the term). Polito (2012: 49 n. 37) calls δόγμα a 'thematic word' from (Antiochus' contemporary) Aenesidemus onwards. The Latin term *decretum* is (like *responsum*) used of the pronouncements of authorities like jurists and augurs; see Wieacker (1988: 560–3) and the references collected by Driediger-Murphy (2019: 39 n. 151).

With δόγματα *quorum nullum sine scelere prodi poterit* (as well as *proditur...proditur* in the next sentence), cf. *Luc.* 133: *scelus enim dicebas esse, Luculle, dogma prodere*.

In its rejection of the Academic arguments, this part of the section (cf. above on §26: *tamenne in ista prauitate perstabitis?*) also goes from epistemology to ethics (*et amicitiarum proditiones et rerum publicarum*, and earlier *sine scelere*); the phrase *lex recti uerique* captures both. Obdrzalek (2012: 377) distinguishes a pragmatic and an evidential *apraxia* argument and sees the former in play here.

For the requirements placed on the sage's *decreta* here, see the commentary on *Luc.* 24 above, as well as *Ac.* 1.40–2.

In the last sentence of the paragraph *uisa* is used in the veridical sense, in reported speech giving the perspective of the Academics on the dogmatist view: the Academics deny that *uisa* differ in some way from *falsa*. Both terms refer to impressions only here, not also to states of affairs and purported states of affairs; this is a consequence of the focus on *decreta*. In stating that *decreta* are rejected by the Academics (*talia autem neque esse neque uideri possunt eorum ratione...*), Lucullus is talking about the *decreta* of the dogmatist. In §29 the (rather different) question will be raised if 'nothing can be known' ought to be acknowledged by the Academics as a *decretum* of theirs. And cf. *Luc.* 109–10 on the kind of *decreta* the Academics feel entitled to claim for themselves.

With the asyndeton *stabile fixum ratum*, cf. *Luc.* 23...*nihil haberet comprehendi percepti cogniti constituti*, § 43, §141 *certum comprehensum perceptum ratum firmum fixum*, and on *Ac.* 1.41. *Quicquam* is an internal accusative with *interesse*, adverbial in force. On *ratione qui illa uisa*, see the more detailed account of the evidence from A, B, and V in Plasberg[1] (p. 81).

§§28–29

Luc. 28–9 (= LS 68N) makes reference to three individuals: Hortensius, the Antiochian among the three main speakers in the *Catulus*; the Stoic Antipater, who was a contemporary opponent of Carneades; and Antiochus himself. All three are united in the demand that the Academics, given their avowal of the proposition that nothing can be known (ἀκαταληψία, *nihil posse percipi*), should make the second-order concession that they know at least that, i.e. that nothing can be known. The passage has been subjected to detailed and imaginative analysis by Alleemudder (pp. 150–6); Burnyeat (1997: 280–300); Castagnoli (2010: 308–29); and Polito (2012).

What precisely each of the three took the final consequence of such an admission to be is not clearly stated, and §29 *fin*. only concludes generically that enough has been said about Academic *inconstantia* (a term whose meanings include 'fickleness of view, wavering, sc. between alternatives' and 'inconsistency', i.e. the simultaneous commitment to incompatible options; see n. below). However, that is the Antiochian Lucullus' appraisal, and not necessarily the upshot of Antipater's move against Carneades (Antipater, as we shall see, held a minority view).

Illud in *ex hoc illud est natum* at the beginning of §28 is likely to be a backward reference to the discussion of the previous day. The purported original readership will thus have been able to supply the grounds cited for Hortensius' demand from the *Catulus*. (While *illud* does not unequivocally refer back to the *Catulus*, Hortensius as a character has too little presence in *Luc*. for the pronoun to mean no more than 'that well attested/widely known demand of Hortensius'.) The overall structure of the section is rhetorical, building up to the supposed coup de grâce administered by Antiochus. As a consequence, both Hortensius and Antipater get short shrift.

Cicero's reply to the present passage in *Luc*. 109–10 replicates this rhetorical structure, in that it omits Hortensius completely, engages with Antipater's point only superficially and dismissively, and takes Antiochus as the main opponent to be dispatched.

One might think that Hortensius, as a recent convert to philosophy (in the *Hortensius*; see section 9.5), might have made no more than the common-sensical yet powerful point that Academics argue for ἀκαταληψία so consistently, arrive at conclusions inductively supportive of general ἀκαταληψία so routinely that they appear to have apprehended it, and if that was so, they should admit it. What tells against this interpretation, and at the same time accords a considerable degree of appreciation of the nature of the debate between the Academics and Antiochus to the character Hortensius, is the emphasis that the argument is being conducted with reference to the (Stoic) sage (*perceptum a sapiente diceretis*).[102] Burnyeat (1997: 284–5) explains the salience of this point and the likely overall nature of the argument:

> Well, notice first that the demand made by Hortensius and Antipater is a response to the Academic's conclusion 'Nothing can be perceived'.... Very likely, the Academic has also taken the next step, standard since Arcesilaus, viz. that the sage will suspend judgement about everything.... How does the sage get into the act unless through the Academic going on to argue that, because nothing can be perceived, the (Stoic) sage will suspend judgement about everything?... The justification for Hortensius' demand would be that the sage gives or withholds assent on the basis of how things are, epistemologically speaking, and if the way things are, epistemologically

---

[102] In this respect §28 picks up from the preceding sections of course.

speaking, is that nothing can be perceived, the sage must have a correct appreciation of that fact (cf. *Luc.* 53). Once the Academics invoke the Stoic sage, they must accept that so ideally rational a person would not suspend judgement about everything unless they perceived that nothing can be perceived. And this, Hortensius will argue, is a self-refuting position to end up in.

The self-refutation would consist in the inconsistency of perceiving that nothing can be perceived. According to §28 Carneades agreed that, *if* one were to hold that one perceives that nothing can be perceived, *then* one's position would be inconsistent (i.e. not *consentaneum*) and self-refuting—but Carneades disagrees that this is the position in which the Academics find themselves. Rather, Cicero argues in *Luc.* 110, 'nothing can be known' is for the Academics a *probabile non perceptum* just like any other proposition.

Antipater claimed, against everyone else, that it *is* consistent (*consentaneum*) to say that nothing can be perceived except that one proposition. What is not spelt out in the text is on what grounds he argued for this view, why he demanded that the Academics admit that they perceive this one thing, and why he thought the admission would be detrimental to the Academic position. That he did intend to attack Carneades rather than assist him is plain on general grounds. In any case, Carneades resisted his demand (*Carneades...resistebat*).

Only Burnyeat (1997) has so far ventured an explanation of how Antipater's line of argument might be intended to undermine the Academic position, and I do not have a better one to suggest.[103] He argues that, while it was generally accepted in antiquity that statements like 'nothing can be known' would apply to themselves, Antipater must have held that 'nothing can be known' does not apply to itself, so that knowledge of that proposition at least is possible without inconsistency. This would be detrimental to the Academic argument not because their position is self-refuting but because their intended conclusion—that nothing can be known—is never obtained and consequently universal ἐποχή unwarranted. The brisk dismissal which Antipater receives would either be bluster or the sign of a lack of appreciation of the originality of Antipater's suggestion. In particular, the argument for ἀκαταληψία is by its nature inductive. One can show, time and again, that for any true impression there could be one just like it which is false, and one can make a general claim to that effect (as the Academic core argument does, cf. *Luc.* 40-4), but one cannot show this to be so for every impression in a complete induction. Burnyeat also draws attention to other evidence that Antipater was an innovator in the field of logic and points out that the so-called 'Elusive Argument' (διαλεληθὼς λόγος; cf. Plut., *Prof. Virt.* 75c), on which Chrysippus had written a book, might have provided an inspiration for Antipater. According to this argument, a προκόπτων may acquire all the items of knowledge required for the state of wisdom (while not retaining any false beliefs), and yet will not achieve wisdom because the items of knowledge do not entail the further second-order knowledge that he is now wise, which is, however, required for wisdom to have confidence in herself (as urged in the immediately preceding §27). Burnyeat goes on

---

[103] Cf., however, Castagnoli (2010: 322-3) for an additional suggestion.

to point out that Socrates is invoked as a hero by both the Academics and the Stoics/Antiochus, all of whom can be assumed to agree contra Antipater that the simple 'I know that I know nothing', often ascribed to Socrates, is self-refuting. He shows that a plausible case can be made that none of the passages which invoke Socrates in the *Academica*, whether they are Academic or Antiochian, land Socrates with this self-refuting statement,[104] and that the only character who claims to know that he knows nothing—the younger Catulus in *Luc.* 148—does so from a standpoint of mitigated scepticism, which involves qualified and self-aware assent rather than dogmatic Stoic assent.

In §29 Antiochus' view is presented. Like Hortensius and Antipater he demands that the Academics admit that they know that nothing can be known. Like Hortensius but unlike Antipater he thinks that this admission would lead to inconsistency (and thus self-refutation). Antiochus claims that the Academics held ἀκαταληψία as a 'doctrine' (*decretum* = δόγμα, cf. also *Luc.* 27, with n. on the precise sense of the term). This would seem to differ from Antipater's stance in that the latter claimed that the Academics had failed to rule out the possibility that something can be known (namely that nothing can be known), whereas Antiochus argues that the Academics had committed themselves to knowledge (according to the standards applied by the Stoics and without acknowledging it) of at least this one thing, that nothing can be known. However, it should not be taken to mean that the Academics themselves, or a faction of them, would have termed ἀκαταληψία a *decretum* of theirs unprompted.[105]

Why did Antiochus argue like this? After all, one might think that he, as a former Academic sceptic himself, knows precisely how the Academics conceive of their stance regarding ἀκαταληψία and how they are going to respond to the charge. The most natural explanation is that Antiochus cited the evident attachment of the Academics to ἀκαταληψία, which suggests that it is more for them than a general proposition which they happen to find borne out time and again by arguments about particular matters.[106] On this reading Antiochus may have come to doubt, perhaps while he was still a sceptic himself, that it is an apt description of the Academics' actual epistemic behaviour that ἀκαταληψία has merely the status of a *probabile* and is not treated as what the Stoics would call a *decretum*.

If that is Lucullus'/Antiochus' rationale, then one cannot but concede that work is needed to extract it from the text. I shall retrace the argument of *Luc.* 29. Antiochus is said to have approached the same *locus 'pressius'*, more closely. The adverb has been read (i) in terms of a contrast with Antipater, who did not argue face to face with Carneades but instead chose to write against him, leaving close direct engagement (sc. of Academics, not of Carneades) to Antiochus, and (ii) in terms of a wrestling metaphor, according to which Antiochus engages more closely, or grapples, with his Academic opponent. Neither of these readings is without problems: Lucullus says

---

[104] On Socrates in *Acad.*, see section 7.3.

[105] In §109 *fin.*, where Cicero replies to §29, he does claim *decreta* (plural) for the Academic, but these are *decreta* arising from Clitomachean approval, not from dogmatic assent, and the Cicero character is manifestly reacting to the challenge posed in *Luc.* 28–9.

[106] Thus also Castagnoli (2010: 324): 'The only explanation for them holding their principle of ἀκαταληψία so dearly must be that they have apprehended it.'

that it is a *locus* that is being advanced on, not an individual, whereby *locus* is most naturally read in the rhetorical sense of 'recurrent (type of) argument'. To obtain sense (ii), one would have to assume that *locus* is used in the sense of 'wrestler's stance' or 'position' and used metonymically of the person. The introductory sentence of the paragraph thus only offers vague guidance. Lucullus then shifts to indirect speech, apparently reporting what Antiochus said. Since the Academics embrace ἀκαταληψία as a doctrine, which must mean that they do so as a matter of observable (or inferable) psychological fact rather than that they say so, they must not waver (*fluctuari*) on this as they do on everything else. By 'wavering' Antiochus must mean a failure to commit (cf. *cuiusquam...nihil approbantis* near the end of the paragraph); of this failure to commit the Clitomachean position could be accused because it rejects assent, or indeed mitigated scepticism in that it rejects dogmatic assent and thus does not fully commit. A particular reason why the Academics must commit to ἀκαταληψία is that it is the *summa* of their position—another polysemous term, which, in the absence of disambiguating contextual cues, may be taken to mean 'key concept, main idea' (it cannot mean 'conclusion' here, e.g., of the core argument). *Hanc in hanc enim esse regulam* has then forward reference: any kind of philosophy had the establishment (*constitutio* used as a genuine *nomen actionis*) of what is true and false, apprehended and not apprehended, as a guiding rule (*regula*; κριτήριον). This sounds like a mere assertion from a dogmatist's point of view, but if we take the following *quam rationem quoniam susciperent*...as evidence cited to back up the assertion and *docereque uellent* as explicative of the preceding colon, then the nature of the argument made changes: Lucullus cites, without naming it, the Carneadean πιθανόν as evidence for the fact that the Academics do allow for and encourage (*accipi oporteret...repudiari*) discrimination between impressions, and based on it acceptance and rejection, and then argues a fortiori (*...certe hoc ipsum...*) that they must perceive their own *regula*.

Brittain (2006: 19 n. 37, cf. p. xxxiv) suggests that Antiochus' argument 'relies on the view that philosophical "schools" are individuated by a set of specific doctrines, attested in Diogenes Laertius *Lives* 1.18–20.'[107] While this may indeed be a background assumption, compatible with the account just given, I note that Lucullus/Antiochus fails to state explicitly that the Academics' claim to *being a school* turns on having at least one doctrine. The Academics would not have agreed with this criterion for counting as a school, but they would certainly have claimed to represent one (i.e. 'the Academy').

From *etenim duo esse* the sage is once more (cf. §28) used to frame the argument. How does he re-enter the scene? It is tempting to think that the entrance is facilitated by the Carneadean πιθανόν alluded to in the preceding sentence. One may see here an indication of how Lucullus assumes, for the present purpose, the πιθανόν to function within a larger argumentative strategy. Assume that the πιθανόν forms part of an argument designed to challenge the indispensability of the cataleptic impression and thus takes its place while the rest of the Stoic doctrinal framework in which it is embedded is retained, so that the Stoics are implicitly urged to concede that many,

---

[107] On this view, see also Polito (2007), who, however, discusses it with respect to the self-conception of Pyrrhonism.

possibly all, of the things they want to achieve philosophically are as achievable with the πιθανόν as with the cataleptic impression *by their own standards*: then Lucullus' reply is that this is not so, on the grounds that the sage is supposed to be certain of his judgement as well as certain of the goals he pursues in his actions. This he can only be if he is certain of something: ἀκαταληψία, the Academic *regula*, or so Lucullus suggests. Since the Academics reject this, they are guilty of *inconstantia* (see n. below). On this reading, Antiochus is not disputing the possibility of dialectical argument, in the sense of an argument offered 'for the sake of the argument', i.e. without the endorsement of the speaker, or of an argument relying on premises endorsed by the opponent. What he is disputing is that it is possible to use the πιθανόν (rather than something better) as a criterion of truth and action, dialectically or otherwise, without relying on ἀκαταληψία as a firm *regula* and *decretum*.

One might wonder if the text was open to an alternative reading, viz. that, if the sage accepts a πιθανόν, what he actually does is accept the corresponding impression as true.[108] If that was meant, it would be unclear how ἀκαταληψία as a (dogmatically held) *regula* operating in the background would be fitted in and where in the text *this* inconsistency would be observed and criticized.[109]

Polito (2012: 39–54) revisits and rejects a number of widely held assumptions regarding Antiochus' secession from the Academy and doctrinal development. Part of his argument is that Antiochus may not have been satisfied with showing why he regards the Academic position as self-refuting. Rather, he may in addition have wanted to urge his former fellow-Academics to understand how he came to embrace apprehension—and quite possibly to follow him. The reasoning would have been that, once apprehension of anything is acknowledged (in this case the proposition that nothing can be known), the possibility of apprehension in principle has been established.

Ex hoc illud est natum...nihil posse percipi: the linking sentence reveals what is apparent for other reasons, too, that in §28 Hortensius and even more so Antipater mainly serve the rhetorical function to set up Antiochus in §29: it is Antiochus' spokesman Lucullus who stresses the requirement for δόγματα in §27, and it is Antiochus who deploys δόγματα with, or so Lucullus suggests, devastating effect in §29.

The imperfect in *postulabat* suggests that Hortensius made the point persistently, or that he pursued it for some time. See the general note above on the likely rationale of Hortensius' objection, and how this rationale would have helped to shape the view the readership of the *Catulus* had of Hortensius: enthusiastic dilettante, or unwittingly devastating naïf, or serious and substantial contributor to the discussion. If the latter, this would lend support to the view that the introduction of the Varro character did not lead to a substantial expansion of the material relayed by Varro in *Ac.* 1.15–42. On Hortensius' retention of the focus on the sage, see the general note above.

---

[108] In this case Cicero would be making the reverse point at the beginning of §105 (*Non enim lucem...*).
[109] The Cicero character suggests in §§99–100 that in cases where there really is nothing better available than the πιθανόν (sc. on the Academic view) the Stoics still posited assent to a cataleptic impression—of the form 'It is reasonable that *p*', I argue ad loc. A Stoic/Antiochus might of course claim that this is entirely different from going by a πιθανόν as the Academics construe it since the modifier is located within the proposition.

Sed Antipatro hoc idem postulanti…comprehendi et percipi ullo modo posse: on Antipater, see also the commentary on *Luc.* 17b–18a. Burnyeat (1997: 280–90) makes a plausible case that the image of Antipater in *Acad.* is strongly influenced by a caricature of him created by his opponents: that of a philosopher not nimble enough to tackle Carneades closely and compete with him in face-to-face exchange, and who instead kept a distance and wrote treatises against his Academic opponent. That Antiochus, a Stoic in the field of epistemology for all we know, would buy into the attacks on Antipater, not just on this narrow issue but in general, given that Antipater must have been an important source of anti-Academic arguments for Antiochus, allows us a glimpse of how Antiochus might have countered the charge that, as an Old Academic, he was rather too reliant on the Stoics—by distinguishing between earlier and later Stoics, and approving those closer to the original source (Socrates and Plato), while dismissing the ἐπίγονοι.

Carneades' rejoinder is described as *acutius*, sc. than Antipater's argument (called *pingue* = 'thick, stupid' in §109 by the Cicero character), even though Carneades' was the Academic response one would have expected. If Antipater's attack was both original and acute, Lucullus does not acknowledge this. Already Reid[1] (p. 209) compared passages in Sextus which speak to the self-bracketing of Pyrrhonist formulae; consider *P.H.* 1.14: οὕτως καὶ ἡ 'οὐδὲν μᾶλλον' μετὰ τῶν ἄλλων καὶ ἑαυτήν φησι μὴ μᾶλλον εἶναι καὶ διὰ τοῦτο τοῖς ἄλλοις ἑαυτὴν συμπεριγράφει, 'So also the phrase "no more" claims that itself, like all the others, is "no more (this than that)", and thus cancels itself along with the rest'; 1.206: περὶ πασῶν γὰρ τῶν σκεπτικῶν φωνῶν ἐκεῖνο χρὴ προειληφέναι, ὅτι περὶ τοῦ ἀληθεῖς αὐτὰς εἶναι πάντως οὐ διαβεβαιούμεθα, ὅπου γε καὶ ὑφ' ἑαυτῶν αὐτὰς ἀναιρεῖσθαι λέγομεν δύνασθαι, συμπεριγραφομένας ἐκείνοις περὶ ὧν λέγονται, 'For with respect to all the sceptical phrases, we must grasp first the fact that we make no firm statement as to their unqualified truth, since we say that they may possibly be refuted by themselves, as they are themselves included in the things about which they are said'; *M.* 8.480–1.

On the anticipation error which gave rise to the intrusion *consentaneum esse*, see Plasberg[1] (p. 81). On the concessive use of *ut* (*ut alia non possent*), see Kühner-Stegmann ii.251; Burnyeat (1997: 280 n. 10) regards an epexegetic use ('namely, that other things cannot') as possible, too.

§29

Antiochus ad istum locum pressius uidebatur accedere…percipere eos debuisse: some of the interpretative difficulties raised by *pressius* have been discussed in the general note above. In *Luc.* 109–10 Cicero replies and dismisses the suggestion that Antiochus' attack was conducted in a manner which was *pressius* (quoting the word), but no light is shed on its use beyond the fact that Cicero finds it inapplicable. In *Fin.* 4.24 the adverb occurs twice, again in an exchange, but any metaphorical association is hard to gauge, and the pairing of *pressius* at the second occurrence with *subtilius* perhaps tells against the wrestling metaphor ('*Sed ut propius ad ea, Cato, accedeam quae a te dicta sunt, pressius agamus eaque quae modo dixisti cum iis conferamus quae tuis antepono*'…'*Mihi uero…placet agi subtilius et, ut ipse dixist, pressius.*'). In *Tusc.*

4.14 the adverb seems to be used to mark a definition as more precise than another one: *sed omnes perturbationes iudicio censent fieri et opinione. Itaque eas definiunt pressius, ut intellegatur, non modo quam uitiosae, sed etiam quam in nostra sint potestate*. A combat- rather than wrestling-related use of ἐπιβρίθω 'I exercise pressure' is in Theocr. *Id.* 22.93 δειδιότες μή πώς μιν ἐπιβρίσας δαμάσειε, 'Fearing that in that confined space (the adversary huge as Tityus) would keep pressing and defeat him' (transl. Hopkinson), where the idea is to confine the opponent so as to neutralize any skill or agility advantage; pressure in this sense may well be applied to a location or area (*locus*), even if the ultimate target is the opponent.

Regarding *in suo decreto*, Lucullus asserts that the Academics had a *decretum*, i.e. that nothing can be known. Given that the term and its counterpart δόγμα had only been mentioned in §27, it seems much more likely that, through the parenthesis *sentitis enim...*, Lucullus is intending to underline the provocative nature of his claim than that he is remarking how astonishing a stance to take this is for the Academics—that is, he is *imputing* on the Academics the view that they had a *decretum*. (Even if a mitigated sceptic takes impressions he has assented to, as always qualifiedly, to be δόξαι, it would seem baffling and unnecessary to call one such δόξα a δόγμα/*decretum*. This is a fortiori so for impressions which a Clitomachean has 'approved'. See, however, on *Luc.* 109–10.) There is no precise parallel for the suggestion that the Academics ought to hold *as their sole* δόγμα that nothing can be known (cf., though, Aug., *Contra Acad.* 2.5.11 = t. 24 on it being a δόγμα: *et omnia incerta esse non dicebant solum uerum etiam copiosissimis rationibus affirmabant*). However, Plutarch describes the related Academic universal suspension of judgement as something that others 'did not move' or 'dislodge' (*Adv. Col.* 1122a, avoiding a categorizing label for the stance), and there are texts claiming or implying that the Academics held dogmatic views on a wide range of subjects and merely pretended to be sceptics; see appendix 1, including e.g. the report on Aenesidemus' views on the Academics in Photius, *Bibl.* 212, 169b18–170b3; on *Luc.* 60 and *Luc.* 148.

The verb *fluctuare/fluctuari* denotes a failure to commit, a wavering (*OLD* s.v. 4a), *pace* Reid[1] ('to be at sea'). A similar demand to commit, but without a use of *fluctuare* or a synonym, is made in §43 in the course of the dilemma argument. Cf. also *Tusc.* 5.33, discussed in the general note on *Luc.* 7b–9a, for a statement by an Academic speaker that their views are held *in diem*; *Att.* 13.25.3 (= SB 333): *o Academiam uolaticam*. Reid[1] (p. 209) prints *fluctuare*, on the grounds that the deponent does not appear in Latin before Livy (it was in ω).

With *praesertim cum in eo summa consisteret*, cf. *Fin.* 2.86: *quoniam igitur omnis summa philosophiae ad beate uiuendum refertur...*, where, however, *summa philosophiae* seems best translated as 'the whole aim of philosophy' (so Woolf), which would not fit our passage. Here 'upshot', 'outcome', perhaps with a trace of the mathematical sense 'sum-total' (*OLD* s.v. *summa* no. 3), seems preferable.

With *quae uisa accipi oporteret* Reid[1] compares *Ac.* 1.40: *uisa...quasi accepta sensibus*, where, however, something else is at issue (which shows a degree of flexibility in Cicero's technical vocabulary): the present passage is about which impressions the mind should assent to, whereas *Ac.* 1.40 is about impressions which are being entertained (*accepta*) by the senses, without having (yet) received assent.

Hanc esse regulam refers forward. *Hoc ipsum* refers back to the purported *decretum*. *Iudicium* in *ueri falsique iudicium* is best taken as the act of judging, given the attribute *omne*; regarding Cicero's flexibility in using κριτήριον-related terminology, see on §18 *iudicium incogniti et cogniti*, and the general note above on *constitutio ueri falsi*. I have translated *ratio* as 'mechanism' partly because it picks up from the preceding *constitutionem*, but a loser translation ('rationale') would be possible, too.

Etenim duo esse haec maxima in philosophia...abhorrere a sapientia plurimum: see the general note above. On *nec sapientem posse esse*, instances of the sequence *esse posse* substantially outnumber those of *posse esse*.

Lucullus states that having a criterion and a highest good is the essence of philosophy, and then resumes and glosses the pairing twice with a change in formulation: *iudicium ueri* ~ *cognoscendi...initium* ~ *unde proficiscatur*; *finem bonorum* ~ *extremum expetendi* ~ *quo peruenriendum sit*. In *haec autem habere dubia...* he then refers to both criterion and highest good respectively. See Reid¹ (p. 210) on the variation *haec...iis*.

With *moueri*, cf. κινεῖσθαι in Greek; see Janáček (1972: 50). In the *appendix critica* I have not ascribed the reading *possint (abhorrere)* to a particular corrector since it arises from the erasure of one minim; it cannot be excluded that the exemplar of B actually read *possint* and that the scribe performed the erasure.

I have translated *duo maxima* as 'reference points' because of *aut unde...perveniendum sit* below.

Hoc igitur modo potius erat ab his postulandum...perceptum esse dicerent: Academics, whatever their particular stance, refused to concede that they apprehended that nothing can be known. I have argued above that no Academic would have called 'nothing can be known' a δόγμα unprompted (sc. in the sense at issue in these paragraphs); *Luc*. 109–10 is a reply. A mitigated sceptic would have called it a δόξα, using the originally Stoic term in the modified, self-aware sense characteristic for that position. A Clitomachean would have called 'nothing can be known' something he approves of but would have had no noun to designate the views which resulted from acts of approval. See also Castagnoli (2010: 324–6).

Sed de inconstantia...sit ut opinor dictum satis: on the emendation *est* for *sit*, proposed by Ernesti, see Plasberg¹ (p. 82). Reid¹ (p. 210) assembles parallels for the deliberative or concessive subjunctives next to *ut opinor*. Schäublin et al. (p. 213 n. 77) comment: 'Die Ausdrucksweise ist unklar. Wahrscheinlich will Lucullus mit *inconstantia* sowohl die begriffliche Inkompatibilität gewisser Merkmale charakterisieren, die den Begriff des Weisen in akademischer Sicht ausmachen, als auch den selbstwidersprüchlichen Charakter der Behauptung "Nichts ist erkennbar".' I think the clue to what exactly *inconstantia* is are the criticism of wavering (*fluctuari*) and the immediately preceding demand that the Academics admit that they have apprehension of 'nothing can be apprehended'. *Inconstantia* primarily means 'changeableness in mood, attitude, etc., fickleness, inconstancy' (*OLD* s.v. no. 2a), and the fickleness lies in repeatedly arguing that nothing can be apprehended and yet not accepting it as a *decretum*, i.e. *inconstantia* resides in the Academics' 'actual' as opposed to their avowed position; cf. e.g. *Tusc.* 4.76: *inconstantia mutabilitasque mentis*; *Div.* 2.38. This position is also inconsistent and thus self-refuting (*OLD* s.v. no. 2b) since 'nothing can be apprehended' and 'I apprehend something, viz. that nothing can be apprehended' are incompatible.

§§30–31

This section begins in a manner which signals a new departure, but then revisits in quick succession many of the topics covered in §§19–27, with which the present section naturally links up (§§28–9 is a digression). The crucial difference (and the new departure) is that, whereas the earlier survey was systematic, the one alluded to here is teleological in that it presents the highly successful design of human beings as part of nature's plan (cf. Cicero's reply in *Luc.* 87; and the relevant section in Varro's survey of Old Academic physics, at *Ac.* 1.28–9). Nature's plan is governed by a divine intellect on the Stoic view.[110]

The initially baffling opening is to be explained against that background. Earlier scholars have taken the phrase *sequitur disputatio copiosa* to gesture to the opening scene in Alexandria (Alleemudder p. 157 n. 1), with its debates lasting several days, or to an Antiochian source used by Cicero (Reid[1] p. 210; Haltenhoff p. 169).[111] The former would seem to require a past tense rather than the present (*sequitur*); cf. *Luc.* 49:…*Antiochus quidem et permulta dicebat et erat de hac una re unius diei disputatio*. The latter would unnecessarily break the fiction of Lucullus as spokesman of Antiochus, who relies on his memory.

No *copiosa disputatio* is actually provided, and the section is in fact functionally equivalent to a rhetorical *praeteritio*. It is preferable to take the introductory sentence as a metaliterary remark that now, in the natural sequence of topics, there follows a detailed discussion, but one which is more recondite and the domain of natural philosophy, at least up to a point (*aliquantum*). No reference to a particular source or discussion needs to be intended.[112]

A passage in the second book of *N.D.*, written soon after *Acad.*, illuminates the reference to *physica*. There Q. Lucilius Balbus offers a defence of Stoic theology, in the course of which he presents an extensive argument from design.[113] That the world is governed by divine reason in a providential way is apparent from its well-orderedness. Examples gradually build towards human beings and their capacities, via topics like the constellations (from 2.104) and plant life (2.120). From 2.140 human sense organs are described in physiological terms. From 2.145 human eyes and their use for various arts are discussed, leading to man's divine gift for reason in 2.147–9. It is this last section which exhibits several clear points of contact with

---

[110] Peripatetic thought has been detected in our passage by some, including in the conception of teleology; see below.

[111] An interpretation of *sequitur disputatio copiosa*…in terms of sources would then take §§28–9 as an intrusion into a section (§§19–27, 30–1) which is derived from or even renders a continuous Greek text; thus Haltenhoff (p. 170).

[112] See also section 9.3.

[113] Cf. Sedley (2007: 205–38) on the Stoic use of the argument from design.

Luc. 30–1 (to be documented in the nn. below), which similarly starts from *animal omne* and arrives at man, and the human mind (i.e. the ἡγεμονικόν) in particular.

The sources of Balbus' speech in *N.D.* 2 have been discussed extensively and inconclusively by generations of scholars (see the survey in Pease 1955-8: 45–8). Suggestions include Posidonius and Panaetius (as well as the combination of multiple sources), but not Antiochus. Indeed, while *N.D.* 2 and our passage helpfully illuminate each other at particular points of contact, they are different in their concerns, notably their argumentative aims: whereas in *N.D.* the argument cites evidence from the human sphere to support a particular conception of the divine, the situation is the other way around in our passage where the goal remains to show that there are cataleptic impressions.

The passage is also significant because it raises various questions as evidence for Antiochian thought. First, there is the question of whether §§30–1 really is just a restatement of what was said in §§19–27 or whether there is a material difference; some of those who assume the latter have suggested that in §§30–1 Antiochus shifts to a Peripatetic conception of the mind and of the interrelation of the senses. It would be odd if Antiochus now adopted a stance which was different from that of §§19–27, and it would also require particular interpretative decisions in §§30–1 which cannot convince.[114] Second, if we assume that in the field of epistemology Antiochus was an unequivocal empiricist and a dogmatic Stoic in particular;[115] and if we further assume that the survey of Old Academic views in the field of epistemology, provided by Varro in *Ac.* 1.30–2 (see the comm.), is historical (in the sense that Antiochus himself does not posit Forms however construed), then the question arises how the Zenonian view on sense perception, impressions, and κατάληψις, discussed by Varro in *Ac.* 1.40–2 (see the comm.) and, on this reading, adopted by Antiochus,[116] can count as a correction (*Ac.* 1.43) and thus modification of Old Academic views. These questions are discussed in Reinhardt (2018), where it is suggested that already *Ac.* 1.30–2 offers a conceptualist interpretation of the Forms and that the notion of reason in evidence in *Luc.* 30–1 can reasonably be presented as a development of such a view.[117]

---

[114] Fladerer's attempt (1996: 86–94) to find an amalgam of Platonic, Peripatetic, and Stoic thought in *Luc.* 30–1 has been plausibly rejected by Glucker (2002: 292), who shows that Fladerer's supplementation in *Ac.* 1.30 *hanc* (sc. *mentem*) *illi ἰδέαν apellabant, iam a Platone ita nominatam* (p. 86 n. 260) is impossible, and by Brittain (2012: 113–18), who shows that, despite certain similarities between *Luc.* 30–1 and the summary of Peripatetic epistemology in *M.* 7.217-26 (= Theophrastus frg. 301A FHS & G), on which see also Huby (1999: 94), the former passage does not provide evidence for Antiochus' epistemology being 'centred on the decidedly non-Stoic process of the higher mind evaluating its perceptual inputs'. Chiaradona (2013: 35) merely notes the notion of *similitudo*/ὁμοιότης as a point of contact between *Luc.* 30 (erroneously quoted as '*Luc.* 39') and Sext., *M.* 7.220. See esp. the n. on §30 *mens enim ipsa...* below

[115] Cicero remarks in *Luc.* 142–3 that, as far as his view on the criterion was concerned, Antiochus was a Stoic and not a follower of Plato, who was not an empiricist, nor a follower of Xenocrates or Aristotle. If Antiochus had endorsed Platonic forms (on a conceptualist interpretation and a fortiori on a non-conceptualist interpretation), Cicero would no doubt have used this as an opening for an attack.

[116] Lucullus does show awareness of younger Stoics, who responded to Carneades, and he does seem to accept their constraint on a cataleptic impression's winning assent (that it must be 'unimpeded', cf. section 6.4), but that constraint is intended to operate on the basis of the Zenonian definition and does not represent a modification of it.

[117] It would be compatible with this scenario if the source for Lucullus' speech predated that for *Ac.* 15–42: the assumption would be that on this point Antiochus' view did not significantly change over time. See section 7.2.

It is argued further that the thread which connects the Old Academy and Stoicism is that the senses and the mind need to work together to achieve knowledge, that the difference between the two positions lies in the power and reliability accorded to the senses (in part due to different views about the objects of the senses), and that Plato's *Theaetetus* is alluded to in *Ac.* 1.30–2, in 1.40–2, as well as here so as to act as a link and Platonic warrant underwriting the development from Old Academy to Stoa.

Sequitur disputatio copiosa…lucem eripere conetur: see the general note above on *sequitur disputatio*….

That matters of natural philosophy are obscure, and that attempts to explain nature often involve especially unfounded dogmatic assumptions, is a commonplace in *Acad.* itself; see the commentary on *Luc.* 14, 116. *Libertas* and *licentia*, when used in combination by Cicero (cf. e.g. *Rep.* 1.68, 3.23), typically mark behaviour that is reprehensible and detrimental to the greater good; here Lucullus is concerned about granting the opponent space he does not deserve and which he will exploit: he who tries to rob humans of the light is at an advantage when dealing with obscure subjects (*nam quid eum facturum…?*). For the Academics, any argument from design relies on undemonstrable dogmatic assumptions, as Lucullus acknowledges, and the Academics are on record with rejections of the notion of divine providence (*Luc.* 87, 119–21; *N.D.* 1.4, 2.73, 3.65–85). Lucullus is explicitly expounding a background consideration for his belief in κατάληψις which he knows will not impress his opponents.

Passages which say that the Academics 'steal the daylight', cover with darkness matters that are clear vel sim. (cf. Reid[1] pp. 210–11; Alleemudder p. 144 n. 4 on passages in Plato and Aristotle which link reason or the intellect with light): *Luc.* 16 (*clarissimis rebus tenebras obducere*), 26 (*ratio omnis tollitur, quasi quaedam lux lumenque uitae*), 38 (*animus eripitur*), 61 (a more extended allegory), 103 (*sensus eripere*); *N.D.* 1.6; cf. Sext., *P.H.* 1.20. §32 uses similar imagery for a radical version of scepticism; see ad loc. Naturally it is not the Academics but their opponents who deploy the imagery of total darkness and sensory deprivation: it is the Stoics who *define* perception as assent to a cataleptic impression (cf. *Luc.* 108), and who accord to cataleptic impressions supreme validity and to non-cataleptic ones none at all, whereas the Academics claim that one can discriminate between impressions in all kinds of respects, yet without ever arriving at a determinate category of cataleptic impressions. There is thus a sense, as Allen (1997) has shown, in which the most extreme form of scepticism found in the Academy, characterized by its pessimism about the prospects of human progress towards knowledge, is not one of the positions entertained or held at different times by the Academy, but the kind of scepticism imputed on the Academics by the Stoics or Antiochus. See also on §31 *de temeritate* below.

For *physicis* derived from *physica* (pl.) rather than *physici*, cf. *Ac.* 1.6; so also Reid[2]; Brittain (2006); contrast Schäublin et al. (p. 43): '…ist von den Naturphilosophen bezogen.'

Sed disputari poterat subtiliter…intenderemus: *disputari poterat*, counterfactual in sense despite the indicative (cf. Kühner-Stegmann i.171), makes the *praeteritio* character of the section (see the general note above) plain.

For *natura* operating *artificio* as well as *quae uis esset in sensibus*, cf. respectively *N.D.* 2.57–8: *Zeno igitur naturam ita definit, ut eam dicat ignem esse artificiosum ad gignendum progredientem uia. Censet enim artis maxume proprium esse creare et gignere, quodque in operibus nostrarum artium manus efficiat id multo artificiosius naturam efficere, id est ut dixi ignem artificiosum magistrum artium reliquarum. Atque hac quidem ratione omnis natura artificiosa est, quod habet quasi uiam quandam et sectam quam sequatur; ipsius uero mundi, qui omnia complexu suo coërcet et continet, natura non artificiosa solum sed plane artifex ab eodem Zenone dicitur, consultrix et prouida utilitatum opportunitatumque omnium*; 2.142: *Quis uero opifex praeter naturam, qua nihil potest esse callidius, tantam sollertiam persequi potuisset in sensibus?* Cf. the passages collected under SVF ii.1127–31 and ii.1132–40. On our passage Inwood (2012: 190–1) notes that Aristotle 'typically avoids explicit language of craftsmanship such as we see here in the *Lucullus* ('quanto quasi artificio natura fabricata esset')'; this is one of several instances where details which in principle admit of a Peripatetic or of a Stoic interpretation upon closer examination point to the latter rather than the former.

Lucullus then describes briskly the handling of impressions by us (or more specifically our minds), starting with the impressions themselves (*quem ad modum prima uisa pellerent*), which gives rise to impulse (*deinde appetitio ab his pulsa sequeretur*; ὁρμή; see on §24), followed by a 'directing' of the senses towards the object of perception (*ad res percipiendas intenderemus*). This last step in the series is somewhat peculiar: on the one hand we are clearly dealing with the recapitulation of a process covered earlier (so that nothing substantially new ought to be introduced here), on the other it is not clear what is meant by this directing of the senses. That it is not just a manner of speaking is clear from the restatement in the next sentence (*intendit ad ea…*; *alia uisa… arripit* below is, by contrast, about something else). The phenomenon of selective attention, suggested by Alleemudder (pp. 160–1), is unlikely to be the point of reference, since action had already been triggered, which would presuppose the mind's focusing on something within a person's ken, and impressions are not mental pictures to be scrutinized. Perhaps what is meant is a continuing inclination to obtain further impressions (cf. §26: *nam quaerendi initium ratio attulit…*): in that case, the suggestion would not be that the mind attends, as it were after the event, to the very impressions which have already triggered action, but that the mind would actively seek to obtain *the kind of* impression which gave rise to action earlier. This would explain why there is an incremental process leading towards rationality and, in the case of the sage, wisdom. Cf. Brittain (2012: 116–17) for an interpretation of the passage which is similar to the one offered here. Brittain goes on to reject Fladerer's reading of the passage (1996: 86–8), which posits that it contrasts 'initial sensory inputs and subsequent judgements or apprehensions', on the grounds that such a distinction cannot be found in the passage itself and that it would turn Antiochus into the worst kind of syncretist—unable or unwilling to reconcile the components of his view, following the Stoics in §§23–5 and the Peripatetics in §§30–1.

With *uisa pellerent*, cf. *Ac.* 1.40: *de sensibus…, quos iunctos esse censuit e quadam quasi impulsione oblata extrinsecus, quam ille φαντασίαν, nos uisum appellemus licet*; *uisa* 'strike' us or our minds, which may sound somewhat peculiar given that impressions are supposed to be formed by the mind as a result of the world impinging on us. However, to the native speaker *uisa* will not just be a stand-in for φαντασίαι but will have a sense of 'sights'. See section 10.

I print the transmitted reading *prima*, rather than the emendation *primum* found in *deteriores*, or Lambinus' emendation *primo*, in *quem ad modum prima uisa nos pellerent*; see also Plasberg¹ (p. 82). It is true that the sequence *primum... deinde... tum* is frequent in Cicero (thus Brittain 2012: 117), but in that case *utrum in alterum* points to *prima* being right unless it yields unsatisfactory sense. In fact both *prima* and *primum* (*primo*) produce a satisfactory text: the former suggests a chronological progression (from early childhood onwards, when we receive our first impressions), the latter reading gives a synchronic picture.

Mens enim ipsa... e quibus memoria oritur: on the central role of the mind, cf. the Stoic context in *Fin.* 5.34: *animumque ita constitutum* (sc. *esse*), *ut et sensibus instructus sit et habeat praestantiam mentis, cui tota hominis natura pareat, in qua sit mirabilis quaedam uis rationis et cognitionis et scientiae uirtutumque omnium*, with Brittain (2012: 128–9 n. 48). Cf. also Sen., *Dial.* 7.8.4.

For general statements on the relationship between the mind and the senses, see Aët. 4.8.1 (= *SVF* ii.850), 4.23.1 (= *SVF* ii.854 = LS 53M); D.L. 7.159 (= *SVF* ii.837) in particular, and the passages collected under *SVF* ii.834–49 and ii.850–61 in general. The Stoics used various images to illustrate the relationship of the soul's ruling part with the senses (see the relevant entries in Rolke 1975), of which the image found in our passage (*sensuum fons*) is arguably superior in capturing the relationship of the mind and senses envisaged by the Stoics. For the mind as a fountain head, cf. Chalcidius *in Tim.* ch. 220 (= *SVF* ii.879 = LS 53G): *uelut e capite fontis*, which would be consistent with the mind being called itself a *sensus* in our passage; ibid. the image of the branches of a tree and the threads of a spider's web; cf. also Reed (2002: 171–2), who observes that Chrysippus' primary purpose in this fragment seems to be to give a materialist account of the soul. The senses are likened to the tentacles of an octopus in Aët. 4.21 (= *SVF* ii.836 = LS 53H). All of these passages have previously been assembled by Alleemudder (p. 159 n. 3). Add, however, and crucially, Plt., *Tht.* 184d–e (with Burnyeat 1976), where it is claimed that the soul, while using the senses as instruments or tools (ὄργανα) to obtain perceptual data (cf. §31 below: *sensibus utitur*), accounts for the unity of consciousness (184d–e); on Antiochus' use of *Tht.* to devise an account of epistemology in the Academic tradition, see Reinhardt (2018).

The sentence *itaque alia uisa sic arripit...* gives the impression that some impressions are 'used' immediately, while others—and only them—are stored away and result in memory. Alleemudder (p. 162) rightly observes that this is implausible: one would think that impressions which are 'used' and register with us in some stronger sense would then give rise to memory, while those which never enter into full consciousness would give rise to memories only in exceptional cases. So *alia... alia* should not refer to mutually exclusive classes of impressions, but to roughly the same class of impressions under two different descriptions. This use is not recognized by the dictionaries and grammars, but cf. Cic., *Fin.* 4.28 (a reference owed to Barnaby Taylor): *Chrysippus autem exponens differentias animantium ait alias earum corpore excellere, alias autem animo, nonnullas ualere utraque re*, 'In his exposition of the different animal species, Chrysippus says that some excel in body, others in mind; and some flourish in both aspects' (transl. Woolf), where each *alias* refers to a set of creatures (those which excel in body, and those which excel in mind), with explicit overlap between the two sets (it is possible to excel in both)—just as in our passage, each *alia* denotes a set of impressions (those which are used at once, and those which are stored away), between which two sets one would expect there to be at least overlap (it should be possible for both to be used at once and to be stored away).

For the absence of attraction in **mens...**, *quae sensuum fons est atque etiam* **ipsa** [emended to *ipse* by Ernesti] *sensus est*, see Kühner-Stegmann i.39.

Cetera autem similitudinibus...προλήψεις uocant: the subject of *construit* is *mens*. Beyond that this sentence poses several difficulties. First, there is the semantically almost empty *cetera*; the reference must be to the next phase in the progression towards full-fledged reason, which rules out that *cetera* resumes *uisa* from the previous sentence. Rather, *cetera* are generically the items associated with the next stage, which later in the sentence are revealed to be conceptions. Second, the phrase *similitudinibus construit*: Reid[1] (p. 213) cites the Ciceronian fragment *ap. Diomed.* 2 p. 421 Keil: *ars est praeceptionum* (*perceptionum* Reid) *exercitarum constructio ad unum exitum utilem uitae pertinentium* (cf. Sext., *P.H.* 3.188, of the Stoics: τέχνην δὲ εἶναί φασι σύστημα ἐκ καταλήψεων συγγεγυμνασμένων, τὰς δὲ καταλήψεις γίγνεσθαι περὶ τὸ ἡγεμονικόν); this confirms both *construit*, which had been suspected by earlier editors, and suggests that the assemblage of general conceptions out of καταλήψεις is at issue. Third, the ablative *similitudinibus*: as Alleemudder (p. 164) observes contra Reid, given how the sentence continues, Cicero cannot here be thinking of secondary concept formation by similarity and analogy (καθ' ὁμοιότητα; κατ' ἀναλογίαν), whereby e.g. the concept of a centaur arises from combining the concepts 'horse' and 'man' (cf. *Fin.* 3.33 = *SVF* 3.72 = LS 60D; Sext., *M.* 8.58-60, 11.250; D.L. 7.52-3 = LS 40P, Q). Instead, he must be thinking that a series of similar impressions—e.g. a series of impressions of human beings—giving rise to a general concept 'human being'. Thus *similitudines* means either 'items which are alike' (*OLD* s.v. no. 2a), with the ablative being instrumental (cf. Aët. 4.11 = *SVF* ii.83 on ἐμπειρία: τὸ τῶν ὁμοειδῶν φαντασιῶν πλῆθος), or *similitudinibus* means 'with reference to similar features'. The former would make the word a more straightforward antecedent for *ex quibus* (Cicero would have written exceedingly carelessly if *ex quibus* resumed *uisa* from the preceding sentence). Fourth, while in §22 *notitiae* was identified as a rendering for ἔννοιαι, the suggestion here is that it could stand for either ἔννοιαι or προλήψεις. This may seem arbitrary, but could also reflect the fact that the former are held to be articulations of the latter; see Aët. 4.11.1-4 (quoted above) and Dyson (2009: 60-71). However, Cicero is certainly capable of not drawing this distinction at least when the point he is making lies elsewhere (as in *Top.* 31: *Notionem appello quod Graeci tum* ἔννοιαν *tum* πρόλημψιν. *Ea est insita et ante percepta cuiusque cognitio enodationis indigens*, where he also uses the term *notio* rather than *notitia* as here; see §27 *init.* for *notio* in a different sense). On Cicero's various renderings of the two Greek terms, see Hartung (1970: 78-101), Reid[1] (pp. 213-14).

A passage which can plausibly be seen as Antiochian and which might appear to offer a different account of concept formation—*Fin.* 5.59—is discussed by Brittain (2012: 123–30).

Eo cum accessit ratio argumentique conclusio...ad sapientiam peruenit: for the human ability to reason and use logic, cf. *N.D.* 2.147: *Quo enim tu illa modo diceres, quanta primum intellegentia, deinde consequentium rerum cum primis coniunctio et comprehensio esset in nobis; ex quo uidelicet iudicamus quid ex quibusque rebus efficiatur idque ratione concludimus singulasque res definimus circumscripteque conplectimur, ex quo scientia intellegitur, quam uim habeat qualis⟨que⟩ sit, qua ne in deo quidem est res ulla praestantior.*

Perceptio eorum omnium apparet poses a problem, as Brittain (2012: 118) notes. If *perceptio* stands for κατάληψις, then it would be peculiar if apprehension appeared so late in the process and not already when conceptions were formed. He proposes two possible solutions: either *perceptio* does not stand for 'apprehension' but for a more general form of knowledge (cf. *scientia* in §31, which he glosses 'understanding knowledge' or 'synoptic knowledge'), or *perceptio* means 'apprehension', and the progression is from common conceptions (and the apprehension involved in forming them) to a 'technical conception of things such as horses, dogs, god'.

I also think that *perceptio* denotes apprehension, but that the second-order apprehension of one's perfected reason which completes the journey to and secures wisdom is meant; cf. §27: *(sapientia)...neque de se ipsa dubitare debet...*, and §§28–9, where the issue is also in the background. On this reading the passage combines, like the previous section §§19–27, an account of progress towards rationality as it applies to ordinary people with a perspective on sagehood, the ultimate goal of this progression, achieved by very few if any. This strengthens the case for the view that §§30–1 is intended to restate from a teleological angle what preceded. Changes in perspective (sage vs non-sage as reference point) are an expository device used §§19–27 (see the commentary passim). The tense of *peruenit* I take to be perfect (i.e. *peruēnit*). *Res* in *rerum innumerabilium* is as close as Cicero comes to using the word to mean 'facts', 'states of affairs' in a technical sense; cf. *Fin.* 2.113; *Tusc.* 1.57. *Eorum omnium* refers somewhat sweepingly to the three elements in the *cum*-clause: reason (*ratio*), the capacity for reasoned argument (*argumenti conclusio*), the apprehensions arising from exposure to *rerum innumerabilium multitudo*. For *uirtus* as *rationis perfectio*, cf. e.g. *Fin.* 4.35. See Reid[1] (p. 214) on attempts to emend *perfecta* to *profecta* and *progressa*.

§31

Ad rerum igitur scientiam uitaeque constantiam...tum etiam propter usum: a summary sentence, shifting the focus back to the cataleptic impression and apprehension as the basis for rationality. It is for emphasis that the Greek term is once more (*ut dixi*) given along with its precise Latin rendering (*uerbum e uerbo* seems to signal the morpheme-by-morpheme translation of a compound; cf. Adams 2003: 460). The reasons for the signalling of such Greek/Latin correspondences vary and merit investigation in each case.

For the connection between *constantia* and apprehension, see on *Luc.* 23. Two reasons are named for the mind's pursuit of apprehension: apprehensions represent or contain truths, which are inherently worth seeking, and they are useful. Cf. *Fin.* 3.17 on the first point, where apprehensions are said to be *propter se asciscendae* (= *per se amat* here).

Cognitio can be used as one of the Latin terms for κατάληψις (cf. *Luc.* 17), but is not so used here as *istam* makes clear; I have opted for 'cognition' as a translation, Brittain (2006) translates 'knowledge', Schäublin et al. 'Erkenntnis'.

The future tense of *dicemus* is striking next to the acknowledgement that the translation *comprehensio* was already introduced in §17 (*ut dixi*), but Reid[1] (p. 214) assembles parallels in type. Note also that Varro comes very close to making the equation in *Ac.* 1.41, which is likely to have had a counterpart in *Catul.*, given what we know from the fragments about the relationship of the two editions.

Quocirca et sensibus utitur…ex qua re una uita omnis apta sit: the grammatical subject remains *mens hominis*. There is no precise parallel for the claim that the arts are *quasi sensus alteri*, which looks like a category mistake, but the connection with §20 and the way in which artistic knowledge leads to a refinement and enhancement of the senses is plain enough: arts are, on one level of description, dispositions of the human mind (i.e. the artist's mind), and as such they account for increased perceptiveness.

Brittain (2006: 20 n. 41) notes that the Stoic and Antiochian models for the 'process leading from our natural love for apprehension to the development of the sciences and eventually to a coherent life—i.e., wisdom' are explained in *Fin.* 3.17–21 and 5.41–5, respectively.

The notion that concepts arising from perceptual experience are constituent parts of crafts is also present in *N.D.* 2.148: *ex quibus collatis inter se et comparatis artes quoque efficimus partim ad usum uitae, partim ad oblectationem necessarias*, 'out of these apprehensions, gathered together and compared, we also fashion crafts which are necessary partly for the practical benefits of life and partly for entertainment.'

For the participial force of *apta*, see OLD s.v. *aptus* no. 1. The relative clause beginning with *ex qua* describes the effect virtue has if implemented rather than its actual current function in the world. *Philosophia* earlier in the sentence is philosophy done in an approved manner, but Lucullus does not generally deny the Academic position the status of being philosophy.

Ergo ei qui negant quicquam posse comprehendi…perinde ut causa postulat dicere: a similar address of and turn to the Academics in *N.D.* 2.147: *Quanta uero illa sunt, quae uos Academici infirmatis et tollitis, quod et sensibus et animo ea, quae extra sunt, percipimus atque comprehendimus*.

The etymological connection of *animal* and *anima* is conventional (*Tusc.* 2.21; *N.D.* 1.26 and 3.36; Sen., *Ep. mor.* 113.2), but has particular force in Lucullus' speech, given that he has consistently stressed how natural his position is, incl. in virtue of being consistent with the implicit assumptions of ordinary language; see Reinhardt (2019). Alleemudder (p. 168) speculates on analogous wordplay Cicero might have found in his Greek source and, given that ζῷον and ψυχή do not allow for it, wonders if the source used the term ἔμψυχον. It seems, however, equally possible that Cicero has Lucullus expand out of his own resources on a theme which was present in the source. See on §37, where I think *animal* means 'rational being' rather than just 'living being'; this may well be the sense here, too, given that animals do not have the kind of mind which allows them to experience apprehension.

With *totam uitam euertunt*, cf. τὸ ζῆν ἀναιροῦσιν in Plut., *Adv. Col.* 1108d, cf. 1119d; D.L. 9.104; *Luc.* 99 below.

On *temeritas*, see Alleemudder (pp. 167–8) and Lévy (2018). The charge of *temeritas* is in Cicero's writings deployed by dogmatists and sceptics alike, but they mean different things by it. *Temeritas* can (i) denote 'rash assent', i.e. assent given in situations where the impression at issue is non-cataleptic or false; as such, it is a charge levelled by sceptics against dogmatists, who, or so the sceptics argue, assent to all kinds of obscure matters (i.e. their doctrines), or by dogmatists against ordinary people (i.e. everyone who is not a sage). When used by the dogmatist against the sceptic, as here, it is (ii) rashness in the sense of obliviousness to the consequences of one's position (see n. above at §30 *Sequitur disputatio copiosa*...on whether the Academics would recognize this criticism). For (i), cf. on *Luc.* 68, 108; *Ac.* 1.42 (within the report of Zeno's views on epistemology, *temeritas* features in a list of intellectual vices which the sage avoids); *N.D.* 1.1; cf. Sext., *P.H.* 1.20. The Stoic term for *temeritas* in this sense is προπέτεια (D.L. 7.46 = *SVF* ii.130 = LS 31B), a 'tendency to fly forward', whose contrary is the privative noun ἀπροπτωσία, 'non-precipitancy', defined as the 'science of when to give assent and when not' (ἐπιστήμη τοῦ πότε δεῖ συγκατατίθεσθαι καὶ μή); Voelke (1990: 184–6); Long (1996a: 92–3); Salles (2007). For (ii), cf. on *Luc.* 66; *Fin.* 3.72.

Obdrzalek (2012: 370–5) treats the present section as an instance of the ἀπραξία-argument, but as will be explained in the commentary on *Luc.* 37–9, this argument typically turns on the consequences of universal suspension of judgement (ἐποχή), which is not mentioned in the present passage.

On *instrumenta uel ornamenta uitae*, see Reid[1] (p. 215). With *euertunt*, cf. §99 *uitae euersio*.

§32

The section *Luc.* 32–6, marked in §36 *fin.* as still belonging with the defence of κατάληψις, is a *refutatio* of Academic alternatives. Lucullus dismisses an extreme form of scepticism quickly, and then turns to a more moderate alternative which is characterized by the introduction of the Carneadean πιθανόν.[118] In doing so, he employs a careful ambiguity of expression, speaking at times as if he is talking about the same people (the Academics) adopting different argumentative stances at different moments, and at others as if different groups or factions amongst the Academics are meant.[119]

What is plain is that the moderate Academics, or the Academics acting in a moderate way, must comprise both the Clitomachean position and that of mitigated

---

[118] See also section 6 on the πιθανόν.
[119] Cf. the use of διαφωνίαι in *Luc.* 112–46.

scepticism. It is true that at one point (§§34b-35a) a sub-group of the moderate Academics is singled out, which has been identified with Philo since the nineteenth century and with mitigated scepticism in particular by his twenty-first-century interpreters,[120] but this reinforces the impression that outside of this passage Lucullus pointedly makes no distinction between the two (moderate) Academic positions in play in *Acad.*, and indeed he states that the views of the sub-group are vulnerable to the same counterarguments as the moderate Academic view in general. Overall, it is as well to note that it is a fundamental strategy of Lucullus' to minimize differences between varieties of (in the context of the present passage, moderate) Academic scepticism, and that consequently one reads his speech against the grain if one assumes unmarked, and to readers hardly fathomable, shifts between different targets. It is Lucullus not his opponent Cicero who bears the argumentative risk for his argument failing to hit the target, so advancing arguments against the avowed Clitomachean Cicero to which only the mitigated position is vulnerable would be futile.[121] Cf. the commentary on §§43-4, where similar strategies are employed.

Lucullus offers, in varying formulations, one fundamental objection to the πιθανόν: if one wants to achieve anything, morally or cognitively, one will need to rely on true impressions which meet a requirement like that formulated in the third clause of Zeno's definition. Any kind of πιθανόν is subject to the kind of ἀπαραλλαξία consideration which the Academics cited against the Zenonian definition. (To which the Academics would reply that ἀπαραλλαξία is only a problem if one employs the rational standards of the Stoics, which they, however, do not share.)

The Cicero character will later reply (§100) that even the Stoic sage relies on mere πιθανά—a category recognized and originally devised by the Stoics of course—when he has to, but on my reading this is not assumed to be acknowledged by the Stoics or the Lucullus character: thus what Lucullus tells us here is to be seen as a blanket dismissal of πιθανά and a denial of their usefulness even in narrowly circumscribed situations (so that their use would be permitted only for those who are otherwise in possession of all the benefits supposedly bestowed by cataleptic impressions, including the concept of 'true').

The πιθανόν must have featured in the discussions of the previous day, i.e. in the *Catulus* (cf. also on §32: *et hoc quidem... moueri*), and thus any attempt to relate what we learn here to the much more detailed evidence from Sextus should accommodate the fact that the present section, while being Lucullus' main discussion of the subject, presupposes knowledge of an earlier lost one (see the introduction, section 6.5). It would also be most peculiar if this key concept of Academic epistemology had been introduced by an Antiochian character.

---

[120] For references, see ad loc.
[121] Brittain (2001: 103-8) is more confident than I am that one can reconstruct details of the mitigated position (which he calls 'Philonian/Metrodorian') by analysing *Luc.* 32-6, but notes (p. 103 n. 49): 'Antiochus (via Lucullus) takes no pains to distinguish the Clitomachian from the Philonian/Metrodorian Academics; by leaving the notion of the *probabile* largely undefined, he is able to direct his argument against both groups, although at some cost to its effectiveness.' Allen (1997) emphasizes the fact that any post-Carneadean Academic position down to Philo was established as an argumentative option by Carneades. Striker (1997: 260-1) takes §§32-6 to be aimed at Philo, but at the Roman Books view in particular. See also Ioppolo (2009: 193-208).

Nec uero in §32 *init.* marks a sense break (Kühner-Stegmann ii.43), but the air of slight exasperation with which the previous paragraph ended carries over into the present one (conveyed by the almost otiose *aut quid uelint*).[122] Having expressed bafflement over the rationale of the Academic position generally speaking, Lucullus first speaks about an extreme response which he (and/or Antiochus and his followers, and/or the Stoics: *adhibemus*) receive occasionally (*interdum*) when he offers a reasoning (*adhibemus ad eos orationem* suggests studied detachment) to the effect that, if what they are arguing was true, then everything would be uncertain (*incerta*, i.e. ἄδηλα; cf. §54),[123] which he takes to be an absurd consequence. In reply the Academics do not demur, say that they are not responsible, and that it is nature which is to blame, since 'she has hidden truth away in a deep abyss, as Democritus says'. What the dogmatist puts to the Academics is surely the claim that nothing can be known, and the Academics do not resist the inference that it follows that everything is uncertain. Why do they disavow responsibility for this result and instead refer Lucullus to 'nature'? One reason might be that they offer considerations and arguments which do or should enjoy the endorsement of the addressee (i.e. the dogmatist), given his epistemic standards, without endorsing them themselves. Yet in that case one might expect them to say 'blame yourselves and your extreme requirements of what counts as knowledge' rather than 'blame nature'. To reply 'blame nature' becomes intelligible if the Academic adopts the dogmatist's perspective even though the endorsement is not his, so (a) that the Academic purports to, as it were, follow the evidence where it leads on the dogmatist's behalf, or (b) if the Stoic rejection of the πιθανόν as an alternative is already priced in,[124] in which case the Academic might imply that the consequences of rejecting the πιθανόν have to be faced by the dogmatist when κατάληψις has already been eliminated as an option.[125] The notion that everything is uncertain is further characterized a few lines later, in that it is associated with the claim that everything is as uncertain as whether the number of stars is odd or even (see the n. below). This dovetails with Democritus' remark about truth, in that truth was said to be hidden but in existence—the number of stars may well be taken to be either odd or even, but humans have no way of ascertaining which. The reference to Democritus itself is, as is observed by Brittain and Palmer (2001: 54), partly dialectical: he was an early thinker whom the dogmatists respected and whose views (and even more so, pronouncements) on the subjects are not easily dismissed. The Democritean statement as well as its use by the Academics can be paralleled (see n. below).

Most scholars take this part of the paragraph to refer to a particular group of people. In view of the radical nature of the scepticism, only a small number of candidates fit the bill, and Aenesidemus, sometimes named, is much less likely to be

---

[122] Contrast—including on *quid uelint*—Schäublin et al. p. 215 n. 85: 'Dieser Passus könnte direkt an das Ende von §29 anschließen: Lucullus wunderte sich über die Unempfindlichkeit der Akademiker ihrer eigenen Inkonsistenz gegenüber; nun fragt er sich, was sie eigentlich vor Augen haben bzw. was sie wollen.'
[123] See the n. on ἄδηλον below.
[124] The second option is proposed by Allen (1997: 244).
[125] One might reply that the πιθανόν is linked to the alternative response which is discussed next. However, if what Lucullus rehearses here is, or is at least partly, types of reply rather than replies advanced by different groups of people, this objection will be less powerful.

referred to than Arcesilaus and his followers, given that Aenesidemus is no recognizable presence in *Acad.* at all and that Lucullus had announced in §12 that he would be addressing 'Arcesilaus and Carneades'.[126] Allen (1997) has observed that Carneades could conceivably have defended both this and the view which is discussed next at different times (and without commitment), and argues that the text does not warrant an interpretative preference for different groups of Academics at issue as opposed to Academics arguing in different modes at different times. Both ways of looking at the passage are not just encouraged by it but also consistent with each other, and the Clitomachean position, mitigated scepticism, and the 'Roman Books' view all had a credible claim to being Carneadean, in that they arise from argumentative options first advanced dialectically by Carneades.[127]

The other view, with which Lucullus will actually engage, is then ascribed to a different group of people (*alii autem*) who are said to argue *elegantius*. This seems an oddly aesthetic description and is probably meant to sound condescending, given how comprehensively the πιθανόν is dismissed eventually. In any case, on this 'more elegant' view there is a difference between what cannot be apprehended (*quod percipi non potest*) and what is unclear (*incertum*). The former, or an instance of it, is the πιθανόν, which impressed Lucullus' interlocutors, sc. on the previous day, i.e. in the *Catulus* (see above). Still, Lucullus turns to it here for the first time explicitly, glossing it as *quasi ueri simile*. The phrasal term here partly serves a polemical purpose (*quasi* functions like *aliquid* above), in that Lucullus goes on to argue (§33) that the Academics are not entitled to it because they have no credible way of explaining how they come by the concept of the true (and the false).[128] The Academics are said to use the πιθανόν as a *regula*, which must correspond to κριτήριον but is only in §33, in the course of a counterargument, expanded to *regula ueri et falsi*: the Academics may have called the πιθανόν a 'criterion', but the further step that they called it a 'criterion of truth' is unwarranted, especially in a context where the position at issue (which we may, on the evidence of §12, associate with Carneades generally speaking) ranges over the Clitomachean position and that of mitigated scepticism.[129]

The Academics are said to use the πιθανόν as a criterion *et in agenda uita et in quaerendo ac disserendo*. The first use relates to everyday decision-making and will involve but not be confined to the use of perceptual impressions, given that the recognition of objects within one's ken will fall under it, but also, e.g., deliberation about alternative courses of action. The second must relate to philosophical investigation and the discussion of dogmatic views. Cicero famously recommends the *disputatio in utramque partem* with a view to the emergence of the *ueri simile* as a method of

---

[126] Those who have seen Arcesilaus as the target here include Brittain (2001: 96).

[127] There are also passages in Cicero's speech where he characterizes the Academic posture as reactive, i.e. as more defensive and appreciably more radical while under attack, and more expansive and 'optimistic' at other times; see e.g. on *Luc.* 98.

[128] Cf. Aug., *Contra Acad.* 3.18.40 (= t. 60).

[129] In *Luc.* 103, in a section that purports to use a work by Clitomachus as a source, he is reported as denying that the πιθανόν can be used as a criterion of truth. Brittain (2001: 17, 96, 107) holds that *Luc.* 32–3 represents evidence that what he calls the 'Philonian/Metrodorians' did regard the πιθανόν as a criterion of truth. Other passages quoted ibid. p. 96 n. 34 which seem to provide evidence for a quasi-dogmatic, criterial use of the πιθανόν I would interpret as distorting like the present passage, i.e. Photius, *Bibl.* 212, 170a.17–21 (cf. *Anon. in Theat.* col. 61.10–46); *Anon. Prol.* 7; and Galen, *PHP* 9.7.3; see appendix 1.

philosophy, and one cannot but conclude that this is what he has in mind here. Notably, this use of the πιθανόν is ascribed to the broader category of less extreme Academics, and thus the passage discourages both the view that this use of the πιθανόν was associated with mitigated scepticism in particular *and* the view that that the use of disputation on either side with the possible emergence of the *ueri simile* is a Ciceronian innovation on the more sceptical argumentative practices of his teacher Philo.[130] What Cicero has Lucullus say here about the use the second group of Academics makes of the πιθανόν is consistent with what the Clitomachean character Cicero says about his philosophical practices in *N.D.* 1 (see also the introduction, p. clii).

That the radical and the moderate views introduced by Lucullus should be associated with Arcesilaus and Carneades respectively is not just suggested by *Luc.* 12, but also by a similar distinction in Numenius (frg. 26 Des Places = Eus., *Praep. Ev.* XIV.7.15; cf. appendix 2):

Μεθ' οὓς Καρνεάδης ὑποδεξάμενος τὴν διατριβὴν τρίτην συνεστήσατο Ἀκαδημίαν, λόγων μὲν οὖν ἀγωγῇ ἐχρήσατο ᾗ καὶ ὁ Ἀρκεσίλαος· καὶ γὰρ αὐτὸς ἐπετήδευε τὴν εἰς ἑκάτερα ἐπιχείρησιν καὶ πάντα ἀνεσκεύαζε τὰ ὑπὸ τῶν ἄλλων λεγόμενα· μόνῳ δ' ἐν τῷ περὶ τῆς ἐποχῆς λόγῳ πρὸς αὐτὸν διέστη, φὰς ἀδύνατον εἶναι ἄνθρωπον ὄντα περὶ ἁπάντων ἐπέχειν· διαφορὰν δ' εἶναι ἀδήλου καὶ ἀκαταλήπτου καὶ πάντα μὲν εἶναι ἀκατάληπτα, οὐ πάντα δ' ἄδηλα.

After these [sc. Lacydes and Euander] Carneades took over the school and established the Third Academy, employing the same manner of argumentation as Arcesilaus. For he, too, deployed the technique of arguing on either side and sought to refute everything argued for by others. He differed from him only in his rationale concerning suspension of judgement, saying that it is impossible for human beings to suspend judgement about everything, and that there was a difference between the uncertain and the inapprehensible, in that everything was inapprehensible, but not everything uncertain.

What is different here, or rather what this text does not pronounce on, is how Arcesilaus would have responded to the charge that his entirely destructive approach would have dire consequences if found to be warranted.

§32

Nec uero satis constituere possum…quid uelint: = LS 68R. See above (p. 408) on the links with §29 and the immediately preceding paragraph. Reid[1] (p. 215) suggests that *quid uelint* is tautological, which is strictly true; as argued above, the fullness of expression may convey the mood of the speaker here. See Hofmann (1951[3]: 70–102) on 'affektische Übertreibungen und Abundanzen'. *Consilium* suggests purpose as well as strategy; contrast e.g. *Academiae ratio* in §7 to designate an overall approach.

---

[130] See sections 4 and 6.6.

Interdum enim...penitus abstruserit: clues to the meaning of *incertum* are the general context here, the example of an *incertum* given below ('whether the number of stars is odd or even'), and the identification of the Latin term with Greek ἄδηλον in *Luc.* 54 (see ad loc.). The latter was a technical term used by Epicureans, Stoics, and Pyrrhonists, which can in principle be applied to objects/issues and impressions thereof; see Usener (1977: 10–11) and Barnes (2014a: 313), (1980: 177–8), and Cortassa (1975) respectively; and earlier Gomperz (1933) and Gernet (1956). One way in which Sextus uses the term ἄδηλα is in contrast with φαινόμενα when he wishes to contrast subjectively clear appearances and the realities underlying them; but for him φαινόμενα *are* ἄδηλα if the former are understood to be supremely clear appearances as the dogmatist construes them. The evidence on Academic scepticism does not suggest that φαινόμενα was used as a technical or semi-technical term in the debate with the Stoics, and consequently one would expect the use of the term ἄδηλα in that debate not to map exactly on that in Sextus' works.

Ἄδηλος means 'non-evident' or 'non-manifest'. *Incertus* is not usually used to describe the quality of phenomenal experiences (see, however, *OLD* s.v. no. 11b and Verg., *A.* 6.270: *per incertam lunam*). The larger context here, where the *probabile* and its use for practical and theoretical purposes is contrasted and where the example of the stars is cited, suggests that an *incertum* (i) provides nothing 'to go on' for practical and theoretical purposes and (ii) is such that it or an impression of it neither invites nor discourages endorsement by the perceiving subject (see Sext., *M.* 7.243 quoted below). For Lucullus it is absurd that everything is supposed to be non-evident. Presumably the character takes this view not just because he assumes cataleptic impressions to provide the base case for perception (which is usually successful), but also because impressions of perceptible objects experienced under normal circumstances are not, as a matter of fact, such that they do not invite endorsement. Hence calling everything *incertum* seems to involve a counterintuitive claim about the phenomenal properties and subjective feel of perceptual experience.

The import of the question *quid ad nos?* could conceivably be 'we are not to blame' or 'this does not concern us', but *num nostra culpa est?* suggests that the former is meant.

Brittain and Palmer (2001: 53–8), in their study of the New Academy's appeal to the Presocratics, interpret this passage plausibly as a primarily dialectical appeal to the respect which Democritus enjoys among the Stoics; this section of my note draws on their findings. They observe that in *Luc.* 73, during Cicero's own speech, Democritus' views are presented in an apparently different way, i.e. as more extreme: *atque is non hoc dicit quod nos, qui ueri esse aliquid non negamus, percipi posse negamus; ille esse uerum plane negat [esse]; sensus quidem non obscuros dicit sed tenebricosos (sic enim appellat eos)*. Whereas in §32 the truth appears as hidden but existent according to Democritus, in §73 the view that it does not exist at all is ascribed to him. Prima facie it is peculiar that the more extreme position is ascribed to Democritus in Cicero's own speech, and not here where supposedly extreme Academics are cited (or impersonated) and dismissed. §§32 and 73 cohere with each other in that in both places the Academics are said to hold that there are truths, but that they cannot be apprehended. They are in apparent disagreement only on the view ascribed to Democritus. In §73 Cicero's purpose is to enlist support from

Democritus on the one hand, but to represent his position as different from and more extreme than the Academic, and specifically Clitomachean one, on the other: accordingly, Democritus is presented as a radical sceptic, as he is in Sextus' collection of his *dicta* (*M.* 7.136-7), in line with the sceptical Academy's reading of Democritus. Here in §32, where Lucullus is placing an invocation of Democritus in the mouth of some Academics, there may be no substantially different interpretation of Democritus intended. Note also Arist., *Met.* Γ5, 1009b11-12, where both views at issue are ascribed to Democritus alongside one another (διὸ Δημόκριτός γέ φησιν ἤτοι οὐθὲν εἶναι ἀληθὲς ἢ ἡμῖν γ' ἄδηλον), so that the apparent disagreement may have a basis in the transmitted record. The view that the references to Democritus in §§32 and 73 are not supposed to be inconsistent is further supported by what the character Cicero says in *Ac.* 1.44:...*ut Democritus,* **in profundo ueritatem esse demersam,** *opinionibus et institutis omnia teneri,* **nihil ueritati relinqui,** *deinceps omnia tenebris circumfusa esse dixerunt.* For the abyss motif, see also D.L. 9.72 (= DK 68B117): Δημόκριτος... 'ἐτεῇ δὲ οὐδὲν ἴδμεν· ἐν βυθῷ γὰρ ἡ ἀλήθεια'.

On the possible identity of the radical Academics (if they are indeed to be viewed as a group of people) see the general note above. For Arcesilaus, see section 7.5 and on *Ac.* 1.44-6. Long and Sedley (ii.1987: 441) identify the group of 'hard-line Academics' with 'philosophers like Aenesidemus'; see also Lévy (1992: 24) for earlier proponents of this view. As Brittain and Palmer (2001: 54-5 n. 20) note, 'Cicero nowhere mentions Aenesidemus or shows any familiarity with the Pyrrhonian revival'; for what Cicero does say about Pyrrho, see on *Luc.* 130.

Disputentur has been suspected: Manutius emended to *disputent*, Kayser cited by Baiter to *disputentur ab iis*.

Alii autem elegantius...docere conantur eaque distinguere: for Cicero invoking 'elegance' in philosophical contexts, cf. *Luc.* 146: *Num minus haec inuidiose dicuntur? Nec tamen minus eleganter: illa subtilius*; the passages collected by Kühner (1853: 105) on *Tusc.* 1.55, where 'elegant' philosophical argument as advanced by Socrates and Plato is compared to that of *plebeii philosophi*.

Note that Lucullus began the paragraph by reporting a reaction he receives 'sometimes' (*interdum*) from 'those people' (*ad eos*), i.e. the Academics in general, in response to his suggestion that, if they are right, everything will be non-evident. He now reports that others, i.e. a sub-group of Academics, respond differently to the general accusation. The tension between the same group saying different things at different times and different groups of people saying different things is not resolved. *Eos* is not equivalent to *se* and is not strictly speaking indirectly reflexive, i.e. does not exclusively refer to *alii* at the beginning of the sentence/main clause, but refers to the Academics in general (who include the *alii*); cf., however, Kühner-Stegmann i.610 for the indirectly reflexive use of *is* (and *ille*).

Cum his igitur agamus...quasi desperatos aliquos relinquamus: Lucullus now turns back to the more extreme view, which does involve saying, or at least not denying, that all things are *incerta*. The use of *dicunt* is tendentious.

'The number of stars is odd' and 'the number of stars is even' appear in some texts as the kind of claims which are non-evident (e.g. Sext., *P.H.* 2.90, 97), in others as the kind of claims which are neither πιθανόν nor the opposite (e.g. Sext., M. 7.243, from a Stoic division of impressions using the criterion of πιθανότης). As Reid[1] (p. 216) notes, the indefinite pronoun *aliquos* 'conveys a touch of contempt'.

Volunt enim...in quaerendo ac disserendo: this is the first explicit mention of the *probabile* in *Luc.*, but see on §§28–9. (Aug., *Contra Acad.* 2.7.16 may be drawing on its counterpart in *Ac.* 3.) The parenthesis probably refers to the discussion of the previous day, i.e. *Catul.*, rather than exposure which Lucullus had to Academics at some point in his life, including at Alexandria; a reference to something previously mentioned is also suggested by *aliquid*. By stating that the Academics posit or 'want there to be' a *probabile* the speaker ignores the fact that the πιθανόν was a recognized category in Stoic thought (see section 6.4), albeit one not available for use to the Stoic sage.

On the πιθανόν and its connection with the *probabile* in Cicero, see *Luc.* 98–111; Reinhardt (2018a); and sections 6.5 and 6.6. The *probabile* is not just what deserves approval (as its etymology might suggest), but what seems plausible to rational people on grounds of consistency with antecedently held beliefs as well as possible additional properties (like its clarity).

Hermann (1851: 16) was the first to suggest that, while the *probabile* corresponded to the πιθανόν, *ueri simile* must have had a terminological counterpart in Greek other than paraphrases and that Philo must have distinguished something which he called εἰκός (presumably a species of the πιθανόν). In recent times this hypothesis has been supported by Glucker (1995: 126–7; 2004: 149–50) and entertained by Obdrzalek (2006: 269–71). Against it there stands the fact that the term is completely absent from the Greek record on the sceptical Academy and that the discussion of the πιθανόν in Sext. M. 7 does speak of πιθανά 'appearing true', which can plausibly be rendered *ueri simile* and makes the assumption of the use of an otherwise unattested term uneconomical; see section 6.3.

A *regula* is originally a ruler (unlike a κριτήριον, which is an unspecified instrument), a sense which remains present even in *Acad.*; cf. the first fragment from the *Academicus secundus* (Nonius pp. 162–3 M. = t. 9): *atqui si id crederemus, non egeremus perpendiculis non normis non regulis*, where the tricolon lists similar but different items. Cf. also Lucr. 4.513–17: *Denique ut in fabrica, si prauast regula prima, | normaque si fallax rectis regionibus exit, | et libella aliqua si ex parti claudicat hilum, | omnia mendose fieri atque obstipa necesse est, | praua cubantia prona supina atque absona tecta...*, 'Lastly, as in a building, if the original rule is warped, if the square is faulty and deviates from straight lines, if the level is a trifle wrong in any part, the whole house will necessarily be made in a faulty fashion and be falling over, warped, sloping, leaning forward, leaning back...' (transl. Smith). On Ciceronian renderings of κριτήριον, see Hartung (1970: 39–43), who notes that phrasal terms involving *iudicium* are much more frequent (e.g. *Luc.* 33: *iudicium*; 142: *Plato autem omne iudicium ueritatis...*). See also the fundamental study by Striker (1996a).

The phrase *uitam agere* denotes the conduct of life, from the processing of perceptual information arising from one's surroundings to deliberation about practical problems; cf. e.g. Cic., *Fin.* 4.69: *Admirantes quaeramus ab utroque quonam modo uitam agere possimus, si nihil interesse nostra putemus, ualeamus aegrine simus, uacemus an cruciemur dolore, frigus famem propulsare possimus necne possimus*; *Luc.* 109 *fin.* For the πιθανόν as a 'criterion for the conduct of life' (an expression which sounds Pyrrhonian, cf. Brittain 2001: 154 n. 37), see also Sext., *M.* 7.166: κριτήριον πρός τε τὴν τοῦ βίου διεξαγωγὴν καὶ πρὸς τὴν τῆς εὐδαιμονίας περίκτησιν. However, the phrase *in quaerendo ac disserendo* represents a significant expansion and must relate to philosophical inquiry and debate; cf. the same juxtaposition in *Luc.* 147, in connection with inquiry into the *dissensiones* amongst philosophers; in *Or.* 206, where an inquiry into a fairly recondite matter of rhetorical theory is at issue. The verb *disserere* is also sometimes used in phrasal terms rendering the Greek λογική (e.g. *Fat.* 1), as is the collocation with *quaerere*; cf. *Fin.* 1.22: *Iam in altera philosophiae parte, quae est quaerendi ac disserendi, quae* λογικὴ *dicitur*.... See also Reinhardt (2003: 189–94). Lucullus ascribes here, without any suggestion that he wants to be controversial, to the more restrained Academics in general, i.e. those who follow Carneades, the use of the πιθανόν in connection with philosophical problems; contra Brittain (2001: 17), who holds that one should see a reference, or ultimately intended reference (see his p. 103 n. 49), to the 'Philonian/Metrodorian view'.

§§33–34a

Having briefly introduced the Academic *regula*, Lucullus now moves to criticism: it would be a strange *regula ueri et falsi* if we had no concept of the true and the false.[131]

This sounds as if the Academics had claimed that the πιθανόν was their criterion of truth, and Lucullus observes that they are not entitled to such a criterion, since he who rejects cataleptic impressions forfeits the claim to the concepts of the true and the false, which on the Stoic account of concept formation arise from cataleptic impressions.[132]

Alternatively, the Academics claimed that the πιθανόν was their criterion, sc. without claiming that it was a criterion *of truth*, and Lucullus' point is that there can be no such thing as a criterion which is not a criterion of truth, followed by the point on concept formation. Or indeed it is Lucullus' claim that the Academics as a matter of fact *use* the πιθανόν as one would use a criterion (cf. *uti* in §32 *fin.*).

The latter interpretation is recommended by the unqualified use of *regula* in the report in §33 *fin.*, as well as by the fact that the followers of Carneades in general are at issue—at best a species of them, if at all, can be credited with laying claim to a criterion of truth.[133]

---

[131] See Striker (1997: 261) on the merits of the argument. Görler (1994: 863) ascribes a related argument to Cicero: that one cannot claim to be in possession of the *ueri simile* without knowing the *uerum*. I do not believe that a version of this argument is to be found in Cicero's extant works, but *Contra Acad.* 3.18.40 (= t. 60) suggests that it featured in the lost parts of the final edition. See the commentary ad loc.

[132] For concept formation, see on *Luc.* 30.

[133] In Sextus' survey of epistemological views the πιθανόν is in *M.* 1.166 introduced as Carneades' 'criterion for the conduct of life and for the attainment of happiness' (κριτήριον πρός τε τὴν τοῦ βίου διεξαγωγὴν καὶ πρὸς τὴν τῆς εὐδαιμονίας περίκτησιν). Overall Sextus presents the Academics as dogmatists who merely pretend to be sceptics, i.e. his aims are somewhat different from Lucullus'; nonetheless, I would argue that Sextus is foisting the term κριτήριον onto the Academics. Cf. also *M.* 7.173, 176, 184. Further, the section features scenarios in which subjects give 'assent' and impressions are 'true'.

Anti-sceptical arguments which arise from the combination of the claims (i) that the sceptic cannot be in possession of concepts and (ii) that concepts are required if the sceptic is to understand the dogmatist, in particular the terms he uses ('proof', e.g.), or if he is to be able to think or 'investigate' (σκέπτεσθαι)—the hallmark of the sceptic—form a significant stratum in the debate between the Pyrrhonists and the dogmatists, but are largely absent from the record on the debate between Academics and Stoics/Antiochus.[134] In *P.H.* 1.23–4 Sextus replies with some dogmatic-sounding assumptions: the sceptic is in possession of concepts because he acquired them as a child, prior to developing the faculty of assent, i.e. his concepts are not the result of acts of assent. Had the Academics given this response, Antiochus would no doubt have welcomed it and would have interpreted it as a concession on the point which he is emphasizing at least here: that there are cataleptic impressions.

So if we do possess the concept of the true and the false, Lucullus argues, there must be a difference between the true and the false. If there is no difference, there will be no criterion, no way of making judgements, and no mark of truth (*nota ueritatis*). Expressions like *nota ueritatis* have given rise to a debate as to whether Antiochus was still using an orthodox Stoic conception of cataleptic impressions. See the survey of all relevant passages below and section 10.2.

Lucullus then offers an analogy: when the Academics say that the only thing they do not accept, sc. in Zeno's definition of the cataleptic impression, is the stipulation contained in the third clause, this is as if someone who deprives a person of the use of their eyes were to say that he does not take away the objects, sc. in the world which are there to be seen (*cerni*, a word that is used with preference for 'veridical seeing'). For just as we see the objects with our eyes, we see everything else by means of impressions which bear the mark of truth, not a mark that indicates truth as much as falsehood. Once more this is said from the perspective of Stoic thought: perception (αἴσθησις) is *defined* as assent to a cataleptic impression. That is why Lucullus can compare the loss of our eyes to giving up on the cataleptic impression, whereas Cicero will later say that his perceptual experience affords him, in terms of representational content, with everything that is available to the Stoic (*Luc.* 105a).

Lucullus adds at the very end of the paragraph that, whether one uses the plain *probabile* or one which has been subjected to some kind of test, one must always return to the cataleptic impression, sc. because any kind of *probabile*, however scrutinized, will be subject to the ἀπαραλλαξία charge. §34a then restates and emphasizes the need for a distinctive feature in any *uisum* one might want to use.

Some Academics might have replied that they are advancing their arguments or offering the πιθανόν dialectically, in the sense that what they say is either endorsed by their dogmatic opponents or ought to be endorsed by them, given their standards of rationality and their acknowledgement that cataleptic impressions are not available all the time, but the Cicero character's commitment to the *probabile* is not purely dialectical; see on *Luc.* 98–111, esp. 104–5, and sections 4 and 6, where I argue that the Clitomachean position and that of mitigated scepticism represented in *Acad.* are in many ways very similar but differ sharply on what kind of belief (in a non-terminological sense, not in the sense of Stoic δόξα) they permit.

---

[134] See also on §22 above.

Excursus: Did Antiochus regard the cataleptic impression as a sign?

It is not a given that Antiochus, although he was dubbed a Stoic by his critics (Cic., *Luc.* 132; Sextus, *P.H.* 1.235), adopted Stoic doctrine without modifications (sc. in the field of epistemology). Expressions like *ueritatis nota* (*Luc.* 33) have given rise to a debate: was Antiochus (1) still using an orthodox Stoic conception of the cataleptic impression, and notably of the distinctive feature which marked such impressions out as self-warranting (not necessarily in a manner that was consciously available to the perceiving subject), or had he (2) modified the doctrine by interpreting (2a) the cataleptic impression itself, or (2b) its distinctive feature, as a sign from which the perceiving subject, independently of the content of the impression (representational or propositional), can infer that the propositional content of the impression in question is true?

On option (2) Antiochus would have reinterpreted the Stoic doctrine. Striker (1997: 262–5) proposed option (2a) and suggested that Cicero used *nota* and *signum* for the Greek σημεῖον (rather than ἰδίωμα), which, so the argument, he found in his Antiochian sources, and that he used both terms (with one exception, *Luc.* 58) to refer to the cataleptic impression rather than to its distinguishing feature.[135] Brittain (2012: 118–20), in proposing to evaluate this suggestion, in fact considered the question of whether *notae* and *signa*, assuming the terms were used to refer to the distinguishing feature rather than the impression itself, could be interpreted as signs.

In order to be evaluated, option (2b) requires an appraisal of what Cicero generally says about cataleptic impressions in *Acad*. Brittain (2012: 118–20) provides this and concludes plausibly that other passages (where *signum* or *nota* do not feature) are naturally read as presupposing the interpretation of the cataleptic impression as a natural criterion, i.e. as delivering truths directly and without an inference. Option (2a) can be tested by surveying all passages in which the relevant terms (*nota*, *signum*) feature; this I propose to do in what follows.

The Greek term ἰδίωμα is attested for the younger Stoics (Sextus, *M.* 7.252 and 408), who used it to refer to the distinctive feature of cataleptic impressions, but it is not one of the terms used to denote a 'sign' in the inferential sense. While it is true that *nota* and *signum* can both mean 'sign' in the inferential sense as e.g. in Cic., *Div.* 1.127 (as well as have other meanings peculiar to themselves), I do not believe that *nota* and *signum* are used as exact synonyms or interchangeably by Cicero in *Luc.*, nor do I think that both terms render the Greek term σημεῖον, as Striker (1997: 262 n. 7) assumes following Plasberg² (pp. 117, 122). Rather, it seems more likely that Cicero found one Greek term in his Greek sources, probably ἰδίωμα, chose to render it *nota*, and used *signum* in the sense of 'impression' to reference a particular property of impressions, viz. that they represent an object minutely. I survey the relevant passages here and provide more detailed explanation in the commentary ad loc. in each case.[136]

---

[135] Striker (1997: 265) regards this as an Academic interpretation of the Stoic doctrine, akin to how the Carneadean scheme conceptualized πιθανά.

[136] I do not include §48 *nulla in uisis distinctio appareat*, since I do not believe *distinctio* to refer to the distinctive feature of purported cataleptic impressions.

Luc. 33: *Si nihil interest, nulla regula est, nec potest is, cui est uisio ueri falsique communis, ullam habere iudicium aut ullam omnino ueritatis notam.*

Here *iudicium* refers to the criterion, i.e. the cataleptic impression, which is threatened by ἀπαραλλαξία (cf. *uisio ueri falsique communis*). For *nota* to mean 'impression', the second disjunct would have to be explicative of the first. *Nota* is better taken to mean 'mark' here.

Luc. 33: *Vt enim illa oculis modo agnoscuntur, sic reliqua uisis, sed propria ueri, non communi ueri et falsi nota.*

The presence of *uisis*, and the fact that *nota* is singular, makes 'mark' the natural interpretation of *nota*.

Luc. 34: *...ad uisum illud de quo agimus tibi erit reuertendum. In eo autem, si erit communitas cum falso, nullum erit iudicium, quia proprium in communi signo notari non potest.*

Here *eo* clearly resumes *uisum* in the preceding sentence. *Communitas cum falso* is yet another phrasal term related to ἀπαραλλαξία (which is a property of actual or purported impressions). The repetition of *in* (*in eo* ~ *in communi signo*) suggests that *signum* refers to an impression here; if *signum* meant 'sign', one would expect it to be instrumental ablative; cf. Aug., *Contra Acad.* 2.5.11: *his signis uerum posse comprehendi, quae signa non potest habere quod falsum est*. *Notare* is a *uerbum sentiendi* and means 'to recognize' (*OLD* s.v. no. 6). *Signo* is generic singular.

Luc. 35: *Non enim urguent ut coarguant neminem ulla de re posse contendere nec asseuerare sine aliqua eius rei quam sibi quisque placere dicit certa et propria nota.*

Here I feel less confident than in the earlier cases. Because of the relative clause attached to *rei*, *nota eius rei* is not a straightforward parallel of *illius rei signum* in *Luc.* 36. *Certa et propria* seem more natural attributes of the distinguishing 'mark' in this context: *propria* means 'peculiar to the impression/kind of impression'.

Luc. 36: *Vt enim confidant, notum iis esse debebit insigne ueri; quo obscuro et oppresso quod tandem uerum sibi uidebuntur attingere? Quid autem tam absurde dici potest quam cum ita loquuntur: 'Est hoc quidem illius rei signum aut argumentum, et ea re id sequor, sed fieri potest ut id quod significatur aut falsum sit aut nihil sit omnino.'*

Confidence (sc. in an impression) comes from being familiar with or having access to the *insigne ueri*; for this not to be circular, the *insigne ueri* must be the distinguishing feature (*insigne* as a noun is rare; cf. *Luc.* 101 for the adjective). The direct speech at the end of the extract is difficult (see ad loc.), but on balance it most likely amounts to a statement put into the mouth of the Academic that there is a detailed impression that *p*, that the speaker therefore follows it, but that it can happen that what is represented in the impression turns out to be false or non-existent. Cf. also *Luc.* 45: *perspicuitas... magnam habet uim, ut ipsa per sese ea quae sint nobis ita ut sint indicet.*

Luc. 57: ...*de quo omnis hic sermo est, cum ei res similes occurrant quas non habeat dinotatas.*

Dinotare is attested only here in classical Latin, but is readily understood and not suspicious. The passage speaks to Cicero's (and Lucullus') conception of the *nota* as used of the distinctive feature of cataleptic impressions, in that a *nota* is apparently not a feature which can be perceived independently of the content of an impression. Rather, things are marked out in an impression in a distinctive way. Cf. the other Antiochian speaker's, Varro's, characterization of the distinctive feature in *Ac.* 1.41 as *propriam quandam... declarationem earum rerum quae uiderentur.*

Luc. 58: *Quasi uero non specie uisa iudicentur, quae fidem nullam habebunt sublata ueri et falsi nota.*

Here the presence of *uisa* precludes the possibility that *nota* could refer to an impression.

Luc. 69: *Quis [quam] enim iste dies illuxerit, quaero, qui illi ostenderit eam quam [quam] multos annos esse negitauisset, ueri et falsi notam.*

Cicero says in the same speech (§77 *fin.*) that the dispute over the third clause of Zeno's definition was the remaining one between dogmatists and Academics, and the distinguishing feature is of course linked to that clause. On the most natural reading *nota* denotes that feature here.

Luc. 71: *Dionysius ille Heracleotes utrum comprehendisset certa illa nota qua assentiri dicitis oportere....*

The passage could be pressed to yield that one apprehends through a *nota*, where *nota* stands for the impression: it is the cataleptic impression, in virtue of having a special feature, which causes assent, not the special feature itself, but the latter claim, if intended, could also be a loose way of expressing the first one.

Luc. 77: *Tum illum ita definisse, ex eo quod esset sicut esset impressum et signatum et effictum.*

This passage is not drawn on in the argument made by Striker (1997) since *signare* and cognates as they feature in definitions of the cataleptic impression and related statements are for her not connected with instances of *signum*, but it is part of my argument that *signum*, where it has the reference of 'impression', does not mean 'sign' but means 'impression' in the literal sense (unlike *uisum*, which means 'appearance').

Luc. 84: *incidebat in eius modi uisum quod percipi non posset, quia nulla nota uerum distinguebatur a falso... agnoscendo eius modi notam quae falsa esse non possit?... tamen non ea nota iudicabis qua dicis oportere ut non possit esse eiusdem modi falsa.*

On its first occurrence, given the presence of *uisum* earlier in the sentence and the fact that the true is said not to have been distinguished from the false by means of a *nota*, *nota* must refer to the feature. On the other two occasions, a reference to the impression would seem more natural, given that *falsa* is an attribute of *nota* in both cases (to assume that *falsus* means 'not genuine' here rather than 'false', to enable the reading 'mark', is unattractive). Since Cicero is evidently talking about the same issue throughout, looseness of expression (cf. *Luc.* 71), rather than a substantial difference in the conception of the cataleptic impression, seems the most natural explanation. This is also suggested by the variation between §35 *certa et propria nota* and §103 *ueri et certi notam*, where surely no material difference is intended. Note finally that *Luc.* 84 responds to *Luc.* 58 above, where *nota* clearly means 'mark'.

Luc. 101: ...*ut ei uera multa uideantur, neque tamen habere insignem illam et propriam percipiendi notam.*

Whether *uera multa* go together (with *uideantur* as a full verb) or *uera* is a complement (see ad loc.), *habere...notam* is only open to one reading here, i.e. many impressions appear true / many true impressions appear but appear not to have a peculiar feature. With *insignem*, cf. the noun *insigne* in *Luc.* 36 above.

Luc. 103 *fin.*: [Academics do not deny the existence of colour, taste, and sound] ... *illud sit disputatum, non inesse in iis propriam, quae nusquam alibi esset, ueri et certi notam.*

Nota is here an inherent feature of things the Academics profess they perceive, too.

Luc. 110: *Sed ut illa habet probabilia non percepta, sic hoc ipsum, nihil posse percipi. Nam si in hoc haberet cognitionis notam, eadem uteretur in ceteris.*

Here the *nota cognitionis* is said to be 'in' the propositional content of an impression (or in the impression). Thus *nota* denotes the feature.

Luc. 111: *nam tam uera quam falsa cernimus. Sed probandi species est, percipiendi signum nullum habemus.*

The epigrammatic second sentence is again difficult. *Species* is most likely the 'look' of an impression, and the sentence might mean that Academics recognize a look of impressions which gives rise to approval, but that they do not have the sign, i.e. distinguishing feature, which signals (or gives rise to) apprehension. However, if one does not approach the passage with the preconception that *signum* means 'sign, distinguishing feature', and reads it in the light of earlier passages, the contrast may be between a vague look warranting approval and an ex hypothesi uniquely detailed impression (imprinted on the mind) which leads to apprehension.

I conclude that there is no linguistic evidence (as per option 2a above) suggesting that Antiochus, as represented by Lucullus in *Luc.*, thought that a cataleptic impression functioned as a sign which allowed the human subject to infer the truth of the underlying proposition. *Luc.* 57 is especially significant in this connection, in that it appears to illuminate how Cicero conceives of the distinguishing feature: he does so in a manner which is entirely consistent with the interpretation of the cataleptic impression as a natural criterion. There is a certain looseness with respect to the term *nota*, which is used of the distinguishing feature cataleptic impressions supposedly have as well as of such impressions themselves—metonymically, I think, rather than in a way which expresses a substantial philosophical position.[137] The term *signum*, in relevant contexts, does not actually mean 'sign', but means 'impression' in a literal sense which relies on the etymological connection with *signare* as it features on Cicero's rendering of the Zenonian definition of the cataleptic impression. The use of *signum* to denote a representation of an object (e.g. a painting or a bust representing an individual) is in the background, too.[138] A Latin native speaker who was steeped in the works of Cicero would later take *nota* and *signum* to come apart in a comparable way in a relevantly similar context; see Magee (1989: 49–63, esp. 63) on Boethius' use of *nota* and *signum* in his translation of Aristotle's *Int*.

Quae ista regula est ueri et falsi...aut ullam omnino ueritatis notam: with the dilemmatic structure of the argument—either we have a *notio ueri et falsi* or we do not; if the former, then one should accept the Stoic criterion; if the latter, then one has no criterion at all—cf. §§43–4, where the same device is used.

On the possible significance of *regula* in §33 *fin*. being resumed by *regula... ueri et falsi*, and on references to the πιθανόν as a criterion in the Carneadean section in Sextus, *M*. 7, see the general note above. Reid[1] (p. 217) notes: 'The insertion of these words [*regula ueri et falsi*] here (though they follow below) is emphatic and intentional', and cross-refers to §43: *illa uera definitio*. The term *regula* enables the play on *rectum et prauum*; by contrast, *iudicium* can have the connotation of the power to judge (see *OLD* s.v. no. 5, cf. 11a). For *notio* = ἔννοια, cf. §30; in §21 Lucullus used *notitia*, and *notio* in a different sense (§27).

For *internosci*, see the discussion of discrimination terminology in section 5.3; and cf. Hor., *Epist*. 2.2.44–5: *Adiecere bonae paulo plus artis Athenae, scilicet ut uellem curuo dinoscere rectum atque inter siluas Academi quaerere uerum*.

The pairing *rectum et prauum* alludes to the primary sense of *regula*, 'ruler'; *regula* derives from *rego*, of which *rectus* is originally the perfect participle. There is thus an etymological argument hinted at as to why a criterion can only be a criterion of truth as opposed to merely being a useful guide which helps one to get things right most of the time: rulers, which are invariably completely straight, are used to verify if something else is straight or bent. Cf. Lucr. 4.513:...*si prauast regula prima* (the larger context is likewise the subject of the criterion).

---

[137] The argument could be strengthened further by considering relevant Ciceronian evidence from outside *Acad*., e.g. *N.D*. 1.12: *Non enim sumus ii quibus nihil uerum esse uideatur, sed ii qui omnibus ueris falsa quaedam adiuncta esse dicamus tanta similitudine ut in iis nulla insit certa iudicandi et assentiendi nota*, 'For we are not those to whom nothing true appears, but rather those who say that to all true (impressions) certain false ones are attached of such similarity that in them there is no certain mark for judging and assenting.' Here the reference to ἀπαραλλαξία (*ueris falsa...adiuncta*) makes it clear that impressions and a mark attaching to them is at issue. Dyck (2003: 69) glosses 'reliable mark (as a basis) for judging and assenting', but the gerund in the genitive may also signal a purpose; see Kühner-Stegmann i.737–8.

[138] Cf. *OLD* s.v. no. 9a: 'a typical or representative sign, emblem, symbol, token'; no. 12a: 'a sculptured figure, commonly a deity, statue, image.'

Given Cicero's use of *uisum* elsewhere (see section 10 and Reinhardt 2016), including in passages which turn on the correspondence with Greek terminology and thus stand out as programmatic (cf. *Luc.* 18; *Ac.* 1.40), one may wonder if **uisio** *ueri falsique communis* is meant to be subtly different in meaning from *uisum* here. Note also that the Carneadean πιθανόν is called a *uisio probabilis* later in this very paragraph, in a context where *uisum* features in the immediately preceding sentence as well as later in the same sentence. Quint. 6.2.29 suggests that he at least regarded *uisio* as a straightforward rendering of φαντασία: *Quas* φαντασίας *Graeci uocant (nos sane uisiones appellemus), per quas imagines rerum absentium ita repraesentantur animo ut eas cernere oculis ac praesentes habere uideamur, has quisquis bene ceperit is erit in affectibus potentissimus.* The term *uisio* can denote something in the world (i.e. an 'appearance' in that sense) as well as an experience had (and thus a mental item); cf. *OLD* s.v. no. 2. Here it is tempting to suspect that *uisio* is something like the faculty of φαντασία, because of the general statement about the existence of a criterion and the *datiuus possessoris* (*cui*), which would not be natural if the mere having of an impression was meant; thus also Hartung (1970: 33–4), who renders *uisio* as 'Erkenntnisfaehigkeit'. In §49 *uisiones inanes* are 'vacuous impressions'; in §90 the force of *uisio* as a *nomen actionis* is actualized once again in that the term is used to describe the mind's activity in having *inanes uisiones*.

See above, p. 417 for my reading of *Si nihil interest…ueritatis notam* as evidence for Antiochus' interpretation of the doctrine of the cataleptic impression and for the use of *nota* in the sense of 'mark'; on Cicero's uses of *nota*, see also section 10.2. *Omnino* reinforces *ullam*: 'any mark of truth at all'; cf. the discussion of *omnino* in §12: *negat Academicos omnino dicere*. The distinguishing feature is clarity, and Lucullus' point is that, if true and false impressions could be equally clear, clarity could not be the feature which marks out cataleptic impressions. There is no suggestion that on the line of reasoning introduced by Lucullus an impression that *p* could also be an impression that not-*p*; cf. Striker (1997: 263).

Lambinus deleted the first occurrence of *ueri et falsi* and was followed by some later editors, but the repetition seems emphatic and deliberate.

Nam cum dicunt hoc se unum tollere…sed propria ueri, non communi ueri et falsi nota: for *tollere* = ἀναιρεῖν, cf. *Luc.* 26, 144, 146, 148. For the transmitted *ut quicquam possit ita uideri* Manutius wrote *quicquam ⟨uerum⟩*, and Baiter *ut quicquam possit ita ⟨uerum⟩ uideri*, dubbed 'not improbable' by Reid[1], who prints the transmitted text, and adopted by Plasberg[1] and Plasberg[2]; however, there are enough instances of veridical *uideri* to make any insertion unnecessary.

One difference between the position characterized here and the Roman Books view (cf. on §18) is that the former pointedly contrasts impressions which meet the first two clauses of the Zenonian definition with cataleptic impressions. That the entire debate from Arcesilaus onwards was about the third clause is stated in §78 *init.*

For the analogy offered from *Quo enim…*, cf. Sext., *M.* 7.260 (= end of LS 40K; a Stoic context): Ἄτοπον οὖν ἐστι τοσαύτην δύναμιν ἀθετεῖν καὶ τὸ ὥσπερ φῶς αὐτῶν ἀφαιρεῖσθαι. ὃν γὰρ τρόπον ὁ χρώματα μὲν ἀπολείπων καὶ τὰς ἐν τούτοις διαφοράς, τὴν δὲ ὅρασιν ἀναιρῶν ὡς ἀνύπαρκτον ἢ ἄπιστον, καὶ φωνὰς μὲν εἶναι λέγων, ἀκοὴν δὲ μὴ ὑπάρχειν ἀξιῶν, σφόδρα ἐστὶν ἄτοπος (δι' ὧν γὰρ ἐνοήσαμεν χρώματα καὶ φωνάς, ἐκείνων ἀπόντων οὐδὲ χρῆσθαι δυνατοὶ χρώμασιν ἢ φωναῖς), οὕτω καὶ ὁ τὰ πράγματα μὲν ὁμολογῶν, τὴν δὲ φαντασίαν τῆς αἰσθήσεως, δι' ἧς τῶν πραγμάτων ἀντιλαμβάνεται, διαβάλλων τελέως ἐστὶν ἐμβρόντητος, καὶ τοῖς ἀψύχοις ἴσον αὐτὸν ποιῶν, 'It is absurd, then, to reject so great a capacity [sc. of impression] and to deprive ourselves of the light (as it were). For in the same way as the person who admits colors and the differences among them, but does away with sight as unreal and untrustworthy, and who says that there are sounds, but maintains that hearing is not real, is totally absurd (for if the things through which we conceive colors and sounds are not there, we are not capable of experiencing colors and sounds), so too the person who accepts objects, but attacks sensory appearance, through which one grasps objects, is completely deranged and is putting himself on a par with inanimate things' (transl. Bett).

Reid[1] (p. 217) discusses the grammar of the sentence beginning *ut si quis*.... Dismissing a suggestion by Madvig (1876: 523) that *ut* has the force of 'for example' and that *si quis*... functions as a protasis to the preceding sentence ending in *negant* with reference to the tense of *priuauerit*, Reid holds instead that 'the passage...belong(s) to a very numerous class, in which the illustrative *ut* is followed by a conditional clause, without any apodosis.' It is not clear that the two syntactical phenomena to which Reid refers can be separated neatly. The mood of *priuauerit* is due to the fact that the *si*-clause is cast in the independent potential subjunctive, its tense is determined by the rules of the sequence of tenses; *possent* below replicates the pattern in historical sequence depending on *ademisse*. See also Plasberg[1] (p. 84).

With *propria ueri...nota* 'peculiar mark of truth', cf. *Ac.* 1.41:... *iis* [*uisis*] *solum quae propriam quandam haberent declarationem earum rerum quae uiderentur*, and above, p. 417; the juxtaposition suggests that the *nota* is not 'some additional feature, like a blue ribbon or perhaps a watermark' (to borrow a phrase from Striker 1997: 272), but is simply the manner in which an impression represents its object. See also on §84.

Quam ob rem siue tu probabilem uisionem...ad uisum illud de quo agimus tibi erit reuertendum: on *uisum* vs *uisio*, see on *quae ista regula* above. An impression which is 'unimpeded' is an impression which has survived scrutiny; cf. the tests referred to in §36 *init.*, the similar criticism in §§44 and 59, Cicero's reply in §§104–9, and sections 6.1 and 6.5. Sextus says in *P.H.* 1.229 that the philosophers of the New Academy preferred the πιθανά which had been tested to the simple πιθανόν; in *M.* 7.184–5 the plain πιθανόν is said to be reserved for trivial matters or for situations in which there is no time for a detailed appraisal. This is consistent with what is reported for Carneades here. *Reuerti* means 'to return to' both for the purpose of everyday life and in terms of doctrinal commitment.

§34a

In eo autem, si erit communitas cum falso...non possit item falsum uideri: see above, p. 417 for my interpretation of the sentence. As argued in the introduction (section 5), ἀπαραλλαξία (sc. of supposed cataleptic impressions and false ones just like it) does not mean 'indistinguishability', but 'non-distinctness'. The term *communitas* of the true and the false is one of Cicero's renderings, suggesting that he appreciated the precise force of the term; cf. §42 *fin.*, where it is said that every true impression has a false one just like it *adiunctum*, and §54: *nec sit in duobus aut pluribus nulla re differens ulla communitas*.

Reid¹ (p. 218) wonders if an *ei* has dropped out before *erit communitas*. *Regula* above might have been replaced by *iudicium* here to convey the notion of a 'power of judgement'.

With *notare* 'to recognize', cf. Cic., *Div.* 1.34 *signis notatis* 'recognized signs' and Lucr. 1.699–700: *Quid nobis certius ipsis | sensibus esse potest, qui uera ac falsa notemus?* Schäublin et al.: '...da das Eigene anhand eines gemeinschaftlichen Zeichens nicht festgestellt werden kann.' For *notare in aliqua re*, cf. *De orat.* 3.186. *OLD* s.v. *noto* no. 1a lists our passage under 'to put an identifying or distinguishing sign on, mark'. For the future tense (*erit...erit*) used to express a possibility which the speaker regards as counterfactual, see Kühner-Stegmann i.142.

§§34b–35a

Speaking as if he was talking about Academics arguing in a certain way, rather than about a different group of Academics (cf. §32: *interdum...alii*), Lucullus now considers a position which involves 'labouring under a similar kind of mistake' (*simili in errore uersantur*)—the mistake must be the positing of a kind of impression which does not come up to the standard of the καταληπτικὴ φαντασία. For Lucullus any such impression would be worthless because it would be open to the same ἀπαραλλαξία-considerations which the Academics themselves cite against the cataleptic impression.

The impression at issue is called the *perspicuum* (ἐναργές) and is characterized as satisfying the first two clauses of the Zenonian definition but not the third one. Since the nineteenth century it has been suspected by some that this position is to be associated with Philo, and with the Roman Books view in particular, which has of course been reconstructed in different ways. Others have ascribed the view to a minor faction within the Academy, and yet others to Carneades, as a position offered for the sake of the argument.[139] Some of the grounds which have been cited for the connection with Philo appear in fact to rest on a misunderstanding: there are two passages which ascribe to Philo a weakening of the Academic position under pressure (cf. *conuicio ueritatis coacti* here), in contexts which are in one case more plausibly and in the other unequivocally associated with the position of Philo's Roman Books,[140] but neither of them invites connection with §34b. The Roman Books view shares with the one under discussion here in §34 that it accepted the first two clauses of the Zenonian definition, but differed from it in that it called the resulting impression cataleptic.[141] What is more, the Roman Books view is explicitly left aside in Lucullus' speech (*Luc.* 12; see, however, on §18).

---

[139] A collection of pronouncements on the subject is in Allen (1997: 238–9); see also the note in Reid¹ (p. 219).

[140] The first passage is Numenius frg. 28 Des Places (= Eus., *Praep. Ev.* XIV.9.1–3), discussed in the general note on §18 (and see appendix 2), which ascribes a change of Philo's position to the clarity and consistency of his experiences; the second passage is *Luc.* 18, which talks about Philo yielding to pressure which arises from what people say about Academic intransigence.

[141] For the Roman Books view, see on *Luc.* 18.

The *perspicuum* must be a variety of the πιθανόν rather than an alternative to it, given that Lucullus is still recounting the views of the less extreme Academics identified as a worthy target in §32, who were generically identified through their allegiance to the πιθανόν. In general, it is widely agreed that the Academics who followed Carneades articulated their positions as versions of the πιθανόν. The Stoics took ἐνάργεια, rendered *perspicuitas* in *Acad.*, to be peculiar to cataleptic impressions; cf. *Luc.* 17, 45, 51 (Lucullus speaks); 87, 99, 105 (Cicero speaks); *Ac.* 1.41: *declaratio rerum* (Varro speaks). On the difference between the Academic and the Stoic construction of clarity, see section 6.[142]

In §35a we return to the theme of §§28–9, but the scope is broader: whereas there the question was whether the Academics would not have to concede that they apprehend at least one tenet, i.e. that nothing can be known, the suggestion here is that they might be asked with respect to any statement they make (*quicquid dixerint*) whether they apprehend it. Given that Lucullus connects this with what precedes with *ex hoc*, the dogmatist's question must aim at whether any proposition or corresponding impression which is classed as *perspicuum* by the Academics can then count as apprehended (so as to make the point that, if not, the *perspicuum* is open to the same objections as other varieties of the πιθανόν; cf. on §§43–4 for the underlying rationale); see n. below. The Academics laugh this objection off, on the grounds that they are not committed to defending the Stoic criterion.

Simili in errore uersantur...percipi ac comprehendi posse: on the force of *simili in errore*, see the general note above. Reid[1] (p. 219) assembles parallels for the metaphorical use of *conuicium* with dependent genitives, which in Cicero tends to denote sustained and vocal clamour, not a one-off complaint; for the emendation *conuicio* (sc. *ueritatis*), see Madvig (1826: 145). The colon *uerum illud quidem impressum in animo atque mente* renders the first two clauses of the Zenonian definition. For the significance of the collocation *animo atque mente*, see the commentary on §§37–9. Reid[1] (p. 219) assumes two corruptions to the archetypal reading: (i) he modifies the transmitted *percipi ac comprehendi* to...*atque*...('Cic. most certainly did not write *ac* before a guttural'), but Plasberg[1] (p. 84) refers to the substantial collection of instances in TLL s.v. *atque, ac* cols 1048.84–1049.6 (which cannot all be corrupted); (ii) following Harl.2 he deems it possible that *et* has dropped out before *impressum in animo atque mente*.

---

[142] Brittain (2001: 104–8) makes the case for the view that what he calls the 'Philonian/Metrodorian position' adopted the *perspicuum* as its hallmark and it is thus the target here; in the process, he dismisses, at p. 105 n. 50, the view promoted by Allen (1997: 237–43) that Carneades himself, i.e. a position formulated by Carneades dialectically, is engaged with here. I think that, if *perspicua* were embraced by Philo, they are not to be linked with mitigated scepticism, which—again on my view—Philo never promoted, and if *perspicua* are to be linked with mitigated scepticism, they cannot be connected with Philo (but should rather be associated with the position held by Catulus in *Acad.*). However, *N.D.* 1.12 is a context in which the Clitomachean narrator appears to link the commitment to universal ἐποχή to very clear (= *perspicua*?) but not cataleptic impressions: *Non enim sumus ii, quibus nihil uerum esse uideatur, sed ii, qui omnibus ueris falsa quaedam adiuncta esse dicamus tanta similitudine,* **ut in iis nulla insit certa iudicandi et assentiendi nota.** *Ex quo exsistit et illud multa esse probabilia, quae, quamquam non perciperentur, tamen, quia uisum quendam haberent* **insignem et illustrem,** *his sapientis uita regeretur.*

Quo enim modo perspicue dixeris...neque perspicuum ullum relinquitur: Lucullus argues that it flies in the face not just of the Stoic conception of clarity but of any reasonable conception of clarity embedded in normal usage that an object could be 'called' (*dixeris*) 'clearly white' when it is in fact black, or that certain objects could be said to be represented clearly in our experience or imprinted (sc. on our mind) in minute detail when it is uncertain whether our mind is set in motion by an actually obtaining state of affairs (*uere*) or is experiencing a vacuous impression (with *inaniter*, cf. §47: *cum animi inaniter moueantur eodem modo rebus iis quae nullae sint ut iis quae sint*). Supremely clear (i.e. cataleptic) impressions, according to the Stoics, meet the third clause of Zeno's definition and normally move the mind to assent. While *moueatur* must relate to movement of the mind towards assent, Lucullus avoids using the latter term here, perhaps because his discussion is compartmentalized in such a way that the discussion of assent only follows in §§37–9. Nor does he differentiate between mere action (as opposed to complete inaction) and successful goal-directed action.

Earlier editors have toyed with inserting a word for 'mind' in various places in this sentence. While *impressa subtiliter* seems perfectly intelligible without such an insertion especially given *impressum in animo atque mente* in the immediately preceding sentence, *moueatur* in the *cum*-clause without a subject is less straightforward but not suspicious; Reid[1] (p. 221) refers to impersonal *sentiatur* in §21, Plasberg[1] (p. 85) holds that *mens* can be readily supplied given *impressa*.

The sentence beginning *Ita neque...*, deliberately monotonous in its structure, is meant to hammer home the point that those Academics who posit *perspicua* leave us in as bad a state cognitively and epistemically as other Academics (cf. §32, where the moderate Academics were said to argue—merely—*elegantius* than the extreme ones who are immediately dismissed): if *perspicua* are still subject to ἀπαραλλαξία, then there *is* no colour (only the appearance of it), no object sc. in front of us as a bearer of colour (since the object we perceive may not be there), no truth, no proof, no perception, and nothing clear. This is cast as a general statement (but the Stoics/Antiochus *define* perception and clarity in specific ways); Cicero rejects the claim in §103 by saying that the Academics do not abolish sound, taste, and colour, but only that the corresponding impressions had the distinctive feature posited for cataleptic impressions.

Reid[1] (p. 221) suggests that *inaniter* means 'deceptively'; this is plausible, given the contrast with *uere*. If *inaniter* meant 'vacuously', i.e. referred to being moved by an impression which is not caused by an object, then false impressions which are nonetheless caused by an object would be unaccounted for. *Corpus* for *res* in the sense of 'external object' was presumably chosen because of the juxtaposition with *color*; cf. the use of *corpus* in *N.D.* 1.49 (an Epicurean context).

§35

Ex hoc illud...certa et propria nota: Hirzel (1883: 254 n. 2) regards this part of the text as an interpolation (blamed on copyists, 'Abschreiber'), on the grounds that it does not connect with §34 and instead resumes the subject of §§28–9; see the general note above on how I interpret *ex hoc*, and Plasberg[1] (p. 85).

The sentence from *Non enim urguent...* is difficult. The verb *urgere* or *urguere* means 'to stress, to press in argument' (*OLD* s.v. no. 9a). *Coarguere* means 'to prove a charge or an allegation' (*OLD* s.v. no. 2) not 'to show (a statement, belief etc.) to be false, refute' (*OLD* s.v. no. 4); but see below. And let us call *p* the proposition 'nobody can claim anything without a *nota*'.

If the subject of *urguent* is 'the Academics (who embrace *percepta*)', then the sentence means 'they place no emphasis on proving *p*'; the Academics would be laughing because once more they are misunderstood. If the subject of *urguent* is 'the dogmatists' (a possibility raised by Schäublin et al. p. 219 n. 99), then the sentence means 'the dogmatists do not press the Academics to show that *p*'; the Academics would be laughing because the dogmatist attack is weak and ineffectual, and Lucullus may be implying that he is rather more effective. A favourable distinction between Antiochus' arguments against the Academics and earlier ones of broadly similar type is drawn in §§28–9.

Schäublin et al. assume that *coarguere* has the meaning rejected above; they translate: 'Denn sie bestehen nicht auf einer Widerlegung des Satzes, daß man nichts feststellen noch behaupten könne, wenn die Sache, die einer je vertritt, nicht gewissermaßen ein klares und eigenes Kennzeichen aufweist.'

On the meaning and use of *nota*, see the general note on *Luc*. 33–34a, and cf. *certa et propria nota* here with §103 *ueri et certi notam*, which I do not take to be materially different.

§§35b–36

By way of a conclusion to the section on the *probabile* (*OLD* s.v. *igitur* no. 4), Lucullus now poses the question of the nature of *uestrum probabile*, only to find it wanting once more. The pronoun *uestrum* may refer to 'the Academics' in general, or to Cicero and the younger Catulus alike, the proponents of the Clitomachean position and mitigated scepticism respectively in the first edition of *Acad.* The groups of Academics who were distinguished from §32 were introduced in the third person as it were and so would not naturally be referred to by *uestrum*. It would be most peculiar, and very hard for a reader (contemporary or modern) to pick up, if mitigated sceptics alone were meant. Indeed, it would go against the grain of the entire passage, which is, as indicated, a concluding remark on the *probabile* in general.[143]

Lucullus then mentions the unexamined, basic *probabile*, which it would be rash to use, as well as the *probabile* which has undergone testing (see the nn. below, as well as on §33: *Quam ob rem siue tu probabilem uisionem...*, above). The latter may come very close to being true, which here is best taken to mean that individual *probabilia* are numerically likely to be true (or that the class of tested *probabilia* contains more true impressions than false ones; see on *magnam partem*). Nonetheless, Lucullus has

---

[143] This general nature of the section is also the reason for the third-person plural in *(id se) dicent (sequi)* and *ut solent dicere*; given that these points were probably made in *Catul.*, one might have expected second-person plural (or singular) here. It is less likely that the Lucullus character intends to cast doubt on the credibility of the younger Catulus or Cicero as representatives of the Academy.

two objections: first, however close it comes to the truth, it will be vulnerable to the charge of ἀπαραλλαξία; second, the true will remain beyond the Academics' grasp because, given that the invariably true and its distinctive feature are shrouded in darkness, they will never be able to have unqualified confidence in their impressions (*ne... quidem... confidere sibi poterunt*). The confidence at issue is confidence in a given *probabile* in any particular situation, not abstract confidence in the philosophical construct.

It is explicitly stated by Lucullus that the assumed reference point of the Academics is the sage. For Lucullus the sage does not just have access to the distinctive feature of cataleptic impressions, but also second-order awareness of his state of wisdom.

Sextus, *M*. 7.435-8, offers the same arguments and illuminates §§35b-36 in a number of ways. Thus the question of whether one can have confidence in any impression which is a mere tested *probabile* corresponds to whether φαντασίαι are πισταί, it is plain that individual impressions encountered are at issue, and the phrase *aut argumentum* in the present passage (see n. below) has no counterpart.

Quod est igitur istuc uestrum probabile...confidere sibi poterunt: this programmatic passage raises numerous questions, all covered in the introduction (section 6); they include: what accounts for the *probabilitas* of *probabilia*, unexamined as well as examined; how does the evidence from Cicero line up with that from Sextus; how exactly do the Latin terms for tests to which *probabilia* can be subjected (*circumspectio*, *consideratio*) relate to the Greek evidence, and do they carry connotations all their own; in what way can the *probabile* be related to modern conceptions of probability. See also on §§104-105a.

Quod is the adjectival interrogative; see Kühner-Stegmann i.655. With the *primo quasi aspectu probabile*, cf. Sext., *M*. 7.185-6, where the use of πιθανά which have not been subjected to testing is linked to situations which require swift decisions. For *exitum non habebunt*, 'they will have no argumentative way out', cf. §27 (the subject is *philosophia*):...*quem habebit exitum*.

The considerations cited even against the tested *probabile* are marked by (i) *primum* and (ii) *deinde*, although the second point is really subordinate to the first (see the general note above). The main clause is *confidere sibi potuerunt*, which derives its negation from the embedded conditional ⟨*ne*⟩ *si magnam...; cum dicant...absit longissime* ⟨*a*⟩ *uero* is the corresponding subordinate clause. *Fidem abrogare* is a standard phrase of legal/rhetorical terminology, which arguably determines how *fides* should be interpreted here (see, however, on §19: *dum aspectus ipse fidem faciat sui iudicii*); cf. Plaut., *Trin*. 1048; *Rhet. Her*. 1.17; Sen., *Ben*. 6.8.2.

Regarding *magnam partem* (= ὡς ἐπὶ τὸ πολύ) and *quam proxime*, the similarity between the true and the πιθανόν is discussed in section 6, where expressions which indicate that it is a matter of statistical or quasi-statistical likelihood that the πιθανόν is true are also touched on (section 6.3). Moreover, the persuasiveness of a πιθανόν is in part determined by the perceiving subject's sensorimotor interaction with the external world; it can thus inherently function as (fallible) evidence. Brittain (2001: 108) comments that 'the conception of the *pithanon* as providing "the truth or its best approximation" plainly marks this as Philonian/Metrodorian.' As argued above, that Lucullus is giving a characterization of the *probabile* in general tells against the identification of the mitigated position as the particular target of §36; that identification is also made by Hankinson (1997: 190). Madvig (1826: 148) supplied *ne*.

Vt enim confidant...aut nihil sit omnino: Lucullus now elaborates on the need to have confidence in a given impression. This can arise only when the mark of truth, i.e. the distinctive feature which marks the impression out as an instance of the class of self-warranting impressions, is *notum*, 'familiar'—a term which by itself seems to be neutral to the distinction between cognitive availability below the level of conscious awareness and conscious awareness (in §§22, 25, and 27 Lucullus talks about the sage's ability to 'discern'—*discernere*—cataleptic impressions). If that mark is obscured, then what truth (*quod* is again the adjectival interrogative, cf. §35b *quod est igitur*..., and is an attribute to *uerum*) can perceiving subjects deem to 'reach' (*attingere*), or so the question for the Academics is. *Videri* in *sibi uidebuntur attingere* is a doxastic use. *Attingere* is not terminological in *Acad.* of any mental act or event; see *OLD* s.v. *attingo* no. 11, and cf. *Tusc.* 4.47. On *insigne* as a noun, see *TLL* s.v. col. 1901.5-6; in *Luc.* 101 Cicero responds and uses the corresponding adjective: *neque tamen habere insignem...notam.*

The absurdity of having an *insigne* which is not familiar in the relevant sense is then made plain by a statement put into the mouth of the Academics (in direct speech), on which see also p. 417. One question here is the meaning of *signum*, another that of *argumentum*. If *aut argumentum* is authentic, then it cannot mean 'argument' and must mean 'a piece of evidence' (*OLD* s.v. no. 1a; thus Brittain 2006: 23) and go with *illius rei* like *signum*. (For such an unusual use of a term frequently deployed in a different sense in *Acad.*, cf. the use of *notio* in a sense other than 'concept, conception' in §§27, 85.) *Signum* might be a variation of *insigne* above, but the genitive *illius rei* 'of such and such a thing' could equally refer to the content of an impression, and *sequor* in the next colon typically has an impression not a sign as its grammatical and logical object (see section 10.3). Thus I am inclined to think that *signum* refers to an 'impression' in the literal sense here (on this use see p. 418), and that the sentence draws out the implication of relying on an impression whose *nota* is 'obscured' rather than restates the point. The presence of *ea re* would seem to support this reading: the Academic may well follow a detailed impression that *p*, but less so a mere sign that *p*. *Quod significatur*, surely deliberately chosen because it is related to *signum*, does not settle the issue, in that *quod significatur* could be what is indicated by a sign and what is represented by an impression; with the latter use, cf. collocations of *significare* and *declarare* in Cicero (e.g. *Sest.* 122; *Mil.* 4; *De orat.* 3.49 and 3.220; *Phil.* 14.6) and *Ac.* 1.41 *declarationem rerum*. Whether a sign or an impression is meant by *signum*, *aut argumentum* would seem to represent an unnecessary addition at best and to introduce a distraction at worst; note also that *id quod significatur* precedes the disjunction in the final part of the sentence rather than forms part of the first disjunct, as one might expect if the two disjuncts were to go distributively with *signum* and *argumentum*. It is possible that *aut argumentum* is an interpolation by a scribe who had read *Ac.* 1.32 (or its counterpart in the *Catulus*): *post argumentis quibusdam et quasi rerum notis ducibus utebantur ad probandum et ad concludendum id quod explanari uolebant.* See also the different interpretations by Burnyeat (1982a: 235) and Sedley (1982: 256).

Aut falsum sit aut nihil sit omnino must refer to false impressions (caused by an external object, but not representing it veridically) and vacuous impressions (not caused by an external object, and false); *nihil* in this specific sense is not recognized by *OLD* s.v.

Lucullus' report on what the Academics say makes reference to the sage (*dicant posse accidere **sapienti***). As far as the issue of confidence in what either outlook— Academic or Stoic/Antiochian—posits as the best kind of impression obtainable is concerned, the Academics would not assume a categorical difference between sage and non-sage, whereas the dogmatist thinks the distinctive feature of cataleptic impressions is consciously available to the sage only. Whether the feature is consciously available ought to have an effect on the degree of subjective confidence a human being has in a purported cataleptic impression.

Obscurato, an emendation by Lambinus, was printed by Reid[1] among others for the transmitted *obscuro*; Davies wondered about *obruto*.

Sed de perceptione hactenus...ueritas se ipsa defendet: Reid[1] (p. 222) assembles parallels for the expression that the truth (or some other inanimate thing) speaks for itself. The formulation fits with the naturalistic tendencies in Lucullus' speech (see Reinhardt 2019): to him the theory which he expounds is not just a theory, still less a scholastic construction, but read off and in tune with reality in a way in which the opponent's position is not. Walker cited by Davies wanted to emend *absentibus* to *tacentibus*, but as Reid[1] (p. 222) observes, *abesse* next to *defendere* evokes the legal sense of 'to decline a brief'. Plasberg[1] has the same division as my text, while Plasberg[2] makes this section a separate short paragraph.

§§37–39

Having formally concluded his discussion of κατάληψις (which began in §19) at §36 *fin.*, Lucullus now turns to the subject of assent.[144] Under this heading he discusses, without introducing the Greek term, the so-called ἀπραξία-argument, one of the main anti-sceptical strategies employed by the Stoics (and Antiochus), and one of the driving forces behind the evolution of the Academic stance from Arcesilaus onwards.

The term ἀπραξία means 'inactivity' or 'inaction'. The basic form of the argument, likened to the Gorgon's head (sc. shown to the Academics) in Plut., *Adv. Col.* 1122a, is that holding nothing to be true entails inactivity or is incompatible with activity (πρᾶξις), whereby 'activity' can mean a range of different things, from the elementary (movement of any kind, unlike a plant, which is stationary) over actions which only a rational being can perform to actions in accordance with virtue as only the sage can perform them.[145]

---

[144] The Stoic concept of assent is discussed in *Ac.* 1.40–2; see ad loc. For the competing Academic concepts of approval and self-aware assent, see on *Luc.* 104–105a and 148, respectively.

[145] Not all varieties of the argument are in evidence in *Acad.* or in other sources which provide information on the debate between Academics and Stoics. (The ἀπραξία-charge is also engaged with by Pyrrhonists.) For a more complete list, see Vogt (2010a: 166). On 'moral turpitude' as a consequence of ἀπραξία on the Stoic view (because of suspension of judgement about obligations), see Obdrzalek (2012: 382). See also Aug., *Contra Acad.* 2.5.12 (which, however, provides rather less information than *Luc.* 37–9).

Since activity in these senses is held to be impossible, the argument functions as a *reductio*.

On the Stoic view, belief is required for any kind of action, and belief arises from assent, i.e. from taking an impression to be true. Thus universal suspension of judgement—ἐποχή—is the specific target. This is so whether the impression is true (or even cataleptic) or false, but actions arising from assent to cataleptic impressions, and especially the actions of the sage (who assents only to cataleptic impressions), do of course have a special status, given that his every action is performed in accordance with virtue (cf. e.g. Stob. II.7, pp. 85.18–86.4 Wachsmuth = LS 59B4).

Our main sources for the ἀπραξία-charge levelled by the Stoics and Academic responses to it are *Acad.* (esp. the present passage, 61–2, 104), Plut., *Adv. Col.* 1122a–d, and Sextus, both in his own voice (*P.H.* 1.23–4) and in his account of the views of various philosophers on the criterion (*M.* 7.150–8 on Arcesilaus, 7.159–89 on Carneades); cf. LS 69. Of these *Acad.* is of course the earliest substantial text on the subject, but we know that already Arcesilaus addressed the charge, and rejected that assent is required for action.[146]

I shall now review the argument of §§37–9 and the interpretative problems the section poses. Lucullus proposes to cover the subject of assent, giving the Greek term as well as *assensio* and *approbatio* as apparent synonyms. He wants to do so briefly, not because the subject he is presenting is not large, but because the basis for its coverage had been laid before: when apprehension was at issue up to this point in Lucullus' speech, it had been assumed to be secured by assent, i.e. in the entire section beginning with §19. That assent and sensation go together in a way to be specified is indeed an assumption in what immediately follows; this may be one implication of *deinde* in *Deinde cum inter inanimum et animal*..., which marks a next step rather than a completely new beginning.

The argument down to... *neque assentiri uolunt* then is (I use an ambiguous formulation first and then review the prospects for disambiguation):

(i) Action requires *sensūs* and assent.
(ii) The difference between an *inanimum* and an *animal* is that the latter acts (*agit aliquid*).
(iii) Either one takes away *sensūs* as well (sc. if one already rejects assent, as the Academics do) or one grants (sc. to *animalia*) the faculty of assent (sc. in addition to *sensūs*).
(iv) The *animus* is taken from those (*animalia*) that are granted neither assent nor *sensūs* (i.e. they become *inanima*).

The issue here is the scope of the argument, specifically who it is about. On the basis of (ii), where *inanimum* is an emendation but almost certainly correct (see n. below), one might assume that an *animal* is any living being, or perhaps slightly more

---

[146] Scholarly discussions include Striker (1996b), who also touches on the earliest example of this kind of argument in Aristotle (see below); Frede (1997); Brittain (2001: 233–5, 267–73); Brittain (2006: xxv–xxx); Corti (2009: 29–55), exclusively on Pyrrhonism; Perin (2010a: 86–113), mainly on Pyrrhonism; Vogt (2010a); Brittain (2012: 120–3); Obdrzalek (2012).

narrowly any living being capable of movement in response to a stimulus (i.e. 'animals' in English).[147] The problem with this interpretation is that it appears to grant to animals so understood the faculty of assent, whereas on the standard Stoic view assent is a faculty of a mind, i.e. of a soul which has reason. If one does not want to posit a confusion on Cicero's part, there are two ways of resolving this difficulty.

The first is to assume that Lucullus' argument quite deliberately encompasses *animalia* which neither have reason nor the faculty of assent proper. The Stoic position on concept formation required an ability on the part of children to form conceptions by means of cataleptic impressions prior to becoming rational and developing the faculty of assent. Relatedly, young children were assumed to have quasi-speech and quasi-emotions, and the same thing was assumed for (certain) animals.[148] (That humans but not animals would go on to develop assent offers a way of explaining how they can be responsible for their actions.) There are traces of a notion of non-rational yielding (εἶξις),[149] and some scholars have wondered if one should regard this as, or assume a related notion of, quasi-assent; cf. Inwood (1985: 75); Brittain (2014: 349). The scope of the argument would be from *animalia* requiring quasi-assent to quasi-impressions in order to act to sages requiring assent to cataleptic impressions in order to act virtuously. A slightly different version of this reading would invoke what the Antiochian Piso says, in opposition to Stoic doctrine, in *Fin.* 5.38: *Sunt autem bestiae quaedam in quibus inest aliquid simile uirtutis, ut in leonibus, ut in canibus, ⟨ut⟩ in equis, in quibus non corporum solum, ut in subus, sed etiam animorum aliqua ex parte motus quosdam uidemus. In homine autem summa omnis animi est et in animo rationis, ex qua uirtus est, quae rationis absolutio definitur, quam etiam atque etiam explicandam putant.* Here the mental and cognitive faculties lead to something like virtue, but the claim only relates to the *bestiae quaedam* named, whereas our passage seems to be more general (on the reading under consideration). In any event, the suggestion would be that the categories for action which is virtue-related and action which is not would be blurred. On this reading Lucullus would be returning to animal behaviour of the most general type (*tollit is omnem actionem e uita*) at the end of §39, having just before touched on the very specific type of human behaviour which is action in accordance with virtue. What tells against this interpretation is that time and again *Acad.* is concerned with the possibility of dogmatic assent and lesser forms of endorsement (like Clitomachean approval, cf. *Luc.* 104–105a) as given by rational human beings. Relying on recherché notions like yielding without signalling it clearly would place excessive demands on the reader.

The second is to assume that the entire argument is in fact about human behaviour, i.e. the behaviour of beings that have a mind.[150] The difficulty which this reading faces is that some of the apparently rather general terms in the argument would have to be taken in a specific way for the interpretation to be sustained. Thus an *animal* would need to be a rational being, an *inanimum* a being which does not have a

---

[147] Thus e.g. Inwood (1985: 76–7); Brittain (2012: 121–2); Obdrzalek (2012: 371 n. 7, 377).
[148] See Varro, *LL* 6.56; Sen., *De ira* 1.3.7; Plut., *Soll. An.* 960f, 961e–f; Porphyry, *Abst.* 3.21–2 (all cited by Brittain 2014: 349 n. 37); Inwood (1985: 72–81). See also Brittain (2002: 256–74) on the Stoic theory of non-rational cognition.
[149] Cf. D.L. 7.51 (= LS 39A = *SVF* ii.61).
[150] Thus e.g. Vogt (2010a: 168).

rational soul (as opposed to no soul at all), *animus* in (iv) would need to mean 'reason', and the verb *agere* would denote the kind of action rational beings perform. It is arguable that there are enough footholds for these more specific senses in the context of Lucullus' speech, whereas, as indicated, animal behaviour has not been at issue up to now. Rather, in §31, at the end of the teleological argument for κατάληψις, *animal* as well as *animus* are used in the required sense in an etymological argument: he who denies that there are things which can be apprehended deprives the *animal* of its *animus* (*ipsumque animal orbant animo*); cf. (iv). The terms *mens* and *animus* feature as synonyms in §34 (...*uerum illud quidem et impressum in animo atque mente*...), and *inanimum* is a sufficiently rare term to owe the precise meaning the reader gives to it in §37 to its opposition with *animal*. The phrase *in **nostra** potestate* also suggests that it is not just any kind of *animal* that is at issue, as does the gender of the relative pronoun in §38: *animus*... *eripitur iis **quos** neque sentire neque adsentiri uolunt*. See n. below.[151]

In §38 Lucullus employs the image of a pair of scales, in order to back up (*enim*) the point that those who deny to *animalia* sense perception and assent deprive them of their *animus*: just like a scale must necessarily go down if a weight is placed upon it, so the mind (*animus*) must yield (*cedere*) to *perspicua*, supremely clear (i.e. cataleptic) impressions.[152] Two questions arise here: first, how did we get from *sensūs* (perhaps the ability to perceive, or more narrowly, or so I argued, the ability to have rational impressions) to receiving *perspicua*? Did *sensūs* denote the ability to have cataleptic impressions all along? This seems a straightforward way to make sense of the text, for otherwise the argument would be less than compelling: what is true of the *species* is not thereby true of the *genus*.[153] Second, one might wonder if *cedere* is something less than assent, so that the point made would be that one cannot fail to be moved in the direction of assent by cataleptic impressions, but the next sentence resumes *cedere* by means of *approbare*, which, coming from Lucullus, can only denote assent. This raises the question of how the passage can be read coherently, for it seems self-contradictory to say both that assent is like the yielding of a scale to a weight that is placed upon it and *in nostra potestate* at least on some readings of the latter phrase.

I note first of all what Lucullus' argumentative aim is: to show that universal suspension of judgement is impossible,[154] and that it is *normal* for human beings to

---

[151] One might wonder if Lucullus' reference point in this section could not be rational beings (= humans) but a species of them, namely sages (thus Reid¹ p. 224), but while Lucullus will be talking about virtue shortly (§39), it is not an assumption which is required to make sense of the text; contrast also *Luc.* 23–5, where the significance of κατάληψις for virtuous action is at issue, and where the sage is very overtly mentioned as reference point. This line of argument could be developed further: e.g. *agere* is a term which can naturally denote 'rational action' but is by itself not an obvious term for virtuous action.

[152] Brittain (2014: 351–2) discusses the passage with the question of whether the Stoics took assent to be compulsive in mind.

[153] Cf. *Luc.* 37 (i.e. just above): *Nam cum uim quae esset in sensibus explicabamus, simul illud aperiebatur, comprehendi multa et percipi sensibus, quod fieri sine assensione non potest*, and 108 (from Cicero's reply): *Alterum est quod negatis actionem ullius rei posse in eo esse, qui nullam rem assensu suo conprobet. Primum enim uideri oportet, in quo est etiam assensus (dicunt enim Stoici sensus ipsos assensus esse, quos quoniam appetitio consequatur, actionem sequi)—tolli autem omnia si uisa tollantur*, with Stob., *Ecl.* I.50, p. 474.18–19 Wachsmuth (= FDS 295): Οἱ Στωικοὶ πᾶσαν αἴσθησιν εἶναι συγκατάθεσιν καὶ κατάληψιν.

[154] Cf. *Luc.* 107: *Primum enim negatis fieri posse ut quisquam nulli rei assentiatur*.

assent to impressions, notably cataleptic impressions. This does not necessarily mean that it invariably happens, although the scales image by itself can suggest that. In Cicero's own speech Chrysippus' advice on how to deal with soritical arguments is referred to, and this advice does seem to assume that occasionally the human mind will not assent to a cataleptic impression (*Luc.* 93-4; see also 53, 94, 107). Moreover, in Sextus 'younger Stoics' are cited who respond to a Carneadean argument by interpreting a Carneadean scenario in such a way that a cataleptic impression ends up failing to win the assent of the perceiving subject.[155] There would seem to remain room for the possibility that Antiochus diverged from the Stoics by positing automatic and invariable assent to cataleptic impressions, but it is difficult to see how this could have been perceived as an attractive move. The same image occurs in a related text—Plut., *Adv. Col.* 1122b-c—but in a way which does not decisively illuminate the point at issue in our passage: in both cases the Academic assumption of impulse without assent is at issue, and it would appear as if Plutarch uses a Stoic image for Academic purposes, but no firm conclusions are possible about the Stoic use of the allegory. (See the n. below for further evidence.) Overall, the most plausible explanation is that Cicero has Lucullus overstate his case somewhat, by presenting assent as the necessary rather than normal consequence of cataleptic impressions experienced by humans. A piece of evidence *in the text* which points in this direction is the suggestion that an *animal* cannot fail to have an impulse towards something that appears suited to its nature: 'what appears suited to the nature of an *animal*' is a general class of things, but obtaining particular elements of this class may not be appropriate or desirable in every case and always; cf. Brittain (2014: 351-2), who observes that 'animals at pasture would burst from overfeeding'.

The meaning and use of the phrase *in nostra potestate* has been the object of careful study in recent years, as has its relationship to possible Greek counterparts and the wider issue of freedom and determinism in Stoic philosophy (see n. below). There is no suggestion that the faculty of assent bestows on rational subjects the ability to accept or reject impressions at will irrespective of their properties and the perceiving subject's antecedent dispositions; as Frede (2011: 151-2) puts it, this would come 'rather close to deluding oneself into thinking that one is god'. Rather, assent is 'in our power' in that it is a function of our moral character, which has been shaped by past experiences and past decision-making: if one is a person of a certain kind, then 'accepting what is the case' and 'doing what is right' in a particular situation naturally flows from one's disposition (including one's ability to be able to withhold assent from cataleptic impressions in highly circumscribed situations) and is in that sense emanating from us rather than the environment we encounter. How exactly this scenario allows for the possibility of *blaming* individuals for their bad epistemic and moral decisions (or praising them for good ones) is of course a problem for Stoic philosophy. For if decision-making, epistemic or otherwise, flows from an individual's rational make-up, one is bound to ask at which point the modification of this make-up was in our power.

---

[155] See Sextus, *M.* 7.254-6, with Brittain (2014: 340-1) and Reinhardt (2018b). Brittain (2001: 97 n. 37) rightly sees awareness of the younger Stoic ideas in the present passage.

Another question raised by the section is whom we should take Lucullus' target to be in particular, given that there are at least two Academic positions in play in *Acad.*, the Clitomachean one and that of mitigated scepticism. The latter does envisage the possibility of informed, self-aware assent, i.e. assent given with an awareness that the impression or proposition assented to may be false. Should one then assume that Lucullus' target here is exclusively the Clitomachean position? Not necessarily, since the kind of self-aware assent envisaged by mitigated sceptics is not recognized by the Stoics and Antiochus as assent, given that it is applied at best to impressions which meet the criteria specified in the first two clauses of the Zenonian definition but not that specified in the third clause. Cf. the commentary on *Luc.* 148.

Cicero responds to the argument of *Luc.* 37-9 in §§108-9 of his own speech in particular, although there are other passages in the vicinity which are relevant, too (§§106-7 on the possibility of memory and systematic arts if there is no κατάληψις; §§104-105a on Clitomachean approval, which amounts to non-assent but gives rise to a form of belief). In general, the charge of ἀπραξία arising from ἐποχή is countered by the Academics either by rejecting the need for assent altogether (Arcesilaus) or by introducing forms of endorsement of impressions and, as a consequence, belief, which amount to less than Stoic assent (Carneades according to Clitomachus). Moreover, the Academics reject any notion that, because ἐποχή is a consequence of ἀκαταληψία, their rejection of cataleptic impressions is apt to lead to inaction: this is where the Carneadean πιθανόν comes in.

It has been argued, by Striker (1996b: 99-104) and in considerably more detail by Obdrzalek (2012), that Lucullus' speech provides evidence for an otherwise unattested second version of the ἀπραξία-charge, one which reasons from the Academic claim that nothing can be known (ἀκαταληψία) directly to ἀπραξία, i.e. without positing ἐποχή as a consequence of ἀκαταληψία and the basis for ἀπραξία, in an argument that is applicable to sages and non-sages alike. The evidence cited for this is *Luc.* 24-5, where cataleptic (hormetic), rather than mere hormetic, impressions are presented as a requirement for action, as well as other passages from the same section, e.g. §22, which argues that there could be no conceptions, and no application of conceptions, if there were no cataleptic impressions, without an apparent reference to assent. In fact, none of this evidence supports the notion that ἀκαταληψία directly entails ἀπραξία. In *Luc.* 24-5 the sage is the frame of reference, so that no *general* argument is made, and assent is in fact mentioned (§25: *illud autem quod mouet prius oportet uideri* **eique credi**), albeit in a way which makes a point of not anticipating the discussion in the present section terminologically. As to the apparent absence of references to assent in §§19-36, it is made quite clear in §37 that assent had always been assumed to be part of the picture: *Nam cum uim quae esset in sensibus explicabamus, simul illud aperiebatur, conprendi multa et percipi sensibus, quod fieri sine assensione non potest.* Lucullus (or Cicero) has, evidently for dispositional reasons, avoided overt references to assent in the section concerned with apprehension except for §23 fin.: *nisi iis rebus assensus sit quae falsae esse non possint*. However, there are arguably also implicit references: the verb *percipere*, used frequently in §§19-36, is effective in aspect. Thus the characters in *Acad.* often end up speaking, as it were, about καταλήψεις rather than cataleptic impressions. While *percipere* and καταλαμβάνειν are equivalent in sense, the Latin language does not have the resources to create an exact counterpart for Greek verbal adjectives meaning 'capable of ϕ-ing' (like καταληπτικός); however, no doubt Cicero would have found a way of conveying this notion had he wanted to.

Obdrzalek (2012: 375) notes that the Stoic rejection of ἀκαταληψία denies the possibility of universal ἐποχή, while the ἀπραξία-argument assumes the possibility of universal ἐποχή. This raises the question of the relationship between the two arguments. One might think that, depending on the conception of πρᾶξις involved, the possibility of universal ἐποχή assumed in the ἀπραξία-argument is either a counterfactual one ('As a matter of fact, no rational being stands still') or a real one ('It would be a pity if action in accordance with virtue was not possible'). In the latter case ἀπραξία would emerge as deeply unattractive rather than be rejected by *modus tollens*. Yet while Stoic views regarding the actual existence of sages are a murky subject, it is more likely that they held that sages were extremely rare rather than non-existent and a mere theoretical possibility. If so, then wisdom (and sagehood) is a reality, and the non-existence of action in accordance with virtue is a counterfactual possibility, too. The same holds a fortiori for successful goal-directed everyday action of non-sages.[156] There is, thus, no tension between the different attitudes to ἐποχή taken by the Stoic rejection of ἀκαταληψία and the ἀπραξία argument.[157] It is consistent with this that

---

[156] When Lucullus accuses the Academics of overturning human life by rejecting cataleptic impressions out of *temeritas* (cf. e.g. *Luc.* 31 *fin.*), this (counterfactual) inability to act is one of the undesirable consequences implied by *temeritas*. Cf. Plut., *Adv. Col.* 1122e–f: 'ἀλλὰ πῶς οὐκ εἰς ὄρος ἄπεισι τρέχων ὁ ἐπέχων ἀλλ' εἰς βαλανεῖον, οὐδὲ πρὸς τὸν τοῖχον ἀλλὰ πρὸς τὰς θύρας ἀναστὰς βαδίζει, βουλόμενος εἰς ἀγορὰν προελθεῖν; τοῦτ' ἐρωτᾷς ἀκριβῆ τὰ αἰσθητήρια λέγων εἶναι καὶ τὰς φαντασίας ἀληθεῖς; ὅτι φαίνεται δήπουθεν αὐτῷ βαλανεῖον οὐ τὸ ὄρος ἀλλὰ τὸ βαλανεῖον, καὶ θύρα οὐχ ὁ τοῖχος ἀλλ' ἡ θύρα, καὶ τῶν ἄλλων ὁμοίως ἕκαστον. ὁ γὰρ τῆς ἐποχῆς λόγος οὐ παρατρέπει τὴν αἴσθησιν, οὐδὲ τοῖς ἀλόγοις πάθεσιν αὐτῆς καὶ κινήμασιν ἀλλοίωσιν ἐμποιεῖ διαταράττουσαν τὸ φανταστικόν, ἀλλὰ τὰς δόξας μόνον ἀναιρεῖ χρῆται δὲ τοῖς ἄλλοις ὡς πέφυκεν, ' "But how comes it that the man who suspends judgement does not go dashing off to a mountain instead of to a bath, or why does he not get up and walk to the wall instead of the door when he wishes to go out to the market place?" You ask this when you hold that the sense organs are accurate and sense images true? Why, because what appears to him to be a bath is not the mountain but the bath, and what appears to him to be a door is not the wall but the door, and so with everything else. For the doctrine of suspension of judgement does not deflect sensation or introduce into the non-rational affections and movements themselves a change that disturbs the presentation of sense images; it is only our opinions that it eliminates, whereas it deals with the other parts in accordance with their natural uses' (transl. Einarson and De Lacy).

[157] The earliest attested version of an inactivity argument in Arist., *Met.* Γ4, 1008b2–31, argues from the *rejection* of the principle of non-contradiction on the part of a human subject to a *counterfactual* inactivity scenario. Consider 1008b2–13: ἔτι ἄρα ὁ μὲν ἢ ἔχειν πως ὑπολαμβάνων ἢ μὴ ἔχειν διέψευσται, ὁ δὲ ἄμφω ἀληθεύει· εἰ γὰρ ἀληθεύει, τί ἂν εἴη τὸ λεγόμενον ὅτι τοιαύτη τῶν ὄντων ἡ φύσις; εἰ δὲ μὴ ἀληθεύει, ἀλλὰ μᾶλλον ἀληθεύει ἢ ὁ ἐκείνως ὑπολαμβάνων, ἤδη πως ἔχοι ἂν τὰ ὄντα, καὶ τοῦτ' ἀληθὲς ἂν εἴη, καὶ οὐχ ἅμα καὶ οὐκ ἀληθές. εἰ δὲ ὁμοίως ἅπαντες καὶ ψεύδονται καὶ ἀληθῆ λέγουσιν, οὔτε φθέγξασθαι οὔτ' εἰπεῖν τῷ τοιούτῳ ἔσται· ἅμα γὰρ ταῦτά τε καὶ οὐ ταῦτα λέγει. εἰ δὲ μηθὲν ὑπολαμβάνει ἀλλ' ὁμοίως οἴεται καὶ οὐκ οἴεται, τί ἂν διαφερόντως ἔχοι τῶν γε φυτῶν; ὅθεν καὶ μάλιστα φανερόν ἐστιν ὅτι οὐδεὶς οὕτω διάκειται οὔτε τῶν ἄλλων οὔτε τῶν λεγόντων τὸν λόγον τοῦτον, 'Again, are we to say that he who believes that things are in a certain state, or are not, is in error, while who believes both has the truth? For if he has the truth, what can be meant by saying that the nature of things-that-are is of that kind? If he does not have the truth, but has more truth than the one who believes the former way, then the things-that-are would already be in some state, and that be true and simultaneously also not true. But if everyone equally both is in error and states the truth, there will be nothing for such a person to speak or say; for he simultaneously says this and not this. And if a man believes nothing, but considers it equally so and not so, how would his state be different from a vegetable's? From which it is also quite obvious that nobody actually is in that condition, neither those who state this thesis nor anybody else' (transl. Kirwan).

Lucullus seems to treat universal ἐποχή as impossible as a matter of psychological fact in §29,[158] urging that the Academics need to acknowledge at least one δόγμα of theirs, namely the claim that nothing can be known. A refusal to recognize a kind of acceptance of impressions which is less strong than Stoic assent can also be seen in Lucullus' apparently provocative treatment of the nouns *assensio* and *approbatio* as synonyms (*Luc*. 37 *init*.), given that the latter is the term used by Cicero in his speech for 'approval' (*Luc*. 104). No objection to this reading can be derived from that fact that approval is the subject of a detailed discussion only much later in the text, given that the notion itself must have been introduced in the *Catulus*, with Cicero in his speech providing a second, fully referenced account.

§§37–38a

His satis cognitis...sed paulo ante iacta sunt fundamenta: the use of terminology associated with apprehension (*his satis cognitis*) is perhaps intended to convey the systematicity of Lucullus' exposition.

The Stoic notion of assent, the associated Greek terminology, and the Latin terminology employed by Cicero are discussed in the commentary on *Ac*. 1.40–2, where Varro discusses the Stoic 'corrections' to Old Academic epistemology in his historical survey.

As noted above, Lucullus uses *assensio* and *approbatio* interchangeably and as synonyms, whereas Cicero, notably in the programmatic section §§104–5, where he paraphrases closely a work by Clitomachus, uses *(ap)probare* for Academic approval, pointedly characterized as a type of non-assent. Lucullus may be speaking polemically, implying that there is no meaningful distinction to be drawn between assent and approval. In §43 he will argue that one either accepts a proposition or one does not (and that in the latter case consequences would be disastrous). Alleemudder (p. 198) states that in his speech Cicero distinguishes between *probare* and *approbare*. I do not believe this to be so: rather, Cicero can use *(ap)probare* to mean 'to assent' in contexts where the meaning of clear, and to mean 'to approve, to follow' where a contrast with assent is intended. In what way *fundamenta* for the present subject have already been laid is explained in the next sentence.

Reid[1] (p. 222) comments on *non quo...sed* being slightly anacoluthic for *non quo...sed quia*.

Nam cum uim quae esset...quod fieri sine assensione non potest: Lucullus is referring back to §§19–20, where the powers of discrimination and of appreciating the detail of perceptual experiences were discussed, but for these powers to issue in apprehension, they must yield more than impressions and thoughts merely

---

[158] *Pace* Obdrzalek (2012: 380), who detects no charges of inconsistency in Lucullus' speech. What is more, the Cicero character seems to agree with Lucullus on this point. The former calls himself a *magnus opinator* in *Luc*. 66, meaning that he finds it impossible to suspend judgement all the time although he is committed to ἐποχή theoretically as a Clitomachean. The reason he cites for this is that he is not a sage. Since the assumption has to be that on the character's view very few if any actual human beings are sages, the character comes close to treating ἐποχή as impossible as a matter of psychological fact.

entertained. Rather, such impressions must be taken to be true, which requires assent. What Lucullus says can also be read as a comment on the linguistic expressions *comprehendere* and *percipere*: that they are effective in aspect, i.e. *percipere* means 'to grasp something successfully', which a cataleptic impression by itself is not able to do. Rather, it needs to have been assented to (*quod fieri sine assensione non potest*).

Deinde cum inter inanimum...neque sentire neque assentiri uolunt: *deinde* suggests a step in a sequence rather than a completely new beginning (though no compelling argument may be derived from this), and the immediately preceding sentence was concerned with apprehension and assent; the latter is necessary for apprehension to come to pass.

Inanimum is a conjecture first made in the second *Veneta* of 1496. It is not absurd to say that the difference between the disembodied soul and the embodied soul (or the disembodied mind and the embodied mind) is that the latter acts or is capable of action, and if the corruption was not mechanical, this might have been the rationale for the change, but it is plain from what follows that disembodied souls or minds are not at issue. Cicero contrasts *inanimum* and *animal* elsewhere, but—on my reading of the passage above—in a way which does not clearly deliver the contrast between beings with a mind and beings without mind which I have defended above and for which there are footholds within Lucullus' speech. Cf. *Rep.* 6.28: *Cum pateat igitur aeternum id esse quod a se ipso moueatur, quis est, qui hanc naturam animis esse tributam neget? Inanimum est enim omne quod pulsu agitatur externo; quod autem est animal, id motu cietur interiore et suo, nam haec est propria natura animi atque uis; quae si est una ex omnibus quae sese moueat, neque nata certe est et aeterna est*. Here the overall paradigm is arguably Platonic and a contrast between self-movers and other things is intended. Very similar is *Tusc.* 1.54, again from a context which is overtly Platonic and close to paraphrase. In *N.D.* 2.90 there is no contrast with *animal*. Cf., however, much later Mar. Victorin., *Gen.* 10 (= p. 27 Henry/Hadot): *inanimam ὕλην, inanimum autem dico, quicquid sine intellectuali anima est*.

Assent is said to be *in nostra potestate*, and the apparent tension with the scales allegory has been highlighted in the general note above. In *Ac.* 1.40 Cicero has Varro introduce the Zenonian distinction between an impression passively received and voluntary assent: *sed ad haec quae uisa sunt et quasi accepta sensibus assensionem adiungit animorum, quam esse uult in nobis positam et uoluntariam*. This provides two glosses on *in nostra potestate*, namely that assent 'resides in us' and that it is 'voluntary'. In *Fat.* the claim that assent is *in nostra potestate* is made frequently (see esp. 43; 9, 25, 31, 40–1, 45). It is widely held, and sometimes unequivocally asserted, that *in nostra potestate* translates the Greek ἐφ' ἡμῖν, but the closest our evidence comes to linking Chrysippus with the statement that assent is ἐφ' ἡμῖν is Plut., *Sto. rep.* 1056c–d (where Plutarch argues that Chrysippus contradicts himself in calling fate inexorable on the one hand, and an antecedent not a complete cause on the other), which may be compared with §39 *init*.: πότερον οὖν τὰς συγκαταθέσεις μὴ λέγωμεν ἐφ' ἡμῖν εἶναι μηδὲ τὰς ἀρετὰς μηδὲ τὰς κακίας μηδὲ τὸ κατορθοῦν μηδὲ τὸ ἁμαρτάνειν, ἢ τὴν εἱμαρμένην λέγωμεν ἐλλείπουσαν εἶναι καὶ τὴν πεπρωμένην ἀπεράτωτον καὶ τὰς τοῦ Διὸς κινήσεις καὶ σχέσεις ἀσυντελέστους; 'So then, shall we say that we do not have control over acts of assent or over virtues or vices or right action or wrongdoing; or shall we say that destiny is deficient and determination is indeterminate and the motions and stations of Zeus are frustrate?' (transl. Cherniss). Chrysippus uses other expressions in similar contexts, though not narrowly in connection with assent, in literal quotations from his *On Fate* in Eus., *Praep. Ev.* VI.8.2 (παρ' ἡμᾶς, 'on our side' or 'because of us' = Diogenianus frg. 1 Gercke = *SVF* ii.999) and 6.8.25–6 (ἐξ ἡμῶν, 'from us' = Diogenianus frg. 3 = *SVF* ii.998); see Gourinat (2014) in particular. A general characterization, based on a broad consensus of recent scholarship, of the sense in which assent and as a result actions are *in nostra potestate* has been given above. How Cicero can say that assent 'resides in us' is easy to see, but it is more difficult to free oneself of modern preconceptions about what makes an action 'voluntary' (*assensionem... in nobis positam et uoluntariam*): an act of assent is thus described—stipulatively, it feels to the modern reader—if it emanates from within us and our reason, which has been uniquely shaped by our past experiences and past decision-making. See Bobzien (1998); Frede (2011); and Destrée et al. (2014), in which Frede (2014) offers an epilogue of sorts.

What *in* **nostra** *potestate* and *animus...eripitur iis* **quos**... do suggest is that human beings are at issue, not *animalia* in general or higher mammals (see the general note above).

Reid[1] (p. 223) prints *at uero* in §38 init., but the transmitted *et uero* is a satisfactory marker of transition to the next point. With *sensus adimendus*, cf. §61: *eam philosophiam... orbat sensibus*.

Vt enim necesse est lancem...rem perspicuam non approbare: the Stoics used the image of the scales to describe the mind's reaction to impressions, without it being clear whether the precise *illustrandum* is the movement of the mind in the direction of assent or the result of that movement, i.e. assent itself. See Plut., *Adv. Col.* 1122c (ῥοπή, the standard term for the movement of the scale-pan); *Virt. mor.* 447a; Origen, *De princ.* 3, p. 108 Delarue (= *SVF* ii. 988, p. 288.25); *Sto. rep.* 1045c (ἐπίκλισις as well as ῥοπή) on Chrysippus' use of the image in general. Cf. Carneades' use of it in Sextus, *M.* 7.166–89; *P.H.* 1.226–30. On our passage, see Inwood (1985: 77); Brittain (2014: 351).

General orientation on the passage was provided above. Lucullus seems to be clear, by creating a parallelism between *cedere* and *approbare*, that movement of the mind issuing in assent is meant, but as explained in the general note above, the reference to pursuit of what is suited to one's nature suggests not an automatism but a very strong natural inclination. This would be in line with the Stoic position; Brittain (2014: 340) suggests plausibly that, in the famous statement that the cataleptic impression 'μόνον οὐχί' seizes us by the hair, dragging us towards assent (Sext., *M.* 7.257: αὕτη γὰρ ἐναργὴς οὖσα καὶ πληκτικὴ μόνον οὐχὶ τῶν τριχῶν, φασί, λαμβάνεται, κατασπῶσα ἡμᾶς εἰς συγκατάθεσιν), the adverbial phrase does not serve to soften the metaphor of hair-pulling ('as it were'), but introduces a qualification: 'all but', 'almost'.

The presence of *cedere* (= εἴκειν) in the present context raises the question whether the Stoics assumed, in addition to non-rational yielding, a rational form of yielding, but if they did, then, for the reasons indicated, the present passage provides us with no insight into what it is. Brittain (2014: 335–6) offers further speculation.

On obtaining things which are *naturae accommodatum*, and the Stoic notion of οἰκείωσις, see the commentary on *Luc.* 25.

Given how Cicero has his characters talk about impressions in *Acad.*, the phrase *obiectam rem perspicuam...approbare* strikes the eye, in that *perspicuitas* is a property of impressions not of objects, and that *perspicuam* cannot be a complement. *Res* may just mean 'thing' generically, rather than 'object', but it remains a peculiar expression. (Reid[1] p. 224 writes '*rem*: here = *uisum*, rather awkwardly'.) Perhaps the legal use of *approbare* is asserting itself briefly here (which relates to approval processes of things in the world); cf. the commentary on *Luc.* 104-105a.

Reid[1] (pp. 223-4) suggests that the sage alone is at issue here; this would mean that the frame of reference of the argument immediately preceding is maintained. I assume that the near-compulsion of assent would be posited by the Stoics for non-sages, too, whose primary epistemic problem was that they do not withhold assent from many non-cognitive impressions, although it was recognized by the younger Stoics that antecedently held false beliefs may block assent to cataleptic impressions (see p. xcix).

Quamquam, si illa de quibus disputatum est uera sunt...assentitur statim: Lucullus seems to be referring back to §§19-29 generically (so that the present sentence and the following one stand in a general-particular relationship); the alternative—that Lucullus refers only to, say, §§19-21—is less attractive.

In §§19-29 Lucullus discussed human faculties and intellectual achievements which would be impossible without κατάληψις, and κατάληψις involves assent. That is the import of *qui enim quid percipit...* (not that assent follows cataleptic impressions *statim*): *percipere* means 'to apprehend' (i.e. have a cataleptic impression and assent to it), not 'to experience a cataleptic impression'.

Reid[1] (p. 224) thinks *omnino* modifies *nihil*, but word order suggests it goes with *loqui*.

Sed haec etiam secuntur...in eo qui rei nulli assentietur non erit: as indicated in the previous n., by *Sed haec etiam secuntur...* Lucullus seems to be detailing what he referred to generically in the previous sentence (*Quamquam, si illa de quibus disputatum est...*). *Sequi* means 'to be entailed', sc. as a consequence of universal suspension of judgement, and is not a metatextual remark like §30: *Sequitur disputatio copiosa* (*pace* Reid); thus Alleemudder (p. 204 n. 3).

Lucullus then resumes the idea (and formulation) from §37 that assent is in *nostra potestate* and observes that the 'most important thing' for human beings, namely what lies *in nostra potestate*, will not reside in the person who assents to nothing. Put differently, universal ἐποχή deprives human beings of freedom understood in a certain way, namely of freedom to be the owner of one's epistemic and moral choices.

The sentence from *idque...* is facing two ways. Syntactically, it is marked as an addendum to the former rather than a freestanding step of an argument, but it is the basis of the consideration offered in §39 *init*.

In §22 Lucullus argued that *memoria* is not possible without apprehension. Here he argues that *memoria* is not possible without assent. Assent was arguably implicit as a second necessary condition, jointly sufficient with the experience of individual cataleptic impressions, for the creation of individual memory items in §22 (see previous n.).

§39

Vbi igitur uirtus...eique quod uisum sit assentiatur: if the faculty of assent is what makes human beings free, then virtue is abolished if assent is abolished. And it will be absurd to castigate people for their vices, but to deny them praise for their virtues.

Lucullus may here be invoking normal human behaviour (and thus continue some of the naturalistic arguments he offered before): ordinary people want to and do blame people for their mistakes, and it is inconsistent to do that but not to praise people for virtuous behaviour (thus Alleemudder pp. 206–7).

In addition (rather than alternatively), Lucullus may be aiming at the Academics in particular, who accused dogmatists of rashness when they gave assent to obscure matters (*Luc.* 66; *Ac.* 1.45; D.L. 9.49; Sext., *M.* 9.49) but, the argument goes, inconsistently withheld praise for virtuous behaviour which resulted from acts of assent, too.

By *omninoque* Lucullus then seems to signal a move to a more general level. The obvious level would be that of cataleptic impressions received by any human, not just sages (who alone are capable of virtuous behaviour). The former was, as I argued, the level of generality at which the argument in §37 (*Deinde cum inter inanimum...*) was formulated and to which we would be returning. The wording here, about *uisa* issuing in action after assent has been given, is very close to that in §25, but there the context signalled that the sage's behaviour, and not that of human beings in general, was at issue. *Videri* 'to appear' here must have the veridical sense, as Reid[1] (p. 225) noted, too (although he speaks of the 'passive sense', since he assumes that the *uideri* can only be veridical if it is the passive of *uidere* = 'to see veridically').

Lambinus emended *assentiatur* to *assentiri*; see, however, Madvig (1826: 131–2) for the change in construction, and the explanatory note in Plasberg[1] (p. 87). On *hoc idem* without an explicit indication of a contrast, see Reid[1] (p. 225).

Qua re qui aut uisum aut assensum tollit, is omnem actionem tollit e uita: Reid[1] (p. 225) cites a number of parallels from Cicero, none of which is close enough to secure the precise sense of the passage: that actions arising from cataleptic impressions in human beings must be at issue. *Aut...aut...* does have its standard exclusive sense here: cataleptic impressions and assent belong together (without the former invariably necessitating the latter). The sentence concludes the section on apprehension which began in §19, and Cicero and a fortiori Catulus do recognize impressions; hence *uisum* must again have the veridical sense. On inactivity as an actual and as a counterfactual possibility, see p. 435 above.

§§40–62

Having made the case for apprehension, Lucullus turns to *refutatio* in the second half of his speech. In *Luc.* 40–58 he offers responses to the Academic arguments for the non-distinctness (ἀπαραλλαξία) of purported cataleptic and false impressions. In *Luc.* 40-4 Lucullus moves on to the 'core Academic argument',[159] which concludes that cataleptic impressions do not exist given non-distinctness, and Antiochus' general objections to it; in *Luc.* 45-58 he evaluates the two main types of Academic argument for non-distinctness of purported cataleptic and false impressions in the domain of perception.[160] The core argument is likely to have been introduced by one of the Academic speakers in *Catul*.[161]

§§40-44

We know that the Clitomachean position and the position of mitigated scepticism were introduced as philosophical options in the *Catulus*; the latter is clearly attested in *Luc.* 148 and represented by the younger Catulus. Brittain (2001: 130) suggests that at least the arguments of *Luc.* 43-4 must be aimed at what he calls the Philonian/Metrodorian position, on the grounds the Clitomachean position would be immune to them.[162] This has been countered by Glucker (2004: 131-2 n. 47), who holds that there are ways of reading the entire speech as directed against the Clitomachean position (with *Luc.* 34 being a possible exception, in that this paragraph may on Glucker's view be directed against Metrodorus and his pupils).[163]

If it could be shown that some of Lucullus' remarks only make adequate sense if their target is the mitigated position, then this would not just confirm what we know independently, that such a position existed, but it would also bolster the view that the mitigated position, or a version of it like Brittain's Philonian/Metrodorian position, was the official view of the Academy in the late 90s and early 80s BC, given that the target here is not just any argument but the one which had encapsulated Academic scepticism since Arcesilaus.

In the background there is also the question of how Lucullus' and Cicero's speeches fit together and how one would relate either speech to its hypothetical source or sources. Cicero's speech engages with Lucullus' closely, so that someone who thinks of the relationship between the two speeches in terms of texts that informed them may be tempted to argue that the source of Cicero's speech must be a Philonian response to the source of Lucullus' speech—but if that was so, then Cicero's avowedly Clitomachean stance in his speech might be taken to tell against the mitigated position as the prevailing view of the Academy after Philo had abandoned the radical scepticism of the Clitomachean position, and might instead suggest that Philo held

---

[159] The phrasal term was coined by Brittain (2001).
[160] Cf. Brittain (2006: 25 n. 53). See also section 5.6.
[161] In terms of the disposition of the dialogue, it would be peculiar if Cicero had an Antiochian speaker introduce this argument.
[162] See section 4 on how the difference between the Clitomachean position and mitigated scepticism is construed in this commentary, and how Brittain's construal of the Philonian/Metrodorian position differs from my construal of mitigated scepticism.
[163] For Glucker (2004) the Philonian/Metrodorian position as reconstructed by Brittain is no more than a notional possibility, and certainly not the prevailing Academic position for an extended period of time; note in particular his discussion of *Luc.* 148 (Glucker 2004: 129). However, no detailed alternative reading of *Luc.* 43-4 is offered.

two positions only over the course of his life, the Clitomachean one and that of the Roman Books. In this commentary such reasonings are deemed not irrelevant but uncompelling by themselves, not just because Cicero is regarded as perfectly capable of writing a tightly argued response to Lucullus' speech without following any one source closely; see section 9.3.

The question thus arises to what extent both Academic positions in play can be seen as targets in this section of Lucullus' speech, and if so, which strategies the text employs to signal what its specific target is at any one point. Explicit statements in the text on the target(s) of Lucullus' speech offer no immediate help. In *Luc.* 18 Lucullus states he is speaking against 'Arcesilaus und Carneades', which indicates a general aspiration to refute Academic scepticism. The Clitomachean and mitigated positions, like that of the Roman Books which is not being considered in the speech, were of course presented as authoritative interpretations of Carneades' stance by their proponents. However, the names of the two scholarchs in juxtaposition may at least hint at both positions distributively, because of the manner in which the Cicero character claims Arcesilaus as a figurehead for the Clitomachean position.[164]

The focus of the first part of the section (*Luc.* 40–4) is the so-called Academic 'core argument' against the Stoic conception of κατάληψις, which was upheld by Clitomacheans and proponents of the mitigated position (as well as Philo in the Roman Books, as far as the Stoic conception of κατάληψις is concerned). Any argument in support of any one of its premisses will already have been formulated by the Stoics (in the case of the premisses which the Stoics would endorse), Carneades, or the Clitomacheans, but later adopted by mitigated sceptics, too. A rejection of the core argument may thus be directed at the Clitomachean and mitigated position alike if e.g. it questions whether any of the premisses actually obtain. What will differentiate the positions is the attitude taken to the core argument.

If one construes the Clitomachean position in such a way that Clitomacheans are deemed to advance the core argument 'dialectically', i.e. without endorsing the premisses themselves and instead relying on their opponents' endorsement of them, while the mitigated sceptics assented to them in a qualified way, conscious of the fact that premisses they take to be true may in fact be false, but nonetheless 'owning' them, then a riposte to the core argument which turns on whether the Academics are entitled to the premisses and to holding them jointly, given the attitude which they take to them (§44), may be read as directed against the mitigated sceptics while leaving the Clitomacheans untouched.

However, while it is plausible to assume that Academics advanced the core argument in this ad hominem manner at some point, the kind of Clitomacheans Lucullus is engaging did not do this: within *Acad.*, Clitomachean Academics were in fact deemed to approve the core argument in the technical sense of approval discussed in *Luc.* 104–5; see on *Luc.* 43–4 in particular, as well as on *Luc.* 67.[165] Nor is this surprising, given the larger context: having debated the Academics for two centuries, the Stoics and adopters of their epistemological views like Antiochus, on record for

---

[164] See on *Luc.* 66–7 and section 7.5.
[165] Compare Castagnoli (2019: 194–7), who, however, is concerned with Academic argument more generally.

rejecting the the ἀπαραλλαξία of purportedly cataleptic and false impressions including in *Acad.*, would reasonably reject the notion that the core argument could be cited against them ad hominem, because the key premiss in it was not endorsed by them and had, they argued, no rational hold on them. In this situation, their reply to the Academics could reasonably have been that the latter need to endorse the core argument themselves if they want it to go through. I will argue that Lucullus' strategy for rejecting the core argument in fact gives parity to the Clitomachean and mitigated position in the sense that it poses the same challenge to both positions.

§40

See also the general note on §§40–4, p. 441. Lucullus begins by putting his audience in a position to understand what he calls the *fundamenta* of the Academic position. Of these, there are two: first, a detailed division of species of impressions; second, one particular premiss in the core argument, as well as a rider to that premiss. It is peculiar that a division of impressions is assigned a fundamental role here, but that no actual details of the division are given. It seems likely that details of such a division, or perhaps more than one, were provided by Catulus in the *Catulus*; by the same token, one would have expected the core argument to have featured there for the first time. What Lucullus is doing here, then, is to isolate topics of the earlier discussion which he regards as elementary, possibly in a tendentious way. Further, while it is reasonably clear why a premiss in the core argument and a rider to it are singled out as fundamental, no explanation of this status is provided for the division, nor is there an indication as to whether and how the two *fundamenta* are supposed to integrate so as to feature jointly in an argumentative strategy.

A detailed Academic division of impressions is given by Sextus, *M.* 7.166–75 (= LS 69D), in the Carneadean sub-section of his account of Academic epistemology. Notably, it does not include the cataleptic impression (although one could easily add it, as a species of true impressions relative to the object). In *Luc.* 99 Cicero makes reference to another division, also ascribed to Carneades, in which the cataleptic impression features at the top level and is contrasted with impressions which are not cataleptic (the latter divide into persuasive impressions and impressions which are not persuasive/*probabile*).[166] Given that Academics would have no difficulty accepting the definition of the cataleptic impression, while observing that its conditions are never met, there are prima facie good reasons for the claim, which the transmitted text of our passage makes, that the Academic division included the cataleptic impression as a species (sc. defined as the Stoics defined it). However, the transmitted text does pose a grammatical difficulty, which has led Schäublin (1992: 44–5) to insert *quaerentes* before *quale sit id quod percipi et comprehendi possit*, yielding the sense that the purpose of the division was to *enquire* what place the cataleptic impression might have in it (see n. on *componunt igitur*)—and presumably to find that it has none; the division in Sextus could be cited in support of this suggestion. Contrast the division in *Luc.* 99.

---

[166] On both passages, see also section 6.

The Stoics use division mainly as a tool for conceptual analysis (see LS 32), less as a device to aid the formulation of definitions as Plato and Aristotle do, although they are aware of this application; definitions of cataleptic impressions reflect the conceptual distinctions higher up 'loosely or not at all' (Long and Sedley i.1987: 193). Divisions may be used to map out an entire area of knowledge, or to isolate one particular species; a division of the latter kind may thus not include subdivisions of some concepts even though it was understood that further analysis of them was possible. D.L. 7.49 (cf. 7.43) reports that the theory of φαντασία features at the beginning of the exposition on λογική, either in the semantic branch of dialectic or in the treatment of the criterion. This resonates with the description of the division of impressions as a *fundamentum* in our passage. Stoic divisions of impressions—cf. Sextus, *M.* 7.242: τῶν δὲ φαντασιῶν πολλαὶ μὲν καὶ ἄλλαι εἰσὶ διαφοραί—follow various principles, adopting e.g. a top-level distinction between true and false or between persuasive and unpersuasive (see LS 1987: ii.242 on Sextus, *M.* 7.242–6 = part of *SVF* ii.65); such divisions are attested at Aët. 4.9.4; Chrysippus, *Quaest. log.* col. III = *SVF* ii.100–1, fr. 298a; Cic., *N.D.* 1.70; Sextus, *M.* 7.242–7; D.L. 7.46. For a late Stoic division, presumably by Antipater of Tarsus, and helpful general discussion see Backhouse (2000) on *P.Berol.* inv. 16545, first edited by Szymański (1990).

The transmitted text of our passage gives no indication as to what exactly the Academics used the division for. Sextus' discussion of Carneades' epistemology begins with the Carneadean claim that there is no criterion of truth in the strict sense required by the Stoics (*M.* 7.159), followed by an argument to the effect that, if there was a criterion, it would have to be an impression (7.161).[167] At this point the question arises what kind of impression, if not a cataleptic one, could play the role which on the Stoic view only the cataleptic impression can play. Similarly, the Academic core argument concludes that there are no cataleptic impressions, which invariably raises the question what human beings do have to go on. A division is the suitable format for contextualizing the alternative which the Academics would offer to the Stoics, viz. the πιθανόν.

Before I look more closely at the second *fundamentum*, I shall examine the Academic core argument as it features at the end of *Luc.* 40.[168] Lucullus presents this as a *conclusio*, which suggests that he regards it as a formal argument, a proof; he will go on to argue that sceptics are not entitled to use the tools of dogmatic philosophers, like definitions, divisions, and formal arguments (*Luc.* 43–4). Cicero, in his reply, seems to reject this designation and uses the much less formal term *capita* for the individual steps of the argument in *Luc.* 83.

---

[167] For the dependence of the Academic divisions on Stoic ones, see Couissin (1983), first published in 1929; Schäublin et al. (p. 224 n. 118); section 6.

[168] Further discussion of the argument is to be found in *Luc.* 66–7, 77, and 83 (all part of Cicero's reply to Lucullus). The corresponding Greek argument can be derived from Sextus, *M.* 7.150–89, esp. 154–7. Cf. also Photius, *Bibl.* 212, 170a26–38 = Aenesidemus B3 Polito (partial) = LS 71C (partial), quoted and discussed on p. 459 below. See the discussions in Brittain (2001: 12–13, 90–2, 131–2, 152) and Castagnoli (2019: 191–203). One might wonder if the fact that the core argument is set out clearly in *Acad.* while it needs to be assembled from Greek texts suggests that *Acad.* is informed by primary material which reflects a late stage of the debate; the accidents of survival do not seem a more plausible explanation in this case, given the nature of our evidence.

The argument is presented like this:[169]

(i) *eorum quae uidentur alia uera sunt alia falsa.*
Of appearances, some are true and some are false.
(ii) *quod falsum est, id percipi non potest.*
What is false cannot be apprehended.
(iii) *quod autem uerum uisum est id omne tale est ut eiusdem modi falsum etiam possit uideri.*[170]
But everything which is a true appearance is of such a kind that something false which is exactly alike could appear in the same way.
(iv) *quae uisa sint eius modi ut in iis nihil intersit, non posse accidere ut eorum alia percipi possint, alia non possint.*
With respect to appearances without a difference between them, it cannot happen that some of them can be apprehended, and others cannot.
(v) *nullum igitur est uisum quod percipi possit.*
Therefore there is no appearance which can be apprehended.

According to *Luc.* 41, (ii) and (iv) are to be deemed conceded, whereas the Academics advance many arguments for (i) and (iii) and thus do not take these two premisses to be conceded; according to Cicero in *Luc.* 83, (i) is taken to be conceded, too, because the envisaged opponent is the Stoics, who do concede it. One way of explaining this apparent disagreement is to see the core argument in *Luc.* 41 as directed against not just the Stoics but also the Epicureans,[171] whereas Cicero in *Luc.* 83 seeks to combat the Stoics in particular.

A notable feature of the argument, resulting from Cicero's choice to translate φαντασία as *uisum*, is that it is cast so as to be about impressions inasmuch as they represent objects, as opposed to being about impressions only.[172] Earlier interpreters have either assumed that the premisses at times refer to objects and at other times to impressions thereof,[173] or that *uisa* and phrases like *ea quae uidentur* invariably refer to impressions, in the way in which the argument must have been formulated in Greek (Brittain).[174] The latter interpretation would require that such phrases function as mere stand-ins for the Greek term φαντασία and that *quae uisa dicimus*, which looks back to *Luc.* 18 and the earlier discussion in the *Catulus*, acts as a reminder of that function.

---

[169] The English translation 'appearance' is deliberately ambiguous between 'impression' and 'object of the impression', for reasons which will be explained below. 'True' and 'false' might be deemed suitable attributes for impressions only, but the relevant Latin terms are equally applicable to objects, in which case they mean 'real, genuine' and 'not genuine' or 'not obtaining'.

[170] Cf. Sextus, *M.* 7.154:... δεύτερον ὅτι οὐδεμία τοιαύτη ἀληθὴς φαντασία εὑρίσκεται οἵα οὐκ ἂν γένοιτο ψευδής. On the syntactic ambiguity of Cicero's formulation, see the n. below.

[171] Thus Schofield (1999: 338–47); Castagnoli (2019: 214 n. 121). On an *interpretatio Epicurea* adjustments would need to be made to the interpretation of concepts appearing in the premisses (like that of apprehension).

[172] See section 10; Reinhardt (2016) and (2018b) on Cicero's use of *uidere/uideri* to talk about impressions.

[173] See Reid[1] (pp. 226 and 227) on his lines 5 and 14, respectively; Schäublin et al. (p. 224 n. 120).

[174] See the translation in Brittain (2006: 25–6).

Given ordinary Latin usage, the 'object' that is understood when a Latin speaker hears the term *uisum* is not necessarily a particular physical object, but something like a state of affairs, involving a particular and a property, albeit in a truth-neutral way;[175] this is why *uisum* in that sense must be modified by *uerum* if a true impression is meant (cf. premiss iii, with n. below) and when it does not function as the object of a factive verb like *percipere*.[176]

The second *fundamentum* of Academic argument apart from the division of impressions is identified as:

(iv) *quae ita uideantur, ut eorum alia eodem modo uideri possint nec in iis quicquam intersit, non posse eorum alia percipi alia non percipi,*

combined with:

(rider to iv) *nihil interesse autem non modo, si omni ex parte eiusdem modi sint, sed etiam, si discerni non possint.*

It makes no difference whether two appearances are alike in every respect, or whether they cannot be distinguished.

We may combine these so as to obtain:

(iv, and rider to iv)

For a class of *uisa* [impressions/'objects of impressions'] which are all alike, or appear to be alike [rider to (iv)], it cannot be the case that some of its elements can be grasped but others cannot.

'Ability to distinguish' in (rider to iv) can, as elsewhere in *Acad.*, mean a conscious ability to identify features which make an impression self-warranting, or an ability to track the effects which such impressions have on the perceiving subject via a mechanism which is itself non-transparent.

In what sense, then, do (iv) and (rider to iv) represent a *fundamentum* of the Academic position? The text provides two clues: that only premisses (i) and (iv) are cast in the plural, and that (iv) and (rider to iv) are said to 'contain, as it were, the entire issue' (*quae quasi contineant omnem hanc quaestionem*). (iv), like (i), is about the entire class of impressions, while (ii) and (iii) make statements about false and true impressions respectively. Premiss (iv) presupposes (i) and (ii), and in that sense encapsulates the issue (iv is able to presuppose ii because the verb *percipere* is factive). (iv) also captures the issue in another sense: it is not itself contentious

---

[175] Consider Dido's ill-omened sacrifice in Verg., A. 4.450–6 (discussed and translated p. clxxxiii): *tum uero infelix fatis exterrita Dido | mortem orat; taedet caeli conuexa tueri. | quo magis inceptum peragat lucemque relinquat, | uidit, turicremis cum dona imponeret aris, | (horrendum dictu) latices nigrescere sacros | fusaque in obscenum se uertere uina cruorem; | hoc uisum nulli, non ipsi effata sorori*. Here *uisum* refers to the milk going black and the wine turning to gore, not just the milk and the wine.

[176] However, *uisum* by itself can also *mean* 'state of affairs' or rather 'state of affairs apprehended' if the sense of *uidere* at issue is the veridical one (see Reinhardt 2016: 85).

(41; cf. 83). What is under dispute is if the conditions of (iv) are met; these conditions are the subject of (iii).

§40

Nunc ea uideamus…quasi fundamenta cognoscere: Cicero uses the passive *disputari* with a subject, but not the active *disputare* with an object, as Reid[1] (p. 215) observes on *Luc.* 32. The verb can be synonymous with *disserere* to denote careful philosophical and esp. dialectical argument (e.g. *Part. or.* 139), but *disserere* is never modified by adverbial *contra*, only by a prepositional phrase involving *contra* (e.g. *Luc.* 17); in contexts where both words are contrasted (e.g. *Red. Sen.* 14), *disserere* denotes expansive discourse on a subject, whereas *disputare* is to argue a point. Etymologically, *disputare* was associated with purification (Varro, *L.L.* 6.63), *disserere* with sowing and planting (*OLD* s.v. *sero*¹) and thus with careful arrangement (Varro, *L.L.* 6.64); only the former etymology is correct. For *disputare* in the sense of 'merely arguing dialectically or ad hominem' as opposed to making as well as endorsing one's argument, see *Luc.* 78. *His* refers to the Academics in general; cf. *Luc.* 12: *ad Arcesilam Carneademque ueniamus*.

The core argument and the premisses which Lucullus is going to identify as *fundamenta* must have featured in the *Catulus*. So Lucullus is not announcing completely new information, but promises that his interlocutors will be able to see previously covered material in a new light, specifically to appreciate a premiss of the core argument and a rider to it as well as a division of impressions as fundamental; *potestis…cognoscere* (cf. *OLD* s.v. n. 1 or 7) instead of a formulation amounting to 'I will explain to you…' suggests this, too. Reid[1] (p. 225) suggests that *quasi* marks a translation from Greek (cf. Sextus, *M.* 5.50: ὥσπερ θεμέλιος), but it could just signal the metaphorical use of *fundamentum*. *Ratio* may denote the Academics' thinking or argumentative habit, but could also have the more formal sense of 'doctrine'; the latter would be in line with other attempts in the passage to paint the Academic stance as a negatively dogmatic one. Cf. on *Luc.* 7: *Academiae ratio.* On earlier editors' concerns about *potestis*, see Plasberg[1] (p. 87).

Componunt igitur primum artem quandam…totidem uerbis quot Stoici: *componunt* and *definiunt* suggest that the division at issue is drawn up from scratch by the Academics, but it is well recognized (see section 6.4) that the Academics appropriated Stoic divisions, which they modified in places. The two verbs are thus of a piece with other formulations suggesting dogmatic activities for the Academics. The same applies to calling their division an *ars*, which suggests that using it amounts to acting in accordance with an expertise. A division can be called an art by synecdoche. The latter is an ordered body of knowledge relating to a particular subject area. This involves a genus–species division as well as definition of the kinds pertaining to the art; so *definiunt* does mean 'they define' rather than 'they recognize' vel sim. (thus Schäublin 1992: 44 n. 15). That a division 'is' an art in a manner of speaking is, however, acknowledged by *quandam*. For *uisa*, see *Luc.* 18, where there is a backward reference to the *Catulus*, *Ac.* 1.40, and the introduction (section 10.1). *Primum* is picked up by *deinde* below. On Cicero's use of *hic…qui*, see Hofmann and Szantyr (1965: 181).

Schäublin (1992: 44–5) raises concerns about the sentence beginning *in his quale sit id*, with respect to its grammar as well as its content. He regards it as not immediately apparent that *quale sit…comprehendi possit* is a second object to *definiunt* alongside *et uim* and *genera*, with *in his* either providing a generic backward reference to the first part of the sentence (thus Reid) or picking up *genera*; he deems *totidem uerbis quot Stoici* an awkward afterthought. However, his main concern is about the content: he suggests that a definition of the cataleptic impression would be incompatible with the conclusion of the core argument that there are no cataleptic impressions. For these reasons Schäublin et al. print *in his ⟨quaerentes⟩, quale sit id, quod percipi et comprehendi possit, totidem uerbis quot Stoici*, which would make *genera* the natural reference of *in his* and would make the cataleptic impression the subject of inquiry. However, as Schäublin himself notes but regards as irrelevant, cataleptic impressions feature as a category in the Carneadean division mentioned in *Luc.* 99. There no definition is furnished, but this may simply be due to the division given not being as detailed. Crucially, there is no inconsistency in accepting the definition of the cataleptic impression and advancing the core argument, since the Academics could accept that the conditions for knowledge are as set out in the definition, but deny that the conditions are ever met, i.e. regard the class of cataleptic impressions as empty. For the synonym pairing *percipi et comprehendi*, cf. e.g. *Luc.* 22; *N.D.* 2.5: *cognitum comprehensumque*. The phrase *totidem uerbis quot Stoici* must relate to the whole division, not just the element in it which is the cataleptic impression; moreover, the phrase fits with other expressions (*componunt, definiunt*) which represent the Academics as the authors of the division.

Deinde illa exponunt duo…omnem hanc quaestionem: *exponunt* 'they set forth', esp. steps of an argument or the gist of a case or issue, primarily in rhetorical rather than philosophical argument; not used as a translation of τιθέναι in dialectical contexts (contrast *quibus positis* below). Cf. *TLL* s.v. col. 1764.22–40. See the general note above on how the premiss (iv) and (rider to iv) 'encapsulate' (*contineant*) the entire *quaestio* ('Are there self-warranting impressions of things in the perceptible world?'). *Quasi* softens the metaphor.

Quae ita uideantur ut…non posse eorum alia percipi, alia non percipi: cf. 33: *ut quicquam possit ita uideri ut non eodem modo falsum etiam possit [ita] uideri*; 83: *inter quae uisa nihil intersit, fieri non posse ut eorum alia percipi possint alia non possint*. The difficulty of reading this sentence in such a way that the reference shifts between objects and impressions is plain from the explanation offered by Reid[1] (p. 226): presumably because the *figura etymologica* that 'an appearance appears' is found to be difficult (which it should not be), he thinks *quae* refers to objects, as does the first *alia*, but then claims that with *in iis* we have to supply *uisis*. He then takes *eorum* to refer to the objects, which entails that *alia…alia* must be objects, too. I have above made the case for assuming that the argument is phrased with reference to objects as represented in impressions; see also the following n. On the uses of *percipere*, see on *Luc.* 37; section 10.1.

Nihil interesse autem...sed etiam si discerni non possint: on *omni ex parte eiusdem modi sint* Reid comments: 'the real subject is *uisa*'. Given that he took the reference of *alia...alia* in the immediately preceding sentence to be to objects, this seems peculiar; again the difficulty would be solved by assuming a double reference. On the substance of (rider to iv) see the general note above and section 5.3. The two options distinguished in this sentence are identity of objects and consequently impressions (qua imprint, or in terms of representational content) on the one hand, and non-identity of objects and consequently impressions but indistinguishability of objects and consequently impressions (qua imprint, or in terms of representational content) on the other. What is meant by indistinguishability is not explained, and may mean indistinguishable with respect to any feature which is supposed to be peculiar to cataleptic impressions, or indistinguishable with respect to behaviour (broadly speaking) only they are supposed to give rise to. The sentence plainly does not contrast indistinguishability on grounds of identity of objects and impressions (qua imprint, in terms of representational content, or in any other way) on the one hand, and indistinguishability in spite of non-identity of objects and impressions (qua imprint, in terms of representational content, or in any other way) on the other. All this shows that the written record of the debate between Stoics and Academics retained an awareness that the initial objection to Zeno's definition turned on the epistemic possibility of the identity of a purported cataleptic impression and a false one, that ἀπαραλλαξία means 'non-distinctness', and that considerations of awareness and availability entered the debate at a later stage and were recognized to be different from the ἀπαραλλαξία charge proper. See section 5.6.

Quibus positis unius argumenti conclusione...conclusio sic est: the 'core argument' is announced. *Ponere* as often of the 'setting down' of premisses (*OLD* s.v. n. 20; cf. Cic., *Tusc.* 5.50), originally performed by the respondent in dialectical discussion, by answering 'yes' to a πρότασις offered by the questioner. *Vnius* contrasts with *tota*. *Argumenti conclusio* suggests formal argument or proof (cf. *Luc.* 26), a tool of dogmatic philosophers to which the Academics are not entitled according to 43; Cicero, in his reply in 83, pointedly uses the informal *capita* to refer to the steps of the core argument. *Causa* probably has one of its legal senses, referring to 'the case', i.e. the entire debate. On the force of *comprehenditur*, cf. also the translation by Reid[2]: '...they put their whole case in the compass of a single demonstration.'

Eorum quae uidentur, alia uera sunt, alia falsa: Reid[1] (p. 226) glosses *eorum quae uidentur* '= *uisorum*', which seems inconsistent given his reading of *quae ita uideantur...non posse eorum alia percipi* reported above, and raises the question of why Cicero did not simply write *uisorum*. (Reid proceeds to explain 'the general drift of the argument', apparently despairing of how exactly it is to be extracted from the Latin.) Comparison with Numenius frg. 27, p. 77.28–9 Des Places, which is about premiss (i) of the core argument, too, suggests that Cicero's wording, which brings objects as represented in impressions into view, may be a deliberate attempt to do justice to the Greek formulation of the argument (the subject is 'Carneades'): τὸ γὰρ ἀληθές τε καὶ τὸ ψεῦδος ἐν τοῖς πράγμασιν ἐνεῖναι συγχωρῶν, ὥσπερ ξυνεργαζόμενος τῆς ζητήσεως τρόπῳ παλαιστοῦ δεινοῦ λαβὴν δοὺς περιεγίγνετο ἔνθεν, 'For by conceding that there is true and false in all things, as if he was joining in with the enquiry, he allowed himself to be grabbed in the manner of a clever wrestler in order to gain the upper hand from that position'; see appendix 2 for the passage in context. On the Academic attitude to premiss (i)—whether it was offered dialectically, approved, or assented to—see n. below on *Luc.* 41: *Reliqua uero multa... quale etiam a falso possit esse.*

Et quod falsum est id percipi non potest: this is premiss (ii) of the core argument; on *et* for the more contrastive *atqui* in the *assumptio*, see *N.D.* 1.110; *OLD* s.v. *et* no. 2c. The sentence can be read so as to be about false impressions (which are said to be incapable of being grasped), but it may be less plain how it can be read as being about objects in the perceptible world which cannot be grasped. On this point, cf. *Luc.* 77, where Cicero writes: *nullum tale esse uisum a uero ut non eiusdem modi a falso possit esse*, where *a falso* means 'from a purported state of affairs which does not actually obtain'; this involves a particular (an object in the world) and a predicate that does not actually apply to the particular. On *percipere* as a factive verb, see the general note on *Luc.* 21–2.

Quod autem uerum uisum est id omne tale est ut eiusdem modi falsum etiam possit uideri: premiss (iii) of the core argument, again formulated so as to refer to objects as they are represented in impressions. *Verum uisum* is either the complement to *quod* as in my translation, or *uerum* is an attribute to *quod*; *uerum* cannot be a complement to *uisum est* (appearance of object/impression *as* true or false is not at issue here); *Luc.* 34: *id enim quaero quod ita mihi uideatur uerum ⟨ut⟩ non possit item falsum uideri* is different due to *ita... ut*. Likewise, *falsum* is the subject of the *ut*-clause (and *eiusdem modi* a complement to *uideri*). Ἀπαραλλαξία is normally presented as the claim that for every purportedly cataleptic impression there could be a one just like it which is false (see section 5.6); on the phrase *eiusdem modi esse* or *uideri* as a rendering of ἀπαράλλακτον εἶναι, see the appendix to section 5. In Sextus, *M.* 7.154 (...δεύτερον ὅτι οὐδεμία τοιαύτη ἀληθὴς φαντασία εὑρίσκεται οἵα οὐκ ἂν γένοιτο ψευδής), γένοιτο is a full verb (i.e. 'of which kind no false impression could arise' rather than 'as could not turn into a false one').

Et 'quae uisa sint eius modi...nullum igitur est uisum quod percipi possit': premiss (iv) of the core argument. The relative clause allows for two constructions, depending on whether *uisa* is taken as part of the subject with *quae* or as part of the complement (with *quae* alone as subject). On both constructions the clause and the rest of the sentence is best read as being about objects as represented in impressions. Pace Reid, *ut in iis nihil intersit* is not a clumsy way to render that the impressions are ἀπαράλλακτοι, but one which captures the Greek notion with precision. Some earlier editors emended to *sunt* and *potest* because the other premisses were introduced in direct speech, but Plasberg[1] (p. 87) notes 'sed uariatur oratio' and cites parallels.

Nullum igitur est uisum quod percipi possit: the conclusion of the core argument. *Nullum* is raised for emphasis and an attribute of *uisum* (i.e. *uisum* does not function as a complement).

§41

See also the general note on §§40–4. In this section Lucullus reviews the premisses of the core argument with a view to whether the Academics cite arguments for them or regard them as simply conceded because nobody objects to them.

Whether or not the Academics themselves endorse the premisses is an entirely separate question, which is not overtly touched on (see also n. on *quae autem sumunt...* below) and to which the paragraph does not speak; thus on the most natural reading Lucullus is at this point targeting the core argument in general, and not as advanced from a particular Academic position (it being understood that the key difference between the Clitomachean and mitigated positions is the kind and degree of endorsement given to the premisses of the argument by the person advancing it; see section 4).[177]

Premisses (i) and (iii) are said to be supported with arguments, while (ii) and (iv) are uncontroversial. With this one may compare *Luc*. 83, where Cicero, in his reply to Lucullus from a Clitomachean point of view, states that premiss (i) is deemed to be conceded, too, since the current disagreement was with the Stoics, and premiss (i) was only disputed by the Epicureans, who held that all perceptions are true. This is a reason for thinking that here in §41 Lucullus is introducing a version of the core argument which is supposed to have applicability beyond the Stoic school.[178] Another is the very general formulation for the acceptance which premisses (ii) and (iv) enjoy (*neque enim quisquam repugnat*), which would be a peculiar way of putting it if the issue was merely that no Stoic, or neither the Stoics nor Antiochus, objected to them. The choices Cicero made as a 'translator', viz. that the argument makes reference to impressions to the extent that they represent objects, a reading which is encouraged by the comparison with Numenius (see n. on §40: *eorum quae uidentur, alia uera sunt, alia falsa*), also enable a gesture towards the Epicurean conception of truth, according to which what is true is what is the case; cf. Sextus, *M*. 8.9 (= frg. 244 Usener):

ὁ δὲ Ἐπίκουρος τὰ μὲν αἰσθητὰ πάντα ἔλεγεν ἀληθῆ καὶ ὄντα. οὐ διήνεγκε γὰρ ἀληθές εἶναί τι λέγειν ἢ ὑπάρχον· ἔνθεν καὶ ὑπογράφων τἀληθὲς καὶ ψεῦδος 'ἔστι' φησὶν 'ἀληθὲς τὸ οὕτως ἔχον ὡς λέγεται ἔχειν', καὶ 'ψεῦδός ἐστι' φησὶ 'τὸ οὐχ οὕτως ἔχον ὡς λέγεται ἔχειν'.[179]

---

[177] According to Numenius frg. 27, p. 77.28-9 Des Places, cited on *Luc*. 40: *eorum quae uidentur alia uera sunt alia falsa*, above (and see appendix 2), Carneades conceded premiss (i) only for the sake of the argument and in order to gain an argumentative handle on his opponents (noted by Brittain 2001: 130 n. 1). Nothing in §41 points the reader of Cicero's text to that interpretation, and there is evidence in Cicero's speech later in *Luc*. suggesting that within *Acad*. Carneades, when read as a radical (Clitomachean) sceptic, is deemed to approve the core argument (in the technical sense of approval discussed in *Luc*. 104–5); see on *Luc*. 67 and 103–105a.

[178] See p. 445 above. Haltenhoff (p. 195) suggests implausibly that premiss (i) was defended 'with a view to premiss (iii)', in order to show that there were instances of false impressions which one might have regarded as true.

[179] The connection with the Epicurean conception of the true is made by Alleemudder (pp. 214–15 n. 4). On *M*. 8.9 and its interpretation, see also Bown (2016a).

But Epicurus said that all perceptible things are true and existent. For there is no difference between saying that something is true and that it is 'subsisting'. For that reason they also say, when describing the true and the false, that true is what is in such a way as it is said to be, and false what is not in such a way as it is said to be.

The Epicureans feature as a target of Academic arguments in *Luc.* 79–80, as well as 101. In the latter passage Cicero combines premiss (i) of the core argument with what he calls an Epicurean 'tenet' (*caput*), namely 'if any sense impression is false, nothing can be apprehended', to obtain 'nothing can be apprehended'.[180] Vogt (2014: 492–3) has suggested that the Carneadean scheme of the πιθανόν can be read as a dialectical response not just to Stoic but also to Epicurean opponents.

The expansiveness of the exposition here is notable. Given that the core argument must have featured in the *Catulus* already and that it was set out in some detail in §40, one wonders why Lucullus did not refer back rather than restate the premisses. An explanation would be that Lucullus performs the precision and accuracy to which only dogmatists are entitled according to §42.

Quae autem sumunt...neque enim quisquam repugnat: *his* has forward reference. On *sumere* (λαμβάνειν) as a technical term for the positing of a premiss (originally as the questioner in a dialectical exchange), see *OLD* s.v. n. 17. *Id quod uolunt* does not by itself suggest endorsement of the conclusion by the Academics: in order to advance an argument at all, one needs to want to obtain its conclusion at least in some sense; see also on *Luc.* 42: *Diuidunt enim in partis et eas quidem magnas...ulla res percipi possit*. *Neque...repugnat* suggests that arguments for 'there are true and false impressions' are offered not because the Academics are committed to it (although they might be), but because the Epicureans dispute it.

Ea sunt haec...alia ut non possint: premisses (ii) and (iv) of the core argument are repeated with slight variation from above. *Visa* again of objects represented in impressions. *Falsa* does not restrict the reference of *uisa* to impressions only, as is suggested inter alia by *a uero* and *a falso* below. Walker cited by Davies proposed to delete *alterum*.

Reliqua uero multa...quale etiam a falso possit esse: premisses (i) and (iii), repeated with slight variation from §40, are said to be defended in great detail; see the general note above. On *a uero* and *a falso* used to render ἀπὸ ὑπάρχοντος and ἀπὸ μὴ ὑπάρχοντος, see section 5.1 and 5.2. The preposition *a/ab* is open to a causal and a representational sense like ἀπό in Greek; see also on §105: *qua a sole collucet*.

---

[180] See also Sedley (2019: 107–8) on *Fat.* 23–8.

§42

See also the general note on §§40–4, p. 441. According to §42, the Academics do not just argue for premisses (i) and (iii) of the core argument in detail, but are also said to 'develop' them (*dilatare*). This development consists in a division into parts, which we might call domains of knowledge, and arguments to the effect that in these various domains there are true and false impressions, and that the former are 'just like' the latter. The domains are 'the senses', 'what is derived from the senses and from common experience', as well as 'rational method and inference'; see the nn. below for details.

The tripartite division is a recurrent structuring device in the *Academica*, as Brittain (2006: 26–7 n. 56) observes: 'The three parts of the Academics' argument structure Lucullus' defence of apprehension in *Ac.* 2.19–27 (*Ac.* 2.19–20 covers the senses, *Ac.* 2.21–2 their products, and *Ac.* 2.22–7 reason). They also structure Cicero's attack in *Ac.* 2.79–98.... Chrysippus' use of this division is attested in *Ac.* 2.87.' This last point is significant for the economy of the dialogue (see ad loc.): in *Luc.* 87 we learn, and there is independent evidence to make it very plausible, that Chrysippus attacked the possibility of knowledge in the various domains, often more convincingly than he defended it (elsewhere), and thus provided Carneades with his armoury. So Cicero is later coolly pointing out to Lucullus that the Academics can claim to stand in the tradition of Chrysippus.

Cicero's attack in *Luc.* 79–98 is more loosely based on the tripartite division, which nonetheless remains discernible enough: §§79–82 deal with the senses and §§91–8 with reason, while §§83–90 focus on the core argument and issues relating to premiss (iii) in particular.

Given that most of the evidence on arguments from ἀπαραλλαξία turns on perceptual impressions, and non-distinctness with respect to representational content in particular, it is at this stage not obvious what non-distinctness with respect to non-perceptual impressions would consist in, which is described here in terms familiar from descriptions of ἀπαραλλαξία of perceptual impressions. Clarification on this point will follow in §§43–4.

Haec duo proposita...diligentiam: in line with Lucullus' tendency to present the Academic argument as a formal proof (cf. the instances of *conclusio* in *Luc.* 40), *propositum* is best given the formal sense of 'premiss' here (*OLD* s.v. 4b, not 4a, where the present passage is cited). In *Fat.* 4 the term renders θέσις, which is not the sense at issue here. Cf. also Cic., *Inv.* 1.70: *cum aut proponimus aut assumimus sine approbatione*, where *proponere* involves obtaining approval for a premiss. *Praeteruolare* appears only twice in Cicero's philosophical works. In *Fin.* 5.77 it is used absolutely, of the speech skating over a point which needs to be obtained through argument. For *dilatare*, cf. *Parad.* 2, where the Stoic brand of concise oratory is characterized (*quae* [sc. *hairesis*] *nullum sequitur florem orationis neque dilatat argumentum, minutis interrogatiunculis quasi punctis, quod proposuit, efficit*).

Diuidunt enim in partis, et eas quidem magnas...ulla res percipi possit: the phrase *eas quidem magnas* may hint at the fact that this division functions as an organizational principle of Lucullus' and Cicero's speeches. The section corresponding to *primum in sensus* (= *in ea quae ad sensum pertinent*) in Lucullus' *confirmatio* is *Luc.* 19–20. With *quae ducuntur a sensibus et ab omni consuetudine*, cf. *Luc.* 21–2. For the meaning of *consuetudo*, see on *Luc.* 75 and *Luc.* 87.

On the unobjectionable passive infinitive *obscurari*, see Reid[1] (p. 228). The Academics are also said to try to rob human beings of daylight (*Luc.* 30), to overturn life in its foundations (*Luc.* 31), and to deprive human beings of their eyesight by analogy (*Luc.* 33).

No distinction is drawn between Academics who, while arguing against the Stoic conception of knowledge, differ in their particular stance.

The intention of the Academics referred to in *uolunt* might in principle cover an ad hominem argument apt to show that the Stoics are not entitled to their philosophical beliefs on their own terms; one needs to want to advance such an argument, or else one would not make it. Alternatively, Antiochus may have held that, at least as far as the core argument and its immediate implications was concerned, and at this late stage in the debate, there was no such thing as an Academic argument which only relied on the commitments of the opponent as well as premises which ought to have a rational claim on him (cf. the introductory note to *Luc.* 43–4), and that in that sense the Academics themselves must be wanting to advance the argument; this is my preferred reading. A third interpretation would be Antiochus, himself a former Academic, attempted to paint the Academics as negative dogmatists, either to misrepresent them or because he took them to be negative dogmatists without it being apparent to them, in which case the argument would be properly theirs, deliberately advanced. Cf. also *uolunt efficere* in §43 below and §44: *omnia non tam esse quam uideri uolunt*.

On the domain relating to apprehension *ratione...et coniectura*, cf. *Luc.* 22–9 in Lucullus' *confirmatio*, and 91–8 for Cicero's reply. Dialectic (as understood by the Stoics) is the target of the latter section, and the sorites and the Liar are discussed. This suggests that *ratio* here relates to formal methods of proof, whereas *coniectura* refers to rational methods of inference which are of a lesser standard of cogency (cf. *Tusc.* 1.17; *Div.* 2.16). On *coniectura*, see *TLL* s.v. col. 315.1–11 (the entry has too few subdivisions, and the technical sense associated with divination, which is treated separately, is clearly related to the one at issue in our passage); similarly, the *OLD* entry draws too simple a distinction between sense no. 1 'the inferring (of one fact from another), reasoning' and no. 2 'guesswork, coniecture'.

Haec autem uniuersa concidunt etiam minutius…non posse comprehendi: *uniuersa* are, somewhat vaguely, 'general areas'; cf. *OLD* s.v. *uniuersus*, no. 3c. For *concidunt*, cf. *OLD* s.v. *concīdo*², no. 5. *Vt enim de sensibus hesterno sermone uidistis* refers to arguments which Cicero introduced in *Catul.*, as *Luc.* 79 (Cicero speaking) shows: *idcirco heri non necessario loco contra sensus tam multa dixeram*; see section 9.2 on the reconstruction of the lost parts of both editions. Mansfeld (1997: 53) notes that 'yesterday' the senses only were covered, not 'further inferences' and 'reasoning'/'conjecture'. *Videri* (in *iis omnibus quae uisa sint*) here ranges over perceptual and non-perceptual appearances, as the context makes plain; see on §§43–4 on how non-perceptual ἀπαραλλαξία is construed. With *uolunt efficere* 'they want to conclude', cf. *uolunt* above.

§§43-44

See also the general note on §§40-4, p. 441. §43 initially links back to §42 via the theme of manifold divisions, which for Lucullus are the hallmark of dogmatic philosophizing. Said divisions were in §42 *fin.* mentioned as deployed by the Academics to show that there exists ἀπαραλλαξία beyond the domain of perceptual impressions.

From *Luc.* 43-4 it emerges that non-perceptual ἀπαραλλαξία is characterized by the following claim: for every non-perceptual impression which is true, it is possible that the impression could be false.[181] So understood non-perceptual ἀπαραλλαξία maps exactly onto perceptual ἀπαραλλαξία, the rebuttal of which will be the subject of *Luc.* 47-58.[182]

Lucullus argues in §43 that fine distinctions, statements about similar and dissimilar things, and notably definitions are the tools of dogmatic philosophers who accept the existence of definite truths, not of those 'who clamour that these [the corresponding propositions, notably ones in which a purported *definiens* is predicated of a *definiendum*] are no more true than false' (... *qui clament nihilo magis uera illa esse quam falsa*). In the absence of any indication that a sub-set of Academics is meant to be understood as the grammatical subject of *clament*, this is best seen as a polemically phrased but apt characterization of the Academics in general as those philosophers who insist on ἀκαταληψία, sc. if the Stoic conception of the cataleptic impression is presupposed.

Since the core argument does not feature any propositions in which a definition is predicated of a *definiendum*, it is to be noted that the focus of Lucullus' exposition temporarily turns away from the core argument. However, the points made in the course of discussing such propositions are eventually applied to propositions generally and to those making up the core argument in particular.

Lucullus then poses a question apparently for the Academics in general, which opens up a dilemma.[183] This dilemma is the main structuring device until the end of §44. In my view it poses a challenge to both Clitomacheans and mitigated sceptics, such that the two positions can equally be seen as its target; I will reject an influential alternative reading of the passage on which it is an effective attack on the mitigated position, while leaving the Clitomachean position untouched.[184]

---

[181] Contra Schäublin et al. (p. 227 n. 128), who suggest that impressions which are 'true as well as false' are meant, e.g. Orestes' impression of Electra as a fury (caused by a real object, which is, however, misrepresented); cf. Sextus, *M.* 7.244. They explain: 'Da die Stoiker ihrerseits zugestanden, daß ein und dieselbe Erfahrungssituation von "wahren" und "falschen" Elementen durchsetzt sein könne, bemühten sich die Akademiker, plausibel zu machen, daß die Situation des Mit- und Nebeneinanders von Wahrem und Falschem nicht nur in solchen eng spezifizierten Kontexten gegeben sei, sondern für sämtliche Bereiche typisch sei, bzw. nicht ausgeschlossen werden könne.' The instances cited are once again perceptual impressions, and hard to reconcile with the well-documented and well-understood instances of ἀπαραλλαξία, to the point where the consistency of the entire concept would be threatened if this interpretation was correct.

[182] See section 5.8.

[183] On anti-sceptical dilemmas more generally, see Castagnoli (2010: 160-86, 278-307, 324 n. 52); on §§43-4 in its historical context, Mansfeld (1988: 243).

[184] See Brittain (2001: 129-38).

The question is if a definition put forward in a proposition by the Academics can be transferred to another subject,[185] i.e. whether it is possible that it can be truly predicated of another subject. Then the two possible replies are considered:

(A) If the answer is 'yes', then the Academics will have no grounds for calling the definition true in the first place.
(B) If the answer is 'no', then the Academics will have to confess that they apprehend the subject the definition offers a conceptual analysis of.

Lucullus adds that the Academics are reluctant to make the claim (*quod minime ille uolunt*) that they apprehend the *definiendum* at issue as per option (B).[186] This means that, as per the dilemma, they are committed to holding that for the impression corresponding to the proposition at issue, it is possible that it could be false. This is the ἀπαραλλαξία claim.

In §44 init. Lucullus then moves from propositions in which a *definiens* is predicated of a *definiendum* to propositions which feature in an argument,[187] and as he proceeds, it becomes clear that he is thinking of the propositions which make up the core argument in particular. He does this by introducing a second dilemma building on the first, with the horns in reverse order:

(b) If the Academics say that they 'see clearly through' (*perspicere*) what they are conversing about and without impediment from 'the commonality of (true and false) impressions' (i.e. ἀπαραλλαξία), then they will be confessing that they apprehend.[188]
(a) If they deny that true impressions can be distinguished from false ones, they will not be able to proceed (sc. from one step to the next when advancing an argument).

Option (b) gestures to the Carneadean πιθανόν/*probabile* through the use of the verb *perspicere*; *perspicua* had been introduced as a sub-class of *probabilia* in §34.[189] Option (a) overtly refers back to the core argument: if true impressions are held to be indistinguishable from false impressions given premiss (iii),[190] then this will stop any argument in its tracks, since progression from one premiss to the next will be halted.

---

[185] The Latin text does not clearly indicate whether definitions newly formulated by the Academics are meant or also definitions formulated by dogmatists; given the general nature of the context, the reference is likely to be to both. Moreover, the text does not specify whether only certain types of definition are meant, e.g. those of natural kinds as opposed to those of philosophical concepts, like the cataleptic impression.

[186] Cf. *Luc.* 28–9 and 35 on whether the Academic apprehends, or ought to apprehend, (some of) his own statements.

[187] Note §43 *fin.*: *eadem dici poterunt in omnibus partibus*. The step from definitions to other propositions is not simply a generalization (which would be uncompelling); rather, that the other propositions feature as premisses *in an argument* and *are endorsed in some form* is crucial.

[188] Contrast *Luc.* 105a, which makes the corresponding claim from the Academic point of view: *Non enim lucem eripimus, sed ea quae uos percipi comprehendique, eadem nos si modo probabilia sint uideri dicimus*.

[189] The Academics assume the premisses and the conclusion of the core argument to be *probabilia*.

[190] See on §40: *Nihil interesse autem, non modo...si discerni non possint*.

The next sentence (*Nam concludi argumentum... nulla possint esse*) elaborates that an argument can only be brought to a conclusion if its premises have been 'approved' (*ita probatis*) in such a way that there cannot be false ones just like it.[191] If the argument does so proceed, it will issue in the conclusion that nothing can be apprehended. Lucullus then reformulates the point about the need for unequivocal endorsement as true (cf. *ita probatis...*) with reference to the Stoic definition of scientic proof: if a proof is to conclude something that is not evident from something that is evident, then what is all the Academic talk that everything is not so much the case as appears to be the case (and as such not unequivocally endorsed)?

Finally, Lucullus moves on to another self-contradiction. This is said to occur when one holds premises (i) and (iii) of the core argument simultaneously. The problem, as Brittain (2001: 130–1) following Couissin (1983: 63 n. 52; 1929a: 273 n. 1) observes, is on what grounds someone who endorses (iii) in some form could also endorse (i), i.e. what one's endorsement of (i) and specifically of the claim that some impressions are true could be based on given one's commitment to (iii). Additional light is cast on this point by Cicero's reply in §111, where we are told that this particular line of criticism troubled Philo greatly according to Antiochus while the Cicero character claims to be unperturbed by it.[192] This raises the question if Cicero's position was different from Philo's.

A position from which one could reject these charges of inconsistency is one which involves putting forward the core argument for consideration ad hominem, such that any endorsement would be given, or would be expected to be given because of the opponent's commitment to rationality, by the other side. Someone who adopted this stance could reply that he does not 'own' any definition (with reference to the first dilemma) and that he takes no view on the premises which make up the core argument. Brittain (2001: 130) construes the Clitomachean position as a radically sceptical stance, reliant solely on ad hominem argument. He concludes that Lucullus is here not arguing against the Clitomachean position, but against mitigated sceptics who advance the core argument while giving qualified assent to its premises and to its conclusion; for only they would be vulnerable to Lucullus' objection.[193] Another piece of evidence which is marshalled for this purpose is the formulation used in §44 *init.* in continuation of horn (A) of the dilemma: ... *ea de quibus disserent se dilucide perspicere....* It had been suspected since Herrmann (1851) and (1855) that *perspicuitas* (i.e. ἐνάργεια) was a hallmark of a position of Philo's, and since we know that the Roman Books view would call the relevant impressions 'cataleptic' and that it is not at issue in Lucullus' speech, Cicero has been held to refer to the

---

[191] On the nature of the endorsement referred to by *probatis*, see below.

[192] Brittain (2001: 130) also states that premisses (i) and (iii) are not formally inconsistent. As emerges from §111, Antiochus was aware that ἀπαραλλαξία means 'non-distinctness' and took premiss (iii) to assert that true and false impressions are the same thing, not that they are indistinguishable (see section 5.6), as Brittain (2001: 131) and Couissin (1983: 63 n. 52; 1929a: 273 n. 1) assume. However, as is clear from §44a, Antiochus did press on the issue of access (*sin autem negabunt... distingui*), viz. the grounds for endorsement.

[193] See also Numenius frg. 27, p. 77.28–9 Des Places, cited in the n. on §40: *eorum quae uidentur alia uera sunt alia falsa*, above.

mitigated position in particular.[194] *Luc.* 111 is treated as supporting the notion that Philo was a mitigated sceptic while Cicero himself was a Clitomachean.

In my view, this interpretation of *Luc.* 40-4, viewed as directed at mitigated scepticism only, misconstrues the nature of Clitomacheanism as represented in Cicero's works, and quite possibly also of Clitomacheanism in general at the end of the second century BC.[195] Evidence from Cicero's speech later in the *Lucullus* (*Luc.* 67), delivered from a Clitomachean position, suggests that the Clitomacheans were not deemed to advance the core argument in a purely dialectical way, relying solely on the dogmatists' endorsement of several of the premises. Rather, they are assumed to approve it, in the technical sense explained in *Luc.* 104–5. Approving *p* is incompatible with approving not-*p* at the same time.[196] According to *Luc.* 104–105a, approving is a form of not giving assent: a Clitomachean who approves a premiss in an argument nonetheless withholds assent to it. However, the core argument is one which the Academics had consistently used over two centuries, routinely arriving at the same conclusion. This being so, the claim that the approval of the premisses amounts to suspension of judgement must have looked unconvincing at best. Relatedly, the Stoics and Antiochus never accepted the ἀπαραλλαξία thesis. They may have taken the view, two centuries into the debate, that Academics who want to obtain the conclusion that there are no cataleptic impressions or that nothing is apprehensible must provide the endorsement themselves. Finally, in terms of the arrangement of *Acad.*, and given that Cicero was in all three editions the main Academic speaker and was, here as elsewhere, a Clitomachean in particular, it would be odd if Lucullus' objection to the core argument had been formulated in a way which did not touch the Clitomachean position.[197] These considerations provide reasons for thinking that the choice between the two horns of the dilemma is, on Antiochus' view, one which Clitomacheans face if they approve of definitory propositions, as well as propositions generally and the premisses of the core argument. But if the Clitomacheans face it, then the mitigated sceptics face it a fortiori, since they can reasonably be taken to assent to the propositions at issue, even if it is in a qualified fashion which allows for the possibility that the corresponding impression assented to may actually be false. It is a function of Lucullus' approach and the deployment of the dilemma device that any mode of endorsement short of dogmatic assent, i.e. approval or qualified assent, is given parity of treatment.[198]

That the second dilemma uses the term *perspicere* in manifest reference to certain *probabilia* does recall the distinction between *percepta* and *perspicua* in §34, but as I explain ad loc., while it is possible that *perspicua* were claimed by Philo, the conceptual category was most likely formulated by Carneades and thus in principle common property among later Academics, and there is no compelling reason to associate

---

[194] See Brittain (2001: 133); and the commentary on *Luc.* 34.
[195] See section 4; and on *Luc.* 103–105a.
[196] See also Castagnoli (2019: 197) on this point.
[197] The bearer of the argumentative risk of an *ignoratio elenchi* is the person who makes the argument, not the person at whose position it is mistakenly directed.
[198] Cf. *Luc.* 59 *init.*, where *sequi probabilia* is branded impossible by Lucullus given ἀπαραλλαξία.

it with the mitigated position exclusively or primarily, and some evidence for linking it to the developed Clitomachean position.[199]

In *Luc.* 111 Cicero reports on what Antiochus said about Philo's reaction to Antiochus' claim of incompatibility between premises (i) and (iii) of the argument. It is unclear if the Cicero character intends to cast doubt on Antiochus' report (of which he appears to have learnt only when he had contact with Antiochus or was able to read his writings), or if the character is engaging in self-characterization, implying that he inhabited the Clitomachean position in a profound way, so much so that he was able to rebut challenges to it which had troubled Philo himself (sc. while he held the same view). What the Cicero character does not say is that Antiochus' point did not affect him since he was advancing the core argument ad hominem. Rather, he responds as if Lucullus' argument was pertinent to his view but mistaken: the Academics do discern both true and false impressions, i.e. are entitled to endorsing premiss (i) in some way, but this does not mean that any of their impressions carry the sign which marks them out as self-warranting and which would warrant dogmatic assent. Therefore, the Clitomacheans (note that Cicero uses the first-person plural: *non facimus... cernimus*) 'approve' them.

There is one further piece of evidence which needs to be integrated with my discussion: Photius, *Bibl.* 212, 170a26–38 = LS 71C (partial),[200] which resembles parts of the present section, in places down to particular formulations. This text has been taken as evidence for the 'Philonian/Metrodorian position' and for its canonical status for a substantial period of Philo's tenure as scholarch (prior to the formulation of the Roman Books view). It has also been deployed to support the interpretation of *Luc.* 43–4 which assumes that Lucullus is targeting the 'Philonian/Metrodorian position' from the very beginning and exclusively:

τὸ δὲ μέγιστον, οἱ μὲν περὶ παντὸς τοῦ προτεθέντος διαποροῦντες τό τε σύστοιχον διατηροῦσι καὶ ἑαυτοῖς οὐ μάχονται, οἱ δὲ μαχόμενοι ἑαυτοῖς οὐ συνίασι· **τὸ γὰρ ἅμα τιθέναι τι καὶ αἴρειν ἀναμφιβόλως**, ἅμα τε φάναι κοινῶς ὑπάρχειν ⟨ἀ⟩κατάληπτά [ἀ- suppl. Hirzel 1883: 232-3], μάχην ὁμολογουμένην εἰσάγει, ἐπεὶ πῶς οἷόν τε γινώσκοντα τόδε μὲν εἶναι ἀληθὲς τόδε δὲ ψεῦδος ἔτι διαπορεῖν καὶ διστάσαι, καὶ οὐ σαφῶς τὸ μὲν ἑλέσθαι τὸ δὲ περιστῆναι; **εἰ μὲν** γὰρ ἀγνοεῖται ὅτι τόδε ἐστὶν ἀγαθὸν ἢ κακόν, ἢ τόδε μὲν ἀληθὲς τόδε δὲ ψεῦδος, καὶ τόδε μὲν ὂν τόδε δὲ μὴ ὄν, πάντως ὁμολογητέον ἕκαστον ἀκατάληπτον εἶναι· **εἰ δ' ἐναργῶς** κατ' αἴσθησιν ἢ κατὰ νόησιν **καταλαμβάνεται**, καταληπτὸν ἕκαστον φατέον.

The chief point is that those who are aporetic about every matter [i.e. the Pyrrhonists] maintain consistency and are not in conflict with themselves, whereas

---

[199] Brittain (2001: 131, 76–82) also holds that only 'Philonian/Metrodorians' treat the πιθανά as *evidence*, or delivering evidence, as opposed to treating πιθανά as psychological self-reports, so that the question of the grounds on which they accept the two premises at issue affects their position in ways in which it would not affect the Clitomachean position. I am working with a different reconstruction of the Carneadean πιθανόν (see section 6) and believe it to be inherent in it that it is interpretable as evidence (i.e. πιθανότης is in part a function of its, or the perceiving subject's, relationship with the world), and that such an interpretation could be actualized by modes of endorsement other than assent (qualified or not).

[200] The text is also part of Aenesidemus B3 in Polito (2014), who, however, prints a different text in place of ἅμα τε φάναι κοινῶς ὑπάρχειν ⟨ἀ⟩κατάληπτά. See also appendix 1.

[the Academics] are in conflict with themselves but do not realize it; **for to assume and reject things unambiguously**, and, at the same time, to say that they are generally non-cataleptic, introduces an obvious conflict. How can someone who knows that this is true and that false still be unclear and undecided, and not plainly choose the former and reject the latter? For *if* it's not known that this is good or bad, or that this is true and that false, and this existent and that is non-existent, it should be agreed that each of them is not subject to *catalepsis* [non-cataleptic]. But *if* it is **clearly apprehended** through perception or thought, it should be called subject to *catalepsis* [cataleptic].' (transl. as in Brittain 2001: 134 and 134 n. 3)

Luc. 44 *init.*: **Si enim** ea, de quibus disserent, se **dilucide perspicere** nec ulla communione uisorum impediri, **comprehendere** ea se fatebuntur. **Sin autem** negabunt uera uisa a falsis posse distingui, qui poterunt longius progredi?

The verbal correspondences with §44 *init.* were noted by Brittain (2001: 134 n. 8), as was the dilemmatic structure (although Brittain construes the latter's effect and role differently as noted earlier). The highlighted τὸ γὰρ ἅμα τιθέναι τι καὶ αἴρειν ἀναμφιβόλως (cf. the earlier occurrence in Photius, *Bibl.* 212, 169b39–40 = Aenesidemus B2 Polito), which the Academics are said to do while saying that nothing is apprehensible (inconsistently), is for Brittain (2001: 135) evidence that the 'Philonian/Metrodorians' are at issue (sc. in what is presented as a general characterization of the Academics): 'The Philonian/Metrodorians seem to take the reasons they adduce for their provisional beliefs as evidence sufficient to justify holding them "unambiguously".' While this is a possible interpretation of the expression found in Photius' report, one cannot but observe that the report is not cast in terms of (provisional) assent given to impressions, or in terms of beliefs held, but that it instead uses expressions reminiscent of the terminology of dialectical exchanges in question and answer, where saying 'yes' to a proposition offered by means of a yes/no-question is called τιθέναι.[201] And saying 'yes' in a dialectical exchange is used as an illustration not of assent, provisional or dogmatic, but of Clitomachean approval in *Luc.* 104 (see ad loc.). The degree to which Photius' report gives Aenesidemus' exact wording cannot be assessed, but the relevant terms occur twice in the report. It is entirely conceivable that Aenesidemus talked about Clitomacheans like Cicero, or that he talked about the Academics in general and used a formulation sufficiently general to cover Clitomachean approval as well as qualified assent (which was, on the evidence of *Luc.* 148, a key component of a position held by some Academics, but was, or so I believe, never the official position of the Academy).[202]

---

[201] The effect of a successful argument against a proposition 'B is A', performed by the questioner in a dialectical exchange, is called ἀναιρεῖν or ἀνασκευάζειν (both semantically similar to αἴρειν); see Reinhardt (2000: 62).

[202] As noted above (p. 458), approving *p* is incompatible with approving not-*p* at the same time and could thus be called τιθέναι…ἀναμφιβόλως by someone intent on presenting the Academics as dogmatists.

§43

Hanc ego subtilitatem...remotissimam: as Reid[1] (p. 96) notes on *Ac.* 1.7, 'not "subtlety", but "minute accurate treatment" '; cf. *OLD* s.v. 4a: 'attentiveness (of a person) to finer points of distinction, minute thoroughness, subtlety, etc.' In *Fat.* 3 *subtilitas* is cited as a hallmark of Academic argument, but the context seems more general there. In arguing that the Academics are not entitled to *subtilitas* which is most befitting for philosophy, Lucullus is not trying to deny that their position can be called a philosophical one, or their argumentative practice philosophy; cf. the Pyrrhonist stance, which is the third type of philosophy recognized by Sextus in *P.H.* 1.4 (dogmatism, negative dogmatism, and inquiry). *Causa* denotes the case under dispute as construed by the Academics (hence *eorum*); cf. *Luc.* 40: *tota ab his causa comprehenditur.* Reid[2] translates: '...most alien to the *principles* of those who thus argue' [my emphasis]. There is no suggestion that only Academics of a particular bent (e.g. mitigated sceptics) are meant.

Definitiones enim et partitiones et horum luminibus utens oratio...certa esse quae tutentur: the grammatical subject of this sentence extends from *definitiones* to *distinctio*. It is well recognized that there is a sense break after *oratio*, marked by *tum* (cf. *OLD* s.v. no. 9 for this use). On *definitio* and *partitio* and their relationship to conceptual analysis, see *Top.* 26-4, with Reinhardt (2003) ad loc.; and Brittain (2005: 200-9). Here *definitiones* and *partitiones* are presumably phrasal terms which feature in sentences (this is suggested by their being able to function as *lumina* in discourse, *oratio*); if *definitiones* meant 'definitory statements', sentences in which a definition is predicated of a *definiendum*, it is difficult to see how *partitiones* could be something analogous. These sentences, or so the wider context suggests, feature as premisses in arguments. It is peculiar that definitions and partitions are presented as mere stylistic flourishes of Academic speech: *lumina* are 'figures' (σχήματα), and Reid[1] (p. 229) rightly refers to *De orat.* 3.202-8; *Brut.* 69; and *Or.* 134-8; see also *TLL* s.v. col. 1820.48-9. (§107: *Sed illa sunt lumina duo* is different.) If there is polemical intent in this, it is not easy to describe with precision; Lucullus may be hinting at a 'lack of investment' on the part of the Academics (cf. *non eorum qui clament...quam falsa* below, and the first horn of the dilemma, *si posse dixerint...*): definitions do not actually mean anything for the Academics, they are just philosophically sounding flourish with which they adorn their speech. In the second part of the subject, *similitudines dissimilitudinesque* is best taken to refer not to similarities and differences, but to things which are similar or dissimilar (cf. *OLD* s.v. *similitudo* no. 2a). This would give readily intelligible sense to *tenuis et acuta distinctio*, and would fit with objects (as opposed to impressions thereof) coming into view occasionally in what follows (e.g. *illa uera definitio transferri possit in falsum*); cf. p. lii for the sense of 'objects' at issue. By itself *tutari* (cf. *OLD* s.v. *tutor*[2] no. 2) could suggest that the proponent of an argument is endorsing it just as an advocate would when he is acting on behalf of a client (cf. *Fin.* 1.6: *sed tuemur ea quae dicta sunt ab iis qui probamus*), but *fidentium...illa uera et firma et certa esse* provides crucial qualification. The archetype omitted *dissimilitudines* (retaining only *-que*), correctly restored by the shared source of V and S (ξ). On the emendation *harum* for *horum (luminibus)* printed by Lambinus, see Reid[1] (p. 228) and Plasberg[1] (p. 88).

Non eorum qui clament nihilo magis uera illa esse quam falsa: the formula οὐ μᾶλλον is typically associated with pre-Hellenistic sceptical arguments (Leucippus and Democritus; Theophrastus) and with Pyrrhonian scepticism (see e.g. Sextus, *P.H.* 1.188–91); see the summary in Kechagia (2011: 313–21) and Schofield (2002), and Castagnoli (2010: 258–72), respectively. Earlier informative studies include de Lacy (1958); Graeser (1970); Makin (1993); and more generally Brennan (1998). In Sextus the formula is deployed with a degree of flexibility, which Castagnoli (2010: 261) aims to capture in the following way: 'For every pair of conflicting unclear matters *p* and *q* which *I* have examined, *p appears to me now* as persuasive as *q*, and therefore, being unable to assent to either of them, *I* can believe neither the one nor the other (*I* suspend judgement).' Other characterizations of its Sextan use assume that the formula turns on the applicability of predicates in particular; thus Kechagia (2011: 313 n. 3): 'In a "no more *x* than *y*" statement *x* and *y* stand for any predicate (e.g. "object A is no more a horse than a chair"); but it can also be the case that *y* is the opposite of *x*, that is *non-x* (e.g. "object A is no more hot than cold").' In our passage Lucullus is thinking primarily of impressions whose content is non-perceptual; on how non-perceptual ἀπαραλλαξία is conceived, see the general note above and section 5.8. Moreover, one need not commit Lucullus to the assertion that the Academic would find the two second-level propositions at issue—'*r* is true' and '*r* is false'—equally persuasive. The Academic and Pyrrhonian use of the formula may be coming apart on this point; see, however, Svavarsson (2014), esp. p. 366. Only two other texts associate the οὐ μᾶλλον formula with the Academics. They are Numenius frg. 27.33–7 Des Places (see appendix 2): παραλαβὼν γὰρ ἀληθεῖ μὲν ὅμοιον ψεῦδος, καταληπτικῇ δὲ φαντασίᾳ καταληπτὸν ὅμοιον καὶ ἀγαγὼν εἰς τὰς ἴσας, οὐκ εἴασεν οὔτε τὸ ἀληθὲς εἶναι οὔτε τὸ ψεῦδος, ἢ οὐ μᾶλλον τὸ ἕτερον τοῦ ἑτέρου ἢ μᾶλλον ἀπὸ τοῦ πιθανοῦ, 'For he would take the true together with something false resembling it, and an apprehensible object together with a (sc. supposedly) cataleptic impression and show that there are equally good reasons for both, and would not admit that there was truth or falsehood, or that one was more than the other, one more than the other on the basis of persuasiveness'; and Hippolytus, *Ref.* 1.23.3: οἱ μὲν οὖν τῶν Ἀκαδημαϊκῶν λέγουσι μὴ δεῖν τὴν ἀρχὴν περὶ μηδενὸς ἀποφαίνεσθαι, ἀλλ' ἁπλῶς ἐπιχειρήσαντας ἐᾶν· οἱ δὲ τὸ ⟨οὐ⟩ μᾶλλον προσέθεσαν, λέγοντες οὐ μᾶλλον τὸ πῦρ ⟨πῦρ⟩ εἶναι ἢ ἄλλο τι· οὐ μέντοι ἀπεφήναντο αὐτὸ ⟨τὸ⟩ τί ἐστιν, ἀλλὰ τὸ τοιόνδε, 'Some followers, then, of the Academics say that one ought not to make plain an opinion on the principle of anything, but simply endeavour to give it up; whereas others added the formula "no more this than that", saying that the fire is no more fire than anything else. But they did not declare what this is, but what kind it is.' The latter passage appears to confuse Academic scepticism and Pyrrhonism, as the preceding text (not quoted) suggests; in any event, it ascribes a centrality to the formula which it, for all we know, did not have for the Academics. The former passage provides a close verbal parallel to our passage here. Reid[1] (p. 229) draws attention to Seneca, *Ep. mor.* 88.44: *Nausiphanes ait ex his quae uidentur esse nihil magis esse quam non esse.*

Quid enim agant...num illa definitio possit in aliam rem transferri quamlibet: the question which sets up the dilemma is directed at all Academics without recognizable distinction. 'The transfer of a definition to another thing' must mean the predication of the predicate in a proposition of the form 'B is A', where A is a purported definition, of a subject other than B (C), such that 'B is A' is false. What cannot be meant is—*pace* Reid—that the predicate could be predicated truly of C as well as B; for the problem which Lucullus is confronting is the alleged possibility of non-perceptual ἀπαραλλαξία (see §44: *quae ad concludendum sumpta... ut falsa eiusdem modi nulla possint esse*). The subject B, despite *in aliam rem*, cannot be a particular, for it is supposed to be amenable to conceptual analysis (§43: *quod ea definitione explicetur*).

Si posse dixerint, quid [enim] dicere habeant cur illa uera definitio sit: this sentence introduces the first horn of the dilemma. See the general note above: neither horn of the dilemma is apt to threaten someone who is not endorsing his own argument in any way, but the wider context suggests that this is not part of the underlying scenario in any case. The present subjunctive marks this first option out as genuine rather than counterfactual possibility. *Vera definitio* is tendentious, but not in a harmful way: any kind of endorsement of a definitory proposition *p* will involve the rejection of, or disinclination to accept, the notion that the same definition can be applied to a different subject. *Enim* was repeated from *quid enim agant* above. On *habeo* with the infinitive, see Reid[1] (p. 229) and Reinhardt (2010: 210–11).

Si negauerint...Quod minime illi uolunt: the second horn of the dilemma is introduced; see the general note above. *Falsum* refers to the alternative *definiendum* (cf. *alia res*), of which the definition cannot be truly predicated. On *explicare* of conceptual analysis by means of a definition, see *Top.* 27, with Reinhardt (2003: 263–5) and Brittain (2005: 200–4). The transmitted *uel illa uera (definitio)* has been suspected by many. Some *recentiores* and Davies deleted *uel*; the defence mounted by Reid[1] (p. 229), viz. that it means 'even' here, does not convince, since sense neither requires nor admits of modification by 'even'. Kayser cited by Baiter proposed to bracket *uel illa*; Halm excluded *uel* and *uera*. It is possible that all of *uel illa uera* has been interpolated, or rather that *uel* signalled the insertion of *illa uera* as a possibility. Plasberg[1] prints *uel illa uera* like Reid[1], but Plasberg[2] places *cruces* around the three words.

Eadem dici poterunt in omnibus partibus: Reid[1] (p. 230) glosses 'at every step of the controversy', but the reference is more likely to be to the areas of knowledge distinguished in §42 (where *pars* occurs several times in the required sense, whereas it would be an unusual term to denote a step in an argument). *Eadem* must refer to both horns of the dilemma, given that the next two sentences return to them in chiastic order. *Poterunt* is a correction first made by the correcting hand in M; M had *poterint*. The future tense is suggested by *dicent* below, but the reading of ζ cannot be dismissed.

§44

Si enim dicent ea de quibus disserent...comprehendere ea se fatebuntur: Lucullus now proceeds to a second dilemma, modelled on the first, with the horns in reverse order. At issue now are not definitory statements, but any claim advanced in a formal argument which the speaker endorses in some form himself. On the connection between *dilucide perspicere* and the Academic distinction between *perspicua* and *percepta* in §34, see the general note above; contrast Lucullus' own use of *perspicere* in §53: *a perspiciendo*. Reid[1] (p. 230) rightly connects *communio uisorum* with ἐπιμιξία, which he regards as a synonym of ἀπαραλλαξία (see his note on *Luc.* 34: *in eo autem (sc. uiso) si erit communitas cum falso*); see also *OLD* s.v. *communio*[2] no. 2, *TLL* s.v. col. 1961.12–13. Given the uses of *communio* and the fact that the phrase *communio uisorum* stands in the ablative, the term cannot be used of the συνδρομή of impressions discussed in Sextus' report on the Carneadean πιθανόν (*M.* 7.176–81), although the notion of impedance is connected with the syndrome, too: an impression is unimpeded if none of the impressions in the syndrome associated with it appears false (see section 6.1). *Fatebuntur* is used extensionally (*OLD* s.v. *fateor* no. 4a): the Academics will reveal that they apprehend as a matter of fact, while presumably refusing to acknowledge that this is so. Contrast *Luc.* 105a, where Cicero claims that everything will 'appear' to him in a specific sense which the dogmatist claims he apprehends.

Sin autem negabunt uera uisa a falsis posse distingui, qui poterunt longius progredi: turning to the other horn of the dilemma, which envisages that any claim advanced in an argument might as well be false, Lucullus asserts that no argument can proceed from its premises to its conclusion on this assumption, because such progression requires a firm commitment to the propositions on the part of the person making the argument. This claim only makes sense if it is assumed that the other side would withhold endorsement (i.e. resist an ad hominem argument) and would not be impressed by an argument which is intended to transfer πιθανότης from the premises to the conclusion (cf. Brittain 2001: 132 on this point). I explain in the general note above why I think Lucullus feels entitled to adopt this posture here.

There is no reason to suspect that Lucullus intends to declare it impossible to bring an argument to a conclusion which includes premises endorsed not by the speaker but by the opponent at whom it is directed (or by third parties in the spirit of 'one might argue'); this would include normal refutations, which arise from an opponent's assumption(s). Rather, or so I assume, Lucullus is making a more narrow point on the conditions under which the core argument could have force at the end of the long debate between Stoics and Academics (see the general note above). Cicero replies in *Luc.* 111.

The evidence for the view that Lucullus' dilemma is posed on the assumption that any Academic will want to endorse the core argument somehow consists in what we are told about the corollary to the core argument in *Luc.* 67 for the Clitomachean position, and in the readiness to express qualified assent shown by Catulus in *Luc.* 148 for mitigated scepticism. The remark in §41 *init.* that the Academics 'want' to arrive at the conclusion of the core argument (*sumunt ut concludant id quod uolunt*) does not appear to impute to them just the minimal intent needed to make an argument as opposed to staying silent, but seems to ascribe a firmer intent to 'want' to make the argument.

One might wonder why Lucullus speaks in terms of the possibility of distinguishing or discriminating (*uera uisa a falsis posse distingui*) as opposed to identity/non-identity of true and false impressions; I believe that this is because attitudes taken to the impressions or corresponding propositions matter in the present context. See below on *Nam concludi...esse*.

Occurretur enim, sicut occursum est: the sentence sounds like a proverb, but there is no evidence that it was a standing expression. Lucullus is referring back to §27 *init.*, where he stated that ἀπαραλλαξία would prevent any proof from being concluded. For Pyrrhonist attacks on the dogmatic conception of proof, see Barnes (1980). Reid[1] (p. 230) notes the Greek equivalent ἀπαντᾶν. Cf. *Luc.* 46; *N.D.* 3.70; *Off.* 2.7; and Heumann-Seckel s.v. *occurrere* no. 4 for a legal use.

Nam concludi argumentum non potest...ut falsa eiusdem modi nulla possint esse: this sentence concludes the consideration of the horn (a) of the second dilemma. *Probare* must stand for endorsement of any kind here, i.e. assent or Clitomachean approval. The expressions meaning 'to assent' could not readily have been deployed in the same way, but conversely, Cicero could have made Lucullus use them had he wanted to do so. *Ita* signals inter alia that approval as characterized in *Luc.* 104 is not meant exclusively. Grammatically the *ut*-clause here reflects the attitude of the endorsing subject: endorsement is given in such a way that it is thereby *assumed by the subject* that there cannot be a proposition like the one at issue which is false; see Kühner-Stegmann ii.249. Trivially, endorsement of whatever kind cannot *make* a proposition invariably true. A proof or demonstration could do that, and *probare* can mean 'to prove', but the notion that propositions are to be demonstrated would come out of nowhere and would be impossible to integrate into an overall interpretation of the passage. See *OLD* s.v. *sumo* no. 17 for the use of premises posited in a formal argument; Reid[1] (p. 230) refers to the use of *sumptio* (λῆψις) and *assumptio* (πρόσληψις) for first and second premiss in *Div.* 2.108.

Ergo si rebus comprehensis et perceptis nisa et progressa ratio hoc efficiet, nihil posse comprehendi, quid potest reperiri quod ipsum repugnet magis: the text returns to horn (b) of the dilemma and to the core argument: if the premises in the latter are taken to be true (and thereby apprehended, as per the principle formulated in the first sentence of §44), then the proponent of the argument ends up in an inconsistent and self-refuting position upon reaching the conclusion. *Nisa* as in the *deteriores* (e.g. Neap.3) must be right, and the transmitted *uisa* the result of minim confusion.

Cumque ipsa natura...quam uideri uolunt: Lucullus continues with what he regards as the absurdities associated with horn (b). If one advances formal arguments, and in a way which gives the propositions featuring in them the status of *perspicua*, then what one actually offers is a proof as the Stoics define it (cf. *Luc.* 26). This being so, the conception of argument used by those who (sc. make such arguments but) say with respect to everything that it appears to be the case rather than is the case must be deemed absurd. On attempts made by both Lucullus and Cicero to present their stance as not just correct but natural—cf. the personification of the *natura accuratae orationis*—see Reinhardt (2019). Reid[1] (p. 230) notes that *patefacere* recalls attributes typically attached to proofs in Greek texts (ἐκκαλυπτικός, δηλωτικός).

With *qui omnia... uolunt* compare the general characterization of the Academics—before the dilemma is introduced—in *Luc.* 43: *qui clament nihilo magis uera illa esse quam falsa.*

Maxime autem conuincuntur...inter falsa et uera nihil interesse: Lucullus now steps back from the dilemma and ends with a final contradiction into which the Academics in general fall when they advance the core argument and endorse it in some way; see the general note above, which also touches on Cicero's reply in *Luc.* 111, and Brittain (2001: 131 n. 4). *Haec duo* refers to premisses (i) and (iii) of the core argument; for *congruere* used of consistency or compatibility, cf. *Fin.* 2.99. For *repugnare* (= μάχεσθαι) to denote incompatibility or conflict, cf. *N.D.* 1.30; as explained above, the two premisses are not formally incompatible. *Declarare* means 'to announce, declare' (*OLD* s.v. no. 1a) and does not signal unqualifiedly endorsed statements (unlike, say, *affirmare*), but sense requires that the statements at issue are assumed to be endorsed by the speaker in some form.

At primum sumpseras tamquam interesset: ita priori posterius, posteriori superius non iungitur: that someone who accepts premiss (iii) ought to struggle to have confidence in premiss (i) is plain, but it may be less obvious why the reverse should hold. Presumably true and false impressions can be differentiated by e.g. the behavioural outcomes they give rise to, and since these will typically be, respectively, successful and unsuccessful in a relevant sense, this will represent a consideration against (iii).

At the end of the sentence, sense requires that an incompatibility (of holding premisses i and iii) is noted, less so that i and iii 'refute' one another. For the use of *iungere*, see *OLD* s.v. iungo n. 13. Reid[1] (p. 231), who also printed *non iungitur*, may or may not be right in making a connection with συνάρτησις, which characterizes the relationship between antecedent and consequent in conditionals (understood in a certain way); see Bobzien (1996: 185–6). The archetype had the ablatives *priore* and *posteriore*, which could only be retained with Plasberg's *conuincitur*. V[2]'s *non iungitur* would be an outstanding emendation by the Carolingian corrector, not a vertically transmitted reading; see the Oxford Classical Text, p. lxi n. 63.

§§45–46

Having concluded the discussion of the core argument (40–4), and before engaging with the two main types of consideration cited in support of ἀπαραλλαξία in the domain of perception (cf. premiss iii of the core argument), Lucullus discusses two measures one can take in order to make effective use of cataleptic impressions, which—we may assume—all human beings experience regularly and frequently but not invariably, and to retain καταλήψεις arising from them. The first measure is to appreciate the unique clarity (*perspicuitas*) of cataleptic impressions; the second measure is to study and understand sophistic arguments which can be used to argue to the contradictory of the propositional content of καταλήψεις, with a view to dislodging them.

Perspicuitas corresponds to the Greek ἐνάργεια (cf. *Luc.* 17). The Stoics used this term to refer to the unique clarity which cataleptic impressions, i.e. the uniquely clear way in which they present their object (cf. *Ac.* 1.41: *Visis non omnibus adiungebat fidem, sed iis solum quae propriam quandam haberent declarationem earum rerum quae uiderentur*).[203] *Perspicuitas* is to be identified with the mark (*nota*) which only cataleptic impressions have, although that connection is not explicitly made either here or elsewhere in *Acad.*; see section 6 for a detailed discussion and a comparison with clarity as construed by the Academics. The present passage offers insights regarding two important aspects of *perspicuitas*: first, *perspicuitas* is not necessarily a property one is consciously aware of. This is worth noting because one might think that we can readily tell whether our perceptions are clear or not.[204] In fact, however, the conscious appreciation of clarity requires, according to Lucullus, a particular kind of focused attention on the part of the perceiving subject. Second, and relatedly, *perspicuitas* is a quality which an impression has or does not have; while impressions can be placed on a spectrum from unclear to clear, and while human beings are able to appreciate how changes in the conditions of perception (e.g. lighting, distance to object) affect the quality of our impressions, *perspicuitas* seems to denote the property of extreme clarity at the very end of the spectrum. This being so, it is easier to see how one can fail to appreciate consciously that an impression is uniquely clear in the way in which only cataleptic impressions can be, as opposed to being merely very clear indeed.

In *Luc.* 17 various attitudes among Stoics regarding the defence of *perspicuitas* are listed. One is that *perspicuitas* is something which is immediately apparent, and a definition of it could not possibly be more informative than *perspicuitas* itself. Another is that *perspicuitas* should speak for itself, but that arguments in support of it should be mounted if it was attacked with arguments. Lucullus evidently acts on the latter view here.

In the second half of §45 a connection is made with Epicurus; what the connection consists in is not entirely clear. Thus in his translation Brittain (2006) puts the section in brackets and does not translate the *nam* which links it to what precedes. The reasoning involved seems to be the following: someone who is not trained in the art of dialectic and who has no experience in dealing with sophistic argument is likely to let go of true perceptual beliefs when these are directly challenged through sophistic argument. Epicurus is then introduced: he wanted to address cognitive malfunctions which interfere with the cognition of the truth, by positing that all perceptions are true, that 'opinion' is, however, placed on true perceptions, and that opinion itself may be false. This achieved nothing, Lucullus says, because the error of opinion was not removed. The point of contact between Epicurus and what precedes is the notion that humans have true perceptual thoughts which they, however, are unable to use effectively. There is thus, Lucullus holds, a cognitive phenomenon *in re* which the Stoics and Epicurus (the latter but dimly) recognize. Epicurus' analysis of it is wanting, as is suggested by the fact that the supposed error of opinion cannot be

---

[203] 'Conspicuousness', the translation offered by Reid[2], is quite misleading, as is 'Anschaulichkeit' (Schäublin et al.).
[204] Thus Nawar (2014).

conceptually separated, let alone eradicated. *Nam* links the aside on Epicurus to what precedes not by providing evidence or justification, but by giving elaboration and background (see Kroon 1995: 147–8 on this use of *nam*). The equation of Stoic καταλήψεις and Epicurean perceptions which Lucullus makes is questionable (see *Luc.* 79–80 with comm.).

§45

Sed progrediamur...in praeteritis relinquamus: as noted by Reid[1] (p. 231), *assentari* is never used by Cicero as a synonym for *assentiri*. For the formulation *ut nihil assentati esse uideamur*, cf. Cic., *Lael.* 97; *Fam.* 3.11.2 (= SB 65). *Praeterita* are 'things left behind/passed over', cf. the figure of style *praeteritio*. The sentence gestures self-consciously to the methodical approach to philosophical argument to which only the dogmatist is properly entitled; cf. *Luc.* 43.

Primum igitur perspicuitas illa quam diximus...indicet: *perspicuitas* is introduced as the Latin counterpart of ἐνάργεια in *Luc.* 17; the wording there suggests that the connection was not already made in the *Catulus*. Lucullus does not seem to be claiming *perspicuitas* for the Stoics and the Antiochean position here, which he might have done, given that in *Luc.* 34 reference is made to a group of Academics who recognize *perspicua* but claim that these can never be *percepta*; these Academics thus rely on a different conception of *perspicua*. The *ut*-clause might suggest that *perspicuitas* is a feature which is unproblematically consciously available, but *Luc.* 46 shows that this is not so; the term *uis* is here linked to the power of cataleptic impressions to reveal their subject (*indicare* = 'to point out something which is there', like Greek δηλοῦν). Elsewhere they are said to have power in that they are assent-inducing by a quasi-automatic process (see Brittain 2014). Reid[1] (p. 232) notes that *(ut) ipsa* could be feminine (sc. *perspicuitas*) or neuter plural.

Sed tamen...depellamur: the comparatives *firmius et constantius* suggest that Lucullus is not looking to the sage, who would be unshakeable in his καταλήψεις (which would also be ἐπιστῆμαι in his case). The adjective *clarus* is evidently used as a synonym to *perspicuus*; cf. *Ac.* 1.41 *declarationem rerum* (cited with context above). The collocation *praestigiis quibusdam et captionibus* is not necessarily just an instance of stylistic fullness; *praest(r)igia* (or *-ae*), while meaning 'action intended to hoodwink, trick' (*OLD* s.v. n. 1), has a particular association with vision and visual deception (Walde-Hofmann s.v.: 'Blendwerk'; Isid., *Orig.* 8.9.33: *dictum...-um quod praestringit aciem oculorum*), whereas *captio* is especially associated with verbal misleading; cf. Cic., *Fin.* 2.17: *dialecticas captiones*; Sen., *Ep.* 45.8: *idem de istis captionibus dico (quo enim nomine potius sophismata appellem?)*. As usual, Reid[1] (p. 232) suggests that *quasi* marks the conscious rendering of a Greek term (σόφισμα) into Latin, which may in this case be correct.

Nam qui uoluit subuenire erroribus [Epicurus]...sustulit: *perspicuitas illa...nullo modo sustulit* = frg. 223 Usener. Cf. *Luc.* 79–80; Epic. *ad Hdt.* 49–52 (= D.L. 10.49–52);

Sextus, *M.* 8.63-6 (= frg. 253 Usener) on the disagreement between Epicureans and Stoics as to whether there are true impressions only, or true and false impressions. On the force of *nam* and the connection with what precedes, see the general note above. Reid¹ (p. 232) comments on *cognitionem* that 'here the verbal noun conveys the idea of *possibility*' [his emphasis], but for there to be a connection with the preceding context, *cognitio ueri* must refer to the sense organ's actual receiving of an invariably true impression (called ἐναργές by the Epicureans), and *conturbare* to the mishandling of this impression by 'opinion' (δόξα), whereby the latter is something quite different from Stoic δόξα. The sentence *ipsius enim opinionis...sustulit* seems to hint that the Epicurean separation of impression and opinion is useless since errors of opinion can neither be isolated nor prevented. By contrast, the Stoic training in dialectic is able to provide protection against sophistic arguments; the Epicureans famously reject dialectic. For discussions of the issues raised by the Epicurean view, see Taylor (1980); Asmis (1984: 141-66); Annas (1992: 157-73); Asmis (2009).

Baiter excluded *Epicurus* as a gloss. This seems convincing, given that the name is oddly positioned in its transmitted place, where it splits *erroribus* and *iis*, and that the relative clause which begins the sentence works well on its own as a characterization of Epicurus. See also the note in Plasberg¹ (p. 90).

§46

Quam ob rem...contra comparanda: *causa* is clearly not the overall case, but the case of one side, that of the Academics (*OLD* s.v. no. 2). That Cicero can write *rebus* rather than *uisis* suggests that he is not exclusively talking about mental states; cf. the discussion of *Luc.* 40-2. Epict., *Diss.* 1.27.2, promises βοήθεια in a similar context (noted by Reid¹ p. 232).

Aduersantur enim primum...agnoscere: on *defigere*, see *TLL* s.v. *defigo* cols 340.75-341.32, and specifically 340.81-341.6 on *defigere in aliquam rem* (*in ea quae perspicua sunt* goes with both verbs); on *intendere*, cf. *Luc.* 30: *ut sensus ad res percipiendas intenderemus*, and *TLL* s.v. *intendo* cols 2113.47-67 and 2113.68-80 (*sensus*). That one needs to attend to cataleptic impressions in a particular way in order to appreciate their unique clarity consciously dovetails with information provided elsewhere that training is necessary to discriminate between impressions of very similar objects (and indeed between objects); see *Luc.* 57, and section 5.3. Reinhardt (2011) suggests that in Galen we find a theory that impressions carry more perceptual information than enters into conscious awareness, and that this theory is likely to be influenced by Stoic thought. Training amounts to a modification of the amount of perceptual information which is consciously available. Cataleptic impressions are uniquely rich in representational content. In virtue of this quality, they can and will trigger assent even though their richness is not consciously appreciated (there is thus an objective dimension to the Stoic conception of clarity, one which the Academics do not recognize). Non-sages, however, tend to assent to cataleptic impressions as well as to non-cataleptic ones which are not uniquely rich; epistemic progress partly consists in eliminating instances of assent to non-cataleptic impressions. The related topic of selective attention to information within our ken is recognized e.g. by Plotinus 4.4.8.8–13, on which see Brittain (2003: 241–2). To what extent it was recognized by the Stoics is unclear: Seneca writes in *Ep. mor.* 94.59 that, in order to lead a morally good life, it is necessary *in tanto fremitu tumultuque falsorum unam denique audire uocem*, and Socrates says in Plt., *Crit.* 54d2–7, that he listens to the laws of the city in the same way in which the Corybantes listen to the flutes, i.e. in such a way that he does not hear anything else. Both passages suggest an awareness of the phenomenon of selective attention. *Ea quae perspicua sunt* is best taken as objects presented in impressions, i.e. there is reason to limit the reference to either impressions or their objects; *quanta luce ea circumfusa sint* is equally open to both readings, suggesting a shine emanating from an impression or the illumination which an object receives. The transmitted *(circumfusa) sunt* may be an instance of an indirect question with the indicative; see Bräunlich (1920: 100).

Alterum est...a ueritate: a restatement of what was said in the previous paragraph. The interpretation of *conturbare ueri cognitionem* given above is confirmed by *desciscunt a ueritate* here, where *ueritas* is the unsecured (true) perceptual belief which arises from a cataleptic impression that has been assented to. *Desciscere* here simply 'to diverge from' (*TLL* s.v. *descisco* col. 655.68); contrast Reid[2]: 'revolt from the truth', assuming the primary political sense (ibid. col. 654.57). Plut., *Sto. rep.* 1036d, reports Chrysippus' view that uncontrolled use of arguments *in utramque partem* will draw an unprepared audience away from καταλήψεις if they do not have the relevant λύσεις at their disposal; see also on *Luc.* 87b. As to *interrogationibus*, several ancient texts cast sceptical arguments mounted against the Stoics in question-and-answer format; see the commentary on *Luc.* 104. With the use of *dissoluere*, cf. §75.

Oportet igitur...facere constitui: Lucullus looks back to §17 *fin.* and justifies speaking in support of *perspicuitas*. *Quae pro perspicuitate responderi possunt* seem to be the remarks of *Luc.* 45–6, which must be deemed sparse on the nature of *perspicuitas* itself (see also Schäublin et al. p. 232 n. 145 on this point). For measures against sophistic arguments Lucullus refers forward (*deinceps*). *Captio* literally 'a catching' or attempt at a catching; then 'a piece of sophistry'. With *facere constitui*, cf. §43: *dicere habeant*. For *discutere* 'to shatter', see *TLL* s.v. *discutio* col. 1374.4.

§§47–58

In *Luc.* 47–58 Lucullus turns his attention to arguments cited in support of premiss (iii) of the core argument, concerned with ἀπαραλλαξία. Sextus, *M.* 7.401–11 distinguishes two types of such arguments, those from abnormal states of mind and those from very similar objects (see also section 5.6).

§§47–54a

Luc. 47–54a is devoted to the first type of arguments, those from vacuous impressions (*uisiones inanes*), i.e. thoughts which do not arise as a consequence of the standard causal process involving an object. On the evidence of reliable reports on Stoic thought, the Stoics used the term φαντάσματα ('figments') for such impressions, and confined the use of φαντασία to cases where an actually existing object was involved in the creation of the thought in question; cf. D.L. 7.49–51 = *SVF* ii.52, 55, 61 = LS 39A = *FDS* 255.[205]

In §§47–48, Lucullus recounts the Academic arguments pro (sc. ἀπαραλλαξία, from vacuous impressions), in §§49–53a he offers his (or rather Antiochus', or the Stoics') arguments contra.

§47 deals with vacuous impressions which have been created by a divine being; the Academics evidently devised such arguments because the Stoics themselves allowed for impressions created by divine beings, including—under very specific circumstances—false ones. §48 deals with vacuous impressions which are either self-generated or the result of abnormal circumstances (intoxication, madness, dreaming). Sextus only discusses vacuous impressions of the latter type, and there is no other parallel source for the arguments from non-distinctness which turn on divinely generated impressions in particular.

The detail with which Lucullus rehearses here the arguments cited in favour of ἀπαραλλαξία by the Academics raises the question of the distribution of material between the lost *Catulus* and *Luc*. It would be normal expectation that material such as that laid out in *Luc*. 47–8 would be introduced by an Academic rather than a speaker representing Antiochus, perhaps as part of his 'many arguments against the senses' (cf. §79). On the one hand, the detail given here, not on marginal or secondary issues but on central elements of the Academic's anti-Stoic strategy, suggests that our section is the place where these arguments feature for the first time in the *Acad.* On the other hand, there appear to be manifest weaknesses, even on its own terms, in the case for ἀπαραλλαξία as presented by Lucullus; this makes one wonder if the present section can be the first treatment, given Cicero's overall evenhandedness.

In the sub-section §§47–50, Academic arguments which Lucullus himself calls soritical (§49) are first introduced and then rejected. In order to appreciate the nature of these arguments and the grounds on which Lucullus rejects them, one needs to consider briefly the history of the engagement with the sorites in antiquity and its use in the debate between Stoics and Academics. In a second step the actual arguments offered in our passage need to be analysed as well as compared with Academic arguments for the ἀπαραλλαξία of vacuous and purportedly cataleptic impressions which we find elsewhere.

My appreciation of ancient efforts to understand soritical arguments and to solve or at least disarm them owes much to Barnes (1982), who includes in Appendix A a

---

[205] However, on occasion the term φαντασία is used in texts classed as Stoic fragments where one would expect φάντασμα, and some vacuous impressions arise from an object in some form, which, however, is substantially misrepresented in the impression in question, as opposed to having arisen without an object being involved in any way.

list of ancient texts on the sorites (pp. 65–7); Burnyeat (1982b); Williamson (1994: 8–35); Leib (2001); and Bobzien (2002); a revisiting of some of the issues raised by these seminal studies is Hankinson (2007).[206] Bobzien (2002: 217–18) gives the following characterization:

> At the time of the Stoic Chrysippus it was typically presented in the form of a dialectical game of questioning—perhaps as follows: 'Does one grain of wheat make a heap?'—'No'. 'Do two grains of wheat make a heap?'—'No'. 'Do three?'—'No'.—etc. If the respondent switches from 'no' to 'yes' at some point, they are told that they imply that one grain can make a difference between heap and non-heap, and that that's absurd. If the respondent keeps answering 'no', they'll end up denying e.g. that 10,000 grains of wheat make a heap. And, they are told, that's also absurd.

As per the rules of exchanges in question and answer, the respondent in Bobzien's characterization accepts a singular proposition ('One grain of wheat does not make a heap'). The respondent is then led to absurdity by means of a series of *modus ponens* inferences. The singular propositions involved have subjects which form a set ordered on a simple numerical principle, as well as a vague predicate ('makes a heap'; 'are few' is used elsewhere).

This is a (rather untechnical) description of the kind of argument characterized by Bobzien. Burnyeat (1982b) investigates inter alia to what extent philosophers in antiquity would have recognized this description (and more technical ones); as he puts it (p. 316): 'My question is the following: With what degree of abstraction did the ancients grasp the pattern of argument they called sorites? Did they have a general conception of the conditions, formal or material, which an argument must satisfy to count as a sorites?'

While soritical arguments of this kind may give the impression that ancient philosophers broadly meant the same thing as modern philosophers by the term, there are other arguments which point to a looser understanding. Consider the famous Carneadean argument against the existence of God (Sextus, *M.* 9.182–4, cf. Cicero, *N.D.* 3.43–52; the translation is Bury's):[207]

---

[206] See also Cicero's reply in *Luc.* 92–4.
[207] Εἰ Ζεὺς θεός ἐστι, καὶ ὁ Ποσειδῶν θεός ἐστιν·

> τρεῖς γάρ τ' ἐκ Κρόνου ἦμεν ἀδελφεοί, οὓς τέκετο Ῥέα,
> Ζεὺς καὶ ἐγώ, τρίτατος δ' Ἀΐδης ἐνέροισιν ἀνάσσων.
> τριχθὰ δὲ πάντα δέδασται, ἕκαστος δ' ἔμμορε τιμῆς.

ὥστε εἰ ὁ Ζεὺς θεός ἐστι, καὶ ὁ Ποσειδῶν ἀδελφὸς ὢν τούτου θεὸς γενήσεται. εἰ δὲ ὁ Ποσειδῶν θεός ἐστι, καὶ ὁ Ἀχελῷος ἔσται θεός· εἰ δὲ ὁ Ἀχελῷος, καὶ ὁ Νεῖλος· εἰ ὁ Νεῖλος, καὶ πᾶς ποταμός· εἰ πᾶς ποταμός, καὶ οἱ ῥύακες ἂν εἶεν θεοί· εἰ οἱ ῥύακες, καὶ αἱ χαράδραι. οὐχὶ δὲ οἱ ῥύακες· οὐδὲ ὁ Ζεὺς ἄρα θεός ἐστιν. εἰ δέ γε ἦσαν θεοί, καὶ ὁ Ζεὺς ἦν ἂν θεός. οὐκ ἄρα θεοί εἰσίν. καὶ μὴν εἰ ὁ ἥλιος θεός ἐστιν, καὶ ἡμέρα ἂν εἴη θεός· οὐ γὰρ ἄλλο τι ἦν ἡμέρα ἢ ἥλιος ὑπὲρ γῆς. εἰ δ' ἡμέρα ἐστὶ θεός, καὶ μὴν ἔσται θεός· σύστημα γάρ ἐστιν ἐξ ἡμερῶν. εἰ δὲ ὁ μὴν θεός ἐστι, καὶ ὁ ἐνιαυτὸς ἂν εἴη θεός· σύστημα γάρ ἐστιν ἐκ μηνῶν ὁ ἐνιαυτός. οὐχὶ δέ γε τοῦτο· τοίνυν οὐδὲ τὸ ἐξ ἀρχῆς. σὺν τῷ ἄτοπον εἶναι, φασί, τὴν μὲν ἡμέραν θεὸν εἶναι λέγειν, τὴν δὲ ἕω καὶ τὴν μεσημβρίαν καὶ τὴν δείλην μηκέτι.

If Zeus is a God, Poseidon is also a God:
'Brethren three were we, all children of Cronos and Rhea,
Zeus and myself and Hades, the third, with the Shades for his kingdom.
All things were parted in three, and each hath his share of the glory.'
So that if Zeus is a God, Poseidon also, being his brother, will be a God. And if Poseidon is a God, Achelous, too, will be a God; and if Achelous, Neilos; and if Neilos, every river as well; and if every river, the streams also will be Gods; and if the streams, the torrents; but the streams are not Gods; neither, then, is Zeus a God. But if there had been Gods, Zeus would have been a God. Therefore, there are no Gods.—Further, if the sun is a God, day will also be a God; for day is nothing else than sun above the earth. And if day is God, the month too will be God; for it is a composite made up of days. And if the month is God, the year too will be God; for the year is a composite made up of months. But this is not ⟨true⟩; neither then is the original supposition. And besides, they say, it is absurd to declare that the day is God, but not the dawn and midday and the evening.

On this passage, see Burnyeat (1982b: 100–6), who cites modern discussions which see the only link to the sorites proper in the 'polysyllogistic structure' of the two arguments, but who observes that ancient discussions emphasize the potentially unlimited reach of soritical arguments (see ibid. p. 101 n. 33), and notes that many arguments featuring under that heading are not actually instances of the pattern. I note that the subjects involved are not ordered in a series based on a simple numerical principle, and that the predicate—'is a god'—is not vague as 'is a heap' or 'is few' were. This changes the nature of the progression through the argument, in that no general principle is cited on which the applicability of the predicate to every newly introduced subjects rests. Instead, arguments which have force for particular steps only are offered or implied (Zeus and Poseidon are brothers; Archelous and the Nile are rivers, sc. and rivers are traditionally conceived as gods etc.). What enables the first argument is that the various 'deities' which feature as subjects are widely recognized as divine in the context of a polytheistic culture, and in that sense form a natural series of sorts; however, these preconceptions give out once one reaches sufficiently small and humble accumulations of water. The argument starting from 'the sun is a god' seems more far-fetched, and it needs to be appreciated that days, months, and years have divine powers according to rationalizing Stoic explanations of traditional religion (Cic., *N.D.* 1.36). As Cicero comments (*N.D.* 3.44), Carneades' aim was not to argue against the existence of god, but to question rational theology, and Stoic rational theology in particular.[208]

In *Luc.* 47–50 an ordered series of types of impression is relied on passim to construct the soritical or quasi-soritical argument for the ἀπαραλλαξία of vacuous and purported cataleptic impressions, and the possibility of a soritical argument is disputed in Lucullus' argument contra with reference to that series; that this is so is slightly obscured by the fact that Lucullus only once runs through the entire series

---

[208] Cicero uses formally similar arguments against the Peripatetic *tria bona* in *Fin.* 5; cf. 5.84: *tria genera bonorum: procliui currit oratio. Venit ad extremum; haeret in salebra*, discussed by Görler (2011: 346–7).

(*Luc.* 49 *fin.*), but it is clearly in the background throughout. The series of types of impression is:[209]

(i) impressions which are *probabile* (but false);
(ii) impressions which are *ualde ueri simile*;
(iii) impressions which are hard to tell apart from true ones;
(iv) impressions which cannot be told apart from true ones (while being different in some objective respect);
(v) impressions which are no different from true ones.

In *Luc.* 50 (i)–(v) are referred to as *genera* of impressions, but the way in which Lucullus rejects the Academic arguments raises the question of whether the Academics would have regarded this term as tendentious (see below). Moreover, I note that (i)–(v) do not form a 'natural' and widely recognized series (as the deities in the first group of theological arguments above do), nor are the types recognized by Stoic doctrine as species of impressions on the evidence of the divisions which are extant except for type (i) (the argument thus does not rely on Stoic assumptions in the way in which the second group of theological arguments above does).

The Stoics held that gods (and sages) do at times create impressions in the minds of non-sages which are persuasive but false (see the nn. below). This gives rise to the first soritical argument at the end of §47, advanced by the Academics and cited by Lucullus. The starting point is type (i) above, which serves as the subject in a proposition whose predicate is 'can be created by god'. This is a Stoic tenet and marked as such. From this the Academic argument proceeds through *modus ponens* inferences ('if type (i) impressions can be created by god, type (ii) impressions can be created by god; if type (ii) impressions can be created by god, type (iii) impressions…') to the conclusion that type (v) impressions can be created by god. In §48 the argument pattern is modified so as to introduce a new predicate—'can arise as a motion of the mind'—, i.e. a predicate which does not introduce god as the creator of the type of impression in question. In §49 the argument pattern is identified as a sorites and as a serious issue to whose refutation Antiochus devoted considerable effort. Lucullus here restates the argument of §47 *fin.* and observes that he only owns the conclusion if he accepted the premisses, whereas the argument is the Academic's problem if the latter proceeded of his own accord.

Before I consider Lucullus' rejection of the argument in *Luc.* 50, I observe that the argument for the ἀπαραλλαξία of vacuous and purported cataleptic impressions which we find in Sextus does not involve soritical or slippery slope arguments. Rather, a straightforward inference is made from the behaviour (broadly construed) of people whose state of mind is abnormal to their experiencing impressions exactly like purportedly cataleptic ones (*M.* 7.403; see section 5.6). (Interestingly, such

---

[209] That the series of types, and the associated soritical argument, is restated or invoked several times has been noted by Alleemudder (pp. 243–4). Types (i) and (iii)–(v) feature in the second half of §47; types (i), (iv), and (v) in §48 *init.* and §48 *fin.*, types (i)–(v) in the second half of §49, and types (i) or (ii) implicitly, as well as (iv) and (v) overtly in §50.

behaviour is cited as an example for the conclusion of the soritical argument in §48 and thus plays a different argumentative role in our passage.) And as has been mentioned above, steps of the argument pattern are in fact omitted in some of the restatements of the argument in our section. The Academics could equally well have argued from type (i) to type (v) directly ('if god can make up false persuasive impressions, he can make up any kind of false impression, including ones exactly like purportedly cataleptic impressions'). Given further that the types (i)–(v) are neither common sense categories (like what counts as a deity) nor species of impression according to Stoic doctrine with the exception of type (i), and that thus no preconceptions can have existed as to which type of impressions god can create or can arise to the exclusion of others, one wonders if the sorites pattern in this case has been stretched so thin as to qualify not even as a slippery slope argument by ancient standards—and if this is meant to be caricature.

The Stoics did not devise solutions to the sorites; rather, they made suggestions as to how to contain its corrosive effect. Lucullus' response to the Academic arguments in §50 affects to be more than that. He (A) rejects the notion that the argument can even get going, and he (B) dismisses its conclusion as absurd—both with reference to the types of impression (i)–(v). Both of the considerations offered are predicated on a particular reading of the soritical arguments: Lucullus argues as if the Academics argued that—to use the argument of *Luc.* 47 *fin.*—, if god can create a class of persuasive false impressions (impressions of type i), he can turn *that very class*, i.e. the elements of that class, into type (ii) impressions, and if he can turn them into type (ii) impressions, he can turn them into type (iii) impressions, and so on. Upon returning to §47, the reader will find that this may be a possible reading of the Latin text—but will also object that it was more natural to read the argument so as to say that, if god can create type (i) impressions, he will be able to create a different class of impressions, namely type (ii) impressions, and if type (ii) impressions, then type (iii) impressions, and so on.

Lucullus now offers two arguments. The first (cf. A above) is against the progression from step to step in the soritical pattern: objects (including impressions) naturally belong to a *genus*, and it is not possible to transfer them to a different *genus*, as one would by allowing the same impressions to be of type (i) and then of type (ii), and so on. He illustrates this with a comparison: we say that wolves are similar to dogs, but can we thereby say that wolves and dogs are the same thing? By this Lucullus means that we start with two classes of impressions, persuasive false ones and cataleptic ones, whose relationship is gradually reinterpreted as the argument moves from type (i) to type (v); put differently, the designations of types (i)–(v) are explicitly or implicitly relational, and the relationship posited with the class of cataleptic impressions changes from similar to identical through the progression. The second argument (cf. B above) is directed at the conclusion of the soritical argument: if there is a class of false impressions which is identical with a class of purportedly cataleptic impressions, then the impressions in question would belong to two *genera*, which, so Lucullus, is absurd.

This second argument we can connect with Lucullus' repeated statements that the Academics abolish the difference between truth and falsehood (see on *Luc.* 43–4). The Academics would presumably reply that they posit a class of impressions which are exactly like purported cataleptic impressions (with respect to representational content, ability to give rise to action, etc.) except for being false. The first argument may initially seem like wilful misinterpretation of the Academic argument, but one should note that the Stoics (and Antiochus) only ever recognized type (i) impressions as a *genus*. This is what allows Lucullus to argue that it is only that particular class of impressions which is at issue.

§47

Exponam igitur...illi solent non confuse loqui: Lucullus looks back to his earlier remarks on proper method in philosophical discourse (*Luc.* 43): the dogmatists adhere to it and are entitled to it, the Academics adhere to it, too (*non confuse loqui*), but without being entitled to it. The adverb *generatim* indicates that there are different classes of arguments directed at premiss (iii) of the core argument, and in what follows Lucullus signals clearly the 'sub-sections' of his exposition: *primum* at the beginning of the next sentence introduces vacuous impressions caused by god, *deinde* at the beginning of §48 introduces vacuous impressions which have arisen without divine involvement. *Postremo* in §48 *fin.* marks the last element of the series. Reid[1] (p. 233) on *confuse loqui* assembles Ciceronian characterizations on types of philosophical discourse.

Primum conantur ostendere...quae nullae sint ut iis quae sint: this sentence cannot just refer to attempts to show that there are vacuous impressions (i.e. impressions whose coming into being did not involve a physical object), since this was recognized and granted by the Stoics. Brittain (2006: 29 n. 62) notes this and translates *conantur ostendere multa posse uideri esse* as 'tries to show that there are often ⟨persuasive⟩ impressions of things that don't exist at all', without assuming that a word has been lost in the Latin text. How this sense is to be extracted from the Latin requires explanation. We know—Lucullus says so a little later (§52)—that the Stoics denied that vacuous impressions had the same 'force' as those received while awake; this makes it likely that they would have regarded such impressions as less persuasive. And the persuasive is characterized both as 'what leads us in the direction of assent' (D.L. 7.75, where propositions are at issue; the context is the survey of Stoicism) and as 'what appears true' (Sextus, *M.* 7.171, where persuasive impressions according to Carneades are at issue). In the sentence under discussion, the required sense could be obtained by assuming that *esse* in *multa posse uideri esse* means not 'to exist' but 'to be the case' (as it does in Cicero's renderings of the Zenonian definition, cf. section 5.1), thereby yielding 'that many things can appear to be the case/to be true'. For the negation, instead of *non*, in *quae omnino nulla sint* see the note in Reid[1] (p. 233) and *OLD* s.v. *nullus* no. 4d; the philosophical examples cited there all involve a verb of being in the sense of 'to exist', but the veridical sense will surely carry over in the present passage without difficulty. For *inaniter moueri* in a relevant contrast, cf. *Luc.* 34: *cum sit incertum uere inaniterne moueatur*. Notice also that Lucullus speaks of the mind being moved by vacuous impressions, giving an outside description of the perceiving subject's experiences; we find similar expressions in Sextus (see section 5.6.1). *Res* in *rebus iis* clearly means 'thing' in a general sense, so as to include intentional objects, not 'physical object'. *Moueantur... inquiunt* was omitted by V and supplied by V² from the shared source of V and S (ξ); see the Oxford Classical Text, p. lx.

Nam cum dicatis...quae nihil sit omnino: the precise connection of this section with what precedes only becomes apparent at the very end of the paragraph, when the soritical series concludes with the claim that a deity may devise an impression which is not just *probabile* but exactly like a purported cataleptic impression. The syntax of the sentence is awkward—it gives the Academic argument, first in direct speech down to *extis declarentur*, and then in indirect speech dependent on *quaerunt* reported by Lucullus; the main clause begins with *quaerunt*. *Inquiunt* is parenthetical, as is *haec enim—quos contra disputant*. The *cum*-clause is causal, giving the grounds for the Academic line of attack (the fact that the Stoics assume that there are impressions sent by god, notably some false ones). Macrobius, *Somn.* 1.3.2, in a survey of Latin terms for 'dream', notes that Cicero can use *uisum* to render (sc. not just φαντασία but also) φάντασμα; in terms of the semantics of the term, this is unproblematic, but it raises the question whether there is a difference between *uisum* in this sense and *uisio* (cf. *Luc.* 49: *ad has omnes uisiones inanes*, with comm.). The Stoics held that traditional means of obtaining e.g. divine guidance on suitable courses of action (use of auspices, inspection of entrails) were not absurd. However, they were not held to be foolproof as techniques, and they were made possible not because divine powers were deliberately giving humans covert signals on particular issues, but because the universe was arranged according to a providential order, and this order could, within limits, be gleaned; cf. Sen., *N.Q.* 2.32.3-4 and Cic., *Div.* 1.118 (with Algra 2003: 173):

> Sed distinguendum uidetur quonam modo. Nam non placet Stoicis singulis iecorum fissis aut auium cantibus interesse deum (neque enim decorum est nec dis dignum nec fieri ullo pacto potest), sed ita a principio incohatum esse mundum, ut certis rebus certa signa praecurrerent, alia in extis, alia in auibus, alia in fulgoribus, alia in ostentis, alia in stellis, alia in somniantium uisis, alia in furentium vocibus. Ea quibus bene percepta sunt, ii non saepe falluntur; male coniecta maleque interpretata falsa sunt non rerum uitio, sed interpretum inscientia. Hoc autem posito atque concesso, esse quandam uim diuinam hominum uitam continentem, non difficile est, quae fieri certe uidemus, ea qua ratione fiant suspicari. Nam et ad hostiam deligendam potest dux esse uis quaedam sentiens, quae est toto confusa mundo, et tum ipsum, cum immolare uelis, extorum fieri mutatio potest, ut aut absit aliquid aut supersit; paruis enim momentis multa natura aut adfingit aut mutat aut detrahit.

> But it seems that one must determine *how* this is done. For it is not Stoic doctrine that the gods are concerned with every single fissure of livers, with every birdsong (for that is neither appropriate, nor worthy, nor in any way possible), but that the world was created from the beginning in such a way that predetermined signs would precede predetermined events, some in entrails, others in birds, others in

lightning, others in portents, others in the stars, others in the visions of dreamers, and others in the utterances of those inspired. Those who understand these signs well are not often deceived; bad conjectures and bad interpretations prove wrong not because of the reality but because of the lack of skill of the interpreters. Once this has been set down and agreed [that there is a certain divine power which controls the lives of men], it is not hard to imagine by what means those things happen which we clearly see do happen. For a sentient force which pervades the whole world can guide in the choice of a sacrificial victim and at the very moment when you intend to sacrifice, a change of entrails can take place so that something is either added or taken away. For in a brief instant Nature either adds or modifies or removes many things. (transl. Wardle)

Quite separately in terms of the doctrinal context in which the question arises, i.e. in the debate about whether impressions are self-sufficient causes of assent, the Stoics held that gods and sages could at times create persuasive but false impressions; see Plut., *Sto. rep.* 1057a–b; Sextus, *M.* 7.42; Stob., *Ecl.* II.7, p. 111.10 Wachsmuth; Quint. 12.1.38 and Bobzien (1998: 271–4) for an analysis of the argument in which this claim featured. Bobzien notes (p. 273): 'Occasionally, the only way a sage can produce a certain good, desired, or commanded outcome is by producing false impressions in non-wise people... by telling them falsehoods'; the rationale for certain false dreams caused by gods is the same. Lucullus' argument here is not as clear as it might be. Impressions which arise from the inspection of entrails, true or false, are in any case not vacuous in the usual sense of the term. What Lucullus does is combine the notions that impressions are caused by gods and that some dreams are false (but appear true, at the time), in order to arrive at a starting point for his sorites. The verb *declarentur*, used of the way in which the dreams represent their object, helps convey the contention that the dream impressions at issue are like cataleptic impressions; cf. *Ac.* 1.41: *propriam quandam haberent declarationem earum rerum quae uidentur.*

Reid[1] (p. 234) notes that *plane* followed by a superlative is unparalleled in Cicero (though readily intelligible). He places a comma after *quae perdifficiliter* and suggested that a second *internoscantur* may have dropped out; I have adopted this suggestion, since *tamen* in postposition qualifying a point made earlier in the same clause is not documented.

The emendation *accedant* (Lambinus) in favour of the transmitted *accedunt* (printed by Plasberg[2], but not by Plasberg[1]) is compelling, even in a syntactically unusual sentence, as is his supplement *inter-*, given §49: *ut nihil inter hoc et illud intersit*; §50: *nihil inter haec interesse* and *nihil interesset*.

§48

Deinde, cum mens moueatur ipsa per sese...sed ut in iis nihil intersit omnino: the grammatical shape of this section, if not its overall sense, depends on what to print after *furiosis uidentur* and before *ueri simile sit*. The archetype read *non inquam ueri simile sit*; since an Academic argument is being reported, a first-person *uerbum dicendi* cannot be right. Solutions which have been proposed assume that after *furiosis uidentur* the main clause starts, either in the form of a statement or of a rhetorical question. They include: (i) a parenthetical verb of saying or thinking, cast as a rhetorical question; thus Goerenz printed *non, inquiunt, uerisimile sit*...; Plasberg[1] wondered about *non in⟨tellegetis⟩ quam*, which is ingenious but unlikely to be right (a solution which assumes a question but no *uerbum dicendi* or *sentiendi* is *nonne perquam* printed by Schäublin et al.); (ii) a temporal adverb or adverbial phrase meaning 'sometimes' or 'occasionally'; both of these solutions envisage a main clause which is a statement beginning with *ueri simile sit*. Thus *non numquam, (uerisimile est)* proposed by Madvig (1876: 444), adopted by Baiter and Reid[1]; this gives good sense and stays close to the paradosis, but the change from *sit* to *est* is not necessary. See also Plasberg[1] (p. 91) and Brakman (1923: 377).

With *deinde*, Lucullus moves on to a second type of vacuous impressions, those which arise naturally and without divine interference; this is stressed by *mens...ipsa* and *per sese* (cf. *inaniter* in §§34, 47). (On the 'discretive' use of *ipse*, see Pinkster i.1154.) The verb *declarant*, elsewhere in *Acad.* used of the way in which cataleptic impressions make their object plain (*Ac.* 1.41), may be used polemically here by the Academic speaker in a second-order sense (what is made plain is not what an impression is of, but that the mind is moved by itself).

Quae cogitatione depingimus is baffling, in that no other source suggests that impressions we generate by picturing things before the mind's eye—while awake and sane, as seems to be implied—might be exactly like purported cataleptic impressions. That the impressions of people who are asleep or insane have this property is, however, suggested elsewhere. See the note in Reid[1] (p. 235), who refers to *Luc.* 51 and *N.D.* 1.39 for the same phrase and comments: 'Cogitatio, like διάνοια in Greek, is almost the only word in Latin which will render our "imagination".'

In the main clause from *ueri simile sit* to *omnino*, the fictional Academic speaker suggests that vacuous impressions (*uisa illa*) might be type (iv) or type (v) impressions (see above); this implies that in the preceding *cum*-clause they are deemed to be of a different type, most likely type (i), since false persuasive impressions are recognized by the Stoics.

Vt si qui tremerent...⟨inter⟩ intestinum et oblatum: this sentence, a subordinate clause loosely attached to what precedes, illustrates how the absence of a difference between vacuous and purported cataleptic impressions manifests itself. By contrast, the observations cited here for mere illustration are in Sextus' account used to infer ἀπαραλλαξία from (cf. *M.* 7.403). In the present passage the argument structure is provided by the quasi-sorites (see the general note above). On the subject of internally generated impressions, cf. *Div.* 2.139. The phrase ⟨*inter*⟩ *intestinum et oblatum* is peculiar. Neither term makes for a natural noun, and while impressions (*uisa*) are of course very much in the background of our passage, they are not explicitly mentioned in the immediate context and thus harder to supply mentally. Merguet s.v. *offerre* may have been right that the reader is to supply *tremorem et pallorem* from the preceding clause. The closest parallel for adjectival *intestinum* in a suitable sense is Lucr. 2.289-90:...*sed ne mens ipsa necessum* | *intestinum habeat cunctis in rebus agendis*, '...but what keeps the mind itself from having necessity within it in all actions' (transl. Smith), where *necessum* seems to function as a noun (see Fowler

2002: 364–5 ad loc.). On *oblatum*, see *OLD* s.v. *offero* no. 6: 'to bring on or induce (a condition, etc., usu. unpleasant), cause, inflict'. Plasberg[1] (p. 91) discusses the deletion of *ut (esset qui)* and *ut (quicquam)*, reported in the marginal note in 'Lambinus'; Reid[1] (p. 235) cites Ciceronian parallels.

Postremo...nulla in uisis distinctio appareat: *postremo* seems to pick up from §47 *primum* and §48 *deinde*, but what is provided is merely a restatement (once again by means of a quasi-sorites) of what was said at the beginning of the paragraph. The only new consideration is the sage's suspension of judgement while in an abnormal state of mind; this is posited by the Stoics and cited as an acknowledgement of the ἀπαραλλαξία for which the Academics want to argue. I have translated *distinctio* as 'difference'; it is, *pace* Reid[2], who translates 'distinctive stamp', not one of the synonyms of *nota/signum*. On suspension of judgement / the withholding of assent (*sustinere se ab omni assensum* = ἐπέχειν), cf. *Luc.* 59, 104.

§§49–50

See also the general note on §§47–54a, p. 471. In §§49–50 Lucullus identifies by name the type of Academic argument which was reported in §§47–8, i.e. as a sorites.[210] While being dismissive of it because of the malicious intent of its users, Lucullus also claims in §50 that there is something fundamentally wrong with the sorites in that it produces false arguments. Specifically, Lucullus denies that, if a class of impressions is '*probabile* and false', i.e. if predicate (i) applies to a subject designating a class of impressions, then predicates (ii)–(v) (see above, p. 473) will apply to it. That is, he disputes the truth of the conditionals involved in the series of *modus ponens* inferences which constitute the sorites.

However, the grounds on which Lucullus dismisses in §50 the arguments discussed in §§47–8, even if valid (on this point see p. 475 above), would not allow for generalization to other types of argument labelled 'sorites' in antiquity (i.e. those which are typically thus called), some of which involve singular propositions, while others involve changing subjects (the series of possible candidates for being a deity). The text gives no guidance on how to interpret this, and §49 certainly gives the appearance of a general dismissal of the sorites. One wonders if one to read this as an attempted sleight of hand on Lucullus' part.

§49

Ad has omnes uisiones inanes...sed ipsa capita dicenda: Cicero is able to use *uisio* as a mere synonym of *uisum* (e.g. *Luc.* 33), as well as in other epistemological senses, but, as Alleemudder (p. 258) notes, here the use of *uisio*, with *ad* in the sense of 'in response to', is to suggest that the arguments of the Academics are the ravings of

---

[210] On it, see also Castagnoli (2019: 204–5).

madmen (cf. 54: *quod uelle efficere non mediocris insaniae est*; Numenius' term ὀνείρατα for Carneades' arguments, frg. 27.37-8 Des Places (see appendix 2); frg. 25.34 σκιαγραφία; frg. 25.41 φάσματα). That these issues took up a whole day of Antiochus' discussion signals their importance; contrast Sedley (2012b: 83 n. 4), who sees a veiled reference to a source used by Cicero here: 'The text from which Cicero actually drew these arguments was probably Antiochus' reply to Philo's Roman books, in debate with the New Academic Heraclitus, because they include the summary of "a whole day's debate" (*Luc.* 49) about the Academic appeal to empty impressions, and this "day" was clearly one of "*complures dies*" (*Luc.* 12) that the entire Antiochus-Heraclitus debate took up.' For my views on the sources of *Acad.*, see section 9.3. For *capita* 'main points', see *TLL* s.v. *caput* col. 423.4 (this passage in 423.74-5).

Et primum quidem hoc reprehendum...Vitiosum sane et captiosum genus: see the general note above, p. 475. The standard example of the sorites, turning on the question of how many grains make a heap (σωρός), is in Galen, Περὶ τῆς ἰακτρικῆς ἐμπειρίας 17.1, p. 115 Walzer; σωρίτης means 'accumulator'. On the history of the term and its use see (Burnyeat 1982b: 90-4). The argument is also known as ὁ παρὰ μικρὸν λόγος (Galen, Περὶ τῆς ἰακτρικῆς ἐμπειρίας 16.2, p. 115 W.). The transliteration *sorites* is referred to as deeply familiar in Cic., *Div.* 2.11. For *aceruus* in our passage, cf. Hor., *Ep.* 2.1.47: *elusus ratione ruentis acerui*; for *minutatim et gradatim* here, cf. Cic., *Brut.* 285: *et gradus et dissimilitudines*. *Captiosus* means 'designed to ensnare' (*OLD* s.v. no. 1), not 'inherently flawed'. On exchange by question and answer as a standard format of soritical arguments, see p. 472. As to *quod genus minime in philosophia probari solet*, the sorites is a potent attacking device to which dogmatic positions generally are vulnerable. It was therefore a less likely weapon of choice for dogmatists arguing against dogmatists, but was of course used extensively by the Academics against the Stoics. As to the sorites being a *uitiosum genus*, this could mean that it is pernicious in its effects (cf. Cic., *Fin.* 4.50: *sorites ⟨est⟩, quo nihil putatis* [i.e. the Stoics] *uitiosius*) notably on non-sages, but given what follows in §50 and the juxtaposition with *captiosum*, one wonders if the suggestion is not rather that the sorites is an inherently flawed pattern of argument. See Reid[1] (p. 236) on the repetition of the antecedent in *genere...quod genus*.

Sic enim ascenditis...sin ipse tua sponte processeris, tuum: there is no recognized technical sense of *ascendere* in connection with arguments, beyond the sense of advancement from step to step. One might wonder if Cicero wrote *descenditis*, to describe the downward movement through a *diuisio*; but *descendere* is not used in this way, and the five *genera* are construed in §50 as mutually exclusive classes. That Lucullus returns to the first version of arguments from vacuous impressions, the one which involves a divine being creating false dream impressions, may be explicable in terms of the first reply which it enables (see §50 *init.*), but it is peculiar that the argument is restated in its fullest form. Notice that the wording of the argument, with a subject (*uisum obiectum*) explicitly stated only in the first step, suggests that notionally the same impression is at issue throughout, which makes Lucullus' objection in the next paragraph—that the Academics try to place items in more than one *genus*—intelligible. That the respondent 'owns' an argument only if he concedes the premisses offered by the questioner is a familiar rule of dialectical exchanges in question and answer. Reid[1] (p. 237) refers to *N.D.* 1.89 for the technical sense of *peruenire* = 'to arrive at a conclusion through a chain of reasoning', and discusses *primum quidque* = 'each successive step'. On dreaming arguments in the later history of philosophy, see Dunlop (1977); Williams (1978); and Newman (2019: section 3) on Descartes.

§50

Quis enim tibi dederit...ita facturum esse si possit: for *dare* used of the conceding of premisses offered during dialectical exchange, see *OLD* s.v. 16b and Reinhardt (2000a: 61–7) on διδόναι, used like the more common τιθέναι. There are numerous Stoic statements of divine omnipotence (e.g. Cic., *Div.* 2.86), but there were constraints: one is, as Brittain (2006: 30 n. 64) notes, that god is unable to do wrong (Sen., *Ep.* 95.47 = *SVF* ii.1117), which is relevant to the first disjunct. In *N.D.* 3.92 the Academic speaker Cotta raises the issue of divine omnipotence. See also Essler (2014: 118–19). The possibility of an 'evil demon' is not considered, but it is not unheard of in antiquity; see Mansfeld (1981). Plasberg[1] (p. 92) speculates about the reasons for the situation in A.

Quo modo autem sumis...quod e suo genere in aliud genus transferri possit: for *sumere* = 'to treat a premiss as obtained', used of the questioner in dialectical exchange, cf. *OLD* s.v. no. 17, and Greek λαμβάνειν (e.g. Arist., *Top.* B7, 113b17). Lucullus now argues that the Academics are unable to progress through their argument on the grounds that the consequents of the conditionals involved in the *modus ponens* inferences do not follow from their antecedents (*Quo modo...sequatur*). He makes this argument on a higher level of abstraction, by formulating it with reference to the relations which were used to make up the five *genera* of impressions, but without reference to impressions. Rather than to frame his argument with reference to a class of impressions to which different quasi-soritical predicates supposedly apply, he argues that, if a class of items is similar to something, it will not follow that it is difficult to distinguish from it etc. Lucullus' argument assumes that it is the same class of items of which different relational predicates are predicated (cf. the restated Academic argument at the end of §49), and since the relations involved are binary, Lucullus can claim that the Academics want to progress from 'two classes A and B are similar' through a number of steps to 'two classes A and B are identical', or indeed claim that a set of items A would be transferred from one *genus* to another if it was first said to be 'similar to B' and then eventually 'identical to B'.

The similarity of wolves and dogs features in *N.D.* 1.97 in an Epicurean context, as well as in Plt., *Soph.* 231a, where the wider context is concerned with appropriate techniques of division and their pitfalls. The Old Academic Lucullus may be gesturing to a Platonic text in our passage, as I suspect he does in *Luc.* 30; see ad loc. and Reinhardt (2018: 64).

On the similarity of *honesta/non honesta* and *bona/non bona*, see Sen., *Ep.* 120.8, with Inwood (2007: 326). In the letter Seneca argues that analysing such similarities helps us to train our ability to reason so as to be able to act morally. For *non honesta*, cf. *Ac.* 1.39: *non corpus*; for *non bona*, cf. *Fin.* 2.53; and Wackernagel (2009: 730–3). Overall, the evidence suggests that *non artificiosa* are things (items, actions, processes) which carry negative associations, like the products of pretend arts as opposed to the products of mere knacks; cf. the εἴδωλα of arts in Plt., *Grg.* 463e5–466a3.

As to the tone, *quid dubitamus…haec interesse* is evidently a sarcastic question, spoken in the voice of the Academic or at least so focalized. The following *ne…uidemus*, from the same point of view, could be a question or a statement/exclamation. *Repugnantia* are things (including propositions) which stand in conflict (μάχη) and are incompatible; cf. on *Luc.* 44. Kayser (in Baiter) emended to *regugnantiam*, but cf. e.g. *Div.* 2.150.

At si efficeretur…Quod fieri qui potest: having argued that the Academics will not be able to proceed through the series of inferences which make up the sorites, Lucullus now argues that the conclusion, even if it was obtained (*efficeretur*; cf. *Tusc.* 1.77: *in quibus* [sc. *libris*] *uult* [sc. Dicaearchus] *efficere animos esse mortales*), would be absurd: if there was no difference between two *genera*, then there would be some elements (*reperirentur quae*) which are members of both classes. This, it is implied, is incompatible with the Stoic principle of the identity of ἀπαράλλακτα (cf. *Luc.* 54, 56, 58), to which the Academics are not committed. Implicitly, Lucullus is applying this principle to impressions here rather than the objects that give rise to them, but as noted above, the paragraph is formulated on a higher level of abstraction. With *si efficeretur*, cf. §42: *uolunt efficere iis omnibus quae uisa sint*.…

§§51–54a

See also the general note on §§47–54a, p. 471. Lucullus suggests that the way to rebut all arguments from vacuous impressions is to insist that they do not have the same clarity as cataleptic impressions (§51). This position is less ad hoc and less weak than it might appear. Because the clarity of cataleptic impressions, on the Stoic view, is a function of the causal process by which they come about,[211] and because the perceiver's mind represents one link in the causal chain,[212] abnormal states of mind

---

[211] *Ac.* 1.40–1, on Zeno's modifications to the *prima forma* of philosophy formulated by the *ueteres*, moves from a description of the coming into being of an impression cast in causal terms to the *declaratio rerum* cataleptic impressions furnish.

[212] Cf. Sextus, *M.* 7.424 (= *SVF* ii.68 = LS 40L): Ἵνα γε μὴν αἰσθητικὴ γένηται φαντασία κατ' αὐτούς, οἷον ὁρατική, δεῖ πέντε συνδραμεῖν, τό τε αἰσθητήριον καὶ τὸ αἰσθητὸν καὶ τὸν τόπον καὶ τὸ πῶς καὶ τὴν διάνοιαν, ὡς ἐὰν τῶν ἄλλων παρόντων ἓν μόνον ἀπῇ, καθάπερ διάνοια παρὰ φύσιν ἔχουσα, οὐ σωθήσεται, φασίν, ἡ ἀντίληψις, 'Now, in order for a sensory appearance to occur, such as a visual one, five things must come together, according to them: the sense-organ, the thing sensed, the place, the manner, and thought, since if a single one of these is missing while others are present—for example, if thought is in an unnatural state— the apprehension, they say, will not be preserved' (transl. Bett).

would be expected to have an influence on perception, on our ability to experience cataleptic impressions, and on the properties of our impressions. A fortiori, impressions experienced in the absence of an object and while the subject is in an abnormal state of mind cannot have the causal ancestry that would bestow unique clarity on them.

Lucullus cites the fact that upon waking or recovering sanity people (as evidenced by stock scenes in drama) usually recognize their vacuous impressions for what they are (§51 *fin.*). The Academics reply that while in an abnormal state of mind we cannot tell the difference, and this is conceded by Lucullus and the Stoics when they say that the sage will suspend judgement in such situations (§48 *fin.*), as well as while awake if the process which gives rise to impressions is less than optimal (§53 *init.*). At this point the Stoics are occasionally presented as running out of convincing replies, but they do say that, first, the behaviour of people in such states, which suggests that their confidence in their impressions is decreased, does point to a difference in the quality of their impressions (§52), and, second, that the beginning and the end of a period during which one is in an abnormal state of mind is marked, detectable, and usually detected (ibid.). The second point ought to mean that even non-sages are in a position to adopt the sage's policy of suspending judgement during such episodes. What is more, one might hold that the real danger of accepting a vacuous impression is to end up with a false belief, which then causes cognitive and epistemic havoc in our normal waking lives, e.g. because it makes us reject cataleptic impressions on grounds of incompatibility. Lucullus' insistence that we recognize vacuous impressions for what they are once normal conditions are restored speaks to this point, in that beliefs acquired while in an abnormal state of mind are presumably liable to be revised.

The section on Carneades' epistemology in Sextus provides further evidence for arguments from vacuous impressions devised by the Academics. In *M.* 7.406–8 (= part of LS 40H) Heracles, while insane, is said to perform successful actions (using a bow appropriately and effectively) as well as misguided actions (killing his children, having mistaken them for somebody else's), which, the argument goes, would make it reasonable to call the impression of the bow not just true but cataleptic. This line of argument—that while mad human beings experience impressions which give rise to successful action and thus ought to be classified as cataleptic—could be used to question the Stoic view that the causal process which gives rise to cataleptic impressions is compromised in the insane (or drunk). This would entail a refusal to accept the connection which the Stoics make between the objective reality represented by a suitable and specific causal mechanism and the clarity/strikingness of the resulting cataleptic impression. See section 5.6.

A hallmark of the section is the introduction of Academic arguments in direct speech and, as it were, through a fictitious interlocutor. This device, which in poetic texts is associated with diatribe style, is then used to peculiar effect in §53, where Lucullus seems to make the interlocutor confront or at least realise the supposed absurdity of his position.[213]

---

[213] See also *Rhet. Her.* 4.65 and Quint. 9.2.32 on *sermocinatio*.

Omnium deinde inanium uisorum…per insaniam: Lucullus shifts back from *uisiones* in §49 *init.* to *uisorum*. The shift may signal that here vacuous impressions only are meant, i.e. that the suggestion that the Academics arguments themselves are the dreamings of madmen is dropped. The *nomen actionis 'depulsio'* need have no connotation of possibility, *pace* Reid[1] (p. 238); for its use of arguments, see *OLD* s.v. no. 2b. Lucullus accepts the possibility that there may be vacuous impressions which arise from picturing things before the mind's eye while awake (cf. §48: *quae cogitatione depingimus*), but seems to note that these are not usually part of the discussion (*quod fieri solere concedimus*); they represent a point which is easy to concede, and easy to dismiss as irrelevant. For *cogitatio*, cf. §§48, 82; for *per uinum* Cic., *Top.* 75: *per somnum uinum insaniam*.

Nam ab omnibus eius modi uisis…abesse dicemus: cf. *Div.* 2.126 (= *SVF* ii.62): *Praesertim cum Chrysippus, Academicos refellens, permulto clariora et certiora esse dicat, quae uigilantibus uideantur, quam quae somniantibus.* On *perspicuitas*, see on §§45–6; cf. also Nonius p. 139 M. (= t. 26). *Mordicus tenere* also in *Rep.* 1.51; *Fin.* 4.78; on *mordicus*, see Fruyt (1980).

Quis enim…Eadem ratio est somniorum: picturing something before the mind's eye while awake and sane was introduced as one instance of vacuous impressions in §48, although the parallel evidence from Sextus suggests that vacuous impressions are normally confined to those arising during abnormal states of mind. Since in such cases it is especially plain to the perceiving subject that the impression does not have the required *perspicuitas*, Lucullus seems happy to use them as his initial reference point, and to treat dream impressions as analogous in a second step (*eadem ratio est somniorum*). *Se ad se reuocare* means 'to recall oneself from a flight of fancy'.

Num censes Ennium…ego esse mortuom: Lucullus suggests, quoting evidence from the *Annales* and the *Epicharmus* of Ennius, that, when awake, speakers signal that they are recounting dream appearances by using a part of *uideri*, whereas real experiences had while awake are reported in factual terms; see the general note above on the import of his claim and on the Academic reply. In his speech (§§88–9), Cicero cites evidence from poetry in reply in which speakers who suffer from an abnormal state of mind indicate through what they say that at that moment they regard their experiences as real.

Servius Sulpicius Galba lived in a house near or even adjacent to Ennius' on the Aventine Hill, and the two men were known to have shared conversations while out walking; see Ov., *A.A.* 3.409–10; Val. Max. 8.14.1; Plin., *N.H.* 7.114. Zetzel (2007: 10) suggests that Cicero found the reference in Ennius' *Satires*; a conversation during a walk is of course the subject of Horace, *S.* 1.9.

The first quotation comes from the proem of Book 1 of the *Annales* (frg. iii Skutsch) and was part of a report on a dream (see frgs ii–x ibid.) in which Ennius claimed to have encountered Homer, who disclosed to him that he (Ennius) was Homer reincarnate. Skutsch (1985: 147–53) discusses testimonia on the dream which do not include direct quotations. In the commentary on this fragment (frg. iii and l. 3 Skutsch), for which our passage is the only source, Skutsch defends (p. 154) printing the words as the end of a hexameter, as is conventional, but notes that the sequence of third-, fourth-, and fifth-foot trochee is unparalleled except in l. 528, where the rhythm signals speed (which cannot be the explanation in our passage). He wonders, guided by two testimonia (Verg., *A.* 2.270 and Fronto 4.12.4), if Cicero has deliberately rearranged the Ennian quotation, so as to suppress a phrase *in somnis* which, for Skutsch, would have destroyed Cicero's point that the use of *uisus* signals doubt about the reality of the dream appearance; he suggests exempli gratia:

> (in somnis ecce ante oculos mihi) uisus Homerus
> ....adesse poeta.

To me it seems more likely that Cicero has Lucullus quote accurately, since the manipulation envisaged by Skutsch would have been obvious to contemporaries, and thus would have undermined the character Lucullus and his case in a way which would be out of the line with the conventions of Ciceronian dialogue. Moreover, given that Cicero in his reply offers his own choice poetic quotations, notably some from a play from which some of Lucullus' evidence came (§§88–9), his failure to pick up on any truncation of Ennian lines would reflect badly on that character, too. In Ennius *uisus* (*est*) would have been sufficient to signal that a dream was being recounted. The perfect indicative in *cum somniauit* for the pluperfect subjunctive is peculiar, but both the concluding sentence of the paragraph, which offers an inference based partly on the expressions used in the quotations, and §88: *quia cum experrectus esset*... make it clear that Ennius recounted an earlier dream. On Cicero's quotes from the *Annales*, see Elliott (2013: 365–97).

The line from Ennius' *Epicharmus* (*PCG* frg. 281 Kassel and Austin), a septenarius, is only attested here; on this and the other fragments, see Courtney (2003: 30–8), who notes (p. 31): '*uidebar* is common in dream contexts..., but *uidebar somniare* meaning *somniabam* seems odd', but goes on to cite parallels (e.g. Plaut., *Curc.* 260). In *Tusc.* 1.15 Cicero quotes as *Epicharmi sententia* the following line (also a septenarius): *emori nolo, sed me esse mortuum nihil aestimo*, which, as has been noted, would have been a fitting line to precede the one quoted here. In *Div.* 2.111 Cicero reports: *acrostichis...cum deinceps ex primis uersus litteris conectitur, ut in quibusdam Ennianis Q. ENNIVS FECIT.* The line from *Tusc.* 1.15 and ours would yield the letters E and N. Courtney (2003: 32) therefore wonders whether the line quoted here in *Luc.* 51 might be the third of the *Epicharmus*, or the ninth if 'Quintus' was spelled out, too, but I see no grounds for locating the acrostich at the very beginning of the poem. Courtney (ibid.) rightly notes that what we know of the Greek line behind the one translated in *Tusc.* 1.15 suggests that the speaker was not Ennius, but Epicharmus, and making this assumption for our passage, too, would still leave Cicero's point intact.

On the uses of *uidere/uideri*, see section 10 and Reinhardt (2016). On *med ego* (Manutius) for the transmitted *me et ego* and *ego memet* suggested by Leo (1913: 200), see Kassel and Austin (2001: 165) and Courtney (2003: 31–2); on *med* itself, Leumann (1977: 228–9).

Itaque, simul ut experrecti sumus...quae in foro gessimus: for *simul ut*, see Hofmann and Szantyr (1965: 626); for *contemnere* 'to treat as of no importance', see

OLD s.v. no. 2; for *habere* 'to regard', see *OLD* s.v. no. 25. *In foro* is said exempli gratia; the phrase does not mean 'in real life'. *Vt ea*, sc. *facta*.

§52

See also the general notes on §§47–54a and 51–54a, pp. 471 and 483. In §52 the Academic claims that dream impressions have the same look as real ones. Lucullus rejects this notion, asserting that the mind and the senses of those who are asleep do not exhibit the same *uis* and *integritas* as the mind and senses of those who are awake. Detailed reasons would presumably include aspects of the causal story of how cataleptic impressions come into being and how their properties, viz. being uniquely clear and striking, are a function of their genesis; against this background, impressions had while dreaming could not be as clear as cataleptic ones for Lucullus. He further argues that the behaviour of people experiencing vacuous impressions due to being drunk shows they do not take them as seriously while they are in this state, and once recovered they fully understand that the impressions in question were vacuous. Finally, he argues that those on the cusp of going mad or becoming sane again recognize the boundaries between a normal and abnormal cognitive state.

At enim dum uidentur…uidemus: this is the Academic opponent speaking in *oratio recta*. The archetype had *eorum quae uigilantes* or *eorumque uigilantes*. A connective to go with *idem* is needed, though Plasberg in both editions prints the reading of ζ. The supplement *et* made by Lambinus is Ciceronian usage, *eorumque quae* proposed by Hermann (1852: 468) is not; see Hofmann and Szantyr (1965: 478). With *eorum* we need to supply an unspecified 'things' mentally (*uisa uidere* is not used by Cicero). *Species* means 'look' (cf. *OLD* s.v. no. 3: 'visual appearance, look, aspect'; Brittain 2006); see on §58. The following sentence makes this clear: *species* is the aspect or dimension of a visual experience with reference to which it makes sense to attribute (or not) complete clarity (*perspicuitas*) to it. An interesting note on *species* in philosophical Latin is in Fowler (2002: 141–2). There are no grounds for seeing a connection with the *genera* of impressions mentioned in §50 (and earlier).

Primum, interest: sed id omittamus: Lucullus must be gesturing to *perspicuitas* being confined to cataleptic impressions (§45) and wants it to be understood that he is not yielding on the point. See *OLD* s.v. *intersum* no. 6b for the absolute use of *interest*. See Reid[1] (p. 240) on *primum* not being followed up by *deinde* or a similar word.

Illud enim dicimus, non eandem esse uim neque integritatem…nec mente nec sensu: *enim* signals the alternative statement and responds to *omittamus*; this use has been called 'meta-communicative' (Kroon 1995: 195), but it does not seem to be agreement-soliciting. The point made is that the mind and the senses do not function properly while subjects are in a state where their impressions are vacuous. *Vis* and *integritas* are here grammatically the properties of human beings (with the mind and the senses in the ablative of respect); contrast *Div.* 2.126, where properties of impressions are at issue: *praesertim cum Chrysippus Academicos refellens permulto* *clariora et certiora esse dicat quae uigilantibus uideantur quam quae somniantibus*, '…especially since Chrysippus, in his rebuttal of the Academics, says that appearances of people who are awake are much clearer and more specified than those experienced while awake.' *Vis* and *integritas* do not seem to map onto *clariora* and *certiora*. The phrase *integritas mentis* is attested in a fragment of Marcus Antistius Labeo (D. 28.1.2), whose death is usually dated to AD 10 or 11; Lucullus may be appealing to legal categories of unsoundness of mind here.

Ne uinulenti quidem quae faciunt…illa uisa quam leuia fuerint intellegunt: approval (cf. *approbatio*) and assent (cf. *assentire*) are of course technical terms in the debate, but neither is capable of degrees, as are assumed here implicitly (through *eadem approbatione*) or explicitly (through *imbecilius*). ('Weak assent' in the technical Stoic sense, which is not at issue here, is not assumed to be given less emphatically than assent which is not weak.) Lucullus conveys here that any kind of endorsement is reduced in subjects whose state of mind is abnormal. *Intellegunt* at the end of the sentence is emphatic: people in abnormal states exhibit less confidence in their impressions (a fact that a third party can observe), and once they have woken up, *they themselves understand* how weak their impressions were (cf. *sentiant* below). With *leuis*, used of vacuous impressions, contrast *leuitas* in §53, used to dismiss an entire argumentative approach.

Quod idem contingit insanis…cum oculorum aspectu: for the line to be illustrative of Cicero's point, the speaker must be referring to experiences which have the feel of visual ones but arise from no object whatsoever (so as to be vacuous impressions). If *cum oculorum aspectu* seems a slightly paradoxical way to express this, one may compare e.g. Verg., *A*. 2.270-3 (where the narrator speaks, but from the perspective of the dreamer): **in somnis**, ecce, **ante oculos** maestissimus Hector | uisus adesse mihi largosque effundere fletus, | raptatus bigis ut quondam, aterque cruento | puluere perque pedes traiectus lora tumentis. On this passage see also p. clxxxv.

See Jocelyn (1967: 72-5) for the fragments of Ennius' *Alcmeo*. The assignment of the words here (= frg. XVa) and further material quoted in *Luc*. 89 (= frg. XVb) to Ennius, who is not named as author here or there, was first made by Columna in the sixteenth century (see Jocelyn, p. 186). The words here are plausibly taken as part of a trochaic tetrameter whose last two syllables are missing (Jocelyn, p. 198), whereas the material quoted in *Luc*. 89 is in lyrics which are hard to categorize. The latter are in *Luc*. 89 used as evidence by the Academic Cicero that, while in the grip of madness, the speaker regards his experience as real. One might think that dramatically it would work well if Lucullus quoted the beginning of a speech where the character, still using a metre suitable for narrative, feels madness descending (cf. *incipientes furere sentiant* here) and mistrusts his experience, while Cicero replies with evidence from later in the same speech which illustrates his point that, while in the grip of madness, we trust our impressions; the extant remains of Republican tragedy do not furnish a parallel for this scenario, but in Seneca's *Agamemnon* there is a scene (720-74) in which Cassandra notices the beginning of madness, finds it briefly getting dark (726), and then is in propethic trance during which she sees bright light (cf. the references to light in the quotations in *Luc*. 89), all the while speaking in a normal narrative metre (iambic trimeters in this case), only to end her speech with lyrics (759–74). However, both the context here and in *Luc.* 89 suggest that the line is to be regarded as evidence that, once we have recovered, we disown our earlier false impressions. This suggests that the line stood after a speech delivered while in a state of madness and verbalizes the recovery (the change of metre would support this scenario, too); I have translated *cum oculorum aspectu* accordingly. If this was correct, then it should be reflected in the order in which the fragments from the *Alcmeo* are presented in editions of Ennius (thus Ribbeck³ and Vahlen 1903, but not Jocelyn 1968 and Manuwald 2012). See Reid¹ (p. 240) and Plasberg¹ (p. 94) on how to parse *incipientes furere sentiant*. On *cor* in the sense of *animus*, see *OLD* s.v. no. 2.

§53

See also the general notes on §§47–54a and 51–54a, pp. 471 and 485. §52 ended with Lucullus' observation that, while someone is being overcome by madness, they notice and start to mistrust their impressions, and then notice when they recover. A possible rejoinder of the Academic would have been that such distrust disappears once madness has taken hold, and that point is made by Cicero in *Luc.* 88–9. However, Lucullus' fictitious interlocutor introduces a different consideration instead: that even the sage suspends judgement while mad, for fear of accepting something false as true. This notion had featured once before, in §49, to back up the conclusion of the sorites.

The intended force of the Academic argument is not clear. The Stoics would happily concede that true and false impressions experienced while mad cannot be discriminated, but they would resist the suggestion that any impression experienced while in such a state is cataleptic. It may be that an assumption on which the Academic argument relies but which is not stated is that some true impressions experienced while mad have a claim to being classified as cataleptic by the Stoics (cf. Sextus, *M.* 7.406–7).[214] If that was the case, it would support the idea (section 5.8) that what the scenarios of madness, etc. do for the Academic argumentative strategy is to provide stable conditions under which purported cataleptic impressions would be just like false ones.

As it is, Lucullus finds it easy—too easy—to deflect the Academic argument by pointing out that the sage will suspend judgement not just while mad, but in many other circumstances, too. He then launches a counterattack, by observing that the sage's occasional withholding of assent is in fact *evidence* for a difference between true and false impressions. Otherwise the sage would 'withhold assent always or never'; this claim looks back to Lucullus' claim that the Academics are hoping to eradicate the distinction between truth and falsehood.

---

[214] Contrast Brittain (2006: 32 n. 70): 'Although this Academic argument (first alluded to in *Ac.* 2.48 [i.e. *Luc.*]) is not elaborated or defended by Cicero, it may imply that the Stoic sage is supposed to suspend assent even from "apprehensible" impressions under certain conditions, as Cicero argues in *Ac.* 2.94 and 2.107.'

In the second half of the paragraph Lucullus then completely dismisses arguments from the states of mind during which we experience vacuous impressions; he does this by reasoning with the Academics and inviting them to appreciate what absurd scenarios they have ended up debating with the dogmatists.

At enim ipse sapiens sustinet se in furore ne approbet falsa pro ueris: cf. §48 *fin.* The verb *approbare* is clearly not technical here, since the Stoic sage is at issue. On Stoic attitudes to madness and the possibility of the madness of the sage, see Ahonen (2019).

Et alias quidem saepe…temporis breuitate excluditur: the sage will not assent in many cases while awake and sane since an impression received under less than optimal conditions can never be cataleptic. Only an impression which satisfies all the conditions can reveal the truth all by itself; cf. *Luc.* 19 on the process subjects follow to obtain self-warranting impressions *dum aspectus ipse fidem faciat sui iudicii*, Sextus, *M.* 7.258, and Allen (1994: 106). Lucullus' rejoinder makes the Academic argument look implausibly feeble; see the general note above on where its force might have come from. The gerund *perspiciendo* is remarkable in that in other formulations *perspicuitas* appears as a property which some impressions inherently have; the gerund suggests that the perceiving subject, or the subject's mind (cf. §52), plays an active role in bringing about *perspicuitas*.

Quamquam totum hoc…aut semper sustineret aut numquam: Lucullus starts from the assumption that there is a Stoic sage and that he assents to some impressions but not to others—and that this would not be possible on the Academic view. He can do this because the Academics themselves argue that the sage sometimes withholds assent. In doing so, Lucullus construes the claim of ἀπαραλλαξία as extending to the truth values of the propositions associated with impressions—if true and false impressions were exactly alike, impressions would either all be true (in which case the sage would assent to them) or all false (in which case the sage would withhold assent); see also on *Luc.* 43–4.

The archetype had an omission after *uisa*. Sense requires a supplement like V²'s, which is readily furnished by the larger context (cf. e.g. §50 *fin.*: *ut inter uisa differentium generum nihil interesset*). There is no reason to posit that V² drew on a third manuscript on the basis of this passage (see the Oxford Classical Text, p. lxii), but cf. §44 *fin*. However, *uisa* by itself seems somewhat jejune: Plasberg¹ (p. 94) proposed *uisa differentium generum* with reference to *Luc.* 50; Gigon *uisa perspicua et inania*. The resumption of *uera et falsa* from the beginning of the paragraph would make for an effective conclusion on the narrow point; for the phrasing, cf. *Luc.* 44: *inter falsa uisa et uera nihil interesse*, for the word order, cf. *Luc.* 90: *inter uisa uera et falsa*.

Sed ex hoc genere toto…qui omnia cupiunt confundere: Lucullus now begins his general dismissal of the argument from vacuous impressions. If he grasps what philosophical work abnormal states of mind are supposed to do in the Academic scenarios, he keeps it to himself, and affects utter bafflement instead. With *leuitas* (which combines the notions of lack of seriousness and folly; OLD s.v. no. 3), cf. *uisa...leuia* in §52 and *insania* in §54.

Quaerimus grauitatis constantiae...tum nihil interesse: cf. *Luc.* 66: *nihil est enim ab ea cogitatione quam habemus de grauitate sapientis, errore leuitate temeritate diiunctius. Quid igitur loquar de firmitate sapientis?*

Lucullus shifts here from the third-person plural, speaking about 'them', to the first-person plural, only to return to the third-person plural at the beginning of §54. The Lucullus character does not take himself to do anything undesirable out of his own volition but finds himself party to an absurd debate with the Academics, without being responsible for the absurdity. *Quaerimus...iudicium* could be said from a purely Stoic perspective, but Lucullus may also be speaking in good faith and describing the joint project he and the Academic are engaged in. The following *utimur exemplis...ebriosorum* might be interpreted as spoken from a purely Stoic perspective (*utimur* as 'we have to put up with'; so Reid[1], Schäublin et al.), or 'we' again stands for both parties who end up arguing with reference to these scenarios (*utimur* as 'we use', 'we deploy'). The following question is also best read as including both parties, since it cites inconsistency: the sentence beginning *non enim proferremus* mentions first the Stoic then the Academic view on the qualities of impressions experienced under normal and abnormal conditions, respectively. Others assume that Lucullus is here referring to inconsistency within the pronouncements made by the Academics: Reid[1] (p. 241) suggests that Lucullus chooses to treat the Academic appeal to the Stoic sage's suspension of judgement (§53 *init.*) as an acknowledgement that the impressions of the mad and the sane are qualitatively different. Alleemudder (p. 284 and n. 1) thinks Lucullus has the Academic concession in mind that we dismiss dreams once awake (i.e. recognize them to be different then). (However, this point is only made by Cicero in *Luc.* 88.) I think that this reading would make the first-person plural of *proferremus* difficult to explain. The question is satisfactory as transmitted; however, Schäublin (1992: 43) suggests ⟨num⟩ *illud attendimus* (printed in Schäublin et al.), and Gigon prints *illud* ⟨*non*⟩ *attendimus*.

§54a

See also the general notes on §§47–54a and 51–54a, pp. 471 and 485. As his final point, Lucullus argues in 54a that the arguments from vacuous impressions make everything *incertum* (= ἄδηλον), i.e. uncertain. What exactly is meant by that can be elucidated from the context here, and from parallel passages in *Acad.* and elsewhere.[215]

As what follows shows, 'everything becomes uncertain' because, if one argues from vacuous impressions that for every impression which meets the first two clauses of Zeno's definition there could be one just like it which is false, this would give rise to doubt about a subject's sanity at any point in time, sc. including when the subject

---

[215] See the n. on §32: *Interdum enim...penitus abstruserit.*

is awake and sane. Lucullus treats this as an absurd consequence of the Academic arguments, not as the argumentative outcome the Academics are aiming at. This is the closest the ancient discussion gets to modern brain-in-the-vat scenarios used as an argument for external world scepticism, which highlights a fundamental difference between the debate reported and dramatized in the *Acad.* and its *Nachleben* and continuation in the history of philosophy.

For Lucullus, as we have seen, it is not just a piece of doctrine that is at stake because of Academic refusal to accept that there are cataleptic impressions. Perception is defined not as a range of psychological phenomena of varying complexity and accuracy which can be placed on a spectrum, at whose extreme end there is the grasp of a state of affairs afforded by assent to a cataleptic impression—perception *is* assent to a cataleptic impression. This raises the question of how making things 'uncertain' could be worse or different from plunging things into total darkness (see on *Luc.* 30).

Lucullus is presumably appealing here to an *Academic* use of the term. In *Luc.* 32 'some Academics' are referred to who insist that, while everything was inapprehensible, this did not mean that everything was uncertain. This view, whether it is endorsed in some form or advanced for the sake of the argument, assumes that human beings have something to go on even if a cataleptic grasp of things is not available to them (see the commentary on §32; Allen 1997; Ioppolo 2013a: 266; cf. also §110). What Lucullus is suggesting in our passage is that, if we cannot be sure that we are not mad now and if any impression we might have could be a vacuous one, we will have absolutely nothing to go on even on the terms of these Academics.

Ne hoc quidem cernunt…quod nolunt: Lucullus is now making his final point speaking about the Academics, and not including the dogmatists grammatically as in the previous paragraph. Recent editors (Reid[1], Plasberg in both editions, Schäublin et al.) punctuate as a question.

Ea dico incerta…ἄδηλα Graeci: on the Greek term and its uses, see the commentary on *Luc.* 32.

Si enim res se ita habeant…non mediocris insaniae est: the manuscripts read *habeant*. Goerenz emended to *habeat*, on the grounds that *res se…habet* is the typical expression for 'the matter is such and such'. Reid[1] (p. 242) thinks *res* means 'external objects' and therefore retains *habeant*. Yet Lucullus is not here considering how external objects appear to the deranged and the sane. It seems best to follow Goerenz on sense, but reject the notion that this reading requires the singular; we may compare uses like *Att.* 1.19.4 (= SB 19): *urbanae autem res se sic habent*. The subject of *uideatur*, as Reid rightly observes, is a general 'anything'; if one modified to *habeat* above and started with the sense 'if the matter lies in such and such a way', then *res* would rather oddly and retrospectively change meaning to 'external object' here. Lambinus inserted *ut* before *sano*, which the reader certainly has to understand if not actually supply; the expunction of *ut* before *insano* (V[2]) is a different way of smoothing out the text (see the note in the app. crit. of Plasberg[1] p. 95 in addition).

The participle *exploratus* is frequently used by Cicero in the phrase *exploratum habeo*; see Thielmann (1885: 529–31).

Unlike in other passages where Lucullus imputes an intention to achieve certain argumentative goals to the Academics (see on §42: *Diuidunt enim in partes, et eas quidem magnas… ulla res percipi possit*), *quod uelle efficere* here is of a different quality: Lucullus does regard the option at issue as an absurd consequence which the Academics do not actively seek.

§§54b–58

Lucullus proceeds to the discussion of the second main group of arguments for ἀπαραλλαξία, those which turn on similarity. The difference in mode of exposition is striking: while in §§47–54a the arguments from vacuous impressions were self-consciously presented in a natural sequence from first beginnings, so much so that one wondered why the Antiochian speaker Lucullus had been given the material by Cicero rather than an Academic speaker, Lucullus here launches immediately into the polemical engagement with particular aspects of the Academic arguments.[216] This may in part be explicable as a continuation of the polemical approach with which the previous section ended, but it probably also suggests that the two types of argument from ἀπαραλλαξία received quite different treatments in the lost *Catulus*. The discussion in 54b–58 seems to presuppose a more systematic exposition of the arguments as reference point. See section 5.6.2 of the introduction for a discussion of arguments from similar objects in the various sources and an attempt to identify a relative chronology of some central argumentative moves.

Cicero replies in *Luc.* 84–86a, of which §§84–85a is the Academic rejoinder in a nutshell. It turns primarily on the notion of a *nota* by which cataleptic impressions are supposed to be distinguished and on which topic Lucullus ends the discussion of similarity (*nota* is the last word of §58—a neat example of the way in which Cicero's speech very closely engages with Lucullus').[217] In §§84–85a Cicero, far from insisting that there can be two identical objects in the world (contrast 54b *fin.*), uses the metaphysical thesis that every individual is unique to generalise from purported cataleptic impressions of twins to purported cataleptic impressions of any conceivable object.

The Stoics assume that every object in the world, whether a human being or a grain of sand, has a quality which is peculiar to it (see on §56: *singularum rerum proprietates*). This unique quality is assumed to make impressions of objects received under ideal conditions unique in turn. It is not part of the Stoic view, i.e. neither an assumption the Stoics made nor one to which they are or ought to be committed, that human beings, notably non-sages, can always tell when their impressions are cataleptic, as is shown e.g. by the fact that the Stoics assumed that non-sages can be talked out of perceptual beliefs which have arisen from cataleptic impressions.[218] In §58 Lucullus might appear to indicate that the distinctive feature of cataleptic impressions was

---

[216] On this point, see also Alleemudder (pp. 289–90).
[217] See the survey of passages featuring the relevant terminology in the general note on *Luc.* 33–34a.
[218] See section 5 on the theory of the cataleptic impression; and on *Ac.* 1.41.

routinely consciously available to him (*Habeo enim regulam, ut talia uisa uera* **iudicem** *qualia falsa esse non possint*), but actually the passage requires a different explanation.[219] Relatedly, the section shifts between the sage and non-sages as reference point (contrast §57: *illum ipsum sapientem, de quo omnis hic sermo est* with §58: **habeo regulam**), and any interpretation of it will need to be attentive to this kind of variation. §58 means 'I have a criterion available as an argumentative position', not 'I have a criterion at my disposal'—the character Lucullus does not claim to be a sage.

§54b

See also the general note on §§54b–58 just preceding. In 54b Lucullus begins by dismissing the invocation of similarities between certain types of object as childish; this looks back to the criticism of similarities in §50, but the point is not pressed, since similarity features in quite a different way there. Presumably the reader is to come away from this with a general notion that the Academics are fond of conflating similar things. Lucullus then portrays the Academics as not being satisfied with referring to very similar objects, sc. which might give rise to impressions 'just like' a purported cataleptic one but which are false, and as urging the identity of such objects.

In §84 Cicero will reject that the Academics insist on the possibility of identity, but will maintain that it remains a plausible assumption in §85.

Similitudines uero…pueriliter consectantur: with the dismissive tone, cf. §53 *fin.*; §33 for *pueriliter* in a dismissal of an Academic argument. For the examples of twins and the imprints created by seals, see §§84–5. With *similitudines*, cf. the Chrysippean book titles cited on §85.

Quis enim nostrum similitudines…plurimis in rebus appareant: what Lucullus means is that similarity is a deeply familiar phenomenon which, in virtue of its familiarity, is not likely to cause cognitive failure (*appareant* 'are plainly observable' as opposed to merely 'manifest themselves'). The Academics might have replied that they are initially concentrating on a very specific kind of similarity which is indeed likely to give rise to cognitive failure, and that they show then that such cases are hard to contain and delimit.

Sed, si satis est…in duobus aut pluribus nulla re differens ulla communitas: *cur id potius contenditis…singulas proprietates esse* is SVF ii.114. As stated in the general note above, Cicero in §84 does not recognize that the Academics insist on the possibility of identical objects. *Cognitio* is used for Greek κατάληψις here; see section 10.3. On the adverb *praesertim* with absolute ablative constructions, see *TLL* s.v. col. 867.13–22. Reid[1] (pp. 242–3) assembles parallels for the expression *rerum natura…patitur*, which cover a wide range of possible applications of the phrase; see also ibid. on *ulla* rather than *nulla (communitas)*.

---

[219] Note e.g. that in §57 *init.* even the sage is said to withhold assent when faced with objects which have potentially very similar counterparts.

Vt si sint et oua ouorum...tibi uis in geminis: the manuscripts transmit *sibi*, which Plasberg[1] and Plasberg[2] prints with an asterisk and a crux respectively, for *si* (Mueller 1859/60: 24). Formally, the sentence may be read as a tagged-on comparison; cf. e.g. §48: *ut si qui tremerent et exalbescerent...*; Lucr. 6.759. However, the *ut*-clause is also forward-looking, setting up *quid pugnas* as meaning 'why are you urging that' (cf. N.D. 1.75: *illud uideo pugnare te, species ut quaedam sit deorum, quae nihil concreti habeat...*); thus Haltenhoff (p. 213). I assume the corrupt *sibi* to be due to the influence of *tibi*. It is less attractive to assume that Cicero wrote *tibi* in both places. See also Plasberg[1] (p. 95).

Conceditur enim similis esse...quod fieri nullo modo potest: *eosdem esse* is a close rendering of ἀπαράλλακτοί (closer than any translation invoking discernibility); see section 5.6. On the use of the pluperfect *potueras*, see Pinkster i.460.

§55

See also the general note on §§54b–58, p. 493. In §55 Lucullus refers to an Academic argument which relies on the Democritean notion of innumerable worlds to argue, first, that in those worlds there might be countless identical counterparts to objects in our world (the example is Quintus Lutatius Catulus), and second, that as a consequence we should posit the same possibility within our world. For if atoms can assemble to create an identical object anywhere, they will be able do so in our world.

It is striking that the Academics would devise arguments against the Stoics which involved Democritean assumptions and premises. The dialectical nature of Academic arguments is often assumed to manifest itself in the exclusive use of premisses which are 'owned' by the opponent. While next to no extant arguments directed against the Stoics actually meet this description because of the internal consistency of Stoic thought, so that the Academics need at least one premiss which is not itself a Stoic tenet, this one premiss would not normally correspond to a position held by a different dogmatic school. However, we can cite parallels of Carneadean arguments which are assembled from premisses 'owned' by more than one philosophical school, in a way which is more reminiscent of Aristotle's habit of constructing arguments from premisses which are ἔνδοξα, i.e. stand in good repute and enjoy the support of all, many, or certain individuals of some standing; see Allen (1997: 224) on our passage and Warren (2011: 58–9) for a similar case in Sextus. When advancing arguments 'for the sake of the argument', the Academics evidently felt able to use premisses which had some claim to rational purchase, even if they relied on doctrines to which neither they nor their targets subscribed. Somewhat differently Brittain and Palmer (2001: 66–7, at 67): 'The point of this particular appeal [sc. to Democritus] may have been to point out a certain circularity in the Stoics' response to the twins objection, namely that they claim to have a cognitive grasp of one of the very principles they introduce in defending the existence of cognitive impressions, or, perhaps more simply, that they seek to establish something non-apparent on the basis of something even more non-apparent. Neither the

Stoics nor the Academics need accept Democritus' theory for this particular appeal to work.'[220]

Dein confugis ad physicos...itemque homines: = Democritus A81 DK. Brittain (2006: 33 n. 74) notes: 'Elsewhere Democritus is ascribed the views that there are innumerable coexistent, though perishable, worlds and that a type-identical world might recur; see Diogenes Laertius, *Lives* 9.44 (fr. A1 DK), and Hippolytus, *Refutation of All Heresies* 1.13 (fr. A 40 DK), and Simplicius *Commentary on Aristotle's 'On the Heavens'* p. 310 (fr. A 82), respectively. But only Cicero—and perhaps [Hippocrates] *Letter* 10 (Littré 9.322)—suggests that he argued for the existence of innumerable simultaneous and identical worlds.' Cf. Cicero's reply in *Luc.* 125 (which also explains *itemque homines* here); *Fin.* 1.21 and Aug., *Contra Acad.* 3.10.23 on Democritus' innumerable worlds, though not the specific claim made here.

Confugis suggests that the Academics seek succour from an unlikely source, namely Democritean physical doctrines to which they do not themselves subscribe. One must also wonder if Lucullus, rather than drawing on his general knowledge of Academic argument, is referring back to the *Catulus*, i.e. if Democritus was invoked by an Academic speaker there (if so, then the second person verbs do not allow for the identification of a particular speaker); cf. also §56: *me ad Democritum uocas*.

The term *physicus* in the sense of 'natural philosopher' is used already by Lucil. 635 M.; cf. also Varro, *L.L.* 10.55: *de omni natura disputant atque ideo uocantur physici*. For Democritus as a *physicus*, see Cic., *De orat.* 1.49; *physici* are distinguished from *dialectici* in *Fin.* 3.4.

As to *eos qui maxime in Academia irridentur*, this may just be rhetorical flourish. The Academics did invoke certain *physici* in support of some of their arguments (see Brittain and Palmer 2001), and while Carneades attacked all dogmatic philosophers, there is no record of him singling out the atomists in particular. Lucullus may be overreaching polemically and may be thinking of members of Plato's school who lived before the Academy turned sceptical and whose physical/metaphysical views were very different from Democritus', but even in this case we lack evidence to back up the hypothesis. *A quibus ne tu quidem iam te abstinebis* is an over-confident prediction of Lucullus' (and not a breaking of the fiction of the dialogue): Cicero will in fact rehearse the doctrines of the *physici* in *Luc.* 118–19 without much of a comment, noting merely the disagreement among them and that the dogmatist's adoption of one will entail the dismissal of the others. For dismissive references to Democritean and Epicurean atomism in Cicero's works, see Reinhardt (2005: 158–62).

The archetype had the words *et eo quidem innumerabiles itemque homines* after *prorsus intersit*. The point of the *ut*-clause seems to be that the worlds are in all respects identical; *deinde postulas*... then picks up on this claim and moves on to its implications. That there are countless worlds is an unnecessary restatement from above (where also *et quidem* already occurs), and that the same then applies to the people in these worlds seems a tidy-minded secondary gloss inspired by *et in iis quidem innumerabilibus innumerabiles*... below, which becomes less repetitive in

---

[220] On the passage, see also Castagnoli (2019: 205–6).

phrasing and thought if one applies brackets here. Halm, followed by Reid[1] (p. 243), modified *eo* to *eos* but excluded *et eos quidem innumerabiles*. See the detailed note on earlier attempts to heal this passage in Plasberg[1] (p. 96).

Deinde postulas ut si mundus ita sit...ut nihil differat, nihil intersit: without giving a reason at this point, this sentence makes the inference from innumerable (sc. simultaneously existing) identical worlds to the possibility of identical objects in our world.

'Cur enim', inquies, 'ex illis indiuiduis...Catulus alter non possit effici': the Academics ask, or so Lucullus either recalls or intimates, why atoms can assemble so as to form countless identical copies of the same individual in countless parallel worlds, but not one such copy in our world. On *indiuidua* and other Ciceronian terms for atoms, see Reinhardt (2005); apart from *indiuidua* Cicero also uses the more descriptive phrasal term *corpora indiuidua propter soliditatem* (*Fin.* 1.17). Quintus Lutatius Catulus senior was evidently invoked in the *Catulus* by his son and is referred to in *Luc.* elsewhere; cf. §148. On *omnia* and *omne* used to render τὸ πᾶν, see Reid[1] (p. 243), who also cites parallels for the absence of an adversative particle before *in hoc tanto mundo*. The sentence is cast in a potential subjunctive.

§56

See also the general note on §§54b–58, p. 493. In §56 Lucullus replies that he rejects the physical theories of Democritus, and that instead he is following the physical theories of others (the Stoics), who assume that all objects in the world are individuals with unique (if at times very similar) properties. A particular pair of identical twins is cited as evidence: indistinguishable to people unfamiliar with them, they were discernible to relatives (which would be impossible if they were not different from one another).

Primum quidem me ad Democritum uocas...singularum rerum singulas proprietates esse: formal uses of *uocare ad rem/aliquam rem* are collected in *OLD* s.v. no. 4: *me ad Democritum uocas* is probably intended to invoke a summons before an official or other figure of authority (cf. e.g. Cic., *Catil.* 3.5: *praetores... ad me uocaui, rem exposui*), whose pronouncement Lucullus does not recognize (*cui non assentior*); the technical sense of 'to assent' is not primary here, although it is of course in the background (for the argument to have any purchase on Lucullus, he needs to assent to its premisses). Once more one wonders if Lucullus could choose an expression like *me ad Democritum uocas* if Democritus' innumerable worlds had not actually been invoked by an Academic speaker in the *Catulus*.

Atomism was frequently criticized in antiquity, including for its lack of explanatory power; see Furley (1987). The Stoics are the *politiores physici* by comparison. Cf. also Cic., *N.D.* 2.74, where the Stoic Balbus characterizes Epicurus as *hominem sine arte, sine litteris, insultantem in omnes, sine acumine ullo sine auctoritate sine lepore*, although there Balbus does not just have Epicurus' physical theory in mind; see Sedley (2019).

The Stoics assumed that every object in the world was unique and had a property which was peculiar to it: *singularum rerum singulae proprietates* renders ἴδιαι ποιότητες (ἰδίως ποιόν is also used); see *SVF* ii.395, LS 28I; Lewis (1994); Irwin (1996); Brunschwig (2003: 229 with n. 75). Plt., *Tht.* 209c4–9 may have influenced the Stoics when they formulated the notion of a peculiar property.

As to the text from *assentior potius*, the adverb *potius* cannot go with what precedes: although *quidem* followed by an adversative particle is familiar (see the examples in Solodow 1978: 30–3), *potius*, which has an adversative use (*OLD* s.v. no. 4), is not documented in conjunction with *quidem* and would be odd in postposition. By contrast, *potius* does suitably set up a positive attitude, to be contrasted with *non assentior*. V² strikingly restores sense in a manner which makes a word separation error likely as the ultimate source of the corruption (*potiusque refello* 〉 *potius quare fallor*); the text as in V² is adopted by Reid¹, while Plasberg¹ prints *potius qua re fallor* and Plasberg² *potius † quare fallar †*. On the question of whether V² offers vertically transmitted readings not in evidence elsewhere in the tradition see the Oxford Classical Text, p. lxi; Malaspina (2020). In his app. crit. Plasberg¹ (p. 96) proposed a lengthy insertion and rewriting: *cui non assentior potius quam re fallar minime perspicua; inde autem quod efficis id ipsum redarguere atque refellere potest id*.

Primum has no *deinde* (vel sim.) to follow it. Gigon (p. 403) regards it as possible that 'several lines' have dropped out at the beginning of §56, but does not elaborate.

Fac enim antiquos illos Seruilios...minimum quidem similes uiderentur: for *fac* in the sense of 'suppose', see *OLD* s.v. *facio* no. 20b; the following construction is typically an accusative with infinitive, so it is preferable to assume ellipsis of *esse/fuisse* here than that *Seruilios* is object and *similes* its complement.

P. Servilius Geminus was consul in 252 and 248 (*RE* s.n. Servilius no. 62; see Münzer 1923); his twin brother (*RE* no. 63), who did not enjoy an equally distinguished career, was Q. Servilius Geminus (see Münzer 1923a). See also Münzer (1920: 140). Badian (1971: 172–83), cf. Badian (1984: 50), argues that the former is to be identified with the Servilius mentioned by Ennius, *Ann.* 286 Skutsch; Skutsch (1985: 447–8) makes a convincing case that Publius' son, Cn. Servilius Geminus (cos. 217), must be meant. Lucullus' point derives authority from the fact that such a deeply familiar, historical case is cited.

On how the *consuetudo* which would enable one to tell twins apart was theorized, see the following paragraph, and Reinhardt (2011: 313–15).

That *cognoscebantur* is correct is clear from §86 *oua cognosceret* (so Reid¹ p. 244). The insertion in ⟨*ut*⟩ *ne* is necessary since *ne* goes with *quidem* and does not function as a conjunction. Davies mended *uenire* to *uenisse*, possibly correctly, given the tenses of the subjunctives in what follows. Reid¹ (p. 244) may be right that *putassemus* is due to 'I did not expect' = *non putaram* in Latin, but the opinion referred to is chronologically earlier than the ability to discriminate. I doubt, however, that *ne minimum quidem* should be viewed as a 'sarcastic repetition' (ibid.) from the previous paragraph.

§57

See also the general note on §§54b–58, p. 493. In §57 Lucullus concedes that the sage will often suspend judgement when faced with very similar objects, but goes on to argue that through training and experience the sage acquires the skill of being able to discern objects which look identical to the untrained. (However, this skill would presumably still be confined to particular types of object, and not automatically extend to all objects which could occur in pairs or even larger series.) Examples of enhanced ability to discriminate are provided by non-sages: mothers who are able to distinguish their twins or Delian poultry farmers who are able to tell from an egg which of their hens had laid it. The sage will be able to develop such an ability a fortiori.

Given how the cataleptic impression is defined, the Stoic position, on my reading of it, ought to be that an egg perceived under ideal conditions will give rise to a cataleptic impression, even if the perceiving subject's egg discrimination skills are completely undeveloped, even if he or she withheld assent in the face of it on the grounds that he or she was unable to use such an impression, and even if he or she failed to assent to it on other grounds. (This is, however, not stated; it is also not contradicted by §58: *Habeo enim regulam...*, on my reading.) The definition of the cataleptic impression includes no awareness requirement of any kind, i.e. the perceiving subject need neither be aware of an object's peculiar quality nor of any property of the impression which makes it self-warranting. Reinhardt (2011) is an attempt at a reconstruction of the way in which Galen and the Stoics conceived of the process of cognitive development from an inability to discriminate very similar objects to an ability to do so. See also section 5.3.

It must seem beside the point that Delian poultry farmers are not just able to discriminate eggs but can also tell which hen produced a particular egg; if this was not just a misleading manner of saying that such farmers are able to tell if they are looking at this egg rather than that egg, then a possible explanation would be that training and experience is assumed not just to enhance the powers of discrimination, but to enable the perceiving subject to retrieve the causal history of a cataleptic impression at least in part.

How promising a strategy the avoidance of assent to impression of objects which are likely to have very similar counterparts is depends on whether these objects form a neatly circumscribed class (note Lucullus' phrase *ad ceteras res* in the present paragraph). Other sources, though not Cicero's reply in §§84–5, suggest that the Academics pressed precisely this point, by raising the possibility of deliberate deception by means of replicas of objects or of twin brothers of people who were assumed not to have one.

Hic pugnes licet...quale falsum esse non possit: presumably Lucullus does not expect Academic resistance on the possibility of cognitive improvement, but on the relevance of this possibility to the problems of everyday perception. Cicero will reply in §86 that normal perception (sc. as we can observe it around us) requires unlikely levels of expertise on the Antiochian view.

The restriction of the 'entire conversation' to the sage needs to be qualified, in that in §58a non-sages and Lucullus himself come into view before Lucullus appears to return to the level of the sage in §58b; the Cicero character will also frame his reply in terms of an (Academic) sage, but occasionally make 'personal' statements (e.g. §66).

The verb *dinotare* is not otherwise attested, though its sense is clear enough from its formation (consider esp. *OLD* s.v. *noto* no. 6), as is the overall sense of the passage: the sage must have objects which come in very similar multiples marked out through experience in order to discriminate between them consciously (or unconsciously, i.e. in a manner of which he could not give an account). Otherwise he will refrain from assenting. For this to work, the sage must be able to tell in advance if an object within his ken is the kind of thing which might have a 'twin' (or more); whether such determination is invariably possible is contentious. *Nisi quod tale... non possit* gestures at Ciceronian renderings of the definition of the cataleptic impression; cf. *Luc.* 18, 77. The noun *nota* is in *Acad.* used to denote the distinctive feature of cataleptic impressions or such impressions themselves (cf. the general note on §§33–34a; Cicero's terminology for impressions frequently allows for a simultaneous reference to object and impression thereof, and *res dinotatas habere* is consistent with that; on this point see also the discussion of §§40–4). Cf. also *Ac.* 1.41: ... *propriam quandam ... declarationem earum rerum quae uiderentur*; and, for the use of *habere*, Aug., *Trin.* 15.12.17: *quae nota cogitamus, et habemus in notitia etiam si non cogitemus*.

Sed et ad ceteras res...si assueueris: on the difficulty of neatly separating objects which come in very similar multiples and others (*ceterae res*) see the general note above.

Lucullus seems to stop short of positing the need for a proper technical expertise (*ars*, τέχνη) in using cataleptic impressions of ordinary objects to the best effect: *quandam* in *quandam artem* is alienating ('an art of a kind'). Further, with respect to very similar objects even the sage cannot do without experience (*usus*). Reinhardt (2011) examines passages in Galen which conceptualize and dramatize the process of cognitive improvement due to repeated exposure to relevantly similar perceptual information.

For *consuetudo oculorum*, cf. the commentary on *Luc.* 75 and 87. For the use of *ad* (*ceteras res*), see *TLL* s.v. at cols 536.61–537.28.

Videsne...inter se similitudo: for the proverb, see e.g. Sen., *Apoc.* 11: *tam similem sibi quam ouo ouum* and Otto (1890: 261). Apart from eggs, on which see also Sextus, *M.* 7.408–11 and Numenius frg. 27.38–40 Des Places (who mentions a wax egg and thus the possibility of man-made duplicates), similar 'objects' cited in the sources are impressions made by seals (*Luc.* 54 and 84), bees (*Luc.* 54; Plut., *Comm. not.* 1077c = *SVF* ii.112), hairs, grains of corn, copies of statues (*Luc.* 84), snakes (Sextus, loc. cit.), doves, grains of wheat, and figs (Plut., loc. cit.). Alleemudder (p. 291 n. 2) rightly notes that the evidence on ᾠοσκοπία cited by Reid[1] (p. 245) at §58 *satis est* etc. probably pertains to divination by means of eggs, not arguments from similarity.

Tamen hoc accepimus...dicere solebant: cf. Cicero in *Luc.* 86: *quoniam gallinarium inuenisti Deliacum illum qui oua cognosceret*. The context there suggests that the force of *inuenisti* is not that Lucullus invented the Delian poultry farmers, but that he had to work hard to find them (as an example, given that his position is far-fetched and implausible). As a matter of fact, however, there is no exact parallel in the relevant text here for what Lucullus says; Pliny, *N.H.* 10.155 (*traditur quaedam ars gallinarii cuiusdam dicentis, quod ex quaque esset*) probably draws on our passage's counterpart in the final edition (attested in Nonius p. 117 M. = t. 27) rather than independent evidence. The Roman agricultural writers credit the people of Delos with particular expertise in poultry farming, including knowledge about eggs and about the connection between a hen's diet and the quality of the shell of eggs produced by the hen (colour seems to be the prevalent concern, though); see Orth (1913: 2525). For ancient texts on poultry farming more generally see the primary references assembled by Arnott (2007: 9–10) in the article on 'Alektōr'. One may suspect that it was already known in antiquity, at least among poultry farmers, that the body of a hen gets progressively worse at producing homogeneous eggshell the older the animal gets (assuming a stable diet); see Solomon (2010); Tumová et al. (2014). This would make it possible in theory to link the physical appearance of a particular egg with a particular hen. See Reid[1] (p. 245) on the mood of *inspexerant*.

§58

See also the general note on §§54b–58, p. 493. In §58 Lucullus reaffirms that being unable to discriminate very similar objects (or even identical ones if there were any) is not a problem for the dogmatist and for him personally. One will be protected from error if one only judges those impressions to be true which cannot be false. The existence of ἀπαραλλαξία would abolish the difference between truth and falsehood (cf. §§43–4). Lucullus concludes by dismissing the Academic claim that impressions may well be unique qua imprint but identical with respect to their look or appearance (their representational content), on the grounds that impressions are discerned by their look and appearance—even if not everyone may be able to make the relevant discrimination in every particular case: the fact that *someone* is able to do so, usually after training, shows that there is a difference in looks.[221]

On the Stoic and Antiochian view cataleptic impressions put the perceiving subject directly in touch with the object, and the clarity of such an impression, ex hypothesi received under ideal conditions, is due to the fact that the perceived object's features transfer directly to the mind, whether this is conceived of as an imprint on or alteration of the mind, which in turn means that the perceived object's features are in evidence in (or through) an impression's representational content (its *species*). (Whether or not such detail is fully available to conscious experience without training is another matter.) The Academics are not invested in the physical story involving unique objects and the transfer of their properties to the mind by means of a process for which the Zenonian definition uses the imagery of printing and sealing. They are happy to concede, for the sake of the argument, that the imprint or alteration to which an impression amounts on one level of description may match any object uniquely, while suggesting that a true and a false impression's *species*,

---

[221] I believe that this consideration is supplied by the larger context, notably the end of the previous paragraph.

construed purely as a phenomenal quality, could be identical. Lucullus, for the reasons described, could not allow an impression's physical dimension and its *species* to come apart. I assume that the reference point of Lucullus' discussion in §58b is again the sage (cf. §57: *illum ipsum sapientem de quo omnis hic sermo est*, but note the shift to the dogmatists and Lucullus in particular in §58a), since only he judges consciously and routinely by impressions' *species* when he assents.

Neque idem contra nos...interesset: Reid[1] prints (cf. Brittain 2006): *Neque id est contra nos, nam nobis satis est oua illa non internoscere: nihil enim magis adsentiri par est hoc illud esse, quasi inter illa omnino nihil interesset*; Plasberg[1]: *Neque id est contra uos; nam uobis satis esset oua illa non internoscere; nihilo enim magis adsentirer hoc illud esse quam si inter illa omnino nihil interesset*; Schäublin et al.: *Neque idem contra nos; nam nobis satis est oua illa non internoscere; nihilo enim magis adsentirer hoc illud esse, quam si inter illa omnino nihil interesset*. Minim confusion can easily account for *nos/nobis* vs *uos/uobis*, so sense must determine what to print. Davies introduced *par est* into the text, which was adopted by a number of later editors; the finite *assentirer* printed by Plasberg[1] is a clearly superior way of restoring the syntax. *Nihil magis...quam si* where *nihil* modifies *magis* is not well attested; Cic., *Balb.* 26, already cited by Reid[1] (pp. 245–6), is the only good example, and there one relies on the edition by Peterson (1910). *Nihilo magis* is well attested and a simple change (proposed by Lambinus for Cic., *Balb.* 26 as well). Grammatically, a clue as to what to print at the beginning of the paragraph comes from *habeo enim regulam*, which would be insufficiently marked if there was a change in perspective from the second person to the first person here. *Assentiri par est*, like *assentirer* (though the latter to a smaller degree), also does not signal such a change in perspective—all of which suggests that the paragraph began with a first-person point of view. Independently of these considerations, that the Academics are quite content not to be able to discriminate very similar objects is a statement so obvious that it would not seem to be worth making. The train of thought is this: in §56b Lucullus, picking up on Academic arguments from very similar objects, talks about the Servilius twins, who were distinguishable, even though he has the Academic speaker object that people did confuse them. Practice, so Lucullus, enables us to make such discriminations. In §57 he anticipates objections, but signals that he will not fight back: the sage will suspend judgement when facing very similar objects which he has not marked out. (The dogmatist assumes very similar objects are a clearly delineated category, such that one can tell of a particular object if it is an element of this class of objects; the Academic disagrees. Cf. on *Luc.* 84–5.) What is more, one can train the ability to distinguish through practice and craft. But—and this is the beginning of §58—this takes nothing away from the dogmatic position (*nos...nobis*): being unable to discriminate very similar objects and refusing to give assent to impressions of very similar objects is just fine. For the dogmatist/Lucullus in particular has a *regula* such that he judges those impressions to be true which cannot be false (on the import of this sentence, see next n.). Lucullus then ceases to speak about himself and adopts a more general perspective: the Academics' argument that impressions qua imprints may be different but that they might still be identical in respect of their 'look' is to be dismissed. Someone is able to discriminate impressions even of very similar objects, and would do so with reference to their 'look' (for *species* = 'look', see also *Luc.* 52 *init.* and Brittain 2006: 31 n. 68; OLD s.v. no. 3). On the changes of perspective (§57 sage; §58a the dogmatists and Lucullus; §58b the dogmatists in general or the sage and the expert in particular), see also Schäublin et al. (p. 241 n. 180).

The very beginning of the paragraph must refer back to the argument just made, since Lucullus foregoes the option of arguing that the sage will be able to tell eggs apart. This sense is achieved by *id est* or indeed by *idem* ('this very point'), with an ellipsis of *est*. Malaspina (2020: 274 n. 94) gives a slightly different account of the situation in V than I give in the *appendix critica*. It is possible that the intralinear *potest* is in V[2]'s hand, but in my view ink colour suggests it is in V's hand (see f. 119v); note also that the interlinear *potest* writes *-st* as ligature, while the marginal *potest* has it as two letters.

Habeo enim regulam...ne confundam omnia: on the term *regula*, see also the commentary on *Luc.* 32-3. The term can either (i) designate the criterion or (ii) be used in the sense of 'rule, principle' (as in the phrasal term *regula iuris*). The *ut*-clause is open to different readings: it can either (a) spell out the content of the *regula* or (b) it can spell out the effect of being in possession of the *regula* (i.e. the outcome of its application); cf. Schäublin et al. (p. 241 n. 182) on this point. What the sentence certainly cannot mean, because it is phrased in the first person, is that the speaker claims to have at his disposal a piece of doctrine which applies in the idealized world the sage inhabits. Given that the sentence down to *non possint* is supposed to provide justification (*enim*) for the preceding sentence, option (b) would deliver a mere assertion, whereas option (a) would deliver an *explanation* why very similar items pose no problem for Lucullus. And because cataleptic impressions by themselves do not invariably enable the ability to make correct judgements, I prefer option (ii) over option (i): what Lucullus is saying is that he makes it, or is in possession of, a rule that he only judges such impressions to be true (consciously and deliberately) which cannot be false. This rules out, on Lucullus' view, impressions of objects which come in multiples. On this reading the *regula* which Lucullus claims for himself corresponds to the manner in which the sage is said to proceed in §57 (*cum ei res similes occurrant quas non habeat dinotatas*). *Vera* must be a complement on any account rather than an attribute to *talia uisa*.

Full stop after *confundam omnia* is needed (so Reid[1]) rather than after *nihil erit quod intersit* (so Plasberg in both editions, Schäublin et al.); otherwise the following *ut*-clause is hard to integrate syntactically with what follows (Schäublin translates as if it was a main clause). That the last sentence of the paragraph returns to the theme of the apprehension of the true and the false points also suggests that *ueri enim et falsi modo cognitio* marks the beginning of a sense unit. For similar expressions to the apparently proverbial (*ut aiunt*) *non...transuersum...digitum discedere*, see Reid[1] (p. 246).

Veri enim et falsi non modo cognitio...ueri et falsi nota: *cognitio* is here used as a genuine *nomen actionis* ('apprehension') and not as a translation of κατάληψις as elsewhere (disambiguation is achieved by the attribute *ueri...et falsi*); see section 10.

Lucullus interprets the claim of ἀπαραλλαξία as positing the non-distinctness of true and false impressions in every respect (cf. §53), including truth-value (hence *Veri enim et falsi...natura tolletur*), and dismisses as absurd the Academic attempt to prise apart the imprint to which an impression amounts and its representational content (see the general note above). The Academics will reply that the claim of ἀπαραλλαξία does not amount to an abolition of the truth value of impressions (merely to a non-distinctness of true and false impressions in all respects except truth value), to which Lucullus would reply that the Academics are not entitled to the true/false distinction given ἀπαραλλαξία (see *Luc.* 44 *fin.*). *Visa* in *in animos imprimantur* can comfortably have the double reference to object seen and impression had thereof. *Inter ipsas impressiones* contrasts with the following *species* (cf. §52 *init.*); with *impressio*, cf. *signum* in §34. There is no reason to assume a connection with *classes* of impressions, either those distinguished in §47 and called *genera* in §50 (*pace* Reid[1] p. 246 and Schäublin et al. pp. 241–2 n. 184), or with cataleptic impressions as a class (*pace* Striker 1997: 271): Cicero could have used *genera* had he wanted to, and *quasdam formas eorum* would require the singular if a class of impressions was meant (the alienating *quasdam* would be odd, too). Schofield (1999: 346 n. 60) suspects the Greek term ἔμφασις behind *species*, but while it occurs in Stoic texts in connection with impressions and while the Academics are said to have called persuasive impressions ἐμφάσεις (see section 6.1), none of these uses is apt to illuminate our passage. *Fides* must mean 'reliability' or 'trustworthiness' (neither of which is, on Lucullus' view, a property which is capable of degrees). In his reply in §84, Cicero will pick up on the very last point made by Lucullus, the *ueri et falsi nota* which is supposed to characterize cataleptic impressions (*nota* must mean 'mark' given the opposition with *uisa*). He will then argue as if this *nota* was supposed to mark out a class of impressions irrespective of content. See also the general note on §§33–34a on the uses of *nota*.

On this section, see also Alessandrelli (2003). Regarding *natura tolletur*, see Reinhardt (2019) on naturalistic arguments in *Luc.*

§59

The ostensible topic of this paragraph, which together with the following one ends the philosophical part of Lucullus' speech, is the Academic attitude to assent. However, this is used to illustrate the general misguidedness of Academic scepticism. In line with his earlier indication that his speech would be concerned with Arcesilaus and Carneades (§12: *ad Arcesilam Carneademque ueniamus*) he distinguishes between the attitudes of both philosophers. Since they stand for the two main Academic positions in play in *Acad.*, Clitomacheanism and mitigated scepticism, Lucullus can dismiss both positions in this way. This is, on my reading, in line with his approach in *Luc.* 40–4 (esp. 43–4), where both positions are his target.

The previous paragraph ended with Lucullus' insistence that the Academics cannot offer (for the sake of the argument) that a true and a false impression may be different qua imprints on the mind, but identical in terms of their 'look', the implication being that, if the Academics want to argue for ἀπαραλλαξία, they need to posit that it applies in any respect. With this in mind Lucullus looks back to §§32-6 and the discussion of the Carneadean *probabile*, which Academics 'follow' (*sequi*) if it is unimpeded (on the notion of impedance see section 6.5). He asks first how ἀπαραλλαξία cannot be an impedance, and second how there can be a criterion of truth given ἀπαραλλαξία;[222] this looks back to §§43-4. By dismissing 'following', the mode of endorsement of πιθανά which is permitted to the Clitomachean position, Lucullus signals that Clitomacheanism is his target (see on *Luc.* 104-5).

In any event, the considerations cited, Lucullus suggests, necessarily gave rise to suspension of judgement. Arcesilaus adhered to this consistently, while Carneades— as was stated on the previous day, i.e. in the *Catulus*—'said' (*diceret*) that the sage will sometimes hold opinions. *Diceret* is vague as to whether Carneades advanced this view for the sake of the argument or because he approved it (see the n. on *interdum* below). But, Lucullus says, the sage must never assent to non-cataleptic impressions. By introducing 'opining', the mode of holding a view which is permitted to the mitigated position, Lucullus adds the mitigated position to his list of targets (see on *Luc.* 148).[223]

The *probabile* is a concept which, for Cicero as for us, is associated with Carneades but not Arcesilaus, but this is of course not a problem. Arcesilaus is a figurehead for Cicero in *Acad.* since he shares with Arcesilaus the commitment to universal suspension of judgement,[224] while the πιθανόν is used by Cicero, too (see esp. §105a). Moreover, Lucullus' second question above—how there can be a criterion of truth given ἀπαραλλαξία—is sufficient to motivate the inclusion of Arcesilaus.

Illud uero perabsurdum quod dicitis...cum sit commune falsi: cf. §§32-6 on the *probabile*, see section 6 above, Allen (1994); on the unimpeded *probabile*, see also §§101, 104, 105 (where Cicero seems to allude to our passage, insisting that the *probabile* was, following his discussion, completely 'extricated':...*probabili, et eo quidem expedito soluto libero nulla re implicato*), 108-9. For 'following' (*sequi*), see also on §§104-5; qualified assent as practised by the mitigated sceptic is never called 'following'. For ἀπαραλλαξία, perceptual and non-perceptual, see on §§43-4. *Cum (a ueris)* as often 'almost equivalent' to *si*, as Reid[1] (p. 247) notes.

Ex his illa necessario nata est ἐποχή...peccaturum esse sapientem: according to §§66-7, Arcesilaus agreed with Zeno that the sage should never be tricked. However, he disagreed that the standard for knowledge set by the definition of the cataleptic impression could ever be met, and therefore approved that the sage should suspend judgement at all times. In *P.H.* 1.232 Sextus goes further and claims that Arcesilaus

---

[222] Possible Academic replies to both points include that the *probabile* in itself is initially merely the central element of a description of how human beings behave as a matter of fact, that the impedance at issue is conceived as an impression within an impression's syndrome which does not *appear* true and thus does not turn on a reflective attitude regarding the possibility of the actual truth of *probabilia*, and that no Academic claims the *probabile* to be a criterion in the Stoic sense (if any Academic claimed it to be a criterion in any sense); see section 6.

[223] Thus also Brittain (2006: 39 n. 89).

[224] See section 7.5 and on §§65-7; Sextus, *P.H.* 1.232.

declared suspension of judgement the τέλος, which was accompanied by ἀταραξία; seeking ἐποχή unqualifiedly is something Academics do not do.

On the concept of assent, and the competing Academic concept of approval, see the commentary on *Luc.* 37 and 104–5, where the Greek and Latin terminology is discussed, too. *Tollendus assensus est* is a slightly peculiar expression, in that *tollere* is not one of the standard terms for suspension (hence the translation 'abolish'), while suspension of assent is clearly meant (not the abolition of the concept); when Augustine loosely speaks about ἀκαταληψία and ἐποχή (*Contra Acad.* 3.10.22, 2.5.11), he avoids *assensum tollere*.

In the sequence *eo delabi interdum ut diceret opinaturum*, the adverb *interdum* would in terms of word order more naturally go with *delabi* rather than *opinaturum*, in which case Lucullus would be tendentiously implying that, because it is evident that even the sage will sometimes opine, Carneades at times let it 'slip out'; however, in §112 (*diceret ille sapientem interdum opinari*) the adverb can only qualify *opinari*. See Alleemudder (p. 305 n. 2); Schäublin et al. (p. 242 n. 188) for the connection of opining here with mitigated scepticism.

Because Stoicism conceives of virtue as knowledge, cognitive failure, i.e. assent to the non-cataleptic, is also potentially moral failure, since it leaves the subjects with beliefs which may be false. See on *Ac.* 1.42 for a fuller discussion and references; *Luc.* 66, 68; *Fin.* 3.18: *a falsa autem assensione magis nos alienatos esse quam a ceteris rebus quae sint contra naturam arbitrantur*.

Peccaturum, like *delabi* above, is presumably Lucullus' description, which is accurate from the viewpoint of Stoic doctrine, but not necessarily a description which Carneades himself would have chosen or which he would have used with himself as focaliser (as opposed to the Stoics).

Heri audiebamus is a backward reference to the *Catulus*. The point at issue might have first been made in the section corresponding to what has been lost immediately after Varro's speech breaks off in *Ac.* 1.46, but *audiebamus* suggests that the topic came up repeatedly.

Mihi porro non tam certum est…numquam assentiri rei uel falsae uel incognitae: this is a new point, rather than the third in an interconnected sequence, despite *porro* after *primum…deinde* above (noted by Alleemudder p. 305 n. 3). It is peculiar, especially for a Stoic, to rank the two tenets for certainty, and Lucullus seems to be doing it for rhetorical effect. Contrast the formulation in *Ac.* 1.45: *…temeritatem, quae tum esset insignis cum aut falsa aut incognita res approbaretur*; on the import of the variation *aut…aut* vs *uel…uel*, see Schäublin et al. (p. 243 n. 190).

§60

Lucullus now turns to criticism of the Academic method of arguing *in utramque partem* and of the motives behind it. 'They' (i.e. the Academics in general: *dicunt*) claim this is done in order to discover the truth (sc. and not in order to induce suspension of judgement or to prove that nothing is apprehensible). Lucullus wishes to 'see' what they have found in their search. A reply is introduced by an unidentified interlocutor (*inquit*, a device used frequently in the preceding paragraphs):²²⁵ 'We usually do not "show" it.' Lucullus' question and the reply give the impression that the search has yielded something, which the Academics are, however, unwilling to disclose (cf. also *celatis* below). What are these 'mysteries' (*mysteria*), Lucullus enquires further, and why do you conceal your view as if it was something reprehensible? Note here that *sententia* is used, not *opinio*, which was associated with Carneades in the previous paragraph; this suggests that 'a view' of any kind, i.e. presumably arising from whatever kind of endorsement, would satisfy Lucullus. The interlocutor replies: 'in order for those who listen to be guided by (their own) reason rather than authority'. This looks back to what Cicero the character, who then spoke as a Clitomachean, said in the proem (see n. below). Lucullus replies that being guided by a combination of both would be better still, which not by coincidence could serve as a motto for Varro's handling of the Academic tradition in *Ac*. 1. However, there is, he says, one tenet (not characterized by a noun, but merely by a pronoun) which the Academics (the text switches back to the plural in *celant*) do not conceal: that nothing can be apprehended. Lucullus treats this here as elsewhere as a settled view of the Academics (cf. *Luc*. 28–9), rather than the outcome, reached again and again, of their argumentative practice. With respect to this tenet, Lucullus suggests, the Academics do not mind endorsement through authority, although they should. For without Arcesilaus' and especially Carneades' backing nobody would have followed such a manifestly false and absurd claim.

I continue with a report on Augustine's reception of the passage, or rather of its counterpart in the final edition. Alluding to it, he claims in *Contra Acad*. 3.17.38–18.41 that during its sceptical phase from Arcesilaus onwards and down to Plotinus the Academics concealed their adherence to Platonic doctrines, which had in fact been unbroken.²²⁶ Having listed a number of Platonic ontological and epistemological doctrines in 3.17.37.23–32 (though not the theory of Forms), Augustine states that these doctrines were preserved by Plato's successors and guarded as *mysteria*.²²⁷ He then expands on what being treated as *mysteria* means: the teachings in question can only be apprehended by those who have purified or cleansed themselves, and conveying them to just about anyone amounts to a transgression. Augustine continues that, when Zeno came to the Academy while Polemo was head, this raised suspicion,

---

²²⁵ Ancient and modern readers of *Acad*. have felt moved to ask who the subject of *inquit* was; see below.

²²⁶ On the entire passage, see the admirable commentary by Fuhrer (1997: 418–48), who lists earlier allusions within *Contra Acad*. to the thesis of 3.17.38–18.41 on p. 418; Görler (1994: 804); Glucker (1978: 296–329), who refers to *Epistles* 1.1–2 and 118.16 as passages where Augustine adds postscripts to the *Contra Acad*. discussion without drawing on new material (pp. 297 n. 3, 316), but who offers a reading of *Contra Acad*. 3.18.41 in particular (summarized on p. 83) which is quite different from the one adopted here (more on this below); Barnes (1997: 92); Brittain (2001: 68–70). In *Contra Acad*. 3.37.3 Augustine says about his account: *Audite iam... non quod sciam sed quid existimem*. Part of 3.18.41 is my t. 58, on which see the commentary.

²²⁷ In *Contra Acad*. 3.20.43, by contrast, Augustine distinguishes between a secret doctrine taught in the Academy (naming Cicero as his source) and that secret doctrine being Platonic philosophy (noted by Fuhrer 1997: 418). This supports a reading on which the counterpart to *Luc*. 60 in *Ac*. 3 did not provide the inspiration for Augustine's claim that dogmatic teaching continued in the sceptical Academy (a view which, as will be discussed below, is likely to have had an independent history in the Hellenistic period), but instead allowed Augustine to link the notion with *Acad*.

for he was not the kind of man to whom Platonic doctrines could be entrusted,[228] and certainly not before purification. After Arcesilaus had succeeded Polemo and after Zeno had developed his various (from Augustine's point of view, offensive) doctrines, Arcesilaus decided to hide the views of the Academy and attack those who followed misguided teachings, notably materialism. If Zeno had recognized his mistake, the futile controversy between Academics and Stoics would have ended a long time ago. Carneades understood that Arcesilaus' strategy (sc. of speaking against, and for and against, every thesis; see the commentary on *Ac.* 1.45) was seen as wilfully obstructive, and therefore concentrated his attacks on Chrysippus in particular. He countered the charge of inactivity by developing the doctrine of the *probabile* or *ueri simile*, which he could do because as an intellectual descendant of Plato he knew the truth and hence what was similar to it (it is only here that Augustine writes in terms reminiscent of the Forms).[229] However, Carneades still held that the time had not come to disclose the actual truths to the uninitiated, and therefore merely left some clues. In Cicero's day the specious Antiochus tried to infiltrate the Academy as a Stoic (a kind of re-enactment of Zeno's infiltration), at a time when Philo was beginning to 'open the gates' and admit glimpses of previously concealed Platonizing thought. Philo aborted his cautious abandoning of the defensive posture when faced with Antiochus, and resisted him by marshalling one last time the Academic arguments. Philo's cautious move back to the Academy of Plato is universally understood to be a reference to the Roman Books (see on *Luc.* 18), whose rationale Augustine unsurprisingly either deliberately misinterpreted or misunderstood, given the tantalizing references to them in *Acad.*[230]

That in our passage Lucullus as created by Cicero cannot have had anything like this story in mind is quite plain. Platonic doctrines would not emerge from a *disputatio in utramque partem*—they do not need discovering to begin with, or at least discovering in this way. And as Fuhrer (1997: 421 n. 34) points out, Antiochus, whose point of view is given here, cannot both accuse the Academics of breaking away from the tradition of their school and credit them with concealed doctrinal Platonism. However, as noted above, the use of the Academic interlocutor whose interventions are introduced by *inquit*, and the talk of findings made by the

---

[228] Cf. Fuhrer (1997: 425): 'Das Misstrauen der Akademiker gegenüber Zenon wird durch dessen Studium bei fremden Lehrern erklärt...Eine ähnliche Zurückhaltung bezeugt Cic. *Tusc.* 5, 34: *Zeno Citieus, advena quidem et ignobilis verborum opifex, insinuasse se in antiquam philosophiam videtur*...Der Polemik zugrunde liegt wohl die Rivalität zwischen den beiden Polemon-Schülern Zenon und Arkesilaos.'

[229] As Fuhrer (1997: 435) notes, Augustine ignores here that *probabile* is Cicero's primary rendering of πιθανόν, and that his interpretation only works in Latin. However, one might think that the εἰκός/εἴκων of Plt. *Tim.* served as inspiration, too (thus Krämer 1971: 55 n. 212). Glucker (1995: 126–7) and Obdrzalek (2006: 269–71) have posited that εἰκός has dropped out of the record, implausibly (see Reinhardt 2018a: 235–6; section 6.3).

[230] Modern scholars disagree, though, on the import of the move and of its alleged abandonment. Glucker (1978: 83 and 296–329) interpreted the Augustinian passage as evidence that Philo reverted to an earlier sceptical position when the Roman Books were badly received, and that he responded to Antiochus' *Sosus* in writing with a text which informs the speech of the Cicero character in *Luc.*, but, as Brittain (2001: 68–70) has shown, no support for this view can be derived from *Contra Acad.* 3.17.38–18.41: the Roman Books view involved continued rejection of the Stoic criterion, and Augustine speaks of resistance to Antiochus, but not in terms suggestive of an actual book. See on *Luc.* 18.

Academics and their concealment, provided an opening for Augustine's reading.[231] Few modern scholars have read our passage as evidence for the pursuit of dogmatic Platonic philosophy in the sceptical Academy;[232] however, Augustine's suggestion that Philo's Roman Books represented the first step towards a revival of Platonism which was free of Stoic contamination has more modern proponents.[233]

Contra Acad. 3.17.38–18.41 has been studied closely against the wider Platonic tradition, and passages in earlier writers have been identified which shed light on what Augustine says. I will list the most important passages, but will not comment on them, since they do not illuminate *Luc.* 60 substantially.[234] Glucker (1978: 312–13) points out that the *Contra Acad.* passage reveals the influence of two different traditions: one Neoplatonic, which claims an 'unbroken chain' of Platonic dogmatic philosophizing from Plato to late antiquity, which presents Plato as divine and his teachings as akin to knowledge revealed in mystery religions, without, however, pronouncing on how the sceptical phase of the Academy is to be integrated into this picture; and another, older one, which treats Academic scepticism as a front while dogmatism continued in the school, a strategy which is presented positively as cunning by some texts or negatively as cowardice in the face of opponents by others.[235]

The latter group of passages may well reflect notions about the general rationale of Academic scepticism which go back to the Hellenistic period. Certain passages in Platonic texts (the criticism of writing in the *Phaedr.*, hints at esoteric doctrines, as well as the terminology of the mystery cults) will have been enabling (see n. on *quae sunt tandem ista mysteria...* below). Beyond that it must have been hard to accept that the philosophical school with the grandest tradition of all should have done away with the teachings of its founder and should have replaced it with an argumentative practice which was seemingly nihilist, unproductive, and not obviously able to contribute to the ethical advancement which the dogmatic schools aimed for.

To return to *Luc.* 60 itself, it would not seem in line with the general even-handedness of Cicero the author if the Lucullus character foisted a remark like *non solemus ostendere* in reply to 'what have you found?' on the other side *ex nihilo*. And if one discards the possibility that one of the Academic speakers made it but referred to substantial doctrines dogmatically held, what could have been meant? There would seem to be four possibilities: (i) views which meet the revised definition of

---

[231] On the Academic practice of concealing one's own views in certain circumstances, see below.
[232] See the bibliography collected by Lévy (1978: 336 n. 6); Fuhrer (1997: 423).
[233] See Tarrant (2018), which looks back to earlier publications by the same author and the scholarly reaction they prompted.
[234] Important discussions of ancient texts suggesting that there was esoteric dogmatizing in the sceptical Academy or that Platonic doctrines continued to be upheld include Krämer (1971: 53–8, esp. 55 n. 212); Lévy (1978); and Görler (1994: 801–6).
[235] Neoplatonic: Photius, *Bibl.* cod. 242, 151, p. 346a17–19 (= Photius' excerpts from Damascius' *Life of Isidore*); Proclus, *Theologia Platonica* p. 6 Saffrey-Westerink. Scepticism as a front: seen positively (Augustine: Arcesilaus prevented Platonic teachings from being profaned), or negatively (Sextus, *P.H.* 1.234: Arcesilaus tried to test the nature of his students for susceptibility to Platonic doctrine, which is misguided from a Pyrrhonist point of view, since dogmatism is misguided; Numenius frg. 25.75–82 Des Places, reporting a view of Diocles of Knidos which he does not endorse, without mentioning Platonic doctrine explicitly; frg. 27.56–9 and 69–72: the secret doctrine of Carneades). See also Krämer (1972: 55 n. 212) and Görler (1994: 803) for lists of relevant passages.

κατάληψις advanced in the Roman Books; (ii) views which arise from self-aware assent, which is the hallmark of mitigated scepticism as defended by the younger Catulus in *Catul.* and *Luc.* 148;[236] (iii) views held *in diem* as per *Tusc.* 5.33, i.e. ones which appear momentarily plausible in the course of an argument *in utramque partem*, and which attract approval as characterized in *Luc.* 104–105a, but only temporarily so;[237] (iv) views which appear plausible, have emerged from argument *in utramque partem*, attract approval as characterized in *Luc.* 104–105a, but which have—unlike the views under (iii)—turned out not to be transient.

Since it is now universally agreed that the Roman Books play a marginal role in *Acad.*, option (i) can perhaps be eliminated rightaway. I take it that views which emerge as *probabile* temporarily and in a particular discussion as per (iii) do not fall under the Socratic requirement of concealment, on the evidence of Cicero's dialogues,[238] and are thus unlikely to be a target here. (I also think such *probabilia* are not 'lived by' in any sense and are for that reason a less likely target of the Lucullus character, assuming he plays fairly.)

This leaves options (ii) and (iv). The desire not to rely on authority and the use of argument on either side in order to find the truth and obtain if not the truth then *ueri similia* which one might follow or approve of (in the technical sense of *Luc.* 104) is attested in Clitomachean contexts within the Ciceronian corpus in general (see the nn. below) and in *Luc.* in particular (§§7b–9a), where, however, Cicero speaks in the frame. The Cicero character claims for himself *decreta* of a kind in §109 while signalling that these are not *decreta* as the dogmatist would hold them (§111, cf. §§28–9). This would seem to secure option (iv). There is, however, no reason to exclude option (ii). It is one of the contentions of this commentary that (late) Clitomacheans and mitigated sceptics mainly disagreed on the kind of belief (loosely speaking) they permitted; see section 4. I therefore submit that Lucullus here genuinely has both factions in mind (as in the preceding paragraph).[239] Either Cicero or Catulus could have said *non solemus ostendere* and *ut qui... ducantur* in *Catul.*, while speaking not just for themselves but for the other Academic position too.[240] One would expect concealment to apply for both options (ii) and (iv).[241]

---

[236] See Brittain (2001: 112 n. 60); cf. Hirzel (1883: 195–250, 251–341).

[237] Cf. Glucker (1997: 81).

[238] Cf. e.g. *N.D.* 3.95.

[239] Contrast e.g. Brittain (2001: 16–17) on the use of *in utramque partem* argument which is not purely sceptical. Long and Sedley (ii.1987: 440) posit 'Philo as the Academic authority for this heuristic goal'; this seems right, in that I regard Philo as the source of Cicero's Academic influence and—probably unlike Long and Sedley—posit that Philo was a Clitomachean when Cicero first met him. See also Tarrant (2020: 208, 215 n. 47).

[240] Also note *cur celatis quasi turpe aliquid sententiam* **uestram**.

[241] Cf. Socratic (i.e. maieutic or peirastic) argument as ascribed to Arcesilaus in *Ac.* 1.44–6 and featuring e.g. in *Tusc.* 5.11: *Cuius multiplex ratio disputandi rerumque uarietas et ingeni magnitudo Platonis memoria et litteris consecrata plura genera effecit dissentientium philosophorum, e quibus nos id potissimum consecuti sumus, quo Socratem usum arbitrabamur, ut nostram ipsi sententiam tegeremus, errore alios leuaremus et in omni disputatione, quid esset simillimum ueri, quaereremus*; *N.D.* 1.10 (cf. 1.11); *Tusc.* 5.83; cf. *De orat.* 3.67; *Div.* 2.150. The boundary between a 'Socratic' and a non-Socratic use of *in utramque partem* argument can be hard to make out and seems to have been deliberately obscured in some cases; contrast §121, where it is unlikely that any *decretum* of the Cicero character is at stake, with §§134 and 138–9, where the subject is the highest good, a topic on which we have reason to think the historical Cicero changed his mind several times over the course of his life. One way to interpret this somewhat

Restat illud quod dicunt ueri inueniundi causa contra omnia dici oportere et pro omnibus: *restat illud quod dicunt...auctoritate ducantur* is LS 68Q. Cf. §§7b–9a, a general defence of Academic scepticism delivered by a Clitomachean speaker, for the three topics (desire to find the truth, no reliance on authority, use of *in utramque partem* argument to find the truth or the *ueri simile*). The Academic attitude to authority features again in the concluding paragraph of Lucullus' speech (§62), and in the interlude before the Cicero character's speech (§63). He will speak to the theme of the search for truth in §§65–6 (cf. also §76, where Cicero looks back to §60 and seems to promise a disclosure which, however, never comes). For other passages where the distinction between the Cicero character and the speaker in the frame is blurred see on §6.

On the search for the truth as the rationale for the *disputatio in utramque partem*, see Cic., *N.D.* 1.11 (where the speaker Cicero is a Clitomachean as in *Luc.* 7b–9a); Plut., *Sto. rep.* 1037c (see appendix 1, text 2). On *disputatio i.u.p.* as the best method to teach philosophy, see Galen, *Opt. doctr.* 1 (appendix 1, text 1), with Ioppolo (1993).

Volo igitur uidere...ostendere: see the general note above on *decreta* (*Luc.* 109–11) and the policy of concealment. On the use of a fictional interlocutor, see also the general note on §§51–54a; on *inquit* here, see the general note above, Hofmann-Szantyr pp. 417–18.

Quae sunt tandem ista mysteria...quam auctoritate ducantur: for Cicero's use of the term *mysteria*, cf. *Att.* 4.17.1 (= SB 91): *epistulae nostrae...tantum habent mysteriorum, ut eas ne librariis quidem fere committamus*; ironically of the scholastic lore of rhetoricians in *Tusc.* 4.55: *ne rhetorum aperiamus mysteria* (cf. *De orat.* 1.206: *petimus ab Antonio, ut...illa dicendi mysteria enuntiet*). Similarly Plt., *Tht.* 156a. Haltenhoff (p. 220 n. 49), who assembles all these parallels, wonders if the term might for the Roman audience have associations with the Bacchanalian conspiracy (cf. Livius 39.8–19; Cic., *Leg.* 2.35–7), which would motivate *turpe* below. On the use of *mysteria* in the Latin fathers, see Fuhrer (1997: 67–8).

Plato criticizes writing in *Phaedr.* 274–9 and hints at unwritten doctrines in *Rep.* 378a and 509c; *Tht.* 152c8 (of Protagoras) and 180b; *Symp.* 210a, as does 'Plato' in *Ep.* 7, 341b–c. Terminology associated with mystery cults in Plato e.g. at *Phaedo* 62b (ἀπόρρητα); *Tht.* 153e (ἀμύητοι, μυστήρια); see Riedweg (1987: 5–8 and passim). On secret doctrines of Plato, see also Numenius frg. 23 Des Places (from his Περὶ τῶν παρὰ Πλάτωνι ἀπορρήτων), cf. the secret doctrines ascribed to Speusippus and Menedemus (D.L. 4.2 and 2.135). On Arcesilaus' criticism of Zeno's empiricism using Platonic objections, see Plutarch frg. 215a, with von Staden (1978) and Trabattoni (2005).

---

unclear demarcation is as a meta-literary device designed to make the reader exercise judgement. (Whether an Antiochian would recognize such *decreta* as views in an acceptable sense is another matter, and it seems likely that the device used in *Luc.* 43–4, i.e. to attempt to narrow the options to dogmatic endorsement or no endorsement at all, would be deployed.) Note also that Cicero in his speech describes his scepticism as reactive in the sense that under pressure and facing extremist Stoics he will act more defensively than he otherwise would (e.g. *Luc.* 112).

On *ratio* vs *auctoritas*, cf. also Aug., *Ord.* 2.5.16 and 2.9.26, noted by Hagendahl (1967: 63).

Quid si utrumque—num peius est: the reader is surely to think of Antiochus' attitude to the *prima forma* of Platonic philosophy formulated by the *ueteres*, open as it is to 'corrections' from Aristotle, Peripatetics, and Stoics, all after suitable evaluation (see section 7.2); this is on display in Varro's speech in *Ac.* 1, but must have featured, perhaps in shorter form, in the *Catulus*, too. In *N.D.* 3.110 the Stoic Balbus claims to despise authority and follow reason. Reid[1] (p.) prints *utroque* (found in the *deteriores* and proposed by Davies), which carries over the ablative from the preceding sentence.

Vnum tamen illud non celant...quod percipi possit: cf. on *Luc.* 28–9; Velleius at Cic., *N.D.* 1.17: *ambo enim* [sc. Cotta and Cicero] ... *ab eodem Philone nihil scire didicistis*; Sen., *Ep.* 88.44: *Academici, qui nouam induxerant scientiam, nihil scire*.

An in eo auctoritas...multo etiam maior in Carneade et copia rerum et dicendi uis fuisset: see on *Ac.* 1.45 for Arcesilaus' effectiveness in argument, on 1.46 for Carneades'. The phrase *aperte perspicueque* alludes to the philosophical use of *perspicue*: for Lucullus, to follow what is manifestly false is evidence of corrupted reason, and since the term *perspicuum* is also claimed by some Academics (cf. *Luc.* 34), there is also the implied charge that the Academics violate their own standards.

§§61–62

Speeches in Cicero's philosophical dialogues usually have, in line with the rules for epideixis, a conclusion which is of elevated style, exhibits a degree of hyperbole, and includes an exhortation, sometimes to an individual, and sometimes of a more general nature. At the end of *Fin.* 2 Torquatus is encouraged to abandon Epicurean hedonism; *Tusc.* 4 ends with a eulogy of the ethical benefits of pursuing philosophy; at the end of *N.D.* 2 the Academic Cotta invites the Stoic Balbus to adopt his theological views.[242]

A theme of the conclusion here is the incompatibility between Cicero's Academic scepticism, his activity as a writer of philosophical works, and his life as a political operator. The latter in particular, it is suggested, required and involved deeply held convictions, confidence in one's judgement, and in the reliability of evidence. Lucullus alludes to a particular situation in a senate meeting held at the time of the Catilinarian conspiracy (see n. below), which puts the historical Cicero and thereby the character here 'on record' in a relevant way.[243] However, he also raises the wider

---

[242] All noted by Alleemudder (p. 319 n. 3). See also the end of *Div.* 2, with Schofield (1986: 57).

[243] Compare a question which has exercised modern scholars, viz. how Cicero can appear to occupy a position close to an Antiochian one in some works, esp. of the 50s BC, and an avowedly sceptical one in others, notably *Acad.* See the commentary on *Ac.* 1.13–14, section 8 on Cicero's Clitomacheanism, and Gawlick and Görler (1994: 1084–9).

question of how the sceptic can live his scepticism and answer the charge of ἀπραξία, which had already featured earlier in his speech. That ἀπραξία and the connected issue of assent are given prominence in this way may seem surprising, given that the subject of the preceding paragraphs had been ἀπαραλλαξία, but is to be explained by Lucullus' charge that Cicero's life as an author and as a politician ought to be impossible.[244]

One of Cicero's objectives in his character's reply later on is the dismissal of the charge of inconsistency: he will assert that his Clitomachean stance enables him to be a fully functioning person, advocate, and politician without requiring him to accept the extreme standard of the cataleptic impression or the kind of endorsement of impressions which dogmatic assent bestows (see esp. *Luc.* 65-7). He will argue further that, far from being an outlandish view, the kind of detachment he claims for himself is in fact deeply rooted in a proto-sceptical attitude which the Romans had all along and which shows up in various contexts where figures of authority publicly pronounce on matters requiring evaluation and judgement (*Luc.* 146b).[245] His encouragement to pursue philosophy in the *Hortensius* would, it is argued by Lucullus, require dogmatic commitment, but there again the Academics' and the dogmatists' perception of the Academic stance differ radically: while Lucullus presents Academic scepticism as sterile and unworkable negative dogmatism, Cicero would claim that it holds out the same prospects for individual happiness as the dogmatists claim for their outlook.

Academic scepticism is here, as on some other occasions in Lucullus' speech, presented in stark terms: it deprives human beings of the faculty of assent, of their senses, plunges them into total darkness, and makes them unable to move. This 'version' of scepticism is extreme, devised by the dogmatist for argumentative purposes as the outcome of the Academic position (in general) rather than a description which any Academic would recognize (see Allen 1997). The Academics provided an opening for this caricature of their position by stressing the difficulty of epistemic progress, the limitations of our senses (*Luc.* 7), and by claiming that at least some things, notably questions pertaining to the field of physics, were obscure (*Luc.* 32; *Ac.* 1.44).

Finally, one must ask how this conclusion to Lucullus' speech relates to the fact that in *Acad.* two Academic positions are acknowledged, the Clitomachean one and the mitigated one. Cicero is being addressed directly, and his position is avowedly the former. That the abolition of assent, which is constitutive of the Clitomachean position, is explicitly criticized also suggests that this position is primarily targeted. On the other hand, we have found that Lucullus appears to formulate his arguments at times in a way which makes them applicable to either Academic position (cf. e.g. *Luc.* 43-4; 60 on my interpretation), and it is reasonable to expect that the same degree of generality is aspired here, too. Now given that the abolition of assent is so explicitly mentioned, the only way in which the mitigated position could be a secondary target would be if the assent with whose abolition the Academics are credited was Stoic dogmatic assent: Lucullus would not recognize qualified assent

---

[244] On this aspect of *Luc.* 61-2, see also Obdrzalek (2012: 377-8).
[245] Other passages which speak to the issue include *N.D.* 1.12 and *Off.* 2.8.

(self-consciously given in the knowledge that the impression assented to may be false) as assent. From *Luc.* 148 it emerges, at least on my construal of the text, that at least mitigated sceptics viewed the mitigated position as inconsistent with universal ἐποχή.

§61

Haec Antiochus fere...quam est mortuus: see on *Luc.* 11 for a fuller discussion of Antiochus' biography; Görler (1994: 938–45); Blank (2007); Hatzimichali (2012). Antiochus accompanied Lucullus on his second mission to the East, against Mithridates and his father-in-law Tigranes. Plutarch (*Luc.* 28.8) records that Antiochus wrote about a major battle in the war against Tigranes, which took place in October 69 BC and following which Lucullus' forces destroyed Tigranocerta, the new capital of the Armenian kingdom. After these events Lucullus spent time in Gordyene, which lies east of the Tigris; presumably Antiochus died there.

The apparently superfluous detail relayed by Lucullus enhances both his and Antiochus' credibility: Lucullus emphasizes the length of his association with Antiochus and moves the terminus post quem for relevant philosophical discussions significantly towards the dramatic date of the dialogue. And Antiochus' consistency in maintaining his dogmatic stance over a long time is emphasized, which is important because the Academics criticized him for his shift from scepticism to dogmatism (*Ac.* 1.13; cf. Catulus' remark immediately after the Lucullus' speech in *Luc.* 63; and *Luc.* 71).

Sed iam confirmata causa...non dubitabo monere: now that his case has been made (*confirmata causa*) and because he has seniority (by about ten years), Lucullus takes the liberty of advising Cicero. *Dubito* with infinitive is used in its usual sense of 'to hesitate'. That Lucullus speaks about the exhortation to philosophy in the *Hortensius* next may suggest that Cicero qua sceptic is being addressed, rather than as a Clitomachean in particular. Reid[1] (p. 248) notes that the apposition *hominem amicissimum...minorem natu* is best seen as replacing a causal clause (*aliquot...natu* precludes that it could be concessive).

Tune, cum tantis laudibus philosophiam extuleris...orbat sensibus: the *Hortensius*, written just before *Catul.* and *Luc.*, dramatized a conversation which preceded that represented in the *Catulus* and *Lucullus*, involving the same characters, and set at the villa of Lucullus; see section 9.5. Four speakers defended four different fields of study: Catulus poetry, Lucullus historiography, Hortensius rhetoric, and Cicero philosophy. Augustine famously described in his *Confessiones* (3.4.7; cf. *De vita beata* 1.4) how he was turned towards philosophy by *Hort.*; see Schlapbach (2006) on the role accorded to the dialogue in Augustine's work. Already in that work Cicero identified his personal position as Clitomachean, but Hortensius opted for the Old Academy in the fiction of the triptych. It is likely that *Catul.* offered some explanation on this choice.

In the characterization of scepticism (*quae confundit uera cum falsis...orbat sensibus*) Lucullus starts with the most recent subject covered (ἀπαραλλαξία), which via the abolition of a criterion to which it amounts and thus the removal of any basis for assent, leads to the claim of the abolition of the senses. Assent is central to the argument from ἀπραξία in *Luc*. 37–9; Cicero's main reply is given in *Luc*. 102–3, but the hyperbolic claim that humans are plunged into darkness and deprived of their senses is also addressed in *Luc*. 73–4.

See the collection of parallels in Reid[1] (p. 249) for the question type *tune… sequere*. The emendation *omnibus* in V[2] may be correct: *approbatio* is not strictly in need of modification, and in any event *approbatione omni* is better taken to mean 'of any (instance of) approval' rather than 'of any kind of approval' (the abolition of assent is the key consideration). Stylistically it is mildly preferable for the third colon in the enumeration to be the heaviest one.

Et Cimmeriis quidem…ut nos commouere nequeamus: in Hom., *Od*. 11.12–19, the Cimmerians are described as residing in the area beyond Okeanos, where the entry to Hades is situated, and on whom the sun never shines; see the collection of material in Tokhtas'ev (1996). The implication is that Academic scepticism reduces human beings to creatures who are barely sentient and almost infernal. The phrase *ad dispiciendum* means 'so as to glimpse something despite difficulty'; cf. Cic., *Div*. 2.81: *imbecilli animi… uerum dispicere non possint*, 'weak minds are unable to make out the truth'; *Tusc*. 1.45 (on the origin of philosophy): *cum has terras incolentes circumfusi erant caligine, tamen acie mentis dispicere cupiebant*, 'even in the days when they dwelt on earth surrounded by gloom, they nonetheless desired to penetrate it with keen sight'; both passages cited by Haltenhoff (p. 224). With *deus aliquis*, cf. *deus aliqui* in *Luc*. 19; Cicero does not appear to observe a clear distinction between substantival *aliquis* and adjectival *aliqui*; see the note in Reid[1] (p. 249). *Vinculis simus astricti* polemically responds to what Cicero said in *Luc*. 8 of people who follow the first dogmatic school they encounter, without having exercised their own judgement: *Nam ceteri primum ante tenentur astricti quam quid esset optimum iudicare potuerunt*; that, however, was Cicero speaking as narrator in the frame, not as a character. Lucullus passes over the distinction. Plasberg[1] has a more detailed report than my apparatus provides on the situation in ms. B after *natura* and around *uti lumine licebat*. The correction *Cimmeriis* is one important piece of evidence for the evaluation of the nature of correction layer V[2] in V, specifically for the question of whether Lupus of Ferrières can be expected to have known of the Cimmerians and if not whether the correction could only have been achieved through reference to a manuscript other than ξ; see the Oxford Classical Text p. lx. Malaspina (2020: 282–3) considers the question and observes that we know that Lupus had access to texts which mention this group of people (e.g. Gell. 17.8.16).

§62

Sublata enim assensione…sed omnino fieri non potest: Lucullus looks back here to §§24–5 and the account of action: if the rational basis for assent has been taken away because of ἀπαραλλαξία, then there can be no impulse (ὁρμή; *motus animorum*) and as a consequence no action. The reference point is apparently still the Stoic sage

(§57). As to the distinction between *recte fieri* and *omnino fieri*, Lucullus is saying that the Academics will not just be unable to account for action appropriately, but will be unable to explain how the sage can act at all.

V² manifestly emends to *adsensionem*, in order to create a readable text following the error *sublatentem* in VS (ξ); but *sublatenter... adsensionem* cannot be right, since there is nothing stealthy in the Academic abolition of assent. See the note in Reid¹ (p. 250) on *actionem rerum*.

Prouide etiam... a te ipso minuatur auctoritas: the Catilinarian conspiracy of 63 BC is still a recent event, and the present passage is one of those which help identify the dramatic date of the dialogue (approximately 62/1; see Gigon 1962: 230). Cicero reassured the senate in *Catil.* 1.10: *haec ego omnia uixdum etiam coetu uestro dimisso comperi*. From *Att.* 1.14.5 (= SB 14) we learn that Clodius used the phrase against Cicero (*me tantum 'comperisse' omnia criminabatur*), apparently implying that Cicero had suppressed evidence (see Alleemudder p. 321 n. 1); Lucullus and Hortensius were present on that occasion. Cf. also *Fam.* 5.5.2 (= SB 5) to Antonius Hybrida, Cicero's colleague during his consulate: *nam 'comperisse' me non audeo dicere, ne forte id ipsum uerbum ponam, quod abs te aiunt falso in me solere conferri*, 'I dare not say "learnt" in case I might be using the very word which they tell me you often bring up against me untruly' (transl. Shackleton Bailey). The remark was sufficiently familiar to be used by the author of [Sall.] *in Tull.* 3: *denique de eo tibi compertum erat* (see Novokhatko 2009: 155 n. 27 ad loc.).

Cicero is said to have sworn to have 'learnt' about the conspiracy. In *Luc.* 146, near the very end of his speech, Cicero cites conventional affirmative formulations used in court by judges and by witnesses in sworn testimony to make the point that even those are phrased so as to leave scope for the possibility of error. Haltenhoff (p. 225) queries the validity of Cicero's reply, since Cicero's remarks in the senate were not conventional and dictated by set procedures—to which Cicero would presumably reply that what he said in the senate implicitly carried the rider which features in legal standard formulations. Haltenhoff also compares *Font.* 29, directed at the accuser: *qui... illud uerbum consideratissimum nostrae consuetudinis, 'arbitror', quo nos etiam tunc utimur, cum ea dicimus iurati quae comperta habemus, quae ipsi uidimus, ex toto testimonio suo sustulit, atque omnia se 'scire' dixit*, '...but, in the first place that phrase of wholesome discretion which we are accustomed to employ—the phrase "I think"—used by us when we give utterance even on oath to statements of ascertained fact of which we have been eye-witnesses, that phrase had no place in all his evidence; in every case he said "I know"' (transl. Watts).

The phrases/expressions *res occultissimas* (of the conspiracy) and *in lucem protuleris* (of Cicero's investigative activities) reinforce Lucullus' point due to their association with philosophical positions: Cicero the Academic lives and acts like a Stoic, and is in danger of tarnishing his legacy by claiming otherwise. On darkness inflicted by the Academics, cf. *Luc.* 16: *clarissimis rebus tenebras obducere*, 26: *ratio... tollitur, quasi quaedam lux lumenque uitae*, 30: *quid eum facturum putem de abditis rebus et obscuris qui lucem eripere conetur*, 33: *si quis quem oculis priuauerit*, 42: *deinde in ea quae ducuntur a sensibus et ab omni consuetudine, quam obscurari uolunt*; cf. *N.D.* 1.6 *multis etiam sensi mirabile videri eam nobis potissimum probatam esse philosophiam, quae lucem eriperet et quasi noctem quandam rebus offunderet.* For Stoic 'light', cf. in addition 31: *nihil enim est ei ueritatis luce dulcius.*

With the sentiment that Cicero's actions as consul commit him to certain stances, cf. *Fin.* 3.10, where Cato tells Cicero that he (Cic.) can only hold that virtue is the sole good. *Qui ex te illa cognoueram* looks back to §60: Lucullus is happy to accept Cicero's authority (rather than rely on reason only, as the Academics speciously claim); he can do this because Cicero can be relied on to know (contrary to what he says).

Reid[1] (p. 250) wonders if *licebat* (in some *deteriores*) could be corrupted from *liquebat* and compares *N.D.* 1.74, where this change has occurred. That the relative clause is cast in the singular rather than to agree with *ea* tells against it. See also Plasberg[1] (p. 100).

Quae cum dixisset ille, finem fecit: cf. Caes., *BG* 1.46: *Caesar loquendi finem fecit*; Sall., *Catil.* 52.1: *Postquam Caesar dicundi finem fecit.*

§63

This interlude between Lucullus' and Cicero's speeches is hard to evaluate for tone, but the tone is important for the characterization of the speakers. Hortensius responds first—in the *Catulus* he must have been given at least some, possibly all of the historical material on Antiochus' position which in *Ac.* 1 is introduced by Varro,[246] and so it is unsurprising that he gives his strong approval and invites Cicero to join the Antiochian side (possibly in jest, as Cicero notes—this introduces, as a theme of the narrative, a possible disconnect between what the characters say and what they think).

Having Hortensius react first means that the two Academic participants speak in sequence, and Cicero's reaction directly leads into his long speech given in reply. One might wonder if Catulus, who is in *Luc.* associated with the position of mitigated scepticism (§148), is going to say something indicating that *his* position would be affected differently from Cicero's Clitomachean one (considering e.g. that Lucullus' speech ended with a heavy emphasis on the subject of assent, which makes for a dividing line between the two Academic positions).

However, there seems to be no indication in Catulus' remarks that he meant to speak to the different positions: Catulus presents himself and Cicero as on the same side. The most noticeable feature of his remarks is that they are palpably rhetorical and subtly manipulative (at one point he is said to smile): he regards it as possible that Lucullus' speech, which is described in terms that do not turn on the quality of the arguments in it, may have influenced (*flectere*) Cicero (see n. below). A philosopher who prides himself on his *iudicium* (cf. §§8, 60) may read this as a suggestion that, if he is now attracted by the other side, it will be for the wrong reasons. Indeed there follows an admonishment that the one thing Cicero should avoid is being

---

[246] There is nothing to suggest that someone else spoke about the history of the Old Academy in the *Catulus*, but the treatment may not have been as detailed as the one we find in *Ac.* 1; see section 9.2.

moved by Lucullus' *auctoritas* (sc. which would be out of line with the self-perception of the Academics). The *auctoritas*, Catulus intimates, was deployed to threaten Cicero with the possibility of being dragged by the tribunes before the *contio* and being made to account for the apparent contradiction between Cicero's public declarations about his knowledge of the Catilinarian conspiracy and his sceptical stance (cf. §§62, 144). Cicero, he adds, should not be 'terrified' by this prospect. This invites both a refusal to be timid on Cicero the character's part and the reader's observation that Lucullus argued from terrifying prospects for Cicero the politician—prospects which were real, as history proved and the reader knows, and did not require Lucullus' authority to be credible. When Catulus says that it would not surprise him if Cicero went over to the dogmatists because Antiochus had done the same, then Cicero the character, as well as the reader, may regard this as teasing or condescending and in any event intended to secure Cicero's loyalty to the Academic cause (whether that means to 'reason/judgement' or to Catulus). It is difficult to decide whether Catulus' tone is meant to be read as that of banter among friends or whether there is an edge to it.

The substantial reply of the Cicero character follows from §65. Without anticipating what Cicero will say there, we note here that the character, cast as a Clitomachean, gives no indication that he regards himself as not entitled to knowledge claims in the political sphere as he made in connection with his findings on the Catilinarian conspiracy.

Hortensius autem...coepit hortari ut sententia desisterem: that nobody has spoken against the New Academy *subtilius* looks back to §10, esp. Hortensius' expectations for Lucullus' speech (*a Lucullo autem reconditiora desidero*, sc. compared to Hortensius' own remarks in the *Catulus*); the approval signalled by Hortensius shows that Lucullus has met his expectations. Immediately following Catulus praises slightly different features of the speech (*memoriter accurate copiose*).

Punctuation as in Plasberg[1], notably with regard to the two parentheses. The clause *ut sententia desisterem* does not imply that Cicero held opinions (contrary to his stated position) or is committed to sceptical tenets in a negatively dogmatic way: *sententia* just means 'view' here. For *admirari* 'to show admiration', see *OLD* s.v. *admiror* no. 2. On *numquam* positioned away from *dictum esse*, see Reid[1] p. 251. *Academia* here as usual in *Acad.* 'the sceptical Academy'.

Tum mihi Catulus 'Si te...deterrendum puto': for *flectere* used of influencing someone rhetorically and specifically emotionally, see the passages under *OLD* s.v. no. 9; Cic., *Or.* 69: *probare necessitatis est, delectare suauitatis, flectere uictoriae: nam id unum ex omnibus ad obtinendas causas potest plurimum*. None of *memoriter accurate copiose* turns on the quality of the arguments advanced: *accurate* relates to arrangement and organization; cf. Secundus' praise for Aper's *accuratissimus sermo* in Tac., *Dial.* 14.2. On the use of *memoriter*, see Madvig (1876: 73). With *sententiam mutare*, cf. *sententia desistere* immediately above.

Illud uero non censuerim...Hoc, quaeso, caue ne te terreat: see on §60 for the theme of *auctoritas* (vs *iudicium*). *Tantum...monuit* looks back to §61 *monere*. The reference to Publius Clodius Pulcher, who eventually succeeded in getting Cicero exiled for his handling of the Catilinarian conspiracy, makes Catulus' words prescient and menacing, especially after Lucullus had alluded to the issue in much more subtle way; Cicero replies in §§97 and 144 (see ad loc.). On Clodius, see Tatum (1999); on the construction of Clodius in Cicero's works, Berno (2007); Seager (2014).

Quorum uides quanta copia semper futura sit seems oddly expansive and may be making the metaphorical point that there will always be someone who challenges an incompatibility between philosophical position and real-life conduct.

As Reid[1] p. 252 notes, *in contione quaerere* refers to the procedure of summoning someone before a *contio*, usually called *in contionem producere*; the latter is a generic term which covers friendly invitations, too (see Linderski 1986: 2209; Morstein-Marx 2008: 164), whereas what Catulus has in mind is more narrowly called *prensio* (see Kunkel and Wittmann 1995: 577).

On *te comperisse dixisses*, see §62. That Catulus restates this point verbatim adds a certain insistence to what he says. There does not seem to be a suggestion that Cicero would be more entitled to such 'knowledge talk' if he became a mitigated sceptic like Catulus (even mitigated sceptics reject apprehension and do not claim the term). On *ne te terreat*, see the general note above.

Non, first excluded in the Aldina, may be a repetition from the preceding sentence. Reid[1] p. 251, with a degree of hesitation, retains it by turning the whole sentence into a question (i.e. question mark after *dixisses*); see also the note in Plasberg[1] (pp. 100–1). Rackham (1951) keeps *non*, does not translate it, and makes the sentence a statement. *Inquit* in parenthesis modified by a participle is rare. On *censuerim*, see Kühner-Stegmann i.177. For the *idem…idem* repetition Reid[1] (p. 252) cites Cic., *Div.* 2.77; *Phil.* 2.40.

De causa ipsa autem…sententia destitisse: with *De causa ipsa* Catulus turns back to the 'subject that was discussed', as opposed to things extraneous to it like the authority of whoever spoke to it. Catulus gives no indication that he, while of an Academic persuasion, disagrees with Cicero on whether (self-aware) assent is permitted (see on §148). On Antiochus' shift from allegiance to the New Academy to dogmatism, see *Ac.* 1.13; *Luc.* 71; *Luc.* 61 *init*. On the variation in tense between the *cum* and the *simul ac* clause, see Pinkster i.589–90.

Reid (1883: 62) on *Lael.* 2 suggests that the perfect infinitive as opposed to the present infinitive is used when the speaker was not personally witness to the event. We have no positive evidence suggesting that the younger Catulus and Antiochus ever met in person.

Haec cum dixisset Catulus, me omnes intueri: Reid[1] (p. 252) gives cautious endorsement to the suggestion made by Ranitz (1809: 14) that, given how *N.D.* 2 and 3 start, this probably became the beginning of Book 4 in the final edition. The fragment of *Ac.* 4 which comes first in the sequence corresponds to *Luc.* 66 (Aug., *Contra Acad.* 3.14.31 = t. 28).

§64

Cicero's speech responds to Lucullus' on many points,[247] but its structure is only partially determined by it. One reason for this is that the Academic position operates unlike a dogmatic one: it is not committed to tenets, still less to ones which define it, and thus has fewer views of its own to expound, while being ready to scrutinize the views of dogmatists (this explains the presence of the doxographical section §§112–46).

In his speech,[248] Cicero will first describe his position (§§64–6) and his attitude towards ἐποχή (§§66–8), with reference to the sage/non-sage distinction; while assent features as a separate topic in Lucullus' speech (§§37–9), it is less central to the argument, since κατάληψις requires (dogmatic) assent and is an indispensable component of the dogmatist position. §§69–71 is devoted to Antiochus' shift from scepticism to his current position, which raises obvious questions; §18, on the Roman Books view, is a counterpart of sorts, in that it is devoted to a position which was formulated by Philo after he first held a different one. §§72–76a rebuts Lucullus' response to the Academic invocation of the Presocratics as intellectual ancestors of sorts; this must have featured in *Catul.*, as is suggested also by *Ac.* 1.44–6. §§76b–8 is devoted to the initial dispute between Zeno and Arcesilaus relating to the cataleptic position, and about Arcesilaus' and Carneades' stances on the subject. The section thereafter is devoted to ἀκαταληψία (§§79–98), §§79–90 in the domain of the senses, §§91 in the domain of reason. §§98–111 is devoted to the the πιθανόν, the Academic 'alternative' to the cataleptic impression, with §§105–11 addressing Lucullus' suggestion that apprehension was indispensable for the conduct of practical and intellectual life; §§104–105a is devoted to 'approval', the kind of endorsement of impressions which Carneades permitted according to Clitomachus under general ἐποχή. In §§112–44 Cicero reviews the διαφωνίαι among the views held by the dogmatic philosophers; for the Academics, these should undermine anyone's confidence that one can find the correct view on philosophical matters and have complete confidence in it. §§145–6 then argues that the Stoic standard for knowledge, which the sage alone possesses, is so extreme that even the greatest experts in particular field of expertise would have to count as not being in possession of knowledge. The general conclusion to the book is another exchange between the interlocutors, which crucially illuminates Catulus' position (§148), i.e. that of mitigated scepticism.

Cicero uses various devices to present the speech in its situational context as similar to a forensic one (see the nn.). However, he does make it clear that he will be speaking out of sincere conviction, in contrast to Lucullus, who accepted the role given to him but came close to disavowing it as a statement of his views.[249] The

---

[247] Glucker (1978: 391–406), who demonstrates how closely Cicero's speech is geared to Lucullus', infers from this that Cicero's speech must be drawing on a source which had been written in response to the Lucullus' source (see also Glucker 2004: 112–13). I regard this inference as unwarranted, on the grounds that Cicero was easily capable of composing 'his' speech with reference to, but not closely following, a range of Academic sources available to him. See also section 9.3 on the sources of *Acad.*

[248] Cf. the structural analyses in Reid¹ (pp. 79–83); Schäublin et al. (pp. lxxiv–lxxxv); and Brittain (2006: lv–lvii).

[249] Cf. *Luc.* 10: *non laboro quam [quam] ualde ea quae dico probaturus sim.... Dicam enim nec mea nec ea, in quibus non si non fuerint non uinci me malim quam uincere*; see Görler (2004c: 268–9 n. 1) on the attitudes interlocutors in Ciceronian dialogues signal with respect to their subjects. And in general, Leonhardt (1999) for an approach to Cicero's dialogues which privileges the forensic paradigm.

speech begins in a measured, urbane, and reasonable way, which contrasts with Catulus' immediately preceding provocative remarks.

Tum ego non minus commotus...sum exorsus: Reid[1] (p. 252) assembles passages from Cicero which state that the orator needs to be moved in order to perform at his best (*Div.* 1.80), or that at the beginning of an important case the orator is so moved (*Deiot.* 1; *Div. Caec.* 41; *Clu.* 51; *De orat.* 1.121). As the parallels from speeches show, such nervousness is not by itself indicative of a deeper investment on the part of the speaker. Cicero may also be hinting at the 'seniority' of Lucullus. There is no reason to view Cicero's urbanity as cocky. The ablative *quadam oratione* is unobjectionable; Lambinus emended to *quandam orationem*, construing the phrase as an object to *sum exorsus* (cf. *OLD* s.v. *exordior* no. 2c).

Me, Catule, oratio Luculli de ipsa...nisi tu opposuisses non minorem tuam: Cicero seems to correct Catulus tacitly: *mouere* but not *flectere* (cf. §63) was the effect of Lucullus' speech; he stresses the comprehensive nature of Lucullus' speech whereas Catulus praised secondary virtues, but, as he says, he is not shy (*diffidere*) to reply (Catulus had raised the possibility that Cicero might have been intimidated by Lucullus' words). The point about authority is countered, too, in a polite way. The omission of *me* with *respondere* was addressed by *respondere* ⟨*me*⟩ (Davies) and *responderi* (Lambinus 1566); but see Reid[1] (p. 327) on §128 *considerare*.

Aggrediar igitur...quasi de fama mea dixero: parallels suggest that *fama mea* is only slightly stronger than 'me': *Off.* 2.1: *dicere aggrediar...si pauca prius de instituto ac de iudicio meo dixero*; *N.D.* 3.5: *ante quam de re, pauca de me*. See Reid[1] (p. 253) on the pattern of present subjunctive or future plus *si* with future perfect, as well as variation between *si* and *cum*.

§65

Cicero offers '*pauca...de fama mea*' as announced in §64. He stresses his sincerity, his deep commitment to his stance and to the pursuit of truth, his limitations (by noting twice that the debate with Lucullus is about the sage, which Cicero acknowledges he is not), and he rejects any suggestion that he could be motivated by vanity or cantankerousness. The nature of Cicero's position is characterized in subsequent paragraphs.

This plea resonates on several levels. First, it looks back to the attitude adopted by Lucullus at the beginning of his speech,[250] when he indicated his approval of but lack of deep investment in the subject he was going to cover in his speech.[251] One might

---

[250] Cf. *Luc.* 10, quoted in n. 249.
[251] Görler (2004c: 268 n. 1) assembles a number of passages from Cicero's dialogues in which characters signal something other than sincere conviction regarding the subject they are speaking on. These form a rather disparate set and show Cicero's nuance of characterization: *Rep.* 3.7–8 (Philus speaking) is a disavowal of ownership which contrasts in different ways with the present passage and with Lucullus'

think that Cicero as author is handing himself as character a dramatic advantage here, compared to his other creation Lucullus, but one may equally observe that, for all we know, the role accorded to philosophy and to a particular stance in the lives of the two men is fairly represented, and that the first-person speaker of the frame, whose date is the same as the date of composition of the dialogue, did not, for all we know, have an outlook which was different from that of the historical Cicero around the dramatic date of *Luc.* in the relevant respect. Nonetheless, one should not on the basis of this assume an uncomplicated continuity between Cicero the man and the various first-person speakers one encounters in the Ciceronian corpus.[252] Second, Cicero is rejecting accusations, either made by Lucullus or attested elsewhere as dogmatists' criticism of sceptics (Academic or Pyrrhonian), that the Academic practice was purely destructive and dubiously motivated, or—more fundamentally—that it did not amount to a philosophical stance, since dogmatic philosophical schools were individuated e.g. with reference to the highest good posited, a requirement the Academics had no desire to meet. However, the insistence that a Clitomachean like Cicero takes himself to be pursuing the truth points to limits to the type of scepticism Cicero upholds in his speech. Third, the phrase *de fama mea* also evokes sections in forensic speeches *de uita ac moribus* either of the advocate or of the client,[253] and thus encourages readers to approach *Luc.* with at least some of the expectations usually applied to adversarial oratory. In Roman lawcourts, where physical evidence played a limited role for obvious reasons, many arguments relied on considerations of plausibility given the main players' character and known earlier conduct. Image transfer from advocate to client was a frequently deployed strategy, and the advocate himself routinely assured juries of the purity of his motivation and commitment to shared values.

Not just the subject but also the manner of its introduction is reminiscent of oratory. Cicero argues that, if various charges which Lucullus had dropped into his speech were justified, then this would cast doubt not just on Cicero's case but on him as a person. Such charges belie his life to date and, if warranted, would be evidence of self-delusion. By means of a *praeteritio* and a comparison with political life, Cicero raises the possibility that he could swear to his desire to find the truth and to his sincerity in general. And by not addressing the point made by Lucullus in §62 and by Catulus in §63, viz. that the historical Cicero made unqualified knowledge in public settings in connection to the conspiracy of Catiline, the Cicero character gives the impression that the historical Cicero was entitled to them.

The Cicero character's desire to find the truth, on which see also *Luc.* 7b–9a (itself part of the 'frame'), requires further comment. In the following paragraphs, as is

---

statement in §10 quoted above (*praeclaram uero causam ad me defertis, cum me improbitatis patrocinium suscipere uultis*); in *N.D.* 3.95 the Academic Cotta states that he has merely discussed a set of views and is happy to be defeated with respect to them (*ego uero et opto redargui me...et facile me a te uinci posse certo scio*); in *Tusc.* 3.46 the speaker expresses happiness in the event of being be defeated by the truth, but the context is an exposition of aspects of Epicurean doctrine (*cupio refelli: quid enim laboro, nisi ut ueritas in omni quaestione explicetur?*); *Tusc.* 3.51, from the same section, verbalizes a similar happiness to cede to those who speak the truth, should they be forthcoming (*uerum dicentibus facile cedam*).

[252] See section 8.
[253] Noted by Griffin (1997: 10–11 n. 40).

widely recognized, the speaker is very clear on the position he adopts: it is a position of radical scepticism associated with Clitomachus' interpretation of Carneades, not a position of mitigated scepticism as claimed for the Catuli (father and son) in §148.[254] In the proem of N.D. (1.11), i.e. in the framing section of another dialogue, Cicero refers to *Acad.* as giving the rationale for his philosophical stance and states that Academics speak on either side of every question in order to find the truth. Thus N.D. 1.11 would appear to confirm the connection of the commitment to finding the truth with the particular stance Cicero adopts in *Luc.* (in the frame and as a character). This in turn seems to preclude a stance which aims solely at the refutation of views endorsed by an opponent, either from premises held in a negatively dogmatic way (e.g. 'nothing can be known') or from premises held by the opponent which the Academic adopts for the sake of the argument. Such a stance is, however, associated with radical Academic scepticism by some ancient sources as well as some modern scholars.[255] This should not lead us to conclude that radical scepticism so conceived did not exist, but it does suggest that radical scepticism ought to be construed as admitting of richer and less rich conceptions, with the former showing many of the hallmarks associated with what is conventionally called mitigated scepticism, and that Cicero's Clitomacheanism is in that sense 'rich'.

In what way a Clitomachean might claim to be searching for the truth will be pursued further in the commentary on §§66–8.[256] Here I note that the present passage, and in general Cicero's aspiration to search for the truth as a Clitomachean, seem at variance with Sextus' famous division, in *P.H.* 1.1–4, of philosophers into dogmatists ('Aristotle, Epicurus, the Stoics'), negative dogmatists ('those who declare matters to be inapprehensible, like Clitomachus, Carneades, and the other Academics'), and sceptics ('who keep on searching', i.e. the Pyrrhonists). Striker (2001) argues that the division is best viewed as a piece of philosophical polemic, that the self-identification of the Pyrrhonists as 'searchers' may in fact be the result of an appropriation of an Academic self-characterization, and that the actual argumentative practices of Academics and Pyrrhonists warrant calling the former 'searchers' rather than the latter; on the relationship between Academic scepticism and Pyrrhonism, see also section 7.5. Why Sextus described Clitomachus as someone who declares matters to be inapprehensible, when the Clitomachean position is characterized by the rejection of assent, will be discussed elsewhere; see on §§66, 104, section 8, as well as the discussion of passages assembled in appendix 1.

---

[254] See also on *Luc.* 78, seen by some as evidence for mitigated scepticism within the Academy; section 4.

[255] Cf. e.g. Chrysippus on the destructive nature of Academic scepticism in Plut., *Sto. rep.* 1035f–1036a (= SVF ii.127 = LS 31P, 1–2; text 2 in appendix 1), with Görler (1994: 805), as well as Lucullus in his speech in *Luc.*; and some modern representatives of the purely dialectical interpretation of Arcesilaus and Carneades, including Couissin (1929); Striker (1996b); Frede (1987b); and Long and Sedley (i.1987: 446–8), who, however, should not be taken to regard *Cicero* as a radical sceptic in this sense. Moreover, whether or not someone who argues in a purely ad hominem manner aims only at refutation depends on whether meta-philosophical considerations are deemed to motivate the dialectical practice, and on their exact nature.

[256] See also on §§7b–9a and §§77–8.

Ego enim si aut ostentatione aliqua adductus...mores et naturam condemnandam puto: *ostentatio* is behaviour that is 'put on', and which does not reflect the real person and his convictions; cf. its pairing with *simulatio* in *Off.* 2.43 in the pursuit of *ficta* rather than *uera gloria* (see also Dyck 1996: 424 ad loc.), or *De orat.* 2.333 where the proper conduct during senate meetings is at issue (a display of one's *ingenium* is frowned upon). See Corbeill (2004: 132) on the uses of the term in Cicero's speeches and philosophical writings more generally, and Hellegouarc'h (1972: 376 n. 5) on its use in late Republican political discourse.

For *studium certandi* (φιλονεικία) as misguided motivation, see the passages collected by Reid[1] (pp. 156–7) on *Ac.* 1.44 *non pertinaciā* (where the text continues *aut studio uincendi*), who lists accusations against Socrates in Platonic dialogues, charges against interlocutors in other works by Cicero, as well as accusations against the Academics in *Acad.* For the use of *ego enim*, see *OLD* s.v. *enim*, no. 7b.

Nam si in minimis rebus pertinacia reprehenditur...aut frustrari cum alios tum etiam me ipsum uelim: for *pertinacia*, see the previous n. Reid[1] (p. 253) rightly comments that the legal sense of 'slander' is present in *calumnia*; it is evoked by *coercetur*, which suggests legal redress. Cicero urges that, given societal disapproval of stubbornness and even more so of slander, and the importance of the issue, it is implausible to suggest that he would seek a conflict for nothing or indeed delude himself. Schäublin (1993: 158–9) notes that *uelim* ought to be potential rather than dubitative subjunctive, and that the absence of an interrogative is peculiar. He thus inserts *cur* before *ego de omni statu* (*ego* is an emendation for the stemmatically transmitted *ergo*). In Suet., *Gramm.* 14.3, *ego* is likely corrupted to *ergo* after preceding *cur* (*cuR ego* ⟩ *cuR eRgo*); cf. Kaster (1992: 88).

Itaque, nisi ineptum putarem in tali disputatione id facere...me et ardere studio ueri reperiendi et ea sentire quae dicerem: *ineptum* signals lack of suitability or appropriateness for the context. Reid[1] (pp. 253–4) plausibly suggests that Cicero is referring to a particular situation: in the year of Cicero's consulship (63 BC), Q. Caecilius Metellus Nepos became *tribunus plebis* in December and denied Cicero as outgoing consul the traditional final speech before the people, during which the consul would review his year in office and defend his record. Instead, he only allowed Cicero to take the usual oath 'that he had not acted against the laws' (cf. Plin., *Paneg.* 65: *et abiturus consulatu iurasti te nihil contra leges fecisse*; Cass. Dio. 53.1; see Mommsen 1876: 606 n. 2). Cicero responded by making an addition to the conventional phrase, viz. that he had saved the Republic (*Fam.* 5.2.7 = SB 2, addressed to Metellus Celer, the tribune's brother; *Att.* 6.1.22 = SB 115, responding to a letter by Atticus sent on the anniversary of the oath; cf. *Pis.* 3); in reply, the people swore that he had sworn the truth. In §62 Lucullus had alluded to the Catilinarian conspiracy, in a manner which was joking in tone but intended to be close to the bone, and Catulus in §63 had resumed both the topic and the ambiguous tone. By the same token, the character Cicero is striving to sound urbane here, but conveys profound seriousness about his views at the same time. This would presumably mean that his avowed endorsements in that context arose from carefully considered approval (see on *Luc.* 104), clothed in conventional parlance, rather than that they were instances of rash assent, i.e. opining.

The force of *sentire* raises a question in a context in which types of belief, degrees of endorsement, and differences of epistemic commitment are among the very subjects at issue. Given that this is the very beginning of Cicero's exposition, and that *sentire* is not used as a technical term in *Acad.* to denote a particular conception of belief, it seems best to take this as signalling 'I mean what I say' in a non-terminological, pre-theoretical sense. *Quae dicerem* is the result of attraction (= *quae nunc dico*), as Reid[1] (p. 254) notes.

§§66–67

§65 ended, if in *praeteritio*, with an oath affirming Cicero's commitment to search for the truth (as opposed to, say, ostentation or pointless belligerence) as the rationale for Cicero's (and the Academy's) argumentative practice. *Enim* in the rhetorical question which opens §66 links back to the 'oath': given that Cicero is glad when he finds something that is *simile ueri*, how could he not desire to find the truth? This is of course a reference to the Carneadean πιθανόν, which Cicero qua Clitomachean uses for the conduct of everyday life and also in the evaluation of philosophical doctrines.[257] The term *simile ueri* (rather than *probabile*) is used to make the a fortiori argument work which is implied by the rhetorical question (this is also the reason for the inverted word order of the phrasal term), but Cicero also seems to be implicitly rejecting arguments that the Academics are not entitled to the notion of a *ueri simile* given that they dispute the existence of impressions which cannot be false and are thus in no position to identify a class of impressions which are truth-like.[258] If Cicero was adopting here the position of a radical sceptic who purely argues ad hominem, he could say that he does not need to endorse the notion of a true impression as long as his opponent does, and that he can introduce truth-like impressions as something his dogmatic opponents should (and do, in certain contexts) accept by their own standards of rationality. Yet this is not what he does, which sheds further light on the nature of his Clitomacheanism.[259]

The following sentence then explains what is at stake in advancing beyond the discovery of the *ueri simile*: being able to see the truth (the phrase *uera uidere* is capable of a number of readings, see n. below) is the most beautiful thing in Cicero's view. (The verb *iudicare* is not terminological in *Acad.* Thus Cicero is not using a term which signals assent or approval, or which marks his view as a *decretum*/δόγμα.) By contrast, the most shameful thing is to approve something false while taking it to be true. This is introduced as a factual statement, not as Cicero's judgement; by changing the expression Cicero signals not a different kind of commitment to the content of the main clause, but rather that both clauses express his view *and* are undisputed between him and Lucullus. For it is the Stoic view that the sage should only assent to cataleptic impressions and that assenting to non-cataleptic impressions is a sin.

---

[257] See sections 6 and 8; and on *Luc.* 32–6.
[258] The extant parts of *Acad.* do not contain an instance of this line of argument, but see Aug., *Contra Acad.* 3.18.40 (= t. 60), which is likely to draw on a lost part.
[259] Cf. also on *Luc.* 109–10, where Cicero claims *decreta* of a kind for the Academic sage; §60.

There follows a personal note of the Cicero character, a statement about him as opposed to the sage (Academic or Stoic): he does approve, he does assent, and he does (as a consequence) hold opinions (i.e. beliefs which arise from accepting non-cataleptic impressions as true). The context makes it plain that this is to be taken at face value: what Cicero claims for himself is what to the Stoics is the assent of the fool.[260] So in calling himself a *magnus opinator* Cicero is confessing to a human failing with regret, even though it has fairly been observed by Gawlick and Görler (1994: 1117) that the phrase itself does not obviously suggest this and that the exact nuance is hard to judge. I opt for disarming self-deprecation ('a right old opiner').[261]

I noted just above that the Cicero character agrees with the dogmatist that assent to what is not true or might not be true is shameful. If his scepticism was confined to ad hominem arguments against others, without any meta-philosophical convictions or intuitions underwriting or motivating this practice, then he should not see it as an epistemic failing to assent to what is or could be false. But even if he had such intuitions, they would not necessarily explain why it is a moral failure, rather than, or in addition to, an epistemic one, to assent in such circumstances. Pointing to similarities with the modern 'ethics of belief' debate,[262] Wynne (2018: 95–9) has made a connection with the Stoic view, discussed in *Off.* 1.13 and, chronologically closer to *Acad.*, *Fin.* 3.17–18, that human beings naturally aspire to finding the truth and obtaining truths, which makes it a betrayal of our rational nature to accept as true what is or what could be false. I regard it as more likely that the Clitomachean position was informed by and invoked Arcesilaus' stance (cf. *Ac.* 1.45: *... neque hoc quicquam esse turpius quam cognitioni et perceptioni assensionem approbationemque praecurrere*) and, at a further remove, points made by Socrates in Plato's dialogues (see the commentary on *Luc.* 148, where Plato, *Rep.* 506c is briefly discussed). Since giving self-aware assent as permitted by mitigated sceptics is incompatible with a policy of universal ἐποχή (see again on §148), one can be reasonably certain that Cicero is here touching on a feature that was peculiar to Clitomacheanism.

The first part of the sentence beginning *ego uero ipse...* speaks to the Cicero character's actual practice of endorsement. The second part (from *et meas cogitationes*) speaks to the epistemic status of the impressions Cicero relies on, by means of an analogy from navigation and seafaring (note *et... et*). He ends with an acknowledgement of the limitations of his approach (*ut errem et uager latius*), which are a function of his

---

[260] One might wonder if assent is here intended to be dogmatic assent, i.e. assent in the Stoic sense, or the self-aware assent which the mitigated sceptic accepts (cf. *Luc.* 148), i.e. acceptance of an impression as true but with an awareness that one may be mistaken. Given the deep commitment of the Cicero character to the claim that nothing can be known, the larger context suggests the latter; §141 provides confirmation. This would not preclude that the Cicero character accepts things as true unqualifiedly on occasion, i.e. that he is momentarily unable to deploy suitable provisos. However, Academics, whether mitigated sceptics or Clitomacheans, are also committed to reviewing what beliefs and quasi-beliefs they hold (see sections 4 and 6), which makes it unlikely that momentarily dogmatic beliefs would remain such for long. See also the n. on §66: *pro ueris probare falsa* below.

[261] So also Wynne (2014: 256–7). Brittain (2016: 12–13) holds that the *magnus opinator* claim indicates that Cicero is torn between radical and mitigated scepticsm. There is no evidence that Cicero ever thought that something other than universal ἐποχή could be permitted as a matter of policy. However, already in *Inv.* 2.10 he seemed to hint at doubts about the achievability of complete suspension of judgement (*quoad facultas feret*).

[262] See further Clifford (1999), first published in 1877; and Chignell (2018).

opining and of the epistemic status of the impressions used (*errare* and *uagari* do not form a hendiadys). These limitations are, however, unavoidable in the Cicero character's view and ultimately negligible since he usually gets to where he wants to and thus ends up doing the right thing. Cicero caps the analogy by reiterating that the normal frame of reference for the debate with Lucullus is the sage (cf. §57).

The analogy itself contrasts the use of two different constellations for the purpose of navigation:[263] one is hard to make out but enables the sailor to steer a direct course to the intended destination (the Little Bear or *Cynosura*, preferred by the Phoenicians), while the other is easier to discern, but affords a less direct course (the Great Bear or *Septemtriones*, preferred by the Greeks). Cicero follows the latter. In a context in which (Clitomachean) scepticism is contrasted with the Stoic view, the two constellations are best taken to stand for the cataleptic impression and the πιθανόν respectively.[264] This is also suggested by the fact that Zeno of Citium, who first devised the doctrine of the cataleptic impression, was reportedly of Phoenician descent.

This may be the extent of what the analogy is supposed to illustrate. However, there are grounds for thinking that it is meant to deliver a little more. Further points to note include: (i) the Little Bear must be understood to include the star which is crucial for navigation (the star closest to the celestial pole, i.e. the North Star), whereas the Great Bear can merely be used to work out either a general direction or where the North Star, itself not part of the constellation, is. I believe that this difference is used to symbolize the different ways in which Stoics and Academics construe privileged perceptual experiences (cataleptic impressions and πιθανά, or a subset of them, respectively), viz. experiencing an impression which contains in itself all relevant information vs experiencing one which is in fact part of a chain of interrelated impressions which need to be appreciated jointly; (ii) while there is a difference in effectiveness between the two constellations, both of them represent means of reaching one's destination which are superior to conceivable alternatives; (iii) given that Cicero introduces the analogy having just spoken about his all-too-human tendency to opine, one wonders if he wishes to convey that the clarity of persuasive impressions (*clarissimos Septemtriones*) helps explain this tendency; (iv) there is a view defended by some that Clitomacheans accord to persuasive impressions the status of psychological self-reports, whereas mitigated sceptics take them as evidence for states of affairs in the external world. I argue elsewhere (section 6) that the latter view was inherent in the Academic conception of the πιθανόν and capable of being actualized as soon as persuasive impressions were not exclusively cited ad hominem, and observe here only that the constellation which Cicero claims to use for guidance appears to represent useable evidence for a world outside of our own consciousness.

In *Visa enim ista…nec possum resistere*, if *ista* is taken to refer to the class of impressions corresponding to the *Septemtriones*,[265] Cicero invokes strikingness, a

---

[263] I provide more material on the analogy in the nn. below and discuss it in more detail in Reinhardt (forthcoming).

[264] A different interpretation is advanced by Görler (2016: 247–9): he argues that Cicero opts for 'lofty, far-reaching thoughts' ('erhabene, weitreichende Gedanken') rather than a safe, unambitious course which follows the shoreline. Yet navigating by the Little Bear does not involve the latter.

[265] Thus correctly Brittain (2006); contrast Schäublin et al. (p. 244 n. 196); and see n. below.

property of persuasive impressions other than clarity,[266] as the reason why he sometimes assents to them (despite his avowed commitment to suspension of judgement). *Accipere* must denote a form of endorsement below assent, given that assent is set apart as an occasional response (*interdum*). Yet when assenting, Cicero says, he does not apprehend, i.e. end up with a belief which cannot turn out to be false; for apprehension he regards as impossible (*arbitror* is another term which has no settled terminological force in *Acad.*). And once more he invokes his weakness qua non-sage: sometimes he cannot resist non-cataleptic impressions (but even the Academic sage has nothing better to go on).

After the digression on Cicero's behaviour qua non-sage (*Nec tamen ego is sum…uisis cedo nec possum resistere*), the speech returns to the sage (*Sapientis autem hanc censet…*), and to pronouncements made by Arcesilaus on him. The wider context, as I said, is a programmatic one, explaining and justifying Cicero's own stance as a Clitomachean among other things. This being so, the impression arises that Arcesilaus is employed as a figurehead for Clitomacheanism, who is invoked to create a lineage for a particular version of the Academic stance. Arcesilaus is said to take the view (*censet*), agreeing with Zeno (*Zenoni assentiens*), that the sage is uniquely capable to ensure that he is not caught out, to see to it that he is not deceived. That Cicero does not just aim to provide a piece of historical information but cites a view of continuing significance is suggested by the present tense of *censet* and the following general remark in his own voice that error and misguided assent are incompatible with sage's *grauitas*. The participle *assentiens*, used in the sense of 'agreeing' with a personal object, admits of more than one interpretation: it might indicate no more than that Arcesilaus accepts, for dialectical purposes and without endorsing it himself, a view of Zeno's; or it might mean that Zeno advanced a view with which Arcesilaus agreed either because he antecedently held it himself, or because he found it convincing on the spot. What follows in §67 (*Hanc conclusionem Arcesilaus…primum et secundum*) suggests that one of the latter options is what Cicero has in mind; this is in line with Cicero's account of Arcesilaus' response to Zeno in *Ac.* 1.44–6 (see ad loc.). Cicero continues with a rhetorical question that there is nothing to say about the sage's steadfastness (*firmitas*), for the sage, Lucullus concedes to Cicero (cf. §66 init.), holds no opinions. The easy shift between 'agreements' between Zeno and Arcesilaus on the one hand and Lucullus and Cicero on the other support the suggestion made above that Arcesilaus was invoked as a philosophical authority for Cicero's own stance. As to *firmitas*, this has been held to refer to the sage's ability to resist, i.e. not to assent to, persuasive impressions which are not cataleptic (Brittain 2006: 39). However, the use of cognate and semantically similar terms in *Acad.* suggests that *firmitas* is the disposition of the sage which makes his (invariably true) beliefs unshakeable by argument (see n. below); this disposition is settled and invulnerable to argument because it is wholly consistent and includes no (false) opinions. The agreement between himself and Lucullus on the sage's foregoing of opinions leads into Cicero's invitation to consider the force of an argument 'back to front' (*praepostere*), i.e. without following the natural order of topics, or that suggested by Lucullus' speech.

---

[266] Cf. §66:…*acriter mentem sensumue pepulerunt*.

The argument, set out in §67 *init.*, is the corollary argument, which brings the conclusion of the core argument ('nothing is apprehensible' or 'there are no cataleptic impressions') to bear on the view that the sage will not opine:

(i) Si ulli rei sapiens assentietur umquam, aliquando etiam opinabitur.
(ii) Numquam autem opinabitur.
(iii) Nulli igitur rei assentietur.

This way of formulating the argument only yields the conclusion if ἀκαταληψία is assumed, e.g. because has been antecedently established by the core argument. Yet Cicero does not spell this out immediately and only touches on it at the end of the paragraph. This suggests what is plausible on independent grounds anyway, that not just the core argument but also the corollary argument featured already in the *Catulus* and that Cicero highlights rather than introduces the latter here. Contrast the way in which the same argument is introduced in Sextus' survey of epistemological views, in the section on Arcesilaus (*M.* 7.156-7), and specifically the way in which ἀκαταληψία is repeatedly referred to:

> Πάντων ὄντων ἀκαταλήπτων διὰ τὴν ἀνυπαρξίαν τοῦ Στωικοῦ κριτηρίου, εἰ συγκαταθήσεται ὁ σοφός, δοξάσει ὁ σοφός· μηδενὸς γὰρ ὄντος καταληπτοῦ εἰ συγκατατίθεταί τινι, τῷ ἀκαταλήπτῳ συγκαταθήσεται, ἡ δὲ τῷ ἀκαταλήπτῳ συγκατάθεσις δόξα ἐστίν. ὥστε εἰ τῶν συγκατατιθεμένων ἐστὶν ὁ σοφός, τῶν δοξαστικῶν ἔσται ὁ σοφός. οὐχὶ δέ γε τῶν δοξαστικῶν ἐστιν ὁ σοφός (τοῦτο γὰρ ἀφροσύνης ἦν κατ' αὐτούς, καὶ τῶν ἁμαρτημάτων αἴτιον)· οὐκ ἄρα τῶν συγκατατιθεμένων ἐστὶν ὁ σοφός.

> Given that everything is incognitive, owing to the non-existence of the Stoic criterion, then if the wise person assents, the wise person will hold opinions. For given that nothing is cognitive, if he assents to anything, he will assent to the incognitive, and assent to the incognitive is opinion. So if the wise person is among those who assent, the wise person will be among those who hold opinions. But the wise person is certainly not among those who hold opinions (for they [sc. the Stoics] claim this to be a mark of folly and a cause of wrongdoing). Therefore the wise person is not among those who assent. (transl. Schofield 1999: 326)

Because he endorsed (*confirmabat*) premises (i) and (ii), Arcesilaus is said to have 'approved' (*probabat*) *hanc conclusionem*, i.e. not the conclusion (iii) *pace* Schäublin, but the entire argument (cf. §66 *fin.*: *haec... conclusio*); thus Brittain (2006: 40). This means that Cicero is assuming that Arcesilaus approved the core argument, too, without which the corollary argument does not lead to its conclusion, which in turn shows that Arcesilaus is not construed by Cicero as someone who advanced the core and corollary arguments without endorsing them himself, relying on actual endorsement of the argument by the Stoics or on endorsement which the Stoics ought to provide, given their own standards of rationality.[267] Further, as noted above,

---

[267] Thus also Castagnoli (2019: 195).

Arcesilaus appears to serve as a figurehead for Clitomacheanism, without it being plain so far how exactly Cicero would conceptualize the differences between Arcesilaus' stance and his own, beyond the obvious fact that Arcesilaus did not have the Carneadean πιθανόν at his disposal (*Acad.* makes no reference to Arcesilaus' εὔλογον, and Cicero shows no awareness of it elsewhere),[268] and what the nature of the endorsement is. If, as is reasonable to assume, Cicero construes the Clitomachean position in a way which also involves some kind of endorsement of the core and corollary arguments, then Antiochian counterarguments like those advanced in *Luc.* 43–4, which only make sense if the opposite side endorses the core argument to some degree and in some way, need not be directed at mitigated scepticism only. This, indeed, makes sense, given that mitigated scepticism is a view of secondary importance in *Acad.* Cicero will offer his own view in §68.

Cicero then reports on Carneades. He 'gave' (*dabat*—a term which offers no indication of whether the premiss was provided for the sake of the argument or because it was Carneades' view; see n. below) as second premiss (*secundum*) the antecedent of the conditional which serves as the first premiss. Thus the consequent follows: the sage will sometimes opine, which Antiochus and the Stoics reject (and Cicero as a Clitomachean agrees). He adds that the first premiss of the corollary argument is held to be false by the Stoics and Antiochus, since it is predicated on ἀπαραλλαξία obtaining: for the sage, according to the Stoics and Antiochus, is able to distinguish true and false impressions, as well as cataleptic and non-cataleptic ones.

§66

Qui enim possum non cupere uerum inuenire...si simile ueri quid inuenerim: *possum* has present subjunctive sense as usual (Kühner-Stegmann i.171); *cum* is causal. By *simile ueri* Cicero means the Carneadean πιθανόν, but the term *probabile* would have obscured the argument; the inverted word order, which emphasizes *simile*, facilitates the a fortiori reasoning. It has been suggested by some (Glucker 1995: 126–7; Obdrzalek 2006: 269–71) that the occurrence of the term *ueri simile* in Cicero points to Philo using εἰκός for a particular conception of the πιθανόν, who, however, acknowledge that there is no evidence for this in the Greek record; yet Sextus says that persuasive impressions 'appear true' (e.g. *M.* 7.169: (φαντασία) φαινομένη ἀληθής), and the distribution of the term *ueri simile* in Cicero discourages a particular Philonian conception of the πιθανόν behind it, too; see also section 6. No domain restriction (e.g. to perceptual impressions) is given here, and Cicero seems to be speaking generally. For the antisceptical argument that recognition of the truth-like presupposes a grasp of the true, which is possibly alluded to here, see on Aug., *Contra Acad.* 3.18.40 (= t. 60).

Sed ut hoc pulcherrimum esse iudico...pro ueris probare falsa turpissimum est: *uera uidere* is (innocuously) ambiguous between 'seeing something (sc. in the world) which is the case' and 'having a perceptual or visual thought which is true, i.e.

---

[268] See section 7.5.

represents correctly a state of affairs in the world'. (See Reinhardt 2016 on the different uses of *uidere* in *Acad*.) For the kind of meta-philosophical commitments which make seeing the truth beautiful, see the general note above; Wynne (2018: 100 n. 17). With the main clause, cf. *Ac*. 1.45: (*Arcesilaus censet*)... *neque hoc quicquam esse turpius quam cognitioni et perceptioni assensionem approbationemque praecurrere*, and the n. on *sapientis autem hanc censet Arcesilas uim* below. Cicero signals common ground between himself qua Clitomachean and the Stoics here; a mitigated sceptic would allow for assent to the non-cataleptic, provided the subject was aware that what was being assented to could be false (cf. *Luc*. 148), and such assent would not be shameful if it turned out that it had been given to a false impression. *Pro ueris probare falsa* means 'to approve false things as if they were true' (*OLD* s.v. *pro* no. 9c), not 'to approve false things in place of true things' (*OLD* s.v. *pro* no. 6a), as Thorsrud (2012: 148 n. 4) notes. The correction *iudico* was made by Ernesti; Plasberg[1] prints the transmitted *iudicem* and adds in support of it: '...sed nescio an subaudiatur *si uideam*.'

Nec tamen ego is sum...sed quaerimus de sapiente: for *tamen* preceded by a copulative or adversative particle, see *OLD* s.v. no. 2b. 'Approval' in the technical sense (cf. *Luc*. 104) is available to Cicero and indeed to the sage as construed by Clitomachus, and it does not result in 'opinion' (which is assent to the non-cataleptic). So *approbare* cannot be the technical term here and means, like *probare* in the previous sentence, acceptance in some looser sense; *assentiar* would then appear to specify the kind of endorsement at issue with more precision. The point is that Cicero is prone to accept impressions, even to assent to them, and to end up with an opinion; see also the general note above. He does not here, at the beginning of his speech, enter into the rather fine-grained distinctions between different types of acceptance, which would also obscure the point of the constellation analogy which follows. Cicero's opinions are plainly marked as those of someone who is not wise, as per the Stoic framework; a mitigated sceptic would claim opinions for the sage, with the proviso that the sage was aware that his opinions might be false. Thorsrud (2012: 140-1) thinks that Cicero was a mitigated sceptic, and that his view was that Stoic sages do not hold opinions, while real-life sages do; however, in the present context, Cicero does not cast himself as a real-life sage, and opining is not associated with sagehood. On the Academic sage see Neuhausen (1987).

Ego uero ipse et magnus quidam sum opinator...sed de sapiente quaeritur: through *et...et* the sentence speaks first to the issue of endorsement of impressions and then to the epistemic status of impressions; the latter is then illustrated by means of the navigation allegory. However, while the part of the sentence concerned with endorsement describes what the Cicero character sees as a human failing, viz. his habit of assenting which runs counter to his avowed position (formulated with reference to the figure of the sage), the second part of the sentence from *et meas cogitationes* is not so qualified: an Academic of any particular persuasion could so characterize the impressions they endorse in some way, including 'Academic sages'.

I have given my reading of the tone of the *magnus opinator* claim in the general note above. That the term *opinator* has a technical sense offers little help: it denotes an official charged with the evaluation and collection of corn contributions to be made by farmers (cf. *TLL* s.v. col. 713.49–78; Landgraf 1896: 405; Lammert 1939). Given the date of the evidence, Cicero more likely coined the term here rather than appropriated it. Its 'Ciceronian' use did not catch on in extant texts which are known to have drawn on Cicero, but Augustine writes in *Contra Acad.* 3.14.31 (= t. 28): *Clamat Cicero se ipsum magnum esse opinatorem, sed de sapiente se quaerere.* This shows the continuity on this point between the first and final edition of *Acad. Clamat* might gesture at the perceived confessional mode of Cicero's statement or could just mean 'proclaim, state plainly' (cf. *OLD* s.v. *clamo* no. 5a). *Magnus* is perhaps best taken to hint at frequency, though as an attribute modifying nouns in -*tor* it can of course convey other nuances, too; cf. e.g. Plaut., *Menaechm.* 268 (*magnus amator*); Cic., *Brut.* 32 (*magnus orator*); Sen., *Ben.* 7.1.4 (*magnus luctator*); Sen., *Ep. mor.* 30.3 (*magnus gubernator*).

The obvious Greek counterpart of *opinator* is δοξαστής, in itself not a frequently used term, and there is one particularly striking occurrence of it in Plt., *Tht.* 208e5 (the wider context there must have played some role in the formulation of the definition of the cataleptic impression; see on *Ac.* 1.30–2 and Reinhardt 2018: 46–8 and 62–3): Socrates says that he who, in addition to having a correct judgement about a thing, grasps its difference from the rest, has become an ἐπιστήμων of the thing when he was a δοξαστής before. Cicero's constellation analogy which follows immediately seems to contrast the use of the cataleptic and persuasive impressions respectively; this would map onto the difference between ἐπιστήμων and δοξαστής.

Cicero says that following, metaphorically speaking, the *Septemtriones* rather than the *Cynosura* guides his *cogitationes*. At the very least, the latter term suggests that he is not just talking about perceptual impressions: thought or decision-making processes of some kind are meant. It is likely that Cicero did not just have practical deliberations in mind but also evaluations of philosophical doctrines; the latter do certainly occur in the body of his speech. Cf. also e.g. *Off.* 1.19: *omnis...cogitatio motusque animi...in consiliis capiendis de rebus honestis...uersabitur;* 1.132: *cogitatio in uero exquirendo maxime uersatur; Tusc.* 1.6. On *dirigo*, Reid[1] (p. 254) aptly cites Sen., *Ep. mor.* 95.45:*...finem summi boni ad quem nitamur, ad quem omne factum nostrum dictumque respiciat; ueluti nauigantibus ad aliquod sidus dirigendus est cursus.* In addition *cogitationes* may hint at the self-reflective attitude Academics think one should adopt with respect to one's impressions.

On the Greek and Latin terms used for the Little Bear (*Cynosura, Ursa minor, Arctus minor,* Κυνόσουρα, Ἄρκτος μικρά, Φοινίκη) and for the Great Bear (*Septemtriones, Arctus maior,* Ἄρκτος μεγάλη, Ἄμαξα, Ἑλίκη), see Le Boeuffle (1977: 90–2 and 82–9); Bishop (2016: 162–5). The two quotations come from Cicero's translation of Aratus' Φαινόμενα, which are cited with their context in *N.D.* 2.106 (= frg. 7 Soubiran) in the course of an argument that the well-orderedness of the universe, observable in the night sky, supports a providential, Stoic conception of god. Cicero has adjusted both lines at the beginning to fit them into his sentence, and the relative pronouns stand in place of *haec* and *nam*, respectively. That the two constellations were used by Phoenicians and Greeks respectively was a τόπος; see Callimachus, frg. 191, ll. 52–5 Pfeiffer (= D.L. 1.23), whose 'source' is assumed to have been Maiandrios of Miletus (492F18 *FGrHist*). In Latin literature, cf. e.g. Manil. 1.299–302; Sen., *Med.*

694-9, which makes reference to another constellation in the area, *Draco*; Lucan, 8.165-92, with Tracy (2010). For Zeno of Citium being of Phoenician descent, cf. Cic., *Fin.* 4.56 *tuus ille Poenulus*, with Franko (1994: 155 n. 11) and Brunschwig (2002: 14-16), D.L. 7.1-3; this facilitates the association of *Cynosura* and the cataleptic impression.

Today navigation by means of either constellation in the northern hemisphere crucially involves the North Star (Polaris). Since it is very close to the celestial pole and thus does not appear to rotate around it, it can be used to identify north and consequently other directions. How high it stands in the sky gives an indication of latitude, although this is less noticeable in the Mediterranean where the distances involved are fairly short. Longitude is famously difficult to determine using the stars alone. The Little Bear and the Great Bear help with finding Polaris in different ways: Polaris is part of the Little Bear, located at the end of its 'handle', so in identifying the Little Bear, one finds Polaris; however, as the ancient poetic trope says, the Little Bear is not very bright. The Great Bear is used by identifying the constellation as a whole, then focusing on the two stars which form the back of the wagon (Merak and Dubhe, or *Beta Ursae Maioris* and *Alpha Ursae Maioris*, respectively), and extending an imaginary line through them; Polaris is located along this line, at about five times the distance between Merak and Dubhe. One will have gone too far if one reaches the constellation *Cassiopeia*. A useful source of information on such matters is the *Nautical Almanac*, published annually in the United Kingdom by HM Nautical Almanac Office since 1767.

In the Hellenistic period, thanks to axial precession, Polaris was not the star within the Little Bear which was closest to the celestial pole. Instead, it was Kochab (Beta Ursae Minoris, β UMi, β Ursae Minoris), another star in the Little Bear. It is most likely this star which was named as the north star by Eudoxus of Cnidus; others disagreed. See Le Boeuffle (1997: 92-3). Kochab is probably the star to which the noun *axis* refers in Lucan 8.175; that *axis* there refers to a star (rather than the pole, *pace* Housman 1926: 277) is suggested by its attribute *clarissimus* (and by line 170). See also *OLD* s.v. *axis*[1] no. 4.

Failure in the attempt to use the Little Bear would arise from not identifying or misidentifying the entire constellation since finding it and consequently the North Star is hard to begin with. The Great Bear is a less reliable guide to one's destination, but misusing it is harder.

As indicated above, I believe that Cicero's purpose was to fill the poetic motif with additional, philosophical content. Against the foundationalist convictions of the Stoics, according to which a cataleptic impression is a self-contained item whose content represents the object uniquely, thus making the impression self-warranting and supremely persuasive, the Academics argued that an impression is always one element in an endless chain of impressions, which jointly account for the persuasiveness of the impression. Sextus explains, in his report on Carneades' views on the criterion (*M.* 7.166-89), that, just as a doctor makes a diagnosis on the basis of a concurrence (a 'syndrome') of symptoms (*M.* 7.175-82), so any perceiving subject holds that this is e.g. Socrates on the basis of a series of interconnected impressions which each have another feature—by itself, not uniquely—associated with Socrates as its subject. One of the terms Lucullus uses for the Academic practice of scrutinizing impressions—*consideratio* in *Luc.* 36—was etymologized in antiquity as the metaphorical gathering together of particular stars which make up a constellation (*sidus*). It would appear that Cicero replaced Sextus' image of the syndrome with that of a constellation; see section 6.5. One might object that as per the analogy cataleptic impressions have coordinated impressions, too, viz. the stars other than Kochab in the Little Bear. One way of resolving this problem is by observing that cataleptic impressions may fail to win or retain assent if the perceiving subject's antecedent beliefs, which have arisen from impressions, are incompatible with them; see Sextus, *M.* 7.253 with Reinhardt (2018a: 241).

On *rationes has latiore specie, non ad tenue limatas*, the noun means most likely 'pattern' (cf. *OLD* s.v. *ratio* no. 13a), of the stars making up the Great Bear; Reid[1] (p. 255) wonders if Cicero wrote *latiores* but does not print it. For *specie* without an attribute as an ablative of respect, cf. §99: *specie probabile*. Manil. 1.300 comments on the smallness (not just faintness) of *Cynosura* compared to *Ursa maior*. *Limare* has its secondary meaning 'to explore' (cf. Nonius p. 333.36–7 M.: '*limare*' *exquirere et delenire secundum consuetudinem a lima* [*aliam*: codd.] *dictum*; Cic., *Off.* 2.35). *Ad tenue* is unparalleled but not objectionable, and Plasberg[1] (p. 102) cites similar expressions; the adjective means 'thin' not 'smooth', and the phrase refers to the point of arrival of the mental search for the North Star. *Errem*, in a passage rich in Stoic terminology, of rash assent (cf. *Ac.* 1.41). *Latius uagari* of the less direct path the Great Bear affords. Contrast Görler (2016: 248), who takes the two verbs to form a hendiadys. One might wonder if a temporal adverb like *interdum* should be expected with *errem*, but arguably the *eo fit ut* construction obviates the need for it. For further detail, see Reinhardt (forthcoming).

I adopt *quidam* (Manutius) for the transmitted *quidem*; as Plasberg[1] (p. 102) argues, for *quidem* to stand, one would either have to delete the preceding *et* or re-order to *sum opinator et magnus quidem* (both inferior in terms of sense). On *sed Helicen* rather than *sed ad Helicen* (as the corrector of A would have it), see Reid[1] (p. 254). Boot (1895: 211) proposed to delete *id est...eliminatas*.

Visa enim ista...nec possum resistere: this section still belongs to Cicero's personal remarks about how he himself operates. By *uisa...ista*, Cicero is referring to those impressions (corresponding to the *Septemtriones*) on which he does act and whose strikingness accounts for his acceptance of them, and even occasional assent to them—Cicero is still explaining why he is a *magnus opinator*. Schäublin et al. translate 'your impressions', on the grounds that impressions are a piece of Stoic doctrine which Academics need not necessarily accept (p. 244 n. 196); yet the Cicero character does accept impressions (cf. e.g. §105a). On the strikingness of cataleptic impressions (not at issue here), their being πληκτικός, see Lefebvre (2007) and Brittain (2014: 339). For *cedere* (εἴκειν), see Reid[1] (p. 224) on *Luc.* 38:...*sic animum perspicuis cedere*. Cicero must mean that he cannot invariably resist, not that he can never resist. On Cicero's uses of *mens*, here simply contrasted with 'the senses', see Brittain (2014: 128 n. 48).

Sapientis autem hanc censet Arcesilas uim...Quem quidem nihil opinari tu quoque, Luculle, concedis: the Cicero character makes three substantial references to Arcesilaus (here, in *Luc.* 77, and in *Ac.* 1.44–6); these are considered together in the introduction (section 7.5). In *Ac.* 1.44–6 Arcesilaus is credited with two views (of uncertain status), without a reference to Zeno: that nothing can be known and that one should not allow one's acceptance of views to outrun apprehension; one may thus wonder why Arcesilaus is here said to 'agree' with Zeno that the sage should not be tricked. Possible explanations include Cicero's different agendas in both passages (addressed in the introduction) and the fact that here the sage in particular is at issue. For the Stoic requirement that the sage be infallible, and how it was conceptualized, see on *Ac.* 1.40–2. For the different senses in which *temeritas* is employed in *Acad.*, see on *Luc.* 31; and more generally Lévy (2018).

There is a certain fullness of expression, as well as noticeable artistic intent, in what Cicero says: Reid[1] (p. 255) notes the chiasm in *cauere ne capiatur, ne fallatur uidere*, and the tricolon *errore leuitate temeritate* is striking, too (though it is partly functional, since the terms denote one-off mistakes, a lack of caution, and rashness). The Cicero character seems to be speaking here with feeling and setting out his personal commitments, even though the ostensible subject is Arcesilaus. See also on *Ac.* 1.40–2 for the Stoic conception of failure. On *firmitas*, which has been interpreted in different ways (see the general note above), cf. on *Ac.* 1.42 and *Luc.* 23:…*sapientiam*…*quae ipsa ex sese habeat constantiam*. Lucullus' commitment to the avoidance of opinion is a function of his overall position; *opinari* renders δοξάζειν (see e.g. the Chrysippean book title Ἀποδείξεις πρὸς τὸ μὴ δοξάζειν τὸν σοφόν α′ 'Proofs that the wise man will not have opinions, one book' in D.L. 7.201 = *SVF* ii.17).

Quod quoniam a te probatur…haec primum conclusio quam habeat uim considera: *praepostere* means 'the wrong way around' (of two alternatives) or 'in the wrong order' (see *OLD* s.v.), either because Cicero discusses the corollary argument before the core argument (discussion of the latter follows in §83), or because he does not follow the structure of Lucullus' speech (note that Cicero concludes §71 with *nunc ad ea quae a te, Luculle, dicta sunt*). The term *conclusio* refers to the whole argument.

§67

Si ulli rei sapiens assentietur umquam…nulli igitur rei assentietur: as indicated in the general note above, this is the first occurrence of the corollary argument in the extant parts of *Acad.*, but it is very likely to have featured in the *Catulus* already in the course of an outline on Academic strategy. This is also suggested by the fact that no reference is made to the conclusion of the core argument that nothing can be known, even though ἀκαταληψία needs to have been established for the argument in Cicero's formulation to go through; contrast the formulation in Sextus, *M.* 7.155–7, quoted above. Reid[1] (p. 256) suggests a common source for *M.* 7.155–7 and our passage, 'probably…Clitomachus'; I think the differences between the two passages are more remarkable than the similarities, though Reid may be right about the ultimate source. On the corollary argument see Brittain (2001: 13), Brittain (2006: xxii–xxiii and xxviii–xxx), Brittain (2008a: section 3.1); Striker (1996b: 109–10).

Assent at some unspecified point in the future will constitute opinion; hence future rather than future perfect in the protasis.

V has left a blank space of four and a half lines after *opinabitur* (f. 121 recto, 2nd column) and of the first four lines of the first column of f. 121 verso), but no text is missing. Plasberg[1] (p. 103) wanted to discuss it in the preface to the *editio maior* (which was never published), and Plasberg[2] makes no reference to it.

Hanc conclusionem Arcesilas probabat…et primum et secundum: *conclusio* is the entire argument (cf. §66 *fin.*: *haec…conclusio*); *primum* and *secundum* must here refer to the first and the second premiss. Whether or not *probabat* denotes approval in the technical sense discussed in §104, *confirmare* would not be a suitable term to denote mere advancement for the sake of the argument without some degree of commitment on Arcesilaus' part (cf. §78, where *disputare* is contrasted with *probare*), which in turn requires commitment to the core argument; see the commentary ad loc. and section 7.5. Thus also Castagnoli (2019: 195). This is consistent with the account Cicero gives of Arcesilaus in *Ac.* 1.44–6. *Confirmare* is also unlikely to have a connotation of 'to endorse after someone else', given the chronology of Arcesilaus and the fact that the Stoics are said to regard the first premiss as false at the end of the paragraph.

Carneades non numquam…et recte, ut mihi uideris: Carneades' alternative second premiss (*secundum* used as above) affirms the antecedent of the first premiss rather than to deny its consequent, thus using *modus ponens* rather than *modus tollens* and arriving at a different conclusion ('the sage will (sometimes) opine', as opposed to 'the sage will not assent to anything'). This second premiss is marked as introduced for the sake of the argument: *dabat* suggests a mere putting forward as opposed to 'confirmation' above, and this reading is encouraged by *non numquam* (a second premiss actually held by Carneades would need to be offered routinely). On the use of διδόναι in dialectical exchanges, see Reinhardt (2000: 66).

Some *recentiores* as well as editors delete *secundum* (see Reid[1] p. 256; Plasberg[1] p. 103), but it is well motivated by what precedes and secured by parallel passages. Schäublin (1992: 51–2) and Schäublin et al. (p. 88) inserted *opinari sed* after *non numquam*, an unnecessary clarification. See also Glucker (2004: 127); Ioppolo (2007: 240–1).

The different interpretations of the spirit in which the alternative second premiss was supplied by Carneades—for the sake of the argument or endorsed by qualified assent—are referenced in *Luc.* 59, 148, as well as 78, which, however, raises particular problems of interpretation (see ad loc.).

Sed illud primum…ab iis quae possint distinguere: the Stoics disputed, with reference to the sage, that assent invariably led to opinion in at least some instances, since they rejected the core argument and notably the claim of ἀπαραλλαξία. For them, the first premiss of the corollary argument was false, presumably, because the antecedent did not 'contain' the consequent; for this understanding of a conditional, see Sextus, *P.H.* 2.110–12 and Reinhardt (2018a: 229–30). With Antiochus as *Stoicorum adstipulator*, OLD s.v. no. 2 'one who supports an opinion' (the primary legal sense is 'accessory party to a promise'; Kaser 1971: 660), cf. *Luc.* 132: *germanissmus Stoicus*, 137: *Stoicus perpauca balbutiens*; and section 7.2 on Antiochus' Stoicism. Reid[1] (p. 256) rightly notes that with *opinaturum* one needs to understand *fuisse*, not *esse*. Cicero quite carefully distinguishes between the two types of impressions which are not cataleptic, false and incognitive ones. The reading *esse* ⟨*et*⟩ *Stoici* (ξ) may be correct. V²'s attempt to fill the lacuna in ξ (omission of *percipi ab iis quae possint*) is illuminating, in that it is an intelligent attempt at emendation which shows no sign of being influenced by input from a lost manuscript (let alone from F after correction); see Malaspina (2020: 272 n. 87) and the Oxford Classical Text, p. lxi.

§68

The section continues the account of Cicero's position in his speech, with particular reference to the issue of assent; it characterizes a posture that Cicero aspires to and to which he is rationally committed, as opposed to his actual practice as a non-sage who cannot help being a *magnus opinator* (cf. §66). While both the Stoic and the Academic sage are idealized reference points for a valorized set of attitudes and patterns of behaviour, Academics including Cicero are not on record saying that there are not and have never been actual sages.

I take *nobis* to contrast with the Stoics and Antiochus, since they were the last individuals named and the ability to distinguish cataleptic impressions from others was the last issue mentioned in §67 (the clause beginning *etiam si* introduces a—hypothetical—concession on this point).

Cicero notes that, even if there were cataleptic impressions, getting into the habit of assenting to them would be 'dangerous and slippery' (*periculosa...et lubrica*).[269] Once one gets into this habit, the chance of assenting to non-cataleptic impressions is increased. The emphasis on *consuetudo* may be linked to the Stoic assumption that the overwhelming majority of our impressions is cataleptic, so that a habit of assenting is a normal component of our cognitive behaviour. The attitude Cicero seeks to foster is one of habituated scrutiny of any impression experienced (which is the opposite of rash acceptance, cf. *ne praecipitet si temere processerit*).

As it is, Cicero holds that there are no cataleptic impressions, and he has the Stoics' and Antiochus' (and Lucullus') concession that the sage should not opine: hence the sage should suspend judgement universally. This, he continues, leaves Lucullus with a dilemma (clearly a rejoinder to the latter's deployment of that figure of argument in *Luc.* 43–4):[270] either to accept universal suspension of judgement for the sage or to accept that the sage will opine. He predicts that Lucullus will reject both options because he does not accept ἀκαταληψία, and so Cicero concludes that the dilemma which he has posed rests on ἀκαταληψία obtaining. Thus the entire debate is about this question.

On this point Cicero would have been in complete agreement with Arcesilaus, for all we know about him and as Cicero construes him.

---

[269] As Brittain (2006: 40 n. 92) notes, this is a veiled threat of a sorites argument against assent; cf. §92:...*ad soritas, lubricum sane et periculosum locum.* I shall discuss in the commentary on §92 how exactly such a sorites would be mounted. It is not obvious that the threat would have been recognizable in its specificity for a contemporary reader at this point.

[270] As is shown by the extant works of Sextus, the dilemma is very much a sceptical device: Cicero is reclaiming it.

Nobis autem primum...periculosa esse uidetur et lubrica: that cataleptic impressions are a frequent phenomenon according to the Stoics and that they usually attract assent (which is required for them to play the role accorded to them in human life according to the Stoics) emerges e.g. from §§19–26 of Lucullus' speech; see also Brittain (2014). Cf. §92:...*ad soritas, lubricum sane et periculosum locum*. Reid[1] (p. 256) notes *primum* without *deinde*.

Quam ob rem...si temere processerit: Cicero once again distinguishes carefully between assent to what is false and assent to what is incognitive (cf. §67 *fin*.). The injunction to avoid falling headlong (*praecipitare*), which is a metaphor for allowing assent to outrun the required quality of the impression assented to (cf. *Ac*. 1.45: *neque hoc quicquam esse turpius quam cognitioni et perceptioni assensionem approbationemque praecurrere*), corresponds to the requirement for ἀπροπτωσία (ἐπιστήμη τοῦ πότε δεῖ συγκατατίθεσθαι καὶ μή, 'knowledge of when to assent and when not' in D.L. 7.46 = *SVF* ii.130; διάθεσις ἀσυγκατάθετος πρὸ καταλήψεως, 'a disposition not prone to assent before apprehension' in *P.Herc.* 1020 = *SVF* ii.131; and on *Ac*. 1.42b). For *temere*, cf. on *temeritas* in §31. Reid[1] (p. 256) explains *quicquam* as similar to *nihil* with *assentati* in *Luc*. 45 (and observes that it is used instead of *aliquid* because *uitiosum* creates a negative context); Plasberg[1] (p. 103) views the accusative as an object in a construction analogous to that of *approbare*. On *ne praecipitet si* my apparatus offers a summary account; Plasberg[1] (pp. 103–4) gives more detail.

Ita enim finitima sunt falsa ueris...non debeat se sapiens committere: Cicero is arguing here from within the Stoic position, as he makes clear in the parenthesis: the Stoics themselves ought to see his point. The adjective *finitima* may be spatial in sense: in §§93–4 Chrysippus is asked how he would deal with a series of impressions (whose propositional content involves a vague predicate) which at one point features a cataleptic impression right next to a false one. With the phrase *in praecipitem locum*, cf. of course the English expression 'slippery slope', apparently not attested before the nineteenth century; *praeceps locus* not of an argument e.g. Sen., *Troad*. 1110.

The insertion of *iis quae possunt* (Lambinus), compelling given the parenthesis, heals a lacuna due to a *saut du même au même*. See Reid[1] (p. 257) on the word order of *tam in praecipitem*. See Plasberg[1] (p. 104) on *iam enim uidebimus* in A.

Sin autem omnino nihil esse quod percipi possit...an aliquid opinaturum esse sapientem: for *a me sumpsero* Reid[1] (p. 257) plausibly refers to expressions like *ab aliquo sumere (dare, soluere) pecuniam* for comparison (§23 *ex sese habeat* is quite different). These would suggest that Cicero has something stronger in mind than the mere supplying of a premiss for argumentative purposes and without endorsement. Rather, the implication is that a premiss that is in some sense owned by Cicero is supplied. This would be consistent with the notion that, like Arcesilaus, Cicero approves the core argument. *Mihi das* marks a concession, made because Lucullus endorses the premiss (whereas *secundum illud dabat* in §67 just means the introduction of a premiss without endorsement by Carneades).

'Neutrum', inquies 'illorum'...omnis est controuersia: the dilemma and the shared assumption allows Cicero to focus on the single issue of whether something can be known (cf. §78 *init*. on whether the third clause of Zeno's definition obtains: *haec est una contentio quae adhuc permanserit*). However, various other issues intrude, notably historical ones, in the immediately following sections. Given that it is in B and V, the duplication of *nitamur* must have been in the archetype. For the use of *nitor*, see *OLD* s.v. no. 9: 'to strive in argument; (w. acc. and inf.) to endeavour to prove, contend (that)', and the fine note in Reid[1] (p. 257).

§§69–71

§§69–71 are devoted to Antiochus and a key source of information on several central aspects of his life, notably his break with the sceptical Academy and his adoption of Stoic epistemology.[271] Within Cicero's speech, the section serves, in line with the conventions of forensic oratory, to cast doubt on the credentials and motivation of the opposing side:[272] Antiochus' *inconstantia* diminishes his *auctoritas* while Lucullus' character is unassailable (note the distinction implied in §69 *init.*: *prius pauca cum Antiocho* and §71 *fin.*: *nunc ad ea quae a te, Luculle, dicta sunt*).

D.L. offers no biography of Antiochus (his account of the Academic succession ends with Clitomachus in 4.67). There is a section on Antiochus in Philodemus' *Index Acad.* (col. xxxiv.34–xxxv.16), but of the biographical part only the section on the end of his life is preserved.[273] There are also some pertinent remarks in Plutarch's biographies of Cicero (*Cic.* 4.1–2) and Lucullus (*Luc.* 42.3–4).

Antiochus' date of birth of approximately 130 BC is reconstructed on the basis of information on his philosophical teachers (see below).[274] He is assumed to have died in 68 or 67, on the grounds that he is said to have accompanied Lucullus in the East (Cic., *Luc.* 4), that in a work of his he made reference to Lucullus' defeat of Tigranes in the battle of Tigranocerta in 69 (Plut., *Luc.* 28.8), which is usually taken to refer to first-hand experience, and that the *Index Acad.* states that he died 'in Mesopotamia in the service of Lucullus' (col. xxxiv.39–42; cf. Cic., *Luc.* 61); Lucullus was replaced in 67 and returned to Rome in 66. In 79 Antiochus lectured in the Ptolemaeum, a public gymnasium in Athens, where Cicero, Atticus, and Quintus Cicero heard him (Cic., *Fin.* 5.1; *Brut.* 315).[275]

Political turmoil due to the Romans' war against Mithridates caused Philo to leave Athens for Rome in 88, along with other members of the Academy. The scene in

---

[271] Important discussions include Glucker (1978: 15–21); Görler (1994: 941–2); Barnes (1997: 68–70); Tarrant (2007); Hatzimichali (2012); Polito (2012); see also Brittain (2001: 55–6); Lévy (2010: 91); Bonazzi (2020: 251–4); Tarrant (2020: 215 n. 50). *Luc.* 69–71 is part of F5 Mette for both Philo and Antiochus; see also the translations of testimonia on both philosophers in Brittain (2001: 351–2) and Sedley (2012c: 342). A new edition of Philod. *Index Acad.* by Kilian Fleischer is forthcoming.

[272] See e.g. Stroh (1975: 250–62).

[273] See the modern editions by Dorandi (1991) and Blank (2007); Blank's latest thinking on the text is reflected in Sedley (2012c: 335–6); see also Fleischer (2015).

[274] Cf. also the commentary on *Luc.* 1–4, concerned with Lucullus' biography.

[275] We do not know when exactly Antiochus returned to Athens; see Hatzimichali (2012: 25).

Alexandria in which Antiochus received a copy of Philo's Roman Books (*Luc.* 11–12) must be dated to 87. We do not know if Antiochus had left for Rome, too, when Philo and other Academics, as well as pro-Roman Athenians, left Athens, but soon moved on to Alexandria, or whether he moved directly to Alexandria. The latter is much more likely.

There is a view, articulated by Polito (2012), that Antiochus set up his 'Old Academy' only after the end of the Academy as an institution in 88 BC (so that there was no longer an institution from which he could secede, and no competition with the Academy proper), and that he formally departed from scepticism only at a late stage, too. While I shall be arguing that this view does not provide the most natural explanation of the evidence, and offer a version of the majority opinion that Antiochus left the Academy in the 90s, possibly after a period of dissatisfaction with Academic scepticism rather than overt rejection of it, Polito's argument involves making a number of salutary points about spots of vagueness or ambiguity in §§69–71, and about possible chronological discontinuities in the account of events.

I shall retrace §69 and point out the interpretative choices to be made. Cicero begins by stating that none of Philo's pupils had studied for longer 'those very matters' which he is defending (*haec ipsa quae a me defenduntur*) than Antiochus, that Antiochus wrote most acutely about them, and that 'in his old age' (*in senectute*) he attacked them with more alacrity than he had previously mustered in defence. Which matters are meant and when did the attack happen? Given that the Roman Books view is dismissed in *Luc.*, there are three options: Cicero is referring to (a) the Clitomachean view, (b) the position of mitigated scepticism, or (c) the reference is to Academic scepticism in general. Prima facie (a) is the most attractive option, given that in §68 characterized himself as a Clitomachean, whose commitment to suspension of judgement is unequivocal. Conversely, option (b) is the least attractive one, since mitigated scepticism as characterized by self-aware assent is never defended by Cicero in *Acad.* (or elsewhere). However, (c) cannot be dismissed either, since in the present context the force of Cicero's point might seem slightly reduced if he drew attention to the fact that there were two Academic positions and that he only represented one; on the other hand, if the one he represented was the official position of the Academy whereas mitigated scepticism was a minority view not held by the (or any) scholarch, then there would be no need to include mitigated scepticism within the scope of the statement. I favour option (a) because of the content of the section preceding §69 and highlight that I hold on independent grounds (see section 8) that Philo was a Clitomachean until he devised the Roman Books view some time after his arrival in Rome.[276]

Antiochus' attack, so we are told, took place when he was *in senectute*. Given Antiochus' likely date of birth, he was by most definitions (see n. below) not a *senex* in the 90s when the majority of scholars posit his giving up on scepticism (whether that meant leaving the Academy or not). This is one of the reasons Polito (2012: 40) cites for assuming that Antiochus' public departure from scepticism postdates the

---

[276] Brittain (2001: 181) favours what I call option (c): '...these views [sc. *haec ipsa quae a me defenduntur*] are clearly not the Roman views, but the "Academic views" in the restricted sense of the arguments of Arcesilaos and Carneades (whether in the Clitomachean or Philonian/Metrodorian interpretation).'

end of the Academy as an institution. Yet to calculate how old Antiochus was in the 90s BC is perhaps the wrong response to the text: Cicero's point is that Antiochus was a loyal pupil of Philo's for a very long time, and that his change of mind came very late indeed. This is, quite possibly hyperbolically, expressed as 'in his old age'. By the same token, the reference to the sharpness of Antiochus' attacks (*acrius*; cf. Polito 2012: 41–2) may be designed to emphasize the completeness of the volte-face, rather than to mark a phase in Antiochus' life which postdates the mild-manneredness which he still shows in 87 BC until the Roman Books arrive (*Luc.* 11: *lenissimus*).

In any case, Antiochus' *inconstantia* damages his *auctoritas*; *auctoritas* is a watchword for the dogmatist, whereas the Academics stress their *iudicium* and valorize changes of mind under suitable circumstances (see on *Luc.* 60, cf. 7b–9a; *Tusc.* 2.4–5). Cicero then probes Antiochus' motivation for the shift, mostly by posing a series of sarcastic questions. He first asks what kind of special day brought the illumination which consisted in appreciating the distinctive feature of cataleptic impressions that had so far eluded Antiochus. Then, modifying the suggestion slightly, he asks whether Antiochus himself arrived, by philosophical reflection (*Excogitauit aliquid?*), at his new position. By exclaiming 'he says the same thing as the Stoics', Cicero dismisses both suggestions as implausible, given that Antiochus miraculously ended up with the Stoic position; the present tense conveys an appeal to the audience (the other characters participating in the discussion) and also to the reader to attend to Lucullus' speech, which reflected Antiochus' mature post-conversion thinking. Cicero then asks if Antiochus had been embarrassed by his earlier views or felt regret over them (*illa* cannot refer to the most recent view named). If he did, why did he not join another school, notably the Stoics, who properly owned the divergent position Antiochus had now adopted? (An implication is presumably that the untenability of the Academic position ought to have made it undesirable to be an Academic of any description, including an 'old' Academic.) Moreover, one wonders what the implied contrast is, i.e. what Antiochus actually did on Cicero's account: is it assumed at this point that he established a new school (in some sense), or that he failed to leave the Academy? Polito (2012: 33) is right to note that the latter is the more likely reading, especially given what we hear later, that Antiochus remained 'with Philo' until he had pupils of his own. However, the most economical view on this implication would be that Antiochus remained in the Academy for a while when he already had doubts, but that he left while the Academy was still a functioning institution.[277]

An important reason for thinking that Cicero assumes Antiochus' conversion to have taken place in the 90s while the Academy was still a functioning school, i.e. prior to 88, is the reference to Mnesarchus and Dardanus: they were the leaders of the Stoics (i) 'at the time' (sc. when Antiochus embraced the epistemological view described earlier in the paragraph and (ii) 'in Athens' (*qui erant Athenis tum principes Stoicorum*).[278] Independent evidence for the dates of the two Stoics is consistent

---

[277] A notion that Antiochus' departure from scepticism might have preceded his institutional secession from the Academy is entertained e.g. by Görler (1994: 941) and Barnes (1997: 68–70).

[278] This is stressed by Brittain (2001: 55–6), who also notes that *Luc.* 111, about Antiochian anti-sceptical arguments which supposedly perturbed Philo, appears to require Philo and Antiochus to be in the same place (viz. Athens before 88 BC).

with this account; see n. below. Beyond that, two things are remarkable: it is again left vague what precisely Antiochus did beyond adopting the Stoic position, i.e. whether he set up a new school or formed a splinter group within the Academy; and the Stoic view is presented as the divergent view, when one might think that the Stoic view was primary and the Academic position a response to it. The latter is due to Cicero preparing the ground for a topic of the next paragraph, viz. who is entitled to the name 'Academy'. The information that Antiochus did not leave Philo until he had pupils of his own, if it is not intended to present him as underhand, suggests less than full conviction on his part and the desire to play it safe.[279] The men who are with Antiochus in the Alexandrian scene in *Luc.* (§11) are usually and plausibly seen as his pupils, so that it is assumed that Antiochus must have 'left Philo' before 87. What does *a Philone discessit* mean, precisely? It may mean that Antiochus left the Academy, either to set up his own school or to set up something less formal than a school, but 'Philo' might also stand for Academic scepticism, so that the sentence would describe his shift of allegiance rather than changes to his institutional affiliation: if we assume that Antiochus did not wake up a Stoic one morning, but started out as someone who had doubts about Academic scepticism, then the sentence might mean that Antiochus turned from doubts about scepticism to active opposition once his critical stance had won him pupils.[280] Still, even in this case one would assume that the moment to depart institutionally had to come at some point before 88 BC, despite the Academy's tradition of being pluralist and tolerant: it is inconceivable that Antiochus taught and endorsed the doctrine of the cataleptic impression in Philo's Academy.

Having ended §69 with a reference to Antiochus, his pupils, and their departure from Philo (however interpreted), it may seem natural to read the question at the beginning of §70 (*Vnde autem subito uetus Academia reuocata est?*) as enquiring about the reason Antiochus claimed the title 'Old Academy' for himself and his pupils once they had left the Academy, although they had no right to use the designation. This reading is initially encouraged by Cicero's report that some claim Antiochus wanted to retain the honour of the name (*nominis dignitas*) although he had defected from 'the thing itself'—again this could be literal or metaphorical, or both. However, as one reads on, this interpretation runs into difficulties. First Cicero reports the views of others that Antiochus may have been motivated by a desire for *gloria* and that he may have been hoping that his followers would call himself 'Antiochians'. This rather suggests that the initial question was more about the rationale for creating the entity called 'Old Academy', and that the name of the grouping, while obviously functional, was not salient. This impression is confirmed when Cicero continues that Antiochus could not withstand the combined assault of all the other philosophers, which he follows up with a simile that likens Antiochus to traders on the forum who could not bear the heat in places exposed to the sun.

§71 then provides a testimonium, not otherwise attested, for an argument which Antiochus advanced while he was still an Academic sceptic (there is no indication of

---

[279] In §70 Antiochus will be presented as acting under external pressure.
[280] The chronology favoured by Polito (2012) *requires* that the name 'Philo' in *a Philone discessit* stands metaphorically for Academic scepticism.

what the ultimate source of this information is). Dionysius of Heraclea started out as a Stoic but later shifted to Cyrenaic philosophy: hence Cicero says that he first deemed the honourable to be the highest good, and later pleasure. Antiochus, so Cicero says, used this to argue—against the Stoics, one assumes—that every impression is susceptible to ἀπαραλλαξία considerations. Once he became a dogmatist at least as far as the Stoic conception of the cataleptic impression is concerned, the very same argument was applied to him by other people.

The issue is plainly not that Dionysius was not a sage and that he should therefore serve as a warning to all other non-sages that one's καταλήψεις are not secure and remain mere δόξαι until one becomes a sage, and that this holds even for the most central tenet of Stoic philosophy—for this is something the Stoics could not just accommodate but would warmly embrace.

How exactly can a change of mind and of philosophical allegiance be seen as an instance of the ἀπαραλλαξία of true and false impressions, from the perspective of a sceptical Academic? Here one must look back to §§43–4, where Lucullus invoked a notion of non-perceptual ἀπαραλλαξία, which could be characterized by the following claim: for every non-perceptual impression which is true, it is possible that the impression could be false. Here in §71 Cicero says that Antiochus argued on the basis of Dionysius' change of view that nothing could be imprinted on our minds from something 'uerum' which could not equally be imprinted from something 'falsum' (*nihil ita signari in animis nostris a uero posse quod non eodem modo possit a falso*). For 'uerum' and 'falsum' to create imprints in this way (rather than *be* imprints on the mind), the terms must refer to states of affairs and merely supposed states of affairs in the world, respectively. The natural way to read the text is to assume that, on the argument made, for Dionysius during his Stoic phase 'the honourable is the highest good' arose from a state of affairs (*uerum*), whereas he viewed it as arising from a *falsum* once he changed his view to pleasure being the highest good.[281] Antiochus' critics then turned this argument against him once he had adopted his new position.

Glucker (2004: 114 n. 22) has argued that §§69–70 are harshly polemical in a manner which would not befit the Cicero character but would be appropriate in a comment of Philo's which reflects his personal disappointment with Antiochus. Put differently, the present passage has been cited as evidence that Cicero followed a Philonian source. If this was correct, then this Philonian source would have to pre-date the formulation of the Roman Books view, given the Clitomachean stance adopted by the Cicero character, or else one would have to assume, in the absence of any supporting evidence, that Philo reverted to the Clitomachean position after the failure of the Roman Books; see section 9.3.

Finally, it should be recognized that §69 appears to speak to an issue on which the record is otherwise almost completely silent, namely which experiences or considerations caused Antiochus to develop doubts about the Academic stance and to accept the definition of the cataleptic impression.[282] Cicero speaks of a moment of

---

[281] See also section 5.8 on non-perceptual ἀπαραλλαξία.
[282] The reasons cited by Plut., *Cic.* 4.2 for Antiochus' conception of the Old Academic view, viz. that he was 'overwhelmed by clarity and his sense impressions', resemble those cited by Numenius (frg. 28 Des

enlightenment and theorization (*excogitauit aliquid?*) of this insight. However, both of these suggestions (if they do not belong together) are to be taken with a pinch of salt, in that they suggest the creative and independent formulation of a view on the one hand, but on the other do so primarily to set up the punchline that Antiochus actually adopted a pre-existing position. We have no way of knowing whether one day Antiochus came to the view that a sub-set of his perceptual experiences was supremely clear and never false, or whether he came to think that his interactions with the world were largely successful and that this was best explained by assuming that there are self-warranting perceptual experiences, to name just two possible scenarios.[283]

§69

Sed prius pauca cum Antiocho…quam antea defensitauerat: Gell. 10.28.1 is conventionally cited on who counted for a *senex* in Rome (…*eosque ad annum quadragesimum sextum 'iuniores' supraque eum annum 'seniores' appellasse*…), but there was no legal definition, it is not a given that any such definition would be applicable to Antiochus, and it is easy to point to contexts in which a *senex* is taken to be substantially older than 46 (the plots of Roman comedy, e.g.). In any case, as argued above, whether an age in the mid-30s would have warranted calling Antiochus a *senex* is probably not the question to ask. Differently Barnes (1997: 69 n. 75): 'Has Cicero slipped? Is he exaggerating wildly? No: he says not that Antiochus *converted* in his old age but that he attacked Philo in old age—and we need not infer that these senile attacks were the first he essayed.'

For the reference of *haec ipsa…defenduntur*, see the general note above. *Defensitare*, which is rare in Cicero, means 'to defend time and again'. Given that there is a degree of disagreement among scholars whether *a Philone discedere* below means 'to part with scepticism' rather than with the man (and the school whose head he was), one cannot but note that the name cannot be ambiguous in the phrase *discere apud Philonem*. The anti-sceptical argument which Antiochus made according to §71 may or may not have featured in the work(s) referred to here (*scripsit…acutissime*). For *cum Antiocho*, see *OLD* s.v. *cum* no. 14a, cf. §71 *fin.*: *cum hoc*.

Quamuis igitur fuerit acutus…Excogitauit aliquid: on the different status accorded to the authority of philosophical forebears (and teachers) and judgement, see on *Luc.* 60: *Vt qui audient…ratione potius quam auctoritate ducantur*, which looks back to *Luc.* 7b–9a. On *leuatur*, see *OLD* s.v. *leuo* no. 4a: 'to reduce in force, potency, etc., lessen.' *Illucescere*, with a word for 'day' as subject, is intransitive (*OLD* s.v. no. 2: 'to begin to grow light, dawn, break'). The subject of the suggested illumination is described rather narrowly as the *ueri et falsi nota*; the phrase does not describe the

---

Places; see appendix 2) for *Philo*'s abandonment of universal ἐποχή, sc. when he formulated the Roman Books view. This makes them uninformative, as Brittain (2001: 133 n. 6) notes.

[283] It is a notable feature of Lucullus' speech in *Luc.* that it withholds any insight into this issue, and presents not just Stoic epistemology but also standard Stoic defensive postures as Antiochian.

criterion in general, but refers, in the terminology of *Acad.*, to the distinctive feature of cataleptic impressions which makes them self-warranting (see the general note on *Luc.* 33–34a for a survey of passages where *nota* and related terms feature in the relevant sense). Elsewhere Cicero credits Antiochus with a more comprehensive appropriation of Stoic doctrine (*Luc.* 132). Such passages are not at variance with the present one, where the appreciation of the one topic on which the entire debate still hinges (see §78 *init.*) is at issue, and **eadem dicit quae Stoici** seems to suggest agreement beyond a single (if salient) point. With *negitare* 'to deny repeatedly', cf. *defensitare* above.

The image of illumination may suggest a sudden change of opinion rather than a gradual development from dissatisfaction to fundamental change of mind. *Excogitauit aliquid* does not reinforce this reading (while *excogitare* means 'cogitando inuenire' as *TLL* s.v. col. 1274.74 has it, the instances listed there do not support a connotation of *sudden* discovery). However, the suggestion may be one of initial sudden insight followed by more careful articulation. The two points jointly or individually set up *eadem...Stoici*: it is a strange coincidence that Antiochus ended up with the pre-existing Stoic position. The absence of *-ne* with *excogitauit* may convey a degree of exasperation. The B reading before correction was *negitauisse* followed by the ampersand.

Eadem dicit quae Stoici...principes Stoicorum: on the force of the plural *eadem* in *eadem dicit*, see the previous n. above; the present tense of *dicit* signals exasperation. Cicero intimates regret over his Academic views as Antiochus' motivation, a wish that he had not adopted them in the first place (see Kaster 2005: 66–83 on *paenitentia*). That transfer to another school, and to the Stoics in particular, is mentioned as an option foregone could in principle imply the foundation of a new school *at this point*, but the notice that Antiochus remained with Philo until he had pupils of his own discourages such a reading.

On Mnesarchus and Dardanus, see Glucker (1978: 19–20) and Barnes (1997: 69–70); Goulet (1994) on Dardanus; and Goulet (2005) on Mnesarchus. Goulet summarizes judiciously the complex arguments for their respective dates. It is widely agreed that referring to the pair as *principes Stoicorum* makes best sense if the speaker has the 90s in mind; Barnes (1997: 70 n. 76) entertains the possibility that by this time the two were 'in their thriving sixties', but most scholars assume them to be older. The important point is that, if one assumes, on the basis of our text, Antiochus' secession around or not long after the time when Mnesarchus and Dardanus were leaders of the Stoics, then a date in the 90s for this event remains the most plausible (*Athenis tum* by itself delivers a terminus ante quem of 88 BC; see the general note above). Antiochus is named as a pupil of Mnesarchus by Eus., *Praep. Ev.* XIV.9.3 (= T1 Mette = Numenius frg. 28 Des Places), as well as by Aug., *Contra Acad.* 3.18.41 (= frg. 8a Mette = my t. 58). Reid[1] (p. 258) found the notion of a teacher–pupil relationship dubious, but Augustine's source was likely a lost section of the final edition of *Acad.*, and Puglia (2000: 18–19) has plausibly suggested that Philodemus provided this information, too (*Index Acad.* col. xxxiv.22–4; see also Fleischer 2015). Reid[1] (p. 258) compares *sensit* in *Ac.* 1.23 with *sensisse* here; within *Acad.*, the verb means 'having a view' without clear indication of the manner in which it is held (though in

Ac. 1.23 and here a dogmatically held view is at issue). With *dissensio* supplement *a Philone*.

Reid[1] (p. 258) puts a question mark after both instances of *quid* (as well as after *paenitebat* and *Dardani*). The earlier sentence question without *-ne* warrants this, although it does not make it compelling. On uses of *quid* in conversational or colloquial speech, see Ricottilli (2003: 191–2). The question of whether the present context alludes to the teacher–pupil relationship of Mnesarchus and Antiochus is neutral to the punctuation issue, as Fleischer (2015: 2 n. 5) notes.

Numquam a Philone discessit...qui se audirent habere: for the force of *a Philone*, see the general note above. On *qui se audirent* = *auditores* in the sense of 'pupils', see Reid[1] (p. 258). According to *Luc.* 12, which recounts the arrival of the Roman Books in Alexandria in 87 BC, there were present on that occasion Aristus, Antiochus' brother, as well as Aristo and Dio. The latter two are mentioned as students of Antiochus in *Index Acad.* col. xxxv.7–10. While *Luc.* 12 does not refer to them as students but as people Antiochus 'valued especially', and while both came from Alexandria, it is not unreasonable to assume that they were his pupils already at that point, and did not become his pupils only later; that, however, at best provides a terminus ante quem for the teacher–pupil relationship (note that the validity of this reasoning is disputed by Polito 2012: 33). *Numquam...nisi* for *non...nisi* is emphatic.

§70

Vnde autem subito uetus Academia reuocata est...Antiochii uocarentur: given the immediately preceding remark that Antiochus left Philo when he had pupils of his own, and if one interprets 'Philo' as designating the man rather than metonymically Academic scepticism (in line with the occurrence of 'Philo' in §69 *init.*), it is a natural assumption that Antiochus did leave eventually, before the upheaval caused by the Mithridatic war (cf. Hatzimichali 2012: 14).

While the phrase 'Old Academy' is not attested before Antiochus' time, this may be due to the accidents of survival: Sextus, *P.H.* 1.220–1, who refers to earlier divisions, uses it with reference to the Academy from Plato to Polemo, without associating it with Antiochus (who is also mentioned and 'whose school is counted by some as the fifth Academy'). That the notion of a 'New Academy' already existed emerges from *Ac.* 1.45: *Hanc Academiam nouam appellant...*; see n. ad loc. for other references in Cicero. 'Old Academy' was thus probably claimed rather than coined by Antiochus; it is also attested in the account of Antiochus' life in Philodemus' *Index Acad.* col. xxxv.15–16 (see Blank 2007: 89). For ancient divisions/typologies of 'the Academy' generally, see on *Ac.* 1.18 and 1.46.

The suggestion by some that Antiochus was hoping his pupils would call themselves 'Antiochians' raises the question if Antiochus' school was not immediately called 'Old Academy', as the naming would have made any such move less likely, whereas temporary namelessness could be seen to invite it; see also the general note above. On our passage, see also Glucker (1978: 27 n. 49); on who was included in the 'Old Academy' see section 7.2.

For a desire for fame as Antiochus' suspected motivation, cf. also Aug., *Contra Acad.* 2.6.15: *Antiochus qui, ut nonnullis uisus est, gloriae cupidior quam ueritatis in simultatem adduxit Academiae utriusque sententias.*

Reuocare means 'to call back' in the sense of 'to restore, bring back into existence' (*OLD* s.v. nos 10–12; *Luc.* 11: ... *ista philosophia, quae nunc prope dimissa reuocatur*) and is mildly sarcastic. The import of *cum a re ipsa desciceret* is not entirely clear: the suggestion may be that he left the Academy qua institution or parted with scepticism (which Cicero of course views as the Academy's official position), or that Antiochus is not credible as an Old Academic (cf. the accusations in Aug., *Contra Acad.* 3.18.41: *faeneus ille Platonicus*, that he is like a dummy stuffed with straw, not a real Platonist). See also Galen, *Plac. Hipp. et Plat.* 2.1.2 (p. 102 De Lacy) and Aug., *C.D.* 18.41 (both already cited by Reid[1] p. 258) on the kind of attempted image transfer ascribed to Antiochus.

The relative pronoun *quod* resumes the preceding clause as a whole and functions as the object of *facere* within the relative clause beginning with *qui*. The emendation *facere dicerent* (Camerarius) for the transmitted *facerent* is compelling; see Reid[1] (p. 258).

Manutius (1541–60) emended *reuocata* to *renouata*, but the parallel from *Luc.* 11 tells against it; see also Plasberg[1] (p. 104). *Enim* for *etiam*, proposed by Davies, would not improve sense, since, as indicated above, the claiming of the name 'Old Academy' sits oddly with Antiochus wanting his followers to call themselves 'Antiochians'.

Mihi autem magis...concursum omnium philosophorum: a new sentence should begin with *mihi*, given that Cicero offers his own opinion. That Antiochus was unable to stand up to the 'combined assault' of all philosophers and thus shifted his stance for a dubious reason appears to be a rejoinder to Lucullus' claim about Philo's shift to the Roman Books position (*Luc.* 18: *Philo autem dum noua quaedam commouet quod ea sustinere uix poterat quae contra Academicorum pertinaciam dicebantur...*). *Sustinere* is a military term ('to bear up against'), as Reid[1] (p. 258) notes; so is *concursus* (*OLD* s.v. no. 2 'charge, attack, encounter').

Etenim de ceteris sunt...nemo probet: Cicero's rhetorical point depends on the complete isolation of the Academics (*sententia* probably means their stance in general rather than any particular tenet, or their argumentative practice, which would more naturally be called *ratio*), but one still wonders if Cicero could have written this if he had been aware of nascent Pyrrhonism. See also on *Luc.* 130.

Itaque cessit...Academicorum umbram secutus est: the simile illustrates Antiochus' inability to withstand the heat of philosophical criticism directed at the Academics, not his choice of name for his school, as the beginning of the paragraph might suggest. A secondary implication may be that Antiochus' stance is determined by external forces (corresponding to the sun) to which he responds, rather than by his independent decision on where to position himself. Reid[1] (p. 295) lists all relevant illustrative parallels: for *sub Nouis*, cf. Varro, *L.L.* 6.59 (*sub nouis dicta pars in foro aedificiorum, quod uocabulum ei peruetustum*). The *Maeniana* were timber balconies attached to the upper storeys of buildings, in this case the *tabernae* lining the Forum, from which one could watch games and spectacles and whose shade fell on the ground underneath; cf. Ebert (1928); Platner and Ashby (1919: 504–5); Lehman-Hartleben (1938); Oakley (2005: 111) on Liv. 9.7.8. Cicero writes *Academicorum* rather than *Academiae* either to create the jingle with *Maenianorum*, or to imply that Antiochus is hiding behind the individuals representing the Old Academy.

§71

Quoque solebat...uoluptatem esse summum bonum: *solebat* suggests repeated use of the argument in either debate or writing, but may just be tendentious. Antiochus' scepticism is characterized by 'his holding the view' (*placebat*) that nothing can be known. Cicero could have referred to the period in which Antiochus argued for this view; that he does not do so does not suggest that he is presenting Antiochus as someone who endorsed that nothing can be known in some form (which leaves it open if he was mitigated sceptic or a Clitomachean—*placere* is ambiguous between assent or approval).

As Brittain (2006: 42 n. 98) notes, 'conversions from one philosophical school to another by established philosophers were rare', and an instance of conversion from the Stoa to another dogmatic school suited the Academic case particularly (thus Reid¹ p. 259); see also §106 (on Polyaenus' conversion). On Dionysius of Heraclea, called ὁ μεταθέμενος for his change of school, see D.L. 7.166–7; Cic., *Fin.* 5.94; *Tusc.* 2.60 and 3.19 (collected along with other evidence in *SVF* i.422–34); von Arnim (1903); Guérard (1994). Born c.330–325, he was a pupil of Zeno, and became a Cyrenaic (D.L. 7.167) or Epicurean (Athen. 7.281) in his old age, on the grounds that painful medical conditions made it impossible for him to continue to regard pain as an indifferent (Cic., *Tusc.* 2.60).

On the *nota*, the distinctive mark of cataleptic impressions, see on §84, the survey of passages at the end of the general note on §§33–34a, and section 10.2. Cf. Cic., *N.D.* 1.11 for the connection with assent posited by the Stoic theory (Cicero is characterizing his stance as Academic sceptic): the distinctive feature allows for conscious discrimination (*iudicandi...nota*) as well as has causal efficacy, in that it usually though not invariably gives rise to assent (*assentiendi nota*); cf. Brittain (2014), who examines whether cataleptic impressions were held to trigger assent invariably and concludes that they do not. Given the examples which Cicero cites, which are propositions identifying the highest good in Stoicism and in Epicureanism/Cyrenaic thought respectively, Cicero is thinking about non-perceptual impressions here, but he does not explain, and it is in general undertheorized in *Acad.*, how one would construe the distinctive feature of cataleptic impressions in cases where the impression is not perceptual. Non-perceptual clarity or distinctness are not intuitive concepts.

With the *honestum* as an *inane nomen*, cf. *Luc.* 140; Cic., *Fin.* 2.48; *Tusc.* 3.42, which translates a passage from Epicurus' Περὶ τέλους; Morel (2015: 93). On the syntax of the whole sentence, see the note by Reid¹ (p. 259). For *defensitare*, see on §69 above.

Qui ex illius commutata sententia...ex eo ceteri sumerent: on the notion of having something imprinted on the mind *a uero* or *a falso*, see the general note above.

Chrysippus is reported to have criticized his Stoic predecessors for describing an impression as an imprint on the mind; he suggested 'alteration' as a better term (see section 5.2), on the grounds that multiple imprints on top of one another would end up being not discrete. There is no reason to think that the material on which Cicero draws, or his own thinking on the subject, sided with the earlier Stoics since it may have been understood by everyone that 'seal' or 'imprint' were just metaphors. On *curauit ⟨ut⟩ quod* (Lambinus), see Plasberg[1] (p. 105).

Sed cum hoc alio loco...dicta sunt: it is not clear what the reference is; Plasberg[1] (p. 105) suggests §§113 and 133, Schäublin et al. (p. 245 n. 203) §98 (where Antiochus' entire position is dismissed). Cf. also §87: *sed de physicis mox*. With *cum hoc*, cf. §69 init.: *cum Antiocho*.

§§72–76a

Cicero now examines the political analogy used by Lucullus in §13 to discredit the New Academy's invocation of the Presocratics; *Luc.* 13 in turn responded to the counterpart of *Ac.* 1.44–6 in the *Catulus*. Issues raised by this section include how *Ac.* 1.44–6 and *Luc.* 72–76a relate to one another, i.e. if the latter passage is a continuation or possibly elaboration of the material presented in the former section, or if there is a discontinuity between the two, possibly reflective of the sources used or of an inherent tension within the Academic stance.[284]

The Academics, so Lucullus suggested in §13, are like populist sectarians who invoke as spiritual ancestors venerable politicians of the past who were supportive of the people. In §72 Cicero rejects the analogy on two grounds: first, the sectarians invoke the blameless ancients as cover for their own morally reprehensible words and actions (*res ⟨non⟩ bonas tractent*), whereas the disagreement between Academics and dogmatists has no moral dimension from his point of view (the dogmatists would disagree); second, the ancients invoked by the sectarians were in fact moderate, whereas the Presocratics can be seen as more extreme than the Academics in that their pronouncements corresponded to beliefs of theirs as opposed to mere apperances (*uideri...placuisse*). He also criticizes a double standard employed by the dogmatists: the latter hold the Presocratics in high regard, despite their extremism compared to the Academics, but it is the latter whom they malign.

The first Presocratic philosopher discussed is Anaxagoras, but before one examines what the Cicero character says about him, one must attend more closely to the manner in which he is introduced. In the sentence *nos autem ea dicimus nobis uideri quae uosmet ipsi nobilissimis philosophis placuisse conceditis*, it is not obvious what is referred to by *ea...quae*, and where the concession made by the dogmatists is supposed to have occurred.[285] I suggest that the reference is to the kind of sceptical pronouncements Presocratics including Anaxagoras are invoked for in *Ac.* 1.44; to the

---

[284] See section 7.1.
[285] Only Schäublin et al. (pp. 245–6 n. 204) recognize the problem, but their solution is different from mine.

extent that an Academic and a Clitomachean in particular would endorse them, these are not his settled views but merely what appears to him to be the case. The concession referred to was made by Lucullus in *Luc.* 14b (*et tamen isti*...), although there Lucullus appears to put down the sceptical pronouncements to moments of frustration. However, he says in the immediately following sentence (ibid.) that the Presocratics were if anything too dogmatic in their statements, and Cicero may, in a somewhat lawyerly move, be connecting this with their sceptical remarks rather than their positive theory building notably on physical matters. Importantly, this speaks to the issue of continuity between *Ac.* 1.44–6 and the present passage; if this is not appreciated, it is harder to understand the rationale of Cicero's handling of Anaxagoras.

Without a clearly signalled connection with what precedes, Cicero states that Anaxagoras said that snow was black.[286] His point must be that 'snow is black' is, like the sceptical proclamations referenced in the previous sentence, absurd from Lucullus' point of view, and yet Anaxagoras enjoys excellent repute (with Lucullus/Antiochus inter alios, one assumes), whereas if Cicero qua Academic held this view, this would prompt outrage.[287] In §100, while characterizing the sage, Cicero will return to the theme of beliefs vs appearances and point out that the Academic sage 'approves' that snow is white, whereas Anaxagoras 'denied' that, because he knew snow consisted of water and water was black, snow appeared white to him (or: he denied that it appeared to him to be the case that snow is white). This means a shift of focus from the manner in which views are held to their content: Cicero stresses that his appearances are, in terms of content, like those of the dogmatist (he just does not regard them as invariably true), whereas someone as respected (by the dogmatist) as Anaxagoras goes so far as to claim that his appearances are modified by his dogmatically held views. The sage, so the implication, can be guided by impressions provided he does not regard them as invariably true, but dogmatically held views (like Anaxagoras', but also like the Stoics' with their exalted standards of what counts as an impression on which action can be based) can get in the way of the ability to conduct one's life.

In §73 Cicero proceeds to Democritus, another early thinker held in high esteem by the dogmatists (the first-person plural in *cum eo conferre possumus* is functional and supposed to include Cicero's addressees and himself).[288] He begins by engaging more closely, and slightly differently than in §72, with a point made by Lucullus in §14, where the latter sought to show that the scepticism of the Presocratics was specific and limited: their statements about the unknowability of things and the limitations of human experience were rare and not considered opinions, but rather outbursts of frustration, while overall their real problem was one of overconfidence about what they could affirm and pronounce on. Cicero cites what he calls an introductory statement of Democritus', which addresses the supposed rarity of sceptical pronouncements made by the Presocratics and does not appear to be an outburst: that he (Democritus) proposes to speak *de uniuersis*, about everything. There follows

---

[286] See the discussion in Brittain and Palmer (2001: 51–3).
[287] It is because of this connection that my text does not begin a new paragraph with *Anaxagoras*.
[288] See the discussion in Brittain and Palmer (2001: 53–8).

what seems to be a somewhat gratuitous dismissal of Stoics, including Chrysippus, as second-rate thinkers compared to Democritus; if there is a connection, it could be the implied charge that the Stoics split hairs where Democritus is not afraid to tackle the big questions. Cicero then resumes a point from the previous paragraph: Democritus is in a crucial respect more extreme than the Academics, in that the latter do not deny that there is something true, just that it could be apprehended without fail, whereas Democritus—so Cicero infers from a Democritean statement about sense perception—denies the existence of the true altogether. This is worth noting in part because Cicero (sc. who is a Clitomachean) claims that he accepts (in some sense) that there are true impressions; this is further evidence for the view, defended in the commentary on *Luc.* 43-4, that Lucullus is right to treat the first premiss of the core argument as one which Academics of any colour endorse themselves in some way. Whereas Democritus' attitude to sense perception was inferred by Cicero, he ends with an actual quote from Metrodorus of Chios, billed as an admirer of Democritus', apparently in an effort to drive home the point about the extremism of Democritus' scepticism.

§74 continues with Empedocles. Lucullus had invoked him in §14 to support his point that the Presocratics' sceptical pronouncements were due to momentary fits of frustration rather than considered attitudes. Cicero's rejoinder that Empedocles speaks appropriately given his subject matter is a tantalizing snippet of literary criticism, and presumably his own view as a cultured and educated Roman of a particular kind. The implication is that Empedocles' sceptical statements cannot be dismissed on the grounds Lucullus cites. Cicero then resumes the theme of the double standard applied by the dogmatists (cf. §72): have any of the hyperbolic charges typically levelled at the Academics ever been directed at Empedocles? For the evidence the Academics might have cited in support of the view that Empedocles was a sceptic, see n. below.

Cicero then turns to Parmenides and Xenophanes, inferior poets compared to Empedocles (but not, it is implied, inferior philosophers). Their angry frustration is acknowledged, but, it is suggested, was in fact directed at those making excessive knowledge claims; this reactive dimension of their scepticism, we are to understand, aligns them with the Academics.

Plato and Socrates feature next.[289] Cicero refers back to §15, where Lucullus wanted to separate both from those who 'deny that anything can be known or apprehended', Plato because he had a fully elaborated doctrinal system, Socrates because he used irony and apparently hid what view or views he had. (Lucullus in turn responded to the counterpart of *Ac.* 1.45-6 in the *Catulus*.) When he would not advance any opinions of his own and instead aim to refute the positions taken by his interlocutors, this was, for Antiochus/Lucullus, a deliberate strategy of concealment rather than evidence that Socrates did not actually hold any views. So for Lucullus Socrates' and Plato's (positive) dogmatism separated them from the Presocratics. Cicero observes first of all that he can speak with confidence about both, since he has read so many Socratic dialogues; this aligns him with Arcesilaus, whose Socratic

---

[289] See sections 7.3 and 7.4.

posture came, on Cicero's view,[290] about in the same way, and it reinforces the impression which arises from §§66–7, that Arcesilaus is deployed by Cicero as a figurehead for Clitomacheanism in particular. From Socratic dialogues Cicero takes it to be plain that it appeared to Socrates that he knew nothing, except this one thing (see n. below on the exact import of this formulation of Socratic ignorance as well as the fact that an explicit statement to this effect features in one influential passage of Plat. *Apol.*; Cicero's formulation here suggests an impression of Socrates' attitude formed on the basis of his behaviour in dialogues, or of the outcome of aporetic dialogues). As to Plato, Cicero suggests that Plato would not have presented Socrates' way of interacting with interlocutors as governed by a notion that nothing can be known (except this one thing) if Plato had not approved of that notion. For nobody could reasonably adopt someone else's ironic posture, least of all consistently so. For Cicero it makes no sense at all that a dogmatist would deploy a literary character who hides his dogmatism behind the front of a master dialectician.[291] The notion that the Socrates *persona* of the dialogues may serve a didactic purpose, whether or not this would be an accurate representation of the historical Socrates, does not even receive a hearing.

In §75, by way of a concluding remark on his invocation of the Presocratics, Cicero restates that unlike people like Saturninus (cf. §14) he does not merely name models, but genuinely imitates them, and that the models invoked are (by universal agreement) invariably distinguished and noble (so that following them has to be a good thing).

If, however, he just wanted to be awkward, sc. when selecting his philosophical models, so Cicero says in *praeteritio*, he could invoke dialecticians whose eristic arguments, while insubstantial, pose real difficulties for the dogmatist. And if he wanted to be even more awkward, he could deploy writings by Chrysippus himself, in which he attacked the senses, only to defend them later, apparently for didactic purposes. He has a fictitious interlocutor—a technique which Lucullus deployed, too—reply that the solutions offered by Chrysippus were superior to the arguments cited against the senses, to which Cicero replies that he did not share that view. However, he allows for the possibility that Chrysippus found such solutions (in line with his earlier statement that he does not dispute the existence of the truth, just that one can ever be certain about any particular truth), but notes that Chrysippus would not have assembled so many arguments against the senses if he had not realized how hard to resist they are.

The remark that Chrysippus argued against the senses (as well as dismantled his own arguments to that effect) is elucidated by evidence from Plutarch. In *Sto. rep.* 1035f–1036e Plutarch reports that Chrysippus did not completely reject the practice

---

[290] This is not stated in *Acad.*, but see *De orat.* 3.67: *Arcesilas primum, qui Polemonem audierat, ex uariis Platonis libris sermonibusque Socraticis hoc maxime arripuit, nihil esse certi quod aut sensibus aut animo percipi possit; quem ferunt eximio quodam usum lepore dicendi aspernatum esse omne animi sensusque iudicium primumque instituisse—quamquam id fuit Socraticum maxime—non quid ipse sentiret ostendere, sed contra id, quod quisque se sentire dixisset, disputare.*

[291] I argue in section 7.3 that the Cicero character assumes Lucullus' claim in §15 to be that Socratic irony concealed dogmatic beliefs—and that he contests this claim.

of arguing for and against a thesis, but warned of its dangers when used in the instruction of pupils, whose beliefs are not firm and mutually secured like those of the sage. In such cases it is, according to Chrysippus, advisable to use the technique only to undermine the plausibility of the view which the speaker rejects. Plutarch criticizes this practice from his Platonist standpoint as that of a lawyer whose only aim is to destroy the opposition's argument rather than that of a philosopher striving for truth. He further reports that Chrysippus often argued against the views which he approved with such zeal and conviction that his actual attitude was not easy to discern. His publications against συνήθεια (= *consuetudo*) and sense perception were held by his followers to include arguments so powerful as to outdo anything Carneades formulated.[292] Unfortunately, so Plutarch, his arguments in favour of sense perception and common experience were weaker than those against (cf. also *Luc.* 87: *ab eo* (sc. *Chrysippo*) *armatum esse Carneadem*), and so Chrysippus ended up in violation of his own injunctions, unsettling his followers' beliefs. In 1036d-e a warning of Chrysippus' about the careless use of arguments on either side is cited verbatim. According to Sotion (D.L. 7.183-4),[293] Chrysippus attended the Academy (παραγενόμενος ἐν Ἀκαδημείᾳ), where he 'engaged in philosophy jointly with Arcesilaus and Lacydes' (τέλος δ' Ἀρκεσιλάῳ καὶ Λακύδῃ, καθά φησι Σωτίων ἐν τῷ ὀγδόῳ, παραγενόμενος ἐν Ἀκαδημείᾳ συνεφιλοσόφησε). The text continues (without it being clear whether it is Sotion's report or interpretation, or D.L.'s interpretation) that Chrysippus argued against and for συνήθεια 'for that reason' (δι' ἣν αἰτίαν καὶ κατὰ τῆς συνηθείας καὶ ὑπὲρ αὐτῆς ἐπεχείρησε). This information has given rise to quite different interpretations (surveyed by Glucker 1996: 106–7 n. 4). Babut (2003) has carefully weighed the possibilities of misreporting and distortion, malicious or otherwise, and concludes that Chrysippus will indeed have sought contact with the Academy, towards the end of Arcesilaus' tenure, in order to study Academic arguments.[294]

Lucullus had cited the Cyrenaics in §20 as evidence that the notion of a criterion which lies in the senses, and which furnishes 'impressions' one cannot be mistaken about, is not peculiar to the Stoics and Antiochus. In §76a Cicero replies, validly and substantially, that the Cyrenaics operate such a narrow conception of perceptual content that their position offers more support for his view that ordinary phenomenal content cannot be apprehended.[295] Cyrenaic perceptual content is not

---

[292] The catalogue of Chrysippus' works includes two relevant entries (D.L. 7.198): Κατὰ τῆς συνηθείας πρὸς Μητρόδωρον α´β´γ´δ´ε´ς´ and Περὶ τῆς συνηθείας πρὸς Γοργιππίδην α´β´γ´δ´ε´ς´ζ´; on περί, transmitted and printed by Dorandi in favour of Cobet's emendation ὑπέρ, which earlier editors had adopted, see Babut (2005: 85).

[293] For Sotion, see the general note on *Luc.* 118–26.

[294] Cf. also Bénatouïl (2007: 86): 'Chrysippe pourait en effet être allé à l'Académie pour se perfectionner en matière de dialectique, dont la connaissance lui était indispensable pour défendre les doctrines stoïciennes.'

[295] See O'Keefe (2011: 34): 'The Epicureans mock the Cyrenaics' notion that we can have knowledge only of our own states of awareness and not of their causes (*Adv. Col.* 1120d). The Cyrenaics use their contorted neologisms in order to avoid entirely any reference to objects or states of affairs beyond the content of the *pathê* themselves. This is because their project is to give an analysis of our awareness of our own internal states, which gets us down to what is immediately given. The Cyrenaics wish to get down to what is immediately given because they share the criteria of other Greek epistemologists as to what can be

representational and as such unsuitable for bringing the perceiving subject in touch with the external world and forming beliefs about it.

For the overall interpretation of the relationship of the passages which deal with the Academic view on the history of philosophy (*Ac.* 1.44–6; *Luc.* 13–15, Lucullus' reaction to the counterpart of *Ac.* 1.44–6 in the *Catulus*; *Luc.* 72–76a) see section 7.1.

§72

Et primum quod initio dixisti...placuisse conceditis: in *illi cum res ⟨non⟩ bonas tractent*, the pronoun *illi* refers to seditious politicians who invoke earlier 'popular' ones as political ancestors (*initio* refers to §13). *Bonas* without *non* could only be correct if it was focalized by the seditious politicians; yet they are not idealists who are merely misguided, but wickedly manipulative. This rules them out as focalizers of *bonas*, and Cicero, the alternative focalizer, agrees with Lucullus that the machinations of these politicians are not good. The choice between the emendation on offer from later manuscripts (⟨*non*⟩ *bonas*) or scholars (*nouas* for *bonas* without *non*, proposed by Faber 1611) is not easy, but there does not seem to be a third obvious solution. The redistribution of property which is usually part of the programme of the seditious politicians envisaged could only be accomplished by a political upheaval so great that *res nouae* would be a fitting description. I have opted for *res ⟨non⟩ bonas* since it fits better with *tractare*: new political circumstances are normally striven for rather than treated of.

The adjective *popularis* is here without negative connotation (*OLD* s.v. no. 6: 'liked or admired by the general public; popular'), although Cicero's point in part depends on the audience's awareness of the contentious use of the term; see also the discussion in Hellegouarc'h (1972: 518–41).

For the reference of *ea...quae* (viz. sceptical pronouncements like those ascribed to the Presocratics in *Ac.* 1.44 and presumably its counterpart in the *Catulus*) see the general note above. Cicero's point about the unequal treatment of Presocratics and Academics by the dogmatists by itself could work if *uideri* and *placuisse* were just designations for very similar or even identical attitudes (thus the translation in Brittain 2006), but the passage yields better sense if Cicero sets up a contrast between the tentatively held views of the sceptic and the negative dogmatism of the Presocratics. One of the general points which emerge from his remarks is that he is not seeking to equate certain Presocratics and Academic sceptics: rather, the latter are presented as holding a less extreme, more nuanced view. The tense of *solerent* is due to *dixisti*, as Reid[1] (p. 260) notes. For *nominare*, cf. §75.

Anaxagoras...et grauitatis et ingenii gloria: the evidence for Anaxagoras' statement and modern literature on him is cited on *Luc.* 100. Here it just serves as an instance

apprehended, and they think that a proper analysis of our *pathê* will show that the *pathê*, and the *pathê* alone, meet these criteria.... The Cyrenaics think that our *pathê* can be characterized in ways which strip away any purported representational content referring to objects external to the perceiver—in ways that refer only to what is immediately given. So characterized, their content is both self-evident to the perceiver, and sincere statements which report this content are infallible.'

of an obviously counterintuitive view which nonetheless did not dent its creator's standing among the dogmatists. Reid[1] (p. 260) notes the striking ellipsis after *Tu* (sc. *non ferres*) and gives parallels; *dubitare* in *ne si dubitarem* must mean 'to entertain in a doubtful manner'. What is meant by *sophistes* in the present passage is helpfully glossed by Cicero himself; other notable references to sophists include *Fin.* 1.7, 2.2; *N.D.* 1.63. The final sentence of the paragraph must contrast with what precedes: as a matter of fact Anaxagoras enjoyed an outstanding reputation. See Reid[1] (p. 261) on the absence of an adversative particle. It is left open whether this tells against his being a sophist, or whether this represents evidence for the unfair treatment of the Academics (sc. if even sophists are held in higher regard), but Anaxagoras is not usually classed as a sophist in antiquity (or modern scholarship), even though his interests overlapped with those of known sophists. Some *deteriores* and earlier editions emend to *philosophabantur*.

§73

Quid loquar de Democrito...potest extra uniuersa: cf. Sextus, *M.* 7.265 (= DK 68B165): Δημόκριτος δὲ ὁ τῇ Διὸς φωνῇ παρεικαζόμενος, καὶ λέγων τάδε περὶ τῶν ξυμπάντων, 'But Democritus, who compared himself to the voice of Zeus, and spoke in this manner about all things...', as well as Simpl. *in Arist. Cael.* p. 295.20-2 Heiberg (= DK 68A37 *fin.* = Arist. frg. 208 Rose) (a quote from Aristotle's lost work on Democritus; the grammatical subject is Democritus): λέγει δὲ τὴν γένεσιν καὶ τὴν ἐναντίαν αὐτῇ διάκρισιν οὐ μόνον περὶ ζῴων, ἀλλὰ καὶ περὶ φυτῶν καὶ περὶ κόσμων καὶ συλλήβδην περὶ τῶν αἰσθητῶν σωμάτων ἁπάντων, 'He describes creation and its opposite, dissolution, not just in the case of animals, but also of plants and of worlds and of perceptible bodies generally.' On the implied contrasts with the Academic approach see the general note above.

Quid introducing a question could conceivably mean 'why' (*OLD* s.v. *quis*[1] no. 16), but 'why' would give inferior sense here: Democritus has featured in the discussion before, and the question is what Cicero makes of Lucullus' angle on him (§14).

Quis hunc philosophum non anteponit...quintae classis uidentur: on the possible rationale for the blanket dismissal of the Stoics, see the general note above. The term *classis* alludes to Servius Tullius' division of Roman citizens into classes; see Reid[1] (p. 261) for a collection of early passages on the subject, as well as Kübler (1899) and Liebenam (1901). Assignment to a class depended on wealth; during votes in the late Republic the *prima classis* voted first and had as a block equal weight to the other classes, which, however, contained more people. Moreover, the political weight of the *prima classis* was relatively larger since they voted first under a system where the casting of ballots ceased when a majority had been reached. Overall the term *classis* is suggestive more of significance than of quality.

Atque is non hoc dicit...sic enim appellat eos: cf. Sextus, *M.* 7.137-9 (= DK 68B11) for the distinction between σκοτίη γνῶσις and γνησίη γνῶσις, 'dark' and 'genuine' *cognitio*, by means of the senses and reason, respectively. No semantic difference between *tenebricosus* and *obscurus* is apparent from uses elsewhere (cf. Fordyce 1961: 94 on *Cat.* 3.11), but the former is obviously choicer, not a standard epistemological term in *Acad.* and beyond, and meant to render the equally unusual σκότιος.

Brittain and Palmer (2001: 56–8) address an apparent contradiction between *Luc.* 32, where Lucullus attributes the view to Democritus that nature has hidden the truth from us, and the present passage, where Democritus is said to have made the stronger claim that nothing is true (cf. earlier Reid[1] p. 262). They offer three possible explanations: first, the record on Democritus may have included statements which were at variance with each other; second, different Academics may have appealed to Democritus in different ways, which may be reflected in the two passages; third, and this is the option plausibly favoured by Brittain and Palmer, the Academics may have opted for a stronger reading of the Democritean evidence, according to which the true character of things is hidden from humans in principle. They cite the series of Democritean *dicta* in Sextus, *M.* 136–7 (DK 68B9, 10, 6, 7, 8), which do allow for such a strong reading. It would suit Lucullus' and Cicero's respective rhetorical purposes if the former delimited Democritus' scepticism, while the latter made it out to be all-encompassing and dogmatic; see next n.

One of the two *esse* needs to be deleted, and sense/required emphasis seems better served by deleting the second *esse* with Halm (in his apparatus) than the first with Davies.

Is qui hunc maxime est admiratus...sitne aliquid an nihil sit: Brittain and Palmer (2001: 58) observe that Metrodorus, who is absent from the list of sceptical ancestors in *Ac.* 1.44–5 and *Luc.* 14, is cited in support of the strong reading of Democritus (see previous n.) which is favoured by the Academics.

On Metrodorus of Chios (fourth century BC), whose testimonies and fragments are collected as DK 70, see Goulet (2005b); Brunschwig (1996), who surveys and discusses the versions of Metrodorus' statement reported by various authors; and Brunschwig (1999: 237–40), who places what little we know about Metrodorus in the wider context of Hellenistic epistemology. Burnyeat (1978: 204) regards it as likely that the 'upside-down back-to-front sceptic' of Lucretius 4.469–72 is Metrodorus.

With the quotation here, which comes from the beginning of Metrodorus' work (so Eusebius, quoted below), cf. the following parallels (assembled by Brunschwig 1996: 22–3): Epiphanes, *Adv. haer.* 3.2.9 (= DK 70A23, DG p. 590.35): μηδένα μηδὲν ἐπίστασθαι, '(he said) that nobody knew anything'; Philodemus, *Rhet.* frg. inc. 3.1, vol. ii p. 169 Sudhaus (= DK 70A25): μὴ [εἰδέ]ναι μηδ' αὐτὸ τοῦ[το, '(he said) he knew nothing and not even that'; D.L. 9.58 (= DK 69A2, 72A1): ἔλεγε μηδ' αὐτὸ τοῦτ' εἰδέναι, ὅτι οὐδὲν οἶδε, 'he said that he did not even know that, that he knew nothing'; Sextus, *M.* 7.88 (= DK 70A25): οὐδὲν ἴσμεν, οὐδ' αὐτὸ τοῦτο ἴσμεν ὅτι οὐδὲν ἴσμεν, 'we know nothing, and do not even know that, that we know nothing'; Eus., *Praep. Ev.* XIV.19.9 (= DK 70B1): οὐδεὶς ἡμῶν οὐδὲν οἶδεν, οὐδ' αὐτὸ τοῦτο, πότερον οἴδαμεν ἢ οὐκ οἴδαμεν (see below for the translation options). Brunschwig gives the text of our passage as in DK 70B1, with an insertion of *scire* as A[a] and B[a] have it, and with a division (i)–(iii) for ease of reference: (i) *nego scire nos sciamusne aliquid an nihil sciamus*, (ii) *ne id ipsum quidem nescire aut scire ⟨scire⟩ nos*, (iii) *nec omnino sitne aliquid an nihil sit*.

With respect to the Eusebius passage Brunschwig (1999: 237 n. 24) points out an ambiguity: 'The sentence seems to admit of two grammatically possible construals: (a) one...takes αὐτὸ τοῦτο to refer to the initial proposition ("none of us knows anything") and to serve proleptically as object of the verbs οἴδαμεν ἢ οὐκ οἴδαμεν; (b) αὐτὸ τοῦτο could also be read as second object of οἶδεν and taken to refer to the indirect question, πότερον οἴδαμεν ἢ οὐκ οἴδαμεν; the translation would then be: "None of us knows anything, not even this, viz. whether we know or do not know".' Brunschwig opts plausibly for the first of the two readings, on the grounds that the indirect question appears syntactically incomplete if the verbs do not have an object.

Thus construed, Metrodorus' statement is a disavowal of first-order knowledge, as well as a disavowal of second-order knowledge of the speaker's epistemic state, and it is possible to explain the other Greek testimonies as alternative formulations of the statement as presented by Eusebius (Sextus), in two cases compressed (D.L.; Philodemus), or else the result of a truncation of the statement (Epiphanes).

The formulation in Cicero is, on the face of it, quite different from what we find in Eusebius. Clause (iii) in Brunschwig's division has no immediately obvious counterpart in the parallel evidence, and clause (i) is concerned with second-order rather than first-order knowledge. The object of that second-order knowledge in (i) is grammatically an indirect disjunctive question (*sciamusne aliquid an nihil sciamus*, formally comparable to Eusebius' πότερον οἴδαμεν ἢ οὐκ οἴδαμεν, who, however, had Metrodorus disavow first-order knowledge beforehand); contrast Sextus' formulation (οὐδ' αὐτὸ τοῦτο ἴσμεν ὅτι οὐδὲν ἴσμεν).

Cicero's clause (ii) poses a number of problems. Brunschwig (1996: 33–4) shows how their precise identification and solution was pushed yet further beyond reach by the fact that some of Metrodorus' interpreters viewed Cicero's text through the prism of Diels-Kranz's unsatisfactory re-translation into Greek. Given that *nescire aut scire* stand in disjunction while the clause as a whole, in virtue of *ne...quidem*, ought to offer another disavowal of knowledge, the insertion of *scire* has obvious attraction, but it places *nescire aut scire* in stylistically awkward parenthesis (note the translation in Brittain 2006, who renders it as if it is an indirect question). Moreover, one encounters a problem similar to the one which Brunschwig identified with respect to the evidence from Eusebius: that an absolute use of *nescire* and *scire* is unsatisfactory. The solution to this would be to treat *ne id ipsum quidem* as resumptive as well as the object of *nescire* and *scire* (analogous to οὐδ' αὐτὸ τοῦτο in the Greek texts); thus Dal Pra (1975[2]: i.52): '[Io affirmo]...che non sappiamo neppure se sappiamo o non sappiamo questa cosa stessa.'

This leaves two problems: clause (ii) retains a complexity and awkwardness which serves no positive purpose, and it refers back to clause (i) which was about second-order knowledge. Brunschwig (1996: 35–6) thus notes the attractiveness of a suggestion made by Langerbeck (1935: 122): *nescire* (or rather *nescire aut*) might be a misguided insertion. Langerbeck, however, thought this insertion was made by Cicero himself, whereas I suspect an interpolator. The text resulting from excluding *nescire aut*, which would not require the insertion of *scire*, would yield the same sense much more smoothly: *ne id ipsum quidem scire nos*. The disjunctive question in the previous clause might have prompted an early insertion of *nescire aut*. On either reading, however, clause (ii) would provide something that is missing from the

Greek evidence: a disavowal of third-order knowledge. This distinguishes Metrodorus' position from that of the Academics and makes it more extreme; cf. Brittain and Palmer (2001: 58 n. 24), although they accept a different text. On the correctors' (or corrector's) addition of *scire* and its import for the evaluation of the correction layers in A and B see also Reinhardt (forthcoming).

Brunschwig (1996: 37) concludes his discussion with the plausible suggestion that clause (iii), still governed by *nego scire* at the beginning of the sentence, should be viewed as a delayed and somewhat full disavowal of first-order knowledge. Contrast Tor (2013: 13 n. 26), who holds that 'Cicero's formulation does not seem to include an explicit *first-order* denial of knowledge at all'. See *OLD* s.v. *sum* no. 8a for *esse* 'to be the case' (as opposed to 'to exist', as e.g. Reid² p. 60 has it). For the position of *Chius* see Reid¹ (p. 338) on *Luc.* 137.

§74

Furere tibi Empedocles uidetur...sonum fundere: cf. on *Luc.* 14 on the *persona* of the Empedoclean narrator in the extant fragments. *Dignissimum...sonum fundere* might sound jarring given the lack of control suggested by the verb, but mimics oracular expressions: Cic., *N.D.* 1.66: *haec ego nunc physicorum oracula fundo*; Catul. 64.321: *talia diuino fuderunt carmine fata*; Lucr. 5.110: *fundere fata*. See also *TLL* s.v. *fundo²*, col. 1566.45–84.

Brittain and Palmer (2001: 58–60) identify statements by Empedocles which might have given rise to his inclusion in a list of sceptical predecessors drawn up by the Academics: DK 31B8 is cited by Colotes according to Plut., *Adv. Col.* 1111f–1112a as evidence that Empedocles robs humans of a criterion with respect to the senses; Sextus, *M.* 7.120–5 rejects the notion that Empedocles was sceptical about the senses, but cites what is DK 31B2 as apparent evidence that Empedocles rejected the senses in favour of ὀρθὸς λόγος as a criterion. D.L. 9.71–3 quotes from the same fragment (lines 7–8a and 5) 'in a review of the purported forerunners of Pyrrhonism...These verses may ultimately lie behind Cicero's report of the Academic view that Empedocles denied that the senses can serve as reliable criteria for judging the truth of the things he speaks of in his poem; they might also support the claim that he likewise rejected reason as a criterion' (Brittain and Palmer 2001: 60).

Num ergo is excaecat...quae sub eos subiecta sunt iudicanda: on the complaint about the double standard—the Academics are accused of holding outlandish views (or views which have outlandish consequences; §30: *lucem eripere*, §61: *confundit...sensibus*) while certain Presocratics, who are in some ways more extreme, are admired by the dogmatists, see the general note above.

With *subicere sub aliquam rem*, cf. the alternative *subicere alicui rei* in *Ac.* 1.31: *subiectae sensibus* (so Reid¹ p. 263, who also refers to the discussion of *subicere* in Madvig 1876: 228–9 on *Fin.* 2.48).

Parmenides, Xenophanes...audeant se scire dicere: the supposed *ira* of Xenophanes and Parmenides is presumably to be distinguished from the *furor* which Lucullus diagnoses in Empedocles' case. While it is not difficult to detect indignation in Xenophanes' *persona*, it is less apparent in the case of Parmenides', which may suggest that the latter is here conflated with the former because of their teacher–pupil relationship (cf. *Luc.* 129). The discussion by Brittain and Palmer (2001: 60-3) provides an insightful guide, to which this n. is indebted. Both Xenophanes and Parmenides are presented as assuming that nothing can be known (*cum sciri nihil possit*), and their anger arises from knowledge claims made by others.

In the case of Xenophanes the evidence which could be cited in support of the Academic view are the criticism of conventional conceptions of divinity (DK 21B1.21-4, B10-12, B14-16) as well as an apparent profession of scepticism (Sextus, *M.* 7.49 = DK 21B34); on the latter passage see also Tor (2013):

> καὶ τὸ μὲν οὖν σαφὲς οὔτις ἀνὴρ ἴδεν, οὐδέ τις ἔσται
> εἰδὼς ἀμφὶ θεῶν τε καὶ ἅσσα λέγω περὶ πάντων·
> εἰ γὰρ καὶ τὰ μάλιστα τύχοι τετελεσμένον εἰπών,
> αὐτὸς ὅμως οὐκ οἶδε· δόκος δ' ἐπὶ πᾶσι τέτυκται.

> And that which is clear no man has seen, nor will there be anyone
> who knows what I say about the gods and all matters;
> for even if someone happened to succeed in speaking what has come
>   to pass,
> he nonetheless does not know; opinion is wrought over all.

Sextus states in the immediately preceding context that Xenophanes had declared all things to be non-cognitive. Brittain and Palmer note a particular affinity with the Academics, in that Xenophanes' claim that, even if one succeeded in saying something 'perfect', one would not know, can be compared with Cicero's remark that the Academics do not deny that there is a truth, just that it can be apprehended (§73: *nos, qui ueri esse aliquid non negamus, percipi posse negamus*). Sextus illustrates the point with the analogy of people feeling their way around a dark room which contains a golden treasure (*M.* 7.52): they will think they may be touching the gold when they touch something, but will not be certain that they do even when they are in fact touching the gold. B34 is a general statement; contrast Lucullus' claim (§14) that the Presocratics make sceptical pronouncements occasionally *cum haerent aliquo loco*. See also Vassallo (2015).

How exactly Parmenides was used is less clear, and the present passage is all one has to go on in Cicero (in addition to the even briefer reference in Lucullus' speech). Sextus states that Parmenides renounced the senses (*M.* 7.114 *fin.*; cf. Aëtius in DK 28A49). This impression can be derived from DK 28B7.3-5 (Sextus, *M.* 7.111) and the suggestion of the 'instability and uncertainty of human νόος' in DK 28B16 (Arist., *Met.* Γ5, 1009b22-5); so Brittain and Palmer (2001: 61), who go on to discuss evidence from Plut., *Adv. Col.* 1121f-1122a (= LS 68H) on Arcesilaus' appeal to Parmenides and Heraclitus—evidence which is at variance with what is reported in *Acad.* in a number of ways (Arcesilaus is said to have attributed ἀκαταληψία as well as ἐποχή to them). They conclude that the notice in Plutarch may be about the representation of Parmenides and Heraclitus in Plato's dialogues and not involve a direct engagement with their texts. On Plato's *Parm.* as a text which the Academics might have invoked to justify their stance see also Glucker (1978: 40-7).

Parmenides' poetry is usually noted for its obscurity and rich use of metaphors rather than for its inferiority, but cf. Plut., *De aud.* 13, p. 45a (= DK 28A16), cited first by Davies: μέμψαιτο δ' ἄν τις Ἀρχιλόχου μὲν τὴν ὑπόθεσιν, Παρμενίδου δὲ τὴν στιχοποιίαν ('verse-making'), Φωκυλίδου δὲ τὴν εὐτέλειαν, Εὐριπίδου δὲ τὴν λαλιάν, Σοφοκλέους δὲ τὴν ἀνωμαλίαν; Wöhrle (1993) for a modern discussion. On the Presocratics who wrote verse in general, cf. Philo of Alexandria, *De prov.* 2.39: *optimi quidem uiri—poetae tamen non felices* (Aucher's Latin translation from the Armenian translation of the lost Greek original). On *quamquam...sed tamen*, see Rudolph (1996: 226-9); Mikkola (1957: 108) [*non vidi*]. Madvig (1876: 726-7) notes on *Fin.* 5.68 that Cicero omits the verb of the *quamquam* clause only if it is the same as that of the main clause (here *increpant*).

The resumptive pronoun *illi* is strictly redundant, as Reid[1] (p. 263) noted, but not suspect in the dialogue format which admits of colloquial features more freely. The ablative *illis* is attractive, in that it would place more emphasis on the verses (and their content). Schäublin (1992: 45-6) proposed the insertion of *et* before *illi*.

Et ab iis aiebat...nihil amplius: cf. §15: *Quorum e numero tollendus est et Plato et Socrates*. Lucullus, as noted above, gave reasons then, so Cicero's 'Why?' signals his resistance. With the metaphorical use of 'living with someone' = 'being deeply familiar with them' contrast the literal use in §115 on Diodotus.

Reid[1] (p. 264) is right to note that *sermones* could in principle refer to Socratic dialogues rather than just Platonic ones featuring Socrates, but given that Plato's representation of Socrates is salient for the dismissal of Antiochus' ironic, dogmatist Socrates, perhaps the more narrow reference is intended here; certainly no attempt is made to argue against Plato from other authors' representations of Socrates.

The force of *perscribere* is not clear: the word may just mean 'to write down', but it may also be suggestive of the dialogues being records of actual conversations, or of them being detailed records of such conversations (cf. on *Ac.* 1.16: *perscripti*).

Socrates' profession of ignorance in *Apol.* 21b4-5 was a philosophical commonplace already in antiquity; however, the passage cannot be straightforwardly rendered as 'I know that I know nothing', since σύνοιδα ἐμαυτῷ does not simply mean 'I know', and 'to be wise' (σοφὸς ὤν) is suggestive of expertise or craft knowledge (broadly construed): 21b4-5: ἐγὼ γὰρ δὴ οὔτε μέγα οὔτε σμικρὸν σύνοιδα ἐμαυτῷ σοφὸς ὤν; cf. 21d4-7: ἀλλ' οὗτος μὲν οἴεταί τι εἰδέναι οὐκ εἰδώς, ἐγὼ δέ, ὥσπερ οὖν οὐκ οἶδα, οὐδὲ οἴομαι· ἔοικα γοῦν τούτου γε σμικρῷ τινι αὐτῷ τούτῳ σοφώτερος εἶναι, ὅτι ἃ μὴ οἶδα οὐδὲ οἴομαι εἰδέναι. Burnyeat (1997: 290-300), having shown that 'I know that I know nothing' was recognized as self-refuting in the Hellenistic period and that Socrates is treated as a 'philosophical hero' in the sceptical Academy (who ought not to make self-refuting statements), examines references to Socrates in *Acad.* (*Ac.* 1.16, 1.44-5, where the phrase *confessio ignorationis* features; *Luc.* 15; and the present passage), arguing, largely persuasively, that these passages do not commit Socrates to the self-refuting 'I know that I know nothing' but rather to the consistent statement 'I know nothing except that one proposition, viz. that I know nothing'. (*Luc.* 15 is in fact merely compatible with this reading, and in my view the Cicero character places a different reading on it, see section 7.3 and below.)

'I know nothing...viz. that I know nothing' is what Cicero reports here in the resumption (*Excepit unum tantum, 'scire se nihil scire', nihil amplius*), which, as Burnyeat shows (1997: 297–300), ought to be viewed as a less-than-nuanced summary of a weaker initial formulation, in that...*quin Socrati nihil sit uisum sciri posse* and the wider context are suggestive of numerous qualifications: it (merely) *appeared* to Socrates that nothing could be known (sc. by *him*), since his conversations are at issue, and even these conversations covered only a sub-set of possible issues one might discuss (thus Burnyeat takes *nihil* to be implicitly qualified, too, i.e. restricted to the subjects which Socrates has investigated; with *excepit* one then has to supply 'explicitly'). The Academics, following Arcesilaus, did in any event drop even the one negative knowledge claim (*Ac.* 1.45).

Nihil amplius suggests that the Cicero character takes Lucullus to have implicitly ascribed further knowledge claims to Socrates in §15, a notion which Cicero would reject; see next n. *Aiebat* rather than *aiebas* may be read as indicating an indignant turn towards a larger audience (viz. all interlocutors present).

Quid dicam de Platone...nulla fuit ratio persequi: Cicero turns to Plato, but is in fact speaking about both Socrates and Plato. In §15 Lucullus had suggested that Socrates deployed irony, leaving it vague whether behind it he concealed knowledge of various matters which he took himself to have or only the one item of second-order knowledge mention here in §74. Cicero here does two things: (i) he rejects the notion that Socrates as presented in Plato was ironic. The point that Plato would have had no reason to represent Socrates' ironic posture consistently suggests that the Cicero character takes Lucullus to have implied in §15 that Socrates did conceal knowledge of various matters; to create a character who dissimulates in this way and to sustain him over many works would be without rationale, whereas sustaining a character who makes but one second-order knowledge claim would be less peculiar. (ii) He states that Plato himself approved *haec*, which presumably means Socrates' disavowals of knowledge (not 'these doctrines', as Rackham 1951 has it).

Burnyeat (1997: 298) argues that the Cicero character accepts that Socrates is ironic, translating *ironiam enim alterius...* as '*otherwise* there was no reason...' [my emphasis]; similarly Rackham (1951). *Enim* cannot mean 'otherwise'.

For the concept of irony, see on *Luc.* 15. Reid[1] (p. 264) notes that in *Luc.* 15 Cicero is likely to have written the word εἰρωνεία in Greek letters, whereas here he opted for a transliteration; in §15 code-switching occurs because what is at issue is how the Greeks express themselves, whereas here Cicero deploys in his own voice what has become a standard term of literary criticism (cf. *De orat.* 2.270). The manuscript evidence is usually not a reliable guide on whether Greek letters or transliteration was used; see O'Sullivan (2019) and (2021). For *persequi*, see *OLD* s.v. *persequor* no. 9: 'to conform steadfastly to (a pattern, a rule, or sim.).'

§75

Videorne...nisi nobilem: cf. §14:...*neque Saturninus, ut nostrum inimicum potissimm nominem*. The contrast between *nominare* and *imitari* is 'merely name for show / actually follow'. See Reid[1] (p. 264) on Cicero's use of sentence questions with -*ne* inviting the answer 'no'. On conjectural activity around *imitari numquam*, see Plasberg¹ (p. 107).

Atqui habebam molestos uobis...conclusiunculae: Diodorus Cronus (died c.284 BC; cf. Dorandi 1999: 52) and Stilpo (died c.280 BC; see ibid.) were reportedly teachers of Zeno's (D.L. 7.16 = *FDS* 108; D.L. 2.114, 120; 7.2, 24), and Alexinus, who was slightly younger (died c.265 BC), wrote against Zeno (D.L. 7.163). All three are associated with the Megarian school, or with the Dialectical School, which either derived from the former or formed a sect within it. As a group they shared an interest in dialectical skill, logic, the formulation of paradoxes, and their resolution. The paradoxes continued to preoccupy the Stoics after there ceased to be Dialecticians around the middle of the third century BC (see §§92–8 on the sorites and the Liar; only the latter is attested to have been studied by the Megarians). See Sedley (1977); Bobzien (2011); Allen (2019).

An *acus* is a needle or pin; the term is used in various figurative senses, incl. in standing phrases, e.g. *acum in mentibus relinquere*, 'to leave one's sting behind, sc. in the minds of the audience' (*OLD* s.v. no. 3e), which may have influenced Cicero's choice of *aculeatus* (on which see also Plasberg¹ p. 108), given that many sophisms leave the audience with a baffling conclusion upon the acceptance of apparently innocuous premises. On the technical sense of σόφισμα, see Barnes, Bobzien, and Mignucci (1999: 157): 'A false argument is an argument which either has something false in its premisses or is formally incorrect (D.L. VII.79). What makes a false argument a sophism is that its conclusion is evidently false and it is not clear on what the falsity of the conclusion depends (Gal., *Pecc. Dig.* 5.72–3).' Reid¹ (p. 265) suggests that Cicero 'interposed' the word *cauillatio* in the final edition of *Acad.*, with reference to Sen., *Ep.* 111.1: *Quid uocentur Latine sophismata quaesisti a me. Multi temptauerunt illis nomen imponere, nullum haesit; uidelicet, quia res ipsa non recipiebatur a nobis nec in usu erat, nomini quoque repugnatum est. Aptissimum tamen uidetur mihi quo Cicero usus est: 'cauillationes' uocat*. There is no second occurrence of σόφισμα in Cicero's extant writings. I give the term in Greek letters, since it is an unfamiliar one, which the speaker is quoting.

Minutus just means 'small, insignificant', not 'small-minded, ignoble' (*OLD* s.v. no. 2b), given *sed* rather than *et*.

Sed quid eos colligam...non facile posse: on Chrysippus sustaining the Stoa singlehandedly, cf. the famous line in D.L. 7.183: εἰ μὴ γὰρ ἦν Χρύσιππος, οὐκ ἂν ἦν στοά, 'If Chrysippus had not been there, there'd have been no Stoa', and Carneades' equally famous reply (4.62): εἰ μὴ γὰρ ἦν Χρύσιππος, οὐκ ἂν ἦν ἐγώ, 'If Chrysippus had not been there, there'd have been no me.' See the general note above on the substance of the reference to Chrysippus. The sentence *At dissoluit idem* (sc. the arguments against the senses and *consudetudo*) is a fictional intervention by the opponent (Lucullus used the same technique to structure his argument, which introduces quasi-dialogue into a speech). Cicero disagrees that Chrysippus rebutted anything, but grants the point for the sake of the argument (going so far as to say that he is 'taken in'—*fallere*—by them), insisting only that Chrysippus must have felt the force of the arguments contra, or else he would not have assembled them. For *consuetudo*, see on *Luc.* 87b. Reid¹ (p. 265) on *uideret* for the pluperfect subjunctive and on *in consuetudine probari*; *TLL* s.v. *probo* col. 1474.7–23, esp. ll. 11–15.

§76a

Quid Cyrenaici tibi uidentur...sed tantum sentire affici se quodam modo: see on *Luc.* 20 for the interpretation of the Cyrenaic position, the notion of 'internal touch', and primary references. The Cyrenaics were one of the Socratic schools, and thus in principle candidates for a role of some kind in Antiochus' and Philo's competing histories of the Academic tradition. With *quo quid colore...*, Sextus, *M.* 7.191 (about colour and sweetness, rather than colour and sound); see Tsouna (1998: 154–6). On *quid tibi uidentur* for *quales tibi uidentur*, see Reid¹ (p. 265). I print *Cyrenaici*, but it is not impossible that Cicero wrote *Cyrenai* here and *Cyrenaici* in *Luc.* 20; see also Plasberg¹ (p. 108).

§§76b–78

Cicero concludes the section which began in §72 *init.* by stating that enough has been said about authorities, sc. invoked by either party in support of their views. He then proposes to rely 'shortly', i.e. from §79 *init.*, on Lucullus as a judge to establish whether a question the latter had raised in §15 should be answered in the affirmative: whether so many brilliant minds investigating assiduously over a long period of time have been able to uncover something. The question in §15 had been: *...nihilne tot saeculis summis ingeniis maximis studiis explicatum putamus?* This is not quite the same as asking whether something true has been discovered (as noted by Schäublin et al. p. 247 n. 210), although it is arguable that the verb *explicare* is factive and thus presupposes that there is something that is the case to be uncovered. The issue on which Cicero will let Lucullus be the judge is in due course (§78 *fin.*) identified as whether the condition specified in the third clause of Zeno's definition of the cataleptic impression is ever met.

Cicero proceeds to give a potted account of why Arcesilaus came to engage with Zeno almost exclusively; cf. *Ac.* 1.44: *Cum Zenone...ut accepimus Arcesilas sibi omne certamen* **instituit.**[296] With the theme of the search for the true, successful or otherwise, established, Arcesilaus is introduced as someone who engaged Zeno in argument, not in order to disparage, but because he wanted to find the true. §77 then introduces a reason why Zeno in particular was selected as an interlocutor. He made two very original statements (which, one may suspect, resonated with the two views Arcesilaus had formed, according to *Ac.* 1.44–5, prior to engaging with Zeno: that nothing can be known, and that as a consequence one should not form opinions):[297]

---

[296] On §77 as part of the Arcesilaus narrative, see section 7.5; on its role as evidence for the doctrine of the cataleptic impression and in particular its representation in *Acad.*, see section 5, esp. 5.1. For a discussion of §77 and its reception in Augustine from the viewpoint of epistemological terminology, see Reinhardt (2018b).

[297] I take these two views of Arcesilaus to be general, i.e. not formulated with reference to any particular conception of knowledge.

that it is possible to live without opinions, and that for the sage this is not just possible, but actually incumbent upon him. Arcesilaus' two antecedently held views would be compatible with a human life in which the subject is reduced to mere opinion, however undesirable and reprehensible this would be held to be. Zeno's two statements offer the hope of something better, notably for the sage, who is a Stoic conception and does not feature in Arcesilaus' antecedently held views which arose from the *obscuritas rerum*.

The two statements 'appear to Arcesilaus to be true, honourable, and fitting for the sage'. Cicero does not say that he assented to them: Arcesilaus is strongly associated with universal suspension in *Acad.*, and Cicero is a Clitomachean. Nor does Cicero *say* that Arcesilaus responded to them with a lesser form of endorsement; however, the evaluative terms used do suggest an attraction felt by Arcesilaus which goes, quantitatively and qualitatively, beyond e.g. approval as it would be given by answering 'yes' in a dialectical exchange (cf. *Luc.* 104).

Cicero then provides a piece of stylized dialogue between Arcesilaus and Zeno. Arcesilaus 'perhaps' posed a question: *fortasse* is less likely to signal limited confidence in any source used than to draw attention to the fictional quality of the exchange—'it may have happened like this' (see also the two instances of parenthetical *credo* further into the paragraph).[298] The dialogue dramatizes inter alia how, given his general, pre-theoretical views, Arcesilaus could end up debating with Zeno what seems a very narrow point within Stoic philosophy, and one predicated on Stoic doctrine (which assumes e.g. entities like impressions). What the section does not aim to provide is (a) the actual introduction of Zeno's definition into the debate (it featured already in §18 of Lucullus' speech, and presumably in the historical section of the *Catulus* which corresponded to *Ac.* 1.40–2), or (b) a fictional account of how the definition as a whole came about, even though the text might seem to encourage a reading according to which Zeno formulates the entire definition on the spot in response to Arcesilaus' questions. However, the section does seem intended to explain why Zeno added a third clause to an earlier version of the definition which only had the first two clauses.

Arcesilaus asked Zeno what would happen if nothing could be apprehended and the sage was not to have opinions. Given how the dialogue then unfolds, it is reasonable to read this as Arcesilaus' attempt, genuine or not, to bring his antecedently held conviction that nothing can be known (sc. on any construal of knowledge) to bear on Zeno's stipulation that the sage must not hold opinions. Cicero has Zeno reply that on his view there is something which affords apprehension, an impression, and one which meets the requirements of the first and the second clause of the definition of the cataleptic impression (the definition is in this case presented in such a way that first and second clause are combined). Arcesilaus then asks about the possibility of a false impression 'of the same kind' (*eius modi*) as a true (and, it is implied, supposedly cataleptic) impression. The likeness of true and false impression envisaged must relate to the property described in the second clause of the definition, since the first

---

[298] Compare Brittain (2006: 45 n. 110): 'This passage should probably be read as a "philosophical reconstruction" rather than the record of an actual debate, since our other evidence suggests that the Stoic response to Arcesilaus came from Zeno's students rather than their leader.'

clause stipulates that a cataleptic impression be true. Zeno is said to have been acute in seeing that no apprehension is possible if true and false impressions can share the property described in the second clause, and therefore added the third clause. Arcesilaus 'agreed' with the addition of the third clause but proceeded to argue—by means of arguments from ἀπαραλλαξία—that the condition thus imposed is never met by any impression.

At the beginning of §78 Cicero identifies the debate about the third clause as the one issue which has remained live until the present day, sc. of the two mentioned in §77. The issue of whether the sage will ever assent is said to be unrelated. This is so because (i) Cicero can rely on Lucullus' agreement that,[299] if apprehension is impossible, the sage will not opine and (ii) some Academics accept that, if apprehension is impossible, the sage will opine irrespective of what the Stoics think. The latter relates to an inner-Academic dispute which arose after Zeno and Arcesilaus and is marked as a side issue by Cicero (who is debating Lucullus).[300]

On (ii): to some within the Academy it has been permissible (*licebat*) to apprehend nothing and yet hold opinions (as a result of assent to incognitive impressions). Carneades is said to have 'approved' this view (*a Carneade probatum dicitur*); Cicero, however, follows the Carneades interpretation of Clitomachus rather than that of 'Philo or Metrodorus' (*Philoni aut Metrodoro*), in that he thinks that Carneades 'argued' for this view (*disputatum*) rather than 'approved' it himself (*probatum*). Carneades could have 'argued' for the view in question on the grounds that it ought to have a claim on the Stoics given their own standards of rationality and e.g. the possibility that the sage finds himself in a situation in which there is nothing better to be had than a merely persuasive impression. 'Approving' the same view would have meant a degree of endorsement on the part of Carneades.

§78, which is 69H in Long and Sedley (1987), Carneades F5 Mette, and test. XXV in Brittain (2001: 358), has played an important role in influential reconstructions of the views available in the post-Carneadean Academy and, as a consequence, in the history of philosophical scepticism generally.[301] Brittain (2001) combines the evidence of the present passage with that of *Luc.* 148, where the Catulus character gives his self-aware assent to the proposition that nothing can be known. Self-aware assent, the hallmark of mitigated scepticism, is like dogmatic assent in terms of the endorsement given to an impression, viz. it is taken as true, but it differs from assent through the attitude with which assent is given, viz. with an accompanying second-order belief that the impression in question may be false.[302] On the assumption that §78

---

[299] Cf. §68: *quod tu mihi das, accepero, sapientem nihil opinari*; so if he succeeds in showing that the condition set out in the third clause is never met, then he can rely on Lucullus' concession that one should suspend judgement universally.

[300] See also on *Luc.* 59 and 66-7 which also mention this argumentative option.

[301] Relevant discussions include Hirzel (1883: 316-18); Lörcher (1911: 241, 260-2); Glucker (1978: 64-88); Lévy (1992: 267); Görler (1994: 870, 873); Striker (1996b: 93-4); Burnyeat (1997: 300-9); Görler (2004c: 277, 288); Glucker (2004: 118-33); Lévy (2005: 70-6); Thorsrud (2012: 138-42); Ioppolo (2013: 251-6, 266-7); Wynne (2014: 250-1); Allen (2018: 190-1); Bonazzi (2019: 247-51). Before Brittain (2001), the interpretative options arising from this passage were fully appreciated only by Frede (1987b), who, however, does not think that mitigated scepticism was ever the official position of the Academy (pp. 212-13, 221). A detailed rebuttal of Brittain's reading of *Luc.* 78 is included in Glucker (2004).

[302] I take self-aware assent to be incompatible with general ἐποχή, but there is a textual problem in §148 which obscures this; see ad loc.

and §148 speak about the same view, Brittain identifies mitigated scepticism as a position of Philo's, which the latter adopted after he gave up Clitomacheanism and before he formulated the Roman Books view. He further argues that mitigated scepticism was not just a position Philo adopted qua scholarch but that it became the official position of the Academy for a period, embraced not by all members of the school but by a substantial group which he calls the 'Philonian/Metrodorians'. Evidence from later writers which casts the Academics as dogmatically committed to their sceptical views is marshalled in support of the suggestion that the 'Philonian/Metrodorians' came to determine the reception of sceptical Academy.

In this commentary I argue that independent evidence suggests that Philo never was a mitigated sceptic.[303] I also do not believe that the evidence warrants the assumption that there ever was a discernible group of mitigated sceptics whom one could characterize as 'Philonian/Metrodorians',[304] although §148 provides good evidence that mitigated scepticism was a position of some standing in the Academy.[305] Nor do I think that reports on the sceptical Academy in other authors support the notion that the mitigated position ever was the official position of the Academy, or the one which determined the the later 'construction' of Academic scepticism.[306] Much of the evidence cited for Philonian/Metrodorian thinking from the Ciceronian corpus does in fact come from passages where the speaker is Clitomachean or where the Clitomachean position can plausibly be seen as a target.[307] As for §78, I observe that Philo's and Metrodorus' names are linked by the exclusive 'or' (*aut*), suggesting less that they shared a view than that they held different views which converged on the narrow issue on which the paragraph turns: that the sage is permitted (or 'will') assent to the non-cataleptic.

Given that §78 primarily aims to speak to the remaining disagreement from the time of Arcesilaus and Zeno (cf. §77), the possibility needs to be seriously considered that Philo and Metrodorus are independently linked with positions which *within the Stoic framework* would be characterized as assent to the non-cataleptic. On this reading, the Carneadean alternative to the corollary argument would not directly issue in a programmatic statement of an avowed position (or rather, given *aut*, positions) but would function as a description of it from the Stoics' point of view. Such positions are Philo's Roman Books view and the only position attested for Metrodorus, respectively.

For the former see on *Luc.* 18, from which it emerges that Roman Books κατάληψις arises from an impression which meets the first two clauses of Zeno's definition and

---

[303] I argue in section 8 that Philo's being a mitigated sceptic (or promoting the Roman Books view) when Cicero first met him would sit oddly with the narrative of Cicero's philosophical formation contained in his works. §69 *init.* strongly suggests that Philo was a Clitomachean when Antiochus was his pupil (see ad loc.).

[304] See also Glucker (2004) on this point.

[305] I speculate in the commentary on *Luc.* 18 how Catulus' familiarity with it might have been explained in the first edition of *Acad.*

[306] I discuss this evidence in appendix 1 and attempt to show that the kind of position Cicero adopts in his philosophical works—which retains the commitment to universal suspension of judgement while allowing for 'approval' of (some) persuasive impressions (§104)—could just as easily have given rise to Academic scepticism's reception as mitigated scepticism.

[307] This is an issue pursued in the commentary passim.

which has been assented to. For the biographical information on Metrodorus, who unusually for an Academic started out as an Epicurean, see on *Luc.* 16-17a; for the evidence for his philosophical views, see the n. below. The evidence for his position comes from Philodemus and Augustine (as well as *Luc.* 78). According to the former, he claimed to have understood Carneades better than anyone else; this would have sounded immodest in the mouth of the scholarch, which he was not, and must have appeared provocative. His views, if the conventional chronology holds, must have been formulated when Philo was by universal agreement a Clitomachean. It thus seems unlikely that Philo would have seen or would have cared to present him as an ally, or that Cicero would have done this on his behalf. This supports the notion that §78 is intended to cite two independent individuals whose views converged on a narrow point. Both authors agree that Metrodorus claimed that not everything was non-cataleptic. Only Augustine reports that Metrodorus added that the thesis of ἀκαταληψία was merely a weapon against the Stoics, taken up 'out of necessity'. On the most natural reading, this is not a disavowal of ἀκαταληψία as far as the Stoic criterion is concerned, but an explanation of it, and the context here in §78 encourages such a reading inasmuch as the views of Philo and Metrodorus are by implication predicated on ἀκαταληψία (sc. on the Stoic conception of κατάληψις). The evidence does not tell us how Metrodorus' positive account of definition of knowledge looked like, but it is striking that Metrodorus's position seems to share two significant features with Philo's Roman Books view, i.e. the claiming of the term κατάληψις, and the combination of a doctrinal claim with a historical one (he introduced his view as the correct interpretation of Carneades' stance). This might seem to raise the question of the extent to which Antiochus' anger over the Roman Books could have been sincere (see on *Luc.* 11), but more importantly for present purposes, it makes it economical to assume that §78 is, as far as Metrodorus is concerned, about the same view mentioned elsewhere, notably about assent involved in his alternative conception of κατάληψις attested in Philodemus and Augustine (which would, from the Stoic point of view, be a δόξα). Otherwise one has to posit that §78 provides the sole evidence for a second position of Metrodorus' or else find reasons to discard the evidence from at least one of the three authors.[308] If §78 can refer to a position of Metrodorus' which is, on a suitably general level of description, like Philo's Roman Books position, it can refer to the latter as well.[309]

---

[308] Brittain (2001: 215 n. 74), cf. (2006: xxviii n. 47), holds that the evidence from Augustine conflicts with *Luc.* 78: 'Cicero ascribes to Philo and Metrodorus provisional beliefs under the condition of *acatalepsia* in *Ac.* 2.78, while Augustine seems to suggest in *Contra Ac.* 3.41 that Metrodorus anticipated the acceptance of catalepsis, i.e. the central innovation of the Roman Books.' He proposes to reject the evidence from Augustine. Glucker (2004: 124-7) thinks the evidence from §78 conflicts with that from Philodemus and Augustine, in that the latter two passages ascribe a notion of κατάληψις to Metrodorus, whereas §78 says 'but only by implication' that Metrodorus upheld ἀκαταληψία. He proposes to discard the evidence from *Luc.* and thinks that Cicero corrected himself in the final edition on which Augustine relied. As indicated, I think the three pieces of evidence are consistent if one assumes that Metrodorus, like Philo as per his Roman Books view, posited a notion of κατάληψις under general ἀκαταληψία as far as the Stoic criterion was concerned.

[309] Those who assume that the position of mitigated scepticism represented by Catulus in §148 is the same as Philo's referenced here in §78 face their own challenges of reconciliation, in that the evidence for Metrodorus cannot be credibly linked to mitigated scepticism.

I do not think Metrodorus' view and Philo's Roman Books view involved rejection of the core and alternative to corollary arguments, but that both embraced these arguments as part of an explanation why their views had credible Academic credentials.[310] An explanation along these lines is hinted at in Philodemus' evidence on Metrodorus' view (see n. below), in that his view appears to have been presented as a superior interpretation of statements made by Carneades.

However, one might still wonder why Cicero would refererence the Roman Books view and a similar Metrodorean view here, as opposed to the position of mitigated scepticism which Catulus represents in the dialogue. That the Roman Books view is avowedly not the subject of debate in *Luc.* (cf. §18) is not a problem, in that the issue of opining is very clearly marked as an aside in *Luc.* 78. Brittain (2001: 154–8) has plausibly argued that assent as envisaged by Philo's Roman Books view was dogmatic assent.[311] This raises the possibility that the view formulated by Metrodorus involved the same assumption. If so, it would be natural to group both views together here and not to make reference to mitigated scepticism as represented by Catulus. The kind of assent the latter envisaged was presumably not recognized by the dogmatist as assent.[312]

If Philo never was a mitigated sceptic, then it might not have occurred to Cicero that from §78 and §148 the impression could arise that Philo was one. To be sure, a mitigated sceptic would have described his position in the terms on offer in §78 (though he would not have linked it to Metrodorus', for all we know); but, given what we know about Catulus the father's interaction with Philo over the Roman Books (§§12, 18), it seems that he did not see Philo as the source of the mitigated interpretation. He accused Philo of lying, not of changing his mind.

§76b

Satis multa de auctoribus: this clearly marks the end of the section which began in §72. On the relevant sense of *auctor*, see *OLD* s.v. no. 4d; here as normally the term need not imply a model that is to be followed in every respect and whose views and attitudes are identical to one's own. For the Academic preference for *iudicium* over *auctoritas*, see *Luc.* 60. Reid[1] (p. 266) expresses surprise that Pyrrho has not been mentioned here, who is named by Cicero in §130 (see ibid.), but only as a moralist. Bett (2014: §2) comments on Cicero as a source on Pyrrho: 'Cicero refers to Pyrrho about ten times, and Cicero is, in general, a responsible reporter of other people's views. Unfortunately his information about Pyrrho appears to be very incomplete, and…the impression he conveys of him may very well be inaccurate. With one exception, he never mentions him except in conjunction with the Stoics Aristo and (sometimes) Erillus, and the remarks in question always concern the same one or

---

[310] Brittain (2006: xxx–xxxi) holds that Philo's Roman Books view involved a rejection of the Academic alternative to the corollary argument.

[311] See on *Luc.* 18 and 148.

[312] Lucullus' arguments in §§43–4 suggest this, in that they are designed to force the Academic to choose between unqualified commitment to propositions and corresponding impressions and no commitment at all.

two points in ethics; it looks as if his knowledge of Pyrrho derives almost entirely from a single source that conveyed little or nothing about Pyrrho individually, and nothing at all about any views of his in metaphysics or epistemology.'

Quamquam ex me quaesieras…te ipso quidem iudice: cf. *Luc.* 16 for the question, which was about progress made by the Academics since the time of Arcesilaus. Cicero paraphrases it, tendentiously, as enquiring about whether *uerum* has been discovered since then (*uerum* seems to be carefully ambiguous between 'the truth' and 'something true'). Lucullus had not gone as far as applying a dogmatist's standard of incremental progress marked by the discovery of truths to the Academics. On the pluperfect of *quaesieras*, where one might have expected perfect tense, cf. Kühner-Stegmann i.139–40. Reid[1] (pp. 266–7) wonders if the personification in *studiis quaerentibus* is not objectionable, and if it is the result a copyist's addition of *-que* (without which *quaerentibus* becomes an attribute of *ingeniis*, with *tantis studiis* in the instrumental ablative). However, Cicero makes Lucullus sound polemical in indirect speech here, and the personification may have been intended to convey that. Schäublin (1992: 46) deletes *studiis*.

To 'let the opponent be the judge' is a topos of forensic oratory (cf. *Caec.* 48: *te ipsum habebo iudicem*). *Videro* may point to the doxographical section from §116 (thus Plasberg[1] p. 109), or to the Carneadean πιθανόν (§§98b–101b), or to '§§ 91 sq.' (so Reid[1] p. 267), if the reference is not meant to be to 'what follows' generally.

Arcesilam uero…uerum inuenire uoluisse sic intellegitur: on the spelling *Arcesilam*, see p. lxxiv of the Oxford Classical Text. In dismissing that Arcesilaus engaged Zeno *obtrectandi causa* Cicero is still looking to what Lucullus said in §16 (*Arcesilas Zenoni ut putatur obtrectans*); however, the false charge of antagonism for the sake of it also serves to characterize Arcesilaus, because the same was said of Socrates by numerous interlocutors in Plato's dialogues. The Academic commitment to search for the truth (on which see at §§7b–9a) can of course be traced to Socrates, too; see e.g. Plut., *Adv. Col.* 1117d (Socrates' claim that he is searching for the truth, coupled with his disavowal of knowledge, amounts to ἀλαζονεία). Against this background, it is fitting that Arcesilaus and Zeno are about to engage in *dialogue*.

§77

Nemo umquam superiorum…honesta et digna sapienti: on the contrast between *exprimere* and *dicere*, 'carefully formulate' vs 'say', see Reid[1] (p. 267). The view Zeno is credited with here is prima facie reminiscent of the Pyrrhonist's life without beliefs or opinions, but unlike the Pyrrhonist Zeno holds that to sages as well as non-sages something better than belief is available, i.e. κατάληψις. That assumption, however, is not shared by Arcesilaus. That Zeno's view appeared 'not just true' to Arcesilaus, but 'honourable and fitting for the sage' is notable for two reasons: first, given that Arcesilaus advocated universal suspension of judgement, what does it mean that he adopted this attitude to Zeno's *sententia*? In §67 Arcesilaus is said to have 'approved' (arguably in the terminological sense of *Luc.* 104) the corollary argument, and Zeno's *sententia* 'appearing true' to Arcesilaus may be pointing in the same direction. That the *sententia* appears also 'honourable and fitting for the sage' may then suggest that approval, while invariably involving detachment of the perceiving subject, is susceptible to further categorizations. If the explanation given at §104—that approving is like saying 'yes' to a proposition offered in a dialectical exchange—is correct, then one can see why this might be so: even propositions which share the feature of being true may vary in appeal. While one might think that variations in appeal are a function of what views the subject holds antecedently, a Clitomachean would presumably reply that no antecedently held view enjoys more endorsement than is bestowed by approval. The Stoic might reply that this is a plausible account of our cognitive life only if one posits that views which are problematized, which become the object of our focus, can plausibly count as approved, whereas unproblematic background assumptions function like a dogmatist's beliefs. The Academic would presumably respond that a reactive conception of one's set of beliefs is sufficient for his purposes, viz. the possibility that any belief which is momentarily deeply unproblematic may be problematized. The second notable point is that, just as in §67, Arcesilaus is unproblematically credited with views here, whereas other evidence has him conceal, in the Socratic manner, whether he has any views, preferring to interrogate others about their views; see section 7.5.

Quaesiuit de Zenone fortasse…quod percipi posset: Reid[1] (p. 267) notes on *quaesiuit* that *Luc.* 67 and 68 'should be closely compared'. In a wider context which has Cicero commit himself to the Clitomachean position, §67 presents Arcesilaus as approving the corollary argument which concludes that judgement is to be suspended; in §68, where Cicero's position is treated as if it was continuous with Arcesilaus', Cicero identifies whether anything can be known as the sole contentious issue between Lucullus and him, signalling his support for universal ἀκαταληψία. In terms of relative chronology, §77 dramatizes an earlier point in Arcesilaus' argumentative engagement with Zeno, i.e. the formulation of the third clause of Zeno's definition.

On *fortasse*, the first in a series of distancing devices (two instances of *credo* follow), see the general note above; cf. Striker (1997: 265): 'In an anecdote that is no doubt too good to be true…'.

For reasons explained in the general note above, one should not read the text as recounting the moment when Zeno devised the entire conception and definition of an impression which affords apprehension. Nor should one assume that Arcesilaus is being introduced to that conception. Rather, he draws it out of Zeno, as is his Socratic way. On the dates of Zeno and Arcesilaus, see Gourinat (2018) and Dorandi (1989a). Brittain (2006: xiii) suggests that Arcesilaus' challenge to Zeno happened during the latter's lifetime 'though probably after his retirement'.

Quid ergo id esset? 'Visum', credo: syntactically the question depends on *quaesiuit* above. The subject of *credo* is Cicero, not Zeno (cf. the immediately preceding sentence). Reid[1] (p. 267) holds that *uisum* means 'cataleptic impression' here, without providing an explanation. While *uisum* can have this meaning, i.e. reflect the veridical sense of *uidere/uideri* (see section 10.1), and while the absence of an indefinite pronoun modifying *uisum* might suggest this, the immediately following question rather suggests that Zeno's reply is, or is taken to be by Arcesilaus in the fictional dialogue, 'an impression', i.e. that Zeno does not fully answer the question in his initial reply.

Quale igitur uisum...quale uel falsum: whether or not *uisum* in Zeno's initial reply meant 'cataleptic impression' or 'impression', what the question *quale igitur uisum?* cannot be aiming at is elucidation on what an impression is. Morever, as a Latin word *uisum* pre-existed *Acad.* and is not a term of art newly coined (just like the term φαντασία existed before it was used by the Stoics, even though its meaning was different); see Reinhardt (2018b: 310 n. 18, 312 n. 23). The question is what kind of *uisum* it is, sc. that affords apprehension.

If it is correct that Arcesilaus is presented as extracting from Zeno a definition which the latter had formulated earlier, then *definisse* must refer to the putting forward of a definition in the exchange, not the devising of it on the spot.

The actual definition given here, for which cf. the earlier passage in *Luc.* 18 (as well as §§41 *fin.* and 112), runs together the first and the second clause of the Zenonian definition. Its first clause (ἀπὸ ὑπάρχοντος) corresponds to *ex eo quod esset* **sicut esset**; the highlighted words make it plain that the present passage takes the first clause to stipulate that cataleptic impressions be true (i.e. present an object truthfully as being such-and-such) rather than merely come from an object. No comma should be placed after *quod esset*. Because Cicero shifts to indirect speech from *quale igitur uisum*, I have not printed quotation marks thereafter.

For the stamping and impressing imagery in *impressum et signatum et effictum* (corresponding to κατ' αὐτὸ τὸ ὑπάρχον ἐναπομεμαγμένη καὶ ἐναπεσφραγισμένη), cf. the slightly different formulations in §§18 (*impressum effictumque*), which confirms the emendation by Manutius here, and 112 (*quod impressum esset e uero*). More fundamentally on the definition, see section 5.1, also on passages in Plt. *Tht.* as a possible inspiration for it. See also the entry on §77 in the survey of passages relating to the distinctive feature of cataleptic impressions in the general note on *Luc.* 33–34a.

In *uisum uerum quale uel falsum* the term *uisum* has the attribute because of the contrast with false impressions (i.e. the presence of the attribute does not settle either way what *uisum* at its first occurrence meant). For *quale* **uel** *falsum* (repeated below), cf. §18: *quod est tale quale uel falsum esse possit*; but *Fin.* 5.76: *percipiendi uis ita definitur a Stoicis ut negent quidquam posse percipi nisi tale uerum quale falsum esse non possit*.

Hic Zenonem...posset esse: cf. Sextus, *M.* 7.252: τὸ δὲ 'οἷα οὐκ ἂν γένοιτο ἀπὸ μὴ ὑπάρχοντος' προσέθεσαν, ἐπεὶ οὐχ ὥσπερ οἱ ἀπὸ τῆς Στοᾶς ἀδύνατον ὑπειλήφασι κατὰ πάντα ἀπαράλλακτόν τινα εὑρεθήσεσθαι, οὕτω καὶ οἱ ἀπὸ τῆς Ἀκαδημίας, 'they added the clause "of such a kind as could not arise from what is not the case" because the Academics did not, as the Stoics did, regard it as impossible that a presentation exactly alike in all respects could be found. ' This passage differs from *Luc.* 77 in two respects: first, reference is made to the Academics in general and not to Arcesilaus; second, the addition of the third clause is presented as a clarification for the benefit of the Academics rather than an additional requirement (see section 5.4 on the weak and the strong interpretation of the third clause, and the fact that parallel evidence, including from Sextus as just cited, reveals the weak interpretation to be the official Stoic position). This being so, the present passage shows once more its fictional nature, in that it states misleadingly that it was acumen on Zeno's part in the face of Arcesilaus' question which led to the addition of the third clause. The recognition on Zeno's part that the Academics failed to see eye to eye with the Stoics on this point would not be thus described. For the emendation *cuius (modi)*, see Plasberg[1] (p. 109).

Recte consensit Arcesilas...si esset tale quale uel falsum: *recte* qualifies *additum* and stands at the head of the sentence for emphasis. Reid[1] (p. 268) considers various punctuations for the sentence, none of which is preferable to the one he actually prints (also adopted here). *Consentire* is not a technical term in *Acad.* and therefore not straightforward to place among the various expressions denoting different modes of endorsement. That interlocutors agree with propositions offered in dialectical exchanges is familar enough, but I note that it had been Arcesilaus (modelled on Socrates) asking the questions, and that it is normally the respondents who agree or fail to agree with propositions offered in the form of questions (whereby 'agreement' does not entail that the questioner himself endorsed the proposition he offered; cf. Brown 2018a on ὁμολογεῖν in Plato). Arcesilaus' reported agreement is thus unusual in a dialectical scenario. Whether it is given, on the fiction of the passage, on the basis of approval posited for Arcesilaus (like his approval of the corollary argument in §67) or for the sake of the argument is not stated.

That, given ἀπαραλλαξία, neither the true *nor the false* could be apprehended (*percipi*), is a striking formulation, given that *percipere* is normally used factively in *Acad.*, but the point seems to be the perfectly intelligible one that ἀπαραλλαξία is symmetrical; thus true impressions may be false and false impressions true.

On the force of *a uero*, see section 5.1; the parallels assembled by Reid[1] (p. 302) on §105 *a sole* are a mixed bag. With §77 generally, cf. Aug., *Contra Acad.* 3.9.21 and 2.6.14 (neither of which, however, provides close verbal correspondences).

Incubuit autem in eas disputationes...a falso possit esse: having accepted Zeno's definition as correct, Arcesilaus proceeded to show that the conditions it stipulates are never met. *Vt* introduces a purpose clause, but the exact nature of the intention (i.e. its grounds) is not captured by the grammatical categorization. The *eiusdem modi* formulation is one of several which captures accurately that ἀπαραλλαξία does not mean 'indistinguishability' but 'non-distinctness'; see section 5.6.

§78

Haec est una contentio...nihil ad hanc controuersiam pertinebat: = LS 69H = Carneades F5 Mette = test. XXV in Brittain (2001: 358). The scope of *adhuc* is most naturally taken to be 'the present point in time', i.e. the dramatic date of the dialogue. The implication is that all Academic positions until then agreed on ἀκαταληψία as far as the Stoic criterion is concerned. For *contentio*, cf. §140; *Fin.* 3.41. By means of *illud* Cicero refers back to the second conjunct in §77: *quaesiuit...quid futurum esset, si nec percipere quicquam posset sapiens nec opinari sapientis esset.*

Licebat enim nihil percipere...Sed id omittamus: Cicero is our only source for Carneades' pronouncement or view that the sage may opine, as well as for the two inner-Academic interpretations of it distinguished here, i.e. that Carneades advanced it for the sake of the argument and that he held it (see also on §§59, 66–7, 148), which themselves are used to classify further interpretations.

For Cicero's Clitomachean position, see section 8 and on §§7b–9a, 65–7; for Philo's Roman Books view, see on §18. Metrodorus of Stratonicea (we do not know which city of that name), on whom see Görler (1994: 905–6); Fuhrer (1997: 441–2); Brittain (2001: 117 n. 68, 214–15, 313); Glucker (2004: 118–33); Dorandi (2005b); Lévy (2005); and Fleischer (2019a), who dates his birth 'kaum später als 170 v.Chr.' (p. 126), stands somewhat apart in Lucullus' survey in §17 (see ibid.), where he is but briefly mentioned (cf. *De orat.* 1.45). With the information provided in *Luc.* 17, cf. *Index Acad.* xxvi.9: ἔφη Καρνεάδου παρακηκοέναι πάντας, 'he said that everyone else had misunderstood Carneades.' The *Index* continues with Metrodorus' assertion that Carneades did not in fact regard everything as inapprehensible (οὐ γὰρ ἀκα[τάλη]|πτα ν[ε]νομικέναι πά[ντα); cf. Aug., *Contra Acad.* 3.18.41 = t. 58 (on which see also the commentary): *Metrodorus...primus dicitur esse confessus non decreto placuisse Academicis nihil posse comprehendi, sed necessario contra Stoicos huius modi eos arma sumpsisse.* Augustine's information will come from a lost section of the final edition of *Acad.* and is not difficult to isolate from the Platonist interpretation which Augustine places on it (see especially Glucker 2004: 124–5, *pace* Brittain 2001: 215). It is remarkable for two reasons: first, Metrodorus' claim is in outline close to, quite possibly identical with, Philo's philosophical thesis in the Roman Books (see on §18 below; and Sextus, *P.H.* 1.235, in particular of the primary evidence). This raises the question of whether Antiochus' surprise and outrage over the Roman Books was appreciably histrionic and spurious from an informed reader's point of view. However, a charitable interpretation is possible: Antiochus' reaction may have been aimed at the historical claim alone, though in this case one would have to note that Metrodorus credits Carneades himself with the view that not everything is inapprehensible, i.e. is making a historical claim, too, if a less far-reaching one; and Metrodorus' construal of acceptable κατάληψις may well have been articulated quite differently, despite the similar general characterization. Second, here in *Luc.* 78 Philo and Metrodorus, or rather 'Philo *or* Metrodorus', are linked with the possibility of holding opinions, i.e. giving assent to non-cataleptic impressions, while rejecting κατάληψις. If Metrodorus did hold two positions, then it is not clear how they would be reconciled; however, I suggested in the general note above that Cicero is more likely to be making a narrow point about Metrodorus' acceptance of assent (so that there would be no need to posit two different Metrodorian positions and multiply unknowns).

On the most natural reading of *Philoni aut Metrodoro*, i.e. as referring to two different views held by two individuals which converged on the point at issue, see Glucker (2004: 120), who aptly refers to *Luc.* 113 *Aristoteles aut Theophrastus*, 137 *Aristoteles aut Xenocrates*, and 139 *Epicuro aut Aristippo*; similarly Lévy (2010: 86–7). These pairings also discourage: (i) the notion that Cicero might have given one name only, Metrodorus' (which is less familiar), and that a reader in antiquity could have supplied that of Philo from the wider context (e.g. §69); moreover, readers tend to signal alternatives suggested in the margins of manuscripts with *uel*; (ii) the notion that *aut* is self-correcting and intended to indicate that Cicero is unsure if Philo or Metrodorus is to be credited.

The tense of *licebat* suggests a licence of longer standing, as would be appropriate for views which, once formulated, are 'available'. *Enim* in *licebat enim* is either justifying or 'meta-communicative' like German 'ja' (see Kroon 1995: 195); I incline towards the latter since the possibility of opining under general ἀκαταληψία had been touched on before in *Luc.* and *Catul.*

Illud certe opinatione et perceptione sublata...tu concedas numquam assensurum esse: Lucullus would agree that, if there is no apprehension, the sage (*sapientem* supplied with *assensurum*, see Plasberg¹ p. 110) will have to withhold assent always. It is striking that Cicero opts for three *nomina actionis*, two of them quite rare in *Acad.*, in this concluding remark to the section (*opinatio, perceptio, assensionum retentio*). This may be intended to provide some stylistic *grauitas*; see also on *Ac.* 1.42.

§§79–98

The overarching subject of this section is that nothing can be apprehended; cf. §78 *init.* This is argued in §§79–90 for possible apprehension by the senses, and in §§91–8 for reason.[313]

§§79–82 is devoted to the unreliability of the senses and replies to §§19–20 in Lucullus' speech, §83 turns to the core argument (which concludes that nothing can be apprehended, cf. §§40–4), §§84–90 cite arguments in support of the crucial premiss of the core argument which introduces the ἀπαραλλαξία consideration. §§84–90 is bipartite: §§84–7 uses arguments from similar objects to make the point that supposedly cataleptic impressions do not carry a distinctive feature, or if they did, that it would be of no cognitive use for human beings (this section is a reply to §§54–8); at the same time, Lucullan counterarguments are considered and addressed. §§87–90 advances arguments from abnormal mental states, to show that supposedly cataleptic and non-cataleptic impressions are equally assent-inducing (this section is a reply to §§47–54).

§§91–8 begins with a section which characterizes dialectic as conceived by the Stoics (and Antiochus); cf. Lucullus on the role of reason in §§22–9, in particular §26 on proof. Cicero then cites the sorites as a fundamental threat to any dogmatic position (§§92–4) and argues in a section devoted to the Liar (§§95–6) that that paradox casts doubt on the principle of bivalence and the validity of *modus ponens* (sc. a fundamental Stoic inference). §97 argues that Epicurus' response to an argument for determinism implies that he did not accept that a disjunction formed from a contradictory pair of propositions was true, in which case no disjunction would be true; this is to cast doubt on arguments which have disjunctions as their first premiss. §98a is a concluding remark on the sceptic's attitudes to dialectic, while the defence of the Carneadean πιθανόν begins in §98b.

---

[313] See also Bringmann (1971: 261–5) and Glucker (1978: 399–405) for discussions of how exactly Cicero's speech responds to that of Lucullus.

From the close tie-in between Lucullus' and Cicero's speech little can be gleaned about sources used, given Cicero's overall grasp of the material and occupation as a leading advocate.[314]

§§79–80a

The section begins with a question which is an effective indication of the topic and studiedly vague at the same time. The reliability of the deliverances of the senses is the issue, but the wording of the *si*-clause leaves it open which possibility exactly is held up for consideration (i.e. whether none of our perceptual experiences is true, or only some).

In §§19–20 Lucullus defended the senses with a commonplace (*communi loco*), a possibility which Cicero had tried to forestall on the previous day (i.e. in the *Catulus*) by advancing 'so many' (*tam multa*) arguments against the senses at a point of the discussion where such fullness was uncalled for. The contrast between the singular *communi loco* and the plural *tam multa* is striking: unless the former is generic, Cicero is suggesting that Lucullus offered a sweeping statement rather than detailed arguments and thus failed to engage on a crucial issue. This reading is encouraged by the report of Lucullus' dismissal of the arguments from conflicting appearances, the broken oar and the neck of the dove,[315] which Lucullus did indeed dismiss (§19)—too quickly, Cicero suggests: Lucullus had said (ibid.), with reference to these two stock examples, that he is not someone who holds that everything is as it appears (*Non enim is sum qui quidquid uidetur tale dicam esse quale uideatur*), a view he takes the Epicureans to be committed to (unfairly so; see ad loc. and below). Cicero picks up on precisely this sentence, using in a first-person statement a verb (*sentio*) which signals awareness on his part, too, that the oar only appears bent, and the dove's neck only appears to have more than one colour.[316] This suggests that from Cicero's point of view the issue is a different one—as is stated at the end of §80a,[317] it is how one distinguishes between a true and a false impression. That is, how does one *know* that the oar is not bent and that the impression at issue fails to represent a state of affairs in the world? If the answer was that the perceiving subject knows as a matter of fact that oars are never bent, not even exceptionally, then this would be implausible in itself.[318] If the answer was that such an impression of a bent oar could not, as a matter of fact, be as clear and distinct as an impression of a straight oar that is not half-submerged under ideal conditions, then this would seem to require the strong interpretation of the third clause of Zeno's definition of the cataleptic impression.[319]

---

[314] See, however, section 9.3.1.
[315] On Stoic and Epicurean analyses of the problem of the dove's neck, see Ierodiakonou (2015), who also discusses the evidence from *Luc.* She lists passages which offer similar examples on p. 228 n. 1.
[316] On the—in my view, less appealing—possibility that the first-person speaker of this sentence is the opponent, see the n. below.
[317] *Tu uero, qui uisa sensibus alia uera dicas esse alia falsa, qui ea distinguis?*
[318] Why such an impression would not win assent would be readily explained within the horizon of Stoic theorizing; see e.g. Frede (1994: 51); Brittain (2014: 352–3); Reinhardt (2018a: 241).
[319] See section 5.4.

Cicero follows up with another question about all the other points he made (*deinde... diximus?*)—if these retain validity (and they will if Lucullus does not even engage with them), then Lucullus' entire case will lie defeated.[320] Cicero continues with another careful ambiguity: he, i.e. Lucullus, says that his senses are truthful, which can mean that his senses deliver the truth most of the time, or invariably. What Lucullus had said was (§19): *Meo autem iudicio ita est maxima in sensibus ueritas*. In a somewhat lawyerly move, Cicero suggests to Lucullus that he might recognize an authority in Epicurus, who held that, if any sense ever did 'lie', then one should never trust any visual experience again. On this point Cicero offers his sarcastic encouragement.

Timagoras (for the identification see the n. below) is introduced to illustrate the absurdity of the Epicurean dogma that all perceptions are true, to which he is committed. Specifically, he is an example of those who exhibit unshakeable confidence in their witnesses (in an Epicurean's case, the senses) and thus insist on their own perversity. Timagoras looked at a lamp while pressing on his eyeball with his finger, which must have caused him, like everyone else, to see double. He denied that he *saw* (veridically) two flames,[321] on the grounds that he held all perceptions to be true and took the two flames which appeared to him to be the result of 'opinion' distorting the invariably accurate deliverances of the senses. Cicero dismisses this reply as beside the point, since the question was not what is the case, but what appeared to him. For, we may surmise, it is impressions which put us in touch with the external world, as in the case of the bent oar.

Cicero is quite likely to have appreciated that, when the Epicureans say all perceptions are true, they mean by perceptions something quite different than the Stoics have in mind when they talk about impressions, but it was Lucullus who opened the door to the avoidance of such nuance by making a casual reference to Epicurus in §19 and by invoking the Cyrenaics in support of his own view in §20 (see the commentary on both passages).

Quid ergo est... communi loco defendis: for the notion that the senses act as reporters, sc. to the mind, see Calcidius 220 (= LS 53G = *SVF* ii.879), with Reed (2002: 171-3). Cicero can rely on his opponent's acceptance of the notion that the senses, if anything, will yield apprehension.

See the general note above for the reference and the singular of *communi loco*. The phrasal term is used in the familiar sense of 'rhetorical commonplace' (*OLD* s.v. *communis* no. 4b), not in one of the more specialized senses also found in Cicero; see Reinhardt (2003: 27-9).

Quod ne id facere posses... commoueri: if the transmitted text is retained, then *quod* is the mildly adversative connective 'whereas' (German 'indes'), cf. *quod si*, *quod quoniam*, *quod utinam*. Hofmann-Szantyr (p. 571) cite as an instance of a 'rein anknüpfendes *quod* sogar vor dem Relativ' Cic., *Phil.* 10.9: *quod qui... abducit*

---

[320] See n. below on the textual and punctuation problems raised by this passage.
[321] There is disagreement on the meaning of *esse uisas*; see the lemmatized n. below.

exercitum..., praesidium...adimit rei publicae, and refer to our passage as a less extreme case. So also Reid[1] (p. 269), with a degree of hesitation, and Plasberg[1] (p. 110), who lists in his app. crit. earlier attempts to explain the presence of both *quod* and *id* (along the same lines as Reid), or indeed to remove it (Manutius suggested deleting *id*, 'Lambinus' emended it to *tu*, Durand wrote *quamquam ne id*; Plasberg[1] p. 110 wonders about *quod ne ita*, suggested by Mueller). The sentence as a whole aims at emphasis through fullness; cf. the strictly unnecessary *idcirco* at the beginning of the main clause.

On *non necessario loco*, correctly Reid[1] (p. 45): 'Yet these arguments must have occupied some considerable space in Cicero's speech, although foreign to its main intention'; similarly Mansfeld (1997: 52-3 n. 19), who observes that the phrase as a whole is without a good parallel but assembles relevant instances of *necessarius* and *locus*. Lörcher (1911: 263) interprets the phrase from the standpoint of *Quellenforschung*. The two sceptical speakers in the *Catulus*, Catulus iunior and Cicero, needed to establish the larger picture first, as well as provide a historical background for it; the *Lucullus* was evidently conceived as the place for detailed philosophical argument. For the two examples cited see on §19; Ierodiakonou (2015: 228) for a list of further examples preserved in ancient texts; §105 on the changing colour of the sea.

The emendation *inflexo* (Bentley in Davies) is motivated by §19: *remo inflexo*. Plasberg[1] (p. 110) notes that Lucretius uses *refracta* and *reflexa* interchangeably (4.440 and 442). I translate as 'bent' on the assumption that the oar looks broken but still attached.

Primum cur...nec esse plus uno: *sentire*, here used, as the context suggests, to describe awareness without doctrinal commitment and without a claim to certainty, is not an established technical term in *Acad.*; cf. the instances in *Luc.* 52, 65 *fin.*, and 125 *fin.* One might wonder if the entire sentence *nam et in... nec esse plus uno* should be placed in quotation marks, i.e. be viewed as a statement given to Lucullus, restating what was said in §19 (I noted the verbal correspondence above). This seems less attractive precisely because it would be a mere restatement from above and as such somewhat redundant in its fullness, whereas the Cicero character's signalling agreement with Lucullus implies that something else is the issue. Moreover, parallel evidence suggests that the Stoics did think the dove's neck had one colour, whereas the Epicureans assumed that it had more than one, viz. all the ones which appeared; see Ierodiakonou (2015). Thus Cicero would here be signalling agreement here with Lucullus on a point on which he might have taken a different view.

Deinde, nihilne praeterea diximus...iacet ista causa: the two clauses following the question must logically form a conditional, with the first clause functioning as the protasis: if all the other arguments advanced by Cicero in the previous day remain intact (cf. *OLD* s.v. *maneo* no. 8c), then *that* (i.e. Lucullus') case is overturned in some sense. (See Ricottilli 2003: 254-6; Nutting 1903.) The problem is the predicates. While the normal mood/tense patterns for conditionals are no guide, it would seem that either both predicates should be indicative or both subjunctive. *Lacerare* cannot be used absolutely or intransitively (Plasberg prints *lacerat* in 1908 and †*lacerat* in

1922), and so would have to be passive; in addition, the metaphor would seem too strong. Arguably, the subjunctive in both cases yields a nonchalant tone which suits the surrounding context better than the indicative. I have opted for the transmitted *maneant* and *iaceat* as found in e.g. Cant.2 (noted by Reid[1]) and favoured by Madvig (1826: 175); the latter gives good sense (*OLD* s.v. *iaceo* no. 4 'to lie on the ground, lie in ruins') and is palaeographically easy to explain. The next sentence moves on to a new point; thus there should be no colon after *causa* (*pace* Reid[1] p. 270). Plasberg[1] and Plasberg[2] place all of *maneant… sensus dicit* ⟨*Epicurus*⟩ in quotation marks, but only *ueraces suos…* could conceivably be put in the mouth of the opponent (and is not, see next n.). See also Schäublin (1993: 167–8).

Veraces suos esse sensus dicit…nulli umquam esse credendum: the insertion of *Epicurus* after *sensus dicit*, ascribed to unidentified individuals by Halm and to Reitzenstein by Plasberg[1], is mistaken. No argument in favour of it can be derived from *igitur*. Cicero is referring to *Luc.* 19: *meo autem iudicio ita est maxima in sensibus ueritas*, using the dismissive third-person *dicit* (see Reid[1] p. 270 for an extensive collection of parallels). It is only on the back of this paraphrasing sentence that Cicero makes reference to a possible *auctor* for Lucullus, who then emerges to be Epicurus.

The suggestion that Lucullus might use Epicurus as an *auctor* alludes to the association of the dogmatists with *auctoritas* (of intellectual ancestors) and of the sceptics with *ratio* or *iudicium* (the reliance on their own critical faculties); cf. *Luc.* 60, and 7b–9a. For the Epicurean doctrine that all perceptions are true, see the commentary on *Luc.* 19. One might wonder if 'to speak falsely' is to be preferred as a translation of *mentitus sit*, since the senses cannot be credited with intentions, but rhetorical effect is better served by the translation 'to lie'. On the force of *eo… demittit* and the following conditional clause being explanatory of *si* and used for *ut, si… credendum sit*, see Reid[1] (p. 270), as well as *OLD* s.v. *demitto* no. 8b.

§80a

Hoc est uerum esse…in prauitate insistere: at the beginning of the sentence, the question is whether the text makes reference to a person ('that is what it means that someone is *uerum*') or to a view or attitude ('that is being *uerum*', 'that is what being *uerum* means'). In the former case, *uerum* would mean 'true to oneself' or 'genuine' (*OLD* s.v. *uerus* no. 1). The latter option is favoured by Schäublin et al. ('Darauf also beruht offenbar "das Wahre" …'), but it is a problem that in the immediately preceding sentence truth is only an implied topic, and that the earlier statement that 'the senses are truthful' (*ueraces suos esse sensus dicit*) does not actually employ the adjective *uerus*. Further, it is hard to see how *confidere suis testibus…* can be a gloss on *uerum* in the sense of 'true'. Some have thought that a person is referred to here but that *uerum* is corrupt: according to Plasberg[1] (p. 111), Madvig suggested *uirum* for *uerum* ('a real man'), while Orelli, Baiter, and Halm (1861: 29) suggested *certum* (presumably 'to be confident, sc. in one's perceptions' rather than 'to be reliable'). More likely, as Reid[1] (p. 271) and Brittain (2006) assume, a person is meant and *uerum* ('true to oneself') is to be retained. In that case the following two infinitives represent a description of the consequences of someone upholding that, if any sense ever 'lied', none could be trusted ever again (cf. the immediately preceding sentence). *Confidere suis testibus* is unproblematic: someone who is confident in his witnesses declares them to be veridical. This fits with Timagoras' statement below that his eyes do not lie. The second colon is obviously corrupt: *inportata* is nonsensical. *In prauitate* (Reid[1] p. 271) is very plausible, in sense (Cicero is about to brand Timagoras' insistence that his eyes do not lie as absurd), because it would represent a fitting polemical comeback to *Luc.* 26 (*Quid quod, si ista uera sunt, ratio omnis tollitur, quasi quaedam lux lumenque uitae? Tamenne in ista prauitate perstabitis?*), and because it is a commonplace to dismiss Epicurean views on non-ethical subjects as not just false but morally depraved (outrage about the Epicurean theory of pleasure colours the criticism in other areas of philosophy; see Reinhardt 2005: 174). *In importunitate* (entertained in the app. crit. by Plasberg[1] p. 111) in the sense of 'with such brazenness, with such insolence' is slightly less attractive, but formally closer to what is transmitted; cf. also *inportune* (in F in the corrector's hand). Schäublin (1993: 168–9) defends Gulielmius' *in porta*.

Itaque Timagoras…non quid uideatur: discussions of the passage include Schäublin et al. (p. 249 n. 222); Verde (2010: 306–7); and Sedley (2018: 111–12). The key difficulty is the force of *esse uisas*; the main possibilities are (i) a veridical sense, i.e. either prototypical seeing (thus Rackham 1951: 'Timagoras…denies that he has ever really seen two little flames…'; similarly Reid[2]) or veridical appearing, (ii) phenomenal appearing (thus Schäublin et al.: 'Timagoras [muß] behaupten, niemals seien ihm…zwei Flämmchen aus einer Lampe erschienen'), and (iii) epistemic appearing (amounting to that 'he has never been misled into thinking that there were two flames'; Sedley 2018: 111, cf. Verde 2010: 304 n. 57). The wider context would seem to demand option (i), viz. the Epicurean insistence that all perceptions are true, Timagoras' reported insistence that his eyes were not lying (an instantiation of the Epicurean dogma), and crucially the fact that Cicero dismisses Timagoras on the grounds that the question was not what is the case, but what appears to him to be the case. In order to read *esse uisas* as the perfect passive of veridical *uidere*, one must take *sibi* to be a *datiuus auctoris*, which is grammatically unproblematic (see Kühner-Stegmann i.324). Veridical appearing seems discouraged when the example is manifestly one from the sense modality of vision. Epistemic appearing (iii above) is not veridical; see Reinhardt (2015: 69). Prototypical seeing, i.e. *uideo* plus object (x), involves two component senses or two claims made at the same time: 'there is x' and 'I have a visual appearance of x', both of which Timagoras denies in denying that he is seeing two flames. See Reinhardt (2016), section 10.1.

One might wonder if Cicero's meaning would be clearer if he had used an active verb. *Negat se umquam cum oculum torsisset duas ex lucerna flammulas uidisse* would arguably have been ambiguous, too, because *uidere* can denote phenomenal as well as veridical (prototypical) seeing. *Cernere* would also have posed problems; it often denotes veridical seeing, but with an added connotation of seeing (multiple) things within one's ken distinctly. That Cicero refers to Timagoras' statement as answering the question *quid sit* while characterizing the question which was at issue with an expression (*quid uideatur*) which is superficially closer to Timagoras' reported wording (if quite different in sense) may have confused some readers, but it allows Cicero to specify with almost lexicographical precision which sense he had in mind in the case of *esse uisas*. Reid[1] (p. 272) assembles Greek and Latin parallels, incl. Lucr. 4.447–52, for the visual effect at issue; these parallels, which are quite varied in formulation, tend the describe the effect in terms of 'mere' phenomenal appearance. For Anaxagoras' 'denial' of the evidence from his senses, see on *Luc*. 72.

Timagoras is an obscure figure. He is introduced here as a proponent of the conventional Epicurean dogma, even if his response to the challenge arising from the optical illusion was apparently unusual. It has been suggested by various scholars that he is to be identified with Timasagoras, an Epicurean of the second century BC who likely lived in Rhodes and is attacked by Philodemus for his innovations (over Epicurus himself) in the understanding of emotions as well as in the field of perception (see Monet 1996 on *P.Herc*. 19/698). Verde (2010: 285–9), who assumes that Cicero meant Timasagoras here, cites all relevant earlier literature and attempts to show how our passage and Aët. 4.13.6 (on sight), where Timagoras is said to have replaced Epicurean εἴδωλα with 'effluences' (ἀπόρροιαι), mutually illuminate each other; see also also Verde (2016: 1194–5). However, while the case for emending the name in Aëtius to Timasagoras is persuasive, given the heterodoxy cited there, there is less of a case for modifying the transmitted name in our passage, although the possibility that Timasagoras is right cannot be dismissed.

Torquere is here used of pressing action on the eye which causes the effect of double vision. Reid[1] (p. 272) rightly notes that *mendacium* cannot be the subject of *(quid) sit*.

Sic hic quidem…domi nobis ista nascuntur: *maiorum similis* does not signal that Timagoras was unorthodox, but that he essentially took the general Epicurean view even if his insistence on the truth of his perceptions under the exceptional circumstances described stretched credulity particularly. Cicero then refocuses on the crucial question (which Lucullus had left unanswered when he dismissed oar and dove): given that he recognizes a difference between true and false impressions, how does he distinguish between the two? Reid[1] (p. 272) correctly notes that *desinere* with separative ablative is not idiomatic, but the expression can be viewed as short for *desine communibus locis sensus defendere* (Plasberg[1] p. 111). The context, an outburst of sorts, can help explain an unusual ellipsis, but the suggestion that Cicero may have written *desiste* (Reid[1] p. 272), which takes the simple ablative, merits consideration. On the proverb, see Otto (1888: 8–9): '…ich habe selbst etwas in eigenem Besitze, brauche es nicht von anderen zu entlehnen'; cf. e.g. Cic., *Fam*. 9.3.2 (= SB 176); *Att*. 1.19.3 (= SB 19) and 10.14.2 (= SB 206); Tac., *Dial*. 9: *hi enim* [sc. *uersus*] *Basso domi nascuntur*.

§§80b–82

There follows a plea with Lucullus to end the use of commonplaces. Given that Cicero has just dispatched the Epicurean Timagoras whom he had introduced, this plea would seem to have a forward reference (hence the paragraphing of the Latin text), i.e. to the god who appears and offers better senses (cf. Lucullus' use of the device in §19). This god would be presented by Cicero with a long list of dissatisfactions.

The Cicero character enters into a fictional exchange with Lucullus, who is made to introduce new considerations as something that the deity might or would say, with Cicero responding in each case. Towards the end of §81 the discussion moves from the insufficient acuity and reach of the senses to frequently cited examples of illusion: a ship seen by the interlocutors out at sea will appear to stand still, while to those on it the villa where the dialogue takes place will seem to move. Lucullus, so Cicero, can investigate the reasons for this phenomenon, but he will likely not succeed, and even if he did, all he would have achieved is to provide an explanation for his false impression, and not certainty that a particular impression (sc. which appears true) is truthful (this, it is implied, ought to be his ultimate aim, and one he can never reach). Illusions appear true but are 'known' to be false; the problem is separating them from impressions which appear true and are true in virtue of an intrinsic feature (as Stoic foundationalism would require).

§82 is a polemical cap to the section on the senses, although the reintroduction of Epicurus makes it a less personal attack on Lucullus than it might have been (perceived improprieties of tone are sometimes plausibly cited as evidence that Cicero must locally be working closely from a source).[322] The basic point is the introduction of a choicer case of conflicting appearances: the sun, its actual size and how big it appears, as well as that it appears to stand still when it moves through the universe at enormous speed. This is combined with a swipe at Epicurus, who made pronouncements on the size of the sun which seem at variance with his commitment to the tenet that all perceptions are true. Epicurus, however, was only declared an *auctor* for Lucullus by Cicero.

'Si', inquis, 'deus te interroget...quid respondeas': see §19 on the *deus* device. Grammatically, the mood suggests an actual possibility.

Vtinam quidem roget...male ageret: the transmitted *agerent* cannot be right given that a verb in the singular is needed as well as a different tense if one reads *audies* at the beginning of the sentence; see Plasberg[1] (p. 111) for the solutions which have been proposed. I retain the unobjectionable *audies* and adopt the emendation *egerit*.

Vt enim uera uideamus...O praeclarum prospectum: *ut enim* is clearly concessive, and the concession rhetorical; the use of *uidere* = 'project the gaze' (cf. *intendi acies* below) in the second occurrence here is not recognized by the OLD.

Cicero describes what he sees when he looks north from Bauli (the location of Hortensius' *uilla*) across the land in the direction of Cumae, and what he sees when he looks in a south-eastern direction across the gulf towards Pompeii. The transmitted text was first suspected by Lipsius (see Plasberg[1] p. 111), who proposed deletion of the

---

[322] See section 9.3.

first *cerno* and modified *regionem* to *e regione* = 'in a straight line, directly'. Halm deleted *regionem uideo*, taking it to be an intruded gloss on *Pompeianum non cerno*. Plasberg¹ agreed there was a problem but thought that the transmitted text was more likely to contain a lacuna (he printed: *ego Catuli Cumanum ex hoc loco cerno; regionem ⟨Pompeiani, ipsum⟩ Pompeianum non cerno*, which Schäublin et al. adopt). Reid¹ inserts *et* and adopts Lipsius' *e regione*, punctuating after *uideo* (...*Cumanum ex hoc loco cerno et e regione uideo, Pompeianum*). The contrast between *cerno* = 'to discern, make out' and generic *uidere* seems too apt to be the result of an intruded gloss. Further, a contrast between the general area of Pompeii and a particular *uilla* is entirely germane to the general point Cicero is making (note also the similar point made about Puteoli below). The phrase *e regione*, applied to the gaze towards Cumae in the north, is pointless, especially alongside the generic *uideo*. Plasberg's idea of the required sense is convincing, but his insertion produces a hyperclarity which seems unwarranted. I have thus repunctuated the transmitted text and assume that *regionem* would be easily intelligible as *regionem*, sc. *Pompeiani*. The villa in question is either Cicero's *Pompeianum* (cf. *Luc.* 9) or Catulus'; see Griffin (1997: 17 n. 64).

For the *uillae* alluded to here, see the commentary on *Luc.* 9b–10; for *aciem intendere*, cf. *OLD* s.v. *intendo* no. 6c.

Prospectus here means either 'the ability or opportunity of seeing before one' (*OLD* s.v. no. 1a) or 'that which is seen, a prospect, view' (*OLD.* s.v. no. 2a). If it means the former (and the sentence immediately preceding would suggest this), it will be sarcastic; if it means the latter (and the sentence immediately following would suggest this), it will be a genuine if theatrical expression of admiration (genuine because we know from other statements that Cicero, like many, enjoyed the scenery of this coast, cf. Reid¹ p. 273).

Puteolos uidemus...non uidemus: on C. Avianius Flaccus, see Cic., *Fam.* 13.35.1 (= SB 306), which provides the *cognomen*, and 13.74.1–2 (= SB 269), revealing him as a well-connected businessman in the grain trade. By the time Cicero wrote *Acad.*, Avianius was dead, as may be inferred from *Fam.* 13.79 (= SB 276), in which Cicero describes the two sons of Avianius as his *necessarii* and urges the proconsul of Sicily to aid their commercial interests. See D'Arms (1972: 209–10). Plasberg¹ (p. 112) comments that the Avianius mentioned was not necessarily the *frumentarius*, but it is a reasonable assumption, given conventions of reference (see Adams 1978: 145), that an abbreviation of a *praenomen* was given, and there is no good evidence that Cicero wrote 'P.' Thus like Reid¹ I print 'C.'

A *porticus Neptuni* in Puteoli is not otherwise documented, but there were baths of Neptune, which may have had a *porticus* adjoined.

§81

At ille nescio qui...non esse contentum: on *schola* in the sense of 'lecture', see *OLD* s.v. no. 1a; Cic., *Div.* 2.31; *Fin.* 2.67. Sextus, *P.H.* 1.81–4, provides the kind of list of instances of unusual abilities in individuals which Cicero must have in mind. A *stadium* corresponds to 185 metres, and Cicero uses the term elsewhere, though usually in 'Greek' contexts (e.g. Cic., *Fam.* 16.2.1 = SB 146); the Romans otherwise tended to specify distances in *milia passuum*, the unit used for purposes like road building. The mood of *quod abesset* is due to it being a generic consecutive clause.

The birds may be eagles, as Reid[1] (p. 273) suggests with reference to Sen., *Ben.* 2.29, where eagles are mentioned for their eyesight in a list of sceptical dissatisfactions with human faculties.

Quaedam...longius could equally be part of the fictional intervention. The number *octingenta* has been suspected on the basis of a variant in M (*octoginta*) and Plin., *N.H.* 7.85; see Plasberg[1] (p. 112).

Dicit me acrius uidere...aer crassus offunditur: Cicero suggests that the opponent would cite the inferior position of fish, which see less than humans due to living in a denser medium than air. *Fortasse* precludes that an Antiochian did say something to this effect in *Catul.* and makes the emendation *dicet* unnecessary; see Hofmann-Szantyr p. 307 on *praesens pro futuro*. Cicero replies that this means that their situation is *analogous* to that of humans rather than worse, in that something impedes their vision, even if the medium human beings live in is less dense than water.

Reid[1] (p. 274) notes: 'The diver in fragm. 10 is in the same position as the fishes here.' Nonius p. 474 M. (t. 34 = no. 10 Reid) states that a submerged (human) diver does not see what is above the waterline, or only unclearly: in other words, when humans are put into the position of fish, their sight is not comparatively keener. Rather than being an alternative reply to the one which Cicero gives here in *Luc.*, the fragment appears designed to secure the essential analogy of humans and fish which Cicero points out in our passage. It is reasonable to assume that t. 34, on which see the commentary, offers a glimpse of the rationale of the second edition at least on the particular point at issue here: Cicero did not just recast the dialogue with new speakers but added further argumentative content in particular places. Another fragment which suggests this is t. 51.

For the notion of thick air in Cicero, cf. *N.D.* 2.17 with Pease (1955–8: 592), who offers an exhaustive collection of parallels. Democritus claimed that we could see an ant in the sky if there was no intervening air (Arist., *De anim.* B7, 419a15 = DK 68A122). Sentences ending with *fortasse* are well documented. I take the Cicero character's reply to begin with *qui neque uidentur* and thus punctuate strongly after *fortasse*.

At amplius non desideramus...lumen putas: the first sentence is another intervention by the opponent. In reply, Cicero compares the opponent to a mole, which was thought of as blind and thus not desirous of something it has not the slightest awareness of (contrast the translation by Brittain 2006: 47): *that*, Cicero intimates, is why Lucullus is not looking for more than the senses he has. The suggestion that Lucullus is like a mole has bite, not just because he had extolled the power of the senses humans are endowed with (§§19–20), notably vision, but also because he accuses the Academics of depriving human beings of the senses with their arguments (§61, cf. §30; and Cicero's reply §105).

Proverbial expressions turning on the mole's blindness are collected by Otto 1890: 340; using one of them, the astronomer Cleomedes called Epicurus πολὺ τῶν ἀσπαλάκων τυφλότερος (2.1; cited by Reid[1] p. 274). See also Steier (1930).

Neque tam[en] quererer cum deo…moueri haec uilla: Cicero now returns to the subject of illusions, this time of movement. The phenomenon, which was familiar enough to give rise to the poetic topos of 'moving landscapes' (see Cardauns 2001), features in *Div.* 2.120: *nam et nauigantibus moueri uidentur ea quae stant*; Lucr. 2.308–11, 4.386–8; Sen., *N.Q.* 7.25.7; Arist., *De insomn.* 2, 460b26–7; Sextus, *P.H.* 1.107 and *M.* 7.414; see also Reinhardt (2016: 68–9). Cf. also *Luc.* 123 below on Hicetas of Syracuse, who stated that the motion of the night sky was explicable in two ways: either it or the earth moves. *Viderem* is used of phenomenal seeing, i.e. having a visual experience that does not correspond to a state of affairs in the world; see Reinhardt (2016: 64–5). *Stare* means 'to ride at anchor' (Reid[1] p. 274).

Quaere rationem cur ita uideatur…falsum testimonium dicere ostenderis: the imperative of *quaere* (sc. an explanation for the illusion) is blunt and gives the impression of a dare. Even if Lucullus succeeded, all he would have achieved is an explanation for his false impression rather than a way of telling it apart from a true one (cf. §80: *tu uero, qui uisa sensibus alia uera dicas esse alia falsa, qui ea distinguis?*).

For the senses, or an impression in particular, as a witness, cf. §80. Reid[1] (p. 275) comments on *ostenderis*: 'The word is carefully chosen to indicate that the statement in question can only have the force of a declaration, not of a proof', but this seems at variance with the uses of the verb; rather, Cicero is making a rhetorical concession (even a compelling explanation of the false impression will be epistemically worthless).

§82

Quid ego de naue…maiora fortasse quaeris: Cicero proposes facetiously to leave both ship and oar behind and move on to something bigger. Cf. the anecdote in *Brut.* 197 (written in 46 BC), which compares a jurist's argumentative strategy to a boy finding a rowlock on the beach and dreaming of building a matching boat.

Quid potest ⟨esse⟩ sole maius…Mihi quidem quasi pedalis: cf. the notes by Reid[1] (pp. 274–5) and Brittain (2006: 48 n. 120), as well as Reid[1] (p. 286) on §91, where the question is cited as a problem in physics to whose resolution dialectic has nothing to contribute. Aët. 2.21, on which see Mansfeld and Runia (2009: 534–46), assembles views on the question; cf. the general note on §§118–26.

For Cicero's line of argument it is important that the size of the sun is assumed to be a given, but he may simply be proceeding like this for the sake of the argument. It is not clear whether *confirmant* means 'they confirm' or 'they give assurance'. The size named here—eighteen times larger than the earth—is not the one posited by leading ancient astronomers or mathematicians (*mathematicus* can mean both, and it is not clear from Cicero into whose field of expertise he took such questions to fall primarily); cf. Heath (1913: 337–50); Barnes (1989); Carmman (2014). *Luc.* 128 suggests it was a figure accepted by the Stoics. This view is ascribed to the geographer Serapion of Antioch (*Anecd. Par.*, vol. i, p. 373.25–7 Cramer), whose work was known to Cicero (*Att.* 2.4.1 = SB 24; 2.6.1 = SB 26) and was cited in Achilles Tatius' commentary on Aratus (pp. 319 and 445 Maass; the latter passage cites μαθηματικοί as source). For the view that the sun is 'about' (*quasi*; cf. *OLD* s.v. no. 8) the size of a foot, interjected probably not because Cicero has a considered opinion on the subject but to illustrate that other views are possible, cf. Arist., *De an.* Γ3, 428b2–4.

Epicurus autem posse putat...Vbi igitur illud est 'semel': Cicero argues that Epicurus' pronouncements on the size of the sun sit oddly with his claims that all perceptions are true and that, if any sense ever delivered a false report (*semel*), none should ever be trusted again (§79 *fin.*). In particular, the fact that Epicurus did not assert that the sun was exactly the size we perceive it to be, but either that or a little less or a little more, is criticized.

The main evidence is D.L. 10.91 (from the letter to Pythocles; I give Dorandi's text with an embedded scholion citing Book 11 of Epicurus' Περὶ φύσεως;[323] τοῦτο καὶ...διάστημα οὐθέν ἐστι is frg. 81 Usener): Τὸ δὲ μέγεθος ἡλίου τε καὶ τῶν λοιπῶν ἄστρων κατὰ μὲν τὸ πρὸς ἡμᾶς τηλικοῦτόν ἐστιν ἡλίκον φαίνεται· (τοῦτο καὶ ἐν τῇ ια' Περὶ φύσεως· 'εἰ γάρ', φησί, 'τὸ μέγεθος διὰ τὸ διάστημα ἀπεβεβλήκει, πολλῷ μᾶλλον ἂν τὴν χρόαν'). ἄλλο γὰρ τούτῳ συμμετρότερον διάστημα οὐθέν ἐστι. κατὰ δὲ τὸ καθ' αὑτὸ ἤτοι μεῖζον τοῦ ὁρωμένου ἢ μικρῷ ἔλαττον ἢ τηλικοῦτον (οὐχ ἅμα). οὕτω γὰρ καὶ τὰ παρ' ἡμῖν πυρὰ ἐξ ἀποστήματος θεωρούμενα κατὰ τὴν αἴσθησιν θεωρεῖται. καὶ πᾶν δὲ εἰς τοῦτο τὸ μέρος ἔνστημα ῥᾳδίως διαλυθήσεται ἐάν τις τοῖς ἐναργήμασι προσέχῃ, 'The size of the sun and the remaining stars relatively to us is just as great as it appears. [This he states in the eleventh book 'On Nature'. For, says he, if it had diminished in size on account of the distance, it would much more have diminished its brightness; for indeed there is no distance more proportionate to this diminution of size than is the distance at which the brightness begins to diminish.] But in itself and actually it may be a little larger or a little smaller, or precisely as great as it is seen to be. For so too fires of which we have experience are seen by sense when we see them at a distance. And every objection brought against this part of the theory will easily be met by anyone who attends to plain facts' (transl. Hicks); cf. Aët. 2.21.5 (= frg. 345 Usener); Cic., *Fin.* 1.20: *Sol Democrito magnus uidetur* (= DK 87 68A), *quippe homini erudito in geometriaque perfecto, huic* (sc. *Epicuro*) *pedalis fortasse; tantum enim esse censet quantus uidetur, uel paulo aut maiorem aut minorem* (Cicero highlights the disagreement between Epicurus and his intellectual ancestor Democritus, just as he contrasts the Epicurean view with that of the *mathematici* in our passage). Lucr. 5.564–91 is too long to quote here. The beginning of Book 2 of Cleomedes' Μετέωρα is devoted to anti-Epicurean polemics, incl. on the size of the sun. See further Essler (2011: 249).

Lucr. provides detail on the argument from analogy briefly mentioned in D.L. 10.91 above and expanded from size to colour in the scholium. He reasons that because fires which are properly burning and which are perceived clearly appear to be similarly sized from close distance and from afar, the stars (like the sun and the moon) must be of the same size as it appears to have, or of only a slightly different one. Bailey (1947: 1408–9) speculates about the physical explanation which might

---

[323] Dorandi prints the scholion in the main text on the grounds that it was already embedded in Diogenes' source (see Dorandi 2013: 51–2).

account for the appearance. The wording used by Epicurus in D.L. 10.91 (ἐάν τις τοῖς ἐναργήμασι προσέχῃ) shows that he thinks of our viewing the sun as a case of straightforward perception, if from a distance; so also Bailey (1947: 1408), who, however, fails to appreciate that *ut oculi aut nihil mentiantur [tamen] aut non multum* in our passage is Cicero's biased gloss (which looks back to §80: *opinionis enim esse mendacium, non oculorum*). The distance of the sun might be invoked in an explanation of why the actual size of the sun and how it appears to us may be somewhat at variance: the εἴδωλα emitted by the sun may suffer ever so slightly in transit, even though they fully translate into perceptual experience (and thereby provide an instance of the view that all perceptions are true as the Epicureans construe it); see Asmis (1984: 313).

Tamen, given that it is in A and B before correction by A^a and B^a, respectively, was in the archetype but omitted by the common source of VS. Plasberg^1 (p. 113) prints *aut nihil mentiantur [tamen] aut non multum—mentiantur ⟨tamen⟩*, assuming that *tamen* is in the record and thus likely to have had a place somewhere. It is possible that *tamen* was pulled forward by an anticipation error caused by the double occurrence of *mentiantur*. For the use of *ne...quidem*, see Reid^1 (p. 93) on *Ac.* 1.5.

Sed ab hoc credulo...tamen nobis stare uideatur: Epicurus is dismissed with a final counterexample to the notion that all perceptions are true: the sun appears stationary when it is known to be moving at high speed. Cicero may also be implying that he needs to move on from Epicurus because time is passing quickly.

Some considerations regarding the speed of the heavens are discussed in Cleomedes' Μετέωρα, 2.155–83 Todd (on Cleomedes' Stoicizing outlook, see the introduction of Bowen and Todd 2004). He cites a line of heralds deployed by a Persian king in intervals of shouting distance, who took a night and a day to relay a message from Athens to Sousa, and infers that the heavens, which covered a much larger distance in the same period, must move many times faster. Moreover, he invokes the authority of Homer, *Il.* 5.770–2, according to which the distance a man is able to take in with his gaze while sitting on a promontory and looking out to sea is equivalent to one stride of the Sun's chariot (which consequently must be moving very fast). See also Reid^1 (p. 276).

§83

Having completed the rebuttal of the claim that the senses are truthful, the Cicero character refocuses by inviting Lucullus to consider how small their disagreement is. He restates the conclusion of the core argument, i.e. that nothing can be known, and lists the argument's four premisses, not so much with a view to *advancing* the argument again, but in order to consider the premisses as to whether they are contentious: Cicero calls them *capita* here, which inter alia marks them out as (potential) individual subjects for debate (see the n. below).[324] The premiss which claims

---

[324] Alleemudder (p. 212) suggests that Cicero speaks of *capita* because he is hesitant to call the core argument a proof (*argumenti conclusio*, cf. *Luc.* 26).

ἀπαραλλαξία of true and false impressions is then identified as the remaining point of dispute (cf. §78 *init.*, where the same point is made).

There are minor variations compared to the way in which the individual premisses of the core argument are formulated in §40. By pulling forward the conclusion and inverting the order of the third and fourth premisses, Cicero is able to end on the contentious premiss. More significantly, perhaps, Cicero appears to restrict one premiss, and thereby the argument, to perceptual impressions (noted also by Alleemudder p. 220). I put the versions in §40 and here side by side in the order presented in the text (they are cast in direct and indirect speech respectively):[325]

§40	§83
	(v) Nihil esse quod nosci percipi comprehendi possit.
(i) Eorum quae uidentur, alia uera sunt, alia falsa.	(i) Esse aliquod uisum falsum.
(ii) Quod falsum est id percipi non potest.	(ii) Non posse id percipi.
(iii) Quod autem uerum uisum est id omne tale est ut eiusdem modi falsum etiam possit uideri.	(iv) Inter quae uisa nihil intersit, fieri non posse ut eorum alia percipi possint alia non possint.
(iv) Quae uisa sint eius modi ut in iis nihil intersit, non posse accidere ut eorum alia percipi possint, alia non possint.	(iii) Nullum esse uisum uerum a sensu profectum cui non appositum sit uisum aliud quod ab eo nihil intersit quodque percipi non possit.
(v) Nullum igitur est uisum quod percipi non possit.	

The argument is formulated with reference to Stoic doctrine through the use of *percipere* and synonyms (*noscere, comprehendere*); contrast *Ac.* 1.45, where Arcesilaus' view that nothing can be known is phrased in a way which does not tie it to a particular conception of knowledge by avoiding the technical terms for κατάληψις (*negabat esse quicquam quod sciri posset... neque esse quicquam quod cerni aut intellegi posset*). This being so, it may be surprising that according to Cicero some of the premisses of the core argument are universally accepted. While this tells us little about the Academics and the attitude they take to their anti-Stoic arguments, because they may simply choose to offer e.g. the premiss that there are true and false impressions ad hominem (or indeed give Clitomachean approval or self-aware assent, as the case may be), it does suggest that nobody (including Epicurus) would question the Stoic framework which is relied on by the argument (e.g. by claiming that our perceptual experiences are misdescribed as Stoic impressions). This is the result of a presentational choice, i.e. to present the dispute between Stoics and Academics as without alternative. Cf. also *Luc.* 112, where Cicero says that dealing with a Peripatetic would be straightforward for him since a Peripatetic would not insist on the third clause of the Zenonian definition.

---

[325] See also the comparison of the two versions in Schäublin et al. (p. 250 n. 228).

Sed ut minuam controuersiam...quam in paruo lis sit[is]: *Luc.* 83–5 is, with omissions, LS 40J. The disingenuous transition, given that it was Cicero who choose Epicurus as a target, is self-consciously ironized by the overtly lawyerly language; see Reid[1] (p. 277) on phrases like *controuersiam minuere* in legal and quasi-legal contexts. Durand's emendation *in paruo lis sit* (Durand 1740) for the transmitted *in paruolis sitis* is compelling; Reid[1] (p. 276) assembles parallels, exact and in type, for substantivated *paruum*. On the point itself, cf. §78 *init.*: *Haec est una contentio quae adhuc permanserit*.

Quattuor sunt capita...de quo haec tota quaestio est: see Ernesti (1797: 48–51) s.v. *caput*; Quint. 3.11.27, who surveys the rhetorical uses of *caput*/κεφάλαιον; D'Ancona (2012: 51 n. 52) on philosophical uses of κεφάλαιον. The subjunctive *concludant* is due to the consecutive clause: 'of such a kind as to conclude', 'which are apt to conclude'. On the cluster of synonyms in the conclusion of the argument, see the general note above, and cf. *Luc.* 23:...*comprehensi percepti cogniti constituti*; contrast *Ac.* 1.44: *qui nihil cognosci nihil percipi nihil sciri posse dixerunt*, where *sciri* seems to secure that any conception of knowledge could be meant.

E quibus primum est...percipi non possit: Reid[1] (p. 277) suggests that *a sensu* corresponds to *a uero* (which occurs in the resumption of premiss iii in §41), in an evident desire to harmonize the two versions of the argument, but *sensus* cannot denote a sense object (which represents or causes an impression; for the use of the preposition *a/ab*, see section 5.1).

It is not obvious how exactly the Latin *uisum falsum non percipitur* translates a Greek sentence meaning 'a false impression is not cataleptic'. If the archetypal *uisum percipere* means 'to grasp something [a state of affairs] as it appears', due to the dual reference of *uisum* to object seen and impression thereof (see section 10.1 and Reinhardt 2016: 84–5), then the addition of the attribute *falsum* would not—as far as the meaning of the Latin phrase is concerned—by itself remove the dual reference (since *falsus* can mean both 'not genuine' and 'false'). (The dual reference of *uisum* is in evidence in §84.) However, the context here is clearly an argument about impressions, and it is in this way that *uisum falsum* comes to be restricted to mean 'false impression'. The technical term *percipere* is used as a factive verb in *Acad.*: it can only be used of truths or states of affairs (see the general note on *Luc.* 21–2; Reinhardt 2019: 156–7).

Cicero's *cui non appositum sit* for ἀπαράλλακτος captures well that ἀπαραλλαξία means 'non-distinctness' rather than 'indistinguishability' (similarly §40), but fails to convey that the 'juxtaposed' non-distinct but false impression is notional: there is no suggestion e.g. that everyone, including people we know well and whom we know to be only children, might have a twin. What is also not apparent from the Latin wording (or its Greek counterparts) is that ἀπαραλλαξία can be construed in a generic sense, i.e. one can say of two different impressions with different representational and propositional content that they are ἀπαράλλακτοί with respect to their assent-inducing capacity (see also section 5.6).

Horum quattuor capitum...id quoque conceditis: interlocutors can 'concede' premisses for a range of reasons, and no immediate inference to a particular rationale for such concessions is possible, but the claim of universal acceptance is striking (see the general note above). *Epicurus non dat* is the language of dialectical exchanges, where the granting of a premiss put forward as a question is called διδόναι and τιθέναι (see on §104 and Reinhardt 2000: 61–7). Here as elsewhere in *Acad.* (cf. *Luc.* 19, 79; see also Schäublin et al. p. 250 n. 229) it is not acknowledged that the Epicurean conception of an αἴσθησις is quite different from a Stoic φαντασία. *Pugna* resumes *tota quaestio* above.

§§84–87a

Cicero moves straight into the discussion of the first type of ἀπαραλλαξία-consideration, which involves very similar objects.[326] *Igitur* creates a backward reference to §56, where the Servilii twins were introduced as frequently mistaken for one another by strangers but easily distinguished at home, i.e. by their *familia*. This means that Cicero assumes from the beginning that the Servilii are very similar in appearance but not identical. It probably also means that the perceiving subject featuring in his example is assumed to be aware of the fact that there are two Servilii.

Cicero argues that in a situation where a perceiving subject has looked at Publius Servilius Geminus but ended up believing that he was looking at Quintus Servilius, the impression of Publius Servilius cannot have carried the distinctive feature (*nota*) which in the present case supposedly distinguished the true impression and the false impression.[327] Once the distinction between cataleptic impressions marked by a *nota* and others is removed, then, Cicero suggests, the same perceiving subject could not be certain when looking at Gaius Cotta, who was consul twice with Publius Servilius (and who has no twin brother, one must supply), that it was him, in the absence of a *nota* marking out the invariably true impression.

Rather than clarifying this last move, e.g. by explaining why apparently obvious rejoinders (see below) are not available to the Stoics, Cicero then turns to a claim typically made by them in response to arguments from the ἀπαραλλαξία of impressions arising from very similar objects: that such objects are never identical, however similar they are, and that consequently they give rise to slightly different impressions. The introduction of this claim casts Cicero's opponents as being on the back foot in two ways: first, that the Servilii were not identical was already clear from Lucullus' remark about them; second, Cicero had made a second step (to Cotta), to which the Stoic reply is not pertinent. In proceeding as he does, he dramatizes the slowfootedness of his dogmatic opponents. He addresses the metaphysical claim by acknowledging somewhat condescendingly that the opponent is putting up a fight when advancing it, but observes that he is not resisting: rather, he grants the uniqueness of every thing in the world, implicitly allows for it to transfer to impressions qua alterations of or imprints on the mind arising from a causal process, but notes that

---

[326] On the order in which the two main types of ἀπαραλλαξία-arguments feature in our sources, see section 5.7.

[327] On terminology relating to the distinctive feature of cataleptic impressions, see the general note on *Luc.* 33–34a, as well as section 10.2.

things which may be different in their nature may appear (epistemically) to us to be identical. And, he submits, once a similarity has led us astray (as in the case of the Servilii), everything is thrown into doubt (as in the case of Cotta). For even if one forms a true perceptual belief about the identity of the object one is looking at, one will not have done so on the basis of a *nota* which marks the impression out as cataleptic. In §85a Cicero then restates his argument (for the benefit of his somewhat slow opponent, one may surmise): if one can mistake one unique twin for another very similar but equally unique twin, this will be so because there was no *nota* marking out an impression arising from the first twin, and if there was none in this case, one cannot claim there to be one in the case of another unique individual, Cotta. Even if one has a true impression of him, one will not have gone by a distinctive feature.

How exactly does the generalizing move from the Servilii to Cotta work? Three considerations are in play. The first two are Stoic views: that every thing in the world is unique, and that cataleptic impressions carry as a class a distinctive feature which marks them out.[328] The third is the observation that one can mistake one object for one very similar to it. Once this has happened (Cicero uses the imperfect indicative) with respect to one unique object, no object can be claimed to be identified by means of an impression carrying this distinctive feature. Without the metaphysical assumption about the uniqueness of each thing Cicero could reason from inevitable confusion about twins to inevitable confusion about, say, grains of sand, and even to inevitable confusion of objects which one can replicate to near-perfection (i.e. of all these objects one could not have a cataleptic impression), but there would remain objects which are unique and which cannot be credibly replicated (e.g. Cotta).

Hirzel once argued that Cicero's speech was based on a source to which the source on which Lucullus' speech is based had already replied,[329] so I shall briefly examine how exactly Cicero responds to *Luc.* 54–8. In §§54–5 Lucullus initially argues against Academic arguments to the effect that there are, or could be, identical objects in the world (some of these must have featured in Catulus' and Cicero's contributions on the previous day); so when Cicero in §84 introduces his opponent as someone who goes on and on about this point, this is warranted by the structure of Lucullus' exposition. In §56 Lucullus turns to the Servilii—they appear to be newly introduced into the debate—and cites their family's ability to tell them apart as evidence for their essential difference; as I had argued above, Cicero makes this his initial assumption rather than a point of contention in §84. In §57a Lucullus acknowledges that a problem arises from similar pairs or multiples of objects and suggests that the strategy for dealing with them is to withhold judgement; this of course requires an ability to determine in advance when one is faced with such an object. In §84 Cicero does not

---

[328] This holds whether one assumes the weak or the strong interpretation of the third clause of Zeno's definition; see section 5.4.

[329] See Hirzel (1883: 251–341); his thesis is conveniently summarized by Glucker (1978: 393): 'Hirzel's theory, in a nutshell, is that Lucullus' speech is based on Antiochus' speech in the *Sosus*, and that Cicero's speech—although it is officially an answer to Lucullus'—is in fact based on Philo's Roman books, the very books to which the *Sosus* (and, by its derivation from that work, Lucullus' speech) was an answer.' For an examination of Hirzel's thesis, see Glucker (1978: 391–420); pp. 401–3 is devoted to *Luc.* 84–7.

press on this point, as he might have, and instead starts from a scenario in which the misidentification has already occurred. In §57b training is discussed, which will enable someone to discern very similar objects, but in §58 Lucullus restates that withholding judgement remains advisable. In §58b Lucullus introduces the Academic argument, 'made occasionally', that impressions qua alterations of the soul's ruling part may differ but may appear the same—a suggestion he rejects on the grounds that impressions are judged by their appearance (see the comm. ad loc.). And he ends by noting that one can have no confidence in any impression once one has abolished (i.e. disputed) the *nota ueri et falsi*. Cicero's reply in §84 very fittingly focuses on this *nota*. Overall, Cicero's reply is adroit, relevant, and clearly a reaction to Lucullus' arguments.

The corresponding section in Sextus' account of Academic arguments from ἀπαραλλαξία in *M.* 7.408-11, devoted to non-distinctness with respect to 'stamp and impress' (κατὰ χαρακτῆρα καὶ κατὰ τύπον), differs from the account here in Cicero in that it only argues from non-distinctness of very similar objects. That is, the Stoic assumption about the identity of indiscernibles is not clearly presupposed (the phrase used is ἐπὶ γὰρ τῶν ὁμοίων μὲν κατὰ μορφήν, διαφερόντων δὲ κατὰ τὸ ὑποκείμενον), let alone flagged if presupposed, and the generalizing move to Cotta is not made. However, in 7.411 *init.* Sextus still draws a general conclusion, i.e. that the cataleptic impression possesses no feature which marks it out from the false and non-cataleptic impression.[330] This should caution against a hypothesis which might otherwise be tempting: that Sextus' discussion is based on material which is, in terms of relative chronology, earlier and less complex than Cicero's source material. When discussing *Luc.* 88-90, we shall also see that Sextus' discussion of the other type of arguments from ἀπαραλλαξία, from abnormal states of mind, in the same section, offers at least one argument which is more complicated than its counterpart in Cicero and thus could appear relatively later.

Allen (1997: 248-9) rightly notes that none of the arguments offered in this section aim to show that 'human beings are in dire epistemic straits'. Rather, the purpose of the argument is to show that this would be so if the Stoics were right. Allen goes on to show that the most obvious rejoinders one might give to the inference from mistaking the identity of P. Servilius to being unable to be certain that one is seeing Cotta involve precisely the kind of considerations which are available to the Academics in virtue of their relying on the Carneadean πιθανόν while they are not

---

[330] Perin (2005: 515 n. 21) comments: 'Sextus Empiricus, M. 7.408-410 is full of confusion. For Sextus reports there that if two objects A and B are perceptually indiscernible, then a cognitive impression of A will be indiscernible from a false impression of A. But if A and B are perceptually indiscernible, then no impression of A or of B will be a cognitive impression. And of course if the Stoic cannot distinguish A from B, then she will not assent to any impression of the form "This is A" or "This is B"; she will suspend judgment about the identity of the objects in question.' In order to see confusion or at least distortion (thus LS i.252) here, one must assume that, if one experiences a cataleptic impression, one will be able to discriminate the object on the basis of it. By contrast, I am assuming that the Stoics are committed to the possibility of experiencing a cataleptic impression of any object under ideal conditions (whether the impression is useable, allows for discrimination, and should and will win assent is another matter); see section 5.3 and Reinhardt (2011). I am further assuming that, when Sextus talks about 'cataleptic impressions', he means '*purported* cataleptic impressions', 'impressions which are supposed to be cataleptic on the Stoic account'.

available to the Stoics. The Stoic cannot reply that he knows that Cotta does not have a twin brother, since the corresponding belief can have no bearing on an impression's catalepticity according to Stoic foundationalist convictions (while it would correspond to one impression in the syndrome of impressions an impression with the propositional content 'this is Cotta' is associated with on the Carneadean view). If the Stoic were to reply that he can *see* that this is Cotta (and not someone completely different), he would have to enumerate all the features which mark out Cotta as well as state that they appear to him with unique clarity—that is, he would either just do what the Academics do when they consider the syndrome of impressions (see section 6.1) and verify the clarity of each impression in it, or he would in the last analysis have to invoke the *nota* on which he cannot rely according to the argument. That is why Cicero claims in §85 *init*. that Lucullus would have no answer to the question of why Cotta could not appear to him as someone he is not.

This leads us to another question: does Cicero's argument rely on the weak or on the strong interpretation of the third clause of Zeno's definition (see section 5.4)? If he relied on the strong interpretation, then this would either represent evidence that Lucullus (and thus Antiochus) did so, too, or it would represent an *ignoratio elenchi* on Cicero's part (sc. if Lucullus himself relied on the weak interpretation). For this move of Cicero's there could then be various explanations. If one construed, as entertained as a possibility for Antiochus by Striker (1997: 272), the difference between the weak and the strong interpretation in such a way that on the former clarity is a function of how phenomenal content is represented, while on the latter it is a property which can be considered entirely divorced from content, then it might appear that only on the latter construal the argumentative step from the Servilii to Cotta was possible, given the acknowledged uniqueness of Cotta. However, on any interpretation of the third clause cataleptic impressions form a distinct class of impressions, and this fact is all that Cicero is relying on: if, under ideal conditions, one can fail to have a true impression which cannot be false when faced with one individual, then it will be possible to have a false impression of any individual.

In §§85b–86a, having presupposed the Stoic view that every thing is unique in §§84–85a, Cicero reaffirms that his argument is able to accommodate it, but then goes on to point out that, while it may be plausible for some things, it is much less plausible for others (like multiple copies of the same statue). If the Stoic view was false, then two objects could of course give rise to impressions which are identical in every respect. The mocking suggestion that Lucullus may want to recruit an expert to deal with impressions arising from such objects leads into the charge (in §86b) that Lucullus' remark in §20—experts are able to access more information contained in sense impressions than laymen—turns perception into an art which requires extreme skill levels and practice (as opposed to being something humans are naturally endowed with). §§86 *iam illa praeclara*...to §87a (*...uideare mentitus*) dismisses Lucullus' praise of nature as the supreme artist (§30) as unsupported by actual evidence (sc. which meets the standards the dogmatists themselves require).

Qui igitur P. Seruilium Geminum uidebat...quae falsa esse non possit: *Luc.* 83–5 is, with omissions, LS 40J. For this use of *igitur*, see *OLD* s.v. no. 4. Allen (1997: 250 n. 33) posits 'certain confusions' in this section down to ...*distinguebatur a falso*;

he writes: 'But there is no need to cite here the principle according to which an impression that is not characterized by a *propria nota* of true impressions cannot be cognitive, because the impression is false and already non-cognitive on that account. The principle is needed to show that a true impression is not cognitive because indistinguishable from this false impression.' I think the key to interpreting this passage lies in appreciating how exactly Cicero talks about impressions and their objects in Latin. If one reads *uidebat* as 'looked at' (sc. at P. Servilius qua object in the world; see section 5.6.2, as well as Reinhardt 2016: 64–5, 86–7 on relational seeing and the gazing sense of *uidere*) and the following *uidere* in the same way (it is *putabat* which indicates that now a false perceptual belief about an object is at issue), then *uisum* resumes *uidebat/uidere* and means 'object seen' (cf. *OED* s.v. 'appearance' no. 14a) rather than just 'impression', with *incidebat in* (which describes the happening upon an object more naturally than the experiencing of an impression) pointing in the same direction. This 'object seen' could not be apprehended, because 'the true' is not distinguished from 'the false' by any *nota*. *Verum* and *falsum* are more naturally attributes of impressions rather than objects (or states of affairs), and the reader should probably privilege at *this* point the notion that impressions are being talked about, but the adjectives can qualify the objects/states of affairs, too, and then mean 'actually obtaining' and 'not obtaining'. Another important point is that there are two impressions at issue here, one true which the perceiving subject could not apprehend (to mimic Cicero's expression) in the absence of a *nota* and which did not give rise to a perceptual belief, and the false one he ended up with. Conversely, *that* there are two impressions at issue is suggested by the content of the *quia*-clause: the *nota* is supposed to mark impressions which are not merely true but cataleptic, so Cicero's talk of a *nota* which fails to distinguish the true from the false only makes sense if the frame of reference is two impressions, a true one and a false one.

On whether *nota* should be translated as 'sign' rather than 'distinctive mark', see the general note on *Luc.* 33–34a and section 10.2. On *qua distinctione sublata*, Reid[1] (p. 278) cross-refers to §86 and glosses 'possibility of distinguishing'; alternatively, it simply means 'a distinction (made between)', cf. *OLD* s.v. no. 2b. For *in C. Cotta* = 'in the case of C. Cotta', see *OLD* s.v. *in* no. 42. C. Aurelius Cotta (*RE* s.n. Aurelius no. 94; cos. 252 and 248 BC) is of course not to be confused with his descendant of the same name, who was a follower of the New Academy and features as an interlocutor in Cicero's *De orat.* and *N.D.* On *agnoscendo* (gerundive with *C. Cotta*), it is not obvious whether 'to recognize, know again, identify' (*OLD* s.v. no. 1) is the intended sense, or 'to become or be aware of, come to recognize, discern' (no. 7), but the latter seems preferable, since whether or not there is such a *nota* is the salient point. To speak of a *nota* which could not be false, as opposed to an impression marked by a *nota* which could not be false, is imprecise and cannot be paralleled in the Greek record, but cf. the comparable boldness in the phrase *certa iudicandi et assentiendi nota* in *N.D.* 1.12. On the tense of *possit*, see Plasberg[1] (p. 105).

Negas tantam similitudinem in rerum natura esse...fallet igitur sensum: cf. §54:...*cur id potius contenditis, quod rerum natura non patitur, ut non suo quidque genere sit tale quale est, nec sit in duobus aut pluribus nulla re differens ulla communitas?* See ad loc. on the Stoic metaphysical principle that every thing in the world is a unique individual; and §85. With the teasing *pugnas omnino…*, cf. §57 *init.*: *Hic pugnes licet, non repugnabo*. On concessive *omnino* followed by *sed*, see Shackleton Bailey (1960: 14). With *aduersario facili*, cf. §12: *minus…acer…aduersarius* and *aduersarius lenior* (of Philo, who is generally dismissed for the historical claim made in the Roman Books): Cicero is of course making Philo's case here. For elliptical *ne sit*, cf. §102.

Et si una fefellerit similitudo…esse eiusdem modi falsa: Cicero's point is not that, once one similarity (sc. between objects) has led us astray, we should suspect another similarity to do the same thing at any time, but that our confidence in our impressions is in general undermined after a similarity has lead us astray. To reply that Cotta has no twin would be beside the point. And even if one gets it right, this will be down to pure luck, rather than the use of a *nota* as a point of reference.

Nota is also the grammatical subject of the *ut*-clause (which is consecutive and picks up on *ea nota*; hence the negation with *ut non*); with this peculiar expression, cf. …*notam quae falsa esse non posset* above. *Videris* denotes relational seeing ('gazing') as at the beginning of the paragraph. Reid[1] (p. 278) clarifies the grammar: with *agnosci* a generic *aliquem* is to be supplied, with *oportere* not *te iudicare* but *iudicari*, and *ipse* is used for *is ipse*. For the uses of *iudicium*, see on *Ac.* 1.30. Plasberg[1] (p. 114), unusually, glosses *si ipse erit quem uideris qui tibi uidebitur* as καὶ ἐὰν αὐτὸς ὁ ὁρώμενος ᾖ ὁ δοκῶν ὁρᾶσθαι; Greek texts on the subject tend to use parts of φαίνεσθαι to maintain the etymological connection with φαντασία.

§85a

Quando igitur potest tibi P. Geminus Quintus uideri…quod non est: *quando* is causal. For the expression *quid habes explorati*, cf. §129: *quid habemus in rebus bonis et malis explorati?* The subjects of the *quando igitur…* and *cur non possit…* clauses are *P. Geminus* and *qui non sit* (sc. *Cotta*), respectively, while *Quintus* and *Cotta* are complements.

Quod non est is according to Reid[1] (p. 279) to be expanded to *quod non est id quod esse uidetur*; I assume, because of the shift to the neuter, *esse* and *est* to be parts of the full verb (meaning here 'to be the case') rather than the copula with an ellipsis.

§85b

Omnia dicis sui generis esse…nullum granum: *Stoicum est quidem…nullum granum* is *SVF* ii.113. On the Stoic view itself, cf. apart from the passages in Lucullus' speech (§§54, 57) Sextus, *M*. 7.241–52 (= *SVF* ii.65) as well as 7.409–10; Plut., *Comm. not.* 1077c-e (= *SVF* ii.112 = LS 28O), with Long and Sedley (i.1987: 27–8); Sen., *Ep. mor.* 113.16, with Inwood (2007: 283). Reid[1] (p. 279) draws attention to the Stoic book title Περὶ τῶν ὁμοίων, attested for Chrysippus and Sphaerus (D.L. 7.178 and 199). Remarkably, Lucr. 2.333–80 upholds the principle, too, assuming minute variations in the atomic composition of objects as well as that two individuals must be composed of different atoms. This shows that the principle, or some version of it, had wider acceptance (rather than showing influence of Stoic on Epicurean thought).

Various emendations have been proposed for *Stoicum sedem*. To have a reference to the Stoics or Stoic philosophy at all seems warranted by the implicit contrast with the preceding sentence: Cicero makes a point of observing that the principle upheld by Lucullus is simply a Stoic tenet. *Stoicum* delivers this unproblematically, but Ciceronian usage would be consistent with *Stoicorum*, too (cf. e.g. *Fin.* 4.33: *tale enim uisum est ultimum Stoicorum*). I print *id* rather than *istud*, since a smaller word is better warranted by the paradosis.

Haec refelli possunt...etiam si differat: Cicero insists one more time that he does not wish to contest the metaphysical principle, as it makes no difference to his argument (see the general note on §§84–85a) whether the identity of objects is actual or merely perceived. The distinction between ἀπαραλλαξία qua non-distinctness and indistinguishability is clearly drawn; see section 5.6.

Sed si hominum similitudo tanta esse non potest...Qua igitur notione discerneres: Cicero now observes that the metaphysical principle, while not implausible in some cases, is less compelling in others; multiple copies of statues (*signa*) are a case in point.

The example cited, Lysippus, predates the age of what is deemed genuine mass production, but Cicero's list of the specificities of the manufacturing process makes his point clear: *temperatio* denotes the mixture of the ingredients of the *aes* (cf. Cic., *Ver.* 2.4.98), the *caelum* is a metal tool (*OLD* s.v. *caelum*[1]). Reid[1] (p. 279) argues that *aqua* arose from a corruption of *atque*: 'The reading *aqua* originated with a copyist who took *caelo* to be "sky"..., and also probably *aere* to be "air", and *temperatione* to be "climate".' Yet Plasberg[1] (p. 114) explains that *aqua* refers to βάψις, i.e. tempering. For *eiusdem modi facere* = 'to copy', cf. Cic., *Ver.* 4.4; the similarity with ἀπαραλλαξία-terminology is unlikely to be coincidental.

Lysippus, whose *floruit* is usually given as the last quarter of the fourth century BC but who was active for an unusually long time (in or not long after 372 BC he is reported to have created a statue of Troilus, a victorious charioteer), produced statues of gods, heroes, and men (notably Alexander and his generals). His statues had smaller heads and more delicate physiques than those of his predecessor Polyclitus. There existed countless copies of his most famous works. See Moreno (1994: 23–123) and Edwards (1996); Reid[1] (p. 279) collects references in Latin literature.

Notio in *qua igitur notione* can mean neither 'concept' (as in *Ac.* 1.32) nor 'investigation' (as in *Luc.* 27), but while the juxtaposition with *discerneres* makes it tempting to see it as just a synonym to *nota*, Reid[1] (p. 279) is probably right to resist: 'Here related to *nota* as *uisio* to *uisum* (§33), marking rather the general process than the individual act.' Cf. *OLD* s.v. no. 2b.

I print *Alexandrūs* rather than *Alexandros* since the former is *difficilior* and possible (*-um* was probably the reading of the archetype).

§§86a–87a

Quid? Si in eius...cognosceret: on freestanding interrogative *quid* preceding sentence questions and functioning as an expression of disbelief, see Pinkster i.317; the present case of a constituent question is no different. For *distinctio*, see on §84 *qua distinctione sublata*; *agnoscendo* is also resumed from there. On *anularius aliqui*, see Reid¹ (p. 249) on *aliquis* vs *aliqui* (there is no reason to suspect the text here). The noun is rare (cf. *TLL* s.v. col. 193.34–40) but attested in inscriptions referencing actual craftsmen (*CIL* XI.1235, XII.4456), so it is unlikely that Cicero is coining a new term here. In any case, the polemical point is to ask whether Lucullus would draw on a ring expert to tell apart impressions in wax made by the same seal or signet ring. Talk of invention in connection with the Delian farmer who can tell from the egg which hen had laid it is polemical, too: as explained at §57 (where Lucullus speaks of *complures*), agricultural writers did credit Delian poultry farmers with particular expertise. However, Cicero's basic point stands again, despite the hyperbole. *Oua cognoscere* is vague, but there is no reason to think that Cicero is now talking about discriminating one egg from another, as opposed to what Lucullus did in fact claim.

Sed adhibes artem aduocatam etiam sensibus...carmen agnoscitur: Reid¹ (p. 280) comments on the legal metaphor in *aduocare* (*OLD* s.v. no. 4a: 'to employ as counsel, have plead one's case'), with which *sensibus* goes as a *dat. commodi*; the implication is that Lucullus' argument was lawyerly and far-fetched. Cicero is not here distinguishing between a knack gained through experience and technical expertise in the stronger sense; cf. §22 *fin.* with n.

Cicero is referring to the examples cited in §20. If the explanation given there of the recognition of musical accompaniment of a play is correct, then *a perito carmen adnoscitur* does not refer to recognizing a particular piece of music (which is possible for anyone who is familiar with it, τεχνίτης or not) but to recognizing a new composition which has been created so as to fit with the characters and nature of a certain play.

Quid? Hoc nonne...nec uidere nec audire possimus: already Hirzel (1883: 331) noted that in §20 Lucullus did not claim that the senses were only able to deliver veridical perception if one had acquired a special expertise. Reid¹ (p. 280) glosses *magnis* as 'difficult', but 'elaborate' comes closer to the required sense. Given Lucullus' repeated claims that the Academics are depriving human beings of their senses, the infinitives *uidere* and *audire* should perhaps be taken as 'to see' and 'to hear' in general, rather than just veridically.

Iam illa praeclara...[§87a] cur non extimescam opinandi temeritatem: see *OLD* s.v. *iam* no. 8a for the use in marking the transition to a new topic. The reference is to the brief praise of nature as an artist in §30. *Praeclara* is ironic (cf. *N.D.* 3.40: *omitto illa, sunt enim praeclara*) and must be neuter plural, with the sentence from *quanto* in apposition. The mood of *artificio esset* indicates that Cicero is relating Lucullus' view. With *constructio hominis* and *quae fabricata sit hominem* below, cf. *N.D.* 2.133:

hominis fabricatio. For the uses of *temeritas* in *Acad.*, see on *Luc.* 31 *fin.* Here Cicero is thinking of rash assent, i.e. assent given to the non-cataleptic (in which case 'opinion' results): for him, any account of nature's providential organization of the world involves assent to obscure and unverifiable claims.

Etiamne hoc affirmare potes...quando cur quo modo: Cicero briefly assumes the role of an advocate interrogating an accused or witness. For a question introduced by *etiamne*, see *Tusc.* 5.111 and the examples collected by Pinkster i.324; formally, this is a genuine request for information. *Affirmare* has the technical sense of 'affirm' on the basis of assent. *Scilicet* is ironical. *Fabricari* is used in *Luc.* 30 (*tuo uerbo* here). Cf. *N.D.* 1.19, which leads into a similar cluster of questions: *Quibus enim oculis animi intueri potuit uester Plato fabricam illam tanti operis, qua construi a deo atque aedificari mundum facit? Quae molitio, quae ferramenta, quae uectes, quae machinae, qui ministri tanti muneris fuerunt?*

Tractantur ista ingeniose...ne tu, qui id me facturum paulo ante dixeris, uideare mentitus: Cicero pointedly evaluates the argument esthetically and stylistically, since it has no substance. *Ne affirmentur modo* 'provided they are not affirmed' is peculiar not because the restriction placed on the main clause is unusual, but because *modo* normally precedes *ne* (see Kühner-Stegmann ii.446–8); Reid[1] (p. 281) cites three examples from comedy. The Stoics of course do affirm these claims.

Lucullus had said in §55 *init.* (cf. *qui id...dixeris* here) that Cicero was seeking refuge with the *physici* in defending his claims about ἀπαραλλαξία and that he would not be able to stay away from them, sc. in his speech. Cicero replies here that he will come to them eventually (i.e. in §116; divine creation is discussed in §§119–21; cf. also §§127–8), but only to prevent Lucullus from being guilty of lying, thus implying that they do not merit engagement. Here, however, Cicero has temporarily shifted to a different topic, the well-orderedness of the world.

§87b

Having briefly mentioned physical matters as a subject to be treated in due course, Cicero now proposes to turn to subjects which are less obscure (*clariora*) than *physica*. He foregrounds what follows from §88 *init.* by saying that many of the arguments at issue were furnished by Chrysippus himself. What follows from §91 could be informed by Chrysippean discussions of logical fallacies (cf. §90 *fin.*: *Sed abeo a sensibus. Quid est quod ratione percipi possit?*). The senses, logic, and reason are, from the Academic point of view, *clariora* than physical matters relatively speaking.

With §87b, cf. the commentary on *Luc.* 75, where Chrysippus is reported as having argued for and against the senses. For making the argument contra Chrysippus was presented as an enabler of Carneades, which was evidence of his argumentative mastery to some, and of his misguidedness to others (on the grounds that he himself allowed the inferiority of the Stoic position to become plain); see Plut., *Sto. rep.* 1036b–c. In the context of these reports, reference is made to Chrysippus' works against συνήθεια (cf. on *Luc.* 75 for details), in connection with which the Stoics remarked that Chrysippus' arguments against the senses easily outshone those of Carneades. This gives us the Greek term corresponding to *consuetudo* mentioned here in §87b and makes it plain that the term had a distinct application in the field of epistemology, as our passage here suggests, too (συνήθεια in the fields of ethics and linguistic theory is to be distinguished). Plutarch, *Comm. not.* 1059b, reports that Arcesilaus was the first to attack συνήθεια, which suggests, together with the wider context, that the technical epistemological concept predates Chrysippus. However, within Stoic texts, the term occurs only in the fragments of Chrysippus, who is reported to have written several books for and against συνήθεια. No definition of the term is preserved. The most detailed study of the concept to date is Glucker (1996). Using evidence from D.L. relating to Timon (9.105), an early sceptic associated with Pyrrho and a contemporary of Arcesilaus and later Chrysippus, as well as from Sextus (*P.H.* 1.92, 1.120),[331] on how training may enhance the powers of our senses, and combining it with passages from *Acad.* where the term *consuetudo* is used in connection with the same kind of training (*Luc.* 57), Glucker (1996: 114) suggests that συνήθεια/*consuetudo* 'is there to correct...or to perfect...what is given us by "bare" sense-perception.'[332] He adds a historical hypothesis which is to account for the state of the evidence: that the relative sparsity of the term in our sources, and the absence of a definition, is to be explained by the fact that Carneades devised a devastating objection to it, after which συνήθεια was mentioned in records of the debate only for completeness.

I believe that evidence from *Acad.* suggests that *consuetudo* is a broader notion, which may cover the effects training has on our ability to be appreciative of our impressions but is not confined to it, and that the historical hypothesis rests on false assumptions.

In *Luc.* 20 Cicero has Lucullus use the very example in connection with which D.L. mentions the notion of συνήθεια (and on which Sextus sheds further light): experience with paintings makes the observer appreciate the two-dimensional devices which painters use to create three-dimensional effects. With suitable training one does not mistake the former for genuine three-dimensional phenomena. Other instances of being able to do more with one's impressions after training are a musician's ability to identify a certain type of music from just a few notes (also *Luc.* 20), the ability to tell very similar physical objects apart, a chicken farmer's ability to tell which of his hens had laid a given egg, and a mother's ability to tell her twins apart (all §57).[333] The cognitive processes involved in these examples are quite different from one another and would be analysed and described in different ways. This suggests that *consuetudo*/συνήθεια are general terms, capable of encompassing non-technical and technical familiarity;[334] for issues relating to either there is specialized terminology not related to *consuetudo*/συνήθεια and cognate terms.

---

[331] See Clayman (2009) and (2016).
[332] See also Glucker (1996: 214): 'On the level of perception, then, συνήθεια seems to carry on from where αἴσθησις and ἐνάργεια have supplied us with the "rare materials", and to ensure that we are careful in giving our συγκατάθεσις in each case.'
[333] That Lucullus links of an enhanced ability to use one's impressions to technical expertise and craft knowledge (e.g. *Luc.* 20, 57) prompts the Academic rejoinder that he is turning everyday perception into a specialized skill requiring unlikely levels of expertise (*Luc.* 86).
[334] The Greek record is consistent with this. In *Sto. rep.* 1036e (= *SVF* ii.109 = part of LS 31P) Chrysippus is said to have warned against mounting arguments directed at positions which one actually endorses when dealing with non-sages, ἐπεὶ καὶ οἱ κατὰ τὴν συνήθειαν καταλαμβάνοντες καὶ τὰ αἰσθητὰ

Moreover, there are reasons for thinking that *consuetudo* (and συνήθεια) extends beyond training in the use of impressions. First, 'the senses', *consuetudo*, and reason provide an organizational principle in *Acad.* (see the commentary on *Luc.* 42). In one of the sections where this tripartite division is the main structuring device, there is a section on concept-formation and becoming rational in the place where one would expect *consuetudo* to be dealt with (*Luc.* 21–2); while the actual term is not used in this paragraph, it is plain that *consuetudo* would have a readily intelligible application in this connection, although it would refer to 'use' of impressions in quite a different sense than before. On the Stoic view, human beings experience cataleptic impressions before they become rational in the proper sense, and the very reliability of cataleptic impressions helps account for concept formation and memory.[335] Everyday experience in this sense, and everyday cognitive operations, are a natural topic to follow after a treatment of 'the senses' proper. Second, there is the way in which Cicero talks about *consuetudo*: in *Luc.* 42 Lucullus reports that the Academics divide the subject matter they discuss *primum in sensus, deinde in ea quae ducuntur a sensibus et ab omni consuetudine*; in *Luc.* 75 Chrysippus is said to have argued *multa…contra sensus,…multa contra omnia quae in consuetudine probantur*. The first passage points, through *in ea quae ducuntur a sensibus*, to products of the senses (like concepts or memory) and would oddly return to the theme of the senses and their use with *ab omni consuetudine* if that was meant by the phrase here. As to *in consuetudine probari*, this would seem to be a mystifying expression for approval on the basis of trained sense perception.

Glucker (1996: 117) holds that the paucity of evidence on συνήθεια is due to the fact that cognitive improvements as a consequence of training could no longer be cited once (a) Carneades had introduced the argument from ἀπαραλλαξία, which he seems (b) to interpret as 'indistinguishability' and (c) to associate with arguments from abnormal states of mind exclusively. On the interpretation followed in this commentary, none of the assumptions (a)–(c) is correct, even though it is to be acknowledged that arguments from abnormal states of mind, i.e. one type of ἀπαραλλαξία arguments, are especially associated with Carneades in our texts.[336] It is in any case hard to see how the possibility of training could lose its argumentative relevance in the way posited by Glucker:[337] arguments to the effect that we might be mad or dreaming now, common in modern discussions of scepticism inter alia, featured in the debate between Stoics and Academics only as absurd consequences, held to be evidently unacceptable to everyone (*Luc.* 54).[338] Abnormal states of mind were demonstrably cited in a different connection, as a reply to the claim that cataleptic

---

καὶ τὰ ἄλλα ἐκ τῶν αἰσθήσεων ῥᾳδίως προίενται ταῦτα, 'because those who grasp in accordance with συνήθεια both perceptible objects and what arises from those perceptions easily let go of them', sc. because their beliefs are not mutually secured like those of the sage. Here κατὰ τὴν συνήθειαν καταλαμβάνειν is an untutored grasping from which one can easily be diverted.

[335] See Frede (1994).
[336] Thus Ioppolo (1993: 199–200 n. 60).
[337] Lucullus in *Luc.* certainly does not give the impression that the possibility of training was a consideration which the debate had left behind, and the character Cicero dismisses it for reasons which are unconnected with arguments from ἀπαραλλαξία citing abnormal states of mind.
[338] There is also no record of an argument to the effect that we cannot rely on memory because the impressions which gave rise to it were experienced while the subject was in an abnormal state of mind.

impressions possess a unique causal property which normally triggers assent to them; cf. Sextus, *M*. 7.405 and Brittain (2014).

Sed ut ad ea, quae clariora sunt ueniam...itaque ab eo armatum esse Carneadem: what follows is *clariora* compared to physics (cf. *Luc*. 19: *altera de natura et rebus occultis*), to which Cicero will return in *Luc*. 116 (the subject of divine creation is discussed in *Luc*. 119–21).

Res iam uniuersas profundam is a peculiar expression in a number of ways. On *uniuersas* Schäublin et al. (p. 254 n. 248) comment: 'Was mit *res universae* gemeint ist, läßt sich vielleicht nicht bündig entscheiden. Vielleicht will Cicero sagen, daß er nun nicht "im Einzelnen" (*in singulis rebus*, vgl. §42) zeigen will, daß nichts erfaßt werden kann, sondern sich auf einige klassische Fälle beschränken will.' Alternatively, the word is meant to capture the scope of Chrysippus' arguments contra (*contra sensus et perspicuitatem contraque omnem consuetudinem contraque rationem*), which informs the disposition of what follows until §98 at least up to a point (*ratio* would relate to arguments in particular). *Profundam* would fit with this; our passage is cited under *OLD* s.v. *profundo* no. 4b: 'to make known or publish copiously'; notice the following relative clause. *Iam*, whose position suggests that it modifies *uniuersas* rather than being a temporal adverb modifying the whole clause, would be 'at this stage or point (in a development) / (implying that the latest stage is in some way contrary to expectation)' (*OLD* s.v. no. 7b).

The evidence for Chrysippus' writings on the subject (*de quibus uolumina...*) is collected on *Luc*. 75. We are unable to specify which Academics in particular are meant by *nostris*; the most likely candidate is Clitomachus. With *de quo queri solent Stoici* cf. §75:*...Chrysippum qui fulcire putatur porticum Stoicorum*. To present the opponent as someone who 'complains' is standard polemics (cf. §§32, 144).

In *contra sensus et perspicuitatem* both elements belong together, and the double *-que* accounts for the articulation. In *contraque omnem consuetudinem* 'omnem' suggests that *consuetudo* is a term with wide-ranging application. On *contraque rationem*, see the general note above and §91 *init*.

With *ipsum sibi respondentem inferiorem fuisse*, cf. Plut., *Sto. rep*. 1036c–d:*...ἐκεῖνο δ' ἀληθές, ὅτι βουληθεὶς αὖθις συνειπεῖν τῇ συνηθείᾳ καὶ ταῖς αἰσθήσεσιν ἐνδεέστερος γέγονεν αὐτοῦ καὶ τὸ σύνταγμα τοῦ συντάγματος μαλακώτερον*, '...this is true, that, when later he desired to speak on the side of common experience and the senses, he fell short of his own achievement and the second treatise was feebler than the first' (transl. Cherniss).

§§88–90

In this section Cicero advances arguments for ἀπαραλλαξία arising from abnormal states of mind.[339] In doing so, he rebuts Lucullus criticism of such arguments in §§51–4.

---

[339] On the order in which different types of ἀπαραλλαξία arguments feature in our sources, see section 5.7.

There Lucullus made use of the device of an imaginary interlocutor, who introduced points made by the Academics in direct speech. To what extent these interventions picked up on what was said in the *Catulus* is impossible to say in any particular case, but it is likely on general grounds that they did expand on points previously made, considering the reference to Cicero's 'many arguments against the senses' in §79, and also that it is unlikely that Cicero the author gave the first substantial statement on these matters to an Antiochian speaker. I survey briefly what Lucullus said there:

- in §51 Lucullus gave his main reply: that the impressions received by people in abnormal states of mind do not have the same *perspicuitas* as cataleptic impressions received under ideal conditions. The evidence cited is (a) that, when we wake up or recover, we disown our earlier impressions. Lucullus would presumably have endorsed the implication that it is *our* fault that we did not recognize the absence of *perspicuitas* at the time.
- §52 *init.* introduced the opponent as saying that, while we are disturbed, our impressions have the same representational content in type as impressions experienced under ideal conditions while awake (Cicero says the *species* of the impressions is the same in both cases). Lucullus said there was a difference, but he would not now go into it, and then he cited counterevidence (b): even while in an abnormal state, we hesitate or else notice that our impressions are somehow wanting. Again the implication seemed to be that, when we do not hesitate, it is our fault.
- in §53 the opponent pointed out to the Stoics that they stipulate that their wise man will withhold judgement while insane, precisely because impressions experienced then are like impressions experienced in a normal state. The opponent took this as an implicit endorsement of his position. Here Lucullus' replied (c) that that it was rather proof of his point that the sage is sometimes justified to suspend and sometimes not. If there was no difference between impressions, he would never suspend judgement (if every impression was true) or always (if every impression was false). The Academics would retort that they do not deny the existence of true and false impressions (and in that sense recognize a difference), but dispute that truth does ever correlate with other features (notably ones which are in some sense available to us).
- in §54 Lucullus argued (d) that, if the Academics were right, one might be in a state of insanity now. This was treated as an absurd consequence of the Academic arguments, rather than something they seek to make plausible or prove.

Cicero's strategy in reply is to press the point that, while we are in an abnormal state of mind, we cannot tell the difference (i.e. he addresses a above). He bolsters the point by observing (citing evidence from Pacuvius' *Iliona*) that, even when subjects have woken, they sometimes retain the notion that their impressions were true. Cicero shifts to addressing (b) only in the middle of §89 and disarms the point by quoting lines from the same play which Lucullus had quoted, which illustrate that even the speaker who expressed doubt about his impressions was a little later clearly misled and took his impressions for real. Point (c) is passed over in silence, and point (d) addressed only indirectly: Cicero does wish to generalize from his arguments and observes that true and false impressions are equally capable of triggering assent, but he does not acknowledge and recognize that this implies that we might be dreaming or insane now. Instead, he repeats his reply to (a).

The way in which Cicero replies to Lucullus is somewhat surprising, in that his reply heavily emphasizes a single point. One may explain this by assuming that, in this particular area, a kind of argumentative stalemate had been reached. In such a situation it is reasonable to give prominence to the strongest consideration one can cite against the opponent. Moreover, in the ebb and flow of the debate over the two books on the first edition, this is Cicero's final pronouncement on the matter, so is reasonable for him to emphasize what he takes to be his strongest point by way of *peroratio*.

I had observed in connection with the other type of argument from ἀπαραλλαξία (§§84–7) that the corresponding section in Sextus' discussion of such arguments seemed to lack a natural 'next' argumentative step which was in evidence in Cicero, raising the question of whether it reflected chronologically earlier material on the Academic arguments. It is thus notable that in *M.* 7.405–7, the section covering the same ground as §§88–90, Sextus offers an argument which gives the impression of being 'later' in terms of relative chronology: he argues that Heracles, while struck with madness, acted both successfully (i.e. seized his bow, shot, and hit his target) and unsuccessfully (i.e. mistook his own children for Eurystheus). This is taken as evidence that purported cataleptic impressions and false impressions equally give rise to assent.[340] In §89 we get a brief glimpse of Cicero's source material: there Cicero briefly diverges from his practice of citing Latin poets in support of his points and instead talks about Euripides' *H.F.* from which the scenario in Sextus is derived, but only to argue that all the impressions which made Heracles, while insane, perceive his children, his wife, and his father as other individuals moved him in the same way as purportedly cataleptic impressions experienced while in a sane state would have.

With that exception Lucullus and Cicero use quotations from Roman epic and drama where Sextus' discussion invokes scenarios from Euripidean tragedies (*Alc.*, *H.F.*). In the present section Cicero makes use of a number of strategies in order to counter Lucullus' arguments: in §88 he repeats Lucullus' arguments for the 'weakness' of vacuous impressions, which turned on quotations from Ennius, with an expansiveness which contrasts with crisper cross-referencing elsewhere, but only to dismiss these arguments as beside the point. In this case there is a polemical edge to Cicero's mode of exposition: he ostentatiously rehearses the opponent's argument, only to dispatch it in an instant. He then cites evidence from some poets to bolster what he presents as the salient point: that, while deranged, subjects take their impressions to be true. In same cases (§88 *fin.*), this feeling persists even after subjects have woken up. The quotations from Ennius' *Alcmeo* in §89 seem to be selected to

---

[340] To this the Stoic might reply that no impression received while insane could qualify as a cataleptic impression because the causal process which gives rise to it was compromised. To the Academic this would be a dogmatic assertion.

illustrate not just the realistic feel of vacuous impressions in general, but also quite specifically that they are as rich and colourful as impressions experienced while awake.

Cicero comments on his practice of using poetic quotations in philosophical contexts in *Tusc.* 2.26; see Spahlinger (2005: 188-96).

§88

Ea sunt eius modi...uigilantium siccorum sanorum: *ea sunt eius modi* resumes §87 *init.*: *ea quae clariora sunt*. The adjectives *uinulentus* and *uinosus* are of course standard terms for 'drunk' since no alcoholic drinks other than wine were available in antiquity. Other terms are associated with wetness, e.g. *madere*, which is, however, of a lower stylistic level (unlike its opposite *siccus*; cf. the passages assembled by Reid[1] p. 283 on *siccorum sanorum*). On Lucullus' (and Antiochus' and the Stoic) view, cataleptic impressions arise from a causal process which involves, among other factors, the mind, and if the mind is blunted or deranged, this causal process is compromised, which results in impressions being 'weaker' (*imbecilliora*) than they otherwise would be (cf. §52:...*illa uisa quam leuia fuerint intellegunt*); see next n. The reference of *tractata sunt* is the section from §46; *dicebas* refers back to §52.

Quo modo...'sed mihi ne utiquam cor consentit...'. Similia de uinulentis: the question *quo modo?* enquires about the nature of the weakness of the impressions. Cicero then restates the points made by Lucullus in §§51 and 52 (see ad loc. for interpretation and references) before attacking them from *Quasi quisquam neget...* below. The weakness has two dimensions: such impressions lack the *perspicuitas* which is peculiar to cataleptic impressions (cf. §51), as is suggested by the scenario at the beginning of Book 1 of Ennius' *Ann.*; and it relates to a deficiency in the 'strikingness' of such impressions, i.e. in their ability to trigger assent, as is suggested by the *Alcmeo* passage cited (cf. §52: *imbecillius assentiuntur*). Reid[1] (p. 282) glosses *uisum esse* 'sc. uidere', but the quote in §51 (*uisus Homerus adesse poeta*) suggests that *Homerum* replaces *se* as subject accusative in the second half of the sentence and that the sense 'to merely appear' of *uideri* is at issue. Plasberg[1] (p. 115) wonders about *sed uisum esse* ⟨*adesse*⟩, but the change of subject would be less harsh if Cicero had written *sed* ⟨*Homerum*⟩ *uisum esse*.

Quasi quisquam neget et qui experrectus sit...quo modo uiderentur, id quaeritur: Cicero happily concedes, as he implies anyone would, that people disown their impressions once they have woken up or recovered their sanity. The transmitted *somniare* cannot be correct and has prompted various emendations. The insertion of *non* before *somniare* (Plasberg[1]) does not help, because, as *sed non agitur...* below shows, a reference to how things appeared while the subject was dreaming is required. A change to *somniasse*, as suggested by Lambinus, with *putare* later in the sentence assumed to be functioning ἀπὸ κοινοῦ, would not do, since *putare* takes the accusative with infinitive. *Somniasse se* (Müller) addresses this problem, gives good sense, and is idiomatic as well as reasonably close to the paradosis; the perfect infinitive itself is encouraged by the way in which Lucullus introduces the quotation from the *Annals* in §51: *At, cum somniauit, ita narrauit*... The reading *somniasse ⟨se sentire⟩*, adopted by Schäublin et al., offers a neatly idiomatic (within the specialized context of *Acad.*) use of *sentire* (cf. §79: *in remo sentio non esse id quod uideatur*), but seems uneconomical compared to *somniasse se*. Likewise *eum somnia[re] ⟨sua uisa putare⟩*, suggested by Halm in the apparatus. *Somnia re⟨ri⟩* (Reid[1]) would be slightly elliptic, in that one would have to understand a demonstrative in the neuter plural. Brittain (2006: 114) opted for *somnia[re] ⟨ea putare⟩*. One might be tempted to combine these two suggestions (*somnia re⟨ri ea⟩*), but Cicero never uses *reri* (although other parts of the verb are attested).

For the sequence *non id agitur—id quaeritur*, cf. Cic., *Div.* 1.86: *Cur fiat quidque quaeris. Recte omnino; sed non nunc id agitur; fiat necne fiat, id quaeritur*. Reid[1] (p. 283) cites parallels for the emphatic *id*.

Nisi uero Ennium non putamus...dormienti uero aeque ac uigilanti probantur: *O pietas animi* is frg. v (l. 4) Skutsch of Ennius' *Annals*; Skutsch (1985: 157): 'Cicero's *totum illud audiuisse* seems to indicate that this was the beginning of Homer's main speech, though not necessarily his first utterance.' Cicero's implication is that Homer's speech and appearance must have felt like a waking experience to Ennius at the time; *nisi uero*, here used like *nisi forte*, marks the ironical entertaining of a suggestion, actual or hypothetical, which is deemed absurd. Reid[1] (p. 283) glosses *uisa* as φαντάσματα, which is strictly correct in terms of Stoic terminology (cf. D.L. 7.50), but Sextus also uses the term φαντασία freely in cases where strictly φαντάσματα are at issue. One must either supply *falsa* (with Reitzenstein *apud* Plasberg[1]) or *inania* after *uisa*, or delete *et* before *somnia* (with Lambinus); Davies's *esse* (for *et*) would be in the wrong place. The participle *dormienti* corresponds to a temporal clause in the indicative, while *uigilanti* corresponds to a counterfactual conditional clause.

Quid? Iliona somno illo...quam uigilantes fidem: on Pacuvius' *Iliona*, see Schierl (2006: 312–41). The subject of this tragedy is the myth of Polydorus, son of Priam. Unlike in the versions of the myth presupposed in Euripides' *Hecuba* and Vergil's *Aeneid* (3.22–68), Polydorus is not murdered by the Thracian king Polymestor, but survives because his sister, Iliona, who is Polymestor's wife, swaps him with her own son Deipylus (cf. Hygin., *Fab.* 109). Deipylus is murdered by Polymestor and, near the beginning of the play but after a prologue or initial expository dialogue (see Schierl 2006: 315), appears to his mother in a dream, begging her for a proper burial. *Mater te appello*...is the beginning of an octonarius; the line continues...*tu, quae curam somno suspensam leuas*. In *Tusc.* 1.106 Cicero cites the entire line and the following four (= frg. 146 Schierl = ll. 197–201 Ribbeck[3] = ll. 227–31 D'Anna), in which Deipylos describes the condition of his unburied corpse in gruesome detail:

> mater, te appello; tu, quae curam somno suspensam leuas,
> neque te mei miseret, surge et sepeli natum ⟨...⟩
> prius quam ferae uolucresque ⟨...⟩
> neu reliquias semesas sireis denudatis ossibus
> per terram sanie delibutas foede diuexarier.

> Mother, I call you; you, who eases her care with sleep's relief,
> and who does not take pity on me, rise and bury your son...
> before wild animals and birds...
> and do not let my half-eaten remains with bones stripped
> along the ground besmeared with blood be foully torn apart.

In *Tusc.* 1.106 Cicero refers to all five lines as *septenarii*, but two of them are *octonarii*, one can be plausibly emended to an *octonarius*, and two lines are incomplete; substantial interference would be necessary to arrive at five septenarii (Lambinus 1566 emended Cicero's *septenarios* to *octonarios*).

Cicero uses *mater te appello* in *Sest.* 126 (given in 56 BC), where the sudden appearance of Appius Claudius Pulcher at public games is likened to the appearance of Deipylus. Hor., *Sat.* 2.3.60–2, recalls a performance of *Iliona* at which the actor playing Iliona was drunk and missed his entry, at which point the audience called him using these words. Evidently the play was frequently restaged and could be assumed to be familiar to Cicero's listeners and readers.

The words of Iliona quoted by Cicero as evidence that she took Deipylus' dream appearance to be real even after waking up are frg. 147 Schierl (= l. 202 Ribbeck³ = ll. 232–3 D'Anna). Cicero quotes *iteradum...mihi* in *Tusc.* 2.44 and *Att.* 14.14.1 (= SB 368), without indicating the origin of the words; it is our passage which provides *age...audi* as the immediately preceding context, assigns the words to the *Iliona*, and places them after the five lines beginning with *mater te appello*. It is, however, not clear whether Deipylos continued his speech beyond what is known of it. On the change from *credit* to *crederet*, see Reid¹ (p. 284).

§89

Quid loquar de insanis...quam is putabat quae uidebantur: Sempronius Tuditanus (*RE* s.n. Sempronius no. 89), son of C. Sempronius Tuditanus (cos. 129 BC; *RE* s.n. Sempronius no. 92), exhibited deranged behaviour in his old age; cf. Cic., *Phil.* 3.16 (...*qui cum palla et cothurnis nummos populo de rostris spargere solebat*), Val. Max. 7.8.1 (on his behaviour and his will), with Hopwood (2007), and Lact., *Inst.* 3.23.7. On the dress worn by him (that of a dramatic actor), see Hor., *A.P.* 278–89. Presumably Tuditanus is not just cited as an instance of someone who was mentally ill; rather, his peculiar attire and activity—presupposed as familiar here—are meant to be suggestive of a particular situation in which he took himself to be.

On *quisquam sanissimus...*, Reid¹ (p. 284) cites Verg., *A.* 1.48–9: *Et quisquam numen Iunonis adorat | praeterea aut supplex aris imponet honorem?* As here, this is a sentence question rather than the use of *quisquam* as an interrogative, and the speaker exhibits a degree of exasperation (on this point, see also Austin 1971 ad loc.). Here *uidere* vs *uideri* is clearly the contrast between veridical seeing and mere appearance; see section 10.1 and Reinhardt (2016: 63–72).

Quid ille qui 'uideo, uideo te'...cum omnino non uideret: the quotation, an iambic senarius, must come from an Ajax tragedy, where it was spoken by the raging hero (cf. Soph., *Ai.* 214–62); it is *trag. inc.* 47 Ribbeck[3]. We know of three relevant tragedies, cf. Jocelyn (1968: 178): one by Ennius, Pacuvius' *Armorum iudicium*, and a play by Accius of the same name. The line cannot be securely assigned. In *De orat.* 3.162 Cicero quotes our line (with *uiue* for *uiuum* transmitted in the *Luc.* manuscripts) and the words immediately following: *oculis postremum lumen radiatum rape!* The wider context is an evaluative survey of more and less successful metaphors. Ennius had featured with a different metaphor earlier in the same paragraph, which was, however, found to be wanting. The quote from the Ajax tragedy is then given without a prefatory remark, but afterwards Cicero praises the metaphorial use of *rape*. Wisse et al. (2008: 215–16) wonder ad loc. whether Cicero, having criticized Ennius whom he otherwise holds in very high regard, was eager to balance a less successful metaphor with a very good one by the same author.

The key point for Cicero's argument is that the speaker exclaims that he sees Odysseus when he is in fact delusional; in the *cum*-clause, *omnino* emphasizes *non*, and *uideret* is 'to see veridically'. Ajax evidently does have a visual experience, and there is no suggestion that it does not feel real.

Like Reid[1] (p. 284) and Plasberg[1]/Plasberg[2] I do not put a question mark after *Quid* (in *quid ille*). This necessitates a question mark after *dum licet* and that a new sentence begins with *Nonne*....Contrast the structure of *Quid? Ipse Alcmaeo...qui negat...nonne...oritur?* below.

Quid? Apud Euripidem...ut ueris moueretur: on the general import of this section, which suddenly turns to Greek tragedy (*H.F.* 921–1015), and for a comparison with Sextus, *M.* 7.405–7, see the general note above. In *M.* 7.249 a scenario from *H.F.* is used, too, but there the subject is not ἀπαραλλαξία, but that Heracles has an impression caused by the city of Thebes, but not as Thebes. The verbs *mouebatur* and *moueretur* make it clear that the capacity of false impressions to trigger action by inducing assent to suitable impressions is at issue; see on §90 and Brittain (2014).

Quid? Ipse Alcmeo tuus...me expetunt: see on §52: *Quod idem contingit insanis...cum oculorum aspectu*. The Cicero character now cites Ennius against Ennius (and Lucullus): the same Alcmeo who appeared to profess a mistrust in his perceptual experiences (cf. §52) made other statements, apparently in the same scene (*ibidem* may mean that, rather than just 'in the same play'), which gave every indication that he took his perceptual experiences to be real. However, since both in §52 and here the line on the disagreement of the *cor* and the *oculi* is cited as evidence that we doubt the impressions we experienced while deranged once we have recovered, we should assume, with Ribbeck (1897: 21–2) and Vahlen (1903: 123–4), that the line followed after the speech of Alcmeo cited by the Cicero character here. For the use of *cor*, see *OLD* s.v. no. 2.

A commentary on all quotations in this paragraph is provided by Jocelyn (1968: 198–202). Alcmeo killed his mother because she had betrayed his father Amphiaraus. Like Orestes he fled from one city to another from the furies, against whom he was protected by Apollo. The speech which Cicero quotes here in instalments describes an assault by the furies, who—for our passage to make sense—cannot have been visible on stage and were thus recognizably figments of Alcmeo's mind, as well as his rescue by Apollo and Diana (both equally imagined). Regarding *unde haec flamma oritur*, see Jocelyn (1968: 199) on seeing fire as a conventional sign for the onset of madness (see also on §52); *incitare* in *incitato furore* is thus more likely to be ingressive rather than effective in aspect. The transmitted double imperative *incede* was emended to double *incedunt* by Orelli, Baiter, and Halm (1861), but is protected by expressions like ἔμβα ἔμβα (Eur., *El.* 113, 128), cited by Vahlen (1903: 27). The duplication of *adsunt* is not sufficiently motivated by the fact that it can be paralleled in another Ennian fragment (cited by Cic. in *Div.* 1.66). *Adesse* is technical of the presence of the deity (*OLD* s.v. *adsum* no. 13), though the presence is usually felicitous. Pinkster i.965 regards *illa deinceps* as a substantival use of the adverb; if so, his translation '...and those following words...' would be preferable to mine.

Quid cum uirginis fidem implorat...Diana facem iacit a laeva: Jocelyn (1968: 167) notes that *uirginis fidem implorare*, while containing 'nothing foreign to Cicero's usage', looks 'as if he [Cicero] is echoing tragic Alcmeo's address to a person unknown'; *fides* here has the ancient sense of 'protective power' (*TLL* s.v. col. 665.73–666.28; cf. 663.25: *deorum uel hominum tutela atque praesidium*). (It is not uncommon for poetic quotes in Cicero to bleed into the context where they are embedded.) Jocelyn goes on to suggest that from the address the *uirgo* appears to be Alcmeo's social superior and could be a priestess of Apollo (who, as god of healing, plays a similar role in Alcmeo's myth as in Orestes'); and that *flammiferam...uim* might refer to the torches of the furies or to the fever felt by Alcmeo (Jocelyn 1968: 200).

The dissatisfaction with the transmitted text felt by Colonna (1707: 284) is likely to have been caused by the other references to fire in the vicinity, and *angui* is consistent with standard imagery. However, *caeruleae* as an attribute of the furies is supported by parallels given by Colonna himself (*Orph. H.* 70.6–7: κυανόχρωτες ἄνασσαι, ἀπαστράπτουσαι ἀπ' ὄσσων δεινὴν ἀνταυγῆ φάεος σαρκοφθόρον αἴγλην). When Cicero chose to cite these lines, too, part of his purpose must have been to give evidence for the vivid colours in impressions experienced by the insane; the continuation of the quote (*intendit...*) is presumably given because it is a detailed description (reflecting the detail of the impression). *Luna innixus*, deemed unintelligible by Reid[1] (p. 285), seems unproblematic; see *OLD* s.v. *innitor* no. 1a.

§90

Qui magis haec crederet...Apparet enim iam 'cor cum oculis consentire': the rhetorical question compares a hypothetical situation (*crederet*), in which Alcmeo is sane, with an ex hypothesi actual one (*credebat*), viz. the situation Alcmeo was in while deranged. In the introduction I suggest that, while the Academics want to show that we cannot trust our impressions while awake, they invoke abnormal states of mind because they provide stable conditions in which humans routinely have highly realistic but false impressions (see section 5.8). With the contrast between *si essent* and *quia uidebantur*, cf. §80: *Quasi quaeratur quid sit, non quid uideatur*.

A situation in which someone's *cor* agrees with their eyes is clearly one in which they trust them. It is striking that *apparere/apparet* is not used more frequently in *Acad.*

Omnia autem haec proferuntur...sed qualis uisio fuerit aut furentium aut somniantium tum cum mouebantur. Sed abeo a sensibus: Cicero makes it clear that through the arguments just presented the Academics want to draw a general conclusion about the ἀπαραλλαξία of true and false impressions, specifically about the capacity of either class of impressions to induce assent. Brittain (2014: passim, esp. 350) shows that one should not infer from this that the Stoics, older as well as younger, took cataleptic impressions to trigger assent invariably and automatically, only that they took assent to be the normal consequence. Cicero offers no rebuttal of the suggestion made in §54 *init.* that, if the Academics are right, we should be uncertain of our mental state now, even though the natural place to offer it would have been here; this is striking, given how influential such scenarios have been in the later history of philosophy. Unlike Reid[1] (p. 286), I would assume *uel furiosorum uel somniantium* to depend on *falsa* rather than *recordatione*. The absence of *uisa* is tolerable, but Reid's suggestion that it may be hiding behind the first *uel* is tempting; however, support for *uel...uel* may be derived from *aut...aut* below.

From *uos autem...*Cicero turns to refutation; with *nihil agitis* and *non...id quaeritur*, cf. §88: *sed id non agitur*. *Recordatio* may not just be 'recollection' in the usual sense (i.e. recollection of a past event/earlier state), but also recollection in the sense of 'reacquisition of one's faculties' (cf. *OED* s.v. recollection[1], no. 2): there may be a hint of an etymological argument turning on *cor* in the quotation adapted at the beginning of the paragraph (*cor cum oculis consentire*).

Visio more naturally denotes (cf. *OLD* s.v. *uisio* no. 1) the capacity to experience *uisa* (cf. LSJ s.v. φαντασία no. II) rather than meaning *uisum* here (in which case it would be a generic singular); cf. on *Luc.* 49 and section 10.2.

§§91–98a

Having argued that nothing can be apprehended by means of the senses, Cicero proceeds to argue in §91 that nothing can be apprehended by reason, i.e. nothing that could be true or false can be judged to be one or the other with certainty by means of what the Stoics call διαλεκτική in any field outside logic itself.[341]

Barnes (1997a: 146–7) comments that 'Cicero is right to reject the claim that is "arbiter and judge of the true and the false"—if the claim means that logical expertise is sufficient (and necessary) to determine the answer to any factual question', adding in a note: 'But surely no logician ever made so absurd a claim?'

However, at least one of the questions cited here by Cicero as left unanswered by dialectic—'what is the highest good?'—is a theoretical question. If Cicero the character was committing his opponent Lucullus to an absurd claim, it would be because

---

[341] Discussions of the passage include Bénatouïl and El Murr (2010: 73–4); Castagnoli (2010a: 162); Aubert-Baillot (2019: 259–60); and Castagnoli (2019: 172–3).

Cicero the author has put him in a position to do so. In §26, having completed the argument for apprehension arising from perceptual impressions, Lucullus proceeded to reason (*ratio*) as a source of apprehensions, drawing attention to linguistic usage as evidence that it is universally recognized that there is such a thing as apprehension. Reason was cited there quite generally as driving enquiry and issuing in discovery. The section ended with the Stoic definition of proof (ἀπόδειξις). By saying pointedly *plus autem pollicebatur*, Cicero indicates, or at least affects, that he is picking up on unfulfilled promises made by the Stoics, although it is left vague what precisely was promised. In §26 Lucullus did not explicitly claim that logic would deliver the answer to factual questions, either in the sense that the questions with which *ratio* would help would invariably or mostly be factual ones or in the sense that scientific proofs are about obtaining the answers to factual questions (as opposed to, say, presenting scientific knowledge antecedently arrived at), or that it would answer theoretical questions. The relative generality of §26 arguably creates the opening for Cicero's attack. Moreover, whether Cicero's point should not actually be taken to be more modest—that if logic is to be accepted and if logic is to earn its status as a constituent part of philosophy (cf. the commentary on *Ac*. 1.19, Varro speaking), it ought to contribute something to the resolution of questions which turn on the position of human beings in the world, whether they belong to the domain of physics or of ethics, and whether they are factual or theoretical (cf. the last sentence of §91)—, depends on how fundamental the assault on logic in the following paragraphs is going to be. If Cicero were to argue that the most elementary forms of inference cannot be relied on, then there would be less reason to charge him with *ignoratio elenchi* regarding the intended purpose of logic.[342]

In the second half of §91 Cicero arrives by elimination at the area in which διαλεκτική functions as an arbiter and judge: διαλεκτική itself. Reid[1] (p. 286) notes the similarity with Plt., *Grg*. 453d–458b, where Socrates identifies the domain of rhetoric by a process of elimination and Cic., *Div*. 2.10, on the domain of divination. The latter is marked as a Carneadean argument, and it resembles our passage closely in technique and examples used.[343] Whether we glimpse details of Cicero's source here or his ability to use an Academic mode of argument (which could be paralleled from the speeches) is impossible to say. There is no strong reason to assume direct recourse to Plato *Grg*. in §91, i.e. recourse made by Cicero himself.[344]

In §§92–98a, under the general heading of the rejection of reason (sc. as conceived by the Stoics),[345] and dialectic in particular, as a path towards non-perceptual apprehension, Cicero discusses the sorites (§§92–4) and the Liar paradox (§§95–6). Both

---

[342] A discussion of the arguments advanced by Sextus in various places against the Stoic conception of proof is Barnes (1980).

[343] *Eadem in litteris ratio est reliquisque rebus quarum est disciplina. Num censes eos qui diuinare dicuntur posse responderet sol maiorne quam terra sit an tantus quantus uideatur, lunaque suo lumine an solis utatur, sol luna quem motum habeat, quem quinque stellae, quae errare dicuntur? Nec haec qui diuini habentur profitentur se esse dicturos, nec eorum quae in geometria describuntur, quae uera quae falsa sint: sunt enim ea mathematicorum, non hariolorum.*

[344] The possibility of other Platonic intertexts, notably *Rep*. 7, is considered by Bénatouïl and El Murr (2010: 73–4).

[345] The Academic takes himself and his approach to be rational and governed by reason.

of these paradoxes could be invoked to argue against the principle of bivalence and the validity of *modus ponens*; however, Cicero indicates that only the discussion of the Liar is supposed to have that import. Thus one can either assume that Cicero failed to identify the purpose of the sorites discussion properly or that the upshot of the sorites discussion is intended to be different from that of the Liar discussion.[346] In what follows, I shall argue for the latter view and suggest that the two sections are practical and theoretical, respectively: in the sorites section, Cicero's point is that the devastating effect of the sorites cannot be contained and can potentially threaten any dogmatically held view, while in the Liar section the aim is to show that the paradox threatens the principle of bivalence and the validity of *modus ponens* (which, if shown not to apply once, cannot be relied on ever). In §97 Cicero uses the Epicurean response to the so-called 'Truth-to-Necessity Argument' (Bobzien 1998: 79) for an attack on the validity of another type of Stoic arguments: those which have a disjunction as first premiss. §98a is a concluding remark.

In §92 *init.* Cicero begins with the ominous remark that dialectic, in which the Stoics put so much stock, might turn against them. Then, in self-conscious allusion to the fact that sorites arguments are also known as 'little-by-little' arguments (e.g. Gal., Περὶ τῆς ἰατρικῆς ἐμπειρίας xvi.2, p. 115 Walzer: ὁ παρὰ μικρῶν λόγος), Cicero goes through various subjects covered under the heading of dialectic step by step, only to arrive at a subject previously identified by Lucullus as harmful: the sorites.[347] The study of paradoxes was part of the treatment of dialectic.[348] Because the Academic deployment of the sorites is liable to attract the charge of captiousness, Cicero asks whose fault the harmfulness of the sorites is, and proceeds to locate it in the *natura rerum*, which has failed to establish clear boundaries for many terms which can function as soritical predicates. This comes close to identifying vagueness as the phenomenon which enables the sorites and is in part a rejoinder to Lucullus' earlier naturalistic arguments for the view that the third clause of Zeno's definition receives support from factive expressions (cf. §22 and Reinhardt 2019); ordinary language, Cicero intimates, provides footholds for the Academic position, too. (See also Epicurus' citation of the *natura rerum* in §97.) By stating that no subject is safe from the sorites and by providing a series of terms which can give rise to it Cicero implies that the phenomenon is not confined to a few, or a narrowly defined set of, terms, but the scope of his claim is not plain at this point: is Cicero speaking hyperbolically, is he suggesting that the sorites presents a threat to any dogmatic claim because vagueness is pervasive, or does he hold that not all predicates are susceptible to vagueness

---

[346] Cf. Barnes (1999: 148): 'Now precisely these two threats [sc. to *modus ponens* and the principle of bivalence] are raised in *Luc.* 95–8, so that it is tempting to think that our text does not divide at 95 and that the sorites determines the course of the argument up to 98. But no sorites is mentioned in *Luc.* 95–8; and I am unable to construct a single train of thought which starts in 92 and ends in 98. I conclude, lamely, that Cicero has not made of the sorites all that he might have done'; Brittain (2006: 52 n. 134): 'Both sections can be construed as attacks on the principle of bivalence (see *Ac.* 2.95) and the validity of basic Stoic inferences, i.e., of *modus ponens*'; Hankinson (2007: 353) suggests that the sorites section attacks *modus ponens*, and the Liar section the principle of bivalence. On modern attempts to provide unified treatments of both paradoxes (none of which offer inspiration for Cicero's discussion), see Hyde (2014: section 4).

[347] Introductory material on the sorites is assembled in the general note on *Luc.* 47–50. With our passage, cf. Sextus, *P.H.* 2.253–5 and *M.* 7.416–21 on Chrysippus' handling of the sorites.

[348] See Barnes, Bobzien, and Mignucci (1999: 157–76).

while operating a broader conception of what counts as a soritical argument (cf. *Luc.* 47 and the general note on §§47–54a)?

One noteable feature of the manner in which Cicero discusses these matters is that he writes as if there was no need to spell out how exactly a sorites looks like and how exactly it can be deployed to undermine dogmatic claims, assuming evidently that his audience is able to supply this information. *Luc.* 47–50 is similar in this respect, which raises the question of whether one of the Academic speakers in the *Catulus* had introduced the sorites as a kind of signature move of the Academics.

In §93 Cicero then uses the familiar device of a fictional interlocutor (cf. e.g. §§51–54a), who makes interventions in direct speech, and as in §§84–5, he goes over the same ground twice (in §§93 and 94), letting the opponent describe the same strategy of how he proposes to deal with the sorites in two different ways. Presentationally, this puts Cicero in a position to highlight different aspects of the opponent's position on the two occasions, and to offer different rejoinders, thus giving the impression that he is able to close down every attempt to diffuse the harmful potential of the sorites. At the same time, he offers a glimpse of the history of the debate, in that the dogmatist and the sceptic are revealed to be not just Lucullus and Cicero, or Antiochus and Philo, but also Chrysippus and Carneades. In §98 he then cites Antiochus as his teacher in the field of dialectic, just as Carneades had Diogenes of Babylon as a teacher. Cicero thus continues to hone his Clitomachean *persona*, having earlier invoked Arcesilaus as a significant ancestor (§§65–7).

For the first intervention by the opponent (*at uitiosi sunt soritae*) to have a point, *uitiosus* must not mean 'detrimental', but 'flawed' (see n. below). Cicero challenges the opponent to solve it and remarks that inconvenience will arise if he is not careful (*nisi cauetis*). Exploiting the ambiguity of *cauere*, the opponent replies that he is careful, in that Chrysippus decided he would, when confronted with a series of soritical questions 'whether three is few or many', '"rest" (*quiescere*, ἡσυχάζειν) some time (*aliquanto*) before he gets to "many".' Carneades then suggests that resting is no solution (the dogmatist could even 'snore' if he liked), because when 'awakened' and confronted with the next question in the soritical series, he would have to go on (and on, it is implied—*progrediere rursus quoad uidebitur* would be a peculiar way of describing advancement by just one step).

What do we learn, and equally importantly, what do we not learn? The exchange is primarily an enactment of a principle we find explicitly stated in some parallel sources, a principle which, as we know, the Stoics accepted, and which is here deployed against the dogmatic position: 'one [further step in the soritical series] does not make a difference.'[349] Chrysippus' strategy of 'resting' is ineffectual because the principle allows the sceptic to push beyond any point at which the sceptic chooses to 'rest'.

We further learn that the dogmatist will stop 'some way' before getting to 'many', i.e. before a positive answer to a question of the form '*n* is few' amounts to assent to a falsehood. What is left unspecified is what precisely 'resting' amounts to beyond 'falling silent' (*conticuisti*), i.e. whether it is a mere refusal to answer or also a refusal to assent, how the point at which Chrysippus suggests rest is to be characterized beyond

---

[349] Cf. Gal., Περὶ τῆς ἰατρικῆς ἐμπειρίας xvii.3, xx.3; Sextus, *M.* 1.69; and see Bobzien (2002: 236 with n. 64).

'some point before getting to *multa*', and the nature of the soritical series as a whole e.g. is there a clear cut-off point such that two adjacent impressions corresponding to two subsequent propositions in the soritical series end up having different truth-values?

Having had Carneades make the point that the dogmatist can be woken from his state of rest and be made to proceed further, Cicero suggests that he needs to say no more, sc. to prove his point (*Quid plura?*). For the dogmatist has shown himself to have no clear sight of the last proposition '*n* is few' which is true and the first one which is false—as is plain from the fact that he can be 'raised' and made to go on and answer 'yes' on the grounds that it appears right to him (cf. *quoad uidebitur*). Cicero ends on the cryptic remark that the effect of the sorites cannot be limited, thus emphasizing its potentially universal applicability rather than the fact that it threatens fundamental principles of Stoic logic.[350]

§94 begins with a restatement of the dogmatist's strategy against the sorites, again in direct speech and this time cast in the simile of a charioteer approaching a precipice and stopping in good time. This restatement clarifies a couple of points which were left open in the previous paragraph, but the overall amount of clarification achieved is modest; one thus wonders if, as in §§84–5, the twofold treatment is intended to signal a certain slowmindedness on the part of the dogmatist. The dogmatist's simile involves a boundary and a precipice, which implies a clear cut-off point; in principle, this could be a boundary between true and false propositions (corresponding to impressions arising from questions), or it could be the boundary between cataleptic and non-cataleptic impressions. What follows suggests that the latter is meant (see below).[351] In speaking of the restraining of the horses (*equos sustinebo*), a term is employed which is in *Acad.* associated with the suspension of judgement; this is confirmed by what we learn below.

In his reply, Cicero then uses a dilemma structure, but, as Brittain (2014: 344–5) has noted, the deployment of the dilemma is unusual in that the dogmatist is not confronted with two choices which ought to be equally unpalatable to him and of which he would rather choose neither: in this case, it is known and acknowledged that he opts for one, and Cicero's suggestion is that he is not entitled to it. The choices are: *either* (i) the dogmatist 'has a clear view' and yet fails to answer, in which case he is acting arrogantly, *or* (ii) he does not have a clear view. Given the wider context and the terminology used in *Acad.* (*liquet*, glossed indirectly by *ne...quidem perspicis* in the second horn), 'having a clear view' must mean experiencing a cataleptic

---

[350] Contrast Sextus, *P.H.* 2.254, where the sorites is characterized as a threat to the principle of bivalence and *modus ponens*: Καὶ ἡμεῖς μὲν ἀδοξάστως ἀπὸ τῆς βιωτικῆς τηρήσεως ὁρμώμενοι τοὺς ἀπατηλοὺς οὕτως ἐκκλίνομεν λόγους, οἱ δογματικοὶ δὲ ἀδυνάτως ἕξουσι διακρῖναι τὸ σόφισμα ἀπὸ τοῦ δεόντως δοκοῦντος ἐρωτᾶσθαι λόγου, εἴγε χρὴ δογματικῶς αὐτοὺς ἐπικρῖναι, καὶ ὅτι συνακτικόν ἐστι τὸ σχῆμα τοῦ λόγου καὶ ὅτι τὰ λήμματά ἐστιν ἀληθῆ ἢ οὐχ οὕτως ἔχει, 'And whereas we, by starting undogmatically from the observation of practical life, thus avoid these fallacious arguments, the Dogmatists will not be in a position to distinguish the sophism from the argument which seems to be correctly propounded, seeing that they have to pronounce dogmatically that the form of the argument is, or is not, logically sound and also that the premisses are, or are not, true' (transl. Bury).

[351] Cf. also Sextus, *M.* 7.416–21, who is very clear about the soritical series being made up of declarative sentences which correspond to cataleptic and non-cataleptic impressions.

impression arising from a question inviting acceptance or rejection of a proposition; 'not having a clear view' should then mean to experience a non-cataleptic impression. If the dogmatist was to opt for (ii), then Cicero would accept the answer (it is the one he would give), but, as he acknowledges, this is not the dogmatist's position. Rather, the dogmatist proposes to halt in the area where things are clear (that the area rather than the last clear impression is meant is suggested by the plural ⟨in⟩ illustribus rebus) and before entering the area where things are obscure (again the plural ad obscura). The chariot simile had also spoken of 'holding the horses before one reaches the boundary' (priusquam ad finem ueniam) rather than at the boundary. Silence (i.e. 'resting'), Cicero suggests, achieves nothing, for it makes no difference to a sceptic who wants to ensnare the dogmatist whether he catches him silent or speaking. Here one might think that a distinction is relied on between assenting and not disclosing that one does assent, and assenting and saying so; the implication would be that the dogmatist *must* assent in the face of a cataleptic impression. In fact, the Stoics do posit that assent to the cataleptic, while normal, is not inevitable, and Cicero glosses 'to be silent' below as *a certis illustrioribus cohibere assensum*; thus assenting but not disclosing that one does assent cannot be meant. Cicero's stated objection to the strategy of 'falling silent' is that it is arrogant (*superbe*) and hypocritical, in that the dogmatist claims the right to withhold assent in the face of what he recognizes as supremely clear, while denying suspension of judgement in the face of the obscure to the Academic (not just in soritical situations).[352] It is arguable that Cicero's more fundamental point is that the dogmatists have no grounds for suspension *given their own standards of rationality and foundationalist convictions*: a non-sage may fail to assent to a cataleptic impression if he holds a false belief which is inconsistent with the propositional content of said impression, but no such consideration can be cited here, and a sage has no false beliefs ex hypothesi. And while it is true that neither sages nor non-sages are required to assent to all cataleptic impressions (the missing of epistemic opportunities is not culpable, and their practical interests may lie elsewhere in a given situation), one would have assumed the dogmatist to be sufficiently engaged in an exchange in question and answer to make suspension of judgement in the face of the cataleptic look rather ad hoc. The concluding remark to the section is a paraphrase of the penultimate sentence of the previous paragraph, which fits with the notion that in some respects §93 and §94 go over the same ground twice.

Cicero's discussion assumes, and implies that it was Chrysippus' view, that in a soritical series there is a clear cut-off point of some kind ('the precipice') and that its precise location is obscure to us, i.e. that we cannot tell where exactly it is. The clear

[352] This charge of hypocrisy on the part of the Stoics is also made by Sextus, *P.H.* 2.253: Καὶ εἴγε οἱ περὶ τὸν Χρύσιππον δογματικοὶ ἐν τῇ συνερωτήσει τοῦ σωρίτου προϊόντος τοῦ λόγου φασὶ δεῖν ἵστασθαι καὶ ἐπέχειν, ἵνα μὴ ἐκπέσωσιν εἰς ἀτοπίαν, πολὺ δήπου μᾶλλον ἂν ἡμῖν ἁρμόζον εἴη σκεπτικοῖς οὖσιν, ὑποπτεύουσιν ἀτοπίαν, μὴ προπίπτειν κατὰ τὰς συνερωτήσεις τῶν λημμάτων, ἀλλ' ἐπέχειν καθ' ἕκαστον ἕως τῆς ὅλης συνερωτήσεως τοῦ λόγου, 'And if the Dogmatists of the school of Chrysippus declare that when the "Sorites" is being propounded they ought to halt while the argument is still proceeding and suspend judgement, to avoid falling into absurdity, much more, surely, would it be fitting for us, who are Sceptics, when we suspect absurdity, to give no hasty approval of the premisses propounded but rather to suspend judgement about each until the completion of the whole series which forms the argument' (transl. Bury).

cut-off point is between cataleptic and non-cataleptic impressions arising in an interlocutor's mind when questions inviting acceptance or rejection of a declarative sentence featuring a vague predicate are posed. That cataleptic and non-cataleptic *impressions* are meant is strongly suggested by the association of declarative sentences which are indubitably true with clarity, and ones which are not indubitably true with obscurity. Within the context of *Acad.*, it would be highly misleading to introduce a different conception of clarity at this point without signalling it or explaining it. If the impressions corresponding to the questions in a soritical series are either cataleptic or non-cataleptic, it follows that there must be a clear boundary between them at which the last cataleptic and the first non-cataleptic impression come to lie side by side, for an impression has to be either cataleptic or non-cataleptic. That Chrysippus took the location of this boundary to be not discernible to us is suggested by the injunction to come to 'rest' within (rather than at the end of) the zone where the answer to the questions is still clearly 'yes'. Cicero the character also observes that the Stoics de facto admit that they cannot specify the last number which should count as 'few' and the first which should 'count as many' (i.e. not few) (§93 *fin.*). Since the cataleptic/non-cataleptic distinction is not the same as the true/false distinction, I take Cicero's point to be that uncertainty about the former *entails* the inability to pinpoint the end of the series of true statements and the beginning of the series of false statements. This does not require that the two series are directly adjacent, i.e. they may or may not be separated by a series of questions in between where there is no one 'fact of the matter'. That the former of these two options introduces a second boundary—that between questions where there is no fact of the matter and ones where the answer is 'no'—is not troubling if it was right to assume that the 'precipice' is the boundary between cataleptic and non-cataleptic impressions. Either scenario raises the question why Chrysippus did not issue an instruction to stop at the last cataleptic impression. He may have held that the last cataleptic impression, whose clarity qua cataleptic impression is an objective property independent of 'context' (given Stoic foundationalist convictions), could nonetheless not be recognizable as cataleptic due to its neighbouring non-cataleptic impression.[353] Given that the Stoics have a need to explain why humans in general often fail to appreciate a cataleptic impression for what it is,[354] and that even the sage requires domain-specific training and will not be able to appreciate every cataleptic impression, this explanation would not be ad hoc.[355]

---

[353] Thus Brittain (2014: 345–6): 'The point of comparing the two cases—50 versus 10,000 with 50 versus 51—is presumably to show that one's reaction to an impression is partially dependent on the context in which one receives it. But given Chrysippus' theory of cataleptic impressions, he can't think that our contextual beliefs or expectations make any difference to the objective features of the impressions, since that would be to surrender to the coherentist view Carneades espoused. So Chrysippus must think that it is possible to become unclear or confused about whether or not a particular impression is cataleptic; and for that reason he recommends falling silent, or suspending assent, before one reaches the end of the sequence of cataleptic impressions that "n is few."'

[354] See section 5.4 and Reinhardt (2011).

[355] The present passage makes no reference to the sage and seems to provide guidance for anyone faced with a soritical argument. I would thus assume that no difference between the sage's and the non-sage's ability to discern boundaries (of whatever kind) is assumed.

Williamson (1994: 8–35) suggested that the ancient evidence on Chrysippus' response to the sorites suggested that he was an epistemicist, i.e. that he held that the statements posed as questions in the soritical series were either true or false, but that we cannot know where the boundary is between the last true and the first false statement. Partly in reply, Bobzien (2002: 218–22) observed that the Stoics recognized declarative sentences which do not have a corresponding proposition and which as a consequence have no truth-value,[356] and that they made use of this possibility in their responses to other paradoxes and sophisms. This suggests that the Stoics were not epistemicists in general, although it does not preclude the possibility that Chrysippus posited a clear cut-off point between declarative sentences corresponding to true propositions and those corresponding to false propositions in a soritical series. While the deployment of declarative sentences which do not have a corresponding proposition is not attested in the record on Chrysippus' handling of the sorites, Bobzien suggests that it is more likely that Chrysippus' response to the sorites involved the assumption that the questions in a soritical series begin with declarative statements which are true, pass through a zone where the declarative statements have no truth-value, and ends with declarative statements which are false.

One concern one might have about Bobzien's argument is that Chrysippus, on the evidence of our passage, had offered no solution to the sorites. If he assumed that a soritical series includes declarative sentences to which no proposition corresponds, he might have argued that the sorites breaks down once it reaches instances of *modus ponens* whose first premiss is neither true nor false, in virtue of the fact that neither the antecedent nor the consequent is true or false. Yet in our passage Cicero dares Chrysippus to 'break' the sorites if he can, implying that he did not do so (cf. *Div.* 2.11, where Cicero describes Chrysippus' treatment of the sorites as 'resistance' rather than 'solution'). However, Chrysippus is also presented as committed to the principle that 'one does not make a difference', which threatens any boundary or cut-off point.

I proceed to §§95–6; see p. 610 on the connection of this section with what precedes and what follows. The Liar paradox was probably invented by Eubulides; cf. D.L. 2.108 (DM frg. 50, 51A, 64). A version of it was known to Aristotle, who discusses it in *S.E.* 25, 180b2–7 (see Crivelli 2004); see also the development of Aristotle's discussion in [Alex. Aphr.] *in Arist. S.E.* p. 171.16–20 Wallies (cf. *FDS* 1210). Theophrastus devoted a work in three books to it (cf. D.L. 5.49). Chrysippus devoted numerous works to the Liar; titles of relevant books are listed in D.L. 7.196 (= *FDS* 194 = *SVF* ii.15), and Rüstow (1910: 63–5) speculates plausibly that yet further works by Chrysippus may have touched on it. The Liar was also mentioned in the *Quaestiones logicae* (*P.Herc.* 307, cols ix–xi; see *FDS* 698). Modern studies include Cavini (1993); Barnes (1997: 148–60); Barnes, Bobzien and Mignucci (1999: 163–70); Mignucci (1999); and Papazian (2012).

I trace the train of thought in §§95–6 in this general note and justify particular interpretative and textual choices in the nn. below. Assuming Cicero's example is:

Si te mentiri dicis, mentiris an uerum dicis?

---

[356] See also Crivelli (1994).

then *mentior* (= 'I speak falsely' rather than 'I lie', i.e. speak falsely and intend to do so),[357] contained in the protasis, would yield a paradox for the reason the simple declarative sentence 'This statement is false' yields a paradox. In uttering 'I speak falsely' I may be taken to state something, namely that 'I speak falsely'. But if what I state is true, then it is false, and if what I state is false, it is true. Hence what I state is not either true or false, since it is either both true and false or neither true nor false.[358] Cicero does not immediately spell out the paradox if we read the text given above: he may have felt he does not have to since he relies on its most basic form.

Such arguments, Cicero continues, are termed 'insoluble' by the Stoics,[359] and Cicero complains once more in *praeteritio* that the Stoics regard themselves as entitled to such classifications while the Academics may not call things 'not apprehended'. Returning to his main theme, he presents declarative statements like *mentior* as a threat to the principle of bivalence. He then continues:

Rebus sumptis adiungam ex iis sequendas esse alias improbandas quae sint in genere contrario.

Once certain assumptions are made, I will add that other things must follow from them which are to be rejected—which properties (i.e. having to follow and having to be rejected) are contradictory.

The sentence as given is what is transmitted.[360] It makes no formal reference to what precedes e.g. through a pronoun modifying *rebus*, although it cannot just be forward-looking either. Barnes (1997) calls it 'transitional': Cicero evidently thinks, for reasons which he does not spell out, that the problem of *mentior* affects the two arguments in §96 in which *mentior* occurs in some way. In these the conclusion both follows and is to be rejected.

In §96 Cicero performs the same maneouvre twice: an instance of *modus ponens* is cited, which Chrysippus accepts, followed by a second, similar one (with respect to the simple propositions involved), which, however, involves an occurrence of *mentior* and which Chrysippus does not accept. Cicero argues on the basis of this that one either approves an elementary inference (*modus ponens*) always or the art of dialectic is non-existent. The arguments are:

---

[357] See Mignucci (1999: 57): '...let us pause to examine our translation of the verb *mentiri*. It is normally rendered as "to lie", which is, of course, a possible translation. But one might also render the Latin as "speaking falsely"—as the Greek ψεύδεσθαι, which is behind the Latin, allows. The advantage of this translation is that we avoid all the problems connected with the psychological act of lying. We may lie when we say something that is the opposite of what we believe, and what we say by lying may be true if our beliefs are false. By taking *mentiri* as "speaking falsely" we are faced with the simpler situation of someone who utters false propositions, and this is a necessary condition for building up the paradox.' I submit that there is nothing in Cicero's text which tells against this reading of *mentiri*. On Greek ψεύδεσθαι (and ἀληθεύειν), see also Crivelli (2004a: 51 n. 24).

[358] Cf. Barnes (1997: 152 with n. 41).

[359] See below on evidence from elsewhere suggesting that Chrysippus may have thought at some point that he had solved the Liar; Cicero's argument here assumes that the Liar defeated Chrysippus.

[360] Numerous changes have been proposed; see the lemmatized n. below.

(A) Si dicis nunc lucere et uerum dicis, lucet.
Dicis autem nunc lucere et uerum dicis.
Lucet igitur.

(B) Si dicis te mentiri uerumque dicis, mentiris.
Dicis autem te mentiri uerumque dicis.
Mentiris igitur.

(C) Si lucet, lucet.
Lucet autem.
Lucet igitur.

(D) Si mentiris, mentiris.
Mentiris autem.
Mentiris igitur.

The Stoics accept argument (A), and the type of inference argument (A) is an instance of, and teach it as the first indemonstrable, according to Cicero. He continues that the Stoics can either accept every instence of this type of inference or there is no art of dialectic. However, Cicero continues, Chrysippus did not accept argument (B), even though it is his example, albeit one which he did not solve. Argument (C), Cicero suggests (plausibly), Chrysippus would again accept: if one accepts the antecedent of the conditional, one must accept the consequent. Yet argument (D) poses problems once more, in that Chrysippus neither accepts it nor rejects it. This seems a slightly different reaction than the one Chrysippus showed regarding argument (B), but the main point is again Chrysippus' refusal to accept (D); cf. Barnes (1997: 157) on this point. Cicero concludes the section by restating that, if the type of inference is to be valid, Chrysippus should treat arguments (C) and (D) in the same way. Cicero will restate this last point in §98a.

The overall structure of the argument is plain, and we have to take Cicero's word that Chrysippus rejected arguments (B) and (D). The latter's rationale for doing so is not reported here or elsewhere. It is plausible to assume that Chrysippus thought, or at least that Cicero took Chrysippus to think, that the first premises in arguments (B) and (D) are vitiated by the inclusion of *mentior* in them, quite possibly by inheriting the same problem which arises from the basic *mentior*. As Barnes (1997: 155) puts the principle which seems to underlie Chrysippus' attitude to (B) and (D):

If f(A) is a complex statement containing the statement A as a component, then if A is not either true or false, f(A) is not either true or false,

and with respect to (D) (p. 158):

Find a problematical Liar sentence Σ, and the conditional 'If Σ, Σ' will inherit the problem.

Barnes (1997: 159–60) goes on to suggest that Chrysippus held that arguments like (B) and (D) are valid if the conditional which serves as their first premiss is true. If the first premises of both arguments have no truth-value in virtue of the principle, the arguments are not valid.

Plut., *Comm. not.* 1059d-e (= LS 37I) claims that Chrysippus solved the Liar paradox but that his solution involves the discarding of fundamental assumptions he otherwise made in the field of logic. Plutarch's brief remark is developed into reconstructions by Cavini (1993: 103–7) and Mignucci (1999: 62–8); with the latter cf. Barnes, Bobzien, and Mignucci (1999: 167–70). Cicero was either unaware of this (cf. *Div.* 2.11) or suppressed it. That Plutarch is an Academic of sorts might suggest the latter, but would Cicero have omitted a reference to a solution proposed by Chrysippus which could be regarded as self-undermining?

In §97 Cicero adds a postscript to §§95–6: the Stoics demand that unsolvable arguments should be treated as exceptions rather than be deemed to undermine dialectic itself—a demand which Cicero is no mood to accept.

He then continues the line of argument that the validity of elementary Stoic inferences is in doubt by citing the Epicurean response to an argument which is itself not given in full or assigned to an individual or a school. This response he interprets as implying that disjunctions generally, which the Stoics and Antiochus employ as first premiss of fourth and fifth indemonstrables, are false.

Epicurus, whose anachronistic appearance in the present context is partly motivated by his general rejection of dialectic (in the sense of a formal theory of argument),[361] would not have approved:

Either Hermarchus will be alive tomorrow or he will not be alive

even though 'the dialecticians' (i.e. the Stoics) claim that a complex proposition of the form:

Either p or not-p

was not just true but necessary. For if Epicurus accepted that either p or not-p was necessary, then, if p was 'Hermagoras will be alive tomorrow', Hermagoras would either be necessarily alive tomorrow or would be necessarily not alive tomorrow.[362] This could not be so because there was no necessity in nature with respect to future events, as Epicurus is reported as saying. This posed a problem for the Stoics, Cicero concludes: if a disjunction whose two component propositions are a contradictory pair could be false, then no disjunction was true, and arguments which rely on disjunctions as first premisses would be useless.

Bobzien (1998: 75–84) has offered a reconstruction of the argument to which Epicurus originally responded and of his response, drawing on our passage, *Fat.* 21, 28, 37, and *N.D.* 1.70. Bobzien comments (p. 76) that 'similarities between these passages are so strong that it is plausible to assume that each time Cicero draws from the same discussion, in which Epicurus rejected a certain argument by some logicians.'[363]

---

[361] Chrysippus was a child when Epicurus died.

[362] On future contingents cf. *Fam.* 9.6 (= SB 181); *Fat.* 37; and *Div.* 1.127.

[363] Bown (2016) covers some of the same ground as Bobzien (1998). He is more confident than Bobzien that the evidence from Cicero allows us to form a view on Epicurus' attitudes to the principle of bivalence and to different versions of the law of excluded middle, and unlike Bobzien he does not think that bivalence was a concern of the Stoics and that its appearance in these Epicurean contexts is due to Cicero, either out of confusion or because Cicero wanted to create a dialogue between the Epicurean and Stoic views. However, he regards §97 as muddled or corrupt; see the lemmatized n. below on *alterutrum concessero necessarium esse*. Light is also shed on §97, specifically on the grounds cited by Epicurus (according to Cicero's report) for his rejection of *necessitas*, by Sedley (2019: 105–8).

If this was correct, it would raise the question of whether §97 is informed by the same source as §§92–6 or whether we can witness Cicero combining material that is likely to come from different sources in §§91–8.

The argument is given in *Fat.* 21 in this form:

(1) Si enim alterum utrum ex aeternitate uerum sit, esse id certum, (2) et si certum etiam necessarium: (3) ita et necessitatem et fatum confirmari putat.

Bobzien (1998: 78) supplies the Law of Excluded Middle as a first premiss and omits *ex aeternitate uerum* in (1) and *et fatum* in (3) as likely additions made by Cicero to create a kind of dialogue between Epicurus and Chrysippus (whose concern is with fate)[364] to arrive at:

(P1) Of every contradictory pair either one or the other is true.
(P2) If one of every contradictory pair is true, it is also certain.
(P3) If it is certain, it is also necessary.
(C) Therefore, of every contradictory pair one is necessary.

The argument holds for future propositions and events as well as for any others, and 'truth, certainty, and necessity are all tied to the present'; to signal this, Bobzien provides the following versions of (P1) and (C):

(P1′) Of every contradictory pair either one or the other is true *now*.
(C′) Therefore, of every contradictory pair one is necessary *now*.

Bobzien calls this the 'Truth-to-Necessity Argument' and observes:

That is, it concludes that whatever happens, including what will be the case in the future, is already now necessary. The argument assigns truth, certainty, and necessity to the same—unspecified—entities. There can be little doubt that in the *De fato* version it starts out with propositions. So somewhere in the argument a switch from propositions to events would be expected (and depending on where this happens, a deterministic presupposition is there smuggled in). But the argument is too fragmentary for one to decide where.[365]

Bobzien (1998: 80) goes on to note a similarity of the Truth-to-Necessity argument with the so-called Mower argument ($\theta \epsilon \rho i \zeta \omega \nu$ $\lambda \acute{o} \gamma o s$), which is likely to have been devised in the Megaric-Dialectic school.[366] I quote Bobzien once more (who in turn draws on Seel 1993; the primary sources are Amm. *in Arist. Int.* p. 131.27–8 Busse for

---

[364] Contrast Bown (2016: 243–4) on this point.
[365] On the Epicurean ascription of truth to events, see Bown (2016a).
[366] This is where one would expect the Truth-to-Necessity argument to originate as well, which, as Sedley (2019: 105–8) shows, seems to reflect Aristotle's discussion of future contingents in *Int.* 9: that this Aristotelian discussion is the ultimate reference point for Epicurus, which need not have been transparent to Epicurus himself, is suggested by the latter's preoccupation with contradictory pairs (a concern inherited from *Int.*, because its primary intention was to aid dialectical exchanges in question and answer, which feature contradictory pairs as $\pi \rho o \tau \acute{a} \sigma \epsilon \iota s$; on this point, see Whitaker 1996).

P1, and Stephanus, *Int.* pp. 34.36–35.5 Hayduck for the rest of the argument except C1, which comes from Anon. *in Arist. Int.*, Cod. Par. Gr. 2064, pp. 54.8–55.5 Tarán = *FDS* 1253):

(P1) Necessarily, either you will mow or you will not mow.
(P2) If you will mow, you will not perhaps mow, perhaps not mow, but you will certainly mow.
(P3) If you will not mow, you will not perhaps mow, perhaps not mow, but you will certainly not mow.
(P4) But 'certainly' introduces 'necessarily'.
(C1) Therefore you will either necessarily mow or necessarily not mow.
(C2) Therefore, the contingent will be destroyed.

Cicero shows no explicit awareness of this argument. If his immediate source knew it, it may have aided—given its first premiss—the repurposing of Epicurus' reply (see below) to the Truth-to-Necessity argument as an attack on Stoic disjunctions, but equally Cicero's source would likely not have required the inspiration of the Mower argument to make this connection.

Epicurus' reply to the Truth-to-Necessity is only given in our passage, i.e. *Luc.* 97: it is that such necessity, viz. that Hermagoras either lives tomorrow or does not live tomorrow, does not lie 'in the nature of things'.[367] This amounts to a rejection of the conclusion of the argument,[368] and I note that once more a naturalistic consideration is invoked in what in the Ciceronian context is an anti-dogmatic argument (cf. §92 on the sorites, where the phenomenon of vagueness is put down to the *rerum natura*, in the Cicero character's own voice, however). Because of his rejection of the conclusion of the Truth-to-Necessity argument, Epicurus needs to reject (at least) one of its premisses, and he rejects some version of the Law of Excluded Middle.[369] Here in *Luc.* 97, Epicurus is presented as holding that no complex proposition of the form 'either *p* or not-*p*' is necessary (cf. *N.D.* 1.70) and that no proposition of this form is true. This entails the invalidity of the Principle of Bivalence for simple future propositions.[370]

Cicero does not make this point. Thus as in the discussion of the sorites Cicero foregoes an opportunity to make the connection with Principle of Bivalence. Some will see this as further evidence that his, or his source's, grasp on the material in section §§92–7 is tenuous. Others will see method: the discussion of the sorites is practical (the dogmatist is defenceless against soritical arguments), that of the Liar theoretical (it attacks the Principle of Bivalence and the validity of *modus ponens*), while the present section is intended to extend the attack to disjunctions and arguments which rely on them.

Whether Cicero is here drawing on a source by Philo which had Antiochus as its target or an earlier post-Carneadean Academic source aimed at the Stoics, one might

---

[367] On the import of this point within the horizon of Epicurean theorizing, see the lemmatized n. below.
[368] This point is contentious; see n. below.
[369] See Bown (2016: 254 and 269) on the specific version of the Law of Excluded Middle rejected.
[370] See Bobzien (1998: 82) and Bown (2016: 254) on this point.

ask why Academics thought that the dogmatists including Antiochus should be impressed by an argument with the kind of history and genesis which the one presented in this paragraph has. Could they not have replied that they did not recognize Epicurus as an opponent, still less as a critic of Stoic dialectic? Note that there is no suggestion that Cicero is rehearsing arguments advanced by later Epicureans. The assumption seems to be that the argument as assembled ought to have a rational claim on the dogmatist, in virtue of the plausibility of the assumptions it makes and the nature of the reasoning it employs. For Carneadean arguments which rely on premisses that 'belong' to different schools and are apparently used for their 'endoxic' quality, see on *Luc.* 101; Sedley (2020).

In the conclusion to his attack on dialectic (§98a), Cicero suggests that the dogmatists are not engaged in a dispute with him but with themselves, in two senses. First, some of the arguments which he has rehearsed in fact derive (ultimately) from Stoic works devoted to paradoxes; these Stoic works offered no solutions at least in some cases, and must instead have discussed the destructive potential of the arguments in question. Second, Cicero suggests that (at least some of) his arguments rely on inferences recognized by the Stoics. This is also the upshot of the Carneadean anecdote.

The anecdote also serves a purpose in the construction of Cicero the character's philosophical persona. As a Clitomachean, he can claim Arcesilaus as an intellectual hero in a way in which a mitigated sceptic cannot (cf. *Luc.* 65–7), but at the same time he is Carneades to Antiochus' Diogenes of Babylon. Cicero quite deliberately plays with the disjointed timelines which arise from the multi-layered debate and the fact that protagonists at one point in time invoke others at a different time as models; cf. Schäublin et al. (p. 261 n. 281) on §98b *Antiochea ista corruent uniuersa*: 'Cicero unterstellt, daß Karneades' Position der Sache nach als eine Vorauswiderlegung der Position des (späteren) Antiochos anzusehen sei. Später wird Cicero geltend machen, daß Antiochos in Kenntnis der Einwände des Karneades nicht so hätte argumentieren dürfen, wie er es tat (§102).'

Of all the points made in the previous section, he singles out for restatement the attack on *modus ponens* arising from the Liar.

§91

Quid est quod ratione percipi possit … quid habet ut queat iudicare: cf. phrases like *sensibus percipere* in *Luc.* 21. Given the manifold uses of the noun *ratio*, it is not obvious by itself what *ratione percipere* means here: in principle, it could mean 'to grasp with the mind', but the mind is involved in perception through the senses as well (it is to the mind that the senses report e.g. in the image used in §79: *Quid ergo est quod percipi possit, si ne sensus quidem uera nuntiant?*). Cicero could be using *ratione* in *ratione percipi* emphatically, so as to mean 'through the mind alone' or 'through the mind primarily'. However, in §26, to which the present paragraph is the beginning of a reply, *ratio* meant 'reason', i.e. a power and capacity, and expressions like §42 *tum perueniunt ad eam partem ut ne ratione quidem et coniectura ulla res percipi possit* suggest that *ratio* is not the organ, as it were, by means of which apprehension is achieved, or the place where it is achieved, but rather the capacity or even the capacity enacted. Therefore *ratio*, on the most natural reading, means 'reason' or 'reasoning' here. There are no closely analogous Greek formulations (*SVF* ii.108 = Origen, *Contra Celsum* 7.37, vol. ii p. 187.22 Kötschau: αἰσθήσεσιν καταλαμβάνεσθαι τά καταλαμβανόμενα, which might be regarded as corresponding to *sensibus percipere*, is unlikely to reflect Stoic usage accurately). The initial question, then, enquires what can be apprehended by reason.

The immediately following sentence does then not offer a direct reply but draws in dialectic as a field or skill from where an answer to the question might be derived. Comparison of Cicero's characterization of dialectic with others suggests that he opted to emphasize the role of dialectic as a judge or arbiter in some sense. 'Characterizations' (sometimes called 'definitions' by modern scholars) of dialectic tend not to emphasize this aspect, making it 'the science of arguing or speaking well', or the 'science of what is true and what is false and what is neither' (*SVF* ii.48 = D.L. 7.41: τήν τε ῥητορικὴν ἐπιστήμην οὖσαν τοῦ εὖ λέγειν περὶ τῶν ἐν διεξόδῳ λόγων καὶ τὴν διαλεκτικὴν τοῦ ὀρθῶς διαλέγεσθαι περὶ τῶν ἐν ἐρωτήσει καὶ ἀποκρίσει λόγων· ὅθεν καὶ οὕτως αὐτὴν ὁρίζονται, ἐπιστήμην ἀληθῶν καὶ ψευδῶν καὶ οὐδετέρων). However, with our passage compare D.L. 7.47 (*SVF* ii.130 = LS 31B); Gal., *De animis peccatis dignoscendis*, p. 56.7–12 Marquardt (*SVF* ii.272); Sextus, *P.H.* 2.229 (= *FDS* 1200), all briefly discussed by Aubert-Baillot (2019: 258–60) alongside the present paragraph and all stressing dialectic's role in judgement and discrimination. Especially the Sextus passage is ideologically similar to Cicero's point here. The noun *disceptatrix* is rare, and Cicero uses it only here, but it need not be a neologism, and it need not be designed to sound dismissive; *disceptator* is an established legal term for 'arbitrator' (see Heumann-Seckel s.v.), and *disceptatrix* is attested in legal texts of, ultimately, uncertain date (e.g. Cod. Iust. 3.26.7: *colonis...grauitatem tuam...disceptatricem esse*; cf. *TLL* s.v. *disceptatrix* col. 1293.44–50). *Disceptatrix* and *iudex* (of truth and falsehood) probably reflect Greek διαγινώσκεσθαι and διευκρινεῖσθαι, used to describe dialectic in D.L. 7.47; consider, however, also the adjective διακριτική in Sextus *P.H.* 2.229. *Quasi* may qualify the whole phrase which follows and signal that this is Cicero's interpretation of dialectic's role; Reid[1] (p. 286) thinks it marks a rendering from Greek and goes with *disceptatricem* only.

The question *Cuius ueri et falsi...* asks for a generic description of the kind of truth and falsehood dialectic judges, whereby 'judging truths and falsehoods' functions like the phrase 'to judge the innocent and the guilty', i.e. such judgement involves considering items of some kind and classifying them as either true or false; contrast e.g. 'to judge the living and the dead'. *Et in qua re* then asks for domains.

Cicero then considers and dismisses different areas in which dialectic might act as a judge in the way described, i.e. geometry, literature, and music. From there he proceeds to *philosophia* and claims that dialectic cannot help answer central questions in the fields of physics and ethics. On the size of the sun, see §82 above; on the highest good, see §§129–41 below.

On the mode of argument by means of which the purpose of dialectic is to be identified, see the general note above.

On *quid ad illum*, 'what does it matter to him?', Reid[1] (p. 286) compares §94 *Quid enim ad illum qui te captare uolt...*, but there *ille* is a hypothetical opponent of

Lucullus', whereas here *ille* is either Lucullus (in which case Cicero's tone would be quite strident), or Antiochus, or a generic representative of his position ('the Stoic'). The scribe of V omitted *quasi…falsi et*, supplied by the corrector V² except for *et*; that S lacks *et* as well is one piece of evidence suggesting that V² used ξ rather than an unknown lost manuscript. See Malaspina (2020: 272 n. 87) on this point.

Quid igitur iudicabit…non est satis: Cicero suggests that what remains as a possible domain in which dialectic might function as a judge is the consideration of broadly speaking logical relationships (the truth conditions for complex propositions, viz. conjunction, disjunction, conditional, and the study of incompatibility), as well as of types of ambiguity. If all dialectic can be used for is the consideration of such matters, it will, Cicero suggests, merely judge itself and not deliver on what Lucullus promised (see the general note above on the reference to §26). In suggesting this, Cicero relies on a false dichotomy, according to which dialectic enables one either to answer factual or theoretical questions conclusively or merely to study said logical relationships.

Reid[1] (p. 286-7) assembles parallels from Cicero (and elsewhere) on the Latin terms used to refer to complex propositions, incompatibility, and ambiguity; see also Merguet. Cicero clearly intends to give a general characterization of what is comprised by dialectic (see on *Ac.* 1.19), and one which is not to be pressed too much on the details. *Coniunctio* corresponds to *quid sequatur quamque rem*, and *disiunctio* to *quid repugnet*. This suggests that *coniunctio* does indeed correspond to συνημμένον ἀξίωμα, and not to συμπεπλεγμένον, as it might (thus the translation by Brittain 2006; cf. *Fat.* 12: *haec quoque coniunctio est ex repugnantibus: et est Fabius, et in mari Fabius morietur*). It would also be peculiar to place the comparatively marginal conjunction at the very beginning, and to have it precede the disjunction, given that a negated conjunction features as first premiss of third indemonstrables. In the light of this, it is not significant that Cicero later in *Luc.* refers to conditionals by a different term (§§96, 143: *connexum*). On conditionals, see D.L. 7.71 (= *SVF* ii.207), with Frede (1974: 80-93); on disjunctions, see D.L. 7.71, and Frede (1974: 93-6); on conjunctions, see Gal., *Introd.* 4, pp. 10.13-11.13 Kalbfleisch (= *SVF* ii.208). The notion of incompatibility (μάχη) is characterized in *Anecd. Gr.* p. 484 Bekker (= *SVF* ii.176). On ἀμφιβολία, see D.L. 7.62, and Atherton (1993: 131-74).

On the import of the concluding sentence, which states that logic ought to help answer the kind of questions which arise *in philosophia*, see the general note above. Reid[1] (p. 287) assembles on *de se ipsa* critical ancient statements on dialectic. Of these Hortensius frg. 30 Müller (= frg. 54 S.-Z. = frg. 25 Grilli = Nonius p. 81 M.) stands out, which compares dialectic to an animal that eats itself (*se ad extremum pollicetur prolaturum ⟨feram⟩ [suppl. Grilli; ⟨bestiam⟩ suppl. Plasberg] quae se ipsa comest: quod efficit dialecticorum ratio*); cf. Plut., *Comm. not.* 1059d-e, where the same image occurs, and Stob., *Ecl.* II.2, p. 23 Wachsmuth, who reports, more specifically, that Carneades compared dialectic to an octopus that eats its own limbs (see Castagnoli 2019: 176-8 for a discussion of these passages). One wonders if there are intratextual references to *Hort.* in *Luc.* 91-8 which are no longer retrievable.

§92

Sed quoniam tantum in ea arte ponitis...uitiosum interrogandi genus: §§92–6...*ne ab ipso quidem soluta* is LS 37H. The Stoics characterized dialectic as an art (τέχνη; cf. the book title by Zeno's pupil Sphaerus recorded by D.L. 7.178), as a science (ἐπιστήμη, e.g. in D.L. 7.42 = *SVF* ii.48), and as a virtue (D.L. 7.46 = *SVF* ii.130; cf. Menn 1995), depending on the level of description and whether the reference point was the sage or the non-sage.

For *nasci* in the sense of 'to arise', see *OLD* s.v. no. 4a; Reid[1] (p. 287) wondered if *nata* was interpolated, on the grounds that *contra aliquem esse* is a standing phrase (cf. §58). One might think that *festiue* in juxtaposition with *progressu* is suggestive of a public, formal procession, but *progressus* does not mean 'procession'; *festiue* has its ironic sense of 'jolly' here. For the subject areas comprised by dialectic and ways of characterizing them in Latin, see the commentary on *Ac.* 1.19. With *paucis additis*, cf. *minutatim* below; §93: *gradatim*. *Locus* is ambiguous between 'place' and 'commonplace', and the clause alludes to a proverb; cf. Fronto p. 161 Naber: *facilis ad lubrica lapsus est*, with Otto (1890: 196).

The backward reference (...*quod tu modo dicebas*...) is to §49; see the commentary on §47 for the connection with series of questions. Hankinson (2007: 352) sees an allusion to a possible application of the sorites to itself here, but such a recherché suggestion would be unlikely in an introductory passage. See also Castagnoli (2010: 296 n. 139): 'Hankinson (2007: 365) nicely stresses that the phrase itself "by a series of small additions" (*paucis additis*) seems to hint at some sort of soritical progression. I interpret this, however, as the generic progression from the safe ground of the principles of Stoic dialectic to the advanced and controversial area of the paradoxes, and not as Hankinson's specific "meta-Sorites", which starting from the Stoic's acceptance of the validity of the first indemonstrable concludes the validity of very long chains of first indemonstrables, such as the Sorites itself ("simple *modus ponens* leads, inexorably, to the Sorites; logic destroys itself" (367)). Hankinson's interpretation rests on a quite strained reading of *ratio concludendi* as Cicero's Latin counterpart of συνακτικὸς λόγος ("conclusive argument"), and as a direct reference to the Stoic first indemonstrable in particular. Moreover, on that interpretation Cicero would be locating the core of the Sorites difficulty in its logical syntax, rather than the semantic issue of identifying which of the various (apparently epistemically indistinguishable) conditional premisses is materially false, and this seems to me difficult to square with the rest of Cicero's passage (*Luc.* 93–4) and with the ancient evidence on the Sorites.' Plasberg[1] (p. 118) notes that *elementa loquendi* appears to correspond to τὰ τοῦ λόγου στοιχεῖα.

Quid ergo? Istius uitii num nostra culpa est...quanto aut addito aut dempto certum respondeamus, non habemus: for *quid ergo*, see Reid[1] (p. 106) on *Ac.* 13. The genitive with *culpa* is conventional.

For the citation of *rerum natura*, which continues a theme in *Luc.*, see the general note above, and Reinhardt (2019). This is the closest any ancient text comes to locating the origin of the sorites in the vagueness of predicates. *Cognitio finium* means 'grasp of the boundaries' (*pace* Reid[1] p. 287, who sees here and in §45 the sense of 'possibility of knowing' in play), and Cicero may be relying on the technical usage *cognitio* = 'apprehension' (cf. §31); the Stoics did not claim human beings had such a grasp, but Cicero implies that they ought to be able to have it given Stoic commitments. Cf. Persius 6.79–80: *Depunge ubi sistam,* | *inuentus, Chrysippe, tui finitor acerui*, 'Make me a mark where I am to stop, Chrysippus, the person who determines the boundary of your heap has been found.'

For the elliptic *in re statuere...quatenus*, cf. Cic., *Or.* 73: *in omnibusque rebus uidendum est quatenus*. On *minutatim interrogare*, see the previous n. On indirect sentence questions without an interrogative conjunction (*diues pauper...*), see Kühner-Stegmann ii.501–3; Hofmann-Szantyr p. 544. The predicates assembled are all obviously susceptible to vagueness, but *nulla omnino in re* suggests that they are merely illustrative, and that any predicate might give rise to a sorites; see the general note above on the scope of Cicero's claim. *Certum* in *certum respondere* is an internal object, so the phrase means 'to give a definite answer'. Reid[1] (p. 288) suggests that the ablative in *quanto aut addito aut dempto* is one of place; alternatively, it is to be classed as an ablative *mensurae/discriminis*. Madvig (1834: i.508) noted that the sense does not require *non* in *non habemus*.

§93

'At uitiosi sunt soritae'...nisi cauetis: 'defective' (cf. §98: *si recte conclusi...sin uitiose...*) is the more elementary sense of *uitiosus* compared to 'detrimental', and the dare issued by Cicero to solve them has more point if the former sense is intended; cf. ἄποροι λόγοι in Greek, arguments which not afford a way out. (I have found no instance in Cicero or other relevant texts where *uitiosus* means 'invalid' as used of arguments.) The term corresponding to *frangere* is λύειν (cf. the general note on §§95–6 below). The clear implication here is that Chrysippus was unable to solve the sorites (see the general note above). *Nisi cauetis* just means 'if you are not careful'; but see next n.

'Cautum est', inquit....quod ab his dicitur ἡσυχάζειν: *cautum est* is legal terminology (used passim by Cicero in legal contexts, as well as in legal texts like D.) and alludes to the *cautio* (cf. Berger 1953 s.v.: '[*Cautio*] denotes the obligation assumed as a guaranty for the execution of an already existing obligation or of a duty which is not protected by the law'), but this presents the dogmatist's reply in a bad light, in that such a guarantee needs to be given and accepted (the Academic refuses to do the latter). *Interrogetur* may be impersonal, or its subject may be Chrysippus, as Reid[1] (p. 288) notes. *Anne multa* is slightly peculiar, in that the sorites format envisages yes/no questions in which the predicate remains the same. *Aliquanto* signals that resting is to be adopted 'some time' before the answer to a soritical question is clearly false; the next paragraph clarifies that one is to stop answering while a positive reply is still evidently correct (see §94: *illustribus igitur rebus insistis*, where the plural is functional) and the corresponding impressions cataleptic.

Id est quod ab his dicitur ἡσυχάζειν is ambiguous between 'that is what is said by them: ἡσυχάζειν' and '"resting" is called ἡσυχάζειν by them', but either interpretation would give sense. Cf. Sextus, *P.H.* 2.253: δεῖν ἵστασθαι καὶ ἐπέχειν (clarifying that suspension of judgement is meant by 'resting'); *M.* 7.416 ὁ σοφὸς στήσεται καὶ ἡσυχάσει (making the sage the explicit reference point, unlike our passage); Epict., *Diss.* 2.18.18 calles the sorites the ἡσυχάζων, sc. λόγος (cf. D.L. 7.197 *fin.*).

'Per me uel stertas licet'...progrediere rursus, quoad uidebitur: *stertere* can mean 'to be disengaged' or 'to daydream' and is thus used in various standing expressions (see the commentaries on Lucr. 3.1048), but in Carneades' joke it must just mean 'to snore'. *Vel* in *uel stertas* means 'even' (*OLD* s.v. no. 5).

The little scene dramatizes the principle 'one does not make a difference' (see the general note above), on which the Academic operates and which the dogmatist deems unproblematic as long as he is assenting. *Sed quid proficit* enquires what the benefit sc. of the policy of resting is, so τὸ ἡσυχάζειν must be the subject of *proficit* (thus Reid[1] p. 289). *Progrediere rursus quoad uidebitur* suggests that the respondent has no grounds for saying 'no' other than the arbitrary decision to 'rest'; *quoad uidebitur* 'solange es dir eben gut scheint' (Schäublin et al.) rather than 'bis es Dir "viel" erscheint' (Gigon).

Quid plura...ut non uideam quo non possit accedere: *quid plura*, sc. *dicam*, i.e. the consequences of the situation are plain: Chrysippus' strategy (and behaviour upon being roused) is owed to the fact that he cannot see 'the end of few' and 'the beginning of many' (the plural is due to questions in the soritical series being envisaged); see the general note above on the disagreement between Williamson (1994) and Bobzien (2002) as to whether Chrysippus assumed a cut-off point between 'few' and 'many', i.e. whether he thought that the last declarative sentence expressing a true proposition and the first one expressing a false were adjacent, with it being unclear to human beings where the boundary was. What Cicero says here is by itself open to this reading but need not mean it.

As at the end of §92, Cicero implies that the sorites could affect any predicate and hence any declarative sentence. On *manat*, see *TLL* s.v. *mano*, col. 322.10-17; Reid[1] (p. 289) glosses it correctly as '*late patere, serpere*'. Reid[1] (p. 289) also identifies the right sense of *respondere*: 'to put something into an answer'.

§94

'Nihil me laedit'...'nec diutius captiose interroganti respondeo': the dogmatist is now made to restate his strategy (see the general note above), using the image of the charioteer stopping before reaching a precipice. Cicero alludes to a line from Lucilius (= l. 1305 Marx = l. 1249 Warmington = l. 1321 Krenkel): *Sustineas currum ut bonus saepe agitator equosque*, which he quotes in *Att.* 13.21 (= SB 351), a letter in which he discusses different renderings of ἐποχή (see below); the line is also on his mind in *Lael.* 63. Cf. Soph., *El.* 735, with Finglass (2007: 327), which raises the question of whether Cicero's source deployed a line of Greek poetry in some form, which Cicero chose to render through the Lucilian allusion. Fuhrer (1997: 162-3) discusses Ciceronian and Augustinian ἐποχή-terminology on *Contra Acad.* 2.5.12: *refrenationem et quasi suspensionem assensionis.*

The notion of a precipice (*finis, locus praeceps*) is not accounted for by the poetic allusion and thus most likely to form part of the philosophical substance of the point made. The nature of the precipice, i.e. whether it is the true/false or the cataleptic/non-cataleptic boundary, is discussed in the general note above. The clause *prius quam ad finem ueniam* illuminates *aliquanto prius quam ad multa perueniat* in §93. The adverb *captiose* must characterize the interlocutor's intent, given that the dogmatist is unable to find fault with the sorites.

Att. 13.21 (= SB 351 = T33 in my collection) dismisses *inhibere* as a term for ἐποχή (or ἐπέχειν), and Lucilius is quoted in support of the superior *sustinere*, which we obviously read in *Luc.* 94. (There are also several other instances of *sustinere* in this sense in *Luc.*, used elliptically or with an object.) This is further evidence that Cicero must be talking about suspension of judgement in our passage (see the debate referenced in Brittain 2014: 344 n. 27). The letter also tells us that Carneades used the charioteer's stopping and the boxer's defence position as images for suspension (*semperque Carneades προβολὴν pugilis et retentionem aurigae similem facit ἐποχῇ*). Finally, the letter speaks to a change relating to *inhibere/sustinere* which Cicero made after handing over the final edition to Varro and which he then regretted; see the discussion in section 9.1, p. clxvi. All the evidence on Cicero's assent terminology is collected by Hartung (1970: 102–12).

Cf. also Sextus, *P.H.* 1.196: Τὸ δὲ 'ἐπέχω' παραλαμβάνομεν ἀντὶ τοῦ 'οὐκ ἔχω εἰπεῖν τίνι χρὴ τῶν προκειμένων πιστεῦσαι ἢ τίνι ἀπιστῆσαι', δηλοῦντες ὅτι ἴσα ἡμῖν φαίνεται τὰ πράγματα πρὸς πίστιν καὶ ἀπιστίαν. καὶ εἰ μὲν ἴσα ἐστίν, οὐ διαβεβαιούμεθα· τὸ δὲ φαινόμενον ἡμῖν περὶ αὐτῶν, ὅτε ἡμῖν ὑποπίπτει, λέγομεν. καὶ ἡ ἐποχὴ δὲ εἴρηται ἀπὸ τοῦ ἐπέχεσθαι τὴν διάνοιαν ὡς μήτε τιθέναι τι μήτε ἀναιρεῖν διὰ τὴν ἰσοσθένειαν τῶν ζητουμένων, 'The phrase "I suspend judgement" we adopt in place of "I am unable to say which of the objects presented I ought to believe and which I ought to disbelieve", indicating that the objects appear to us equal as regards credibility and incredibility. As to whether they are equal we make no positive assertion; but what we state is what appears to us in regard to them at the time of observation. And the term "suspension" is derived from the fact of the mind being held up or "suspended" so that it neither affirms nor denies anything owing to the equipollence of the matters in question' (transl. Bury). For how suspension of judgement is conceptualized within Academic scepticism, see on *Luc.* 104–105a.

Si habes, quod liqueat, neque respondes, superbe…ne tu quidem perspicis: for the argumentative device of a dilemma, see §§43–4 and 68, and the general note above on the peculiar way it is used here. The phrase *quod liqueat* is easy enough to align with other terminology used in *Acad.* to refer to cataleptic impressions, but it does not occur elsewhere; however, the way in which it is resumed later in the paragraph, including in the other horn, arguably establishes its meaning. Reid[1] (p. 289) cites parallels from *N.D.*, but none of them is technical of cataleptic impressions.

The adverb *superbe* may have a resonance in Aug., *Contra Acad.* 3.7.14 (*superbe nonnullis resistere uideamur*), where, however, it is not used with an ellipsis (cf., though, *quatenus* in §92, and *si id* below). *Percipis* and *perspicis*, for which cf. *Luc.* 17 (e.g.), would give good sense (cf. Sextus, *M.* 7.417), but the latter is more likely to be what Cicero wrote, given the paradosis.

Si quia obscura...⟨in⟩ illustribus igitur rebus insistis: *in illustribus rebus insistere* is, after *quod liqueat* above, another expression which is suggestive of 'halting while still amongst the things which appear clearly in cataleptic impressions', but whose meaning is only secured by the context (*a certis et illustrioribus cohibes assensum* below). For *insistere* in this sense, cf. also §107.

Si id tantum modo, ut taceas...hoc idem me in obscuris facere non sinis: that 'silence for the sake of it', dismissed as an option here, cannot mean 'actually assenting but keeping silent about it' is discussed in the general note above. Rather, the strategy is dismissed as mere standoffishness, not compatible with the Stoic's own standards of rational behaviour. *Sin autem*...continues to explore the same horn of the dilemma, so *autem* is not contrastive. On the disambiguating force of *a certis et illustrioribus cohibes assensum*, see the previous n. Reid[1] (p. 290) cites parallels for the coupling of a positive with a comparative. For the complaint about a double standard employed by the dogmatist see the general note above.

Nihil igitur te contra soritas ars ista adiuuat...quid aut primum sit aut postremum docet: effectively a restatement of the concluding sentence of the preceding paragraph. The 'art' would, if at all, help by *solving* the sorites. Reid[1] (p. 290) adopts Halm's conjecture *nec augentis nec minuentis*, which must refer to the questioner conducting the exchange, but the gerund, denoting the act of adding and (as the case may be) reducing, sc. performed by the questioner, seems unproblematic to me. See also Plasberg[1] (p. 119).

§95

Quid? Quod eadem illa ars quasi Penelopae telam...utrum ea uestra an nostra culpa est: the art of dialectic is like Penelope, weaving her tapestry by day and unravelling it by night; cf. the suggestion at the beginning of §92 that dialectic, in covering various subject areas, step by step (like a sorites) reaches the study of paradoxes, which then undermines dialectic itself, and the probably Carneadean image of dialectic as an octopus (discussed on §91: *Quid igitur iudicabit?*...). In particular, Cicero's point is that one part of dialectic—the Liar paradox—undermines dialectic's basis, the Principle of Bivalence (thus also Castagnoli 2010: 295-7). As in §92, Cicero speaks as if, by treating of it, the Stoics owned the problematic type of argument.

The same idea, and the same simile, seem to have been on Cicero's mind in *De orat.* 2.158 (note also the occurrence of *ad extremum*, as in our passage meaning 'at the end', cf. *OLD* s.v. *extremum* no. 2a), on which Leeman, Pinkster, and Rabbie's (1989: 97) comment that the sentence's convoluted structure suggests that the Stoic way of speaking is being mocked: *Nam et omne, quod eloquimur sic, ut id aut esse dicamus aut non esse, et, si simpliciter dictum sit, suscipiunt dialectici, ut iudicent, uerumne sit an falsum, et, si coniuncte sit elatum et adiuncta sint alia, iudicant rectene adiuncta sint et uerane summa sit unius cuiusque rationis, et ad extremum ipsi se compungunt suis acuminibus et multa quaerendo reperiunt non modo ea, quae iam non possint ipsi dissoluere, sed etiam quibus ante exorsa et potius detexta prope retexantur.*

Nempe fundamentum dialecticae est…aut uerum esse aut falsum: I take this sentence to be a statement (*OLD* s.v. *nempe* no. 1), but it could also be a question expecting the answer 'yes' (ibid. no. 2). See the texts collected in *SVF* ii.193–8; this passage down to *quod aut uerum aut falsum sit* is *SVF* ii. 196, down to *inexplicabilia esse dicitis*, *FDS* 1212. Cicero could not be clearer that *effatum* is intended to render ἀξίωμα, but one wonders if his choice of translation was informed by Stoic pronouncements on the relationship between ἀξιώματα and λεκτά; cf. e.g. Sextus, *P.H.* 2.104 (= LS 35C2): καὶ τὸ μὲν ἀξίωμά φασιν εἶναι λεκτὸν αὐτοτελὲς ἀποφαντὸν ὅσον ἐφ' ἑαυτῷ, 'And the proposition, they say, is a complete sayable, which, so far as it itself is concerned, can be asserted' (transl. Long and Sedley). A sayable is that which a proposition states (cf. *pronuntiatum* in the quote from *Tusc.* below); this makes the perfect participle *effatum* apt to render ἀξίωμα. Seneca will cite *effatum* as a translation used by some for λεκτόν; cf. *Ep.* 117.13: '…*corpus est quod uideo, cui et oculos intendi et animum. Dico deinde: Cato ambulat. Non corpus*' inquit '*est quod nunc loquor, sed enuntiatiuum quiddam de corpore, quod alii effatum uocant, alii enuntiatum, alii dictum.*' On the spelling *effatum* over *ecfatum*, see the Oxford Classical Text, p. lxxiii.

With the description of the principle as a *fundamentum*, cf. *Tusc.* 1.14: *An tu dialecticis ne imbutus quidem es? In primis enim hoc traditur: omne pronuntiatum* (sic enim mihi in praesentia occurrit ut appellarem ἀξίωμα, —*utar post alio, si inuenero melius*), *id ergo est pronuntiatum, quod est uerum aut falsum.*

Quid igitur? Haec uera an falsa sunt…mentiris an uerum dicis: the sentence which introduces the Liar is preceded by a question: *haec uera an falsa sunt*? The plural, as Barnes (1997: 152 with n. 42) suggests and some earlier editors must have assumed, 'intimates' that the following example involves more than one declarative statement. This has given rise to the various supplements recorded in the *appendix critica*. However, Barnes himself notes that in *Ac.* 1.41 Varro seeks acceptance for his translation of one term (καταληπτόν)—*comprehendible*—by asking *feretis haec?*, which Reid (1878: 152) glosses in his apparatus as '*talia qualia hoc est*'. That this generic sense is at issue in our passage, too, is suggested by *haec scilicet inexplicabilia esse dicitis* below, where one might otherwise have expected *talia* for *haec*, since Stoic *inexplicabilia* are not confined to sentences involving the Liar in some form.

There is thus no compelling reason to look for two declarative sentences to follow the introductory *haec uera an falsa sunt*. If we are initially guided by sense alone, then we will look for the most powerful way to set up the paradox, attested elsewhere in antiquity, namely the Latin equivalent for 'this statement is false'. This is achieved through:

Si te mentiri dicis [idque uerum dicis], mentiris ⟨an⟩ uerum dicis?

The deletion of *idque uerum dicis* was considered by Mignucci (1999: 57), who claimed to have found it in Plasberg's app. crit. (apparently misreading it), but he dismissed it, on the grounds that it involved an unlikely process of corruption; cf. Mignucci (1999: 57): 'But this is a strange way to fill a gap [sc. between *mentiris* and *uerum dicis*] by deleting an expression attested by all the MSS. There is no palaeographical reason to erase "idque verum dicis", and we must, on the contrary, be suspicious about "et" [in place of *an*].' (Cf. also Barnes, Bobzien, and Mignucci 1999: 164–5.) None of these reasons contra is compelling. The rationale for the deletion of *idque uerum dicis* has nothing to do with the later lacuna; rather, the problem is that the paradox is blunted and that the text with *idque uerum dicis* requires further, substantial additions (considered by Barnes 1997: 153–5). Nor is *idque uerum dicis* to be deleted on palaeographical grounds (whatever these could be), and if the question was how *idque uerum dicis* could have intruded here, then the answer is simple: a scribe supplied these words from §96 below (*Si dicis te mentiri uerumque dicis, mentiris*), where they do give good sense (see the general note above). In general, §§95–6 exhibit (cf. the app. crit.) an unusually bad text by the standards of *Acad.*, so that the assumption of an interpolation is not egregious; however, the errors admittedly consist mostly in omissions due to *sauts du même au même*, i.e. are down to carelessness rather than deliberate interference.

Barnes (1997: 155) also wondered whether the most basic (and at the same time most compelling) form of the sentence from which the paradox arises had been avoided by Cicero at this stage because it might have presented the Liar as a marginal, self-contained problem, i.e. one that was not likely to undermine the whole of dialectic. However, §96 is intended to show how the problems arising from the basic paradox infect more complex arguments and *modus ponens* itself. This makes beginning with the narrow, self-contained point a natural expository strategy.

The immediately preceding question *haec uera an falsa sunt?* provides encouragement, if not a reason, to retain the unconnected but transmitted *uerum dicis* after *mentiris* and to connect it to the latter with *an*, so as the end up with a question. See also the long note in Plasberg¹ (p. 120) on these words. To the solutions cited there add the one proposed by Powell (2001: 224): *Si te mentiri dicis, idque uerum dicis, mentiris; ⟨sin mentiris⟩, uerum dicis*.

Haec scilicet inexplicabilia esse dicitis…quod aut uerum aut falsum sit: on Stoic classifications of paradoxes and sophisms, see Barnes, Bobzien, and Mignucci (1999: 157–63, esp. 157–8) and Atherton (1993: 407–70), who writes on ἄποροι λόγοι, an unclearly defined sub-group of sophisms (p. 436 n. 43): 'The list "deficient and ἄποροι and conclusive" at D.L. 7.44 ([LS] 37C) is hard to square with the introduction of the Veiled, Elusive, Sorites, Horned, and No-man arguments as all ἄποροι, D.L. 7.82 (37D); it is hard to believe that Stoics would admit that some arguments—even the Liar—are ἄποροι in that they are insoluble or intractable, as accepted, uneasily and with qualifications, by Ebbesen 1981a [1981]: I: 42ff.; cf. Barnes 1982: 41, n. 64. At D.L. 7.82 the word seems to mean no more than "puzzling" or "problematic". A different, and more precise, meaning would be likely at 7.44, but what it was remains puzzling itself.' Barnes, Bobzien, and Mignucci (1999: 159) observe: 'This [that certain arguments are called ἄποροι λόγοι or *inexplicabilia*] does not mean that ancient logicians, and in particular the Stoics, were pessimistic about the solution of some paradoxes. The number of works dedicated by Chrysippus to the Liar paradox may show that in some cases he was not happy with his own solution, but not that the Liar or any other important paradox was considered unsolvable by him. The aporetic character ascribed to certain sophisms depended primarily on the impression they made on people to whom they were directed. Aporetic arguments were those in which it is very difficult for the answerer to see where the fallacy lies, since both the premisses and the logic of the argument appear to be acceptable, although something wrong is derived. In the very end it may be that the difficulty for the answerer to get free of the paradoxes becomes a difficulty also for the experienced logician who tries to solve the paradoxes and detect their fallacies. But it is not because of this that some paradoxes received their qualification as aporetic.' See also Bobzien (2012: 166-7).

The adjective *odiosus*, as Reid[1] (p. 281) notes, means 'vexatious' rather than 'hateful'. For the implicit complaint about a double standard, cf. §94: *Hoc idem me in obscuris facere non sinis*.

The use of the plural continues all the way from *haec uera an falsa sunt* above, through the generalizing *haec scilicet inexplicabilia...*, on to the return to the threat to bivalence posed by the Liar (see the previous n.).

On the use of *definitio*, see Barnes (1997: 150): 'It may define and determine the boundaries of the concept. In effect, the word *definitio* indicates that the fundamental thesis is an equivalence rather than a one-way conditional.' OLD s.v. *iudicium* no. 11c comes closest to the sense employed here. Reid[1] (p. 291) on *ubi est*: 'Like οὐδαμοῦ εἶναι.'

Rebus sumptis adiungam...quae sint in genere contrario: see the general note above for my reading of this sentence (in its transmitted form). I take it to be a general and vague statement on the relationship between the issue of bivalence which precedes and that of *modus ponens* which follows, with reference to the two arguments in §96 which Chrysippus does not accept (not to all four featuring in that paragraph). A consideration telling against modifying *rebus* by a pronoun (*his, quibus*) is that the premisses in the arguments in question are syntactically more complex than just the proposition or statement in relation to which the issue of bivalence is raised. *Alias* is the subject accusative in the accusative with infinitive, and *sequendas* its complement. *Improbandas* is an attribute to *alias*. *Quae sint in genere contrario* refers to the properties expressed by the two gerundives, an interpretation opted for also by Barnes (1997: 159). *Adiungere* just 'to add', not 'to infer' (*pace* Gigon; Barnes 1997: 159); it is easy to parallel in Cicero in this use. There is no close Ciceronian parallel for *in genere contrario* in the sense assumed here, but cf. *Fin.* 4.78.

Reid[1] adds a second *alias* after the first (which he found in Oxford, Lincoln College lib., Lat. 38 = Linc); this insertion is unnecessary if one interprets *sequi* just as 'to follow' and not as 'to follow and to be accepted' and if one takes the sentence to be concerned only with arguments which are not accepted (by Chrysippus). For a defence of Reid's supplement, see e.g. Brittain (2006: 55 n. 143). Long and Sedley (ii.1987: 226) print a supplement by Sedley: *Rebus sumptis adiungam ex iis ⟨eiusdem generis conclusionibus quarum una sit recta, ceteras ex his⟩ sequendas esse, alias inprobandas quae sint in genere contrario*, which they translate as (i.1987: 225): 'To my premisses I shall add this one, that of ⟨inferences of the same type one of which is valid, the remainder⟩ should be accepted, while others, of a contradictory type, should be rejected.' Plasberg[1] (p. 120) has a longer note, in the course of which he proposes his solution, which involves two supplements: *rebus sumptis adiungam ⟨alias, deinde concludam rationum summas, eodem in omnibus conclusionis genere;*

tamen alias uincam⟩ *ex iis sequendas esse alias inprobandas* ⟨*cum uos dicatis eas conclusiones omnes sequendas esse, in quibus id quod summae contrarium sit pugnet cum conexione sumptionum, eas autem inprobandas*⟩ *quae sint in genere contrario.* (The three longer supplements proposed by Sedley and Plasberg are formulated in such a way that the corresponding lacunae would be explicable with a *saut du même au même.*)

§96

Quo modo igitur hoc conclusum esse iudicas…traditis: *quo modo…*enquires about the validity and is answered by *rectissime conclusum dicitis* below. The supplement by Manutius, which remedies a *saut du même au même*, is compelling; see also Plasberg[1] (p. 121). On *genus* in *probatis certe genus*, see Bobzien (1996: 134–6) on the 'modes' (τρόποι) or 'classes' of indemonstrables (indemonstrables themselves are particular arguments). *Traditis* may seem to be a direct address to the Stoics, but cf. §98: *quas didici ab Antiocho*; accordingly *in docendo* most likely = 'when you lecture'.

Aut quidquid igitur eodem modo concluditur…aut ars ista nulla est: Cicero will draw the same conclusion after the second set of arguments below. *Ars nulla est* means 'the art is worthless' (Reid[1] p. 292). On *igitur*, see Plasberg[1] (p. 121).

Vide ergo hanc conclusionem…cum probaueris eiusdem generis superiorem: Manutius' emendation *uide* for the transmitted *uideo* is once more compelling, given the indirect question. *Conclusio* means 'argument' rather than 'conclusion'. *Probare* is not technical (of 'approval') here.

Haec Chrysippea sunt, ne ab ipso quidem dissoluta: on the most natural reading, these are actual Chrysippean examples (cf. §87b); alternatively, *haec* is once more generic (cf. on §95 above), and the suggestion is that Chrysippus 'owns' the Liar as he owns the sorites, in virtue of discussing both and not solving them. For *dissoluta*, here and in *Div.* 2.11 (where it is implied again that the Liar was not solved), cf. the Chrysippean book-title Περὶ ψευδομένου λύσεως (in three books; D.L. 7.197); see the general note above. Long and Sedley (ii.1987: 227) comment on the line (which is the end of their text 37H): 'It is probably a mistake, then, to look for any definitive solution Chrysippean solution to the Lying Argument. One is sometimes claimed at *Quaest. log.* III, 10.12–18 (*SVF* 2, pp. 106–7), but there is insufficient context there to justify the claim, and the aporetic nature of the work as a whole…is against it.' The adjective *Chrysippeus* is not used elsewhere by Cicero.

Quid enim faceret huic conclusioni…cogit inferius concedere: on *conclusioni*, see n. above, and the note in Reid[1] (p. 292) on the dative. The remark about the *ratio conexi* is probably not intended to make a deeper point about the nature of the kind of conditional issue (Chrysippus posited a 'connection'—συνάρτησις—between antecedent and consequent in a conditional; cf. Sextus, *P.H.* 2.111, with Bobzien 1996:

185-6); contrast §91 *coniunctio* (with n.). *Superius* and *inferius* render the Stoic standard terms for antecedent and consequent, τὸ ἡγούμενον and τὸ λῆγον (see e.g. Sextus, *M.* 8.110).

Quid ergo haec ab illa conclusione differt…qui igitur magis illud: see the general note above on whether Cicero is signalling a slightly different attitude on the part of Chrysippus compared to his reaction to the second argument of the paragraph.

Si ars si ratio si via…eadem est in utroque: the string of alterative protaseis is obviously rhetorical. Cicero does not want or need to be precise here, but I have tried to capture the differences between the four terms in the translation.

§97

Sed hoc extremum eorum est: postulant ut excipiantur haec inexplicabilia: see n. on §95 *inexplicabilia* above, incl. on which arguments were ἄποροι according to the Stoics. Reid[1] (p. 292) cites the many instances of *hoc extremum alicuius est*, 'this is the length someone goes to', in the letters. On *excipere*, see the next n.

Tribunum aliquem censeo uideant; a me istam exceptionem numquam impretrabunt: Cicero is referring to the procedures associated with a private trial. Cf. Berger (1953) s.v. *exceptio*: 'A defense opposed by the defendant to the plaintiff's claim to render it ineffective and exclude the defendant's condemnation as demanded by the plaintiff in the *intentio* of the procedural formula. Formally the *exceptio* was a clause in the formula containing an assertion of the defendant who, without denying the plaintiff's claim in principle, opposed to it a legal provision…or a fact not alleged by the plaintiff.' When no *exceptio* was granted, the defendant could appeal to the *tribunus plebis*, who could enforce it using his *ius auxilii*; see Thommen (1989: 233-41), who lists the eight known instances in the late Republic (pp. 236-7).

One can infer that the invocation of one of the *tribuni* was rarely successfully made, so Cicero is implying that Lucullus should not be too hopeful that he will obtain an *exceptio* from anyone. In §14 the Academics had been likened to populist demagogues by Lucullus, many of whom acted while serving as *tribunus plebis*. Partly because of that, the tribunate was viewed with suspicion by aristocrats and their followers. It is thus meant to be read as ironic that Cicero is now following procedure meticulously and recommending an appeal to the tribune.

Videant has better manuscript authority and is unobjectionable (see Plasberg[1] p. 121); *adeant* is not routinely used of the approach to the tribunes, but Reid[1] (p. 292) notes Liv. 40.29.12: *scriba tribunos plebis adit*.

Etenim cum ab Epicuro…totam enim euertit dialecticam: my punctuation in the second half of this paragraph differs in places from Reid[1] and Plasberg[1], without there being material differences in the parsing of the text.

For a sentence with similarly disjointed syntax, cf. §18. Evidence and bibliography on the Stoic and Epicurean views at issue is cited in the general note above; see ibid. for the artificiality, chronological and otherwise, of the scenario. On the Epicurean attitude to dialectic, see Sedley (2019).

With *effabimur*, cf. *effatum* in §95. With *cautus* ('circumspect'), which contrasts with *tardus* ('slow-witted'), cf. *cauetis* and *cautum est* in §93; Reid[1] (p. 293) wonders if Cicero wrote *bardus* not *tardus*, cf. *Fat.* 10. Cicero calls logicians in general *dialectici*; cf. *Luc.* 143 and Ebert (1991: 26). *Dialectici* are glossed as 'Antiochus and the Stoics' because otherwise one might think of members of the Dialectical School (noted by Reid[1] p. 294).

Hermarchus was Epicurus' pupil and successor as head of the Garden; see Erler (1994); Dorandi and Queyrel (2000). Cic., *Fin.* 2.96, preserves a letter to him by Epicurus. The example may well be Epicurus', as is suggested by the fact that it represents an instance of 'a special type of future-tensed utterance' which picks out a particular state of affairs obtaining at a particular time (Bown 2016: 252). *N.D.* 1.70 has another instance, viz. 'Epicurus will be alive tomorrow'.

If *concedere* was only used of premises, as posited by Long and Sedley (i.1987: 111) and Bown (2016: 256), then the passage could not be read coherently with the other evidence for the Truth-to-Necessity argument. Long and Sedley (i.1987: 111) suggest that sense would be restored if the text offered *uerum* in place of (*alterutrum concessero*) *necessarium*, apparently assuming a mistake on Cicero's part rather than textual corruption. However, *concedere* can be used of concessions of any kind, including of conclusions; cf. §18 of the conclusion of the core argument; §66 of the conclusion of the corollary argument. I thus follow Bobzien (1998: 79 n. 45) in assuming that what is (hypothetically) being conceded is the conclusion of an argument; see the general note above. A conventional term for conceding premises is *dare*.

As for the claim that no *necessitas* resides *in natura rerum*, this is obviously not elaborated here. Sedley (2019: 107–8) argues, contra Bobzien (1998: 75–86), that Epicurus anticipated Chrysippus in positing a connection between the 'logical premiss' (a) that it is 'true now that such and such a future event will take place' and the 'causal thesis' (b) that 'there are now existing causes sufficient to bring that event about'. Epicurus, so the argument, did not infer (b) from (a) like Chrysippus, but the falsehood of (a) from the falsehood of (b). Evidence for the Epicurean reasoning is located in *Fat.* 26–8.

Nam si e contrariis disiunctio...nulla uera est: for the meaning of *e contrariis disiunctio*, which Cicero himself helpfully glosses, see the general note; cf. *Fat.* 37. Plasberg[1] (p. 122) correctly glosses as ἐξ ἐναντίων (uel ἀντικειμένων) διεζευγμένον. With *alterum aiat, alterum neget*, cf. §104 with n.; *Top.* 49. See also Barnes (2005), and Cicero's discussion of Stoic indemonstrables in *Top.* 53–7.

In line with his general purpose, viz. the attack on dialectic, Cicero ends by attempting to generalize: if a disjunction formed from a contradictory pair of propositions (or possibly, given the context, formed from a contradictory pair of propositions of the kind at issue in §97) is false, then no disjunction will be true.

§98a

Mecum uero quid habent litium...haec autem merces erat dialecticorum: cf. Plaut., *Truc.* 897: ⟨*Ec*⟩*quid, Astaphium, litiumst? Disciplina* does not mean 'school of thought' or 'sect' here, *pace* Glucker (1978: 197).

Carneades' epigram is modelled on the story of Corax and Tisias; cf. Suda κ, no. 171 (cf. *Proleg. syll.* pp. 26-7 Rabe and the context there): Κακοῦ κόρακος κακὸν ᾠόν· ταύτην τὴν παροιμίαν οἱ μὲν ἀπὸ τοῦ πτηνοῦ ζῴου φασὶν εἰρῆσθαι, ὅτι οὔτε αὐτὸ βρωτόν ἐστιν οὔτε τὸ ᾠόν, ὃ ἔχει. οἱ δὲ ἀπὸ τοῦ Κόρακος τοῦ Συρακουσίου ῥήτορος, πρῶτον διδάξαντος τέχνην ῥητορικήν. ὑπὸ γὰρ τούτου, ὥς φασι, μαθητής, Τισίας ὄνομα, μισθὸν ἀπαιτούμενος εἰς τὸ δικαστήριον εἶπεν· εἰ μέν με νικήσειας, οὐδὲν μεμάθηκα· εἰ δὲ ἡττηθῇς, οὐ κομίσῃ τοὺς μισθούς. θαυμάσαντες οἱ δικασταὶ τὸ σόφισμα τοῦ νεανίου ἐπεφώνουν· κακοῦ κόρακος κακὸν ᾠόν, 'From a bad crow comes a bad egg. Some say this proverb comes from the winged animal of the same name because neither it nor its egg is edible. But others say it comes from Corax the Syracusan, who was the first to teach the art of rhetoric. For they say that a pupil of his, named Tisias, taken to court by him for his fee, said: "If you win, I have not learnt anything; but if you lose, you will not get your fee." The judges were astonished by the young man's sophistry and said: "From a bad crow comes a bad egg".' The story is also told elsewhere without the judges' condemnation of both parties; in any case, it would have been rather Carneadean to rely on the self-mocking subtext. See also Usher (2006) on Carneades' apparent fondness for playing with literary culture.

For the sense and absolute use of *teneo*, see *OLD* s.v. no. 16b: 'to maintain successfully, uphold (an argument)'; there is no reason to insert *te* before *teneo*, as suggested by Davies. Cf. also on *Luc.* 104 *alterum placere...alterum tenere* on the uses of the verb. Reid[1] (p. 294) compares *Luc.* 16: *Carneades diu tenuit*, but there *Academiam* seems the implied object. With *uitiose* cf. §93: *at uitiosi sunt soritae*, above.

On Diogenes of Babylon, Carneades' fellow ambassador during the famous embassy of 155 BC, see Guérard et al. (1994); cf. §137. Otherwise Carneades' careful study of the *writings* of Chrysippus is of course well documented (cf. *Luc.* 87 with comm.). *Diogenes mihi* (Halm) for the transmitted *Diogeni* is compelling.

Sequor igitur eas uisas...ne illud quidem iudicabo: cf. the nn. on §97, of which what Cicero says here is a restatement, down to the details about the same *conexum* in both arguments, which ought to ensure equal treatment. The emendation by Plasberg[1] *hoc ut illud* delivers the required sense; *iudicare hoc et illud* would mean 'to pass judgement on both this and that'.

§98b

Having concluded the discussion of dialectic with a stereotypical dismissal of dialectic as nitpicking, Cicero moves on to the discussion of 'who we (Academics) really are'—a discussion of Academic views on their own terms. This, he suggests, will achieve what destructive argument by itself may not achieve: the crumbling of Antiochus' doctrinal edifice.

Unusually, Cicero identifies his source by author, title, and book, so as to remove himself as a potentially distorting mediator. This still leaves the possibility of course that his immediate source was Philo who in turn relied on the cited work by Clitomachus, presented here as a devoted and punctilious follower of Carneades.

Embedded quotations and paraphrases from philosophical texts are of course usually signalled by Cicero,[371] but where a source plays a structural role within Cicero's own argument, as opposed to serving as 'evidence' or being itself the explicit object of analysis, it is not normally identified (hence the existence of *Quellenforschung*). In the present case, it is not altogether clear how Clitomachus is used, directly or mediated, after the initial point of entry in §99. In §103 translation of Clitomachean material is resumed and clearly marked in §102, but the section in between is less clear-cut. I shall be pursuing this issue below.

Sed ut omnes istos aculeos...Antiochea ista corruent uniuersa: the sentence is a typical instance of one 'facing both ways', with the *ut*-clause concluding the previous section, and the main clause beginning the new one.

Aculeus denotes primarily the sting of insects and other animals, and has various transferred and metaphorical uses in addition. With *aculeos et totum tortuosum genus disputandi*, cf. §75: *contorta et aculeata* σοφίσματα; and *Fat.* 16: *multa genera sunt enuntiandi nec ullum distortius...contortiones orationis*. Görler (2004c: 271) comments on the image: '...is taken from difficult terrain: the preceding arguments are likened to a thicket of thorny shrubs where one cannot proceed but cautiously and slowly, in difficult windings and turns.' Görler goes on to note that the simile reappears in §12, where Cicero, having addressed a finer point about the problems of the core argument, promises that 'from now on' he will 'roam happily and freely in a much wider field'.

The transmitted *Antioche*, if not simply the result of mechanical corruption, would be a baffling address to Antiochus. *Antiochea* is most likely to be correct (cf. *Chrysippea* in §96). Reid[1] (p. 295) prints *Antiochi* (as in F after correction).

Nec uero quicquam ita dicam...sunt sumpta de primo: *fingi* hints at Antiochus' claim that Philo 'lied' (§18), sc. in the Roman Books, which are not at issue here. For Clitomachus, whose Carthaginian name was Hasdrubal (Ἀσδρούβας; Philod., *Index Acad*. col. xxv.1-2), see the commentary on *Luc.* 16-17a. On Carthaginian cleverness, which need not be malicious but often carries a connotation of trickery, see e.g. Plaut., *Poen*. 1125; Colum. 1.3.8: *acutissimam gentem Poenos*; Cic., *Fin*. 4.56: *Poenulus...homo...acutus* (of Zeno: *scis enim Citieos...e Phoenica profectos*; see also on *Luc.* 66-7). On *ut Poenus* justifying the attribute *acutus*, see Pinkster ii.276.

It would be peculiar to begin a new sentence with *et quattuor...*, and deleting *et* without inserting another particle is not attractive. Dorandi (1994: 425) and Görler

---

[371] See e.g. DeGraff (1940); Görler (1989: 253-6); Long (1995); Reinhardt (2005); more secondary literature is assembled by Gawlick and Görler (1994: 1057-8). A monograph devoted to the topic is Spahlinger (2005). See also section 9.3 on the sources of *Acad*.

(1994: 902) plausibly suggest that Clitomachus' work, of which we know only from the present passage, was called Περὶ ἐποχῆς. In Greek texts which report on Pyrrhonism or Academic scepticism the plural of ἐποχή is not used of individual acts of suspension (contrast the manner in which συγκαταθέσεις is used of individual acts of assent), but it is still striking that Cicero, who had the resources to translate the title in a way which preserves a singular (cf. §59: *assensionis retentio*), opted not to do so.

I ascribe the omission of *quae* to ξ in the apparatus because it was first deleted by the scribe of V through underlining and the deletion then reinforced through expunction by V². Since we know that V² (like V) had ξ available for comparison and since *quae* is missing in S, the word was most likely not in ξ. Thus also Malaspina (2020: 271 n. 83).

§§99–101

Having announced that he will draw on the first book of Clitomachus' Περὶ ἐποχῆς (§98b) for the *Carneadis sententia*, Cicero begins his report on (or even translation of) Clitomachus: on Carneades' view there were two divisions of impressions. The two sentences giving the divisions are in indirect speech, and Cicero continues in indirect speech until...*ut autem probatio, multa* below (still §99). This raises the question of whether at that point Cicero ceases to follow Clitomachus, or whether Clitomachus himself ended the report on Carneades' views and reverted to direct speech and to speaking in his own voice. What is clear from §102 *explicaui paulo ante Clitomacho auctore*...is that by that point Cicero was no longer closely following Clitomachus (he quotes him again, though apparently not the same work, from §103 *init.*, then rendering what Clitomachus said in indirect speech), and the argument which precedes this remark from §101b, with its combination of Stoic and Epicurean premises, is very similar in strategy to earlier passages (§§79–80, 97) which we have no reason to link with Clitomachus and the work cited in §98, although we know that the strategy goes back to Carneades.[372]

The question, then, is whether Clitomachus informs what Cicero says from §99 *Etenim contra naturam esset*...down to §101a...*aliter se habere ac sensibus uideantur*. It is plain that, minimally, there are Ciceronian insertions in the section, like the reference to the setting in §100, the backward reference in §99 *quam tu Luculle commemorabas*, and possibly the concluding sentence of §101a which is cast in the first-person plural, but e.g. the vignette of the Academic sage in §101 would fit naturally into a Clitomachean work on the suspension of assent, as would the argument of §99 *fin.* that even the Stoic sage will find himself in situations where he cannot assent since he has less to go on than cataleptic impressions but will need to put to sea nonetheless.

In §102 the Cicero character clearly speaks in his own voice, including on the use of Clitomachean texts. In §103 Cicero avowedly reports—in indirect speech— Clitomachus' further thoughts on the nature of *probabilia* within a divisional

---

[372] See section 9.3 on the sources of *Acad.*

framework. This could be taken to suggest that the quotation from Clitomachus in §99 gives out where the indirect speech ends (i.e.: ...*ut autem probatio, multa*) and resumes in §103 *init*. However, §103 *Itaque ait uehementer errare*...proves that Clitomachus did not just provide a division, and the manner in which Cicero indicates that he is in §103 quoting from a Clitomachean work dedicated to Lucilius suggests that he is no longer relying on Περὶ ἐποχῆς. See the general note on §102 below.

According to §99, Clitomachus reported that Carneades distinguished two different ways of dividing the genus 'impression', either into cataleptic and non-cataleptic ones (the latter class comprises true and false impressions), or into persuasive impressions (called *probabilia* in Latin) and those which are not persuasive. All arguments against the senses and clarity (*perspicuitas*) were directed against the former way of classifying impressions, while the latter division was untouched by them. Thus there were impressions upon which 'approval' (treated as a counterpart of 'apprehension', i.e. either the mechanism/process or the outcome, and looking forward to §104) was attendant. It is well recognized that the Carneadean πιθανόν drew on an existing Stoic division,[373] and we may compare the one in Sextus, *M*. 7.242–52 (*SVF* ii.65 = LS 39G [7.242–6] = part of *FDS* 273), ascribed by Sextus to 'the Stoics' and listed by von Arnim under Chrysippus' fragments.[374] There φαντασίαι are divided into πιθαναί and ἀπίθανοι, then the former into true and false impressions, and then true impressions into cataleptic and non-cataleptic ones. In our passage, by treating the *probabile/non probabile* and cataleptic/non-cataleptic distinctions as alternatives, Carneades is presented as taking no explicit stance on the connection of *probabilia* with truth; however, this may just be due to the focus of the passage being elsewhere.

The discussion of the *probabile* here is the third one in the first edition of *Acad*. The second one was Lucullus' discussion in §§32–6, which provided inter alia terms for the testing procedures *probabilia* are supposed to be subjected to (§35 *fin*.). These must have featured in the first discussion in the *Catulus*, which was most likely provided by Catulus (see section 9.2 on the probable distribution of roles in that book).

Cicero continues (in indirect speech) by resisting the Stoic move to define perception as commonly understood as assent to a cataleptic impression (cf. §108) and to

---

[373] See the classic discussion in Couissin (1983: 44–51), originally published in 1929; Burnyeat (unpublished); Reinhardt (2018a) and this volume, section 6.1; Alessandrelli (2019).

[374] Another division is attested in *P.Berol*. inv. 16545, first edited by Szymański (2000) and re-examined by Backhouse (2000). In the papyrus, the division is almost certainly credited to a philosopher called Antipater, most likely Antipater of Tarsus (see the commentary on *Luc*. 28). The division does not employ persuasiveness as a categorizing feature, and instead divides impressions into those οὐκ ἀπό τινος (glossed as διάκενοι), which are false, and those ἀπό τινος, which subdivide into impressions κατ' αὐτὰ τὰ ὄντα, which are true, and παρατυπωτικαί, which are false. As Backhouse explains, the division employs whether an impression comes from an actually existing object as a categorizing feature, and can thus be linked with a minority interpretation of the Zenonian definition of the cataleptic impression which interprets its first clause as 'from an existing object' and which assumes that veridicality is stipulated by the second clause (see sections 5.1 and 5.2). Backhouse makes a case for identifying impressions κατ' αὐτὰ τὰ ὄντα as cataleptic impressions, but much of the terminology in the fragment is non-standard, and impressions κατ' αὐτὰ τὰ ὄντα might also be non-cataleptic true impressions, a category otherwise absent from the division (cataleptic impression would then be assumed to have featured in an immediately following section which has not come down to us). The interpretation of Zeno's definition presupposed consistently in *Acad*. assumes that the first clause stipulates veridicality.

present, as a consequence, opposition to the cataleptic impression as the total overturning of life (cf. §53: *omnia confundere*). As Allen (1997: 244-6) shows, the kind of scepticism which the Stoics devise as a characterization of the Academic position is the most extreme form found in antiquity, one which is predicated on the extremism of the Stoic view, and, as Cicero suggests, a caricature of the actual position of the Academics. In a move which functions as a gesture to Lucullus' earlier naturalistic arguments (§§22, 26) but which may nonetheless go back to Clitomachus,[375] Cicero asserts that it would be unnatural for there to be no *probabile* as he conceives of it.[376] What is absent, though, according to him is any feature in an impression which guarantees its truth.

Cicero proceeds that the sage (sc. as he construes him) will use what is *probabile* in appearance (*specie*) and unobstacled (see n. below), and that life in all its aspects will be governed by it. *Omnis ratio uitae* is not precise in scope, but it would seem artificial to insist that Cicero only means practical matters and not also philosophical problems. He then pointedly turns from his conception of the sage to the Stoic one (*is quoque qui a uobis sapiens inducitur*) and states in factual terms that the Stoic sage acts in the same way on non-cataleptic impressions and without assenting to them, citing as an instance a sea voyage where it is 'merely' *probabile* that he will arrive safely. Although this is not explicit from what Cicero says, he is unlikely mean that the Stoics *concede* that sometimes the sage is guided by *probabilia* without assenting to them; it would have been highlighted if there was a localized concession by the Stoics on this point, who did not waver on the principle that assent is required for action and that the sage assents to cataleptic impressions only. Rather, the suggestion must be that, given what the world is like and contrary to what the Stoics are prepared to concede, even the Stoic sage will encounter situations in which approving *probabilia* is the best and all he can do. I am therefore hesitant to treat the passage as evidence that the Stoics allowed themselves to be guided by πιθανά without assenting to them under certain circumstances, however narrowly circumscribed. A text that has been cited in support of such a reading of *Luc.* 99 is Philod., *De Signis* col. vii.26-38 De Lacy (with the alterations proposed by Sedley 1982: 249 n. 25), in which the Stoic Dionysius replies to Epicurean counterarguments:[377]

Ἔτι δὲ λε|γόν[τω]ν ὡς καὶ τὰ τερατώδη | πρός
[τιν᾽ ὅ]μοια 'κατ᾽ αὐτοὺς εἰ | μὴ τ[ὰ π]αρ᾽ ἡμῖν ὅμοια
τούτοις | οὐχ [ὑπά]ρχειν ἀποκόψομεν,' τῶι | τε κ[ατ᾽
ἀ]νασκευὴν ἀποκό[ψ]ειν | φησ[ίν. οὐ] μὴν ἀλλ᾽ ἐπαρ-
κε[ῖν] ἡμῖν [τό τε] πεπεῖσθαι περὶ τ[ο]ύ|τω[ν καὶ π]ερὶ
τῶν ἐκ τῆς πε[ί]ρας | κατ[ὰ τὴν] εὐλογίαν, ὃν τρόπον |
ὅτι [γενη]σόμεθα πλέοντες | θέρ[ους] ἐν ἀσφαλεῖ [ ]
.Ω | TH[ ]POY ἔχ[οντες.

---

[375] On Lucullus' 'naturalistic' arguments and Cicero's response to them, see also Reinhardt (2019).
[376] Cicero takes himself, or the Clitomacheans, to be describing human cognitive behaviour as it actually is.
[377] The Dionysius in question is most likely Dionysius of Cryene, pupil of Diogenes of Babylon and Antipater of Tarsus; see Dorandi (1994f).

Again, when our people [the Epicureans] say that according to them even freaks bear resemblances in some respects—unless we are going to abolish the existence of the things in our experience which resemble them!—he [Dionysius] says, first, that the abolition will be by the elimination method; but that anyway it is sufficient, concerning these things and concerning those which derive from experience, for us to be convinced in accordance with reasonableness, just as when we sail in summer we are convinced that we will arrive safely. (transl. Sedley, modified)

Unlike in *Luc.* 99, here we have a Stoic speaking in his own voice, who acknowledges that the Stoics take sea voyages in situations when they are (merely) 'convinced' (πεπεῖσθαι), sc. that they will arrive safely, acting in accordance with reasonableness (εὐλογία).[378] However, it is not evident, *pace* Sedley (1982: 250) and Tielemann (1996: 266–7), that πεπεῖσθαι has to be a reference to the πιθανόν here. Rather, as Barnes (1985: 459–60) suggests, the phrase 'in accordance with εὐλογία' seems to introduce the main consideration, which points towards a different way of explaining how Stoics behave in the sea voyage scenario, and one which does not require the jettisoning of the principles that the sage assents to cataleptic impressions only and that any action on his part requires an act of assent. The Stoics allowed for non-perceptual cataleptic impressions whose propositional content can be formulated as 'It is reasonable (εὔλογον) that *p*', where *p* could be something like 'I will arrive safely when I make this crossing on a well-maintained ship, with a competent crew, and while the breeze is light'.[379] For such impressions to give rise to action, the sage would assent to them, and he would not have assented rashly and 'opined' (i.e. assented to the non-cataleptic) if he suffered shipwreck, since 'it is reasonable that *p*' would have been true whatever the outcome. If Cicero (whether via Clitomachus or not) knew about the Stoic use of reasonable impressions, he may have felt that it is specious to envisage it but to reject approval (= non-assent, cf. *Luc.* 104) of πιθανά as an explanatory model for the same scenario. However, he gives no indication that he knew about the relevant use of reasonable impressions, and he does envisage the Stoic sage to act without assent (*multa sequitur probabilia...neque assensa*) in such situations.[380]

---

[378] That *Luc.* 99 refers to the sage while Philodemus refers to 'the Stoics' does not seem significant.

[379] See Brennan (1996: 318–25) on D.L. 7.177 (= *SVF* i.625) and Athenaeus 354E (= *SVF* i.624, part), both of which are combined in LS 40F.

[380] Seneca sides not with the Stoics of the Hellenistic period but with the Clitomachean Cicero, in conscious imitation of these passages in *Acad.* (cf. not just §100, but also §109a: ...*in nauigando et in conserendo, in uxore ducenda, in liberis procreandis*...). However, he does not pronounce on the issue of assent, and his point of reference is not the sage. Cf. *Ben.* 4.33.1–4, on whether one should wait in conferring a benefit until one knows if the recipient is ungrateful or not: '*Quid? Si*' inquit '*nescis, utrum ingratus sit an gratus, expectabis, donec scias, an dandi beneficii tempus non amittes? Expectare longum est (nam, ut ait Plato, difficilis humani animi coniectura est), non expectare temerarium est.*' *Huic respondebimus numquam expectare nos certissimam rerum comprehensionem, quoniam in arduo est ueri exploratio, sed ea ire, qua ducit ueri similitudo. Omne hac uia procedit officium: sic serimus, sic nauigamus, sic militamus, six uxores ducimus, sic liberos tollimus; cum omnium horum incertus sit euentus, ad ea accedimus, de quibus bene sperandum esse credidimus. Quis enim pollicetur serenti prouentum, nauiganti portum, militanti uictoriam, marito pudicam uxorem, patri pios liberos? Sequimur qua ratio, non qua ueritas traxit. Expecta ut nisi bene cessura non facias et nisi comperta ueritate nil noueris: relicto omni actu uita consistit. Cum ueri similia me in hoc aut in illud impellant, non uera, ei beneficium dabo, quem ueri simile erit gratum esse.*

Having illustrated his point with a reference to the setting of the dialogue (§100 *init.*), Cicero continues his argument against the charge of *omnis uitae euersio* to which the Academic position supposedly leads. Unlike Anaxagoras, who had unwarranted dogmatic views (*sciret*) about the colour of water being black and therefore refused to accept what his impressions suggested (that snow was white), the sage will be more amenable (*facilior*) and 'approve' that snow is white. Notice how Cicero, having apparently shifted his gaze to the Stoic sage in §99 *fin.*, continues with the same subject through §100, implicitly claiming that the supposedly unerring Stoic sage, who never assents to a non-cataleptic impression, in reality and as a matter of fact behaves as the Academics construe him.

In §101a Cicero broadens the theme that the sage is *facilis* to a general description: the sage is not sculpted from rock or carved from oak, and will be moved if he receives persuasive impressions as long as they are unimpeded.[381] Reid[1] (p. 297) suggests that this is intended to contrast with the rigid conception of the sage which the Stoics employ. It is true that the *constantia sapientis* is proverbial, and that the steadfastness of the Stoic sage is absolute (resulting from his only ever assenting to cataleptic impressions and having no false beliefs to begin with). However, Cicero's point here is not just that the sage as he sees him will review and change his mind when there is new information, but also that the Academic sage is recognizably a human being, sane, and sensible. When Stoics want to appear reasonable, they can sound remarkably like Cicero; cf. Sen., *De Constantia Sapientis* 10.4 (on the suffering sage): *Alia sunt quae sapientem feriunt, etiam si non peruertunt, ut dolor corporis et debilitas aut amicorum liberorumque amissio et patriae bello flagrantis calamitas: haec non nego sentire sapientem;* **nec enim lapidis illi duritiam ferriue adserimus.** *Nulla uirtus est quae non sentias perpeti. Quid ergo est? Quosdam ictus recipit, sed receptos euincit et sanat et comprimit, haec uero minora ne sentit quidem nec aduersus ea solita illa uirtute utitur dura tolerandi, sed aut non adnotat aut digna risu putat.* Cicero continues that the sage is of such a constitution and has the faculties as to be able receive impressions (cf. Sextus, *M.* 7.161-2), but while many impressions appear true to him (see n. below), none appears to carry the mark of apprehension supposedly peculiar to cataleptic impression. Therefore the sage will, as is the Clitomachean position, withhold assent because of the ever-present threat of ἀπαραλλαξία. Cicero ends by reinforcing the point that little separates Academics and Stoics: both assume that there are many false impressions, which present things differently to how they are. This 'agreement' provides a link with §101b, where the dissenting Epicureans feature with their view that all perceptions are true.

In §101b Cicero draws the Epicureans into the debate, for reasons which only become apparent in §101b *fin.*: rejecting the notion that there is *either* Stoicism which enables the conduct of life *or* the complete overturning of the human existence which the Academic position amounts to, he suggests that the Stoic (or Lucullus/Antiochus) engages with Epicurus, with whom there is substantial disagreement, rather than with the Academics, with whom there is discernible common ground. The manner in which the passage pointedly links back to what precedes (*hoc*

---

[381] See the lemmatized n. below for a parallel in Sextus.

autem si ita sit...) suggests that Cicero is attempting to turn the tables on the Stoics: their assumption that there are false impressions, which *he* regards as entirely reasonable, could lead to a complete overturning of life, just like the Academic assumption of ἀπαραλλαξία allegedly does. In both cases, or so Cicero implies, the line of argument is equally absurd. The argument is obviously polemical, which makes it unlikely that Cicero is still drawing on Clitomachus, whose works are presented in §102 *fin.* in a manner which suggests a handbook-type summary.

Making a point of removing himself from the argument, Cicero uses an Epicurean premiss ('If any perceptual presentation is ever false, nothing can be known') and a Stoic premiss ('There are false impressions') to conclude by *modus ponens* that nothing can be known.[382] Then, using the device of the fictional interlocutor again, Cicero has the Stoic reply that he does not accept the Epicurean premiss, i.e. the conditional. This prompts Cicero's invitation to quarrel with Epicurus rather than the Academics. For the technique of combining premisses 'owned' by different schools, which goes back to Carneades, see on §97. Here, unlike in some other cases where an Academic combines Epicurean premisses with others, one cannot say that the Epicurean premiss ought to have a claim on the Stoics on rational grounds.

§99

Duo placet esse Carneadi genera uisorum...alia non probabilia: *esse* means 'to have currency' (*OLD* s.v. *sum* no. 3b); see the general note above on the two *genera* being alternatives rather than species of a superordinate genus '*uisum*' (Plasberg[1] p. 123 glosses *genera* '*quaestionis*' and 'σχέσεις'). *Visa* must here denote impressions qua mental items only; on *uisum percipere* and related phrases see section 10.1; Reinhardt (2018b). *Visa quae (percipi) non possint* are ἀκατάληπτα. Cf. the Stoic division in D.L. 7.45, in which impressions are divided into cataleptic and acataleptic. Elsewhere the Stoics treat cataleptic impressions as a species of persuasive impressions; cf. Sextus, *M.* 7.242-7, with Backhouse (2000: 26-7).

In *M.* 7.169-75 Sextus discusses the Academic division of impressions. In §169 presentations are divided into those which appear true (πιθανότης, πιθανὴ φαντασία; ἔμφασις) and those which do not appear true (ἀπειθής or ἀπίθανος φαντασία). The ἀπίθανος φαντασία is here the contradictory not the contrary of the πιθανὴ φαντασία as in Stoic divisions of πιθανά; such impressions either fail to be persuasive or are positively unpersuasive. The class of impressions which appears true is then divided further into impressions which intensely appear true (§171), which may serve as the criterion, and ones which are 'dim' (ἀμυδρός, ἔκλυτος, both opposites of ἐναργής, but that term is not repeated here from §161). See Reinhardt (2018a: 221) and section 6.1.

Plasberg[1] (p. 123) gives a fuller account of the situation in ABV around the lacuna than my summary apparatus. A good supplement was furnished by A[a] and V[2] independently (but the latter was guided by V[m]).

---

[382] Given that the conditional is clearly marked as Epicurean in content, Cicero cannot be thinking of the Stoic definition of αἴσθησις as 'assent to a cataleptic impression' (see on §108).

Itaque quae contra sensus contraque perspicuitatem...ut autem probatio, multa: *dicantur,* sc. *ab Academicis.* Arguments against the cataleptic impression can only be treated by the Stoics as the abolition of the senses because they define perception as assent to a cataleptic impression; see *Ac.* 1.40-2. On *probatio,* see §104, but the noun (rather than *approbatio*) is only used here; the variation does not seem to carry any particular meaning beyond highlighting the etymological connection with *probabilia.* On the tense of *consequeretur,* see Plasberg[1] (p. 123). *Oportere* perhaps of an injunction of reason in particular.

Etenim contra naturam esset...commemorabas euersio: cf. §97: *in natura rerum;* here and there Cicero rebuts Lucullus' naturalistic arguments. Lucullus made the claim of *tota euersio* in §31.

Reid[1] (p. 295) suggests that Cicero breaks off the quotation from Clitomachus at the end of the preceding sentence, but *et sequitur...euersio* could just be a Ciceronian insertion, with the paraphrase of Clitomachus resuming in the following sentence. Reid also notes that *commemorare* is a verb of speaking, not a verb of remembering (cf. *TLL* s.v. col. 1830.77-80), viz. 'to call to mind something that is familiar' (hinting that the accusation was not an original one). A number of earlier editors do not insert *si,* supplied by the corrector of F, and print *etenim contra naturam esset probabile nihil esse,* but an accusative with infinitive which has the force of the protasis of a conditional would be problematic; see Plasberg[1] (p. 123).

Itaque et sensibus probanda multa sunt...quale not etiam falsum nihil ab eo differens possit: another of Cicero's many formulations which characterizes ἀπαραλλαξία as the absence of an objective difference rather than indistinguishability; see Reid[1] (p. 242) on *cur id...communitas* and the introduction (section 5.6). *Sensibus,* an instrumental ablative or an impersonal use of the *datiuus iudicantis* (on which see Pinkster 2005: 244), signals that perceptual impressions are at issue; there is no suggestion that the senses as opposed to the mind could give approval. Plasberg[1] (p. 123) correctly observes that *et utetur iis sapiens* is to be supplied mentally after *multa sunt.*

Sic quidquid acciderit specie probabile...sic omnis ratio uitae gubernabitur: with *specie,* cf. not §66 as quoted by Reid[1] (p. 295) nor εἶδος, *pace* Striker (1997: 271), but §58 *fin.: quasi uero non specie uisa iudicentur, quae fidem nullam habebunt sublata ueri et falsi nota;* §111 *fin.*; also ἔμφασις in *M.* 7.169 quoted above, with section 6.1 and 6.2, and Reinhardt (2018a: 221-3, 228-31); with *acciderit,* cf. τὸ προσπῖπτον in *M.* 7.179 *fin.* On the notion of an 'impedance' to persuasiveness, see §105: *Sic igitur inducto et constituto probabili...*below, §36 *init.,* section 6.5, and Reinhardt (2018a: 222-8). See the general note above on the conception of the sage, and Cicero's suggestion that he is construing the Stoic sage as he ought to be construed, rather than devising an alternative Academic sage; and in general the close parallel in *N.D.* 1.12, where *alio loco* probably refers to our passage here: *Nec tamen fieri potest, ut, qui hac ratione philosophentur, hi nihil habeant quod sequantur. Dictum est omnino de hac re alio loco diligentius, sed quia nimis indociles quidam tardique sunt, admonendi uidentur saepius. Non enim sumus ii, quibus nihil uerum esse uideatur, sed ii qui omnibus* *ueris falsa quaedam adiuncta esse dicamus tanta similitudine, ut in iis nulla insit certa iudicandi et assentiendi nota. Ex quo exsistit et illud, multa esse probabilia, quae, quamquam non perciperentur, tamen, quia uisum quendam haberent insignem et illustrem, his sapientis uita regeretur.*

See the introduction (section 6.1) and Reinhardt (2018a: 218) on the question of what accounts for initial *probabilitas* prior to any testing for impedances or obstacles (*si…contrarium* corresponds to ἀπερίσπαστος and/or διεξ- or περιωδευμένος). Note also that Cicero's formulation here suggests that the initial *probabile* and the tested *probabile* are the same thing, as opposed to testing creating a new *probabile* of the same propositional content as the untested one; this is in keeping with the notion that testing routines test for properties which account for πιθανότης/*probabilitas* to begin with.

Etenim is quoque…omnis uita tollatur: = LS 42I (down to §100: *esse saluum*). See the general note above: this is the Academic's interpretation of how the Stoic sage is bound to behave willy-nilly, and not a description which the Stoics would recognize, not even for certain narrowly circumscribed situations. For the Stoics, there is no action of the sage without assent to cataleptic impressions, and no action of anyone without assent to an impression.

For *sequi* as synonym for *approbare*, cf. §§8, 36, 59, 104 (twice in the translated quotation from Clitomachus), 107, 108, 109; ἕπεσθαι occurs in the Greek record. (On εὐδοκεῖν, which is used by Sextus to refer to the Pyrrhonist's acceptance of impressions, see Frede 1987g: 193–4; Fine 2000: 84–8; and Morison 2019: §3.4.) That *sequi* and *approbare* are treated as equivalents is important because it suggests, against the background of the explanation of approval in *Luc.* 104, that 'following' is not, as it has sometimes been characterized, a going-along-with in the sense of a passive acquiescence to certain impressions, a being left with a view as the result of an impression, although approval like assent may presumably sometimes be unconscious. (I also think that 'following' is conceptualized differently by Academics and Pyrrhonists; see on §§104–105a.) Rather, the paradigm case for (Academic) 'following', i.e. Clitomachean approval, is conscious acceptance; in that respect, I do not take approval to be different from dogmatic assent as construed by the Stoics. *Sequi* is not attested as a synonym for self-aware assent as given by the mitigated sceptic (cf. on §148).

Inducitur is theatre terminology and means 'is brought on the stage', as Reid[1] (p. 296) notes. For *omnis uita tollatur*, see above on *omnis uitae…euersio*. Reid[1] (p. 296) also glosses *sapiens* as *tamquam sapiens sit*; this is incorrect, as Cicero's point depends on the *sapiens* as conceived by the Stoics being meant. For the same reason, I am not attracted by *nobis* (S, as well as early editions) for *uobis*.

§100

Quid enim…probabile uideatur se illuc uenturum esse saluum: for the phrase *ex sententia*, cf. §146:…*qui primum iurare 'ex sui animi sententia' quemque uoluerunt*, but there the sense is that he who takes on oath places a restriction on what he says.

I have translated *sapiens* as 'your sage' since I take Cicero to be contesting an assumption the dogmatists make or are committed to. Reid[1] (p. 296) notes that *Quid enim?* is always followed by another question; see also Kroon (1995: 189) on the use of *enim* in rhetorical questions.

For the Stoic conception of 'reasonable impressions', used to explain such scenarios, see the general note above. Reid[1] (p. 296) notes the thematic similarity with *Anth. Gr.* 11.162 by Nicarchus (first century AD), in which a seer when asked about a safe crossing gives an answer full of hedges:

Εἰς Ῥόδον εἰ πλεύσει, τις Ὀλυμπικὸν ἦλθεν ἐρωτῶν
τὸν μάντιν, καὶ πῶς πλεύσεται ἀσφαλέως.
χὠ μάντις· 'Πρῶτον μέν,' ἔφη, 'καινὴν ἔχε τὴν ναῦν,
καὶ μὴ χειμῶνος, τοῦ δὲ θέρους ἀνάγου.
τοῦτο γὰρ ἂν ποιῇς, ἥξεις κἀκεῖσε καὶ ὧδε,
ἂν μὴ πειρατὴς ἐν πελάγει σε λάβῃ.'

One came to ask the prophet Olympicus if he should take
ship for Rhodes and how to sail there safely. And the prophet said:
'First have a new ship and don't start in winter, but in summer. If you
do this you will go there and back, unless a pirate catches you.'
(transl. Paton)

Evidently scenarios like the ones considered here by Cicero were commonly cited instances of the human inability to anticipate future events completely.

On the use of *si iam* to introduce considerations for the sake of the argument, see Kühner-Stegmann ii.428. Lévy (1992: 5) argues that the example of the sea voyage suggests that the dismissal of the notion that Carneades was a probabilist by Burnyeat (unpublished) needs to be qualified: 'Ce *probabile* est certes un sentiment subjectif, mais il exprime dans la conscience du sujet tous les facteurs physique et humains qui définissent la probabilité objective, statistique.' I explain in Reinhardt (2018a: 234–9) and the introduction (section 6.3) why the totality of the evidence on the Carneadean πιθανόν and on the Ciceronian *probabile* does not suggest that considerations of statistical likelihood account for persuasiveness, even though this modern interpretation can yield plausible readings for *probabilia* relating to similar actions undertaken frequently or even regularly by the same individual ('it is probable that I will arrive safely since I have arrived safely in similar conditions *x* number of times before'); see also the examples referred to in §109a *fin*.

Huius modi igitur uisis…albam ipsam esse ne uideri quidem: the ἀπραξία-argument of §§37–9 is rejected, in that the sage is not condemned to inactivity and is able to act or to refrain from acting, depending on whether his persuasive impressions are impeded or not. Following on from the seafaring example, this appears to be a claim about practical action, although moral action would be explained on the same model; see section 6.1 on πιθανότης depending on coherence within the 'syndrome' of impressions, and Reinhardt (2018a: 249). Reid[1] (p. 296) notes that *facilis* ('amenable', cf. *TLL* s.v. *facilis* col. 62.22–75) with an *ut*-clause is unusual (*TLL* s.v. col. 64.29–30 names only Apul., *Flor.* 12: *dum facile os psittaci uti conformetur* as a parallel), and that a prepositional construction (*ad, in*) with gerund would be standard.

For Anaxagoras' claim that snow is not and does not even appear white, on the grounds that water is black and that snow is frozen water, see Sextus, *P.H.* 1.33 (which is, together with our passage, DK 59A97). Cicero cites him in §72 to point out that Anaxagoras is well respected by the dogmatists, yet is permitted to make counterintuitive claims on the basic of dubious dogmatic convictions. Brittain and Palmer (2001: 51–2) comment on §72: 'We might call this a defensive appeal to Anaxagoras: when confronted by his opponents with the purported absurdity of withholding assent on the most obvious matters, the Academic introduces a figure whose authority his opponents acknowledge and who goes even farther than he himself is willing to in opposing what is supposedly so obvious. The appeal thus serves in a somewhat indirect way the Academics' general position that the senses do not furnish a criterion of truth.' In §100 Cicero turns this into a positive statement: the Academics are more accommodating (*facilior*) than the well-respected Anaxagoras, in that they approve that snow is white, while refraining from assenting to an impression to that effect, which would commit them unqualifiedly.

§101

Et quaecumque res eum sic attinget…mouebitur: since Cicero seems to be speaking generally here rather than about action, *mouebitur* must relate to being moved to follow or to approve, rather than being moved to action. *Res* means 'matter' in a general sense rather than 'object, sc. in the world', but *res* and *uisum* are not 'equivalent' here (*pace* Reid[1] p. 297). On the unimpeded *probabile* see §99:…*si nihil se offeret quod sit probabilitati illi contrarium*, §33, and section 6.5.

Since *mouebitur* is passive, the clause *quaecumque…impeditum* stands in place of an *ablatiuus causae*. The subject of the *ut*-clause is *uisum illud*.

Non enim est e saxo sculptus aut e robore dolatus…cuius modi hoc uerum: see the general note above, and the survey of passages in *Luc.* which speak of the distinctive feature of cataleptic impressions (general note on §§33–34a). With *insignem… propriam percipiendi notam*, cf. §36: *insigne ueri*; §34 init.

Cicero, as a Clitomachean or possibly even paraphrasing Clitomachus, seems to state here without compunction that many truths appear to him, i.e. that he receives many true impressions, albeit with the usual qualification (*neque tamen habere…*); *pace* Reid[1] (p. 297) on *mente…sensibus*, who reads *multa uera* with the Aldina. My reading, however, requires that *uideantur* is a full verb whereas *uideantur* to be understood in the second half of the sentence is an auxiliary (given *habere*). Yet the alternative construal, on which *uera* (pulled forward for emphasis) is a complement to *uideantur* rather than an attribute to *multa*, is discouraged by the wider context: *cuius modi hoc uerum* below refers back to this sentence, and *uerum* there is unqualified. Note also how the present passage ends with the claim that Stoics and Academics see eye to eye as far as false impressions, rather than impressions which appear false, are concerned. Cf. §111, where the question arises if Philo's concern about Antiochus' objection that he was not entitled to claim that there are true and false impressions given his (Philo's) commitment to ἀπαραλλαξία only makes sense if Philo is construed as a mitigated sceptic. I argue ad loc. that the Clitomachean position as articulated in *Acad.* would be as vulnerable to the charge as one of mitigated scepticism, partly on the grounds that in the present passages Cicero as a Clitomachean lays claim to premiss (i) of the core argument.

Mente...sensibus relates to non-perceptual and perceptual impressions, since perceptual impressions are evaluated by the mind, too (within the framework presupposed here).

For the characterization of the sage as conceived by the Academics, cf. Hom., *Od.* 19.163: οὐ γὰρ ἀπὸ δρυός ἐσσι παλαιφάτου οὐδ' ἀπὸ πέτρης, '(But even so, tell me who you are, and the place where you come from); you were not born from any fabulous oak, or a boulder' (transl. Lattimore), which Sextus cites in a similar though not identical context ('suspension of judgement does not leave the sceptic unfeeling, he just does not entertain unhelpful second-order beliefs about the badness of pain') in *M.* 11.161, where he adds the half-line: ἀλλ' ἀνδρῶν γένος ἦεν. Reid[1] (p. 297) overstates the similarity and overreaches when he says that Sextus' passage must come 'from the same Greek source' (similarly Lévy 1992: 175). The line had a broad reception in antiquity; see Watkins (1995: 161–4) on the Greek side, and e.g. Verg., *Aen.* 8.315; Stat., *Th.* 3.560 and 4.340. *Lael.* 48, the second passage in the Ciceronian corpus where the Homeric line is on Cicero's mind, is rather closer to the context in Sextus. Cf. also *Luc.* 141, where Cicero insists that the impression certain arguments make on him is the same as that experienced by Lucullus.

For ἀπαραλλαξία-related expressions involving the phrase *eiusdem modi*, see on §84: *sed si hominum similitudo.*

The fragment containing the reading *robore* is my t. 35. On Lambinus' emendation *habet* for *habere (insignem illam...)*, Plasberg[1] (p. 124) comments: '...sed habere uisa negantur non sapiens.'

Neque nos contra sensus...longeque aliter se habere ac sensibus uideantur: see the previous n. on the possible connection with *Luc.* 111, which responds to §44, in particular (of the Academics): *sumunt...primum, esse quaedam falsa uisa (quod cum uolunt, declarant quaedam esse uera).*

Hoc autem si ita sit...posse sensibus: the issue is the possibility of a single false impression, not that a true impression might be deemed false by the perceiving subject; thus *falsum* is an attribute of *unum* (so my translation) not a complement. *Praesto est* may be, like §99 (*sapiens*) *inducitur*, theatre terminology (cf. Ter., *Phorm.* 51, 267, 561).

Ita nobis tacentibus ex uno Epicuri capite...comprehensio tollitur: with *nobis tacentibus*, cf. §36: *absentibus nobis ueritas se ipsa defendet.* For the term *caput* used of a premiss, see §83 *quattuor sunt capita* (with n.).

Quod est caput Epicuri...'nihil posse percipi': the fact that Epicurean αἰσθήσεις are quite different from Stoic φαντασίαι is glossed over elsewhere, too (cf. §§79, 83). The phrasal term *sensus uisa* cannot signal awareness of this, since it is repeated in the Stoic premiss; rather, the argument is confined to perceptual impressions. The 'conclusion which speaks for itself' may signal that neither an Epicurean nor a Stoic would accept the argument. *Vt taceam* is a purpose clause rather than concessive. Reid[1] (p. 298) notes that, when the subject is personified (like *conclusio* here), *loqui* is preferred to *dicere*. The Aldina and some later editors including Reid re-order to *percipi potest*.

Non concedo, inquit, Epicuro...tibi assentior: the change from second-person address (*uestrum*) to the third person gives the scene a stagy feel. *Assentior alicui aliquid* is not the technical term, and given that the disvowal of assent is not currently at issue, it means no more than 'agree with someone on something' here.

§102

Cicero continues that nothing puzzles him more than that 'those things' (*ista*) are said against the Academics, notably by Antiochus, to whom 'what I said a little earlier' (*quae paulo ante dixi*) was deeply familiar. The latter is a reference to the *probabile*, which allows the sage as the Academic conceives of him to navigate life, as is clarified by what immediately follows. The former relates to claims that a denial of the existence of cataleptic impressions amounts to a profession that one sees and hears nothing (restated as *nihil igitur cernis, nihil audis, nihil tibi est perspicuum* below). Remarks to that effect are made on several occasions by Lucullus; see e.g. §31 *fin.*[383] Criticism for rejecting cataleptic impressions would have been less serious, if what the Academics offer in its place was recognized, namely the *probabile*. But that is not the case.

Nothing is known about the considerations which prompted Antiochus to abandon Academic scepticism and adopt Stoic epistemology, and the only partial comparandum which we have is Philo's relinquishing of Clitomacheanism.[384] Brittain (2012) has made a powerful case for the view that Antiochus' Stoicism was—in the field of epistemology—materially orthodox.[385] What is more, and startling, is that on the evidence of Lucullus' speech Antiochus did not just adopt Stoic doctrines but also the extremist postures which go with it, notably the claim that the Academics deprive human beings of their senses (which was also levelled against Academics in Clitomachus' day, as we learn in §103: *Itaque ait uehementer errare eos*..., and indeed

---

[383] Schäublin et al. (p. 265 n. 294) suggest that *ista* relates to §§37–8, i.e. the ἀπραξία-argument and the suggestion that universal ἐποχή will lead to a complete reversal of life. However, while the charge that the Academics deprive human beings of their senses is made in that passage, Cicero—relying on Clitomachus—will only make the point that human beings can manage without assent in §104. §103, located in between, deals with divisions of impressions and the place of *probabilia*. So it seems preferable to think that *ista* relates to arguments which turn on *probabilia* being unsatisfactory in virtue of their epistemic status and irrespective of assent.

[384] See also on *Luc.* 69–71.

[385] This is compatible with Antiochus having devised a narrative on how he arrived at his views which emphasized Stoic epistemology's origins in Platonic thought.

by Aristo of Chios in the third century BC).³⁸⁶ It seems unlikely that Antiochus could have had a sudden epiphany that the Stoics were right about everything all along, given his nuanced ethical views. If Antiochus' change of opinion came as a result of a gradual acceptance of the notion that there might actually be cataleptic impressions, on which in turn much of what the Stoics call dialectic relies, then one might think that he would have regarded—and presented—the Academic position as second-best and wanting but not as *omnis uitae euersio* (*Luc.* 99). However, there is no evidence of this in Lucullus' speech, which for various reasons ought to be regarded as Antiochus' developed view.³⁸⁷ The Cicero character merely hints at the issue (see the first n. below).

Immediately after the report on Lucullus' claim that the Academics do not see or hear anything, Cicero returns to Clitomachus, evidently to illustrate what it is that the Academics see or hear. §103 reports Clitomachus' views on persuasive impressions, §104 (said to draw on the same work as §103: *quae cum exposuisset adiungit...*) formally deals with assent and approval. Given the similarity of topic, one might wonder if §103 is based on the same work as used earlier, *De sustinendis assensionibus* in four books mentioned in §98b, where book 1 was cited as the source for Carneades' remarks on divisions of impressions. However, the manner in which Cicero indicates here in §102 that he is quoting from a work dedicated to Lucillius suggests that a different work is at issue.³⁸⁸ That two different works of such similar content are cited in close vicinity is made less peculiar by the fact that a third work 'on the same issues' dedicated to L. Censorinus is also mentioned.³⁸⁹ If this is not miscellaneous detail which is added for colour, its implication might be that Romans had been familiar with Academic philosophy for quite some time, so that Lucullus ought to know that he is misrepresenting the Academics. Cicero also provides a brief characterization of his source as an introductory work.

Quamquam nihil mihi tam mirum uidetur...quae paulo ante dixi notissima: for the reference of *ista* and *ea quae paulo ante dixi*, see the general note above. Cicero finds the objection *mirum* ('odd') because he deems it obviously unwarranted, and

---

³⁸⁶ See D.L. 7.163: Πρὸς δὲ τὸν φάμενον Ἀκαδημεικὸν μηδὲν καταλαμβάνειν 'ἆρ' οὐδὲ τὸν πλησίον σου καθήμενον ὁρᾷς;' εἶπεν· ἀρνησαμένου δέ,

τίς ⟨δέ⟩ σ' ἐτύφλωσεν—ἔφη—, τίς ἀφείλετο λαμπάδος αὐγάς;

When some Academic alleged that he apprehended nothing, (Aristo) said: 'Do you not even see the person sitting next to you?' When he denied it, he asked: 'Who can have blinded you? Who robbed you of luminous eyesight?' (transl. Hicks, modified). The second and third questions, which invite the answer 'no one' and allude to Hom. *Od.* 9, is Cratinus frg. 459 Kock = frg. 157 Kassel-Austin.

³⁸⁷ See section 7.2 and 9.3.

³⁸⁸ Von Fritz (1921: 658) also thought that §§103–4 draw on the work dedicated to Lucilius, while *De sustinendis assensionibus*, quoted *uerbatim* in §99, is a different work; similarly Dorandi (1994: 425).

³⁸⁹ Ioppolo (2007: 229–30) suggests that all of §§98b–109 *fin.* is based on Clitomachus' Περὶ ἐποχῆς, 'con alcune interpolazioni di Cicerone' (Sedley 1983a: 26 n. 52, whom Ioppolo cites in support, is concerned with a different issue). However, as indicated, in §103 Cicero is probably using a different work, and from §105b down to 111 Cicero replies to Lucullus' speech (i.e. §§22–44). While this does not preclude the possibility that he draws on Clitomachus in places (e.g. when he likens Carneades to Hercules for extirpating assent in §108), his main focus in §§105–9 is no longer on ἐποχή, which was the subject of the, in my view, two works by Clitomachus which Cicero cites. See also Brittain (2006: 58 n. 148).

thinks that Antiochus ought to be able to appreciate this; the implication is that he acts as if he does not. On *quamquam* used to introduce a main clause see *OLD* s.v. no. 3a.

Licet enim haec quiuis arbitratu suo reprehendant…satis esse uobis: the reproach is *leuior* because the Academics have not left human beings with nothing: they do posit *probabilia*. So do the Stoics, and the reason they are dissatisfied is because of the use to which the Academics put them, and because they feel the can be guided by them without assent (see also Brittain 2006: 60 n. 152). On Stoic πιθανά, see section 6.4. See Reid[1] (p. 298) on *tamen* 'but, putting that aside'; Plasberg[1] (p. 125) on how to structure the sentence.

Ne sit…nihil tibi est perspicuum: *ne sit* is concessive and means '(Granted) it may not be that'; cf. Pinkster i.509–10, who cites *Tusc.* 2.14: *Quare ne sit sane summum malum dolor, malum certe est*. Cf. also *Luc.* 84: *Ne sit sane, uideri certe potest*.

Illa certe… is a restatement of the claims referred to by *ista* at the beginning of the paragraph, cf. §§31, 105a. For Clitomachus see on §17 *init*.

Explicaui paulo ante Clitomacho auctore…sed scriptum est ita: for Clitomachus see on *Luc.* 17. Carneades left no writings, hence his sayings were explained *Clitomacho auctore*; see Görler (1994: 849–51). The reference is to the alternative divisions of 'impression' in §99 *init.*, which Cicero used to make the point that arguments against *perspicuitas* only pertain to the first of them.

Clitomachus' statement on the subject, probably intended to be consistent with Carneades' views, is then quoted from §103 *init*. It would have been easy for Cicero to acknowledge that he is quoting from the same work cited earlier. Instead the reference to the dedication to the satirical poet Lucilius as an identifying property suggests a different work. Lucilius mentions Carneades in 1.31 Marx, transmitted in Lactantius (*Inst.* 5.14.3): an intractable problem could not be solved even if the (notoriously skilled dialectician) Carneades was returned from the Orcus (*…non Carneaden si ipsum Orcus remittat*; Carneades died in 129/8 BC); on the line, see Goh (2018). Büttner (1893: 136–43) has argued that Lucilius was a follower of the Academy, but this seems unwarranted by the evidence.

We also learn that an earlier work on the same subject had been dedicated to Lucius Marcius Censorinus (cos. 149; cens. 147; *RE* s.n. Marcius no. 46). That three Clitomachean works on the same subject are cited is put into context by D.L. 4.67: Clitomachus wrote 'over four hundred books'.

There is no further evidence on these dedications in Cicero or elsewhere. Given that Clitomachus was Carthaginian (§98), that he is known to have written a consolation to his fellow citizens after the destruction of Carthage at the end of the third Punic war in 146 BC, and that Censorinus played a major role in the military campaign (*Tusc.* 3.54), one wonders if the dedication was made some time before 146 BC. Scholars disagree whether Clitomachus accompanied Carneades during the philosophical embassy of 155 BC (cf. *Luc.* 137, where Cicero claims to have read about the subject in a work of Clitomachus'), when Lucilius could have made his acquaintance (Gratwick 1982: 166), or whether Lucilius travelled to Greece and met

Clitomachus there (Cichorius 1908: 11–12, 41). Clitomachus may have chosen to dedicate works on this subject because to him it encapsulated the central idea of Academic scepticism (alongside ἀκαταληψία).

Obbink and Vander Waerdt (1991: 378–9) suggest that Cicero's *prima institutio et quasi disciplina*, glossed by Reid[1] (p. 298) as 'a double rendering of some Greek term', translates σύστημα. If so, it would presumably be a deliberate Clitomachean (and possibly Carneadean) appropriation of a Stoic term; on it, see Bronowski (2019: 49–80). However, the characterization may also be Cicero's, who gives his reasons in parenthesis for why he selected the work in question in particular. While the phrase is general, it encourages the notion that more material in the section from §§99 up to here comes from Clitomachus' work than just the division in §99 *init*. The two terms are juxtaposed also in *Q.fr.* 1.1.19 (= SB 1), where, however, they do not form a unit (*haec institutio atque haec disciplina*).

§103

Drawing on the Clitomachean work dedicated to Lucilius which was mentioned in the previous paragraph, Cicero reports that Clitomachus said that the Academics hold as a view (*placere*) that objective differences between things account for the fact that some impressions appear persuasive while others appear not persuasive. This can be elucidated with reference to Sextus' discussion of Carneades' 'views on the κριτήριον' (*M.* 7.178–9): we form a persuasive impression of Socrates based on his customary qualities (appearance, built, attire, location), whereby all these properties correspond to impressions in a 'syndrome' of impressions which cohere with one another.[390] If Socrates was wearing a new coat, this would presumably make an impression of his unpersuasive. Incidentally, this is further evidence for the fundamental continuity between the account of the Carneadean πιθανόν in Sextus and what Cicero says about the *probabile*. And yet, Cicero continues, that this is so can never mean that there is apprehension of the content of an impression or the state of affairs it represents.[391]

I have discussed elsewhere how Cicero's impression-related terminology allows him to shift perspective between object represented and impression had (of an object);[392] cf. Greek φαινόμενον. Cicero deploys this facility in the present paragraph: the Academics hold that there are differences between things, and that these differences account for the fact that some impressions appear persuasive, while others do not. 'Persuasiveness', being *probabile*, is a property of impressions, not of objects or states of affairs in the world.

Against the background of the remarks on the nature of the *probabile*, Clitomachus rejects the dogmatists' claim that the Academics remove sense perception altogether

---

[390] In the wider context, Sextus also provides evidence to suggest that the clarity of persuasive impression was, in the Carneadean scheme, construed as a function of the perceiving subject's relationship with objects in the world; see section 6.1 and Reinhardt (2018a).

[391] In any event, external world criticism was not a feature of ancient scepticism; see §54 *init*. on the possibility—dismissed as absurd—that one might be dreaming *now*.

[392] See section 10.1.

and that their view on the nature of perceptual impressions commits them to the claim that there is no colour, no taste, and no sound (presumably to be construed as secondary properties attached to suitably generally conceived *res* in the world), which would mean that an Academic's subjective perceptual experience is different from that of the dogmatist (see the general note to §102).

With this compare §111, where Cicero in his Clitomachean persona claims to be entitled to holding that there are true and false impressions, i.e. to being able to discriminate between them, with the same caveat as is made here that a feature which marked out the object of the impression as securely apprehended, or the impression as enabling such apprehension, did not exist.[393] *Probabilia* are impressions which appear true.

The Clitomachean position, also referred to as radical scepticism, is in the scholarship usually associated with dialectical or ad hominem argumentation, as well as a corresponding interpretation of Carneadean argumentative practice. By contrast, the Cicero character in *Acad.* (and arguably elsewhere in the Ciceronian corpus, see section 8) clearly feels entitled to 'approve' impressions (in the technical sense at issue in *Luc.* 104) and to hold views which result from approval (§109 *fin.*). It is to be noted that the material rendered in the present paragraph does not give the impression of having the status of a dialectical alternative to a Stoic division of impressions (note the use of *placere*); in that respect it seems comparable to e.g. the Pyrrhonist explanation of the kind of δόγμα the sceptic holds or is permitted to hold. This suggests that Cicero's Clitomachean *persona* is rooted in Clitomachean writings, which would either require a distinction between two types of Clitomacheanism or a reinterpretation of Clitomacheanism, such that its hallmark would no longer be dialectical or ad hominem argumentation.[394] Any philosopher, dogmatist or sceptic, will of course argue dialectically on occasion, and a more nuanced reconstruction of the patterns of the use of this mode of argument may be required to characterize Clitomachus' posture and strategies with precision.

Lucullus' speech is primarily directed at the Clitomachean position, or perhaps a version of it, but occasionally targets a position of mitigated scepticism, too; it is explicitly not directed at the Roman Books view. If it is not misguided to look at *Acad.* in terms of underlying sources, then a desire to avoid multiplying unknowns *praeter necessitatem* would lead one to conclude that Antiochus' developed view, as exhibited in Lucullus' speech, was formulated at a time when Philo's position was the kind of Clitomacheanism in evidence in *Acad.* This would be consistent with the assumption that mitigated scepticism was never the official view of the Academy, let alone for a longer period like all of the 90s BC, and with the assumption that Antiochus seceded from the Academy in the 90s.[395] If the material for Lucullus' speech postdated the Roman Books and was directed at Clitomacheanism because Antiochus took it to be the main form of Academic scepticism, then one would have

---

[393] Numenius frg. 27.19–32 Des Places (see appendix 2) suggests that Carneades did not actually accept the distinction between true impressions but conceded it to the Stoics in order to gain the upper hand in the debate.
[394] On the second option, see Castagnoli (2019).
[395] See on §§69–71 and 78; section 8 *fin.*

to assume either that Cicero's speech does not draw on a source in a sustained way or that Philo reverted to the kind of Clitomacheanism we find in *Acad.* after the failure of the Roman Books (yet there is no evidence that Philo replied to the *Sosus*). Another possibility is, of course, that Cicero used sources much more freely and that we cannot glimpse the philosophical outlook of these sources on the basis of either Lucullus' or Cicero's speech.[396]

Academicis placere...aliae contra: see the general note above. In the work which Cicero translates here, Clitomachus was evidently ready to speak about views of the Academics in general, rather than just Carneades' as in the earlier report. This need not imply that the views of the Academics differed from Carneades' on Clitomachus' view—Clitomachus may have distinguished between direct quotations and paraphrases, summaries, or faithful interpretations.

The use of *contra* in *aliae contra* is standard, but the expression is ambiguous as to whether *probabilia* are contrasted with their contrary (cf. *Fin.* 3.50) or their contradictory (cf. *Part. or.* 17); §99 *non probabilia* meant the latter, and the two passages should be read so as to be consistent.

Id autem non esse satis...perceptum et cognitum possit esse: the last clause features as premiss (ii) of the core argument in §83. Clitomachus addresses the question of why *probabilia* cannot be identified as cataleptic impressions: many *probabilia* are false, and false impressions cannot be apprehended. This would theoretically leave room for a sub-class of *probabilia* to be cataleptic impressions (as a Stoic division might have it), but ἀπαραλλαξία, referred to at the end of the paragraph, precludes this possibility, too. Note that Clitomachus has no compunction to speak of false impressions outside of a dialectical context; see the general note above, and cf. §§101, 111.

Itaque, ait, uehementer errare eos...ueri et certi notam: *ait*, sc. *Clitomachus*. The claim regarding the abolition of the senses (see on §102) sits naturally next to the ἀπραξία-charge, which gave rise to Carneades' initially dialectical formulation of the πιθανόν according to Sextus, *M.* 7.166 (cf. *Luc.* 99). For an earlier Academic response to the ἀπραξία-charge, see section 7.5.

Cicero ends with a forceful assertion that *probabilia* will never have the distinctive feature supposedly peculiar to cataleptic impression. The unusually full formulation is in keeping with the point functioning as an interim conclusion here, before Cicero moves on to the issue of approval, i.e. the manner of acceptance Academics are permitted. Note how the Zenonian definition is referenced through the notions of truth [clause 1 and 2], peculiarity [= clause 2], and certainty [clause 3]. The formulation is slightly redundant in that *propriam* gestures to the third clause, as does *et certi*; no material difference from §35 *certa et propria nota* can be intended.

With the expression which claims no attachment of a *nota* to the properties listed earlier in the sentence (*aut colorem aut saporem aut sonum*), cf. *Luc.* 57 *res...quas*

---

[396] These possibilities are weighed in section 9.3.

non habeat dinotatas and *Ac.* 1.41...*propriam quandam declarationem earum rerum quae uiderentur*: the distinguishing feature is not conceived as something that can be observed independently of an impression's content. Rather, it would manifest itself in the manner in which it represents the object and its properties. See also the general note on *Luc.* 33–34a for Cicero's *nota*-terminology.

With the remark about properties cf. also §105 for a statement to the same effect, but in Cicero's own voice; and t. 13 (Nonius p. 162 M.) from the second book of the second edition.

See Hofmann-Szantyr p. 438 on the *constructio ad sensum* of *Academia...a quibus*; Reid[1] (p. 299) on the adversative asyndeton of *illud*.

§§104–105a

In this section Cicero formally introduces the so-called distinction between assent and approval.[397] He does this indirectly, by distinguishing two senses of the sentence 'the sage withholds assent.' The distinction was presumably made by Carneades, and Cicero's account is based on Clitomachus' explanation of it. This section concludes the close report from the work dedicated to Lucilius (cf. §102).

The larger argumentative context to which the distinction belongs is the various Academic responses to the ἀπραξία-charge (see on *Luc.* 37–9);[398] a different Academic response to the same charge is attested in *Luc.* 148, viz. self-aware assent. The two passages need to be considered alongside each other in any event even though there is disagreement among scholars about their exact relationship.[399]

An interpretation of the passage should accommodate the following considerations (see the nn. below for details):[400]

(i) As is clear from the correspondence between *ut aut **approbet** quid aut improbet* and *neque tamen omnia eius modi uisa **approbari** sed ea quae nulla re impedirentur* below, *approbare* (approve) is something that the Academic sage does, not something he refrains from.

(ii) In giving approval and when he approves, the Academic sage withholds assent (e.g. *qui de omnibus rebus contineat se ab assentiendo...dum sine assensu*).

(iii) The two ways of saying yes/no in Latin which occur in the passage (*ut neque neget aliquid neque aiat*; *aut 'etiam' aut 'non' respondere possit*) are not equivalent. The former denotes a definitive yes/no, while *etiam* may be described grammatically as an incomplete affirmative (see n.).

---

[397] Substantial discussions include Hirzel (1883: 162–7); Frede (1987b); Long and Sedley (i.1987: 454–5) and (ii.1987: 449–50); Bett (1990); Striker (1996b: 98, 110–13); Burnyeat (1997: 300–9); Brittain (2001: 74–6); Görler (2004c: 287); Obdrzalek (2006); Ioppolo (2007) and (2017); Thorsrud (2012: 142–5).
[398] See e.g. Burnyeat (1997: 302); Vogt (2010a: 170–1).
[399] See also the commentary on §148.
[400] Cf. Long and Sedley (ii.1987: 450) on the Latin text from *quae cum exposuisset*: 'The general sense of the Latin is easier to make out than some of the linguistic details.'

(iv) The contrast between *placere* and *tenere* in *alterum placere...alterum tenere* is one between accepting a rule of some kind in theory and accepting it in practice. *Alterum...alterum* is due to the fact that here Cicero is talking about two different senses of the rule in question, i.e. 'the sage withholds assent' taken as a normative statement. (This leaves open a number of possibilities of how the distinction between theory and practice is to be conceived of and articulated.)

(v) What the highlighted explicative *ut*-clause in *altero, cum se a respondendo,* **ut aut approbet quid aut improbet***, sustineat, ut neque neget aliquid neque aiat* explicates is not entirely obvious (note: text given as transmitted). It could explicate *respondendo*, in which case 'the Academic sage refrains from *approbare* (and *improbare*)' would be one of the two senses of 'the Academic sage withholds assent'. Alternatively, it could explicate the whole of *a respondendo sustineat*, so that the sentence would translate 'in the other sense (it is said that the sage withholds assent) when he checks himself from responding in such a way that (sc. in checking himself from responding) he either approves or disapproves, so that he says neither "yes" nor "no" definitively.' On this reading, expressing approval or disapproval is a checking oneself from responding, which would be acceptable if *respondere* had a strong sense of being the response of the Stoic sage. It is, however, used below (in *aut 'etiam' aut 'non' respondere possit* and *respondere possimus sequentes tantum modo, quod ita uisum sit, dum sine assensu*) of the Academic's response.

If one appreciates (iv) and (v) but not (i)–(iii), then *Luc.* 104–5 *init.* may appear to introduce three different forms of acceptance: the two which are distinguished indirectly in the course of setting out two senses of 'the sage withholds assent', and the one which features in the positive characterization of what the sage does. Such a reading of the passage has been adopted by Plasberg[1] (p. 126) in the apparatus ('*scilicet non omnino a respondendo se sustinet sed ab his duobus generibus*'), by Frede (1987b: 215), and by Obdrzalek (2006: 264–5).

However, as per (i) above, it would be unfortunate if Cicero had used the same terminology to characterize assent which is withheld in the second sense and the kind of acceptance which the Academic sage can exercise, and it seems desirable to opt for a reading of the passage which does not require this assumption. Hence most scholars assume instead that there are only two types of acceptance in play in 104–5 *init.*, but at the same time want to hold that *ut aut approbet quid aut improbet* explicates *respondendo* (cf. v). These interpreters try to achieve their desired result by construing the *placere...tenere* contrast in such a way that the first term means 'to adopt as a dogma' (sc. in a suitably qualified sense), used of the policy of assent withheld, while *tenere* is rendered as 'to hang on to', used of approval (*approbare*);[401] this is hard to reconcile with (ii) and (iii) above and would make the second *ut*-clause (*ut neque neget aliquid neque aiat*) redundant.

A reading of the passage which acknowledges that approving or disapproving is something the Academic sage does *and* a way of withholding assent has so far only

---

[401] See e.g. the translations by Long and Sedley (1987) and Brittain (2006); Striker (2010: 200), who cites Brittain.

been advanced by Burnyeat (1997: 300–4).⁴⁰² In his case, however, it is unclear how the interpretation is to be extracted from the standard Latin text, which he accepts. There are two conceivable ways to achieve this sense. The first is to assume that *ut aut adprobet quid aut inprobet* explicates the whole of *a respondendo sustineat* (cf. v). The second *ut*-clause—*ut neque neget aliquid neque aiat*—would on this reading restate for clarity that approval and disapproval are deemed to be ways of withholding assent ('qualified non-assent', as Burnyeat 1998: 304 puts it), and it would add a rider similar to the two clauses/phrases in (ii) above. What the Academic sage does when he says 'yes' to an impression would twice be characterized as *approbare*. But Burnyeat's translation shows that he does not opt for this reading. The second way of achieving this sense would be to emend to *a respondendo…⟨non⟩ sustineat* while assuming that *ut aut adprobet quid aut inprobet* explicates *respondendo* only. The translation would then be: '…in the other sense (it is said that the sage withholds assent) when he does not check himself from responding in such a way that he either approves or disapproves, so that he says neither "yes" nor "no" definitively.' With this text, the Academic sage does give, or rather not withhold, a response of approval or disapproval, which is, however, given the second *ut*-clause, still a way of withholding assent. It would be easy to explain how *non* might have dropped out here: it may well have baffled a thinking scribe that giving a response of approval or disapproval is supposed to be a way of saying neither 'yes' nor 'no'. Nor can mechanical corruption be ruled out: after capital scripts dropped out of use, *non* would have been represented as a small *n* topped by an abbreviation mark. On this reading the Academic responds by not withholding approval or disapproval while withholding assent. No contortions on the sense (or use) of *respondere* would be required.

To return to (iv) above, one can now see how *tenere* can mean following a policy of assent withheld in line with the parallels for *placere/tenere* and yet secure the notion of approval for the Academics (cf. i). According the *diuisio* in play here is this one, 'the sage withholds assent' has two senses, 'the sage withholds assent completely' and 'the sage withholds assent but approves or disapproves'.

That 'approval or disapproval' is a type not of assent but of non-assent is an insight which can be brought to bear on Bett's influential article about Carneades' distinction between assent and approval (Bett 1990). He contends that human attitudes to action-guiding impressions can be placed on a spectrum which he characterizes in the following way (Bett 1990: 10–11):

(1) A person takes a left turn, while en route to a certain house. The action is intentional but is not the result of any conscious deliberation.

(2) The person is not familiar with the route. She wonders whether to take a left turn, in light of evidence afforded by her map, prominent landmarks, etc.; having considered the matter, she takes the left turn. In doing so, she thinks to herself 'it seems to me plausible that this is the route'; she does not think to herself 'Yes; this really is the right way to go.'

---

⁴⁰² Ioppolo (2007: 267 n. 94) professes agreement with Burnyeat on the point that approval is 'qualified non-assent', but claims in her interpretation of *Luc.* 104 (p. 232) that Clitomachus rejects the second kind of suspension of judgement ('Clitomaco accoglie il primo modo e respinge il secondo e ne spiega le ragioni').

(3) The same as in (2), except that she does think to herself 'Yes; this really is the right way to go' (and not, or not only, 'it seems to me plausible that this is the route').

Based on this set of scenarios, Bett proceeds to argue that Carneades's distinction was designed to criticise the Stoic notion of assent as too broad, on the grounds that it included cases like (1) and (2) as well as, of course, (3) under 'assent' when actually Stoic assent ought to be confined to (3).[403] And having developed this argument in the abstract, Bett then finds support for it in our passage, with its statement that 'the sage withholds assent' is ambiguous. Bett suggests that Carneades took the Stoic notion of assent and divided it into assent as the Stoics ought to construe it on the one hand, and approval on the other.

One problem with this analysis is that, as shown above, there is no division of non-assent into complete non-assent (see also n. on *uno modo, cum hoc intelligatur, omnino eum rei nulli assentiri*) and non-approval or approval withheld in *Luc.* 104–5 *init*. Only this, however, would be the division whose positive counterpart is a division of assent as the Stoics do define it into assent as the Stoics ought to define it on the one hand and approval on the other. Bett's interpretation is not compatible with the evidence of 104–5 *init*.

However, the three scenarios are nonetheless convenient for exploring where the disagreement between the Stoics and Carneades is likely to have been situated. The scenarios arguably run together two issues to whose distinctness Carneades would have been sensitized by e.g. Stoic theory, with which he was deeply familiar: the question of whether we regard or treat impressions, action-triggering or factual, as true or persuasive, and the question of whether our reaction to these impressions is explicit and conscious or not. Bett argues that in situations like (1) the Stoics posit that assent must have been given for the perceiver to act in a certain way, a claim which Carneades would be likely to question, since he does not subscribe to the Stoic theory of action and the theory of mind it employs; rather, the argument continues, only when we consciously and explicitly accept something as true can we be said to assent in the proper sense. It is according to Bett only in cases of type (3) that explicitness of assent and acceptance of an impression as true simultaneously obtain for Carneades, which is why Carneades suggests that 'assent' be applied to such cases only.[404] One might reply that everyday experiences can also be invoked to make sense of the notion of non-explicit assent which involves taking an impression as true. That being so, there is no need to suspect, in particular, Carneades' refusal to accept the obscure descriptions of mental events of Stoic philosophy of mind as his motivation. If, to employ an example which Sextus uses when reporting on Carneades' views (*M.* 7.187–8), one enters a dark room, glimpses a coiled rope on

---

[403] Later Bett (1990: 14) recasts the three scenarios as a twofold distinction: 'There are, on the one hand, (A) cases where people do explicitly commit themselves, with greater or less conviction, to the truth of certain propositions (both practical and theoretical ones). There is, on the other hand, (B) a great range of cases in which no such explicit commitment takes place. Very often, people simply act without thinking; and even when they do deliberate about what they do, they will often draw their conclusions in a tentative, non-committal fashion (as in example (2) above).'

[404] While it is easy to agree that in cases like (3) the explicitness of assent and one's regarding of the impression in question as true coincide, it is less easy to see why the connection between the two should be necessary.

the floor, mistakes it for a snake, and jumps into the air as a consequence, then no conscious decision need have been involved, but the fact that one jumped could be seen as evidence that one really thought there was a snake on the floor, as opposed to e.g. entertaining a hypothetical belief to that effect (see below).[405] Regarding scenario (2), the Stoics themselves would have classified the final decision about the right way as an act of assent, viz. as assent to an impression that it is reasonable that this is the right way (see on §100). As far as the explicitness of approval is concerned, I would assume, in the absence of evidence to the contrary, that the Academics would want, as an argumentative option, exactly the same spectrum of options as that posited for Stoic assent: conscious and deliberate endorsement as the paradigm case, with implicit endorsement as a possibility.[406]

Approval conferred upon *probabilia* is in fact characterized positively in our passage.[407] There are arguably three different clues regarding its nature. Two of these represent Cicero's attempts to elucidate the concept using the resources of the Latin language, while one allows us to glimpse behind the Latin text an illustration which Clitomachus must have used in the text from which Cicero worked. First, there are the compounds *approbare* and *improbare*, whose *uerbum simplex* had been used earlier in the text to characterize a Clitomachean acceptance of an impression (see esp. §67).[408] By themselves, these terms do of course have a fairly broad application, but given that Cicero quite specifically aligns the attitude the sceptic takes to impressions with that of judges to the verdicts they pass as something *quod uidetur* to them (*Luc.* 146), and given that this very usage occurs here in *Luc.* 105 *init.* in a contrasting comparison of the Academic and the Stoic attitude to impressions, it seems legitimate to ask how *approbare* and *improbare* are used in legal contexts. Some of these uses are linked to the actions of judges. Typical applications in this field are to the admission of individuals as witnesses and to the acceptance of documents connected with a lawsuit. These uses are suggestive of a rational process, of the verification of compliance with certain formal criteria, which is, however, by its nature divorced from the realities which underlie a case or to which a legal document refers, of which the judge does not have direct knowledge and could obtain it only with great difficulty or not at all. Another application is connected with the final approval of a craftsman's job by the person who commissioned it. Here one can judge, so to speak, the outward appearance, the basic functionality etc., but one cannot really be certain if every part of the e.g. well to be constructed has been executed with the same care and attention, and one will not know until something goes wrong if there has been a problem all along.[409] This would be consistent with what we learn from Sextus about

---

[405] See Brennan (2005: 59): 'When we assent to an impression, we swing the whole weight of our actions and beliefs behind it, like jumping to grab a rope that will rescue us from a balcony. From there out, unless we reconsider it, we will act as though that impression is solid and reliable, and will make plans based on it. Not assenting, or withholding assent, by contrast, means not endorsing, not jumping.'

[406] So also Obdrzalek (2006: 263).

[407] *Probabilia* are rationally persuasive items like Carneadean πιθανά (see sections 6.1 and 6.5): they are the kind of items rational agents would regard as deserving of approval, because they exhibit no inconsistency with concurrent *probabilia* or with antecedent beliefs, and in addition no unclarity in the case of perceptual *probabilia*.

[408] *Probare* and compounds must have been introduced in some form in the *Catulus*.

[409] See the lemmatized nn. below for detail.

the scrutiny to which πιθανά are subjected according to Carneades, and also with his distinction of two different σχέσεις of a presentation (*M.* 7.168–9), one turning on the relation between object and presentation, according to which an impression is true or false, and one on that between presentation and the perceiving subject, according to which an impression is apparently true or apparently false.[410] The Academic is concerned with the latter and does not firmly pronounce on the former.

Second, the two ways of saying 'yes' and 'no'. As indicated above, *etiam*, which amounts to saying 'yes' understood as approval, is either used as weak affirmative or as an incomplete affirmative; the evidence on the former use is hard to pin down but consistent with the third point to be discussed below, while the latter use is better documented (see n. below). *Etiam* as an incomplete affirmative, one which suggests that the speaker's positive response is not the last word on a subject, would fit with a feature of the Carneadean πιθανόν: that, however much it has been scrutinized, it is still open to revision at any point if new information becomes available.[411]

Third, approval is compared to saying 'yes' in a dialectical exchange by question and answer (*interrogati in utramque partem respondere possimus*). As I have argued elsewhere,[412] it emerges from Aristotle's *Top.* that dialectical exchanges can only work if the propositions used in them owe their status not to being backed by authority of one kind or another (although they will be backed by authority), but to appearing true on rational grounds, which means that they cohere with other propositions which appear true to us, possibly imply them or are implied by them, possibly make them more intelligible, and so on. At the same time, it is the exception, only briefly considered by Aristotle, rather than the norm, that the propositions which we accept in a dialectical exchange are what we personally hold to be true and in that sense our beliefs (consider *Top.* Θ5, 159b25–9 against the wider context in Θ5).[413] Normally, the propositions involved in a dialectical exchange appear true to us on the grounds cited above, without us therefore judging them to be true or accepting them as true as we would if we assented to them. What distinguishes them from beliefs is the dialectician's attitude of detachment: he brings his rational faculties to bear on them, and on their relationship with other propositions, but without making them thereby 'his' beliefs. This, however, does not mean that, as far as the explicitness of approval is concerned, giving approval means a passive acquiescing as in scenario (1) formulated by Bett (see above): the respondent in a dialectical exchange has to answer, quite explicitly, 'yes' or 'no' for the exchange to proceed (see below). Arriving at the answer is a conscious, rational process, not an unconscious process whose outcome one can explain after the event.[414] This is not to say that there cannot be unconscious rational approval; rather, as with dogmatic assent the descriptive perspective chosen, and the paradigm case, is conscious and deliberate approval.

---

[410] See on §103 regarding the extent to which Clitomachus permits objective differences between things in the world to influence the persuasiveness of impressions thereof.
[411] See Allen (1994: 97–8).
[412] See Reinhardt (2015).
[413] See also Smith (1997: 132) and Brunschwig (2007: 284–5) ad loc.
[414] Contrast Ioppolo (2007: 232, cf. p. 260): 'Condizione di una vita razionale infatti è la capacità di *giustificare* le proprie azioni rispondendo positivamente o negativamente, se interrogati. Questa pretesa si fonda sul fatto che esistono rappresentazioni tali che *inducono* ad agire e altre che *inducono* a rispondere, se interrogati, seguendo ciò che appare probabile a ognuno' (my emphasis).

The first point on *approbare* might seem to pose a problem, though. Is there not a sense in which a judge who passes a verdict thereby expresses a belief or beliefs? If that was so, one would have to wonder if legal *approbare* would not be a better illustration for the mitigated position rather than the Clitomachean one (assuming that a belief involves, as per the standard conception, taking something to be true).[415] Yet, although there is unfortunately no ancient text which problematizes the matter, it seems entirely conceivable that a judge's verdict was construed to be the result of his having discharged his, among others, epistemic duties appropriately without thereby amounting to an expression of his belief. Indeed, one could argue *e contrario* that in *Luc.* the author Cicero is quite clear about the difference between the Clitomachean and the mitigated position, and that he, whose character 'Cicero' is himself a Clitomachean, refers to the pronouncements of judges for illustration, must have had such a reading in mind.[416]

The recognition that approval is a way of not assenting or happens under suspension is likely to influence one's view on the relationship between the Clitomachean position and the mitigated one, according to which the Academic sage does assent and form opinions. There are two views which merit consideration. On the first, both positions were initially advanced dialectically by Carneades at different points in time, and some Academics unlike Clitomachus adopted the mitigated position.[417] On the second, the two positions represent different interpretations of an initial Carneadean distinction between two kinds of assent.[418] That approval is a species of non-assent here in §104 would seem to tell against the second possibility. Moreover, in the absence of positive evidence to support this view, positing a third, original form of weaker acceptance alongside approval and self-aware assent (cf. *Luc.* 148) for Carneades would complicate the picture *praeter necessitatem*.

---

[415] See Schwitzgebel (2019).

[416] Roman legal texts from the early and high Empire do not usually, partly as a function of their literary format, engage in theorizing the actions of a judge, but in the following extract from *Ep.* 77.11 Ambrosius of Milan expounds John 5:30: 'I can do nothing on my own; as I hear, I judge' in the light of his own experiences as a judge: *Non possum a me facere quidquam; iustitia in iudicando, non potentia est in iudicando. Ego non iudico, sed facta tua de te iudicant: ipsa te accusant, et ipsa condemnant. Leges te adiudicant, quas iudex non conuerto, sed custodio....Secundum quod audio, iudico, non secundum quod uolo; et ideo iudicium meum uerum est, quia non uoluntati indulgeo, sed aequitati* 'I can do nothing on my own; justice is what lies in the giving of judgements, not power. I do not judge you, your own actions pass judgement on you; they accuse you and they condemn you. The laws sit in judgement on you, which I as a judge do not adapt but safeguard.... I judge according to what I hear, not according to my own will; and thus my judgement is just [lit. true], because I do not act in accordance with my wishes but with what is right.' On the passage, see Harries (1989: 216–17), whose translation I have quoted. See also Daube (1956: 77): 'It is an interesting paradox that a judgement, with its caution and moderation, enjoys a higher degree of recognition than the censor's unqualified verdict. The finding 'he appears to have done so and so' is objective, the person of the judge has nothing to do with it. Within its self-imposed limits, it is essentially of permanent validity. By contrast, the statement 'You have done so and so' expresses the censor's personal view. It contains no reservations, it claims more than is necessarily warranted. But it is essentially valid only for the period of the *lustrum*.'

[417] Thus Burnyeat (1997: 306); Brittain (2006: xxviii). Burnyeat thought that the mitigated position was held by Philo at one point, while Brittain associated it with Philo and Metrodorus. In this commentary I recognize the existence of the mitigated position but hold that neither Philo nor Metrodorus can plausibly be associated with it (see on *Luc.* 78).

[418] Thus Frede (1987b: 213–15).

According to the passage under discussion the Clitomachean position posits that the Academic sage does not have beliefs (assuming that belief requires taking something to be so, to be true). If it involves approval and hypothetical beliefs (a notion which represents one way of conceptualizing what an Academic sage ends up with having given approval), then these are at best assent of a kind and beliefs of kind respectively—which are in certain respects comparable to assent and belief without being species of either.[419]

The possibility that an act of approval leaves the Academic sage with a hypothetical belief has been considered by various scholars,[420] and it has been noted that for both this view and for the mitigated position Carneades would have been able to invoke passages from Platonic dialogues for illustration.[421] Yet while the notion of a hypothetical belief is intelligible and unproblematic, it is less clear that someone could only have hypothetical beliefs, or that larger numbers of interconnected hypothetical beliefs could be entertained without being set against a background of genuine beliefs. This is arguably what the model of a scientist working on the basis of or investigating a hypothesis would suggest.[422] One could devise a model of human cognitive behaviour which is responsive in the sense that any belief, i.e. anything that passes for a belief within the confines of the model for the time being, could be problematized and have its hypothetical nature raised to consciousness, but our Clitomachean evidence gives out on this point.

Clitomachean approval has sometimes been compared with Pyrrhonist εὐδοκεῖν, the mode of acceptance by which the latter acquires what Sextus calls δόγματα in P.H. 1.13. While the question of how Sextus' view is to be understood is itself contentious, I only state here that in my view Carneadean πιθανά qua rationally persuasive impressions are different from Sextan φαινόμενα (see section 6.1), both intrinsically and with respect to what kind of contents are permitted for πιθανά (e.g. philosophical views), and that approval, conceived as saying 'yes' in a dialectical exchange where what appears true is at stake, is quite different from εὐδοκεῖν.[423]

§104 is continuous, including as a translation or close report, with §103, which spoke of Academics' views (*placere*). As has been recognized,[424] the section thus gives the appearance of an explanation of the Academics' approach as opposed to a 'dialectical' response to the ἀπραξία-charge which comes without endorsement and is offered to the dogmatist as a mere alternative to his own account of human behaviour. This tells against reducing Clitomacheanism to ad hominem argument and against viewing it as a mere extension of Carneadean argumentative practice.[425] The Cicero character, in *Acad.* and beyond, feels entitled to 'own' approval in any case.

---

[419] Contrast Brittain (2001: 16 n. 23, 270). See also Striker (1996b: 112–13) on why the difference between the Clitomachean and the mitigated position is not merely verbal.
[420] Roughly, someone who has the hypothetical belief that *p* treats *p* as if it was true.
[421] See Vogt (2010: §3.2, sub-section iii) and the commentary on §148.
[422] See e.g. Perin (2010: 148–50).
[423] A summary of the discussion about εὐδοκεῖν is in Morison (2019: §3.4).
[424] See Brittain (2001: 270).
[425] Ioppolo (2017) offers an overall interpretation of what it meant for Clitomachus to 'follow the probable'. The article builds on substantial earlier studies of hers and offers interpretations of *Luc.* 98–108, 104–5, as well as of Sextus' report on the Carneadean πιθανόν in *M.* 7.166–89 (see section 6 of the introduction). I note some major points of disagreement here and add further detail in the lemmatized nn.:

Quae cum exposuisset...assensus sustinere sapientem: in §103 Cicero had rejected the suggestion that the Academics do away with the senses and their objects completely, insisting that what impressions lacked was a mark of truth. From this he naturally proceeds to two ways of withholding assent, the second of which amounts to approval. Cicero's formulation suggests that he is drawing on his source continuously, but we have no way of knowing if he used Clitomachus directly or a source which itself used Clitomachean works. The Greek for *assensus sustinere* is plain ἐπέχειν, not συγκατάθεσιν ἐπέχειν, as already Reid[1] (p. 299) noted. Cicero does not use *sustinere* absolutely, i.e. without an object. (More material on assent terminology in the commentary on §94.) Hirzel (1883: 168 n. 1) was troubled by the occurence of *assensus* in the superordinate term of the *diuisio*, and the suggestion by Bett (1990) that Clitomachus intended to divide Stoic assent as it was conceived into Stoic assent as it should be conceived and approval (see above), is partly prompted by it. Passages on the Academic sage used as a construct in dialectical arguments are discussed in Neuhausen (1987). For the use of *dupliciter dicere* in connection with ambiguity, cf. e.g. Cic., *Tusc.* 4.17; Reid[1] (p. 299) on the tense pattern *exposuisset...adiungit*.

Vno modo, cum hoc intellegatur, omnino eum rei nulli assentiri: on the interpretation given above, acts of non-assent in the second sense below are *instances* of non-assent in the sense at issue here. Bett (1990: 15) translates *omnino eum rei nulli assentiri* as 'not giving one's entire assent to anything', taking *omnino* with *assentiri* rather than *rei nulli* (p. 20 n. 32). However, *omnino* typically goes with the negation or negative phrase in such contexts (see Hofmann-Szantyr p. 453; Orlandini 2005: 170–2; Wackernagel 2009: 744). See also *qui de omnibus rebus contineat se ab assentiendo* below (n.), which arguably speaks to the matter; Burnyeat (1997: 302 n. 63).

Altero, cum se a respondendo, ut aut approbet quid aut improbet, ⟨non⟩ sustineat, ut neque neget neque aiat: on the insertion of *non* and on how to read the text coherently if one does not want to insert *non*, see the general note above. Davies proposed to delete *ut aut approbet quid aut inprobet*, on the grounds that neither sense nor style required it; this suggestion has not found favour with more recent scholars but was adopted by Lévy (1992: 269 n. 80), who explains: 'Carnéade accepte

---

(i) Ioppolo argues that one can discern significant differences between the πιθανόν-schema as reported in Sextus and the references to the *probabile* in the Clitomachean section *Luc.* 98–108. More generally, she assumes that Carneadean and Clitomachean thinking came apart in non-trivial ways (p. 210). My account above (and in section 6) assumes that the Sextan and the Ciceronian account can be reconciled, that the former is not at variance with Clitomachean thinking and may actually go back to a Clitomachean source (which has been modified so as to make the schema sound more dogmatic), and that ancient evidence claiming that Clitomachus was faithful in recording Carneadean thought is to be believed. (ii) Ioppolo takes *Luc.* 104, on the two ways of suspending judgement, to be concerned with Clitomachus' theory of action exclusively. I take it to be concerned with theory of action as well as responses to philosophical claims. This issue largely turns on how one interprets *Luc.* 104 *interrogati in utramque partem* and whether one takes *Luc.* 104 to align with *Luc.* 32: *Volunt enim...probabile aliquid esse et quasi ueri simile, eaque se uti regula et in agenda uita et in quaerendo ac disserendo*. (iii) Ioppolo regards 'following' and 'approval' as a 'passively adhering' (p. 216) to what appears in the 'phenomenological sense' (p. 209). I have explained in section 6 why I think that for the Academics persuasive impressions are persuasive primarily in virtue of their propositional content, and above why I think that approval is mischaracterized as passive adhering (or acquiescing or 'mere going along with').

la suspension totale de l'assentiment, mais refuse la seconde interpétation de l'ἐποχή, qui impliquerait de sa part l'aphasie.' As indicated above, I take Clitomachus to embrace rather than reject the second type of non-assent. With *respondendo* compare *respondere* (twice explicitly, and implied in other places) below. The second *ut*-clause makes it plain that approval happens under the proviso of assent withheld. On *nego/ aio* as the '*absolute* "no" and "yes"', see Reid[1] (p. 300), as definitive declarations either of opinion or intent made in the course of legal procedures, see Lévy-Bruhl (1932) and Manthe (2002). Cf. Aug., *Contra Acad.* 3.4.9, which appears to be informed by the counterpart to the present passage in *Ac.* 4, as Hagendahl (1967: 65–6) notes.

Id cum ita sit…alterum tenere: does *tenere* mean 'to hang on to' (sc. the opposite of the second sense of 'to withhold assent'; cf. *OLD* s.v. 13a) or does it mean 'to keep, observe (rules, etc.)' (cf. *OLD* s.v. 15c)? It cannot mean the former, given that the text explicitly describes approval as occurring while assent is withheld (ii above); on the latter sense see also Gawlick and Görler (1994: 1111–12). On *placere* and *tenere* to refer to the adoption of a general principle in two slightly different ways, see also Burnyeat (1997: 302 n. 66).

Vt sequens probabilitatem, ubicumque haec aut occurrat aut deficiat, aut 'etiam' aut 'non' respondere possit: that '*following*' *probabilitas* is here equated with replying *etiam* precludes the possibility that the Academic acquiesces in *probabilia*, at least if that is meant to involve an impassive going-along-with; even if the endorsement given to a *probabile* is qualified in the manner characterized above, this places no restriction on the explicitness or force of the acceptance. The verb *sequi* by itself can be used of acceptance upon careful consideration like the English 'to follow (sc. someone else's view)' in legal contexts. See the collection of synonyms and related terms in Striker (1996b: 98 n. 23).

Etiam as an affirmative puzzled Thesleff (1960: 35), given its semantic weakness. Occurrences in comedy and Cicero's letters, where there are frequent fictional exchanges between Cicero and the addressee, suggest that *etiam* is weak not in terms of the endorsement it signals ('I suppose so') but because it is incomplete: *etiam* is typically used as an initial positive response to a question which either prompts the interlocutor to solicit further information (Plaut., *Most.* 999) or the speaker to submit it (Ter., *Hec.* 811; Cic., *Att.* 2.6.2 = SB 26). This would fit well with the notion that a *probabile*, once approved, remains open to revision. That the Academic's saying *etiam* or *non* is called *respondere* here represents, in my view, a reason for the insertion of *non* before *sustineat* above. Hofmann-Szantyr (p. 452) call *non* used in the sense of 'no' colloquial, but 'conversational' seems more suitable, given its connection with interpersonal exchange.

At the end of this sentence ms. V gives out. Plasberg[1] and Plasberg[2] used ms. N to replace V. I give the reconstructed reading of V (*v*) from here onwards. The relationship of most of the manuscripts which can be used to reconstruct V was established by Malaspina (2019).

Nam cum placeat…agere aliquid: as Reid[1] (p. 300) observes, the line of thought is continuing from the previous sentence, with the beginning of the sentence likely echoing *id cum ita sit* in sense. So a connective followed by a causal conjunction is needed. In terms of sense, there is little to choose between *nam cum* ('Lambinus'), *et cum* (Davies), and *etenim cum* (Reid[1]), but the emendation by 'Lambinus' is marginally closer to what is transmitted. Plasberg[1] (p. 126) seems unnecessarily troubled. For *placeat*, see n. on *alterum placere...* above. The Academics make the assumption (itself a *probabile*; cf. Burnyeat 1997: 302 n. 64) that someone who withholds assent in the Stoic sense nonetheless can act and answer questions on theoretical matters. *Se continere* is synonymous with *se sustinere* above, while the whole clause *qui de... assentiendo* illuminates *omnino eum nulli rei assentiri* (see n.).

By itself, the phrase *moueri tamen et agere aliquid* is open to a reading whereby the agents envisaged are moved by impressions and act on them in a rationally blind way, without engaging consciously with their impressions. However, such a conception of what acting on *probabilia* is would not counter the ἀπραξία-charge on several conceptions of πρᾶξις (see Vogt 2010a: 166). Moreover, given that Cicero invokes legal decision-making as a model for illustrating the Academic sage's behaviour (see *Luc.* 146, the general note above, and *uideri dicimus* below), this interpretation is strongly discouraged.

Reliquit eius modi uisa, quibus ad actionem excitemur: indirect speech in what precedes and in what follows (*neque tamen omnia...*) provides reasonable grounds for thinking that *relinqui*, conjectured by Davies, is correct, but a shift into *oratio recta* and back would not be unparalleled. Whether or not Cicero casts Clitomachus' thoughts into reported speech grammatically, he is still reporting his views here (as opposed to drawing inferences from what Clitomachus said and thereby interpreting him): that, because he who withholds assent is still moved and capable of action, impressions 'remain' (i.e. need to be posited) which give rise to action (or allow the Academic sage to respond on theoretical matters; see next n.). It is not spelt out here how the possibility of action without assent is established, nor how Clitomachus would define the Academic equivalent of Stoic φαντασίαι ὁρμητικαί, impressions which give rise to action (*Luc.* 23–5). See on §§37–9.

Item ea quae interrogati in utramque partem respondere possimus: having dealt with *uisa* which give rise to action without having been assented to, Cicero proceeds to *uisa* on theoretical matters; cf. *Luc.* 32: *uolunt enim...probabile aliquid esse et quasi ueri simile, eaque se uti regula et in agenda uita* **et in quaerendo ac disserendo**, where *uti regula* suggests conscious engagement with *probabilia*. Cicero can and does of course talk about *in utramque partem* **disserere** (or *dicere* or *disputare*; see Aubert-Baillot 2019: 256–8, 263, and passim) on occasion, whereby the hope or the effect may be that the *ueri simile* will emerge. Here his point is a different one: approving a theoretical *uisum* is like responding 'yes' in an exchange by question and answer. Thus *in utramque partem* must go with *interrogati* (thus Brittain 2006: 61) rather than *respondere* (Reid[1] p. 301; Long and Sedley i.1987: 454–5; Schäublin et al. p. 135; Gigon p. 221).

This is confirmed by the following consideration: *interrogati in utramque partem* can be compared to Alexander of Aphrodisias's expression εἰς ἑκάτερον μέρος ἐπιχείρησις (*in Top.* p. 27.11–12 Wallies; cf. p. 584.9–11), which is the skill that dialectic aims to foster: the ability of the questioner to attack (= mount a dialectical syllogism to the contradictory of) the thesis chosen by the respondent when confronted with the initial πρόβλημα. For Aristotle's use of ἐπιχείρημα in the required sense, see e.g. *Top.* Θ 11, 162a15–16; Θ3, 158a31–2. In *Top.* Θ5 Aristotle distinguishes the normal case of dialectical exchanges where the respondent answers in a detached way in accordance with what appears true (159a25–159b25) from a situation where he answers in accordance with his own beliefs (159b25–7); see Reinhardt (2015: 230–8). Approving theoretical *uisa* is comparable to the former situation; this is very similar to the notion that approving leads to hypothetical beliefs (Striker 1996b: 112). While it is unlikely that Cicero had read Aristotle's *Top.*, in *Tusc.* 1.7–17 he shows familiarity with dialectical procedures very similar to those described by Aristotle, as Moraux (1968: 300–7) has shown. It is a consequence of the fact that dialectical exchanges provide the framework for conceptualizing approval that approval can be given to theoretical (or 'philosophical') propositions. For these are the material of dialectical exchanges. Note also that in *Top.* Aristotle sought to codify a practice of question-and-answer λόγοι already existing in the Academy rather than to create it ex nihilo. Passages in Plato's dialogues which characterize belief-formation, or rather what immediately precedes belief-formation, in terms of a question-and-answer exchange do not constitute relevant comparanda, since they tend to be about a dialogue of the soul with itself (cf. e.g. *Phileb.* 38b12–39a7; *Theaet.* 189e6–190a6; *Soph.* 263e3–264a2, with Moss 2014: 217–20), quite apart from the fact that they can be linked more credibly with the emergence of the concept of assent.

Eius modi uisa above and *omnia eius modi uisa* below would seem to suggest that *uisa* is to be understood after *item ea*, which, however, is not easy to accommodate grammatically. One would need to assume that *quae* is an accusative of respect with *respondere*, which is not in line with Ciceronian usage; alternatively, *uisa* is not to be supplied, and *ea quae* are 'those things' which one can give in response (cf. the translation in Brittain 2006: 61). These 'things' do, however, ultimately correspond to impressions.

Sequentes tantum...dum sine assensu: for the force of *sequi*, see above on *sequens probabilitatem*. *Ita* means *ita ut respondemus*, as Reid[1] (p. 301) notes. *Dum sine assensu*, sc. *respondeamus*. This is the third time that approval is said to involve the withholding of assent after *ut neque neget aliquid neque aiat* and *qui de omnibus rebus contineat se ab assentiendo*. See Kühner-Stegmann ii.446–8 on this use of *dum*.

Neque tamen omnia eius modi uisa approbari, sed ea quae nulla re impedirentur: cf. *Luc.* 33 and 35–6 on *probabilia* 'which are not impeded'; section 6.5, p. cv. That the kind of *uisa* at issue is specified in this way determines the sense of *uideri* below. Hirzel (1883: 165–6) found it problematic that there should be a larger class of *probabilia* which can give rise to action, a species of which the Academic will rely on; he thus proposed to delete *eius modi* as repeated from above, assuming that there was only one type of *probabile* and that it was defined as 'a *uisum* which was not impeded' ('...und das seien solche Vorstellungen, die, *weil sie mit keiner anderen im*

Widerspruch stünden, uns als wahrscheinlich gälten' [my emphasis]). However, *Luc.* 35-6 distinguishes a *probabile primo quasi aspectu* and a *probabile* which is not impeded, which shows that *eius modi* must be retained; thus also Reid[1] (p. 301) and Plasberg[1] (p. 126).

§105a

Haec si uobis non probamus…non enim lucem eripimus: the shift in narrative perspective appears to mark the end of the report from Clitomachus, but §105a is entirely consistent with the report and could still be more loosely informed by it. On *sane* with the concessive subjunctive, see Reid[1] (p. 301).

In *M.* 7.159-62 Sextus reports how Carneades argued that, if anything could serve as a criterion, it would have to be an impression. In *M.* 7.163 this is stated, and the originally Stoic comparison of an impression with light, which reveals itself and its cause (Aët. 4.12 = *SVF* II.54 = LS 39B), is used. See further on §102 for the anti-sceptical argument that the Academics remove the senses completely.

Sed ea quae uos percipi comprehendique…uideri dicimus: *si modo probabilia sint* signals that the sense of *uideri* must be loaded, i.e. amount to more than just 'to appear' (so also Schäublin et al. pp. 268-9 n. 303): unimpeded *probabilia* must be at issue for them to be pitted against cataleptic impressions. The claim is that the same kind of thoughts which the Stoics regard as cataleptic impressions are held to be *probabilia* (which have been found to be unimpeded) by the Academics. Cf. Gal., *Plac. Hipp.* 9.7.3 (p. 778 Kühn = p. 586 De Lacy) and 9.9.37 (p. 802 Kühn = p. 606 De Lacy), who equates the περιωδευμένη φαντασία of the 'New Academics', said to be like the πιθανὴ φαντασία and the ἀπερίσπαστος φαντασία, with the cataleptic impression of the Stoics. Cicero's point is that Academics and Stoics seek to characterize materially the same impressions; Galen's point may either be the same or that the Academics, for all their caveats, act as if the impressions which they privilege are cataleptic impressions (so that the dispute is revealed to be purely terminological). For the latter reading see Tielemann (2011: 86-7).

Daube (1956: 73-4) analyses the technical legal use of *quod uidetur* in the formula employed by judges announcing their verdict (cf. *Luc.* 146), which Cicero has adopted here (recognized by *OLD* s.v. *uideo* no. 22): 'First, the…phrase acknowledges the possibility of an error.…Secondly…the pronouncement "he appears" and so on claims to be the result of investigation and evaluation.…Thirdly, by saying "he appears" and so on instead of "he has done" or "he has not done", a judge keeps aloof from and above the matter. His is a well-considered, sober utterance. An unrestrained "he has done" might come from the mouth of an accuser or a critic, a "he has not done" from the accused or his defence.'

The absence of impedance in connection with approval is itself a legal concept, a fact that was surely not lost on the contemporary readership: a piece of craftsmanship was deemed to have received approval (*approbatio*) if no objection had been raised during final inspection. At that point liability passed from the craftsman to the party represented by the inspector. See Zimmermann (1996: 404-6).

§105b

Having covered the subject of approval, the kind of endorsement recognized by Carneades (on Clitomachus' account) and which functions together with the *probabile*, Cicero returns to the latter, evidently no longer drawing directly on Clitomachus. Cicero restates with a concrete example (the colour of the sea which forms part of the setting of the dialogue) the point previously made in §103, where Cicero was directly reporting Clitomachus: that objects in the world differ from each other and that these differences account for the persuasiveness or lack of persuasiveness of the impressions they give rise to,[426] but that the impressions nonetheless do not give us a certain grasp of the properties of these objects. And even if the Stoics had a theory which would explain why the sea can apparently change colour, such a theory would not enable them to claim that a particular impression at a given point in time was true.

Cicero says that the defence of clarity lies defeated. By this he means two things. First (cf. *Sic igitur inducto et constituto probabili…*), the existence of the *probabile* and its useability as a criterion of sorts shows that the cataleptic impression is not, as Lucullus had suggested, without alternative and that it must be accepted for that reason. Second (cf. the rest of the paragraph), cataleptic impressions have been shown to be non-existent.

By stressing that the *probabile* was to be 'untethered', Cicero indicates that he is singling out the tested *probabile* which featured in §36. That the terms used for testing there (*consideratio, contemplatio*) are not even alluded to here, whereas the opposing side did mention them, suggests that they were introduced and explained by one of the Academic speakers on the previous day, i.e. in the *Catulus*.

When describing how the sea appears differently at different points in time, Cicero talks as if he is confronting an Academic conception of the sage with the Stoic one (to make the point that he is assuming that they look at the same sea and have the same visual experience, with the only difference being that the Stoic sage's visual experience is held to be cataleptic). Elsewhere it suits his argumentative purpose better to write as if there is one sage only, of whom the Stoics conceive in one way, and the Academics in a different way (cf. §100).

Sic igitur inducto et constituto probabili…tuum perspicuitatis patrocinium: with *inducto*, cf. §99: *a uobis sapiens inducitur* with n.; for *constituere* in an abstract sense of 'to establish', see *OLD* s.v. no. 11. *Expeditus* is originally a military term, of troops unencumbered by heavy luggage; see sections 6.1 and 6.5 on how the absence of impedance is conceptualized in the Carneadean scheme. For *iacēre* 'to lie defeated' cf. §79: *iacet ista causa*. See the general note above on §36: *ex circumspectione aliqua et accurata consideratione*. *Illud tuum patrocinium* may be contrasting with §17: *Philone autem uiuo patrocinium Academiae non defuit*. The counterpart of this passage in the final edition was on Augustine's mind in *Contra Acad.* 2.5.12.

---

[426] §103 by itself may give the impression that differences between objects *alone* account for differences in persuasiveness, but the parallel evidence from Sextus (*M.* 7.171–3 and 183) suggests that this is not to be interpreted narrowly, so that e.g. the conditions under which one perceives something are included among differences between objects for the present purpose; cf. also *qua a sole collucet* in the present paragraph. See further section 6, p. lxxxvii; Reinhardt (2018a: 226–7).

Isdem enim hic sapiens...sentiet: on the device of confronting the Academic and the Stoic sage, rather than saying that the latter is mischaracterized, see the general note above. On *intueri* and *tueri* 'to look at' contrasted with other *uerba uidendi*, see García-Hernández (1996). For *sub sensum cadere*, cf. *Ac.* 1.31, and 1.40:...*sed quia nihil quod cadere in eam* [sc. *comprehensionem*] *relinqueret*. The Academic sage's perceptual experience is exactly like that of the Stoic; cf. *Luc.* 141, where a similar point is made about the attitude taken to arguments.

Cicero aims for a degree of stylistic elevation here, as the asyndeton *caelum terram mare* suggests; cf. *Fin.* 5.9 (on the Peripatetics): *Natura sic ab iis inuestigata est, ut nulla pars caelo mari terra, ut poëtice loquar, praetermissa sit.* Cf. Enn., Medea ll. 234–6 Jocelyn: *Iuppiter tuque adeo summe Sol qui res omnis inspicis | quique tuo lumine mare terram caelum contines | inspice hoc facinus prius quam fit.* With *iisdem... oculis*, cf. D.L. 9.62 and 104 (cited by Reid[1] p. 301).

Mare illud...non possis id uerum esse, quod uidebatur oculis, defendere: Cicero readily talks about objects in the world and refers to them with deictic pronouns; see on §103 above: *Academicis placere esse rerum eius modi dissimilitudines, ut aliae probabiles uideantur aliae contra.* Reid[1] (pp. 301–2) has various good notes on the colour terminology and related expressions, some of which have poetic resonance like the asyndeton in the previous sentence.

Cf. t. 13 from *Ac.* 2: *Quid? Mare nonne caeruleum? At eius unda cum est pulsa remis, purpurascit, et quidem aquae ⟨corpus⟩ tinctum quodam modo et infectum.* While the many almost *uerbatim* correspondences between fragments of *Ac.* 3 and 4 on the one hand and *Luc.* on the other show that Cicero did not rewrite the latter systematically for the final edition, t. 13 demonstrates that in some places Cicero made significant alterations. See also t. 47 and t. 51.

Lucr. 2.757–87 offers explanations of the changes of colour in the sea within his own methodological framework.

With the present passage cf. D.L. 9.62 (part of Pyrrho test. 6 Decleva Caizzi = Aenesidemus test. B6 Polito) and 104–5 on Pyrrho (part of Aenesidemus test. B5 Polito). In the first passage Diogenes says that Pyrrho reportedly acted like a man who was blind and deaf, never relying on the senses, and that his friends had to keep him out of harm's way. However, Aenesidemus rejected this caricature: Αἰνεσίδημος δέ φησι φιλοσοφεῖν μὲν αὐτὸν κατὰ τὸν τῆς ἐποχῆς λόγον, μὴ μέντοι γ' ἀπροοράτως ἕκαστα πράττειν, 'Aenesidemus...said that Pyrrho philosophised according to the line of reasoning of suspension of judgement, but that he did not do anything without foresight' (transl. Polito). 9.104–5 is another parallel to our passage with different examples: Πάλιν οἱ δογματικοί φασιν καὶ τὸν βίον αὐτοὺς ἀναιρεῖν, ἐν ᾧ πάντ' ἐκβάλλουσιν ἐξ ὧν ὁ βίος συνέστηκεν. οἱ δὲ ψεύδεσθαί φασιν αὐτούς· οὐ γὰρ τὸ ὁρᾶν ἀναιρεῖν, ἀλλὰ τὸ πῶς ὁρᾶν ἀγνοεῖν. καὶ γὰρ τὸ φαινόμενον τιθέμεθα, οὐχ ὡς καὶ τοιοῦτον ὄν. καὶ ὅτι τὸ πῦρ καίει αἰσθανόμεθα· εἰ δὲ φύσιν ἔχει καυστικὴν ἐπέχομεν. καὶ ὅτι κινεῖταί τις βλέπομεν, καὶ ὅτι φθείρεται· πῶς δὲ ταῦτα γίνεται οὐκ ἴσμεν. μόνον οὖν, φασίν, ἀνθιστάμεθα πρὸς τὰ παρυφιστάμενα τοῖς φαινομένοις ἄδηλα. καὶ γὰρ ὅτε τὴν εἰκόνα ἐξοχὰς λέγομεν ἔχειν, τὸ φαινόμενον διασαφοῦμεν· ὅταν δ' εἴπωμεν μὴ ἔχειν αὐτὴν ἐξοχάς, οὐκέτι ὃ φαίνεται ἕτερον δὲ λέγομεν, 'Again the dogmatists maintain that they [the Sceptics] even do away with life, since they dismiss all that life consists in. But the Sceptics say that this is false. For they say that they do not abolish vision. Rather they do not know how vision takes place. Indeed we posit that which appears, but we do not posit that it is such as it appears. We do experience the fact that fire burns, but we suspend judgement as to whether it has a caustic nature. We see that a thing comes to be and passes away, but how these processes take place we do not know. Thus, they say, we only oppose non-evident entities underlying appearances. And when we say that a painting has depth and distance, we are describing that which appears, but if we say that it does not possess them we are no longer stating that which appears, but something else' (transl. Polito). Unlike §103, neither passage speaks to how changes in objects might affect appearances.

Quodque = et quia, as Reid[1] (p. 302) notes.

§§106–107a

In §22 Lucullus had argued that the existence of concepts in the mind requires the existence of cataleptic impressions, and that the faculty of memory as well as the existence of arts (= τέχναι) are inconceivable without the assumption that there are cataleptic impressions.[427] With respect to memory, he asked: *Quae potest enim esse memoria falsorum, aut quid quisquam meminit quod non animo comprehendit et tenet?* On a charitable reading, Lucullus did not claim that human beings cannot have recollections of situations in which they have experienced false impressions, or of the content (representational or propositional) which these impressions had. Rather, his point was a linguistic one: when we say 'I have a memory that *p*' or 'I remember that *p*', we tend to use 'to have a memory of' and 'to remember' in a factive way, of truths, and of certain truths at that. This shows, so Lucullus, that the— correct, to his mind—assumption that there are certain truths is encoded into normal linguistic usage.

Cicero's summary of this argument as *Vnde memoria si nihil percipimus?* is not unfair: that Lucullus' argument turns on linguistic usage is not obvious from §22 itself, but is suggested by §26, where the factivity of *inuenire* is invoked in an analogous argument (...*inuenta dicuntur*). In his reply Cicero interprets Lucullus' suggestion as meaning that 'person A remembers that *p*' entails both (i) *p is* invariably true and (ii) person A *regards p* as invariably true. He then pursues a two-pronged strategy: he uses a first example, Polyaenus, to show that (ii) need not be entailed by 'person A remembers that *p*' (this point is made in the section *Meminisse uisa nisi...oblitus est?*). He then uses the example of Siron to show that (i) need not be entailed by 'a person remembers that *p*' (this point is made in the section *Atqui falsum quod est...comprehensio perceptioque nulla sit*). Neither of his arguments makes a positive case for grounding memory in unimpeded *probabilia*; instead, he concludes that memory is possible in the absence of apprehension. However, beliefs resulting from apprehension and from approval exhaust the notional possibilities for the Academic (cf. §99 *init.*; §105a); this is the background assumption which grounds the argument.

---

[427] A fuller discussion of Lucullus' argument and Cicero's response is in Reinhardt (2019).

First, Cicero questions rhetorically that memory of what seemed to someone to be the case at some point is impossible unless we had apprehension of it. He refers to Polyaenus, who had absorbed the system of geometry, then became a follower of Epicurus, and—since the Epicureans reject geometry—came to regard that system, sc. which he remembered, as false. Now on the Stoic view geometry is an art, and the items of knowledge which constitute it are καταλήψεις irrespective of whether one regards them as true. If one ends up dismissing them because they prove incompatible with false beliefs (like Epicurean tenets) which one has, then all this shows is that one is not a sage. Cicero's point must be a different one, then, and he appears to mean that, for a proposition p to be the content of a memory, it is not necessary that it be regarded as true by the subject; rather, it suffices if the proposition at issue is true as a matter of fact. Thus Polyaenus' geometrical memories, while being dismissed by him, are still memories (that seems to be the implication of ...*num illa etiam, quae sciebat, oblitus est?*).

For his second example, Cicero cites the Epicurean Siron, who 'remembers' tenets of Epicurean philosophy. This would be acceptable for Cicero (who is not committed to the view that one can only say 'I remember that p' when p is true and cannot be false), but not for Lucullus (who is an Antiochian or, for epistemological purposes, a Stoic). A committed Epicurean might say something like 'I remembered that "the world is made up of atoms and void" [p]', taking p to be true.

While this shows that expressions like 'I remember that p' can be used when p is false, contra Lucullus, and that his inference from linguistic usage to how things 'really' are was open to objection, Lucullus might in turn object that language is used for communication, and that a non-Epicurean might charge the Epicurean with using 'to remember' in a deviant way. Cicero could reply that, for a use of 'I remember that p' to be deemed non-deviant by a set of interlocutors, it suffices if everyone regards p as true.

In §107a Cicero dismisses, somewhat abruptly, the suggestion that technical expertise (τέχνη) is inconceivable without the existence of apprehension.[428] He suggests that there are at least two kinds of technical expertise which do not rely on apprehension, so-called stochastic arts and those which are made up of items of knowledge which do not amount to apprehensions but to what appears to be the case (i.e. *probabilia*). The former are typically characterized by the contingency of their outcomes, not by a difference to their constitution qua ordered body of knowledge or to the epistemic status of the individual items of knowledge in it. As for the latter, Cicero's point may be that such arts exist because all arts ultimately need to be so described (cf. §105 *init.*, where Cicero says that the Academics call those very impressions which the Stoics regard as cataleptic *probabilia*: ...*sed ea, quae uos percipi comprehendique, eadem nos, si modo probabilia sint, uideri dicimus*). In §146 Cicero suggests that Zeuxis, Phidias, and Polyclitus would be unlikely to accept the notion that they are not in possession of their respective arts, but would be content if they were told that arts presuppose apprehension as defined by the Stoics (a notion they would dismiss as absurd, Cicero implies). It is less likely that Cicero is thinking

---

[428] In Reinhardt (2019: 170) I argue that Lucullus derives this claim from a linguistic observation, viz. that 'X is an *artifex*' presupposes that X is in possession of truths which cannot be falsehoods.

of something like empiricist medicine, discussed in §122 in an epistemological context, as Brittain (2001: 161) suggests. Empiricist medicine does not operate the same conception of an art as everyone else while merely assigning a different epistemic status to the items of knowledge an art is made up of.

'Unde memoria, si nihil percipimus?' Sic enim quaerebas: the reference is to §22. Reid[1] (p. 302) notes the unusually harsh transition.

Quid? Polyaenus...oblitus est: *Polyaenus...credidit* is frg. 229a Usener. Cf. §71, where Cicero invokes another thinker who changed allegiance, Dionysius called ὁ μεταθέμενος. Polyaenus (Πολύαινος) was one of the four 'masters' (καθηγεμόνες) of the Epicurean school alongside Metrodorus, Hermarchus, and Epicurus himself; on him see Clay (2009: 12-3); Dorandi (2012); and the collection of fragments by Tepedino Guerra (1991), which lists *Polyaenus qui...oblitus est* as frg. 39 (and *Fin.* 1.20 *Ne illud quidem...etiam ipsum dedocere* as frg. 40). He was born at Lampsacus, and trained and wrote as a mathematician. He must have come into contact with Epicurus' during the latter's stay in Lampsacus between 311/10 and 307/6 BC, gave up mathematics for Epicurean philosophy, and moved to Athens where he died in 278/7 BC. Cicero refers to him also in *Fin.* 1.20. The Epicurean rejection of geometry is also alluded to in *Ac.* 1.6.

Polyaenus rejected geometry because of his commitment to theoretical *minima*; see Sedley (1976: 23): 'That Epicurus believed in a minimal unit of measure out of which not only atoms but also all larger lengths, areas and volumes are composed, is nowadays widely accepted; and most would also agree that it is not merely a physical minimum, contingent upon the nature of matter, but also a theoretical minimum, than which nothing smaller is conceivable. Others before and since Epicurus have been seduced by similar theories without being led to reject conventional geometry. Yet this is precisely the penalty which a theory of minimal parts should carry with it, for one of its consequences is to make all lines integral multiples of a single length and therefore commensurable with each other, whereas incommensurability of lines in geometrical figues had been recognized by Greek mathematicians since the fifth century. Moreover the principle of infinite divisibility lay at the heart of the geometrical method commonly called "method of exhaustion", which was fruitfully developed by Eudoxus in the fourth century.' See also Mueller (1982: passim, but esp. 92-5), who is primarily concerned with Sextus' arguments against geometry in *M.* 3, but notes continuities between sceptical and Epicurean attacks on the subject, and considers possible cross-influences; White (1989).

The first consideration cited by Cicero ends with *oblitus est*. The principles of geometry do not cease to count among Polyaenus' memories because he came to regard them as false. See the general note above on Cicero's construal of Lucullus' view of memory.

Atqui falsum quod est...etiam si comprehensio perceptioque nulla sit: the first sentence is a restatement of premiss (ii) of the core argument (see §83), which the Stoics themselves endorse as Cicero observes. Cf. *Luc.* 22: *Quae potest...esse memoria falsorum...* The phrase *perceptarum comprehensarumque rerum* is a complement to *est*, not an attribute to *memoria*. Cf. Aug., *Contra Acad.* 3.4.10: *placuit inter nos, quod etiam inter omnes ueteres interque ipsos Academicos, scire falsa neminem posse.*

Reid¹ (p. 302) comments on *Si igitur...* that there is a 'precisely similar argument' made against the dogmatists in Sextus, *P.H.* 2.4–5. In fact, that argument is not concerned with memory, and rejects the dogmatist's suggestion that the sceptic apprehends a dogmatic tenet in merely entertaining it. Cicero's point here is not that Siron merely entertains *Epicuri dogmata*, and he derives the absurd conclusion that Epicurean tenets are true from the fact that Siron remembers them, using Lucullus' assumptions. See Reid¹ (p. 302) on *nunc* in *uera igitur nunc sunt omnia*.

Siron (on the spelling see Haupt 1866: 40–1), mentioned by Cicero also in *Fin.* 2.119 alongside Philodemus as a *familiaris* and in *Fam.* 6.11.2 as an *amicus*, is famously mentioned as Vergil's teacher by Servius on *E.* 6.13 and *A.* 6.264; see also *Catalepton* 5.9–10 and 8. He lived in Naples. See Crönert (1906: 125) on *P.Herc.* 125; Erler (1994a: 274–5). His fragments are collected by Gigante (1990).

For the term *dogma*, here less clearly marked as a code-switch than in §27 and hence transliterated in my text, see ibid. and on §109.

Why is the Academic happy to accept that the Epicurean 'remembers' his doctrines, which, after all, must appear to be prime examples of groundless dogmatism to him? One reason is that he does not share Lucullus' assumptions about the factivity of 'to remember' (see on §§21–2): *nothing* follows from the Epicurean speaking in this way. Another is that he is not invested in the dispute, in the sense that testing Lucullus' argument is his aim. There is no *pars construens* here.

Cicero ends the point with another dilemma-type argument (cf. §§43–4; 68, 94): either give up on the notion of memory altogether (*memoriam...remittas*) or grant that there is room for it even if there is no such thing as κατάληψις.

On *fateare*, see Reid¹ (p. 303) and Plasberg¹ (p. 127).

§107a

'Quid fiet artibus?'...istam artem uestram qua uera et falsa diiudicent: the reference is still to §22. See the general note above for the identification of the two types of τέχνη which are introduced as counterexamples to Lucullus' claim that arts require apprehension. The distinction between arts which are rigidly methodical and achieve their outcome invariably, and others which involve conjecture (στοχασμός), is quite old; cf. e.g. Plt., *Phileb.* 55e–56c and *Grg.* 464c. The latter passage comes closest to what Cicero might seem to need here, in that it distinguishes arts which rely on γιγνώσκειν and others which involve στοχάζειν (464c6: οὐ γνοῦσα λέγω ἀλλὰ στοχασαμένη). See further Auffret (2019). An art was assumed to proceed methodically towards a particular kind of worthwhile goal, to reach this goal invariably, and to be different from a knack in that it was able to account for its successes and failures; see Barnes (2015b). While this model works well for practical arts (carpentry, housebuilding), it poses a problem e.g. for medicine, where outcomes cannot be guaranteed, or for intellectualist accounts of virtuous living which use craft knowledge as a model; on the latter, see Striker (1996c). The uncertainty of outcomes could threaten, in the case of medicine, the τέχνη-status of the field, and the model of a stochastic art, which measured success not by final outcomes but by adherence to the standards and procedures of the art, was deployed to address this problem. See Alex. Aphr. *in Arist. Top.* pp. 32.12–34.5 Wallies; *Quaest.* p. 61.1–28 Bruns; Ierodiakonou (1995); Setaioli (2018). As indicated above, a τέχνη's status as a stochastic art was not normally conceptualized in terms of an inferior epistemic status of the items of knowledge which jointly constitute it. Cf., however, Cic., *Div.* 1.24: *artium quae coniectura continentur et sunt* **opinabiles**. *Videri* in *id quod uidetur* may be the technical sense of §105a: Cicero has no reason to be dismissive of arts and needs to accommodate (and account for) their existence.

§§107b–109a

In §§107b–109a Cicero turns to the issue of assent, specifically to whether it is possible to suspend assent invariably (§107b) and whether a successfully implemented policy of suspending judgement makes action impossible (§§108–109a). However, as we shall see, assent is not being considered completely separately from the question of the nature of the impressions involved.

§§108–109a is a reply to §§37–9 (cf. §§24–5; 59), where Lucullus advances the inactivity argument. §107b is not in the same way a direct reply to a particular section in Lucullus' speech, but we know that the Stoics held that cataleptic impressions normally compel assent, and Cicero concedes in §66 that he—a committed Clitomachean who is, however, not a sage—will often assent. This suggests that the claim to which Cicero is responding is that the sage cannot possibly be conceived in such a manner that he assents to nothing, as was assumed in §104 where Cicero reported Clitomachus' view on approval,[429] and it is consistent with this that Cicero reasons from Panaetius to the sage in §107b. So Cicero seems to be rejecting not a point made in Lucullus' speech, but the reply an Antiochian would give to what he himself said in §104. One can only speculate what the Antiochian reply to §104 might have been: e.g. that even if it was possible to take the kind of attitude to which approval amounts to some impressions, one could not possibly take them to all impressions, since mere approval of some impressions is only possible if one holds many genuine and deeply unproblematic beliefs.[430]

Cicero's reply cites instances of suspension of judgement in some cases and then posits that they show that universal suspension is possible. First, he draws attention to Panaetius' doubts about divination, which earlier Stoics accepted as true, and argues that, if Panaetius as a non-sage can suspend judgement about central tenets and domains of Stoic doctrine, the sage can suspend judgement about everything a fortiori. (Cicero must be thinking of §108 and the superhuman—Herculean, in fact—effort required to suspend judgement, which the sage is more likely to manage than the non-sage.) Second, he asks if there is any view which, once it is set forth, the sage can only accept or reject, but not be doubtful about. A positive answer does not

---

[429] Thus also Schäublin et al. (p. 272 n. 310).
[430] See the general note on §§104–105a.

quite give Cicero what he needs: even if it was granted that the sage can suspend judgement about anything, it does not follow that he can suspend judgement about everything. However, here we need to remember that as a Clitomachean Cicero feels entitled to regard all of the sage's views as merely 'approved', and that approval is a form of non-assent (cf. §§104–105a). Third, he cites the fact that the Stoics themselves want non-sages (this is the implication of the second person in *poteris* and *uoles*) to suspend judgement when confronted with a soritical series of questions, sc. while the impressions which arise from the questions are cataleptic, but do not want to allow the sage to suspend judgement about everything else. This, Cicero concludes, is especially baffling given that the sage—the sage as Cicero conceives of him—can be guided by the *ueri simile* without assenting to it (this was Cicero's interpretation of the seafaring scenario in §100, referred to also in §109a; the Stoic reading of such events would be different, see the comm. ad loc.).

In §§108–109a Cicero turns to Lucullus' claim that action required assent. Lucullus had first made this claim in §§23–5, where the reference point was the sage: all *his* actions arise from assent to cataleptic impressions, and the sage seems to be the reference point in the present passage, too (cf. §107: *ille in reliquis rebus non poterit*..., with no change of logical subject since then). (Non-cataleptic impressions can issue in action according to the Stoics, but only in non-sages.) Cicero reports that 'the senses themselves are assents' for the Stoics, alluding to the fact that perception is defined as assent to a cataleptic impression. Thus, the report continues, the whole nexus of cataleptic impression, assent, and action goes if cataleptic impressions are removed.

Much could be said about the subject, Cicero suggests in 108a *fin.*, but he feels he can be brief. By saying that he regards suspending assent as 'the greatest action', Cicero is implying that the Stoic account of action relies on a gratuitous stipulation of what action is (§108 *fin.*): avowedly leaving possible disputes about what qualifies as an *actio* aside, Cicero tries to question assumptions about the relative plausibility of the two explanatory models by asking why action could not simply follow if there was no obstacle to acting (i.e. if there was an unimpeded *probabile* which was approved). The dogmatists' reply is given in direct speech in §109 *init.*: the fact that the Academics themselves claim that the *probabilia* on which he acts are inapprehensible. Cicero lets the reader draw the inference that the dogmatist is a prisoner within his own rigid framework. He is able to give himself the last word: inapprehensible impressions are no obstacle to action, and anyone who goes on a sea voyage, works the land, gets married or fathers children has nothing better to go on. The Stoics would disagree (see §59 *fin.*, and the commentary on §100).

Sed illa sunt lumina duo quae maxime causam istam continent: *lumina* are crisp statements or even *sententiae* which encapsulate the case (*causa*); cf. Tac., *Dial.* 22.3 (on Cicero's style, which it is argued left something to be desired): *tarde commouetur, raro incalescit; pauci sensus apte et cum quodam lumine terminantur.*

Primum enim negatis fieri posse...cur id sapiens de reliquis rebus facere non possit: on *enim* used in the explanation of an antecedent demonstrative, see Kühner (1853: 359) on *Tusc.* 4.45. *Res* in *nulli rei* means just 'thing' rather than 'object, sc. in the world'. Brittain (2006) rightly treats *at id quidem perspicuum est* as a main clause, and an intervention by the dogmatist: it functions as confirmation that the dogmatists are denying that one can suspend judgement about everything, a claim which might otherwise seem foisted upon the opponent by Cicero. Reid[1] (p. 303) attaches it to *assentiatur*, which requires two changes to what is transmitted (*et* for *ad*, *esse* for *est*); see the rebuttal in Plasberg[1] (p. 128). *Perspicuum* is of course used polemically.

On Panaetius, see Steinmetz (1994: 646–69); Gourinat and Alesse (2012). His fragments were edited by Van Straaten (1946); Alesse (1997), who lists *Primum enim...facere non possit?* as testimonium 136; and Vimercati (2002). His 'doubts' about divination are also mentioned in *Div.* 1.6 (= FDS 462): *Sed a Stoicis uel princeps eius disciplinae, Posidoni doctor* (= Posidonius T10 Edelstein-Kidd), *discipulus Antipatri, degenerauit Panaetius, nec tamen ausus est negare uim esse diuinandi, sed dubitare se dixit. Quod illi in aliqua re inuitissumis Stoicis Stoico facere licuit, id nos ut in reliquis rebus faciamus a Stoicis non concedetur? Praesertim cum id, de quo Panaetio non liquet, reliquis eiusdem disciplinae solis luce uideatur clarius*; cf. 1.12, 2.88, 97; D.L. 7.149 (= FDS 463; context: Stoic views on divination): ὁ μὲν γὰρ Παναίτιος ἀνυπόστατον αὐτήν φησιν 'Panaetius says divination does not have real existence'. See also Long (1982: 168–9); Steinmetz (1994: 652–4). Disagreements between leading Stoics are also at issue in §126.

As to *seque ab assensu sustineat*, it is not possible to determine on the basis of the evidence whether Panaetius suspended judgement (i.e. engaged in ἐποχή) and professed doubt in a manner which consciously invoked the Academic practice or was even informed by Academic, notably Carneadean, arguments against divination. The formulation in D.L. 7.149 suggests that this need not be so, and Cicero is of course looking for precedents for suspension of judgement as he conceives of it by Stoics about core Stoic doctrines; on the issue see the discussion in Alesse (1997: 268–70). See also on §94 for Cicero's ἐποχή-related terminology. The supplement *responsa* by Ernesti is compelling, and the phrasal term frequent in Cicero.

An est aliquid...dubitare non possit: by means of a rhetorical question Cicero suggests that there is no impression which demands either acceptance or rejection, but does not permit doubt; this is a precondition for his claim that suspension of judgement about everything is possible. *Vel...uel* is used in the exclusive sense of *aut...aut* here; cf. Kühner-Stegmann ii.110.

Approbare and its opposite do not seem to be used in the technical sense of §104, given that Cicero's overall aim is to show that one can suspend judgement rather than withhold approval about everything.

It is an implication of what Cicero says that approval in the technical sense of §104 is given not unless there is no doubt but because there is always the possibility of doubt. This possibility of doubt cannot function as an obstacle or impedance of the *probabile*, since it always obtains (or so Cicero argues), and there *are* unimpeded *probabilia*. Contrast §109 *init.*, where the dogmatist is introduced as saying that what impedes *probabilia* is that they are not apprehended by the Academic's admission.

An tu in soritis poteris hoc...ipsam ueri similitudinem non impeditam sequi: in connection with the sorites (§§93–4), the Stoics counsel suspension of judgement when faced with a cataleptic impression (sc. in a particular context). Cicero suggests that, if one can do it once, one will be able to do it always, esp. given the possibility of following the *probabile* (here called *ueri similitudo*, cf. Sextus, *M.* 7.169). That Cicero occasionally uses *ueri simile* or similar expressions instead of *probabile* should not be taken as evidence that Academics used the term εἰκός alongside πιθανόν, or for πιθανόν the interpreted in a particular way; see section 6.3 and Reinhardt (2018a: 235–7). *Poteris*, sc. *facere*.

§108a

Alterum est quod negatis actionem ullius rei posse in eo esse qui nullam rem assensu suo comprobet...si uisa tollantur: the second *lumen* announced in §107 *sunt lumina duo*. The Stoics assumed that non-cataleptic impressions often attract assent and give rise to action, sc. in the non-sage, so if the present passage assumes that the impressions which give rise to action are invariably cataleptic, this requires explanation. In §§24–5, to which §108a is a reply, the same assumption was made, and I had suggested in the commentary that this must be so because the frame of reference there is the sage's behaviour. The sage is here referred to in the last sentence of §107b (...*ille in reliquis rebus non poterit*...).

Actionem **ullius rei** is probably intended to cover action which issues in e.g. mere movement as well as moral action; cf. §62: *sublata enim assensione omnem et motum animorum et actionem rerum sustulerunt*. With *nullam rem assensu suo comprobet*, cf. §138:...*mihi uerenti ne labar ad opinionem et aliquid asciscam et comprobem incognitum*, where assent is at issue, too.

When Reid[1] (p. 304) glosses *uideri* in as 'the true passive', he means that the use is veridical as in §25; cf. Reinhardt (2016: 84–5). This use carries over into *uisa* in *uisa tollantur* below. For the definition of perception (αἴσθησις) as assent to the cataleptic see the commentary on *Ac.* 1.40–2; Aët. 4.8.12 (= *SVF* ii.72) and 4.9.4 (= *SVF* ii.78). For *appetitio* = ὁρμή, see *Luc.* 24–5. This is one of four passages in *Luc.* where *comprobare* is used of endorsement given; the term is not technical and modified (cf. *assensu* here) in §§126 and 148 (in §146 unspecified acceptance is meant). I take *dicunt*...to be parenthetical, but *tolli autem*...depends on *dicunt*.

Passages in Augustine which appear to be informed by the counterpart of *Luc.* 108a in *Ac.* 4 are *Contra Acad.* 2.5.12 and 3.18.40 (= t. 60).

§§108b–109a

Hac de re in utramque partem...sed breui res potest tota confici: this is Cicero's reply to the issue raised in §108a; see the general note above. On the group of arguments which fall under the heading ἀπραξία, see §§37–9 and Vogt (2010a).

Vide superiora seems an obvious gloss, and I have followed the deletion made by Davies. Plasberg[1] (p. 129) marks the passage as a crux (with an asterisk in the margin) and wonders if Cicero wrote: *scripta multa, et oratione quidem multo ut uides uberiore*. Stroux (1937: 111) argues that the gloss is a reader's backward reference to the *Catulus* (*superiore*, sc. *libro*).

Ego enim etsi maximam actionem puto repugnare uisis...qui probabilia sequitur nulla re impediente: on the polemical point that one might posit a different conception of πρᾶξις (*actio*) compared to the Stoics, see the general note above. Hercules was at times invoked by the Stoics, so likening Carneades to Hercules for dragging assent from human minds like a wild beast from its lair is polemical, too. Clitomachus' remark may derive either from the work cited in §99 or the one used in §§103-4 or indeed a third one (see on §102), but *ita scribenti* suggests that Cicero is not just reporting a bonmot conventionally ascribed to him. With *repugnare uisis*, cf. *Fin.* 3.31 (giving the view of the *Academici*): *summum munus sapientis obsistere uisis assensusque suos firme sustinere*. With *assensus lubricos*, cf. §68 *init.*, where the habit (*consuetudo*) of assenting is called slippery. Cicero uses *exanclare* 'to endure' (see Walde-Hofmann s.v. *anclo*: 'schöpfen...aus gr. ἀντλεῖν') in the philosophical works and his poetic works; the distribution beyond Cicero (comedy; tragic fragments; Lucilius; Apuleius) suggests that it was felt to be archaic. *Assensio* juxtaposed with *opinatio* and *temeritas* denotes the habit of assenting; cf. *Ac.* 1.42 *fin.*; *Luc.* 66 for *temeritas*.

In *ut ea pars defensionis relinquatur*, Cicero gives up his opposition to the Stoic conception of action, allowing suspension of judgement to be merely what Lucullus called a *motus animorum* in *Luc.* 62. However, he still asks why action as the Stoics understand it should require assent, and why following unimpeded *probabilia* should not be equally possible. See Reid[1] (p. 304) on *etsi...tamen*.

§109a

'Hoc' inquit 'ipsum impediet...posse percipi': the dogmatist is made to reply, picking up on the double occurrence of *impedire* in the previous sentence, that what blocks action without assent is that the Academic claims that impressions he approves are not cataleptic. See on §107b: *An est aliquid...dubitare non possit?*, above.

Iam istuc te quoque impediet...in quibus nihil sequere praeter probabile: Cicero replies that this would prevent action on the Stoic's part in a whole range of areas of activity in which Stoics would engage, too, and where nothing more than *probabile* is to be had.

§§109b-110

Cicero now turns to the rebuttal of §§28-9, where Hortensius, Antipater, and Antiochus were introduced as demanding that the Academics, even if they hold that nothing can be known, should admit 'as their δόγμα (*decretum*)' that they know (i.e. apprehend) at least one thing, namely that nothing can be known. The likely rationale for this line of argument included that the notion that philosophical schools are identified by their doctrines, and that such doctrines underpin arguments made by representatives of a given school in a particular way, i.e. as first principles of a kind (see Allen 1997: 219–21). However, to claim that one knows that nothing can be known is inconsistent, the dogmatist argues.

While in §29 Lucullus could be read as imputing on the Academics that 'nothing can be known' was their δόγμα (sc. with all that this entails on his view), Cicero's reply—'Surely the sage has more than one *decretum* and cannot live without them'—suggests that he is quite happy to adopt the term and embrace the notion that his life is guided by δόγματα, but with the qualification that 'nothing can be known' is just one among many and that none of them is apprehended (thus rejecting the inconsistency charge as well as the dogmatic notion of a δόγμα).[431]

Cicero continues that relying on *probabilia* does not conflate everything and turn it into *incerta* (like the question of whether the stars are odd and even). Rather, *probabilia* allow the sage to act and to give replies, i.e. take a view under proviso, in philosophical discussion (with *nec quid respondeat*, cf. §104: *quae interrogati in utramque partem respondere possimus sequentes tantum modo quod ita uisum sit*). Lucullus had referred to a distinction, first drawn by Carneades, between *perspicua* and *percepta* in §§32–4: if an impression is *non perceptum*, it is not therefore an *incertum* but may well be a *perspicuum* (§34:...*conantur ostendere esse aliquid perspicui, uerum illud quidem impressum in animo atque mente, neque tamen id percipi atque comprehendi posse*). Cicero is relying on that distinction here.

Brittain (2001: 105) suggests that the *perspicuum* was appropriated by the mitigated sceptics (his 'Philonian/Metrodorians') and takes Allen (1997: 237–43) to task for failing to appreciate that there could be a distinction between the Carneadean concept, devised for the sake of the argument, and its adoption as part of the framework of mitigated scepticism. In Brittain (2006: 64 n. 165) he notes (on the passage under discussion) that 'Cicero's easy acceptance of Academic ethical "principles" [δόγματα] over and above the Academic's experience may reflect the mitigated sceptical position....' For the 'ethical principles', see n. on §110: *Itaque non metuit...nec quid faciat nec quid respondeat*, below.

This amounts to the suggestion that Cicero is defending here against Lucullus not his own Clitomachean position (which had been particularly prominent from §98 onwards), but either a hybrid stance which combines elements of Clitomacheanism with those of the mitigated position or indeed the mitigated position alone. (Brittain also holds that in the immediately following §111 Philo qua mitigated sceptic is referenced.) Alternatively and, I think, more plausibly, the present section is to be taken at face value: as a statement of the stance which the kind of Clitomachean that Cicero is could take.[432] I shall be resuming the consideration of this issue in the commentary on §111.

The Pyrrhonist's claim to δόγματα (Sextus, *P.H.* 1.13), on which see p. 661 above, is superficially similar to Cicero's claim here, but is in fact apt to illustrate the substantial differences between Academic πιθανά and Pyrrhonist φαινόμενα as well as between Clitomachean approval and Pyrrhonist εὐδοκεῖν.

---

[431] Cf. also the occurrences of *placere* in the Clitomachean quotation in §104, with Burnyeat (1997: 302 n. 64): 'The verb *placere* unavoidably suggests *placita*, ἀρέσκοντα.'

[432] Apart from the question of whether the *perspicuum* is a hallmark of mitigated scepticism, the construal of Clitomacheanism offered in this commentary is predicated on a particular interpretation of the nature of the πιθανόν (see section 6), of the nature of approval (see on §§104–105a), and of the ability of the Clitomachean to hold views of a kind (see section 8).

Et tamen illud usitatum...⟨si quicquam comprehendi posse⟩ dicatur: on *et tamen*, 'and putting that aside', see Reid[1] (p. 305). *Repudiare* means 'to reject' rather than 'to reject successfully', i.e. refute. *Pressius* occurred as an Antiochian quote in §29; see ad loc. On the likely rationale of Antipater's point see the commentary on §28 and the general note above. *Affirmaret* indicates strong endorsement and reflects the viewpoint of the dogmatist. On *pinguis* 'stupid' like English 'thick', see *OLD* s.v. no. 7a; πυκνός, of people and when not meaning 'overweight', is not so used and means 'shrewd'. The subject of *putat* is Antiochus. For *decretum*, see *Luc.* 27. The different supplements in F after correction and *v* (the latter likely due to V² given the evidence of S) are suggestive of independent attempts to address the same problem; see the Oxford Classical Text, p. lxi.

Illo modo potius putat...fateretur esse perceptum: the *ut*-clause (*ut hoc ipsum quidem decretum*) follows on *illo modo urguendum fuisse* and is consecutive: Antiochus thinks one should exercise pressure so that Carneades makes the confession that he has apprehended at least one *decretum*. That is, Antiochus is trying to hold Carneades to the dogmatist's standard. The transmitted text with *qui* requires that a finite verb be supplied in the relative clause; Plasberg[1] (p. 129) printed *ut hoc ipsum decretum qui sapientis esse* ⟨*diceret*⟩, *nihil posse percipi, fateretur esse perceptum*. Reid[1] modified the paradosis by emending *qui* to *quidem* and inverting the order of *decretum* and *qui(dem)*. I think the latter text is superior because it is a fairer representation of Antiochus' charge in §§28–9: he wants to extract agreement that the Academic requires his sage to hold one *decretum* dogmatically, and while the Academic may have said all along that he permits the sage to have *decreta* (sc. as he defines them), he will not have given 'nothing can be known' privileged status. This way of restoring the text also gives Cicero's rejoinder slightly more punch. However, the inversion is a major interference, and it would be preferable if the content of the *decretum* was characterized as 'nothing can be known' only, without the sage being referenced in the *decretum* itself. Hence the text I print; cf. e.g. Davies. The corrector of F is to be credited with *quod* for the transmitted *qui* and *esset* for the transmitted *esse*.

Proinde quasi sapiens...uitam agere possit: for *proinde quasi* = 'as if', see Kühner-Stegmann ii.453. Reid[1] (p. 306) explains why the transmitted text must be maintained (Lambinus changed *et* to *nec*); cf. the sentence immediately following. The Clitomachean's claim to *decreta* arising from approval is not entirely ad hoc: cf. the use of the pairing *placere/tenere* in §104, and see the general note above for the Pyrrhonist parallel. Reid[1] (p. 305) is also good on the force of *nullum aliud*, which does not imply a claim to other *decreta* of the kind the dogmatist is seeking to impute, but a claim to *decreta* of a different kind. Cf. §110 init. and the last sentence of *N.D.* 1.12.

§110

Sed ut illa habet probabilia...nihil posse percipi: *illa* refers to the sage's other *decreta*, which he regards as *probabilia non percepta* (the phrase functions as a complement to *illa*). 'Nothing can be apprehended' has the same status. Reid[1] (p. 306) aptly cites Sextus' claim that the Academics are negative dogmatists (*P.H.* 1.226; see appendix 1 for a translation): Οἱ δὲ ἀπὸ τῆς νέας Ἀκαδημίας, εἰ καὶ ἀκατάληπτα εἶναι πάντα φασί, διαφέρουσι τῶν σκεπτικῶν ἴσως μὲν καὶ κατ' αὐτὸ τὸ λέγειν πάντα εἶναι ἀκατάληπτα (διαβεβαιοῦνται γὰρ περὶ τούτου, ὁ δὲ σκεπτικὸς ἐνδέχεσθαι καὶ καταληφθῆναί τινα προσδοκᾷ).... While Cicero would feel misrepresented, it seems plain that what is said in *Luc.* 109b–110a would be sufficient to give rise to statements like Sextus'. Qualified self-aware assent, as is characteristic for mitigated scepticism (§148), need not be a privileged target of statements of this kind.

Nam si in hoc haberet cognitionis notam...utitur probabilibus: for *cognitionis nota*, the distinctive feature which on the dogmatist's view attaches to cataleptic impressions only (cf. *N.D.* 1.12: *certa iudicandi et assentiendi nota*), cf. §84 and the discussion of all related expressions in *Acad.* in the general note on *Luc.* 33–34a. *Vti* primarily of conscious use, but it need not be so restricted; I argue at 104–105a that the paradigmatic case for approval (as for dogmatic assent) is conscious acceptance.

Itaque non metuit...nec quid faciat nec quid respondeat: with *confundere omnia*, cf. §53, and with *incerta*, cf. §32, where the issue of the number of the stars features, as well as §54 *init.*, where the corresponding Greek term is cited. Cicero claims of the use of the *probabile* not just for practical matters, but also for moral action (*de officio*) and for philosophical debate (note the correspondence between...*nec quid respondeat* here and §104:*...ea quae interrogati in utramque partem respondere possimus...*). Cf. also §32:*...probabile aliquid esse et quasi ueri simile, eaque se uti regula et* **in agenda uita et in quaerendo ac disserendo**.

On some reconstructions of the πιθανόν the question arises of how it can be capable of enabling or guiding moral action given that πιθανότης is assumed to arise from the phenomenal properties of an impression; see also Brittain (2001: 269–73) on the issue. Given that what is persuasive is primarily determined by considerations of coherence (see the introduction, section 6.1, and Reinhardt 2018a: 238–9 and passim), the fact that the context of our lives provides us with certain goals and conditions us to a high level would seem to allow for the moral action guided by the πιθανόν. The mechanism would be similar to the acquisition and enactment of medical expertise on an empiricist model; cf. also the way in which the Pyrrhonist is guided by φαινόμενα, with Striker (2010: 202–7). One reason why Cicero may have been satisfied with such an account of moral action (rather than to, say, dismiss it as the extension of the animal model of action to human beings) is the heavily traditional nature of Roman society.

§111

In this paragraph Cicero addresses a report by Antiochus that Philo was troubled by an objection which Antiochus had levelled against the core argument, which Arcesilaus had first formulated. Antiochus' objection is reported in §§43–4 (see ad loc.). For convenience I reproduce the core argument as it features in *Luc.* 40:[433]

---

[433] For the slightly different formulations of the core argument in *Acad.* see the introduction (end of section 5). The version quoted in §40 uses a formulation for premiss (iii) which allows for equivalence in

(i) eorum quae uidentur alia uera sunt alia falsa.

Of appearances, some are true and some are false.

(ii) quod falsum est, id percipi non potest.

What is false cannot be apprehended.

(iii) quod autem uerum uisum est, id omne tale est ut eiusdem modi falsum etiam possit uideri.

But any true appearance is of such a kind that something false which is exactly alike could appear in the same way.

(iv) quae uisa sint eius modi ut in iis nihil intersit, non posse accidere ut eorum alia percipi possint, alia non possint.

With respect to appearances without a difference between them, it cannot happen that some of them can be apprehended, and others cannot.

(v) nullum igitur est uisum quod percipi possit.

Therefore there is no appearance which can be apprehended.

Antiochus' objection was that the Academics cannot both claim (i) and (iii) on the grounds that they are incompatible, viz. Antiochus took premiss (i) to amount to the claim that there are true and false impressions, and premiss (iii) to amount to the claim that there is no difference between true and false impressions, i.e. to be an identity claim. Here in §111 Cicero indicates that Antiochus' objection relies on an incorrect interpretation of premiss (iii).

As explained in detail in the commentary on §44, Couissin (1983: 63 n. 52; 1929a: 273 n. 1) and Brittain (2001: 130–1) have argued as follows: anyone who advanced the core argument dialectically would introduce premiss (i) ad hominem, as one the Stoic opponent is committed to. If Philo was assumed to advance the argument dialectically, there would be no issue of incompatibility in any event, and no explanation for his concern regarding Antiochus' point. If, by contrast, he was a mitigated sceptic, who assents to the premisses of the core argument qualifiedly, then a different problem of incompatibility would arise: on what grounds could he give his qualified assent to (i), given that he also assents to (iii)? Therefore the reference must be to a concern Philo had while his position was that of the mitigated scepticism referenced in *Luc.* 148.[434]

There is, however, a third possibility regarding the position Philo occupied when he supposedly expressed his concern. He may have been the kind of Clitomachean the Cicero character is cast as in *Luc.*, which would mean inter alia that he approves of the core and corollary arguments in the technical sense of *Luc.* 104; cf. *Luc.* 66–7 (with comm.).[435] This position could be deemed as vulnerable to Antiochus'

---

type and in terms of representational content, but not with respect to the physical nature of an impression (imprint, alteration), which may be explained by the fact that the dogmatist allows only for a notional distinction between an impression qua imprint/alteration and its *species* (cf. §58 *fin.*). In §40 the ability to distinguish impressions which are equivalent as envisaged in premiss (iii) is explicitly introduced as a separate consideration.

[434] Cf. also Brittain (2006: 64 n. 165).
[435] §111 is itself evidence that Cicero approves the core argument in the technical sense.

objection as a position of mitigated scepticism, for even though it does not involve taking premisses (i) and (iii) as true, approving *p* is incompatible with approving not-*p*, and the issue of the grounds for approval would again arise.

If Cicero's own stance involved advancing the core and corollary arguments dialectically, he could simply have said that, whatever Philo's concerns were, he had no reason to share them. Here there would have been an opportunity to show the superiority of Cicero's position over that adopted by the younger Catulus in *Luc.* 148. Instead he claims to be entitled to the distinction drawn in premiss (i),[436] which suggests that he sees himself in the same boat as Philo (note also the first-person plural of *facimus* and *cernimus*).

In particular, Cicero replies here that the two premisses at issue, i.e. 'there are false (and consequently true) impressions' and 'there is no difference between true and false impressions', are not incompatible in that he was capable of discerning true and false impressions, thus rejecting the notion that as per premiss (iii) true and false impressions were the same thing, viz. members of a class whose elements share all properties.[437] The final sentence of the paragraph then looks back to the dilemma in §44a, where Lucullus had tried to argue that, for an argument to go through, the person who makes it must apprehend the premisses: this is not so according to Cicero, for (sc. true) impressions, corresponding to said premisses, only warrant approval but do not have the distinctive feature of cataleptic impressions. This fits with earlier sections where Cicero freely claimed that the Academic experiences true impressions (§101) and that many *probabilia* 'are' false (§103, a translation from Clitomachus). He can do this because the πιθανόν or *probabile* is even in the hands of a Clitomachean, or a Clitomachean of the kind Cicero is, not just a report of the Academic's subjective experience, but also indicative of and dependent on how things are in the external world; see §105b and section 6.6.

Philo's concern is introduced here as something Antiochus repeatedly remarked on. If Cicero's speech is informed by a Philonian source, it would be difficult to see how it could have included this information, given how casually Cicero dismisses it. It is more likely that Cicero himself is supplying this information. How would Cicero know what concerns Antiochus claimed Philo had? 'Antiochus used to say' suggests Cicero knows this from personal communication. He did not meet Antiochus until he studied with him in Athens in 79 BC, a decade after he heard Philo lecture in Rome.[438] At that point it might have featured in an account of the self-destruction of Academic scepticism, as a supposedly powerful objection to Clitomacheanism of the kind found in *Acad.*,[439] which in turn could have been presented as having given rise to the position of the Roman Books (however unperturbed Cicero affects to be in

---

[436] Cf. also *Luc.* 119: *uides enim iam me fateri aliquid esse ueri.*

[437] There is an inference involved, from their distinguishability to their difference; see sections 5.3 and 5.6.

[438] If Philo had mentioned such a concern while lecturing in Rome (cf. *Ac.* 1.13), e.g. to explain why he wrote them, then Antiochus would presumably not be cited for the information. Cicero could vouch for it himself.

[439] If these were the circumstances in which Cicero learnt of Philo's concern about Antiochus' objection, then it would seem fair to assume that from Antiochus' point of view Clitomacheanism and mitigated scepticism suffered from similar flaws.

our passage). If that position was fallibilist, as the most plausible reconstruction has it, it would not have been open to Antiochus' objection, but it would have posed other problems. It is not impossible in itself that, in placing himself 'in the same boat' as Philo, Cicero is suppressing that he and Philo (the latter at the unspecified time at issue) held different positions, if ones which were equally open to the Antiochian objection, but there seem to be no considerations in favour of this reading arising from the present context.

There are also some other considerations which need to be borne in mind in treating §111 as evidence on Philo. First, the Lucullus character is capable of presenting anti-Academic arguments which are of limited force and sophistication as devastating (see on §§43–44a). Second, the reference to Antiochus' distinction (*nec mirum...nobilis*) may be mildly sarcastic rather than straightforward (the Cicero character shifts between these two attitudes in his speech in *Luc.*), in which case Cicero would be signalling doubt about Antiochus' claim.[440] Third, if Cicero was cast as answering for and on behalf of Philo from the standpoint of a position shared by them, then this would not need to be interpreted negatively as suggesting that Cicero was the better Clitomachean, but could just be a part of the narrative which casts Romans as natural Clitomacheans (see on §146), or Cicero as a genuine representative of Academic scepticism.

Whatever qualifications one wishes to make, §111 does of course also represent evidence on Antiochus. We have no reason to doubt that he claimed that Philo was worried by his line of argument. Since the argument is made from the dogmatist standpoint in §§43–4, and since Philo and Antiochus did not, for all we know, meet again after the siege of Athens, the passage represents evidence that Antiochus' conversion took place in the 90s BC. This point is well made by Brittain (2001: 56) and only occasionally appreciated in earlier scholarship;[441] see also on §§69–71. If Clitomacheanism of the kind represented by Cicero in *Acad.* is a credible target in §111, then this fits with the assumptions about Philo's philosophical development advanced in this commentary, viz. that there were only two positions Philo adopted over time, the Clitomachean one and that of the Roman Books.

Ne illam quidem praetermisisti, Luculle...Philonem maxime perturbatum: cf. §44. *Ne...quidem* may already hint that Cicero regards Antiochus' point as less than powerful; given *ne...quidem*, it is more natural to understand *Antiochus* rather than *reprehensio* with *nobilis* (*pace* Brittain 2006: 64). *Antiochi* is subjective genitive, as Reid[1] (p. 306) notes. *Solebat dicere* does not naturally suggest that Antiochus made the point repeatedly in a book which Cicero read. Reid[1] (p. 306) is right to stress against Hirzel (1883: 315) that the aside on Antiochus' remark does not allow for the inference that Cicero was relying on a Philonian source in §§90–148. It is, however, likely on other grounds that a Philonian source or sources informed Cicero's speech; see section 9.3. On the ambiguity of the parenthesis, see the general note above.

---

[440] See also Striker (1997: 261–2).
[441] E.g. by Goedeckemeyer (1905: 103 n. 102); contrast Glucker (1978: 15 n. 7).

Cum enim sumeretur unum...nihil tam repugnare: for the interpretation of Antiochus' criticism, see the commentary on §§43–4, and section 5.6 on the various points of reference which the ἀπαραλλαξία-charge can have (truth-value itself is not among them; rather, true and false impressions are held to be non-distinct with respect to other things). The subject accusative which has to be supplied with *attendere* is *Philonem*. The verb *repugnare* refers to the concept of incompatibility, μάχη; see Reinhardt (2003: 232–7) on *Top.* 19–21. I explain in the general note above how Antiochus interpreted premisses (i) and (iii) for them to be incompatible; they could not possibly be formally incompatible if ἀπαραλλαξία is interpreted as 'indistinguishability' and if premiss (iii) is deemed to invoke ἀπαραλλαξία in this sense. From the *editio Romana* of 1471 onwards editors have frequently printed *ea re ⟨a se⟩*; thus also Reid[1] (p. 307).

Id ita esset...percipiendi signum nullum habemus: as indicated in the general note above, an Academic advancing the core argument ad hominem such that premiss (i) was assumed to be endorsed by the opponent would be invulnerable to Antiochus' objection however premiss (iii) is interpreted exactly. So Antiochus' objection is directed against Academics who endorse (in some manner) the core argument.

Cicero responds as if Antiochus' point was that premiss (iii) is an identity claim. If it was, it would be inconsistent with premiss (i), and it would be unclear in addition on what grounds one could endorse (i) given one's endorsement of (iii). The suggestion that premiss (iii) is an identity claim is not entirely unreasonable given that ἀπαραλλαξία means 'non-distinctness' (mirrored in various expressions used by Cicero in *Acad.*; see section 5.6). The reply, then, is that premiss (iii) does not altogether abolish 'the true' (sc. in impressions, hence *uerum* not *ueritatem*). Cicero continues that the Academics 'discern' true as well as false impressions, which presumably means that they recognize the conceptual distinction *and* discriminate between true and false impressions routinely as a matter of fact, just not with certainty and on the basis of a distinctive feature (on the issue of access see section 5.3). Cf. *N.D.* 1.12: *Non enim sumus ii quibus nihil uerum esse uideatur, sed ii qui omnibus ueris falsa quaedam adiuncta esse dicamus tanta similitudine, ut in iis nulla insit certa iudicandi et assentiendi nota.*

The phrase *probandi species* is hard to understand by itself but receives some illumination when juxtaposed with expressions like *percipiendi signum* as here. Note, however, that the two gerunds denote different kinds of things: apprehension is the result of an act of assent; approval is a kind of acceptance. A *signum percipiendi* (cf. *N.D.* 1.12: *certa...nota* quoted above) is a mark indicating that apprehension of the object is possible through this particular impression. Similarly, a *species probandi* is a 'look' which lead to or merits approval. For the sense of *species*, cf. §58 *fin.*: *quasi uero non specie uisa iudicentur*. *Species* probably renders ἔμφασις, which means 'appearance' but was also used by the Academics as a synonym for 'persuasive impression' (cf. Sextus, *M.* 7.169); see section 6.1 and 6.2. Reid[1] (p. 307) has further instances, including non-philosophical ones, of such a loose connection between head and gerund depending on it. See also the general note on *Luc.* 33–34a on *nota*-related terminology.

§§112-15

Luc. 112-15 has a number of functions. It is transitional, capping the responses (§§105b-111) to various points made by Lucullus in his speech and providing a commentary on why such detailed rebuttal was required on the one hand but was distracting from broader issues on the other, thus offering reflections on the nature of the debate from the Cicero character's viewpoint. The broader issues include the appraisal of the variety of philosophical views in the fields of physics (§§116-28), ethics (§§128-41), and logic (§§142-6). In §147 Cicero concludes this doxographical section with further thoughts on the theme of 'broader issues vs narrow dialectical argument'. At the same time, §§112-15 offer insights into how Cicero construes his Clitomacheanism in *Acad.*[442]

In §112 Cicero begins by observing that he has been proceeding in too austere a fashion and that he has allowed himself to be forced into the narrow corners and inhospitable thicket that is the province of the Stoics, when his speech might better have roamed freely (this connects with imagery first used in §98b; see n. below on *etiam nunc*). In the immediately preceding paragraph, he had dealt with an Antiochian objection to the *Academic* core argument which encapsulates the Academic opposition to the Stoic doctrine of the cataleptic impression.[443] In dubbing his own approach austere, Cicero is thus observing that it is—partly; see below—a function of the approach of the opponent he is up against. This is confirmed by Cicero's next point: if he was debating with a (sc. contemporary) Peripatetic, who Cicero suggests would employ a definition of an impression which affords apprehension that amounts to the Zenonian definition minus the third clause,[444] then he would be dealing with a straightforward man and would not put up much of a fight. That the epistemological position of contemporary Peripatetics could be characterized in such terms is noted also in *Fin.* 5.76 and is at least consistent with certain remarks Sextus makes about Peripatetic epistemology; see below on both passages.[445] Cicero says he would not put up much of a fight, which suggests that he would put up some fight.[446]

---

[442] On the construal of the Clitomachean position in *Acad.* and the Ciceronian corpus, see section 8 and, relatedly, section 7.5 on Arcesilaus.

[443] Görler (2004c: 273) calls §111 a 'thematic aberration', but it was simply the last in a series of replies to Lucullus (and to §§43-4 in particular).

[444] In *quod impressum esset a uero*, the phrase *a uero* is suggestive of the first clause of Zeno's definition, *quod impressum esset* of the second clause. By using the verb *percipere*, Cicero allows the impression to arise that he is talking about a Peripatetic conception of κατάλημψις. Whether this is innocuous or a tendentious *interpretatio Stoica* (or *Antiochea*) will need to be considered.

[445] Cicero does not acknowledge the fact that in outline this position was equivalent to the one defended by Philo in the Roman Books, which, however, are avowedly not the subject of the discussion in *Luc.* (§12b); see Görler (2004c: 281 n. 20). However, the Lucullus character comments on the merit of the epistemological claims of the Roman Books (§18) and dismisses its historical claims as a lie (§12), apparently agreeing on the latter point with the elder Catulus; and see the commentary on §78, where I argue that in that passage the Roman Books view is referenced in an aside to a larger argument concerned with something else.

[446] Thus also Brittain (2001: 186): 'We cannot extract a positive approbation of these "Peripatetic" doctrines from Cicero's measured negatives.' For a different view, see Glucker (2004: 126 n. 39).

If the Cicero character was purely arguing ad hominem and from assumptions which the opponent actually makes or ought to find compelling, then one would expect him to test any claim to knowledge with equal vigour. However, Cicero is not a Clitomachean so construed and behaves in a number of ways as only a mitigated sceptic would (on some construals of mitigated scepticism; see section 4). The Academics never denied that the first two clauses of Zeno's definition can be met and are often met (cf. e.g. Sextus, *M.* 7.402), and in what precedes he had claimed the right to posit that there are true impressions (most recently §111) while in §109b he claimed the right to *decreta*, sc. under Clitomachean approval (cf. §§104–105a). When Cicero says here that he would provide limited resistance to the Peripatetic, this suggests that his sceptical posture is not fully reactive and is instead expanding and contracting as it were depending on who the opponent is. He refrains from characterizing any of his commitments positively here, but the issue at hand is not what he would do if he acted completely on his own terms, and addressing them would have been a distraction given what immediately follows.

Cicero continues: if *he* made the claim that nothing can be apprehended, and *the Peripatetic* claimed that the sage will sometimes opine, then he would put up no resistance, especially given that Carneades 'put up no particular resistance on this point' (cf. *Luc.* 59, 67, 78). This raises several questions: what is the conception of apprehension employed in Cicero's claim? What is the nature and illustrative purpose of a hypothetical scenario in which Cicero and his contemporary Peripatetic would each contribute a claim to an overall position? (e.g. should one think of e.g. §101, where an Epicurean and a Stoic premiss yield the conclusion that nothing can be apprehended?) Why is it the Peripatetic who is contributing the claim about opining, when his conception of apprehension has just been at issue? What stance, if any, is Cicero taking here with respect to the inner-Academic dispute about Clitomacheanism versus mitigated the scepticism of the younger and elder Catulus (cf. *Luc.* 148),[447] characterized by the claims that 'nothing can be known' (sc. on the Stoic conception of knowledge) and 'the sage will sometimes opine' (i.e. assent to non-cataleptic impressions)? And do we have any reason to think that contemporary Peripatetics would formulate their epistemological views with reference to the sage (*diceret ille sapientem interdum opinari*), as Stoics and as a consequence Academics do?

This last point is perhaps key to the understanding of that part of the sentence (from *atque etiam si*): we have no such reason. Cicero is restating, with concrete examples, the general point with which he started, i.e. that his posture in part depends on that of his opponent. On this reading, the claim which Cicero advances is the conclusion of the core argument, i.e. 'nothing can be known' if one presupposes the Stoic conception of knowledge, and the Peripatetic is made to introduce 'the sage will sometimes opine' on the Stoic conception of δόξα. What changes everything is that the Peripatetic is *simplex*.

That this is an overstatement for rhetorical effect is suggested by Cicero's reaffirmation of 'nothing can be known' and 'the sage does not opine' at the end of §113. §112 concludes with a question which implies that no such sensible approach is open to

---

[447] *Luc.* 78, on my reading, does not represent evidence for the mitigated position.

Cicero, given how things actually are. Considering how overt and focused the engagement with Lucullus and the Antiochian position is in §112, I am hesitant to derive from the paragraph that the difference between a universal commitment to ἐποχή and mitigated scepticism, crucially characterized by the permission of qualified assent, is a lesser issue in Cicero's eyes. The section does not seem intended to speak to this matter, nor is it relevant that Cicero confesses to the human failing of opining frequently qua non-sage (§66). The Peripatetic may have been 'given' the claim that the sage will opine because he *is* a dogmatist and thus in need of a conception of belief, or one recognizable as such within the terms of the debate (Sextus, discussed below, sheds light on how the Peripatetic could be credited with opining). Another consideration which discourages a reading of §112 on which it minimizes the difference between Clitomacheanism and mitigated scepticism is the justification which Cicero offers for his commitment to ἐποχή: suspending judgement is a moral imperative for him.[448]

While §112 spoke of the constraints imposed by dealing with Stoic doctrine, §113 turns to the historical claims which provide the background to Antiochus' epistemology.[449] Cicero implies that he was able to speak of *Stoic* 'thickets' because Antiochus' views on the subject are taken over without modification from the Stoics (and from them alone). Truth-seeking Academic that he is (cf. *Luc.* 7b–9a, 76 *fin.*), Cicero asks what can be apprehended. Aristotle or Theophrast do not speak to the matter, nor do Xenocrates and Polemon: in other words, their thinking on the subject of knowledge was simply not concerned with the question of what can be apprehended. Rather, only a 'younger' one (most likely Zeno; see n. below) replies: 'a truth of such a kind as cannot be false.'[450] Yet Cicero finds no instance of such an impression, and so he assents—i.e. cannot help assenting (cf. §66 on Cicero as *magnus opinator*)—to the incognitive, sc. as a non-sage. He adds that the Peripatetics and the Old Academics permit this, presumably because they do not pronounce on the subject, whereas Antiochus bans it. After an expression of personal fondness for Antiochus, Cicero reasserts by means of a rhetorical question that before Zeno nobody had stated that only such impressions were cataleptic which could not be false and that the sage would not opine. He ends by expressing his approval of both claims, saying that he regards them both as true. This signals that he is now moving to engage the Stoics/Antiochus again.

The manner in which Cicero shifts in §§112–13 from hypothetical engagement with a contemporary Peripatetic to the consideration of views held by historical figures (Aristotle and Theophrastus; Polemo and Xenocrates) to hypothetical engagement with the latter (*hoc mihi... concedit*) and back to the presentation of their views

---

[448] Note especially §66: *pro ueris probare falsa turpissimum est*, which is a general statement whose categorical nature seems unconnected to the extreme standard set by Zeno's definition; §77.

[449] I do agree with Leonhardt (1999: 51) that already §112 implies a historical claim. This reading leads Leonhardt to the view that Cicero is claiming historical continuity between himself and the Peripatetics: 'Er [Cicero] stelle also im Grunde eine Kontinuität der Akademiegeschichte her, die den mit Arkesilaos eingetretenen Bruch leugnet.' Cicero's attested strategies for dismissing such a rupture are quite different: he claims continuity of Arcesilaus' with Socrates and Plato, and by and large ignores the Old Academics and Aristotle (*Luc.* 74).

[450] On the text after *aut Polemo*, see the n. below.

as historical (*...quis umquam **dixit**...*) is one reason why the passage is obscure and difficult, but that these shifts are performed seems plain enough. In *Fin.* 5.76 Cicero ascribes to Peripatetics, and most plausibly contemporary ones, what appears to be the same view as in §112 regarding an impression enabling apprehension, i.e. the acceptance of something like Zeno's definition minus the third clause,[451] and makes a similar point overall: that he rejects apprehension *as defined by the Stoics*. There is no precise parallel for the claim which Cicero makes about the epistemological stance of contemporary Peripatetics, but Sextus' discussion in his survey of the different views held on the criterion ascribes to 'Aristotle, Theophrastus, and the Peripatetics' the view that the criterion in the realm of the senses is τὸ ἐναργές and goes on to discuss the notion of φαντασία in terms loosely based on Aristotle's *De anim.* (see *M.* 7.216-26 = Theophrastus frg. 301A Fortenbaugh).[452] On the basis of this discussion one can see both how within the terminological parameters set by the Stoics the position ascribed to the Peripatos could be characterized as positing impressions which are rational, true, and clear as a criterion in the realm of perception, *and* why Cicero can say that the early Peripatetics (and the Old Academics) did not speak to the issue of apprehension.[453] What is notable is that the term κατάληψις is not used (instead the question is what the Peripatetic criterion is), and the sage as a reference point does not occur and instead human perception generally is at issue. However, the Peripatetics are credited with a conception of 'opinion' (δόξα) which arises from 'assent'; unlike in the Stoic system and according to Antiochus, however, the arts are said to be constituted by such δόξαι (*M.* 7.225).[454] §114 then identifies what to Cicero is a jarring contradiction: while banning Cicero from assenting to the incognitive and while regarding all opining as reprehensible and a sign of blind rashness, Antiochus engages in theory building on a grand scale, with respect to all areas of philosophy and consequently all aspects of life.[455] In all of these areas certainty is, or so the Academics have argued for centuries, not to be had, and so Cicero regards it as bizarre that he is to avoid opining by adopting Antiochus' system. Cicero ends the paragraph by calling it presumptuous on Antiochus' part to think that the abandoning of Academic scepticism would lead to the adoption of his system, given that there are many other schools to choose from. This provides the rationale for the review of conflicting views in the doxographical section §§116-47; see the general note on §116.[456]

---

[451] *Fin.* 5.76: '*Non est ista,*' inquam, '*Piso, magna dissensio. Nihil enim est aliud, quam ob rem mihi percipi nihil posse uideatur, nisi quod percipiendi uis ita definitur a Stoicis, ut negent quicquam posse percipi nisi tale uerum, quale falsum esse non possit. Itaque haec cum illis est dissensio, cum Peripateticis nulla sane. Sed haec omittamus; habent enim et bene longam et satis litigiosam disputationem*'; see also the note in Annas (2001: 143).

[452] Apart from the commentary in Huby (1999: 93-9), see Annas (1992b) and Gottschalk (2004). Annas (1992b: 207) sees Antiochus behind the Sextus passage; contra Brittain (2012: 108-13). Huby's claim (1999: 101) that 'it seems likely that Cicero is drawing his material [sc. in *Luc.* 112-13] from Antiochus' is implausible on more than one account. Tarrant (1985: 12 and n. 22-4) regards the fact that Sextus uses τὸ ἐναργές of both perceptual and non-perceptual impressions as evidence that the account in Sextus is influenced by Philo; I can see no basis for this, either.

[453] Cf. the comment by Annas (1992b: 208): 'The...passage...gives us an interesting example of what happens when a theory is interpreted in terms of concerns which are absent or peripheral in it.'

[454] On Aristotle's conception of belief in its historical context, see e.g. Moss and Schwab (2019).

[455] That many of Antiochus' doctrines were on Cicero's view not devised by him is here not at issue.

[456] See Algra (1997: 133-4).

§115 begins with the concession that not all dogmatic schools are equally attractive to Cicero: he feels no temptation to join the Peripatetics or the Epicureans. No reasons are cited, and instead Cicero gives characterizations of both schools: the former claim a particular affinity with rhetoric, as well as a history of producing leading politicians, while among Cicero's associates there are many Epicureans, they are good people, and devoted to each other. The last point alludes to the value Epicureans place on friendship, while their being good people gestures to an anti-Epicurean topos: that they take pleasure to be the highest good, and this invalidates everything else they say. Cicero counters this view politely by speaking of *tam boni*, while at the same time hinting that this is the reason why Epicureanism holds no attraction for him. This raises the question whether the characterization of the Peripatos given, which would normally be taken for praise when coming from Cicero, serves here to suggest that the Peripatetics are relative lightweights (see the n. below). The Stoics are represented by Diodotus, who lived in Cicero's house for many years—but who rejected Antiochus' ideas (what precisely he rejected is not clear from *illa Antiochia*). At this point Cicero has Lucullus (or Antiochus) interject in direct speech and with a hint of petulance that 'only' his view is true. Cicero dryly replies that this would have to be so since there cannot be several truths which are incompatible with each other.[457] He insists that it is not immodest to want to avoid error by suspending judgement with respect to obscure dogmatic claims, but arrogant to claim for oneself to know everything. Here the dogmatist is made to intercede again, saying that it is the sage who is deemed to know everything. To that Cicero has two replies. First, he observes that the dogmatist's claims about what the sage knows cannot be relied on if the dogmatist is not a sage. This may seem facile, but it conveys an important point: the Stoic sage is an unattainable ideal, which creates an issue of legitimacy for doctrines formulated by προκόπτοντες, while the Academic redescription of the sage offers a model for attainable real-life behaviour. Second, he agrees to continue to conduct the discussion with reference to the sage, who had been named as reference point in Lucullus' and Cicero's speech repeatedly. This may seem peculiar given what had just been said about non-sages pronouncing on sages and their beliefs.[458] However, Cicero (the character) has no reason to avoid the sage as a reference point, since the disagreements among the dogmatic philosophers which he is about to review are, or so he argues, apt to induce suspension of judgement of the sage (however conceived), and a fortiori of the non-sage.

§112

Ac mihi uideor...compellimus: *etiam nunc* refers back to §98b: *sed ut omnes istos aculeos...*, where Cicero ends the discussion of Academic objections to Stoic

---

[457] Cf. *Luc.* 147, which concludes the section beginning in §112:...*ut, cum plus uno uerum esse non possit, iacere necesse sit tot tam nobiles disciplinas*. In what immediately follows Cicero resumes the topic of the constraining effect which the Stoics have on the debate.
[458] Cf. Schäublin et al. (pp. 281–2 n. 336).

dialectic. *Ieiunitas* is abstinence from food and drink; *ieiune* then metaphorically of actions which are barren and needlessly confined; cf. *Or.* 118; *Fin.* 3.19. In *campus...exsultare possit oratio*, the speech is likened to a horse; cf. Hor., *C.* 3.11.9-10: *equa...campis ludit exsultim*, which compares a girl to a filly (see Nisbet and Rudd 2004: 154-5 ad loc.). A related image of a ship sailing on the open sea as opposed to being pushed along by oars is in *Tusc.* 4.9. See Görler (2004d: 211). The *angustiae* are in the context implied to arise from the very strong conception of knowledge operated by the Stoics, which forces (*compellimus*) the Academic to mount the kind of argument which is the reference point of Antiochus' criticism in §111. For *dumeta* 'thicket', cf. *N.D.* 1.68 (to the Stoics): *in dumeta correpitis*; Aug., *Contra Acad.* 2.2.6 (an allegory, but the context is not narrow technical argument); *spinae* is used in *Fin.* 4.6 of the stylistic austerity of Stoic speech, and in *Tusc.* 4.9 of Stoic division and definition.

Si enim mihi cum Peripatetico res esset...Nunc quid facere possum: §112: *si enim mihi cum Peripatetico*—§113: *magno opere defensum est* is Theophrastus frg. 302 FHS&D. See the general note above on further evidence for the Peripatetic conception of knowledge derived from the senses (and on the difficulty of treating §§112-13 as a fragment of Theophrastus). There is no positive evidence for Carneadean engagement with (contemporary) Peripatetic epistemology (from which, however, one should not infer lack of interest on Carneades' part; his engagement with the doctrines of schools other than the Stoa is well documented). On Carneades' claim that the sage will sometimes opine (§78), assumed to be advanced ad hominem by the Clitomacheans (§67) and as his own qualified opinion by mitigated sceptics (§148), see also §59, where the speaker is Lucullus. Cicero is being very measured in describing the different attitude he would take when dealing with a 'straightforward Peripatetic' (*simplex* is not pejorative; cf. *OLD* s.v. no. 8a): he would not put up resistance (contrast §148: *uehementer assentior*; the younger Catulus speaking), and Carneades 'did not resist much'. *Nunc* signals the end of the description of the counterfactual scenario. Görler (2004c: 276) paraphrases (*ille sapientem interdum*) *opinari* 'succumbs to opinions'; if the Stoic conception of opinion is in play, as I have argued above, this is not unwarranted, i.e. the opinions in question would still be conceptualized as epistemic failures. *Quod impressum esset e uero* runs together the first and the second clause of Zeno's definition while making it plain that the first clause is interpreted as stipulating veridicality. On the relevant sense of *accessio* 'addition', see *OLD* s.v. no. 4a; and §78 *init.* on the significance of the third clause. Reid[1] (p. 307) compares the shift from *e uero* to *a falso* with that from *e* to *de* in §11 (*e Philone audiuisset/audiuisse de Philone*); he also prints *adhiberet* (p. 307), following the Veneta of 1494 or 1496 (see Hunt 1998: 276 on both), for the transmitted *adhaerere*; given that a stipulation made (or rather not made) as opposed to an inherent property of the *definiendum* is at issue, that *adhaerere* is intransitive, and that the corruption would be easy to explain palaeographically, this seems right. Plasberg[1] (p. 131) prints *adhaerere* and assumes that it was Cicero who phrased the sentence poorly. See also Görler (2004c: 274 n. 11). *Quia* for *qui id* is in S as well as N and Nicc (the other *v* mss read *qui* without *id*).

§113

Quaero enim...Nihil eius modi inuenio: having ended the hypothetical encounter with a contemporary Peripatetic in the previous sentence, Cicero now speaks as the truth- and knowledge-seeking Socratic. For the Peripatetics and the role accorded to them in Antiochus' construction of the Old Academy, see *Ac.* 1.33–9; section 7.2 for the Antiochian views on the history of philosophy more generally; and *Luc.* 69–71 for related criticism of Antiochus by the Cicero character.

As to the text after *Polemo*, the archetype seems to have read *sed mihi minorem* or *minores*. *Minorem* does not construe, and another *mihi* would be redundant and undeserving of emphasis, since the issue is who replies, not to whom the reply is given (*mihi* as an ethical dative would be a mere filler word). Plasberg[1] emends to *hi minores*; on this reading *mihi* could either be an anticipation of the first syllable of *minor* or perseveration from *respondet mihi* above. However, given that the definition of the cataleptic impression is so firmly associated with Zeno in *Acad.* (cf. §77) and that the context is historical, the plural *minores*, which would either mean the Stoics in general or run Zeno and Antiochus together, is unattractive. Reid[1] (p. 308) suggests that *mihi* displaced a relative, printing *sed qui minor est* (so the hyparchetype m, possibly as the result of an emendation by William of Malmesbury; see Malaspina 2015; Reid cited Cant2, one of the two contributing manuscripts). This is attractive (provided one makes Zeno the reference point, not Antiochus like Reid), yields a text with the right emphases, and is closer to the paradosis than e.g. *sed minor quidam*. For a similar attitude attitude to Zeno, cf. *Tusc.* 5.34; see also on *Ac.* 1.43. I take *minor* to be free of pejorative connotation, given that §113 ends with an endorsement of Zeno on two specific points. See also Schäublin et al. (p. 278 n. 327), who, however, print Plasberg's text.

After *tale* one may have to understand *uisum* as in *Fin.* 5.76 (thus Reid[1] p. 308) or Cicero meant to write no more than 'such a truth'. *Nihil eius modi inuenio* signals that Cicero can find no instantiations of the definition, of which he approves at the end of the paragraph; so also Sextus in *M.* 7.154, in his discussion of Arcesilaus.

Itaque incognito nimirum assentiar...politissimum et acutissimum omnium nostrae memoriae philosophorum: Lambinus' restoration is compelling. On *incognito* Reid[1] (p. 308) notes the rarity of the 'dative singular of the substantival participle'. The singular is generic, given the previous sentence. On the general point, cf. §68. The singular *concedit* is unobjectionable after *Academia* given *Peripatetici*; see Pinkster i.1252. For further evidence of the affection in which Cicero held Antiochus, see Hatzimichali (2012: 25); sometimes Cicero sounds more dismissive, perhaps when he is following a source more closely (see section 9.3). With *ita iudico* cf. §108: *Clitomacho ita scribenti*.

A quo primum quaero...Certe nemo: Reid[1] (p. 308) notes the tendency in Greek and Latin for rhetorical questions to receive a reply. The *Academia* is Antiochus' Old Academy here.

Horum neutrum ante Zenonem...sed ita plane probo: for Zeno as the creator of these two positions, cf. §77, but *magno opere* signals a qualification which is absent from the earlier passage: the implication is that in a vague, loose, and quite possibly differently conceived form the notions that nothing can be apprehended and the sage should not opine *had* been upheld previously; cf. section 7.1 on the attested Academic construals of the history of philosophy. 'Nothing could be known', if not on the Stoic conception of knowledge, was traced back to the Presocratics, and certain Platonic dialogues, e.g. the *Euthyphro* and the *Ion*, could be cited as assuming knowledge, and knowledge only, among experts at least in the relevant domain; the injunction not to opine can be linked to *Rep.* 506c and Socrates. See on *Ac.* 1.44–6 and *Luc.* 148.

Arcesilaus' approval of the propositions which are the conclusions of the core and corollary arguments is referenced in §§66–7 and 77, and if the former passage already suggested that Arcesilaus is construed as a particularly important intellectual ancestor for the Clitomachean position, then the present passage represents further evidence for this. For *temporis causa* = 'for the sake of expediency', cf. *Tusc.* 4.8. On the use of *ita* (or *sic*) in place of a neuter pronoun functioning as an object, see Reid (1882: 65) on *Sen.* 16: ...*et tamen sic a patribus accepimus*.

The use of *probo* in its context illustrates that 'approval', while being used interchangeably with *sequi* and while rendering inter alia ἕπεσθαι (see on §104; Striker 1996b: 98 n. 23), is not paradigmatically a passive acquiescing. In contexts where philosophical questions are at issue approval issues from a rational attitude, in which one consciously says 'yes', arguably with varying degrees of conviction for a number of reasons. Görler (2004b: 70–1) argues that by rendering ἕπεσθαι as *probare* Cicero modifies the concept of approval itself (because of the different associations of the two terms), but *Luc.* 104, which is presented as a translation from Clitomachus, suggests otherwise. *Plane* most naturally signals the degree of endorsement, sc. within the limits set by approval (*OLD* s.v. no. 3), as opposed to the endorsement being unguarded (Brittain 2006: 66: 'openly') or deliberate (Rackham 1951: 613: 'it is my deliberate judgement').

§114

Illud ferre non possum...et artificium traditurum: for *illud ferre non possum*, cf. §136. *Vetare* as usual 'to ban, sc. from doing' rather than 'to object that something is occurring or being done', *pace* Schäublin et al. (p. 147): 'Während du dagegen Einspruch erhebst, dass ich Nichterkanntem zustimme....' For the Stoic condemnation of assent to non-cataleptic impressions as *temeritas*, see *Ac.* 1.42. *Disciplina sapientiae* = 'doctrinal system'; see Glucker (1978: 193–206) for the use of *disciplina* in the sense of 'sect'. Sometimes both senses are in play; *exponas* disambiguates here. The rest of the sentence indicates what is encompassed by the phrase. Reid[1] (p. 309) cites parallels for the characterizations of the different fields of philosophy. Cicero combines expressions which suggest an analysis of the given (*naturam rerum...euoluas*) with others which suggest stipulation (*mores fingas*); the former is implied to be presumptuous because humans lack the relevant insight, the latter because it is interfering and insufficiently warranted. Dialectic's claim to enhancing understanding is dismissed in §§91–8. *Artificium* stands for an art qua system of rules which one can learn and use; it is neutral in tone like *ars*. The product of an art cannot be meant here.

For *temeritas*, see on *Luc.* 66 and *Ac.* 1.42. The similarity of *fines...malorumque* with the full title of *Fin.* (deployed after Cicero abandoned the idea of naming the component books after individuals, as he did in the case of *Acad.*) is striking, but the phrase means something different here, since only one school is at issue.

Cum (me incognito) is adversative or concessive. On the punctuation of the sentence, see the note in Plasberg[1] (p. 132).

Perficies ut ego...si ab hac abstraxeris: with *labar* and the notion that an act of assent to the incognitive amounts to a 'slip' or indeed sets up a general slide (in that false beliefs wreak havoc on one's assent patterns), cf. §108: *assensus lubricos sustinere*, §139: *labor eo ut assentiar Epicuro aut Aristippo*, §68:...*ipsa consuetudo assentiendi periculosa esse uidetur et lubrica*, §59: (on Carneades, but Lucullus is speaking) *Carneadem...heri audiebamus solitum esse ⟨eo⟩ delabi interdum ut diceret opinaturum, id est peccaturum, esse sapientem*, as well as the related image (§68)...*sustinenda est potius omnis assensio, ne* **praecipitet** *si temere processerit*. See Görler (1974: 189–91) for related passages from other Ciceronian works, and the commentary on *Ac.* 1.42 for the assent-related Stoic 'virtues'. Reid[1] (p. 309) suspects *deducas* and wants to emend to the future *deduces*, but at the same time explains how the subjunctive would give good sense.

Vereor...ad suam quisque rapiet: with *subarroganter*, cf. §126: *arroganter*. The prefix is presumably softening ('somewhat arrogant'; cf. *subdolus, subsimilis*), but I could find no precise parallel.

§115

Age, restitero Peripateticis...'Nostra', inquies, 'sola uera sunt': logically the sentences beginning *restitero...* and *sustinuero* have the force of the protasis in a conditional (*Diodoto quid faciam...* is then the apodosis); the deliberative subjunctive has the force of a simple future. See Kühner-Stegmann ii.164–6.

For the characterization of the Peripatetics, see Görler (2004d: 195). Theophrastus collected laws from various city states (*Fin.* 5.11), Dicaearchus continued Aristotle's collection of constitutions (*Leg.* 3.14; *Att.* 2.16.3 = SB 36), and Demetrius of Phaleron ruled Athens for ten years (*Leg.* 3.14; *Brut.* 37). Cicero presents himself sometimes as reuniting political oratory and philosophy in a Peripatetic fashion (*Fam.* 15.4.16 = SB 106; *Tusc.* 1.7; *Div.* 2.4; *Off.* 1.3), and one wonders if Aristotle was somehow invoked by Philo when he taught rhetoric in Rome. However, the rhetorical interests of the Peripatetics are also occasionally invoked to present them as lightweight, as in the story about the transfer of Aristotle's books to Skepsis, which reduced his school to θέσεις ληκυθίζειν (Strab. 13.1.54), and here the context would seem to require at least a hint as to why the Peripatetics hold no attraction for Cicero. *Dicant* appears significant in this respect, in that it marks a failure on Cicero's part to endorse the Peripatetic claims. *Cognatio* denotes a blood relationship in its primary sense, so the Peripatetics claim more for themselves than an interest or an expertise in oratory.

Cicero's best-known *familiaris* who followed Epicureanism was of course Atticus, who was closely involved with the editorial process of *Acad.* and features as an interlocutor in the final edition; others include L. Manlius Torquatus, C. Trebatius Testa, and Lucius Saufeius (on whom see Gilbert 2019). Dismissing Epicureanism and its followers out of hand would not have been an option. However, the statement that Cicero's Epicurean *familiares* are *boni* needs to be read against the hostility directed elsewhere against the theory of pleasure, which in antiquity often prevents the fair consideration of Epicurean doctrines outside the field of ethics; see Reinhardt (2005: 161 and passim) and e.g. *N.D.* 1.66, where the claim that the bedrock of reality is atoms is dismissed as *flagitia*, or Aug., *Contra Acad.* 3.10.23, where atoms are likened to prostitutes. On the role of friendship in Epicureanism, see *Fin.* 1.65, 2.81; Brown (2009: 182–91); and Konstan (2014).

Having said that he will resist the Peripatetics and the Epicureans, Cicero does not actually state how he would deal with the Stoics, citing his personal relationship with and affection for Diodotus, only to report on Diodotus' attitude to Antiochus, which was very negative. Diodotus instructed Cicero in Stoic logic (*Brut.* 309; cf. *N.D.* 1.6, where he is named as one of his four philosophical teachers alongside Philo, Antiochus, and Posidonius) and died in 59 BC (*Att.* 2.20 = SB 40; cf. *Brut.* 309), i.e. a couple of years after the dramatic date of *Luc.*; see McDermott and Heesen (1975). Reid[1] (p. 310) observes that *mecum uiuit* is illuminated by *qui habitat apud me*; the former does not mean 'lived in the same house' by itself. *Diodoto* is perhaps best explained as an ablative of respect; cf. Reid[1] (p. 292) on §96: *quid enim faceret huic conclusioni*. The phrase *ista Antiochea* is too vague to take a view on what Diodotus was dismissing: presumably not epistemology and logic, but ethics, or the *disciplina* as a whole complete with its assumed history.

Certe sola, si uera...discrepantia esse non possint: the same principle is alluded to in §§117, 147. With *discrepare*, originally used of jarring sounds, cf. *repugnantia* in §50; *discrepare* of philosophers disagreeing in *Luc.* 147; *Tusc.* 4.61.

Vtrum igitur nos impudentes...scire se solos omnia: on *labi*, see *labar* in the previous paragraph (with n.). Reid[1] (p. 310) quotes Hor., *Ep.* 2.1.87 (to Augustus, on people who are as ignorant as everyone else about archaic song but claim a fondness for it): *quod mecum ignorat, solus uolt scire uideri*.

Non me quidem...a non sapiente explicari sapientiam: in §66 Cicero as Clitomachean draws the corresponding distinction between himself and the Academic sage. On ironic or sarcastic *optime*, see *OLD* s.v. no. 1b. What follows is short for *Nempe dicis ista sapientem scire...disciplina*; on *nempe*, see *OLD* s.v. no. 1a. With *hoc quale est* = 'what are we to make of this?', cf. *Leg.* 1.1:...*aut quale est istuc quod poetae serunt*, with Dyck (2004: 60). Reid[1] (p. 311) refers to *Ac.* 1.39 *non corpus*; see also Wackernagel (2009: 730–2). The shift from plural *illi* to singular *inquit* is not unusual; it can be read as a slightly exasperated turn towards the internal audience. Note also *inquies* above.

Sed discedamus...omnis haec quaestio est: *discedere* is often used of the parting with a character in the text, cf. §82: *ab hoc credulo discedamus*; *Tusc.* 2.33: *a te malo discedere*. Both Lucullus (e.g. §§23, 57) and Cicero (e.g. §§66, 105) reaffirm in various places that the sage's behaviour is under discussion.

§§116–17

§§116–17 serve as an 'epistemological preface to the physics section' (Brittain 2006: 67 n. 173).[459] §128b fulfils a similar function for the section on ethics, while drawing on considerations developed in §§116–128a (the issue of the size of the sun recurs, too): the reasoning there is that by affirming—irrationally, as the Academic thinks—their physical doctrines the dogmatists also lose authority over matters which are less obscure, like ethical doctrines. This is because their methodological framework does not allow them to calibrate their responses; instead, everything is affirmed in the same manner (sc. through dogmatic assent).

Cicero refers to the division of the three branches or parts of philosophy into physics, ethics, and logic, and announces that he will begin with enquiries into nature, i.e. physics. By means of a rhetorical question he expresses bafflement that anyone should be so misguided as to persuade himself that he has knowledge in the area. He states that he is not looking for reasonings which depend on conjecture, which can in debate be influenced one way or another, and which do not rely on necessary persuasion that such-and-such is the case.[460] Rather, the geometers should supply their reasonings (*prouideant*, sc. *rationes*; cf. §117: *geometricis rationibus*), which they claim are not merely persuasive but compelling;[461] what is more, these proofs are recognized by the dogmatist. As a concession, Cicero undertakes to refrain from questions about principles of geometry, which are a standard target of the sceptics, as is plain from Sextus' attack on them in *M*. 3.[462] A scenario is then devised in which the sage witnesses the geometer conduct a proof of the size of the sun, in line with his exacting methodology and whose subject belongs with the realm of physics. The question is how the sage would react to the proof once it is concluded. The options are presented as a dilemma: if he accepts the proof, he will show contempt for a divine being, i.e. the sun (this contempt consists in assuming it to be a definite size, or to be measurable like an ordinary physical object; cf. §126); if the sage does not accept the proof, sc. conducted by the most rigorous standards and on a subject to do with physics, he will have no grounds whatsoever to believe arguments advanced by philosophers in the same domain.

Alternatively, if he was prepared to accept the arguments advanced by philosophers, whose in particular should he adopt (sc. given that they all say different

---

[459] Other editors paragraph the text slightly differently: Plasberg¹ (p. 133) breaks after §117 *nec plus uno poterit* and runs §118 on at the end of the section, while Schäublin et al. (p. 150) break after §117 *quorum potissimum* and again at the end of §117.

[460] Note *Luc*. 127: *indagatio ipsa rerum cum maximarum tum etiam occultissimarum habet oblectationem; si uero aliquid occurrit quod ueri simile uideatur, humanissima completur animus uoluptate*. Strikingly, when Seneca discusses natural philosophy in the *N.Q.*, he quite overtly adopts a methodology which draws on the *probabile* and Cicero's *Acad*. in particular; see Armisen-Marchetti (2000).

[461] See Tielemann (2008: 50–3) on Galen's invocation of geometry as a methodological model for medicine.

[462] See Mueller (1982) for a discussion of the anti-geometrical strategies employed in Sextus, *M*. 3, and the shorter account in Cambiano (1999: 590–5) and Betegh (2015: 157–71). Mueller is avowedly interested in explaining the issues raised by Sextus, and not in investigating sources, but it is plausible to assume that Sextus was able to draw on Academic arguments against geometry, just as he probably drew, as Mueller shows, on anti-geometrical Epicurean arguments (cf. the commentary on *Luc*. 106). See also Bénatouïl and El Murr (2010).

things)? As a next step Cicero exploits the fact that the Stoics formulate doctrines with reference to the sage, but assume that actual sages are exceedingly rare or non-existent (cf. §115 *fin.*). Someone who is yet to choose a physical doctrine or system to follow can only do so while not yet being a sage (the implication being that part of the sage's wisdom is being in possession of such a doctrine). He therefore chooses as an *insipiens* as Cicero pointedly says, having used the neutral phrasal term *non sapiens* in §115 *fin.* (it is of course the *Stoic* view that anyone who is not a sage on the Stoic conception of sagehood is a fool). And, Cicero continues, even if the *insipiens* had a divine talent, whose position should he approve? There are so many, and he can only approve one. As a concession, Cicero proposes not to pursue open-ended questions, but the fairly narrow issue of physical principles. I shall discuss the question of the origin of the doxographical material used in what follows, and its sceptical repurposing, in the general note to §§118–26.[463]

§116

In tres igitur partes...distributa sapientia est: the first occurrence of the division in the second edition is in *Ac.* 1.19 (*iam accepta a Platone philosophandi ratio triplex*); it is then used as an organizational principle for Varro's speech. In the first edition it must have occurred in the *Catulus* for the first time. That Cicero uses *sapientia* here for *ratio philosophandi* could be more than *uariatio*, given how he employs the concept of sagehood against the dogmatist in §117 *fin.* Reid[1] (p. 311) compares the subjunctive in *si placet...uideamus* with that in §29: *sit, ut opinor, dictum satis.*

Primum ergo si placet...ut sibi illa scire persuaserit: if the transmitted text after *uideamus* is correct, it needs to be parsed as a self-correction (*uel*), followed by a metatextual purpose clause with ellipsis (*ut illud ante*, sc. *dicam*), followed by strong punctuation. Reid[1] (p. 311) suggested that the manuscript reading *uelut* is the result of gloss on an original *at* (*uel 'ut'*).

With *inflatus errore*, cf. *Off.* 1.91:...*cum homines inflati opinionibus turpiter irridentur et in maximis uersantur erroribus*. On the connotation of arrogance which *inflatus* often carries, see Kaster (2006: 157–8). The rhetorical question overall aims at the unlikelihood of achieving knowledge in the domain of physics (*illa*), and it consequently being presumptuous to regard one's beliefs as knowledge.

Non quaero rationes eas...nullam adhibent persuadendi necessitatem: *rationes* is as so often difficult to pin down, but 'reasonings' or 'proofs' (i.e. arguments offered as proofs) seems to capture its sense best. *Coniectura* does in Cicero and other Latin writers correspond to στοχασμός, but one should perhaps not see a reference to stochastic arts in the narrow sense (see §107 *init.*), because the context is too unspecific

---

[463] I merely note here, and discuss in more detail in the commentary on the doxographical section, that within the tradition of the *placita* mathematics features in one of the main sources (Stob., *Ecl.* I.1, pp. 15–22 Wachsmuth) as a propedeutic subject before the discussion of physical tenets begins; cf. Lévy (1996: 112–14). Diels (1879) did not include the prefatory sections in his reconstruction of Aëtius.

to suggest reasoning in accordance with an art and the application of craft knowledge: the *rationes* at issue seem to cover non-deductive inference generally. For the connection of *coniectura* with waywardness, cf. *Div.* 2.147: *coniectura quae in uarias partes duci possit*, but an important addition here is *disputationibus*: argumentative scrutiny drags or, as we would say, pushes around results achieved by *coniectura*.

Nullam adhibent persuadendi necessitatem is ambiguous. It could mean that as a matter of fact the reasonings in question are not compelling, or it could mean that they carry no claim to being compelling. When Seneca wrote the following in *N.Q.* 1.4.1, he may have had the former reading of Cicero in mind: *Rationes, quae non persuadent sed cogunt, a geometris afferuntur,* **nec dubium cuiquam relinquitur,** *quin arcus imago solis sit male expressi ob uitium figuramque speculi: nos interim temptemus alias probationes, quae de plano legi possint,* 'The proofs offered by geometers are not only persuasive but compelling, and nobody is left with any doubt that a rainbow is an image of the sun, imperfectly represented because of the flawed shape of the mirror; let us attempt other proofs in the meantime, the kind that can be picked up in the open.'

Necessitas renders ἀνάγκη (e.g. D.L. 7.77 = *SVF* ii.238), while *cogere* below is reminiscent not just of ἀναγκάζειν but also of συνάγειν (D.L. 7.78 and Sextus, *M.* 8.411 = *SVF* ii.239), which, however, is used of the bringing together of the premises in a conclusion and does not denote an effect on an audience.

Geometrae prouideant...⟨altitudine⟩ carentem: with *geometres, -ae,* m. (γεωμέτρης; contrast the nominative singular *geometra* in *CIL* III.6041), cf. Quint. 2.14.4: *Ne pugnemus igitur, cum praesertim plurimis alioqui Graecis sit utendum; nam certe et philosophos et musicos et geometras dicam, nec uim adferam nominibus his indecora in Latinum sermonem mutatione*; *TLL* s.v. col. 1907.39–40: 'nom. *-es* optimi stili est' (examples follow).

Prouideant (sc. *rationes* supplied from the previous sentence, cf. *geometricis rationibus* in §117 *init.*) not 'to see to' or 'to watch out for' (Plasberg[1] p. 132: '(=) caveant'; Schäublin et al. p. 151: 'in Acht nehmen'), but 'to provide, to furnish' (cf. *OLD* s.v. *prouideo* no. 5). On *cogere*, see previous note. *Vobis*, as Reid[1] (p. 311) rightly notes, is emphatic: the Stoics and Antiochus accept the proofs, but not the Academics. With *describunt* (of geometrical drawings), cf. *Div.* 2.10: *quae in geometria describuntur*; *TLL* s.v. *describo* col. 657.13–52.

Quaerere ex aliquo with an object 'to ask someone about something', with *his* referring to the geometers. On the geometer's habit of making or positing but not defending basic assumptions (*initia* here), see *Tusc.* 5.18; *Off.* 3.33. For *digitus* as a minute amount by which one must not yield in arguments, proofs, or courses of action cf. §58: *ab hac mihi non licet transuersum, ut aiunt, digitum discedere.*

As mentioned in the general note above, much of the attack on geometry in Sextus, *M.* 3, is devoted to these basic concepts or principles (Cicero's *initia* here, corresponding to στοιχεῖα, which is usually rendered *elementa*; for the equation *initia = elementa* see *Ac.* 1.26). Cicero's order of 'point, surface, line' is, as Reid[1] (p. 311) notes, 'unnatural', but his point does not depend on it. Several of the terms feature here for the first time in Latin, but their occurrence in e.g. Vitruvius or the *gromatici* suggests that this is due to the accidents of survival. Cf. Sextus, *P.H.* 3.39: σημεῖον μὲν γάρ φασιν οὗ μέρος οὐθέν, γραμμὴν δὲ μῆκος ἀπλατές, ἐπιφάνειαν δὲ μῆκος μετὰ πλάτους, 'For they say that the point is that which has no parts, that the line is a length without width, and that the surface is a length with width', for all three terms. On *punctum*, cf. M. 9.283 (cf. 377): ἐπεὶ κατ' αὐτοὺς ἡ γραμμὴ ἐκ στιγμῶν συνεστῶσα νοεῖται, 'since according to them the line is understood to be composed of points'; Cic., *Tusc.* 1.40. *Extremitas* corresponds to ἐπιφάνεια (cf. Sextus, M. 9.415: ἡ δὲ ἐπιφάνεια πέρας σώματος 'the surface is the boundary of the solid'); in *Tim.* 33b Plato speaks of the τελευταί of a sphere, which Cicero renders as *extremitas* in his translation, but τελευταί does not seem to have caught on with mathematical writers. The phrase *et quasi libramentum* is added to indicate that a plane surface is at issue (Greek ἐπιφάνεια is not so restricted); *quasi* probably signals that the term is unusual or unusually applied here by Cicero, and its later occurrences in that sense suggest that *libramentum* was not mathematical standard terminology (Sen., *Ben.* 5.6.4; *N.Q.* 1.12.1—both passages probably influenced by Cicero). With *nulla crassitudo*, cf. Sextus, *P.H.* 3.43: μῆκος καὶ πλάτος ἄβαθες, '(in connection with solid one cannot imagine) length and width without depth'. The final colon in this tricolon of geometrical terms poses a textual problem. In the transmitted *lineamentum sine ulla latitudine carentem* the last word does not construe, and would need to be emended if a lacuna was posited before it. Reid[1] (p. 312) deletes *carentem* and writes [his emphasis]: 'Symmetry requires that the line should be described *by a negation merely*, like the point and the surface. The words *sine latitudine* are a rendering of ἀπλατές in the ordinary Euclidian definition of γραμμή as μῆκος ἀπλατές.' Against this, one could cite first that the symmetry of the passage is flawed in any case due to the inverted sequence of surface and line, and that it would be quite natural to end what is a tricolon on a somewhat fuller definition. Gellius 1.20 cites Varro's definition of the line as *linea est longitudo quaedam sine latitudine et altitudine*. This probably inspired Usinus' insertion of *longitudinem* after *lineamentum* (coupled with deletion of *sine ulla*), and certainly the insertion of *atque omni altitudine* (Plasberg[1] p. 133) before *carentem* (which Plasberg combined with *longitudinem* proposed by Ursinus 1581). Reid's observation that there is a formal principle in play which involves a negation offers some protection to *sine ulla*; moreover, if Cicero had written *lineamentum longitudinem latitudine carentem* and *longitudinem* had dropped out, inserting *sine ulla* secondarily (rather than emending *carentem* to *carens*) would have been a peculiar move. Following sense, I print a text inspired by Varro's definition, which Cicero may have used or which he may have formulated independently (given the terminological constraints, it is in this case conceivable that two writers might end up with very similar translations). This seems preferable to assuming e.g. that *carentem* derives from a marginal remark which introduced the notion of an absence of depth. Cicero's mentioning of *lineamentum* in *De orat.* 1.187 predates the occurrence here by about a decade, but includes no definition. For the spelling *lineamentum* over the transmitted *liniamentum*, see *TLL* s.v. *lineamentum* cols 1438.67–1439.5.

Haec cum uera esse concessero...iuraturum putas: the phrase *ius iurandum adigere aliquem* means 'to cause someone to take an oath'. The *cum*-clause is temporal, its tense is the future perfect, as is the tense of the verb in the *priusquam*-clause. *Putas* is genuine present tense rather than *praesens pro futuro* (which is not uncommon in conditionals; see Kühner-Stegmann i.119–20), since the question is what Lucullus now thinks the sage will do (*iuraturum*) under the circumstances envisaged. *Inspectare* is used in its basic intransitive sense, 'to look on, watch'.

On the issue of the size of the sun, cf. §§82 and 126–7 (which concludes the physics section), as well as Aët. 2.21 (with Mansfeld and Runia 2009: 534–46). As Brittain (2006: 68 n. 175) notes, there is no evidence that Archimedes worked on the problem of the size of the sun himself, but his famous work Ψαμμίτης is devoted to the question of how many grains of sand fit into the universe. This required an estimation of the size of the universe, for which Archimedes must have drawn on Aristarchus of Samos' calculations on the size of the sun. Archimedes is probably named here as a famous geometer.

Reid[1] (p. 312) rightly rejects earlier editors' attempts to remove the negation *nec (prius)* and refers to §123: *nec ille iurare possit*. On the uses of *adigere* and *adicere*, see Madvig (1873: 251–2).

Si fecerit...contempserit: the tense pattern (future perfect in protasis and apodosis) emphasizes that in the act of giving assent under oath the sage will have revealed himself to be in contempt of god. That the sun is a divine being for the Stoics is stated in §126, where measuring it 'as if with a surveyor's rule' is dismissed as absurd.

§117

Quod si geometricis rationibus non est crediturus...aut si est crediturus, quorum potissimum: *ne* is the affirmative particle ('truly'), not the negation, and *ille* is subject of *aberit* ('he will be far from...'), which is in personal construction. Pace Reid[1] (p. 313), who takes *aberit* to be impersonal, 'as the usage of Cic. and the best writers requires', and *ille* to be the subject to *credat* (i.e. *ille* would have been pulled in front). Reid is correct that the impersonal construction of *abest* with *ut* is much more frequent, but it seems dogmatic to read our passage as well as e.g. *Fin.* 2.54, where the word order would be yet more extreme, as an impersonal construction: *Is enim qui occultus et tectus dicitur tantum abest ut se indicet, perficiet etiam ut dolore alterius improbe facto uideatur*. Personal construction with a prepositional phrase (*absum ab aliqua re*) is more common (e.g. Cic., *Ver.* 2.60: *a qua suspicione ille aberat plurimum*). **Vim afferre in docendo** means 'to carry demonstrative force'. Whether *argumentis* should be rendered 'proofs' or 'arguments' depends on who is deemed to be the focalizer here: for Cicero, they are (mere) 'arguments', for the subject envisaged, 'proofs'. With the criticism implied in *quorum potissimum* Reid[1] (p. 313) aptly compares Sextus, *P.H.* 1.88 and *M.* 11.173. *Philosophi* is used for contrast with geometers; in the next sentence Cicero speaks more narrowly of *physici*, philosophers (or thinkers) who have pronounced on physical matters.

Omnia enim physicorum licet explicare...quaero tamen quem sequatur: on the shift from *philosophi* to *physici*, see above. See Reid[1] (p. 313) on the indicative of *longum est* as well as the possibility that *omnia* is a corruption of *somnia* (cf. §121).

Finge aliquem nunc fieri sapientem...⟨et⟩ disciplinam: the *proficiens* (προκόπτων) is becoming a sage (*fieri sapientem*), hence the need to choose a physical doctrine:

the sage ought to have a physical doctrine, which is part of his wisdom. *Disciplinam* as complement of *sententiam* would suggest that the *disciplina* consisted in the one *sententia* (which, when *disciplina* is in the vicinity, would naturally be taken to mean 'tenet'), so an insertion is needed. There is not much to choose between the emendations *aut* and *et*; the latter may be taken to convey better that in selecting a *sententia* one selects the *disciplina* to which it belongs.

Etsi quamcumque eliget…Nec plus uno poterit: by shifting from the phrasal term *non sapiens* in §115 *fin.* to *insipiens*, Cicero alludes to the Stoic view that all non-sages are fools (cf. Cic., *Parad.* 27–32) and that their choices are consequently unreliable. Stoic thought does not admit of non-sages who are superior due to *ingenium diuinum*; this is an Academic concession for the sake of the argument. With *nec plus uno poterit*, cf. §147: *cum plus uno uerum esse non possit*; §115: *plura enim uera discrepantia esse non possunt*.

Non persequor quaestiones infinitas…Est enim inter magnos homines summa dissensio: in rhetorical contexts, a *quaestio infinita* is a general question (i.e. a θέσις), and it is no coincidence that the questions which Cicero names as instances of *quaestiones* in *Inv.* 1.8 feature in the doxographical tradition: 'are the senses true?' is Aët. 4.9, 'what is the shape of the cosmos?' is 2.2, 'what is the size of the sun?' is 2.21. Cf. also Runia (2010: 277). The rhetorician Hermagoras appropriated a pre-existing sense of the term θέσις (= 'general question') and claimed that rhetoric was concerned with particular questions, ὑποθέσεις (again *Inv.* 1.8 = frg. 6a Matthes). However, this does not mean, *pace* Reid[1] (p. 313), that in the present passage *quaestiones infinitae* are 'θέσεις as opposed to ὑποθέσεις': the restriction to the subject of the principles (*principia*, ἀρχαί) does not amount to a particular question in the rhetorical sense (i.e. one which is definite with respect to people involved, time, place, etc.), nor is there a general question which would correspond to it. *Quaestiones infinitae* are θέσεις in the less determinate older sense. The relative clause *e quibus omnia constant* narrows down the sense of *principia* to material principles (on this use of *principium*, see *TLL* s.v. cols 1311.43–1312.2). *Dissensio* will be a recurrent theme in the doxographical section; cf. §§126, 129, 134, 147.

§§118–26

In the section §§118–28 Cicero argues from the disagreement of the *physici* on a range of subjects that there are no rational grounds for assenting to any physical tenet advanced by the dogmatists, or the Stoics (here equated with Antiochians) in particular. The passage has, along with similar ones in *N.D.* 1.25–41 (on who or what has been identified as a divine being) and *Tusc.* 1.18–24 (on the nature of the soul), been studied in connection with investigations into the so-called doxographical tradition.

Building on earlier studies, including by his teacher Hermann Usener, Diels (1878) argued on the basis of extensive agreements between Ps.-Plutarch's *Placita philosophorum* (second century AD), Stobaeus' *Florilegium* (fifth century AD), and

Theodoretus' *Curatio affectionum Graecarum* (fifth century AD) that all three texts must go back to a common source, compiled by Aëtius, dated to the first or early second century AD.[464] He reconstructed Aëtius through overlap between his sources, printing Ps.-Plutarch and Stobaeus in columns side by side, which makes agreements plain, and by assigning section numbers to the double columns, continuing in some cases where only one of the texts was available. Diels also argued that an earlier collection of *placita* was available in the first century BC, dubbed the *Vetusta Placita* by him, and that Cicero (as well as others) had access to it. He identified various tributaries to the collection as a whole, chief among whom he took to be works by Theophrastus, because of correspondences between pieces of information on various Presocratics marked as coming from Theophrastus in Simplicius' commentary on Aristotle's *Physics* on the one hand, and Aëtius on the other.[465] Since Theophrastus was deemed to be a supremely reliable source, Diels felt licensed to build later editorial projects, notably that of the fragments of the Presocratic philosophers, on the theoretical foundation laid in *Doxographi Graeci* and the reconstructed Aëtius in particular.[466]

Initially separately and later in collaboration, Jaap Mansfeld and David Runia have tested and confirmed Diels's hypothesis about a shared source of Ps.-Plutarch and Stobaeus, whose authors they, too, take Aëtius to be. However, they have shown that the pre-Aëtius phase of the tradition is more complex and less easy to pin down than Diels allowed for,[467] and that in cases where tenets in Aëtius can be compared with their ultimate sources, it is plain that Aëtius delivers streamlined and adapted material. Mansfeld and Runia have also extended the evidence base for the doxographical tradition by identifying, or noting the significance of, texts not considered, or merely touched on, by Diels. They have made significant progress on the patterns and techniques of organization of the *placita* which recur in the tradition, and have traced some of them back beyond Theophrastus to Aristotle.[468] Finally, they have tried to delineate the limits of the analogy between analysing the manuscript tradition of a text by means of the stemmatic method and analysing the *placita* tradition, by observing that there is small core of material—usually just tenets and the names of their originators—which is susceptible to such analysis, situated in a sea of much more fluid context whose nature depends on the purposes of a given writer and his use of the *placita* material, as well as on further models or intertexts used to enrich it.[469] Moreover, even said core material may have been, qua evidence for particular Presocratics, subject to the streamlining described above.

---

[464] The name Aëtius is mentioned in Theodoretus only; cf. *Cur. aff. Graec.* 4.31.

[465] See Diels (1879: 132–44). The occurrence of some of this information in Cicero, Philodemus, and Clement represents evidence for the pre-Aëtian history of the tradition; cf. Diels (1879: 119–32).

[466] Diels (1878) offers a rationale of his methods and outcomes in the Latin preface. Accessible summary accounts of his methodology include Frede (1999a); Mansfeld (1999) and (2013).

[467] See Mansfeld (1990: 3058–9) on additions to a pre-existing body of material during the Hellenistic period.

[468] See esp. Mansfeld (1999) and (2010b: 8–10).

[469] Apart from numerous individual works which we will cite by author and date, their research has been published under the title *Aëtiana* in four volumes. Of these, vol. 1 and the two-part vol. 2 will be cited as Mansfeld and Runia (1999) and (2009) respectively. Vol. 3—Mansfeld and Runia (2010)—includes articles by both scholars, which I will cite individually by author and date. Mansfeld and Runia have been criticized for following Diels too closely in their methods (by Lévy 1996) or not closely enough (by Zhmud 2001); rebuttals include Mansfeld (2002) and (2010b), respectively. See also Reydams-Schils (2011); Bottler (2014).

For the purposes of a commentary on *Acad.*, this means that the text can be analysed at several levels of increasing relevance to the main task. First, the question is what the ultimate source of the information on the views of a given natural philosopher is; thus e.g. some of the information provided in §118 probably goes back to Theophrastus, as already Diels (1878: 119–21) showed and Mansfeld (1989: 136–7) confirmed. Second, one can ask which of the views cited and engaged with by Cicero are likely to form part of an antecedently existing collection, and whether the organization and presentation of the views reveals any ideological purpose; thus it has been suggested, e.g. by Festugière (1949: 363), and is now widely accepted that parts of the *placita* tradition show an arrangement which does not just assemble and classify views but pits them against each other, so as to reveal a disagreement among their originators, and that this sort of arrangement is probably due to the sceptical Academy,[470] whose representatives had an obvious use for a collection arranged in this fashion (cf. *Ac.* 1.45 *fin.*, on Arcesilaus: *Huic rationi quod erat consentaneum faciebat, ut contra omnium sententias disserens de sua plerosque deduceret…*).[471] The same mode of presentation is still recognizable in Aëtius. Mansfeld (1989a) has identified a fragment of Chrysippus preserved in Galen which shows engagement with a body of *placita* arranged in this way;[472] this suggests that the sceptical arrangement goes back to the Academy of Arcesilaus and his followers.[473] However, there are further organizational principles in play (by succession, or geographical/intellectual affinity). The question of whether Cicero uses material from an antecedently existing collection can of course also be illuminated by asking what points of contact there are between Cicero's discussion and Aëtius, or the sources used to reconstruct Aëtius, even though these texts are later than Cicero; it is very unlikely that Latin texts fed back into the Greek tradition of the *placita*. However, in such cases issues of form and content need to be attended to carefully.[474] Third, there is the issue of thematically related doxographical passages in Cicero, and near-contemporary ones in other Roman writers like Lucretius and, less tangibly, Varro.[475] Should one assume that

---

[470] Festugière (1949: 363): 'Ainsi donc le modèle académicien du *Lucullus*—c'est, en dernière analyse, Carnéade—emploie les doxographies dans un dessein particulier: l'histoire de la philosophie ne lui sert pas à construire (comme faisait, par exemple, Aristote dans le premier livre des *Métaphysiques*), mais à détruire, ou du moins il en tire argument pour incliner les esprits à l'$\dot{\epsilon}\pi o\chi\acute{\eta}$.' See Mansfeld (1989: 133); also Riedweg (1994: 109–15) on the use of the 'Widerspruchsargument' in Ps.-Iustinus.

[471] Such disagreements were already noted e.g. by Plat., *Soph.* 246a4–5 and Xenoph., *Mem.* 1.1.13.

[472] Cf. Mansfeld (1990: 3167–77).

[473] Runia (1999: 232) observes that the subject discussed by Chrysippus is one on which various doctors had pronounced and that their not being mentioned suggests that medical material, i.e. *placita* formulated by or ascribed to doctors, had not yet entered the tradition.

[474] Apart from correspondences in tenets reported by name, it is striking that in Stobaeus the doxographical material is preceded by a section on mathematics (I.1, pp. 15–22 Wachsmuth, noted by Lévy 1996: 112), just as the report of views on the principles in *Luc.* 118 is preceded by a section on geometry in *Luc.* 116. However, the discussions in Cicero and Stobaeus then differ in intent and purpose: in Stobaeus mathematics is presented as a propaedeutic subject, whereas Cicero notes that the Stoics act in a self-undermining way when they demand the same unqualified endorsement for the results of geometrical proofs and for the outcomes of physical enquiry. See also Mansfeld (2010b: 19–20).

[475] For Lucretius, see Runia (1997), the commentary on book 1.635–920, devoted to principles like *Luc.* 118, by Piazzi (2005); and Montarese (2012). For Varro, see Censorinus, *De die natali* 4.7–9.3, with Diels (1878: 186–99) and Mansfeld (1990: 3179–83). The use of 'political' doxography in Cic. *Off.* is studied by Schmitz (2017).

these come from the same proximate source, or do they draw on the same tradition while relying on different configurations of the material? Any answer one might give has bearings on the question of the sources of *Luc.* and of how they inform Cicero's text. Fourth, it is also desirable to read the text against the grain of the doxographical material as it were, i.e. to read it immanently with an eye to the *intentio operis* of *Luc.*, treating the doxographical material on a par with its surrounding context, as well as to look for other texts to which Cicero may be alluding, thereby giving the doxographical material a new context and repurposing it for his own agenda, or indeed reviving its allusive potential in cases when he spots and references the original source for a piece of doxographical information in addition to its immediate source.

I set out the structure of §§118–26 and indicate by name the philosophers cited across the section:[476]

§118: Material principles proposed by different *physici*.	Thales, Anaximander, Anaximenes, Anaxagoras, Xenophanes, Parmenides, Leucippus, Democritus, Empedocles, Heraclitus, Melissus, Plato, Pythagoreans.[477]
§§119–21: The question of the providential organization of the world and attendant issues.	§119: 'The Stoics', Aristotle; §120: 'you' (the Antiocheans, the Stoics); §121: Strato, (Democritus invoked by Strato).
§122: The obscurity of some objects and their workings in the domain of physics.	Empiricists; § ends with unassigned views on the position of the earth in the universe.
§123: Particular disagreements: a couple of implausible claims and the impossibility of being certain either way.	Xenophanes [probably erroneously], Hicetas of Syracuse, Plato, Epicurus, Socrates, Aristo of Chios.
§124: 'Soul and body' as a further area of disagreement.	Dicaearchus, Plato, Xenocrates.
§125: The Antiocheans are disingenuous in claiming that they want the Academics to adopt *a* dogmatic position, as is plain from their (presumed) reaction to the possibility that an Academic might opt for the entirely respectable Democritean view.	Democritus.
§126: Rather, they want the Academics to be Stoics. However, Stoic views are implausible, and the Stoics disagree amongst themselves.	'The Stoics'; Zeno, Cleanthes.

---

[476] Schäublin et al. (pp. lxxxi–lxxxii) subdivide the entire physics section down to §128a as follows: (a) §§116–17 the basic issue; (b) §§118–26 disagreement among philosophers, i.e. §118 principles of natural philosophy, §§119–21 relationship of god and world, §§122–4 problems of natural philosophy and the weakness of the human mind, §§125–6 the Academic and the disagreement of philosophers; (c) §§127–128a the Academic and the Stoic sage. Brittain (2006: lvi–lvii) subdivides: §§116–17 results inconclusive, §§117–21 disagreements about first principles, §§122–4 other disagreements, §§125–128a reasons against any one choice, §128b equal warrant argument.

[477] The same list of thirteen, in the same order, is in Aug., *Contra Iul.* 4.15.75, as Hagendahl (1967: 67–8).

The section can be divided into units, with 118–21 and 124–5 mapping onto discernible parts of the *placita* tradition (as reconstructed), while the other sections seem connected to the tradition in a looser way.

§118 assembles views on material principles, beginning with Thales; cf. Aët. 1.3 in Diels (1878: 276–88).[478] The second view in the survey, Anaximander's, is introduced with the remark that Thales' view did not persuade Anaximander (*At hoc Anaximandro...non persuasit*). As a result, the remaining views featuring in the paragraph can naturally be read as in disagreement with all the others. At the end of the paragraph Cicero concludes—apparently implying that he has introduced a jointly exhaustive set of options—that the Stoic will select one thinker's view (and presumably integrate it into his own physical theory),[479] while he dismisses everybody else's views, despite esteem and reputation (including in the eyes of the Stoic; see on §§72–6) of the proponents.[480]

As to the principles posited themselves, Mansfeld (1989: 134) comments: 'In 118 werden die Meinungen der Philosophen über die Prinzipien einander u.a. in einer Weise gegenübergestellt, dass sich daraus ergibt, die einen sagten, das Prinzip sei eins, die anderen, es sei mehr als eins, und dass die einen sagten, das eine Prinzip sei unendlich, andere dagegen, es sei es nicht. In einigen Fällen wird ausserdem darauf hingewiesen, das Prinzip sei unbewegt bzw. unveränderlich, während es sich in anderen Fällen unmissverständlich um ein bewegtes bzw. veränderliches Prinzip (oder Prinzipien) handelt. In einem Fall wird sogar explizit die Welterschaffung durch den Gott angesprochen.' He goes on to reinvestigate the question raised by Diels of whether there are traces of Theophrastus' *Phys. op.* in Cicero.[481] Diels had come to this conclusion because of correspondences between Cicero's report here, and fragments and paraphrases of Theophrastus in Simplicius' commentary on Aristotle's *Phys*. After a re-examination of the evidence and some corrections to Diels's list of correspondences, Mansfeld concludes that the Theophrastean material is more likely to come from Theophrastus' *Physics* than from the large doxographical *Phys. op.* (p. 257). However, this would be its ultimate origin, the source at several removes from any material used by Cicero, and the source for the individual views rather than the arrangement in which we find it in Cicero. For the sense of *tot homines quot sententiae* which the reader gets from Cicero's organization is, as Mansfeld also shows by comparing the organization of lists of principles from Aristotle onwards, due to the implementation of the arrangement κατὰ διαδοχήν: first there is a Ionian line (Thales, Anaximander, Anaximenes), then an Eleatic line (Xenophanes, Parrmenides, Leucippus, Democritus), whose beginning is signalled through an indication of chronology (*Xenophanes, paulo etiam antiquior*). There follow Empedocles and Heraclitus, which also in parallel texts (see below) of similar organization are unassigned. The last three *physici* (Melissus, Plato, and the Pythogoreans)

---

[478] See also Aët. 2.4 (εἰ ἄφθαρτος ὁ κόσμος) with Mansfeld and Runia (2009: 347–66).
[479] Cf. Schäublin et al. (p. 286 n. 359): 'Es ist nicht klar, mit welchem Recht Cicero findet, dass der stoische Weise aus dem Arsenal der vorliegenden Auffassungen (§118) auswählen (*eliget*) müßte.'
[480] The Stoics posited two principles, an active and a passive one, a view which can be traced to Plato's *Tim.*; cf. on *Ac*. 1.24–5. In §118 Cicero does allude to the *Tim.*, but only for the passive principle.
[481] Cf. Rösler (1973: 50–4), who conducts a similar investigation for the section on Heraclitus in Lucr. 1.635–704.

are added without affiliation. The plural *Pythagorei* might hint at an Italic line which is not executed. Traces of arrangement by date, teacher-pupil relationship, etc. are in evidence in the Theophrastean fragments which have been extracted from Simpl. *in Phys.*, but the developed pattern of organization is associated with Sotion, who between 200 BC and 170 BC wrote a work entitled Διαδοχαὶ τῶν φιλοσόφων which was quoted by D.L., if probably not used directly, as well as by Sextus Empiricus, Athenaeus, and Eunapius.[482] As a consequence of the arrangement by succession, other plausible ordering principles (moved or unmoved, one or many, finite or infinite) are foregone.[483] Given that arrangements of doxographical material which highlight disagreement are attested early as well as widely, there are no good grounds for crediting Cicero himself with this arrangement, and it has long been held that at least §§118–21 must be reflecting an Academic source,[484] which is plausible but tells us nothing about Cicero's immediate source (e.g. whether it was a work by Philo, and if so whether it is drawn upon for more than just §§118–21). Clearly an Academic could have availed himself of the organizational principle which served his purpose (i.e. that of succession) without it being originally intended to emphasize disagreements.

§§119–21 move on to another issue, whether the world is providentially organized or not.[485] Specifically, §119 asks whether the universe is providentially organised *and* has a beginning as well as an end. The Stoics hold that the world is intelligent, divine, and that it will end one day in a conflagration. Cicero comments that this may be true and adds a reference to §111 where he addressed the question of whether the Academics (i.e. the Clitomacheans) are entitled to the claim that there are true and false impressions; however, he goes on to observe ibid. that the Stoic view or set of views cannot count as apprehended. He then imagines a scene in which the Stoic sage stops dictating his views to Antiochus,[486] because Aristotle appears and offers his view on the world, which is at variance with that of the Stoics.[487] Since Aristotle's intervention is presented as rhetorically exuberant (so that the reference cannot be to the treatises) and since his lost dialogue *De philosophia* is used as source in *N.D.*, editors have included the second half of §119 among the fragments of the *De philosophia* (see the n. below). Aristotle claims that the world is intelligently organized, he makes no reference to the divine, and he posits that the world has neither a beginning nor an end. Cicero's opponent, or so he suggests, will have to reject Aristotle's view as if his life and reputation depended on it. To Cicero this is less rational than acknowledging the doubt he feels, in an area where certainty is not to be had. §120 begins with a reference to two ideologically charged terms which featured earlier in the debate, the rashness (*temeritas*) of the dogmatist, who assents when assent is not warranted, and the freedom (*libertas*) of the Academic who is without dogmatic

---

[482] On Sotion, see Mansfeld (1999: 23–5) and Schneider (2016a).
[483] Cf. Mansfeld (1990: 3157–61) on lists of principles according to number; Riedweg (1994.ii: 229–31).
[484] See e.g. Diels (1878: 119).
[485] Cf. Aët. 2.3 with Mansfeld and Runia (2009: 337–46).
[486] On the legitimacy of the suggestion that in the field of physics Antiochus straightforwardly adopted Stoic teachings, see the commentary on *Ac.* 1.24–9, 1.39, and Brittain (2006: xxxii–xxxiii).
[487] Pitting the Stoics and Aristotle against each other in this way also has the effect of casting doubt on Antiochus' claim that the Old Academy and the Peripatetics were in substantial agreement with each

constraints.[488] Cicero hails the latter. He asks, first, how the Stoic notion that the world is providentially organised by a divine being for the benefit of humans can be reconciled with the existence of plenty of animals on land and sea which are deadly to human beings. And second, he suggests that the organization of the world down to the level of detail would require a divine being to have attended to all these—from a certain point onwards, trivial—matters, which is at variance with the majesty of the divine that one ought to assume. §121 begins with the introduction of the opponent's view that nothing could come about without god. The scope of this very general claim becomes clear from the position with which it is confronted, that of the Peripatetic Strato of Lampascus, who succeeded Theophrastus as head of the Peripatos. He holds that the world requires no divine interference neither for its creation nor for its maintenance and continuation; rather, everything occurred because of 'natural weights and movements'.[489] In holding this view Strato takes himself (*censet*) to disagree with Democritus, who also thought that no divine being was involved in creating the world and in keeping it going, but for different reasons.[490] Strato's view is hailed by Cicero as liberating god and himself in equal measure—him because he does not need to be in awe of god if human beings are of no concern to god, and because he does not have to worry that any misfortune which befalls him might be justified divine punishment. This sounds as if Strato's view as reported here might be called Cicero's view. However, he immediately adds that he gives his assent neither to Strato nor to his opponent, on the grounds that either view appears to him more *probabile* than the other at different times. This is more plausibly read as qualifying the nature of the endorsement just given to Strato's view, rather than as a withdrawal of that endorsement: for now Strato's view *is* more *probabile* to Cicero.[491]

It is again Mansfeld (1989: 134–6) who notes that in reports on the tenth trope of Aenesidemus (Sextus, *P.H.* 1.145; D.L. 9.83; Phil., *Ebr.* 198) reference is made to disagreement among the δογματικαὶ ὑπολήψεις (thus Sextus and D.L.) which is apt to induce ἐποχή. The treatment in these writers is shorter than in Cicero in terms of the range of views cited, and no names are assigned, but all three authors mention physical principles *as well as* the providential organization of the world as areas where there is such disagreement. Cicero's reference to a *deus sempiternus* also creates an internal connection between principles and providence, whereas the subjects appear merely juxtaposed in the other sources. The reference to the *deus sempiternus* in §118 *fin.* also makes for a smooth transition to §119, which starts with the view that there is providence. So there is reason for thinking that in *Luc.* 118–21 we get a fuller version of the kind of collection merely referred to by the other texts. At the same time, the parallels do show that the arrangement and sequence which we find in

---

other; cf. the digression in the general note on *Ac.* 1.15–18 and section 7.2. However, this need not mean that the arrangement is Cicero's.

[488] See on *Luc.* 7b–9a and the notes below.

[489] Brittain (2006: xxxii–xxxiii) notes that §§119–21 allow for no inferences as to Antiochus' physical views since they deal with disagreements between Stoics and dissident Peripatetics.

[490] Strato and Democritus are juxtaposed in several doxographical texts on various subjects; see the nn. below.

[491] See section 8 for further passages where the Cicero character expresses views. Given the infrequency with which physical matters are discussed in the corpus, there are no comparanda in this case.

Cicero cannot be his, and one way of explaining this would be that the other texts had sight of similar material. However, for reasons explained above, this need not have been Cicero's proximate source.

A related passage in Cicero is the historical survey of theological views in *N.D.* 1.25-41, which partially overlaps with *Luc.* 118-21. There are significant correspondences in the sequence of *physici* named, with omissions and additions on both sides, but as far as the substance of the views reported is concerned, the overlap is limited (therefore it will be documented in the nn. below, rather than in a table). This is so because the two passages have different subjects and correspond to different sections in Aëtius. What overlap there is can be explained by observing that the *placita* tradition relies on—with variations—a recurrent sequence of thinkers whose views are given and by the fact that the subjects of principles and gods are not completely unrelated (e.g. some principles are deemed to be divine). I would thus be hesitant to posit the same proximate source for both passages (i.e. an Academic one), which does not preclude the possibility that the source informing the *N.D.* passage was at an earlier point subject to Academic rearrangement: the principle of succession is in evidence to a degree, and in some places disagreements between *physici* are drawn attention to, or indeed internal inconsistencies in the views of one and the same speaker are pointed out (as in the case of Plato). There is a possibility that in *N.D.* Cicero's immediate source is Philodemus' *De pietate*;[492] this would be compatible with the immediate source of the section in *Luc.* being Philonian, or with it being derived from a Clitomachean source of which Cicero availed himself for the physical section, since the same larger body of material may lie behind both passages (*N.D.* and *Luc.*) at several removes.

§§122-3 is more loosely related to doxographical material, i.e. introduces fewer views but engages more substantially with them. The relevant sections in Aëtius are 3.10 (περὶ σχήματος γῆς) and 3.11 (περὶ θέσεως γῆς; Ps.-Plut. 895d-e only, since Stobaeus is missing for this section);[493] cf. also 2.23-9 on the moon. The empiricist doctors who feature in §122 do not feature in the doxographical tradition with the views cited by Cicero.

In §122 Cicero leaves the subject of providence behind and turns to the obscurity of objects broadly speaking within the domain of physics. Anything in the sky or within the earth is beyond the reach of human cognitive faculties. This is so a fortiori since we do not even know our own bodies, viz. the location of all their parts and the function of these parts. For this reason doctors opened up bodies so that such matters might become plain (see the n. on *uiderentur*). However, as the Empiricists observed, this did not provide illumination, since the act of opening up might change

---

[492] The text we refer to as Philodemus' *De pietate*, transmitted in *P.Herc.* 1428 (as well as *P.Herc.* 1077 and 1098; see Obbink 1996: 24-31), is itself so-called largely by convention, since the papyrus only preserves the first letter of the author's name. Correspondences between that text and *N.D.* 1.25-41 are listed by Diels (1879: 529-50). For the evaluation of the correspondences, and observations on differences in arrangement, see Henrichs (1974: 8-10); Obbink (1996: 96-9); Obbink (2001) with Auvray-Assayas (2001); and Vassallo (2018). For Cicero's personal familiarity with Philodemus, see *Fin.* 2.119 and *Fam.* 6.11 (= SB 224).

[493] Cf. Mansfeld (2010a: 194-5).

the nature of the object. From here Cicero returns to the nature of the world and the universe, observing that the 'opening up' and physical 'dividing' which proved unproductive in the case of bodies is not even possible in the case of the world, whose anchoring and position in the universe is wholly inaccessible to us.

In §123 Cicero assembles a number of outlandish views on the moon and the sun advanced by particular thinkers, eventually ending with Socrates and Aristo of Chios, who both held that knowledge is not be had in this area. Antiochus' view of Socrates is that of secret dogmatist who concealed his views using irony (see on *Luc.* 15 and section 7.3) cannot consistently be a secondary target here. Aristo was a pupil of Zeno,[494] and reference to him allows Cicero to imply that there is disagreement amongst the Stoics themselves about physical doctrines (cf. §126), which makes it all the more unreasonable that his opponent requires Cicero to accept *his* view (cf. §126 *init.*).

In §124 a return to the subject of 'the soul and the body' is announced. The body and difficulties in investigating its parts and functions featured in §122, but the soul was not explicitly mentioned there. From our ignorance of the nature of muscles and veins/arteries Cicero moves on to a doxography on the soul. Here the views are merely juxtaposed (contrast §118 *init.*). The first view assigned by name is Dicaearchus' that the soul does not exist and that any role one might ascribe to it is a function of the physical make-up of the body. The next view is Plato's tripartite division of the soul into parts, followed by Xenocrates', who takes the soul to have no parts and to be a number. The final issue, which can be supported either way, is whether the soul is mortal or eternal; here no proponent is cited by name. The moral Cicero draws from this is that the Stoic sage settles for one of the options which have been or could be distinguished, whereas the Academic cannot even identify one as *probabile*. Rather, the considerations which can be cited for the various views are equipollent.

Luc. 124 shows similarities with another doxographical passage, *Tusc.* 1.18–24; both can be connected with the same section in Aëtius (4.2.1–4.4.7). A conspicuous shared feature is what Mansfeld has dubbed the 'question types',[495] questions which facilitate the imposition of order on a complex body of material, in a manner that is akin to rhetorical στάσις-doctrine, which shares a common ancestor with the question types, i.e. Aristotelian methods of organizing material.[496] Unsurprisingly, Cicero handles the question types with flexibility and dexterity, which makes doxographical sections so organized less straightforwardly relatable to similar material. However, unlike the questions associated with the στάσεις, which are used to structure material but are themselves usually not mentioned in speeches except in overtly metarhetorical passages, the question types are stated explicitly. As such they function as a generic marker of doxographical material. In *Tusc.* the context is whether death is an evil, which raises the question of what happens to the soul when human beings die, which then prompts the survey of views on the soul. As to the correspondences themselves, while they are sufficient in extent to signal shared material, the order is

---

[494] See section 7.5.
[495] See Mansfeld (1990: 3063).
[496] The evidence is summarized in Mansfeld (2010b: 8–10).

different, in that the *Luc.* passage inserts a couple of thinkers with a very brief summary in parenthesis among the question types, while the *Tusc.* passage presents them in a more natural position in the sequence, and with a fuller statement of their view. If we ask once again if any of this gives us an indication of Cicero's proximate source, then the answer will have to be negative. The fact that §124 announces a 'return' to the subjects of the soul and the body when only the body featured before might suggest that what we are dealing with is the seam between two sources (though whether it was Cicero who did the splicing is a separate matter), and that the fuller discussion in *Tusc.* is logically if not chronologically the primary location for this material. However, this would not preclude the possibility of one Philonian text as proximate source for §§118–26.

Lévy (1996: 115–19) shows how other authors like Philo and Seneca who draw on doxographical material relating to the soul and organised by question types arrange it freely and in a manner that is in keeping with their own agenda, too. He further observes that in *Tusc.* Cicero can be seen to be alluding, in these very passages, to particular sections in Plato's *Apology* and *Phaedo*,[497] as in general *Tusc.* 1 is full of references to Plato.[498] From this one can derive the insight that individual recipients of doxographical material may choose to enrich it through intertextual allusion. In such cases the intertext selected may at the same time be the point of material origin for the tenet(s) in question, or at least a plausible candidate for it. This does nothing to undermine the notion that the target text ought to be viewed as drawing on the doxographical tradition, but it does suggest that this tradition was not viewed by ancient authors as an inert body of tralaticious material. Rather, it was read as having rich allusive potential, whose individual tenets are capable of sending author and reader alike 'back' to the ultimate source.

In §125 Cicero disingenuously entertains the possibility that his opponent wants him to accept *a* view rather than the one he himself holds. He affects to opt for Democritus, who enjoyed considerable prestige among the Stoics. This triggers an incredulous direct speech by the opponent, who lists the many implausible assumptions made by Democritus; for the technique of a fictitious interlocutor making interventions in direct speech see on §53. The opponent concludes by saying that no definite stance is better than following Democritus. §125 seems to move on from the subject of §124 but may be loosely inspired by the same body of doxographical material on which *Tusc.* 1.18–24 draws. There Democritus features, if in *praeteritio* (1.22 *fin.*), as someone who wants even the soul to be constituted from atoms.

The dogmatist's speech in §125 about the absurdity of Democritus' views allows Cicero to claim in §126 that his opponent will not be satisfied if he (or the Academics) merely accept *a* view. After rejecting several central Stoic doctrines as unpersuasive while acknowledging that matters may nonetheless be as the Stoics say, Cicero fastens on a disagreement between Zeno and Cleanthes—on whether *aether* or the sun is the highest god—and concludes that he must be forgiven for suspending judgement under the circumstances.

---

[497] Also noted by Kleijwegt (1966: 362–3); see also Auvray-Assayas (1996) on *N.D.* and Plt. *Tim.*
[498] See Reinhardt (2018: 33–9).

§118

Princeps Thales...constare omnia: cf. DK 11A12 (= Arist., *Met.* A3, 983b18–33) and 11A13 (Simpl. *in Arist. Phys.* p. 23.21–9 = Theophrastus, *Phys. Dox.* frg. 1 in Diels 1879: 475–6 = part of frg. 225 FHS&G); Aët. 1.3.1; Cic., *N.D.* 1.25 (cf. Aët. 1.7.11), adding a report on Thales' views on the divine: *Thales enim Milesius, qui primus de talibus rebus quaesiuit, aquam dixit esse initium rerum, deum autem eam mentem, quae ex aqua cuncta fingeret: si dei possunt esse sine sensu; et mentem cur aquae adiunxit, si ipsa mens constare potest uacans corpore?* A compressed list of views on principles is in Sextus, *P.H.* 3.30–2.

Thales as chronologically the first of the *physici* is a recurrent pattern in the *placita* tradition. The relative clause alludes to a story in which Thales received, after initially rejecting it, the gift of a tripod intended for 'the wisest' from the other sages; cf. D.L. 1.28. See also Dyck (2004: 330) on Cic., *Leg.* 2.26. In other accounts it is Solon who ends up as 'the wisest'.

Reid[1] (p. 313) aptly compares the use of indeclinable number term *septem* as a noun with *XII* (for the law of the Twelve Tables). For *primas* (sc. *partes*), see *OLD* s.v. *primus* no. 15b.

At hoc Anaximandro...e qua omnia gignerentur: cf. DK 12A1 (= D.L. 2.1–2) and 12A9 (Simpl. *in Arist. Phys.* p. 24.13–21 = Theophrastus, *Phys. Dox.* frg. 2 in Diels 1879: 476 = part of frg. 226A FHS&G); Aët. 1.3.3; Cic., *N.D.* 1.25 (cf. Aët. 1.7.12).

Popularis designates a member of the same community, i.e. the city of Miletus (cf. *OLD* s.v. *popularis*[2]). *Sodalis* suggests equality in rank, but Anaximander is usually deemed to be a generation younger than Thales. On the presentation of their difference of opinion as a disagreement (*non persuasit*) see the general note above (p. 704). For *natura* in the sense of οὐσία or ὕλη, see *Ac.* 1.28: *in omni natura*; 1.27 for *omnia* = τὸ πᾶν.

Post eius auditor Anaximenes...tum ex iis omnia: cf. DK 13A1–3, 4 (= Arist., *Met.* A4, 984a5–7), 5 (Simpl. *in Arist. Phys.* pp. 24.26–25.1 = Theophrastus, *Phys. Dox.* frg. 2 in Diels 1879: 476 = part of frg. 226A FHS&G; Aët. 1.3.4; Cic., *N.D.* 1.26 (cf. Aët. 1.7.13).

Post signals succession, not just being the next in the enumeration. For *auditor* 'pupil', cf. Greek ἀκροατής. For *definita* = πεπερασμένα cf. Cic., *Top.* 79. The determinate things which arise in sequence are first earth, water, and fire, and then the things of our experience (*omnia*), as Reid[1] (p. 314) notes. The process of condensation and rarefaction which accounts for this is mentioned in DK 13A5 (see above) and 13A7 (Hippol., *Haer.* 1.7.1–3).

Anaxagoras materiam infinitam...adductas mente diuina: cf. DK 59A43 (= Arist., *Met.* A3, 984a11–6), A45 (= Arist., *Phys.* Γ4, 203a19–24); B11 (Simpl. *in Arist. Phys.* p. 164.22–4), 12 (ibid., pp. 164.24–165.4), 13 (ibid., pp. 300.27–301.1); Aët. 1.3.5; Cic., *N.D.* 1.26–7 (cf. Aët. 1.7.15): *Inde Anaxagoras, qui accepit ab Anaximene disciplinam, primus omnium rerum discriptionem et motum mentis infinitae ui ac ratione designari et confici uoluit. In quo non uidit neque motum sensu iunctum et* *continentem infinito ullum esse posse, neque sensum omnino, quo non ipsa natura pulsa sentiret. Deinde si mentem istam quasi animal aliquod uoluit esse, erit aliquid interius, ex quo illud animal nominetur; quid autem interius mente? Cingatur igitur corpore externo; quod quoniam non placet, aperta simplexque mens nulla re adiuncta, quae sentire possit, fugere intellegentiae nostrae uim et notionem uidetur*; Lucr. 1.830–44.

Cicero makes no overt attempt to relate Anaxagoras to Anaximenes, but *materiam infinitam, sc. posuit* (resuming *infinitum aera* from Anaximenes) seems to serve the same function as *qui accepit ab Anaxemene disciplinam* in *N.D.* 1.26: it presents Anaxagoras' view as a modification of Anaximenes'. Reid[1] (p. 314) notes that the verb to be supplied mentally after *materiam infinitam* must be *posuit* or *excogitauit*. The *particulae similes inter se minutae* must be the ὁμοιομέρη, which Lucretius famously refused to render into Latin in 1.830 (although he then explains the concept in 1.834–42). Reid[1] (p. 314) suggests *eas* is added for emphasis, but it is not obvious why emphasis would be needed at this point—unless its function was to signal that Cicero is paraphrasing the very beginning of Anaxagoras' work (Simpl. *in Arist. Phys.* p. 155.26–7 = part of DK 59B1: δηλοῖ διὰ τοῦ πρώτου τῶν Φυσικῶν λέγων ἀπ᾽ ἀρχῆς 'ὁμοῦ χρήματα πάντα ἦν ἄπειρα καὶ πλῆθος καὶ σμικρότητα...'). On the *mens diuina*, see *N.D.* 1.26–7 quoted above.

Xenophanes...conglobata figura: cf. DK 21A30 (= Arist., *Met.* A5, 986b18–27), A31 (= Simpl. *in Arist. Phys.* pp. 22.22–23.20 = Theophrastus frg. 224 FHS&G), B23–6 (25 and 26 are Simpl. *in Phys.* pp. 23.19 and 22.9); Aët. 1.3.12, cf. 4.5, names earth as Xenophanes' principle; Cic., *N.D.* 1.28: *Tum Xenophanes, qui mente adiuncta omne propterea quod esset unum et infinitum deum uoluit esse, de ipsa mente item reprehendetur ut ceteri, de infinitate autem uehementius, in qua nihil neque sentiens neque coniunctum potest esse.*

Paulo etiam antiquior signals the new beginning after the end of the Milesian series (see the general note above). With *neque natum umquam*, cf. §119: *neque enim ortum*. Fragments on the nature of the Xenophanean god include DK 21B23–6, but see also Timon *ap.* Sextus, *P.H.* 1.224: θεὸν ἐπλάσατ᾽ ἴσον ἀπάντῃ (noted by Reid[1] p. 314).

Parmenides ignem...quae ab eo formetur: on earth and fire as Parmenides' principles, cf. DK 28A1 (= D.L. 9.21–3), A7 (= Alex. Aphr. *ad* Arist. *Met.* A3, 983b3, *in Arist. Met.* p. 31.7–12); contrast B8 on the unmoveable being; no entry in Aët. 1.3; Cic., *N.D.* 1.28 has different material germane to its own purpose (for which cf. Aët. 1.7.26). With *moueat terram*, cf. Arist., *Met.* A3, 984b6–7: χρῶνται γὰρ ὡς κινητικὴν ἔχοντι τῷ πυρὶ τὴν φύσιν.

Leucippus plenum et inane. Democritus...uberior in ceteris: the sources frequently mention both *physici* together. For the ascription of the two principles to Leucippus, cf. DK 67A7 (= Arist., *De gen. et corr.* A8, 324b35–325a6), 67A1 (= D.L. 9.31–3), concerned with cosmogony; Aët. 1.3.15; cf. Cic., *N.D.* 1.66 (on the unlikelihood of the world being made up of atoms which collide randomly; void is not at issue). For Democritus, see e.g. DK 68A57 (= Plut., *Adv. Col.* 1110f–1111a) on atoms and 67A19 on void (= Arist., *Phys.* Δ6, 213b4–22). On both, and the principles and cosmogony

67A6 (= Arist., *Met.* A4, 985b4–19). Aët. 1.3.16 on Democritus; there is no exact parallel in Cic., *N.D.* 1. The equation of 'the full' (τὸ πλῆρες) with atoms is conventional.

Empedocles haec peruolgata et nota quattuor: cf. DK 31B6; Simpl. *in Arist. Phys.* p. 25.19–24 (= Theophrastus, *Phys. Dox.* frg. 3 in Diels 1879: 477–8 = part of frg. 227A FHS&G); Aët. 1.3.20; Cic., *N.D.* 1.29: *Empedocles autem multa alia peccans in deorum opinione turpissime labitur. Quattuor enim naturas, ex quibus omnia constare censet, diuinas esse uult; quas et nasci et extingui perspicuum est et sensu omni carere* (without counterpart in Aët. 1.7); Lucr. 1.712–829.

Heraclitus ignem: cf. DK 22B30 (= Clem., *Strom.* 5.104.2), B64 (= Hippol., *Haer.* 9.10.7), B66 (ibid.); Aët. 1.3.11; Heraclitus does not feature relevantly in *N.D.* 1; Lucr. 1.635–711.

Melissus hoc…et fuisse semper et fore: cf. DK 30A5 (= Ps.-Arist. *XMG* 1.2), 30A8 (= Arist., *Phys.* Δ6, 213b12–14 and *De gen. et corr.* A8, 325a2–16); 20B1 (= Simpl. *in Arist. Phys.* p. 162.24–6); Arist., *Met.* A5, 986b19–21. Melissus' view presupposes Parmenides' on being; see Schofield (2012: 158–60) on Arist., *Met.* A5 and 986b8–987b2 in particular. Melissus does not feature in Aët. 1.3, or in Cic. *N.D.* 1 and Lucr.

Plato ex materia…censet a deo sempiternum: the parallel section in Aëtius (1.3.21) ascribes to Plato three principles, god, matter, and Form. In *N.D.* 1.30 the Epicurean Velleius notes contradictory statements on Plato's part, but makes no reference to Form like *Luc.* 118 (though conceivably this could be due to the different subject in that passage, the nature of the divine being): *Iam de Platonis inconstantia longum est dicere, qui in Timaeo patrem huius mundi nominari neget posse, in Legum autem libris, quid sit omnino deus, anquiri oporteret non censeat. Quod uero sine corpore ullo deum uult esse* (ut Graeci dicunt ἀσώματον), *id, quale esse possit, intellegi non potest: careat enim sensu necesse est, careat etiam prudentia, careat uoluptate; quae omnia una cum deorum notione conprehendimus. Idem et in Timaeo dicit et in Legibus et mundum deum esse et caelum et astra et terram et animos et eos, quos maiorum institutis accepimus. Quae et per se sunt falsa perspicue et inter se uehementer repugnantia.*

To posit two and not three principles is consistent with the physical section of Varro's speech in *Ac.* 1, esp. 1.24, as well as with the apparent treatment of Forms as equivalent to conceptions in the mind in the epistemological section of the same speech (*Ac.* 1.30–2); see also Reinhardt (2018: 39–53). While the assumption of two principles, god and matter, is reminiscent of the Stoics, Sedley (2002: 42) observes that it is a view which Theophrastus ascribed to Plato evidently on the basis of an interpretative reading of the *Timaeus* (Simpl. *in Arist. Phys.* p. 26.7–15 = Theophrastus, *Phys. Dox.* frg. 9 in Diels 1879: 484–5 = frg. 230 FHS&G). He goes on to argue that *Ac.* 1.24–9, on the physics of the Old Academy, draws on physical views of Polemo in particular and make a plausible and credible case for the affinity of Old Academic and Stoics physics; see the commentary ad loc. Contra Inwood (2012). A more complex picture of how Plato, and Plato interpreted in a certain way, might have influenced Stoic physics is provided by Ademollo (2012). Reydams-Schils (2013) points out that it is necessary to distinguish, and that Theophrastus frg. 230 does distinguish, between positing forms in the realm of physics and as items of first philosophy. However, it is not a given that Cicero and his contemporaries interpreted Forms as transcendental entities when they did posit them; cf. Boys-Stones (2012: 222); Reinhardt (2018). In any case, in the present context Cicero has no reason to modify doxographical source material which names three principles so as to end up with a view that is closer to Antiochus' of the Old Academy as reported in *Ac.* 1. Rather, his source is likely to have named two principles only.

With *ex materia in se omnia recipiente*, cf. *Ac.* 1.24: ...*ut eam* (sc. *naturam*) *diuiderent in res duas, ut altera esset efficiens,* **altera autem quasi huic se praebens, ex eaque efficeretur aliquid**; Plt., *Tim.* 51a7. Reid[1] (p. 315) notes that the end position of *sempiternum* makes it emphatic: '...so as to be everlasting.'

Pythagorii...proficisci uolunt omnia: cf. e.g. Philolaus' views in DK 44B11, and Sextus, *M.* 10.277–83, for general illustration; Aët. 1.3.8; Cic., *N.D.* 1.27–8 (cf. Aët. 1.7.18) does not overlap with the present passage. As noted above, the plural of *Pythagorei* may be seen to hint at an Italic line. Aët. 1.3.8 shifts between Πυθαγόρας and Πυθαγόρειοι; Philolaus features in 1.3.10. Volk (2016) is a study of the significance of Pythagoras for the self-conception of Roman philosophy. For *mathematicorum initia*, cf. §116. It is likely that *ex* was supplied by V² given its absence from S (and AB).

Ex iis eliget uester sapiens...condemnatique discedent: that the sage should select from the options rehearsed (*ex iis*) one as his position may seem a peculiar notion. For one would assume it be to part of his sagehood to have a position on physical matters, including on the principles. The scenario is that the Antiochian sage is being constructed and has to choose; see Sedley (2002: 50 n. 21). Of the views which have been set out the Platonic one would be the obvious candidate for a sage who is a Stoic in the field of epistemology, and harder to characterize with respect to his physical and ethical views (Cicero simplifies in saying *quoniam Stoicus est* in the next paragraph).

The selection of one view entails the rejection of all the others (Reid[1] p. 315 notes the quasi-legal sense of *discedere*, 'to come off, sc. after a vote'; cf. *OLD* s.v. no. 4b); *sequi aliquem* implies unqualified endorsement (cf. §117: *quaero...quem sequatur*) and is different from *sequi* (with 'views' as logical and/or grammatical object) = (*ap*)*probare* as in §104 (noted by Algra 1997: 134 n. 63). For someone who prizes *auctoritas* if necessary over judgement (cf. *Luc.* 59), the dismissal of all these respectable *physici* ought to pose a problem.

§119

Quamcumque uero sententiam probauerit...et omnia moderetur mouet regat: *probare* means 'to accept' in a looser sense rather than the technical one of *Luc.* 104. The overall argument is similar to that of the equal warrant consideration of §128:

the uncompromising view of the Antiochian about assent means that he is required to give the same kind of endorsement in the obscure field of physics as in the relatively more straightforward field of ethics. Similarly, here the suggestion is that the sage gives the same kind of endorsement to perceptual impressions (*nunc lucere*) as he gives to (Stoic) physical *sententiae*.

§119 init.—*deflagret* is *SVF* ii.92. Cf. Aët. 1.7.33; Cic., *N.D.* 2.39: *Est autem nihil mundo perfectius, nihil uirtute melius; igitur mundi est propria uirtus. Nec uero hominis natura perfecta est, et efficitur tamen in homine uirtus; quanto igitur in mundo facilius; est ergo in eo uirtus. Sapiens est igitur et propterea deus. Atque hac mundi diuinitate perspecta tribuenda est sideribus eadem diuinitas; quae ex mobilissima purissimaque aetheris parte gignuntur neque ulla praeterea sunt admixta natura, totaque sunt calida atque perlucida, ut ea quoque rectissime et animantia esse et sentire atque intellegere dicantur;* 2.57–8; and cf. the hostile report in 1.36. See also D.L. 7.147 (= *SVF* ii.1021).

The clause *quoniam Stoicus est* is aimed at Antiochus, but is polemical in that Antiochus did not, as Cicero knew, adopt Stoic physics without modification in the way in which he adopted Stoic epistemology; see on *Ac.* 1.24–9. On *ipsum* in the phrase *et se et ipsum* in the sense of *id ipsum*, see Reid[1] (p. 278). With *fabricata sit*, cf. §§87 and 120 *fin*.

The asyndeton *moderetur moueat regat* might be intended to sound dismissive; cf. the asyndetic string of celestial bodies in the next sentence.

Erit ei persuasum etiam solem lunam...ut omnis hic mundus ardore deflagret: cf. Cic., *N.D.* 1.36 (see previous note), and 2.39–44 (= *SVF* ii.684). For the divinity of sun, moon, stars, and the parts of the earth, see Aët. 1.7.33 (= *SVF* ii.1027). With *animalis intelligentia*, cf. *natura sentiens* in *Ac.* 1.28; for *permanet*, Sen., *Dial.* 12.8.3 (*Cons. Helv.*): *spiritus per omnia maxima ac minima aequali intentione diffusus*. Hic in *omnis hic mundus* is deictic, 'the world around us'. On conflagration, see e.g. Origen, *Contra Celsum* 4.68 (= *SVF* ii.626), with Long (1985).

Sint ista uera...comprehendi ea tamen et percipi nego: in §§43–4 Lucullus had disputed that an Academic can consistently endorse that there are true and false impressions, and that true and false impressions are non-distinct, i.e. subject to ἀπαραλλαξία. Cicero's parenthesis is aimed at Lucullus' suggestion (*iam* goes with *uides*, not with *fateri*), to which he had responded in §111.

To say that that the Stoic *sententiae* just mentioned may well be true but are not apprehended means that they may be contingently true, but are not necessarily true (contrast the conclusions of geometrical proofs, cf. §§116–17). They do not meet the requirement stated in the third clause of Zeno's definition; cf. §§77–8. It does not mean that they may be true, but we cannot tell—if that was the issue, Cicero would have had the resources to say it. On *sint ista*, see Reid[1] (p. 316).

Cum enim tuus iste Stoicus sapiens syllabatim...ut hic ornatus umquam dilapsus occidat: = Arist., Περὶ φιλοσοφίας frg. 20 Ross (= frg. 22 Rose[3] = frg. 20 Walzer); cf. Lact., *Inst.* 2.10 under the same rubric. In *N.D.* Cicero cites from Περὶ φιλοσοφίας on related topics; cf. 1.33: *Aristotelesque in tertio De philosophia libro multa turbat a* *magistro suo Platone dissentiens; modo enim menti tribuit omnem diuinitatem, modo mundum ipsum deum dicit esse, modo alium quendam praeficit mundo eique eas partes tribuit ut replicatione quadam mundi motum regat atque tueatur.* (See Barnes 1997c: 47–8 on Cicero's knowledge of the *De philosophia*.) Aët. 2.4.4 gives Aristotle's views on whether the universe is ensouled and governed by providence, in line with the present passage. Cf. also Lucr. 2.1023–39, where Lucretius relies on another fragment from the same Aristotelian dialogue, connected with our passage through the motif of the world in its outstanding beauty; on the passage see Rumpf (2003: 149–52).

The ascription of the information presented here to Aristotle's dialogue is uncertain. In its content it agrees with Arist., *Cael.* A3, 270b1–4, but it is doubtful if Cicero had knowledge of the esoteric works, and the reference to Aristotle's speech as a *flumen aureum* points to a dialogue. The thematic similarity to passages like *N.D.* 1.33 then leads to the ascription. See Flashar, Dubielzig, and Breitenberger (2007: 145); and Flashar (2004: 268–71). Plut., *Cic.* 24, might reflect this passage in *Luc.*, in which case it would be another rare piece of evidence for the early transmission of the dialogue, but other explanations are possible; see Plasberg[1] (p. 135).

The force of *syllabatim*—'syllable by syllable'—is not obvious. Reid[1] (p. 316) holds that it signals dictation (thus *Att.* 13.25.3 = SB 333), in which case Cicero is implying again that Antiochus simply took over the Stoic view on physics; Durand emended *dixerit* to *dictauerit* (noted already by Plasberg[1] p. 135). However, that point was already made in *quoniam Stoicus est* above. Alternatively, *syllabatim* contrasts with the praise of Aristotle's style, and Cicero is alluding to the stylistic inadequacy of Stoic rhetoric and style; cf. Cic., *Fin.* 4.7, and Atherton (1988). For *fundere* of exuberant speech, see Reid[1] (p. 263).

The noun *inceptio* only here in Cicero, but cf. Lact., *Inst.* 7.5.5: *suorum operum inuentione, inceptione, perfectione.* With *nouo consilio* and the rejection of the notion that the divine mind was changeable and thus able to resolve on the creation of the world when there was none before, cf. Lucr. 5.168: *quidue noui potuit tanto post ante quietos* (sc. *deos*) | *inlicere ut cuperent uitam mutare priorem?* See also Cic., *N.D.* 1.21–2, on the absurdity of the suggestion that the gods built the world 'having slept for countless centuries'. With *undique aptum*, cf. *Fin.* 4.53: *omnia inter se apta et conexa.* Reid[1] (p. 317) notes that *motus mutationemque* seems intended to capture both senses of κίνησις, motion and change. With *ornatus* = κόσμος, cf. *Fin.* 1.20; *N.D.* 2.115; Varro, *Men. Sat.* frg. 420 Astbury: *appellatur a caelatura caelum, Graece ab ornatu* κόσμος, *Latine a puritia mundus*; Vitr. 9.1.3; as well as *pulchritudo* in *Cato mai.* 81 and *Tusc.* 1.45.

The arrangement of §119—the Stoic view and Aristotle's 'response' to it—is paralleled in Philo, *De aeternitate mundi* §§9–11; cf. Runia (2010: 293–5). One can thus exclude that the arrangement here is Cicero's.

Tibi hoc repudiare...mihi ne ut dubitem quidem relinquatur: *illud superius* refers to the Stoic view laid out earlier in the paragraph. For *caput* alongside *fama*, 'life and reputation', cf. e.g. Cic., *Quinct.* 8; *Lael.* 61. Cicero implies that there are no grounds for favouring the Stoic over the Aristotelian view, which makes committing unequivocally to one of the two less rational than exercising doubt and committing to neither. The correction of the transmitted *quid* to *quidem* is probably right, since the Stoics do not deny the right to doubt, i.e. suspend judgement, sometimes.

§120

Vt omittam leuitatem temere assentientium…non mihi necesse esse quod tibi: on *leuitas* and rash assent, i.e. dogmatic assent when unqualified endorsement is unwarranted, cf. §66:…*quam habemus de grauitate sapientis, errore leuitate temeritate diiunctius*, with n. Reid[1] (p. 317) on the genitive plural participle *assentientium*. See also his note on the infinitive construction explicative of *libertas*.

The freedom which Cicero praises in an exclamation is precisely not to be compelled by doctrinal constraints to take a view when reason suggests otherwise; cf. §§7b–9a (and Lucullus' reply in §§61–2). *Non mihi necesse esse* looks back to *necesse erit* in the previous paragraph and must not be separated from *quanti libertas ipsa aestimanda est* by punctuation. The relative clause *quod tibi* is not in need of a verb, and thus I follow Schäublin (1993: 162) in punctuating after *tibi* and modifying the transmitted *est* to *estne*. The mood of the question which follows requires it to be indirect, and it is more economical to assume the corruption of *estne* to *est* than to make *est* the predicate in the relative clause, and insert *quaero* before *cur* with Reid[1] (p. 317), followed by Plasberg[1] (p. 136). Halm printed *quod tibi est, respondere, cur deus…*.

Est⟨ne⟩ cur deus…cur mortifera tam multa ⟨ac⟩ perniciosa terra marique disperserit: see previous n. regarding the textual problem at the beginning of the lemma. Lact., *Inst.* 7.4.11 (= t. 42) quotes *cur…disperserit* from the final edition.

Nostra causa is unobjectionable, and the emendation *nostri*, found in later manuscripts, unnecessary; for the notion that animals are created to be used by humans, cf. Cic., *N.D.* 2.120–33 (primarily on intelligent design, but note 131:…*ut semper et nouitate delectemur et copia*) and 2.157–62. *Voltis* refers to the Stoics and Antiochus, and on the point at issue there is no reason to think that their views differed. *Natrix* 'water snake' and *uipera* 'viper' stand in for genera of snakes, as in Sen., *Dial.* (*De ira*) 4.31.8. Generic terms for 'snake' in Latin (*anguis, serpens*) have particular literary or stylistic associations. Cf. Verg., *G.* 2.153–4 (on the absence of snakes, or large snakes, from Italy) and 3.435–9 (on the Calabrian watersnake).

Cicero points to harmful creatures as an argument against providential design of the world by a divine intellect. That a god would have to be responsible for those, too, is a rhetorical move; a notion that an evil demiurge might have designed the world so that it is bad was not adopted by anyone in the first century BC (see Mansfeld 1981). For the argument, cf. Carneades in Porph., *De abst.* 3.20 (= frg. 8b Mette): καὶ μὴν εἰ πρὸς ἀνθρώπων χρῆσιν ὁ θεὸς μεμηχάνηται τὰ ζῷα, τί χρησόμεθα μυίαις, ἐμπίσι, νυκτερίσιν, κανθάροις, σκορπίοις, ἐχίδναις, 'But if god created animals for the use of men, in what way do we use flies, lice, bats, beetles, scorpions, and vipers.'

Similarly, Lucretius argues against providence by observing that the world is evil (5.198–9 = 2.180–1): *nequaquam nobis diuinitus esse paratam | naturam rerum: tanta stat praedita culpa*. In 5.200–34 Lucretius goes on to point out that large parts of the world are uninhabitable.

Chrysippus made minor concessions concerning the point in hand when he allowed that minor flaws in the universe are like husks and wheat getting lost in an otherwise perfectly managed house (Plut., *Sto. rep.* 1051c) and that there has to be some evil for the good to exist, just as the existence of truth requires the existence of falsehood (Plut., *Comm. not.* 1065, parts of which are *SVF* ii.1181). See also Gell., *N.A.* 7.1.7-13 (= *SVF* ii.1170).

Reid[1] (p. 318) quotes further passages bearing on the debate about providence. Runia (2010a) is a study of Aët. 1.7.1-10, which is devoted to the question of who the deity posited by various thinkers is and which begins with some who claimed that there exist no gods at all. The first three philosophers in Aëtius' list also occur in Cic., *N.D.* 1.117-19, and Sextus, *M.* 9.50-8. Cicero evidently had access to an *Atheistenkatalog*, which, however, while being thematically related, does not overlap with our passage here. Winiarczyk (1976) follows Diels (1879: 58-9) in arguing that the lists reflected in Cic., *N.D.* 1.117-19, and Sextus, *M.* 9.50-8, go back to a work by Clitomachus, who in turn drew on earlier material.

Negatis haec tam polite tamque subtiliter effici potuisse...Myrmecides aliquis minutorum opusculorum fabricator fuisse uideatur: cf. Cic., *N.D.* 2.157-62 and 2.120-33, for the claim that an intelligent being must have expended thought on the design of animals, many of which can only be intended for use by human beings. *Haec* has backward reference, so the point is that even animals detrimental to humans exhibit careful design; contrast Reid[2] (p. 80): 'the world', Schäublin et al. (p. 120). *Deducere* may mean 'to mislead, lead astray', as Reid[1] (p. 318) suggests, but sense would be better served by 'to stretch thin': Cicero suggests that it is hard to reconcile the majesty of the divine that the deity should attend to things as small as bees and ants, a point he drives home by suspecting a Myrmecides among the gods.

For Myrmecides, a quasi-mythical creator of miniature works of art, see Plut., *Comm. not.* 1083d-e, on a sesame seed inscribed with lines from Homer (also Ael. *V.H.* 1.17); Pliny, *N.H.* 7.85 and 36.43, on miniature ships and chariots which an insect could cover with its wings. See Squire (2011: 287-8) with further references. Myrmecides was presumably chosen as an example because of the etymological connection of his name with Greek ant (μύρμηξ); cf. *formica* here. For a collection of ancient sources on the question of whether animals are endowed with reason, see Newmyer (2010: 3-26). *Fabricator* was probably chosen over *artifex* because it denotes more clearly a creator of objects, and over *opifex* because artistic skill is involved; cf. also §87.

Reid[1] (p. 318) notes the reminiscence of our passage, or rather its counterpart in the second edition, in Aug., *C.D.* 7.2: [if gods are called *di maiores* because of the importance of their functions] *non eos inuenire debuimus inter illam quasi plebeiam numinum multitudinem minutis opusculis deputatam.*

Brittain (2001: 135 n. 9) on *Luc.* 120-1 speculates how mitigated sceptics might have used species-teleological arguments, as opposed to arguments from human design by a deity, to explain why humans' generally successful interaction with the world justifies their treating persuasive impressions as true or truth-like and as evidence for states of affairs in the world. In this commentary, persuasive impressions are construed as inherently able to be treated as evidence (see section 6), and

Clitomacheans, or a Clitomachean of the kind who Cicero is, would be as able to cite arguments of the kind in question as mitigated sceptics. On Cicero's Clitomacheanism, see section 8.

§121

Negas sine deo posse quicquam: *negas sine...et me timore* is Strato frg. 32 Wehrli. Repici (1988: 121–8) discusses §121 with a view to whether Strato was in disagreement with Aristotle (cf. §119). For *posse = fieri posse*, see Hofmann-Szantyr p. 422. The shift from second-person plural in §120 (*negatis, deducitis*) to second-person singular (*negas*) seems to be mere *uariatio*.

Ecce tibi e transuerso Lampsacenus Strato...quanto est aequius habere ipsos deos: *ecce tibi...ponderibus et motibus* is Democritus frg. DK 68A80. On Strato, see the commentary on *Ac.* 1.34. The phrase *e transuerso* means 'unexpectedly' (*OLD* s.v. *transuersus* no. 3a), and may be hinting at the fact that a leading early Peripatetic who rejects the providential organization of the world poses a problem for the construction of an Old Academy as envisaged by Antiochus.

Cf. the parallel in *N.D.* 1.35 (= frg. 33 Wehrli) on the role accorded, or rather not accorded, to the divine: *Nec audiendus eius auditor Strato, is qui physicus appellatur, qui omnem uim diuinam in natura sitam esse censet, quae causas gignendi, augendi, minuendi habeat, sed careat omni et sensu et figura.* Lact., *De ira dei* 10.1 (= frg. 34 Wehrli) interprets N.D. 1.35 in line with *Luc.* 121: *Qui nolunt diuina prouidentia factum esse mundum, aut principiis inter se temere coeuntibus dicunt esse concretum aut repente natura exstitisse; naturam uero, ut ait Strato, habere in se uim gignendi et minuendi, sed eam nec sensum habere ullum nec figuram, ut intelligamus omnia quasi sua sponte esse generata, nullo artifice nec auctore.* Cf. Plut., *Adv. Col.* 1115b (= frg. 35 Wehrli).

The relative clause *qui det* is consecutive: 'whose view is such that he...'. Reid[1] (p. 338) assembles passages which feature the sequence epithet/name as in *Lampsacenus Strato*. See Mommsen (1905: 249–51) on the *uacatio militiae* and the *uacatio muneris publici* of priests. Reid[1] prints Goerenz' *et cum* for the transmitted *sed cum*, but the latter can connect as well as contrast; see also Plasberg[1] (p. 136).

Negat opera deorum...haec esse dicat interiecto inani: Strato is introduced as denying that he posits divine help in his account of the creation of the world. Rather, everything comes about 'naturally', in a manner which is quite different from Democritus' account, who accounts for the world in terms of the interaction of atoms endowed with certain primary qualities and void. Strato himself posited elemental, material qualities like 'the hot' and 'the cold' as principles; the evidence is reviewed and interpreted by Keyser (2010). Strato and Democritus are also elsewhere juxtaposed in the doxographical tradition; cf. e.g. Ps.-Gal., *De hist. phil.* 108, and below on *somnia censet....*

Cf. Cic., *N.D.* 1.66, for the primary qualities of atoms:...*corpuscula quaedam leuia, alia aspera, rutunda alia, partim autem angulata et hamata, curuata quaedam et quasi adunca, ex iis effectum esse caelum atque terram nulla cogente natura, sed concursu quodam fortuito*; t. 44 (Nonius p. 189 M.), which shows that the present passage was not modified in the final edition; Arist., *Met.* A4, 985b4–22. The terms used to characterize the primary qualities of atoms can also be paralleled in Lucr., except for *uncinatus* (*-que* marks *uncinatis* as a synonym of *hamatis*, added for stylistic fullness in an *et... et* series); cf. 2.333–729 and Epic., *Ep. ad Hdt.* 42 (which is not Lucretius' direct model), Reinhardt (2005). However, this need not mean that Cicero used Lucretius, since none of the terms is very choice. The subjunctive in *dicat*, if it is not due to *attractio modi*, suggests that (sc. according to Cicero) Strato compared himself to Democritus, and favourably so. See Plasberg[1] (p. 136) on ⟨*ex*⟩ *asperis* (Reid[1] p. 319).

Somnia censet haec esse Democriti...sed optantis: Reid[1] (p. 319) shows that *somnium* is a standard term of philosophical controversy (and everyday disparagement). However, it is striking that in the doxographical tradition Democritus and Strato are juxtaposed on the subject of dreams; cf. Diels (1879: 416) and Mansfeld and Runia (2020: 1772) on Aët. 5.2.1–2: Δημόκριτος τοὺς ὀνείρους γίνεσθαι κατὰ τὰς τῶν εἰδώλων παραστάσεις. Στράτων ἀλόγῳ φύσει τῆς διανοίας ἐν τοῖς ὕπνοις αἰσθητικωτέρας μέν πως γινομένης, παρ' αὐτὸ δὲ τοῦτο τῷ γνωστικῷ κινουμένης, 'Democritus says that dreams are formed by the occurrence of images. Strato, that the irrational part of the soul, which during sleep becomes more perceptive, is moved by the rational part.' For the loaded sense of *optare* of 'wishful thinking', cf. *Tusc.* 2.30; *Fat.* 47; *docere* of the teaching or demonstration of truths (*OLD* s.v. no. 3a).

Ipse autem singulas mundi partes persequens...et deum opere magno liberat et me timore: *persequi* must mean 'to pursue in discovery and explanation' (cf. *Tusc.* 2.1), as the following clause shows. In the absence of information about the level of description at which Strato took causal forces to operate, the present passage leaves the difference between his and Democritus' view unclear. One would assume that *motūs* arise from the *pondera* of matter (cf. *Fin.* 1.18 *fin.* on atoms), but cf. e.g. *Fat.* 22 (on the swerve): *Itaque tertius quidam motus oritur extra pondus et plagam*, 'Thus a third type of movement arises in addition to weight and impulse.'

For Strato's theory of weights, see frgs 50–3 Wehrli, esp. Simpl. *in Arist. Cael.* p. 269.4–6 (= frg. 50) and Stob., *Ecl.* I.14, p. 143 Wachsmuth (= frg. 51). See Berryman (2009: 106–14) on the *Mechanica* ascribed to Aristotle, and p. 108 on the question of whether Strato might be its author.

For the affirmative *ne* followed by indicative, paralleled in comedy and a colloquial element in Cicero's philosophical dialogues, see Ricottilli (2003: 135–6).

Quis enim potest...extimescere ne id iure euenerit: cf. Cic., *N.D.* 1.54: *Quis enim non timeat omnia prouidentem et cogitantem et animaduertentem et omnia ad se pertinere putantem curiosum et plenum negotii deum?* Further related passages are assembled by Pease (1955–8: 338) ad loc. For *et dies et noctes*, 'all the time', see Cic., *Att.* 12.46.1 (= SB 287).

Nec Stratoni tamen assentior...modo illud probabilius uidetur: Cicero defends his general, Clitomachean policy of universal ἐποχή with respect to the views which have just been laid out. The section does not include a clear statement to the effect that Cicero approves Strato's view (in the technical sense of §104), but it is tempting to think that Cicero gives his qualified endorsement from *Ne ille et deum*.... If so, the comment that Cicero finds *modo hoc modo illud* more persuasive would mean that, for now, he finds Strato's view more persuasive, but knowing himself, he knows that new information or experiences might make him warm to the Stoic view. Reid[1] (p. 320) assembles numerous passages on Academic wavering between positions; I discuss this aspect of the Academic posture in section 8. On *probabilitas* as plausibility, and the manner in which perceptual and non-perceptual *probabilia* are treated as akin, see sections 6.1 and 6.5.

§122

Latent ista omnia...terram intrare possit: the statement is stylized, with *crassis* and *tenebris* mimetically enclosing *occultata et circumfusa*, and *penetrare in caelum* in chiastic arrangement with *terram intrare*. The intended effect is not clear. Davies (p. 194) notes that *crassis...tenebris* is a *uersus heroicus*, which he ascribes to Cicero ('e Ciceronis enim nec opinantis calamo uidetur effluxisse'). Goerenz (pp. 218–19) suspected an allusion to an archaic Roman poet, and it is possible that a choral ode in a tragedy might have included words to similar effect (not necessarily in a sceptical pronouncement). Cicero may also be alluding to the sceptical pronouncements of Presocratics who wrote poetry (cf. *Ac.* 1.44; *Luc.* 72-5), implying that his stance on physical matters is that of the *physici* themselves (sc. as he construes them). For the notion that the air thickens at times of darkness, cf. Lucr. 4.348-50.

Contrast the Stoic context in *N.D.* 2.153: *Quid uero hominum ratio non in caelum usque penetrauit? Soli enim ex animantibus nos astrorum ortus, obitus cursusque cognouimus, ab hominum genere finitus est dies, mensis, annus, defectiones solis et lunae cognitae praedicataeque in omne posterum tempus, quae, quantae, quando futurae sint.*

In the fourth book of the final edition (Mart. Cap. 5.517, where the vocative *Luculle* is replaced with *Varro*; t. 45), *crassis occultata* was changed to *magnis obscurata*. See Hunt (1998: 24–5), who notes that Mart. Cap. just cited is the last reference to *Acad.* in antiquity. With *circumfusa tenebris*, cf. *Ac.* 1.44, and contrast *Luc.* 46: *luce...circumfusa*.

Corpora nostra non nouimus...quam uim quaeque pars habeat ignoramus: the statement seemed Reid[1] (p. 320) so sweeping and pessimistic that he wondered if Cicero had written *habitus* 'normal condition' rather than *situs*, but the context is rhetorical, and the overall purpose is to argue for ignorance in physical matters a fortiori, including the issue of the position of the earth. Since dissection of human corpses was not practised in Republican Rome, let alone exploratory experiments on living humans as Herophilus of Alexandria had conducted them (see next n.), it is also conceivable that even issues like the positions of main organs were not held to be settled. Note in this connection §124: *Satisne tandem ea nota...quae uenarum?*

Itaque medici ipsi...ut patefacta et detecta mutentur: famous doctors who opened up human bodies, corpses as well as reportedly the living bodies of convicted criminals, in order to discover their workings, include Herophilus of Alexandria (see von Staden 1989) and Erisistratus (see Fraser 1969); see von Staden (1992). With our passage, cf. *Tusc.* 1.46. On Cicero's knowledge of medical theory, see Gourevitch (1984: 439–62).

On the Empiricist school of medicine, which prized observation and experience arising from past successful treatment but resisted medical theorizing, see Frede (1987d); von Manz (2005). *Corpora nostra...patefacta et detecta mutentur* is frg. 66 in Deichgräber (1965²: 130). For the objection made here, cf. Celsus 1.pr.40-4, esp. 41; Tert., *De anim.* 10.4: *ipsa morte mutante quae uixerant*, with Waszink (2010²: 185); Gal., *De sectis ingredientibus* §10. See Deichgräber (1965²: 286); Lloyd (1982: 144–5); Cosans (1997: 42–5).

The Empiricists feature only once, on the subject of 7-month-old embryos, among the medics whose views entered the doxographical tradition at some point; see Runia (1999: 207).

The emphasis delivered by *ipsi* is explained in the latter part of the sentence: the doctors have a special interest and privileged insight. Veridical seeing must be meant by *uiderentur*. *Detecta* is a compelling early conjecture for the transmitted *deiecta(m)*; Reid¹ (p. 321) mentions but dismisses *desecta*.

Sed ecquid nos eodem modo rerum naturas persecare...et quasi radicibus suis haereat an media pendeat: a reasoning from one relatively accessible object of physical enquiry to less accessible ones. *Rerum naturae* and *radicibus haerere* are paralleled in Lucr. (for the latter, cf. 3.25; 5.554), and in the former case *res* would have sufficed, as Reid¹ (p. 321) notes. Arist., *Cael.* B13–14, surveys views on the position and shape of the earth.

The first view is ascribed to Xenophanes in Aët. 3.9.4 (subject of the section is περὶ γῆς): Ξενοφάνης ἐκ τοῦ κατωτέρω μέρους εἰς ἄπειρον [μέρος] ἐρριζῶσθαι, ἐξ ἀέρος δὲ καὶ πυρὸς συμπαγῆναι, 'Xenophanes says (the earth) is rooted from its lower part down to an unlimited depth, and made out of compacted air and fire'; cf. Arist., *Cael.* B13, 294a22–4. If the view was so assigned in Cicero's source material, too, this might explain why he could attribute the next tenet in §123 to Xenophanes erroneously. (For a different explanation see Mansfeld and Runia 2009: 583–4.) The omission of the name here, however, appears deliberate and may thus offer a glimpse of how Cicero adapted his source. For the alternative considered here—the earth in the centre of the universe—cf. *Tusc.* 1.40 and the collection of parallels in Reid¹ (p. 321); Zhmud (2006: 254). On the use of *ecquid*, see Pinkster i.335.

§123

Habitari ait Xenophanes...neque ego non ita: cf. Lact., *Inst.* 3.23.12. §122: *Sed ecquid...urbium et montium* is DK 21frg. 47 (Xenophanes). However, the view presented here is assigned to Anaxagoras in D.L. 2.8: Οὗτος ἔλεγε...τὴν δὲ σελήνην οἰκήσεις ἔχειν, ἀλλὰ καὶ λόφους καὶ φάραγγας, 'He said [something about the sun]...and that there were houses on the moon, as well as hills and ravines'; see previous n. Anaxagoras is also reported to have held, possibly in addition to his view on the moon, that there are other worlds inhabited by humans like us, with suns and moons of their own; cf. Simpl. *in Arist. Phys.* pp. 156.2–157.16 (= part of DK 59B4). See also Aët. 2.23–9 on the moon.

For *portenta* used of wild claims, esp. in philosophical polemics, *Fin.* 4.70; *N.D.* 1.18 (*portenta et miracula non disserentium philosophorum, sed somniantium*); similar terms are *somnia* (§121), *monstra* (*Tusc.* 4.54). With *iurare*, cf. §116 *fin.*, but also §146 (where it is pointed out that oaths in court involve a rider acknowledging human fallibility, a notion not present here).

Vos etiam dicitis esse e regione nobis…desipere uos arbitrantur: the Stoics accepted the notion, which was Platonic as well as Aristotelian, that all things tend towards the centre of the universe; cf. Stob., *Ecl.* I.19, p. 166 Wachsmuth on Zeno (= *SVF* i.99); Plut., *Sto. rep.* 1054e on Chrysippus (= *SVF* ii.550); Cic., *N.D.* 2.115–16 (= *SVF* ii.549). The world's location in the centre of the universe, its sphericity (Aët. 3.10.1= *SVF* ii.648), the assumption that the antipodean parts of the two temperate zones were habitable (D.L. 7.156 = *SVF* ii.649), and the existence of antipodes are a natural function of this notion. The claim that there are antipodes is not otherwise explicitly attested for the Stoics, although Manil. 1.238–41 might qualify as a sufficiently Stoicizing context. Lucr. 1.1052–82 dismisses the notion that things tend to the centre, and the idea that there are antipodes from 1061; Bailey (1947) interprets this as directed against the Stoics, but Lucretius may equally be reaching beyond the Stoics, in line with his practice of inheriting his philosophical targets from his philosophical models (see Sedley 1998: 78–82). Here Stoic views and Antiochian ones are once more simply equated (*uos*), but there is no independent evidence that the latter pronounced on the subject.

For the term ἀντίπους, cf. Plt., *Tim.* 63a3; Arist., *Cael.* Δ1, 308a20. From the inflection *antipodas* it is not plain whether Cicero did not actually use Greek letters which were normalized in the process of transmission (Greek letters in *TLL* s.v. *antipodes* col. 173.37; other writers used the Latinized *antipodae, -arum*, see ibid. col. 173.38–46). In the case of an unusual term this would have been more in line with his practice than transliteration (let alone transliteration and inflection like a Latin word, as in cases like *dialectica*; see on *Ac.* 1.25).

The phrase *e regione* has its usual sense of 'directly, in a straight line' and thus functions together with the following colon, from which it should not be separated by a comma. Reid[1] (p. 321) notes that t. 46 (preserved in Nonius Marcellus) has *in contraria parte*, while Aug., *C.D.* 16.9 has *a contraria parte*; neither should be selected over the reading transmitted here. *Vestigium* is presumably intended to have its primary sense of 'footprint', given *antipodas*.

The question beginning with *cur* illustrates once more that Cicero's point is rhetorical: having selected an especially implausible—at least in the eyes of some (e.g. the Epicureans)—claim, he suggests that the Academic's suspension of judgement ought to be preferable to the Stoics/Antiochians than the hostile rejection by other dogmatists. With *non aspernor*, cf. *Luc.* 148.

Hicetas Syracosius…quae si stante terra caelum moueretur: Hicetas of Syracuse was a Pythagorean; see Centrone (2000).

Elsewhere Hicetas is associated with standard Pythagorean doctrines. D.L. 8.85 ascribes to him the view that the earth moves in a circle (*pace* Brittain 2006: 72 n. 188), noting that others ascribe it to Philolaus. In Aët. 3.9.1–2 Hicetas is associated with the traditional Pythagorean doctrine of a counterworld (ἀντίχθων). Both views, as well as that the earth moves around a central fire (rather than rotating around its axis, as envisaged here), in Arist., *Cael.* B13, ascribed to the Pythagoreans.

Hicetas Syracosius...paulo obscurius is frg. Theophrastus frg. 240 FHS&D. Diels (1879: 492–3) printed *Hicetas Syracusius...terra caelum moueretur* as *Phys. op.* frg. 18, but as Mansfeld (1989: 133–4 and passim) observes, the mentioning of the name 'Theophrastus' as a source should not lead to the conclusion that the Theophrastean material of *Luc.* 118, shown to be such through agreements with reports on Theophrastus in Simpl. *in Arist. Phys.*, and the present passage reflect the same tradition.

Seneca touches on the question of whether the heavens or the earth turn on *N.Q.* 7.2.3. For the kind of illusion of movement which probably gave rise to such questions, cf. *Luc.* 81. On our passage, see also Cardauns (2001: 123–4). On the decausative use of *(rem ullam in mundo) moueri*, see Pinkster i.231.

Atque hoc etiam Platonem...sed paulo obscurius: the reference is to *Tim.* 40b8–c3, and specifically the participle ἰλλομένην: γῆν δὲ τροφὸν μὲν ἡμετέραν, ἰλλομένην δὲ τὴν περὶ τὸν διὰ παντὸς πόλον τεταμένον, φύλακα καὶ δημιουργὸν νυκτός τε καὶ ἡμέρας ἐμηχανήσατο, πρώτην καὶ πρεσβυτάτην θεῶν ὅσοι ἐντὸς οὐρανοῦ γεγόνασιν, 'Earth he devised to be our nurturer, and, because it is packed around the axis that stretches throughout the universe, also to be the maker and guardian of day and night. Of the gods that have come to be within the heavens, Earth ranks as the foremost, the one with the greatest seniority' (transl. Zeyl). The question is whether ἰλλομένην means 'compacted' or 'winding' (for the two senses, see LSJ s.v. εἴλω, B and C), and if the latter—but this issue was not debated in antiquity—whether the reading εἰλλομένην transmitted in some manuscripts should be printed. That the earth is said to be winding around its axis was the minority view in antiquity; cf. Proclus *in Plat. Tim.* 3.137–8, citing Arist., *Cael.* B13, 293b31, and Heraclides Ponticus (frg. 105 Wehrli) as proponents of it. See Cornford (1935: 120–36) and Zeyl (2000: xlix–l).

Quid tu, Epicure...et ipsi illum uicissim eluditis: it is impossible to say whether Epicurus comes in here because Cicero mentioned him earlier or because he was in Cicero's source. The former seems more likely.

The piece of dialogue with Epicurus poses a textual problem. Cicero asks Epicurus if he really takes the sun to be 'as small as that', i.e. as small as he takes it to be (cf. §82). The reply is transmitted as *egone uobis quidem tantum* in AB, which suggests that this is what the archetype read. Cicero ends the exchange by observing that both sides deride one another. That Epicurus should begin his reply with a question amounting to 'are you talking to me?', i.e. *egone?*, seems compelling, as does the suggestion that he should then make reference to what he thinks rather than to what his opponent thinks—this would tell against the transmitted *uobis* and in favour of a first-person pronoun. The question is then whether sense requires that Epicurus spells out what his view is, as Plasberg[1] (p. 138) assumed when he speculatively suggested *nobis quidem ⟨tantulum, reapse uel paulo maiorem quam uidetur aut minorem uel⟩ tantum* (cf. D.L. 10.91 = Epic., *Ep. ad Pyth.*), or whether his response should signal that dissatisfaction over the size of the sun which he does posit is unwarranted (such dissatisfaction would be conveyed by the diminutive *tantulum*). The latter is much more plausible, given that the topic of the size of the sun and Epicurus' view on it had featured before and that Cicero is building up to a section break, with Socrates' and Aristo's view about to serve as a punchline of sorts. Thus I print Faber's *nobis quidem tantum* (see Davies p. 198), an appropriately epigrammatic reply to 'do you take the sun to be as small as that?': 'We take it to be of such a size as previously indicated, sc. which is quite large enough', as the resumption of *tantulum* by *tantum* can easily convey. Cf. *Att.* 15.27.3 (= SB 406) for a slightly different play on *tantum* and *tantulum*. Confusion of *nos/uos* or *nos/uobis* is of course trivial. The specific point made by Cicero in §82—that the Epicurean pronouncement on the size of the sun could be seen to be in disagreement with the view that all perceptions are true, due to its hedging nature—, which Plasberg seeks to introduce here, is not at issue. For a different view, see Brittain (2006: 72 n. 190). *Eludere* is here plainly intended as a synonym of *irridere* and means 'to mock, ridicule', not 'to trick'. Two different verbs are merely used for *uariatio*.

Liber igitur a tali irrisione Socrates...qui nihil istorum sciri putat posse: with *liber*, cf. §120 *init.*: *quanti libertas ipsa aestimanda est*: the freedom to judge for oneself results in freedom from ridicule for being forced into absurd positions by one's dogmatic commitments. The implication is that two philosophers whom Antiochus either wants to claim for his Old Academy or ought to be able to accommodate within it felt licensed to act as an Academic would: Socrates, whom Antiochus took to be ironic in his professions of ignorance (*Luc.* 15), and Zeno's contemporary Aristo. At the same time, Cicero is appealing to their authority, *auctoritas* being another Antiochian watchword (cf. §60).

Aristo is reported to have rejected physics and logic in D.L. 7.160 (= *SVF* i.351) on the grounds that the former is beyond human beings and the latter does not affect them (τόν τε φυσικὸν τόπον καὶ τὸν λογικὸν ἀνῄρει, λέγων τὸν μὲν εἶναι ὑπὲρ ἡμᾶς, τὸν δ' οὐδὲν πρὸς ἡμᾶς, μόνον δὲ τὸν ἠθικὸν εἶναι πρὸς ἡμᾶς, 'he wished to discard both logic and physics, saying that physics was beyond our reach and logic did not concern us: all that did concern us was ethics', transl. Hicks); Sextus, *M.* 7.12, for the claim that physics is useless. See Ioppolo (1980: 78 n. 53, 87) for further references; Ranocchia (2011: 342); Ioppolo (2012). Grammatically the relative clause only characterizes Aristo's view (there is no case for emending to *putant*); Socrates' rejection of physics was deeply familiar (cf. *Ac.* 1.15).

§124

Sed redeo ad animum et corpus...quae uenarum: cf. §90: *abeo a sensibus* as a formula for finishing with a subject. The human body was dealt with in §122, but not the soul; see the general note above on the possible import of this. Cicero then resumes the subjects of body and soul chiastically, expanding on the latter; however, it cannot be ruled out that *animum et* is an interpolation. In that case Cicero would have announced a return to the body, would in fact be returning to the subject briefly, and would proceed to the related subject of the soul. For the claim that we do not really know about muscles (*nerui*; cf. *N.D.* 2.139: *neruos a quibus artus continentur*) and veins/arteries (*uenae* covers both), cf. the pessimistic statement in §122: *corpora nostra non nouimus...quaeque pars habeat ignoramus*. A distinction between veins and arteries was first made by Praxagoras in the fourth century BC. *Satisne* = *num*, as Reid[1] (p. 323) observes; see also Pinkster i.341–2.

Tenemusne quid sit animus...ne sit quidem ullus: on this use of *tenere* ('to grasp'), see *OLD* s.v. no. 23. With the 'question types', cf. *Tusc.* 1.18: *Quid sit porro ipse animus aut ubi aut unde, magna dissensio est*; Lucr. 3.176–7 (with Mansfeld 1990: 3149–51); Philo, *De somniis* 1.30; Sen., *Ep. mor.* 121.12; and the general note above (p. 708). Important Aristotelian passages which illustrate the origin of the organizational technique include *Top.* A11, 104b1–8, A14, 105a35–b25; *An. Post.* B1, 89b24–35. The soul is the subject of Aët. 4.2–23.

For the use of the same technique in *N.D.* 1.2 and 1.65, where, however, the subject is not the soul, see Mansfeld (1990: 3207–8).

Cicero inserts the reference to Dicaearchus' view (see frgs 7–8k Wehrli) here (*Tenemusne...quidem ullus?* is frgs 8f Wehrli) in short parenthesis, whereas in *Tusc.* it features later in the sequence in greater detail (1.21 = frg. 7 Wehrli), ascribed to an interlocutor in Dicaearchus' dialogue Κορινθιακοί, thus affording a glimpse of the nature of the material available to Cicero and discouraging any notion that for him the views relayed were just tralaticious material stripped of a larger context. Cf. *Tusc.* 1.41 (= frg. 8d Wehrli); Aët. 4.2.7.

Si est, trisne partes habeat...mortale sit an aeternum: *si simplex...numerus nullo corpore?* is Xenocrates frg. 201 Isnardi Parente. (i) Plato (cf. Aët. 4.4.1) and (ii) Xenocrates (cf. Aët. 4.2.4) feature in reverse order in *Tusc.* 1.20: (ii) *Xenocrates animi figuram et quasi corpus negauit esse ullum, numerum dixit esse, cuius uis, ut iam ante Pythagorae uisum erat, in natura maxima esset* (= Xenocrates frg. 199 Isnardi Parente). (i) *Eius* [sc. *Xenocratis*] *doctor Plato triplicem finxit animum, cuius principatum, id est rationem, in capite sicut in arce posuit, et duas partes parere uoluit, iram et cupiditatem, quas locis disclusit: iram in pectore, cupiditatem supter praecordia locauit.* For Plato's conception of a tripartite soul, see *Rep.* 4, 436a–41c. See Isnardi Parente (1981) frgs 165–212 for Xenocrates' psychology in general as well as Arist., *De anim.* A2, 404b27–8. In other doxographical texts the question of whether the soul is corporeal or not is an explicit sub-division; cf. e.g. Sen., *Ep.* 88.34: *innumerabiles quaestiones sunt de animo tantum...utrum corpus sit an non sit*. This division is hinted at in both *Tusc.* 1.20 (*...et quasi corpus negauit esse ullum...*) and in our passage (*numerus nullo corpore*). See Mansfeld and Runia (2009: 57). *Tusc.* 1.20 confirms (and probably informs) Bentley's emendation of *mens* to *numerus* (noted by Davies); Plasberg[1] (p. 139) added *merus* to accommodate the paradosis, in a manner which is in line with his tendency to diagnose corruptions as due to omissions and heal them with supplements. See also *Ac.* 1.39. Reid[1] (p. 323) notes that Cicero fails to report that Xenocrates regarded the soul as a number which is self-moving.

The unassigned views briefly mentioned are that the soul is (a) fire, (b) *anima* (most likely πνεῦμα), and (c) blood. For (a), see *SVF* i.120 (= Stob., *Ecl.* I.25, p. 213; contrast Aët. 4.3.7, where the view is assigned to Leucippus): Ζήνων...φησι...δύο γὰρ γένη πυρός, τὸ μὲν ἄτεχνον καὶ μεταβάλλον εἰς ἑαυτὸ τὴν τροφήν, τὸ δὲ τεχνικόν, αὐξητικόν τε καὶ τηρητικόν, οἷον ἐν τοῖς φυτοῖς ἐστι καὶ ζῴοις, ὃ δὴ φύσις ἐστὶ καὶ ψυχή, 'Zeno...says...there are in fact two kinds of fire, one non-artificial and which transforms its nourishment into itself, the other artificial, which determines growth and preservation, like that found in plants and animals. And that fire is nature and soul.' For (b), see *SVF* i.235 (= D.L. 7.157) on the soul as πνεῦμα ἔνθερμον (ascribed to 'the Stoics' in Aët. 4.4.3). Given that both (a) and (b) are ascribed to Zeno, they may also be different formulations of the same view. For (c) cf. Aët. 4.5.8, according to which Empedocles situates the leading part of the soul in the blood (ἐν τῇ τοῦ αἵματος συστάσει; DK 31A97). All three views (as well as others) are mentioned, unassigned, in *Tusc.* 1.24.

Nam utramque in partem...in plerisque contrariarum rationum paria momenta: contemporary texts which reflect the debate about the mortality of the soul include *Tusc.* 1, Lucr. 3, esp. the long series of arguments in favour of the mortality of the soul (3.417–828), and the Ps.-Platonic dialogue *Axiochus*. See on §137.

Reid[1] (p. 323) refers to *Ac.* 1.46, where the Academic practice of arguing on either side is mentioned, but Cicero's point here is that the issue is keenly contested among dogmatists. Assuming as at the end of §118 that a survey of views on the soul would be exhaustive, Cicero suggests that the Stoic or Antiochian would regard one of them as certain (cf. §118: *Sint ista uera...percipi nego*), whereas the Academic would not even be able to say which position is most *probabile*. This is so because the arguments in favour of one of the other views are equally persuasive; cf. *paria...momenta* in *Ac.* 1.45, *rationis momenta* in *N.D.* 1.10. *Ita* is not inferential but modifies *paria*. On the circumstances in which *in utramque partem* argument can issue in a view according to Cicero, see section 8. *Occurrit*, a near-synonym of a verb of appearing here, is probably perfect tense, as Reid[1] (p. 327) notes.

§125

Sin agis uerecundius et me accusas...quem potissimum, quem: on *uerecundius*, cf. Kaster (2005: 27): '*verecundia*, as an emotion, animates the art of knowing your proper place in every social transaction and binds the free members of a civil community, exerting its force both vertically, across the different ranks of society, and horizontally, among members of comparable status.' The Cicero character's reference is to §114, which described Lucullus'/Antiochus' as making unreasonable demands (and thus violating *uerecundia*); cf. also §§115, 126. §§132–3 restates that Lucullus/Antiochus demanded that the Academics select a position rather than suspend judgement (cf. *quod nullis* here). With reference to Plut., *Adv. Col.* 1124a, where it is suggested that, given the well-documented disagreements among philosophers, assenting to a view was odd, not suspending judgement over all of them, Schäublin et al. (p. 291 n. 389) speculate that Antiochus may have held that it was not possible for human beings to suspend judgement with respect to all philosophical views in a given domain. A conviction of this kind, arrived at over time as a result of introspection, could conceivably be part of an explanation of how Antiochus gave up Academic scepticism and became a dogmatist. See also on *Luc.* 69–71.

Reid[1] (p. 323) collects parallels for *uincam animum* 'I will suppress my feelings, will overcome my natural inclination'. With *deligam*, cf. §118 *fin.*: *eliget*; and with *quem potissimum* as a question §117: *quorum potissimum*. With the insistent follow-up question *quem?* cf. e.g. *quid?* in §106 *init*. Cicero may have written *quemnam* in the follow-up question, as Reid[1] (p. 324) suggests with reference to Aug., *Contra Acad*. 3.15.33 *quid? quidnam?*

Democritum:...studiosus nobilitatis fui: Antiochus had inherited the Stoic respect for Democritus; cf. §14: *Democriti uerecundia*. Cicero's point depends on him selecting a figure whom the opponent is known to rate; this is ironic, in that Cicero now affects to go by *auctoritas* (cf. §60), since a rational choice based on *iudicium* is impossible (so also Schäublin et al. p. 291 n. 390). At the same time, Cicero is commenting ruefully on his lifelong political allegiance; see Griffin (1997: 9). As Reid[1] (p. 324) notes, it is the wrong question to ask whether Democritus was held to be of aristocratic descent. For the citation of Democritus in the present context, cf. *Tusc*. 1.22 *fin*. (cited below).

Vrgebor iam omnium uestrum conuicio: for *conuicium*, cf. §34, where Reid[1] (p. 219) quotes Zumpt (1859) on *Mur.* 13: 'Non unum maledictum appellatur conuicium sed multorum uerborum quasi uociferatio.' Here there is also an implication of a failure to advance a genuine argument. Adamietz (1996: 108) on *Mur.* 13 notes that the antithesis of well-founded accusation and mere abuse was conventional; cf. *Cael.* 6, *Cael.* 30; *Planc.* 30; *Font.* 37; Dem., *Coron.* 123 (κατηγορία, λοιδορία). See also Schäublin et al. (p. 291 n. 391).

Tune aut inane quicquam putes esse...rem ullam effici posse praeclaram: Cicero now gives, addressed to himself, the opponent's *conuicium*, prompted by his choice of Democritus as the *physicus* whom he follows. The *conuicium* is a quick survey of central Democritean doctrines, initially punctuated by three instances of *aut*. The opponent questions first that there is void, by confronting the notion with the Aristotelian rejection of void. He then questions that there are atoms, endowed with primary qualities only, which account for the perceptible world in all its detail, i.e. are apt to give rise to secondary qualities. Thirdly, he questions that the world, complex and well-organized as it is, could be the result of something other than an intellect's planning and organization.

Aristotle discusses the notion that bodies are able to move because of the movement of other bodies rather than the existence of void in *Phys. Δ*7, 214a16–18 *fin.*; see the commentary by Hussey (1993). Lucr. rejects it in 1.370–97; see Bailey (1947: 658–63), who cites further evidence on the ancient debate. See also on *Luc.* 55–6 and 119–21 for further arguments against Democritean views.

The text after *conferta sint omnia* has long been suspected (see the long app. crit.). That Cicero must have written *ut et* is clear. Beyond that the question is what perspective the text takes on an event which involves two notional objects interacting (on the view at issue, there is no void, only bodies displacing one another). The verb *mouebitur*, which is passive rather than medio-passive on the most natural reading, has as its grammatical subject an object that is affected by another object rather than actively affecting ('moving') other objects. The second *et*-colon then describes the consequence of the object referred to in the first colon being moved. The text is ⟨*ut*⟩ *et quod mouebitur corporum cedat et quā quidque cesserit aliud ilico subsequatur*, which is unobjectionable grammatically and in sense: '...that both any body which is moved gives way and something else follows immediately (*ilico*) in the direction in which whatever it was yielded'. For *quā* 'in which direction?', see *OLD* s.v. no. 1b.

On atoms Reid[1] (p. 324) writes: 'The point of the criticism seems to be that, on the atomic theory, *all* things are unlike their elements, while, on the orthodox theory of the four elements, only some are unlike.' *Dissimillimum* suggests that this is at least part of it, but there may also be a concern that it is unintelligible how ongoings on the atomic level, somehow determined by the primary qualities of atoms, could at all explain events in the perceptible world, even if the theory was correct. By the same token, a neuroscientist's explanation of what an emotion 'is' may seem unsatisfactory. There are good grounds for assuming that Lucretius was aware of the alienating effect of Epicurean physics and that he sought to address it by talking about atoms in metaphorical language; see Wardy (1988). The third point alludes to the 'argument from design', on which see Sedley (2007: 82–6).

We cannot know why Cicero opted for Democritus in §125, given that he is only introduced for the sake of the argument (cf. §55, though), but I note that the survey of views on the soul in *Tusc.* 1, which represents a parallel for *Luc.* 124, Democritus features as well, in *praeteritio* and because of his misguided attachment to atoms (*Tusc.* 1.22 *fin.*): *Democritum enim, magnum illum quidem uirum, sed leuibus et rotundis corpusculis efficientem animum concursu quodam fortuito, omittamus; nihil est enim apud istos, quod non atomorum turba conficiat.*

Et cum in uno mundo ornatus hic tam sit mirabilis...iisdem de rebus disputantes: see the commentary on §55, where Cicero suggests, as here, that Democritus did not just posit type-identical innumerable worlds co-existing but token-identical ones; *Fin.* 1.21; *N.D.* 1.73; Aug., *Contra Acad.* 3.10.23. Other Presocratics assumed successive innumerable worlds, e.g. Xenophanes (D.L. 9.19) or Anaximander (Cic., *N.D.* 1.25); see the full collection of parallels in Mansfeld and Runia (2009: 320–2). *Videamus* is an instance of the gazing sense of *uidere*; see Reinhardt (2016: 64–5) on 'relational seeing'.

With *ornatus* 'splendour' contrast the use in §119. *Eiusdem modi* in *alios eiusdem modi esse* may allude to Cicero's standard way of saying that two impressions are ἀπαράλλακτοι; cf. §77 *fin.* and again §55. The passage corresponding to *et ut nos...uideamus* is t. 47 in the final edition, adapted to the new setting of the dialogue; see the commentary ad loc.

Et, si nunc aut si etiam dormientes aliquid animo uidere uideamur...irrumpere: the dogmatist objects to the notion that hallucinations or daydreams, or dreams experienced while asleep, are due to εἴδωλα emitted by external objects and impinging on our minds physically. For the theory, see Plut., *Quaest. conv.* 734f–735b (= DK 68A77); Cic., *Div.* 2.120. For *animo uidere*, i.e. having a visual experience without seeing in the proper sense, cf. *Tusc.* 1.37 and 62; cf. *OLD* s.v. *uideo* n. 7 for *uidere* alone in this sense. For the locution *uidere uideor*, conventional of apparitions and dreams, see Haffter (1934: 39–41); Reinhardt (2016: 75 n. 28). On *imago* and related terms as a rendering for εἴδωλον in Cicero, see Reinhardt (2005: 156). Cf. the proem of Lucr. 4 and 4.1011–1106 (on dreams). The phrase *per corpus*, in Cicero only here but cf. Lucr. 2.266 (there meaning 'throughout the body'), probably does not mean 'through physical contact', but rather that the images may come through any part of the body in order to register with the mind.

Tu uero ista...nihil sentire est melius quam tam praua sentire: the conclusion to the speech given to the dogmatist interlocutor; §125 began with the raising of the possibility that the dogmatist objects not to the Academic's not adopting his view, but to his not adopting any view. Now the dogmatist has been shown to find Cicero's 'choice' unacceptable. *Ne* with perfect subjunctive as a standard prohibition. *Asciscere* in the quasi-legal sense of 'to accept, adopt'. For *commenticius* 'made up, fanciful', used dismissively of philosophical views, see *Fin.* 1.19; Reid[1] (p. 325) has further references. Cf. *somnia* in §121, *portenta* in §123. *Sentire* is a non-technical term for holding a view in *Acad.*; cf. *Ac.* 1.23: *Itaque omnis illa antiqua philosophia sensit in una uirtute esse positam uitam beatam.*§126

Non ergo id agitur...cum ista tua mihi ne probabilia quidem uideantur: the text has been suspected of being lacunose after *comprobem* by some; cf. the app. crit. The overall sense is clear enough: the dogmatist's harangue over the choice of Democritus has made plain that, contrary to what he said earlier, he will not be satisfied with the Academic just adopting any position. The natural corollary of this is that for the dogmatist only the Stoic position will do. The question is how the latter point is made in the text. The solution by Madvig (1826: 187–8), adopted by Reid[1] (p. 325), relies on the transmitted text, punctuated in a certain way. On this reading, *quae* elliptically refers to the corollary (cf. §72: *Ferres me si ego id dicerem? Tu ⟨sc. non ferres⟩ ne si dubitarem quidem*). That demand would be importunate, not just arrogant, because (some) Stoic doctrines strike Cicero as not even *probabilia*. The solution of Plasberg[1] (p. 140) and versions of it like Schäublin's assume that in a lacuna after *comprobem* the corollary view was explicitly gestured to. I print the transmitted text with Madvig and Reid, since the unusual elliptical use of *quae tu* can be paralleled in type in Cicero's speech and since it would help create a tone of mild exasperation. *Ista...probabilia* below protects the plural *quae* (as opposed to Davies's *quod*).

With *arroganter*, cf. §114 *tantum tibi arroges*, of Stoic-Antiochian grand theory building; with *impudenter*, cf. the aspiration in §126 *fin.* to be *uerecundior*; for both cf. §115: *Vtrum igitur nos imprudentes, qui labi nolumus, an illi arrogantes, qui sibi persuaserint scire se solos omnia?*

Nec enim diuinationem...atque haud scio an ita sit: *probatis* conflates the Stoics and Antiochus. In §107 Cicero notes that Panaetius suspended judgement over divination, against the standard view in the Stoic school (on which see also *Luc.* 47). *Contemnere* conveys indifference rather than contempt (cf. Sen., *Ben.* 2.34.3: *fortitudo est uirtus pericula iusta contemnens*); the Academic does not feel bound by fate; contrast §119. *Existimo* is, in *Acad.*, another non-standard term for taking a view.

Reid[1] (p. 325) observes that *atque* connects contrasting clauses (= *et tamen*). *Haud* is a local negation of *scio* in this case (see Pinkster i.689): Cicero is claiming ignorance on the point.

Sed cur rapior in inuidiam: *rapior* might suggest that Cicero's own *inuidia* is at issue but the larger context suggests it is the opponents'. *Inuidia* is 'angry disapproval', not 'envy'; cf. §105: *inuidiosa certe non sunt*. Cf. also §144: *in inuidiam uocare aliquem* = 'to bring someone into disrepute', i.e. present him in a way which makes him the object of other people's anger; §146.

Licetne per uos nescire…cum iis non licebit: cf. *N.D.* 1.84: *confiteri potius nescire quod nescires*; *Tusc.* 1.60: *nec me pudet, ut istos, fateri nescire quod nesciam*. Suspending judgement is an admission of ignorance. *Disceptare* is suggestive of considered, often legal argument: an implication is that the dogmatists converse rationally amongst each other but get stroppy with Cicero.

For the disagreements among the Stoics, which are inconsistently permitted, cf. §§107, 143; *Div.* 1.6; *Off.* 3.91; Sen., *N.Q.* 4.3.6. See Mansfeld and Runia (2009: 473 n. 295) on disagreements among Stoics highlighted in Aëtius. Reid[1] (p. 325) wonders if a dative (*nobis, mihi*) has dropped out before *non licebit*.

Zenoni et reliquis fere Stoicis…solem dominari et rerum potiri putat: for Zeno's view, cf. Cic., *N.D.* 1.36 (= *SVF* i.154), for Cleanthes', D.L. 7.139 (*SVF* i.499). However, it is not clear that Cleanthes and Zeno were in genuine disagreement on the subject; cf. D.L. 7.147 (= *SVF* ii.1021): Θεὸν δ' εἶναι…ὥσπερ πατέρα πάντων κοινῶς τε καὶ τὸ μέρος αὐτοῦ τὸ διῆκον διὰ πάντων, ὃ πολλαῖς προσηγορίαις προσονομάζεται κατὰ τὰς δυνάμεις….Ζῆνα δὲ καλοῦσι παρ' ὅσον τοῦ ζῆν αἴτιός ἐστιν ἢ διὰ τοῦ ζῆν κεχώρηκεν, Ἀθηνᾶν δὲ κατὰ τὴν εἰς αἰθέρα διάτασιν τοῦ ἡγεμονικοῦ αὐτοῦ, Ἥραν δὲ κατὰ τὴν εἰς ἀέρα, καὶ Ἥφαιστον κατὰ τὴν εἰς τὸ τεχνικὸν πῦρ, καὶ Ποσειδῶνα κατὰ τὴν εἰς τὸ ὑγρόν, καὶ Δήμητραν κατὰ τὴν εἰς γῆν· ὁμοίως δὲ καὶ τὰς ἄλλας προσηγορίας ἐχόμενοί τινος οἰκειότητος ἀπέδοσαν, 'The god…is, as it were, the father of all things, both in general and with respect to the part of him that permeates all things, which is referred to by many terms depending on its function.…They call him Zeus inasmuch as he is the cause of life and present in all that is alive, Athena because his ruling part extends to the aether, Hera because it extends to the air, and Hephaestus because it extends to the technical fire, and Poseidon because it extends to the wet, and Demeter because it extends to the earth. In the same way they gave the other designations to him because of a particular affinity.' See Mansfeld (1999a: 455–62).

On the subject, cf. also *Ac.* 1.29. *Summus deus* is attested in Caecil. l. 259 Ribbeck; cf. on *radiatus* below. In keeping with the tone thus evoked, *maiorum gentium*, as Reid[1] (p. 325) notes, is sarcastic: Cicero applies it elsewhere to the superior gods (*Tusc.* 1.29: *ipsi illi maiorum gentium dii qui habentur hinc nobis profecti in caelum reperientur*). For *auditor* = 'pupil', cf. *Luc.* 118; *Ac.* 1.34.

Ita cogimur dissensione sapientium dominum nostrum ignorare...quasi malis architectis, mensurae uestrae nego credere: not knowing the divine leads potentially to religious transgressions or at least sins of omission, and may also interfere with the process of οἰκείωσις.

Radiatus is used in poetry and poeticizing contexts in prose, and may serve, together with *summus deus* above and the subject of the appropriate treatment of the divine in the previous sentence, to give the passage a mock-dramatic tone. References to the time of day, and e.g. to sunrise at the beginning of a play (e.g. Soph., *Ant.* 100), are frequent in drama; cf. *De orat.* 3.209: *his autem de rebus sol me ille admonuit*, a self-conscious remark in a contribution of Crassus'. With *sol...ille*, cf. *hic* here.

That a transposition is the ultimate cause of the situation in the manuscripts was already recognized by Manutius. The key step to reordering the text as I have printed it was taken by Madvig (1826: 188–90). Reid[1] (p. 326) plausibly explains the situation in the manuscripts: 'The disturbances in the MSS probably arose thus. In the archetype the scribe omitted the words *permensi refertis ego* and placed them on the margin; he denoted the place from which they were omitted by some mark, and put the same mark on the margin with the word *hic*, meaning "at the place where this mark is, insert the words *permensi refertis ego.*" Succeeding scribes treated *hic* as part of the omission, and inserted all the words after *nego*, where they got partially corrupted, *hic* to *hoc* and *ego* to *ergo*.' Residual disagreements have related to the demonstratives: Reid[1] (p. 326) prints *huic me quasi malis...*, which Plasberg[1] (p. 141) also links with attempted correction of an earlier omission. See his detailed note ibid. The reading of 𝒱 in the short app. crit. is more 'reconstructed' than usual: the contributing manuscripts exhibit various minor *lectiones singulares*. The personal apposition of *malis architectis* to the impersonal *mensurae uestrae* is somewhat harsh.

Dubium est igitur...uerecundior: if we assume that Cicero is returning to the theme of arrogance and impudence which featured at the beginning of §126, *ut leuiter dicam* indicates that he wants to speak more calmly, viz. in terms of respect or lack of it. (Changing *leuiter* to *leniter* is unnecessary, as Mueller 1878: xiii shows; see also Plasberg[1] p. 141.) The emendation *inuerecundius* would more obviously resume the negative terms from the beginning of the paragraph, and Reid[1] (p. 326) is right that omission of *in* happens often in manuscripts, but *uerecundius* is tenable.

Cicero may also be hinting that how to deal with claims of the *physici*, notably conflicting ones, is not strictly a matter of *uerecundia*. For *uerecundia* (cf. §125 *init.*) is only ever at issue in one's relationship with others, whereas for Cicero the application of judgement in the evaluation of impressions concerns the individual who is supposed to take a view. Still, or so Cicero suggests, if the invitation to commit to a physical view is seen as predicated on the involvement of two parties, then *uerecundia* is shown by withholding assent when one is unconvinced, not by giving it rashly when it is unwarranted. See also Schäublin et al. (p. 292 n. 396).

§§127–28

The dismissal of the possibility that any physical view advanced by a dogmatist was apt to attract assent might give the impression that Clitomachean Academics regard physical inquiry in general as futile and a waste of time. This is a notion which Cicero seeks to counter in §127, by offering an encomium on physical enquiry as a profoundly human endeavour. The encomium is of such a kind that a dogmatist could write or endorse it, except for one qualification: on Cicero's construal, the endeavour culminates in encountering a view or set of views which is *probabile* or *ueri simile*. Cicero's opponent would not accept this of course.

In §128a recasts this difference between the dogmatist and the Clitomachean approach with reference to the competing conceptions of the sage: both look for what is materially the same thing (i.e. a *probabile*; see n. below), but the dogmatist assents to it, taking it to be a cataleptic impression, whereas the Clitomachean does not assent and 'is already pleased when he finds something that is *ueri simile*' (no mode of endorsement is specified, but it can be assumed to be approval as explained in *Luc.* 104). The Clitomachean's enthusiastic pursuit of physical enquiry flows from his commitment to search for the truth, which is highlighted in several passages of programmatic import (*Luc.* 7; *N.D.* 1.11).[499] There is no mention of the practice of argument *in utramque partem* here, but the notion that physical claims and the arguments which support them are to be evaluated against each other is present in the preceding section (cf. §124 *fin.*: *paria momenta*), and *dissensio*/διαφωνία is an organizational principle for parts of the section (see the general note on §§118–26). That it is, as a matter of fact, rare for a physical view to emerge as *probabile* is not inconsistent with the Clitomachean's desire to bring about such situations, nor would it be peculiar if physical views which are deemed *probabile* are more likely to lose the subject's approval than others.[500]

In §127 the study of nature is said to serve an intellectual need (it is a *animorum pabulum*), to elevate the spirit, to induce a beneficial indifference to human affairs which comes from pondering the universe, and to be enjoyable.[501] The dogmatist would agree.[502] There is no particular model for the *laudes physicae*, but there are a

---

[499] *Off.* 1.13 also speaks to the human drive to seek knowledge and truth.

[500] Contrast Brittain (2008a: section 3.3) on the difference between mitigated scepticism and radical scepticism: 'These mitigated skeptics thus took the persuasiveness of perceptual impressions under the right perceptual and coherence conditions as defeasible, but rational, *evidence* for their truth, rather than as merely the ground for their acceptance. We find a similar move in the case of non-perceptual impressions: some mitigated skeptics construed the standard Academic practice of arguing on either side of philosophical questions as a means of rationally evaluating arguments in order to establish which side is more likely to be true. These mitigated skeptics thus changed the status of argument on either side from a critical and, in effect, destructive practice into a positive method for rationally confirming and, indirectly, teaching philosophical conclusions.' The present passage, an unequivocally Clitomachean context (and thus evidence for 'radical scepticism'), makes no reference to teaching, in this case, physical subjects, but otherwise matches Brittain's description of mitigated scepticism. This suggests that the evidence from *Acad.* militates against a dichotomy between purely destructive radical scepticism and cautiously constructive mitigated scepticism. On the construal adopted in this commentary of the kind of Clitomacheanism the Cicero character represents in *Acad.*, the Clitomachean is able to use *in utramque partem* argument in the hope of establishing which view appears more *probabile* (see on §§104–105a), and the *probabilitas* of an impression is inherently external-world related and as such capable of being viewed as evidence in Brittain's sense, in general and a fortiori outside of strictly ad hominem contexts (see section 6.6).

[501] When Cicero composed *Luc., N.D.* and probably also the partial translation of Plato's *Timaeus* were not yet in existence. This means that Cicero had written only the passage corresponding to Ac. 1.24–9 in the *Catulus* on physical matters. See further on *Luc.* 147.

[502] Cf. also *Luc.* 101 on the Academic' subjective experience and cognitive responses being, notwithstanding the caveat about apprehension, no different from those of a non-Academic.

number of texts which exhibit points of contact with our passage, notably praises of engagement with a subject which falls under the broader heading of physics.[503] Texts which extol the contemplative life, or rather a subset of them which emphasizes reflective engagement and active scrutiny over detachment and a withdrawal from public life, form a wider background.[504] In *Part. anim.* A5 Aristotle famously claims that the study of living beings which are subject to coming-to-be and perishing is as attractive and deserving of attention as the study of beings which are ungenerated and imperishable, i.e. the heavenly bodies, which are the subject of *Cael.*[505] In *Cael.* B12, 291b27, he speaks of 'thirst for philosophy' ($\phi\iota\lambda o\sigma o\phi\acute{\iota}\alpha s$ $\delta\acute{\iota}\psi\alpha$) as a motivating force for enquiry. Seneca, *Ep. mor.* 95.10, is one of the passages in which an interest in ethics is presented as continuous with an interest in physics, especially cosmology: *Philosophia autem et contemplatiua est et actiua: spectat simul agitque. Erras enim si tibi illam putas tantum terrestres operas promittere: altius spirat. 'Totum' inquit 'mundum scrutor nec me intra contubernium mortale contineo, suadere uobis aut dissuadere contenta: magna me uocant supraque uos posita'.*[506] Cf. *De otio* 5.8. Manilius 1.40–52 and 2.105–25 combine a historical survey of the origins of *astronomia* with a praise of the subject and the activity.[507] In *Rep.* 1 Cicero gives a brief history of the reception of Greek philosophy and science in Rome, and in §23 he explains how a legate's knowledge of Greek astronomy enabled him to explain an eclipse and avoid a panic within the Roman army before the battle of Pydna in 168 BC. Compare also *Fin.* 4.12: *Inest in eadem explicatione naturae insatiabilis quaedam e cognoscendis rebus uoluptas, in qua una confectis rebus necessariis uacui negotiis honeste ac liberaliter possimus uiuere.*

In §128b Cicero announces the shift to the subject of ethics, only to dwell on the problems of arriving at certainty on physical matters for another paragraph. Since the dogmatist allows for one type of acceptance only in both fields—dogmatic assent to cataleptic impressions—, the readiness to give assent in the area of physics casts doubt on assent given in what is supposedly a less obscure area, ethics.[508] This is illustrated with examples from everyday experience on the one hand, and divination and physics (the size of the sun) on the other: dogmatic assent given to impressions pertaining to the latter casts doubt on assent given to impressions relating to the

---

[503] A more general eulogy to philosophy is in *Tusc.* 5.5–11; see Hommel (1968).

[504] For the distinction between $\theta\epsilon\omega\rho\acute{\iota}\alpha$ that is purely theoretical and one serving a practical (i.e. moral or political) purpose in its cultural context, see e.g. the introduction of Wilson Nightingale (2004); see also the collection on $\theta\epsilon\omega\rho\acute{\iota}\alpha$ in Hellenistic and post-Hellenistic philosophy by Bénatouïl and Bonazzi (2012). For the general human desire to understand the *locus classicus* is Arist., *Met.* A1, on which see Cambiano (2012).

[505] Consider e.g. *Part. anim.* A5, 645a8–10: Καὶ γὰρ ἐν τοῖς μὴ κεχαρισμένοις αὐτῶν πρὸς τὴν αἴσθησιν κατὰ τὴν θεωρίαν ὁμοίως (sc. as the study of 'divine things'; mss. have ὅμως) ἡ δημιουργήσασα φύσις ἀμηχάνους ἡδονὰς παρέχει τοῖς δυναμένοις τὰς αἰτίας γνωρίζειν καὶ φύσει φιλοσόφοις, 'For even in the study of animals unattractive to the senses, the nature that fashioned them offers immeasurable pleasures in the same way to those who can learn the causes and are naturally lovers of wisdom' (transl. Balme). See the commentaries by Balme (1972: 122–4) and Kullmann (2007); Moreau (1959).

[506] Important but too long to quote here is Sen., *N.Q.* 1.pr.1–4. Cf. Chrysippus on theology as the τέλος of instruction, following on from logic and ethics, in *Sto. rep.* 1035a–b (= *SVF* ii.42 = LS 26C). Chrysippus is also reported to have rejected the merely contemplative life, i.e. the quiet life of scholarship (Plut., *Sto. rep.* 1033c–d = *SVF* iii.702).

[507] See Landolfi (2004).

[508] Compare the similar section in §§116–17, as well as §§141 and 147.

former.⁵⁰⁹ What the dogmatist ought to want, or so Cicero suggests, is a way of calibrating his endorsements, of allowing for apprehension to come in degrees,⁵¹⁰ but that is precisely what he cannot allow (*omnium rerum una est definitio comprehendendi*).

§127

Nec tamen istas quaestiones exterminandas puto: *exterminare* usually 'to drive away, banish', of people (e.g. kings), or 'to dismiss', of ideas; see *OLD* s.v. nos. 1–2. The term is not used of political procedure, e.g. the suppression of questions in meetings. Rather, the implication is that such questions arise naturally for human beings, and that the Academics do not act against human nature by dismissing them.

Cicero's phrasal term *quaestiones physicorum* may be hinting at the ad hominem nature of (much of) Academic dialectic; contrast Seneca's *naturales quaestiones*.

Est enim animorum...consideratio contemplatioque naturae: for *quoddam quasi*, cf. *Ac.* 1.40: *e quadam quasi impulsione*. Of the various parallels for expressions meaning 'nourishment for the soul' assembled by Reid¹ (p. 326), *Tusc.* 5.66 *pastus animorum* and *Att.* 12.6.2 *scire...quo uno animus alitur* (= SB 306) connect the motif with science and enquiry. For physical and theoretical study on the one hand and ethical study on the other being inextricable and mutually beneficial, cf. *Leg.* 1.58–63; *Fin.* 3.73 and 4.11; *Tusc.* 5.71; Sen., *Ep.* 65.16, 88.28, 117.19 (again, see Reid¹ p. 326). The Stoic sage need not be an expert in everything, e.g. every conceivable expertise, but part of his wisdom must be discursive knowledge in the area of physics (see Brouwer 2014: 7–50); it is only to be expected that the competing conception of the Academic sage is no different in this respect. Hirzel (1878: 293–301) suggests that Cicero must be relying on Philo rather than Clitomachus here (p. 294): 'Das Wahrscheinliche das uns dort begegnet [sc. in Sextus' account of Carneades], ist von anderer und viel geringerer Art: denn im besten Falle ist es nur das Ergebnis reiflicher Ueberlegung, aber nicht erhabener Speculation und tiefgehender Forschung und verräth ausserdem zur Naturphilosophie gar keine Beziehung sondern ist ganz der Praxis des Lebens zugewandt.' Against this one can point to passages in which Cicero qua Clitomachean is speaking about his commitment to a search for the truth (*Luc.* 7b–9a; *N.D.* 1.11), and one can refer to *Luc.* 104, where Clitomachus, in his report on Carneades' account of suspension of judgement, envisages approval of non-perceptual impressions as they arise from propositions discussed in a dialectical question-and-answer λόγος.

Consideratio contemplatioque is a collocation favoured by Cicero, cf. *Off.* 1.153; *Rep.* 1.19; *Tusc.* 5.9; *Fin.* 5.11 and 58 (assembled by Reid¹ p. 327); but see below for its earlier history. The terms themselves are discussed in detail in connection with the scrutiny procedures for persuasive impressions (*Luc.* 36: *circumspectio, consideratio*) in section 6.5; see also Reinhardt (2018a: 247 n. 73).

---

⁵⁰⁹ On the passage, see also Brittain (2001: 166 with n. 53).
⁵¹⁰ Cf. §§133–4, 141, 146; and the similar Academic argument in Sextus, *M.* 7.421–2.

Erigimur, elatiores fieri uidemur...humanissima completur animus uoluptate: Cicero now describes the effect of the nourishment provided by physical enquiry. On the metaphorical quality of *erigimur*, which entails that the change of *elatiores* (itself a modification of the reading of the archetype) to *altiores* in what follows is to be rejected, see Reid[1] (p. 327); contra Plasberg[1] (p. 141), who prints *altiores*. *Humana despicimus* is a topos associated with the contemplative life and the ὁμοίωσις θεῷ (but see below); to the parallels assembled by Reid[1] (p. 327), mainly from Stoic contexts, add Cic., *Off.* 3.100; Sen., *Cons. ad Marc.* 24-5, on the afterlife as a time when the soul is freed from the constraints of an earthly and bodily existence. Cf. also the epigram *A.Gr.* 9.577, ascribed to the celebrated astronomer Ptolemy, i.e. Claudius Ptolemaeus: Οἶδ', ὅτι θνατὸς ἐγὼ καὶ ἐφάμερος· ἀλλ' ὅταν ἄστρων | μαστεύω πυκινὰς ἀμφιδρόμους ἕλικας, | οὐκέτ' ἐπιψαύω γαίης ποσίν, ἀλλὰ παρ' αὐτῷ | Ζανὶ θεοτρεφέος πίμπλαμαι ἀμβροσίης, 'I know that I am mortal, a creature of a day; but when I search into the multitudinous revolving spirals of the stars my feet no longer rest on the earth, but, standing by Zeus himself, I take my fill of ambrosia, the food of the gods' (transl. Paton). See Page (1981: 112-13).

With *haec nostra*, cf. *haec* in §120. For the pronoun in *indagatio ipsa*, cf. Cic., *Rep.* 1.19: *cognitio ipsa rerum consideratioque delectat*; *Tusc.* 5.70; *Luc.* 120: *ipsa libertas*. However, it is not just inquiry itself which is satisfying, but also success in the hunt, i.e. hitting upon something *probabile*. That this is said to induce *humanissima uoluptas* seems, after verbal gestures towards the contemplative life as envisaged by the dogmatist, like a deliberate veering away from ὁμοίωσις θεῷ.

§128a

Quaeret igitur haec...si in eius modi rebus ueri simile quod sit inuenerit: the sentence poses a number of problems of interpretation, relating to the meaning of *quaeret*, the reference of *haec*, and the nature of the two *ut*-clauses. *Quaerere* might mean 'to enquire into, examine, consider' (*OLD* s.v. no. 9a), in which case *res cum maximae tum etiam occultimissimae* or *quaestiones physicae* (cf. §127 *init.*) would be its logical object. Or *quaerere* means 'to pose questions', with *haec* being an internal object and referring logically to *quaestiones physicae* only. Or it means 'to look for', in which case *haec* must refer to *ueri similia* = *probabilia* mentioned in the previous sentence; so Schäublin et al. (p. 167). The latter seems to me the most natural reading, given what immediately precedes: the suggestion is that Academic and dogmatist set out to find impressions corresponding to claims in the domain of physics which are *probabile* (cf. §105a), the implication being that there is nothing better to find in such a search. *Et... et* points in the same direction, since emphasizing that both Stoic and Academic sage pursue *haec* has more point if the idea is that both are after what is materially the same thing. The difference between dogmatist and Academic is described in two *ut*-clauses (*ut assentiatur... ut uereatur*). The latter cannot be a purpose clause, given its content, *pace* Gigon (p. 247): fearing that one might opine is not something one can intend. It seems desirable, though not necessary, for both *ut*-clauses to be equivalent in type. So I take both to be consecutive: assent is the consequence of the dogmatist's enquiry, whereas the Academic's leads to wariness that he might be in danger of opining, and satisfaction when he does find a *ueri simile*. Note that, on the reading favoured here, Cicero's Academic, in a straightforwardly Clitomachean context, is searching for the *probabile* in the domain of physics.

For *temere opinari*, see *Luc*. 66. Reid[1] (p. 327) on *praeclareque agi secum*, cf. the personal construction in §80: *nobiscum male ageret*. *Inuenerit* is perfect subjunctive replacing the non-existent subjunctive of the future perfect in primary sequence.

§128b

Veniamus nunc ad bonorum malorumque notionem…et paulum ante dicendum est: see the general note on §§127–8 above. For *notio*, cf. *Luc*. 30, but here the issue is a theoretical conception, not one naturally, or only naturally, acquired; cf. also *Fin*. 3.21. *Et* is mildly contrastive; see *OLD* s.v. no. 14a, Plasberg[1] (p. 142).

Non mihi uidentur considerare…si quae illustriores uideantur, amittere: the transmitted *physici* arose most likely from an intruded gloss, since the opinions of the *physici* (= thinkers advancing physical tenets) are not at issue; rather, it is Cicero's opponents', the dogmatists', reaction to such tenets. Reid[1] (p. 328) rightly notes that the emendation *physica* (made in the Aldina) is uncompelling, since *physica affirmare* is not Latin for 'to affirm physical tenets', but the intrusion may have started out as *physica*, intended to illuminate *ista*; contrast Plasberg[1] (p. 142). With *illustriores*, cf. §94: *illustribus…rebus insistis*, as here of 'clear' non-perceptual impressions, the difference being that here relatively higher clarity, as obtains even on the Academic's view in the field of ethics, is at issue, whereas in §94 a Stoic injunction to refrain from assent to cataleptic impressions is meant. (On clarity, see sections 5.2 and 6.1; *Ac*. 1.41.) On the omission of *se* in the accusative with infinitive depending on *considerare*, see Kühner-Stegmann i.700–1.

Non enim magis assentiuntur neque approbant lucere nunc…plus quam duodeuiginti partibus maiorem esse quam terram: *assentiri* and *approbare* are here used for stylistic fullness; approval in the sense discussed in §104 is not at issue. Cicero's gives two examples of cases where the dogmatist's acceptance of one kind of endorsement only—dogmatic assent—is self-undermining, (i) an impression that it is day attracts the same endorsement as one that the cawing of the crow amounts to an injunction to do something or a prohibition not to do something, and (ii) an impression that a statue is of a fixed height is assented to after measuring it, just as an impression that the sun is *x* times larger than the earth is assented to, even though it cannot be measured. Cf. §119 *init*. for the same type of argument. With *cornix*, cf. Cicero on *diuinatio* as not furnishing *probabilia* in §126, and Panaetius' doubts about divination in §107. *Illud* in *signum illud* is deictic and refers to the setting in which the dialogue is conducted. On the size of the sun, cf. §§82, 126; §128 represents evidence for the Stoic view on the subject, as Brittain (2006: 75 n. 200) notes. For *partes* used to denote multiples, cf. §116 *multis partibus*.

Ex quo illa conclusio nascitur...nullam rem percipit: cf. the arguments offered by Cicero in §§97, 101. Cicero casts his objection in the form of a first indemonstrable, while hinting through *nascitur* that it imposes itself.

Respondebunt posse percipi quantus sol sit...una est definitio comprehendendi: for the indirect question *quantus sol sit*, cf. §91. Cicero will not resist because he thinks the dogmatist is threatening his entire position through his own absolutism; for Lucullus using the phrase differently, cf. §57. Reid[1] (p. 328) observes that *omnium rerum* does not directly depend on *definitio*, so that it would be combined with a gerund/gerundive in the singular, but that *una definitio comprehendendi* is, as word order shows, to be parsed as one unit, on which *omnium rerum* depends; see also his parallels. Schäublin et al. (p. 293 n. 401) suggest that the success of Cicero's attack depends on the extreme demands which the Stoics make for the sage's state of ἐπιστήμη, but in fact Cicero's point depends on the unqualified endorsement which assent amounts to for sages and non-sages alike.

§§129–41

In §§129–41 Cicero shows that in the field of ethics, just as in the field of physics, there is widespread disagreement among the dogmatists, and that, differences in *probabilitas* between various positions notwithstanding, there are no grounds for dogmatic assent to any position.

The structure of the section is as follows.[511] In §129 Cicero restates that a conception of the highest good is necessary to determine whether particular things are good or bad, and that on no issue the *dissensio* is larger. He lists some completely obsolete views in §129 and adds further apparently less contemptible but still obsolete views in §130. While some of the names featured are peculiar to the present context, the group of Aristo, Pyrrho, and Erillus features elsewhere in Cicero as thinkers whose views have been rejected (*Fin.* 5.23: *explosae...sententiae*; *Off.* 1.6).[512] They have in

---

[511] Cf. Schäublin et al. (pp. lxxxiii–lxxxiv) analyse the section thus: §§129–31 disagreement about the highest good, comprising §§129–30 on views long obsolete, and §131 on views which have been prevalent for some time; §§132–41 are devoted to the Academics and disagreements among philosophers, with §132 being concerned with the incompatibility of Old Academic and Stoic ethics, §§133–4 with the disagreement between Antiochus and the Stoa, §§135–7 with disagreements between Antiochus and the Old Academy, and §§138–40 to there being only three possibilities of what the highest good could be according to Chrysippus; §141 is a conclusion. Algra (1997: 107) writes: 'The section on the *diaphonia* of philosophical *doxai* in ethics in its turn falls into three parts. First, after a brief review of more or less obsolete views on the End (e.g. those of the Megarians and of Aristo), there is a discussion of the famous *Carneadea divisio* (131), an overview of possible conceptions of the *telos*. Next comes a section which deals with the differences between the Stoics and Antiochus (132–7). Finally, Cicero discusses Chrysippus' way of dealing with the various views on the *telos* (138–41).' Brittain (2006: lvii), in his articulated table of contents, divides the section into §§129–31 'disagreements about ends', §§132–7 'Old Academics vs. Stoics', §§138–41 'Chrysippus on ends'.

[512] Aristo had no followers within the Stoic school, but as we shall see, his fundamental objection to Zeno's doctrine was invoked in Carneades' as well as Antiochus' anti-Stoic arguments.

common that they assume that no rational choice can be made between things which are not entirely good or bad and that looking at the basic natural attachments of human beings is of no use in determining what the final end of human action is and should be.[513] In §131 Cicero introduces a division of highest goods which individuate ethical theories. Seven highest goods are distinguished:

(1) *uoluptas* (upheld by Aristippus, Cyrenaics, Epicurus);
(2) *uoluptas* & *honestas* (Callipho);
(3) *uacare molestia* (Hieronymus, a Peripatetic);
(4) *uacare molestia* & *honestas* (Diodorus, a Peripatetic);
(5) *honeste uiuere* & *frui iis rebus quas primas homini natura conciliet* (Old Academy, Polemo, Aristotle and his followers);
(6) *frui iis rebus quas primas homini natura conciliet* (Carneades for the sake of the argument, in order to attack the Stoics);
(7) *honeste uiuere* (Zeno).

This is the, or rather a, *Carneadea diuisio*, but the term is not used here.[514] Rather, it occurs in Piso's speech in *Fin.* 5 (see the discussion below). What matters for the present purpose is how Cicero deploys this division of mutually exclusive options against Lucullus, i.e. so as to unpick the historical construction of Antiochus' Old Academy as a doctrinal edifice developed by the successors of Plato in the Academy, embraced by Peripatetics, and de facto by Stoics, too, who, however, use different terminology.[515] He proclaims to be attracted by the Stoic view: would he be allowed to adopt it or would if not Aristotle (who posits a different end and is invoked by Antiochus) then Antiochus permit this? Antiochus was a genuine Stoic,[516] Cicero says, which implies that he ought to support acceptance of the Stoic view. However, as the division makes plain, Antiochus avowed a view which is different from Zeno's. So the sage as a theoretical reference point is either an Old Academic or a Stoic: he cannot be both since the views are different. This point is then expanded to create oppositions between philosophers whom Antiochus tries to capture under the one banner of the Old Academy: Polemo vs the Stoics, Zeno vs Old Academics and Peripatetics. In §133 Cicero then drives home the significance of the disagreements he has pointed out: given that he and Lucullus agree that the sage should not opine and assent to the incognitive, making any decision in an area where there is disagreement might mean just that. He draws attention to one so-called Stoic paradox—that all transgressions are equal (see Cic., *Parad.* 20-6)—which Antiochus does not endorse, and suggests that, if Antiochus cannot accept some Stoic positions, he—Cicero—is entitled to be wary of accepting others. §134 is devoted to another

---

[513] Cf. Annas (2007: 191–3); Ioppolo (2016), who shows how these supposedly obsolete views continue to play a role in anti-Stoic arguments; and Cic., *Fin.* 5.23 (cited and discussed on §129).
[514] On *diuisio* as a device to structure rhetorical arguments, see Quint. 5.10.64–70.
[515] This point was made by Carneades, as Cicero knows (see *Fin.* 3.41), and before that by Aristo of Chios (Sextus, *M.* 11.61-7 = *SVF* i.361), as Cicero appears to have known; see Ioppolo (2016: 167–8).
[516] In modern discussions of Antiochus this statement of Cicero's is often used as straightforward evidence of how Antiochus was viewed 'in antiquity'; this is to ignore the highly tendentious context in which Cicero makes the remark.

supposed disagreement between Antiochus and the Stoics: Zeno holds virtue to be sufficient for happiness, while Antiochus holds virtue to be sufficient for the *uita beata*, which is capable of further enhancement by what to the Stoics are indifferents so as to become the *uita beatissima*. The Antiochian view involves, so Cicero, a contradiction: happiness is supposed to remain possible for the wise man despite misfortune. Zeno's view is admirable but does not take human nature into account. Both views are *probabile*, and one is more persuasive (to Cicero) than the other at different times. And if neither view is correct, then virtue falls altogether (see n. ad loc.). The last sentence of §134 signals the end of the review of disagreements. §135 then turns to common ground, viz. the view that the sage does not experience emotions, a view proverbially ascribed to the Stoics, with qualified justification. This view Antiochus ought not to accept, given his other commitments, or so Cicero argues, and he goes on to cite the Old Academic Crantor, who wrote a famous book on grief. This is taken as evidence that at least one certified Old Academic did assign emotions to the sage—and Crantor's work was recommended to Tubero by the Stoic Panaetius. The Old Academy did also teach that certain emotions were of benefit to human beings, so that Cicero can conclude in §136 *init*. that he fails to see when the harshness which Antiochus claims for it should have entered the Old Academy. Cicero continues in §136 by pointing out the unpersuasiveness of further Stoic views apparently not rejected by Antiochus and the lack of nuance of Antiochus' historical account, which becomes apparent when one tries to locate said views in it. These are so-called Stoic paradoxes, which Cicero correctly traces to Socrates, but which—he observes—were not endorsed and would not have been endorsed by Aristotle and Xenocrates. The discussion becomes quite rhetorical here, in that Cicero reduces the paradoxes ad absurdum by drawing out their implications in terms which are specific to Roman ('only the sage can be consul') or Greek circumstances ('Solon's laws were not laws'). However, Cicero continues in §137, given that Antiochus has wholeheartedly embraced Stoicism, he must give unqualified support to the paradoxes, whereas Cicero is free to mount a (non-dogmatic) defence only of those views which appear persuasive to him. He illustrates this with an anecdote connected with the philosophical embassy of 155 BC: Carneades was treated as a negative dogmatist about perception by A. Albinus and asked if he—Albinus—did not appear as a praetor to him, or Rome not as a city, and the people of Rome not as the city's population. Carneades, rather than to say that his perceptual experience is the same as that of Albinus (cf. §105b), replied that these were the impressions of the Stoic Diogenes of Babylon next to him (sc. who is committed to the paradoxes mentioned in §136). Aristotle and Xenocrates would have sided with Carneades, Cicero submits, but Antiochus is a real Stoic and only occasionally lapses into a stammer, i.e. either fails to endorse Stoic views or fails to show total commitment to them. In §138 *init*. Cicero resumes with the idea that he is concerned about lapsing into error (by assenting to the incognitive)—so what to do? Here Chrysippus is invoked; this is not explicitly motivated, but the reason may be that Chrysippus qua Stoic ought to be acceptable as an aide to the *germanissimus Stoicus* Antiochus. Chrysippus is shown to reduce a larger list of ends to three: virtue, pleasure, and the combination of virtue and pleasure. These, he thought, were the only ones which carried some persuasiveness. In §139 Cicero responds by acknowledging that Chrysippus may be right (in positing that the three ends are persuasive), but immediately professes to find nothing more *probabile* than the view of 'Polemo, the Peripatetics, and Antiochus'. He then talks about the attractiveness of the two positions of Chrysippus' three which the latter did not favour, thereby dramatizing the vagaries of *probabilitas*, and ends up dismissing the one composite view Chrysippus allowed for. §140 is devoted to the battle between pleasure and virtue. Chrysippus thought there was no contest, but Cicero spends the first half of the paragraph citing arguments against pleasure as the highest good, and the second citing arguments against virtue as the highest good. The implication seems to be that both can be persuasively attacked.[517] In the concluding paragraph §141 Cicero steps back and states that such arguments and others like them do not leave him unmoved (cf. §101): he is a human being with a mind, and in principle impressions (and propositions) which appear persuasive to Chrysippus will move him, too. Yet while Lucullus assents dogmatically as if he was a sage (so that his apprehensions are deemed to be unshakeable by argument; see n. ad loc.), Cicero, even in cases where he assents because he cannot help it (cf. on §66: *magnus...opinator*), does so aware that nothing assented to is such that it could not be false.[518] Here one might think that the Stoic would stand by their view which they 'recognize' as right rather than be affected by the persuasiveness of competing positions, but what Cicero says here is predicated on Chrysippus' view reported in §138 *fin.*: Chrysippus held that three views can be defended persuasively, including the Stoic position (there cast as 'virtue is the end'), even though the latter is assumed to be correct.

§§129–41 shows Cicero making the case for suspension of judgement about the τέλος and the associated theories being rational given the *tot homines quot sententiae* on the subject. Nothing he says in the section is inconsistent with the Clitomachean stance he expressly adopts in the speech as a whole. What is not furnished by Cicero here, although he could have provided it e.g. by pitting it against Lucullus'/Antiochus' favoured theory (for the sake of the argument, to show that it is at least as persuasive as the dogmatist's favoured theory, or as his view under Clitomachean approval, cf. §104), is an indication of how the Clitomachean would live his scepticism in situations when moral action is required.[519]

In *Luc.* 138 (= *SVF* iii.21) Cicero recounts what has become known as the *Chrysippea diuisio*, although Cicero himself does not use the term. This division itself is the product of a process of reduction and elimination to which a longer list of views individuated by simple and composite ends is subjected. Chrysippus starts from three views characterized by a simple end:

(1) virtue (called *honestas* here);
(2) pleasure (*uoluptas*);
(3) freedom from pain (*uacuitas modestiae*).

---

[517] Algra (1997: 130–2) is right to dismiss the interpretation of Michel (1968: 118–19) and Lévy (1992: 344–5) on which Chrysippus' division is deployed by Cicero to make a view emerge as the most persuasive. However, Cicero does allow for different views *being* persuasive (to someone) to different degrees at particular points in time (see on §139).

[518] The passage speaks to the question of how Cicero relates his Clitomachean position to that of mitigated scepticism; for full discussion, see on §148, §§66–7, §§112–15.

[519] See, however, *Off.* 2.7–8 and 3.17, with Dyck (1996: 516–17); note 2.8: *affirmandi arrogantia*.

He also recognizes three views characterized by a composite end:

(4) virtue & pleasure;
(5) virtue & freedom from pain;
(6) virtue & the first advantages of nature (*prima naturae*).

Chrysippus, or so Cicero tells us, was able to reduce these six views to a set of three, which make up the *Chrysippea diuisio* in the narrow sense.

(i) virtue;
(ii) pleasure;
(iii) virtue & pleasure.

The process of reduction, mentioned in *Luc.* 138, turns on the assumption that (the pursuit or obtainment of) pleasure is merely verbally different from freedom from pain, a move which Epicureans would find easier to accept than others. View (3) thus comes down to (2). When we come to the composite views (4)–(6), then (5) and (6) are treated as equivalent to (4), which is in line with the earlier reduction of (3) to (2), while freedom from pain is held to be merely verbally different from the (pursuit or obtainment of) *prima naturae*. Thus only (1 = i), (2 = ii), and (4 = iii) remain, which, or so Cicero says, Chrysippus deemed *probabile*.

Before I turn to the likely wider context in which Chrysippus used this division, some observations. First, Chrysippus' division is not intended as a synthetic one from first principles; rather, it first assembles a list of actually held views and then eliminates options through a process of reduction (which posits equivalences of views). This is e.g. the reason why the notion of *prima naturae* can come in in connection with a composite view (6), without there being a position which is characterized by the simple goal of pursuit or obtainment of the *prima naturae*—nobody held this, or so is the implicit assumption. (This matters because in the *Carneadea diuisio* the Stoic position is characterized differently, i.e. by the avowed simple end of pursuit of the *prima naturae* as well as by the de facto end of virtue & pursuit of *prima naturae*.) Second, parallels secure what is reasonably clear from *Luc.* 138 (despite the use of the term *honestas*): the Stoic view is in *Luc.* 138 deemed to be characterized by the simple end of virtue.[520] Third, the inclusion of view (6), which, as we have no reason to doubt, is original, shows that what became the Antiochian view was very much a historical reality in Chrysippus' day: Chrysippus was perhaps thinking of the Peripatetics.[521] Finally, we can fill in from elsewhere how Chrysippus dealt with the three views which emerged as *probabilia*. (iii) can be dismissed by positing that

---

[520] Cf. *Fin.* 2.44 (= *SVF* iii.22).
[521] See on *Ac.* 1.19–23. Even if it was true that Polemo's view of the τέλος would fit the description of the Peripatetic one, the view had, for all we know, no proponents who identified as Academics in Chrysippus' day (sc. when the Academy was sceptical). Lévy (1992: 357) has suggested that the view ascribed to the Old Academics in the *Carneadea diuisio* is an addition of Antiochus' (alongside two others); see Algra (1997: 124–6) contra. Yet if it already was a consideration for Chrysippus, if only to be reduced away, then it is more likely that Carneades himself included it. For further observations on inherent tensions of the *Carneadea diuisio*, see Görler (1994: 880); Annas (2007: 191–6).

pleasure invariably compromises any composite view it forms part of (cf. *Fin.* 5.22 for the Antiochian Piso deploying this 'tainting' consideration), while (ii) can be dismissed by means of anti-hedonistic arguments. The Stoic view (1 = i) is thus left standing.

It has plausibly been suggested by Algra (1997: 111-15) that the *Chrysippea diuisio* is to be linked with certain reports on Chrysippus' teaching methods. He is said to have recommended arguments *in utramque partem* as a way of fastening already existing καταλήψεις of his pupils (see Plut., *Sto. rep.* ch. 10; Benatouïl 2007: 81-91, and the commentary on *Luc.* 87b, 75), by inducing suspension of judgement about rival theories and destroying their πιθανότης (cf. *Luc.* 138: *ita tres relinquit sententias quas putet probabiliter posse defendi*). The division would provide a natural framework for such an approach, and that Chrysippus accords persuasiveness to views he is bound to dismiss eventually is suggestive of a connection.[522]

A text typically cited for comparison with *Luc.* 131 and its wider context is *Fin.* 5.15-23, where the Antiochian speaker Piso (see on *Ac.* 1.19-23) introduces what he calls the *Carneadea diuisio*. Cicero uses related divisions in a number of other passages, in contexts which need to be appreciated for their peculiarity in each case, but the discussion in *Fin.* 5 is the most detailed, and only there the phrasal term *Carneadea diuisio* is actually attached to it. Some think that *Fin.* provides the division in its original form, in which case other divisions can be analysed and described as derivations from it, while others think that it is incoherent and thus probably not Carneades' original division (see above). In the latter case, the question arises whether Piso's account nonetheless allows us to reconstruct the division. Looking at the section itself will allow us to take a view on these matters as well as illuminate the use of such divisions, including in Cicero's speech here in *Luc.*

Having reviewed Peripatetic attitudes to ethics in 5.12-14, and having established that there was significant variation within the Peripatetic school regarding the highest good as well as interest taken in ethics generally, Piso asserts in §14 *fin.* that Antiochus followed the *sententia antiquorum* closely, which is then glossed as Aristotle's and Polemon's at the same time. With the reader thus expecting the exposition of that *sententia*, §15 is devoted to the central role which the *summum bonum* plays in any ethical theory, where it serves as a reference point for the *uitae uia* and for the conception of appropriate action (*officium*). In §16 the *Carneadea diuisio* is introduced. The stated reason for its introduction is the widespread disagreement (*magna dissensio*) among philosophers about the highest good, and we learn that Antiochus was fond of using it. Both statements taken together are presumably intended to if not baffle then intrigue, given that the demonstration that such *dissensio* obtains was the obvious use to which Carneades put the division.[523] Given how

---

[522] See also Mansfeld (1989a) on Chrysippean arguments arising from a doxographical survey of views on the soul; Algra (1997: 111). On the Stoic use of πιθανά for argumentative purposes, see also Sedley (1982: 252), who refrains from 'suggesting that Chrysippus had a separate and systematic theory of extralogical discourse', and Brunschwig (1991: 95), who suggests that the Stoics engaged in ethical argument *more Aristotelico*, i.e. from commonly held views, alongside their argument 'from a particular view of the place of human beings in divine cosmic nature'.

[523] Alternatively, Carneades may have used the division to defend the view that the obtainment of the *prima naturae* is the end. This is the view assigned to him in the division, as one which he advanced for the

Carneades almost proverbially relies on assumptions and devices owned by his dogmatic opponents, Antiochus is implicitly characterized as turning the tables on him. The use of the division is then cited as the reason why Antiochus was aware (*ille igitur uidit*) not just of *summa bona* which had been posited, but also of those which could conceivably be posited. This, trivially, creates the impression that the division will be exhaustive, and makes it a natural assumption that already Carneades added these hypothetical options. However, the point immediately following seems to be at odds with the notion that the division will be exhaustive, in that Piso terms what he calls *prudentia* the art of living, comparing *prudentia* to crafts which are concerned with goals that do not arise from the craft itself and lie outside it (thus medicine is the *ars ualetudinis*). That moral knowledge or virtue is relevantly like an art was a widely but not universally held view.[524] Note also that Piso's exposition appears to lose focus slightly in that talk about the *summum bonum* is replaced with vaguer expressions (*quae ipsa a se proficisceretur*; *in se uersari*; *quod propositum sit arti*). A way of explaining this is to assume that 5.16 *Negabat igitur ullam esse artem* marks the beginning of the exposition proper, and that Piso is beginning with an indication of the general context, from which then notions like the highest goal and the *prima inuitamenta* (see below) are allowed to emerge. §17 begins with the observation that it is recognized among 'almost all' that *prudentia* is concerned with and seeks to obtain what is in accordance with nature due to an internal impulse of the subject (*appetitus*, ὁρμή). The qualification 'almost all' is striking, given the impression given earlier that Carneades' division would be exhaustive: while it is true that a form of naturalism was the basis of all major Hellenistic ethical theories, it was not a universal one, which seems to be acknowledged here.[525] The next sentence (*Quid autem sit quod ita moueat...*) then moves closer to the main issue: Piso observes that different schools have different views what the impulse is directed at, and from that (*deque eo*) stems the disagreement about the *summum bonum*. Here the object of the initial impulse and the final good emerge as separate entities also terminologically, although of course what one thinks about the former minimally has an effect on what one thinks about the latter. The next sentence makes it plainer that what Piso has in mind is that there is a direct link between the *prima inuitamenta* and the *summum bonum*:

> Totius enim quaestionis eius, quae habetur de finibus bonorum et malorum, cum quaeritur, in his quid sit extremum et ultimum, fons reperiendus est, in quo sint prima inuitamenta naturae [i.e. the objects of the initial impulse]; quo inuento omnis ab eo quasi capite de summo bono et malo disputatio ducitur.
>
> The origin of the whole dispute about the highest goods and evils, and the question of what among them is ultimate and final, is to be found by asking what the basic

---

sake of the argument. If this was true, it would make Antiochus' fondness for using the division no less intriguing. However, in Piso's hands the division is used to eliminate hedonist views (see below), and the view ascribed to Carneades as the one which he advanced for the sake of the argument would fall under that heading. One would thus have to assume a recontextualization of the division by Piso/Cicero.

[524] On the probable origin of the notion of *prudentia* as a craft, and why it is introduced here, see below, p. 747. Aubert-Baillot (2015) is an analysis of Cicero's uses of *prudentia*.

[525] One can exclude the possibility that the reference is to the kind of naturalism which makes the *prima naturae* part of the τέλος, coupled with the claim that not everyone holds *that* view.

natural attachments are. Discover these, and you have the sources from which the rest of the debate about the supreme good and evil can be traced. (transl. Woolf)

This 'direct link', introduced in a low-key manner, is notable: on one influential modern interpretation the form of naturalism which the *Stoics* claimed for themselves did not envisage it. Rather, they assumed that in the course of their development human beings would eventually come to recognize virtue as the sole good even though it was not included among the items of value humans seek to obtain at or near the beginning of their lives.[526]

In §17 *fin.* Piso lists three different objects of the initial impulse (called *prima inuitamenta naturae*, which are, as becomes clear at once, not the same as the *prima naturae*); given a naturalist framework,[527] the list of three is intended to be a jointly exhaustive set of possibilities (as is stated in §18). The three objects are given as (a) *uoluptatis appetitus et depulsio doloris*, (b) *uacuitas doloris et declinatus dolor*, and (c) *prima secundum naturam* (i.e. bodily integrity, freedom from pain, vigour, beauty; and their counterparts in the sphere of the soul, notably the first seeds of virtue, *uirtutum igniculi et semina*).[528] Of these, (a) is presumably to be parsed in such a way that freedom from pain is a necessary condition for the unhindered experience of pleasant sensations, whereas in (b) the two phrasal terms appear to function as a hendiadys. In §18 *fin.* the notion of *prudentia* reappears as having to do with (*uersari in*) either (a), (b), or (c), thus confirming that when it occurred above Piso was not yet talking about the *summum bonum*.

§19 then explains how we get from *prima inuitamenta* to (some) conceptions of the *summum bonum*: from those three things which are the objects of impulse a conception of what is right and good can be derived, which Piso stipulatively calls the *honestum*. This is the reason why the list of three *inuitamenta* can issue in three corresponding conceptions of the *summum bonum* (and three conceptions of the *honestum*). As the emphatic last word of the paragraph—*obtinenda*—makes clear, the first three conceptions of the *summum bonum* thus derived envisage the actual securing of either pleasure, or freedom from pain, or the *prima secundum naturam*, rather than just the striving for these things.

In §20 Piso then discloses who defended the three views which have thus emerged (*frui* resumes *obtinere*) and proceeds to explain how a second set of three *summa bona* can be derived from the *prima inuitamenta* by assuming that the goal is not to obtain the latter but to strive for them (note the use of *expetere*). The first two options (striving for pleasure; striving for freedom from pain) have not been held by anyone, whereas the third one is ascribed to the Stoics. As we shall see, the Stoics reappear a

---

[526] Klein (2016: 154–9) offers a characterization of the two competing reconstructions and of the manner in which they invoke the primary evidence. He also traces the genesis of both views in modern scholarship.

[527] On naturalism in the Hellenistic ethical debates, see White (1979: 144, 146–7); Annas (1993: 135–41); Striker (1996d: 221–31); on the Epicurean and Stoic 'cradle arguments', see Brunschwig (1986) and Inwood (2016).

[528] That seeds of virtue should be included among the *prima inuitamenta* is consistent with the kind of naturalism posited in §17, but is Antiochian, not Stoic doctrine; see Striker (1996d: 262 n. 29). This would appear to be a second instance where the way is being paved for Piso's eventual argumentative goal. See also Annas (2007: 191 n. 7 and 194).

little later as committed to a composite *summum bonum* and being in substantial agreement with Antiochus (while adopting a pointlessly different terminology). So Piso's point here must relate to the position the Stoics take avowedly as opposed to— from his point of view—de facto; since the two views at issue represent genuine alternatives, there is no inconsistency in having them both in the *diuisio*. However, what is more striking is that in Chrysippus' own division (reviewed above) the Stoic τέλος is 'virtue' (*honestas*) rather than pursuit of the *prima naturae*. What must have happened here is that Carneades has exploited the debate about the right τέλος *formula* and has selected one (i.e. Antipater's) which does not overtly feature virtue.[529] While Carneadean arguments are attested which could have been used to dismiss virtue as a simple end,[530] Carneades evidently chose to represent the Stoics' avowed position as a different one.

In §§21–2 Piso moves on to composite goals, of which only three were upheld and are actually possible: *honestas*, i.e. virtue, and pleasure (upheld by Callipho and Dinomachus), *honestas* and freedom from pain (upheld by Diodorus), and *honestas* and the pursuit of the *prima naturae* (upheld by the *antiqui*, i.e. the Old Academics and the Peripatetics). Then Piso begins the process of elimination, starting with the views characterized by a simple end. Pleasure is dismissed on the grounds that human

---

[529] Noted already by Madvig (1876: 638). Several Stoic τέλος-formulae are attested. Zeno, Cleanthes, and Chrysippus said that the goal of life was living in accordance with nature. Diogenes of Babylon said that the goal was 'rational behaviour in the selection of what is natural' (εὐλογιστεῖν ἐν τῇ τῶν κατὰ φύσιν ἐκλογῇ; D.L. 7.88 = *SVF* iii.45). (For an attempt to trace them back to the Old Academy, see Görler 1994: 955.) Antipater said that it was 'doing everything in one's power, constantly and unwaveringly, to obtain the primary natural things' (πᾶν τὸ καθ' αὑτὸν ποιεῖν διηνεκῶς καὶ ἀπαραβάτως, πρὸς τὸ τυγχάνειν τῶν προηγουμένων κατὰ φύσιν; Stob., *Ecl.* II.7, p. 76.11-13 Wachsmuth = part of *SVF* iii.57), where προηγουμένων appears to be optional (see Striker 1996c: 300 n. 3). These have been studied extensively; see in particular Hirzel (1882: 230–57); Rieth (1934); White (1978: 173–8); Striker (1996c) and (1996d: 239–48); Ioppolo (2016: 176–80 and 192–7). The relative dates of Carneades and Diogenes make it likely that Diogenes' formula predates Carneades' criticism, but already before Diogenes a distinction between the selection and the obtainment of things of value was operative. If what virtue does consists in the rational selection of things of value, but the things selected are actually indifferent (so that obtaining them is a matter of indifference), the distinction is already assumed. Antipater's formula, by contrast, probably postdates Carneades. From Plut., *Comm. not.* ch. 26, 1070f-1071b, Striker (1996d: 241–2) has reconstructed a Carneadean challenge to the Stoics which made reference to Diogenes τέλος-formula: 'Carneades' attack... was focused on the two propositions (i) that the goal of life is the reasonable selection of things in accordance with nature, and (ii) that virtue is the craft of selecting things in accordance with nature.... Carneades confronted the Stoics with a dilemma: on the Stoic theory, either there will have to be two goals of life, namely the acquisition of the "natural" things on the one hand, and the selection itself on the other; or the goal will be distinct from the reference point of all action. Both alternatives were unacceptable for the Stoics.... The crucial move in this argument is the assumption that a selection can only be reasonable if it aims at something that has value for, or is identical with, the goal of life. Since the Stoics did not want to make attainment of things in accordance with nature part of the goal, they could refute this argument only by showing that it is not unreasonable to select things that do not contribute to the final good.' Antipater, on Striker's reconstruction, did this by arguing that virtue was like a stochastic art, i.e. an art whose τέλος is formulated in such a way that it is achieved if one does everything in one's power in accordance with the art; thus the τέλος of the stochastic art of medicine would be to act in the treatment of a patient in complete accordance with the rules of the art, whether or not the patient ends up being cured (which is ultimately a matter beyond one's control). Antipater appears to have illustrated this suggestion through the analogy of an archer (cf. *Fin.* 3.22), whose ultimate success in hitting the target depends on circumstances beyond his control, but who will have reached the τέλος of the art of archery if he has acted in accordance with the art's rules.

[530] Cf. the argument made in *Fin.* 4.26, 4.32, and 4.41 that the Stoics reduce human beings to their minds.

beings are born for higher things, and freedom from pain because it is for most purposes equivalent to pleasure, and the same is claimed in §22 *init.* for the view upheld by Carneades for the sake of the argument, that the end was the obtainment of the *prima naturae* (which include—cf. §18—freedom from pain). None of these theories could accommodate duty, virtues, and friendship. When Piso then turns to the composite ends, he dismisses those which combine *honestas* with pleasure or freedom from pain, on the grounds that the former is tainted in such combinations. This leaves the view which combines virtue and the *prima naturae* in a composite telos. Piso ascribes it to the Old Academics and the Peripatetics, and also to the Stoics, whom he takes, in the Antiochian vein, to adopt this view while modifying the terminology pointlessly. While this represents a dogmatic use of the *diuisio* (after the elimination of competing views the preferred view is left standing), it raises questions: from the account of the *Chrysippea diuisio* it would seem to follow that Chrysippus reduced the view Antiochus claims for the Old Academy to one which adopts a composite end made up from virtue and pleasure, by reducing *prima naturae* to pleasure. He then posited that the involvement of pleasure taints virtue. *Fin.* 5.22 features the reduction of a theory involving *prima naturae* as a simple end to one involving pleasure as a simple end, which is then dismissed, and the dismissal of composite ends featuring pleasure (and freedom from pain). These are precisely the steps Chrysippus is reported to have taken to eliminate options. One thus wonders how Antiochus could have upheld the view of the Old Academy, given that it is open to the same counterarguments in virtue of its inclusion of the *prima naturae.* Evidently Antiochus veered away from the sceptical use of the *Carneadea diuisio* at this point; however, he does so in a manifestly transparent way, so that it is difficult to avoid the impression that the *Carneadea diuisio*—a favoured presentational device of his, as pointed out above—retained its sceptical potential even in his hands.

In 5.23 Piso touches on a number of positions which can be dismissed on the grounds that they lie outside the ambit (*orbis*) chosen.[531] The framework, as Piso explains, is predicated on the naturalist assumption that the question about the highest good starts from what is in accordance with nature and the first direct object of appetition. The section concludes with the observation that now all possible views have been considered and that only that of the *ueteres* (and of the Stoics at the same time) retains validity.

To conclude the section on the two types of *diuisiones* in Cicero: there is no reason to doubt what has emerged as the standard view amongst scholars,[532] that the so-called *Chrysippea diuisio* of actually upheld ethical τέλη (and, by implication, of ethical theories individuated by their ends) inspired the *Carneadea diuisio* of conceivable (whether upheld or not) τέλη. However, I have added the qualification that the latter division is not simply the result of an expansion of the Chrysippean one, since the Stoic view is represented by a different entry in Carneades' division.[533] I have also identified the ideological import of the repurposing of a pre-existing division first by Carneades and then by Antiochus. As far as one can tell, the division in the narrow

---

[531] On these figures, see Ioppolo (2016).
[532] See e.g. Glucker (1978: 54); Giusta (2012²: 224).
[533] *Pace* Algra (1997: 123).

sense (i.e. the set of options) in *Fin.* 5, the fullest report of the (or 'a', as one should say; see below) *Carneadea diuisio*, was not subject to manipulation by Antiochus or Cicero.[534] That the sceptical import of the division runs away even with Antiochus is best put down to the inherent nature of the division than seen as something the latter would have engineered himself. That the avowed Stoic view is de facto eliminated on the grounds that it amounts to hedonism may seem a Carneadean rather than an Antiochian move, at least in a context where the division is used to demolish the τέλη of all positions captured by the division.

It is worth asking, though, how the naturalist preface (5.16–17; cf. 23) as well as the conception of *prudentia* as an *ars uiuendi* (5.16 *fin.*) relate to the division in the narrow sense. Are these addenda which are extraneous to the *diuisio* itself likely to have been secondarily attached by Antiochus to advance his particular argumentative purposes, or should one assume that these 'belong with' the *diuisio* and go back to Carneades?

That *prudentia* conceived as a craft needs to have a goal outside of itself is reminiscent of the argument Chrysippus cited against Aristo of Chios' view.[535] Aristo's view is among those dismissed as obsolete in *Fin.* 5.23. It would have suited Carneades, whether his aim was to argue against any theory or to argue for his alternative moral theory (which assumes that the end is obtainment of the *prima naturae*), as it suited Antiochus, to reduce the list of contenders by introducing this consideration, and hence it is reasonable to assume that it was Carneades who made the point originally. That it fails to do justice to some of the views classified in the *Carneadea diuisio* would have troubled neither Carneades nor Antiochus.[536]

The commitment to naturalism which bookends the account of the division does make something explicit which is inherent in all the views assembled, at least as they are presented in it, viz. the notion that a human being's first natural impulses inform and are connected with what emerges as the formal final end in the developed moral theory. It also provides a secondary rationale for the exclusion of the views of *Fin.* 5.23, as we shall see. It is at this point that we should briefly consider some other instances of *diuisiones* of ends in *Fin.*[537] These share the feature of placing the Stoic view *outside* of the division in virtue of the fact that Stoicism relies on a different type of naturalism from the other views (i.e. it relies on a kind of naturalism, but posits a disconnect between first natural impulses and final goals). Depending on whether the speaker is an Academic or a Stoic, this is either seen as a weakness of Stoicism or as a strength. The question thus arises if these parallels can tell us which set of views precisely we should call the *Carneadea diuisio* or if it is wrong to look for just one. In *Fin.* 3 Cato defends the Stoic theory, and in 3.30 Cato introduces a division featuring six ends, three simple and three composite, with the simple view assigned to the Stoics in *Fin.* 5.20 *fin.* being absent while the view advanced for the sake of the argument by Carneades in 5.20 is present (i.e. the actual obtainment of the *prima naturae*). All six are dismissed, and only the Stoic one, characterized in 3.31 *fin.* by three

---

[534] Note, however, the addition of the 'seeds of virtue' in 5.18, on which see Striker (1996d: 262 n. 29).
[535] See Plut., *Comm. not.* 1071f–1072a, with Striker (1996d: 233–4).
[536] To the best of my knowledge, no Epicurean text on an ethical subject employs the craft analogy.
[537] See also Döring (1893); Lévy (1992: 337–76, esp. 360–72); Annas (2007: 201–13). On *Fin.* 2.35, not discussed here, see Algra (1997: 119).

familiar formulae (including Diogenes, but not Antipater's), is accepted.[538] Annas (2007: 198–201) has shown that Cato's crucial assumption is that the views classified in the *diuisio* are united by a strong form of naturalism, i.e. strong in the sense that 'primary natural advantages' are not just supposedly observable starting points for action in humans when they are young but actually enter into the final end of the respective theory—this kind of naturalism is of course the background assumption in *Fin.* 5.15–23.[539] The naturalism inherent in Stoicism, or so Cato thinks, is different in that it provides a starting point and directs initial impulses, but is eventually replaced by a different end, virtue. In *Fin.* 4, where Cicero is arguing against Stoic ethics, he relies on the same set of six options (4.49–51), and broadly the same assumptions, but this is seen to lead to a position which either collapses into that of Aristo (which leads to inaction in that rational choice becomes inexplicable if what Zeno would call preferred indifferents have no value) or is no different from the Old Academic one which combines virtue and the *prima naturae* into a composite end.

The natural conclusion to draw from all this is that there is not one particular *Carneadea diuisio* (the occurrence of the phrasal term in *Fin.* 5 is no mark of originality) but minimally two related *diuisiones* (in *Fin.* 5, and *Fin.* 3 and 4) which can be deployed according to argumentative need and context.[540] In the background of these divisions stands the issue of moral naturalism, but even this cashes out differently in different contexts: in *Fin.* 5 what is salient is that the theories gathered within the *diuisio* are all predicated on *a* form of naturalism, namely what we can identify as the strong form of naturalism, but the distinction between weak and strong naturalism is not invoked in the passage, and those theories which are dismissed for being obsolete are not expressly identified as non-naturalistic (although we can supply from elsewhere that this is one of their inherent common features). This involves claiming the Stoics for strong naturalism, a move made possible by selecting a τέλος-formula to identify them which turns on what is selected by virtue viewed as a disposition: the items selected by fully developed moral agents are indeed traceable to the *prima naturae*. In *Fin.* 3 and 4, by contrast, different types of naturalism are at issue, and only one of them—the stronger form—represents a shared assumption for the views gathered in the *diuisio*. Antiochus, who used to be a sceptical Academic, and Cicero, who was a historically aware sceptical Academic as well as a gifted advocate, would readily be able to formulate and draw out the naturalistic assumptions

---

[538] See Ioppolo (2016: 172–4), who wants to retrace the *diuisio* in *Fin.* 3.30–1 to Chrysippus, on the grounds that it includes, uniquely among the passages featuring *diuisiones*, a dismissal of sceptical Academics which is not easily credited to Carneades. In my view, this reasoning overlooks Cicero's role in supplying the characters of his dialogues with powerful and relevant arguments.

[539] See also Lévy (1992: 355–6 and 438); Annas (1993: 184–6); Ioppolo (2016: 183); and more generally the comparison between Stoic and Antiochian οἰκείωσις in Gill (2016).

[540] This possibility, raised by Malcolm Schofield, is considered and dismissed by Algra (1997: 121 n. 38; cf. 127 n. 52), who writes: 'Here again we should remember that Carneades did not leave anything in writing, and that it is not very likely that various versions of his division were transmitted orally in their original form.' In my view, the flexible handling of a number of related divisions is as easily transmittable orally as it can be taught and practised in classroom scenarios, nor is it unlikely that such divisions were documented in writing by Clitomachus, known to have recorded Carneadean arguments extensively. However, Algra (1997: 108) also observes that at each occurrence a distinction must be made between the views captured in a given division and the overall purpose to which it is put; on the same point, see Annas (2007: 196).

underlying a given version of the *diuisio* in a particular context. I see no reason to favour the *diuisio* of *Fin.* 5 over that of *Fin.* 3 and 4, but rather hold that they reflect—even in the hands of the interlocutor Cato—Carneadean flexibility in handling a device which could be employed within the context of different strategies as required. As to whether the naturalistic frame around the discussion of the division in *Fin.* 5 is 'original', it clearly suited Antiochus' purpose there to stress the common ground between the theories represented in the division, but we also saw how easy it would have been for the argument to end in the rejection of *all* the views assembled, or indeed in the promotion of the view which Carneades advanced for the sake of the argument (= obtainment of the *prima naturae* as the end). Thus on balance it is plausible to assume that the version of the *diuisio* used in *Fin.* 5 carried naturalistic prefatory material already in Clitomachus' writings (which we may suspect as a source at some removes, but not as the proximate source).

Various non-Ciceronian texts have been examined with a view to whether they represent parallel evidence for the *Carneadea diuisio* as configured and used in Piso's speech in *Fin.* 5.[541] The majority of them either exhibit limited points of contact with the evidence from Cicero (Stob.), or else present material which resembles pieces of information provided by Cicero within a sea of doxographical material not offered by him (Clem. Alex.), so as to make any suggestion of a shared source precarious or uninformative.[542] There is, however, one text—[Archytas'] Περὶ παιδεύσεως ἠθικῆς (*On Ethical Education*)—in which a *diuisio* occurs which resembles that of *Fin.* 5. and which is deployed in a manner reminiscent of Piso's strategy in *Fin.* 5.[543] After stating that life needs to have a τέλος (cf. *Fin.* 5.15), [Archytas] introduces four views which also feature in the division in *Fin.* 5 (pleasure; freedom from pain; the combination of each with virtue) while replacing two (Carneades' and the Old Academic view are replaced with the εὐπάθεια of the body and 'virtuous activity coupled with external prosperity').[544] He then eliminates the four as well as one of the 'new' positions so as to leave a position standing which resembles that of the Old Academy. We cannot be sure if [Archytas] used Carneades' division directly (possibly as relayed by Clitomachus) or mediated through Antiochus, but the fact that the 'Carneadean' view (i.e. the one Carneades defended for the sake of the argument) does not feature and that the view which emerges as superior resembles Antiochus suggests the latter. This being so, [Archytas] gives out nothing regarding the question of whether the prefatory material preceding the *Carneadea diuisio* in *Fin.*, notably the idea that life needs to have a τέλος, is Carneadean or Antiochian.

The case of Varro's *De philosophia*, on which Augustine draws in *C.D.* 19.1–3, is discussed in the general note on *Ac.* 1.19–23.

---

[541] See Algra (1997: 120–1 n. 37); Madvig (1876: 837–48); Glucker (1978: 52–63); Giusta (2012²: 217–429).

[542] On Stobaeus (*Ecl.* II.7, pp. 47.12–48.5 Wachsmuth), which parallels the three *inuitamenta naturae* in *Fin.* 5.17–18, see Döring (1893: 179–80) and Giusta (2012²: 77–94); on Clement (*Strom.* 2.127–33), Döring (1893: 180–98).

[543] See the discussion in Burkert (1972: 30–40) and Annas (2007: 214–23), who assembles the recent editions and scholarship on [Archytas] on p. 214 n. 30. The most recent scholarly edition of the text is Giani (1993).

[544] See Burkert (1972: 31) on these divergences.

The views on moral ends which feature in Cicero's works, not just in the contexts in which *diuisiones* are expressly at issue, have also been drawn on by Giusta (2012²: 57–105) in his attempt to demonstrate that there was a doxographical tradition of ethical views similar to that first reconstructed in detail by Diels for physical views. His main hypothesis has not commanded assent because the correspondences he has been able to identify are not nearly as close and extensive as those between Stobaeus and Ps.-Plutarch.[545] His discussions of the Ciceronian passages which concern us here, while offering helpful observations on points of detail, are driven by a desire to identify a common Peripatetic source and do not aim to construct the *intentio operis* of the dialogues in question.

§129

Sed quod coeperam...summa referatur: Cicero refers back to §128b: *Veniamus nunc ad bonorum malorumque notionem.* For *quid...explorati*, cf. §85; for the sentiment, cf. Sextus, *P.H.* 3.175. On *nempe*, see Pinkster i.310: 'The interactional particle *nempe* "you mean" checks the attitude of the (putative) addressee with respect to a certain state of affairs.' With *summa bonorum* (= *summum bonum*), cf. *Fin.* 4.43, 46; and Schäublin et al. (pp. 280 n. 331 and 293 n. 403) on Greek and Latin terminology relating to the highest good.

Qua de re igitur...quae relicta uidentur: for *maior dissensio*, cf. §134 init. Reid¹ (p. 328) wonders if *relicta* is a corruption for *reiecta* (citing §130 and *Fin.* 2.43). Plasberg¹ (p. 142) holds *et*, deleted by Madvig (1826: 201), on the grounds that it has the force of *et quidem*.

Erillum...non multum a Platone: for the spelling *Erillus* instead of *Herillus*, see Madvig (1876: 206) on *Fin.* 2.35 and Leeman, Pinkster, and Wisse (1996: 242) on *De orat.* 3.62: even if it was correct to print Ἥριλλος in D.L. 7.165 (as Dorandi 2013 does), the manuscripts in the various places where Cicero gives his name suggest that he wrote *Erillus*. On Erillus, 'philosophe stoïcien hétérodoxe, disciple de Zénon de Citium', see Ioppolo (1985); Guérard (2000); and the texts collected as *SVF* i.409–21 (*Omitto illa... a Platone* here is frg. i.413). The insertion of *ut* before *Erillum* (Davies) is mildly discouraged by the shift from *illa* in the previous sentence to a person.

The most detailed account of his view is in D.L. 7.165: Ἥριλλος δ' ὁ Καρχηδόνιος τέλος εἶπε τὴν ἐπιστήμην, ὅπερ ἐστὶ ζῆν ἀεὶ πάντ' ἀναφέροντα πρὸς τὸ μετ' ἐπιστήμης ζῆν καὶ μὴ τῇ ἀγνοίᾳ διαβεβλημένον. εἶναι δὲ τὴν ἐπιστήμην ἕξιν ἐν φαντασιῶν προσδέξει ἀνυπόπτωτον ὑπὸ λόγου. ποτὲ δ' ἔλεγε μηδὲν εἶναι τέλος, ἀλλὰ κατὰ τὰς περιστάσεις καὶ τὰ πράγματ' ἀλλάττεσθαι αὐτό, ὡς καὶ τὸν αὐτὸν χαλκὸν ἢ Ἀλεξάνδρου γινόμενον ἀνδριάντα ἢ Σωκράτους. διαφέρειν δὲ τέλος καὶ ὑποτελίδα· τῆς μὲν γὰρ καὶ τοὺς μὴ σοφοὺς στοχάζεσθαι, τοῦ δὲ μόνον τὸν σοφόν. τὰ δὲ μεταξὺ ἀρετῆς καὶ κακίας ἀδιάφορα εἶναι, 'Herillus of Carthage declared the end of action to be knowledge, that

---

[545] See Kerferd (1967); Mansfeld (1968).

is, so to live always as to make the scientific life the standard in all things and not to be misled by ignorance. Knowledge he defined as a habit of mind, not to be upset by argument, in the acceptance of presentations. Sometimes he used to say there was no single end of action, but it shifted according to varying circumstances and objects, as the same bronze might become a statue either of Alexander or of Socrates. He made a distinction between end-in-chief and subordinate end: even the unwise may aim at the latter, but only the wise seek the true end of life. Everything that lies between virtue and vice he pronounced indifferent' (transl. Hicks). Cicero usually groups Erillus together with Aristo and Pyrrho who feature in the next paragraph (in addition to the passages named below, see e.g. *Fin.* 2.35; *Tusc.* 5.85; *Off.* 1.6), which seems at variance with the division here between §129 devoted to the truly obsolete and §130 to the still obsolete who, however, nonetheless enjoy and deserve some credit. Cf. in particular *Fin.* 5.23: *Iam explosae eiectaeque sententiae Pyrrhonis, Aristonis, Erilli quod in hunc orbem, quem circumscripsimus, incidere non possunt, adhibendae omnino non fuerunt. Nam cum omnis haec quaestio de finibus et quasi de extremis bonorum et maiorum ab eo proficiscatur, quod diximus naturae esse aptum et accommodatum, quodque ipsum per se primum appetatur, hoc totum et ii tollunt, qui in rebus iis, in quibus nihil [quod non] aut honestum aut turpe sit,* **negant esse ullam causam, cur aliud alii anteponatur, nec inter eas res quicquam omnino putant interesse***, et Erillus, si ita sensit, nihil esse bonum praeter scientiam, omnem consilii capiendi causam inuentionemque officii sustulit*. The highlighted sentence gives the reason for the dismissal of these philosophers: their view of the good does not allow for rational choice and consequently precludes appropriate action. Cf. also *Fin.* 2.43, which adds that Chrysippus conclusively dealt with Erillus: *Quae quod Aristoni et Pyrrhoni omnino uisa sunt pro nihilo, ut inter optime ualere et grauissime aegrotare nihil prorsus dicerent interesse, recte iam pridem contra eos desitum est disputari. Dum enim in una uirtute sic omnia esse uoluerunt, ut eam rerum selectione expoliarent nec ei quicquam, aut unde oriretur, darent, aut ubi niteretur, uirtutem ipsam, quam amplexabantur, sustulerunt. Erillus autem ad scientiam omnia reuocans unum quoddam bonum uidit, sed nec optimum nec quo uita gubernari possit. Itaque hic ipse iam pridem est reiectus; post enim Chrysippum non sane est disputatum*. In *Fin.* 5.73 Piso seems to explain Erillus' view as due to an overinterpretation of Aristotle's and Theophrastus' praise of *scientia*.

The reference to Plato in our passage (*quam non multum a Platone*) is illuminated by what Cicero says in §142, where he appears to ascribe to Plato a view which downgrades perceptual information (required to select things of value) relative to the status accorded to it by Varro in *Ac*. 1.30-2 (see ad loc.), where, however, the view of the *antiqui* (the Old Academics and the Peripatetics) is given.

Erillus' view is compared to Aristo's in Long and Sedley (i.1987: 359). Dyck (2004: 170) discusses passages in which these *sententiae explosae* feature with a view to whether Cicero is speaking in Stoic or Antiochian mode. On succession as a principle of organizing doxographical material, see the general note in §§118–26.

Megaricorum fuit nobilis disciplina ... et simile et idem semper: *Megaricorum ... qua uerum cerneretur* = test. 26A Döring; *Megaricorum ... multa a Platone* = SSR II a 31 Giannantoni. Cf. Boys-Stones and Rowe (2013: 62 n. 12): 'The claim that Xenophanes, then Parmenides and Zeno, "founded" the Megarian school amounts to no more than the claim that the school lay in a tradition of thought initiated by them.' This historical claim is found only here; *ut scriptum uideo* seems intended to signal a recherché fact (Reid[1] p. 329 assembles parallels, but they are disparate and require individual assessment). (The backward reference regarding Xenophanes is to §§118 or 123.) That Euclides availed himself of the writings of Parmenides is also reported by D.L. 2.106 (= frg. 24 Döring), which, moreover, provides further information on the ethical interpretation of the Eleatic One (*quod esset unum et simile et idem semper*): Εὐκλείδης... καὶ τὰ Παρμενίδεια μετεχειρίζετο, καὶ οἱ ἀπ' αὐτοῦ Μεγαρικοὶ προσηγορεύοντο, εἶτ' ἐριστικοί, ὕστερον δὲ διαλεκτικοί, οὓς οὕτως ὠνόμασε πρῶτος Διονύσιος ὁ Χαλκηδόνιος διὰ τὸ πρὸς ἐρώτησιν καὶ ἀπόκρισιν τοὺς λόγους διατίθεσθαι. πρὸς τοῦτόν φησιν ὁ Ἑρμόδωρος ἀφικέσθαι Πλάτωνα καὶ τοὺς λοιποὺς φιλοσόφους μετὰ τὴν Σωκράτους τελευτήν, δείσαντες τὴν ὠμότητα τῶν τυράννων. οὗτος ἓν τὸ ἀγαθὸν ἀπεφαίνετο πολλοῖς ὀνόμασι καλούμενον· ὁτὲ μὲν γὰρ φρόνησιν, ὁτὲ δὲ θεόν, καὶ ἄλλοτε νοῦν καὶ τὰ λοιπά. τὰ δ' ἀντικείμενα τῷ ἀγαθῷ ἀνῄρει, μὴ εἶναι φάσκων, 'Euclides...applied himself to the writings of Parmenides, and his followers were called Megarians after him, then Eristics, and at a later date Dialecticians, that name having first been given to them by Dionysius of Chalcedon because they put their arguments into the form of question and answer. Hermodorus tells us that, after the death of Socrates, Plato and the rest of philosophers came to him, being alarmed at the cruelty of the tyrants. He held the supreme good to be really one, though called by many names, sometimes wisdom, sometimes god, and again mind, and so forth. But all that is contradictory of the good he used to reject, declaring that it had no existence' (transl. Hicks). The phrase characterizing the One is reminiscent of descriptions of Forms, too (*Ac.* 1.31: *id quod semper esset simplex et unius modi et tale quale esset*), perhaps implying that the Socratic Euclides equated the One and Socrates' ἰδέα τοῦ ἀγαθοῦ.

Euclides is mentioned only here, but individual Megarians feature elsewhere, not for their ethical views, but because of their cleverness and interest in argument; Cicero's fullest statement on the various Socratics is in *De orat.* 3.62, on which see Leeman, Pinkster, and Wisse (1996: 238–44). With *Euclides... unum et simile et idem semper*, cf. Lact., *Inst.* 3.12.9 (= test. 26B Döring = my t. 49). Plasberg[1] (p. 143) posits a lacuna before *itaque ab his Eleatici*, but it can be assumed to have been familiar where Parmenides and Zeno were from.

Hi quoque multa a Platone...sed opinor explicata uberius et ornatius: *a Menedemo... ornatius* is Menedemus frg. 17 (= SSR III F 17), along with D.L. 2.129: Πρὸς δὲ τὸν εἰπόντα πολλὰ τὰ ἀγαθὰ ἐπύθετο [sc. Menedemus] πόσα τὸν ἀριθμὸν καὶ εἰ νομίζει πλείω τῶν ἑκατόν, 'Of one who affirmed that there were many good things, he inquired how many, and whether he thought there were more than a hundred' (transl. Hicks), and Plut., *De virt. mor.* 2, 440e: Μενέδημος μὲν ὁ ἐξ Ἐρετρίας ἀνῄρει τῶν ἀρετῶν καὶ τὸ πλῆθος καὶ τὰς διαφοράς, ὡς μιᾶς οὔσης καὶ χρωμένης πολλοῖς ὀνόμασι· τὸ γὰρ αὐτὸ σωφροσύνην καὶ ἀνδρείαν καὶ δικαιοσύνην λέγεσθαι, καθάπερ βροτὸν καὶ ἄνθρωπον, 'Menedemus of Eretria removed the notion that there were many virtues and the differences between them, on the grounds that there was one for which many designations are used; for the same thing is called prudence, fortitude and justice, like mortal and human being'. On Menedemus, see his life in

D.L. 2.125-44 and Goulet (2005a). In *De virt. mor.* Plut. proceeds to Aristo (see §130 below with n.). For a discussion of Menedemus' and Aristo's view on virtue see Cooper (1999a: 90-6). This is the only reference to Menedemus of Eretria in Cicero, who, however, mentions the *Eretrici* [sic] in *De orat.* 3.62 (see previous note). Their views on the nature of the mind are not otherwise attested.

Hi quoque, sc. like Erillus. Reid[1] (p. 330) prints *ex Eretria*, unnecessarily. His emendation *Elii* for the non-sensical *ulli* cannot be dismissed (see Brittain 2006: 76 n. 205), but *Erilli* (nom. pl.) seems secured by its occurrence in *De orat.* 3.62, and as Plasberg[1] (p. 143) notes, it would be peculiar for Cicero to return to a chronologically earlier group. *Erilli* is a spelling variation of *Herilli*, which was proposed by Madvig (1826: 202-3).

§130

Hos si contemnimus...despicere debemus: as noted above, in Cicero Erillus features several times together with Aristo and Pyrrhon, so the grounds for separating the latter two here from the philosophers named in §129 are not immediately apparent. Brittain (2006: 76 n. 206) comments: 'The second group of abandoned views— which usually includes Erillus' elsewhere in Cicero—have the distinction of being useful for discussing and criticizing the function of "indifferents" in Stoic ethics.' Perhaps Cicero's first-person plural is slightly patronizing, and his point is that the followers of Antiochus may dismiss the factually obsolete figures of §129 but ought to regard Aristo and Pyrrho as deserving of consideration, since their views were invoked by Antiochus himself as the reason why the Stoic view on preferred indifferents was untenable: it *either* amounted to the view of Aristo and Pyrrho *or* to the Peripatetic/Antiochian view which classed preferred indifferents as goods. This is suggested by the argument of *Fin.* 4.60b, where Aristo is aligned with Pyrrho as in our passage and the Antiochian topos of equivalence in substance but difference in terminology between the Antiochian and the Stoic position occurs. With *abiectos*, cf. *Fin.* 2.35 *abiecti*; *Off.* 1.6 *explosa* (of their *sententia*).

Aristonem...ἀδιαφορία ab ipso dicitur: = *SVF* i.362. On Aristo of Chios see, *SVF* i.333-403; Ioppolo (1980); Schofield (1984); Guérard (1989); on his theory of action and its possible constructive role for Chrysippean doctrine, see Ioppolo (2012).

Aristo's view is introduced here with a polemical inversion of the Antiochian topos (see previous note) that the Stoics held the Old Academic view but used different terminology: Aristo actually took the view to which Zeno only paid lip-service: he regarded virtue as the only good, its opposite as the only vice. (Aristo himself is said to have called indifferents goods in all but name; see Sextus, *M.* 11.61-7 = *SVF* i.361, with Ioppolo 2016: 168.) As to things in between, called *media* here, what significance Zeno wanted to attach to them Aristo regarded as non-existent. The highest good according to Aristo consisted in a state in which these *media* gave rise to no inclination either way at all.

See Dyck (2004: 170) on the different deployment of Aristo in Cicero depending on whether he is invoked in support of or to embarrass the Stoics.

Elsewhere Cicero translates ἀδιάφορον as *indifferens* when he wants to signal the equivalence to his bilingual readers or capture the Greek term with precision (e.g. *Fin.* 3.53). Otherwise he uses *medium* in line with the well-attested terminological use of μέσον. See Hartung (1970: 160–3).

For Aristo's view that rational choice between indifferents is impossible because preferability is not an intrinsic feature but context-dependent, see on *Ac.* 1.35–7; Sextus, *M.* 11.64–7 (= *SVF* i.361 = LS 58F); the Ciceronian texts collected under *SVF* i.364, notably *Fin.* 2.43, as well *Fin.* 3.50 (= *SVF* i.365), where Cicero criticizes Aristo's view; 5.73 (= *SVF* 5.73). That it is Zeno's position rather which is inconsistent is argued for in *Fin.* 4.68–73. Reid[1] (p. 330) notes that *momenta* corresponds to ἀξίαι or *aestimationes*.

The highest good of ἀδιαφορία is described here in terms which leave it open whether indifference was a strategy to be pursued or a state which follows upon achieving perfect virtue. The latter interpretation is defended by Benatouïl (2007: 183–91). Striker (1996d: 231–9) discusses Chrysippus' response to Aristo's challenge, notably the former's rejection of the latter's conception of indifference as the goal of life as reported by Plut., *Comm. not.* 1071f–1072a (= *SVF* iii.26); see also Klein (2015: 238 n. 17).

I had observed above that Aristo's position appears to be excluded from the *Carneadea diuisio* in *Fin.* 5.15–23 because it is deemed not to be grounded in a relevant naturalist view of nature, notably human nature. This, however, is the critic's perspective on Aristo, who in Sen., *Ep.* 94.8 (= part of *SVF* i.359), is presented as committed to living in accordance with nature just like other Stoics.

Reid[1] (p. 278) on §84 summarizes Madvig (1876: 297–9) on *Fin.* 2.93 about the uses of *ipse* vs *is ipse* (cf. *ab ipso* here).

Pyrrho autem...multumque defensa sunt: = Pyrrho frg. 69a Decleva Caizzi. With ἀπάθεια here, cf. Eus., *Praep. Ev.* XIV.18.26. Ἀταραξία is attested, too; cf. ibid., XIV.18.1–4.

For the position ascribed to Pyrrho here, cf. *Fin.* 2.43 and 4.43. Both passages connect his view with Aristo's like the present. In *Fin.* 2.43 Cicero writes: *Quae quod Aristoni et Pyrrhoni omnino uisa sunt pro nihilo, ut inter optime ualere et grauissime aegrotare nihil prorsus dicerent interesse, recte iam pridem contra eos desitum est disputari. Dum enim in una uirtute sic omnia esse uoluerunt, ut eam rerum selectione exspoliarent nec ei quicquam, aut unde oriretur, darent, aut ubi niteretur, uirtutem ipsam, quam amplexabantur, sustulerunt.*

On the question of why Cicero, here as elsewhere (e.g. *De orat.* 3.62), ascribes an ethical position to Pyrrho but seems unaware or does not assume that he was a sceptic see Decleva Caizzi (1992), who also addresses the question of why Aenesidemus of Cnossos is not mentioned by Cicero even though he dedicated his Πυρρωνίων λόγοι in eight books to Cicero's *familiaris* L. Aelius Tubero (cf. Phot., *Bib.* 169b30–5 and Cic., *Lig.* 21): her suggestion is that the book dedicated to Tubero while the latter served as a legate to Quintus Cicero in Asia minor (61–58 BC) represented the beginning of a movement not yet in existence; Bett (2000: 102–5), who suggests that what Cicero knew of Pyrrho is derived from the supplementary material he received together with the *Carneadea diuisio* from his philosophical teachers (*Fin.* 5.23);

Polito (2014: 4–10); and earlier Glucker (1978: 116–17). Cooper (2006: 169 n. 2) shows that behind ἀπάθεια here there cannot lie the sceptical 'life without belief' familiar from Sextus' writings. Passages in Cicero which have been seen as influences of Pyrrhonism can be explained differently, e.g. *Off.* 2.7, on which see Griffin and Atkins (1991: 65 n. 3).

§131

Alii uoluptatem finem esse uoluerunt...de ipsa uoluptate consentiens: in this paragraph Cicero surveys the different views on the τέλος which are collected in the *Carneadea diuisio* in *Fin.* 5.17–21, without an indication of the origin of the division; see the general note above. In *Fin.* the immediately implausible and/or obsolete positions, which here in *Luc.* precede the *diuisio*, follow in 5.23. Further texts in Cicero where all or part of the *diuisio* is engaged with, are *Fin.* 2.19, 2.34–5, 4.49–50, 5.21, 5.73–4; *Tusc.* 5.84–8; see also the general note above, where scholarly discussions of these passages are cited.

This first part of §131 is Aristippus frg. 178 Giannantoni. On Aristippus of Cyrene, founder of the Cyrenaic school, see Caujolle-Zaslawsky (1989). Cicero makes plain that the division is reductive, in that it assembles views under the same heading (i.e. those of the Cyrenaics and of Epicurus) which are not identical. Cf. *Fin.* 2.35: *Epicurus autem cum in prima commendatione uoluptatem dixisset, si eam, quam Aristippus, idem tenere debuit ultimum bonorum, quod ille.* On the difference between the Cyrenaic and the Epicurean conception of pleasure, see *Fin.* 2.18–21 and 2.39–41. On Epicurus' view, see below, §§138 and 140.

The evidence on the Cyrenaic school is assembled in the second volume of Giannantoni (1990). See also Tsouna (1998); Long (1999a: 632–9); O'Keefe (2002); Warren (2013); Lampe (2015). See also Dyck (1996: 646) on *Off.* 3.116. Epicurean texts on pleasure, which make occasional reference to the Cyrenaics, are collected under no. 21 in Long and Sedley (1987). On Cicero's handling of material relating to the conceptions of pleasure of the Cyrenaics and Epicurus, see Graver (2002: 195–201). For the Cyrenaics, cf. also *Luc.* 20, 142 (both passages are concerned with the criterion).

Voluptatem autem et honestatem...Callipho censuit: what little is known about Callipho is assembled by Goulet (1994a), who suspects that Cicero knew him only as 'pures références doxographiques' via the *Carneadea diuisio* passed on by Antiochus. While I agree that Callipho was merely a name for Cicero, it is less plausible to assume that Cicero is here in *Luc.* drawing on Antiochian source material: rather, the present context, more likely to be informed by sceptical Academic material, suggests that Antiochus did indeed receive the division via such material as well (so that Cicero had encountered the *diuisio* in Antiochian as well as Academic sources and teaching).

See also §139; *Fin.* 2.19, 2.34, 4.50, 5.21 (alongside the equally obscure Dinomachus), 5.73; *Tusc.* 5.85 (with Dinomachus), 5.87; *Off.* 3.119 (with Dinomachus). Callipho und Dinomachus also feature, along with Epicurus, Hieronymus, Diodorus, and the Cyrenaics, in a doxographical passage in Clement, *Strom.* II, cap. XXI, 127.3 Stählin (*pace* Schäublin et al. p. 296 n. 416, who claim that Cicero is our only source for Callipho). See Reid[1] (p. 331) on the spelling of *Callipho*.

Vacare omni molestia Hieronymus: cf. *Fin.* 5.14: *quem iam cur Peripateticum appellem nescio*, which is a comment on his view, not an expression of doubt that he was actually a member of the Peripatetic school. His fragments are collected in Wehrli (1969); see esp. frgs 8a–10e. See Schneider (2000); and Dalfino (1993) on the view for which he is cited here. Cf. also *Fin.* 2.19, 35, 41, but he is referred to in passing by Cicero on numerous other occasions. *Vacare molestia* renders ἀοχλησία (cf. Sen., *Ep. mor.* 92.6).

Hoc idem cum honestate Diodorus, ambo hi Peripatetici: once more, Cicero shifts from a simple τέλος to a compound which adds one new component. On Diodorus, see Wehrli (1969: 85–91); Goulet (1994b). In Cicero he does not feature outside of doxographical sections mostly on the *summum bonum*, but see *De orat.* 1.46.

Honeste autem uiuere fruentem rebus iis quas primas homini natura conciliet...et Aristoteles eiusque amici huc proxime uidentur accedere: cf. *Fin.* 5.21: *Nam aut uoluptas adiungi potest ad honestatem, ut Calliphonti Dinomachoque placuit, aut doloris uacuitas, ut Diodoro, aut prima naturae, ut antiquis, quos eosdem Academicos et Peripateticos nominauimus*, which does not strike the note of caution inherent in *huc proxime... accedere*. This part of §131 is 'Baustein' 4.2a in Dörrie (1987: 96–7). For Antiochus' 'Old Academic' view and the role accorded to Polemo see *Ac.* 1.19–23. *Conciliare* 'to commend' rather than 'to procure' (*OLD* s.v. no. 3 and 4a, respectively). For Aristotle's view, see on *Ac.* 1.19:*...finem bonorum adeptum esse omnia e natura et animo et corpore et uita*. On *amici* 'followers', including later ones, see Reid[1] (p. 332).

Introducebat etiam Carneades...quas primas natura conciliauisset: cf. *Fin.* 5.20: *Expositis iam igitur sex de summo bono sententiis trium proximarum hi principes: uoluptatis Aristippus, non dolendi Hieronymus, fruendi rebus iis quas primas secundum naturam esse diximus Carneades, non ille quidem auctor, sed defensor disserendi causa fuit*. The phrase *disserendi causa* glosses *non quo probaret* here, in that Carneades mounted an argument in support of this τέλος for the sake of the argument and apparently in order to fill an empty position in the grid of actual and conceivable ends. In §139 Cicero mentions that Carneades, sc. in other contexts defended Callipho's view with enthusiasm, so that the question arose if he actually endorsed it. On the phrasal term prima naturae, its variations, and the underlying doctrine, see on *Ac.* 1.22; compare also Bénatouïl (2007: 219–43), who contrasts the Stoic and the Antiochian conception of the use of what the Stoics call indifferents (a sub-set of which are the *prima naturae*). *Frui* recurs in all passages where Cicero talks about this Carneadean 'position'; cf. *Fin.* 2.35: *frui principiis naturalibus*, 5.20; *Tusc.* 5.84: *naturae primis aut omnibus aut maximis frui*; and Pfligersdorffer (1971). On *conciliare*, see the previous note. *Opponere* is not used absolutely with a dative in the sense of 'to oppose someone': the following accusative with infinitive functions as an object to opponeret (cf. *TLL* s.v. *oppono* col. 765.80–4).

Honeste autem uiuere...qui inuentor et princeps Stoicorum fuit: cf. *Fin.* 5.20: *At uero facere omnia, ut adipiscamur, quae secundum naturam sint, etiam si ea non assequamur, id esse et honestum et solum per se expetendum et solum bonum Stoici dicunt.* In this characterization of the Stoic end, Piso characterizes the Stoic view by using Antipater's τέλος-formula (πᾶν τὸ καθ' αὑτὸν ποιεῖν διηνεκῶς καὶ ἀπαραβάτως, πρὸς τὸ τυγχάνειν τῶν προηγουμένων κατὰ φύσιν, 'To do everything in one's power continuously and undeviatingly with a view to obtaining the predominating things which accord with nature', transl. Long and Sedley; Stob., *Ecl.* II.7, p. 76.11–13 Wachsmuth = part of *SVF* iii.57 = part of LS 58K), which focuses on exercising rational choices (sc. with respect to indifferents) as the natural activity of virtue, and thus on living in accordance with nature; see above, p. 745 n. 529. (In 5.22 Piso will claim that the Stoics agree substantially with the Old Academy, but use different and unnecessarily novel terminology.)

Here in *Luc.* the Stoic end is characterized as living virtuously (*honeste uiuere*). *Conciliatio naturae* is one of Cicero's translations for οἰκείωσις; see the commentary on *Ac.* 1.23. One of Antiochus' main objections against the Stoic view was that it involved a reorientation of human beings as they develop, from the *prima naturae* to the categorically distinct end of virtue, and that this undermined any claim the Stoics had to a naturalist foundation of their view. The subjunctive of *ducatur*, which marks the derivation of virtue from the *conciliatio naturae* as Zeno's view (discussed in *Fin.* 3), is functional.

Reid[1] (p. 332) notes the instances of *inuentor et princeps* in Cicero. On Zeno's contributions in the field of ethics from an Antiochian point of view, see *Ac.* 1.35–9.

§132

Iam illud perspicuum est...malorum fines esse contrarios: the sentence concludes the paragraph but with a new point, marked by *iam* (see Reid[1] p. 280 on *Luc.* 86). Schäublin et al. (p. 299 n. 427) observe that Cicero is hinting that the scale of the underlying disagreements would be plainer if the *malorum fines* were added. Since a τέλος in Greek can only be a positive thing, *malorum fines* in Greek would presumably be the ἐναντία of τέλη.

Ad uos nunc refero...Nihil potest dici inconsideratius: *ad uos refero* is reminiscent of the procedural language of the assembly or the courts; cf. e.g. Livy 34.22. In the background is what Stoics/Antiochus and the Academics, or rather the Clitomacheans, are agreed on: that the sage should not assent to the non-cataleptic, i.e. opine (see the end of the paragraph). This is why the dogmatist's reply is not just foolish but shows lack of education and consideration.

The same rhetorical figure ('Whom should I choose?'), cf. *Luc.* 125, 126. With *inconsideratius*, cf. the list of cognitive vices identified by Zeno in *Ac.* 1.42 *fin.* and one of the terms associated with the Academic scrutinizing of persuasive impressions, *consideratio* (*Luc.* 36 *init.*).

Cupio sequi Stoicos...per ipsum Antiochum: *cupio* is perhaps less indicative of Cicero's affinity to Stoic ethics (sc. under Academic proviso) documented elsewhere (*pace* Lévy 1992: 342, 344–5) than intended to aid the dramatization, viz. it hints at the synthetic nature of the construct which is Antiochus' Old Academy: the Stoics pull *strongly* in one direction, Antiochus (and Aristotle) in another. Görler (2004c: 283–4) sees in *cupio sequi Stoicos* 'strong personal conviction' but concludes: '...in the end there seems to be equilibrium between the competing views.' See also Görler (2011: 347) on similar expressions in Cicero (e.g. *Fin.* 5.77: *ego uero uolo in uirtute uim esse quam maximam*); Görler (2016); and section 8. Reid[1] (p. 333) compares Sextus, *P.H.* 1.88, where, however, general disagreements of the dogmatists are at issue.

Omitto per Aristotelem means 'I leave aside "as far as Aristotle is concerned...".' For similar generic praise of Aristotle, cf. *Tusc.* 1.22; *Fin.* 5.7; *Leg.* 1.15, 2.39; *Rab. post.* 23. However, Aristotle's being invoked here tells against the suggestion (cf. p. 123) that it was Cicero rather than Antiochus who played up the Peripatetic element in Antiochus' ethics.

With *Aristotelem...prope singularem*, cf. the generic praise in *Tusc.* 1.22; *Fin.* 5.7; *Leg.* 1.15 and 2.39, but *singularem* may have a polemical edge: he would militate against subsumption under the Old Academy (sc. if he was not omitted by *praeteritio*).

Qui appellabatur Academicus...germanissimus Stoicus: the sentence or indeed the half-sentence in which Antiochus is called a most genuine Stoic sometimes features in general discussions of Antiochus, as Cicero's view on him; see e.g. Striker (1996d: 269); Görler (2004a: 91). Yet while Cicero is writing here and while the character Cicero is speaking, the context in this paragraph, and even in this sentence (with Antiochus being dubbed an *Academicus*, unusually meaning—see Glucker 1978: 104—an Old Academic rather than an Academic sceptic), is polemical; see e.g. Grilli (1975: 77); Lévy (1992: 52). Even *si perpauca mutauisset* is polemical, in that it alludes to and inverts the Antiochian claim that the Stoics merely 'corrected and modified' Old Academic thought (cf. *Ac.* 1.40 *init.*: *plurima autem* [sc. *Zeno*] *in illa tertia philosophiae parte mutauit*; 1.43, where Cicero speaks more accommodatingly, replying to Varro: *horum esse autem arbitror, ut Antiocho, nostro familiari, placebat, correctionem ueteris Academiae potius quam aliquam nouam disciplinam putandam*).

Cf. *Luc.* 69: *eadem dicit quae Stoici* (and 67), 137: [Antiochus as] *Stoicus perpauca balbutiens*, 'a Stoic who is stammering on a few points'; Barnes (1997: 78–9).

See also the rather similar remark in Sextus, *P.H.* 1.235 (= F1 in Sedley 2021c = LS 68T), included with translation and commentary in appendix 1; Dörrie (1987: 196–205). Further Eus., *Praep. Ev.* XIV.9.2 (= Numenius frg. 28 Des Places; see appendix 2); Aug., *Contra Acad.* 3.18.41.

Academicus is normally reserved for sceptical Academics in Cicero (and *Academia* for the New Academy); see Glucker (1978: 103–6 and 206–25), and the qualifications made by Tarrant (1980: 113–17). One might have expected *fuisset* for *erat*, but the indicative is owed to the antithesis with *appellabatur*.

Erit igitur res iam in discrimine...de tota possessione contentio: Cicero notes that the point he just made is not a mere matter of terminology or suitable historical perspective: given the standards that apply for the sage, all of whose beliefs (loosely speaking) are true and therefore consistent with each other, there is no scope for more than one highest good, or for reconciliation between two different ones. For *in discrimine esse* 'to be at a decisive stage', cf. e.g. *Fam.* 5.21.3 (= SB 182). *Constituere* means 'to install' (see Heumann-Seckel s.v. *constituere*, sense e), preparing for the metaphorical *possessio* below; *Stoicus* and *ueteris Academiae* are not intended to function as complements to *sapiens*, but are attributes of it (here and below Cicero speaks in terms of two different sages, not of one conceived in different ways). For a different, earlier use of the legal metaphor (*possessio*), relating to the dispute between Zeno and the Old Academy over the highest good, cf. *Leg.* 1.55 (with Dyck 2004: 216 ad loc.). Elsewhere in *Luc.* the Stoic/dogmatist and the Academic/sceptical sage are compared; cf. e.g. §§65–7. *Sapiens ueteris Academiae* is resumed by *Polemonius sapiens* below.

Nam omnis ratio uitae...de omni uitae ratione dissident: see the general note above for the idea that moral theories are individuated by the τέλος posited. Cf. also *Fin.* 5.14 (immediately before the *Carneadea diuisio* is introduced), 3.41; and Aug., *C.D.* 19.1 (citing the same point from Varro's *De philosophia*).

Non potest igitur uterque esse sapiens...Academicos Peripateticosque dicenda: if the sage on the Old Academic construal justifiedly assents to his end, the Stoic sage will be in error, and vice versa. However, both sides, Lucullus and Cicero, are in agreement that the sage must never assent to a falsehood.

There is no evidence that the historical Polemo formulated his moral theory with reference to a conception like the sage. Lucullus' speech in *Luc.* states explicitly that the reference of the exposition is usually the sage (e.g. §57), but while he is not mentioned in *Ac.* 1.19–23, Piso makes occasional reference to him in *Fin.* 5 (e.g. 5.32, 66). Cicero thus arguably had licence to proceed as he does here, even though to speak of a *Polemonius sapiens* is tendentious. It is impossible to establish to what extent Antiochus took himself to be placing a slightly anachronistic interpretation on the Old Academic evidence available to him.

For the view that the sage does not opine, agreed between Lucullus/the Stoics and Cicero/Clitomachean Academics, see *Luc.* 65–7, 77. *Veteres Academicos Peripateticosque* spells out *ueteris Academiae* above. The emendation *uos quidem* in V gives good sense while remaining close to the paradosis; a question beginning with *num quidem*, inviting the answer 'no', would not fit. Reid[1] (p. 333) prints *namque idem*, where *idem* seems superfluous.

Hic igitur neutri assentiens, si numquam uter ⟨sit sapiens apparebit, nonne utroque⟩ est prudentior: the transmitted text is *hic igitur neutri assentiens si numquam uter est prudentior*. The sequence of words as a whole does not construe. *Hic* could mean 'here' or be the demonstrative pronoun. *Vter est prudentior* may seem sound by itself but does not fit with what precedes: a finite verb earlier in the sentence would be required, to name but one issue. *Si numquam* may suggest that a verb is to be supplied mentally, but if so, the verb would not likely be a part of *assentiri* since this would involve a shift between two different uses and senses of the verb (*assentiri alicui* 'to agree with someone' vs *assentiri alicui rei* or *assentiri* used absolutely meaning 'to assent'). *Assentiens* may be a corruption of *assentietur*, e.g. by perseveration from above, but emending it to *assentietur* can at best be part of a solution.

Editors have printed quite different texts: *hic igitur neutri assentiens, si numquam uter ⟨sit sapiens apparebit, nonne utroque⟩ est prudentior* (Lambinus); *hic igitur neutri assentiens multo quam uester est prudentior* (Christ); *hic igitur neutri assentietur? Sin, inquam, uter est prudentior?* (Reid cited by Halm in his app.); *hic igitur neutri assentiens tu effigies turpitudinem; ego si numquam* (sc. *assentior*), *uter est prudentior?* (Plasberg[1] in his app. crit.; he prints the transmitted text with a crux/asterisk after *assentiens*). Schäublin et al. set the whole line in cruces and posits a lacuna after *uter*. Reid[1] (p. 334) regards *uter est prudentior* as certainly correct, while Plasberg[1] (p. 145) holds that the *prudentia* of a third party which is invited to make a choice is at issue, not of the Stoic or Polemonian sage or their followers. He also holds that *hic* and *numquam* correlate as 'now' and 'never'.

Of these points, I take Plasberg's first one to be correct. Like him and like Lambinus, I think that a third party, expected to make a choice, is introduced here, that it is cast as refusing (or unable) to choose, and that it is therefore deemed to be prudent. Cicero is here talking about the tensions within Antiochus' Old Academy, which is, thanks to the mutual incompatibility of the *fines* involved, prised apart if either the Polemonian or the Stoic end is endorsed. Hence it ought to be in Lucullus' interest that the person invited to choose refrains from endorsing either, behaving like an Academic in the process. *Hic igitur neutri* strongly suggests that, after the Polemonian and the Stoic sage, a third figure is introduced, who agrees with neither (*assent-* neutri*). At the end of the sentence, the idea can only be that this third figure is *prudentior* than either of the two sages who featured just before. The connection between both ideas is provided by the notion of a failure to err: that is what his superior *prudentia* consists in. The question at the end cannot be which of the two is *prudentior*, since the relative *prudentia* of *Polemonius sapiens* and *Stoicus sapiens* is not at issue, and comparing the third figure introduced by *Hic igitur...* with one of the two is futile. Lambinus' solution is capable of reflecting all these considerations while explaining what is transmitted plausibly as the result of a *saut du même au même*. Other reconstructions, equivalent in sense, are conceivable (*Hic igitur ⟨qui⟩ neutri assentietur, ⟨non peccabit⟩. Si ⟨non⟩* (sc. *peccat*), *inquam, ⟨nonne⟩ utroque est prudentior?*), but they require an unlikely process of corruption.

§133

Quid? Cum ipse Antiochus...probanda esse sapienti: the indignant (or baffled) question *quid?* functions as a structuring device, introducing the next point (cf. §106 init.). Cicero now asks if Antiochus' disagreements with the Stoics, even on comparatively minor issues, do not wreak havoc on his precarious construct of an Old Academy, in that they introduce disagreements on the level of description of the sage.

Reid[1] (p. 334) observes that *iudicare* is often used of people who make admissions to their own detriment; cf. *Quinct.* 31; *Tusc.* 5.61. *Probare* means generically 'to endorse' and here refers to the dogmatic assent Antiochus envisages (contrast *Luc.* 104).

Placet Stoicis omnia peccata esse paria...uehementissime displicet: for the Stoic doctrine, grounded in the view that any transgression arises from an act of assent which should not have been given, and thus introduces a false belief in the subject's mind, see D.L. 7.120 (= *SVF* i.224), where Diogenes also mentions two Stoics, one of them a pupil of Antipater, who disagreed with the view; Sextus, *M.* 7.422; Cic., *Mur.* 61 and *Parad.* 20–6; Hor., *S.* 1.3.76–124, esp. 96 (all also under *SVF* i.224); Cic., *Fin.* 3.32, 3.48, 3.69. Objections to the view are given in *Fin.* 4.74–7 and *Mur.* 60–6; the former passage in particular may be informed by what Cicero knew about Antiochus' views. See also *Ac.* 1.42 *fin.* for a list of epistemic failures which are assent-related.

Liceat tandem mihi considerare...aliquando quidlibet: *tandem* cannot be concluding, but is assertive ('really; after all'; *OLD* s.v. no. 1). On the colloquial *praecide* ('cut it short'), see Reid[1] (p. 334), who cites Cic., *Att.* 8.4.2 (= SB 156).

For the device of introducing the opponent in direct speech, cf. e.g. §101. Not naming him, i.e. not specifying a subject, and referring to him in the third-person singular sounds slightly contemptuous; cf. §79: *Veraces suos esse sense dicit*, with Reid[1] (p. 270).

Quid...quod mihi tecum est dogma commune: Cicero now drives home his point: he professes that the Stoic and the Antiochian view on the relative weight of all sins are equally well supported. Should he thus not exercise caution for fear of falling into error? Then he cites Lucullus' view that one must not abandon a dogma (cf. §27), as well as identifies the shared dogma that the sage should not assent to the incognitive (see §66). This tenet is of course only a dogma in the technical sense, i.e. the result of dogmatic assent, for Lucullus; in §§109 *fin.*–110 Cicero claims *decreta* for the Academic sage (which, however, do not arise from dogmatic assent).

My text at the beginning of the section is that of Plasberg[1] (p. 146), with different punctuation and spelling; see his note. Reid[1] (p. 334) prints *quid quod quae dicuntur* ('What of the fact that...'), which cannot be dismissed. The phrase *in utramque partem* is best taken with *dicuntur*; it looks slightly stranded because *quae dicuntur* is pulled forward for emphasis. The two views at issue form a contradictory pair, so Cicero is thinking of the arguments in support of each pole.

I use the Latin spelling *dogma* not because of the manuscript evidence (which does not help), but because the context does not call for a marked code-switch (unlike §27; cf. also §106).

§134

Ecce multo maior etiam dissensio...sed non beatissimam: Cicero proceeds to a more significant disagreement between Antiochus and the Stoics: both regard virtue as necessary and sufficient for the happy life, but Antiochus holds that this state can be enhanced to the 'happiest life' by the presence of bodily and external goods; see the general note on §§129–41 above for further evidence for the Antiochian view and its justification. On *etiam* for 'yes' in Latin, see Dickey (2015: 119).

Deus ille...partim etiam necessaria: the contrast *deus...homuncio* is found as early as Ter., *Eun.* 590–1; cf. Cic., *N.D.* 3.76. *Deus* is used of a philosopher (Plato) by Cicero in *N.D.* 2.32. The phrase *deus ille* of human beings occurs in various prominent contexts, e.g. Lucr. 5.8; Verg., *E.* 5.64; *A.* 5.391, as well as in various later passages alluding to one of these texts. See also the note in Santorelli (2013: 163–4) on Iuv. 5.132–3.

The *homuncio*'s (i.e. Antiochus') position is formulated in a way which hints at its (perceived) incoherence: that the goods which account for the difference between the happy and the happiest life should be *necessaria* (sc. *ad uitam beatissimam*) undermines the claim that virtue should be necessary and sufficient for happiness.

Sed ⟨et⟩ ille uereor...si sapiens sit: I follow Plasberg[1] (p. 146) in adding *et* between *sed* and *ille*, and then setting only a comma before *et hic metuo...* below. Having expressed admiration for Zeno's view, Cicero now observes that it places exceedingly strenuous demands on human beings. To illustrate this, he cites Theophrastus (= frg. 492 FHS&G), who went so far as to claim that virtue is not sufficient for happiness (a move condemned by Varro in *Ac.* 1.33, 35; cf. the doubts expressed over the sufficiency of virtue for happiness in *Fin.* 5.24–5, 5.77, 5.85–6; *Tusc.* 5.24–5). This then allows him to shift the gaze back to Antiochus, who implausibly claimed that the sage could be happy while being positively afflicted by *mala* of the body as well as external ones. Reid[1] (p. 335) rightly glosses *qui in his omnibus sit* as 'who is surrounded by these, and no others', comparing Hor., *Ep.* 1.5.2: *holus omne prandere*.

Distrahor...Verum in his discrepant: with *distrahor* as a first-person report on being in (at least) two minds, cf. Sen., *Dial.* 7.19.3. With *iacere* 'to lie defeated, collapsed', cf. *Luc.* 79: *iaceat ista causa*. Cicero does not elaborate why virtue falls if neither Zeno nor Antiochus is right. Both views at issue assume that virtue is necessary and sufficient for happiness, unlike Theophrastus'. Views like Aristo's (see on §129) are not under consideration here and on that count alone do not present a third option, but Cicero may also be thinking that Aristo's view does not deliver an adequate account of virtuous action, even though it makes virtue the sole good; see Ioppolo (2012). A complex end which involves virtue on the one hand and pleasure or freedom from pain on the other would presumably be deemed reducible to hedonism. With *tum hoc...tum illud*, cf. §121: *modo hoc modo illud* (and *Att.* 13.25.3 = SB 333: *O Academiam uolaticam*). On *uerum...discrepant*, Reid[1] (p. 335) refers to *ergo haec animorum* in *Ac.* 1.21, which similarly marks section ending.

§135

Quid? Illa, in quibus consentiunt...numquam dolere: from points of disagreement between the Stoics and Antiochus Cicero moves to issues which are agreed but on his view anything but persuasive. Interrogative *quid*, as in §133 *init.*, is used to signal bafflement as well as a new point. The position of *num* late in the sentence (see Reid[1] p. 335) allows Cicero to put the new topic at the head. The qualification of *probare* by *pro ueris* suggests that endorsement of any kind or indeed dogmatic endorsement are meant; Clitomachean approval (§104) would not satisfy the opponent, but might be invoked in an a fortiori consideration.

For the four elementary types of emotion (ἐπιθυμία, ἡδονή, φόβος, λύπη), cf. D.L. 7.110 (= Hecaton frg. 9 Gomoll), rendered in Cic., *Tusc.* 4.11–13 as *laetitia gestiens* or *nimia, libido, aegritudo,* and *metus*; cf. Verg., *A.* 6.733; Hor., *Ep.* 1.6.12. In our passage Cicero has opted for *cupiditas* over *libido*. *Ecferri* seems intended to capture that a passion is literally a motion of the soul.

Having introduced as incapable of commanding approval the notion that *cupiditas* and *laetitia* will not move the sage, Cicero concedes rhetorically that it might be persuasive, only to continue that this is most definitely not true of the corresponding negative passions, which cannot but affect human beings.

Sapiensne non timeat…uenisse doleat: the sage's lack of emotion is introduced as an instance of agreement between Antiochus and the Stoics on what is unpersuasive: an implausible position in itself, it has a degree of justification in Stoic thought, where nothing but virtue is a good, but is less justifiable in the context of Antiochus' theory, where goods other than virtue are recognized, and where consequently future evils should give rise to fear, and past evils to pain or sorrow. Further, Cicero feels that Antiochus' historical claims are particularly dubious in this area, and cites a doctrine of 'mean states' (*mediocritates*; see below) approved by the Old Academics, as well as the Old Academic Crantor's famous consolation against grief as evidence. He also refers to a view of the Old Academics that emotions serve a positive benefit, with e.g. fear making us circumspect, and anger brave.

There is no non-Ciceronian evidence that Antiochus agreed with the Stoics on the ἀπάθεια of the sage, but given that—on the evidence of Lucullus' speech—Antiochus appears fully committed to Stoic moral psychology, there is no reason to doubt Cicero here. In *Ac.* 1.38b–39 Varro, in discussing Zeno's modifications to Old Academic teaching in the field of ethics, mentions that Zeno held that the sage should be free of passions altogether, and gives a brief account of the Stoic view of emotion: earlier philosophers (here called *superiores,* not *ueteres*; see ad loc.) held that the soul had parts and that the passions were to be ascribed to the non-rational part of the soul. By contrast, Zeno held that the soul had one part only, namely reason, i.e. the ruling part (τὸ ἡγεμονικόν), and that passions were due to assent given to impressions which categorised things as truly bad when they were in fact indifferent. The resulting false beliefs gave rise to (or were identical with) what is commonly called the passions; see esp. *Tusc.* 3.24–5 and 4.22. Passions thus conceived are voluntary because they arise from acts of assent, and assent is in our power (see *Luc.* 37–9). Varro does not state explicitly that Antiochus accepted Zeno's modification, but it is very likely that he did; contra Karamanolis (2006: 78–9). Brittain (2006: 79 n. 218) notes on *Luc.* 135: 'In *Fin.* 5.32 he [i.e. Antiochus] allows that the sage is moved by grievous circumstances, but *Fin.* 5.95 suggests that this is not a full-blown emotion.' The Stoic view is also spelt out in *Fin.* 3.35 and defended in *Tusc.* 3–4.

See the texts collected as *SVF* i.205–15, iii.377–490; no. 65 in Long and Sedley (1987). Important studies include Frede (1986); Striker (1996d: 270–80); Brennan (1998a); Cooper (2005); Graver (2007).

Reid[1] (p. 336) gives some parallels for short rhetorical questions followed by answers supplied by the speaker, but none of them is precisely equivalent (the question here is incredulous, not a response to an injunction).

Cicero here directly responds to Stoic assertions; cf. Plut., *Stoicos absurdiora poetis dicere* 1057d: ἄφοβος δὲ μένει καὶ ἄλυπος καὶ ἀήττητος καὶ ἀβίαστος, τιτρωσκόμενος ἀλγῶν στρεβλούμενος, ἐν κατασκαφαῖς πατρίδος ἐν πάθεσιν οἰκείοις, '[Subject: The Stoics' Lapithes]...remains without fear, without regret, invincible when tortured, feeling pain, tormented, when his city's walls are undermined, when suffering befalls his house'; Sen., *Ep. mor.* 74.31 and 85.29 (with Inwood 2007: 234). The issue of course has resonance for the interlocutors as well as for Antiochus.

With *durum sed*...Reid[1] (p. 336) compares *Tusc.* 1.107: *durum hoc sane*. Nisbet and Hubbard (1970: 288) list Greek poetic parallels for the figure of thought in Hor., *C.* 1.24.19: *durum sed leuius fit patientia*.

The subjunctive in *metuat* and *doleat* is due to their being dependent on *necesse est*. For Antiochus' acceptance of the Peripatetic *tria bona* scheme, see the commentary on *Ac.* 1.19–23.

Sed quaero quando...uolebant esse quendam modum: the *ut*-clause is explanatory of *ista*. Old Academics are, as Cicero says, not on record for denying that the sage feels fear with respect to imminent evil or pain with respect to past or present evil. Nor do they use the conception and presentational device of the sage.

The transmitted *dunttia* has been plausibly emended to *duritia* by Glucker (1978a). In minuscule script *ri* can easily be mistaken for *n*. The emendation requires the further change of *fuerint* to *fuerit*; *fuerint* would be assumed to have arisen if not mechanically then from the mistaken notion that *dunttia* is a plural term. However, *Academia uetere* cannot be a bare ablative, *pace* Plasberg[1] (p. 147), who takes it to be temporal. The readings *decreta* and *dicta* (with *fuerint* earlier, and *in* or *ab* if *dicta* is read, or *in* if *decreta* is read) are not impossible; both are instances of Carolingian emendation (probably of V[2] in the case of *dicta*). The theme of harshness occurs earlier in the paragraph (*durum*) as well as in §136 *init.* (*atrocitas*). This does not secure the reading *duritia*, though, since Cicero may have opted for *uariatio*. What does support *duritia* is the verb of saying (*negarent*) in the *ut*-clause, which is better motivated if its logical antecedent does not itself denote a pronouncement, as both *dicta* and *decreta* do. Schäublin et al. print *Academiae ueteri inculcata* for *Academia uetere dunttia*, retaining *fuerint*.

The term *mediocritates* can either refer to the Aristotelian doctrine of the mean (cf. Cic., *Off.* 1.89, 130, 2.59–60) or to a doctrine of μετριοπάθεια, which Cicero associates with Peripatetics (e.g. *Tusc.* 3.22) and Old Academics, without it becoming quite clear if and how he takes the conceptions of the two schools to differ. The Peripatetic doctrine of μετριοπάθεια probably first appeared in the *Magna Moralia* (see Inwood 2014a: 26). However, despite Piso's stressing of the Peripatetic credentials of his Antiochian speech in *Fin.* 5, *mediocritates* do not feature there (see *Fin.* 5.31 and 5.53, though), or in Varro's summary of Old Academic ethics in *Ac.* 1.19–23. This raises the question of whether μετριοπάθεια was, however credited, part of Antiochus' construction of the Old Academy—it seems more likely that Cicero's familiarity with the concept comes from a tradition separate from Antiochus.

Μετριοπάθεια is, by Cicero as well as others, associated with Crantor (mentioned just below). See [Plut.], *Cons.* 102c–d = Crantor frg. 3a Mette; cf. Cic., *Tusc.* 3.12. See Bett (2000a: 90); Knuuttila (2006: 88–9); Gill (2012: 42–3); Bonazzi (2012: 328–9), who thinks the passage constitutes evidence that Antiochus tried to reconcile Stoic ἀπάθεια and Old Academic μετριοπάθεια. For the term *mediocritates*, cf. also *Tusc.* 3.11, 74. Dillon (2003: 227 n. 123) states: 'The actual term *metriopatheia*, as opposed to *apatheia*, is not attested before Philo of Alexandria (whose reflections on Abraham's moderated grief at the loss of Sarah at *Abr.* 255–7 may well owe something to Crantor's work), but we cannot be sure that it does not go back to the earliest phase of Academic opposition to Stoic *apatheia*', which is predicated on the correspondence between the Greek term and Cicero's *mediocritates* being not certain. The plural is functional in that it relates to a multitude of states. Schäublin et al. (p. 302 n. 442) seem to think that a more general attitude of moderation is meant rather than a particular doctrine. *Permotio* is synonymous with *commotio animi* in *Tusc.* 4.61.

Legimus omnes Crantoris...ad uerbum ediscendus libellus: Crantor is cited as an instance that the Old Academy recognized emotions as natural provided they stayed within limits (the *mediocritates* just referred to). This fact is presented as widely familiar (*legimus omnes*). It is not entirely clear if Crantor is also meant to serve as an instance of the point introduced just below from *Atque illi quidem*, given the shift to a plural subject and the expansion beyond the emotion of grief. Cf. *Tusc.* 4.38–47 on the views of the opponents of the Stoic view that the best life is without emotion (argued for in 4.34–8), with the Peripatetics featuring in 4.38–42 and the Old Academics 4.43–7; see the commentary by Graver (2002: 163–7).

On Crantor, cf. also Cic., *Tusc.* 1.115, 3.12; Mette (1984: 8–40). His Περὶ πένθους (= *de luctu* here), a short treatise or epistle (it was reported to have been dedicated to a Hippocles on the occasion of the death of his sons; cf. [Plut.], *Cons.* 114c–e = Crantor frg. 6a Mette), is likely to have informed (Plin., *N.H.* praef.22) the consolation Cicero composed after the death of his daughter Tullia (*Att.* 12.14.3 = SB 251). Some of the content of Crantor's work can be reconstructed from the correspondences between Cicero's *Tusc.* 3–4 and the work named by [Plut.]; see the texts assembled in Mette (1984: 32–6). On Crantor, see also Krämer (1983: 113–29); Dorandi (1994b); on his contribution to the consolatory tradition, Johann (1968: passim); Graver (2002: 187–94); Tulli (2005).

While Crantor's *On Grief* was an important text for Cicero personally, outside of contexts in which the debate between the Academy and the Stoa/Old Academy was at issue, there is no evidence for a Carneadean, Clitomachean, or Philonian interest in him. Cicero may well have supplemented whatever source material informed his speech with a well-taken point of his own.

Crantoris, sc. *librum* (cf. *Ac.* 1.13 *contra Philonis*, which, however, seems a reference to claims or views rather than a work). Reid[1] (p. 336) notes the double diminutive *aureolus...libellus* and calls it colloquial, but it is better characterized as emotive; see Chahoud (2010: 62–4). In §118 Cicero speaks of Aristotle's *flumen aureum*, meaning the stylistic brilliance of the dialogues; if a judgement on style is not intended here as well (thus Krämer 1971: 36 n. 146), then the suggestion is that Crantor's work, while small in scale, is valuable. With the reference to Panaetius' advice, cf. Cic., *Fin.* 4.23, about a work of his dedicated to Tubero on the endurance of pain; *Off.* 3.63 on Hecato dedicating a work to Tubero.

Atque illi quidem etiam…recte secusne, alias uiderimus: the notion that emotions are associated with virtues or can enable virtuous behaviour is part of the Roman martial tradition (ambiguously reflected e.g. in Verg., *A.* 12.107–8, where Servius takes *saeuus* to mean *fortis*; cf. Wright 1997: 178), as well as has a philosophical history and context.

See the previous n. on the shift to *illi* as subject. Cicero may be thinking of the Old Academics generally, or of the Peripatetics (cf. the *illi* referred to in connection with *mediocritates* above). The latter reading gains support from the apparent reference (*recte secusne alias uiderimus*) to *Tusc.* 4.43 (the choice expression *fortitudinis…cotem* provides the specific link, as does *utiliter a natura…datas*; for the latter see also 4.79): *Quid, quod idem Peripatetici perturbationes istas, quas nos extirpandas putamus, non modo naturales esse dicunt, sed etiam utiliter a natura datas? Quorum est talis oratio: primum multis uerbis iracundiam laudant, cotem fortitudinis esse dicunt, multoque et in hostem et in improbum ciuem uehementioris iratorum impetus esse, leuis autem ratiunculas eorum, qui itam cogitarent: 'proelium rectum est hoc fieri, conuenit dimicare pro legibus, pro libertate, pro patria'; haec nullam habent uim, nisi ira excanduit fortitudo.* The specificity of these correspondences suggests that *Tusc.* was in a stage of advanced planning when Cicero wrote *Luc.* (the former is generally deemed to have been composed between July and August 45 BC; see e.g. Graver 2002: xiv–xv), after Cicero had completed work not just on the first but also on the final edition of *Acad.* It is unlikely that Cicero went back to the first edition and inserted a forward reference once he had composed *Tusc.*

The Peripatetics are also said to have ascribed an indispensable role to emotions by Philodemus, *De ira* (= Arist. frg. 95 Bonitz = Volum. Herculan. P. I Oxon. 1824 f. 64 = Coll. alt. t. I Neap. 1861 f. 54 = Indelli 1988: 88), cited already by Reid[1] (p. 337): ἔνιοι γοῦν τῶν Περιπατητικῶν…διὰ προσώπων ἐκτέμνειν τὰ νεῦρα τῆς ψυχῆς φασι τοὺς τὴν ὀργὴν καὶ τὸν θυμὸν αὐτῆς ἐξαιροῦντας, 'Some Peripatetics say…that those who want to remove anger and spirit from the soul cut out its sinews', with Flashar et al. (2006: 208). Philodemus is critical of this supposed Peripatetic view; see Tsouna (2011: 185–6).

For the metaphorical uses of *cos* (cf. Greek κῶνος), see *TLL* s.v. col. 1083.10–25. The metaphor is fully brought out by Flor., *Epit.* 1.19.3: *quasi cote quadam…ferrum suae uirtutis acuebat.* Seneca (*De ira* 1.9.2, 1.17.1, 3.3.1) ascribes very similar statements to Aristotle, but Graver (2002: 166) on *Tusc.* 4.43 suggests that the phrase *cos fortitudinis* (or its Greek counterpart) is Crantor's, apparently on the basis of *Luc.* 135. Given the change of subject here to *illi*, that seems unlikely, unlike the suggestion was that Crantor cited the Peripatetics (with approval?), summing up their view as 'anger is the whetstone of courage'.

§136

Atrocitas quidem ista…nescio: this is the concluding sentence to the point made in §135. *Ista tua* is addressed to Lucullus in the first instance. One may think that the harsh tone would be more suitable if used by Philo against his renegade pupil Antiochus, but it is most unlikely that Cicero is following one Philonian source in his speech, and §135 just above seemed to be supplied from Cicero's own resources; see section 9.3 on sources. *Atrocitas*, while hyperbolic and pejorative, is not one of the standard terms Cicero uses to dismiss positions as implausible (cf. e.g. §121: *somnia*, §123: *portenta*); rather, it aims at the harshness of the Stoic/Antiochian attitude to emotions (cf. §135: *durum*), which according to Cicero had no place in Old Academic thought (and was inserted violently into it; cf. *irruperit* 'broke in').

Illa uero ferre non possum...hos enim quasi eosdem esse uultis: the text from here to *essent sapientium* below is *SVF* iii.599. Cicero now turns to the so-called Stoic paradoxes, to which he sees Antiochus committed; while these are admirable up to a point (cf. *Parad.* 4 quoted below), especially so because they are traceable to Socrates, there is no evidence that Xenocrates or Aristotle even touched on the views in question (let alone endorsed them). In this way he continues the argument for the synthetic nature of Antiochus' Old Academy. The sentence is somewhat out of balance in the way in which it introduces the topic, referred to proleptically through *ista*, in a parenthesis.

The paradoxes spell out implications of Stoic moral theory for sages, non-sages, or both. Thus they are paradoxes in the sense that commonly held views (δόξαι) are at variance with them (cf. *Parad.* 4: *admirabilia contraque opinionem omnium*); such δόξαι will also be opinions in the technical Stoic sense, i.e. beliefs resulting from assent to non-cataleptic impressions (cf. *Ac.* 1.41 *fin.*). For the Stoics the supposed paradoxes are 'simply true' (Annas cited by Inwood 2005a: 74 n. 40). However, the Stoics held at the same time that these claims, which initially appeared as paradoxical, were in agreement with the preconceptions human beings acquire naturally, provided these preconceptions were properly articulated and understood; this is the serious philosophical concern underlying Cicero's *Parad.* (see Mehl 2002 on this point). The evidence suggests that the Stoics themselves used the term παράδοξα from very early on; see *Gnomologion Monac.* 196 (= *SVF* i.281) on Zeno; Epict., *Diss.* 4.1.173 (= *SVF* i.619) on Cleanthes; cf. again *Parad.* 4.

No complete collection of them is extant. The three sets of paradoxes Cicero introduces here §136 overlap only partially with those treated in his own *Paradoxa Stoicorum* (§§6–15: 'only virtue is the good'; §§16–19: 'The virtuous person has everything needed for a happy life'; §§20–6: 'all transgressions and all right actions are equivalent'; §§27–32: 'all non-sages are insane'; §§33–41: 'all sages are free, all non-sages slaves'; §§42–52: 'the sage alone is rich'), or else can be paralleled from other Ciceronian and non-Ciceronian texts (see below).

Cicero acknowledges that many of these paradoxes were traced to Socrates (cf. *Parad.* 4, 23; *Tusc.* 3.10), predicated as they are on an intellectualist view of virtue; see also Gourinat (2016). Vogt (2008: 129) observes: 'Claims of the form "Only the sage is an X" do not add to our picture of the sage by telling us that he is, in addition to being all-knowing, virtuous, and wise, also an X. Rather, these claims become understandable and interesting elements of the Stoic theory only if we see that the explanatory direction is the other way around: *A thesis of the form "Only the sage is X" redefines X as involving wisdom (or knowledge, or virtue).*' See also Brown (2006).

Cf. the expression in §114: *illud ferre non possum*. *Hos* is best taken to refer to Aristotle and Xenocrates, and not the Stoics as well (even though Antiochus took all of them to be in substantial agreement), but to refer to the same set of individuals by *hos* and *illi* in subsequent sentences is unusual.

Reid[1] (p. 337) comments: 'A curious admission that Xenocrates was not a close follower of Socrates', referring to *Ac.* 1.17 and *Luc.* 143. But here Cicero the Clitomachean is speaking, who acknowledged Socrates' role both as an ancestor for Academic scepticism via Arcesilaus and as an influence on Stoicism, while the Old Academics played, for all we know, no prominent role in the sceptical Academy's construction of the history of philosophy. What is more striking is that Xenocrates is here mentioned at all, given that Old Academic ethics is construed by Antiochus with reference to Polemo in particular (see on *Ac.* 1.19–23). It may be the relative affinity between Polemo's and Zeno's ethical thinking which made Xenocrates a rhetorically more effective example here: he can more plausibly be assumed to have said no such thing. Passages in which an *Antiochian* perspective on Xenocrates is given seem of no help in illuminating the present passage; cf. e.g. *Fin.* 4.15–18, with Dillon (2003: 137–8); on Antiochus' construction of Xenocrates, see also Sedley (2012: 96–8); Inwood (2012: 205–6), as well as section 7.2.

Illi umquam dicerent sapientes…quemquam nisi sapientem: as is explained in Cic., *Fin.* 3.75–6 (cf. *Parad.* 42–52), the sage alone is a king, since he rules himself through reason (unlike Tarquinius, who ruled neither himself—for he gave in to his vices—nor his people). The sage alone is beautiful because beauty can only reside in the fully rational soul. Everything is his property since only he knows how to make use of things. Cicero ends with Romanized positions of authority, supposedly the sole preserve of the sage, but mocks the view by adding the role of the *quinqueuir* (in charge of policing and fire services at night; cf. D. 1.2.2.31), which likewise only the sage can fill properly.

Dicerent is genuinely counterfactual; Cicero suppresses a protasis along the lines of 'if they were here'. For the primary parallels relevant to this paragraph, see also Brittain (2006: 80 n. 220).

Postremo solum ciuem…furiosos: cf. Stob., *Ecl.* II.7, p. 103.9–23 Wachsmuth (= *SVF* iii.328): Λέγουσι δὲ καὶ φυγάδα πάντα φαῦλον εἶναι, καθ' ὅσον στέρεται νόμου καὶ πολιτείας κατὰ φύσιν ἐπιβαλλούσης. Τὸν γὰρ νόμον εἶναι…σπουδαῖον, ὁμοίως δὲ καὶ τὴν πόλιν. Ἱκανῶς δὲ καὶ Κλεάνθης περὶ τὸ σπουδαῖον εἶναι τὴν πόλιν λόγον ἠρώτησε τοιοῦτον· Πόλις μὲν ⟨εἰ⟩ ἔστιν οἰκητήριον κατασκεύασμα, εἰς ὃ καταφεύγοντας ἔστι δίκην δοῦναι καὶ λαβεῖν, οὐκ ἀστεῖον δὴ πόλις ἐστίν· ἀλλὰ μὴν τοιοῦτόν ἐστιν ἡ πόλις οἰκητήριον· ἀστεῖον ἄρ' ἔστιν ἡ πόλις, 'They maintain that every foolish man is an exile, in that he does not have the law and the city according to nature. For the law is…good, and so is the state. About the thesis that the state is good Cleanthes posed this question quite appropriately: if the state were an agglomeration of buildings in which one can find refuge, submit to and seek justice, would it not be good? But the state is just that, and therefore it is good.'

On the kinds of communities discussed by the Stoics, notably the one in which the paradoxes are obviously true, see Vogt (2008: 65–110).

Denique scripta Lycurgi...nisi quae essent sapientium: Plasberg[1] (p. 136) punctuates so as to make *denique* go with *furiosos*, but the inconsistency of having subsequent steps in an argument or enumeration by *postremo* and *denique* is not unparalleled, and as Reid[1] (p. 338) notes, *denique* may be emphatic rather than concluding.

For the notion that only sages can follow the (real) law, see Cic., *Rep.* 3.27 Powell (= 4.33). The definition of *ciuitas* presupposed is given by Dio Chrys., *Or.* 36.20 (= *SVF* iii.329): τὴν πόλιν φασὶν εἶναι πλῆθος ἀνθρώπων ἐν ταὐτῷ κατοικούντων ὑπὸ νόμου διοικούμενον, 'They call a state a large number of people who live together and who are subject to law'; cf. Cic., *Parad.* 27.

In *Leg.* 2.59 Cicero states that he had to memorise the law of Twelve Tables as a schoolboy *ut carmen necessarium*, but this was no longer the practice now (i.e. at the dramatic date of the dialogue). On its status as a cultural monument, see the collection of passages in Wieacker (1988: 299 n. 70). For the sense of *scriptum*, see *OLD* s.v. no. 2c; emendation to *praescripta*, entertained by Reid[1] (p. 338), is unnecessary.

§137

Haec tibi, Luculle,...bono modo, tantum quantum uidebitur: with *tam...moenia*, cf. §§8 and 119 where Cicero also mentions the inflexible commitments Lucullus has entered into in virtue of the Stoic element in Antiochian thought. For the expression *bono modo* ('with moderation'), 'conversational' in stylistic level, cf. e.g. *Att.* 13.23.3 (= SB 331) with the note by Shackleton Bailey (1966: 378). The phrase may be intended to convey the notion that Academic restraint is in keeping with the Roman way; see on *Luc.* 146.

Legi apud Clitomachum...Stoico non uideris: for the overall import of the anecdote, see also the general note above. Reid[1] (p. 339) quotes Quint. 12.2.24, which fits with the question directed at Carneades (but not with Carneades' answer) and supports his deletion: *Pyrrhon quidem quas in hoc opere* (the training of the orator) *partes habere potest, cui iudices esse, apud quos uerba faciat, et reum pro quo loquatur, et senatum in quo sit dicenda sententia, non liquebit?* See also Epict., *Diss.* 5.6–7; Eus., *Praep. Ev.* XIV.19.3; Aug., *Contra Acad.* 3.10.22; Brittain (2006: 80 n. 221).

With *legi*, cf. §129: *ut scriptum uideo*. There is no reason to doubt that Cicero read about this episode in a work by Clitomachus, but given what Cicero tells us about the subject and the nature of Clitomachus' works (see on §§99 and 102), it does not seem likely that Cicero is referring to the same work as in §102, *pace* Reid[1] (p. 338). (It is in any event plausible on independent grounds, see section 9.3 on sources, that Cicero uses a number of Academic sources to inform his speech in reply to Lucullus.) See also on §102 for the question of whether the information provided here provides grounds for thinking that Clitomachus accompanied Carneades to Rome during the embassy of 155 BC. Obbink and Vander Waerdt (1991: 390–3) regard it as possible that Cicero is here relying on the work by Clitomachus referenced in §102. They also argue against athetizing *quia sapiens non sum*: 'If Carneades intended to suspend judgement on the external existence of the praetorship and city, why would

Carneades then turn, as he immediately does, to attribute the doctrine to *Diogenes*?' Carneades is no external world sceptic, and the point of the exchange is that, when he is taken to be one (like Pyrrho in Quint. 12.2.24 quoted above is), he does not just demur, but instead invokes unrealistic Stoic claims about the sage. In the background there is of course the allegation that the Academics subvert everyday life (see on §102), as well as the natural affinity the Romans felt to Stoic doctrine, which is often seen to articulate intuitively held moral convictions the Romans had traditionally.

For the anecdote to deliver the desired effect, the praetor's words must be ambiguous between phenomenal and doxastic/epistemic appearing, the former must be intended by him, but Carneades opts for the latter reading, viz. Albinus intends 'praetor that I am, I do not appear to you' (cf. D.L. 7.163, quoted p. 649 n. 386), and Carneades responds to 'I do not appear to you to be praetor'.

Powell (2013) re-examines the evidence on the philosophical embassy of 155 BC and concludes plausibly that Carneades would have failed to honour his political obligations and undermined the purpose of the entire mission if he had delivered speeches for and against justice even while off-duty. This does not mean that Cicero did not draw on Carneadean arguments, relayed most likely by Clitomachus, in *Rep.* 3, but it does suggest that the element of literary fiction in Cicero's reports on the events in 155 BC (to our passage here add *De orat.* 2.157–60; *Tusc.* 4.5) is much larger than is often allowed for; see, however, also Ferrary (1977) and Glucker (2001). In *Att.* 12.23.2 (= SB 262 = *FGrH* 244 T8), dating from early 45 BC, Cicero asked Atticus about the historical circumstances of the embassy (and notes that he obtained the information, now included here, on who the consuls of 155 BC were from Atticus' *Liber Annalis*). Powell (p. 240) aptly comments: 'In other words, when Cicero had written in the *De re publica* about Carneades' visit to Rome, his imagination was uninhibited by any specific knowledge of the actual occasion of the embassy or of the arguments used by the ambassadors. Thus he would not appreciate that, in making Carneades argue both for and against justice in international relations, he was making him undermine his own position as ambassador.'

On Aulus Postumius Albinus (praet. 155 BC; cos. 151 BC; *RE* Postumius no. 31) see Münzer (1953). The negative reports on him in Polyb. 39.12.1–12 are arguably due to bias, given that the historian held him responsible for the extension of his exile by five years (33.1.5). With the characterization here, cf. *Brut.* 81: *et litteratus et disertus*; cf. also *Att.* 13.32.5 (= SB 305). On Publius Cornelius Scipio Nasica Corculum (cos. 162 and 155 BC; *RE* Cornelius no. 353) see Münzer (1901). His speeches were not known directly to Cicero (*Brut.* 79). Plut., *De inimic. util.* 3, quotes him as commenting on the fall of Carthage and the subjugation of Greece that Rome was now entirely safe, since it did not need to feel fear regarding the former nor shame regarding the latter. On Marcus Claudius Marcellus (cos. 166, 155, and 152 BC; *RE* Cornelius no. 225), see Münzer (1899). For Diogenes of Babylon, see on §98.

See Reid[1] (p. 338) on *ad senatum stare* = 'to be in waiting on the senate'; ibid. on the vocative *Carneade* (cf. 89 *Ulixe*).

Aristoteles aut Xenocrates…Stoicus perpauca balbutiens: *sequi uolebat* = 'affected to follow'; see Madvig (1876: 313) on *Fin.* 2.102. *Balbutire* means to speak with a speech impediment (like a stammer or a lisp), suggesting either that when Antiochus does not sound entirely Stoic, it is a matter of delivery rather than substantial disagreement (cf. §132: *germanissimus Stoicus*), or that even his Stoicism is 'put on', i.e. simply taken over (cf. §§69–71); on either reading, this is a moment where the tone is more suggestive of the disappointed scholarch of the Academy than of the respectful pupil Cicero (see section 9.3). With *Aristoteles aut Xenocrates*, cf. §78: *Philoni aut Metrodoro*; Cicero may be implying here that, coming from their somewhat different viewpoints, both would have agreed that Albinus was a praetor etc. *Noster* = 'our friend', as Reid[1] (p. 339) notes contra the emendation *uester* (suggested by Davies). Plasberg[1] (p. 148) suggests that *perpauca* sc. *Academica*; I take *perpauca* to be an internal accusative. On possessive adjectives functioning as head of a noun phrase (*noster*), see Pinkster i.945.

§138

Vos autem mihi uerenti...quid consilii datis: Cicero states again, in words a Stoic could have used, that he is concerned about lapsing into error by assenting to the non-cognitive (cf. §66), sc. concerning the highest good. His question of who to turn to motivates the introduction of Chrysippus. *Mihi* goes with *quid consilii datis*; Reid[1] (p. 339) observes that *uereri alicui* 'to fear for someone' is not Ciceronian. The coupling of *asciscere* and *(com)probare*, also in *Fin.* 1.23 (*sciscat et probet*) and 3.70 (*ascisci aut probari*); the mode of endorsement as issue must be dogmatic assent. For *quid consilii datis*, cf. §25: *quid officii sui sit*.

Testatur saepe Chrysippus...circumcidit et amputat multitudinem: *testatur...posse defendi* is *SVF* iii.21 (which includes §140: *Unum igitur...simulatioque uirtutis* as well). *Testatur* is less specific than §137 *legi* and §129 *ut scriptum uideo*, but this need not mean that Cicero obtained the information in a different way: *testari* may also be intended to bestow authority. Reid[1] (p. 339) notes that *solus* for 'only' is common with numerals in Cicero, and lists parallels for the coupling *circumcidere et amputare*, to which add Colum. 7.5.13 (probably closest to the original application of the coupling). *De* in *de finibus bonorum* is partitive as in *homo de plebe*.

For the mechanism of reduction employed by Chrysippus, see the general note on §§129–41 above; see also Schäublin et al. (p. 303 n. 452). Cicero also uses the set of three in *Cael.* 41 (56 BC), on a rare occasion where philosophical considerations are overtly mentioned in a forensic speech. On §138, see also Lévy (1980: 244–5).

Aut enim honestatem esse finem...utrum⟨que⟩: in §131 these three ends are associated with Zeno, Aristippus or Epicurus, and Callipho, respectively. The characterization of Callipho's view there (*uoluptatem autem et honestatem finem esse Callipho censuit*) secures the emendation to *utrum⟨que⟩* here. On *honestas* (and the more common *honestum*) as a translation for τὸ καλόν, see Dyck (1996: 69); Glucker (2015: 49–52). In other contexts the Stoic end is presented—by non-Stoics—not as the possession of virtue, but as the pursuit of *prima naturae*; see p. 741 above.

One way in which Chrysippus argued for his preferred view is reported in *Fin.* 4.28 (= *SVF* iii.20), where, however, Antiochian influence is likely, since the Stoic view is presented as reducing human beings to their minds. On this passage, see also Ioppolo (2016: 179–80).

Nam qui summum bonum dicant id esse...prima naturae commoda adiungerent: in §131 these views are associated with Hieronymus, Diodorus, and Polemo (i.e. the Old Academy), respectively. It is not stated if *Chrysippus* thought of the Old Academy or the Peripatetics as the proponents of the composite end of virtue and pursuit of the *prima naturae*. On Chrysippus treating pursuit of the *prima naturae*, freedom from pain, and pleasure as relevantly similar, see p. 741 above. For a discussion of the *prima naturae*, see on *Ac.* 1.22; Reid[1] (p. 340) on *id esse si*.

Ita tris relinquit sententias quas putet probabiliter posse defendi: the statement that the three positions which are the outcome of Chrysippus' reductive review can be 'persuasively defended' provides a plausible link to reports that Chrysippus deemed it useful to argue for or against competing views once students had developed a κατάληψις of the correct Stoic view; see above, pp. 553, 742.

§139

Sit sane ita...sensibus nostris blandiatur: *sit sane ita* 'that may be so' signals hesitant approval of the notion that only Chrysippus' three possible views can be persuasively defended (which is not quite the same as conceding the point for the sake of the argument; so Algra 1997: 132). Yet from *quamquam*...Cicero gives a consideration against: the Antiochian position—which is not among Chrysippus' three—nonetheless has a hold on Cicero. Then the pull of pleasure is acknowledged, but virtue calls Cicero back. So Cicero considers if he should take up the intermediate position of Callipho: the *honestum* and pleasure as the composite end. Yet 'reason' opposes, on the grounds that it wants the *honestum* to consist in spurning pleasure.

For *sit sane ita*, cf. *Brut.* 279; and *Leg.* 1.2, where the word order is *sit ita sane* (followed by *uerum* as here); Hofmann and Szantyr (1965: 332). While granting persuasiveness to the other options which follow, Cicero seems to signal relatively stronger attachment to the Antiochian view here through *non facile diuellor* and *nec quicquam habeo adhuc probabilius*. *Diuellere* is not used elsewhere in Cicero for the detachment of a subject from a view. *Adhuc* is purely temporal, as Reid[1] (p. 340) rightly notes.

That the persuasiveness of hedonism is presented as purely non-verbal and non-argumentative is rhetorical stylization. Presumably some contrast is intended, too, with the manner in which virtue 'acts' and pulls Cicero back with her hand below. *Finibus* refers the highest good and the worst evil, as opposed to multiple ends.

Labor eo...hominem iungit deo: cf. §59 *delabi*, §114 *labar*, but in both cases the error of unwarranted assent / opining is meant, whereas here the overall context suggests that Cicero just means the effect of the persuasiveness of the view in question. A collection of passages in which Cicero uses related imagery (slipping, falling) is in Gawlick and Görler (1994: 1109–11). For Aristippus' and Epicurus' view, see §131, where, however, they are said not to be equivalent. A more detailed version of the criticism levelled against hedonism is in *Fin.* 2.39–41. Reid[1] (p. 340) assembles parallels for the metaphor of an abstract entity, or a person in a metaphorical sense, physically restraining someone. For the followers of pleasure as animals, cf. Cic., *Pis.* 37: *Epicure noster, ex hara producte, non ex schola*, with Nisbet (1961: 98) ad loc.; and, most famously, Hor., *Epist.* 1.4.16: *Epicuri de grege porcum*; pleasure as bestial in *Off.* 1.105–6. Davies emended *iungit* to *iungi*.

Possum esse medius ... recta ratio mihi obuersetur: see *OLD* s.v. *medius* no. 8 for the sense ('in the middle between two extremes') at issue here. Elsewhere the fact that humans have a soul and a body is cited in support of Antiochus' position; see *Fin.* 4.17, 25–8, and pp. 141, 212. For Callipho, see §131 above; *ut* before *Calliphontem*, deleted by Lambinus, is resumed because of the length of the sentence. *Quidem* correlates with *sed* below, but the sentence is overlong and out of shape, beginning as it does with an assertion and ending in a question.

Cicero might be deemed to be gesturing here at the inner-Academic debate about whether Carneades suspended judgement unqualifiedly or allowed for qualified assent (see on on §148; Reid[1] p. 340 on *uideretur; cuius quidem sententiam ... Carneadi probaretur* is LS 69L). On that reading, he would be suggesting how the notion that Carneades accepted qualified assent took hold: Carneades could argue for the sake of the argument so powerfully that he appeared to be committed, even to his pupil Clitomachus, who took him to suspend judgement unqualifiedly. However, the parenthesis from *quamquam* discourages such a reading: Clitomachus said he could not tell what Carneades 'approved'. If Carneadean 'approval' is to be regarded as possible in principle by Clitomachus, it must here have the technical sense of §104 (Clitomachus construed Carneades as committed to universal suspension of judgement). Note also that in the *Carneadea diuisio* Carneades is associated with a different, not actually held, position which he defended for the sake of the argument (obtainment of the *prima naturae* as the end; cf. *Luc.* 131; *Fin.* 5.20). Callipho's position was an attractive one to defend for Carneades because it was deemed to be beyond the pale by Chrysippus; cf. also *Off.* 3.119–21.

It is not obvious what *ueritas et grauis et recta ratio* is. *Fin.* 4.55 (and the immediately following point here) suggest that it is an appeal to Lucullus' view and/or Stoic right reason: *Sensus enim cuiusque et natura rerum atque ipsa ueritas clamabat quodam modo non posse adduci, ut inter eas res, quas Zeno exaequaret, nihil interesset.* Cf. also *Luc.* 34: *conuicio ueritatis*. Plasberg[1] (p. 149) prints *seueritas* and *grauitas*, noting that the two nouns are paired elsewhere. For *obuersetur*, see *OLD* s.v. no. 2.

Tune, cum honestas ... tamquam hominem cum belua copulabis: Reid[1] (p. 341) rejects the translation 'consists in' (adopted by Brittain 2006: 81) for *consistat* and suggests 'takes her stand'; cf. *Phil.* 1.18: *Pompeii consulatus ... constitit in legibus*; cf. Schäublin's 'auf ... beruht'.

A similar image, applied to the same view, in *Off.* 3.119: *... si cum honestate uoluptatem tamquam cum homine pecudem copulauissent*, 'if they coupled pleasure with honourableness, as if man with beast.' Callipho's position makes Seneca (*Ep. mor.* 92.9) think of Scylla, a notion encouraged by *belua* here (though not by *pecudem* in *Off.* 3.119). On *tune*, which is frequent in Cicero, see Reid[1] (p. 341).

§140

Vnum igitur par...non magna contentio: *unum igitur...simulatio uirtutis* is the second part of *SVF* iii.21 (§138 above was the first part). *Depugnet* suggests that the earlier options have been eliminated, or rather have eliminated one another by bringing their persuasiveness to bear on the view they are pitted against in the sequence. Cf. *Fin.* 2.44 (= *SVF* iii.22): *totumque discrimen summi boni in earum* [sc. *uirtutis et uoluptatis*] *comparatione positum putat*. See *OLD* s.v. *par*³.

For the phrase *magna contentio*, cf. *Brut.* 313; *Fin.* 3.41. Plasberg suggests in the app. crit. that between *non* and *magna* something like *pauca acute disputata estque inter illas* has dropped out, but it seems that Cicero intends to say that for Chrysippus there is no contest between virtue and pleasure (even though he cites arguments against Chrysippus' view in the second half of the paragraph); thus also Algra (1997: 111). This reading receives support from *quantum ego sentio*, which is not an indication that Cicero has read about this somewhere (contrast e.g. *ut scriptum uideo* in §129), but appears to give his view on what Chrysippus thought in the end. *Chrysippo* is a *datiuus iudicantis*. Schäublin et al. (p. 305 n. 460) is the fullest statement of the case for a lacuna. On *reliquus* vs *relicuus*, see Leumann (1977: 136).

Alteram si sequare...sed fallax imitatio simulatioque uirtutis: Algra (1997: 116) surveys Chrysippean book-titles suggesting anti-hedonistic polemics (see D.L. 7.202). More specifically, cf. Plut., *Sto. rep.* 15, 1040d (= *SVF* iii.157), 'although the rest of Plutarch's chapter indicates that this is a crude summary of his position' (Brittain 2006: 82 n. 225). The Plutarch passage engages with a piece of anti-Platonic polemic advanced by Chrysippus (crisply explored by Irwin 2011: 287 n. 9). Schäublin et al. (p. 305 n. 462) comment on our passage: 'Die Ausdrucksweise "Scheinbild der Tugend" hat einen Platonischen Klang und erinnert an die Unterscheidung zwischen dem, was Tugend selbst wirklich ist, auf der einen Seite, und dem, was Menschen meinen, daß sie sei, auf der anderen Seite.' Michel (1968: 119) holds that Cicero is giving his own views here. Reid[1] (p. 341) notes the attraction in *quae uoluptate* for *quod*.

Audi contra illos...quid in uita sequeretur habiturum: = Epicurus frg. 400 Usener. Cf. *Ac.* 1.7:...*quod bonum quale sit negat omnino Epicurus sine uoluptatibus sensum mouentibus ne suspicari* ⟨*quidem*⟩, and *Fin.* 2.48 (with *populari fama gloriosum* there, cf. *quod gloriosum sit in uolgus* here, a hint at the baseness of Epicurean thought). For pleasure as the ethical criterion (*norma, regula*; κανών) cf. *Fin.* 1.30; D.L. 10.129 = Epic., *Ep. ad Men.* That the source of all goods should reside in the body means no more than that the body needs to be involved for pleasure (however conceived) to be experienced.

With the introduction of the Epicurean view by *audi*, cf. the same device in Sen., *Contr.* 1.7.2: *Audite nouam captiui uocem*....

With the polemical claim made by the Epicureans that they do not even know what *honestas* means (sc. as used by their opponents), compare *Fin.* 1–2, where the Epicureans present themselves as plain speakers who call things by their names (which is one reason why they do not require definitions; see Taylor 2016; Sedley

2019: 108–13), unlike their opponents. Cf. *Fin.* 1.15, 1.61; 2.6–7, 48–9, 75; and *Tusc.* 5.73.

§141

Nihil igitur me putatis...neque me minus hominem quam ⟨te⟩ putaueris: one might wonder why Cicero should assume that Lucullus should think that Cicero was unmoved by what persuasiveness these various positions hold. What Cicero is responding to here is the caricature of his position as negative dogmatism (cf. §§28–9, 101–2, 109b) which assumes as a dogma that nothing can be known; cf. with the present passage §101, of the Academic sage: *non enim est e saxo sculptus aut e robore dolatus, habet corpus habet animum, mouetur mente mouetur sensibus....* Lucullus, in turn, is assumed to be moved by the persuasiveness of the various positions just rehearsed, since §138 *fin.* had ended with Chrysippus' declaration that there are three views which can be persuasively defended; this carries implied criticism, for Lucullus attaches himself unequivocally to the Antiochian view while rejecting all others. For the notion that the same impressions (in type) affect the Academic and the Antiochian, which, however, the latter takes to issue in apprehension while former does not, cf. §66b: *Visa enim ista cum acriter mentem sensumue pepulerunt, accipio, iisque interdum etiam assentior, nec percipio tamen; nihil enim arbitror posse percipi*; §105a. Reid[1] (p. 342) notes the shifts from *audi* to *putatis* to *tu*, with parallels.

Tantum interest...praesertim cum iudicia ista dialecticae nulla sint: Cicero now focuses on the difference between Lucullus and himself: Lucullus assents to certain impressions and fully commits to them, whereas Cicero, even when he assents (which represents a failing on his part qua Clitomachean, cf. §66), does so in the knowledge that true impressions are not marked off from false ones by a difference in look and that he will consequently assent to false impressions on occasion. Cicero and Lucullus are not sages. So when Cicero says that as a result of assenting the opponent will end up with beliefs which he cannot be made to give up by argument (*deque eo nulla ratione...moueri potes*; cf. §145 and *Ac.* 1.41:...*et si ita erat comprehensum ut conuelli ratione non posset, scientiam*), this merely sounds as if the sage's ἐπιστήμη (= *scientia*) is at issue and actually illustrates the dogmatist's stubborn and, from the Academic point of view, irrational commitment (cf. §8 *fin.*), stylistically signalled by the two clusters of near-synonyms. The Academic disputes that any of the properties *certum...fixum* attaches to impressions, including ones which meet the first two clauses of Zeno's definition.

I take *es commotus* to be the sole predicate of the *cum*-clause, and *asciscis...approbas, uerum illud...potes* and *ego nihil...saepe falso* to be syntactically coordinate. *Verum illud* is appropriately rendered 'your "truth"' by Reid[2] (p. 88), and the focalization by the dogmatist is enabled by *uis*; the asyndetic series *certum...fixum* functions as a complement to *uerum illud*. *Fuisse uis* has given rise to emendations, but Plasberg[1] (p. 150) explains it well, as '*nunc ais tum fuisse cum assensus es*'. Cf. §128a, a passage which also functions as a hinge between sections.

With *ratum firmum fixum*, cf. §27: *stabile fixum ratum*, and Diomedes I, p. 377.11–15 K. (= t. 57); with *certum comprehensum perceptum*, cf. §23:...*nihil haberet comprehensi percepti cogniti constituti*. For relevant uses of *certus*, see the survey of *nota*-related terminology in the general note on §§33–34a.

Ἀπαραλλαξία is once more cited as the reason why Cicero refrains from assent, and as elsewhere Cicero chooses a formulation which characterizes it as an objective equivalence between impressions rather than indiscriminability, sc. for the subject: *uera a falsis nullo [insin] discrimine separantur*. The emendation *uisi* for the non-sensical *insin* (Plasberg[1] p. 150) may be correct and would be easily explicable as due to minim confusion; the main argument for deletion is that sense requires a word for 'look' here, which Cicero renders *species* elsewhere (§§99, 111 *fin*.), in which case someone other than Cicero supplied *uisi* which was then corrupted. Yet 'no difference in appearance' would not be impossible.

Assensus sim...assentiar stand in for future perfect / future in a non-dependent clause (see Kühner-Stegmann ii.181–2), but as Schäublin (1993: 162–3) note, one might think that protasis and apodosis refer to simultaneous events or indeed the same event. Cicero seems to be speaking generically of impressions which lack a *nota*; Schäublin et al. suggest that he wrote *cui si ⟨uero semel⟩* to clarify this. Reid[1] (p. 342) observes that *falso* is used as a noun, like *incognito* in §133. For *si* 'even if', see *OLD* s.v. no. 9a.

Iudicia may mean 'criteria' as in §142, i.e. be intended as a recognizable loan translation, or denote more loosely 'judgements', i.e. instances or acts of judgement. See on §§91–7; Schäublin et al. (p. 205 n. 45); Hartung (1970: 39–43).

§§142–47

Having covered disagreements among the dogmatists in the fields of physics (§§118–28) and ethics (§§129–41), Cicero now turns to the field of logic (i.e. λογική, including epistemology and theory of argument).[546] This section is much shorter than the preceding ones.[547] This is partly due to the fact that the central question of epistemology, i.e. whether there are cataleptic impressions, occupies large parts of the first half of Cicero's speech and underpins the physical and ethical sections (see §§116–17, 128); see also §147.

In §142 Cicero introduces four different views of the criterion (*iudicium*), Protagoras', the Cyrenaics', Epicurus', and Plato's. In the first instance, these are just meant to illustrate the range of views which existed (none of which corresponds to Antiochus'), but the paragraph raises further questions: is there any rationale to Cicero's selection, beyond the views in question being at variance with each other, or because they are in some sense significant for the Academic stance? How does Plato's

---

[546] Schäublin et al. (p. lxxxv) divide the section thus: §§142–6 'the Stoicism of Antiochus', §§144–6 'there is no knowledge, only conjecture'. Brittain (2006: lvii) takes §§142–6 to be devoted to disagreements about criteria, §143 to disagreements about conditionals, and §§144–6 to Stoics vs Academics on knowledge (2.144–6).

[547] An important body of related material is Sextus, *M*. 7 and 8, devoted to λογική.

view of the criterion as reported here compare to Varro's account of the Old Academic view prior to Zeno's *correctiones* (*Ac.* 1.30-2)? I shall pursue these questions below.

In §143 introduces Antiochus. He accepts none of the views introduced in §142, nor indeed one of his 'ancestors" (*maiores*). By this Cicero does, prima facie surprisingly, not mean Plato, introduced in §142, but Xenocrates and Aristotle.[548] So Cicero is once more taking aim at the synthetic nature of Antiochus' Old Academy. Antiochus is in fact presented as a close follower of Chrysippus in the area of λογική (cf. §132).[549] Next Cicero asks 'how come "we" are called Academics' (note genuine passive in *appellamur*; see the n. below), and whether the use of the term is justified. Here 'we' needs to be taken to refer to anyone who is called Academic (whether Cicero thinks the label is justified or not), i.e. Antiochus *and* the sceptics, the implication being that neither side has grounds to follow anyone.[550] For this to make sense, Cicero cannot be suggesting that one might follow all (or any one, on the dogmatist's principle of 'follow *someone*', cf. §132) of those named in §142. Rather, the backward reference must be to the philosophers just mentioned in §143, who are subsumed under Antiochus' Old Academy but disagree amongst themselves.[551]

Cicero then repeats the pattern of first pointing out disagreements among the dogmatists in general and then amongst philosophers supposedly included in Antiochus' Old Academy. Those who have pronounced on the truth conditions of conditionals disagree among each other: Diodorus, Philo, and Chrysippus each have a different view (presumably only Chrysippus would fall under Antiochus' Old Academy). And within the Stoic school, Chrysippus often disagreed with his teacher Cleanthes (sc. over dialectical matters in general rather than the truth conditions for conditionals), and Antipater and Archidemus disagreed with each other. The problem posed by such disagreements remains the same: any view along with all the considerations that can be cited in its favour has at least enough weight to make assent unwarranted, and probably enough to discourage approval.

---

[548] The role accorded to Plato in Varro's speech in *Ac.* 1 is quite carefully constructed: the body of doctrines which represents the teachings of the Old Academy (the *prima forma* of philosophy) is presented as arrived at by Plato's successors and early Peripatetics through interpretation, specifically an interpretation which they took to correspond to Plato's intentions. In that sense, Plato 'himself' or his texts and their contents are at one remove from the philosophy of the Antiochian Old Academy, at least in the eyes of someone who is not himself an Old Academic; see section 7.2 and the commentary on *Ac.* 1.30-33a as well as on 1.15-17. According to Varro the *prima forma* was later 'corrected' by Zeno (1.40-2). In the commentary on 1.30-2, I suggest that Old Academic epistemology is presented there in a manner which makes Zeno's epistemology look like a genuine modification of the *prima forma* (rather than a completely new theory). Others think that Zeno's epistemology, even on Varro's account, completely supplants that of 1.30-2 (see below). That Cicero excludes Plato from Antiochus' intellectual ancestry here in §§142-3 does not directly confirm this aspect of my interpretation of the historical constructions of Varro's speech, since Cicero has every reason to posit a radical break between Plato and the key figures of Antiochus' Old Academy, or between their *prima forma* and Zeno. Glucker (1978: 397) states: 'Surely, this appeal to Xenocrates and Aristotle must come from someone like Philo, not from a consistent Carneadean sceptic', but Xenocrates and Aristotle are invoked dialectically.

[549] The link between Antiochus and Chrysippus may itself have a polemical point, in that Varro exclusively invokes Zeno in *Ac.* 1.40-2.

[550] Both sides, Old Academic and Clitomachean, are of course equally committed to not falling into error; cf. *Luc.* 67 and 77.

[551] *Sequi* is in any event best taken to be used non-terminologically, i.e. not of Clitomachean approval (cf. §104).

In §144 Cicero turns to the subject of τέχναι, intending to show that the concept of καταληψις is unable to do the philosophical work the dogmatist requires it to do, and that only ἐπιστήμη, the sole province of the sage, will do. Lucullus claimed that the Academics abolish the possibility of technical expertise (§22), since the items of knowledge on which technical expertise relies and which constitute it are, on the Stoic view, καταλήψεις, whose existence the Academics deny. Cicero addressed this point first in §107 and compares it here to being dragged into the *contio* by a seditious tribune who shuts down, in a politically motivated move, the shops of the craftsmen. His first reply, facetious but already hinting at the serious point he will make next, is that the *contio* would not be pleased to be told by Antiochus that they are all exiled, slaves, and insane because they do not have knowledge (qua non-sages, cf. §136). The dogmatist's rejoinder that he does grant καταληψις to the non-sage is then dismissed as not addressing the problem.

§145, the famous passage featuring Zeno illustrating epistemological concepts with his hands, is intended to explain why, given the dogmatist's own assumptions, nobody has knowledge and why, as a consequence, it is actually the dogmatist who is committed to the view that technical expertise does not exist: because the standards for knowledge that p which the dogmatist employs are so high that no ordinary human being can meet them, in that knowledge that p is only to be had by someone who does not have a single false belief. Consequently, Cicero concludes, Catulus does not know that it is day, nor Hortensius that the conversation takes place in his villa. So given Antiochus' commitments, neither a mitigated sceptic like Catulus nor an Antiochian like Hortensius has knowledge. Rather, even Antiochians ought to end up as the negative dogmatists as which Antiochus and the Stoics paint the Academics.[552] And while Cicero may be turning to Catulus and Hortensius simply for effect, i.e. to recruit them to his cause against Lucullus, the address would be even more pointed if Hortensius had—in the *Catulus*—introduced the material, or a shorter version of it, which is given to Varro in *Ac.* 1.

In §146 Cicero concedes that it—the last point made in §145 *fin.*—was unsophisticated and that 'the one made earlier' (*illa*) was more subtle: the reference must be to the claim that the dogmatist's standard for knowledge is so high that it is never met, for it is this notion which is then pursued further.[553] Just as Lucullus had challenged Cicero earlier by arguing that technical expertise required καταλήψεις as a basis and could not be grounded in *probabilia*, so Cicero now responds that as per the opponent's commitments nothing short of ἐπιστῆμαι (i.e. καταλήψεις as only the sage has them) will do. This position Cicero then reduces ad absurdum, by arguing that the most celebrated artists in antiquity would not meet this standard,[554] which would

[552] See Allen (1997) on the economy of the debate between Stoics and Academics.
[553] The overall force of Cicero's argument partly depends on how one construes craft knowledge; e.g. is it possible to be a non-sage and yet enact one's knowledge of a particular craft within its domain in such a way as the sage would make use of his wisdom, recognizing all his apprehensions for what they are and knowing that he is wise?
[554] Görler (2004c: 280–1) comments: 'To be sure, this is rhetoric, and Lucullus would not have failed to answer (had he been given an occasion) that his school after all did grant "perceptions" to ordinary people and a fortiori to artists.' If that had been Lucullus' reply, it would not have addressed Cicero's point, which is that even καταληψις should not suffice *by the dogmatist's own standards*. The point that 'perceptions' are granted to ordinary people *is* made in §144 *fin.*, but only to bring out its ineffectiveness against the Academic argument.

give rise to indignation among them, or so Cicero imagines, until they are assured that the claim was in fact not true and that the *probabilia* which the Academics grant them are perfectly sufficient to explain their expertise (or indeed to act on it). This last point Cicero then supports by arguing that the *maiores*, the Roman ancestors, can in fact be shown to be proto-sceptics in that it can be inferred from standard formulations recurrent in legal procedure that they, too, did not believe in infallible knowledge and instead operated with *probabilia*. This argument ties in with a theme which is present in both speeches of *Luc.*, i.e. a contest about whose position is more 'natural', a fairer reflection of how things really are.[555] By being able to show that caution about knowledge claims was encoded into legal procedure, perceived to be an original cultural achievement of the Romans rather than a foreign import like philosophy or rhetoric, Cicero is able to imply that the Romans have always been Academics *avant la lettre*.

In §147 Cicero concludes his speech and the whole doxographical section. The interlocutors must break up and leave. Next time more time still should be devoted to physics and ethics, but not to the arguments against the senses, or to paradoxes and fallacies with which the Stoics tie themselves in knots. What is more, he implies (cf. §112) that the case for the Academic position is best made not by getting bogged down on very narrow issues like the third clause of Zeno's definition of the cataleptic impression, but by looking at substantial views held with conviction by dogmatists and by the recognition that there are no rational grounds for assenting to any of them. Another interpretation of §147, on which it is a programmatic statement on future planned dialogues, is discussed in the nn. below.

I proceed to discussing some issues of wider import arising from the section. The first is the reference to Plato's view of the κριτήριον. The Academic view of Plato is that he was a sceptic (see *Ac.* 1.46), whereas here he is cited as a dogmatist of some description. So Cicero introduces Plato in the manner in which he is interpreted by others. This, however, need not mean that he introduces him as Antiochus construes him—any credible view of Plato as a dogmatist (sc. as long as Plato's view is different from Chrysippus') will do. As indicated above (p. 779, n. 548), I do not think that *Ac.* 1.30-2 directly provides Antiochus' view of Plato's thought in the area of λογική; instead, it provides Antiochus' view of how the *antiqui* construed Plato's thinking. Still, one must ask if *Luc.* 142 and *Ac.* 1.30-2 offer materially the same construal of Plato, and if they do not, whether §142 envisages that (a) Plato relied on a conceptualist interpretation of forms but posited a sharper divide between the deliverances of the senses on the one hand and concepts and thought on the other, or that (b) Plato adopted a two-world view as in Plato's *Tim.* and assumed that there were transcendental forms.

Some scholars find view (b) in *Ac.* 1.30-2, but as I argue ad loc., I do not regard it as an interpretation which can be sustained there. It may be intended here, but I submit that Cicero could have made it much plainer that Plato is positing forms qua transcendental entities had he wanted to.[556] Sedley (2012b), who assumes that a two-world view is ascribed to Plato in *Ac.* 1.30-2, holds that we can discern two

---

[555] See Reinhardt (2019).
[556] See also the commentary on *Ac.* 1.33b, where *Luc.* 142 is compared with *Fin.* 4.42.

phases of Antiochian reconstruction of the Old Academy, one harmonizing and in evidence in *Fin.* 4.8–10, which predates Philo's Roman Books, and one more ready to acknowledge discontinuities in the Academic tradition, for which the main evidence is Varro's speech in *Ac.* 1 and which postdates the Roman Books. Sedley assumes that in *Luc.* 142 we see Philo's response to Antiochus' post-Roman Books construction of the Old Academy (p. 87 n. 13): 'It seems that this [i.e. *Luc.* 142–3: *Plato autem... noster Antiochus?*] reflects Philo's own response to Antiochus' move, pointing out how far he has now distanced himself from Plato.' While the argument for the view that Cicero's works provide evidence for two different Antiochian reconstructions of the Old Academy is attractive, I hesitate to see *Philo's* response here, given that the passage is loosely speaking doxographical, that for chronological reasons it is unlikely that Cicero used one continuous Philonian source for 'his' speech in *Luc.*, and that we have no evidence whatsoever of any Philonian reply to an Antiochian reply to the Roman Books.[557] I believe, for reasons of economy, that option (a) is what Cicero actually intends here, thus not assuming the carefully calibrated role given to the senses in *Ac.* 1.30–2,[558] but it is possible that option (b) is meant.[559]

Zeno's use of hand gestures to illustrate aspects of doctrine is well documented, but unlike the symbolic representation of rhetoric as an open palm and of dialectic as a closed fist,[560] §146 happens to be unparalleled elsewhere.[561] Good observations on various points of detail have been made.[562] Thus the progression from the open palm to the clenched fist secured by the other hand does not straightforwardly represent a chronological sequence ('one impression's journey to knowledge'),[563] because assent and apprehension coincide such that apprehension arises in and through the act of

---

[557] Glucker (1978: 415) offers a different kind of argument for the view that Cicero's speech in *Luc.* is based on a Philonian reply to the *Sosus*: 'If Philo's reply to the *Sosus* is the source, one could understand the severe and magisterial tones in which Antiochus is reprimanded in passages like 69–70; 98; 102; 132; 133–4; 143. *In propria persona*, Cicero is full of respect for Antiochus (4; 111; 113). The passages of reproof for Antiochus, especially 69–70 and 102, are those of a master who has recently been touched on the raw by the public defection of an old and favourite pupil.' This is a significant consideration, but as indicated elsewhere (see section 9.3), the assumption that Philo returned to the Clitomachean position after the failure of the Roman Books is highly problematic. Moreover, the harsh tone in a fictional address to a Greek philosopher who has been dead for more than a generation (or to politician and general who had been dead for more than ten years) is to be judged differently from, say, the tone which Cicero employs in his asides to Cato and Servius Sulpicius Rufus in the *Pro Murena*.

[558] On my reconstruction the material Varro presents in his speech in *Ac.* 1 was presented by Hortensius in the *Catulus*, although an expansion in the final edition is conceivable, given that Varro is a much more credible presenter e.g. of the intricate section 1.19–29 than Hortensius.

[559] The apparent emphasis on the complete rejection of true opinion is peculiar to *Luc.* 142, but it is separate from the distinction between options (a) and (b).

[560] See Cic., *Or.* 113; *Fin.* 2.17; Sextus, *M.* 2.7 (= *SVF* i.75); and Atherton (1988). The Stoics also used the closed fist to represent the πως ἔχον (Sextus, *M.* 7.39 = *SVF* ii.132 = *FDS* 324) and an extended finger to symbolize something that is neither προηγμένον nor ἀποπροηγμένον (D.L. 7.104 = *SVF* iii.119 = LS 58B2).

[561] However, Cicero himself appears to foreshadow it in *Ac.* 1.41 (*...comprehensionem appellabat, similem iis rebus quae manu prehenderentur*).

[562] See Stroux (1965: 72–85); Annas (1980: 86); Ioppolo (1984: 329–34); Long and Sedley (i.1987: 256–9); Ioppolo (1990: 435–6); Schäublin et al. (p. 308 n. 480); Görler (2004f: 1–8), who reviews important items of earlier scholarship. I have not seen Dumont (1967–8).

[563] *Pace* e.g. Graeser (1975: 51 n. 31): 'Anders fassen die durch Cicero, *Ac. Post.* 1, 41 and *Ac. Pr.* 2, 145 vermittelten Bestimmungen nicht den Vollzug des Erkenntnisaktes ins Auge, sondern den Prozeß der Bildung von Erkenntnisinhalten.' Correctly e.g. Rolke (1975: 124).

assent.⁵⁶⁴ It has also been observed that the 'stages' corresponding to different positions of the hand are not all equivalent in kind: assent would seem to be an act performed by the mind, whereas ἐπιστήμη would seem to be a state, i.e. one of the sage's uniquely secured individual καταλήψεις or the totality of his ἐπιστῆμαι in the first sense.⁵⁶⁵ Further and trivially, there is a sense in which the hand corresponds to the human mind, which, when the outside world impinges on it, is mostly reactive (although the conceptualization of perceptual information on the outside world requires an active contribution from the mind even in the event of an impression that is merely entertained), symbolized in the open palm, the hand's natural position at rest, whereas the acts or states beyond the passive affection of an impression require an active agency of the mind.⁵⁶⁶ It is thus surprisingly difficult to capture in a simple phrase what Zeno is illustrating; e.g. both 'stages of cognition' and 'kinds of cognition' are slightly misleading.⁵⁶⁷

§§144–6 is remarkable inter alia for its artful composition. The Stoic 'fragment' sits at its centre: that Cicero is able to cite it characterizes him as someone who knows the opponent's position intimately. It also functions as an undistortable piece of evidence (but it is Cicero who derives the key point contra the dogmatist from it). Before and after the fragment, there stand scenarios in which the dogmatist and the Academic vie for the approval of experts. The quasi-*contio* resumes earlier imagery, intended to dismiss Cicero's position by pointing out that it would attract ridicule and dismay when exposed to public scrutiny—a suggestion Cicero counters by suggesting that it is the dogmatist who is committed to denying the craftsmen skill and expertise. In §146a, the device of false closure is used; having secured the intended takeaway, Cicero introduces a new audience of even greater experts, whom the dogmatist must deny knowledge, too.⁵⁶⁸

Cicero's position throughout his speech in *Luc.* is that of a Clitomachean.⁵⁶⁹ Is there any reason to think that §§142–7 are different, e.g. that he is making a deliberate effort to formulate a conclusion for his speech which refutes Antiochus not just

---

⁵⁶⁴ The passage also assumes that knowledge is never reached since there are no sages, but this point does not seem part of the Stoic 'fragment'.

⁵⁶⁵ On the second sense, see Brunschwig (1994b: 146): 'Knowledge in the second sense is a σύστημα, a totality whose elements are conjoined and indissociable, as is probably indicated by the last stage in the famous lesson by gestures that Zeno had delivered on the theory of knowledge: at this point, the left hand moved across to fasten upon the right, which was already clenched into a fist.'

⁵⁶⁶ See Striker (1996b: 111), with reference to *Luc.* 145 (inter alia): 'This distinction [between the act of accepting a presentation as true from the mere "having" an impression] has become part of the European tradition, its latest prominent descendant being perhaps Frege's distinction between the mere grasping of a thought and the judgement that the state of affairs expressed by a proposition is a fact.' Stroux (1965: 72) thinks one can go beyond observing that the hand corresponds to the mind: 'Bei der geöffneten Hand veranschaulichen die fünf Finger die fünf Sinne, die Handfläche das Hegemonikon, mit dem die Sinne durch das gemeinsame stoffliche Substrat des Seelenpneumas verbunden sind und an das sie ihre Eindrücke weitergeben. Im Hegemonikon laufen die einzelnen Sinneseindrücke zusammen und vereinigen sich zu einem Gesamteindruck, der "Erscheinung" des Objekts. Die ausgestreckten Finger verdeutlichen, daß in den Sinnen eine nach außen gerichtete Spannung enthalten ist.' Burnyeat (1979: 102) observes that the 'idea of perception as a firm grasp of an object is some sort of antithesis to the window model', on which perceiving things in the world is being directly presented with the world as if looking out through a pane-less window.

⁵⁶⁷ See Long and Sedley (ii.1987: 254). 'Kinds of cognition' is used by Kerferd (1978: 254).

⁵⁶⁸ See further Reinhardt (2021).

⁵⁶⁹ See section 8.

from a Clitomachean standpoint but also from that of mitigated scepticism (and possibly even the view of the Roman Books), just as Lucullus seemed at times to formulate arguments against the Academic view in a manner which was apt to target the Clitomachean view as well as mitigated scepticism, defended by the second Academic speaker, Catulus (see on §§43–4)?

In order to answer this question, one should distinguish between destructive argument, intended to demonstrate that the opponent's position is untenable, and constructive argument, an outline of a position of one's own under proviso.[570] Any Academic, whether Clitomachean or mitigated sceptic, could advance a destructive argument turning on the lack of agreement amongst the dogmatists, and any Academic would marshal arguments against the extreme standard required for sagehood, which in turn would bolster the Academic position. Thus when Cicero says in §145 *fin.* that by Antiochus' standards Catulus does not know that it is day, nor Hortensius that the group is staying at his villa, he means that neither could by Antiochus' standards claim knowledge of these everyday facts, even though both might make such claims using the term 'to know' non-terminologically (just like Cicero). Cicero addresses this remark to the Antiochian Hortensius and the mitigated sceptic Catulus for effect, it being understood that Antiochus would deny such 'knowledge' to the Clitomachean in any case.

When Cicero turns to the famous artists who would not have knowledge on the Antiochian view (and would not be offended once it was explained to them what ἐπιστήμη entailed), he says that they would not direct anger towards the Academics 'because they merely abolished what did not exist anyway and left behind what was sufficient for their purposes'. The same *ratio* is then said to be in evidence in the caution about knowledge claims found in standard legal formulations, notably the loaded sense of *uideri* which features in the standard wording with which judges issue their verdicts. Which Academic position is best captured by these statements? One might think that Cicero's remark points to the Roman Books,[571] which effectively amounted to calling impressions cataleptic which met the first two clauses of Zeno's definition but not the third (and claiming that this had been the Academic position all along), but then even Cicero in Clitomachean mode is happy to concede that persuasive impressions often meet the first two clauses of the Zenonian definition but never the third one, and that all that remains of the debate with the Stoics is the dispute over the third clause.[572] What makes it likely that Cicero is firmly

---

[570] An Academic may offer a positive position purely for the sake of the argument, but *Luc.* 104–105a suggests that the Cicero character permits himself 'approval'.

[571] This possibility is entertained by Striker (1997: 274 with n. 18): 'Why not...follow ordinary life and redraw the line between knowledge and mere opinion so as to separate well-founded judgements from superficial beliefs? I would suggest that this was the consideration that led Philo to his Roman innovations. He concluded, plausibly enough, that the Stoics had set their standards too high. It was unnecessary modesty on the part of the Academics to concede that all they could hope for was opinion, not knowledge.'

[572] Striker (1996b: 107 n. 51) derives a more general point from *Luc.* 146: 'Carneades also tried to show that nothing absurd follows if we drop the disputed premisses—in fact, as Cicero puts it (*Acad.* II 146), the sceptic only throws out what is never the case, but leaves everything that is needed.' Görler (2004c: 281) thinks that Cicero is attempting a synthesis of sorts: '"...leave to them what is sufficient (146)." This is nearly Cicero's last sentence within his speech proper. It is clearly ironical in character: one should not

remaining in Clitomachean mode is the reference to standard wordings used in legal procedure, notably said loaded sense of *uideri*, which is associated with Clitomachean approval of *probabilia* in §105a (...*eadem nos si modo probabilia sint uideri dicimus*).[573]

§142

Venio enim iam ad tertiam partem philosophiae...quod cuique uideatur: the section down to §143...*a Chrysippo pedem nusquam* is 'Baustein 20.3b' in Dörrie (1987: 200–1). Cf. the earlier *diuisio* in *Luc.* 116: *in tres igitur partes et a plerisque et a uobismet ipsis distributa sapientia est*, and the section beginning in §128: *ueniamus nunc ad bonorum malorumque notionem*. The division must also have been used in the *Catulus*; cf. *Ac.* 1.19. The physical and ethical sections of the doxographical part of Cicero's speech each had an epistemological preface of sorts (§§116–17, 128).

Protagoras is elsewhere cited by Cicero alongside other sophists without reference to any particular view of his (*De orat.* 3.128; *Brut.* 30, 46, 292), or for his agnostic views on the gods (*N.D.* 1.2, 1.29, 1.63, 1.117). See also Wisse, Winterbottom, and Fantham (2008: 122–3) on *De orat.* 3.128.

The view ascribed to him here is given in Plt., *Tht.* 152a, and Sextus, *M.* 7.60 (DK 80B1) as: Πάντων χρημάτων μέτρον ἐστὶν ἄνθρωπος, τῶν μὲν ὄντων ὡς ἔστιν, τῶν δὲ οὐκ ὄντων ὡς οὐκ ἔστιν, 'Man is the measure of all things, of those that are, that they are, and of those that are not, that they are not.' According to Plato, *Tht.* 161c, it featured at the beginning of Protagoras' work Ἀλήθεια; Sextus cites the work under a different title, Καταβάλλοντες ('The Down-Throwers'). Burnyeat (1976a: 45–7) observes that Protagoras' statement introduces a form of relativism, i.e. things are for someone as they appear to someone, whereas the bulk of the ancient tradition, including Sextus, take Protagoras' to be a statement of subjectivism, i.e. the view that every judgement is true absolutely, not just for the person whose judgement it is. He notes on our passage (p. 46 n. 3): 'Otherwise, the only exception to a uniformly subjectivist record seems to be Cicero, *Academica* II.142, which means that the Academic Sceptic whom Cicero is reproducing (probably Clitomachus or Philo of Larissa) took the trouble to state Protagoras' view correctly.' See Reid[1] (p. 343) on *putet* here but *putant* later.

---

quarrel about words as long as there is agreement in substance; it does not matter much how to call what a good artist must have at his disposition; be it "knowledge" or a set of "perceptions" or "probable views". Amazingly, Cicero's final remark fits both sides. He had mentioned the Stoic notion of "knowledge", reserved to the sage but unavailable to ordinary people. And as the Stoics were not sure whether, so far, there had been a wise man at all, in a way "knowledge" (as they defined it) may be said to be "nowhere".... What is "left" is perception in the case of the Stoics, "probable views" with the Academics: both schools "leave" what is sufficient for arts, crafts, and everyday action. The specific terms are faded out, and that is hardly accidental: Cicero, here, does not want to point to the controversial issues any longer, here the stress is on what both sides have in common.' What tells against this reading is that Cicero continues with the 'Academic' argument in §146, i.e. after making the points Görler cites.

[573] On §§144–6, see also Brittain (2001: 160–3 and 272 n. 35), who offers interpretations of the different attitudes to crafts (τέχναι) which the Clitomachean, mitigated, and Roman view entailed—interpretations predicated in part on his view, not shared in this commentary, that Clitomacheans and mitigated sceptics construed the πιθανόν in different ways. See section 6.6 and Reinhardt (2018a).

Aliud Cyrenaicorum...putant esse iudicii: the Cyrenaics were invoked by Lucullus in *Luc.* 20 as evidence for the reliability of the sense of touch and the verifiability of its deliverances (see n. there), as well as by Cicero in *Luc.* 76 as better suited to advance his case rather than Lucullus', on the grounds that the perceiving subject cannot proceed beyond the bare sense of being affected (πάθος = *perturbatio*) towards a secure grasp of the world and what it is like. Here they are cited for positing a criterion which is different from everybody else's (and, possibly, which is vaguely like an impression). For *iudicium* in the sense of κριτήριον, see the n. in *Ac.* 1.30.

Aliud Epicuri...et in uoluptate constituit: = frg. 245 Usener. Epicurus is invoked by both parties in *Luc.* (e.g. 19, 45; 79, 83, 101). Here Cicero lists the three different things recognized by Epicurus as criterial, reinforcing the impression of a wide variety of opinions on the subject. Cf. D.L. 10.31 (frg. 35 Usener = LS17A): (ἐν τοίνυν τῷ Κανόνι λέγων ἐστὶν ὁ Ἐπίκουρος) κριτήρια τῆς ἀληθείας εἶναι τὰς αἰσθήσεις καὶ προλήψεις καὶ τὰ πάθη, 'Thus Epicurus, in the *Kanōn*, says that sensations, preconceptions and feelings are criteria of truth' (transl. Long and Sedley). See Asmis (1984: 91–100); Long and Sedley (i.1987: 88–90); and Striker (1996a: 29–51) on the Epicurean understanding of their criteria.

Plato autem omne iudicium...mentis esse uoluit: on the relationship of this statement, *Ac.* 1.30–2, and *Fin.* 4.42, see the general note above. For the notion that any judgement resides in or is a matter for *cogitatio* and *mens*, cf. *Ac.* 1.30: *mentem uolebant rerum esse iudicem*, but on my reading ibid.: *Quamquam oriretur a sensibus, tamen non esse iudicium ueritatis in sensibus* gives a slightly more substantial role to the senses than *omne iudicium ueritatis ueritatemque ipsam abductam...a sensibus...uoluit* here. Comparable with *Ac.* 1.30 in this respect is the characterization of Plato's view on the criterion in Sextus, *M.* 7.141 (quoted and discussed in the general note on *Ac.* 1.30–33a), which goes on to cite *Tim.* 27d as evidence (see below); Brittain (2012: 108–13) argues plausibly that it is unlikely that Antiochus was Sextus' source in *M.* 7. In the commentary on *Ac.* 1.30–2 I argue that *Tht.* 182–6 is Varro's main reference point in his exposition.

The brevity of the present passage makes it difficult to identify Platonic intertexts with any degree of precision. Opsomer (1998: 54 n. 109) sees a possible reference to *Phaed.* 99e here, specifically for the notion of λόγος as the criterion. *Tim.* 27d–28a, the statement on the two-world view, is arguably relevant, too (as it is in *Ac.* 1.30–33a, where I cite and discuss it). However, there is no clear sense of a *realm* or *world* of opinion here in *Luc.* 142 (despite *ab opinionibus*), and Reid[1] (p. 343) aptly comments: 'It is surprising to find no reference to ἰδέαι here'; cf. ibid. pp. 54–5. See the commentary on *Ac.* 1.30–33a and 33b for the view that there forms qua transcendental entities are not at issue either.

§143

Num quid horum probat noster Antiochus? Ille uero ne maiorum quidem suorum: *horum* refers back to the thinkers named in §142. Plato is evidently not treated as one of the *maiores*, given *enim* below: Plato's successors in the Academy and Aristotle and the early Peripatetics had views of their own, but these are not here treated as an interpretation of Plato which they took to be Plato's view (the *forma* of philosophy discussed in *Ac.* 1.17, cf. *Ac.* 1.33a; see the commentary on these passages and section 7.2; the general note above). Cicero—the author and the character—may just be reflecting the attribution of views in his source material, but he also has no reason to entertain Antiochus' historical constructions and good reason to separate Plato, the Old Academics, Aristotle and the Peripatetics, as well as the Stoics.

Reid[1] (p. 343) compares *num quid horum* with *contra ea Philonis* in *Ac.* 1.13 (where I print *contra Philonis*); cf. also *Luc.* 133: *Legimus omnes Crantoris ueteris Academici de luctu*. The use of the genitive is clearly the same, but here Cicero is probably speaking of views rather than written works (a reading that is also possible in *Ac.* 1.13, where the views of the Roman Books may be at issue). *Probare* is used of the holding of a view (and not in the technical sense of *Luc.* 104).

In addition, there seems to be a slight change of subject after... *Antiochus?*, since §142 was concerned with the criterion (which of course falls under λογική), while Xenocrates below is cited for his views on logic, i.e. theory of argument. The reference to Aristotle is ambiguous and could, out of context, single him, and in particular his dialogues, out for his stylistic qualities, but that Chrysippus rather than Zeno is then cited shows that the focus on logic is retained.

Vbi enim [et] Xenocratem sequitur...nihil est acutius, nihil politius: from Cicero's references to Xenocrates it is not plain how much he knew of the latter's interests in theory of argument and related issues. The fragmentary evidence which has been assembled by modern scholars presents him as standing firmly in the Academic tradition which Aristotle seeks to codify and impose order on in his *Topics*. Cicero's reference here seems to be to Περὶ τὸ διαλέγεσθαι πραγματεία in fourteen books (D.L. 4.13, which lists book titles), though this need not have been transparent to Cicero. That διαλέγεσθαι relates to question-and-answer exchanges is suggested by Xenocrates' definition of the term in Sextus, *M.* 2.6 (= frg. 13 Heinze = frg. 90 Isnardi Parente):...ἐν συντομίᾳ κείμενον κἂν τῷ λαμβάνειν καὶ διδόναι λόγον διαλεκτικῆς ἐστιν ἔργον, τὸ δὲ λέγειν ἐν μήκει καὶ διεξόδῳ θεωρούμενον ῥητορικῆς ἐτύγχανεν ἴδιον, '['Speaking' in a rhetorical context differs in sense from dialectical discussion since]... speaking which is concise and consists in giving and receiving an account is the task of dialectic, but to speak on a given subject at length and with detailed exposition is the special characteristic of rhetoric' (transl. Bury). Here λαμβάνειν καὶ διδόναι λόγον designate the roles of questioner and respondent in a dialectical exchange, in line with the terminology used in Arist. *Top.* Cf. also the beginning of Arist. *Rhet.*, which characterizes rhetoric with reference to dialectic and the beginning of *Top.* Discussions of Xenocrates' views on λογική include Krämer (1971: 14–58); Isnardi Parente (1981: 309–20); Krämer (1983: 48–51); Dillon (2003: 150–3). Cicero had some knowledge of Academic dialectic in this sense, as is clear from parts of *Tusc.* (the relevant section begins in 1.7; see Moraux 1968: 304–7), but Xenocrates is not mentioned in that connection.

The reference to Aristotle's polish (*politius*) might point to the dialogues, elsewhere referred to by Cicero for their stylistic brilliance (cf. *Att.* 2.2.1 = SB 22), but such a reference would make no sense in the present context, and *acutius* points in a different direction. We have no grounds for thinking that Cicero had more than superficial familiarity (if any) with Aristotle's *Top.* and *Rhet.*, and he shows no familiarity at all with the other treatises which make up the Aristotelian *Organon*. In particular, when he talks about logic in the sense of formal theory of argument, he invariably thinks of Stoic propositional logic, not of the theory of *An. Pr.* Similarly, when scientific demonstration is at issue, Stoic doctrine is the reference point. See also Barnes (1997c: 44–63) on the question of whether Cicero reveals knowledge of any esoteric works.

A Chrysippo pedem nusquam: Reid[1] (p. 343) collects the evidence for the proverbial expression (and for similar ones), often with ellipsis of the verb as here, but cf. e.g. *Fam.* 10.31.6 (= SB 368): *nullum enim uestigium abs te discessurus sum*. Chrysippus rather than Zeno appears to be named since it was him who formulated most of Stoic logic.

Qui ergo Academici appellamur? An abutimur gloria nominis: for the use of *qui* see *OLD* s.v. *qui*[2] no. 1; the Aldina emended to *quid*. I punctuate so as to give the second question equal weight to the first one. Contrast Plasberg[1] (p. 151).

One might expect the second-person singular here given the reference to Chrysippus in the previous sentence and the fact that Cicero disputes Antiochus' claim to the title *Academicus* (see on *Luc.* 132). Patronizing first-person plural for second-person singular ('how are we feeling today?') is not attested in Latin, and in any case *appellamur* would have to be 'autocausative' (i.e. 'we call ourselves'; see Pinkster i.260–7) rather than passive for such a reading to be enabled, which it cannot be (cf. the *TLL* entry, which does not recognize autocausative uses of *appellor*). So Cicero must be including himself for rhetorical effect and then asks whether either of them is entitled to using the title (*OLD* s.v. *an*[2] no. 3). This is followed up with a rhetorical question suggesting that neither of them is compelled to follow people who disagree amongst themselves (since, presumably, both sides are equally committed to avoiding error). For *gloria nominis* = *glorioso nomine*, cf. the similar passages in *Fin.* 1.61: *honestum, non tam solido quam splendido nomine*; *Tusc.* 2.33: *quid philosophiae nomine gloriosi sumus?*

While Cicero (the character) takes himself to stand in the tradition of certain Presocratics, Socrates and Plato (interpreted in a certain way), and Arcesilaus and Carneades, he is not 'following' any one of them; see on §§7b–9a.

Aut cur cogimur…Chrysippo aliter placet: *in hoc ipso…placet* is *SSR* II F23. For *aut* introducing a new point, often with the air of self-correction, see *OLD* s.v. no. 6b. *Aut cur cogimur…* sets up what follows, i.e. the disagreement about the truth conditions for conditionals, whereas just before the legitimate use of the term *Academicus* was at issue. In the background there is the desire, shared by dogmatist and Academic, to avoid the lapse into error, i.e. assent to the non-cataleptic; cf. e.g. *Luc.* 114. Disagreement among otherwise recognized authorities ought to induce caution, or so Cicero suggests; cf. e.g. *Luc.* 129.

For the phrase *elementa* 'elementary teachings', cf. e.g. Lucr. 1.81; Quint. 1.1.23; Diels (1899: 70). On the uses of the term *dialecticus*, cf. *Luc.* 91. For *connexum* of a conditional, cf. *Luc.* 96; *Fat.* 12; but see *coniunctio* in *Luc.* 91. For Diodorus, see on *Luc.* 75. On Philo of Megara / Philo the dialectician, see Döring (1998); Muller (2012). On the Megaric school and the question of whether there was a Dialectical school, see Allen (2019).

In *P.H.* 2.110-12 Sextus discusses truth-conditions for conditionals; on the passage see also section 6.2. Four types are distinguished. The first two are truth-functional and associated with Philo of Megara and Diodorus Cronus respectively. The third one is not assigned by name but is likely to be Chrysippus'. It is not truth-functional and assumes a 'connection' (συνάρτησις) between antecedent and consequent, which means that a conditional of the type at issue is true if the antecedent and the contradictory of the consequent are incompatible (see e.g. Bobzien 1996: 185-7). The fourth type, which is otherwise unattested, is described in the following terms (*P.H.* 2.112-13): 'And those who judge by ἔμφασις say that a conditional is true when its consequent is contained implicitly in its antecedent (ἐν τῷ ἡγουμένῳ περιέχεται δυνάμει). According to them, "if it is day, it is day", and every duplicated conditional statement, will no doubt be false; for it is impossible for anything to be contained in itself (αὐτὸ γάρ τι ἐν ἑαυτῷ περιέχεσθαι ἀμήχανον).' As Frede (1974: 92) notes, Plutarch's collocation of συνάρτησις and ἔμφασις in a Stoicizing context (*De E apud Del.* 387a) suggests that the fourth type of conditional is Stoic. He interprets it as an attempt to clarify the kind of connection between antecedent and consequent which the third type posits, which turns on the semantic content of the simple propositions involved. The independent evidential value of our passage is limited, but strengthens the case for the third view being Chrysippus'; cf. also Döring (2010a: 273 n. 20): 'Einziges nichtsextianisches Zeugnis ist eine Bemerkung bei Cicero (...) [*Luc.* 143], die nicht mehr besagt, als dass Diodor, Philon und Chrysipp bezüglich der Frage der Richtigkeit der Konditionalaussage unterschiedlicher Meinung waren.'

Quid? Cum Cleanthe...in rebus dissentiunt: *quid?* marks a new point as elsewhere. Cicero must now be thinking about disagreements in the field of λογική generally. One such disagreement was over the appropriateness of the wax-block image used by Zeno to characterize impressions; see Sextus, *M.* 7.228-31 (= *SVF* ii.56; Chrysippus favoured the idea that an imprint should be seen as an 'alteration'). Another, cited by Brittain (2006: 83 n. 233), is over the appropriate response to Diodorus Cronus' so-called 'Master Argument'; see Epict., *Diss.* 2.19.1-5 (*SVF* ii.283); Cic., *Fat.* 14. Cf. also D.L. 7.179 (= *SVF* ii.1) on Chrysippus' disagreeing with Cleanthes in general, *Luc.* 107 and 126 for other disagreements amongst the Stoics.

On Antipater, see *Luc.* 17, 28; and Nonius p. 65 M. (= t. 8). Plut., *Sto. rep.* 4, 1034a refers to a work by Antipater, devoted to the difference between Cleanthes and Chrysippus (= *SVF* iii.66). Little is known of Archidemus (see *SVF* iii for his fragments), but he is frequently mentioned together with Antipater (D.L. 7.68 and 84; Epict., *Diss.* 2.19.7); both came from Tarsus.

The transmitted *opiniosissimi* has been suspected. It is unexampled except for one passage in Tertullian (*adv. Marc.* 4.35), where our passage or its counterpart in the final edition probably served as a source, but this does not preclude an early corruption. Sense is rather well served by the transmitted reading—assuming it means 'very opinionated'—in a passage where disagreements are at issue, while *spinosissimi*

(Hermann 1852: 475), printed by Plasberg[1] (p. 151), seems beside the point (although dialectical arguments and dialecticians may be 'thorny' or 'spiky' of course, cf. e.g. *Or.* 115; *Fin.* 3.3); Georges's *ingeniosissimi* (Georges 1913–18 s.v. *opiniosus*) seems flat.

§144

Quid me igitur, Luculle...occludi tabernas iubes: Cicero envisages a scenario where the dogmatist, cast as a seditious tribune, holds a *contio* and summons him to hold him to account (*in contionem uocare*), while forcing the closure of workshops (*tabernae*) in the city. The loss of earnings arising from closure would dispose the *opifices* negatively towards the man summoned (even before they are told that on that man's view there was no such thing as the crafts which earn them a living). Griffin (1997: 9) observes that 'the teasing about the tribunate...shows them [i.e. Cicero and Lucullus] sharing good Optimate attitudes'. For what makes the tribunes *seditiosi* is not just their malicious intent (in the eyes of *optimates*) but also the fact that the cessation of all public business (*iustitium*) was supposed to be imposed by edict by the highest-ranking magistrate in Rome, and in the late Republic usually only upon a decision taken by the senate (see Liv. 3.3.6); on the conventions around *iustitium*, see Golden (2013: 87–103). Nonetheless, closure of the shops was apparently not a frequent event; see *Dom.* 54 and 89 (relating to a particular event early in 58 BC), with Schneider (1932: 1170) and especially Russell (2016); Cic., *Catil.* 4.17 (with Dyck 2008: 232 ad loc.).

In *Luc.* 13 Lucullus had compared the Academics, who draw attention to sceptical pronouncements made by Presocratics, to *seditiosi ciues* who invoke great politicians from the Roman past in support of their populist cause. Cicero had rejected the analogy in §72, noting that his cause was a good one and that the intellectual ancestors invoked by him normally enjoy the respect of the dogmatist. In §63 Catulus had warned that an *improbus tribunus plebis* might seize him and interrogate him in the *contio* about how he could consistently argue (qua Academic) that nothing certain can be found and yet use an expression like *comperi*, which seems to signal a confident knowledge claim as well as also echoes a remark Cicero famously made about the 'facts of the case' during the Catilinarian conspiracy; see ad loc.

The expression *in contionem uocare* is conventional, and the men thus summoned were called *in contionem producti*; see the material assembled by Morstein-Marx (2004: 164). With *in inuidiam uocare* 'to make the object of disdain or hatred', cf. Cic., *Caec.* 65; *Rab. Perd.* 20; and the catalogue of passages in which *inuidia* is aroused in formal or informal settings in Kaster (2005: 96–7). For *tabernas occludere*, cf. again *Catil.* 4.17.

Quo enim spectat illud...facile contra uos incitabuntur: Lucullus had asserted that τέχναι can only exist if there are καταλήψεις, which Cicero rebutted in §107. *Artificium* can mean the craft itself (cf. §30) as well as the product of the craft, but *tolli* is more naturally used of the ἀνασκευή of theoretical conceptions than of declaring the products of an art to be non-existent. Reid[1] (p. 345) cites Cic., *Flacc.* 18: *opifices et tabernarios...quid est negotii concitare?*; Sall., *Iug.* 73.6: *plebes sic accensa ut* *opifices agrestesque... relictis operibus frequentarent Marium*, and notes that the *opifices* include the celebrated artists named in §146.

Expromam primum illa inuidiosa... insanos esse dicatis: the theme of tit-for-tat which started with *concitentur–incitabuntur* is continued with *inuidiosa* (cf. *in inuidiam... uocas* above). For the Stoic paradox that every non-sage is an exile, a slave, and insane, cf. §§136–7; *Fin.* 4.74, where Cicero comments on his use of the paradoxes to discredit his opponent, the younger Cato, in his speech for Murena. *Expromere* functions as a meta-rhetorical term here, implying that Cicero's rhetorical prowess would enable him to turn the assembled *tabernarii*; cf. Cic., *Leg.* 2.17–18. On confrontations in the *contio*, see the passages collected by Matexaki-Mitrou (1985).

Deinde ad illa ueniam... etiam insipientem multa comprehendere: a similar turn from the argument for the attention of the many (*multitudo*) to the interlocutors in the dialogue (*qui adestis*) in *Fin.* 4.74 (see previous n.).

Stoics and even Academics use verbs of knowing when there is no need to be precise about the nature and degree of endorsement a given claim receives; see e.g. §148. So when Cicero says that on Zeno's and Antiochus' view none of the interlocutors knows anything, the fictional interlocutor is not cast as obtuse when he replies that the non-sage 'apprehends many things': for most contexts it is not unreasonable to say that, in granting apprehension to the non-sage, the Stoics and Antiochus grant knowledge.

Cicero uses the exchange to signal that he is now talking about the Stoic technical sense of ἐπιστήμη, which the Stoics and Antiochus reserve for the sage. Craft knowledge, so the argument goes, ought to require ἐπιστήμη rather than κατάληψις, since any κατάληψις of the non-sage is in fact mere δόξα and ἄγνοια. Cf. Sextus, *M.* 7.153 (part of which is *SVF* i.69), on apprehension of sage and non-sage: Ταῦτα δὴ λεγόντων τῶν ἀπὸ τῆς Στοᾶς ὁ Ἀρκεσίλαος ἀντικαθίστατο, δεικνὺς ὅτι οὐδέν ἐστι μεταξὺ ἐπιστήμης καὶ δόξης κριτήριον ἡ κατάληψις. Αὕτη γὰρ ἥν φασι κατάληψιν καὶ καταληπτικῆς φαντασίας συγκατάθεσιν, ἤτοι ἐν σοφῷ ἢ ἐν φαύλῳ γίνεται. ἀλλ᾽ ἐάν τε ἐν σοφῷ γένηται, ἐπιστήμη ἐστίν, ἐάν τε ἐν φαύλῳ, δόξα, καὶ οὐδὲν ἄλλο παρὰ ταῦτα ἢ μόνον ὄνομα μετείληπται, 'This is what the Stoics say, and Arcesilaus rebutted them by showing that apprehension is no criterion between knowledge and opinion. For what they call apprehension, and assent to an apprehensive appearance, takes place either in a wise or in an inferior person. But if it takes place in a wise person, it is knowledge, and if in an inferior person it is opinion, and beyond these nothing has been substituted other than a mere name' (transl. Bett); *P.H.* 2.83 on the true being accessible to sage and non-sage alike, but truth only to the sage. See also Meinwald (2005).

Sextus, *M.* 7.432–4, as Brittain (2006: 84 n. 236) notes, advances an argument very similar to Cicero's here and notes that it enables the sceptics to cite against the Stoics the arguments which the Stoics conventionally cite against them. However, Sextus speaks about knowledge claims generally rather than the status of apprehensions which form part of a τέχνη.

§145

At scire negatis...Zeno gestu conficiebat: §144 *Negat enim uos...* §145 *sapientem esse neminem* is *SVF* i.66; *at scire negatis...sapientem esse neminem* is LS 41A; §144 *quo enim spectat...* §145 *in tua uilla nos esse* is *FDS* 369.

As indicated in the general note above, §145 is often described as Zeno's illustration of the stages or types of cognition, so it is as well to note that Cicero introduces it as showing that only the sage has knowledge. Reid[1] (p. 345) draws attention to the use of *conficere* in Aug., *Contra Acad.* 3.7.15-16 (t. 51); and *Fin.* 2.26, where, however, showing something in or through an argument is at issue (cf. *OLD* s.v. no. 6; *TLL* s.v. col. 200.67-81). The imperfect tense of *conficiebat* (maintained in the paragraph) suggests that Zeno used the illustration habitually ('used to show').

There is no Greek parallel evidence for §145, although of course there is ample evidence on each of the concepts illustrated by Zeno. Cicero himself alludes the illustration by hand in *Ac.* 1.41: *...comprehensionem appellabat, similem iis rebus quae manu prehenderentur*. A second illustration by hand gesture is attested for Zeno, viz. the likening of rhetoric to the open palm and of dialectic to the fist; cf. Cic., *Fin.* 2.17, *Or.* 113; Quint. 2.20.7; Sextus, *M.* 2.7 (all *SVF* i.75). Unlike here, there is no clear sense that in this second illustration the hand corresponds to the mind; rather, one is reminded of the notion that good rhetorical argument should be relevantly like philosophical argument (cf. Plt. *Phaedr.*), or that rhetoric is a counterpart of dialectic (cf. the beginning of Arist. *Rhet.*).

The passage is rightly classified as a fragment, but it seems unlikely that Zeno would present himself in this manner in a treatise of his own, i.e. in an apparent teaching scenario, and combining description and direct speech. It is more likely that a series of comparisons was stylized in this way by someone else. *Fin.* 1.39, composed at about the same time as *Luc.*, is an interestingly similar passage, in which Torquatus relays how his father described a statue of Chrysippus' on the Ceramicus, taking the philosopher to illustrate with his outstretched hand an argument, likewise introduced in direct speech; on the passage, see Warren (2016: 56-9). On the reconstructed statue, see Andreae (2001: 99-100); interpretative observations on it informed by *Fin.* 1.39 inter alia in Zanker (1995: 98-102). It is tempting to speculate that also in *Luc.* 145 statuary representations are an intertext. The notion that according to the Stoics only the sage has knowledge is used by Aug., *Soliloq.* 1.4.9, as Hagendahl (1967: 69) notes.

Nam cum extensis digitis...assensus huius modi: with *aduersam manum* 'the hand opposite the other person or audience', cf. the use of *aduersus* in §123: *aduersis uestigiis*. For *uisum* as a rendering for impression, see *Luc.* 18; *Ac.* 1.40; section 10.1; Reinhardt (2016). For the role of assent, see *Ac.* 1.40-1 and *Luc.* 38. *Contrahere* is the standard term for the retraction of fingers; cf. Cic., *N.D.* 2.150: *digitorum...contractio porrectio*. Receiving an impression is passive in a relevant sense, even though the mind plays an active role in the conceptualization of the object prior to assent, whereas giving assent is construed as within the subject's power; see the general note above.

Tum cum plane compresserat...κατάληψιν imposuit: for the Greek term and its Latin renderings, see the commentary on *Ac.* 1.41. For all we know Cicero may be correct in noting that the *nomen actionis* was first applied or even coined by Zeno to designate apprehensions, but the verb καταλαμβάνειν was used before in a suitably similar sense (Long 2002: 118 notes Arist., *Top.* E3, 131a30). As an Academic Cicero has no particular interest in emphasizing the continuities between the Stoics, Plato, and Aristotle.

Cum autem laeuam manum...compotem nisi sapientem esse neminem: for the notion of *scientia* = ἐπιστήμη, see on *Ac.* 1.41. The progression from fist to secured fist suggests that by *scientia* one securely fastened apprehension is meant, rather than the state of having only securely fastened apprehensions. Zeno appears to be presented as right-handed here. The correction *admouerat* 'moved up close' is compelling; as Reid[1] (p. 345), Cicero uses *aduertere* only in the phrase *animum aduertere*. By printing -*mo*- in *admouerat* in italics, Plasberg[1] indicates that he does not think that the corrections of A[a] are due to vertical transmission.

Sed qui sapiens...in tua uilla nos esse: the Stoics do not name sages past and present, and they would in any case not recognize the Antiochian Hortensius or the mitigated sceptic Catulus as sages. Repurposing the Antiochian/Stoic argument that anyone who denies the existence of apprehension plunges human beings into darkness and deprives them of their sense altogether (cf. §§30, 102), Cicero concludes that neither Hortensius nor Catulus can be said to know everyday empirical facts. This does not imply that either of them (as a character in Cicero's dialogue) claimed knowledge in some technical sense (contrast the way in which Philo apparently sought to appropriate the term κατάληψις in the Roman Books; see on *Luc.* 18), but does suggest that they might have used e.g. verbs of knowing in a non-technical sense without hesitation (like Cicero himself). Cicero turns to those two rather than addressing Lucullus because he is seeking their approval for his argument; similarly, it is customary for orators to address not just the judges but also the *corona* near the end of their speech. See also Schäublin et al. (p. 308 n. 481).

Parallels from original Stoic and Roman texts are assembled by Brittain (2006: 84 n. 237) and Reid[1] (pp. 345–6). Chrysippus disputed that he himself or one of his fellow Stoics including his teachers was a sage; cf. Plut., *Sto. rep.* ch. 31, 1048e (= *SVF* iii.662) and Quint. 12.1.18 ('Zeno, Cleanthes, and Chrysippus were not sages'). Sextus notes that 'up to now' no sage has materialized (*M.* 7.432; 9.132); cf. Cic., *Div.* 2.61; Sen., *Ep.* 42.1. Cic., *Lael.* 18–19 is a fuller statement to the effect that according to the Stoics no sage had arisen so far and that the great Romans of the past would not have been deemed sages by them. See Brouwer (2014: 92–135). For the setting (*tua uilla*), see on *Luc.* 9b.

§146

Num minus haec...illa subtilius: *haec* refers back to the last sentence of the previous paragraph, and Cicero suggests that the charge is as invidious to Lucullus as the corresponding charge was to the Academic position when delivered by Lucullus in §30. He then dismisses it as inelegant and calls an earlier consideration 'more subtle'—this must be the argument advanced from §144 *init.*, which is now continued. Contrast Schäublin et al. (p. 308 n. 482): 'Cicero scheint mit *illa subtilius* auf seine Unterscheidung zwischen der "Menge" und den Anwesenden [§144 *fin.*: *ad illa ueniam, quae iam non ad multitudinem, sed ad uosmet ipsos, qui adestis, pertinent*]...zurückzuverweisen'. With *illa subtilius*, cf. Cic., *Tusc.* 5.93: *non nimis fortasse subtiliter, utiliter tamen.*

Sed quo modo tu...refero artem sine scientia esse non posse: cf. Sextus, *M.* 7.433 (context: a similar argument to the one made in §§144b–145; see p. 781 above): Τούτου δὲ οὕτως ἔχοντος ἀπολείπεται τὰ ὑπὸ τῶν Στωικῶν πρὸς τοὺς ἀπὸ τῆς σκέψεως λεγόμενα παρὰ μέρος καὶ ὑπὸ τῶν σκεπτικῶν πρὸς ἐκείνους λέγεσθαι, 'And since this is the case, the things said by the Stoics against the skeptics are available to be said, in turn, by the skeptics against them' (transl. Bett).

The reference of *dicebas* is to *Luc.* 22 where Lucullus disputed that crafts can exist when there are no apprehensions; see also Schäublin et al. (p. 309 n. 483). This implies that *probabilia* are insufficient to ground an *ars* (the Clitomachean Cicero disagrees, cf. §107a, as would mitigated sceptics). Reid[1] (p. 346) assembles parallels for *quo modo...sic.* For *referre* 'to retort', see *OLD* s.v. no. 12d.

An pateretur...tanta sollertia: for Zeuxis (painter; *c.*450–380 BC), Phidias (sculptor, painter, and architect; *c.*465–425 BC), and Polyclitus (sculptor; *c.*480–410 BC), see Gschwantler (1978), Lippold (1938), and Lippold (1952), respectively. *Luc.* 146 is *DNO* 1050 (Phidias), as well as 1761 (Zeuxis). The three artists, mentioned here as supreme proponents of their crafts, feature elsewhere in Cicero in various contexts, including to illustrate points of philosophical argument, but none of these parallels is closely relevant to the present context. Cf. *De orat.* 3.26 (*DNO* 1762); *Parad.* 5; *Or.* 8–9 (*DNO* 948; discussed on *Ac.* 1.30–2); *Fin.* 2.115 (*DNO* 1759) and 4.34; *Tusc.* 1.34 (*DNO* 900). On *Brut.* 70, where Phidias seems to be omitted for effect (thus illustrating how well known he was), see Innes (1978).

Quod si eos docuisset aliquis...quod autem satis essent ipsis relinquere: see the general note above on it being the *probabile* (referred to earlier in the paragraph) which is left standing by the Academics but which is sufficient (sc. to account for the existence of crafts). A similar argument, directed at the Epicureans, is in Plut., *Adv. Col.* 1118b. For *tollere* and *relinquere*, see *Luc.* 26 and 34 *fin.*, respectively, with the notes in Reid[1] (p. 347); Hor., *S.* 1.10.51: *tollenda relinquendis.* For *nusquam esse* = 'to be non-existent', cf. Cic., *Div.* 1.117: *quo modo...uates...ea uideant quae nusquam etiam tunc sint.*

Quam rationem maiorum etiam...sed ut 'uideri' pronuntiaretur: that *diligentia maiorum* is a familiar phrase cannot be coincidental (cf. *Verr.* 2.4.9; *Caec.* 34; *Leg. agr.* 2.73; and Hellegouarc'h 1972[2]: 251–2), but the circumspection is normally political, not epistemic.

The conventional formulation of an oath referred to here is: *Ex mei animi sententia (iuro), ut ego...(faciam); si sciens fallo fefellerove, tum me Iuppiter...(faxit)*, 'To the best of my belief (I swear) that I will...do; if I knowingly mislead or have misled, then Jupiter shall render me....' (On *si sciens fallo*, see Hickson 1993: 126.) The punishment to be inflicted by Jupiter in the event of a false oath would be inserted before *faxit*; cf. *teneri* 'to be held liable' here. Cf. e.g. Liv. 22.53; *CIL* II.172; and Jordan (1881: 236). The possibility of failure due to circumstances beyond the subject's control as well as of honest mistakes is emphasized. Oath formulae were highly conventional, so Livy's date as well as that of the inscription (AD 37) do not tell against Cicero crediting the *maiores*. Cf. also *De orat.* 2.260, where the same formula is referenced. Cf. also *Off.* 3.44 on the oath of the *iudex* in criminal proceedings and private cases; Roloff (1938: 103–4).

For the cautious *arbitror* in witness statements, cf. Cic., *Font.* 19; Liv. 3.13.3, 26.33.7 (noted by Reid[1] p. 347). *Arbitror* was also used by officials in public pronouncements, when, however, it would not invariably be meant to qualify; see Heumann-Seckel s.v. *arbitrari*, *TLL* s.v. col. 416.6–48.

For *fecisse uidetur* / *non uidetur* as the phrase with which judges pronounced on the truth of the charge, see Mommsen (1899: 448–9), elaborated on by Daube (1956: 73–7); *OLD* s.v. *uideo* no. 22: '(pass., in legal and other technical contexts) to appear after due consideration, or sim., be deemed.' Cf. *Luc.* 105a. The supplement by Plasberg[1] (p. 152) seems pragmatically necessary; Manutius printed *ut ea non esse facta sed ut uideri pronuntiarent*, which captures either possible outcome under not being the case but appearing to be the case. This is not impossible in terms of sense and Latinity, but less easy to explain relative to the paradosis.

§147

Verum quoniam non solum...sit mihi perorandum: see *Luc.* 9b on Lucullus' and Cicero's travel plans for the day. *Insusurrare* is typically used of the whispering of people; to make *Fauonius* its grammatical subject signals mild stylistic elevation (but the compound verb itself, unlike its simplex, is not poetic). On *sit mihi perorandum*, see next note.

Posthac tamen...quas plagas ipsi contra se Stoici texuerunt: *summi uiri* alludes to the dogmatist's appreciation of *auctoritas* whereas the Academic promotes *iudicium*, 'judgement'; cf. *Luc.* 7b–9a and *N.D.* 1.10. Aug., *Contra Acad.* 2.5.11, seems informed by the counterpart of this section in *Ac.* 4.

For *obscuritas rerum*, cf. *Ac.* 1.15, 1.44. For the notion that of the many possibilities only one view can be true, cf. *Luc.* 115, 117; *De orat.* 2.30; *N.D.* 1.5; Aug., *C.D.* 19.2 (the report on Varro's *De philosophia*; see the general note on *Ac.* 1.19–23). For *iacēre* 'to lie defeated', of a view, cf. *Luc.* 79. For the senses as liars, cf. *Luc.* 79, 80, 82, and the commentary on 19–20; *oculi* is used metonymically of the sense of sight. For the sorites, cf. *Luc.* 49 (where different designations are discussed, too), 92–5, 107; for the liar, §§95–6. With *plagas*, cf. §112: *Stoicorum dumeta*.

In the general note above I have suggested that Cicero is here making a metaphilosophical statement on the debate between dogmatists and Academics; on this reading, Cicero is here, as one would expect in a *peroratio* (cf. *sit mihi perorandum*), taking a step back from the subject matter of *Acad.* as a whole: λογική (i.e. issues touched on in §§142–6, those passed over in the section but covered in *Luc.* 92–6, as well as the epistemological problems which take up the bulk of the work, here represented by *mendacia oculorum sensuumque reliquorum*) is ultimately a less productive area to discuss than physics and ethics. 'Next time let us do *y*' would be a literary flourish rather than expression of intent on the part of Cicero (the character or the author). Similarly Brittain (2006: 85 n. 239), who cross-refers to *Luc.* 112: 'Cicero suggests that his arguments against Stoic apprehension (*Ac.* 2.64–111) were purely defensive: the fundamental case for scepticism derives from the disagreements of dogmatic philosophers (*Ac.* 2.112–46). The latter were the staple of both Academic and Pyrrhonian sceptical arguments.' See also Griffin (1997: 4–7).

Alternatively, it has been suggested e.g. by Bringmann (1971: 112 n. 5 and 137 n. 87) and Steinmetz (1990: 147) that Cicero is here hinting at further works (i) involving the same speakers (cf. the first-person plural verbs) and (ii) to be devoted to physics and ethics. As is acknowledged, Cicero ended up changing the interlocutors already in the intermediate edition of *Acad.*; he did not use the interlocutors featuring in *Luc.* in later works; and *N.D.* covers at best some subjects which would fall under the heading of physics (while *Fin.* is the major ethical work to follow), unless the fragmentary work to which the translation of *Tim.* belongs could be seen as covering physics (so Steinmetz 1990: 149; on the date of *Tim.*, see Marinone 2004^2: 215 and Sedley 2013). So any plan for further works hinted at here would soon have been substantially amended. Could the passage be both meta-philosophical comment on the debate and announcement of future plans (albeit plans soon to be modified)? It emerges from letters to Atticus that the *Catulus* and the *Lucullus* were completed on or just before 13 May 45 BC and that *Fin.* 1, which of course uses different speakers, was completed in draft on or just before 29 May 45 BC (see section 9.1). Even granting the enormous speed with which Cicero wrote, it seems unlikely that he had not already decided on the basic plan for *Fin.* as well as interlocutors when he completed *Luc.* (Thus also Griffin 1997: 4.) This tells against reading *Luc.* 147 as an announcement of future plans. On Lucullus' reply (§148 *init.*) to Cicero's concluding remark see the n. ad loc.

Tamen, which was in the archetype but was already excluded by A^a, could have displaced an *iterum*, as Plasberg^1 (p. 153) suggests. In the edition Greek terms are represented in Greek letters rather than Latin transliteration when the context suggests that an overt code-switch is intended. The present passage, viz. *sorites* and *pseudomenos*, is a borderline case, given that *Stoici* is the subject of the following relative clause.

§148

In §147 the Cicero character had ended his speech by playing down the significance and merit of the subject of λογική (and consequently the author's accomplishment in presenting it). Lucullus replies that he enjoyed the discussion and that the group might indeed convene more frequently e.g. on their Tusculan estates to discuss matters which occur to them, politely not endorsing the suggestion that the subject should better be physics or ethics next time. The Cicero character then invites a comment from the two other characters, Catulus and Hortensius. Catulus states that he is returning to his father's view, whom the latter dubbed Carneadean, that nothing could be apprehended but that the sage would (sc. sometimes) assent to the non-cataleptic, but with an awareness that he was opining and that nothing could be apprehended. The beginning of the sentence after *percipi possit* is corrupt, and two possibilities are conceivable in principle:[574] that Catulus stated that he 'assented strongly' to the proposition that nothing can be known while either (i) rejecting or (ii) accepting universal suspension of judgement. Cicero replies with an acknowledgement, stating that he does not object strongly. Hortensius then gives his view with one word, which is open to two readings: that it is time to go and that assent is to be done away with. Since he had been an Antiochian in *Catul.* and *Luc.*, one is to understand either that the second meaning was not intended or that he is signalling a conversion, whether seriously or not. In any event, Cicero's reply turns on the second meaning: he states that this is the Academy's position. Lucullus and Cicero depart while Catulus remains behind (sc. with Hortensius, cf. §9).

On the reading defended here, §148 furnishes clear evidence that in the *Catul.* Catulus, the second Academic speaker in the first edition of *Acad.*, represented a position which was different from the Cicero character's Clitomachean one, in that it permitted self-aware assent to the incognitive ('mitigated scepticism'). Moreover, we learn that in the dialogue his father held the same position, which he called 'Carneadean'; in the present context, this must mean that the elder Catulus took it to be Carneades' view, rather than something which Carneades advanced for the sake of the argument. This much is accepted by most scholars.[575] There is also broad agreement on one way in which the position of mitigated scepticism could arise, viz. from what Brittain (2006: xxviii) has called the 'new corollary argument', taken as a statement of Carneades' view (see section 4, and below).

Beyond that, the import and significance of §148 as evidence for the sceptical Academy depends on how its relationship with other texts is interpreted as well as on the resolution to the above-mentioned textual problem. Of the passages which make reference to the new corollary argument (*Luc.* 59, 67, 78, 112), *Luc.* 78 stands out for a number of reasons. While the other three passages refer to the sage's opining as an argumentative option against the background of a different view (the commitment to universal suspension of judgement represented by the Cicero character), Cicero records an inner-Academic disagreement in §78: believing Clitomachus rather than 'Philo or Metrodorus', he holds that Carneades suggested that the sage might opine for the sake of the argument, as opposed to this being his view. On one view, Catulus in §148 holds the very position presented as Philo's or Metrodorus's in §78, i.e. a position of mitigated scepticism which, the assumption is, Philo adopted as scholarch of the Academy after giving up the Clitomachean position early in the 90s BC

---

[574] Recent detailed discussions, with references to earlier scholarship, include Schäublin (1993: 163–7); Görler (2004c: 286 n. 29); Burnyeat (1997: 300–9); Brittain (2001: 80–1).
[575] Those who disagree either dispute that there is a difference between the positions held by the Cicero character and by the younger Catulus (see below), or they assume that the younger Catulus defended the Roman Books view in the *Catulus* and is here claiming to return to his father's mitigated position (thus Mansfeld 1997: 57), as opposed to holding this position throughout; see the lemmatized n. below on *reuoluor*.

and before formulating the view of the Roman Books.[576] Metrodorus would be referenced because he is credited with co-formulating or, given his dates,[577] possibly instigating the view at issue. On another view—the one argued for in this commentary—, §78 refers to two distinct views, Philo's Roman Books view and a similar view of Metrodorus', which can both be characterized as permitting assent but maintaining ἀκαταληψία, sc. on the Stoic construal of κατάληψις.[578] On this reading §78 and §148 come apart in an important respect, and only in §148 mitigated scepticism features as a distinct position (namely that of the Catuli), whereas it appeared as a 'for the sake of the argument' option in §§59, 67, and 112. Mitigated scepticism, on this reading, had some currency but was never adopted by the scholarch and thus was never the official Academic position. On either of these interpretations self-aware assent is incompatible with a continued commitment to universal ἐποχή, i.e. self-aware assent is still assent (I will explain presently how self-aware assent could at all be thought to be consistent with universal ἐποχή).[579]

The second passage against which §148 has been read intratextually is §§104–105a, where Cicero translates from a work by Clitomachus, who distinguished two senses of the 'the wise man will suspend judgement', one where it just means that the wise man will not assent, and another where it means that he will not assent but will approve, i.e. will approve under universal ἐποχή. Reid[1] (p. 348) thinks that the same distinction is at issue in §148, which cannot be right, because approval and self-aware assent would collapse into one.[580] Others think that §§104–105a and §148 introduce relevantly analogous distinctions, such that, if approval is possible under universal ἐποχή, so is self-aware assent.[581] I shall explain below why I do not think this to be the case and instead favour a third option, viz. that §148 stands on its own as evidence for mitigated scepticism and that Catulus endorses ἀκαταληψία but gives up on ἐποχή.[582]

Another set of passages, in this case non-Ciceronian, has been connected with §148;[583] they are assembled and discussed in appendix 1. Their shared feature is that they present the Academics as negative dogmatists in some sense. If one takes §78 to refer to the same position as §148, namely Philo's after he had given up the Clitomachean position and before he formulated the Roman Books view, which by

---

[576] Thus Hirzel (1883: 162–80); Striker (1996b: 93), first published in 1980; Long and Sedley (ii.1987: 451); Görler (1994: 871), on §148: '…im wesentlichen die Deutung Metrodors…'; Burnyeat (1997: 300–9); Brittain (2001: 11–12, 14–15, 84–9) and elsewhere; Bonazzi (2003: 103–9).

[577] See Dorandi (2005b).

[578] However, there is sound evidence that both Philo and Metrodorus posited a different, non-Stoic conception of κατάληψις; see the commentary on §§78, 18.

[579] Frede (1987b: 213) takes Catulus' position to be a heterodox one, but thinks self-aware assent is possible under universal ἐποχή.

[580] This may seem an attractive option to those who claim that Cicero, in the frame and as a character, is a Clitomachean in *Acad.* and a mitigated sceptic in other works. I do not think such a shift in position is in evidence in the Ciceronian corpus; see section 8. Glucker (2004: 129, cf. 121–2), who contests the suggestion that there was a distinct group of 'Philonian/Metrodorians' who were mitigated sceptics (thus Brittain 2001), dismisses §148 (as well as §78) as evidence for this group, and also interprets §148 so as to cohere with §104. Similarly Thorsrud (2012: 146, 148 n. 25).

[581] Thus Schäublin (1993: 163–7); this reading requires the corrupt sentence beginning to say that Catulus endorses ἐποχή.

[582] It is possible that the code-switch to the Greek term ἐποχή marks a reference to §104, but if so, the intention is to signal disagreement; see the lemmatized n. below.

[583] See Frede (1987b: 218–20); Brittain (2001: 88–90).

universal agreement was an immediate and inconsequential failure, then such passages may be deemed further evidence for the notion that mitigated scepticism was for a time the official position of the Academy and as such determined the reception of Academic scepticism for a long time. In this commentary, I opt for a different interpretation. First, the distinction between assent and approval is not straightforward to conceptualize, to the point where many modern interpreters speak of §104 as distinguishing two types of assent; consequently, the Clitomachean position, construed as including a licence to give approval when appropriate, is sufficient to account for the evidence. Second, a number of the sources have reasons of their own to misrepresent Academic scepticism, e.g. in order to claim that the Academics are not credible generally speaking, or not credible sceptics (thus the Pyrrhonists, who thereby become the true proponents of scepticism). Third, on the side of the dogmatic opponents, too, there is evidence for thinking that the nuance inherent in approval under ἐποχή would be elided on purpose; cf. the dilemmatic argument in Luc. 43–4. There is, however, no reason to deny that mitigated scepticism may be a reference point, or an additional reference point, for some of the passages assembled in appendix 1; crucially, such a reference is not required to account for the evidence.

Two considerations in favour of the view that self-aware assent is incompatible with universal ἐποχή are (i) the correspondences and emphases in the apparently accurately transmitted parts of the relevant two sentences here in §148 and (ii) the manner in which Cicero qua non-sage speaks about his own cognitive habits elsewhere in Luc. Ad (i): the sentence *egone...percipi possit* introduces in sequence two main propositions, that according to the view at issue nothing can be apprehended and that the sage will (sometimes) opine. In the sentence which begins with the corruption the former view is referred to in the unobjectionable second part, which makes it likely that the corrupt beginning of the same sentence (however it is to be restored in detail) referred to the other main proposition, by rejecting universal ἐποχή. Regarding the emphases, Long and Sedley (ii.1987: 451) observe: 'The favoured emendation *quare* [before *epochen*] makes Catulus say that he both approves of *suspension of assent* about all things and vehemently *assents* to the view that nothing is cognitive. So blatant a contradiction seems unlikely unless we take Catulus to be exploiting Clitomachus' distinction between two kinds of assent... [§§104–105a], as suggested by Reid...[see above]. But there is no hint in the text that any such equivocation is intended, and, if it were, it would be incredible that Catulus should use *vehementer adsentior* to express the *weaker* kind of assent, as this interpretation would require.' Ad (ii): the Cicero character, who is committed to universal ἐποχή as a Clitomachean, professes that he is frequently unable to stick to his avowed policy, such that he gives his assent on many occasions (§§65–6). He also makes it clear that his assent is self-aware, i.e. is exactly the sort of assent which is permitted to the mitigated sceptic (§141), which one would assume in any event on independent grounds, given the deep commitment to ἀκαταληψία.[584] And yet, in

---

[584] In the commentary on §§66–7 I consider the possibility that the Cicero character's assent, cast as a human failing, might be momentarily dogmatic, i.e. given in an oblivious way and without attending to any proviso. I do not believe that this option, even if it was entertained as a possibility by Cicero, would alter the situation.

§§65–6 there is no suggestion that his assent allows him to escape censure (or self-censure) in virtue of being unlike dogmatic assent; rather, in virtue of giving the kind of assent that he does give he is revealed as flawed and weak.[585]

How exactly self-aware assent was construed by mitigated sceptics as well as Clitomacheans who recognized it as a real-life possibility is not evident from our passage, but e.g. the elaborate account of the πιθανόν in Sextus *M.* 7 or the section on approval in *Luc.* 104–105a suggest by analogy that the notion was articulated in some detail, too. The only substantial reconstruction to date is by Brittain (2001: 83–94),[586] who starts from the clause spelling out the qualification under which assent is permitted to the Academic sage and consequently to everyone: ... *opinaturum ... sed ita ut intellegat se opinari sciatque nihil esse quod comprehendi et percipi possit*. Brittain (p. 85) identifies two provisos under which self-aware assent is permitted and formulates them as follows:

(1) that the subject is aware that the impression to which he is assenting is non-cataleptic (or not such that the impression might not be false); and
(2) that the subject recognizes that no impression is such that it might not be false, and hence that there are no conditions under which it is rational to assert knowledge of (the propositional content of) an impression.

He argues that, first, proviso (1) cannot be intended to stand as 'another, co-ordinate belief' to the belief at issue, since this would make the second proviso redundant qua generalization of the first one; and, second, that, if the subject is committed to provisos (1) and (2), then the co-ordinate belief would itself require another co-ordinate belief (i.e. 1), and so on. He also rules out the possibility (p. 86) that the provisos qualify the content of the belief at issue in such a way that it is understood as a 'possibility or (statistical) probability', on the grounds that even in that case the assent given would endorse the proposition in question so modified as true. Thus, by a process of elimination, Brittain concludes that the provisos must be operative 'on the assent of the subject, or on the way in which the subject holds (individually) the beliefs he has.' The first of these two possibilities is, however, not intended to entail that self-aware assent is possible under universal ἐποχή.

I agree that the proviso cannot be meant to qualify the content of the belief for the reasons cited, but do wonder if the provisos could not function as co-ordinated beliefs in a different way. Proviso (2) is arguably primary and secured inductively by the many considerations in favour of ἀπαραλλαξία which the Academics have cited over two centuries; as such, *it* is not in need of another co-ordinated belief like (1).[587] Proviso (1) flows in the case of each belief from proviso (2). On this construal, the basic cognitive act of acceptance or endorsement which assent represents would be

---

[585] See the *appendix critica* of the edition for the ways in which different editors have restored the text in §148.
[586] See, however, also Burnyeat (1997: 305).
[587] I take this to be compatible with the fact that proviso (2) is about a recognition with regard to the conclusion of the core argument, viz. a prime example for the sort of proposition to which the mitigated sceptic would give self-aware assent (as opposed to approval, like a Clitomachean of the kind the Cicero character is).

the same for dogmatic and self-aware assent, i.e. it would not be modified by the provisos.

Clitomachean approval is not in some sense passive, acquiescing, a mere going-along-with, as I argue in the commentary on *Luc.* 104–105a. Rather, approval is ex hypothesi given to what appears true (without thereby being taken to be true) under full conscious and deliberate deployment of one's rational faculties, which makes it unsurprising that the Cicero character can call his approval something that is given *plane*, 'fully' or 'absolutely' (§113 *fin.*). What about the fact that Catulus' assent is given *uehementer* here, i.e. does this reveal something about the nature of self-aware assent? One might think that the basic act of endorsement, of accepting an impression or proposition as true, issues from a binary choice and is as such not capable of calibration. *Assentiri* is of course a verb which has pre- and non-philosophical uses, notably in the political sphere, and in those contexts modification by an adverb like *uehementer* would be entirely unremarkable; it would be in keeping with the customary bonhomie in the 'frames' of Ciceronian (and Platonic) dialogues if the philosophical use here in §148 shaded into the non-philosophical one, in which case there would be nothing that could be learnt about self-aware assent from the modification *uehementer* in the present passage. Alternatively one may wonder if it is helpful to think of self-aware assent as given to impressions which can themselves be placed on a graded scale; in this case calling a particular instance of self-aware assent 'vehement' would be slightly loose talk. Thus to the mitigated sceptic impressions assented to are πιθανά or *probabilia*, which differ in their πιθανότης in virtue of their subject, contextual circumstances, one's antecedently held beliefs (understood in a suitable way), and possibly the perceiving subject's long-standing and momentary practical interests.[588] The considerations which account for the relative persuasiveness of a given impression may be construed as *reasons* of varying strength for self-aware assent when it is given.[589]

One way to tell the story of the emergence of mitigated scepticism is, as mentioned above, with reference to the different attitudes taken to the new corollary argument, i.e. to assume that Carneades advanced it as a view of his own rather than for the sake of the argument. This, however, tells us little about the underlying rationale: given that Academics prized independent judgement over following authority (see on *Luc.* 7b–9a), those who adopted this view will have felt a need to explain their shift away from the Clitomachean position. We may be seeing a glimpse of these explanations in Cicero's profession that it is very difficult to adhere to a policy of universal suspension of judgement, which sits awkwardly with the Clitomachean self-representation as deploying realistic and achievable standards and categories compared to the Stoics (*Luc.* 65–7; 144–6). Moreover, as noted at §§104–105a, while it is an entirely intuitive notion that one can 'merely' approve some impressions, it is more difficult to assume this for all one's impressions and quasi-beliefs.[590] Finally,

---

[588] See section 6.1 and Reinhardt (2018a).
[589] Thus self-aware assent is reason-responsive in a way which is analogous to the reason-responsiveness of dogmatic assent; see Coope (2016) on the reason-responsiveness of dogmatic assent.
[590] In this commentary the difference between late Clitomacheanism as represented by Cicero and mitigated scepticism is assumed to turn on the narrow issue of what conception of belief either stance operates. This makes the reconstruction of the pressures which led some Academics to give up

some members of the school may have shifted in their meta-philosophical attitude to opining, which the Clitomacheans shared with the Stoics and derived from Arcesilaus (cf. *Luc.* 77).[591]

A Platonic passage which strikingly juxtaposes key aspects of the rationale for the Clitomachean and the mitigated position and which therefore could conceivably have been invoked by Academics is Plato, *Rep.* 506c, where Socrates, in response to the question of what he thinks the good is, refuses to reply on the grounds that it is wrong to talk about things one does not know as if one did. His interlocutor Glaucon counters the point by saying that this need not be so provided one puts forward beliefs as mere beliefs rather than knowledge. Yet Socrates insists that belief without knowledge is disgraceful and blind at best, enabling the subject merely to get things right by accident even if everything goes well. A Clitomachean might have derived encouragement from this outcome of the exchange.[592]

Tum Lucullus 'Non moleste...requiremus': Lucullus' reply to Cicero's concluding remark gives out little for the question of whether §147 was hinting at further planned dialogues; see ad loc. Reid[1] (p. 347) takes *in Tusculanis nostris* to be a reference to *Tusc.*, whose subject matter seemed to be on Cicero's mind in §135 *fin*. In section 9.5 the question is considered whether Lucullus' *Tusculanum* was the setting for *Hort.*; if so, the reference could be a closural device for the triptych of dialogues. For *conferre* 'to discuss', see *OLD* s.v. no. 13).

'Optime', inquam, 'sed quid Catulus sentit, quid Hortensius?': see Reid[1] (p. 289) on §94 *superbe*, where, however, the ellipsis is more marked than here. For the roles played by the younger Catulus and Hortensius, see section 9.2 and on *Luc.* 63–4. *Sentire* is as elsewhere in *Luc.* generic, i.e. does not designate belief or quasi-belief in one of the senses discussed in the dialogue.

Tum Catulus, 'Egone?...uehementer assentior': the section is part of Carneades F5, 189–93 Mette = LS 69K. *Egone* is conversational, frequent in comedy, and conveys mild surprise, whether genuine or not; if the reader is to picture Catulus as genuinely surprised, then it will be because the second Antiochian was not asked for his view first. *Reuoluor*, for which see *OLD* s.v. *reuoluo* no. 4, could in principle either signal a substantial shift of position (thus Mansfeld 1997: 57), who assumes that Catulus endorsed the Roman Books view in *Catul.* and is now returning to his father's mitigated position, or it could convey no more than that Catulus was tempted by Cicero's case for the Clitomachean outlook but decides to remain committed to the mitigated view associated with his father (thus Barnes and Görler *per litteras*, reported by

---

Clitomacheanism in favour of mitigated scepticism more straightforward than if one assumes e.g. that both stances relied on quite different interpretations of the πιθανόν (thus Brittain 2001: 94–128, cf. Frede 1987b: 214) or were associated with fundamentally different practices (e.g. purely destructive argument vs moderate theory-building under proviso).

[591] Thus Striker (1996b: 97): 'If one does not hold, like the Stoics that errors are sins, there seems to be no good reason left why one should not hold an opinion with the express proviso that it might be wrong. And this is just what Carneades is said to have maintained (*Acad.* II 148).'

[592] See the general note on *Luc.* 66–7 on the Clitomachean's evidentialist convictions, and Wynne (2016) on how the Clitomachean view may be interpreted in terms of the modern 'ethics of belief' debate.

Mansfeld 1997: 57 n. 26; see also the discussion in Lévy 1999: 120–1). I think the latter must be meant, for a number of reasons. First, in §63 after Lucullus' speech Catulus raises the possibility that Cicero might be so impressed by it as to be turned by it, so that it would be natural for him to resume this theme of a possible conversion here with respect to himself. Second, the Roman Books view is dismissed in §18; if Catulus had endorsed it in *Catul.*, it would amount to a loss of face for the character to give it up here without further explanation and to just revert to his father's position; note also Catulus' easy, slightly arrogant confidence in §63. Third, given that the elder Catulus is cast as challenging Philo robustly on the claims of the Roman Books (§18), the younger Catulus endorsing the view would in my view not show independence of mind, but an inclination towards rebellion without a cause. Fourth, *habeo... aspernor* below would be insufficient as an acknowledgement of a change of stance on Catulus' part.

Mansfeld (1997: 52) states that it would have made the younger Catulus a 'mere *fils à papa*' if he had confined himself in *Catul.* to reporting what his father had said to Philo, and that this would also make it hard to explain why the dialogue was named *Catulus*. I agree that the latter fact indicates a substantial role for the younger Catulus, but also think that the manner in which Roman aristocrats construed father-son-relationships would have made it entirely unobjectionable for the son to uphold the father's view.

On the Carneadean credentials of the mitigated position, see the general note above. The elder Catulus' repeated insistence (note tense of *dicebat*) that the view was Carneadean might narrowly relate to with what is reported in §18, i.e. that he put to Philo that the Roman Books view was not Carneadean, but the point might also have been presented in *Catul.* as a broader one: it would amount to an insistence on the credentials of the mitigated position at a time when the majority view and, on my construal Philo's, was the kind of Clitomacheanism represented by Cicero in his works (in 'frames' and as a character) as well as by Cotta in *N.D.*

The assent of the Academic sage would issue in δόξα/ἀγνοία on Stoic terms irrespective of any provisos the Academics wish to make; see the general note above, and the commentary on *Ac.* 1.41 with Meinwald (2005). However, to the mitigated sceptic the provisos make all the difference of course.

Regarding the two verbs of knowing *intellegat... sciatque*, it is clear from other passages (§67) where the new corollary argument features that *aliquando* (or *interdum*) is to be supplied with *opinaturum*: Catulus is not talking about a state of opining (analogous to the Stoic sage's state of ἐπιστήμη), but about individual acts of assent leading to individual *opiniones*. *Intellegere* signals an awareness of the nature of such individual *opiniones*; in *Acad.* it is not a term which incurs or reveals particular ideological commitments. On my reading, the use of *-que* shades into the explanatory (*OLD* s.v. no. 6): it is not the case, or not necessarily the case, that the Academic sage understands that a given *opinio* is such that it could be false because of an intrinsic property which it has or fails to have, i.e. because of a conscious awareness of the absence of the supreme clarity which is supposed to mark out cataleptic impressions. Rather, that understanding is derived from the 'knowledge' that there is nothing which can be apprehended, which in turn has been secured inductively (see the general note above). That *scire* is used by an Academic who disavows knowledge (understood in a certain way) has troubled some editors (Reid[1] p. 348 suggests emendation to *sentiat*), but only in §145 *fin.* the Cicero character had made the point in a *reductio* that, given Stoic stipulations of what knowledge is and how knowledge terminology is to be used, Catulus did not 'know' that it was day. For *scire* and *intellegere* in interaction, cf. *Fin.* 2.13.

In the general note above, I explain why I think that Catulus must be rejecting universal ἐποχή here. However, one cannot be confident about what exactly Cicero wrote. The suggestion by Lambinus that *per (ἐποχὴν illam)* results from a perseveration error, i.e. *percipi possit per* or *percipi possit percipi* followed by incomplete deletion of the second *percipi*, seems correct to me, and preferable to assuming that *per* has displaced a different word. (The notes at the end of the text in 'Lambinus' state that he excludes *per* as well as assumes that *enim* has dropped out.) *Improbare* occurs several times in *Luc.*, while *non probare* is not used, nor does it occur in other parts of the Ciceronian corpus.

It is striking that Cicero did not use one of the Latin renderings for 'assent' which he deploys elsewhere; instead, he either wrote ἐποχήν in Greek letters or in transliteration. I have printed the former, since it seems more likely that Cicero marked the unusual word in this way. The reason for the code-switch is not obvious, though. That ἐποχήν is modified by *illam* and by *omnium rerum* may suggest that there is a reference to §104 *init.* (*assensus sustinere sapientem... omnino eum nulli rei assentiri*) here, where the Greek term does not feature, but which is marked as a translation from a Greek original. If so, the connection would not be one of those considered in the general note above; rather, Catulus would be signalling that he disagrees on the sage's commitment to suspension of judgement.

Nihil esse quod percipi possit is apt and not otiose; Schäublin (1993: 163–7) deletes it as a misguided explanatory gloss because he takes *sententia* to refer to the second sense of 'the sage suspends judgement' distinguished in §104 (*altero, cum se a respondendo... sustineat*).

On the questions raised by *uehementer*, see the general note above. Mansfeld (1997: 56 n. 25) has assembled instances of *uehementer assentiri* in Cicero: *De orat.* 1.110 and 262; *Fin.* 3.17 and 57; *N.D.* 3.65; *Div.* 1.105; *Fam.* 11.21.5 (= SB 411). Scholarly discussions of the instance here include Frede (1987b: 213); Brittain (2001: 86–8); and Bonazzi (2003: 106 n. 28).

'Habeo', inquam, '...Hortensi': for the use of *habere*, see *TLL* s.v. col. 2434.8; Nonius Marcellus glosses it as *audire* (p. 318.8 M. = p. 498.21 Lindsay). One might be tempted to take *nec... admodum aspernor* as evidence that Cicero is playing down the disagreement with Catulus, and the significance of the difference between Clitomacheanism and mitigated scepticism, but as Görler (2004c: 287 n. 30) observes, the Cicero character uses the same phrase in §123 to signal an attitude to a view which he must have thought rather unlikely, viz. that there may be 'antipodes who stand such that the soles of their feet face ours'. The concluding section of a dialogue is a place where disagreements tend to be played down.

Tum ille ridens 'Tollendum': on the two senses of *tollere* at issue and the way in which the pun works, see the general note above; for 'to weigh the anchor', see *OLD* s.v. no. 1c, for '= ἀνειρεῖν' no. 14 and e.g. §59: *tollendus assensus est*. See also Schäublin et al. (p. 310 n. 488). In the translation I use 'away with it' (like Brittain 2006: 86), intended to allude to the nautical command 'aweigh the anchor', out of which, however, no suitably ambiguous expression can be formed. Another passage where Cicero plays on the ambiguity of *tollere*, if in a slightly different way, is *Fam.* 11.20.1 (= SB 401): *laudandum adulescentem, ornandum, tollendum* (of Octavian); cf. Vell. Pat. 2.62.6. Reid[1] (p. 348) and Brittain (2006: 86 n. 242) state that *Att.* 13.21.3 (= T33), which comments on assent terminology in Latin, relates to the present passage; I think it speaks to §94, since the two candidates in play in the letter for rendering ἐπέχειν are *sustinere* and *inhibere*.

'**Teneo te**', inquam, 'nam ista Academiae propria sententia': for the use of *teneo*, see *OLD* s.v. no. 22b: 'to hold (by ties of allegiance, or sim.; also, by ties of affection)'. In calling the commitment to universal ἐποχή the *propria sententia* of the Academy, Cicero signals agreement with Hortensius (and Lucullus) that judgement is to be suspended in the absence of apprehension. The Roman Books view is dismissed in *Acad.* even though it was advanced by Philo while he was scholarch, but one wonders if Cicero could have spoken about suspension of judgement as he does here if Philo himself had ever been a mitigated sceptic. Reid[1] (p. 348) draws attention to the title of a Varronian *satura* (ἔχω σε; no. 172 in Cebè and in Astbury), which would have given this ending additional resonance in the final edition; see on Aug., *Contra Acad.* 3.7.15–6 (t. 51).

Ita sermone confecto Catulus remansit; nos ad nauiculas nostras descendimus: cf. §9: Catulus remains with Hortensius, Lucullus and Cicero leave. *Nauicula* may be equivalent to *nauis*; see Adams (2016: 515).

APPENDIX 1

Non-Ciceronian Texts on the Sceptical Academy

For the texts assembled in this section I have usually compared the standard edition as well as the text in collections of fragments and testimonia; I name an editor when the work may be difficult to identify without it.

Texts

1. Galen, *Opt. doctr.* 1 (= LS 68V = Favorinus t. 28 Barigazzi, p. 179.1–21 = F33–6 Amato); 3 (Favorinus t. 28 Barigazzi, pp. 182.27–183.3); 3 (Favorinus t. 28 Barigazzi, pp. 183.13–17)

(1) (a) Τὴν εἰς ἑκάτερα ἐπιχείρησιν ἀρίστην εἶναι διδασκαλίαν ὁ Φαβωρῖνός φησιν. Ὀνομάζουσι δ᾽ οὕτως οἱ Ἀκαδημαϊκοὶ καθ᾽ ἣν τοῖς ἀντικειμένοις συναγορεύουσιν. Οἱ μὲν οὖν παλαιότεροι τελευτᾶν αὐτὴν εἰς ἐποχήν ὑπολαμβάνουσιν, ἐποχὴν καλοῦντες τὴν ὡς ἂν εἴποι τις ἀοριστίαν, ὅπερ ἐστὶ περὶ μηδενὸς πράγματος ὁρίσασθαι μηδ᾽ ἀποφήνασθαι βεβαίως. (b) Οἱ νεώτεροι δ᾽—οὐ γὰρ μόνος ὁ Φαβωρῖνος—ἐνίοτε μὲν εἰς τοσοῦτον προάγουσι τὴν ἐποχήν ὡς μηδὲ τὸν ἥλιον ὁμολογεῖν εἶναι καταληπτόν, ἐνίοτε δ᾽ εἰς τοσοῦτον τὴν κρίσιν ὡς καὶ τοῖς μαθηταῖς ἐπιτρέπειν αὐτὴν ἄνευ τοῦ διδαχθῆναι πρότερον ἐπιστημονικὸν κριτήριον. Οὐδὲ γὰρ ἄλλο τί ἐστιν, ὃ Φαβωρῖνος εἴρηκεν ἐν τῷ 'Περὶ τῆς Ἀκαδημαϊκῆς διαθέσεως', ὃ 'Πλούταρχος' ἐπιγέγραπται... . Καὶ μέντοι κἀν τῷ μετὰ ταῦτα γραφέντι βιβλίῳ, τῷ 'Ἀλκιβιάδῃ' τοὺς Ἀκαδημαϊκοὺς ἐπαινεῖ συναγορεύοντας μὲν ἑκατέρῳ τῶν ἀντικειμένων ἀλλήλοις λόγων, ἐπιτρέποντας δὲ τοῖς μαθηταῖς αἱρεῖσθαι τοὺς ἀληθεστέρους. (c) Ἀλλ᾽ ἐν τούτῳ μὲν εἴρηκε πιθανὸν ἑαυτῷ φαίνεσθαι, μηδὲν εἶναι καταληπτόν, ἐν δὲ τῷ Πλουτάρχῳ συγχωρεῖν ἔοικεν εἶναί τι βεβαίως γνωστόν. Ἄμεινον γὰρ οὕτως ὀνομάζειν τὸ καταληπτὸν ἀποχωροῦντας ὀνόματος Στωικοῦ.

Context: the beginning of the treatise, in which Galen attacks Favorinus.
On the text of ἐπαινεῖ συναγορεύοντας ... αἱρεῖσθαι τοὺς ἀληθεστέρους, see Ioppolo (1983: 192 n. 34).

(3) Ἀλλ᾽ ἴσως φησὶ μηδὲν εἶναι τοιοῦτον ἐν φιλοσοφίᾳ καὶ δόγμασι. Μὴ τοίνυν ἔτι προσποιοῦ γιγνώσκειν τι μηδ᾽ ἀποφάναι μηδ᾽ ἀποδίδρασκε τὴν ὑπὸ τῶν πρεσβυτέρων Ἀκαδημαϊκῶν εἰσαγομένην ἐποχήν, μηδὲ σεμνύνου γραμματικοῦ ποιῶν ἔργον, ἅπερ εἰρήκασιν οἱ πρόσθεν ἐκμεμελετηκώς. Ὅτι δ᾽ αὐτῶν ὑγιές ἐστιν οὐδέν, εὔδηλον ἐννοῶ. ... Εὔδηλος οὖν ἐστιν ὁ Φαβωρῖνος αἰδούμενος μὲν ἀνατρέπειν πάντα καὶ ἀγνοεῖν ὑπάρχον ὁμολογεῖν, ὃ δῆθεν ὑπάρχειν οἱ πρόσθεν ἔλεγον Ἀκαδημαϊκοί τε καὶ Πυρρώνειοι, προσποιούμενος δ᾽ ἐπιτρέπειν τὴν κρίσιν τοῖς μαθηταῖς, ἣν οὐδ᾽ ἑαυτοῖς ἐπέτρεψαν οἱ πρὸ αὐτοῦ.

2. Plutarch, *Sto. rep.* 10, 1037b–c (= SVF ii.129 = LS 31P)

Ἵνα τοίνυν μηδ᾽ ἀντίρρησιν ἀπολίπῃ τοῦ τὰ ἐναντία λέγειν, ἐν μὲν ταῖς Φυσικαῖς Θέσεσι ταῦτα γέγραφεν· 'ἔσται δὲ καὶ καταλαμβανόντας τι πρὸς τὰ ἐναντία ἐπιχειρεῖν, τὴν ἐνοῦσαν συνηγορίαν ποιουμένους· ποτὲ δ᾽ οὐδέτερον καταλαμβάνοντας εἰς ἑκάτερον τὰ ⟨ἐν⟩όντα [suppl. Jones] λέγειν'. ἐν δὲ τῷ Περὶ τῆς τοῦ Λόγου Χρήσεως εἰπών, ὡς οὐ δεῖ τῇ τοῦ λόγου δυνάμει πρὸς τὰ μὴ ἐπιβάλλοντα χρῆσθαι καθάπερ οὐδ᾽ ὅπλοις, ταῦτ᾽ ἐπείρηκε· 'πρὸς μὲν γὰρ τὴν τῶν ἀληθῶν εὕρεσιν δεῖ χρῆσθαι αὐτῇ καὶ πρὸς τὴν τούτων συγγυμνασίαν, εἰς τἀναντία δ' οὔ, πολλῶν ποιούντων τοῦτο, πολλοὺς δὴ λέγων ἴσως (C) τοὺς ἐπέχοντας. ἀλλ' ἐκεῖνοι μὲν οὐδέτερον καταλαμβάνοντες εἰς ἑκάτερον ἐπιχειροῦσιν, ὡς εἴ τι καταληπτόν ἐστιν οὕτως ἂν μόνως ἢ μάλιστα κατάληψιν ἑαυτῆς τὴν ἀλήθειαν παρέχουσαν· σὺ δ', ὁ κατηγορῶν ἐκείνων, αὐτὸς τἀναντία γράφων οἷς καταλαμβάνεις περὶ τῆς συνηθείας ἑτέρους τε τοῦτο ποιεῖν μετὰ συνηγορίας προτρεπόμενος ἐν ἀχρήστοις καὶ βλαβεροῖς ὁμολογεῖς τῇ τοῦ λόγου δυνάμει χρώμενος ὑπὸ φιλοτιμίας νεανιεύεσθαι.

Context: an attack on Chrysippus, who fell foul of his own stipulations regarding arguments on either side and ended up arguing more powerfully against common sense than for it.

In the absolute accusative construction ὡς εἴ τι ... τὴν ἀλήθειαν παρέχουσαν, the word ὡς could in principle introduce a subjective comparison ('as if') or a subjective rationale ('their idea being'); see Kühner-Gerth ii. 87-90 and 90-1. In the former case the apposition might give Plutarch's view, whereas in the latter it has to give the Academics' rationale as they see it. That the latter must be intended is clear from the overall train of thought: Plutarch criticizes Chrysippus for making the Academics seem more rigid than they are, noting that they had a use for argument on either side which was not intended to lead to stalemate, whereas Chrysippus himself, by arguing on either side and getting carried away due to his arrogance, used reason in a harmful manner.

3. Sextus, *P.H.* 1.220-35, with omissions (1.232-4 = LS 68I; 1.235 = LS 68T)

(220) Φασὶ μέντοι τινὲς ὅτι ἡ Ἀκαδημαϊκὴ φιλοσοφία ἡ αὐτή ἐστι τῇ σκέψει· διόπερ ἀκόλουθον ἂν εἴη καὶ περὶ τούτου διεξελθεῖν. Ἀκαδημίαι δὲ γεγόνασιν, ὡς φασὶ⟨ν οἱ⟩ πλείους [ἤ], τρεῖς, μία μὲν καὶ ἀρχαιοτάτη ἡ τῶν περὶ Πλάτωνα, δευτέρα δὲ καὶ μέση ἡ τῶν περὶ Ἀρκεσίλαον τὸν ἀκουστὴν Πολέμωνος, τρίτη δὲ καὶ νέα ἡ τῶν περὶ Καρνεάδην καὶ Κλειτόμαχον· ἔνιοι δὲ καὶ τετάρτην προστιθέασι τὴν περὶ Φίλωνα καὶ Χαρμίδαν, τινὲς δὲ καὶ πέμπτην καταλέγουσι τὴν περὶ [τὸν] Ἀντίοχον.

(226) Οἱ δὲ ἀπὸ τῆς νέας Ἀκαδημίας, εἰ καὶ ἀκατάληπτα εἶναι πάντα φασί, διαφέρουσι τῶν σκεπτικῶν ἴσως μὲν καὶ κατ' αὐτὸ τὸ λέγειν πάντα εἶναι ἀκατάληπτα (διαβεβαιοῦνται γὰρ περὶ τούτου, ὁ δὲ σκεπτικὸς ἐνδέχεσθαι καὶ καταληφθῆναί τινα προσδοκᾷ), διαφέρουσι δὲ ἡμῶν προδήλως ἐν τῇ τῶν ἀγαθῶν καὶ τῶν κακῶν κρίσει. Ἀγαθὸν γὰρ τί φασιν εἶναι οἱ Ἀκαδημαϊκοὶ καὶ κακὸν οὐχ ὡς ἡμεῖς, ἀλλὰ μετὰ τοῦ πεπεῖσθαι ὅτι πιθανόν ἐστι μᾶλλον ὃ λέγουσιν εἶναι ἀγαθὸν ὑπάρχειν ἢ τὸ ἐναντίον, καὶ ἐπὶ τοῦ κακοῦ ὁμοίως, ἡμῶν ἀγαθόν τι ἢ κακὸν εἶναι λεγόντων οὐδὲ μετὰ τοῦ πιθανὸν εἶναι νομίζειν ὅ φαμεν, ἀλλ' ἀδοξάστως ἑπομένων τῷ βίῳ, ἵνα μὴ ἀνενέργητοι ὦμεν. (227) Τάς τε φαντασίας ἡμεῖς μὲν ἴσας λέγομεν εἶναι κατὰ πίστιν ἢ ἀπιστίαν ὅσον ἐπὶ τῷ λόγῳ, ἐκεῖνοι δὲ τὰς μὲν πιθανὰς εἶναί φασι τὰς δὲ ἀπιθάνους.

Εἰ δὲ καὶ πείθεσθαί τισιν οἵ τε ἀπὸ τῆς Ἀκαδημίας καὶ οἱ ἀπὸ τῆς σκέψεως λέγουσι, (230) πρόδηλος καὶ ἡ κατὰ τοῦτο διαφορὰ τῶν φιλοσοφιῶν. Τὸ γὰρ πείθεσθαι λέγεται διαφόρως, τό τε μὴ ἀντιτείνειν ἀλλ' ἁπλῶς ἕπεσθαι ἄνευ σφοδρᾶς προσκλίσεως καὶ προσπαθείας, ὡς ὁ παῖς πείθεσθαι λέγεται τῷ παιδαγωγῷ· ἅπαξ δὲ τὸ μετὰ αἱρέσεως καὶ οἱονεὶ συμπαθείας κατὰ τὸ σφόδρα βούλεσθαι συγκατατίθεσθαί τινι, ὡς ὁ ἄσωτος πείθεται τῷ δαπανητικῶς βιοῦν ἀξιοῦντι. Διόπερ ἐπειδὴ οἱ μὲν περὶ Καρνεάδην καὶ Κλειτόμαχον μετὰ προσκλίσεως σφοδρᾶς πείθεσθαί τε καὶ πιθανὸν εἶναί τί φασιν, ἡμεῖς δὲ κατὰ τὸ ἁπλῶς εἴκειν ἄνευ προσπαθείας, καὶ κατὰ τοῦτο ἂν αὐτῶν διαφέροιμεν.

(235) Οἱ δὲ περὶ Φίλωνά φασιν ὅσον μὲν ἐπὶ τῷ Στωικῷ κριτηρίῳ, τουτέστι τῇ καταληπτικῇ φαντασίᾳ, ἀκατάληπτα εἶναι τὰ πράγματα, ὅσον δὲ ἐπὶ τῇ φύσει τῶν πραγμάτων αὐτῶν,

καταληπτά. Ἀλλὰ καὶ ὁ Ἀντίοχος τὴν Στοὰν μετήγαγεν εἰς τὴν Ἀκαδημίαν, ὡς καὶ εἰρῆσθαι ἐπ' αὐτῷ ὅτι ἐν Ἀκαδημίᾳ φιλοσοφεῖ τὰ Στωικά· ἐπεδείκνυε γὰρ ὅτι παρὰ Πλάτωνι κεῖται τὰ τῶν Στωικῶν δόγματα. Ὡς πρόδηλον εἶναι τὴν τῆς σκεπτικῆς ἀγωγῆς διαφορὰν πρός τε τὴν τετάρτην καὶ τὴν πέμπτην καλουμένην Ἀκαδημίαν.

Context: in a survey of schools which might be deemed sceptical, Sextus devotes a substantial amount of space to the Academics, showing that their outlook is different from that of the Pyrrhonists, with the partial exception of Arcesilaus. 1.221–5 deal with Plato, 1.226–31 with the 'New Academics', and 1.232–4 with Arcesilaus.

4. Gellius, *N.A.* 11.5.1–8 (= Favorinus fr. 26 Arrighetti [11.5.1–8] = F32 Monte [11.5.1–5])

De Pyrrhonis philosophis quaedam deque Academicis strictim notata; deque inter eos differentia.

1. Quos Pyrrhonios philosophos uocamus, hi Graeco cognomento σκεπτικοί appellantur; 2. id ferme significat quasi 'quaesitores' et 'consideratores'. 3. Nihil enim decernunt, nihil constituunt, sed in quaerendo semper considerandoque sunt, quidnam sit omnium rerum, de quo decerni constituique possit. 4. Ac ne uidere quoque plane quicquam neque audire sese putant, sed ita pati afficique quasi uideant uel audiant, eaque ipsa, quae adfectiones istas in sese efficiunt, qualia et cuiusmodi sint, cunctantur atque insistunt; omniumque rerum fidem ueritatemque mixtis confusisque signis ueri atque falsi ita imprensibilem uideri aiunt, ut, quisquis homo est non praeceps neque iudicii sui prodigus, his uti uerbis debeat, quibus auctorem philosophiae istius Pyrrhonem esse usum tradunt: οὐ μᾶλλον οὕτως ἔχει τόδε ἢ ἐκείνως ἢ οὐθετέρως. Indicia enim rei cuiusque et sinceras proprietates negant posse nosci et percipi, idque ipsum docere atque ostendere multis modis conantur. 5. Super qua re Favorinus quoque subtilissime argutissimeque decem libros composuit, quos Πυρρωνείων τρόπων inscribit.

6. Vetus autem quaestio et a multis scriptoribus Graecis tractata, an quid et quantum Pyrrhonios et Academicos philosophos intersit. Vtrique enim σκεπτικοί, ἐφεκτικοί, ἀπορητικοί dicuntur, quoniam utrique nihil affirmant nihilque comprehendi putant. Sed ex omnibus rebus proinde uisa fieri dicunt, quas φαντασίας appellant, non ut rerum ipsarum natura est, sed ut affectio animi corporisue est eorum, ad quos ea uisa perueniunt. 7. Itaque omnes omnino res, quae sensus hominum mouent, τῶν πρός τι esse dicunt. Id uerbum significat nihil esse quicquam, quod ex sese constet, nec quod habeat uim propriam et naturam, sed omnia prorsum ad aliquid referri taliaque uideri esse, qualis sit eorum species, dum uidentur, qualiaque apud sensus nostros, quo peruenerunt, creantur, non apud sese, unde profecta sunt. 8. Cum haec autem consimiliter tam Pyrrhonii dicant quam Academici, differre tamen inter sese et propter alia quaedam et uel maxime propterea existimati sunt, quod Academici quidem ipsum illud nihil posse comprehendi quasi comprehendunt et nihil posse decerni quasi decernunt, Pyrrhonii ne id quidem ullo pacto uerum uideri dicunt, quod nihil esse uerum uideatur.

Context: indicated by the heading given in the manuscripts of Gellius (reproduced above).

5. Anon., *Proleg. in Plat.* 7.10–14 Westerink

Διαφέρουσι δ' οἱ τῆς νέας Ἀκαδημίας τῶν ἐφεκτικῶν τῷ τοὺς μὲν ἐφεκτικοὺς ὁμοίως λέγειν διὰ πάντων τῶν ὄντων πεφοιτηκέναι ⟨τὴν ἀκαταληψίαν⟩, τοὺς δὲ τῆς νέας Ἀκαδημίας οὐχ ἁπάντων ὁμοίως, ἀλλ' εἶναί τινα τῶν πραγμάτων ἃ σαίνουσι τὴν ἡμετέραν ψυχὴν πρὸς συγκατάθεσιν μετρίαν.

Context: philosophical schools before Plato and after him, with the New Academy being kept separate from Plato properly understood.

6. Anon., *Proleg. in Plat.* 10 *init.* Westerink

Ἀλλὰ καὶ τὴν τῶν νέων Ἀκαδημαϊκῶν ὑπερέβαλεν φιλοσοφίαν τῷ ἐκείνην ἀκαταληψίαν πρεσβεύειν, δεῖξαι δὲ τοῦτον ὡς εἰσὶν ἐπιστημονικαὶ καταλήψεις τινές. Λέγουσι δέ τινες συνωθοῦντες τὸν Πλάτωνα εἰς τοὺς ἐφεκτικούς τε καὶ τοὺς Ἀκαδημαϊκοὺς ὡς καὶ αὐτοῦ ἀκαταληψίαν εἰσάγοντος· καὶ κατασκευάζουσι τοῦτο ἐκ τῶν εἰρημένων αὐτῷ ἐν τοῖς συγγράμμασιν αὐτοῦ.

Context: the survey of philosophical schools continues, with the author showing in each case why Plato was superior.

7. Phot., *Bibl.* 212, 170a14–17 (= part of LS 71C = Aenesidemus A3 Polito)

Οἱ δ' ἀπὸ τῆς Ἀκαδημίας, φησί, μάλιστα τῆς νῦν, καὶ Στωϊκαῖς συμφέρονται ἐνίοτε δόξαις, καὶ εἰ χρὴ τἀληθὲς εἰπεῖν, Στωϊκοὶ φαίνονται μαχόμενοι Στωϊκοῖς.

Context: in the course of his summaries of books, Photius speaks of the contents of Aenesidemus' *Pyrrhonist Discourses*. Having characterized the Pyrrhonists on their own terms, he turns to the Academics.

8. Phot., *Bibl.* 212, 170a17–38 (= part of LS 71C = Aenesidemus B3 Polito)

Δεύτερον περὶ πολλῶν δογματίζουσιν. Ἀρετήν τε γὰρ καὶ ἀφροσύνην εἰσάγουσι, καὶ ἀγαθὸν καὶ κακὸν ὑποτίθενται, καὶ ἀλήθειαν καὶ ψεῦδος, καὶ δὴ καὶ πιθανὸν καὶ ἀπίθανον καὶ ὂν καὶ μὴ ὄν, ἄλλα τε πολλὰ βεβαίως ὁρίζουσι, διαμφισβητεῖν δέ φασι περὶ μόνης τῆς καταληπτικῆς φαντασίας. Διὸ οἱ μὲν ἀπὸ Πύρρωνος ἐν τῷ μηδὲν ὁρίζειν ἀνεπίληπτοι τὸ παράπαν διαμένουσιν, οἱ δ' ἐξ Ἀκαδημίας, φησίν, ὁμοίας τὰς εὐθύνας τοῖς ἄλλοις φιλοσόφοις ὑπέχουσι, τὸ δὲ μέγιστον, οἱ μὲν περὶ παντὸς τοῦ προτεθέντος διαποροῦντες τό τε σύστοιχον διατηροῦσι καὶ ἑαυτοῖς οὐ μάχονται, οἱ δὲ μαχόμενοι ἑαυτοῖς οὐ συνίσασι· τὸ γὰρ ἅμα τιθέναι τι καὶ αἴρειν ἀναμφιβόλως, ἅμα τε φάναι κοινῶς ὑπάρχειν ⟨ἀ⟩καταληπτά [ἀ- suppl. Hirzel 1883: 232–3], μάχην ὁμολογουμένην εἰσάγει, ἐπεὶ πῶς οἷόν τε τὰ γινώσκοντα τόδε μὲν εἶναι ἀληθὲς τόδε δὲ ψεῦδος ἔτι διαπορεῖν καὶ διστάσαι, καὶ οὐ σαφῶς τὸ μὲν ἑλέσθαι τὸ δὲ περιστῆναι; Εἰ μὲν γὰρ ἀγνοεῖται ὅτι τόδε ἐστὶν ἀγαθὸν ἢ κακόν, ἢ τόδε μὲν ἀληθὲς τόδε δὲ ψεῦδος, καὶ τόδε μὲν ὂν τόδε δὲ μὴ ὄν, πάντως ὁμολογητέον ἕκαστον ἀκατάληπτον εἶναι· εἰ δ' ἐναργῶς κατ' αἴσθησιν ἢ κατὰ νόησιν καταλαμβάνεται, καταληπτὸν ἕκαστον φατέον.

Context: runs on immediately from text 7.

A list of the ways in which the text between ἅμα τε φάναι κοινῶς ... μάχην ὁμολογουμένην εἰσάγει has been constituted, along with a justification for an emendation by Sandbach which yields the same sense as Hirzel's (ἅμα τε φάναι κοινῶς ⟨μὴ⟩ ὑπάρχειν καταληπτά), is in Long and Sedley (ii.1987: 460). A much fuller, but ultimately open-ended discussion is provided by Polito (2014: 125–30). See also the general note on *Luc.* 43–4.

Translations

1. Galen, *Opt. doctr.* 1

(1) (a) Favorinus says that arguing on either side of a thesis is the best method of teaching. This is the designation the Academics give to their arguments for opposite conclusions. The older ones assume that it ends in suspension of judgement, calling suspension of judgement what one might call indeterminateness, which means making no determination or firm pronouncement on any subject. (b) The younger ones—not only Favorinus—sometimes take suspension of judgement so far as to not even grant that the sun is apprehensible, but at other times they carry the exercising of judgement to the point where they even entrust it to their pupils without educating them first on the scientific criterion. For what Favorinus said in his 'On the Academic Stance', which is entitled 'Plutarch', is no different. . . . Yet in his later book entitled 'Alcibiades' he praises the Academics for speaking in favour of both sides in opposing arguments, but leaving it to the pupils to select the truer ones. (c) Here he has said that it seems persuasive to him that nothing is apprehensible, but in his 'Plutarch' he seems to concede that something is firmly knowable; it is in fact better that we call the apprehensible that (i.e. 'firmly knowable'), diverging from the Stoic expression.

(3) But perhaps he (Favorinus) says there is no such thing (as a criterion) in philosophy and with respect to doctrines. In that case do not pretend to know anything, make no affirmative pronouncements, and do not run away to the suspension of judgement introduced by the older Academics, and do not act proud and like a grammarian, being fastidious about what they said. That none of what they say is sound is obvious to any sensible person. . . . It is obvious that, while Favorinus is ashamed to overturn everything and to agree that he does not know if it (i.e. the criterion) exists—though that it does not exist is what the older Academics and the Pyrrhonists said—, he pretends to allow his students to make a judgement, which his predecessors did not even allow themselves.

2. Plutarch, *Sto. rep.* 10, 1037b–c

In order to leave no possibility of denying that he contradicts himself, he has written this in his *Physical Theses*: 'Even for those who have apprehension of something it will be possible to argue to the contrary by mounting such a case as the subject allows for and sometimes to state the case inherent to each side, although they have apprehension of neither.' And yet in his treatise *On the Use of Reason*, [Chrysippus], after having said that the faculty of reason must not be used for unsuitable purposes just like weapons must not be so used, he added: 'For one must make use of it in order to find truths and in order to use truths in combination, but not for opposite ends, although many people do this as a matter of fact', and by 'many people' he probably means those who suspend judgement. (C) But they mount arguments on either side, having apprehension of neither, their idea being that, if there was such a thing as the apprehensible, only or primarily in this way would the truth yield an apprehension of itself. But you, who speak against them, when on the subject of common experience you write the opposite of what you apprehend and encourage others to do this with an air of advocacy, you do yourself confess that due to ambition you make a display by using the faculty of reason in ways which are unproductive and harmful.

3. Sextus, *P.H.* 1.220–35

(220) Some indeed say that the philosophy of the Academy is the same as scepticism [i.e. Pyrrhonism]; therefore it would appear to be our next task to treat of that, too.

According to most people there have been three Academies, the first and oldest being the one of the school of Plato, the second and middle one of the school of Arcesilaus, the pupil of Polemo, and the third and most recent one that of the School of Carneades and of Clitomachus; yet some add as a fourth one the school of Philo and Charmadas, and some even name a fifth one, that of Antiochus.

(226) The members of the New Academy, even though they say that all things are inapprehensible, differ from the sceptics, precisely with respect to that statement, that all things are inapprehensible (for they make a firm statement about it, whereas the sceptic regards it as a possibility that some things may be apprehended), but they differ from us plainly in the judgement of things good and bad. For the Academics call something 'good' and 'bad' not in the way we do, but on the basis of being convinced that it is more persuasive that what they call good really is good than the opposite, and equally about the bad, whereas we do not describe anything as good or evil with the assumption that it is persuasive, but simply fall in with life undogmatically so that we are not inactive. (227) And regarding impressions, we say that they are equal with respect to the convincingness they have or do not have (as far as the argument goes), whereas they say that some of them are persuasive, others unpersuasive.

And although the adherents of the Academy and of sceptical philosophy say they go along with some things, the difference between the two philosophies also in this area is manifest (230) For 'going along' is said in different senses, in that sometimes it means not straining against and simply going along without strong inclination and preference, as the boy is said to go along with the teacher; but then again it means on the basis of a choice and a certain sympathy assenting to something in accordance with a strong wish, as the dissolute man goes along with someone who demands extravagant living.

(235) The followers of Philo say that, as far as the Stoic criterion is concerned, i.e. the cataleptic impression, things are inapprehensible, but as far as the nature of things themselves is concerned, they are apprehensible. But Antiochus introduced the Stoa into the Academy, so that it was even said of him that he teaches Stoic philosophy in the Academy; for he tried to show that the doctrines of the Stoics are already present in Plato. Consequently it is quite plain how the sceptic way is different from the fourth and the fifth Academy.

4. Gellius, *N.A.* 11.5.1–8

Some brief notes in the Pyrrhonists and the Academics; on the difference between them.

1. Those whom we call the Pyrrhonist philosophers are designated 'sceptics' with the Greek name; 2. that means roughly the same as 'those who investigate and examine things'. 3. For they decide nothing, they establish nothing, but are always engaged in investigating and examining what there is amongst the totality of things about which one can determine and establish something. 4. And they hold that they do not see or hear anything clearly, but that they are so affected as if they see and hear, and they hesitate as to the kind and nature of the things which give rise to these very affections in them, and they are stuck on them; they say that the reliability and truth of all things is, given that the marks of the true and the false are mixed up and confused, so inapprehensible, that any man who is not rash and hasty in his judgement must use those expressions which according to them the founder of that philosophy Pyrrho used: 'this matter is no more this way than it is that way or neither.' They deny that the marks and genuine properties of each thing can be known and perceived, and they try to show this and bring this out in many ways. 5. On this subject Favorinus, too, has composed ten books with great subtlety and cleverness, which he entitled 'The Pyrrhonist Modes'. 6. It is an ancient question, and one discussed by many Greek authors, whether and to what extent the Pyrrhonist and the Academic philosophers are different. For both groups are called 'sceptics',

'withholders of judgement', 'those who are at a loss', since they both affirm nothing and believe that nothing can be apprehended. But they say that from all things there arise appearances, which they call 'impressions', not according to the nature of things themselves, but according to the affection of soul and body is of those to whom these appearances come. 7. Therefore they say that all things which move the senses of human beings are amongst the 'things relative to something'. This phrase means that there is nothing which is what it is in and of itself and which has a quality and nature peculiar to it, but that all things are related to something and appear in such a way as their look is while they are seen, and such as they are formed by our senses which they reach, not by themselves from the things from which they have come. 8. But although the Pyrrhonists and the Academics say very similar things about these matters, they have been held to differ both because of other matters and particularly because the Academics quasi-apprehend that claim itself, that nothing can be apprehended, whereas the Pyrrhonists say that not even that appears true in any way because nothing appears to be true.

5. Anon., *Proleg. in Plat.* 7.10–14 Westerink

The followers of the New Academy differ from those who suspend judgement in such a way that the latter say that inapprehensibility permeates all things to an equal degree, while the former say it did not apply to all things in equal measure, but that there are some things which beguile our souls into a moderate kind of assent.

6. Anon., *Proleg. in Plat.* 10 *init.* Westerink

But he also surpassed that philosophy of the New Academics in that they cultivate that so-called inapprehensibility, while he [Plato] showed that there are some apprehensions which confer knowledge. Some, running Plato together with those who suspend judgement and the New Academics, say that it was him who introduced the notion of inapprehensibility; and they make the case for this on the basis of his statements in his works.

7. Phot., *Bibl.* 212, 170a14–17 (= A3 Polito)

But those who belong with the Academy, he says, in particular those of the present day, are sometimes in agreement with Stoic tenets, and, to tell the truth, appear to be Stoics fighting Stoics.

8. Phot., *Bibl.* 212, 170a17–38 (= B3 Polito)

Second, they form dogmatic views about many things. For they introduce virtue and folly, and posit good and bad, and truth and falsehood, and the persuasive and the unpersuasive, that which is and that which is not, and they determine many other things firmly, and say their dispute is solely about the cataleptic impression. For this reason the followers of Pyrrho remain absolutely above criticism in that they determine nothing, but the followers of the Academy, he says, are subject to the same kind of criticism as other philosophers; especially, those who are in a state of aporia about every thesis maintain consistency and are not in conflict with themselves, but those (i.e. Academics) are in conflict with themselves and are not aware that this is so. For to say that something is so and to say that something is not so unequivocally on the one hand, and to say that things generally are non-apprehensible on the other, introduces an undeniable conflict; for how can one recognize this as true and that as false and yet maintain confusion and doubt, and not select one and avoid the other? For if it is not known that this is good or bad, or that this true and that is false, and that this is and that is not, one must agree in every way that each thing is inapprehensible; but if apprehension clearly takes place through perception or thought, then each thing must be said to be apprehensible.

Commentary

The texts assembled here have been taken to offer some insight into how the sceptical Academy was perceived after the Academy as a school became defunct and consequently also, at another remove, into the philosophical outlook of the Academy in its final phase. Several of them feature contributions to a long-standing point of debate—what the difference was between Academics and Pyrrhonists[1]—and address related questions, like whether the Academics held views dogmatically. Where such holding of views is assumed, inconsistency with the commitment to inapprehensibility is sometimes explicitly claimed or implied. I survey them against the cumulative findings of the commentary, viz. that there was (i) a Clitomachean position (as represented by Cicero) which exhibited many of the features conventionally associated with mitigated scepticism, (ii) a position of mitigated scepticism, held by some Academics without ever being the official position of the school, which differed from developed Clitomacheanism primarily and possibly exclusively with respect to the type of belief or quasi-belief permitted, as well as (iii) Philo's view articulated in the Roman Books and in outline but not in its detailed articulation anticipated by Metrodorus.

In text 1, Galen reports that Favorinus called arguing on either side the best method of teaching.[2] Cicero's entire practice of composing dialogues featuring speeches for and against is arguably informed by the same attitude.[3] Favorinus distinguished between older Academics and younger Academics. The former used argument on either side in such a way that it ended in suspension of judgement; this leaves it open whether Favorinus took the older Academics to end up suspending judgement routinely as a matter of fact or to have set out to suspend judgement. The younger Academics either behave in quite different ways at different times or fall into (at least) two groups which act in quite different ways; the formulation suggests the former.[4] The two types of behaviour are: first, suspending judgement on everyday matters (as opposed to philosophical problems) which are genuinely plain; second, allowing pupils to form judgements in response to arguments on either side, without proper instruction on the 'criterion'.[5] In his book 'Alcibiades' Favorinus praised the Academics for letting them select the 'truer' argument of a set of opposing arguments.[6] In the same work he apparently called it

---

[1] See Polito (2014: 90–1), who comments that 'the question was to become a topos in the early second century AD.'
[2] On Favorinus in general, see Barigazzi (1993); Holford-Strevens (1997); Follet (2000); and the editions by Barigazzi (1996) and Amato (2005); on him as an Academic, see Glucker (1978: 280–93); on our set of extracts in their larger context, see Ioppolo (1983); Opsomer (1997) and (1998: 213–40); Lévy (2010: 96–8).
[3] See Cic., *Fin.* 1.6, and section 8.
[4] Cf. *Luc.* on 32–4, where Cicero shifts between formulations which suggest different groups of Academics say different things, and ones suggesting that the Academics say different things at different times.
[5] On the most natural reading, this means that the Academics permit judgements of some kind without positing a formal criterion, not that they have such a criterion but do not instruct their pupils to use it or use it adequately.
[6] Most modern scholars have suspected that the Alcibiades of the title is the imperial official P. Aelius Alcibiades; see Amato (2010: 155–9). Amato (ibid.) makes the case for assuming that the work in question

'persuasive' that nothing can be known, but elsewhere, viz. in the 'Plutarch', he even recognized the possibility of there being something which Galen calls firmly knowable. Whether Favorinus himself used the terms 'the apprehensible' (τὸ καταληπτόν) or 'firmly knowable' (βεβαίως γνωστόν) is not clear.[7]

The passage speaks to the evidence from Cicero in that it makes it very likely that the use of argument on either side with a view to the emergence of the *probabile* was not a Ciceronian invention, as has been claimed by some.[8] The notion that pupils should be invited to form their own view is paralleled in Cicero, too (see on *Luc.* 7b–9a); the invitation to select the 'truer' view arguably discourages rather than encourages the interpretation that endorsement of a view as true was meant. Text 1 is consistent with the evidence from Cicero in that Galen's report is open to a reading on which it was Clitomacheans like Cicero who acted like Favorinus' younger Academics.[9] There are no grounds for thinking that the reference of any piece of information offered here is to mitigated sceptics exclusively (assuming a conception of mitigated scepticism as outlined above), but the possibility of such a reference need not be excluded either.[10]

In text 2, Plutarch points out contra Chrysippus that there were Academics who argued on either side on the assumption that truth might be found in this way, a fact which he regards as evidence that the Academics were not entirely destructive in their use of the technique, as Chrysippus appears to have asserted. This stops short of the claim that what is persuasive might be the outcome of such an argument,[11] and might mean that argument on either side was undertaken in genuine search of the truth (for the latter idea see again on *Luc.* 7b–9a). We have reason to think that Plutarch had access to *Acad.*, but text 2. should be taken as independent evidence.

The selections assembled as text 3 come from a passage in which Sextus discusses the difference between Academics and Pyrrhonists.[12] Sextus' manifest interest is to present the Pyrrhonists as—in some sense—genuine sceptics, and everyone else who might conceivably be deemed a sceptic as wedded to dogmatic convictions in one way or another.[13] In 1.220 Sextus reviews divisions of the Academy: some posit three Academies, while others add two more, apparently without revising the division of three (see on *Ac.* 1.18). That Carneades and his, by all accounts, faithful pupil Clitomachus are listed as representatives of the third Academy is unsurprising, but that Philo and Charmadas represent the fourth is less easily

---

was a dialogue in which Alcibiades and Socrates featured. This seems an attractive suggestion, given that the topic at issue—the need to think for oneself—features in the *Alcibiades I* at 114e, which may well have informed such a dialogue. See Coope (2019) on *Alc. I* 114e and its reception in Olympiodorus.

[7] The phrasal term βεβαίως γνωστόν is favoured by Galen himself in *De dign. puls.* VIII.771 K.
[8] Thus Görler (1994: 1089–1118).
[9] On text 1, see also Lévy (2010: 96–8) and Tielemann (2011: 85–7). For Galen's equation of the cataleptic impression with the tested persuasive impression of the 'New Academics' (see *Plac. Hipp.* 9.7.3 = p. 778 Kühn = p. 586 De Lacy; 9.9.37 = p. 802 Kühn = p. 606 De Lacy), which illuminates his views on the sceptical Academy, see on *Luc.* 105a.
[10] Brittain (2001: 93), cf. (2007: 301–4), sees evidence for three Academic epistemological views in the passage: '(1) the (Clitomachean) advocay of universal *epoche*; (2) the (Philonian/Metrodorian) position that it is *pithanon* that nothing can be known; and (3) the (almost Roman Philonian) position that it is *pithanon* that there is *catalepsis*.' I believe that the view at issue in (2) equally characterizes the Clitomachean position in its developed form represented by Cicero and that the evidence for (3), i.e. the information on the 'Alcibiades', is also open to other readings (see e.g. on *Luc.* 112).
[11] *Pace* Brittain (2001: 112 n. 58, 226–7).
[12] On ancient and modern discussions of this question, see Striker (1996f) and (2010); Bonazzi (2012a); on the evidence from Sextus, see Ioppolo (2009: passim).
[13] Thus e.g. Brunschwig (1999: 233): 'Later, the Neopyrrhonists refer to the sceptical Academy only to distance themselves from it, ascribing to the Academy a negative meta-dogmatism—which they seem to have invented for their own purposes.'

explained, both in terms of their relative chronology and given what we know of their views. If Philo deserved separation from Carneades and Clitomachus because of his Roman Books, then the coupling with Charmadas requires an explanation; if Charmadas and Philo were grouped together because they were, or Sextus took them to be, mitigated sceptics of some description at some point,[14] then the division would leave the Roman Books view unaccounted for (yet the Roman Books view features in 1.235, which also ties back to the division). In 1.226–227a, a difference between Pyrrhonists and Academics is identified: the Academics deem certain statements that they make persuasive, i.e. that something is good or bad, or that nothing is apprehensible. About the latter claim they even make a firm statement. And relatedly, they regard some impressions as persuasive, and others as unpersuasive, unlike the Pyrrhonists. Here the question is which particular Academic position should be seen as the reference point of Sextus' remarks. While it would be a serious misrepresentation, though hardly one which Sextus would not be capable of, to say that Academics arguing strictly ad hominem were open to Sextus' objection, both Clitomacheans of the type Cicero represents and mitigated sceptics like Catulus in *Luc.* 148 may be charged with endorsing some of their impressions as persuasive.[15] The difference between self-aware assent and approval would surely be a negligible one—for Sextus.[16] Nor should we assume that Sextus would be averse to conflating Academic positions if it suited his argumentative purpose, assuming he was fully alive to the differences between them. 1.229b–230 focuses more specifically on positive responses to impressions: the Pyrrhonist follows, as a schoolboy follows the teacher's instructions, without an investment or inclination, and without taking a view on what the impression leads him to do; the Academic by contrast positively opts for and 'assents to' (persuasive) impressions out of a certain sympathy. Does the characterization of the Academic mark him out as a mitigated sceptic, who after all is capable of assenting vehemently but with an awareness that the impression he is assenting to may be false (cf. again *Luc.* 148)? The possibility can certainly not be excluded. However, even if assent, and qualified assent at that, was in 1.230 associated with the Academy, it would still not be straightforward to infer from this e.g. that mitigated scepticism was something like the official position of the Academy at any point. The evidence from *Acad.* suggests that mitigated scepticism was the stance of a group within the Academy, and probably not of Philo (see sections 4, 8; and on *Luc.* 78); this being so, one wonders if Sextus might not have fastened on one group within the Academy which suited his argumentative aims. However, there is also the possibility that he is not talking about mitigated sceptics, but about Clitomacheans of the Ciceronian type.[17] Again, approval would be treated as assent; as I argue in the commentary on *Luc.* 104, approval and assent are not distinguished with reference to the vehemence of the endorsement. Cicero—in Clitomachean character—remarks in *Luc.* 101 that Academics are not made of rock or hardwood: they respond to impressions, and many of them appear true to them. It is no leap from such an attitude to Sextus' concept of sympathy: there is a natural affinity between persuasive impressions and the physical and mental make-up of human beings, or so the claim would be.[18] Finally, I note in section 6 that the account of the πιθανόν in *M.* 7.166–89 describes it as a (or: the) criterion and

---

[14] According to Cic., *Or.* 51, Carneades described Charmadas as the pupil of his who in content and form came closest to his own teaching; according to *De orat.* 1.84 (Antonius speaking) Charmadas 'refuted everyone'.

[15] *Pace* Brittain (2001: 276 n. 43), who thinks that 'Sextus falsely attributes this Philonian/Metrodorian interpretation of the *pithanon* to Carneades and Clitomachus; his mistake is clear from Cicero's account of Clitomachus (*Ac.* 2.98–109).'

[16] Note e.g. the Cicero character's claim to *decreta* in *Luc.* 109 *fin.*

[17] Clitomacheanism 'of the Ciceronian type' can be traced back to Clitomachus himself at least in part; see on *Luc.* 103–105a.

[18] On the passage, see also Striker (2010: 204–5).

assumes that acceptance of it is assent. To some this will be evidence that Sextus' discussion reflects the viewpoint of a mitigated sceptic, to me it is a parallel for Sextus' tendency to make the Academics look more dogmatic than they were.

1.235 provides information on Philo which is usually linked with the Roman Books; see the full discussion on *Luc.* 18 and looks back to the five-fold division of the Academy in 1.220. Thus Sextus seems to be associating the Roman Books view of Philo with Charmadas. In this he may simply be mistaken;[19] alternatively, Philo may have invoked Charmadas in claiming that the Roman Books view had been the position of the Academy all along.[20]

Text 4, after a description of the Pyrrhonist position (11.5.1–4), turns to the subject of text 3. It is not entirely clear if Gellius is still drawing on Favorinus here, but this is usually assumed.[21] §§5–7 report on common ground between the Academics and Pyrrhonists.[22] §8 is crucial for our purposes, but it is, again, vague.[23] Talk of quasi-apprehension would prima facie suggest that Philo's Roman Books view is at issue, given that it apparently allowed for a form of apprehension and claimed the term, but then one might think that this view seems to have had little impact on the later tradition overall and would thus be an unlikely candidate for 'the' Academic view in contradistinction to the Pyrrhonist one.[24] Beyond that it is again difficult to see grounds for asserting with conviction that only a position like Cicero's or only one like Catulus' in *Luc.* 148 is the reference point.[25] If Gellius or his source viewed quasi-apprehension of the claim that nothing can be apprehended as self-refuting, he did not say so.

Text 5 is very late but appears well informed in some respects, e.g. on the supposed indications of Plato's sceptical stance found in his dialogues (announced in text 6 and detailed in the immediately following section which I have not quoted).[26] In this case the question is what is meant by 'moderate assent', which is not an established technical term. On one plausible reading, this could be assent, i.e. acceptance as true, which is, however, less forcefully given than usual or than it might be. If so, then this would be at odds with *Luc.* 148, where Catulus is capable of giving self-aware assent *uehementissime*. Approval as in *Luc.* 104 might be at issue. Again it is difficult to say with conviction which form of Academic scepticism is meant, although it does seem clear that a variety is meant which allowed for some kind of endorsement of impressions.

Texts 7 and 8 appear to provide an insight into the reasons which one of the two high-profile renegades during Philo's leadership of the Academy cited for his departure (the other being Antiochus).[27] Aenesidemus' departure probably took place in the 90s BC, like

---

[19] Thus Brittain (2001: 54). The collocation of Philo and Charmadas is also in Eus., *P.E.* XIV.4.16 (= Numenius frg. 23 Des Places); see appendix 2. See also Glucker (1978: 344–56, esp. 345–6).
[20] Thus also Tarrant (2018: 83).
[21] Most recently Amato (2010) treats 11.5.1–5 as informed by Favorinus.
[22] Favorinus, if it is him, applies the terms σκεπτικοί and ἐφεκτικοί (i.e. 'withholders of assent') to both Pyrrhonists and Academics, and attributes to both the claim that everything is 'relative'. Bonazzi (2011: 21–4) considers the evidence for, and dismisses the possibility of, a Pyrrhonist interpretation of Plato.
[23] With our reading contrast Brittain (2001: 89–90, 96 n. 34, 210–12) and (2007: 302–3).
[24] I note, however, that Sextus, *P.H.* 1.235 also appears to make the Roman Books view the one which marked the end of the sceptical Academy, as well as makes it the one view Philo is associated with, which implies that it was 'the' Academic view for a time if one assumes that the scholarch determines the school's outlook.
[25] If *nihil posse decerni quasi decernunt* was suggestive of the etymological connection between *decernere* and *decretum*, then one could once again cite *Luc.* 110, where the Cicero character lays claim to *decreta*.
[26] See the introduction and notes on the translation in Westerink (1962) and Westerink et al. (1990), as well as Lévy (2010: 93); Layne (2018).
[27] See Polito (2014: 50–1 and 74–134).

Antiochus'.²⁸ In the two texts he criticizes the Academics, 'especially those living now', for appearing to be Stoics fighting Stoics, 'except for the cataleptic impression', and for 'dogmatizing', i.e. presumably having dogmatic beliefs rather than formulating doctrines. Again the question is what one can infer from this about the Academy in the 90s BC. If the qualification 'especially those living now' is to be taken seriously, then Academics have been open to Aenesidemus' accusation for some time, but contemporary ones are open to it to a higher degree. The character Cicero states in *Luc.* 78 that the only contentious issue which remained, sc. between dogmatists and the Academy, was the cataleptic impression. The Academics Aenesidemus objects to make firm determinations on a range of subjects, but their claim that there are no apprehensible things is, so he argues, at variance with that: either one makes firm determinations or one regards everything as inapprehensible. (For a similar point levelled against the Academics by Antiochus, and Cicero's reply from a Clitomachean point of view, see on *Luc.* 27–9 and 111.)²⁹ It is true that Aenesidemus may still be aiming at mitigated sceptics, though in this case one need not infer that their view was the standard Academic position at the time. Rather, if the view had some currency and was known to have gained traction later than the Clitomachean one, this would suffice to trouble someone like Aenesidemus as another ominous step in the wrong direction (witness the hint at a gradual emergence of the problem).³⁰ Alternatively, Aenesidemus may be thinking of Clitomacheans like Cicero who feel able to give approval—and he may be refusing to recognize the distinction between it and self-aware assent.

---

²⁸ See Brittain (2001: 56–7).
²⁹ See ad loc. and Castagnoli (2010: 308–29).
³⁰ See, however, Polito (2014: 51) on μάλιστα τῆς νῦν.

APPENDIX 2

Numenius on the Academy

I give the text as in the edition by Des Places, with light modifications signalled ad loc. and occasionally different punctuation; I have also compared Leemans (1939) as well as Wyss (2005), and have adopted the latter's style of embedding references to collections of fragments and testimonia in the text.

Texts

Frg. 24 Des Places (Eus., *Praep. Ev.* XIV.4.16–5.9, pp. 727a–729b Viger; II, pp. 268.11–271.6 Mras)

Τοιαύτη μέν τις ἡ αὐτοῦ Πλάτωνος ὑπῆρξε διαδοχή. Ὁποῖοι δὲ γεγόνασιν οἴδε τὸν τρόπον, λαβὼν ἀνάγνωθι τὰς ὧδε ἐχούσας Νουμηνίου τοῦ Πυθαγορείου φωνάς, ἃς τέθειται ἐν τῷ πρώτῳ ὧν ἐπέγραψε Περὶ τῆς τῶν Ἀκαδημαϊκῶν πρὸς Πλάτωνα διαστάσεως·

(5.1) Ἐπὶ μὲν τοίνυν Σπεύσιππον (frg. 30 Isnardi Parente) τὸν Πλάτωνος μὲν ἀδελφιδοῦν, Ξενοκράτη (frg. 77 Isnardi Parente) δὲ τὸν διάδοχον τὸν Σπευσίππου, Πολέμωνα (frg. 3 Gigante) δὲ τὸν ἐκδεξάμενον τὴν σχολὴν παρὰ Ξενοκράτους ἀεὶ τὸ ἦθος διετείνετο τῶν δογμάτων σχεδὸν δὴ ταὐτόν, ἕνεκά γε τῆς μήπω ἐποχῆς ταυτησὶ τῆς πολυθρυλήτου τε καὶ εἰ δὴ τινων τοιούτων ἄλλων. Ἐπεὶ εἴς γε τὰ ἄλλα πολλαχῇ ⟨τὰ μὲν⟩¹ παραλύοντες, τὰ δὲ στρεβλοῦντες, οὐκ ἐνέμειναν τῇ πρώτῃ διαδοχῇ. ἀρξάμενοι δὲ ἀπ᾽ ἐκείνου καὶ θᾶττον καὶ βράδιον διίσταντο προαιρέσει ἢ ἀγνοίᾳ, τὰ δὲ δή τινι αἰτίᾳ ἄλλῃ οὐκ ἀφιλοτίμῳ ἴσως. (5.2) Καὶ οὐ μὲν βούλομαί τι φλαῦρον εἰπεῖν διὰ Ξενοκράτη, μᾶλλον μὴν ὑπὲρ Πλάτωνος ἐθέλω. Καὶ γάρ με δάκνει ὅτι μὴ πᾶν ἔπαθόν τε καὶ ἔδρων σῴζοντες τῷ Πλάτωνι κατὰ πάντα πάντῃ πᾶσαν ὁμοδοξίαν. Καίτοι ἄξιος ἦν αὐτοῖς ὁ Πλάτων, οὐκ ἀμείνων μὲν Πυθαγόρου τοῦ μεγάλου, οὐ μέντοι ἴσως οὐδὲ φλαυρότερος ἐκείνου, ᾧ συνακολουθοῦντες σεφθέντες τε οἱ γνώριμοι ἐγένοντο πολυτιμητίζεσθαι αἰτιώτατοι τὸν Πυθαγόραν.

(5.3) Τοῦτο δὲ οἱ Ἐπικούρειοι οὐκ ὤφελον μέν, μαθόντες δ᾽ οὖν ἐν οὐδενὶ ὤφθησαν Ἐπικούρῳ ἐναντία θέμενοι οὐδαμῶς, ὁμολογήσαντες δὲ εἶναι σοφῷ συνδεδογμένοι καὶ αὐτοὶ διὰ τοῦτο ἀπέλαυσαν τῆς προσρήσεως εἰκότως· ὑπῆρξέ τε ἐκ τοῦ ἐπὶ πλεῖστον τοῖς μετέπειτα Ἐπικουρείοις μηδ᾽ αὐτοῖς εἰπεῖν πω ἐναντίον οὔτε ἀλλήλοις οὔτε Ἐπικούρῳ μηδὲν εἰς μηδέν, ὅτου καὶ μνησθῆναι ἄξιον· ἀλλ᾽ ἔστιν αὐτοῖς παρανόμημα, μᾶλλον δὲ ἀσέβημα, καὶ κατέγνωσται τὸ καινοτομηθέν. Διὸ τοῦτο οὐδεὶς οὐδὲ τολμᾷ, κατὰ πολλὴν δὲ εἰρήνην αὐτοῖς ἠρεμεῖ τὰ δόγματα ὑπὸ τῆς ἐν ἀλλήλοις αἰεί ποτε συμφωνίας. Ἔοικέ τε ἡ Ἐπικούρου διατριβὴ πολιτείᾳ τινὶ ἀληθεῖ, ἀστασιαστοτάτῃ, κοινὸν ἕνα νοῦν, μίαν γνώμην ἐχούσῃ· ἀφ᾽ ἧς ἦσαν καὶ εἰσί καί, ὡς ἔοικεν, ἔσονται φιλακόλουθοι.

(5.4) Τὰ δὲ τῶν Στωϊκῶν (SVF ii.20) ἐστασίασται, ἀρξάμενα ἀπὸ τῶν ἀρχόντων καὶ μηδέπω τελευτῶντα καὶ νῦν. Ἐλέγχουσι δὲ ἀγαπώντως ὑπὸ δυσμενοῦς ἐλέγχου, οἱ μέν τινες αὐτῶν ἐμμεμενηκότες ἔτι, οἱ δ᾽ ἤδη μεταθέμενοι. Εἴξασιν οὖν οἱ πρῶτοι ὀλιγαρχικωτέροις, οἳ δὴ διαστάντες ὑπῆρξαν εἰς τοὺς μετέπειτα πολλῆς μὲν τοῖς προτέροις, πολλῆς δὲ τῆς ἀλλήλοις ἐπιτιμήσεως αἴτιοι, εἰσί τε ἑτέρων ἕτεροι Στωϊκώτεροι καὶ μᾶλλον ὅσοι πλεῖον περὶ τὸ τεχνικὸν ὤφθησαν μικρολόγοι· αὐτοὶ γὰρ οὗτοι τοὺς ἑτέρους ὑπερβαλλόμενοι τῇ τε πολυπραγμοσύνῃ τοῖς τε σκαρ⟨ι⟩φηθμοῖς² ἐπετίμων θᾶττον.

---

¹ Suppl. Wyss. ² Suppl. Dindorf.

(5.5) Πολὺ μέντοι τούτων πρότερον ταὐτὰ ἔπαθον οἱ ἀπὸ Σωκράτους (SSR 1 H 11) ἀφελκύσαντες διαφόρους τοὺς λόγους, ἰδίᾳ μὲν Ἀρίστιππος (frg. 126 D Mannebach), ἰδίᾳ δὲ Ἀντισθένης καὶ ἀλλαχοῦ ἰδίᾳ οἱ Μεγαρικοί τε καὶ Ἐρετρικοὶ ἢ εἴ τινες ἄλλοι μετὰ τούτων. (5.6) Αἴτιον δέ, ὅτι τρεῖς θεοὺς τιθεμένου Σωκράτους (SSR 1 C 462) καὶ φιλοσοφοῦντος αὑτοῖς ἐν τοῖς προσήκουσιν ἑκάστῳ ῥυθμοῖς, οἱ διακούοντες τοῦτο μὲν ἠγνόουν, ᾤοντο δὲ λέγειν πάντα αὐτὸν εἰκῇ καὶ ἀπὸ τῆς νικώσης αἰεὶ προστυχῶς ἄλλοτε ἄλλης τύχης ὅπως πνέοι.

(5.7) Ὁ δὲ Πλάτων πυθαγορίσας (ᾔδει δὲ τὸν Σωκράτην μηδαμόθεν ἢ ἐκεῖθεν δὴ τὰ αὐτὰ ταῦτα εἰπεῖν καὶ γνόντα εἰρηκέναι), ὧδε οὖν καὶ αὐτὸς συνεδήσατο τὰ πράγματα, οὔτε εἰωθότως οὔτε δὴ εἰς τὸ φανερόν· διαγαγὼν δ᾽ ἕκαστα ὅπῃ ἐνόμιζεν, ἐπικρυψάμενος ἐν μέσῳ τοῦ δῆλα εἶναι καὶ μὴ δῆλα, ἀσφαλῶς μὲν ἐγράψατο, αὐτὸς δ᾽ αἰτίαν παρέσχε τῆς μετ᾽ αὐτὸν στάσεώς τε ἅμα καὶ διολκῆς τῆς τῶν δογμάτων, οὐ φθόνῳ μὲν οὐδέ γε δυσνοίᾳ· ἀλλ᾽ οὐ βούλομαι ἐπὶ ἀνδράσι πρεσβυτέροις εἰπεῖν ῥήματα οὐκ ἐναίσιμα. (5.8) Τοῦτο δὲ χρὴ μαθόντας ἡμᾶς ἐπανενεγκεῖν ἐκεῖσε μᾶλλον τὴν γνώμην, καὶ ὥσπερ ἐξ ἀρχῆς προυθέμεθα χωρίζειν αὐτὸν Ἀριστοτέλους καὶ Ζήνωνος, οὕτως καὶ νῦν τῆς Ἀκαδημίας, ἐὰν ὁ θεὸς ἀντιλάβηται, χωρίζοντες ἐάσομεν αὐτὸν ἐφ᾽ ἑαυτοῦ νῦν εἶναι Πυθαγόρειον· ὡς νῦν μανικώτερον ἢ Πενθεῖ τινι προσῆκε διελκόμενος πάσχει μὲν κατὰ μέλη, ὅλος δ᾽ ἐξ ὅλου ἑαυτοῦ μετατίθεταί τε καὶ ἀντιμετατίθεται οὐδαμῶς. (5.9) Ὅπως οὖν ἀνὴρ μεσεύων Πυθαγόρου καὶ Σωκράτους, τοῦ μὲν τὸ σεμνὸν ὑπαγαγὼν μέχρι τοῦ φιλανθρώπου, τοῦ δὲ τὸ κομψὸν τοῦτο καὶ παιγνιῆμον ἀναγαγὼν ἀπὸ τῆς εἰρωνείας εἰς ἀξίωμα καὶ ὄγκον καὶ αὐτὸ τοῦτο κεράσας Σωκράτει Πυθαγόραν, τοῦ μὲν δημοτικώτερος, τοῦ δὲ σεμνότερος ὤφθη.

Frg. 25 Des Places (Eus., *Praep. Ev.* XIV.5.10–6.14, pp. 729b–733d Viger; II, pp. 271.7–277.9 Mras)

(5.10) Ἀλλ᾽ οὐ γάρ τοι ταῦτα διαιτήσων ἦλθον, μὴ περὶ τούτων οὔσης νῦν μοι τῆς ζητήσεως, ἃ δὲ προυδέδοκτο· καὶ εἶμι ἐκεῖσε ᾗ δὴ φροῦδος ἀναδραμεῖν δοκῶ μοι, μὴ καί που ἀποκρουσθῶμεν τῆς ὁδοῦ τῆς φερούσης.

(5.11) Πολέμωνος δὲ ἐγένοντο γνώριμοι Ἀρκεσίλαος (T2 Mette = F88 Vezzoli) καὶ Ζήνων (SVF i.11)· πάλιν γὰρ αὐτῶν μνησθήσομαι ἐπὶ τέλει. Ζήνωνα μὲν οὖν μέμνημαι εἰπὼν Ξενοκράτει, εἶτα δὲ Πολέμωνι φοιτῆσαι, αὖθις δὲ παρὰ Κράτητι κυνίσαι· νυνὶ δὲ αὐτῷ λελογίσθω ὅτι καὶ Στίλπωνός τε μετέσχε καὶ τῶν λόγων τῶν Ἡρακλειτείων. (5.12) Ἐπεὶ γὰρ συμφοιτῶντες παρὰ Πολέμωνι ἐφιλοτιμήθησαν ἀλλήλοις, συμπαρέλαβον εἰς τὴν πρὸς ἀλλήλους μάχην ὁ μὲν Ἡράκλειτον καὶ Στίλπωνα ἅμα καὶ Κράτητα (SSR V H 39), ὧν ὑπὸ μὲν Στίλπωνος ἐγένετο μαχητής, ὑπὸ δὲ Ἡρακλείτου αὐστηρός, κυνικὸς δὲ ὑπὸ Κράτητος· ὁ δ᾽ Ἀρκεσίλαος Θεόφραστον ἴσχει καὶ Κράντορα (T3 Mette) τὸν Πλατωνικὸν καὶ Διόδωρον (DM frg. 106 = II F 4 SSR), εἶτα Πύρρωνα (T 33 Decleva Caizzi), ὧν ὑπὸ μὲν Κράντορος πιθανουργικός, ὑπὸ Διοδώρου δὲ σοφιστής, ὑπὸ δὲ Πύρρωνος ἐγένετο παντοδαπὸς καὶ ἴτης καὶ οὐδέν. (5.13) Ὅ⟨θεν⟩>[3] καὶ ἐλέγετο περὶ αὐτοῦ ᾀδόμενόν τι ἔπος παραγωγὸν καὶ ὑβριστικόν (SVF i.343 = DM frg. 107; cf. Hom., *Il.* 6.181)·

πρόσθε Πλάτων, ὄπιθεν [δὲ][4] Πύρρων, μέσσος Διόδωρος

Τίμων δὲ καὶ ὑπὸ Μενεδήμου (SSR III F 22) τὸ ἐριστικόν φησι λαβόντα ἐξαρτυθῆναι, εἴπερ γε δή φησι περὶ αὐτοῦ (SH no. 805)·

τῇ μὲν ἔχων Μενεδήμου ὑπὸ στέρνοισι μόλυβδον
θεύσεται ἢ Πύρρωνα τὸ πᾶν κρέας ἢ Διόδωρον.

(5.14) Ταῖς οὖν Διοδώρου, διαλεκτικοῦ ὄντος, λεπτολογίαις τοὺς λογισμοὺς τοὺς Πύρρωνος καὶ τὸ σκεπτικὸν καταπλέξας διεκόσμησε λόγου δεινότητι τῇ Πλάτωνος φλήναφόν τινα

---

[3] Suppl. Leemans.   [4] Secl. Casaubon.

κατεστωμυλμένον καὶ ἔλεγε καὶ ἀντέλεγε καὶ μετεκυλινδεῖτο κἀκεῖθεν κἀντεῦθεν ὁποτέρωθεν τύχοι, παλινάγρετος καὶ δύσκριτος καὶ παλίμβολός τε ἅμα καὶ παρακεκινδυνευμένος· οὐδέν τι εἰδώς, ὡς αὐτὸς ἔφη γενναῖος ὤν· εἶτά πως ἐξέβαινεν ὅμοιος τοῖς εἰδόσιν, ὑπὸ σκιαγραφίας τῶν λόγων παντοδαπὸς πεφαντασμένος. (6.1) (Arcesilaus F89 Vezzoli) Τοῦ τε Ὁμηρικοῦ Τυδείδου ὁποτέροις μετείη ἀγνοουμένου (οὔτε εἰ Τρωσὶν ὁμιλέοι οὔτε εἰ καὶ Ἀχαιοῖς) οὐδὲν ἧττον Ἀρκεσίλαος ἠγνοεῖτο. Τὸ γὰρ ἕνα τε λόγον καὶ ταὐτόν ποτ᾽ εἰπεῖν οὐκ ἐνῆν ἐν αὐτῷ, οὐδέ γε ἠξίου ἀνδρὸς εἶναί [πω]⁵ τὸ τοιοῦτο δεξιοῦ οὐδαμῶς. Ὠνομάζετο οὖν (TGrF 323 Nauck²)

δεινὸς σοφιστής, τῶν ἀγυμνάστων σφαγεύς.

(6.2) Ὥσπερ γὰρ αἱ Ἔμπουσαι ἐν τοῖς φάσμασι τοῖς τῶν λόγων ὑπὸ παρασκευῆς τε καὶ ὑπὸ μελέτης ἐφάρματτεν, ἐγοήτευεν, οὐδὲν εἶχεν εἰδέναι οὔτε αὐτὸς οὔτε τοὺς ἄλλους ἐᾶν· ἐδειμάτου δὲ καὶ κατεθορύβει καὶ σοφισμάτων γε καὶ λόγων κλοπῆς φερόμενος τὰ πρῶτα κατέχαιρε τῷ ὀνείδει καὶ ἡβρύνετο θαυμαστῶς, ὅτι μήτε τί αἰσχρὸν ἢ καλὸν μήτε ἀγαθὸν μήτε αὖ κακόν ἐστι τί ᾔδει, ἀλλ᾽ ὁπότερον εἰς τὰς ψυχὰς πέσοι τοῦτο εἰπὼν αὖθις μεταβαλὼν ἀνέτρεπεν ἂν πλεοναχῶς ἢ δι᾽ ὅσων κατεσκευάκει. (6.3) Ἦν οὖν Ὕδραν τέμνων ἑαυτὸν καὶ τεμνόμενος ὑφ᾽ ἑαυτοῦ, ἀμφότερα ἀλλήλων δυσκρίτως καὶ τοῦ δέοντος ἀσκέπτως, πλὴν τοῖς ἀκούουσιν ἤρκεσεν, ὁμοῦ τῇ ἀκροάσει εὐπρόσωπον ὄντα θεωμένοις· ἦν οὖν ἀκουόμενος καὶ βλεπόμενος ἥδιστος, ἐπεί γε προσειθίσθησαν ἀποδέχεσθαι αὐτοῦ τοὺς λόγους ἰόντας ἀπὸ καλοῦ προσώπου τε καὶ στόματος οὐκ ἄνευ τῆς ἐν τοῖς ὄμμασι φιλοφροσύνης. (6.4) Δεῖ δὲ ταῦτα ἀκοῦσαι μὴ ἁπλῶς, ἀλλ᾽ ἔσχεν ὧδε ἐξ ἀρχῆς· συμβαλὼν γὰρ ἐν παισὶ Θεοφράστῳ, ἀνδρὶ πράῳ καὶ οὐκ ἀφεῖ τὰ ἐρωτικά, διὰ τὸ καλὸς εἶναι ἔτι ὢν ὡραῖος τυχὼν ἐραστοῦ Κράντορος τοῦ Ἀκαδημαϊκοῦ, προσεχώρησε μὲν τούτῳ, οἷα δὲ τὴν φύσιν οὐκ ἀφυὴς τρεχούσῃ χρησάμενος αὐτῇ ῥᾳδίᾳ γε θερμουργῷ ὑπὸ φιλονεικίας, μετασχὼν μὲν Διοδώρου (DM frg. 106) εἰς τὰ πεπανουργημένα πιθανὰ ταῦτα τὰ κομψά, ὡμιληκὼς δὲ Πύρρωνι (T 34 Decleva Caizzi) (ὁ δὲ Πύρρων ἐκ Δημοκρίτου ὥρμητο ἀμόθεν γέ ποθεν) οὕτως μὲν δὴ ἔνθα ⟨κἄνθεν⟩ καταρτυθείς, πλὴν τῆς προσρήσεως, ἐνέμεινε Πυρρωνείως τῇ πάντων ἀναιρέσει. (6.5) Μνασέας γοῦν καὶ Φιλόμηλος καὶ Τίμων οἱ σκεπτικοὶ σκεπτικὸν αὐτὸν προσονομάζουσιν, ὥσπερ καὶ αὐτοὶ ἦσαν, ἀναιροῦντα καὶ αὐτὸν τὸ ἀληθὲς καὶ τὸ ψεῦδος καὶ τὸ πιθανόν.

Λεχθεὶς οὖν ἂν αἰτίᾳ τῶν Πυρρωνείων Πυρρώνειος, αἰδοῖ τοῦ ἐραστοῦ ὑπέμεινε λέγεσθαι Ἀκαδημαϊκὸς ἔτι. Ἦν μὲν τοίνυν Πυρρώνειος, πλὴν τοῦ ὀνόματος· Ἀκαδημαϊκὸς δ᾽ οὐκ ἦν, πλὴν τοῦ λέγεσθαι. (6.6) Οὐ γὰρ πείθομαι τοῦ Κνιδίου Δι⟨και⟩οκλέους⁶ φάσκοντος ἐν ταῖς ἐπιγραφομέναις 'Διατριβαῖς' Ἀρκεσίλαον φόβῳ τῶν Θεοδωρείων (frg. 254A Mannebach = SSR IV H29) τε καὶ Βίωνος τοῦ σοφιστοῦ ἐπεισιόντων τοῖς φιλοσοφοῦσι καὶ οὐδὲν ὀκνούντων ἀπὸ παντὸς ἐλέγχειν, αὐτὸν ἐξευλαβηθέντα, ἵνα μὴ πράγματα ἔχῃ, μηδὲν μὲν δόγμα ὑπειπεῖν φαινόμενον, ὥσπερ δὲ τὸ μέλαν τὰς σηπίας προβάλλεσθαι πρὸ ἑαυτοῦ τὴν ἐποχήν. Τοῦτ᾽ οὖν ἐγὼ οὐ πείθομαι.

(6.7) Οἱ δ᾽ οὖν ἔνθεν ἀφορμηθέντες, ὅ τε Ἀρκεσίλαος καὶ Ζήνων, ὑπὸ τοιούτων ἀρωγῶν, ἀμφοτέροις συμπολεμούντων λόγων, τῆς μὲν ἀρχῆς ὅθεν ἐκ Πολέμωνος ὡρμήθησαν ἐπιλανθάνονται (Hom., Il. 12.86, 4.447–9, 13.131, 4.472, 450–1),

διαστάντες δέ γε καὶ σφέας αὐτοὺς ἀρτύναντες
σὺν δ᾽ ἔβαλον ῥινούς, σὺν δ᾽ ἔγχεα καὶ μένε᾽ ἀνδρῶν
χαλκεοθωρήκων· ἀτὰρ ἀσπίδες ὀμφαλόεσσαι
ἔπληντ᾽ ἀλλήλῃσι, πολὺς δ᾽ ὀρυμαγδὸς ὀρώρει.
Ἀσπὶς ἄρ᾽ ἀσπίδ᾽ ἔρειδε, κόρυς κόρυν, ἀνέρα δ᾽ ἀνὴρ ἐδονοπάλιζεν.
Ἔνθα δ᾽ ἅμ᾽ οἰμωγή τε καὶ εὐχωλὴ πέλεν ἀνδρῶν
ὀλλύντων τε καὶ ὀλλυμένων

τῶν Στωϊκῶν· (6.8) οἱ Ἀκαδημαϊκοὶ γὰρ οὐκ ἐβάλλοντο ὑπ᾽ αὐτῶν, ἀγνοούμενοι ᾗ ἦσαν ἁλῶναι δυνατώτεροι. Ἡλίσκοντο δὲ τῆς βάσεως αὐτοῖς σεισθείσης, εἰ μήτε ἀρχὴν ἔχοιεν μήτε μάχεσθαι ἀφορμήν. Ἡ μὲν δὴ ἀρχὴ ἦν τὸ μὴ Πλατωνικὰ λέγοντας αὐτοὺς ἐλέγξαι· τὸ δὲ μηδὲ ἔχειν τινὰ

---

⁵ Secl. Wilamowitz.   ⁶ Δι⟨και⟩οκλέους Wilamowitz Διοκλέους codd.

ἀφορμὴν ἦν, εἴπερ μόνον ἕν τι μετέστρεψαν ἀπὸ τοῦ ὅρου τοῦ περὶ τῆς καταληπτικῆς φαντασίας ἀφελόντες. (6.9) Ὅπερ νῦν μὲν οὐκ ἔστι μηνύειν μοι ἐν καιρῷ, μνησθήσομαι δ' αὐτοῦ αὖθις ἐπὰν κατὰ τοῦτο μάλιστα γενέσθαι μέλλω.

Διαστάντες δ' οὖν εἰς τὸ φανερὸν ἔβαλλον ἀλλήλους οὐχ οἱ δύο, ἀλλ' ὁ Ἀρκεσίλαος τὸν Ζήνωνα (SVF i.12). Ὁ γὰρ Ζήνων εἶχε δή τι τῇ μάχῃ σεμνὸν καὶ βαρὺ καὶ Κηφισοδώρου τοῦ ῥήτορος οὐκ ἄμεινον· ὃς δὴ ὁ Κηφισόδωρος, ἐπειδὴ ὑπ' Ἀριστοτέλους βαλλόμενον ἑαυτῷ τὸν διδάσκαλον Ἰσοκράτην ἑώρα, αὐτοῦ μὲν Ἀριστοτέλους ἦν ἀμαθὴς καὶ ἄπειρος, ὑπὸ δὲ τοῦ καθορᾶν ἔνδοξα τὰ Πλάτωνος ὑπάρχοντα οἰηθεὶς κατὰ Πλάτωνα τὸν Ἀριστοτέλην φιλοσοφεῖν, ἐπολέμει μὲν Ἀριστοτέλει, ἔβαλλε δὲ Πλάτωνα καὶ κατηγόρει ἀρξάμενος ἀπὸ τῶν ἰδεῶν, τελευτῶν εἰς τὰ ἄλλα, ἃ οὐδ' αὐτὸς ᾔδει, ἀλλὰ τὰ νομιζόμενα ἀμφ' αὐτῶν ἢ λέγεται ὑπονοῶν. (6.10) Πλὴν οὕτως μὲν ὁ Κηφισόδωρος, ᾧ ἐπολέμει μὴ μαχόμενος, ἐμάχετο ᾧ μὴ πολεμεῖν ἐβούλετο. Ὁ μέντοι Ζήνων καὶ αὐτός, ἐπειδὴ τοῦ Ἀρκεσιλάου μεθίετο, εἰ μὲν μηδὲ Πλάτωνι ἐπολέμει, ἐφιλοσόφει δήπου ἐμοὶ κριτῇ πλείστου ἀξίως, ἕνεκά γε τῆς εἰρήνης ταύτης. Εἰ δ' οὐκ ἀγνοῶν μὲν ἴσως τὰ Ἀρκεσιλάου, τὰ μέντοι Πλάτωνος ἀγνοῶν, ὡς ἐξ ὧν αὐτῷ ἀντέγραψεν ἐλέγχεται, [ὅτι] ἐποίησεν ἐναντία καὐτός, μήτε ὃν ᾔδει πλήττων ὅν τε οὐκ ἐχρῆν ἀτιμότατα καὶ αἴσχιστα περιυβρικώς, καὶ ταῦτα πολὺ κάκιον ἢ προσήκει κυνί. (6.11) Πλὴν διέδειξέ γε μὴν μεγαλοφροσύνῃ ἀποσχόμενος τοῦ Ἀρκεσιλάου. Ἤτοι γὰρ ἀγνοίᾳ τῶν ἐκείνου ἢ δέει τῶν Στωϊκῶν (Hom., Il. 10.8)

πολέμοιο μέγα στόμα πευκεδανοῖο

ἀπετρέψατο ἄλλῃ, εἰς Πλάτωνα· ἀλλὰ καὶ περὶ μὲν τῶν Ζήνωνι εἰς Πλάτωνα κακῶς τε καὶ αἰδημόνως οὐδαμῶς νεωτερισθέντων εἰρήσεταί μοι αὖθίς ποτε, ἐὰν φιλοσοφίας σχολὴν ἀγάγω· μή ποτε μέντοι ἀγάγοιμι σχολὴν τοσαύτην, τούτου οὖν ἕνεκεν, εἰ μὴ ὑπὸ παιδιᾶς.

(6.12) Τὸν δ' οὖν Ζήνωνα ὁ Ἀρκεσίλαος ἀντίτεχνον καὶ ἀξιόνικον ὑπάρχοντα θεωρῶν τοὺς παρ' ἐκείνου ἀποφερομένους λόγους καθῄρει καὶ οὐδὲν ὤκνει. (6.13) Καὶ περὶ μὲν τῶν ἄλλων ἃ ἐμεμάχητο ἐκείνῳ οὔτ' ἴσως εἰπεῖν ἔχω εἴ τε καὶ εἶχον οὐδὲν ἔδει νῦν αὐτῶν μνησθῆναι· τὸ δὲ δόγμα τοῦτο αὐτοῦ πρώτου εὑρομένου καὐτὸ καὶ τὸ ὄνομα βλέπων εὐδοκιμοῦν ἐν ταῖς Ἀθήναις, τὴν καταληπτικὴν φαντασίαν, πάσῃ μηχανῇ ἐχρῆτο ἐπ' αὐτήν. Ὁ δ' ἐν τῷ ἀσθενεστέρῳ ὢν καὶ ἡσυχίαν ἄγων οὐ δυναμένου ἀδικεῖσθαι, Ἀρκεσιλάου μὲν ἀφίετο, πολλὰ ἂν εἰπεῖν ἔχων, ἀλλ' οὐκ ἤθελε, τάχα δὲ μᾶλλον ἄλλως, πρὸς δὲ τὸν οὐκέτι ἐν ζῶσιν ὄντα Πλάτωνα ἐσκιομάχει καὶ τὴν ἀπὸ ἁμάξης πομπείαν πᾶσαν κατεθορύβει, λέγων ὡς οὔτ' ἂν τοῦ Πλάτωνος ἀμυναμένου ὑπερδικεῖν τε αὐτοῦ ἄλλῳ οὐδενὶ μέλον, εἴ τε μελήσειεν Ἀρκεσιλάῳ, αὐτός γε κερδανεῖν ᾤετο ἀποτρεψάμενος ἀφ' ἑαυτοῦ τὸν Ἀρκεσίλαον. Τοῦτο δὲ ἤδη καὶ Ἀγαθοκλέα τὸν Συρακόσιον ποιήσαντα τὸ σόφισμα ἐπὶ τοὺς Καρχηδονίους. (6.14) Οἱ Στωϊκοὶ δὲ ὑπήκουον ἐκπεπληγμένοι· 'ἁ μοῦσα γὰρ αὐτοῖς οὐδὲ τότε ἦν φιλόλογος οὐδ' ἐργάτις' χαρίτων, ὑφ' ὧν ὁ Ἀρκεσίλαος τὰ μὲν περικρούων, τὰ δὲ ὑποτέμνων, ἄλλα δ' ὑποσκελίζων κατεγλωττίζετο αὐτοὺς καὶ πιθανὸς ἦν. Τοιγαροῦν πρὸς οὓς μὲν ἀντέλεγεν ἡττωμένων, ἐν οἷς δὲ λέγων ἦν καταπεπληγμένων, δεδειγμένον πως τοῖς τότε ἀνθρώποις ὑπῆρχε μηδὲ εἶναι μήτ' οὖν ἔπος μήτε πάθος μήτε ἔργον ἐν βραχὺ μηδὲ ἄχρηστον ⟨ἢ⟩[7] τοὐναντίον ὀφθῆναί ποτ' ἄν, εἴ τι μὴ Ἀρκεσιλάῳ δοκεῖ τῷ Πιταναίῳ· τῷ δ' ἄρα οὐδὲν ἐδόκει οὐδ' ἀπεφαίνετο οὐδὲν μᾶλλον ἢ ῥηματίσκια ταῦτ' εἶναι καὶ φόβους.

Frg. 26 Des Places (Eus., *Praep. Ev.* XIV.7.1–15, pp. 734a–737a Viger; II, pp. 277.12–281.8 Mras)

(7.1) Περὶ δὲ Λακύδου (T3 Mette) βούλομαί τι διηγήσασθαι ἡδύ. Ἦν μὲν δὴ Λακύδης ὑπογλισχρότερος καί τινα τρόπον ὁ λεγόμενος οἰκονομικός, οὗτος ὁ εὐδοκιμῶν παρὰ τοῖς πολλοῖς, αὐτὸς μὲν ἀνοιγνὺς τὸ ταμεῖον, αὐτὸς δ' ὑποκλείων. Καὶ προῃρεῖτο δὲ ὧν ἐδεῖτο καὶ ἄλλα τοιαῦτα ἐποίει πάντα δι' αὐτουργίας, οὔ τί που αὐτάρκειαν ἐπαινῶν οὐδ' ἄλλως πενίᾳ χρώμενος οὐδ' ἀπορίᾳ δούλων, ᾧ γε ὑπῆρχον δοῦλοι ὁπόσοι γοῦν· τὴν δὲ αἰτίαν ἔξεστιν εἰκάζειν.

---
[7] *Suppl. Des Places.*

(7.2) Ἐγὼ δὲ ὃ ὑπεσχόμην τὸ ἡδὺ διηγήσομαι. Ταμιεύων γὰρ αὐτὸς ἑαυτῷ τὴν μὲν κλεῖδα περιφέρειν ἐφ᾽ ἑαυτοῦ οὐκ ᾤετο δεῖν, ἀποκλείσας δὲ κατετίθει μὲν ταύτην εἴς τι κοῖλον γραμματεῖον· σημηνάμενος δὲ δακτυλίῳ τὸν μὲν δακτύλιον κατεκύλιε διὰ τοῦ κλείθρου ἔσω εἰς τὸν οἶκον μεθιείς, ὡς δὴ ὕστερον, ἐπειδὴ πάλιν ἐλθὼν ἀνοίξειε τῇ κλειδί, δυνησόμενος ἀνελὼν τὸν δακτύλιον αὖθις μὲν ἀποκλείειν, εἶτα δὲ σημαίνεσθαι, εἶτα δ᾽ ἀναβάλλειν ὀπίσω πάλιν ἔσω τὸν δακτύλιον διὰ τοῦ κλείθρου. (7.3) Τοῦτο οὖν τὸ σοφὸν οἱ δοῦλοι κατανοήσαντες, ἐπειδὴ προΐοι Λακύδης εἰς περίπατον ἢ ὅποι ἄλλοσε, καὶ αὐτοὶ ἀνοίξαντες ἂν κἄπειτα, ὥς σφιν ἦν θυμός, τὰ μὲν φαγόντες, τὰ δ᾽ ἐμπιόντες, ἄλλα δὲ ἀράμενοι ἐκ περιόδου ταῦτα ἐποίουν, ἀπέκλειον μέν, ἐσημαίνοντο δέ, τὸν δακτύλιον πολλά γε αὐτοῦ καταγελάσαντες εἰς τὸν οἶκον διὰ τοῦ κλείθρου ἠφίεσαν. (7.4 = Arcesilaus F90 Vezzoli) Ὁ οὖν Λακύδης πλήρη μὲν καταλιπών, κενὰ δὲ εὑρισκόμενος τὰ σκεύη ἀπορῶν τῷ γιγνομένῳ, ἐπειδὴ ἤκουσε φιλοσοφεῖσθαι παρὰ τῷ Ἀρκεσιλάῳ τὴν ἀκαταληψίαν, ᾤετο τοῦτο ἐκεῖνο αὐτῷ συμβαίνειν περὶ τὸ ταμεῖον, ἀρξάμενός τ᾽ ἔνθεν ἐφιλοσόφει παρὰ τῷ Ἀρκεσιλάῳ, μηδὲν μήτε ὁρᾶν μήτε ἀκούειν ἐναργὲς ἢ ὑγιές· καί ποτε ἐπισπασάμενος τῶν προσομιλούντων αὐτῷ τινα εἰς τὴν οἰκίαν ἰσχυρίζετο πρὸς αὐτὸν ὑπερφυῶς, ὡς ἐδόκει, τὴν ἐποχήν, καὶ ἔφη· 'Τοῦτο μὲν ἀναμφίλεκτον ἐγώ σοι ἔχω φράσαι, αὐτὸς ἐπ᾽ ἐμαυτοῦ μαθών, οὐκ ἄλλου πειραθείς.' (7.5) Κἄπειτα ἀρξάμενος περιηγεῖτο τὴν ὅλην τοῦ ταμείου συμβᾶσαν αὐτῷ πάθην. 'Τί οὖν ἄν', εἶπεν, 'ἔτι Ζήνων λέγοι πρὸς οὕτως ὁμολογουμένην διὰ πάντων φανεράν μοι ἐν τοῖς τοιοῖσδε ἀκαταληψίαν; ὃς γὰρ ἀπέκλεισα μὲν ταῖς ἐμαυτοῦ χερσίν, αὐτὸς δὲ ἐσημηνάμην, αὐτὸς δὲ ἀφῆκα μὲν εἴσω τὸν δακτύλιον, αὖθις δ᾽ ἐλθὼν ἀνοίξας τὸν μὲν δακτύλιον ὁρῶ ἔνδον, οὐ μέντοι καὶ τὰ ἄλλα, πῶς οὐ δικαίως ἀπιστοῦντως τοῖς πράγμασιν ἕξω; οὐ γάρ πω φήσω, εἰπεῖν, ἔγωγ᾽ ἐπελθόντα τινὰ κλέψαι ταῦτα ὑπάρχοντος ἔνδον τοῦ δακτυλίου.' (7.6) Καὶ ὃς ἀκούων, ἦν γὰρ ὑβριστής, ἐκδεξάμενος τὸ πᾶν ὡς ἔσχεν ἀκοῦσαι, μόλις καὶ πρότερον ἑαυτοῦ κρατῶν, ἀπέρρηξε γέλωτα καὶ μάλα πλατὺν γελῶν τε ἔτι καὶ καγχάζων διήλεγχεν ἅμα αὐτοῦ τὴν κενοδοξίαν. Ὥστε ἔκτοτε Λακύδης ἀρξάμενος οὐκέτι μὲν τὸν δακτύλιον ἔσω ἐνέβαλλεν, οὐκέτι δὲ τοῦ ταμείου ἐχρῆτο ἀκαταληψίᾳ, ἀλλὰ κατελάμβανε τὰ ἀφειμένα καὶ μάτην ἐπεφιλοσοφήκει.

(7.7) Οὐ μέντοι ἀλλὰ οἵ γε παῖδες φόρτακες ἦσαν καὶ οὐ θατέρα ληπτοί, οἷοι δὲ οὗτοι οἱ κωμῳδικοί [τε καὶ][8] Γέται τε καὶ Δακοὶ κἀκ τῆς Ἀττικῆς[9] λαλεῖν στωμυλήθρας κατεγλωττισμένοι, ἐπεί γε τοῖς Στωϊκοῖς τὰ σοφίσματα ἤκουσαν, εἴτε καὶ ἄλλως ἐκμαθόντες, εὐθὺ τοῦ τολμήματος ᾖσαν καὶ παρελύοντο αὐτοῦ τὴν σφραγῖδα καὶ τοτὲ μὲν ἑτέραν ἀντ᾽ ἐκείνης ὑπετίθεσαν, τοτὲ δὲ οὐδὲ ἄλλην, διὰ τὸ οἴεσθαι ἐκείνῳ γε ἀκατάληπτα ἔσεσθαι καὶ οὕτω καὶ ἄλλως. (7.8) Ὁ δ᾽ εἰσελθὼν ἐσκοπεῖτο· ἀσήμαντον δὲ τὸ γραμματεῖον θεωρῶν ἢ σεσημασμένον μέν, σφραγῖδι δ᾽ ἄλλῃ, ἠγανάκτει· τῶν δὲ σεσημάνθαι λεγόντων, αὐτοῖς γοῦν τὴν σφραγῖδα ὁρᾶσθαι τὴν αὐτοῦ, ἠκριβολογεῖτ᾽ ἂν καὶ ἀπεδείκνυε· τῶν δ᾽ ἡττωμένων τῇ ἀποδείξει φαμένων, εἰ μή τι ἔπεστιν ἡ σφραγὶς αὐτὸν ἴσως ἐπιλελῆσθαι καὶ μὴ σημήνασθαι, καὶ μὴν αὐτός γε ἔφη σημηνάμενος μνημονεύειν καὶ ἀπεδείκνυε καὶ περιῄει τῷ λόγῳ καὶ ἐδεινολογεῖτο πρὸς αὐτούς, οἰόμενος παίζεσθαι, καὶ προσώμνυεν. (7.9) Οἱ δ᾽ ὑπολαβόντες τὰς προσβολὰς ἐκείνου αὐτοί γε ᾤοντο ὑπ᾽ αὐτοῦ παίζεσθαι, ἐπεὶ σοφῷ γε ὄντι δεδόχθαι τῷ Λακύδῃ εἶναι ἀδοξάστῳ ὥστε καὶ ἀμνημονεύτῳ· μνήμην γὰρ εἶναι δόξαν· ἔναγχος γοῦν τοῦ χρόνου ἔφασαν ἀκοῦσαι ταῦτα αὐτοῦ πρὸς τοὺς φίλους. (7.10) Τοῦ δ᾽ ἀναστρέφοντος αὐτοῖς τὰς ἐπιχειρήσεις καὶ λέγοντος οὐκ Ἀκαδημαϊκά, αὐτοὶ φοιτῶντες εἰς Στωϊκῶν τινος τὰ λεκτέα ἑαυτοῖς ἀνεμάνθανον κἀκεῖθεν ἀρξάμενοι ἀντεσοφίστευον καὶ ἦσαν ἀντίτεχνοι κλέπται Ἀκαδημαϊκοί· ὁ δὲ Στωϊκῶς ἐνεκάλει· οἱ παῖδες δὲ τὰ ἐγκλήματα παρέλυον αὐτῷ ὑπὸ ἀκαταληψίας οὐκ ἄνευ τωθασμῶν τινων. (7.11) Διατριβαὶ οὖν ἦσαν πάντων ἐκεῖ καὶ λόγοι καὶ ἀντιλογίαι· καὶ εἰ οὐδὲν ἐν τῷ μέσῳ κατελείπετο, οὐκ ἀγγεῖον, οὐ τῶν ἐν ἀγγείῳ τιθεμένων, οὐχ ὅσα εἰς οἰκίας κατασκευὴν ἀλλ᾽ ἔστι συντελῆ.

(7.12) Καὶ ὁ Λακύδης τέως μὲν ἠπόρει, μήτε λυσιτελοῦσαν ἑαυτῷ θεωρῶν τὴν τοῖς ἑαυτοῦ δόγμασι βοήθειαν εἴ τε μὴ ἐξελέγχοι πάντα ἀνατρέψεσθαι ἑαυτῷ δοκῶν, πεσὼν εἰς τἀμήχανον τοὺς γείτονας ἐκεκράγει καὶ τοὺς θεούς, καὶ ἰοῦ ἰοῦ καὶ φεῦ φεῦ καὶ νὴ τοὺς θεοὺς καὶ νὴ τὰς θεὰς ἄλλαι τε ὅσαι ἐν ἀπιστίαις δεινολογουμένων εἰσὶν ἄτεχνοι πίστεις, ταῦτα πάντα ἐλέγετο βοῇ ἅμα καὶ ἀξιοπιστίᾳ. (7.13) Τελευτῶν δέ, ἐπεὶ μάχην εἶχεν ἀντιλεγομένην ἐπὶ τῆς οἰκίας, αὐτὸς μὲν ἂν δήπουθεν ἐστωϊκεύετο πρὸς τοὺς παῖδας, τῶν παίδων δὲ τὰ Ἀκαδημαϊκὰ

---

[8] Secl. Mras.   [9] Ἀττικῆς Hirzel: Δακικῆς codd.

ἰσχυριζομένων, ἵνα μηκέτι πράγματα ἔχοι, οἰκουρὸς ἦν φίλος τοῦ ταμείου προσκαθήμενος. Οὐδὲν δ' εἰς οὐδὲν ὠφελῶν ὑπιδόμενος οἷ τὸ σοφὸν αὐτῷ ἔρχεται, ἀπεκαλύψατο· 'Ἄλλως,' ἔφη, 'ταῦτα, ὦ παῖδες, ἐν ταῖς διατριβαῖς λέγεται ἡμῖν, ἄλλως δὲ ζῶμεν.'

(7.14) Ταῦτα μὲν καὶ περὶ τοῦ Λακύδου. Τούτου δὲ γίνονται ἀκουσταὶ πολλοί, ὧν εἷς ἦν διαφανὴς ὁ Κυρηναῖος Ἀρίστιππος, ἐκ πάντων δ' αὐτοῦ τῶν γνωρίμων τὴν σχολὴν αὐτοῦ διεδέξατο Εὔανδρος καὶ οἱ μετὰ τοῦτον. (7.15 = Arcesilaus F91 Vezzoli) Μεθ' οὓς Καρνεάδης (T2 Mette) ὑποδεξάμενος τὴν διατριβὴν τρίτην συνεστήσατο Ἀκαδημίαν, λόγων μὲν οὖν ἀγωγῇ ἐχρήσατο ᾗ καὶ ὁ Ἀρκεσίλαος· καὶ γὰρ αὐτὸς ἐπετήδευε τὴν εἰς ἑκάτερα ἐπιχείρησιν καὶ πάντα ἀνεσκεύαζε τὰ ὑπὸ τῶν ἄλλων λεγόμενα· μόνῳ δ' ἐν τῷ περὶ τῆς ἐποχῆς λόγῳ πρὸς αὐτὸν διέστη, φὰς ἀδύνατον εἶναι ἄνθρωπον ὄντα περὶ ἁπάντων ἐπέχειν· διαφορὰν δὲ εἶναι ἀδήλου καὶ ἀκαταλήπτου καὶ πάντα μὲν εἶναι ἀκατάληπτα, οὐ πάντα δὲ ἄδηλα. Μετεῖχε δ' οὗτος καὶ τῶν Στωϊκῶν λόγων, πρὸς οὓς καὶ ἐριστικῶς ἱστάμενος ἐπὶ πλέον ηὐξήθη, τοῦ φαινομένου τοῖς πολλοῖς πιθανοῦ ἀλλ' οὐ τῆς ἀληθείας στοχαζόμενος· ὅθεν καὶ πολλὴν παρέσχε τοῖς Στωϊκοῖς ἀηδίαν.

Γράφει δ' οὖν καὶ ὁ Νουμήνιος περὶ αὐτοῦ ταῦτα.

Frg. 27 Des Places (Eus., *Praep. Ev.* XIV.8.1–15, pp. 737b–739a Viger; II, pp. 281.11–284.9 Mras)

(8.1) Καρνεάδης (T2 Mette = Arcesilaus F92 Vezzoli) δ' ἐκδεξάμενος παρ' Ἡγησίνου χρεὼν φυλάξαι ὅσ' ἀκίνητα καὶ ὅσα κεκινημένα ἦν, τούτου μὲν ἠμέλει, εἰς δ' Ἀρκεσίλαον, εἴτ' οὖν ἀμείνω εἴτε καὶ φαυλότερα ἦν, ἐπανενεγκὼν διὰ μακροῦ τὴν μάχην ἀνενέαζε.

(8.2) Καὶ ἑξῆς ἐπιλέγει·
Ἦγε δ' οὖν καὶ οὗτος καὶ ἀπέφερεν ἀντιλογίας τε καὶ στροφὰς λεπτολόγους συνέφερε τῇ μάχῃ ποικίλων ἐξαρνητικός τε καὶ καταφατικός τε ἦν κἀμφοτέρωθεν ἀντιλογικός· εἴ τε που ἔδει τι καὶ θαῦμα ἐχόντων λόγων, ἐξηγείρετο λάβρος οἷον ποταμὸς ῥοώδης, [σφοδρῶς ῥέων,]¹⁰ πάντα καταπιμπλὰς τὰ τῇδε καὶ τἀκεῖθι, καὶ εἰσέπιπτε καὶ συνέσυρε τοὺς ἀκούοντας διὰ θορύβου. (8.3 = Arcesilaus F93 Vezzoli) Τοιγαροῦν ἀπάγων τοὺς ἄλλους αὐτὸς ἔμενεν ἀνεξαπάτητος, ὃ μὴ προσῆν τῷ Ἀρκεσιλάῳ (T2 Mette). Ἐκεῖνος μέν γε περιερχόμενος τῇ φαρμάξει τοὺς συγκορυβαντιῶντας ἔλαθεν ἑαυτὸν πρῶτον ἐξηπατηκὼς μὴ ᾔσθησθαι, πεπεῖσθαι δ' ἀληθῆ εἶναι ἃ λέγει, διὰ τῆς ἁπαξαπάντων ἀναιρέσεως χρημάτων. (8.4) Κακὸν δὲ ἦν ἂν κακῷ ἐπανακείμενον, ὁ Καρνεάδης τῷ Ἀρκεσιλάῳ, μὴ χαλάσας τι σμικρόν, ὑφ' οὗ οὐκ ἄπρακτοι ἔμελλον ἔσεσθαι, κατὰ τὰς ἀπὸ τοῦ πιθανοῦ λεγομένας αὐτῷ θετικάς τε καὶ ἀρνητικὰς φαντασίας τοῦ εἶναι τόδε τι ζῷον ἢ μὴ ζῷον εἶναι. (8.5) Τοῦτο οὖν ὑπανείς, ὥσπερ οἱ ἀναχάζοντες θῆρες βιαιότερον καὶ μᾶλλον ἑαυτοὺς ἱεῖσιν εἰς τὰς αἰχμὰς καὐτοὺς ἐνδοὺς δυνατώτερον ἐπῆλθεν· ἐπεί τε ὑποσταίη τε καὶ εὖ τύχοι, τηνικαῦτα ἤδη καὶ οὗ προυδέδοκτο ἑκὼν ἠμέλει καὶ οὐκ ἐμέμνητο. (8.6) Τὸ γὰρ ἀληθές τε καὶ τὸ ψεῦδος ἐν τοῖς πράγμασιν ἐνεῖναι συγχωρῶν, ὥσπερ ξυνεργαζόμενος τῆς ζητήσεως τρόπῳ παλαιστοῦ δεινοῦ λαβὴν δοὺς περιεγίγνετο ἔνθεν. Κατὰ γὰρ τὴν τοῦ πιθανοῦ ῥοπὴν ἑκάτερον παρασχὼν οὐδέτερον εἶπε βεβαίως καταλαμβάνεσθαι. Ἦν γοῦν λῃστὴς καὶ γόης σοφώτερος. (8.7) Παραλαβὼν γὰρ ἀληθεῖ μὲν ὅμοιον ψεῦδος, καταληπτικῇ δὲ φαντασίᾳ καταληπτὸν ὅμοιον καὶ ἀγαγὼν εἰς τὰς ἴσας, οὐκ εἴασεν οὔτε τὸ ἀληθὲς εἶναι οὔτε τὸ ψεῦδος, ἢ οὐ μᾶλλον τὸ ἕτερον τοῦ ἑτέρου ἢ μᾶλλον ἀπὸ τοῦ πιθανοῦ. (8.8) Ἦν οὖν ὀνείρατα ἀντὶ ὀνειράτων, διὰ τὸ ὁμοίας φαντασίας ἀληθέσιν εἶναι τὰς ψευδεῖς, ὡς ἀπὸ ᾠοῦ κηρίνου πρὸς τὸ ἀληθινὸν ᾠόν. (8.9) Συνέβαινεν οὖν τὰ κακὰ καὶ πλείω. Καὶ μέντοι λέγων ὁ Καρνεάδης ἐψυχαγώγει καὶ ἠνδραποδίσατο. Ἦν δὲ κλέπτων μὲν ἀφανής, φαινόμενος δὲ λῃστής, αἱρῶν καὶ δόλῳ καὶ βίᾳ τοὺς καὶ πάνυ σφόδρα παρεσκευασμένους. (8.10) Πᾶσα γοῦν Καρνεάδου διάνοια ἐνίκα καὶ οὐδεμία ἡτισοῦν ἄλλων, ἐπεὶ καὶ οἷς προσεπολέμει ἦσαν εἰπεῖν ἀδυνατώτεροι.

(8.11) Ἀντίπατρος (SVF iii.6) γοῦν ὁ κατ' αὐτὸν γενόμενος ἔμελλε μὲν καὶ ἀγωνιῶν¹¹ τι γράφειν, πρὸς δ' οὖν τοὺς ἀπὸ Καρνεάδου καθ' ἡμέραν ἀποφερομένους λόγους οὔποτε ἐδημοσίευσεν, οὐκ ἐν ταῖς διατριβαῖς, οὐκ ἐν τοῖς περιπάτοις οὐδὲν εἶπεν οὐδ' ἐφθέγξατο οὐδ' ἤκουσέ τις αὐτοῦ, φασίν, οὐδὲ γρῦ· ἀντιγραφὰς δ' ἐπανετείνετο καὶ γωνίαν λαβὼν βιβλία

---

¹⁰ Secl. Viger.   ¹¹ ἀγωνιῶν Viger: ἀγωνιᾶν codd.

κατέλιπε γράψας τοῖς ὕστερον, οὔτε νῦν δυνάμενα καὶ τότε ἦν ἀδυνατώτερα πρὸς οὕτως ἄνδρα ὑπέρμεγαν φανέντα καὶ καταδόξαντα εἶναι τοῖς τότε ἀνθρώποις τὸν Καρνεάδην.

(8.12) Ὅμως δέ, καίτοι καὐτὸς ὑπὸ τῆς Στωϊκῆς φιλονεικίας εἰς τὸ φανερὸν κυκῶν, πρός γε τοὺς ἑαυτοῦ ἑταίρους δι' ἀπορρήτων ὡμολόγει τε καὶ ἠλήθευε καὶ ἀπεφαίνετο ἃ κἂν ἄλλος τῶν ἐπιτυχόντων.

(8.13) Εἶτα ἑξῆς φησι·
Καρνεάδου δὲ γίνεται γνώριμος Μέντωρ μὲν πρῶτον, οὐ μὴν διάδοχος· ἀλλ' ἔτι ζῶν Καρνεάδης ἐπὶ παλλακῇ μοιχὸν εὑρών, οὐχ ὑπὸ πιθανῆς φαντασίας οὐδ' ὡς μὴ κατειληφώς, ὡς δὲ μάλιστα πιστεύων τῇ ὄψει καὶ καταλαβὼν παρῃτήσατο τῆς διατριβῆς. Ὁ δὲ ἀποστὰς ἀντεσοφίστευε καὶ ἀντίτεχνος ἦν, ἐλέγχων αὐτοῦ τὴν ἐν τοῖς λόγοις ἀκαταληψίαν.

(8.14) Καὶ πάλιν ἐπιφέρει λέγων·
Ὁ δὲ Καρνεάδης, οἷον ἀντεστραμμένα φιλοσοφῶν, τοῖς ψεύμασιν ἐκαλλωπίζετο καὶ ὑπ' αὐτοῖς τὰ ἀληθῆ ἠφάνιζε. Παραπετάσμασιν οὖν ἐχρῆτο τοῖς ψεύμασι καὶ ἠλήθευεν ἔνδον λανθάνων καπηλικώτερον. Ἔπασχεν οὖν πάθημα ὀσπρίων, ὧν τὰ μὲν κενὰ ἐπιπολάζει τε τῷ ὕδατι καὶ ὑπερέχει, τὰ χρηστὰ δὲ αὐτῶν ἐστι κάτω καὶ ἐν ἀφανεῖ.

Ταῦτα καὶ περὶ Καρνεάδου λέγεται. Διάδοχος δ' αὐτοῦ τῆς διατριβῆς καθίσταται Κλειτόμαχος, μεθ' ὃν Φίλων[12] (T VI Brittain), οὗ πέρι ὁ Νουμήνιος μνημονεύει ταῦτα·

Frg. 28 Des Places (Eus., *Praep. Ev.* XIV.9.1–4, p. 739b–d Viger; II, pp. 284.11–285.3 Mras)

(9.1) Ὁ δὲ Φίλων[13] (T XXIII Brittain) ἄρα οὗτος ἄρτι μὲν ἐκδεξάμενος τὴν διατριβὴν ὑπὸ χαρμονῆς ἐξεπέπληκτο καὶ χάριν ἀποδιδοὺς ἐθεράπευε καὶ τὰ δεδογμένα τῷ Κλειτομάχῳ ηὖξε καὶ τοῖς Στωϊκοῖς (Hom., *Il.* 7.206)

ἐκορύσσετο νώροπι χαλκῷ.

(9.2) Ὡς δὲ προϊόντος μὲν τοῦ χρόνου, ἐξιτήλου δ' ὑπὸ συνηθείας οὔσης αὐτῶν τῆς ἐποχῆς, οὐδὲν μὲν κατὰ τὰ αὐτὰ ἑαυτῷ ἐνόει, ἡ δὲ τῶν παθημάτων αὐτὸν ἀνέστρεφεν ἐνάργειά τε καὶ ὁμολογία. Πολλὴν δῆτ' ἔχων ἤδη τὴν διαίσθησιν ὑπερεπεθύμει εὖ ἴσθ' ὅτι τῶν ἐλεγξόντων τυχεῖν, ἵνα μὴ ἐδόκει (Hom., *Il.* 8.94)

μετὰ νῶτα βαλών

αὐτὸς ἑκὼν φεύγειν. (9.3) Φίλωνος[14] δὲ γίνεται ἀκουστὴς Ἀντίοχος (T1 Mette = T1 Sedley), ἑτέρας ἄρξας Ἀκαδημίας. Μνησάρχῳ γοῦν τῷ Στωϊκῷ σχολάσας ἐναντία Φίλωνι[15] τῷ καθηγητῇ ἐφρόνησε μυρία τε ξένα προσῆψε τῇ Ἀκαδημίᾳ.

(9.4) Ταῦτα καὶ παραπλήσια τούτοις μυρία τῆς Πλάτωνος πέρι διαδοχῆς μνημονεύεται.

Translations

frg. 24[16]

Such were the successors of Plato himself. For their character receive and read the remarks of Numenius the Pythagorean, which he has set down in a book with the title 'About the dissension of the Academics from Plato':

---

[12] Φίλων Estienne: Φιλίων codd.   [13] Φίλων Estienne: Φιλίων codd.
[14] Φίλωνος Estienne: Φιλίωνος codd.   [15] Φίλωνι Estienne: Φιλίωνι codd.
[16] I have compared the translations by Des Places (1973), Wyss (2005), as well as where applicable Boys-Stones (2018).

(5.1) Under Speusippus, Plato's nephew, Xenocrates, the successor of Speusippus, and Polemo, who had taken over the leadership of the school from Xenocrates, the character of the school as far as doctrine was concerned roughly remained the same, because that well-worn 'suspension of judgement' and all the rest did not yet exist. But because they often dropped some tenets and twisted others, they did not stick with the earlier position of the school. After this beginning they continued to step away from Plato's teachings, sometimes faster, sometimes more slowly, deliberately or out of ignorance, in other cases also for a different reason (ambition may have played a role). (5.2) I have no intention of saying anything dismissive about Xenocrates, but I want to speak up for Plato. For it is painful to me that they were not prepared to suffer and do anything in order to maintain the complete agreement with Plato's doctrine on all points. And yet Plato deserved this of them. He was not better than the great Pythagoras, but perhaps not inferior to him either. Pythagoras' successors venerated him and, as his pupils, were responsible for the high esteem bestowed upon him.

(5.3) The Epicureans did not need to learn this, but they did so, and nobody ever saw them claim anything other than Epicurus had claimed, they showed themselves in unison to be of the same opinion as the sage (i.e. Epicurus) and accordingly they themselves profited from the designation. And this was indeed so with the later Epicureans that they contradicted neither one another nor Epicurus on any point which would be worth mentioning. For this counts among them as lawless, indeed even sacrilege, and innovations (sc. in doctrine) are treated as crimes. Therefore none of them has ever dared to do this, and the doctrines of the master have rested with them in great peace, since there was always agreement amongst them. The school of Epicurus resembles the true republic, which is free of rebellions, characterized by a common spirit and one opinion. Therefore they were and are and, it seems to me, will be zealous followers (sc. of Epicurus).

(5.4) The school of the Stoics by contrast consists of many factions, which have continued to exist since the time of the founders without interruption. They lay into one another with great gusto and malicious criticism. Some of them maintain the original view, others have already changed their mind. The Stoics of the first generation resembled oligarchs, who became, through their quarreling, the cause of criticism and rebuke for their successors, with respect to their predecessors, as well as amongst themselves, and some were more Stoic than the others, particularly those who were regarded as especially small-minded about technical matters. For these, who outdid the other ones in hyperactivity, were quick to find fault in others.

(5.5) Much earlier than the Stoics the successors of Socrates experienced the same thing, who had derived their different doctrines from him, each in his own way: Aristippos and Antisthenes, somewhat differently the Megarians and Eretrians or whoever else was to be counted among them. (5.6) The cause for this was that the listeners, when Socrates put forward the account of the three gods and philosophized about each of them in an appropriate style, did not understand this, but thought he was saying this in a random manner and depending on accidental circumstances soon in this way, then in that way, as the wind was turning.

(5.7) But Plato philosophized in the manner of Pythagoras (he knew that Socrates derived what he said from precisely this place and with complete awareness of this), and so he too brought his subjects together, in a manner that was neither usual nor in plain sight. He covered each as he saw fit and hid (sc. the results) right in the middle of the completely clear and the utterly unclear. He wrote everything down in safety, but provided an opening for dissension after him and for disagreement about his teachings, but not out of jealousy or malice. But I do not want to make detracting remarks about ancient and venerable men. (5.8) With this knowledge we must direct our attention elsewhere. And as we had planned from the beginning to separate him from Aristotle and Zeno, so we separate him (sc. Plato) now also from the Academy, with the help of god, and allow him to be a Pythagorean for himself. For now he is suffering since he is being torn apart limb by limb, more furiously than any Pentheus deserved, althoug taken as a whole he never changes back and forth. (5.9) As a man who occupies a position in the middle between Pythagoras and Socrates, he reduced and turned the eminent dignity of the one into approachable kindness, and elevated the acumen and the wit of the other away from irony in the direction of respect and dignity. He combines Pythagoras with Socrates in such a way that he appears more accessible than the one, and more venerable than the other.

frg. 25

(5.10) I have not come to tell you about this—that is not the purpose of my current inquiry—, but will rather talk about what I was planning to talk about: I will return to the place from which, it seems, I was diverted, so that I do not lose sight of my chosen path.

(5.11) Arcesilaus and Zeno became Polemo's pupils. I will mention them again at the end. I remember I said already that Zeno attended lectures with Xenocrates and then with Polemo and then was introduced to Cynicism by Crates. Now it also needs to be credited to his account that he was interested in Stilpo's and Heraclitus' discourses. (5.12) For after Arcesilaus and Zeno had regularly attended Polemo's lectures, they began to enter into a rivalry. For this battle Zeno took Heraclitus, Stilpo and Crates as allies: under Stilpo's influence he became combative, under Heraclitus' serious and severe, and through Crates a cynic. By contrast, Arcesilaus sided with Theophrastus, the Platonist Krantor, Diodorus and Pyrrho. Under Krantor's influence he learned to persuade easily, under that of Diodorus to argue cleverly, and through Pyrrhon to be agile, irreverent and elusive. (5.13) Therefore someone coined the following mocking and outrageous line about him:

Plato in front, Pyrrho at the back, Diodorus in the middle.

(5.14) Timon by contrast claimed that Arcesilaus had equipped himself by adopting from Menedemus the eristic technique, if indeed it is about him that he wrote: 'With Menedemus' leaden weight under his breast, he (sc. Arcesilaus) will run either to the very muscular Pyrrho or to Diodorus'. Arcesilaus now combined with the clever arguments of the dialectician Diodorus the reasonings of Pyrrho and his sceptical attitude, augmented his non-sensical babble with Plato's impressive style, spoke for and against, rolled this way and that as chance determined, took back what he had said, was hard to judge, inconsistent and ready to take risks at the same time, without knowing anything, as he himself conceded. So he came out looking similar to those who actually know something, showed himself to be many things through his words, like the outlines (sc. of a shadowplay). (6.1) You knew with Arcesilaus as little as you did with the Homeric Diomedes on whose side he was, whether that of the Trojans or that of the Greeks. For to stick to one and the same argument was not given to him, and he regarded this as in no way the mark of a right-thinking man. Accordingly he was called:

Mighty sophist, slayer of the untrained.

(6.2) For he stupefied and cast a spell like the Empusae with his phantom arguments, having prepared himself and practiced appropriately. Neither could he himself know anything, nor could he let others know something, he caused fear and terror, made noise and disrupted, and when he had won the prize in clever argument and verbal trickery, he delighted in this shameful title. He gloried immensely in knowing neither what is ugly or beautiful, or good or bad, but after saying whichever thing came into his head, he would change again and reject his argument, removing everything in more ways than he had prepared it. (6.3) He was a Hydra beheading himself and being beheaded by himself (both activities can hardly be distinguished), without any regard to whether that was right: yet to the listeners it was enough to look at the attractive orator while listening. He was very pleasant when one heard and saw him, especially given that his audience had got used to hearing his arguments since they came from an attractive-looking speaker with a fetching gaze. (6.4) This is not something to be taken lightly, for he was like this from the beginning. As an adolescent Arcesilaus encountered Theophrastus, this gentle man, who was not untalented in the field of love. Still a young man, he encountered the Academic Krantor, who became his lover due to his beauty. Arcesilaus joined Krantor, but since he was not untalented by his natural disposition, he used that disposition easily and with burning ambition, and took over these clever arguments from Diodorus in order to be wickedly persuasive, but also spent time with Pyrrho (who himself was influenced by Democritus in some way or other) and thus equipped himself from here and from there. Except for the designation he remained a Pyrrhonist through the pursuit of the refutation of all knowledge in the Pyrrhonist way. (6.5) The sceptics Mnaseas, Philomelos and Timon called him a sceptic, as they themselves were, since he too was someone who removed true, false, and persuasive.

One might have called him a Pyrrhonist because of his Pyrrhonist arguments, but out of respect for his lover he tolerated it to be called an Academic. But he was a Pyrrhonist, except in name; Academic he was not, except in name. (6.6) For I do not believe what Dikaiokles of Knidos writes in his work with the title *Diatribes*:[17] out of fear of the followers of Theodorus and the sophist Bion, who moved against the philosophers and did not hesitate to refute them completely, Arcesilaus carefully ensured that, in order not to get into trouble, he did not appear to state any tenet openly, but distributed suspension of judgement carefully around himself, like a cuttlefish its black ink. This I do not believe.

(6.7) So Arcesilaus and Zeno, who came from the same starting point, forgot, because of such auxiliaries, i.e. the arguments helping both sides in the war, where they originally came from, namely from Polemo,

drawing apart, they armed themselves,
clashed hides together, and lances and the force of men
in brazen breastplates, but their bossed shields met one other, and a great noise arose,
shield pressed against shield and helmet against helmet, and man against man did battle,
then went forth together the wailing and boasting of men,
of the slaying and the slain

who were the Stoics. (6.8) For the Academics were not touched by the Stoics since one could not know where best to grab them. The Academics might have been grabbed and their foundation shaken, if they had had neither a firm foundation nor a starting point for their fight. But the foundation was to refute the Stoics where they did not say what Plato said, the starting point was that the Stoics would have nothing at all if they had modified and removed only a single point in the definition of the cataleptic impression. (6.9) But now is not the right moment for me to say something about it. I will return to it when I come to address this topic specifically.

They positioned themselves openly against one another and attacked, not both in the same way, but Arcesilaus attacked Zeno. For Zeno had a certain dignity and seriousness in combat, and was as ineffective as the orator Kephisodorus: when he saw that his own teacher Isocrates was being attacked by Aristotle, he waged war on Aristotle (of whom he knew nothing at all). But since he realized how famous Plato's philosophy was and assumed that Aristotle did philosophy like Plato, he was at war with Aristotle, but hit Plato. He made accusations against him by beginning with Forms and ending with the rest, of which he had no understanding, but made guesses on the basis of what people said. (6.10) However, in this manner Kephisodorus did not fight against the man his battle was with, but against the man with whom he did not want to engage in battle. If Zeno himself, after leaving Arcesilaus to one side, had not waged war on Plato, he would have shown himself an excellent philosopher, if only for keeping the peace. But if he acted with knowledge of Arcesilaus' views but in ignorance of Plato's, as is evidenced by the work he had composed against Plato, he achieved the opposite (sc. of what he wanted) by, on the one hand, not striking the one he knew well, and, on the other, mistreating in an ignominious and shameful way the one whom he should not have struck, treating him much worse than a dog deserves. (6.11) In failing to engage with Arcesilaus, he made

---

[17] See Des Places (1973: 68).

a display of his arrogance. For he turned against someone else, either out of ignorance or out of fear of the Stoics,

<blockquote>war's wide-open jaws of bitter peril,</blockquote>

namely against Plato. But about Zeno's bad and shameless innovations against Plato I will talk some other time if I ever have a break from philosophy. Though I would never want to have that much spare time, except as a game.

(6.12) But Arcesilaus, when he realized that Zeno was an opponent who was matched in skill and capable of winning, set about refuting the arguments cited by him and did not hesitate on one of them. (6.13) And on the other topics about which he fought with Zeno I have, perhaps, nothing to say, but if I had something to say, it would be unnecessary do so now: because he saw that the thesis which Zeno was the first to develop, the issue itself and the designation 'cataleptic impression', were popular in Athens, he used every means at his disposal against it. But Zeno, who was in the weaker position but could not suffer damage if he remained calm, ignored Arcesilaus, against whom he would have had many things to say but he did not want to (unless there was some other reason). Instead, he took to shadow-boxing with Plato, who was no longer among the living, and he caused disarray in the entire procession from his chariot, thinking, on the one hand, that Plato could no longer defend himself, on the other, that nobody was taking up his defence. If, however, it became Arcesilaus' task to see to that defence, then, Zeno thought, this would be his gain, since he would have turned Arcesilaus away from himself. (He knew that this trick had also been used by the general Agathocles of Syracuse against the Carthaginians.) (6.14) The Stoics listened and were surprised. For at the time 'their Muse was neither a lover of language' nor 'even active for the Graces' (cf. Pind., *Isthm.* 2.6). With the Graces' help Arcesilaus shut up the Stoics, by tackling them from all sides, cutting off their path or tripping them up—and he was persuasive. And so those against whom Arcesilaus cited his arguments were defeated, and those with whom he spoke were paralysed. To the people alive then it became plain that nothing exists—neither word nor feeling, nor could any small and inconsequential action ever be deemed the opposite— unless Arcesilaus of Pithane thought that it did. Yet he had no opinion and proved nothing beyond the fact that these were just captious words and fears.

frg. 26

(7.1) About Lacydes I now want to tell a funny story. Lacydes, well-liked amongst the many, was somewhat stingy and the proverbial housekeeper; he opened the larder himself, locked it up himself, took out what he needed, and did everything himself in the same manner, not because he had made being autonomous his maxim, also not because he might have been poor or he might have been lacking slaves, of whom he actually had rather a large number; no, for a reason which is now easy to guess. (7.2) But I want to recount now that good story that I promised. For although he managed his household himself, he did not regard it as necessary to carry the key around; rather, when he locked up, he placed it into an unfilled writing tablet. After he had sealed it with the ring, he pushed the ring through the lock into the chamber, on the reasoning that he could later, when he returned and opened the room again with the key, pick up the ring, lock up again, then seal the tablet again and push the ring through the lock once more. (7.3) His slaves had seen through this trick: whenever Lacydes went for stroll or otherwise left the house, they unlocked the door, ate and drank as much as they liked, took other things with them and then did the following in this order: they locked up, sealed the writing tablet and pushed, having made fun of Lacydes, the ring through the lock into the chamber. (7.4) Now Lacydes, when he found the pots empty which he had left behind full, was unable to explain what had happened, and since he had heard that inapprehensibility was being philosophized about under Arcesilaus, he thought that this was no different than what had happened in his larder. And so he started at that point and engaged in philosophy with Arcesilaus, holding that everything which we see and hear is confused and mere appearance. And once when he had brought an acquaintance home he impressed on him very strongly, as he thought, the need to suspend judgement and said: 'I may perhaps call this indisputable since I had experienced it myself and had not learned it from someone else.' (7.5) And then he began and told him everything, what had happened with his larder. 'What', he continued, 'could Zeno say in the face of an inapprehensibility which was acknowledged by everyone and manifest through all circumstances, as the one at issue here? For when I locked the door with my own hands, impressed the seal himself and pushed the ring through the lock, and on my return found the ring on the inside, but not what else was contained in the larder, do I not have the right to be doubtful about the reality of things? For I shall be unable to say that someone came and stole the things, since the ring was still on the inside.' (7.6) When his friend heard this—he had a wicked sense of humour—he waited first until he had heard everything and then broke into laughter, although he could hardly contain himself earlier, and while he was still laughing he also refuted his view, baseless as it was. As a consequence Lacydes no longer pushed the ring through the lock from here onwards and no longer cited the inapprehensibility of the larder, but apprehended what he had lost, and his philosophizing had been in vain.

(7.7) But the slaves were tricksters and not easy to catch with one hand, rather like the Getes and Dakians of comedy who owe their loquacity to the Attic way with words, because they had either heard or otherwise learned dialectical tricks from the Stoics. They embarked without compunction on the execution of the cheeky assault and removed the seal, put a different one in its place, or else no seal at all, since they thought it would be inapprehensible to him anyway. (7.8) When he then came home, he checked; and when he found the tablet unsealed or sealed with a different seal, he got angry; and when they explained that it was sealed, given that they were seeing the same seal, he was irate and offered a meticulous proof to the contrary. And when they had to give way in the light of this proof and say that, if a seal was not on it, he must have forgotten it and not sealed the tablet, then he replied that he recalled that he sealed the tablet himself, and demonstrated this in a cumbersome disquisition and rebuked them because he believed they were mocking him, and swore (to what he had said). (7.9) But they took their cue from his accusation and said in return that they were being taken for a ride by him; for as a wise man Lacydes held no beliefs according to his own view, and accordingly had no memory, for a memory was a belief, too; at least that is, they said, what they had heard him say to his friends recently. (7.10) When he then rejected their attacks and cited many considerations which were not Academic, they attended classes with a Stoic and learned what they should say, and after this began to counter him with sophisms and to rival him in technical argument as Academic thieves. When he reproached them for this as a Stoic would, the slaves demonstrated how untenable his accusations were on the basis of inapprehensibility, which did also involve a degree of ridicule. (7.11) As a consequence there were lengthy debates, speeches and counterspeeches, and nothing remained, no vessel, nor their content, nor what else was part of the household.

(7.12) Lacydes was at a loss for a long time, since he saw that he was not deriving benefit from the help of his doctrines and that, if he did not succeed in refutation, everything would be ruined for him, or so he thought; so he screamed in despair to his neighbours and the gods, and 'woe, woe', 'alas, alas', and 'by the gods' and 'by the goddesses', and what other untechnical steps there are with which one indignantly tries to secure credence having been met with distrust; all of those he mustered with a loud voice and a sincere expression. (7.13) But finally, since he was tired of objections based on his own views, he played the Stoic when dealing with his slaves, but when the slaves stuck to their Academic position, he positioned himself as a trusty guard in his larder so as to avoid having further difficulties. But since all of this offered little help, he made the following confession out of fear where his wisdom might lead to: 'Slaves', he said, 'we talk about such things one way in school, and a different way in real life.'

(7.14) So much for Lacydes. Many became his pupils, one of them the famous Aristippus of Cyrene. From amongst his many students Euandrus took over his school and his many pupils. (7.15) After him Carneades took over the leadership of the school, who then set up the third

Academy. He used the same method of argument as Arcesilaus. For he, too, engaged in enquiry on either side and refuted everything advanced by others. He took a position that was different from Arcesilaus' only with respect to suspension of judgement. He said it was impossible for a human being to suspend judgement over everything. For there was a difference between what was unclear and what was inapprehensible. Everything was inapprehensible, but not everything unclear. He also engaged with Stoic arguments: by presenting himself as ready for a fight with respect to them, he only grew larger, and aimed at what seems persuasive to the many, but not at truth. This is why he caused much grief to the Stoics.

Numenius wrote this about him, too.

frg. 27

(8.1) Although Carneades, when he had taken over (sc. the leadership) from Hegesinus, should have kept as it was what had never been changed by him as well as what had been changed, he failed to do that, but derived everything, for better or worse, from Arcesilaus, and renewed after a long time the battle (sc. between Stoa and Academy).

(8.2) And so Numenius continued:

He, too, guided the philosophical discussion in this direction and that; he brought counter-speeches and subtle about-turns into the battle, spoke cleverly, denied and affirmed, and was adept in contradicting from the other side. And when speeches were necessary, even far-fetched ones, he rose with might like a river in flood, which drenches everything on this side and on the other, and leapt upon the audience and carried them with him by means of his roaring swell. (8.3) So he distracted the others, without being deceived himself, an ability which Arcesilaus had lacked. He (sc. Arcesilaus) ensnared his enrapt followers with his drugs; however, due to an unintended self-deception he was, without noticing it, convinced of the truth of what he was saying, because he had refuted everything completely. (8.4) Evil seemed to have been heaped upon evil, Carneades upon Arcesilaus. He (sc. Carneades) never gave way even on the smallest point, unless his opponents would be reduced to being inactive, by exploiting as persuasive what he called impressions which stated or denied something, e.g. that this is an animal or not. (8.5) After such a concession he would retreat a little, like wild animals who then advance mightier and stronger on the lances (sc. of the enemy), and after giving in attack again with more force. When he held up well and had success, then immediately he no longer cared for what appeared right to him previously, and forgot it. (8.6) For by conceding that there is true and false in all things, as if he was joining in with the enquiry, he allowed himself to be grabbed in the manner of a clever wrestler in order to gain the upper hand from that position. And by setting out both sides according to the weight of persuasiveness, he said that neither was apprehended securely. He was a robber and a magician more clever (sc. than Arcesilaus). (8.7) For he would take something false which was like the true on the one hand, and an apprehensible object together with a (sc. supposedly) cataleptic impression on the other, and put them on the balanced pans of the scale. And he would not admit that there was truth or falsehood, or that one was more the case than the other, or that one was more so than the other on the basis of persuasiveness. (8.8) So dreams followed dreams because false and true impressions were similar, as a waxen egg resembles a genuine one. (8.9) Further evil outcomes came to pass: Carneades affected his listeners' souls as he was speaking to them and enslaved them. He was an invisible thief, a manifest robber, he seized with trickery and force even those who were well prepared. (8.10) Every opinion of Carneades' was victorious, then, and none advanced by anyone else, since those against whom he argued were rhetorically less gifted than he was.

(8.11) His contemporary Antipater was eager to write something against him, but against the arguments which Carneades advanced on a daily basis he took no action publicly; neither in lectures nor in the public walks did he say anything, did he make noise of any kind; nobody heard of him, as they say, as much as a peep. He kept threatening written rebuttals, withdrew to a corner and left books behind which he had written for posterity; they are without power today and were even less effective back then against a man like Carneades, who showed himself to be so very great and enjoyed such high prestige amongst his contemporaries.

(8.12) Although he (sc. Carneades) caused turmoil in public through his rivalry with the Stoics, he upheld doctrine in front of his associates and in secret, told the truth, and disclosed his view like anyone else.

(8.13) Then Numenius added:

Mentor was a student of Carneades' at first, but he was not his successor: for during his lifetime Carneades had caught him with his mistress. Not on the basis of a persuasive impression, and not as if he had no cataleptic impression at his disposal, but with full confidence in his sense of sight Carneades apprehended the situation and expelled him from the school. As a renegade Mentor made counterarguments and was a rival, refuting the inapprehensibility in Carneades' arguments.

(8.14) And then he continued with the following words:

Carneades, who practised a philosophy of contradictory arguments, wore the lies like an ornament and made the truth disappear under them. He now used false doctrines as a cover and spoke inside the shop secretly the truth as a common trader would. Thus what happens to beans happened to him: the hollow ones rise in water to the top and float there, the useable ones stay down and are not seen.

(8.15) This is what was said of Carneades. His successors as head of the school were Clitomachus, then Philo, about whom Numenius said the following.

frg. 28

(9.1) This Philo now, who had just taken over the leadership of the school, was beside himself with joy, showed himself appreciative and showed respect to (sc. his predecessor) Clitomachus, honoured the latter's views and

> armed himself with gleaming steel

against the Stoics. (9.2) But as time went on, due to familiarity their suspension of judgement faded, and he no longer held the view which he had held before, but the clarity and consistency of his experiences made him change his mind. Given his already significant power to discriminate, he wanted at any price (we know why) encounter some who would refute his views, in order to avoid the impression

> that he was turning his back

and withdrawing of his own accord. (9.3) A pupil of Philo's became Antiochus. He founded another Academy. He attended lectures of the Stoic Mnesarchus and was of a completely different view than his teacher Philo. He added countless alien ideas to the Academy.

(9.4) This and many similar reports on Plato's succession are given by Numenius.

Commentary

Numenius,[18] who wrote around the middle of the second century AD, is occasionally used by scholars to put evidence on the sceptical Academy from Cicero, Sextus, and elsewhere into

---

[18] On Numenius, see Frede (1987f); Fuentes González (2005); Wyss (2005: 95–159); Staab (2013); Karamanolis (2016) with further literature.

context.[19] In many ways, he pursues an agenda which is different from Sextus', who mainly wants to distinguish Pyrrhonists from Academics,[20] from Cicero's, who endeavours to present the Academy in its own right, mostly through Academic speakers in his dialogues, or from Plutarch's, who is a more conventional Platonist and as such has some use for the Academy's anti-Stoic arguments, given that their target is dogmatic empiricism.[21] Numenius aims to show that the Academics betrayed their philosophical heritage (cf. the title of his work, cited in Eus., *P.E.* XIV.5.1), which he identifies as a dogmatic Platonism with Pythagorean tendencies, and to define a particular version of Platonism.[22]

Morever, his writing is full of striking similes, literary references and poetic quotations, clever turns of phrase, and even vignettes whose similarity to standard plot lines of comedy or satire has been noticed.[23] This literary quality is drawn attention to in a self-conscious way in the text itself (XIV.7.7). The style varies across the relevant fragments, and it is tempting to suspect that Numenius' treatment is informed, directly or indirectly, by more than one source; if so, there may be a meaningful distinction to be drawn between Numenius' overall bias and the bias of the presumed underlying source material. Anyone attempting to extract information on the Academy's history, on particular positions adopted by individual philosophers, and on Numenius' familiarity with arguments advanced in the course of the debate will need to bear these constraints in mind. It is also to be noted that Numenius seems less well informed on or interested in the sceptical Academy after Carneades.

Frg. 24 begins with a survey of philosophical schools, partly guided by the consideration of internal cohesion and faithfulness to what is deemed true doctrine in each case. The immediate successors of Plato were somewhat inept custodians of Plato's thought, although they did not set out to distort. The Pythagoreans recognized Plato for who he was, sc. on Numenius' view. The school of Epicurus, otherwise rarely deemed deserving of praise by Platonists, is singled out for its cohesiveness and its well-informed loyalty to Epicurus and his teachings. By contrast, strife characterizes the Stoic school, where everyone disagrees with everyone, and where the authority of the founders means little. The Socratics were in similar disagreement, who, however, are a loose grouping not a school. Moreover, their disagreements were due to them all following Socrates, who said different things at different times. Numenius then returns to Plato, who was a Pythagorean (as Socrates had been, who influenced him), which can be inferred from his writings, although he did write in a way which makes it understandable that there were different interpretations of his work. There are a couple of striking comparisons, of the early Stoics with oligarchs (14.5.4) or of Plato with Pentheus (14.5.8), who was torn to pieces like Plato has been by his many interpreters, but overall the tone of the passage is by Numenius' standards matter-of-fact and plain.

Frg. 25 marks the preceding chapter out as a digression, and Numenius avowedly returns to his main topic, viz. how the Academics diverged from Plato. The first important representative of this divergence is Arcesilaus. Numenius begins with a well-known parodic description of Arcesilaus' stance as a composite of the various philosophical influences he was exposed to. On this account Arcesilaus' association with the Academy and Plato is a front, his argumentative dexterity is due to dialectical influences, and his commitment to suspension of judgement

---

[19] Notably by Tarrant (1981) and (1985); Görler (1994); Brittain (2001) and (2007); and Wyss (2005); see also Boys-Stones (2018), texts 1F and 1G.
[20] See especially Sext. *P.H.* 1.220–35, cf. Gell., *N.A.* 11.5.1–8 (both in appendix 1). Modern contributions to the genre are Striker (1996f) and (2010).
[21] See Opsomer (1998: passim). [22] Cf. Brittain (2001: 254 n. 66).
[23] See Hirzel (1883) on frg. 26 Des Places, devoted to Lacydes.

to Pyrrho.[24] This leads into a description of Arcesilaus' style of argument (5.14–6.3): he baffles, fails to commit, states that he knows nothing, so that one could not tell whose side he was on, but his speech was beguiling, and so he had very considerable impact. In 6.4–5 the narrative returns to philosophical influences, with the added suggestion that amorous impulses (sc. rather than philosophical ones as assumed in *Acad.*) determined these associations. In 6.6 Numenius considers and dismisses the option that Arcesilaus merely concealed actual beliefs he had and deployed suspension of judgement as a defensive strategy (see on *Luc.* 60). In 6.7 the confrontation between Arcesilaus and Zeno comes into view. The former's motivation for engaging Zeno is said to have been that he wanted to show up Zeno for misinterpreting Plato, with Arcesilaus being the aggressive party. However, Zeno is said to have had similar motivations, which would have been laudable, had he not been misguided about what Plato's doctrines were, and had he not gone on to write against Plato. When Arcesilaus attacked Zeno over the cataleptic impression, which was their main point of dispute, Zeno refused to engage further after a while, perhaps hoping that his own attacks on Plato would lead Arcesilaus to desist from pursuing him.[25] In any event, to contemporaries it appeared as if Arcesilaus came out on top, although he had no opinion himself and only created the appearance of substance through clever argument.

Frg. 25 differs in style from the preceding one, notably through the deployment of poetic quotations to communicate and illustrate points Numenius wishes to make (striking metaphors—Arcesilaus as Empusa or Hydra in 6.2–3—represent continuity). The emphasis on personal relationships as an explanation of philosophical positions is reminiscent of a certain type of philosophical biography, and the chapter has a somewhat synthetic feel because personal relationships are invoked twice (5.11–13, 6.4–5). And while, as noted above, Numenius thought that Arcesilaus was genuinely without opinion and not a crypto-dogmatist who concealed his beliefs behind suspension of judgement (6.6), the account of Carneades in frg. 26 *fin.* and 27 draws a distinction between Arcesilaus' and Carneades' stance which, if at all consistent with frg. 25, suggests that frg. 25 minimally omits important qualifications and detail regarding Arcesilaus' position, and may even be at variance with frg. 27 (see below). There is no indication that Arcesilaus' scepticism was a reasoned and philosophically substantial position, notably not one which arose from reflection on the model of Socrates, as is suggested by Cic. *Ac.* 1.44–6, but the terms in which his approach to argument is characterized are suggestive of Socrates' (6.14); this raises the question of whether Numenius suppressed information contained in his source material. Numenius, in line with one strand of the tradition on Arcesilaus (see section 7.5 and on *Ac.* 1.44–6) and contra the Life of Arcesilaus in D.L., does assume that Arcesilaus' conflict was with Zeno (not Aristo) and over the cataleptic impression, and that it was the biggest philosophical event of its day.

Frg. 26 moves on to Lacydes,[26] Arcesilaus' successor, except that when we encounter him, he is not yet an Academic but a small-minded head of a household who devises barmy schemes to prevent (or uncover) theft from his larder. When his slaves subvert his scheme, he is so baffled that he seeks instruction from Arcesilaus, whose 'inapprehensibility' seems germane to the inexplicable problem Lacydes is facing. With Arcesilaus he debated the thesis that 'everything we see and hear is confused and mere appearance', which was never a thesis argued

---

[24] Cf. Sextus, *P.H.* 1.234 (= *SVF* i.343 (Aristo) = LS 68E2 = Arcesilaus F86 Mette and Vezzoli); D.L. 4.33; and section 7.5.
[25] Given Zeno's reported lack of interest in continuing the dispute after a while, Wyss (2005: 130–1) raises the question of whether Numenius had access to both extant traditions on Arcesilaus, the one which pits him against Zeno (represented mainly by Cicero), and the one which pits him against Aristo (represented by D.L.); see also section 7.5.
[26] See on *Luc.* 16; Görler (1994: 830–4).

for by the Academics, but rather a caricature, promoted by dogmatists, of the import of their argumentative practice.[27] Lacydes is attracted by Arcesilaus' teachings and especially the policy of suspension of judgement, which Lacydes relays to a visitor as an appropriate response to the miraculous disappearance of items from his larder. The visitor ridicules Lacydes, who abandons his schemes to protect the contents of his larder and becomes disillusioned with philosophy. Yet this proves to be a false closure, in that Lacydes is presented as continuing his larder protection schemes, and the slaves as continuing to subvert them (7.7). When the slaves refuse to acknowledge the evidence of interference, Lacydes starts arguing like a dogmatist and cites his clear memory of sealing the larder (7.8). This gives rise to a swap of argumentative positions, with the slaves now arguing from inapprehensibility. Lacydes falls into despair, takes up permanent residence in his larder, and announces that school debate is one thing, and real life quite another (7.13), a gesture to the anti-sceptical objection that the sceptic cannot live his scepticism.[28] Hankinson (1995: 92-4) suggests that Lacydean arguments for memory scepticism are reflected in this story. One might also be tempted to identify its historical-philosophical core as the claim that Academic scepticism did not solidify under Arcesilaus and that his immediate successor struggled to sustain their sceptical position, not just because of what we learn here, but also because in frg. 27 Carneades is said to have renewed the debate with the Stoics (8.1).[29] However, we are not actually told what Lacydes' outlook was when he became scholarch, though he is said to have had many pupils, one of whom, Euandrus, became his successor (7.14).

In 7.15 Carneades is introduced, but it is not clear if this transitional passage should be credited to Eusebius rather than be treated as part of the Numenian fragment as Des Places, whose arrangement I have reproduced, has it.[30] If the former, which is more likely given other transitional passages in Eusebius' report, then one would nonetheless have to assume that a source containing information on the Academy, and possibly Numenius himself, informed Eusebius' paragraph. Thus it seems advisable to evaluate every piece of information in 7.15 on its own merit. That Carneades marked a new departure in that he 'set up the Third Academy' can be paralleled elsewhere, but only here do we find a fourfold division.[31] Carneades is explicitly aligned with Arcesilaus, through his method of argument: arguing on either side and arguing against theses advanced by dogmatists. (The former technique is, of course, more frequently associated with Carneades elsewhere, notably in Cicero.)[32] What distinguishes him from Arcesilaus, we are told, is that his position on suspension of judgement is different: he said that it was impossible for humans never to assent,[33] and offered an explanation for it, i.e. that not everything was unclear, even though everything was inapprehensible. We have solid grounds for thinking, on the basis of the Ciceronian evidence (esp. *Luc.* 103-8), that Carneades never abandoned the commitment to universal ἐποχή, and this is suggested by frg. 27 as well, so what we are told here is either incompatible with other evidence or requires reconciliation. Note that Carneades is not presented as arguing from the sage, but instead cites human behaviour in general; so the point Carneades is credited with may be that it is human to assent on occasion, albeit a failing (cf. *Luc.* 66, where Cicero claims to be a *magnus opinator* while being

---

[27] See on *Luc.* 102.
[28] A shorter and less pointed version of this story features in D.L. 4.59. Hirzel (1883) suspected the summary of a comedy plot behind it; Görler (1994: 833) thinks of contemporary satire.
[29] Cf. Lévy (2005: 58-9).   [30] Noted by Brittain (2007: 311 n. 30).
[31] According to frg. 28 (9.5) Antiochus founded 'another Academy'. See on *Ac.* 1.18 for such divisions; Görler (1994: 780-1) for a discussion of the one here in Eusebius' report.
[32] See, however, D.L. 4.28 on Arcesilaus; Plut., *Sto. rep.* 1037b-c (= text 2 in appendix 1) has Academics prior to Carneades argue on either side.
[33] Cf. *Luc.* 38 (Lucullus speaking) and 66 (Cicero speaking as a Clitomachean and non-sage).

committed to suspension of judgement). Carneades' main opponents are said to have been the Stoics, and he aimed for what is persuasive rather than true.

In frg. 27 *init*. Numenius suggests that Carneades consciously invoked and followed the model of Arcesilaus (8.1). Even more than him (apparently), he was dexterous and elusive in argument, but unlike Arcesilaus he was not convinced of the truth of his own arguments (8.3).[34] This claim gives pause, for in frg. 25 there was no indication to that effect. It is true that Arcesilaus was likened to a self-decapitating Hydra, which has been interpreted as conveying the same point metaphorically,[35] but the image more likely relates to arguments for and against the same view.[36] Note also that according to frg. 25 Arcesilaus had no consistent opinion (certainly not one that comes up to knowledge) (6.14 *fin*.), which in the absence of a scope restriction ought to include no consistent opinion on whether nothing can be known; that his commitment to suspension of judgement was complete; and that he was de facto a Pyrrhonist (6.5). If Arcesilaus as per frg. 27 was enthralled by his own arguments, then this state might have manifested itself in a form of endorsement below the level of assent, but the text gives us no indication that this is meant.[37] Here one does wonder about the consistency of frgs 25 and 27.

Carneades' technique was not to yield except in cases where his momentary yielding allowed him a better grip on his opponent (8.5). A case in point was his accepting—for the sake of the argument—that there were true and false impressions (8.6). Sections 8.7 and 8.8 deal with Carneades' deployment of ἀπαραλλαξία-considerations without mentioning the term; esp. 8.8 must have seemed cryptic to someone without antecedent knowledge of the debate. 8.9–8.11 extol the dialectical and rhetorical prowess of Carneades: nobody was able to withstand him, and the attempts of Antipater of Tarsus to combat him in writing were ineffectual and feeble. (This is not quite the picture which emerges from *Acad.*, where his writing is rated; see on *Luc*. 28–9.) In 8.12 it is suggested that Carneades in fact held views in secret and would disclose them to select associates. The views themselves are not characterized further but their disclosure 'inside the shop' suggests that philosophical views rather than views on everyday matters are meant. Accusing Academics of crypto-dogmatism is an old strategy, but there is no mediation between the accusation and the earlier claim that Carneades only ever argued for the sake of the argument. In 8.13 there is then a counterpart to the story about Lacydes and his slaves: when Carneades found his mistress cheating on him with a pupil, he suddenly had apprehension of the situation and expelled him from the Academy.[38] 8.14 is a conclusion to the treatment of Carneades, which ties together his practice of arguing on either side with his supposed concealed dogmatism (the latter remains vague with respect to the actual views Carneades supposedly held dogmatically). The three paragraphs 8.12–14 clearly form a unit, but as indicated, they do not cohere well with the preceding text up to 8.11, and

---

[34] A modern version of this interpretation is advanced by Görler (1994: 804, 816–19).
[35] Thus Wyss (2005: 119–20; cf. 133), who observes that 'beheading the Hydra' is a proverbial expression for resolving difficulties and that at Plt., *Euthyd*. 297c, Socrates is likened to a Hydra.
[36] Thus Castagnoli (2010: 300–1).
[37] I see no possibility of aligning the Arcesilaus/Carneades differentiation with the difference that the speaker Cicero in *Acad*. posits for Socrates and Arcesilaus (i.e. that the latter disavowed all knowledge except for one second-order knowledge claim, that he knows nothing).
[38] With 8.13 compare the account of Carneades' dealing with Mentor in D.L. 4.63–4, analysed by Usher (2006): according to the account in D.L., Carneades challenged Mentor with a cento composed from two lines derived from Homer *Od*. and one from Soph. *Ant*., to which Mentor replied with a line from the *Iliad*. The lines quoted allude in ingenious ways to the debate about the Carneadean πιθανόν and concepts associated with it, while 8.13 reads like an addendum to the Carneades-Mentor exchange from a dogmatic point of view.

they do again raise the question of how much weight the evidence from Numenius is actually capable of bearing. Numenius provides the connecting remark on Clitomachus and Philo in 8.15, but does not mention the somewhat complicated succession of Carneades (see on *Luc.* 16), nor does he devote a separate section to Clitomachus.

Frg. 28 begins with the suggestion that after becoming scholarch Philo initially continued to uphold Clitomachus' position. That in so doing he 'gave thanks' suggests that his Clitomachean outlook was one of the reasons for his election. He continued the fight with the Stoics (9.1). 9.2 is then concerned with a dramatic change of position. (i) It occurred after some time has passed, (ii) a main feature of the new position that is singled out was the abandoning of suspension of judgement, (iii) the clarity and consistency of Philo's impressions gave rise to the change, and (iv) Philo was looking for opponents so that his change of position would not appear to have been enacted of his own accord. The last point only makes sense if the attacks Philo was hoping for were to be targeted at his old, not his new position. For only then could they provide adequate cover for his deliberate withdrawal. (It is not obvious, though, why changing position under duress is preferable to modifying one's position upon independent reflection.) The change is usually assumed to be the move to the Roman Books position,[39] but it is characterized by the abolition of ἐποχή, not by the introduction of an alternative conception of κατάληψις; however, a shift in the evaluation of the content of impressions prior to the instigation of the change is mentioned ('with his already significant power to discriminate', πολλὴν δῆτ' ἔχων ἤδη τὴν διαίσθησιν).[40]

Antiochus departed from the Third Academy and established another one, was taught by the Stoic Mnesarchus, and introduced alien, i.e. apparently Stoic, notions into the Academy.

Finally, one must ask in what way the evidence from Numenius speaks to the interpretative problems raised by *Acad*. For Numenius, the Academics from Arcesilaus to Philo form a group, sc. of deviants from the Academic tradition proper. This implies that Philo remained a sceptic throughout, and did not become a Platonist of some description even after his change of position. Antiochus was no Platonist for a different reason, viz. the degree to which he embraced Stoicism. Nor, however, was he an Academic. Carneades used the first premiss of the core argument 'for the sake of the argument', rather than endorsing it. And he is said (frg. 26, XIV.7.15) to have drawn a distinction between ἄδηλα and ἀκατάληπτα which Cicero has Lucullus mention in *Luc.* 34 and which Lucullus ascribes to an unspecified group of people.[41] Philo was a Clitomachean when he was elected scholarch, but later performed one significant change of position. His new position allowed for assent.

These points are consistent with the evidence from *Acad.* as I read it. In particular, if Philo never was a mitigated sceptic and if *Luc.* 78 references the view of the Roman Books, as I argue ad loc. on independent grounds, it would help explain why the latter could be characterized by the abandonment of ἐποχή: it would be the view by whose adoption Philo abandoned ἐποχή. It is likely that Carneades himself advanced the core argument in an ad hominem manner, although it does not follow that a Clitomachean, or the kind of Clitomachean the character Cicero is, would do the same. Like Cicero, Numenius shows no awareness of two substantial

---

[39] See e.g. Glucker (1978: 67); Lévy (1992: 48, 267 n. 75). Differently Brittain (2001: 133 n. 6, cf. 12 n. 16), who unlike Glucker and Lévy posits three Philonian phases: 'Numenius' comment probably refers to Philo's change to *Roman* position, but what he gives here is an explanation of Philo's rejection of *epoche*, i.e., in the first instance, of his change to the Philonian/Metrodorian position' [his emphasis].

[40] The reasons cited for Philo's change of position in (iii) do not by themselves enable a decision as to whether the envisaged doctrinal point of arrival was mitigated scepticism or the Roman Books view.

[41] See Allen (1997: 218–23), who connects *Luc.* 32-4 with Carneades (without drawing on evidence from Numenius); see ad loc.

changes of position rather than one on Philo's part,[42] but he also fails to speak to aspects of the evidence from *Acad.*, notably the modified Clitomacheanism which Cicero adopted there and throughout his works and which allowed for approval in the technical sense. I discuss the contribution of frg. 28 to our evidence for the Roman Books in the commentary on *Luc.* 18 in more detail.

---

[42] Cf. also the badly damaged later part of col. xxxiii in Philodemus' *Index Acad.*

Bibliography

Adamietz, J. (1960) *Ciceros 'De Inventione' und die Rhetorik 'ad Herennium'*, Marburg (diss. phil.).
Adamietz, J. (1996²) *Marcus Tullius Cicero—Pro Murena*, Darmstadt.
Adams, J. N. (1978) 'Conventions of Naming in Cicero', *Classical Quarterly* 28, 145–66.
Adams, J. N. (1995) *Pelagonius and Latin Veterinary Terminology in the Roman Empire*, Leiden.
Adams, J. N. (2003) *Bilingualism and the Latin Language*, Cambridge.
Adams, J. N. (2003a) '*"Romanitas"* and the Latin Language', *Classical Quarterly* 53, 184–205.
Adams, J. N. (2013) *Social Variation and the Latin Language*, Cambridge.
Adams, J. N. (2016) *An Anthology of Informal Latin, 200 BC—AD 900*, Cambridge.
Adamson, P. (2010) 'Posterior Analytics 2.19: A Dialogue with Plato?', *Bulletin of the Institute for Classical Studies* 107, suppl.: Aristotle and the Stoics Reading Plato, 1–19.
Ademollo, F. (2012) 'The Platonic Origins of Stoic Theology', *Oxford Studies in Ancient Philosophy* 43, 217–43.
Ademollo, F. (2018) 'On Plato's Conception of Change', *Oxford Studies in Ancient Philosophy* 55, 35–83.
Ahl, F. (1984) 'The Art of Safe Criticism in Greece and Rome', *American Journal of Philology* 105, 174–208.
Ahonen, M. (2019) 'Ancient Philosophers on Mental Illness', *History of Psychiatry* 30, 3–18.
Alessandrelli, M. (2003) 'Cic. Acad. II 58: a proposito di un passo controverso', *Elenchos* 24, 399–416.
Alessandrelli, M. (2019) '$Περιφάνεια$ e $πίστις τῆς καταλήψεως$: la risposta neo-stoica a Carneade', *Antiquorum Philosophia* 13, 127–56.
Alesse, F. (1997) *Panezio di Rodi—Testimonianze*, Naples.
Alesse, F. (2008) 'Alcuni esempi della relazione tra l'etica Stoica e Platone', in C. Helmig and M. Bonazzi (eds), *Platonic Stoicism—Stoic Platonism: The Dialogue between Platonism and Stoicism in Antiquity*, Leuven, 23–39.
Alfonsi, L. (1967) 'Studi sulle *Tusculane*', *Wiener Studien* 89, 147–55.
Algra, K. (1990) 'Chrysippus on Virtuous Abstention from Ugly Old Women (Plutarch, SR 1038E–109A)', *Classical Quarterly* 40, 450–8.
Algra, K. (1997) 'Chrysippus, Carneades, Cicero: The Ethical *Divisiones* in Cicero's *Lucullus*', in B. Inwood and J. Mansfeld (eds), *Assent and Argument—Studies in Cicero's 'Academic Books'*, Leiden, 107–39.
Algra, K. (2003) 'Stoic Theology', in B. Inwood (ed.), *The Cambridge Companion to Stoics*, Cambridge, 153–78.
Algra, K. (2017) 'The Academic Origins of Stoic Cosmo-Theology and the Physics of Antiochus of Ascalon—Some Notes on the Evidence', in Y. Z. Liebersohn, I. Ludlam, and A. Edelheit (eds), *For a Skeptical Peripatetic: Festschrift in Honour of John Glucker*, Sankt Augustin, 158–76.
Alleemudder, A. (1979) *A Philosophical Commentary on Cicero, 'Academica Priora' II, 1–62*, London (PhD thesis, University of London). URL = <https://qmro.qmul.ac.uk/xmlui/handle/123456789/1361>.
Allen, J. V. (1994) 'Academic Probabilism and Stoic Epistemology', *Classical Quarterly* 44, 85–113.
Allen, J. V. (1997) 'Carneadean Argument in Cicero's *Academic Books*', in B. Inwood and J. Mansfeld (eds), *Assent and Argument—Studies in Cicero's 'Academic Books'*, Leiden, 217–56.
Allen, J. V. (2001) *Inference from Signs*, Oxford.

Allen, J. V. (2011) 'Antiochus of Ascalon', in *The Stanford Encyclopedia of Philosophy* (Winter), Edward N. Zalta (ed.), URL = <http://plato.stanford.edu/archives/win2011/entries/antiochus-ascalon/>.
Allen, J. V. (2012) 'Carneades', in *The Stanford Encyclopedia of Philosophy* (Winter), Edward N. Zalta (ed.), URL = <https://plato.stanford.edu/archives/win2012/entries/carneades/>.
Allen, J. V. (2014) 'Aristotle on the Value of "Probability", Persuasiveness, and Verisimilitude, in Rhetorical Argument', in V. Wohl (ed.), *Probabilities, Hypotheticals, and Counterfactuals in Ancient Greek Thought*, Cambridge, 47–64.
Allen, J. V. (2018) '*Aporia* and the New Academy', in G. Karamanolis and V. Politis (eds), *The Aporetic Tradition in Ancient Philosophy*, Cambridge, 172–91.
Allen, J. V. (2019) 'Megara and Dialectic', in T. Bénatouïl and K. Ierodiakonou (eds), *Dialectic after Plato and Aristotle*, Cambridge, 17–46.
Allen, J. V. (2022) 'Radicalism and Moderation', *Phronesis* 67, 133–60.
Amato, E. (2005) *Favorinos D'Arles—tome I: Introduction générale. Témoignages. Discours aux Corinthiens. Sur la Fortune*, Paris.
Amato, E. (2010) *Favorinos D'Arles—tome III: fragments*, Paris.
Amory, F. (1981) 'Aristotle, Horace, and the Ironic Man', *Classica et Medievalia* 33, 49–80.
Andreae, B. (2001) *Skulptur des Hellenismus*, Munich.
André, J.-M. (1964) 'Cicéron et Lucrèce. Loi du silence et allusions philosophiques', in P. Gros and J.-P. Morel (eds), *Mélanges de philosophie, de littérature et d'histoire ancienne offerts à Pierre Boyancé*, Paris, 21–38.
Angeli, A. (2018) 'Zénon de Sidon', in R. Goulet (ed.), *Dictionnaire des philosophes antiques*, vol. 7, Paris, 400–15.
Angeli, A. and Colaizzo, M. (1979) 'I frammenti di Zenone Sidonio', *Cronache Ercolanesi* 9, 47–133.
Annas, J. (1980) 'Truth and Knowledge', in M. Schofield, M. Burnyeat, and J. Barnes (eds), *Doubt and Dogmatism—Studies in Hellenistic Epistemology*, Oxford, 84–104.
Annas, J. (1990) 'Stoic Epistemology', in S. Everson (ed.), *Companions in Ancient Thought 1—Epistemology*, Cambridge, 184–203.
Annas, J. (1992) *Hellenistic Philosophy of Mind*, Berkeley, Los Angeles, and London.
Annas, J. (1992a) 'Plato the Sceptic', in J. C. Klagge and N. D. Smith (eds), *Methods of Interpreting Plato and his Dialogues*, Oxford Studies in Ancient Philosophy, suppl. vol., Oxford, 43–72.
Annas, J. (1992b) 'Sextus Empiricus and the Peripatetics', *Elenchus* 13, 203–31.
Annas, J. (1993) *The Morality of Happiness*, Cambridge.
Annas, J. (1993a) 'Virtue as the Use of Other Goods', *Apeiron* 26, 53–66.
Annas, J. (1997) 'Cicero on Stoic Moral Philosophy and Private Property', in M. Griffin and J. Barnes (eds), *Philosophia Togata I*, Oxford, 151–73.
Annas, J. (2001) *Cicero—On Moral Ends*, Cambridge.
Annas, J. (2007) 'Carneades' Classification of Ethical Theories', in A. M. Ioppolo and D. N. Sedley (eds), *Pyrrhonists, Patricians, Platonizers*, Naples, 187–223.
Annas, J. (2008) 'The Sage in Ancient Philosophy', in F. Alesse et al. (eds), *Anthropine Sophia: Studi di Filosofia e Storiografia Filosofica in Memoria di Gabriele Giannantoni*, Naples, 11–27.
Armisen-Marchetti, M. (2001) 'L'imaginaire analogique et la construction du savoir dans les "Questions naturelles" de Sénèque', in M. Courrént and J. Thomas (eds), *Imaginaire et modes de construction du savoir antique dans les textes scientifiques et techniques: actes du colloque de Perpignan, 12–13 mai 2000*, Perpignan, 155–74.
von Arnim, H. (1890) 'Über einen stoischen Papyrus in der Herkulanensischen Bibliothek', *Hermes* 25, 473–95.
von Arnim, H. (1894) 'Antipatros 26', in *RE* I.2, 2515–16.
von Arnim, H. (1903) 'Dionysios 119', in *RE* V.1, 973–4.
von Arnim, H. (1921) 'Kleitomachos', in *RE* XII.1, 656–9.

Arnott, W. G. (2007) *Birds in the Ancient World from A to Z*, London.
Asmis, E. (1984) *Epicurus' Scientific Method*, Ithaca and London.
Asmis, E. (2009) 'Epicurean Empiricism', in J. Warren (ed.), *The Cambridge Companion to Epicureanism*, Cambridge, 84–104.
Astbury, R. (1974) 'Misapplication of the "lex Lindsay" in Nonius Marcellus', *Hermes* 102, 625–7.
Astin, A. E. (1958) *The Lex Annalis before Sulla*, Brussels.
Astin, A. E. (1967) *Scipio Aemilianus*, Oxford.
Astin, A. E. (1978) *Cato the Censor*, Oxford.
Atherton, C. (1988) 'Hand over Fist: The Failure of Stoic Rhetoric', *Classical Quarterly* 38, 392–47.
Atherton, C. (1993) *The Stoics on Ambiguity*, Cambridge.
Atkins, J. W. (2013) *Cicero on Politics and the Limits of Reason: The Republic and Laws*, Cambridge.
Aubert-Baillot, S. (2009) 'Stoic Rhetoric between Technique and Philosophy: The Example of Diogenes of Babylon', in F. Woerther (ed.), *Literary and Philosophical Rhetoric in the Greek, Roman, Syriac and Arabic Worlds*, Hildesheim, 95–117.
Aubert-Baillot, S. (2015) 'De la $\phi\rho\acute{o}\nu\eta\sigma\iota\varsigma$ à la *prudentia*', *Mnemosyne* 68, 68–90.
Aubert-Baillot, S. (2019) 'Terminology and Practice of Dialectic in Cicero's Letters', in T. Bénatouïl and K. Ierodiakonou (eds), *Dialectic after Plato and Aristotle*, Cambridge, 254–82.
Auffret, T. (2019) 'Approximation, métrétique et stochastique: le modèle platonicien de la médecine', in C. Crignon and D. Lefebvre (eds), *Médecins et philosophes. Une histoire*, Paris, 19–50.
Austin, R. G. (1971) *P. Vergilii Maronis Aeneidos Liber Primus*, Oxford.
Auvray-Assayas, C. (1996) 'La constructions doxographiques du *De natura deorum* et la reflexion Ciceronienne sur la physique', in C. Lévy (ed.), *La concept de nature à Rome—la physique*, Paris, 67–83.
Auvray-Assayas, C. (2001) 'Relire Cicéron pour comprendre Philodème. Réponse à Dirk Obbink', in C. Auvray-Assayas and D. Delattre (eds), *Cicéron et Philodème: La polémique en philosophie*, Paris, 227–34.
Ax, W. (1938) *M. Tullius Cicero: De Divinatione, De Fato, Timaeus*, Stuttgart.
Babut, D. (2003) 'Chrysippe à l'Académie: Diogène Laërce VII, 183–184', *Philologus* 147, 70–90.
Babut, D. (2005) 'Sur les polémiques des anciens stoïciens', *Philosophie Antique* 5, 65–91.
Backhouse, T. (2000) 'Antipater of Tarsus on False "Phantasiai" (PBerol inv. 16545)', *Papiri Filosofici: Miscellanea di studi* 3, 7–31.
Badian, E. (1964) 'Caesar's *Cursus* and the Intervals between Offices', in *Studies in Greek and Roman History*, Oxford, 140–56.
Badian, E. (1971) 'Ennius and his Friends', in *Ennius, Entretiens Fondation Hardt* 17, Vandœuvres, 151–208.
Badian, E. (1984) 'The House of the Servilii Gemini: A Study in Misuse of Occam's Razor', *Papers of the British School at Rome* 52, 49–71.
Baier, T. (1997) *Werk und Wirkung Varros im Spiegel seiner Zeitgenossen—von Cicero bis Ovid*, Stuttgart.
Bailey, C. (1947) *Titi Lucreti 'De Rerum Natura'*, 3 vols, Oxford.
Bake, J. (1842) *M. Tullii Ciceronis 'De Legibus' libri tres*, Leiden.
Balbo, A. (2013) 'Marcus Junius Brutus the Orator: Between Philosophy and Rhetoric', in C. E. W. Steel and H. van der Bloom (eds), *Community and Communication: Oratory and Politics in Republican Rome*, Oxford, 315–28.
Balme, D. M. (1972) *Aristotle—'De Partibus Animalium' I and 'De Generatione Animalium' I*, Oxford.
Banateanu, A. (2001) *La théorie Stoïcienne de l'Amitié: Essai de Reconstruction*, Fribourg.
Baraz, Y. (2012) *A Written Republic—Cicero's Philosophical Politics*, Princeton.

Barigazzi, A. (1996) *Favorino di Arelate, Opere. Introduzione, testo critico e commento*, Florence.
Barigazzi, A. (1993) 'Favorino di Arelate', *Aufstieg und Niedergang der Römischen Welt* II.34.1, 556–81.
Barnes, J. (1980) 'Proof Destroyed', in M. Schofield, M. Burnyeat, and J. Barnes (eds), *Doubt and Dogmatism—Studies in Hellenistic Epistemology*, Oxford, 161–81.
Barnes, J. (1982) 'Medicine, Experience and Logic', in J. Barnes, J. Brunschwig, M. Burnyeat, and M. Schofield (eds), *Science and Speculation: Studies in Hellenistic Theory and Practice*, Cambridge, 24–68.
Barnes, J. (1985) 'ΠΙΘΑΝΑ ΣΘΝΗΜΜΕΝΑ', *Elenchos* 6, 453–67.
Barnes, J. (1989) 'The Size of the Sun in Antiquity', *Acta Classica* 25, 29–41.
Barnes, J. (1997) 'Antiochus of Ascalon', in M. Griffin and J. Barnes (eds), *Philosophia Togata I*, Oxford (2nd edn with corrections), 51–96.
Barnes, J. (1997a) 'Logic in *Academica* I and the *Lucullus*', in B. Inwood and J. Mansfeld (eds), *Assent and Argument—Studies in Cicero's 'Academic Books'*, Leiden, 140–60.
Barnes, J. (1997b) 'The Beliefs of a Pyrrhonist', in M. F. Burnyeat and M. Frede (eds), *The Original Sceptics: A Controversy*, Indianapolis, 58–91.
Barnes, J. (1997c) 'Roman Aristotle', in J. Barnes and M. Griffin (eds), *Philosophia Togata II— Plato and Aristotle at Rome*, Oxford, 1–69.
Barnes, J. (2003) *Porphyry—Introduction*, Oxford.
Barnes, J. (2005) 'What Is a Disjunction?', in D. Frede and B. Inwood (eds), *Language and Learning: Philosophy of Language in the Hellenistic Age*, Cambridge, 274–98.
Barnes, J. (2014) *Proof, Knowledge, and Scepticism: Essays in Ancient Philosophy III*, Oxford.
Barnes, J. (2014a) 'Epicurean Signs', in Barnes (2014), 307–54.
Barnes, J. (2015) *Mantissa—Essays in Ancient Philosophy IV*, Oxford.
Barnes, J. (2015a) 'Ancient Plato', in Barnes (2015), 204–43.
Barnes, J. (2015b) 'Is Rhetoric an Art?', in Barnes (2015), 80–105.
Barnes, J., Bobzien, S., and Mignucci, M. (1999) 'Logic', in K. Algra, J. Barnes, J. Mansfeld, and M. Schofield (eds), *The Cambridge History of Hellenistic Philosophy*, Cambridge, 77–176.
Barthel, B. (1903) 'Über die Benutzung der philosophischen Schriften Ciceros durch Lactanz, Teil 1', *Beilage zum Programm des königlichen Gymnasiums in Strehlen (Schles.)*, Strehlen.
Barwick, K. (1957) 'Widmung und Entstehungsgeschichte von Varros De Lingua Latina', *Philologus* 101, 298–304.
Behler, E. (1998) 'Ironie', in *Historisches Wörterbuch der Rhetorik* 4, 599–624.
Bénatouïl, T. (2007) *Faire usage: la pratique du Stoïcisme*, Paris.
Bénatouïl, T. (2016) 'Structure, Standards and Stoic Moral Progress in *De Finibus* 4', in J. Annas and G. Betegh (eds), *Cicero's 'De Finibus'—Philosophical Approaches*, Cambridge, 198–220.
Bénatouïl, T. (2016a) 'Aristotle and the Stoa', in A. Falcon (ed.), *Brill's Companion to the Reception of Aristotle in Antiquity*, Leiden, 56–75.
Bénatouïl, T. and Bonazzi, M. (2012) *Theoria, Praxis, and the Contemplative Life after Plato and Aristotle*, Leiden.
Bénatouïl, T. and El Murr, D. (2010) 'L'Académie et les géomètres: usages et limites de la géométrie de Platon à Carnéade', *Philosophie antique* 10, 41–80.
Benveniste, E. (1993) *Noms d'agent et noms d'action en indo-européen*, Paris.
Berger, A. (1953) *Encyclopedic Dictionary of Roman Law*, Philadelphia.
Bergmann, M. (2006) *Justification without Awareness: A Defence of Epistemic Externalism*, Oxford.
Berno, F. R. (2007) 'La "Furia" di Clodio in Cicerone', *Bolletino di Studi Latini* 37, 69–91.
Berryman, S. (2009) *The Mechanical Hypothesis in Ancient Greek Natural Philosophy*, Cambridge.
Betegh, G. (2015) '"Body" *M* 9.359–440', in K. Algra and K. Ierodiakonou (eds), *Sextus Empiricus and Ancient Physics*, Cambridge, 130–83.

Bett, R. (1989) 'Carneades' *Pithanon*: A Reappraisal of its Role and Status', *Oxford Studies in Ancient Philosophy* 7, 59–94.
Bett, R. (1990) 'Carneades' Distinction between Assent and Approval', *The Monist* 73, 3–20.
Bett, R. (2000) *Pyrrho, his Antecedents, and his Legacy*, Oxford.
Bett, R. (2005) *Sextus Empiricus—Against the Logicians*, Cambridge.
Bett, R. (2014) 'Pyrrho', in *The Stanford Encyclopedia of Philosophy* (Winter 2014), Edward N. Zalta (ed.), URL = <http://plato.stanford.edu/archives/win2014/entries/pyrrho/>.
Bishop, C. (2016) 'Naming the Roman Stars: Constellation Etymologies in Cicero's *Aratea* and *De Natura Deorum*', *Classical Quarterly* 66, 155–71.
Blank, D. (1998) *Sextus Empiricus—Against the Grammarians*, Oxford.
Blank, D. (2007) 'The Life of Antiochus of Ascalon in Philodemus' *History of the Academy* and a Tale of Two Letters', *Zeitschrift für Papyrologie und Epigraphik* 162, 87–93.
Blank, D. (2012) 'Varro and Antiochus', in D. N. Sedley (ed.), *The Philosophy of Antiochus*, Cambridge, 250–89.
van der Blom, H. (2010) *Cicero's Role Models: The Political Strategy of a Newcomer*, Oxford.
Bobzien, S. (1996) 'Stoic Syllogistic', *Oxford Studies in Ancient Philosophy* 14, 133–92.
Bobzien, S. (1998) *Determinism and Freedom in Stoic Philosophy*, Oxford.
Bobzien, S. (1999) 'Logic: The Stoics (part 2)', in K. Algra, J. Barnes, J. Mansfeld, and M. Schofield (eds), *The Cambridge History of Hellenistic Philosophy*, Cambridge, 106–8.
Bobzien, S. (2002) 'Chrysippus and the Epistemic Theory of Vagueness', *Proceedings of the Aristotelian Society* 102, 217–38.
Bobzien, S. (2011) 'Dialectical School', in *The Stanford Encyclopedia of Philosophy* (Fall 2011), Edward N. Zalta (ed.), URL = <http://plato.stanford.edu/archives/fall2011/entries/dialectical-school/>.
Bobzien, S. (2012) 'How to Give Someone Horns—Paradoxes of Presupposition in Antiquity', *Logical Analysis and History of Philosophy* 15, 159–84.
Boland, V. (1996) *Ideas in God according to St Thomas Aquinas: Sources and Synthesis*, Leiden.
Bolisani, E. (1937) *I Logistorici Varroniani*, Padova.
Bonazzi, M. (2003) *Academici e Platonici: Il dibattito antico sullo scetticismo di Platone*, Milan.
Bonazzi, M. (2007a) 'Eudorus' Psychology and Stoic Ethics', in M. Bonazzi and C. Helmig (eds), *Platonic Stoicism—Stoic Platonism*, Leuven, 109–32.
Bonazzi, M. (2011) 'A Pyrrhonian Plato? Again on Sextus on Aenesidemus on Plato', in D. E. Machuca (ed.), *New Essays on Ancient Pyrrhonism*, Leiden, 11–26.
Bonazzi, M. (2012) 'Antiochus and Platonism', in D. N. Sedley (ed.), *The Philosophy of Antiochus*, Cambridge, 307–33.
Bonazzi, M. (2012a) 'Plutarch on the Difference between Academics and Pyrrhonists', *Oxford Studies in Ancient Philosophy* 43, 271–98.
Bonazzi, M. (2015) *À la recherche des idées: Platonisme et philosophie hellénistique d' Antiochus à Plotin*, Paris.
Bonazzi, M. (2018) 'Héraclite, l'Académie et la platonisme: une confrontation entre Cicéron et Plutarque', in S. Franchet d'Espèrey and C. Lévy (eds), *Les présocratiques à Rome*, Paris, 129–42.
Bonazzi, M. (2019) 'L'Académie hellénistique et l'héritage sceptique de Platon', in B. Collette-Ducic, M.-A. Gavray, J.-M. Narbonne (eds), *L'esprit critique dans l'Antiquité I: Critique et licence dans la Grèce antique*, Paris, 237–58.
Bonazzi, M. (2020) 'The End of the Academy', in P. Kalligas, C. Balla, E. Baziotopoulou-Valavani, and V. Karasmanis (eds), *Plato's Academy—Its Workings and its History*, Cambridge, 242–55.
Bonazzi, M. and Helmig, C. (2007) *Platonic Stoicism—Stoic Platonism*, Leuven.
Boot, I. C. G. (1895) 'Coniectanea Tulliana', *Mnemosyne* 33, 199–220.
Bos, A. P. (1989) *Cosmic and Meta-Cosmic Theology in Aristotle's Lost Dialogues*, Leiden.

Bos, A. P. (2003) *The Soul and its Instrumental Body: A Reinterpretation of Aristotle's Philosophy of Living Nature*, Leiden and Boston.
Bottler, H. (2014) *Pseudo-Plutarch und Stobaios: eine synoptische Untersuchung*, Göttingen.
Bowen, A. C. and Todd, R. B. (2004) *Cleomedes' Lectures on Astronomy: A Translation of the Heavens*, Berkeley and London.
Bown, A. (2016) 'Epicurus on Bivalence and the Excluded Middle', *Archiv für Geschichte der Philosophie* 98, 239–71.
Bown, A. (2016a) 'Epicurus on Truth and Falsehood', *Phronesis* 61, 463–503.
Boys-Stones, G. (2005) 'Alcinous, *Didaskalikos* 4: In Defence of Dogmatism', in M. Bonazzi and V. Celluprica (eds), *L'Eredità Platonica: Studi sul Platonismo da Arcesilao a Proclo*, Naples, 201–34.
Boys-Stones, G. (2012) 'Antiochus' Metaphysics', in D. N. Sedley (ed.), *The Philosophy of Antiochus*, Cambridge, 220–36.
Boys-Stones, G. (2018) *Platonist Philosophy 80 BC to AD 250—An Introduction and Collection of the Sources in Translation*, Cambridge.
Boys-Stones, G. and Rowe, C. (2013) *The Circle of Socrates: Readings in the First-Generation Socratics*, Indianapolis.
Bräunlich, A. F. (1920) *The Indicative Indirect Question in Latin*, Chicago (PhD thesis 1913, University of Chicago).
Brakman, C. (1923) 'Observationes Criticae in Ciceronis Academica', *Mnemosyne* 51, 376–80.
Bremi, J. H. (1798) *M. Tulli Ciceronis 'De Finibus Bonorum et Malorum' libri quinque*, vol. 1, Zurich.
Brennan, T. (1996) 'Reasonable Impressions in Stoicism', *Phronesis* 41, 318–34.
Brennan, T. (1998) 'Pyrrho on the Criterion', *Ancient Philosophy* 18, 417–34.
Brennan, T. (1998a) 'The Old Theory of the Emotions', in Sihvola, J. and Engberg-Pedersen, T. (eds), *The Emotions in Hellenistic Philosophy*, Dordrecht, 21–70.
Brennan, T. (2003) 'Stoic Moral Psychology', in B. Inwood (ed.), *The Cambridge Companion to the Stoics*, Cambridge, 257–94.
Brennan, T. (2005) *The Stoic Life—Emotions, Duty, and Fate*, Oxford.
Bringmann, K. (1971) *Untersuchungen zum späten Cicero*, Göttingen.
Bringmann, K. (2012) 'Cicero über seine *Philosophica*. Zu Überlieferung und Interpretation einer umstrittenen Selbstaussage in Att. 12,52,3', *Hermes* 140, 25–36.
Brink, C. O. (1961) Review of Ruch (1958), *Journal of Roman Studies* 51, 215–22.
Brink, C. O. (1971) *Horace on Poetry: The 'Ars Poetica'*, Cambridge.
Brittain, C. (2001) *Philo of Larissa—The Last of the Academic Sceptics*, Oxford.
Brittain, C. (2003) 'Attention Deficit in Plotinus and Augustine: Psychological Problems in Christian and Platonist Theories of the Grades of Virtue', *Proceedings of the Boston Area Colloquium in Ancient Philosophy* 18, 223–63.
Brittain, C. (2005) 'Common Sense: Concepts, Definition and Meaning in and out of the Stoa', in D. Frede and B. Inwood (eds), *Language and Learning—Philosophy of Language in the Hellenistic Age*, Cambridge, 164–209.
Brittain, C. (2006) *Cicero—On Academic Scepticism*, Indianapolis.
Brittain, C. (2006a) 'Plato and Platonism', in G. Fine (ed.), *The Oxford Handbook to Plato*, Oxford, 526–52.
Brittain, C. (2007) 'Middle Platonists on Academic Scepticism', *Bulletin of the Institute of Classical Studies*, suppl. no. 94, 297–315.
Brittain, C. (2008) 'Arcesilaus', *The Stanford Encyclopedia of Philosophy* (Fall 2008), Edward N. Zalta (ed.), URL = <http://plato.stanford.edu/archives/fall2008/entries/arcesilaus/>.
Brittain, C. (2008a) 'Philo of Larissa', *The Stanford Encyclopedia of Philosophy* (Fall 2008), Edward N. Zalta (ed.), URL = <http://plato.stanford.edu/archives/fall2008/entries/philo-larissa/>.

Brittain, C. (2011) 'Augustine as a Reader of Cicero', in R. C. Taylor, D. Twetten, and M. Wreen (eds), *Tolle Lege: Essays on Augustine and Medieval Philosophy in Honor of Roland J. Teske, SJ*, Milwaukee, 81–114.
Brittain, C. (2012) 'Antiochus' Epistemology', in D. N. Sedley (ed.), *The Philosophy of Antiochus*, Cambridge, 104–30.
Brittain, C. (2014) 'The Compulsions of Stoic Assent', in M.-K. Lee (ed.), *Strategies of Argument—Essays in Ancient Ethics, Epistemology, and Logic*, Oxford and New York, 332–55.
Brittain, C. (2016) 'Cicero's Sceptical Methods: The Example of the *De Finibus*', in J. Annas and G. Betegh (eds), *Cicero's 'De Finibus': Philosophical Approaches*, Cambridge, 12–40.
Brittain, C. and Palmer, J. (2001) 'The New Academy's Appeal to the Presocratics', *Phronesis* 46, 38–72.
Brochard, V. (1887) *Les sceptiques grecs*, Paris.
Bronowski, A. (2019) *The Stoics on Lekta: All There Is to Say*, Oxford.
Brouwer, R. (2002) 'Sagehood and the Stoics', *Oxford Studies in Ancient Philosophy* 23, 181–224.
Brouwer, R. (2007) 'The Early Stoic Doctrine of the Change to Wisdom', *Oxford Studies in Ancient Philosophy* 33, 285–315.
Brouwer, R. (2014) *The Stoic Sage—The Early Stoics on Wisdom, Sagehood and Socrates*, Cambridge.
Brown, E. (2006) 'Socrates in the Stoa', in S. Ahbel-Rappe and R. Kamtekar (eds), *A Companion to Socrates*, Oxford, 275–84.
Brown, E. (2009) 'Politics and Society', in J. Warren (ed.), *The Cambridge Companion to Epicureanism*, Cambridge, 179–96.
Brown, J. (2018) *Fallibilism: Evidence and Knowledge*, Oxford.
Brown, L. (2018a) 'Rethinking Agreement in Plato', in D. O. Brink, S. S. Mayer, and C. Shields (eds), *Virtue, Happiness, Knowledge: Themes from the Work of Gail Fine and Terence Irwin*, Oxford, 18–32.
Brunschwig, J. (1980) 'Proof Defined', in M. Schofield, M. Burnyeat, and J. Barnes (eds), *Doubt and Dogmatism—Studies in Hellenistic Epistemology*, Oxford, 124–60.
Brunschwig, J. (1986) 'The Cradle Argument in Epicureanism and Stoicism', in M. Schofield and G. Striker (eds), *The Norms of Nature*, Cambridge, 113–44.
Brunschwig, J. (1991) 'On a Book-Title by Chrysippus: On the Fact that the Ancients Admitted Dialectic along with Demonstrations', *Oxford Studies in Ancient Philosophy*, suppl. vol., 81–95.
Brunschwig, J. (1994) 'The Stoic Theory of the Supreme Genus and Platonic Ontology', in *Papers in Hellenistic Philosophy*, Cambridge, 92–157.
Brunschwig, J. (1994a) 'Rhétorique et Dialectique, *Rhétorique* et *Topiques*', in D. J. Furley and A. Nehamas (eds), *Aristotle's Rhetoric: Philosophical Essays*, Princeton, 57–96.
Brunschwig, J. (1994b) 'The Conjunctive Model', in *Papers in Hellenistic Philosophy*, Cambridge, 72–91.
Brunschwig, J. (1996) 'La fragment DK 70B1 de Métrodore de Chio', in K. A. Algra, P. W. van der Horst, and D. T. Runia (eds), *Polyhistor: Studies in the History and Historiography of Ancient Philosophy, Presented to Jaap Mansfeld on his Sixtieth Birthday*, Leiden, 21–38.
Brunschwig, J. (1999) 'Introduction: The Beginnings of Hellenistic Epistemology', in K. Algra, J. Barnes, J. Mansfeld, and M. Schofield (eds), *The Cambridge History of Hellenistic Philosophy*, Cambridge, 229–59.
Brunschwig, J. (2002) 'Zeno between Kition and Athens', in T. Scaltsas and A. S. Mason (eds), *The Philosophy of Zeno*, Larnaka, 13–26.
Brunschwig, J. (2003) 'Stoic Metaphysics', in B. Inwood (ed.), *The Cambridge Companion to the Stoics*, Cambridge, 206–32.
Brunschwig, J. (2007) *Aristote, 'Topiques'. Tome II: Livres V–VIII*, Paris.

Brunt, P. A. (2013) *Studies in Stoicism*, edited by M. Griffin, A. Samuels, and with the assistance of M. Crawford, Oxford.
Brunt, P. (2013a) 'Panaetius in *De Officiis*', in Brunt (2013), 180–242.
Bryan, J., Wardy, R., and Warren, J. (2018) 'Introduction: Authorship and Authority in Ancient Philosophy', in J. Bryan, R. Wardy, and J. Warren (eds), *Authors and Authorities in Ancient Philosophy*, Cambridge, 1–19.
Buchwald, W. (1966) '*Musae Varronis*', *Museum Helveticum* 23, 215–17.
Buck, C. D. and Petersen, W. (1944) *A Reverse Index of Greek Nouns and Adjectives, Arranged by Terminations with Brief Historical Introductions*, Chicago.
Bultmann, R. (1948) 'Zur Geschichte der Lichtsymbolik im Altertum', *Philologus* 97, 1–36.
von Büren, V. (2019) 'Nonius Marcellus, *De compendiosa doctrina*: une entreprise carolingienne', *Aevum* 93, 287–351.
Burkert, W. (1959) '$\Sigma TOIXEION$—eine semasiologische Studie', *Philologus* 103, 167–97.
Burkert, W. (1972) 'Zur geistesgeschichtlichen Einordnung einiger Pseudopythagorica', in K. von Fritz (ed.), *Pseudepigrapha I: Pseudopythagorica, Lettres de Platon, littérature pseudépigraphique juive*, Geneva, 23–55.
Burkert, W. (1972a) *Lore and Science in Ancient Pythagoreanism*, Cambridge, MA.
Burnyeat, M. F. (1976) 'Plato on the Grammar of Perceiving', *Classical Quarterly* 26, 29–51.
Burnyeat, M. F. (1976a) 'Protagoras and Self-Refutation in Later Greek Philosophy', *Philosophical Review* 85, 44–69.
Burnyeat, M. F. (1978) 'The Upside-Down Back-To-Front Sceptic of Lucretius IV 472', *Philologus* 122, 197–206.
Burnyeat, M. F. (1979) 'Conflicting Appearances', *Proceedings of the British Academy* 65, 69–111.
Burnyeat, M. F. (1980) 'Aristotle on Learning to be Good', in A. O. Rorty (ed.), *Essays on Aristotle's 'Ethics'*, Berkeley and London, 69–92.
Burnyeat, M. F. (1982) 'Idealism and Greek Philosophy: What Descartes Saw and Berkeley Missed', *Philosophical Review* 91, 3–40.
Burnyeat, M. F. (1982a) 'The Origins of Non-Deductive Inference', in J. Barnes, J. Brunschwig, M. Burnyeat, and M. Schofield (eds), *Science and Speculation: Studies in Hellenistic Theory and Practice*, Cambridge, 315–38.
Burnyeat, M. F. (1982b) 'Gods and Heaps', in M. Schofield and M. Nussbaum (eds), *Language and Logos*, Cambridge, 315–38.
Burnyeat, M. F. (1990) *The Theaetetus of Plato*, Indianapolis.
Burnyeat, M. F. (1997) 'Antipater and Self-Refutation: Elusive Arguments in Cicero's *Academica*', in B. Inwood and J. Mansfeld (eds), *Assent and Argument: Studies in Cicero's Academic Books*, Leiden, 277–310.
Burnyeat, M. F. (1999) 'Plato on Why Mathematics is Good for the Soul', in T. Smiley (ed.), *Mathematics and Necessity: Essays in the History of Philosophy*, Oxford, 1–81.
Burnyeat, M. F. (unpublished) 'Carneades was no probabilist'.
Bury, R. G. (1935) *Sextus Empiricus—Against the Logicians*. Cambridge, MA.
Büttner, R. (1893) *Porcius Licinus und der litterarische Kreis des Quintus Lutatius Catulus*, Leipzig.
Cambiano, G. (1999) 'Philosophy, Science and Medicine', in K. Algra, J. Barnes, J. Mansfeld, and M. Schofield (eds), *The Cambridge History of Hellenistic Philosophy*, Cambridge, 585–613.
Cambiano, G. (2012) 'The Desire to Know: Metaphysics A1', in C. Steel and O. Primavesi (eds), *Aristotle's Metaphysics Alpha*, Oxford, 1–42.
Camerarius, I. (1552) *In M. Tul. Ciceronem Annotationes*, Lyon.
Campos-Daroca, F. J. (2019) 'Epicurus and the Epicureans on Socrates and the Socratics', in C. Moore (ed.), *Brill's Companion to the Reception of Socrates*, Leiden, 237–65.

Cappello, O. (2019) *The School of Doubt: Skepticism, History and Politics in Cicero's 'Academica'*, Leiden.
Cardauns, B. (1978) 'Varro und die römische Religion. Zur Theologie, Wirkungsgeschichte und Leistung der *Antiquitates Rerum Diuinarum*', *Aufstieg und Niedergang der Römischen Welt* II.16, 80–103.
Cardauns, B. (2001) 'Bewegte Landschaft—die poetische Verwendung einer Sinnestäuschung in der römischen Dichtung', *Rheinisches Museum für Philologie* 144, 123–39.
Cardauns, B. (2001a) *Marcus Terentius Varro—Einführung in sein Werk*, Heidelberg.
Carman, C. C. (2014) 'Two Problems in Aristarchus' Treatises *On the Sizes and Distances of the Sun and the Moon*', *Archive for History of Exact Sciences* 68, 35–65.
Carruthers, M. (2008[2]) *The Book of Memory*, Cambridge.
Castagnoli, L. (2010) *Ancient Self-Refutation: The Logic and History of the Self-Refutation Argument from Democritus to Augustine*, Cambridge.
Castagnoli, L. (2010a) 'How Dialectical Was Stoic Dialectic?', in A. Nightingale and D. N. Sedley (eds), *Ancient Models of Mind: Studies in Human and Divine Rationality*, Cambridge 153–79.
Castagnoli, L. (2019) 'Dialectic in the Hellenistic Academy', in T. Bénatouïl and K. Ierodiakonou (eds), *Dialectic after Plato and Aristotle*, Cambridge, 168–217.
Caston, V. (1999) 'Something and Nothing: The Stoics on Concepts and Universals', *Oxford Studies in Ancient Philosophy* 17, 145–213.
Caujolle-Zaslawsky, F. (1989) 'Aristippe de Cyrène', in R. Goulet (ed.), *Dictionnaire des philosophes antiques*, vol. 1, Paris, 370–5.
Caujolle-Zaslawsky, F. and Goulet, R. (1989) 'Ariston d'Alexandrie', in R. Goulet (ed.), *Dictionnaire des philosophes antiques*, vol. 1, Paris, 396–7.
Cavini, W. (1993) 'Chrysippus on Speaking Truly and the Liar', in K. Döring and T. Ebert (eds), *Dialektiker und Stoiker—Zur Logik der Stoa und ihrer Vorläufer*, Stuttgart, 85–109.
Cebè, J.-P. (1972–99) *Varron, Satires ménippées*, 13 vols, Rome.
Cebè, J.-P. (1998) *Varron, Satires Ménippées. 12. Sexagessis—Testamentum*, Rome.
Celkyte, A. (2020) 'The Soul and Personal Identity of Early Stoicism: Two Theories?', *Apeiron* 53, 463–86.
Centrone, B. (2000) 'Hicétas de Syracuse', in R. Goulet (ed.), *Dictionnaire des philosophes antiques*, vol. 3, Paris, 681.
Chahoud, A. (2007) 'Antiquity and Authority in Nonius Marcellus', in J. H. D. Scourfield (ed.), *Texts and Culture in Late Antiquity: Inheritance, Authority, and Change*, Swansea, 69–96.
Chahoud, A. (2010) 'Idiom(s) and Literariness in Classical Literary Criticism', in E. Dickey and A. Chahoud (eds), *Colloquial and Literary Latin*, Cambridge, 42–64.
Chahoud, A. (2016) '*Quid ago? Quid facimus?* "Deliberative" Indicative Questions from Early to Late Latin', in J. N. Adams and N. Vincent (eds), *Early and Late Latin Continuity or Change?*, Cambridge, 217–45.
Chappell, T. (2004) *Reading Plato's Theaetetus*, Sankt Augustin.
Chiaradonna, R. (2013) 'Platonist Approaches to Aristotle: From Antiochus of Ascalon to Eudorus of Alexandria (and Beyond)', in M. Schofield (ed.), *Aristotle, Plato and Pythagoreanism in the First Century B.C.*, Cambridge, 28–52.
Chiaradonna, R. (2014) 'Galen on What Is Persuasive (pithanon) and What Approximates to Truth', *Bulletin of the Institute of Classical Studies*, suppl. 114: *Philosophical Themes in Galen*, 61–88.
Chignell, A. (2018) 'The Ethics of Belief', *The Stanford Encyclopedia of Philosophy* (Spring), Edward N. Zalta (ed.), URL = <https://plato.stanford.edu/archives/spr2018/entries/ethics-belief/>.
Cichorius, C. (1908) *Untersuchungen zu Lucilius*, Berlin.
Cichorius, C. (1922) *Römische Studien*, Berlin.

Clausen, W. (1994) *Virgil—Eclogues*, Oxford.
Clay, D. (2009) 'The Athenian Garden', in J. Warren (ed.), *The Cambridge Companion to Epicureanism*, Cambridge, 9–28.
Clayman, D. L. (2009) *Timon of Phlius*, Berlin and New York.
Clayman, D. L. (2016) 'Timon de Phlionte', in R. Goulet (ed.), *Dictionnaire des philosophes antiques*, vol. 6, Paris, 1226–30.
Clifford, W. K. (1999) 'The Ethics of Belief', in T. Madigan (ed.), *The Ethics of Belief and Other Essays*, Amherst, MA, 70–96.
Cohn, L. (1905) *Antipater von Tarsos*, Berlin.
Coleman, R. (1977) *Vergil—Eclogues*, Cambridge.
Coleman, R. (1999) 'Poetic Diction, Poetic Discourse and the Poetic Register', in J. N. Adams and R. G. Mayer (eds), *Aspects of the Language of Latin Poetry*, Proceedings of the British Academy no. 93, 21–93.
Colonna, G. (1707) *Q. Ennii Poetae Vetustissimi Fragmenta*, Amsterdam.
Conte, G. B. (1992) 'Proems in the Middle', *Yale Classical Studies* 29, 147–59.
Coones, P. (1983) 'The Geographical Significance of Plutarch's Dialogue, Concerning the Face Which Appears in the Orb of the Moon', *Transactions of the Institute of British Geographers* 8, 361–72.
Coope, U. (2016) 'Rational Assent and Self-Reversion: A Neoplatonist Response to the Stoics', *Oxford Studies in Ancient Philosophy* 50, 237–88.
Coope, U. (2019) 'Free to Think? Epistemic Authority and Thinking for Oneself', *Journal of the British Academy* 7, 1–23.
Cooper, J. M. (1970) 'Plato on Sense-Perception and Knowledge ("Theaetetus" 184–6)', *Phronesis* 15, 123–46.
Cooper, J. M. (1985) 'Aristotle on the Goods of Fortune', *Philosophical Review* 94, 173–96.
Cooper, J. M. (1996) *Reason and Emotion—Essays on Ancient Moral Psychology and Ethical Theory*, Princeton.
Cooper, J. M. (1996a) 'The Unity of Virtue', in Cooper (1996), 76–117.
Cooper, J. M. (2005) 'The Emotional Life of the Wise', *Southern Journal of Philosophy* 43, suppl. vol., 176–218.
Cooper, J. M. (2006) 'Arcesilaus: Socratic and Sceptic', in V. Karasmanes and L. Judson (eds), *Remembering Socrates: Philosophical Essays*, Oxford, 169–87.
Corbeill, A. (2004) *Nature Embodied—Gesture in Ancient Rome*, Princeton.
Corbeill, A. (2017) 'Anticato', in L. Grillo and C. Krebs (eds), *The Cambridge Companion to the Writings of Julius Caesar*, Cambridge, 215–22.
Cornford, F. M. (2000) *Plato's Cosmology*, London.
Cortassa, B. (1975) '*ΤΟ ΦΑΙΝΟΜΕΝΟΝ* e *ΤΟ ΑΔΗΛΟΝ* in Sesto Empirico', *Rivista di Filologia e di Istruzione Classica* 103, 276–92.
Corti, L. (2009) *Scepticisme et Langage*, Paris.
Cosans, C. E. (1997) 'Galen's Critique of Rationalist and Empiricist Anatomy', *Journal of the History of Biology* 30, 35–54.
Couissin, P. (1929) 'L'origine et l'évolution de l'ἐποχή', *Revue des Études Grecques* 42, 373–97.
Couissin, P. (1929a) 'Le Stoïcisme de la Nouvelle Académie', *Revue d'histoire de la philosophie* 3 (1929), 241–76.
Couissin, P. (1983) 'The Stoicism of the New Academy', in M. Burnyeat (ed.), *The Skeptical Tradition*, Berkeley and Los Angeles, 31–63 [first published as Couissin (1929a)].
Courtney, E. (2003) *The Fragmentary Latin Poets*, Oxford (rev. edn).
Cramer, J. A. (1839) *Anecdota Graeca e codd. manuscriptis Bibliothecae Regiae Parisiniensis*, Oxford, vol. i.
Crawford, M. H. (1996) *Roman Statutes*, 2 vols, London.

Crivelli, P. (1994) 'Indefinite Propositions and Anaphora in Stoic Logic', *Phronesis* 39, 187-206.
Crivelli, P. (2004) 'Aristotle on the Liar', *Topoi* 23, 61-70.
Crivelli, P. (2004a) *Aristotle on Truth*, Cambridge.
Croissant, J. (1984) 'Autour de la quatrième formule d'implication dans Sextus Empiricus, Hyp. Pyrrh., II, 112', *Revue de Philosophie Ancienne* 2, 73-120.
Crönert, W. (1906) *Kolotes und Menedemos*, Leipzig.
Dahlmann, H. (1935) 'M. Terentius Varro', in *RE* suppl. VI, 1172-1277.
Dahlmann, H. (1973) 'Varroniana', *Aufstieg und Niedergang der Römischen Welt* I.3, 3-25.
Dahlmann, H. (1978) 'Silent diuitius Musae Varronis quam solebant', in J. Collart (ed.), *Varron: Grammaire antique et stylistique latine*, Paris, 85-9.
Dahlmann, H. and Heisterhagen, R. (1957) *Varronische Studien I: Zu den Logistorici*, Akademie der Wissenschaften und der Literatur, Abhandlungen der geistes- und sozialwissenschaftlichen Klasse no. 4, Mainz.
Dahlmann, H. and Speyer, W. (1959) *Varronische Studien II*, Akademie der Wissenschaften und der Literatur, Abhandlungen der geistes- und sozialwissenschaftlichen Klasse no. 11, Mainz.
Dalfino, M. C. (1993) 'Ieronimo di Rodi: la dottrina della *vacuitas doloris*', *Elenchos* 14, 277-304.
D'Ancona, C. (2012) 'The Textual Tradition of the Graeco-Arabic Plotinus. The Theology of Aristotle, Its "ru'ūs al-masā'il", and the Greek Model of the Arabic Version', in J. Oppenraaij and R. Fontaine (eds), *The Letter before the Spirit: The Importance of Text Editions for the Study of the Reception of Aristotle*, Leiden, 37-71.
D'Arms, J. H. (1970) *Romans on the Bay of Naples—A Social and Cultural Study of the Villas and their Owners from 150 B.C. to A.D. 400*, Cambridge, MA.
D'Arms, J. H. (1972) 'CIL X, 1792: A Municipal Notable of the Augustan Age', *Harvard Studies in Classical Philology* 76, 207-16.
Daube, D. (1956) *Forms of Roman Legislation*. Oxford.
Davies, J. (1725) *M. Tullii Ciceronis Academica*, Cambridge.
De Allio, J. C. (1743) *M. Tulli Ciceronis Academica*, Venice.
De Lacy, P. (1984^3) *Galen: On the Doctrines of Hippocrates and Plato*, vol. i, Berlin.
Decleva Caizzi, F. (1992) 'Aenesidemus and the Academy', *Classical Quarterly* 42, 176-89.
DeFilippo, J. G. (2000) 'Cicero vs. Cotta in De natura deorum', *Ancient Philosophy* 20, 169-87.
DeGraff, T. B. (1940) 'Plato in Cicero', *Classical Philology* 35, 143-53.
Deichgräber, K. (1965^2) *Die griechische Empirikerschule*, Berlin and Zurich.
Del Pra, M. (1975^2) *Lo scetticismo greco*, Rome and Bari.
Della Corte, F. (1970) *Varrone, il terzo gran lume Romano*, Firenze.
Denk, J. (1906) 'Zur Itala', *Archiv für lateinische Lexikographie und Grammatik* 14, 279-81.
Derolez, A. (2003) *The Palaeography of Gothic Manuscript Books from the Twelfth to the Early Sixteenth Century*, Cambridge.
DeRose, K. (1991) 'Epistemic Possibilities', *The Philosophical Review* 100, 581-605.
Desclos, M. L. and Fortenbaugh, W. W. (2010) *Strato of Lampsacus*, New Brunswick.
Destrée, P., Salles, R., and Zingano, M. (2014) *What Is Up to Us? Studies on Agency and Responsibility in Ancient Philosophy*, Sankt Augustin.
Deufert, M. (2001) 'Zur Datierung des Nonius Marcellus', *Philologus* 145, 137-49.
Develin, R. (1978) '*Provocatio* and Plebiscites. Early Roman Legislation and the Historical Tradition', *Mnemosyne* 31, 45-60.
Develin, R. (1979) 'The Political Position of C. Flaminius', *Rheinisches Museum für Philologie* 122, 268-77.
Dickey, E. (1997) '*Me autem nomine appellabat*: Avoidance of Cicero's Name in his Dialogues', *Classical Quarterly* 47, 584-8.

Dickey, E. (2015) *The Colloquia of the Hermeneumata Pseudodositheana*, Vol. 2: *Colloquium Harleianum, Colloquium Montepessulanum, Colloquium Celtis, and Fragments*, Cambridge.
Diels, H. (1879) *Doxographi Graeci*, Berlin.
Diels, H. (1888) 'Zu Aristoteles' Protreptikos und Cicero's Hortensius', *Archiv für Geschichte der Philosophie* 1, 477–97.
Diels, H. (1899) *Elementum—eine Vorarbeit zum griechischen und lateinischen Thesaurus*, Leipzig.
Diggle, J. (2004) *Theophrastus—Characters*, Cambridge.
Dillon, J. (1993) *The Handbook of Platonism*, Oxford.
Dillon, J. (2003) *The Heirs of Plato—A Study of the Old Academy (347–274 BC)*, Oxford.
Dillon, J. (2011) 'The Ideas as Thoughts of God', *Études platoniciennes* [online], 8 | 2011, published online on 16 December 2014, accessed 6 April 2019, URL: = <http://journals.openedition.org/etudesplatoniciennes/448>; DOI: 10.4000/etudesplatoniciennes.448.
Dillon, J. (2016) 'The Reception of Aristotle in Antiochus and Cicero', in A. Falcon (ed.), *Brill's Companion to the Reception of Aristotle in Antiquity*, Leiden and Boston, 183–201.
Dillon, J. (2020) 'Polemo, *grosser Schatten* of the Old Academy', in P. Kalligas, C. Balla, E. Baziotopoulou-Valavani, and V. Karasmanis (eds), *Plato's Academy—Its Workings and its History*, Cambridge, 188–99.
Dodds, E. R. (1959) *Plato—Gorgias*, Oxford.
Dodds, E. R. (1968) review of Edelstein (1967), *Journal of the History of Ideas* 29, 453–7.
Döderlein, Ludwig von (1852^2) *Handbook of Latin Synonymes*, London.
Doherty, K. F. (1960) 'Location of the Platonic Ideas', *The Review of Metaphysics* 14, 57–72.
Doignon, J. (1981) 'Cicéron a-t-il comparé Épicure à Liber? (*Academicorum fragm.*, apud Augustinum, *C. Acad.* 3, 7, 16)', *Revue des Études Latines* 59, 153–63.
Doignon, J. (1983) 'Un éclairage nouveau du fragment 104 (Grilli) de l' "Hortensius" de Cicéron', *Hermes* 111, 458–64.
Donini, P. (1988) 'Tipologia degli errori e loro correzione secondo Galeno', in P. Manuli and M. Vegetti (eds), *Le opere psicologiche di Galeno*, Naples, 65–116.
Donini, P. (2011) 'Le fonti medioplatoniche di Seneca: Antioco, la conoscenza e le idee', in P. Donini and M. Bonazzi (eds), *Commentary and Tradition: Aristotelianism, Platonism, and Post-Hellenistic Philosophy*, Berlin and New York, 297–313.
Donini, P. (2011a) 'Platone e Aristotele nella tradizione pitagorica secondo Plutarco', in P. Donini and M. Bonazzi (eds), *Commentary and Tradition: Aristotelianism, Platonism, and Post-Hellenistic Philosophy*, Berlin and New York, 359–73.
Donini, P. and Inwood, B. (1999) 'Stoic Ethics', in K. Algra, J. Barnes, J. Mansfeld, and M. Schofield (eds), *The Cambridge History of Hellenistic Philosophy*, Cambridge, 675–738.
Dorandi, T. (1989) 'Antiochos d'Ascalon', in R. Goulet (ed.), *Dictionnaire des philosophes antiques*, vol. 1, Paris, 216–19.
Dorandi, T. (1989a) 'Arcésilas di Pitane', in R. Goulet (ed.), *Dictionnaire des philosophes antiques*, vol. 1, Paris, 326–30.
Dorandi, T. (1991) *Filodemo. Storia dei filosofi: Platone e l'Academia*, Naples.
Dorandi, T. (1991a) *Ricerche sulla Cronologia dei Filosofi Ellenistici*, Stuttgart.
Dorandi, T. (1994) 'Cleitomaque de Carthage', in R. Goulet (ed.), *Dictionnaire des philosophes antiques*, vol. 2, Paris, 424–5.
Dorandi, T. (1994a) 'Charmadas', in R. Goulet (ed.), *Dictionnaire des philosophes antiques*, vol. 2, Paris, 297–8.
Dorandi, T. (1994b) 'Crantor de Soles', in R. Goulet (ed.), *Dictionnaire des philosophes antiques*, vol. 2, Paris, 482–3.
Dorandi, T. (1994c) 'Cratès de Thria', in R. Goulet (ed.), *Dictionnaire des philosophes antiques*, vol. 2, Paris, 500–1.

Dorandi, T. (1994d) 'Carnéade de Cyrène', in R. Goulet (ed.), *Dictionnaire des philosophes antiques*, vol. 2, Paris, 224–6.
Dorandi, T. (1994e) 'Dion d'Alexandrie', in R. Goulet (ed.), *Dictionnaire des philosophes antiques*, vol. 2, Paris, 839–40.
Dorandi, T. (1994f) 'Dionysius de Cyrène', in R. Goulet (ed.), *Dictionnaire des philosophes antiques*, vol. 2, Paris, 865–6.
Dorandi, T. (1994g) 'Cleitomache de Carthage', in R. Goulet (ed.), *Dictionnaire des philosophes antiques*, vol. 2, Paris, 424–5.
Dorandi, T. (1994h) 'Cratès de Thria', in R. Goulet (ed.), *Dictionnaire des philosophes antiques*, vol. 2, Paris, 500–1.
Dorandi, T. (1999) 'Chronology', in K. Algra, J. Barnes, J. Mansfeld, and M. Schofield (eds), *The Cambridge History of Hellenistic Philosophy*, Cambridge, 31–54.
Dorandi, T. (2000) 'Héraclite de Tyr', in R. Goulet (ed.), *Dictionnaire des philosophes antiques*, vol. 3, Paris, 628.
Dorandi, T. (2000a) 'Euandros de Phocée', in R. Goulet (ed.), *Dictionnaire des philosophes antiques*, vol. 3, Paris, 243.
Dorandi, T. (2000b) 'Hégésinos', in R. Goulet (ed.), *Dictionnaire des philosophes antiques*, vol. 3, Paris, 529–30.
Dorandi, T. (2005) 'Lacydès de Cyrène', in R. Goulet (ed.), *Dictionnaire des philosophes antiques*, vol. 4, Paris, 74–5.
Dorandi, T. (2005a) 'Melanthios de Rhodes', in R. Goulet (ed.), *Dictionnaire des philosophes antiques*, vol. 4, Paris, 383–4.
Dorandi, T. (2005b) 'Métrodore de Stratonicée', in R. Goulet (ed.), *Dictionnaire des philosophes antiques*, vol. 4, Paris, 518.
Dorandi, T. (2012) 'Polyen de Lampsaque', in R. Goulet (ed.), *Dictionnaire des philosophes antiques*, vol. 5b, Paris, 1253–4.
Dorandi, T. (2016) 'Staséas de Naples', in R. Goulet (ed.), *Dictionnaire des philosophes antiques*, vol. 6, Paris, 556.
Dorandi, T. and Queyrel, F. (2000) 'Hermarque de Mytilène', in R. Goulet (ed.), *Dictionnaire des philosophes antiques*, vol. 3, Paris, 633–7.
Döring, A. (1893) 'Doxographisches zur Lehre vom τέλος', *Zeitschrift für Philosophie und philosophische Kritik* 101, 165–203.
Döring, K. (1972) *Die Megariker. Kommentierte Sammlung der Testimonien*, Amsterdam.
Döring, K. (1979) *Exemplum Socratis: Studien zur Sokrates-Nachwirkung in der kynisch-stoischen Popularphilosophie der frühen Kaiserzeit und im frühen Christentum*, Wiesbaden.
Döring, K. (1998) 'Diodoros Kronos, Philon, Panthoides', in H. Flashar (ed.), *Grundriss der Geschichte der Philosophie. Die Philosophie der Antike*, Bd. 2/1, Basel, 221–30.
Döring, K. (2010) *Kleine Schriften zur antiken Philosophie und ihrer Nachwirkung*, Stuttgart.
Döring, K. (2010a) 'Die kleinen Sokratiker und ihre Schulen bei Sextus Empiricus', in *Kleine Schriften zur antiken Philosophie und ihrer Nachwirkung*, Stuttgart, 263–89.
Dörrie, H. (1967) 'Xenokrates Nr. 4', in *RE* IX A2, 1512–28.
Dörrie, H. (1987) *Der Platonismus in der Antike: Grundlagen—System—Entwicklung. Die geschichtlichen Wurzeln des Platonismus. Bausteine 1–35: Text, Übersetzung, Kommentar*, Stuttgart-Bad Cannstatt.
Driediger-Murphy, L. (2019) *Roman Republican Augury*, Oxford.
Dumont, J.-P. (1967–8) 'L'âme et la main. Signification du geste de Zénon', *Revue de l'enseignement philosophique* 19.4, 1–8.
Dunlop, C. E. M. (1977) *Philosophical Essays on Dreaming*, Ithaca.
Dyck, A. R. (2003) *Cicero—'De Natura Deorum' Book 1*, Cambridge.
Dyck, A. R. (2004) *A Commentary on Cicero, 'De Legibus'*, Ann Arbor.

Dyck, A. R. (2008) *Cicero—Catiliarians*, Cambridge.
Dyson, H. (2009) *Prolepsis and Ennoia in the Early Stoa*, Berlin and New York.
Ebbesen, S. (1981) *Commentators and Commentaries on Aristotle's 'Sophistici Elenchi'*, Leiden, 3 vols.
Ebert, F. (1928) 'Maenianum', in *RE* XIV.1, 245–7.
Ebert, T. (1991) *Dialektiker und frühe Stoiker bei Sextus Empiricus: Untersuchungen zur Entstehung der Aussagenlogik*, Göttingen.
Eble, F. X. (1846–7) *Über den Sosus des Antiochus von Ascalon*, Progr. Offenburg.
Eckerman, C. (2013) 'Lucretius' Self-Positioning in the History of Roman Epicureanism', *Classical Quarterly* 63, 785–800.
Edelstein, L. (1967) *The Idea of Progress in Classical Antiquity*, Baltimore.
Edwards, C. M. (1996) 'Lysippos', *Yale Classical Studies* 30, 130–53.
Elkins, N. T. (2017) 'Aequitas and Iustitia on the Coinage of Nerva: A Case of Visual Panegyric', *Numismatic Chronicle* 177, 93–106.
Elliott, J. (2013) *Ennius and the Architecture of the Annales*, Cambridge.
Emonds, H. (1941) *Zweite Auflage im Altertum: kulturgeschichtliche Studien zum Studium der antiken Literatur*, Berlin.
Erler, M. (1994) 'Hermarchus', in H. Flashar (ed.), *Grundriss der Geschichte der Philosophie. Die Philosophie der Antike*, Bd. 4/1: *Die hellenistische Philosophie*, Basel, 227–34.
Erler, M. (1994a) 'Siron', in H. Flashar (ed.), *Grundriss der Geschichte der Philosophie. Die Philosophie der Antike*, Bd. 4/1: *Die hellenistische Philosophie*, Basel, 274–5.
Ernesti, J. C. G. (1797) *Lexicon technologiae latinorum rhetoricae*, Leipzig.
Essler, H. (2011) *Glückselig und unsterblich: epikureische Theologie bei Cicero und Philodem, mit einer Edition von PHerc. 152/157, Kol. 8–10*, Basel.
Essler, H. (2014) 'Zum Fragment aus Chrysipps *De Divinatione* (PHerc. 152/157, Kol. 7, 26—Kol. 8, 5)', *Cronache Ercolanesi* 44, 117–28.
Faes de Mottoni, B. (1982) 'Lattanzio e gli Academici', *Mélanges de l'Ecole française de Rome, Antiquité* 94, 335–77.
Falcon, A. (2012) *Aristotelianism in the First Century BCE: Xenarchus of Seleucia*, Cambridge.
Farrell, J. (2001) *Latin Language and Culture*, Cambridge.
Farrell, J. (2008) 'The Six Books of Lucretius' *De rerum natura*: Antecedents and Influence', *Dictynna* 5, accessed 19 April 2019, URL = <http://journals.openedition.org/dictynna/385>.
Fedeli, P. (1961–4) 'Un problema di tradizione indiretta: Nonio e il "De Officiis" di Cicerone', *Ciceroniana* 3–6, 105–54.
Fedeli, P. (2005) *Properzio: Elegie, Libro II. Introduzione, testo e commento*, Cambridge.
Ferenczy, E. (1989) 'Über die Quellen der historischen Werke Varros unter besonderer Berücksichtigung der Antiquitates rerum humanarum', *Klio* 71, 353–60.
Ferrary, J.-L. (1977) 'Le discours de Philus (Cicéron, *De Re Publica* III, 8–31) et la philosophie de Carnéade', *Revue des Études Latines* 55, 128–56.
Ferri, R. and Probert, P. (2010) 'Roman Authors on Colloquial Language', in E. Dickey and A. Chahoud (eds), *Colloquial and Literary Latin*, Cambridge, 12–41.
Fessler, F. (1913) *Benutzung der philosophischen Schriften Ciceros durch Laktanz*, Leipzig and Berlin.
Festugière, A. J. (1949) *La Révélation d'Hermès Trismégiste. II: Le Dieu Cosmique*, Paris.
Fine, G. (1993) *On Ideas: Aristotle's Criticism of Plato's Theory of Forms*, Oxford.
Fine, G. (2000) 'Sceptical *Dogmata*: Outlines of Pyrrhonism I 13', *Méthexis* 13, 81–105.
Fine, G. (2003) 'Sextus and External World Scepticism', *Oxford Studies in Ancient Philosophy* 23, 341–85.
Fine, G. (2008) 'Does Socrates Claim to Know That He Knows Nothing?', *Oxford Studies in Ancient Philosophy* 35, 49–88.

Fine, G. (2014) *The Possibility of Inquiry—Meno's Paradox from Socrates to Sextus*, Oxford.
Fine, G. (2017) 'Plato on the Grades of Perception: *Theaetetus* 184-186 and the *Phaedo*', *Oxford Studies in Ancient Philosophy* 53, 65-109.
Finglass, P. J. (2007) *Sophocles: Electra*, Cambridge.
Fladerer, L. (1996) *Antiochos von Askalon—Hellenist und Humanist*, Graz.
Flashar, H. (2004) 'Aristoteles, *Über die Philosophie*', in A. Bierl, A. Schmitt, and A. Willi (eds), *Antike Literatur in neuer Deutung*, Munich and Leipzig, 257-73.
Flashar, H., Dubielzig, U., and Breitenberger, B. (2006) *Aristoteles—Fragmente zur Philosophie, Rhetorik, Poetik, Dichtung*, Berlin.
Fleischer, K. (2014) 'Der Akademiker Charmadas in Apollodors "Chronik" (PHerc. 1021, Kol. 31-32)', *Cronache Ercolanesi* 44, 66-75.
Fleischer, K. (2015) 'Der Stoiker Mnesarch als Lehrer des Antiochus im Index Academicorum', *Mnemosyne* 68, 413-23.
Fleischer, K. (2015a) 'Die Schüler des Charmadas (PHerc.1021, XXXV 32—XXXVI 14)', *Cronache Ercolanesi* 45, 49-53.
Fleischer, K. (2016) 'New Readings in Philodemus' *Index Academicorum*: Dio of Alexandria (P. Herc. 1021, col. XXXV, 17-19)', *Proceedings of the 27th International Congress of Papyrology, The Journal of Juristic Papyrology*, suppl. vol. 28, 459-70.
Fleischer, K. (2017) 'Starb Philo von Larisa im Alter von 63 Jahren?', *Archiv für Papyrusforschung und verwandte Gebiete* 63, 335-66.
Fleischer, K. (2017a) 'The Pupils of Philo of Larissa and Philodemus' Stay in Sicily (PHerc. 1021, col. XXXIV 6-19)', *Cronache Ercolanesi* 47, 73-85.
Fleischer, K. (2017b) 'New Evidence on the Death of Philo of Larissa (PHerc. 1021, cols. 33,42-34,7)', *The Cambridge Classical Journal* 63, 69-81.
Fleischer, K. (2019) 'Carneades: The One and Only', *Journal of Hellenic Studies* 139, 116-24.
Fleischer, K. (2019a) 'Zur Abstammung der akademischen Philosophen Melanthios von Rhodos und Metrodor von Stratonikeia (PHerc. 1021, Kol. 23,10-20)', *Archiv für Papyrusforschung* 65, 124-32.
Fleischer, K. (2020) *The Original Verses of Apollodorus' 'Chronica'*, Berlin and Boston.
Fleischer, K. (2022) 'Philo or Philio of Larissa?', *Classical Quarterly* 72, 1-11.
Fleischer, K. (forthcoming) *Philodems Geschichte der Akademie*.
Fögen, T. (2000) *Patrii Sermonis Egestas—Einstellungen lateinischer Autoren zu ihrer Muttersprache*, Munich and Leipzig.
Follet, S. (2000) 'Favorinus d'Arles', in R. Goulet (ed.), *Dictionnaire des philosophes antiques*, vol. 3, Paris, 418-22.
Fordyce, C. J. (1961) *Catullus: A Commentary*, Oxford.
Fortenbaugh, W. W. et al. (1992) *Theophrastus of Eresus. Sources for his Life, Writings, Thought and Influence. Part Two: Psychology, Human Physiology, Living Creatures, Botany, Ethics, Religion, Politics, Rhetoric and Poetics, Music, Miscellanea*, Leiden.
Fox, M. (2007) *Cicero's Philosophy of History*, Oxford.
Franko, G. F. (1994) 'The Use of *Poenus* and *Carthaginiensis* in Early Latin Literature', *Classical Philology* 89, 153-8.
Fraser, P. M. (1969) 'The Career of Erisistratus of Ceos', *Rendiconti del Istituto Lombardo* 103, 518-37.
Frede, D. (1989) 'The Soul's Silent Dialogue: A Non-Aporetic Reading of the *Theaetetus*', *Proceedings of the Cambridge Philological Society* 35, 20-49.
Frede, D. (1996) 'The Philosophical Economy of Plato's Psychology: Rationality and Common Concepts in the *Timaeus*', in M. Frede and G. Striker (eds), *Rationality in Greek Thought*, Oxford, 29-58.
Frede, D. (1996a) 'How Sceptical were the Academic Sceptics?', in R. H. Popkin (ed.), *Scepticism in the History of Philosophy*, Dordrecht, 1-26.

Frede, M. (1986) 'The Stoic Doctrine of the Affections of the Soul', in M. Schofield and G. Striker (eds), *The Norms of Nature—Studies in Hellenistic Ethics*, Cambridge, 93–110.
Frede, M. (1987) *Essays in Ancient Philosophy*, Oxford.
Frede, M. (1987a) 'Observation on Perception in Plato's Later Dialogues', in *Essays in Ancient Philosophy*, Oxford, 3–8.
Frede, M. (1987b) 'The Skeptic's Two Kinds of Assent and the Question of the Possibility of Knowledge', in *Essays in Ancient Philosophy*, Oxford, 201–22.
Frede, M. (1987c) 'Stoics and Sceptics on Clear and Distinct Impressions', in *Essays in Ancient Philosophy*, Oxford, 151–76.
Frede, M. (1987d) 'The Ancient Empiricists', in *Essays in Ancient Philosophy*, Oxford, 243–60.
Frede, M. (1987e) 'The Original Notion of Cause', in *Essays in Ancient Philosophy*, Oxford, 125–50.
Frede, M. (1987f) 'Numenius', *Aufstieg und Niedergang der Römischen Welt* II.36.2, 1034–75.
Frede, M. (1987g) 'The Skeptic's Beliefs', in *Essays in Ancient Philosophy*, Oxford, 179–200.
Frede, M. (1988) 'A Medieval Source of Modern Scepticism', in R. Claussen and R. Daube-Schackat (eds), *Gedankenzeichen. Festschrift für Klaus Oehler zum 60. Geburtstag*, Tübingen, 65–70.
Frede, M. (1994) 'The Stoic Conception of Reason', in K. Boudouris (ed.), *Hellenistic Philosophy II*, Athens, 50–63.
Frede, M. (1997) 'The Sceptic's Beliefs', in M. Burnyeat and M. Frede (eds), *The Original Sceptics: A Controversy*, Indianapolis, 1–24.
Frede, M. (1999) 'Stoic Epistemology', in K. Algra, J. Barnes, J. Mansfeld, and M. Schofield (eds), *The Cambridge History of Hellenistic Philosophy*, Cambridge, 295–322.
Frede, M. (1999a) Review of Mansfeld and Runia (1997), *Phronesis* 44, 135–49.
Frede, M. (1999b) 'On the Stoic Conception of the Good', in K. Ierodiakonou (ed.), *Topics in Stoic Philosophy*, Oxford, 71–94.
Frede, M. (2005) 'La théologie Stoïcienne', in G. Romeyer Dherbey and J.-B. Gourinat (eds), *Les Stoïciens*, Paris, 213–32.
Frede, M. (2011) *A Free Will—Origins of the Notion in Ancient Thought*, Oxford.
Frede, M. (2014) 'The *eph' hêmin* in Ancient Philosphy', in P. Destrée, R. Salles, and M. Zingano (eds), *What Is Up to Us? Studies on Agency and Responsibility in Ancient Philosophy*, Sankt Augustin, 351–63.
Friedman, J. (2017) 'Why Suspend Judging?', *Noûs* 51, 303–26.
Frisk, H. (1966) 'Über den Gebrauch des Privativpräfixes', in *Kleine Schriften zur Indogermanistik und zur griechischen Wortkunde*, Göteborg, 183–229.
von Fritz, K. (1921) 'Kleitomachos', in *RE* XI.1, 656–9.
von Fritz, K. (1952) 'Polemon 8a', in *RE* XXI.2, 2524–9.
von Fritz, K. (1972) 'Zenon von Sidon', in *RE* X.A, 122–38.
Fruyt, M. (1980) 'L'origine de latin *mordicus*', *Revue belge de philologie et d'histoire* 58, 47–52.
Fuentes González, P. P. (2005) 'Nouménios d'Apamée', in R. Goulet (ed.), *Dictionnaire des philosophes antiques*, vol. 5b, Paris, 724–40.
Fuhrer, T. (1992) 'Das Kriterium der Wahrheit in Augustins *Contra Academicos*', *Vigiliae Christianae* 46, 257–75.
Fuhrer, T. (1993) 'Der Begriff *veri simile* bei Cicero und Augustin', *Museum Helveticum* 50, 107–25.
Fuhrer, T. (1997) *Augustin, Contra Academicos (vel De Academicis), Bücher 2 und 3*, Berlin and New York.
Furley, D. J. (1987) *The Greek Cosmologists*, Vol. 1: *The Formation of the Atomic Theory and its Earliest Critics*, Cambridge.
Fussl, M. (1999) 'Disciplinae liberales', in *Augustinus-Lexikon* vol. 2, fasc. 3/4, 472–85.

Gaertner, J. F. (2005) *Ovid, Epistulae ex Ponto, Book 1*, Oxford.
Gaertner, J. F. (2007) 'Tum und Tunc in der Augusteischen Dichtersprache', *Rheinisches Museum für Philologie* 150, 211-24.
García-Hernández, B. (1996) 'Lat. *tueor*. Del análisis estructural a la investigación histórica', in Bammesberger, A. and Heberlein, F. (eds), *Akten des VIII. Internationalen Kolloquiums zur Lateinischen Linguistik*, Heidelberg, 385-400.
Gatti, P. (2011) 'Nonio Marcello e la *Compendiosa Doctrina*', in R. Ferri (ed.), *The Latin of Roman Lexicography*, Pisa and Rome, 49-62.
Gawlick, G. and Görler, W. (1994) 'Cicero', in H. Flashar (ed.), *Grundriss der Geschichte der Philosophie, Die Philosophie der Antike* 4, *Die Hellenistische Philosophie, Zweiter Halbband*, Basel, 991-1168.
Gelzer, M. (1926) 'L. Licinius Lucullus [104]', in *RE* 13.1, 376-414.
Gendler, T. S. and Hawthorne, J. (2006) 'Introduction: Perceptual Experience', in T. S. Gendler and J. Hawthorne (eds), *Perceptual Experience*, Oxford, 1-30.
Georges, H. (1913-18) *Ausführliches lateinisch-deutsches Handwörterbuch*, Hanover.
Gernet, L. (1956) 'Choses visibles et choses invisibles', *Revue Philosophique de la France et de l'Étranger* 146, 79-86.
Gersh, S. (1986) *Middle Platonism and Neoplatonism: The Latin Tradition*, 2 vols, Notre Dame.
Geymonat, M. (2009) 'Arithmetic and Geometry in Ancient Rome: Surveyors, Intellectuals, and Poets', *Nuncius* 24, 11-34.
Giani, S. (1993) *Pseudo-Archita. L'educazione morale*, Rome.
Giannantoni, G. (1991) *Socratis et Socraticorum Reliquiae*, 4 vols, Naples.
Gieré, A. (1986) *Hippodromus und Xystus—Untersuchungen zu römischen Gartenformen*, Zürich (diss. phil.).
Gigante, M. (1976) 'Polemonis Academici Fragmenta', *Rendiconti della Accademia di Archeologia, Lettere e Belle Arti* 51, 93-144.
Gigante, M. (1990) 'I frammenti di Sirone', *Paideia* 45, 175-98.
Gigon, O. (1962) 'Die Szenerie des ciceronischen Hortensius', *Philologus* 106, 222-45.
Gigon, O. (1988) 'The Peripatos in Cicero's *De Finibus*', in W. W. Fortenbaugh and R. W. Sharples (eds), *Theophrastean Studies (RUSCH 3)*, New Brunswick and London, 259-71.
Gilbert, N. (2019) 'Lucius Saufeius and his Lost Prehistory of Rome: Intellectual Culture in the Late Republic (Servius *Ad Aen.* 1.6)', *Classical Philology* 114, 25-46.
Gildenhard, I. (2007) *Paideia Romana: Cicero's Tusculan Disputations*, Cambridge.
Gildenhard, I. (2013) 'Of Cicero's Plato: Fictions, Forms, Foundations', in M. Schofield (ed.), *Aristotle, Plato and Pythagoreanism in the First Century B.C.—New Directions for Philosophy*, Cambridge, 225-75.
Gildenhard, I. (2013a) 'Cicero's Dialogues: Historiography Manqué and the Evidence of Fiction', in S. Föllinger and G. M. Müller (eds), *Der Dialog in der Antike: Formen und Funktionen einer literarischen Gattung zwischen Philosophie, Wissensvermittlung und dramatischer Inszenierung*, Berlin and New York, 235-74.
Gill, C. (2012) 'The Transformation of Aristotle's Ethics in Roman Philosophy', in J. Miller (ed.), *The Reception of Aristotle's Ethics*, Cambridge, 31-52.
Gill, C. (2016) 'Antiochus' Theory of *oikeiōsis*', in J. Annas and G. Betegh (eds), *Cicero's 'De Finibus'—Philosophical Approaches*, Cambridge, 221-47.
Gill, M. L. (1987) 'Matter and Flux in Plato's Timaeus', *Phronesis* 32, 34-53.
Giusta, M. (1969) 'Due edizioni originali delle *Tusculane*?', *Atti della Accademia delle Scienze di Torino, Classe di Scienze Morali, Storiche e Filologiche* 103, 437-99.
Giusta, M. (1976) 'L'opusculo pseudogalenico Ὅτι αἱ ποιότητες ἀσώματοι (edizione critica, traduzione e note)', *Memorie dell'Accademia delle Scienze di Torino*, serie 4a, 34, Turin.
Giusta, M. (2012²) *I Dossografi di Etica*, 2 vols, Turin (1st edn published in 1964).

Glidden, D. (1979) '*Sensus* and Sense Perception in *De Rerum Natura*', *California Studies in Classical Antiquity* 12, 155-81.
Glucker, J. (1978) *Antiochus and the Late Academy*, Göttingen.
Glucker, J. (1978a) 'Dunttia (Cicero Lucullus 135)', *Classical Philology* 73, 47-9.
Glucker, J. (1988) 'Cicero's Philosophical Affiliations', in J. Dillon and A. A. Long (eds), *The Question of 'Eclecticism'*, Berkeley and Los Angeles, 34-69.
Glucker, J. (1994) 'The Origin of ΥΠΑΡΧΩ and ΥΠΑΡΞΙΣ as Philosophical Terms', in F. Romano and D. P. Taormina (eds), *Hyparxis e Hypostasis nel Neoplatonismo*, Firenze, 1-23.
Glucker, J. (1995) '*Probabile*, *Veri Simile*, and Related Terms', in J. G. F. Powell (ed.), *Cicero the Philosopher*, Oxford, 115-43.
Glucker, J. (1997) 'Socrates in the Academic Books and other Ciceronian Works', in B. Inwood and J. Mansfeld (eds), *Assent and Argument: Studies in Cicero's Academic Books*, Leiden, 58-88.
Glucker, J. (2001) 'Carneades in Rome: Some Unsolved Problems', in J. G. F. Powell and J. North (eds), *Cicero's Republic, Bulletin of the Institute of Classical Studies*, suppl. no. 76, London, 57-82.
Glucker, J. (2002) review of Fladerer (1996), *Gnomon* 74, 289-95.
Glucker, J. (2004) 'The Philonian/Metrodorians: Problems of Method in Ancient Philosophy', *Elenchos* 25, 99-154.
Glucker, J. (2012) 'Cicero's Remarks on Translating Philosophical Terms—Some General Problems', in J. Glucker and C. Burnett (eds), *Greek into Latin from Antiquity into the Nineteenth Century*, London and Turin, 37-96.
Glucker, J. (2015) 'Cicero as Translator and Cicero in Translation', *Philologica* [Kyoto] 10, 37-53.
Goebel, G. H. (1989) 'Probability in the Earliest Rhetorical Theory', *Mnemosyne* 42, 41-53.
Goedeckemeyer, A. (1905) *Geschichte des griechischen Skeptizismus*, Leipzig.
Goerenz, J. A. (1810) *M. T. Ciceronis Philosophica Omnia*, Leipzig and London, 3 vols.
Goh, I. (2018) 'Scepticism at the Birth of Satire: Carneades in Lucilius' *Concilium Deorum*', *Classical Quarterly* 68, 128-42.
Golden, G. K. (2013) *Crisis Management during the Roman Republic: The Role of Political Institutions in Emergencies*, Cambridge.
Goldschmidt, V. (1972) 'ὑπάρχειν e ὑφεστάναι dans la philosophie stoïcienne', *Revue des Études Grecques* 85, 331-44.
Gomoll, H. (1933) *Der stoische Philosoph Hekaton: seine Begriffswelt und Nachwirkung unter Beigabe seiner Fragmente*, Berlin.
Gomperz, H. (1933) 'ΟΨΙΣ ΤΩΝ ΑΔΗΛΩΝ ΤΑ ΦΑΙΝΟΜΕΝΑ', *Hermes* 68, 341-3.
Görler, W. (1974) *Untersuchungen zu Ciceros Philosophie*, Heidelberg.
Görler, W. (1980) Review of Straume-Zimmermann (1976), *Gnomon* 52, 123-30.
Görler, W. (1989) 'Cicero und die "Schule des Aristoteles"', in W. W. Fortenbaugh and P. Steinmetz (eds), *Cicero's Knowledge of the Peripatos*, New Brunswick and London, 246-63.
Görler, W. (1994) 'Älterer Pyrrhonismus—Jüngere Akademie—Antiochus aus Askalon', in H. Flashar (ed.), *Grundriss der Geschichte der Philosophie, Die Philosophie der Antike* 4, *Die Hellenistische Philosophie, Zweiter Halbband*, Basel, 721-989.
Görler, W. (1995) 'Silencing the Troublemaker: *De Legibus* 1.39 and the Continuity of Cicero's Scepticism', in J. G. F. Powell (ed.), *Cicero the Philosopher*, Oxford, 85-113.
Görler, W. (2004) *Kleine Schriften zur hellenistisch-römischen Philosophie*, Leiden and New York.
Görler, W. (2004a) 'Antiochus von Askalon ueber die "Alten" und ueber die Stoa. Beobachtungen zu Cicero, *Academici Posteriores* I 24-43', in *Kleine Schriften zur hellenistisch-römischen Philosophie*, Leiden and New York, 87-104.
Görler, W. (2004b) 'Ein sprachlicher Zufall und seine Folgen. "Wahrscheinliches" bei Karneades und bei Cicero', in *Kleine Schriften zur hellenistisch-römischen Philosophie*, Leiden and New York, 60-75.

Görler, W. (2004c) 'Cicero's Philosophical Stance in the *Lucullus*', in *Kleine Schriften zur hellenistisch-römischen Philosophie*, Leiden and New York, 268-89.
Görler, W. (2004d) 'Cicero und die "Schule des Aristoteles"', in *Kleine Schriften zur hellenistisch-römischen Philosophie*, Leiden and New York, 193-211.
Görler, W. (2004e) 'Zum *virtus*-Fragment des Lucilius (1326-1338 Marx) und zur Geschichte der stoischen Güterlehre', in *Kleine Schriften zur hellenistisch-römischen Philosophie*, Leiden and New York, 105-35.
Görler, W. (2004f) 'ΑΣΘΕΝΗΣ ΣΥΓΚΑΤΑΘΕΣΙΣ—Zur stoischen Erkenntnistheorie', in *Kleine Schriften zur hellenistisch-römischen Philosophie*, Leiden and New York, 1-15.
Görler, W. (2011) 'Cicero, *De finibus bonorum et malorum*, Buch 5. Beobachtungen zur Quelle und zum Aufbau', *Elenchos* 32, 329-54.
Görler, W. (2012) review of Sedley (2012b), *Elenchos* 33, 376-83.
Görler, W. (2016) 'Erwünschtes Irren—Überlegungen zu einem provozierenden Bekenntnis Ciceros', in P. Galand and E. Malaspina (eds), *Vérité et apparence: mélanges en l'honneur de Carlos Lévy offerts par ses amis et ses disciples*, Turnhout, 245-55.
Gorman, R. (2005) *The Socratic Method in the Dialogues of Plato*, Stuttgart.
Gottschalk, H. B. (2004) 'Peripatetic Reactions to Hellenistic Epistemology', in W. W. Fortenbaugh and S. A. White (eds), *Lyco of Troas and Hieronymus of Rhodes—Text, Translation, and Discussion*, New Brunswick and London, 375-88.
Goulet, R. (1994) 'Dardanos d'Athènes', in R. Goulet (ed.), *Dictionnaire des philosophes antiques*, vol. 2, Paris, 613-14.
Goulet, R. (1994a) 'Calliphon', in R. Goulet (ed.), *Dictionnaire des philosophes antiques*, vol. 2, Paris, 176-7.
Goulet, R. (1994b) 'Diodoros de Tyr', in R. Goulet (ed.), *Dictionnaire des philosophes antiques*, vol. 2, Paris, 795.
Goulet, R. (2005) 'Mnésarque d'Athènes', in R. Goulet (ed.), *Dictionnaire des philosophes antiques*, vol. 4, Paris, 538-42.
Goulet, R. (2005a) 'Ménédème d'Érétrie', in R. Goulet (ed.), *Dictionnaire des philosophes antiques*, vol. 4, Paris, 443-54.
Goulet, R. (2005b) 'Métrodore de Chios', in R. Goulet (ed.), *Dictionnaire des philosophes antiques*, vol. 4, Paris, 506-8.
Gourevitch, D. (1984) *Le triangle hippocratique dans le monde gréco-romain. Le malade, sa maladie et son médecin*, Paris.
Gourinat, J.-B. (2000) *La dialectique des Stoïciens*, Paris.
Gourinat, J.-B. (2009) 'The Stoics on Matter and Prime Matter: "Corporealism" and the Imprint of Plato's *Timaeus*', in R. Salles (ed.), *God and Cosmos in Stoicism*, Oxford, 46-70.
Gourinat, J.-B. (2014) '*Adsensio in nostra potestate*: "from us" and "up to us" in Ancient Stoicism—a Plea for Reassessment', in P. Destrée, R. Salles, and M. Zingano (eds), *What Is Up to Us? Studies on Agency and Responsibility in Ancient Philosophy*, Sankt Augustin, 141-50.
Gourinat, J.-B. (2016) 'Les paradoxes stoïciens sont-ils "socratiques"? (Cicéron, Lucullus, 136)', *Antiquorum philosophia* 10, 47-65.
Gourinat, J.-B. (2018) 'Zénon de Citium', in R. Goulet (ed.), *Dictionnaire des philosophes antiques*, vol. 7, Paris, 364-93.
Gourinat, J.-B. and Alesse, F. (2012) 'Panétius de Rhodes', in R. Goulet (ed.), *Dictionnaire des philosophes antiques*, vol. 5a, Paris, 131-8.
Gow, A. S. F. (1952^2) *Theocritus*, 2 vols, Cambridge.
Gowers, E. (2012) *Horace—Satires Book 1*, Cambridge.
Graeser, A. (1970) 'Demokrit und die skeptische Formel', *Hermes* 98, 300-17.
Graeser, A. (1975) *Zenon von Kition—Positionen und Probleme*, Berlin and New York.

Gratwick, A. (1982) 'The Satires of Ennius and Lucilius', in E. J. Kenney and W. V. Clausen (eds), *The Cambridge History of Classical Literature*, Vol. 2: *Latin Literature*, Cambridge, 156–72.
Graver, M. (2002) *Cicero on the Emotions: Tusculan Disputations 3 and 4*, Chicago.
Graver, M. (2007) *Stoicism and Emotion*, Chicago.
Graver, M. (2016) 'Honor and the Honorable: Cato's Discourse in De Finibus 3', in J. Annas and G. Betegh (eds), *Cicero's 'De Finibus': Philosophical Approaches*, Cambridge, 118–46.
Green, W. M. (1970) *Sancti Aurelii Augustini Contra Academicos, De Beata Vita, De Ordine, De Magistro, De Libero Arbitrio*, Turnhout.
Griffin, M. T. (1989) 'Philosophy, Politics, and Politicians at Rome', in M. Griffin and J. Barnes (eds), *Philosophia Togata*, Oxford, 1–37.
Griffin, M. T. (1995) 'Philosophical Badinage in Cicero's Letters', in J. G. F. Powell (ed.), *Cicero the Philosopher*, Oxford, 325–46.
Griffin, M. T. (1997) 'The Composition of the *Academica*—Motives and Versions', in B. Inwood and J. Mansfeld (eds), *Assent and Argument—Studies in Cicero's Academic Books*, Leiden, 1–35.
Griffin, M. T. and Atkins, E. M. (1991) *Cicero: On Duties*, Cambridge.
Grilli, A. (1975) 'Cicerone tra Antioco e Panezio', *Ciceroniana* 2, 73–80.
Grilli, A. (2010²) *Marco Tullio Cicerone: Ortensio*, Bologna.
Gruen, E. (1965) 'The Lex Varia', *Journal of Roman Studies* 55, 59–73.
Gschwantler, K. (1978) 'Zeuxis no. 1', in *RE* S XV, 1481–8.
Guérard, C. (1989) 'Ariston de Chios', in R. Goulet (ed.), *Dictionnaire des philosophes antiques*, vol. 1, Paris, 400–3.
Guérard, C. (1994) 'Denys d'Héraclée', in R. Goulet (ed.), *Dictionnaire des philosophes antiques*, vol. 2, Paris, 724–5.
Guérard, C. (2000) 'Hérillos', in R. Goulet (ed.), *Dictionnaire des philosophes antiques*, vol. 3, Paris, 631–2.
Guérard, C., Dumont, J.-P., Delattre, D., and Flamand, J.-M. (1994) 'Diogène de Séleucie, dit le Babylonien', in R. Goulet (ed.), *Dictionnaire des philosophes antiques*, vol. 2, Paris, 807–12.
Guérard, C. and Puech, B. (1989) 'Antipatros de Tarse', in R. Goulet (ed.), *Dictionnaire des philosophes antiques*, vol. 1, Paris, 219–23.
Guillaumin, J.-Y. (2003) 'Géometrié et arpentage. Le *geometres* à l'époque néronienne d'après Sénèque, *ad Luc.* 88, §§10–13', in M. Garrido-Hory and A. Gonzales (eds), *Histoire, espaces et marges de l'Antiquité: hommages à Monique Clavel-Lévêque*, vol. i, Besançon, 109–32.
Gundel, W. (1933) 'Mond', in *RE* XVI.1, 76–105.
Gurd, S. (2007) 'Cicero and Editorial Revision', *Classical Antiquity* 26, 49–80.
Gutas, D. (2016) 'Théophraste d'Érèse', in R. Goulet (ed.), *Dictionnaire des philosophes antiques*, vol. 6, Paris, 1034–1121.
Gwyn Morgan, M. (1974) 'Three Notes on Varro's *Logistorici*', *Museum Helveticum* 31, 117–28.
Habermehl, P. (2006) *Petronius, 'Satyrica' 79–141: ein philologisch-literarischer Kommentar*, Berlin and New York.
Habets, A. C. J. (1997) *A History of the Division of Philosophy in Antiquity*, Leiden.
Hadot, P. (1969) 'Vorgeschichte des Begriffes "Existenz"—ΥΠΑΡΧΕΙΝ bei den Stoikern', *Archiv für Begriffsgeschichte* 13, 115–27.
Haffter, H. (1934) *Untersuchungen zur altlateinischen Dichtersprache*, Berlin.
Hagendahl, H. (1967) *Augustine and the Latin Classics*, Vol. 1: *Testimonia*, Vol. 2: *Augustine's Attitude*, Göteborg.
Hahmann, A. (2015) 'Epikur über den Gegenstand der Wahrnehmung', *Archiv für Geschichte der Philosophie* 97, 271–307.
Hahmann, A. (2015a) 'Epicurus on Truth and Phantasia', *Ancient Philosophy* 35, 155–32.
Halla-Aho, H. and Kruschwitz, P. (2010) 'Colloquial and Literary Language in Early Roman Tragedy', in E. Dickey and A. Chahoud (eds), *Colloquial and Literary Latin*, Cambridge, 127–53.

Haltenhoff, A. (1998) *Kritik der akademischen Skepsis—ein Kommentar zu Cicero, Lucullus 1-62*, Frankfurt a.M.
Hankinson, R. J. (1994) 'Usage and Abusage: Galen on Language', in S. Everson (ed.), *Language*, Cambridge, 166-87.
Hankinson, R. J. (1995) *The Sceptics*, London.
Hankinson, R. J. (2007) 'Self-Refutation and the Sorites', in D. Scott (ed.), *Maieusis: Essays in Ancient Philosophy in Honour of Myles Burnyeat*, Oxford, 351-73.
Hardie, P. R. (2007) 'Lucretius and Later Latin Literature in Antiquity', in S. Gillespie and P. R. Hardie (eds), *The Cambridge Companion to Lucretius*, Cambridge, 111-27.
Hardie, P. R. (2013) 'Trojan Palimpsests: The Archeology of Roman History in Aeneid 2', in J. Farrell and D. P. Nelis (2013) *Augustan Poetry and the Roman Republic*, Oxford, 107-23.
Harries, J. (1989) 'Constructing the Judge: Judicial Accountability and the Culture of Criticism in Late Antiquity', in R. Miles (ed.), *Constructing Identities in Late Antiquity*, London, 214-33.
Hartung, H.-J. (1970) *Ciceros Methode bei der Übersetzung griechischer philosophischer Termini*, Hamburg (diss. phil.).
Hatzimichali, M. (2011) *Potamo of Alexandria and the Emergence of Eclecticism in Late Hellenistic Philosophy*, Cambridge.
Hatzimichali, M. (2012) 'Antiochus' Biography', in D. Sedley (ed.), *The Philosophy of Antiochus*, Oxford, 9-30.
Haupt, M. (1866) 'Analecta', *Hermes* 1, 21-46.
Haynes, H. (2004) 'Tacitus's Dangerous World', *Classical Antiquity* 23, 33-61.
Heath, T. (1913) *Aristarchus of Samos: The Ancient Copernicus*, Oxford.
Heinze, R. (1925) 'Auctoritas', *Hermes* 60, 348-66.
Hellegouarc'h, J. (1972) *Le vocabulaire latin des relations et des partis politiques sous la république*, Paris.
Helmig, C. (2007) 'Plato's Arguments against Conceptualism. *Parmenides* 132B3-C11 Reconsidered', *Elenchos* 28, 303-36.
Helmig, C. (2010) 'Proclus' Criticism of Aristotle's Theory of Abstraction and Concept Formation in *Analytica Posteriora* II 19', in F. A. J. de Hass, M. Leunissen, and M. Martijn (eds), *Interpreting Aristotle's Posterior Analytics in Late Antiquity and Beyond*, Leiden, 27-54.
Helmig, C. (2012) *Forms and Concepts: Concept Formation in the Platonic Tradition*, Berlin and Boston.
Hendrickson, G. L. (1939) 'Brutus *De virtute*', *American Journal of Philology* 60, 401-13.
Henrichs, A. (1974) 'Die Kritik der stoischen Theologie in *PHerc*. 1428', *Cronache Ercolanesi* 4, 5-32.
Hermann, C. (1851) *Disputatio de Philone Larissaeo*, Göttingen.
Hermann, C. (1855) *De Philone Larissaeo Disputatio Altera*, Göttingen.
Hermann, K. Fr. (1852) 'Beiträge zur Kritik von Cicero's Lucullus', *Philologus* 7, 466-76.
Heumann, H. G. (1891) *Handlexikon zu den Quellen des römischen Rechts*, Jena.
Hickson, F. V. (1993) *Roman Prayer Language: Livy and the Aeneid of Vergil*, Stuttgart.
Hine, H. (2016) 'Philosophy and *philosophi* from Cicero to Apuleius', in G. D. Williams and K. Volk (eds), *Roman Reflections—Studies in Latin Philosophy*, Oxford, 13-29.
Hirsch, T. (forthcoming) *Cicero—'De Inventione' Book 1*, Oxford.
Hirzel, R. (1876) 'Über den Protreptikos des Aristoteles', *Hermes* 10, 61-100.
Hirzel, R. (1877) *Untersuchungen zu Cicero's philosophischen Schriften, I. Theil: 'De Natura Deorum'*, Leipzig.
Hirzel, R. (1882) *Untersuchungen zu Cicero's philosophischen Schriften, 2. Theil: 'De Finibus', 'De Officiis'*, Leipzig.
Hirzel, R. (1883) *Untersuchungen zu Cicero's philosophischen Schriften, III. Theil: 'Academica Priora', 'Tusculanae Disputationes'*, Leipzig.

Hirzel, R. (1883a) 'Ein unbeachtetes Komödienfragment', *Hermes* 18, 1-16.
Hirzel, R. (1895) *Der Dialog*, vol. i, Leipzig.
Hobein, H. (1929) 'Staseas', in *RE* III A 2, 2153-58.
Hoffer, S. E. (2007) 'Cicero's "Stomach": Political Indignation and the Use of Repeated Allusive Expressions in Cicero's Correspondence', in R. Morello and A. D. Morrison (eds), *Ancient Letters: Classical and Late Antique Epistolography*, Oxford, 87-106.
Hoffman, D. C. (2008) 'Concerning *Eikos*: Social Expectation and Verisimilitude in Early Attic Rhetoric', *Rhetorica* 26, 1-29.
Hoffmann, E. (1899-1900) *Sancti Aurelii Augustini episcopi 'De Civitate Dei' libri XXII*, Vienna.
Hofmann, J. B. (1951^3) *Lateinische Umgangssprache*, Heidelberg.
Hofmann, J. B. and Szantyr, A. (1965) *Lateinische Syntax und Stilistik*, Munich.
Holford-Strevens, L. (1997) 'Favorinus. A Man of Paradoxes', in M. Griffin. and J. Barnes (eds), *Philosophia Togata II—Plato and Aristotle in Rome*, Oxford, 188-217.
Hollis, A. S. (2007) *Fragments of Roman Poetry c. 60 BC-AD 20*, Oxford.
Hommel, H. (1968) *Ciceros Gebetshymnus an die Philosophie, Tusculanen V 5*, Heidelberg.
Hopwood, B. (2007) 'The Testament of Sempronius Tuditanus', *Antichthon* 41, 1-12.
Horsfall, N. (1972) 'Varro and Caesar: Three Chronological Problems', *Bulletin of the Institute of Classical Studies* 19, 120-8.
Housman, A. E. (1926) *M. Annaei Lucani Belli Civilis Libri Decem*, Oxford.
van den Hout, T. (1999) *A Commentary on the Letters of M. Cornelius Fronto*, Leiden and Boston.
Huby, P. (1999) *Theophrastus of Eresus. Commentary Vol. 4: Psychology (Texts 265-327)*, Leiden.
Hülsemann, F. (1806) *M. T. Ciceronis Academica, seu academicorum ueterum disputationes de natura et imperio cognitionis humanae*, Magdeburg.
Hülser, K. (1987-8) *Die Fragmente zur Dialektik der Stoiker*, Stuttgart-Bad Cannstatt.
Hunt, J. M. (1981) 'On Editing the Letters of Cicero', *Classical Philology* 76, 215-24.
Hunt, T. J. (1998) *A Textual History of Cicero's 'Academici Libri'*, Leiden.
Hussey, E. (1993^2) *Aristotle—Physics Books III and IV*, Oxford.
Hutchinson, D. S. and Johnson, M. R. (2005) 'Authenticating Aristotle's Protrepticus', *Oxford Studies in Ancient Philosophy* 29, 193-294.
Hyde, D. (2014) 'Sorites Paradox', in *The Stanford Encyclopedia of Philosophy* (Winter), Edward N. Zalta (ed.), URL = <http://plato.stanford.edu/archives/win2014/entries/sorites-paradox/>.
Hyman, M. D. (2005) 'Terms for "Word" in Roman Grammar', in Th. Fögen (ed.), *Antike Fachtexte—Ancient Technical Texts*, Berlin, 155-70.
Ierodiakonou, K. (1993) 'The Stoic Division of Philosophy', *Phronesis* 38, 57-74.
Ierodiakonou, K. (1995) 'Alexander of Aphrodisias on Medicine as a Stochastic Art', in Ph. van der Eijk et al. (eds), *Ancient Medicine in its Socio-cultural Context*, Amsterdam, 473-85.
Ierodiakonou, K. (2012) 'The Notion of *Enargeia* in Hellenistic Philosophy', in B. Morison and K. Ierodiakonou (eds), *Episteme, etc.: Essays in Honour of Jonathan Barnes*, Oxford, 60-73.
Ierodiakonou, K. (2015) 'Hellenistic Philosophers on the Phenomenon of Changing Colours', in B. Holmes and K.-D. Fischer (eds), *The Frontiers of Ancient Science—Essays in Honor of Heinrich von Staden*, Berlin and New York, 227-50.
Indelli, G. (1988) *Filodemo: L'ira*, Naples.
Innes, D. C. (1978) 'Phidias and Cicero', *Classical Quarterly* 28, 470-1.
Inwood, B. (1985) *Ethics and Human Action in Early Stoicism*, Oxford.
Inwood, B. (2005) *Reading Seneca—Stoic Philosophy at Rome*, Oxford.
Inwood, B. (2005a) 'Politics and Paradox in Seneca's *De Beneficiis*', in Inwood (2005), 65-94.
Inwood, B. (2005b) 'Rules and Reasoning in Stoic Ethics', in Inwood (2005), 95-131.
Inwood, B. (2005c) 'Getting to Goodness', in Inwood (2005), 271-301.
Inwood, B. (2007) *Seneca—Selected Philosophical Letters*, Oxford.

Inwood, B. (2012) 'Antiochus on Physics', in D. N. Sedley (ed.), *The Philosophy of Antiochus*, Cambridge, 188–219.
Inwood, B. (2014) 'Ancient Goods—the *Tria Genera Bonorum* in Ethical Theory', in M.-K. Lee (ed.), *Strategies of Argument—Essays in Ancient Ethics, Epistemology, and Logic*, Oxford and New York, 255–80.
Inwood, B. (2014a) *Ethics after Aristotle*, Cambridge, MA.
Inwood, B. (2016) 'The Voice of Nature', in J. Annas and G. Betegh (eds), *Cicero's 'De Finibus': Philosophical Approaches*, Cambridge, 147–66.
Inwood, B. and Mansfeld, J. (1997) *Assent and Argument: Studies in Cicero's Academic Books*, Leiden.
Ioppolo, A. M. (1980) *Aristone di Chio e lo stoicismo antico*, Naples.
Ioppolo, A. M. (1983) 'The Academic Position of Favorinus of Arelate', *Phronesis* 38, 183–213.
Ioppolo, A. M. (1984) 'Doxa ed epoché in Arcesilao', *Elenchos* 5, 317–63.
Ioppolo, A. M. (1985) 'Lo Stoicismo di Erillo', *Phronesis* 30, 58–78.
Ioppolo, A. M. (1986) *Opinione e scienza: Il dibattito tra Stoici e Accademici nel III e nel II secolo a.C.*, Naples.
Ioppolo, A. M. (1990) 'Presentation and Assent: A Physical and Cognitive Problem in Early Stoicism', *Classical Quarterly* 40, 433–49.
Ioppolo, A. M. (1993) 'The Academic Position of Favorinus of Arelate', *Phronesis* 38, 183–213.
Ioppolo, A. M. (1995) 'Socrate nelle tradizioni accademica-scettica e pirroniana', in G. Giannantoni et al. (eds), *La tradizione socratica—Seminario di studi*, Naples, 89–123.
Ioppolo, A. M. (1996) 'Fidelity to Zeno's Theory', in E. A. Moutsopoulos (ed.), *Chypre et les origines du Stoïcisme, Actes du Colloque: Paris 12–13 Mai 1995*, Paris, 62–73.
Ioppolo, A. M. (2007) 'L'assenso nella filosofia di Clitomaco: un problema di linguaggio', in A. M. Ioppolo and D. Sedley (eds), *Pyrrhonists, Patricians, Platonizers—Hellenistic Philosophy in the Period 155–86 BC*, Naples, 227–67.
Ioppolo, A. M. (2009) *La testimonianza di Sesto Empirico sull'Accademia scettica*, Naples.
Ioppolo, A. M. (2012) 'Chrysippus and the Action Theory of Aristo of Chios', in B. Inwood and R. Kamtekar (eds), *Virtue and Happiness: Essays in Honour of Julia Annas*, Oxford Studies in Ancient Philosophy, suppl. vol., Oxford, 197–222.
Ioppolo, A. M. (2013) *Dibattiti Filosofici Ellenistici—Dottrina delle Cause, Stoicismo, Accademia Scettica*, ed. B. Centrone, R. Chiaradonna, D. Quarantotto, E. Spinelli, Sankt Augustin.
Ioppolo, A. M. (2013a) 'Arcésilas dans le *Lucullus* de Cicéron', in Ioppolo (2013) 251–70.
Ioppolo, A. M. (2016) '*Sententia explosa*: Criticism of Stoic Ethics in *De Finibus* 4', in J. Annas and G. Betegh (eds), *Cicero's 'De Finibus': Philosophical Approaches*, Cambridge, 167–97.
Ioppolo, A. M. (2017) 'Clitomachus on what it means to follow the "probable"', in Y. Z. Liebersohn, I. Ludlam, and A. Edleheit (eds), *For a Skeptical Peripatetic—Festschrift in Honour of John Glucker*, Sankt Augustin, 192–219.
Ioppolo, A. M. (2018) 'Arcesilaus', in D. E. Machuca and B. Reed (eds), *Skepticism from Antiquity to the Present*, London, 36–50.
Irwin, T. (1986) 'Stoic and Aristotelian Conceptions of Happiness', in M. Schofield and G. Striker (eds), *The Norms of Nature—Studies in Hellenistic Ethics*, Cambridge, 205–44.
Irwin, T. (1996) 'Stoic Individuals', *Noûs* 30, suppl.: Philosophical Perspectives, 10, Metaphysics, 459–80.
Irwin, T. (2007) *The Development of Ethics*, Vol. I: *From Socrates to the Reformation*, Oxford.
Irwin, T. (2012) 'Antiochus, Aristotle and Stoics on Degrees of Happiness', in D. N. Sedley (ed.), *The Philosophy of Antiochus*, Cambridge, 151–72.
Isnardi Parente, M. (1980) *Speusippo: Frammenti*, Naples.
Isnardi Parente, M. (1981) *Senocrate—Ermodoro: Frammenti*, Naples.
Isnardi Parente, M. (2016) 'Speusippe de Myrrhinonte', in R. Goulet (ed.), *Dictionnaire des philosophes antiques*, vol. 6, Paris, 528–39.

Isnardi Parente, M. (2018) 'Xénocrate de Chalcédoine', in R. Goulet (ed.), *Dictionnaire des philosophes antiques*, vol. 7, Paris, 194–208.
Janáček, K. (1971) *Sextus Empiricus' Sceptical Methods*, Prague.
Janko, R. (1984) *Aristotle on Comedy: Towards a Reconstruction of Poetics II*, London.
Jenkins, F. W. (1985) *Ammianus Marcellinus' Knowledge and Use of Republican Latin Literature*, Urbana, PhD thesis.
Jenkyns, R. (2013) *God, Space, and City in the Roman Imagination*, Oxford.
Jocelyn, H. D. (1968) *The Tragedies of Ennius*, Cambridge.
Jocelyn, H. D. (1977) 'The Ruling Class of the Roman Republic and Greek Philosophers', *Bulletin of the John Rylands Library* 59, 323–66.
Joffre, M. D. (2005) 'Les conditions morphosyntaxiques de l'ambiguïté volontaire—l'emploi de *videor* dans les chants II et III de l'Énéide', in L. Basset and F. Biville (eds), *Les jeux et les ruses de l'ambiguïté volontaire dans les textes grecs et latins*, Lyon, 91–9.
Johann, H.-T. (1968) *Trauer und Trost: eine quellen- und strukturanalytische Untersuchung der philosophischen Trostschriften über den Tod*, Munich.
Johansen, T. K. (2012) *The Powers of Aristotle's Soul*, Oxford.
Jolivet, V. (1987) 'Xerxes togatus: Lucullus en Campanie', *Mélanges de l'Ecole française de Rome, Antiquité* 99, 875–904.
Jordan, H. (1881) 'Altlateinische Inschrift aus Rom', *Hermes* 16, 225–60.
Kalligas, P., Balla, C., Baziotopoulou-Valavani, E., and Karasmansis, V. (2020) *Plato's Academy: Its Workings and its History*, Oxford.
Kalligas, P., Balla, C., Baziotopoulou-Valavani, E., Karasmansis, V. (2020a) 'Philodemus' History of Philosophers: Plato and the Academy (*PHerc* 1021 and 164)', in Kalligas et al. (eds), *Plato's Academy: Its Workings and its History*, Oxford, 276–383.
Kany-Turpin, J. and Pellegrin, P. (2010) *Cicéron: Les Académiques, Academica*, Paris.
Karamanolis, G. (2006) *Plato and Aristotle in Agreement? Platonists on Aristotle from Antiochus to Porphyry*, Oxford.
Karamanolis, G. (2016) 'Numenius', in *The Stanford Encyclopedia of Philosophy* (Winter), Edward N. Zalta (ed.), URL = <https://plato.stanford.edu/archives/win2016/entries/numenius/>.
Kaser, M. (1971) *Das römische Privatrecht*, Munich.
Kaser, M. and Hackl, K. (1996) *Das römische Zivilprozessrecht*, 2nd edn, Munich.
Kassel, R. and Austin, C. (2001) *Poetae Comici Graeci (PCG)*, Vol. I: *Comoedia Dorica, Mimi, Phlyaces*, Berlin and New York.
Kaster, R. A. (1992) *Studies on the Text of Suetonius, 'De Grammaticis et Rhetoribus'*, Atlanta.
Kaster, R. A. (1995) *C. Suetonius Tranquillus—'De Grammaticis et Rhetoribus'*, Oxford.
Kaster, R. A. (2005) *Emotion, Restraint, and Community in Ancient Rome*, New York and Oxford.
Kaster, R. A. (2006) *Cicero—Speech on Behalf of Publius Sestius*, Oxford.
Katzoff, R. (1973) 'Where Was Agrippina Murdered?', *Historia* 22, 72–8.
Keaveney, A. (1992) *Lucullus. A Life*, London.
Kechagia, E. (2011) *Plutarch against Colotes: A Lesson in the History of Philosophy*, Oxford.
Kendeffy, G. (2016) 'L'appropriation des arguments néoacadémiciens par Lactance', in A.-I. Bouton-Touboulic and C. Lévy (eds), *Scepticisme et religion: constantes et évolutions de la philosophie héllenistique à la philosophie médiévale*, Turnhout, 137–55.
Keppie, L. (2011) '"Guess Who's Coming to Dinner": The Murder of Nero's Mother Agrippina in its Topographical Setting', *Greece and Rome* 58, 33–47.
Kerferd, G. (1967) 'Review of vol. i of Giusta (1964 [i.e. 2012^2])', *Classical Review* 17, 156–8.
Kerferd, G. (1978) 'The Problem of Synkatathesis and Katalepsis in Stoic Doctrine', in J. Brunschwig (ed.), *Les Stoïciens et Leur Logique*, Paris, 251–72.

Keyser, P. T. (2010) 'Elemental Qualities in Flux—a Reconstruction of Strato's Theory of Elements', in M. L. Desclos and W. W. Fortenbaugh (eds), *Strato of Lampsacus*, New Brunswick, 293–312.
Kidd, I. G. (1997) 'What Is a Posidonian Fragment?', in G. W. Most (ed.), *Collecting Fragments—Fragmente sammeln*, Göttingen, 225–36.
Kienast, D. (1954) *Cato der Zensor: seine Persönlichkeit und seine Zeit*, Heidelberg.
Kirwan, C. (1993) *Aristotle—Metaphysics, Books Γ, Δ and E*, Oxford.
Kleijwegt, A. J. (1966) 'Philosophischer Gehalt und persönliche Stellungnahme in *Tusc*. I 9–81', *Mnemosyne* 19, 359–88.
Klein, J. (2014) 'Review of A. G. Long (ed.), *Plato and the Stoics*, Cambridge 2013', *Notre Dame Philosophical Reviews* 2014.09.34.
Klein, J. (2015) 'Making Sense of Stoic Indifferents', *Oxford Studies in Ancient Philosophy* 49, 227–81.
Klein, J. (2016) 'The Stoic Argument from *oikeiōsis*', *Oxford Studies in Ancient Philosophy* 50, 143–200.
Kleve, K. (1978) 'The Philosophical Polemics in Lucretius: A Study in the History of Epicurean Criticism', in *Entretiens sur l'antiquité classique* no. 24: *Lucrèce*, Geneva, 39–71.
Kleve, K. (1983) 'Scurra Atticus: The Epicurean View of Socrates', in *ΣΥΖΗΤΗΣΙΣ: Studi sull' Epicureismo Greco e Romano offerti a Marcello Gigante*, Naples, vol. 2, 227–53.
Knuuttila, S. (2006) *Emotions in Ancient and Medieval Philosophy*, Oxford.
Kondratieff, E. (2015) 'Finding Libo', *Historia* 64, 428–66.
Konstan, D. (2014) 'Epicurus', *The Stanford Encyclopedia of Philosophy* (Summer), Edward N. Zalta (ed.), URL = <http://plato.stanford.edu/archives/sum2014/entries/epicurus/>.
Kotrč, R. (1981) 'The Dodecahedron in Plato's *Timaeus*', *Rheinisches Museum für Philologie* 124, 212–22.
Kragelund, P. (2001) 'Dreams, Religion, and Politics in Republican Rome', *Historia* 50, 53–95.
Krämer, H.-J. (1971) *Platonismus und Hellenistische Philosophie*, Berlin and New York.
Krämer, H.-J. (1983) 'Die Ältere Akademie', in H. Flashar (ed.), *Grundriss der Geschichte der Philosophie, Die Philosophie der Antike 3, Ältere Akademie—Aristoteles—Peripatos*, Basel, 1–174.
Kramer, J. (1998) *Die Sprachbezeichnungen* Latinus *und* Romanus *im Lateinischen und Romanischen*, Berlin.
Kraner, F., Dittenberger, W., and Meusel, H. (1960) *C. Iulii Caesaris Commentarii de Bello Gallico*, Berlin.
Krenkel, W. (1997) 'Zur Chronologie der Menippeen des Varro', *Myrtia* 11, 9–15.
Krische, A. B. (1845) *Ueber Cicero's Akademika*, Göttingen.
Kroll, W. (1913) *M. Tullii Ciceronis Orator*, Leipzig.
Kronenberg, L. (2009) *Allegories of Farming from Greece and Rome—Philosophical Satire in Xenophon, Varro, and Virgil*, Cambridge.
Kroon, C. (1995) *Discourse Particles in Latin—A Study of 'Nam', 'Enim', 'Autem', 'Vero' and 'At'*, Amsterdam.
Kübler, B. (1895) 'Ueber die Bedeutung von *iudicium* und *formula* bei Cicero und in den übrigen Quellen der republikanischen Zeit', *Zeitschrift der Savigny-Stiftung für Rechtsgeschichte, Romanistische Abteilung* 16, 137–80.
Kübler, B. (1899) 'Classis 2', in *RE* III, 2630–2.
Kühner, R. (1853) *M. Tullii Ciceronis Tusculanarum Disputationum Libri Quinque*, Jena (4th edn).
Kullmann, W. (2007) *Aristoteles—Über die Teile der Lebewesen*, Berlin.
Kumaniecki, K. (1962) 'Cicerone e Varrone. Storia di una conscienza', *Athenaeum* 40, 219–43.
Kunkel, W. (1952) *Herkunft und soziale Stellung der römischen Juristen*, Weimar.

Kunkel, W. and Wittmann, R. (1995) *Staatsordnung und Staatspraxis in der Römischen Republik*, Handbuch der Altertumswissenschaft. Rechtsgeschichte des Altertums. Band X, 3.2.2, Munich.

Kupreeva, I. (2003) 'Qualities and Bodies: Alexander against the Stoics', *Oxford Studies in Ancient Philosophy* 25, 297-344.

Kupreeva, I. (2009) 'Stoic Themes in Peripatetic Sources?', in R. Salles (ed.), *God and Cosmos in Stoicism*, Oxford, 135-70.

Kupreeva, I. (2012) 'Polémon d'Athènes', in R. Goulet (ed.), *Dictionnaire des philosophes antiques*, vol. 5b, Paris, 1190-4.

Lachapelle, G. F. de (2011) *Publilius Syrus—Sentences*, Paris.

Laks, A. (1997) 'Du témoigne comme fragment', in G. W. Most (ed.), *Collecting Fragments—Fragmente sammeln*, Göttingen, 237-72.

Lammert, F. (1939) 'Opinator', in *RE* XVIII.1, 681-3.

Lampe, K. (2015) *The Birth of Hedonism. The Cyrenaic Philosophers and Pleasure as a Way of Life*, Princeton.

Landgraf, G. (1896) 'Glossographie und Wörterbuch', *Archiv für Lateinische Lexikographie und Grammatik mit Einschluss des älteren Mittellateins* 9, 355-446.

Landolfi, L. (2004) 'Ovidio, Manilio, e le *laudes astronomiae*', *Vichiana* 6, 232-52.

Landolfi, L. (2018) 'Il significato del termine σύγγραμμα', *Glotta* 94, 213-33.

Langenberg, G. (1959) *M. Terenti Varronis 'Liber de philosophia'—Ausgabe und Erklärung der Fragmente*, Xanten (diss. phil.).

Langerbeck, H. (1935) *ΔΟΞΙΣ ΕΠΙΡΥΣΜΙΗ: Studien zu Demokrits Ethik und Erkenntnislehre*, Berlin.

Langslow, D. R. (2000) *Medical Latin in the Roman Empire*, Oxford.

Latte, K. (1968) '*Augur* und *Templum* in der varronischen Auguralformel', in *Kleine Schriften*, Munich, 91-105.

Layne, D. A. (2018) 'The Anonymous Prolegomena to Platonic Philosophy', in H. Tarrant, D. A. Layne, D. Baltzly, and F. Renaud (eds), *Brill's Companion to the Reception of Plato in Antiquity*, Leiden and Boston, 533-54.

Le Boeuffle, A. (1977) *Les noms latins d'astres et de constellations*, Paris.

Leach, E. W. (1999) 'Ciceronian "*Bi-Marcus*": Correspondence with M. Terentius Varro and L. Papirius Paetus in 46 B.C.E.', *Transactions of the American Philological Association* 129, 139-79.

Leach, E. W. (2014) 'M. Atilius Regulus—Making Defeat into Victory: Diverse Values in an Ambivalent Story', in C. Pieper and J. Ker (eds), *Valuing the Past in the Greco-Roman World*, Leiden, 243-68.

Leavy, S. A. (1997) 'Commentary on "The Stoic Conception of Mental Disorder"', *Philosophy, Psychiatry, and Psychology* 4, 295-6.

Lee, R. W. (1940) '*Ut Pictura Poesis*: The Humanistic Theory of Painting', *The Art Bulletin* 22, 197-269.

Leeman, A. D., Pinkster, H., and Rabbie, E. (1985) *M. T. Cicero: 'De Oratore' Libri III. 2. Band: Buch I, 166—Buch II, 98*, Heidelberg.

Leeman, A. D., Pinkster, H., and Rabbie, E. (1989) *M. T. Cicero: 'De Oratore' Libri III. 3. Band: Buch II, 99-290*, Heidelberg.

Leeman, A. D., Pinkster, H., and Wisse, J. (1996) *M. T. Cicero: 'De Oratore' Libri III. 4. Band: Buch II, 291-367; Buch III, 1-95*, Heidelberg.

Leemans, A.-E. (1937) *Studie over den Wijsgeer Numenius van Apamea met Uitgave der Fragmenten*, Brussels.

Lefebvre, D. (2016) 'Aristotle and the Hellenistic Peripatos: From Theophrastus to Critolaus', in A. Falcon (ed.), *Brill's Companion to the Reception of Aristotle in Antiquity*, Leiden and Boston, 11-34.

Lefebvre, D. (2017) 'Aristote, Theophraste, Straton et la "philosophie des êtres divins"', in F. Baghdassarian and G. Guyomarc'h (eds), *Réceptions de la théologie Aristotélicienne d'Aristote à Michel d'Ephèse*, Leuven, 59-88.

Lefebvre, D. (2017a) 'Théophraste sur les principes physiques de Platon dans le fr. 230 FHS and G et dans sa *Métaphysique*', in M.-A. Gavray and A. Michalewski (eds), *Les principes cosmologiques du Platonisme: origines, influences et systématisation*, Turnhout, 63-89.

Lefebvre, R. (2007) 'Représentation et évidence: Les Stoïciens face à leurs adversaires de l'Académie', *Elenchos* 28, 337-67.

Lehmann, Y. (1985) 'La dette de Varron à l'égard de son maître Lucius Aelius Stilo', *Mélanges d'Archéologie et d'Histoire de l'École Française de Rome* 97, 515-25.

Lehmann-Hartleben, K. (1938) 'Maenianum and Basilica', *American Journal of Philology* 59, 280-96.

Leib, E. J. (2001) 'On the $\Sigma\omega\rho\iota\tau\eta s$: Towards a Better Understanding of Chrysippus', *Ancient Philosophy* 21, 147-59.

Leo, F. (1913) *Geschichte der römischen Literatur*, Vol. 1: *Die archaische Literatur*, Berlin.

Leonhardt, J. (1999) *Ciceros Kritik der Philosophenschulen*, Munich.

Leumann, M. (1977) *Lateinische Laut- und Formenlehre*, Munich.

Lévy-Bruhl, H. (1932) 'Le formule vindicatoire', *Revue historique de droit français et étranger* 11, 205-26.

Lévy, C. (1978) 'Scepticisme et dogmatisme dans l'Académie: "l'ésotérisme" d'Arcésilas', *Revue des Études Latines* 56, 335-48.

Lévy, C. (1992) *Cicero Academicus. Recherches sur les Académiques et sur la philosophie Cicéronienne*, Paris.

Lévy, C. (1992a) 'Cicéron créateur du vocabulaire latin de connaissance: essai de synthèse', in P. Grimal (ed.), *La langue latine—langue de la philosophie*, Rome, 91-106.

Lévy, C. (1993) 'La Nouvelle Académie a-t-elle été antiplatonicienne?', in M. Dixsaut (ed.), *Contre Platon*, vol. 1, Paris, 139-56.

Lévy, C. (1996) 'Doxographie et philosophie chez Cicéron', in C. Lévy (ed.), *La concept de nature à Rome—la physique*, Paris, 109-23.

Lévy, C. (1999) 'Philon et Antiochus dans le *Catulus*', *Archives de Philosophie* 62, 117-26.

Lévy, C. (2003) 'Cicero and the "Timaeus"', in G. Reydams-Schils (ed.), *Plato's 'Timaeus' as a Cultural Icon*, Notre Dame, 95-110.

Lévy, C. (2005) 'Les petits Académiciens: Lacyde, Charmadas, Métrodore de Stratonice', in M. Bonazzi and V. Celluprica (eds), *L'Eredità Platonica—Studi sul Platonismo da Arcesilao a Proclo*, Naples, 51-77.

Lévy, C. (2008) 'Cicéron, le moyen platonisme, et la philosophie romaine: à propos de la naissance du concept latin de *qualitas*', *Revue de métaphysique et de morale* 57, 5-20.

Lévy, C. (2010) 'The Sceptical Academy: Decline and Afterlife', in R. Bett (ed.), *The Cambridge Companion to Ancient Scepticism*, Cambridge, 81-104.

Lévy, C. (2012) 'Other Followers of Antiochus', in D. N. Sedley (ed.), *The Philosophy of Antiochus*, Oxford, 290-306.

Lévy, C. (2018) 'De la rhétorique à la philosophie: le rôle de la temeritas dans le pensée et l'œuvre de Cicéron', in G. M. Müller and F. Mariani Zini (eds), *Philosophie in Rom—Römische Philosophie?*, Berlin and Boston, 285-303.

Lévy, C. (2018a) 'Quelques remarques sur la place des présocratiques dans les conceptions cicéroniennes de l'histoire de la philosophie', in S. Franchet d'Espèrey and C. Lévy (eds), *Les présocratiques à Rome*, Paris, 117-28.

Lewis, E. (1994) 'The Stoics on Identity and Individuation', *Phronesis* 40, 89-108.

Liebenau, W. (1901) 'Comitia', in *RE* IV, 679-715.

Lilla, S. (1990) 'Die Lehre von den Ideen als Gedanken Gottes im griechischen patristischen Denken', in H. Eisenberger (ed.), *EPMHNEYMATA—Festschrift für Hadwig Hörner zum sechzigsten Geburtstag*, Heidelberg, 27-50.

Lilla, S. (2003) 'Die Lehre von den Ideen als Gedanken Gottes im byzantinischen Denken', *Römische historische Mitteilungen* 45, 181-90.
Linderski, J. (1986) 'The Augural Law', *ANRW* II.16.3, 2146-312.
Linderski, J. (1986a) 'Watching the Birds: Cicero the Augur and the Augural *Templa*', *Classical Philology* 81, 330-40.
Linderski, J. (1995) *Roman Questions*, Stuttgart.
Linderski, J. (1995a) 'Garden Parlors: Nobles and Birds', in J. Linderski, *Roman Questions*, Stuttgart, 44-6 (with addenda on p. 633 and further addenda in Linderski 2007: 610-11).
Linderski, J. (2007) *Roman Questions II*, Stuttgart.
Lindsay, W. M. (1901) *Nonius Marcellus' Dictionary of Republican Latin*, Oxford.
Lindsay, W. M. (1902) 'De fragmentis scriptorum apud Nonium servatis', *Rheinisches Museum für Philologie* 57, 196-204.
Lindsay, W. M. (1903) *Nonii Marcellii De Compendiosa Doctrina*, Leipzig.
Lintott, A. W. (1967) 'Popular Justice in a Letter of Cicero to Quintus', *Rheinisches Museum für Philologie* 110, 65-9.
Lintott, A. W. (1968) *Violence in Republican Rome*, Oxford.
Lippold, G. (1933) 'Myrmekides von Milet', in *RE* XVI.2, 1105.
Lippold, G. (1938) 'Pheidias no. 2', in *RE* XIX.2, 1919-35.
Lippold, G. (1952) 'Polykleitos no. 10', in *RE* XXI.2, 1707-18.
Lloyd, G. E. R. (1982) 'Observational Error in Later Greek Science', in J. Barnes, J. Brunschwig, M. Burnyeat, and M. Schofield (eds), *Science and Speculation: Studies in Hellenistic Theory and Practice*, Cambridge, 128-64.
Long, A. A. (1982) 'Astrology: Arguments Pro and Contra', in J. Barnes, J. Brunschwig, M. Burnyeat, and M. Schofield (eds), *Science and Speculation: Studies in Hellenistic Theory and Practice*, Cambridge, 165-92.
Long, A. A. (1985) 'The Stoics on World-Conflagration and Everlasting Recurrence', *The Southern Journal of Philosophy* 23, 13-37.
Long, A. A. (1986) 'Diogenes Laertius, Life of Arcesilaus', *Elenchos* 7, 429-49.
Long, A. A. (1989) 'Socrates in Hellenistic Philosophy', *Classical Quarterly* 38, 150-71.
Long, A. A. (1995) 'Cicero's Plato and Aristotle', in J. G. F. Powell (ed.), *Cicero the Philosopher*, 37-61.
Long, A. A. (1996) *Stoic Studies*, Berkeley and Los Angeles.
Long, A. A. (1996a) 'Dialectic and the Stoics Sage', in A. A. Long (ed.), *Stoic Studies*, Berkeley and Los Angeles, 85-106.
Long, A. A. (1996b) 'The Harmonics of Stoic Virtue', in A. A. Long (ed.), *Stoic Studies*, Berkeley and Los Angeles, 202-23.
Long, A. A. (1998) 'Theophrastus and the Stoa', in J. M. van Ophuijsen and M. van Raalte (eds), *Theophrastus: Reappraising the Sources*, New Brunswick, 355-83.
Long, A. A. (1999) 'Stoic Psychology', in K. Algra, J. Barnes, J. Mansfeld, and M. Schofield (eds), *The Cambridge History of Hellenistic Philosophy*, Cambridge, 560-84.
Long, A. A. (1999a) 'The Socratic Legacy', in K. Algra, J. Barnes, J. Mansfeld, and M. Schofield (eds), *The Cambridge History of Hellenistic Philosophy*, Cambridge, 617-41.
Long, A. A. (2002) 'Zeno's Epistemology and Plato's *Theaetetus*', in T. Scaltsas and A. Mason (eds), *The Philosophy of Zeno*, Larnaca, 115-30.
Long, A. A. (2005) 'Review of Dillon (2003)', *Classical Review* 55, 60-1.
Long, A. A. (2010) 'Socrates in Later Greek Philosophy', in D. R. Morrison (ed.), *The Cambridge Companion to Socrates*, Cambridge, 355-79.
Long, A. A. (2018) 'In and Out of the Stoa: Diogenes Laertius on Zeno', in J. Bryan, R. Wardy, and J. Warren (eds), *Authors and Authorities in Ancient Philosophy*, Cambridge, 242-62.
Long, A. A. and Sedley, D. N. (1987) *The Hellenistic Philosophers*, 2 vols, Cambridge.

Long, A. G. (2013) *Plato and the Stoics*, Cambridge.
Lörcher, A. (1911) *Das Fremde und das Eigene in Ciceros Büchern De Finibus Bonorum et Malorum und den Academica*, Halle.
Lorenz, H. (2009) 'Ancient Theories of Soul', *The Stanford Encyclopedia of Philosophy* (Summer), Edward N. Zalta (ed.), URL = <http://plato.stanford.edu/archives/sum2009/entries/ancient-soul/>.
Luque Moreno, J. (1996) '*Voces*. La clasificación de los sonidos en el mundo antiguo: I: Los gramáticos', *Voces* 7, 9–44.
Lurie, M. (2014) 'Der schiffbrüchige Odysseus oder: wie Arkesilaos zum Skeptiker wurde. Zu Timon von Phleius Fr. 806 SH (32D)', *Philologus* 58, 183–6.
Luschnat, O. (1958) 'Das Problem des ethischen Fortschritts in der alten Stoa', *Philologus* 102, 178–214.
MacGillivray, E. D. (2015) 'Epitomizing Philosophy and the Critique of Epicurean Popularizers', *Journal of Ancient History* 3, 22–54.
Machuca, D. E. (2017) 'Again on Sextus on Persuasiveness and Equipollence', *Archiv für Geschichte der Philosophie* 99, 212–28.
Maconi, H. (1988) '*Noua Non Philosophandi Philosophia*: A Review of Anna Maria Ioppolo, *Opinione e Scienza*', *Oxford Studies in Ancient Philosophy* 6, 231–53.
MacRae, D. (2017) '"The Laws of the Rites and of the Priests": Varro and Late Republican Roman Sacral Jurisprudence', *Bulletin of the Institute of Classical Studies* 60, 34–48.
Madvig, J. N. (1826) *Emendationes in Ciceronis Libros Philosophicos I*, Copenhagen.
Madvig, J. N. (1834) *Opuscula Academica*, Copenhagen, 2 vols.
Madvig, J. N. (1860) *Emendationes Liuianae*, Copenhagen.
Madvig, J. N. (1873) *Adversaria critica at scriptores Graecos et Latinos*, vol. 2, Copenhagen.
Madvig, J. N. (1876³) *M. Tullii Ciceronis De Finibus Bonorum et Malorum Libri Quinque*, Copenhagen.
Magee, J. (1989) *Boethius on Signification and Mind*, Leiden and New York.
Makin, S. (1993) *Indifference Arguments*, Oxford.
Malaspina, E. (2015) 'In Anglia invenitur: come Guglielmo di Malmesbury leggeva e soprattutto correggeva Cicerone nel XII secolo', *Studi e ricerche del Dipartimento di Lettere e Filosofia* 13, Università degli Studi di Cassino e del Lazio Meridionale, 31–52.
Malaspina, E. (2018) '*Recentior non deterior*: Escorial R.I.2 e una nuova *recensio* del *Lucullus* di Cicerone', *Paideia* 73, 1969–85.
Malaspina, E. (2019) 'A Tradiçao Manuscrita do *Lucullus* de Cícero: do *Corpus Leidense* a William of Malmesbury e à Fortuna no Período Humanístico', in I. T. Cardoso and M. Martinho (eds), *Cícero: obra e recepção*, Cohimbra, 19–53.
Malaspina, E. et al. (2014) 'I manoscritti del *Lucullus* di Cicerone in Vaticana: valore filologico e collocazione stemmatica', *Miscellanea Bibliothecae Apostolicae Vaticanae* 20, 589–620.
Mankin, D. (2011) *Cicero, De Oratore Book III*, Cambridge.
Mansfeld, J. (1968) 'Review of vol. i of Giusta (1964 [i.e. 2012²])', *Mnemosyne* 21, 436–8.
Mansfeld, J. (1981) 'Bad World and Demiurge. A "Gnostic" Motif from Parmenides and Empedocles to Lucretius and Philo', in R. van den Broek and M. J. Vermaseren (eds), *Studies in Gnosticism and Hellenistic Religions Presented to Gilles Quispel on the Occasion of his 65th Birthday*, Leiden, 261–314.
Mansfeld, J. (1985) 'Review of Ioppolo (1980)', *Mnemosyne* 38, 209–15.
Mansfeld, J. (1988) 'De Melisso Xenophane Gorgia: Pyrrhonizing Aristotelianism', *Rheinisches Museum für Philologie* 131, 239–76.
Mansfeld, J. (1989) 'Gibt es Spuren von Theophrasts *Phys. op.* bei Cicero?', in W. W. Fortenbaugh and P. Steinmetz (eds), *Cicero's Knowledge of the Peripatos*, New Brunswick, 133–58.
Mansfeld, J. (1989a) 'Chrysippus and the *Placita*', *Phronesis* 34, 311–42.

Mansfeld, J. (1990) 'Doxography and Dialectic: The Sitz im Leben of the "Placita"', in *Aufstieg und Niedergang der Römischen Welt W* II.36.4, 3056–229.
Mansfeld, J. (1997) 'Philo and Antiochus in the Lost *Catulus*', *Mnemosyne* 50, 45–74.
Mansfeld, J. (1999) 'Sources', in K. Algra, J. Barnes, J. Mansfeld, and M. Schofield (eds), *The Cambridge History of Hellenistic Philosophy*, Cambridge, 3–30.
Mansfeld, J. (1999a) 'Theology', in K. Algra, J. Barnes, J. Mansfeld, and M. Schofield (eds), *The Cambridge History of Hellenistic Philosophy*, Cambridge, 452–78.
Mansfeld, J. (2002) 'Deconstructing Doxography', *Philologus* 146, 277–86.
Mansfeld, J. (2010a) 'Physical *doxai* in the *Phaedo*', in J. Mansfeld and D. T. Runia (2010), 183–201.
Mansfeld, J. (2010b) 'Doxographical Studies, *Quellenforschung*, Tabular Presentation and Other Varieties of Comparativism', in J. Mansfeld and D. T. Runia (2010), 183–201, 3–31.
Mansfeld, J. (2013) 'Doxography of Ancient Philosophy', in *The Stanford Encyclopedia of Philosophy* (Winter), Edward N. Zalta (ed.), URL = <http://plato.stanford.edu/archives/win2013/entries/doxography-ancient/>.
Mansfeld, M. and Runia, D. T. (1999) *Aëtiana: The Method and Intellectual Context of a Doxographer*, Vol. I: *The Sources*, Leiden.
Mansfeld, M. and Runia, D. T. (2009) *Aëtiana: The Method and Intellectual Context of a Doxographer*, Vol. II: *The Compendium*, Leiden.
Mansfeld, M. and Runia, D. T. (2010) *Aëtiana: The Method and Intellectual Context of a Doxographer*, Vol. III: *Studies in the Doxographical Traditions of Greek Philosophy*, Leiden.
Mansfeld, M. and Runia, D.T. (2020) *Aëtiana V: An Edition of the Reconstructed Text of the 'Placita' with a Commentary and a Collection of Related Texts*, Leiden.
Manthe, U. (2002) '*Agere* und *aio*: Sprechakttheorien und Legisaktionen', in M. J. Schermaier, J. M. Rainer, and L. Winkel (eds), *Iurisprudentia universalis: Festschrift für Theo Mayer-Maly zum 70. Geburtstag*, Köln and Vienna, 431–44.
Mantovani, D. (1999^2) *Le formule del processo privato Romano—Per la didattica delle Istituzioni di diritto romano*, Padova.
Manuwald, G. (2011) *Roman Republican Theatre*, Cambridge.
Manuwald, G. (2012) *Tragicorum Romanorum Fragmenta*, Vol. ii: *Ennius*, Göttingen.
von Manz, H. G. (2005) 'Empiriker-Schule', in W. E. Gerabek et al. (eds), *Enzyklopädie Medizingeschichte*, Berlin and New York, 352–3.
Marinone, N. (2004^2) *Cronologia Ciceroniana*, 2nd edn, Bologna.
Mariotti, I. (1966) *Aristone di Alessandria*, Bologna.
Marshall, A. J. (1968) 'Cicero, Ad Quintum Fratrem ii.10.1', *Classical Review* 18, 16–17.
Marzotto, T. (2012) *Polemone l'Ateniense, Scolarca dell' Academia Antica. Testimonianze*, Paris (diss. phil.).
Maso, S. (2008) *Capire e dissentire: Cicerone e la filosofia di Epicuro*, Naples.
Maso, S. (2016) 'L'atomo di Lucrezio', *Lexicon Philosophicum* 4, 173–82.
May, J. M. and Wisse, J. (2001) *Cicero—On the Ideal Orator*, New York and Oxford.
McConnell, S. (2014) *Philosophical Life in Cicero's Letters*, Cambridge.
McConnell, S. (2019) 'Why Latin *spectrum* is a Bad Translation of Epicurus' $ΕΙΔΩΛΟΝ$', *Mnemosyne* 72, 154–62.
McConnell, S. (2019a) 'Cicero and Socrates', in C. Moore (ed.), *Brill's Companion to the Reception of Socrates*, Leiden, 347–66.
McCracken, G. (1942) 'The Villa and Tomb of Lucullus at Tusculum', *American Journal of Archaeology* 46, 325–40.
McDermott, W. C. and Heesen, P. T. (1975) 'Cicero and Diodotus', *Classical Bulletin* 52, 38–41.
Mehl, D. (2002) 'The Stoic Paradoxes According to Cicero', in C. Damon, J. F. Miller, and K. S. Myers (eds), *Vertis in Usum: Studies in Honour of Edward Courtney*, Munich, 39–46.

Meillet, A. (1925) 'A propos de *qualitas*', *Revue des Études Latines* 3, 214-20.
Meinwald, C. (2005) 'Ignorance and Opinion in Stoic Epistemology', *Phronesis* 50, 215-31.
Meinwald, C. (2011) 'Two Notions of Consent', *Oxford Studies in Ancient Philosophy* 40, 361-80.
Mejer, J. (1998) 'A Life in Fragments: *The Vita Theophrasti*', in J. van Ophuijsen and M. van Raalte (eds), *Theophrastus: Reappraising the Sources*, New Brunswick and London, 1-28.
de Melo, W. D. C. (2019) *Varro—De Lingua Latina*, 2 vols, Oxford.
Menn, S. (1995) 'Physics as a Virtue', *Proceedings of the Boston Area Colloquium in Ancient Philosophy* 11, 1-34.
Menn, S. (2010) 'On Socrates' First Objections to the Physicists (*Phaedo* 95e8-97b7)', *Oxford Studies in Ancient Philosophy* 38, 37-68.
de Meo, C. (1983) *Lingue techniche del Latino*, Bologna.
Messina, M. T. (2011) 'Filosofi e filosofia nelle "Saturae menippeae" di Varrone Reatino', *Acme* 64, 265-79.
Metaxaki-Mitrou, F. (1985) 'Violence in the Contio during the Ciceronian Age', *L'Antiquité Classique* 54, 180-7.
Mette, H. J. (1984) 'Zwei Akademiker heute. Krantor von Soloi und Arkesilaos von Pitane', *Lustrum* 26, 7-94.
Mette, H. J. (1985) 'Weitere Akademiker heute. Von Lakydes bis zu Kleitomachos', *Lustrum* 27, 39-148.
Mette, H. J. (1986-7) 'Philon von Larissa und Antiochus von Askalon', *Lustrum* 28-9, 9-63.
Michael, H. (1874) *De Ammiani Marcellini studiis Ciceronianis*, Breslau (diss. phil.).
Michel, A. (1968) 'Doxographie et histoire de la philosophie chez Cicéron (Lucullus, 128 sq.)', in J. Harmatta (ed.), *Studien zur Geschichte und Philosophie des Altertums*, Budapest and Amsterdam, 113-20.
Mikkola, E. (1957) *Die Konzessivität bei Livius. Mit besonderer Berücksichtigung der ersten und fünften Dekade*, Helsinki.
Miller Jones, R. (1929) 'The Ideas as the Thoughts of God', *Classical Philology* 21, 317-26.
Miltner, F. (1952) 'Pompeius 12', in *RE* XXI.2, 2056-8.
Modrak, D. (2010) 'Nominal Definition in Aristotle', in D. Charles (ed.), *Definition in Greek Philosophy*, Oxford, 252-85.
Mommsen, T. (1876²) *Römisches Staatsrecht*, vol. 1, Leipzig.
Mommsen, T. (1899) *Römisches Strafrecht*, Leipzig.
Mommsen, T. (1905) *Gesammelte Schriften*, vol. i, Berlin.
Monet, A. (1996) '[Philodème, *Sur les sensations*] PHerc. 19/698', *Cronache Ercolanesi* 26, 27-126.
Montarese, F. (2012) *Lucretius and his Sources: A Study of Lucretius, 'De Rerum Natura' I 635-920*, Berlin and New York.
Moore, T. J. (2012) *Music in Roman Comedy*, Cambridge.
Moraux, P. (1963) 'quinta essentia', in *RE* XXIV.1, 1174-1263.
Moraux, P. (1968) 'La joute dialectique d'après le huitième livre des Topiques', in G. E. L. Owen (ed.), *Aristotle on Dialectic*, Oxford, 277-311.
Moraux, P. (1974) *Der Aristotelismus bei den Griechen*, vol. 1, Berlin.
Moreau, J. (1959) 'L'éloge de la biologie chez Aristote', *Revue des Études Anciennes* 61, 57-64.
Morel, P. (2015) 'Cicero and Epicurean Virtues (*De Finibus* 1-2)', in J. Annas and G. Betegh (eds), *Cicero's 'De Finibus': Philosophical Approaches*, Cambridge, 77-95.
Morel, P. (2018) 'Démocrite chez Cicéron', in S. Franchet d'Espèrey and C. Lévy (eds), *Les Présocratiques à Rome*, Paris, 41-56.
Moreno, P. (1994) *Scultura Ellenistica*, Rome.
Moreschini, C. (1979) 'Osservazioni sul lessico filosofico di Cicerone', *Annali della Scuola Normale Superiore di Pisa, Classe di Lettere e Filosofia* 9, 99-178.

Morgan, L. (2007) 'Natura narratur: Tullius Laurea's Elegy for Cicero (Pliny, Nat. 31.8)', in S. J. Heyworth (ed.), *Classical Constructions: Papers in Memory of Don Fowler, Classicist and Epicurean*, Oxford, 113-40.

Morgenstern, K. (1800) *Oratio de litteris humanioribus, sensum veri, honesti et pulchri excitantibus atque acuentibus, publice habita in aud. max. Athenaei Gedanensis*, Leipzig and Gdansk.

Morillon, P. (1974) *Sentire, sensus, sententia. Recherche sur le vocabulaire de la vie intellectuelle, affective et physiologique en latin*, Lille (diss. Paris.).

Morison, B. (2008) 'Language', in R. J. Hankinson (ed.), *The Cambridge Companion to Galen*, Cambridge, 116-56.

Morison, B. (2019) 'Sextus Empiricus', in *The Stanford Encyclopedia of Philosophy* (Fall), Edward N. Zalta (ed.), URL = <https://plato.stanford.edu/archives/fall2019/entries/sextus-empiricus/>.

Moss, J. (2014) 'Plato's Appearance-Assent Account of Belief', *Proceedings of the Aristotelian Society* 114, 213-38.

Moss, J. and Schwab, W. (2019) 'The Birth of Belief', *Journal of the History of Philosophy* 57, 1-32.

Most, G. W. (1997) *Collecting Fragments—Fragmente sammeln*, Göttingen.

Mras, K. (1914) 'Varros menippeische Satiren und die Philosophie', *Neue Jahrbücher für das Klassische Altertum* 33, 390-420.

Mueller, C. F. W. (1859/60) *Coniecturae Tullianae*, Königsberg.

Mueller, I. (1982) 'Geometry and Scepticism', in J. Barnes, J. Brunschwig, M. Burnyeat, and M. Schofield (eds), *Science and Speculation—Studies in Hellenistic Theory and Practice*, Cambridge, 69-95.

Mueller, I. (1991) 'On the Notion of a Mathematical Starting Point in Plato, Aristotle, and Euclid', in A. C. Bowen (ed.), *Science and Philosophy in Classical Greece*, London and New York, 59-97.

Muller, R. (2000) 'Euclide de Mégare', in R. Goulet (ed.), *Dictionnaire des philosophes antiques*, vol. 3, Paris, 272-7.

Muller, R. (2012) 'Philon (de Mégare)', in R. Goulet (ed.), *Dictionnaire des philosophes antiques*, vol. 5.1, Paris, 438-9.

Münzer, F. (1899) 'Claudius 225', in *RE* III.2, 2758-60.

Münzer, F. (1901) 'Cornelius 353', in *RE* IV.1, 1497-1501.

Münzer, F. (1909) 'Flaminius 2', in *RE* VI.2, 2496-502.

Münzer, F. (1920) *Römische Adelsparteien und Adelsfamilien*, Stuttgart.

Münzer, F. (1923) 'P. Servilius Geminus', in *RE* II.A.2, 1795-6.

Münzer, F. (1923a) 'Q. Servilius Geminus', in *RE* II.A.2, 1796.

Münzer, F. (1953) 'Postumius 31', in *RE* XXII.1, 902-8.

Murphy, T. (2004) 'Valerius Soranus and the Secret Name of Rome', in A. Barchiesi, J. Rüpke, and S. Stephens (eds), *Rituals in Ink: A Conference on Religion and Literary Production in Ancient Rome*, Stuttgart, 127-40.

Mutschmann, H. (1911) 'Die Stufen der Wahrscheinlichkeit bei Karneades', *Rheinisches Museum für Philologie* 66, 190-8.

Nardelli, M. L. (1984) 'L'ironia in Polistrato e Filodemo', in *Atti del XVII Congresso Internazionale di Papirologia*, Naples, 525-36.

Nawar, T. (2014) 'The Stoic Account of Apprehension', *Philosophers' Imprint* 14, no. 29, 1-21.

Nehamas, A. (1975) 'Plato on the Imperfection of the Sensible World', *American Philosophical Quarterly* 12, 105-17.

Németh, A. (2016) 'Excerpts versus Fragments', in A. Grafton and G. W. Most (eds), *Canonical Texts and Scholarly Practices: A Global Comparative Approach*, Cambridge, 253-74.

Nesselrath, H.-G. (1990) *Die attische mittlere Komödie—ihre Stellung in der antiken Literaturkritik und Literaturgeschichte*. Berlin and New York.
Netz, R. (1999) *The Shaping of Deduction in Greek Mathematics*, Cambridge.
Neubecker, A. J. (1956) *Die Bewertung der Musik bei Stoikern und Epikureern*, Berlin.
Neuhausen, K. A. (1987) '*Academicus sapiens*: Zum Bild des Weisen in der Neuen Akademie', *Mnemosyne* 40, 353–90.
Neuhausen, K. A. (1992) *M. Tullius Cicero—Laelius*, Einleitung und Kommentar, Lieferung 3, Heidelberg.
Newman, L. (2019) 'Descartes' Epistemology', in *The Stanford Encyclopedia of Philosophy* (Spring), Edward N. Zalta (ed.), URL = <https://plato.stanford.edu/archives/spr2019/entries/descartes-epistemology/>.
Newmyer, S. (2010) *Animals in Greek and Roman Thought*, Abingdon.
Nicolas, C. (2005) *Sic enim appello: essai sur l'autonymie terminologique gréco-latine chez Cicéron*, Louvain and Paris.
Niehoff, M. (2007) 'Did the *Timaeus* create a Textual Community?', *Greek, Roman, and Byzantine Studies* 47, 161–91.
Nisbet, R. (1961) *In L. Calpurnium Pisonem Oratio*, Oxford.
Nisbet, R. and Hubbard, M. (1970) *A Commentary on Horace, Odes, Book 1*, Oxford.
Nisbet, R. and Rudd, N. (2004) *A Commentary on Horace, Odes, Book III*, Oxford.
Norberg, D. (1943) *Syntaktische Forschungen auf dem Gebiete des Spätlateins und des frühen Mittellateins*, Uppsala.
Nordenfelt, L. (1997) 'The Stoic Conception of Mental Disorder: The Case of Cicero', *Philosophy, Psychiatry, and Psychology* 4, 285–91.
Novokhatko, A. (2009) *The Invectives of Sallust and Cicero: Critical Edition with Introduction, Translation, and Commentary*, Berlin and New York.
Van Nuffelen, P. (2010) 'Varro's *Divine Antiquities*: Roman Religion as an Image of Truth', *Classical Philology* 105, 162–88.
Nutting, H. C. (1903) 'The Order of Conditional Thought', *American Journal of Philology* 24, 149–62.
Oakley, S. (2005) *A Commentary on Livy, Books VI–X*, Oxford.
Obbink, D. (1996) *Philodemus—On Piety*. Part 1: *Critical Text and Commentary*, Oxford.
Obbink, D. (2001) 'Le livre I du *De natura deorum* de Cicéron et le *De pietate* de Philodème', in C. Auvray-Assayas and D. Delattre (eds), *Cicéron et Philodème: La polémique en philosophie*, Paris, 203–25.
Obbink, D. and Vander Waerdt, P. (1991) 'Diogenes of Babylon: The Stoic Sage in the City of Fools', *Greek, Roman and Byzantine Studies* 32, 355–96.
Obdrzalek, S. (2006) 'Living in Doubt: Carneades' *Pithanon* Reconsidered', *Oxford Studies in Ancient Philosophy* 31, 243–80.
Obdrzalek, S. (2012) 'From Skepticism to Paralysis: The *Apraxia* Argument in Cicero's *Academica*', *Ancient Philosophy* 32, 369–92.
Ogilvie, R. M. (1978) *The Library of Lactantius*, Oxford.
O'Keefe, T. (2002) 'The Cyrenaics on Pleasure, Happiness, and Future-Concern', *Phronesis* 47, 395–416.
O'Keefe, T. (2011) 'The Cyrenaics vs. the Pyrrhonists on Knowledge of Appearances', in D. E. Manchuca (ed.), *New Essays on Ancient Pyrrhonism*, Leiden and Boston, 27–40.
Opsomer, J. (1998) 'Favorinus versus Epictetus on the Philosophical Heritage of Plutarch. A Debate on Epistemology', in J. Mossman (ed.), *Plutarch and his Intellectual World*, London and Swansea, 17–39.
Opsomer, J. (1998a) *In Search of the Truth—Academic Tendencies in Middle Platonism*, Brussels.

Opsomer, J. (2004) 'Plutarch's *de animae procreatione in Timaeo*: Manipulation or Search for Consistency', in P. Adamson, H. Baltussen, and M. F. Stone (eds), *Philosophy, Science and Exegesis in Greek, Arabic and Latin Commentaries*, BICS suppl. 83.1, vol. 1, London, 137–62.

Orlandini, A. (2005) 'Fonctions adverbiales dans des structures corrélatives en latin', in P. Carvalho and F. Lambert (eds), *Structures parallèles et corrélatives en grec et en latin actes du colloque de linguistique grecque et latine: Bordeaux, 26-7 Septembre 2002*, Saint-Étienne, 159–81.

Orth, A. (1913) 'Huhn', in *RE* viii/2, 2519–35.

Osorio, P. (2021) 'Reconstructing Brutus' *De Virtute*: Consolation and Antiochean Fundamentalism', *Phronesis* 66, 52–83.

O'Sullivan, N. (2019) 'Manuscript Evidence for Alphabet-Switching in the Works of Cicero: Common Nouns and Adjectives', *Classical Quarterly* 68, 498–516.

O'Sullivan, N. (2021) 'Manuscript Evidence for Alphabet-Switching in the Works of Cicero: Proper Nouns and Adjectives', *Classical Quarterly* 70, 677–90.

Otto, A. (1888) 'Kleidung und Wohnung im Sprichwort', *Archiv für Lateinische Lexikographie und Grammatik mit Einschluss des älteren Mittellateins* 5, 1–15.

Otto, A. (1890) *Die Sprichwörter und sprichwörtlichen Redensarten der Römer*, Leipzig.

Page, D. L. (1981) *Further Greek Epigrams*, Cambridge.

Paparazzo, E. (2013) 'Viewing the World from Different Angles: Plato's *Timaeus* 54E–55A', *Apeiron* 46, 244–69.

Papazian, M. (2012) 'Chrysippus Confronts The Liar: The Case for Stoic Cassationism', *History and Philosophy of Logic* 33, 197–214.

Pappas, G. (2014) 'Internalist vs. Externalist Conceptions of Epistemic Justification', in *The Stanford Encyclopedia of Philosophy* (Fall), Edward N. Zalta (ed.), URL = <http://plato.stanford.edu/archives/fall2014/entries/justep-intext/>.

Pârvulescu, A. (1980) 'Latin *Considerare* and *Desiderare*', *Zeitschrift für vergleichende Sprachforschung* 94, 159–65.

Patzig, G. (1979) 'Cicero als Philosoph, am Beispiele der Schrift *De finibus*', *Gymnasium* 86, 304–22.

Pearce, Z. (1810[6]) *M. Tullii ad Q. Fratrem Dialogi Tres De Oratore*, New York.

Pease, A. S. (1913) 'The Conclusion of Cicero's *de Natura Deorum*', *Transactions of the American Philological Association* 44, 25–37.

Pease, A. S. (1935) *Publi Vergili Maronis Aeneidos Liber Quartus*, Cambridge, MA.

Pease, A. S. (1955–8) *M. Tulli Ciceronis De Natura Deorum*, 2 vols, Cambridge, MA.

Perin, C. (2005) 'Academic Arguments for the Indiscernibility Thesis', *Pacific Philosophical Quarterly* 86, 493–517.

Perin, C. (2006) 'Review of Brittain (2006)', *Notre Dame Philosophical Reviews* 2006.10.06.

Perin, C. (2010) 'Scepticism and Belief', in R. Bett (ed.), *The Cambridge Companion to Ancient Scepticism*, Cambridge, 145–64.

Perin, C. (2010a) *The Demands of Reason—An Essay on Pyrrhonian Scepticism*, Oxford.

Perin, C. (2013) 'Making Sense of Arcesilaus', *Oxford Studies in Ancient Philosophy* 45, 313–40.

Petrucci, F. M. (2018) 'Review of Bonazzi (2015)', *Mnemosyne* 71, 351–64.

Petrucci, F. M. (2021) 'Authority beyond Doctrines in the First Century B.C.: Antiochus' Model for Plato's Authority', in M. Erler, J. E. Heßler, and F. M. Petrucci (eds), *Authority and Authoritative Texts in the Platonist Tradition*, Cambridge, 89–114.

Pfligersdorffer, G. (1971) 'Zu den Grundlagen des augustinischen Begriffspaares *uti-frui*', *Wiener Studien* 5, 195–224.

Philippson, R. (1932) 'Das erste Naturgemäße', *Philologus* 87, 445–66.

Philippson, R. (1939) 'Tullius Cicero: Philosophische Schriften', in *RE* II.13, 1104–92.

Piazzi, L. (2005) *Lucrezio e i Presocratici—un commento a 'De rerum natura'* 1, 635–920, Pisa.

Pilar García Ruiz, M. (2014) '*Aequor*: The Sea of Prophecies in Virgil's *Aeneid*', *Classical Quarterly* 64, 694–706.
Pinkster, H. (2005) 'The Language of Pliny the Elder', in T. Reinhardt, M. Lapidge, and J. N. Adams (eds), *Aspects of the Language of Latin Prose*, Oxford, 239–56.
Des Places, E. (1973) *Numénius—fragments*, Paris.
Plasberg, O. (1892) *De M. Tulli Ciceronis Hortensio dialogo*, Leipzig.
Platner, S. B. and Ashby, T. (1929) 'Tabernae circum Forum', in *A Topographical Dictionary of Ancient Rome*, London, 504–5.
Plezia, M. (1936) 'De Ciceronis *Academicis* dissertationes tres', *Eos* 37, 425–49.
Plezia, M. (1937a) 'De Ciceronis *Academicis* dissertationes tres', *Eos* 38, 10–30.
Plezia, M. (1937b) 'De Ciceronis *Academicis* dissertationes tres', *Eos* 38, 169–86.
Plezia, M. (1989) 'M. Tulli Ciceronis Prooemiorum volumen', *Meander* 44, 3–19.
Pohlenz, M. (1940) *Grundfragen der stoischen Philosophie*, Göttingen 1940.
Polito, R. (2007) '"Was Scepticism a Philosophy?" Reception, Self-Definition, Internal Conflicts', *Classical Philology* 102, 333–62.
Polito, R. (2012) 'Antiochus and the Academy', in D. N. Sedley (ed.), *The Philosophy of Antiochus*, Cambridge, 31–54.
Polito, R. (2014) *Aenesidemus of Cnossus*, Cambridge.
Powell, J. G. F. (1988) *Cicero: Cato Maior De Senectute*, Oxford.
Powell, J. G. F. (1995) 'Cicero's Translations from Greek', in J. G. F. Powell (ed.), *Cicero the Philosopher*, Oxford, 273–300.
Powell, J. G. F. (2001) 'Review of Inwood and Mansfeld (1997) and Hunt (1998)', *Journal of Roman Studies* 91, 224–5.
Powell, J. G. F. (2006) *M. Tulli Ciceronis De Re Publica, De Legibus, Cato Maior De Senectute, Laelius De Amicitia*, Oxford.
Powell, J. G. F. (2013) 'The Embassy of the Three Philosophers to Rome in 155 B.C.', in C. Kremmydas and K. Tempest (eds), *Hellenistic Oratory: Continuity and Change*, Oxford, 219–47.
Preisigke, F. (1915) *Fachwörter des öffentlichen Verwaltungsdienstes Ägyptens in den griechischen Papyrusurkunden der ptolemäisch-römischen Zeit*, Göttingen.
Primavesi, O. (1996) *Die Aristotelische Topik—ein Interpretationsmodell und seine Erprobung am Beispiel von Topik B*, Munich.
Pucci, G. C. (1966) 'Echi lucreziani in Cicerone', *Studi Italiani di Filologia Classica* 38, 70–132.
Puelma, M. (1986) 'Die Rezeption der Fachsprache griechischer Philosophie im Lateinischen', *Freiburger Zeitschrift für Philosophie und Theologie* 33, 45–69.
Puglia, E. (2000) 'Le biografie di Filone e di Antioco nella *Storia dell' Academia* di Filodemo', *Zeitschrift für Papyrologie und Epigraphik* 130, 17–28.
Rackham, H. (1951²) *Cicero De Natura Deorum Academica*, Cambridge and London.
Radermacher, L. (1951) *Artium Scriptores (Reste der voraristotelischen Rhetorik)*, Vienna.
Ramelli, I. and Konstan, D. (2009) *Hierocles the Stoic: Elements of Ethics, Fragments, and Excerpts*, Atlanta.
Ramsey, J. T. (2003) *Cicero—Philippics I–II*, Cambridge.
Ranitz, A. C. (1809) *De libris Ciceronis academicis commentatio*, Leipzig.
Ranocchia, G. (2011) 'Aristone di Chio in Stobeo e nella Letteratura Gnomologica', in G. Reydams-Schils (ed.), *Thinking through Excerpts: Studies on Stobaeus*, Turnhout, 339–86.
Rapp, C. (2002) *Aristoteles—Rhetorik*, 2 vols, Berlin.
Reid, J. S. (1882) *M. Tulli Ciceronis Cato Maior de Senectute*, Boston, New York, and Chicago.
Reid, J. S. (1883) *M. Tullii Ciceronis Laelius De Amicitia*, Cambridge.
Reid, J. S. (1925) *Cicero De Finibus—Books I and II*, Cambridge.

Reed, B. (2002) 'The Stoics' Account of the Cognitive Impression', *Oxford Studies in Ancient Philosophy* 23, 147-80.
Reed, B. (2012) 'Fallibilism', *Philosophy Compass* 7/9, 585-96.
Reinhardt, T. (2000) 'Rhetoric in the Fourth Academy', *Classical Quarterly* 50, 531-47.
Reinhardt, T. (2000a) *Das Buch E der aristotelischen Topik—Untersuchungen zur Echtheitsfrage*, Göttingen.
Reinhardt, T. (2003) *Cicero's Topica*, Oxford.
Reinhardt, T. (2005) 'The Language of Epicureanism in Cicero', in T. Reinhardt, M. Lapidge, J. N. Adams (eds), *Aspects of the Language of Latin Prose*, Proceedings of the British Academy no. 129, Oxford, 151-77.
Reinhardt, T. (2007) 'Techniques of Proof in 4th Century Rhetoric: Ar. *Rhet.* 2.23-4 and Pre-Aristotelian Rhetorical Theory', in D. C. Mirhady (ed.), *Influences on Peripatetic Rhetoric*, Leiden and Boston, 87-104.
Reinhardt, T. (2008) 'Epicurus and Lucretius on the Origins of Language', *Classical Quarterly* 58, 127-40.
Reinhardt, T. (2010) 'Syntactic Colloquialism in Lucretius', in E. Dickey and A. Chahoud (eds), *Colloquial and Literary Latin*, Cambridge, 203-28.
Reinhardt, T. (2010a) 'Plausibility in Plato's *Phaedrus* and the *Rhetorica ad Alexandrum*', *Museum Helveticum* 67, 1-6.
Reinhardt, T. (2011) 'Galen on Unsayable Properties', *Oxford Studies in Ancient Philosophy* 40, 297-317.
Reinhardt, T. (2015) 'On *Endoxa* in Aristotle's *Topics*', *Rheinisches Museum für Philologie* 158, 225-46.
Reinhardt, T. (2016) 'To See and To Be Seen: on Vision and Perception in Lucretius and Cicero', in G. D. Williams and K. Volk (eds), *Roman Reflections: Studies in Latin Philosophy*, New York, 63-90.
Reinhardt, T. (2018) 'Antiochus of Ascalon on Epistemology in the Academic tradition', in C. Lévy and J. B. Guillaumin (eds), *Plato Latinus—Actes de Diatribai di Gargnano*, Turnhout, 31-67.
Reinhardt, T. (2018a) '*Pithana* and *Probabilia* in Sextus and Cicero', in T. Bénatouïl and K. Ierodiakonou (eds), *Dialectic after Plato and Aristotle*, Proceedings of the XIIIth Symposium Hellenisticum, Cambridge, 218-53.
Reinhardt, T. (2018b) 'Cicero and Augustine on Grasping the Truth', in G. M. Müller and F. M. Zini (eds), *Philosophie in Rom—Römische Philosophie? Kultur-, literatur- und philosophiegeschichtliche Aspekte*, Berlin and Boston, 305-23.
Reinhardt, T. (2019) 'Linguistic Naturalism in Cicero's *Academica*', in G. Pezzini and B. Taylor (eds), *Language and Nature in the Classical Roman World*, Cambridge, 153-70.
Reinhardt, T. (2021) 'Zenons Hand (Cicero, *Lucullus* §§144-6)', in M. Grandl and M. Möller (eds), *Wissen en miniature: Theorie und Epistemologie der Anekdote*, Wiesbaden, 41-50.
Reinhardt, T. (2021a) 'Cicero's Academic Scepticism', in T. Bénatouïl and J. Atkins (eds), *The Cambridge Companion to Cicero's Philosophy*, Cambridge, 103-19.
Reinhardt, T. (forthcoming) 'Navigating Cognitive Success (and Failure): Cicero, *Lucullus* 66'.
Renaud, F. and Tarrant, H. (2015) 'Prereception and Early Reception', in F. Renaud and H. Tarrant, *The Platonic Alcibiades I: The Dialogue and its Ancient Reception*, Cambridge, 85-152.
Repici, L. (1988) *La natura e l'anima: saggi su Stratone di Lampsaco*, Turin.
Reydams-Schils, G. (1999) *Demiurge and Providence: Stoic and Platonist Readings of Plato's 'Timaeus'*, Turnhout.
Reydams-Schils, G. (2010) 'Seneca's Platonism: The Soul and its Divine Origin', in A. Nightingale and D. N. Sedley (eds), *Ancient Models of Mind: Studies in Human and Divine Rationality*, Cambridge, 196-215.

Reydams-Schils, G. (2011) *Thinking through Excerpts—Studies on Stobaeus*, Turnhout.
Reydams-Schils, G. (2013) 'The Academy, the Stoics and Cicero on Plato's *Timaeus*', in A. G. Long (ed.), *Plato and the Stoics*, Cambridge, 29–58.
Ribbeck, O. (1897) *Scaenicae Romanorum Poesis Fragmenta*, Leipizg, 3rd edn.
Rich, A. N. M. (1954) 'The Platonic Ideas as Thoughts of God', *Mnemosyne* 7, 123–33.
Richlin, A. (2017) *Slave Theater in the Roman Republic*, Oxford.
Ricottilli, L. (2003³) *Johan Baptist Hofmann: La lingua d'uso Latina*, Bologna.
Riedweg, C. (1987) *Mysterienterminologie bei Platon, Philon, und Klemens von Alexandrien*, Berlin and New York.
Riedweg, C. (1994) *Ps.-Justin (Markell von Ankyra?) ad Graecos de Vera Religione (bisher 'Cohortatio ad Graecos')*, 2 vols, Basel.
Riesenweber, T. (2009) 'Eine stoische Tugenddefinition. Zur Überlieferung von Cic. Inv. 2, 159–167', *Rheinisches Museum für Philologie* 152, 265–91.
Rieth, O. (1934) 'Über das Telos der Stoiker', *Hermes* 69, 13–45.
Riggsby, A. M. (2010) *Roman Law and the Legal World of the Romans*, Cambridge.
Rispoli, G. M. (1983) 'La sensazione scientifica', *Cronache Ercolanesi* 13, 92–101.
Rispoli, G. M. (1983) 'Sensazione, esperienza, giudizio tecnico. Testimonianze su origine e sviluppi di una concezione estetica', *Annali della Facoltà di Lettere e Filosofia della Università di Napoli* 24, 105–19.
Ritschl, F. (1845) *Parerga zu Plautus und Terenz*, vol. 1, Berlin.
Ritschl, F. (1848) 'Die Schriftstellerei des M. Terentius Varro', *Rheinisches Museum für Philologie* 6, 481–560.
Robinson, L. (1976) 'Marcus Terentius Varro, *Sexagesis*, or Born Sixty Years Too Late', in *Atti del Congresso Internazionale di Studi Varroniani*, vol. 2, Rieti, 477–83.
Rolke, K.-H. (1975) *Bildhafte Vergleiche bei den Stoikern*, Hildesheim and New York.
Roloff, H. (1938) *Maiores bei Cicero*, Göttingen (diss. phil.).
Rösch-Binde, C. (1998) *Vom 'δεινὸς ἀνήρ' zum 'diligentissimus inuestigator antiquitatis'—Zur komplexen Beziehung zwischen M. Tullius Cicero und M. Terentius Varro*, Munich.
Roskam, G. (2005) *On the Path to Virtue—The Stoic Doctrine of Moral Progress and its Reception in (Middle-) Platonism*, Leuven.
Rösler, W. (1973) 'Lukrez und die Vorsokratiker: Doxographische Probleme im 1. Buch von De rerum natura', *Hermes* 101, 48–64.
Ruch, M. (1950) 'A propos de la chronologie et de la genèse des "Academica" et du "De Finibus"', *L'antiquité classique* 19, 13–26.
Ruch, M. (1958) *L'Hortensius de Cicéron: histoire et reconstitution*, Paris.
Ruch, M. (1958a) *Le préambule dans les œuvres philosophiques de Cicéron—Essai sur la genè et l'art du dialogue*, Paris.
Ruch, M. (1969) 'La *disputatio in utramque partem* dans le Lucullus et ses fondements philosophiques', *Revue des Études Latines* 47, 167–79.
Ruch, M. (1970) 'Observations sur le texte et le sens de quelques passages des *Academica Posteriora*', *Revue de Philologie, de Littérature et d'Histoire Anciennes* 44, 76–83.
Rudolph, E. (1996) *Contrast—Adversative and Concessive Expressions on Sentence and Text Level*, Berlin and New York.
Rühl, M. (2018) *Ciceros Korrespondenz als Medium literarischen und gesellschaftlichen Handelns*, Leiden and Boston.
Rumpf, L. (2003) *Naturerkenntnis und Naturerfahrung—zur Reflexion epikureischer Theorie bei Lukrez*, Munich.
Runia, D. T. (1997) 'Lucretius and Doxography', in K. A. Algra, M. H. Koenen, and P. H. Schrijvers (eds), *Lucretius and his Intellectual Background*, Amsterdam, 93–103.

Runia, D. T. (1999) 'The *Placita* ascribed to Doctors in Aëtius', in P. J. van der Eijk (ed.), *Ancient Histories of Medicine—Essays in Medical Doxography and Historiography in Classical Antiquity*, Leiden, 191–250.
Runia, D. T. (2010) 'Philo and Hellenistic Doxography', in J. Mansfeld and D. T. Runia (eds), *Aëtiana—The Method and Intellectual Context of a Doxographer*, Vol. 3: *Studies in the Doxographical Traditions of Ancient Philosophy*, Leiden, 271–312.
Runia, D. T. (2010a) 'Atheists in Aëtius—Text, Translation and Comments on *De Placitis* 1.7.1-10', in J. Mansfeld and D. T. Runia (eds), *Aëtiana—The Method and Intellectual Context of a Doxographer*, Vol. 3: *Studies in the Doxographical Traditions of Ancient Philosophy*, Leiden, 343–73.
Russell, A. (2016) 'Why Did Clodius Shut the Shops?', *Historia* 65, 186–210.
Rüstow, A. (1910) *Der Lügner: Theorie, Geschichte und Auflösung*, Leipzig.
Salles, R. (2007) 'Epictetus on Moral Responsibility for Precipitate Action', in C. Bobonich and P. Destrée (eds), *Akrasia in Greek Philosophy: From Socrates to Plotinus*, Leiden, 249–63.
Sandbach, F. H. (1930) 'ΕΝΝΟΙΑ and ΠΡΟΛΗΨΙΣ in the Stoic Theory of Knowledge', *Classical Quarterly* 24, 44–51.
Sandbach, F. H. (1971) 'Phantasia kataleptike', in A. A. Long (ed.), *Problems in Stoicism*, London, 9–21.
Santorelli, B. (2013) *Giovenale, 'Satira' V*, Berlin and New York.
Santorelli, B. (2014) *[Quintiliano], Il ricco accusato di tradimento. Gli amici garanti (Declamazioni maggiori, 11; 16)*, Cassino.
Scade, P. (2010) 'Stoic Cosmological Limits and their Platonic Background', in V. Harte, M. M. McCabe, R. W. Sharples, and A. Sheppard (eds), *Aristotle and the Stoics Reading Plato*, London, 143–83.
Scarsi, M. (1986) 'Due note agli *Academica* di Cicerone', *Studi Noniani* XI, 179–90.
Schäublin, C. (1992) 'Kritisches und Exegetisches zu Ciceros "Lucullus"', *Museum Helveticum* 49, 41–52.
Schäublin, C. (1993) 'Kritisches und Exegetisches zu Ciceros "Lucullus" II', *Museum Helveticum* 50, 158–69.
Schierl, P. (2006) *Die Tragödien des Pacuvius*, Berlin and New York.
Schlapbach, K. (2003) *Augustin Contra Academicos (uel De Academicis), Buch 1*, Berlin and New York.
Schlapbach, K. (2006) 'Hortensius', in C. Mayer et al. (eds), *Augustinus Lexikon* 3, 3/4, 425–36.
Schmidt, O. E. (1899) *Ciceros Villen*, Leipzig.
Schmidt, P. L. (1978-9) 'Cicero's Place in Roman Philosophy: A Study of his Prefaces', *Classical Journal* 74, 115–27.
Schmidt, P. L. (2001) 'The Original Version of the *De re publica* and the *De legibus*', in J. G. F. Powell (ed.), *Cicero's Republic, Bulletin of the Institute of Classical Studies Supplement*, London, 7–16.
Schmitt, C. B. (1972) *Cicero Scepticus: A Study of the Influence of the Academica in the Renaissance*, The Hague.
Schmitz, P. (2017) 'ΟΙΚΟC, ΠΟΛΙC and ΠΟΛΙΤΕΙΑ: Das Verhältnis von Familie und Staatsverfassung bei Aristoteles, im späteren Peripatos und in Ciceros *De officiis*', *Rheinisches Museum für Philologie* 160, 9–35.
Schmitz, T. A. (2000) 'Plausibility in the Greek Orators', *American Journal of Philology* 121, 47–77.
Schneider, J. P. (2000) 'Hiéronymos de Rhodes', in R. Goulet (ed.), *Dictionnaire des philosophes antiques*, vol. 3, Paris, 701–5.
Schneider, J. P. (2016) 'Straton de Lampsaque', in R. Goulet (ed.), *Dictionnaire des philosophes antiques*, vol. 6, Paris, 614–30.

Schneider, J. P. (2016a) 'Sotion d'Alexandrie', in R. Goulet (ed.), *Dictionnaire des philosophes antiques*, vol. 6, Paris, 521-6.
Schneider, J. P. (2016b) 'Théophraste d'Érèse', in R. Goulet (ed.), *Dictionnaire des philosophes antiques*, vol. 6, Paris, 1034-1120.
Schneider, K. (1932) 'Taberna', in *RE* II.4a, 1163-72.
Schofield, M. (1984) 'Ariston of Chios and the Unity of Virtues', *Ancient Philosophy* 4, 83-95.
Schofield, M. (1986) 'Cicero for and against Divination', *Journal of Roman Studies* 76, 47-65.
Schofield, M. (1999) 'Academic Epistemology', in K. Algra, J. Barnes, J. Mansfeld, and M. Schofield (eds), *The Cambridge History of Hellenistic Philosophy*, Cambridge, 323-51.
Schofield, M. (2002) 'Leucippus, Democritus and the οὐ μᾶλλον principle', *Phronesis* 47, 253-63.
Schofield, M. (2003) 'Stoic Ethics', in B. Inwood (ed.), *The Cambridge Companion to the Stoics*, Cambridge, 233-56.
Schofield, M. (2012) 'Pythagoreanism: Emerging from the Presocratic Fog', in C. Steel (ed.), *Aristotle's Metaphysics Alpha*, Oxford, 141-66.
Schofield, M. (2012a) 'The Neutralizing Argument: Carneades, Antiochus, Cicero', in D. N. Sedley (ed.), *The Philosophy of Antiochus*, Cambridge, 237-49.
Schofield, M. (2012b) 'Antiochus on Social Virtue', in D. N. Sedley (ed.), *The Philosophy of Antiochus*, Cambridge, 173-87.
Schofield, M. (2012c) 'Writing Philosophy', in C. E. W. Steel (ed.), *The Cambridge Companion to Cicero*, Cambridge, 73-87.
Schofield, M. (2017) 'Cicero's Plato', in T. Engberg-Pedersen (ed.), *From Stoicism to Platonism: The Development of Philosophy, 100 BCE-100 CE*, Cambridge, 47-66.
Schofield, M. (2018) 'Cicero on *Auctoritas*', in J. Bryan, R. Wardy, and J. Warren (eds), *Authors and Authorities in Ancient Philosophy*, Cambridge, 278-95.
Schrenk, L. P. (1991) 'Faculties of Judgement in the "Didaskalikos"', *Mnemosyne* 44, 347-63.
Schröder, B.-J. (1999) *Titel und Text: Zur Entwicklung lateinischer Gedichtüberschriften, mit Untersuchungen zu lateinischen Buchtiteln, Inhaltsverzeichnissen und anderen Gliederungsmitteln*, Berlin and New York.
Schultz, F. (1856^3) *Lateinische Synonymik zunächst für die oberen Klassen der Gymnasien*, Paderborn.
Schulz-Falkenthal, H. (1976) 'Die Kyniker und ihre Erkenntnistheorie', *Klio* 58, 535-42.
Schulze, W. (1904) *Zur Geschichte lateinischer Eigennamen*, Berlin.
Schulze, W. (1958) *Orthographica et Graeca Latina*, Rome.
Schumacher, H. (1966) *Der Akademiker Polemon. Kommentierte Sammlung der Testimonien zu Leben und Lehre*, Tübingen (diss. phil., unpublished).
Schwameis, C. (2014) *Die Praefatio von Ciceros De Inventione*, Munich.
Schwitzgebel, E. (2019) 'Belief', in *The Stanford Encyclopedia of Philosophy*, Edward N. Zalta (ed.), URL = <https://plato.stanford.edu/archives/fall2019/entries/belief/>.
Schwyzer, E. (1953) *Griechische Grammatik. Erster Band: Allgemeiner Teil, Lautlehre, Wortbildung, Flexion*. Munich.
Seager, R. (2014) 'The (Re/De)Construction of Clodius in Cicero's Speeches', *Classical Quarterly* 64, 226-40.
Sedley, D. N. (1976) 'Epicurus and the Mathematicians of Cyzicus', *Cronache Ercolanesi* 6, 23-54.
Sedley, D. N. (1977) 'Diodorus Cronus and Hellenistic Philosophy', *Proceedings of the Cambridge Philological Society*, 23: 74-120.
Sedley, D. N. (1981) 'The End of the Academy', *Phronesis* 26, 67-75.
Sedley, D. N. (1982) 'On Signs', in J. Barnes, J. Brunschwig, M. Burnyeat, and M. Schofield (eds), *Science and Speculation—Studies in Hellenistic Theory and Practice*, Cambridge, 239-72.
Sedley, D. N. (1982a) 'The Stoic Criterion of Identity', *Phronesis* 27, 255-75.

Sedley, D. N. (1983) 'Epicurus' Refutation of Determinism', in G. Pugliese Carratelli (ed.), *SUZHTHSIS: Studi sull'epicureismo greco e romano offerti a Marcello Gigante*, Naples 11–51.
Sedley, D. N. (1983a) 'The Motivation of Greek Skepticism', in M. Burnyeat (ed.), *The Skeptical Tradition*, Berkeley and Los Angeles, 9–29.
Sedley, D. N. (1985) 'The Stoic Theory of Universals', *Southern Journal of Philosophy* 23, 87–92.
Sedley, D. N. (1996) 'Three Platonist Interpretations of the *Theaetetus*', in C. Gill and M. M. McCabe (eds), *Form and Argument in Late Plato*, Oxford, 79–103.
Sedley, D. N. (1996a) 'Alcinous' Epistemology', in K. Algra, P. W. van der Horst, and D. T. Runia (eds), *Polyhistor: Studies in the History and Historiography of Ancient Philosophy*, Leiden, 300–12.
Sedley, D. N. (1997) 'Philosophical Allegiance in the Greco-Roman World', in M. Griffin and J. Barnes (eds), *Philosophia Togata I*, Oxford (2nd edn with corrections), 97–119.
Sedley, D. N. (1997a) 'The Ethics of Brutus and Cassius', *Journal of Roman Studies* 87, 41–53.
Sedley, D. N. (1997b) 'Plato's *Auctoritas* and the Rebirth of the Commentary Tradition', in J. Barnes and M. T. Griffin (eds), *Philosophia Togata II*, Oxford, 110–29.
Sedley, D. N. (1998) *Lucretius and the Transformation of Greek Wisdom*, Cambridge.
Sedley, D. N. (2002) 'The Origins of Stoic God', in D. Frede and A. Laks (eds), *Traditions of Theology. Studies in Hellenistic Theology, its Background, and its Aftermath*. Leiden and New York, 41–83.
Sedley, D. N. (2002a) 'Zeno's Definition of *phantasia kataleptike*', in T. Scaltsas and A. S. Mason (eds), *The Philosophy of Zeno*, Larnaka, 135–54.
Sedley, D. N. (2003) 'The School, from Zeno to Arius Didymus', in B. Inwood (ed.), *The Cambridge Companion to the Stoics*, Cambridge, 7–32.
Sedley, D. N. (2004) *The Midwife of Platonism*, Oxford.
Sedley, D. N. (2007) *Creationism and its Critics in Antiquity*, Berkeley, Los Angeles, and London.
Sedley, D. N. (2012) *The Philosophy of Antiochus*, Cambridge.
Sedley, D. N. (2012a) 'Introduction', in D. N. Sedley (ed.), *The Philosophy of Antiochus*, Cambridge, 1–8.
Sedley, D. N. (2012b) 'Antiochus as Historian of Philosophy', in D. N. Sedley (ed.), *The Philosophy of Antiochus*, Cambridge, 80–103.
Sedley, D. N. (2012c) 'Appendix—a Guide to the Testimonies for Antiochus', in D. N. Sedley (ed.), *The Philosophy of Antiochus*, Cambridge, 334–46.
Sedley, D. N. (2013) 'Cicero and the *Timaeus*', in M. Schofield (ed.), *Aristotle, Plato, and Pythagoreanism in the First Century B.C.*, Cambridge, 187–205.
Sedley, D. N. (2014) 'Horace's *Socraticae chartae* (*Ars poetica* 295–322)', *Materiali e discussioni per l'analisi dei testi classici* 72, 97–120.
Sedley, D. N. (2018) 'Epicurean Theories of Knowledge from Hermarchus to Lucretius and Philodemus', *Lexicon Philosophicum*, Special Issue: Hellenistic Theories of Knowledge, 105–21.
Sedley, D. N. (2019) 'Epicurus on Dialectic', in T. Bénatouïl and K. Ierodiakonou (eds), *Dialectic after Plato and Aristotle*, Proceedings of the XIIIth Symposium Hellenisticum, Cambridge, 82–113.
Sedley, D. N. (2020) 'Carneades' Theological Arguments', in P. Kalligas et al. (eds), *Plato's Academy—Its Working and its History*, Cambridge, 220–41.
Seel, G. (1993) 'Zur Geschichte und Logik des θερίζων λόγος', in K. Döring and T. Ebert (eds), *Dialektiker und Stoiker*, Stuttgart, 291–318.
Senore, C. (2017) 'Il ruolo di El Escorial, V.III.6 e dei suoi discendenti nella tradizione manoscritta del *Lucullus*', *Ciceroniana on line* I.1, 157–91.
Setaioli, A. (2018) 'Divinazione e arti congetturali. Quinto e Marco (e Posidonio) nel *De divinatione* ciceroniano', in E. Gavoille and S. Roesch (eds), *Divina Studia. Mélanges de religion et de philosophie anciennes offerts à François Guillaumont*, Bordeaux, 13–28.
Shackleton Bailey, D. R. (1960) *Towards a Text of Cicero: 'Ad Atticum'*, Cambridge.

Shackleton Bailey, D. R. (1965) *Cicero's Letters to Atticus*, Vol. 1: *68-59 B.C., 1-45 (Books I and II)*, Cambridge.
Shackleton Bailey, D. R. (1966) *Cicero's Letters to Atticus*, Vol. 5: *48-45 B.C., 211-354*, Cambridge.
Shanzer, D. (2007) 'Augustine's Disciplines: *Silent diutius Musae Varronis?*', in K. Pollmann and M. Vessey (eds), *Augustine and the Disciplines: From Cassiciacum to 'Confessions'*, Oxford, 69-112.
Sharples, R. W. (1991) *Cicero: On Fate (De Fato) and Boethius: The Consolation of Philosophy IV.5-7, V (Philosophiae Consolationis)*, Warminster.
Sharples, R. W. (2010) *Peripatetic Philosophy, 200 BC to AD 200. An Introduction and Collection of Sources in Translation*, Cambridge.
Sharples, R. W. and Sorabji, R. (2007) *Greek and Roman Philosophy 100 BC-200 AD*, 2 vols, London.
Shogry, S. (2019) 'What Do our Impressions Say? The Stoic Theory of Perceptual Content and Belief Formation', *Apeiron* 52, 29-63.
Sigsbef, D. L. (1976) 'The *Paradoxa Stoicorum* in Varro's Menippeans', *Classical Philology* 71, 244-8.
Silverman, A. (1990) 'Plato on Perception and "Commons" ', *Classical Quarterly* 40, 148-75.
Smith, M. F. (1993) *Diogenes of Oinoanda: The Epicurean Inscription*, Naples.
Smith, R. (1997) *Aristotle: Topics I and VIII*, Oxford.
Solodow, J. B. (1978) *The Latin Particle 'quidem'*, University Park.
Solomon, S. E. (2010) 'The Eggshell: Strength, Structure, and Function', *British Poultry Science* 51, 52-9.
Spahlinger, L. (2005) *Tulliana Simplicitas—Zu Form und Funktion des Zitats in den philosophischen Dialogen Ciceros*, Göttingen.
Spinelli, E. (2008) 'Sextus Empiricus, l'experiénce sceptique et l'horizon de l'éthique', *Cahiers Philosophiques* 115: 29-45.
Spinelli, E. (2016) 'Sextus Empiricus', in R. Goulet (ed.), *Dictionnaire des philosophes antiques*, vol. 6, Paris, 265-300.
Squire, M. (2011) *The Iliad in a Nutshell: Visualizing Epic on the 'Tabulae Iliacae'*, Oxford.
Staab, G. (2013) 'Numenios', in *Reallexikon für Antike und Christentum* vol. 25, 1172-97.
von Staden, H. (1978) 'The Stoic Theory of Perception and its "Platonic" Critics', in P. K. Machamer and R. G. Turnbull (eds), *Studies in Perception—Interrelations in the History of Philosophy and Science*, Columbus, 96-136.
von Staden, H. (1989) *Herophilus—The Art of Medicine in Early Alexandria*, Cambridge.
von Staden, H. (1992) 'The Discovery of the Body: Human Dissection and its Cultural Context in Ancient Greece', *The Yale Journal of Biology and Medicine* 65, 223-41.
von Staden, H. (1999) 'Celsus as a Historian', in P. J. van der Eijk (ed.), *Ancient Histories of Medicine—Essays in Medical Doxography and Historiography in Classical Antiquity*, Leiden, 251-94.
Stärk, E. (1995) *Kampanien als geistige Landschaft: Interpretationen zum antiken Bild des Golfs von Neapel*, Munich.
Steel, C. E. W. (2013) 'Structure, Meaning and Authority in Cicero's Dialogues', in S. Föllinger and G. M. Müller (eds), *Der Dialog in der Antike—Formen und Funktionen einer literarischen Gattung zwischen Philosophie, Wissensvermittlung und dramatischer Inszenierung*, Berlin and New York, 221-34.
Steier, A. (1930) 'Maulwurf', in *RE* XIV.2, 2338-42.
Steinmetz, P. (1989) 'Beobachtungen zu Ciceros philosophischem Standpunkt', in W. W. Fortenbaugh and P. Steinmetz (eds), *Cicero's Knowledge of the Peripatos (RUSCH 4)*, New Brunswick, 1-22.
Steinmetz, P. (1990) 'Planung und Planänderung der philosophischen Schriften Ciceros', in P. Steinmetz (ed.), *Beiträge zur hellenistischen Literatur und ihrer Rezeption in Rom*, Stuttgart, 141-53.

Steinmetz, P. (1994) 'Die Stoa', in H. Flashar (ed.), *Grundriss der Geschichte der Philosophie, Die Philosophie der Antike 4, Die Hellenistische Philosophie, Zweiter Halbband*, Basel, 495–716.

Stojanoviç, P. (2019) 'Zeno of Citium's Causal Theory of Apprehensive Appearances', *Ancient Philosophy* 39, 151–74.

Van Straaten, M. (1946) *Panétius. Sa vie, ses écrits et sa doctrine avec une édition des fragments*, Amsterdam.

Strasburger, H. (1990) *Ciceros philosophisches Spätwerk als Aufruf gegen die Herrschaft Caesars*, Hildesheim, Zurich, and New York.

Straume-Zimmermann, L. (1976) *Ciceros Hortensius*, Frankfurt.

Straume-Zimmermann, L. (1997²) *Marcus Tullius Cicero: Hortensius, Lucullus, Academici libri*, edited, translated with commentary by L. Straume-Zimmermann, F. Broemser, and O. Gigon, Munich and Zurich.

Striker, G. (1995) 'Cicero and Greek Philosophy', *Harvard Studies in Classical Philology* 97, 53–61.

Striker, G. (1996) *Essays in Hellenistic Epistemology and Ethics*, Cambridge.

Striker, G. (1996a) 'Κριτήριον τῆς ἀληθείας', in Striker (1996), 22–76.

Striker, G. (1996b) 'Sceptical Strategies', in Striker (1996) 92–115.

Striker, G. (1996c) 'Antipater, or the Art of Living', in Striker (1996), 298–315.

Striker, G. (1996d) 'Following Nature: A Study in Stoic Ethics', in Striker (1996), 221–80.

Striker, G. (1996e) 'Ataraxia: Happiness as Tranquility', in Striker (1996), 183–95.

Striker, G. (1996f) 'On the Difference between Pyrrhonists and Academics', in Striker (1996), 135–49.

Striker, G. (1997) 'Academics fighting Academics', in B. Inwood and J. Mansfeld (eds), *Assent and Argument—Studies in Cicero's 'Academic Books'*, Leiden, 257–76.

Striker, G. (2001) 'Scepticism as a Kind of Philosophy', *Archiv für Geschichte der Philosophie* 83, 113–29.

Striker, G. (2010) 'Academics vs. Pyrrhonists, reconsidered', in R. Bett (ed.), *The Cambridge Companion to Ancient Scepticism*, Cambridge, 195–207.

Striker, G. (2016) 'Philon (3), of Larissa, last undisputed head of the Academy, 159/158–84/83 BCE', *Oxford Classical Dictionary*. Retrieved 18 September 2021, URL = <https://oxfordre.com/classics/view/10.1093/acrefore/9780199381135.001.0001/acrefore-9780199381135-e-5005>.

Stroh, W. (1975) *Taxis und Taktik: Die advokatische Dispositionskunst in Ciceros Gerichtsreden*, Stuttgart.

Stroh, W. (1982) 'Die Nachahmung des Demosthenes in Ciceros Philippiken', in *Éloquence et Rhetorique chez Cicéron*, Vandœuvres-Genève, 1–31.

Stroud, B. (2014) 'Scepticism while Tracking the Truth', *teorema* 33, 171–9.

Stroux, J. (1937) 'Das Schlußwort zu Ciceros Lucullus', *Philologus* 92 n.s. 46, 109–11.

Stroux, L. (1965) *Vergleich und Metapher in der Lehre des Zenon von Kition*, Heidelberg (diss. phil.).

Sullivan, F. A. (1941) 'Cicero and Gloria', *Transactions and Proceedings of the American Philological Association* 72, 382–91.

Sutton, R. F. (2009) 'The Invention of the Female Nude: Zeuxis, Vase-Painting, and the Kneeling Bather', in J. H. Oakley and O. Palagia (eds), *Athenian Potters and Painters*, vol. 2, Oxford, 270–9.

Svavarsson, S. H. (2009) 'Plato on Forms and Conflicting Appearances: The Argument of Phd. 74A9-C9', *Classical Quarterly* 59, 60–74.

Svavarsson, S. H. (2010) 'Pyrrho and Early Pyrrhonism', in R. Bett (ed.), *The Cambridge Companion to Ancient Scepticism*, Cambridge, 36–57.

Svavarsson, S. H. (2014) 'Sextus Empiricus on Persuasiveness and Equipollence', in M.-K. Lee (ed.), *Strategies of Argument—Essays in Ancient Ethics, Epistemology, and Logic*, Oxford, 356–73.

Szymański, M. (1990) 'P. Berol. inv. 16545: A Text on Stoic Epistemology with a Fragment of Antipater of Tarsus', *Journal of Juristic Papyrology* 20, 139–41.
Talon, O. (1547) *Academia. Eiusdem in Academicum Ciceronis fragmentum explicatio, item in Lucullum commentarii*, Paris.
Tarán, L. (1975) *Academica: Plato, Philip of Opus, and the Pseudo-Platonic 'Epinomis'*, Philadelphia.
Tarán, L. (1987) 'Cicero's Attitude towards Stoicism and Scepticism in the *De Natura Deorum*', in K. Selig and R. Somerville (eds), *Florilegium Columbianum: Essays in Honor of Paul Oskar Kristeller*, New York, 1–22.
Tarrant, H. (1980) 'Academics and Platonics', *Prudentia* 12, 109–18.
Tarrant, H. (1981) 'Agreement and the Self-Evident in Philo of Larissa', *Dionysius* 5, 66–97.
Tarrant, H. (1982) 'Two Fragments of Cicero *Ac.* 1', *Liverpool Classical Monthly* 7.2, 21–2.
Tarrant, H. (1985) *Scepticism or Platonism*, Cambridge.
Tarrant, H. (2007) 'Antiochus: A New Beginning?', in R. W. Sharples and R. Sorabji (2007), vol. 2, 317–32.
Tarrant, H. (2018) 'Philo of Larissa', in D. E. Machuca and B. Reed (eds), *Skepticism from Antiquity to the Present*, London, 81–92.
Tarrant, H. (2020) 'One Academy? The Transition from Polemo and Crates to Arcesilaus', in P. Kalligas, C. Balla, E. Baziotopoulou-Valavani, and V. Karasmansis (eds), *Plato's Academy: Its Workings and its History*, Oxford, 200–19.
Tarver, T. (1997) 'Varro and the Antiquarianism of Philosophy', in J. Barnes and M. T. Griffin (eds), *Philosophia Togata*, Vol. II: *Plato and Aristotle at Rome*, Oxford, 130–64.
Tatarkiewicz, W. (1963) 'Classification of Arts in Antiquity', *Journal of the History of Ideas* 24, 231–40.
Tatum, W. J. (1999) *The Patrician Tribune—Publius Clodius Pulcher*, Chapel Hill.
Taub, L. (2009) 'Cosmology and Meteorology', in J. Warren (ed.), *The Cambridge Companion to Epicureanism*, Cambridge, 105–23.
Taylor, B. (2016) 'Definition and Ordinary Language in Cicero, De Finibus 2', *Classical Philology* 111, 54–73.
Taylor, C. C. W. (1980) ' "All Perceptions are True" ', in M. Schofield, M. Burnyeat, and J. Barnes (eds), *Doubt and Dogmatism—Studies in Hellenistic Epistemology*, Oxford, 105–24.
Tepedino Guerra, A. (1991) *Polieno—Frammenti*, Naples.
ter Beek, L. J. (2006) 'Ciceros Bericht über die Einführung der Rechtsmittel gegen Arglist (*dolus malus*) durch Aquilius Gallus', in A. P. M. H. Lardinois, M. G. M. van der Poel, and V. J. C. Hunink (eds), *Land of Dreams—Greek and Latin Studies in Honour of A. H. M. Kessels*, Leiden and Boston, 327–38.
Testard, M. (1958) *Saint Augustin et Cicéron*, 2 vols, Paris.
Theiler, W. (1964) *Die Vorbereitung des Neuplatonismus*, 2nd edn. Berlin.
Thesleff, H. (1960) *Yes and No in Plautus and Terence*, Helsingfors.
Thesleff, H. (1999) *Studies in Plato's Two-Level Model*, Helsinki.
Thiel, D. (2006) *Die Philosophie des Xenokrates im Kontext der Alten Akademie*, Munich and Leipzig.
Thielmann, P. (1885) 'Habere mit dem Part. Perf. Pass.', *Archiv für Lateinische Lexikographie und Grammatik mit Einschluss des älteren Mittellateins* 2, 509–49.
Thomas, R. F. (2000) 'A Trope by Any Other Name: "Polysemy", Ambiguity and Significatio in Virgil', *Harvard Studies in Classical Philology* 100, 381–407.
Thomas, Y. (1984) 'Se venger au forum: Solidarité familiale et procès criminal à Rome (Premier siècle av.–deuxième siècle ap. J.C.)', in R. Verdier and J.-P. Poly (eds), *La Vengeance: Études d'ethnologie, d'histoire et de philosophie*, vol. 3, Paris, 65–100.
Thommen, L. (1989) *Das Volkstribunat der späten römischen Republik*, Stuttgart.
Thorsrud, H. (2009) *Ancient Scepticism*, Stocksfield.

Thorsrud, H. (2010) 'Arcesilaus and Carneades', in R. Bett (ed.), *The Cambridge Companion to Ancient Scepticism*, Cambridge, 58–80.
Thorsrud, H. (2012) 'Radical and Mitigated Scepticism in Cicero's *Academica*', in W. Nicgorski (ed.), *Cicero's Practical Philosophy*, Notre Dame, 133–51.
Thurneysen, R. (1905) 'Senium und desiderium', *Archiv für Lateinische Lexikographie und Grammatik* 14, 179–84.
Tielemann, T. (1996) *Galen and Chrysippus on the Soul. Argument and Refutation in the 'De Placitis' Books II–III*, Leiden.
Tielemann, T. (2008) 'Methodology', in R. J. Hankinson (ed.), *The Cambridge Companion to Galen*, Cambridge, 49–65.
Tielemann, T. (2011) 'Galen on Perception', *Antiquorum Philosophia* 5, 83–97.
Todd, R. B. (1973) 'Chrysippus on Infinite Divisibility (Diogenes Laertius VII.150)', *Apeiron* 7, 21–9.
Togni, P. (2013) 'Plato's Soul-Book Simile and Stoic Epistemology', *Méthexis* 26, 163–85.
Tokhtas'ev, S. (1996) 'Die Kimmerier in der antiken Überlieferung', *Hyperboreus* 2, 1–46.
Tor, S. (2013) 'Sextus Empiricus on Xenophanes' Scepticism', *International Journal for the Study of Skepticism* 3, 1–23.
Trabattoni, F. (2005) 'Arcesilao platonico?', in Mauro Bonazzi and Vincenza Celluprica (eds), *L'eredità platonica: Studi sul platonismo da Arcesilao a Proclo*, Naples, 13–50.
Trabattoni, F. (2022) 'Antiochus of Ascalon's "Platonic" Ethics', *Elenchos* 43, 85–103.
Tracy, J. (2010) '"Fallentia Sidera": The Failure of Astronomical Escapism in Lucan', *American Journal of Philology* 131, 635–61.
Traglia, A. (1971) 'Note su Cicerone traduttore di Platone e di Epicuro', in *Studi filologici e storici in onore di Vittorio de Falco*, Naples, 307–40.
Tronci, L. (2013) 'Verbal Adjectives', in *Encyclopedia of Ancient Greek Language and Linguistics*, Managing Editors online edn, consulted online on 19 April 2019, DOI: 10.1163/2214-448X_eagll_COM_00000366.
Tröster, M. (2008) *Themes, Character, and Politics in Plutarch's 'Life of Lucullus'—The Construction of a Roman Aristocrat*, Stuttgart.
Tschiedel, H. J. (1977) 'Caesar und der berauschte Cato', *Würzburger Jahrbücher für die Altertumswissenschaft* 3, 105–13.
Tschiedel, H. J. (1981) *Caesars 'Anticato': Eine Untersuchung der Testimonien und Fragmente*, Darmstadt.
Tsouna, V. (1998) *The Epistemology of the Cyrenaic School*, Cambridge.
Tsouna, V. (2011) 'Philodemus, Seneca and Plutarch on Anger', in J. Fish and K. R. Sanders (eds), *Epicurus and the Epicurean Tradition*, Cambridge, 183–210.
Tsouni, G. (2012) 'Antiochus on Contemplation and the Happy Life', in D. N. Sedley (ed.), *The Philosophy of Antiochus*, Cambridge, 131–50.
Tsouni, G. (2018) 'The Emergence of Platonic and Aristotelian Authority in the First Century BCE', in J. Bryan, R. Wardy, and J. Warren (eds), *Authors and Authorities in Ancient Philosophy*, Cambridge, 263–77.
Tsouni, G. (2018a) 'The "Academy" in Rome: Antiochus and his *uetus Academia*', in G. M. Müller and F. M. Zini (eds), *Philosophie in Rom—Römische Philosophie? Kultur-, literatur- und philosophiegeschichtliche Aspekte*, Berlin and New York, 139–49.
Tsouni, G. (2019) *Antiochus and Peripatetic Ethics*, Cambridge.
Tulli, M. (2005) 'Der *Axiochus* und die Tradition der *consolatio* in der Akademie', in K. Döring, M. Erler, and S. Schorn (eds), *Pseudoplatonica: Akten des Kongresses zu den Pseudoplatonica vom 6.–9. Juli 2003 in Bamberg*, Stuttgart, 255–71.
Tumová, E., Gous, R. M., and Tyler, N. (2014) 'Effect of Hen Age, Environmental Temperature, and Oviposition Time on Egg Shell Quality and Egg Shell and Serum Mineral Contents in Laying and Broiler Breeder Hens', *Czech Journal of Animal Science* 59, 435–43.

Ursinus, F. (1581) *In omnia opera Ciceronis notae*, Antwerp.
Usener, H. (1884) *Epicurea*, Leipzig.
Usener, H. (1901) 'Italische Volksjustiz', *Rheinisches Museum für Philologie* 56, 1–28.
Usener, H. (1977) *Glossarium Epicureum*, ed. M. Gigante and W. Schmid, Rome.
Usher, M. D. (2006) 'Carneades' Quip: Orality, Philosophy, Wit, and the Poetics of Impromptu Quotation', *Oral Tradition* 21, 190–209.
Vahlen, J. (1903²) *Ennianae Poesis Reliquiae*, Leipzig.
Vander Waerdt, P. A. (1987) 'The Justice of the Epicurean Wise Man', *Classical Quarterly* 37, 402–22.
Vasaly, A. (2014) 'The Composition of the *Ab Urbe Condita*: The Case of the First Pentad', in B. Mineo (ed.), *A Companion to Livy*, Chichester, 217–29.
Vassallo, C. (2015) 'Senofane e lo Scetticismo antico. *PHerc.* 1428, fr. 12 e il contesto dossografico di DK 21 B34', in V. Gysembergh and A. Schwab (eds), *Le Travail du Savoir / Wissensbewältigung*, Trier, 165–93.
Vassallo, C. (2018) 'The "Pre-Socratic" section of Philodemus' *On Piety*: A New Reconstruction', *Archiv für Papyrusforschung* 64, 98–147.
Verde, F. (2010) 'Ancora su Timasagora Epicureo', *Elenchos* 31, 285–317.
Verde, F. (2016) 'Timasagoras de Rhodes', in R. Goulet (ed.), *Dictionnaire des philosophes antiques*, vol. 6, Paris, 1192–7.
Verde, F. (2017) 'Plato's Demiurge (NF 155 = YF 200) and Aristotle's Flux (Fr. 5 Smith): Diogenes of Oinoanda on the History of Philosophy', in J. Hammerstaedt, P.-M. Morel, and R. Güremen (eds), *Diogenes of Oinoanda: Epicureanism and Philosophical Debates*, Leuven, 67–87.
Verde, F. (2018) 'Ancora sullo statuto veritativo della sensazione in Epicuro', *Lexicon Philosophicum*, Special Issue, 79–104, URL = <http://lexicon.cnr.it/index.php/LP/article/view/562/415>.
Vezzoli, S. (2016) *Arcesilao di Pitane—L'origine del platonismo neoaccademico*, Turnhout.
Vimercati, E. (2002) *Panezio—Testimonianze e Frammenti*, Milan.
Voelke, A.-J. (1990) 'Soigner par le logos: la thérapeutique de Sextus Empiricus', in A.-J. Voelke (ed.), *Le Scepticisme Antique—Perspectives Historiques et Systématiques*, Geneva, Lausanne, Neuchâtel, 181–94.
de Vogel, C. J. (1953) 'On the Neoplatonic Character of Platonism and the Platonic Character of Neoplatonism', *Mind* 62, 43–64.
Vogt, K. M. (2004) 'Die frühe stoische Theorie des Werts—eine Skizze', in F. J. Bormann and C. Schröer (eds), *Abwägende Vernunft: praktische Rationalität in historischer, systematischer und religionsphilosophischer Perspektive*, Berlin and New York, 61–77.
Vogt, K. M. (2006) 'Skeptische Suche und das Verstehen von Begriffen', in C. Rapp and T. Wagner (eds), *Wissen und Bildung in der antiken Philosophie*, Stuttgart, 333–47.
Vogt, K. M. (2008) *Law, Reason, and the Cosmic City: Political Philosophy in the Early Stoa*, Oxford.
Vogt, K. M. (2009) 'Sons of the Earth: Are the Stoics Metaphysical Brutes?', *Phronesis* 54, 136–54.
Vogt, K. M. (2010) 'Ancient Skepticism', *The Stanford Encyclopedia of Philosophy* (Winter), Edward N. Zalta (ed.), URL = <http://plato.stanford.edu/archives/win2011/entries/skepticism-ancient/>.
Vogt, K. M. (2010a) 'Scepticism and Action', in R. Bett (ed.), *The Cambridge Companion to Ancient Scepticism*, Cambridge, 165–80.
Vogt, K. M. (2012) *Belief and Truth: A Skeptic Reading of Plato*, Oxford.
Vogt, K. M. (2014) 'The Hellenistic Academy', in J. Warren and F. Sheffield (eds), *The Routledge Companion to Ancient Philosophy*, New York, 482–95.
Vogt, K. M. (2015) 'Ancient Skepticism', in *The Stanford Encyclopedia of Philosophy* (Fall), Edward N. Zalta (ed.), URL = <http://plato.stanford.edu/archives/fall2015/entries/skepticism-ancient/>.

Vogt, K. M. (2015a) 'Why Ancient Skeptics Don't Doubt the Existence of the External World', in G. D. Williams and K. Volk (eds), *Roman Reflections: Studies in Latin Philosophy*, New York, 260–74.
Vogt, K. M. (2016) 'All Sense-Perceptions are True: Epicurean Responses to Skepticism and Relativism', in J. Lezra and L. Blake (eds), *Lucretius and Modernity*, New York, 145–59.
Volk, K. (2016) 'Roman Pythagoras', in G. D. Williams and K. Volk (eds), *Roman Reflections: Studies in Latin Philosophy*, New York, 33–49.
Volk, K. (2019) 'Varro and the Disorder of Things', *Harvard Studies in Classical Philology* 110, 183–212.
Volkmann, H. (1955) 'P. Valerius Publicola (Poplicola)', in *RE* 8A, 178–88.
Volkmann, R. (1869) *Leben, Schriften und Philosophie des Plutarch von Chaeronea, Zweiter Theil: Plutarchs Philosophie*, Berlin.
Voss, B. R. (1966) 'Tusculum oder Neapolitanum? Der Ort des Gesprächs in Ciceros Hortensius', *Hermes* 94, 505–6.
Wackernagel, J. (2009) *Lectures on Syntax, with Special Reference to Greek, Latin, and Germanic*, edited with notes and bibliography by David Langslow, Oxford.
Walde, A. and Hofmann, J. B. (1938³) *Lateinisches etymologisches Wörterbuch*, 3 vols. Heidelberg.
Wardle, D. (2006) *Cicero on Divination: De Divinatione, Book I*, Oxford.
Wardy, R. (1988) 'Lucretius on What Atoms Are Not', *Classical Philology* 83, 112–28.
Warren, J. (2002) 'Socratic Scepticism in Plutarch's *Adversus Colotem*', *Elenchos* 23, 333–56.
Warren, J. (2002a) *Epicurus and Democritean Ethics: An Archaeology of Ataraxia*, Cambridge.
Warren, J. (2011) 'What God Didn't Know: Sextus Empiricus AM 9.162-6', in D. Machuca (ed.), *New Essays on Ancient Pyrrhonism*, Leiden, Brill: 41–68.
Warren, J. (2013) 'Epicureans and Cyrenaics on Pleasure as a *pathos*', in S. Marchand and F. Verde (eds), *Épicurisme et Scepticisme*, Rome, 85–103.
Warren, J. (2013a) 'Plutarch's *Adversus Colotem* and the Cyrenaics: 1120C–1121E', URL = <https://journals.openedition.org/aitia/706>.
Warren, J. (2016) 'Epicurean Pleasure in Cicero's *De Finibus*', in J. Annas and G. Betegh (eds), *Cicero's De Finibus: Philosophical Approaches*, Oxford, 41–76.
Wassmann, H. (1996) *Ciceros Widerstand gegen Caesars Tyrannis—Untersuchungen zur politischen Bedeutung der philosophischen Spätschriften*, Bonn.
Waszink, J. H. (2010²) *Quinti Septimi Florentis Tertulliani De Anima*, Leiden.
Watkins, C. (1995) *How to Kill a Dragon: Aspects of Indo-European Poetics*, Oxford.
Wehrli, F. (1969) *Hieronymos von Rhodos; Kritolaos und seine Schüler; Rückblick: Der Peripatos in vorchristlicher Zeit; Register*, Die Schule des Aristoteles, vol. 10, 2nd edn, Basel and Stuttgart.
Weische, A. (1972) *Ciceros Nachahmung der attischen Redner*, Heidelberg.
Welsh, J. T. (2012) 'The Methods of Nonius Marcellus' Sources 26, 27 and 28', *Classical Quarterly* 62, 827–45.
Westerink, L. G. (1962) *Anonymous Prolegomena to Platonic Philosophy*, Amsterdam.
Westerink, L. G., Trouillard, J., and Segonds, A. Ph. (1990) *Prolégomènes à la philosophie de Platon*, Paris.
Whitaker, C. W. A. (1996) *Aristotle's De Interpretatione: Contradiction and Dialectic*, Cambridge.
White, F. (1975) 'Plato on Geometry', *Apeiron* 9, 5–14.
White, M. J. (1989) 'What to Say to a Geometer', *Greek, Roman and Byzantine Studies* 30, 297–311.
White, N. (1979) 'The Basis of Stoic Ethics', *Harvard Studies in Classical Philology* 83, 143–78.
Whittaker, J. (1990) *Alcinoos—Enseignement des Doctrines de Platon*, Paris.
Wichert, G. H. R. (1856) *Die lateinische Stillehre*, Königsberg.

Wieacker, F. (1988) *Römische Rechtsgeschichte. Quellenkunde, Rechtsbildung, Jurisprudenz und Rechtsliteratur. Erster Abschnitt: Einleitung, Quellenkunde, Frühzeit und Republik*, Munich.
von Wilamowitz-Moellendorff (1881) *Antigonos von Karystos*, Berlin.
Wildberger, J. (2006) *Seneca und die Stoa: der Platz des Menschen in der Welt*, 2 vols, Berlin and New York.
Williams, B. (1978) *Descartes: The Project of Pure Enquiry*, New York.
Williamson, T. (1994) *Vagueness*, London and New York.
Willink, C. W. (1989) *Euripides—Orestes*, Oxford.
Wilson Nightingale, A. (2004) *Spectacles of Truth in Classical Greek Philosophy—Theoria in its Cultural Context*, Cambridge.
Winiarczyk, M. (1976) 'Der erste Atheistenkatalog des Kleitomachus', *Philologus* 120, 32–46.
Winterbottom, M. (1994) *M. Tulli Ciceronis De Officiis*, Oxford.
Wiseman, T. P. (1994) 'The Necessary Lesson', in T. P. Wiseman, *Historiography and Imagination: Eight Essays on Roman Culture*, Exeter, 86–9.
Wiseman, T. P. (2009) 'Cicero and Varro', in T. P. Wiseman, *Remembering the Roman People: Essays on Late-Republican Politics and Literature*, Oxford, 107–29.
Wiseman, T. P. (2009a) 'Marcopolis', in T. P. Wiseman, *Remembering the Roman People: Essays on Late-Republican Politics and Literature*, Oxford, 131–51.
Wisse, J., Winterbottom, M., and Fantham, E. (2008) *M. Tullius Cicero, De Oratore Libri III, A Commentary on Book III, 96–230*, vol. 5, Heidelberg.
Wöhrle, G. (1993) 'War Parmenides ein schlechter Dichter? Oder: Zur Form der Wissensvermitllung in der frühgriechischen Philosophie', in W. Kullmann and J. Althoff (eds), *Vermittlung und Tradierung von Wissen in der griechischen Kultur*, Tübingen, 167–80.
Woolf, R. (2015) *Cicero—The Philosophy of a Roman Sceptic*, London and New York.
Wright, M. R. (1997) 'Ferox uirtus', in S. M. Braund and C. Gill (eds), *The Passions in Roman Thought and Literature*, Cambridge, 169–84.
Wynne, J. P. F. (2014) 'Learned and Wise: Cotta the Sceptic in Cicero's *On the Nature of the Gods*', *Oxford Studies in Ancient Philosophy* 47, 245–73.
Wynne, J. P. F. (2018) 'Cicero', in D. E. Machuca and B. Reed (eds), *Skepticism from Antiquity to the Present*, London, 93–101.
Wynne, J. P. F. (2019) *Cicero on the Philosophy of Religion*, Cambridge.
Wyss, B. (2005) *Akademie, Akademiker und Skeptiker: Studien zur Rezeption der Akademie in der lateinischen und griechischen Natur des zweiten Jahrhunderts nach Christus*, Freiburg, Switzerland (diss. phil.).
Zanker, P. (1995) *Die Maske des Sokrates: das Bild des Intellektuellen in der antiken Kunst*, Munich.
Zetzel, J. E. G. (1998) '*De re publica* and *De rerum natura*', in P. E. Knox and C. Foss (eds), *Style and Tradition: Studies in Honor of Wendell Clausen*, Stuttgart and Leipzig, 230–47.
Zetzel, J. E. G. (2007) 'The Influence of Cicero on Ennius', in W. Fitzgerald and E. Gowers (eds), *Ennius perennis: The 'Annals' and Beyond*, Cambridge, 1–16.
Zetzel, J. E. G. (2016) 'Philosophy Is in the Streets', in G. D. Williams and K. Volk (eds), *Roman Reflections: Studies in Latin Philosophy*, New York, 50–90.
Zeyl, D. (1975) 'Plato and Talk of a World in Flux: *Timaeus* 49a6–50b5', *Harvard Studies in Classical Philology* 79, 125–48.
Zeyl, D. (2000) *Plato—Timaeus*, Indianapolis.
Zhmud, L. (2001) 'Revising Doxography: Hermann Diels and his Critics', *Philologus* 145, 219–43.
Zhmud, L. (2006) *The Origin of the History of Science in Classical Antiquity*, Berlin and New York.
Zimmermann, R. (1996) *The Law of Obligations—Roman Foundations of the Civilian Tradition*, Oxford.
Zumpt, A. W. (1959) *M. Tullii Ciceronis Oratio pro M. Murena*, Berlin.

Addenda to the Bibliography

Dyck, A.R. (1996) *A Commentary on Cicero, 'De Officiis'*, Ann Arbor.
Lévy, C. (1980) 'Un problème doxographique chez Cicéron: Les indifférentistes', *Revue des Études Latines* 58, 238–51.
Malaspina, E. (2020) 'Lupo e "Hadoardo" nel Lucullus di Cicerone: congetture carolinge e tradizioni perdute nel Corpus Leidense', *Rationes Rerum* 16, 251–88.

General Index

Acad.:
  Catulus (dialogue) section 9.2 xxv, xxx, lxxix,
    cv, cxv, cxxi, clxvii, clxxii, clxxvi, clxxviii, 91,
    115, 119, 131, 175, 238–9, 265–74, 286, 295,
    303, 305, 309, 317–19, 321, 323, 326, 328, 344,
    348, 352, 354, 356, 359, 370, 374, 379, 389–90,
    394, 407, 409, 428, 436, 441, 443, 445, 447,
    452, 468, 471, 493, 496–7, 506, 512, 514,
    517–18, 529, 535, 549, 551, 554, 564, 575, 577,
    601, 611, 638, 658, 667, 696, 732, 778, 780,
    783, 794
  characters in the three editions clxxi
  composition section 9.1
  date xxix
  editions section 9 294
  as evidence for Academic scepticism xlviii
  format xxxiii
  interpretations xlviii
  missing parts section 9.2 265
  prefaces cxlviii, 295
  and the Roman Books view section 4.3 xxv, xl,
    xli, xliii, xlv, xlvi, xlix, clv, clvi, clvii, clxix,
    clxx, clxxi, clxxiv, clxxv, 115, 124, 288, 325,
    350, 354, 357, 407, 421, 423, 457, 459, 508,
    520, 540, 543, 545, 567, 568, 685, 795, 796,
    800, 803
  significance xxi
  sources section 9.3
  status among Cicero's works section 3
  title(s) section 9.4
  tripartite division of ethics, logic,
    physics cxvii, 149
  tripartite division of senses, their products,
    reason 358, 453, 599
  and work on *Tusc.* xix
Academic scepticism:
  not *ad hominem* already in Clitomachus'
    day (?) 652
  affinity to Roman attitudes 792
  ἀκαταληψία l, clxx, 253, 260, 292, 325, 328–9,
    349, 353–5, 357, 365, 390–4, 434–5, 455, 506,
    520, 529, 535, 537, 559, 567, 570, 572, 574,
    651, 797, 807, 808, 821, 823
  ἀπαραλλαξία section 5.5 xxiii, xxxviii, xl, li, lx,
    lxi, lxiv, lxv, lxvi, lxvii, lxviii, lxix, lxx, lxxii,
    lxxiv, lxxiv, lxxv, lxxviii, lxxix, cxxxv, cxxxvi,
    cxxxvii, clxxii, clxxxiv, clxxxv, clxxxviii, 242,
    289, 291, 384, 387, 407, 415, 417, 420, 422–3,
    425, 427, 441, 443, 449, 450, 453–8, 462, 463,
    464, 465, 466, 470–1, 473, 474, 479, 480, 490,
    493, 501, 504–5, 513, 514, 515, 530, 536, 543,
    565, 572, 574, 587–9, 591, 595, 597, 599, 600,
    602, 606, 608, 641–3, 647, 653, 684, 714, 776,
    798, 834
  ἀπαραλλαξία, non-perceptual section 5.5
    lxxviii, 454, 455, 462, 463, 505, 543
  'approval' xlii, xlvi, cvii, cxxxi, cxxxv, cxxxvii,
    cxl, clxxvi, cxci, cxcii, 273, 300–1, 431, 434,
    436, 458, 460, 465, 506, 520, 525, 548, 570,
    640, 644, 653, 654–66, 674, 682, 686, 692, 732,
    740, 763, 773, 782, 796–9, 814
  argument against a thesis xxxv, xxxvii, xxxviii
  arguments from premisses 'owned' by more than
    one school 495
  argument *in utramque partem* xlix, lxxx, c,
    cxlvi, clv, 124, 251, 257, 259, 263, 306, 409,
    470, 506, 508, 510–11, 732, 742
  Clitomacheanism sections 4.1, 8
  conflicting appearances clxviii, 267, 268, 271–4,
    291, 359, 361, 366, 575, 581
  core argument xl, xli, lxxviii, lxxix, cxxxv,
    cxxxviii, clxxiii, 391, 393, 441–66, 470, 476,
    529, 530, 535–8, 551, 574, 586–7, 634, 636,
    653, 671, 680–1, 684–6, 798, 835
  corollary argument xl, xli, cxxxv, cxxxvi,
    cxxxviii, 529, 530, 535–6, 568, 569, 570, 572
  corollary argument, alternative to xli, 566, 568,
    795, 799, 801
  criterion, views on 776
  and *decreta*/δόγματα 389
  and Stoic dialectic 608
  'dialectical' argument xxxix
  divisions of impressions lxxxiii, lxxxv, lxxxviii,
    lxxxix, xcix, ciii, 443–4, 642
  dogmatism, secret or esoteric 507–11
  dreams, arguments citing section 5.6.1 487
  endorsement xxxix
  Fin. and Clitomacheanism cli
  'following' cxlix, cxcii, 104, 301, 333, 369, 374,
    381, 398, 426, 439, 458, 505, 631, 644, 663,
    665, 692, 713, 757, 770, 777
  freedom cxlvii, cliii, 277, 298–9, 300, 302, 314,
    439, 705, 716, 724
  and geometry 695

GENERAL INDEX

Academic scepticism (*Cont.*)
 groupings (?) 407
 historical narrative associated with it section 7.1
 intention in advancing arguments 454
 Metrodorean view section 4.4
 mitigated scepticism sections 4.2, 6.6 xxiv,
  xxxix, xl, xliii, xlix, xlix, l, cxxxiv, cxlix, cl, clv,
  clvi, clvii, clxx, clxxiii, clxxiv, clxxvi, 114, 267,
  273, 301, 311, 323–4, 326, 340, 343, 346, 354,
  393, 396–7, 407, 409, 410, 424, 426, 428, 434,
  441, 442, 457–8, 505, 510, 519–20, 530, 531,
  540, 566, 568, 647, 652, 660, 678, 681–2, 687,
  690, 732, 778, 782–3, 795–6
 mitigated scepticism determining the reception
  of the New Academy (?) appendix 1
 naturalism cii
 oar, broken 271, 359
 in *Off*. cliii
 οὐ μᾶλλον formula 462
 on perceptual experience generally 491
 'Philonian/Metrodorian view' xli, xlv, 301, 314,
  350, 407, 409, 414, 424, 427, 441, 459, 460,
  540, 566, 678, 796–7, 814
 and physics 695
 and Presocratics section cix
 probabile (πιθανόν), emergence of section 6
 probabile, not entitled to (?) 289
 rationale section 4
 and 'real life' 512
 Roman Books view section 4.3 xxv, xl, xli, xliii,
  xlv, xlvii, xlix, clv, clvi, clvii, clxix, clxx, clxxi,
  clxxiv, clxxv, 115, 124, 288, 325, 350, 354, 357,
  407, 421, 423, 457, 459, 508, 520, 540, 543,
  545, 567, 568, 685, 795–6, 800, 803
 search for the truth xxxviii, xlii, xlvi, xlix,
  cxxxviii, cl, clv, clxxxi, 249, 273, 276, 289, 298,
  301, 313, 316–17, 339, 341, 388, 506, 510–11,
  521, 523, 525, 569, 732, 734, 813
 on the senses 575
 'stealing the daylight' of human beings by
  rejecting apprehension 400, 454
 Stoic terminology, use of xxxix
 invoking the *Theaetetus* lxiv, 191, 250
 ueri simile see probabile
 uerba sciendi, use of 516
 see also Arcesilaus; Carneades; Clitomachus; Philo
  (or Philio) of Larissa; Marcus Tullius Cicero
Academy:
 defections xxiv, xlvi, cxxiv, 539, 780, 815
 divisions (periods) of 117, 133
 sceptical phase xxiii
 tolerant xliii
Academy, Old (= Plato's successors):
 Antiochus' interpretation section 7.2
 ethics 135
 Philo's interpretation cviii
 physics 162
Academy, 'Old' (Antiochus'), *see* Antiochus
Academy, sceptical, *see* Academic scepticism
Lucius Aelius Stilo 83, 105
Aenesidemus 408, 412
 criticism of Academics 396, 444, 460, 816
 date 754
 defection from the Academy 815
 and Pyrrho 668, 754
 see Antiochus
Aeschines of Naples (Academic) 344
Ajax (Roman tragedy) 605
Alcinous:
 on epistemology 195, 237
Amafinius (Epicurean) 87, 99, 101
Anaxagoras cx, cxii, 254, 280, 549–50, 554, 580,
 641, 646, 703, 710–11, 721
Anaximander 703, 704, 710, 728
Anaximenes 703, 704, 710, 711
ancestors xxxv, cii, cxi, cxv, 204, 330, 332–3, 338,
 340, 354, 520, 549, 554, 556, 777, 779, 788
Anonymus *in Theatetum, see* Index Locorum
Antiochus:
 abandoning Academic scepticism cl, 117, 123,
  325, 394, 539, 546, 688
 Academic tradition, claim to cxx, 119
 Alexandrian scene cxi, clxviii, clxxviii, 113, 248,
  321, 328, 331, 542
 ἀντακολουθία, of virtues 214
 antiqui (*ueteres*) cxvi, cxvii, cxviii, cxix, cxxi, cxxiii,
  cxxiv, clix, clxxv, 104, 140, 161–3, 165–6, 169,
  171, 183, 189, 192, 199, 216, 228, 745, 751, 779
 ἀπάθεια of the sage 763
 and ἀπαραλλαξία 457
 appropriate action 138
 Aristotelian texts, use of 146
 Aristotle, invocation of 123
 on the cataleptic impression section 5 234, 416
 contact with Cicero cxlvi, 119
 date 321–30, 514
 and Democritus 727
 desire for fame (?) 547
 disagreement with the Stoics on the end 761
 dismissed Roman Books view xxv, 322
 on emotions 227
 end (τέλος), Antiochian, in the *Carneadea
  diuisio* 142
 end (τέλος), views on 136, 142
 ethics, from a historical point of view 135
 forms, views on 171, 190
 goods, external 141
 history of philosophy, views on section 7
 history of the sceptical Academy, views on 340
 λογική, from a historical point of view 188

and μετριοπάθεια 764, 765
and Middle Platonism xxxii, 173, 198
on the mind 399
and naturalism 270, 429, 504
and naturalism, ethical 136-8, 143, 747
officium 160
οἰκείωσις, views on 141, 159
physics in the Old Academy, views on 162
Platonic texts, reference to 146, 170, 191, 231
and Polemo 139, 143
prima forma, concept of cxiii, cxviii, cxix, cxx, cxxi, cxxv, cxxviii, clxxv, cxciv, 120, 125, 130, 160, 170, 183, 189, 201, 205-7, 215, 219, 226, 228-9, 231-3, 237, 241, 244-5, 483, 512, 777
prima naturae 137, 140-1, 148, 158-9, 212, 741, 745-7, 756
providential organization of the world 187, 477, 718
retaining aspects of the sceptical posture (?) 320
sign, cataleptic impression interpreted as 416
Sosus xxx, cxxi, clxxi, clxxii, clxxiii, clxxv, clxxvii, clxxviii, 116, 118-19, 123, 169, 252, 322-3, 325, 328, 331-2, 508, 590, 653, 780, 850
on *temeritas* 406
terminology, changes in section 7.2 283, 342
tria bona 137, 140-2, 147
see also Aristotle; Peripatetics; Philo (or Philio) of Larissa; Marcus Tullius Cicero
Antipater of Tarsus xxiii, cxx, 212, 269, 346, 348, 389-95, 677, 679, 761
date xxiii
division of impressions, author of (?) 444, 638
on the end 159, 745, 748, 757
anti-sceptical arguments 123, 276, 289, 380, 541, 544, 666, 833
concepts, related to 415
dilemma 455
no entitlement to 'the true' 313
see ἀπραξία
Marcus Antistius Labeo 488
ἀπαραλλαξία xxiii, xxxviii, xl, li, lx, lxi, lxiv, lxv, lxvi, lxvii, lxviii, lxix, lxx, lxxii, lxxiv, lxxiv, lxxv, lxxviii, lxxix, cxxxv, cxxxvi, cxxxvii, clxxii, clxxxiv, clxxxv, clxxxviii, 242, 289, 291, 384, 387, 407, 415, 417, 420, 422-3, 425, 427, 441, 443, 449-50, 453-8, 462-6, 470-1, 473, 474, 479-80, 490, 493, 501, 504-5, 513-15, 530, 536, 543, 565, 572, 574, 587-9, 591, 595, 597, 599-600, 602, 606, 608, 641-3, 647, 653, 684, 714, 776, 798, 834
basic contention lxxviii
'approval' 654-66
ἀπραξία 429-40
in Aristotle 435
arising from ἀκαταληψία 434
and assent 429, 673

and the πιθανόν 508
see also Arcesilaus; Clitomacheanism
L. Appuleius Saturninus 330-1, 333-4
Arcesilaus section 7.5 342, 569
ἀπαραλλαξία objection section 5.6 xxliii, li
ἀπραξία charge, response to cxxxv
and Aristo of Chios cxl
commitments cxxxviii
date xxiii, 570
disavowal of knowledge 253
dogmatism, secret 507
εὔλογον lxxx, cxxxv, cxxxix, 530
figurehead for the Clitomachean position cxxix, cl, 442, 505, 528, 530
interaction with Zeno section 5 cxxxi, 563
interpretations of section 7.5
opposition to dogmatists in general 249, 257
'Plato in front...' cxl, 825
modelling himself on Socrates cxxxiii
'views' 250
see also Academic scepticism; Carneades; Philo (or Philio) of Larissa; Marcus Tullius Cicero
argument from design 398, 400, 728
argument on either side (*in utramque partem*) xlix, cxlvi, clv, clxv, cxcvi, 124, 251, 257, 259, 306, 312, 409, 470, 508, 510-11, 726, 732, 742
Aristippus 230, 755
end, view on 738, 756
Aristo of Alexandria 329
Aristo of Chius:
and Arcesilaus cxl
ethics 737
on indifferents 754
and Pyrrho 753
rejecting logic and physics 724
on terminology 738
Aristotle:
and Antiochus 123-5
element, fifth 165, 170, 183, 214, 229
end, view on 738
forms, particular 164
on forms, Platonic 206, 215
on inactivity/ἀπραξία 435
man as a political animal 155
De philosophia 714
on rhetoric and dialectic 204
role in Antiochus' construction of philosophy cxvii, 122, 123, 130
on void 727
see also Antiochus; Critolaus; Peripatetics; Staseas
Aristus (brother of Antiochus) 113, 546
art (craft; *ars*, τέχνη):
division of 375
and memory 669

assent:
  Academic attitude to 504
  and approval 654
  and ἀπραξία 429, 674
  faculty of animals (?) 431
  movement of the soul's ruling part lv
  to the non-cataleptic lv
  in nostra potestate 432, 433, 437–9
  and the Roman Books view xlvii
  self-aware, of the mitigated sceptic 794
  in Stoic thought 657
  and sub-virtues of dialectic 246
  terminology 239
Marcus Atilius Regulus 379
atomism 497, 596
atoms 101, 497, 694
  primary qualities 718–19, 727–8
attention, selective 401, 467, 470
Augustine:
  as evidence for *Acad.* 266
  theory of esoteric Platonism 507
Gaius Aurelius Cotta (interlocutor in
  N.D.) xxxv, cxlvi
  Clitomachean xli, xliv, cvi, cxliii, cxlvii, cliii,
    cliv, clvi, clxiii, 299, 343, 355, 482, 522
  authority cx, cli, 121, 129, 215, 218–19, 316, 326,
    516, 539, 541, 568, 724, 727, 793
Gaius Avianus Flaccus 582

belief:
  and 'belief' xlvii
  Latin expressions section 10.3 cvii
  see also assent; 'approval'
Brutus, *see* Iunius

Callipho (Peripatetic):
  end, view on 738, 745, 755–6, 771–3
Carneades:
  Clitomachus as a witness to his views xlii
  corollary argument xl, xli, cxxxv, cxxxvi,
    cxxxviii, 529, 530, 535–6, 568, 569–70, 572
  countering the ἀπραξία objection lxxxi
  date xxiii
  diuisio, Carneadea 140, 212
  embassy to Rome clix, 324, 650, 739,
    769, 770
  end (τέλος), Antiochian, in the Carneadea
    diuisio 142, 738
  interpretations of section 4
  the only Academic of that name 343
  on the πιθανόν section 6
  rhetorical abilities 263
  scope of argument practice 262
  significance xlii
  Stoa, debt to 274, 340, 562

theorising, moral 147
see also Academic scepticism; persuasiveness
Lucius Cassius Longinus Ravilla 332
cataleptic impressions section 5
  ἀπαραλλαξία section 5.5 xxiii, xxxviii, xl, li, lx,
    lxi, lxiv, lxv, lxvi, lxvii, lxviii, lxix, lxx, lxxii,
    lxxiv, lxxiv, lxxv, lxxviii, lxxix, cxxxv, cxxxvi,
    cxxxvii, clxxii, clxxxiv, clxxxv, clxxxviii, 242,
    289, 291, 384, 387, 407, 415, 417, 420, 422–3,
    425, 427, 441, 443, 449–50, 453–8, 462–3,
    464–6, 470–4, 479–80, 490, 493, 501, 504–5,
    513–15, 530, 536, 543, 565, 572, 574, 587–9,
    591, 595, 597, 599, 600, 602, 606, 608, 641–3,
    647, 653, 684, 714, 776, 798, 834
  ἀπαραλλαξία, non-perceptual section
    5.5 lxxviii, 454–5, 462–3, 505, 543
  'approval' xlii, xlvi, cvii, cxxxi, cxxxv, cxxxvii,
    cxl, clxxvi, cxci, cxcii, 273, 300, 301, 431, 434,
    436, 458, 460, 465, 506, 520, 525, 548, 570,
    640, 644, 653, 654–66, 674, 682, 686, 692, 732,
    740, 763, 773, 782, 796–9, 814
  ἀπό causal or representational lii
  apprehension of the non-sage as ignorance 235
  clarity li, liv, lv, lvii, lviii, lix, lx, lxi, lxii, lxv, lxvii,
    lxxi, lxxx, lxxxi, lxxxii
  constraint on winning assent/'fourth
    clause' xxiii, xcix, 362, 399
  content, representational or phenomenal li, liv,
    lv, lvi, lviii, lix, lxvii, lxx
  counterarguments from abnormal states of
    mind lxvi, lxxi
  counterarguments from similar objects lxvi
  definitions lii–liv
  and being able to discriminate them lix,
    lxxi, 382
  discrimination terminology section 5.3 382
  distinctive feature liv, lxiii, lxx, lxiii, lxxiv
  epistemological optimism xcvii
  expert vs non-expert lviii, 364
  imprint or alteration li, lv, lviii, lxxii, 238
  imprint vs phenomenal content lv, lvi, 501
  internalist vs externalist interpretation
    section 5.3
  discussed in Latin section 10.1
  Little Bear, allegorically 527
  their 'object' lviii
  perceptual or also non-perceptual section 5.5
  and Plato's *Theatetus* section 5.6
  richness (in content) lxxxvi
  and sage lvii, lviii
  second clause of definition section 5.2
  strikingness lv
  third clause of definition section 5.4
  training in how to use them lviii, 364, 469
  ὑπάρχειν lii

Catilinarian conspiracy 307, 318, 512, 516, 518–19, 522, 524, 788
Cato, *see* Porcius
Catulus (dialogue) section 9.2 xxv, xxx, lxxix, cv, cxv, cxxi, clxvii, clxxii, clxxvi, clxxviii, 91, 115, 119, 131, 175, 238–9, 265, 267–8, 270–1, 274, 286, 295, 303, 305, 309, 317–19, 321, 323, 326, 328, 344, 348, 352, 354, 356, 359, 370, 374, 379, 389, 390, 394, 407, 409, 428, 436, 441, 443, 445, 447, 452, 468, 471, 493, 496–7, 506, 512, 514, 517, 518, 529, 535, 549, 551, 554, 564, 575, 577, 601, 611, 638, 658, 667, 696, 732, 778, 780, 783, 794
    speakers 91
Catulus, *see* Lutatius
Charmadas (Academic) xlviii, 344, 350
    evidence from Sextus xlvii, 351, 810, 813–15
    pupil of Carneades xlii
    on rhetoric 344
    see also Academic scepticism; Carneades; Philo (or Philio) of Larissa
Chrysippus:
    and the Academy xliii, c, 274, 470, 523, 806
    Chrysippea diuisio 741, 751, 771
    on conditionals xc, 787
    date xxiii
    on 'disappearing argument' lxviii, 380, 391
    role in debate over the cataleptic impression liii, liv, lv, 549, 638
    end, view on 140, 737, 739, 772
    indifferents as 'goods' (?) 137
    on the Liar 616–18, 630
    on λογική 777
    on physics 244
    and the *placita* 702
    presence in *Acad.* xxv
    on *prima naturae*, pursuit of 745–6
    sceptical pronouncements cxiii, 552
    senses, arguing against 552, 599
    on the sorites cvii, 284, 433, 611
    on the soul 402
    on συνήθεια 366, 562, 597–8
Cicero, *see* Tullius
Cimmerians 515
clarity:
    according to the Academics section 6
    according to the Stoics section 5
Cleanthes 188, 730
    end, view on 703, 745
Clitomacheanism, *see* Academic scepticism; Carneades; Marcus Tullius Cicero; Clitomachus
Clitomachus 343, 769
    Carthaginian 636
    Περὶ ἐποχῆς 344, 636, 649
    faithful chronicler of Carneades' arguments xliii

    position section 4.1, 4.2
    pupil of Carneades xxiv
competition:
    cultural xxxv
    contio 302, 310, 331, 518, 519, 778, 781, 788–9
conversion 548, 795
    Hortensius' (in *Hort.*) clxxvi, clxxx, 305
    Antiochus' 114, 124, 275, 325, 350
Publius Cornelius Scipio Numantinus Africanus minor 332
Cotta, *see* Aurelius
Crantor 219, 220, 337
    Περὶ πένθους 739, 763, 765
Cratippus (Peripatetic) xxxii, 329
criterion 776
    see also cataleptic impression
Critolaus 137, 139
    tria bona 151
Cyrenaics cxiii, 543
    end, view on 738
    and Epicurus on pleasure 755
    epistemology clxxxviii, 365, 368–72, 553, 563, 784

Dardanus (Stoic) 541, 545
dedications 96
    Cicero to Varro clxiii, clxiv, 79, 90
    Clitomachus to Romans 650
    of *Fin.* to Brutus clxii
    Varro to Cicero clxii, 80
Delian poultry farmer lvii–lx, 265, 499–501, 596
    see also cataleptic impression
delusion liii, 606
    see also cataleptic impression
demiurge, evil 716
Democritus 281, 331, 411–12, 703
    invoked by Academics cx, cxii, 254, 551, 555
    involved by dogmatists cxi, cxxix
    cited contra Epicurus 101
    and οὐ μᾶλλον 462
    presented as sceptic 334
    on physics 704, 709, 711, 718, 727
demon, evil 482
dialectic (theory of argument):
    conditionals xc, 787
    elusive argument 391
    Liar 615
    like an octopus 623
    like Penelope 628
    sorites 472
    sub-virtues of dialectic 246
    Stoic, and Academic criticism 608
Dialectical school 562, 634, 787
dialogue:
    as a literary format xxi, cxlviii, 309
    with or without preface 79

Dicaearchus xxix, 693, 708, 725
Dinomachus 745, 755
Dio (student of Antiochus') 329
Diodorus Cronus xc, 562, 787
Diodorus (Peripatetic):
    end, view on 738, 745, 756, 772
Diogenes of Babylon 739
    in *Acad.* 621
    and Antipater xxiii, 348
    embassy to Rome xxxv, 635
    end, view on 745
    teacher of Carneades 611
    themes featuring in his fragments xxiii
Dionysius of Heraclea 543, 548
dreams section 5.6.1

eggs lvii, lix, lx, lxvi, lxviii
Electra lii, 455
elegance:
    in philosophical contexts 412
embrace:
    as a greeting 79, 93
emotion 763
Empedocles cx, cxii, 254, 334–5, 551, 558–9, 704, 712, 726
empiricism sections 5 and 6
Empiricist medicine 671, 707, 721
    syndrome lxxxv
Quintus Ennius:
    Alcmeo 488, 489, 602–3, 606–7
    Andromacha 367
    Annals 604
    and dreams 485
    Epicharmus 485–6
Epicureanism:
    on definition 348
    easy to render into Latin 82
    on ἐνάργεια 353
    and geometry 670
    on λογική 199
    on perception 361
    in Rome xxxv, 82, 99
Epicurus:
    criterion 784
    and Cyrenaics on pleasure 755
    end, view on 738
    on law of excluded middle 618, 620
    on principle of bivalence 620
    'truth-to-necessity' argument 619
ἐποχή xxxvii, xxxviii, xlii, xlv, cxl, cxlv, cl, clvi, cxciii, 116, 140, 239, 247, 253, 257, 292, 344, 377, 391, 406, 410, 424, 430, 434–6, 439, 505–6, 514, 520, 526, 544, 559, 565, 626–7, 637–8, 648, 649, 663, 668, 675, 687, 702, 706, 719, 796–8, 802–3, 805, 819, 821–3, 833, 835

Erillus cxl, 216, 568, 737, 750–1, 753
Euandrus of Phocaea 343
Eubulides 615
Euclid 698, 752
Eurystheus lxx, lxxvii, 58, 602
externalism section 5.3

factivity 371
fallibilism:
    and the Roman Books view xxv, xlviii, l, 355
Gaius Fannius 339
fifth element, *see* Aristotle
fish:
    vision 583
Gaius Flaminius 332
forms:
    according to Antiochus cxviii, cxxii, cxxiii, 125, 145, 168, 171–2, 189, 192–3, 195, 196, 199–202, 206, 208–9, 216
    as thoughts of god 173

Hagnon 344
Hegesinus 343
Heracles lxx, lxxi, lxxvii, xcix, 362, 484, 602, 606
Heraclitus of Ephesus 253, 559, 703–4, 712, 825
Heraclitus of Tyre clxxviii, 123, 321, 325, 481
Hermagoras of Temnos 700
Hermarchus 634, 671
Herophilus of Alexandria 720
Hicetas of Syracuse 584, 703, 722
Hieronymus:
    end, view on 738, 755–6, 772
history:
    constructions of section 7
Hortensius (dialogue) section 9.5
    dramatic date 318
    setting 91
Quintus Hortensius Hortalus 517
    role in *Catulus* section 9.2 305, 778

illusion liii, lxxxv, 359, 580–1, 584, 723
impressions, *see* cataleptic impression; clarity; persuasiveness
internalism section 5.3
Gaius Iulius Caesar:
    Anticato xxviii, xxxiii, clx
Marcus Iunius Brutus xxx, 112
    interlocutor in the intermediate edition of *Acad.* clxiii, clxv, clxvii, clxix
    Περὶ τοῦ καθήκοντος 112
    De patientia 112
    De virtute 108, 112

knowledge, *see* cataleptic impression; persuasiveness

Lacydes:
   contact with Chrysippus 553
   in division of Academy 134, 342, 410
   features in satirical story cxl, 343, 832–4
Latin:
   as a medium for writing about physics 101, 102
   as a medium for writing about Stoicism 103
Leucippus 462, 703–4, 711, 726
Liar:
   and principle of bivalence 610–16
L. Licinius Crassus Divus Mucianus 333
Lucius Licinius Lucullus:
   Antiochus, acquaintance with 304
   biography 296
   character's attitude to Antiochian material 318
   character vs historical individual 302
   father 303
   library 307
   and Mithridates 304
Gaius Lucilius:
   Academic leanings (?) 324
   and Carneades 650
Lupus of Ferrières 515
Quintus Lutatius Catulus (= Catulus the elder):
   back story in *Catul.* xlv, clvi, 91, 115, 295, 324
   historical individual 309, 497
   and mitigated scepticism xlv
   and Philo 323, 328, 352, 568
   source of authority on Academic scepticism 324, 344
Quintus Lutatius Catulus Capitolinus (= Catulus the younger):
   character in *Catul.* and *Luc.* xxiv, xxv, xlix, cix, cx, cl, clxii, clxx, 317, 517–19, 794
   and mitigated scepticism xxiv, xliv, 392, 441, 510, 565, 794
   role in *Catul.* cix, cxiv, cxlix, clxvii–viii, clxix, clxxvi, 323
Lysippus 595

madness lxvi, lxix, lxxii, lxxvi, 471, 488, 602
L. Marcius Censorinus 649
medicine 211, 364, 671–2, 721, 743, 745
   knowledge of muscles 725
   see also Empiricist medicine
Megarian school 562, 752
Melanthius of Rhodes 344
Melissus 704, 712
memory 358, 369, 371, 374, 434, 599, 669–70, 672
   art of 305–6
Menedemus of Eretria 753
Q. Caecilius Metellus Nepos 524
Metrodorus of Chios 551, 556, 649
Metrodorus of Stratonicea section 2, 4.4 345, 565
   and mitigated scepticism xxiv, xli, 795

and Philo xlv, 566
position sections 2, 4.4 xliii, cvi, 288, 322, 566–74
mitigated scepticism section 4.2
   evidential basis clvii, appendix 1
Mnesarchus (Stoic) 269, 288, 388, 541
mole 583
moving landscapes 584
Mower argument 619–20
Publius Mucius Scaevola 333
Myrmecides 717

naturalism:
   in Hellenistic ethical debate 748
Publius Nigidius Figulus xxxii

opinion, *see* δόξα; *opinio*

Orestes lii, 455, 606, 607

Marcus Pacuvius:
   Antiopa 367
   Iliona 601, 604–5
Panaetius:
   on divination 673, 675
Parmenides cxi, 253, 334, 551, 559, 560, 711, 752
perception:
   and expert knowledge lviii
   and Latin expressions section 10.1
   see also cataleptic impression; persuasiveness
Peripatetics:
   δόξα 688
   knowledge, conception of xlviii, 687
   tria bona 137, 140–2, 147, 151, 153, 157–9, 222, 473, 764
   see also Aristotle; Critolaus; Staseas
persuasiveness (πιθανότης):
   applicability 409
   as a 'criterion' lxxxii
   as a 'criterion for the conduct of life' 414
   different Academic interpretations section 6.6
   in divisions of impressions 638
   and τὸ εἰκός xciv–xcvi, 413, 530
   as 'evidence' section 6.6
   Great Bear, allegorically 527
   and ideal conditions lxxxviii
   'levels' lxxxii
   and 'for the most part' xciv
   non-perceptual, Stoic xcviii
   and plausibility section 6.1
   rational section 6.1 ci, cvii, 658
   as self-report section 6.6
   and syndrome lxxxii, lxxxv–viii, xcii, xciii
   and testing section 6.1
   as conceived by the Stoics section 6.4
   unified conception section 6.6

Phidias 173, 670, 792
Philo (or Philio) of Larissa:
    and Antiochus xxiii–iv
    and the Clitomachean position xxiv, xliii, cxliii
    date of unveiling of the Roman Books view xxv, 118, 324
    and Metrodorus xlv, 565
    and mitigated scepticism 565
    or Philio (?) 326
    no return to an earlier position xxv
    see also Acad.; Academic scepticism; 'Philonian/Metrodorian position'
Philo of Megara xc, 787
'Philonian/Metrodorian position' xli, xlv, clxv, clxxvi, 11, 252–3, 301, 314, 327, 350–1, 407, 409, 414, 424, 427, 441, 459, 460, 530, 540, 543, 566, 678, 682–3, 707, 709, 765, 767, 780, 796, 813–14, 835
philosophy:
    progress 335
πιθανόν:
    see Academic scepticism, persuasiveness
placita tradition cx, 700
    and Aenesidemus 706
    and mathematics 696
    and question types 708–9, 725
    and scepticism 702
    and Theophrastus 704
Plato section 7.4
    Academic reading of 258, 260, 552
    antiqui, not one of Antiochus' 132–3
    criterion 779
    invoked by Antiochus 552
    mystery cults, use of language related to 511
    open to many interpretations 129–30
    positing two principles (?) 168
    principles 712
    tripartite soul 708. 725
    ubertas cxvii, cxix, 122, 131, 201, 205, 228, 233
Polemo:
    Antiochus, invoked by 140, 143
    end, view on 738, 772
    ethics, views on 143–4
    forms, views on 145–6
    goods, views on 144
    naturalism 145–6
    and οἰκείωσις 144
    and the sage 759
    teacher of Zeno xxiii, cxxii, 220
Polyaenus 548, 669–71
Polyclitus 595, 670, 792
pomegranates lxxvii
Gnaeus Pompeius Magnus 306
Marcus Porcius Cato:
    on Greek language and culture 308

Marcus Porcius Cato Uticensis
    interlocutor in the intermediate edition of *Acad.* clxii–iii, clxv
Aulus Postumius Albinus 739, 770–1
poverty topos 81–2, 86
Presocratics:
    invoked by Academics cxi
    knowledge of, in Rome 33
Protagoras 511, 776, 783
Pseudo-Archytas:
    diuisio 759
Pyrrho 668, 737, 754
    similarity with Arcesilaus cxl, cxli
    similarity with Arcesilaus according to Sextus cxxiv
    and Aristo 751, 753
    mentioned as a moralist by Cicero 568
    moral views 751
Pyrrhonism:
    and Academics as property sceptics clxxxv
    on Academic scepticism 301
    on concepts 415
    difference from Academics 317, 350
    on δόγματα 652, 678
    εὐδοκεῖν 644, 661
    formulae 395
    ἰσοσθένεια 258
    on proof 465
    self-conception 252, 461
    tranquility 313
    and φαινόμενα 680
Pythagoreans 334, 723, 831

quaestio infinita 1450
question-and-answer λόγοι:
    as conceptual framework for approval 665

Rabirius (Epicurean) 99
rationality:
    acquisition of 401, 404
Regulus, *see* Atilius
Roman Books view section 4.3
    and assent xlvii
    in the different editions of *Acad.* 119
    evidence from Sextus xlvii
    interpretations l, 291, 349
    and κατάληψις xlviii, l
    launch date clv–clvi
    and Peripatetic views xlvii, 685
    see also Academic scepticism

Sceptical arguments:
    insanity, arguments invoking 1060
    vacuous impressions, against arguments turning on 1050
    see also ἀπαραλλαξία

Lucius Scribonius Libo clxv, 96
Gaius Selius 327
Publius Selius 327
Sempronius Tuditanus clxi, 605
Servilius twins lxxiv, lxxv, lxxvi, 498, 502, 589–92
Sextus Empiricus:
    on Academics appendix 1
Siron 669–70, 672
Socrates section 7.3
    invoked by Academics section 7.3
    and Antiochus section 7.3
    and Epicureans 337
    irony 337
    and Pythagoreanism 125
sorites cvii, 472, 481, 610–12, 620, 624
    terminology 481
    vagueness 610, 620, 624–5
sources:
    of *Acad.* section 9.3 clxxii
Speusippus:
    role in Antiochus' construction of
        philosophy cxvi, 130–1, 219
Staseas of Naples 139
Stilpo 562, 825
Strato of Lampsacus cxxiii
    ethics, dismissal of 210
    physics, interest in cxxiii, 184, 210, 706, 718
Stoics:
    and Academics xxi–ii
    on antipodes 722
    debate over cataleptic impression section 5
    disagreement with Antiochus on the end 761–2
    disagreement amongst Stoics 730
    elusive argument 391
    ἔννοιαι 369–70, 375
    growing argument 163
    on ignorance 235
    indifferents cxxiii, 137, 141, 144, 148, 152, 211, 222, 224, 754
    on individuals lxxiv, 164, 593
    infinite divisibility 184
    moral psychology 378
    on πάθη 227
    παράδοξα 739, 767
    paradoxes 562, 610, 615, 630
    on progress (προκοπή) lvii, 154
    on sagehood lvii, 226, 404, 435, 531, 696
    τέλος formulae 745
    on *temeritas* 406, 435
    'all transgressions are equal' 71, 738, 767
    on the world 722
    writing in Latin 87
    younger Stoics xxiii, xcix, c, 362, 399, 416, 433, 439
Servius Sulpicius Galba 485

sun:
    size 581, 584–6, 699–700, 724
suspension of judgement, see ἐποχή

Marcus Terentius Varro:
    Antiquitates 83
    character in *Academici libri* xxv, clxiii, 80
    character on writing philosophy in Latin 98
    Disciplinae 94
    Laudationes 83
    De lingua Latina 80
    Logistorici 84
    Menippean satires 83
    and naturalism, ethical 136
    Old Academic commitments 81
    relationship with Atticus 89
    relationship with Cicero 88
    works and interests xxvi
Tetrilius Rogus (?) 327
Thales 704, 710
Theophrastus:
    changes to the *prima forma* 209
    οἰκειότης and οἰκείωσις 138
    on Plato positing two principles 168
Timagoras (or Timasagoras?) 576, 579–80
Timon of Phlius cxli, 125, 339, 598, 825
translation:
    uerbum e uerbo 242, 348
Marcus Tullius Cicero:
    Antiochian for a period (?) cxlvi, 114
    Antiochus, personal contact with 682
    and belief clv
    Clitomachean section 8
    comperire, use of 516
    and ἐποχή clv
    on ethics 737
    as evidence for the sceptical Academy xlviii
    four uses of 'Cicero' cxlii
    Hortensius section 9.5
    letters, coverage of xxx
    Latin, writing philosophy in 86, 296
    magnus opinator 285, 301, 436, 526, 531, 534, 537, 687, 833
    and mitigated scepticism xliv–v
    and the Old Academy 113, 114
    and Philo's position cxliii, 118
    and Philodemus' *De pietate* 707
    objects to the designation 'New Academy' 251
    on physics 731
    prefaces of philosophical dialogues xxxii
    and the *probabile* section 6.5
    purpose of philosophical writing section 3
    sceptic and politician 512
    on the Stoic and Antiochian τέλος cliv
    Timaeus xxxii

Marcus Tullius Cicero (*Cont.*)
  Torquatus clxi, clxxix
  on true impressions 551, 682
  on Varro's philosophy writing 97
  uolumen prooemiorum xxviii, 91, 275, 298
  works of the 50s section 3
  works of the 40s section 3
  see also *Acad.*; Academic scepticism; Antiochus, Philo (or Philio) of Larissa
twins:
  and ἀπαραλλαξία section 5.6.2 lvii, lx, lxviii, 499, 589
  and *consuetudo* 4 98
  and eggs lxvi

Publius Valerius Publicola 769
Varro, *see* Terentius
verisimilitude, *see* persuasiveness
villas:
  Catulus' at Cumae xxx, 318
  Catulus' at Pompeii 582
  Cicero's at Cumae 79, 93, 281
  Cicero's at Pompeii 582
  Hortensius' near Bauli 318, 581
  Lucullus' at Bauli xxx
  Lucullus' at Tusculum xxx
  Varro's at Cumae 92, 281

wisdom 109, 166, 187, 377, 379, 380, 404, 692, 696

Xenocrates:
  on creation story in Plato's *Tim.* 184

division of philosophy 136, 149
on goods 145
on λογική 150, 198, 785
role in Antiochus' construction of philosophy cxvii–iii, 122, 130–1, 219
on the soul 169, 170, 230, 725
Xenophanes cix, cxi, 334, 551, 558–9, 704, 711, 721, 728, 751–2

Zeno of Citium:
  appropriate action 225
  changes to the *prima forma* 209, 230
  correcting Plato's immediate successors 230
  date xxiii, 220
  definition of the cataleptic impression section 5.1
  on emotions 227
  end, view on 738, 744
  on epistemology 230
  ἐπιστήμη 778
  on goods 137
  hand used for illustration 778
  on ignorance 243
  neologisms, use of 86
  on physics 730
  pupil of Polemo xxiii
  role in debate with the Academics section 5 xxiii
  statue as an intertext 790
  virtue as a disposition 227
Zeno of Sidon (Epicurean) 262
Zeuxis cxliv, 670, 792

Index Locorum

Aenesidemus (ed. Polito)
  A3 808
  B2 460
  B3 444, 459, 808
  B5 668
  B6 668

Aëtius, *Plac.*
  1.3 704, 711
  1.3.1 710
  1.3.3 710
  1.3.4 710
  1.3.5 710
  1.3.8 713
  1.3.11 712
  1.3.12 711
  1.3.15 711
  1.3.16 712
  1.3.20 712
  1.3.21 712
  1.7 712
  1.7.1–10 717
  1.7.11 710
  1.7.12 710
  1.7.13 710
  1.7.15 710
  1.7.18 713
  1.7.26 711
  1.7.29 169, 175, 187
  1.7.30 173, 182
  1.7.33 714
  1.10 200
  2.2 700
  2.3 705
  2.4 704
  2.4.4 715
  2.21 584, 699
  2.21.5 585
  2.23–9 707, 722
  3.5.5 361
  3.9.1–2 723
  3.9.4 721
  3.10 707, 722
  3.11 707
  4.2–23 725
  4.2.1–4.4.7 708
  4.2.4 725
  4.2.7 725
  4.3.7 726
  4.4.1 725
  4.4.3 726
  4.5.8 726
  4.8 lv, 242
  4.8.1 402
  4.8.12 clxxxiv, 676
  4.9 700
  4.9.4 clxxxiv, 444
  4.9.17 clxxxvi
  4.11.1–4 369, 403
  4.12 xcii, 666
  4.13.6 580
  4.21 402
  5.2.1–2 719

Alexander of Aphrodisias
  Quaest. (ed. Bruns)
    p. 61.1–28 673
  in S.E. (ed. Wallies)
    p. 171.16–20 675
  in Top. (ed. Wallies)
    p. 1.10–11 100
    p. 27.11–12 124, 664
    pp. 32.12–34.5 673
    p. 584.9–11 124, 664

Ambrosius of Milan
  Ep. 77.11 660

Ammonius
  in Arist. Int. (ed. Busse)
    p. 131.27–8 619

Anaxagoras
  DK 59A97 646

Anonymus *in Arist. Int.* (ed. Tarán)
  Cod. Par. Gr. 2065, pp. 54.8–55.5
    620

Anonymus *de phil. Plat.* (ed. Westerink)
  4.15.1–9 130
  7.10–14 807
  10.1–46 260
  10 *init.* 808

Anonymus *in Platonis Theaetetum*
    (ed. Bastianini and Sedley)
  col. 54.38–55.13 191, 259
  col. 59.19–21 259
  col. 61.10–46 409

Anonymus Seguerianus (ed. Graeven)
  pp. 28.15–29.3 xcv
Anthologia Graeca
  9.577 755
  11.162 645
Apuleius
  Florida 12 646
  Met. 8.6 clxxxix
Aristotle
  An. Post.
    A2, 71b17–22 386
    B19 208, 216, 217
  An. Pr.
    B27, 70a2–6 xcv
  De anim.
    B7, 419a15 583
  Cael.
    B12, 291b27 733
  E.E.
    H6, 1214a30–3 137
  Met.
    A4, 985b4–22 712, 719
    A6, 987a32–b1 201
    A7, 988a7–11 174
    A9 208
    Γ4, 1008b2–13 435
    Γ5, 1009b11–12 412
    Δ19–20, 1022b1–14 227
  N.E.
    A6 208
    A6, 1097b22–1098a20 227
    B1, 1103a17 153
    B7, 1108a17–19 178
    B7, 1108a19–23 337
    Z13 213
    Z13, 1144b33–4 226
  Part. anim.
    A5 733
  Phys.
    Δ7, 214a16–18 727
    H2, 246a13–6 154
  Poet.
    6, 1449b38 127
  Rhet.
    A1, 1354a1–6 204
    B23, 1397b12–27 xcv
    B23, 1397b18–20 xcv
    B23, 1397b24–5 xcv
  S.E.
    25, 180b2–7 615
    34, 183b6–8 125
  Top.
    A5, 102a18–19 liv
    A11, 104b1–8 725
    A14, 105a35–b25 725
    A14, 105b19–29 149
    B10, 115a6–24 xcv
    Θ3, 158a31–2 665
    Θ5, 159a38–b25 cviii
    Θ5, 159b25–9 cviii, 659, 665
    Θ5, 159b25–7 665
    Θ11, 162a15–16 665
Athenaeus
  354E 640
Augustinus
  C.D.
    4.22 83
    6.2 108
    7.17 123
    7.28 174
    7.35 83
    19.1–3 136, 142, 749
    19.2 793
    19.3 138, 142, 144, 155–7
  Confessiones
    3.4.7 514
  Contra Acad.
    1.2.7 clxxxii
    1.3.7 cxlviii
    1.4.10–1.5.14 276
    1.9.24 276
    2.5.11 273, 356–7, 396, 417, 506, 793
    2.5.12 273, 429, 626, 667, 676
    2.6.14–15 cxiv
    2.6.14 248, 572
    2.6.15 279, 547
    2.7.16 413
    2.8.21 292
    2.10.24–2.13.30 285
    2.11.26 285
    3.4.9 663
    3.4.10 672
    3.7.14 292, 627
    3.7.15–16 clxii, clxv, 266, 790, 803
    3.9.21 572
    3.10.22 506, 769
    3.10.23 283, 496, 694, 728
    3.11.26 361
    3.14.31 cxlvii, cl, clxxxxii, 273, 519, 532
    3.15.34–3.16.36 276
    3.16.35 clxxx, 281
    3.17.37.23–32 149, 507
    3.17.38–18.41 294, 507–9
    3.18.41 clxxvii, 114, 269, 345, 355, 507, 545, 547, 573, 758
    3.20.43 cli, 257, 291, 300, 507
  Ord.
    2.5.16 512
    2.9.26 512

Soliloq.
  1.4.9 790
Trin.
  10.7.10 386
  15.11.21 361
De vita beata
  1.4 514

Callimachus (ed. Pfeiffer)
  frg. 191.52–5 532

C. Cassius Hemina (FRHist)
  Ann. frg. 35 98

C. Cassius Longinus
  Cic., *Fam.* 15.19.1 clxxxviii

Cato, *see* Porcius

Censorinus
  De die natali 4.7–9.3 702

Chalcidius, *in Tim.*
  ch. 220 372, 402

Cicero, *see* Tullius

A. Cornelius Celsus, *De medicina*
  8.10.1 civ

Corpus Inscriptionum Latinarum
  I².1423 clxxxiv
  II.172 793
  III.6041 697

Clemens, *Strom.* (ed. Stählin)
  1.14.64.1 134
  1.17.82.6 lxxiv
  2.22.133.7 144
  4.12.85.2 lxxiv
  5.14.97.6 cxx
  6.14.121.4 385
  7.6.32.9 144

Cleomedes
  Μετέωρα (ed. Todd)
    2.1 583
    2.155–83 586

Cratinus (ed. Kock)
  frg. 459 649

Digesta
  1.2.2.6–7 132
  1.2.2.31 768
  28.1.2 488
  50.14.3.1 ciii

Dio Chrysostomus
  Or. 36.20 769

Diogenes Laertius
  1.14 134
  1.19 134
  2.19 339
  2.21 126

2.37 127
2.106 752
2.108 615
2.129 752
3.52 259
3.56 149
3.70 181
4.18 144
4.28–45 cxxxix
4.28 cxxxi, 257, 833
4.33 cxl, 832
4.59 134, 342, 833
4.62 263, 274, 340, 562
4.63–4 263, 834
5.30 137, 151, 155
5.59 212
7.2 562
7.41 622
7.45 386, 642
7.46–7 246
7.46 li, 406, 444, 538, 624
7.47 243, 622
7.49 358, 444
7.49–51 lxxxix, 471
7.50 lii, 238, 604
7.51 431
7.52 lv, 242, 403
7.71 623
7.75 xcviii, 476
7.77 697
7.88 745
7.104–5 222, 780
7.106 224
7.110 xcviii, 763
7.120 761
7.125 379
7.134 167
7.139 186, 730
7.147 714, 730
7.149 675
7.160 724
7.162 lxxvi, cxli
7.163 562, 649, 770
7.165 243, 750
7.177 dust jacket; lxxvi, lxxxvi, 640
7.178 594, 624
7.183–4 562, 553
7.196 615
7.198 lxviii, 553
7.199 594
7.201 535
7.202 774
9.58 556
9.62 668

Diogenes Laertius (*Cont.*)
  9.71–3 558
  9.72 254, 412
  9.86 361
  9.104–5 406, 668
  9.104 668
  10.6 103
  10.31 784
  10.91 585–6, 724
  10.147 359
Donatus
  De com. 8.11 365, 367
  Ad Ter. Herc. 77.2 94
XII tabulae (ed. Crawford)
  tab. VIII.13 82
Empedocles (ed. Diels and Kranz)
  31B2.1 254
  31B112 335
  31B115 335
Ennius
  Ann. (ed. Skutsch)
    309 90
  Medea (ed. Jocelyn)
    ll.234–6 668
Epictetus
  Diss.
    1.7.25 347
    1.27.15 347
    2.6.9 211
    2.10.5–6 211
    2.18.18 626
    2.19.1–5 787
    4.5.1–4 337
Epicurus
  Ep. ad Hdt.
    42 719
    49–52 468
Epiphanes
  Adv. haer. 3.2.9 556
Euripides
  El. 113 607
  H.F. 921–1015 602, 606
Eusebius
  Praep. Ev.
    VI.8.2 438
    XIV.19.9 556
Gaius, *Inst.*
  4.30 132
  4.60 132
Galen
  De animis peccatis dignoscendis (ed. Marquardt)
    p. 56.7–12 622

De exp. med. (ed. Kühn)
  XVI.1–2 cvii
  XVI.2 610
  XVII.3 611
  XVII.102 cvii
  XX.3 611
De locis affectis
  VIII.187–8 xciv
In Hippocr. de med. officina
  XVIIIb.649–50 373
Introductio logica
  (ed. Kalbfleisch)
  4, pp. 10.13–11.13 623
Plac. Hipp. (ed. De Lacy)
  2.1.2 547
  5.3 369
  9.7.3 c, 666, 813
  9.9.37 c, 666, 813
De plenitudine
  VII.554–5 lxxxv
  VII. 560 xciv
[Galen]
  Hist. phil. 3 262
  De qualitatibus incorporeis
    (ed. Giusta)
    11.109–61 184
Gellius, *Noctes Atticae*
  1.20 698
  2.21.1–11 civ
  7.1.7–13 717
  10.28.1 544
  11.5.1–8 807, 831
  11.5 250
  13.5 217
  17.8.16 515
Gnomologion Monacense
  196 767
Hieronymus
  C. Ioann. Hieros. 35 361
Hippolytus
  Ref. 1.23.3 462
Homer
  Il.
    5.576 xc
    5.770–2 586
    6.181 cxl, 818
    11.654 90
  Od.
    8.515 xc
    9.21 lxxxiv
    11.12–19 515
    11.523 xc
    19.163 647

Horace
  A.P.
    291 96
    310 129
    323–32 82
  Epist.
    1.4.16 219
    2.2.44–5 420
  S.
    1.5.43 93
    2.3.33 327

Lactantius, *Div. Inst.*
  1.6.7 83
  3.4.10–11 289
  3.6.7–12 cxxxviii, 248, 290
  3.6.10 342
  3.14.15 298
  3.28.10–13 254, 268
  5.14.3 650
  6.24.1 266, 298

Livy
  22.53 793
  34.22 757

Lucan
  8.165–92 533

Lucilius (ed. Marx)
  31 650
  784–90 182
  1305 626

Lucretius
  1.370–97 727
  1.832 86
  2.180–1 716
  2.333–729 719
  2.683–5 360
  2.757–87 668
  2.801–5 361
  3.260 86
  4.353–7 clxxxix
  4.440–2 361
  4.513–17 513
  5.198–9 1481
  6.960 360
  6.984–5 360

T. Maccius Plautus
  Cas. 843 101
  Curc. 260 486
  Menaechm. 268 532
  Mil. 455 363
  Most. 999 663
  Poen. 1125 636
  Trin. 1048 427
  Truc. 897 635

Macrobius
  Somn. 1.3.2 239

Manilius
  1.40–52 733
  1.299–302 532
  2.105–25 733

Marius Victorinus
  Gen. (ed. Henry and Hadot)
    10 437

Nemesius
  De natura hom.
    7 361

Nonius Marcellus
  p. 65 Mercier clxxvii, 347, 787
  pp. 65–6 79, 92
  p. 81 623
  p. 117 501
  p. 139 485
  p. 162 654
  pp. 162–3 413
  p. 170.22 clxxxi
  p. 189 719
  p. 193.11 clxxxi
  p. 318.8 802
  p. 333.36–7 534
  p. 474 583

Numenius (ed. Des Places)
  frg. 24:
    Eus. *P.E.* 14.5.1 cxl
  frg. 25:
    Eus. *P.E.* 14.6.3 cxxxviii, cxl
    Eus. *P.E.* 16.6.6 cxl
  frg. 26:
    Eus. *P.E.* 14.7.1–13 342, 350
    Eus. *P.E.* 14.7.4 cxl
    Eus. *P.E.* 14.7.15 134, 410
  frg. 27:
    Eus. *P.E.* 14.8.1–15 250
    Eus. *P.E.* 14.8.3 cxxxviii, cxl
  frg. 28:
    Eus. *P.E.* 14.9.1–4 802
    Eus. *P.E.* 14.9.3 134, 269, 288, 545
  frg. 25.75–82 509
  frg. 27.19–32 652
  frg. 27.28–9 449, 451
  frg. 27.33–7 462
  frg. 27.37–8 481
  frg. 27.38–40 500
  frg. 27.47–56 269
  frg. 27.56–9 509
  frg. 27.69–72 509
  frg. 28 clvii

Olympiodorus
  in Plat. Gorg. (ed. Jahn)
    pp. 53–4 371
Origen
  Contra Celsum
    4.45.16 lxxxiv
    4.68.9 714, lxxxiv
    7.12.11 lxxxiv
    7.37 622
    8.51 137
Orph. H.
    70.6–7 607
P. Berol.
    inv. 16545 liv, 444, 638
Persius
    6.79–80 625
Philo Alexandrinus
  De mundi opificio (ed. Wendland)
    §166, vol. i p. 58.9 238
  Ebr.
    182 361
Philodemus
  Index Acad.
    col. xiv.3–10 144
    col. xxi.37–42 134, 342
    col. xxiii.4–6 344
    col. xxiv.9–16 345
    col. xxv.1–2 326, 636
    col. xxvi.8–11 288, 345
    col. xxvi.9 xli, 573
    col. xxxi.3–12 344
    col. xxxiii clvii, 326, 836
    col. xxxiii.42–xxxiv.7 345
    col. xxxiv–v 83
    col. xxxiv.16 325
    col. xxxiv.23–4 269, 288, 545
    col. xxxv.1–14 329
    col. xxxv.2–3 113
    col. xxxv.2–16 329
    col. xxxv.7–10 546
    col. xxxv.15–16 546
  Rhet. (ed. Sudhaus)
    frg. inc. 3.1 (vol. ii, p. 169) 556
  De signis (ed. De Lacy)
    col. vii.26–38 639
  De vitiis (ed. Jensen)
    col. xx.20–2 127
Photius, *Bibl.*
    212, 169b18–170b3 396
    212, 169b39–40 460
    212, 170a14–17 808
    212, 170a17–38 808
    212, 170a26–38 409, 444, 459
    242, 346a17–19 509

Plato
  Alc. 1
    114e 299, 813
    129e–130c 151
  Apol.
    20e–21d 121
    21a 127
    21b 121, 127, 560
    21d4–7 560
  Crit.
    54d2–7 470
  Euthyd.
    278e–282d 137, 337
    281e 337
    288d–292e 155
    297c 834
  Gorg.
    453d–458b 609
    458a cliv
    463e5 483
    464c 672
    501c5 239
  Men.
    87c–89a 137
  Parm.
    129d 193
  Phaedr.
    273d–274a xcv
  Phd.
    72e–78b 194
    78d 200
    96a 254
  Phileb.
    38b12–39a7 233, 665
    55e–56c 672
  Rep.
    443d–444c 213
    506c 526, 692, 800
    602c–603b 366
  Soph.
    231a 482
    246a4–5 702
    247d8–e4 174
    254b–58e 193
    263e3–64a2 233, 665
  Symp.
    204d–206e 146
    211b 200
  Tht.
    145c–e lxiv, 235
    150c4–7 259
    152a 783
    182–7 191, 192
    182a 179
    184a–186 192, 232, 236
    184c–185a 191

184d3 191
184d–e 402
185e1–2 192, 200
186d2–5 191
187a1–6 192
189e6–190a6 232–3, 235, 665
191a–195b lii, lxiv, 217
194d4 lxv, 236
196d1–200c6 217
206c2–210a9 lxv
208b12–210b3 234
208e4 lxv
208e5 532
209b10–c2 234
209c6–7 lxv
Tim.
  27d–28a 190, 194, 196–8, 202, 784
  29c–d 351
  33b 698
  39e 173
  40b8–c3 723
  47b 104
  52a8–b5 177
  52c6–8 167, 177
  92c 171
[Plato]
  Def. 414b7–9 149
'Plato'
  Ep. 7, 341b–c 511
Plautus, *see* Maccius
C. Plinius Secundus, *N.H.*
  10.155 265–6, 278, 501
  31.6–8 92
C. Plinius Caecilius Secundus
  Ep. 3.12.2 clx
Plutarch
  Adv. Col.
    1108d 406
    1110f–1111a 711
    1111f–1112a 361, 558–9
    1115b 553
    1117d 569
    1118b 792
    1120d 553
    1121f–1122a cix, cxxxiv, 253, 258–9
    1122a–c 382
    1122a–d 430
    1122a 888
    1122b–c 433
    1122c 438
    1122e–f 435
    1124a 726
  De aud.
    13, p. 45a 560

Cic.
  4.2 350, 539, 543
  40 clxxix, 239, 265, 302–3, 370, 379
Comm. not.
  1059d–e 618, 623
  1065 717
  1069e–1070b 145
  1069e 160
  1070a 223
  1070b–1071b 148, 745
  1071f–1072a 7 47, 754
  1073b xci
  1077c 500, 594
  1083b–c 244
  1083d–e 717
  1122a–c 382
  ch. 26 158
  ch. 36 lxvi
De E apud Del.
  387a xc, 787
frg. (ed. Sandbach)
  215 385
Garr.
  514c–d 269
Luc.
  2 304, 306, 321, 322
  4.2 304
  20 306
  42 clxxix, clxxx, 239, 265, 302, 539
  61 539
Prof. Virt.
  75c 391
Prov.
  200e 344
Quaest.
  734f–735b 729
Soll. An.
  960f 431
  961e–f 431
Stoicos absurdiora poetis dicere
  1057d 764
Sto. rep.
  1034c 213
  1035a–b 733
  1035f–1036a 523
  1035f–1036e 523
  1036c–d 600
  1036d–e c, 553
  1036d 470
  1036e 598
  1037b–c 805, 833
  1037b xliii
  1037c xliii, 313, 317, 511
  1040d 774
  1048a 137
  1048e 791

Plutarch (*Cont.*)
   1051c 717
   1056c–d 437
   1057a–b 478
  Virt. mor.
   440e 752
   441a 212
   441c–d 227
   441d 229

Polybius
  6.47.7–10 lxxxiii
  39.12.1–12 770

M. Porcius Cato
  Agr. 34.2 103

Porphyry
  Abst.
   3.20 716
   3.21–2 431

Proclus
  Theologia Platonica (ed. Saffrey-Westerink)
   p. 6 509

Propertius
  1.1.13 112
  2.6.27–30 clxxxiii, 238

Publilius Syrus (ed. Ribbeck)
  282 314

Quintilian
  5.10.64–70 738
  8.3.83–4 xc
  12.1.18 791
  12.1.38 478

Rhet. ad Alexandrum
  1428a25–6 xcv

Rhet. ad Herennium
  1.3 366
  1.17 427
  2.30 clxxxvii
  3.33 clxxxvii
  4.4–9 cxliv
  4.15 180
  4.45–6 180
  4.61 100, 180
  4.65 484
  4.67 xci
  4.69 100

Scholia
  in Arist. Nub. 114 127

Seneca
  Agamemnon
   720–74 488
  Apoc.
   11 500

Ben.
  4.33.1–4 640
  5.6.4 698
De constantia sapientis
  10.4 641
De ira
  1.3.7 431
De otio
  5.8 733
Dial.
  7.8.4 402
Ep. mor.
  30.3 532
  71.7 125–6
  74.22 341
  74.31 764
  79.14 334
  85.29 764
  88.44 462
  92.6 756
  92.9 773
  92.14 159
  94.59 470
  95.10 733
  95.45 532
  99.9 149
  113.2 405
  113.16 594
  117.6 300
  117.13 629
  121.12 725
Medea
  694–9 533
N.Q.
  1.pr.1–4 733
  1.2.3 359
  1.3.9–10 359
  1.3.9 361
  1.4.1 697
  1.5.6 361
  1.12.1 698
  1.17.2 359
  2.32.3–4 477

Sextus Empiricus
  Adversus Mathematicos
   1.69 611
   2.6 785
   2.7 780, 790
   3 671, 695, 697
   7.16 149
   7.39 780
   7.42 478
   7.49 559
   7.52 559
   7.60 783

INDEX LOCORUM 903

7.88 556
7.135 254
7.137–9 555
7.141–260 196, 366
7.141–4 196, 198
7.141 784
7.151–2 243
7.151–7 lviii
7.151 243
7.152 lii
7.153 789
7.154 445, 450, 691
7.155 cxxxiii
7.155–7 535
7.156–7 529
7.159–62 666
7.161–2 641
7.161 444
7.162 196
7.163 666
7.166–89 xliv, lxxxi, lxxxii, clxviii, 285, 438, 533, 661, 814
7.166–75 443
7.166 lxxxi, 414, 653
1.168–9 659
7.169–75 642
7.169–70 xci, 530, 643, 676, 689
7.171–3 lxxxvii, xci, 667
7.171 476
7.172 lxxxi, cvii
7.173 xciii, 289, 414
7.175–81 533
7.176 414
7.177 lxxxvi
7.178–9 651
1.179 643
7.180 lxxxi, lxxxviii
7.181–2 xcvi
7.183 lxxxvii, 667
7.184–5 422
7.184 414
7.187–8 657
7.188 lxxxi
7.198 272
7.216–26 688
7.217–26 217, 399
7.224 375
7.228–31 lv, 787
7.241–51 xcviii, 594
7.242–52 638
7.242–7 444, 642
7.242 xcviii, 444
7.243 411, 413
7.244 361, 455
7.248–51 244

7.248 li, 356
7.252 liii, 416, 571
7.253 xcix, 534
7.253–4 362
7.253–5 xcix, c
7.253–7 xxiii, xcix
7.254–5 lv, 433
7.257 lv, 438
7.258 360, 490
7.260 421
7.265 555
7.344–7 370
7.346–7 372
7.373 374
7.401 xcvi
7.402–11 lxvi, 470
7.402 lii, 686
7.403 lxix, lxxii, 361, 474, 479
7.405 lxx, 600
7.405–7 lxx, 489, 602, 606
7.406–8 484
7.406 lxx
7.407 lxx, lxxi
7.408–11 500, 591
7.408 liv, lxix, lxxii, 240, 416
7.409 l x, lxviii, lxxii, lxxiii
7.409–10 594
7.411 lxviii, lxxii, lxxiv, lxxv, 591
7.413 272
7.414 584
7.416–21 610, 612
7.416 626
7.421–2 734
7.422 761
7.424 483
7.426 lii
7.432–4 789
7.432 791
7.433 792
7.435–8 lxxxi, 427
7.438 lxv
8.9 451
8.58–60 403
8.67 lii
8.85–6 lii
8.192–6 lxxxiv
8.314 386
8.385 386
9.182–4 472
9.283 698
9.332 175
9.377 698
10.300 lxxxix, xc
11.8–11 373
11.61–7 738, 753

Sextus Empiricus (*Cont.*)
    11.161 647
    11.162–4 lxxxiv
    11.183 li
    11.250 403
    Pyrrhoniae hypotyposes
    1.1–4 523
    1.13 661, 678
    1.14 395
    1.33 646
    1.44 272
    1.55 273
    1.92 366, 598
    1.100–11 267
    1.100–17 272
    1.118–23 270, 361, 363
    1.119 361
    1.120 361, 366, 598
    1.145 706
    1.188–91 462
    1.196 627
    1.198 272
    1.206 395
    1.220–35 350, 806, 831
    1.220–1 134, 546
    1.220 xlvii, 262, 350, 813, 815
    1.221–5 259, 807
    1.226–30 438, 807
    1.226 cxxxiii, 250, 317
    1.227–30 lxxxi
    1.228 lxxxviii
    1.228–9 lxxxviii
    1.229 422, 814
    1.232–4 cxxxiv, 806
    1.232 505
    1.234 cxl, 509, 832
    1.235 xlvii, cxx, 320, 329, 350–1, 416, 573, 758, 814, 815
    2.4 lii, 672
    2.48–69 267
    2.83 789
    2.90 412
    2.97 412
    2.104 629
    2.110–12 xc, 536, 787
    2.112 xc, xci, 787
    2.253 610, 613, 626
    2.254 612
    3.39 697
    3.43 698
    3.188 403

Sylloge Inscriptionum Graecarum³
    838 lxxxvii

Simplicius (CAG)
  in Arist. Cael. (ed. Heiberg)
    p. 295.20–2 555
  in Arist. Phys. (ed. Diels)
    p. 26.5–15 168
    pp. 156.2–157.16 722

Sophocles
  El. 735 626

Stephanus
  in Arist. Int. (ed. Hayduck)
    pp. 34.36–35.5 620

Stephanus of Byzantium (ed. Meineke)
    132.3 328

Stob. *Ecl.* (ed. Wachsmuth)
    I.1, pp. 15–22 696
    I.1, p. 26.4 188
    I.14, p. 143 719
    I.19, p. 166 722
    I.25, p. 213 726
    I.50, p. 474.18–19 432
    II.2, p. 23 623
    II.7, p. 42.11–13 149
    II.7, pp. 46–8 151
    II.7, p. 46 151, 154
    II.7, pp. 47.12–48.5 749
    II.7, pp. 47.20–48.1 159
    II.7, pp. 55.5–7 130
    II.7, pp. 59.4–5 227
    II.7, pp. 73.19–74.14 243
    II.7, p. 74.16 235
    II.7, pp. 76.11–13 745, 757
    II.7, p. 76.22–3 150
    II.7, pp. 84.18–24 577
    II.7, pp. 85.13–86.4 225
    II.7, pp. 85.18–86.4 224, 430
    II.7, p. 88 378
    II.7, pp. 94.21 156
    II.7, p. 99.2–7 227
    II.7, p. 103.9–23 768
    II.7, p. 108.12–15 337
    II.7, p. 111.10 478
    II.7, p. 111.20–1 243
    II.7, p. 117 153

Strabo
    8.3.17 lxxxiii
    10.2.12 lxxxiv
    13.1.54 693

Suda
  κ
    no. 171 635
  λ
    no. 72 134, 342
  π
    1707 343

Suetonius
  Dom. 4.4.1 252

Synesius
  De insomn. 136c 361
Terence
  Hec. 811 663
Tertullian
  De an.
    10.4 721
    17 361
    17.2 271
Theocritus
  5.23 135
  22.93 396
Theodoretus
  Cur. aff. Graec. (ed. Raeder)
    4.31 701
Timon of Phlius (ed. Lloyd-Jones and Parsons)
  frg. 799 339
  frg. 806 cxli
Tryphon (*Rhet. Gr.* III ed. Spengel)
  p. 199.15–20 xc
M. Tullius Cicero
  Ac. 1
    1.1–46 section 9.3.2, clxxv
    1.5–6 86, 87
    1.7 xxxiii, xxxvi
    1.11 xxvi, xxxiii, xxxiv, 309
    1.13 xlvii, cxlvi, 180, 215, 258, 327, 354, 514, 519, 682, 765, 785
    1.14 clxxv
    1.15–42 cxv, 116, 394
    1.15–17 cxvi, cxvii, cxxi, cxxiv, 189, 198, 204, 255, 316, 336, 706, 777
    1.24–6 cxxi, clxxv, 82, 102, 120, 124, 143, 145, 173, 201, 207, 210, 236, 704, 705, 712, 732
    1.33 cxviii, cxxiii, cxxv, 120, 122, 125, 142, 152, 173, 183, 233, 245, 252, 691, 762, 779, 785
    1.40–2 xxiii, xxxix, li, cxiii, cxxv, cxxxii, cxlix, clxviii, 98, 179, 191, 194, 201, 303, 341, 348, 375, 389, 436, 535, 564, 643, 676, 777
    1.40 li, liv, cxxxv, 205, 220, 228, 356, 396, 401, 421, 668, 734, 758
    1.41 lv, lvi, lvii, clxxxiv, cxc, cxci, 103, 380, 418, 422, 424, 428, 467–8, 478, 479, 493, 500, 534, 629, 654, 736, 767, 775, 780, 790, 791, 801
    1.42 lvii, clxviii, 119, 120, 202, 219, 233, 235–6, 286, 373, 506, 535, 692, 761
    1.43 cx, cxiii, cxv, cxix, cxxx, 191, 207, 293, 311, 399, 691, 758
    1.44–6 xxii, xxxviii, cix, cx, cxii, cxxviii, cxxx, cxxxv, cxxxviii, cxl, clxxvi, clxxviii, 115, 128, 268, 286, 292, 330, 343, 354, 412, 510, 520, 528, 535, 549, 554, 692, 832
    1.44 cix, cxi, clxxi, 104, 116, 119, 253, 258, 262, 268, 298, 312, 333, 341, 412, 513, 524, 554, 563, 588, 720, 793
    1.45 xxviii, cx, cxxxi, cxxxv, cxxxix, cxl, cli, cxciii, 242, 249–50, 263, 341, 440, 506, 508, 512, 515, 526, 531, 538, 546, 561, 587, 702, 726
    1.46 cxi, cxxviii, clxviii, clxxi, 133, 258, 262, 506, 512, 546, 726, 779
Aratea (ed. Soubiran)
  frg. 7 532
Arch.
  6 93
Att.
  1.5 cxlvi
  1.14.5 516
  2.2.1 785
  2.3.3 cxlvi
  2.6.2 663
  4.14(16) 89, 107
  4.16.2 clxi
  4.16.5 298
  4.16(17) 89
  4.17.1 511
  4.19(21) 90
  5.11.3 89
  5.19.3 311
  6.1.22 524
  12.12.2 clviii, 4
  12.23.2 4, 118, 770
  12.52.3 clxxvii, 6
  13.16.1–2 clix, clxxix, 8, 295, 318, 328
  13.3.1–2 7, 268, 271, 278, 283
  13.12(24) clxxix, 7, 89, 95–7, 104, 112, 123
  13.13.1 xxix, clxxix, 88, 310
  13.13–14(25) 91, 112
  13.16.1–2 clvi, clxxix, 8, 89, 91, 295, 318
  13.19.35 clvi, clxxix, 8, 89, 91, 295, 318
  13.21 91, 294, 327, 626–7, 803
  13.24(35) 10, 90
  13.25(36) cl, 11, 90–1, 112, 247, 283, 396, 715, 762
  13.30 xxix, clxi
  13.32.2–3 xxix, cxlviii, clxviii, clxxviii, clxxix, 265, 275, 295–6, 770
  13.33a clxiv, 10, 84, 90
  13.48.2 xxix, 84
  14.16.1 92
  16.6.4 xxix, clxxix, 14, 91, 276–7, 287, 298
Brut.
  10 94
  11 94
  12 112
  19 94
  26 97
  30 783
  31 125–6

M. Tullius Cicero (*Cont.*)
    32 532
    37 693
    44 131
    46 783
    60 107
    62 106
    69 461
    70 792
    79 770
    81 770
    97 332
    121 217
    173 98
    197 584
    204 217
    205 clvi, 105, 107, 150
    207 105
    232 154
    236 98
    250 112
    255 215
    279 772
    285 481
    292 cxxvii, 337, 339, 783
    298–9 337
    299 339
    300 clxix
    306 xxvii, cxlv, clvi, 118, 321
    309 694
    313 774
    315 119, 539
    322 104
    330 112
    332 113
Caec.
    51 86
Cael.
    41 771
Clu.
    177 93
De opt. gen. orat.
    18 111
De orat.
    1.42 134
    1.43 257, 345
    1.45 344, 345, 573
    1.46 269, 756
    1.47 344
    1.49 217, 496
    1.50 131
    1.57 216
    1.83 269
    1.84 814
    1.96 206
    1.110 802
    1.121 521
    1.155 111
    1.163 182
    1.187 698
    1.206 511
    1.248 126
    1.262 802
    2.16 319
    2.26 319
    2.28 156
    2.30 793
    2.45 263
    2.136 130
    2.157–60 770
    2.158 628
    2.161 263
    2.171 229
    2.266 284
    2.267 269
    2.233 135
    2.256 205
    2.260 793
    2.261 205
    2.270 337, 339, 561
    2.333 524
    2.348 378
    2.351–60 305
    2.359 305
    2.360 344
    2.365 344
    3.21 303
    3.26 792
    3.49 428
    3.56–73 128
    3.62 368, 750, 752–4
    3.67 130, 134, 220, 250, 255, 257, 258, 510, 552
    3.68 263
    3.76 305
    3.80 257
    3.102 365, 367
    3.109 131
    3.114 205
    3.115 154
    3.121 131
    3.128 783
    3.144 319
    3.148–70 180
    3.149 180
    3.154 180
    3.162 606
    3.179 182
    3.185 152
    3.186 423

3.202-8 461
3.209 731
3.220 428
3.222 240
Div.
  1.2 *fin.* 240
  1.6 675, 730
  1.7 cxlii
  1.8 317
  1.9 115, 309
  1.24 281, 673
  1.34 423
  1.61 228
  1.66 607
  1.80 521
  1.82 311
  1.86 604
  1.87 262
  1.105 248, 802
  1.111 272
  1.117 792
  1.118 477
  1.125 188
  1.125-6 188
  1.127 416, 618
  2.1 xxxi, xxxiv, cxlviii, clxxix, clxxxi, 14, 85, 91, 309, 310
  2.3-4 97
  2.3 310
  2.4 xxxiv, 693
  2.6-7 310
  2.6 112
  2.8 clii
  2.10 609, 697
  2.11 481, 615, 618, 632
  2.16 454
  2.28 clii
  2.31 582
  2.38 398
  2.49 188
  2.61 791
  2.77 519
  2.81 515
  2.86 482
  2.100 311
  2.108 465
  2.111 486
  2.120 729
  2.126 485, 487
  2.139 479
  2.147 697
  2.150 313, 483, 510
Div. Caec.
  41 521
  64 ci, 110

Dom.
  14-15 clxiv
Fam.
  3.11.2 468
  4.4.1 337
  4.5 112
  4.6.2 112
  5.2.7 524
  5.5.2 516
  5.15.4-5 5
  5.17.1 93
  5.21.3 759
  6.11 707
  6.11.2 672
  9.1-7 clxv, 90
  9.1 xxviii,
  9.2.4-5 xxx, 96
  9.2.5 xxvii
  9.3 135
  9.3.2 580
  9.6 618
  9.6.4-5 104
  9.8 clviii, clxxvi, 10, 79, 80, 97, 247-8, 322, 330
  9.8.1 96, 133
  9.18.3 135
  9.26.4 clviii
  10.5.2 240
  10.31.6 786
  11.20.1 803
  11.21.5 802
  13.35.1 582
  13.79 582
  15.4.16 104, 693
  15.15.4-5 5
  15.16-19 88
  15.16.1-2 clxxxviii, 88
  15.17.1 93
  15.19.1 88
  15.21.2 240
  15.21.4 220
  16.2.1 583
  16.22.1 95
Fat.
  1 xliii, 149, 199, 414
  2 94, 128
  3 461
  4 453
  9 437
  10 634
  12 623, 787
  14 787
  16 636
  20 188
  21 618-19

M. Tullius Cicero (*Cont.*)
    22 719
    23-8 452
    23 262
    25 437
    26-8 634
    28 618
    31 437
    37 618, 634
    40-1 437
    43 437
    45 437
    46 101, 238
    47 719
  Fin.
    1.1-12 xxxv, 84
    1.1 79, 308
    1.2 xxx, clxxx, 12, 110, 275, 309
    1.6 cli, clii, 98, 105-6, 117, 269, 461, 812
    1.8-10 87
    1.10 xxxiv, 86
    1.12 cli
    1.14 88, 94
    1.17 101, 497
    1.20 101, 585, 671, 715
    1.30 347
    1.39 790
    2.17 106, 149, 468, 780, 790
    2.18-21 755
    2.26 790
    2.33 144, 159
    2.34 143-4, 159
    2.39-41 755, 773
    2.43 cxlii, 216, 750-1, 754
    2.54 699
    3.3 82, 88, 101, 180, 788
    3.4 xxxvi, 180, 496
    3.5 86, 179-80, 203, 285
    3.7-8 307
    3.15 179, 224, 311, 348
    3.17-18 158, 242, 348, 405, 526, 802
    3.17-21 405
    3.18 361, 506
    3.22 160, 745
    3.33 403
    3.41 138, 160, 310, 572, 738, 774
    3.45 152, 384
    3.51 86
    3.51-7 222
    3.68 311
    4.2 130
    4.3-10 cxxii
    4.8-10 116, 195, 198, 199, 201, 237, 780
    4.10 88
    4.12 149, 229, 733
    4.17 154, 773
    4.20 223
    4.24 395
    4.25-8 773
    4.26 cxxiii, 138, 745
    4.27 161
    4.28 402, 771
    4.32 cxxiii, 138, 745
    4.41 cxxiii, 138, 745
    4.42 173, 200, 207-8, 779, 784
    4.45 cxxiii
    4.51 143
    4.55 773
    4.60 753
    4.72 148, 159
    5.1 119, 539
    5.7 117, 134, 220, 758
    5.8 113, 139, 140
    5.9-74 139
    5.9 140, 668
    5.10 106
    5.11 693, 734
    5.15-23 742, 748, 754
    5.15 749
    5.16 142, 151, 211
    5.17-21 755
    5.17 148, 150, 749
    5.18 151, 159
    5.20 140, 747, 756-7, 773
    5.22 140, 747, 756-7, 773
    5.23 161, 737-8, 747, 751, 754
    5.34-6 151
    5.34 212, 402
    5.36 152, 153
    5.38 431
    5.41-5 405
    5.45 138
    5.66 155
    5.67 213, 226
    5.68 150, 157, 160, 560
    5.71-2 138, 145, 152, 159
    5.72-3 cxxiii
    5.76 571, 685, 688, 691
    5.81 cxxiii, 210
    5.83-95 142
    5.86 732
    5.84 128, 151
    5.87 126
    5.88-91 cxxiii
    5.96 119
  Font.
    29 1110
  Hort. (ed. Grilli)
    frg. 2 clxxx

frg. 5 clxxx
frg. 8 clxxx
frg. 11 clxxx
frg. 17 311
frg. 18 clxxx
frg. 19 clxxx
frg. 25 623
frg. 26–32 clxxxi
frg. 30 clxxxi
frg. 32 clxxxi
frg. 51 xxxi, cxlviii, clxxxi, 297
frg. 58 clxxxi
frg. 59 clxxxi
frg. 67 clxxxi
frg. 78 clxxxi
frg. 82 clxxxi
frg. 93 clxxxi
frg. 107 xxxi, cxlviii, clxxxi, 297
frg. 110 clxxxi
frg. 112 clxxxi
frg. 114 cx
frg. 115 clxxxi

Inv.
1.51 128
1.61 128
1.70 453
2.1–10 cxliv
2.9 xlvii, cxlvi, cxlvii, cxlix, clvi, 114, 118, 323
2.10 132, 314, 526

Lael.
32 215

Leg.
1.36 cxlvii, 314
1.39 114, 154
1.54 xxx
1.55 cxxiii, 130, 759
1.62 150, 199
2.59 105, 769
3.14 693

Luc.
1–148 clxxii
9 276, 582, 791, 793
10 303, 384, 520
12 xxv, xlv, xlvii, xlix, cxxix, clxx, clxxiii, 83, 116, 169, 269
13–15 cix, cx, cxii, cxv, 253, 312
14 cix, cx, cxii, cxxv, cxxvi, cxxviii, cxxix, 254, 400, 550, 558
15 cx, cxv, cxvi, cxix, cxxi, cxxii, cxxiv, cxxvi, cxxvii, cxxviii, clxxiv, clxxviii, 122–3, 127, 133, 198, 218–19, 248, 253, 259, 290, 336, 560, 708, 724
16 xxiii, xlii, 120, 288–9, 351, 400, 516, 567, 635–6, 882
17 xxv, clxxvii, cxci, 80, 242, 277, 326, 395, 405, 424, 447, 467, 573, 627, 650, 787
18 xlv, xlvii, xlviii, l, liv, ci, cxiv, clvi, clxviii, clxx, clxxiii, clxxxiv, 115, 118, 234, 238, 277, 298, 322–3, 328, 421, 423, 445, 500, 508, 547, 566, 571, 791, 815
23 cxci, 242–3, 335, 389, 405, 432, 535, 588
27 xxv, cxciii, 287, 392, 595, 679, 816
28 xxiii, cxliii, clxvii, clxxi, 123, 256, 348, 359, 387, 456, 507, 512, 638, 834
33 xlvi, lx, lxi, lxxiv, cv, clxxxix, cxc, cxci, 160, 234, 238, 413, 416–17, 426, 454, 480, 493, 545, 571, 589, 593, 654, 665, 680, 684
34 lxv, 220, 417, 441, 450, 458, 464, 468, 476, 512, 773, 835
35–6 lxxxi, ciii, civ, cv, 177, 267, 417, 666
40–58 lxvi, 440
40 xl, xlvi, lxvi, lxxiv, ciii, 250, 391, 469, 504, 680
41 356
42 clxviii, 302, 452, 599
46 lv, lvii, 465, 468, 720
48 lxv, lxx, lxxi, lxxiii, clxvi, 228, 238
51 lxxi, 479, 486
52 lxxi, clxxxix, cxcii, 201, 291, 503, 577
54 lxxi, 242, 411, 483, 500, 599
57 lix, lxviii, cxc, 265, 278, 364, 418–19, 469, 598, 653
58 lv, lvi, lxxiv, ciii, clxxxviii, cxc, 372, 416, 418–19
59 xli, xlv, clxviii, 239, 458, 480, 536, 565, 686, 713, 795
61 clxxx, clxxxi, 326, 513, 519, 539
63–4 clxx, 800
65–7 xxv, xli, cxxix, clxviii, 247, 250, 311, 312, 505, 513, 573, 611, 621, 759, 799
66 xxxix, xl, civ, cxxx, cxxxiv, cxl, cxlv, cxlviii, cl, cxcii, 96, 104, 150, 245, 273, 276, 285, 300–1, 406, 436, 440, 442, 444, 491, 506, 519, 636, 677, 681, 693, 736, 800, 833
69–71 xxiv, cxxx, 113, 117, 288, 648, 727
69 clvi, 288, 418, 758
71 cxc, 418–19, 514, 519
72 cix, 251, 254, 293, 331, 335, 549, 554, 580, 720
73 411, 515
74 cxvi, cxxvi, 122, 127, 255, 258, 291, 336, 687
75 cxiii, 366, 454, 500, 597, 599, 787
76 cxxxi, cl, 249, 317, 341, 368, 784
77 xxiii, xl, li, lii, liii, liv, lxv, lxvii, lxxviii, cxxxvii, cxli, clxvii, 249, 252, 294, 342, 356, 357, 418, 450, 534, 571, 800

910 INDEX LOCORUM

M. Tullius Cicero (*Cont.*)
  78 xxiv, xl, xli, xliii, xlv, xlviii, xlix, l, cxxxv,
    cl, clxxiii, 213, 228, 267, 345, 355, 447, 523,
    565, 568, 795
  79 clxviii, clxxi, 270, 274, 318, 326, 330, 359,
    374, 454, 762, 793
  81 279, 287, 723
  83–5 lxxiii, 588
  84 lxxiv, lxxv, clxxxiv, 164, 234, 245, 418, 493,
    500, 590, 650
  86 lix, 265, 366–7, 500, 598, 757
  88–9 lxvi, lxxi, 489, 591
  90 clxxxix, 490
  94 clxvi, cxclii, 91, 239, 627
  99 xliii, ciii, cv, clxxiii, cxc, cxcii, 406, 443,
    448, 639, 649, 653
  103–4 cxcii
  104–5 xlii, xlvii, cvii, cxlviii, 239, 300, 302,
    314, 384, 442, 451, 458, 505, 655, 657
  105 lxxxi, c, clxxxv, cxc, 270–2, 285, 314, 354,
    415, 456, 464, 658, 793, 813
  108 clxxii, clxxxiv, 400, 676
  109–10 300, 388–90, 395–7, 525, 535
  110–11 cxxx, 123
  111 cxxxviii, cxc, 290, 419, 458–9, 464, 466,
    541, 647
  112 cliii, 88, 286, 511, 587, 794, 813
  132 cxx, 142, 166, 221, 320, 416, 536, 545, 786
  135 xxix, xxxi, clxi, 97, 213, 220, 763, 766
  139 xlii, 230, 291, 344
  142–3 cxii, 207, 399, 780
  146 xxxv, cii, ciii, cvii, cxliv, clxx, 240, 286,
    371, 412, 513, 516, 658, 664, 666, 769,
    782, 792
  147 xxxi, 414, 689, 694, 732, 794
  148 xxiv, xxxix, xli, xliii, xliv, xlv, xlviii, xlix, l,
    lxxxii, cvii, cxiv, cxxxv, cxlv, cxlviii, cxlix,
    cl, clv, clvii, clxviii, clxix, clxx, clxxiii,
    clxxvi, cxcii, 251, 273, 301, 314, 323, 326,
    344, 350, 392, 396, 434, 441, 460, 464, 505,
    510, 514, 526, 531, 565, 654, 660, 681–2,
    686, 692, 722, 814–15
Marc.
  13 xxxvi
N.D.
  1.6 xxvii, cxlvi, 106, 311–12, 342, 400,
    516, 694
  1.8 86
  1.9 xxxii, xxxiv, 13, 112
  1.10–12 301
  1.10 314, 316, 510, 726, 793
  1.11 xxxi, cxxxii, cxlviii, clxxix, 13, 257–8,
    262, 302, 312, 511, 523, 548, 732, 734
  1.12 lxv, clii, clxxxix, cxci, 420, 424, 513, 593,
    643, 679, 680, 684

  1.17 clvi, 512
  1.25–41 700, 707
  1.33 216, 715
  1.35 331, 718
  1.39 187–8, 479
  1.61 cliv
  1.66 101, 558, 694, 711, 718
  1.97 482
  2.39 714
  2.47 xxxii, 104
  2.57–8 401
  2.84 186, 229
  2.95–6 216
  2.104–49 398
  2.145 364, 366
  2.147 404, 405
  2.148 405
  2.153 720
  3.7 cliv
  3.43–52 472
  3.95 cliii, cliv, 510, 522
  3.110 512
Off.
  1.1–3 xxxv
  1.3 693
  1.6 106, 737, 751, 753
  1.13 273, 526, 732
  1.19 225, 532
  1.40 302
  1.153 109
  2.3–4 309
  2.5 104
  2.7–8 14, 313, 740
  2.8 xxxi, clxxix, 257, 513
  2.43 524
  3.20 313
  3.99–115 379
  3.117 161
  3.119–21 773
  3.119 755, 773
Or.
  8–10 173–4, 193, 200
  51 xlii, 344, 814
  113 100, 780, 790
  114 204
  148 xxx, xxxi, clviii
  237 xxx
Parad.
  2 453
  4 767
  5 792
  16 379
  20–6 738, 761
  23 767
  27–32 700

27 769
42–52 768
Phil.
  2.102–5 91
  2.105 105
Q. fr.
  1.1.19 651
  2.10.1 clxiv
  2.10.3 334
  2.11 clxiv
  3.5.1 xxvii
  3.7.3 111
Rab. perd.
  16 306
  18–24 334
  20 788
  22 332
Rep.
  1.1–23 xxxiv
  1.8 309
  1.15 125
  1.16 108, 126
  1.17 94, 307
  1.19 94, 734
  1.51 485
  1.68 400
  2.34 105
  2.51 131, 206
  2.53 332
  2.54 332
  2.55 332
  3.7–8 521
  3.8 cxlvii, 313
  3.23 400
  3.27 769
  5.1 254
  5.5 101
  6.1 93
  6.17 187
  6.28 437
Sest.
  23 132
  93 302
  96–135 331
  102 97
  122 240, 428
  126 605
Tim.
  1 xxxi
  52 104
Top.
  58 102
  97 101
Tusc.
  1.1–8 xxxiv
  1.5 xxxiv, 82, 88, 102

  1.6 87, 95, 532
  1.7–17 cvii, 665
  1.7 693
  1.8 xliii
  1.14 629
  1.18–24 700
  1.20 228, 725
  1.22 101, 182–3, 229, 727–8, 758
  1.40 698, 721
  1.45 515
  1.54 437
  1.55 412, 715
  1.56–8 193, 200, 202, 245
  1.57 404
  1.58 201
  1.59 305
  1.106 604
  2.1 clxxxi, 112, 719
  2.4 xxxi, clxxix, 12, 309, 541
  2.5 314
  2.7 99
  2.9 xliii, 124, 206, 257, 313, 317
  2.67 361
  3.46 217, 312, 522
  3.51 252, 522
  3.80 229
  4.1–7 xxxiv
  4.4 cliv
  4.6–7 87–8, 99
  4.7 99, 102, 314
  4.43 766
  4.55 511
  5.5–11 733
  5.10 xxxii, 125, 126
  5.11 cxxvii, 313, 510, 693
  5.24 217, 524, 762
  5.33 cliii, 300, 396, 510
  5.34 129, 285, 691
  5.68 150
  5.71 378, 734
  5.76 151, 154
  5.83 cliii, 300, 510
  5.84–5 755, 756
  5.120 138, 160
Ver.
  2.60 699
Varro
L.L.
  5.18 105
  5.153 164
  6.56 431
  6.59 547
  6.63 447
  6.64 447
  7.2 105

Varro (*Cont.*)
   7.9 civ
   10.6 225
   10.55 496
  Men. Sat. (ed. Buecheler)
   frg. 36 89
   frg. 225 90
   frg. 420 715
   frg. 505 108
   frg. 556 89
  R.R.
   1.1.3 83
   3.1.9 96
   3.17.9 318

Vergil
  A.
   2.270–3 clxxxv
   2.772–3 clxxxv
   4.450–6 clxxxviii
   12.107–8 766

Vitruvius
  5.11.4 319
  7.pr.11 366
  9.pr.4 160

Xenophon
  Ap. 14 121, 127
  Mem. 1.1.13 334, 702

Index of Greek Terms

ἄγνοια 235, 243, 789, 801
ἄδηλος 386–7, 408, 410–12, 491–2, 668, 835
ἀδιαφορία 753
ἀδιάφορον 210, 222, 754
ἄθροισμα lxxxv, xciv, 369, 374–5
αἵρεσις 133, 222, 339
αἰσθανεσθαι 237
αἴσθησις lv, lxvi, clxxxiv, 191, 231–3, 238, 242, 260, 359, 367, 379, 415, 432, 589, 598, 642, 647, 676, 784
Ἀκαδημικὴ σύνταξις clxii, clxxix
ἀκαταληψία 1, clxx, 253, 260, 292, 325, 328–9, 349, 353–5, 357, 365, 390–4, 434, 435, 455, 506, 520, 529, 535, 537, 559, 567, 570, 572, 574, 651, 797, 807–8, 821, 823
ἀλαζονεία 337, 569
ἀληθεύειν 435, 616
ἀματαιότης 246
ἀμετάπτωτος 379
ἀμυδρός lxxxiii, lxxxvii, xcii, 360, 642
ἀμφιβολία 623
ἀναιρεῖν 374, 384, 395, 421, 460, 627, 668, 819
ἀναίρετος lxxxiv
ἀναισθησία lxvi, 177
ἀναλαμβάνειν clxxxv
ἀναλογία 403
ἀναλογίσματα 191, 192
ἀναμφιβόλως 459–60, 808
ἀνασκευάζειν 460
ἀνασκευή 788
ἀναφέρειν 151, 246, 750
ἀνεικαιότης 246
ἀνελεγξία 246
ἀντίληψις clxxxiv, 483
ἀντίπους 722
ἀξίωμα xcviii
ἀπαντᾶν 465
ἀπαράλλακτος li, liii, lv, lxv, lxx, 450, 483, 495, 571, 588, 728
ἀπαραλλαξία xxiii, xxxviii, xl, li, lx, lxi, lxiv, lxv, lxvi, lxvii, lxviii, lxix, lxx, lxxii, lxxiv, lxxiv, lxxv, lxxviii, lxxix, cxxxv, cxxxvi, cxxxvii, clxxii, clxxxiv, clxxxv, clxxxviii, 242, 289, 291, 384, 387, 407, 415, 417, 420, 422–3, 425, 427, 441, 443, 449, 450, 453–8, 462, 463–6, 470–4, 479, 480, 490, 493, 501, 504–5, 513–15, 530, 536, 543, 565, 572, 574, 587–9, 591, 595, 597, 599–600, 602, 606, 608, 641, 642–3, 647, 653, 684, 714, 776, 798, 834

ἀπαραλλάττω lxvi
ἀπειθής lxxxiii, 642
ἀπεμφαίνειν lxxxiii
ἀπέμφασις lxxxiii–lxxxiv
ἀπερίσπαστος xciii, xcvi, c, civ, 644, 666
ἀπιθανός lxxxiii, lxxxv, lxxxviii, lxxxix, xci, xcviii, xcix, 638, 642
ἄπιστος xcix, c, 362
ἀπό lii
ἀπόγραφα clxi, clxii, clxxvii
ἀποδεικνύναι 384
ἀπόδειξις 373, 383–6, 535, 609
ἀποπροηγμένα 224, 780
ἄποροι λόγοι 625, 630, 633
ἀπόρροιαι 580
ἀπραξία xxxviii, xl, lxvi, lxxxi, ciii, cxxxv, 160, 374, 378, 382, 406, 429–30, 434–5, 513, 515, 645, 648, 653–4, 661, 664, 676
ἀπροπτωσία 246, 406, 538
ἀρχή 217
ἀταραξία xxxvii, lxvi, 506, 754
αὐτόπιστος 376

βέβαιος 361, 379

γιγνώσκειν 672
γνώμων 245, 270
γνῶσις 385, 555
γραμμή 698

δηλοῦν 468, 627
δηλωτικός 465
διαζωγραφεῖν 185
διάθεσις 100, 227
διάκρισις lx, lxxii, 197, 555
διάνοια xcviii, 373, 479, 483, 627
διδόναι 482, 536, 589, 785
διεζευγμένον 634
διεξοδεύειν civ
διεξοδικός 151
διορίζειν lx, lxxii, lxxiii, lxxv
δόγμα cxx, cxciii, 287, 387–9, 392, 394, 396–7, 436, 525, 652, 661, 677–8
δοκιμασία lxxxvii, ciii
δόξα xxv, xxix, xli, xlvi, lxv, xci, cxxxv, clv, cxci, cxcii, 171, 194, 213, 228, 235, 243–4, 246, 299, 396, 397, 415, 469, 543, 567, 686, 688, 767, 789, 801
δοξάζειν 191, 233–4, 535

914 INDEX OF GREEK TERMS

δοξάστης 532
δόσις xc, clxxxvi

εἴδωλον clxxxviii, clxxxix, 729
εἴκειν 438, 534
εἰκός xciv, xcv, 289, 413, 508, 530, 676
εἶξις 431
εἴρων cxxx, 127, 337, 339
εἰρωνεία 337, 561
εἰσοχαί 366
ἐκκαλύπτειν 386
ἐκκαλυπτικός 465
ἔκλυτος lxxxiii, lxxxvii, xcli, 642
ἔκτυπος liv
ἐμπειρία 217, 376, 403, 481, 610
ἐμφαίνεσθαι lxxxiii, xc, xcii, 113, 130
ἔμφασις sections 6.1, 6.2 504, 642–3, 684, 787
ἐναργεία liv, lxxi, lxxxii, cxli, 46–8, 196–7, 240, 341, 346–8, 353, 355, 424, 457, 598
ἐναργής liv, lxix, lxxxiii, 100, 423, 438, 459, 469, 642, 688
ἔννοια clxviii, 193, 201, 235, 369–70, 372, 375, 385, 403, 420
ἐννόημα 195, 209
ἔντονος liv
ἐξοχαί 366, 668
ἕπεσθαι 644, 692
ἐπέχειν cxxxiii, 410, 435, 480, 613, 626–7
ἐπιβρίθω 396
ἐπίκλισις 438
ἐπισκοπεῖν 192, 200
ἐπιστήμη xlviii, c, cii, cxci, cxciii, 100, 149, 191–2, 197, 201, 217, 226–7, 235, 240, 243–6, 255, 260, 336, 361, 375, 377, 379–80, 386–7, 406, 468, 538, 622, 624, 737, 750, 775, 778, 781–2, 789, 791, 801
ἐπιφάνεια 698
ἐπιχείρημα 665
ἐπιχείρησις 664
ἐποχή xxxvii, xxxviii, xlii, xlv, cxl, cxlv, cl, clvi, cxciii, 116, 140, 239, 247, 253, 257, 292, 344, 377, 391, 406, 410, 424, 430, 434–6, 439, 505, 506, 514, 520, 526, 544, 559, 565, 626–7, 637–8, 648–9, 663, 668, 675, 687, 702, 706, 719, 796–8, 802–3, 805, 819, 821–3, 833, 835
ἑτεροίωσις lv
ἐτυμολογία 203
εὐδοκεῖν 644
εὐλογία 639, 640
εὔλογον lxiv, lxxx, cxxxv, cxxxix, 225, 530, 640
ἐφάπτεσθαι clxxxv·
ἐφεκτικός 815

ζήτησις 383, 385, 449, 818, 822

ἡσυχάζειν 611, 625–6

θέσις 453, 700
θεωρία 126, 733

ἰδέα cxvii, 189–93, 200–2, 215, 221, 399, 752, 784
ἴδια ποιότης 234, 236, 244, 341
ἰδίωμα liv, lxi, lxii, lxiii, lxvii, lxviii, lxix, lxx, lxxiii, lxxiv, lxxvi, lxxvii, 240, 244, 416
ἰσοσθένεια 258

καλαμοβόας 269, 348
καλός 221, 771
καταλαμβάνειν clxxxv, clxxxvi, clxxxvii, 241, 348, 360, 386, 434, 459, 598–9, 622, 649, 791, 805
καταληπτικὴ φαντασία section 5 li, lii, lxv, lxxii, xcix, cxxxiii, clxxxvi, 244, 329, 350, 356, 362, 423, 462, 789, 806, 808, 820, 822
καταληπτικός clxxxv, clxxxvi, clxxxviii, 240, 348, 435
καταληπτός clxxxv, clxxxvi, 240
κατάληψις xxii, xxiii, xxv, xli, xlvii, xlviii, l, lv, cxxxiii, cxxxvii, cxli, clxviii, clxx, clxx, clxxxvi, clxxxvii, clxxxviii, 115, 190, 216, 234–5, 239, 241, 242, 270, 276, 284, 293, 303, 312, 323, 336, 346–9, 354–5, 358, 372, 376–7, 379, 380, 384–6, 388, 399–400, 404–6, 408, 429, 432, 434, 439, 442, 494, 503, 520, 566–7, 569, 573, 587, 672, 685, 688, 772, 778–9, 791, 796, 835
κινεῖσθαι 397
κοινά 191–3, 200, 231–2, 236
κοσμόπολις 155
κόσμος 130, 171, 175, 704, 715
κρίνειν 192, 197, 376
κριτήριον (τῆς ἀληθείας) lxv, lxxxi, 189, 195, 198–9, 245, 357, 361–2, 397, 409, 413–14, 651, 779, 784, 789

λαμβάνειν cxcii, 357, 452, 482, 785
λεκτόν 629
λῆψις 465
λόγος xliii, lxv, lxviii, cvii, cxxxvii, 163, 197, 229, 234, 243, 246, 383, 386, 391, 481, 558, 610, 619, 624, 626, 734, 784
λύειν 625
λύσις 632

μάχεσθαι 144, 373, 459, 466
μάχη 483, 623, 684, 808
μονοειδής lxxxiv, 200

ξυστός 319

οἴησις 246
ὁμοιομερία 86
ὁμοιότης 399
ὁμολογεῖν 572, 805

INDEX OF GREEK TERMS 915

ὁρμή 40, 222, 377-8, 385, 401, 515, 676, 743
ὁρμητικὴ φαντασία 378, 664

παραλλάττειν lxvi
περιληπτός 194, 196-7, 284
περιοδεύειν civ
περισπᾶν c
περίστασις xcix, c, 272, 362
πιθανόν section 6 *passim* xxiii, xxvi, xlii, xliii, xliv, xlvi, clv, clxviii, clxx, 267-8, 284, 289, 291, 314, 393-4, 406-10, 413-15, 420-2, 424, 427, 434, 444, 452, 459, 464, 505, 508, 520, 525, 527, 530, 569, 574, 591, 638, 640, 651, 653, 659, 661-2, 676, 678, 680, 682, 783, 800, 805-6, 808, 814, 819, 834
πιθανότης lxxx, lxxxiii, lxxxvii, xciii, xciv, xcvii, xcviii, xcix, c, cvi, 413, 459, 464, 642, 644-5, 680, 742, 799
πιστεύειν lxxxiv, lxxxvi, 626
πιστός xciv
πλάτος xcii, xciii
πληκτικός liv, 534
ποιότης 163, 178-9, 234, 236, 244, 341
πρᾶξις 160, 374, 429, 435, 664, 677
πρόβλημα 110, 149, 665
προηγμένα 224-5, 780
προκοπή 154
προπέτεια 406
προκόπτων lix, c, 227, 391, 699
προσλαμβάνειν clxxxv
πρόσληψις 465
προσπίπτον lxxv, lxxxvi
πρότασις xcv, 449
πρότασις ἔνδοξος xcv
πυξίς 273

ῥοπή 438

σημεῖον lxv, lxvi, xcv, 234, 385, 416, 697
σκέπτεσθαι 415
σκεπτικός 327, 395
σκηνογραφία 366
σκιαγραφία 481, 819
στοιχεῖον 182
στοχάζειν 672
στοχασμός 672, 696
συγκατάθεσις lxx, lxxxix, xcviii, cxxxiii, cxcii, 239, 243-4, 358, 379, 432, 437-8, 529, 598, 637, 662, 789, 807
συμπεπλεγμένον 623
συνάρτησις xc, 466, 632, 787

συνδρομή lxxxii
συνειδέναι 127
συνήθεια 366, 553, 597-600, 806, 823
συνημμένον ἀξίωμα 623
σύνθεσις 372, 373
σύνταγμα clx, 144, 600
σύνταξις clx, clxii, clxxix
σύστημα 133, 371, 374-5, 403, 472, 651, 781
σχῆμα 132, 461, 612, 707
σχολή cliii, 817, 820

τεκμήριον lxix
τελευτή 698, 752
τέχνη lix, 133, 148, 217, 226, 364, 366, 369, 371, 374-6, 403, 500, 624, 635, 670, 672-3, 789
τιθέναι 448, 459-60, 482, 589, 627, 808
τρανής liv, 361
τριβή 376
τριγένεια 157
τύπωσις lv

ὕλη 160, 162, 168, 176, 437, 710
ὑπάρχειν lii, liii, lxxxiv, 162, 168, 176, 197, 437, 710
ὑπογραφή 346
ὑπόθεσις 560
ὑπόληψις 246, 706
ὑπόμνημα clx
ὑποτύπωσις 132

φαίνεσθαι clxxxiii
φαινόμενον clxxxiii
φαίνειν xc
φαντασία lxxxv, lxxxix, xc, xcii, xciii, xcvi, xcviii, cxxxiii, clxxxii, clxxxiv, clxxxiv, clxxxvi, clxxxvii, clxxxix, 237-9, 289, 350, 356, 358-62, 378, 401, 402, 421, 427, 444-5, 471, 477, 571, 589, 594, 604, 608, 638, 642, 647, 666, 688, 807
φάντασμα li, lxviii, lxx, lxxxiii, lxviii, lxxxix, 375, 471, 477, 604
φάσμα 481
φιλένδοξος clxiii
φιλονεικία 524
φυσικός 331

χαρακτήρ lxix, lxxii, 591

ψεύδεσθαι 616

ὡς ἐπὶ τὸ πολύ xciv, xcv, 427

Index of Latin Terms

abscedentia 366
Academicus clxx, 327, 758, 786
accipere cxviii, 150, 165, 185, 241, 528
actio 677
aculeus 636
acus 562
adducere 102, 103, 253
adiuncta (falsa ueris) lxv, lxxix, cxci, 420, 424, 684
adiungere 240, 631
aduersarius 322, 330, 354, 594
aduocare 596
aequor 270-1, 281
aer 181, 186, 280, 583
aes 595
aestimatio 211-12, 223, 754
affigere 287
affirmare cxxxii, cxlix, 259, 301, 313-14, 335, 466, 597, 679, 736
affirmatio 132, 259
agnoscere 327
aiare 634, 654-6, 664, 665
alabaster 273
amplexari cxviii, 173, 216
angustiae 690
animal 278, 372, 399, 405-6, 430-1, 433, 437-8
animus 111, 166-7, 230, 233, 383, 430, 432, 489, 725, 734-5
apertus 355, 386, 512
appellare 777, 786
appetitio 381, 385, 676
apponere lxxiv, 587-8
approbare 607, 1372
approbatio cxcii, 432, 438-9, 490, 531, 644, 654-6, 660, 665, 675, 736
aqua 272, 595
arbitrari cii, 793
argumentum 362, 386, 428, 457, 465
ars 500, 501
ascendere 481
asciscere 729, 771
aspectus clxxxix, 240, 360, 362-3, 388
assensio cxxxi-ii, cxcii, 239, 246, 256, 430, 436-8, 526, 531, 574, 649, 677
assensus clxxxiv, cxcii, 239, 506, 662, 677, 802
assentire cxxxiv, 528
assentiri 228, 529, 648, 662, 759-60, 800
atrocitas 764, 767

auctoritas cx, cli, 121, 129, 215, 218-19, 316, 326, 516, 539, 541, 568, 724, 727, 793
audax 277
audire 313, 546, 596, 802
auditor 218, 546, 710, 730
aut 573, 771
axis 533

balbutire 536, 758, 770
biennium 96

caecus 286
caelestia 126
caelum 595
caeruleus 607, 668
calumnia cxi, cxxix, 252, 307, 334, 524
cantus 367
captio 468, 470
captiosus 481, 626
caput 452, 481, 588, 647, 715
cauere 611
causa 102, 107, 110, 188, 216, 674
cautus 634
cedere lxi, 240, 432, 438, 534
censere cxxx, cxxxi, cxxxv, cxciii, 256
cernere 189, 192, 200, 217, 240, 256, 335, 376, 579
certamen cxxx, 248, 252, 563
certus 361, 776
cessare 95
circumspectio ciii, civ, clxviii, 427, 667, 734
citro 165, 185, 186
classis 555
cogere 697
cogitatio 207, 245, 479, 485, 526, 531-2, 784
cognitio civ, cxcii, 241, 242, 256, 312, 376, 378-9, 405, 469, 494, 503, 526, 555, 624, 680
cognoscere cx, 242, 254, 447, 498, 500, 506
colloquium 310
color 272, 368, 425, 563, 653
commemorare 637, 643
communio 460, 464
communitas (cum falso) lxv, 417, 422-3, 464, 494
commutatio 120, 205, 231, 237, 246
complere 131
componere 132
comprehendere clxxxvi, clxxxviii, 241-2, 356, 372, 380, 386, 389, 448, 587, 669, 737, 789

INDEX OF LATIN TERMS 917

comprehendibilis clxxxvi–vii, 234, 240, 242, 629
comprehensio clxxxvi–vii, cxci–ii, 234, 235, 241–2, 669, 671, 790
comprobare 676
concedere 632, 634
conciliare 756
conciliatio 221, 757
concinere 283–4
conclusio 383, 386, 404, 444, 449, 453, 529, 535–6, 632
concursus 547
confessio 253, 560
conficere 369, 376, 560
confidere 427, 578–9
confirmare 536
congruere 129, 161, 466
coniectura 454, 621, 673, 696–7
coniunctio 180, 623, 787
connexum 623, 786
consideratio ciii, civ, cv, 667, 734, 757
consilium 410
consonare 284
constantia xxxiii, xxxvi, 83, 104, 252, 377, 379, 380, 405, 491, 641
constituere 242, 410, 667, 759
constitutio 393, 397
consuetudo 133, 153, 179, 364, 454, 498, 500, 537, 553, 598–9, 677, 693
contemnere 110, 486, 730
contemplari civ
contemplatio civ, 667, 734
contentio 313, 539, 572, 588, 774
conticescere 94, 611
contra 653
contrahere 790
conuicium 424, 727
corpus 163, 166, 183, 186, 230, 272, 425, 483, 729
corpusculum 101
corrigere 117, 220
cos 766
credo cxli, 244, 252, 564, 570
cupere 530, 757
curator 131
Cynosura 527, 532–4

dare 113, 538, 634
declarare 240, 428, 466
declaratio lvii, clxxxvi, 234, 238, 240, 348, 361, 418, 422, 424, 428, 483, 500, 654
decretum cxciii, 248, 289, 348, 387–9, 392, 394, 396, 397, 510, 525, 677, 678, 679, 815
deducere 109, 228, 257, 702, 717
defectio 248, 293
defensitare 544–5, 548
defigere 469

definitio 203, 461–2, 631
delabi 506, 693, 772
delectatio 112
delitescere 338
depingere 479
depugnare 277, 347
depulsio 485
descendere 481
describere 697
descriptio cxvii, 132, 160
desciscere 248, 470, 547
dialecticus 634
dicta cli, 323, 328, 764
diffidere 521
digladiari 269, 281, 347
dilatare 453
diligentia 219, 453, 792
dilucidus 457, 460, 464
dinotare cxc, 418, 500, 503, 654
discedere 544, 694, 697, 713
disceptare 202, 730
disceptator 622
disceptatrix 622
discernere lxxix, 375, 377, 381–2, 446, 449
disciplina cxii, cxiv, cxv, cxvi, cxvii, cxix, cxxi, cxxii, cxxv, cxxvi, cxxviii, 95, 122, 133, 191, 203, 205, 207, 215, 218, 247–8, 336, 338–9, 635, 651, 675, 689, 692, 694, 699–700, 751
discrimen 759
discidium cx, cxxx, 247, 248, 292–3
discrepare 230, 694
disputare 447, 536, 664
disputatio cxviii, cxlix, 205–6, 398, 400, 511
dissensio xxxvii, 231, 546, 725, 731–2, 737, 742, 750, 761
disserere 220, 414, 447, 664
dissimulatio 336, 337
distinctio 593, 596
diuellere 772
diuinus cxviii, 173, 209, 215, 216, 700
dogma 672
dubitatio 133, 287
dumetum 690
dupliciter 662

effari 634
effatum 180, 629
efficere 162, 174, 176, 185, 230, 483
egestas 86, 179
eius modi (esse) liii, lv, lxv, lxxviii, 445, 564, 587, 681
elementum 182
eligere 700, 704, 713, 727
eminentia 366
error 245, 268, 273, 276, 491, 535, 696, 716

918 INDEX OF LATIN TERMS

esse 642
etiam 663
exanclare 677
exceptio 633
excogitare 541, 544–5
exercitatio 363, 366
existimare 118, 730
existimator 311
expeditus 667
explanare 428
explicare 338, 463, 563
explicatrix 204
exponere 206, 274
exprimere cxlix, 165, 185, 569
exquirere 316
exterminare 734
extremitas 698
extrinsecus 238

facere 498
facilis 256, 312
facinerosus 277
facultas cxliv
faeneus 547
fama 715
familiaris 325, 672
fateri 464
fidenter 380
fides 240, 362–3, 388, 427, 504, 607
firmitas 528, 535
fixus 29, 287
flectere 518, 521
fluctuare/fluctuari 393, 396, 397
forma cxiii, cxviii, cxix, cxx, cxxi, cxxv, cxxviii, clxxv, 120, 125, 130, 160, 170, 183, 189, 201, 205–7, 215, 219, 226–9, 231–3, 237, 241, 244–5, 483, 512, 77
formula cxvii, cxviii, cxix, cxxii, 122, 131–3, 198, 205
fortasse cxli, 252, 564, 570, 583
fortuna 166, 188
frangere 218, 625
frui 144, 756
frumentarius 582
fundamentum 444–7, 629
fundere 558, 715

geometres 697
germanus 758, 771
granum 594

haesitare 338
homuncio 762
honestas 745–6, 771
honestum 140, 221, 548, 744, 771–2
hui clxv

iacere 577–8, 667, 762, 793
ieiunus 690
ignorantia 246
ignoratio 359, 458
illucescere 544
improbare 655, 658, 802
immutatio cxviii, 120, 204–5, 252
implorare 327, 607
impressio 151, 504
impulsio liv, 237–8, 401, 734
inanimum 430–2, 437, 440
inaniter 220, 425, 476
inceptio 715
incertus 411
includere 89
incognitus 242
inconstantia 390, 397, 541
indocilis 305
indicare 468
indiuiduum 497
inducere 644
induere se 356
inexplicabile 629–31, 633
infectus 272
inflexus 271
infractus 271
ingenium 153, 303
inhibere clxvi, 12, 627, 803
initium 386, 401
inopia 86
inquisitio 273
inquisitor 285
inscientia 235, 240, 243–4
insigne 290, 417, 428, 646
inspectare 699
instituere cxxx, 96, 252
instituta 254
institutio 161, 205, 651
intellegentia 367, 404
interesse lv, lxxix, 388, 446, 449, 466, 490, 502
internoscere lx, lxxi, 420, 478, 502
interrogare lxxx, 659, 664, 678
interrogatio 100, 470
intestinus 238, 479
intexere clxi
inuenire 385–6, 530, 545, 669
inuitamentum 150, 743, 744, 749
inuoluere 386
iudicium clii, 189, 199, 357, 397, 413, 417, 420, 423, 541, 568, 594, 776, 784, 793
iudicium ueritatis 189, 199, 207
iungere 466

labefactare 208, 215–16, 341
labi 693

INDEX OF LATIN TERMS

leuitas 246, 490, 535, 716
libertas 400, 705, 716, 735
libramentum 698
licentia 400
lima 96
limare 534
lineamentum 698
lis 588
lumen 109, 384, 400
lumina 461, 674

manare 626
manus 95
materia 162, 176
mediocritas 764, 765
mentiri 329, 616
minutus 562
mirificus 208, 216
mordicus lxxi, lxxvii, 485
moueri 890
multiplex 122, 127, 129, 131
Musae 94
mysteria 300, 507, 509, 511

nasci 338, 624
natura 162
naturae 229
negare cxxx, cxxi, cxciii, 118, 255
nempe 629, 694, 750
norma 270
nota section 10.2 lxxv, 416, 548, 589, 594
notare 423, 500
notatio 203
notio clxviii, 120, 189, 191, 193–4, 202, 236, 245
notitia clxviii, 369–70, 373–4, 388, 403, 420

oblatus 238, 479, 480
oblectatio 112
obscurari 429, 454
obscuritas cx, cxi, cxxx, cxxxii, 249, 250, 253, 255, 312, 793
obtinere 357, 744
obtrectare 341–2, 569
occurrere 465
odiosus 631
officium 160, 212, 225
omnino 104, 126, 329, 421, 439–40, 594, 662
opifex 285, 717
opinabilis 202, 203
opinatio 246, 574, 677
opinator 526, 531–2, 534, 537
opinio cxci, cxcii, 228–9, 235, 243, 801
optare 719
orator 100, 111
ornatus 715, 728
ostendere 479, 509, 510

paenitentia 545
pars 202
particula 711
percipere lxxiv, cx, clxxxiv, clxxxv, clxxxvii, 201, 242, 434, 437, 439, 446, 448, 450, 572, 588, 621, 642
percontari 94
persequi cxxvi, 104, 561, 719
perspicere 456–8, 464
perspicuitas lxxi, 240, 348, 417, 424, 439, 457, 466–8, 470, 485, 487, 490, 601, 603, 638, 650
perspicuus lvii, lxi, 240, 381, 423–5, 432, 439, 456, 458, 464, 468, 678
pertinacia 252, 524
perturbationes 227–8, 784
peruenire 482
philosophia 97
physicus 331, 496, 727
pinguis 395, 679
piscinarius 303
placere 548, 651–2, 655, 661, 663, 678, 679
Poenus 291, 344, 636
ponere 449
popularis 330, 333, 554, 710
portentum 722
postulare 394, 496
potestas 276–7
praeposita 223, 224
praepostere 528, 535
praescribere 160, 314
praescriptio 314
praest(r)igia(e) 468
prauitas 384, 578–9
pressius 392, 395–6, 679
prima naturae 137, 140–1, 148, 158–9, 212, 741, 745–6, 747, 756
probabile section 6.5 xxv, 110, 778
probare xlii, ci, clii, cxcii, 436, 465, 531, 632, 692, 713, 760, 767, 785
probatio cxcii, 637–8
procurare 187
proficisci 699
prominentia 366
prospectus 582
prudentia 743
pueriliter 494
punctum 698
pyxis 273

quaerere 414, 519, 697, 735
qualitas 163, 178, 179
quasi 131
quiescere 611

ratio 199, 243, 256, 298, 311, 621
recordatio 608

refellere 127, 314, 485, 487, 498
referre 792
regula 393-4, 397, 409, 413, 414, 420, 423, 502
reiecta 223-4
relinquere 117, 219, 562, 792
reprehensor 311
repudiare 679
repugnare 466, 684
requirere 97, 363
res 199, 202
respondere 626, 655-6, 659, 663-4, 678
restat 296, 309, 311
reuocare 485, 547
reuoluere 800
rhetor 100
robor 646

sapientia 109, 166, 187, 377, 379, 380, 404, 692, 696
saxum 315
schola 582
scientia xlviii, cii, cxci, 189, 231, 235, 240, 243-4, 255, 311, 379, 404, 775, 791-2
scire cx, cxci, 255, 557, 801-2
scriptum 327, 769
sensus 201, 230, 232, 235, 358, 360, 430, 434, 578, 600
sententia 112, 121, 128, 139, 239, 249, 257-8, 518, 570, 644, 700, 714, 803
sentire 229, 368, 525, 577, 604, 729, 800
Septemtriones 527, 532
sequi cxlix, cxcii, 104, 301, 333, 369, 374, 381, 398, 426, 439, 458, 505, 631, 644, 663, 665, 692, 713, 757, 770, 777
series 372
sidus civ, cv, 532, 534
significare 428
signum section 10.2 416-20, 428, 480, 684
simpliciter 103
societas 156
sophistes 555
species section 10.2 lv, ciii, cxviii, 21, 190, 201, 206, 215, 216, 419, 432, 487, 501, 502, 503, 504, 684, 776
spectra clxxxviii, 88
spoliare 217
stella civ
stomachari 269, 326
successor 131

sumenda 211, 223
sumere 452, 482, 538
superiores 165, 169, 213-14, 219, 226, 227, 229, 230, 763
sustinere clxvi, 355, 547, 627, 662, 664

tardus 634
temeritas xxxvi, xxxvii, 245-6, 256, 406, 677, 692, 693, 705
temperatio 595
tenere 157, 366, 386, 635, 655-6, 663, 679, 725
tibicen 365-7
tinctus 272
tollere 384, 421, 506, 792, 802
torquere 580
tractare cxii, 114, 117, 180, 554
tueri clii, 117, 668
tutari 461

uagari 527, 534
uarius cxvi, 122, 127, 129, 131
ubertas cxvii, cxix, 122, 131, 201, 205, 228, 233
uehementer 215, 638, 648, 653, 690, 799-800, 802
uerecundia cxi, 334, 726, 727, 731
uerus 578
uidere section 10.1 361, 593
uideri section 10.1 lxxix, cii, cvii, cxii, 152, 202, 238, 378, 381-3, 421, 434, 440, 445, 450, 476, 486, 549, 594, 603, 605, 665-6, 676, 783, 792
uinosus 603
uinulentus 603
uirtutis usus 144, 227
uisio section 10.2 238, 417, 421-2, 477, 480, 595, 608
uisum section 10.1 cxci, 237-8, 241, 356, 363, 378, 421-2, 440, 445, 446, 450, 477, 480-1, 570-1, 588, 593, 595, 608, 642, 646, 665, 790
uita beata 141, 143, 159, 160
uita beatissima 141, 143, 159, 160
uitiosus 611, 625
ultro 165, 185, 186
umbrae 366
uniuersus 454
uocabulum 225
usus 155, 227, 363, 366, 500
uulgaris sermo 81, 101

xystus 319